University Casebook Series

June, 1991

ACCOUNTING AND THE LAW, Fourth Edition (1978), with Problems Pamphlet (Successor to Dohr, Phillips, Thompson & Warren)

George C. Thompson, Professor, Columbia University Graduate School of Business.

Robert Whitman, Professor of Law, University of Connecticut.

Ellis L. Phillips, Jr., Member of the New York Bar.

William C. Warren, Professor of Law Emeritus, Columbia University.

ACCOUNTING FOR LAWYERS, MATERIALS ON (1980)

David R. Herwitz, Professor of Law, Harvard University.

ADMINISTRATIVE LAW, Eighth Edition (1987), with 1989 Case Supplement and 1983 Problems Supplement (Supplement edited in association with Paul R. Verkuil, Dean and Professor of Law, Tulane University)

Walter Gellhorn, University Professor Emeritus, Columbia University.

Clark Byse, Professor of Law, Harvard University.

Peter L. Strauss, Professor of Law, Columbia University.

Todd D. Rakoff, Professor of Law, Harvard University.

Roy A. Schotland, Professor of Law, Georgetown University.

ADMIRALTY, Third Edition (1987), with Statute and Rule Supplement

Jo Desha Lucas, Professor of Law, University of Chicago.

ADVOCACY, see also Lawyering Process

AGENCY, see also Enterprise Organization

AGENCY—PARTNERSHIPS, Fourth Edition (1987)

Abridgement from Conard, Knauss & Siegel's Enterprise Organization, Fourth Edition.

AGENCY AND PARTNERSHIPS (1987)

Melvin A. Eisenberg, Professor of Law, University of California, Berkeley.

ANTITRUST: FREE ENTERPRISE AND ECONOMIC ORGANIZATION, Sixth Edition (1983), with 1983 Problems in Antitrust Supplement and 1990 Case Supplement

Louis B. Schwartz, Professor of Law, University of Pennsylvania.

John J. Flynn, Professor of Law, University of Utah.

Harry First, Professor of Law, New York University.

BANKRUPTCY, Second Edition (1989), with 1990 Case Supplement

Robert L. Jordan, Professor of Law, University of California, Los Angeles.

William D. Warren, Professor of Law, University of California, Los Angeles.

BANKRUPTCY AND DEBTOR–CREDITOR LAW, Second Edition (1988)

Theodore Eisenberg, Professor of Law, Cornell University.

BUSINESS ASSOCIATIONS, AGENCY, PARTNERSHIPS, AND CORPORATIONS (1991)

William A. Klein, Professor of Law, University of California, Los Angeles.
Mark Ramseyer, Professor of Law, University of California, Los Angeles.

BUSINESS CRIME (1990)

Harry First, Professor of Law, New York University.

BUSINESS ORGANIZATION, see also Enterprise Organization

BUSINESS PLANNING (1991)

Franklin Gevurtz, Professor of Law, McGeorge School of Law.

BUSINESS PLANNING, Temporary Second Edition (1984)

David R. Herwitz, Professor of Law, Harvard University.

BUSINESS TORTS (1972)

Milton Handler, Professor of Law Emeritus, Columbia University.

CHILDREN IN THE LEGAL SYSTEM (1983) with 1990 Supplement (Supplement edited in association with Elizabeth S. Scott, Professor of Law, University of Virginia)

Walter Wadlington, Professor of Law, University of Virginia.
Charles H. Whitebread, Professor of Law, University of Southern California.
Samuel Davis, Professor of Law, University of Georgia.

CIVIL PROCEDURE, see Procedure

CIVIL RIGHTS ACTIONS (1988), with 1990 Supplement

Peter W. Low, Professor of Law, University of Virginia.
John C. Jeffries, Jr., Professor of Law, University of Virginia.

CLINIC, see also Lawyering Process

COMMERCIAL AND DEBTOR–CREDITOR LAW: SELECTED STATUTES, 1990 EDITION

COMMERCIAL LAW, Second Edition (1987)

Robert L. Jordan, Professor of Law, University of California, Los Angeles.
William D. Warren, Professor of Law, University of California, Los Angeles.

COMMERCIAL LAW, Fourth Edition (1985), with 1991 Case Supplement

E. Allan Farnsworth, Professor of Law, Columbia University.
John Honnold, Professor of Law, University of Pennsylvania.

COMMERCIAL PAPER, Third Edition (1984), with 1991 Case Supplement

E. Allan Farnsworth, Professor of Law, Columbia University.

COMMERCIAL PAPER, Second Edition (1987) (Reprinted from COMMERCIAL LAW, Second Edition (1987))

Robert L. Jordan, Professor of Law, University of California, Los Angeles.
William D. Warren, Professor of Law, University of California, Los Angeles.

COMMERCIAL PAPER AND BANK DEPOSITS AND COLLECTIONS (1967), with Statutory Supplement

William D. Hawkland, Professor of Law, University of Illinois.

UNIVERSITY CASEBOOK SERIES—Continued

COMMERCIAL TRANSACTIONS—Principles and Policies, Second Edition (1991)

Alan Schwartz, Professor of Law, Yale University.
Robert E. Scott, Professor of Law, University of Virginia.

COMPARATIVE LAW, Fifth Edition (1988)

Rudolf B. Schlesinger, Professor of Law, Hastings College of the Law.
Hans W. Baade, Professor of Law, University of Texas.
Mirjan P. Damaska, Professor of Law, Yale Law School.
Peter E. Herzog, Professor of Law, Syracuse University.

COMPETITIVE PROCESS, LEGAL REGULATION OF THE, Revised Fourth Edition (1991), with 1989 Selected Statutes Supplement

Edmund W. Kitch, Professor of Law, University of Virginia.
Harvey S. Perlman, Dean of the Law School, University of Nebraska.

CONFLICT OF LAWS, Ninth Edition (1990)

Willis L. M. Reese, Professor of Law, Columbia University.
Maurice Rosenberg, Professor of Law, Columbia University.
Peter Hay, Professor of Law, University of Illinois.

CONSTITUTIONAL LAW, Eighth Edition (1989), with 1990 Case Supplement

Edward L. Barrett, Jr., Professor of Law, University of California, Davis.
William Cohen, Professor of Law, Stanford University.
Jonathan D. Varat, Professor of Law, University of California, Los Angeles.

CONSTITUTIONAL LAW, CIVIL LIBERTY AND INDIVIDUAL RIGHTS, Second Edition (1982), with 1989 Supplement

William Cohen, Professor of Law, Stanford University.
John Kaplan, Professor of Law, Stanford University.

CONSTITUTIONAL LAW, Eleventh Edition (1985), with 1990 Supplement (Supplement edited in association with Frederick F. Schauer, Professor, Harvard University)

Gerald Gunther, Professor of Law, Stanford University.

CONSTITUTIONAL LAW, INDIVIDUAL RIGHTS IN, Fourth Edition (1986), (Reprinted from CONSTITUTIONAL LAW, Eleventh Edition), with 1990 Supplement (Supplement edited in association with Frederick F. Schauer, Professor, Harvard University)

Gerald Gunther, Professor of Law, Stanford University.

CONSUMER TRANSACTIONS, Second Edition (1991), with Selected Statutes and Regulations Supplement

Michael M. Greenfield, Professor of Law, Washington University.

CONTRACT LAW AND ITS APPLICATION, Fourth Edition (1988)

Arthur Rosett, Professor of Law, University of California, Los Angeles.

CONTRACT LAW, STUDIES IN, Fourth Edition (1991)

Edward J. Murphy, Professor of Law, University of Notre Dame.
Richard E. Speidel, Professor of Law, Northwestern University.

CONTRACTS, Fifth Edition (1987)

John P. Dawson, late Professor of Law, Harvard University.
William Burnett Harvey, Professor of Law and Political Science, Boston University.
Stanley D. Henderson, Professor of Law, University of Virginia.

CONTRACTS, Fourth Edition (1988)

E. Allan Farnsworth, Professor of Law, Columbia University.
William F. Young, Professor of Law, Columbia University.

CONTRACTS, Selections on (statutory materials) (1988)

CONTRACTS, Second Edition (1978), with Statutory and Administrative Law Supplement (1978)

Ian R. Macneil, Professor of Law, Cornell University.

COPYRIGHT, PATENTS AND TRADEMARKS, see also Competitive Process; see also Selected Statutes and International Agreements

COPYRIGHT, PATENT, TRADEMARK AND RELATED STATE DOCTRINES, Third Edition (1990), with 1989 Selected Statutes Supplement and 1981 Problem Supplement

Paul Goldstein, Professor of Law, Stanford University.

COPYRIGHT, Unfair Competition, and Other Topics Bearing on the Protection of Literary, Musical, and Artistic Works, Fifth Edition (1990), with 1991 Statutory and Case Supplement

Ralph S. Brown, Jr., Professor of Law, Yale University.
Robert C. Denicola, Professor of Law, University of Nebraska.

CORPORATE ACQUISITIONS, The Law and Finance of (1986), with 1990 Supplement

Ronald J. Gilson, Professor of Law, Stanford University.

CORPORATE FINANCE, Third Edition (1987)

Victor Brudney, Professor of Law, Harvard University.
Marvin A. Chirelstein, Professor of Law, Columbia University.

CORPORATION LAW, BASIC, Third Edition (1989), with Documentary Supplement

Detlev F. Vagts, Professor of Law, Harvard University.

CORPORATIONS, see also Enterprise Organization and Business Organization

CORPORATIONS, Sixth Edition—Concise (1988), with 1990 Case Supplement and 1990 Statutory Supplement

William L. Cary, late Professor of Law, Columbia University.
Melvin Aron Eisenberg, Professor of Law, University of California, Berkeley.

CORPORATIONS, Sixth Edition—Unabridged (1988), with 1990 Case Supplement and 1990 Statutory Supplement

William L. Cary, late Professor of Law, Columbia University.
Melvin Aron Eisenberg, Professor of Law, University of California, Berkeley.

CORPORATIONS AND BUSINESS ASSOCIATIONS—STATUTES, RULES, AND FORMS (1990)

CORRECTIONS, SEE SENTENCING

CREDITORS' RIGHTS, see also Debtor-Creditor Law

CRIMINAL JUSTICE ADMINISTRATION, Fourth Edition (1991)

Frank W. Miller, Professor of Law, Washington University.
Robert O. Dawson, Professor of Law, University of Texas.
George E. Dix, Professor of Law, University of Texas.
Raymond I. Parnas, Professor of Law, University of California, Davis.

CRIMINAL LAW, Fourth Edition (1987)

Fred E. Inbau, Professor of Law Emeritus, Northwestern University.
Andre A. Moenssens, Professor of Law, University of Richmond.
James R. Thompson, Professor of Law Emeritus, Northwestern University.

CRIMINAL LAW AND APPROACHES TO THE STUDY OF LAW, Second Edition (1991)

John M. Brumbaugh, Professor of Law, University of Maryland.

CRIMINAL LAW, Second Edition (1986)

Peter W. Low, Professor of Law, University of Virginia.
John C. Jeffries, Jr., Professor of Law, University of Virginia.
Richard C. Bonnie, Professor of Law, University of Virginia.

CRIMINAL LAW, Fourth Edition (1986)

Lloyd L. Weinreb, Professor of Law, Harvard University.

CRIMINAL LAW AND PROCEDURE, Seventh Edition (1989)

Ronald N. Boyce, Professor of Law, University of Utah.
Rollin M. Perkins, Professor of Law Emeritus, University of California, Hastings College of the Law.

CRIMINAL PROCEDURE, Third Edition (1987), with 1990 Supplement

James B. Haddad, Professor of Law, Northwestern University.
James B. Zagel, Chief, Criminal Justice Division, Office of Attorney General of Illinois.
Gary L. Starkman, Assistant U. S. Attorney, Northern District of Illinois.
William J. Bauer, Chief Judge of the U.S. Court of Appeals, Seventh Circuit.

CRIMINAL PROCESS, Fourth Edition (1987), with 1990 Supplement

Lloyd L. Weinreb, Professor of Law, Harvard University.

DAMAGES, Second Edition (1952)

Charles T. McCormick, late Professor of Law, University of Texas.
William F. Fritz, late Professor of Law, University of Texas.

DECEDENTS' ESTATES AND TRUSTS, See also Family Property Law

DECEDENTS' ESTATES AND TRUSTS, Seventh Edition (1988)

John Ritchie, late Professor of Law, University of Virginia.
Neill H. Alford, Jr., Professor of Law, University of Virginia.
Richard W. Effland, late Professor of Law, Arizona State University.

DISPUTE RESOLUTION, Processes of (1989)

John S. Murray, President and Executive Director of The Conflict Clinic, Inc., George Mason University.
Alan Scott Rau, Professor of Law, University of Texas.
Edward F. Sherman, Professor of Law, University of Texas.

DOMESTIC RELATIONS, see also Family Law

DOMESTIC RELATIONS, Second Edition (1990)

Walter Wadlington, Professor of Law, University of Virginia.

UNIVERSITY CASEBOOK SERIES—Continued

FAMILY LAW, see also Domestic Relations

FAMILY LAW Second Edition (1985), with 1991 Supplement

Judith C. Areen, Professor of Law, Georgetown University.

FAMILY LAW AND CHILDREN IN THE LEGAL SYSTEM, STATUTORY MATERIALS (1981)

Walter Wadlington, Professor of Law, University of Virginia.

FAMILY PROPERTY LAW, Cases and Materials on Wills, Trusts and Future Interests (1991)

Lawrence W. Waggoner, Professor of Law, University of Michigan.
Richard V. Wellman, Professor of Law, University of Georgia.
Gregory Alexander, Professor of Law, Cornell Law School.
Mary L. Fellows, Professor of Law, University of Minnesota.

FEDERAL COURTS, Eighth Edition (1988), with 1990 Supplement

Charles T. McCormick, late Professor of Law, University of Texas.
James H. Chadbourn, late Professor of Law, Harvard University.
Charles Alan Wright, Professor of Law, University of Texas, Austin.

FEDERAL COURTS AND THE FEDERAL SYSTEM, Hart and Wechsler's Third Edition (1988), with 1989 Case Supplement, and the Judicial Code and Rules of Procedure in the Federal Courts (1989)

Paul M. Bator, Professor of Law, University of Chicago.
Daniel J. Meltzer, Professor of Law, Harvard University.
Paul J. Mishkin, Professor of Law, University of California, Berkeley.
David L. Shapiro, Professor of Law, Harvard University.

FEDERAL COURTS AND THE LAW OF FEDERAL–STATE RELATIONS, Second Edition (1989), with 1990 Supplement

Peter W. Low, Professor of Law, University of Virginia.
John C. Jeffries, Jr., Professor of Law, University of Virginia.

FEDERAL PUBLIC LAND AND RESOURCES LAW, Second Edition (1987), with 1990 Case Supplement and 1990 Statutory Supplement

George C. Coggins, Professor of Law, University of Kansas.
Charles F. Wilkinson, Professor of Law, University of Oregon.

FEDERAL RULES OF CIVIL PROCEDURE and Selected Other Procedural Provisions, 1991 Edition

FEDERAL TAXATION, see Taxation

FIRST AMENDMENT (1991)

William W. Van Alstyne, Professor of Law, Duke University.

FOOD AND DRUG LAW, Second Edition (1991)

Peter Barton Hutt, Esq.
Richard A. Merrill, Professor of Law, University of Virginia.

FUTURE INTERESTS (1970)

Howard R. Williams, Professor of Law, Stanford University.

FUTURE INTERESTS AND ESTATE PLANNING (1961), with 1962 Supplement

W. Barton Leach, late Professor of Law, Harvard University.
James K. Logan, formerly Dean of the Law School, University of Kansas.

UNIVERSITY CASEBOOK SERIES—Continued

GOVERNMENT CONTRACTS, FEDERAL, Successor Edition (1985), with 1989 Supplement

John W. Whelan, Professor of Law, Hastings College of the Law.

GOVERNMENT REGULATION: FREE ENTERPRISE AND ECONOMIC ORGANIZATION, Sixth Edition (1985)

Louis B. Schwartz, Professor of Law, Hastings College of the Law.
John J. Flynn, Professor of Law, University of Utah.
Harry First, Professor of Law, New York University.

HEALTH CARE LAW AND POLICY (1988)

Clark C. Havighurst, Professor of Law, Duke University.

HINCKLEY, JOHN W., JR., TRIAL OF: A Case Study of the Insanity Defense (1986)

Peter W. Low, Professor of Law, University of Virginia.
John C. Jeffries, Jr., Professor of Law, University of Virginia.
Richard C. Bonnie, Professor of Law, University of Virginia.

INJUNCTIONS, Second Edition (1984)

Owen M. Fiss, Professor of Law, Yale University.
Doug Rendleman, Professor of Law, College of William and Mary.

INSTITUTIONAL INVESTORS, (1978)

David L. Ratner, Professor of Law, Cornell University.

INSURANCE, Second Edition (1985)

William F. Young, Professor of Law, Columbia University.
Eric M. Holmes, Professor of Law, University of Georgia.

INSURANCE LAW AND REGULATION (1990)

Kenneth S. Abraham, University of Virginia.

INTERNATIONAL LAW, see also Transnational Legal Problems, Transnational Business Problems, and United Nations Law

INTERNATIONAL LAW IN CONTEMPORARY PERSPECTIVE (1981), with Essay Supplement

Myres S. McDougal, Professor of Law, Yale University.
W. Michael Reisman, Professor of Law, Yale University.

INTERNATIONAL LEGAL SYSTEM, Third Edition (1988), with Documentary Supplement

Joseph Modeste Sweeney, Professor of Law, University of California, Hastings.
Covey T. Oliver, Professor of Law, University of Pennsylvania.
Noyes E. Leech, Professor of Law Emeritus, University of Pennsylvania.

INTRODUCTION TO LAW, see also Legal Method, On Law in Courts, and Dynamics of American Law

INTRODUCTION TO THE STUDY OF LAW (1970)

E. Wayne Thode, late Professor of Law, University of Utah.
Leon Lebowitz, Professor of Law, University of Texas.
Lester J. Mazor, Professor of Law, University of Utah.

JUDICIAL CODE and Rules of Procedure in the Federal Courts, Students' Edition, 1989 Revision

Daniel J. Meltzer, Professor of Law, Harvard University.
David L. Shapiro, Professor of Law, Harvard University.

UNIVERSITY CASEBOOK SERIES—Continued

JURISPRUDENCE (Temporary Edition Hardbound) (1949)

Lon L. Fuller, late Professor of Law, Harvard University.

JUVENILE, see also Children

JUVENILE JUSTICE PROCESS, Third Edition (1985)

Frank W. Miller, Professor of Law, Washington University.
Robert O. Dawson, Professor of Law, University of Texas.
George E. Dix, Professor of Law, University of Texas.
Raymond I. Parnas, Professor of Law, University of California, Davis.

LABOR LAW, Eleventh Edition (1991), with 1991 Statutory Supplement

Archibald Cox, Professor of Law, Harvard University.
Derek C. Bok, President, Harvard University.
Robert A. Gorman, Professor of Law, University of Pennsylvania.
Matthew W. Finkin, Professor of Law, University of Illinois.

LABOR LAW, Second Edition (1982), with Statutory Supplement

Clyde W. Summers, Professor of Law, University of Pennsylvania.
Harry H. Wellington, Dean of the Law School, Yale University.
Alan Hyde, Professor of Law, Rutgers University.

LAND FINANCING, Third Edition (1985)

The late Norman Penney, Professor of Law, Cornell University.
Richard F. Broude, Member of the California Bar.
Roger Cunningham, Professor of Law, University of Michigan.

LAW AND MEDICINE (1980)

Walter Wadlington, Professor of Law and Professor of Legal Medicine, University of Virginia.
Jon R. Waltz, Professor of Law, Northwestern University.
Roger B. Dworkin, Professor of Law, Indiana University, and Professor of Biomedical History, University of Washington.

LAW, LANGUAGE AND ETHICS (1972)

William R. Bishin, Professor of Law, University of Southern California.
Christopher D. Stone, Professor of Law, University of Southern California.

LAW, SCIENCE AND MEDICINE (1984), with 1989 Supplement

Judith C. Areen, Professor of Law, Georgetown University.
Patricia A. King, Professor of Law, Georgetown University.
Steven P. Goldberg, Professor of Law, Georgetown University.
Alexander M. Capron, Professor of Law, University of Southern California.

LAWYERING PROCESS (1978), with Civil Problem Supplement and Criminal Problem Supplement

Gary Bellow, Professor of Law, Harvard University.
Bea Moulton, Professor of Law, Arizona State University.

LEGAL METHOD (1980)

Harry W. Jones, Professor of Law Emeritus, Columbia University.
John M. Kernochan, Professor of Law, Columbia University.
Arthur W. Murphy, Professor of Law, Columbia University.

ix

LEGAL METHODS (1969)

Robert N. Covington, Professor of Law, Vanderbilt University.
E. Blythe Stason, late Professor of Law, Vanderbilt University.
John W. Wade, Professor of Law, Vanderbilt University.
Elliott E. Cheatham, late Professor of Law, Vanderbilt University.
Theodore A. Smedley, Professor of Law, Vanderbilt University.

LEGAL PROFESSION, THE, Responsibility and Regulation, Second Edition (1988)

Geoffrey C. Hazard, Jr., Professor of Law, Yale University.
Deborah L. Rhode, Professor of Law, Stanford University.

LEGISLATION, Fourth Edition (1982) (by Fordham)

Horace E. Read, late Vice President, Dalhousie University.
John W. MacDonald, Professor of Law Emeritus, Cornell Law School.
Jefferson B. Fordham, Professor of Law, University of Utah.
William J. Pierce, Professor of Law, University of Michigan.

LEGISLATIVE AND ADMINISTRATIVE PROCESSES, Second Edition (1981)

Hans A. Linde, Judge, Supreme Court of Oregon.
George Bunn, Professor of Law, University of Wisconsin.
Fredericka Paff, Professor of Law, University of Wisconsin.
W. Lawrence Church, Professor of Law, University of Wisconsin.

LOCAL GOVERNMENT LAW, Second Revised Edition (1986)

Jefferson B. Fordham, Professor of Law, University of Utah.

MASS MEDIA LAW, Fourth Edition (1990)

Marc A. Franklin, Professor of Law, Stanford University.
David A. Anderson, Professor of Law, University of Texas.

MUNICIPAL CORPORATIONS, see Local Government Law

NEGOTIABLE INSTRUMENTS, see Commercial Paper

NEGOTIATION (1981) (Reprinted from THE LAWYERING PROCESS)

Gary Bellow, Professor of Law, Harvard Law School.
Bea Moulton, Legal Services Corporation.

NEW YORK PRACTICE, Fourth Edition (1978)

Herbert Peterfreund, Professor of Law, New York University.
Joseph M. McLaughlin, Dean of the Law School, Fordham University.

OIL AND GAS, Fifth Edition (1987)

Howard R. Williams, Professor of Law, Stanford University.
Richard C. Maxwell, Professor of Law, University of California, Los Angeles.
Charles J. Meyers, late Dean of the Law School, Stanford University.
Stephen F. Williams, Judge of the United States Court of Appeals.

ON LAW IN COURTS (1965)

Paul J. Mishkin, Professor of Law, University of California, Berkeley.
Clarence Morris, Professor of Law Emeritus, University of Pennsylvania.

PENSION AND EMPLOYEE BENEFIT LAW (1990)

John H. Langbein, Professor of Law, University of Chicago.
Bruce A. Wolk, Professor of Law, University of California, Davis.

PLEADING AND PROCEDURE, see Procedure, Civil

POLICE FUNCTION, Fifth Edition (1991)

Reprint of Chapters 1–10 of Miller, Dawson, Dix and Parnas's CRIMINAL JUSTICE ADMINISTRATION, Fourth Edition.

PREPARING AND PRESENTING THE CASE (1981) (Reprinted from THE LAW-YERING PROCESS)

Gary Bellow, Professor of Law, Harvard Law School.
Bea Moulton, Legal Services Corporation.

PROCEDURE (1988), with Procedure Supplement (1991)

Robert M. Cover, late Professor of Law, Yale Law School.
Owen M. Fiss, Professor of Law, Yale Law School.
Judith Resnik, Professor of Law, University of Southern California Law Center.

PROCEDURE—CIVIL PROCEDURE, Sixth Edition (1990), with 1991 Supplement

Richard H. Field, late Professor of Law, Harvard University.
Benjamin Kaplan, Professor of Law Emeritus, Harvard University.
Kevin M. Clermont, Professor of Law, Cornell University.

PROCEDURE—CIVIL PROCEDURE, Fifth Edition (1990)

Maurice Rosenberg, Professor of Law, Columbia University.
Hans Smit, Professor of Law, Columbia University.
Rochelle C. Dreyfuss, Professor of Law, New York University.

PROCEDURE—PLEADING AND PROCEDURE: State and Federal, Sixth Edition (1989), with 1990 Case Supplement

David W. Louisell, late Professor of Law, University of California, Berkeley.
Geoffrey C. Hazard, Jr., Professor of Law, Yale University.
Colin C. Tait, Professor of Law, University of Connecticut.

PROCEDURE—FEDERAL RULES OF CIVIL PROCEDURE, 1991 Edition

PRODUCTS LIABILITY AND SAFETY, Second Edition, (1989), with 1989 Statutory Supplement

W. Page Keeton, Professor of Law, University of Texas.
David G. Owen, Professor of Law, University of South Carolina.
John E. Montgomery, Professor of Law, University of South Carolina.
Michael D. Green, Professor of Law, University of Iowa

PROFESSIONAL RESPONSIBILITY, Fifth Edition (1991), with 1991 Selected Standards on Professional Responsibility Supplement

Thomas D. Morgan, Professor of Law, George Washington University.
Ronald D. Rotunda, Professor of Law, University of Illinois.

PROPERTY, Sixth Edition (1990)

John E. Cribbet, Professor of Law, University of Illinois.
Corwin W. Johnson, Professor of Law, University of Texas.
Roger W. Findley, Professor of Law, University of Illinois.
Ernest E. Smith, Professor of Law, University of Texas.

PROPERTY—PERSONAL (1953)

S. Kenneth Skolfield, late Professor of Law Emeritus, Boston University.

PROPERTY—PERSONAL, Third Edition (1954)

Everett Fraser, late Dean of the Law School Emeritus, University of Minnesota.
Third Edition by Charles W. Taintor, late Professor of Law, University of Pittsburgh.

UNIVERSITY CASEBOOK SERIES—Continued

PROPERTY—INTRODUCTION, TO REAL PROPERTY, Third Edition (1954)

Everett Fraser, late Dean of the Law School Emeritus, University of Minnesota.

PROPERTY—FUNDAMENTALS OF MODERN REAL PROPERTY, Second Edition (1982), with 1985 Supplement

Edward H. Rabin, Professor of Law, University of California, Davis.

PROPERTY, REAL (1984), with 1988 Supplement

Paul Goldstein, Professor of Law, Stanford University.

PROSECUTION AND ADJUDICATION, Fourth Edition (1991)

Reprint of Chapters 11–26 of Miller, Dawson, Dix and Parnas's CRIMINAL JUSTICE ADMINISTRATION, Fourth Edition.

PSYCHIATRY AND LAW, see Mental Health, see also Hinckley, Trial of

PUBLIC UTILITY LAW, see Free Enterprise, also Regulated Industries

REAL ESTATE PLANNING, Third Edition (1989), with Revised Problem and Statutory Supplement (1991)

Norton L. Steuben, Professor of Law, University of Colorado.

REAL ESTATE TRANSACTIONS, Revised Second Edition (1988), with Statute, Form and Problem Supplement (1988)

Paul Goldstein, Professor of Law, Stanford University.

RECEIVERSHIP AND CORPORATE REORGANIZATION, see Creditors' Rights

REGULATED INDUSTRIES, Second Edition, (1976)

William K. Jones, Professor of Law, Columbia University.

REMEDIES, Second Edition (1987)

Edward D. Re, Chief Judge, U. S. Court of International Trade.

REMEDIES, (1989)

Elaine W. Shoben, Professor of Law, University of Illinois.
Wm. Murray Tabb, Professor of Law, Baylor University.

SALES, Second Edition (1986)

Marion W. Benfield, Jr., Professor of Law, University of Illinois.
William D. Hawkland, Chancellor, Louisiana State Law Center.

SALES AND SALES FINANCING, Fifth Edition (1984)

John Honnold, Professor of Law, University of Pennsylvania.

SALES LAW AND THE CONTRACTING PROCESS, Second Edition (1991)

(Reprinted from Commercial Transactions, Second Edition (1991)
Alan Schwartz, Professor of Law, Yale University.
Robert E. Scott, Professor of Law, University of Virginia.

SECURED TRANSACTIONS IN PERSONAL PROPERTY, Second Edition (1987) (Reprinted from COMMERCIAL LAW, Second Edition (1987))

Robert L. Jordan, Professor of Law, University of California, Los Angeles.
William D. Warren, Professor of Law, University of California, Los Angeles.

SECURITIES REGULATION, Sixth Edition (1987), with 1990 Selected Statutes, Rules and Forms Supplement and 1990 Cases and Releases Supplement

Richard W. Jennings, Professor of Law, University of California, Berkeley.
Harold Marsh, Jr., Member of California Bar.

SECURITIES REGULATION, Second Edition (1988), with Statute, Rule and Form Supplement (1988)

Larry D. Soderquist, Professor of Law, Vanderbilt University.

SECURITY INTERESTS IN PERSONAL PROPERTY, Second Edition (1987)

Douglas G. Baird, Professor of Law, University of Chicago.
Thomas H. Jackson, Dean of the Law School, University of Virginia.

SECURITY INTERESTS IN PERSONAL PROPERTY (1985) (Reprinted from Sales and Sales Financing, Fifth Edition)

John Honnold, Professor of Law, University of Pennsylvania.

SELECTED STANDARDS ON PROFESSIONAL RESPONSIBILITY, 1991 Edition

SELECTED STATUTES AND INTERNATIONAL AGREEMENTS ON UNFAIR COMPETITION, TRADEMARK, COPYRIGHT AND PATENT, 1989 Edition

SELECTED STATUTES ON TRUSTS AND ESTATES, 1991 Edition

SOCIAL RESPONSIBILITIES OF LAWYERS, Case Studies (1988)

Philip B. Heymann, Professor of Law, Harvard University.
Lance Liebman, Professor of Law, Harvard University.

SOCIAL SCIENCE IN LAW, Second Edition (1990)

John Monahan, Professor of Law, University of Virginia.
Laurens Walker, Professor of Law, University of Virginia.

TAXATION, FEDERAL INCOME (1989)

Stephen B. Cohen, Professor of Law, Georgetown University

TAXATION, FEDERAL INCOME, Second Edition (1988), with 1990 Supplement (Supplement edited in association with Deborah H. Schenk, Professor of Law, New York University)

Michael J. Graetz, Professor of Law, Yale University.

TAXATION, FEDERAL INCOME, Seventh Edition (1991)

James J. Freeland, Professor of Law, University of Florida.
Stephen A. Lind, Professor of Law, University of Florida and University of California, Hastings.
Richard B. Stephens, late Professor of Law Emeritus, University of Florida.

TAXATION, FEDERAL INCOME, Successor Edition (1986), with 1991 Legislative Supplement

Stanley S. Surrey, late Professor of Law, Harvard University.
Paul R. McDaniel, Professor of Law, Boston College.
Hugh J. Ault, Professor of Law, Boston College.
Stanley A. Koppelman, Professor of Law, Boston University.

TAXATION, FEDERAL INCOME, OF BUSINESS ORGANIZATIONS (1991)

Paul R. McDaniel, Professor of Law, Boston College.
Hugh J. Ault, Professor of Law, Boston College.
Martin J. McMahon, Jr., Professor of Law, University of Kentucky.
Daniel L. Simmons, Professor of Law, University of California, Davis.

TAXATION, FEDERAL INCOME, OF PARTNERSHIPS AND S CORPORATIONS (1991)

Paul R. McDaniel, Professor of Law, Boston College.
Hugh J. Ault, Professor of Law, Boston College.
Martin J. McMahon, Jr., Professor of Law, University of Kentucky.
Daniel L. Simmons, Professor of Law, University of California, Davis.

TAXATION, FEDERAL INCOME, OIL AND GAS, NATURAL RESOURCES TRANSACTIONS (1990)

Peter C. Maxfield, Professor of Law, University of Wyoming.
James L. Houghton, CPA, Partner, Ernst and Young.
James R. Gaar, CPA, Partner, Ernst and Young.

TAXATION, FEDERAL WEALTH TRANSFER, Successor Edition (1987)

Stanley S. Surrey, late Professor of Law, Harvard University.
Paul R. McDaniel, Professor of Law, Boston College.
Harry L. Gutman, Professor of Law, University of Pennsylvania.

TAXATION, FUNDAMENTALS OF CORPORATE, Third Edition (1991)

Stephen A. Lind, Professor of Law, University of Florida and University of California, Hastings.
Stephen Schwarz, Professor of Law, University of California, Hastings.
Daniel J. Lathrope, Professor of Law, University of California, Hastings.
Joshua Rosenberg, Professor of Law, University of San Francisco. .

TAXATION, FUNDAMENTALS OF PARTNERSHIP, Second Edition (1988)

Stephen A. Lind, Professor of Law, University of Florida and University of California, Hastings.
Stephen Schwarz, Professor of Law, University of California, Hastings.
Daniel J. Lathrope, Professor of Law, University of California, Hastings.
Joshua Rosenberg, Professor of Law, University of San Francisco.

TAXATION OF CORPORATIONS AND THEIR SHAREHOLDERS (1991)

David J. Shakow, Professor of Law, University of Pennsylvania.

TAXATION, PROBLEMS IN THE FEDERAL INCOME TAXATION OF PARTNER-SHIPS AND CORPORATIONS, Second Edition (1986)

Norton L. Steuben, Professor of Law, University of Colorado.
William J. Turnier, Professor of Law, University of North Carolina.

TAXATION, PROBLEMS IN THE FUNDAMENTALS OF FEDERAL INCOME, Second Edition (1985)

Norton L. Steuben, Professor of Law, University of Colorado.
William J. Turnier, Professor of Law, University of North Carolina.

TORT LAW AND ALTERNATIVES, Fourth Edition (1987)

Marc A. Franklin, Professor of Law, Stanford University.
Robert L. Rabin, Professor of Law, Stanford University.

TORTS, Eighth Edition (1988)

William L. Prosser, late Professor of Law, University of California, Hastings.
John W. Wade, Professor of Law, Vanderbilt University.
Victor E. Schwartz, Adjunct Professor of Law, Georgetown University.

TORTS, Third Edition (1976)

Harry Shulman, late Dean of the Law School, Yale University.
Fleming James, Jr., Professor of Law Emeritus, Yale University.
Oscar S. Gray, Professor of Law, University of Maryland.

TRADE REGULATION, Third Edition (1990)

Milton Handler, Professor of Law Emeritus, Columbia University.
Harlan M. Blake, Professor of Law, Columbia University.
Robert Pitofsky, Professor of Law, Georgetown University.
Harvey J. Goldschmid, Professor of Law, Columbia University.

TRADE REGULATION, see Antitrust

TRANSNATIONAL BUSINESS PROBLEMS (1986)

Detlev F. Vagts, Professor of Law, Harvard University.

TRANSNATIONAL LEGAL PROBLEMS, Third Edition (1986) with 1991 Revised Edition of Documentary Supplement

Henry J. Steiner, Professor of Law, Harvard University.
Detlev F. Vagts, Professor of Law, Harvard University.

TRIAL, see also Evidence, Making the Record, Lawyering Process and Preparing and Presenting the Case

TRUSTS, Sixth Edition (1991)

George G. Bogert, late Professor of Law Emeritus, University of Chicago.
Dallin H. Oaks, President, Brigham Young University.
H. Reese Hansen, Dean and Professor of Law, Brigham Young University.
Claralyn Martin Hill, J.D. Brigham Young University.

TRUSTS AND ESTATES, SELECTED STATUTES ON, 1991 Edition

TRUSTS AND WILLS, See also Decedents' Estates and Trusts, and Family Property Law

UNFAIR COMPETITION, see Competitive Process and Business Torts

WATER RESOURCE MANAGEMENT, Third Edition (1988)

The late Charles J. Meyers, formerly Dean, Stanford University Law School.
A. Dan Tarlock, Professor of Law, IIT Chicago-Kent College of Law.
James N. Corbridge, Jr., Chancellor, University of Colorado at Boulder, and Professor of Law, University of Colorado.
David H. Getches, Professor of Law, University of Colorado.

WILLS AND ADMINISTRATION, Fifth Edition (1961)

Philip Mechem, late Professor of Law, University of Pennsylvania.
Thomas E. Atkinson, late Professor of Law, New York University.

WRITING AND ANALYSIS IN THE LAW, Second Edition (1991)

Helene S. Shapo, Professor of Law, Northwestern University
Marilyn R. Walter, Professor of Law, Brooklyn Law School
Elizabeth Fajans, Writing Specialist, Brooklyn Law School

University Casebook Series

EDITORIAL BOARD

FOOD AND DRUG LAW

Cases and Materials

SECOND EDITION

By

PETER BARTON HUTT
Covington & Burling, Washington, D.C.

and

RICHARD A. MERRILL
Albert C. Tate, Jr. Professor of Law, University of Virginia

New York, New York
FOUNDATION PRESS
1991

COPYRIGHT © 1980 FOUNDATION PRESS
COPYRIGHT © 1991 By FOUNDATION PRESS

        395 Hudson Street
        New York, NY 10014
        Phone Toll Free 1–877–888–1330
        Fax (212) 367–6799
        fdpress.com

Library of Congress Cataloging-in-Publication Data

Hutt, Peter Barton, 1934–
    Food and drug law : cases and materials / by Peter Barton Hutt and
Richard A. Merrill. — 2nd ed.
      p.   cm. — (University casebook series)
    Includes index.
    ISBN 0-88277-863-3
    1. Food law and legislation—United States—Cases. 2. Drugs—Law
and legislation—United States—Cases. I. Merrill, Richard A.
II. Title. III. Series.
KF3868.F66 1991
344.73'04232—dc20
[347.3044232]   91–8967

6th Reprint — 2001

Dedicated to
Louise Fraser Hutt
and
Elizabeth D. Merrill

And to the thousands of dedicated women and men who
have worked at the
Food and Drug Administration since its creation

*

PREFACE TO THE 1980 EDITION

Food and drug law is a long-recognized specialized field of legal practice and the oldest arena of federal consumer protection legislation. The Food and Drugs Act of 1906, with the Meat Inspection Act of the same year, comprised Congress' first major efforts to protect consumers legislatively. The 1906 Act predated by nearly a decade creation of the Federal Trade Commission and by a full half-century the establishment of other agencies—such as the Environmental Protection Agency and the Consumer Product Safety Commission—that have a consumer protection role. Thus, lawyers have been involved advising or representing private clients and government officials on food and drug law questions from the early days of this century.

Notwithstanding this comparatively ancient lineage, until the 1970's food and drug law did not command the attention of a large number of laywers. It has been taught in only a few law schools, and only recently has it begun to generate substantial serious scholarship. The small number of practitioners can be attributed to the geographic concentration of the practice in two or three cities and to the comparatively modest resources of the Food and Drug Administration. The inattention paid by the law school community, we suspect, is a function also of earlier failure to recognize the richness of the issues presented by government regulation of these important consumer products.

Food and drug law deals with government's attempts to protect public health and individual welfare in the development and marketing of essential commodities. The scope of these commercial activities is impressive. On any day few Americans escape exposure to drugs or cosmetics, and all of us require food. By a rough estimate, more than 25 cents of every consumer dollar is spent for products that fall within the categories regulated by FDA. But it is not only the personal and economic importance of the products FDA controls that justifies serious study of the process and substance of food and drug regulation. The subject merits, and now receives, the attention of students and scholars for additional reasons.

First, FDA's continuing efforts to come to grips with its regulatory responsibilities comprise a mini-history of American administrative law. . . .   Many judicial decisions that are accepted as part of the corpus of administrative law have involved FDA. FDA has been responsible for major innovations in administrative procedure, and in the agency's experience one can discern the intimate interrelationship between administrative procedure and regulatory substance. In short, the subject provides an excellent vehicle for understanding the American administrative process.

Second, over the past two decades regulation of food, drugs, and related products has presented some of the most challenging illustrations of the tense interplay between law and science. FDA has been at the forefront of government efforts to identify, evaluate, and control human exposure to potentially harmful substances. This responsibility, extending well beyond implementation of the famous Delaney Clause, has forced it to determine the reliability of animal test results, explore the limits of techniques for chemical analysis, and evaluate modern biostatistical methods for estimating human risk. The agency was the first to grapple with the threat of skin cancer posed by fluorocarbon reduction of the ozone layer. It has been involved in some of the most controversial issues of preventive medicine, such as the swine flu immunization program, and in development of medical technology, such as computerized tomographic (or CT) scanning. And as government has assumed an increasing share of the cost of medical care, FDA has become a quality control expert for public health care programs.

Third, because of the growing complexity of its responsibilities and the potential clash between public objectives, FDA has also been forced to experiment with a wide variety of innovative administrative procedures for deciding controversial law-science issues. It has been the first federal agency to use a "science court" model for decisionmaking. It has been one of the most successful at exploiting the scientific expertise of advisors from the academic community—and in the process grappled with the constraints of federal conflict of interest legislation and faced accusations that it was abdicating its responsibility. And FDA has experimented with various approaches to trade-off analysis, ranging across the spectrum of cost-effectiveness, cost-benefit, and risk-benefit formulations.

Finally, and not unimportantly, we find the story of federal efforts to regulate the marketing of foods and drugs fascinating as history. The creation and experience of any regulatory agency undoubtedly mirrors strong political and economic currents, but few other agencies regulate products or activities that play so intimate a role in the lives of citizens. The visibility of foods and drugs, the concern of individuals for their health, and the expectations they have for those charged with protecting them, have made FDA a resonant amplifier of American social history.

No single volume can capture all of these facets of FDA regulation. We do not pretend to have compiled either a text on administrative law or a history of the American market for consumer goods. This is a coursebook in food and drug law, intended primarily for law students. The materials included, the organization used, and the issues dealt with reflect this focus. We hope that the book will also prove useful in teaching students and professionals in other fields, such as nutrition, medicine, and public administration. We also believe that the book will be helpful to practitioners of food and drug law. In most instances the statutes referred to and the cases reproduced reflect legal requirements prevailing in 1980. The changes in this field, however, are so rapid that no coursebook can provide the sort of coverage of FDA requirements that a practitioner could confidently rely upon to the exclusion of other, more current, sources. Our organization of materials and bibliographic assistance should help frame the pertinent questions and identify many of the relevant sources, but no careful lawyer should fail to consult the standard legal publications that can provide the most current coverage.

Selection of Materials

A variety of considerations have influenced our selection of primary materials, which consist mainly of four types: judicial opinions; documents published in the Federal Register, including notices, proposed regulations, final regulations, and other final orders; articles from legal and other journals; and congressional sources, including reports of the General Accounting Office (GAO) and the Office of Technology Assessment (OTA). Obviously, economy of space is one important criterion in the choice of material to explain a subject or illuminate issues. A major problem for the editors of course materials in any regulatory field is the sheer volume of printed pages available. Legal requirements for regulatory agencies to be more explicit in explaining decisions and to analyze a growing range of effects of regulatory actions, such as those on the environment and economy, have generated a paperwork burden for scholars and practitioners alike. The difficulty is not simply that there are more words to read and evaluate, but that it is increasingly difficult to capture the reality of the regulatory process without reproducing materials in the same quantities the participants are accustomed to encountering them. The most authentic course materials in administrative law may not be bound between two covers but are probably cramped into a four-drawer file cabinet or a shelf of looseleaf binders.

Judicial opinions, too often maligned as teaching materials, provide one way of responding to this problem. The opinions of conscientious judges engaged in reviewing administrative action are often the best summaries of the labyrinthine proceedings and complex factual issues underlying a regulator's decisions. In many of them the judge has had to condense the entire history in order to determine how the case should be decided. In the food and drug field, moreover, there is another important reason to feature judicial decisions. Until perhaps 1970, most substantive law was reflected in court rulings. From the earliest days of federal regulation of food and drugs until the last decade, FDA relied mainly on court enforcement of loosely defined statutory standards to make new law. Furthermore, because the risk of adverse publicity provides a powerful incentive for most manufacturers of food and drugs, ground-breaking judicial decisons have generated both immediate interest and a high degree of voluntary compliance. Thus, in many areas, the substance of food and drug law is expressed in a series of well-accepted judicial precedents.

In the last decade FDA's regulatory style has changed. Confronted with a growing number of firms making regulated products and increasingly complex substantive issues, FDA has turned toward rulemaking as the principle technique for explaining and defining legal requirements. Most of the major issues that confronted FDA in the 1970's it attempted to resolve through administrative, rather than court, action. Thus the Federal Register has become the primary vehicle for official discussion and resolution of food and drug problems. Accordingly, we have included numerous excerpts from this source, now the principal "library" of both regulators and private practitioners.

Our use of congressional materials cannot be explained in terms of economy, for committee reports and particularly hearing records tend to be prolix and unfocused. But they can be useful summaries of problems and, more important, they reflect legislative perceptions that significantly influence FDA officials and, thus, the firms whose products the agency regulates. This influence, if anything, increased during the 1970's. One seeking to understand the focus and intensity of FDA regulation during this period must appreciate the impact of congressional action in considering new legislation and overseeing enforcement of existing laws.

Throughout the book, in addition to primary original sources, we have included detailed Notes. These have multiple objectives. The Notes attempt, first, to bring the reader up to date on a subject and supply historical background missing from primary sources. Second, they raise questions about the policies reflected in agency decisions or judicial rulings. And third, the Notes attempt to provide bibliographic assistance to the reader who wishes to pursue a subject in depth. Our listings of secondary sources, though often lengthy, are only illustrative. Our listings of Federal Register documents are intended to . . . permit the reader to trace the development of regulatory policy from its inception.

The full text of the Federal Food, Drug, and Cosmetic Act of 1938, 21 U.S.C. §§ 301 *et seq.* (the Act or FD&C Act), currently the governing federal statute in this area, and other statutes referred to in the book, are reproduced separately in a paperback supplement. . . . .

PREFACE TO THE 1991 EDITION

Any authors who allow eleven years to elapse between editions of a casebook owe their readers some explanation. We will absolve ourselves by saying simply that other matters have claimed our attention. Still a sense of guilt has led us to search for advantages in so long a hiatus, and we believe there are some real ones. First, the passage of time may allow greater objectivity in our assessment of policies that we once had a hand in formulating. Furthermore, 1991 affords a better vantage from which to anticipate the direction of food and drug regulation in the last decade of the 20th century than would, say, 1985, and lapse of a full decade surely permits a richer account of this important field of government activity.

To be entirely candid, however, we resumed work on this book with a sense that not much had happened since the 1980 edition was published. We felt confident that our basic structure was sound, and that view has not changed. But we also believed that there would be relatively little new material to add. We could think of only a handful of cases we would excerpt, rather than merely cite. The Reagan Administration's efforts to curb the issuance of regulations meant that the Federal Register would provide a thinner vein to mine for material. And the policy issues that drew public attention during the 1980s seemed at first glance to represent continuations of old stories. But the work of preparing this second edition yielded much more of interest and importance than we had anticipated, and convinced us that a second edition was indeed overdue.

Despite changes in the political climate and some loss of organizational independence, FDA has lost no importance since the first edition was published. Public interest in the agency's work and its performance has never been higher. Challenges to the safety of foods (remember EDB and Alar?), concerns over the testing and approval of drugs to treat AIDS and other much less common diseases, mounting commercial interest in uses of biotechnology to produce new foods and therapeutic and diagnostic agents, and scandals in the review and approval of generic drugs—to mention only a few issues of the 1980s—have kept the agency busy and, if anything, heightened appreciation of its critical role in consumer protection. Happily, public awareness of FDA's responsibilities was not accompanied by a loss of confidence in its ability to perform them. Gallup Poll surveys at the end of the decade showed no significant decline in public admiration for the agency. What did trouble many observers was the slow erosion of its budget, and consequent reduction in the agency's workforce during a period of rising expectations.

The growth in expectations for FDA could be dramatized by listing the crises it faced during the 1980s—which typically generated demands that it more effectively or more rigorously enforce the authorities that Congress had already delegated to the agency. But unlike the 1970s when the Medical Devices Amendments of 1976 provided the agency's only new powers, the decade of the 1980s witnessed several significant legislative additions to the agency's responsibilities. Between 1980 and 1990, Congress enacted 26 laws enlarging FDA's duties. These included the establishment of standards for infant formulas, the identification of promising therapies for rare diseases, the accelerated approval of generic drugs and identification of those therapies whose patents should be extended, the first revision of food labeling requirements since 1938, and substantial refinements of the medical device provisions, to mention just a few. Occasionally FDA was given additional resources and personnel to handle the new responsibilities; more often, it was asked to take on new chores with the same, or often fewer, resources.

Many of these themes are explored in detail in the pages that follow. We identify them here simply to demonstrate, if demonstration is needed, that the issues involved in regulating food, drugs, medical devices, and related technologies for which FDA has responsibility are, if anything, more interesting and challenging in 1990 than they were a decade ago. It seems clear that legal practice in this field has grown and become more complex. We are also pleased that more law schools are offering courses that deal with Federal regulation of food and drugs. The challenge facing us as we began work on this revised edition was to encompass both the fascinating history of the field and the excitement of contemporary problems within a volume of reasonable length.

We should reemphasize that we have not made major changes in the basic structure of the 1980 edition, which, like this one, consisted mainly of chapters dealing with more or less discrete product categories regulated by FDA. All of the original ten chapters are included. Several of these chapters reflect restructuring. Perhaps Chapters II and III, dealing with food and with drugs, have undergone the most significant change as we sought a more easily understood analytic structure, at some sacrifice of our illustration of the historical evolution of FDA policy. Chapter VI, on devices, includes much new material as we have fleshed out the account of FDA's implementation of the 1976 Medical Device Amendments, an activity really just beginning as the first edition went to press.

The most significant additions, however, are two new chapters. Chapter VIII deals, largely in historical sequence, with FDA's efforts to frame a policy for regulating carcinogens—substances shown to cause cancer in animals but not yet associated, and perhaps never associatable, with cancer in humans. In this important field, FDA policy evolved centrally, if not always coherently. What one part of the agency decided directly and sometimes profoundly influenced what other parts thought and did. And each important decision, e.g., about how to estimate human risk from animal data, clearly reflected earlier actions, and influenced those soon to follow. Furthermore, in this area perhaps more than any other, FDA has influenced practice in other agencies and has worked with sister agencies to develop common approaches. Since 1978 Presidents and their science advisors have sought to exert some centralizing control over decisionmaking about carcinogens by the agencies chiefly involved—EPA, OSHA, USDA, CPSC, as well as FDA. A historical account of FDA's evolving approach thus seemed potentially appropriate.

We had another goal in the creation of new Chapter VIII, which draws material from several of our original ten chapters, notably those dealing with food, animal drugs, and cosmetics. FDA's struggle to regulate carcinogens in the shadow of the Delaney Clause illustrates the influence and evolution of quantitative risk assessment in the regulation of environmental carcinogens generally. FDA's efforts to devise a coherent policy is a microcosm of the broader, less cohesive efforts that preoccupied federal health regulators for the entire decade of the 1980s.

Our second new chapter deals with biotechnology. It examines the methods and commercial promise of "gene splicing" techniques for producing conventional FDA-regulated products and explores some of the challenges for FDA presented by the use of recombinant DNA methods in the production of new foods (e.g., a tomato containing its own insecticide) or the achievement of previously unachievable therapeutic and diagnostic objectives. Rather than an account of a history like Chapter VIII, new Chapter IX is an introduction to FDA's dealings with the newest science.

In most other respects, the second edition resembles the first, although it is, with the assent of the publisher, a good deal longer. We have reedited some cases and other excerpts to omit *less* material from the original, and we have added a good deal of new material. Much of the new material is from official sources, such as GAO reports, NAS studies, and legislative documents. There are relatively few new cases because relatively few important new cases were decided during the 1980s.

There were even fewer major new regulations, and this departure from the pattern established in the 1970s deserves some comment. One might speculate that by 1980 FDA longtimers had grown tired of the pace of new regulations and impatient with making policy through rulemaking rather than enforcement. It could also be said that many of FDA's regulations were relatively fresh, and that implementation rather than formulation of policy properly claimed the attention of agency managers. Whether either of these explanations has any power, however, it is clear that more important forces slowed the development of regulations generally, and altered the content of those that did emerge.

Most significantly, Ronald Reagan's election as President commenced a decade of increased executive control over agencies exercising regulatory authority. While active White House oversight of agency rulemaking began in the Ford and Carter Administrations, President Reagan's issuance of Executive Order 12291 on February 17, 1981, marked a new era for FDA and other executive branch agencies. Agency regulations have thereafter confronted an additional, formidable obstacle in the form of OMB review. Almost as important from FDA's perspective was the contemporaneous decision by HHS Secretary Richard Schweiker to withdraw the agency's authority to propose and promulgate regulations without departmental approval. For several decades the FDA Commissioner, alone among subordinate officers of the Department, had exercised such authority and many observers, within and outside the agency, believed it provided essential assurance of FDA's independence—or at least insulation—from partisan politics. Whether or not this perception was accurate, FDA's need after 1981 to convince the Secretary's staff of the need for, or wisdom of, each important rule undoubtedly slowed, and in some cases clearly frustrated, the development of new regulations. For the authors of the "Reagan Revolution," of course, this was the intended, wholly benign result.

Citation Format

Though our citation forms generally follow the current edition of the "Blue Book," *A Uniform System of Citation* (16th ed. 1988), as in the first edition we have adopted some distinctive practices of our own, sometimes to save space that would be wasted if we endlessly repeated the prescribed form.

As before, all of our statutory references are to sections of the 1938 FD&C Act, as amended, or to sections of other laws as enacted, such as the Public Health Service Act, and not to the United States Code. We have not, however, substituted statutory references for Code citations in original sources, such as judicial opinions. Determining the proper U.S. Code citation for most sections of the FD&C Act is straightforward. By dropping the middle digit and inserting a "3" in front of the two digits remaining, one can usually derive the U.S.C. section. For example, section 401 of the Act is codified as 21 U.S.C. § 341.

We have again used certain short forms for sources that are cited frequently. Thus, we use "FDC L.J." to denote works published in the Food, Drug, Cosmetic Law Journal, the periodical in which many of the articles published in this field have appeared. "OTA" is our routine description for the Office of Technology Assessment of the U.S. Congress, and "GAO" is our colloquial, as well as official, reference to the U.S. Government Accounting Office.

Another departure from form is our inclusion of the month and day as well as the year in all citations to the Federal Register. This additional information can be helpful in locating a document in both printed and microform volumes of the Register. And our practice allows the reader to discern temporal connections between formal regulatory announcements and related scientific discoveries or political events.

In citations accompanying principal cases and other materials that form primary readings, we pay only lip service to Blue Book form, preferring instead either the customary form of Foundation Press (for cases) or our own style for such sources as the Federal Register. In no case, however, do we omit material that the Blue Book would require. Our references to books and articles and legislative materials likewise betray small departures from form, chiefly in typography.

In quoted original sources, such as cases, we have routinely omitted citations and footnotes without any notation in the text. Footnotes included retain their original numbering. We have also omitted, again without notation, most organizational designations, such as headings and paragraph numbers. With one exception, all omissions of text are disclosed by elipses appearing in the middle, or as appropriate, at the end of sentences or paragraphs. Three elipses at the end of a paragraph denote the omission of the balance of that paragraph. Four elipses at the end of a paragraph denote the omission of at least one full paragraph, and on occasion omissions from the paragraph itself. Paragraphs omitted from the beginning of an excerpted source, however, are not noted. As in 1980, errors in spelling or grammar in original Federal Register documents are corrected without notation because they are routinely corrected by the Office of the Federal Register in subsequent issues or when published in the Code of Federal Regulations. Errors in other original sources are denoted by [sic], in the conventional fashion.

Disclosure of Interests

In the 1980 edition of this book, our obligation to users led us to draw attention to our prior service as successive Chief Counsels to the Food and Drug Administration. Mr. Hutt served from 1971 to 1975; Mr. Merrill succeeded him and served until 1977. Our concern then was that our involvement in, and no doubt intellectual attachment to, many of the policies adopted and defended by FDA during the 1970s might influence our assessment of their merits. In any case, we believed that readers were entitled to know about our backgrounds so they could judge for themselves whether we had fairly depicted the agency's history.

In 1990 such disclosures might seem less important, for neither of us has had any official responsibility for fashioning or defending any FDA policy or decision for more than a dozen years. But we have retained this revised disclosure statement for two reasons. First, many of the policies framed during our adjacent periods of service remain firmly in place while others are undergoing reassessment. Second, in the intervening period each of us had more than a few occasions, as authors, as members of advisory groups assembled to review and critique food and drug regulatory policies, and, in Mr. Hutt's case, as a regular advisor to firms regulated by FDA to take positions in support of, or adverse to, those adopted by FDA. Accordingly, we have no better claim to recognition as detached observers of food and drug regulation today than we had in 1980; at most we can hope to be considered fair and complete in our efforts to illustrate the issues FDA has confronted and the solutions it has attempted to implement.

Appreciation

As in 1980, we owe a considerable debt to several former and current University of Virginia law students who helped us assemble and edit these materials. The contribution to the first edition of Robert Ewers, '81, still merits mention because the book he worked on comprises the core of this one. More recently, Michael Beverly, Mary Dunbar, Charles Durant, Jill Gillenwater, Laura Gillespie, Virginia Griffin, Robyne Lau, Tony Lim, and John Palmer aided us in preparing the current manuscript. Jim Czaban of the Class of '92 and Karen Rosenthal of the Class of '93 provided the critical help during the final months of preparation and earned our special thanks. Two Covington & Burling paralegals, Marilynn Whitney, who was with us originally, and Katherine MacRae, discovered and helped organize materials that cannot be found in conventional libraries. The founding librarian of the Food and Drug Library at Covington & Burling, Meg Gleason, and the current librarian, Dorothy Donahoe, have facilitated our work by maintaining the country's most comprehensive collection of food and drug law materials in easily accessible form. The typing of the 1600-page manuscript was done at Covington & Burling by Beth Vida and Carol Gibson, and at the University of Virginia School of Law by Madeline Branch, Cathy Burton, Evelyn Gray, and Leslie Yowell. Ms. Branch is due our special appreciation because she helped type the first edition and has labored with this project almost as long as we have.

Professor Merrill was supported in his work on this edition by the generosity of the donors to the Albert C. Tate, Jr. Professorship of Law at the University of Virginia, including Mrs. Elvira Tate, Mr. Lurton Massee, Jr., and partners of the law firm of Kilpatrick & Cody.

Once again, we express fond appreciation to our patient and forgiving wives, Ellie Hutt and Lissa Merrill.

PETER BARTON HUTT
Washington, D.C.

RICHARD A. MERRILL
Charlottesville, Virginia

ACKNOWLEDGEMENTS

We acknowledge the courtesy of the following publishers, journals, law reviews, and authors who have permitted us to reprint excerpts from their publications:

(1) Food Drug Cosmetic Law Journal and the Food and Drug Law Institute, which gave us blanket permission to reproduce or quote from articles appearing in the Journal, and to whom we owe a special debt of thanks.

(2) Annual Review of Nutrition: Hutt, *Government Regulation of the Integrity of the Food Supply*, 4 Annual Review of Nutrition 1 (1984).

(3) Association of Food and Drug Officials: Austern, *Federalism in Consumer Protection: Conflict or Coordination?*, 29 Q. Bull. A. of Food & Drug Off. 148 (1965); Hutt, *FDA Court Actions and Recent Legal Developments*, 39 Q. Bull. A. of Food & Drug Off. 11 (1975); Hutt, *Public Information and Public Participation in the Food and Drug Administration*, 36 Q. Bull. A. of Food & Drug Off. 212 (1972); Miller, *The Saga of Chicken Little and Rambo*, 51 J.A. of Food & Drug Off. 196 (1987).

(4) Banbury Center: Fields, et al., eds., Genetically Altered Viruses and the Environment (Report No. 22, 1985).

(5) Business Lawyer: Goodrich, *The Coming Struggle Over Vitamin-Mineral Pills*, 20 Bus.Law. 145 (1964).

(6) Columbia Law Review: Merrill and Collier, *"Like Mother Used to Make": An Analysis of FDA Food Standards of Identity*, 74 Colum.L.Rev. 561 (1974).

(7) Cosmetic Toiletry and Fragrance Association Cosmetic Journal: Hutt, *Reconciling the Legal, Medical, and Cosmetic Chemist Approach to the Definition of a "Cosmetic,"* 3 CTFA Cosm.J., No. 3, 1971.

(8) Drug Information Journal: Mattison and Richard, *Post-Approval Research Requested by the FDA at the Time of NCE Approval, 1970–1984*, 21 Drug Info.J. 309 (1987).

(9) Federation of American Societies for Experimental Biology: A Review of Foods For Medical Purposes: Specially Formulated Products For Nutritional Management of Medical Conditions (June, 1977).

(10) Food Technology: Hutt, *Regulating the Misbranding of Food*, 43 Food Technology 288 (Sept., 1989).

(11) George Washington Law Review: Merrill, *Risk-Benefit Decision-Making by the Food and Drug Administration*, 45 Geo.Wash.L.Rev. 994 (1977).

ACKNOWLEDGEMENTS

(12) Georgetown Law Journal: Note, *Drug Efficacy and the 1962 Drug Amendments*, 60 Geo.L.J. 185 (1971).

(13) Harvard Law Review: *Developments in the Law—The Federal Food, Drug, and Cosmetic Act*, 67 Harv.L.Rev. 632 (1954).

(14) Health Scan: Hutt, *Landmark Pharmaceutical Law Enacted*, 1 Health Scan, No. 3 (1984).

(15) Kellogg Nutrition Foundation: Hutt, *Health Claims For Foods—An American Perspective*, Symposium 1986.

(16) Institute of Medicine: Computed Tomographic Scanning (1977); Their, *New Medical Devices and Health Care*, New Medical Devices: Invention, Development and Use (1988).

(17) Journal American Academy of Dermatology: Elder, *The Cosmetic Ingredient Review—A Safety Evaluation Program*, 11 J.Am.Acad. of Dermatology 1168 (1984).

(18) Journal of the Association of Analytical Chemists: Hutt, *The Importance of Analytical Chemistry to Food and Drug Regulation*, 68 J.A. of Analytical Chemists 147 (1985).

(19) Journal of Law and Economics: Temin, *The Origin of Compulsory Drug Prescriptions*, 22 J. of Law & Econ. 91 (1979).

(20) Journal of Public Law: Marquis, *Fair Packaging and Consumer Protection*, 18 J. of Public Law 61 (1969).

(21) Law and Contemporary Problems: Cavers, *The Food, Drug, and Cosmetic Act of 1938: Its Legislative History and Its Substantive Provisions*, 6 Law & Contemp. Probs. 2 (1939); Hayes & Ruff, *The Administration of the Federal Food and Drugs Act*, 1 Law & Contemp. Probs. 16 (1933).

(22) Legal Times of Washington: Hutt, *FDA Reduces Economic Regulation of Food Industry*, August 30, 1981; Hutt, *Laetrile Decision Ignores Constitutional Question*, July 2, 1979.

(23) National Academy Press: Olson, Biotechnology: An Industry Comes of Age (1986).

(24) National Research Council: Board on Agriculture, Designing Foods: Animal Product Options in the Marketplace (1988).

(25) New York Times: Kolata, *An Angry Response to Action on AIDS Spurs FDA Shift*, June 26, 1988.

(26) Saint Louis University Law Journal: Baynes, *Liability for Vaccine Related Injuries: Public Health Considerations and Some Reflections on the Swine Flu Experience*, 21 St. Louis U.L.J. 44 (1977).

(27) Science, copyright by the American Association for the Advancement of Science: Editorial, *Food Additives and Hyperactivity*, 199 Science 516 (1978); Mortimer, *Immunization Against Infectious Disease*, 200 Science 902 (1978); Wade, *Division of Biologics Standards: In the Matter of J. Anthony Morris*, 175 Science 861 (1972); Wade, *Divi-*

ACKNOWLEDGEMENTS

sion of Biologics Standards: Scientific Managements Questioned, 175 Science 966 (1972); Wade, *Division of Biologics Standards: The Boat That Never Rocked,* 175 Science 1225 (1972); Wade, *DBS: Agency Contravenes Its Own Regulations,* 176 Science 34 (1972); Wade, *Ice Cream: Dairymen Imperiled by FDA's Recipe,* 197 Science 844 (1977).

(28) George F. Stickley Company: Janssen, *The Gadgeteers,* chapter 16 of Barrett and Knight, The Health Robbers (1980).

(29) Syracuse Law Review: Comment, *The Federal Food, Drug and Cosmetic Act as an Experiment in Quality Control,* 20 Syracuse L.Rev. 883 (1969).

(30) Texas Law Review: Hamilton, *Rulemaking on a Record by the Food and Drug Administration,* 50 Tex.L.Rev. 1132 (1972).

(31) Time Magazine: *Drugs from the Underground,* July 10, 1989.

(32) Virginia Law Review: Merrill, *Compensation for Prescription Drug Injuries,* 59 Va.L.Rev. 1 (1973).

(33) Wall Street Journal: *How a PR Firm Executed the Alar Scare,* October 3, 1989.

(34) Washington Post: Kinsley, *The FDA: Too Cautious, Not Too Bold,* August 10, 1989; Russell, *Temporary Heart Implanted: Tucson Operation Lacked FDA Approval,* March 7, 1985; Specter, *Food Labels Often Light on Nutrition Information,* July 23, 1989.

(35) Yale Law Journal and Fred B. Rothman, Inc.: Note, *Federal Regulation of Deceptive Packaging: The Relevance of Technological Justifications,* 72 Yale L.J. 788 (1963).

*

SUMMARY OF CONTENTS

Appendices

*

TABLE OF CONTENTS

TABLE OF CONTENTS

TABLE OF CONTENTS

CHAPTER VII. COSMETICS

TABLE OF CONTENTS

TABLE OF CONTENTS

Appendices

TABLE OF CASES

Principal cases are in italic type. Non-principal cases are in roman type. References are to Pages.

lxix

*

FOOD AND DRUG LAW

Cases and Materials

*

Chapter I

HISTORICAL BACKGROUND

A. EARLY REGULATION OF FOOD AND DRUGS

PETER BARTON HUTT, GOVERNMENT REGULATION OF THE INTEGRITY OF THE FOOD SUPPLY

4 Annual Review of Nutrition 1 (1984).

For centuries, government has had an essential role in assuring the integrity of the food supply. The focus of the regulatory function has, of course, evolved over the years. It originated essentially as a means to protect against fraud in the marketplace. Very quickly, it expanded into a mechanism for preventing the sale of unsafe food. As the science of nutrition has developed, it has assumed the role of protecting the nutritional integrity of the food supply as well.....

Ancient Times ....

The first great botanical treatise on plants as a source of food and medicine, the *Enquiry Into Plants* written by Theophrastus (370–285 BC), reported on the use of artificial preservatives and flavors in the food supply even at that early date. Theophrastus noted that "even uncompounded substances have certain odors which men endeavor to assist by artificial means even as they assist nature in producing palatable tastes." He reported that items of commerce, such as balsam gum, were mixed with adulterants for economic reasons. The treatise *On Agriculture* by Cato (234–149 BC) recommended the addition to wine of boiled-down must, salt, marble dust, and resin, and included a method "to determine whether wine has been watered."

Pliny the Elder (23–79 AD) found widespread adulteration throughout the food supply. He described, for example, the adulteration of bread with chalk, vegetable meals, and even cattle fodder. He pointed out that pepper was commonly adulterated with juniper berries. Indeed, his *Natural History* is replete with so many references to adulteration of the natural food and drug supply that he observed: "So many poisons are employed to force wine to suit our taste—and we are surprised that it is not wholesome!" Pliny, describing "the remedies that are in the control of a man's will," stated that "the greatest aid to health is moderation in food." He urged the value of a kitchen garden for "harmless" market supplies. Galen (131–201 AD), a renowned Roman physician who followed the philosophical tradition of the School

1

of Hippocrates, similarly warned against the adulteration of common food products, such as pepper.....

The Roman civil law reflected the concern expressed by these early writers about preserving the integrity of the food supply. Fraud in the sale of merchandise not only gave rise to a private right of action, but also constituted the offense of *stellionatus,* which included the adulteration of food: "And, where anyone has substituted some article for another; or has put aside goods which he was obliged to deliver, or has spoiled them, he is also liable for this offense." Although *stellionatus* was technically not a crime, it was comparable to a civil offense under present law, subject to government prosecution, and resulted in such punishment as condemnation to the mines or temporary exile.

The English Experience, 1200–1875

... At the end of the Dark Ages ... concern about the food supply once again emerged. Nowhere is this more evident than in the experience reflected in the laws of England at that time.

Initial governmental concern came in the form of regulating the price of bread, and perhaps other staple food products as well. It did not take long for the English government to realize that the price of food could be regulated only in relation to the quality of that food. Accordingly, the early English regulatory statutes prohibited the adulteration of any staple food that was also subject to price controls.

These regulatory enactments, called assizes, were codified by Parliament in 1266. The 1266 statutes prohibited the sale of any "corrupted wine" or of any meat, fish, bread, or water that was "not wholesome for Man's body" or that was kept so long "that it loseth its natural wholesomeness." These laws, with periodic amendments, continued in effect throughout England until 1844. They were supplemented, from time to time, with additional statutes directed at other food commodities that became a source of commerce, such as butter, cheese, and spices.

In addition to the statutes enacted by Parliament, local cities enacted their own ordinances to prevent food adulteration. The judicially-created common law, reflecting the principles underlying the statutes and ordinances, created both a civil cause of action for damages for any aggrieved party, and a criminal offense as well. Numerous examples of early enforcement actions against the purveyors of adulterated food may be found in the records of the City of London.

Finally, the trade guilds ... also performed a major regulatory function. These guilds covered every important food category, including the bakers, butchers, cooks, grocers, fruiters, poulters, and salters. Using their power to search all premises and to seize all unwholesome products, the guilds exercised a relatively strong regulatory power in policing the marketing of food to the public.

The Development of Chemistry and the Accum Treatise

As the Renaissance emerged out of the Middle Ages, a few pioneers in the newly developing discipline of "chymistry" broke away from the philosophic mysticism of alchemy and initiated modern scientific inquiry. While earlier analyses of food adulteration depended almost completely upon taste and sight, the new science of chemistry, led particularly by Boyle, slowly began to develop chemical methods of analysis. . . . .

By the beginning of the 19th century . . . chemical analysis had advanced to the point where at least qualitative methods had become available for detecting many common food adulterants. In 1820, a German-born chemist, Frederick Accum, working in England, published his landmark *Treatise on Adulterations of Food and Culinary Poisons.* . . . Accum undertook to describe both the numerous kinds of adulteration practiced at that time and the various methods available to detect them. His treatise was an immediate and worldwide success. . . . The treatise spawned a generation of books on food adulteration in England, the United States, and Europe. Ultimately, it resulted in the modern era of food regulatory statutes.

. . . [T]he English Parliament enacted statutes in 1860, 1872, and 1875, replacing the assizes that had been repealed in 1844, to assure strong regulatory authority to protect the integrity of the food supply.

As would be expected, these English statutes reflect only the state of scientific, medical, and nutritional knowledge at that time. There is no specific mention in those statutes of nutrition. Instead, they broadly prohibited any form of food adulteration, thus assuring that food would reach the marketplace and the consumer in its natural and most nutritious state. Indeed, the prohibitions against adulteration contained in these statutes encompass the same prohibitions contained in our most modern food regulatory statutes, and were in fact the models for the 1906 and 1938 legislation enacted in the United States.

The American Experience

The people who settled in the American colonies brought with them the tradition of food regulation established in England. Early colonial laws were, indeed, indistinguishable from those that prevailed in England at the time. American common law similarly developed on the basis of English precedent.

The American Revolution did not change food regulation. Early state laws continued to follow the English law. As the United States emerged from a rural economy and urban centers developed that depended more heavily on commerce in food products, additional statutes and ordinances were enacted by cities, counties, and states to assure the integrity of those products. Following Lemuel Shattuck's landmark report on public health and sanitation in 1850, which urged the establishment of local boards of health to control, among other things, the wholesomeness of the food supply, the enactment of state laws accelerated in the last half of the 19th century.

Congress created a Department of Agriculture in 1862, and included within it a Division of Chemistry that was later to be the focal point for all food protection activities and for the initial departmental interest in nutrition. In 1883, Congress enacted its first specific food protection law, to prevent the importation of adulterated tea. This was followed in 1896 by the oleo-margarine statute and in the 1890s by laws intended to prevent the import or export of adulterated food.

Throughout the last quarter of the 19th century, however, there was a growing realization of the need for a truly comprehensive and national regulatory statute governing the food supply. Following the appointment of Dr. Harvey W. Wiley as Chief Chemist, the US Department of Agriculture issued a number of reports documenting in detail the widespread adulteration of common foods found in the marketplace. In 1906, Congress responded by enacting the Food and Drugs Act, the first federal statute broadly prohibiting the misbranding or adulteration of food.

NOTE

For detailed discussions of early food and drug laws, *see, e.g.,* Hart, *A History of the Adulteration of Food Before 1906,* 7 FDC L.J. 5 (1952); Hutt, *Criminal Prosecution for Adulteration and Misbranding of Food at Common Law,* 15 FDC L.J. 382 (1960); Hutt and Hutt II, *A History of Government Regulation of Adulteration and Misbranding of Food,* 39 FDC L.J. 2 (1984); Janssen, *America's First Food and Drug Laws,* 30 FDC L.J. 665 (1975).

B. STATUTORY AND INSTITUTIONAL HISTORY

1. THE FOOD AND DRUG ADMINISTRATION

The history of food and drug regulation in the United States is chronicled both in congressional enactments and in the development and growth of an institution, the Food and Drug Administration (FDA). The origins of FDA (and its predecessors) date from the creation of the U.S. Department of Agriculture (USDA) in 1862. Hutt, *A Historical Introduction,* 45 FDC L.J. 17 (1990), summarizes the institutional chronology:

YEARS	NAME	DEPARTMENT
1862–1890	Chemical Division	USDA
1890–1901	Division of Chemistry	USDA
1901–1927	Bureau of Chemistry	USDA
1927–1930	Food, Drug, and Insecticide Administration	USDA
1930–1940	Food and Drug Administration	USDA

YEARS	NAME	DEPARTMENT
1940–1953	Food and Drug Administration	Federal Security Agency
1953–1979	Food and Drug Administration	Dept. of Health, Education, and Welfare
1979–	Food and Drug Administration	Dept. of Health present and Human Services

The organization that is now FDA has been a functioning, integrated, regulatory agency for most of this century. It has grown in size as the federal government has grown, assuming larger responsibilities as private ordering gave way to regulation in many areas and Washington supplanted the states as the primary locus of regulatory activity. Some few current FDA employees can recall the pre-HEW era. The last of those who were working for the agency at the time of the enactment of its organic statute, the Federal Food, Drug, and Cosmetic Act of 1938 (FD&C Act), retired in 1979.

Throughout its history FDA has had essentially the same assignment: to assure that the products it regulates are safe and truthfully labeled. This statement obviously oversimplifies the agency's current responsibilities, which encompass a much larger role in the development, testing, introduction, and marketing of these products, but it conveys an important truth. By Washington, D.C., standards, FDA is a venerable institution, whose employees have long memories and a tradition of dedicated, sometimes single-minded public service—in sum, a strong commitment to the job of regulation. Senior FDA employees still recall an era when the agency's activities centered on enforcement of clear-cut statutory prohibitions rather than choosing among closely balanced alternatives in controlling advanced technologies. Their long memories and vigorous commitment continue to influence the agency's regulatory style, and in recent years have sometimes produced ambivalence in its response to the more complex issues of the late 20th century.

This is not a book about FDA as an institution. Our focus is on the legal requirements of the FD&C Act and related laws and their impact on consumers, medical professionals, and producers and distributors of regulated products. But one cannot fully understand the current regulatory system without some appreciation of the history of the agency responsible for the law's administration.

NOTES

1. *Patent Office Agricultural Division.* Prior to 1862, examinations of agricultural products were conducted by the Commissioner of Patents, an office originally based in the Department of State and transferred to the Department of Interior when it was created in 1849. Such examinations were first authorized by Congress in 9 Stat. 284, 285 (1848), which appropriated $1,000 for the "expenses of chemical analyses of vegetable substances produced and used for the food of man and animals in the United States." Professor Lewis C. Beck, M.D., who two years earlier had published the first American treatise on

adulteration of food and drugs, was recruited to conduct these analyses. *See* Beck, *Report on the Breadstuffs of the United States,* in "Annual Report of Commissioner of Patents for the Year 1848," H.R. Exec. Doc. No. 59, 30th Cong., 2d Sess. 11–12, App. 1 at 245 (1849). When the Department of Agriculture was created by Congress in 1862, the legislation transferred the Patent Office's Agricultural Division to the new department and the chemical laboratory became the Chemical Division.

2. *FDA Annual Reports.* FDA and its predecessor agencies issued formal annual reports from 1862 through 1974. The annual reports from 1862 through 1906 can be found in the USDA annual reports for those years. The annual reports from 1907 through 1974 are reprinted in Food Law Institute, FEDERAL FOOD, DRUG, AND COSMETIC LAW: ADMINISTRATIVE REPORTS, 1907–1949 (1951), and Food and Drug Administration, FOOD AND DRUG ADMINISTRATION ANNUAL REPORTS 1950–1974 (1976). Since 1974, the agency's activities have been summarized by the FDA Office of Planning and Evaluation in the FDA QUARTERLY ACTIVITIES REPORT.

3. *Organizational Growth.* The organizational history of FDA since 1906 is traced in Brannon, *Organizing and Reorganizing FDA* in SEVENTY–FIFTH ANNIVERSARY COMMEMORATIVE VOLUME OF FOOD AND DRUG LAW 135 (Food and Drug Law Institute 1984).

4. *Historical Sources.* Useful general histories of FDA include G. Weber, THE FOOD, DRUG, AND INSECTICIDE ADMINISTRATION (1928), and S. Wilson, FOOD AND DRUG REGULATION (1942). Numerous articles chronicling the agency's history may be found in the Food Drug Cosmetic Law Journal (FDC L.J.), which has been published since 1946. *See, e.g.,* Dunbar, *Memories of Early Days of Federal Food and Drug Law Enforcement,* 14 FDC L.J. 87 (1959); and the five-part series by Linton, *Leaders in Food and Drug Law,* 4 FDC L.J. 451 (1949), 5 FDC L.J. 103, 326, 479, 771 (1950).

---

2. THE EVOLUTION OF FEDERAL FOOD AND DRUG LEGISLATION

A single statute, the FD&C Act of 1938, as amended, establishes the basic legal framework controlling the activities of producers of food, drugs, cosmetics, and medical devices. This statute is the successor to an earlier federal food and drug law, and it has been frequently revised and expanded since its enactment. FDA has also been delegated responsibility for administering other important regulatory laws applicable to these four categories of products. Thus, in truth, FDA's current statutory armamentarium is an amalgam of provisions enacted by Congress over a period of almost ninety years.

a. State and Local Laws in the 19th Century

Colonial America was an agrarian economy. People consumed the food and herbal drugs they produced at home. Even those who lived in small towns kept livestock and maintained their own gardens. As urban centers grew, local food markets were established to serve them. In his classic study, T.F. De Voe traced the history of the public markets of the City of New York from the origin of the West India Company's store in the 1630s through the 1840s. THE MARKET BOOK: A HISTORY OF THE PUBLIC MARKETS OF THE CITY OF NEW YORK (1862). As these markets were established, the City of New York adopted various requirements to regulate them. These requirements largely reflected the English common and statutory law.

Although many of these early laws were aimed at specific commodities or narrow problems, a number were directed more generally at preventing any form of adulteration. As cities grew larger, concern about public health expanded. Lemuel Shattuck's landmark report on public health in 1850 documented the decrease in average life expectancy at birth in America's large urban centers and identified the adulteration of food and drugs as a matter of public health concern. Shattuck recommended the establishment of local boards of health which would "endeavor to prevent the sale and use of unwholesome, spurious, and adulterated articles, dangerous to the public health, designed for food, drink, or medicine." REPORT OF THE SANITARY COMMISSION OF MASSACHUSETTS 220 (1850).

In 1867, De Voe published another study in which he noted the great expansion in public trade and the need for increased regulation to protect *both* the producer and the consumer:

> The producer is often hundreds of miles in one direction, while the consumer may be as many hundred in another, from the *mart* at which the productions were sold and purchased....
>
> A great trade has imperceptibly grown upon us (particularly in New York), which I have sometimes thought, would have been more profitable to both producer and consumer, if proper laws, and practical, honest heads, had been placed over these vast interests, which so much affect the general health and comfort, as well as the *pockets* of our over-taxed citizens....

THE MARKET ASSISTANT 9 (1867). Following Shattuck's report and this expansion in trade, boards of health were established in cities, counties, and states throughout the country. Congress initially enacted food and drug legislation for the District of Columbia in 1888 and substantially strengthened it in 1898.

---

b. Enactment of the First Federal Laws

Although Congress during the 1800s enacted a short-lived statute to assure a safe and effective supply of smallpox vaccine, 2 Stat. 806 (1813), repealed 3 Stat. 677 (1822), and several statutes to regulate foreign commerce in food and drugs (*e.g.,* 9 Stat. 237 (1848) (imported drugs); 22 Stat. 451 (1883) and 29 Stat. 604 (1897) (imported tea); 26

Stat. 414 (1890), 26 Stat. 1089 (1891), 30 Stat. 151, 210 (1897), and 30 Stat. 947, 951 (1899) (imported and exported food)), no 19th century federal legislation dealt generally with the safety or effectiveness of food and drugs marketed throughout the United States.

At the same time that De Voe was documenting the growth of public food markets, the English and American authors who followed Accum were warning the public about adulteration of food and drugs. Campaigns were mounted by *Frank Leslie's Illustrated Newspaper* beginning in 1858, and by the *New York World* beginning in 1868, to publicize this problem. By 1879, there was a full-fledged public outcry against adulteration of food and drugs in the United States. In January of that year, Dr. E.R. Squibb, in a major address to the Medical Society of the State of New York, proposed enactment of a nationwide food and drug law. He began his remarks with a strong statement on the need for uniform national regulation of these articles:

> It is self-evident that a law to be most effective in prevent-ing the adulteration of food and medicine should be general or national in order to secure universality and uniformity of action. . . .

Only ten days later, the first comprehensive food and drug bill was introduced in Congress. Because of strong sentiment that this was properly a matter for state and local regulation, federal legislation languished in Congress from 1879 to 1906.

Throughout this time, the need for national uniformity in regula-tion of food and drugs was an important argument in favor of federal legislation. The Director of the Bureau of Chemistry of the New York State Department of Health argued for uniform national regulation of food and drugs in 1903:

> . . . [I]t is very certain that the widely differing statutes relat-ing to our food supply in the different States have worked much mischief, been the cause of much confusion, and serious-ly embarrassed some useful industries. I think all who have studied the matter will be inclined to admit that uniformity in our food laws is much to be desired. . . .

W. Tucker, FOOD ADULTERATION: ITS NATURE AND EXTENT, AND HOW TO DEAL WITH IT 21 (1903).

As has often happened in the history of food and drug regulation, a tragedy intervened to spur the enactment of the first national statute. The Biologics Act of 1902, 32 Stat. 728, was enacted in response to the distribution in St. Louis of tetanus-infected diphtheria antitoxin that resulted in the death of several children. The law required that biological drugs sold in interstate commerce must be licensed and must be produced in licensed establishments.

The USDA Division of Chemistry played an important role in the investigation of food adulteration that ultimately led to enactment of the Federal Food and Drugs Act of 1906. When Peter Collier became

Chief Chemist in 1879, the Division began a major investigation of food and drug adulteration. Collier was succeeded by Dr. Harvey W. Wiley, who served as Chief Chemist from 1883 to 1912. In 1883, the Division of Chemistry began to publish bulletins containing the results of its investigations. Bulletin 13, issued in 10 parts and 1417 pages from 1887 to 1902, dealt extensively with adulteration of common food products. After the Department of Agriculture was made an Executive Department in 1889, Congress appropriated funds "to enable the Secretary of Agriculture to extend and continue the investigation of the adulteration of food, drugs, and liquors." The appropriations continued through enactment of the 1906 Act and permitted USDA to conduct extensive work in this area.

Perhaps the most dramatic work of the Division of Chemistry involved food preservatives. After extensive study of their chemistry, Congress specifically appropriated funds in 1900 "to investigate the character of proposed food preservatives and coloring matters; to determine their relation to digestion and health; and to establish the principles which should guide their use." A "poison squad" of twelve USDA employees acted as human subjects to test the safety of boric acid and borax, salicylic acid and salicylates, sulfurous acid and sulfites, benzoic acid and benzoates, and formaldehyde, during 1902–1904. Each member complied with a strict dietary regimen on which detailed records were kept, and was subject to extensive examination respecting the effects of the preservatives included in the diet. The results, published in five parts during 1904–1908, provoked interest throughout the country.

LAUFFER HAYES & FRANK RUFF, THE ADMINISTRATION OF THE FEDERAL FOOD AND DRUGS ACT

1 Law & Contemporary Problems 16 (1933).

The [1906] Act forbids interstate commerce in adulterated and misbranded food and drugs. It provides criminal penalties for violation and also authorizes the seizure of offending products. In the case of standard drugs, the United States Pharmacopoeia and the National Formulary were resorted to by Congress for the purpose of establishing standards of purity and quality which the drug manufacturers were enjoined to follow—unless they declared standards of their own on the labels of their products.... In the case of foods, standards were not available, and in their stead, the draftsmen of the Act resorted to generalities proscribing the intermixture or substitution of substances reducing quality, the abstraction of valuable constituents, the concealment of damage or inferiority, the addition of deleterious ingredients, and the use of spoiled animal or vegetable products. Misbranding was confined chiefly to the making of false or misleading statements regarding a food or drug on the package or label thereof. The sale of an imitation was forbidden, but this was accompanied by provisos which relieved mixtures or compounds not in themselves harmful when sold under "their own distinctive names" or when labeled with the word "compound," "imitation" or "blend," from the operation of both the misbranding and adulteration provisions of the Act. Aside from the latter, the only affirmative labeling requirements were the disclosure of the presence and quantity of enumerated narcotic drugs and the declaration of the net weight of foods when sold in package form.

NOTES

1. *1906 Act History.* The legislative and administrative histories of the 1906 Act are chronicled in A. Greeley, THE FOOD AND DRUGS ACT (1907); H. Wiley, THE HISTORY OF A CRIME AGAINST THE FOOD LAW (1929); H. Wiley, AN AUTOBIOGRAPHY (1930); *Legislation: The Consumer's Protection Under the Federal Pure Food and Drugs Act,* 32 Colum. L. Rev. 720 (1932); Symposium, *The Protection of the Consumer of Food and Drugs,* 1 Law & Contemp. Probs. 1 (1933); Symposium, *The Fortieth Anniversary of the Original Federal Food and Drugs Act of 1906,* 1 FDC L.Q. 285 (1946); Anderson, *Pioneer Statute: The Pure Food and Drugs Act of 1906,* 13 J. Pub. L. 189 (1964); Young, *From Oysters to After–Dinner Mints: The Role of the Early Food and Drug Inspector,* 42 J. Hist. Med. & Allied Sci. 30 (1987); J.H. Young, PURE FOOD: SECURING THE FEDERAL FOOD AND DRUGS ACT OF 1906 (1989).

2. *Decisions Under the 1906 Act.* FDA's administrative decisions under the 1906 Act were compiled through mid–1914 in C. Gwinn, FOOD AND DRUGS ACT (1914), and were issued by FDA in periodic regulations, food inspection decisions, and service and regulatory announcements. Court decisions under the 1906 Act were compiled through mid–1934 in M. White and O. Gates, DECISIONS OF COURTS IN CASES UNDER THE FEDERAL FOOD AND DRUGS ACT (1934).

---

c. The Federal Food, Drug, and Cosmetic Act of 1938

1917 REPORT OF THE USDA BUREAU OF CHEMISTRY

It is perhaps impossible for any one correctly to estimate the general effect of the Food and Drugs Act. To state that more than six thousand cases have been terminated in the courts during the first decade since the enactment of the act; that manufacturers have been cited to hearing more than forty thousand times, that many thousands of factory inspections have been made, that more than seven hundred and fifty thousand shipments of food and drugs, both domestic and imported, have been examined, gives but an imperfect indication of results....

The Food and Drugs Act was among the first of that group of laws which today would be classed as laws for the prevention of unfair competition. The suppression of fraud upon the consumer and of unfair competition among business rivals are but the two faces of the same coin. In consequence the food industries are sincerely and effectively supporting and helping the Bureau of Chemistry to enforce the law. Indeed, the Bureau is not infrequently appealed to by the industries to compel the cessation of unfair practices and to encourage the standardization of products when the industry is incapable by itself of bringing about these results.....

The Food and Drugs Act's chief contributions to the safeguarding of the peoples' health have been its effect upon the drug and patent medicine industry, upon the control of the traffic in polluted, decomposed or filthy foods and upon the elimination from foodstuffs of contamination with poisons such as lead and arsenic which entered the product because of the use of impure reagents in the process of manufacture, or of utensils constructed of improper materials.

While the accomplishments of the Food and Drugs Act have been considerable, it must be admitted that it has its serious limitations. Especially conspicuous ones are the lack of legal standards for foods, of authority to inspect warehouses, and of any restriction whatever upon the use of many of the most virulent poisons in drugs; the limitations placed upon the term "drug" by definition which render it difficult to control injurious cosmetics, fraudulent mechanical devices used for therapeutic purposes, as well as fraudulent remedies for obesity and leanness; the limitation of dangerous adulterants to those that are added so that the interstate shipment of a food that naturally contains a virulent poison is unrestricted. Furthermore, the law fails to take cognizance of fraudulent statements covering foods or drugs which are not in or upon the food or drug package. Greater flexibility to prescribe the disposition of imports is also desirable. The Secretary of Agriculture has at one time or another recommended legislation to fill most of these gaps in the law. It should also be noted that at present there is no Federal law which prohibits unregistered or unlicensed persons from sending into interstate commerce medicinal agents, poisons, and the like, although they can not be sold locally by them nor indiscriminately even by registered or licensed pharmacists or physicians.

1933 REPORT OF THE FOOD AND DRUG ADMINISTRATION

Demand for a complete overhauling of the outworn mechanism of 1906 received a new impetus during the year through the interest of the President of the United States and the sympathy and cooperation of the Secretary and Assistant Secretary of Agriculture. A bill to supplant the present measure was drafted in the Department, reviewed and approved by the Department of Justice, and introduced in the Senate on June 12, by Senator Royal S. Copeland, of New York, as S. 1944.

The new draft preserves all of the worthy features of the present law. Its principal additional features are as follows:

1. Cosmetics are brought within the scope of the statute.

2. Mechanical devices intended for curative purposes, and devices and preparations intended to bring about changes in the structure of the body are also included within the purview of the law.

3. False advertising of foods, drugs, and cosmetics is prohibited.

4. Definitely informative labeling is required.

5. A drug which is, or may be, dangerous to health under the conditions of use prescribed in its labeling is classed as adulterated.

6. The promulgation of definitions and standards for foods, which will have the force and effect of law, is authorized.

7. The prohibition of added poisons in foods or the establishment of safe tolerances therefor is provided for.

8. The operation of factories under Federal permit is prescribed where protection of the public health cannot be otherwise effected.

9. More effective methods for the control of false labeling and advertising of drug products are provided.

10. More severe penalties, as well as injunctions in the case of repeated offenses, are prescribed.

———

Five years passed before Congress enacted and President Roosevelt, on June 25, 1938, signed the FD&C Act. In structure, the Act is a catalogue of definitions elaborating two basic concepts: "adulteration" and "misbranding." Most of the Act's operative provisions describe circumstances under which a food, drug, cosmetic, or device will be considered adulterated or misbranded under the law and thus subject to FDA enforcement action. For example, section 402(a) of the Act does not forthrightly forbid the marketing of food that is decomposed or filthy; it specifies that food that is decomposed or filthy shall be "deemed adulterated." Then section 301 enumerates a series of "prohibited acts," among them the shipment, distribution, or sale of any adulterated food. In short, much of the statute is devoted to ascribing the labels "adulterated" or "misbranded" to products whose composition, production, or labeling fails to meet substantive requirements that are the real focus of the law. In this respect, the Act's basic format has not changed since 1906. Rather, changes in the scope of FDA's responsibilities have generally been reflected in the addition of new definitions of adulteration and misbranding.

We examine the enforcement remedies available to FDA in Chapter XI. The principal statutorily authorized sanctions remain those provided in 1938: criminal prosecution of individuals and firms guilty of prohibited acts, injunction against such acts, and seizure of adulterated or misbranded goods. Of these authorized judicial remedies, seizure is by far the most common. From the beginning, however, FDA has also relied on informal remedies not explicitly provided in the Act, such as publicity, recalls, and regulatory letters, which now comprise the primary routine enforcement tools of the agency.

NOTE

On the legislative history of the 1938 Act, *see* C. Jackson, FOOD AND DRUG LEGISLATION IN THE NEW DEAL (1970); Kleinfeld, *Legislative History of the Federal Food, Drug, and Cosmetic Act*, 1 FDC L.Q. 532 (1946); Symposium, *The New Food, Drug, and Cosmetic Legislation*, 6 Law & Contemp. Probs. 1 (1939). The legislative history is collected in part in C. Dunn, FEDERAL FOOD, DRUG, AND COSMETIC ACT (1938), and in full in FDA, A LEGISLATIVE HISTORY OF THE FEDERAL FOOD, DRUG, AND COSMETIC ACT AND ITS AMENDMENTS, Vols. 1–24 and Apps. A–J (1979).

---

d. Post–1938 Amendments

The FD&C Act has been amended many times since 1938. Some of the changes made by Congress can fairly be described as technical or remedial. The more noteworthy amendments have typically extended the coverage of the Act or, even more commonly, enlarged FDA's substantive authority over products already within its jurisdiction. Examples of such legislation include the Miller Pesticides Amendment of 1954, which empowered FDA to establish tolerances for pesticides on agricultural commodities; the Food Additives Amendment of 1958, which required premarket approval of new food ingredients and many food contact articles; and the Color Additive Amendments of 1960, which established a premarket approval system for colors used in food, drugs, and cosmetics.

Two of the most significant amendments to the basic Act occurred in 1962 and 1976. The Drug Amendments of 1962 fundamentally restructured the way in which FDA regulated new medicines, transforming a system of premarket notification into one that requires individual premarket approval of the safety and effectiveness of every new drug. The 1962 Amendments also thrust FDA into a greater role in regulating prescription drug promotion and clinical testing of new agents. With the passage of this legislation, the regulation of drugs became the single most controversial, and perhaps the most important, of FDA's activities.

In 1976 Congress enacted the most recent comprehensive changes to the basic FD&C Act, the Medical Device Amendments. Unlike the 1962 changes in the law governing drugs, the Medical Device Amendments were the culmination of fifteen years of study and debate, not only within Congress and the agency, but also among representatives of clinical medicine, biomedical engineering, device manufacturers, and consumer groups. While the 1976 Amendments did not significantly enlarge FDA's jurisdiction over devices, they transformed its approach to regulation of these products and substantially enlarged the array of regulatory tools available to it.

The 1980s have been punctuated by additional single-purpose or narrowly focused amendments, including the Infant Formula Amendments of 1980 and the Drug Price Competition and Patent–Term Restoration Act of 1984. In 1988, Congress created FDA by statute. Congress enacted two more major statutes in 1990, the Nutrition Labeling and Education Act and the Safe Medical Devices Act.

But the history of federal food and drug legislation has not been an unbroken succession of enlargements of regulatory power. In 1976 FDA also saw the first of a series of enactments intended to curtail its authority, perhaps reflecting the growing congressional skepticism of regulation generally as well as specific solicitude for the targets of recent FDA attention. The most significant of these were the Vitamin–Mineral Amendments of 1976, which limited FDA's authority to regulate the composition and promotion of dietary supplements—marking a rejection of the agency's decade-long efforts to control high potency nutritional products and health foods. A year later Congress passed the first of a series of laws forestalling any FDA action to ban the use of saccharin in food. In 1977 it also adopted a rider to unrelated legislation that directed FDA to refrain from implementing a proposed system for controlling the sanitation of shellfish harvested in U.S. waters until the Department of Commerce had completed a predictably alarming assessment of the economic impact.

While these (and other) periodic expressions of congressional disagreement on specific issues depart from the general pattern of federal food and drug legislation, they do not appear to represent a fundamental shift in legislative policy. Over the past three decades both houses of Congress have displayed strong support for vigorous regulation of food, drugs, and other medical products.

---

3. OTHER LAWS ENFORCED BY FDA

While the much-amended FD&C Act forms the agency's basic regulatory framework, FDA also administers several other statutes applicable to one or more categories of products within its jurisdiction. It has been delegated authority to enforce the Biologics Act, 42 U.S.C. § 262, originally enacted in 1902. This statute provides the agency's primary authority to regulate biological products, such as vaccines, products derived from human blood, and drugs produced by the recent advances in biotechnology. FDA relies on section 361 of the Public Health Service Act, 42 U.S.C. § 264, to regulate sanitation in food service establishments and on interstate carriers, as well as to address more unusual, arguably less significant problems, such as the transmission of disease by pet turtles. Another important law delegated to

FDA is the Radiation Control for Health and Safety Act of 1968, 82 Stat. 1173, now recodified by the Safe Medical Devices Act of 1990, 104 Stat. 4511, as section 531 *et seq.* of the FD&C Act, under which it regulates X-ray machines, microwave ovens, ultrasound equipment and other products capable of emitting potentially harmful radiation.

NOTES

1. *Authorities Delegated to FDA.* For a listing of statutory functions delegated to FDA, *see* 21 C.F.R. § 5.10 and Appendix B.

2. *Attempted Recodification.* In 1950, the House Committee on the Judiciary introduced a revision of the FD&C Act designed simply to codify the existing provisions in clearer language. After four years of consideration, the bill ultimately passed both houses of Congress. President Eisenhower withheld his approval, however, because the bill did not appear to achieve its objective of avoiding substantive change in the current law. *See* H.R. Rep. No. 906, 84th Cong., 1st Sess. (1955). Although the legislation was subsequently revised, it was never able to overcome that Presidential disapproval and subsequently died.

3. *Food Legislation.* A summary of food legislation enacted or considered by Congress may be found in Hutt, *Food Legislation in Perspective,* 34 FDC L.J. 590 (1979).

C. FDA'S STRUCTURE AND ORGANIZATION

FDA's legal authority is outlined in detail by the FD&C Act and related laws, but the agency's structure is not described in any statute, *see* 21 C.F.R. § 5.100. In fact, although it has a long institutional history, the agency was not recognized in legislation until 1988. *See* 102 Stat. 3048, 3120–22 (1988). Similarly, the agency's top office, that of the Commissioner of Food and Drugs, was a creature of administrative regulation until 1988. Formal legal responsibility for administering the FD&C Act, as well as the other statutes that FDA administers, lies with the Secretary of HHS.

Every FDA Commissioner who took office before 1988, though perhaps approved by the White House, was appointed by the Secretary and thus not subject to Senate confirmation. Under Section 903(b)(1) of the FD&C Act, added by the 1988 statute, Commissioners must now be appointed by the President with the advice and consent of the Senate. In formal organizational terms, the Commissioner ranks below the Assistant Secretaries of HHS in the fourth tier of the Department. In fact, the job is more prominent than many ostensibly higher ranking HHS offices, and it attracts individuals of national reputation. FDA's visibility and the potential sensitivity of its decisions always have given the Commissioner a direct line to the Secretary of HHS and, sometimes, to the White House as well.

As its organizational location reveals, FDA does not have the same independence of Presidential control that agencies like the FTC and

CPSC ostensibly enjoy. A Commissioner of Food and Drugs is subject to direction and may be removed from office by the Secretary (now by the President) for any or no reason. Furthermore, the agency is headed by a single administrator. Its decisions represent collegial judgments only to the extent that the Commissioner relies on collegial support. Deliberative meetings among agency officials are frequent, informal, unannounced, and not ordinarily open to the public. The Government in the Sunshine Act, 90 Stat. 1241 (1976), thus has no application to FDA's internal deliberations, though of course the agency's numerous expert advisory committees hold open meetings as required by the Federal Advisory Committee Act, 86 Stat. 770 (1972).

FDA's location in the Department of HHS might suggest that the agency is subject to substantial political influence. For several reasons, however, this has not been the customary pattern. First, the evident scientific basis for most of FDA's decisions has helped insulate it from many of the customary forms of political pressure. Second, the visibility of FDA's programs has given the agency, and thus the Commissioner, a public standing that frequently blunts pressure from within any incumbent administration. Finally, the agency's relatively low rank in the bureaucratic hierarchy means that few jobs have been subject to political appointment. As a technical matter, only two positions in FDA—that of the Commissioner and the Deputy Commissioner—have been formally subject to Secretarial or, now, Presidential appointment. A change in administrations has not usually resulted in numerous resignations or reassignments among the agency's middle and upper-level managers, even though it may abruptly terminate the service of a Commissioner. Accordingly, for most of its existence FDA has operated with considerable decisional independence and enjoyed continuity in the service of employees who hold middle-management positions and staff its several field offices.

FDA's total full-time workforce numbered 7395 in 1989, a majority of whom are located at its headquarters in the Washington, D.C. area. Most of the remainder—inspectors, compliance officers, and laboratory scientists—work in one of ten regional offices or in additional district offices and resident posts around the country. FDA's headquarters personnel are dispersed among almost two dozen different buildings in and around Washington. They are divided among eight primary components: the Commissioner's office and central administrative staff, which includes several Associate Commissioners, budget officers, and personnel experts; field operations, which consist of regional, district, and local offices throughout the country that carry on FDA's inspectional and enforcement activities, all of which are coordinated by the Associate Commissioner for Regulatory Affairs; and five centers (formerly "bureaus") which are responsible for one or more categories of products within FDA's jurisdiction. In descending order of number of employees, these are the Center for Drug Evaluation and Research, the Center for Biologics Evaluation and Research, the Center for Food Safety and Applied Nutrition, the Center for Devices and Radiological

Health, and the Center for Veterinary Medicine. The heads of each of these entities—center directors—report to the Commissioner. The eighth component is the National Center for Toxicological Research, established in 1971 in the converted facilities of the former biological warfare project in Jefferson, Arkansas.

A key organization in FDA's regulatory operations, but not formally a part of the agency, is the Chief Counsel's office—officially the Food and Drug Division of the Office of the General Counsel of the Department of Health and Human Services. FDA's Chief Counsel is thus an employee of the Secretary of HHS, not of the Commissioner of Food and Drugs. In practice, however, the office functions more as an active component of the agency than as the representative of the Department. The FDA Chief Counsel in fact serves as the Commissioner's lawyer.

FDA's 7400 employees are responsible for regulating the products of several large and diverse industries. FDA fared relatively well in maintaining its budget during the general reductions of the 1980s. For FY 1989, the agency budget was $487 million, compared with $295 million in 1979. But even this figure is dwarfed by the activities of the firms whose products FDA regulates; approximately 25 cents of every consumer retail sales dollar is spent for products within the agency's jurisdiction. As the following chapters reveal, the scope of FDA's authority over this heterogeneous universe varies widely, ranging from comprehensive premarket approval responsibility for new drugs, food additives, and certain life-supporting types of medical devices, to the policing activities applicable to cosmetics. Furthermore, within the several industries and many thousands of establishments over which FDA has some measure of regulatory control, there is enormous diversity among individual firms. They range in size from giant nationwide food processors and distributors to small warehousemen, from multinational chemical companies to small partnerships among biomedical engineers engaged in the development of a single type of device, and from the nation's largest cattle feed lots to contract laboratories engaged in preclinical testing of new food ingredients.

The placement of FDA within the executive branch has been the subject of continuous study. The Hoover Commission initially concluded that FDA should be split in two, with the responsibility for food regulation transferred to USDA and the responsibility for drug regulation transferred to a new Union Medical Administration. A Task Force of the Hoover Commission then recommended that the pesticide regulatory functions of the Department of Agriculture be transferred to FDA and the animal biologics regulatory functions of the Department of Agriculture be combined with the human biologics regulatory functions of the National Institutes of Health, without referring to the earlier proposal. The 1955 Hoover Commission Report concluded that the matter should be decided by administrative determination and took no action on it. In January 1971, the President's Advisory Council on Executive Reorganization recommended that consideration be given to transferring FDA to a new Federal Trade Practices Agency. The Ash

Council Report, also in January 1971, proposed that FDA be made part of a new Department of Human Resources. A 1977 report by the Senate Committee on Governmental Affairs recommended transfer of USDA food regulatory functions to FDA. A 1978 White House Study, never released, recommended consolidation of the food regulatory functions of FDA and USDA but did not resolve where the new organization would be located. A 1984 OTA study recommended that regulation of animal vaccines be transferred from USDA to FDA.

D. THE REGULATORY ENVIRONMENT

Experienced practitioners in any regulatory field appreciate the need to understand the background and motives of the agency with which they are dealing, and sophisticated observers of federal regulation have often commented on the influence of history, personality, and style on the regulatory process. It is not possible, however, to describe the style or atmosphere of an eighty-year old agency in a few pages. Our examination of FDA's formulation and enforcement of substantive legal requirements does, however, attempt to convey some sense of the forces that drive FDA regulation and the political and scientific environment in which it functions. And it is therefore appropriate at the outset to identify some features on the FDA landscape that cast long shadows over its administration of the law.

While most federal agencies frequently come under close public and journalistic scrutiny, even by Washington standards FDA has been an intensely watched agency. It seems to us unlikely that any other agency—and certainly none of those involved in health and safety regulation—has been the subject of as frequent study as FDA during the last three decades. The most current, yet only partial, catalogue of external and internal studies of the agency's performance appears in Hutt, *Investigations and Reports on the Food and Drug Administration,* in TWENTY–FIFTH ANNIVERSARY COMMEMORATIVE VOLUME OF FOOD AND DRUG LAW 27 (Food and Drug Law Institute 1984). As this volume went to press, two national committees were studying FDA, the National Committee to Review Current Procedures for Approval of New Drugs for Cancer and AIDS, established in 53 Fed. Reg. 46942 (November 21, 1988) at the request of President Bush, and the Advisory Committee on the Food and Drug Administration, established in 54 Fed. Reg. 51236 (December 13, 1989) at the request of HHS Secretary Louis Sullivan. The number of studies of FDA's performance is certainly evidence of the high degree of public interest in its work, but it also betrays the persistence of a belief among some in Washington that the agency is not doing its job well enough or fast enough, a skepticism that contributes to the self-doubt that has periodically beset agency employees. This skepticism, however, has not generally been shared by the public at large which, according to repeated public surveys, rates FDA among the federal agencies in which they have the greatest confidence.

FDA's persistent fascination as a subject of study by official and quasi-official bodies mirrors congressional interest in its work. In recent years, FDA has been the subject of a degree of congressional attention unsurpassed by any other regulatory agency. Between September 1971 and July 1977, FDA officials were called to testify before congressional committees a total of 198 times. The inauguration of a Democratic President in 1977 and appointment of a new Commissioner did not measurably diminish congressional interest in overseeing FDA's performance. The arrival of a Republican President in 1981, combined with the change in party control of the Senate, did, however, significantly reduce congressional oversight, but congressional pressure resumed following the Senate elections in 1986.

The number of congressional hearings involving FDA tells only part of the story. Fewer than 20 percent of its appearances deal with legislation affecting the agency. In most years no more than two appearances concern the agency's budget. The remainder, an average of almost thirty hearings a year, are "oversight" hearings in the conventional sense. Our purpose is not to argue that FDA *should be* left alone to do its work, but simply to document that it *is not* left alone. The agency is controversial. Its decisions are closely watched. Numerous congressional committees critique its performance, very often concluding that it has been reckless in approving new products or insufficiently vigorous in acting against old ones. The message conveyed by both the intensity and attitude of congressional oversight has had enormous influence on both the content of FDA's requirements and the thrust of its enforcement efforts.

RICHARD A. MERRILL, RISK–BENEFIT DECISIONMAKING BY THE FOOD AND DRUG ADMINISTRATION

45 George Washington Law Review 994 (1977).

... Historically, the agency devoted its primary energies to combatting unsanitary food production and preventing the marketing of deficient drugs, principally through instituted product recalls and court enforcement actions halting or punishing distribution of adulterated and misbranded products. FDA rarely had difficulty determining whether a process was deficient or a product mislabeled; the agency's major problems were the detection and prevention of individual violations.

Although policing activities still comprise a major part of FDA's work, the agency's regulatory agenda has expanded and shifted. Both the passage of legislation regulating food additives, color additives, and human and veterinary drugs and mounting public concern about environmental hazards have broadened the nature of FDA decision-making. The agency increasingly is required to determine the level of risk acceptable in products that are properly manufactured and used as intended. Rather than measuring the practices of individual manufacturers against well-established standards of conduct, FDA now must prescribe the standards of safety and, in some instances, the standards of performance particular products must meet before they reach the public. . . .

Only in the last generation has FDA begun to act like a modern "regulatory agency"—a body responsible for routine monitoring of the operations of several industries and exercising comprehensive authority to prescribe how they must make and market products. However, FDA brings to this modern responsibility history and experience that still influence the attitudes of agency officials about the appropriate role of a health regulatory agency. Many FDA employees have devoted their lives to gathering proof of statutory violations in preparation for court enforcement proceedings, and this adversary experience has engendered suspicion of regulated firms. This suspicion has in turn produced a desire to devise requirements that cannot be escaped or subverted.

But FDA's modern responsibilities have forced the agency to become less suspicious and more inventive. As we discuss more fully in Chapters XI and XII, *infra,* it has shifted its emphasis from court enforcement against individual violators to the establishment of generic requirements through rulemaking. In the process, FDA has assumed a larger role in determining the content of regulatory policy. Whenever Congress establishes a regulatory program it necessarily must allow the responsible agency some authority to fashion the precise requirements that apply to regulated firms. Administrative discretion is, of course, characteristic of the regulatory process, but FDA has enjoyed unusual freedom to adopt and revise regulatory approaches. Other health regulatory agencies, such as OSHA, NHTSA, EPA, and CPSC, are creatures of modern organic statutes, which typically reflect more explicit legislative choices among available regulatory techniques. The FD&C Act, by contrast, is comparatively old-fashioned. Many of its most important provisions are couched in general language, which FDA has had the responsibility and opportunity to adapt to contemporary problems.

NOTE

For discussions of the effects of congressional oversight of FDA, *see* Austern, *Drug Regulation and the Public Health: Side Effects and Contraindications of Congressional Committee Post Hoc Medical Judgments,* 19 FDC L.J. 259 (1964); Hutt, *Balanced Government Regulation of Consumer Products,* 31 FDC L.J. 592 (1976).

E. FDA'S MISSION AND RESOURCES

AGRICULTURE, RURAL DEVELOPMENT, AND RELATED AGENCIES APPROPRIATION BILL, 1990

Senate Report No. 101-84, 101st Congress, 2d Session (1989).

The mission of the Food and Drug Administration (FDA) is to ensure that (1) food is safe, pure, and wholesome; (2) cosmetics are safe; (3) human and animal drugs biological products, and therapeutic devices are safe and effective; and (4) radiological products and use procedures do not result in unnecessary exposure to radiation.

Under the foods program, FDA sets food standards; evaluates food additives and packaging for potential health hazards; conducts research to reduce food-borne disease, to determine specific health impacts of hazardous substances in food and to develop methods for detecting them in foods; and maintains surveillance over foods through plant inspections, laboratory analyses, and legal action where necessary.

The drugs program includes the premarket review of human drugs and biological products in order to ensure their safety and efficacy, and the postmarketing monitoring of drug experience. FDA conducts manufacturer inspections and sample examinations to ensure industry compliance. Included under this program activity is the similar regulation of animal drugs, devices, and feeds as well as a program to assure the safety of animal derived human foods.

The devices and radiological products program conducts premarket review and postmarket surveillance of medical devices to determine their safety and efficacy, and sets standards for the manufacture and use of radiological products to protect the public from unnecessary exposure to radiation. FDA monitors experience with medical devices, and conducts inspections of manufacturing plants and tests of radiological products to ensure compliance with regulations and standards.

For these three major product-oriented programs, the agency utilizes a wide variety of scientific skills to deal with the many types of products regulated and the many scientific decisions FDA must make. These skills range from field investigators, all of whom must have education in the physical or biological sciences, to chemists, microbiologists, engineers, medical officers, and scientists from many other disciplines. Similarly, FDA utilizes a variety of laboratory facilities, both to test products for safety and to conduct the research necessary to evaluate health hazards and to develop the means to detect product hazards and prevent them.

In addition, the National Center for Toxicological Research in Jefferson, AR, serves as a specialized resource for FDA's other program elements by advancing the science of toxicology. This facility conducts research to improve the base of scientific knowledge on which the agency makes decisions in assessing the risks of potentially toxic substances.

SALARIES AND EXPENSES

Appropriations, 1989 .... $487,344,000
Budget estimate, 1990 .... [1]442,671,000
House allowance 550,171,000
Committee recommendation 581,871,000

1. The budget proposed that $56,941,000 of this amount be appropriated to the Office of the Assistant Secretary for Health for AIDS research and education.

. . .

The Committee recognizes the need for sufficient staff to carry forward the mission of the Food and Drug Administration assuring the safety of foods and the safety and efficacy of drugs, medical devices, and biologics—roughly one-fourth of all consumer products in the marketplace. In the past 10 years, 23 new laws have expanded FDA authorities, yet today FDA has 800 fewer employees to accomplish these important tasks that it did in 1979. Resources for the agency must be substantially increased if FDA is to meet the burgeoning demands for approval and inspection of foods, human and animal drugs, therapeutic and diagnostic products for various diseases, bloodbanks, and radiological products on a routine and emergency basis, and if FDA is to make advances in treatments and cure of serious illnesses, such as AIDS and cancer. . . .

Chapter II

FOOD

A. DEFINITION OF "FOOD"

The statutory requirements for food differ from those for drugs or other products regulated by FDA. Accordingly, the classification of a product as a food or a drug—or sometimes both—can determine its legality.

FOOD, DRUGS, AND COSMETICS
Senate Report No. 361, 74th Congress, 1st Session (1935).

It has not been considered necessary to specify that the definitions of food, drug, and cosmetic shall not be construed, other than to the extent expressly provided, as mutually exclusive. The present law does not have such a clause relating to the definitions of food and drug and there has never been a court decision to the effect that these definitions are mutually exclusive, despite the fact that repeated actions have been brought, for example, against filthy foods bearing unwarranted therapeutic claims, alleging these products to be adulterated as food because of their filth, and misbranded as drugs because of their false and fraudulent therapeutic claims.

The use to which the product is to be put will determine the category into which it will fall. If it is to be used only as a food it will come within the definition of food and none other. If it contains nutritive ingredients but is sold for drug use only, as clearly shown by the labeling and advertising, it will come within the definition of drug, but not that of food. If it is sold to be used both as a food and for the prevention or treatment of disease it would satisfy both definitions and be subject to the substantive requirements for both. The manufacturer of the article, through his representations in connection with its sale, can determine the use to which the article is to be put. For example, the manufacturer of a laxative which is a medicated candy or chewing gum can bring his product within the definition of drug and escape that of food by representing the article fairly and unequivocally as a drug product.

23

NUTRILAB, INC. v. SCHWEIKER

United States Court of Appeals, Seventh Circuit, 1983.
713 F.2d 335.

CUMMINGS, Chief Judge.

Plaintiffs manufacture and market a product known as "starch blockers" which "block" the human body's digestion of starch as an aid in controlling weight. On July 1, 1982, the Food and Drug Administration ("FDA") classified starch blockers as "drugs" and requested that all such products be removed from the market until FDA approval was received. . . .

The only issue on appeal is whether starch blockers are foods or drugs under the Federal Food, Drug, and Cosmetic Act. Starch blocker tablets and capsules consist of a protein which is extracted from a certain type of raw kidney bean. That particular protein functions as an alpha-amylase inhibitor; alpha-amylase is an enzyme produced by the body which is utilized in digesting starch. When starch blockers are ingested during a meal, the protein acts to prevent the alpha-amylase enzyme from acting, thus allowing the undigested starch to pass through the body and avoiding the calories that would be realized from its digestion.

Kidney beans, from which alpha-amylase inhibitor is derived, are dangerous if eaten raw. By August 1982, FDA had received seventy-five reports of adverse effects on people who had taken starch blockers, including complaints of gastro-intestinal distress such as bloating, nausea, abdominal pain, constipation and vomiting. Because plaintiffs consider starch blockers to be food, no testing as required to obtain FDA approval as a new drug has taken place. If starch blockers were drugs, the manufacturers would be required to file a new drug application pursuant to 21 U.S.C. § 355 and remove the product from the marketplace until approved as a drug by the FDA.

The statutory scheme under the Food, Drug, and Cosmetic Act is a complicated one. Section 321(g)(1) provides that the term "drug" means

> * * * (B) articles intended for use in the diagnosis, cure, mitigation, treatment, or prevention of disease in man or other animals; and (C) articles (other than food) intended to affect the structure or any function of the body of man or other animals; and (D) articles intended for use as a component of any article specified in clauses (A), (B), or (C) of this paragraph; but does not include devices or their components, parts, or accessories.

The term "food" as defined in Section 321(f) means

> (1) articles used for food or drink for man or other animals, (2) chewing gum, and (3) articles used for components of any such article.

Section 321(g)(1)(C) was added to the statute in 1938 to expand the definition of "drug." The amendment was necessary because certain articles intended by manufacturers to be used as drugs did not fit within the "disease" requirement of Section 321(g)(1)(B). Obesity in particular was not considered a disease. Thus "anti-fat remedies" marketed with claims of "slenderizing effects" had escaped regulation under the prior definition....

It is well established that the definitions of food and drug are normally not mutually exclusive; an article that happens to be a food but is intended for use in the treatment of disease fits squarely within the drug definition in part B of Section 321(g)(1) and may be regulated as such. Under part C of the statutory drug definition, however, "articles (other than food)" are expressly excluded from the drug definition (as are devices) in Section 321(g)(1). In order to decide if starch blockers are drugs under Section 321(g)(1)(C), therefore, we must decide if they are foods within the meaning of the part C "other than food" parenthetical exception to Section 321(g)(1)(C). And in order to decide the meaning of "food" in that parenthetical exception, we must first decide the meaning of "food" in Section 321(f).

Congress defined "food" in Section 321(f) as "articles used as food." This definition is not too helpful, but it does emphasize that "food" is to be defined in terms of its function as food, rather than in terms of its source, biochemical composition or ingestibility. Plaintiffs' argument that starch blockers are food because they are derived from food—kidney beans—is not convincing if Congress intended food to mean articles derived from food it would have so specified. Indeed some articles that are derived from food are indisputably not food, such as caffeine and penicillin. In addition, all articles that are classed biochemically as proteins cannot be food either, because for example, insulin, botulism toxin, human hair and influenza virus are proteins that are clearly not food.

Plaintiffs argue that 21 U.S.C. § 343(j) specifying labeling requirements for food for special dietary uses indicates that Congress intended products offered for weight conditions to come within the statutory definition of "food." Plaintiffs misinterpret that statutory Section. It does not define food but merely requires that if a product is a food and purports to be for special dietary uses, its label must contain certain information to avoid being misbranded. If all products intended to affect underweight or overweight conditions were *per se* foods, no diet product could be regulated as a drug under Section 321(g)(1)(C), a result clearly contrary to the intent of Congress that "anti-fat remedies" and "slenderizers" qualify as drugs under that Section.

If defining food in terms of its source or defining it in terms of its biochemical composition is clearly wrong, defining food as articles intended by the manufacturer to be used as food is problematic. When Congress meant to define a drug in terms of its intended use, it explicitly incorporated that element into its statutory definition. For example, Section 321(g)(1)(B) defines drugs as articles "intended for use" in, among other things, the treatment of disease; Section 321(g)(1)(C) defines drugs as "articles (other than food) intended to affect the structure or any function of the body of man or other animals." The definition of food in Section 321(f) omits any reference to intent.... Further, a manufacturer cannot avoid the reach of the FDA by claiming that a product which looks like food and smells like food is not food because it was not intended for consumption....

Although it is easy to reject the proffered food definitions, it is difficult to arrive at a satisfactory one. In the absence of clearcut Congressional guidance, it is best to rely on statutory language and common sense. The statute evidently uses the word "food" in two different ways. The statutory definition of "food" in Section 321(f) is a term of art and is clearly intended to be broader than the common-sense definition of food, because the statutory definition of "food" also includes chewing gum and food additives. Food additives can be any substance the intended use of which results or may reasonably result in its becoming a component or otherwise affecting the characteristics of any food. Paper food-packaging when containing polychlorinated biphenyls (PCB's), for example, is an adulterated food because the PCB's may migrate from the package to the food and thereby become a component of it.... Yet the statutory definition of "food" also includes in Section 321(f)(1) the common-sense definition of food. When the statute defines "food" as "articles used for food," it means that the statutory definition of "food" includes articles used by people in the ordinary way most people use food—primarily for taste, aroma, or nutritive value. To hold as did the district court that articles used as food are articles used solely for taste, aroma or nutritive value is unduly restrictive since some products such as coffee or prune juice are undoubtedly food but may be consumed on occasion for reasons other than taste, aroma, or nutritive value....

This double use of the word "food" in Section 321(f) makes it difficult to interpret the parenthetical "other than food" exclusion in the Section 321(g)(1)(C) drug definition. As shown by that exclusion, Congress obviously meant a drug to be something "other than food," but was it referring to "food" as a term of art in the statutory sense or to foods in their ordinary meaning? Because all such foods are "intended to affect the structure or any function of the body of man or other animals" and would thus come within the part C drug definition, presumably Congress meant to exclude common-sense foods. Fortunately, it is not necessary to decide this question here because starch blockers are not food in either sense.* The tablets and pills at issue are

---

* The FDA urges an interpretation of the statute that would allow drug regulation of a product if, for example, an appetite suppressant were added to a recognized food. According to the FDA, addition of the drug might make it a "component" and therefore subject to regulation as a statutory "food". As such, the literal language of Section 321(g)(1)(C) would preclude regulation as a drug because the product would qualify as a statutory "food". Even if Section 321(g)(1)(C)

not consumed primarily for taste, aroma, or nutritive value under Section 321(f)(1); in fact, as noted earlier, they are taken for their ability to block the digestion of food and aid in weight loss. In addition, starch blockers are not chewing gum under Section 321(f)(2) and are not components of food under Section 321(f)(3). To qualify as a drug under Section 321(g)(1)(C), the articles must not only be articles "other than food," but must also be "intended to affect the structure or any function of the body of man or other animals." Starch blockers indisputably satisfy this requirement for they are intended to affect digestion in the people who take them. Therefore, starch blockers are drugs under Section 321(g)(1)(C) of the Food, Drug, and Cosmetic Act.

Affirmed.

NOTE

In another case brought at the same time in New York City, *American Health Prods. Co., Inc. v. Hayes,* 574 F. Supp. 1498 (S.D.N.Y. 1983), FDA advanced an argument not discussed by the *Nutrilab* court—that a product for which a physiological effect is claimed, but for which no therapeutic claim is advanced, falls outside the food exclusion in section 201(g)(1)(C):

> In deciding whether the FDA's determination that starchblockers are drugs is "in accordance with law," the FDA's interpretation merits substantial deference. A court must only ensure that the agency's action was "governed by an intelligible statutory principle." Here the government contends that subsection (g)(1)(C) contemplates dual classification; in addition to classifying as drugs all those products that affect bodily structure or functions and are not common foods, the Act is said also to classify as drugs within the part (C) definition even a "food" product, if it is sold with specific representations as to its physiological effects. The manufacturers argue, on the other hand, that the definition of "food" in subsection (f), which refers to common usage, governs the reach of the parenthetical exclusion in part (C). Therefore, they urge, if an article is a "food" under subsection (f), it cannot be regulated as a drug under subsection (g)(1)(C) regardless of any representations as to its structural or functional effects made in connection with its sale.
>
> The government's contention is untenable. Though most sections of the Act countenance dual classification, no other contains a parenthetical like that Congress inserted in part (C). Ignoring that parenthetical would render meaningless the distinctions Congress has attempted to delineate. Nevertheless, the government is correct in claiming that starchblocker pills are a "drug" under the Act, because the pills are not a "food" in any sense cognizable under the statute....

> meant only to exclude common-sense foods, an article might still be considered food unless addition of an appetite suppressant so changed its nature that it was no longer used primarily for taste, aroma or nutritional value. The FDA submits that a drug manufacturer could easily escape drug regulation by simply adding the drug to a food.

> It is not necessary to resolve this problem in order to resolve this case. We merely note the possibility that the word "component" might be interpreted to exclude substances specifically added to a food to avoid bringing the substance within the drug definition, and, as noted above, a food may lose its food character if a drug is added.

... [I]f an article affects bodily structure or function by way of its consumption as a food, the parenthetical precludes its regulation as a drug notwithstanding a manufacturer's representations as to physiological effect. The Act evidences throughout an objective to guarantee accurate information to consumers of foods, drugs, and cosmetics. The presence of the parenthetical in part (C) suggests that Congress did not want to inhibit the dissemination of useful information concerning a food's physiological properties by subjecting foods to drug regulation on the basis of representations in this regard.

Whether or not the parenthetical of section 321(g)(1)(C) incorporates the entire technical definition of food in section 321(f), however, and whether or not section 321(g)(1)(C) contemplates dual classification, the manufacturers cannot prevail here. Notwithstanding the government's contention that the FDA could regulate their products as a food if it chose to do so, the manufacturers cannot demonstrate that starchblockers are a food in any sense cognizable under the statute.....

An example offered by the manufacturers illustrates well the consequences of the dual classification dispute, but demonstrates at the same time its irrelevance to the case of starchblocker pills. Coffee is often consumed as a stimulant, but is also commonly drunk for its taste and aroma, if not its nutritional value. Were the parenthetical read to preclude dual classification, the common usage of coffee as a food would place it beyond the reach of the part (C) drug definition even though a manufacturer might promote its coffee exclusively for its use in staying awake. (A doctor who testified at the hearing on behalf of the FDA stated that such a coffee would remain a food notwithstanding such promotional claims.) This result is unavailable to the manufacturers of starchblockers, however, because they cannot demonstrate that their products are commonly used for food. The manufacturers simply cannot bring their products within the parenthetical of part (C).

Though it affirmed the district court, the Second Circuit specifically stated that "we do not reach the issue whether dual classification is appropriate under section 321(g)(1)(C)." *American Health Prods. Co. v. Hayes,* 744 F.2d 912 (2d Cir. 1984) (per curiam).

FDA has traditionally classified vitamin and mineral products as foods unless therapeutic claims are made for them. In the early 1970s, however, the agency was confronted with reports of human toxicity from large doses of vitamins A and D, which were endorsed in books by a self-proclaimed nutritional expert, Adelle Davis, who advocated a "natural" approach to good health. Vitamins A and D are fat-soluble nutrients, i.e., they accumulate in fatty tissue, and thus ingestion of excess quantities may lead to serious harm.

To meet this problem, FDA promulgated regulations, 37 Fed. Reg. 26618 (December 14, 1972), 38 Fed. Reg. 20723 (August 2, 1973), classifying preparations providing more than 10,000 international units

(IU) of vitamin A or 400 IU of vitamin D per daily serving as drugs and requiring further that they be sold only on prescription. The regulations were initially upheld, *National Nutritional Foods Ass'n v. Weinberger,* 376 F. Supp. 142 (S.D.N.Y. 1974), but the court of appeals concluded that the administrative record was incomplete and remanded the case with instructions to the district court to inquire into the full bases for the Commissioner's ruling. 512 F.2d 688 (2d Cir. 1975). After conducting the mandated hearing, the district court again upheld the regulations. 418 F. Supp. 394 (S.D.N.Y. 1976).

NATIONAL NUTRITIONAL FOODS ASS'N v. MATHEWS

United States Court of Appeals, Second Circuit, 1977.
557 F.2d 325.

Robert P. ANDERSON, Circuit Judge:

Plaintiffs-appellants, producers and vendors of vitamin preparations, appeal the dismissal of their action seeking declaratory and injunctive relief against regulations promulgated by the Food and Drug Administration (FDA) which classified preparations of Vitamins A and D in excess of 10,000 IU (international units) per dosage unit and 400 IU per dosage unit, respectively, as "drugs" under § 201(g)(1) of the Federal Food, Drug and Cosmetic Act, and which restricted them to prescription sale under § 503(b)(1) of the Act.

When this case was previously remanded by us to the district court, we said, " ⟨.. a serious question is raised as to whether the Commissioner, in concluding that the higher level dosage forms of Vitamins A and D are 'drugs,' acted 'in accordance with law.'⟩ The relevant portions of § 201(g) of the Act define a drug as:

> "(g)(1) the term 'drug' means (A) articles recognized in the official United States Pharmacopoeia, official Homoeopathic Pharmacopoeia of the United States, or official National Formulary, or any supplement to any of them; and (B) articles intended for use in the diagnosis, cure, mitigation, treatment or prevention of disease in man or other animals ..."

In the statement announcing the proposal of the Vitamins A and D regulations and in the one accompanying their adoption, the Commissioner did not rely upon the recognition of these preparations in the above named publications as the basis of the drug classification. Rather, the Commissioner determined that the circumstances surrounding the use of Vitamins A and D at the regulated levels indicated an intended therapeutic use under § 201(g)(1)(B). The vendors' intent in selling the product to the public is the key element in this statutory definition.

In determining whether an article is a "drug" because of an intended therapeutic use, the FDA is not bound by the manufacturer's subjective claims of intent but can find actual therapeutic intent on the basis of objective evidence. Such intent also may be derived or inferred from labeling, promotional material, advertising, and "any other relevant source." In remanding this case, this court expressly indicated that evidence that Vitamins A and D at the regulated levels were used "almost exclusively for therapeutic purposes" when coupled with lack of a recognized nutritional use, would be sufficient to show that high dosage Vitamins A and D products were intended for use in the treatment of disease.

In proposing the regulations, the Commissioner emphasized the potential for toxicity and the widespread promotion of the intake of high doses of Vitamins A and D to cure a variety of ills. To show objective therapeutic intent, the Commissioner's affidavit submitted on remand relied upon three factors: (1) widespread promotion to the public in the use of high potency Vitamins A and D preparations for the treatment of various ailments; (2) lack of recognized nutritional usefulness; and (3) potential for toxicity from the ingestion of large doses of these vitamins over extended periods of time....

Plaintiffs assert that toxicity is irrelevant to the issue of therapeutic intent and, although the key element in determining that a drug should be limited to prescription use under § 503(b) of the Act, it has no bearing upon whether an article is a drug. The Government argues, on the other hand, that toxicity is relevant to therapeutic intent and that the Commissioner must make the decision of whether there should be a regulation which classifies an article as a food or as a drug, for the purposes of the Act. Although an article may be recognized as a food, this does not preclude it from being regulated as a drug. The determination that an article is properly regulated as a drug, however, is not left to the Commissioner's unbridled discretion to act to protect the public health but must be in accordance with the statutory definition. Toxicity is not included as an element in the statutory definition of a drug. It is relevant as a factor supporting the Commissioner's classification under § 201(g)(1)(B), but only to the extent that it constitutes objective evidence of therapeutic intent. Toxicity is cited by the Commissioner as constituting objective evidence of "something more" than lack of nutritional usefulness.... Such evidence, however, only presents a further indication that the excessive intake of Vitamins A and D may not be nutritionally useful and does not provide the objective evidence of therapeutic intent necessary to support these regulations.

There is no evidence in the administrative record that the manufacturers and vendors of Vitamins A and D preparations, at the regulated dosages, represent through labeling, promotional materials, or advertising that these products are effective in the cure or treatment of disease. They are sold as "dietary supplements." ...

The main issue on this appeal is whether the evidence of the extensive use of large doses of Vitamins A and D to treat or prevent diseases and the promotion of such usage by persons not associated with the manufacturers or vendors establishes such widespread therapeutic use at the regulated levels as to overcome the plaintiffs' claim of the lack of an intended use to cure or prevent disease and thus justifies the Commissioner's determination.

The Commissioner admits that below the stated levels of potency, Vitamins A and D are foods. The evidence relied upon to show therapeutic intent, therefore, must be related to the potency level chosen to differentiate between the use of Vitamins A and D as foods and the use of these vitamins as drugs. The administrative record clearly establishes that the factors involved in choosing the levels at which Vitamins A and D become drugs were solely related to the Commissioner's fear of potential toxic effect and his belief that the ingestion of vitamins at levels above the U.S. RDA is not nutritionally useful. No further record evidence has been produced on the remand to show that the 10,000 IU and 400 IU levels were chosen because at those potencies, consumption of them is almost exclusively for therapeutic purposes. A sampling of the comments submitted to the FDA after publication of the proposed regulations reveals that people believe that a wide range of doses of these vitamins are therapeutically useful. A large group of individuals indicated that they ingested these vitamins at various dosages solely to supplement their daily diet in the belief that more Vitamins A and D were needed to maintain optimal health than the upper limits in the U.S. RDA.

In remanding this case, this court suggested that proof in the record demonstrating that, at the 10,000 IU and 400 IU levels, respectively, these vitamins were taken "almost exclusively" for therapeutic purposes, would tend to show that the regulations were not arbitrary or capricious. There was no evidence, however, supporting the Commissioner's conclusion that, when sold at the regulated, *i.e.* prescription, levels, therapeutic usage of these vitamins so far outweighed their use as dietary supplements, it showed an objective intent that these products were used in the mitigation and cure of diseases. This claim furnished no contradiction to the charge that the FDA's regulations are arbitrary and capricious and not in accordance with law....

The Commissioner also seeks to justify the Vitamins A and D regulations on the basis of § 201(g)(1)(A), which defines as drugs, articles "recognized" in the United States Pharmacopoeia (USP) or National Formulary (NF). Both Vitamins A and D are included in the USP and NF.... To construe § 201(g)(1)(A) so as to grant the Commissioner the power to regulate as drugs every item mentioned in the USP and NF solely on the basis of such inclusion would give the FDA virtually unlimited discretion to regulate as drugs a vast range of items.... An administrator's decision under a regulatory statute, such as the Food, Drug, and Cosmetic Act, must be governed by an intelligible statutory principle. If § 201(g)(1)(A) defines as drugs every item included in the USP and NF, the FDA is not being consistent in its treatment of other items similarly recognized. The Commissioner, therefore, has not applied the § 201(g)(1)(A) definition to every item in the compendia. Rather he has singled out for drug classification items included in the USP and NF on the basis of factors, such as toxicity in this case, that are not relevant to the statutory criteria in § 201(g).

The Commissioner admitted in his affidavit that mere inclusion in the USP and NF is an insufficient basis for drug classification after the decision in *National Nutritional Foods Ass'n v. FDA, supra* (504 F.2d 761). He attempts to distinguish that case on the ground that Vitamins A and D are recognized at therapeutic dosages in the compendia and are regulated as drugs in this case only at levels in excess of the recognized food levels in the USP. Other articles, however, are recognized in the compendia at therapeutic levels and not regulated as drugs, for example Vitamin C. The Commissioner must, therefore, show that the conflicting treatment in the regulations of items similarly classified in the USP and NF is not arbitrary under the applicable criteria. The FDA regulates Vitamin C preparations at the USP's therapeutic level as food. To justify the regulation of Vitamins A and D as drugs by relying on § 201(g)(1)(A) the Commissioner would have to distinguish his treatment of Vitamin C as food.

In proposing and adopting these regulations for Vitamins A and D, the Commissioner did not rely upon or cite the recognition of these vitamins in the USP and NF. He may not at this late hour on appeal rely upon them as the basis for his drug classification because it is sheer *post hoc* rationalization....

NOTES

1. *Subsequent Proceedings.* Following this decision, FDA revoked the regulations in 43 Fed. Reg. 10551 (March 14, 1978).

2. *Once a Drug?* In *United States v. Articles of Drug ... Neptone,* Food Drug Cosm. L. Rep. (CCH) ¶ 38,240 (N.D. Cal. 1983), FDA contended that the seized product was a drug and was granted summary judgment based on the following reasoning:

... Claimant Aquaculture Corporation markets in the United States a product called Neptone, which is freeze-dried, homogenized, powdered New Zealand green mussel (Perna canaliculus) in capsule form. In 1976, claimant received from the Food and Drug Administration ("FDA") an Investigational Exemption for New Drug ("IND") for Neptone. The purpose of this exemption is to permit claimant to conduct clinical investigations into Neptone's safety and effectiveness.

Neptone is sold in health food stores and by mail order. Claimant advertises in various health food magazines. Since 1980, claimant has also promoted Neptone through several brochures, magazine reprints, and a scientific paper. These were available on request and were sent to mail order customers. FDA Consumer Safety Officer Paul J. Sage was one such customer. In general, claimant's advertising extols the green mussel (and Neptone) as being high in mucopolysaccharides, which are claimed to help prevent diseases commonly associated with aging, such as arthritis and hardening of the arteries....

... The Court finds that the claimant's promotional claims clearly show that it intended Neptone to be used "in the diagnosis, cure, mitigation, treatment, or prevention of disease in man." The so-called "brown brochure" is the most flagrant example, but even the so-called "blue brochure" claims, among other things, that Neptone helps to repel infection, prevent blood clots, and maintain the elasticity of the arteries. . . .

The Court does not view this opinion as establishing for all time that Neptone is a drug. The determination that Neptone is a drug rests entirely on the pattern of promotion used by claimant in the several years immediately preceding the instant seizure. Should Neptone again be marketed after some hiatus and a change in labelling, this order will not necessarily work an estoppel on whether that batch of Neptone is a drug.[4] The answer will turn on the relationship between the future sales and the offensive labelling. Clearly, this opinion cannot work any estoppel on the issues of misbranding and safety and effectiveness. . . . .

The Court recognizes that not applying collateral estoppel to future batches of Neptone might allow it to be marketed without its having been established as safe and effective. Fault for this lies with the drafters of this statute for conditioning the safety and effectiveness requirements on labelling. As noted above, claimant brought the regulatory scheme down upon itself through its labelling and promotional brochures; this Court will not take the further step of saying that now claimant can never get out from under the regulatory scheme.

3. *Other Cases.* *See also* the following cases in which the courts held that products ordinarily regarded as foods are properly classified as drugs because of the claims made for them: *United States v. 250 Jars . . . "Cal's Tupelo Blossom U.S. Fancy Pure Honey"*, 344 F.2d 288 (6th Cir. 1965), *United States v. 24 Bottles . . . "Sterling Vinegar and Honey"*, 338 F.2d 157 (2d Cir. 1964); *United States v. Hohensee*, 243 F.2d 367 (3d Cir. 1957) (tea); *United States v. 500 Plastic Bottles . . . "Wilfley's Bio Water,"* Food Drug Cosm. L. Rep. (CCH) ¶ 38,143 (D. Or. 1989) (water); *United States v. Kollman,* Food Drug Cosm. L. Rep. (CCH) ¶ 38,342 (D. Or. 1985 & 1986) (blue-green algae harvested from Klamath Lake, Oregon).

4. *Evidence of Intended Use.* In determining whether a product is to be classed as a food or a drug, oral and written promotional statements from any source are relevant. *See, e.g., United States v. Hohensee*, 243 F.2d 367 (3d Cir. 1957); *United States v. Millpax, Inc.*, 313 F.2d 152 (7th Cir. 1963); *Nature Food Centres, Inc. v. United States*, 310 F.2d 67 (1st Cir. 1962); *United States v. Article of Drug Designated B–Complex Cholinos Capsules*, 362 F.2d 923 (3d Cir. 1966).

5. *No Longer "Fit" Food.* A product is a food under the Act if it is generally regarded as food when sold in food form, even if it is decomposed or otherwise unfit for food at the time FDA institutes legal action against it. *See, e.g., United States v. H.B. Gregory Co.*, 502 F.2d 700 (7th Cir. 1974); *Otis McAllister & Co. v. United States*, 194 F.2d 386 (5th Cir. 1952); *United States v. O.F. Bayer & Co.*, 188 F.2d 555 (2d Cir. 1951); *United States v. 52 Drums Maple*

---

4. This reasoning does not apply to any Neptone now in existence that is not currently under the *in rem* jurisdiction of this Court. The Court has found that claimant's promotions over the past few years reveal Neptone's intended use as a drug. These promotional claims presumably apply to the Neptone that was effectively seized as well as to the Neptone that was [not] effectively seized.

Syrup, 110 F.2d 914 (2d Cir. 1940); *United States v. Technical Egg Products, Inc.,* 171 F. Supp. 326 (N.D. Ga. 1959); *United States v. Thirteen Crates of Frozen Eggs,* 215 Fed. 584 (2d Cir. 1914). *See also* Annotation: *What is "Food" Within Meaning of Statute,* 17 A.L.R. 1282 (1922).

6. *Migrating Food–Contact Materials.* The statutory definition of food includes substances that migrate from food packaging, *Natick Paperboard Corp. v. Weinberger,* 525 F.2d 1103 (1st Cir. 1975), and substances that migrate to food from dinnerware, *United States v. Articles of Food Consisting of Pottery ... Labeled Cathy Rose,* 370 F. Supp. 371 (E.D. Mich. 1974).

7. *Dual Food and Drug Classification.* Not only may a product be classified as both a food and a drug, but a product currently marketed as a food may at the same time undergo clinical investigation for drug uses (in compliance with the FDA investigational drug requirements, p. 513 *infra*). *See, e.g.,* "Nutrition Education—1973: Phosphate Research and Dental Decay," Hearings before the Senate Select Comm. on Nutrition and Human Needs, 93d Cong., 1st Sess. 549 (1973).

8. *Food Regulatory History. See generally* Hutt and Hutt II, *A History of Government Regulation of Adulteration and Misbranding of Food,* 39 FDC L.J. 2 (1984); *Symposium on Fifty Years of Food Regulation Under the Federal Food, Drug, and Cosmetic Act,* 45 FDC L.J. 17 (1990).

SPECIFIC FOOD CATEGORIES

Several categories of food products are subject to specific regulatory requirements.

Meat, Poultry, and Eggs. These products are regulated by the United States Department of Agriculture (USDA) under the Federal Meat Inspection Act, 21 U.S.C. § 601 *et seq.,* the Poultry Products Inspection Act, 21 U.S.C. § 451 *et seq.,* and the Egg Products Inspection Act, 21 U.S.C. § 1031 *et seq.* USDA has ceded to FDA jurisdiction over any food containing less than two percent of meat or poultry. The jurisdiction of USDA and FDA over these three categories of food products is otherwise complex and uncertain. FDA has exclusive regulatory jurisdiction over live animals intended to be used for food. *United States v. Tomahara Enterprises, Ltd.,* Food Drug Cosm. L. Rep. (CCH) ¶ 38,217 (N.D.N.Y. 1983). USDA has exclusive jurisdiction over the slaughter of food animals and over the subsequent processing of meat and poultry, except that USDA and FDA have joint jurisdiction over the use of food additives in meat and poultry. After processing, USDA and FDA have joint jurisdiction over the distribution of meat and poultry up to the retail establishment where it is sold. FDA has exclusive jurisdiction over retail food establishments. *D & W Food Centers, Inc. v. Block,* 786 F.2d 751 (6th Cir. 1986), held that a central kitchen making pizza containing meat was not subject to the continuous inspection requirements of the Federal Meat Inspection Act. *See generally Food Regulation: A Case Study of USDA and FDA,* in "Study on Federal Regulation: Regulatory Organization," Senate Comm. on Governmental Affairs, 95th Cong., 1st Sess., Vol. V, at Ch. 4 (Comm. Print 1977).

Alcoholic Beverages. The Bureau of Alcohol, Tobacco, and Firearms (BATF) of the Department of the Treasury has jurisdiction over alcoholic beverages under the Federal Alcohol Administration Act, 49 Stat. 977 (1935), codified in 27 U.S.C. § 201 *et seq.* BATF regulates all beer products regardless of their alcohol content. 51 Fed. Reg. 39666 (October 30, 1986). In contrast, BATF regulates only those wine products that contain 7 percent alcohol or more, and FDA regulates all wine products containing less than 7 percent alcohol. FDA Compliance Policy Guide No. 7101.05 (October 1, 1980). Attempts to amend the Federal Alcohol Administration Act to extend BATF jurisdiction to wine products containing as little as 0.5 percent alcohol have been unsuccessful. Accordingly, wine coolers, which have an alcohol content of less than 7 percent, are regulated by FDA rather than BATF. A court has held that the labeling of alcoholic beverages is subject only to BATF jurisdiction and is exempt from the labeling requirements of the FD&C Act, *Brown–Forman Distillers Corp. v. Mathews,* 435 F. Supp. 5 (W.D. Ky. 1976). In other respects, however, alcoholic beverages are regulated as food by FDA. *See* Cooper, *The FDA, the BATF, and Liquor Labeling: A Case Study of Interagency Jurisdictional Conflict,* 34 FDC L.J. 370 (1979); Hancock, *Federal Jurisdictional Disputes in the Labeling and Advertising of Malt Beverages,* 34 FDC L.J. 271 (1979); *Symposium on Alcoholic Beverage Control,* 7 Law & Contemp. Probs. 543 (1940). FDA has adopted Compliance Policy Guide 7101.04, 54 Fed. Reg. 38559 (September 19, 1989), governing the labeling of dealcoholized wine and malt beverages.

Chewing Gum. Section 201(f)(2) of the FD&C Act specifically classifies chewing gum as food. As a result, FDA has taken the position that, when snuff is included in a masticatory carrier base, which has the appearance of a piece of confectionary, it is properly regulated as a food. *See* Letter from FDA Associate Commissioner for Regulatory Affairs J.M. Taylor to S.M. Pape (April 11, 1988).

Water and Ice. Under the Safe Drinking Water Act, 88 Stat. 1660 (1974), general responsibility for the purity of drinking water was placed in EPA, but section 410 was added to the FD&C Act to preserve FDA's jurisdiction over bottled drinking water. The agency also has jurisdiction over ice. *See* Felix, *Ice—the Forgotten Food,* 53 J. AFDO 19 (July 1989). Water used to process food or as an ingredient in food is subject to the same requirements under the FD&C Act as any other food constituent.

CULTURAL INFLUENCES ON FOOD REGULATION

The authors are indebted to Lewis A. Segall for pointing out the current debate on the origin and meaning of dietary practices and the problems they create for FDA. M. Sahlins, CULTURAL AND PRACTICAL REASON (1976), argues that western societies eat cattle but not dogs, not because of the difference in their worth as foodstuffs, but because of the difference in the degree to which they are identified with humanity. M. Harris, CULTURAL MATERIALISM: THE STRUGGLE FOR A SCIENCE OF CULTURE (1979), contends that food decisions are made solely on the basis of material factors. Dogs are bred for hunting and companionship and are not used for food because many other meat sources exist. These opposing views illustrate Segall's point:

[F]requently attitudes toward different foods may have less to do with rational instrumental reasoning than with cultural meaning. Contemporary fears of cancer are from this perspective an interesting case. On the one hand, cancer is a serious threat to health, and it is rational to want to avoid foods which may cause it. On the other hand, the public appears to have somewhat irrational attitudes toward cancer-causing food, failing to realize the greater danger from natural than from artificial substances, and generally having great difficulty in comparing levels of risk and acting accordingly. Public attitudes toward cancer and food seem neither solely material or cultural.

The case of alar on apples seems a good example of how cultural meanings (in this instance the possibility of cancer in the school lunchbox) may play a significant role in shaping regulatory policy.... [O]ne of the fascinating aspects of food regulation is precisely the interaction of these two realms: a federal agency concerned with safety and health, and basing its decisions on scientific grounds, is charged with regulating a part of society which is fraught with nonrational cultural attitudes, prejudices, and allegiances.... [F]ood regulation ... operates in a world of cultural meanings. The point is not that these cultural meanings are wrong or misguided, much less that they should determine regulatory decisions. Rather it is that accounting for culture may give a fuller account of the dynamics of regulatory policy.

Letter from L. A. Segall to P. B. Hutt (April 12, 1990).

B. REGULATION OF FOOD LABELING

This part focuses on government efforts to protect the economic expectations of both consumers and food distributors. It begins with a historical overview, to place the various FDA policies that relate to food misbranding in their broader context, and then proceeds to analyze each of those policies in greater detail. It covers all of the FD&C Act's mandatory food labeling requirements except for the name of the food itself. Part C covers both standards of identity for food and the requirement that every food be labeled with its own common or usual name, including the requirement that an imitation food be labeled as such. Part D covers the application of the basic food labeling provisions set forth in Parts B and C to the regulation of the nutrient content of food. Part E covers specific requirements applicable to vitamin-mineral products.

1. HISTORICAL OVERVIEW

Section 403 of the Act itemizes the circumstances under which a food will be considered "misbranded" and thus subject to enforcement action. Most of the varieties of "misbranding" specified in section 403 relate to information included in, or omitted from, the "label" or "labeling" of food products. In various ways, these definitions of misbranding are designed to force food suppliers to tell the truth about their products. Section 403(a) thus prohibits label statements that are "false or misleading in any particular." Additional provisions are aimed at other types of affirmative deceptions respecting quality, quantity, or identity. Other provisions force manufacturers to provide information that they might otherwise omit—such as the complete ingredients of a product. These affirmative requirements thus make assumptions about the types of information that consumers need to make wise choices.

PETER BARTON HUTT, REGULATING THE MISBRANDING OF FOOD

43 Food Technology 288 (September 1989).

The statutory provisions enacted by Congress in 1938 to regulate food misbranding have remained virtually unchanged.... This history therefore reflects evolving administrative policy implemented by FDA, not statutory changes adopted by Congress. This history is split into two eras, divided by the White House Conference on Food, Nutrition, and Health held in December 1969. The Conference report and the new FDA leadership that was committed to implementation of the regulatory policy recommended in that report profoundly changed FDA's approach to food regulation and permitted the full use of modern food technology.

1939–69

Following enactment of the FD&C Act in 1938, FDA relied primarily upon five statutory provisions to regulate food misbranding: (1) the mandatory information required by the statute to appear on all food labels, (2) mandatory standards of identity for food products, (3) the labeling of imitation food, (4) nutrition information for special dietary food, and (5) the prohibition of any false or misleading claims.

1. *Mandatory Food Labeling.* Under Section 403 of the FD&C Act, every food label must bear, at the very minimum, the following four categories of information: the name of the food; a statement of the ingredients; the net quantity of contents; and the name and address of the manufacturer or distributor. Under the 1906 Act, as it was originally enacted, none of this information was required. The Gould Amendment of 1913 for the first time required that the net quantity of contents be labeled on food packages.....

2. *Standards of Identity for Food.* Ancient botanists, beginning with Theophrastus (370–285 B.C.), established "standards" by describing the available food supply and warning against its adulteration with other substances. Standards of identity for bread were established in the Roman Empire and in medieval England, to assure the integrity of the food supply. The same approach has been pursued to the present.

Even before enactment of the 1906 Act, FDA had established some 200 informal food standards. Although Congress declined to include legal authority for mandatory food standards in the 1906 Act, FDA continued with this work until the FD&C Act was enacted in 1938. Section 401 of the FD&C Act authorized FDA to promulgate definitions and standards of identity for any food product in order to "promote honesty and fair dealing in the interest of consumers." Because of its long interest in food standards, FDA promptly moved to implement this new authority.... By 1970, it was estimated that half of the American food supply was subject to an FDA food standard.

When these early food standards were adopted, modern food technology was just beginning to flourish. Some functional food ingredients (*e.g.*, preservatives, emulsifiers, thickeners, and so forth) were in use, but many staple foods remained quite simple and had not yet undergone the transformation that later occurred. Moreover, at this time FDA had no independent statutory authority to require premarket testing and approval of new food additives for safety. Accordingly, FDA adopted the policy of establishing "recipe" standards of identity, under which every permitted ingredient was specifically listed in the standard. Under this policy, no new ingredient could be used until the standard was amended to include it. Accordingly, all progress in food technology for standardized foods depended upon amendment of the applicable food standards. With enactment of the Food Additives Amendment of 1958 and the Color Additive Amendments of 1960, and the rapid development of food technology, use of recipe standards was no longer warranted. FDA initially experimented with a new, broader form of standard, which permitted any "safe and suitable" functional ingredient, in the 1960s, but did not move to broaden all of the existing standards.

One particular aspect of food standards, not specifically mentioned in the statute, became a principal focus of this activity. Developing knowledge about essential vitamins and minerals during the 1930s led the American Medical Association's Council on Food and Nutrition to adopt a policy that food fortification should be reserved for exceptional cases where there is convincing evidence of a need for the vitamin or mineral and where the food to be fortified is a suitable carrier. When FDA announced public hearings in 1940 to establish a standard of identity for flour, both AMA and the National Academy of Sciences recommended that the standard establish appropriate levels for enrichment with vitamins and minerals. The enriched flour standard of identity became effective on January 1, 1942, and set a pattern for numerous subsequent standards for enriched food.

To prevent indiscriminate food fortification, FDA issued a statement in July 1943 setting forth the agency policy on addition of vitamins and minerals to food. Following World War II, however, food fortification continued to grow. By the early 1960s, FDA was convinced that a more restrictive regulatory approach was necessary to prevent overfortification of the American food supply. FDA proposed to limit fortification to eight classes of food, with 12 essential nutrients....

3. *Imitation Food.* The 1906 Act had prohibited imitation food. Section 403(c) of the FD&C Act provided, however, that any imitation food must be labeled as an imitation. FDA initially sought to apply this statutory provision to control the development of new substitute food products. It argued that any imitation of a standardized product was inherently illegal, but the Supreme Court overruled the agency on this point in 1951. When a substitute ice cream was made from soybeans and marketed as "Chil–Zert," FDA brought a successful legal

action to require that it be labeled as an imitation ice cream. This was, however, the high point of FDA's use of the imitation provision to inhibit the marketing of new food products. As food technology progressed, and more substitute products were marketed, the agency did not institute legal action to prevent their sale.

Nonetheless, FDA did adhere tenaciously to the position that the name of a standardized food could not be used as part of the name of a nonstandardized substitute product. The Supreme Court had ruled in 1943 that, once FDA had established a standard of identity, the standard could not be evaded by adding nonpermitted ingredients and revising the name of the food to reflect that change....

... FDA took no administrative action to clarify its position on the imitation provision. Several states therefore brought action against new substitute food products under comparable provisions in their state laws....

4. *Special Dietary Food Labeling.* Under Section 403(j) of the FD&C Act, FDA was authorized to promulgate regulations to require label information concerning the vitamin, mineral, and other dietary properties of food represented for special dietary uses. In November 1941, following a public hearing, FDA promulgated regulations governing vitamin-mineral supplements, fortified food products, and such other special dietary foods as infant food, hypo-allergenic food, and food used in weight control.

Because these were labeling requirements and imposed no limit upon other claims or permissible formulations, the types of special dietary products marketed, and the claims made for them, proliferated. In spite of numerous court actions and educational approaches, FDA could not bring these products under control.... As a result, FDA concluded that the only reasonable approach to this matter would be through revision of the 1941 regulations. As part of the proposed regulations to restrict food fortification already discussed above, FDA proposed to limit the number of permitted formulations of dietary supplements of vitamins and minerals and to ban common labeling claims for these products that the agency regarded as false or misleading.....

5. *Prohibition of False or Misleading Claims.* Like the 1906 Act, Section 403(a) of the FD&C Act prohibited any false or misleading statement in food labeling. Most fraudulent or outrageous food claims had long since disappeared as a result of FDA regulatory action taken under the 1906 Act. With the advent of food fortification and vitamin-mineral supplements, and the gradual unfolding of scientific evidence about the relationship of diet and health, new regulatory problems emerged.

... FDA readily permitted general health claims for food products, but sought to prohibit any specific claim that a food or food component would prevent a particular disease. Following publication of a major report to the American Heart Association in August 1957 recommending a reduction in dietary cholesterol and saturated fats, labeling and advertising claims for common food products made reference to this new information. Faced with these claims, FDA sought to prohibit any reference to cholesterol or saturated fat, considering such reference as "nutritional quackery." As time wore on, however, and the scientific evidence became more compelling, increased pressure was placed on the agency to change its position. By the late 1960s, FDA continued to adhere to its policy in public, but took relatively little legal action to enforce it.

The White House Conference on Food, Nutrition, and Health

President Nixon announced a White House Conference on Food, Nutrition, and Health in May 1969. . . . Although the White House Conference was convened in response to charges of hunger and malnutrition in America, and not to consider regulatory issues, its conclusions had a dramatic and unexpected impact on FDA policy in regulating food misbranding. The highly restrictive approach to food standards, imitation labeling, special dietary foods, and nutrition claims that was the subject of the formal public hearing conducted by FDA during 1968 and 1969 was thoroughly criticized and rejected. The White House Conference report emphasized the need for sound nutrition, the capability of modern food technology to provide products to fill that need, and the use of increased public information about nutrition, rather than the problems of nutrition quackery. . . .

1969–89

The White House Conference represented the end of the restrictive approach to food regulation proposed by FDA during the 1960s. In its place emerged a number of new regulations, based largely on food labeling requirements rather than on rigid standards for product composition.

1. *Mandatory Food Labeling Information.* The same four statutory categories of mandatory information remain. In two respects, however, they have been changed to reflect the new emphasis on provision of adequate information to consumers rather than on establishing rigid standards for product composition.

Under the FD&C Act, a standardized food is not required to include on the label any mandatory ingredient in the food, and is required to include on the label only those optional ingredients that are specified as required to be labeled under the standard. Pursuant to its policy of encouraging full labeling for all food products, FDA urged food manufacturers and distributors to include in the statement of ingredients both mandatory and optional ingredients and began systematically to amend all existing food standards to make as many "mandatory" ingredients optional as possible and to require the labeling of all optional ingredients.

FDA also promulgated new regulations governing the names to be used on the labels for food products. The new regulations emphasized that a food name must accurately identify or describe the basic nature of the food or its characterizing properties or ingredients, and distinguish the food from different foods. Related regulations provided for inclusion, as part of the food name, the percentage of any characterizing ingredients, or a statement that the food does not contain ingredients that might otherwise be expected....

2. *Food Standards.* In the early 1970s, FDA began a systematic amendment of all existing food standards to eliminate the old "recipe" approach and to permit any "safe and suitable" functional ingredient. Accordingly, it is no longer necessary to amend existing food standards to permit the use of new food additives and color additives once they have been approved as safe for use.

Since 1970, FDA has not proposed or promulgated new food standards. In a number of instances where food standards had been proposed in the past, they were replaced with regulations that simply establish the name of the food, pursuant to the regulations discussed above. This approach has permitted greater flexibility in food labeling and food formulation.

As a related policy, FDA has abandoned its old position that any resemblance of a new food to a traditional standardized food, or any reference to a standardized food in the name for a new food, automatically renders the new food illegal. For example, FDA has stated that "raisin bread made with enriched flour" does not violate the raisin bread standard; "enriched macaroni products with fortified protein" does not violate the enriched macaroni standard; "tomato juice enriched with vitamin C" does not violate the tomato juice standard; and "goat's milk yogurt" does not violate the yogurt standard....

The limitation of fortification to listed foods, within specified levels, was totally abandoned. Fortification of standardized foods was permitted, where no enrichment standard already existed....

Finally, FDA adopted new regulations governing nutrition labeling for all food. Except for bread products that must be enriched under state laws, it is not mandatory that any food product either be enriched with vitamins or minerals or bear labeling relating to its nutritional value. FDA therefore promulgated a requirement that, if any nutrient is added to a food, or any nutrition claim is made for a food, the product must bear full nutrition labeling in the format established by FDA....

FDA made a conscious trade-off in adopting this new approach. It substantially reduced the restrictions on formulation and composition imposed by food standards and other regulations, and correspondingly increased the labeling requirements for all food. The food industry was thus free to pursue the benefits of modern food technology, but only at the price of providing far more information to consumers through food labeling.

3. *Imitation Food.* To eliminate the confusion and resulting barrier to innovation in the food industry caused by the lack of a clear policy relating to the imitation labeling provision, FDA in 1973 promulgated a regulation defining "imitation" solely in terms of nutritional inferiority.... FDA emphasized that a new food product, rather than being called "imitation," should bear its own descriptive name under the rules already discussed above.

4. *Special Dietary Foods.* When FDA abandoned its restrictive approach to food fortification, it retained limitations upon the composition and potency of vitamin-mineral supplements. In 1974, however, the courts remanded part of these regulations for further action, and in 1976 Congress amended the FD&C Act to add a new Section 411 which significantly curtailed FDA's authority to restrict the composition of dietary supplements....

In all other areas relating to special dietary foods, however, FDA has successfully completed its modernization of the regulations. Final special dietary food regulations have now been promulgated for hypo-allergenic food, infant food, weight-control food, diabetic food, and low-sodium food.

5. *Prohibition of False or Misleading Claims.* As part of its new approach to more expansive food labeling, FDA adopted in the early 1970s a distinction between the provision of specific information relating to food composition, and the use of specific health claims based upon that composition. FDA took the position that product composition information was lawful, as permitted by nutrition labeling, but that any specific claim that the composition of a product would help prevent a particular disease was unlawful. Thus, FDA permitted cholesterol and fatty acid information as an optional part of nutrition labeling, but prohibited any claims linking that information to a potential reduction in heart disease.

In March 1985, however, FDA announced a major change in this policy. Under the new FDA policy, specific claims about prevention of disease are permitted if they are recognized as valid by qualified experts, they emphasize that good nutrition is a function of the total diet, the claims are reasonably uniform within the marketplace, and they do not result in dietary "power" races....

6. *Slack Fill and Deceptive Packaging.* Although Congress considered amending the 1906 Act to prohibit slack fill and deceptive packaging, such a provision was not enacted until the FD&C Act. In large part because FDA lost every contested case under this provision, Congress included in the Fair Packaging and Labeling Act of 1966 discretionary authority for FDA to establish regulations governing nonfunctional slack fill. After a decade of study, however, FDA concluded that slack fill did not represent a major problem, and thus no such regulations have been promulgated....

JURISDICTION OVER FOOD ADVERTISING

The Wheeler–Lea Amendments of 1938, 52 Stat. 111, 114, confirmed the authority of the Federal Trade Commission to regulate advertising for foods, while FDA retained primary responsibility for their labeling. This division of jurisdiction was a point of sharp controversy during Congressional consideration of the FD&C Act during 1933–1938, and the FTC's retention of jurisdiction was viewed as a victory for the industries that produced and marketed these products. The bifurcation of authority has meant that considerable attention has been focused on defining the outer limits of FDA jurisdiction over "labeling."

---

2. SCOPE OF "LABELING"

The cases immediately following deal with the jurisdictional reach of FDA's labeling requirements. All of them involve health food products against which FDA took action because of their therapeutic claims. The terms "label" and "labeling," defined in section 201, have the same meaning for all products covered by the FD&C Act.

KORDEL v. UNITED STATES

Supreme Court of the United States, 1948.
335 U.S. 345.

Opinion of the Court by Mr. Justice DOUGLAS, announced by Mr. Justice REED.

Kordel was charged by informations containing twenty counts of introducing or delivering for introduction into interstate commerce misbranded drugs. He was tried without a jury, found guilty, and fined two hundred dollars on each count. This judgment was affirmed on appeal.

... Since 1941 [Kordel] has been marketing his own health food products, which appear to be compounds of various vitamins, minerals and herbs. The alleged misbranding consists of statements in circulars or pamphlets distributed to consumers by the vendors of the products, relating to their efficacy. The petitioner supplies these pamphlets as well as the products to the vendors. Some of the literature was displayed in stores in which the petitioner's products were on sale. Some of it was given away with the sale of products; some sold independently of the drugs; and some mailed to customers by the vendors.

It is undisputed that petitioner shipped or caused to be shipped in interstate commerce both the drugs and the literature. Seven of the counts charged that the drugs and literature were shipped in the same cartons. The literature involved in the other counts was shipped separately from the drugs and at different times—both before and after the shipments of the drugs with which they were associated. The question whether the separate shipment of the literature saved the drugs from being misbranded within the meaning of the [FD&C] Act presents the main issue in the case.

. . . The term labeling is defined in § 201(m) to mean "all labels and other written, printed, or graphic matter (1) upon any article or any of its containers or wrappers, or (2) accompanying such article." . . . In this case the drugs and the literature had a common origin and a common destination. The literature was used in the sale of the drugs. It explained their uses. Nowhere else was the purchaser advised how to use them. It constituted an essential supplement to the label attached to the package. Thus the products and the literature were interdependent. . . . .

It would, indeed, create an obviously wide loophole to hold that these drugs would be misbranded if the literature had been shipped in the same container but not misbranded if the literature left in the next or in the preceding mail. The high purpose of the Act to protect consumers who under present conditions are largely unable to protect themselves in this field would then be easily defeated. The administrative agency charged with its enforcement has not given the Act any such restricted construction. . . . Accordingly, we conclude that the phrase "accompanying such article" is not restricted to labels that are on or in the article or package that is transported.

The first clause of § 201(m)—all labels "upon any article or any of its containers or wrappers"—clearly embraces advertising or descriptive matter that goes with the package in which the articles are transported. The second clause—"accompanying such article"—has no specific reference to packages, containers or their contents as did a predecessor statute. It plainly includes what is contained within the package whether or not it is "upon" the article or its wrapper or container. But the second clause does not say "accompanying such article in the package or container," and we see no reason for reading the additional words into the text.

One article or thing is accompanied by another when it supplements or explains it, in the manner that a committee report of the Congress accompanies a bill. No physical attachment one to the other is necessary. It is the textual relationship that is significant. . . . . Moreover, the fact that some of the booklets carried a selling price is immaterial on the facts shown here. . . . The Act cannot be circumvented by the easy device of a "sale" of the advertising matter where the advertising performs the function of labeling.

Petitioner points out that in the evolution of the Act the ban on false advertising was eliminated, the control over it being transferred to the Federal Trade Commission. We have searched the legislative history in vain, however, to find any indication that Congress had the purpose to eliminate from the Act advertising which performs the function of labeling. Every labeling is in a sense an advertisement. The advertising which we have here performs the same function as it would if it were on the article or on the containers or wrappers. As we have said, physical attachment or contiguity is unnecessary under § 201(m)(2)....

[The dissenting opinion of Justice Black, in which Justice Frankfurter, Justice Murphy and Justice Jackson joined, is omitted.]

NOTE

The defendant in *Kordel* was responsible for the shipment of both the products and the descriptive pamphlets, even though the two acts were divorced in time. But the possibility that the Court's expansive interpretation of the Act's definition of "labeling" might have been influenced by the facts of the case was laid to rest by its decision in *United States v. Urbuteit*, 335 U.S. 355 (1948), decided the same day. In *Urbuteit*, a seizure action, the Court similarly found that leaflets shipped at a different time than the medical devices nonetheless accompanied the devices:

> ... [T]he common sense of the matter is to view the interstate transaction in its entirety—the purpose of the advertising and its actual use. In this case it is plain to us that the movements of machines and leaflets in interstate commerce were a single interrelated activity, not separate or isolated ones. The Act is not concerned with the purification of the stream of commerce in the abstract. The problem is a practical one of consumer protection, not dialectics. The fact that the false literature leaves in a separate mail does not save the article from being misbranded. Where by functional standards the two transactions are integrated, the requirements of § 304(a) are satisfied, though the mailing or shipments are at different times.

UNITED STATES v. 24 BOTTLES "STERLING VINEGAR & HONEY," ETC.

United States Court of Appeals, Second Circuit, 1964.
338 F.2d 157.

LUMBARD, Chief Judge.

Balanced Foods, Inc., appeals from an order of the District Court for the Southern District of New York condemning a number of bottles of Sterling Vinegar and Honey and a number of copies of two books, "Folk Medicine" and "Arthritis and Folk Medicine." Balanced Foods wholesales health foods and related products. The books and Vinegar and Honey were seized in its warehouse in New York City and condemned as misbranded drugs ... on the ground that the books were "labeling" for the Vinegar and Honey and are misleading....

Vinegar and Honey seems to have been one of the minor ephemera characteristic of the health and diet food trade. That it gained shelf space among boxes of sunflower seed, wheat germ and healing grasses can be attributed to the wide reading of Dr. D. C. Jarvis' first book, "Folk Medicine," subtitled "A Vermont Doctor's Guide to Good Health." ...

Prominent among Dr. Jarvis' remedies is a mixture of cider vinegar and honey, which is prescribed for a wide variety of maladies. Inevitably some people found it burdensome to mix the vinegar with the honey, and, true to the traditions of free enterprise, several companies responded by producing a pre-mixed product. Among them was Sterling. "Folk Medicine" and its sequel, "Arthritis and Folk Medicine," mention Sterling cider vinegar by name as suitable for medicinal use, and the two books certainly have promoted the sale of Sterling's Honey and Vinegar. In addition, Balanced Foods stocked both and sold both to a number of retailers. The question is whether the sum of these relationships constitutes labeling. We do not think that it does.

The Vinegar and Honey bottles bear a label, which claims no more than that they contain one pint of "aged in wood cider vinegar blended with finest honey." The labeling subject to the Act is not limited to this common form of label.... On the other hand, labeling does not include every writing which bears some relation to the product. There is a line to be drawn, and, if the statutory purpose is to be served, it must be drawn in terms of the function served by the writing.

... Advertising and labeling overlap; most labels advertise as well. They are not identical, however, and material which serves only as an advertisement is not covered by the Act. The distinguishing characteristic of a label is that, in some manner or another, it is presented to the customer in immediate connection with his view and his purchase of the product. Such a connection existed at both wholesale and retail levels in Kordel....

We need not consider whether or under what circumstances integrated use of written material and a drug product by a retailer would by itself allow condemnation of the goods in the hands of the wholesaler, for there is no evidence of such use of "Folk Medicine" or "Arthritis and Folk Medicine" with Vinegar and Honey at either level. Balanced Foods sold both, and the government presented some evidence that it took special steps to promote "Folk Medicine." There was no evidence of any joint promotion of either book with Vinegar and Honey, however. It perhaps could be inferred that the officers of Balanced Foods realized that sale of the books would tend to promote sale of Vinegar and Honey. But there can be no inference that it sold the books for that purpose. It first ordered "Folk Medicine" almost two years before it began carrying Vinegar and Honey; it sold over 7,000 copies of "Folk Medicine" at $2.00 each wholesale and fewer than 2,000 pint bottles of Vinegar and Honey. There was, in sum, no basis for finding that Balanced Foods did more than carry two related products....

"Folk Medicine" ... made broad claims for a vinegar and honey mixture, which led ultimately to Sterling's marketing Vinegar and Honey. It is not disputed that these claims were misleading, but the Federal Food, Drug and Cosmetic Act was not intended to deal generally with misleading claims....

The judgment of the district court is reversed.

NOTES

1. *Books as Labeling. Compare United States v. 250 Jars ... "Cal's Tupelo Blossom U.S. Fancy Pure Honey"*, 344 F.2d 288 (6th Cir. 1965), in which the court held that a booklet was labeling because it was shown to an FDA inspector acting as a prospective purchaser of the honey. In *United States v. 8 Cartons, More or Less, Molasses*, 97 F. Supp. 313 (W.D.N.Y. 1951), the court declined to hold that a book constituted labeling for a food solely upon a showing that the book was shipped simultaneously with the food. The court stated that the determination whether the book constitutes labeling depends upon "the use to which the book was put in connection with marketing the molasses," not upon shipment. After FDA amended its complaint, however, the court held that the book did constitute labeling because it was displayed with the molasses and customers were referred to the book when purchasing the molasses. Responding to the claim that the seizure of a book violates the First Amendment, the court observed:

> The Administrator by resorting to the seizure provisions of the Act does not undertake to interfere with the publication or circulation of the publisher's book. The seizure has not interfered with the bona fide sale of the book. The publisher may continue to sell its books wherever it finds a market, even in food stores, and even in stores where "Plantation" blackstrap molasses is sold. The seizure relates not to books offered for bona fide sale but to copies of the book claimed to be offending against the Act by being associated with the article "Plantation" Blackstrap Molasses in a distribution plan in such a way as to misbrand the product.

103 F. Supp. 626, 627 (W.D.N.Y. 1951).

2. *Compliance Policy.* In 1982, FDA initiated seizure of an unapproved drug, DMSO, and copies of an accompanying book about the drug. After the author's widow challenged the seizure of the book on the ground that the Supreme Court had extended the First Amendment to commercial speech, FDA issued Compliance Policy Guide No. 7153.13 (December 1, 1982) determining that, where labeling does not include books FDA will continue to seize both the offending product and the labeling, but where the labeling is in the form of a book the agency will seize only the product and will request an injunction to halt, after a hearing, the misuse of the book. On the basis of this policy, the book was released to the author's widow and the court denied her motion to intervene. *United States v. An Article of Drug on the Premises of DMSO, Inc.*, 1983–1984 FDLI Jud. Rec. 1 (W.D.N.Y. 1983).

3. *Other Authority.* For other cases construing the scope of labeling *see Seven Cases of Eckman's Alternative v. United States*, 239 U.S. 510 (1916); *United States v. Guardian Chemical Corp.*, 410 F.2d 157 (2d Cir. 1969); *United States v. Diapulse Mfg. Corp.*, 389 F.2d 612 (2d Cir. 1968); *United States v. Article of Drug Designated B–Complex Cholinos Capsules*, 362 F.2d 923 (3d Cir. 1966); *United States v. 47 Bottles, More or Less, Jenasol RJ Formula "60"*, 320 F.2d 564 (3d Cir. 1963); *Nature Food Centers, Inc. v. United States*, 310 F.2d 67 (1st Cir. 1962); *United States v. 353 Cases Mountain Valley Mineral Water*, 247 F.2d 473 (8th Cir. 1957); *V.E. Irons, Inc. v. United States*, 244 F.2d 34 (1st Cir. 1957); *United States v. Hohensee*, 243 F.2d 367 (3d Cir. 1957); *Alberty Food Products v. United States*, 194 F.2d 463 (9th Cir. 1952); *Alberty Food Products Co. v. United States*, 185 F.2d 321 (9th Cir. 1950); *Alberty v. United States*, 159 F.2d 278 (9th Cir. 1947); *United States v. Research Laboratories, Inc.*, 126 F.2d

42 (9th Cir. 1942); *United States v. Articles of Drug ..., Foods Plus, Inc.,* 239 F.
Supp. 465 (D.N.J. 1965); *United States v. "Vitasafe Formula M,"* 226 F. Supp.
266 (D.N.J. 1964); *United States v. Articles of Drug ... Century Food Co.,* 32
F.R.D. 32 (S.D. Ill. 1963); *United States v. 40 Cases CDC Capsules,* 204 F. Supp.
280 (E.D.N.Y. 1962); *United States v. Vitamin Industries, Inc.,* 130 F. Supp. 755
(D. Neb. 1955).

4. *State–Mandated Warnings.* Do posters or other public notices bearing
warnings required by state statute constitute "labeling" that is preempted
under federal law? One court has held that a poster warning required by
Michigan was labeling and thus was preempted. *American Meat Institute v.
Ball,* 550 F. Supp. 285 (W.D. Mich. 1982), *aff'd sub. nom. American Meat
Institute v. Pridgeon,* 724 F.2d 45 (6th Cir. 1984). Three other cases have held
that similar public notices are not labeling and thus are not preempted.
Grocery Manufacturers of America, Inc. v. Gerace, 755 F.2d 993 (2d Cir. 1985);
New York State Pesticide Coalition, Inc. v. Jorling, 874 F.2d 115 (2d Cir. 1989);
D–Con v. Allenby, 728 F.Supp. 605 (N.D. Cal. 1989).

5. *Commentary.* See Link, *Judicial Interpretation of the Words "Accompanying Such Article" Contained in the Federal Food, Drug, and Cosmetic Act,* 2
FDC L.Q. 207 (1947).

UNITED STATES v. ARTICLES OF DRUG ...
CENTURY FOOD CO.

United States District Court, Southern District of Illinois, 1963.
32 F.R.D. 32.

MERCER, District Judge.

This case is a libel of information by the United States against
divers vitamin and mineral compounds offered for sale by Century Food
Company after shipment in interstate commerce, alleging that each
such article of drug is misbranded. Misbranding is alleged to arise
from the fact that various pamphlets and articles of literature accompanying the several drug products contain false and misleading representation as to medical guidance for the use of vitamins and minerals in
the cure of serious diseases. One such book alleged to constitute a false
labeling of the drug products is a paper back book entitled, "Eat, Live
and be Merry," written by the intervenor, Carlton Fredericks....

Paragraph 3 of the answer alleges, in summary, that the intervenor had no knowledge of the nature of the seized drug articles or of
the operation of Century, that Century's use of intervenor's book to sell
or promote the seized articles was not authorized by intervenor, that
intervenor had no knowledge of the efficacy of the seized articles for the
treatment of any disease, and that over 20,000 copies of intervenor's
book have been sold through book stores and other outlets to the public.

Each of those averments of fact is completely irrelevant to any
issue in this case. In fact, a fair reading of the libel imports the
implication that intervenor was not culpable in the premises alleged.

Certainly there is no allegation in the libel that intervenor had any knowledge of Century's operation, or drug products, or that intervenor's book was used as labeling for those products by his authority. If it be assumed that intervenor had no knowledge of Century's operation, and had not authorized Century's use of his book as labeling for its drug products, copies of intervenor's book would, nevertheless, be subject to seizure to the extent that they were used and are being used as false labeling for Century's products. And the fact of the matter as to whether one copy, twenty thousand copies, or twenty million copies of intervenor's book have been sold to the public is a fact which is simply wholly alien to the case at bar. . . . .

Intervenor's second affirmative defense avers that the seizure of intervenor's book in connection with this case constitutes a prior restraint in violation of the First Amendment to the Constitution of the United States. . . .

The Act prohibits false labeling and misbranding, and authorizes the seizure of articles which are so misbranded. Certainly, the Act contemplates that a book, as well as any other type of representation, may be so used as to become a label for an article offered for sale. It was so held in *United States v. 8 Cartons, etc., Molasses,* in which the court entered a judgment of condemnation against a book to the extent that it was used as a label for the sale of a brand of black strap molasses. The same case resolved the issue of the constitutionality of that seizure, the court holding that the First Amendment does not prohibit the seizure and condemnation of a book which was being used as prohibited labeling. The court was careful there to point out that the condemnation related to the use of the book for that purpose, only, and that it could not operate as a restraint upon the sale of the book through book stores or other outlets. As the court there suggested, the condemnation did not prohibit the sale of the book in food stores, and even in stores in which the brand of molasses involved was offered for sale, so long as the book was not offered in conjunction with the product as a label for the product. . . .

NOTES

1. *Religious Tracts as Labeling.* In *Founding Church of Scientology v. United States,* 409 F.2d 1146 (D.C. Cir. 1969), p. 738 *infra,* FDA seized as misbranded certain items of electrical equipment used by adherents of the Scientology religion. The agency claimed that the items were "devices" under the Act for which false and misleading curative claims had been made. To prove its case, the FDA cited claims contained in religious tracts published by the church. Judge Wright expressed concern about the constitutionality of the government's attack on the truth of what the claimant argued were essentially assertions of religious belief.

2. *Commercial Speech.* Although no case has squarely confronted the issue, the free speech guarantee of the First Amendment presumably limits the power of government to regulate the content of labeling for food and similar products. Space does not permit an extended examination of the current limits on governmental regulation of so-called "commercial speech," but the broad

outlines of doctrinal development are evident. In *Valentine v. Chrestensen*, 316 U.S. 52 (1942), the Supreme Court suggested that the First Amendment imposed no constraints on government regulation of "purely commercial advertising." More recent cases, however, have undercut this dictum by sustaining constitutional objections to specific forms of government regulation of economically-inspired expression. *See Bates v. State Bar of Arizona*, 433 U.S. 350 (1977) (invalidating local restrictions on advertising by lawyers); *Bigelow v. Virginia*, 421 U.S. 809 (1975) (invalidating restrictions on the advertising of legal abortions). *See also National Com'n on Egg Nutrition v. FTC*, 570 F.2d 157 (7th Cir. 1977); *Beneficial Corp. v. FTC*, 542 F.2d 611 (3d Cir. 1976).

Probably the leading case is *Virginia State Bd. of Pharmacy v. Virginia Citizens Consumer Council, Inc.*, 425 U.S. 748 (1976), in which the Court struck down a statute that prohibited pharmacists from advertising the prices of prescription drugs. The Court emphasized the public interest in intelligent decision-making by consumers:

> ... To this end, the free flow of commercial information is indispensable.... [E]ven if the First Amendment were thought to be primarily an instrument to enlighten public decisionmaking in a democracy, we could not say that the free flow of [commercial] information does not serve that goal.

But the Court went on to emphasize that some forms of commercial speech regulation are permissible:

> Untruthful speech, commercial or otherwise, has never been protected for its own sake. Obviously, much commercial speech is not provably false, or even wholly false, but only deceptive or misleading. We foresee no obstacle to a State's dealing effectively with this problem.

A footnote in the decision attempts to delineate the contours of permissible regulation of commercial expression:

> ... [T]he greater objectivity and hardiness of commercial speech may make it less necessary to tolerate inaccurate statements for fear of silencing the speaker. They may also make it appropriate to require that a commercial message appear in such a form, or include such additional information, warnings, and disclaimers, as are necessary to prevent its being deceptive. They may also make inapplicable the prohibition against prior restraints.

The Supreme Court enunciated what appears to be the current test for government regulation of commercial speech in *Central Hudson Gas & Elec. Corp. v. Public Service Com'n of New York*, 447 U.S. 557, 566 (1980):

> At the outset, we must determine whether the expression is protected by the First Amendment. For commercial speech to come within that provision, it at least must concern lawful activity and not be misleading. Next we ask whether the asserted governmental interest is substantial. If both inquiries yield positive answers, we must determine whether the regulation directly advances the governmental interest asserted, and whether it is not more extensive than is necessary to serve that interest.

See also Board of Trustees of the State University of New York v. Fox, 492 U.S. 469 (1989) (legislative and executive branches need not adopt the least restrictive means of regulating commercial speech); *Posadas De Puerto Rico Assoc. v.*

Tourism Co., 478 U.S. 328 (1986) (legislature may determine whether counter-speech would be as effective as restriction on advertising).

3. *Commentary.* For detailed discussion of the potential limitations of the First Amendment on government regulation of product claims, *see, e.g.,* Elman, *Advertising and the First Amendment,* 33 FDC L.J. 12 (1978); Jackson and Jeffries, *Commercial Speech: Economic Due Process and the First Amendment,* 65 Va. L. Rev. 1 (1979); Kozinski and Banner, *Who's Afraid of Commercial Speech,* 76 Va. L. Rev. 627 (1990); Reich, *Consumer Protection and the First Amendment: A Dilemma for the FTC?,* 61 Minn. L. Rev. 705 (1977).

3. LABELING REQUIREMENTS OF SECTION 403

Section 403 contains two quite different types of provisions: those that prohibit certain types of representations, and those that require disclosure of specified information.

a. Prohibited Representations

Section 403(a) prohibits statements in labels or labeling that are "false or misleading in any particular," repeating language of the original 1906 Act. Proponents of the 1938 Act were successful in resisting the addition of qualifying terms, such as the insertion of the word "material" before "particular," although one has difficulty finding a case in which FDA successfully attacked labeling representations to which that qualifier would not have applied. *See United States v. 432 Cartons . . . Candy Lollipops,* p. 54 *infra. See also* Cavers, *The Food, Drug, and Cosmetic Act of 1938: Its Legislative History and Its Substantive Provisions,* 6 Law Contemp. Probs. 2 (1939).

UNITED STATES v. NINETY–FIVE BARRELS OF . . . APPLE CIDER VINEGAR

Supreme Court of the United States, 1924.
265 U.S. 438.

Mr. Justice BUTLER delivered the opinion of the Court.

This case arises under the Food and Drugs Act of June 30, 1906. The United States filed information in the District Court for the Northern District of Ohio, Eastern Division, for the condemnation of 95 barrels of vinegar. Every barrel seized was labeled:

"Douglas Packing Company
Excelsior Brand Apple Cider Vinegar Made
from Selected Apples
Reduced to 4 Percentum
Rochester, N.Y."

The information alleged . . . that the vinegar was made from dried or evaporated apples, and was misbranded in violation of § 8, in that the statements on the label were false and misleading, and in that it was an imitation of and offered for sale under the distinctive name of another article, namely apple cider vinegar....

... Section 8 provides, "That the term 'misbranded,' as used herein, shall apply to all ... articles of food, or articles which enter into the composition of food, the package or label of which shall bear any statement, design, or device regarding such article, or the ingredients or substances contained therein which shall be false or misleading in any particular, ... That for the purpose of this Act an article shall also be deemed to be misbranded: ... In the case of food: First. If it be an imitation of or offered for sale under the distinctive name of another article. Second. If it be labeled or branded so as to deceive or mislead the purchaser, ... Fourth. If the package containing it or its label shall bear any statement, design, or device regarding the ingredients or the substances contained therein, which statement, design, or device shall be false or misleading in any particular...."

The statute is plain and direct. Its comprehensive terms condemn every statement, design and device which may mislead or deceive. Deception may result from the use of statements not technically false or which may be literally true. The aim of the statute is to prevent that resulting from indirection and ambiguity, as well as from statements which are false. It is not difficult to choose statements, designs and devices which will not deceive. Those which are ambiguous and liable to mislead should be read favorably to the accomplishment of the purpose of the act. The statute applies to food, and the ingredients and substances contained therein. It was enacted to enable purchasers to buy food for what it really is.

The vinegar made from dried apples was not the same as that which would have been produced from the apples without dehydration. The dehydration took from them about 80 percent of their water content—an amount in excess of two-thirds of the total of their constituent elements. The substance removed was a part of their juice from which cider and vinegar would have been made if the apples had been used in their natural state. That element was not replaced. The substance extracted from dried apples is different from the pressed out juice of apples.... While the vinegar in question made from dried apples was like or similar to that which would have been produced by the use of fresh apples, it was not the identical product. The added water, constituting an element amounting to more than one-half of the total of all ingredients of the vinegar, never was a constituent element or part of the apples. The use of dried apples necessarily results in a different product.

If an article is not the identical thing that the brand indicates it to be, it is misbranded. The vinegar in question was not the identical thing that the statement "Excelsior Brand Apple Cider Vinegar made from selected apples," indicated it to be.... [T]he words, "apple cider vinegar made from selected apples" are misleading. Apple cider vinegar is made from apple cider. Cider is the expressed juice of apples and is so popularly and generally known. It was stipulated that the juice of unevaporated apples when subjected to alcoholic and subsequent acetous fermentation is entitled to the name "apple cider vinegar." The vinegar in question was not the same as if made from apples without dehydration. The name "apple cider vinegar" included in the brand did not represent the article to be what it really was; and, in effect, did represent it to be what it was not,—vinegar made from fresh or unevaporated apples. The words "made from selected apples" indicate that the apples used were chosen with special regard to their fitness for the purpose of making apple cider vinegar. They give no hint that the vinegar was made from dried apples, or that the larger part of the moisture content of the apples was eliminated and water substituted therefor. As used on the label, they aid the misrepresentation made by the words "apple cider vinegar."

The misrepresentation was in respect of the vinegar itself, and did not relate to the method of production merely. When considered independently of the product, the method of manufacture is not material. The act requires no disclosure concerning it. And it makes no difference whether vinegar made from dried apples is or is not inferior to apple cider vinegar.

The label was misleading as to the vinegar, its substance and ingredients. The facts admitted sustain the charge of misbranding.

NOTES

1. *Misbranding and Economic Adulteration.* The several food misbranding provisions of the Act are to some extent duplicative, as the charges in the *Apple Cider Vinegar* case suggest. Indeed, they also overlap the economic adulteration provisions in section 402(b). In most such cases, FDA relies only upon the basic prohibition of deception in section 403(a). The *Apple Cider Vinegar* case is one of the very few in which FDA has explicitly relied on the prohibition, now found in section 403(b), against offering a food for sale "under the name of another food." Like the economic adulteration provisions, which are essentially designed to prevent the marketing of debased foods, section 403(b) requires a court to identify a standard against which to compare the product involved, *i.e.*, the "other" food that the seized product is charged with imitating. The need for a standard of comparison is common to statutory as well as common law theories that are concerned primarily with "passing off" offenses. The economic adulteration provisions of the Act are discussed beginning at p. 88 *infra*.

2. *Proving Product Identity.* In addition to the problem of identifying the standard for comparison in such cases, there may be technical difficulties in proving that a food product is not, in fact, what it is represented to be. *See* Crawford, *Technical Problems in Food and Drug Law Enforcement,* 1 Law & Contemp. Probs. 36 (1933).

UNITED STATES v. 432 CARTONS ... CANDY LOLLIPOPS

United States District Court, Southern District of New York, 1968.
292 F. Supp. 839.

MANSFIELD, District Judge.

The article of food in question consists of about 432 cartons each containing six lollipops. On the outside the carton is labeled on top "Candy * * * for one with Sophisticated Taste," on one side, "A. Freed Novelty, Inc., N.Y.C.," and on the other side, "Ingredients: Sugar, corn syrup, citric acid, natural and artificial flavors." The inside of the box contains the legend, "Liquor Flavored Lollypops," and the slogan, "Take Your Pick of a Liquor Stick." In addition the lollipops themselves are labeled, both in the box and on the cellophane in which they are individually wrapped as "Scotch," "Bourbon," and "Gin."

The Government contends that the internal labeling is false or misleading [in violation of Section 403(a)] in that it implies and represents that "the article is flavored with liquor, which it is not." In response claimant does not allege that the lollipops are flavored with liquor, but by way of affirmative defenses contends that they are not misbranded because the cartons are clearly labeled "candy" and the ingredients are distinctly set forth, and that the ordinary purchaser would not read or understand it to represent that the lollipops contain any alcohol or liquor.

In approaching the question of whether the labeling here was false and misleading within the meaning of the statute, we recognize that the statute does not provide for much flexibility in interpretation, since it requires only that the labeling be false or misleading "*in any particular.*" (emphasis supplied). This represents a stricter substantive standard than that applied with respect to false advertising, which in order to be prohibited must be "misleading in a *material respect.*" (emphasis supplied) 15 U.S.C. § 55(a). Furthermore the statute says "false *or* misleading." ...

The issue of whether a label is false or misleading may not be resolved by fragmentizing it, or isolating statements claimed to be false from the label in its entirety, since such statements may not be deemed misleading when read in the light of the label as a whole. However, even though the actual ingredients are stated on the outside of a carton, false or misleading statements inside the carton may lead to the conclusion that the labeling is misleading, since a true statement will not necessarily cure or neutralize a false one contained in the label. Furthermore, the fact that purchasers of a product have not been misled, while admissible on the issue of whether the label is false or misleading, would not constitute a defense.

Applying these principles here, it cannot be concluded as a matter of law that no material issue exists with respect to the alleged false and misleading character of the label here before us. Although the labeling on the inside of each box of "candy," when read alone, might be misleading, the detailed description of the contents of the box listed on the outside of the carton could convince a jury, when the labeling or literature is read as a whole, that it is not "misleading in any particular." ...

... The Government's motion for a judgment on the pleadings is therefore denied.

NOTES

1. *"All Meat" Frankfurters.* In *Federation of Homemakers v. Butz,* 466 F.2d 462 (D.C. Cir. 1972), the Court of Appeals upheld a lower court ruling invalidating a USDA regulation which permitted frankfurters containing up to 15 percent water, filler, and spices, to be labeled "All Meat." The court agreed that the regulation was not a legitimate exercise of the Secretary's authority to prescribe labels and labeling for meat products in order to avoid the use of labels which would be false or misleading to the consumer:

> Do the words "All Meat" mean to an ordinary consumer, as distinguished from an expert, that a frankfurter in a package on which these words appear contains 85 percent meat and other components, and not 81 1/2 percent meat and other components? We think the answer to the question is plain, that the words do not convey that meaning and distinction, and that the Secretary could not reasonably conclude that they do.

USDA has explained how to differentiate between added and nonadded water in 52 Fed. Reg. 30925 (August 18, 1987), 55 Fed. Reg. 7294 (March 1, 1990).

2. *Oral Representations.* In *Weeks v. United States,* 245 U.S. 618 (1918), the Court held that oral misrepresentations could constitute misbranding under the 1906 Act's prohibition against offering a food for sale under the name of another article.

3. *Wine Labeling. Wawszkiewicz v. Department of the Treasury,* 480 F. Supp. 739 (D.D.C. 1979), invalidated regulations governing the labeling of wine on the ground that the permitted labeling would be misleading. The unlawful regulations permitted wine labels to carry the name of a single grape variety without disclosing that other grape varieties may compose up to 25 percent of the volume; to represent that the product is made from grapes grown entirely within one geographic region with no disclosure that up to 25 percent of the volume may be grown in other regions; and to represent that a winery "produced" the product even though it fermented as little as 75 percent of the volume.

4. *Disclaimers Ineffective.* Disclaimers have generally been held insufficient to cure otherwise misleading labeling. *See, e.g., United States v. 24 Unlabeled Cans ... "Compound Vegetable Butter Brand ... ",* 1969–1974 FDLI Jud. Rec. 32 (E.D. Mich. 1969) ("Not a dairy product" insufficient to overcome misleading use of the word "butter").

5. *Misleading Brand Name.* While a product's brand name may be held misleading, *United States v. 70 ½ Dozen Bottles ... "666",* 1938–1964 FDLI Jud. Rec. 89 (M.D. Ga. 1944), courts are reluctant to sustain orders that would require abandonment of a brand name, *Jacob Siegel Co. v. FTC,* 327 U.S. 608 (1946); *FTC v. Algoma Lumber Co.,* 291 U.S. 67 (1934).

UNITED STATES v. AN ARTICLE OF FOOD ...
"MANISCHEWITZ ... DIET THINS"

United States District Court, Eastern District of New York, 1974.
377 F. Supp. 746.

JUDD, District Judge.

The government initiated this action in 1972 when 423 cases of Diet Thins were seized in Baltimore, Maryland. The government contended that the name Diet–Thins prominently displayed on the label's front panel conveyed to consumers the misleading impression that the matzos were lower in caloric content than other matzos and were useful in weight control diets. Claimant asserts that the label is not misleading because Diet–Thins have several dietary uses other than weight control and that the present label incorporates changes requested by the Food and Drug Administration (FDA) in 1963....

Originally the Diet–Thins were thinner than the regular matzos manufactured and marketed by the claimant. Sometime during the mid–60's, however, the thickness of the regular matzos were reduced, so that at the time of the seizure the Diet–Thins was identical with other matzo crackers made by claimant, except that the Diet–Thins were made with enriched flour rather than ordinary flour. The Diet–Thins furnish the same number of calories as plain matzo crackers and have no greater value in weight control diets than claimant's ordinary matzo crackers.... Although matzos contain less calories than many other crackers on the market, their caloric content is substantially the same as Melba toast, wholewheat crackers, and certain other crackers....

In order to sustain a seizure, the government need not prove that all the label representations are both false and misleading. A food is misbranded if it appears that any *one* representation is false *or* misleading..... [T]he test is not the effect of the label on a "reasonable consumer," but upon "the ignorant, the unthinking and the credulous" consumer. Even a technically accurate description of a food or drug's content may violate 21 U.S.C. § 343 if the description is misleading in other respects....

Purchasers of diet products are often "pathetically eager" to obtain a more slender figure. There can be no doubt that the weight-conscious consumer may be led to believe that Diet–Thin Matzos are lower in calories than ordinary matzo crackers. The exchange of affidavits, and the depositions and discovery sought by the claimant have no bearing on this basic issue.

Claimant may have a right to assert that ordinary matzo crackers have value in diet and weight control. If this were the issue, further discovery and cross-examination of the government's deponents might be useful. Since it is sufficient that only one label statement may be misleading in any particular, the use of the phrase "Diet–Thins" violates the statute.

This does not appear to be a case where the label reference to Diet–Thins can be clarified by an explanatory phrase as was true in *Potato Chip Institute v. General Mills, Inc.* The function of the court is merely to determine whether the existing label is misleading, not to tell the Food and Drug Administration what amendments may be appropriate in order to rectify the situation....

It is ordered that the government's motion for summary judgment be granted, and that a decree of condemnation be entered, and that defendants' motions be denied.

NOTES

1. *Analogous Case.* Compare *United States v. 88 Cases ... Bireley's Orange Beverage*, 187 F.2d 967 (3d Cir. 1951), p. 88 *infra*, an economic adulteration case.

2. *Consumers to be Protected.* The courts have articulated a variety of standards for determining whether statements in labeling are "misleading." In *United States v. 62 Packages ... Marmola Prescription Tablets*, 48 F. Supp. 878 (W.D. Wis. 1943), the court stated that the purpose of the FD&C Act is "to protect the public, the vast multitude which includes the ignorant, the unthinking and the credulous who, when making a purchase, do not stop to analyze." By contrast the court in *United States v. Pinaud, Inc.*, 1938–1949 FDLI Jud. & Admin. Rec. 526, 529 (S.D.N.Y. 1949), stated that the proper standard was "purchasers who are of normal capacity and use that capacity in a common sense way." The standard was characterized as the "ordinary person" in *United States v. 1 Device ... Radiant Ozone Generator*, 1949–1950 FDLI Jud. & Admin. Rec. 139, 143 (W.D. Mo. 1949), and *United States v. Vrilium Products, Co.*, 1949–1950 FDLI Jud. & Admin. Rec. 210, 214 (N.D. Ill. 1950). But in *United States v. Article Consisting of 216 Cartoned Bottles ... "Sudden Change"*, 409 F.2d 734 (2d Cir. 1969), the court concluded that the law should protect "the ignorant, the unthinking and the credulous." Another court characterized the standard as the "often unthinking and gullible consumer" in *United States v. An Article of Food ... "Schmidt's Blue Ribbon"*, 1969–1974 FDLI Jud. Rec. 139 (D. Md. 1973).

3. *Vitamin–Mineral Products.* Until the 1970s litigation over the "misleading" character of the labeling of food products, and particularly vitamin-mineral supplements and other health food products, was commonplace. Such litigation has since virtually ended for two related reasons. First, FDA has sought to reclassify these products as drugs, based on the therapeutic claims made for them, and then has sought to have then condemned as illegal new drugs, marketed without an approved NDA. *See* p. 207 *infra.* Second, the regulations promulgated by FDA in the early 1970s for special dietary foods reduced the potential for misleading labeling. Occasionally, however, FDA brings an action solely under the food misbranding provisions. *See, e.g., United States v. Earthquest Oriental Ginseng*, Food Drug Cosm. L. Rep. (CCH) ¶ 38,043 (N.D. Ga. 1980), holding misleading a claim that a vitamin and mineral supplement would increase hair growth. With the popularity of specific disease prevention claims for food products, the potential for deception has re-emerged. *See* p. 180 *infra.*

4. *Sell or Use Dates.* Some food manufacturers voluntarily include on their labels a specific date by which it is recommended that the product be sold or used. FDA has considered, but never proposed, regulations governing this type of disclosure. For an analysis of the issues involved, *see* OTA, OPEN SHELF–LIFE DATING OF FOOD, No. OTA–F–94 (August 1979).

SPECIAL LABELING ISSUES

USDA Food Grade Labeling. Under the Agricultural Marketing Act of 1946, 60 Stat. 1082, 1087, codified in 7 U.S.C. § 1621 *et seq.*, USDA is authorized to establish a voluntary system of food grading, inspection, and certification. The regulations governing this program appear at 7 C.F.R. part 51 *et seq.* Under the program, producers who desire to participate must request, and pay for, the USDA inspection and grading service. The USDA quality standards, which are established by notice-and-comment rulemaking, relate to food quality and include such factors as color, size, shape, flavor, texture, maturity, and defects. The USDA grade assigned to a lot of food can then be used by the producer in labeling. Thus, the USDA grading system serves two purposes. First, it allows an independent quality determination on the basis of which wholesale buyers establish prices. Second, it provides useful information to retail consumers. *See* GAO, FOOD LABELING: GOALS, SHORTCOMINGS, AND PROPOSED CHANGES, Ch. 5, No. NWD–75–19 (January 19, 1975). Although use of USDA grade labeling is subject to section 403(a) of the Act, FDA has never participated in this program or objected to inclusion of grade information in food labels.

Kosher Labeling. Section 403(a)'s prohibition against false or misleading labeling applies to any statement made in food labeling. FDA has stated in 21 C.F.R. § 101.29 that a food may lawfully be described as "kosher" only if it meets the applicable religious dietary requirements. The agency has discouraged use of the phrase "kosher style" because it may mislead purchasers into believing that the product is in fact kosher. It has explained the two label symbols used to signify compliance with Jewish dietary laws in FDA, SYMBOLS ON FOOD LABELS, DHEW Pub. No. (FDA) 76–2021 (Rev. December 1975):

> The symbol which consists of the letter "J" inside the letter "O" is one whose use is authorized by the Union of Orthodox Jewish Congregations of America, more familiarly known as the Orthodox Union, for use of foods which comply with the Jewish dietary laws. Detailed information regarding the significance and use of this symbol may be obtained from the headquarters of that organization at 116 E. 27th St., New York, New York 10016.

> The symbol which consists of the letter "K" inside the letter "O" is one whose use is authorized by "O.K." Laboratories, 105 Hudson St., New York, New York 10013, to indicate that the food is "Kosher," that is, it complies with the Jewish dietary laws, and its processing has been under the direction of a rabbi.

Food Origin Labeling. For almost a century federal regulatory officials have worried about false or misleading claims about the origin of food products. A 1902 statute provided that no person may sell "any dairy or food product which shall be falsely labeled or branded as to the State or Territory in which they are made, produced, or grown ... " 32 Stat. 632 (1902), now codified in 21 U.S.C. § 16. FDA found it unnecessary to issue regulations implementing this statute prior to 35 Fed. Reg. 9214 (June 12, 1970), 36 Fed. Reg. 9444 (May 25, 1971), when the agency promulgated 21 C.F.R. § 1.15(c) in response to both domestic and foreign complaints.

The United States Customs Service has long required, under section 304 of the Tariff Act of 1930, 19 U.S.C. § 1304, that food imported into the United States must be labeled with the country of origin pursuant to regulations established in 19 C.F.R. Part 134. *See National Juice Products Ass'n v. United States,* 628 F. Supp. 978 (CIT 1986). In 51 Fed. Reg. 7285 (March 3, 1986), 51 Fed. Reg. 23045 (June 25, 1986), 51 Fed. Reg. 27195 (July 30, 1986), 53 Fed. Reg. 20836 & 20869 (June 7, 1988), 54 Fed. Reg. 24168 (June 6, 1989), 54 Fed. Reg. 29540 (July 13, 1989), the Customs Service implemented this requirement with respect to imported fruit juice products. For a discussion of extending country-of-origin labeling to all food containing an imported ingredient, *see* "Country-of-Origin Labeling Requirements for Imported Meat and Other Food Products," Hearing before the Subcomm. on Trade of the House Comm. on Ways and Means, 100th Cong., 2d Sess. (1988).

"NATURAL" AND "ORGANIC" FOOD CLAIMS

As foods have become increasingly processed, claims that a product is "natural," or contains only "natural ingredients," or contains no "preservatives" or other additives, or has been grown under "organic" conditions, without the use of fertilizers or pesticides, have become common. These sorts of representations have led four federal regulatory agencies and a voluntary industry organization to establish enforcement policies in this area.

1. *FDA.* FDA initially took the position that the only food products that could lawfully be characterized as "natural" were raw agricultural commodities that were sold in their natural state, without any processing. Faced with growing numbers of such claims, however, the agency concluded not to expend the resources that would be necessary to enforce this policy or to promulgate regulations defining these terms. Beginning in the mid–1970s, FDA concluded that it would prohibit use of the term "natural" only on products containing artificial color, artificial flavor, or synthetic ingredients such as chemical additives. It has taken no position regarding use of the word "natural" in relation to the processing of food products. In Compliance Policy Guide 7120.06 (October 1, 1980), FDA sought to provide general guidance with respect to designation of food as "fresh," and in 56 Fed. Reg. 5694 (February 12, 1991) the agency announced its intention to issue proposed regulations to govern the use of this term.

2. *FTC.* In a trade regulation rule (TRR) governing nutrition claims in food advertising proposed in 39 Fed. Reg. 39842 (November 11, 1974), and debated for nearly ten years, the FTC would have prohibited use of the terms "natural" and "organic." The Commission later proposed to require advertisers to state the precise facts applicable to the food (*e.g.,* that the food contains no artificial preservatives or artificial fertilizers). The agency eventually abandoned that position and agreed to permit a food to be represented as "natural" if it had not undergone more than "minimal processing" after harvest or slaughter and contained no artificial flavor, color additive, chemical preservative, or other artificial or synthetic ingredient. Appreciating the uncertainty of the "minimal processing" standard, however, the Commission concluded in 48 Fed. Reg. 23270 (May 24, 1983) to abandon the entire proceeding.

3. *USDA.* For many years, USDA simply banned any claim using the term "natural" or referring to the absence of preservatives or other additives of any kind on the premise that such claims were inherently misleading. In 1980, faced with a new form of packaging (retortable pouches) that required no preservatives, USDA relented slightly and permitted labeling statements linking the absence of preservatives to the new type of packaging. In Policy Memorandum No. 055 issued in November 1982, the Department went further and provided that the term "natural" could be used if the product does not contain any artificial flavor, color, chemical preservative, or other artificial or synthetic ingredient, and the product and its ingredients are not more than minimally processed. The USDA policy memorandum defined minimal processing. It required that all products claimed to be natural must be accompanied by a brief statement which explains what is meant by the term "natural," *i.e.*, it contains no artificial ingredients and is only minimally processed. The agency explained that it was adopting the approach endorsed by the FTC. Although the Commission subsequently abandoned this approach in May 1983, USDA has never withdrawn its policy memorandum. In the Organic Foods Production Act of 1990, 104 Stat. 3359, 3935, Congress directed USDA to establish national standards for the certification of foods as "organic." *See also* Institute of Food Technologists, *Organically Grown Foods,* 44 Food Tech. 26 (June 1990).

4. *BATF.* Following the FTC approach, BATF proposed to adopt a formal definition of the term "natural" in 45 Fed. Reg. 83530 (December 19, 1980). It took the position that a "natural" alcoholic beverage was one that had been minimally processed and contained no artificial additives. After the FTC abandoned this approach, however, BATF withdrew its proposal. 50 Fed. Reg. 960 (January 8, 1985).

5. *NAD.* In 1971, the advertising industry established a system of self-regulation through the National Advertising Division (NAD) of the Council of Better Business Bureaus. In October 1984 the NAD issued a special report summarizing thirty NAD cases relating to "natural" and "no artificial ingredient" food advertising claims between June 1975 and September 1984. In general, the NAD has applied a flexible rule that allows the advertiser to define the scope of the term "natural" or, failing that, holds the advertiser to the broadest meaning of that term. *See, e.g.,* Smithies, *Nutritional Issues in Advertising,* 31 Cereal Foods World 464 (1986).

---

b. Affirmative Disclosures

Section 403 explicitly mandates affirmative disclosure of five types of information on every food label: the name of the food; the name and place of business of the manufacturer; a statement of ingredients; the net quantity of contents; and nutrient content. In addition, section 201(n) provides that, in determining whether labeling is misleading, "there shall be taken into account" not only the representations made about the product but also the extent to which the labeling fails to reveal material facts. Since the early 1970s FDA has exploited this provision to prescribe, by regulation, additional requirements for affirmative disclosure of information in food labeling.

Section 403(f) speaks to the prominence and legibility of label information required by the other provisions of the section. From 1938 until 1973 FDA enforced this requirement based solely on the subjective impressions and informed judgment of agency compliance personnel. Very few cases were ever litigated. One of the few suits brought to enforce section 403(f), *United States v. 46 Cases, More or Less, "Welch's Nut Caramels"*, 204 F. Supp. 321 (D.R.I. 1962), evoked the following response from the court:

> The net weight and ingredient statements are printed on the label in a distinctive silver color that is not employed for any other statements appearing on said package. Both statements are printed in the same size type which the evidence establishes as being easily readable at a distance of approximately 29 inches by the average person. The Act prescribes no minimum specific standard as to how prominent such statements should be. It would seem that the requirements of said section 403(f) are met in a particular case if such statements are prominent enough to be seen and understood by the ordinary individual who is interested in discovering and learning the information disclosed thereby, and who makes a minimum examination of the package to determine its net weight and the ingredients of the candy contained in said package.

FDA obviated reliance on section 403(f) by promulgating general regulations, 38 Fed. Reg. 2124 (January 19, 1973), 38 Fed. Reg. 6950 (March 14, 1973), now codified in 21 C.F.R. § 101.2, to standardize the location and type size for mandatory information on food labels.

FOOD LABELING
21 C.F.R. Part 101.

§ 101.1 Principal display panel of package form food

The term "principal display panel" as it applies to food in package form and as used in this part, means the part of a label that is most likely to be displayed, presented, shown, or examined under customary conditions of display for retail sale. The principal display panel shall be large enough to accommodate all the mandatory label information required to be placed thereon by this part with clarity and conspicuousness and without obscuring design, vignettes, or crowding. Where packages bear alternate principal display panels, information required to be placed on the principal display panel shall be duplicated on each principal display panel. For the purpose of obtaining uniform type size in declaring the quantity of contents for all packages of substantially the same size, the term "area of the principal display panel" means the area of the side or surface that bears the principal display panel....

§ 101.2 Information panel of package form food

(a) The term "information panel" as it applies to packaged food means that part of the label immediately contiguous and to the right of the principal display panel as observed by an individual facing the principal display panel with the following exceptions:

(1) If the part of the label immediately contiguous and to the right of the principal display panel is too small to accommodate the necessary information or is otherwise unusable label space, e.g., folded flaps or can ends, the panel immediately contiguous and to the right of this part of the label may be used.

(2) If the package has one or more alternate principal display panels, the information panel is immediately contiguous and to the right of any principal display panel.

(3) If the top of the container is the principal display panel and the package has no alternative principal display panel, the information panel is any panel adjacent to the principal display panel.

(b) All information required to appear on the label of any package of food pursuant to ... this chapter shall appear either on the principal display panel or on the information panel, unless otherwise specified by regulations in this chapter.

(c) All information appearing on the principal display panel or the information panel pursuant to this section shall appear prominently and conspicuously, but in no case may the letters and/or numbers be less than one-sixteenth inch in height unless an exemption pursuant to paragraph (f) of this section is established....

[Numerous exemptions from the type size requirements are omitted.]

(d)(1) All information required to appear on the principal display panel or on the information panel pursuant to this section shall appear on the same panel unless there is insufficient space. In determining the sufficiency of the available space, any vignettes, design, and other nonmandatory label information shall not be considered. If there is insufficient space for all of this information to appear on a single panel, it may be divided between these two panels except that the information required pursuant to any given section or part shall all appear on the same panel. A food whose label is required to bear the ingredient statement on the principal display panel may bear all other information specified in paragraph (b) of this section on the information panel....

(e) All information appearing on the information panel pursuant to this section shall appear in one place without other intervening material.

(f) If the label of any package of food is too small to accommodate all of the information required by ... this chapter, the Commissioner may establish by regulation an acceptable alternative method of disseminating such information to the public, *e.g.*, a type size smaller than one-sixteenth inch in height, or labeling attached to or inserted in the package or available at the point of purchase. A petition requesting such a regulation, as an amendment to this paragraph shall be submitted pursuant to Part 10 of this chapter.

NOTE

For a caustic commentary on this regulation, *see* Austern, *The Regulatory Gospel According to Saint Peter,* 29 FDC L.J. 316 (1974).

---

4. DECEPTIVE PACKAGING

RUTH LAMB, AMERICAN CHAMBER OF HORRORS
(1936).

In a recent survey by State authorities in Alabama, six samples of black pepper showed a fill of container from 82 per cent to as low as 43 per cent of what the housewife might reasonably expect. Coffee and chicory compounds ranged from 67 to 80 per cent, the average being about 70, and one sample of tea was hardly more than half full. An attractive basket of fancy sealed pecans, thanks to a false bottom, was only 77 per cent filled. Three samples of salt showed fills of 72, 75 and 80 per cent respectively....

... A candy box one of the inspectors told me about was big enough to hold a pound; but it had a false bottom occupying a quarter of the space, and such other structures that there was room actually for only six ounces. Candy boxes holding no more than fifteen ounces are common.

And Mr. W. R. M. Wharton, Chief of the Eastern District, has a story about a cheese manufacturer who, on finding competition keen, reduced the quantity of cheese in his package from the conventional eight ounces to six by putting in a false bottom. But a competitor went him one better by putting in two layers of false bottom, thus reducing the quantity to four ounces. And then came another competitor who chiseled away yet another ounce by adding a third false bottom! ...

It was in response to practices such as these that Congress included in the 1938 Act section 403(d), which declares a food misbranded "if its container is so made, formed, or filled as to be misleading." *See generally* Hutt, *Development of Federal Law Regulating Slack Fill and Deceptive Packaging of Food, Drugs, and Cosmetics,* 42 FDC L.J. 1 (1987).

UNITED STATES v. 116 BOXES ...
ARDEN ASSORTED CANDY DROPS

United States District Court, Massachusetts, 1948.
80 F. Supp. 911.

WYZANSKI, District Judge.....

Each box measures in inches: 3 ¾ x 2 ½ x 1 ¼. A box is intended to sell at retail at five cents. Each bears a legend stating the name of the drop and showing the weight of the box as 1 1/2 ounces.... There is no statement as to the number of pieces of candy. Most of the boxes contain 17 pieces. Some, however, contain 18 or 19. When 17 pieces are in the box and a reasonable time has elapsed since manufacture, the candy settles so that there is an average air space in the box of 33%.

Each box in evidence was packaged by a standard packaging machine, manufactured by a third party, of the type used by a majority of leading concerns packaging candy or cough drops intended to retail at five or ten cents. Such a packaging machine is made with only slight variations necessary for each concern. The machine works in conjunction with a conveyor belt. The belt carries a flat piece of cardboard to the machine, which folds it into a box with an opening left at one end. The machine then inserts wax paper, turns the folded box into an upright position and passes it under a rotary disk. Above this disk pieces of candy are placed. The disk has twenty apertures which may be plugged up to regulate the number of pieces which will drop into each box. Back of the place where the box stands under the disk is an agitator which jars the box during the time candy pieces are falling through the disk. This aids the candy to settle in the box so that more pieces can fall into the box. After being under the disk, the box moves to a finger-like contraption which folds over the wax paper and closes the box.

The process of manufacture is supervised by an operator who watches for spillage as the candy falls to the floor from the disk or the box. The operator discards boxes which are overpacked. He does not add drops by hand. If he were to do so, he could often make the box contain at least 20 drops of the present style. Without such additions by hand, it is admittedly practical to set the disk for at least 17 such drops. If the disk is set at 18 such drops, the machine occasionally jams. Moreover, at 18 drops the number of boxes which are overpacked and must be discarded is between 5% and 10% of the total number of boxes filled. There was no evidence as to how many pieces of candy any consumer would expect to receive from a box of the type here involved.

Upon the basis of the foregoing facts and for the following reasons I conclude as a matter of law that the shipment did not violate § 403(d) of the Act and that the libel should be dismissed without costs and the boxes delivered to the shipper.

The Act (which incidentally has not been interpreted by any official regulation or administrative pronouncement) prohibits the shipment of a package of candy which is in fact so slack-filled as to be misleading, even if the package correctly states the weight of the contents....

... I do not go so far as to accept the argument, advanced by the Government, that the question is whether the package is so filled as to mislead an average five-year old child who might expect the box to be filled to overflowing. Infantile anticipation is not the test. Rather it is what would be expected by an ordinary person—not necessarily an adult—who had been led to expect and desire machine-packing. Such a customer knows machine-packing is more sanitary than hand-packing. He knows it results in economies of mass production and that these economies are in some measure likely to be passed on to the ultimate consumer. Moreover, from buying various types of five-cent candies, cough drops and lozenges packed by machine in standard rectangular containers, he has come to expect some slack or air space. Indeed, he recognizes that tight packing would often solidify into a mass pieces which he prefers to have separate. It is the expectations of a person who has that common degree of familiarity with our industrial civilization which furnish the standard which Congress intended to be applied....

In the case at bar no evidence was introduced as to what an ordinary non-infantile purchaser would expect. But in my view he would not expect any particular number of lozenges. So long as he received ordinary lozenges not obviously so eccentric in shape as to result in peculiar packing difficulties, and so long as he received approximately as many of these lozenges as could conveniently be packed in a standard rectangular carton by machine, he would not in my opinion be misled.

UNITED STATES v. 174 CASES ... "DELSON THIN MINTS"

United States Court of Appeals, Third Circuit, 1961.
287 F.2d 246.

BIGGS, Chief Judge.

There are two ways in which a trial court may hold for the claimant in cases such as that at bar. First, the court can find as a fact that the accused package is not made, formed, or filled in such a way that it would deceive the ordinary purchaser as to the quantity of its contents. Alternatively, the court may find as a fact that even though the form or filling of the package deceives the ordinary purchaser into thinking that it contains more food than it actually does, the form and filling of the package is justified by considerations of safety and is reasonable in the light of available alternative safety features....

... [T]he court below did not find that the Delson package did not deceive the ordinary purchaser by making him think that it contained more than it actually did contain. The court stated in respect to this issue: "The case is, in my opinion, lacking in adequate proof that the average adult, of normal intelligence, would be induced by the exterior appearance of the accused containers to buy a box of Delson mints with the expectation that it would contain any particular number of individual candies." This statement is beside the point. The question was not whether the ordinary purchaser would expect to find a particular number of individual candies in the box but whether such a purchaser would expect to find more of the Delson box filled.... People do not think in terms of the number of individual mints when buying them in containers.

... [E]vidence introduced by the United States tended to show that only 44% of the total volume of the accused container and that only 75% of its practical volume was filled with mints; that the remainder of the usable space was taken up with hollow cardboard dividers and hollow end pieces. The United States introduced substantial uncontradicted evidence to show that purchasers of the mints, opening the boxes, expected to find far more mints in them than were there. In view of this it is obvious, if there were nothing more in the case, that the containers might well fall within the interdiction of the statute.

But, and this is a point which we must emphasize, a showing by the United States that the ordinary purchaser, on viewing a container, will believe that it contains significantly more food than in fact it does contain, and was deceived, cannot be dispositive of the issues of such a case as that at bar. A claimant may go forward and show, as the claimant has attempted to do here, that the circumstantial deception was forced upon it by other considerations such as packaging features necessary to safeguard its product. But safety considerations, before they can be held to justify a slack package must be shown to be reasonably necessary in the light of alternative methods of safeguarding the contents....

... The court has to find that the container's efficacy outweighs its deceptive quality. Further, it has to find that the available alternative efficacious means are not less deceptive than those actually employed....

NOTES

1. *Subsequent Proceedings.* On remand, 195 F. Supp. 326 (D.N.J. 1961), the district court held that the package was not deceptive, and that even if it were the available alternative means of packaging were no less deceptive and the efficacy of the present package outweighed any deception.

2. *Economic Adulteration. See also United States v. 738 Cases ... Jiffy-Lou Vanilla Flavor Pudding,* 71 F. Supp. 279 (D. Ariz. 1946), which held 55% slack fill lawful. *But cf. United States v. 149 Cases ... "Silver Brand ... Dried Black Eyed Peas,"* 1938–1964 FDLI Jud. Rec. 1289 (D. Colo. 1953), in which FDA prevailed on a charge of economic adulteration under section

402(b)(2) on the ground that excess packing material had been substituted for the peas.

3. *Commentary.* *See* Depew, *The Slack–Filled Package Law,* 1 FDC L.Q. 86 (1946); Forte, *Food and Drug Administration, Federal Trade Commission and the Deceptive Packaging of Foods,* 21 FDC L.J. 205 (1966); Martin, *Section 403(d)—Containers So Made, Formed or Filled as to be Misleading,* 8 FDC L.J. 663 (1953); Thompson, *Functional Slack–Fill in the Manufacture and Packaging of Confections,* 27 FDC L.J. 779 (1972).

4. *Enforcement of 403(d).* Section 403(d)'s prohibition against misleading packaging has rarely been the basis for enforcement proceedings by FDA. Between 1938 and the enactment of the Fair Packaging and Labeling Act in 1966 the agency had not prevailed in a single contested case under section 403(d). One obstacle to successful enforcement was the lack of legislatively prescribed criteria of deception and FDA's failure to develop criteria by regulation. Thus, according to one court, "[t]here is no hard and fast rule as to what would constitute slack-filling. Whether or not over 50 per cent space in a particular package of candy was slack-filling is a question of fact for the district court to decide." *United States v. Cataldo,* 157 F.2d 802, 804 (1st Cir. 1946). Furthermore, courts vacillated over whether it was incumbent upon the FDA to introduce evidence of actual consumer deception. Courts appeared reluctant to find a package misleading without such evidence, perhaps because the Act requires the net contents to be disclosed on the label.

NOTE, FEDERAL REGULATION OF DECEPTIVE PACKAGING: THE RELEVANCE OF TECHNOLOGICAL JUSTIFICATIONS

72   Yale Law Journal 788 (1963).

... [F]or some consumers in some circumstances, the net weight may be an adequate guide to an intelligent purchase; for others, however, this may not be the case. A Government survey of consumer behavior has indicated that a significant number of purchases are based largely on size. Moreover, the net weight may be presented in such a way as to preclude calculation of unit cost by the consumer. For example, if the larger of two packages contains 10 5/8 ounces and costs 39 cents and the smaller package contains 11 ¾ ounces of the same commodity and costs 42 cents, which is the better buy? Without a slide rule the calculation is not easy, and the frustrated consumer may well turn to package size as a more useful criterion for choice. Finally, the usefulness of net weight as a criterion depends largely on the objective of the consumer. If a purchaser is primarily interested in the number of units in a package, rather than in the total weight of all the units, size is a very rational guide for selection.....

... Because of the highly competitive atmosphere of the supermarket aisle, some manufacturers have tended to increase the size of their package without increasing the quantity of its contents, so that their product will " 'reach out' from the blur of boxes" more effectively than their competitors'.... If all instances of slack filling could be explained solely in terms of packager activities of this sort, then they would appear to be totally unjustified....

However ... the *Delson* case and the packaging hearings identified two other explanations for slack filling which frequently involve benefits for consumers. One of these explanations, with which the *Delson* case was directly concerned, involves product protection and preservation.... The second explanation for slack filling which may be associated with consumer benefits involves machine packaging. Mechanical handling and processing may yield economies of scale that drastically reduce the cost to the consumer of many food items. They may also be partly responsible for the marketing of products in a variety of quantities and in various stages of preparation, thus increasing the range of consumer choice and perhaps effecting additional economies for the consumer by preventing waste. Yet, because of technological problems, slack filling may inevitably accompany these benefits of machine packaging....

HAROLD MARQUIS, FAIR PACKAGING AND CONSUMER PROTECTION
18 Journal of Public Law 61 (1969).

One approach that would avoid the complexities of promulgating standards of fill for individual commodities would be to require a conspicuous disclosure of fill for commodities when the regulatory authorities thought consumer deception was occurring. Regulations, on a commodity-by-commodity basis, could require the disclosure when the fill was below a certain percentage of the maximum fill possible. This disclosure requirement might be satisfied by a "___% Full" statement, or a "Filled to Here" line, or by a transparent window that allows the consumer to view the content level. Less technical information would be needed to draw this type of regulation on a commodity-by-commodity basis than would be necessary to establish a standard of fill, as a manufacturer would not be forced to meet a minimum standard of fill, regardless of expense.

The disclosure approach not only circumvents the technological arguments raised by industry against fill standards, but could exert some pressure on industry to overcome major technological obstacles to full packaging. At the least, it should neutralize attempts by manufacturers to use slack fill to obtain a competitive advantage at the expense of consumers....

NOTES
1. *Fill of Container Standards.* Section 401 authorizes FDA to issue "reasonable standards of fill of container," and the agency has issued such standards for many canned foods. *See* 21 C.F.R. Parts 145 *et seq.*

2. *FPLA.* In 1966, Congress enacted the Fair Packaging and Labeling Act, 80 Stat. 1296, 15 U.S.C. §§ 1451–61, a law primarily designed to facilitate price comparisons by consumers between competing products. The core of this Act is a requirement that packages of consumer commodities bear a legible, prominent label statement of net quantity of contents (in terms of weight, measure or numerical count). In addition, the FPLA authorizes FDA to adopt regulations "to prevent the nonfunctional-slack-fill of packages containing" foods, drugs, devices, or cosmetics. FDA has not proposed or even seriously considered promulgating such regulations, which would be governed by the formal rulemaking requirements of section 701(e) of the FD&C Act.

3. *California Requirements.* Although the California statutes governing slack fill and deceptive packaging are the same as the Federal statutes, on the basis of *Hobby Industry Association of America, Inc. v. Younger,* 101 Cal.App.3d 358, 161 Cal. Rptr. 601 (Ct. App. 1980), the state took the position that all nonfunctional slack fill is inherently illegal whether or not there is evidence of deception. California applied this standard both to the fill of the immediate container and to the fit of the immediate container in an outer package. The state adopted Slack Fill Enforcement Guidelines (April 21, 1988), setting forth 14 principles for determining when exterior packaging and immediate product containers may be considered as not slack filled.

FOOD TAMPERING

Although the initial tampering incident with a product subject to FDA jurisdiction involved a nonprescription drug, Extra Strength Tylenol, p. 614 *infra,* there have been numerous reports of tampering with food products since then. *E.g.,* "Tampering-Related Arrest," FDA Talk Paper No. T86–37 (May 30, 1986). In many cases the manufacturer has been forced to take action without knowing whether a tampering threat is true or false. *E.g.,* "Sugar-Free Jello—Cyanide Threat," FDA Talk Paper No. T86–51 (July 10, 1986); "Lemon-Lime Slice—Cyanide Threat," FDA Talk Paper No. T86–52 (July 11, 1986); "Foremost Dairy Threat," FDA Talk Paper No. T86–55 (July 23, 1986); "Acme Milk Products," FDA Talk Paper No. T87–14 (February 25, 1987). In at least two instances, however, ingestion of cyanide in food resulted in death. *E.g.,* "Camden, N.J., Death," FDA Talk Paper No. T89–1 (January 4, 1989). The most widely reported food tampering, however, involved the discovery by FDA, HHS News No. P89–10 (March 6, 1989), of two grapes apparently contaminated with trace amounts of cyanide in a large shipment of fruit from Chile. All Chilean fruit was detained until FDA completed further inspections, which found no evidence of contamination. The temporary detention, however, had a severe impact on the Chilean economy. HHS News Nos. P89–11 (March 13, 1989), P89–13 (March 17, 1989), P89–15 (March 21, 1989), and P89–19 (April 14, 1989).

---

5. WEIGHT LABELING

The requirement in section 403(e) of net weight labeling originated with the Gould Amendment to the 1906 Act, 37 Stat. 732 (1913). Although straightforward in concept, implementation of the requirement has presented two difficult problems, both of which involve the moisture content of food.

a. Gain and Loss of Moisture

Food packaged in a dry climate will gain moisture, and thus weight, when it is stored and marketed in a moister climate, and conversely food packaged in a moist climate will lose weight when marketed in a dry climate. Accordingly, rules must be developed to govern the gain or loss of moisture during transportation and storage. When California adopted its own rules, which differed slightly from those followed by FDA and USDA, the Supreme Court held them preempted in *Jones v. Rath Packing Co.*, 430 U.S. 519 (1977), p. 1009 *infra*. Following the *Rath* decision, FDA held public hearings, 42 Fed. Reg. 55227 (October 14, 1977), to reconsider its policy, and together with USDA published proposed new regulations in 45 Fed. Reg. 53002, 53023 (August 8, 1980). Under these proposed regulations, the two agencies would have established maximum allowable variations below the declared net weight for categories of food products.

For many years, the National Bureau of Standards (now the National Institute of Standards and Technology, or NIST) in the Department of Commerce has published handbooks governing determination of the net weight of consumer products. Following the August 1980 FDA and USDA proposals, the National Conference on Weights and Measures (NCWM), an organization of state and local officials supported by NIST, became the principal forum for building a consensus on determining the net weight of food products. Based upon the work of NCWM, NIST has issued revised versions of its two handbooks on weights and measures, No. 44, SPECIFICATIONS, TOLERANCES AND OTHER TECHNICAL REQUIREMENTS FOR WEIGHING AND MEASURING DEVICES, and No. 133, CHECKING THE CONTENTS OF PACKAGED GOODS, which establish acceptable maximum allowable variances for moisture loss for food products. USDA therefore withdrew its August 1980 proposal and proposed to adopt the NIST handbooks in 54 Fed. Reg. 9370 (March 6, 1989). The agency's preamble states that FDA intends to adopt the same approach.

---

b. Drained Weight

Many food products naturally contain juice or moisture or are traditionally packed in some type of liquid. At the same time FDA was considering the problem of moisture loss, it also confronted the issue of proper net weight declaration for these other food products as well.

DRAINED WEIGHTS FOR
PROCESSED FRUITS AND VEGETABLES
40 Federal Register 52172 (November 7, 1975).

... Consumers Union of United States, Inc.... filed a petition [38 Fed. Reg. 33512 (December 5, 1973)] proposing establishment of regulations, or the amendment of existing regulations, in 21 CFR Part 1, to require that all processed fruits and vegetables packed with sugar or other syrup, water, brine, or their own juice, bear on their labels a statement of the drained weight of the solid food content of the container....

... Containers of the same product marked with the same net weight, were found to vary considerably in drained weight from packer to packer. Furthermore, many private label as well as brand name products are obtained from contract canners who may vary the fill of fruit or vegetable as commodity prices rise. Hence, petitioner contended, the lack of drained weight labeling totally frustrates the consumer's attempt to obtain the most fruit or vegetable for his money. Consumers Union was of the opinion that the value of providing drained weight labeling would far exceed the costs such a regulation would entail.....

Thirteen comments opposed drained weight labeling of processed fruits and vegetables because of the inability to determine accurately a figure for the drained weight of the processed food prior to processing and storage. This inability to predetermine a value for the drained weight of the food was reported to result from differences in maturity of the food, differences in variety, variations within a particular variety resulting from growth conditions, differences due to seasonal changes, grade, and shape and size of the individual pieces.....

Comments were received from manufacturers and two trade associations regarding the added costs of drained weight declaration. All indicated that there would be cost increases and that, in most cases, the increases would be passed on to the consumer....

The Commissioner believes the wisdom of a proposal to require drained weight labeling ultimately depends on the dollar value to the consumer of any benefit of knowing drained weight, when buying food, in relation to any increase in the product cost resulting from manufacturers' costs being passed on to the consumer.... Any final decision about a drained weight labeling regulation will depend primarily on an analysis of the economic information ultimately available to the Commissioner....

The Consumers Union Petition. The Consumers Union petition called for drained weight labeling of all processed, i.e., frozen and canned, fruits and vegetables. Ascertaining drained weight levels was to be done through lot testing. Using the National Canners Association (NCA) estimate of 1 cent per unit to comply with the drained weight requirement proposed by Consumers Union results in an estimated cost impact of $92 million....

The "Label Disclosure" Approach. One option for instituting a drained weight requirement would be to apply the provisions of the Consumers Union petition only to canned fruits and vegetables. This would avoid the problem of ascertaining drained weight for frozen foods, where appropriate testing techniques would have to be developed. The cost estimate for industry compliance under this second option is

$74 million, calculated by multiplying the annual volume of canned products covered by a drained weight requirement by $0.01 per unit.

The Commissioner's proposal. The key difference between the Commissioner's proposal and the other two is that it would permit a processor to label cans based on fill-of-container standards, where they exist. Where such a standard does not exist, a processor would have to undertake lot testing and label drained weight based on lot average. Where fill-of-container standards exist, a processor would have the option of labeling cans based on the standard, or undertaking lot testing and labeling with the lot average.

In the aggregate, the reduction in anticipated cost impact from permitting the use of a fill-of-container standard should be substantial. Fill-of-container standards specifying minimum average drained weights are being proposed for 78 percent of the total production of all products for which drained weight labeling would be required. Consequently, the cost impact from complying with the Commissioner's proposal should only be applied to the 22 percent of canned fruits and vegetables amenable to a drained weight requirement but for which there would be no fill-of-container standard. This cost would amount to about $16 million, derived by multiplying 7.4 billion (annual production of canned goods with drained weight required) by $0.01 (cost per unit) by .22 (percent of no fill-of-container standard)....

DRAINED WEIGHT OR SOLID CONTENT WEIGHT FOR CANNED FRUITS AND VEGETABLES

42 Federal Register 62282 (December 9, 1977).

In a comment dated May 5, 1976 on the drained weight proposal, the National Canners Association (NCA) ... proposed a regulation to require the declaration of the solid content weight as an alternative to the declaration of the drained weight..... In support of its proposal to require solid content labeling, NCA stated that the costs of compliance with drained weight labeling of canned fruits and vegetables had been estimated by Touche Ross and Co., San Francisco, CA, for NCA at $104.2 million annually, an amount that NCA considers to be prohibitive.....

Battelle Columbus Laboratories (Battelle), Columbus, Ohio was commissioned by FDA to review the cost information submitted in comments on the drained weight proposal and to interview canners to obtain an independent cost estimate for drained weight labeling.... They estimated the cost of compliance with drained weight labeling ... at $74 million annually with an initial capital investment of $44.3 million.....

To further support solid content labeling, NCA cited a consumer survey conducted for NCA by Opinion Research Corp. (ORC), Princeton, NJ, in which more than half of the consumers polled would not be willing to support a drained weight regulation costing 1 cent per can and still fewer consumers would support a regulation at greater expense.

The Commissioner notes that consumer surveys sponsored by Consumers Union in Detroit, MI, and Denver, CO, found that more than half of consumers polled would be willing to pay increased costs for drained weight labeling. Among those willing to pay for drained weight information, a majority of consumers polled in both cities would pay as much as 1 cent per can (41 percent in Detroit v. 63 percent in Denver). . . . .

On November 12, 1976, NCA announced that food canners would begin to declare voluntarily the solid content weight (fill weight) in addition to the net weight on labels of canned fruits and vegetables; NCA said that the new weight information would assist consumers in making food buying selection. Further, NCA contended that it would give consumers, at far less cost, information as meaningful as the drained weight.

Based on industry estimates, the NCA announcement estimated the total cost of solid content labeling for canned fruits and vegetables at $10 million annually. A similar estimate made by Battelle from information obtained during the study on the cost of drained weight labeling indicated that the cost of solid content labeling would range between $3.9 and $8.1 million annually. The Commissioner notes that using either of these estimates, the per unit cost for solid content labeling based on current production data for canned fruits and vegetables would be 0.1 cent or less as compared to 0.7 to 1.2 cents for drained weight labeling. . . .

In that announcement, NCA stated that it has recommended that individual canners keep fill weight records and make these records available on a voluntary basis to FDA upon written request, for compliance purposes. . . . . In the past, FDA has not considered proposing a requirement for declaration of the solid content weight (fill weight) because of the lack of effective means to determine compliance with the fill weight before canning. Since the weight of the solid contents of many canned fruits and vegetables changes after processing, FDA has no means of determining the accuracy of a fill weight declaration unless an FDA inspector is present at the time of processing to check the fill weights or, alternatively, unless canners make fill weight records available. . . .

The Commissioner has considered the comments received on the drained weight proposal including the comments by NCA proposing solid content labeling, which was represented as a more practical alternative to drained weight labeling. He is not fully convinced that solid content labeling, although admittedly less costly, is superior to drained weight labeling. However, he is of the opinion that the voluntary solid content labeling program announced by NCA will provide a good opportunity to test the merits of solid content labeling. He is proposing an exemption from the clear space requirement to permit canners to declare either the solid content weight (fill weight) or drained weight in conjunction with the net weight before he makes a final decision on this new proposal for drained weight or solid content (fill weight) labeling and the November 7, 1975 drained weight labeling proposal....

NOTES

1. *Voluntary Solid Content Labeling.* The National Canners Association (now the National Food Processors Association) implemented its voluntary solid content labeling program. FDA has taken no further action on its November 1975 or December 1977 proposals.

2. *Metric Declaration.* Following Congress' enactment of the Metric Conversion Act of 1975, 89 Stat. 1007, it was anticipated that the United States would rapidly convert to use of the metric system for weights and measures. Although that expectation has not been realized, FDA has issued Compliance Policy Guide No. 7150.17, 52 Fed. Reg. 8534 (March 18, 1987), to establish an acceptable approach to the use of the metric system in declaring the net contents on the labels of FDA-regulated products. Because section 5164 of the Omnibus Trade and Competitiveness Act of 1988, 102 Stat. 1107, 1451, designates the metric system as the preferred system for trade and commerce, its use in labeling may increase.

3. *Descriptive Weight or Size Labeling.* Section 4(b) of the FPLA prohibited the use of "qualifying words or phrases" in conjunction with the net quantity of contents statement, but permitted such words to be used elsewhere in labeling. Section 5(c)(1) authorized FDA to establish standards for characterizing the size of packages, but this authority has not been exercised. Both of these provisions were designed to deal with the common practice of characterizing the size of consumer product packages with such terms as "giant" or "jumbo."

4. *Package Size.* Section 5(d) of the FPLA authorized the Secretary of Commerce to establish voluntary product standards governing the sizes of retail packages to prevent "undue proliferation" in package sizes that "impairs the reasonable ability of consumers to make value comparisons." This provision, designed to preclude odd package sizes that hinder price comparison, requires use of the voluntary product standard procedures in 15 C.F.R. Part 10. Following an opinion of the Department of Justice that permitted the private formulation of package size standards without adherence to the Department of Commerce's formal procedures, several industries voluntarily established standard package sizes.

6. INGREDIENT LABELING

FDA has issued numerous regulations to explain and amplify the requirements for ingredient labeling in sections 403(i) and 403(k) of the Act. *See* 21 C.F.R. §§ 101.4, 101.22–.35. The basic rule can be stated simply: All of the ingredients of a food must be listed, in descending order of predominance. Listing is to be by chemical name, rather than by class or function (*e.g.*, sweeteners or emulsifiers), except that spices, flavorings, and uncertified colorings *may* be listed generically. Chemical preservatives are the only class of food ingredient that must be declared both by chemical name and by function.

In recent years, attention has focused on the consumer's ability to identity and avoid specific ingredients, but in 1938, the new requirement of ingredient declaration was viewed primarily as a matter of economics.

DAVID F. CAVERS, THE FOOD, DRUG, AND COSMETIC ACT OF 1938: ITS LEGISLATIVE HISTORY AND ITS SUBSTANTIVE PROVISIONS

6 Law and Contemporary Problems 2 (1939).

... Deception with respect to foods is most frequently effected through creating the impression that a product is a commonly-known food when it does not in fact contain the ingredients which may properly be expected of that food. The tactic may result in both adulteration and misbranding. Suppose tea-seed oil is added to olive oil and the mixture labeled "olive oil." Here both offenses are clearly present. Yet tea-seed oil is harmless and its presence cannot easily be detected. It should be possible to market such a compound so long as the public is not deceived.

The old Act had sought to escape this difficulty by providing that harmless "mixtures or compounds" might be offered for sale under their own "distinctive names," provided that an article was not "an imitation of or offered for sale under the distinctive name of another article" and, in the case of a compound, imitation or blend of foods not sold under a distinctive name, that the word "compound," "imitation" or "blend" plainly appear on the label. This solution provided a convenient loophole for evasion of the Act. To return to the example given above, adulterated olive oil could be sold as, say, "Spanola—For Salads," in an olive-hued can resembling those used for genuine olive oil, and an undiscriminating public would purchase it without any awareness that the distinctive name meant an inferior product....

FOOD ADDITIVES AND HYPERACTIVITY

199 Science 516 (1978).

For the past 5 years, many members of the public have been intrigued by a theory that food additives cause hyperactivity. This theory was put forth in 1973 by Ben F. Feingold, an allergist at the Kaiser–Permanente Medical Center in San Francisco. Feingold developed a diet in which foods containing synthetic colors, synthetic flavors, and salicylates are banned. He reported that 50 percent of hyperactive children dramatically improved their behavior when they followed his diet.

Last year, in response to the huge acclaim for the Feingold diet, J. Preston Harley and his associates at the University of Wisconsin tested the effects of the diet with a controlled clinical trial. Forty-six hyperactive boys who participated were observed for 8 weeks by parents, teachers, neurologists, and trained observers. Some of the children followed an additive-free diet and some did not, but neither the children, their parents nor the other observers knew which child followed which diet....

The results of this study failed to confirm Feingold's claims. In fact, Harley and his associates report no effects of the additive-free diet on hyperactivity of school-age children.....

Many parents still swear by the Feingold diet, and their experience cannot necessarily be dismissed. Some psychologists suggest that children's behavior improves not because of the diet, but because of the increased attention paid to the children when they are on the diet. Of course, it remains possible that the diet does help some children. Keith Connors of the University of Pittsburgh has some evidence that the behavior of a small fraction of hyperactive children might improve with the diet. He finds that the behavior of most children, however, is not affected by it....

NOTES

1. *Ingredients of Standardized Foods.* Under section 403(g), as it was enacted in 1938, the label of a standardized food need not declare any mandatory ingredients and need declare only those optional ingredients that are prescribed by the standard. For many years food standards required the labeling of only a few optional ingredients. In 37 Fed. Reg. 5120 (March 10, 1972), 38 Fed. Reg. 2137 (January 19, 1973), FDA issued 21 C.F.R. § 101.6, which *urged* that the labels of standardized foods be revised to declare all ingredients. At the same time the agency undertook to revise existing standards to mandate labeling of all optional ingredients. It took the position that where a standard permitted more than one form of a mandatory ingredient the form chosen was to be considered "optional," thus in effect requiring full ingredient disclosure. The 1990 Nutrition Labeling and Education Act amended section 403(g) to require the listing of all ingredients in standardized food.

2. *Chemical Preservatives.* In 38 Fed. Reg. 20745 (August 2, 1973), 39 Fed. Reg. 5627 (February 14, 1974), FDA promulgated 21 C.F.R. § 101.22(j), interpreting section 403(k) to require that a preservative be declared in the statement of ingredients both by its chemical name and by a separate description of its function.

3. *Flavorings.* Generic declaration of flavors in the ingredient statement is permitted by section 403(i)(2) of the Act. In addition, however, FDA has promulgated complex regulations in 21 C.F.R. § 101.22(g) governing prominent label disclosure of natural and artificial flavoring. *See* 38 Fed. Reg. 2139 (January 19, 1973), 38 Fed. Reg. 20718 (August 2, 1973), 38 Fed. Reg. 27622 (October 5, 1973), 38 Fed. Reg. 33284 (December 3, 1973). *See also* the USDA

flavor regulations for meat food products promulgated in 52 Fed. Reg. 30922 (August 18, 1987), 55 Fed. Reg. 7289 (March 1, 1990), codified in 7 C.F.R. § 317.2(f)(1)(i).

4. *Colors.* Section 403(i)(2) as it was enacted in 1938, also permitted generic declaration of all colors in the statement of ingredients. On January 3, 1978, FDA Commissioner Kennedy wrote to the 100 largest manufacturers and distributors of packaged foods, requesting that they voluntarily label the specific colors used in their foods:

> This Agency believes that all colors added to a food product should be identified by name in the list of ingredients appearing on the product. Only through full ingredient disclosure can the consumer exercise in full measure the fundamental right to choose to be informed, and to be assured of safety. I believe that label declaration of colors, in particular, is essential to individuals who may be sensitive to certain color additives or who, for various reasons, wish to avoid products containing them. These individuals should be given the means to make an informed choice....

FDA proposed to allow the declaration of specific color additives in abbreviated form, by deleting the prefix "FD&C" in 50 Fed. Reg. 23815 (June 6, 1985), and explicitly permitted the use of abbreviated names pending publication of a final regulation, but as of June 30, 1990 had issued no final regulation. The Nutrition Labeling and Education Acts of 1990 amended section 403(i)(2) to require the declaration of all colors not required to be certified under section 706(c), *i.e.*, all FD&C color additives.

5. *Percentage Ingredient Labeling.* FDA proposed a uniform method for declaration of the percentage of any ingredient in the ingredient statement, where this is done voluntarily by the manufacturer, in 39 Fed. Reg. 20885 (June 14, 1974). The proposal was withdrawn in 51 Fed. Reg. 15653 (April 25, 1986).

6. *Legislative Proposals.* Proposals to amend section 403(i) to require specific labeling of colors, flavorings, and spices have been before Congress for several years. In 44 Fed. Reg. 75990 (December 21, 1979) FDA reiterated its intention to seek legislative authority to require label declaration of the specific identity of colors and spices, but not of flavors because the number of flavors in a single processed food may exceed 40. The agency said it would also again seek to repeal the proviso in section 403(k) which exempts butter, cheese, and ice cream from label declaration of added artificial color. The 1990 Act, however, amended section 403(i) only to require the declaration of colors required to be certified; it left section 403(k) unchanged.

7. *Reconditioning After Condemnation.* The requirement that all ingredients be labeled can have unforeseen consequences. After a product labeled "honey" was condemned as misbranded because it was in fact table syrup rather than honey, the court in *United States v. An Article of Food ... Pure Raw Honey,* 550 F.Supp. 15 (W.D. Okl. 1982), upheld FDA's refusal to allow the product to be relabeled because the distributor could not prove that there were no undeclared additional ingredients present in the food.

8. *Ingredient Nomenclature.* Although 21 C.F.R. § 101.4(a) and (b) require that a food ingredient be declared on the label by a "specific" common or usual name, the regulations do not specify how that name is to be determined. In practice, FDA determines the specific name for food ingredients when it has promulgated standards of identity and food additive or GRAS regulations.

Where a food manufacturer wishes to shorten or simplify the chemical name for a food ingredient for purposes of label declaration, FDA has customarily permitted use of the shortened version in parentheses following the full chemical or biological name of the ingredient for a period of time, and ultimately allowed use of the shortened version alone. For example, the agency's initial GRAS affirmation regulation for rapeseed oil with a low erucic acid content, 47 Fed. Reg. 35342 (August 13, 1982), 50 Fed. Reg. 3745 (January 28, 1985), specified the name "low erucic acid rapeseed oil." The petitioners requested use of the specific name "canola oil" but FDA replied that this term had no meaning in the United States and suggested that it be used in parentheses following the name the agency had designated. Several years later, 53 Fed. Reg. 36067 (September 16, 1988), 53 Fed. Reg. 52681 (December 29, 1988), FDA changed the name to "canola oil." 21 C.F.R. § 184.1555(c). *See also* 43 Fed. Reg. 54238 (November 21, 1978) and 49 Fed. Reg. 22796 (June 1, 1984), establishing the specific name "cocoa butter substitute primarily from palm oil" for "1–palmitoy/1–2–oleoyl–3–stearin" without ever requiring that the former be used in parentheses following the latter. Because food ingredient nomenclature has a low priority at FDA, it has been suggested that the designation of specific names for food ingredients should be undertaken by the National Academy of Sciences (which publishes the Food Chemicals Codex) or a consortium of organizations like those responsible for designating United States Adopted Names (USAN) for drugs, *see* p. 454 *infra*.

INGREDIENT LABELING FOR ALCOHOLIC BEVERAGES

For many years FDA took the position that alcoholic beverages were "food" within the meaning of the FD&C Act but did not insist that their labels comply with section 403 of the Act, instead deferring to the Bureau of Alcohol, Tobacco, and Firearms (BATF) of the Department of Treasury, which administers the Federal Alcohol Administration Act, 27 U.S.C. § 201 *et seq.* BATF had never required labeling of ingredients in distilled spirits, wine, or beer. As FDA became convinced of the desirability of complete ingredient labeling of foods it began to pressure BATF to require such labeling for alcoholic beverages. When BATF eventually concluded that ingredient labeling was likely to be costly for the industry and not useful for consumers, 40 Fed. Reg. 52613 (November 11, 1975), FDA announced that it was abandoning its historical posture and would require compliance by all alcoholic beverages with the labeling requirements of the FD&C Act, including section 403(i), 40 Fed. Reg. 54455 (November 24, 1975).

In a suit brought in Owensboro, Kentucky by producers of distilled spirits and wine, alcoholic beverages were held exempt from the labeling requirements of the FD&C Act. *Brown–Forman Distillers Corp. v. Mathews*, 435 F. Supp. 5 (W.D. Ky. 1976). The Department of Justice declined to allow FDA to appeal this ruling after BATF agreed to initiate rulemaking to require at least partial ingredient labeling of alcoholic beverages. That proposal was published in 44 Fed. Reg. 6740 (February 2, 1979). After issuance of this proposal the *Brown–Forman* plaintiffs unsuccessfully asked the court to hold FDA and its Commissioner in contempt of the earlier order because of their efforts to pressure BATF into requiring ingredient labeling under the FAA Act. *Brown–Forman Distillers Corp. v. Califano*, Food Drug Cosm. L. Rep. (CCH) ¶ 38,245 (W.D. Ky. 1979).

The *Brown–Forman* decision holds that the labeling requirements of the FD&C Act are supplanted by the product-specific provisions of the FAA Act.

Other cases, however, have held that the adulteration provisions of section 402(a) do apply to alcoholic beverages. *United States v. 1,800.2625 Wine Gallons of Distilled Spirits,* 121 F. Supp. 735 (W.D. Mo. 1954); *United States v. Commonwealth Brewing Corp.,* Food Drug Cosm. L. Rep. (CCH) ¶ 50,051.43 (D. Mass. 1945). *See* Cooper, *The FDA, the BATF, and Liquor Labeling: A Case Study of Interagency Jurisdictional Conflict,* 34 FDC L.J. 370 (1979).

Following the February 1979 proposal, the alcohol beverage industry sought unsuccessfully to obtain a directive in BATF's pending appropriations legislation prohibiting the use of funds to require ingredient labeling for alcoholic beverages. BATF then published final regulations requiring alcoholic beverage ingredient labeling in 45 Fed. Reg. 40538 (June 13, 1980). After review under the standards of Executive Order No. 12291, however, it rescinded the regulations, 46 Fed. Reg. 24962 (May 4, 1981), 46 Fed. Reg. 55093 (November 6, 1981). This action was held unlawful in *Center for Science in the Public Interest v. Department of the Treasury,* 573 F. Supp. 1168 (D.D.C. 1983), and BATF thereupon reinstated the regulations, 48 Fed. Reg. 10309 (March 11, 1983); and subsequently proposed to reconsider the entire matter in 48 Fed. Reg. 27782 (June 17, 1983). In this new rulemaking, BATF determined that the only ingredient whose labeling could be justified on health grounds was FD&C Yellow No. 5, and it therefore again revoked its ingredient labeling regulations except for that color additive. 48 Fed. Reg. 45549 (October 6, 1983). Meanwhile, the Court of Appeals held that the original issue was moot. 727 F.2d 1161 (D.C. Cir. 1984).

The district court once again held that BATF failed to provide a reasoned explanation for its refusal to mandate ingredient labeling. However, the court of appeals reversed and determined that the BATF decision was reasonable and supported by the record, 797 F.2d 995 (D.C. Cir. 1986).

BATF has subsequently required the disclosure of sulfites on alcoholic beverage labels, 50 Fed. Reg. 26001 (June 24, 1985), 51 Fed. Reg. 34706 (September 30, 1986), based on a health concern, but has not otherwise moved to require ingredient labeling for alcoholic beverages.

As FDA has moved in the direction of insisting that all food ingredients be specifically labeled in order of predominance, it has been pressed to address the practical difficulties confronting manufacturers who adjust the composition of their products in response to changes in the price and seasonal fluctuations in the character of basic ingredients.

FOOD LABELING: INGREDIENT LABELING EXEMPTIONS
42 Federal Register 43095 (August 26, 1977).

In the FEDERAL REGISTER of January 6, 1976 (41 FR 1156), FDA promulgated regulations amending § 101.4 concerning the manner in which ingredients are to be declared on the labels of finished foods. One of the results of the promulgation of these regulations is that Trade Correspondence Number 94 (TC–94) was revoked in its entirety. TC–94 had provided that manufacturers of bakery products using ingredients acting as leavening, yeast nutrients and dough conditioners could declare these ingredients as such on labels of bakery products in place of the specific common or usual names of these ingredients.

In a final rule published in the FEDERAL REGISTER of February 12, 1976 (41 FR 6242), FDA issued amendments to the definitions and standards of identity for bakery products and required label declaration of all optional ingredients.....

The American Bakers Association (ABA) ... has submitted two petitions requesting relief.... One petition proposes that the Commissioner of Food and Drugs amend § 101.4 to permit all ingredients that act as leavening agents, yeast nutrients, or dough conditioners in bakery products to be listed together in order of predominance in parentheses following the appropriate collective term that describes the ingredients' function.

The second petition requests that the Commissioner amend the definition and standard of identity for bread in § 136.110 to permit the declaration of dough conditioners (other than potassium iodate or calcium iodate) that may be added to bakery products so that the label declaration would be the same whether or not specific dough conditioners were present in the finished food, provided that such declarations are followed by the statement "used as needed." ...

In its petition to amend the standard of identity for bread, ABA states that bakers have found it necessary to add certain safe and suitable ingredients from time to time, depending on raw material variations. For example, if a wheat crop is "weak," it may be necessary to add additional dough strengtheners to obtain a uniformly high quality product. Although bakers know that these ingredients may be needed to produce an acceptable food, they find it impossible to predict in advance what ingredients will be needed at any particular time. The petitioner contends that no legitimate interest would be harmed by granting bakers the right to disclose such ingredients on an "as needed" basis in the ingredient declaration because each of the ingredients involved has already been determined by FDA to be safe and suitable for its intended purpose and all ingredients present will be disclosed on the label. The petitioner contends that the declaration of dough conditioners on an "as needed" basis will provide necessary flexibility in the labeling of bakery products and avoid higher labeling costs that may result in increased prices to the consuming public....

The Commissioner has considered both of the petitions submitted by ABA and concludes that the petitions contain sufficient grounds to warrant publication of a proposed regulation. The Commissioner is of the opinion, however, that the requested exemption should not be limited to products conforming to a definition and standard of identity for bakery products. Consequently, the Commissioner is proposing an amendment to § 101.4 to provide that ingredients that act as dough conditioners, yeast nutrients, or leavening agents may be listed by their specific common or usual names in the ingredient statement in parentheses following the appropriate collective names "leavening," "yeast nutrients," or "dough conditioners." The exemption stated in this manner will apply to all foods utilizing these functional ingredients....

On the assumption that the manufacturers are unable to predict in advance the specific dough conditioners, yeast nutrients, and leavening agents to be used in a particular food and they are unable to maintain a uniform quantity of these ingredients in a formulation because of raw material variation, the Commissioner is proposing that the specific dough conditioners, yeast nutrients, and leavening agents need not be listed in descending order of predominance.

In addition, the Commissioner is proposing that ingredients that act as dough conditioners, yeast nutrients, or leavening agents in foods, but which are used intermittently in foods, may be declared in the ingredient statement even though they may not be present in the finished food, provided the ingredients are identified by words indicating that they may not be present, such as "dough conditioners (ammonium chloride and/or L-cysteine)" or "dough conditioners (one or more of the following: Ammonium chloride, L-cysteine, potassium bromate)." . . .

The Commissioner is of the opinion that the proposed exemption from ingredient labeling for foods will provide sufficient flexibility for the baking industry while retaining complete ingredient disclosure for consumers. Furthermore, because the proposed exemption is a general labeling provision applicable to both standardized and nonstandardized foods, there is no need to amend individual standards of identity....

NOTES

1. *Collective Ingredient Labeling.* FDA promulgated final regulations, 21 C.F.R. § 101.4(b)(16)-(18), in 43 Fed. Reg. 24518 (June 6, 1978). Similarly, in 43 Fed. Reg. 16347 (April 18, 1978), 48 Fed. Reg. 8053 (February 25, 1983), FDA permitted the labeling of firming agents in food to be declared in an ingredient statement by the collective name "firming agents" followed in parentheses by the specific name of each firming agent used but not in descending order of predominance. The agency has, however, since expressed concern that consumers who are allergic to particular ingredients may not be able to protect themselves adequately if alternative ingredient declaration were permitted on a widespread basis.

2. *Order of Predominance. See also* 43 Fed. Reg. 14677 (April 7, 1978), in which FDA proposed to permit manufacturers of bakery products to list ingredients present in their products at levels of 2 percent or less by weight at the end of the ingredient statement in other than descending order of predominance. The proposal was designed to enable manufacturers to respond to seasonal variations and changes in raw materials. FDA issued regulations expanding this proposal to include all food products in 51 Fed. Reg. 2405 (January 16, 1986), 55 Fed. Reg. 17431 (April 25, 1990).

3. *Consumer Understanding.* Apparently most consumers do not understand that food ingredients are listed in descending order of predominance. FDA has considered the possibility of requiring a label statement of this fact. For an economic analysis of this approach, *see* A.D. Little, Inc., ECONOMIC

IMPACT ANALYSIS OF A DECLARATION THAT INGREDIENTS ARE LIST-
ED IN DESCENDING ORDER OF PREDOMINANCE, Report to FDA under
HHS Contract No. 223–79–8052 (May 19, 1981).

4. *Exempt Ingredients.* Incidental additives that are present in a food at
insignificant levels and do not have any technical or functional effect in the
food are exempt from declaration in ingredient labeling under 21 C.F.R.
§ 101.100(a)(3). In the only case interpreting this provision, *Sea Snack Foods,
Inc. v. United States,* Food Drug Cosm. L. Rep. (CCH) ¶ 38,062 (D.D.C. 1987),
the court upheld FDA's determination that the processing aid involved served a
functional purpose in the finished food and thus must be declared on the label.
In part to clarify that sulfites are not incidental additives when used in food,
FDA promulgated regulations requiring the declaration of sulfites as part of
ingredient labeling in 50 Fed. Reg. 13306 (April 3, 1985), 51 Fed. Reg. 25012
(July 9, 1986).

---

7. LABEL WARNINGS

The FD&C Act contains no specific authority for FDA to require
warning statements on food labels. Until relatively recently, such
warnings were uncommon. In 38 Fed. Reg. 6191 (March 7, 1973), 40
Fed. Reg. 8912 (March 3, 1975), FDA promulgated a regulation, now
codified in 21 C.F.R. § 101.17, establishing food label warnings under
section 201(n) of the FD&C Act. Since then, the number of warnings
required by regulation or by statute as well as provided voluntarily by
manufacturers has increased significantly. And this trend can be
expected to continue.

Safe Use. The original regulation prescribed warnings against
unsafe use of aerosolized containers for food products by inhaling the
propellant or incinerating the container.

Allergic Reactions. Many individuals are allergic to even very
common food ingredients. The primary rationale for Congress' decision
to mandate ingredient labeling was to permit consumers to avoid the
ingredients to which they are allergic. Based upon reports of allergic
reactions to FD&C Yellow No. 5, FDA published a regulation in 42 Fed.
Reg. 6835 (February 4, 1977), 44 Fed. Reg. 37212 (June 26, 1979), 45
Fed. Reg. 60419 (September 12, 1980), codified in 21 C.F.R.
§ 74.705(d)(2), requiring label disclosure of this color additive, but the
agency rejected an outright ban. When it approved FD&C Yellow No.
6, 51 Fed. Reg. 41765 (November 19, 1986), FDA also required specific
label declaration of this color. The Certified Color Manufacturers
Association objected on the grounds that there was insufficient evidence of allergic reactions to the color additive and that FDA had failed
to provide an opportunity for public comment. After the agency
rejected these objections in 52 Fed. Reg. 21505 (June 8, 1987), the
CCMA contested the requirement in court. Rather than litigate the
issue, FDA agreed to suspend this requirement, 53 Fed. Reg. 49138

(December 6, 1988), and then to withdraw it unless imposed by notice-and-comment rulemaking.

Based upon new information indicating allergic reactions to sulfiting agents in food, FDA took action in 50 Fed. Reg. 13306 (April 3, 1985), 51 Fed. Reg. 25012 (July 9, 1986), codified in 21 C.F.R. § 101.100(a)(4), requiring label declaration of sulfites in food if they can be detected using an analytical method specified by FDA and sensitive to 10 parts per million.

As a result of its experience with allergic reactions to Yellow 6, aspartame, and sulfites, FDA established an ad hoc advisory committee initially to review hypersensitivity to sulfites and, later, all food constituents in 49 Fed.Reg. 15021 (April 16, 1984). Based upon an internal report by Tollefson, A COMPUTERIZED MONITORING SYSTEM FOR RECORDING AND ASSESSING ADVERSE REACTIONS TO FOOD PRODUCTS AND ADDITIVES REGULATED BY THE FOOD AND DRUG ADMINISTRATION (July 1985), FDA created Form 2516 for reporting complaints of injury from food products. Physicians and other health professionals were asked to inform FDA of "any severe and well-documented non-microbiologic reactions associated with food" in an article published in 15 FDA Drug Bulletin 34 (December 1985). *See* Tollefson, *Monitoring Adverse Reactions to Food Additives in the U.S. Food and Drug Administration,* 8 Reg. Tox. & Pharmacol. 438 (1988). For an overview of food allergy, *see* Sampson *et al., Food Allergy,* 258 J.A.M.A. 2886 (November 27, 1987).

FDA has made no attempt to specify the frequency of adverse reactions that will require declaration of an ingredient or justify a ban. Allergic reactions to food are common, affecting up to 8 percent of children and 2 percent of adults. Metcalfe, *Diseases of Food Hypersensitivity,* 321 N.E.J.M. 255 (July 27, 1989).

Inborn Errors of Metabolism. Many individuals are born with natural metabolic defects that require them to avoid specific food constituents. For example, phenylketonurics must avoid the amino acid phenylalanine. Accordingly, 21 C.F.R. § 172.804(e)(2) requires that any food containing the sweetener aspartame must bear the following prominent statement: "Phenylketonurics: contains phenylalanine." Similarly, a diet beverage containing a combination of nutritive and nonnutritive sweeteners is required under 21 C.F.R. § 100.130(d)(3) to bear the statement: "Contains sugar(s); not for use by diabetics without advice of a physician."

Toxicity. Section 403(*o*) of the FD&C Act requires any food containing saccharin to bear the following statement: "Use of this product may be hazardous to your health. This product contains saccharin which has been determined to cause cancer in laboratory animals." In the Alcoholic Beverage Labeling Act of 1988, 102 Stat. 4181, 4518, codified in 27 U.S.C. § 213 *et seq.,* Congress required the following statement on the container of every alcoholic beverage: "GOVERNMENT WARNING: (1) According to the Surgeon General, women should not drink alcoholic beverages during pregnancy because of the risk of birth defects. (2) Consumption of alcoholic beverages impairs your ability to drive a car or operate machinery, and may cause health problems." BATF has implemented this statute with regulations published in 54 Fed. Reg. 7160 (February 16, 1989), 55 Fed. Reg. 5414 (February 14, 1990).

In the mid–1970s, low calorie protein-based diets were marketed for rapid weight loss. Following reports of illness and death associated with these products, FDA required label warnings in 42 Fed. Reg. 61285 (December 2, 1977), 45 Fed. Reg. 22904 (April 4, 1980). Two courts determined that FDA failed to justify the specific warnings. *National Nutritional Foods Association v. Goyan,* 493 F. Supp. 1044 (S.D.N.Y. 1980); *Council for Responsible Nutrition v. Goyan,* Food Drug Cosm. L. Rep. (CCH) ¶ 38,057 (D.D.C. 1980). On remand, FDA amended the regulations in 47 Fed. Reg. 25379 (June 11, 1982), 49 Fed. Reg. 13679 (April 6, 1984), codified in 21 C.F.R. § 101.17(d). Both the required warnings and the requirement that they appear on the principal display panel were subsequently upheld. *Council for Responsible Nutrition v. Novitch,* Food Drug Cosm. L. Rep. (CCH) ¶ 38,281 (D.D.C. 1984); *National Nutritional Foods Ass'n v. Novitch,* 589 F. Supp. 798 (S.D.N.Y.1984); *National Nutritional Foods Ass'n v. Young,* 598 F. Supp. 1107 (S.D.N.Y. 1984).

Side Effects. Many food ingredients produce undesirable physiological effects in humans. Food labels bear warnings about many of these side effects. For example, 21 C.F.R. § 184.1835(e) requires that any food whose reasonably foreseeable consumption may result in a daily ingestion of 50 grams of sorbitol shall bear the statement: "Excess consumption may have a laxative effect." More than 50 common food substances are also used as active ingredients in nonprescription drug products. *See, e.g.,* 50 Fed. Reg. 2124, 2132 (January 15, 1985), discussing the use of fiber as both an active ingredient in OTC laxative drugs and an ingredient in high fiber food products. The labeling for foods containing these ingredients can be expected to bear appropriate label warnings comparable to the warnings used when they are included in a nonprescription drug.

C. REGULATION OF FOOD IDENTITY AND QUALITY

1. PREMISES OF REGULATION

CAROLENE PRODUCTS CO. v. UNITED STATES

Supreme Court of the United States, 1944.
323 U.S. 18.

Mr. Justice REED delivered the opinion of the Court.

... The corporate petitioner sells the products mentioned in the indictment which are manufactured for it by another corporation from skim milk, that is, milk from which a large percentage of the butterfat has been removed. The process of manufacture consists of taking natural whole milk, extracting the butterfat content and then adding cottonseed or coconut oil and fish liver oil, which latter oil contains vitamins A and D.... The compound is sold under various trade names in cans of the same size and shape as those used for evaporated milk. The contents of the can are practically indistinguishable by the buying public from evaporated whole milk, but the cans are truthfully labeled to show the trade names and the ingredients.

The indictment charged the petitioner corporation and the individual petitioners, its president and vice president, with violation of the [Federal Filled Milk Act]....

Filled milk is defined in § 1(c) of the act as any milk, "whether or not condensed, evaporated, concentrated, powdered, dried, or desiccated, to which has been added, or which has been blended or compounded with, any fat or oil other than milk fat, so that the resulting product is in imitation or semblance of milk ..., whether or not condensed, evaporated, concentrated, powdered, dried, or desiccated." The petitioner's compounds, it is agreed, fall within this definition. But, petitioners contend, they do not fall within its spirit, since the vitamins which cause deficiency have been restored and that therefore the act is inapplicable to the enriched compounds....

Petitioners' position as to the legislative purpose of the act was not accepted by the trial or reviewing court. We agree with those courts. While, as we have stated above, the vitamin deficiency was an efficient cause in bringing about the enactment of the Filled Milk Act, it was not the sole reason for its passage. A second reason was that the compounds lend themselves readily to substitution for or confusion with milk products. Although, so far as the record shows, filled milk compounds as enriched are equally wholesome and nutritious as milk with the same content of calories and vitamins, they are artificial or manufactured foods which are cheaper to produce than similar whole milk products. When compounded and canned, whether enriched or not, they are indistinguishable by the ordinary consumer from processed natural milk. The purchaser of these compounds does not get evaporated milk. This situation has not changed since the enactment of the act. The possibility and actuality of confusion, deception and substitution was appraised by Congress. The prevention of such practices or dangers through control of shipments in interstate commerce is within the power of Congress. The manner by which Congress carries out this power, subject to constitutional objections which are considered hereinafter ... is within legislative discretion, even though the method chosen is prohibition of manufacture, sale or shipment. Congress evidently determined that exclusion from commerce of filled milk compounds in the semblance of milk was an appropriate method to strike at evils which it desired to suppress. Although it now is made to appear that one evil, the nutritional deficiencies, has been overcome, the evil of confusion remains and Congress has left the statute in effect. It seems to us clear, therefore, that there is no justification for judicial interference to withdraw these assumedly non-deleterious compounds from the prohibitions of the act....

The petitioners urge another reason why the act does not cover their compounds. This ground is that the compounds are not "in imitation or semblance" of milk within the meaning of the act's definition of filled milk....

Petitioners rely upon the admitted fact that no ingredient is added to the skim milk, oil and vitamins to alter the appearance of the compound. Accepting the evidence that the compounds are indistinguishable from whole milk products by purchasers, it is urged that they cannot be held to be in "imitation or semblance" of milk unless the manufacturer purposefully adds something to make the mixture simulate milk....

... [A]s determinative of the intention of Congress to include compounds whose resemblance to milk products arises from their ingredients and not from conscious effort, we note the fact that compounds of this innocent character were specifically included by name in the list of compounds which the Congressional reports pointed out as products which were covered by the proposed act. Petitioner's compounds were themselves so named. The addition of vitamins does not affect their physical likeness to milk products.

If the Filled Milk Act is applicable to the compounds whose shipment was the basis of the indictment in this case, as we have just concluded, petitioners assert that the act, as thus applied, violates the due process clause of the Fifth Amendment. Their argument runs in this manner. Since these enriched compounds are admittedly wholesome and sold under trade names with proper labels without the commission of any fraud by petitioners on the public, Congress cannot prohibit their interstate shipment without denying to petitioners a right protected by the due process clause, the right to trade in innocent articles....

... Under the first point of this opinion, we have determined that the avoidance of confusion furnished a reason for the enactment of the Filled Milk Act.... The reports show that it was disputable as to whether wholesome filled milk should be excluded from commerce because of the danger of its confusion with the condensed or evaporated natural product or whether regulation would be sufficient. The power was in Congress to decide its own course. We need look no further....

In the action of Congress on filled milk there is no prohibition of the shipment of an article of commerce merely because it competes with another such article which it resembles.... Here a milk product, skimmed milk, from which a valuable element—butterfat—has been removed is artificially enriched with cheaper fats and vitamins so that it is indistinguishable in the eyes of the average purchaser from whole milk products. The result is that the compound is confused with and passed off as the whole milk product in spite of proper labeling.

When Congress exercises a delegated power such as that over interstate commerce, the methods which it employs to carry out its purposes are beyond attack without a clear and convincing showing that there is no rational basis for the legislation; that it is an arbitrary fiat. This is not shown here. . . .

Affirmed.

NOTES

1. *Related Case.* In an earlier decision, *United States v. Carolene Prods. Co.*, 304 U.S. 144 (1938), the Supreme Court upheld the application of the Filled Milk Act to a version of this product that was not fortified with vitamins to make it as nutritious as milk.

2. *Rationale for Regulation.* The Supreme Court has sanctioned prohibition of foods to prevent injury or deception, but it has generally rejected other grounds for regulation. In *Minnesota v. Barber*, 136 U.S. 313 (1890), the Court struck down a Minnesota statute that prohibited the importation of meat from animals slaughtered in other states, holding that no state can bar the interstate shipment of products fit for human food. In *Schollenberger v. Pennsylvania*, 171 U.S. 1 (1898), the Court also struck down a Pennsylvania statute prohibiting the importation of all oleomargarine.

> This does not interfere with the acknowledged right of the State to use such means as may be necessary to prevent the introduction of an adulterated article, and for that purpose to inspect and test the article introduced, provided the state law does really inspect and does not substantially prohibit the introduction of the pure article and thereby interfere with interstate commerce. It cannot for the purpose of preventing the introduction of an impure or adulterated article absolutely prohibit the introduction of that which is pure and wholesome.

Similarly, in *Collins v. New Hampshire*, 171 U.S. 30 (1898), the Court overturned a New Hampshire statute that required all margarine to be colored pink, on the ground that the statute was "prohibitory" in nature and thus fell within the rule established in *Schollenberger*. The practical limits on state power, however, sometimes prove illusory. For example, in *Hebe Co. v. Shaw*, 248 U.S. 297, 302 (1919), the Court upheld a state law prohibiting a properly labeled, wholesome food, condensed skim milk, on the ground that the states have a right "to save the public from the fraudulent substitution of an inferior product that would be hard to detect."

3. *Substantive Due Process.* Judicial reluctance to invoke "substantive due process" as a limitation on state or federal economic regulation has resulted in judicial validation of a wide range of laws that impinge on the food and drug area. Restrictions in almost every state on the sale of products that compete with traditional dairy foods—such as milk, cream, and butter—have been routinely upheld. *But see Milnot Co. v. Richardson*, 350 F. Supp. 221 (N.D. Ill. 1972), p. 115 *infra*. Judicial doctrines that have permitted wide latitude in legislative choice to aid consumers whom the market would not otherwise protect have likewise allowed legislative schemes whose primary effect, and perhaps purpose, has been to protect established producers from competition. This result has not gone uncriticized. *See, e.g.* Mashaw, *Constitu-*

tional Deregulation: Notes Toward a Public, Public Law, 54 Tul. L. Rev. 849 (1980).

In *The Theory of Economic Regulation,* 2 Bell J. of Econ. & Mgt. Sci. 3 (1971), Professor George Stigler argues:

... [A]s a rule, regulation is acquired by the industry and is designed and operated primarily for its benefit....

The most obvious contribution that a group may seek of the government is a direct subsidy of money....

The second major public resource commonly sought by an industry is control over entry by new rivals....

We propose the general hypothesis: every industry or occupation that has enough political power to utilize the state will seek to control entry. In addition, the regulatory policy will often be so fashioned as to retard the rate of growth of new firms....

A third general set of powers of the state which will be sought by the industry are those which affect substitutes and complements. Crudely put, the butter producers wish to suppress margarine and encourage the production of bread....

---

2. ECONOMIC ADULTERATION

UNITED STATES v. 88 CASES ... BIRELEY'S ORANGE BEVERAGE

United States Court of Appeals, Third Circuit, 1951.
187 F.2d 967.

HASTIE, Circuit Judge.

Pursuant to its libel charging economic adulteration of certain food within the meaning of Section 402(b)(4) of the Federal Food, Drug and Cosmetic Act, the United States seized for condemnation 88 cases of an article of food labeled "Bireley's Orange Beverage." [2] The charges thus asserted were tried to a jury in the District Court for the District of New Jersey with a resultant finding of adulteration and a decree of condemnation....

In this case the United States charged and undertook to prove that the "food" in question—Bireley's Orange Beverage—was "adulterated" within the meaning of the statute in that "substances—particularly, yellow coal tar dyes, sugar, lactic acid, and orange oil—had been "added thereto or mixed therewith * * * so as to make it appear better or of greater value than it is." ...

2. The article is described in the libel, in detail, as follows: "88 cases, more or less, each containing 24—6 fluid ounce bottles of an uncarbonated beverage labeled:

(crown cap) "Bireley's Orange Beverage Contains water, orange pulp & juice, lemon pulp & juice, sug-

ar, lactic acid, orange oil, artificial color Bireley's, Inc., Phila., Pa."

(bottle label) "Enjoy Bireley's Daily for Real Fruit Taste, Bireley's, Inc., Phila., Pa., 6 fl. ozs. Noncarbonated."

Preliminarily, we consider an argument that the types of processing and manufacture covered by Section 402(b)(4) should be limited by a strict grammatical application of the words of the statute. Such an approach suggests that the noun "food" used in the introductory line of the section, and the articles and adverbs referring back to it be applied precisely and consistently to denote either an adulterated end product or an unadulterated original food. Further, it is argued that the statutory description of adulteration in terms of substances "mixed with" or "added to" a "food" limits the application of the section to situations in which the process of manufacture has been the modification of a basic identifiable and unadulterated article of food through the introduction of some additive.

We reject this restrictive analysis. In Section 402(b)(4) we think Congress has employed a very brief text, informally phrased in non-technical language, to cover generally a very considerable and diverse, but not precisely delimited, field of processing and fabrication. We view the language of the section as a comprehensive, if not always grammatically precise and consistent, description applicable to the manufacture and processing of foods generally, whether a recognized food is altered or sundry ingredients are combined or compounded to make what is essentially a new article of manufacture....

Such broad and non-technical construction of the language in question is supported by the only two cases which have come to our attention where Courts of Appeals have had to consider the scope of the section. In *United States v. Two Bags* Poppy Seeds, 6 Cir. 1945, 147 F.2d 123, the product seized was white poppy seeds which had been artificially colored with charcoal. The result was that they looked like naturally dark poppy seeds. The market for the naturally dark seeds was substantially better than that for white seeds. The court held that the product, artificially colored white seeds, was adulterated under 402(b)(4) because it appeared to be the naturally dark seeds although in fact it was not. "Food" in the introductory line of the section under this construct thus meant the artificial product. The Court in effect held that the processed article, artificially colored white poppy seeds, is an adulterated product because it is made by mixing with white poppy seeds (the base food) an additional product, charcoal, to cause the white poppy seeds to appear to be naturally dark poppy seeds, and thus better or of greater value than they, the white poppy seeds, in fact are. Under no technically grammatical reading of Section 402(b)(4) could this result have been reached. Yet, under no circumstances could it be considered an unfair, improper, or surprising conclusion as to the meaning of the section in relation to the facts of the case.

In the context of the present case, it is our conclusion that the language of Section 402(b)(4) covers a situation in which the challenged process of manufacture was the inclusion of one or more designated ingredients among the primary integral components of a distinct fabricated article. It is not important whether the final product has been achieved by a direct dilution of orange juice, or, as here, by a more complex process of fabrication.

More difficult questions arise in construing and applying the requirement of the statute that admixture shall have made the food "appear better than it is." To whom must the food appear better than it is? And how is it to be determined whether the food "appears better than it is"?

With reference to the first question, the trial judge charged the jury as follows: "Your function in this case is to determine whether any part of the public, the vast multitude which includes the ignorant, the unthinking and the credulous, and those who do not stop to analyze in making a purchase would be so misled." We have found nothing else in the charge which modifies the impression created by this statement. The jury was told that deceptive appearance to "any part" of the public sufficed and the significance of "any part" was emphasized and underlined by the accompanying reference to "the ignorant, the unthinking and the credulous." This was error.

The correct standard was the reaction of the ordinary consumer under such circumstances as attended retail distribution of this product. When a statute leaves such a matter as this without specification, the normal inference is that the legislature contemplated the reaction of the ordinary person who is neither savant nor dolt, who lacks special competency with reference to the matter at hand but has and exercises a normal measure of the layman's common sense and judgment. What constitutes the norm of common sense and judgment is peculiarly the province of the jury.... Congress has indicated no extraordinary standard in this section under consideration and we find no basis for imposing one.

In Section 403(f) of the Act which deals with misbranded food, it is expressly stated that the branding must be such as is "likely to be read and understood by the ordinary individual under customary conditions of purchase and use." It would be unreasonable to conclude that an abnormal and more burdensome standard results from the fact that Congress did not deem it necessary to specify a test in Section 402(b)(4). We think that essentially the same standard should be applied to the determination of consumer reaction under both sections.

This formulation also disposes of an issue that has arisen whether such matters as bottling, labeling and retail price, as well as the taste and physical appearance of the food, constitute appearance under the statute. In our view, all customary circumstances of retail acquisition and consumption are relevant. Thus, the bottling and labeling of the libeled article are properly considered unless it is shown that some considerable part of the retail trade acquires the beverage without such packaging. Of course, consumer habits in observing or not observing details of packaging are relevant and may be weighed by a jury in determining the effect of container markings upon the consumer.

We next consider what is meant by a description of food as appearing "better than it is" and what criteria are applicable to the determination of such apparent superiority over actual quality....

The parties agree that Bireley's orange drink contains about 6% orange juice, 2% lemon juice, 87% water, and small quantities of various other harmless substances. Undoubtedly, any percentage increase in the orange juice content with a corresponding decrease in water content would represent some improvement in food value. Hence, literally the product appears better than it is if it appears to the consumer to contain more than 6% orange juice.

But here we encounter serious difficulties of vagueness. The statutory test in Section 402(b)(4) is unreasonable and unenforceable if it requires manufacturers in first instance to anticipate and the trier of fact thereafter to measure anything so speculative or even whimsical as the customer's guess whether an artificial beverage contains five, six, seven, or some other percentage of orange juice. Popular judgments as to degree of dilution, more or less than actuality, are in our view too vague and speculative for meaningful guidance or fair and practical administration of a prohibition against the introduction of otherwise unobjectionable food into commerce. The difficulty with this entire approach is that the "adulterated" food is made to serve as its own only standard.

The solution to the problem and the correct construction of the statutory language are to be found in the rationale of the legislative exclusion of products from commerce for economic adulteration where no hygienic adulteration exists. In such cases a product is recognized as wholesome but is excluded from commerce because of the danger of confusing it with something else which is defined, familiar, and superior. There is no evidence to indicate a legislative intent to bar from the market foods which are wholesome merely because they may in fact be of relatively little value. So long as they are not confused with more wholesome products, their presence does no harm. Without a finding that a marketable inferior product is likely to be confused with a specified superior counterpart, we think there can be no appearing "better than it is" within the scope of disapproval of a section patently concerned only with confusion. Thus, in the case before us, proof of violation of the statute requires first description and definition of the superior counterpart, and second, proof that the consumer is likely to mistake the inferior for the superior....

In the instant case, undiluted orange juice is the only defined and familiar food pointed out in the libel and in evidence as possibly to be confused with Bireley's Orange Beverage. We therefore agree with the claimant that the issue on this aspect of the case is squarely this: Would the ordinary consumer confuse claimant's product with undiluted orange juice?

Legislative consideration of the problem of standards under the Act gives further support to our conclusion that Section 402(b)(4) is not applicable if the allegedly adulterated food is its own only standard. The inability of the government to establish enforcible standards for fabricated foods, considerably hampered the work of enforcement of the 1906 Act. The solution to this problem suggested in the course of legislative consideration of the 1938 bill, and in due course adopted, was the enactment of provisions giving the Secretary of Agriculture power to promulgate standards of identity for foods....

Questions of various permissible degrees of dilution which were regarded below as relevant and in issue are peculiarly appropriate for disposition by this administrative technique. Under the required administrative procedure, the whole industry can participate in the determination whether orange-flavored soft drinks are capable of satisfactory definition, how their composition should be restricted, and even whether such a food as orange drink, or any of its variants, should be permitted in commerce.

However, we agree with the government that it is not necessary that this channel be used. We agree that the statute does not foreclose the procedure used here. But as already indicated, we think the procedure used here permits condemnation only where there is confusion with a defined superior product. If the government would go further it must undertake the formulation of standards of identity in this area.

The trial court's instruction to the jury did not ask simply and directly whether the Bireley product could be confused with undiluted orange juice. Nor did it ask anything sufficiently close so that we can say that the issue was in effect determined.... In a new trial that issue should be made entirely clear to the jury....

NOTES

1. *Concealment of Inferiority.* In *United States v. 36 Drums of Pop'n Oil,* 164 F.2d 250 (5th Cir. 1947), the majority sustained a charge of economic adulteration under section 402(b)(3) and (b)(4) against artificially colored and flavored mineral oil. The product was marketed, with truthful labeling, principally to movie theaters for use in making popcorn. Although at trial the government disavowed any charge that the mineral oil was deleterious or harmful, the author of the opinion suggested this possibility as a ground for decision. The concurring judge, though agreeing with the dissent's assertion that "zeal for enforcement ... is here outrunning common sense and the true intent of the law," reluctantly concluded that the product was adulterated under (b)(3) because its inferiority had been concealed by making it look like butter, and under (b)(4) because mineral oil had been colored to make it appear of greater value than it was. Compare the "ordinary consumer" standard applied in the *Bireley's* case with the various standards applied in the misbranding cases cited in note 2 at p. 57 *supra.*

2. *Ineffectiveness of Truthful Labeling.* In the *Pop'n Oil* case, the product was intended for use in a way that consumers could never know its composition, *i.e.*, on popcorn sold at movie theaters without ingredient labeling. Under the *Pop'n Oil* rationale would all fabricated food sold at restaurants or other food service institutions without ingredient labeling violate section 402(b)? If

ingredient information had been provided to consumers in this case should the result have been different? *See United States v. 55 Cases Popped Corn,* 62 F. Supp. 843 (D. Idaho 1943), posing the same issue as the *Pop'n Oil* case in the context of a consumer product that bore full ingredient labeling disclosing the presence of mineral oil and coloring. FDA contended the product was not popcorn because neither melted butter nor vegetable oil was used. The court rejected this contention because "there is no exact formula used in the preparation of popcorn for the market" and "the consumer was fully advised as to the contents of the various packages." *But see United States v. 716 Cases ... Del Comida Brand Tomatoes ...,* 179 F.2d 174 (10th Cir. 1950), holding that truthful labeling cannot cure economic adulteration.

3. *Vagueness of Standard.* The court in *United States v. Fabro, Inc.,* 206 F. Supp. 523 (M.D. Ga. 1962), declared section 402(b)(1) unconstitutionally vague as applied to a nonstandardized food. *Van Liew v. United States,* 321 F.2d 674 (5th Cir. 1963), held that an indictment charging a violation of sections 402(b)(2) and (4) was impermissibly vague because it did not specify in detail what valuable constituent was omitted from the defendants' orange drink product, what substance was substituted therefor, or how it was made to appear better or of greater value than it was.

4. *1906 Act Cases.* The central economic adulteration decision under the 1906 Act was *United States v. Ten Cases ... Bred Spred,* 49 F.2d 87 (8th Cir. 1931). There the court held that a strawberry flavored spread containing less than half the strawberries found in traditional strawberry jam was not adulterated:

> The mere fact that the product contained fewer strawberries than some other product, e.g., jam, does not show that Bred Spred was inferior to jam; nor does it show that a comparison with jam was called for by the statute unless Bred Spred was being palmed off on the public as jam. No showing of this kind was made.

Other economic adulteration cases under the 1906 Act include *United States v. Seven Hundred and Seventy-Nine Cases of Molasses,* 174 Fed. 325 (8th Cir. 1909); *Libby, McNeill & Libby v. United States,* 210 Fed. 148 (4th Cir. 1913); *F.B. Washburn & Co. v. United States,* 224 Fed. 395 (1st Cir. 1915); *United States v. Schider,* 246 U.S. 519 (1918); *United States v. Krumm,* 269 Fed. 848 (E.D. Pa. 1921); *United States v. 154 Sacks of Oats,* 283 Fed. 985 (W.D. Va. 1922), 294 Fed. 340 (W.D. Va. 1923); *W.B. Wood Mfg. Co. v. United States,* 292 Fed. 133 (8th Cir. 1923); *United States v. Nesbitt Fruit Prods., Inc.,* 96 F.2d 972 (5th Cir. 1938).

5. *USDA Regulation.* *See Chip Steak Co. v. Hardin,* 332 F. Supp. 1084 (N.D. Cal. 1971), upholding a USDA ban on preservatives in cooked sausage on the ground that such additives "conceal inferiority and damage and make the product appear better than it actually is."

6. *Commentary.* *See* Forte, *The Food and Drug Administration and the Economic Adulteration of Foods,* 21 FDC L.J. 533 (1966); Kushen, *The Significance of Section 402(b),* 10 FDC L.J. 829 (1955); Nelson, *What Standard for the Non-standardized Food?,* 8 FDC L.J. 425 (1953).

In Trade Correspondence 381 (January 23, 1942), FDA recounted that it had historically considered foods in which saccharin was substi-

tuted for sugar to be adulterated. The agency did not renounce this
position though it did acknowledge that "products which contain saccharin and are for special dietary uses may be legally manufactured
and sold under the restrictions laid down by the regulations under
Section 403(j) of the Act."

UNITED STATES v. 1200 CANDY BARS ... "STA–TRIM"

United States District Court, Northern District of California, 1964.
1965–1968 FDLI Jud. and Ad. Rec. 148.

SWEIGERT, District Judge.

On the issue of adulteration, the amended libel alleges that the
Sta–Trim bars are adulterated within the meaning of 21 U.S.C. § 342(d),
in that they are confectionery and contain saccharin and sodium
cyclamate, which are alleged to be non-nutritive substances. This
section reads in pertinent part as follows: "A food shall be deemed to
be adulterated ... (d) If it is confectionery, and it bears or contains any
alcohol or non-nutritive article or substance except authorized coloring,
harmless flavoring...."

The ... question is therefore presented whether Section 342(d) is to
be construed as prohibiting the use in confectionery of non-nutritive
substances which are not harmful or inedible.

When Congress enacted the Food and Drug Act in 1906, its obvious
purpose was to eliminate from confectionery certain non-nutritive substances which were poisonous or deleterious ingredients.... When
Congress enacted the present law in 1938, the section was broadened to
omit references of specific harmful substances and there was substituted the general phrase, "non-nutritive substance," with certain specific
exceptions in regard to authorized coloring and harmless flavoring.....
[But] Section 342(d), when read in light of its predecessor Section 7 of
the 1906 Act, embodies a legislative purpose to prohibit non-nutritive
ingredients which are either harmful or inedible....

The use of artificial sugars, such as saccharin and sodium cyclamate in the manufacture of a confection may possibly give rise to
questions relating to a statutory standard of identity, Section 343(g), or
problems of misbranding, Section 343. But, as far as adulteration,
within the meaning of Section 342(d) is concerned, we hold that the
statutory phrase, "non-nutritive substances," means only non-nutritive
substances that are harmful or inedible.

If Section 342(d) were to be read to prohibit the addition of
harmless non-nutritive substances, such as saccharin and sodium cyclamate, into confectionery, this section would conflict with Section 343(j)
which permits the sale of special dietary foods, when properly labeled,
including foods containing saccharin and sodium cyclamate. Interpretations that result in such conflicts should be avoided as far as reasonably possible....

NOTES

1. *Subsequent Proceedings.* The district court later reaffirmed this ruling, released for publication in 1964 but clearly issued much earlier, but ultimately held the product misbranded. Because the government prevailed on the misbranding charge, FDA's appeal was dismissed as moot but the court of appeals stated that "[s]o much of the judgment below as dealt with the issue of adulteration is vacated and set aside, and the same is and shall be without further force and effect." *United States v. 1200 Candy Bars . . . "Sta-Trim,"* 1938–1964 FDLI Jud. Rec. 1833 (N.D. Cal. 1961), *vacated as moot*, 313 F.2d 219 (9th Cir. 1963).

2. *Statutory Amendments.* Section 402(d)(1) and (3) were amended to their present form by 80 Stat. 231 (1966), which signaled the end of FDA's traditional opposition to the use of nonnutritive sweeteners in ordinary foods.

3. *Confectionery Containing Alcohol.* From its enactment in 1938 the provision that is now section 402(d)(2) prohibited confectionery containing any alcohol in excess of 0.5 percent derived solely from the use of flavoring extracts. This provision was amended by the Comprehensive Smokeless Tobacco Health Education Act of 1986, 100 Stat. 30, 35, to permit confectionery containing alcohol to be shipped to states where such products are lawful. By 1986 eleven states had enacted laws specifically permitting the sale of candy containing alcohol, 132 Cong. Rec. 1862 (February 6, 1986), and efforts to enact such laws continue in others. FDA has interpreted the 1986 statute to authorize the importation of candy containing alcohol if it is to be sold in a state that allows sale of such products. Letter from FDA Center for Food Safety and Applied Nutrition Director S.A. Miller to National Confectioners Association President R.T. O'Connell (May 27, 1986). For FDA enforcement policy in other states, *see* 48 Fed. Reg. 18896 (April 26, 1983), 50 Fed. Reg. 8677 (March 4, 1985).

4. *Mixtures of Candy and Trinkets.* FDA initially took the position that the sale of trinkets mixed with candy and sold in vending machines violated original section 402(a). After this interpretation was overruled in *Cavalier Vending Corp. v. United States,* 190 F.2d 386 (4th Cir. 1951), legislative proposals to ban the practice were unsuccessful. When section 402(d)(1) was enacted in its present form, 80 Stat. 231 (1966), it prohibited only those trinkets that are partially or completely embedded in food. Nonetheless, FDA continues to express concern about the mixing of trinkets with confectionery in vending machines and recommends that the trinkets be "physically separated from candy or gum by some form of wrapping as a safety precaution." Compliance Policy Guide No. 7105.04 (October 1, 1980).

5. *Nonnutritive Decoration.* Under the 1906 Act, nonnutritive decorations on candy did not violate the law. *French Silver Drageè Co. v. United States,* 179 Fed. 824 (2d Cir. 1910); *United States v. R.C. Boeckel & Co.,* 221 Fed. 885 (1st Cir. 1915). The courts interpreted the 1906 Act to prohibit any amount of the nonnutritive substances specifically prohibited by name in the statute, but to prohibit only harmful amounts of other nonnutritive substances. The use of silver dragees was similarly permitted by FDA under the 1938 Act. TC No. 239 (April 11, 1940).

6. *Nonenforcement of 402(b).* Applied literally, the economic adulteration provisions of the FD&C Act would render most modern food technology problematic. Many functional ingredients—color additives, preservatives, emulsifiers—are intended to improve the appearance of the product and thus could be challenged as making food appear better than it is. Food producers would

claim that these ingredients in fact improve the food and only make it appear to be as good as it genuinely is. Without purporting to resolve this debate, FDA has virtually abandoned enforcement of section 402(b) except in cases of outright fraud. The agency has embraced, though never publicized, the philosophy that, notwithstanding the proper legal interpretation of the statute, informative labeling can cure "economic adulteration."

---

3. FOOD STANDARDS OF IDENTITY

DEVELOPMENTS IN THE LAW—THE FEDERAL FOOD, DRUG, AND COSMETIC ACT

67 Harvard Law Review 632 (1954).

One of the greatest weaknesses of the 1906 Act was its failure to provide for mandatory standards of identity and quality for food, which would have the force of law in prosecutions for adulteration and misbranding. The Secretary could and did establish standards for his own guidance in deciding when to proceed against a food as adulterated or misbranded, but in each prosecution he had to reestablish the validity and reasonableness of the standard from which he claimed the offending food departed. . . . There were individual statutes authorizing the establishment of mandatory standards for certain types of food, and the McNary–Mapes Amendment of 1930 empowered the Secretary to promulgate standards of "quality, condition and/or fill of container" for almost all canned foods, requiring foods that fell below such standards to be appropriately labeled. But in large and important areas of the food industry there was no provision for mandatory standards. . . .

Before any standard for a food . . . can be issued [under the 1938 Act] the Secretary must publish the proposal in general terms, together with notice of the hearing which is required by Section 701(e) of the Act. Any interested person may appear and offer testimony at the hearing, and all relevant and material evidence is to be accepted, without regard to common law rules of admissibility. . . . Every detail of the standard as finally promulgated must be supported by "substantial evidence of record," and detailed findings of fact must be set out in the order, covering not only all ingredients included in the standard, but also those not included although suggested at the hearing.

Hearings have tended to grow longer; those on the proposed bread standard spanned ten years and amassed a record of 17,000 pages. In view of the ponderousness of the procedure and time wasted in putting into the record evidence as to which there is no disagreement, it was proposed in Congress [in 1953] that hearings be dispensed with in cases where there is no objection to the standard or amendment proposed by the Secretary. The present hearing procedure would be retained for cases where there was such objection, but would apply only to those parts of the standard which were actually in dispute. . . . Of course this bill * . . . will have no effect on the time required to dispose of contested issues; in these cases there would still be no limit on introduction of evidence or cross-examination of witnesses. . . .

---

a. Operation of Food Standards

FEDERAL SECURITY ADM'R v. QUAKER OATS CO.
Supreme Court of the United States, 1943.
318 U.S. 218.

Mr. Chief Justice STONE delivered the opinion of the Court.

The Federal Security Administrator, acting under §§ 401 and 701(e), promulgated regulations establishing "standards of identity" for various milled wheat products, excluding vitamin D from the defined standard of "farina" and permitting it only in "enriched farina," which was required to contain Vitamin B_1, riboflavin, nicotinic acid and iron. The question is whether the regulations are valid as applied to respondent. The answer turns upon (a) whether there is substantial evidence in support of the Administrator's finding that indiscriminate enrichment of farina with vitamin and mineral contents would tend to confuse and mislead consumers; (b) if so, whether, upon such a finding, the Administrator has statutory authority to adopt a standard of identity, which excludes a disclosed non-deleterious ingredient, in order to promote honesty and fair dealing in the interest of consumers; and (c) whether the Administrator's treatment, by the challenged regulations, of the use of vitamin D as an ingredient of a product sold as "farina" is within his statutory authority to prescribe "a reasonable definition and standard of identity." . . .

Respondent, The Quaker Oats Company, has for the past ten years manufactured and marketed a wheat product commonly used as a cereal food, consisting of farina as defined by the Administrator's regulation, but with vitamin D added. Respondent distributes this product in packages labeled "Quaker Farina Wheat Cereal Enriched with Vitamin D," or "Quaker Farina enriched by the Sunshine Vitamin." The packages also bear the label "Contents 400 U.S.P. units of Vitamin D per ounce, supplied by approximately the addition of 1/5 of 1 percent irradiated dry yeast."

Respondent asserts, and the Government agrees, that the Act as supplemented by the Administrator's standards will prevent the marketing of its product as "farina" since, by reason of the presence of vitamin D as an ingredient, it does not conform to the standard of identity prescribed for "farina," and that respondent cannot market its product as "enriched farina" unless it adds the prescribed minimum quantities of vitamin B_1, riboflavin, nicotinic acid and iron. Respon-

---

* [The bill was enacted, 68 Stat. 54 (1954).
See also 70 Stat. 919 (1956).]

dent challenges the validity of the regulations on the grounds sustained below and others so closely related to them as not to require separate consideration.

As appears from the evidence and the findings, the products of milled wheat are among the principal items of the American diet, particularly among low income groups. Farina, which is a highly refined wheat product resembling flour but with larger particles, is used in macaroni, as a breakfast food, and extensively as a cereal food for children. It is in many cases the only cereal consumed by them during a period of their growth. Both farina and flour are manufactured by grinding the whole wheat and discarding its bran coat and germ. This process removes from the milled product that part of the wheat which is richest in vitamins and minerals, particularly vitamin B_1, riboflavin, nicotinic acid and iron, valuable food elements which are often lacking in the diet of low income groups. In their diet, especially in the case of children, there is also frequently a deficiency of calcium and vitamin D, which are elements not present in wheat in significant quantities. Vitamin D, whose chief dietary value is as an aid to the metabolism of calcium, is developed in the body by exposure to sunlight. It is derived principally from cod liver and other fish oils. Milk is the most satisfactory source of calcium in digestible form, and milk enriched by vitamin D is now on the market.

In recent years millers of wheat have placed on the market flours and farinas which have been enriched by the addition of various vitamins and minerals. The composition of these enriched products varies widely. There was testimony of weight before the Administrator, principally by expert nutritionists, that such products, because of the variety and combination of added ingredients, are widely variable in nutritional value; and that consumers generally lack knowledge of the relative value of such ingredients and combinations of them.

These witnesses also testified, as did representatives of consumer organizations which had made special studies of the problems of food standardization, that the number, variety and varying combinations of the added ingredients tend to confuse the large number of consumers who desire to purchase vitamin-enriched wheat food products but who lack the knowledge essential to discriminating purchase of them; that because of this lack of knowledge and discrimination they are subject to exploitation by the sale of foods described as "enriched," but of whose inferior or unsuitable quality they are not informed. Accordingly a large number of witnesses recommended the adoption of definitions and standards for "enriched" wheat products which would ensure fairly complete satisfaction of dietary needs, and a somewhat lesser number recommended the disallowance, as optional ingredients in the standards for unenriched wheat products, of individual vitamins and minerals whose addition would suggest to consumers an adequacy for dietary needs not in fact supplied....

... Taking into account the evidence of public demand for vitamin-enriched foods, their increasing sale, their variable vitamin composition and dietary value, and the general lack of consumer knowledge of such values, there was sufficient evidence of "rational probative force" to support the Administrator's judgment that, in the absence of appropriate standards of identity, consumer confusion would ensue.

Respondent insists, as the court below held, that the consumer confusion found by the Administrator affords no basis for his conclusion that the standards of identity adopted by the Administrator will promote honesty and fair dealing. But this is tantamount to saying, despite the Administrator's findings to the contrary, either that in the circumstances of this case there could be no such consumer confusion or that the confusion could not be deemed to facilitate unfair dealing contrary to the interest of consumers. For reasons already indicated we think that the evidence of the desire of consumers to purchase vitamin-enriched foods, their general ignorance of the composition and value of the vitamin content of those foods, and their consequent inability to guard against the purchase of products of inferior or unsuitable vitamin content, sufficiently supports the Administrator's conclusions....

Both the text and legislative history of the present statute plainly show that its purpose was not confined to a requirement of truthful and informative labeling. False and misleading labeling had been prohibited by the Pure Food and Drugs Act of 1906. But it was found that such a prohibition was inadequate to protect the consumer from "economic adulteration," by which less expensive ingredients were substituted, or the proportion of more expensive ingredients diminished, so as to make the product, although not in itself deleterious, inferior to that which the consumer expected to receive when purchasing a product with the name under which it was sold. The remedy chosen was not a requirement of informative labeling. Rather it was the purpose to authorize the Administrator to promulgate definitions and standards of identity "under which the integrity of food products can be effectively maintained," and to require informative labeling only where no such standard had been promulgated, where the food did not purport to comply with a standard, or where the regulations permitted optional ingredients and required their mention on the label.

The provisions for standards of identity thus reflect a recognition by Congress of the inability of consumers in some cases to determine, solely on the basis of informative labeling, the relative merits of a variety of products superficially resembling each other. We cannot say that such a standard of identity, designed to eliminate a source of confusion to purchasers—which otherwise would be likely to facilitate unfair dealing and make protection of the consumer difficult—will not "promote honesty and fair dealing" within the meaning of the statute.

Respondent's final and most vigorous attack on the regulations is that they fail to establish reasonable definitions and standards of identity, as § 401 requires, in that they prohibit the marketing, under the name "farina," of a wholesome and honestly labeled product consisting of farina with vitamin D added, and that they prevent the addition of vitamin D to products marketed as "enriched farina" unless accompanied by the other prescribed vitamin ingredients which do not co-act with or have any dietary relationship to vitamin D. Stated in another form, the argument is that it is unreasonable to prohibit the addition to farina of vitamin D as an optional ingredient while permitting its addition as an optional ingredient to enriched farina, to the detriment of respondent's business.

... We must reject at the outset the argument earnestly pressed upon us that the statute does not contemplate a regulation excluding a wholesome and beneficial ingredient from the definition and standard of identity of a food. The statutory purpose to fit a definition of identity of an article of food sold under its common or usual name would be defeated if producers were free to add ingredients, however wholesome, which are not within the definition. As we have seen, the legislative history of the statute manifests the purpose of Congress to substitute, for informative labeling, standards of identity of a food, sold under a common or usual name, so as to give to consumers who purchase it under that name assurance that they will get what they may reasonably expect to receive. In many instances, like the present, that purpose could be achieved only if the definition of identity specified the number, names and proportions of ingredients, however wholesome other combinations might be. The statute accomplished that purpose by authorizing the Administrator to adopt a definition of identity by prescribing some ingredients, including some which are optional, and excluding others, and by requiring the designation on the label of the optional ingredients permitted.

Since the definition of identity of a vitamin-treated food, marketed under its common or usual name, involves the inclusion of some vitamin ingredients and the exclusion of others, the Administrator necessarily has a large range of choice in determining what may be included and what excluded. It is not necessarily a valid objection to his choice that another could reasonably have been made. The judicial is not to be substituted for the legislative judgment. It is enough that the Administrator has acted within the statutory bounds of his authority, and that his choice among possible alternative standards adapted to the statutory end is one which a rational person could have made....

We cannot say that the Administrator made an unreasonable choice of standards when he adopted one which defined the familiar farina of commerce without permitting addition of vitamin enrichment, and at the same time prescribed for "enriched farina" the restoration of those vitamins which had been removed from the whole wheat by milling, and allowed the optional addition of vitamin D, commonly found in milk but not present in wheat. Consumers who buy farina will have no reason to believe that it is enriched. Those who buy enriched farina are assured of receiving a wheat product containing those vitamins naturally present in wheat, and, if so stated on the label, an additional vitamin D, not found in wheat....

Reversed.

COLUMBIA CHEESE CO. v. McNUTT
United States Court of Appeals, Second Circuit, 1943.
137 F.2d 576.

CHASE, Circuit Judge.

The administrative proceedings which led to the issuance of the order here under review began in August of 1939 with the object of establishing a definition and standard of identity for cream cheese; and these resulted in a proposed order which was issued on September 28, 1940, with findings of fact and a proposed regulation. But on application of the petitioners, who filed exceptions to the order, the hearing was reopened and consolidated with a hearing on proposals for standards for neufchatel, cottage and creamed cottage cheeses. This hearing resulted in a final order of December 22, 1942, which substantially rejected petitioners' arguments in favor of standards which would allow lower fat and higher moisture content in the manufacture of these cheeses....

The Administrator found that there are produced and marketed various cheeses of a soft uncured nature, but that these cheeses, while they have similar characteristics, have separate and distinct identities....

One of the problems in the manufacture of cream cheese has been the leakage of moisture, which renders the cheese less attractive and correspondingly less merchantable.... [F]ollowing the discovery that gum could be used to prevent leakage it became the practice of many manufacturers to heat the gum and curd together so as to disperse the gum in the curd, by homogenization, and it became possible by this "hot-pack" process to raise the moisture and lower the fat content of the cheese without losing the appearance and texture of cream cheese....

Consumers, it was found, cannot readily distinguish between the cream cheese made by the older process and the lower-fat, higher-moisture cheese made by the "hot-pack" process; and since fat content is the chief item of expense in such cheeses retailers sometimes sold the cheaper product as "cream cheese".... The cheaper product being sold consumers was found by the administrator to be more closely akin to neufchatel cheese, which was found to be the common or usual name of a cheese made by the same process as cream cheese, but having a fat content of a minimum of 20% and a moisture content of a maximum of

65%. This type of cheese, prior to about 1920, was marketed in substantial quantities, but gradually the market declined until it almost vanished because of a progressive cheapening of the product in quality....

One of petitioners' chief objections to the regulations promulgated by the Administrator is that a substantial portion of the cheese manufactured by them must be designated as neufchatel cheese.... And they suggest that the Administrator would have done better if he had used the designation cream cheese with some sort of qualification such as Grade B or No. 2. But it is not our function, as has been pointed out before, to substitute our judgment of what might be a proper name for that of the Administrator. He chose the designation neufchatel; and there was substantial evidence to support such a choice.... The fact that neufchatel had fallen into disrepute in the 1920's is of no particular significance so long as he could find, as he did, that cheese made with a fat content of below 33% and with a moisture content of above 55% was not the product cream cheese as it was traditionally known. Nor does petitioners' assertion that these standards of identity will create a monopoly for one manufacturer make the order unlawful. If they continue to make the product they now make, they can sell it as neufchatel; and if they want to make a product that they can sell as cream cheese, they need only comply with the standards of the product that the Administrator has identified as cream cheese....

SWAN, Circuit Judge (dissenting in part).

For many years cheese having less than 33% of milk fat has been sold as "cream cheese." Almost every one in the industry, with the exception of the Kraft Cheese Co., objects to the requirement that such cheese hereafter be called "neufchatel." The statute authorizes the Administrator to promulgate regulations "establishing for any food, under its common or usual name so far as practicable, a reasonable definition and standard of identity," etc. There is no finding that it is impracticable to use the common name and distinguish between cheese of different milk fat content by adjectives, for example, light cream cheese or heavy cream cheese. Without at least a finding of impracticability, I think it unreasonable to deprive the bulk of the industry of their good will in the commonly used name.

NOTE

Compare Brunetto Cheese Mfg. Corp. v. Celebrezze, 356 F.2d 874 (2d Cir. 1966), which upheld FDA's decision to authorize the use of the name Mozzarella for two types of standardized cheese, one described as "Low Moisture Mozzarella."

———

RICHARD A. MERRILL & EARL M. COLLIER
"LIKE MOTHER USED TO MAKE":
AN ANALYSIS OF FDA FOOD STANDARDS OF IDENTITY

74 Columbia Law Review 561 (1974).

... From the very beginning, Congress conceived that standards of identity would resemble "recipes" for foods. Legislators explicitly analogized processed foods purchased in the market to their home-made counterparts.... Starting from this initial conception—that standards of identity should define foods in terms of "time-honored" home recipes—the FDA began promulgating standards that prescribed the composition of foods in detail. The first standards fixed every ingredient in a food, but gradually FDA "recipes" began not only to specify mandatory ingredients but to allow certain optional ingredients as well. Nevertheless, until the early 1960's virtually all identity standards faithfully followed the basic "recipe" concept, leaving manufacturers comparatively little choice among ingredients and affording consumers practically no information about the composition of standardized foods.

Fruit preserves, canned foods, and other similar traditional products were among the first to undergo standardization, but the FDA's affection for the device soon extended to more complicated, less obvious foods. As the agency's range broadened, however, it became increasingly difficult to identify those characteristics of particular foods that most consumers could be said to expect, or to capture the name by which all consumers recognized the product. Furthermore, the proliferation of new food products resulted in numerous, narrowly-drawn, individual standards rather than in any relaxation of existing requirements for traditional foods.

Two objectives explain the FDA's prolonged adherence to its original recipe format: (1) a desire to preclude any modifications of basic food formulas that could contribute to consumer deception, and (2) a concern to restrain the growing use in food production of chemical additives whose safety had not been demonstrated....

... Recipe standards would not have dramatically affected the availability of substitutes for traditional foods if the FDA had not simultaneously espoused an expansive reading of the "purports to be or is represented as" language in section 403(g). A broad reading obviously imperils more products than a narrow one, for any product that "purports to be or is represented as" a standardized food must meet FDA's compositional requirements.... An expansive reading thus contributes to product homogeneity in those food markets for which standards have been adopted.

The FDA has never formally announced general criteria for determining whether a new product is subject to an existing food standard, i.e., whether a product does, or if marketed would, purport to be the standard food.... The few reported cases ... demonstrate an early consistency of purpose by the FDA to apply section 403(g) to reach most substitutes for standardized foods, sometimes even when there was no risk that consumers would confuse a challenged product with the standard item. Moreover, they reflect the courts' willingness to support the FDA's initial broad reading of that provision.... [60] ...

Any use of the appropriated name, whether or not accompanied by other qualifying language, would appear to be sufficient to support a finding that a product "purports to be or is represented as" the standard item. Absent such use, a court—and traditionally the FDA—would look to similarities in appearance, packaging, and taste....

Most important, the cases make clear that truthful labeling will not save a product that is challenged as "purporting to be" a standard food. Where a product's label consists simply of a fanciful name accompanied by full disclosure of ingredients, one might well doubt that the "ordinary consumer" would always distinguish the product from the standard food. But were a manufacturer to (1) eschew the standard name in favor of his own non-deceptive product description, (2) disclose all of his ingredients, and (3) also declare that the product fails to meet the FDA standard in a specific respect while nonetheless promoting it as a substitute, one would have difficulty imagining a serious risk of consumer confusion. The case law under section 403(g) affords no assurance, however, that such a product could be sold....

Even if the FDA had read "purports to be" more narrowly, however, the use of recipe standards would itself have significantly restricted the range of substitutes for standard foods. For instance, by fixing the amount of fruit that "jam" must contain, the FDA's recipe standard for that food prevents marketing as "jam" other products that contain less fruit. Of course, a relaxed construction of section 403(g) would allow a manufacturer of a low-fruit product to establish a separate market identity without altering its labeling or appearance so substantially that it could not compete with "jam." ...

NOTES

1. *Commentary.* Among the most insightful analyses of FDA's early approach to food standards are two articles by H. Thomas Austern, *The*

60. The first important case under section 403(g) is *Libby, McNeill & Libby v. United States,* 148 F.2d 71 (2d Cir. 1945), in which the FDA successfully enforced its 1940 standard for "tomato catsup," which did not allow for the inclusion of benzoate of soda as an ingredient. The product's label plainly stated that the "tomato catsup" contained therein did not satisfy the FDA standard:

> [T]he product does not conform to government standard for catsup, and contains 1/10 of 1% of benzoate of soda.

Nevertheless, the FDA contended that the product purported to be catsup but failed to meet the standard, and the Second Circuit agreed....

... [O]ne should note *United States v. 20 Cases ... Buitoni 20% Protein Spaghetti,* 130 F. Supp. 715 (D. Del. 1954), *aff'd,* 228 F.2d 912 (3d Cir. 1956) (per curiam), which dramatically demonstrates the difficulty of retaining a separate market identity for non-conforming substitutes once the FDA has standardized a food. For more than 100 years the claimant had marketed its product, which contained *more* gum gluten than the FDA's 13 percent ceiling in protein was intended to permit. Neither this marketing history nor the claimant's truthful label saved the product, whose similarities in size, color, packaging, general appearance, composition, and use convinced the court that it purported to be standard "spaghetti." ...

F–O–R–M–U–L–A–T–I–O–N of Mandatory Food Standards, 2 FDC L.Q. 532 (1947), and *Food Standards: The Balance Between Certainty and Innovation,* 24 FDC L.J. 440 (1969), where Austern recounted:

> ... The original concept was that the label name would be standardized and listing of the basic ingredients would not be required. The important optional ingredients would alone have to be disclosed. Underlying that approach was possibly the quaint idea that the American consumer would be able to read the *Federal Register,* or that with well-known simple foods a full ingredient listing would be superfluous....
>
> The first departure was to fission a food, and to provide that the same food for regulatory purposes could become two foods if it was differently made. As a simple illustration, sliced peaches became one form of food, and peach halves another....
>
> ... What clearly evolved ... was that the label name, appropriated to a given basic composition, overtook the original concept. Instead of having a standard built on basic ingredients *not* labeled, and optional ingredients separately labeled, standards were built on *optional forms* of the same basic ingredients....
>
> ... [T]he developed approach made it more and more difficult to standardize any but the simplest foods. Efforts to do so led to strong dissent, to insistence that the law be amended to permit product development, and thus to limit standardization to basic ingredients and to permit any manufacturer to innovate additionally so long as he plainly labeled his innovation....

2. *Multiple Standards of Quality.* In 1938 Congress declined to give FDA authority to establish multiple standards of quality for a single food. It can be argued, however, that the agency has sometimes circumvented the limits on its authority simply by establishing individual identity standards for different "grades" of the same product, *e.g.,* for "cream cheese" and "neufchatel." Most identity standards include requirements that are designed to maintain the quality of the standardized food, such as minimum limits on important constituents.

3. *Peanut Butter.* In *Corn Prods. Co. v. Department of HEW,* 427 F.2d 511 (3d Cir. 1970), the court upheld FDA's infamous standard requiring 90% peanuts in peanut butter, rejecting the claim that 87% peanuts should be sufficient. This demonstrates that a standard of identity may raise the "quality" of existing foods. Prior to the adoption of FDA's standard of identity for peanut butter, would anyone have seriously suggested that a product containing only 87 percent peanuts and 13 percent other ingredients was adulterated under section 402(b)?

4. *Court Challenges to Food Standards.* Because of the economic impact of food standards, they have been frequently challenged in court. Other important cases include *A.E. Staley Mfg. Co. v. Secretary of Agric.,* 120 F.2d 258 (7th Cir. 1941); *Twin City Milk Producers Ass'n v. McNutt,* 122 F.2d 564 (8th Cir. 1941), 123 F.2d 396 (8th Cir. 1941); *Land O'Lakes Creameries v. McNutt,* 132 F.2d 653 (8th Cir. 1943); *United States Cane Sugar Refiners' Ass'n v. McNutt,* 138 F.2d 116 (2d Cir. 1943); *Willapoint Oysters, Inc. v. Ewing,* 174 F.2d 676 (9th Cir. 1949); *Cream Wipt Food Products Co. v. Federal Security Admin.,* 187 F.2d 789 (3d Cir. 1951); *Atlas Powder Co. v. Ewing,* 201 F.2d 347 (3d Cir.

1952); *Reade v. Ewing,* 205 F.2d 630 (2d Cir. 1953); *Pineapple Growers Ass'n of Hawaii v. FDA,* 673 F.2d 1083 (9th Cir. 1982).

5. *Colors in Standardized Foods.* In promulgating a standard of identity FDA confronts decisions about the permitted composition of a food that might otherwise go unexamined. An example is the use of color additives, which can result in economic adulteration and in violations of section 706(b)(6) of the Act. In 39 Fed. Reg. 32753 (September 11, 1974), 41 Fed. Reg. 6242 (February 12, 1976), 41 Fed. Reg. 45540 (October 15, 1976), 43 Fed. Reg. 22785 (May 26, 1978), Food Drug Cosm. L. Rep. (CCH) ¶ 38,240 (April 4, 1979), 48 Fed. Reg. 51448 (November 9, 1983), 49 Fed. Reg. 1982 (January 17, 1984), and 49 Fed. Reg. 13690 (April 6, 1984), FDA promulgated standards of identity for egg bread and other bakery products containing eggs. The major issue, requiring a full evidentiary hearing, related to the use of ingredients capable of imparting a yellow color that could mislead consumers into believing the product had a higher egg content than it did.

6. *Challenges to Nonconforming Products.* Cases involving the failure of a product to conform to a standard of identity are seldom litigated. A rare illustration is *United States v. Articles of Food ... [Concentrated Orange Juice],* Food Drug Cosm. L. Rep. (CCH) ¶ 38,152 (W.D. Tex. 1981) (products labeled "concentrated orange juice for manufacturing" or "orange juice" failed to comply with applicable standards). In *Stauffer Chemical Co. v. FDA,* Food Drug Cosm. L. Rep. (CCH) ¶ 38,065 (C.D. Cal. 1980), the court declined to entertain a challenge to a letter from FDA stating that use of a processing aid for the canning of tuna would violate the standard of identity on the grounds that the matter was not yet ripe for judicial review and the company had failed to exhaust its administrative remedies. The court indicated, however, that it agreed with FDA's position on the merits.

7. *Revocation of Food Standards.* FDA has revoked only one food standard. The standard for soda water (soft drinks), which had been promulgated in 28 Fed. Reg. 9988 (September 14, 1963), 31 Fed. Reg. 1066 (January 27, 1966), 31 Fed. Reg. 5490 (April 7, 1966), was revoked in 52 Fed. Reg. 18922 (May 20, 1987), 54 Fed. Reg. 398 (January 6, 1989), 54 Fed. Reg. 18651 (May 2, 1989).

8. *Statutory Standards of Identity.* Congress has defined by statute three food products: butter, 42 Stat. 1500 (1923), 21 U.S.C. § 321a; oleomargarine, 64 Stat. 20 (1950), 15 U.S.C. § 55(f); and nonfat dry milk, 70 Stat. 486 (1956), 21 U.S.C. § 321c.

9. *Commentary. See also* Beacham, *Why and How—Standard Making,* 6 FDC L.J. 167 (1951); Burditt, *The Need for New Uses of the Regulatory Power to Establish Food Standards,* 20 FDC L.J. 165 (1965); Cody, *Food Standards and the White House Conference on Food and Nutrition,* 26 FDC L.J. 347 (1971); Crawford, *Ten Years of Food Standardization,* 3 FDC L.Q. 243 (1948); Goodrich, *Food Standardization Past, Present and Future,* 24 FDC L.J. 464 (1969); Hegsted, *Food Standards,* 24 FDC L.J. 384 (1969); Holeman, *The Role of the States in Establishing Food Standards,* 20 FDC L.J. 159 (1965); Kaplan, *Food Standard Making Procedures,* 20 FDC L.J. 149 (1965); Kleinfeld, *Reflections on Food Standards,* 22 FDC L.J. 100 (1967); Stephens, *et al., Do FDA's Present Food Standards and Standard Making Policy Best Serve the Consumer?,* 20 FDC L.J. 180 (1965).

b. Effects of Food Standards

FDA has promulgated nearly 300 standards of identity, which at their maximum reach covered about 45 percent of the wholesale value of food shipped in interstate commerce, excluding fresh fruits and vegetables. 44 Fed. Reg. 75990 (December 21, 1979).

LABEL DECLARATIONS ON STANDARDIZED AND NONSTANDARDIZED FOODS: NOTICE OF DENIAL OF PETITION

37 Federal Register 5131 (March 10, 1972).

A notice of proposed rule making was published in the FEDERAL REGISTER of May 12, 1971 (36 F.R. 8738), in response to a petition filed by Label, Inc., concerning disclosure, on the label, of all ingredients contained in standardized and nonstandardized foods....

The Commissioner ... concludes that he does not have legal authority to promulgate the requested regulation and that the petition must therefore be denied, as follows:

The statutory language of sections 401 and 403(g) and (i) of the act defines two categories of food: Standardized and nonstandardized. Congress explicitly provided distinct labeling requirements for each category. It specifically and deliberately did not require that all foods be labeled with a list of all ingredients.... For standardized food, the statute requires that the label must bear only the common name of each optional ingredient (other than spices, flavoring, and coloring) included in the definition and standard of identity and specifically designated in the standard to be named on the label. Failure to comply with these labeling requirements is a misbranding violation. There is no statutory authority to require that the label bear the name of each mandatory ingredient contained in a standardized food or the name of each spice, flavoring, or coloring contained in any food. If Congress had intended to require full disclosure of all ingredients contained in all food, instead of different labeling requirements for different foods, it would have so provided in the statute.

The lack of statutory authority to require complete ingredient disclosure is clearly indicated by the statute's legislative history and confirmed by the decision of the U.S. Supreme Court in *Federal Security Adm'r v. Quaker Oats Co.* ...

Although the Commissioner lacks legal authority to require complete ingredient disclosure, there is nothing in the act prohibiting manufacturers, packers, and distributors from voluntarily making such disclosure, and there is published elsewhere in this issue of the FEDERAL REGISTER, a notice to that effect.

NOTES

1. *Court Review.* In *Label, Inc. v. Edwards,* 475 F.2d 418 (D.C. Cir. 1973), the court of appeals sustained this order.

2. *Voluntary Ingredient Disclosure.* In 37 Fed. Reg. 5120 (March 10, 1972), 38 Fed. Reg. 2137 (January 19, 1973), codified in 21 C.F.R. § 101.6(b), FDA urged food manufacturers to label voluntarily all ingredients in standardized foods and announced it would amend existing standards to require the maximum ingredient disclosure permitted by law. *See* note 1, p. 76 *supra.* For an analysis of the cost of providing this information, *see* A.D. Little, Inc., COST IMPACT ANALYSIS OF LISTING OF OPTIONAL INGREDIENTS IN STANDARDIZED FOOD, Report to FDA under HHS Contract No. 223–79–8052 (December 19, 1981).

3. *Statutory Amendment.* The 1990 Nutrition Labeling and Education Act amended section 403(g) to require the declaration of all ingredients in standardized foods.

ROBERT W. HAMILTON, RULEMAKING ON A RECORD BY THE FOOD AND DRUG ADMINISTRATION

50 Texas Law Review 1132 (1972).

The following tables illustrate the delays in § 701(e) proceedings of the past decade:

	Notice to Order (Months)	Order to Notice of Hearing (Months)	Days of Hearing/ Pages of Transcript	Notice of Hearing to Proposed Findings (Months)	Proposed Findings to Final Order (Months)	Total Time Elapsed (Months)
Orange Juice I	40	9	27/3434	23	11½	83½
Orange Juice II	9½	4	8/874	15½	7	36
Breaded Shrimp I	25	7½	9/1308	12	2½	47
Cheddar Cheese I	8	5	4/490	12	9	34
Cold Pack Cheese Foods/Spreads	7½	8½	4/527	9	5	30
Fruit Jellies	2½	6½	2/234	27	19	55
Jelly	5	6½	2/399	36	10	57½
Peanut Butter	29	45½	30/7736	26½	8	109
Foods for Special Dietary Uses	48	21½	247/32,405	—	—	—

NOTES

1. *Impact of Formality.* The advantages and disadvantages of the formal hearing requirement of section 701(e) for establishing food standards are explored at p. 1271 *infra.* For a vigorous defense of the requirement, *see* Austern, *Food Standards: The Balance Between Certainty and Innovation,* 24 FDC L.J. 440 (1969).

2. *Statutory Amendment.* The 1990 Nutrition Labeling and Education Act amended section 701(e) to exclude all standards of identity except for the amendment or repeal of standards for dairy products and maple sirup.

COMMENT, THE FEDERAL FOOD, DRUG AND COSMETIC ACT AS AN EXPERIMENT IN QUALITY CONTROL

20 Syracuse Law Review 883 (1969).

The FTC found ... a more rapid rate of decline in the number of food manufacturers than in any other major food industry with indications of an increasing decline with each census taken since 1947. From 1947 to 1961 the total number of food manufacturers declined from 40,000 to 32,000, while in 1947 there were 31 food manufacturers with assets in excess of $50 million and in 1961 there were 68 such manufacturers. In 1966 the 50 largest food manufacturers accounted for 50 percent of the total industry assets and 60 percent of the industries' profits. The reason for the increased profits by the large food manufacturers does not necessarily lie in increased economies of scale in manufacturing, for it was generally found that efficiency in plant operation is achieved at relatively small outputs.... Instead, it should be realized that with rigid standards of identity, the differentiation between similar food items is nil....

While it may be unjustifiable to place the emergence of food standards as even the main cause of increasing concentration in the food industry, there is at least some evidence that food standards can be partially blamed. As was pointed out, the standards of identity minimize product differentiation among the foods so covered, at least as the standards are now administered. While manufacturers of standardized foods are permitted to produce a food which exceeds the standard's minimum quality level, they can only do this by using higher quality ingredients.... Thus faced with the problem of little product differentiation and competitive pricing, it is understandable why the food producers turned to advertising to manufacture product differentiation....

TEMPORARY MARKETING PERMITS

To facilitate the development of new foods varying from a standard of identity, FDA has established a system of temporary permits for test marketing of such products pending amendment of the standard. 21 C.F.R. § 130.17. Recognizing the difficulty of securing amendments to existing standards, the agency has increasingly liberalized this temporary permit system to allow continuous marketing during consideration of a pending amendment. *See* 37 Fed. Reg. 26340 (December 9, 1972), 40 Fed. Reg. 21721 (May 19, 1975). Nonetheless, the temporary permit system remains a major barrier to product innovation because FDA has adopted the policy that, when the agency approves a permit, it must approve the entire label of the product and not just the variation from the standard.

c. Alternative Approaches to Food Standards

Following enactment of the 1958 Food Additives Amendment, and the 1960 Color Additive Amendments, FDA concluded that it could permit greater flexibility in food standards. In 30 Fed. Reg. 2860 (March 5, 1965), FDA promulgated its first food standard permitting the use of any "safe and suitable" functional ingredients rather than specifying each functional ingredient that could be used in the food.

FROZEN RAW BREADED SHRIMP
21 C.F.R. § 161.175.

(a) Frozen raw breaded shrimp is the food prepared by coating one of the optional forms of shrimp specified in paragraph (c) of this section with safe and suitable batter and breading ingredients as provided in paragraph (d) of this section. The food is frozen.

(b) The food tests not less than 50 percent of shrimp material as determined by the method prescribed in paragraph (g) of this section, except that if the shrimp are composite units the method prescribed in paragraph (h) of this section is used....

(d) The batter and breading ingredients referred to in paragraph (a) of this section are the fluid constituents and the solid constituents of the coating around the shrimp. These ingredients consist of suitable substances which are not food additives ... or if they are food additives ... they are used in conformity with regulations established pursuant to section 409 of the act....

NOTE

This innovation was later characterized in the following way:

> In its practical impact, the breaded shrimp standard of identity represents a very modest deviation from traditional FDA regulation. It retains a minimum-content platform for the valuable ingredient, restricts, though loosely, the nature of other allowable ingredients, and provides consumers no additional information about product composition. Nevertheless, despite these similarities to traditional recipe standards, the "breaded shrimp" standard marks a significant shift in approach. Rather than prescribe all of the ingredients in the food, the FDA was content to narrow its focus to the essential constituents....

Merrill and Collier, "*Like Mother Used to Make*": *An Analysis of FDA Food Standards of Identity*, 74 Colum. L. Rev. 561 (1974).

"SAFE AND SUITABLE" FOOD INGREDIENTS: GENERAL DEFINITION
39 Federal Register 17304 (May 15, 1974).

In the FEDERAL REGISTER of April 26, 1973 (38 FR 10274), the Commissioner of Food and Drugs proposed a new § 10.1(d) [now

§ 130.3(d)] which defines the phrase "safe and suitable" as it describes food ingredients. This phrase has been variously defined in numerous food standard regulations, and it was the intent of the Commissioner in his proposal to avoid repeating the same or similar definitions in every individual food standard in the future where it might be applicable....

The Commissioner concludes that there is no advantage to repeatedly define certain terms, such as "safe and suitable," which appear in many individual food standards. In the process of promulgating food standard regulations, all ingredients will be considered under the "safe and suitable" definition. Those ingredients which are deemed not suitable for a particular product will be excluded from the standard....

§ 130.3 Definitions and interpretations

(d) "Safe and suitable" means that the ingredient:

(1) Performs an appropriate function in the food in which it is used.

(2) Is used at a level no higher than necessary to achieve its intended purpose in that food.

(3) Is not a food additive or color additive as defined in section 201(s) or (t) of the Federal Food, Drug, and Cosmetic Act as used in that food, or is a food additive or color additive as so defined and is used in conformity with regulations established pursuant to section 409 or 706 of the act....

NOTES

1. *Modernizing Food Standards.* Beginning in 1972, FDA undertook to modernize all important food standards to (1) require full ingredient labeling, (2) permit use of any safe and suitable functional food ingredients, and (3) adopt any appropriate aspects of the international food standards developed by the FAO/WHO Codex Alimentarius Commission. *See, e.g.,* the revision of the standards for milk and cream, 37 Fed. Reg. 18392 (September 9, 1972), 38 Fed. Reg. 27924 (October 10, 1973); flour, 38 Fed. Reg. 2334 (January 24, 1973), 38 Fed. Reg. 32787 (November 28, 1973); margarine, 38 Fed. Reg. 10952 (May 3, 1973), 38 Fed. Reg. 25671 (September 14, 1973); bakery products, 39 Fed. Reg. 32753 (September 11, 1974), 41 Fed. Reg. 6242 (February 12, 1976). This was part of the FDA policy to eliminate all labeling differences between standardized and nonstandardized food.

2. *Codex Standards.* FDA adopted a procedure for review of all Codex Alimentarius food standards, 37 Fed. Reg. 21102 (October 5, 1972), 38 Fed. Reg. 12396 (May 11, 1973), codified in 21 C.F.R. § 130.b, and has since published several such standards for consideration. *See, e.g.,* 37 Fed. Reg. 21106 (October 5, 1972), 39 Fed. Reg. 3541 (January 28, 1974), 39 Fed. Reg. 33663 (September 19, 1974) (new standard for frozen peas); 37 Fed. Reg. 21112 (October 5, 1972), 39 Fed. Reg. 5760 (February 15, 1974), 40 Fed. Reg. 30940 (July 24, 1975) (amending standard for canned corn); 39 Fed. Reg. 35809 (October 4, 1974) 43 Fed. Reg. 16991 (April 21, 1978), 50 Fed. Reg. 2693 (January 18, 1985) (proposal and withdrawal of new standard for frozen strawberries); 44 Fed. Reg. 10724 (February 23, 1979), 44 Fed. Reg. 60314 (October 19, 1979) (termination of

consideration of standard for table olives); 46 Fed. Reg. 60625 (December 11, 1981), 47 Fed. Reg. 41580 (September 21, 1982) (termination of consideration of standard for fructose); 49 Fed. Reg. 8627 (March 8, 1984), 49 Fed. Reg. 29804 (July 24, 1984) (termination of consideration of standard for quick-frozen shrimps or prawns); 53 Fed. Reg. 8512 (March 15, 1988), 54 Fed. Reg. 14396 (April 11, 1989) (termination of consideration of standard for dessert mousse). The Codex standards have had a larger impact on dairy products than in any other area. *See, e.g.,* 42 Fed. Reg. 37006 (July 19, 1977), 43 Fed. Reg. 19834 (May 9, 1978) (amendments to standards for nonfat dry milk and related products); 42 Fed. Reg. 37013 (July 19, 1977), 43 Fed. Reg. 21668 (May 19, 1978) (amendments to standards for evaporated milk and related products); and 42 Fed. Reg. 29919 (June 10, 1977), 46 Fed. Reg. 9924 (January 30, 1981) (establishing standards for cultured and acidified dairy products). Consideration of virtually all other Codex standards has been terminated by FDA without action, but publication of the Codex standards in the Federal Register has served the useful purpose of notifying the United States food industry about the existence and details of food standards that are often adopted and enforced elsewhere in the world.

The following reaction to the Codex standard for pickled cucumbers, which was published in 49 Fed. Reg. 17519 (April 24, 1984) and consideration of which was subsequently terminated in 49 Fed. Reg. 36870 (September 20, 1984), is typical of the U.S. food industry reaction to most Codex standards:

> In a time when the Reagan administration has promised that government would control its fervor for regulations, an attempt has been made to regulate every good hamburger's sidekick—the pickle.

> But as you might expect, the pickle packers of America don't exactly relish the idea. In fact, they are clearly sour on the Food and Drug Administration's five-page proposal for standardization of pickled cucumbers.

> Clausen's Pickle Co., an Oscar Meyer division, and Pickle Packers International (PPI), a trade association, the only organizations to file comments to the pickle proposals published by the FDA this spring, turned thumbs down on the idea.

> PPI objected to language that dictated the shape of cucumbers used in the pickling process and standards for the thickness and angle of sliced versions.

> Pickled cucumbers "have been produced since the dim dawn of history all over the world and in the United States since early colonial times, and no one in this country has ever seen the need to establish a standard for them," PPI observed.

> The trade association noted that half the fun of pickles is that they are an "infinitely variable food" in terms of size, shape and flavoring.

> Clausen's Pickle Co. contended that the government may appropriately address itself only to the issue of food safety and that safety has already been covered by the U.S. Agriculture Department.

> The pickle proposal was conceived by the Codex Alimentarius Commission, a U.N. organization that seeks to standardize foods sold internationally.

Gregg, *Regulatory Pickle,* Washington Post, September 4, 1984, at A17.

3. For the extensive literature on the work of the Codex Alimentarius, *see* Beacham, *Current Codex Alimentarius Activities*, 28 FDC L.J. 79 (1973); Kimbrell, *Food Composition Regulation and Codex Standards*, 33 FDC L.J. 144 (1978); bibliographies by Zimmerman in 26 FDC L.J. 303 (1971) and 31 FDC L.J. 229 (1976).

When FDA applied a liberalized approach to the standard of identity for ice cream, 39 Fed. Reg. 27144 (July 25, 1974), 42 Fed. Reg. 19127 (April 12, 1977), 42 Fed. Reg. 35152 (July 8, 1977), however, it encountered fierce and unexpected opposition.

NICHOLAS WADE, ICE CREAM: DAIRYMEN IMPERILED BY FDA'S RECIPE

197 Science 844 (1977).

The FDA's proposed standard for "America's number one fun food," as the ice cream maker's chief lobbyist touts it, would allow manufacturers to use more casein and whey in their mixes and less milk powder. Casein is the principal protein of milk, and is found mainly in milk. Whey is the even more highly nutritious product left over when milk is converted to cheese.... Where is the harm in that?

"This is a terrible, terrible thing that should happen," Pat Healy, chief lobbyist of the National Milk Producers Federation, moans about his dairy industry colleagues, the ice cream makers. "For a group of people operating on the fringes of the industry to take the chance of destroying an industry which is a valuable national asset in order to make a couple of cents extra per gallon of ice cream—I think it is a despicable act by short-sighted, quick-buck artists who have no thought for the long-range impact of their actions."

"The FDA is proposing a technologized frozen dessert product filled with chemicals and dairy waste products—the leftovers of the dairy manufacturing process. This is a matter which is seriously and radically altering one of America's favorite foods," Congressman Frederick Richmond (D–N.Y.) declaimed at a house hearing held on 2 August.

"We want ice cream to stay the real thing," stated Congressman Charles Rose (D–N.C.). "I think what we are concerned about is that America does not go the way of Hitler's Germany in World War II where ersatz became a by-word of products that were sold to its people out of economic necessity." ...

What has happened is that a new regulatory philosophy ... holds that the agency should not prevent food producers making use of new technologies as long as the nutritional standards of the products are maintained. The doctrine is perfectly in accord with the principles of the free market, but it has opened the way for head-on collision with sectors such as the milk producers, whose approach to maintaining their market share rests not on technological adaptation but on protective measures backed by political clout....

Ice cream at present may be made from milk powder (nonfat dried milk), whey, and 11 other milk-derived products including casein, but there are limits on the amounts of whey and casein that ice cream makers may use. The proposed new standards would lift the limits on whey and casein, stipulating only a minimum protein percentage and leaving manufacturers to choose whatever mix of dairy products they pleased to meet it.

Casein, whey, and nonfat dried milk are all highly nutritious substances. In the FDA's view, there would be no loss of quality in an ice cream made with more whey and casein and less milk powder. "Casein is a chemical product made with acid in foreign countries," sneers a staff member of Associated Milk Producers, Inc. But casein is a foreign product not because the American cow differs in her physiology from any other cow but because ... American farmers find it more profitable to sell their milk powder at the government-guaranteed support price than to convert it to casein.

Imported casein is a far cheaper product than American-protected milk powder. So too is whey, a surplus by-product of the burgeoning cheese industry. Under the FDA's proposed changes, ice cream makers would have a strong incentive to substitute as much whey and casein for milk powder as possible. Consumer preferences and other factors impose limits on the extent of this substitution.... The cost savings to manufacturers would eventually, through competition, be passed on to the consumer, amounting to a reduction of 2 percent in the retail price of ice cream....

Against this background, the milk producers' heated reaction to the ice cream issue becomes immediately comprehensible. The milk powder displaced by the FDA's proposed new standards would have to be bought by the government at an estimated cost of $183 million, according to USDA. Coming on top of the support program's expected doubling in cost, the extra $183 million could be a very damaging shock, not to say the final straw that breaks the program's political support in Congress....

NOTE

In 43 Fed. Reg. 4596 (February 3, 1978), FDA announced that it was revoking the controversial provisions of its proposed ice cream standard:

... When it issued these standards, FDA did not expect that there would be measurable nutritional differences between ice cream made under the new standard and that made under the present one. But the agency's studies determined that under the new standard some ice cream formulations could have lesser amounts of some nutrients than under the current standard....

MILNOT CO. v. RICHARDSON

United States District Court, Northern District of Illinois, 1972.
350 F. Supp. 221.

ROBERT D. MORGAN, District Judge.

This is an action for declaratory judgment ... asking the court to declare that the product known as "Milnot," manufactured by the plaintiff, is not within the purview of the provisions of 21 U.S.C. §§ 61–64 [The Filled Milk Act]; or, in the alternative, to declare that Act unconstitutional on the ground that it violates the provisions of the Fifth Amendment to the Constitution of the United States....

... The substance involved in this case, Milnot, is a food product which basically is a blend of fat free milk and vegetable soya oil, to which are added vitamins A and D. In the production of this product cream is skimmed from whole fresh milk. The cream contains the butterfat content of the milk including the fat-soluble vitamins A, D and E. To the portion of the milk which remains after the skimming process, plaintiff adds, *inter alia,* soybean oil as well as vitamins A and D. This restores the liquid to a milk-like consistency and composition. The mixture is then evaporated so as to remove a portion of the water content. That Milnot is wholesome, nutritious, and useful as a food source is clear from the record.

The Filled Milk Act, promulgated by Congress in 1923, prohibits interstate shipment of filled milk products. Following enactment of that statute, plaintiff, then known as Carolene Products Company, violated it and was convicted. After much litigation, the United States Supreme Court twice upheld the validity of the statute.... At least since affirmance of its second conviction, plaintiff has limited its distribution of Milnot to intrastate commerce in the several states where it is produced....

It is further undisputed that through technical advancements since 1944, and a proliferation of treatments, including breakdowns, build-ups, and various reconstitutions of whole fluid milk, several food products have appeared on the market in competition with Milnot, which are permitted to be shipped in interstate commerce, subject to regulation by defendant, and which are commonly known as imitation milk or imitation dairy products, as distinguished from filled milk products. Content analyses reveal that certain of these products are produced in part by combining skim milk with vegetable oil, while others are made by combining sodium caseinate with water and vegetable oils. It is clear and undisputed that sodium caseinate is a soluble white powder which is produced primarily by treating skim milk with an acid....

... It seems clear ... that the Filled Milk Act does by its terms prohibit interstate shipment of the present-day product known as Milnot.

... Plaintiff suggests, and this court agrees, that the appearance and continued existence of new products on the market and in interstate commerce which are quite similar in composition to and competitive with Milnot, and also in imitation or semblance of milk as fully as is Milnot (even though perhaps not "filled milk" in a technical sense under the statutory definition), creates a new factual situation upon which the court should reconsider the constitutionality of the Filled Milk Act as applied to Milnot....

The measuring stick to which legislative acts must conform in order to satisfy due process has been stated in the previous *Carolene* decisions. That is, regulatory legislation affecting ordinary commercial transactions is not to be pronounced unconstitutional unless, in light of the known facts, it is of such a character as to preclude the assumption that it rests upon some rational basis within the knowledge and experience of the legislators. And as previously stated, the constitutionality of a statute predicated upon the existence of a particular state of facts may be challenged by showing to the court that those facts have ceased to exist.

From the undisputed facts in the record here, it appears crystal clear that certain imitation milk and dairy products are so similar to Milnot in composition, appearance, and use that different treatment as to interstate shipment caused by application of the Filled Milk Act to Milnot violates the due process of law to which Milnot Company is constitutionally entitled. No useful purpose is served by listing such products here by name or otherwise, or by discussing the dairy market conditions and dangers of confusion which led to the passage and judicial upholding of the Filled Milk Act many years ago. Suffice it to say that this court finds that the latter have long since ceased to exist.[1]

... The possibility of confusion, or passing off, in the marketplace, which justified the statute in 1944, can no longer be used rationally as a constitutional prop to prevent interstate shipment of Milnot. There is at least as much danger in this regard with imitation milk as with filled milk, and actually no longer any such real danger with either....

NOTES

1. *Agency Response.* Following this decision FDA published the following announcement in 38 Fed. Reg. 20748 (August 2, 1973):

> The court in the *Milnot* case concluded that, since other substitute milk and dairy products may lawfully be shipped in interstate commerce, the prohibition against interstate shipment of filled milk products was an unconstitutional discrimination against these products. The White House Conference on Food, Nutrition and Health recommended in 1969 that the Filled Milk Act be repealed, and the Food and

---

1. It is not insignificant in this regard that some eleven states which passed filled milk acts have since discarded them—five by repeal and six by court action. By far the majority of states now permit wholesome and properly labeled filled milk products. It is worth noting, also, that when the Federal Filled Milk Act was passed by Congress and upheld by the Supreme Court, the presently accepted dangers of "cholesterol" in animal fat were almost unknown.

Drug Administration has concurred in that recommendation. Accordingly, it has been concluded that the decision in the *Milnot* case will not be appealed. On February 1, 1973, a protective notice of appeal filed in the case was withdrawn, and the appeal was dismissed.

This notice will serve to inform the public that, pursuant to the court decision in this case, the Filled Milk Act will no longer be enforced. Henceforth, filled milk products may lawfully be shipped in interstate commerce and will be regulated under the provisions of the Federal Food, Drug, and Cosmetic Act, just as any other foods.

In conjunction with this statement of enforcement policy, the agency proposed the establishment of a common or usual name for "filled milk." The agency subsequently withdrew the proposed common or usual name regulation and proposed a standard of identity for filled milk and other substitute dairy products in 43 Fed. Reg. 42118 (September 19, 1978).

2. *State Filled Milk Laws.* Several state filled milk statutes have also been held invalid, generally under state constitutional provisions. *E.g., General Foods Corp. v. Priddle,* 569 F. Supp. 1378 (D. Kan. 1983), *Strehlow v. Kansas State Board of Agriculture,* 232 Kan. 589, 659 P.2d 785 (1983), *Milnot Co. v. Douglas,* 452 F. Supp. 505 (S.D. W.Va. 1978), *Milnot Co. v. Arkansas State Bd. of Health,* 388 F. Supp. 901 (E.D. Ark. 1975).

3. *Narrowed Application.* In *Dean Foods Co. v. Wisconsin Dept. of Agriculture, Trade and Consumer Protection,* 478 F. Supp. 224 (W.D. Wis. 1979), the district court granted a preliminary injunction against enforcement of a state statute prohibiting the sale of any food which purports to be or is represented as milk and which contains any fat or oil other than milkfat. The state proposed to prohibit the sale of "Choco–Riffic," a nondairy beverage that resembles chocolate milk. The court concluded that a plaintiff had a reasonably good chance to prevail on its contention that a ban of a healthy, nutritious product unduly burdens interstate commerce and thus enjoined an outright prohibition of sale while allowing the state to explore less restrictive measures. On reargument, the court withdrew its initial determination that the product "purports to be" a dairy product and stated that this would depend not upon mere physical resemblance but upon whether, in light of all circumstances, a substantial portion of consumers believe that the product is a dairy product. 504 F. Supp. 520 (W.D. Wis. 1980).

---

4. FOOD NAMES

Section 403(i)(1) of the FD&C Act requires that a nonstandardized food bear on the label its "common or usual name." Since 1938, names for many foods were officially established by standards of identity. In the early 1970s, however, in response to the proliferation of new foods that did not conform to an established standard of identity, FDA adopted a new policy. First, FDA officials concluded that the agency should essentially cease adoption of new standards of identity. Second, the agency decided to interpret the "purports to be" language in section 403(h) narrowly, thus restricting the application of standards of identity to products labeled or otherwise clearly represented as specific standardized foods. The third element of this new policy was reliance on informative common or usual names. FDA established general criteria for all common or usual names for food products and established a separate procedure for adopting common or usual names by regulation.

COMMON OR USUAL NAMES FOR
NONSTANDARDIZED FOODS

38 Federal Register 6964 (March 14, 1973).

In the FEDERAL REGISTER of June 22, 1972 (37 (FR 12327), the Commissioner of Food and Drugs proposed a procedure for the establishment by regulation of common or usual names for foods. The Commissioner also proposed to establish a common or usual name for seafood cocktails, to include the percentage of the characterizing seafood ingredient(s)....

Twenty-eight requests were made that the proposal be expanded to include additional labeling requirements such as the percentage of all ingredients for all foods; the percentage of primary ingredients for all foods; the percentage of fats, carbohydrates, and proteins; the vitamin and mineral content; and the specific source of ingredients.

The Commissioner concludes that percentage labeling of ingredients should be restricted to situations where this information has a material bearing on price or consumer acceptance of the food, or where such information may prevent deception. Labeling the percentage of all ingredients would be extremely costly and would provide no proven benefits to consumers. A mechanism for establishing a regulation requiring labeling of the percentage of all "primary" ingredients that have a material bearing on the price or consumer acceptance is provided for in this regulation....

Common or usual names will not be established ... for all nonstandardized foods. Such names will be established by such regulation only when it is necessary fully to inform the consumer, or where different names are used for the same product by different manufacturers.

Common or usual names for "like" or "similar" products, where none now exists, may be proposed under the provisions of this regulation and will reflect the reasonable expectations of consumers. The name itself will accurately identify or describe the basic nature or characterizing properties of the food in a way that will distinguish it from other foods.

A food that purports to be a standardized food does not cease purporting to be a standardized food merely because its label bears the percent of characterizing ingredients. The label of a food which neither purports to be nor is represented as being a standardized food must bear on the label its common or usual name, which may not be false or misleading. Nor may a manufacturer avoid a standard merely by adding an ingredient not permitted in the standard unless that ingredient substantially changes the nature or characteristics of the food.... Use of a new method or process, with or without an added artificial sweetener, to produce a substantial reduction in calories would, on the other hand, result in the new product not purporting to be the standardized food when a distinctive descriptive name is used and the food is not an "imitation" under proposed new § 1.8(e)....

Eight respondents contended that other factors such as count, size, and quality may be factors of equal or greater importance in determining value than the percentage of the characterizing ingredient. The Commissioner agrees that characteristics other than percentage may influence both price and consumer acceptance. The establishment of informative common or usual names will make new information available to the consumer without subtracting from, or otherwise affecting, any other information or means by which the consumer judges acceptability. Nothing in this regulation precludes the use of such information in labeling or excuses labeling from the requirement that it not be false or misleading in any particular....

COMMON OR USUAL NAME FOR NONSTANDARDIZED FOODS
21 C.F.R. Part 102.

§ 102.5 General principles

(a) The common or usual name of a food, which may be a coined term, shall accurately identify or describe, in as simple and direct terms as possible, the basic nature of the food or its characterizing properties or ingredients. The name shall be uniform among all identical or similar products and may not be confusingly similar to the name of any other food that is not reasonably encompassed within the same name....

(b) The common or usual name of a food shall include the percentage(s) of any characterizing ingredient(s) or component(s) when the proportion of such ingredient(s) or component(s) in the food has a material bearing on price or consumer acceptance or when the labeling or the appearance of the food may otherwise create an erroneous impression that such ingredient(s) or component(s) is present in an amount greater than is actually the case....

(c) The common or usual name of a food shall include a statement of the presence or absence of any characterizing ingredient(s) or component(s) and/or the need for the user to add any characterizing ingredient(s) or component(s) when the presence or absence of such ingredient(s) or component(s) in the food has a material bearing on price or consumer acceptance or when the labeling or the appearance of the food may otherwise create an erroneous impression that such ingredient(s) or component(s) is present when it is not, and consumers may otherwise be misled about the presence or absence of the ingredient(s) or component(s) in the food....

§ 102.26 Frozen "heat and serve" dinners

(a) A frozen "heat and serve" dinner:

(1) Shall contain at least three components, one of which shall be a significant source of protein and each of which shall consist of one or more of the following: meat, poultry, fish, cheese, eggs, vegetables, fruit, potatoes, rice, or other cereal based products (other than bread or rolls).

(2) May also contain other servings of food (e.g., soup, bread or rolls, beverage, dessert).

(b) The common or usual name of the food consists of all of the following:

(1) The phrase "frozen 'heat and serve' dinner," except that the name of the predominant characterizing ingredient or other appropriately descriptive term may immediately precede the word "dinner" (e.g., "frozen chicken dinner" or "frozen heat and serve beef dinner"). The words "heat and serve" are optional. The word "frozen" is also optional, provided that the words "Keep Frozen" or the equivalent are prominently and conspicuously placed on the principal display panel....

(2) The phrase "containing (or contains) _____" the blank to be filled in with an accurate description of each of the three or more dish components listed in paragraph (a)(1) of this section in their order of descending predominance by weight (e.g., ham, mashed potatoes, and peas), followed by any of the other servings specified in paragraph (a)(2) of this section contained in the package (e.g., onion soup, enriched white bread, and artificially flavored vanilla pudding) in their order of descending predominance by weight. This part of the name shall be placed immediately following or directly below the part specified in paragraph (b)(1) of this section.... The words "contains" or "containing" are optional.

(3) If the labeling implies that the package contains other foods and these foods are not present in the package, e.g., if a vignette on the package depicts a "serving suggestion" which includes any foods not present in the package, the principal display panel shall bear a statement that such foods are not present....

§ 102.32 Diluted orange juice beverages

(a) The common or usual name of a noncarbonated beverage containing less than 100 percent and more than 0 percent orange juice shall be as follows:

(1) A descriptive name for the product meeting the requirements of § 102.5(a) (e.g., diluted orange juice beverage or another descriptive phrase) and

(2) A statement of the percent of orange juice contained in the product.... The percent of orange juice shall be declared in 5–percent increments, expressed as a multiple of five not greater than the actual percentage of orange juice in the product, except that the percent of orange juice in products containing more than 0 percent but less than 5–percent orange juice shall be declared in the statement as "less than 5" percent....

§ 102.41 Potato chips made from dried potatoes

(a) The common or usual name of the food product that resembles and is of the same composition as potato chips, except that it is composed of dehydrated potatoes (buds, flakes, granules, or other form), shall be "potato chips made from dried potatoes." ...

§ 102.54 Seafood cocktails

The common or usual name of a seafood cocktail in package form fabricated with one or more seafood ingredients shall be:

(a) When the cocktail contains only one seafood ingredient, the name of the seafood ingredient followed by the word "cocktail" (e.g., shrimp cocktail, crabmeat cocktail) and a statement of the percentage by weight of that seafood ingredient in the product....

(b) When the cocktail contains more than one seafood ingredient, the term "seafood cocktail" and a statement of the percentage by weight of each seafood ingredient in the product....

AMERICAN FROZEN FOOD INSTITUTE v. MATHEWS

United States District Court, District of Columbia, 1976.
413 F. Supp. 548, *aff'd* 555 F.2d 1059, 1977.

AUBREY E. ROBINSON, Jr., District Judge.

By this action Plaintiff American Frozen Food Institute (AFFI) challenges the innovative attempt by the Food and Drug Administration (FDA) to regulate labeling in certain areas of the food industry through establishing "common and usual names" for nonstandardized foods. AFFI contends that two recent rulings from FDA which establish common and usual names for seafood cocktails and frozen heat and serve dinners must be set aside by this Court on the grounds that they were promulgated in a manner excessive of agency authority, establish an unlawful presumption, violate the First Amendment and are arbitrary and capricious without sufficient support in the record.... [T]he Court concludes that the FDA acted within its statutory authority and that the defendants are entitled to summary judgment....

... FDA has established common and usual names for certain of these foods under its general rulemaking authority, Section 701(a) of the Act. The regulations were prompted by a concern expressed by the White House Conference on Food Nutrition and Health, regarding the lack of informative food labeling....

The Plaintiff contends that FDA lacks authority to *create* common and usual names through substantive rulemaking.... In the alternative, AFFI contends that even if FDA has authority to establish common and usual names through its general rulemaking authority, these two specific regulations exceed that authority....

... Under the general rulemaking provision of the governing statute set forth in 21 U.S.C. § 371(a), FDA is authorized to "promulgate regulations for the efficient enforcement of [the Act]." Plaintiff contends that despite the broad mandate reflected by this provision, FDA is restricted to two methods for establishing common and usual names. AFFI's position is that FDA can either recognize an already established common and usual name in the context of a Section 701 proceeding (establishing a definition and standard of identity) or may bring a judicial action pursuant to the sanctions set forth in 21 U.S.C. §§ 331–334 for violations of the Act, during which the Court can recognize the common and usual name of a particular food....

The Court is not persuaded that the Act should be read so narrowly. Plaintiff's first argument ignores significant case law which by analogy supports the FDA's authority to proceed by substantive lawmaking in this case. The cases are legion in which Courts have recognized the preference of substantive rulemaking by an agency over the time consuming and often unfair process of case by case adjudication....

By the action challenged herein, FDA is attempting to provide consumers with relevant buying information on food labels of nonstandardized products. It is not attempting to eradicate economic adulteration nor to prescribe food composition. As stated earlier, the label of a standardized food bears only optional ingredients. The nonstandardized foods for which FDA has established common and usual names by the procedure challenged herein will bear on the label such information deemed appropriate by the agency in light of the purpose of the Act.

Although there is nothing in the legislative history which clearly indicates that FDA has the authority to provide this consumer information pursuant to its rulemaking authority by establishing common and usual names, there is nothing in the legislative history of Section 701(a) or (e) which indicates that it cannot....

Next the Court must determine whether the two specific regulations challenged by this action have additional infirmities requiring this Court to set them aside. The thrust of Plaintiff's attack directed at the common and usual name for frozen heat and serve dinners is that this regulation ... is actually a definition and standard of identity because it includes components as part of the name. Plaintiff contends that it must be set aside because it was not promulgated pursuant to a Section 701(e) proceeding....

Although the Court recognizes that this name appears to be more than just a name, Plaintiff's argument that it is a definition and standard of identity is not persuasive. This regulation controls use of the term "dinner" and requires an accurate description of each component in order of descending predominance. As the regulation makes clear, all the specific ingredients are optional. Only categories are mandatory. Therefore, to require a definition and standard of identity, which normally sets forth a "recipe" for a food, would be inappropriate since there *are* no specific mandatory ingredients for frozen heat and serve dinners. Therefore, it cannot be said that this particular regulation is actually a definition and standard of identity.

Lastly, Plaintiff challenges that portion of the regulation for seafood cocktails ... which requires that the percentage of seafood ingredients be plainly stated on the label. Plaintiff argues strongly that FDA's authority to enforce such percentage of ingredient labeling requirements was specifically deleted from the statute when originally enacted. However, the Court is influenced by the subsequent inclusion of Section 201(n) which authorizes the Commissioner to consider "the extent to which the labeling fails to reveal facts material in the light of such representations" in determining whether a label is false or misleading.

FDA's reasoning for the general principle of requiring disclosure of the percentage of characterizing ingredients for certain foods is that such information may be a "material fact" which must be disclosed to prevent a food label from being misleading....

The Court also notes that the record support for this regulation indicates the materiality of the percentage of characterizing ingredient in this particular product. Virtually all of the consumer responses heartily supported the general principle proposed, and several consumers indicated express approval of disclosure of percentage of ingredients for seafood cocktails as a necessary device for comparative food shopping. In light of the materiality of the information required to be disclosed by this regulation, the Court is not persuaded that the Commissioner has exceeded his statutory authority in requiring that the label of seafood cocktail reveal the percentage of seafood ingredients therein....

NOTES

1. *Peanut Butter versus Peanut Spread.* Compare the standard of identity for "peanut butter" in 21 C.F.R. § 164.150, which requires at least 90% peanuts,

see note 3, p. 105 *supra*, with the common or usual name for "peanut spread" in 21 C.F.R. § 102.23, promulgated in 40 Fed. Reg. 51052 (November 3, 1975), 42 Fed. Reg. 36452 (July 15, 1977), which merely requires label declaration of the percent of peanuts in products containing between 10% and 90%.

2. *Infant Foods.* In 41 Fed. Reg. 37593 and 37595 (September 7, 1976), FDA proposed two regulations for infant food. One would establish a common or usual name that would include the percent of the characterizing ingredient or ingredients. The other, based on section 403(j) of the Act, would require the percent declaration of each ingredient present at a level of 5% or more by weight. Both of these proposals were withdrawn in 51 Fed. Reg. 15653 (April 25, 1986) and reinstated in 51 Fed. Reg. 39546 (October 29, 1986). *See* Hutt, *Food Legislation in Perspective,* 34 FDC L.J. 590 (1979); S. 1652, 96th Cong., 1st Sess. (1979).

3. *Procedures for Establishing Food Names.* The fact that a common or usual name can be established through notice-and-comment rulemaking does not mean that the process is necessarily easy or speedy. Following promulgation of the regulation requiring that any diluted orange juice beverage declare the percent of orange juice, 21 C.F.R. § 102.32, FDA promulgated a comparable regulation for all other diluted fruit or vegetable juices in 39 Fed. Reg. 20908 (June 14, 1974), 45 Fed. Reg. 39247 (June 10, 1980), codified in 21 C.F.R. § 102.33. After the agency rejected a petition for reconsideration, 45 Fed. Reg. 80497 (December 5, 1980), and extended the time for compliance, 47 Fed. Reg. 13003 (March 26, 1982), 48 Fed. Reg. 2735 (January 21, 1983), its action was upheld, *Processors Council of the California–Arizona Citrus League v. FDA,* Food Drug Cosm. L. Rep. (CCH) ¶ 38,186 (C.D. Cal. 1982). Opponents of the regulation remained adamant, however, and FDA first proposed amendments, 49 Fed. Reg. 22831 (June 1, 1984), and then proposed its revocation, 52 Fed. Reg. 26690 (July 16, 1987). This proposal, in turn, provoked efforts to salvage the regulation, 55 Fed. Reg. 3266 (January 31, 1990), which continued as this book went to press. The 1990 Nutrition Labeling and Education Act attempted to resolve this controversy by amending section 403(i) to require that a beverage containing a fruit or vegetable juice must declare the percent of juice on the label.

4. *Other Proposed Names.* FDA proposed names for main dish products, 39 Fed. Reg. 20906 (June 14, 1974); formulated meal replacements, 39 Fed. Reg. 20905 (June 14, 1974); fruit-flavored sweetened spreads, 40 Fed. Reg. 52616 (November 11, 1975); and substitutes for margarine and butter, 41 Fed. Reg. 36509 (August 30, 1976). But all of these proposals were withdrawn in 51 Fed. Reg. 15653 (April 25, 1986).

5. *Commentary.* For discussion of the concept of a "common or usual name," *see* Harvey, *"Common or Usual Name,"* 14 FDC L.J. 555 (1959); Kleinfeld, *"Common or Usual Name"—Its Meaning, If Any,* 16 FDC L.J. 513 (1961); Sayer, *A Rose by Any Other Name,* 30 FDC L.J. 415 (1975).

In 41 Fed. Reg. 46851 (October 26, 1976), FDA issued a final standard of identity for "enriched raisin bread." The standard permitted the same quantity of nutrients required by the standard for enriched bread and the same quantity of raisins required by the standard for raisin bread, which did not provide for the use of enriched flour.

Formal objections to the new standard were filed, resulting in a stay of its effective date. Rather than hold the necessary evidentiary hearing to resolve the objections, FDA concluded that the new standard could be rendered unnecessary by "providing advice" on the appropriate labeling for raisin bread made with enriched flour:

> The Commissioner ... advises that a raisin bread conforming to the requirements of § 136.160 except that it is made with enriched flour, enriched brominated flour, or a combination, as the sole farinaceous ingredient may be sold as a nonstandardized bread under a suitable name, e.g., "raisin bread made with enriched flour." Many breads are sold as nonstandardized foods when they contain and are named to identify ingredients not provided for in the standard for bread that provide a distinctive flavor, color, or other feature important to consumers, e.g., rye bread. If a raisin bread has been enriched to the nutrient levels in § 136.115, (with additional amounts of nutrients added to compensate for the flour displaced by the raisins), the food may be sold as "enriched raisin bread." Either raisin bread so labeled must also bear nutrition labeling in accordance with § 101.9.

43 Fed. Reg. 43456 (September 26, 1978).

NOTES

1. *Enriched Standardized Foods. See also* 43 Fed. Reg. 11695 (March 21, 1978) ("enriched macaroni with fortified protein" does not purport to be standardized "enriched macaroni"); 39 Fed. Reg. 31898 (September 3, 1974) ("tomato juice enriched with vitamin C" does not purport to be standardized "tomato juice").

2. *Use of Standardized Name on Nonstandard Products.* In 44 Fed. Reg. 3964 (January 19, 1979) FDA stated that "[t]he existence of a standard of identity for a particular food does not necessarily preclude the use of the standardized name in connection with the name of a nonstandardized food, and 'in some cases it may be necessary to include a standardized name in the name of a substitute food in order to provide the consumer with accurate, descriptive, and fully informative labeling,'" citing 38 Fed. Reg. 20703 (August 2, 1973). Manufacturers of traditional foods covered by standards of identity have, however, strenuously objected to the use of those food names as part of the names for new substitute foods and have argued that entirely new fanciful names should be adopted for these new products. *See, e.g.,* 43 Fed. Reg. 42118 (September 19, 1978), in which FDA described a National Cheese Institute petition proposing the name "Golana" ("analog" spelled backward) rather than "substitute," "alternate," or even "imitation" cheese. In 49 Fed.Reg. 27796 (June 1, 1984), FDA adopted "cocoa butter substitute primarily from palm oil" as the common or usual name for a substitute product, rejecting the contention that it has no authority to establish a common or usual name that utilizes the name of a traditional food.

3. *Dairy terms for Margarine.* In *Anderson, Clayton & Co. v. Washington State Dept. of Agriculture,* 402 F.Supp. 1253 (W.D.Wash.1975), a Washington statute prohibiting the use of dairy terms in labeling or advertising for margarine was declared unconstitutional. In *Lever Bros. Co. v. Maurer,* 712

F.Supp. 645 (S.D.Ohio 1989), the court declared unconstitutional an Ohio statute that prohibited the word "butter" in labeling or advertising a reduced calorie product containing 50 percent butter. FDA objected to the specific common or usual name used for the product, however, and prepared the following affidavit for use in the event of litigation:

> ... [M]anufacturers in the United States market margarines and other table spreads which are flavored with butter, but which do not purport to be butter and do not meet the requirements of the butter standard of identity set forth at 42 Stat. 1500. With respect to such products, FDA has not objected to statements such as "Contains ___% butter" as part of the identity statement as long as the butter in the product is present in a significant amount.

> The FDA has no objection to the use of the word "butter" as part of a descriptive name of a product that does not comply with the standard of identity, as long as that name describes how the product differs from butter in all significant respects. With respect to the Lever Brothers Company ("Lever") product currently named "Dairy-brook Reduced Calorie Butter Product," the product's name does not comply with this general requirement because the name does not make clear that the product consists, to a significant degree, of something other than butter. While we do not object to the term "reduced calorie" when used in compliance with 21 CFR § 105.66, that term, as used in the current name of Lever's product, is insufficient to adequately distinguish the product from standardized butter or properly identify the product.

> Therefore, FDA has objected in writing, to Lever, to the use of the phrase "Reduced Calorie Butter Product" as part of the product's identity statement.

Rather than litigate the case, the company changed its label.

The labeling of new dairy products that do not meet all of the requirements of existing standards of identity continues to challenge FDA's ingenuity. In 1986 the agency was asked to sanction distribution of "goat's milk yogurt," a product that conformed to the standard of identity for yogurt except for the source of milk. It responded:

> It is our conclusion that "goat's milk yogurt" is sufficiently distinctive as an identity statement under Section 403(i)(1). It is sufficiently different from yogurt so as not to purport or represent the product as the standardized food under Section 403(g) of the Federal Food, Drug, and Cosmetic Act. We therefore agree that it can be used as a statement of identity.

Letter from L. R. Lake to P. B. Hutt (November 25, 1986).

But in 1988 the agency rejected suggestions that yogurt and ice cream-like products sweetened with aspartame could be marked as "Reduced Calorie Yogurt" and "Reduced Calorie Ice Cream."

> These products would not be yogurts because they do not comply with the yogurt standards. These are yogurt substi-

tutes or alternatives, not yogurts. Furthermore, these are not reduced calorie products because sweeteners are optional ingredients in yogurts, not mandatory, and yogurt-type products sweetened with aspartame are not calorie reduced at all when compared to the unsweetened standardized yogurts....

Your advice on non-standardized frozen desserts is contrary to the standards of identity because you state that the standards of identity do not preclude the use of aspartame, and that frozen desserts sweetened with aspartame can use the name "ice cream", as shown in your examples of "Diet ice cream— Calorie Reduced" or "Reduced Calorie Ice Cream." We disagree because your advice is not consistent with the standard of identity for ice cream. There is a good analogy which involves a precedent set some years ago. A GRAS affirmation regulation was issued under 21 CFR 184.1835 which permitted sorbitol to be used in frozen desserts. Sorbitol is a nutritive sweetener but, like aspartame, is not an ingredient permitted by the standard. There are a number of sorbitol sweetened frozen desserts on the market, and they are labeled as "frozen desserts" or "frozen dairy desserts" but not "ice cream" because the manufacturers realize they cannot be called by any of the standardized names.

Letter from L. R. Lake to G. Witte (August 10, 1988).

The naming of fish species has likewise become controversial as federal health officials, members of Congress, and the seafood industry have sought to encourage increased consumption of fish. *See, e.g.,* GAO, DEVELOPING MARKETS FOR FISH NOT TRADITIONALLY HARVESTED BY THE UNITED STATES: THE PROBLEMS AND THE FEDERAL ROLE, Rep. No. CED–80–73 (May 7, 1980); GAO, SEAFOOD MARKETING: OPPORTUNITIES TO IMPROVE THE U.S. POSITION, Rep. No. RCED–87–11BR (October 22, 1986). In 33 Fed. Reg. 19007 (December 20, 1968), now codified in 21 C.F.R. § 102.57, FDA found it necessary to prohibit use of the term "halibut" as a substitute for "Greenland turbot." 21 C.F.R. part 102 contains common or usual names for fish sticks or portions made from minced fish, Pacific Whiting, Bonito, fried clams made from minced clams, crabmeat, seafood cocktails, and nonstandardized breaded composite shrimp units. In 54 Fed. Reg. 12284 (March 24, 1989), FDA announced the availability of THE FDA GUIDE TO ACCEPTABLE MARKET NAMES FOR FOOD FISH SOLD IN INTERSTATE COMMERCE, which was developed jointly with the National Marine Fisheries Service.

The 1980s have witnessed the growing use of "surimi," a minced fish product that can be obtained from a number of different types of fish, to make products that resemble other seafood products. FDA announced the following policy regarding this practice in 50 Fed. Reg. 30523 (July 26, 1985).

COMPLIANCE POLICY GUIDE NO. 7108.16
June 3, 1985.

Surimi is an intermediate processed seafood product used in the formulation/fabrication of a variety of finished seafood products. It is normally traded in 10 kg. frozen blocks which are individually wrapped in waxed cardboard boxes. Surimi is minced fish meat (usually pollock) which has been washed to remove fat and undesirable matters (such as blood, pigments, and odorous substances), and mixed with cryoprotectants (such as sugar and/or sorbitol for a good frozen shelflife). In formulating finished seafood products, surimi is thawed and blended with other ingredients and additives such as natural shellfish meat, and/or shellfish flavoring, salt, water, and starch and/or egg white; and processed by heat for making fibrous, flake, chunk, and composite-molded consumer products. The finished products are marketed frozen or unfrozen and may be breaded.

The following guidance is in response to inquiries FDA has received regarding the proper labeling for surimi-based seafood products.

1. If the surimi-based product purports to be or is represented as any specific type of natural seafood, including shape or form representations, but is nutritionally inferior to that seafood, it must be labeled as imitation in accordance with 21 CFR 101.3. To date FDA has not encountered any surimi-based product in which nutritional equivalency has been achieved.

2. An additional statement of product identity must appear on the principal display panel such as "A Blend of Fish with _____." The blank is to be filled in with the common or usual name of the ingredient or component, such as "snow crab." Because the fish used in the surimi-base has been decharacterized, the word "fish" is adequate for the statement of product identity....

3. The specific names of all seafoods used in the product shall appear in the ingredient statement in descending order of predominance ("pollock" must be used as opposed to "white fish"; "snow crab" rather than "crab"). All other ingredients present must also be declared in descending order of predominance....

4. Products that are not purported or represented to be a specific type of seafood or seafood body part, need not be labeled imitation, but may be marketed if the label properly reflects their composition.

5. Labeling of surimi-based products may suggest use in recipes in place of the natural seafood products by a generalized statement such as, "use like crabmeat, lobster, or shrimp in all seafood recipes," or a similar statement.

NOTE

In *Mrs. Paul's Kitchens, Inc. v. Califano*, 1978–1980 FDLI Jud. Rec. 685 (E.D. Pa. 1978), the court was required to confront a labeling issue posed by the requirements of high speed food processing and uniform portion sizes. The company cut uniform portions of fish from frozen blocks of fish filets in a way that there could be no assurance that the individual portion consisted of a piece of only one fish. The court overruled FDA's position that the proper name for the product was "fish portion" or "pieces of filet" and instead held that "fish filet" is a proper common or usual name for the product and is not false or misleading.

---

5. "IMITATION" LABELING

62 CASES OF JAM v. UNITED STATES

Supreme Court of the United States, 1951.
340 U.S. 593.

Mr. Justice FRANKFURTER delivered the opinion of the Court.

The proceeding before us was commenced in 1949 in the District Court for the District of New Mexico. By it the United States seeks to condemn 62 cases of "Delicious Brand Imitation Jam," manufactured in Colorado and shipped to New Mexico. The Government claims that this product "purports" to be fruit jam, a food for which the Federal Security Administrator has promulgated a "definition and standard of identity." The regulation specifies that a fruit jam must contain "not less than 45 parts by weight" of the fruit ingredient. The product in question is composed of 55% sugar, 25% fruit, 20% pectin, and small amounts of citric acid and soda. These specifications show that pectin, a gelatinized solution consisting largely of water, has been substituted for a substantial proportion of the fruit required. The Government contends that the product is therefore to be deemed "misbranded" under § 403(g). . . .

According to the Federal Food, Drug, and Cosmetic Act, nothing can be legally "jam" after the Administrator promulgated his regulation in 1940, unless it contains the specified ingredients in prescribed proportion. Hence the product in controversy is not "jam." It cannot lawfully be labeled "jam" and introduced into interstate commerce, for to do so would "represent" as a standardized food a product which does not meet prescribed specifications.

But the product with which we are concerned is sold as "imitation jam." Imitation foods are dealt with in § 403(c) of the Act. In that section Congress did not give an esoteric meaning to "imitation." It left it to the understanding of ordinary English speech. . . .

In ordinary speech there can be no doubt that the product which the United States here seeks to condemn is an "imitation" jam. It looks and tastes like jam; it is unequivocally labeled "imitation jam." The Government does not argue that its label in any way falls short of the requirements of § 403(c). Its distribution in interstate commerce would therefore clearly seem to be authorized by that section. We could hold it to be "misbranded" only if we held that a practice Congress authorized by § 403(c) Congress impliedly prohibited by § 403(g).

We see no justification so to distort the ordinary meaning of the statute. Nothing in the text or history of the legislation points to such a reading of what Congress wrote. In § 403(g) Congress used the words "purport" and "represent"—terms suggesting the idea of counterfeit. But the name "imitation jam" at once connotes precisely what the product is: a different, an inferior preserve, not meeting the defined specifications. Section 403(g) was designed to protect the public from inferior foods resembling standard products but marketed under distinctive names. Congress may well have supposed that similar confusion would not result from the marketing of a product candidly and flagrantly labeled as an "imitation" food. A product so labeled is described with precise accuracy. It neither conveys any ambiguity nor emanates any untrue innuendo, as was the case with the "Bred Spred" considered by Congress in its deliberation on § 403(g). It purports and is represented to be only what it is—an imitation. It does not purport nor represent to be what it is not—the Administrator's genuine "jam." . . .

Reversed.

Mr. Justice DOUGLAS, with whom Mr. Justice BLACK concurs, dissenting.

The result reached by the Court may be sound by legislative standards. But the legal standards which govern us make the process of reaching that result tortuous to say the least. We must say that petitioner's "jam" purports to be "jam" when we read § 403(g) and purports to be not "jam" but another food when we read § 403(c). Yet if petitioner's product did not purport to be "jam" petitioner would have no claim to press and the Government no objection to raise.

NOTE

In *United States v. 856 Cases . . . "Demi"*, 254 F. Supp. 57 (N.D.N.Y. 1966), the government seized as misbranded the claimant's "imitation margarine," a product that failed to conform to FDA's standard of identity for margarine. The government unsuccessfully attempted to distinguish *62 Cases of Jam* by arguing that Congress intended all products made in semblance of butter to be called "margarine," and that FDA had in effect defined the only marketable imitation of butter in its standard of identity for margarine.

UNITED STATES v. 651 CASES . . . CHOCOLATE CHIL-ZERT

United States District Court, Northern District of New York, 1953.
114 F. Supp. 430.

BRENNAN, Chief Judge.

The problem here involves the construction and application of [section 403(c) of the FD&C Act]. . . .

Imitation is initially a question of fact, but both parties agree that there are no material facts in dispute, and the question becomes one of law.

[Chil–Zert] ... is a comparatively new product, having been offered for sale in only two cities. It contains the usual ingredients of chocolate-flavored ice cream in approximately the same proportions, except that soy fat and soy protein are used therein in place of milk fat and milk protein. The product is similar in taste and appearance to chocolate ice cream. It has the same characteristics such as color, taste, texture, body and melting qualities. It is manufactured substantially in the same manner as chocolate flavored ice cream, and with the use of similar machinery. It is appropriate for use for the same purposes for which ice cream is used and is packaged and offered for sale in containers or cartons of the same size, shape and description as those used in the packaging and selling of ice cream. The retail price of pint packages of chocolate Chil–Zert is substantially lower than the average retail price of a pint of ice cream, as shown by Labor Department statistics for 1951, cited by the claimant.

The food sought to be condemned is packaged in pint carton containers with the words "Rich's Chocolate Chil–Zert" prominently printed on the four sides of the container and on the top and bottom thereof. Immediately below the words quoted above and in prominent letters the words "not an ice cream" appear, and on two sides of the carton there also appears [sic] the words "contains no milk or milk fat!" The ingredients are printed on two sides of the carton, and the product is referred to as "The Delicious New Frozen Dessert!" ... [T]here is no claim made here as to deceptive or misleading statements as to the advertising of the product.

The government contends that Chocolate Chil–Zert is an imitation of another food; to-wit, chocolate ice cream, and is, therefore, misbranded, since the word "imitation" followed by the name of the food imitated does not appear upon the container in which the food is packed, shipped and offered for sale. The claimant contends that Chocolate Chil–Zert is a new distinctive product composed of natural rather than artificial ingredients; that, as labeled, no element of deception is involved, and it is, therefore, not an imitation within the meaning of the statute. Claimant further contends that, since no legal standard has been promulgated for chocolate ice cream, the test of imitation may not be applied.

Congress has not defined the word "imitation." ... Judicial precedent does not define its meaning within a rigid mould. Ordinary understanding of the term appears to be the test of its meaning....

It is plain that no all-inclusive test of imitation can be prescribed. Resemblance and taste are elements.... Smell is included as one of the elements. The word connotes inferiority in the sense that it is cheapened by the substitution of ingredients. Resemblance alone is not enough to constitute imitation. It would seem that imitation is tested not by the presence or absence of any one element of similarity, but rather by the effect of a composite of all such elements. As indicated above, Chil–Zert is identical with ice cream in its method of manufacture, packaging and sale. It is similar, in taste, appearance, color, texture, body and melting qualities. It has identical uses; its composition differs only from ice cream in the substitution of a cheaper ingredient; namely, vegetable oil in place of milk products. It is, therefore, something less than the genuine article chocolate ice cream. It is inescapable that the ordinary understanding of English speech would denominate it as an imitation of ice cream....

Claimant does not purport to pass off its product as ice cream. The labeling of the product in language negates any such contention. It may be debatable whether or not the words "not an ice cream" will act as a warning or as a snare for the unwary purchaser. In any event, it is not for the claimant to choose the means or method to advise the public that his product is not in fact the one which is imitated. The statute in explicit terms makes a provision therefor. It may be that the requirement of the statute would be less effective than the means adopted by the claimant. Such an argument is one for Congress and not for the Court. Truthful labeling does not exempt Chil–Zert from the requirement of the statute. Neither is deception nor intent to mislead necessary to establish that claimant's product is an imitation. The Court is impressed that claimant's argument proceeds as if the distinctive name provision of the 1906 Act is still in force, and claimant seeks to use the fanciful name of Chil–Zert with informative labeling to escape the provisions of the present statute. (The distinctive name provision was eliminated in the 1938 Act.)

Claimant's contention to the effect that chocolate ice cream is not imitated by Chil–Zert because no legal standard has been promulgated therefor will be briefly referred to. In other words, it is contended that a food may not be imitated until it is defined. A short answer to such an argument is that the statute does not refer to an imitation only of foods for which a standard has been set. If Congress had intended to so limit the law, it is reasonable to conclude that it would have so stated. The statutory provisions as to adulterations apply to non-standardized food. The same reasoning would seem to apply to the misbranding provisions of the law.

Research fails to disclose that the section of the statute invoked here has been extensively used. In fact, no case has been cited by either counsel in which Section 343(c) of Title 21, U.S.C. has been invoked under circumstances comparable to those which exist here. The Court has tried to keep in mind the beneficial purposes of the statute and at the same time not to unduly restrict the marketing of the many variations of well known food products. It is difficult to conceive that the statute invoked has any purpose unless it is applicable here. It is concluded that the claimant's motions are denied, and the libelant's motion for a summary judgment is granted....

NOTES

1. *Enforcement of Section 403(c).* The *Chil–Zert* case was the first FDA brought based solely on section 403(c). Perhaps surprisingly, the agency brought no other enforcement actions based solely on section 403(c), and it failed to challenge as "imitations" a wide variety of foods made from vegetable oil marketed as substitutes for dairy products such as whipped toppings and coffee whiteners. *Compare United States v. Schider,* 246 U.S. 519 (1918).

2. *State Enforcement.* Numerous state regulatory bodies have challenged vegetable oil-based substitutes for dairy products under state laws restricting "imitations." Most recent cases have refused to suppress the marketing of such products when truthfully labeled. *Coffee–Rich, Inc. v. Kansas State Bd. of Health,* 192 Kan. 431, 388 P.2d 582 (1964), is illustrative:

> ... Coffee–Rich is a manufactured product and not a natural product. It is a wholesome food, and is generally sold in quart containers which truthfully list the ingredients of the product. Immediately below the trade name on the containers appears the words "CONTAINS NO MILK OR MILK FAT," and immediately below those words are the words "A VEGETABLE PRODUCT." The product is basically a vegetable fat emulsion; it is artificially colored and its sole ingredients are vegetable fats, corn syrup solids, sodium caseinate, sodium citrate, carrogeenin, sorbitan, monastearate, polysorbate 60, pure beta carotene and water. Coffee–Rich contains no cream, no half-and-half, no milk, and no dairy products. The product was designed primarily to enrich the taste and lighten the color of coffee, although it is also suitable for use on fruits, breakfast cereals, and desserts, and in soups and sauces.

> As a vegetable fat product, Coffee–Rich is an original development, and it was never plaintiff's intention to imitate cream, or half-and-half, or any other dairy product. Rather, it intended to create and produce a product which would not have the inherent defects of cows' cream and other dairy products when used for purposes for which Coffee–Rich was designed. Cream and half-and-half are natural products. Coffee–Rich is distributed in a frozen state whereas dairy products are distributed in a liquid state. It does not taste like cows' cream, neither does it have the same aroma nor the same texture as cows' cream. The color of Coffee–Rich is yellowish white or possibly a tannish color and it is constant and never changes, whereas the color of cream varies at times during the year depending upon the diet of the cows producing the cream. It is a product uniform in flavor whereas cows' cream varies in flavor. It can be stored for longer periods than cream; it has less bacterial organisms than cream, and it will remain sweet and fresh longer than cream. Coffee–Rich contains no cholesterol, whereas cows' cream contains cholesterol, and it has a lower caloric value or content than cream. Coffee–Rich is resistant to "oiling off" and "feathering," whereas cream exhibits those tendencies....

> ... Courts, common usage, and dictionary definitions are agreed that "imitation" connotes an inferior quality or watered-down version of the imitated item. The implication is that imitations contain some of the imitated substances and are of lesser quality or quantity.... "Cream" and "imitation" are contradictory words. An imitation cannot be genuine; the two terms are antithetical. By implication or

otherwise, Coffee–Rich contains no milk, cream or butter fat, nor any other characteristic or distinctive ingredient of cows' cream. The label expressly declares that it "contains no milk or milk fat," but instead, is a "vegetable product." Its taste is discernibly different from cows' cream. While it has uses similar to cream and does somewhat resemble cream, that alone does not make it an imitation. The fact that sometimes it is used as a substitute for cream or half-and-half without being declared to be such, would not justify its being condemned under the act. . . .

See also *Coffee–Rich, Inc. v. Michigan Dept. of Agriculture,* 1 Mich.App. 225, 135 N.W.2d 594 (1965). In *Coffee–Rich, Inc. v. Commissioner of Public Health,* 348 Mass. 414, 204 N.E.2d 281 (1965), the Massachusetts Supreme Judicial Court held that there is no rational basis for prohibiting the sale of Coffee–Rich and thus declared the state law prohibiting the product unconstitutional.

MEAT FOOD NAMES

Although USDA and FDA formally share jurisdiction over meat food labeling, *see* p. 34 *supra,* USDA exercises primary jurisdiction in this area and many important meat food names are established in standards of identity that it has promulgated in 9 C.F.R. Parts 317 and 319.

Armour & Co. v. Freeman, 304 F.2d 404 (D.C. Cir. 1962), held invalid a USDA regulation that required meat packers who added moisture to ham during the curing process to use the label "Imitation Ham." The court concluded that the required labeling was false and deceptive and thus inconsistent with USDA's own statute, the Federal Meat Inspection Act. Judge Prettyman, concurring with the court's decision, declared: "Everybody knows that a ham made of the cured thigh of a hog and otherwise unaltered save by the addition of a bit of water is not an imitation of some product other than ham. . . . As a matter of plain fact, such a ham is not even an imitation ham. It is a real ham, a ham by definition and by universal common acceptance." In *American Meat Institute v. United States Dept. of Agriculture,* 646 F.2d 125 (4th Cir. 1981) (per curiam), the court, reversing the district court, upheld a USDA regulation permitting cured turkey to be labeled as "turkey ham" with the additional qualifying phrase "cured turkey thigh meat."

In *National Pork Producers Council v. Bergland,* 631 F.2d 1353 (8th Cir. 1980), *cert. denied,* 450 U.S. 912 (1981), the court upheld a USDA regulation permitting nitrate-free and nitrite-free meat products to be sold under the product names traditionally reserved for food containing these preservatives as long as the word "uncured" appeared as part of the product name and the label stated that no nitrate or nitrite had been added and that refrigeration was required.

Even where USDA has changed its mind about the proper labeling for a standardized meat food product, its ultimate decision has been upheld. The agency initially determined that mechanically deboned meat could lawfully be used in processed meat food products without any special labeling. After *Community Nutrition Institute v. Butz,* 420 F. Supp. 751 (D.D.C. 1976), overturned this ruling, USDA promulgated regulations requiring that the product be identified in the ingredient statement as "mechanically processed [species] product" and that the presence of the ingredient also be emphasized by two prominent qualifying phrases next to the common or usual name of the food: "With mechanically processed [species] product" and "Contains up to _____ percent powdered bone." On the basis of an industry petition, and following the change in the Administration, USDA revised the regulation to require that the product be declared in the ingredient statement as "mechanically processed [species]," to repeal the requirement that the common or usual name refer to the ingredient, and to replace the powdered bone statement with a requirement that the label state the percent of the U.S. RDA of calcium in a serving. These changed requirements, codified in 9 C.F.R. § 317.2(j)(13), were upheld in *Community Nutrition Institute v. Block*, 749 F.2d 50 (D.C. Cir. 1984).

USDA's efforts to grapple with the naming of pizza products have gained considerable notoriety. Pizza without a meat component is subject to the exclusive jurisdiction of FDA. Pizza containing pepperoni or any other meat component is subject to USDA jurisdiction. FDA has established no regulations or guidelines governing pizza labeling, but USDA has established a standard of identity in 9 C.F.R. § 319.600. In 38 Fed.Reg. 16363 (June 22, 1973), USDA proposed to establish a minimum of 12 percent cheese for any pizza product subject to its jurisdiction. In the face of industry objections to this requirement and support for the use of substitute cheese ingredients, the agency published a request for additional comments in 44 Fed.Reg. 71417 (December 11, 1979). It published another proposal in 48 Fed.Reg. 35654 (August 5, 1983) requiring that any substitute for cheese be labeled as a "cheese substitute" (or, if it is nutritionally inferior, "imitation cheese") as part of the name of the food. Manufacturers opposed this proposal on the ground that the use of cheese substitutes is made known through the statement of ingredients. Based upon these comments, USDA withdrew the proposed regulations in 52 Fed.Reg. 11828 (April 13, 1987). Legislation was then introduced to require any pizza containing a substitute cheese product be labeled as "contains imitation cheese" (rather than "substitute cheese") and came close to enactment. *See* "Labeling of Meat Food Products to Reflect the Inclusion of Imitation or Alternate Cheese; The Effects of Consumption of Tropical Oils on the Soybean Program," Joint Hearing before the Subcomm. on Livestock, Dairy, and Poultry and the Subcomm. on Wheat, Soybeans, and Feed Grains of the House Comm. on Agriculture, 100th Cong., 1st Sess. (1987); GAO, FOOD MARKETING: FROZEN CHEESE PIZZA—REPRESENTATIVE OF BROADER FOOD LABELING ISSUES, No. RCED-88-70 (March 1988).

D. REGULATION OF THE NUTRIENT CONTENT OF FOOD

FDA efforts to regulate the nutrient content of food merit separate treatment for several reasons. Good nutrition is a matter of both intense individual and public concern. It is closely related to individual physical and mental development and to the avoidance of disease and has been made a priority objective by administrations from both political parties. Accordingly, FDA programs relating to the nutritional value of food comprise one of the agency's most important functions.

Until the 1970s, FDA relied largely upon the statutory provisions and concepts already discussed in this Chapter. The agency vigorously pursued misleading nutritional claims in food labeling under section 403(a) and promulgated standards of identity for enriched food to assure the nutritional quality of basic staples since 1938. In addition, shortly after the Act was passed FDA issued regulations governing food claims for "special dietary uses," as specifically authorized by section 403(j), which are discussed in Part E, p. 204 *infra*. But during the 1970s, faced with increasing concern about the relation between diet and health and greater public demand for information about food and nutrition, the agency created entirely new regulatory programs based on provisions that have been in the Act from the beginning. For an overview, *see* Hutt, *Government Regulation of Health Claims in Food Labeling and Advertising*, 41 FDC L.J. 3 (1986).

---

1. NUTRITIONAL STATUS OF AMERICANS

Through the 1950s and 1960s, FDA food policy rested on the assumptions that Americans could get proper nourishment from ordinary foods and that most were in fact adequately nourished. These assumptions came under serious question in the late 1960s. Several events were responsible for undermining these assumptions, but none was more important than the investigations of the Senate Select Committee on Nutrition and Human Needs, chaired by Senator George McGovern.

THE FOOD GAP: POVERTY AND MALNUTRITION IN THE UNITED STATES

Staff Report of the Senate Committee on Nutrition and Human Needs,
91st Congress, 1st Session (1969).

The national nutrition survey, supported by the Department of Health, Education, and Welfare, . . . is studying the extent of malnutrition in low-income census districts in 10 states. . . . [T]he survey has found an alarming prevalence of those characteristics that are associated with undernourished groups. More specifically, seven cases of marasmus and kwashiorkor—cases of caloric and protein starvation— were identified and clinically validated; one-third of the children under 6 years and 15 percent of the total sample population were found to be anemic, to have hemoglobin levels in the "unacceptable range"; 3.5 percent of the children X-rayed showed evidence of retarded bone growth; vitamin A, essential for the formation of cells and for normal vision, was found to be at unacceptable levels for 33 percent of the children under 6 [years of age] and 13 percent of the population; vitamin C, important for normal tooth and bone formation, wound healing, and resistance to infection was found at less than acceptable levels in 12 to 16 percent of all age groups; vitamin D, necessary for the absorption of calcium and the normal development of bones, was found to be at less than acceptable levels for 3.7 percent of all children under 6 years. . . .

In the spring of 1965, the Department of Agriculture conducted its customary nationwide survey of food consumption, covering 7,500 households. The results of this survey tend to corroborate the preliminary results of the national nutrition survey. Half of the households surveyed had diets that failed to meet the recommended dietary allowances set by the Food and Nutrition Board of the National Academy of Sciences–National Research Council for one or more nutrients. About one-fifth of the sample had "poor" diets—their food intake provided less than two-thirds of the NRC allowance for one or more nutrients.

Of greater significance, the number of "good" diets fell 10 percent from 1955 to 1965, while the number of "poor" diets rose 6 percent in the same period. Although southern and north-central households had higher concentrations of "poor" diets, urban and rural households yielded similar proportions of diets below the allowances for one or more nutrients.

As incomes rose, adequacy of diets also rose. While nearly two-thirds or 63 percent of the households with incomes under $3,000 had diets that did not meet the allowances for one or more nutrients, only 37 percent of the households with incomes over $10,000 had such diets....

These and other surveys lead to one clear, general conclusion: Clinically validated malnutrition not only exists in the United States but is a serious problem.... The evidence is by no means complete, and further scientific surveying is necessary if we are to have an understanding of the real extent of hunger and malnutrition in America. But the tip of the iceberg has been exposed. We know enough now to warn us that there is a demonstrably high incidence of nutritional deficiency, detected clinically by medical and biochemical examinations, particularly among infants, preschool and schoolchildren from low-income families and among the general population with incomes under $5,000 per year in four States....

NOTES

1. *FDA Responsibility.* Many nutrition programs are beyond the budget or the authority of the FDA to implement. Yet its regulatory policies can affect the success of other programs. *See, e.g.,* Hutt, *Regulatory Implementation of Dietary Recommendations,* 36 FDC L.J. 66 (1981). A recurrent question is whether the FDA efforts to help consumers eat wisely aid or impede efforts to combat malnutrition.

2. *Consumer Understanding.* FDA must make some assumptions about the extent of consumer information and understanding—not to mention consumer concern—in devising food regulations. Can it safely assume that most consumers are aware that they need only the RDAs of essential nutrients, should limit their consumption of saturated fats, and ought to watch closely their daily intake of calories? Or should the agency assume that such nutritional decisions are too important to be left to consumers, and fashion regulatory policies to assure that "good" foods are readily available and widely consumed?

According to Dr. Jean Mayer and other nutritionists, ignorance about nutrition is by no means confined to low income groups. The rich, Mayer once suggested to a Senate investigating committee, are as unaware of what constitutes good nutrition as the poor. The Washington Post, December 6, 1972, § D, at 3. In 1972, three Colorado pediatricians reported a surprising incidence of physical retardation caused by zinc deficiency among some Denver schoolchildren. "All of the children were from families in the middle and upper socio-economic group ... not poor, unhealthy, malnourished youngsters ... "; yet 9 of 10 were below average in height and weight and in most the sense of taste was impaired. Dr. Mayer speculated that the explanation for this deficiency, which apparently can be remedied by zinc supplementation, was "our methods of milling and enriching grain products." Zinc is present in whole wheat but is mostly eliminated during processing and not replaced by enrichment. The Washington Post, February 1, 1973, § H, at 12.

3. *Nutrition Update.* Twenty years after the McGovern investigations, the reports of hunger and malnutrition continue. *See, e.g.,* Physician Task Force on Hunger in America, HUNGER IN AMERICA: THE GROWTH EPIDEMIC (1985); "Oversight on Nutritional Status of Low–Income Americans in the 1980's," Hearing Before the Subcomm. on Nutrition of the Senate Comm. on Agriculture, Nutrition, and Forestry, 98th Cong., 1st Sess. (1983).

4. *Nutrition Monitoring.* Repeated attempts since 1977 to enact legislation to establish a coordinated national nutrition monitoring and research program culminated in the passage of the National Nutrition Monitoring and Related Research Act of 1990, 104 Stat. 1034.

2. NUTRITION LABELING

The White House Conference on Food, Nutrition and Health, held in December 1969, is a watershed in the development of FDA food policy. Many recommendations were made to revise existing FDA policy, and in particular to place greater regulatory emphasis on the nutritional quality of food and on label information to inform consumers about the nutritional characteristics of food. Five individuals who participated actively in the White House Conference within two years had assumed positions at FDA, as Deputy Commissioner, Director of the Bureau of Foods, Director of the Division of Nutrition, Deputy Director of the Division of Nutrition, and Chief Counsel. The cornerstone of the new policy was the now-familiar nutrition labeling that in 1991 appears on the labels of foods comprising well over half of all packaged food sales.

NUTRITION LABELING
38 Federal Register 2125 (January 19, 1973).

In the FEDERAL REGISTER of March 30, 1972 (37 FR 6493), the Commissioner of Food and Drugs proposed a new section on nutrition labeling under Title 21....

Mandatory nutrition labeling. Some 290 consumers and 15 consumer groups believe that nutrition labeling should be mandatory for all foods. The Commissioner has concluded that insufficient information is known about the nutrient content and variability of some foods, and that the analytical methodology and capability of some food manufacturers, processors, and distributors is inadequate to permit adoption of a requirement at this time that all foods bear nutrition labeling. Experience under this new regulation is required before expansion to all foods on a mandatory basis can be considered.

Applicability of nutrition labeling. Numerous comments requested clarification of the circumstances under which nutrition labeling will and will not be applicable, and particularly the relationship between nutrition labeling and special dietary food labeling.... The final regulation clarifies both of these points.

Except for some standardized foods, the decision to add a vitamin or mineral to or make a nutritional claim for, a food is entirely voluntary. The Commissioner has therefore concluded that, where a nutrient is added to a food, e.g., the addition of vitamin C to a breakfast drink, or a claim or information with respect to nutritional properties of a food is included in labeling or advertising, e.g., the amount of vitamin C, or a general or specific reference to the caloric or fat content of a food, or any other representation that a food is useful in the daily diet because of any of the nutrient qualities covered in this regulation, the full nutrition labeling established in this regulation must be utilized. Only by having available this full nutrition labeling for a food to which such a nutrient is added or for which such claim or information is provided can such claim or information be evaluated and understood, and the food properly used in the diet. Without full nutrition labeling such claims or information would be confusing and misleading for lack of completeness, and could deceive consumers about the true nutritional value of the food, its over-all nutritional contribution to the daily diet, and its nutritional weaknesses as well as strengths. Since addition of nutrients and use of nutrition claims or information is voluntary in most cases, the application of this new regulation on nutrition labeling is also voluntary. A manufacturer who does not wish to use nutrition labeling need not add nutrients to his products or refer to their nutritional properties in labeling or advertising.

All food standards providing for addition of nutrients or labeling of nutritional qualities have been reviewed. For most food standards, the addition of nutrients is optional and nutrition labeling is therefore entirely appropriate because the manufacturer is not required to add nutrients or to label nutritional properties. For those few food standards where the addition of nutrients and/or the labeling of nutritional properties is mandatory, the Commissioner has concluded that no hardship will be imposed by the application of nutrition labeling. Accordingly, none of these standardized foods is exempted from nutrition labeling....

For some products, general nutrition labeling ... is inappropriate and very specific special dietary food labeling is retained. These foods are exempted . . . in this final regulation. Such exempted foods include certain infant foods; . . . dietary supplements of vitamins and minerals; . . . any food intended for use as the sole item of the diet (for which specific special dietary food labeling, including in some cases amino acid composition is appropriate) . . .; and foods represented for use solely under medical supervision in the dietary management of specific diseases and disorders (such as foods for the dietary management of inborn errors of metabolism, for which specific special dietary food labeling is also more appropriate). . . . In each of these instances, the broad approach adopted for nutrition labeling, which is clearly desirable for general consumer use, is inappropriate because of the need for more detailed and specific information and because the type of product involved is more readily susceptible to precise quality control of the nutrient levels. . . .

As already explained, any reference in labeling or advertising to protein, fat, carbohydrates, or calories will result in a requirement that the food bear full nutrition labeling. . . .

Sodium declaration. Several authorities indicated the value of continuing to list sodium content of foods, without listing other nutrients, for those on a sodium-controlled diet. This need has been met by permitting the listing of sodium in milligrams per serving, without subjecting the label to the requirements of nutrition labeling. . . .

Cholesterol declaration. Because of the interest of many individuals and medical authorities, the Commissioner has concluded that it is in the best interest of the consumer to permit listing of cholesterol content without subjecting the label to the requirement of full nutrition labeling. . . .

Standardized format. The Food and Drug Administration proposed a standardized format for listing seven commonly analyzed nutrients. This proposal was well received by consumers, consumer groups, and most professionals and teachers. The intense interest of consumer groups in inclusion of all seven nutrients in the standardized format has been reiterated several times. Industry, however, strongly opposed listing nutrients that were not present, emphasizing that this is a negative approach to nutrition labeling and referring to it as "negative labeling." Recognizing the validity of both views, the Commissioner has concluded that it is reasonable to require a standard seven-nutrient format unless a food contains less than 2 percent of the U.S. RDA for four or more of the seven nutrients. In the latter case, the manufacturer or distributor may list no more than three nutrients without listing the seven required by the standard format. Where the standard seven-nutrient format is not used, it is necessary to add the statement "contains less than 2 percent of the U.S. RDA of _____," listing whichever of the seven nutrients for which specific levels have not been declared.

The original proposal indicated that quantities of nutrients at levels less than 5 percent of the RDA would be considered insignificant and would have to be labeled to show consumers this fact. Suggestions were made that levels of nutrients less than the lowest increment be designated by an asterisk opposite the given nutrient or nutrients in the standard seven-nutrient format with a reference statement "less than _____ percent of the RDA." After careful consideration of these comments, the regulation has been changed to provide that nutrients present in amounts less than 2 percent of the U.S. RDA may be indicated by a zero, or by an asterisk referring to another asterisk placed at the bottom of the table and followed by the statement "contains less than 2 percent of the U.S. RDA of this (these) nutrient (nutrients)." . . .

Fortification guidelines and nutritional claims. The subject of labeling increments and "negative labeling" is inextricably involved with the problem of "nutrient races" and promiscuous fortification. . . .

With the selection of smaller increments (2 percent) below the 10 percent level, there is concern that claims of nutrient superiority of one food over another based solely on small differences could become a problem. The smaller increments were selected in order to provide more useful nutrition labeling for consumers, because otherwise the cumulative amounts of low nutrient levels would not be known (e.g., it is estimated that 20 percent to 40 percent of the daily nutrient supply is obtained from foods containing less than 5 percent of the U.S. RDA in a serving); the small increments are not intended to suggest that a 2 percent or 5 percent difference in one food is itself significant. When making claims of nutrient superiority of one food over another, a difference of less 10 percent of the U.S. RDA is not considered significant. Thus, any label claims for nutritional superiority, or claims that a product makes a significant contribution to the daily allowances of a nutrient(s), will be evaluated by this 10 percent standard.

Compliance levels. The setting of practical limits of variation in nutrient levels for compliance purposes was the subject of extensive comments by some trade associations and manufacturers. . . .

The Commissioner realizes that manufacturers can exert varying degrees of control over the nutrient content of food products. Considerable control can be exerted over the nutrient levels when individual nutrients are added as specific substances. When discrete nutrients consisting of vitamins, minerals, and/or protein are added for the purposes of increasing the nutrient claims as a percent of the U.S. RDA, it is reasonable to require that compliance procedures be rigid. The compliance procedures set forth below for foods to which nutrients are so added require relatively exact nutrient levels in relation to label claims. Less variation in nutrient level is expected in a nutrient that is added to a food than in a naturally occurring (indigenous) nutrient in a food. . . .

Therefore, nutrients in foods will be divided generally into two classes for compliance purposes. These two classes are:

Class I. Added nutrients in fortified or fabricated foods.

Class II. Naturally occurring (indigenous) nutrients....

Complete assurance that a lot is or is not in compliance with the labeled nutrient values would of course require destructive analysis of the entire lot. Therefore, a statistical approach involving analysis of a representative sample from the lot is required. Any such approach entailing examination of only a portion of the lot is subject to the possibility of an incorrect compliance decision. However, the differentiation between Class I and Class II nutrients, linked to a valid sampling plan, permits the derivation of a logical compliance procedure, which reduces the chance of an incorrect decision to a tolerable level....

In order to assure that the average nutrient level of a lot meets the label declaration for that nutrient, according to statistical projection, the following criteria shall be met:

Class I. The nutrient content of the composite shall be at least equal to the value for that nutrient declared on the label.

Class II. The nutrient content of the composite shall equal at least 80 percent of the value of that nutrient declared on the label.

Although the greater variability of Class II nutrients requires a different statistical approach, the average nutrient content of the lot will nonetheless be the same as for a Class I nutrient....

Representative values. Some 22 companies and 21 trade associations felt that "representative" values based upon averages of surveys made over the years, rather than actual analytical values based on current testing of lots of the manufacturer's product, should be permitted as a basis for labeling for many foods. The consumer groups generally favored use of current analytical values.

... At the present time, however, the data available from survey averages are incomplete, and thus unsuitable as a basis for labeling claims. Moreover, processes of various manufacturers differ enough that comprehensive data may never provide a single representative "industry average" for processed foods. The consumer has a right to expect that nutrition labeling will honestly represent the food in the package. It is therefore essential that "representative" data be checked at this time by analysis of sufficient individual lots to give assurance that the labeled value adequately represents the product offered, at least until accurate and complete data are available on an industry-wide, regional, and manufacturer basis....

NOTES

1. *Final Regulations.* FDA published additional modifications in the nutrition labeling regulations, 38 Fed. Reg. 6951 (March 14, 1973). The final regulations appear at 21 C.F.R. § 101.9.

2. *Fresh Fruits and Vegetables.* The final nutrition labeling regulations promulgated by FDA in 1973 applied to fresh fruits and vegetables. When suit was brought by the fresh fruit and vegetable industry to challenge this application, however, FDA exempted these products pending further study of

the issues involved, 38 Fed. Reg. 32786 (November 28, 1973). Based upon the proviso in section 401 that no standard of identity may be established for fresh fruits or vegetables except in limited circumstances, the court in *National Nutritional Foods Ass'n v. FDA,* 504 F.2d 761, 806–807 (2d Cir. 1974), p. 215 *supra,* enjoined application of FDA's vitamin-mineral regulations to fresh fruits and vegetables. FDA subsequently issued a new proposal respecting nutrition labeling for fresh fruits and vegetables, 40 Fed. Reg. 8214 (February 26, 1975), but withdrew the proposal in 48 Fed. Reg. 27266 (June 14, 1983) on the ground that the costs outweighed the benefits.

3. *Serving Size.* A critical element of nutrition labeling is the "serving size" of the food on the basis of which the nutrient content is declared. Because of variances among serving sizes used in labeling for identical food products, FDA proposed a procedure for standardizing serving sizes in 39 Fed. Reg. 20887 (June 14, 1974) and a specific serving size for soft drinks in 40 Fed. Reg. 4315 (January 29, 1975), but it withdrew both proposals in 51 Fed. Reg. 15653 (April 25, 1986). An FDA survey has indicated that, as a result of increased consumer concern about such problem nutrients as sodium, fat, cholesterol, and calories, food manufacturers have reduced the labeled serving sizes to minimize the declared amounts of these nutrients. Heimbach, *et al. Declared Serving Sizes of Packaged Foods, 1977–86,* 44 Food Tech., No. 6, at 82 (June 1990).

4. *Abbreviated Format.* In an effort to simplify nutrition labeling, FDA proposed in 39 Fed. Reg. 8621 (March 6, 1974) to permit a short format for foods which are not meaningful sources of nutrition by allowing statements such as "contains no vitamins or minerals." Because the comments reflected a wide disparity of views, the proposal was withdrawn in 42 Fed. Reg. 27261 (May 27, 1977).

5. *Coverage of Nutrition Labeling.* A 1978 FDA survey determined that 40 percent of the leading national brands, 25 percent of the remaining national brands, and 44 percent of chain store private label brands, used nutrition labeling for packaged processed foods. This amounted to about 40 percent of the retail sales value of this category of food. *See* Schucker, A SURVEILLANCE OF NUTRITION LABELING IN THE RETAIL PACKAGED FOOD SUPPLY (1978). A decade later, according to FDA, "about 60 percent of FDA-regulated packaged foods bear nutrition labeling." 54 Fed. Reg. 32610, 32612 (August 8, 1989).

6. *Consumer Education.* From the inception of nutrition labeling, FDA stated that use of this new information by the public would depend upon supportive educational efforts that are beyond the agency's mandate and resources. Some efforts have been undertaken, *see* National Nutrition Consortium, NUTRITION LABELING: HOW IT CAN WORK FOR YOU (1975), and USDA, NUTRITION LABELING: TOOLS FOR ITS USE, Agric. Info. Bull. 382 (1975), but the government has never mounted a major educational campaign. One study found that the attitude of consumers towards nutrition labeling was "highly positive" but comprehension was "low" and thus more consumer education is "essential." Daly, *The Response of Consumers to Nutrition Labeling,* 10 J. of Consumer Affairs 170 (1976). *See also* Smith, *Consumer Attitudes Toward Food Labeling and Other Shopping Aids,* USDA Agric. Econ. Rep. No. 439 (1979).

7. *Commentary. See generally* Grant, *Nutrient Labeling,* 27 FDC L.J. 271 (1972); Hegsted, *Nutrition Labeling: Not All Good—Not All Bad,* 29 FDC L.J.

412 (1974); Johnson, *Nutrition Labeling—A Foremost Concern*, 28 FDC L.J. 108 (1973); Littlefield, *Nutritional Labeling Revisited—Regulatory Considerations*, 29 FDC L.J. 331 (1974); Peterson, *Consumer Nutrition Advocacy*, 32 FDC L.J. 423 (1977); Roberts, *Nutrition–Labeling Compliance*, 30 FDC L.J. 89 (1975); Schmidt, *Nutrition Labeling and the Consumer: Feast or Famine?*, 29 FDC L.J. 414 (1974); Somers, *Quality Control Problems in Nutritional Labeling*, 27 FDC L.J. 287 (1972); Stokes, *The Consumer Research Institute's Nutrient Labeling Research Program*, 27 FDC L.J. 249 (1972); Thompson, *FDA—They Mean Well, But ...*, 37 J. AFDO 185 (1973); Wells, *The Consumer Research Institute's Nutrient Labeling Research*, 27 FDC L.J. 40 (1972). For a discussion of the impact of FDA's nutrition labeling on USDA and the FTC, *see* Mussman, *USDA Nutritional Labeling Regulations and the Growth of Voluntary Nutritional Labeling on Meat*, 29 FDC L.J. 425 (1974); Rosch, *Nutrition Information and Nutrition Advertising*, 29 FDC L.J. 429 (1974).

8. *Labeling Format.* FDA's prescribed format has never satisfied all critics. *See, e.g.,* Cimons and Jacobson, *How to Decode a Food Label*, Mother Jones Magazine, p. 32 (March 1978); Specter, *Food Labels Often Light on Nutrition Information*, The Washington Post, July 23, 1989, at A1.

9. *Exemptions.* In order to encourage experimentation in nutrition labeling, FDA established a procedure under which exemptions from the current labeling requirements may be granted in 45 Fed. Reg. 58880 (September 5, 1980) and 48 Fed. Reg. 15236 (April 8, 1983), codified in 21 C.F.R. § 101.108.

CHOLESTEROL AND FAT LABELING

No aspect of nutrition labeling has occasioned more debate than disclosure of cholesterol and fat composition. The issues raised in this area include the manner in which the fat in any fabricated food is declared in the statement of ingredients, label declaration of the amount of cholesterol in a food and the fatty acid composition of that food, and labeling claims relating to the potential relationship of cholesterol and fatty acid composition to heart disease.

Shortly after enactment of the 1938 Act, FDA issued various trade correspondence permitting the declaration of individual fats and oils in the ingredient statement of fabricated foods under generic terms such as "shortening" or "vegetable oil." *See* TC–62 (February 15, 1940), TC–94 (February 21, 1940), and TC–209 (March 21, 1940). At that time, no nutritionally significant difference was thought to exist among the various fats and oils used in food. In the 1950s, however, some scientific research indicated that there may be a correlation between blood cholesterol levels and heart disease. Scientific research also showed that saturated fat tends to increase blood cholesterol and polyunsaturated fat tends to decrease blood cholesterol. Concerned that this preliminary information might prompt unwarranted claims in food labeling, FDA published a statement of policy, 24 Fed. Reg. 9990 (December 10, 1959), stating that the role of cholesterol in heart disease had not been established, that the advisability of making extensive changes in the nature of the dietary fat intake had not been demonstrated, and that any labeling claims related to heart disease would be regarded as illegal. FDA interpreted this statement to prohibit use of the term "cholesterol" and any related claims.

In May 1964 the agency reported the results of a consumer survey which showed that food labels referring to "polyunsaturated" or "cholesterol" misled many people to believe that the foods would reduce blood cholesterol and thus treat heart disease. It therefore reaffirmed its earlier policy statement. In response, prominent physicians requested FDA to permit labeling statements that would assist physicians in recommending a proper diet for patients and to assist patients in following that diet. Accordingly, in 30 Fed. Reg. 6984 (May 25, 1965), FDA proposed to retain its earlier policy statement but at the same time to permit factual declaration of the fatty acid content of foods (*i.e.*, the number of grams of saturated fatty acids, monounsaturated fatty acids and polyunsaturated acids, in an ordinary serving and in 100 grams of the food). This proposal was withdrawn in 31 Fed. Reg. 3301 (March 2, 1966), pending further study.

By the 1970s, interest in the dietary fat issue had intensified. In 36 Fed. Reg. 11521 (June 15, 1971), FDA published two new proposals to replace the 1965 proposal. First, the agency proposed to revoke the old TCs and to require in the statement of ingredients declaration of the specific name of each individual fat or oil ingredient in the order of predominance. Second, it offered two alternative proposals to replace its 1965 proposal respecting cholesterol/fatty acid labeling. The first proposal involved retention of the 1959 policy statement with the addition of a prohibition of any labeling use of the terms "polyunsaturated," "monounsaturated," or "saturated," except as specifically permitted by FDA regulation. The second proposal would have established a form for the voluntary declaration of the fatty acid composition of any food containing 10 percent or more fat and not less than 3 grams of fat in an average serving.

As part of its final nutrition labeling regulations, FDA established rules governing cholesterol/fatty acid labeling in 36 Fed. Reg. 11521 (June 15, 1971), 38 Fed. Reg. 2132 (January 19, 1973), now codified in 21 C.F.R. § 101.25. The agency made cholesterol and fatty acid composition labeling an optional, rather than a mandatory, part of nutrition labeling. Where this information is provided, it must conform to the format specified by FDA. The principal display panel of the label may state "cholesterol (fat) information appears ___," the blank to be filled in with a phrase stating where the information is contained on the label, but only in small size type. The 1959 policy statement was revoked as obsolete. The new regulation was modified in 38 Fed. Reg. 6961 (March 14, 1973) and in 38 Fed. Reg. 20071 (July 27, 1973). FDA added an additional paragraph to make it clear that no statements relating to cholesterol or fatty acid content may be made in labeling other than those specifically permitted in the regulation.

In 39 Fed. Reg. 20888 (June 14, 1974), FDA took action on its proposal respecting specific declaration of fats and oils in the ingredient statement for fabricated food. FDA adopted the approach described above, revoking the old TCs and requiring specific individual declaration of fats and oils, but permitting declaration of alternative ingredients to allow flexibility in food formulation. The final regulation was published in 41 Fed. Reg. 1156 (January 6, 1976), now codified in 21 C.F.R. § 101.3(b)(14). A subsequent modification, 41 Fed. Reg. 52481 (November 30, 1976), 43 Fed. Reg. 12856 (March 28, 1978), substituted the term "hydrogenated" for "saturated" in describing fats and oils. In 42 Fed. Reg. 6834 (February 4, 1977), 45 Fed. Reg. 37420 (June 3, 1980), FDA amended its regulations to permit dairy products to declare fat content as part of the ingredient statement without providing full nutrition information.

As public reports during the 1980s emphasized the relationship between serum cholesterol and heart disease, consumer demand grew for information about the cholesterol and fatty acid composition of food products. FDA responded in 51 Fed. Reg. 42584 (November 25, 1986) by proposing to define the terms "cholesterol free," "low cholesterol," and "cholesterol reduced," to require that both cholesterol and fatty acid composition be included as a part of nutrition labeling whenever either is declared, and to delete the provision currently found in 21 C.F.R. § 101.25(d) requiring the label statement that "information on fat and cholesterol content is provided for individuals who, on the advice of a physician, are modifying their dietary intake of fat and cholesterol." The proposal stopped short of making information about cholesterol and fatty acid composition a mandatory part of nutrition labeling or of revoking the regulation that permits alternative "and/or" declaration of fats and oils in a statement of ingredients. FDA commissioned economic analyses of its policy regarding ingredient labeling of fats and oils and its policy on fat composition information as a part of nutrition labeling. A.D. Little, COST OF COMPLIANCE AND ECONOMIC IMPACT OF SPECIFIC SOURCE DECLARATION OF FATS AND OILS IN FOODS, Report to FDA under HHS Contract No. 223–79–8052 (May 1981); A.D. Little, COST IMPACT ANALYSIS OF DECLARATION OF FATTY ACID AND CHOLESTEROL CONTENT IN FOODS, Report to FDA under HHS Contract No. 223–79–8052 (October 1981). FDA published a tentative final regulation in 55 Fed.Reg. 29456 (July 19, 1990), but passage of the 1990 Nutrition Labeling and Education Act will necessitate reconsideration by the agency.

SODIUM LABELING

When the special dietary food regulations were promulgated in November 1941, they contained no provision relating to sodium labeling. In 18 Fed. Reg. 7249 (November 14, 1953), 19 Fed. Reg. 2767 (May 13, 1954), and 19 Fed. Reg. 3999 (July 1, 1954), FDA promulgated a special dietary food regulation under section 403(j) requiring that a food represented as a means of regulating the intake of sodium or salt be labeled with the number of milligrams of sodium in 100 grams of the food and in an average serving of the food. As part of its wholesale revision of the regulations during the 1960s, FDA revised the sodium regulation in 27 Fed. Reg. 5515 (June 20, 1962), 31 Fed. Reg. 8521 (June 18, 1966), and when most of the revisions were stayed by objections the agency included the revised sodium regulation in the 1969 hearing even though no specific issues were raised about it. The final regulation, promulgated in 37 Fed. Reg. 9763 (May 17, 1972) and codified in 21 C.F.R. § 105.69, retained the 1954 requirement and added some clarifying details. Adopted at the same time, FDA's nutrition labeling regulations specified that sodium labeling in accordance with section 105.69 would not trigger full nutrition labeling.

The association between sodium and hypertension was not widely accepted in 1972. Indeed, the FTC later entered consent orders prohibiting any representation for salt substitute products that there is "a causal connection between sodium intake and high blood pressure or water retention, or that a reduction in the level of sodium intake will promote or maintain good health." *Morton–Norwich Prods., Inc.,* 86 F.T.C. 299 (1975); *Nagle, Spillman & Bergman, Inc.,* 88 F.T.C. 244 (1976). By the early 1980s, however, scientific opinion on this matter had changed dramatically. FDA commissioned an economic analysis of options for expanded sodium labeling, A.D. Little, Inc., COST OF COMPLIANCE AND ECONOMIC IMPACT OF SODIUM/POTASSIUM LABELING REGULATORY ALTERNATIVES, (December 1981), and in 47 Fed. Reg. 26580 (June 18, 1982), 49 Fed. Reg. 15510 (April 18, 1984), the agency promulgated new regulations governing sodium labeling of food, which reflected three significant changes. First, although sodium labeling alone still did not trigger full nutrition labeling, sodium content became a mandatory part of nutrition labeling. Second, FDA defined the terms "sodium free," "very low sodium," "low sodium," and "reduced sodium." To be labeled as reduced in sodium, a food had to achieve a 75 percent reduction. Third, section 105.69 of the special dietary food regulations was revised to state that, where a food is represented as a means of regulating the intake of sodium or salt, the label must either bear full nutrition labeling or, at the very least, a statement of the number of milligrams of sodium in a specified serving. As a practical matter, most food labels that declare the sodium content do so as part of nutrition labeling.

An attempt to enact legislation mandating sodium labeling for all food failed in the 98th Congress. *See* "Sodium in Food and High Blood Pressure," Hearing Before the Subcomm. on Investigations and Oversight of the House Comm. on Science and Technology, 97th Cong., 1st Sess. (1981); "Sodium in Food and High Blood Pressure," Report Prepared by the Subcomm. on Investigations and Oversight of the House Comm. on Science and Technology, 97th Cong., 1st Sess. (Comm. Print 1981). Three years later a suit to force FDA to institute a rulemaking to prescribe sodium labeling for all food products, rather than a part of nutrition labeling, was dismissed. *Center for Science in the Public Interest v. Novitch,* Food Drug Cosm. L. Rep. (CCH) ¶ 38,275 (D.D.C. 1984).

---

3. OTHER NUTRITION INFORMATION

As part of its complete revision of the 1941 special dietary food regulations, *see* p. 212 *infra,* FDA in the 1962 proposal and the June 1966 "final" order included changes in the regulations governing labeling of infant food, hypoallergenic food, low sodium food, and food for which caloric claims are made. All of these regulations were considered during the 1968–1969 special dietary food hearings, although only the regulation respecting caloric claims was the subject of any significant interest.

Following those hearings, FDA published the infant food regulations in 35 Fed. Reg. 16737 (October 29, 1970) and 36 Fed. Reg. 23555 (December 10, 1971), now codified in 21 C.F.R. § 105.65. The regulations for hypoallergenic food and for low sodium food, which were not contested, were published in 37 Fed. Reg. 9763 (May 17, 1972), now codified in 21 C.F.R. §§ 105.62 and 105.69.

In 42 Fed. Reg. 37166 (July 19, 1977) and 43 Fed. Reg. 43248 (September 22, 1978), FDA promulgated its final regulations respecting caloric claims for food. In spite of the major commercial importance of these regulations, they were not challenged in court pursuant to section 701(f), and thus became effective.

PETER BARTON HUTT & ELIZABETH SLOAN
FINAL REGULATIONS GOVERNING LABEL STATEMENTS
FOR FOODS REPRESENTED AS USEFUL IN REDUCING
OR MAINTAINING CALORIC INTAKE OR BODY WEIGHT

Nutrition Policy Issues, No. 2, November 1978.

1. *Mandatory Label Statements For All Foods Making Weight Control Claims.* This category of foods must bear nutrition labeling (unless otherwise exempt) and a statement of the dietary usefulness of the food (i.e., "low calorie" or "reduced calorie" or "for calorie restricted diets"). Certain terminology (e.g., "diet," "dietetic," "artificially sweetened") may be used only if the food qualifies for labeling as low calorie or reduced calorie....

Use of the terms "sugar free," "sugarless," or "no sugar" are limited to foods properly labeled as low calorie or reduced calorie with one exception. The exception occurs when the term is used to designate a specified purpose other than weight control (e.g., sugarless gum), in which case the term must be accompanied by an appropriate explanatory statement such as "not for weight control" or "useful only in not promoting tooth decay."

Any weight control food which uses a nonnutritive sweetener must state that fact. If the food contains both nutritive and nonnutritive sweeteners, the presence of both must be declared. A weight control food which uses another nonnutritive ingredient to achieve its dietary usefulness must declare on its label the presence of that nonnutritive ingredient and its percentage by weight.

2. *"Low calorie" foods.* A food may claim to be "low calorie" only if a serving of the food contains no more than 40 calories and the food has a caloric density of no more than 0.4 calories per gram as consumed.... The final regulations retain the provision that a food which is naturally low calorie must be labeled in order to make that clear (i.e., "celery, a low calorie food," not "low calorie celery")....

3. *"Reduced calorie" foods.* A food is a reduced calorie food if it is not nutritionally inferior to the compared food and it has a caloric reduction from the compared food of at least one-third. The label of a reduced calorie food must describe the comparison upon which the weight control claim is based, either by identifying a specific food having at least 150 percent of the calories for which the reduced calorie food can substitute or by indicating that the reduced calorie claim is based on a comparison with the same food without the change that results in the reduction in calories. This statement must include a comparison between the caloric content of a specified serving of the food and an equivalent serving of the compared food.

If the reduced calorie food is similar in all of its organoleptic properties to the compared food, it must be labeled as "reduced calorie" or "reduced in calories" or "a reduced calorie food." If the reduced calorie food is not similar in all its organoleptic properties to the compared food, those terms may not be used in juxtaposition to the name of the food, but those terms or other appropriate terms may be used elsewhere on the label to indicate its comparative dietary usefulness as long as the statement indicates the material differences in organoleptic properties between it and the compared food.

4. *Foods "for calorie restricted diets."* The final regulations permit virtually all food to make some type of label claim for weight control purposes. In addition to claims that meet the requirements for "low calorie" or "reduced calorie," any other food may be represented for use in "calorie restricted diets" or as "useful for weight control" as long as the basis for the claim is conspicuously and clearly stated in conjunction with the claim. . . .

HYPOALLERGENIC FOOD CLAIMS

Although the special dietary food regulations, 21 C.F.R. § 105.62, provide for the labeling of hypoallergenic food, such claims are rarely made. In early 1989, however, in accordance with the requirements of the Infant Formula Act of 1980, 94 Stat. 1190, codified as section 412 of the FD&C Act, FDA undertook a review of the labeling claims for existing infant formulas. The agency concluded that the claims for hypoallergenicity, *i.e.*, "usefulness in the management of severe food allergies, sensitivity to intact protein and galactosemia (inability to metabolize one milk sugar)," were not supported by "a convincing body of evidence." "Infant Formula Claims," FDA Talk Paper No. T89–18 (March 27, 1989); "Update on Good Start Formula," FDA Talk Paper No. T89–31 (May 10, 1989).

---

4. DEFINITION OF "IMITATION"

REPORT ON THE WHITE HOUSE CONFERENCE ON FOOD, NUTRITION AND HEALTH

Panel III–2: New Foods (1969).

Presently, new foods are often required by Government regulatory agencies to be called "imitation" products. The "imitation" label has been regarded as equally applicable when the new product is inferior to the old as it is when the new product is superior to the old. Thus, the use of such over simplified and inaccurate words are [sic] potentially misleading to consumers, and fail[s] to inform the public about the actual characteristics and properties of the new product. . . .

Under existing law, Government agencies could . . . require an informative and descriptive generic name for every food. The existing legal prohibitions against false or misleading labeling and advertising could be utilized to prevent the use of any terminology that could mislead consumers about the identity or characteristics of the new product.... Such a policy ... would provide more accurate and useful information for consumer[s] about the identify of foods than is presently the situation. It would also encourage the development and marketing of variations of traditional foods and of completely new foods that can provide consumers a greater variety of acceptable, higher quality, and more nutritious food products at lower prices....

IMITATION FOODS, APPLICATION OF TERM "IMITATION": PROPOSED RULEMAKING
38 Federal Register 2138 (January 19, 1973).

Vast strides in food technology have taken place since section 403(c) of the act was enacted, and there are now on the market many new wholesome and nutritious food products, some of which resemble and are substitutes for other, traditional foods. Significantly, it is no longer the case that such products are necessarily inferior to the traditional foods for which they may be substituted.

There has been some uncertainty as to the proper scope of the term "imitation" in this modern context. The term clearly fails to inform the public of the actual characteristics and properties of a new food product.... To apply automatically the term "imitation" to new substitute food products which are not nutritionally inferior would be a disservice to consumers and would be contrary to the common understanding that the word "imitation" connotes inferiority. Section 403(c) of the act would then present a serious obstacle to the development and marketing of modified products with improved nutritional content. Indeed, because of the traditional connotation of inferiority, application of the term "imitation" to a substitute food product which is not inferior could be misleading to the consumer, in violation of section 403(a) of the act.

Accordingly, the Commissioner of Food and Drugs has concluded that it is in the interest of consumers and consistent with the general intent of Congress to restrict required application of the term "imitation" to a substitute food which is nutritionally inferior to the food for which it is a substitute.

The consumer, however, must be protected from unwitting purchase of a product which is different, although not inferior, from what he may reasonably expect. The Commissioner concurs with the further recommendation of the White House Conference that the "name of a food should accurately describe, in as simple and direct terms as possible, the basic nature of the food or its characterizing properties or ingredients." Accordingly, in order to avoid "imitation" status, a substitute food product which is not nutritionally inferior must also bear a label which clearly states the common or usual name of the product and which is not false or misleading....

The Commissioner has considered whether there may be basis for imitation labeling other than nutritional inferiority. In reviewing this matter, it appears that nutritional inferiority is the only type of inferiority that is quantifiable on an objective basis. All other potential aspects of inferiority involve essentially subjective judgment which may vary from person to person.... The Commissioner has concluded that it is not the function of the Food and Drug Administration to attempt to arbitrate between the likes and dislikes of different individuals or between the different economic considerations that motivate different producers of agricultural commodities or different manufacturers and distributors of foods. The function of the Food and Drug Administration is solely to assure the safety of all foods and to prevent misleading labeling....

NOTE

In promulgating the final regulation, 21 C.F.R. § 101.3(e), FDA noted that "[n]o comment was able to articulate or even suggest objective standards constituting inferiority in addition to nutritional inferiority." 38 Fed. Reg. 20702 (August 2, 1973). Under the regulation, "nutritional inferiority" was defined as a reduction of 2% or more of the U.S. RDA of protein or any essential nutrient but not of fat or caloric content.

FEDERATION OF HOMEMAKERS v. SCHMIDT

United States Court of Appeals, District of Columbia Circuit, 1976.
539 F.2d 740.

TAMM, Circuit Judge.

The Food and Drug Administration (FDA) recently promulgated a regulation which, for the first time, attempted to define an imitation food subject to section 403(c) of the Federal Food, Drug, and Cosmetic Act. The appellants in this case challenge the new regulation as contrary to the terms of the Act and as arbitrary and capricious. We affirm the district court's finding that the regulation fulfills the objectives of the statute in question and is a reasonable exercise of the regulatory power of the FDA.... The Federation of Homemakers, a national consumer group, filed suit to enjoin enforcement of the new definition by the FDA, but on cross motions for summary judgment, District Judge Joseph C. Waddy held that the regulation is consistent with the statute and Congressional intent. *Federation of Homemakers v. Schmidt*, 385 F. Supp. 362 (D.D.C. 1974)....

... Beginning with the Supreme Court's admonition in *62 Cases of Jam v. United States* that "imitation" must be "left ... to the understanding of ordinary English speech," appellants call our attention to cases in which texture, smell, taste, appearance, manufacture, packaging and marketing all contribute to a determination of whether the food in question must be labeled an imitation.[8] While it is true that these judicial definitions may be reasonable ones, we do not believe that they prevent the promulgation of an equally reasonable definition by the agency charged with administering the Act. Congress chose not to define the parameters of its imitation label requirements; our deference to the enforcing agency's interpretation limits our review to determining only whether the regulation violates the language of the statute or is arbitrary and capricious. Neither the legislative history of the companion section regarding standardized foods, 21 U.S.C. § 341 (1970), nor the undefined use of "imitation" in the statute leads us to conclude that a food nutritionally equivalent to the ordinary food and clearly labeled with a common name established by regulation or with a descriptive term violates Congressional objectives if it is marketed without the imitation label. Indeed, the new regulation successfully reconciles the need to alert the public to inferior products with the proscription in subsection 343(a) against false or misleading labels.

As to the arbitrary and capricious issue raised by the Federation of Homemakers, we are convinced that the FDA regulation is well within the zone of reasonableness required of agency rulemaking. We note first that appellant's primary complaint with the regulation is that the FDA has not decided to issue standards of identity for all new foods, but instead has promulgated regulations which provide for developing new common names as well as for employing standards of identity and imitation labeling. . . .

This regulatory scheme satisfies prior criticisms that the imitation requirement as interpreted by courts had unduly deterred the development of new food products, desirable for consumers, because the manufacturer's product, even if superior, was subject to the disparagement intimated by the imitation label. *See, e.g.,* Report of Panel III–2; White House Conference on Food and Nutrition, *Final Report* (Dec. 24, 1969). In addition, the FDA reasonably expects this more flexible approach to encourage greater emphasis on nutritional value and consumer knowledge about purchased food products. Furthermore, the regulation provides a safety valve for specific cases arising later in which nutritional equivalency and descriptive labeling do not adequately protect consumers from food substitutes which are inferior in other ways.

This regulation, directed at the laudable aims of encouraging manufacture of nutritional food products and of better informing consumers so that they may exercise a knowledgeable choice of differing

---

8. In response to criticisms that the new regulation considers only nutritional equivalency, the FDA pointed out that by defining an imitation as a *substitute,* the characteristics previously noted by courts are still applicable in reaching this threshold finding.

Nutritional inferiority is not the only criterion involved in defining "imitation" status. An evaluation of the over-all impression conveyed by the food must first establish that the food is a substitute for and resembles another food.

Response to Comments, 38 Fed. Reg. 20202 (1973). . . .

foods within general categories, lies well within the bounds of discretion which the FDA may exercise. The judgment of the trial court is hereby Affirmed.

NOTES

1. *Collateral Challenges.* In *National Milk Producers Federation v. Harris,* 653 F.2d 339 (8th Cir. 1981), the court rejected the plaintiffs' claim that FDA violated section 403(c) by failing to require cheese substitutes to be labeled as imitations and upheld the agency's definition of "imitation." In *Grocery Mfrs. of America, Inc. v. Gerace,* 755 F.2d 993 (2d Cir. 1985), a trade association challenged a New York statute requiring all food products that resembled or are intended to substitute for cheese be labeled as imitation cheese. The court of appeals held that the FDA definition of an imitation food was reasonable, that the New York statute was in direct conflict with the federal regulation and thus was preempted insofar as it applied to food labeling, but that the New York statute was not preempted insofar as it applied to signs and menus that do not constitute labeling.

In *Dyson v. Miles Laboratories, Inc.,* 57 A.D.2d 197, 394 N.Y.S.2d 86 (1977), the court refused to dismiss New York's complaint that Morningstar Farms Breakfast Links and similar soy-based substitutes for sausage and bacon were misbranded under local law because they failed to bear "imitation" labeling. The court acknowledged the existence of the FDA regulation sustained in the *Federation of Homemakers* case, but concluded that New York could constitutionally apply its own standard, which is based on the *Chil–Zert* decision.

A decade after it promulgated its regulation defining "imitation" in terms of nutritional inferiority, FDA reaffirmed that decision and rejected alternative approaches in 48 Fed. Reg. 37665 (August 19, 1983).

2. *Substitutes for Standardized Foods.* For discussion of the special considerations involving application of section 403(c) to a new food that is intended to substitute for a standardized food, *see* p. 126 *supra.*

3. *USDA Policy.* In *In re Castleberry's Food Co.,* USDA FMIA Dkt. No. 36 (January 3, 1980), a Department of Agriculture Administrative Law Judge ruled that USDA had improperly required a product that varied from its standard for corned beef hash to be labeled "imitation." The ALJ's opinion documented substantial inconsistency in USDA labeling practices and endorsed the FDA approach. It found that the product was properly labeled with its own descriptive phrase and a statement of how it varied from the standard. Although the USDA Judicial Officer overruled the ALJ and determined that the product was an imitation, his decision stated that the FDA definition of imitation was used by USDA in the case-by-case approval of meat food labels. 40 Agric. Dec. 1262, 1277–78 (1981). *See also Grocery Mfgrs. of America, v. Gerace, supra* at 1001–02, where USDA represented that it had adopted the FDA definition of imitation.

In *Armour & Co. v. Freeman,* 304 F.2d 404 (D.C.Cir.1962), the court held that USDA could not lawfully require smoked ham containing added moisture of up to 10 percent to be labeled as "imitation ham," because that would be a "false or deceptive name" prohibited by the Federal Meat Inspection Act. The same court prohibited USDA from permitting frankfurters containing up to 15 percent nonmeat ingredients to be labeled "All Meat." *Federation of Homemakers v. Butz,* 466 F.2d 462 (D.C.Cir.1972).

Swift & Co., Inc. v. Walkey, 369 F.Supp. 1198 (S.D.N.Y. 1973), upheld application of New York's "imitation" labeling requirement—essentially identical to section 601(n)(3) of the Federal Meat Inspection Act—to "All American Fun–Links," a product made in link form from meat, isolated soybean, flavorings, water, and curing agents. The product's label had been approved by USDA, which apparently relied on the White House Conference recommendations.

4. *Commentary.* The controversy over required and permissible "imitation" labeling has inspired a large literature. *See* Austin, *The Jam Standard Case—Its Social Significance,* 6 FDC L.J. 919 (1951); Burditt, *Imitation,* 19 FDC L.J. 72 (1964); Hankin, *Quality Aspects of Imitation and Artificial Foods,* 24 FDC L.J. 368 (1969); Harvey, *Imitation Dairy Products,* 8 FDC L.J. 527 (1953); Hensel, *Dietary Version of a Standardized Food—Is It an Imitation?,* 13 FDC L.J. 172 (1958); Lambert, *New Foods and Old Laws: Conflict or Accommodation?,* 26 FDC L.J. 644 (1971); Markel, *The Law on Imitation Food,* 5 FDC L.J. 145 (1950); Myers, *The Wet Ham Controversy and New Concepts in Federal Food Regulation: Armour v. Freeman,* 19 FDC L.J. 196 (1964); Olsson, *New Foods—Another Viewpoint,* 26 FDC L.J. 652 (1971); Rubenstein, *The Bugaboo of Imitation Foods,* 7 FDC L.J. 266 (1952); Williams, *What Price Imitation,* 5 FDC L.J. 185 (1950).

---

5. COMMON OR USUAL NAMES

In establishing names for new fabricated foods, FDA has been forced to devote as much attention to the nutritional quality of the new food as to the terminology to describe it.

PETER BARTON HUTT & ELIZABETH SLOAN, FDA REGULATION OF VEGETABLE PROTEIN PRODUCTS
Nutrition Policy Issues, No. 3, January 1979.

During the 1960's a substantial amount of developmental work was undertaken by the food industry on extraction of protein from numerous vegetable sources and use of that protein in the fabrication of new food products.... Many were intended to resemble and substitute for traditional foods, such as meat, seafood, poultry, eggs, and cheese, that are regarded as "major protein foods." ...

In the FEDERAL REGISTER of June 14, 1974 (39 Fed. Reg. 20892), FDA concluded that, because the technology of new protein sources was still in a very active stage of development and because the most important public issue involved the accurate and informative labeling of final food products made from these new vegetable proteins, the proposed standard of identity should be abandoned. Instead, FDA proposed to establish descriptive "common or usual names" for food products containing vegetable protein as extenders or replacements for five "major protein foods"....

... FDA issued a tentative final regulation in the FEDERAL REGISTER of July 14, 1978 (43 Fed. Reg. 30472). The tentative final regulation would establish both (1) common or usual names for vegetable proteins that are processed so that some portion of the nonprotein constituents of the vegetable is removed, and thus that can be made into or become part of finished food products, and (2) common or usual names for finished food products that are intended to be substitutes for the five designated major protein foods and that contain vegetable protein as a protein source....

1. *Vegetable protein.* This portion of the regulation would establish common or usual names for three categories of vegetable protein. A vegetable protein containing less than 65 percent protein by weight would include the name of the source of the protein and the term "flour" and/or a term which describes the physical form of the product (e.g., "soy flour," "soy granules," or "soy flour granules"). The word "protein" could not be included in the name of this type of product. A vegetable protein containing 65–90 percent protein by weight would be a "protein concentrate" (e.g., "soy protein concentrate"). A term that describes the physical form of the product could be included.... A vegetable protein containing 90 percent or more protein by weight would be a "protein isolate" or "isolated protein" (e.g., "soy protein isolate" or "isolated soy protein"). A term that describes the physical form of the product could be included. In all three cases, the words "textured" or "texturized" could be part of the name.

2. *Substitutes for major protein foods (meat, seafood, poultry, eggs, and cheese) which contain vegetable protein).* This portion of the regulation would establish both nutrition and labeling requirements for any finished food product that contains vegetable protein as a source of protein and that resembles and substitutes for one of the five major protein foods.

3. *Nutritional requirements.* In order to avoid being labeled as "imitation," a finished food product containing any vegetable protein intended for use as a source of protein must be nutritionally equivalent to the type of food for which it substitutes....

4. *Labeling.* The tentative final regulation proposes two separate labeling rules depending on whether the vegetable protein is the sole source of protein or is mixed with one of the other traditional sources. If the finished food contains only vegetable protein and is intended to substitute for one of the five major protein foods, the common or usual name of that food would be required to include the term "vegetable [or "plant"] protein product." It could also include the terms "textured" or "texturized" and/or a term that describes the physical form of the product. In addition, proper flavor representations and other product characteristics could be included....

If the finished food contains a combination of vegetable protein and one of the five major protein foods, the common or usual name of that food would be required to include the name of both constituents in descending order of predominance and in the same size type. For example, a combination of tuna and a vegetable protein product, in which the tuna was the predominant ingredient by weight, would properly be labeled as "tuna and artificial tuna-flavored vegetable protein product."

The name of a finished multicomponent food that contains a characterizing component food that is made in whole or in part of vegetable protein and that substitutes for one of the five major protein foods must be accompanied by a statement such as "contains " or "made with,"the blank to be filled with the name of the component containing the substitute food. For example, a food substituting for "fish chowder" in which the fish component is wholly replaced by vegetable protein would properly be labeled as "chowder made with artificially fish-flavored vegetable protein product." Similarly, a food resembling "macaroni and cheese" in which vegetable protein substitutes for part of the cheese would properly be labeled as "macaroni casserole, made with cheese and vegetable protein product." ...

NOTES

1. *History.* The earlier history of FDA's efforts to regulate plant protein products is reflected in 32 Fed. Reg. 14237 (October 13, 1967), 34 Fed. Reg. 11423 (July 10, 1969), 35 Fed. Reg. 18530 (December 5, 1979).

2. *USDA Adherence.* Although FDA has taken no final action on the July 1978 proposal as of June 30, 1990, USDA has required that all vegetable protein products used in child nutrition programs conform to the FDA tentative final regulation in 48 Fed. Reg. 775 (January 7, 1983), codified in 7 C.F.R. Parts 210, 225, and 226, App. A.

3. *Butter and Margarine Substitutes.* See also the nutritional considerations involved in the FDA proposal to establish common or usual names for substitutes for margarine and butter, 41 Fed. Reg. 36509 (August 30, 1976), subsequently withdrawn in 51 Fed. Reg. 15653 (April 25, 1986).

In the early 1970s, FDA made the decision to apply the same policy on common or usual names to standardized and nonstandardized foods. Previously the agency had taken the position that any new substitute for a standardized food was required to be labeled as an imitation but a new substitute for a nonstandardized food was not required to be so labeled. Dressings for salad illustrate the impact of this policy. FDA had promulgated a standard for French dressing, 21 C.F.R. § 169.115, but not for Italian or Russian dressing. Under its traditional policy a reduced calorie version of French dressing had to be labelled as "imitation" French dressing, but a reduced calorie version of Italian or Russian dressing could be described as "reduced calorie" Italian or Russian dressing. Under its new policy FDA took the position that the common or usual name for a nonstandardized food could *include* the name of a standardized food, as long as the difference between the products was made clear, *see* note 2, p. 125 *supra*. This new policy was intended to prevent standards of identity from operating as barriers to the development of new food products, especially new versions of traditional foods with macronutrient composition modified to meet national nutrition goals. Food producers responded by developing dozens of new products with a reduced content of calories, sodium, cholesterol, and fat.

A decade later, however, FDA reverted to the pre–1970 approach. Modified versions of standardized foods were required to be designated as "alternative" or "substitute" products. If a modified product had its own standard of identity, however, the "alternative" or "substitute" language could be omitted. In substance, the agency substituted the terms "alternative" or "substitute" for the older "imitation" as a way of differentiating between standardized and nonstandardized versions of the same product.

The dairy industry has been a major battlefield in the war over names for modifications of or substitutes for traditional foods. For decades, the dairy industry sought to inhibit modified or substitute products through laws such as the Filled Milk Act, p. 84 *supra*. When the courts began to allow the marketing of new products bearing truthful labeling, the dairy industry sought to require coined names, or in any event to prohibit the use of dairy terms, for modified or substitute products. In 43 Fed. Reg. 42118 (September 19, 1978), FDA proposed to establish standards of identity for substitutes for milk, cream, and cheese. The resulting comments revealed a wide and deep divergence of views, and the agency decided to abandon any effort to standardize modifications of or substitutes for traditional dairy products and to pursue instead the development of guidelines for common or usual names.

SUBSTITUTES FOR MILK, CREAM, AND CHEESE; WITHDRAWAL OF PROPOSED STANDARDS OF IDENTITY
48 Federal Register 37666 (August 19, 1983).

In response to the proposal, FDA received 1,393 letters of comment.... The principal objection to the proposal was to the use of the names of traditional and standardized dairy foods in the names of the milk, cream, cheese, and cheese product substitutes. Most of these comments contended that the proposed names are confusingly similar to those of traditional dairy products and, as such, have the potential for misleading consumers, particularly when the substitute foods are packed in materials similar to those of traditional dairy products and are displayed in close proximity to dairy products in supermarkets. Some comments stated that all such foods should be labeled "imitations", whether or not they are nutritionally equivalent to the foods simulated. Others stated that substitute foods should be marketed under their own distinctive names which make no reference to the foods simulated as is done in the case of mellorine and margarine.

Comments from dairy farmers and persons or organizations representing dairy farmers contended that the proposed regulations were unfair to dairy farmers and should be withdrawn because they could have an adverse economic impact on them. One comment expressed the opinion that the use of dairy terms in the names of these foods will, over time, cloud the distinction in consumers' minds between dairy and nondairy products, resulting in economic losses to the dairy industry.

Several comments from manufacturers of substitute foods objected to the proposed compositional requirements because some of their products would have to be reformulated in order to comply and thus avoid the "imitation" designation in the name. Some also objected to the need to change the name of existing products that have had many years of consumer acceptance under their current names and requested that exemptions be granted for these products.

Some comments rejected the proposed nutrition profiles because certain minor constituents of traditional dairy products, for which no U.S. recommended daily allowances (RDA) have been established, were not included. Others opposed the "averaging concept" used to establish minimum levels of nutrients in these substitute foods because it would result in lower levels of some nutrients in some substitutes than are present in the foods simulated. The comment from [the National Cheese Institute] contained an alternative proposal for a standard of identity for cheese and cheese product substitutes under the name "Emarine". . . .

Several comments from manufacturers of cheese and cheese product substitutes opposed coined names such as "Golana", "Cheesana", or "Emarine" because such names are not meaningful to consumers and their adoption would require extensive advertising to establish name recognition. Some comments also stated that the term "substitute" is not meaningful to consumers, and in particular, when the term is used in conjunction with the term "imitation" as proposed for substitute products which are nutritionally inferior to the foods they simulate.

As the comments evidence, there is a lack of agreement regarding the most appropriate nomenclature for milk, cream, and cheese substitutes. Under these particular circumstances, the agency believes that honesty and fair dealing are best served by the withdrawal of the proposal and the termination of the rulemaking proceedings. Milk, cream, and cheese substitutes will continue to be governed by the regulations in 21 CFR 101.3(e) regarding the use of the term "imitation" and in 21 CFR 102.5 that set forth the general principles for common or usual names for nonstandardized foods. A food made in semblance of a milk, cream, cheese, or cheese product will be deemed to be an imitation and thus subject to the requirements of section 403(c) of the Federal Food, Drug, and Cosmetic Act if it is nutritionally inferior to the milk, cream, cheese, or cheese product simulated. If it is not nutritionally inferior, it must bear a common or usual name that complies with the provisions of 21 CFR 102.5 which is not false or misleading in any particular or, in the absence of an existing common or usual name, an appropriately descriptive name which is not false or misleading. The label may, in addition, bear a fanciful name that is not misleading.

To ensure that the name of a substitute food is not misleading, the name should ordinarily not include the name of a product subject to a standard of identity unless (1) it complies with the standard of identity, or (2) it is nutritionally inferior to the food simulated and is labeled with the term "imitation". However, in some cases, it may be reasonable and appropriate to include the name of a standardized food or other traditional food in the name of a substitute food in order to provide the consumer with an accurate description. When this is done, the name of the food must be modified such that the nature of the substitute food is clearly described and is clearly distinguished from the food which it resembles and for which it is intended to substitute. The modification of the traditional or standardized food's name must be descriptive of all differences that are not apparent to the consumer. Thus, the procedure for naming these foods will depend on the nature of the substitute food and the manner and extent to which it differs from the food it simulates.

NOTES

1. *Application of Guidelines.* In applying these guidelines, FDA has treated standardized and nonstandardized products differently. For example, FDA promulgated standards of identity for yogurt, lowfat yogurt, and nonfat yogurt, in 21 C.F.R. §§ 131.200, 131.203, and 131.206. The agency also promulgated a standard of identity for low sodium cheddar cheese in 21 C.F.R. § 133.116. In no instance was one of these standardized modified products required to be labeled as a "substitute" or "alternative." When manufacturers began to market nonstandardized versions of other dairy products, however, FDA issued the following letters.

> This replies to your letter of November 20, 1986 concerning a "sour cream product" which conforms to the standard for sour cream in 21 CFR 131.160 except that it contains 8% milkfat whereas the standard requires not less than 18% milkfat..... [O]ne of our concerns with your client's proposed product is that 8% milkfat is not significantly different from standardized sour half and half under 21 CFR 131.185. This standard requires not less than 10.5% milkfat with an absolute minimum of 8.4% milkfat if bulky ingredients are added. You indicated that your client was interested in FDA's position on a 4% milkfat substitute for sour cream.

> Our other concern has been with the word "product" as part of the identity statement. Although we understand that many dislike the word "substitute," we have decided after consideration that "product" is not fully informative in this situation.....

> If your client's proposed product contained only 4% milkfat and were labeled as you proposed in your letter with the change from 8% to 4% milkfat and from "product" to "alternative" the label would read:

> > "Reduced milkfat sour cream alternative
> > contains four percent milkfat
> > regular sour cream contains 18% milkfat."

We would not object to such a label designation. We believe, however, the top line should appear in letters of equal type size and prominence.

Letter from L. R. Lake to P. B. Hutt, February 27, 1987.

... [W]e continue to maintain that the statements "Colby Reduced Fat Cheese," and "Swiss Reduced Fat Cheese", "Mild Cheddar Reduced Fat Cheese", and "Monterey Jack Reduced Fat Cheese" are inappropriate as statements of identity of your products.....

As you know, the fat content, which affects taste and other characteristics, is a major component of the standards of identity for cheeses. In fact the minimum fat content is specified by most cheese standards. Consequently, we believe it is inappropriate for a nonstandardized cheese to bear a reduced fat claim on its label while still using the name of the standardized food if the fat is reduced below the minimum for the standard. This would be of particular concern if the reduction is obtained by substituting, in whole or in part, for mandatory ingredients specified in the standard of identity. This practice does not adequately inform consumers of the differences between the nonstandardized product and the standardized food. Furthermore, a product made in semblance of cheddar cheese but with lower fat than required by the standard for cheddar cheese could easily have characteristics that differ from the standardized product. Consequently the product may not bear both a reduced fat claim and the unmodified standardized name because it would no longer be cheddar cheese. In order to assure that consumers are not confused, some further modification of the name such as "substitute" or "alternative" after the standardized name is necessary.

Appropriate identity statements for [your] nonstandardized cheese products are as follows:

(1) Assuming that these cheeses are nutritionally equivalent to the products they are intended to simulate, i.e., Monterey Jack cheese, Swiss cheese, Cheddar cheese, and Colby cheese, they may be identified as "Monterey Jack cheese substitute," "Swiss cheese substitute," "Cheddar cheese substitute," and "Colby cheese substitute," respectively. The word "alternative" may be used in place of "substitute". We would also be willing to consider other terms that would clearly inform consumers that these are not the standardized cheeses.

(2) On the other hand, if these cheeses are nutritionally inferior and bear the traditional names, such names shall be immediately preceded by the word "imitation" in type of uniform size and prominence.....

Letter from S. A. Miller to J. E. Thompson (July 9, 1987). FDA has also concluded that the name "nonfat ice cream" is illegal. Letter from F. R. Shank to M. S. Thompson (March 13, 1990).

In each instance FDA made clear that the common or usual name it rejected for the nonstandardized version would be acceptable it if were established by a standard of identity. To underscore this policy, FDA has issued temporary permits for the marketing of "light eggnog" in 54 Fed. Reg. 35725 (August 29, 1989), "lite sour cream" in 54 Fed. Reg. 43989 (October 30, 1989), and "light ice cream" in 55 Fed. Reg. 3772 (February 5, 1990).

2. *Sour Cream Dressings.* In 43 Fed. Reg. 11150 and 11226 (March 17, 1978), FDA revoked a stayed standard of identity for sour cream dressing and

repealed the standard of identity for sour half-and-half dressing on the ground that the use of the word "dressing" was insufficient to inform consumers of the difference between the previously standardized products and the new versions of those products.

---

6. NUTRIENT FORTIFICATION OF FOOD

Food fortification began in the 1830s when a French chemist observed the need to add iodine to salt to prevent goiter. It was not until 1917, however, that the use of iodized salt was adopted in the United States. During World War I, Denmark added vitamin A concentrate from fish liver oil to margarine in order to prevent vitamin A deficiency. Irradiation of milk to increase its vitamin D content began in this country about 1930.

The American Medical Association (AMA) Council on Foods and Nutrition spearheaded the early drive to fortify food products. In the early 1930s the AMA endorsed the addition of vitamin D to milk and of iodine to table salt. Later it recommended that fortification should be reserved for exceptional cases where there was convincing evidence of a need for enhanced amounts of the vitamin or mineral in the general food supply and the food vehicles proposed for fortification were suitable and appropriate. 107 J.A.M.A. 39 (1936). Subsequently, it issued a formal statement of policy, 113 J.A.M.A. 681 (1939), which opposed indiscriminate fortification but recognized the addition of vitamin D to milk, vitamin A to substitutes for butter, iodine to table salt, and calcium and iron to cereal products. This statement also encouraged the restoration of vitamins and minerals to natural levels after processing, which led to experimentation with the addition of vitamins to flour and bread.

In mid–1940, the National Academy of Sciences (NAS) established a Subcommittee on Medical Nutrition, which later grew into the Food and Nutrition Board, whose recommendations had a major impact on food fortification. The Board immediately endorsed enrichment of flour and bread with thiamine, iron, and nicotinic acid, and in 1941 added iron, and then calcium and vitamin D, as optional nutrients for enrichment. The Board published its first recommended dietary allowances in 1943. The most recent edition, the 10th, was published in 1989.

Simultaneously FDA was beginning to implement its new authority to promulgate food standards under the FD&C Act. In 5 Fed. Reg. 2746 (August 3, 1940), FDA announced public hearings on proposed standards of identity for flour. At the hearings, the AMA and NAS fortification recommendations were supported by industry witnesses, who urged that FDA standards should mandate fortification of appropriate foods. The enriched flour standard was promulgated in 6 Fed. Reg. 1729 (April 1, 1941), 6 Fed. Reg. 2574 (May 27, 1941). This established the regulatory approach to food fortification that has continued to this day.

During World War II, the War Food Administration was given authority over all food distributed in the United States. War Food Order No. 1 required the enrichment of all bread and rolls. 7 Fed. Reg. 11105 (December 13, 1942). Since the FDA enriched flour standards had already become effective, and many bakers voluntarily enriched their bread, this order reinforced generally existing industry practice. In response to the growing interest in fortified food, FDA issued the following statement of policy.

STATEMENT OF POLICY WITH RESPECT TO THE ADDITION OF NUTRITIVE INGREDIENTS TO FOODS

8 Federal Register 9170 (July 3, 1943).

The labeling or advertising of a food as enriched with vitamins and minerals is an implied promise to consumers that it contains, in addition to the normal constituents of the unenriched food, sufficient vitamins and minerals to make a substantial contribution to the nutritional welfare of persons eating the enriched food in customary amounts. In order to promote honesty and fair dealing by fulfilling this implied promise, it is necessary that the kinds and quantities of enriching ingredients be determined in the light of deficiencies of the various nutritional factors in the diets of the population in general and of significant population groups, the place occupied by the food in such diets, and the suitability and effectiveness of the food as a carrier of the enriching ingredients without undue separation or loss before consumption.

Honesty and fair dealing will best be promoted if such enriched foods as are available to consumers serve to correct such deficiencies and furnish a reasonable margin of safety. Enrichment above the levels required to accomplish this end is wasteful and contrary to the interest of most consumers.... Enrichment of foods with nutrients that are supplied in adequate quantities by the diets of all significant population groups is not only wasteful but tends to confuse consumers as to their nutritional needs.....

Because of the lack of adequate production of a number of foods high in certain nutrients and the lack of consumer knowledge of nutrition, appropriate enrichment of a few foods widely consumed by the population in general or by significant population groups will contribute substantially to the nutritional welfare of consumers and to meeting their expectations of benefit. Enrichment of those foods which are not a substantial part of the diet of any significant group tends to confuse and mislead consumers through giving rise to conflicting claims of nutritional values and by creating an exaggerated impression of the benefits to be derived from the consumption of such foods.

If the customary process of manufacturing a staple food refines it so as to remove significant quantities of nutritive factors present in the natural product from which the food is made, and if the refined food is a suitable and efficient carrier of the factors so removed, some nutritionists advocate the restoration of such factors to the levels of the natural product as the most desirable basis of enrichment. To the extent that restoration serves to correct deficiencies of such factors, it is consistent with the promotion of honesty and fair dealing that refined foods be enriched on a restoration basis. However, when the evidence shows that the restoration levels are too low to correct deficiencies, or that deficiencies exist in other factors for which the refined food is an efficient carrier, the promotion of honesty and fair dealing may require the inclusion of corrective quantities of nutritive factors in the enriched food even though such factors are present in smaller quantities or wholly lacking in the natural product from which the food is made. Similar considerations may require the enrichment of unrefined foods....

Following World War II, food fortification flourished. State laws made enrichment of flour and bread mandatory in most states. The standard of identity for enriched bread, which had been postponed at the request of the War Food Administration, was promulgated in 13 Fed. Reg. 6024 (October 14, 1948), 15 Fed. Reg. 5102 (August 8, 1950), 17 Fed. Reg. 4453 (May 15, 1953). FDA also established standards of identity for other enriched foods such as dairy products, macaroni and noodle products, and margarine. *See* 21 C.F.R. Parts 131, 139, 166.

In 1961, the AMA and NAS issued a joint statement on "General Policy on Addition of Specific Nutrients to Foods," 178 J.A.M.A. 1024 (1961). The statement endorsed fortification where the addition of a particular nutrient to a given food is shown to be advantageous for a significant segment of the consumer population, the food involved is an effective vehicle, and the nutrient addition would not prejudice the achievement of a sound diet.

By the early 1960s, FDA had become concerned about possible overfortification of food. The agency concluded that aggressive enforcement against misleading or blatantly false claims was insufficient. Its proposed revision of the special dietary food regulations in 27 Fed. Reg. 5815 (June 20, 1962) would have permitted the use in fortified food only of specific listed nutrients recognized as both essential in human nutrition and appropriate for supplementation. The comments on this proposal and the decision in the *Dextra Sugar* case, p. 165 *infra*, convinced FDA that an even more restrictive approach was necessary to stem the tide of indiscriminate food fortification. Thus, the regulations it published in 31 Fed. Reg. 8525 (June 18, 1966), 31 Fed. Reg. 15730 (December 14, 1966) included a novel standard of identity which would have drastically limited the number of foods that could lawfully be fortified.

Encouraged by FDA's use of their 1961 statement to support its 1966 approach to restricting food fortification, the AMA and the NAS issued another joint policy statement in 205 J.A.M.A. 868 (1968) to clarify their position. This statement distinguished between modification of traditional foods and fortification of new and formulated foods. It endorsed the addition of nutrients to new and formulated food so that their nutritional value would at least equal the nutritional value of the foods they replace.

Ultimately, a political event transformed public attitudes about food fortification. The Report on the White House Conference on Food, Nutrition and Health in December 1969 contained several recommendations for fortification of existing and new food products which cut directly against FDA's prevailing approach. Agreeing with this conclusion, a special report to the AMA Board of Trustees, 213 J.A.M.A. 272 (1970), stated that malnutrition is probably more prevalent than hunger, although not as dramatic, and noted that half of the households studied by USDA in 1965 failed to meet the NAS recommended dietary allowances for one or more nutrients. The officials who had designed the restrictive strategy of the 1960s had left FDA, and been succeeded by individuals who had helped prepare the Report of the White House Conference. Accordingly, FDA in its 1973 regulations explicitly abandoned its attempt to control food fortification through standards of identity. Instead, the agency developed a new approach, based largely upon requirements for affirmative label disclosure of the nutritional value of foods.

NOTES

1. *AMA and NAS Policy.* The most recent report of the AMA respecting food fortification appears at 242 J.A.M.A. 2335 (1979). For some of the important NAS reports on food fortification, *see* THE PROBLEM OF CHANGING FOOD HABITS, NRC Bull. No. 108 (1943); INADEQUATE DIETS AND NUTRITIONAL DEFICIENCIES IN THE UNITED STATES, NRC Bull. No. 109 (1943); ENRICHMENT OF FLOUR AND BREAD, NRC Bull. No. 110 (1944); THE FACTS ABOUT ENRICHMENT OF FLOUR AND BREAD (1944); CEREAL ENRICHMENT IN PERSPECTIVE (1958); PROPOSED FORTIFICATION POLICY FOR CEREAL–GRAIN PRODUCTS (1974); TECHNOLOGY OF FORTIFICATION OF FOODS (1975). *See also* Miller and Vorist, *Chronologic Changes in the Recommended Dietary Allowances,* 54 J. Am. Dietetic Ass'n 109 (1969); GAO, NATIONAL NUTRITION ISSUES, No. CED–78–7 (1977).

2. *Commentary. See generally* Boudreau, *The Food and Nutrition Board of the National Research Council,* 1 FDC L.Q. 144 (1946); Gunderson, *Improvement in Nutritive Value of Foods,* 7 FDC L.J. 128 (1952); Jolliffe, *The Enrichment Program for White Flour and Bread,* 1 FDC L.Q. 66 (1946); King, *Contributions of Technology to the Nutritional Value of Food,* 16 FDC L.J. 8 (1961); Stare, *Nutrition, Health, and the Law,* 2 FDC L.Q. 382 (1947); Wilder, *The Nutritional Quality of Food and Standards of Identity,* 2 FDC L.Q. 73 (1947); Williams, *Modern Progress in Food Enrichment,* 8 FDC L.J. 357 (1953);

Williams, *The Relationship of the Work of the Food and Nutrition Board, National Research Council, to Food–Law Enforcement,* 10 FDC L.J. 197 (1955); Wilson, *Influence of the Council on Foods and Nutrition, American Medical Association, for Voluntary Food–Industry Standards to Protect and Improve Public Health,* 10 FDC L.J. 140 (1955).

UNITED STATES v. 119 CASES ...
"NEW DEXTRA BRAND FORTIFIED CANE SUGAR"

United States District Court, Southern District of Florida, 1963.
231 F. Supp. 551.

CHOATE, District Judge.

... [T]he Government alleges that the label of the seized article of food contains statements which represent, suggest, and imply:

(a) That the American diet is deficient in vitamins and minerals and that Dextra Sugar will correct this implied deficiency;

(b) That the nutritional content of diets generally is significantly improved by the use of the seized article;

(c) That Dextra Sugar when used in the ordinary diet is significantly more nutritious than any other sugar;

(d) That the article under seizure is of significant value because it restores vitamins and minerals lost in the refinement of cane juice;

(e) That all of the vitamins and minerals in the article are present in nutritionally significant amounts for special dietary use.

The label complained of has the following statements:

(on the front panel of the label)

"New!"

"Dextra Brand Fortified Sugar"

"Fortified with Vitamins and minerals"

(on the backside panel of the label)

"Now, at long last, many of the vitamins and Minerals lost in the refinement of cane juice have been restored to DEXTRA Fortified Cane Sugar."

"Almost any diet can be nutritionally improved by the use of DEXTRA Fortified Cane Sugar in place of sweetening agents containing only "empty" calories—calories unaccompanied by nutrients."

"MORE NUTRITIOUS THAN ANY OTHER SUGAR!"

The representations above referred to are also made by listing 19 ingredients of the seized sugar and *comparing* the amounts of each of these ingredients in the seized sugar with the amounts present in ordinary sugar.

Considering each of these allegations of mislabeling in turn as set forth below, the Court finds as follows:

(a) *That the American diet is deficient in vitamins and minerals and that Dextra Sugar will correct this implied deficiency.* There is no persuasive evidence of any kind that consumers would construe the label statements referring to the fact that the Dextra Brand product is "fortified with vitamins and minerals" to represent, suggest or imply that the "American diet," or their own diets, are significantly deficient in vitamins and minerals, and that use of this product would overcome such a deficiency. The record establishes that consumers are familiar with many food products labeled as vitamin fortified or enriched, including flavorings made largely from sugar, and foods enriched pursuant to standards promulgated by the Federal Food and Drug Administration. In addition, vitamin and mineral supplements, labeled as such, are sold on an unrestricted basis in many types of retail outlets. The Government disclaimed the notion that the mere disclosures on the labels of these products of their fortification with vitamins and minerals are likely to be construed by consumers to involve representations with respect to deficiencies of vitamins and minerals in the food supply. No adequate basis was presented for holding that consumers would react differently to the label of Dextra Brand Fortified Sugar....

(b) *That the nutritional content of diets generally is significantly improved by the use of the seized article.* The Government contends that the added nutrients in Dextra Brand Fortified Sugar are not nutritionally significant because adequate amounts of these nutrients are available in the average "American" diet, and that the added nutrients in the product would be excreted and of no value.... As heretofore noted, a wide variety of vitamin and mineral supplements and vitamin-and mineral-fortified food products are sold in this country, and admittedly the diet of a small but significant portion of our population is deficient in vitamins. The Government and its witnesses do not assert that the offering of these products is per se deceptive to consumers because the vitamins and minerals added therein are of no nutritive value. If the Government's contention were valid, any vitamin-fortified product could be singled out and challenged on the ground that the added vitamins and minerals in any particular food are of no value inasmuch as these nutrients are available elsewhere in the food supply, and the consumers' requirements are met....

(c) *That Dextra Sugar when used in the ordinary diet is significantly more nutritious than any other sugar.* The disclosures of the fact that the product is fortified do not misrepresent the product's nutritional value in comparison with ordinary sugar. The Government has not seriously disputed the fact that the product contains appreciable amounts of vitamin B$_1$ (thiamine), vitamin B$_2$ (riboflavin), vitamin B$_6$ (pyridoxine), niacin, vitamin A, vitamin C, iron and iodine. Nor is there any question that these vitamins and minerals are highly important in human nutrition.... The Government's witnesses have further acknowledged that Dextra Brand Fortified Sugar is an effective carrier of these vitamins and minerals contained in the product and that their potency is in no way diminished by their association with this sugar. On the other hand, ordinary sugar is commonly referred to in the nutritional literature as "empty calories" because of its complete lack of nutrients. The product, when considered in comparison with ordinary sugar, is clearly more nutritious in view of the addition of these important nutrients and is honestly labeled to reflect this fact.

(d) *That the article under seizure is of significant value because it restores vitamins and minerals lost in the refinement of cane juice.* ... Sugar in its natural state is found in sugar cane and sugar beet plants. These plants contain substantial quantities of the vitamins and minerals listed. However, in the refining of sugar, these nutrients are completely lost. The end product, white granulated sugar, is devoid of any vitamins and minerals; it consists entirely of pure carbohydrates.

The process of fortifying sugar with vitamins and minerals was created by a biochemist, John Paul Bartz. Over a fifteen-year period, he developed a method of refining sugar to retain the vitamins and minerals found in natural sugar plants. He also developed a process of adding these vitamins and minerals to ordinary sugar essentially to duplicate the product obtained by use of his refining methods. Claimant uses this latter method for making fortified sugar at this time, inasmuch as the Bartz refining process requires large-scale production to be economically feasible. The implication italicized above rather than false or misleading seems to be true in all respects....

(e) Finally, the Government contends that the labels falsely imply, "That all of the vitamins and minerals in the article are present in nutritionally significant amounts for special dietary use." However, the label makes no specific therapeutic or health claims. The label states "Almost any diet can be nutritionally improved" by using the product "in place of sweetening agents containing only 'empty' calories—calories unaccompanied by nutrients." The Government has failed to show that this statement is factually in error. Moreover, the record affirmatively establishes that the product is nutritionally superior to ordinary sugar which, by the testimony of the Government's own witnesses, is regarded as "empty calories," and that many diets could be improved through the use of this product. On this record, such an innocuous statement, accurate in its terms especially when applied to a significant part of our population, cannot be regarded as false or misleading to consumers. . . .

Although the foregoing disposes of the specific allegations of mislabeling, the Government's principal contention is that the offering of a sugar fortified with vitamins and minerals and labeled to disclose such facts is "per se" false and misleading to consumers. Specifically, the Government charges that the mere mention on the labels of such product that it is fortified with vitamins and minerals infers contrary to fact that (1) the diet available to the American consumer is vitamin deficient; (2) such product might promote the increase of sugar as a part of the American diet contrary to sound nutritional practice; and (3) sugar is not an effective or preferable vehicle of vitamin supplementation. This is the actual thrust of the Government's case to which they have devoted themselves assiduously. . . .

However, the Government failed to present any valid factual support for its principal objection. It introduced no authoritative studies or other data to show that American consumers are receiving all the nutrients they need and that the added vitamins and minerals would be of no value to them. Instead, it relied on the vague opinions of several expert witnesses regarding the adequacy of the nutrients in the average "American diet." This cannot be regarded as persuasive proof. Whatever the usefulness of the concept, "average American diet," in nutritional planning, it is not appropriate for determining allegations of product misbranding. In the first place, the use of an average implies that some persons may be getting more nutrients and others less. Further, such broad measures of nutritional adequacy bear little relationship to the needs of any single individual or groups of individuals.

Moreover, the opinion testimony of the Government's witnesses on this point was not persuasive. The Government's witnesses testified, and claimant did not dispute, that the food supply available to consumers contains adequate amounts of all the vitamins and minerals contained in Dextra Brand Fortified Sugar. But the Government did not establish that consumers were taking full advantage of this availability. Its witnesses testified merely that vitamin and mineral consumption in the United States had risen to the point where *diseases* caused by vitamin deficiencies, such as scurvy and rickets, had virtually disappeared. However, Dextra Brand Fortified Sugar is not sold as a drug to cure or prevent these deficiency diseases, and the evidence established that the consumption levels of vitamins and minerals recommended for good nutrition are considerably higher than the levels required to prevent disease.

Moreover, it was established at the trial that there are a large number of studies, including those published by the United States Government, which disclose that appreciable segments of the population in all parts of the country, and in various economic and age groups, consume substantially less than the allowances of vitamins and minerals recommended by the Food and Nutrition Board of the National Research Council, which allowances are regarded as the standard by most nutritionists....

The testimony of the Government's witnesses disclosed that the real basis of the Government's objection to the sale of fortified sugar is the notion that sugar is not a preferable vehicle for distributing vitamins and minerals. Two Government witnesses expressed the belief that the fortification of sugar might lead to its increased use in place of other foods, which would be contrary to "sound nutritional teachings." Even if this were true, and no proof to the effect that such was the case was offered, it would not justify condemnation of the product. The implementation of sound nutritional principles, and the encouragement or discouragement of the consumption of particular foods in accordance with these principles, are matters for consumer education, not for legal enforcement pursuant to the seizure provisions of the Federal Food, Drug, and Cosmetic Act....

The basic flaw in the Government's case against the product is that it is seeking, under the guise of misbranding charges, to prohibit the sale of a food in the marketplace simply because it is not in sympathy with its use. But the Government's position is clearly untenable. The provisions of the Federal Food, Drug, and Cosmetic Act did not vest in the Food and Drug Administration or any other federal agency the power to determine what foods should be included in the American diet; this is the function of the marketplace....

The court does not undertake to constitute itself an arbiter of nutritional problems involved in determining more or less desirable agents for vending vitamin and mineral supplements to the consumer. The Congress did not provide the necessity for such determination. Neither will the Court permit a federal agency to appoint itself such an arbiter under the guise of prosecuting an action under the Act in question. Plainly, only Congress can or should regulate the use of vitamins and then only to prevent public injury....

NOTE

In affirming the district court, the court of appeals stated only that:

In light of the fact that any purchaser of food products could elect to maintain his present "average" diet with sufficient nutrients in it, or, if he wished, change to a different diet and substitute dextra fortified cane sugar for some other item, we conclude that the trial court was not in error in finding as a fact that the challenged statement was not false and misleading.

United States v. 119 Cases, More or Less, 334 F.2d 238, 239 (5th Cir. 1964) (per curiam).

IMPROVEMENT OF NUTRIENT LEVELS OF ENRICHED FLOUR, ENRICHED SELF–RISING FLOUR, AND ENRICHED BREADS, ROLLS OR BUNS

38 Federal Register 28558 (October 15, 1973).

A notice of proposed rulemaking was published in the FEDERAL REGISTER of April 1, 1970 (35 FR 5412) [doubling the permitted level of iron in enriched flour and bread]....

Three respondents, all physicians, opposed the proposal on the grounds that increased iron in the diet, especially in the case of males, could lead to excessive iron storage and such diseases as cirrhosis of the liver and hemochromatosis or to an increased prevalence of iron storage disorders. As the 1969 White House Conference on Food, Nutrition and Health, the Food and Nutrition Board, National Academy of Sciences–National Research Council, and the Council on Foods and Nutrition, American Medical Association had all recommended increasing the iron content in the diet, the Commissioner deemed it advisable to pursue the matter further....

Accordingly, a notice of proposed rulemaking was published in the FEDERAL REGISTER of December 3, 1971 (36 FR 23074), in which the Commissioner, on his own initiative, made an alternate proposal that the standards of identity for enriched flour, enriched self-rising flour, enriched farina, and enriched bread, rolls or buns be amended to revise the requirements, not only for iron, but also for calcium and vitamins....

The only major opposition to the proposal concerned the increase in iron enrichment. The principal reasons for concern expressed by those opposing the increase in iron enrichment and the Commissioner's conclusions are as follows:

(1) *It was asserted that higher iron intakes might result in chronic iron toxicity in males, manifested by an increase in the prevalence and/or severity of iron storage disorders, particularly hemochromatosis.* On the basis of the comments received, the comprehensive report from FASEB, the AMA review statement and other information, the Commissioner concludes that the proposed increase in the iron content of enriched flours and enriched bread, rolls or buns will not jeopardize the health of normal males (or females), and that the additional iron will not increase the incidence of hemochromatosis or other hereditary iron storage disorders. Regarding the hypothesis that additional dietary iron may accelerate the accumulation of iron in the latent or undiagnosed hemochromatotic, the Commissioner concludes that there is no substantial evidence to prove or disprove the hypothesis....

(2) *Doubts were expressed as to the need for or efficacy of the iron enrichment as proposed.* ... The Commissioner initiated reexaminations of each of these questions within the Food and Drug Administration to determine if the stated conclusions of such groups as the AMA Council on Foods and Nutrition, the NAS–NRC Food and Nutrition Board, and the White House Conference on Food, Nutrition, and Health remained valid. The Commissioner's conclusions are discussed below:

(a) There has been a steadily increasing number of studies on specific population groups indicating substantial prevalences of iron deficiency anemia in various sex, age, and physiologic groups. There have been no studies to the contrary....

(b) There is general agreement that severe iron deficiency anemia is debilitating and, in rare cases, that it can be extremely serious and even fatal; that sufficient dietary iron leads to a maximum hemoglobin level generally thought of as being optimal for good health; and that marked iron deficiency is harmful to both pregnant women and the newborn.... There remains a considerable lack of precise knowledge in the area of the clinical significance of mild to moderate anemia.... Nevertheless, most (but not all) efforts to explore this area have indicated adverse effects of mild to moderate anemia.

(c) ... The Commissioner realizes that a fixed degree of bioavailability for any specific source of iron does not exist because of individual variability from person to person and extensive variations due to the effect of the composition of the total diet on bioavailability.... The Commissioner concludes that there is a need to define sources of iron with reasonable bioavailability characteristics, but does not feel that it is in the public interest to delay publication of these regulations to await the outcome of evaluation of the single matter of acceptable sources of iron. This matter will be handled as a separate action upon completion of the evaluation....

(e) Concerning the matter as to whether cereal products generally are the most suitable vehicles for iron enrichment, the Commissioner notes that cereal-based foods, particularly bread and other products made from wheat flour, continue to be the most uniformly consumed major foods in the American diet (except for meat, poultry and fish which are not amenable to enrichment).... The Commissioner also notes that specific target population groups such as adult women during their menstrual life continue to consume significant quantities of bread, rolls and biscuits. There also are no other classes of foods the consumption of which is characteristically high in specific target groups except for milk and milk-based products in infancy and childhood....

Accordingly, having considered the comments received and other relevant information, the Commissioner concludes that it will promote honesty and fair dealing in the interests of consumers to rule jointly on the proposals published in the FEDERAL REGISTERS of April 1, 1970 (35 FR 5412), and December 3, 1971 (36 FR 23074), by adopting the proposed amendments as modified....

IRON FORTIFICATION OF FLOUR AND BREAD: TENTATIVE ORDER

42 Federal Register 59513 (November 18, 1977).

Thirty objections to the final order were received, leading the Commissioner to conclude in his order published in the FEDERAL REGISTER of February 11, 1974 (39 FR 5188), that, in light of questions regarding the public health raised by members of the medical profession opposing the increase in added iron content of flour and bread, a formal evidentiary public hearing on the matter was justified.... Having considered the evidence received at the hearing, the Hearing Examiner's Recommended Decision and all the written arguments that were filed, the Commission is issuing this tentative order to withdraw the stayed provisions of the amendments.

One respondent ... challenged the authority of the Commissioner to promulgate any identity standards whose purpose is to correct for dietary deficiencies unrelated to the standard. The basis for Dr. Crosby's argument is the contention that the only purpose of standards promulgated pursuant to section 401 is to prevent consumer fraud. Although the purpose of the present document is to withdraw the stayed augmented-iron provisions of the regulation, the Commissioner is not basing the withdrawal upon this theory. On the contrary, to read section 401 so narrowly would be counter to the purposes of the act as a whole....

The first major contested issue at the hearing was the need for additional iron in the diet. The Food and Drug Administration produced a number of witnesses and studies which, it argues, point to the conclusion of need for additional iron in the diet....

The Commissioner concludes that, whereas available data show that there is a need for additional iron for two well-defined groups (preschool infants and pregnant women), the need has not been proven to be as great or as general as the proponents of the amendments have argued. In addition, the Commissioner concludes that there are far better ways of reaching those persons in need of additional iron than through fortification of bread. Bread is not particularly effective as a supplement to the diet of women of child-bearing age and preschool children, the groups most in need of additional iron. Surely, it would be more effective to reach people in need, once these people have been identified, by directing education programs to them, by improving their overall diet, and by encouraging their use of foods naturally high in iron or foods specially designed for them. Additional fortification of bread, which would subject the entire population, including those voluntarily exposed, to increased dietary iron, would seem to be an inefficient and—in light of unresolved safety questions—a possibly more dangerous approach to take....

Drs. Goldsmith and Darby testified that, in their opinions, additional iron enrichment in bread will be effective in improving the iron balance of those people who are iron-deficient. On the other hand, Dr. Finch frankly stated that he did not know how effective the increased fortification would be. A study conducted by Dr. P. C. Elwood, in Cardiff, Wales, showed little effect from iron enrichment of bread. In light of the small iron quantities involved in his inquiry, as compared to the amounts with which bread would be fortified under the stayed provisions of the present regulation, this study cannot be given much weight. However, the Elwood study, as the only human efficacy study on the record involving iron-fortified bread, is not contradicted by adequate studies showing the effectiveness of iron fortification of bread on the iron balance of those who are iron-deficient....

Therefore, the Commissioner concludes that, before he can make a finding of efficacy, more studies will have to be done. The issue of efficacy is rendered all the more important in light of the issue of safety.

A substantial number of experts who made their views known on the record at the hearing testified that (a) in their view the augmentations are not safe or (b) have not been proven safe....

The Food and Drug Administration adduced testimony to the contrary from other distinguished physicians, such as Drs. William Darby, Richard MacDonald, and Grace Goldsmith. Nevertheless, the Commissioner finds that, with respect to some of the safety concerns voiced by the opponents of the stayed provisions of the regulations, the data on the record and the testimony at the hearing do not establish the safety of the iron augmentation....

This hearing was most concerned about two groups, both of which are small in proportion to the population—those in need of additional iron and those who may be harmed by increased iron in their diet. Assuming, arguendo, the effectiveness of iron fortification of bread, the issue becomes whether government policy should promote involuntary exposure in order to ameliorate iron deficiency. In balancing benefits against risks, the defenselessness of those potentially at risk from iron overage due to involuntary exposure must be weighed heavily, in view of the availability of an alternative strategy: selective targeting of those in need.

The Commissioner concludes that, on the present record, the increased iron levels should not be approved, since, among other things, the burden of proving them safe has not been satisfied. Better data must be obtained before what amounts to an uncontrolled study on the United States population is attempted. The Commissioner emphasizes that in his view the increased iron levels have not been proven unsafe either; but enough serious questions have been raised to prevent his approval of the increased levels at this time.

NOTES

1. *Further Proceedings.* In 43 Fed. Reg. 38575 (August 29, 1978), FDA issued findings of fact, conclusions, and a final order. The Commissioner sought to relieve concern that his tentative order would deter further research in iron fortification:

> The Commissioner has no intention to discourage research, and no control over the research budgets of food manufacturers. If, as seems likely, this exception is intended to present the Commissioner with an opportunity to narrow the scope of his final order, he accepts the opportunity to do so. The order in this proceeding results from the finding that a proposed fortification has not been proven to be safe, effective, or needed. In another situation, if the evidence supporting the safety, effectiveness, or necessity of the fortifying ingredient is more favorable to the proposed change, the Commissioner may decide another way....

> The requirement of "adequate studies" in the tentative order should be seen as applying in situations where serious concern about the safety of a proposed ingredient has been voiced and where the needed amount of that ingredient is in dispute. Also, this requirement will apply especially in cases where the food in question is a widely eaten staple product....

The Commissioner also rejected criticism of his proposal for attempting to "supplement" only the diets of individuals known to be at risk:

> The Commissioner believes that this idea cannot be rejected until it has been tried, although he recognizes that there may be difficulties with it. Where there are safety questions of the sort set forth in the tentative order, educational programs for people at risk and the promotion of iron supplementation or the consumption of high-iron-content foods present possible alternatives to the assumption of involuntary risks by others....

2. *Anemia in Child–Bearing Women.* In 53 Fed. Reg. 51009 (December 19, 1988), FDA announced the establishment of a study by the Federation of American Societies for Experimental Biology (FASEB) on how iron deficiency anemia in women of childbearing age can be managed without "possible harmful effects of ingestion of large amounts of iron-rich foods or dietary supplements."

After FDA decided in 1973 to abandon its 1966 attempt to restrict food fortification through food standards, it published in 39 Fed. Reg. 20900 (June 14, 1974) proposed regulations establishing principles governing the addition of nutrients to food. Based on comments on this proposal and information from hearings on food labeling and nutrition which it had conducted in 1978, FDA issued its final food fortification policy in 45 Fed. Reg. 6314 (January 25, 1980), codified in 21 C.F.R. § 104.20. The agency expressed concern that, in the absence of a unifying set of principles, random and arbitrary fortification of foods is likely. This may result in overfortification with some nutrients which are inexpensive and easy to add, and underfortification with others. Yet promulgation of standards of identity for fortification of all foods would be unnecessarily inflexible. Accordingly, FDA decided to adopt a statement of general principles respecting food fortification.

The June 1974 proposal had incorporated enforcement mechanisms to assure compliance with the fortification principles. FDA had proposed that any fortified food that did not comply with the proposed policy would be required to bear the statement that "the addition of ____ to this product has been determined by the U.S. government to be unnecessary and inappropriate and does not increase the dietary value of the food." Claims that a product has been fortified would have been prohibited unless the fortification amounted to at least 10 percent of the U.S. RDA in a serving. The final policy statement, however, eliminated these restrictions because, according to FDA, a substantive rule covering all aspects of fortification and labeling of fortified foods was not feasible at that time. Thus, the 1980 policy statement represents only guidelines that are not directly enforceable by FDA as legal requirements.

The 1980 policy acknowledges that fortification can be an effective way of maintaining and improving the nutritional quality of the food supply, but it emphasizes that FDA considers fortification of the following foods inappropriate: fresh produce; meat, poultry, or fish products; sugar; and snack foods such as candies and carbonated beverages. The agency states that snack foods are not considered by the public as components of meals or as making a nutritional contribution to the diet, and neither the public nor the scientific community has considered snack foods to be appropriate carriers for added nutrients. The statement then enunciates five principles for appropriate food fortification.

1. *To correct dietary insufficiency.* FDA states that any of 22 listed nutrients may appropriately be added to a food to correct a dietary insufficiency recognized by the scientific community to exist and known to result in nutritional deficiency disease. Although food manufacturers are free to implement this principle on their own, they are urged to contact FDA before doing so. FDA states that the addition of specific nutrients to food may continue to be important in preventing

nutrient deficiency diseases where sufficient information is available to identify a nutritional problem, to define affected population groups, and to designate suitable foods to act as vehicles.

2. *To restore lost nutrients.* FDA recognizes that it is appropriate to add any of the 22 listed nutrients to a food to restore them to levels representative of the food prior to storage, handling, and processing, but only if they have been lost in a "measurable amount," *i.e.*, at least 2 percent of the U.S. RDA per serving. If restoration is undertaken, all measurably depleted nutrients are to be restored.

3. *To balance calories with nutrients.* In the most controversial portion of its policy statement, FDA states that addition of nutrients is appropriate to balance the vitamin, mineral, and protein content with the total caloric content of the food. For purposes of implementing this principle, FDA adopts a standard daily caloric intake of 2000 kilocalories as contrasted with 2800 kilocalories that had been reflected in the 1974 proposal. Three important limitations are placed upon this principle. First, this principle applies only where a serving of the food contains at least 40 kilocalories. Second, each of the 22 listed nutrients must be added in the amount necessary to achieve nutrient balance (except that vitamin D, iodine, and protein, are optional because of the relatively narrow range of safety for vitamin D and because iodine and protein are already consumed in sufficient quantities in the average diet). Third, only the amount needed to achieve the proper nutrient density is to be added.

4. *To avoid nutritional inferiority.* Under current FDA regulations, p. 150 *supra,* a new food that resembles, and is intended to substitute for, another food must be labeled as an "imitation" if it is nutritionally inferior. This principle encourages the common practice of adding nutrients to new substitute foods in order to avoid the "imitation" label.

5. *To comply with other regulations.* This principle permits nutrient addition to comply with any requirements found in existing standards of identity, nutrition quality guidelines, and regulations establishing common or usual names for foods.

NOTES

1. *Protein–Nutrient Balance.* For an alternative proposal to permit balanced fortification on the basis of protein rather than calories, *see* Lachance, *Nutrification: A Concept for Assuring Nutritional Quality by Primary Intervention in Feeding Systems,* 20 J. Agric. Food Chem. 522 (1972); Lachance *et al., Balanced Nutrition through Food Processor Practice of Nutrification,* 26 Food Tech., No. 6, at 30 (1972). *See also* Johnson, *Rationale for Constraints on Nutrient Additions,* 34 FDC L.J. 426 (1979).

2. *Congressional Oversight.* The application of the FDA's 1980 food fortification policy statement to the fortification of flour and bread was explored in "Fortification of Cereal Grains with Essential Vitamins and Minerals," Hearing Before the Subcomm. on Natural Resources, Agriculture Research, and Envi-

ronment of the House Comm. on Science and Technology, 97th Cong., 2d Sess. (1982).

3. *Fortification of Orange and Grapefruit Juice.* In 52 Fed. Reg. 31667 (August 21, 1987), FDA issued an advisory opinion on whether standardized orange juice or grapefruit juice may lawfully be fortified in a manner not provided for in the standard of identity. The agency opined that the product could lawfully be fortified as long as the labeling did not represent it as the standardized food and the addition of the nutrients was consistent with the 1980 fortification policy.

FDA REGULATION OF INFANT FORMULAS

FDA's original special dietary food regulations included provisions for the labeling of infant food, including infant formulas. Proposed revisions of those regulations, 27 Fed. Reg. 5815 (June 20, 1962), 31 Fed. Reg. 8521 (June 18, 1966), were the subject of the 1968–1969 FDA hearings, and final regulations were promulgated in 35 Fed. Reg. 16737 (October 29, 1970), 36 Fed. Reg. 23553 (December 10, 1971), now codified in 21 C.F.R. § 105.65.

In mid–1979, Syntex Laboratories recalled three soy protein-based infant formulas that, because of an inadequate level of chlorine, resulted in a number of cases of metabolic alkalosis, an abnormal condition generally characterized in infants by a failure to thrive. "Infant Formulas Being Recalled," FDA Talk Paper No. T79–34 (August 2, 1979). Following a public meeting, 45 Fed. Reg. 6702 (January 29, 1980), FDA published interim guidelines for the nutrient composition of infant formulas in 45 Fed. Reg. 17206 (March 18, 1980). Not satisfied with this response, Congress enacted the Infant Formula Act of 1980, 94 Stat. 1190, adding Section 412 to the FD&C Act. Section 412(g) enacted the FDA interim guidelines into law, with slight modifications. The 1980 Act also enlarged FDA's regulatory authority over infant formulas.

Pursuant to the 1980 Act, FDA established reporting requirements in 45 Fed. Reg. 77136 (November 21, 1980); quality control procedures in 45 Fed. Reg. 86362 (December 30, 1980), 47 Fed. Reg. 17016 (April 20, 1982); recall requirements in 47 Fed. Reg. 2331 (January 15, 1982), 47 Fed. Reg. 18832 (April 30, 1982); exemptions in 48 Fed. Reg. 31875 (July 12, 1983), 50 Fed. Reg. 48183 (November 22, 1985); labeling requirements in 48 Fed. Reg. 31880 (July 12, 1983), 50 Fed. Reg. 1833 (January 14, 1985); and nutrient requirements in 49 Fed. Reg. 14396 (April 11, 1984), 50 Fed. Reg. 45106 (October 30, 1985).

The quality control and recordkeeping requirements of these regulations were unsuccessfully challenged by a consortium of citizen organizations in *Formula v. Heckler*, 779 F.2d 743 (D.C. Cir. 1985). The organizations then turned to Congress for relief. Section 4014 of the Anti–Drug Abuse Act of 1986, 100 Stat. 3207, amended section 412 of the FD&C Act to add additional requirements. FDA has implemented the 1986 Amendments by amending the recall regulations in 52 Fed. Reg. 30171 (August 13, 1987), 54 Fed. Reg. 4006 (January 27, 1989), and 54 Fed. Reg. 11518 (March 21, 1989), and by proposing detailed new microbiological testing and record retention requirements in 54 Fed. Reg. 3783 (January 26, 1989). The infant formula regulations are codified in 21 C.F.R. Part 107.

7. NUTRITIONAL QUALITY GUIDELINES

In 1970, FDA Commissioner Charles Edwards announced a new agency initiative in regulating the nutritional quality of foods:

> We proposed to establish ... nutritional guidelines for selected classes of foods.... [T]entatively we have in mind formulated main dishes; new foods, such as analogs for meat products, dairy products and fruit juices; staples that are important in the diet of ethnic groups in which malnutrition has been found through the surveys.

> We do not plan to set formal standards of nutritional quality. If guidelines are issued, this should be accomplished within a very small number of years, in part, because it will be done on a class basis rather than an individual food basis. We would then expect that commercial pressures would cause processors to use the guidelines in formulating and designing their products. If they do so extensively, there will be no reason to consider a mandatory mechanism.

"Regulatory Policies of the FDA," Hearings Before a Subcomm. of the House Comm. on Government Operations, 91st Cong., 2d Sess. (1970).

NUTRITIONAL QUALITY GUIDELINES FOR FOODS
21 C.F.R. Part 104.

§ 104.5 General Principles

(a) A nutritional quality guideline prescribes the minimum level or range of nutrient composition (nutritional quality) appropriate for a given class of food.

(b) Labeling for a product which complies with all of the requirements of the nutritional quality guideline established for its class of food may state "This product provides nutrients in amounts appropriate for this class of food as determined by the U.S. Government." ...

(d) No claim or statement may be made on the label or in labeling representing, suggesting, or implying any nutritional or other differences between a product to which nutrient addition has or has not been made in order to meet the guideline, except that a nutrient addition shall be declared in the ingredient statement....

(f) A product within a class of food for which a nutritional quality guideline has been established and to which has been added a discrete nutrient either for which no minimum nutrient level or nutrient range or other allowance has been established as appropriate in the nutritional quality guideline, or at a level that exceeds any maximum established as appropriate in the guideline, shall be ineligible to bear the guideline statement provided for in paragraph (b) of this section, and such a product shall also be deemed to be misbranded under the act unless the label and all labeling bear the following prominent and conspicuous statement: "The addition of ___ to" (or "The addition of ___ at the level contained in") this product has been determined by the U.S. Government to be unnecessary and inappropriate and does not increase the dietary value of the food," the blank to be filled in with the common or usual name of the nutrient(s) involved....

§ 104.47 Frozen "heat and serve" dinner

(a) A product, for which a common or usual name is established in § 102.26 of this chapter, in order to be eligible to bear the guideline statement set forth at § 104.5(b), shall contain at least the following three components:

(1) One or more sources of protein derived from meat, poultry, fish, cheese, or eggs.

(2) One or more vegetables or vegetable mixtures other than potatoes, rice, or cereal-based product.

(3) Potatoes, rice, or cereal-based product (other than bread or rolls) or another vegetable or vegetable mixture.

(b) The three or more components named in paragraph (a) of this section, including their sauces, gravies, breading, etc.:

(1) Shall contribute not less than the minimum levels of nutrients prescribed in paragraph (d) of this section.

(2) Shall be selected so that one or more of the listed protein sources of paragraph (a)(1) of this section ... shall provide not less than 70 percent of the total protein supplied by the components named in paragraph (a) of this section.

(c) If it is necessary to add any nutrient(s) in order to meet the minimum nutrient levels prescribed in paragraph (d) of this section, the addition of each such nutrient may not result in a total nutrient level exceeding 150 percent of the minimum level prescribed. Nutrients used for such addition shall be biologically available in the final product.

(d) Minimum levels of nutrients for a frozen "heat and serve" dinner are as follows:

Minimum Levels for Frozen "Heat and Serve" Dinner

Nutrient	For Each 100 Calories (kcal) of the Total Components Specified Nutrient in Par. (a)	For the Total Components Specified in Par. (a)
Protein, grams	4.60	16.0
Vitamin A, IU	150.00	520.00
Thiamine, mg	.05	.2
Riboflavin, mg	.06	.2

Nutrient	For Each 100 Calories (kcal) of the Total Components Specified Nutrient in Par. (a)	For the Total Components Specified in Par. (a)
Niacin, mg	.99	3.4
Pantothenic acid, mg	.32	1.1
Vitamin, B^6, mg	.15	.5
Vitamin, B^{12}, mcg	.33	1.1
Iron, mg	.62	2.2

(1) A frozen "heat and serve" dinner prepared from conventional food ingredients listed in paragraph (a) of this section will also contain folic acid, magnesium, iodine, calcium, and zinc....

(3) When technologically practicable, iodized salt shall be used or iodine shall be present at a level equivalent to that which would be present if iodized salt were used in the manufacture of the product.

(4) When technologically practicable, product components and ingredients shall be selected to obtain the desirable calcium to phosphorus ratio of 1:1....

NOTES

1. *Compared to Standards of Identity.* How does this regulation differ from a standard of identity?

2. *Other Proposed Guidelines.* In addition to the nutrition quality guideline for frozen convenience dinners, FDA proposed guidelines for breakfast beverage products, 39 Fed. Reg. 20895 (June 14, 1974); fortified hot breakfast cereals, 39 Fed. Reg. 20896 (June 14, 1974); fortified ready-to-eat breakfast cereals, 39 Fed. Reg. 20898 (June 14, 1974); formulated meal replacements, 39 Fed. Reg. 20905 (June 14, 1974); and main dish products, 39 Fed. Reg. 20906 (June 14, 1974). The agency initially announced that it was holding these proposals in abeyance pending publication of a final food fortification policy, which appeared at 45 Fed. Reg. 6314 (January 25, 1980), but later withdrew them all in 51 Fed. Reg. 15653 (April 25, 1986).

---

8. DISEASE PREVENTION CLAIMS

Since 1938, a major FDA enforcement priority has been to prevent false or misleading nutrition claims in food labeling. As illustrated at p. 204 *infra*, a key component of the agency's strategy has been to classify disease prevention claims as drug claims, thus permitting summary disposition of enforcement actions based on expert affidavits that the challenged product is not "generally recognized" as safe and effective. Where a manufacturer made no explicit disease prevention claim, however, this gambit often did not work. And as the evidence of the important relationships between diet and disease has mounted, the agency has had to reconsider even its traditional ban on specific disease prevention claims for food.

PETER BARTON HUTT,
GOVERNMENT REGULATION OF HEALTH CLAIMS IN
FOOD LABELING AND ADVERTISING

41 Food Drug Cosmetic Law Journal 3 (1986).

... In February 1964, President Johnson announced the formation
of a Commission on Heart Disease, Cancer, and Stroke with the mission
of recommending "steps to reduce the incidence of these diseases
through new knowledge and more complete utilization of the medical
knowledge we already have." Ten months later, the Commission issued
its report, recommending major new research on these three diseases.
The source paper on athlerosclerosis stated that "diet, particularly the
amount and kind of fat in it, is considered to have a major influence on
atherogenesis." It noted that research suggested that "modification of
the American diet can be an effective way to reduce the incidence of
coronary heart disease."

Following the report of the Commission, further research and study
on the relation of diet to health was stimulated throughout the country.
The results became apparent with publication of the first edition of
"Dietary Goals for the United States" by the Senate Select Committee
on Nutrition and Human Needs in February 1977. Similar reports
immediately followed:

—The Second Edition of the Senate Committee's Dietary Goals.

—The Report of the DHEW Task Force on Prevention.

—Recommendations for a Prudent Diet by the American
Health Foundation.

—The DHEW Surgeon General's Report on "Healthy People."

—The DHEW Conference on Objectives for the Nation in
Promoting Health and Preventing Disease.

—The National Cancer Institute's Statement on Diet, Nutrition and Cancer.

—The American Medical Association's Concepts of Nutrition
and Health.

—The Department of Agriculture's (USDA) Hassle–Free Guide
to a Better Diet.

—The Consensus Papers of the American Society for Clinical
Nutrition.

—The Joint USDA/DHEW Dietary Guidelines for Americans.

—The National Academy of Sciences (NAS) Food and Nutrition
Board's Report on Healthful Diets.

These reports in turn fostered a deeper interest in federal research on
diet and health and nutrition education. The Comptroller General of
the United States, through the General Accounting Office (GAO),

strongly urged federal agencies to adopt and implement a coordinated national nutrition policy.

... This information on the relationship between diet and health had an impact on Congress as well as FDA. In 1976, Congress enacted the National Consumer Health Information and Health Promotion Act. Under this statute, the Secretary of Health and Human Services (HHS) was required to implement a wide variety of programs designed to prevent disease and promote health. Education relating to nutrition was explicitly included. In 1984, Congress established an Office of Disease Prevention and Health Promotion in the Office of the HHS Assistant Secretary for Health, to implement these requirements.

In 1978, as part of the Biomedical Research and Research Training Amendments, Congress added section 301(b)(3) to the Public Health Service Act to require research and studies on the role of human nutrition in the prevention and treatment of disease:

(3) The Secretary shall conduct and may support through grants and contracts research and studies on human nutrition, with particular emphasis on the role of nutrition in the prevention and treatment of disease and on the maintenance and promotion of health, and programs for the dissemination of information respecting human nutrition to health professionals and the public. In carrying out activities under this paragraph, the Secretary shall provide for the coordination of such of these activities as are performed by the different divisions within the Department of Health and Human Services and shall consult with entities of the Federal Government, outside of the Department of Health and Human Services, engaged in comparable activities.

The Assistant Secretary for Health had already delegated to FDA all functions under section 301 of the Public Health Service Act which relate to the functions of FDA, and thus FDA was equally responsible for carrying out the provisions of this statute. As part of the Health Services and Centers Amendments of 1978, Congress also required the Secretary of Health and Human Services to submit to Congress every three years a "national disease prevention data profile" which must include "the behavioral determinants of health of the population of the United States including ... nutritional and dietary habits."

Beginning in 1946, Congress has also enacted a wide variety of statutory provisions relating to the use of food to prevent or treat disease, as part of the National School Lunch Act of 1946 and the Child Nutrition Act of 1966. Pursuant to these statutory provisions, USDA administered six major food programs, one of which (the Child Nutrition Program) includes six substantial programs. Each of these embodied a congressional determination of the importance of sound nutrition to good health. The Nutrition Education and Training Program, however, is of particular importance to the matter of health claims for food.

In 1975, Congress amended the Child Nutrition Act to authorize and direct "projects to teach schoolchildren the nutritional value of foods and the relationship of nutrition to human health." As part of the National School Lunch Act and Child Nutrition Amendments of 1977, Congress enacted a broad program for nutrition education and training. This statute established a program of nutrition education for school children, school food service personnel, parents, and teachers. The law broadly authorized education about "the relationship between food, nutrition, and health." The program was specifically defined to include information to allow individuals to "maximize their well-being through food consumption practices" and to understand "the relationship between food and human health."

That same year, as part of the Food and Agriculture Act of 1977, Congress established a national food and human nutrition research program in USDA. Congress found that:

> [T]here is increasing evidence of a relationship between diet and many of the leading causes of death in the United States; that improved nutrition is an integral component of preventive health care; that there is a serious need for research on the chronic effects of diet on degenerative diseases and related disorders.

———

PETER BARTON HUTT, HEALTH CLAIMS FOR FOODS—AN AMERICAN PERSPECTIVE

Kellogg Nutrition Symposium, Toronto, Canada.
April 1986.

For purposes of analysis, it is useful to differentiate among three separate types of health claims for food products: implicit health claims, general health claims, and explicit health claims. Implicit health claims are made whenever labelling refers to the nutrient content of a food, whether that content results from nutrients that are naturally present in the food or nutrients that are added through fortification. Nutrition labelling, in short, is an inherent health claim. General health claims can, and often are, made in a wide variety of ways. Statements that a food is nutritious, or good for you, or will promote health, are examples of general health claims frequently found in labelling and advertising. Explicit health claims, in contrast, have infrequently been found in food labelling and advertising until quite recently. Explicit health claims include statements that a food will help prevent specific diseases, such as heart disease and cancer.

... FDA has long approved implicit health claims for food products in the form of accurate information about the composition of food. Such information includes not just the ingredients, but specific information about the micronutrient and macronutrient content as well. Nor has FDA sought to prevent general health claims, that a food is nutritious or healthful. But for many years, FDA drew the line at explicit health claims.

The primary driving force behind this policy was, of course, the prevention of fraud. With the long history of unwarranted claims for dietary supplement and food products, FDA was all too familiar with the regulatory problems that could occur if explicit health claims were permitted.....

The FDA prohibition against explicit health claims in food labeling meant that the United States public received its information on diet and health from other, usually more unreliable, sources.... Beginning in the 1960s, books with false and even harmful information about nutrition flooded the market. Misinformation was disseminated through every conceivable medium except the ones over which the government does in fact have control—food labelling and advertising. Only if a specific book was used as promotional material to sell a product did the government have jurisdiction to regulate the content of that book, and even then the precise contours of that regulatory authority remained uncertain in light of the constitutional right to a free press.

Thus, FDA was faced, in the early 1980s, with two choices. First, it could continue its prohibition against explicit health claims, and thus allow books, newspapers, television, and other media to remain the sole source of information to the United States public on diet and health. Second, it could modify that position, but retain regulatory control over the type of explicit health claims that could be made, and thus assure that at least some of the explicit health claims made to the United States public are reliable, accurate, and truthful.

As often occurs in this kind of situation, the decision was made for FDA, by outside forces, and not by FDA itself. Throughout the 1970s, the FTC had sided with FDA in its continuing opposition to explicit health claims. With the change of administration in the early 1980s, however, the FTC began to change its position on this matter. Convinced that truthful advertising is not only protected under the Constitution but also is genuinely beneficial to the public, the FTC concluded that explicit health claims for food should be permitted where they are in fact accurate and truthful.

The first test of this issue in the United States occurred when Kellogg began to promote its All–Bran Cereal product to reduce the risk of cancer, in October 1984. This claim, based upon authoritative reports issued in 1982 and 1984 by two of the most respected scientific organizations in the United States—the National Academy of Sciences and the National Cancer Institute—was neither false nor misleading. It was, in fact, specifically endorsed by the National Cancer Institute. Seizing the occasion, representatives of the FTC made numerous speeches, in the fall of 1984, endorsing this approach and encouraging a wide range of explicit health claims designed to educate the United

States public about the relationship between diet and health. Faced with responsible claims, specific NCI endorsement, and then FTC encouragement, FDA could do nothing. The matter had been taken out of its hands.

In March 1985, FDA announced a new policy. No longer would it oppose all forms of explicit health claims for food. The Agency was prepared to permit such claims, for the first time, as part of the disease prevention programs of the United States Public Health Service. FDA recognized that food labelling could properly be used as a means of conveying health messages to the United States public, as long as the Agency's ability to regulate health fraud was not diminished or compromised.

To implement this new policy, FDA adopted four general enforcement principles. First, explicit health claims must be based upon a consensus of medical and scientific information. Second, explicit health claims must emphasize that good nutrition is a function of total diet. Third, the wording of explicit health claims should be reasonably uniform from product to product in order to make it more understandable and less confusing to consumers. Fourth, dietary "power races" should be prevented. Within these four principles, FDA said that it was prepared to allow explicit health claims....

FOOD LABELING; PUBLIC HEALTH MESSAGES ON FOOD LABELS AND LABELING
52 Federal Register 28843 (August 4, 1987).

FDA believes that it is worthwhile to consider new ways to inform and educate the general public or target subpopulations concerning the relationship between diet and health. The agency believes that, if proper criteria are followed, it is possible to use the food label to communicate more explicit health-related information. The agency acknowledges that in the past, foods labeled with information of this type could have been viewed as subject to action under 21 CFR 101.9(i) and the new drug provisions of the act. The agency's current view is that appropriate health messages would not be inconsistent with either of these provisions.....

The agency's criteria for evaluating health-related claims and information on food labeling are as follows:

1. Information on the labeling must be truthful and not misleading to the consumer. The information should not imply that a particular food be used as part of a drug-like treatment or therapy oriented approach to health care. Information on food labeling must not over emphasize or distort the role of a food in enhancing good health. The term "health" includes specific health problems, including disease.

2. The information should be based on and be consistent with valid, reliable, scientific evidence that is publically [sic] available (prior to any health related claim being made), including data derived from clinical and other studies performed and evaluated by persons qualified by experience and training to evaluate such studies, and should conform to generally recognized medical and nutritional principles. Preliminary findings should be confirmed. Conclusions supported by a less-than-clear data may prove in time to be correct, but are not appropriate for use on food labeling if they do not reflect the weight of scientific evidence. . . .

3. Available information regarding the relationship between nutrition and health shows that good nutrition is a function, not of specific foods, but of total diet over time. Appropriate information on food labeling should describe the role of a specific food or a specific ingredient in terms that are consistent with generally recognized medical and nutritional principles for a sound total dietary pattern. The dietary characteristics of the food must be consistent with the message being used.

4. The use of health-related information constitutes a nutritional claim that triggers the requirements of FDA's regulations regarding nutrition labeling. Therefore, any product bearing health-related information must comply with the nutrition labeling requirements found in 21 CFR 101.9. However, the use of health-related information in conformity with the agency's criteria will not be deemed misbranding within the meaning of 21 CFR 101.9(i) and will not be deemed to invoke the new drug provisions of the act.

Manufacturers may make health-related claims on food labels that conform to these guidelines without prior approval, with the understanding that, if a manufacturer fails to adhere to the criteria, the product and the manufacturer's activity may be subject to regulatory action. FDA welcomes discussions with any manufacturer who wishes to consult with the agency on health-related claims before making changes in existing labeling.

NOTES

1. *Authoritative Reports.* The most authoritative current statements on the relationship of diet to health and disease are the SURGEON GENERAL'S REPORT ON NUTRITION AND HEALTH, DHHS (PHS) Pub. No. 88–50210 (1988), and National Academy of Sciences, DIET AND HEALTH: IMPLICATIONS FOR REDUCING CHRONIC DISEASE RISK (1989). HHS is currently engaged in a project to set national health objectives for the year 2000. *Health Objectives for the Nation,* 38 Morbidity and Mortality Weekly Rep. 629 (September 22, 1989).

2. *Congressional Action.* Following hearings at which FDA explained its new policy, "FDA Proposals to Permit the Use of Disease–Specific Health Claims on Food Labels," Hearing Before a Subcomm. of the House Comm. on Government Operations, 100th Cong., 1st Sess. (1987), the subcommittee issued

a critical report "Disease–Specific Health Claims on Food Labels: An Unhealthy Idea," H.R. Rep. No. 100–561, 100th Cong., 2d Sess. (1988).

3. *1990 Statute.* FDA reproposed its regulations in 55 Fed.Reg. 5176 (February 13, 1990), but the new provisions of the 1990 Nutrition Labeling and Education Act, p. 200 *infra*, will require that they be reconsidered.

FTC REGULATION OF FOOD ADVERTISING

Section 5 of the Federal Trade Commission Act, 38 Stat. 717 (1914), 15 U.S.C. § 45, provides that "unfair or deceptive acts or practices in or affecting commerce, are declared unlawful." The Wheeler–Lea Amendments of 1938, 52 Stat. 111, added sections 14 and 15, which expressly prohibit any food advertisement, other than labeling, which is "misleading in a material respect." From its inception, the FTC regarded false or misleading labeling and advertising of food products as unfair acts or practices which violate section 5, and the courts have upheld that position. *E.g., Fresh Grown Preserve Corp. v. FTC,* 125 F.2d 917 (2d Cir. 1942), *FTC v. Good-Grape Co.,* 45 Fed.2d 70 (6th Cir. 1930); *Royal Baking Powder Co. v. FTC,* 281 F. 744 (2d Cir. 1922). For an overview of the FTC regulation of food advertising, *see* Hutt, *Government Regulation of Health Claims in Food Labeling and Advertising,* 41 FDC L.J. 3, 9–20 (1986).

The FTC has issued three important policy statements describing the circumstances under which an advertising claim will be found to violate the FTC Act. In a letter to Congress in December 1980, reprinted in 104 F.T.C. 1070 (1984), the Commission stated that, to constitute an illegal "unfair act or practice," an advertisement must be evaluated to determine whether it results in substantial consumer injury, violates public policy, or constitutes unethical or unscrupulous conduct. In October 1983, in another letter to Congress, reprinted in 103 F.T.C. 174 (1984), the Commission stated that, in evaluating whether an advertisement violates the FTC Act, it will be examined "from the perspective of a consumer acting reasonably in the circumstances." And in a 1984 policy statement, reprinted in 104 F.T.C. 839 (1984), the Commission reaffirmed the requirement that advertisers must "have a reasonable basis for advertising claims before they are disseminated" and stated that "what constitutes a reasonable basis depends, as it does in an unfairness analysis, on a number of factors relevant to the benefits and costs of substantiating a particular claim." *See, e.g.,* "FTC's Authority over Deceptive Advertising," Hearing Before the Subcomm. for Consumers of the Senate Comm. on Commerce, Science, and Transportation, 97th Cong., 2d Sess. (1982); "Deception: FTC Oversight," Hearing before the Subcomm. on Oversight and Investigations of the House Comm. on Energy and Commerce, 98th Cong., 2d Sess. (1984); Schechter, *The Death of the Gullible Consumer: Towards a More Sensible Definition of Deception at the FTC,* 1989 U. Ill. L. Rev. 751.

Based upon these policies, the FTC encouraged what it regarded as nondeceptive disease prevention claims when they first appeared in food advertising in the mid–1980s. The preamble to reproposed regulations on disease prevention claims for food, 55 Fed. Reg. 5176, 5186 (February 13, 1990), attempted to reconcile the obvious disparity between the flexible FTC "reasonable basis" standard for advertising claims and FDA's more stringent standard of scientific proof for labeling claims in the following terms.

FDA is not convinced that [FTC's "reasonable basis"] standard is adequate for determining the appropriateness of claims on the food label. As several comments pointed out, it is important that consumers maintain confidence in the food label. Consumers view food labeling as more reliable and trustworthy than food advertising. The existence of this dichotomy in consumer perception of the information from these two sources is supported by the results of several surveys and confirmed by a number of experts in the area of advertising and communication.

Food labeling has a high degree of acceptance among the general public. For example, when asked in a 1984 Roper Survey what sources of information about the nutritional content of food they thought most useful, labels on food packages were the most widely used source, mentioned by 57 percent of the public. Advertisements were considered the most useful source by only 4 percent. These results are essentially unchanged from a 1976 survey. Similarly, a 1980 FDA survey indicated that the perceived honesty/integrity/truthfulness of the food label is very high. Only 1 percent of respondents reported ever having bought a food product that was falsely labeled. In a 1981 survey about what FDA activities were most worthwhile, the two highest rated activities (tied for first) were "making sure food is safe to eat" and "making sure food labeling is honest."

---

9. MEDICAL FOOD

A REVIEW OF FOODS FOR MEDICAL PURPOSES: SPECIALLY FORMULATED PRODUCTS FOR NUTRITIONAL MANAGEMENT OF MEDICAL CONDITIONS

Federation of American Societies for Experimental Biology.
June 1977.

Several investigators have characterized the important properties of specially formulated complete diets for use under medical supervision in terms of their nutritional and physiological impact on the patient. They included a number of properties that should be considered in effective dietary management of various diseases:

- *High Nutritional Efficacy:* Preparations can provide 3000 kcal or more daily and at least 25 percent of the water requirement for extended periods. Nutritionally complete products would supply, in addition to caloric needs, adequate amounts of essential fatty acids, minerals and vitamins, and essential and nonessential nitrogen.

- *Uniform Composition:* Use of chemically identifiable ingredients provides control of product uniformity, allowing modification or supplementation to meet special nutritional needs of individual patients as required. However, deletion, substitution, or reduction of certain nutrients is not possible with commercial preparations.

- *Low Residue:* Most products contain little or no fiber or complex carbohydrates; consequently, gastrointestinal contents and fecal volume are reduced considerably.

- *Ease of Digestibility:* Dietary components may be supplied as readily digestible low molecular weight substances. Absorption in the duodenum and jejunum occurs readily....

- *Microbial Flora Alterations:* Qualitative and quantitative changes in fecal flora suggest that gastrointestinal microbial flora may be altered by consumption of special dietary foods....

- *Alteration of Serum Lipid Levels:* While the nature and amount of carbohydrate or other components in the product may affect the rate of decrease, reduction of serum cholesterol levels has been observed.

- *Reduction of Blood Pressure:* Decreased systolic and diastolic blood pressure levels have been reported in normal subjects maintained several days on special dietary products. Blood pressure levels returned to baseline values after normal diets were resumed.

- *Gastric Effects:* Consumption of such diets reduces gastric acid secretions and delays gastric emptying.

- *Hypoallergenicity:* The ability to eliminate protein components or alter their composition provides a convenient method of supplying nonallergenic nutrients to patients with food allergies.

- *Water Solubility or Dispersibility:* Liquid preparations allow either tube feeding or consumption without mastication which can be important in pediatric and geriatric patients and in patients with oral, dental and other head and neck surgical problems. Some can be administered through extremely small (No. 4 French) feeding tubes.

- *Stabilization of Nutritional State:* The uniformity of types of special dietary products facilitates establishing a stable nutritional status and accurate measurements of the intake of all nutrients.....

Exact definition of these types of products is difficult because of their composition and manner of use. Many currently available products and formulas include widely used foods, food ingredients, and substances that are generally recognized as safe. Similarly, a broad array of regular dietary items is useful in feeding patients with disorders amenable to dietary management. On the other hand, some nutritionally complete products were developed originally to facilitate digestion, provide less bulk and thus lower fecal volume, and at the same time, provide nutrients in amounts equivalent to the estimated requirements of a normal adult. In current practice, these latter formulations are being used in such diverse conditions as obesity and weight reduction, acute and chronic pancreatitis, preoperative preparation for intestinal surgery, enteral nutrition of cancer and terminally ill

patients, extensive body burns, radiation enteropathy, and the short
bowel syndrome.

Regardless of composition or use, products prepared for dietary
management of diseases, disorders or related medical conditions are
types of foods for special dietary use. The term, food for special dietary
use, or colloquially, special dietary foods, is an umbrella term for any
food intended to be used as the sole item of the diet, as a supplementary
source of nutrients to increase total dietary intake of the nutrients, or
to supply a special dietary need that exists by reason of a physical,
physiological, pathological, or other condition, including but not limited
to the condition of disease, convalescence, pregnancy, lactation, infancy,
allergic hypersensitivity to food, underweight, overweight, or the need
to control the intake of sodium.....

While each of the terms in current usage has some advantages, for
purposes of this report the term "medical foods" has been used and it is
defined as follows:

> *Medical Foods* are foods that are specially formulated or pre-
> pared products consumed or administered enterally under di-
> rect or indirect medical supervision in the dietary management
> of individuals with specific diseases, disorders, or medical con-
> ditions in which the existence of associated special nutritional
> requirements is established by medical evaluation.

Regardless of composition, medical foods are foods for use by patients
who require professional medical counsel and supervision to meet
special or unique nutritional requirements. Use of the term, "medical
foods," should connote reference to special dietary foods intended for
use solely under medical supervision to meet nutritional requirements
in specific medical conditions which may be potentially life-threatening
or critically disabling.....

Since 1962, investigational new drug data have been required for
vitamin and mineral preparations promoted for use as drugs; and
notwithstanding the nutritional purposes of use, some special dietary
products were considered drugs because they were originally regulated
to ensure their use under medical supervision. However, in 1972 the
FDA reclassified these types of special dietary foods from *drugs* to *foods
for special dietary use* to enhance their development and availability.
This policy covers all special dietary foods that are intended for use
under medical supervision to meet the nutritional requirements of
patients who require professional counsel to meet their specialized or
unique nutritional requirements because of specific medical conditions.
These products are referred to as "medical foods"; however, the term
was not precisely defined.....

Research, clinical experience, and technical development during
the past three decades have established the value of medical foods in
patient nutrition and dietary management of a wide variety of diseases
and disorders. Additional research and clinical experience can be
expected to provide a basis for continued evolution of products that

meet special nutritional requirements of a broader array of diseases and disorders. Similarly, evolving concepts in health care delivery and long-term maintenance of patients with chronic diseases suggest that applications of medical foods will expand substantially.

NOTES

1. *Orphan Medical Food.* FDA announced the availability of a report on evaluation of incentives for development of "orphan" medical foods in 55 Fed. Reg. 11439 (March 28, 1990). The term "medical food" is defined in section 5(b) of the Orphan Drug Act, 21 U.S.C. § 360ee(b).

2. *Commentary. See generally* Hutt, *Government Regulation of Health Claims in Food Labeling and Advertising,* 41 FDC L.J. 3 (1986); Miller and Scarbrough, *Foods as Drugs,* 21 Drug Info. J. 221 (1987); Symposium: *Medical Foods: Their Past, Present, and Future Regulation,* 44 FDC L.J. 461 (1989).

---

10. FUTURE ISSUES

DIETARY GOALS FOR THE UNITED STATES: SECOND EDITION

Senate Select Committee on Nutrition and Human Needs.
95th Congress, 1st Session (1977).

During this century, the composition of the average diet in the United States has changed radically. Foods containing complex carbohydrates and "naturally occurring" sugars—fruit, vegetables and grain products—which were the mainstay of the diet, now play a minority role. At the same time, consumption of fats and refined and processed sugars has risen to the point where these two macro-nutrients now alone comprise at least 60 percent of total caloric intake, an increase of 20 percent since the early 1900s.

... [T]hese and other changes in the diet amount to a wave of malnutrition—of both over- and under-consumption—that may be as profoundly damaging to the Nation's health as the widespread contagious diseases of the early part of the century.

The over-consumption of foods high in fat, generally, and saturated fat in particular, as well as cholesterol, refined and processed sugars, salt and/or alcohol has been associated with the development of one or more of six to ten leading causes of death: heart disease, some cancers, stroke and hypertension, diabetes, arteriosclerosis and cirrhosis of the liver....

At the same time, current dietary trends may also be leading to malnutrition through undernourishment. Fats are relatively low in vitamins and minerals, and refined sugar (cane and beet) and most processed sugars have no vitamins or minerals. Consequently, diets with reduced caloric intake to control weight and/or save money, but which are high in fats and refined and processed sugars, may lead to vitamin and mineral deficiencies....

... Dr. Briggs provided an analysis of the cost of poor nutritional status which contributes to some of the diseases in the United States. The potential annual savings in nutrition related costs, "based on the more conservative end of the range of current scientific opinion," were as follows:

	Billions
Dental diseases	$ 3
Diabetes	4
Cardiovascular disease	10
Alcohol	20
Digestive diseases	3
Total	$40

It should be noted that this analysis does not include cancer, kidney disease due to mismanagement of hypertension, or the long-term cost associated with low birth weight babies due to maternal malnutrition.

Beyond the monetary savings, it is obvious then that improved nutrition also offers the potential for prevention of vast suffering and loss of productivity and creativity.

One in three men in the United States can be expected to die of heart disease or stroke before age 60 and one in six women. It is estimated that 25 million suffer from high blood pressure and that about 5 million are afflicted by diabetes mellitus.

Given the wide impact on health that has been traced to the dietary trends outlined, it is imperative, as a matter of public health policy that consumers be provided with dietary guidelines or goals for macro-nutrients that will encourage the most healthful selection of foods....

U.S. DIETARY GOALS

1. To avoid overweight, consume only as much energy (calories) as is expended; if overweight, decrease energy intake and increase energy expenditure.

2. Increase the consumption of complex carbohydrates and "naturally occurring" sugars from about 28 percent of energy intake to about 48 percent of energy intake.

3. Reduce the consumption of refined and processed sugars by about 45 percent to account for about 10 percent of total energy intake.

4. Reduce overall fat consumption from approximately 40 percent to about 30 percent of energy intake.

5. Reduce saturated fat consumption to account for about 10 percent of total energy intake; and balance that with poly-unsaturated

and mono-unsaturated fats, which should account for about 10 percent of energy intake each.

6. Reduce cholesterol consumption to about 300 mg. a day.

7. Limit the intake of sodium by reducing the intake of salt to about 5 grams a day.

THE GOALS SUGGEST THE FOLLOWING CHANGES IN FOOD SELECTION AND PREPARATION

1. Increase consumption of fruits and vegetables and whole grains.

2. Decrease consumption of refined and other processed sugars and food high in such sugars.

3. Decrease consumption of foods high in total fat, and partially replace saturated fats, whether obtained from animal or vegetable sources, with poly-unsaturated fats.

4. Decrease consumption of animal fat, and choose meats, poultry and fish which will reduce saturated fat intake.

5. Except for young children, substitute low-fat and non-fat milk for whole milk, and low-fat dairy products for high fat dairy products.

6. Decrease consumption of butterfat, eggs and other high cholesterol sources. Some consideration should be given to easing the cholesterol goal for pre-menopausal women, young children and the elderly in order to obtain the nutritional benefits of eggs in the diet.

7. Decrease consumption of salt and foods high in salt content....

NOTES

1. *Debate Over Dietary Goals.* These dietary goals have not been uncontroversial. For an instructive debate over the wisdom of implementing them, *compare* Harper, *What Are Appropriate Dietary Guidelines?*, Food Tech., September 1978, at 48, *with* Hegsted, *Rationale For Change In The American Diet,* Food Tech., September 1978, at 44. *See also* National Nutrition Consortium, GUIDELINES FOR A NATIONAL NUTRITION POLICY (1974); AMA Council on Scientific Affairs, *American Medical Association Concepts of Nutrition and Health,* 242 J.A.M.A. 2335 (1979); Council for Agricultural Science and Technology, *Dietary Goals for the United States: A Commentary,* Rep. No. 71 (1977). For a discussion of changes in the food supply that would be needed to meet these dietary goals, *see* Peterkin, *The Dietary Goals and Food on the Table,* Food Tech., February 1978, at 34. Two reports by the National Academy of Sciences, TOWARD HEALTHFUL DIETS (1980), and DIET, NUTRITION, AND CANCER (1982), which echoed many of the conclusions of the Senate Select Committee, were sufficiently controversial that eleven numbers of Congress requested a GAO review of the Academy's committee selection procedures and objectivity. *See* GAO, NATIONAL ACADEMY OF SCIENCES' REPORTS ON DIET AND HEALTH—ARE THEY CREDIBLE AND CONSISTENT?, Rep. No. RCED–84–109 (August 21, 1984).

2. *Current Dietary Goals.* Despite controversy, however, the proposed dietary goals have gained substantial credence. The third edition of

NUTRITION AND YOUR HEALTH: DIETARY GUIDELINES FOR AMERI-CANS, published by USDA and DHHS in 1990, offers the following guidance:

1. Eat a variety of foods.
2. Maintain healthy weight.
3. Choose a diet low in fat, saturated fat, and cholesterol.
4. Choose a diet with plenty of vegetables, fruits, and grain products.
5. Use sugars only in moderation.
6. Use salt and sodium only in moderation.
7. If you drink alcoholic beverages, do so in moderation.

DESIGNING FOODS:
ANIMAL PRODUCT OPTIONS IN THE MARKETPLACE
Board on Agriculture, National Research Council (1988).

The nutrition-related health problems experienced by a large segment of the U.S. population today arise from the overconsumption of fat, saturated fatty acids, and cholesterol. For another group the main dietary problems center around underconsumption of iron, calcium, and calories. The incidence of nutrition-related health problems is significant, affecting either directly or indirectly nearly every American family. For example, it has been estimated that 34 million adults in the United States are overweight; nearly 1 million adults die each year of cardiovascular disease; 15 million to 20 million adults are afflicted by osteoporosis; 8 million adults and 12 million children go hungry due to inadequate diets; and iron deficiency has been cited as the most common form of childhood anemia....

... New policies are now needed to sustain the positive trends evident among consumers and throughout the animal product industries, trends like nutrition education programs in supermarkets, closer retail trim of meats, and the growing array of lower fat animal product options. The committee's goals are to provide consumers the opportunity to exercise personal choice in the marketplace, to encourage the development of a range of products consistent with those choices, and to ensure sufficient consumer education and information to make those choices informed decisions. The starting point is for producers and their industry associations to recognize the need to understand marketplace trends and the role of foods in a healthy diet and to implement appropriate animal feeding, breeding, and selection programs....

The Grading System. The committee makes several recommendations regarding the current [USDA] grading system. First, it supports the recent change in the name of the Good grade to Select, to provide the beef industry with an opportunity for improved marketing of beef with less marbling than is found in Prime or Choice. The objectives in adopting grading system changes should be to provide consumers with

clearer, more accurate information about the meat products they purchase and to send to producers and packers distinct economic signals on
the types of products consumers prefer. The current system fails on
both counts.

Second, the committee recommends that the U.S. Department of
Agriculture (USDA) carefully study the potential benefits of changes in
regulations to allow hot-fat trimming at slaughter—removal of the
subcutaneous fat from the carcass immediately after slaughter....
Such a change from current regulations would mean that price would
be determined from the pounds of carcass remaining after trimming, in
effect penalizing the producer for additional fat....

Labeling and Standards of Identity. Three of the committee's
policy recommendations involve labeling and standards of identity.
First, the committee agrees with the Food and Drug Administration
(FDA) that regulations should not restrict truthful information at the
point of purchase or on food product packaging. Second, the committee
recommends that use of the term *Natural* for meat products be standardized in a manner similar to the current FDA effort to standardize
use of terms in cholesterol labeling..... Finally, the committee recommends that the USDA restrict use of the terms *Light, Lite,* or *Lean* to
products in the form that would be presented to the retail consumer....

*Information and Consumer Education.. .*The committee recommends that the FDA encourage the development of point-of-purchase
information programs (additional nutrition education information beyond that mandated by law) in light of the continued growth in
popularity of these programs and the demonstrated willingness of
retailers and processors to supply information beyond that given on the
label. This could be done by issuing specific guidelines for providing
factual nutrition data without judgment or comment. The committee
also recommends that restaurants be encouraged to provide point-of-
purchase information to their customers....

... Currently, there are no standards for serving sizes; consistency
would facilitate comparisons among products, labels, point-of-purchase
information, and federal and private data bases. The committee further recommends the establishment of standards governing serving
sizes. This is important in terms of nutrition education and research
and for a wide range of data base users.

Probably no policy issue has received more attention from regulators, consumer advocacy groups, and food manufacturers than claims
of health promotion and disease prevention. Aside from the fact that
such claims may initiate mandatory nutrition labeling, the most recurrent problem is the inability of manufacturers to document them. The
committee recommends that the private sector seriously consider developing advertising and promotional guidelines that would restrict or
eliminate the use of misleading claims or claims that specific foods are
cures for, or preventers of, diseases....

... The committee recommends that federal agencies strive to reach consensus positions that would enable them to speak with one voice on nutrition and health issues.

One piece of information that is essential to making dietary recommendations is the level of fat consumed by the typical American. In the past, government data sources may have inaccurately estimated the amount of fat consumed, particularly fat of animal origin. Attempts are currently under way within the USDA to improve dietary survey methodologies to more accurately reflect actual intake.... In addition, the federal government should take steps to more accurately distinguish and monitor the fatty acid composition of fats consumed in the diet.....

Preharvest Technology. Several of the committee's recommendations center on technologies that could be applied before slaughter to alter the composition of the animal during growth. These recommendations include identifying the cellular and molecular mechanisms that control partitioning of feed nutrients into fat or lean tissues and altering the fatty acid composition and the lean to fat ratio of meat, milk, and eggs through breeding, nutrition, and management. In addition, the committee recommends implementing available technologies for determining the fat and protein contents of live animals and carcasses.

Research is also recommended to determine the extent of genetic variation in the cholesterol content of animals, the reduction of oxidative rancidity of animal products through feeding or management, and the development of more cost-effective methods of efficiently producing low-fat animal products by integrated production management systems.

Postharvest Technology. Postharvest technologies to reduce fat in animal products can be used satisfactorily in many situations. However, these technologies are not without costs and are usually associated with some change in product characteristics such as texture, flavor, and shelf life....

One of the main research recommendations echoes a previously discussed policy change: the adoption of standards of identity that would reflect today's technology and consumer needs. Less prescriptive standards could permit beneficial applications of new technologies to reduce the fat content of animal products in new ways. The committee also recommends the use of technologies to remove fat at the earliest possible state in processing and to improve methods to evaluate and monitor the resulting fat content of the product after processing. The use of non-fat or low-fat ingredients are recommended to simulate the textural and quality characteristics and properties of fat and to alter the fatty acid composition of processed animal products.

Several of the committee's recommendations center around altering the cholesterol content of animal products during processing. These include the use of molecular genetics and other biotechnologies to generate new microorganisms to reduce the cholesterol content of products through fermentation and the use of selective extraction to reduce both the cholesterol and fat contents of processed animal products.

Sodium chloride plays a critical role in delaying microbial growth, providing flavor, and contributing to the functional characteristics of many processed products, but it is also cited as being excessive in the American diet. The committee recommends that methods be developed to safely and organoleptically ... reduce or replace sodium in manufactured animal products.

MICHAEL SPECTER, FOOD LABELS OFTEN LIGHT ON NUTRITION INFORMATION

The Washington Post, July 23, 1989, at A1.

Realizing that a walk down a supermarket aisle can be a trip into the twilight zone, consumer groups have spent years trying to force a fundamental revision of food-labeling practices.... Current nutrition labels were designed when federal health officials thought that vitamin and mineral contents were the most important aspect of food. But these days, vitamin deficiencies are rare in this country. Instead, the repeated message from doctors and public health officers is that we should increase fiber intake and cut back on eating fat, particularly saturated fat.

In the past year, two major reports, from the surgeon general and the National Academy of Sciences, said that by cutting back on fat Americans can vastly reduce the incidence of heart disease and, possibly, certain types of cancer. Marketing surveys have shown that consumers have received the message but have run into major roadblocks at the grocery store. Fat content, for example, is usually listed in grams, a measure rarely used and poorly understood in this country. Saturated fat is almost never even noted on most processed food packages. Calories are often listed per portion, but many portion sizes are misleading. A 50-cent bag of pretzels bought out of a machine, for instance, is usually listed as containing 1.65 servings although it was clearly intended as a snack for one person.

MODEL LABEL OF UNSPECIFIED FOOD

CURRENT LABEL

NUTRITION INFORMATION

SERVING SIZE ....12 OZ.
SERVINGS PER BOX 1

PER SERVING
CALORIES 320
PROTEIN ....19 g
CARBOHYDRATES ....39 g
FAT ....10 g
SODIUM ....700 mg

**PERCENTAGE OF U.S.
RECOMMENDED DAILY ALLOWANCES
PER SERVING**
PROTEIN 40%
VITAMIN A 160%
VITAMIN C ....*
VITAMIN B1 ....30%
VITAMIN B2 ....25%
NIACIN 20%
CALCIUM 5%
IRON 15%

*contains less than 2%

IMPROVED LABEL I

Nutrition Information Per Serving

Serving Size ....12 OZ.
Servings per Container 1

Calories 320

Total Fat ....High (10 g)
  Cholesterol
  Raising Fat ....Medium (4 g)
Cholesterol ....Low (10 mg)
Sodium ....High (700 mg)

Starch ....High (35 g)
Dietary Fiber ....Low (1 g)
Sugar ....Low (3 g)

Other Nutrients and % of USRDA

Protein ....High (40%)
Vitamin A ....High (160%)
Vitamin C ....(0%)
Calcium ....Low (5%)
Iron ....Medium (15%)

IMPROVED LABEL II

NUTRIENTS PER 12 OZ. SERVING

320 Calories

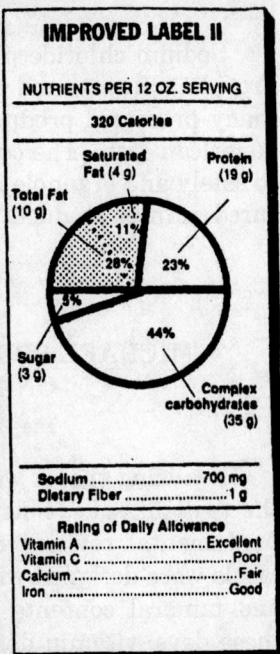

Sodium ....700 mg
Dietary Fiber ....1 g

Rating of Daily Allowance
Vitamin A ....Excellent
Vitamin C ....Poor
Calcium ....Fair
Iron ....Good

CURRENT INGREDIENT LABEL

INGREDIENTS: WHEAT FLOUR, SUGAR, SHORTENING (CONTAINS ONE OR MORE OF THE FOLLOWING: HYDROGENATED SOYBEAN OIL AND/OR COCONUT OIL AND/OR BEEF FAT), CORN SYRUP, DEXTROSE, GUM ARABIC, SALT, HYDROLYZED VEGETABLE PROTEIN, FARM FRESH EGGS, ARTIFICIAL COLOR (INCLUDING YELLOW #5) AND FLAVOR, THIAMINE MONONITRATE, PYRIDOXINE HYDROCHLORIDE, FRESHNESS PRESERVED WITH BHT.

SUGGESTED IMPROVED INGREDIENT LABEL

MAJOR INGREDIENTS: Sugars 50% (sugar, corn syrup, dextrose), White flour (30%), Hydrogenated soybean oil (10%), Coconut fat (5%; a saturated fat).

OTHER INGREDIENTS: Gum arabic, Salt, Hydrolyzed vegetable protein (contains MSG), Egg, Artificial colors including Blue 2 and Yellow 5, Artificial flavors, Vitamins B-1 and B-6, BHT (preservative).

[G636]

FOOD LABELING

54 Federal Register 32610, (August 8, 1989).

Although the food label has been the subject of considerable study and revision over the past 20 years, FDA believes it appropriate now to consider significant new improvements in food labeling.

Several factors underscore this belief. First, the recent "The Surgeon General's Report on Nutrition and Health" and the National Academy of Sciences' report entitled "Diet and Health: Implications for Reducing Chronic Disease Risk" provide authoritative current views on the evidence linking dietary patterns and health. Second, surveys demonstrate that consumers themselves want to play a more active role in self-care and that, specifically, they seek more useful and easily understood information about the nutritional characteristics of the foods they eat. Third, recognizing this interest by consumers, both consumer and industry groups have been striving to design what they consider to be more informative food labels; food manufacturers have also expressed increasing interest in using food labels to convey the relationship between diet and certain diseases. Finally, numerous bills have recently been introduced in Congress and in State legislatures that would amend the current food labeling requirements (e.g., mandatory nutrition labeling, cholesterol content, label identification of vegetable oils, and sodium and potassium content)......

The food label has developed so that it has several possible components, all of which are intended to convey accurate, useful information to consumers. The remainder of this notice solicits comments in the following five areas:

1. *Nutrition Labeling*—Nutrition labeling includes the list of a food's nutritional value—calories, protein, carbohydrate, fat, sodium, vitamins, and minerals. Because the basic nutrition labeling regulations were developed almost 20 years ago, FDA believes this may be an appropriate time to review the regulations to determine if certain required elements could be made voluntary (e.g., some vitamins) or if elements that are currently voluntary should be made mandatory (e.g., saturated fats) to ensure uniformity. Moreover, because nutrition labeling is voluntary for most foods, FDA is seeking comment on whether nutrition labeling should be mandatory for more foods and how this could best be accomplished.

2. *Nutrition Label Format*—FDA has long recognized that the current nutrition label might not be in the optimal format for conveying useable information to consumers. Industry and consumer groups have also argued that the information on the label should be in an easier-to-understand format so that consumers can readily identify

foods suitable for their individual diets. FDA is seeking comment on
how the current label format might be improved.

3. *Ingredient Labeling*—FDA seeks comment on whether the current ingredient labeling requirements that are not mandated by the act
should be amended and whether legislative changes should be sought
for mandated requirements (e.g., for more detailed ingredient information). The agency is also seeking comments on whether and how the
format for ingredient labeling should be revised.

4. *Descriptions of Food*—There are a number of ways in which the
food label is used to describe foods—names established by standards of
identity, common or usual names, imitation or substitute foods, and
descriptor labeling such as "low calorie." FDA has several regulations
in each of these areas and standards are specifically provided for by
law. Among the issues the agency is seeking comment on are: (1) The
usefulness of food standards in assuring consumers that commonly
purchased foods meet certain standards of identity and composition;
and whether revisions should be made in specific standards themselves
or in the procedures by which standards are adopted or amended; and
(2) whether FDA should define, in a manner analogous to current
regulatory definitions for "low sodium," other labeling such as "low
fat" and "lite" that are being used by manufacturers.

5. *Health Messages*—There has been increasing use of food labels
to impart health messages to consumers about such things as the
relationship between high fiber food and colon cancer risks, low cholesterol foods and heart disease, and high calcium foods' impact on
osteoporosis. FDA has traditionally determined that foods may not
make such "medical" claims; in recent years, however, scientific evidence has accumulated that may support certain claims. The agency is
seeking public comment on how such messages can be properly conveyed to consumers.

THE NUTRITION LABELING AND EDUCATION ACT OF 1990

As this book went to press, FDA had proposed new nutrition labeling
regulations and Congress had just enacted new legislation relating to the
labeling of the nutrient content of food.

1. *FDA Proposals.* Based on the preceding Federal Register notice and
four public hearings, 54 Fed. Reg. 38806 (September 20, 1989), 54 Fed. Reg.
43183 (October 23, 1989), FDA published proposed regulations in 55 Fed. Reg.
29476 (July 19, 1990) that would: (1) make nutrition labeling mandatory for
virtually all food; (2) substitute RDIs (Reference Daily Intakes) for the U.S.
RDAs; (3) prescribe labeling of calories, calories from fat, saturated fat, cholesterol, carbohydrate, fiber, protein, sodium, vitamin A, vitamin C, calcium, and
iron; and (4) allow labels to include a "nutrition profile" table showing the
percent of a "daily reference value" (DRV) for fat, saturated fat, cholesterol,
carbohydrate, fiber, and sodium. To solve the problem of inconsistent and
shrunken serving sizes described in note 3 p. [143] *supra,* FDA proposed in 55
Fed. Reg. 29517 (July 19, 1990) to establish uniform serving sizes for 159 food
product categories. In considering these proposals, FDA will have the benefit

of a concurrent study by the Institute of Medicine, NUTRITIONAL LABEL-ING: ISSUES AND DIRECTIONS FOR THE 1990s (1990).

2. *Congressional Action.* Congress seized the initiative from FDA in the effort to reform nutrition labeling late in the fall of 1990 by enacting the Nutrition Labeling and Education Act, 104 Stat. 2353, which President Bush signed into law on November 8, 1990.

Nutrition Labeling. The Act adds a new section 403(q), which requires nutrition labeling for virtually all FDA regulated food products. The new statutory requirements will supplant FDA's current nutrition labeling regulations, 21 C.F.R. § 101.9, and require modification of its proposed new requirements published in July 1990, though in many respects the new statutory requirements are similar to FDA's proposal.

Nutrition information must appear on the label or in accompanying labeling of a food. FDA is to specify a uniform format, which must include the serving size and the number of servings per container. The serving size for a food shall be the amount customarily consumed, expressed in a common household measure appropriate to the food. FDA is directed to establish standards for serving sizes for food.

The statute requires information, on a per serving basis, about the amount of the following nutrients:

Calories

Calories from fat

Total fat

Saturated fat

Cholesterol

Sodium

Total carbohydrates

Complex carbohydrates

Sugars

Dietary fiber

Total protein

Such vitamins and minerals as FDA specifies

FDA may add to or subtract from this list based upon its determination whether the information will assist consumers in maintaining healthy dietary practices. But it may not prohibit the voluntary declaration of nutrients by the manufacturer. FDA may require any information in nutrition labeling to be highlighted by larger type, bold type, or contrasting color.

The new requirements apply to all foods intended for human consumption that are offered for sale. As written, the provision does not apply to unlabeled foods, but it seems clear that Congress intended to include bulk food and fresh fruits, vegetables, and fish as well. The following foods are specifically exempted: foods sold in restaurants and other food service establishments, foods prepared in retail stores for consumption off the premises, infant formula, medical foods, foods in small packages, foods containing insignificant amounts of all mandatory nutrients and making no nutrition claims, all food sold by small businesses (less than $500,000 per year gross sales or $50,000 per year food sales and no nutrition claims), and foods sold by a food distributor to restaurants or other food service establishments. Vitamin/mineral products are subject to whatever specific labeling requirements FDA may impose. Sellers of fresh fruit, vegetables, and seafood are provided an opportunity to implement nutrition labeling on a voluntary basis which, if unsuccessful, will become mandatory.

To implement these, and the other requirements imposed by the Act, FDA must propose regulations within 12 months. The agency must promulgate final regulations within 24 months, or the proposal automatically becomes final. The final regulations become effective six months after all nutrition labeling regulations are promulgated, but FDA can postpone this deadline for one additional year.

Nutrient Descriptors. The new statute adds a new section 403(r), which establishes new requirements for nutrient descriptors. A nutrient descriptor is defined as a claim that characterizes the level of a nutrient present in a food, such as "low calorie" or "high fiber." No nutrient descriptor may be used unless FDA has defined it and the use conforms with that definition. FDA is specifically required to define the following nutrient descriptors: "free," "low," "light" or "lite," "reduced," "less," and "high." Only infant formulas and medical foods are exempt from the provisions governing nutrient desciptors.

The statute imposes several limits on the use of specific descriptors. Claims may be made about the absence of a nutrient that is usually present in the food or a substitute, or if the nutrient is usually not present but FDA determines that the claim will assist consumers. FDA may prohibit any nutrient descriptor that is misleading. Any use of a nutrient descriptor on the label or in labeling must be accompanied by the statement: "See [*e.g.*, side panel] for nutrition information." If the food contains a nutrient at a level FDA has determined increases the risk of disease, this statement must also refer to that nutrient.

The new statute applies to nutrient descriptors even if they are contained in trademarks or brand names. If an undefined nutrient descriptor was used in a brand name prior to October 25, 1989, it may continue to be used. If a descriptor has been defined by FDA regulation, however, the food must meet that definition but will be given an additional six months to do so. Existing diet soft drinks are exempt as long as they are labeled to comply with current FDA regulations. Special rules will apply to vitamin-mineral products.

Any person may petition FDA to define a nutrient descriptor. FDA has 100 days to reject the petition or to accept it for filing. If it is rejected, the petition is not publicly disclosed. If it is accepted for filing, FDA must act on it within 90 days.

Disease Prevention Claims. New section 403(r) also governs disease prevention or health claims, such as "helps reduce the risk of heart disease." A food bearing a claim that meets the requirements of new section 403(r) is specifically excluded from the statutory definition of a drug.

No disease prevention claim may be made in food labeling unless it conforms with a regulation promulgated by FDA. Any regulation authorizing a disease prevention claim must be based on the totality of publicly available scientific evidence, including well-designed studies conducted in accordance with generally recognized scientific procedures and principles, on the basis of which there is significant scientific agreement among qualified experts that the claim is supported. No disease prevention claim may be made for a food, however, if it contains any nutrient at a level that FDA has determined increased the risk of disease, unless FDA specifically permits the claim and the label bears a statement referring to the problematic nutrient.

The statute specifically requires FDA to consider adopting regulations addressing the relationship between the following nutrients and diseases:

Calcium and osteoporosis

Fiber and cancer

Lipids and cardiovascular disease

Lipids and cancer

Sodium and hypertension

Fiber and cardiovascular disease

Disease prevention claims for vitamin/mineral products are to be subject to separate standards to be established by FDA. The following relationships between vitamin/mineral products and diseases must also be considered by FDA:

Folic acid and neural tube defects

Antioxidant vitamins and cancer

Zinc and immune function in the elderly

Omega-3 fatty acids and heart disease

Any person may petition FDA to authorize a disease prevention claim. FDA has 100 days within which to reject the petition or to accept it for filing. If the agency rejects the petition, it is not publicly disclosed. If it is accepted for filing, FDA must act on it within 90 days.

New Labeling Provisions. The statute contains additional provisions that add to, or revise, current food labeling requirements in the FD&C Act. (1) Vegetable and fruit juice beverages must bear the percent of each juice on the information panel of the label. (2) All ingredients in standardized food products must be included in the label statement of ingredients in the future. (3) All certified color additives must be named in the list of ingredients. (4) With two exceptions, food standards henceforth may be established, amended, or repealed through informal rulemaking. Standards for dairy products and maple sirup may only be amended in accordance with the formal procedures in section 701(e).

National Uniformity and State Enforcement. The 1990 Act added novel provisions to assure national uniformity in food labeling and to allow states to participate in the enforcement of federal labeling requirements. These provisions are examined in Chapter X.

E. REGULATION OF VITAMIN–MINERAL SUPPLEMENTS

1. DECEPTIVE MARKETING PRACTICES

V.E. IRONS, INC. v. UNITED STATES

United States Court of Appeals, First Circuit, 1957.
244 F.2d 34.

MAGRUDER, Chief Judge.

V.E. Irons, Inc. and V. Earl Irons in his individual capacity stand convicted, after a three-week trial, on a six-count information for causing the introduction into interstate commerce of misbranded food and drugs....

Count I of the information charged that the defendants (appellants herein) caused to be introduced into interstate commerce articles of food, known as Vit–Ra–Tox 21A (raw veal bone, defatted wheat germ, and the concentrate of juices of young, green cereal shots) and Vit–Ra–Tox 21B (garlic derivative, wheat germ, and lecithin as emulsifiers), which were misbranded under § 343(j) in that they "purported to be and [were] represented as a food for special dietary uses by man by reason of [their] vitamin and mineral content and [their] label[s] failed to bear such information concerning [their] vitamin and mineral properties as has been determined to be and by regulations prescribed as necessary in order fully to inform purchasers as to [their] value for such uses."

Count II charged that the appellants caused to be introduced into interstate commerce articles of drug known as Vit–Ra–Tox 21A and Vit–Ra–Tox 21B ... which were (a) misbranded under 21 U.S.C. § 352(a) in that their accompanying labeling—consisting of certain leaflets and various issues of a newsletter—falsely represented "when viewed in [their] entirety as well as through specific claims * * * that nearly everyone in this country is suffering from malnutrition or in danger of such suffering because of demineralization and depletion of soils and the refining and process of foods, that particularly all illnesses and diseases of mankind are due to improper nutrition, that said article[s] possessed nutritive properties superior to any other vitamin and mineral supplement, that said article[s] would be effective in the cure, treatment, and prevention of the ills and diseases of mankind," including certain specific diseases; and which were (b) misbranded under § 352(f)(1) in that their labeling failed to bear adequate directions for the use of which they were intended, namely, for treatment of the specific diseases which appellants represented that the drugs could cure or prevent....

At the conclusion of the trial the jury returned a verdict of guilty against both defendants on all six counts. The court sentenced V. Earl Irons to one year of imprisonment on each of the six counts, the sentences to run concurrently; and imposed upon the defendant corporation a fine of $1,000 on each count. Appeals were duly taken by both defendants. . . .

Since appellants make no serious argument with respect to Count I, it may be dealt with summarily. The label on the carton introduced into evidence by the government states that Vit–Ra–Tox No. 21A retains "Nature's vitamins, living enzymes, synergists, and activating materials (except Vitamin D); a rich natural source of Carotene (pro-vitamin A) and the complete natural complexes of Vitamins B, C, E, F, and K with the P fractions of the C complex and the Wulzen factor of the F complex, plus the living enzymes, synergists and mineral activa-tors. It contains organic iron, calcium, phosphorus, iodine and a host of other minerals in trace amounts * * * ." The label thus represents that the product has special dietary use for man, by reason of its vitamin and mineral properties, within the scope of the Administrator's regula-tions ... and because there is no claim that the label satisfied the requirements of the regulations, it is quite clear that there was a violation of the Act, so far as Count I is concerned. . . .

In determining whether such labeling contained "false or mislead-ing" statements, we must be careful not to read the literature with the eyes either of experts in nutrition or of overly skeptical buyers. What is pertinent is the effect the claims would have on those to whom they are addressed, namely, prospective purchasers and actual customers of appellants, who cannot be presumed to have special expertness or to be unduly cautious, but who are more likely than not to be persons who are pathetically eager to find some simple cure-all for the diseases with which they are afflicted or who are susceptible to luridly painted scare literature as to the prospect of being disease-ridden unless they consist-ently partake of the vaunted drug product. . . .

When appellants' labeling is examined in this light and in its entirety, it readily appears that the government introduced at least sufficient evidence to warrant submission to the jury of the issues whether appellants made the representations charged against them, and whether these representations were false or misleading. . . . [M]any representations are made that, fairly interpreted, provide adequate support for the government's charges. There are, first of all, numerous assertions that "all human ailments" can be traced to nutritive defi-ciencies and that various specific ills are caused thereby. For example, there is the statement:

> "The evidence is overwhelming! That we Are what we Eat. That practically All Human ailments are traceable to our food. From the times we are conceived until we reach 150 lbs;

> "It's the Material Out of Which we are built that deter-mines the structure. If that material is faulty the structure Breaks Down. If it is Not Faulty, it does Not Break Down * * * It's our Food, that makes us sick or well."

Similarly, in one of appellants' pamphlets it is stated: "We believe that practically all the ailments that beset our civilized world are caused by deficient foods which can lower one's resistance."

With respect to specific diseases, the literature quotes from the writings of one Dr. Sutherland [6] that:

"At the present time many conditions are considered as essentially deficiency diseases and are associated in one's thought with the classical Beri–Beri, Pellagra, Rickets and Scurvy. Such conditions are Infantile Scorbutus, Marasmus, Dentition Difficulties and Imperfect Teeth in Children and Adults, Dyspepsias, Indigestions, Diarrhoeas and Constipation, Obesity, Inability to Nurse Children, Diabetes, Neuroses, Infantile Paralysis, Certain Myalgias or 'Rheumatism,' Dementia Praecox, and even Tuberculosis and Cancer. The list can be extended but it is already a formidable one." ...

At another point appellants modestly state in an unqualified way that "It [Vit–Ra–Tox No. 21] is the One Hope for suffering humanity." And again, that "'This Product' *alone* of all products now on the market has *all* the vitamins, minerals, enzymes, coenzymes, mineral activators and synergists (co-workers or helpers) needed by the human body except Vitamin D)."

Apart from these general representations about the value of their product, the record discloses that appellants claimed the power to cure or ameliorate specific diseases..... [I]t is true that most of the representations in the literature relating to diseases are more indirect; virtues of appellants' products are juxtaposed with descriptions of the symptoms or cures of various diseases, although no statement is made overtly correlating the products with the diseases....

... The record discloses many other illustrations of references to specific diseases cleverly coupled with boosts for or information concerning Vit–Ra–Tox. On the basis of this record it is not at all surprising that a lay jury reading the literature came to the conclusion that special curative or at least preventive powers for the diseases mentioned were claimed by appellants for their Vit–Ra–Tox line.[8] And

6. The literature employs quotations from the writings of others. It is obvious that so long as these writings are quoted with approval, they become the representations of appellants and can be used by the government to sustain its charges.

8. On its cartons and in one or two of appellants' newsletters or pamphlets, one may find disclaimers such as the following:

"Important—We do not diagnose or prescribe

"Neither we nor our Vit–Ra–Tox Distributors are doctors. We do not attempt to diagnose or prescribe. We do not approach our customer's health problem from the standpoint of specific ailments. We are, however, interested in teaching them how, to the extent possible through nutritional influences, we can help them. * * *

"Our sales talk and theory of body building through nutritional elements are not to be interpreted as entering the field of medicine or as violating a doctor's prerogative. Since, therefore, we try only to improve the nutritional vitality of our customers, if any dangerous acute conditions exist, or are suspected, a physician should be consulted."

if such was the impression made upon the jury, it seems more than likely that a prospective purchaser, hoping finally to obtain relief from a long-endured disease, would not read appellants' literature with any skeptical literalness. Bearing in mind the broadly remedial purposes of the Act in preventing deception, the Congress must be taken to have meant to strike not only at palpably false claims but also at clever indirection and ambiguity in the creation of misleading impressions....

NOTES

1. *Double-Barrel Attack.* The principal case demonstrates FDA's use of the Act's overlapping definitions of "food" and of "drug" to attack products marketed to prevent nutritional deficiencies and other diseases. In attempting to identify the criteria for determining whether a product is subject to the "drug" requirements of the Act, consider the following excerpt from *United States v. Nutrition Service, Inc.,* 227 F. Supp. 375 (W.D. Pa. 1964):

> Certain evidence was presented by the plaintiff that the defendants here claimed for Mucorhicin antibiotic qualities by reason of a relationship with penicillin.... While in fact it may be true that mold growth exists naturally in certain foods and that such foods are sold regularly there is essentially this difference, that such foods are sold only as foods and not for treatment, mitigation and prevention of disease. If cheese were to be sold by any processor for the cure, treatment, mitigation and prevention of disease under the classification of food, within the provisions of the Food and Drug Act, it would be necessarily a drug.
>
> ... The real test is how was this product being sold? If as a food, was it for the furnishing of energy and body building? Or was it being sold for the treatment and mitigation of disease? ...

2. *Enforcement History.* The *Irons* case is illustrative of literally hundreds of court actions that FDA instituted against false or misleading nutritional claims in product labeling under both the food and drug sections of the Act. At least prior to 1970, FDA and the FTC undoubtedly expended more enforcement resources in the area of nutrition than in any other single field. The failure of this case-by-case approach to stem the tide of deception explains why both agencies turned to rulemaking. *See* p. 212 *infra.*

UNITED STATES v. "VITASAFE FORMULA M"

United States District Court, District of New Jersey, 1964.
226 F. Supp. 266.

LAND, District Judge.

The United States alleges that the Vitasafe capsule, *as an article of food* within the meaning of 21 U.S.C. § 321(f), is misbranded under 21 U.S.C. § 343(a) in that:

Such disclaimers occur only rarely. And even when they appear in conjunction with some of the literature found to be false or misleading, they should not be regarded as conferring any immunity on appellants, so long as the literature in its entirety is reasonably understood by readers to make the curative claims alleged by the government.

I. Its labeling, when viewed as a whole, represents, suggests and implies that the nutritional needs for men and women differ, and that the "Formula M" capsules are designed to satisfy the special needs of men as contrasted to the "Formula W" capsules which are designed to satisfy the special needs of women, which representations, suggestions, and implications are contrary to fact;

II. The listing on the label of, and references in the labeling to, certain ingredients implies and suggests that the nutritional value of Vitasafe capsules is enhanced by the presence of such ingredients, when in fact such implications and suggestions are false and misleading in that the presence of these ingredients is of no nutritional significance for dietary supplementation....

IV. The overall impression suggested and implied by the statements in the labeling concerning the large amounts of common foods that must be consumed in order to furnish quantities of nutrients equal to the quantities of such nutrients present in one Vitasafe capsule is false and misleading since such large quantities of food would not be needed to supply the necessary dietary requirements for these nutrients and since the labeling does not list all the various nutrients furnished by the stated quantities of food designated in the labeling.

It is further alleged that the Vitasafe capsule, *as a drug* within the meaning of 21 U.S.C. § 321(g), is misbranded under 21 U.S.C. § 352(a) in that:

V. Its labeling contains false and misleading representations, suggestions, and implications that the article is an adequate and effective treatment for depression, tension, weakness, nervous disorders, lethargy, lack of energy, lassitude, impotence, aches and pains, aging, impaired digestion, loss of appetite, skin infections, lesions and scaliness, night blindness, photophobia, fatigue, headache, insomnia, diarrhea, edema of the legs, hypersensitivity to noise, swelling, redness, soreness and burning of the tongue, impairment of memory, inability to concentrate, dermatitis, cracking of the lips, lesions at the corners of the mouth, growth failure in children, sore, swollen and bleeding gums, defective calcification of the bones, lowered resistance to disease and lowered vitality, which representations, suggestions, and implications are false and misleading since the article is not an adequate and effective treatment of the disease conditions and symptoms as stated and implied.

VI. Its labeling contains false and misleading representations, suggestions, and implications that practically everyone in this country is suffering from or is in danger of suffering from a dietary deficiency of vitamins, minerals and proteins which is likely to result in specific deficiency diseases, such as scurvy, as well as a great number of nonspecific symptoms and conditions, which threatened deficiency is represented as being due to loss of nutritive value of food by reason of the soil on which the food is grown, and the storage, processing, and cooking of the foods, which representations, suggestions, and implications are false and misleading since they are contrary to fact. . . .

A study of all the exhibits and the expert testimony . . . leads this court to the following conclusions:

1. The labeling of the seized article, when viewed as a whole, does represent, suggest and imply that a woman, because of sex alone, has different nutritional needs than a man, and "Vitasafe Formula W" will satisfy these special needs of women as contrasted to "Vitasafe Formula M" which will satisfy the special needs of men.

These representations are false and misleading since there is no difference in the nutritional requirements of non-pregnant non-lactating women as compared to men, except for iron in women of childbearing age, which need is adequately satisfied by the normal diet readily available and normally consumed. With the exception of iron, nutritional need is the same for men and women. . . .

2. The labeling of the seized *res,* when viewed in its entirety, does represent, suggest and imply that the nutritional value of Vitasafe capsules is enhanced by the presence in these capsules of the following ingredients . . . :

Vitamin K (Menadione) . . . [quantities deleted]
Monopotassium Glutamate
L-lysine Monohydrochloride
Sodium Caseinate (protein)
Leucin
Lysine
Valine
Histidine
Isoleucine
Phenylalamine
Threonine
Tryptophan
Manganese
Potassium
Zinc
Magnesium
Calcium
Phosphorous
Choline Bitartrate
Inositol
Lemon Bioflavonoid

Sulfur

Royal Jelly

The evidence produced at trial proves that the normal or ordinary diet supplies amounts of the above-listed ingredients greatly in excess of those necessary for good nutrition. Furthermore, with the exception of the fat soluble vitamins A and D, vitamins ingested in excess of those required are excreted and make no nutritional contribution. The evidence further proves that the following ingredients represented to be present in the Vitasafe product have no nutritional value whatever, namely rutin, lemon bioflavonoid, monopotassium glutamate, sulfur, choline bitartrate, inositol and royal jelly. Other ingredients, such as all the amino acids are in such small quantities as to be of no significant value when compared to the quantities of such ingredients which are required and which are present in the average diet. Because the ingredients here designated are either of no nutritional significance per se or are contained in the Vitasafe product in such minute quantities, these ingredients do not enhance the nutritional value of the Vitasafe capsules. Consequently, the representation and suggestion referred to in this finding is false and misleading....

4. Although correct if read literally and carefully, the labeling of the seized *res* represents and suggests to the ordinary reader that it is necessary to eat enormous quantities and varieties of foods in order to obtain the variety of vitamins and minerals in the amounts provided by one Vitasafe capsule. This representation is false and misleading because the variety and quantity of foods referred to in the labeling of the seized *res* provide many times the amounts of nutrients as well as additional nutrients than are supplied by one Vitasafe capsule.

5. The labeling of the seized *res* represents, suggests, and implies that Vitasafe capsules are an adequate and effective treatment of or preventive for the following symptoms and conditions ... [repeating the government's Charge V].

This representation is false and misleading. The evidence produced at trial conclusively proves that the above designated symptoms or conditions are caused by and associated with a great number of serious pathological diseases. Further, although some of these symptoms may be associated with vitamin and mineral deficiencies, the likelihood of their being caused by or associated with vitamin or mineral deficiencies in the United States today is very small. There is a danger involved in the use of this type of labeling insofar as a person having one or more of the above-listed symptoms may resort to a Vitasafe product as a cure. Such a person may continue taking this vitamin product for a long continued period, as he is urged to do in the labeling of this product and thereby fail to obtain competent medical help to correct his physical illness.....

7. The article under seizure is both a food within the meaning of 21 U.S.C. § 321(f) because its labeling recommends its use as and represents it to be of value as a dietary and nutritional supplement,

and also a drug within the meaning of 21 U.S.C. § 321(g) because its labeling recommends its use as and represents it to be of value as a curative or preventive of disease conditions in man affecting the structure and function of the body of man....

NOTE

See also United States v. An Article of Food ... Nuclomin, 482 F.2d 581 (8th Cir. 1973), which held the labeling of a dietary supplement was misleading because it featured ingredients that "were either not needed in the human diet or ... the amount of the ingredient was so small that it would have no value." The court emphasized that "the fact that no purchasers have actually been misled is not a defense under the Act. *Compare United States v. 119 Cases ... "New Dextra Brand Fortified Cane Sugar,"* 231 F. Supp. 551 (S.D. Fla. 1963), *aff'd*, 334 F.2d 238 (5th Cir. 1964), p. 165 *supra*, where FDA unsuccessfully pursued the same legal theory against a fortified food.

----

2. FDA'S VITAMIN–MINERAL REGULATIONS

RUTH LAMB, AMERICAN CHAMBER OF HORRORS

(1936).

And finally there are the frauds which arise from incomplete knowledge. Such is the overzealous exploitation of the vitamins. All the vitamins have a popular appeal, but our knowledge of them is still chaotic.... Of them all, vitamin D is the most widely exploited....

Under the right sort of food-and-drugs act the Government would have authority to compel products which do not contain enough of the vitamin to be of value in preventing rickets to say so frankly on the package, and to forbid claims in the advertising which are not borne out by facts....

DAVID F. CAVERS, THE FOOD, DRUG, AND COSMETIC ACT OF 1938: ITS LEGISLATIVE HISTORY AND ITS SUBSTANTIVE PROVISIONS

6 Law & Contemporary Problems 2 (1939).

... With the requirement that ingredients of fabricated foods be disclosed, S. 1944 coupled a broad grant of power to the Secretary to require by regulation "such further information" on labels "as he may deem necessary to protect the public from deception." In S. 2000 this power was narrowed and directed against the specific field where the need for it was greatest: foods offered for special dietary uses....

Shortly after enactment of the 1938 Act, FDA established detailed labeling requirements for foods marketed for "special dietary uses" pursuant to section 403(j). 5 Fed. Reg. 3565 (September 5, 1940), 6 Fed. Reg. 3304 (July 8, 1941), 6 Fed. Reg. 5921 (November 22, 1941). These requirements remained unchanged until FDA undertook a general revision of its special dietary food regulations, a project that began in 1962 and was interrupted both by court challenges to the agency's policies and procedures and by Congressional restriction of its substantive authority.

The original special dietary food regulations established quantitative "minimum daily requirements" (MDR) for individual nutrients. The label for any product represented for special dietary use because of its vitamin or mineral properties was required to declare the percent of the MDR in the amount of the product consumed during one day. For nutrients for which no MDR existed, the label was required to state that "The need for _____ in human nutrition has not been established." By 1962, FDA had concluded that these requirements were insufficient to control the claims made for vitamin-mineral products. In 27 Fed. Reg. 5815 (June 20, 1962), it published a proposal to revise the regulations completely. The "minimum daily requirements" were to be replaced with "daily requirements" for purposes of labeling. The proposal also stated that the label of a dietary supplement could declare "only those nutrients recognized by competent authorities as essential and of significant dietary-supplement value in human nutrition and that are present in amounts that are consistent with the nutritional requirements for such nutrients." FDA went on to specify the nutrients that it considered essential and the amounts believed nutritionally appropriate, as well as other nutrients not regarded as appropriate for supplementation. Within a short time, however, the agency decided that the June 1962 proposal did not go far enough.

WILLIAM D. GOODRICH, THE COMING STRUGGLE OVER VITAMIN–MINERAL PILLS *

20 Business Lawyer 145 (1964).

A little over two years ago—in June 1962—FDA announced a proposed revision of the regulations for the labeling of foods for special dietary uses. . . .

What was proposed was to eliminate some of the basic causes of confusion and misrepresentation so that the unwary consumer would be spared the snares which now influence his purchase. . . .

1. Formulations of vitamin-mineral tablets which contain many times the "minimum daily requirement" of the nutrients, designed to appeal to the layman's belief that if a little is good to satisfy his "minimum" daily requirement, then much more than that minimum would be much better for his health.

---

* [Mr. Goodrich was then FDA Chief Counsel.]

2. Formulations based on no rational nutritional principles at all, for example, those which might have one-tenth of the minimum daily requirement of an expensive nutrient and ten times the minimum daily requirement of the cheaper ones.

3. So-called "shotgun" preparations, which contain not only all the vitamins and minerals which might possibly play a part in improving the nutritive well being of the customer, but also all the other nutrients so far discovered, regardless of the fact that there is no evidence whatever to support a belief that they are needed in human nutrition....

4. And finally, formulations to support promotional efforts based on the four great myths of nutrition: (a) that our soils are so depleted that ordinary foods do not contain the expected nutrients; (b) that modern processing and storage of food strips them of virtually all important nutritive values; (c) that it is essentially impossible to obtain from our daily diets the nutrients we require; (d) and that as a result almost every one is now or will soon be suffering from a subclinical nutritional deficiency which may be the cause of some serious condition of ill health.

Our own out-dated regulations have contributed to the confusion by requiring that nutrients be declared in terms of percentage of the "minimum daily requirement," and that the need in human nutrition for others has not been established. The classification of vitamin-mineral pills as special dietary foods, rather than as drugs, resulted in the anomalous situation in which all the ingredients of these pills and tablets had to be declared on the label, even the inert ingredients which could not contribute anything of nutritional value. Our drug regulations specifically forbid the declaration of inert ingredients when this may mislead the consumer. To the uninitiated, all this carried the message that a product supplying ten times the "minimum daily requirement" was a superior product, even though it was a well-established scientific fact that the particular vitamins involved were water soluble, not stored in the body, and the excess would be promptly excreted as unneeded nutrients. The "not yet established" legend seemed to promise that the evidence was just around the corner—else why would the manufacturer include this nutrient as an ingredient at all....

––––––

In 31 Fed. Reg. 8521 (June 18, 1966), FDA issued its "final" revision of the special dietary food regulations. The MDRs became "recommended dietary allowances" (RDAs). To solve the problems Goodrich described, the final regulations included four new elements: (1) a standard of identity limiting the nutrients and their levels in dietary supplements; (2) a novel standard of identity specifying the foods to which nutrients could be added; (3) a prohibition of any representation resembling Goodrich's "four great myths of nutrition;" and (4) a requirement that the main panel of every dietary supplement label bear the following so-called "crepe" statement:

> Vitamins and minerals are supplied in abundant amounts by the foods we eat. The Food and Nutrition Board of the National Research Council recommends that dietary needs be satisfied by foods. Except for persons with special medical needs, there is no scientific basis for recommending routine use of dietary supplements.

This order precipitated an avalanche of objections which automatically stayed the regulations and led to an evidentiary hearing lasting much of 1968 and 1969.

ROBERT W. HAMILTON, RULEMAKING ON A RECORD BY THE FOOD AND DRUG ADMINISTRATION

50 Texas Law Review 1132 (1972).

Several problems plagued the hearings. As in the *Peanut Butter* proceeding, the actual hearing commenced with no clear delineation of the issues. The notice of public hearing had set forth the "issues" in general statutory language: "Whether it will promote honesty and fair dealing in the interest of consumers" to provide full information to consumers as to the value of foods for special dietary uses; whether [a] ... "crepe label" is a "necessary means of fully informing consumers of the value" of dietary supplements, and so forth. The hearing examiner's inexperienced evidentiary rulings, particularly during the early part of the hearing, invited technical objections and wrangling among the attorneys. Also, a number of nonlawyers, particularly one medical doctor, actively participated and cross-examined Government witnesses at great length.

As the hearings progressed, several procedural innovations were attempted. These innovations improved the efficiency of the hearing, although several attorneys complained that they were prejudiced by them. These changes includes: (1) submitting direct testimony in written form; (2) prohibiting cross-examination on cross-examination, or on other participants' cross-examination; (3) limiting the use of scientific texts and treatises to the contradiction of direct testimony, and requiring the cross-examiner to specify precisely the testimony to be contradicted and the contradicting passage; (4) limiting colloquy of counsel and legal argument unless specifically requested; (5) striking or limiting cumulative testimony of experts; and (6) prohibiting parties (other than the Government) from cross-examining witnesses of other nongovernmental parties without submitting a written statement to show that testimony was adverse to the opponent's interest....

Despite the restrictions, most of the hearing consisted of repetitious and cumulative cross-examination of Government witnesses....

When the hearing ground to a halt in May 1970, its tangible products had reached Brobdingnagian proportions. Testimony of Government witnesses accounted for about 25,000 pages of transcript—slightly more than two-thirds of the total. The Government and the industry participants had proffered testimony of 162 witnesses and more than 2,000 pieces of documentary evidence....

———

In the interim, the problem of "hunger in America" was publicized in the news media and by the White House Conference on Food, Nutrition and Health. The FDA drive to restrict the use of vitamin-mineral products was therefore substantially blunted. The agency's tentative final and final regulations, 38 Fed. Reg. 2143, 2152 (January 19, 1973), 38 Fed. Reg. 20708, 20730 (August 2, 1973), reflected a major shift in approach, but still did not escape court challenge. The regulations adopted "recommended daily allowances" (RDAs) and continued to require products to be labeled with the percent of the RDAs in a day's serving. Representations exploiting the "myths" of nutrition were banned, but the agency abandoned the "crepe statement." Of primary interest, FDA abandoned any limitations on food fortification, but it did establish standards of identity for four types of dietary supplements: (1) all vitamins and minerals, (2) all vitamins, (3) all minerals, and (4) all vitamins plus iron. The agency set the floor for including nutrients in these standard products at 50 percent of the RDA and the ceiling at 150 percent of the RDA. It also ruled that any product containing amounts in excess of 150 percent of the RDA would be a drug. The regulations were immediately challenged in court.

NATIONAL NUTRITIONAL FOODS ASS'N v. FDA

United States Court of Appeals, Second Circuit, 1974.
504 F.2d 761.

FRIENDLY, Circuit Judge:

We have here 15 petitions under § 701(f) of the Federal Food, Drug and Cosmetic Act to review two final regulations of the United States Food and Drug Administration ... relating to vitamin and mineral supplements sold as foods. One regulation [is] entitled Part 125—Label Statements Concerning Dietary Properties of Food Purporting To Be Or Represented For Special Dietary Uses.... The other, entitled Part 80—Definitions And Standards Of Identity For Food For Special Dietary Uses, embodies a new concept in regard to this type of "food." ... The primary statutory authority invoked for the Regulations lies in the first sentence of § 401 ... and in § 403(j)....

As indicated, the novelty of the regulations lies in the FDA's invoking, with respect to the many vitamins and minerals and the myriad combinations thereof, its power to prescribe a standard of identity under § 401.....

The hardest issues in the case are (1) whether the FDA has power to set standards of identity for dietary supplements in such a way that vitamin and mineral products containing vitamins and/or minerals in nonstandardized combinations or whose daily dosage of any nutrient as specified in their labels exceeds the upper limit of the U.S. RDA's will be deemed misbranded under § 403(g), if they are offered for sale as foods; and, if so, (2) whether there was substantial evidence to support what the agency did.....

We begin by rejecting the argument of some petitioners that the FDA could not proceed simultaneously under §§ 401 and 403(j).... This argument finds support neither in the language of the statute nor in its legislative history. In sharp contrast to § 403(i), nothing in § 403(j) restricts its applicability to cases where no standard of identity has been prescribed. The fair reading of the statute is rather that, in the case of foods for special dietary uses for which standards of identity have been prescribed, Congress wished to authorize the FDA to require label disclosures not only of optional properties, as in the case of other foods with standards of identity, but of mandatory ones as well. Nothing in the legislative history is persuasive to the contrary....

The evidence supporting the need for both a qualitative and a quantitative standard of identity was impressive.... [T]he agency had ample evidence to conclude that a consumer seeking a dietary supplement of a given vitamin or mineral, whether singly or in combination with others, is faced with a dazzling array of recommended daily dosages and that a consumer seeking a multiple supplement is faced with an equally dazzling array of combinations; that neither consumer is given any basis for intelligent selection; and that it would "promote honesty and fair dealing in the interest of consumers," to promulgate the qualitative and quantitative standards of identity of new Part 80....

The FDA considers, with what seems to us, at least in general, entirely sufficient reason, that neither the new label requirements nor additions that might be made to these will suffice to eliminate consumer confusion. The subject matter is simply too recondite and the offering of products too diverse for a label alone to be "clear enough so that, in the words of the prophet Isaiah, 'wayfaring men, though fools, shall not err therein'...." Thus ... we hold the agency was justified, as a matter of good sense, in concluding that the stated purposes of § 401 would be furthered by promulgating qualitative and quantitative standards of identity in this area so as to allow for some 30-odd products (each with limited variability of daily dosages) rather than the hundreds now on the shelves of food and drug stores.....

Concededly ... the consumer who is disappointed by not being able to obtain precisely the dosage or combination he seeks in the standardized products is likely to find his costs somewhat increased if he sets about achieving the same result by purchasing larger numbers of a particular type of pill, or even by purchasing a little of this and a little of that. Such an increase in effective price, and the likely consequential decrease in unit sales by the manufacturers, is, however, a paradigmatic example of the kind of consideration the agency may find outweighed by public needs. . . .

Despite all this we are concerned that the all-or-nothing attitude adopted by both sides in this long and bitter controversy may have led the FDA into proscribing some combinations whose sale should be permitted under the standards of § 401 and into prescribing some maxima where a good case can be made for allowing an excess. . . .

. . . In regard to the maxima, the agency did attempt . . . to update in scientific terms what was then the latest edition of the RDA's with respect to particular nutrients, and there was also other sporadic testimony pro and con with regard to the upper limits for particular ingredients. But the agency made no effort to draw the parties into a comprehensive study of the possibility of raising some upper limits and particularly of raising them even if scientific considerations were somewhat against it simply because such moves in selected cases might not meet real and not altogether irrational market demands without contributing appreciably to consumer confusion, nor any particular effort to deal in its findings with such testimony on particular upper limits as did happen to arise. . . .

With respect to combinations of less than all essential ingredients, the agency itself apparently recognized that it had given at most sporadic consideration to the possibility that some exceptions might be in order. . . .

In light of all these considerations, we direct that § 80.1(b)(4) be modified to permit upward revisions in the maxima for particular vitamins or minerals and that the criteria be broadened to conform to the standards of § 401. We also believe the agency should receive and deal explicitly with applications for increases in particular upper limits and applications under the present § 80.1(b)(4) before the regulations become effective. . . . . To this end we think it necessary to stay the regulations in their entirety, and not just those parts establishing the standard of identity, since, for example, a stay affecting only the standard of identity would force a B-complex manufacturer to change over to the new label imposed by the new regulations while knowing full well that if his § 80.1(b)(4) application was denied his line would be off the shelves when the limited stay expires. . . .

In determining whether it is "reasonable" to deny a particular application, the primary consideration must of course be the degree of increase in potential consumer confusion. . . . Moreover, against any danger of slight increases in confusion should be weighed such factors as the following: (1) how large is the consumer demand for the product at present, and how widespread any expert belief that it is not an irrational product for a significant number of consumers; (2) how effectively could any potential confusion with respect to the particular product be reduced or eliminated by requiring on the label (A) with respect to a high dosage product, a legend to the effect that the FDA has determined this product contains quantities of such-and-such nutrient not normally essential to human health, or (B) with respect to a combination, a legend to the effect that the FDA has determined this product does not contain all the nutrients essential to human health; and (3) in the case of applications to exceed the upper limits, how dependable, if this can be determined, is the particular NSA [sic] RDA on which the upper limit is based relative to other RDA's....

... Section 125.1(c) recognizes that, in addition to the 12 vitamins and 7 minerals approved as mandatory or optional ingredients, two other vitamins and six other minerals are essential to human nutrition. Nevertheless, because no U.S. RDA's have yet been established for them, these are banned "for addition to general purpose foods or dietary supplements of vitamins and minerals," although they "may be added to such other foods for special dietary use as infant formulas, and foods represented for use solely under medical supervision to meet nutritional requirements in specific medical conditions." If this language left open any possibility that these vitamins and minerals could be separately sold as foods, this would be foreclosed by §§ 80.1(b)(1) and (2), and 80.1(f)(1), which effectively ban the sale as dietary supplements of any vitamins or minerals not on the approved list.

We see no sufficient basis for such drastic treatment.... Assuming *arguendo* that bans on separate sale of nontoxic individual nutrients may at times be within the agency's statutory authority, the agency has articulated no basis for invoking such an extreme remedy here—particularly when it is not invoked as to the § 125.2(b)(5) elements, which the agency considers of far lower, indeed of negligible, nutritional rank.

... [W]e shall enjoin enforcement of so much of the regulations as prohibits the inclusion of the vitamins and minerals listed in § 125.1(c) in general purpose foods, or as optional ingredients in dietary supplements, including dietary supplements for separate sale under § 80.1(b)(2)....

Petitioners also object, both as a matter of statutory authority and as a question of substantial evidence, to § 125.1(h), providing, with certain exceptions intended to conform to the standard of identity exemptions in § 80.1(e), that preparations containing more than the upper limits of the U.S. RDA per serving are drugs....

The FDA's decision to handle as drugs all vitamin and mineral products in excess of the upper limits of the U.S. RDA's rested essentially on the thought expressed in paragraph 12 of the preamble to Part 125: "The hearing record discloses no known food or nutrition use of nutrients at such high levels, and no such uses were shown in the exceptions." We believe that this mischaracterizes the record.... [A] significant number of persons have indisputable nutritional need for potencies exceeding the upper limits; in particular, and by no means exclusively, this includes the large number of women taking oral contraceptives. In light of this, it cannot be said even as an objective matter that a given bottle of pills, each containing more than the upper limit of one or more nutrients, is not being used for nutritional purposes.

A *fortiori* it follows that the vendor of such a product can in good faith intend it for nontherapeutic use. Section 201(g)(1)(B) makes the vendor's intent the crucial element in the definition of "drug" here at issue, and the cases consistently have read that language for its plain meaning. While we agree that a factfinder should be free to pierce all of a manufacturer's subjective claims of intent and even his misleadingly "nutritional" labels to find actual therapeutic intent on the basis of objective evidence in a proper case, such objective evidence would need to consist of something more than demonstrated uselessness as a food for most people. We therefore hold that § 125.1(h) is invalid.[35] ...

... [T]he U.S. RDA's serve two different purposes in the FDA's regulatory scheme. One is the requirement, § 125.3(a), that "the label shall bear a statement of the percentage of the U.S. RDA of such vitamins and minerals, as set forth in § 125.1(b), supplied by such food when consumed in a specified quantity during a period of 1 day." The other consists of the substantive provision, § 80.1(c)(1), that "dietary supplements described in this section shall contain in the specified daily quantity no less than the lower limit nor more than the upper limit of any nutrient specified in paragraph (f) of this section for the group(s) for which the supplement is offered."

There is little controversy over the label requirement.... Similarly ... there is, and probably could be, no serious and separate objection, on an evidentiary basis or otherwise, to so much of § 80.1(c)(1) as proscribes the sale of a dietary supplement containing less than the lower limits of the U.S. RDA's. In contrast there are violent objections to the use of the RDA's to prescribe upper limits....

Perhaps the central evidentiary attack on the maxima, which are generally 150% of the U.S. RDA's, is that the FDA misapprehended the purpose of the National Academy of Sciences in promulgating the NAS RDA's on which the U.S. RDA's are based.... All the "appropriate uses" of the RDA's envisioned by the NAS involve evaluation of adequacy of food supplies or consumption patterns over a large population, and not for individuals.... By way of demonstrating that the RDA's are objectively inappropriate for uses other than these envisioned by the NAS, petitioners also emphasize that, on the basis of the FDA's own findings, RDA's provide an adequate intake of essential nutrients only for "essentially all of the normal healthy persons in the United States," more specifically 95% to 99% of the "normal healthy" populations; that even this 95–99% range is apparently derived by excluding certain needs which petitioners regard as nutritional but the

35. While we thus reach this holding as a question of insufficient evidence, we must agree with petitioners that an administrative interpretation in such direct conflict with a legislative definition must also be invalidated on the ground of exceeding the agency's statutory authority.

FDA considers therapeutic (e.g., increased needs for vitamins and/or minerals on the part of women taking oral contraceptives and persons who do not absorb vitamins well), and is derived by partially ignoring what is now a fairly widespread if minority belief that the "optimal" level of nutrition considerably exceeds that necessary to avoid clinical deficiencies; and that the experimental and other methods for developing the RDA's are admittedly far from perfect and the state of current knowledge far from complete.

If the FDA had sought to prohibit ingestion of more than the maxima insofar as it could . . . we should indeed have found it impossible to sustain the regulations. But the agency has done nothing of the sort. Beyond the possibility that some applications for relief from the upper limits will be granted . . . . anyone who is not satisfied with the quantity of a vitamin or mineral permitted in a combination or in a separate pill can take as many more tablets as he likes. He will doubtless find this more expensive, but, as previously suggested, the additional payment required in such cases had to be weighed by the agency against the savings from useless expenditures by purchasers of supplements containing far higher potencies than they require. . . . .

As earlier noted, several petitioners do not object to the basic requirement of § 125.3(a), that "the label shall bear a statement of the percentage of the U.S. RDA of such vitamins and minerals, as set forth in § 125.1(b), supplied by such food when consumed in a specified quantity during a period of 1 day," to which we have referred at the beginning of Part IV. In any event we see no infirmity in it. . . .

In contrast, there is a chorus of objections concerning the requirements of § 125.2(b) with respect to . . . [representations relating to beliefs about nutrition that FDA had previously characterized as "myths." Judge Friendly upheld the agency's prohibitions against (1) disease treatment claims; (2) claims that a balanced diet cannot supply adequate amounts of nutrients (except for iron); (3) claims that foods grown in poor soil may be deficient; (4) statements that processing or cooking of food can result in dietary inadequacies; (5) using unneeded substances in ways that may imply they have nutritional value; and (6) statements that there are differences between natural and synthetic nutrients.]

———

In addition to challenging its regulations in court, FDA's critics continued their efforts to prevent any official limitations on the formulation and sale of dietary supplements through legislation. On April 22, 1976, President Ford signed the Health Research and Health Services Amendments of 1976, 90 Stat. 401. Title V of this legislation, 90 Stat. at 410, a rider adopted on the Senate floor with the objective of constricting the authority on which FDA had relied in adopting its controversial vitamin and mineral regulations, added a new section 411 to the FD&C Act, which significantly curtailed FDA's authority to restrict the composition of dietary supplements under sections 201(n), 401, or 403. At the same time it curtailed FDA's power, the 1976 law gave the agency limited authority to regulate the advertising of dietary foods. The pertinent changes in the Act appear in sections 201(n), 303(d), 304(a)(3), 403(a)(2), and 411. Congress added section 303(d) to exempt such advertising from the Act's criminal sanctions. In section 304(a) it added language to restrict seizures charging misbranding based on advertising for a dietary supplement to those instances where the advertising was disseminated and paid for by the establishment where the product is seized.

The 1976 legislation included a new section 707 of the FD&C Act which, in substance, requires FDA to defer to the FTC before seeking to enforce its new advertising authority. This new authority was considered by some members of Congress to be compensation for the agency's loss of its more important authority over composition and labeling of dietary foods. FDA has not used this new authority since it was conferred, however, and the procedural restrictions imposed by section 707 are likely to assure that the authority is rarely invoked.

HEALTH RESEARCH AND HEALTH SERVICES AMENDMENTS OF 1976

Conference Report No. 94–1005, 94th Congress, 2d Session (1976).

Under the conference substitute, products subject to its provisions are defined as safe human foods for special dietary use which are or contain any natural or synthetic vitamin or mineral and which are intended for ingestion in tablet or capsule form or in small units of liquid measure. In addition, such foods not intended for ingestion in tablet, capsule, or liquid form are subject to the provisions of the substitute only if they do not simulate conventional foods, if they are not represented to be conventional foods, and if they are not represented for use as the sole item of a meal or of the diet....

Except with respect to products defined above, the conference substitute does not alter existing provisions of the Federal Food, Drug, and Cosmetic Act with respect to foods and drugs. The Secretary retains his current authority to regulate the nutritional formulation and composition of, and potency of vitamins, minerals and other ingredients in conventional foods such as milk, enriched bread and enriched rice, as well as in products which simulate conventional foods such as soybased protein substitutes for meats and poultry. The Secretary also retains his current authority to regulate the nutritional formulation and composition of, and potency of vitamins, minerals and other ingredients in foods represented by labeling, advertising, or other promotional materials for use as the sole item of a meal or of the diet....

... [T]hree significant restrictions would be imposed on the Secretary with regard to the regulation of products subject to the conference substitute. First, new section 411(a)(1)(A) of the Act prohibits the Secretary from using his existing authority under sections 201(n) or 403 of the Act (relating to misbranding) or under section 401 of the Act (relating to standards of identity) to impose maximum limits on the potency of safe vitamins and minerals contained in products subject to the conference substitute. This provision would not restrict the Secretary from prescribing minimum potency levels for vitamins or minerals in such products in order to prevent the addition of insignificant or useless amounts.

Second, new section 411(a)(1)(B) of the Act prohibits the Secretary from classifying as a drug a natural or synthetic vitamin or mineral, offered by itself or in combination, solely because it exceeds the level of potency that the Secretary determines is nutritionally rational or useful.

Third, new section 411(a)(1)(C) of the Act prohibits the Secretary from using his authority with respect to misbranding or establishment of standards of identity to limit the combination or number of any safe vitamin, mineral or other ingredient of food in products subject to the conference substitute....

... [T]he limitations on the Secretary, described above, do not apply with respect to a product otherwise subject to the provisions of the conference substitute where such product is represented for use by (1) individuals in the treatment or management of specific diseases or disorders, (2) children, or (3) pregnant or lactating women....

Except as specifically provided, the conference substitute does not alter the drug or food provisions of the Federal Food, Drug, and Cosmetic Act. If a product containing vitamins, minerals or other ingredients is a drug within the meaning of section 201(g) of the Act, the Secretary may, with respect to such product, exercise his authority under Chapter V of the Act. For example, the Secretary may bring an action for misbranding of a product which purports to be or is represented as a drug (within the meaning of section 201(g) of the Act) if its labeling fails to bear adequate directions for its purported use or for the use for which it is represented (within the meaning of section 502(f)(1) of the Act)....

The Secretary also has the authority to regulate the composition or potency of a product subject to the provisions of the conference substitute on the basis of safety. If a high potency preparation of a vitamin or mineral is a drug as defined by section 201(g) of the Act and the Secretary determines that, within the meaning of section 503(b) of the Act, it is not safe for use except under the supervision of a physician, such a high potency preparation is subject to regulation as a prescription drug under the Act.

Similarly, if any vitamin, mineral or other food ingredient is not generally recognized as safe by qualified experts and meets the other criteria of the definition of a "food additive" under section 201(s) of the Act, it would be subject to regulation under section 409 of the Act....

It is on precisely this basis that the Secretary has, by regulation, restricted the potency of the vitamin folic acid that may be added to a food....

The conference substitute provides that a food to which the conference substitute is applicable shall not be deemed misbranded under section 403 of the Act solely because its label bears a listing of all of the ingredients in the food, or solely because its advertising contains references to ingredients in the food that are not vitamins or minerals. Thus, for example, if a tablet or capsule of vitamin C contains rutin, a substance that the Secretary has concluded has no dietary usefulness, the list of ingredients as well as the advertising for the product may refer to rutin without causing the food to be deemed misbranded. However, because of the conferees' concern that consumers not be misled into a belief that such substances have nutritional value, the conference substitute provides that the labeling so [sic] such a product may not list ingredients that are not vitamins or minerals except as a part of a list of all the ingredients of the food, in accordance with applicable regulations promulgated by the Secretary pursuant to section 403 of the Act....

Responding to Judge Friendly's ruling in *National Nutritional Foods Ass'n*, FDA reopened the proceedings, 40 Fed. Reg. 23244 (May 28, 1975), 40 Fed. Reg. 44857 (September 30, 1975). Congress enacted the Vitamin–Mineral Amendments before the agency could complete the rulemaking. In 41 Fed. Reg. 46156 (October 19, 1976) and 42 Fed. Reg. 20292 (April 19, 1977), FDA issued final revised regulations that it believed responded to the Court of Appeals' ruling and complied with the limitations imposed by Congress. But it did not invite further public comment on the impact of the new legislation before completing its rulemaking, concluding, pursuant to 5 U.S.C. § 553(b)(B), that it had good cause for dispensing with this step.

NATIONAL NUTRITIONAL FOODS ASS'N v. KENNEDY
United States Court of Appeals, Second Circuit, 1978.
572 F.2d 377.

FRIENDLY, Circuit Judge.

This is the latest but, unfortunately, probably not the last chapter in the bitter battle between the Food and Drug Administration (FDA) and manufacturers and vendors of pills and liquids containing vitamins and minerals and citizens allied with the latter. While the manufacturers and vendors have obvious private interests as well, the battle reflects what appears to be a sincere sentiment on the part of many citizens that daily ingestion of a substantial quantity and variety of vitamins and minerals in the form of pills or liquids, in addition to those furnished by ordinary diet, is needed for good health, especially because of the increasing consumption of "the modern food fads—sweet drinks, junk foods, heavy sugar diets" and "wheat germ-free bread and nutritionally inadequate breakfast foods," 121 Cong. Rec. S.21856 (daily ed. Dec. 11, 1975) (Sen. Proxmire), and the FDA's equally sincere belief that the promotion of what, on a previous review, this court called a "dazzling array" of recommended daily dosages and combinations, is causing consumers to waste millions of dollars annually in the purchase of vitamin and mineral preparations which they either do not need at all or do not need in the potencies or combinations that are being bought. The battle began nearly a generation ago. . . .

After the Supreme Court had denied petitions for certiorari by those who had been petitioners here, the Commissioner published in the Federal Register of May 28, 1975, 40 F.R. 23244–50, a paper bearing on the labelling of vitamin and mineral preparations. However, we are convinced that in failing to give notice of proposed rulemaking and to accord an opportunity for public participation in the process, as provided in 5 U.S.C. § 553(b) and (c), the Commissioner violated the mandate of Congress. . . .

The legislative history of the Administrative Procedure Act demonstrates that Congress intended the exceptions in § 553(b)(B) to be narrow ones. . . .

. . . [T]he Commissioner relies much more heavily on the claim that public participation was unnecessary; he argues that since Congress had spoken, there was nothing more for the public to say and the agency's duty was simply to excise portions of the proposed regulations that Congress had placed beyond its power. But the agency's task went beyond a mere wielding of scissors. While the 1976 legislation withdrew old powers, it also imposed new duties, notably with respect to labelling, see § 411(b)(2). . . . Moreover, the problem created by the 1976 amendment went deeper than the Commissioner would have it. His promulgation of a standard of identity for vitamin and mineral preparations had rested primarily not on considerations of safety but on the need to lessen confusion among consumers. . . . By the 1976 legislation Congress pronounced that it was not concerned about this for the public in general or, at least, that it considered the costs incident to reducing consumer confusion for the entire public by the FDA's proposed standard of identity to be too high in relation to the benefits to be achieved. While Congress permitted the agency to impose a standard of identity in the three instances cited in § 411(a)(2), it did not require this. Presumably it wished the agency to consider whether to impose a standard and, if so, what standard for the three permitted cases. The record which we found to have furnished substantial evidence to support the standard of identity previously prescribed thus might not serve the same office with respect to the limited applications now permitted. At least those who did not believe so were entitled to an opportunity to present their views, with the agency and other opposing interests, if unpersuaded, then having an opportunity to show why these were wrong. . . .

On the other hand the Commissioner properly rejected the petitioners' claim that further trial type procedures under § 701(e) were required. . . .

Petitioners contend that the Commissioner erred in retaining the minimum potency requirements for dietary supplements. . . . . The fact that the new legislation may prevent the Commissioner from excluding from dietary supplements compounds he thinks worthless in no way undermined his authority, which Congress specifically preserved, to prescribe minimum potencies for vitamins and minerals. . . . We hold to our previous opinion that the limits the Commissioner has set are "clearly within the language and purpose of § 401." . . . .

NOTES

1. *Subsequent Proceedings.* FDA revoked its various vitamin-mineral regulations in 44 Fed. Reg. 16005 (March 16, 1979), and has taken no further action in response to this decision. Thus, the agency repealed even those regulations that were upheld by the court of appeals and were not required to be changed by the 1976 statute.

2. *OTC Vitamin–Mineral Products.* In 44 Fed. Reg. 16126 (March 16, 1979) FDA also published the report of its advisory panel on OTC vitamin-mineral drugs. This report embodied the results of a four-year evaluation of the safety and effectiveness of vitamins and minerals sold as OTC drugs, conducted pursuant to the OTC Drug Review discussed at p. 588 *infra.* Perhaps by coincidence, the proposed monograph for OTC vitamin-mineral drugs was published in the same issue of the Federal Register as the revocation of the vitamin-mineral food regulations. FDA was deluged with objections from individuals and organizations who concluded that the agency was renewing its offensive against vitamin-mineral products. To avoid further confrontation, and to permit further study of the impact of the Vitamin–Mineral Amendments of 1976 on the FDA regulation of OTC vitamin-mineral drugs, FDA withdrew the proposed monograph in 46 Fed. Reg. 57914 (November 27, 1981). The agency had taken no further action as of June 30, 1990.

---

3. REGULATION OF HAZARDOUS NUTRIENTS

In the regulations FDA promulgated following Judge Friendly's first remand, the agency included a provision, since revoked, which asserted the power to regulate vitamins and minerals under the food safety provisions of the Act. Predictably, this provision also came under attack when the case went back before the Second Circuit.

NATIONAL NUTRITIONAL FOODS ASS'N V. KENNEDY
United States Court of Appeals, Second Circuit, 1978.
572 F.2d 377.

FRIENDLY, Circuit Judge.

... Petitioners focus on the paragraph that follows:

(8) Any vitamin or mineral which is included in a dietary supplement and which is not generally recognized, among experts qualified by scientific training and experience to evaluate its safety, as having been adequately shown to be safe under the conditions of its intended use is a food additive within the meaning of section 201(s) of the act; and pursuant to sections 402(a)(2)(C) and 409 of the act, such inclusion is illegal in the absence of a food additive regulation approving such inclusion. A listing of some of the vitamin and/or mineral properties which are generally recognized as safe, and which thus may lawfully be included in a dietary supplement without a food additive regulation, appears at Subpart F of Part 182 of this chapter.

Petitioners say that having been foiled by us, and by Congress, in his effort to classify high potency vitamins and minerals as drugs, the Commissioner is now seeking to reach essentially the same goal by threatening to treat added quantities as food additives....

Petitioners contend that vitamins and minerals are foods within § 201(f), ... and that in the nature of things a "food" cannot be a "food additive," especially when it is just more of the same. Recognizing that the Commissioner must have power to prevent the sale of vitamin and mineral preparations of such high potency as to be dangerous, they say the Commissioner must proceed under more general provisions relating to adulteration on a case by case basis, see, e.g. § 402(a)(1), (3)-(7), (b), rather than the more readily enforceable provisions relating to food additives....

... We do not believe a substance gains immunity from this criterion merely because it also qualifies as a food.... Congress has vested the Commissioner with broad "authority to promulgate regulations for the efficient enforcement" of the Food, Drug and Cosmetic Act, § 701(a), and we see no reason why we cannot determine that too much of even a good thing may come within the definition of a "food additive."

Still more important, Congress, which most likely was aware of the May 1975 regulations, seems to have held that view. The Senate decided not to include in the 1976 legislation a provision prohibiting FDA from regulating safe vitamins, minerals, and associated ingredients as food additives, stating in the report on the bill:

This was not done for two reasons. First of all, it is unnecessary. It would be inappropriate and contrary to the intention of this Title for the FDA to treat vitamins, minerals, and their associated ingredients about whose safety there currently is no doubt, as food additives. There are those who considered vitamins and minerals essentially foods with a long history of safe use. The authors rejected that course of action on grounds that there was insufficient evidence to support such a course of action at this time.

Second, there are some nutrients and ingredients or natural chemicals which are tangentially a part of vitamins or minerals which currently may be considered food additives because of their potential toxicity. We did not wish to prevent the FDA from acting in these circumstances. For the agency to do so based on the policies on potency and combinations which this amendment endorses, however, would be inappropriate.

S. Rep. No. 94–509, 94th Cong., 1st Sess. 40–41 (1975). And the House Conference Report observed ... [here Judge Friendly quoted the passage from the Conference Report set out at p. 221 *supra.*].

NOTES

1. *Mineral Toxicity.* In October 1975, FDA issued a 231–page analysis of the toxicity of the essential minerals. The agency has taken no action on the basis of the report, apparently waiting instead for the results of the GRAS list review, p. 334 *infra*, and the OTC drug review, note 2 p. 225 *supra*.

2. *Actions Against Toxic Nutrients.* FDA has previously restricted the use of several nutrients because of toxicity. *See* 21 C.F.R. § 170.45 (flourine); 25 Fed. Reg. 6633 (July 14, 1960), 25 Fed. Reg. 8224 (August 27, 1960), 28 Fed. Reg. 4768 (May 11, 1963), 28 Fed. Reg. 7425 (July 20, 1963), 36 Fed. Reg. 6843 (April 9, 1971), 38 Fed. Reg. 20725, and 20750 (August 2, 1973), codified in 21 C.F.R. § 172.345 (folic acid); 37 Fed. Reg. 6938 (April 6, 1972), 38 Fed. Reg. 20036 (July 26, 1973), codified in 21 C.F.R. § 172.30 (amino acids). FDA denied a food additive petition for menadione (vitamin K), thus precluding its use in dietary supplements or in food, in 28 Fed. Reg. 3051 (March 28, 1963), 28 Fed. Reg. 7262 (July 16, 1963).

3. *L-tryptophan.* As a result of its association with an outbreak of eosinophilia heyalgia syndrome (EMS), FDA banned L-tryptophan except when used as part of a balanced protein product. *See* HHS Press Release P89–49 (November 17, 1989); "Update on L–Tryptophan," FDA Talk Paper No. T89–76 (December 5, 1989); "Answers on the L–Tryptophan Recall and Warning," FDA Talk Paper No. T90–16 (March 29, 1990); "L–Tryptophan Update: Company Link Suggested," FDA Talk Paper No. T90–18 (April 26, 1990).

FDA REGULATION OF VITAMINS A AND D

Vitamins A and D (as well as vitamins E and K) are fat soluble and stored in the body. At the same time, high dosages of A and D have been heavily promoted for disease prevention, as discussed at p. 28 *supra*, and thus for many years FDA has been concerned about their indiscriminate use. Although both vitamins were included by FDA in the original list of generally recognized as safe (GRAS) food substances under the Food Additives Amendment of 1958, 24 Fed. Reg. 9368 (November 20, 1959), FDA first proposed to restrict use of vitamin D as a food additive because of concern about its toxicity in 30 Fed. Reg. 11140 (August 28, 1965). This proposal was later withdrawn, 33 Fed. Reg. 9783 (July 6, 1968). A few years later based upon "widespread promotion to the laity of excessive quantities of [vitamin A and vitamin D] for prophylaxis and treatment of a variety of diseases and disorders," the agency promulgated regulations, 37 Fed. Reg. 26618 (December 14, 1972), 38 Fed. Reg. 20723 (August 2, 1973), ruling that vitamin A in excess of 10,000 international units (IU) and vitamin D in excess of 400 IU per day would be restricted to prescription sale only. A preliminary injunction was denied in *National Nutritional Foods Ass'n v. Weinberger,* 366 F. Supp. 1341 (S.D.N.Y.), *aff'd,* 491 F.2d 845 (2d Cir. 1973). The regulations were initially upheld on their merits, 376 F. Supp. 142 (S.D.N.Y. 1974), but then remanded to the agency by the court of appeals in order to develop a more complete administrative record on the issue of drug classification, 512 F.2d 688 (2d Cir. 1975). (That remand was a result of the same court's earlier decision invalidating FDA's attempt to classify any product providing more than the upper limit of the U.S. RDA as a drug, *National Nutritional Foods Ass'n v. FDA, p. 215 supra.*)

On remand, FDA supplemented the administrative record by an affidavit containing further justification for classifying high levels of vitamin A and vitamin D as drugs. Based upon the supplemented record, the district court once more upheld the regulations, 418 F. Supp. 394 (S.D.N.Y. 1976). The court of appeals however, held the regulations invalid because FDA had failed to demonstrate an "objective intent" that high levels of vitamins A and D are for therapeutic (drug) rather than nutritional (food) purposes, 557 F.2d 325 (2d Cir. 1977), p. 29 *supra.* Following this decision, FDA revoked the regulations in 43 Fed. Reg. 10551 (March 14, 1978). Since then, FDA has affirmed the GRAS status of vitamin A and vitamin D for purposes of food fortification in 21 C.F.R. §§ 184.1930 and 184.1950, and it continues to list the two vitamins as GRAS (rather than as affirmed as GRAS) for dietary supplement use in 21 C.F.R. §§ 182.5930 and 182.5950.

F. FOOD SANITATION
PETER BARTON HUTT, THE IMPORTANCE OF ANALYTICAL CHEMISTRY TO FOOD AND DRUG REGULATION
68 Journal of the Association of Analytical Chemists 147 (1985).

Ancient Greece and Rome. Adulteration of the food and drug supply was rampant in the ancient world. Numerous Greek and Roman writers documented this adulteration over several centuries....

But knowledge of extensive adulteration of food and drugs, and laws to prohibit it, are useless unless they are enforceable.... The ancient treatises that have survived through the centuries do reveal substantial discussion of analytical methodology. Cato (234–149 B.C.) suggested a method "to determine whether wine has been watered." After his description of widespread adulteration, Pliny contended that "these adulterations can be detected ... by smell, color, weight, taste, and the action of fire." Together, Pliny and Dioscorides described several dozen methods of detecting adulteration, all of which depended solely or partly on the qualitative judgment of the individual person conducting the analysis. Galen suggested methods for determining whether such common articles as pepper were adulterated.

It is all too easy, in this day of scientific sophistication, to dismiss these ancient beginnings of analytical chemistry as sheer speculation. No less an authority than C.A. Browne, who served as president of AOAC in 1925, stated in an article published in 1909 that those in the ancient world who relied on "sense perceptions" to determine adulteration "were unquestionably better judges of the purity of many articles of food than we are today." Browne also concluded that the flame test, ring test, color reactions, and other physical detection methods identified by Pliny and Dioscorides had clear scientific underpinnings and reflected "a large amount of reliable chemical knowledge." ...

The Dark Ages and Middle Ages. After the fall of Rome, nontheological scholarship was discontinued, and the scientific progress begun in Greece and Rome was lost for centuries. The adulteration of food and drugs continued, however, and thus required the use of analytical methods and regulatory controls to contain it. Throughout the Dark Ages and Middle Ages, there was a thriving spice trade, originating among the Mediterranean countries and ultimately reaching England. Then even more than now, spices were extraordinarily valuable and presented an irresistible opportunity for fraudulent profit. Government inspectors—called "garblers"—were therefore employed to remove both natural and artificial adulterants from spices. Although the origin of garbeling is now lost in history, records from the very early 1300s demonstrate that the practice was already well established in England at that time....

As the centuries progressed, adulteration became more sophisticated and thus even more difficult to detect. Because of the lack of detection methods, only gross contamination could be prevented, such as the inclusion of stones, charcoal, dust, and straw in particular products, or the putrefaction of fish and meat. This lack of effective detection methodology, and the resulting poor enforcement of the laws prohibiting food and drug adulteration, was a source of continuing problems and complaints.... In 1592, the Grocers of London submitted a petition to the Lord Mayor of London complaining that the garbelers were doing an inadequate job of enforcement, and suggesting specific standards and procedures that should be followed to improve their regulatory efforts.

The Emergence of Chemistry from Alchemy. In its purely technological (as contrasted with philosophical and theological) aspects, alchemy was the origin of the field of chemistry. But it took the work of Paracellsus in the 16th century and Robert Boyle in the 17th century to break away from the mysticism of alchemy and establish the foundations of modern experimental chemistry.

One year before he died, Boyle wrote the first modern tract on the use of analytical chemistry to detect the adulteration of food and drugs. This work, published in 1690, used the principle of specific gravity to determine "How by the Weight that divers Bodies, us'd in Physick, have in Water; one may discover Whether they be Genuine or Adulterate." In effect, Boyle did no more than apply the principle of specific gravity used by Archimedes to determine the adulteration of gold, for the purpose of determining the adulteration of food and drugs. In so doing, however, he established a scientific foundation for food and drug regulation. A test for adulteration relying on the specific gravity of a substance no longer depended on individual opinion, as did most of the earlier tests identified by Pliny and Dioscorides. On the basis of Boyle's work, other chemists soon made substantial progress in chemical analysis.

The Accum Treatise. Frederick Accum, a German-trained scientist working in England, published a landmark treatise on chemical methods of analyzing adulteration of food and drugs in 1820. Accum not only documented extensive adulteration of the food and drug supply, but offered detailed chemical methods for their detection..... Shortly after, Arthur Hassall began his extensive investigations of food and drug adulteration in England. By introducing use of the microscope (which had been invented two centuries earlier) into food and drug analysis, Hassall led regulation into a new era. Forms of adulteration that could not be detected in any other way were easily found....

Wiley and the 1906 Act. The work undertaken by Hassall in England was mirrored in the United States by Harvey W. Wiley and the Division (later Bureau) of Chemistry in the United States Department of Agriculture..... The 1906 Act was the result largely of the development of extensive documentation of the adulteration of the American food and drug supply. This evidence, which ultimately overwhelmed the congressional reluctance to enact the legislation, resulted from the painstaking and persistent work of the Division of Chemistry and the AOAC.

The Past 35 Years. It is undoubtedly true that there has been more progress in the field of analytical chemistry in the past 35 years than in the prior 20 centuries. Our more detailed understanding of the chemical composition of the food and drug supply has compelled major changes in the regulation of food and drugs.

————

RUTH LAMB, AMERICAN CHAMBER OF HORRORS
(1936).

Common foods are sometimes produced under sanitary conditions that beggar description. Even when processing removes any immediate health menace, there remains a background of filth to make the product repulsive to self-respecting consumers....

... Butter that looked perfectly clean and wholesome to the naked eye disclosed a history of filth leading all the way back to the farm. Hay; fragments of chicken feathers; maggots; clumps of mold—blue, green, white and black; grasshoppers; straw chaff; beetles; cow, dog, cat and rodent hairs; moths; grass and other vegetable matter; cockroaches; dust; ants; fly legs; broken fly wings; metallic filings; remains of rats, mice and other animals were revealed to the astonished eye—all impregnated with yellow dye from the butter.... In a single pound of packing-stock butter consigned to a candy factory, so many maggots were found that if they had been placed end to end their length would have approximated eleven feet, nine inches.... Examination of the cream at stations everywhere—North, East, South and West—yielded some strange and wonderful prizes. Flies and their maggots were the most common find; but mice, rats, cats and chickens in various stages of decomposition were by no means rare....

FEDERAL FOOD INSPECTIONS ARE LAGGING

The New York Times, December 20, 1971, p. 1.

... Dozens of incidents such as the following cases are turned up each month by F.D.A. inspectors:

Some 3,982 cases of Beech–Nut baby food manufactured in Rochester were found to contain cockroach fragments. Federal agents supervised the destruction of all the product. About $2,400 worth of Italian macaroni was confiscated when inspectors found it contaminated with "insects, insect fragments, human hair, paint and metal fragments and other foreign materials." In Seattle inspectors seized an unspecified quantity of frozen shrimp because it had been prepared and packed under unsanitary conditions. Laboratory tests showed it to contain live staphylococci bacteria....

Dr. Virgil Wodicka, director of F.D.A.'s Bureau of Foods, concedes that although there were 355 food recalls and 267 seizures through the courts last year, his inspections turned up only a fraction of the existing violations.... Another indication of the magnitude of the food hazard problem is the count of reported food poisoning cases, ranging from the rare fatal botulism to the vastly more common cases of mild nausea and vomiting caused by Clostridium perfringens, a bacterial cousin of the microbe that causes botulism, Clostridium botulinum. Although the number of reports received by the Federal Center for Disease Control hovers around 25,000 from year to year, public health experts say that because most cases are never reported, the true magnitude of food poisoning is far greater. Estimates range from two million to 10 million cases annually....

Such facts, viewed against the background of recent food scares, suggest that food is less safe today than it was years ago. There is, in fact, no clear evidence that this is the case.... There are even reasons to believe that in some areas food is safer today. This is because more food is manufactured with the aid of automated quality-control equipment than ever before and because, under a new Federal law, many of the inadequate meat inspection programs run by state governments have either been upgraded to meet Federal standards or have been taken over by Federal inspectors....

FDA OVERSIGHT–FOOD INSPECTION

Hearings Before the Subcommittee on Public Health and
Environment of the House Committee on Interstate and
Foreign Commerce, 92d Congress, 1st Session (1971).

FDA Commissioner Charles Edwards.... Every time an emergency situation or a natural disaster occurs, it is necessary for us to suspend food inspections, suspend planned food analyses and our normal program operations. For example, in the Bon Vivant case, the 125 man-years consumed by this emergency effort to date could have been used to inspect 2,300 food plants. This means that in this fiscal year, FDA will probably not inspect 2,300 plants which might otherwise have been investigated and their products sampled and analyzed.....

... [O]ne of our problems in the food field is not unlike the problem in the drug field. We have no registration system, so when a new firm is established and a new product marketed, we have no idea it is happening unless we just happen to run on to it....

Mr. Roy. How many food plants are presently subject to your inspection?

Dr. Edwards. We figure there are approximately 60,000 food establishments which come under our jurisdiction. Now, of that 60,000 about 30,000 of them are manufacturers, per se. Others might be packagers or processors. But there are 60,000 total in terms of our responsibility.

Mr. Roy. And you presently have 250 inspectors in the field? ...

Mr. Rogers. Doctor, what is your need for manpower to do an effective job in inspecting the 60,000 food plants coming within your jurisdiction; 1,500 inspectors, is that a sufficient figure?

Dr. Edwards. I think in that order of magnitude; yes....

Mr. Rogers. That would amount to how much money?

Dr. Edwards. $75 to $85 million.

Mr. Rogers. About the amount of your total budget now?

Dr. Edwards. It is getting fairly close; yes....

NOTES

1. *FDA Inspection Force.* In FY 1971–1972, FDA employed 588 inspectors, 242 of whom handled food inspections. In FY 1979–1980, the agency had

992 inspectors of whom 413 were assigned for food activities. A decade later FDA had a smaller force of inspectors, who were devoting proportionately less time to food-related inspections.

2. *Commentary.* For additional discussion of food sanitation, *see* GAO, DIMENSIONS OF INSANITARY CONDITIONS IN THE FOOD MANUFAC- TURING INDUSTRY, Rep. No. B–164031(ii) (April 18, 1972); GAO, PRO- CESSED FRUITS AND VEGETABLES: POTENTIALLY ADULTERATED PRODUCTS NEED TO BE BETTER CONTROLLED AND SANITATION IN SOME PLANTS NEEDS IMPROVEMENT, Rep. No. B–164031(ii) (February 21, 1973); GAO, LEGISLATIVE CHANGES AND ADMINISTRATIVE IMPROVE- MENTS SHOULD BE CONSIDERED FOR FDA TO BETTER PROTECT THE PUBLIC FROM ADULTERATED FOOD PRODUCTS, Rep. No. HRD–84–61 (September 26, 1984); GAO, EVALUATION OF SELECTED ASPECTS OF FDA'S FOOD MANUFACTURING SANITATION INSPECTION EFFORTS, Rep. No. HRD–84–65 (August 30, 1984); GAO, FOOD INSPECTIONS: FDA SHOULD RELY MORE ON STATE AGENCIES, Rep. No. HRD–86–2 (February 19, 1986); GAO, DOMESTIC FOOD SAFETY: FDA COULD IMPROVE IN- SPECTION PROGRAM TO MAKE BETTER USE OF RESOURCES, Rep. No. HRD–89–125 (September 1989).

The problem of food sanitation has two distinct aspects. First, there is the aesthetic problem of "filth" in food. Although filth was once regarded as a potential indicator of contamination by pathogenic microorganisms, and thus evidence of a potential health hazard, mod- ern food technology allows products to be processed in a way that eliminates any risk of disease. Nonetheless, even sterilized filth, how- ever harmless, is prohibited on aesthetic grounds alone. Second, all food contains microorganisms. And insanitation can facilitate the growth of pathogenic microorganisms that present a substantial risk to human health.

1.　AESTHETIC ADULTERATION

a.　Filth

UNITED STATES v. 484 BAGS, MORE OR LESS

United States Court of Appeals, Fifth Circuit, 1970.
423 F.2d 839.

GODBOLD, Circuit Judge.

This case concerns whether molded green coffee is adulterated, within the meaning of ... 21 U.S.C. § 342(a)(3)....

The coffee was imported from Brazil, admitted to the United States, and stored in a warehouse in New Orleans. Three or four days after arrival in September, 1965 it was damaged by water during Hurricane Betsy. In an effort to impede the growth of mold on the beans the consignee had them run through a dryer and resacked.....

After an evidentiary hearing the District Court found that the beans were fit for food, under the standards of the New York Coffee Exchange, and were neither contaminated nor injurious to health....

The District Court used an erroneous standard in concluding that the coffee was in compliance with the Act and need not be destroyed....

21 U.S.C. § 342(a)(3) provides that a food is deemed adulterated "if it consists in whole or in part of any filthy, putrid or decomposed substance, or if it is otherwise unfit for food." The District Court read the first clause of the quoted provision as being elucidated by the second so that the amount of decomposition made unlawful thereby is that "which would, with reasonable certainty, render the article unfit for food." This court, along with others, has long held that the two clauses are independent and complementary, so that a food substance may be condemned as decomposed, filthy, or putrid even though it is not unfit for food, or condemned as unfit for food even though not decomposed, filthy or putrid....

We turn to consideration of the standards to be used in determining if coffee beans are adulterated. The appellee contends that the statute lays down a rule of reason, allowing seizure and condemnation of only foods which deviate from the norm of purity to the extent of going beyond fair and safe standards. We recognize that "It [the first phrase of § 342(a)(3)] sets a standard that if strictly enforced, would ban all processed food from interstate commerce. A scientist with a microscope could find filthy, putrid, and decomposed substances in almost any canned food we eat." But the majority, in fact almost unanimous, rule is that the Act confers the power to exclude from commerce all food products which contain in any degree filthy, putrid or decomposed substances....

Unjustifiably harsh consequences of a completely literal enforcement are tempered by discretion given the Secretary.... He is allowed to adopt administrative working tolerances for violations of which he will prosecute.[1] The courts may accept the administrative tolerance as a proper judicial measure of compliance with the Act.

Part of the government's evidence at the evidentiary hearing, after the claimant has sought to bring the coffee into compliance with the Act, was that it permitted a tolerance of ten per cent moldy beans in coffee, and that the percentage in tested samples of this coffee averaged 15.1. It is undisputed that the claimant had no actual notice of the administrative tolerance and that it had not been published in the Federal Register. The claimant insists that the government may not employ in support of condemnation an unpublished standard of allow-

---

[1]. In some instances the courts have softened the impact of literal enforcement by imposing a *de minimis* qualification on the statute. *United States v. 133 Cases of Tomato Paste*, 22 F. Supp. 515 (E.D. Pa. 1938). It has been recognized that the allowed administrative tolerances may be themselves an acceptable administrative determination of what is *de minimis*.

able tolerances, known only to itself and sprung upon the unsuspecting merchant at a condemnation hearing and after efforts to rehabilitate the food substance. His complaint is not without equity, if for no other reason than that the provisions of § 334(d) governing release of goods to the owner to be brought into compliance with the Act require that rehabilitation be under the supervision of the government and with the expense of supervision paid by the owner.

In view of the disposition which we make of the case, and of amendments to the Administrative Procedure Act the effect of which have not been considered or briefed by the parties, we do not reach the issue of publication.[3]

We remand the case to the District Court for it to determine under a correct reading of the statute whether the coffee is adulterated. It may accept as a judicial standard the allowable tolerances now permitted by the Secretary, whether published or not. A court may apply a stricter standard than the Secretary and hold a food substance adulterated though within the Secretary's tolerances. Considering the positive command of the statute, the power of the court to allow a greater departure from purity than the administrative tolerances is less certain.[*]

For all future purposes of this case the claimant is entitled to be told what the allowable tolerances are. . . .

DE MINIMUS FILTH

As the principal case indicates, some courts have been skeptical about giving section 402(a)(3) as broad an interpretation as its language would permit. In *United States v. 1,500 Cases . . . Tomato Paste*, 236 F.2d 208 (7th Cir. 1956), for example, the court questioned the majority view of the provision, a view that has since become accepted law:

> We find it impossible to agree with the accepted interpretation of Section 342(a)(3), without ignoring completely the word "otherwise" therein. . . It has . . . been suggested that Congress wanted to protect "the aesthetic tastes and sensibilities of the consuming public," and therefore intended that food containing "any filthy, putrid, or decomposed substance" be deemed adulterated whether it was "unfit for food" or not. Congress may also have wanted to set a standard of purity well above what was required for the health of the consuming public, knowing that not every food product can be individually inspected. If the standard is set at the level of what is "fit for food" or not injurious to health, the occasional substandard item that slips by both industry and Government scrutiny will be hazardous to the health of the consumer. A minimum standard of purity above what is actually the level of danger will, however, allow fewer products to drop below that level. A high standard will also have the same effect by

---

3. In his dissent in *United States v. 449 Cases, Etc.*, 212 F. 2d 567, 575 (2d Cir. 1954), Judge Frank urged that unpublished tolerances violated the Administrative Procedure Act, 5 U.S.C. § 551 et seq.

* [On remand, the district court adopted FDA's tolerance and determined that the coffee beans were within that tolerance. 1969–1974 FDLI Jud. Rec. 76 (E.D. La. 1971).]

encouraging more careful industry inspection. Therefore, we prefer to follow the general rule in interpreting Section 342(a)(3), although admitting that we are unable to answer ... why Congress put the word "otherwise" in the section.

The interpretation we have chosen has one serious disadvantage which most courts have recognized. It sets a standard that if strictly enforced, would ban all processed food from interstate commerce. A scientist with a microscope could find filthy, putrid, and decomposed substances in almost any canned food we eat. (The substances which it is claimed render the respondent "adulterated" were visible only through a microscope.) The conclusion is inescapable that if we are to follow the majority of the decisions which have interpreted 21 U.S.C. § 342(a)(3), without imposing some limitation, the Pure Food and Drug Administration would be at liberty to seize this or any other food it chose to seize.....

... The Food and Drug Administrator with industry cooperation has arrived at a tolerance for tomato paste which is expressed as 40 per cent under the Howard Mold Count method of measurement. The Administration has announced that it will not seize tomato paste on the basis of mold count alone unless that count is over 40 per cent. We, in our search for standards in this area, accept this administrative tolerance as a proper measure of what approximate amount of decomposition is allowable in tomato paste....

The record in this case does not disclose any established tolerances for what is termed "filth" in tomato paste: worm fragments, insects and insect fragments, fly eggs, etc. We can only judge on the basis of the testimony of experts as to what amounts are usual or unavoidable..... The highest worm fragment count shown on exhibit 102 is 6. Insect fragments were in the same general range, and the other examinations made do not show worm and insect fragments in "I" codes appreciably different from those in exhibit 102. The record fully supports the trial court's finding that these counts "were so low that they are regarded by this Court as insignificant and of no consequence."

See also *United States v. 133 Cases of Tomato Paste*, 22 F. Supp. 515 (E.D. Pa. 1938):

... [T]he claimant argues that [section 402(a)(3)] ... is directed only to filth which is perceptible by the consumer.... To so interpret this section of the statute would largely deprive the public of the protection it seeks to give. The consumer ordinarily requires no government aid to protect him from the use of food products the filthy adulteration of which he can see, taste, or smell. What he really needs is government protection from food products the filthy contamination of which is concealed within the product.

In 1972, faced with a request under the Freedom of Information Act, FDA made public all of its "filth guidelines," which it renamed "unavoidable natural defect guidelines." The Director of FDA's Bureau of Foods was quoted as stating, somewhat defensively, that if food were required to be totally pure, "there would be no food sold in the United States." The Washington Post, March 29, 1972, at B2.

NATURAL OR UNAVOIDABLE DEFECTS IN FOOD FOR HUMAN USE THAT PRESENT NO HEALTH HAZARD: PUBLIC AVAILABILITY OF INFORMATION
37 Federal Register 6497 (March 30, 1972).

... Objective findings of such levels without evidence of the history of the production of the food render the product adulterated, even though no health hazard is presented. Thus, appropriate regulatory action is taken whenever the stated defect levels are exceeded. Whether the level of defect in the food was acquired during the growth, processing, storage, or shipment is immaterial. When evidence of insanitary conditions of production or storage is known, action may be taken against products with lower defect levels.... Few foods contain no natural or unavoidable defects. Even with modern technology, all defects in goods cannot be eliminated. Foreign material cannot be wholly processed out of foods, and many contaminants introduced into foods through the environment can be reduced only by reducing their occurrence in the environment.... The defect levels set by the Commissioner of Food and Drugs represent a level below which the defect is both unavoidable under current technology and presents no health hazard. The Commissioner has concluded that the public is entitled to this information....

§ 128.10 Natural or unavoidable defects in food for human use that present no health hazard

(a) Some foods, even when produced under current good manufacturing and/or processing practices, contain natural or unavoidable defects at lower levels that are not hazardous to health. The Food and Drug Administration establishes maximum levels for such defects in foods produced under good manufacturing and/or processing practices and uses these levels for recommending regulatory actions....

(c) Compliance with defect action levels does not excuse failure to observe either the requirement in section 402(a)(4) of the Federal Food, Drug, and Cosmetic Act that food may not be prepared, packed, or held under insanitary conditions or the other requirements in this part that food manufacturers must observe current good manufacturing practices. Evidence obtained through factory inspection indicating such a violation renders the food unlawful, even though the amounts of natural or unavoidable defects are lower than the currently established action levels....

NOTES

1. *Illustrative Action Levels.* The following defect action levels for spices are illustrative of those disclosed by FDA in 1972:

Product	Defect Action Level
Bay (laurel) Leaves	Average more than 5% moldy pieces by weight; or average more than 5% insect infested pieces by weight; or average of 1 milligram excreta per pound after processing.
Cloves	Average of more than 5% stems by weight.
Curry Powder	Average of more than 100 insect fragments per 25 grams or average of more than 8 rodent hairs per 25 grams.
Hops	Average of more than 2500 aphids per 10 grams.

2. *Effects of Disclosure.* Was FDA wise to reveal its enforcement criteria? What was likely to be the effect on public confidence in the nation's food supply or in FDA, or on the willingness of food processors to seek further reductions in filth?

3. *Current FDA Practice.* FDA makes available upon request its current "filth guidelines" and periodically announces in the Federal Register new or revised requirements for specific foods. *See, e.g.,* 53 Fed. Reg. 1520 (January 20, 1988) (insect fragments in wheat flour other than durum wheat flour and in macaroni and noodle products); 51 Fed. Reg. 31840 (September 5, 1986) (mold in catsup and rot fragment count in tomato products); 51 Fed. Reg. 12931 (April 16, 1986) (mold, insect filth, and rodent filth in ground paprika); 49 Fed. Reg. 3140 (January 25, 1984) (thrips in sauerkraut); 46 Fed. Reg. 39221 (July 31, 1981) (decomposition in imported canned and cooked or frozen shrimp); 42 Fed. Reg. 35899 (July 12, 1977) (guideline lowered from 1 rodent excreta pellet per pint of wheat to 9 mg. of rodent excreta pellets per kg. or approximately 0.4 mouse excreta pellets per pint).

4. *Judicial Review of Action Levels.* After initially upholding the FDA defect action level for garlic in *Caribbean Produce Exchange, Inc. v. Department of Health and Human Services,* Food Drug Cosm.L.Rep. (CCH) ¶ 38,100 (D. Puerto Rico, 1988), on rehearing the court reversed its position, Food Drug Cosm.L.Rep. (CCH) ¶ 38,110, determining that the test used to establish violation of the defect action level was arbitrary and capricious and was illegally adopted as a substantive regulation without compliance with the requirements of the Administrative Procedure Act. The case was later remanded, 893 F.2d 3 (1st Cir.1989).

5. *Procedure for Adoption.* In 47 Fed. Reg. 41637 (September 21, 1982), FDA announced that it would allow a one-year period for comment on any new or revised defect action levels, during which the announced levels were effective on an interim basis. The agency revised this procedure in 51 Fed. Reg. 12931 (April 16, 1986), shortening to 60 days the time for comment but suspending enforcement of new or revised levels during this period. FDA had made no statement about the impact on this procedure of the *Caribbean Produce* decision, note 4 *supra,* as of June 30, 1990.

UNITED STATES v. CAPITAL CITY FOODS, INC.

United States District Court, District of North Dakota, 1972.
345 F. Supp. 277.

VAN SICKLE, District Judge.

This is a criminal prosecution by information, based on a claimed violation of [t]he Federal Food, Drug and Cosmetic Act. Specifically, the defendants are charged with having introduced, or delivered for introduction, into interstate commerce, food that was adulterated. The food is claimed to be adulterated because it consisted in part of a filthy substance, i.e., insect fragments. . . .

I apply § 342(a)(3) disjunctively. . . . That is, I do not require that the food is, by virtue of filth, unfit for human consumption. But, the presentation of this case has squarely raised these problems:

1. Since the Food and Drug Administration has not promulgated standards of allowable foreign matter in butter, is that not in itself a standard of zero allowance of foreign matter?

2. If the standard is zero allowance of foreign matter, is such a standard reasonable?

3. In any event, has the government proved sufficient foreign matter to raise its proof above the objection of the maxim de minimis lex? . . .

. . . [I]n its "Notice of Proposed Rule Making On Natural or Unavoidable Defects in Food for Human Use that Present No Health Hazard," of the Food and Drug Administration . . . the introduction language includes this:

"Few foods contains no natural or unavoidable defects. Even with modern technology, all defects in foods cannot be eliminated. Foreign material cannot be wholly processed out of foods, and many contaminants introduced into foods through the environment can be reduced only by reducing their occurrence in the environment."

I accept as a rational, workable approach, the reasoning of the writer in 67 Harv. L. Rev., 632 at 644:

"Indeed, if the section were interpreted literally, almost every food manufacturer in the country could be prosecuted since the statute bans products contaminated "in whole or in part." This undesirable result indicates that the section should not receive so expansive a reading. In fact, in several cases judicial common sense has led to recognition that the presence of a minimal amount of filth may be insufficient for condemnation."

The foreign matter found was mainly miniscule fragments of insect parts. They consisted of 12 particles of fly hair (seta), 11 unidentified insect fragments, 2 moth scales, 2 feather barbules, and 1 particle of rabbit hair. The evidence showed that some of these parties were visible to the naked eye, and some, the fly hair, would require a 30x microscope to see. They were identifiable with the aid of a 470x microscope. The only evidence as to size showed that there was one hair, 1½ millimeters long, and one unidentified insect fragment 0.02 millimeters by 0.2 millimeters. In all, 4125 grams (9.1 lbs.) of butter were checked and 28 miniscule particles were found. This is an overall ratio of 3 miniscule particles of insect fragments per pound of butter.

Thus, there having been no standard established, and no showing that this number of miniscule fragments is excludable in the manufacturing process, I find that this contamination is a trifle, not a matter of concern to the law.

The defendants are found not guilty. Judgment will be entered accordingly.

PREDACEOUS INSECTS

In July 1988 the Director of Compliance of FDA's Center for Food Safety and Applied Nutrition wrote the following response to an inquiry from a Texas grain storage facility:

> This responds to your letter of March 28, 1988, concerning predaceous insects added to stored grain.....
>
> ... The [statutory] word "filth" includes insects and insect related contaminants such as insect excreta and insect fragments. The presence of insects in the food constitute adulteration whether or not the insects attack the food product itself. We recognize that certain low levels of natural and unavoidable defects such as field insects may be present in certain foods even if handled in a sanitary manner. The deliberate addition of insects to food is, however, neither natural nor unavoidable. We have not, therefore, endorsed the practice of intentionally adding "beneficial" insects to foods to control insect pests. Indeed we have considered this simply as either substituting one adulterant for another, or as changing the nature of the adulteration....
>
> Please note that because the intended use of these insects is to kill other insects, such use may be considered a pesticide by EPA....
>
> We emphasize that whether these insects are considered to be pesticides or food additives, the laws enforced by both FDA and EPA require the submission of adequate scientific data to support premarket approval for "substances" added to food. If EPA determines that these insects are not pesticides and you submit a food additive petition containing safety and efficacy data, FDA would be willing to consider approval of the use of predaceous insects.

Following a highly critical story on March 25, 1990 on CBS's "60 Minutes," FDA reversed this decision. *See* EPA's proposed exemption from a tolerance, 56 Fed.Reg. 234 (January 3, 1991).

b. Decomposition

UNITED STATES v. AN ARTICLE OF FOOD ... 915 CARTONS OF FROG LEGS

United States District Court, Southern District of New York, 1981.
Food Drug Cosmetic Law Reports (CCH) ¶ 38,102.

CANNELLA, J. M., District Judge.....

Charles Cardile, an FDA chemist, testified that on December 13, 1977, he and Albert Weber, another trained FDA organoleptic examiner, conducted a joint organoleptic analysis of the eighteen subsamples to determine whether the shrimp were decomposed.[5] Their analysis consisted of thawing the eighteen subsamples, selecting 100 shrimp from each subsample, and then breaking the flesh of each shrimp and smelling it. On the basis of their training and pursuant to FDA Guidelines, the examiners then classified each shrimp as either class one, good commercial shrimp, class two, decomposed shrimp, or class three, shrimp in advanced stages of decomposition. Under the FDA Guidelines establishing tolerances for decomposition, a subsample is classified as decomposed if (1) five percent or more of the shrimp tested is class three, (2) twenty percent or more of the shrimp tested is class two, or (3) the percentage of class two shrimp plus four times the percentage of class three shrimp equals or exceeds twenty percent. The FDA will take legal action against the entire shipment when four or more of the eighteen subsamples are found to be decomposed. Based upon their examination of the eighteen subsamples at issue, Cardile and Weber found seven of the eighteen subsamples to be decomposed....

Since the results of the FDA's joint organoleptic analysis revealed that seven of the subsamples tested contained more than the 20% decomposition tolerated by the FDA, with at least two subsamples scoring as high as 100% and 170%, the Court concludes that more than a *de minimis* amount of decomposition was present in the frozen shrimp and that it is "adulterated" within the meaning of 21 U.S.C. § 342(a)(3).....

NOTES

1. *Decomposition After Shipment.* In *United States v. Allbrook Freezing & Cold Storage, Inc.,* 194 F.2d 937 (5th Cir. 1952), the court upheld a seizure of decomposed and filthy berries after shipment from Louisiana to Mississippi, rejecting the contention that the reprocessed berries in Mississippi were a different food that had not themselves been shipped in interstate commerce.

5. It has been said that decomposition, like drunkenness, "is easy to detect, but hard to define." *United States v. 1,200 Cans, Etc., Pasteurized Whole Eggs,* 339 F. Supp. 131, 137 (N.D. Ga. 1972). Decomposition is "a bacterial separation or breakdown in the elements of the food so as to produce an undesirable disintegration or rot." It is well recognized that organoleptic analysis of food, whereby the examiner relies upon his trained sense of smell to detect different types of offensive food, if honestly administered, is a valid scientific test for decomposition.

2. *Proof of Decomposition.* In *Bruce's Juices, Inc. v. United States,* 194 F.2d 935 (5th Cir. 1952), the court held that, when FDA proves that a food is decomposed, it need not also prove that the food is unfit for human consumption. The court also held that, in a decomposition case, the claimant had no right to have the jury taste and smell the product because decomposition "was not a matter cognizable by the senses."

---

c. Insanitary Conditions

UNITED STATES v. 1,200 CANS ... PASTEURIZED WHOLE EGGS, ETC.

United States District Court, Northern District of Georgia, 1972.
339 F. Supp. 131.

SIDNEY O. SMITH, Jr., Chief Judge.

These five actions were brought in different parts of the United States ... to condemn and destroy as adulterated various lots of pasteurized frozen whole eggs and sugar yolks processed and introduced into interstate commerce by the Golden Egg Products, Inc.... [T]he government contends that the lots were "adulterated" in one or more of the definitions prescribed by Congress in 21 U.S.C. § 342[(a)(1), (3), and (4)]....

Golden Egg is a so-called frozen egg breaking plant, the purpose of which is to remove eggs from their shells, process the egg magma, and package and freeze it in a variety of combinations for sale to manufacturers. Its principal use is in the baking, dairy products and vegetable oil industries.....

Salmonella itself is a well-recognized pathogen. There are some 1400 types, all felt by medical scientists to be deleterious. As such, salmonella constitutes a serious threat to public health, particularly to the old, the young, and the sickly.... The presence of salmonella in frozen eggs is a deleterious and poisonous additive which is dangerous to health within the meaning of 21 U.S.C. § 342(a)(1). Such fact is stipulated here. Accordingly, Lot 1941 is subject to condemnation under this section....

... [A] food substance may be condemned under the present statute as decomposed, filthy, or putrid even though it is not unfit for food. The removal of this requirement has in fact, rendered the legal inquiry more difficult. Experts and laymen are more likely to agree upon a common meaning of "fitness for food", than upon the meaning of the words "filthy, putrid or decomposed" in a literary vacuum.... [U]nder the absolute language of the statute, there must exist actual filth, putridity, or decomposition.... [I]n this instance, the facts must be judged in the absence of a workable standard of fitness for food, (removed by the courts) or a measurable tolerance (omitted by the Secretary.) ...

As to definition, the court sought an acceptable consensus through-out the trial. Even when pressed, however, the experts on this issue had no ready answer..... However, all agree that decomposition involves a bacterial separation or breakdown in the elements of the food so as to produce an undesirable disintegration or rot....

Indicative of this attribute is the almost universal acceptance of organoleptic tests for determining decomposition. All of the experts in this case agree that, honestly administered, they are valid.... Organoleptic smell tests have worked extremely well on unpasteurized egg products for years. The product is either "passable" or "rejected." However, the pasteurization process, which basically arrests decomposition, has posed a new problem.

The pasteurization process, universal since 1966, plus refinements in the freezing process have masked decomposition odors and made the test much more difficult. In the drilling process for microbiological samples, an examiner uses an electric drill, and a sanitized bit ... and bores into the frozen product to the bottom of the can. As it is extracted, the shavings are collected in a pre-sterilized spoon and placed into a sterile whirl-pack bag or jar. Then it is rushed in dry ice to cold-storage facilities for later laboratory examination. The heat generated by the bit gives a brief opportunity for organoleptic testing during the drilling process. As thawing or heating regenerates the decomposition process, the use of organoleptic examination from the sample bags at a later date is effective only under exacting conditions. Usually, one can get only one smell upon opening the bag. Thus, it is extremely difficult to effect a satisfactory organoleptic test on lots of pasteurized frozen eggs. Conversely, however, the presence of a test failure under these conditions would be strong evidence of decomposition.

In this case, only two lots (Can Codes 1935 and 1937) were subjected to and failed such tests. In most lots, two subsamples for laboratory use were taken from ten random cans for a total of 20 subsamples in each lot. Lot 1935 had two such series taken.... In them, a competent organoleptic examiner found two clear rejects in each series. Out of ten subsamples in Lot 1937, another competent examiner found two passable, five rejects, and three possibles, or borderlines.

Recognizing the validity of the tests and the accuracy of the results, the court is concerned only with the quantum of the proof.... What, if any, percent of the total lot must be shown to be decomposed to condemn the entire lot? ... Perhaps the soundest approach is an early one: "—there is no room for controversy over percentages under the statute itself, for it excludes all. Or course, where the entire product is not inspected or tested, the proof must go far enough to satisfy the court or jury that the adulteration extends to the whole product sought to be condemned." ... Recognizing that the trend is to order condemnation if the lot is decomposed "to any degree", the court is still not satisfied that the organoleptic evidence is sufficient to conclude that the entire lots in question are decomposed.....

Because of these difficulties and the fact that not all decomposition is discoverable under organoleptic tests, interested parties have for years sought a more scientific method for establishing and measuring decomposition..... [T]he government here relies on evidence of Direct Microscopic Count (DMC) alone.

There can be little dispute that the presence of large numbers of bacteria in a product indicates a greater possibility of activity than a small number. Accordingly, the DMC tests proceed on the basis of ascertaining the actual count in any given product by random sampling. Under acceptable AOAC [Association of Official Agricultural Chemists] methods, a precise amount of the product is spread on a slide over a given area, stained, and placed under a high-powered microscope. Then, one field of view is examined and the bacteria, both dead and alive, are counted. By applying the mathematical factors in the relationship of the field to the sample and the power of the microscope, the total count per gram can be projected. If the count is 3,000,000 or less, then 30 fields are counted; if more, then 20 fields are counted to obtain a representative result. Years of testing has [sic] indicated that DMC counts of 5,000,000 or more coupled with the presence of certain acid measurement are proof of decomposition in unpasteurized eggs.... The combination of the 5,000,000 count plus positive acid tests is legally acceptable to defendant's experts and, at least, to one court.

Here, however, the government seeks to establish the reliability of a DMC count alone. The evidence presented at trial convinces the court that this standard is not acceptable. Firstly, the DMC count if scientifically accurate only measures the presence of both live and dead bacteria and not their activity (as do the acid tests). Inasmuch as chemical breakdown is the proof positive of decomposition, it cannot be ascertained from a DMC alone whether those bacteria present have or are actively producing the breakdown. Thus the total numbers of bacteria by themselves, while useful for other purposes or in conjunction with acid tests, are not exclusively significant in determining the presence of actual decomposition. Moreover, by reason of the irregular distribution of bacteria throughout frozen eggs and the inherent difficulty in counting those actually observed through the microscope, the DMC is subject to significant variances in different tests run on the same sample.... Thus on the unconvincing original premise that a DMC result may prove actual decomposition under Section (a)(3) and on the substantial test variances on the lots in question, the court concludes that the government's case on this basis fails....

While there are many similarities between (a)(3) and (a)(4) proceedings, the legislative thrust of the latter is entirely different.... [T]he (a)(4) section allows the condemnation of foods processed under insanitary conditions, whether they have actually decomposed or become dangerous to health or not. The objective of (a)(4) is to "require the observance of a reasonably decent standard of cleanliness in handling of food products" and to insure "the observance of those precautions which consciousness of the obligation imposed upon producers of perishable food products should require in the preparation of food for consumption by human beings." It almost reaches the aim of removing from commerce those products produced under circumstances which would offend a consumer's basic sense of sanitation and which would cause him to refuse them had he been aware of the conditions under which they were prepared. . . .

Again, it would be helpful if there were specific plant standards or tolerances to guide the court. . . . Some argument has been made that the [FDA's good manufacturing practice] regulations promulgated in 1969 answer this purpose. With a few exceptions, they are inadequate to do so in that they fail to specify just what is "necessary", "needed", "effective", "sufficient", or the like. . . .

In the absence of particular standards, the question must be determined from the totality of the circumstances as revealed by the evidence. In this regard, it is not necessary that the evidence of insanitary conditions absolutely coincide with the dates of processing provided they are not too remote in time or space. The proof should, however, justify the inference that such conditions actually existed on the dates in question.

Measured by the above, the test has been met in this case. Reviewing the evidence as a whole, the court must conclude that the conditions existing at the Golden Egg plant on the critical dates were exactly those the Congress sought to prevent by the passage of (a)(4). . . . While some extreme dates such as the 1969 inspections some 6–12 months before processing ought to be eliminated, the evidence during 1970 compels the finding of insanitary conditions. This evidentiary history reveals a consistent unsuccessful effort by the Food and Drug Administration enforcement officials over a long period of time to eliminate an intolerable situation at this plant. . . .

. . . [I]n varying degrees the following conditions existed at the times in question: improper refrigeration in the transportation and storage of breaking stock; the use of fiber filler flats in the breaking room; no segregation of breaking stock prior to presenting it to the breaker for breaking; the regular failure to wash, sanitize, and candle the breaking stock before it was sent to the breaking room; the regular breaking of unsanitized and unwashed eggs; the breaking of leaking eggs and eggs with maggots, adhering fecal, and other foreign matter on the shells; ineffective instruction with regard to personal and equipment sanitation; breakers with uncovered open sores breaking eggs; the breaking of eggs without even a sniff to detect rotten eggs; instances where breakers failed to sanitize their hands after handling insanitary objects while breaking eggs; failure to reject rotten eggs; improperly maintained breaking trays that did not permit the breaker to properly observe broken eggs before they dropped into the collecting buckets; paper and rusty parts used on the breaking tray that consistently came into contact with the liquid egg magma; dirty shells in the breaking room strainer; flies, in varying numbers, in the breaking and transfer rooms; evidence of mice in the plant; and improper cleanup and maintenance.

That such conditions still existed on the dates of production is amply borne out by the evidence obtained in the July 24, 1970, FDA inspection, the July 15, 1970, National Sanitation Institute inspection, and the testimony of plant employees presented by both sides at trial.....

Moreover and perhaps most importantly, the DMC evidence in the case is convincing on the question of insanitary conditions and resulting filth. While there is considerable doubt in the court's mind about the valid use of manufacturing conditions to establish decomposition under (a)(3) by the DMC method as advocated by the government, the reverse is assuredly true. The claimant's own experts agree that a high DMC count is scientific proof of the exposure of the product to filth and of production under insanitary conditions.... All together, the evidence amply authorizes the inference of insanitary production conditions to a degree prohibited by the Act. Accordingly, the court finds that all lots are subject to condemnation under Section (a)(4).....

UNITED STATES v. CERTIFIED GROCERS CO–OP.

United States Court of Appeals, Seventh Circuit, 1976.
546 F.2d 1308.

TONE, Circuit Judge.

In this food-adulteration prosecution ... the government appeals under 18 U.S.C. § 3731 from a judgment of acquittal entered after a bench trial. The defendants, relying upon that section's provision that "no appeal shall lie where the double jeopardy clause of the United States Constitution prohibits further prosecution," have moved to dismiss the appeal for lack of jurisdiction. The question of jurisdiction, under the standard set forth in *United States v. Jenkins,* 420 U.S. 358 (1975), is intertwined with the merits. On the authority of that case we dismiss the appeal.

The defendants, Certified Grocers Co-op and two of its principal officers, were charged in a two-count information with violating § 301(k).... by permitting flour held in their warehouse to become adulterated and permitting it to become exposed to adulteration.... The court found the following facts: ...

A Food and Drug Administration inspection on September 19 and 29, 1972, while these 252 bags were being held for sale in the warehouse, disclosed that at least eight of them contained holes gnawed by rodents. These holes were approximately evenly divided between the

General Mills flour described in Count I and the Pillsbury flour described in Count II. Only two of the individual two-pound bags were actually sampled, one from each lot. The General Mills bag contained two rodent excreta pellets and one rodent hair; the Pillsbury bag contained 10 rodent excreta pellets. Near the bales and elsewhere in the warehouse were several hundred rodent excreta pellets and several rodent bait boxes, one of which showed "recent rodent activity." Two dead rodents were "lying about outside the packaged food." There were numerous rodent burrows in the ground near the outside of the warehouse walls.

On September 20, 1972, after FDA inspectors had discovered the conditions just described, defendants voluntarily destroyed the 252 bags of flour, acknowledging in a written statement signed in the presence of the inspectors, "This flour was destroyed because they [the bales and bags] were rodent chewed."

Notwithstanding the foregoing findings, the court acquitted the defendants. With respect to actual contamination (§ 342(a)(3)), the judge concluded that the government had not proved when the rodent activity in the warehouse occurred or whether the two packages which actually contained excreta were breached and contaminated before or after they arrived at the warehouse. . . .

With respect to the possibility of contamination (§ 342(a)(4)), the judge found that the presence, while the flour was being held in the warehouse, of "the gnawed holes and the rodent pellets and hairs and the two dead rodents lying about the packaged food . . . was no doubt an insanitary condition,' " but that "there was no reason to suppose that any of these things could or would enter the packages." He "attach[ed] somewhat less importance" to the lack of evidence of when the rodent activity occurred than he had with respect to the (a)(3) issue, and said "it may be inferred that some significant portion of that activity" occurred while the flour was present. . . .

Recognizing that the standard required for conviction under (a)(4) . . . is whether the insanitary conditions made it "reasonably possible" that the flour would become contaminated, the judge stated that "one might conclude that insanitary conditions . . . made it reasonably possible that a mouse would enter [two packages of flour] . . . and deposit therein . . . rodent excreta pellets and one rodent hair. . . ." Because of the "elusive" nature of the conviction standards, he then stated that "the ultimate question appears to be how the word 'contaminated' in § 342(a)(4) is to be construed, in conjunction with 'reasonably possible.' " He construed "contaminated," as he had the language of (a)(3), to permit the presence of contaminants within a "range of tolerance contemplated by the statute." He concluded that the filth described in the findings, which he calculated were the product of "about seven full mouse-days, so to speak," and was contained in a 100,000–square–foot warehouse, was within that range of tolerance.

Despite our misgivings about the District Court's interpretation of the statute [5] and the acquittal itself, we conclude that we are required to dismiss the appeal for want of jurisdiction.... The double-jeopardy clause precludes review..... However clear it may appear to us that the inference of a reasonable possibility of contamination should have been drawn, that inference could only be drawn by the trier of fact....

NOTES

1. *Government's Burden of Proof.* In *Berger v. United States,* 200 F.2d 818 (8th Cir. 1952), the court held that under section 402(a)(4) FDA must establish a "reasonable," not just a "mere possibility," that the insanitary condition will result in contamination. For an illustration of the difficulty of demonstrating that particular sanitation practices violate sections 402(a)(3) and (a)(4), in the absence of regulations prescribing specific good manufacturing practices, *see United States v. General Foods Corp.,* 446 F. Supp. 740 (N.D.N.Y.), *aff'd,* 591 F.2d 1332 (2d Cir. 1978). There the court refused to find that geotrichum mold on equipment for processing canned green beans demonstrated that the beans had been processed under such conditions as to present a reasonable possibility that they could have become contaminated with filth, relying heavily on testimony that mold is common in such facilities. The court also rejected FDA's charge under section (a)(3):

> ... There is little or no evidence whatsoever to show that the levels of Geotrichum discovered in defendants' finished product were avoidable through the use of current good manufacturing practices, as exist within the industry. Finally, it is uncontroverted that Geotrichum, at the levels with which we are dealing, is not harmful when consumed by humans. This Court therefore finds that, while the Geotrichum found in samples of defendant's frozen french-style green beans constitutes filth, the amount is *de minimis,* and does not therefore constitute an (a)(3) violation.

2. *Compliance Policy.* Following the adverse rulings in the *General Foods* case and a similar case, FDA sent a directive to its field force in January 1979 limiting future legal action under section 402(a)(4):

> Inspections that do not involve pathogens can be developed as 402(a)(4) cases based on observed sanitary conditions concerning visible filth....

> In all 402(a)(4) situations other than those involving pathogens, inspections will be conducted using inspectional observations of organoleptically detectable (by sight and/or smell) filth and collection of physical filth exhibits. For the present, we are not prepared to approve cases based on conditions demonstrable only by bacteriological analysis....

---

5. ... The Act does not provide for the setting of tolerances under (a)(4) as it does with respect to poisonous or deleterious substances under (a)(1) and (2), and §§ 346 and 346(a). The Secretary is vested, however, with the discretion not to prosecute, or even not to institute libel or injunctive proceedings against, "minor violations" of the statute. 21 U.S.C. § 336. Although we would prefer that this broad discretion be regulated by administratively promulgated standards governing industry practices, "there would seem no authority for us to waive statutory violation perhaps beyond the principal of *de minimus.* ... " *United States v. 449 Cases, Containing Tomato Paste.* Thus, subsections (a)(3) and (4) do not appear to incorporate a "tolerance," permitting some minimal level of filth contamination in food....

3. *Microbiological Quality Standards.* In 37 Fed. Reg. 20038 (September 23, 1972), FDA proposed to establish "quality" standards for two foods by prescribing limits for nonpathogenic microorganisms under section 401 of the Act. It published final regulations in 38 Fed. Reg. 20726 (August 2, 1973), which it then stayed in response to objections and requests for hearing, 41 Fed. Reg. 33249 (August 9, 1976). *See* Farquhar, *The Role of Microbiology in the Integrity of Foods,* 31 FDC L.J. 17 (1976). FDA withdrew both proposals in 43 Fed. Reg. 9272 (March 7, 1978), but has not abandoned this approach. In 45 Fed. Reg. 37422 (June 3, 1980), FDA announced it would issue microbiological standards of quality as recommendations rather than as regulations. It announced microbiological defect action levels for raw breaded shrimp in 48 Fed. Reg. 43223 (September 22, 1983), and withdrew levels for langostinos in 54 Fed. Reg. 51079 (December 12, 1989).

4. *FDA/USDA Cooperation.* In AN EVALUATION OF THE ROLE OF MICROBIOLOGICAL CRITERIA FOR FOODS (1985), the National Academy of Sciences recommended establishment of a committee to review microbiological quality standards for food. In cooperation with FDA, in 52 Fed. Reg. 43216 (November 10, 1987), USDA announced the establishment of this committee, now named the National Advisory Committee on Microbiological Criteria for Foods, which has been meeting since.

5. *Reconditioning.* FDA announced a guideline for reconditioning food adulterated under section 402(a)(4) in 54 Fed. Reg. 32395 (August 7, 1989). Damaged food is often sold to the food salvage industry, which either reconditions it for human use or sells it for other purposes. *See, e.g.,* GAO, NEED FOR REGULATING THE FOOD SALVAGE INDUSTRY TO PREVENT SALE OF UNWHOLESOME AND MISBRANDED FOODS TO THE PUBLIC, No. MWD–75–64 (May 20, 1975); GAO, FOOD SALVAGE INDUSTRY SHOULD BE PREVENTED FROM SELLING UNFIT AND MISBRANDED FOOD TO THE PUBLIC, No. HRD–79–32 (February 14, 1979). In cooperation with the Association of Food and Drug officials, FDA developed a model food salvage code, announced in 44 Fed. Reg. 74921 (December 18, 1979), 49 Fed. Reg. 31952 (August 9, 1984). For a discussion of FDA authority to require reconditioning as part of the salvage of adulterated food *see United States v. 1,638 Cases of Adulterated Alcoholic Beverages,* 624 F.2d 900 (9th Cir. 1980).

6. *Permanent Injunction.* For an example of a consent decree of permanent injunction against a bakery operating under insanitary conditions, *see United States v. Manhattan Bakery,* Food Drug Cosm. L. Rep. (CCH) ¶ 38,163 (N.D. Ga. 1982).

7. *Case Law.* For other decisions interpreting sections 402(a)(3) and (4), *see United States v. Gel Spice Co., Inc.,* 773 F.2d 427 (2d Cir. 1985), *aff'g* 601 F.Supp. 1205 (E.D.N.Y. 1984); *Salamonie Packing Co. v. United States,* 165 F.2d 205 (8th Cir. 1948); *United States v. 1851 Cartons ... H. & G. Famous Booth Sea Foods Whiting Frosted Fish,* 146 F.2d 760 (10th Cir. 1945); *A.O. Andersen & Co. v. United States,* 284 Fed. 542 (9th Cir. 1922); *Dade v. United States,* 40 App. D.C. 94 (D.C. Cir. 1913); *United States v. Manhattan Bakery,* Food Drug Cosm. L. Rep. (CCH) ¶ 38,163 (N.D. Ga. 1982); *United States v. 1800 Cases ... "Field's 'World's Best' Pecan Pie ... ",* Food Drug Cosm. L. Rep. (CCH) ¶ 38,098 (N.D. Tex. 1981); *United States v. Corbi,* Food Drug Cosm. L. Rep. (CCH) ¶ 38,040 (D. Md. 1979); *United States v. 900 Cases Peaches,* 390 F. Supp. 1006 (E.D.N.Y. 1975), *aff'd without opinion sub nom. United States v. Noroian,* 556 F.2d 562 (2d Cir. 1977); *United States v. An Article of Food ... 51 Cases,* 1969–1974 FDLI Jud. Rec. 145 (E.D. La. 1973); *United States v. 233 Tins ... "Grove Brand * * ***

Whole Blakemore Strawberries," 175 F. Supp. 694 (W.D. Ark. 1959); *United States v. Roma Macaroni Factory,* 75 F. Supp. 663 (N.D. Cal. 1947); *United States v. 184 Barrels Dried Whole Eggs,* 53 F. Supp. 652 (E.D. Wis. 1943); *United States v. 1,375 Cases of Tomato Paste,* 1938–1964 FDLI Jud. Rec. 13 (D. Conn. 1942).

8. *Commentary.* Representative articles on food sanitation include Beacham, *Organoleptic Examination of Processed Foods,* 5 FDC L.J. 400 (1950); Foster, *An Evaluation of the Salmonella Problem,* 25 FDC L.J. 60 (1970); Jensen, *Bacterial Food Poisoning,* 11 FDC L.J. 631 (1956); Larrick, *Enforcement of the Sanitation Provisions of the Federal Food, Drug, and Cosmetic Act,* 3 FDC L.Q. 237 (1948); Larrick, *Comments on the Food and Drug Administration's Sanitation Program,* 3 FDC L.Q. 510 (1948); Larrick, *The Challenge: Improving Controls in Frozen Foods,* 19 FDC L.J. 290 (1964); Milstead, *FDA Enforcement Problems in the Fishery Industry,* 16 FDC L.J. 274 (1961).

9. *Transport Sanitation.* For discussions of the problems of sanitation in railroad cars used to transport food, *see* 29 FDC L.J. 492 *et seq.* (1974). The Sanitary Food Transport Act of 1990, 104 Stat. 1213, authorizes the Department of Transportation to issue regulations to prevent the contamination of food and other FDA-regulated products by nonfood substances during shipments.

------

d. Otherwise Unfit for Food

UNITED STATES v. 298 CASES ... SKI SLIDE BRAND ASPARAGUS

United States District Court, District of Oregon, 1949.
88 F. Supp. 450.

McCOLLOCH, District Judge.

Defendant is an asparagus packer. One of his products is the center cut of the asparagus. This retails for 20¢ per can (1 lb. 3 oz.) containing 95 to 100 cuts, as compared with 40 to 45 cents per can for the choicer tips. The Government contends that defendant's center cuts are fibrous and woody beyond the permissible limits set up by the Federal Food, Drug and Cosmetic Administration. Three witnesses for the Government said that they had eaten a can (or attempted to) of defendant's cuts. The composite of their testimony was that 25% or more of the cuts were inedible, and the Government's witnesses condemned them as a food product.

On the other hand, the Director of Mary Cullen's Cottage found only 5 or 6 pieces out of 100 that she had to lay aside. Confronted with this conflict in testimony, I obtained counsels' consent to eat a can. This I have done, although I confess had I understood all the difficulties of the undertaking, I might not have been so bold.

To eat a can of asparagus, hand-running, as the saying is, is quite a chore. I took three days to eat the can. That, I can now state, is as much as an old protein user should attempt on his first venture into herbalism. I suspect the Government witnesses tried to eat their cans all at one time, and that may explain the severity of their judgment about defendant's asparagus. I can see where after 50 or 60 cuts, eaten without spelling oneself, one might become very particular.

My test more than confirmed Miss Laughton's good opinion of the cuts. She found 5 or 6 per cent inedible, whereas I ate all of my can, and felt that I was helped by it. There was one runty, tough piece and two or three slivers, but I treated them as de minimis. I agree with the Director of Mary Cullen's Cottage that this is an excellent product, particularly considering its low price. Not everybody in this country can "keep up with the Joneses" and eat only asparagus tips. Indeed it seems strange to me that the Government should be interested in keeping from the market a moderately priced, wholly nutritious food product. I should think in this period of declining income the Government's interest would be the other way. If Mr. Prendergast will prepare appropriate findings, I will give his client's center cuts a clean bill of health. They deserve it.

NOTES

1. *Other Authority.* See also United States v. 24 Cases, More or Less, 87 F. Supp. 826 (D. Me. 1949) (in order for food to be unfit it "must be proved to be so tough and rubbery that the average, normal person, under ordinary conditions, would not chew and swallow it").

2. *Fish Protein.* FDA has frequently been confronted with proposals to market foods from sources that may affront the sensibilities of many consumers.

In the 1950's scientists began exploring means to more effectively exploit marine sources of protein for human food. In 1961 FDA published a proposal to establish a standard of identity for "fish protein concentrate, whole fish flour," a product made by processing intact fish. 26 Fed. Reg. 8641 (September 15, 1961). Comments on the proposal objected that the product would include the viscera, intestines, and other portions of the fish that are not normally used for food. The agency's final standard permitted the product to be made only from edible species of cleaned fish, after discarding "the heads, tails, fins, viscera, and intestinal contents." 27 Fed. Reg. 740 (January 25, 1962). Objections to the standard resulted in a stay pending a public hearing.

Before a hearing could be held, the entire matter was referred to a committee of the National Academy of Sciences, which eventually endorsed the concept of protein concentrate, or flour, being made for human consumption from whole fish. Its report implied that requiring cleaning of the fish prior to processing would be so expensive as to jeopardize the economic viability of this technology for producing a very cheap source of protein.

Accordingly, in 1967, FDA published a regulation authorizing the production and sale under the Food Additives Amendment of whole fish protein concentrate:

> The Commissioner of Food and Drugs, taking cognizance of the findings relative to the suitability of fish protein concentrate ... deems it desirable to make this economical source of protein available for consumers. Individual consumers are entitled to the opportunity of

choice in the matter of whether they desire to include this item in
their diets; therefore, the product, to be readily distinguishable, should
be more properly identified as "whole fish protein concentrate," and
for domestic distribution it should be packaged for household use in
consumer sized units not exceeding 1 pound net weight.

The regulation permitted processing "without removal of heads, fins, tails,
viscera, or intestinal contents." 32 Fed. Reg. 1173 (February 2, 1967).

3. *Worms.* On April 26, 1977, FDA's Bureau of Foods replied to an
inquiry that probed the limits of the "otherwise unfit for food" language of
section 402(a)(3):

Pat L. Smith

Smitty's Worm Hatchery

1005 S. College Avenue

College Place, WA 99324

Worms are not commonly recognized as a source of food in the United
States. We believe the vast majority of consumers would view them as
aesthetically objectionable in food or as food, just as insects are viewed
aesthetically objectionable by most people. There are certain specialty
items, such as fried agave worms, baby beees [sic], and chocolate
covered fried ants that have been sold in this country for many years,
but such products are not widely accepted or consumed and are viewed
primarily as novelty items. We have not objected to the sale of such
items when properly labaled [sic] and otherwise in compliance with the
law, because the purchaser is aware of the nature of the items
purchased and because they have been consumed with apparent safety....

From an aesthetic viewpoint, we would probably view the sale of
worms or products derived from them in the same manner we view
these spacialty [sic] items mentioned above. However, before worms or
products derived from them could be marketed as food in this country,
we would have to insist that they be considered under the food additive
provisions of the FD&C Act to assure that consumption of these
products would be safe....

4. *DES Residues.* Faced with the difficulty of proving that a trace
amount of DES in beef was an added poisonous or deleterious substance that
may render the food injurious to health, the government tried the additional
argument that the DES residue rendered the product "unfit for food." The
court ruled in *United States v. 2,116 Boxes of Boned Beef,* 516 F. Supp. 321 (D.
Kan. 1981), that "[t]he allegation of unfitness must be independent of the
allegation of injuriousness" and that "unfit for food" includes such conditions
as discoloration or a bad smell but does not include intentional additions of
substances to food. The government did not appeal. *See also Millet, Pit and
Seed Co., Inc. v. United States,* 436 F. Supp. 84 (E.D. Tenn. 1977), holding that
apricot kernels naturally containing amygdalin are not "unfit for food" because
FDA failed to prove that they were "inedible for the average person under
ordinary conditions."

5. *Commentary. See generally* Steffy, *"Otherwise Unfit for Food"—A New
Concept in Food Adulteration,* 4 FDC L.Q. 552 (1949).

e. An Alternative Approach

MELVIN J. HINICH AND RICHARD STAELIN, REGULATION OF THE U.S. FOOD INDUSTRY

VI   Study on Federal Regulation,
Senate Document No. 96–14, 96th Congress, 1st Session (1978).

... How much effort should be spent guaranteeing that our food is processed using ingredients and under conditions which are "sanitary" (even though bacteria associated with unsanitary conditions are rendered harmless when the food is later processed correctly), versus guaranteeing that the food is free from substances which cannot be rendered harmless by the proper processing by the manufacturer or consumer? Instead of taking legal action related to aesthetic adulteration, what would happen if all producers were required to affix a label which indicated the level of aesthetically unpleasant contamination? This label probably would be in terms of grades although it could also be more explicit by detailing the exact levels of contamination. If a firm felt that a lower grade label would be detrimental to the marketability of its produce, it would take the necessary steps to insure that its ingredients and manufacturing process met the higher standards. On the other hand, the firm might believe that consumers did not want to pay for extra protection since the food is safe (this occurs during the normal processing). In this case the firm may want to reduce costs (and price) and not meet the higher FDA sanitation grading standards. Consequently, consumers could use the presence or absence of such a label as an indication of the level of sanitation in the plant....

... [C]onsumers are not now getting "pure" food since such food would be prohibitively expensive. The question then is should the FDA ban food when it exceeds the admittedly arbitrary defect action levels or should they allow "informed" consumers to make the choice? (Remember exceeding the allowable levels does not usually imply any safety hazard.) This is particularly important if the FDA tightens the sanitation standards since they would in effect be banning foods which before the new standards were acceptable to both the FDA and the consumer. Moreover, these limits can have deleterious side effects. For instance Professor Donald Kennedy of Stanford University [later FDA Commissioner] after a four year study on insecticide adulteration sponsored by the National Research Council pointed out that the FDA's DAL requirements for insect infestation in fruits and vegetables have caused farmers to use increased amounts of insecticide....

In summary then there would seem, on theoretical grounds, to be some benefit to the labeling approach versus banning since the labeling would allow the consumer to make the ultimate choice with respect to aesthetic adulteration. However, the approach has some drawbacks.

First as mentioned above, the lower grades may not be in high demand, thus consumers would in reality still be offered just one grade. Also institutions, etc. may buy the lower-graded product and serve unknowing customers.... Finally, unless the FDA was given the power to require the producer to affix such a label without going through a legal procedure, the label probably would not be any more cost effective than present regulatory procedures which now require the FDA to go to the judiciary to confiscate contaminated foods. However, it represents an interesting combination of standards and consumer information....

NOTE

Compare Hutt, *The Basis and Purpose of Government Regulation of Adulteration and Misbranding of Food*, 33 FDC L.J. 505, 520–22 (1978).

---

2. THE ISSUE OF "BLENDING"

Section 110.99(d) of FDA's regulations provides:

The mixing of a food containing defects above the current defect action level with another lot of food is not permitted and renders the final food unlawful regardless of the defect level of the final food....

FDA's opposition to "blending" of above and below-tolerance lots of contaminated food represents a longstanding policy which has recently come under reexamination.

SUGARMAN v. FORBRAGD

United States District Court, Northern District of California, 1967.
267 F. Supp. 817.

ZIRPOLI, District Judge.

... These coffee beans were being transported from Colombia to Japan when a fire aboard the ship MS Gunhild Torm required the Captain to change his course and enter a distress port at Long Beach, California..... The unloading of the coffee began on March 28 and was completed by April 3. The bags of coffee were torn, ripped, and split at the seams due to the swelling of the cargo and the coffee beans were therefore unloaded in bulk, commingled with other cargo; at that time the coffee beans were blackened, heated, and in a steaming condition....

On April 11, 1966, Petitioner Sugarman, together with three other joint venturers, purchased "the damaged coffee beans for salvage" for the sum of $600. The coffee beans were then transported to Turlock, California, where they were "cleaned" and sacked and thereafter offered for import.... On March 30, 1967, Respondent Forbragd wrote to the attorney for the Petitioner, incorporating verbatim the following

letter which Mr. Forbragd had received from the Food and Drug
Administration in Washington, D.C.:

> "We agree that the claimant's proposal to salvage this article
> under detention by grinding and blending it with other ground
> coffee is completely unacceptable, since this would amount to
> nothing more than diluting a legal article of food with an
> article which is unfit for food to make a low grade unfinished
> product.
>
> Although you have approved the claimant's application to
> attempt to salvage a portion of this article either by extracting
> the caffeine or by processing into soluble coffee, we doubt that
> a satisfactory soluble coffee can be produced.... If this coffee
> is to be utilized in making soluble coffee the firm should not
> blend this with other coffee beans to prepare the soluble
> coffee....

[The court's discussion of the procedures available to importers of
food and of the availability of judicial review appears at p. 1084 *infra*.]

Petitioner's real objective appears to be an effort to parlay an "as
is" $600 investment "for salvage" plus additionally incurred expendi-
tures for transportation, reconditioning and storage, into a gross return
of some $40,000 at the expense of the ultimate consumer, by mixing
these damaged beans with normal beans in the production of blended
coffee....

At the administrative hearing, Petitioner offered the testimony of a
witness whose work related to the blending of various coffee beans
which would result in an "acceptable" drink. Regarding the problem
of preparing a blend with the charred beans in question, the witness
said:

> In this case, *this particular coffee with its changed profile,
> represented a, one might say, challenge.* [Emphasis added]

This is a remarkable circumlocution and understatement, since the real
issue was how to disguise these damaged beans through a blend and
grind with normal coffee beans so that the public might think the
finished product is coffee. The witness met the "challenge" by proposing a blend of 10 per cent "reconditioned coffee" and 90 per cent
Brazilian coffee....

Petitioner's proposal to blend the charred coffee beans with normal
coffee beans is in reality a proposal to adulterate the good coffee beans,
by substituting in part a cheapened and worthless commodity for
genuine coffee beans. It is as though the proposal were to make a
blend of *used coffee grounds* with freshly ground coffee. No doubt a
skillful "blending" of the charred coffee beans with genuine coffee
beans, or of used coffee grounds with freshly ground coffee, would
enable a coffee producer to palm off the finished product on an
unsuspecting public as coffee....

Under these circumstances, the agency action in question cannot be said to be "arbitrary or capricious." If Petitioner's request to make a coffee blend had been granted, the Food and Drug Administration would have been grossly derelict in the performance of its duties....

NOTE

McNamara, *Some Legal Aspects of Providing a Sufficient Food Supply for a Hungry Population,* 30 FDC L.J. 527 (1975), argues:

... [A]s we insist upon purer and cleaner food and reject that which does not meet our standards, we thereby reduce the available food supply and increase its cost....

... Particularly where the level has been exceeded through no fault of a manufacturer or processor (and assuming that no health hazard exists), it may become more difficult in the future to justify condemnation of food which violates a defect action level when such food might be blended with other food to produce a level of contaminant below the action figure.

See also Hutt, *The Basis and Purpose of Government Regulation of Adulteration and Misbranding of Food,* 33 FDC L.J. 505 (1978):

... This policy was pursued by the Agency because of the fear that condoning the practice of "blending" would discourage sound sanitation practices and would result in great quantities of good food being blended with poor food, thus resulting in a general esthetic debasement of the food supply....

... Competing concerns about the availability and cost of food to feed the world must, however, also be considered. Perhaps it would be possible to permit blending at least for animal feed, or under other limited circumstances, in order to determine the impact that any change in this policy would in fact have. Blind adherence to this longstanding policy is, in any event, no longer justifiable.

In 1978 FDA confronted a situation in the southeastern United States that caused it to relax its opposition to "blending" in the face of genuine concerns about food safety. Heavy rains during the 1977 harvesting season resulted in above-tolerance levels of aflatoxin contamination on as much as 40 percent of the region's corn crop. On January 30, 1978, FDA Commissioner Kennedy responded to one commodity dealer's request for permission to blend several contaminated lots with below-tolerance corn for use as animal feed:

... Tolerances and action levels for poisonous or deleterious substances such as aflatoxin apply only to unavoidable levels of contamination. Intentional blending of a violative article with an uncontaminated article is wholly avoidable and not authorized by such tolerances or action levels. Accordingly, the law does not permit you to blend adulterated corn with unadulterated corn as proposed in your letter....

We recognize that farmers and elevator operators in the southeastern United States face an unusual and economically-devastating problem with respect to aflatoxin contamination in the 1977 corn harvest. It appears that over half of the 1977 corn crop in the southeastern United States (Alabama, Florida, Georgia, Mississippi, North Carolina, South Carolina, and Virginia) may exceed the 20 ppb action level.... Since it may be difficult for farmers in this area to find adequate supplies of corn for use in feeding animals if the law is enforced fully, the Commissioner has determined that he will not recommend regulatory action for violation of the FD&C Act with respect to blending of such corn for use as animal feed if *all* of the following conditions are met:

(1) A technically feasible plan for blending must be provided, the plan to be approved by the FDA district office in Atlanta, Georgia, before blending operations commence.... The blending must be accomplished under Federal or State supervision, and ... [i]t must be demonstrated to the satisfaction of the supervising Federal or State authority that the aflatoxin level of the blended lot is below 20 ppb.

(2) The aflatoxin-contaminated corn must not have been shipped in interstate commerce prior to FDA approval of the blending plan....

(3) The blended lot must be offered for use only for animal feed for mature poultry, swine and beef animals other than milk-producing animals.... Because aflatoxin is such a potent carcinogen, FDA will not under any circumstances authorize the blending for human consumption of corn exceeding the aflatoxin action level.

(4) This approval for limited blending applies only to corn harvested in the southeastern United States (Alabama, Florida, Georgia, Mississippi, North Carolina, South Carolina, and Virginia) during the 1977 harvest....

The decision, subsequently published in 43 Fed. Reg. 14122 (April 4, 1978) in accordance with 21 C.F.R. § 109.4(b)(2), was issued without rulemaking. FDA sanctioned blending a second time under similar circumstances in 46 Fed. Reg. 7447 (January 23, 1981).

The latter action triggered a lawsuit by the Community Nutrition Institute, which argued that FDA's action levels for aflatoxin were unlawful because they had not been established through formal rulemaking under section 406 or even through notice-and-comment rulemaking. CNI also claimed that blending constituted a violation of the FD&C Act. The Court of Appeals' holding that FDA had no legal authority to substitute action levels for formal tolerances under section 406, *Community Nutrition Institute v. Young*, 757 F.2d 354 (D.C. Cir. 1985), was reversed by the Supreme Court, 476 U.S. 974 (1986), p. 304

infra. On remand, the Court of Appeals, 818 F.2d 943, 949–950 (D.C. Cir. 1987), p. 1254 *infra,* held that:

> ... The *intentional* blending of contaminated corn obviously cannot in reason be considered unavoidable. Surely there can be little doubt that blended corn therefore stands branded as "adulterated" for purposes of the FDC Act..... But as FDA goes on to point out, a conclusion that a particular food product is 'adulterated,' in the abstract, means little other than that FDA could choose to initiate enforcement proceedings ...

> Upon analysis, therefore, the gravaman of CNI's complaint is that FDA failed to initiate enforcement proceedings. But as the Supreme Court held in *Heckler v. Chaney* [p. [1057] *infra*], FDA enjoys complete discretion not to employ the enforcement provisions of the FDC Act, and those decisions are not subject to judicial review.

When FDA was again faced with widespread aflatoxin contamination, *see* "Aflatoxin Contamination," FDA Talk Paper No. T88–73 (October 4, 1988), "Drought Increases Aflatoxin Problem for Farmers, Processors," FDA Talk Paper No. T89–13 (February 27, 1989), the agency announced that it was retaining its 20 ppb action level for human food but raising its action levels for animal feed. Explaining that action levels constitute only guidance and not binding requirements, FDA announced the following policy on blending.

CORN SHIPPED IN INTERSTATE COMMERCE FOR USE IN ANIMAL FEEDS; ACTION LEVELS FOR AFLATOXINS IN ANIMAL FEEDS—REVISED COMPLIANCE POLICY GUIDE

54 Federal Register 22622 (May 25, 1989).

... Such blended corn is adulterated within the meaning of section 402(a)(2)(A) of the act. To deal with possible higher than normal levels of aflatoxins in the 1988 corn harvest, however, FDA has decided to exercise its enforcement discretion to refrain from objecting to the blending of corn containing aflatoxins with noncontaminated corn to produce a total level of aflatoxin contamination in the final blended corn that is below one of the action levels for animal feed use only. This policy applies only to corn from the 1988 harvest that contains aflatoxins and is considered necessary because of the severe climate conditions that occurred in many corn-producing states this past summer. The conditions were highly conducive to the formation of the molds that produce aflatoxins. Allowing blending in this situation is intended to provide an acceptable means of using corn that contains aflatoxin and that could not otherwise be lawfully shipped in interstate commerce. For FDA not to object to such blending, however, the following conditions should be met:

1. A technically feasible plan for blending has been reviewed and found acceptable by the FDA Regional Office before blending opera-

tions begin. It should provide assurance that blending conducted in accordance with the plan can reasonably be expected to result in a finished lot of corn containing not more than 20, 100, 200, or 300 ppb of aflatoxins, depending upon the class of food-producing animals for which the blended corn is intended. The blending should be accomplished under Federal or State supervision, and the finished lot should be approved by Federal or State authorities before shipment in interstate commerce. It should be demonstrated to the satisfaction of the supervising Federal or State authority that the aflatoxin level of the blended lot is not above the intended level.

2. The aflatoxin-containing corn has not been shipped in interstate commerce before FDA reviewed the blending plan and found it acceptable. (If the corn could be shipped in interstate commerce before FDA reviewed the blending plan and found it acceptable, there would be an unacceptable risk that some persons might ship contaminated corn in interstate commerce and blend *only* if the contaminated shipments were detected by Federal or State authorities.)

3. The blended corn containing 20 ppb or less aflatoxins is for use as feed for all animals but not for human food use. The blended corn containing 100 ppb or less aflatoxins is for use as feed for only breeding beef cattle, breeding swine, and mature poultry. The blended corn containing 200 ppb or less aflatoxins is for use as feed for only finishing beef cattle or finishing swine. The blended corn containing 300 ppb or less aflatoxins is for use as feed for only finishing beef cattle.

NOTE

In Compliance Policy Guide No. 7120.14 (October 1, 1980), FDA took the position that the deliberate mixing of adulterated food with good food renders the finished product adulterated regardless of the final concentration of contaminants in the finished food. When FDA promulgated its final food GMP regulations, 51 Fed. Reg. 22458, 22474 (June 19, 1986), it specifically declined to revise 21 C.F.R. § 110.110(d), which prohibits the blending of food to achieve an action level for defects that present no health hazard. Now that the agency has sanctioned the blending of food contaminated with a potent carcinogen, even if limited to food used as animal feed, should it continue to prohibit all blending of aesthetically contaminated human food when there is no risk to human health?

---

3. PATHOGENIC MICROORGANISMS

All food contains microorganisms. Most are harmless. Nonpathogenic microorganisms are an essential part of the bacterial fermentation process needed to produce such common food products as cheese, yogurt, and pickles. As described at p. 249 *supra*, FDA has considered establishing standards for harmless microorganisms to protect food quality. With rare exceptions, however, FDA takes regulatory action against any food containing any detectable level of a pathogenic microorganism. For example, Compliance Policy Guide No. 7106.08 (August 1, 1986) authorizes seizure of any dairy product containing any detectable amount of salmonella, campylobacter jejuni, campylobacter coli, yersinia enterocolitica, or listera monocytogenes, or greater than a specified level of escherichia coli. With the unexpected discovery of widespread contamination of food products with listeria in 1982, USDA adopted the same zero tolerance level, 52 Fed. Reg. 7464 (March 11, 1987), 54 Fed. Reg. 22345 (May 23, 1989). In 53 Fed. Reg. 44148 (November 1, 1988), FDA took the unusual step of publishing a revised methodology for detecting and confirming the presence of listeria in food, and in 55 Fed. Reg. 2556 (January 25, 1990) CDC invited proposals to develop tests for the rapid and specific detection of listeria in food.

SANFORD A. MILLER, THE SAGA OF CHICKEN LITTLE AND RAMBO

51 J. Ass'n of Food & Drug Officials, 196 (1987).

Thus far we have tended to focus our attention on the chemical problems associated with our food environment.... Yet, to a significant extent, the most perplexing and hazardous problems of food safety remain today as they always have been, problems of assuring microbiological safety.

For example, there was in 1980 alone, more than one million cases of acute diarrhea in children under five in the developing world. These children died at a rate of ten diarrheal deaths every minute of every day of every year. The majority of these illnesses are caused by food, directly by microbial contamination and indirectly by reducing nutritional status in marginally nourished children. When, to this total, is added the nondiarrhetic foodborne diseases, such as botulinum, typhoid and parasitism, as well as the chronic effects of chemical contamination of foods, the number of people affected and the impact of food contamination on function, well being and economic status is appalling.

Even in the industrialized countries, foodborne diseases are a significant cause of morbidity. Relatively high standards of environmental sanitation, personal hygiene and refrigerator storage of food in most homes has virtually eliminated several serious foodborne diseases, such as typhoid fever. Nonetheless, major outbreaks of such diseases do occur occasionally. Indeed, the incidence of such diseases appears to be on the increase in these countries, in part due to transformation of organisms thought to be benign to those having characteristics which current practices may not entirely protect against. Outbreaks of relatively less serious illness, such as salmonellosis, are not uncommon, usually as the result of an error at one or more stages in the chain of food processing, preparation, distribution and storage in commercial enterprises, public institutions and private homes.

... [O]f much greater concern is the apparent, sudden appearance of a new generation of pathogenic organisms in the food supply. For

affects people w/ weak immune systems

example, a decade ago, organisms such as *Campylobacter jejuni, Aeromonas hydrophilia, Listeria monocytogenes, Yersinia* sp., *Shiigilla* sp., enteropathogenic and hemorrhagic serotypes of E. *coli,* rotoviruses and several protozoans were thought to be rare causes of disease in developed countries. Today, they are among the most common pathogens associated with foods. There are many reasons for this. Among these may be better methods of detection and identification, changing environmental conditions, normal transformation processes, improper use of antibiotics, etc. What is certain, however, is that the pathogenic environment in food is changing. While it appears that current good manufacturing practices involving appropriate and rigorously applied sanitation as well as the proper use of pasteurization and other thermal processing techniques will control these organisms, it is also true that there is not much "forgiveness" in the system....

These concerns are not only of academic interest. For example, scientists at the Center for Food Safety and Applied Nutrition of the USFDA estimated that as many as 81 million or more cases of diarrhea disease of foodborne origin occurs in the United States each year. They also estimated that the average cost for such food-associated illnesses falls close to 164 billion dollars per year. If one adds indirect costs to the economy resulting from such illnesses, they may equal or even double these direct patient-related costs....

It is the acute effects of such illnesses that are generally considered to be the most significant outcomes of their presence. Recent research, however, has emphasized the fact that virtually all of these organisms can also produce or contribute to chronic disorders of many kinds. Thus, certain salmonella, in addition to producing acute enteric disease, may also be associated with the development of rheumatoid problems of various kinds. Certain other organisms may also be associated with the development of neoplasia in the gastrointestinal tract....

There is a parenthetical issue that needs to be addressed. Have we devoted too large a share of our treasure to the problems of chemical contamination of the food supply thus effectively ignoring the considerable problem of microbiological hazard? Public *perception* implies that we have not overreacted. Indeed there are many who say we haven't committed enough to deal with chemical hazards. Recent studies of nearly 1600 food chemicals by the CFSAN of FDA provides an interesting, even "eye opening" perspective on the problem. Among other factors, CFSAN scientists calculated what we call the "Assurance of Safety ratio, 'R' ". This ratio relates exposure to potency as determined by appropriate animal tests. Three observations emerge.

First, the R value (or margin of safety) most likely to be found in this group of food chemicals was 10^5 or a 100,000 fold margin of safety. Second, more than 99% of the values fall above a margin of safety of 1000. Third, for most compounds, only the simplest studies may be required to establish safety since, on the basis of the structure, exposure and potency data obtained in short-term tests, they fall into concern categories that predict high margins of safety. Since the 1600 compounds studied represent that part of the food chemical inventory having the highest probability of significant toxicity, it is likely that the remaining compounds are of even less concern. Based on these and other analysis the time has come, I believe, for a renewed emphasis of microbial issues and some reduction in concern with food chemicals.

NOTES

1. *Cost of Foodborne Disease.* In *Preliminary Estimates of Costs of Foodborne Disease in the United States,* 52 J. Food Protection 595 (1989), Ewen Todd concluded:

> Although the full economic impact of foodborne diseases has yet to be measured, preliminary studies show that the cost of illness, death, and business lost is high indeed. This impact is probably greatest in developing countries, but few facts are known. For the United States, preliminary estimates are 12.6 million cases costing $8.4 billion. These may seem excessive but other authors have postulated even higher case and dollar figures. Microbiological diseases (bacterial and viral) represent 84% of the United States' costs, with salmonellosis and staphylococcal intoxication being the most economically important diseases (annually $4.0 billion and $1.5 billion, respectively.) Other costly types of illnesses are toxoplasmosis ($445 million), listeriosis ($313 million), campylobacteriosis ($156 million), trichinosis ($144 million), *Clostridium perfringens* enteritis ($123 million), and *E. coli* infections including hemorrhagic colitis ($223 million). Botulism has a high cost per case ($322,200), but its total impact is only $87 million because relatively few cases occur (270). This is because the food industry has been able to introduce effective control measures. Salmonellosis, however, is much more widespread (2.9 million cases) and affects all sectors of the food industry.

See also "Foodborne Illnesses and Deaths," Hearing Before the Senate Comm. on Agriculture, Nutrition, and Forestry, 100th Cong., 1st Sess. (1987); *Foodborne Disease Outbreaks, 5–Year Summary, 1983–1987,* 39 Morbidity & Mortality Weekly Rep., No. SS–1 (March 1990).

2. *Sociogenic Illness.* Not all apparent food poisoning episodes are real. Hysteria can also trigger false reports of public illness. *See, e.g., Mass Sociogenic Illness in a Day–Care Center—Florida,* 39 Morbidity & Mortality Weekly Rep. 301 (May 11, 1990).

3. *Basis for Legal Action.* Although the presence of pathogenic microorganisms in food can be the subject of regulatory action by FDA under sections 402(a)(3) and (4), it can also violate section 402(a)(1)'s prohibition against any "poisonous or deleterious substance." The D.C. Circuit declared in *American Public Health Ass'n v. Butz,* 511 F.2d 331 (D.C. Cir. 1974), that "the presence of salmonellae in meat does not constitute adulteration" because the American consumer understands that meat is not sterile and can cause illness if not handled properly, but eight years later the same court determined in *Continental Seafoods, Inc. v. Schweiker,* 674 F.2d 38 (D.C. Cir. 1982), that salmonella in shrimp constitutes an "added substance" that results in adulteration under section 402(a)(1).

4. *Salmonella.* Salmonella contamination of food in general, and of poultry and eggs in particular, has been a major problem. *See, e.g.,* GAO,

SALMONELLA IN RAW MEAT AND POULTRY: AN ASSESSMENT OF THE PROBLEM, No. B–164031(2) (July 22, 1974); *Update: Salmonella enteritidis Infections and Grade A Shell Eggs—United States,* 1989, 38 Morbidity & Mortality Weekly Rep. 877 (January 5, 1990). USDA has undertaken major programs to reduce the problem in poultry and eggs, 55 Fed. Reg. 5576 (February 16, 1990).

———

Even basic food products may be the source of pathogenic microorganisms. Milk was consumed raw before Louis Pasteur discovered that heat treatment destroys bacteria and the dairy industry began in the 1920s to apply this principle through pasteurization of milk. Over the ensuing decades, pasteurized milk gradually drove raw milk out of the market. When FDA revised the food standards for milk and cream in 37 Fed. Reg. 18392 (September 9, 1972) and 38 Fed. Reg. 27924 (October 10, 1973), it required that all fluid milk products moving in interstate commerce be pasteurized. In response to an objection contending that certified raw milk was safe and should not be banned, FDA stayed the pasteurization requirement for certified raw milk, but not for all other fluid milk products, in 39 Fed. Reg. 42351 (December 5, 1974), pending the required administrative hearing.

In response to a petition from the Health Research Group, FDA announced a hearing in 49 Fed. Reg. 31065 (August 3, 1984) to determine whether to permit the continued marketing of certified raw milk. After being ordered to respond, *Public Citizen v. Heckler,* 602 F. Supp. 611 (D.D.C. 1985), FDA denied the petition.

PUBLIC CITIZEN v. HECKLER

United States District Court, District of Columbia, 1986.
653 F. Supp. 1229.

NORMA HOLLOWAY JOHNSON, District Judge. . . .

From 1974 to 1982 the FDA collected and evaluated scientific and medical information to determine if the outbreak of certain diseases was associated with the consumption of certified raw milk. The FDA worked closely with the Center for Disease Control ("CDC"), a branch of HHS, and encouraged the states to test milk and milk products for bacteria or microorganisms and to report outbreaks of milk-borne disease to the CDC. The process of collecting and reviewing data and information led the FDA to conclude that the consumption of certified raw milk and all forms of raw milk and raw milk products was linked to the outbreak of serious disease. In 1982, the FDA began drafting a proposed regulation banning the interstate sale of all raw milk and raw milk products. . . .

[O]n October 11 and 12, 1984, an informal hearing was held by HHS on two issues: (1) whether the consumption of raw milk is a public health concern; and (2) if so, whether requiring pasteurization of all raw milk is the most reasonable regulatory option..... The October hearing resulted in a 330 page transcript and well over 300 comments totalling approximately 4000 pages. Those testifying against any Federal regulation of certified raw milk and certified raw milk products pointed out that many other foods (for example, raw meat) against which no Federal action was contemplated, are also sources of exposure to harmful microorganisms. It was made clear, however, that those other unregulated food products are normally cooked before consumption, and the cooking process kills the salmonella bacteria.

Comments opposing a pasteurization requirement included several witnesses' testimony that in the absence of a definitive case-control study, there was no way to determine whether the apparent association between drinking raw milk and being infected by harmful microorganisms was causal and encouraged HHS to sponsor such a study. Other proponents of raw milk testified that raw milk offers nutritional benefits that are destroyed by pasteurization and that raw milk tastes better than pasteurized milk.

The American Academy of Pediatrics, the National Association of State Departments of Agriculture, the Association of State and Territorial Health Officials, the United States Conference of Local Officials, the National Conference for Food Protection, the American Veterinarians Medical Association, the National Milk Producers Associations, the National Conference on Interstate Milk Shipments, the Association of Food and Drug Officials, the National Dairy Council, the American Society for Microbiology, the Milk Industry Foundation, the Mid–American Dairymen's Association, and others, all supported the pasteurization requirement. These witnesses argued that the risks associated with the consumption of raw milk, even certified raw milk, heavily outweigh any benefits from its consumption.....

On January 29, 1985, the FDA again urged the Secretary to "require the pasteurization of all milk and milk products moving in interstate commerce" because such a requirement "is supported by the administrative record compiled as a result of the [October 1984] hearing." The FDA transmitted to the Secretary a proposed rule banning interstate sales of raw milk and supported this proposed rule by stating that "there is a strong association between the consumption of certified raw milk and the outbreak of disease."

The Secretary rejected the FDA's recommendation and directed the FDA to deny Public Citizen's petition in its entirety. By letter dated March 15, 1985, the Commissioner of the FDA denied the petition, stating that the agency would not ban either interstate or intrastate sales of raw milk. The letter acknowledged that "raw milk, including certified raw milk, is a vehicle for the transmission and spread of numerous diseases" and there is no "scientifically confirmed benefit established for the consumption of raw milk, including certified raw milk." The FDA concluded that "a federal ban would not be the most effective or appropriate means of dealing with the health problems posed by unpasteurized milk and milk products....".....

The crux of the Secretary's explanation for her decision to deny plaintiff's petition is that since a greater amount of raw milk is marketed and consumed locally, rather than shipped interstate, and most illness occurs within the producing locality, the problem is one more appropriately dealt with at the state level. The Secretary claims that interstate sales of certified raw milk are "negligible". There is evidence that most raw milk is produced and consumed locally (mainly in California and Georgia) consistent with state law that permits the sale of unpasteurized milk. The record also shows that there is a serious risk of illness resulting from the consumption of that raw milk which does travel across state lines. The risk is not at all diminished merely because the amount of milk which is sold outside of the producing state is smaller than that sold intrastate. The Secretary failed to recognize that although the relative amount of raw milk that is shipped interstate may be small, the chance of out-of-state residents becoming seriously ill from drinking raw milk remains quite high.

Federal regulation is warranted regardless of the absolute volume of certified raw milk sold interstate. Residents of non-producing states near the producing states do not have access to, and are not represented in, the producing state's political process. A resident of Nevada, for example, who is at risk of becoming ill from the consumption of certified raw milk produced in California and sold in Nevada, cannot turn to a California Congressperson for recourse through the political process.... While an interstate ban on all raw milk might not solve the problem the producing state faces if intrastate sales are permitted, the residents of the producing state are able to turn to the local political process for redress.

The Secretary's reason for her decision has no rational connection to the undisputed facts in the record. As such, her decision cannot be upheld. *See State Farm.* Nothing in the record supports a conclusion that state regulation would be superior to federal regulation. Evidence in the record clearly reflects that the states have been unsuccessful in their individual attempts to regulate the sale of raw milk. The individual states do not have the authority to prohibit sales of raw milk beyond their own boundaries. Only the federal government, under its commerce clause power, may institute a nationwide ban. Even in light of the deferential review this Court must perform, in this case, the action of the Secretary was clearly arbitrary and capricious and must be reversed.

A remand to the agency for further proceedings would serve no purpose and would only add to the delay already encountered. HHS has spent over thirteen years studying the matter and gathering evidence and a hearing has been held. It is undisputed that all types of raw milk are unsafe for human consumption and pose a significant health risk. The appropriate remedy in this case, therefore, is an order compelling the agency to promulgate a regulation prohibiting the interstate sale of certified raw milk and certified raw milk products, and non-certified raw milk and raw milk products. . . .

Public Citizen asks this Court to compel the agency to promulgate a rule banning both interstate and intrastate sales of raw milk. While we must agree that a rule banning the interstate sale of raw milk is appropriate, at this time there is no indication that a rule banning the intrastate sale of raw milk is necessary to effectuate the interstate ban. Accordingly, the Court declines to order the promulgation of a rule banning intrastate sales of raw milk. Assuming the interstate ban is effective without an intrastate ban, it is up to the individual states to decide on such matters of purely local concern. Should it appear that the interstate sale of raw milk continues, it is within HHS's authority at that time to institute an intrastate ban as well. . . .

NOTES

1. *Subsequent Proceedings.* FDA subsequently promulgated a final regulation requiring pasteurization of all milk shipped in interstate commerce, 52 Fed. Reg. 22340 (June 11, 1987), 52 Fed. Reg. 29509 (August 10, 1987), codified in 21 C.F.R. § 1240.61, and at the same time terminated as moot the December 1974 stay of the pasteurization requirement under the standard of identity. Intrastate shipment and sale of certified raw milk remain lawful in those states that permit the product. The regulation FDA promulgated was not based upon section 401 and did not establish or amend the standard of identity for milk. Rather, it was based on the Public Health Service Act, 42 U.S.C. §§ 216, 243, 264, and 271.

2. *Review of Inaction.* This case is one of only two judicial decisions directing FDA to issue a regulation of specified content. Would the court have been prepared to order such relief if the administrative record had not shown that the Secretary of HHS had twice overruled an FDA recommendation to ban all interstate shipment of unpasteurized milk?

FDA COOPERATIVE FOOD SANITATION PROGRAMS

Section 361(a) of the Public Health Service Act, 42 U.S.C. § 264, authorizes FDA to promulgate whatever regulations are "necessary to prevent the introduction, transmission, or spread of communicable diseases . . . " Pursuant to this authority, the Public Health Service (PHS) undertook a number of important food sanitation programs beginning in the 1920s. Administration of these programs was transferred to FDA in 33 Fed. Reg. 9909 (July 10, 1968).

1. *The Pasteurized Milk Ordinance (PMO) and Code.* In 1923, the PHS established an Office of Milk Investigations, and in 1924, in cooperation with state public health officials, it published its first pasteurized milk ordinance. A code of interpretative regulations was added in 1927. Periodically revised, the PMO has been adopted in most states, counties, and cities. *See, e.g.,* the FDA announcement of the 1978 PMO and the related documents that implement it, 44 Fed. Reg. 51337 (August 31, 1979).

To complement the PMO, a National Conference on Interstate Milk Shipments was established to rate farms and milk processing plants for compliance with the PMO. A memorandum of understanding between FDA and the National Conference on Interstate Milk Shipments, establishing the responsibility of both, was published in 42 Fed. Reg. 47261 (September 20, 1977). *See* GAO, FOOD AND DRUG ADMINISTRATION INTERSTATE MILK SHIPPERS PROGRAM, Rep. No. HRD–86–54FS (December 1985).

The PMO has proved generally successful in assuring a sanitary milk supply. Nonetheless, cities, counties, and states have continued to use restrictive sanitation requirements to protect local milk supplies from distant competition. *See, e.g., Dean Milk Co. v. Madison,* 340 U.S. 349 (1951). An attempt to solve this problem through federal legislation, *see, e.g.,* "National Milk Sanitation Act of 1957," Hearings Before a Subcomm. of the House Comm. on Interstate and Foreign Commerce, 85th Cong., 2d Sess. (1958), was unsuccessful. Following the transfer of responsibility for the PMO to FDA in 1968, FDA contemplated codifying the PMO in regulations, *see* Hutt, *FDA Court Actions and Recent Legal Developments,* 39 AFDO Q. Bull. 11, 15 (1975), but abandoned this approach in response to objections by state officials who feared it would undermine federal-state cooperation.

2. *The National Shellfish Sanitation Program (NSSP).* The PHS established the NSSP in 1925 as a cooperative program among the federal and state governments and the shellfish industry to assure sanitary shellfish products. For assessments of the NSSP's success, *see, e.g.,* GAO, PROTECTING THE CONSUMER FROM POTENTIALLY HARMFUL SHELLFISH (CLAMS, MUSSELS, AND OYSTERS), Rep. No. B–164031(2) (March 29, 1973); GAO, NEED TO ASSESS QUALITY OF U.S.-PRODUCED SEAFOOD FOR DOMESTIC AND FOREIGN CONSUMPTION, Rep. No. CED–81–20 (October 15, 1980); GAO, FOLLOWUP ON THE NATIONAL MARINE FISHERIES SERVICE'S EFFORTS TO ASSESS THE QUALITY OF U.S.-PRODUCED SEAFOOD, Rep. No. CED–81–125 (June 22, 1981); GAO, PROBLEMS IN PROTECTING CONSUMERS FROM ILLEGALLY HARVESTED SHELLFISH (CLAMS, MUSSELS, AND OYSTERS), Rep. No. HRD–84–36 (June 14, 1984); GAO, SEAFOOD SAFETY: SERIOUSNESS OF PROBLEMS AND EFFORTS TO PROTECT CONSUMERS, Rep. No. RCED–88–135 (August 10, 1988); "Shellfish Contamination," Hearings Before the Subcomm. on Fisheries and Wildlife Conservation and the Environment of the House Comm. on Merchant Marine and Fisheries, 100th Cong., 2nd Sess. (1988).

Following the transfer of responsibility for the NSSP in 1968, FDA sought to codify the program in regulations. A draft was made available in 38 Fed. Reg. 34353 (December 13, 1973) and regulations were proposed in 40 Fed. Reg. 25916 (June 19, 1975). Although FDA initially stated, 40 Fed. Reg. 58883 (December 19, 1975), that it would repropose the regulations, they were instead withdrawn in 50 Fed. Reg. 7797 (February 26, 1985). Subsequently, FDA and the industry developed an Interstate Shellfish Sanitation Conference (ISSC) patterned after the National Conference on Interstate Milk Shipments, 49 Fed. Reg. 12751 (March 30, 1984). FDA continues periodically to revise and make available the Manual of Operations for the NSSP. *See, e.g.,* 54 Fed. Reg. 7281 (February 17, 1989).

Section 10A of the 1906 Food and Drugs Act, which was added in 48 Stat. 1204 (1934) and amended in 49 Stat. 871 (1935), was the only provision not repealed in 1938. This provision, now codified in 21 U.S.C. § 372a, authorizes FDA, in its discretion, to examine and inspect seafood products upon the payment of a fee. To implement this provision, FDA promulgated regulations codified in 21 C.F.R. part 197 for canned oysters and processed shrimp. Although 90 percent of the canned shrimp packers operated under this program when it began in 1934, only two canneries operated under it in 1957 and the program became inactive at the end of fiscal year 1957 when no firms applied for inspection. HEW ANN. REP. 200 (1957).

The National Marine Fisheries Service (NMFS) of the National Oceanic and Atmospheric Administration (NOAA) in the Department of Commerce operates a voluntary inspection and grading program under 7 U.S.C. § 1622(h) paid for by subscribing members of the fishing industry. In 1983, the NMFS inspection service covered about 18 percent of seafood consumed, but only 11 percent by 1987. The NMFS regulations, codified in 50 C.F.R. Part 260 *et seq.,* include standards for grades for various types of fish products.

Congress has frequently considered legislation to establish a continuous factory inspection program for fish similar to those established for meat, poultry, and eggs. *Compare* "Fishery Products Protection Act of 1967," Hearings before the Consumer Subcomm. of the Senate Comm. on Commerce, 90th Cong., 1st Sess. (1967), and "Wholesome Fish and Fishery Products Act and Assistance Needed to Implement It," Hearings Before the Consumer Subcomm. of the Senate Comm. on Commerce, 90th Cong., 2nd Sess. (1968), *with* "Imported Shrimp," Hearing Before the Subcomm. on Oversight and Investigations of the House Comm. on Energy and Commerce, 100th Cong., 2nd Sess. (1988); "Seafood Safety," Hearing Before the Subcomm. on Oversight and Investigations of the House Comm. on Energy and Commerce, 101st Cong., 1st Sess. (1989); "Seafood Inspection System," Hearing Before the Subcomm. on Fisheries and Wildlife Conservation and the Environment of the House Comm. on Merchant Marine and Fisheries, 101st Cong., 1st Sess. (1989).

Congressional consideration of proposed fish inspection legislation during 1989–1990 pitted FDA, NOAA, and USDA in a struggle over regulatory turf. In an attempt to resolve the matter administratively, FDA and NOAA issued an advance notice of proposed rulemaking in 55 Fed. Reg. 26334 (June 27, 1990) announcing their intent to establish a joint voluntary fish inspection program.

3. *Food Protection Unicode.* In 1935, in cooperation with the Conference of State and Territorial Health Officials and the National Restaurant Code Authority, the PHS prepared a Food Service Sanitation Ordinance, which was later expanded to include a Food Service Sanitation Code of regulations as well. In 1957 the PHS added a Vending of Food and Beverages Ordinance and later a complementary Code. Following transfer of these functions in 1968, FDA prepared in cooperation with the Association of Food and Drug Officials a Retail Food Store Sanitation Code.

Because section 301(k) of the FD&C Act extends FDA jurisdiction to the adulteration of food while held for sale after shipment in interstate commerce, FDA technically has jurisdiction over all restaurants, food vendors, automatic vending machines, and retail food stores in the United States. Lacking the resources to police the hundreds of thousands of establishments involved, however, the agency has concentrated its efforts on food manufacturing, processing, and wholesale warehouses, and has relied on state and local enforcement of the model ordinances and codes to protect against insanitary food conditions at the retail level.

Criticized that it was not doing enough at the retail level, *see, e.g.,* GAO, FEDERAL SUPPORT FOR RESTAURANT SANITATION FOUND LARGELY INEFFECTIVE, Rep. No. MWD–76–42 (December 8, 1975), FDA converted its Food Service Sanitation Ordinance and Code into proposed regulations in 39 Fed. Reg. 35438 (October 1, 1974). But in response to objections that the proposal abridged the understanding between the states and the federal government regarding the regulation of the food service industry, FDA withdrew it in 42 Fed. Reg. 15428 (March 22, 1977) and announced it would instead continue to rely on the development and periodic revision of model sanitation codes.

Over time the distinctions between food service, vending, and retail food stores have become blurred. All three functions are often performed in a single establishment. The Conference for Food Protection in 1986 therefore endorsed the development of a Food Protection Unicode, combining all of the other food protection ordinances and codes. FDA announced this project in 52 Fed. Reg. 11885 (April 13, 1987) and made the draft Unicode available for public comment in 53 Fed. Reg. 16472 (May 9, 1988).

---

4. GOOD MANUFACTURING PRACTICE

During the 1960s FDA experimented with a number of techniques to standardize its enforcement of section 402(a)(4) and to provide food producers better guidance about the requirements of this provision. The agency developed a plant evaluation system (PEV) in which inspectors used standardized forms to evaluate particular segments of the food industry. These forms focused on the sanitation practices with which FDA was principally concerned. Later, FDA issued good manufacturing practice guidelines for specific commodities to guide both its inspectors and manufacturers.

In 32 Fed. Reg. 17980 (December 15, 1967), FDA proposed the first "umbrella" good manufacturing practice (GMP) regulations for the food industry. The agency explained that these regulations were intended to interpret the "insanitary conditions" provisions of section 402(a)(4). FDA issued a reproposal in 33 Fed. Reg. 19023 (December 20, 1968) and ultimately promulgated final GMP regulations, now codified in 21 C.F.R. Part 110, in 34 Fed. Reg. 6977 (April 26, 1969). Those general regulations were not challenged in court. When FDA subsequently adopted GMP regulations for specific food commodities, however, it was forced to defend their legality.

UNITED STATES v. NOVA SCOTIA FOOD PRODUCTS CORP.

United States Court of Appeals, Second Circuit, 1977.
568 F.2d 240.

GURFEIN, Circuit Judge.

This appeal involving a regulation of the Food and Drug Administration is not here upon a direct review of agency action. It is an appeal from a judgment of the District Court for the Eastern District of New York ... enjoining the appellants, after a hearing, from processing hot smoked whitefish except in accordance with time-temperature-salinity (T–T–S) regulations contained in 21 C.F.R. Part 122 (1977).....

Government inspection of appellants' plant established without question that the minimum T–T–S requirements were not being met.

There is no substantial claim that the plant was processing whitefish under "insanitary conditions" in any other material respect. Appellants, on their part, do not defend on the ground that they were in compliance, but rather that the requirements could not be met if a marketable whitefish was to be produced. They defend upon the grounds that the regulation is invalid (1) because it is beyond the authority delegated by the statute; (2) because the FDA improperly relied upon undisclosed evidence in promulgating the regulation and because it is not supported by the administrative record; and (3) because there was no adequate statement setting forth the basis of the regulation. We reject the contention that the regulation is beyond the authority delegated by the statute, but we find serious inadequacies in the procedure followed in the promulgation of the regulation and hold it to be invalid as applied to the appellants herein.* ...

The argument that the regulation is not supported by statutory authority cannot be dismissed out of hand. The sole statutory authority relied upon is § 342(a)(4).... Nor is the Commissioner's expressed reliance solely on § 342(a)(4) a technicality which might be removed by a later and wiser reliance on another subsection. For in this case, as the agency recognized, there is no other section or subsection that can pass as statutory authority for the regulation....

Appellants contend that the prohibition against "insanitary conditions" embraces conditions only in the plant itself, but does not include conditions which merely inhibit the growth of organisms already in the food when it enters the plant in its raw state. They distinguish between conditions which are insanitary, which they concede to be within the ambit of § 342(a)(4), and conditions of sterilization required to destroy micro-organisms, which they contend are not.

It is true that on a first reading the language of the subsection appears to cover only "insanitary conditions" "*whereby* it [the food] may have been rendered injurious to health" (emphasis added). And a plausible argument can, indeed, be made that the references are to insanitary conditions in the plant itself, such as the presence of rodents or insects....

... [S]o far as the category of harmful micro-organisms is concerned, there is only a single provision, 21 U.S.C. § 344, which directly deals with "micro-organisms." ... It may be argued that the failure to mention "micro-organisms" in the "adulteration" section of the Act, which includes § 342(a)(4), means that Congress intended to delegate no further authority to control micro-organisms than is expressed in the "emergency" control of Section 344.

On the other hand ... the manner of processing can surely give rise to the survival, with attendant toxic effects on humans, of spores which would not have survived under stricter "sanitary" conditions. In that sense, treating "insanitary conditions" in relation to the hazard,

* [The portion of the court's opinion discussing the procedural errors made in promulgating the T–T–S regulation is set out p. 1247 *infra*.]

the interpretation of the District Court which described the word "sanitary" as merely "inelegant" is a fair reading, emphasizing that the food does not have to be actually contaminated during processing and packing but simply that "it may have been rendered injurious to health," § 342(a)(4), by inadequate sanitary conditions of prevention....

We do not discount the logical arguments in support of a restrictive reading of § 342(a)(4), but we perceive a larger general purpose on the part of Congress in protecting the public health.

We come to this conclusion, aside from the general rules of construction noted above, for several reasons: First, until this enforcement proceeding was begun, no lawyer at the knowledgeable Food and Drug bar ever raised the question of lack of statutory delegation or even hinted at such a question. Second, the body of data gathered by the experts, including those of the Technical Laboratory of the Bureau of Fisheries manifested a concern about the hazards of botulism....

Lastly, a holding that the regulation of smoked fish against the hazards of botulism is invalid for lack of authority would probably invalidate, to the extent that our ruling would be followed, the regulations concerning the purity of raw materials before their entry into the manufacturing process in 21 C.F.R. Part 113 (1977) (inspection of incoming raw materials for microbiological contamination before thermal processing of low-acid foods packed in hermetically sealed containers), in 21 C.F.R. Part 118 (1977) (pasteurization of milk and egg products to destroy Salmonella micro-organisms before use of the products in cacao products and confectionery), and 21 C.F.R. Part 129 (1977) (product water supply for processing and bottling of bottled drinking water must be of a safe, sanitary quality when it enters the process).

The public interest will not permit invalidation simply on the basis of a lack of delegated statutory authority in this case. A gap in public health protection should not be created in the absence of a compelling reading based upon the utter absence of any statutory authority, even read expansively. Here we find no congressional history on the specific issue involved, and hence no impediment to the broader reading based on general purpose. We believe, nevertheless, that it would be in the public interest for Congress to consider in the light of existing knowledge, a legislative scheme for administrative regulation of the processing of food where hazard from micro-organisms in food in its natural state may require affirmative procedures of sterilization....

Based upon its experience with GMP regulations for specific food commodities, FDA proposed amendments of its umbrella GMP regulations.

CURRENT GOOD MANUFACTURING PRACTICE IN MANUFACTURING, PROCESSING, PACKING, OR HOLDING HUMAN FOOD: PROPOSED RULEMAKING

44 Federal Register 33238 (June 8, 1979).

... FDA's 1977 annual report estimates the overall number of food processing, manufacturing, and warehouse facilities regulated by the agency at 77,000, and FDA conducts approximately 19,000 food establishment inspections annually.... FDA ceased relying exclusively on case-by-case litigation in the late 1960's and adopted a combined policy of promulgating regulations, relying on self-regulation by the industry, and, within the limits of available resources, enforcing regulations when the industry fails to comply with them....

The agency's experience ... has shown that problems to be addressed by those CGMP regulations are common throughout all segments of the food industry, *e.g.*, personnel, plant construction, and sanitation. Accordingly, the agency believes that the most efficient way to proceed now is to revise the umbrella CGMP regulations rather than repetitively to propose identical regulations for numerous segments of the industry....

The CGMP regulations already in effect detail the practices to be followed to ensure (1) that food is manufactured, processed, packed, and held under conditions that are sanitary, and (2) that such food is safe, clean, and wholesome. In general, this notice proposes to revise and update the requirements for plant personnel; plant design and construction; sanitary operations, facilities, and controls; equipment and utensils; regulating and recording controls; processing operations; and coding and recordkeeping.....

Under section 701(a) of the act, FDA has the authority to promulgate regulations for the efficient enforcement of that act, and such regulations have been held to have the force and effect of law. The courts have also expressly held that FDA has the authority to promulgate substantive regulations defining current good manufacturing practices for the food industry. Furthermore, since the promulgation of the CGMP regulations in 1969, the Secretary of Health, Education, and Welfare has delegated authority to exercise the functions vested in the Secretary under section 361 of the Public Health Service Act (42 U.S.C. 264) to the Commissioner of Food and Drugs. Under this provision, the Commissioner is authorized to issue and enforce regulations for any measures that, in the Commissioner's judgment, are necessary to prevent the introduction, transmission, or spread of food-borne communicable diseases from one State to another. Because this authority is designed to eliminate the introduction of diseases such as typhus from one State to another, this authority must of necessity be exercised upon the disease-causing substance within the State where the food is manufactured, processed, or held. Due to the nationwide, interrelated structure of the food industry, communicable diseases may, without proper intrastate food controls, easily spread interstate.... The Commissioner therefore assumes authority to promulgate regulations under the Public Health Service Act to assure that foods are manufactured, processed, packed, or held under sanitary conditions so as to be safe, wholesome, and otherwise fit for food. Regulations promulgated under that statute also have the force and effect of law....

Section 110.19 (21 C.F.R. 110.19) codifies FDA's historical exemption from the "umbrella" CGMP regulations of establishments that are engaged in the harvesting, storage, or distribution of one or more raw agricultural commodities that are ordinarily cleaned, prepared, treated, or otherwise processed before being marketed to the consuming public. Subsequent handlers of the commodities would be subject to the CGMP regulations, and food from those commodities is thus brought into compliance with the act at the later states of the manufacturing, processing, packing, or holding....

... The proposal includes a new subparagraph to explain ways to reduce the possibility of micro-organism, chemical, filth, or other contamination of end products, raw materials, and packaging materials. It recommends separating each step in the operation, from receiving the raw materials, to packing and shipping the end product, to cleaning, sanitizing, and maintaining the operations.....

Section 110.80 (21 CFR 110.80) adds a quality control operation to ensure that all operations in the receiving, inspecting, transporting, packaging, segregating, preparing, processing, and storing of food are conducted in accordance with adequate sanitation principles. This program requirement is based on FDA's experience in conducting approximately 19,000 food establishment inspections annually. Most operations have control procedures of this nature, and quality control procedures of this type help to ensure that raw materials and finished products are fit for food, that packaging materials are safe and suitable, and that all are in compliance with the act.

... [N]ew § 110.91 (21 CFR 110.91) deals expressly with product coding. In § 110.80(i) of the current umbrella GMP regulations, which this proposal would supersede, the agency suggests that meaningful coding of products should be used to enable positive lot identification.... In the past decade, voluntary product recalls by manufacturers have become one of FDA's most useful regulatory tools.... In fiscal year 1975 there were 133 recalls of food products, including misbranding violations, and 163 in fiscal year 1976. These experiences have shown that product coding is an essential element of this regulatory tool.... Many companies are already coding products, and, based upon coding's recognized utility and accepted use in many segments of the food industry, the agency believes product coding should be mandatory for all foods. Accordingly, the agency is proposing, except where specifically exempt, to require permanently legible marks at a readily visible location on each finished food package delivered or displayed to purchasers.....

Section 110.100 (21 CFR 110.100) lists current recordkeeping requirements, amended to conform to those promulgated and upheld in the candy CGMP's. These recordkeeping requirements are correlated with the other CGMP requirements and require the affected parties to maintain (a) records on the results of examinations or copies of supplier guarantees or certifications verifying that the raw materials comply with the basic act and other FDA regulations under proposed § 110.80(a); (b) records of processes that are specified in proposed § 110.80(b) and are intended to destroy or prevent the growth of micro-organisms of public health significance in the foods; and (c) distribution records that identify initial distribution of finished food under proposed § 110.93 to facilitate recalls. The agency proposes that these records be kept for 2 years or for the shelf life of the product, whichever is shorter....

NOTES

1. *Final Regulations.* The regulations based upon this proposal were published in 51 Fed. Reg. 22458 (June 19, 1986).

2. *Shipping Records.* When FDA promulgated the GMP regulations for cocao products and confectionary, 38 Fed. Reg. 32554 (November 26, 1973), 40 Fed. Reg. 24162 (June 4, 1975), the agency included requirements that each shipping container be marked with a code identifying the plant where the candy was packed and its production or packing lot, and that the records of the initial distribution of the candy be kept for a period exceeding its shelf life but not more than two years. These requirements were upheld in *National Confectioners Ass'n v. Califano,* 569 F.2d 690 (D.C. Cir. 1978). FDA's proposed revision of the umbrella GMP regulations included similar requirements for all food products, but the final regulations omitted these provisions, based on the following reasoning:

> The purpose of proposing coding and recordkeeping was to facilitate a manufacturer's recall of suspect products in case such a recall was recommended by FDA. Although such information is potentially useful in determining the production time period which is effected by a recall, thereby limiting manufacturers' risk exposure, it is not needed to protect consumers from products that have been purchased but not ingested. Furthermore, all manufacturers either currently code all their products or keep shipping records in the ordinary course of business, or do both. As these sources can provide most of the information which would have been required in the proposed rule, and all of the information needed for a recall, it is not necessary to impose other economically burdensome recordkeeping requirements. This decision will save manufacturers and consumers approximately $80.5 million annually (1985 dollars) in foregone costs....

> For consumer protection, the most effective safeguard is product, not lot, identification and swift dissemination of such information by mass media....

In addition, the products most likely to involve risk of recall (low acid food) are already subject to coding and recordkeeping requirements.

51 Fed. Reg. 22458 (June 19, 1986).

3. *Revocation of Product Specific GMP Regulations.* Once it decided to revise the umbrella regulations, FDA revoked its GMP regulations for smoked fish, 48 Fed. Reg. 48836 (October 21, 1983), 49 Fed. Reg. 20484 (May 15, 1984); for cocao products and confectionary, 44 Fed. Reg. 52257 (September 7, 1979), 51 Fed. Reg. 22481 (June 19, 1986); and for frozen raw breaded shrimp, 51 Fed. Reg. 22482 (June 19, 1986), 51 Fed. Reg. 41615 (November 18, 1986).

4. *Infant Formula GMPs.* For a discussion of the GMP requirements for infant formula products, *see* p. 177 *supra.*

5. *HACCP.* In the early 1970s, FDA developed the concept of "hazard analysis and critical control point" (HACCP) systems as part of food GMP, to identify aspects of a food manufacturing operation most important to product integrity and safety. USDA announced hearings in 55 Fed. Reg. 21765 (May 29, 1990) to determine how to incorporate HACCP systems into its meat and poultry inspection operations.

6. *PCB Contamination.* Although FDA initially proposed to limit the level of PCBs in sealed electrical equipment in food processing and storage facilities to prevent contamination of food, 45 Fed. Reg. 30984 (May 9, 1980), it subsequently withdrew this proposal, 50 Fed. Reg. 29233 (July 18, 1985), on the ground that controls over PCBs established by EPA adequately protect the public health.

7. *AIDS-Infected Personnel.* Section 110.10(a) of FDA's GMP regulations states that any person who has an illness or infection by which there is a "reasonable possibility of food, food-contact surfaces, or food-packaging materials becoming contaminated" must be excluded from any food operation. Soon after acquired immune deficiency syndrome (AIDS) was first identified in this country, *see* p. 552 *infra,* the question was raised whether individuals infected with the human immunodeficiency virus (originally HTLV and now HIV) should be excluded from employment in food manufacturing and service establishments. The Centers for Disease Control responded by issuing *Recommendations for Preventing Transmission of Infection with Human T-lymphotropic Virus Type III/lymphadenopathy-associated Virus in the Workplace,* 34 Morbidity and Mortality Weekly Rep. 682, 693–94 (November 15, 1985):

> *Food-service workers (FSWs).* FSWs are defined as individuals whose occupations involve the preparation or serving of food or beverages (*e.g.,* cooks, caterers, servers, waiters, bartenders, airline attendants). All epidemiologic and laboratory evidence indicates that blood-borne and sexually transmitted infections are not transmitted during the preparation or serving of food or beverages, and no instances of HBV or HTLV–III/LAV transmission have been documented in this setting.

> All FSWs should follow recommended standards and practices of good personal hygiene and food sanitation (26). All FSWs should exercise care to avoid injury to hands when preparing food. Should such an injury occur, both aesthetic and sanitary considerations would dictate that food contaminated with blood be discarded. FSWs known to be infected with HTLV–III/LAV need not be restricted from work

unless they have evidence of other infection or illness for which any FSW should also be restricted.

> Routine serologic testing of FSWs for antibody to HTLV–III/LAV is not recommended to prevent disease transmission from FSWs to consumers.

This recommendation has not since been changed, and there has been no evidence of AIDS transmission through food. Nonetheless, the House adopted a provision during debate on the 1990 Americans with Disabilities Act permitting the food industry to exclude HIV positive workers from food-handling jobs, 136 Cong. Rec. H2484 (daily ed. May 17, 1990), and the Senate instructed its conferees to accept this amendment, 136 Cong. Rec. S7449 (daily ed. June 6, 1990). In conference, however, the provision was deleted.

8. *Hand Sanitizers.* The use of hand sanitizers is common throughout the food industry to protect against transmission of microorganisms. The legal status of these products, however, requires an understanding of three separate regulatory concepts. Under the Federal Insecticide, Rodenticide, and Fungicide Act (FIFRA), 7 U.S.C. § 136 *et seq.,* the Environmental Protection Agency (EPA) regulates all "pesticides." Although a pesticide is defined under 7 U.S.C. § 136(t) and (u) as any substance that destroys microorganisms, EPA has issued regulations in 40 C.F.R. § 152.8(a) excluding microorganisms "in or on living man or animals." Thus, EPA has narrowed its jurisdiction to exclude FDA-regulated products.

Under section 201(g)(1)(B) of the FD&C Act, a product intended to prevent disease is a drug. Applying this definition, FDA has regulated antimicrobial soap and other topical antimicrobial products as drugs. In the OTC Drug Review tentative final monograph for these products, 43 Fed. Reg. 1210, 1229 (January 6, 1978), FDA set forth its position on proposed labeling claims that these products "disinfected" or "sanitized" the skin:

> The Commissioner realizes that these terms are intended to imply cleansing of human tissue. However, there is some discrepancy between the commonly understood or lay meaning of these terms and their scientific meaning. The Commissioner is concerned that, as he attempts to set general standards in this area, terms and claims not be ambiguous or have dual meanings....

> The Commissioner concludes that to assure clarity and conciseness of the meaning of these claims, as well as to eliminate the confusion caused by the dual meaning, their use should be limited to denoting antimicrobial action only on inanimate objects. Therefore, the above claims (or similar claims) will be considered misleading when applied to the use of topical antimicrobial products on humans.

The food GMP regulations, however, in 21 C.F.R. § 110.10(b)(3) provide as a part of "maintaining cleanliness":

> (3) Washing hands thoroughly (and sanitizing if necessary to protect against contamination with undesirable microorganisms)....

In *Farquhar v. FDA,* 616 F. Supp. 190 (D.D.C. 1985), the district court held that the marketing of a hand sanitizing product for food handlers did not provide a predicate to consideration of the product under the OTC Drug Review, p. 588 *infra.*

9. *National Sanitation Foundation.* The NSF sponsors a voluntary program to establish consensus standards and certification of compliance for food contact equipment and articles. *See* McClelland, *The National Sanitation Foundation: Its Mission, Programs, and Goals,* 48 J. AFDO 93 (1984).

5. EMERGENCY PERMIT CONTROL

FOOD AND DRUG ADMINISTRATION

For Immediate Release
Friday, October 29, 1971

PUBLIC WARNING

The Food and Drug Administration issued an urgent warning today to consumers who may have eaten or have in their homes cans of Stokely–Van Camp Finest French Style Green Beans in eight ounce cans with the code number SB 72/E213D. The suspected code of the product is being recalled by Stokely–Van Camp, Inc., Indianapolis, Indiana.

The Agency warning is based upon preliminary results of tests conducted by the National Center for Disease Control in Atlanta. The tests suggested the presence of botulinum toxin Type B in the serum of an eight-year-old Pensacola, Florida, boy. The boy and his father noticed an off-flavor after each ate two or three beans from a swollen can. Both were then purged at a local hospital. Tests on the serum from the father were negative for botulinum toxin. Neither have developed any symptoms of botulism....

For Immediate Release:
Monday, November 1, 1971

Weekend testing by the Center for Disease Control, Public Health Service, Atlanta, Georgia, has failed to confirm preliminary evidence of botulinum toxin in the blood serum of a Pensacola, Florida boy or in a can of green beans from which the eight-year old and his father ate last Wednesday. FDA, therefore, is rescinding its warning to consumers against eating Stokely–Van Camp Finest French Style Sliced Green Beans, Code Number SB 72/E213D. Recall of the product no longer is considered necessary....

FDA Commissioner Charles C. Edwards, M.D. said: "In dealing with life or death problems like botulism, there are times when the public interest demands action before the scientific case is complete. The decision always must be made in favor of consumer protection. Such decisions are always difficult, both for Government and the industry."

NANCY L. ROSS, REMEMBER THAT VICHYSSOISE?

The Washington Post, June 25, 1972, p. k1.

One year ago next Friday a Bedford, N.Y. banker named Samuel Cochran, Jr. died after eating a poisonous can of Bon Vivant vichyssoise and federal officials feared a national epidemic of deadly botulism. The worst did not happen. Yet the events surrounding that tragedy were to have profound repercussions:

· Mrs. Cochran, who also sampled the soup, was partially paralyzed, and is suing Bon Vivant and Gristede's, the grocery store which sold the soup, for more than one million dollars;

· Bon Vivant Soups, Inc. declared bankruptcy, and is still trying to prove its product is safe to eat to prevent the Food and Drug Administration from ordering the destruction of its entire remaining stock of 1.4 million cans;

· Two major food producers, Campbell Soup and Stokely–Van Camp were involved in botulism scares, the second of which was a false alarm set off by nervous federal officials; ...

· The National Canners Association, shaken by a crisis in consumer confidence, devised stricter regulations to guard against botulism and asked the FDA to enforce them;

· The FDA, embarrassed by the revelation its inspectors had not visited the Bon Vivant plant in six years, made food inspection and safety a priority item, and plans to double the number of inspectors next year;

· Meanwhile, despite official warnings to home canners to prepare food properly, 11 other Americans died in that year from botulism.

When the normally harmless bacterium Clostridium botulinum breeds in an airless, low-acid environment, due to improper cooking of food in vacuum containers, it can be transformed into botulin toxin. A few ounces of this concentrated poison would suffice to depopulate the earth. In the past 50 years 15 people in this country have died from botulism caused by commercially-prepared food, although hundreds more have died from improperly sterilized home-canned products.....

... Bon Vivant's owners, Andrew Paretti, 47, and his wife Maria, appeared most anxious to tell their side of the story to correct what they feel has been biased reporting.... Venomous words like "incredible persecution, unfair treatment, vendetta panic, overreaction" punctuated a two-hour interview. Most of this was aimed at the FDA's action in seizing Bon Vivant's entire inventory and thereby bankrupting his 108–year–old company, which had always had a "clean" record, on the basis of one mistake. No company in FDA history had ever had its entire stock confiscated. That mistake, traced to human error in setting the cooking timer, resulted in one lot of vichyssoise not being thoroughly sterilized—and eventually the death of a man. Botulin toxin was found by FDA chemists in only five cans of vichyssoise, yet his whole line of 90 different products was seized by the agency which claimed it had found an unusually high percentage of abnormal cans. . . .

[The Parettis'] bitterness is aggravated by the government's treatment of the Campbell Soup Company after the firm's labs discovered botulin toxin in a batch of its chicken vegetable. Campbell's was then allowed to effect its own recall of the soup at its own expense—an estimated $5 million. No one became ill. Bon Vivant, on the other hand, could not finance a voluntary recall, so its products were seized by federal marshals. The rest of Campbell's stock remained untouched because inspectors found the plant that produced the poisonous soup to be above reproach. . . .

David McVey, senior vice president of Stokely–Van Camp, the third largest canner in the country, also expressed anger at the false botulism alarm that cost his company millions of dollars in recalls. "When you defame a product label to 200 million people watching television and reading newspapers it takes a long time to rebuild it," he said. . . .

―――――

Section 404 of the FD&C Act authorizes FDA to impose special controls over producers of food subject to microbiological contamination. Following the Bon Vivant, Stokely, and Campbell Soup episodes, FDA issued regulations designed to forestall similar problems in the future. In this instance, the initiative came from the industry itself. The regulations reflect FDA's efforts to avoid the rulemaking procedures of section 701(e) of the Act.

EMERGENCY PERMIT CONTROL

39 Federal Register 3748 (January 29, 1974).

The Commissioner of Food and Drugs published in the FEDERAL REGISTER of May 14, 1973 (38 FR 12716) a final order establishing the requirements and conditions for compliance with, or exemption from, section 404 . . . with respect to thermally processed low-acid foods in hermetically sealed containers.

The Commissioner (38 FR 12720) . . . proposed definitions and procedures to govern implementation of the emergency permit control authority contained in section 404 of the act. . . . .

The Commissioner reaffirms the position that Subpart A of Part 90 is procedural in nature and designed to provide the mechanism for implementation of Part 90 [now 21 C.F.R. Part 108]. Subpart B, which at present consists only of [§ 108.35] relating to thermally processed low-acid canned foods in hermetically sealed containers, contains the substantive requirements established under section 404 of the act for any particular food or class of foods. The Commissioner has concluded that section 702(e)(1) of the act provides an opportunity for a public hearing only on the substantive regulations applicable to a particular food or class of foods authorized by section 404(a) of the act, and that the procedural regulations generally implementing the emergency permit control system of section 404 are authorized by section 701(a) of the act, which does not provide for a public hearing.....

§ 108.19 Establishment of requirements for exemption from section 404 of the act.

(a) Whenever the Commissioner finds after investigation that the distribution in interstate commerce of any class of food may, by reason of contamination with micro-organisms during the manufacture, processing, or packing thereof in any locality, be injurious to health, and that such injurious nature cannot be adequately determined after such articles have entered interstate commerce, he shall promulgate regulations in Subpart B of this part establishing requirements and conditions governing the manufacture, processing, or packing of the food necessary to protect the public health....

(b) A manufacturer, processor, or packer of a food for which a regulation has been promulgated in Subpart B of this part shall be exempt from the requirement for a permit only if he meets all of the mandatory requirements and conditions established in that regulation.

§ 108.5 Determination of the need for a permit.

(a) Whenever the Commissioner determines after investigation that a manufacturer, processor, or packer of a food for which a regulation has been promulgated in Subpart B of this part does not meet the mandatory conditions and requirements established in such regulation, he shall issue to such manufacturer, processor, or packer an order determining that a permit shall be required before the food may be introduced or delivered for introduction into interstate commerce by that person.

(1) The manufacturer, processor, or packer shall have 3 working days after receipt of such order within which to file objections.... If such objections are filed, the determination is stayed pending a hearing to be held within 5 working days after the filing of objections on the issues involved unless the Commissioner determines that the objections raise no genuine and substantial issue of fact to justify a hearing.

(2) If the Commissioner finds that there is an imminent hazard to health, the order shall contain this finding and the reasons therefor, and shall state that the determination of the need for a permit is effective immediately pending an expedited hearing....

(c) Within 5 working days after the hearing, and based on the evidence presented at the hearing, the Commissioner shall determine whether a permit is required and shall so inform the manufacturer, processor, or packer in writing, with the reasons for his decision....

§ 108.7 Issuance or denial of permit.

(a) After a determination and notification by the Commissioner ... that a manufacturer, processor, or packer requires a permit, such manufacturer, processor, or packer may not thereafter introduce or deliver for introduction into interstate commerce any such food manufactured, processed, or packed by him unless he holds a permit issued by the Commissioner or obtains advance written approval of the Food and Drug Administration....

(b) Any manufacturer, processor, or packer for whom the Commissioner has made a determination that a permit is necessary may apply to the Commissioner for the issuance of such a permit. The application shall contain such data and information as is necessary to show that all mandatory requirements and conditions for the manufacture, processing or packing of a food for which regulations are established in Subpart B of this part are met.....

§ 108.6 Revocation of determination of need for permit....

(b) Whenever the Commissioner has reason to believe that a permit holder is in compliance with the mandatory requirements and conditions established in Subpart B of this part and is likely to remain in compliance, he shall, on his own initiative or on the application of the permit holder, revoke both the determination of need for a permit and the permit that had been issued....

In the same issue of the Federal Register that these regulations (Subpart A) appeared, FDA ruled on the objections to its "final" Subpart B regulations governing thermally processed low-acid foods in hermetically sealed containers. Under section 701(e) of the Act, regulations requiring emergency permits for the production of any class of food must be promulgated through formal rulemaking. FDA concluded, however, that none of the objections to Subpart B raised factual issues that justified a formal evidentiary hearing, 39 Fed. Reg. 3750 (January 29, 1974).

SUBPART B—SPECIFIC REQUIREMENTS AND CONDITIONS FOR EXEMPTION FROM OR COMPLIANCE WITH AN EMERGENCY PERMIT

§ 108.35　Thermal processing of low-acid foods packaged in hermetically sealed containers.

(a) Inadequate or improper manufacture, processing, or packing of thermally processed low-acid foods in hermetically sealed containers may result in the distribution in interstate commerce of processed foods that may be injurious to health. The harmful nature of such foods cannot be adequately determined after these foods have entered into interstate commerce.... [A] permit may be required whenever the Commissioner finds, after investigation, that the commercial processor has failed to fulfill all the requirements of this section, including registration and the filing of process information and the mandatory portions of Part 113 [current GMP regulations for thermally processed low-acid foods].....

(c) *Registration and Process Filing.* (1) *Registration.* A commercial processor when first engaging in the manufacture, processing, or packing of thermally processed low-acid foods in hermetically sealed containers ... shall, not later than 10 days after first so engaging, register with the Food and Drug Administration....

(2) *Process filing.* A commercial processor engaged in the thermal processing of low-acid foods packaged in hermetically sealed containers shall, not later than 60 days after registration and prior to the packing of a new product, provide the Food and Drug Administration information as to the scheduled processes ... for each such low-acid food in each container size: *Provided,* That the filing of such information does not constitute approval of the information by the Food and Drug Administration.....

(ii) If a packer intentionally makes a change in a previously filed scheduled process by reducing the initial temperature or retort temperature, reducing the time of processing, or changing the product formulation, the container, or any other condition basic to the adequacy of scheduled process, he shall prior to using such changed process obtain substantiation by qualified scientific authority as to its adequacy. Such substantiation may be obtained by telephone, telegram, or other media, but must be promptly recorded, verified in writing by the authority, and contained in the packer's files for review by the Food and Drug Administration.....

(3) *Process adherence and information.* (i) A commercial processor ... shall process each low-acid food in each container size in conformity with at least the scheduled processes and modifications filed pursuant to paragraph (c)(2) of this section....

(d) A commercial processor ... shall promptly report to the Food and Drug Administration any instance of spoilage or process deviation the nature of which indicates potential health significance where any lot of such food has in whole or in part entered distribution....

(f) A commercial processor ... shall have prepared and in his files a current procedure which he will use for products under his control and which he will ask his distributor to follow, including plans for effecting recalls of any product that may be injurious to health; for identifying, collecting, warehousing, and controlling the product; for determining the effectiveness of such recall; for notifying the Food and

Drug Administration of any such recall; and for implementing such recall program....

(h) A commercial processor ... shall prepare, review, and retain at the processing plant for a period of not less than one year, and at the processing plant or other reasonably accessible location for an additional two years, all records of processing, deviations in processing, container closure inspections, and other records specified in Part 113.... Upon written demand during the course of a factory inspection pursuant to section 704 of the act by a duly authorized employee of the Food and Drug Administration, a commercial processor shall permit the inspection and copying by such employee of these records to verify the adequacy of processing, the integrity of container closures, and the coding of the products....

NOTES

1. *Acidified Food.* FDA has since extended this approach to include acidified food in 41 Fed. Reg. 30442, 30457 (July 23, 1976), 44 Fed. Reg. 16235 (March 16, 1979), codified in 21 C.F.R. Part 114.

2. *Pet Food.* The requirements for low acid canned food apply to pet food as well. *See* 44 Fed. Reg. 48598 (August 17, 1979), codified in 21 C.F.R. Part 507.

3. *USDA Processing Requirements.* USDA has established similar requirements for canned meat and poultry products, 49 Fed. Reg. 14636 (April 12, 1984), 51 Fed. Reg. 45602 (December 19, 1986).

4. *Salmon Contamination.* The importance of extreme care in the production of low acid canned food has never been more dramatically illustrated than by a single incident involving the Alaskan canned salmon industry. In February 1982, a Belgian citizen died of botulism poisoning after eating canned Alaskan salmon. The contamination with botulinum toxin occurred as a result of a hole in the can caused by defective canning equipment. The Alaskan salmon industry undertook a worldwide recall to retrieve other damaged cans, at considerable cost to both the industry and FDA. GAO, FDA'S OVERSIGHT OF THE 1982 CANNED SALMON RECALLS, Rep. No. HRD–84–77 (September 12, 1984).

G. SAFETY OF FOOD CONSTITUENTS

One of FDA's most controversial activities is the regulation of the safety of food constituents—materials that occur naturally in agricultural commodities, that are intentionally added to food during processing, or that accidentally contaminate food as the result of industrial activity. There is no single food safety standard. The food safety provisions of the FD&C Act are an aggregation of authorities enacted over a period of thirty years, each directed at a distinct category of constituents. *See* Merrill *Regulating Carcinogens in Food: A Legislator's Guide to the Food Safety Provisions of the Federal Food, Drug, and*

Cosmetic Act, 77 Mich. L. Rev. 171 (1979); GAO, MONITORING AND ENFORCING FOOD SAFETY—AN OVERVIEW OF PAST STUDIES, No. RCED–83–153 (September 9, 1983).

1. HISTORICAL AND STATUTORY BACKGROUND

The Food and Drugs Act of 1906 declared adulterated any food that contained "any added poisonous or other added deleterious ingredient which may render such article injurious to health." The early law did not deal with hazards posed by constituents that were not "added" to food, a concept that was not defined in the Act but was understood to embrace substances incorporated as ingredients or used during processing.

When Congress wrote the present Act in 1938, it expanded the 1906 Act's controls over toxicants in food. Section 402(a)(1) declares adulterated any food that "bears or contains any poisonous or deleterious substance which may render it injurious to health ...," without apparent limitation to "added" substances. Late in the legislative process, Congress qualified this standard by appending: "but in case the substance is not an added substance such food shall not be considered adulterated under this clause if the quantity of such substance in such food does not ordinarily render it injurious to health." The FD&C Act thus retained the 1906 Act's distinction between substances that are "added" and those that are not, but made the latter subject to FDA regulation for the first time.

The statutory standard applicable to nonadded substances has remained unchanged since 1938. The "ordinarily injurious" test is the legal measure of whether such a substance adulterates food. The test is more permissive of potentially toxic constituents than other provisions of the Act. Because the Act does not define "added," moreover, FDA has exercised broad discretion in determining which food constituents qualify for evaluation under the "ordinarily injurious" test.

Congress also recognized that certain added substances required more comprehensive control than would be achieved under the "may render injurious" test of section 402(a)(1)—a standard it expected FDA to enforce in court. Therefore, section 406 empowered FDA to establish tolerances sufficient to protect the public health for unavoidable or necessary added "poisonous or deleterious" substances, such as pesticide residues on raw agricultural commodities.

The 1938 Act thus contained three standards applicable to potentially toxic substances in food: (1) section 402(a)(1)'s "ordinarily injurious" standard applied to constituents that were not added; (2) section 402(a)(1)'s "may render injurious" standard applied to added constituents that were neither necessary nor unavoidable; and (3) under section 406, FDA could set tolerances "for the protection of public health" for added constituents whose use was "necessary in the production of a food" or whose occurrence was "unavoidable by good manufacturing practice."

This original triad of controls has been augmented by several subsequent amendments to the 1938 Act. Each of these amendments deals with a specific category of the broad class of added food constituents and establishes a system under which FDA is empowered—by administrative order or regulation—to limit the use, or the occurrence, of potentially toxic substances in or on food. The first of these amendments was the Miller Pesticide Amendments of 1954, now section 408 of the Act. This provision was intended to complement the authority then residing in the Department of Agriculture to register pesticides under the Federal Insecticide, Rodenticide, and Fungicide Act (FIFRA). The Amendments provide that a raw agricultural commodity shall be deemed adulterated if it bears any residue of a pesticide that does not conform to a tolerance established under section 408, and establishes an elaborate procedure for the establishment of tolerances. It should be noted that section 408 does not cover pesticides that contaminate foods other than those on which their use is approved, which often occurs as a result of drift during application or persistence in the environment.

In 1958 Congress carved out another category of added constituents of food for special treatment. The Food Additives Amendment, which added section 409 of the Act, establishes a licensure scheme, similar to that for pesticide residues, for substances that are intended to be used as ingredients in formulated foods. The Amendment also applies to substances such as packaging materials that, through use in contact with food, become or "may reasonably be expected to become" components of food. A food that bears or contains a food additive whose use FDA has not approved as "safe," or that contains an approved food additive in a quantity exceeding the limits specified by the agency, is adulterated under section 402(a)(2)(C).

The famous Delaney Clause was added to the Act as part of the Food Additives Amendment. This clause precludes FDA from approving as "safe" any food additive found to induce cancer in man or in animals when administered by ingestion or other appropriate test. Because the Delaney Clause is drafted as a limitation on FDA's approval authority under section 409, however, it technically applies only to substances that fall within the statutory definition of "food additive." That definition does not apply to all intentional ingredients of food or to all substances that may migrate to food. Excepted from its coverage are (1) substances whose use in food is "generally recognized as safe by qualified experts," referred to by the acronym GRAS—an exception that embraces a large number of familiar substances such as sugar and salt—and (2) substances that either FDA or USDA had sanctioned for use in food prior to 1958, so-called "prior sanctions." The issues involved in the regulation of carcinogens are examined in detail in Chapter VIII.

In 1960 Congress addressed the more limited problem of substances used to color foods—as well as colorings for drugs and cosmetics. The Color Additive Amendments apply to all substances used primarily for the purpose of imparting color to food. They contain no exceptions for color additives that may be generally recognized as safe or that were authorized for use prior to 1960. The 1960 Amendments require FDA approval, or "listing," for use of a color additive. A food that bears or contains a color additive whose use has not been approved by FDA, or whose use deviates from the terms of any approval, is adulterated. A second Delaney Clause prohibits the listing of any color additive that has been shown to induce cancer in man or animals.

The last relevant modification of the 1938 Act occurred as part of the Animal Drug Amendments of 1968. After 1958, drugs for food producing animals were regulated under a combination of statutory provisions—either under the Food Additives Amendment coupled with the new drug approval section for drugs administered directly to animals that "could reasonably be expected" to leave residues in human food, or under section 409 alone for compounds incorporated in animal feeds. In 1968, Congress simplified the procedure for evaluating animal drugs by prescribing a unified licensure system under section 512 of the Act. Under the amended Act, no animal drug that is likely to leave residues in edible tissue of livestock may be used, nor may food containing residues be marketed, without prior FDA approval.

Thus, by 1968 Congress had subdivided the universe of added food constituents into several categories subject to special regulatory requirements. In FDA's view, however, the four categories of food constituents to which Congress has given special attention since 1938 do not exhaust the universe of added substances in food. None of the post–1938 Amendments covers exogenous substances, such as PCBs or mercury, whose occurrence in food is unintended and undesired. Such contaminants accordingly are regulated under the provisions of the original 1938 Act.

This part explores the development, implementation, and interpretation of these several food safety schemes. Section 2 considers the statutory distinction between "added" and "nonadded" substances. Section 3 covers the regulation of environmental contaminants under section 406. Section 4 deals with regulation of pesticide residues under section 408. Section 5 describes FDA regulation of ingredients added intentionally to food in order to serve a functional purpose, many of which are subject to the food additive provisions in section 409. Section 6 covers food processing and packaging substances that predictably migrate into food but that otherwise serve no functional purpose in the food itself, many of which are also regulated as food additives. Section 7 deals with color additives, all of which are regulated by FDA under section 706. Section 8 briefly treats animal drug residues, which are regulated by FDA under section 512, whose administration is more fully considered in Chapter IV.

2. POISONOUS OR DELETERIOUS SUBSTANCES

As enacted in 1938, and unchanged since, section 402(a)(1) defines as adulterated any food that contains an "added" poisonous or deleterious substance which may render it injurious to health or a "nonadded" poisonous or deleterious substance which ordinarily renders it injurious to health. The statute, however, contains no definition of the term "added."

a. Added Substances

UNITED STATES v. LEXINGTON MILL & ELEVATOR CO.

Supreme Court of the United States, 1914.

232 U.S. 399.

Mr. Justice DAY delivered the opinion of the court.

The petitioner, the United States of America, proceeding under § 10 of the Food and Drugs Act (June 30, 1906), ... sought to seize and condemn 625 sacks of flour in the possession of one Terry.... The amended libel charges that the flour had been treated by the "Alsop Process," so called, by which nitrogen peroxide gas, generated by electricity, was mixed with atmospheric air and the mixture then brought in contact with the flour, and that it was thereby adulterated under ... § 7 of the act ... in that the flour had been caused to contain added poisonous or other added deleterious ingredients, to-wit, nitrites or nitrite reacting material, nitrogen peroxide, nitrous acid, nitric acid and other poisonous and deleterious substances which might render the flour injurious to health....

The case requires a construction of the Food and Drugs Act. Parts of the statute pertinent to this case are:

"Sec. 7. That for the purposes of this act an article shall be deemed to be adulterated: ...

"In the case of food: ...

"Fifth. If it contain any added poisonous or other added deleterious ingredient which may render such article injurious to health".…

Without reciting the testimony in detail it is enough to say that for the Government it tended to show that the added poisonous substance introduced into the flour by Alsop Process, in the proportion of 1.8 parts per million, calculated as nitrogen, may be injurious to the health of those who use the flour in bread and other forms of food. On the other hand, the testimony for the respondent tended to show that the process does not added to the flour any poisonous or deleterious ingredients which can in any manner render it injurious to the health of a consumer. On these conflicting proofs the trial court was required to submit the case to the jury....

It is evident ... that the trial court regarded the addition to the flour of any poisonous ingredient as an offense within this statute, no matter how small the quantity, and whether the flour might or might not injure the health of the consumer.... The testimony shows that the effect of the Alsop Process is to bleach or whiten the flour and thus make it more marketable. If the testimony introduced on the part of the respondent was believed by the jury they must necessarily have found that the added ingredient, nitrites of a poisonous character, did not have the effect to make the consumption of the flour by any possibility injurious to the health of the consumer....

... [I]n considering this statute, we find that the fifth subdivision of § 7 provides that food shall be deemed to be adulterated: "If it contain any added poisonous or other added deleterious ingredient *which may render such article injurious to health.*" The instruction of the trial court permitted this statute to be read without the final and qualifying words, concerning the effect of the article upon health. If Congress had so intended the provision would have stopped with the condemnation of food which contained any added poisonous or other added deleterious ingredient. In other words, the first and familiar consideration is that, if Congress had intended to enact the statute in that form, it would have done so by choice of apt words to express that intent. It did not do so, but only condemned food containing an added poisonous or other added deleterious ingredient when such addition might render the article of food injurious to the health. Congress has here, in this statute, with its penalties and forfeitures definitely outlined its inhibition against a particular class of adulteration.

It is not required that the article of food containing added poisonous or other added deleterious ingredients must affect the public health, and it is not incumbent upon the Government in order to make out a case to establish that fact. The act has placed upon the Government the burden of establishing, in order to secure a verdict of condemnation under this statute, that the added poisonous or deleterious substances must be such as may render such article injurious to health. The word "may" is here used in its ordinary and usual signification, there being nothing to show the intention of Congress to affix to it any other meaning.... In thus describing the offense Congress doubtless took into consideration that flour may be used in many ways, in bread, cake, gravy, broth, etc. It may be consumed, when prepared as a food, by the strong and the weak, the old and the young, the well and the sick; and it is intended that if any flour, because of any added poisonous or other deleterious ingredient, may possibly injure the health of any of these, it shall come within the ban of the statute. If it cannot by any possibility, when the facts are reasonably considered, injure the health of any consumer, such flour, though having a small addition of poisonous or deleterious ingredients, may not be condemned under the act. This is the plain meaning of the words and in our view needs no additional support by reference to reports and debates, although it may be said in passing that the meaning which we have given to the statute was well expressed by Mr. Heyburn, chairman of the committee having it in charge upon the floor of the Senate:

> "As to the use of the term 'poisonous,' let me state that everything which contains poison is not poison. It depends on the quantity and the combination. A very large majority of the things consumed by the human family contain, under analysis, some kind of poison, but it depends upon the combination, the chemical relation which it bears to the body in which it exists as to whether or not it is dangerous to take into the human system." ...

NOTES

1. *Other Authority.* In *United States v. Forty Barrels and Twenty Kegs,* 241 U.S. 265 (1916), the Court held that caffeine is an added substance in soft drinks and that whether it meets the "may render injurious" standard is a question of fact for the jury. *W. B. Wood Mfg. Co. v. United States,* 286 Fed. 84 (7th Cir. 1923), held that arsenic present as a contaminant in a color additive was an "added" substance but that FDA had failed to establish that the amount present in the food was sufficient to violate the "may render injurious" standard. *Compare Millet, Pit and Seed Co., Inc. v. United States,* 436 F. Supp. 84 (E.D. Tenn. 1977), holding that the amygdalin that occurs naturally in apricot kernels is a nonadded substance and that FDA failed to carry its burden of proving that the amount present was sufficient to render the apricot kernels ordinarily injurious to health.

2. *Codification of Lexington Mill.* When Congress enacted the 1938 Act, reproducing the language of the 1906 statute in the first clause of section 402(a)(1), it clearly intended to incorporate as well the Supreme Court's interpretation of the "may render injurious" standard in *Lexington Mill.* *See Flemming v. Florida Citrus Exchange,* 358 U.S. 153 (1958).

3. *DES Residues.* Even after FDA banned diethylstilbestrol (DES) in food-producing animals, p. 885 *infra,* some ranchers continued to implant cattle with the drug. The government seized the beef from treated cattle, contending that it contained an added poisonous or deleterious substance in violation of the Federal Meat Inspection Act, 21 U.S.C § 601(m)(1), whose language is identical to section 402(a)(1). In *United States v. 2,116 Boxes of Boned Beef,* 516 F. Supp. 321 (D. Kan. 1981), however, the court ruled that the government failed to carry its burden of proving that the levels of DES present in the beef could render the beef injurious to health under the *Lexington Mill* standard, or that the beef was otherwise adulterated. The government did not appeal.

4. *Proof of Hazard.* The key issue under the "may render injurious" standard is the quantity of the added substance in the food. In *United States v. Commonwealth Brewing Corp.,* 1938–1964 F.D.L.I. Jud. Rec. 310 (D. Mass. 1945), the court observed that the quantity of a substance is likely to determine whether it may be harmful and therefore concluded that "quantity would be the test" under section 402(a)(1). Quantity would appear to be an essential element under the "ordinarily injurious" standard as well. The chief distinctions between the two standards in section 402(a)(1) appear to be the greater probability of harm that the government must show to restrict a natural

constituent and its ability, under the "may render" standard, to take account of specially vulnerable segments of the population.

5. *Mixed, Not Added.* The court in *Cavalier Vending Corp. v. United States,* 190 F.2d 386 (4th Cir. 1951), held that the mingling of candy and trinkets in a vending machine did not fall within section 402(a)(1) because the candy did not "contain" the trinkets.

---

b. Nonadded Substances

UNITED STATES v. 1232 CASES AMERICAN BEAUTY BRAND OYSTERS

United States District Court, Western District of Missouri, 1942.
43 F. Supp. 749.

REEVES, District Judge.

This is a proceeding by the process of libel to condemn an alleged adulterated food product. Such food consists of 1232 cases of oysters, each case containing 24 cans, marked "American Beauty Brand Oysters."

As a basis for condemnation, it is alleged by the government that said article "contains shell fragments, many of them small enough to be swallowed and become lodged in the esophagus, and that said shell fragments are sharp and capable of inflicting injury in the mouth."

The provision of the law invoked by the government is section [402(a)]....

The claimant appeared to deny the averments of the libel and assert ownership of the product. The evidence in the case showed that in the processing of oysters for food there is a constant effort to eliminate shells and fragments thereof from the product. For this purpose many means and devices are used to reduce as nearly to a minimum as possible such shells and fragments in the product. The evidence, however, on behalf of both the government and the defense was that with present known means and devices it was impossible to free the product entirely from the presence of part shells and shell fragments.... The shells, therefore, are not artificially added for the purpose of growth or to aid in the processing operations....

[The ... statute ... contemplates that there may be of necessity food products containing deleterious substances] No one who has had the experience of eating either fish or oysters is unfamiliar with the presence of bones in the fish (a deleterious substance) and fragments of shell in the oysters (also a deleterious substance). [The Congress, however, withdrew such foods from the adulterated class "if the quantity of such substance in such food does not ordinarily render it injurious to health."]

The evidence on both sides was that by the greatest effort, and in the use of the most modern means and devices, shell fragments could not be entirely separated from an oyster food product. The government, in its brief, quite aptly and concisely stated its point by using the following language: "It is the character, not the quantity of this substance that controls its ability to injure."

This concession on the part of the government, properly made, upon the evidence removes the case immediately from that portion of the statute which says: " * * * such food shall not be considered adulterated under this clause if the quantity of such substance in such food does not ordinarily render it injurious to health."

Since it is the "character, not the quantity of this substance that controls its ability to injure," as stated by the government, then in the view that it is impossible to eliminate shell fragments in toto from the product, the use of oysters as a food must be entirely prohibited or it must be found that the presence of shell fragments is not a deleterious substance within the meaning of the law and must be tolerated. [T]o reject oyster products as a food is unthinkable. It would be as reasonable to reject fish because of the presence of bones. Even if a greater percentage of shells and shell fragments were found in claimant's product than in that of other processors, yet this fact, under the theory of the government, would not add to the deleterious nature of claimant's product....

Upon the evidence in this case it must be found that the presence of shell fragments in the article sought to be condemned does not ordinarily render it injurious to health....

NOTES

1. *Bone Fragments.* *See also* *Evart v. Suli,* 211 Cal.App.3d 605, 259 Cal.Rptr. 535 (1989), holding that a hamburger containing a piece of bone beef is not adulterated as a matter of law, because the bone is a naturally occurring substance.

2. *Legislative History.* The legislative history of the 1938 Act provides little guidance on the proper interpretation of the second clause of section 402(a)(1). Congress evidently was aware that some foods naturally contain substances that, if consumed in excess, can be harmful, and it obviously intended to establish a demanding standard for FDA enforcement. The court's ruling in *American Beauty Brand Oysters* assumes that, notwithstanding the risk of choking or other injury from oyster shell fragments, Congress would value oysters highly enough to preclude a finding of adulteration. While the Act does not explicitly authorize any weighing of "benefits," the court's approach is consistent with the few illustrations contained in the legislative history of the second clause of section 401(a)(1). The 1906 Act declared food adulterated "[i]f it contain[s] any added poisonous or other added deleterious ingredient which may render such article injurious to health." Most of the early bills to reform the law would have changed that language to define food as adulterated "[i]f it bears or contains any poisonous or deleterious substance which may render it dangerous to health." *See, e.g.,* S. 2000, 73d Cong., 2nd Sess. § 3(a)(1) (introduced January 4, 1934); S. 5, 74th Cong., 1st Sess. § 301(a)(1)

(reported in the House May 31, 1935); S. 5, 75th Cong., 1st Sess. § 11(a)(1) (introduced January 6, 1937). The language Congress ultimately adopted to deal with naturally occurring adulterants appeared in a bill reported on August 14, 1938, as a substitute for the bill (S. 5) passed by the Senate several months earlier. While the House Report, H.R. Rep. No. 213, 75th Cong., 2d Sess. (1938), does not explain why this wording was added, the legislative record of the earlier bills may suggest an answer.

The earliest proposed bills had deleted the word "added" from the language of the 1906 Act to allow the FDA to regulate any food that might present a risk to consumers, whether the deleterious constituent occurred naturally or was put in food by artifice. "Federal Foods, Drugs and Cosmetics," Hearing on S. 2800 Before the Senate Comm. on Commerce, 73d Cong., 2d Sess. (1934). The bills also substituted the word "dangerous" for "injurious." FDA's Walter G. Campbell pointed out that the 1906 Act left such foods as poisonous mushrooms and particularly toxic varieties of West Coast mussels, which acquire their injurious properties naturally, beyond federal control. The word "dangerous" was intended to differentiate "between those products which may be injurious to health in a mild way and those that are unquestionably dangerous to health in a very definite way." "Foods, Drugs, and Cosmetics," Hearing Before a Subcomm. of the House Comm. on Interstate and Foreign Commerce, 74th Cong., 1st Sess. 58 (1935).

The final wording of section 402(a)(1) returned to the word "injurious," but omitted "added" from the second clause—in order to reach naturally occurring poisons. "Injurious" had been the standard for all FDA enforcement actions under the 1906 Act, and Congress was reluctant to change language that the courts had already interpreted. But to prevent over-zealous enforcement against foods that naturally contained a deleterious substance, the House Committee added the proviso requiring the Government to prove that a substance was harmful when consumed in ordinary quantities. Statements during hearings indicate that foods such as coffee, tea, rhubarb (which naturally contains oxalic acid), and cocoa were not to be regulated. Congress wanted to reach only foods such as the poisonous mushrooms, mussels, and "Burma beans" that FDA witnesses had cited as examples of foods that are highly toxic in their natural state.

To facilitate enforcement, FDA has sought to regulate a number of naturally-occurring environmental contaminants of food as "added" rather than "nonadded" substances. Beginning in 1970 FDA established and began to enforce an action level of 0.5 ppm mercury in fish, resulting in a virtual ban of swordfish. Note, *Health Regulation of Naturally Hazardous Foods: The FDA Ban on Swordfish*, 85 Harv. L. Rev. 1025 (1972). This action level was calculated to protect the 99th percentile fish consumers in the country, who eat virtually nothing else, and thus afforded a very wide margin of safety for all other consumers. To clarify the distinction between added and nonadded substances, FDA later promulgated regulations, 39 Fed. Reg. 42746 (December 6, 1974), 42 Fed. Reg. 52814 (September 30, 1977), codified in 21 C.F.R. § 109.3, which took the position that only a substance "that is an inherent natural constituent of the food and is not the result of environmental, agricultural, industrial, or other contamination" is a nonadded substance. Under this definition, all mercury in fish is "added." At the time it proposed these regulations FDA also proposed to establish the 0.5 ppm action level for mercury in fish through informal rulemaking in 39 Fed. Reg. 42738 (December 6, 1974).

UNITED STATES v. ANDERSON SEAFOODS, INC.

United States Court of Appeals, Fifth Circuit, 1980.
622 F.2d 157.

WISDOM, Circuit Judge: ...

In April 1977, the United States sought an injunction against Anderson Seafoods, Inc., and its president, Charles F. Anderson, to prevent them from selling swordfish containing more than 0.5 parts per million (ppm) of mercury, which it considered adulterated under the meaning of § 342(a)(1).... Anderson responded in May 1977 by seeking a declaratory judgment that fish containing 2.0 ppm of mercury or less are not adulterated....

The district court denied the injunction that the government sought. In Anderson's suit, the court also denied an injunction, but issued a declaratory judgment that swordfish containing more than 1.0 ppm mercury is adulterated under § 342(a)(1). In doing so, the court determined that mercury is an "*added* substance" under the Act and rejected Anderson's contention that a level of 0.2 ppm is acceptable. Anderson appealed from the judgment in the class action. The government appealed from the judgment in its enforcement action and cross-appealed in the class action. The government then withdrew its appeal and cross-appeal. This appeal now consists of Anderson's challenge to the way the district court parsed the statute and to the sufficiency of the evidence. We affirm......

In the trial of this case three theories about the meaning of the term "added" emerged. The Food and Drug Administration sponsored the first theory. It argues that an "added substance" is one that is not "inherent".... Under this theory, all the mercury in swordfish is an added substance, because it results not from the creature's bodily processes but from mercury in the environment, whether natural or introduced by man.

Anderson put forward a second theory. A substance, under this theory, is not an added substance unless it is proved to be present as a result of the direct agency of man. Further, only that amount of a substance the lineage of which can be so traced is "added". If some mercury in swordfish occurs naturally, and some is the result of man-made pollution, only that percentage of the mercury in fish proved to result directly from pollution is an added substance.

The district court adopted a third theory. Under the court's theory, if a de minimis amount of the mercury in swordfish is shown to result from industrial pollution, then all of the metal in the fish is treated as an added substance and may be regulated under the statute's "may render injurious" standard. The legislative history and case law, though sparse, persuade us that this is the proper reading of the statute.

Determining that man must appear on the stage before a substance is an added one does not determine the size of the role he must play before it is. The dichotomy in § 342(a)(1) is between two clear cases that bracket the present case. The Act considers added things such as lead in coloring agents or caffeine in Coca Cola. It considers not-added things like oxalic acid in rhubarb or caffeine in coffee. The Act did not contemplate, however, the perhaps rare problem of a toxin, part of which occurs "naturally", and part of which results from human acts. The section is designed, of course, to insure the scrutiny of toxins introduced by man. . . . .

Since the purpose of the "may render injurious" standard was to facilitate regulation of food adulterated by acts of man, we think that it should apply to all of a toxic substance present in a food when any of that substance is shown to have been introduced by man. Anderson argues that this reading of the statute would result "in the anomalous situation where a substance in a food can be 90 percent natural and 10 percent added if the entire substance is considered as added". There is no anomaly, however, in such a situation. The Act's "may render it injurious to health" standard is to be applied to the food, not to the added substance. The food would not be considered adulterated under our view unless the 10 percent increment creates or increases a potentiality of injury to health. If the increment does create or increase such a potentiality, then, because the increment that triggered the potentiality was introduced by man, the Food and Drug Administration ought to be able to regulate it under the standard designed to apply to adulterations of food caused by man. Anderson's argument proves too much. Anderson would argue that if a swordfish contained 0.99 ppm of natural mercury, and 0.99 ppm of mercury from human sources, the fish could be sold although it contained nearly twice as much mercury as the district court found to be a safe level. Such a reading of the statute hardly accords with its "overriding purpose to protect the public health". *United States v. Bacto-Unidisk,* 1969, 394 U.S. 784. The reading we have adopted does accord with this purpose. It may be severe in practice. It may permit the Food and Drug Administration to regulate in some cases where the amount of substance contributed by man—which triggers the potentiality of harm—is minute. But it is the only alternative that fits into the statutory scheme. Congress should amend the statute if our reading produces impracticable results.

In sum, we hold that where some portion of a toxin present in a food has been introduced by man, the entirety of the substance present in the food will be treated as an added substance and so considered under the "may render injurious to health" standard of the Act.

In addition to its attack on the way the district court parsed the statute, Anderson raises a subsidiary argument. There was insufficient evidence to support the conclusion that man's acts contributed "substantial amounts" of mercury to the tissues of swordfish. And, indeed, the court did not find that the amounts were substantial, but rather that they were unknown and perhaps unquantifiable. Under our reading of the statute, however, the amount of mercury that man contributes need not be "substantial". The FDA need show only that some portion of the mercury is attributable to acts of man, and that the total amount may be injurious to health.

There was sufficient evidence to show that some mercury is attributable to the acts of man. There was evidence that mercury is dumped into rivers and washes onto the continental shelf, where some of it is methylated by bacteria and taken up by plankton. It thereby enters the food chain of swordfish, for the plankton is consumed by small organisms and fish, such as copepods, herring, and hake, which are in turn eaten by larger organisms, and eventually by swordfish, a peak predator. This evidence was enough to trigger the Act's "may render injurious to health" standard.*

NOTES

1. *Mercury Action Level.* Following the district court's decision and before the court of appeals ruled, FDA announced in 44 Fed. Reg. 3990 (January 19, 1979) that it would adopt as its own action level the 1.0 ppm level determined by the district court to be safe. (Based upon new methodology, FDA subsequently revised the 1.0 ppm action level to encompass only methyl mercury and not total mercury, 49 Fed. Reg. 45663 (November 19, 1984).) The agency also stated that it would adhere to its own definition of an "added" substance in 21 C.F.R. § 109.3 pending the court of appeals' decision but it has not amended that definition even after the Fifth Circuit rejected it as too broad.

2. *Other Added Substances.* The following substances have been held to be "added": aflatoxin in corn, *United States v. Boston Farm Center, Inc.,* 590 F.2d 149 (5th Cir. 1979); salmonella in shrimp, *Continental Seafoods, Inc. v. Schweiker,* 674 F.2d 38 (D.C. Cir. 1982); and, in two other cases, mercury in swordfish, *United States v. An Article of Food Consisting of Cartons of Swordfish,* 395 F. Supp. 1184 (S.D.N.Y. 1975); *United States v. Globe Fish Co.,* Food Drug Cosm. L. Rep. (CCH) ¶ 38,129 (D. Mass. 1981), ¶ 38,263 (D. Mass. 1984).

3. ENVIRONMENTAL CONTAMINANTS

No provision of the FD&C Act explicitly provides a mechanism for regulating substances that become constituents of food through environmental contamination. Yet such materials—which include mercury, polychlorinated biphenyls (PCBs), polybrominated biphenyls (PBBs), and aflatoxins—may pose serious risks to human health. Controlling

* [The court also affirmed the district court's decision that 1.0 ppm mercury in swordfish does not constitute adulteration. *See* p. 302 *infra.*]

their occurrence in food raises difficult scientific and economic, as well as administrative issues.

Section 402(a)(1) does not specifically provide for the promulgation of implementing regulations. It is a "policing" provision that appears to call for court enforcement. FDA might have relied on the "ordinarily injurious" language of section 402(a)(1) as the basis for court actions to control environmental contaminants, on the premise that since such contaminants are not purposely incorporated in or intentionally used in proximity with food, they should not be considered "added." An alternative would have been to rely exclusively on the first clause of section 402(a)(1), which condemns food containing an added poisonous or deleterious substance if the food "may" be injurious to health. The agency has rejected both approaches. Its objective has been to find a statutory rationale that allows it to determine administratively what level of contamination renders food adulterated. Achievement of this objective would promise uniformity in enforcement and contribute to certainty among sellers of food. Furthermore, it would assign responsibility for evaluation of the health risks posed by a contaminant to the agency's scientific experts rather than to the district courts.

As enacted in 1938, section 406 of the FD&C Act authorized FDA to establish tolerances for added poisonous or deleterious substances that are "required" in the production of food or "cannot be avoided by good manufacturing practice." The level of a tolerance must be set "for the protection of public health." The primary purpose of this provision was to permit FDA to set tolerances for pesticide residues in food. *See, e.g.,* H.R. Rep. No. 2139, 75th Cong., 3rd Sess. 6 (1938). To promulgate a tolerance under section 406, however, the agency was obliged to proceed under section 701(e) which requires that objectors to any regulation be given an opportunity for a formal administrative hearing.

As its first action under section 406, FDA initiated a major rulemaking in 1944 to determine appropriate tolerances for residues of fluorine that remained in food treated with pesticide compounds containing this element. Although the resulting tolerance was upheld, the court effectively nullified it by interpreting it to apply only to elemental fluorine and not to compounds containing fluorine, *Washington State Apple Advertising Comm'n v. Federal Security Administrator,* 156 F.2d 589 (9th Cir. 1946).

After World War II FDA, joined by the American Medical Association, voiced growing concern about the safety of pesticide residues in the food supply and it began preparation for further hearings to establish appropriate tolerances under section 406. *E.g.,* Bellis, *Rule–Making Under Section 406(a) of the Federal Food, Drug, and Cosmetic Act,* 4 FDC L.Q. 488 (1949); Dunbar, *The Food and Drug Administration Looks at Insecticides,* 4 FDC L.Q. 233 (1949); White, *Protection Afforded the Consumer Against Added Chemicals in Foods,* 4 FDC L.Q. 478 (1949); Wilson, *Pesticide Residues in Food as Health Hazards,* 3 FDC L.Q. 561 (1948). When the ensuing hearing had ended in the early

1950s, however, FDA decided that the toxicological evidence was so poor and the record so confusing that the tolerances should be withdrawn. The agency made no other efforts to set tolerances for pesticides until after the enactment of the Miller Pesticide Amendments of 1954, discussed below, p. 306 *infra*.

Beginning in the 1960s, however, evidence of a variety of other contaminants in food began to accumulate. The contaminants that raised the greatest concern other were mercury in fish (resulting from both industrial pollution and natural sources), aflatoxin in nuts, grain, and other food crops, and polychlorinated biphenyls (PCBs) in a variety of foods from industrial disposal and accidents. Remembering its prior unsuccessful efforts to set formal tolerances under section 406, FDA chose instead to establish informal "action levels," *i.e.*, the highest level of contamination that will not trigger court enforcement action. FDA began to rely on action levels in the mid–1960s, and refined their use through regulations that will be discussed further below.

Confronting growing concern over the widespread contamination of food with PCBs, however, FDA decided to establish formal tolerances for this compound under section 406 in 37 Fed. Reg. 5705 (March 18, 1972), 38 Fed. Reg. 18096 (July 6, 1973). After objections to its tolerance for PCBs in paper food packaging material, FDA stayed the tolerance pending a formal hearing, but also announced, 38 Fed. Reg. 22794 (August 24, 1973), that it would seize as adulterated under section 402(a)(1) any packaging material shipped in interstate commerce containing higher than the specified level. This policy was subsequently upheld in *Natick Paperboard Corp. v. Weinberger*, 525 F.2d 1103 (1st Cir. 1975), which held that FDA could establish an action level and institute seizures against paper packaging before the material was used, as long as the agency could demonstrate a likelihood that the material would in fact be used for food packaging. The agency proceeded to deny a hearing on some objections and grant a hearing on others, 40 Fed. Reg. 11563 (March 12, 1975), and subsequently settled the matter without a hearing in 48 Fed. Reg. 37020 (August 16, 1983), 48 Fed. Reg. 45544 (October 6, 1983).

While this administrative proceeding was ongoing, FDA amended the regulations to reduce the tolerance for PCBs in fish in 42 Fed. Reg. 17487 (April 1, 1977), 44 Fed. Reg. 38330 (June 29, 1979). After receiving objections, it conducted a formal hearing, 46 Fed. Reg. 24551 (May 1, 1981). The agency later released the Administrative Law Judge's Initial Decision, Food Drug Cosm. L. Rep. (CCH) ¶ 38,159 (February 8, 1982), and issued a final regulation reducing the tolerance, 49 Fed. Reg. 21514 (May 22, 1984). The tolerances for PCBs, codified in 21 C.F.R. § 109.30, remain the only formal tolerances ever adopted under section 406. *See generally* GAO, FURTHER FEDERAL ACTION NEEDED TO DETECT AND CONTROL ENVIRONMENTAL CONTAMINATION OF FOOD, No. CED–81–19 (December 31, 1980).

POISONOUS OR DELETERIOUS SUBSTANCES IN FOOD: NOTICE OF PROPOSED RULEMAKING

39 Federal Register 42743 (December 6, 1974).

"Added" is a statutory term of art encompassing all ingredients which are not inherent and intrinsic parts of a food..... Although the word chosen implies that the statute is concerned with the act of addition, the legislative history makes clear that the term seeks rather to establish a standard based upon the necessary and inherent normal condition of the food....

The legislative history ... identifies examples of foods naturally containing poisonous or deleterious substances and thus not subject to the "added" provisions of section 402(a)(1) of the act. These examples are Burma beans, which contain a glucoside that yields prussic or hydrocyanic acid; rhubarb, which contains oxalic acid; and coffee and tea. Except for substances whose deleterious nature is inherent to the natural state of the food, and thus similar in origin to these examples, all poisonous and deleterious components are "added" within the meaning of the act. Moreover, when a naturally occurring poisonous or deleterious substance is increased to abnormal levels through mishandling or other intervening act, it is "added" to the extent of such increase....

Section 406 was included in the 1938 act to permit the establishment of tolerances for added poisonous or deleterious substances which are required in the production of food or otherwise cannot be avoided by good manufacturing practice.... Although formal tolerances under section 406 have not been used by the Food and Drug Administration, ... informal action levels have frequently been utilized to implement this provision of the law and a number of those action levels exist today....

The definition of "food additive" established in section 201(s) of the act is not limited to intentional additives. The breadth of the language in section 201(s) of the act includes any food substance and excludes only those substances which cannot reasonably be expected to become a component of food....

When the Food Additives Amendment of 1958 was enacted, the provisions of section 406 of the act were not repealed. Although all added poisonous or deleterious ingredients are food additives, except when they appear in food accidentally and unforeseeably or are exempted under section 201(s) of the act because they are otherwise regulated under the act, the tolerance-setting provisions of section 406 of the act were left intact to deal with those unavoidably added poisonous or deleterious ingredients that could not meet the high standards for issuance of a regulation under the authority of section 409 of the act. A number of added poisonous or deleterious substances, which are also food additives within the meaning of section 201(s) of the act, are unavoidable but cannot meet the requirements for a section 409 regulation because their safety cannot be demonstrated and because they serve no functional purpose. A prominent example is lead, which was one of the contaminants most frequently mentioned in the legislative history of the 1938 act and one of the prime contaminants with which section 406 was enacted to deal. Lead cannot be the subject of a food additive regulation under section 409 of the act even at trivial levels because it serves no functional purpose.* Section 406 of the act, therefore, remains in force to control the use of such substances, since there would otherwise be no statutory means available to recognize their unavoidability and to exercise reasonable control over their presence....

... The Commissioner is not required to establish a tolerance for every added poisonous or deleterious substance, as is indicated by the language of section 406 of the act recognizing that an adulteration charge can be made under section 402(a)(1) of the act when no tolerance is in effect. Section 306 of the act has long been interpreted to permit the Food and Drug Administration to establish action levels in implementing the adulteration provisions of the act....

When the factors required to be considered prior to promulgation of a section 406 tolerance are rapidly changing, it would be inappropriate to set such a formal tolerance. The procedures required by section 406 of the act, including a public hearing and requirement of substantial evidence to support the tolerance, contemplate ample evidence to consider, and a relatively stable situation where the evidence will be of more than transient significance and where the tolerance eventually promulgated will be appropriate for a relatively long period of time....

When it is not appropriate to promulgate a tolerance under section 406 ... the Commissioner will consider promulgating an action level under authority of sections 306, 402(a), and 406 of the act.

Such action levels are similar to a formal tolerance in basis and effect. In setting an action level, the Commissioner considers evidence indicating when the presence of an added poisonous or deleterious substance may render food injurious to health, which is the standard in section 402(a)(1) of the act. In addition, the Commissioner takes into account the question of its unavoidability, a policy embodied in section 406 of the act. Thus, an action level is based on the same criteria as a tolerance, except that an action level is temporary until the appearance of more stable circumstances makes a formal tolerance appropriate....

The proposal also prescribes a method of issuing regulations to deal with foods containing naturally occurring poisonous or deleterious substances. Where appropriate, the Commissioner may identify foods which, because of their inherent components, are deemed to be adul-

* [FDA withdrew this statement as "incorrect" in 44 Fed. Reg. 51233 (August 31, 1979), stating: "The appropriate inquiry into the functionality of such substances is whether they have a purpose in the food-contact article ... not whether they have a purpose of a function in the food."]

terated within the meaning of section 402(a)(1) of the act. These regulations would, of course, not constitute a complete list of such foods....

NOTES

1. *Final Regulations.* FDA's final regulations, 42 Fed. Reg. 52813 (September 30, 1977), codified in 21 C.F.R. Part 109, reflected no significant change in the agency's interpretation of the applicable statutory provisions. The agency elaborated its understanding of the term "added" and concluded that action levels should be established simply by notice in the Federal Register rather than by informal rulemaking.

2. *Contaminant or Food Additive.* The preamble to the final regulations set forth FDA's theory of the relationship between section 406 tolerances (or action levels) and section 409 food additive regulations. The agency stated that a tolerance or action level should not be established for a direct or indirect food additive that is intentionally added to serve a functional purpose unless it is unavoidable in a particular food, but that an action level or tolerance may be established for an intentionally added GRAS or prior sanctioned substance. For example, as discussed at p. 346 *supra,* action levels have been established to control lead migration from pottery and from soldered cans, where the substances containing the lead are intentionally used in the food-contact surface.

In the same December 1974 Federal Register, FDA published a proposed tolerance for aflatoxins in shelled peanuts and peanut products, 39 Fed. Reg. 42748; a proposed tolerance for lead in canned evaporated milk, 39 Fed. Reg. 42740; and a proposed action level for mercury in fish, 39 Fed. Reg. 42738. The mercury proposal, which precipitated the *Anderson Seafood* litigation, p. 293 *supra,* illustrates the agency's approach.

ACTION LEVEL FOR MERCURY IN FISH AND SHELLFISH
39 Federal Register 42738 (December 6, 1974).

Most of man's exposure to mercury arises from the contamination of food and possibly drinking water.... Except in occupational exposure, the contribution of inhaled mercury is insignificant in relation to intake from food. The amount of methylmercury (the most toxic organic form of mercury) found in fruits, vegetables, grains, meat and dairy products is very small. Of all the commodities analyzed for mercury by the Food and Drug Administration (FDA) in a survey of 10 basic foods and in the food commodity classes of the FDA total diet study, fish was the only commodity shown to present a potential hazard to man. Other data show levels of mercury in shellfish (mollusks and crustaceans) similar to the levels in some vertebrate fish. The total human intake of mercury from food sources other than fish and shellfish is insignificant....

Methylmercury and other forms of mercury serve no essential function in fish and shellfish. They are not normal inherent constituents, but are found in aquatic species because of environmental, industrial, and agricultural contamination. The source of methylmercury contamination in fish and shellfish is mercury contamination of the waters. The mercury that contaminates the aquatic environment has come from two principal sources, leaching or volatilization from natural geological source and human activities. Significant amounts of mercury enter the environment from man's agricultural and industrial use (chlor-alkali industry, mercury-based slimicides, mining operations, burning of fossil fuels, etc.)....

Mercury contamination of fish and shellfish is unavoidable. Though further addition of mercury to the aquatic environment from industrial sources can be prevented or at least reduced, at present there are no means of removing the mercury from these waters. Moreover, there is no method of processing fish or shellfish so as to remove or reduce the mercury contamination. Control over mercury intake by consumers of fish and shellfish can be achieved only through regulation of the mercury content of the products sold.

Methylmercury poisoning may lead to progressive blindness, deafness, incoordination, intellectual deterioration, and death. The amount of mercury accumulating in the body is directly related to the methylmercury dose size, and a critical concentration of mercury in brain tissues is required to produce neurological symptoms. Because it requires some time for the brain tissue of exposed individuals to reach such levels, due to the time of passage through the blood-brain barrier and redistribution of mercury in the brain, neurological symptoms are not observed during the early periods of exposure, but may develop several weeks after the exposure. However, it has been established that toxic concentrations of methylmercury in the brain vary very little between different animals. In all mammals, concentrations of 5 to 10 micrograms per gram (mcg/g) of brain tissue may be associated with neurological symptoms....

... [A]n action level of 0.5 ppm permits a daily consumption of 60 grams of fish and shellfish contaminated to that extent, while still maintaining a tenfold margin of safety over the level of mercury intake known to be toxic. The 60 g/day figure is based on a mercury concentration of 0.5 ppm in all fish and shellfish consumed, but because actual concentrations are much less in most fish and shellfish, there is an additional safety margin. In addition, the average consumption of fish and shellfish in this country is regarded as considerably less than 60 grams per day.

A National Marine Fisheries Service (NMFS) survey determined that only 1.8 percent of the population consumes an average of more than 60 grams of fish and shellfish per day. The vast majority of the population is therefore protected by the tenfold margin of safety. Additional protection is provided by the fact that actual concentrations in most fish and shellfish are below 0.5 ppm mercury and the fact that consumption is less than an average of 60 grams per day.

It is not possible, however, to provide this same high level of protection to every person without excluding a great amount of fish and shellfish from the market. The NMFS survey indicated that 1 percent of the participants in the survey consumed an average of 77 grams daily and 0.1 percent consumed 165 grams daily. At the very high consumption of 165 grams per day, the tenfold margin of safety is reduced to less than four; although, it may be increased above that figure by the additional margin resulting from consumption of fish and shellfish with less contamination than 0.5 ppm mercury....

In balancing the unavoidability of mercury in fish and shellfish against the need for protection of the public health, the Commissioner concludes that it would be inappropriate to exclude a vast amount of fish and shellfish from the market in order to provide a large margin of safety for those who consume far more than the average person. The Commissioner notes that a person would have to consume every day the extraordinarily high amount of 600 grams of fish and/or shellfish contaminated at the full 0.5 ppm level to reach the blood levels where symptoms have been known to occur. Thus some margin of safety is still provided for even the largest consumers of these foods....

NOTES

1. *Judicial Review.* In *United States v. Anderson Seafoods, Inc.,* 447 F. Supp. 1151 (N.D. Fla. 1978), *aff'd,* 622 F.2d 157 (5th Cir. 1980), p. 293 *supra,* the court rejected both FDA's 0.5 ppm mercury action level and the industry proposed 2.0 ppm safe level, and determined instead that mercury concentrations of 1.0 ppm or less would not be considered adulterated. While the case was pending appeal, FDA withdrew its December 1974 proposal to establish an action level for mercury and accepted the court-determined level of 1.0 ppm as its new action level in 44 Fed. Reg. 3990 (January 19, 1979). The agency has never withdrawn or adopted its proposed tolerances for aflatoxin in peanuts or lead in evaporated milk, but it has established action levels for these substances.

2. *Analytical and Sampling Guidelines.* To reduce inconsistency among analytical laboratories, FDA announced guidelines for the sampling of imported swordfish for mercury residues in 52 Fed. Reg. 37659 (October 8, 1987).

3. *Regulatory Alternatives.* Note, *Health Regulation of Naturally Hazardous Foods: The FDA Ban on Swordfish,* 85 Harv. L. Rev. 1025 (1972), suggested alternative ways of protecting consumers from excessive levels of mercury:

> ... A crude approach is to advise limited consumption of the food through a frequency warning, as New York has done in recommending that sportfishermen eat their catch only once a week.... A content warning system would provide better protection. It would require that the labels state both the maximum allowable weekly levels of the contaminant and the amount contained in the food in the package. Consumers could keep track of their mercury intake just as many count calories. Though it would be impractical to test each package for its precise concentration, average levels for the food would appear to provide sufficient information to be useful, since the problem is one of average intake over time....

... [There is] a second alternative to a ban for regulating natural-ly toxic foods: food by prescription. One objectionable characteristic of a ban, its denial of the positive health values of regulated foods, would be alleviated by permitting physicians to prescribe such foods, with appropriate dosage instructions, to patients.... Because only long-term intake must be controlled, consumer rationing, the traditional means of controlling access to food in wartime, appears a more reason-able third alternative....

4. *Lead Contamination.* Like mercury, lead is both ubiquitous in the environment and toxic to humans. Lead occurs in food as a result of natural background, environmental pollution, and food processing and packaging (from soldered cans, and foodware articles). FDA has sought to reduce lead residues in food chiefly through two approaches. First, it has attempted to reduce the migration of lead from solder and ultimately to reduce the use of soldered cans themselves, *e.g.,* 39 Fed. Reg. 42740 (December 6, 1974), 44 Fed. Reg. 51233 (August 31, 1979). Second, it has established action levels for migration of lead from food utensils, *e.g.,* 43 Fed. Reg. 58633 (December 15, 1978), 44 Fed. Reg. 47162 (August 10, 1979), 54 Fed. Reg. 23485 (June 1, 1989). *See* "Lead in Housewares," Hearings before the Subcomm. on Oversight and Investigations of the House Comm. on Energy and Commerce, 100th Cong., 2nd Sess. (1988); Groth, *Lead in Canned Food,* III Argic. and Human Values 91 (1986); Johnson, *Perspective Paper: Lead in Canned Food,* III Agric. and Human Values 146 (1986); Austern and Mussman, *Container–Contributed Lead as Part of Environ-mental Exposure to Lead,* III Agric. and Human Values 157 (1986). In compli-ance with the Lead Contamination Control Act of 1988, 102 Stat. 2884, EPA has published lists of drinking water coolers that are not lead free in 54 Fed. Reg. 14320 (April 10, 1989), 55 Fed. Reg. 1773 (January 18, 1990).

5. *Detection of Contaminants.* As the result of improvements in detection methodology and more comprehensive sampling of the food supply, environ-mental contaminants are often found unexpectedly. For example, although FDA had been monitoring the dioxin content of fish, *see* "Dioxin in Fish," FDA Talk Paper No. T81–32 (August 28, 1981) and "Dioxin—the Impact on Human Health," Hearings before the Subcomm. on Natural Resources, Agricultural Research and Environment of the House Comm. on Science and Technology, 98th Cong., 1st Sess. 78, 81 (1983), the agency learned in 1985 that trace amounts were also detectable in paper food packaging and in 1988 discovered that dioxin could migrate from paperboard cartons into milk, "Dioxin Contam-ination of Food and Water," Hearing before the Subcomm. on Health and the Environment of the House Comm. on Energy and Commerce, 100th Cong., 2nd Sess. (1988). FDA's own tests confirmed that the dioxin contamination was "well below 1 part per trillion," and it announced that production changes undertaken by the paper industry would reduce this level so that paper would "contribute essentially no dioxin to the milk and other foods they packaged," HHS News No. P89–38 (September 1, 1989):

> Most contaminant measurements are in parts per million or parts per billion. FDA tests had to be modified to detect the dioxin in the milk, which was found in amounts far below 1 part per trillion. A ppt is 1/1,000,000,000,000, or one part in a millionth of a million, and the dioxin was less than a tenth of that.

See also "Progress in Eliminating Dioxin from Packaging," FDA Talk Paper No. T90–21 (April 30, 1990).

6. *FDA Monitoring.* Since the early 1960s, FDA has conducted yearly monitoring for environmental contaminants in food by chemical analysis of typical diets. *See* Celeste, *F.D.A. Total Diet Program,* 46 J. AFDO 195 (1982).

Although in December 1974 FDA proposed to establish section 406 action levels through notice-and-comment rulemaking, its final regulations, 42 Fed. Reg. 52814 (September 30, 1977), provided only that action levels could be adopted or changed at any time and announced in the Federal Register, with opportunity for comment, as soon as practicable thereafter. In challenging FDA's decision to allow higher levels of aflatoxin in animal feed, p. 257 *supra,* Public Citizen argued that the agencies had authority to implement section 406 only by formal tolerances.

YOUNG v. COMMUNITY NUTRITION INSTITUTE

Supreme Court of the United States, 1986.
476 U.S. 974.

JUSTICE O'CONNOR delivered the opinion of the Court.

We granted certiorari in this case to determine whether the Court of Appeals for the District of Columbia Circuit correctly concluded that the Food and Drug Administration's longstanding interpretation of 21 U.S.C. § 346 was in conflict with the plain language of that provision. We hold that, in light of the inherent ambiguity of the statutory provision and the reasonableness of the Food and Drug Administration's interpretation thereof, the Court of Appeals erred. We therefore reverse....

The parties do not dispute that, since the enactment of the Act in 1938, the FDA has interpreted 21 U.S.C. § 346 to give it the discretion to decide whether to promulgate a regulation, which is known in the administrative vernacular as a "tolerance level." Tolerance levels are set through a fairly elaborate process, similar to formal rulemaking, with evidentiary hearings. On some occasions, the FDA has instead set "action levels" through a less formal process. In setting an action level, the FDA essentially assures food producers that it ordinarily will not enforce the general adulteration provisions of the Act against them if the quantity of the harmful added substance in their food is less than the quantity specified by the action level....

The FDA's longstanding interpretation of the statute that it administers is that the phrase "to such extent as he finds necessary for the protection of public health" in § 346 modifies the word "shall." The FDA therefore interprets the statute to state that the FDA shall promulgate regulations to the extent that it believes the regulations necessary to protect the public health. Whether regulations are necessary to protect the public health is, under this interpretation, a determination to be made by the FDA.

Respondents, in contrast, argue that the phrase "to such extent" modifies the phrase "the quantity therein or thereon" in § 346, not the word "shall." Since respondents therefore view the word "shall" as unqualified, they interpret § 346 to require the promulgation of tolerance levels for added, but unavoidable, harmful substances. The FDA under this interpretation of § 346 has discretion in setting the particular tolerance level, but not in deciding whether to set a tolerance level at all.

Our analysis must begin with *Chevron U.S.A. Inc. v. Natural Resources Defense Council, Inc.*, 467 U.S. 837 (1984). We there stated:

"First, always, is the question whether Congress has directly spoken to the precise question at issue. If the intent of Congress is clear, that is the end of the matter, for the court, as well as the agency, must give effect to the unambiguously expressed intent of Congress. If, however, the court determines Congress has not directly addressed the precise question at issue, the court does not simply impose its own construction on the statute, as would be necessary in the absence of an administrative interpretation. Rather, if the statute is silent or ambiguous with respect to the specific issue, the question for the court is whether the agency's answer is based on a permissible construction of the statute.... [A] court may not substitute its own construction of a statutory provision for a reasonable interpretation made by the administrator of an agency."

While we agree with the Court of Appeals that Congress in § 346 was speaking directly to the precise question at issue in this case, we cannot agree with the Court of Appeals that Congress unambiguously expressed its intent through its choice of statutory language. The Court of Appeals' reading of the statute may seem to some to be the more natural interpretation, but the phrasing of § 346 admits of either respondents' or petitioner's reading of the statute. As enemies of the dangling participle well know, the English language does not always force a writer to specify which of two possible objects is the one to which a modifying phrase relates....

... We find the FDA's interpretation of § 346 to be sufficiently rational to preclude a court from substituting its judgment for that of the FDA.

To read § 346 as does the FDA is hardly to endorse an absurd result. Like any other administrative agency, the FDA has been delegated broad discretion by Congress in any number of areas. To interpret Congress' statutory language to give the FDA discretion to decide whether tolerance levels are necessary to protect the public health is therefore sensible....

Finally, we note that our interpretation of § 346 does not render that provision superfluous, even in light of Congress' decision to authorize the FDA to "promulgate regulations for the efficient enforcement of [the] Act." 21 U.S.C. § 371(a). Section 346 gives the FDA the authority to choose whatever tolerance level is deemed "necessary for the protection of public health," and food containing a quantity of a required or unavoidable substance less than the tolerance level "shall not, by reason of bearing or containing any added amount of such substance, be considered to be adulterated." Section 346 thereby creates a specific exception to § 342(a)'s general definition of adulterated food as that containing a quantity of a substance that renders the food "ordinarily ... injurious to health." Simply because the FDA is given the choice between employing the standard of § 346 and the standard of § 342(a) does not render § 346 superfluous.

For the reasons set forth, the judgment is reversed, and the case is remanded to the Court of Appeals for the District of Columbia Circuit for further proceedings consistent with this opinion.

                                                                    Reversed.

[The dissenting opinion of Justice Stevens is omitted.]

NOTE

The plaintiffs also contended that if FDA were allowed to enforce the Act by means of action levels, they must be established by notice-and-comment rulemaking. The Supreme Court remanded this claim to the court of appeals, which ruled that FDA action levels for poisonous or deleterious substances are legislative rules rather than general statements of policy and therefore must be promulgated through informal rulemaking, *Community Nutrition Institute v. Young*, 818 F.2d 943 (D.C. Cir. 1987), p. 254 *infra*. In response, FDA published a notice, 53 Fed. Reg. 5043 (February 19, 1988), declaring that in the future it would regard action levels as prosecutorial guidelines and not binding rules, and in 54 Fed. Reg. 16128 (April 21, 1989), 55 Fed. Reg. 20782 (May 21, 1990), it amended its regulations to incorporate this policy.

---

4. PESTICIDE RESIDUES

The 1910 Insecticide Act, 36 Stat. 331, regulated the labeling of insecticides. The core of the current Federal Insecticide, Fungicide, and Rodenticide Act (FIFRA), codified in 7 U.S.C. § 136 *et seq.*, was enacted in 61 Stat. 163 (1947) to replace the 1910 Act. FIFRA requires premarket approval ("registration") of all pesticides distributed or sold in the United States. Like the FD&C Act, FIFRA has been amended on several occasions, including three times in the 1970s and again in 1988, and has become an environmental and health protection statute.

Regulation of pesticide residues in food implicates both FIFRA and the FD&C Act. First, no pesticide may be sold for use on food crops or in food processing unless it has been registered under FIFRA. Second, any pesticide intended for use on a raw agricultural commodity must be the subject of a tolerance established under section 408 of the FD&C Act, which was added by the Miller Pesticides Amendment, 68 Stat. 511 (1954). Third, a pesticide sanctioned for use in or on a raw agricultural commodity must also be the subject of a food additive regulation under section 409 of the Act when the raw commodity is used in a processed food *unless,* in accordance with section 402(a)(2)(C) of the FD&C Act (the so-called "pass through" provision), the concentration of the pesticide in the processed food does not exceed the section 408 tolerance. Fourth, where a pesticide is lawfully applied to a "target" commodity but a residue also occurs in another "nontarget" food, *e.g.,* because the wind has transported it, or it has been absorbed from the soil in a later growing season, or by some other route, a section 406 action level must be established to control it.

Administration of FIFRA and the FD&C Act has also been bifurcated. Prior to 1970, USDA was responsible for implementing FIFRA. Reorganization Plan No. 3 of 1970, 84 Stat. 2086, established the Environmental Protection Agency and transferred primary responsibility for pesticide functions to the new agency. EPA and FDA have reached agreement on their mutual responsibilities, 36 Fed. Reg. 24234 (December 22, 1971), 38 Fed. Reg. 24233 (September 6, 1973), 40 Fed. Reg. 25078 (June 12, 1975). Briefly summarized, EPA registers pesticides under FIFRA, establishes pesticide tolerances under section 408, promulgates food additive regulations for concentrated pesticides under section 409, and recommends to FDA action levels for pesticide contaminants. It is FDA that establishes action levels under section 406 and enforces all FD&C Act requirements for pesticide residues in food.

UNITED STATES v. BODINE PRODUCE CO.

United States District Court, District of Arizona, 1962.
206 F. Supp. 201.

BOLDT, District Judge.

The case arose as a misdemeanor criminal action under the Federal Food, Drug, and Cosmetic Act..... [T]he defendant was charged with having violated that Act by causing adulterated lettuce to be introduced and delivered for introduction into interstate commerce at Glendale, Arizona, consigned to Milwaukee, Wisconsin.

The lettuce was alleged to be adulterated within the meaning of 21 U.S.C. § 342(a)(2)(B) in that it was a raw agricultural commodity and it contained a pesticide chemical, namely DDT, which was unsafe within the meaning of 21 U.S.C. § 346a(a) since the quantity of such pesticide chemical on the lettuce was not within the limits of the tolerance for DDT prescribed by regulations of the Secretary of Health, Education, and Welfare. Pertinent regulations of the Secretary, issued by statutory authority, established a tolerance or permissible limit of 7 parts per million for DDT on lettuce.

Upon the evidence adduced at the trial, the jury obviously concluded that the lettuce shipped by the defendant in this instance contained DDT in excess of 7 parts per million. In fact there was substantial evidence to the contrary....

In recent years, Congress has enacted three important amendments to the Federal Food, Drug, and Cosmetic Act: (1) the Pesticide Chemicals Amendment; (2) the Food Additives Amendment; and (3) the Color Additives Amendment....

Each amendment follows essentially the same pattern. In an administrative proceeding, the proponent of the use of a particular chemical or other additive has the burden of establishing the safety of that item for a designated use. The Secretary of Health, Education, and Welfare then evaluates the safety of that item in accordance with legislative standards.*****

If a useful pesticide chemical can be applied safely on fruits and vegetables, it is apparently a guiding principle of the Secretary to limit the permissible residue of that chemical to the amount necessary for the protection of those crops, even if a greater amount might be tolerated safely by humans..... Once the Secretary's regulation became final, the chemicals to which it relates are deemed to be *unsafe* unless their use conforms to the terms of the regulation.... In a judicial proceeding to enforce the regulation, it is only necessary for the Government to prove a violation of the regulation, *not danger to health.* Otherwise this law could not be effectively enforced.

... In the present case, the ... Government does not have the burden of showing that the DDT in this particular shipment of lettuce could be injurious to health. DDT may not be present in lettuce unless it meets a higher standard, namely, conformity to an administrative tolerance which has resulted from a broad and all-inclusive evaluation of DDT and other pesticide chemicals in foods....

The Government's sample of lettuce, upon which analysis revealed the presence of excessive quantities of DDT, was obtained by food and drug inspectors from a conveyor belt that was carrying the lettuce into a freight car for shipment to another State. Defendant contended, however, that the Government's sampling was premature and that the defendant could be convicted only upon a showing that the lettuce contained excessive quantities of DDT after it reached the retail markets at destination....

... Defendant asserts that it is the practice of the retail markets to trim off some of the outer leaves of each head of lettuce before displaying it for sale and that such practice may bring the DDT content below the tolerance. Defendant contends that trimming of this type is a form of "processing" which brings the lettuce within the exemption proviso in 21 U.S.C. § 342(a)(2) and offers a complete defense unless (1)

***** For example, in establishing a tolerance for pesticide chemicals, the Secretary is required to "give appropriate consideration, among other relevant factors, (1) to the necessity for the production of an adequate, wholesome, and economical food supply; (2) to the other ways in which the consumer may be affected by the same pesticide chemical or by other related substances that are poisonous or deleterious; and (3) to the opinion of the Secretary of Agriculture as submitted with a certification of usefulness * * *." [21 U.S.C. § 346a(b)].

the Government obtains samples of the lettuce after it has been trimmed in the retail stores at destination, and (2) an analysis of *those* samples reveals the presence of more than 7 parts per million.

If this were a good defense it is obvious that the law would be completely unenforceable. The general philosophy of this law is to nip the violation in the bud as close to the source as possible. Evidence of allegedly "corrective" action which may be undertaken at destination has no bearing on the issue of whether the product was adulterated when introduced or delivered for introduction into interstate commerce.

The Court is convinced, however, that the exemption proviso does not help the defendant. To see this proviso in proper perspective, it is well to bear in mind that it was enacted in 1958 as a part of the *Food Additives Amendment.* When Congress enacted the *Pesticide Chemicals Amendment* in 1954, it did not expressly include the exemption proviso but the legislative intent was clear from Senate Report No. 1635 which accompanied that amendment prior to enactment. In part, that Report stated:

> "It (the bill) would also include those foods which have been subjected to certain customary post-harvest treatment prior to marketing, such as the washing or coloring of fruits in their unpeeled natural form, *the stripping of the outer leaves of lettuce,* and the preparation of fresh green salads. * * * Food processed by operations such as cooking, freezing, dehydration, or milling would remain subject to section 406 rather than being regulated by this bill." [Emphasis added.]

While Congress in enacting this Amendment in 1954 did not include a statutory exemption proviso for processed foods, it clearly intended to exclude processed foods from the scope of that Amendment. From the emphasized language it is plain Congress contemplated that the stripping of the outer leaves of lettuce *was not a processing* such as would make the lettuce a *processed food* and take it outside the bounds of the statute.

Nor was this Congressional design altered by the Food Additives Amendment in 1958. There, Congress tackled the problems of food additives *in processed foods* in depth. It drew a sharp line between the Food Additives Amendment and the Pesticide Chemicals Amendment. Thus in the definition of "food additive" it excluded pesticide chemicals in or on raw agricultural commodities. The Congressional intent to leave the Pesticide Chemicals Amendment undisturbed is confirmed by the legislative history which also explains the purpose of the exemption proviso.

The exemption proviso was written to deal with the special problem of processed foods made out of raw agricultural commodities that contain pesticide chemicals. Processed foods are subject to the requirements of Sections 346 and 348. Thus, if they contain any pesticide chemical residue derived from a raw agricultural commodity, they violate those sections unless it is permitted by regulations issued under those sections. In a word, the exemption proviso makes such processed foods legitimate articles of commerce (if the conditions of exemption are met) without the need for special regulations under Section 346 or 348.

The exemption proviso simply saves an extra step. Because of this blanket exemption, industry does not have to seek, and the Secretary does not have to issue, a regulation for each such processed food. Obviously, if the apples are legitimate articles of commerce, then the applesauce made from those apples should not be rendered illegal because of the presence of a component permitted in or on the apples. Either by statutory exemption or by regulation, that applesauce must be considered a legal product. Congress chose the statutory exemption technique, *but* (to carry on the same illustration) *only for applesauce made from apples that contained no more than 7 parts per million of DDT.* The exemption does not apply to the apples themselves. They are never permitted to have more than 7 parts per million of DDT and the applesauce made from them must also stay within that limit....

NOTES

1. *FIFRA–FD&C Act Inconsistency.* The interaction among FIFRA and the food safety provisions of the FD&C Act can produce inconsistent results. For example, as explained at p. 955 *infra,* a carcinogenic pesticide may lawfully be registered for food use under FIFRA, be the subject of a tolerance under section 408 (which contains no anticancer clause), occur in processed food in accordance with the pass-through proviso, and be the subject of a section 406 action level, *but* may not be the subject of a food additive regulation for elevated levels in a processed food because section 409 *does* contain an anticancer clause. *See* National Academy of Sciences, REGULATING PESTICIDES IN FOOD: THE DELANEY PARADOX (1987).

2. *EPA Regulations.* In 53 Fed. Reg. 41126 (October 19, 1988) EPA proposed comprehensive new procedural regulations for food additive regulations governing pesticide residues under section 409 of the FD&C Act, and for hearings under sections 408 and 409.

3. *Criteria for Registration. Continental Chemiste Corp. v. Ruckelshaus,* 461 F.2d 331 (7th Cir. 1972), held that failure to have a section 406 tolerance or food additive regulation for a household pesticide likely to leave residues on food stored in the kitchen did not afford a basis for cancellation of registration under FIFRA.

Controlling pesticide residues that occur in food as a result of environmental contamination has proved difficult. Generally FDA has relied upon enforcement of section 406 action levels. On two occasions, FDA attempted to formulate a legal position that would permit enforcement of a residue level for DDT in fish without the sort of challenge that it later encountered to its action level for mercury in swordfish, p. 293 *supra.* In *United States v. Goodman,* 486 F.2d 847 (7th Cir. 1973), the agency successfully argued that, in the absence of a 408 tolerance, any residue of DDT in *raw* fish was illegal and that it could lawfully establish an action level of 5 ppm as an exercise of enforcement discretion under section 306. In the following related case, the agency charged that a residue of DDT in smoked fish (a *processed* food) in excess of the 5 ppm action level was an unapproved "food additive" that was automatically illegal because it was not the subject of an approved food additive regulation.

UNITED STATES v. EWIG BROS. CO.

United States Court of Appeals, Seventh Circuit, 1974.
502 F.2d 715.

STEVENS, Circuit Judge.

There are two ways to state the principal question presented by these appeals. Narrowly, the issue is whether residues of DDT and dieldrin in smoked chubs are "food additives" within the meaning of § 201(s) of the Federal Food, Drug and Cosmetic Act. A somewhat more disturbing way to state the same question is whether all of the fish in the Great Lakes are "adulterated" as a matter of statutory definition. If they are, the [FDA] may have, at least for the present, virtually unbridled power to eliminate all such fish from our food supply. We therefore attach special importance to the additional questions presented in the *Vita Food* appeal. That appeal, unlike the *Ewig Bros.* appeal,[4] requires us to consider the legal significance of an "interim guideline" announced in a press release on April 22, 1969, as well as the district court's findings that the testing methods used by the government's experts were not sufficiently reliable to demonstrate that Vita's smoked chubs contained more DDT than the guideline permits.

A total ban on the future use of DDT would not resolve the problem presented by this case. Although the levels of DDT contamination are declining, we must assume that the chemical, or its derivatives, will survive as an ingredient of all or most foods for some time.

Scientists seem to agree that if the DDT level is high enough, the food should not be consumed by man and, conversely, if the amount is

4. The *Ewig Bros.* case was brought as a companion to complaints filed against five other defendants which distributed raw chubs, as opposed to the smoked chubs distributed by Ewig. In all six cases, the parties stipulated that the quantity of DDT in the chubs exceeded the informal guidelines, and, in the five raw chub cases, that DDT was a "pesticide chemical" and that the fish were "raw agricultural commodities" within the meaning of § 201 of F.D.C.A. In all cases Judge Gordon rejected the defendants' argument that the Administrator was required by statute to establish tolerance limits for DDT in fish before he could claim that the presence of DDT residues resulted in adulteration. In the *Ewig* case, Judge Gordon also held that DDT in the processed chubs is a food additive. . . .

On September 29, 1973, we affirmed the judgments in the five cases involving raw chubs and entered an order holding the *Ewig* appeal for decision with *Vita Food.* See *United States v. Goodman,* 486 F.2d 847, 849 n.10 (7th Cir. 1973). In that case we held that the Administrator is not required to establish by regulation permissible tolerances of DDT and its derivatives before initiating enforcement proceedings or obtaining injunctive relief in such a proceeding. . . . The only contention raised by Ewig Bros. on this appeal is that Judge Gordon erroneously held that DDT residues in smoked chubs are a "food additive."

sufficiently small, ingestion of DDT may be harmless. Danger levels have not been precisely defined. The record demonstrates, however, that in fish levels in the range of 5 parts per million are neither (a) generally recognized among qualified experts as safe, nor (b) demonstrably injurious to health or unfit for human consumption. At the levels disclosed by the record before us, the effect on human health is somewhat uncertain.

Unquestionably DDT is a "pesticide chemical" as that term is defined in § 201(q) of F.D.C.A. Pursuant to statutory procedures, tolerances have been established for its use in or on various raw agricultural commodities, including fruits, vegetables, and meat. Such foods may therefore contain DDT within the prescribed tolerance limits without being "adulterated." ... With respect to the foods for which DDT tolerances have been set, it is reasonable to infer that the rule-making process may have been invoked either by the FDA itself, by manufacturers or distributors of the pesticide, or by farmers or producers who are interested in using DDT as a pesticide. Fishermen, however, have never had any interest in using or selling DDT themselves.... From their point of view, it is not an item which is added to their products; it is a natural component of the fish before it is caught, let alone processed.

In this case the government's claim that defendants' chubs are "adulterated" is not predicated on a claim that the particular fish defendants sell contain a poisonous substance or are otherwise unfit for food pursuant to either subparagraph (1) or subparagraph (3) of § 402[(a)] of the F.D.C.A. Under those subparagraphs the government would have the burden of proving that the fish are actually harmful to man. Instead, the government's claim is predicated on § 402(a)(2)(C), under which it need only prove that "such substance is not generally recognized, among experts qualified by scientific training and experience to evaluate its safety, as having been adequately shown through scientific procedures ... to be safe under the conditions of its intended use...."

It is the government's position that a fair analysis of the statutory scheme Congress has enacted, including the allocation of decisionmaking responsibility between the agency and the judiciary, justifies proceeding under this section. For if, as the government contends, DDT is a food additive, the Food and Drug Administration may itself decide when products containing quantities of DDT should be removed from public consumption, without having to rely upon the decisions—possibly inconsistent with one another—of different federal judges determining danger to health under §§ (a)(1) and (a)(3) on a case-by-case basis. The question, then, is whether DDT and dieldrin in defendants' processed fish are "food additives" within the meaning of § 201(s).....

... The language ... defines a food additive as *any* substance, "the intended use of which results or may reasonably be expected to result, directly or indirectly, in its becoming a component or otherwise affecting the characteristics of any food. . . ." Although Congress was primarily concerned with substances used by a food processor, neither the language nor the history of the 1958 Act limits its application to such substances. The words "the intended use of which" are not confined, as they easily could have been confined, to use in food processing.

Vita has argued that a process, such as smoking, during which nothing new is added to a food, cannot "transmogrify" a preexisting component of a food into an additive. But whether the food be fish, fruit, or meat, if the component is a pesticide chemical, we think that is exactly what Congress intended.

Although it may seem odd to place the label "additive" on a chemical substance which was a component of the raw product and which is not changed by processing, Congress' choice of that label does not result in any "transmogrification." Before processing, DDT is a "pesticide chemical" on a raw product; after processing, it is an "additive." Since there is no tolerance for DDT on fish, both before and after processing the presence of the DDT causes fish to be adulterated without any proof that it is actually unfit as food. Defendant's contention, if accepted, would result in the anomaly that a chemical such as DDT would adulterate all raw fish, but adulteration of processed fish would be determined on an uncertain case-by-case basis. We conclude that such a construction of the statute is illogical and unacceptable. . . . .

Whether we accept the government's evidence at face value . . . [or] whether we assume that the truth lies somewhere in between the views of the respective litigants' experts, or even if we take the defendants' evidence, it is perfectly clear that the limit specified in the 1969 guidelines has been violated. . . .

Vita argues, however, that there really is no significant difference between DDT levels of 5 ppm and levels as high as 8 ppm. But that is an argument that should not be addressed to us; it may properly be asserted as a reason for setting a tolerance at 8 ppm or perhaps even higher. The F.D.A. need not have set its guideline limit at 5 ppm, but it did so, and industry has not seen fit to invoke the statutory procedures for establishing a different tolerance level. In these circumstances, the government has met its burden by proving that the guidelines have been exceeded repeatedly. . . .

NOTES

1. *Current FDA Approach.* FDA has never disavowed the *Ewig Brothers* approach, which certainly facilitates enforcement against nontarget commodities contaminated with pesticide residues. Currently, however, it regulates such residues in the same fashion that it regulates other environmental contaminants, by enforcing action levels based on EPA recommendations. However, *Community Nutrition Institute,* p. 304 *supra,* forced the agency to characterize action levels as enforcement guidelines rather than binding limits.

2. *Proposed Legislation.* Legislation to provide FDA with increased authority to prevent food contamination twice passed the Senate during the 1970s

but never received formal consideration in the House. *See* Hutt, *Food Legislation in Perspective,* 34 FDC L.J. 590 (1979).

Prior to the 1980s, EPA revoked all registrations for pesticides cancelled under FIFRA but generally retained the section 408 tolerances and section 409 food additive regulations as long as residues could occur in food as the result of environmental contamination. With the following notice, however, EPA abandoned this practice.

TOLERANCES AND EXEMPTIONS FROM TOLERANCES FOR PESTICIDE CHEMICALS IN OR ON RAW AGRICULTURAL COMMODITIES
47 Federal Register 42956 (September 29, 1982).

This notice sets forth a policy regarding the revocation of formal tolerances for cancelled pesticides and, where necessary, the establishment of action levels for these pesticides. The Food and Drug Administration (FDA), and the Agricultural Marketing Service (AMS) and Food Safety and Inspection Service (FSIS) of the U.S. Department of Agriculture have reviewed and agreed with the policy statement.....

Food sometimes contains pesticide chemical residues not because of purposeful, direct application, but rather because the pesticide persists in the environment and subsequently contaminates the food. Thus, the presence of the residue in the food cannot be prevented or removed by good agricultural or manufacturing practice. Consequently, residues of pesticides may be present long after cancellation has occurred. In the absence of a tolerance, FDA, FSIS, and AMS rely on an action level recommended by the EPA in determining whether the pesticide chemical is present at levels which make it unsafe and whether regulatory action should be taken. This level is then applied by the FDA, FSIS, and AMS in their regulatory programs.....

When a pesticide's registration for a food or feed use is cancelled because of concern about the safety of the pesticide, the associated tolerance for use or food additive regulation is no longer justified and logically should be revoked. The tolerance revocation should discourage misuse, i.e., the illegal application of a cancelled pesticide, as well as discourage persons in other countries from exporting to the United States food bearing residues of pesticides which can no longer be legally used in the United States because of safety reasons. For pesticides which degrade rapidly in the environment, particularly in the soil, revoking the tolerance should cause no problem because any pesticide residues remaining from applications prior to the cancellation action would not be expected to be present at detectable levels. However, for pesticides which persist in the environment, i.e., which take long periods of time to degrade, crops may contain detectable residues of these pesticides, perhaps even at or near the tolerance levels, for many years after the application of the cancelled pesticide has ceased. Similarly, the meat of animals fed crops containing such residues may also contain such residues. If the formal tolerances for persistent pesticides were revoked and no other action were taken, land to which the cancelled pesticides have been applied could be unavailable for crop use for many years to come. Therefore, in order to avoid unfairly penalizing food producers whose commodities may still contain unavoidable residues of persistent pesticides which can no longer be legally applied, the agencies have agreed to establish action levels to replace formal tolerances that will be revoked. The action levels will be reviewed periodically and lowered as the chemicals dissipate from the environment....

NOTES

1. *EPA Actions on Other Pesticides.* See, e.g., EPA's actions and recommended action levels for DDT, 50 Fed. Reg. 10070 and 10077 (March 13, 1985), 51 Fed. Reg. 46616 and 46658 (December 24, 1986); chlordane, 50 Fed. Reg. 23717 (June 5, 1985), 51 Fed. Reg. 46665 (December 24, 1986); aldrin and dieldrin, 50 Fed. Reg. 10080 (March 13, 1985), 51 Fed. Reg. 46662 (December 24, 1986); carbon disulfide, carbon tetrachloride, and ethylene dichloride, 54 Fed. Reg. 6129 (February 8, 1989); heptachlor, 54 Fed. Reg. 33690 (August 16, 1989); EBDCs, 55 Fed. Reg. 20416 (May 16, 1990).

2. *FDA Action Levels.* FDA's 406 action levels for pesticide residues in food are contained in Compliance Policy Guide No. 7141.01, which is updated regularly to reflect EPA recommendations. See, e.g., reaffirmed action levels for Kepone, 51 Fed. Reg. 11840 (April 7, 1986); revocation of action levels for DBCP, 51 Fed. Reg. 11349 (April 2, 1986); new action levels for aldrin and dieldrin, chlordane, DDT, TDE, and DDE, 52 Fed. Reg. 18025 (May 13, 1987); the revision of the entire guide, 51 Fed. Reg. 34503 (September 29, 1986), 52 Fed. Reg. 2611 (January 23, 1987); and new action levels for heptachlor, 54 Fed. Reg. 50025 (December 4, 1989). In 55 Fed. Reg. 14359 (April 17, 1990), FDA listed all existing pesticide action levels and announced that they represent only enforcement guidelines. For an example of FDA enforcement action, *see United States v. Barnett,* 587 F.2d 252 (5th Cir. 1979).

3. *Monitoring and Enforcement.* Enforcement of pesticide residue limits on imported and domestic food requires analysis of thousands of products. This resource-intensive effort is subject to ongoing reassessment by FDA and the target of critics who claim the agency is not doing enough. *See, e.g.,* "Cancer-Causing Chemicals—Part 2: Chemical Contamination of Food," Hearings before the Subcomm. on Oversight and Investigations of the House Comm. on Interstate and Foreign Commerce, 95th Cong., 2nd Sess. (1978); GAO, BETTER REGULATION OF PESTICIDE EXPORTS AND PESTICIDE RESIDUES IN IMPORTED FOOD IS ESSENTIAL, No. CED–79–43 (June 22, 1979). In 1979 FDA formed an internal study group to recommend improvements in monitoring, analysis, and enforcement, 44 Fed. Reg. 57500 (October 5, 1979). Criticism of the program has continued, however, see, e.g., GAO, PESTICIDES: BETTER SAMPLING AND ENFORCEMENT NEEDED ON IMPORTED FOOD, No. RCED–86–219 (September 26, 1986); GAO, PESTICIDES: NEED TO ENHANCE FDA'S ABILITY TO PROTECT THE PUBLIC FROM ILLEGAL RESIDUES, No. RCED–87–7 (October 27, 1986); "Pesticides in Food," Hearing before

the Subcomm. on Oversight and Investigations of the House Comm. on Energy and Com., 100th Cong., 1st Sess. (1987).

———

Two incidents during the 1980s focused public attention on pesticide residues in food. In 1983, Florida banned the sale of food containing any residues of ethylene dibromide (EDB), even though, based on their assessments of the risk, EPA and FDA had concluded that the problem did not merit action. However, when other states joined Florida by restricting or banning EDB residues, *e.g., American Grain Product Processing Institute v. Department of Public Health,* 392 Mass. 309, 67 N.E.2d 455 (1984), EPA banned its use in 48 Fed. Reg. 46228 (October 11, 1983), 49 Fed. Reg. 4452 (February 6, 1984). Concurrently, FDA established action levels for EDB in food in 49 Fed. Reg. 13195 (April 3, 1984), 49 Fed. Reg. 18624 (May 1, 1984), 50 Fed. Reg. 180 (January 2, 1985). *See generally* "Contamination from Ethylene Dibromide (EDB)," Hearing before the Subcomm. on Toxic Substances and Environmental Oversight of the Senate Comm. on Environment and Public Works, 98th Cong., 2nd Sess. (1984); "Government Regulation of the Pesticide Ethylene Dibromide (EDB)," Joint Hearings before certain Subcomms. of the House Comm. on Government Operations, 98th Cong., 2nd Sess. (1984). For a critical analysis of the government's failure to reassure the public about the insignificance of the risk posed by EDB residues, *see* Sharlin, *EDB: A Case Study in Communicating Risk,* 6 Risk Analysis 61 (1986).

Later in the decade the Natural Resources Defense Council (NRDC) targeted daminozide (Alar), a plant growth regulator, as a health hazard. EPA's denial of a petition to ban the pesticide in 1986 was upheld on procedural grounds in *Nader v. EPA,* 859 F.2d 747 (9th Cir. 1988). In response to claims that it was not protecting the public health, EPA reduced the tolerance for daminozide on apples in 51 Fed. Reg. 12889 (April 16, 1986), 52 Fed. Reg. 1909 (January 16, 1987), 54 Fed. Reg. 6392 (February 10, 1989). Still not satisfied, Massachusetts banned daminozide residues in apples, *see Processed Apples Institute, Inc. v. Department of Public Health,* 402 Mass. 392, 522 N.E.2d 965 (1988).

HOW A PR FIRM EXECUTED THE ALAR SCARE
The Wall Street Journal, October 3, 1989, P. A22.

After this year's stir over use of the chemical Alar on apples, political publicist David Fenton, celebrated the work of his firm in a lengthy memo to interested parties. He wrote of a "sea change in public opinion" that has "taken place because of a carefully planned media campaign, conceived and implemented by Fenton Communications with the Natural Resources Defense Council." Extracts are reprinted below:

"In the past two months, the American public's knowledge of the dangers of pesticides in food has been greatly increased. Overnight, suppliers of organic produce cannot keep up with demand. Traditional supermarkets are opening pesticide-free produce sections....

"Our goal was to create so many repetitions of NRDC's message that average American consumers (not just the policy elite in Washington) could not avoid hearing it—from many different media outlets within a short period of time. The idea was for the "story" to achieve a life of its own, and continue for weeks and months to affect policy and consumer habits. Of course, this had to be achieved with extremely limited resources....

"In October of 1988 NRDC hired Fenton Communications to undertake the media campaign for its report.... The report marked the first time anyone—inside government or out—had calculated children's actual exposure levels to carcinogenic and neurotoxic pesticides. The study showed one of the worst pesticides to be daminozide, or Alar, used primarily on apples and peanuts....

"[L]ast fall, Meryl Streep contacted NRDC, asking if she could assist with some environmental projects. Ms. Streep read the preliminary results of the study and agreed to serve as a spokesperson for it.... It was agreed that one week after the study's release, Streep and other prominent citizens would announce the formation of NRDC's new project, Mothers and Others for Pesticide Limits. This group would direct citizen action at changing the pesticide laws, and help consumers lobby for pesticide-free produce at their grocery stores. The separation of these two events was important in ensuring that the media would have two stories, not one, about this project. Thereby, more repetition of NRDC's message was guaranteed.

"As the report was being finalized, Fenton Communications began contacting various media. An agreement was made with 60 Minutes to "break" the story of the report in late February. Interviews were also arranged several months in advance with major women's magazines like Family Circle, Women's Day and Redbook (to appear in mid-March). Appearance dates were set with the Donahue Show, ABC's Home Show, double appearances on NBC's Today show and other programs.

"On February 26th CBS' 60 Minutes broke the story to an audience of 40 million viewers.... The next morning, NRDC held a news conference attended by more than 70 journalists and 12 camera crews. Concurrently, NRDC coordinated local news conferences in 12 cities around the country also releasing the report.... On March 7 Meryl Streep held a Washington news conference to announce the formation of NRDC's Mothers and Others for Pesticide Limits....

"Coverage of Mothers and Others that week included USA Today (cover); The Today Show on NBC; The Phil Donahue Show (10 million viewers); Women's Day (6 million copies sold); Redbook (4 million); Family Circle (6 million); Organic Gardening (1.5 million); New Woman (1.7 million); People Magazine; USA TODAY Television (200 markets); Entertainment Tonight (18 million viewers); ABC's Home Show (3 million viewers); Cable News Network and numerous radio networks, newspaper chains, broadcast chains, wire services and other media around the nation. In addition, we arranged for Meryl Streep and Janet Hathaway of NRDC to grant 16 interviews by satellite with local tv major market anchors. . . .

"In the ensuing weeks, the controversy kept building. Articles appeared in food sections of newspapers around the country. Columnists and cartoonists took up the story. MacNeil/Lehrer, the New York Times and Washington Post did follow-up stories, as did the three network evening programs and morning shows. Celebrities from the cast of L.A. Law and thirtysomething joined NRDC for a Los Angeles news conference.

"Soon school systems began banning apples (which is not what NRDC intended or recommended). Three federal agencies (EPA, USDA and FDA) issued an unusual joint statement assuring the public that apples were safe (although to children who consume a great deal, these assurances are not entirely true). . . .

"And the industry struck back. NRDC's credibility was, as expected, questioned by industry "front groups" such as the American Council on Science and Health. A major corporate pr firm, Hill and Knowlton, was hired for $700,000 by the apple growers, which also put forward a $2 million advertising budget. Stories began appearing (including a Washington Post cover piece) saying that the levels of Alar in apples were below federal standards, and charging the media with exaggerating the story. . . .

"Usually, it takes a significant natural disaster to create this much sustained news attention for an environmental problem. We believe this experience proves there are other ways to raise public awareness for the purpose of moving the Congress and policymakers."

NOTES

1. *The Alar Ban.* Although EPA and FDA found only low levels of daminozide in apples, "Little Pesticide Residue Found In Foods Children Eat," FDA Talk Paper No. T89–14 (February 27, 1989), "Extremely Low Levels Of Alar Found By Consumers Union," FDA Talk Paper No. T89–19 (March 30, 1989), and attempted to reassure the public, reaction to the NRDC campaign caused EPA to ban daminozide, 54 Fed. Reg. 6392 (February 10, 1989), 54 Fed. Reg. 22558 (May 24, 1989), 54 Fed. Reg. 37278 (September 7, 1989), 54 Fed. Reg. 47492 (November 14, 1989), 55 Fed. Reg. 10218 (March 19, 1990). The impact of the daminozide controversy on public confidence in food safety was examined in "Chemicals and Food Crops," Hearing before the Subcomm. on Toxic Substances, Environmental Oversight, Research and Development of the Senate Comm. on Environment and Public Works, 101st Cong., 1st Sess. (1989); "Produce Safety and Nutrition," Hearing before the Subcomm. on Domestic Marketing, Consumer Relations, and Nutrition of the House Comm. on Agriculture, 101st Cong., 1st Sess. (1989).

2. *EPA Registration Issues.* The statutory requirements for reregistering old pesticides and registering new ones place formidable burdens on EPA. *See, e.g.,* the lists of pesticides required to be reregistered, 54 Fed. Reg. 7740 (February 22, 1989), 54 Fed. Reg. 22706 (May 25, 1989), 54 Fed. Reg. 30846 (July 24, 1989); GAO, PESTICIDES: EPA'S FORMIDABLE TASK TO ASSESS AND REGULATE THEIR RISKS, No. RCED–86–125 (April 1986).

PESTICIDE REGULATION UNDER FIFRA

EPA regulation of pesticides in many ways resembles FDA premarket approval of food additives, color additives, and new drugs. Five distinctive features of FIFRA, however, merit attention.

• FIFRA applies to all pesticides distributed or sold in the United States, including those sold in intrastate commerce.

• FIFRA contains complex provisions governing the disclosure of registration data submitted by the pioneer manufacturer and its use by subsequent "me too" manufacturers, 7 U.S.C. § 136a(c)(1)(D). The "me too" registrant must in some instances compensate the originator for use of the data under 40 C.F.R. Part 152, Subpart E. Disputes relating to data compensation are subject to compulsory arbitration, 29 C.F.R. Part 1440.

• EPA has imposed user fee charges for registration and food additive regulation activities, 51 Fed. Reg. 42974 (November 26, 1986), 53 Fed. Reg. 19108 (May 26, 1988), codified in 40 C.F.R. Part 152, Subpart U. In the FIFRA Amendments of 1988, 102 Stat. 2654, 2663, however, Congress added its own list of user fees, codified in 7 U.S.C. § 136a–1(i), and prohibited imposition of any other user fees before September 30, 1997.

• Under 7 U.S.C. § 136v, a state may forbid the sale or use of a pesticide registered by EPA but may not impose any labeling or packaging requirements in addition to or different from those established by EPA and may not allow any use on food or animal feed that is not lawful under the FD&C Act. Political subdivisions are barred from any form of pesticide regulation, *Maryland Pest Control Ass'n v. Montgomery County, Maryland,* 646 F. Supp. 109 (D. Md. 1986), *aff'd without opinion,* 822 F.2d 55 (4th Cir. 1987). For conflicting views on whether this provision preempts state law tort actions based on inadequate labeling, *compare Ferebee v. Chevron Chemical Co.,* 736 F.2d 1529 (D.C. Cir. 1984), *with Fitzgerald v. Mallinckrodt, Inc.,* 681 F. Supp. 404 (E.D. Mich. 1987).

• Where EPA suspends and subsequently cancels registration of a pesticide, any person who owned any quantity of the pesticide immediately before the suspension notice is entitled to be indemnified under 7 U.S.C. § 136m. *See, e.g.,* 49 Fed. Reg. 49796 (December 21, 1984).

5. INTENTIONAL FUNCTIONAL INGREDIENTS

Before World War II relatively few functional ingredients were used in food. Even then, however, they were viewed with suspicion and concern. *See, e.g.,* O. Folin, PRESERVATIVES AND OTHER CHEMICALS IN FOODS: THEIR USE AND ABUSE (1914). The immediate post-war period saw a proliferation of functional food ingredients and a revolution in food technology. In 1950 Representative Frank B. Keefe

(R-Wisc.) introduced a resolution, 96 Cong. Rec. 8933, to establish a select committee to investigate the use of chemicals in food products. Because he was of the minority party and in poor health, Keefe persuaded Representative James Delaney (D-N.Y.) to sponsor the resolution and serve as chairman of the committee.

INVESTIGATION OF THE USE OF CHEMICALS IN FOODS AND COSMETICS

HOUSE REPORT NO. 2356.
82d   Congress, 2d Session (1952).

At this stage of our civilization, there is a genuine need for the use of many chemicals in connection with our food supply. Many of the chemicals directly added to foods have proved to be of substantial value to the consumer, and constitute a necessary adjunct to modern civilization. Few would quarrel now with the advisability of enriching various staple foods with certain vitamins and minerals, or with the addition of other chemicals which enhance the nutritive value of the products in which they are incorporated..... The progress that has been made in food technology, however, has been attended by a certain degree of hazard, since some quantity of many of the new chemicals utilized in the production and processing of foods is inevitably ingested by the consuming public. It is essential that this risk be kept to a minimum.

... Chemical substances are being introduced into the production, processing, storage, packaging and distribution of food at an ever-increasing rate. There is hardly a food sold in the market place today which has not had some chemicals used on or in it at some state in its production, processing, packaging, transportation, or storage....

The indirect addition of chemicals to our food supply also raises serious problems. For example, cattle are being treated with antibiotic drugs in the control of mastitis, anthrax, and other diseases. There is a question whether the presence of small amounts of antibiotics in milk and milk products has any effect on the consumer; that is, whether the consumer develops a sensitivity or resistance to these chemicals....

The United States Food and Drug Administration, in collaboration with the United States Public Health Service, revealed that approximately 842 chemicals are used, have been used, or have been suggested for use in foods. Of this total, it was estimated that 704 are employed today, and that of these 704 only 428 are definitely known to be safe. Thus, there are approximately 276 chemicals being used in food today, the safety of which has not been established to the satisfaction of many groups concerned with the health and safety of the public.

The Surgeon General of the Public Health Service pointed out that the extent of this problem cannot be fully visualized, because of a lack of adequate information on the chronic effects of chemical substances currently in use. He testified that the toxic effects of many of these chemicals, and of the compounds which they form when introduced into food, are unknown. . . .

***

a. The Food Additives Amendment

Stimulated by the Delaney Committee hearings, Congress enacted the Food Additives Amendment, 72 Stat. 1784 (1958).

FOOD ADDITIVES AMENDMENT OF 1958

SENATE REPORT NO. 2422.
85th Congress, 2d Session (1958).

. . . [U]nder existing law the Federal Government is unable to prevent the use in foods of a poisonous or deleterious substance until it first proves that the additive is poisonous or deleterious. To establish this proof through experimentation with generations of mice or other animals may require 2 years or even more on the part of the relatively few scientists the Food and Drug Administration is able to assign to a particular problem. Yet, until that proof is forthcoming, an unscrupulous processor of foodstuffs is perfectly free to purvey to millions of our people foodstuffs containing additives which may or may not be capable of producing illness, debility, or death.

. . . This huge loophole is 1 of 2 flaws in existing law which, through this measure, we are attempting to fill. This bill, if enacted, will require the processor who wants to add a new and unproven additive to accept the responsibility now voluntarily borne by all responsible food processors of first proving it to be safe for ingestion by human beings.

The second flaw in existing law which has proved detrimental to consumers, to processors, and to our national economy and which this bill seeks to remove is a provision [section 402(a)] which has inadvertently served to unnecessarily proscribe the use of additives that could enable the housewife to safely keep food longer, the processor to make it more tasteful and appetizing, and the Nation to make use of advances in technology calculated to increase and improve our food supplies. Your committee agrees with the Food and Drug Administration that existing law should be changed to permit the use of such additives as our technological scientists may produce and which may benefit our people and our economy when the proposed usages of such additives are in amounts accepted by the Food and Drug Administration as safe. . . .

The legislation also covers substances which may reasonably be expected to become a component of any food or to affect the characteristics of any food. These substances are generally referred to as "incidental additives." . . .

On the other hand, substances which may accidentally get into a food, as for example, paints or cleaning solutions used in food processing plants, are not covered by the legislation.... If accidental additives do get into food, the provisions of the Food, Drug, and Cosmetic Act dealing with poisonous and deleterious substances would be applicable....

The concept of safety used in this legislation involves the question of whether a substance is hazardous to the health of man or animal. Safety requires proof of a reasonable certainty that no harm will result from the proposed use of an additive. It does not—and cannot—require proof beyond any possible doubt that no harm will result under any conceivable circumstances....

In determining the "safety" of an additive scientists must take into consideration the cumulative effect of such additive in the diet of man or animals over their respective life spans together with any chemically or pharmacologically related substances in such diet. Thus, the safety of a given additive involves informed judgments based on educated estimates by scientists and experts of the anticipated ingestion of an additive by man and animals under likely patterns of use....

... We would like ... to call attention to the fact that the Committee on Interstate and Foreign Commerce of the House of Representatives, before bringing the bill to a vote in the House, decided to add to its previously approved bill the [Delaney Clause].... We have no objections to that amendment whatsoever, but we would point out that in our opinion it is the intent and purpose of this bill, even without that amendment, to assure our people that nothing shall be added to the foods they eat which can reasonably be expected to produce any type of illness in humans or animals.... In short, we believe, the bill reads and means the same with or without the inclusion of the clause referred to. This is also the view of the Food and Drug Administration.*

NOTES

1. *Transitional Provisions.* The 1958 Amendment contained transitional provisions under which all food additives were required to be subject to a food additive regulation within two and one-half years. Congress subsequently extended this transitional period in the Food Additives Transitional Provisions Amendment of 1961, 75 Stat. 42, and the Food Additives Transitional Provisions Amendment of 1964, 78 Stat. 1002, to December 31, 1965.

2. *Consideration of Utility.* A major issue during Congressional consideration of the 1958 Amendment was whether an additive should be approved for use if it did not convey some benefit to consumers. The Administration bill would have required a finding by FDA that a food additive has "functional value" in order to be approved, unless the additive was not a poisonous or deleterious substance. H.R. 6747, 85th Cong., 1st Sess. (1957). Industry opposed this approach. A compromise suggested in Oser, *The Functional Value*

* [The Delaney Clause is considered separately in Chapter VIII, p. ___ *infra.*]

of Food Additives, 13 FDC L.J. 131 (1958), under which FDA must find that the additive accomplishes its intended physical or other technical effect, was adopted by the House Committee. H.R. Rep. No. 2284, 85th Cong., 2d Sess. (1958). The Committee stated that this functionality requirement referred to "the objective effect" of the additive and "does not involve any judgment on the part of the Secretary of whether such effect results in any added value to the consumer of such food or enhances the marketability from a merchandising point of view." If no quantitative limitation is required to assure that the use of the additive will be safe, FDA may not consider functionality. Testifying in 1972 on a bill to require that food additives be proved effective and necessary, FDA officials favored the current requirement of functionality and objected to additional requirements that would require the agency to make economic or social decisions. "Nutrition and Human Needs—1972," Hearings before the Senate Select Comm. on Nutrition and Human Needs, 92d Cong., 2d Sess., Part 4B (1972).

3. *Investigational Exemptions.* Section 409(i) requires the Secretary to issue regulations exempting food additives intended solely for investigational use by qualified experts. FDA has never issued such regulations, but has not objected to the investigational use of food additives under conditions similar to those for investigational new drugs.

4. *Proposed Amendments.* The Food Additives Amendment has remained unchanged since 1958. A bill to amend several food safety provisions, including section 409, was introduced with the support of the Reagan Administration, 127 Cong. Rec. 13969 (June 25, 1981), but resulted only in general oversight hearings, "Oversight of Food Safety, 1983," Hearings before the Senate Comn. on Labor and Human Resources, 98th Cong., 1st Sess. (1983).

b. Food Additives

The Act's definition of "food additive" in section 201(s) is the key to understanding the coverage and operation of the premarketing licensure system that Congress established. The term broadly includes all substances that may reasonably be expected to become components of food, but then expressly excludes a substantial portion, probably the majority, of such substances. The substances excluded are those that (1) are generally recognized as safe (referred to as "GRAS"), (2) are subject to a "sanction" given by FDA under the FD&C Act or by USDA under the Federal Meat Inspection Act or the Poultry Products Inspection Act before 1958 (referred to as a "prior sanction"), or (3) fall within specific exceptions for pesticides, color additives, and new animal drugs. Each of these excluded categories is explored below.

For a substance that is a "food additive," as defined by the Act as contrasted with the colloquial meaning of this term, section 409 requires the submission to FDA of a petition demonstrating the substance's safety. Only after FDA has approved the petition and promulgated a food additive regulation may the substance be used in food.

UNITED STATES v. AN ARTICLE OF FOOD

United States Court of Appeals, Seventh Circuit, 1982.
678 F.2d 735.

CUMMINGS, Chief Judge.

... The defendant food comprises numerous cases containing tablets of Aangamik 15.... According to the government's complaint, the tablets are an adulterated food under 21 U.S.C. § 342(a)(2)(C) of the Federal Food, Drug and Cosmetic Act in that they contain a food additive—N,N—Dimethylglycine hydrochloride ("DMG")—which allegedly is unsafe under 21 U.S.C. § 348(a).....

Even though DMG is quite clearly a "substance" that has become a "component" of Aangamik 15, FoodScience [the claimant] would have us read into the definition of "food additive" an exception for substances that become "principal ingredients" of the food to which they are added. Although DMG is the lesser of two active components of the tablets and accounts for less than 4% of each tablet's weight, FoodScience argues that DMG is a "principal ingredient" because the tablets' consumers are particularly hopeful of "the potential usefulness of DMG as a metabolic enhancer (whether or not it is a nutrient in the strict sense) * * *." Since many ordinary additives come in relatively small quantities and food manufacturers often attempt to make their presence inconspicuous, an exception from the definition for "principal ingredients" might agree with the notion of "food additive" used in common parlance. But had Congress intended the Food and Drug Administration and the courts to rely on common parlance it would not have so carefully crafted the foregoing definition of the term.

FoodScience argues it is apparent from the statutory definition that Congress intended to limit the definition of "food additive" to substances that become a component of or affect food in some subtle or incidental fashion, such as substances "intended for use in producing, manufacturing, packing, processing etc." Once again, therefore, important and principal ingredients like DMG in Aangamik 15 should be excepted from the definition, according to FoodScience. The argument is ironic. In drafting Section 321(s), Congress obviously was concerned with creating a very broad definition of food additive that could not be escaped by food purveyors claiming that particular substances were present in too small a quantity or had affected the food too indirectly. FoodScience's argument is that because Congress was concerned with small amounts of unsafe substances, Congress could not similarly be concerned with unsafe substances present in relatively larger quantities. But the definition itself shows the absurdity: "[t]he term 'food additive' means any substance the intended use of which results * * * in its becoming a component * * * of any food * * *." The term "component" of course includes large quantities of unsafe substances as well as small quantities.....

The practical effect of holding that DMG is an additive is to place the burden of showing safety upon FoodScience. In order to avoid the label "food additive," FoodScience must now show that DMG is "generally recognized as safe," whereas if DMG were not an "additive," the Food and Drug Administration would have the burden under 21 U.S.C. § 342 of proving by a preponderance of the evidence that DMG is "injurious to health."....

CUDAHY, Circuit Judge, concurring.

I concur fully in Chief Judge Cummings' conclusion that the government in this case properly condemned defendant's "Aangamik 15" tablets as an adulterated food because they contain an unsafe "food additive"—DMG—for which no exempting regulations have been issued. I write separately only to emphasize that, in my view, characterizing DMG as a "food additive" depends critically on its being added to or sold in combination with other active ingredients. Because FoodScience consistently represented to the public, and maintained throughout the pre-trial stages of this proceeding, that its "Angamik 15" tablets contained *two* active and beneficial ingredients—DMG and calcium gluconate—I agree that the district court properly found DMG to be a "food additive" within the meaning of 21 U.S.C. § 321(s) (1976). I believe, however, as did the district court, that this would be a far different case if DMG were being marketed as a single food ingredient. In that case, the FDA would not be entitled to rely on the "food additive" presumption to condemn plaintiff's product but would instead be obligated to shoulder its normal burden of proving, by a preponderance of the evidence, that DMG was an "adulterated food" within the meaning of 21 U.S.C. § 342(a)(1) (1976) or that the product was "misbranded" under the standards set forth in 21 U.S.C. § 343 (1976).

Limiting the definition of "food additive" to substances which are either added to or sold in combination with other active ingredients not only comports with common usage, but also makes sense from the point of view of informing the consumer. When food substances such as DMG are combined with other "beneficial" ingredients and sold under such unrevealing brand names as "Aangamik 15," "Calcium Pangamate," or "the famous Russian formula," consumers may well be unaware of the presence of, or potential dangers associated with, each of the product's individual ingredients; a broad prophylactic rule such as the burden-shifting "food additive" presumption is therefore appropriate. When substances such as DMG are marketed in pure form, however, *and are properly labeled as such*, consumers can more reasonably be expected to know what they are buying and, thus, can safely be given the opportunity to weigh for themselves the benefits and risks of their purchase. Of course, if DMG is in fact deleterious or dangerous to human health, the FDA may condemn it as an "adulterated food" under 21 U.S.C. § 342(a)(1) (1976)....

FDA may not approve a food additive unless it has been shown to be safe under the conditions of its intended use. Section 409(c)(3)(A) requires a demonstration that, with reasonable certainty, the additive will have no adverse effects on the health of consumers. *See generally* Freedman, *Reasonable Certainty of No Harm: Reviving the Safety Standard for Food Additives, Color Additives, and Animal Drugs,* 7 Ecology L.Q. 245 (1978). FDA is empowered by section 409(c)(1)(A) to prescribe conditions necessary to assure that an additive's use will be safe. Such conditions typically include limitations on the levels of use and can also include restrictions on the foods to which it is added or on the purposes for which it may be used. Occasionally, FDA may also prescribe the form in which an additive may be marketed, *e.g.,* solely as a tabletop sweetener. *See, e.g,* 42 Fed. Reg. 19996 (April 15, 1977) (saccharin); 39 Fed. Reg. 27317 (July 26, 1974) (aspartame). And the act explicitly permits the agency to prescribe labeling for the additive, apparently to provide information to commercial users. In addition, FDA has occasionally prescribed special labeling requirements for the finished foods in which an additive is used. *E.g.,* 21 C.F.R. § 172.110(c) (BHA); 21 C.F.R. § 172.175(b) (sodium nitrite); 21 C.F.R. § 172.375(b) (potassium iodide).

The 1958 Amendment focused on man-made chemicals added to food to perform specific technological functions. There is little evidence suggesting how Congress expected the Amendment to apply to agricultural commodities. Presumably, an apple, sold as such, is not within the reach of the Amendment because it is itself a distinct food, and does not become a "component" of any other food when it is sold in its unprocessed form. When an apple is incorporated in applesauce or in an apple pie, however, it presumably becomes subject to the same analysis under the 1958 Amendment as any other "added" food constituent.

FDA has not published a definitive regulation on this issue, and there is no pertinent case law. However, during the hearings on the 1958 Amendment, "Food Additives," Hearings before a Subcomm. of the House Comm. on Interstate and Foreign Commerce, 85th Cong., 2d Sess. 461–462 (1958), FDA submitted a partial list of GRAS substances which included such common food items as butter, coffee, lemon juice, olive oil, salt, and sugar. In "Nutrition and Human Needs—1972," Hearings before the Senate Select Comm. on Nutrition and Human Needs, 92d Cong., 2d Sess., Part 4B (1972), FDA officials stated that when raw agricultural commodities are used in processed food they become subject to the food additive provisions of the law and thus must be GRAS, prior sanctioned, or the subject of a food additive regulation.

The issue has arisen most directly in FDA's attempts to regulate sassafras tea. In the 1950s agency scientists determined that safrole is an animal carcinogen. The agency therefore prohibited the use of safrole as an ingredient in root beer and other soft drinks, 25 Fed. Reg. 12412 (December 3, 1960). Sassafras tea is made by stripping the bark from the roots of sassafras trees. Sassafras tea beverage is made in the conventional way: the bark is steeped in hot water for several minutes. One of the principal constituents of sassafras bark is safrole.

Following ineluctable logic, FDA concluded that sassafras bark should no longer be permitted to be marketed for use in making sassafras tea. Accordingly, both by regulation and by court enforcement action it banned the product in 38 Fed. Reg. 20040 (July 26, 1973), 39 Fed. Reg. 26748 (July 23, 1974), 39 Fed. Reg. 34172 (September 23, 1974), 41 Fed. Reg. 19207 (May 11, 1976), codified in 21 C.F.R. § 189.180. In *United States v. Articles of Food ... Select Natural Herb Tea, Sassafras, etc.* (C.D. Cal.), 12 FDA Consumer, No. 9, at 32 (November 1978), FDA contended that the product was a food that was, or contained, an unsafe food additive within the meaning of sections 201(s) and 409(a) of the Act. But the agency's claim raised a problem. Safrole in sassafras bark is a natural constituent of a vegetable substance. Many natural foodstuffs contain substances that, if extracted and added to other food, would be both unhealthful and illegal. Spinach, for example, contains oxalic acid. If oxalic acid were extracted from spinach and added to another food, it would be a "food additive," rendering the food to which it was added adulterated. Yet oxalic acid is not regulated as a food additive in spinach. Nor had the agency previously suggested that the addition of spinach to other foods raised food additive issues with respect to the oxalic acid that is necessarily added as part of the spinach.

FDA nonetheless insisted that safrole in sassafras tea was a food additive. While not a food additive as long as it remains in the bark, the agency conceded, safrole becomes a food additive when it emerges into the water. Even if confined to safrole, this view poses problems. Safrole is a natural constituent of a number of food substances, including nutmeg. When nutmeg is added to eggnog, the safrole must emerge from the nutmeg to flavor the eggnog. If safrole were regarded as a food additive in eggnog, presumably cholesterol would be considered a food additive in every food in which milk is used.

To avoid this result, FDA took the position that sassafras bark is not a food in its own right, but serves essentially as a vehicle to convey safrole into water. Nutmeg, although not a food that can be eaten alone, does have food value independent of its safrole content. Likewise spinach and milk are independent foods that can be consumed as such. The components of those foods have no separate legal status in the regulatory scheme for food additives.

Although FDA vigorously pressed these distinctions in the *Select Tea* case, the court declined to rule on the agency's summary judgment motion. In 1977, the judge ordered the case tried. The claimant, over the government's objections, thereupon successfully moved to withdraw its claim. On June 12, 1978, the judge defaulted the tea. Thus, the sassafras tea regulation remains unchallenged.

NOTES

1. *Food Additive Regulations.* FDA food additive regulations are found in 21 C.F.R. Parts 170 *et seq.*

2. *Cyclamate.* After FDA removed cyclamate from the GRAS list in 34 Fed. Reg. 17063 (October 21, 1969) because of evidence of carcinogenicity in animals, the manufacturer continued to test it and eventually petitioned for approval of its use. The agency denied the petition, 41 Fed. Reg. 43754 (October 4, 1976), but granted the manufacturer's demand for a hearing, 42 Fed. Reg. 12515 (March 4, 1977). The Administrative Law Judge likewise ruled that the petition was properly denied, Food Drug Cosm. L. Rep. (CCH) ¶ 38,199 (September 29, 1978), but the Commissioner remanded the matter for further evidence, 44 Fed. Reg. 47620 (August 14, 1979). Frustrated by the lack of progress, the manufacturer successfully sought discovery to determine whether nonstatutory factors were being considered by the agency. *Abbott Laboratories v. Harris,* 481 F. Supp. 74 (N.D. Ill., 1979). The Administrative Law Judge reopened the administrative hearing, took additional evidence, and issued a revised initial decision again upholding the denial of the food additive petition, Food Drug Cosm. L. Rep. (CCH) ¶ 38,026 (February 4, 1980). The district court refused to enjoin the further administrative proceedings because the materials obtained through discovery did not establish that the agency's deliberations had been dominated by political rather than scientific considerations or that it had been acting in bad faith, *Abbott Laboratories v. Harris,* Food Drug Cosm. L. Rep. (CCH) ¶ 38,046 (N.D. Ill. 1980). The court hinted, however, that it would be prepared to compel a prompt disposition of the matter, and the Commissioner issued a final decision denying the food additive petition in 45 Fed. Reg. 61474 (September 16, 1980).

Rather than appeal this ruling the manufacturer undertook yet further studies and analysis and submitted a new food additive petition, 47 Fed. Reg. 51227 (November 12, 1982). In 1984, FDA announced, 49 Fed. Reg. 24953 (June 18, 1984), that the National Academy of Sciences would hold hearings and issue a report on the matter. In "Cyclamate Update," FDA Talk Paper No. T89–35 (May 16, 1989), FDA acknowledged that both its own Cancer Assessment Committee and the Academy had concluded that cyclamate is not a carcinogen, but it also reported that the NAS was unable to determine whether it may be a tumor promoter or a co-carcinogen.

3. *Saccharin.* After FDA proposed to ban saccharin in 42 Fed. Reg. 19996 (April 15, 1977), Congress enacted legislation to suspend any further action, p. 926 *infra.* This statutory moratorium represents the only time Congress has enacted legislation to prevent FDA from banning a food additive. For accounts of the saccharin controversy, *see* "Food Safety: Where Are We?", Senate Comm. on Agriculture, Nutrition and Forestry Comm. Print, 96th Cong., 1st Sess. (1979); Merrill and Taylor, *Saccharin: A Case Study of Government Regulation of Environmental Carcinogens,* III Agric. & Human Values 33 (1986); Whelan and Havender, *Saccharin and the Public Interest,* III Agric. & Human Values 74 (1986); Schultz, *The Bitter Aftertaste of Saccharin,* III Agric. & Human Values 83 (1986).

4. *Aspartame.* The food additive petition for aspartame, 38 Fed. Reg. 5921 (March 5, 1973), was approved and a food additive regulation published in 39 Fed. Reg. 27317 (July 26, 1974). Though FDA initially declined to stay its approval in response to demands for an evidentiary hearing, the agency later reversed itself, 40 Fed. Reg. 56907 (December 5, 1975), because of suspicions

about the reliability of the studies submitted by the manufacturer. After an independent audit validated the study results, FDA announced a hearing before a public board of inquiry in 44 Fed. Reg. 31716 (June 1, 1979), 45 Fed. Reg. 2908 (January 15, 1980). The board's decision, Food Drug Cosm. L. Rep. (CCH) ¶ 38,072 (September 30, 1980), recommended that aspartame not be approved because of unresolved questions regarding aspartame's capacity to cause brain tumors in rodents. The Commissioner, however, reversed the public board of inquiry and approved the additive, 46 Fed. Reg. 3828 (July 24, 1981), 46 Fed. Reg. 50947 (October 16, 1981).

In the years since, FDA has approved additional uses of aspartame in food, which are codified in 21 C.F.R. § 172.804. After approving the sweetener for use in soft drinks, 48 Fed. Reg. 31376 (July 8, 1983), the agency denied requests for an administrative hearing, 49 Fed. Reg. 6672 (February 22, 1984). Its decision was upheld in *Community Nutrition Institute v. Young,* 773 F.2d 1356 (D.C. Cir. 1985). CNI has continued to object to aspartame's approval and FDA has continued to overrule those objections and to deny a public hearing, 53 Fed. Reg. 6595 (March 2, 1988). For discussion of the controversy, *see* GAO, REGULATION OF THE FOOD ADDITIVE ASPARTAME, Rep. No. MWD–76–111 (April 8, 1976); FOOD AND DRUG ADMINISTRATION: SIX FORMER HHS EMPLOYEES' INVOLVEMENT IN ASPARTAME'S APPROVAL, Rep. No. HRD–86–109BR (July 22, 1986); FOOD AND DRUG ADMINISTRATION: FOOD ADDITIVE APPROVAL PROCESS FOLLOWED FOR ASPARTAME, Rep. No. HRD 87–46 (June 18, 1987); " 'NutraSweet'—Health and Safety Concerns," Hearing before the Senate Comm. on Labor and Human Resources, 100th Cong., 1st Sess. (1987).

5. *Radiation.* The definition of a food additive in section 201(s) specifically includes "any source of radiation" in food processing. After years of research, FDA published food additive regulations sanctioning food irradiation in 46 Fed. Reg. 18992 (March 27, 1981), 49 Fed. Reg. 5713 (February 14, 1984), 51 Fed. Reg. 13376 (April 18, 1986), 53 Fed. Reg. 53176 (December 30, 1988), 54 Fed. Reg. 32335 (August 7, 1989). A major point of debate in this proceeding was the need for special labeling to identify irradiated food. FDA determined that food containing an irradiated ingredient would not require special labeling, but that food which itself had been irradiated would require both the international "Radura" logo indicating irradiation and, for two years, in addition a statement that the product has been "treated with radiation" or "treated by irradiation." The obligation to include this statement was subsequently extended to April 1990, 53 Fed. Reg. 4856 (February 18, 1988), 53 Fed. Reg. 12756 (April 18, 1988). In 55 Fed. Reg. 646 (January 8, 1990), 55 Fed. Reg. 14413 (April 18, 1990), FDA made the radiation statement a permanent requirement at least until it can be shown that the logo alone is sufficient to convey to consumers that the product has been irradiated. Members of Congress have taken opposing positions on the practice. *Compare* "The Status of the Technical Infrastructure to Support Domestic Food Irradiation," Hearing before the Subcomm. on Energy Research and Production of the House Comm. on Science and Technology, 98th Cong., 2d Sess. (1984), "Federal Food Irradiation Development and Control Act of 1985," and Hearing before the Subcomm. on Department Operations, Research, and Foreign Agriculture of the House Comm. on Agriculture, 99th Cong., 1st Sess. (1985), *with* "Food Irradiation," Hearing before the Subcomm. on Health and the Environment of the House Comm. on Energy and Commerce, 100th Cong., 1st Sess. (1987).

6. *Biotechnology.* In FOOD BIOTECHNOLOGY: PRESENT AND FU-TURE, Vols. I and II (February 19, 1988), FDA estimated that in 1986–1987 over 150 companies were applying biotechnology to the development of products that would probably require regulation as food additives. In 53 Fed. Reg. 33182 (August 30, 1988), FDA announced that the Federation of American Societies for Experimental Biology (FASEB) would undertake "a study of which scientific concepts and considerations are most appropriately used to determine the regulatory status of foods and food ingredients that are produced by new technologies." For a further discussion of the impact of biotechnology on food and related products, *see* Chapter IX.

7. *Testing Guidelines.* Although FDA established general principles governing toxicity testing for food ingredients as early as the 1940s, Lehman *et al. Procedures for the Appraisal of the Toxicity of Chemicals in Foods*, 4 FDC L.Q. 412 (1949), for many years it resisted issuing specific toxicology guidelines. At the completion of its review of the GRAS list, however, the agency developed a set of toxicological standards for safety evaluation of food additives and color additives, which it subsequently made publicly available in 47 Fed. Reg. 46141 (October 15, 1982).

8. *Accidental Additives.* Compare Gerber Products Co. v. Fisher Tank Co., 833 F.2d 505 (4th Cir. 1987), holding that a liner on the interior of a hot water storage tank used in processing baby foods was an indirect and unapproved food additive, thereby rendering all processed products adulterated, *with Burke Pest Control, Inc. v. Joseph Schlitz Brewing Co.*, 438 So. 2d 95 (Fla. 1983), holding that a pesticide introduced into food during fumigation of the food plant was not a food additive but an accidental additive, whose legal status must be determined under section 402(a)(1) rather than under section 409.

9. *Specifications for Food Additives.* Many food additive regulations contain chemical specifications. FDA has supported the National Academy of Sciences' development of the FOOD CHEMICALS CODEX, a compilation of monographs establishing food grade specifications for food substances. FDA periodically publishes notices providing an opportunity for public comment on changes to Codex monographs, *e.g.,* 50 Fed. Reg. 49131 (November 29, 1985), and adopts the specific specifications adopted for particular substances, *e.g.,* 53 Fed. Reg. 13134 (April 21, 1988), 53 Fed. Reg. 51272 (December 21, 1988) (aspartame).

10. *Diethylene Glycol.* In July 1985, FDA and BATF discovered that some imported wine contained a highly toxic industrial chemical, diethylene glycol—the very chemical that, 48 years earlier, had been used as a solvent in the elixir sulfanilamide product that killed more than 100 people and galvanized Congress to enact the new drug provisions as part of the 1938 Act, *see* p. 476 *supra*. The substance had been deliberately added to sweeten the wine and thus was an illegal food additive. The actions taken by the two agencies to protect against further importation of wine containing diethylene glycol or other contaminants were discussed in "Federal Efforts to Identify and Remove Contaminated Imported Wines," Hearing before a Subcomm. of the House Comm. on Government Operations, 99th Cong., 2nd Sess. (1986).

11. *Cyclic Review.* In the late 1970s, FDA announced its intention to undertake a "cyclic review" of all food additives, to assure that past food safety decisions remained currently justifiable. "Food Additives: Competitive, Regulatory, and Safety Problems," Hearings before the Senate Select Comm. on Small Business, 95th Cong., 1st Sess. (1977). Although originally intended to be

a public process conducted in accordance with formal procedures, Rulis and Ronk, *Cyclic Review—Looking Backward or Looking Forward?*, 36 FDC L.J. 156 (1981), the review has instead been conducted internally without published procedures, timetables, or criteria other than the toxicological standards made publicly available in 47 Fed. Reg. 46141 (October 15, 1982).

12. *GRAS and Prior Sanction Exceptions*. It has often been proposed that regulation of direct food additives should be tightened by eliminating the exclusion of GRAS and prior sanctioned substances. *E.g.*, GAO, NEED FOR MORE EFFECTIVE REGULATION OF DIRECT ADDITIVES TO FOOD, Rep. No. HRD–80–90 (August 14, 1980). When closely scrutinized, however, this proposition has been rejected because of the huge number of raw agricultural commodities and other common food substances that would need to be subjected to animal toxicity tests, the resulting thousands of petitions requiring safety evaluations, and the development of food additive regulations specifying safe conditions of use.

13. *Patent Term Extension*. Under the Patent Term Restoration and Drug Price Competition Act of 1984, p. 485 *infra*, food additives are eligible for patent term extension. *See, e.g.*, 54 Fed. Reg. 28289 (September 15, 1989), relating to extension of the patent life of an indirect food additive.

INTERIM FOOD ADDITIVES

In 35 Fed. Reg. 12062 (July 28, 1970), FDA permitted the continued use of a food additive, brominated vegetable oil (BVO), in fruit-flavored beverages on an interim basis pending additional testing to resolve issues about its safety. This order was upheld in *Jacobson v. Edwards,* Food Drug Cosm. L. Rep. (CCH) ¶ 40,817 (D.D.C. 1971):

> The standard here is not a standard of safety in the sense of absolute, unqualified safety. It is in all of these matters conditional because, obviously, the kind of use, the nature of the use, the amount of the use cannot be dissociated from the absolute question as to whether or not a particular additive may be harmful to animals or harmful to human beings, inasmuch as almost anything is harmful to animals or human beings if used in sufficient quantity and in sufficient concentration.

> I think a fair reading of the Statute as a whole justifies the action that has been taken here in issuing an interim order, inasmuch as the findings contained in the letter of January 5, 1971 make it clear that the Commissioner has determined that the evidence available demonstrates with reasonable certainty that no harm will result from the interim use of BVO, and that the public health is being protected as long as the conditions set forth in that letter are complied with....

The court also concluded that the case had been improperly filed in the district court. The D.C. Circuit affirmed the district court in an unpublished order (December 15, 1972). Subsequently, FDA promulgated criteria and procedures for issuing interim food additive regulations, 37 Fed. Reg. 6207 (March 25, 1972), 37 Fed. Reg. 25705 (December 2, 1972), codified in 21 C.F.R. Part 180.. Section 180.1 of these regulations sets forth the following criteria for an interim food additive regulation.

§ 180.1 General.

(a) Substances having a history of use in food for human consumption or in food contact surfaces may at any time have their safety or functionality brought into question by new information that in itself is not conclusive. An interim food additive regulation for the use of any such substance may be promulgated in this subpart when new information raises a substantial question about the safety or functionality of the substance but there is a reasonable certainty that the substance is not harmful and that no harm to the public health will result from the continued use of the substance for a limited period of time while the question raised is being resolved by further study.

(b) No interim food additive regulation may be promulgated if the new information is conclusive with respect to the question raised or if there is a reasonable likelihood that the substance is harmful or that continued use of the substance will result in harm to the public health.

The interim food additive order for brominated vegetable oil was extended in 1974, 39 Fed. Reg. 14611 (April 25, 1974), 39 Fed. Reg. 36113 (October 8, 1974), and remains in effect, codified in 21 C.F.R. § 180.30, twenty years after it was promulgated.

---

c. GRAS Ingredients

The FD&C Act does not prescribe procedures for determining whether an ingredient is GRAS. The statutory definition of a food additive in section 201(s) is self-executing. In 1958, prior to enactment of the Food Additives Amendment, FDA submitted to Congress a partial list of "chemical food additives" that it would regard as GRAS, including such common food substances as brandy, butter, citric, acid, cloves, coffee, cream, gelatin, lard, margarine, molasses, mustard, paprika, pepper, salt, sugar, vinegar, and wine. Shortly after the passage of the Food Additives Amendment, FDA issued, and from time to time has amended, a nonexclusive list of ingredients that the agency was prepared to acknowledge were GRAS—and therefore could lawfully be used without affirmative approval, e.g., 23 Fed. Reg. 9511 (December 9, 1958), 24 Fed. Reg. 9368 (November 20, 1959), 25 Fed. Reg. 880 (February 2, 1960), 25 Fed. Reg. 7332 (August 4, 1960), and 26 Fed. Reg. 938 (January 31, 1961), now codified in 21 C.F.R. Parts 182 and 184. FDA has stated, 21 C.F.R. § 170.30(d), that the GRAS lists in 21 C.F.R. Parts 182 and 184 "do not include all substances that are generally recognized as safe for their intended use in food" and that "it is impracticable to list all such substances that are GRAS." Thus, FDA has acknowledged that a food manufacturer may determine for itself whether an ingredient that it desires to use can be considered GRAS. 50 Fed. Reg. 27294 (July 2, 1985), 53 Fed. Reg. 16544 (May 10, 1988). *See* Grisanti, *Legal Aspects of Technical Problems and Chemical Additives,* 26 FDC L.J. 588 (1971).

This theoretical freedom of food processors to determine initially which ingredients require FDA licensure has little practical significance for widely used ingredients. Very few processors will purchase ingredients for which the supplier cannot provide documentation of FDA approval or acknowledgement as GRAS. Should a manufacturer independently conclude that an ingredient is GRAS it runs the risk that FDA may disagree and initiate regulatory action against its product. In such an action, however, the agency would have to prove that the ingredient was not GRAS. Neither the ingredient's absence from FDA's GRAS lists nor the manufacturer's failure to consult the agency in advance would be relevant.

Under this system numerous food ingredients have come into common use based on the assumption by manufacturers, sometimes but by no means always endorsed by FDA, that they are GRAS.

UNITED STATES v. AN ARTICLE OF FOOD

United States Court of Appeals, First Circuit, 1985.
752 F.2d 11.

WEIGEL, Senior District Judge.

This is an appeal from the district court's grant of summary judgment. Appellant Coco Rico, Inc., manufactures in Puerto Rico a coconut concentrate called Coco Rico for use as an ingredient in soft drinks. The Coco Rico concentrate sold to beverage bottlers in Puerto Rico contains potassium nitrate, added for the purpose of developing and fixing a desirable color and flavor. On March 10, 1982, the United States instituted *in rem* proceedings against three lots of bottled soft drinks located on the premises of Puerto Rican bottlers. The soft drinks contained Coco Rico concentrate. The government charged that potassium nitrate constitutes an "unsafe" food additive, making the beverages "adulterated" and subject to forfeiture.....

First, Coco Rico claims that Caragay's affidavit is sufficient to show the existence of a factual issue as to whether potassium nitrate is "generally recognized" by qualified experts as having been scientifically shown to be safe. To fall within this exception, the substance must be generally recognized as safe *under the conditions of its intended use.* The burden of proving general recognition of safe use is placed on the proponent of the food substance in question. Caragay's affidavit contained only statements to the effect that she knows of no conclusive scientific evidence that the use of potassium nitrate in beverages is *unsafe,* or that the health effects of potassium nitrate when used in beverages differ from those caused by its use in meats. Even if these allegations are true, they are insufficient to meet Coco Rico's burden of proving that the use of potassium nitrate in beverages is generally recognized by experts as *safe* based on scientific evidence.

For similar reasons, Coco Rico's second argument based on "common use" of potassium nitrate must also fail. Again, a substance may be excluded from classification as a "food additive" only if experience based on common use provides a basis for general recognition by scientists that the substance is safe *under the conditions of its intended use.* The evidence submitted by Coco Rico tends to show that nitrates are naturally present in many foodstuffs, particularly vegetables, and that they have been used for many centuries to cure meats. No evidence was submitted to show that potassium nitrate has long been added to beverages. Consequently, there is no issue of fact as to whether common experience could show that potassium nitrate is not a "food additive" when used in beverages.

NOTES

1. *Lack of GRAS Status.* In *United States v. Articles of Food ... Buffalo Jerky,* 456 F. Supp. 207 (D. Neb. 1978), *aff'd per curiam,* 594 F.2d 869 (8th Cir. 1979), the court concluded that patties made from buffalo (bison) meat, sodium nitrate, sodium nitrite, and other ingredients violated section 409 because nitrate and nitrite are not GRAS and no food additive regulation permitted their use for this purpose, though it recognized that FDA had approved these substances for use in pork products. *See also United States v. An Article of Food,* 678 F.2d 735 (7th Cir. 1982); *United States v. Article of Food ... Orotic Acid,* 414 F. Supp. 793 (E.D. Mo. 1976).

2. *Simplesse.* FDA asked for a GRAS affirmation petition for an ingredient that consisted only of microparticularized egg and milk protein. Eighteen months later the agency affirmed its GRAS status in 55 Fed. Reg. 6384 (February 23, 1990).

3. *Other GRAS Ingredients.* FDA has affirmed the GRAS status of oils from menhaden fish, one of the most widely consumed fish in the world, 54 Fed. Reg. 38219 (September 15, 1989), "Menhaden Oils Recognized as Safe," FDA Talk Paper No. T89–74 (November 30, 1989), and an enzyme, chymosin, produced by recombinant DNA technology for use in making cheese, 55 Fed. Reg. 10932 (March 23, 1990), "Enzyme for Producing Cheese," FDA Talk Paper No. T90–15 (March 26, 1990).

FDA does not have a complete inventory of GRAS ingredients, and it lacks complete information about the extent and levels of their use. Following FDA's action removing cyclamate from GRAS status in 34 Fed. Reg. 17063 (October 21, 1969), President Nixon ordered a complete review of the GRAS list in his Consumer Message of October 30, 1969, "Consumer Protection," 5 Weekly Comp. Pres. Doc. 1516 (November 3, 1969). In response FDA issued a substantial number of regulations establishing the procedures for this review and the criteria for determining GRAS status, as well as regulations codifying the substantive results of the review.

The agency announced National Academy of Science surveys of industry production and use of GRAS substances in 36 Fed. Reg. 20546 (October 23, 1971) and 42 Fed. Reg. 30894 (June 17, 1977). Procedures governing affirmation of GRAS status or determination of food additive status, and establishing interim food additive regulations requiring additional study while a substance remains on the market, were promulgated in 37 Fed. Reg. 6207 (March 25, 1972), 37 Fed. Reg. 25705 (December 2, 1972), now codified in 21 C.F.R. §§ 170.35, 170.38, and 180.1. A comprehensive status report on the GRAS list review was published in 38 Fed. Reg. 20054 (July 26, 1973).

As part of the GRAS list review, FDA concluded that it would be appropriate to include in the resulting regulations limitations on the uses of such substances. Accordingly, the agency undertook to define 43 general food categories and 32 general physical or technical functional effects for which ingredients may be added to foods in 38 Fed. Reg. 20044 (July 26, 1973), 39 Fed. Reg. 34173 (September 23, 1974), now codified as 21 C.F.R. § 170.3(n) and (o). Substances affirmed by FDA as GRAS under this procedure were deleted from the old GRAS list in 21 C.F.R. Part 182 and are identified in new regulations, 21 C.F.R. Part 184.

One of the main issues confronting FDA was determining the criteria for GRAS status. The agency initially adopted GRAS criteria in 35 Fed. Reg. 18623 (December 8, 1970), 36 Fed. Reg. 12093 (June 25, 1971). Five years later it issued revised final regulations.

GENERAL RECOGNITION OF SAFETY AND
PRIOR SANCTIONS FOR FOOD INGREDIENTS
41 Federal Register 53600 (December 7, 1976).

The Commissioner proposed to (1) Require that general recognition of safety through scientific procedures must ordinarily be based upon published literature; (2) Recognize that GRAS status based on scientific procedures requires the same quality and quantity of scientific evidence as would be required for approval of a food additive regulation; (3) Define "common use in food" as used in section 201(s) of the act to mean a substantial history of consumption of a substance by a significant number of consumers in the United States; (4) Recognize that GRAS status based upon common use in food does not require the same quality or quantity of scientific evidence that would be required for approval of a food additive regulation; (5) Recognize three categories of ingredients affirmed as GRAS; (6) Recognize that GRAS affirmation proceedings should consider the manufacturing process involved; and (7) Provide for procedures for considering the applicability of prior sanctions. . . .

One comment . . . argued that longtime use by consumers does not establish safety, and that FDA should not permit use of a substance in food unless it had been established as safe by appropriate scientific studies. . . . The Commissioner notes that the criteria set forth in [§ 170.30] interpret section 201(s) of the act as requiring the same quantity and quality of scientific evidence to establish that a substance is GRAS as is required to establish the safety of a newly used food additive, if the substance was first used in food after January 1, 1958. For substances in common use in food before January 1, 1958, however, the act is explicit in requiring FDA to consider experience based on such use in determining whether a substance is GRAS. Indeed, the act permits a manufacturer to determine that a substance is GRAS considering only experience based on common use in food if the substance was used in food before January 1, 1958. Thus, for those substances that were widely used before 1958, under the terms of the statute FDA must consider available data and may not prohibit use of a substance merely because tests that would be required for new food additives have not been performed....

Comments opposed the criterion ... providing that the benefit contributed by a substance shall be considered in determining whether it is "safe" for use. One comment stated that the social utility of a substance is not to be judged by FDA, but is a determination specifically reserved for the consumer to make in a free and open marketplace....

The Commissioner concludes that it is appropriate to recognize that the benefit contributed by a substance is inevitably a factor to be considered in determining whether a particular substance is "safe" (or generally recognized as "safe") for its intended use. The term "safe" is to be given its ordinary meaning, and in its common usage the term is understood to carry an assessment of benefits and risks. It is true, as the comment states, that minor food additives are not approved at levels that may present a hazard to the normal consumer. This result is required by the act because the benefit of a minor food additive is too small to justify the imposition of a known risk to normal consumers; use of such ingredient at levels that may present a hazard to the normal consumer would not be "safe." However, this result does not necessarily follow in the case of important food additives. For example, if it were found that a major food source such as meat or grain was associated with the development of chronic diseases in normal individuals, it would not necessarily follow that the food was unsafe within the meaning of the act. The ordinary understanding of the term "safe" would require some benefit-to-risk analysis in such circumstances.

Another example relates to the incidence of allergic reactions to particular food ingredients. Adverse reactions caused by allergy are clearly a consideration in determining whether a food ingredient is safe. Ordinarily, the incidence of allergic reactions from a food additive cannot be considered because data and test protocols do not exist. When data exist, however, they may be considered, and an assessment of benefits and risks becomes relevant. For example, if it were determined that both a particular emulsifier and a particular fruit resulted in the same unusually high incidence of allergic reactions, one might reasonably conclude that the emulsifier was not safe but that the fruit was safe. Such conclusions would simply represent common understanding of the concept of safety....

The Commissioner has, however, deleted from the regulations the reference to consideration of benefits on the ground that this separate consideration is legitimately included within the concept of safety as used in the act. Furthermore, explicitly retaining the criterion of benefit in the regulations might be construed as requiring routine formal analysis of a factor that the agency will only occasionally need to take into account, because the agency's general guidelines will result in disapproval of food additives that may cause toxic effects in normal individuals.*

One comment opposed the provision in [§ 181.5(d)] requiring any person who intends to assert or rely on a prior sanction of which the Commissioner is not aware to submit proof of its existence when that prior sanction is inconsistent with a proposed affirmation of GRAS status or a proposed food additive regulation....

The Commissioner concludes that it is necessary for proper functioning of the agency's ingredient review program to require that persons holding prior sanctions make their existence known when the agency is proposing regulations that are inconsistent with the continued use of an ingredient in accordance with a prior sanction.... Several factors support the Commissioner's conclusion: First, it is inequitable if one manufacturer who knows of a prior sanction is permitted to take advantage of it, while his competitors are restrained by regulations arising from the agency's review of ingredient safety. If the prior-sanctioned use is safe, all users should be permitted to rely upon it. If it is not safe, it should be brought to the agency's attention so that appropriate conclusions can be made. Second, enforcement would be highly inefficient if defenses to the agency's conclusions made during rule making are not raised until the time of enforcement.... Third, the issue of whether a prior-sanctioned use continues to be safe should be dealt with in an administrative proceeding, in which all relevant data and information may be economically marshaled and considered, rather than in a judicial trial, which requires the testimony of expert witnesses and in which the finder of fact is a layman....

The Commissioner notes that the specification of manufacturing methods in GRAS affirmation regulations represents a basic difference between GRAS affirmation and food additive regulations, but does not represent an inconsistency. Both food additive and GRAS affirmation petitions require that methods of manufacture be carefully evaluated, as this information may be related to the final purity and safety of the product. Any change in the manufacturing process for a food additive requires a new food additive regulation if the process introduces new substances that are not GRAS into food. Thus, the policy for food additives and GRAS substances is identical. However, in the case of food additives, the manufacturing process is not generally specified in the regulation because under section 301(j) of the act confidential production information may not be disclosed....

NOTES

1. *Legislative History.* In Congressional testimony two years before the Food Additives Amendment was enacted, FDA Commissioner Larrick explained that "[t]here are hundreds of substances in our dietary that have been used for 40, 50, 60, 70, or 80 years, but they have never been tested. There has been no occasion to test them because the common acceptance of them as safe has come

* [FDA Commissioner Donald Kennedy repudiated this discussion in his first decision on DES, 44 Fed. Reg. 54852, 58482–83 (September 21, 1979), p. 888 *infra*.]

about through long usage, but you could not prove through scientific methods whether they are safe or not...." "Federal Food, Drug, and Cosmetic Act (Chemical Additives in Food)," Hearings before a Subcomm. of the House Comm. on Interstate and Foreign Commerce, 84th Cong., 2d Sess. (1956).

2. *Change in Status.* Under section 201(s), a food additive could theoretically become GRAS, thus no longer requiring a food additive regulation. FDA has not yet revoked any food additive regulation on this ground, and is unlikely to do so. Conversely, GRAS status does not permanently exempt a substance from the definition of "food additive." FDA has revoked GRAS determinations on the basis of new data relating to safety. *See, e.g.,* 34 Fed. Reg. 17063 (October 21, 1969) (cyclamate).

3. *Procedural Rights.* An approved food additive enjoys greater procedural protection than GRAS ingredients. Revocation of a substance's GRAS status can be accomplished summarily by court enforcement action or by informal rulemaking to add it to the list of banned food substances, 21 C.F.R. Part 189, created by FDA in 38 Fed. Reg. 20040 (July 26, 1973), 39 Fed. Reg. 34172 (September 23, 1974). Any revocation of a food additive regulation is subject to objection and a demand for a formal evidentiary hearing under section 409.

4. *Applicability of Delaney Clause.* Because GRAS ingredients do not fall within the definition of "food additive," they are not technically subject to the Delaney Clause. In practice, however, before the mid–1970s the Delaney principle prevented the introduction or continued use of a GRAS ingredient that is found in appropriate tests to induce cancer in experimental animals. Such a finding was regarded as undermining any basis for general expert recognition of the safety of the ingredient, thereby rendering it a food additive for which affirmative FDA approval was required. This analysis explains FDA's actions in the case of cyclamate, which prior to 1970 had been widely used based on FDA's determination that it was GRAS. A report by the principal manufacturer that cyclamate might be an animal carcinogen was viewed as destroying its GRAS status, making its continued use unlawful overnight.

Beginning in the mid–1970s, however, as evidence accumulated that virtually all food contains some substances that are carcinogenic in test animals, FDA began to rethink this approach. Although officials continued to state publicly that a carcinogenic food substance would not be regarded as GRAS, the agency has never challenged heretofore GRAS ingredients that have been shown to contain carcinogenic constituents. *See, e.g.,* FDA's responses to questions relating to natural carcinogens in the food supply, "Agriculture, Rural Development and Related Agencies Appropriations for 1984," Hearings before a Subcomm. of the House Comm. on Appropriations, 98th Cong., 1st Sess., Part 4, at 473–77 (1983).

5. *Prior Sanction Status.* The cyclamate episode illustrates an important distinction between ingredients that are excepted from the food additive definition because they are GRAS and ingredients that are permanently exempt because FDA or USDA sanctioned their use prior to 1958. An ingredient's status as GRAS is always vulnerable to the discovery of new evidence casting doubt on its safety. An ingredient that ceases to be GRAS falls automatically within the definition of food additive, and must then be approved by FDA for its use to be lawful.

6. *Limitations on Use.* When FDA initiated the GRAS list review, all of the regulations promulgated in 21 C.F.R. Part 184 affirming particular sub-

stances as GRAS were required to contain specific use level limitations based upon the various NAS food consumption surveys and other information available to the agency. Later FDA revised its regulations, 47 Fed. Reg. 39199 (September 7, 1982), 48 Fed. Reg. 48457 (October 19, 1983), to require that use of all affirmed GRAS substances must comply with current good manufacturing practice, and to allow flexibility in deciding when use limitations need be included in GRAS affirmation regulations.

7. *Indirect Uses.* In 47 Fed. Reg. 27817 (June 25, 1982), 48 Fed. Reg. 48456 (October 19, 1983), FDA clarified that any substance affirmed as GRAS for direct food use is also regarded as GRAS for indirect food use.

8. *Options Open to FDA.* Under 21 C.F.R. § 170.35, upon receiving a GRAS affirmation petition FDA may determine (1) that the substance is GRAS, or (2) that the substance is a safe food additive and promulgate a regulation under section 409, or (3) that the substance is a food additive for which there is inadequate evidence of safety and ban its use. *See, e.g.,* the notice determining that a high intensity sweetener, miracle fruit, is not GRAS and is an unapproved food additive in 42 Fed. Reg. 26467 (May 24, 1977); and the notice determining that a quaternary ammonium chloride combination is not GRAS but is a safe (and approved) food additive, 50 Fed. Reg. 3890 (January 29, 1985).

GRAS STATUS OF SULFITE AND CAFFEINE

1. *Sulfite.* Based upon a FASEB evaluation and report, FDA proposed in 47 Fed. Reg. 29956 (July 9, 1982) to affirm the GRAS status of sulfiting agents in food. After receiving reports of allergic reactions to sulfites, however, the agency announced the formation of an Ad Hoc Advisory Committee on Hypersensitivity to Sulfiting Agents in Food in 49 Fed. Reg. 15021 (April 16, 1984). In 49 Fed. Reg. 27994 (July 9, 1984), the agency announced that it would reconsider the GRAS status of sulfites on the basis of a report to be prepared by a different body, the Ad Hoc Review Panel on the Reexamination of the GRAS Status of Sulfiting Agents. The tentative report of the Ad Hoc Review Panel was made available for comment and public discussion in 49 Fed. Reg. 42984 (October 25, 1984). As an interim measure, FDA notified distributors of shrimp products that shrimp may contain no more than 100 ppm of sulfite and that the presence of sulfite must be declared, 50 Fed. Reg. 2957 (January 23, 1985). After receiving the final report of the Ad Hoc Review Panel, 50 Fed. Reg. 9131 (March 6, 1985), FDA proposed to revoke the GRAS status of sulfite for use on fruits and vegetables intended to be served or sold raw to consumers, 50 Fed. Reg. 32830 (August 14, 1985), 51 Fed. Reg. 25021 (July 9, 1986). The agency proposed also to revoke the GRAS status of sulfite for use in fresh potatoes served or sold unpackaged and unlabeled to consumers, 52 Fed. Reg. 46968 (December 10, 1987), and to place specific limits on the use of sulfites in particular food categories, 53 Fed. Reg. 51065 (December 19, 1988). When FDA revoked the GRAS status of sulfites for use on fresh unlabeled potatoes in 55 Fed. Reg. 9826 (March 15, 1990), the industry initiated litigation that continued as of March 1, 1991.

While FDA was addressing the safety of sulfites, it was concurrently dealing with their labeling. Based upon the advice of the Ad Hoc Advisory Committee, the agency required, 50 Fed. Reg. 13306 (April 3, 1985), 51 Fed. Reg. 25012 (July 9, 1986), codified in 21 C.F.R. § 101.100(a)(4), that any added sulfite that is detectable at 10 ppm or more must be labeled as an ingredient. BATF imposed a similar requirement for alcoholic beverages, 50 Fed. Reg. 26001 (June 24, 1985), 51 Fed. Reg. 34706 (September 30, 1986). FDA has also specifically proposed to extend the labeling requirement to any sulfite in a standardized food, 53 Fed. Reg. 51062 (December 19, 1988). Remarkably, FDA accomplished all this with a single congressional hearing, "Sulfites," Hearing before the Subcomm. on Oversight and Investigations of the House Comm. on Energy and Commerce, 99th Cong., 1st Sess. (1985), and without litigation.

In the first few months of 1983, FDA took the position that, under its three model food sanitation codes, p. 266 *supra*, the use of sulfite on fresh fruits, fresh vegetables, and other raw food is considered safe only if consumers are informed by signs or some other form of public notice. The National Restaurant Association notified its members, who responded by abandoning use of sulfites for salad bars and other related purposes. "Sulfiting Agents Update," FDA Talk Paper No. T83–12 (March 11, 1983); "Sulfiting Agents—Update," FDA Talk Paper No. T83–15 (April 5, 1983).

2. *Caffeine.* FDA placed caffeine on the original GRAS list, 26 Fed. Reg. 938 (January 31, 1961), and it remains listed as of June 30, 1990, 21 C.F.R. § 182.1180. Following a report from FASEB recommending that caffeine no longer be considered GRAS in cola beverages, FDA proposed to revoke its GRAS status and to promulgate an interim food additive regulation requiring additional studies, 45 Fed. Reg. 69816 (October 21, 1980). When FDA allowed additional time for public comments, a consumer group sued to compel the agency to ban caffeine immediately. The court dismissed the action, *Federation of Homemakers, Inc. v. Harris,* Food Drug Cosm. L. Rep. (CCH) ¶ 38,100 (D.D.C. 1981), holding that the FASEB report was not binding on FDA, which in any case was not guilty of undue delay.

FDA subsequently undertook, 46 Fed. Reg. 32453 (June 23, 1981), an audit of the pivotal teratogenicity study on caffeine, which revealed serious flaws. In the meantime, users of caffeine, with the aid of the Freedom of Information Act, scoured FDA archives for correspondence relating to caffeine and found several FDA documents that they claimed supported a prior sanction. On May 20, 1987, FDA proposed to recognize a prior sanction for caffeine in nonalcoholic carbonated beverages, 52 Fed. Reg. 18923. As of June 30, 1990, it had taken no final action on this matter. *See also Caution Light on Caffeine,* 14 FDA Consumer, No. 8, at 6 (October 1980); "Caffeine Content Evaluation Updated," FDA Talk Paper No. T83–42 (October 19, 1983).

FMALI HERB, INC. v. HECKLER

United States Court of Appeals, Ninth Circuit, 1983.
715 F.2d 1385.

FLETCHER, Circuit Judge: ....

Appellant Fmali Herb, Inc., is an importer of Chinese food products. In its business, Fmali wishes to import foods containing herbs traditional in China that have never been widely used in the United States. One such food is a jelly or honey-like product, known as renshenfengwangjiang, that normally contains schizandra seed. The FDA has ruled that renshenfengwangjiang may be sold in the United States only if it does not contain schizandra seed, because schizandra seed has not been scientifically tested and because it was not commonly used in the United States prior to 1958. The FDA held that evidence of long and widespread use of schizandra seed in China is not admissible in aid of establishing that schizandra seed is safe for human consumption.

By promulgating the regulation defining "common use in food" to mean only common use within the United States, the FDA has imposed a restriction not required by the literal terms of the statute. The FDA's reasons for doing so were expressed at the time the regulation was issued:

> The Commissioner believes that the type of experience based on common use in food that will support a GRAS determination must involve use in the United States, and not solely in foreign countries. Reported use in foreign countries often cannot be verified, and in any event the experience based on such use cannot be monitored or evaluated. Food consumption patterns and differences between cultures make it impossible to assess whether a history of use abroad would be comparable to a history of use in the United States.

39 Fed. Reg. 34,195 (1974).

We agree for the most part with the concerns expressed by the FDA. Many residents of areas outside the United States have shorter life expectancies than do Americans. Foreign populations also suffer from higher incidences of some diseases, so that generalizations about the safety of their dietary habits may be unreliable. But it is an illogical and, we think, unwarranted constriction of the statute to rule that evidence of long use of a substance in food outside the United States can *never* provide probative evidence of safety. Counsel for the FDA admitted this point in argument before the district court, when he stated that "there are countries in the world, like West Germany or something, where one might be able to accept" prior use of an ingredient to establish safety, but added that the FDA does not believe that evidence of use in "Guam" or "Southeast Asia" could be accepted. The statute provides no basis for a purely ethnocentric distinction of this kind, divorced from demographic considerations.....

NOTE

Following the *Fmali Herb* case, FDA revised its GRAS regulations in 50 Fed. Reg. 27294 (July 2, 1985), 53 Fed. Reg. 16544 (May 10, 1988), codified in 21 C.F.R. § 170.30(c)(2). The preambles, however, left little doubt about the agency's continued reluctance to accept foreign use as adequate evidence of GRAS status.

d. Prior Sanctioned Ingredients

Section 201(s)(4) constitutes a genuine "grandfather" clause for food ingredients that FDA or the Department of Agriculture had affirmatively approved prior to the enactment of section 409 under the FD&C Act (but not the 1906 Act), the Poultry Products Inspection Act, or the Federal Meat Inspection Act. While prior to 1958 FDA lacked statutory authority to license food ingredients for general use, it routinely responded, as did USDA, to requests for an opinion about the safety of individual ingredients. In addition, FDA exercised premarket control over, and thus approved, ingredients permitted to be used in foods covered by standards of identity. USDA had issued formal regulations describing permitted uses of many ingredients in meat and poultry products, *e.g.*, 13 FDC L.J. 834, 840, 860 (1958), and in some instances FDA formally acknowledged that USDA had sanctioned certain substances for food use. An ingredient's prior sanction status does not depend upon a contemporary evaluation of its utility or its safety, but rests solely on the fact of prior approval by one of the two agencies.

PROPOSAL REGARDING REGULATION OF PRIOR–SANCTIONED FOOD INGREDIENTS

37 Federal Register 16407 (August 12, 1972).

... [A] food ingredient subject to a prior sanction may not be regulated under the food additive provisions of the law. Such an ingredient may, however, be regulated under the general adulteration and misbranding provisions of the Act, and in particular may be banned from food if found to be a "poisonous or deleterious substance" in violation of section 402(a)(1) of the Act.

The Food and Drug Administration, between 1938 and 1958, reaffirmed many sanctions or approvals granted under the Federal Food and Drugs Act of 1906, and also granted additional sanctions and approvals. The U.S. Department of Agriculture has similarly granted many sanctions and approvals. Not all of these sanctions and approvals can be ascertained because of the destruction of old records and the retirement of personnel involved in these matters. The Food and Drug Administration has requested information on prior sanctions (35 F.R. 5810) in an effort to make its files on these matters more complete.

Whether or not a food ingredient is used as a result of a determination that it is GRAS, or pursuant to a food additive regulation, or as a result of a prior sanction, the basis for such use should be a matter of public record. The Commissioner has therefore determined to expand Subpart E under Part 121 [now 21 C.F.R. Part 181] within which will be established regulations governing all prior-sanctioned direct and indirect food ingredients known to the Commissioner.

New scientific information requires, on occasion, that additional limitations be placed on the use of prior-sanctioned ingredients. Accordingly, the Commissioner has concluded that a procedure should also be established under which a regulation in Subpart E stating the existence of a prior sanction may be established or amended to impose limitations upon the use of the ingredient when scientific data justify such limitations.....

NOTES

1. *Final Regulation.* FDA's final regulations, promulgated in 38 Fed. Reg. 12737 (May 15, 1973) and amended in 39 Fed. Reg. 42746 (December 6, 1974) and 42 Fed. Reg. 52814 (September 30, 1977), afford the agency substantial control over prior-sanctioned food ingredients:

§ 181.1 General

(a) An ingredient whose use in food or food packaging is subject to a prior sanction or approval within the meaning of section 201(s)(4) of the act is exempt from classification as a food additive. The Commissioner will publish in this part all known prior sanctions. Any interested person may submit to the Commissioner a request for publication of a prior sanction, supported by evidence to show that it falls within section 201(s)(4) of the act.

(b) Based upon scientific data or information that shows that use of a prior-sanctioned food ingredient may be injurious to health, and thus in violation of section 402 of the act, the Commissioner will establish or amend an applicable prior sanction regulation to impose whatever limitations or conditions are necessary for the safe use of the ingredient, or to prohibit use of the ingredient.

(c) Where appropriate, an emergency action level may be issued for a prior-sanctioned substance, pending the issuance of a final regulation in accordance with paragraph (b) of this section. Such an action level shall be issued pursuant to section 402(a) of the act to identify, based upon available data, conditions of use of the substance that may be injurious to health. Such an action level shall be issued in a notice published in the FEDERAL REGISTER and shall be followed as soon as practicable by a proposed regulation in accordance with paragraph (b) of this section. Where the available data demonstrate that the substance may be injurious at any level, use of the substance may be prohibited. The identification of a prohibited substance may be made in Part 189 of this chapter when appropriate.

2. *Sanctions Under the 1906 Act.* Section 201(s)(4) only recognizes prior sanctions "granted ... pursuant to this [the FD&C] Act," the Poultry Products Inspection Act, and the Federal Meat Inspection Act. Sanctions granted under the 1906 Act and not revoked under the 1938 Act are included, however, if FDA continued to rely upon them after the enactment of the 1938 Act.

3. *Lead in Tin Cans.* In 44 Fed. Reg. 5123 (August 31, 1979), FDA issued an advance notice of proposed rulemaking, requesting evidence of a prior sanction for lead in lead-soldered tin cans as food packaging. As of June 30, 1990, FDA had taken no further action. The most recent discussion of the agency's concern about lead appears in 54 Fed. Reg. 23485 (June 1, 1989), proposing to establish a regulatory limit for lead leaching from ceramic food service pitchers.

4. *Caffeine.* Although FDA proposed in 46 Fed. Reg. 32453 (June 23, 1981) to find that there was no prior sanction for caffeine in soft drinks, it reversed that provision and proposed to find such a prior sanction in 52 Fed. Reg. 18923 (May 20, 1987). *See* p. 340 *supra.*

PRIOR SANCTIONS FOR NITRITE AND NITRATE

Nitrite and nitrate (referred to here by the single term "nitrite") are two of the oldest functional food ingredients. Nitrite has been used to preserve meat since prehistoric times. Early in this century nitrite gained popularity as an agent to impart flavor and color. Nitrite also inhibits the growth of the bacterial spores that cause botulism. In the 1960s, it was discovered that nitrite can combine with amines, substances naturally found in many food products, to produce nitrosamines, some of which cause cancer in laboratory animals. Indeed, the nitrates that occur naturally throughout the human food supply are converted to nitrite and combine with naturally occurring amines to produce nitrosamines in the human gut.

Following congressional hearings, "Regulation of Food Additives and Medicated Animal Feed," Hearings before a Subcomm. of the House Comm. on Government Operations, 92d Cong., 1st Sess. (1971), "Regulation of Food Additives—Nitrites and Nitrates," H.R. Rep. No. 92–1338, 92d Cong., 2d Sess. (1972), FDA proposed to prohibit nonessential uses of nitrite, 37 Fed. Reg. 23456 (November 3, 1972). In this notice the agency stated that "nitrite and nitrate also have prior sanction for use as curing agents in meat and poultry products." (A decade later the FDA Commissioner responsible for this action acknowledged that nitrite had not been banned in November 1972 not only because of its usefulness in preventing botulism, but also "because of its importance in maintaining the characteristics of cured meat that are expected and demanded by consumers." "Oversight of Food Safety, 1983," Hearings before the Senate Comm. on Labor and Human Resources, 98th Cong., 1st Sess. (1983)). The agency subsequently banned the combination of nitrite with spice in curing premixes, 38 Fed. Reg. 19218 (July 19, 1973), because it resulted in nitrosamines.

In 1972 consumer groups petitioned USDA to ban or restrict the use of nitrite in meat. USDA's denial of the petition on the ground that additional information was needed was upheld, *Schuck v. Butz,* 500 F.2d 810 (D.C. Cir. 1974). USDA then created an Expert Panel on Nitrites and Nitrosamines whose recommendations led it to propose modifications in the use of nitrite in meat and poultry products, 40 Fed. Reg. 52614 (November 11, 1975).

Following the 1976 election, USDA reevaluated the status of nitrite, and subsequently advised FDA that there was no prior sanction for nitrite in poultry. FDA therefore issued a statement tentatively determining that nitrite used in poultry products is a food additive and requested information on its safe use, 42 Fed. Reg. 44376 (September 2, 1977). This was followed by a request from USDA in 42 Fed. Reg. 55626 (October 18, 1977) for information on the safe use of nitrite in meat products. Simultaneously, users of nitrite sought a declaratory judgment that a prior sanction for nitrite did exist. In *Tyson Foods, Inc. v. USDA,* Food Drug Cosm. L. Rep. (CCH) ¶ 38,249 (W.D. Ark. 1979), the court held that, because FDA had stated it would take no regulatory action until it made a final decision on the prior sanction issue, the suit was premature.

USDA issued a final regulation in 43 Fed. Reg. 20992 (May 16, 1978), restricting the use of nitrite in bacon and, more important, prohibiting any detectable amount of nitrosamines. A year earlier, a new device for analyzing nitrosamines, called the thermal energy analyser (TEA), had improved the detection sensitivity for nitrosamines by an order of magnitude. The USDA regulation required TEA analysis sensitive to 10 ppb; within one year it had reduced this limit to 5 ppb. Development of the TEA machine had an impact far beyond meat and poultry products, for it detected nitrosamines in other food and consumer products, and indeed in the ambient air in all urban areas.

Faced with these developments, USDA established regulations in 43 Fed. Reg. 18193 (April 28, 1978), 44 Fed. Reg. 48959 (August 21, 1979), permitting meat food products traditionally preserved with nitrite to be prepared without nitrite and to be labeled with the same name with only the addition of the term "uncured." This regulation was later upheld in *National Pork Producers Council v. Bergland*, 631 F.2d 1353 (8th Cir. 1980), *rev'g* 484 F. Supp. 540 (S.D. Iowa 1980).

Through mid–1978, the sole documented scientific concern about nitrite related to the formulation of nitrosamines. In August 1978, however, FDA and USDA announced that an animal feeding study "strongly suggests nitrite produces cancer of the lymphatic system in test animals," HEW News No. P78–28 (August 11, 1978). The two agencies stated that "the need to balance two kinds of health risks—one by taking nitrite out of food and the other by leaving it in—creates a difficult challenge," and made the results of the animal bioassay publicly available for comment. The Department of Justice advised the agencies that if nitrite were determined to be a carcinogen, they had the discretion to adopt timetables and procedures to assure the orderly removal of nitrite from commerce but did not have the discretion to phase out its use over a long period of time. 43 Op. Atty. Gen. No. 19 (March 30, 1979). Producers of meat and poultry products were thus faced with a potentially serious problem. "Nitrite Restrictions on Poultry," Hearing before the Subcomm. on Dairy and Poultry of the House Comm. on Agriculture, 95th Cong., 2d Sess. (1978); "USDA/FDA Announcement on Nitrites and Related Issues," Hearing before the House Comm. on Agriculture, 96th Cong., 2d Sess. (1980).

To resolve mounting questions about the validity of the nitrite bioassay, FDA conducted a public meeting announced in 44 Fed. Reg. 19538 (April 3, 1979). Meanwhile, GAO criticized the agency's delay in resolving the matter, GAO, DOES NITRITE CAUSE CANCER? CONCERNS ABOUT VALIDITY OF FDA–SPONSORED STUDY DELAY ANSWER, Rep. No. HRD–80–46 (January 31, 1980). Furthermore, following USDA's promulgation of its 1978 regulations, consumer groups again challenged the action as inadequate. In *Public Citizen v. Foreman*, 631 F.2d 969 (D.C. Cir. 1980), the court upheld the USDA regulations on the basis of the prior sanction for nitrite as a preservative in cured meat products.

Following the district court decision in *Foreman*, 471 F. Supp. 586 (D.D.C. 1979), which held that the status of nitrite as a color additive must first be presented to FDA before it can be ruled on by the courts, the plaintiffs petitioned the agency to declare nitrite a color additive (and thus unlawful because it lacked either a provisional or permanent listing). FDA initially proposed to determine that nitrite was capable of imparting color to bacon and other red meat, and thus met the threshold criterion of color additive status, but that it was used in bacon solely for purposes other than coloring, 44 Fed. Reg. 75659 (December 21, 1979). This proposal prompted another lawsuit, which was dismissed because of the failure to exhaust administrative remedies, *Public Citizen v. Goyan,* 496 F. Supp. 364 (D.D.C. 1980). FDA's subsequent conclusion that while nitrite "fixes" color, it does not "impart" color either to bacon or other red meat, and thus is not a color additive, 45 Fed. Reg. 77043 (November 21, 1980), was eventually upheld, *Public Citizen v. Hayes,* Food Drug Cosm. L. Rep. (CCH) ¶ 38,161 (D.D.C. 1982).

In 44 Fed. Reg. 75662 (December 21, 1979) FDA had proposed to determine that no prior sanction exists for nitrite in poultry. After another change in administration, however, the agency withdrew this proposal (as well as its November 1972 proposal to ban nonessential uses of nitrite) in 48 Fed. Reg. 9299 (March 4, 1983), based upon USDA's report that a prior sanction did in fact exist for use of nitrite in both cured meat and cured poultry products, 48 Fed. Reg. 1702 (January 14, 1983), codified in 21 C.F.R. §§ 181.33, 181.34.

The prior sanction now recognized for nitrite does not, however, extend to all uses. In *United States v. An Article of Food ... Coco Rico, Inc.,* 752 F.2d 11 (1st Cir. 1985), the court determined that potassium nitrate is not subject to a prior sanction for use in soft drinks.

In the interim, after a complete review of the animal study results that had been released in August 1978, FDA announced in 45 Fed. Reg. 58970 (September 5, 1980) that "insufficient evidence exists to support a conclusion that nitrite induced cancer in rats." *See* Hilts, *The Day Bacon Was Declared Poison,* Washington Post Magazine, April 26, 1981, p. 18, *reprinted in* 127 Cong. Rec. 7980, 13992 (1981). FDA's determination did not end the matter. USDA authorized the use of other additives to inhibit formation of nitrosamines, 50 Fed. Reg. 27573 (July 5, 1985), 51 Fed. Reg. 35630 (October 7, 1986), and has amended its regulations to authorize alternative procedures for controlling the levels of nitrite added to bacon in 51 Fed. Reg. 21731 (June 16, 1986). Most recently, USDA clarified and tightened its restrictions on nitrite in 54 Fed. Reg. 1371 (January 13, 1989), 54 Fed. Reg. 43041 (October 20, 1989).

In the meantime FDA has taken action to control nitrosamines in cosmetics in 44 Fed. Reg. 21365 (April 10, 1979), malt beverages in 45 Fed. Reg. 39341 (June 10, 1980), and rubber baby bottle nipples in 48 Fed. Reg. 57014 (December 27, 1984), 49 Fed. Reg. 26149 (June 26, 1984), 49 Fed. Reg. 50789 (December 31, 1984). EPA took action to control nitrosamines in pesticides in 45 Fed. Reg. 42854 (June 25, 1980), 47 Fed. Reg. 33777 (August 4, 1982).

6. FOOD PROCESSING AND PACKAGING SUBSTANCES

More than 10,000 substances are used in proximity with food—in food packaging, in equipment used to process or store food, in compounds used to clean such equipment—in ways that permit small amounts to migrate to, and become a part of, food. The full requirements of the Food Additives Amendment are applicable to substances that migrate to food from food-contact surfaces.

A migrating food contract material is excluded from food additive classification if it is GRAS or if it is the subject of a prior sanction, and some established packaging materials fall within these exceptions. The basic statutory criteria for approval are the same for indirect and direct food additives. Accordingly, an indirect food additive must be shown, with reasonable certainty, to be safe, and no weight may be accorded the benefits of its use. Similarly, the Delaney Clause squarely applies to indirect food additives.

Many ordinary household articles come into contact with food. These include pots, pans, cooking and eating utensils, home food preparation machines such as blenders and grinders, plates and glasses, and even the surfaces on which food is often laid during the stages of its preparation, such as counter tops. Generally FDA has chosen not to subject these articles to regulation under the Food Additives Amendment. When in the early 1970s the agency learned that high levels of lead were leaching from ceramic pottery into food, however, it initiated a formal compliance program to enforce a limit of 7 ppm on lead migration from pottery to food.

UNITED STATES v. ARTICLES OF FOOD CONSISTING ... OF POTTERY

United States District Court, Eastern District Michigan, 1974.
370 F. Supp. 371.

FEIKENS, District Judge.

The United States has filed a Complaint for Forfeiture against: (a) 668 cases, each containing one 20–piece set, of Cathy Rose pattern pottery, (b) 466 cases, each containing one 45–piece set, of Cathy Rose pattern Pottery, and (c) 187 display sets of Cathy Rose pattern pottery.... In its Complaint for Forfeiture the government alleges that more than 1,000 sets of pottery dinnerware, each containing plates, bowls, cups, and saucers and intended to be used in the service of foods for human consumption, contain a lead substance. The complaint alleges that some or all of this lead, which is unsafe for human consumption, may migrate from the pottery dinnerware to the food which is being served and thus cause harm.

Intervening defendant, Mount Clemens China Company, ... claims in substance that the pottery is not "food" nor can the lead be considered a "food additive" as those terms are defined in the Act.

Intervening defendant's motions must be denied.... The legislative history leading to the Food Additives Amendment of the Act shows a clear Congressional intent that substances which are subject to being ingested by human beings because of migration are "food additives" and thus "foods" within the meaning of the Act....

HOUSEWARES

Following this decision, in 39 Fed. Reg. 13285 (April 12, 1974), FDA proposed to revoke its longstanding "housewares exemption," a policy of not applying the requirements of the Food Additives Amendment to utensils and other articles used for cooking and eating in the home:

Since enactment of the Food Additives Amendment of 1958, letters and oral opinions have at times been issued by personnel of the Food and Drug Administration advising that ordinary houseware articles such as cutting boards, pots and pans, and eating utensils, as well as agents used to clean such housewares, are not subject to regulation under section 409....

The definition of a food additive is extremely broad and easily covers all substances which may reasonably be expected to migrate to food from food-contact articles. Section 201(s) provides ... no basis for an exemption for any houseware, food service, or food dispensing article or cleaning agent, and shows clearly that Congress meant to regulate all substances not generally recognized by experts as having been shown to be safe which become or which may reasonably be expected to become, directly or indirectly, a component of any food unless specifically exempted..... Had Congress meant to exempt specific articles such as dinnerware and cooking utensils from the coverage of the act, therefore, it would have been a simple matter for it to do so....

It is not possible to make an accurate determination of the cumulative effect of an additive without taking into account all means by which that additive may reasonably be expected to enter man's diet. Any reports of adverse effects resulting from migration of unsafe chemical additives from articles such as dinnerware and eating utensils would require prompt regulatory action. Therefore, to exempt dinnerware, eating utensils and other housewares, food service, and food dispensing articles which may reasonably be expected to contribute significant amounts of harmful additives at the final and, arguably, most critical stage of food processing (*i.e.,* immediately before being ingested by the consumer) at the very time when technological advancements have vastly improved methods of detection and evaluation of their effect in man, would be in direct conflict with the express mandate of section 409(c)(5)(B) of the act....

Concern about the burden of processing several hundred food additive petitions caused FDA to vacillate about this proposal. *See* Food Chemical News August 7, 1978, at 2. As of June 30, 1990, FDA has taken no further action on this proposal, and has regulated only the amount of lead migrating from housewares into food.

––––––––

Following enactment of the Food Additives Amendment it was a matter of dispute whether food packaging material falls within the jurisdiction of the FD&C Act before it is actually used to package food. *See, e.g.,* Kuniholm, *Are Empty Containers Food?,* 15 FDC L.J. 637 (1960). After FDA became aware of the widespread contamination of paper food packaging with PCBs, *see* p. ___ *supra*, it took the position that food packaging materials constitute "food" that can be regulated before they are put to their intended use.

NATICK PAPERBOARD CORP. v. WEINBERGER

United States Court of Appeals, First Circuit, 1975.
525 F.2d 1103, *cert. denied*, 429 U.S. 819.

THOMSEN, Senior District Judge.

PCB's are a group of toxic chemical compounds, which find their way into industrial waste, and thence into various products, including recycled paper products. If such a product is used for packaging food, PCB's are likely to migrate into the food unless the food is protected from such migration by an impermeable barrier.

Both plaintiffs manufacture paper and paper products, including paper packaging material from waste paper; [t]hey sell such material in interstate commerce, and some of it is used by their customers to make containers for packaging food. Plaintiffs argue that food packaging material is not "food" within the meaning of the Act, and therefore is not subject to seizure as "adulterated food." ... [Plaintiffs filed a declaratory judgment action to prevent FDA from pursuing its announced intention to recommend seizure of paper food-packaging material containing more than 10 ppm PCB's.]

The affidavits before the district court justify the conclusions that PCB's are toxic, that they tend to migrate from paper packaging material to the contained food by a vapor phase phenomenon, that paper packaging material containing PCB's in excess of 10 ppm is not generally recognized as safe for packaging food for human consumption unless the food is protected from such migration by an impermeable barrier, and that if so used, without such barrier, paper food packaging containing PCB's "may reasonably be expected to result, directly or indirectly, in its becoming a component or otherwise affecting the characteristics of * * * food" within the meaning of sec. 321(s).

Since, therefore, paper food packaging material containing PCB's in excess of 10 ppm will in many instances be an "unsafe food additive" within the meaning of the Act, we proceed to the central issue of this case: whether such material is "adulterated food" under sec. 342 and thus, under sec. 334(a)(1) and (b), subject to seizure by FDA.

... Plaintiffs argue that, although PCB's may be introduced into food by migration from the packaging, such introduction is not intentional and therefore the packaging is not "used for components" of food within sec. 321(f)(3). FDA replies that intentional introduction is not required to meet the definition, and refers to the "food additive" definition in sec. 321(s), ... and to the legislative history....

The protection of the public from unsafe food additives was accomplished by amending sec. 342(a), defining "adulterated food." Among other provisions, a new clause (2)(C) was added to sec. 342(a), stating that a food shall be deemed adulterated *"if it is,* or it bears or contains, *any food additive which is unsafe* within the meaning of section 409" (emphasis added). No other means of prohibiting the unauthorized use of unsafe food additives was provided for in the Amendment; none was needed.[8] We conclude that "unsafe food additives," whether intentional or incidental, are "adulterated food" under sec. 342(a)(2)(C), and, therefore, may be seized, subject to the provisions of sec. 334(a)(1) and (b).

It would defeat the policy of the Act to require, as plaintiffs contend, that FDA must wait until the unsafe food additive has actually entered or come in contact with food before it can be seized; it is enough that FDA has reasonable cause to expect that the additive will be used in such a way as to enter or otherwise come in contact with food. To wait until actual contamination occurs, in the warehouse of the food processor, on the shelf of a grocery store, or in a family kitchen would effectively deny FDA the means to protect the public from adulterated food.

We do not hold, however, that FDA can properly take steps to seize any and all paperboard containing PCB's in excess of 10 ppm wherever it is located and whatever its intended use may be. The district court properly limited its judgment to paper *food packaging* material. We interpret this to mean that the FDA must be able to prove that any paperboard intended to be seized before it has actually been used as a container for food is either in the hands of the packager of food or in transit to, ordered by, or being produced with the intention that it be sold to a packager of food, or that its intended use otherwise meets the test of sec. 321(s). If the packager or other claimant can show that the food placed in or to be placed in the paper container is or will be insulated from PCB migration by a barrier impermeable to such migration, so that contamination cannot reasonably be expected to occur, the paperboard would not be a food additive and would not be subject to seizure under the Act....

With the increasing sensitivity of analytical detection methodology, migration of substances from food-contact articles, and particularly packaging, can be found or predicted at levels as low as 1 part per trillion (ppt). This technical improvement forced FDA to reevaluate both its interpretation of the "may reasonably be expected to result ... in its becoming a component" phrase in section 201(s) and its application of the safety criteria in section 409.

8. Plaintiffs make the argument from syntax: "it," as used in § 342(a)(2)(C), must first be food before it can be adulterated food. However, plaintiffs do not contend that unsafe food additives intended to be introduced into food may not be seized. We see no sound reason to believe that Congress intended to subject to seizure an unsafe substance reasonably expected to become a component of food through intentional mixing but to exempt from seizure an unsafe substance (in this case packaging material containing PCB's) which is likely to affect the characteristics of food by means of migration when such unsafe substance is put to its intended use.

The following landmark court decision on the interpretation of the statutory definition of food additive, as it applies to materials used in contact with food, involved acrylonitrile copolymers used to fabricate plastic beverage bottles. Acrylonitrile was prior sanctioned for some food packaging uses, 39 Fed. Reg. 38907 (November 4, 1974), 41 Fed. Reg. 23940 (June 14, 1976), and had also become widely used in a variety of food contact applications under food additive regulations issued by FDA. In 40 Fed. Reg. 6489 (February 12, 1975), the agency approved a petition to use the material in the production of bottles for nonalcoholic beverages. The following year, because of increased concern about the potential migration of acrylonitrile into foods, FDA issued an interim food additive regulation pursuant to which it required further toxicological study as a condition of continued approval in 41 Fed. Reg. 23940 (June 14, 1976). The Natural Resources Defense Council (NRDC) filed formal objections to this regulation, requesting both a stay of the food additive regulation and a formal evidentiary hearing on the safety of acrylonitrile.

In early 1977, after preliminary reports of the ongoing toxicological studies suggested that acrylonitrile might be carcinogenic, FDA stayed the regulation approving the use of acrylonitrile in producing plastic beverage bottles pending evaluation of the tests in progress, 42 Fed. Reg. 13546 (March 11, 1977). The agency claimed it was acting on the basis of the pending NRDC request for a stay. The manufacturers sought review of this order in the court of appeals, which concluded, in light of the passage of time between the filing of the NRDC objections and the stay order, that FDA had in fact been acting on its own initiative and was obligated to afford the manufacturing parties a prior hearing, *Monsanto Co. v. Gardner*, Food Drug Cosm. L. Rep. (CCH) ¶ 38,098 (D.C. Cir. 1977).

The agency thereupon scheduled a formal evidentiary hearing, 42 Fed. Reg. 17529 (April 1, 1977), to deal with two principal issues: (1) whether beverage containers fabricated from acrylonitrile copolymers were properly considered food additives and (2) whether such containers had been shown, with reasonable certainty, to be safe. The Commissioner's final decision, 42 Fed. Reg. 48528 (September 23, 1977), determined that acrylonitrile was a food additive when used to make plastic beverage bottles and that it had not been shown to be safe for this use. See GAO, FOOD ADDITIVE, ACRYLONITRILE, BANNED IN BEVERAGE CONTAINERS, No. HRD-78-9 (November 2, 1977).

MONSANTO CO. v. KENNEDY

United States Court of Appeals, District of Columbia Circuit, 1979.
613 F.2d 947.

LEVENTHAL, Circuit Judge.

This case arises on a petition for review of a Final Decision and Order of the Commissioner of Food and Drugs [42 Fed. Reg. 48528

(September 23, 1937)] in which he ruled that a substance used to fabricate unbreakable beverage containers, acrylonitrile copolymer, is a "food additive," within the meaning of section 201(s) of the Federal Food, Drug, and Cosmetic Act (the Act).....

The FDA determination that acrylonitrile copolymers used in beverage containers are "food additives" within the statute is based on the finding that such containers invariably retain a residual level of acrylonitrile monomer that has failed to polymerize completely during the manufacturing process and that will migrate from the wall of the container into the beverage under the conditions of intended use. Although the administrative proceedings focused on beverage containers with a residual acrylonitrile monomer (RAN) level equal to or greater than 3.3 parts per million (ppm), the Commissioner made findings and conclusions applicable to all beverage containers manufactured with acrylonitrile, and the Final Order prohibited manufacture of such containers irrespective of their RAN levels.....

At the administrative hearing, petitioners introduced results from tests on a newly developed acrylonitrile beverage container having an RAN level of approximately 3.3 ppm. Tests on the container, employing a detection method sensitive to 10 ppb, detected no migration of acrylonitrile monomer. Nevertheless, the administrative law judge found that acrylonitrile copolymer was a "food additive," since migration had been detected from beverage containers composed of the same chemical compounds, though with higher RAN levels than those present in the "new" container....

This case brings into court the second law of thermodynamics, which C. P. Snow used as a paradigm of technical information well understood by all scientists and practically no persons of the culture of humanism and letters. That law leads to a scientifically indisputable prediction that there will be *some* migration of *any* two substances which come in contact. The Commissioner's Final Decision, which upheld the ALJ's determination is unclear on whether and to what extent reliance was placed on this "diffusion principle" rather than on a meaningful projection from reliable data. At one point in the Final Decision the Commissioner stated: "the migration of any amount of a substance is sufficient to make it a food additive"—a passage evocative of the diffusion principle. Elsewhere, the Commissioner stated that he was able to make a finding of migration based on a projection from actual data—on the assumption that a roughly linear relationship (as a function of time and temperature) existed between the RAN levels in a container and the concentration of acrylonitrile that would migrate into a test fluid. On this premise, though migration from the 3.3 ppm RAN container was itself below the threshold of detectability (10 ppb), it could be projected from the testing data obtained from containers with higher RAN levels.

This was a troublesome aspect of the case. As it was presented to us, the Commissioner had made a projection of migration from 3.3 ppm

RAN containers without the support of any actual data showing that migration had occurred from such containers. One of petitioner's experts put it that the relationship might not be linear at very low RAN levels; but this was dismissed by the Commissioner as "speculative." One could not say that the expert's contention of no migration from very low RAN containers was improbable as a concept of physical chemistry, but it was put to us that the validity of this contention could neither be demonstrated nor refuted for 3.3 ppm RAN containers because, under the conditions of intended use, migration was projected to occur in amounts below the threshold of detectability.

    ... [T]his court requested post-argument memoranda from the parties on whether tests had been performed, or would be feasible, to confirm by actual data the hypothesis that migration occurs from containers with an RAN level of 3.3 ppm. The responses to our inquiry have revealed the probable existence of data unavailable to counsel during the administrative proceedings that bear importantly upon the assumptions made by the Commissioner in reaching his findings and conclusions. This discovery buttressed our earlier conclusion that the Commissioner did not have sufficient support for his decision to apply the "food additive" definition in this case.

    In light of the inadequacy of the agency's inquiry and in light of our view that the Commissioner has a greater measure of discretion in applying the statutory definition of "food additive" than he appears to have thought, we remand this proceeding for further consideration.

    The proceedings at hand are dramatic testimony to the rapid advance of scientific knowledge in our society. At the time of the administrative proceedings, the lowest concentration of acrylonitrile in a test fluid that could be detected with an acceptable degree of confidence was 10 ppb. There are now analytical techniques available that can detect acrylonitrile concentration of 0.1 ppb, an improvement of two orders of magnitude. Thus, on the issue of migration of acrylonitrile monomer it is now possible to generate "hard" data previously unobtainable.

    In his post-argument testimony, Monsanto's expert claims, on the basis of such "hard" data, that the hypothesis which the Commissioner labeled as "speculative" may accurately describe the migration characteristics of containers with very low RAN levels, to wit, that in such containers the acrylonitrile monomer is so firmly affixed within the structure of the copolymer that no migration will occur under the conditions of intended use. If these assertions can be demonstrated to the satisfaction of the Commissioner, a modification of the current regulation is a likely corollary. The actual issuance of a regulation approving the production of a beverage container with an acceptable RAN level would presumably require both a container that had been developed and the appropriate petition. However, the Commissioner would have latitude to issue a statement of policy based upon the results of the proceeding on remand that would specify what in his review was an acceptable RAN level. This would serve a technology-forcing objective.

FDA opposes petitioners' post-argument motion for remand, asserting that the proffered new evidence will not affect the Commissioner's order insofar as that order precludes manufacture of beverage containers with RAN levels equal to or greater than 3.3 ppm—the type of container already tested. FDA points out that the material submitted in response to this court's inquiry affirmatively supports the validity of the Commissioner's findings and conclusions....

... [W]e turn to certain other important questions that ... are ripe for resolution.

... The statutory definition of "food additive" ... contains a two part test. First, the *component* element of the definition states that the intended use of the substance must be reasonably expected to result in its becoming a component of any food. Second, the *safety* element of the definition states that the substance must be not *"generally recognized [as] safe* under the conditions of its intended use."

... Congress did not intend that the component requirement of a "food additive" would be satisfied by a mere recitation of the diffusion principle, a mere finding of any contact whatever with food.... For the component element of the definition to be satisfied, Congress must have intended the Commissioner to determine with a fair degree of confidence that a substance migrates into food in more than insignificant amounts. We do not suggest that the substance must be toxicologically significant; that aspect is subsumed by the safety element of the definition. Nor is it necessary that the level of migration be significant with reference to the threshold of direct detectability, so long as its presence in food can be predicted on the basis of a meaningful projection from reliable data. Congress has granted to the Commissioner a limited but important area of discretion. Although as a matter of theory the statutory net might sweep within the term "food additive" a single molecule of any substance that finds its way into food, the Commissioner is not required to determine that the component element of the definition has been satisfied by such an exiguous showing. The Commissioner has latitude under particular circumstances to find migration "insignificant" even giving full weight to the public health and welfare concerns that must inform his discretion.

Thus, the Commissioner may determine based on the evidence before him that the level of migration into food of a particular chemical is so negligible as to present no public health or safety concerns, even to assure a wide margin of safety. This authority derives from the administrative discretion, inherent in the statutory scheme, to deal appropriately with *de minimis* situations. However, if the Commissioner declines to define a substance as a "food additive," though it comes within the strictly literal terms of the statutory definition, he must state the reasons for exercising this limited exemption authority. In context, a decision to apply the literal terms of the statute, requires nothing more than a finding that the elements of the "food additive" definition have been satisfied.[27]

In the case at hand, the Commissioner made specific rulings that the component element of the definition was satisfied with respect to acrylonitrile beverage containers having an RAN level of 3.3 ppm or more. These rulings were premised on a projection, based on an extrapolation from reliable data, of migration of acrylonitrile monomer in then-undetectable amounts. In light of the supplementary submission made in response to the post-argument inquiry of this court, we find that the determination can be made for the 3.3 ppm RAN containers with an appropriate degree of confidence, and with the support of the required quantum of evidence.

Turning to the safety element of the definition, the Commissioner determined that the scientific community had insufficient experience with acrylonitrile to form a judgment as to safety. Based on this lack of opinion, the Commissioner made a finding that acrylonitrile was not generally recognized as safe within the meaning of the statute. The Commissioner acted within his discretion in making such a finding, but we note that the underlying premise may be affected, perhaps weakened, perhaps strengthened, with time and greater experience with acrylonitrile.[29] This finding on the safety element will be open to reexamination on remand at the discretion of the Commissioner. He would have latitude to consider whether acrylonitrile is generally recognized as safe at concentrations below a certain threshold, even though he has determined for higher concentrations that in the view of the scientific community acrylonitrile is not generally recognized as safe.

Petitioners also made a claim of discriminatory treatment—that the Commissioner is applying policies in the petitioners' case that have not been applied in other similar circumstances. However, there is no claim that the Commissioner was motivated by discriminatory intention to bring the petitioners before the agency and to focus on their product. Petitioners came before the agency in the ordinary course. Once the Commissioner undertook scrutiny, he shifted the lens of his microscope to a higher power—but that is no ground for objection, so long as the final action remains within the legitimate scope of discretion....

NOTES

1. *Subsequent Proceedings.* Following its adoption of the "constituents policy" for carcinogenic components of food additives, p. 915 *infra,* FDA reit-

27. Absent a showing of bad faith or other extraordinary circumstances, a court will not consider meritorious the claim that the Commissioner has abused his discretion in declining to exercise his exemption authority for *de minimis* situations. This is an area of discretion by its nature committed to the informed discretion of the Commissioner.

29. Like the "component" element of the definition, the "safety" element may at times call for more rigorous examination. Thus, the Commissioner has discretion in determining when the statute applies to a given substance, but substances that do fall within its term should be so identified.

erated its conclusion that there is a reasonable expectation of the migration of acrylnitrile to food from plastic nonalcoholic beverage bottles, but at the same time promulgated a food additive regulation establishing the conditions under which acrylonitrile can safely be used in such bottles, 49 Fed. Reg. 36635 (September 19, 1984). The agency later also approved a food additive regulation for plastic containers of alcoholic beverages, 52 Fed. Reg. 33802 (September 8, 1987).

2. *Polyvinyl Chloride.* *See also* FDA's proposal to restrict the use of polyvinyl chloride as an indirect food additive in 40 Fed. Reg. 40529 (September 3, 1975), based on a determination that this polymer contains residual vinyl chloride monomer, a carcinogen, that migrates to food from packaging materials. FDA proposed to prohibit some food contact uses of polyvinyl chloride and to restrict other uses. Following the *Monsanto* decision and its adoption of the constituents policy, FDA withdrew the September 1975 proposal and proposed new regulations for polyvinyl chloride in 51 Fed. Reg. 4173 (February 3, 1986).

3. *Toxicological Insignificance.* For many years, spokesmen for the food packaging industry argued that any migration of a component of food packaging to food at "trace" levels (which ranged at various times from 2 ppm to 2 ppb to the low ppt) should be regarded as "toxicologically insignificant" and thus not subject to the Food Additives Amendment. FDA has thus far declined to accept this approach, although it has acknowledged that some approach to determining a "threshold of regulation" should be established. *See* Heckman, *Fathoming Food Packaging Regulation: A Guide to Independent Industry Action,* 42 FDC L.J. 38 (1987); A.M. Rulis, DE MINIMIS AND THE THRESHOLD OF REGULATION (August 1986).

4. *Structural Similarity.* Based upon adverse toxicity reports, FDA once revoked its approval for an indirect food additive, 39 Fed. Reg. 13667 (April 16, 1974), 44 Fed. Reg. 34513 (June 15, 1979), 52 Fed. Reg. 33929 (September 9, 1987), 54 Fed. Reg. 7188 (Feb. 17, 1989), based solely on its close chemical relationship to another compound that had caused neurological damage in dogs.

5. *Heat Susceptors.* New technology may force FDA to reevaluate existing food additive requirements. Following the development of microwave ovens, makers of food packaging began to incorporate "heat susceptor" components into their products. These components resulted in a higher temperature than used in conventional ovens, thus raising the possibility that previously-approved food packaging materials might migrate into food at higher levels than the agency had anticipated or that migrating substances could degrade into unanticipated byproducts. In 54 Fed. Reg. 37340 (September 8, 1989), FDA requested information on the use and safety of this form of packaging.

6. *Shopping Bags.* Although shopping bags come in contact with food and thus are within FDA jurisdiction, the agency does not regard food contact for such a short period of time to require regulation. "Degradable Commodity Plastics Procurement and Standards Act of 1989," Hearing before the Senate Comm. on Governmental Affairs, 101st Cong., 1st Sess. 21, 23 (1989).

7. *Disposal of Plastic Packaging.* In addition to safety issues, there is increasing public concern about the solid waste problems that plastic packaging materials create. *See, e.g.,* Graff, *The Looming Crisis in Plastic Waste Disposal,* 4 Issues in Science and Technology, No. 2, at 105 (Winter 1988). Because FDA must consider the environmental consequences of its actions, *see* p. 1310 *infra,* these concerns could become a matter of importance for FDA as well.

7. COLOR ADDITIVE REGULATION

a. The 1906 Act

Official concern about the safety of food colorings surfaced as early as 1900, when Congress appropriated funds in 31 Stat. 191, 196, for USDA

> to investigate the character of proposed food preserva-
> tives and coloring matters; to determine their relation
> to digestion and to health, and to establish the princi-
> ples which should guide their use.

USDA commissioned Dr. Bernhard Hesse, a German dye expert, to investigate the toxicity of coal tar colors used in food. Dr. Hesse determined that little was known about the safety of the some 695 coal tar colors then available. Following passage of the 1906 Act, USDA acknowledged only seven coal tar colors as safe for use in food. "Dyes, Chemicals, and Preservatives in Food," FID No. 76 (June 18, 1907). The Department established a program to certify that individual batches of these colors met specifications. "Certificate and Control of Dyes Permissible for Use in Coloring Foods and Foodstuffs," FID No. 77 (September 16, 1907). It was another three years before producers were able to provide colors that qualified for certification. All of these requirements were imposed on the basis of the ongoing work of Dr. Hesse, who eventually published his findings in a remarkable report, COAL TAR COLORS USED IN FOOD PRODUCTS, USDA Bu. Chem. Bull. No. 147 (1912).

Although USDA took the position that its certification program was mandatory, the issue was never tested in court. The agency enforced the safety provisions of the 1906 Act against coal tar color additives by charging a violation of the Act itself rather claiming that a specific additive was not from a certified batch. *E.g., W.B. Wood Mfg. Co. v. United States*, 292 F. 133 (8th Cir. 1923). By 1938 FDA had recognized 15 colors as certifiable for use in food.

---

b. The 1938 Act

Section 406(b) of the original 1938 Act provided that "The Secretary shall promulgate regulations providing for the listing of coal-tar colors which are harmless and suitable for use in foods...." During the following decade unfavorable publicity stemming from the association in the public mind of food colors with "thick, black, sticky" coal tars and the Delaney committee's investigation of the use of chemicals in foods in 1950 caused FDA to tighten its enforcement of this provision. The agency promulgated regulations that required more animal studies with higher feeding levels before it would certify a color additive. More importantly, it redefined "harmless" to mean "substances incapable of producing harm in test animals in any quantity under any conditions." Under this unrealistic definition, eight color additives were delisted between 1956 and 1960, and the status of 19 others was placed in jeopardy. Pressure for a change in the law grew after the Supreme Court upheld the FDA's definition of "harmless" in the following case.

FLEMMING v. FLORIDA CITRUS EXCHANGE

Supreme Court of the United States, 1958.
358 U.S. 153.

Mr. Justice BRENNAN delivered the opinion of the Court.

Commercially grown Florida and Texas oranges have for many years been colored with a red coal-tar color. In 1939 the Food and Drug Administration, after testing and pursuant to § 406(b) of the Federal Food, Drug, and Cosmetic Act, certified this color, FD&C Red No. 32 (hereafter Red 32), to be harmless and suitable for use in food. However, the Secretary ... on November 10, 1955, ordered Red 32 and two other coal-tar colors to be removed from the certified list, after new tests in 1951–1953 cast doubt whether Red 32 was harmless, and after public hearings were held upon the matter on notice published in the Federal Register. The consequence of the Secretary's order was that under § 402(c) of the Act any food bearing or containing such colors would be deemed to be adulterated....

The Secretary did not determine that Red 32 in the quantities used in color-added oranges was harmful for human consumption, but rather determined on the basis of the 1951–1953 tests only that Red 32 and the other suspect coal-tar colors were toxic and therefore not "harmless and suitable for use in food." ...

... The evidence at the hearings held by the Secretary was that the process infuses the peel of an orange with 0.0017% to 0.0034% of Red 32.... It is conceded by the Secretary that there is no evidence that the level of ingestion of Red 32 involved in human consumption of color-added oranges is harmful. However, the evidence at the Secretary's hearing did indicate that Red 32 had a poisonous effect on animals. Feeding the color to rats in quantities as small as 0.1% of their diet was deleterious and often fatal, with liver damage and enlargement of the heart in evidence.... No safe level of administration of Red 32 to the test animals was established....

... The provisions of §§ 402(c) and 406(b) dealing expressly with coal-tar colors were innovations in the Federal Food, Drug, and Cosmetic Act of 1938; there were no counterpart provisions in the original 1906 food and drug legislation.... *United States v. Lexington Mill & Elevator Co.* ... placed the burden upon the Government of establishing that the added substance was such as might render the food to which it was added injurious to health. This rule applied without distinction where coal-tar colors were involved. Congress was aware of the difficulties of this test which required that the questioned food product be evaluated as a whole, and of the existence in this area of an informal certification practice under the 1906 Act under which not food products but the coal-tar colors themselves were subjected to tests to determine their poisonous or harmful character. . . .

It was against this background that the 1938 statute was proposed and enacted. It is obvious to us that an approach different from the rule in *Lexington Mill* was intended by Congress when in § 402(c) and § 406(b) it addressed itself to the severable and narrow problem of coal-tar colors. . . . Section 402(c) provided a separate test: that a food should be deemed adulterated "If it bears or contains a coal-tar color other than one from a batch that has been certified in accordance with regulations as provided by Section 406. . . ." Plainly Congress banned any addition to foods of coal-tar colors not certified by the Secretary. The standard established for the Secretary was set forth in § 406(b): "The Secretary shall promulgate regulations providing for the listing of coal-tar colors which are harmless and suitable for use in food and for the certification of batches of such colors. . . ."

We are not persuaded by the respondents' argument, adopted by the Court of Appeals, that the words "harmless" and "poisonous" are relative words, referring not to the effect of a substance *in vacuo,* but to its effect, taken in a particular way and in particular quantities, on an organic system. Of course this is so, but the question before us certainly does not depend on it. . . . The color substances appear to have been administered at toxicologically significant levels; they played a relatively small part in the diets of the test animals, generally less, and frequently much less, than 1%. Obviously, if the color substances themselves are made an item of diet in the trifling percentages used on the test animals, their effect is poisonous. Congress may have intended "harmless" in a relative sense, but we think it was in relation to such laboratory tests as the ones the Secretary performed that Congress was speaking when it required that coal-tar colors be "harmless." We do not believe that Congress required the Secretary first to attempt to analyze the uses being made of the colors in the market place, and then feed them experimentally only in the proportions in which they appeared in certain of the food products in which the colors were used. . . .

. . . But even if the Secretary's approach of viewing the harmlessness of coal-tar colors in terms of the colors themselves, rather than in their specific applications, is correct, the respondents insist . . . that the Secretary should establish tolerances for the use of colors in food, even though not found to be "harmless." The respondents point to § 406(a) of the Act which allows the Secretary to establish tolerances for poisonous substances added to food where the substance is "required in the production" of the food or "cannot be avoided by good manufacturing practice."

. . . § 406(a) . . . is a prohibition entirely separate and distinct from the prohibitions of § 402(c) on foods containing or bearing uncertified coal-tar colors. The existence of a tolerance is specifically stated in

§ 406(a) only to give sanction to what would otherwise amount to adulteration within the terms of § 402(a)(1). Accordingly it is obvious from the language of the statute that the provisions authorizing the establishment of tolerances apply only to § 402(a)(1) and (2) and do not apply to § 402(c)'s flat prohibition against the use of uncertified colors.... [Congress] evidently took the view that unless coal-tar colors were harmless, the considerations of the benefits of visual appeal that might be urged in favor of their use should not prevail, in the light of the considerations of the public health. In the case of other sorts of added poisons, though only where they were required in the production of the food concerned or could not under good manufacturing practice be avoided, a different congressional policy was expressed in the 1938 enactment....

NOTES

1. *Pre–1938 Law.* Compare W.B. Wood Mfg. Co. v. United States, 286 Fed. 84 (7th Cir. 1923), where the court concluded that the government failed to show that the amount of arsenic in a coal tar color may be injurious to health, noting that when used in food "one would be required to drink 150,000 bottles of soda before he would have consumed a quantity of arsenic sufficient to equal the 'dose' " ordinarily prescribed by physicians.

2. *Immediate Congressional Response.* Following the *Florida Citrus Exchange* decision, Congress passed emergency legislation, 73 Stat. 3 (1959), to permit the use of FD&C Red No. 2 to color oranges until September 1961. By then, the Color Additive Amendments had been enacted.

---

c. The 1960 Amendments

In response to the *Florida Citrus* decision, Congress enacted the Color Additive Amendments of 1960, 74 Stat. 397, codified primarily in section 706 of the Act. While the Amendments apply also to substances used to color drugs, devices, and cosmetics, the following discussion focuses on colors that are used in food.

Section 201(t)(1)(B) defines a color additive as any material which, when added to food, is capable of imparting color, except those which the Secretary, by regulation, determines are used "solely for a purpose or purposes other than coloring." In 26 Fed. Reg. 679 (January 24, 1961), 28 Fed. Reg. 6439 (June 22, 1963), FDA adopted a regulation, 21 C.F.R. § 70.3(g), limiting the circumstances in which the concluding "except" clause might apply:

> For a material otherwise meeting the definition of "color additive" to be exempt from section 706 of the act, on the basis that it is used (or intended to be used) solely for a purpose or purposes other than coloring, the material must be used in a way that any color imparted is clearly unimportant insofar as the appearance, value, marketability, or consumer acceptabili-

ty is concerned. (It is not enough to warrant exemption if conditions are such that the primary purpose of the material is other than to impart color.)

The regulatory requirements applicable to color additives resemble those applicable to food additives, with certain important distinctions. The 1960 Amendments require premarket safety testing and FDA approval of all color additives. The manufacturer or would-be user of a color additive may petition the agency for the issuance of a regulation permitting the color to be used in food. Before it may approve, or "list," a color additive, FDA must find, with reasonable certainty, that the additive poses no risk to human health; that it accomplishes the intended effect; and that its use will not result in deception of consumers. The agency is authorized to impose restrictions on the use of a color to assure that these criteria are satisfied. These restrictions may include limitations on levels of use, a requirement that individual batches of the color be certified by FDA to assure that the color actually used is identical to the substance tested, and specification of the products in which a color may be used.

The Color Additive Amendments contain a Delaney Clause similar in language to the clause that appears in section 409, which is studied closely in Chapter VIII. Because the Amendments do not recognize a category of "generally recognized as safe" colors or exclude substances that were sanctioned or used prior to 1960, section 706 applies to all food coloring agents except those that are only provisionally listed while further safety testing is being conducted.

NOTES

1. *Colors Used in Food Packaging.* Color additives used in food packaging are subject to the food additive provisions of the law, *e.g.,* 44 Fed. Reg. 7149 (February 6, 1979), 53 Fed. Reg. 11402 (April 6, 1988).

2. *Pet Food.* In 44 Fed. Reg. 28418 (May 15, 1979), FDA denied a petition, announced in 42 Fed. Reg. 64440 (December 23, 1977), to prohibit color additives in dog and cat food. The petition alleged that use of color in these products promotes consumer deception in violation of section 706(b)(6) by masking the amount of meat these products contain. FDA stated that section 706(b)(6) generally applies "where the use of color cannot be readily discerned and the use of a label declaration of its presence would not prevent deception of the consumer," citing examples used in the legislative history such as the use of color in food to hide a deficiency. The agency found no evidence that use of color in pet food was deceptive. FDA's subsequent denial of a formal evidentiary hearing, 46 Fed. Reg. 7443 (January 23, 1981), was not challenged.

3. *Drugs Used to Color Poultry.* The use of new animal drugs to provide acceptable pigmentation to poultry poses a similar problem. *See, e.g.,* 47 Fed. Reg. 31429 (July 20, 1982), 49 Fed. Reg. 38193 (September 27, 1984).

4. *Deceptive Coloring of Human Food.* Deceptive use of color additives in human food has been a persistent concern. When FDA updated the standards of identity for bakery products, a major issue was the use of color additives, and of colored butter, margarine, and spices, to impart a yellow color to final bakery products that would suggest a higher butter or egg content. After conducting a

full administrative hearing, 41 Fed. Reg. 6242 (February 12, 1976), Food Drug
Cosm. L. Rep. (CCH) ¶ 38,239 (April 4, 1979), 48 Fed. Reg. 51448 (November 9,
1983), 49 Fed. Reg. 13690 (April 6, 1984), FDA determined that, except for such
color as is naturally present in spices, butter, or margarine, coloring may not be
added as such or as part of another ingredient to standardized bakery products.
See 21 C.F.R. § 136.110(c)(16), (17).

5. *Approval by Product Category.* A color additive must have approval for
each product category in which it is to be used. For example, an additive
approved for cosmetic use cannot be used in a product that is both a cosmetic
and a drug until it has also been approved for drug use. *E.g.,* 52 Fed. Reg.
29664 (August 11, 1987); *United States v. Eight Unlabeled Cases ... Cosmetic,*
888 F.2d 945 (2d Cir. 1989).

6. *Power to Allocate Uses.* Section 706(b)(8) authorizes FDA to ration the
use of a color additive among competing products if safety data do not establish
that exposure from all products would be safe. The only time FDA has
considered this provision potentially applicable, it requested submission on all
uses of FD&C Red No. 3 as a first step toward allocating the allowable safe uses
if this should become necessary, 52 Fed. Reg. 44485 (November 19, 1987).

7. *Commentary.* See *Color Additive Amendments of 1960,* 15 FDC L.J. 432
(1960); Kaplan, *The Color Additive Amendments of 1960 Revisited,* 22 FDC L.J.
553 (1967); Rankin, *Color Additives,* 13 FDC L.J. 772 (1958). For a general
discussion of the use of color in food, *see* National Academy of Sciences, FOOD
COLORS (1971). For an account of color additive regulation since 1900, *see* S.
Hochheiser, SYNTHETIC FOOD COLORS IN THE UNITED STATES: A
HISTORY UNDER REGULATION (U. Wisc. Ph.D. Thesis 1982).

While Congress did not "grandfather" food colors that were already
in use in 1960, it did accord them special status, ostensibly temporarily.
Section 203 of the Color Additive Amendments, which is not part of the
codified Act, authorized FDA "provisionally" to list colors then in use
that were believed to be safe to allow manufacturers time to conduct
the kind of toxicological testing required to support approval under the
new law. The "provisional list" was thus designed to permit an orderly
transition from a situation of bifurcated regulation in which some
colors were subject to little control and others, derived from coal tar,
were unapprovable, to a scheme in which *all* color additives had to be
licensed. Only colors that were in use in 1960 are eligible for provisional listing. Section 203 of the Amendments makes no provision for
adding a post–1960 color to the provisional list to permit continued use
while tests are being conducted to resolve new safety questions. FDA
maintained a list of provisionally approved color additives for almost 30
years, deleting those whose safety came under serious challenge, and
permanently listing others as scientific data were submitted to confirm
their safety.

CERTIFIED COLOR MFRS. ASS'N v. MATHEWS

United States Court of Appeals, District of Columbia Circuit, 1976.
543 F.2d 284.

WILKEY, Circuit Judge.

This appeal is a challenge to the action of the Commissioner of Food and Drugs in terminating provisional approval of the color additive FD&C Red No. 2 pursuant to the Transitional Provisions of the 1960 Color Additives Amendments....

In order to avoid a statutory presumption that all additives not permanently listed at the date of enactment were unsafe, Title II of the Amendments ("Transitional Provisions") provided for the continued use of commercially established additives—such as Red No. 2—on an interim basis. This was allowed only "to the extent consistent with the public health, pending completion of the scientific investigations needed as a basis for making determinations" on the safety of the additive for permanent approval. This provisional listing was to expire on a "closing date" which was established as either 12 January 1963 ("initial closing date"), or such later date as the Commissioner determined. The original closing date could be postponed "if in the [Commissioner's] judgment such action [was] consistent with the objective of carrying to completion in good faith, as soon as reasonably practicable" the investigation needed for making the safety determination.

Throughout this transitional period, while the permanent safety determinations were being made, the Commissioner was granted broad discretionary authority summarily to terminate a provisional listing "forthwith whenever in his judgment such action [was] necessary to protect the public health." During the period following postponement of the closing date, the Commissioner additionally was given broad authority to terminate that postponement "at any time" if he found that, *inter alia,* the basis for the postponement no longer existed because of a change in circumstances....

In the instant case, the Commissioner exercised both of these powers. He terminated the postponement of the closing date of Red No. 2, and additionally terminated its provisional listing.

Red No. 2 is a petroleum derived color additive widely used in this country artificially to create or brighten the white, brown, purple, or red colors of various foods, drugs, and cosmetics.... It has been widely used in this country under federal regulatory control for nearly seventy years. Since the initiation of more sophisticated scientific investigations following enactment of the 1960 Color Additive Amendments, it has failed to receive FDA permanent approval for safety.

Acting pursuant to his authority under the Transitional Provisions, the Commissioner has postponed the closing date a total of fifteen times, either at the request of interested parties or on his own initiative. The most recent postponement occurred 5 January 1976 and was to expire 30 September 1976. A petition for permanent listing pursuant to 21 U.S.C. § 376 has been under active consideration since late 1968, but had not been acted on prior to the action here challenged. At one point the agency was on the verge of affirmatively acting on the petition; before such action could be taken, however, information became available on several studies undertaken in the Soviet Union which raised new concerns over the safety of Red No. 2. One study concluded that amaranth, the generic name for Red No. 2, was poisonous to the reproductive organs of laboratory rats; the remaining studies concluded that amaranth was carcinogenic, that is, it caused cancer.

While FDA scientists questioned the validity of the Soviet tests, the new studies pointed out the absence of information on the effects of Red No. 2 on reproductive physiology and raised concern over its possible carcinogenicity. Accordingly, the FDA undertook its own chronic feeding study over a two-and-one-half year period in which Osborne–Mandel rats were fed Red No. 2 in their diet at concentrations of 3%, 0.3%, 0.003%, and 0%. The duration of that study and the follow-up evaluations have been the primary reason for postponing the closing date of Red No. 2's provisional listing for the last several years. . . .

Following receipt of [a report based on the FDA study concluding that Red No. 2 may be carcinogenic] on 19 January the Commissioner prepared, and gave notice of intent to publish, a regulation to terminate the provisional listing of Red No. 2. . . .

Appellants ... argue that, under the transitional provision, a postponement of the closing date taken to allow for the evaluation of data for a determination of safety may not be terminated on the basis of a change in "circumstances" when in fact the evaluation has not ceased at the time of termination. While this argument is initially appealing, we believe that it is based on a much too confined interpretation of the statute and of the Commissioner's actions. It will be recalled that the statutory authority to grant a postponement is couched in broad, discretionary language and allows for the interplay of judgmental factors. While the statute speaks in terms of completing the necessary "scientific investigations," there is also a pervasive legislative gloss that the postponement must also be consistent with the protection of the public health. . . .

The primary thrust of appellants' statutory argument is that the standard authorizing the Commissioner to act "forthwith whenever in his judgment such action is necessary to protect the public health" requires that there be an actual threat to the public, amounting for all practical purposes to an imminent health hazard. We believe this argument is without foundation. When Congress has intended so to restrict the discretion available to an agency to take regulatory action similar to that involved here, it has not hesitated to indicate that intent by the inclusion of appropriately restrictive language. Here Congress attached no such "qualifiers" and chose instead to provide for a much broader standard, designed, we think, to allow for precautionary or prophylactic responses to perceived risks. There is nothing in the statute or its legislative history to indicate that Congress intended to restrict regulatory action to situations where there was a substantial likelihood of serious harm to the public. The overall Congressional intent appears to be to the contrary....

Our review of the record, in light of the broad discretion conferred on the Commissioner, convinces us that there was no abuse of discretion in terminating the provisional listing of Red No. 2. The information available to him indicated a statistically significant relationship between high dosages of Red No. 2 and the occurrence of cancer in aged female rats. That relationship concededly did not establish conclusive proof that Red No. 2 was a carcinogen, but it was at least suggestive of it, and that statistical analysis was later confirmed, albeit at lower levels of significance. Moreover—and this was the angle from which he was to view these findings—he had been advised that the principal study under evaluation *could not* be used to *establish* safety. Based on this information, he determined in the exercise of his scientific judgment that a question as to the safety of the additive existed sufficient to warrant termination. We cannot say that this was an irrational choice, nor can we say that it was beyond his statutory authority....

Therefore, in light of the broad discretionary authority available to the Commissioner, and our necessarily limited role as judges, we affirm the District Court's holding on this issue. We note, however, that the Commissioner has denied appellants' petition for permanent listing, and we assume that this has triggered a formal proceeding before the agency which will result in a new order being issued based on a complete reevaluation of the evidence. That is a separate proceeding from which there will arise another opportunity to seek judicial review.

Appellants lastly urge that the District Court erred in finding that the notice and comment provisions of the Administrative Procedure Act did not apply to the actions challenged....

The arguments presented in support of this proposition are without merit. The Commissioner is authorized to terminate the postponement of the closing date "at any time" and may terminate a provisional listing "forthwith." Such discretionary authority, expressly designed to avoid any time limitations, are [sic] "so inconsistent with any notice-and-comment requirement as to compel the conclusion that a pre-determination hearing cannot be implied from the terms of the statute." ...

NOTES

1. *Subsequent Proceedings.* The FDA denial of the color additive petition was upheld by the Administrative Law Judge after an administrative hearing, Food Drug Cosm. L. Rep. (CCH) ¶ 38,168 (1978), and affirmed on appeal by the Commissioner, 45 Fed. Reg. 6252 (January 25, 1980).

2. *Sale of Food Containing Delisted Color.* When it has revoked provisional or permanent listing of a color, FDA has generally permitted existing food products containing the color to be marketed and has allowed existing stocks of labeling for the food listing that color to be used up even after the

prohibited color has been removed from the food. *See, e.g.,* 43 Fed. Reg. 45611 (October 3, 1978) (Orange B); 41 Fed. Reg. 41857 (September 23, 1976) (carbon black); 53 Fed. Reg. 26766 and 26768 (July 15, 1988) (D&C Red Nos. 8, 9, and 19, and D&C Orange No. 17). Following FDA's ban of FD&C Red No. 2, however, food containing that color additive was held to be in violation of the Act and was ordered to be destroyed rather than exported even though the color additive remained approved in the country of destination, *United States v. An Article of Food Consisting of 12 Barrels ... Lumpfish Roe,* 477 F. Supp. 1185 (S.D.N.Y. 1979).

3. *Regulation of Cosmetics.* One explanation for FDA's long delay in resolving the status of colors on the provisional list was its attempt to use the Color Additive Amendments to strengthen its controls over the safety of cosmetics. Industry challenges to this attempt took nine years to resolve. *See Toilet Goods Ass'n v. Finch,* 419 F.2d 21 (2d Cir. 1969), p. 860 *infra.*

Sixteen years after enactment of the Color Additive Amendments, FDA realized that the tests previously conducted on most of the colors on the provisional list were out-of-date and it concluded that new testing, using modern protocols, had to be required.

PROVISIONALLY LISTED COLOR ADDITIVES: NOTICE OF PROPOSED RULEMAKING

41 Federal Register 41860 (September 23, 1976).

The Commissioner of Food and Drugs, on [his] own initiative, is proposing to postpone the closing date for the use of certain provisionally listed color additives beyond December 31, 1976. The postponement would be conditioned on the undertaking of appropriate scientific investigations and the submission of data to the Food and Drug Administration (FDA) on a prescribed schedule....

Final determinations have been made on 12 of the 84 provisionally listed color additives on the basis of the Bureau of Foods' review of the petitions seeking "permanent" listing for them.... The available date on 20 of [the remaining] 72 provisionally listed color additives are adequate to support final determinations of safety and regulations "permanently" listing the color additives are being prepared. The Commissioner anticipates that these regulations will be issued before December 31, 1976. The remaining 52 provisionally listed color additives cannot be "permanently" listed at this time because the available data are inadequate to make final determinations. The Commissioner concludes, however, that there are no significant questions of safety regarding any of these 52 color additives, and that continued provisional listing for them presents no risk to the public health....

Under the transitional provisions of the Color Additive Amendments of 1960, however, continued provisional listing of a color additive is appropriate only when studies in progress or under evaluation are capable of demonstrating the safety of the color additives involved.

The Commissioner proposes, therefore, to condition further postponement of the closing dates for the use of these 52 provisionally listed color additives on compliance with specific requirements to be contained in a new § 8.505 of the color additive regulations....

Proposed § 8.505 would require that each of the petitioners agree in writing within 30 days of the effective date of the regulation to undertake the scientific investigations necessary to permit FDA to make final determinations on the color additives, and that the petitioners or other interested persons undertake those scientific investigations, file progress reports with FDA, and submit the final results within fixed time periods prescribed in the regulation. Additionally, the petitioners would be required to notify FDA immediately of any findings that indicate a potential for a color additive to cause adverse effects....

... Of the 72 provisionally listed color additives, 31 cannot be "permanently" listed because the available toxicity data—though suggestive of no adverse effects—are derived from studies that do not meet contemporary standards generally accepted within the scientific community as minimum requirements for the design and conduct of toxicological studies to establish safety....

1. Many of the studies were conducted using groups of animals, i.e., controls and those fed the color additive, that are too small to permit conclusions to be drawn today on the chronic toxicity or carcinogenic potential of the color. The small number of animals used does not, in and of itself, cause this result, but when considered together with the other deficiencies in this listing, does do so. By and large, the studies [used] 25 animals in each group; today FDA recommends using at least 50 animals per group.

2. In a number of the studies, the number of animals surviving to a meaningful age was inadequate to permit conclusions to be drawn today on the chronic toxicity or carcinogenic potential of the color additives tested.

3. In a number of the studies, an insufficient number of animals was reviewed histologically.

4. In a number of the studies, an insufficient number of tissues was examined in those animals selected for pathology.

5. In a number of the studies, lesions or tumors detected under gross examination were not examined microscopically....

The Commissioner advises that FDA is currently evaluating the data that formed the basis for the "permanent" listing of color additives in previous years. It is anticipated that many of the past decisions to list "permanently" color additives were based on data derived from studies that suffer from the same deficiencies as those described above. In that event, the Commissioner will consider what action is appropriate to update those data, including conditioning continued "permanent" listing on the undertaking, over a period of time, of studies of the sort that the Commissioner proposes to require for 31 of the 72 provisionally listed color additives. Should the Commissioner conclude that those data need updating, the Commissioner will take appropriate action. One of the alternatives the Commissioner would seriously consider is publishing regulations proposing a cyclic review of "permanently" listed color additives....

NOTES

1. *Delisting of Red. No. 4.* As part of this decision FDA terminated the provisional listing of FD&C Red No. 4, 41 Fed. Reg. 41852 (September 23, 1976). The Commissioner ultimately upheld the Administrative Law Judge's decision sustaining the agency's action, Food Drug Cosm. L. Rep. (CCH) ¶ 38,208 (November 21, 1978), *aff'd* Food Drug Cosm. L. Rep. (CCH) ¶ 38,238; 48 Fed. Reg. 48533 (October 19, 1983). This left manufacturers of maraschino cherries with a single color capable of producing a stable red color in the product. That color additive, FD&C Red No. 3, is also under attack, p. 372 *infra*.

2. *Red No. 40.* Perhaps no color has received closer scrutiny than FD&C Red No. 40, whose safety has under intense agency review for several years. *See* 42 Fed. Reg. 8005 (February 8, 1977), 42 Fed. Reg. 61630 (December 6, 1977), 43 Fed. Reg. 18258 (April 28, 1978), 44 Fed. Reg. 30437 (May 25, 1979).

Following FDA's final decision to require that most provisionally listed color additives be retested using modern protocols, 42 Fed. Reg. 6992 (February 4, 1977), the Health Research Group began what has so far been an unsuccessful effort to force the agency to remove from the market all those colors for which it had concluded that the existing safety data were inadequate.

HRG initially brought suit in 1977 contending that Congress intended that provisional listing could last no longer than two and one-half years. This argument was rejected in *Health Research Group v. Califano,* Food Drug Cosm. L. Rep. (CCH) ¶ 38,125 (D.D.C. 1977). HRG also filed a petition, 42 Fed. Reg. 33807 (July 1, 1977), requesting immediate revocation of regulations permanently listing six color additives. This petition was denied in 43 Fed. Reg. 54990 (November 24, 1978) on the basis of a detailed analysis of the toxicological information available on each color, and on November 21, 1979, FDA by letter denied a subsequent petition for reconsideration. FDA agreed "that the toxicological data previously considered to support the safety of the color additives may be inadequate by modern-day criteria" but stated that this "general finding" is insufficient to require additional studies for these permanently listed colors. HRG did not challenge this decision in court, but in 1980 it again sued FDA contending that continued provisional listing of any color additive was unlawful.

McILWAIN v. HAYES

United States Court of Appeals, District of Columbia Circuit, 1982.
690 F.2d 1041.

BORK, Circuit Judge: ...

Prior to 1960, color additives used in foods, drugs, and cosmetics could be marketed lawfully unless the Food and Drug Administration ("FDA") tested them and found them unsafe. Because of the FDA's limited resources, Congress believed this testing process likely to be unduly prolonged. In 1960, therefore, the Color Additive Amendments to the Food, Drug, and Cosmetic Act shifted the burden of testing and proof of safety to industry. A color additive is to be deemed unsafe unless industry proves its safety. Recognizing that this would take time with many commercially established additives, Congress provided a grace period of two and one-half years. Additives undergoing testing were to be provisionally listed as available for use. If proven safe, they were to be permanently listed. If not proven safe, the additives were, of course, to be removed from the market.

The present case involves a dispute over the extent and exercise of the power Congress gave the Commissioner of the FDA to postpone the time (the "closing date") by which proof of safety was to be required or the additive delisted and removed from the market. While some additives have been proven safe and permanently listed for use and others have not been proven safe and have been removed from the market, the twenty-three additives in question here have been on the market under provisional listings for over twenty years. The Commissioner of the FDA has repeatedly postponed the closing dates for proof of their safety. On November 4, 1980, the FDA published a proposed rule announcing an intention once more to postpone the closing dates from January 31, 1981, for periods ranging from one to three and one-half years for the various additives. Appellants challenge this latest round of postponements, contending that the Commissioner lacks the authority to keep drugs [sic] not yet proven safe on the market for so many years or that, if he has such authority, he has abused his discretion.

We hold that the Commissioner's latest extensions for proving the safety of these color additives are within his lawful authority and discretion. Undoubtedly, in 1960 many members of Congress anticipated that color additive testing would be completed more rapidly than has been the case with respect to some additives. Just as certainly, however, Congress foresaw that unavoidable delays were possible and provided a statutory mechanism for the Commissioner to cope with such problems. Most significantly, for the issues in this case, Congress provided no limit upon the number of times postponements could be made. The primary reason for the repeated postponements here is that testing technology has evolved and improved so rapidly that, by the time a color additive has been shown to be safe under one series of tests or is still undergoing testing, more sophisticated testing procedures have been devised and the Commissioner orders that the time-consuming testing process begin anew.

It is important to realize what "proving" safety necessarily means. A color additive is subjected to the best tests available and safety is assumed to be shown if no evidence of harm to health is found. We are informed by the Commissioner that no test data supplied so far indicate any problem with the safety of the twenty-three color additives involved here, and it is only the fact that new, more rigorous tests have since become available that makes it possible to say that these products have not yet been conclusively demonstrated to be safe. Under these circumstances, we think it both reasonable and within the express powers conferred upon him by Congress for the Commissioner to postpone the closing dates for the color additives in question. We therefore affirm the judgment of the district court.....

This case is controlled by the plain meaning of sections 203(a)(1) and (2) of the Color Additive Amendments' transitional provisions.... It will be observed that the statute sets no limit upon the number of extensions the Commissioner may grant. Indeed, by using the phrases "from time to time" and "period or periods" in connection with a single, specified additive, it is manifest that Congress contemplated and provided for multiple postponements. The statute also sets no time limit upon provisional listings, a fact that is particularly significant since Congress has set such time limits in analogous statutes.[7]....

Appellants' argument that the Commissioner lacks statutory authority to grant these latest postponements is somewhat difficult to comprehend. The argument does not deny that the Commissioner was given power to postpone closing dates but seems to suggest that the statutory authority has somehow lapsed. Thus appellants state:

> While there may have been a legal basis in the past for extending the provisional list, it is plaintiffs' position that, more than 20 years after the statute's enactment, the FDA no longer has the authority to use the provisional list as a device to allow color additives which have not been proven safe to continue to be sold to the public.

---

7. See section 107(c)(3)(B) of the Drug Amendments of 1962, 76 Stat. 780, which made it unlawful to market, two years after enactment of the statute, any drug for which there was a lack of substantial evidence of effectiveness. Congress provided for a grace period of two years but did not grant the Commissioner authority to extend this period. In *American Public Health Ass'n v. Veneman*, 349 F.Supp. 1311 (D.D.C. 1972), the district court held unlawful the FDA's attempt to permit continued marketing of the drugs beyond the grace period while industry gathered evidence of a drug's efficacy. The 1962 Drug Amendments also made it unlawful to market a drug without FDA approval, after a two-year grace period, unless the drug was recognized as safe and effective. In *Cutler v. Kennedy*, 475 F.Supp. 838 (D.D.C. 1979), the district court held unlawful FDA's Category III regulation which had allowed drugs not yet established as safe and effective to remain on the market past the grace period while industry performed further testing....

The only conceivable basis for this argument is the statement in the statute that provisional listings are to be "on an interim basis for a reasonable period." But a "reasonable period" is defined as the time needed to complete the necessary scientific investigations. Here it appears that much of the delay has been caused by rapidly improving testing procedures so that additive sponsors have had to test and retest. Tests that reflected the best scientific standards when undertaken with FDA approval do not satisfy the more rigorous standards that have since become available. The FDA has been receiving data from the tests done and states that it will end the provisional listing of any additive should test data indicate any safety problem. The Commissioner is given complete power to terminate a provisional listing or a postponement of a closing date whenever he believes that such listing or postponement was mistaken or that any danger to public health appears.

It appears that many and perhaps all of the additives in question here would have been permanently listed as proven safe if the state of testing technology had remained as it stood when testing first began. Only the constant advance of that technology has produced this situation in which additives are tested and retested and now must be tested again. It may be doubted that Congress foresaw that the very advance of science would delay the completion of testing for so long, but it did foresee the possibility of delays well beyond the initial two and one-half year transitional period, and it empowered the Commissioner to use provisional listings to cope with just such unanticipated problems. Under these circumstances, we cannot say that his statutory power has somehow lapsed....

What we have said so far about the Commissioner's statutory authority also largely disposes of the challenge to the exercise of his discretion. Appellants do not contest that the major reason for the length of the provisional listings here is the advance of scientific standards. Nor do they deny the enormous amount of data submitted to the FDA under testing already done fails to show any evidence that these color additives are not safe. Their argument that the Commissioner has abused his discretion is, in fact, fairly characterized as little more than nit-picking. This court has power to set aside the decision of the Commissioner only if it is "arbitrary, capricious, an abuse of discretion, or otherwise not in accordance with law." Given the facts here, we have no choice but to uphold the Commissioner's decision.....

MIKVA, Circuit Judge, dissenting:

By 1960, Congress clearly was dissatisfied with the manner in which the Food and Drug Administration (FDA) was carrying out its mandate to regulate the use of color additives in foods, drugs, and cosmetics. The assignment of the burden of proof, requiring the FDA to show that an additive was unsafe before it could be removed from the market, had caused the law to become largely a dead letter. And so, in the Color Additive Amendments of 1960 (Amendments), Congress shifted the burden of testing color additives from the FDA to industry, forcing industry to prove each additive safe before the additive could be permanently listed and marketed. To manage the problem arising from those additives already on the market, Congress established a provisional listing program that was to end after the additive was proven safe or unsafe, or after a two and one-half year period, whichever came first. Only under exceptional circumstances was it anticipated that any additives already on the market would take more than two and one-half years to be proven safe or removed from the market. Indeed, the major factor that motivated Congress to enact the Amendments was the possibility that if the burden were not shifted, the FDA might take "as much as 20 years" to determine the safety of the existing additives. . . .

Some twenty-two years later, the majority is willing to let the FDA and industry go some more tortured miles to keep color additives that have not been proven safe on the market. The majority has ignored the fact that Congress has spoken on the subject and allows industry to capture in court a victory that it was denied in the legislative arena. The 1960 Color Additive Amendments have been made inoperative by judicial fiat. I dissent. . . .

NOTE

Undiscouraged, HRG sued again, contending that the continued provisional listing for color additives found to be carcinogenic in test animals was illegal. This claim too was rejected in *Public Citizen v. Department of HHS*, 632 F. Supp. 220 (D.D.C. 1986), *aff'd sub. nom. Public Citizen v. Young*, 831 F.2d 1108 (D.C. Cir. 1987). By March 1, 1991, only one color additive remained on the provisional list, FD&C Red No. 3.

FD&C RED NO. 3

The history of FD&C Red No. 3 is complex. The color was permanently listed for food and ingested drug uses in 1969, 34 Fed. Reg. 7446 (May 8, 1969), 34 Fed. Reg. 11542 (July 12, 1969), but its cosmetic and external drug uses were provisionally listed when FDA decided in 1977 to require retesting using modern protocols. When retested FD&C Red No. 3 was found to be carcinogenic, a conclusion that ordinarily would have triggered cancellation. In 48 Fed. Reg. 45237 (October 4, 1983), however, FDA announced that it was uncertain whether FD&C Red No. 3 was a primary or a secondary carcinogen and that therefore it was seeking the advice of the Board of Scientific Councilors of the National Toxicology Program (NTP). *See* 48 Fed. Reg. 6022 (October 11, 1983). Although the NTP report was not officially released, FDA eventually reported, 52 Fed. Reg. 44485 (November 19, 1987), that the Board had concluded that the evidence was insufficient to support a determination that FD&C Red No. 3 was a secondary carcinogen.

In the meantime, 50 Fed. Reg. 26377 (June 26, 1985), FDA had referred the issue to a panel of Public Health Service scientists. The panel concluded that the carcinogenicity of FD&C Red No. 3 is "more likely to be the result of an indirect (secondary) mechanism" and there is "insufficient evidence" of human carcinogenicity "but this possibility cannot be ruled out," 52 Fed. Reg. 29728 (August 11, 1987). *See* note 1, p. 950 *infra*. Anticipating that it might eventually be required to ration the aggregate uses, FDA requested data on specific uses of FD&C Red No. 3, 52 Fed. Reg. 44485 (November 19, 1987).

In 54 Fed. Reg. 27640 (June 30, 1989), however, FDA announced its intention not to allow time for further testing of FD&C Red No. 3. Within days, the House Appropriations Committee included in its report on the agency's budget the following statement:

> The Committee expects the Food and Drug Administration to provide the technical expertise necessary for the development and design of protocols for a long-term study to determine if the secondary mechanism effect can be confirmed for FD&C Red No. 3. Such study shall be financed by the affected industries. The Committee further expects the Food and Drug Administration to review the results of this study, in addition to any other scientifically-based findings which may emerge, prior to making any decision relating to changes in the provisionally or permanently approved uses of this color.

H.R. Rep. No. 101–137, 101st Cong., 1st Sess. 126 (1989). The Senate Appropriations Committee gave FDA no directions on this matter, S. Rep. No. 101–84, 101st Cong., 1st Sess. (1989), but the Conference report both reproduced the statement from the House report and added:

> The managers on the part of the Senate believe that the FDA should reach its final decision on Red Dye No. 3 solely under the standards of the Food, Drug, and Cosmetic Act (21 U.S.C. 376 and the transitional provisions thereto, 74 Stat. 397–203), and section 10(e) of the Administrative Procedure Act, 5 U.S.C. 706.

H.R. Rep. No. 101–361, 101st Cong., 1st Sess. 34 (1989). During the House debate on the agency's budget, Appropriations Committee Chairman Whitten acknowledged, in a response to Representative Weiss, that the statement in the Committee report does not legally require FDA to retain the provisional listing. 135 Cong. Rec. H3836 (daily ed. July 18, 1989). As of March 1, 1991, FDA had revoked the provisional listing for FD&C Red No. 3 in cosmetics and external drugs, 55 Fed.Reg. 3516 (February 1, 1990), but was continuing the provisional listing for food and ingested drugs.

FD&C YELLOW NO. 5: LABELING IN FOOD AND DRUGS FOR HUMAN USE
44 Fed. Reg. 37212 (June 26, 1979).

In the FEDERAL REGISTER of May 8, 1969, the Food and Drug Administration (FDA) issued an order listing FD&C Yellow No. 5 (also commonly known as tartrazine) for use in foods under § 74.705 and for use in ingested drugs under § 74.1705. This action was supported by safety data in a color additive petition and other relevant data.... At the time of listing for food and ingested drug use, no specific restrictions were placed on the use of FD&C Yellow No. 5 other than that it be subject to batch certification by FDA.... Because of mounting evidence of allergic-type reactions to FD&C Yellow No. 5, the agency believes it is now appropriate to require that the presence of the color be specifically identified on the label of products in which it is used.

The evidence concerning the relationship between ingestion of FD&C Yellow No. 5 and allergic-type reactions was discussed in the FEDERAL REGISTER of February 4, 1977 (42 FR 6835), when FDA proposed regulations concerning the use of FD&C Yellow No. 5 in foods and ingested drugs. For food, the proposal would require a label declaration for all foods containing FD&C Yellow No. 5. For ingested drugs, however, FDA set forth two alternative proposals. Drug Proposal I was to require a warning statement on the labels of both over the counter (OTC) and prescription drugs. Drug Proposal II was to ban the use of FD&C Yellow No. 5 in certain categories of OTC and prescription drug products frequently used by persons with allergic disorders and to require a warning statement on the labels of all other OTC and prescription drugs containing FD&C Yellow No. 5....

This final rule requires the label of all foods containing FD&C Yellow No. 5 to declare the presence of the color additive as FD&C Yellow No. 5. In the case of drugs, a slightly different label declaration is required. The presence of FD&C Yellow No. 5 must be declared by both names by which it is known (FD&C Yellow No. 5 and tartrazine) for OTC and prescription drug products which are administered orally, nasally, rectally, or vaginally, but not for topical or other externally applied drug products. In addition, labeling for the prescription drug products subject to the rule will be required to contain a precautionary statement on possible allergic reactions to the use of FD&C Yellow No. 5....

Since FD&C Yellow No. 5 was listed for use in food and ingested drugs, evidence has accumulated of allergic-type responses in humans, not rats, caused by ingestion of foods or drugs containing the color. There have been increasing numbers of reports that these responses to FD&C Yellow No. 5 occur primarily in patients who also have aspirin intolerance. The phenomenon of aspirin intolerance in certain persons with underlying allergic disorders, including bronchial asthma, nasal polyposis, vasomotor rhinitis, and skin allergies to various substances, has been known for over 50 years. Both the aspirin and the FD&C Yellow No. 5 reactions are manifested by asthmatic symptoms, urticaria, angioedema, or nasal symptoms....

Although there is no evidence in the available information on FD&C Yellow No. 5 that demonstrates a significant hazard to the general population at current usage levels, the agency concludes that the evidence of a causal relationship between FD&C Yellow No. 5 and serious allergic-type responses in certain susceptible individuals is sufficient to warrant label declaration. Under the requirements imposed by this regulation, the only broad impact on the general public will be the identification of the color on the label of all foods and most drugs. While some persons may not feel a need for this information, the availability of the information will not interfere with any person's rights....

Many comments favored a complete and absolute ban on the use of FD&C Yellow No. 5 in all foods, drugs, and cosmetics. Some comments suggested a ban of FD&C Yellow No. 5 to the greatest extent possible and appropriate labeling of uses not banned. This approach was carefully considered by the agency before publication of the proposal but was rejected because there was an insufficient basis for that action. The comments received on the proposal did not provide any additional data indicating that a total or partial ban on the use of FD&C Yellow No. 5 was needed to protect sensitive persons. To the contrary, many comments, including several comments from persons sensitive to FD&C Yellow No. 5, suggested that label declaration would be adequate....

The majority of comments were from consumers who supported the proposed label declaration but suggested that FDA should take an even stronger stand and ban FD&C Yellow No. 5. Several comments contended that color additives provide no "benefit" to the public and that their use is purely cosmetic and concluded, therefore, that their use should not be sanctioned by FDA.... Congress has made the judgment that color additives that have been shown to be safe should be permitted in food. The role of FDA under the act is not to make the value judgment about whether color additives are "beneficial," but rather to evaluate the data submitted in support of color additive petitions and to approve for use in foods, drugs, cosmetics, and devices those colors that the agency is reasonably certain are safe. Congress has made the collective judgment that color additives are "beneficial" and should be permitted to be used if shown to be safe.

FDA also advises that "natural" foods and food ingredients are not necessarily safer than artificial ones. Many substances are harmful if ingested in sufficiently large quantities. Additionally, many synthesized ingredients are chemically identical to substances that occur naturally. The notion that natural food ingredients are safer than artificial food ingredients is not supported by scientific data....

At the time of the proposal, FDA had minimal information about the availability of drug products that were in the particular therapeutic categories identified in the proposal and that did not contain FD&C Yellow No. 5. The categories of drugs identified in the proposal for prohibition of the use of the color are those classes of drugs that are most likely to be taken by persons intolerant of FD&C Yellow No. 5 to treat an allergic problem, including those allergic-type conditions that may arise as a result of ingestion of FD&C Yellow No. 5. In view of the information presented, however, it appears that a wide selection of drugs is available in each category that is free of FD&C Yellow No. 5. Therefore, if each drug is appropriately labeled, a physician could prescribe, or a patient could select, if OTC, a drug product free of FD&C Yellow No. 5 from any of these therapeutic categories of drugs....

The agency finds these comments concerning the lack of availability of alternative colors for replacing FD&C Yellow No. 5, along with those concerning the availability of drugs free of FD&C Yellow No. 5, quite persuasive and concludes that FD&C Yellow No. 5 should not be banned from drug products at this time. . . .

FDA . . . concludes that there is no necessity, at this time, for requiring a warning statement on the label of OTC and prescription drugs while requiring only a label declaration on the label of food. FDA also agrees that a label declaration, whether on a food label or a drug label, will achieve the desired notice to sensitive persons. Although several individual comments from some physicians were in favor of the warning statement and/or the ban on FD&C Yellow No. 5, two professional societies of allergists passed resolutions in favor of only the label declaration. To avoid possible confusion concerning the purpose of FD&C Yellow No. 5, however, its presence in drugs, as suggested by one comment, shall be identified on the label as a color additive in a statement such as "Contains FD&C Yellow No. 5 (tartrazine) as a color additive" or "Contains color additives including FD&C Yellow No. 5 (tartrazine)." . . .

The primary basis for this action is section 706(b)(3) of the Federal Food, Drug, and Cosmetic Act, which provides that regulations for the listing of a color additive shall "prescribe the conditions under which such additive may be safely employed for such use or uses (including, but not limited to * * * and directions or other labeling or packaging requirements for such additive)." . . .

NOTES

1. *Yellow No. 6.* FDA's efforts to require label declaration of FD&C Yellow No. 6 because of similar allergic reactions has so far been unsuccessful, *see* p. 82 *supra.*

2. *Legislation.* The 1990 Nutrition Labeling and Education Act mandates that henceforth all certified color additives in a food must be specifically listed among the ingredients.

---

8. ANIMAL DRUG RESIDUES

When a drug is used in a food producing animal (*e.g.*, a cow), some residue of that drug, or a metabolite of the drug, may appear in the food produced by the animal (*i.e.*, the milk or meat). Regulation of animal drugs combines features of both food safety regulation and drug regulation, and the subject is considered more fully in Chapter IV.

---

9. RANKING FOOD RISKS

The assessment by FDA officials of the relative hazards posed by the food supply has not changed significantly in the past two decades. Compare the ranking offered in 1972 by Dr. Virgil Wodicka, Director of the agency's Bureau of Foods, with the estimates in 1989 of Dr. Frank Young, Commissioner of Food and Drugs.

	Wodicka		Young
1.	Food-borne disease	1.	Food-borne disease
[2.	Malnutrition]		
3.	Environmental contaminants	2.	Environmental contaminants
4.	Naturally occurring toxins	3.	Naturally occurring toxins
5.	Pesticide residues	4.	Additives
6.	Deliberate additives	5.	Pesticide residues

See Wodicka, *FDA's Objectives in Food Today,* 27 FDC L.J. 59 (1972); Young, *Weighing Food Safety Risks,* 23 FDA Consumer, No. 7, at 8 (September 1989).

Chapter III
HUMAN DRUGS

A. HISTORICAL BACKGROUND

The first Federal legislation providing for national regulation of all human drugs was the 1906 Food and Drugs Act, but Congress had been concerned about the safety and performance of medications for almost a century before. In 1813 it enacted legislation to assure the dissemination of genuine smallpox vaccine, 2 Stat. 806, and in 1902 it enacted legislation to regulate all biological drugs. *See* Chapter V *infra*. In 1848 Congress passed the following law to prevent the importation of "adulterated and spurious drugs and medicines."

ACT OF JUNE 26, 1848
9 Stat. 237.

Be it enacted by the Senate and House of Representatives of the United States of America in Congress assembled, That from and after the passage of this act, all drugs, medicines, medicinal preparations, including medicinal essential oils, and chemical preparations used wholly or in part as medicine, imported into the United States from abroad, shall, before passing the custom-house, be examined and appraised, as well in reference to their quality, purity, and fitness for medical purposes, as to their value and identity specified in the invoice.

Although passed overwhelmingly by both the House and Senate, the 1848 Act did not have universal support. During the House debate Representative Dickinson expressed doubts which forecast arguments that did not receive serious attention until the 1960s:

Mr. Dickinson said this bill belonged to that class of legislation which attempts to put the bell on the cat. He had no faith in it. The materials would be brought here, and the spurious drugs would be manufactured. If we could stop the compounding of these drugs, interdict patients from taking, and physicians from prescribing, we might do some good. He would not oppose the bill, but he had no faith in this legislation.

Congressional Globe, June 20, 1848, at 858. The 1848 law was not formally supplanted by the 1906 Act, 36 Op. Atty Gen. 311 (July 17, 1907), but ultimately was repealed as part of the enactment of the Tariff Act of 1922, 42 Stat. 858, 989.

JAMES C. MUNCH, A HALF–CENTURY OF DRUG CONTROL
11 Food Drug Cosmetic Law Journal 305 (1956).

... [E]xisting misrepresentations and claims for drugs and drug preparations were so exaggerated as to lead to disrespect for the terms "patent" and "proprietary" remedies, even though many of the manufacturers at that time endeavored to tell the truth and to make proper claims for their products. The series of articles by Edward W. Bok during 1904 and 1905 in the *Ladies' Home Journal* and by Samuel Hopkins Adams in *Collier's* under the title "The Great American Fraud" revealed many of these excessive claims. These publications appear to be the trigger mechanisms stimulating popular and Congressional interest in the passage of suitable control legislation.... Support for [1906] legislation was forthcoming from producers, importers and drug manufacturers, as well as consumers....

Statistical information in FDA annual reports from 1907 through 1939 reveals development of control under the 1906 Act. For the ten years 1930 through 1939, there were 12,016 drug imports detained, of a total of 49,402 offered, or 24 per cent. This may be compared with the data for the four years 1909–1912 (representing drug imports about the time of passage of the 1906 Act, reflecting control under the earlier laws), during which there were 1,350 rejections of a total of 1,931 drug imports offered, or approximately 70 per cent. In the early years, enforcement was largely by prosecution under Section 2; it was necessary to establish rules and regulations for enforcement, and to obtain judicial interpretations of many sections of the Act. Reports show that during the five years 1908–1912, there were 841 prosecutions dealing with drugs, drug products, preparations and medicines, or approximately 25 per cent of the total 3,350 prosecutions. Similar figures for seizure actions under Section 10 were not included in these reports. However, greater use was made of the seizure provisions as enforcement continued. During the last ten-year interval of the 1906 Act, from 1930 through 1939, there were 3,201 prosecutions representing drug control, or 36 per cent of the total 8,804 prosecutions, similarly, there were 3,620 seizures, or 23 per cent of the total 15,666 seizures made. In establishing the project system in 1933, one quarter of the time of the field staff was allocated to drug control projects; percentages for the next seven years ranged from 25 per cent to 33 per cent, averaging 29 per cent.

NOTE

See also Hoge, *The Drug law in Historical Perspective,* 1 FDC L.Q. 48 (1946); Hutt, *Drug Regulation in the United States,* 2 Int. J. of Tech.Assess. in Health

Care 619 (1986); Yakowitz, *The Evolution of the Drug Laws of the United States 1906–1964*, 19 FDC L.J. 296 (1964). For accounts of problems with drugs that led to the 1938 Act, *see* A.J. Cramp, NOSTRUMS AND QUACKERY AND PSEUDO–MEDICINE (1936); M. Fishbein, FADS AND QUACKERY IN HEALING (1932); A. Kallet & F.J. Schlink, 100,000,000 GUINEA PIGS: DANGERS IN EVERYDAY FOODS, DRUGS, AND COSMETICS (1933); R. Lamb, AMERICAN CHAMBER OF HORRORS: THE TRUTH ABOUT FOOD AND DRUGS (1936); J.H. Young, THE MEDICAL MESSIAHS (1967) and THE TOADSTOOL MILLIONAIRES (1961).

B. GENERAL REQUIREMENTS FOR DRUGS
1. DEFINITION OF "DRUG"

The definition of the term "drug" in section 201(g) of the Act expressly excluded "devices," which are separately defined in section 201(h); that exclusion was deleted in 1990. Except for FDA-approved disease prevention claims under the 1990 Nutrition Labeling and Education Act, nothing in section 201(g) precludes FDA from regulating a food as a drug as well. The *V.E. Irons* and *Vitasafe* cases, pp. __ and __ *supra*, demonstrate that FDA has often charged violations of the statutory requirements for both categories of products. Similarly, a product may be both a drug and a cosmetic. Because the statutory requirements for drugs have historically been more rigorous than those for other consumer products, classification has often been the subject of litigation.

UNITED STATES v. 46 CARTONS ... FAIRFAX CIGARETTES
United States District Court, District of New Jersey, 1953.
113 F. Supp. 336.

MEANEY, District Judge.

The claimant introduced into interstate commerce 46 cartons of "Fairfax cigarettes" with 51 accompanying leaflets entitled "How Fairfax Cigarettes may help you." ...

... The libellant contends that the leaflet accompanying the article suggests and represents that the article is effective in preventing respiratory disease, common cold, influenza, pneumonia, acute sinusitis, acute tonsillitis, scarlet fever, whooping cough, measles, meningitis, tuberculosis, mumps, otitis media (middle ear infection), meningopneumonitis psittacosis (parrot fever). Libellant further contends that claimant represents that the smoking of these cigarettes is innocuous for persons suffering from circulatory diseases, high blood pressure and various heart conditions. There is no doubt that the leaflets accompanying the cigarettes fall within the meaning of labeling in the instant case. If there be an indication of intent to use the article for the cure or mitigation, or treatment or prevention of disease in man, then clearly the subject matter of the libel is to be considered a drug within the meaning of the Act....

... If claimant's labeling was such that it created in the mind of the public the idea that these cigarettes could be used for the mitigation or prevention of the various named diseases, claimant cannot now be heard to say that it is selling only cigarettes and not drugs....

Claimant, understandably, does not believe it is selling drugs. It admits that the product has none of the curative or preventive powers implied in the leaflet. But throughout the leaflet claimant has tried to capture a share of the cigarette market by a subtle appeal to a natural and powerful desire on the part of us all to avoid the infectious disease or ailments there in mentioned.... The clear import of the leaflet is at least that the smoking of the cigarettes will make it less likely that the smoker will contract colds or other virus infections. This is enough to bring the product within the statutory meaning of "drug." ...

NOTES

1. *Supporting Authority.* See also *United States v. 354 Bulk Cartons Trim Reducing–Aid Cigarettes,* 178 F. Supp. 847 (D.N.J. 1959).

2. *Tobacco Products.* FDA has taken enforcement action against a number of smoking products on the ground that they fell within one of the categories regulated by the FD&C Act. For example, the agency determined in a letter from FDA Associate Commissioner for Regulatory Affairs J.M. Taylor to S.M. Pape (April 12, 1988) that Masterpiece Tobacs, a snuff product containing tobacco in a masticatory base, was sold in food form and thus was properly regulated as a food under the FD&C Act. In a letter from Assistant to the Director of the Division of Drug Labeling Guidance R.M. Montague to P.N. Georgiades (January 23, 1978), the agency took the position that a chewing gum product containing nicotine and labeled with no therapeutic claims would be regulated as a food and not as a drug. In Regulatory Letter No. 87–HFN–312–06 from Director of the Office of Compliance in the FDA Center for Drugs and Biologics D.L. Michels to Director of Advanced Tobacco Products J.P. Ray (February 9, 1987), FDA stated that Favor Smokeless Cigarettes, a hollow paper tube with nicotine impregnated in the mouthpiece but containing no tobacco, was a drug because it was represented to deliver an amount of nicotine comparable to that of conventional cigarettes and to produce the same nervous system effects. In 1984 FDA approved an NDA for Nicorette, which is indicated "as a temporary aid to the cigarette smoker seeking to give up his or her smoking habit while participating in a behavior modification program under medical or dental supervision." Nicorette is a prescription drug that contains 2 mg nicotine in each piece of chewing gum. PHYSICIANS DESK REFERENCE 1090 (43rd ed. 1989). The agency has classified all smoking deterrent products as drugs, and has published a proposed monograph for nonprescription smoking deterrent drugs as part of the OTC Drug Review in 47 Fed. Reg. 490 (January 5, 1982).

ACTION ON SMOKING AND HEALTH v. HARRIS

United States Court of Appeals, District of Columbia Circuit, 1980.
655 F.2d 236.

On May 26, 1977, Action on Smoking and Health, in conjunction with thirteen other organizations and individuals, filed a citizen petition with the Food and Drug Administration requesting: (1) that the agency assert jurisdiction over cigarettes containing nicotine as a "drug" or a "device"; (2) that the agency regulate cigarettes no less strictly than saccharin; and (3) that the agency restrict the sale of cigarettes to pharmacies.....

Donald Kennedy, Commissioner of Food and Drugs, denied ASH's request that the FDA assert jurisdiction over cigarettes as a drug in a letter memorandum dated December 5, 1977. The Commissioner pointed out initially that FDA jurisdiction could not be predicated upon either evidence of a serious health hazard or the clear absence of authority in any other federal agency to regulate cigarettes. Rather, consistent with the agency's focus upon manufacturers' representations, the FDA has asserted jurisdiction over cigarettes only when health claims were made by the vendors or manufacturers. Absent such claims, the Commissioner stated, cigarettes are not a drug within the meaning of the Act. In answering ASH's contention that cigarettes fall squarely within the statutory definition, the Commissioner stated as follows:

> The petitioners have presented no evidence that manufacturers or vendors of cigarettes represent that the cigarettes are "intended to affect the structure or any function of the body of man ... " 21 U.S.C. § 321(g)(1)(C). Statements by the petitioners and citations in the petition that cigarettes are used by smokers to affect the structure or any functions of their bodies are not evidence of such intent by the manufacturers or vendors of cigarettes, as required under the provisions of 21 U.S.C. § 321(g)(1)(C)....

Unlike petitioners, we do not read these statements to mean either that the Commissioner will never consider evidence of consumer intent on this question or that he simply ignored the evidence presented to him in this petition. Rather, by failing to introduce any evidence of vendors' intent—whether based upon subjective vendor claims or objective evidence such as labeling, promotional material, and advertising— ASH placed itself in the position of having to meet the high standard established in cases where the statutory "intent" is derived from consumer use alone. Clearly, it is well established "that the 'intended use' of a product, within the meaning of the Act, is determined from its label, accompanying labeling, promotional claims, advertising, and any other relevant source." Whether evidence of consumer intent is a "relevant source" for these purposes depends upon whether such evidence is strong enough to justify an inference as to the vendors' intent. This requires a substantial showing....

In cases such as the one at hand, consumers must use the product predominantly—and in fact nearly exclusively—with the appropriate intent before the requisite statutory intent can be inferred. In similar cases involving the determinative intent under section 201(g)(1)(B) of the Act, for example, "articles intended for use in the diagnosis, cure, mitigation, treatment, or prevention of disease ...," courts have accorded limited discretion to the Administration in its attempt to establish the requisite intent based primarily upon consumer use. ASH did not establish, and arguably cannot establish, the near-exclusivity of consumer use of cigarettes with the intent "to affect the structure or any function of the body of man ..." The Commissioner's determination, that this is not the proper case in which some evidence of consumer use, even if demonstrating the appropriate intent, may suffice to establish the requisite statutory intent, was thus neither arbitrary nor capricious. . . .

... [T]he court's remarks in *Federal Trade Commission v. Liggett & Myers Tobacco Co.*, 108 F.Supp. 573 (S.D.N.Y. 1952), *aff'd*, 203 F.2d 955 (2d Cir. 1953), seem as relevant today as they were in 1952:

> Anything which stimulates any of the senses may be said, in some perhaps insignificant degree, to affect the functions of the body of man. Consequently any article which, used in the manner anticipated by the manufacturer thereof, comes into contact with any of the senses may be said to be an article "intended to affect the functions of the body of man". . . .

Surely, the legislators did not mean to be as all-inclusive as a literal interpretation of this clause would compel us to be.

The Administration has also recognized implicit limitations upon the scope of the statutory definition at issue here. In testimony before the Senate, a representative of the Office of the General Counsel, Department of Health, Education, and Welfare, commented on the application of this statutory provision to protective chemical sprays such as "mace." He disagreed with a previous witness on

> whether or not these products could be classified as drugs. We concluded that they could not. They come properly under the Hazardous Substances Act and are not drugs.
>
> I suppose that pistols and bullets are intended to affect the function or structure of the body in the same way these are, but we concluded that the products could not properly be classified as drugs under the definition in the Food, Drug, and Cosmetic Act.

Public Sale of Protective Chemical Sprays: Hearings Before the Consumer Subcomm. of the Senate Comm. on Commerce, 91st Cong., 1st Sess. 37 (1969) (statement of William Goodrich).

The Commissioner demonstrated in his denial letter his awareness of the limitations implicit in the statutory definition of a drug, of case law denying the Federal Trade Commission jurisdiction over cigarettes, and of his own Administration's long-standing interpretation of the scope of its jurisdiction over cigarettes. The Commissioner's restatement of that interpretation cannot be found contrary to law....

NOTES

1. *Cigarette Filters.* In separate petitions filed in 1977 and 1978, ASH also requested FDA to assert jurisdiction over both attached and detached cigarette filters as medical devices, based upon a recommendation by an FDA advisory committee that they be classified in class III under the Medical Device Amendments of 1976, p. 750 *infra.* Following a court order to rule on the petitions, *Action on Smoking and Health v. Food and Drug Administration,* FDLI 1978–1980 Jud. Rec. 862 (D.D.C. 1980), FDA denied both in a letter from Deputy Commissioner M. Novitch to J.F. Banzhaf, III, FDA Dkt. Nos. 77P–0185 & 78P–0338/CP (November 25, 1980). The agency's decision was not challenged in the courts.

2. *Smokeless Cigarette.* In September 1987, R.J. Reynolds Tobacco Co. announced the development of a new cigarette product which heated rather than burned tobacco and thus promised to reduce the products of tobacco combustion. Before Reynolds began test marketing, the Coalition on Smoking or Health submitted two petitions to FDA, one requesting the agency to classify the new product as an "alternative nicotine delivery product" subject to regulation as a drug, and the other requesting classification of all low tar and low nicotine cigarettes as drugs (FDA Dkt. No. 88P–0155/CP001). The American Medical Association submitted a separate petition requesting FDA to assert jurisdiction over the new product, and any similar system that may be developed in the future, as a "nicotine delivery system" that is properly regulated as a drug (FDA Dkt. No. 88P–0155/CP002). Reynolds submitted a response in August 1988 and a month later made public a peer-reviewed summary of the toxicity testing conducted on the product. Test marketing, under the brand name "Premier," began in October 1988 with the primary claim that the product produced a "cleaner" smoke by "substantially reducing many of the controversial compounds found in the smoke of tobacco-burning cigarettes." Four months later Reynolds withdrew the new cigarette after it performed poorly in the marketplace. The *New York Times* editorialized:

> The debacle is likely to please anti-smoking advocates who worry that smokers would seize on the Premier as an excuse not to quit. It will certainly make life easier for the Food and Drug Administration, under pressure to declare Premier a drug delivery system and thus subject to regulation—a decision that would have unleashed the wrath of the tobacco lobby.
>
> But the death of the Premier is no victory for millions of hard-core nicotine addicts who know the risks and smoke anyway. Obviously no smoking is better than smoking, but the best should not be the enemy of the good. There's a strong social case for encouraging manufacturers to develop safer cigarettes that *will* sell.

March 3, 1989, p. A38. In July 1989, FDA concluded that Reynolds' discontinuation of test marketing mooted the dispute; it accordingly declined to rule on the product's legal status or on the status of future similar products.

3. *Lethal Products.* In *United States v. Beuthanasia D Regular,* Food Drug Cosm. L. Rep. (CCH) ¶ 38,265 (D. Neb. 1979), the court upheld an FDA seizure of products intended for euthanasia of animals, rejecting the company's

argument that the products were not drugs and thus were outside the jurisdiction of the FD&C Act. Two years later, FDA rejected a petition to assert jurisdiction over the use of approved pharmaceuticals by state prison officials to accomplish the execution of prisoners sentenced to death. Letter from FDA Commissioner A.H. Hayes, Jr., to D.E. Kendall, FDA Dkt. No. 80P–0513 (July 7, 1981). The Supreme Court ultimately held that the agency's refusal to take enforcement action in this instance was unreviewable. *Heckler v. Chaney*, 470 U.S. 821 (1985).

4. *High–Dose Vitamins.* In the second Vitamin A & D case, *National Nutritional Foods Ass'n v. Mathews*, 557 F.2d 325 (2d Cir.1977), p. 29, *supra,* the Second Circuit held that FDA had failed to justify its conclusion that high dosages of these nutrients were intended by their manufacturers for drug use, and that therefore they could not be limited to sale on prescription. Was the agency's claim against high dosage Vitamin A and D products consistent with its response to the petitions in the *ASH* and *Chaney* cases?

5. *Drug v. Device.* According to Professor David Cavers, *The Food, Drug, and Cosmetic Act of 1938: Its Legislative History and Its Substantive Provisions*, 6 Law and Contemp. Prob. 2 (1939):

> The definition of "drug" in the old [1906] Act was defective in two respects. It did not cover (1) products designed to affect the structure or functioning of the body where disease was not involved or (2) mechanical devices used either for such purposes or in the diagnosis or treatment of disease. Consequently the F&DA was powerless to combat a host of both types of products which appeared on the market under misleading claims and which in some instances were positively dangerous to the user. Accordingly the term "drug" was redefined in S. 1944 so as to include these products. The simple tactic, far from uncommon in statutory definition, of giving a special meaning to an ordinary term, evoked unexpected opposition, and ultimately separate definitions were provided for "drug" and "device." . . .

For a discussion of the problems created by separating these definitions, and the solution ultimately reached in the Medical Device Amendments of 1976, *see* p. 746 *infra.*

6. *Use of Drug Definition to Effect Premarket Approval.* On several occasions, FDA relied on the Act's broad definition of drug to regulate products that would concededly have been subject to the food, device, or cosmetic provisions of the Act. *See, e.g., United States v. An Article of Drug . . . Bacto–Unidisk*, p. 731 *infra; AMP, Inc. v. Gardner*, 275 F. Supp. 410 (S.D.N.Y. 1967), *aff'd*, 389 F.2d 825 (2d Cir. 1968); *United States v. "Sudden Change,"* p. 825 *infra; United States v. "Wilfey's Bio Water",* Food Drug Cosm. L. Rep. (CCH) ¶ 38,143 (D. Or. 1989); and cases noted. In each instance the agency invoked the drug definition in order to demand premarket testing and approval, as the Act does for all "new drugs." In *Bacto–Unidisk*, the Supreme Court sustained FDA's authority to interpret the Act's definitions to accomplish the broad public health objectives of the Act:

> . . . [A]s we have previously held in an analogous situation where the statute's language seemed insufficiently precise, the "natural way" to draw the line "is in light of the statutory purpose." Since the patient will tend to derive less benefit and perhaps some harm from a particular antibiotic if, though the drug itself was properly batch-tested, it was not the proper antibiotic to use, it was entirely reasonable

for the Secretary to determine that the discs, like the antibiotics they serve, are drugs and similarly subject to pre-clearance certification under § 507. . . .

7. *Evidence of Intended Use.* In determining whether a product is intended for use as a drug, FDA will consider representations made by the manufacturer in any forum. In its regulatory letter concerning Favor Smokeless Cigarettes, note 2, p. 384 *supra*, the agency relied upon statements made by the company in submissions to the SEC. In the petition seeking to persuade FDA to regulate Reynolds' new cigarette as a drug, note 2, the petitioners relied upon statements made in the company's patent application.

UNITED STATES v. AN ARTICLE OF DRUG ... OVA II

United States District Court, District of New Jersey, 1975.
414 F. Supp. 660, *aff'd without opinion*, 535 F.2d 1248.

BIUNNO, District Judge.

This case involves the question whether a kit of chemicals and equipment, marketed in interstate commerce by Faraday Laboratories, Inc. under the name "OVA II," is a "drug" within the meaning of the Federal Food, Drug and Cosmetic Act. The kit is marketed with literature indicating its use for the purpose of performing, in the home, a "preliminary screening test" by which a human female, having some reason to suspect that she may be pregnant, may obtain an indication of probability that she is or is not pregnant. . . .

The major difficulty in reaching a decision on the motions arises from the phrasing of the statutory provisions involved. The statutory definition of a "drug," for this purpose, set out in 21 U.S.C. § 321(g)(1), makes use of ordinary words of the language in such peculiar and special senses as to make interpretation an uncertain task.

Three alternative definitions are involved here:

A. "Articles" recognized in the official United States Pharmacopeia, and other identified compendia, are "drugs";

B. "Articles" intended for use in the diagnosis, cure, mitigation, treatment or prevention of disease in man or other animals are "drugs";

C. "Articles" intended to affect the structure or any function of the body of man or other animals are "drugs."

FDA claims that the Ova II kit falls within all three definitions. Faraday claims that it falls within none. Both sides agree that if it comes within any of the definitions of a "drug," it is also a "new drug" as defined by 21 U.S.C. § 321(p), and may not be marketed in interstate commerce without first filing a "new drug application" on the basis of with FDA determines that it is "safe and effective." . . .

Turning to the Ova II kits, the facts are that it consists of two glass vials, and two bottles of solutions. Bottle A contains a solution of hydrochloric acid (HCl). Bottle B contains a solution of sodium hydroxide (NaOH). Use of the kit involves taking a quantity of fresh urine and reacting it with both solutions in the two vials, with differences between them in respect to the number of drops added and the time sequence of the addition. The presence or absence of distinct visual differences in the darkness of the two quantities of urine so treated forms the basis for the indication (distinct differences of color indicates [sic] absence of pregnancy, essentially similar color and saturation indicates pregnancy). This test is in glass, outside the body, using body fluids available by ordinary bodily processes (*i.e., "in vitro"*) to use the technical term). The test does not involve the injection or ingestion of any material in the human body itself (*i.e., "in vivo"*).

Items which are "drugs" as contemplated by the statute fall into two major functional categories. One such category is the "diagnostic" function. The other is the "treatment" function, in the broadest sense that embraces prevention and alleviation of pain or discomfort as well as "cure." Those items related to the treatment function are necessarily "in vivo." Something must be done, or applied to or placed within the body itself to provide treatment. At least in this country, treatment outside the body, as by inserting pins in a doll, is not considered to be treatment. Those items related to the diagnostic function may be either "in vivo" or "in vitro." ...

There is no dispute that FDA has the burden of persuasion. Taking each of the three definitions of a "drug," as set out in 21 U.S.C. § 321(g)(1), it is plain that the Ova II kit does not fall within any of them.

The first definition, *i.e.*, recognition of an item in the U.S. Pharmacopeia, National Formularly, etc., cannot be taken literally. In the first place, none of these compendium publications is more than a privately sponsored set of standards of strength and purity, for medicinal use, which may properly carry labeling such as "U.S.P." or "N.F.," and the like....

These compendiums and pharmacopeiae, being privately published, make changes from time to time. And thus the question arises whether they can have the force of law without running afoul of the principle that a legislative body may not lawfully delegate its functions to a private citizen or organization. Limited delegation of legislative functions to governmental agencies within the boundaries of an expressed norm, standard or guide is well recognized; but a delegation to private groups, and without such boundaries, is quite another matter....

Since the Congress will not be presumed to have enacted an invalid statute, the first definition, *i.e.*, recognition in the U.S.P. or other named compendium must be read to meant that:

(a) an article put into the stream of interstate commerce with the intention that it be used for medicinal purposes, as evidenced by the label designation "U.S.P.," "N.F.," and the like, must meet the privately designated standards for quality and strength, or else be subject to appropriate action for misbranding or adulteration;

(b) the recognition of an item in the U.S.P., etc., by a monograph, coupled with a label indicating compliance with standards, constitutes evidence that the item is a "drug" as a matter of prima facie proof only, calling on the opposing party to come forward with contrary evidence or else risk an adverse ruling; ...

(d) an item recognized in U.S.P., etc., such as sodium hydroxide, hydrochloric acid, or whatever, by name, is not a drug if it is put into the channels of interstate commerce without a label such as "U.S.P.," "N.F." and the like, to imply that it is intended for medicinal use.

Under this interpretation, the Ova II kit is not a drug under 21 U.S.C. § 321(g)(1)(A), despite the fact that it contains sodium hydroxide and hydrochloric acid, since it is not labeled "U.S.P." etc., and is not marketed for medicinal use.

The second definition, namely articles related to the diagnosis of disease, etc., does not apply to the Ova II kit because its purpose is to indicate the existence or non-existence of pregnancy, which is not of itself a disease, and because no other pregnancy test attempts or purports to do anything more than Ova II does.

The third definition, articles intended to affect the structure or any function of the body is obviously not applicable to any article which is used "in vitro," and in no way inserted in, injected in, ingested by or applied to the body....

NOTES

1. *Device Coverage.* With the enactment of the 1976 Medical Device Amendments, products such as Ova II became unequivocally "devices," *see* p. 746 *infra,* but the court's discussion of the "drug" definition retains vitality.

2. *Compendium Listing.* See also *National Nutritional Foods Association v. FDA,* 504 F.2d 761, 788–789 (2d Cir. 1974), and *National Nutritional Foods Association v. Mathews,* 557 F.2d 325, 337–38 (2d Cir. 1977), where the courts held that mere inclusion in an official compendium does not conclusively establish drug status.

---

2. REGULATION OF THERAPEUTIC CLAIMS

Section 502(a) of the Act provides that a drug "shall be deemed to be misbranded ... if its labeling is false or misleading in any particular." Until 1962 this language formed the primary basis for FDA's regulation of therapeutic claims for drugs, and represented an expansion of FDA's authority under the 1906 Act.

Early efforts to regulate drug claims were hampered by narrow interpretations of government authority. In the famous case *American Judicial School of Magnetic Healing v. McAnnulty*, 187 U.S. 94 (1902), the plaintiff was engaged in the business of healing human diseases through appeals to the mind. A large part of the plaintiff's business consisted of providing "treatment" by letter to people throughout the United States. The plaintiff sought an injunction, enjoining the defendant, the local postmaster, from continuing to comply with an order issued by the Postmaster General directing the defendant to return all letters addressed to the school to the original senders with the word "fraudulent" stamped on the outside, and to refuse payment of any postal order drawn to the order of the school. The authority relied on to justify the order was a federal statute granting the Postmaster General discretion to instruct local postmasters to take such preventive steps against any person found to be engaged in a " ... scheme or device for obtaining money through the mail by means of false or fraudulent pretenses, representations or promises...." The lower court sustained the local postmaster's demurrer and dismissed the complaint seeking injunctive relief for insufficiency in law and equity. The Supreme Court, however, reversed in an opinion which questioned the government's authority to regulate the truth of therapeutic claims.

... Just exactly to what extent the mental condition affects the body, no one can accurately and definitely say.... The claim of the ability to cure may be vastly greater than most men would be ready to admit, and yet those who might deny the existence or virtue of the remedy would only differ in opinion from those who assert it. There is no exact standard of absolute truth by which to prove the assertion false and a fraud. We mean by that to say that the claim of complainants cannot be the subject of proof as of an ordinary fact; it cannot be proved as a fact to be a fraud or false pretense or promise, nor can it properly be said that those who assume to heal bodily ills or infirmities by a resort to this method of cure are guilty of obtaining money under false pretenses, such as are intended in the statutes, which evidently do not assume to deal with mere matters of opinion upon subjects which are not capable of proof as to their falsity....

As the effectiveness of almost any particular method of treatment of disease is, to a more or less extent, a fruitful source of difference of opinion, even though the great majority may be of one way of thinking, the efficacy of any special method is certainly not a matter for the decision of the Postmaster General within these statutes relative to fraud. Unless the question may be reduced to one of fact as distinguished from mere opinion, we think these statutes cannot be invoked for the purpose of stopping the delivery of mail matter....

UNITED STATES v. JOHNSON

Supreme Court of the United States, 1911.
221 U.S. 488.

Mr. Justice HOLMES delivered the opinion of the court.

This is an indictment for delivering for shipment from Missouri to Washington, D.C., packages and bottles of medicine bearing labels that stated or implied that the contents were effective in curing cancer, the defendant well knowing that such representations were false....

The question is whether the articles were misbranded within the meaning of § 2 of the Food and Drugs Act of June 30, 1906.... By § 8, the term misbranded "shall apply to all drugs, or articles of food, ... the package or label of which shall bear any statement, design, or device regarding such article, or the ingredients or substances contained therein, which shall be false or misleading in any particular, and to any food or drug product which is falsely branded as to the State, Territory, or country in which it is manufactured or produced...."

It is a postulate, as the case comes before us, that in a certain sense the statement on the label was false, or, at least misleading. What we have to decide is whether such misleading statements are aimed at and hit by the words of the act. It seems to us that the words used convey to an ear trained by the usages of English speech a different aim; and although the meaning of a sentence is to be felt rather than to be proved, generally and here the impression may be strengthened by argument, as we shall try to show.

... [W]e are of opinion that the phrase is aimed not at all possible false statements, but only at such as determine the identity of the article, possibly including its strength, quality and purity, dealt with in § 7....

In view of what we have said by way of simple interpretation we think it unnecessary to go into considerations of wider scope. We shall say nothing as to the limits of constitutional power, and but a word as to what Congress was likely to attempt. It was much more likely to regulate commerce in food and drugs with reference to plain matter of fact, so that food and drugs should be what they professed to be, when the kind was stated, than to distort the uses of its constitutional power to establishing criteria in regions where opinions are far apart. *See School of Magnetic Healing v. McAnnulty.* ...

SEVEN CASES OF ECKMAN'S ALTERATIVE v. UNITED STATES

Supreme Court of the United States, 1916.
239 U.S. 510.

Mr. Justice HUGHES delivered the opinion of the court.

Libels were filed by the United States, in December 1912, to condemn certain articles of drugs (known as "Eckman's Alterative") as misbranded in violation of § 8 of the Food & Drugs Act. . . . Section 8 of the Food & Drugs Act, as amended by the act of August 23, 1912, c. 352, 37 Stat. 416, provides, with respect to the misbranding of drugs, as follows: . . .

> "Third. If its package or label shall bear or contain any statement, design, or device regarding the curative or therapeutic effect of such article or any of the ingredients or substances contained therein, which is false and fraudulent."

The [Sherley] amendment of 1912 consisted in the addition of paragraph "Third," which is the provision here involved.

It is alleged in each libel that every one of the cases of drugs sought to be condemned contained twelve bottles, each of which was labeled as follows:

> "Eckman's Alterative,—contains twelve per cent of alcohol by weight, or fourteen per cent by volume—used as a solvent. For all throat and lung disease including Bronchitis, Bronchial Catarrh, Asthma, Hay Fever, Coughs and Colds, and Catarrh of the Stomach and Bowels, and Tuberculosis (Consumption). . . . Two dollars a bottle. Prepaid only by Eckman Mfg. Co. Laboratory Philadelphia, Penna., U.S.A."

And in every package, containing one of the bottles, there was contained a circular with this statement:

> "Effective as a preventative for Pneumonia." "We know it has cured and that it has and will cure Tuberculosis."

The libel charges that the statement "effective as a preventative for pneumonia" is "false, fraudulent and misleading in this, to-wit, that it conveys the impression to purchasers that said article of drugs can be used as an effective preventative for pneumonia, whereas, in truth and in fact said article of drugs could not be so used"; and that the statement, "we know it has cured" and that it "will cure tuberculosis" is "false, fraudulent and misleading in this, to-wit, that it conveys the impression to purchasers that said article of drugs will cure tuberculosis, or consumption, whereas, in truth and in fact said article of drugs would not cure tuberculosis, or consumption, there being no medicinal substance nor mixture of substances known at present which can be relied upon for the effective treatment or cure of tuberculosis, or consumption."

The principal question presented on this writ of error is with respect to the validity of the amendment of 1912. . . .

. . . [T]he statute is attacked upon the ground that it enters the domain of speculation (*American School of Magnetic Healing v. McAnnulty*, 187 U.S. 94 (1902)) and by virtue of consequent uncertainty operates as a deprivation of liberty and property without due process of law in violation of the Fifth Amendment of the Constitution, and does not permit of the laying of a definite charge as required by the Sixth Amendment. We think that this objection proceeds upon a misconstruction of the provision. Congress deliberately excluded the field where there are honest differences of opinion between schools and practitioners. It was, plainly, to leave no doubt upon his point that the words "false *and fraudulent*" were used. This phrase must be taken with its accepted legal meaning, and thus it must be found that the statement contained in the package was put there to accompany the goods with actual intent to deceive,—an intent which may be derived from the facts and circumstances, but which must be established. That false and fraudulent representations may be made with respect to the curative effect of substances is obvious. It is said that the owner has the right to give his views regarding the effect of his drugs. But state of mind is itself a fact, and may be a material fact, and false and fraudulent representations may be made about it; and persons who make or deal in substances, or compositions, alleged to be curative, are in a position to have superior knowledge and may be held to good faith in their statements. It cannot be said, for example, that one who should put inert matter or a worthless composition in the channels of trade, labeled or described in an accompanying circular as a cure for disease when he knows it is not, is beyond the reach of the law-making power. Congress recognized that there was a wide field in which assertions as to curative effect are in no sense honest expressions of opinion but constitute absolute falsehoods and in the nature of the case can be deemed to have been made only with fraudulent purpose. The amendment of 1912 applies to this field and we have no doubt of its validity. . . .

Judgments affirmed.

NOTE

In spite of the difficulties posed by the *American School of Magnetic Healing* and *Johnson* cases, and by the Sherley Amendment of 1912, 37 Stat. 416 (1912), FDA enforced the drug misbranding provisions of the 1906 Act vigorously and with significant success. *See, e.g., United States v. Antikamnia Chem. Co.,* 231 U.S. 654 (1914); *Simpson v. United States,* 241 Fed. 841 (6th Cir. 1917); *Abbott Bros. Co. v. United States,* 242 Fed. 751 (7th Cir. 1917); *Hall v. United States,* 267 Fed. 795 (5th Cir. 1920); *United States v. Chichester Chem. Co.,* 298 Fed. 829 (D.C. Cir. 1924); *United States v. John J. Fulton Co.,* 33 F.2d 506 (9th Cir. 1929); *United States v. 17 Bottles . . . "B & M",* 55 F.2d 264 (D. Md. 1932); *United States v. William H. Rorer, Inc.,* 27 F. Supp. 671 (E.D. Pa. 1936).

DAVID CAVERS, THE FOOD, DRUG AND COSMETIC ACT OF 1938: ITS LEGISLATIVE HISTORY AND ITS SUBSTANTIVE PROVISIONS

6 Law & Contemporary Problems 2 (1939).

The new Act preserves the broad definition of misbranding contained in the old Act, *viz.*, "false or misleading in any particular." . . .

[I]n the old Act, however, this definition was supplemented by a special requirement, applicable to therapeutic claims, which had been added in 1912 by the Sherley Amendment and which compelled proof that claims were both "false *and* fraudulent." This provision in effect accorded a license to the ignorant nostrum vendor who sold inefficacious drugs in good faith. Moreover, fraud is always difficult to prove, and the F&DA was driven to elaborate investigations and costly trials to secure even the seizure of drugs for which outrageous label claims were made. But since the truth or falsity of therapeutic claims must often rest on opinion evidence and since expert opinion may differ, it was felt essential to provide a criterion of opinion evidence sufficiently definite to avoid the risk that the provision would be held unconstitutional for want of certainty. In S. 1944, therefore, the general definition of misbranding was supplemented, as to drugs, by the following: "if its labeling bears any representation, directly or by ambiguity or inference, concerning the effect of such drug which is contrary to the general agreement of medical opinion." Where no such agreement existed, of course the government's burden of proof could not be sustained. With respect to most claims which called for prosecution, general agreement could normally be anticipated, but recognition of the fact that, as to new products, medical opinion might not have crystallized, resulted in the addition, in S. 2000, of an alternative criterion, "demonstrable scientific facts." This was retained in S. 5 as introduced in 1935, and passed by the Senate that year with minor changes. In S. 5, 1937 model, however, the provision was completely eliminated and did not reappear in the bill.

Concern was not felt that this omission would cause constitutional objection in cases where medical opinion agreed, or scientific fact demonstrated, that the claims at issue were false, but the risk that the defendant might produce one or two experts whose opinion ran counter to the greater weight of scientific opinion was still present. The inclusion of Section 201(n) in S. 5, as reported by the House Committee in 1938, was thought to meet this difficulty....

RESEARCH LABORATORIES, INC. v. UNITED STATES

United States Court of Appeals, Ninth Circuit, 1948.
167 F.2d 410.

GARRECHT, Circuit Judge.

In November, 1944, a libel was filed in the United States District Court for the Western District of Missouri, Western Division pursuant to which there were seized by the United States Marshal about 600 units of Nue–Ovo, each unit containing three bottles.... Pursuant to the same libel there were also seized at the same time stocks of circulars entitled "information on Nue–Ovo and its value in Arthritic and other Rheumatoid symptoms." ...

Summarized, the appellant's attacks upon the judgment below are as follows:

The court below erred in submitting issues to the jury, since every statement in the labeling as to the effectiveness of the product is a statement of opinion, and at the conclusion of the case the record showed nothing more than a difference of opinion among qualified medical experts as to the effectiveness of the product....

As applied by the court the statute is unconstitutional....

It cannot be assumed that the Supreme Court intended to reach out a dead hand over the power of Congress to pass legislation in the future setting up a well-equipped Federal agency capable of arriving at a professional conclusion as to the adulteration or misbranding of drugs "when introduced into or while in interstate commerce." In the *McAnnulty* case the court not only pointed out that "as the case arises on demurrer, all material facts averred in the bill are, of course, admitted," but throughout the opinion doubt was expressed as to the qualifications of a *postmaster general* to pass on medical questions....

In contrast to the meager technical facilities for the determination of medical questions possessed by the Postmaster General—at least at the time that the *McAnnulty* case was decided—we find that the Federal Security Agency has at its disposal almost unlimited professional resources with which to carry out its investigations in the enforcement of the Federal Food, Drug, and Cosmetic Act....

In view of the foregoing, it could well have been reasoned a priori that the impact of the *McAnnulty* case would be carefully limited in later decisions. And that is precisely what has occurred....

Much of the appellee's evidence in the instant case consisted of "controlled clinical studies" conducted by eminently qualified physicians and surgeons.... Testimony of experts that is based upon tests or experiments made by them does not come within the ambit of the *McAnnulty* rule.... It is generally agreed that testimony as to the consensus of medical opinion may be considered in drug-misbranding cases....

In this circuit and elsewhere, it has been held that expert testimony even in its broadest sense—i.e., where the witness has neither tested the product nor purports to report the consensus of medical opinion—is admissible on the question of therapeutic value....

The evidence in this case included the three types that we have discussed hereinabove: Testimony by experts based on (a) tests made of the product itself; (b) the consensus of medical opinion as to the various ingredients used in Nue–Ovo; and (c) the expert witnesses' personal opinions regarding the effectiveness of such ingredients. Altogether, there was ample evidence to support the verdict of the jury....

... [T]he Nue–Ovo labeling contains an "analysis of ingredients," with the prefatory explanation that it is based chiefly on the United Stated Dispensatory, the Pharmacopoeia, and various textbooks on pharmacology. It is here that half-truths enter the picture. While the label's "analysis" followed part of the language of the above named authorities somewhat closely, and sometimes verbatim, there were significant omissions in the excerpts. Here are a few of the deleted portions:

[Ginseng] "The extraordinary medicinal virtues formerly described as [ascribed to] Ginseng had no other existence than in the imagination of the Chinese."

[Horehound] "It has, however, been almost completely abandoned by physicians."

[Salvia or Sage] "For what reasons this condiment was admitted into the N.F. is not obvious. While the ancients say it is highly esteemed, there is no evidence that it possesses therapeutic virtues, and it is practically never prescribed by physicians."

[Lappa or Burdock] "There is not sufficient reason, however, to believe it has any medicinal virtues."

The apocryphal or misleading testimonials and the scientific half-truths in the labeling alone make out a case of actionable misbranding. . . .

It is well settled that the 1938 act was intended to make the provisions against misbranding stricter and not more lenient than they had been in pre-existing laws. The new statute was not designed to provide the misbrander of drugs with additional technical loopholes for escape, but to batten down those already existing. . . . It was to cover precisely such tricky omissions and suppressions that Section 321(n) was designed.

Furthermore, in *any* case where "an article is alleged to be misbranded because the labeling is misleading" in *any* respect, it is made mandatory by § 321(n) itself that the jury "shall" take into account such omissions or suppressions. . . . Accordingly, it was not only not erroneous for the court to instruct the jury on § 321(n), but, under the facts of this case and under the terms of the subsection itself, it was the court's duty to do so. . . .

NOTES

1. *Disclaimers. Research Laboratories* demonstrates that FDA is not disabled from proceeding against misleading claims of therapeutic value masquerading as assertions of opinion. Cases decided under the 1938 Act hold that deception may result from label statements that are technically accurate but misleading in overall impression. Thus, a disclaimer may not be availing. For example, the statement "this preparation does not contain any known therapeutically useful constituent," did not prevent a finding of misbranding in *Pasadena Research Laboratories v. United States,* 169 F.2d 375 (9th Cir. 1948).

2. *Deceptive Names.* The name of a product may impliedly convey a claim of effectiveness that, if false, may render it misbranded. In one case, the use of the term "prophylactics" was sufficient to support the government's seizure upon a finding that several of the claimant's articles contained holes. *United*

States v. 43½ Gross ... "Xcello's Prophylactics," 65 F.Supp. 534 (D. Minn. 1946), p. 1130 *infra.*

3. *Attributed Claims.* Even under the 1906 Act (following passage of the Sherley Amendment) a manufacturer could not escape by attributing false representations of a drug's effectiveness to third parties. In *United States v. John J. Fulton, Co.,* 33 F.2d 506 (9th Cir. 1929), for example, the manufacturer had claimed only that "we have received many letters from physicians reporting" success with this drug. The court characterized such labeling as even more obnoxious than false express claims of therapeutic benefit.

4. *Symptoms v. Underlying Conditions.* Another common deception has been found in labeling for products capable of treating minor ailments such as constipation, whose labeling also proclaims an ability to relieve symptoms that accompany more serious conditions for which the product is of no use whatever. *United States v. Six Dozen Bottles ... "Dr. Peter's Kuriko,"* 158 F.2d 667 (7th Cir. 1947).

5. *Section 201(n).* In addition to providing support for FDA enforcement proceedings based on section 502(a), or section 403(a), in recent years section 201(n) has become significant as a supplementary source of authority for regulations imposing affirmative disclosure requirements. *See National Nutritional Foods Ass'n v. Califano,* p. 1290 *infra; Cosmetic, Toiletry and Fragrance Ass'n, Inc. v. Schmidt,* 409 F.Supp. 57 (D.D.C. 1976). For a discussion of the origin of section 201(n), *see* Williams, *Failure to Reveal Material Facts in Labeling,* 3 FDC L.Q. 64 (1948).

6. *Premarket Approval of Therapeutic Claims.* Court enforcement of section 502(a) no longer plays a major role in FDA's efforts to combat false or misleading therapeutic claims for drugs. The principal explanation for the agency's change of focus lies in the passage of the 1962 Drug Amendments, which gave it authority to demand premarket proof of the effectiveness of all "new drugs," including drugs marketed prior to 1962. For all post–1962 prescription drugs FDA has controlled therapeutic claims through the new drug approval process, where it may force a manufacturer to recast or omit proposed claims before allowing a drug to be marketed. Claims for OTC drugs are subject to FDA regulation under the OTC Drug Review, p. 588 *infra.* For both prescription and OTC drugs, FDA court enforcement actions since 1962 have uniformly charged a violation of the new drug provisions of the Act, rather than, or occasionally in addition to, the misbranding provisions. A claim that a drug is a "new drug" marketed without FDA approval can be sustained based on affidavits that the drug is not *generally recognized* as safe and effective for the claims made. The court need not adjudicate the validity of the claims themselves. *See* pp. 488–92 *infra.*

7. *Advertising Claims.* FDA's use of its licensing authority to regulate label claims in advance of marketing, however, has not obviated scrutiny of the claims made for drugs once they are marketed. FDA has focused its attention on claims made in advertising which, for prescription drugs, falls within its jurisdiction. The agency's customary remedy has been to require the miscreant manufacturer to disseminate "corrective" advertisements through the same channels as the original message. Very rarely has it gone to court. Whether correction is necessary and what form it should take are questions ordinarily worked out in private negotiations with the manufacturer. FDA's regulation of prescription drug advertising is considered in more detail at p. 452 *infra.*

FDA lacks jurisdiction over the advertising of OTC drugs, which is the province of the FTC, and most manufacturers tailor their label claims to minimize the risk of FDA attack. The sheer number of products involved—between 100,000 and 200,000—has generally discouraged both agencies from relying on case-by-case court enforcement.

8. *Priorities for Regulatory Action.* Recognizing that it cannot take action against all illegal drug claims, FDA in Compliance Policy Guide 7150.12 (December 14, 1978) established the following priorities for initiating legal action against "quackery": (1) direct health hazard, (2) indirect health hazard, (3) major economic frauds, and (4) minor economic cheats.

9. *Case Law.* Cases involving false or misleading drug claims under the 1938 Act are legion. Some of the more colorful include *United States v. 11¼ Dozen Packages ... "Mrs. Moffat's Shoo Fly Powders for Drunkenness,"* 40 F. Supp. 208 (W.D.N.Y. 1941); *Empire Oil & Gas Corp. v. United States,* 136 F.2d 868 (9th Cir. 1943); *Pasadena Research Laboratories, Inc. v. United States,* 169 F.2d 375 (9th Cir. 1948); *Colusa Remedy Co. v. United States,* 176 F.2d 554 (8th Cir. 1949); *United States v. Hoxsey Cancer Clinic,* 198 F.2d 273 (5th Cir. 1952); *United States v. Wier,* 281 F.2d 850 (5th Cir. 1960); *United States v. 4 Cases Slim-Mint Chewing Gum,* 300 F.2d 144 (7th Cir. 1962).

10. *Section 502(j).* Although section 502(j) of the Act provides that a drug is misbranded if it is dangerous to health when used in accordance with the labeling, FDA has seldom invoked this provision because violations of other overlapping sections are easier to prove. A case that applies this section is *United States v. 62 Packages ... Marmola Prescription Tablets,* 142 F.2d 107 (7th Cir. 1944).

11. *Commentary.* See also Kaplan, *Therapeutic Claims and the Federal Government,* 11 FDC L.J. 219 (1956); Kuniholm, *Constitutional Limitations on the Regulation of Therapeutic Claims under 1938 Federal Food, Drug, and Cosmetic Act,* 9 FDC L.J. 629 (1954).

---

3. ADEQUATE DIRECTIONS FOR USE

The Act's definitions of "label" and "labeling" apply to foods, drugs, devices and cosmetics without differentiation. Thus the *Kordel* and *Urbuteit* cases, pp. 43–45 *supra,* are germane to the statutory requirements examined in this chapter. Indeed, most of the cases that have dealt with the scope of the Act's requirements for "labeling" have involved drugs.

ALBERTY FOOD PRODUCTS CO. v. UNITED STATES

United States Court of Appeals, Ninth Circuit, 1950.
185 F.2d 321.

BONE, Circuit Judge.

Appellee filed a libel under which it seized appellant's drug here involved (33 botttles of Ri–Co Tablets) charging therein that the drug was "misbranded" in violation of 21 U.S.C. § 352(f)(1) of the Federal

Food, Drug, and Cosmetic Act.... The specific ground of complaint was that the "labeling" of the drug failed to bear adequate directions for use since it did not state the purpose or condition for which the drug was intended. The only directions for use on the label attached to the bottle read as follows: "Three tablets with a cupful of hot water. Take four times daily. Before meals and on going to bed."

At the hearing below two newspaper advertisements from daily publications in large cities were introduced. These ads show that appellant's drug was there represented and recommended by appellant [f]or use in the treatment, mitigation, and cure of arthritis and rheumatism. [One of t]he two advertisements read as follows:

"Rocky Mountain News Tuesday, Oct. 1, 1946

"Arthritis
Rheumatism
Rico Tablets
Another Alberty
Product

"Do you suffer from Arthritis or Rheumatism, two of the most painful ailments that afflict mankind?

"These ailments arise from the same underlying cause— too much acidity that permits deposits of urates in joints or muscles that cause excruciating pain.

"Science has spent many years searching for remedies for these ailments. If you have tried many remedies without relief Try Rico, a formula discovered by a famous Homeopathic physician for relief of the pains of Arthritis and Rheumatism. For over 15 years this formula has been used by many eminent Homeopathic Physicians...."

Appellant appeared as claimant of the drug and filed exceptions to the libel. In essence the exceptions were that the Act does not require the labeling of a drug to state the disease condition for which it is to be used. In this connection it contended that the misbranding here charged was merely a failure to include upon the label of the container information to consumers which was not required by the Act to be included thereon either as directions for its use or otherwise. As a consequence the libel failed to state a cause of action because the alleged misbranding was not a misbranding at all. Appellant's exceptions were overruled by the trial court....

After the answer, appellee filed a motion for summary judgment.... Appellant filed no counter-affidavits, and after hearing the court granted appellee's motion for summary judgment, made and entered Findings and Conclusions and a Decree pursuant thereto....

In appellant's argument ... it says: ...

"*The directions printed on the label* of Ri–Co Tablets are adequate for *their use* in all conditions for which they are prescribed, recommended, suggested, or commonly and effectively used. The Act does not require a label to include *a statement of those conditions* and the decree should accordingly be reversed with instructions to dismiss the libel...." (Emphasis supplied.) ...

As respects the legal sufficiency of the label appearing on its bottle appellant clarifies its position by the further argument: "The Government * * * contends that no information could be more essential to the consumer regarding a drug which he can purchase without prescription than a statement of the conditions for which the drug is used. We agree that no one is likely to purchase a drug without knowing the conditions for which the drug is used. That knowledge, however, *must* be imparted to the consumer by means other than the label. He must have it before he gets close enough to the label to be able to read its fine print. In other words, he will not buy the drug unless he learns of the conditions for which it is used *from sources outside the label,* as by prescription, recommendation, suggestion, or common and effective usage. By the time he sees the label, he needs only to be protected by being told how to use the drug for the condition for which he is purchasing it. If '4 times daily' is an adequate direction for the use of the drug in that condition, the label complies with the Act irrespective of whether it refers to that condition." (Emphasis supplied.)

The foregoing argument conclusively shows that appellant relied exclusively upon these "outside sources," namely, the newspaper advertisements, to provide *all* of the information which could possibly enlighten prospective purchasers of its drug concerning "the conditions" for which the drug was to be used by them....

... Appellant did not resort to the distribution of any sort of "literature" to ultimate purchasers as a "supplement" to its package label. Neither did it distribute such "literature" to purchasers, actual or prospective, to promote sales and to describe and advertise the therapeutic qualities of its drug. Appellant used only the newspaper advertisements and we think that it cannot be said that these advertisements "accompanied" appellant's drug into interstate commerce, and were "distributed" by vendors, or otherwise, to ultimate purchasers of the drug as part of an "integrated distribution program." ...

What we have already said leads us to disagree with appellant's contention that by employing these "remote" newspaper advertisements it fully supplied a legally adequate "labeling" which described the *use* of the drug in the treatment or alleviation of arthritic or rheumatic conditions. It seems to us that supporting appellant's views would be a long and drastic step toward nullifying what we regard as salutary protective features of the act which Congress designed to control and regulate the sale of drugs to a helpless public—helpless because it is uninformed.... The logic of the *Kordel* and *Urbuteit* cases would seem to repel the conclusion that the therapeutic claims made only in random newspaper advertisements, *must* be considered and deemed to be a part of, and to be "accompanying" and "supplementing," the brief dosage statement appearing on the bottles containing appellant's drug. There is no hint in the record that these advertisements were reproduced in pamphlet or leaflet form and shipped with the drug on its interstate journey from appellant to its vendors to be distributed to ultimate consumers. No claim is made that the reading matter in the newspaper advertising appeared in any sort of literature (pamphlet, etc.) which was made available by vendors to purchasers of the drug.

A wholly justifiable inference is that many of those who suffer from pains of arthritis and rheumatism—and they are legion—never heard of Ri–Co Tablets, and undoubtedly never saw, or had a chance to see, appellant's newspaper advertisements. It is certain that as to them, these advertisements gave absolutely no notice of the existence of the drug, its dosage, uses and *therapeutic qualities.* We proceed upon the assumption that the "adequate directions for use" mandate of Sec. 352(f)(1) requires that *all* who might want to use a drug to relieve the pains of arthritis and rheumatism are at least entitled to a chance to somewhere find and examine a "label" which is complete enough to give them information which would lead them to purchase a drug for that purpose, or, in other words, provide sufficient information at the time of purchase upon which intelligent determination might be made as to whether the drug is one which is prescribed, recommended, or suggested for their particular form of arthritic or rheumatic ailment. We are persuaded that the law requires this much.

Since the kind of complete information we have indicated was not made available to the general run of victims of arthritis and rheumatism by a proper and adequate "labeling" of appellant's drug, we must hold that it was "misbranded" under Sec. 352(f)(1) of the Act. This for the reason that what appellant insists is a proper and adequate "labeling" falls far short of legal requirements. It failed to bear "adequate directions for use" since it did not state the purpose or condition for which the drug was intended.

NOTES

1. *Relevance of Advertising Claims.* In *Alberty Food Prods. v. United States,* 194 F.2d 463 (9th Cir. 1952), the company unsuccessfully argued that, if directions for use contained in advertising are insufficient to satisfy section 502(f)(1), advertising claims similarly cannot be considered in determining the intended uses of a drug for which the labeling must bear adequate directions:

> ... This contention fails to grasp the scope and purpose of the inquiry with which the Court was concerned. It is not the truth or falsity of the literature and advertising which is challenged; it is merely consideration, as evidence, of claims promulgated by the manufacturer in measuring whether the information communicated by means of the label adequately describes the diseases or conditions for which the drug was intended as well as relevant facts containing dosage.

In order for the labeling of a drug to bear "adequate directions for use" within the meaning of 21 U.S.C. § 352(f)(1) it must, among other things, state the purposes and conditions for which the drug was intended and sufficient information to enable a layman to intelligently and safely attempt self medication.

While appellants agree with this construction they argue that such fact must be determined from the labeling alone. This contention is without merit. It is not sufficient that the labeling contain a minimum of information and the use of the drug be induced by elaborate collateral representations. To permit the operation of such an escape valve would render the aims and purposes of labeling requirements nugatory....

2. *FDA's "Squeeze Play."* Suppose that Alberty had sought to comply with section 502(f) by including indications for arthritis and rheumatism in its labeling for Ri–Co Tablets. Would FDA have been content with this labeling? Or would it have then claimed that the product was misbranded under section 502(a)? The FDA approach reflected in this case has come to be referred to as the "squeeze play." For additional examples of the "squeeze play," *see V.E. Irons, Inc. v. United States,* 244 F.2d 34 (1st Cir. 1957); *United States v. Hohensee,* 243 F.2d 367 (3d Cir. 1957); *United States v. 38 Dozen Bottles ... Tryptacin,* 114 F. Supp. 461 (D. Minn. 1953); Dickerman, *"Adequate Directions for Use,"* 7 FDC L.J. 738 (1952). *See also* Frailey, *Observations on Section 502(f)(1),* 3 FDC L.Q. 255 (1948); Nelson, *Control of Advertising by Section 502(f)(1),* 7 FDC L.J. 579 (1952).

3. *Relation to New Drug Provisions.* Just like section 502(a), reliance on section 502(f)(1) in FDA court enforcement proceedings has been largely superseded by claims based on the new drug provisions of the Act. *United States v. Articles of Drug,* 625 F.2d 665 (5th Cir. 1980), is thus unusual because there FDA successfully charged a violation of selection 502(f)(1), as interpreted in 21 C.F.R. § 201.5, rather than of section 505. The agency explained that because it had seized the products before they were shipped in interstate commerce it could not bring a new drug charge. Under these circumstances, state authorities may also take action. *DeMarco v. Commonwealth of Pennsylvania,* 40 Pa.Cmwlth. 248, 397 A.2d 61 (1979).

UNITED STATES v. ARTICLE OF DRUG ... DESIGNATED B–COMPLEX CHOLINOS CAPSULES

United States Court of Appeals, Third Circuit, 1966.
362 F.2d 923.

KIRKPATRICK, District Judge.

... The misbranding charged by the Government was that the labeling of the products was not in compliance with Section 352(f)(1) of the Act in that it failed to bear "adequate directions for use." The appellant, Foods Plus, Inc., the manufacturer and owner of the seized articles, filed a claim for them in the District Court.... The trial judge found as a fact that the articles seized (which comprised various quantities of some 43 different formulas of vitamin, mineral and other dietary preparations) were drugs—a finding not now disputed.

The labeling in this case consisted of a catalog of the vitamin and mineral products offered for sale by the claimant, it having been stipulated that its catalogs were labels within the meaning of the Act.

Whether labeling contains "adequate directions for use" of an article necessarily depends upon what it is intended to be used for. In this case, although the catalogs were in a general way suggestive of therapeutic values for the products, they contained nothing whatever to indicate for what diseases or conditions the various preparations were supposed to be beneficial and, in consequence, nothing to show how they were to be used or administered. Since failure to include this information constituted the inadequacy of labeling charged, proof of the intended use of the preparations was a vital part of the Government's case. The Government undertook to show that the claimant intended its vitamin products to be used as medicaments for the prevention, mitigation or cure of various diseases in man, and the Court made a finding to that effect. Whether the evidence was sufficient to support the finding is the point upon which this case turns.

The evidence consisted mainly of transcripts of a series of radio broadcasts by one Carlton Fredericks whom the claimant described in its catalog as an "internationally prominent nutritionist." The broadcasts were commentaries covering the general subject of public health, principally in the field of nutrition, with heavy emphasis being placed upon the therapeutic value of vitamins and of food products fortified by vitamins, the central idea being that many of the ills of man, from simple malaise to serious disease, can be beneficially treated by the use of vitamins and minerals as dietary supplements.

Neither Foods Plus, Inc., nor the trade name of any of its products was mentioned in any of the Fredericks broadcasts. However, advertisements of Foods Plus vitamins were presented in commercials, some of which immediately succeeded the Fredericks programs. Whenever a listener responded to Fredericks' broadcast invitations to write to him for nutritional information, advice or literature, the claimant, which had Fredericks under contract to turn over to it all such letters, would send the listener its catalog.

Fredericks' picture, together with a statement of his academic degree and his fame as a nutritionist, appeared on the first page of the catalog as well as the fact that he was the claimant's "Chief Consultant" and that he had "scientifically formulated the exclusive formulas in this catalog" and that he personally endorsed the product. In addition to the above, it was in evidence that he was employed by the claimant by written agreement as its consultant to (among other things) "aid in the sale and promotion of the products of Foods Plus."
. . .

Upon evidence of the foregoing facts, the Court found that there existed a close relationship between Fredericks and the claimant, that the claimant adopted as its own representation Fredericks' broadcast claims that vitamins were efficacious for the prevention and treatment of human disease, and that the claimant intended its products to be used for the purposes recommended by Fredericks. The facts were practically undisputed and we find no reason to disturb the inference drawn from them by the trial judge or the conclusion that the articles seized in this section were misbranded as alleged in the libel.

The appellant relies strongly upon *United States v. 24 Bottles "Sterling Vinegar & Honey, etc."* [p. 45 *supra*], but that case cannot be taken as a precedent governing the present one. In both cases the issue was simply the sufficiency of evidence to prove a contested issue of fact, namely, an intention or purpose on the part of the claimant of seized goods.... In the present case the question was as to the intention that the articles should be used for a purpose not disclosed by the catalog. The Court held that the evidence offered to show what that intention was was sufficient. In fact there was the strongest kind of evidence that the broadcasts were used to disclose the uses intended....

The appellant sees in the decision of the lower court an expansion of the power and jurisdiction of the Food and Drug Administration into areas of free speech and expresses the fear that such ruling would make independent commentaries broadcast over the radio subject to regulatory control by government agencies. It would seem that this argument is based upon a misconception of what is here decided. There is nothing new or alarming in a ruling that statements made by a lecturer employed by a party and adopted by that party as its own representations may be taken in a civil action as evidence of that party's intention as to matters in which the intention is a material issue. Nor does the fact the representations were made in a radio broadcast affect the situation....

NOTES

1. *FDA Authority Over OTC Drug Advertising.* Does this decision in effect allow FDA to regulate therapeutic claims made in advertising for nonprescription drugs? Would the agency have the same leverage if the product were unequivocally a food, to which section 502(f) would not apply?

2. *Interpretive Regulation.* FDA's current regulation interpreting section 502(f), 21 C.F.R. § 201.5, provides:

> "Adequate directions for use" means directions under which the layman can use a drug safely and for the purposes for which it is intended ... Directions for use may be inadequate because, among other reasons, of omission, in whole or in part, or incorrect specification of:

> (a) Statements of all conditions, purposes, or uses for which such drug is intended, including conditions, purposes, or uses for which it is prescribed, recommended, or suggested in its oral, written, printed, or graphic advertising, and conditions, purposes, or uses for which the drug is commonly used; except that such statements shall not refer to conditions, uses, or purposes for which the drug can be safely used only under the supervision of a practitioner licensed by law and for which it is advertised solely to such practitioner....

3. *Physician's Desk Reference.* In *United States v. Abbott Laboratories,* 1965–1968 FDLI Jud. Rec. 315 (N.D. Ill. 1968), a prosecution for misbranding, FDA charged that the information about a drug that the defendants supplied to the *Physicians Desk Reference* was not "substantially the same" as the FDA-approved package insert, as required by agency regulations. The court held that the PDR is labeling and upheld the FDA regulations against a variety of attacks, but it concluded that FDA had failed to prove beyond a reasonable doubt that the *PDR* monograph differed significantly from the approved labeling. The regulations were subsequently changed in 33 Fed. Reg. 10283 (July 18, 1968), 33 Fed. Reg. 15023 (October 8, 1968), to require that all such labeling contain "the same" information as the approved insert. 21 C.F.R. § 201.100(d)(2).

----

4. PRESCRIPTION DRUG LABELING

a. Limitation to Prescription Sale

Until the end of the nineteenth century, the pharmacy profession exercised predominant control over the compounding of drugs and had equal status with physicians in prescribing their use. In the late 1800s, however, two groups arose to challenge this authority. Commercial companies were organized to manufacture and sell drug products, usually without prescription. Organized medicine also began to assert itself, contending that only a licensed physician was qualified to prescribe drugs, as part of the practice of medicine.

Federal laws enacted by Congress to regulate drugs during the nineteenth century and the first half of this century were designed to assure the integrity of drug products sold to the American public, and did not address the prescription/nonprescription issue. The legislative histories of the short-lived Vaccine Act of 1813 and the later Import Drugs Act of 1848 reveal a congressional concern only with the quality of the drugs made available to Americans. Under the Biologics Act of 1902 and the Food and Drugs Act of 1906, the status of a drug as prescription or nonprescription was left entirely to the manufacturer. Even in the FD&C Act of 1938 Congress made no attempt explicitly to resolve this matter. Only in the Harrison Narcotic Act of 1914 and subsequent statutes controlling narcotics did Congress specifically designate certain drugs as available only on the prescription of a licensed physician.

The concept of mandatory prescription status under federal law was created by FDA in regulations promulgated in 1938. Congress subsequently confirmed FDA's policy in the 1951 Durham–Humphrey Amendments. *See* Hutt, *A Legal Framework for Future Decisions on Transferring Drugs from Prescription to Non-prescription Status,* 37 FDC L.J. 427 (1982).

PETER TEMIN, THE ORIGIN OF COMPULSORY
DRUG PRESCRIPTIONS

22 Journal of Law & Economics 91 (1979).

... The FDA promulgated regulations to enforce the [FD&C Act] before the end of 1938. And among these regulations were those making clear the scope of the exemption from labeling requirements set forth in Section 502(f) of the act.... The FDA said a shipment or delivery of a drug or device was exempt from these requirements:

> If the label of such drug or device bears the statement *"Caution: To be used only by or on the prescription of a* _____ (the blank to be filled in by the word *"Physician," "Dentist,"* or *"Veterinarian,"* or any combination of such words), and all representations or suggestions contained in the labelling thereof with respect to the conditions for which such drug or device is to be used appear only in such medical terms as are not likely to be understood by the ordinary individual, and if such shipment or delivery is made for use exclusively by, or on the prescription of, physicians, dentists, or veterinarians licensed by law to administer or apply such drug or device; but such exemption shall expire when such shipment or delivery, or any part thereof, is offered or sold or otherwise disposed of for any use other than by or on the prescription of such a physician, dentist, or veterinarian. [3 Fed. Reg. 3168 (December 28, 1938)]....

The act said elsewhere (Section 503) that drugs sold by prescription were exempt from the labeling requirements, but it did not say which drugs were to be sold by prescription or that there were any drugs that could not be sold without a prescription. This regulation is different. It says that drugs with certain kinds of labels—*"Warning ... "*—can only be sold by prescription. It allows the drug companies to create a class of drugs that cannot legally be sold without a prescription by putting the appropriate label on them.

This is a stunning change in the ways drugs were to be sold. Before this regulation took effect, consumers could get any nonnarcotic drug they desired without going to see a doctor.... After this regulation became effective, the consumer could no longer buy some drugs without seeing a doctor first and getting his approval. Which drugs were now beyond the consumer's reach? The drug companies would decide, although the FDA could sue them for mislabeling if it disagreed with their choices. The consumers became passive recipients of this decision....

The FDA's assumptions were new to the drug market. Had they arisen from a change in the technology of producing drugs, from the availability of many new and complex drugs? The answer is no. The drug revolution came after 1938..... The FDA's *Annual Report* for

1939 identifies the regulation as the result of "an administrative conclusion of some moment." The conclusion resulted from a conflict the FDA saw within the new law. On the one hand, the law said that all drugs must be labeled adequately, adding that any drug that was dangerous to health when used as the label suggested was automatically misbranded. On the other hand, the report asserted, "Many drugs of great value to the physician are dangerous in the hands of those unskilled in the uses of drugs. The statute obviously was not intended to deprive the medical profession of potent but valuable medicaments."

The conflict was created by the assumption underlying the first of the two sentences quoted. The FDA assumed that adequate directions for self-medication could not be written for some drugs. The reasons for this assumption are not given....

The 1938 regulation does not seem to have aroused much discussion at the time, and its effect on the function of prescriptions was never tested in the courts.... [T]he distinction between prescription and "over-the-counter" drugs was simply accepted....

... [In 1951] Congress ... was considering [the Durham–Humphrey] amendment to the Federal Food, Drug, and Cosmetic Act that would clarify the legal status of prescriptions. The discussion of the amendment centered on the way in which the line was to be drawn between prescription and over-the-counter drugs, but the amendment itself also clarified other ambiguous areas....

The House considered the amendment first. The committee report noted that the existing unamended law allowed the manufacturer to decide whether a drug was to be sold by prescription only or over the counter. The result was that, "Lack of uniformity ... has led to great confusion." The same drug could be classified as a prescription drug by one manufacturer and as an over-the-counter drug by another.... The house committee consequently recommended that the responsibility for designating a drug to be sold over the counter or by prescription only be given to the FDA. The house bill reworded the FDA's regulation to require a prescription for a drug if "its toxicity or other potentiality for harmful effect ... has been determined by the Federal Security Administrator, on the basis of opinions generally held among experts ... to be safe and efficacious for use only after professional diagnosis." The FDA's regulation had acquired a paragraph explaining why certain drugs needed prescriptions, and the House's references to "toxicity or other potentiality for harmful effect" and to drugs that were "safe and efficacious for use" were taken from the regulation....

... A minority report joined the drug manufacturers in opposing this grant of power. The minority report said, ironically in view of its acceptance of the distinction between prescription and over-the-counter drugs, that "the bill as reported jeopardizes the traditional right of self-medication and choice of remedies." It in fact jeopardized the rights of manufacturers, not consumers....

The senate committee reported the controversy over the house proposal to grant new power to the FSA. It reported further that the FDA and FSA had agreed to remove this provision from the amendment and that the manufacturers' associations had been satisfied with this concession.... The senate committee said that its definition of dangerous drugs, that is, drugs requiring prescriptions, was "substantially the same" as the one in the FDA regulation. But a careful look at the senate version of the bill, which became the Durham–Humphrey amendment, shows that the reference to "efficacy" had been removed....

... The most important paradox of the discussion was the apparent absence of controversy on the heart of the matter, the FDA's division of medicinal drugs into two categories....

UNITED STATES v. EL–O–PATHIC PHARMACY

United States Court of Appeals, Ninth Circuit, 1951.
192 F.2d 62.

McALLISTER, Circuit Judge.

This is an appeal from an order of the district court denying permanent injunctions in consolidated cases in which the government sought to restrain appellees from introducing certain allegedly misbranded drugs, known as hormones, into interstate commerce....

It is the claim of the government that it has sustained the burden of proving that the hormones in this case are inherently dangerous; that they are not safe and efficacious for use except under the supervision of a physician; that they are not suitable for self-medication, since a layman could not know when they should be used and when they should not be used; that adequate directions for unsupervised lay use cannot be written; and that such drugs, if sold legally in interstate commerce, must be dispensed only upon prescription of a physician, in accordance with the regulations of the Federal Security Administrator. The government further contends that the proofs disclose that the drugs in question failed to bear adequate directions for use, in that they are offered to the public as efficacious remedies for many conditions which are not mentioned in the labeling or directions for use....

According to the evidence of the government medical expert witnesses, it appears that, from experimental research studies conducted by them, the administration of testosterone inhibits or reduces the activity of the pituitary gland in the production of gonadotrophins, and this, in turn, results in a decrease in the activity of the testes, both in the production of spermatozoa and in the production of testosterone. As a consequence, the administration of testosterone, by upsetting the hormonal balance of the body, tends to produce a condition of infertility or sterility that may continue for months or years, depending upon the amount and duration of administration, and the condition of the reproductive organs....

The great dangers, however, encountered in the administration of testosterone appear, from the evidence, to be concerned with the activation and acceleration of unperceived, dormant, or inactive cancer growths in the human body....

Male hormones, aside from their use in treating cancers in women, are properly prescribed, according to the government medical witnesses, with some minor exceptions, when there is no suspicion of cancer, and only in the rare instances where the patient is suffering from male hormone deficiency—that is, where he is a castrate, or a hypogonad; and only between one to two men out of a thousand who are admitted for hospital treatment are hypogonads. Dr. Huggins testified that only about thirty men in the last eleven years have been treated, at his hospital, for male hormone deficiency. Female hormones, aside from their use in treating cancers in men, are properly prescribed only where there is no suspicion of cancer and where the patient is suffering from the effects of a female hormone deficiency....

Much of the testimony of appellees' medical witnesses—in fact, the whole force of the testimony of two of the three witnesses, who are of the opinion that testosterone has no effect upon male fertility, and who see no danger in its administration to patients suffering from cancer— makes most incongruous appellees' insistent claims in this case that the labels attached to the drugs they distribute adequately warn against the danger of using the drug by anyone who suffers from cancer of the prostate, and caution against its use for the reason that it may result in infertility.

... Moreover, it is to be remarked that appellees' labels themselves set forth that it is impossible for a layman to determine whether he has a male hormone deficiency; that before taking testosterone, a physician should be consulted; that children or young adults must not use the drug except under constant direct supervision of a physician; that it should not be taken by anyone with cancer of the prostate, or defects of spermatogenesis; and that it is for use by adult males deficient in male hormone, when small dosages are prescribed or recommended by a physician. These labels themselves clearly demonstrate that adequate directions for unsupervised use can not be written; and the testimony of the government's medical witnesses, which we accept, only strikingly emphasizes this important and crucial fact. Obviously, in such cases, the direction on the label that "a physician should be consulted," and the directions that the drug be used when dosages are prescribed or recommended by a physician, are not enough to constitute "adequate directions for use" within the meaning of the statute.

Since the drugs in question are inherently dangerous and not safe and efficacious for use except under the supervision of a physician, in view of the fact that a layman would not know when and when not to use them, and since adequate directions for unsupervised lay use can not be written, such drugs, if sold legally in interstate channels, can only be dispensed if the label bears, in accordance with the statute, "adequate directions for use," in the light of the given circumstances. The only adequate instructions for use in such cases would seem to be a caution that it be used only on the prescription of a physician.... [W]e are mindful of the strenuous argument addressed to the court by counsel for appellee to the effect that the only power which the statute confers upon the Administrator to issue regulations in such cases, is authority to issue regulations exempting drugs from the requirement of "adequate directions for use," when that requirement "is not necessary to the protection of the public health," and that, accordingly, the statute gives the Administrator no power to issue regulations providing that drugs be sold only on the prescription of a physician.

... The statute, however, does not state the exemption. It authorizes the formulation of the exemption by regulations. The statute provides that, if the requirement of adequate directions is not necessary to the public health, the Administrator is empowered to promulgate regulations exempting the drug from such requirement. The government takes the stand that the Administrator may exempt the drug from the requirement of adequate directions for use, as not necessary to the public health, *provided* that there be compliance with the regulation requiring the label to state that the drug be used only on the prescription of a physician. Unless contrary to law, arbitrary, or unreasonable, the terms of exemption from adequate directions for use can be prescribed, in the discretion of the Administrator....

A liberal interpretation of the Act, having in mind its background and purposes, requires us to sustain the action of the Administrator on the ground that he was empowered, under the statute, to exempt by regulation the drugs in question from the requirement that the label bear adequate instructions for use, conditioned upon its bearing an inscription that it be used only on the prescription of a physician. Under such construction, the regulation is not contrary to law, arbitrary, or unreasonable....

NOTES

1. *"Consult a Physician."* In this case the court held that the label direction that "a physician should be consulted" does not constitute adequate directions for use. *Compare* the recommendation of the OTC vitamin-mineral panel in 44 Fed. Reg. 16126 (March 16, 1979) that all OTC vitamin-mineral drug products be labeled "For use in the prevention (or treatment) of vitamin (or mineral) deficiency when the need for such therapy has been determined by a physician." The same requirement for physician diagnosis of disease prior to use of an OTC drug has been included in the labeling for cholecystokinetic OTC drugs, 45 Fed. Reg. 9286 (February 12, 1980), 47 Fed. Reg. 37068 (August 24, 1982), 48 Fed. Reg. 27004 (June 10, 1983), and anti-asthmatic OTC drugs, 42 Fed. Reg. 38212 (September 9, 1976), 47 Fed. Reg. 47520 (October 26, 1982).

2. *Section 503(b).* The Durham–Humphrey Amendment, 65 Stat. 648 (1951), added section 503(b) to the Act. *See* Dunn, *The New Prescription Drug Law,* 6 FDC L.J. 951 (1951); Herzog, *Durham–Humphrey—Two Years Later,* 10

FDC L.J. 119 (1955). Note that the act of dispensing a drug in contravention of section 503(b) "shall be deemed to be an act which results in the drug being misbranded while held for sale." Is this language necessary to reach a pharmacist who dispenses a drug without the specified labeling long after it has moved in interstate commerce? *See United States v. Sullivan,* 332 U.S. 689 (1948).

3. *Senate Report.* The Senate Report on the Durham–Humphrey Amendment, S. Rep. No. 946, 82d Cong., 1st Sess. (1951), provides this explanation:

The word "safe," as used in the definition, is intended to have its ordinary meaning. For example, nontoxic drugs like quinidine sulfate, intended for heart disease, or penicillin, for infections, are not safe for self-medication because their unsupervised use may indirectly cause injury or death. The language of the definition clearly shows that toxicity is only one factor to be considered by the courts in determining whether a particular drug is safe for use without medical supervision. The definition requires the court to consider also other potentialities for harmful effect, the method by which the drug is used, and the collateral measures that may be necessary in order to use the drug safely. . . .

In order to give this general definition a more precise meaning so that it may be applied with greater uniformity by the drug trade, the Administrator can exercise the authority he has under section 701(a) of the Federal Food, Drug, and Cosmetic Act to issue interpretative regulations. It is to be understood that the inclusion of the statutory definition does not, of course, in any way derogate from the Administrator's authority to interpret and enforce the definition through the issuance of any regulations necessary or appropriate to protect the public from indiscriminate dispensing of drugs over the counter when they may be unsafe for use without the supervision of a practitioner licensed by law to administer such drugs.

. . . S. 1186 would have authorized the Federal Security Administrator to list by name or class the drugs which he considered within the statutory definition. The grant of such administrative authority was objected to as an unnecessary regulation of the drug industry, and the committee concluded that administrative listing is not necessary at this time. It was felt that the statutory definition, together with the authority to make interpretative regulations, could bring an end to the existing confusion in drug labeling and that uniformity can be achieved through cooperative efforts of the drug industry and the Food and Drug Administration working under the statutory plan.

4. *Authorization to Prescribe Drugs.* Section 503(b) relies upon state law to determine what professional training is required for licensure to administer drugs. *United States v. Shock,* 379 F.2d 29 (8th Cir. 1967), held that a district court should look to state law to determine whether a chiropractor is an authorized practitioner. Practitioners of naturopathy have been unsuccessful in their attempts to force FDA and state agencies to recognize their discipline as a healing art separate from but of equal standing with orthodox medicine. *See Idaho Association of Naturopathic Physicians, Inc. v. FDA,* 582 F.2d 849 (4th Cir. 1978), and cases cited therein.

5. *Reliance on Section 503(b) to Curb Prescribing of Abused Drugs.* In several cases arising before enactment of the Drug Abuse Control Amendments

of 1965, 79 Stat. 226 (1965), and the Controlled Substances Act, 84 Stat. 1242 (1970), 21 U.S.C. § 801 *et seq.*, FDA charged physicians with violating section 503(b) by dispensing amphetamines to persons with whom they did not have a genuine doctor-patient relationship. *See, e.g., DeFreese v. United States*, 270 F.2d 730 (5th Cir. 1959); *Brown v. United States*, 250 F.2d 745 (5th Cir. 1958).

6. *Prescribing of Anabolic Steroids.* FDA has returned to this legal theory to prosecute physicians who distribute anabolic steroids and androgenic hormones to athletes outside a genuine doctor-patient relationship. *See, e.g., Doe v. United States*, 801 F.2d 1164 (9th Cir. 1986); "Five Arrested for Steroid Distribution," FDA Talk Paper No. T87–47 (October 21, 1987); "Steroid Makers in Florida, Coach in South Carolina Charged," FDA Talk Paper No. T89–23 (May 1, 1989); "San Jose Grand Jury Indicts Three For 'Steroids'," FDA Talk Paper No. T89–48 (July 25, 1989). The Anti–Drug Abuse Act of 1988, 102 Stat. 4181, 4230, added section 303(e) to the FD&C Act to prohibit distribution of any anabolic steroid for use in humans other than by prescription for the treatment of disease and provided for imprisonment of up to three years (up to six years for distribution to a minor). Conviction of a violation of section 303(e) is to be treated as a conviction for a violation of the Controlled Substances Act, and thus results in forfeiture of all property used to support the illegal distribution or purchased with the proceeds.

7. *Power to Establish Prescription Status by Rule.* In *National Nutritional Foods Ass'n v. Weinberger*, 512 F.2d 688 (2d Cir. 1975), p. 29 *supra*, FDA's authority to issue substantive regulations restricting an entire class of drugs to prescription sale was in principle upheld.

UNITED STATES v. ARTICLE OF DRUG ... "DECHOLIN"

United States District Court, Eastern District of Michigan, 1967.
264 F. Supp. 473.

FREEMAN, District Judge.

The Government commenced the case by filing a libel of information for condemnation of seventy-three packages bearing approximately ten thousand tablets, each of which contained 250 milligrams (3 3/4 grains) of dehydrocholic acid and was marketed under the trade name "Decholin." Ames Company, Inc., the manufacturer of Decholin, intervened in this in rem proceeding as claimant of the seized articles....

There is only one fundamental issue presented by these motions: is Decholin unsafe as a drug intended for human use without a prescription? Nevertheless, recognizing that in section 503(b)(1)(B) Congress listed a number of ostensibly different reasons why a drug may be unsafe for self-medication and attempting to deal with the parties' arguments in an organized fashion, the motions will be viewed as raising two issues. First, is the pharmacological effect of Decholin such that, unless it is taken pursuant to and in accordance with a physician's directions, reactions sufficient to cause the product to be unsafe may result from its ingestion? This will be called the "toxicity question." Second, does the fact that Decholin may be taken by a person who, although experiencing the indications set out on the label, has an ailment which Decholin cannot cure, coupled with the fact such an individual may postpone a visit to his physician in reliance upon the over-the-counter availability of Decholin, cause the drug to be unsafe? Because the gist of the Government's argument on this issue is that an immediate professional diagnosis to detect the underlying cause of the symptoms in a particular case is a step which must precede or accompany use in order for the drug to be considered safe, this point will be called the collateral measures question....

At the basis of both questions lies the fact that the indications mentioned on the Decholin container can stem from any one of what, for present purposes, will be considered as three types of causes: biliary tract obstruction, organic disease and various minor factors. These last include a host of elements ranging from pregnancy through dietary indiscretions, such as skipping meals, and on to old age. Claimant willingly agrees with the Government that Decholin would not be prescribed by a physician to cure either a tract obstruction or an organic disease.

If the record showed clearly why a practitioner would not order Decholin for a person suffering from an obstruction or an organic disease, the toxicity question could be in better posture for summary disposition. However, the affidavits of the experts suggest different reasons which may be grounded upon conflicting views on a factual issue, the pharmacological effect of the drug. The statements of claimant's authorities suggest that they would not prescribe Decholin in the presence of one of these major ailments primarily, if not exclusively, just because the drug would do no good for the patient. However, these experts are quick to point out that they have never heard of an instance in which a person with either an obstruction or an organic disease sustained any ill effect from self-medication with Decholin; and at least several of them doubt that harm would ever come to an individual who takes the drug under these circumstances....

Even the Government's most helpful spokesman, Dr. Sklar, did not mention that he knew or had heard of a case in which Decholin or any article of similar composition had done harm in any perceptible degree to a layman who had taken the preparation, without consulting a physician upon experiencing the indications listed on the Decholin label. This is not surprising since the Government admitted in answer to interrogatories that it knew of no actual cases of harm attributable to the product.[3] On the other hand, statements made by three of the claimant's experts leave the strong impression that the principal reason why they would consider Decholin safe for self-medication is the fact that their experiences have taught them that a person suffering from an organic disease or a biliary tract obstruction will feel so ill that, as a matter of course, he will seek professional help. Therefore, claimant's

---

3. The record shows that the use of Decholin-type medicines has been extensive. Since 1926, claimant and its predecessor corporations alone have sold over six-tenths of a billion dehydrocholic acid tables under one or another tradename.

experts do not seem to be so much of the opinion that home treatment with Decholin *cannot* cause harm as they do of the view that it *will not;* whereas the Government's affiants stress that Decholin could cause harm to the uninformed lay user, while the Government itself all but concedes that if future unadvised laymen act as their predecessors have, the drug will not be responsible for any serious consequences. . . .

Even if it were apparent from the record that both sides conceded the theoretical possibility of harm from self-medication with Decholin but admitted that, as a practical matter, the likelihood of ill effects is virtually nonexistent, the Court would not feel confident in granting either motion until it has been made aware of the nature of the factors which claimant would say separate the practical order from the theoretical. This is particularly true where, as here and probably in any case of this nature, all conclusions concerning the practical realm depend upon observations of past events, while the Government's purpose in bringing suit is fundamentally to prevent future injury.

The legislative history of the 1951 amendment, which gave birth to section 503(b)(1)(B), shows that Congress did not desire to proscribe self-medication with a product just because under some set of circumstances—and especially hypothetical conditions—the drug may be harmful if taken without professional supervision. . . .

Without presuming to list all the factors which may merit consideration in a section 503(b)(1)(B) action, the following seem especially pertinent here. Probably the single most important element is the seriousness of the effect likely to result under the Government's theory from unsupervised lay use of Decholin. The Government's answers to interrogatories state that the possible aftermath of self-medication by a person suffering from a tract obstruction is jaundice or even death. If it can prove its contention in this regard, no one could maintain that the harm attributable to the drug is not serious. However, in order that the product's true danger can be understood—in order that its theoretical and practical potentials for causing injury can be more clearly distinguished—it would be necessary to know in much more detail the circumstances under which jaundice or death will follow the ingestion of Decholin. For instance, it would be at least helpful, if not actually essential, to understand whether a normal dosage or only a quantity which the reasonable layman is likely to realize constitutes an excessive amount of self-medication will produce the effects. Similarly, a decision would be easier to reach if the record indicated the immediacy of the harmful consequences. Will jaundice or worse result only if a person suffering from an obstruction prolongs his reliance upon Decholin past the point at which the typical individual in his condition would have become convinced of the futility of self-help and have sought professional diagnosis and treatment? If this is the case, what effect would the drug have on the average man? During the period in which he could be expected to take the tablets, would Decholin result in a worsening of his condition to any significant extent beyond the point to which it would have progressed during the time from the onset of the indications until he would probably have consulted a physician had the drug not been available without prescription? If so, would this deterioration actually represent a more serious threat to his life or simply require additional treatment? It would also seem significant if the effects allegedly produced by Decholin cause a noticeable change in a victim's condition with the result that he could be expected to appreciate that the drug is doing him no good and discontinue its use before real harm occurs.

In support of its position that it should be granted summary judgment on the basis of this issue regardless of the outcome of the toxicity question, the Government relies upon the fact that both it and Ames agree that the Decholin indications may be caused by a disease or a disorder (e.g., biliary tract obstruction) which the drug cannot cure. The Government argues that a person suffering from such an obstruction, for instance, is likely to go to the pharmacy, compare his symptoms with the Decholin label, purchase the drug, medicate himself and thereby postpone visiting a physician. Therefore, according to the Government, Decholin is unsafe as a matter of law because the layman is unable to detect the true cause of his discomfort when a differential diagnosis is essential to his well-being, and because his easy access to Decholin is responsible for delaying recourse to the expert qualified to make this all-important determination.

On the other hand, Ames contends that the Government is really saying nothing more than that, in the presence of some types of illness, Decholin is not an efficacious drug and that because of this lack of effectiveness, it should be treated as a prescription drug. This, continues claimant's reasoning, is clearly not a good argument because the action of the House in deleting from the Committee-sponsored bill before it the reference to efficacy as a test of an over-the-counter drug shows that Congress had no intention of having courts consider whether an article is effective or lives up to the claims made for it when they are ruling in cases of this kind.

Claimant oversimplifies the Government's position, and both parties improperly treat the question in too abstract a fashion. While Ames is probably correct in saying that the distribution of a drug was not intended by Congress to be restricted just because it will not serve as a cure in all instances in which it may be taken by a person following the manufacturer's recommendations, the fact that a particular product may be an ineffectual remedy under some circumstances could certainly be a substantial consideration in finding that it is unsafe for self-medication. Conversely, a showing that the drug has a tendency to cause laymen to delay seeking help in determining the natures of their illnesses is not *per se* sufficient to warrant removing it from the over-the-counter market....

Assuming, therefore, that efficacy is not totally unrelated to the question of safety but that the simple fact that inefficacy will result in a postponement in seeking professional assistance is not sufficient to warrant a finding that a product is a prescription drug, the question remains regarding the circumstances in which ineffectiveness, coupled with the likelihood of delay, would serve as the basis for considering a remedy dangerous for unsupervised lay use. The first factor would be the seriousness of the effect that a delay might cause, with the Government's case becoming stronger as its proof tends to show that the consequences of a postponed diagnosis do not merely border on inconvenience as opposed to actual harm. It also seems essential to know how much of a delay will be detrimental, for, in light of the legislative history, it is improper to view the 1951 enactment as a measure designed to protect the stubborn individual who continues to put his trust in self-medication long after the average person would have sought a physician.

A third concern would certainly be the quality of the advice, invariably contained on a drug label, cautioning users to consult a practitioner if certain symptoms develop in addition to those for which the medicine has been recommended by its manufacturer. . . .

The Government in this case has raised the point that a layman cannot determine whether he is suffering from a disorder such as a tract obstruction or a disease like jaundice, although he can compare his symptoms with the indications mentioned on the Decholin label. However, . . . the pertinent question is not whether an individual is able to detect the cause of his ailment, but rather whether the symptoms described on the package as reasons for him to visit a physician are sufficient to alert him to the possibility that his illness may require professional attention. In other words if a serious illness which Decholin cannot cure is the crux of the trouble, will nausea or severe abdominal pain appear along with excessive belching and constipation?

A fourth consideration is closely related to the third because an over-the-counter drug will probably carry, as Decholin does, a warning on its container to the effect that if the indications continue, a physician should be consulted. The issue is whether in a case where a particular drug will not alleviate the cause of an ailment it will, nevertheless, effect a disappearance of the indicative symptoms with the result that a user may have every reason to feel that he has been cured when, in fact, he has not been. In the present record, there is a dispute between Dr. Sklar and all the other experts whose affidavits touched upon this question.

Finally, the previous discussion of Congressional meaning behind the word "safe" and the necessity for distinguishing between the practical and the theoretical in order to do justice to Congressional intent is, of course, as applicable in the context of the collateral measures question as it is in connection with the toxicity issue.

As the foregoing discussion indicates, there are not only differences of opinion in the record concerning pertinent factual issues, but also an absence from the record at this time of evidence relating to many of the factors which must be considered before the outcome of this case can be decided. For these reasons, both motions for summary judgment are denied. An appropriate order shall be submitted.

NOTES

1. *Subsequent Proceedings.* Following the denial of the cross-motions for summary judgment, the case was dismissed with prejudice to FDA and the seized drug was ordered released to Ames, 2 FDA Papers, No. 9, at 34 (November 1968). *See also United States v. General Nutrition, Inc.,* 638 F.Supp. 556 (W.D.N.Y. 1986).

2. *Rx–OTC Switch.* Section 503(b)(1)(C) provides that FDA may require a new drug to be sold only on prescription as part of its decision to approve a new drug application, and section 503(b)(3) authorizes FDA to switch any such drug from Rx to OTC status by regulation. As a practical matter, these provisions now control the status of most drugs. A drug may be switched from Rx to OTC status in three ways. First, the holder of an NDA (or abbreviated NDA) may submit a supplemental application requesting FDA to approve the switch. Second, the manufacturer or in theory any other person may petition FDA under 21 C.F.R. § 310.200. Drugs that FDA has switched to OTC status in response to a petition under this provision are listed in 21 C.F.R. § 310.201. Third, a switch in status may occur through the mechanisms of the OTC drug review established in 21 C.F.R. pt. 330 (subject to the specific conditions established in § 330.13) or by amendment of an established OTC drug monograph. After an OTC drug monograph is established, all Rx–OTC switches of drugs within the class that are not accomplished through a supplemental NDA (or supplemental ANDA) are likely to be effected by amendment of the monograph. The petition procedure and list in §§ 310.200 and 310.201 will thus fall into disuse.

3. *OTC Drug Review Switches.* Since its establishment, the OTC Drug Review process has become the principal means for switching drugs from Rx to OTC status. Both the Nonprescription Drug Manufacturers Association and FDA periodically release lists of drugs switched from Rx to OTC by decisions taken in the course of the OTC Drug Review. Through this process more than 50 active drug ingredients have become available without prescription. *See, e.g.,* the history of FDA's consideration of the switch of hydrocortisone from Rx to OTC status, 55 Fed. Reg. 6932 (February 27, 1990).

FDA's OTC Drug Review regulations provide in 21 C.F.R. § 330.13 that, where an active ingredient was limited to prescription status prior to May 11, 1972 (the date the regulations were promulgated), and an OTC Drug Review panel recommends its switch to OTC status, it may be so marketed following publication of the panel report if FDA does not specifically disagree with the panel recommendation, but that such marketing is subject to the risk that FDA may subsequently disagree and insist that the ingredient remain limited to prescription status. Promethazine hydrochloride illustrates this process. The FDA OTC Cough and Cold Drug Panel recommended it be switched to OTC status, 41 Fed. Reg. 38312 (September 9, 1976), but FDA objected to that recommendation and thus it did not become effective. By the time it published the tentative final monograph, 53 Fed. Reg. 30522 (August 12, 1988), FDA had changed its mind and permitted the OTC marketing of promethazine. However, adverse comments on the tentative final monograph persuaded the agency to reverse field again and in 54 Fed. Reg. 36762 (September 5, 1989) it ruled that OTC marketing should not be permitted until it had studied the matter further.

4. *Benylin Case.* The process of switching an Rx drug to OTC status can be treacherous and contentious. Parke, Davis & Co. initially received FDA approval of an NDA for diphenhydramine hydrochloride (DPH) in 1948 as a prescription expectorant drug under the brand name "Benylin." The OTC Review panel recommended its switch to OTC status in September 1974. Two months later, the company submitted a supplemental NDA seeking approval for the switch. Before FDA acted on the supplemental NDA, however, the company began marketing Benylin as an OTC drug. A year later, in the preamble to the proposed monograph on OTC cough and cold drugs, 41 Fed. Reg. 38312, 38313 (September 9, 1976), FDA stated that the Rx–OTC status of DPH as an antitussive (cough drug) would be decided through the supplemental NDA. A month later, the agency disapproved the supplemental NDA, announced its disagreement with the OTC panel, 41 Fed. Reg. 52536 (November 30, 1976), and offered the manufacturer a hearing on the denial of approval of its supplemental NDA, 41 Fed. Reg. 52537 (November 30, 1976). In an action for declaratory judgment brought by the company, the court held that the FDA enforcement actions against Benylin could not be enjoined. *Parke, Davis & Co. v. Califano,* 564 F.2d 1200 (6th Cir. 1977). When the company did not appear to defend seizures of the product, the actions went by default. *United States v. An Undetermined Quantity of an Article of Drug Labeled as Benylin Cough Syrup,* 583 F.2d 942 (7th Cir. 1978). Following a full evidentiary hearing on FDA's denial of Parke, Davis' supplemental NDA, the Administrative Law Judge determined that Benylin was effective for its recommended use and safe for OTC distribution. In 45 Fed. Reg. 51512 (August 31, 1979), FDA Commissioner Kennedy reversed the Administrative Law Judge and determined that Benylin had not been shown to be effective for use in the treatment of cough. Commissioner Kennedy did not resolve the issue of OTC status, but he did state that, if Benylin were found to be effective, the risks "might not be so severe as to require a prescription." 44 Fed. Reg. at 51523. FDA then proposed to withdraw approval of the existing NDA for DPH in 44 Fed. Reg. 57497 (October 5, 1979). However, after the company submitted evidence of effectiveness of the drug, FDA approved the supplemental NDA for the product as an OTC drug in August 1981 and withdrew the notice of opportunity for hearing, 47 Fed. Reg. 18669 (April 30, 1982). DPH therefore never appeared in the monograph for OTC antitussive drugs, 48 Fed. Reg. 48576 (October 19, 1983), 53 Fed. Reg. 30042 (August 12, 1987), codified in 21 C.F.R. pt. 341, and can now be marketed only pursuant to an abbreviated NDA.

5. *Ibuprofen.* FDA's much-publicized decision in May 1984 to switch ibuprofen from Rx to OTC status, by approving NDAs for Nuprin and Advil, was immediately subjected to two different types of legal challenge. In *Chattem, Inc. v. Heckler,* Food Drug Cosm. L. Rep. (CCH) ¶¶ 38,293, 38,294, and 38,339 (D.D.C. 1984, 1985), *aff'd per curiam,* 1985–1986 FDLI Jud. Rec. 326 (D.C. Cir. 1986), a competitor unsuccessfully challenged FDA's decision to effect this switch by approval of NDAs rather by amendment of the OTC monograph. (Ibuprofen can now be marketed under FDA approval of an abbreviated NDA.) In *McNeilab, Inc. v. Heckler,* Food Drug Cosm. L. Rep. ¶¶ 38,290 & 38,317 (D.D.C. 1984, 1985), the court held that another competitor could challenge the legal basis of FDA's switch of ibuprofen from Rx to OTC but upheld the agency on the merits. As part of its approval of the NDAs, FDA obtained assurances from the two applicants that their advertising would not undercut the approved OTC labeling. McNeilab contended that, since FDA has jurisdiction only over labeling and may only approve a drug for OTC status if it can be safely marketed as *labeled,* the switch from Rx to OTC status was unlawful. The

court held, however, that it was proper for FDA to discuss advertising with the two applicants and that the record demonstrated that it had found ibuprofen to be safe as *labeled.*

6. *Metaproterenol.* FDA has had to be sensitive to the views of physicians and pharmacists when it considers an Rx–OTC switch. Without consulting either the medical profession or the manufacturer, in the tentative final monograph for OTC bronchodilator drugs, 47 Fed. Reg. 47520 (October 26, 1982), the agency announced that metaproterenol sulfate in a metered-dose inhaler for use as a bronchodilator could immediately be switched from Rx to OTC status. Following objections from the medical community and an adverse vote by an advisory committee, the agency rescinded the switch, 48 Fed. Reg. 24925 (June 3, 1983). *See* Hendeles & Weinberger, *Nonprescription Sale of Inhaled Metaproterenol—Deja Vu,* 310 N. Eng. J. Med. 207 (January 19, 1984); "FDA's Prescription to Over–the–Counter Drug Switch," Hearing before the Subcomm. on Oversight and Investigations of the House Comm. on Energy and Commerce, 98th Cong., 1st Sess. (1983).

7. *Future Issues.* Switches of Rx drugs to OTC status are likely to provide most new nonprescription drugs in the future. *See* Hutt, *Drugs for Self–Medication in the Future: Their Source and the Social, Political, and Regulatory Climate,* 19 Drug Info. J. 195 (1985). In the cases discussed, either the pioneer NDA holder or FDA initiated the switch. It is unclear what will happen when the holder of an abbreviated NDA secures approval to market its version OTC and the pioneer NDA holder does not wish to follow suit. Because the Durham–Humphrey Amendment was intended to prevent simultaneous Rx and OTC marketing, arguably FDA would have to withdraw the NDA for the prescription version. A disincentive for switching to OTC status is that a drug ceases to be eligible for reimbursement under Medicare or Medicaid.

PETER BARTON HUTT, A LEGAL FRAMEWORK FOR FUTURE DECISIONS ON TRANSFERRING DRUGS FROM PRESCRIPTION TO NONPRESCRIPTION STATUS

37 Food Drug Cosmetic Law Journal 427 (1982).

... FDA has never enunciated either in published regulations or in other written documents the kind of operational rules that would provide clear policy and result in consistent decisions on the prescription/nonprescription status of drugs in this country. The statutory definition of a prescription drug enacted in the 1951 Amendments has three components: (A) habit-forming drugs listed in section 502(d) of the Act and their derivatives, (B) drugs not safe for use except under a practitioner's supervision, and (C) drugs limited to prescription sale under an NDA.... The first component applies only to the 17 specific habit-forming chemicals listed in section 502(d) or their derivatives. The third component simply covers those new drugs that, because they meet the statutory factors set out in the second component, are limited to prescription status where FDA approves an NDA for the drug. Thus, all future consideration of prescription/nonprescription status is properly limited to the factors set out in the second component of the statutory definition.

In turn, that second component contains three factors to be considered in determining the prescription/nonprescription status of a drug: (1) toxicity, (2) potentiality for harmful effect, and (3) the method of use or collateral measures necessary to use....

1.   Toxicity. The first factor, toxicity, is perhaps the most easily understood and applied. Drugs that have a low margin of safety, and which must therefore be titrated carefully to achieve an adequate level of effectiveness without endangering patient safety, are appropriately placed in prescription status. With increasing scientific sophistication in the field of pharmacology, and the recognition that life-threatening drugs may be needed to treat life-threatening disease, there will undoubtedly always be at least some drugs too toxic for OTC marketing.

At the same time, it must be recognized that the mere possibility that a drug could be misused, with toxic results, is not sufficient by itself to retain that drug in prescription status. As the court recognized in the *Decholin* case, virtually any drug can be misused with some toxic results....

As with all of the factors described in this paper, it is not feasible now, and undoubtedly will not be feasible in the future, to derive operational definitions or empirical formulas for determining appropriate margins of safety. Toxicity, like each of the other factors described below, is simply one factor to be considered as part of an integrated decision....

2.   Other potentiality for harmful effect. The statute does not limit FDA to questions simply relating to toxicity in considering the prescription/nonprescription status of a drug. Rather, FDA is permitted a broad inquiry into other potentiality for harmful effects as well....

It is undoubtedly not feasible to anticipate all of the various possible considerations that fall within this factor of potential for other harmful effects. It is important, however, to note that some considerations that represent valid public health concerns do not properly fall within this factor. Two that immediately come to mind are the potential for tampering with OTC drug products and the possibility that some OTC drug ingredients might be substituted for serious drugs of abuse in counterfeit drug sales on the street....

3.   Method of use and collateral measures necessary to use. Congress intended this factor to have the broadest possible scope. It encompasses all aspects of the circumstances under which a drug is used, including broad questions of social policy. There is perhaps no issue involving drug use that cannot properly be brought into consideration under this factor.

a.   Self-diagnosis. Many people erroneously believe that a drug must be placed on prescription status for any condition for which self-diagnosis is not feasible. In fact, self-diagnosis is not a statutory prerequisite for OTC status and the law has not been applied by FDA in that way. FDA did successfully urge that interpretation upon the court in the *El–O–Pathic* case in 1951, but has not pursued it since that time.

Numerous OTC drugs are presently available for conditions that are not susceptible to self-diagnosis to lay people. The classic example is insulin. No lay person would be trusted to diagnose diabetes. Nor is that an isolated example. Many minor conditions for which OTC drugs are available could be the result of a wide variety of diseases. Differential diagnosis by specialized expert professionals would be required to pinpoint the cause with precision. Upset stomach, after all, could be caused by food poisoning, gastric cancer, too much alcoholic beverage or rich food, excess stomach acid, or an ulcer. Yet no one questions the OTC status of appropriate home remedies for this condition. And analgesics are available for headaches even though no lay person is capable of diagnosing the difference between a headache caused by simple stress and a headache caused by a concussion· or a brain tumor.....

b. Self-treatment and self-care. Another consideration frequently mentioned as a major element in any prescription/nonprescription determination is the need for a doctor to supervise the administration of the drug and to monitor the patient's progress. In earlier days, this might well have been true. Today, it remains one consideration, but not nearly as important as it once was....

With rare exception, self-administration of any drug by a lay person is entirely feasible. It is useful to remember that a major OTC drug, insulin, is administered by injection.....

The vast majority of our population is now fully capable of listening to, understanding, and complying with instructions for self-treatment and self-care. Most people—and particularly those suffering from chronic illness, who must take drugs for long periods of time and perhaps the rest of their lives—are quite capable of appreciating the interaction of daily self-treatment and periodic visits to a physician who can then monitor overall progress.....

c. Adequate labeling. This consideration is receiving more attention than ever before, and undoubtedly will become, with toxicity and abuse potential, the most important consideration in determining prescription/nonprescription status in the future. The quintessential requirement for any OTC drug must be adequate directions for use.

We are just now beginning to face up to the true meaning of that requirement for many products that have long been considered appropriate only for prescription status. It is likely that, with time, OTC drug labeling will become far more lengthy and detailed than it is at the present.....

d. Social policy. Neither the FD&C Act nor its legislative history includes, in specific terms, any reference to broad social policy. It is readily apparent, however, that many determinations of prescription/nonprescription status depend in large measure upon unarticulated principles of social policy.

Societal concerns must always be considered in any decision on prescription/nonprescription status. The panel that considered the prescription/nonprescription status of oral contraceptives, as part of the OTC Drug Review, undoubtedly spent more time discussing broad questions of social policy than narrow questions of toxicity. The status of drugs used to treat venereal disease would undoubtedly raise similar considerations.

The importance of having particular drugs available readily and cheaply for public use is also a major consideration.... The cost of adequate professional care for the poor and the elderly will undoubtedly be a major factor in future decisions about the possibility of transferring drugs used in chronic disease from prescription to OTC status. These are valid considerations, to be encouraged rather than discouraged, as society attempts to come to grips with the need to provide the best possible medical care for its divergent population at the least possible cost.

The concerns of the medical and pharmacy professions must also be considered. Physicians are torn between their concern about permitting important prescription drugs to leave their control, and their realization that many unproductive and unrewarding routine office visits could be avoided if, after a disease was once diagnosed, appropriate medication were readily available on an OTC basis....

Pharmacists, like physicians, are concerned about their eroding position as recognized experts in drug therapy. Ultimately, however, that position must be stabilized and rebuilt not on the basis of a legalized monopoly, but on the basis of demonstrated ability and hard-won public confidence. An increase in the number of drugs transferred from prescription to nonprescription status provides no greater justification for a so-called "third class of drugs," which would be available on an OTC basis only in pharmacies, than did the argument, rejected by FDA and the Department of Justice in 1974, that all OTC drugs with safety warnings should be sold only through pharmacies.

Finally, industry concerns must also be appreciated. The relative profitability of a drug when sold on prescription and nonprescription status will have a significant impact on the approach of the drug industry to any particular decision in this area. The relationship of the drug industry to physicians and pharmacists, and their concern about the potential impact of any prescription nonprescription decision upon that relationship, is too important to be ignored. Nor is the potential change in product liability when a drug is transferred from prescription to prescription status a matter of insignificance....

NOTE

For a broad-ranging discussion of the issues surrounding the switch of drugs from Rx to OTC status, *see The Impact of the Rx–to–OTC Switch Process—Present and Future,* 19 Drug Info. J., No. 2 (1985).

b. Warnings for Prescription Drugs

Section 502(f) of the Act requires, in addition to adequate directions for use, "such adequate warnings against use in those pathological conditions or by children where its use may be dangerous to health, or against unsafe dosage or methods or duration of administration or application, ... as are necessary for the protection of users...." This logical requirement presents difficult problems of implementation. Among these is the distinct possibility that a court may hold that the law governing civil liability may alter or add to the obligations imposed by the Act or by FDA regulations.

In *Stottlemire v. Cawood,* 213 F. Supp. 897 (D.D.C. 1963), a suit to recover for the death of a child who had been given chloromycetin, a drug with a now well-known but rare propensity to cause fatal bone marrow depression, the plaintiff contended that the manufacturer had failed to warn consumers about the risk. Judge Holtzoff rejected the claim:

> It must be borne in mind that this was a prescription drug. It could not be obtained by anyone except on a doctor's prescription, presented at a drugstore. Consequently, there was no reason why there should be a warning of any dangerous possibilities given to the general public.... An entirely different rule would be applicable in connection with drugs sold over the counter to anyone who asked for them.

> There is no proof whatever that no warning or caution was given to members of the medical profession. On the contrary, the only evidence which the plaintiff sought to introduce was to the effect that such literature was issued by the defendant Parke Davis Company....

See also *Magee v. Wyeth Laboratories, Inc.,* 214 Cal. App. 2d 340, 29 Cal. Rptr. 322 (1963), holding that a manufacturer of prescription drugs who adequately warns physicians need not also insure that warning reaches the patients for whom a drug is prescribed. This has come to be known as the "learned intermediary" doctrine. *See* Gilhooley, *Learned Intermediaries, Prescription Drugs, and Patient Information,* 30 St. Louis L.J. 633 (1986); Merrill, *Compensation for Prescription Drug Injuries,* 59 Va. L. Rev. 1 (1973).

The warnings that a manufacturer supplies with a new prescription drug when it is first marketed are specifically prescribed by FDA in the physician package insert that is part of its approval of the NDA. However, information discovered only after a drug has been widely prescribed by physicians may impose an obligation on the manufacturer to provide additional warnings to physicians, even before FDA approves or requires them, or prompt FDA to require changes in the approved labeling.

STERLING DRUG, INC. v. YARROW

United States Court of Appeals, Eighth Circuit, 1969.
408 F.2d 978.

BECKER, Chief District Judge.

This is an appeal by Sterling Drug, Inc. ("Sterling" hereinafter) from a judgment in favor of appellee, a South Dakota housewife and mother of four children, for damages in the sum of $180,000.00 in a civil diversity product liability action. Appellee claimed that her vision had been permanently damaged by use of a prescription drug manufactured and sold by appellant for use in treatment of rheumatoid arthritis and other diseases. . . .

Appellee based her claim for damages on specifications of alleged negligence of the defendant in testing, manufacturing and marketing the drug "Aralen" (also known as "Aralen Phosphate") and in failing to warn the public, appellee, her physician, and retail drug dispensaries from which appellee purchased the drug, of the potential danger to "eyesight and vision" from the use of the drug. . . .

Appellee discontinued the use of the accused drug on October 19, 1964. Therefore, the relevant period concerning the knowledge of its side effects on the human eye is the period prior to October 19, 1964. The evidence is ample to support the findings that during this period appellant knew, or in the exercise of reasonable care should have known, of the following reports: [Here the court describes a series of reports in the medical literature between 1957 and 1963 which documented an association, almost certainly causal, between the use of chloroquine, the main ingredient of Aralen, and irreversible retinal damage.] . . .

These publications were received currently and read carefully by the medical librarians in the medical department of appellant, which also supplied information to physicians and medical information and instruction to detail men trained under the auspices of the Department of Sales Promotion of appellant.

Nevertheless, the detail men who made regular personal calls on prescribing physicians and customers were never, in the relevant period, instructed to invite attention of the physicians and customers to the reported dangers of irreversible retinal damage from prolonged use of the drug by patients. The warnings of side effects in general, and of retinal damage in particular, when given by appellant were limited to the product cards, the Physicians' Desk Reference and the "Dear Doctor" letter dated February 1963, discussed hereinafter. . . .

On this record of the medical reports summarized above, the trial court would have been warranted in holding that the warnings on the product cards and in the Physicians' Desk Reference concerning irreversible retinal damage did not always, in the relevant period, represent the full state of the reported medical knowledge in respect to the percentage of patients affected, the irreversibility of the retinal damage and the toxicity of the recommended drug in affected cases....

Dr. Foley, appellant's Medical Director and Vice–President, testified that in August 1962, because of appearance of additional reports of side effects of chloroquine, that he, and other members of appellant's staff, felt that appellant should add additional information in the literature on the drug. To do so (he testified) appellant's staff consulted with the Food and Drug Administration until January 1963, finally developing the letter, the "Dear Doctor" letter.... Finally in January 1963, through its advertising department, appellant contracted with a mailing service, specializing in mailings to the medical profession, for the mailing of the "Dear Doctor" letter to all physicians and hospital personnel in the United States.... The letter read as follows:

"IMPORTANT DRUG PRECAUTIONS

"Dear Doctor:

"The recent experience of various investigators has shown that Aralen (R) (brand of chloroquine), used alone or as an adjunct to other drugs and therapeutic measures, may be very helpful in the management of patients with lupus erythematosus or rheumatoid arthritis. Although many physicians have found that the incidence of serious side effects is lower than that encountered with other potent agents that are often employed in such patients, certain ocular complications have sometimes been reported during prolonged daily administration of chloroquine. Therefore, when chloroquine or any other antimalarial compound is to be given for long periods, it is essential that measures be taken to avoid or minimize these complications...."

The direct and circumstantial evidence amply supports a finding that, prior to October 19, 1964, Dr. Olson was not aware of the dangers of irreversible retinal damage from prolonged use of the drug. There was ample direct evidence from Dr. Olson, and opinion evidence from qualified professional witnesses, to support the findings that Dr. Olson (and other general practitioners) receive so much literature on drugs that it is impossible to read all of it; that Dr. Olson relied on detail men, medical conventions, medical journals and conversations with other doctors for information on drugs he was prescribing; that Dr. Olson was inundated with literature and product cards of various manufacturers; that a change in literature and an additional letter were insufficient to present new information to Dr. Olson; that detail men visit physicians at frequent intervals and could give an effective warning which would affirmatively notify the doctor of the dangerous side effects of chloroquine phosphate on the retina. These findings of fact were not clearly erroneous....

Appellant contends that in this case the trial court adopted an erroneous view that the law required appellant to warn of dangers of the use of Aralen by the most effective method; that, therefore, the ultimate determination of the fact that appellant breached a duty to warn by the most effective method (by detail men) was induced by application of an erroneous legal standard, a standard higher than the admitted duty to make reasonable efforts to warn. *Amicus curiae* [Pharmaceutical Manufacturers Association] supports appellant by a post-trial extra-record affidavit on the number of detail men on the detail force of 136 companies producing 90% of the output of prescription drugs in the United States. *Amicus curiae* argues that "the trial court has, in effect, asserted that a drug manufacturer should personally notify, by use of detail men, each of the nation's 248,000 physicians of new warning information on a prescription drug"; that this is an unreasonable duty....

... It is clear that the trial court found as a fact that failure to make any effort to instruct its detail force, who promoted use of the drug, to warn the physicians, on whom they were calling, constituted failure to make reasonable efforts to warn the prescribing physicians. To find that reasonable efforts to warn would require appellant to give this warning by detail men in the course of regular calls on physicians whom they had induced to use the drug is not either erroneous, or clearly erroneous, on the record of this case....

This does not mean that every physician in the United States must have been given an immediate warning by a personal messenger. But it does mean that the trial court was justified in finding that it was unreasonable to fail to instruct the detail men, at least, to warn the physicians on whom they regularly called of the dangers of which appellant had learned, or in the exercise of reasonable care should have known....

In its second assignment of error, appellant contends that the finding that detail men present the most effective method of warning the doctor is clearly erroneous.... There was substantial evidence to support the finding....

Some of the evidence which warrants this inference is as follows: Appellant chose the method of personal calls by detail men, armed with special experience, training and literature, to promote the sale and use of its drugs.

It can be inferred that this method was chosen because it was the most effective method of presenting the nature and beneficial effects of appellant's drugs. A reasoning mind could find that this method would also be the most effective way of presenting the dangers of this drug and methods of preventing injury from the use of the drug....

NOTE

FDA has not required the use of detail men to disseminate important drug information. Because of concern about the effectiveness of such information when mailed to physicians, however, it has specified a uniform format for the envelope and type size for the statement of the information, *e.g.*, "Important Drug Warning." 32 Fed. Reg. 7127 (May 11, 1967), 33 Fed. Reg. 12138 (August 28, 1968), codified in 21 C.F.R. § 200.5.

In a line of cases brought by women who have used, and claimed to be injured by, oral contraceptives, the courts have not only rejected or narrowed the "learned intermediary" doctrine but have enunciated a general rule that FDA-mandated warnings represent the minimum, and not necessarily the appropriate, warnings for a prescription drug.

MACDONALD v. ORTHO PHARMACEUTICAL CORP.

Supreme Judicial Court of Massachusetts, 1985.
394 Mass. 131, 475 N.E.2d 65.

ABRAMS, J.

The rule in jurisdictions that have addressed the question of the extent of a manufacturer's duty to warn in cases involving prescription drugs is that the prescribing physician acts as a "learned intermediary" between the manufacturer and the patient, and "the duty of the ethical drug manufacturer is to warn the doctor, rather than the patient, [although] the manufacturer is directly liable to the patient for a breach of such duty." Oral contraceptives, however, bear peculiar characteristics which warrant the imposition of a common law duty on the manufacturer to warn users directly of associated risks. Whereas a patient's involvement in decision-making concerning use of a prescription drug necessary to treat a malady is typically minimal or non-existent, the healthy, young consumer of oral contraceptives is usually actively involved in the decision to use "the pill," as opposed to other available birth control products, and the prescribing physician is relegated to a relatively passive role.

Furthermore, the physician prescribing "the pill," as a matter of course, examines the patient once before prescribing an oral contraceptive and only annually thereafter. . . .

Last, the birth control pill is specifically subject to extensive Federal regulation. The FDA has promulgated regulations designed to ensure that the choice of "the pill" as a contraceptive method is informed by comprehensible warnings of potential side effects. These regulations, and subsequent amendments, have their basis in the FDA commissioner's finding, after hearings, that "[b]ecause oral contraceptives are ordinarily taken electively by healthy women who have available to them alternative methods of treatment, and because of the relatively high incidence of serious illnesses associated with their use, ... users of these drugs should, without exception, be furnished with written information telling them of the drug's benefits and risks." 43 Fed. Reg. 4215 (1978). The FDA also found that the facts necessary to informed decisions by women as to use of oral contraceptives are "too complex to expect the patient to remember everything told her by the physician," and that, in the absence of direct written warnings, many potential users of "the pill" do not receive the needed information "in an organized, comprehensive, understandable, and handy-for-future-reference form." 35 Fed. Reg. 9002 (1970).

The oral contraceptive thus stands apart from other prescription drugs in light of the heightened participation of patients in decisions relating to use of "the pill"; the substantial risks affiliated with the product's use; the feasibility of direct warnings by the manufacturer to the user; the limited participation of the physician (annual prescriptions); and the possibility that oral communications between physicians and consumers may be insufficient or too scanty standing alone fully to apprise consumers of the product's dangers at the time the initial selection of a contraceptive method is made as well as at subsequent points when alternative methods may be considered. We conclude that the manufacturer of oral contraceptives is not justified in relying on warnings to the medical profession to satisfy its common law duty to warn, and that the manufacturer's obligation encompasses a duty to warn the ultimate user. Thus, the manufacturer's duty is to provide to the consumer written warnings conveying reasonable notice of the nature, gravity, and likelihood of known or knowable side effects, and advising the consumer to seek fuller explanation from the prescribing physician or other doctor of any such information of concern to the consumer.

... Because we reject the [trial] judge's conclusion that Ortho had no duty to warn MacDonald, we turn to Ortho's separate argument, not reached by the judge, that the evidence was insufficient to warrant the jury's finding that Ortho's warnings to MacDonald were inadequate. Ortho contends initially that its warnings complied with FDA labeling requirements, and that those requirements preempt or define the bounds of the common law duty to warn. We disagree. The regulatory history of the FDA requirements belies any objective to cloak them with preemptive effect. In response to concerns raised by drug manufacturers that warnings required and drafted by the FDA might be deemed inadequate by juries, the FDA commissioner specifically noted that the boundaries of civil tort liability for failure to warn are controlled by applicable State law. 43 Fed. Reg. 4214 (1978). Although the common law duty we today recognize is to a large degree coextensive with the regulatory duties imposed by the FDA, we are persuaded that, in instances where a trier of fact could reasonably conclude that a manufacturer's compliance with FDA labeling requirements or guidelines did not adequately apprise oral contraceptive users of inherent risks, the manufacturer should not be shielded from liability by such compliance. Thus, compliance with FDA requirements, though admissible to demonstrate lack of negligence, is not conclusive on this issue, just as violation of FDA requirements is evidence, but not conclusive evidence, of negligence. We therefore concur with the plaintiffs' argument that even if the conclusion that Ortho complied with FDA requirements were inescapable, an issue we need not decide, the jury nonetheless could have found that the lack of a reference to "stroke" breached Ortho's common law duty to warn.

The common law duty to warn, like the analogous FDA "lay language" requirement, necessitates a warning "comprehensible to the average user and ... convey[ing] a fair indication of the nature and extent of the danger to the mind of a reasonably prudent person." Whether a particular warning measures up to this standard is almost always an issue to be resolved by a jury; few questions are "more appropriately left to a common sense lay judgment than that of whether a written warning gets its message across to an average person." ....

Ortho argues that reasonable minds could not differ as to whether MacDonald was adequately informed of the risk of the injury she sustained by Ortho's warning that the oral contraceptives could cause "abnormal blood clotting which can be fatal" and further warning of the incremental likelihood of hospitalization or death due to blood clotting in "vital organs, such as the brain." We disagree.... We cannot say that this jury's decision that the warning was inadequate is so unreasonable as to require the opposite conclusion as a matter of law. The jury may well have concluded, in light of their common experience and MacDonald's testimony, that the absence of a reference to "stroke" in the warning unduly minimized the warning's impact or failed to make the nature of the risk reasonably comprehensible to the average consumer. Similarly, the jury may have concluded that there are fates worse than death, such as the permanent disablement suffered by MacDonald, and that the mention of the risk of death did not, therefore, suffice to apprise an average consumer of the material risks of oral contraceptive use.

O'CONNOR, Justice (dissenting).

The court reverses the judgment below and holds Ortho Pharmaceutical Corporation (Ortho) liable to Carole and Bruce MacDonald even though the jury found that Ortho adequately informed Carole MacDonald's physician of the risks associated with the use of its contraceptive pills, and regardless of whether Ortho complied with the applicable Federal Food and Drug Administration (FDA) regulations governing the provision of printed information to users of oral contraceptives. I would hold that, as a matter of law, by adequately informing physicians of the risks associated with its product and by complying with applicable FDA regulations, a contraceptive pill manufacturer fulfills the duty to warn that it owes consumers.....

While I would choose the "prescription drug" rule over the rule announced today by the court, I recognize that the FDA has promulgated regulations governing the provision of printed information to users of oral contraceptives. I would not consider the imposition of tort liability for failure to comply with those regulations, designed to further consumer protection, unfair nor unduly burdensome to contraceptive pill manufacturers. However, in my view, the evidence in this case would not support a finding that Ortho failed to comply with those regulations....

NOTES

1. *Other Cases.* For other oral contraceptive cases, *see, e.g., Odgers v. Ortho Pharmaceutical Corp.,* 609 F.Supp. 867 (E.D. Mich. 1985); *Wooderson v. Ortho Pharmaceutical Corp.,* 235 Kan. 387, 681 P.2d 1038 (1984); *Stanback v. Parke, Davis & Co.,* 502 F.Supp. 767 (W.D. Va. 1980); *Lindsay v. Ortho Pharmaceutical Corp.,* 481 F.Supp. 314 (E.D. N.Y. 1979). *See also Stanton v. Astra Pharmaceutical Products, Inc.,* 718 F.2d 553 (3d Cir. 1983); Note, *A Question of Competence: The Judicial Role in the Regulation of Pharmaceuticals,* 103 Harv. L. Rev. 773 (1990).

2. *Preemption.* Federal preemption principles are examined in Chapter X.

3. *Child Resistant Packaging.* The Poison Prevention Packaging Act of 1970, 84 Stat. 1670, codified in 15 U.S.C. § 1471 *et seq.,* was enacted to prevent poisoning of children through accidental ingestion of toxic household substances, including drugs. Experience, particularly with aspirin, had demonstrated that label warnings were inadequate to prevent such poisonings. Congress therefore authorized the requirement of special "child-restraint" packaging designed to prevent young children from inadvertently obtaining access to dangerous household substances. The Consumer Product Safety Commission (CPSC), which administers the Poison Prevention Packaging Act, has promulgated regulations, 21 C.F.R. §§ 1700.14(a)(10) and 1700.15, requiring essentially all prescription drugs, as well as aspirin and a relatively small number of other nonprescription drugs, to comply with the Act.

BRADLEY v. WEINBERGER

United States Court of Appeals, First Circuit, 1973.
483 F.2d 410.

COFFIN, Chief Judge.

Plaintiffs, 178 physicians who treat diabetes and one diabetes patient who use oral hypoglycemic agents to control the disease by lowering the blood sugar level, brought suit to enjoin the defendants Secretary of Health, Education and Welfare and the Commissioner of the Food and Drug Administration (FDA) from enforcing and the defendant drug companies from complying with the FDA's proposal for altering the labeling of those drugs....

This controversy revolves around a long-term, federally funded study undertaken by the University Group Diabetes Program (hereafter the UGDP study) to determine the effects of oral hypoglycemic agents on vascular complications in patients with adult-onset diabetes. The study, involving twelve clinics and 1200 patients, consisted of four treatment groups: diet alone, diet plus regular insulin doses, diet plus varying insulin doses and diet plus fixed doses of either tolbutamide or phenformin (two hypoglycemic agents). After monitoring the patients for from five to eight years, the study concluded that the combination of diet and either tolbutamide or phenformin was no more effective than diet alone in prolonging life but that those oral agents might be more hazardous than diet or diet plus insulin insofar as cardiovascular mortality was concerned....

After the study received much publicity and criticism ... the FDA concluded that protection of the public required a strong warning to physicians recommending use of an oral agent only if other treatments were inadvisable and noting the UGDP's findings regarding the apparently increased danger of cardiovascular mortality. This evaluation and proposed labeling change was first formally published in the FDA *Drug Bulletin* of June 1971.

On October 7, 1971, the Committee on the Care of the Diabetic, consisting of eminent doctors and experts in the field including some of the plaintiff doctors, submitted through its counsel a petition to the FDA. It asked the FDA to rescind its labeling recommendation, insure that all future FDA comments on the UGDP study include references to its alleged deficiencies and controversial nature, provide petitioners with the complete raw data of the study, and, "in accord with its policy of fair balance," disseminate with equal emphasis and frequency studies and individual expert opinions differing with the study.... The study was primarily criticized for inadequate patient selection controls and use of fixed, rather than variable, doses of the drugs, contrary to allegedly accepted medical practice....

In the May, 1972, *Drug Bulletin,* the FDA published the "Final Labeling Approved for Oral Hypoglycemic Drugs," which proposed changes in the "indications" section of the label and the addition of a "special warning" section. The proposal speaks of "the increased cardiovascular hazard which appears to be associated with oral hypoglycemic agents," notes that the UGDP study was the basis for the change, recites its findings, states that these conclusions apply to all oral agents, not just those employed in the study, and ends with the comment that "Further studies are being undertaken to shed additional light on the role" of the oral agents. On June 5, 1972, the Commissioner formally replied to the Committee's position....

This suit was filed on August 11, 1972 and a temporary restraining order issued that day. After a hearing and submission of affidavits of experts by both sides, the emergency district judge denied the preliminary injunction....

On October 17, 1972, the litigation entered an entirely new phase. On that date, plaintiffs filed a motion for leave to amend their complaint, supported by 13 affidavits by diabetes experts attesting to the controversy over the UGDP study, and new motions for a temporary restraining order and a preliminary injunction. The motions presented for the first time the argument that the FDA's proposed label was itself misleading and thus rendered the drug misbranded in violation of the statute, because it failed to reveal the existence of a "material weight of contrary opinion" among "experts qualified by scientific training and experience" as allegedly required by the agency's own regulation, 21 C.F.R. § 1.3.   After oral argument ... the district court in a Memorandum and Order granted on November 3, 1972, the motions to amend the complaint and for a preliminary injunction....

... Courts are not best equipped, as both sides here readily agree, to judge the merits of the scientific studies and the objections to them. Specialized agencies like the FDA are created to serve that function. In this case, the regulation which, in their motion to amend, plaintiffs contend specifically governs the content of a balanced label, 21 C.F.R. § 1.3, was never presented to the Commissioner nor referred to in the administrative record.   It is the significance of this omission that governs our disposition.

Plaintiffs argue that while this regulation was never mentioned in the administrative proceedings, the concept of "fair balance" which it represents was fully presented and argued by them in their initial petition, was explicitly rejected by the Commissioner in his initial letter, and that the specific statutes under which this regulation was promulgated were mentioned in plaintiffs' letter of response.   While we recognize that the concept was put forward, are fully aware of the disadvantages of further delay, and do not wish to render the exhaustion doctrine a rigid and technical barrier, several factors in this case lead us to insist that the specific argument now pressed be first thrashed out in the administrative arena.

Most significantly, this is an unprecedented argument.   As plaintiffs' counsel readily admitted in oral argument before the district court, there appears to be no prior case in which an FDA drug labeling decision was challenged not by the producer but by concerned medical practitioners, and no case in which the misbranding statutes and regulations were sought to be applied not to the manufacturer's label but to the FDA's proposal for alteration of the label in light of new information....

Now ... the plaintiffs argue that the misbranding statutes and regulation apply.... Implementing [Section 201(n)] ... is regulation 1.3:

> "The existence of a difference of opinion, among experts qualified by scientific training and experience, as to the truth of a representation made or suggested in the labeling is a fact (among other facts) the failure to reveal which may render the labeling misleading, if there is a material weight of opinion contrary to such representation." ...

The Commissioner never considered the meaning of this regulation, its relationship to the substantial evidence test, the intersection of the safety, effectiveness, and misbranding requirements, or the applicability of the misbranding requirements, both statutory and regulatory, to an FDA proposal for re-labeling, for the simple reason that the issue was not presented to him.... [T]he interpretation of even definitional sections in the drug law will often involve expert knowledge and the ability to evaluate the scientific evidence that becomes relevant. Moreover, we have here not only novel issues concerning the interpretation of the statute, which the specialized enforcement agency should first undertake, but also unprecedented inquiries as to the meaning of the agency's own regulations....

Because the plaintiffs failed to exhaust their administrative remedies regarding the issues they now present and, consequently, the district court reviewed the agency decision on something other than the administrative record, we must vacate the injunction....

NOTES

1. *History of Dispute.* Judge Coffin's opinion describes the inception of one of the most contentious episodes in FDA's administration of the federal drug law. *See* Kolata, *Controversy over Study of Diabetes Drugs Continues for Nearly a Decade,* 203 Science 986 (1979).

2. *Physician Opposition.* It is notable, as Judge Coffin points out, that it was a group of physicians, rather than the manufacturers of tolbutamide and phenformin, who initially resisted FDA's efforts to require label warnings about the increased risk of cardiovascular mortality ostensibly revealed by the UGDP study. The opposition of the Committee for the Care of the Diabetic reflected profound disagreement with the findings of the study and suspicion about the way in which it had been conducted. Clinicians specializing in the treatment of diabetes, and known for their espousal of the oral hypoglycemic drugs, believed that the UGDP findings were unreliable, hence their initial demand that FDA provide access to the individual patient records from the study. Committed as they were to continued use of the drugs, the *Bradley* plaintiffs were obviously also concerned about the liability implications of an FDA-prescribed warning cautioning against their routine use and alluding to a heightened risk of cardiovascular disease—a condition that besets many diabetics anyway. Traditionally courts have accorded significant weight to FDA-approved labeling as evidence of at least the minimum standard of physician care in the use of drugs. *See generally* Merrill, *Compensation for Prescription Drug Injuries,* 59 Va. L. Rev. 1 (1973).

3. *UGDP Study Records.* From the earliest reports of the UGDP study the Committee on the Care of the Diabetic had contended that the findings were unreliable and sought access to all of the study records in order to verify their charges. Ultimately this demand was submitted to NIH and FDA in the form of a Freedom of Information Act request, which the agencies denied on the grounds that they did not have custody of the records—which were kept by the study coordinator, Dr. Christian Klimpt, a biostatistician at the University of Maryland Medical School. This denial was upheld in *Forsham v. Califano,* 587 F.2d 1128 (D.C. Cir. 1978). The Court of Appeals expressly left open the question whether FDA could validly prescribe final labeling for the oral hypoglycemic drugs based upon the UGDP findings without affording critics access to the study records. The Court of Appeals' ruling was affirmed by the Supreme Court in *Forsham v. Harris,* 445 U.S. 169 (1980).

The *Bradley* ruling, and FDA's subsequent inability to reach agreement with the plaintiffs on labeling for the drugs, caused the agency to alter its legal approach. As a first step, the agency proposed to revise its regulation interpreting section 201(n) of the Act.

LABELING: FAILURE TO REVEAL MATERIAL FACTS

39 Federal Register 33229 (September 16, 1974).

Section 201(n) was added to the act just prior to congressional passage....

This section is ... offered as a solution to a difficult legal problem. It is a well-known principle of law that a statute providing punishment for the commission of an offense must describe the offense with a reasonable degree of certainty.... If the Congress were to provide that a representation, about the correctness of which qualified opinion differed, would be misleading if the jury agreed with the experts holding one view but not misleading if the jury agreed with the experts holding the other view, it is apparent that the manufacturer would be unable to tell in advance whether his labeling violated the statute. There would therefore exist the kind of uncertainty which would invalidate the statute. But it is undesirable to permit misleading claims to be made simply because a few experts can be found on the occasion of a trial to support them.

One of the important applications of section 201(n) relates to this problem. If only a few experts regard a label statement of curative value as true but the great body of qualified experts in that particular field regard the statement as untrue, then there may be substantial ground for concluding that the curative claim is misleading unless it is qualified in such a way as to show the existence of conflicting opinion as to its truth....

Although there was extensive congressional discussion and debate on the requirements for adequate directions and warnings, there was no suggestion whatever that differing medical opinions about them might be required to be reflected in the labeling. Indeed, from the beginning the legislation required warnings where the drug "may" be dangerous to health. It was nowhere suggested that there be proof of a health hazard before a warning could be required or that, absent such proof, any warning describe varying opinions as to the degree of hazard involved....

... Drug warnings, by their very nature, warn only about possible danger. Although they are often the subject of intense debate, the Food and Drug Administration has never permitted drug labeling to reflect such debate. That debate and disagreement is properly the subject of scientific discussion in professional journals and symposia, but not in drug labeling....

This review demonstrates that 21 CFR 1.3 is inconsistent with relevant statutory requirements and contemporary medical and scientific principles....

Congress has determined that the effectiveness of new drugs and new animal drugs must be established by substantial evidence. Thus, a difference of medical opinion with respect to a labeling claim of effectiveness for these products is legally insufficient and is not a material fact, within the meaning of section 201(n) of the act, unless such opinion is itself supported by evidence which meets the statutory standard. A statement of a difference of medical opinion is no less inconsistent with the misbranding provisions of the act applicable to any drug. It is apparent that a drug is misbranded if any labeling statement represents or suggests that the drug is effective for its intended uses, if in fact it has not been proved to be effective by appropriate scientific data....

... § 1.3 is inconsistent with the statutory standard established in section 502(f) of the act. An adequate warning of possible danger must appear in all such labeling. Without such a warning, a product is misbranded. The statute presupposes a difference of medical opinion since the danger need not be established and absolute, but rather merely potential. Thus, there is no basis to permit warnings to be discounted by an opinion that the warning is really not necessary at all. Providing for medical controversy with respect to a warning undermines the public health impetus of section 502(f) of the act. Where potential danger is the statutory standard, a warning must be unencumbered and unambiguous.

The degree of scientific uncertainty about a possible hazard, or its frequency of occurrence, or other similar related information may, of course, accompany or be part of a warning. It is common for a warning to state the product "may" cause a hazard, where the relationship is not yet conclusively proven, or to point out that the relationship between adverse animal findings and human consequences has not yet been determined. However, presentation of such factual information, which is helpful to the physician in evaluating the significance of a warning, does not permit additional statements of conflicting medical opinion relating to the warning.

... The Commissioner concludes that, where warnings are required, disclamatory opinions necessarily detract from the warning in such a manner as to be confusing and misleading. In this way, differences of medical opinions regarding warnings for foods and cosmetics would render the products to be misbranded within the meaning of section 402(a) and 602(a) of the act....

NOTES

1. *Final Regulation.* The final version of this regulation, 21 C.F.R. § 1.21, was promulgated in 40 Fed. Reg. 28582 (July 7, 1975).

2. *Relabeling of Oral Hypoglycemic Drugs.* At the same time FDA published its final regulation interpreting Section 201(n), it published comprehensive proposed labeling requirements for oral hypoglycemic drugs, 40 Fed. Reg. 28587 (July 7, 1975), and announced a legislative-style public hearing on the issues. Persistent accusations of poor design in the UGDP study and mistakes in recording the experience of patients in the test groups finally led FDA, and the sponsor of the study, NIH, to undertake an audit of the so-called "raw data" of the study, the actual patient records and the transcription of the information for those records for computer analysis. The agencies completed this audit in 1978, concluding:

> ... [W]hile there are certain errors and discrepancies between the data file of the UGDP study and the published reports, none of these appears of sufficient frequency or magnitude to invalidate the finding that cardiovascular mortality was higher in the groups of patients treated with tolbutamide plus diet and phenformin plus diet compared to the groups treated with placebo or insulin.

On November 14, 1978, FDA announced the availability of the audit team's report and reopened the comment period on the proposed labeling. 43 Fed. Reg. 52732. More than five years later, 49 Fed. Reg. 14303, 14441 (April 11, 1984), FDA published its final regulation, codified in 21 C.F.R. § 310.517, establishing a warning for this class of drugs and announced the availability of a class labeling guideline. The prescribed warning stated that oral hypoglycemic drugs have been "reported to be associated with increased cardiovascular mortality as compared to treatment with diet alone or diet plus insulin," citing the UGDP study, and that:

> Despite controversy regarding the interpretation of these results, the findings of the UGDP study provide an adequate basis for this warning. The patient should be informed of the potential risks and advantages of [name of drug] and of alternative modes of therapy.

Finally, the regulation stated that the warning was applicable to all marketed oral hypoglycemic drugs even though only one, tolbutamide, was included in the UGDP study. Because FDA approval of NDAs for glyburide, a new oral hypoglycemic drug of the sulfonylurea class, was held up for a full decade as a result of this controversy, glyburide was granted statutory patent term extension for eight years beyond the May 1, 1984 date of approval, 98 Stat. 3434 (1984).

3. *Banning of Phenformin.* In the interim, separate regulatory action was taken to remove from the market phenformin, the other drug involved in the UGDP study. HEW Secretary Califano suspended marketing of phenformin as an "imminent hazard" on other grounds even before holding an administrative hearing. *See* p. 547 *infra.*

4. *Other Drug Warnings.* Other examples of warnings for prescription drugs imposed by FDA regulations appear in 21 C.F.R. Part 201, Subpart G. The agency formerly prescribed warnings in the Federal Register notices implementing the NAS drug effectiveness study, but now prescribes warnings almost exclusively in the process of approving NDAs.

5. *General Requirements for Physician Labeling.* FDA has established regulations specifying the format and content of the professional package insert for all human prescription drugs. 39 Fed. Reg. 8946 (March 7, 1974), 40 Fed. Reg. 15392 (April 7, 1975), 44 Fed. Reg. 37434 (June 26, 1979), codified in 21

C.F.R. §§ 201.56 and 201.57. *See* Crout, *In Praise of the Lowly Package Insert,* 29 FDC L.J. 139 (1974); Simmons, *FDA Looks at the Package Insert,* 27 FDC L.J. 117 (1972).

6. *Class Labeling.* FDA has long had the goal of achieving uniform, indeed near-identical, labeling ("class labeling") for all identical, similar, or related drugs. This policy was originally implemented by imposing consistent labeling requirements through the DESI program. In the early 1980s, FDA began issuing class labeling guidelines, *e.g.,* 45 Fed. Reg. 76356 (November 18, 1980) (single-entity barbiturates), 46 Fed. Reg. 49205 (October 6, 1981) (topical corticosteroids), 47 Fed. Reg. 29878 (July 9, 1982) (thyroid hormones), and 48 Fed. Reg. 50167 (October 31, 1983) (sodium heparin). The agency has now abandoned this practice and currently pursues the goal of uniformity through the NDA and abbreviated NDA process. FDA has also sought to prescribe similar labeling for competing products used for the same therapeutic purposes, but with less success.

7. *Sample Labeling.* Because of the substantial toxicity, and consequent narrow benefit/risk ratio, of many modern prescription drugs, their labeled contraindications and warnings can be quite frightening.

Accutane (isotretinoin) is a uniquely effective drug in treating severe cystic acne, but is teratogenic (produces deformed babies). As part of a comprehensive program to assure its safe use, *see* p. 635 *infra,* the physician package insert bears the following information:

Avoid Pregnancy

CONTRAINDICATION AND WARNING

Accutane must not be used by females who are pregnant or who may become pregnant while undergoing treatment. There is an extremely high risk that a deformed infant will result if pregnancy occurs while taking Accutane in any amount even for short periods. Potentially all exposed fetuses can be affected.

Accutane is contraindicated in women of childbearing potential unless the patient meets all of the following conditions:

• has severe disfiguring cystic acne that is recalcitrant to standard therapies
• is reliable in understanding and carrying out instructions
• is capable of complying with the mandatory contraceptive measures
• has received both oral and written warnings of the hazards of taking Accutane during pregnancy and the risk of possible contraception failure and has acknowledged her understanding of these warnings in writing
• has had a negative serum pregnancy test within two weeks prior to beginning therapy (It is also recommended that pregnancy testing and contraception counseling be repeated on a monthly basis.)
• will begin therapy only on the second or third day of the next normal menstrual period

Major human fetal abnormalities related to Accutane administration have been documented, including hydro-cephalus, microcephalus, abnormalities of the external ear (micropinna, small or absent external auditory canals), microphthalmia, cardiovascular abnormalities, facial dysmorphia, thymus gland abnormalities, parathyroid hormone deficiency and cerebellar malformation. There is also an increased risk of spontaneous abortion.

Effective contraception must be used for at least one month before beginning Accutane therapy, during therapy and for one month following discontinuation of therapy. It is recommended that two reliable forms of contraception be used simultaneously unless abstinence is the chosen method.

If pregnancy does occur during treatment, the physician and patient should discuss the desirability of continuing the pregnancy.

Accutane should be prescribed only by physicians who have special competence in the diagnosis and treatment of severe recalcitrant cystic acne, are experienced in the use of systemic retinoids and understand the risk of teratogenicity if Accutane is used during pregnancy.

[G635]

Methotrexate is used to treat certain types of cancer and severe psoriasis. FDA's concern about its use for psoriasis before it had been approved for that purpose is discussed at p. 618 *infra*. The physician package insert for the drug bears the following information:

WARNINGS

METHOTREXATE SHOULD BE USED ONLY BY PHYSICIANS WHOSE KNOWLEDGE AND EXPERIENCE INCLUDES THE USE OF ANTIMETABOLITE THERAPY

THE USE OF METHOTREXATE HIGH-DOSE REGIMENS RECOMMENDED FOR OSTEOSARCOMA REQUIRES METICULOUS CARE (see **DOSAGE AND ADMINISTRATION**) HIGH-DOSAGE REGIMENS FOR OTHER NEOPLASTIC DISEASES ARE INVESTIGATIONAL AND A THERAPEUTIC ADVANTAGE HAS NOT BEEN ESTABLISHED

BECAUSE OF THE POSSIBILITY OF SERIOUS TOXIC REACTIONS, THE PATIENT SHOULD BE INFORMED BY THE PHYSICIAN OF THE RISKS INVOLVED AND SHOULD BE UNDER A PHYSICIAN'S CONSTANT SUPERVISION.

DEATHS HAVE BEEN REPORTED WITH THE USE OF METHOTREXATE IN THE TREATMENT OF MALIGNANCY, PSORIASIS, AND RHEUMATOID ARTHRITIS.

IN THE TREATMENT OF PSORIASIS OR RHEUMATOID ARTHRITIS, METHOTREXATE USE SHOULD BE RESTRICTED TO PATIENTS WITH SEVERE, RECALCITRANT, DISABLING DISEASE, WHICH IS NOT ADEQUATELY RESPONSIVE TO OTHER FORMS OF THERAPY, AND ONLY WHEN THE DIAGNOSIS HAS BEEN ESTABLISHED AND AFTER APPROPRIATE CONSULTATION.

1 Methotrexate has been reported to cause fetal death and/or congenital anomalies. Therefore, it is not recommended for women of childbearing potential unless there is clear medical evidence that the benefits can be expected to outweigh the considered risks Pregnant patients with psoriasis or rheumatoid arthritis should not receive methotrexate. (See **CONTRAINDICATIONS**.)

2 Periodic monitoring for toxicity, including CBC with differential and platelet counts, and liver and renal function tests is a mandatory part of methotrexate therapy Periodic liver biopsies may be indicated in some situations. Patients at increased risk for impaired methotrexate elimination (eg, renal dysfunction, pleural effusions, or ascites) should be monitored more frequently (See **PRECAUTIONS**.)

3 Methotrexate causes hepatotoxicity, fibrosis and cirrhosis, but generally only after prolonged use Acutely, liver enzyme elevations are frequently seen; these are usually transient and asymptomatic, and also do not appear predictive of subsequent hepatic disease Liver biopsy after sustained use often shows histologic changes, and fibrosis and cirrhosis have been reported; these latter lesions often are not preceded by symptoms or abnormal liver function tests (See **PRECAUTIONS**.)

4 Methotrexate-induced lung disease is a potentially dangerous lesion, which may occur acutely at any time during therapy and which has been reported at doses as low as 7 5 mg/week It is not always fully reversible Pulmonary symptoms (especially a dry, nonproductive cough) may require interruption of treatment and careful investigation

5 Methotrexate may produce marked bone marrow depression, with resultant anemia, leukopenia, and/or thrombocytopenia

6 Diarrhea and ulcerative stomatitis require interruption of therapy; otherwise, hemorrhagic enteritis and death from intestinal perforation may occur

7. Methotrexate therapy in patients with impaired renal function should be undertaken with extreme caution, and at reduced dosages, because renal dysfunction will prolong methotrexate elimination

8. Unexpectedly severe (sometimes fatal) marrow suppression and gastrointestinal toxicity have been reported with concomitant administration of methotrexate (usually in high dosage) along with some nonsteroidal anti-inflammatory drugs (NSAIDs) (See **PRECAUTIONS, Drug Interactions.**)

METHOTREXATE FORMULATIONS AND DILUENTS CONTAINING PRESERVATIVES MUST NOT BE USED FOR INTRATHECAL OR HIGH-DOSE METHOTREXATE THERAPY   [G634]

c. Patient Labeling for Prescription Drugs

Both FDA's historical practice and court decisions have reinforced the proposition that information about prescription drugs—both indications for use and warnings about possible side effects and adverse reactions—is to be directed to physicians and other medical professionals empowered (by state law) to authorize their dispensing. In the last two decades, however, FDA, with the support of many consumer organizations, has moved in the direction of requiring that more information be provided directly to users of prescription drugs. In 1970, the agency devised the "patient package insert" (PPI), a concept that soon generated a body of secondary literature. *See generally* Barrows, *Prescription Drug Labeling for Patients,* 30 FDC L.J. 98 (1975); Gardner, *Increasing Patient Awareness in Drug Therapy: Ramifications of a Patient Package Insert Requirement,* 66 Geo. L.J. 837 (1978); Guarino, *Patient Package Inserts,* 34 FDC L.J. 116 (1979); Hermann, Herxheimer, and Lionel, *Package Inserts for Prescribed Medicines: What Minimum Information Do Patients Need?,* 2 Brit. Med. J. 1132 (1978); Morris and Halperin, *Effects of Written Drug Information on Patient Knowledge and Compliance: A Literature Review,* 69 Am. J. Pub. Health 47 (1979); Morris *et al., A Survey of Patient Sources of Prescription Drug Information,* 74 Am. J. Pub. Health 1161 (1984).

STATEMENT OF POLICY CONCERNING ORAL CONTRACEPTIVE LABELING DIRECTED TO USERS

35 Federal Register 9001 (June 11, 1970).

On April 10, 1970, there was published in the FEDERAL REGISTER, 35 F.R. 5962, a notice of proposed rule-making to establish new labeling requirements for oral contraceptives which would assure that the user is provided information necessary for her safe use of these drugs. . . .

Organized medicine . . . generally opposed the statement of policy, on the grounds that (1) it would interfere with the physician-patient relationship by introducing a barrier, and by exerting an undue influence on the physician's prescribing decision and the patient's acceptance of the drugs; (2) that it would confuse and alarm the patient to the extent that persons who should take the drugs for health reasons would not do so; (3) that the package insert cannot provide all of the needed information and is not an appropriate means of informing patients; (4) that the physician is the proper person to provide the kind of information to his own patient on an individualized, need-to-know, basis; and (5) that the regulations should not control what information the prescriber gives to the patient by a labeling statement that certain points had been discussed with the patient when the drug was prescribed. . . .

A number of physicians took the opposite view, that information about the hazards of the use of oral contraceptive drugs would serve the cause of patient protection, would enable the patient to make a conscientious choice of this method of contraception, and would not be unduly alarming. . . .

Consumer spokesmen also were divided. Most support much more extensive patient information to assure informed consent to the use of the drugs, but a few spoke of the need to encourage the use of oral contraceptives in family planning among persons for whom unwanted pregnancy would pose a special hazard. . . .

§ 130.45 Oral contraceptive preparations; labeling directed to the patient

(a) The Food and Drug Administration is charged with assuring both physicians and patients that drugs are safe and effective for their intended uses. . . . [T]he Administration has reviewed the oral contraceptive products, taking into account the following factors: The products contain potent steroid hormones which affect many organ systems; they are used for long periods of time by large numbers of women who, for the most part, are healthy and take them as a matter of choice for prophylaxis against pregnancy, in full knowledge of other means of contraception; and there is no present assurance that persons for whom the drugs are prescribed or dispensed are uniformly being provided the necessary information for safe and effective use of the drugs.

(b) In view of the foregoing, it is deemed in the public interest to present to users of the oral contraceptives a brief notice of the nature of the drugs, the fact that continued medical supervision is needed for safe and effective use, that the drugs may cause side effects and are contraindicated in some cases, that the most important complication is abnormal blood clotting which can have a fatal outcome, that the physician recognizes an obligation to discuss the potential hazards of using the drugs with the patient, that he has available for the patient written material discussing the effectiveness and the hazards of the drugs, and that users of the oral contraceptives should notify their physicians if they notice any unusual physical disturbance or discomfort.

(c) The Commissioner agrees that the physician is the proper person for providing use information to his patients, and these regulations will provide him a balanced discussion of the effectiveness and the risks attendant upon the use of oral contraceptives for his use in discussing the drugs with his patients.

(d)(1) . . . [T]he Commissioner concludes that it is necessary in the best interests of users that the following printed information for patients be included in or with the package dispensed to the patient: . . .

Do Not Take This Drug Without Your
Doctor's Continued Supervision

The oral contraceptives are powerful and effective drugs which can cause side effects in some users and should not be used at all by some women. The most serious known side effect is abnormal blood clotting which can be fatal.

Safe use of this drug requires a careful discussion with your doctor. To assist him in providing you with the necessary information, _____ (Firm name) _____ has prepared a booklet (or other form) written in a style understandable to you as the drug user. This provides information on the effectiveness and known hazards of the drug including warnings, side effects and who should not use it. Your doctor will give you this booklet (or other form) if you ask for it and he can answer any questions you may have about the use of this drug.

Notify your doctor if you notice any unusual disturbance or discomfort.

NOTES

1. *Content of Patient Labeling.* This patient package insert (PPI) for oral contraceptives represented a dramatic contraction of the agency's proposed 600–word version, which itself fell far short of the scope and detail of the labeling then directed at physicians. For examples of the current, more comprehensive patient labeling for oral contraceptives and intrauterine devices, *see* 21 C.F.R. §§ 310.501 and 310.502, promulgated in 38 Fed. Reg. 26809 (September 26, 1973), 40 Fed. Reg. 5351 (February 5, 1975), 41 Fed. Reg. 53630 (December 7, 1976), 42 Fed. Reg. 27303 (May 27, 1977), 43 Fed. Reg. 4214 (January 31, 1978), 52 Fed. Reg. 13107, 13132 (April 21, 1987), 54 Fed. Reg. 22585, 22624 (May 25, 1989) (oral contraceptives); 40 Fed. Reg. 27796 (July 1, 1975), 42 Fed. Reg. 23772 (May 10, 1977) (IUDs).

2. *Oral Contraceptive Labeling.* In *Turner v. Edwards*, 1969–1974 FDLI Jud. Rec. 471, 493 (D.D.C. 1970 and 1971), the plaintiffs sought an injunction against FDA's original oral contraceptive PPI regulation on the ground that the short warning was inadequate and requiring that the longer pamphlet be placed in all oral contraceptive packages. The court granted FDA's motion for summary judgment. In *Kushner v. Mathews*, 1975–1977 FDLI Jud. Rec. 537 (S.D.N.Y. 1977), the court declined to order the agency to complete a pending rulemaking to revise the patient labeling for oral contraceptives, despite a claim that the agency had failed to meet commitments for prompter action made before Congress.

3. *Patient Labeling for Other Drugs.* In 1975, FDA was petitioned by a public interest group to prescribe patient labeling for several broad classes of prescription drugs. The agency published the petition in 40 Fed. Reg. 52075 (November 7, 1975) and invited comments on a long list of issues, which suggested a number of then-perceived obstacles to implementation of patient labeling for all prescription drugs.

———

Although no pharmaceutical manufacturer challenged FDA's patient inserts for contraceptives, suit was immediately filed when the agency promulgated a regulation in 41 Fed. Reg. 43108 (September 29,

1976), 42 Fed. Reg. 37636 (July 22, 1977), codified in 21 C.F.R. § 310.515, to require patient labeling for prescription drug products containing estrogens.

PHARMACEUTICAL MANUFACTURERS ASS'N v. FDA *

United States District Court, District of Delaware, 1980.
484 F. Supp. 1179, *aff'd per curiam* 634 F.2d 106.

STAPLETON, District Judge:

The regulation ... outlined several categories of information which must be included in a patient package insert, and required that such an insert be provided to a patient every time the drug was dispensed or administered (i.e. injected).... The agency's action came as a result of several studies published in 1975 which indicated an association between the use of conjugated estrogens and an increased risk of endometrial cancer in women....

Plaintiffs and plaintiff-intervenors raise a number of challenges to the regulation. First, they contend that the FDA lacks statutory authority to require patient packaging inserts for prescription drugs. They next assert that such a requirement is an unconstitutional interference with the practice of medicine. Finally, they challenge the adequacy of the FDA's findings and conclusions embodied in the preamble to the regulation and argue that, based on the administrative record, the regulation is "arbitrary, capricious, an abuse of discretion, or otherwise not in accordance with law." Because I find that the FDA does have statutory authority to require patient labeling, that such a requirement does not interfere with any constitutionality protected rights of physicians, that the agency's reasoning is sufficiently articulated and that the record adequately supports its judgment, I will grant the defendants' motion for summary judgment and deny that of the plaintiffs....

... [Sections 502(a), 502(f), and 201(n) of the FD&C Act], combined with Section 701(a), provide direct support for the challenged regulation. Among other things, they reflect a clear Congressional objective that the users of drugs, whether prescription or non-prescription, shall receive facts "material ... with respect to consequences which may result from the use of the ... [drug] under the conditions of use prescribed in the labeling thereof or under such conditions of use as are customary or usual." The Commissioner, in furtherance of this objective, has seen fit in the challenged regulation to require that information concerning consequences which may result from the use of estrogen drugs be provided to the users thereof on their labeling. I think it clear that Section 701(a) authorizes him to do so....

---

* [An earlier opinion denying a preliminary injunction appears at 1975–1977   FDLI Jud. Rec. 378 (D. Del. 1977).]

While it is true that one of the important applications of Section 201(n) relates to the problem of misleading affirmative claims, nothing in the [1938 House] Report suggests that the section is limited in its application to such claims. Indeed, the text of Section 201(n) itself demonstrates that its scope is not so limited. Plaintiffs focus on that portion of the section which defines as misleading any failure to "reveal facts material in light of ... [the] representations" made on the labeling. But Section 201(n) goes on to require the disclosure of "facts ... material with respect to consequences which may result from the use" of the drug. This language would be rendered meaningless if this Court were to adopt the construction favored by the plaintiffs....

It is ... true that the 1951 exemption of prescription drugs from the requirements of Section 502(f) was enacted with the idea that prescribing physicians would be the primary source of adequate directions for use and adequate warning against misuse or overuse. It does not necessarily follow, however, that Congress meant to strip the Commissioner of the regulatory authority he had possessed for thirteen years over prescription drug labeling. Plaintiffs' argument glosses over the fact that while prescription drugs were exempted from the requirements of Section 502(f) in 1951, they were not exempted from the requirement of Section 502(a) that their labels not be misleading....

While I agree that [section 505(d)], and particularly the addition in 1962 of the sixth ground for disapproval, reflects Congress' continuing concern that drug labeling should be both truthful and complete, I cannot agree that it provides independent support for the challenged regulation. Section 505(d) cannot fairly be read to encompass authority for requiring the delivery of written material to the patient at the time of dispensing. As the FDA itself has explained, the provisions of Section 505, as contrasted with the mislabeling provisions of the Act, "apply only at the moment of shipment in interstate commerce and not to action taken subsequent to shipment in interstate commerce." Notice of Proposed Rule Making, 37 Fed. Reg. 16503 (1972)....

... Plaintiffs argue that the mandatory nature of the regulation interferes with the doctor-patient relationship, and thus with the practice of medicine, by requiring the physician to communicate information emanating from Washington without regard to his or her professional judgment concerning the accuracy of the advice or the desirability of the patient being exposed to it.

To the extent that the plaintiffs' claim of unconstitutional interference with the right to practice medicine is founded on a notion of federalism which reserves all rights over such regulation to the states, it is without merit. It is undisputed that the practice of medicine is subject to the exercise of state police power where such regulation furthers a legitimate state interest....

Turning to plaintiff's view of a physician's right to exercise professional judgment, it is important to focus on what the challenged regulation does not do. The regulation at issue here does not forbid a physician from prescribing conjugated estrogen drugs, or limit the physician's exercise of professional judgment in that regard. Nor does it limit the information the physician may impart to his or her patients concerning estrogens. If the physician disagrees with a perceived "slant" of the labeling provided by the manufacturer, or with the facts stated therein, he or she is free to discuss the matter fully with the patient, noting his own disagreement and views. The sample labeling encourages the patient to have this kind of open discussion with her doctor.

When these limitations on the effect of the challenged regulation are considered, it becomes apparent that the plaintiffs urge recognition not of a right to exercise judgment in prescribing treatment, but rather of a right to control patient access to information.... There simply is no constitutional basis for recognition of a right on the part of physicians to control patient access to information concerning the possible side effects of prescription drugs. The cases cited by plaintiffs do contain language referring to a doctor's right to practice medicine, but the rights there recognized were only those necessary to facilitate the exercise of a right which patients were found to possess. The physician rights discussed are thus derivative of patient rights and do not exist independent of those rights....

The patient rights recognized in the line of cases relied upon by plaintiffs flow from a constitutionally protected right of privacy. As the Supreme Court noted in *Whalen v. Roe* [429 U.S. 589 (1977)], this right encompasses the individual's "interest in independence in making certain kinds of important decisions," as well as his or her "interest in avoiding disclosure of personal matters." To the extent these cases have any bearing on the present issue, then, their rationale would appear to support the challenged regulation....

NOTES

1. *Evaluation of PPIs.* For a critical review of the PPI for estrogens, based upon a survey of women who had received it, *see* Udkow *et al.*, *The Safety and Efficacy of the Estrogen Patient Package Insert*, 242 J.A.M.A. 536 (1979). *See also* Institute of Medicine, EVALUATING PATIENT PACKAGE INSERTS (NAS 1979).

2. *Estrogen PPI.* The PPI for estrogens has since been revised, 52 Fed. Reg. 37802 (October 9, 1987), 55 Fed. Reg. 18722, 18761 (May 4, 1990). In 45 Fed. Reg. 37455 (June 3, 1980) FDA exempted from its patient labeling requirement for progestational drugs any product labeled solely for treatment of cancer. *See Schlieter v. Carlos,* Civ. No. 87–0955 SC (D.N.M. August 31, 1989), holding that medical institutions as well as physicians have a duty to distribute estrogen PPIs to patients.

PRESCRIPTION DRUG PRODUCTS: PATIENT LABELING REQUIREMENTS

44 Federal Register 40016 (July 6, 1979).

The Food and Drug Administration (FDA) is proposing regulations that would require manufacturers to distribute labeling to patients for most prescription drug products for human use, including biological products licensed under the Public Health Service Act of 1944 [42 U.S.C. § 262]. The regulations would require dispensers of prescription drug products to provide the labeling to patients when the products are dispensed. This action is being taken because FDA believes that prescription drug labeling that is directed to patients will promote the safe and effective use of prescription drug products and that patients have a right to know about the benefits, risks, and directions for use of the products....

... [In sections 502(a), 505(d), and (c), and 201(n)] the statute clearly authorizes FDA to take remedial action against a drug product whose labeling is false or misleading in any particular and to compel disclosure of information that is material with respect to consequences that result from the use of the drug product under its labeled conditions, as well as conditions that are customary or usual.

Based upon that authority, the agency proposes to require manufacturers of prescription drug products to disclose information about their products in the form of patient labeling.... [S]tandards for appropriate labeling for drug products must also change as data are compiled about the effects of labeling on patients' safe and effective use of drug products and as patients demand more information about the use and effects of prescription drug products.....

The agency does not believe that patient labeling will significantly increase the incidence of suggestion-induced side effects. So called suggestion effects seem to play a minimal role in causing serious adverse reactions. In any event, it is more likely that beneficial effects will result from an explicit statement of side effects in patient labeling....

... The agency believes ... that providing patients with written information about the proper use of a prescription drug product including information on the benefits and risks the drug product presents to the patient will result in reduced potential liability. This result is likely not only because patients will receive necessary warnings about the product, but also because the availability of written labeling should improve patient compliance with physician directions and improve patient monitoring of adverse reactions, two factors that may actually decrease drug induced injuries. Patient labeling may also reduce the overall number of malpractice actions, because patients will be more aware that certain risks inevitably accompany drug therapy and that not all adverse effects are caused by deficiencies in the drug product or mistakes by the prescriber.

Finally it would be both inappropriate and unreasonable for FDA to base its patient labeling policy on whether patient labeling affected the legal liability of the manufacturer, physician, pharmacist, or other dispenser of the product.....

Patient labeling is not intended to be the sole source of information for patients about prescription drug products. The agency hopes that in most cases it will merely restate and reemphasize the information the physician had told the patient when the product was prescribed....

The proposed regulations set forth general patient labeling requirements that would apply to most prescription drug products. The regulations would require the manufacturer of the product to prepare and distribute patient labeling that physically accompanies the product. The labeling would be written in nontechnical language, would not be promotional in tone or content, and would be based primarily on the physician labeling for the drug product. The patient labeling would contain both a summary of information about the product and more detailed information that identifies the product and the person responsible for the labeling, the proper uses of the product, circumstances under which it should not be used, serious adverse reactions, precautions the patient should take when using the product, information about side effects, and other general information about the proper uses of prescription drug products. The agency would be permitted to exempt the labeling for a particular drug product from any of the specific requirements. The regulations would also establish minimum printing specifications for patient labeling.

FDA would make available guideline patient labeling for many prescription drug products. The manufacturer would be required to provide sufficient patient labeling pieces to the dispenser of a prescription drug product and the dispenser would be required to provide the labeling to the patient....

Patient labeling for a prescription drug product would be required to be based primarily on the physician labeling required for the product under § 201.100(d).... As a legal matter, statements in patient labeling cannot conflict with statements in physician labeling without misbranding the drug product. At the same time, the proposed requirements recognize that there may be substantial differences between the physician and patient labeling for a particular product. For example, the patient labeling may not discuss each of the subjects discussed in the product's physician labeling; and may not contain as thorough a discussion of a subject as the physician labeling. On the other hand, some information that does not appear in physician labeling may be required to appear in patient labeling, such as the consequences of the patient's failure to follow the prescribed regimen....

The patient labeling would also be required to contain a statement that the physician labeling for the drug product (required under § 201.100(c)(1), that is, the drug product's "package insert") is available from the patient's pharmacist or physician. Many persons, including some pharmacists and physicians, erroneously believe that State or Federal law prohibits providing a drug product's official package insert to patients. No such prohibition exists.... Although the package insert for a drug product may be too technical for most patients to easily understand, patients should not be denied access to this information....

On August 30, 1979, the Joint Commission of Pharmacy Practitioners, which represents over 90 percent of the licensed pharmacists in the United States, wrote President Carter to request that he intervene to prevent FDA from issuing a final regulation on patient package inserts. The JCPP contended that the cost of the FDA proposal would be large, and the benefits uncertain, and that a patient education program conducted by the pharmacy profession "can do a better job at lower cost than any Federal patient education program." *See* Demkovich, *FDA in Hot Water Again Over Cost of Proposed Drug Labeling Rule,* National Journal, September 22, 1979, at 1568. In 45 Fed. Reg. 60754 (September 12, 1980), FDA published final regulations establishing requirements and procedures for the preparation and distribution of PPIs for 10 high priority classes of human prescription drugs as a three-year pilot program. The agency promptly began publishing guideline PPIs for the 10 classes of drug products in 45 Fed. Reg. 60785 (September 12, 1980), 45 Fed. Reg. 78514, 78516 (November 25, 1980), 45 Fed. Reg. 80740 (December 5, 1980), 46 Fed. Reg. 28, 160 (January 2, 1981). Within a few months, however, 46 Fed. Reg. 23739, 23815 (April 28, 1981), FDA temporarily stayed the effective dates of the PPI requirements for the five specific drugs for which final guidelines had been published, pending "additional review of these requirements" under President Reagan's Executive Order No. 12291, 46 Fed. Reg. 13193 (February 19, 1981). In April 1981, a consortium of consumer organizations brought suit to set aside that stay. In *Public Citizen v. Department of HHS,* 671 F.2d 518 (D.C. Cir. 1981), the court allowed FDA 30 days to decide its course of action on the matter. The agency then published a notice explaining its stay in 47 Fed. Reg. 1773 (January 13, 1982), outlined the benefits and costs of the program, and stated that the matter was still under regulatory review. A month later, FDA proposed to revoke the PPI regulation, 47 Fed. Reg. 7200 (February 17, 1982), and, following an opportunity for public comment, it issued a final decision.

PRESCRIPTION DRUG PRODUCTS: REVOCATION OF PATIENT PACKAGE INSERT REQUIREMENTS
47 Federal Register 39147 (September 7, 1982).

In the proposal to revoke the final rule, the agency explained that the Commissioner of Food and Drugs had carefully reviewed the entire administrative record of the patient package insert program, the results of a 3–year study conducted under contract for the agency by the Rand Corp. on the effects of prototype PPI's, and information presented at public meetings FDA held on September 30 and October 1, 1981, to solicit views on PPI's.

Based on this review, the proposal noted, the agency believed it could no longer justify the PPI pilot program. First, the agency had been persuaded that the program would not likely have achieved a principal objective, that of enabling FDA to determine whether a mandatory, pharmacy-oriented, drug leaflet program was the most practical way of increasing patient knowledge about prescription drugs. Secondly, the agency pointed out that, since the promulgation of the pilot program, the private sector had provided new initiatives in patient information and was currently developing others. The various private sector initiatives, if effectively implemented, were considered likely to provide consumers with the same type of information about prescription drugs as would have been provided by the agency's pilot program. Moreover, as these initiatives would not be limited to 10 drugs or drug classes, or to pharmacy-distributed leaflets, it was believed possible that they would be capable of providing more information than the agency's pilot program. Also, the agency stressed that cooperation with the private sector would encourage experimentation with diverse systems for delivering patient information, thereby promoting innovation in delivery systems.

 The proposal discussed other aspects of the mandatory program that contributed to the Commissioner's decision. It cited the limited value of providing patient information only at the time of dispensing, the cost of the mandatory program, the strong disagreement about the design and value of the program on the part of the health professionals who would have to implement it, and the need for Federal regulations to be both necessary and cost effective. Based on these factors, the agency tentatively decided to withdraw its mandatory pilot PPI regulation following public comment.

The agency received 602 comments on the proposal.... On the basis of the information in the proposal, a review of the comments, and other information received by the agency through its Committee on Patient Education (COPE), the agency believes that encouraging diverse private sector efforts for providing consumers with adequate prescription drug information is now preferable to implementing a single, mandated Federal program....

The agency agrees with the comments that written information, which the patient can retain and refer to later, is very useful to most patients. It stresses, however, that most current and planned private sector programs will provide this type of written information, to be available either at the pharmacy in the form of pamphlets, tear-off sheets, etc., or directly from the prescribing physician. With respect to special problems of the elderly, private sector efforts appear capable of offering information systems at least as effective as that which the mandatory program might have provided. A mail-order pharmacy service operated by a national organization of retired persons has developed leaflets that are similar to the originally mandated PPI's and that will be mailed with the drugs to patients. Unlike the mandated program, however, this program is able not only to emphasize drugs used mostly by the elderly, but to tailor the information provided in the leaflets to the particular needs of the elderly. These results were not achievable by the 10–drug pilot program, where drugs chosen included many not frequently used by the elderly, and where information had to be directed at a wider audience. It should be noted that FDA actively participated in the preparation of the leaflets to be used in this private program, reflecting an agency commitment to work with the private sector to provide voluntary program with high likelihood of success.

Also, as the proposal states, FDA is aware of a planned effort by the American Medical Association to supply physicians with written drug information that can be given to the patient at the time of prescribing. FDA views this initiative, which would likely not have been undertaken if the mandatory program had remained in effect, as embodying all of the advantages of the mandatory program plus the additional advantage that the information will be provided by the physician. Moreover, it will be provided at the time of prescribing, where the patient can, if he or she wishes, discuss the information more fully with the physician....

The agency is aware of approximately 25 commercially available books that provide readily understandable information about numerous prescription drugs. FDA disagrees with the comments that claimed these books are too costly for consumers. Virtually all of these publications are available in paperback at a reasonable price. Moreover, such books have the recognizable benefit of providing drug information on many drugs in a single retainable volume, which the patient can conveniently refer to with each refill of a prescription. Under the agency's mandatory program, information would have been limited to 10 drugs and would have been given to the patient only when the prescription was initially filled.....

In March 1982, representatives of AMA met with FDA's Committee on Patient Education and announced a timetable for instituting the AMA–PMI program in patient education and also announced that AMA is preparing a public relations campaign to generate public awareness of the PMI's and to use them.

A consortium of major health professional, trade, and consumer groups are forming a National Council on Patient Information and Education. The Council will encourage health professionals to provide more information to patients about prescription drugs, and will sponsor a national advertising campaign that will encourage patients to seek more information about drug use. A Steering Committee, formed to organize the Council, has met twice and has appointed several specific committees to consider activities such as program development and Council membership. The full Council's first meeting will be held before the end of 1982; membership is open to all interested organizations that are involved in disseminating information to patients about prescription drugs, including professional societies, drug manufacturers and their associations, and consumer groups. The Ciba–Geigy Corp. has offered $1 million toward funding and staffing the Council.

Given the resources that have been invested in these and other programs by the private sector in developing alternatives to mandatory PPI's the agency sees no reason to believe that they will fade following revocation of the rule. Although FDA cannot guarantee that all of these programs will ultimately be successful, it is reasonable for the agency to conclude, on the basis of their current development and the statements as to future plans by their sponsors, that these privately sponsored voluntary initiatives represent viable, promising alternatives.....

As the agency stated in the proposal, the regulation requiring PPI's for prescription drugs is a discretionary one.... The legal authority is discussed at length at 45 FR 60758–60759 (September 12, 1980). This authority justified, but did not mandate, the requirement for PPI's for prescription drugs. Because the regulation is a discretionary one, FDA believes it is authorized to revoke it under the same discretionary authority that permitted its issuance.

Revocation of the program will have a reasonable effect. Patients will have access to a variety of programs of drug education and information. Pharmacists will not bear an undue share of the managerial and cost burdens associated with patient information services. At least one alternative program under development—the AMA's—will provide patient information at the time a drug is prescribed. This means of patient education, which is recognized as superior to providing patient labeling at the time of dispensing, would likely not be used if PPI's were Federally mandated.

Revocation of the PPI program is consistent with the law. The argument that absence of PPI's misbrands prescription drugs is based on a misunderstanding of the manner in which FDA utilizes its broad statutory authority in support of specific regulations. A regulation, such as the PPI program, is issued under FDA's authority to promulgate regulations for the efficient enforcement of the Federal Food, Drug, and Cosmetic Act. Such a regulation must also be justified by other, more specific, authority in the act, in this case the prohibition against misbranding. After a regulation is promulgated, failure to adhere to the regulation causes a violation of the specific statutory authority on which the regulation is based. In the absence of the regulation, however, violation of that specific authority does not necessarily occur by conduct that the regulation would have covered. To suggest that it does is tantamount to saying that all regulations issued under section 701(a) of the act are merely interpretive, for substantive regulations would be redundant of the legal requirements inherent in other provisions of the act. This view is plainly wrong. FDA has issued numerous substantive regulations under section 701(a) of the act. Most of these regulations created new legal requirements of general applicability and did not simply explain existing requirements.....

FDA's Committee on Patient Education is an internal FDA Committee, formed to develop and implement a comprehensive plan to encourage voluntary patient information on drugs. The Committee has made coordination with consumer groups a high priority because it believes that active consumer participation is critical to the success of patient information programs. The Associate Commissioner for Consumer Affairs is a member of the Committee and will be representing consumers' interests. The agency will continue to advise consumers of COPE activities and meetings with outside groups through publications and a variety of educational campaigns and efforts. Minutes of all COPE meetings and communications between COPE and the public have been and will continue to be placed on file with FDA's Dockets Management Branch.....

NOTES

1. *Lack of Judicial Challenge.* FDA's decision to suspend its PPI initiative was not contested in the courts. At the same time, FDA revoked the five final guideline PPIs and withdrew the five draft guideline PPIs that had previously been published. 47 Fed. Reg. 39249 (September 7, 1982).

2. *Voluntary PPIs.* Since 1982 pharmaceutical manufacturers have voluntarily distributed PPIs for a number of drugs which present unique safety questions.

3. *PPI Content and Civil Liability.* Throughout the debate it was assumed that a PPI would not contain all of the information required to be included in the physician package insert. However, the failure to provide a consumer with *all* information might well expose a manufacturer to liability for at least compensatory damages, and perhaps also for punitive damages, to any consumer who suffered an injury warned about in the physician package insert but not in the PPI.

4. *FDA Promotion of Voluntary Patient Information Efforts.* FDA's Committee on Patient Education (COPE) has been disbanded but the agency's Office of Consumer Affairs continues to foster and coordinate patient education activities. The National Council on Patient Information and Education (NCPIE) remains active in supporting programs to increase consumer understanding about prescription drugs. AMA Patient Medication Instructions (PMIs) cover more than 80 prescription drugs as of June 30, 1990. An AMA spokesman has estimated that about 10 percent of physicians who write prescriptions are using the AMA PMIs. "How a Federal Policy May Have Contributed to the Accutane Tragedy," Washington Post Health, May 3, 1988, at 7. Beginning in 1980, USP has published a yearly compilation of ADVICE FOR THE PATIENT: DRUG INFORMATION IN LAY LANGUAGE. The PHYSICIAN'S DESK REFERENCE, which contains the full physician's package insert and is republished yearly, is now sold in substantial numbers in bookstores throughout the country.

d. Name of Manufacturer

Section 502(b) of the FD&C Act requires that the label of a drug bear the name and place of business of the manufacturer, packer, or distributor. With the advent of specialized manufacturing techniques in the pharmaceutical industry, this seemingly simple requirement became a matter of some complexity. FDA adopted an informal policy that any of the firms which perform an important manufacturing operation could be identified as *the* manufacturer. In addition, the agency established a "man-in-the-plant" policy, under which a drug company could lease the facilities of, or contract with, another firm to manufacture a drug and still identify itself as the manufacturer if it placed its own employees in the manufacturing facility to supervise production. Both policies came in for criticism. *See* "Competitive Problems in the Drug Industry," Hearings before the Subcomm. on Monopoly and Anticompetitive Activities of the Senate Select Comm. on Small Business, 95th Cong., 1st Sess., Pt. 33 (1977); "Man–in–the–Plant—FDA's Failure to Regulate Deceptive Drug Labeling," Hearings before the Subcomm. on Oversight and Investigations of the House Comm. on Interstate and Foreign Commerce, 95th Cong., 2nd Sess. (1978); "Man–in–the–Plant—FDA's Failure to Regulate Deceptive Drug Labeling, Report together with Separate Views by the Subcomm. on Oversight and Investigations of the House Comm. on Interstate and Foreign Commerce, 95th Cong., 2nd Sess., Comm. Print 95–73 (1978); " 'Man–in–the–Plant' Revisited—A Deceptive Drug Labeling Practice Continues," Hearings before the Subcomm. on Oversight and Investigations of the House Comm. on Interstate and Foreign Commerce, 96th Cong., 2nd Sess. (1980).

Faced with this chorus of criticism, FDA in 1978 proposed a new regulation to clarify who may be considered the "manufacturer" of a drug, 43 Fed. Reg. 45614 (October 3, 1978). After consulting the Department of Justice, FDA reopened the public record for comment on the possible anticompetitive effects of the proposed regulation, 44 Fed. Reg. 37234 (June 26, 1979). *See also* 45 Fed. Reg. 25760 (April 15, 1980), 46 Fed. Reg. 2977 (January 13, 1981). FDA issued its final regulation in 47 Fed. Reg. 24735 (June 8, 1982).

The current complex regulation, codified in 21 C.F.R. § 201.1, abolishes the "man-in-the-plant" policy and allows a firm to be designated as the manufacturer of a drug only if it performs *all* manufacturing operations (with certain limited exceptions, such as encapsulating or sterilizing, that are commonly contracted out). A firm that performs more than half of the important manufacturing operations may be designated as the manufacturer if the label also states that "certain manufacturing operations have been performed by other firms." Alternatively, all firms that contribute to production may be listed as "joint manufacturers," or a single firm may simply be listed as the distributor.

5. PRESCRIPTION DRUG PROMOTION

a. Generic Name Disclosure

From December 1959 until his death in August 1963, Senator Estes Kefauver presided over extensive hearings investigating pricing, promotion, and patent practices of the pharmaceutical industry. The legislation he introduced and pursued to promote competition within the industry was languishing in Congress before it was revived by the reports of the thalidomide tragedy in mid–1962. These grim reports of deformed infants born to many European women who had taken thalidomide during pregnancy revitalized Kefauver's bill, converted it into legislation to increase FDA's authority over the safety and effectiveness of drugs, and assured its enactment in October 1962. *See* R. Harris, THE REAL VOICE (1964); The Insight Team, SUFFER THE CHILDREN: THE STORY OF THALIDOMIDE (1979).

One of the few of Kefauver's original proposals that survived the legislative process was section 502(e)'s requirement that manufacturers disclose the generic name of the active ingredient of their products in labeling and in advertising.

ADMINISTERED PRICES—DRUGS

Senate Report No. 448, 87th Congress, 1st Session (1961).

In addition to patent controls and the vast amounts spent on advertising and promotion, the control of the market by the large drug companies stems from a third source of power; this is their remarkable success in persuading physicians to prescribe by trade names rather than generic names. Where this is done the small manufacturer is automatically excluded from the market, regardless of whether the drugs are patented or nonpatented, and the opportunity for price competition disappears. This state of affairs is furthered by anything which causes the physician to be apprehensive of, or have difficulty in, prescribing by generic names....

The new so-called synthetic penicillin illustrates the problem. The chemical name for this product is alpha-phenoxyethyl penicillin potassium. This set of syllables is also used as a generic name. In addition, there are two other generic names—potassium penicillin 152 and phenethicillin potassium. Since the product is protected by patent, there are only six sellers, each of whom markets under his own trade name. Thus the prescribing physician is bombarded with promotional material for Syncillin, Darcil, Alpen, Chemipen, Dramcillin–S, and Maxipen. All of these are, of course, the same chemical compound....

In this example the busy practitioner is confronted with three generic names, six brand names used as the name of the drug itself, and at least five different colors. Thus, there are 14 different identification symbols for the identical drug. In terms of nomenclature, each product stands isolated: indeed, there is an attempt to conceal the identical nature of the drug....

All ethical drugs, whether marketed under generic or trade names, must meet the minimum standards of the United States Pharmacopoeia or the National Formulary. By law, a drug is deemed to be adulterated if, when sold under or by a name recognized in either compendium, it differs from the standard of strength, quality or purity, as determined by the test laid down in the United States Pharmacopoeia or National Formulary....

———

Pharmaceutical manufacturers strenuously resisted adoption of section 502(e). When the FDA adopted regulations to implement the provision in 1963, the major drug companies promptly took the agency to court. *See* Sweeney, *The "Generic Every Time" Case: Prescription Drug Industry In Extremis,* 21 FDC L.J. 226 (1966). The regulations would have required manufacturer labeling and advertising to disclose the generic name—termed the "established name" in section 502(e)—of the drug each time the trade name was used. The manufacturers sought a declaratory judgment that the regulations were invalid and an injunction against their enforcement in advance of any attempt by FDA to initiate compliance proceedings against any firm or drug. The district court held the regulations invalid. *Abbott Laboratories v. Celebrezze,* 228 F.Supp. 855 (D. Del. 1964). Neither the Court of Appeals for the Third Circuit, which reversed the district court, 352 F.2d 286 (1965), nor the Supreme Court reached the merits of the case. The Court's decision in *Abbott Laboratories v. Gardner,* 387 U.S. 136 (1967), p. 1258 *infra,* remains the seminal judicial discussion of "ripeness" of agency action for judicial review. The Court held that the regulations were reviewable in a preenforcement suit and remanded the case for consideration of the legality of FDA's "every time" requirement.

Following the Supreme Court's remand, the parties reached a settlement a few days before the case was scheduled for reargument before the Third Circuit. The resulting regulation, 21 C.F.R. § 201.10(g), requires that the generic name appear, in type that is at least half the size as the brand name, whenever the brand name is "featured," and at least once when the brand name is used "in the running text."

NOTE

The 1962 Drug Amendments also added section 508 to the Act, which authorizes FDA, when necessary, to prescribe a drug's official name. FDA established a procedure for designating official names in 21 C.F.R. Pt. 299 and initially promulgated a number of official names. The agency revoked these names, however, and adopted the policy of relying upon the drug names established by United States Adopted Names (USAN), 47 Fed. Reg. 31008 (July 16, 1982), 49 Fed. Reg. 37574 (September 25, 1984), 53 Fed. Reg. 5368 (February 24, 1988). USAN is published by a consortium of private organizations, in consultation with FDA and international organizations.

b. Prescription Drug Advertising To Professionals

The 1962 Amendments gave FDA authority to regulate advertising for prescription drugs. Under this grant of authority, in section 502(n), however, regulations must be promulgated in accordance with the formal rulemaking procedures of section 701(e). As a consequence, FDA has issued general regulations for prescription drug advertising on only two occasions, and then only after it agreed to revisions that persuaded the Pharmaceutical Manufacturers Association to withdraw its demand for a formal hearing. *See* Jurow, *Prescription–Drug Advertising—Blight or Light?*, 23 FDC L.J. 242 (1968); Ruge, *Regulation of Prescription Drug Advertising: Medical Progress and Private Enterprise*, 32 Law & Contemp. Probs. 650 (1967).

The original prescription drug advertising regulations were promulgated shortly after enactment of the 1962 Drug Amendments. 28 Fed. Reg. 1448 (February 14, 1963), 28 Fed. Reg. 6375 (June 20, 1963), 28 Fed. Reg. 9837 (September 10, 1963), 28 Fed. Reg. 10993 (October 15, 1963), 29 Fed. Reg. 257 (January 10, 1964). As a result of FDA Commissioner Goddard's personal concern about pharmaceutical advertising, *see* FDA, *Compendium of Medical Advertising*, FDA Pub. No. 40 (June 1967), Goddard, *The Administrator's View*, 22 FDC L.J. 449, 452 (1967), FDA revised those regulations, 32 Fed. Reg. 7533 (May 23, 1967), 33 Fed. Reg. 9393 (June 27, 1968), 34 Fed. Reg. 7802 (May 16, 1969), to prohibit specific practices to which the agency had strong objections.

21 C.F.R. § 202.1

. . .

(6) *Advertisements that are false, lacking in fair balance, or otherwise misleading.* An advertisement for a prescription drug is false, lacking in fair balance, or otherwise misleading, or otherwise violative of section 502(n) of the act if it:

(i) Contains a representation or suggestion, not approved or permitted for use in the labeling, that a drug is better, more effective, useful in a broader range of conditions or patients (as used in this section "patients" means humans and in the case of veterinary drugs, other animals), safer, has fewer, or less incidence of, or less serious side effects or contraindications than has been demonstrated by substantial evidence or substantial clinical experience ... whether or not such representations are made by comparison with other drugs or treatments, and whether or not such a representation or suggestion is made directly or through use of published or unpublished literature, quotations, or other references.

(ii) Contains a drug comparison that represents or suggests that a drug is safer or more effective than another drug in some particular when it has not been demonstrated to be safer or more effective in such particular by substantial evidence or substantial clinical experience.

(iii) Contains favorable information or opinions about a drug previously regarded as valid but which have been rendered invalid by contrary and more credible recent information, or contains literature references or quotations that are significantly more favorable to the drug than has been demonstrated by substantial evidence or substantial clinical experience.

(iv) Contains a representation or suggestion that a drug is safer than it has been demonstrated to be by substantial evidence or substantial clinical experience, by selective presentation of information from published articles or other references that report no side effects or minimal side effects with the drug or otherwise selects information from any source in a way that makes a drug appear to be safer than has been demonstrated.

(v) Presents information from a study in a way that implies that the study represents larger or more general experience with the drug than it actually does.

(vi) Contains references to literature or studies that misrepresent the effectiveness of a drug by failure to disclose that claimed results may be due to concomitant therapy, or by failure to disclose the credible information available concerning the extent to which claimed results may be due to placebo effect (information concerning placebo effect is not required unless the advertisement promotes the drug for use by man).

(vii) Contains favorable data or conclusions from nonclinical studies of a drug, such as in laboratory animals or in vitro, in a way that suggests they have clinical significance when in fact no such clinical significance has been demonstrated.

(viii) Uses a statement by a recognized authority that is apparently favorable about a drug but fails to refer to concurrent or more recent unfavorable data or statements from the same authority on the same subject or subjects.

(ix) Uses a quote or paraphrase out of context to convey a false or misleading idea.

(x) Uses literature, quotations, or references that purport to support an advertising claim but in fact do not support the claim or have relevance to the claim.

(xi) Uses literature, quotations, or references for the purpose of recommending or suggesting conditions of drug use that are not approved or permitted in the drug packaging labeling.

(xii) Offers a combination of drugs for the treatment of patients suffering from a condition amenable to treatment by any of the components rather than limiting the indications for use to patients for whom concomitant therapy as provided by the fixed combination drug is indicated, unless such condition is included in the uses permitted under paragraph (e)(4) of this section.

(xiii) Uses a study on normal individuals without disclosing that the subjects were normal, unless the drug is intended for use on normal individuals.

(xiv) Uses "statistics" on numbers of patients, or counts of favorable results or side effects, derived from pooling data from various insignificant or dissimilar studies in a way that suggests either that such "statistics" are valid if they are not or that they are derived from large or significant studies supporting favorable conclusions when such is not the case.

(xv) Uses erroneously a statistical finding of "no significant difference" to claim clinical equivalence or to deny or conceal the potential existence of a real clinical difference.

(xvi) Uses statements or representations that a drug differs from or does not contain a named drug or category of drugs, or that it has a greater potency per unit of weight, in a way that suggests falsely or misleadingly or without substantial evidence or substantial clinical experience that the advertised drug is safer or more effective than such other drug or drugs.

(xvii) Uses data favorable to a drug derived from patients treated with dosages different from those recommended in approved or permitted labeling if the drug advertised is subject to section 505, 507, or 512 of the act, or, in the case of other drugs, if the dosages employed were different from those recommended in the labeling and generally recognized as safe and effective. This provision is not intended to prevent citation of reports of studies that include some patients treated with dosages different from those authorized, if the results in such patients are not used.

(xviii) Uses headline, subheadline, or pictorial or other graphic matter in a way that is misleading.

(xix) Represents or suggests that drug dosages properly recommended for use in the treatment of certain classes of patients or disease conditions are safe and effective for the treatment of other classes of patients or disease conditions when such is not the case.

(xx) Presents required information relating to side effects or contraindications by means of a general term for a group in place of disclosing each specific side effect and contraindication (for example employs the term "blood dyscrasias" instead of "leukopenia," "agranulocytosis," "neutropenia," etc.) unless the use of such general term conforms to the provisions of paragraph (e)(3)(iii) of this section.

Provided, however, That any provision of this paragraph shall be waived with respect to a specified advertisement as set forth in a written communication from the Food and Drug Administration....

(7) *Advertisements that may be false, lacking in fair balance, or otherwise misleading.* An advertising may be false, lacking in fair balance, or otherwise misleading or otherwise violative of section 502(n) of the act if it:

(i) Contains favorable information or conclusions from a study that is inadequate in design, scope, or conduct to furnish significant support for such information or conclusions.

(ii) Uses the concept of "statistical significance" to support a claim that has not been demonstrated to have clinical significance or validity, or fails to reveal the range of variations around the quoted average results.

(iii) Uses statistical analyses and techniques on a retrospective basis to discover and cite findings not soundly supported by the study, or to suggest scientific validity and rigor for data from studies the design or protocol of which are not amenable to formal statistical evaluations.

(iv) Uses tables or graphs to distort or misrepresent the relationships, trends, differences, or changes among the variables or products studied; for example, by failing to label abscissa and ordinate so that the graph creates a misleading impression.

(v) Uses reports or statements represented to be statistical analyses, interpretations, or evaluations that are inconsistent with or violate the established principles of statistical theory, methodology, applied practice, and inference, or that are derived from clinical studies the design, data, or conduct of which substantially invalidate the application of statistical analyses, interpretations, or evaluations.

(vi) Contains claims concerning the mechanism or site of drug action that are not generally regarded as established by scientific evidence by experts qualified by scientific training and experience without disclosing that the claims are not established and the limitations of the supporting evidence.

(vii) Fails to provide sufficient emphasis for the information relating to side effects and contraindications, when such information is contained in a distinct part of an advertisement, because of repetition or other emphasis in that part of the advertisement of claims for effectiveness or safety of the drug.

(viii) Fails to present information relating to side effects and contraindications with a prominence and readability reasonable comparable with the presentation of information relating to effectiveness of the drug, taking into account all implementing factors such as typography, layout, contrast, headlines, paragraphing, white space, and any other techniques apt to achieve emphasis.

(ix) Fails to provide adequate emphasis (for example, by the use of color scheme, borders, headlines, or copy that extends across the gutter) for the fact that two facing pages are part of the same advertisement when one page contains information relating to side effects and contraindications.

(x) In an advertisement promoting use of the drug in a selected class of patients (for example, geriatric patients or depressed patients), fails to present with adequate emphasis the significant side effects and contraindications or the significant dosage considerations, when dosage recommendations are included in an advertisement, especially applicable to that selected class of patients.

(xi) Fails to present on a page facing another page (or on another full page) of an advertisement on more than one page, information relating to side effects and contraindications when such information is in a distinct part of the advertisement.

(xii) Fails to include on each page or spread to an advertisement the information relating to side effects and contraindications or a prominent reference to its presence and location when it is presented as a distinct part of an advertisement.

(xiii) Contains information from published or unpublished reports or opinions falsely or misleadingly represented or suggested to be authentic or authoritative.

NOTES

1. *Comparative Claims.* In 40 Fed. Reg. 15392 (April 7, 1975), 44 Fed. Reg. 37434 (June 26, 1979), FDA revised its prescription drug advertising and labeling regulations to specify the conditions under which comparative effectiveness claims may be made. The filing of formal objections stayed the effectiveness of the advertising regulations, 44 Fed. Reg. 74817 (December 18, 1979), and they have not been the subject of further FDA action. The labeling amendments, promulgated under section 701(a), became effective six months after publication. *See* Millstein, *FDA Policy on Comparative Prescription Drug Advertising,* 17 Drug Info. J. 63 (1983).

2. *Reminder Advertisements.* Section 202.1(e)(2)(i) of the regulations recognizes a category of "reminder advertisements," which "call attention to the name of the drug product but do not include indications or dosage recommendations. . . ." Such advertisements need not include a summary of information about side effects and contraindications unless the agency has specifically required that a drug's labeling and promotional literature contain a boxed warning relating to a serious hazard associated with its use.

3. *Gifts and Other Promotional Practices.* Following Congressional hearings on unprofessional drug promotion practices, "Examination of the Pharmaceutical Industry, 1973–74," Hearings before the Subcomm. on Health of the Senate Comm. on Labor and Public Welfare, 93rd Cong., 1st & 2nd Sess., Pt. 3 (1974), the Pharmaceutical Manufacturers Association endorsed federal legislation to eliminate such practices as giving gifts to physicians to encourage them

to prescribe specific drugs. "PMA's Positive Program," 36 FDC Reports ("The Pink Sheet"), no. 14, at A1 (April 8, 1974). Criticism of pharmaceutical promotional practices has not abated, however. *See, e.g., Undesirable Marketing Practices in the Pharmaceutical Industry,* 313 N. Eng. J. Med. 54 (July 4, 1985); *One Drug Company's Sales Technique,* 313 N. Eng. J. Med. 270 (July 25, 1985).

4. *Medicare/Medicaid Prohibitions.* The Medicare/Medicaid Anti–Fraud and Abuse Amendments, 91 Stat. 1175 (1977), made it a felony to solicit or receive any remuneration for purchasing any product for which payment may be made under Medicare or Medicaid. In the Medicare and Medicaid Patient and Program Protection Act of 1987, 101 Stat. 680, 681–689, this provision was repealed and a comparable provision reenacted in 42 U.S.C. § 1320a–7b(b). The current version makes it a felony either to pay or to receive any remuneration of any kind to induce the order or purchase of a drug or device for which reimbursement is made under Medicare or Medicaid. Because it is not feasible to determine in advance whether a particular drug will be subject to Medicare or Medicaid reimbursement, all current pharmaceutical industry promotional practices are potentially subject to this provision. Proposed regulations to implement the statute were published in 54 Fed. Reg. 3088 (January 23, 1989).

FDA's current drug advertising regulations are codified at 21 C.F.R. Part 202. Their primary objective, as the portions quoted above suggest, is to curb overstatement in product claims and encourage balanced disclosure of side effects, contraindications, and warnings— the central thrust of section 502(n). However, the primary problems posed by advertising for prescription drugs do not appear easily redressable by the authority to issue regulations or, indeed, by the formal enforcement sanctions provided by the Act.

COMPETITIVE PROBLEMS IN THE DRUG INDUSTRY: SUMMARY AND ANALYSIS

Subcommittee on Monopoly of the Senate Select Committee on
Small Business.

92d Congress, 2d Session (1972).

... In order to obtain sales, drug companies must first make prescribers aware of the existence of the drug.... More important, the successful drug firm must succeed in persuading physicians to choose its products from the multitude of other drugs or drug products which are available to them. To achieve these objectives, drug companies have developed a variety of promotional practices designed to differentiate the products of one company from those of their competitors.

Broadly speaking, promotionally-achieved product differentiation efforts undertaken by pharmaceutical houses encompass many different kinds of activities. For example, the drug industry makes extensive use of trade-names, not only to distinguish one drug from another, but also to differentiate different versions of the same drug from one another. Another feature of the present drug promotion system involves the use of a large number of company salesmen who deal directly and on a personal basis with prescribers and with others in the health community involved in the selection or purchase of prescribed drugs. Companies engage in extensive drug advertising campaigns in professional journals and magazines subscribed to by physicians and other prescribers. Direct mail programs and the distribution of sample products are other ways in which drug companies seek to make practitioners aware of their particular products....

Promotionally-achieved product differentiation efforts are especially effective where consumers, or in this case, physicians, face the difficult task of sorting out competing claims about a variety of products or drugs which often purport to be or do substantially the same thing.....

... [M]anufacturers seeking to increase the overall sales of specific drugs find it in their interest to promote substances as widely as possible and for as many conditions for which the drug can be shown to be indicated. To achieve this objective, critics note that manufacturers tend to emphasize the benefits and good points of particular drugs while, at the same time, minimizing the less desirable and often serious side-effects or adverse reactions that may result from using such drugs.....

If manufacturers are successful in promoting the sale of certain drugs by emphasizing their widest possible uses, they are unlikely suddenly to consider engaging in equally intensive campaigns to point out to prescribers those shortcomings in drugs that would cause physicians to reduce or stop their use of these products. Nor is it realistic to expect manufacturers to emphasize that the competition's newer drugs are either more effective, or less hazardous, than their own products in various prescribing situations....

NOTES

1. *Oral Promotion.* "The amended statute does not specifically give the FDA authority over oral promotional statements made by detail men. These salesmen are also an important source of information about new drugs, making an estimated 18 to 20 million calls a year on doctors and druggists.... The FDA does, however, have jurisdiction over literature left by detailers with doctors...." Ruge, *Regulation of Prescription Drug Advertising: Medical Progress and Private Enterprise,* 32 Law & Contemp. Probs. 650 (1967).

2. *Corrective Advertisements.* In 1972 FDA took issue with a medical journal advertisement for a tranquilizer, which began with the banner headline: "For The Anxiety that Comes from Not Fitting In," followed by this text:

> The newcomer in town who *can't* make friends. The organization man who *can't* adjust to altered status within his company. The woman who *can't* get along with her new daughter-in-law. The executive who *can't* accept retirement.

> These common adjustment problems of our society are frequently intolerable for the disordered personality, who often responds with excessive anxiety.

> Serentil is suggested for *this* type of patient. Not simply because its tranquilizing action can ease anxiety and tension, but because it benefits personality disorders in general. And because it has not been found habituating.

The opposite page depicted a completed jigsaw puzzle with a single piece missing through which stared an anxious face—presumably that of the reader's patient.

FDA found this advertisement deceptive and persuaded the manufacturer to run a corrective version, which appeared under the caption: "Published to Correct a Previous Advertisement which the Food and Drug Administration Considered Misleading."

> The Food and Drug Administration has requested that we bring to your attention a recent journal advertisement for Serentil (mesoridazine) which featured the headline "For the anxiety that comes from not fitting in."

> The FDA considers the advertisement misleading in several respects. For example:

>> The FDA states that the principal theme of the ad suggests unapproved uses of Serentil for relatively minor or everyday anxiety situations encountered often in the normal course of living. THE FACT IS THAT SERENTIL, A PHENOTHIAZINE DRUG, IS LIMITED IN ITS USE TO CERTAIN DISEASE STATES (SEE OPPOSITE PAGE FOR INDICATIONS) IN WHICH THE RISK OF PHENOTHIAZINE THERAPY IS JUSTIFIED IN THE OPINION OF THE PHYSICIAN.

> We have taken steps to withdraw the advertisement in question.

3. *Overpromotion.* In *Love v. Wolf,* 226 Cal. App.2d 378, 38 Cal. Rptr. 183 (1964), the court held that the manufacturer of Chloromycetin, then the only marketed version of the potent antibiotic chloramphenicol, could be held liable for the plaintiff's bone marrow depression if the jury were persuaded that the company's heavy promotion of the drug effectively submerged its own warnings about the hazard:

> ... It appears in evidence that the company knew that many physicians in the United States had been prescribing chloromycetin for conditions less than serious. It does not appear that the detail men were told to attempt to do anything to curtail this. It *was* told them by the company president that "the fact that a drug was administered prior to development of a aplasia is by no means proof that the drug is the offender. At this time, there are absolutely no cases known to us in which such proof is extant." He said that there was "no valid scientific proof" that aplasia resulted from chloromycetin. The detail men were told that this was the position of the company and they were told so to inform the doctors they visited. They were also told (and presumably were told to relay): "Chloromycetin has been officially cleared by the FDA and the National Research Council with no restrictions on the number or the range of diseases for which Chloromycetin may be administered." These statements may have expressed literal truth. They did not, however, express "the whole truth, and nothing but the truth" as a fair warning which, according to plaintiff's

experts, Parke–Davis should have been giving the medical profession....

Following a retrial Parke Davis was found liable for Mrs. Love's injuries and appealed without success. "[T]here was evidence that the overpromotion of chloromycetin by Parke–Davis caused doctors, including Dr. Wolf, to disregard the warnings, even the 1961 warning, and hence Parke–Davis' liability is based more on this overpromotion than on the failure to include in the 1952 warning the matter included in the later warning." 249 Cal. App. 2d 822, 58 Cal. Rptr. 42 (1967). *See also Stevens v. Parke, Davis & Co.,* 9 Cal. 3d 51, 107 Cal. Rptr. 45, 507 P.2d 653 (1973); Cohen, *Stevens v. Parke, Davis & Co.,* 10 U.S.F.L. Rev. 683 (1976).

The dissemination by manufacturers of information about unapproved drugs, or about unapproved uses of an approved drug, has presented vexing problems for FDA. Section 202.1(e)(4) of the agency's advertising regulations, *supra,* provides that advertising cannot recommend or suggest any use that is not in the labeling in an approved NDA. Section 312.7(a) of the IND regulations, on the other hand, though prohibiting any representation "in a promotional context" that an investigational drug is safe and effective, goes on to state:

> This provision is not intended to restrict the full exchange of scientific information concerning the drug, including dissemination of scientific findings and scientific or lay media.

Reconciling these provisions, in an era of near-instantaneous dissemination of new scientific information, has not proved easy.

SPEECH BY KENNETH R. FEATHER*
Annual Meeting of the PMA Marketing Section, March 14, 1989.

Promotional activities for prescription drugs have expanded far beyond the materials traditionally thought of as advertising; i.e. advertisements in journals, mailers, and detail ads. We now see newspaper articles, interviews on TV talk shows, multi-city seminars (traveling road shows), supplements to medical journals, and press conferences being used to promote drugs. This poses new problems for the FDA in its enforcement of the Act and regulations to ensure truthful and complete promotional discussions of prescription drugs.....

We feel the definitions for labeling and advertisements, as found in the Act and in the regulations, can cover virtually all activities disseminating information about a drug which are done by *or on behalf of* the manufacturer. I realize there can be honest debate about that concept, especially since the regulations also tell us (FDA) that we are not to inhibit the "free exchange of scientific information." Let me address this issue.

* [Acting director, FDA Division of Drug
   Advertising and Labeling.]

First, that quoted statement comes from the section of the regulations dealing with IND drugs, not approved, marketed drugs. It is clear that during this investigational phase, information should flow freely between researchers in order to conduct and evaluate more fully, studies and data from this research. To the extent that the promotional regulations restrict information, this provision is clearly meant to remove that restriction in this important special case. We think this means a firm can communicate fully with their researchers; that investigators can publish the results of their research in medical and other scientific journals; and that investigators can present their research in seminars and symposia (more on this later). Does an article in the *Wall Street Journal* fall into this category?

We do not think that section in the regulations means a firm can disseminate any information it wishes simply because they disguise it as a seminar or call it "education." What "scientific" purpose does it serve to hold a press conference for the lay press (or even trade press) to announce the preliminary results of a study....

Many times it appears these activities are designed, not for scientific dialogue, but to try to get a drug used for a wide variety of uses which the company knows they will not get approval for. As an example, for several years information about studies and "logical projections" of the actions of prostaglandins in treating and preventing ulcers have appeared in exhibits, sole sponsored publications, medical press articles, and other materials. This systematically disseminated scientific information discussed these actions in treating and preventing ulcers caused by almost any factor, usually extolling its effectiveness and safety in these areas. It was known these products would not be approved for all of these uses.

This was justified on the basis that the physician must be kept informed so he/she can properly use the drug when approved. But if most of these uses are not going to be adequately studied and proven, how can this information help a physician use the drug "properly?" ... Doesn't this look more like a way to make sure the drug is used for all of these problems, without the company having to do the studies to properly prove them?....

We are often asked if a directly firm sponsored seminar is proper. We have always recommended that seminars and symposia be held under the auspices of a university, a medical school or a professional association, with that body through an editorial board having the responsibility for selecting speakers and perhaps, topics to be discussed. They should also be responsible for editing and disseminating written materials based on this seminar. The sponsoring firm should have little or no influence in this process.....

Of even more concern is [are] similar activities for new uses of currently marketed drugs. Obviously since there is a drug on the market, it can be used for this new purpose. The law prohibits a manufacturer from promoting unapproved uses for an NDA'd drug, so firms turn to these methods of getting this information out....

There's a recent example of discussing a new use for a marketed drug dealing with a press conference.... This involved one short term (6 weeks) small (16 patients) study for a product approved for treating severe acne. The study dealt with using the product to remove or reduce wrinkling and the appearance of aging in the skin. The study was published in a prestigious national medical journal, so the medical/scientific community was made aware of the results of this study. We understand the investigator wanted to have a press conference. He is free to do so. I think it is fair to say that had he called a press conference, very few people would have shown up. The firm paid for a press conference, and this study got national, lay press coverage. By the subject of the study I think you can visualize the headlines resulting from this press conference.... [D]id this serve to promote the product for an unapproved use? The answer to that question is, yes. In fact they can't keep the product on the pharmacy shelves, the demand for it is so high.

The essence of the regulations applying to promotional activities is that the information be accurate, truthful and balanced..... We think these general criteria can be applied to all of these things....

Even though we think most of these activities fall within the jurisdiction of the FDA, it is unlikely we will take action or impose the full range of the regulations if the information is complete and balanced....

NOTES

1. *FDA Policy Statements.* Rather than amend the prescription drug advertising regulations, FDA has issued a number of "policy statements" on various types of advertising and promotional practices that do not fall within the existing regulations.

2. *First Amendment Protection.* Underlying the FDA's concern about restricting dissemination of scientific information, despite its promotional character, is awareness of the First Amendment issues that would arise if it were to attempt to ban discussion of unapproved uses of investigational or approved new drugs.

3. *Journal Articles.* In Compliance Policy Guide 7132b.17 (August 15, 1989), FDA determined that an article about a prescription drug in an independent publication is not to be regarded as advertising (or labeling) for the drug, whether or not the drug is also separately advertised in the same publication, if the manufacturer makes no contribution to the article and does not use the article for promotional purposes.

4. *Commentary. See Symposium on Promotional and Marketing Activities: Preapproval, Time of Approval, Postapproval,* 23 Drug Info. J., No. 4 (1989).

c. Advertising Prescription Drugs to Consumers

With growing governmental interest in promoting prescription drug price competition, FDA concluded in the early 1970s that the prescription drug advertising regulations required revision to allow communication of price comparisons to consumers. In 1975 FDA promulgated new 21 C.F.R. § 200.200 to authorize advertising of consumer prices for prescription drugs as long as no representations are made concerning the safety, effectiveness, or indications of the advertised products. 38 Fed. Reg. 32140 (November 21, 1973), 39 Fed. Reg. 21165 (June 19, 1974), 40 Fed. Reg. 58794 (December 18, 1975).

Nearly a decade later, in a speech to the Pharmaceutical Advertising Council, FDA Commissioner Arthur Hayes appeared to encourage direct advertising of prescription drugs to consumers. Because both section 201(n)(3) of the FD&C Act and the implementing regulations, 21 C.F.R. § 202.1(e), require advertisements to include a "brief summary relating to side effects, contraindications, and effectiveness," broadcast advertisements confront difficulties, but print media do not present the same constraints. The first television advertisement for a prescription drug provoked an immediate regulatory letter. "Rx Advertising to Consumers," FDA Talk Paper No. T83–23 (May 23, 1983). The company revised its advertisement to carry only price information, but went forward with newspaper advertising that carried the full "brief summary" of information, in compliance with FDA regulations. On September 2, 1983, Commissioner Hayes issued a "Statement of Policy" in which he requested a suspension of all advertising of prescription drugs to consumers "in order to permit time for a reasoned assessment of this complex issue."

After an intense public debate and research into the issues, *see, e.g.,* Professional Postgraduate Services, PRESCRIPTION DRUG ADVERTISING TO THE CONSUMER: WHAT ARE THE ISSUES? (1984); "Prescription Drug Advertising to Consumers," Staff Report prepared for the use of the Subcomm. on Oversight and Investigations of the House Comm. on Energy and Commerce, 98th Cong., 2nd Sess., Comm. Pt. 98–DD (1984); Masson and Rubin, *Matching Prescription Drugs and Consumers: The Benefits of Direct Advertising,* 313 N. Eng. J. Med. 513 (August 22, 1985); L. Morris, PRESCRIPTION DRUG ADVERTISING TO CONSUMERS: BRIEF SUMMARY FORMATS FOR TELEVISION AND MAGAZINE ADVERTISEMENTS (FDA, 1984), summarized in Morris and Millstein, *Drug Advertising to Consumers: Effects of Formats for Magazine and Television Advertisements,* 39 FDC L.J. 497 (1984), FDA issued the following statement.

DIRECT–TO–CONSUMER ADVERTISING OF PRESCRIPTION DRUGS; WITHDRAWAL OF MORATORIUM
50 Federal Register 36677 (September 9, 1985).

The Food and Drug Administration (FDA) is withdrawing the voluntary moratorium on direct-to-consumer advertising of prescription drugs first requested in 1983. FDA has concluded that, for the time being, current regulations governing prescription drug advertising provide sufficient safeguards to protect consumers....

The moratorium was intended to allow time for a dialogue among consumers, health professionals, and industry on the issue of direct-to-consumer advertising of prescription drugs. It was also intended to allow time for the conduct and interpretation of research by interested parties on aspects of consumer-oriented drug advertising. These two principal purposes for which FDA sought the voluntary moratorium have now been realized.

----

d. Counterfeit, Imitation, and Diverted Prescription Drugs

From the mid–1960s when it was responsible for enforcement of the Drug Abuse Control Amendments of 1965, 79 Stat. 226 (superseded by the Controlled Substances Act, 84 Stat. 1236, 1242, 1281–1282 (1970), now enforced by the Drug Enforcement Agency), FDA has been concerned about the illicit distribution of legitimate drugs and the distribution of counterfeit drugs. The 1965 Amendments added to the Act section 201(g)(2), defining the term "counterfeit drug," and section 301(i)(2), prohibiting counterfeiting and the distribution of counterfeit drugs. FDA has taken action to enforce these provisions, *see, e.g., United States v. Jamieson–McKames Pharmaceuticals, Inc.,* 651 F.2d 532 (8th Cir. 1981); *United States v. Articles of Drug in Bulk,* Food Drug Cosm. L. Rep. (CCH) ¶ 38,155 (M.D. Fla. 1982); *United States v. All Equipment Including ... An Encapsulating Machine,* 475 F.Supp. 39 (E.D. Mo. 1979); "Counterfeit Drug Cases," FDA Talk Paper, T87–42 (September 30, 1987) (describing cases involving counterfeit contraceptives, analgesic, and antibiotic drug products). *See also* "International Operation Nabs Iranian Dealer and Counterfeit Drugs," FDA Talk Paper T88–55 (August 12, 1988) (recounting undercover operations to stop international trade in counterfeit drugs). *See generally* Hallagan *et al., Anabolic–Androgenic Steroid Use by Athletes,* 321 N.E.J.M. 1042 (October 12, 1989).

Section 502(i)(2), as enacted in 1938, prohibits the sale of any imitation drug. FDA has enforced this provision against a variety of drugs made in imitation of, and sold on the street in substitution for, illegal controlled substances. *See United States v. Articles of Drug,* 633 F. Supp. 316 (D. Neb. 1986); "National Illegal Drug Scheme Halted," FDA Talk Paper No. T86–25 (April 3, 1986) (describing seizure of 24 million tablets and capsules of imitation amphetamines which contained primarily caffeine). On appeal, *United States v. Articles of Drug,* 825 F.2d 1238 (8th Cir. 1987), the court held that a product is an imitation if it is identical in shape, size and color, or similar or virtually identical in gross appearance, or similar in effect to a controlled substance, but not if it is only similar in concept. It sustained an injunction against the marketing practices that resulted in the caffeine-containing product being passed off as controlled substances. For the decision on remand, *see United States v. Articles of Drug,* Food Drug Cosm.L.Rep. (CCH) ¶ 38,089 (D. Neb. 1988). On a second appeal, *United States v. Midwest Pharmaceuticals, Inc.,* 890 F.2d 1004 (8th Cir. 1989), the court of appeals upheld the scope of the injunction broadly prohibiting the marketing of any "look-alike" drugs.

In two early cases courts held that diverted prescription drugs labeled as "physician's sample—not to be sold" did not become misbranded in the possession of wholesalers who obtained them with the intention of selling them to retail druggists to fill prescriptions. *United States v. Various Articles of Drugs Consisting of Unknown Quantities of Prescription Drugs,* 332 F.2d 286 (3d Cir. 1964); *United States v. Various Articles of Drugs Consisting of Unknown Quantities of Prescription Drugs,* 207 F. Supp. 480 (S.D.N.Y. 1962). *See also Miami–Luken, Inc. v. Ohio State Board of Pharmacy,* Food Drug Cosm. L. Rep. (CCH) ¶ 38,106 (Ohio App. 1987). Similarly, a company that repackaged tablets from the manufacturer's original package and resold them was not required to obtain separate FDA approval where the manufacturer already had an approved NDA. *United States v. Kaybel, Inc.* 430 F.2d 1346 (3d Cir. 1970). These decisions made it very difficult for FDA to prevent the adulteration and misbranding of diverted samples.

More recent congressional investigations brought to light a related problem involving pharmaceutical products exported from the United States and later reimported. *See* "Dangerous Medicine: The Risk to American Consumers from Prescription Drug Diversion and Counterfeiting," Report by the Subcomm. on Oversight and Investigations of the House Comm. on Energy and Commerce, 99th Cong., 2nd Sess., Comm. Print 99–Z (1966). In September 1985 FDA adopted a policy of automatic detention of imports of U.S.-produced drugs in order to confirm that they had not become adulterated or misbranded while abroad. 52 Fed. Reg. 706 (January 8, 1987). Because this policy was adopted without the opportunity for public comment it was declared invalid in *Bellarno International Ltd. v. FDA,* 678 F. Supp. 410 (E.D. N.Y. 1988).

In 1987, Congress enacted the Prescription Drug Marketing Act, 102 Stat. 95, which makes the importation of American drugs by anyone other than the manufacturer illegal. It prohibits the sale of drug samples. It also prohibits the resale of drug products initially sold to health care institutions. The Act allows the continued distribution of drug samples by pharmaceutical manufacturers, but only in response to a written request and for which a receipt is obtained. Finally, it requires state licensure of wholesale distributors of prescription drugs. FDA's steps to implement these provisions can be traced in 53 Fed. Reg. 29776 (August 8, 1988), 53 Fed. Reg. 35325 (September 13, 1988), 53 Fed. Reg. 44954 (November 7, 1988), 55 Fed. Reg. 7778 (March 5, 1990).

6.　DRUG PRODUCT SANITATION AND INTEGRITY

In contrast to the food sanitation provisions of the Act, which contain no specific GMP requirement, section 501(a)(2)(B) explicitly declares a drug to be adulterated if it is not manufactured "in conformity with current good manufacturing practice."

UNITED STATES v. AN ARTICLE OF DRUG ...
WHITE QUADRISECT

United States Court of Appeals, Seventh Circuit, 1973.

484 F.2d 748.

PER CURIAM.

... The lower court condemned the shipment because the defendant's production procedure violated the "current good manufacturing practice" (GMP) provision of the Act, 21 U.S.C. § 351(a)(2)(B). Appellant contends that that provision is unconstitutional under the Due Process Clause of the Fifth Amendment because of its alleged vagueness.

The GMP provision stems from congressional concern over the danger that dangerously impure drugs might escape detection under a system predicated only on seizure of drugs shown to be in fact adulterated. In order to insure public safety, Congress determined in 1962 that it was necessary to regulate the means of production themselves.... By ways of implementation, the FDA has promulgated detailed regulations to spell out the precise requirements of the section.

The district court found violations of GMP standards by defendant which include the failure to keep basic production records, inadequate testing of active ingredients before use, and insufficient tests of the finished product prior to shipment. These findings are not contested on appeal and we therefore consider them established....

... We conclude that the term "current good manufacturing practice" adequately defines a standard which the Administrator was authorized to particularize in interpretative regulations. Defendant does not deny that the regulations, which he has plainly violated, were adequate to notify him that his conduct was prohibited.

Defendant's argument is based on attacks on the statutory terms "current" and "good." ... We have no trouble with the use of the words in § 351(a)(2)(B). The term "current" fixes the point in time when the acceptability of the relevant production practices must be determined. Thus, the statute does not permit prosecution for failure to follow safety practices which were not recognized prior to the production of the subject drugs.[4] The term "good" likewise acquires adequate meaning when read in context even though, as defendant observes, a good dictionary lists a good many definitions of the word. Alternative definitions do not create impermissible ambiguity if the relevant definition is capable of interpretation by reference to objective criteria.... The word "good," as used in the GMP provision, is not unduly subjective.

The Constitution requires only a reasonable degree of certainty in statutory language.... Appellant also ignores the detailed regulations promulgated by the FDA which considerably illuminate the statutory language.[5]

In view of the customary presumption of constitutionality and the established high regard for the purposes of the Act, we readily sustain the GMP provision. The language utilized by Congress in this statute is neither less certain nor more difficult to interpret than language elsewhere in the same Act which has been upheld....

Moreover, an argument identical to defendant's was made and rejected in *United States v. Bel–Mar Laboratories, Inc.,* 284 F. Supp. 875 (E.D.N.Y. 1968). Judge Mishler's treatment of the constitutional question in that case is thorough and persuasive; we adopt his views.... We hold that defendant violated reasonably stable, definite, and ascertainable standards of current good manufacturing practice designed to insure the production of unadulterated drugs....

HUMAN AND VETERINARY DRUGS: CURRENT GOOD MANUFACTURING PRACTICE IN MANUFACTURE, PROCESSING, PACKING, OR HOLDING

43 Federal Register 45014 (September 29, 1978).

In the FEDERAL REGISTER of February 13, 1976 (41 FR 6878), the Commissioner of Food and Drugs proposed to revise the CGMP regulations, Parts 210 and 211, issued under section 501(a)(2)(B) of the Federal Food, Drug, and Cosmetic Act, to update them in light of current technology and to adopt more specific requirements to assure the quality of finished drug products....

4. Appellant also argues that even if the section has a definite meaning, it creates a standard subject to such rapid change that a drug manufacturer is unable to ascertain at any point in time what is expected of him. This argument overlooks the interpretative regulations. In our opinion it is appropriate for the statute to authorize changes in regulations to reflect the Administrator's evaluation of "current" practice. We think the GMP standard is sufficiently fixed.

5. "[T]he Secretary's interpretative regulations as to good manufacturing practice for purposes of judging the adequacy of the methods, facilities, and controls would be prima facie evidence of what constitutes current good manufacturing practice in any proceeding involving [§ 351(a)(2)] of the Food, Drug, and Cosmetic Act as amended by the bill." 1962 U.S. Cong. & Admin. News, p. 2890.

A number of comments addressed the so-called "how to" versus the "what" argument; that is, the proposed CGMP regulations describe "how" a particular requirement should be achieved rather than specifying "what" it is that is to be achieved. Many comments recommended that the regulations establish only objectives or specifications and allow each manufacturer to determine the best method of attaining the objective or meeting the specification....

The Commissioner believes that, with relatively few exceptions, the CGMP regulations do describe "what" is to be accomplished and provide great latitude in "how" the requirement is achieved. For example, written records and procedures are required, but FDA will recognize as satisfactory any reasonable format that achieves the desired results. Because of the need for uniformity in certain areas of the CGMP regulations that have presented problems in the past, however, there are some instances where it is desirable to specify the manner in which requirements are to be accomplished.....

The requirement for written procedures is intended to provide additional assurance of effective communication of appropriate information from firm management to line personnel and of regular performance of a firm's established programs and procedures. It is not enough that employees "know their jobs." Key personnel may be absent without warning; personnel substitutions involving less experienced employees may be necessary; and new or revised instructions to employees must be adequately conveyed to those who need to know. These situations are not usual, but may occur frequently. The most appropriate method for reliably relating policies and procedures to those who must know them is to have them set down in writing, readily available, and presented in a manner easily understood. The Commissioner does not believe this is a burdensome requirement....

Several comments argued that § 210.1 should be deleted because it is based on the erroneous proposition that CGMP regulations can be substantive. The comments urged that regulations issued under section 501(a)(2)(B) of the act are only interpretive.

Because of the fervor reflected by these objections and because the Commissioner foresees identical objections being made to proposals to issue binding CGMP regulations for specific classes of drug products in the future, the Commissioner has decided that a lengthy exposition of the basis for his concluding that FDA has legal authority to promulgate such regulations is warranted.....

Based on ... complete review of the legislative history of section 501(a)(2)(B) of the act, the Commissioner concludes that there is no support for the proposition that Congress intended that CGMP regulations should be merely interpretive. At the least, Congress wanted CGMP regulations to have the same force and effect as other regulations issued under section 701(a) of the act. To the extent that a stronger Congressional mandate can be gleaned from the various reports, amendments, and debates, it appears that binding standards were to be issued by FDA and issued through the less cumbersome-notice-and-comment rulemaking procedures of section 701(a) of the act rather than the more complex section 701(e) mechanism. Therefore, the Commissioner rejects the argument that § 210.1 exceeds the authority conferred by Congress under sections 501(a)(2)(B) and 701(a) of the act.....

... [I]f each CGMP requirement has to receive a de novo hearing in each and every enforcement proceeding, the burden of litigation that would result would not be in the public interest, nor would it be equitable to competing manufacturers who were not involved in such litigation.....

... The Commissioner notes that two of the cases [*National Confectioners' Ass'n*, 569 F.2d 690, and *Nova Scotia*, p. 269 *supra*] dealt specifically with the validity of CGMP regulations issued under the statutory standards relating to adulterated foods, which do not explicitly refer to "current good manufacturing practice." It would indeed be anomalous that those regulations could be issued as legally binding if regulations amplifying section 501(a)(2)(B) could not be....

A number of comments suggested, in effect, that whether or not FDA could lawfully "issue" binding CGMP regulations, it would be unwise for the agency to do so.... The Commissioner has evaluated these objections and found that, although some have merit, none is so serious as to outweigh the benefits from making CGMP regulations binding. Recognizing the diversity of manufacturing and control procedures, the Commissioner has endeavored wherever possible to state CGMP regulations in the terms of objectives to be attained, rather than methods of attaining such objectives.... In those few cases where precise procedures are set forth in these regulations, individuals who believe that alternative mechanisms may also be acceptable are invited to petition the Commissioner to amend the specific regulation to permit such alternatives....

With regard to the alleged lack of flexibility in the enforcement of "binding" CGMP regulations, the Commissioner believes that the comments have confused the question of whether a violation exists with the question of whether FDA will take action upon the violation. In numerous areas, FDA has established tolerances for actionable offenses and is currently in the process of establishing regulations setting forth agency policy with regard to prosecutions for violations of the act. It should be noted, however, that even in the absence of any CGMP regulations, whether binding or not, the doing of or failure to do any particular act which is inconsistent with current good manufacturing practice results in the product being legally adulterated, even if no legal action is brought.....

UNITED STATES v. MORTON–NORWICH PRODUCTS, INC.

United States District Court, Northern District of New York, 1978.
461 F. Supp. 760.

MUNSON, District Judge.

This is a criminal action involving three alleged violations of the Federal Food, Drug and Cosmetic Act.... Indictment Number 75–CR–114 ... alleges three violations by both defendants of the Food, Drug and Cosmetic Act, all of which violations involve the interstate shipment of adulterated drugs, in contravention of sections 301(a) and 303 of the Act. Each count, in turn, alleges adulteration in two separate and distinct senses, one falling within section 501(c), in that the purity of the drugs involved differed from that purported, the other coming under section 501(a)(2)(B), contending that the drugs were not manufactured, processed, packaged or held in conformity with current good manufacturing practice so as to assure that they would conform to the Food, Drug and Cosmetic Act requirements as to safety, and would have the strength and identity and meet the quality and purity characteristics which they purported to possess.

The products involved in the three counts of the Indictment are two lots ... of individually packaged gauze pads impregnated with Furacin (trade name for nitrofurazone), an antibacterial dressing....

The gravamen of the charge of adulteration under 21 U.S.C. § 351(c) is that the pads, purported to be sterile according to the labeling found on the foil envelopes in which the pads were to be marketed, were not, in fact, sterile. The charge under 21 U.S.C. § 351(a)(2)(B) relates to several alleged violations of CGMPs, based heavily upon observations made during Food and Drug Administration (FDA) inspections of the defendants' sterile fill facility at Norwich, as well as the actual evidence of product contamination....

Throughout this proceeding, the defendants have attacked ... the introduction into evidence of the results of tests performed by FDA analysts on post-shipment specimens of product taken from the two lots in issue.... The defendants have insisted that their representation of sterility was proper in this case as long as pre-shipment tests, validly conducted by them in accordance with the methods prescribed by the United States Pharmacopoeia (U.S.P.), indicated sterility, despite the fact that later tests revealed the presence of contamination in one or more samples of previously untested product. Secondly, the defendants attack the relevance of post-shipment tests with respect to the issue of sterility at the time of shipment....

In support of their position on this score, the defendants, through various expert witnesses, have proffered definitions of the term "sterility" or "sterile," all of which reject the notion of sterility as being an absolute concept in favor of a definition dependent upon results of probabilistic testing performed upon random samples of the product in accordance with U.S.P. testing methods. Thus, the argument goes, an article is properly labeled as "sterile" if it has passed pre-shipment sterility tests performed pursuant to the U.S.P. method, notwithstanding the fact that some untested product units are in fact contaminated.

The Court rejects the notion that the term "sterile," as contained within the labeling which accompanies the defendants' product, is susceptible of such a narrow interpretation. This Court is of the opinion that the meaning to be ascribed to labeling which accompanies a product is, like beauty, properly in the eyes of the beholder, rather than the manufacturer. A customer who utilizes defendants' furacin gauze or batiste pads, whether he be a doctor, a nurse, or a layman, in this Court's estimation, will interpret the representation of sterility to mean the total lack of contamination of the product. To allow the defendants to avoid liability under the Act merely by testing samples of the product, which samples prove negative for contamination, would be to obliterate the standard of absolute liability imposed by the Food, Drug and Cosmetic Act, and subtly inject into the statute an element of scienter, or conscious awareness of guilt. The Court believes that the relevant inquiry under 21 U.S.C. § 351(c) is whether or not the gauze and batiste pads contained in Lots 705553 and 710749 were, in fact, sterile when shipped, utilizing an absolute definition of sterility....

The clear import of 21 U.S.C. § 331(a) is that in order to prove a violation of that provision, adulteration *at the time the product entered, or was delivered for introduction into, interstate commerce* must be proven beyond a reasonable doubt. Adulteration, of course, may be demonstrated by any logical and convincing means. One manner of proving pre-shipment adulteration is by showing adulteration after receipt at some point in time subsequent to travel in interstate commerce, together with proof that the adulteration necessarily occurred prior to shipment, rather than some later time.

The Court believes that the Government has sufficiently demonstrated that the post-shipment tests performed upon samples of their product are highly probative with regard to the issue of pre-shipment sterility....

The defendants challenge the introduction, as evidence of CGMP violations, of various observations made at the Norwich sterile facility outside of the time frame during which the lots in issue were manufactured. While the Court has indicated that its verdict rests upon finding actual contamination, in violation of 21 U.S.C. § 351(c), rather than a CGMP violation under 21 U.S.C. § 351(a)(2)(B), it nevertheless feels compelled to briefly address this point.

The Court is in agreement that, with respect to CGMP violations, the evidence must relate to conditions as they existed at the time applicable to the Indictment; that is, the time of manufacture of the lots in question. In proving its case, however, the Government should not be limited to use of testimony of observations actually made during the critical time period. Rather, it is proper to consider proof of conditions existing at times reasonably close to those in issue, providing that the Government can demonstrate that, by virtue of the nature of the conditions and the closeness in time, it is reasonable to infer that the same conditions occurred during the critical time period....

NOTES

1. *Drug GMP Cases.* See, e.g., *United States v. Bel–Mar Laboratories, Inc.,* 284 F.Supp. 875 (E.D.N.Y. 1968); *United States v. Lanpar Co.,* 293 F.Supp. 147 (N.D. Tex. 1968); *United States v. Kendall Co.,* 324 F.Supp. 628 (D. Mass. 1971); *United States v. Lit Drug Co.,* 333 F.Supp. 990 (D.N.J. 1971); *United States v. Dianovin Pharmaceuticals, Inc.,* 342 F.Supp. 724 (D. P.R. 1972), aff'd, 475 F.2d 100 (1st Cir. 1973); *United States v. Medwick Laboratories, Inc.,* 416 F.Supp. 832 (N.D. Ill. 1976); *United States v. Articles of Drug ... Labeled ... Colchicine,* 442 F.Supp. 1236 (S.D.N.Y. 1978); *United States v. K–N Enterprises, Inc.,* 461 F.Supp. 988 (N.D. Ill. 1978); *United States v. Jamieson–McKames Pharmaceuticals, Inc.,* 651 F.2d 532 (8th Cir. 1981). GMP problems can also lead to recalls and other forms of voluntary compliance. *See, e.g.,* "Lilly Recalls Drugs Following FDA Inspections," FDA Talk Paper No. T89–55 (September 15, 1989), "Lilly Reaches Compliance Agreement with FDA," FDA Talk paper No. T89–72 (November 3, 1989).

2. *History of Drug GMP Regulations.* The evolution of FDA's regulations may be traced from 28 Fed. Reg. 1459 (February 14, 1963), through 28 Fed. Reg. 6385 (June 20, 1963), 30 Fed. Reg. 932 (January 29, 1965), 34 Fed. Reg. 13553 (August 22, 1969), 36 Fed. Reg. 601 (January 15, 1971), 41 Fed. Reg. 6878 (February 13, 1976), 43 Fed. Reg. 45014 (September 29, 1978), and 54 Fed. Reg. 26394 (June 23, 1989). FDA proposed GMP regulations for large volume parenteral drugs in 41 Fed. Reg. 22202 (June 1, 1976), and at the same time questioned whether similar requirements should apply to small volume parenterals, 41 Fed. Reg. at 22219, but took no further action on this matter. The GMP regulations were held to be enforceable as law in *National Ass'n of Pharmaceutical Mfrs. v. FDA,* 637 F.2d 877 (2d Cir. 1981).

3. *Interpretive Guidelines.* FDA has also issued a number of guidelines interpreting the GMP regulations, including the preparation of compressed medical gases, general principles of process validation, expiration dating and stability testing, computerized drug processing, sterile drug products by aseptic processing, content uniformity testing of tablets and capsules, and parametric release of terminally heat sterilized drug products.

4. *Denial of NDA Approval.* In a relatively unusual action, FDA refused to approve three NDAs for failure to comply with GMPs in 53 Fed. Reg. 18905 (May 25, 1988). The agency has also successfully withdrawn approval of NDAs for failure to comply with GMPs, 52 Fed. Reg. 7318 (March 10, 1987), 52 Fed. Reg. 29274 (August 6, 1987), aff'd, *Copanos and Sons, Inc. v. Food and Drug Administration,* 854 F.2d 510 (D.C. Cir. 1988).

5. *Commentary.* See Elkas, *Revised Good Manufacturing Practice Regulations,* 25 FDC L.J. 78 (1970); Gibbons, *Legal Implications of Good Manufacturing Practice Regulations,* 31 FDC L.J. 473 (1976); Jeffries, *Current Good Manufacturing Practice Compliance—A Review of the Problems and an Approach to Their Management,* 23 FDC L.J. 580 (1968); Jennings, *Revised Good Manufacturing Practice Regulations,* 25 FDC L.J. 107 (1970); Kandle, *Application of Current Good Manufacturing Practices,* 24 FDC L.J. 9 (1969); Roberts, *GMPs—A Statistician's Point of View,* 24 FDC L.J. 9 (1969); Shupe, *GMPs—An Industry Point of View,* 24 FDC L.J. 14 (1969); Williams, *Counsel's Role in*

Current Good Manufacturing Practice, 23 FDC L.J. 71 (1968); Wittick, *Proposed Revisions of the Current GMP Regulations,* 32 FDC L.J. 109 (1977).

6. *Compendial Standards. Morton–Norwich* is one of the few recent cases in which FDA has relied on sections 501(b) and (c) of the Act. At one time, standards set by the three drug compendia recognized by section 501(b) were important regulatory tools. *See* Blake, *The Role of the Compendia in Establishing Drug Standards,* 31 FDC L.J. 276 (1976); Urdang, *The Development of Pharmacopoeias,* 8 FDC L.J. 69 (1953). Although the constitutionality of section 501(b) has been questioned, *see* Christopher, *Validity of Delegation of Power to a Private Agency—The Pharmacopoeia Provisions,* 6 FDC L.J. 641 (1951), the compendial standards were the basis for hundreds of FDA regulatory actions under both the 1906 Act and the 1938 Act. *See, e.g., Woodard Laboratories, Inc. v. United States,* 198 F.2d 995 (9th Cir. 1952); *United States v. King & Howe, Inc.,* 78 F.2d 693 (2d Cir. 1935); *United States v. Lanpar Co.,* 293 F.Supp. 147 (N.D. Tex. 1968). As FDA has relied increasingly upon specifications established through the new drug approval process and bioavailability/ bioequivalence requirements, compendial standards have declined in regulatory importance. Monitoring of drug quality through product analysis, however, remains an important function of the agency. *See* Banes, *The National Center for Drug Analysis,* 25 FDC L.J. 135 (1970).

7. *Establishment Registration and Drug Listing.* The 1962 Drug Amendments added Section 510, which requires the registration of all drug establishments. 76 Stat. 780, 793. The Drug Listing Act of 1972, 86 Stat. 559, added section 510(j), to require the submission to FDA of lists of the drug products made in those establishments. *See* Banse, *Drug Listing Act of 1972,* 28 FDC L.J. 255 (1973). It took almost a decade before the information submitted under this statute became computer-accessible for regulatory purposes. The drug establishment registration and drug product listing regulations are codified in 21 C.F.R. Part 207.

C. FDA LICENSURE OF NEW DRUGS

1. BACKGROUND

Since 1938, the law has required some premarket review by FDA for all new drugs. Under the present Act this process of product licensure necessitates FDA approval of each individual product that falls within the "new drug" definition. The approval process leads to more extensive agency involvement in the decisionmaking of private manufacturers than any other provision of the Act. At the same time, FDA's performance of this function has been the target of persistent criticism, both from proponents who regarded the agency as insufficiently rigorous, and more recently by advocates of reduced regulation who contend that the agency—or the statutory premarket approval requirement—has added to the cost of drug development and delayed the introduction of important new therapies.

DAVID F. CAVERS, THE FOOD, DRUG, AND COSMETIC ACT OF 1938: ITS LEGISLATIVE HISTORY AND ITS SUBSTANTIVE PROVISIONS

6 Law & Contemporary Problems 2 (1939).

[In 1937] ... a tragedy occurred which was directly responsible for adding a new and important proviso to the drug control legislation. At least 73, perhaps over 90, persons in various parts of the country, although chiefly in the South, died as a result of taking a drug known as "Elixir Sulfanilamide," manufactured and sold by the S. E. Massengill Company of Bristol, Tennessee. This product had been prepared in order to render the valuable new drug, sulfanilamide, available in liquid form. Diethylene glycol was used as a solvent. Investigation later showed that the pharmacist on the manufacturer's staff checked the product merely for appearance, flavor, and fragrance. Tests on animals or even an investigation of the published literature would have revealed the lethal character of the solvent.... Yet the only legal basis for the F&DA's intervention was the fact that the preparation was not an "elixir" since that term may properly be applied only to an alcoholic solution. The product was therefore misbranded. The label, incidentally, did not mention the presence of the fatal ingredient, diethylene glycol.

Even if any of the bills ... had been enacted previously it is quite possible that this disaster would have occurred.... Accordingly, Senator Copeland introduced a bill ... which forbade the introduction into interstate commerce of "any drug ... not generally recognized as safe for use" under the conditions prescribed in the labeling thereof "unless the packer of such drug holds a notice of finding by the Secretary that such drug is not unsafe for use." Machinery was provided to enable the Secretary to make such a finding....

DRUG EFFICACY AND THE 1962 DRUG AMENDMENTS

60 Georgetown Law Journal 185 (1971).

... The crux of the [1938 Act's] premarketing review scheme was the designation of certain drugs as "new drugs." A new drug was defined as one not generally recognized by experts "as safe for use under the conditions prescribed, recommended, or suggested in the labeling thereof" or one which had become generally recognized as safe but "which [had] not ... been used to a material extent or for a material time." In order for a new drug to be marketed, it had to be the subject of an "effective" (not disapproved) new drug application (NDA) under section 505(a)....

Within the next decade, two important additions were made to the 1938 Act that bore on the matter of drug efficacy. Section 506, dealing with drugs containing insulin, and section 507, concerning certain antibiotic drugs, bypassed the new drug procedures of section 505 in favor of a batch certification system. Under that system, batches of drugs would be certified for marketing upon determination by the Secretary that the batch had such "characteristics of strength, quality and purity as ... to adequately insure safety and efficacy of use."....

The efficacy provisions of the 1962 Amendments were inserted in the framework of the "new drug" procedure. First, the definition of new drug was extended to comprise drugs not generally recognized as safe and effective. Second ... [t]he data reporting requirements of the new drug procedure were amended to require submission of data showing efficacy. Furthermore, in place of automatic approval of NDAs not disapproved, a positive act of approval is required to make an NDA approved.

The most important changes in section 505, however, occurred in subsections (d) and (e). Under subsection (d), the Secretary ... is now required to refuse approval of any NDA if, after notice and opportunity for hearing, he determines that on the basis of information before him with respect to the drug in question "there is a lack of substantial evidence that the drug will have the effect it purports or is represented to have under the conditions of use prescribed, recommended or suggested in the proposed labeling thereof...." Furthermore, section 505(e) was modified to require the Secretary to withdraw approval of any drug after notice and opportunity for hearing if he finds that "on the basis of new information before him" substantial evidence of efficacy is lacking. Significantly, this subsection also added a proviso permitting the Secretary, in the event of an imminent hazard to health, to withdraw approval of an NDA even before holding a hearing....

2. IMPLEMENTATION OF THE NEW DRUG PRE-MARKET APPROVAL REQUIREMENTS

The complex history of FDA's implementation of the new drug provisions of the Act defies unitary treatment. A chronological account would frustrate legal analysis, while a wholly conceptual structure would obscure recurrent themes. Accordingly, we have combined these approaches. We first summarize the history of FDA's efforts and then examine, through the key materials that document this history, the basic elements of the process for regulating new drugs.

Section 505 of the 1938 Act authorized FDA to permit new drug applications (NDAs) to become effective, but not to affirmatively approve them. By 1941, 4,128 NDAs had been submitted to FDA. Because it was unable to cope with this volume, the agency began in 1942 to examine each application to determine whether the product covered was indeed a "new drug." Manufacturers in turn responded by seeking

FDA's opinion in advance, which ultimately led to a reduction in the number of full NDAs submitted though the agency's workload still remained substantial. By June 30, 1962, NDAs for 9,457 individual products had become effective.

In addition to drug products with effective NDAs, during this period many thousands of similar formulations entered the market as "old drugs." Manufacturers of these products either concluded independently that they were generally recognized as safe (GRAS) because an NDA was in effect for a version manufactured by another company or obtained an opinion from FDA that their drugs were GRAS and thus not "new" or, as they came to be called, "old" drugs. Though the agency kept no record of these "old drug" opinions, it issued several thousand between 1942 and 1962. An original NDA'd drug product came to be referred to as the "pioneer," and all subsequent versions were described as generic or "me-too" drugs. By 1962, for every pioneer drug with an effective NDA, many more me-too copies were on the market.

Congress enacted the Drug Amendments of 1962 hurriedly in the crisis atmosphere of the thalidomide tragedy. In addition to requiring that FDA affirmatively determine that new agents have been demonstrated by "substantial evidence" to be effective, as well as shown to be safe, the Amendments required FDA to review all NDAs that had become effective during the previous twenty-four years to determine whether the products met the new effectiveness standard. No one in the agency or outside fully appreciated the consequences of this requirement when President Kennedy signed the Amendments into law on October 10, 1962, 76 Stat. 780.

Because the 1962 Amendments expanded the coverage of section 505, FDA immediately began to receive an increased volume of NDAs and investigational new drug submissions (INDs), which soon overwhelmed its review capacity. The agency at first did nothing to implement Congress' mandate to review NDAs that had previously become effective. In 29 Fed. Reg. 2790 (February 28, 1964), 29 Fed. Reg. 7019 (May 28, 1964), however, FDA issued regulations requiring reports on those pre–1962 drugs. The major pharmaceutical manufacturers promptly contested the regulations insofar as they might apply to drugs that the firms regarded as grandfathered under the 1962 Amendments. FDA stayed the reporting requirements pending the outcome of the manufacturers' court challenge, 29 Fed. Reg. 12872 (September 12, 1964). Although the companies provided some of the requested information in 1965, they argued that any review of pre–1962 NDAs should be performed by an independent scientific authority, not by the agency. In June 1966, FDA contracted with the National Academy of Sciences (NAS) to conduct such a review. Holders of NDAs were requested to submit information supporting the claims for their products, 31 Fed. Reg. 9425 (July 9, 1966), 31 Fed. Reg. 13014 (October 6, 1966). The manufacturers thereafter withdrew their lawsuit.

The NAS review was performed by thirty panels of experts in specific drug categories. The NAS established guidelines delineating the functions of the panels and identifying the following sources of evidence for evaluation of effectiveness: (1) information available in the scientific literature; (2) information available from FDA, from the manufacturer, or other sources; and (3) the experience and informed judgment of the members of the panels. The NAS also established six ratings to serve as the basis for evaluating each claim made for a drug:

(1) *Effective.*

(2) *Probably effective.* Additional evidence required to be determined. Remedy could be additional research or modification of claims or both.

(3) *Possibly effective.* Little evidence of effectiveness, but possibility of additional evidence should not be ruled out.

(4) *Ineffective.* No acceptable evidence to support claim of effectiveness.

(5) *Effective, but ...* Effective for claimed indication but not approved form of treatment because better, safer or more conveniently administered drugs available.

(6) *Ineffective as a fixed combination.* Combination drugs for which there is no substantial reason to believe that each ingredient adds to the effectiveness of the combination.

The NAS transmitted its first evaluation to FDA in October 1967, and continued to submit monthly reports until midsummer 1968. *See* NAS, DRUG EFFICACY STUDY: FINAL REPORT TO THE COMMISSIONER OF FOOD AND DRUGS (1969). The panels reviewed approximately 4,000 different drug formulations. The panels found roughly seven percent of the drugs ineffective for all claims, many effective for all claims, and the majority somewhere in between. The breakdown of ratings (by claim) was as follows:

Rating	No. of Claims	% of Claims
Ineffective	2,442	14.7
Possibly effective	5,778	34.9
Probably effective	1,204	7.3
Effective	3,159	19.1
Effective, but	3,990	24.0
Total	16,573	100%

As the body with ultimate responsibility for determining drug effectiveness, FDA undertook to review the NAS findings. It refused, however, to release the panel reports before completing its own evaluations.

On January 23, 1968, FDA for the first time addressed the issue of the me-too drugs. At a government-industry conference the agency announced that it would apply the applicable NAS–NRC findings not only to the pioneer NDA's drug but also to all subsequently marketed me-too products. The agency's first implementation notice was published simultaneously, 33 Fed. Reg. 818 (January 23, 1968), covering all bioflavonoid drugs. (Its subsequent withdrawal of approval for these drugs without a hearing was overturned in court, *USV Pharmaceutical Corp. v. Secretary of HEW*, 466 F.2d 455 (D.C. Cir. 1972)). FDA realized that the "old drug" opinions it had issued before 1962 presented a major obstacle to its efforts to exert control over all me-too versions of NDA'd drugs. The agency therefore issued a statement of policy withdrawing all those opinions in 33 Fed. Reg. 7758 (May 28, 1968), now codified in 21 C.F.R. § 310.100. At the same time, it proposed to establish a procedure for determining old drug status, under which presumably many me-too products would be held not to require NDAs, 33 Fed. Reg. 7762 (May 28, 1968).

Following publication of its bioflavonoid notice, FDA turned its attention to fixed dosage combination antibiotic drugs. In 33 Fed. Reg. 12904 (December 24, 1968), the agency proposed to initiate proceedings to withdraw approval of Panalba, the first of many of these drugs that had been rated "ineffective as a fixed combination," and invited submission of pertinent data. In 34 Fed. Reg. 7687 (May 15, 1969), FDA withdrew approval of the drug and offered an opportunity for an administrative hearing. The manufacturer promptly obtained a judicial order enjoining FDA from withdrawing approval of the drug until after it had ruled on the firm's request for a formal evidentiary hearing. *Upjohn Co. v. Finch*, 303 F.Supp. 241 (W.D. Mich. 1969). One month later another manufacturer obtained a similar injunction. *American Home Products Corp. v. Finch*, 303 F.Supp. 448 (D. Del. 1969).

Thus, by mid–1969, FDA confronted the prospect of having to conduct a long series of formal administrative hearings before it could implement the 1962 effectiveness standard. The agency therefore decided to adopt a new policy. In 34 Fed. Reg. 14598 (September 19, 1969), FDA entered an order concluding that Upjohn had failed to show reasonable grounds for an evidentiary hearing and withdrawing approval of Panalba. Simultaneously the agency published regulations embodying two features that became central in its subsequent efforts to implement the 1962 Amendments. The regulations defined the essential elements of an "adequate and well-controlled clinical investigation" necessary to constitute substantial evidence of effectiveness under sections 505(d) and (e), and required the submission of at least two such studies to avoid summary judgment, *i.e.*, withdrawal of approval without a hearing, 34 Fed. Reg. 14596 (September 19, 1969). In the initial court test of its new approach, FDA's order withdrawing approval of Panalba was sustained. *Upjohn Co. v. Finch*, 422 F.2d 944 (6th Cir. 1970).

Meanwhile, the major pharmaceutical manufacturers challenged FDA's regulations defining adequate and well-controlled clinical studies. *Pharmaceutical Manufacturers Ass'n v. Finch*, 307 F.Supp. 858 (D. Del. 1970), held that FDA had violated section 553 of the Administrative Procedure Act by failing to provide an opportunity to comment on the regulations. The agency thereupon reproposed the regulations, 35 Fed. Reg. 3073 (February 17, 1970), and after receiving comments, promulgated them in final form, 35 Fed. Reg. 7250 (May 8, 1970). In *Pharmaceutical Manufacturers Ass'n v. Richardson*, 318 F.Supp. 301 (D. Del. 1970), the regulations were upheld on their merits.

Armed with this decision, which PMA did not appeal, FDA began publishing hundreds of so-called DESI ("drug effectiveness study implementation") notices. The agency also required DESI evaluations to be included in drug labeling and advertising in 35 Fed. Reg. 15761 (October 7, 1970), 36 Fed. Reg. 11022 (June 8, 1971), 36 Fed. Reg. 19978 (October 14, 1971), 37 Fed. Reg. 3176 (February 12, 1972). Orders to withdraw approval of combination antibiotic drugs were upheld in *Pfizer, Inc. v. Richardson*, 434 F.2d 536 (2d Cir. 1970), and *Ciba–Geigy Corp. v. Richardson*, 446 F.2d 466 (2d Cir. 1971). *See also Diamond Laboratories, Inc. v. Richardson*, 452 F.2d 803 (8th Cir. 1972). In two other cases, *American Cyanamid Co. v. Richardson*, 456 F.2d 509 (1st Cir. 1971), and *Bristol Laboratories v. Richardson*, 456 F.2d 563 (1st Cir. 1971), the companies withdrew their appeals after failing to obtain a judicial stay of the agency's withdrawal order. In 36 Fed. Reg. 3126 (February 8, 1971), 36 Fed. Reg. 20037 (October 15, 1971), FDA promulgated regulations codifying its combination drug policy, now found in 21 C.F.R. § 300.50.

FDA also sharpened its policy respecting me-too products. To assure that these drugs would be brought under regulatory control, it created the "abbreviated" NDA, requiring information only on biological availability and manufacturing controls, 34 Fed. Reg. 2673 (February 27, 1969), 35 Fed. Reg. 6574 (April 24, 1970). The agency then issued a general notice in 35 Fed. Reg. 11273 (July 14, 1970) establishing uniform conditions for the marketing of all new drugs covered by a DESI notice, requiring the submission of an NDA or abbreviated NDA for any product whose rating justified continued marketing. In 37 Fed. Reg. 2969 (February 10, 1972), 37 Fed. Reg. 23185 (October 31, 1972), the agency adopted 21 C.F.R. § 310.6, explicitly stating that every DESI notice and notice of opportunity for hearing applies both to the pioneer drug and to all identical, related, and similar me-too drug products. The agency took the position that the failure of the manufacturer of a me-too drug product to respond to a DESI notice or a notice of opportunity for hearing covering the pioneer drug barred any subsequent dispute respecting the status of that drug. *See* Baukin, *Related Drugs Under DESI,* 27 FDC L.J. 124 (1972). Because it was having difficulty learning about me-too drugs, FDA persuaded Congress to enact the Drug Listing Act of 1972, 86 Stat. 559. This legislation, which amended section 510 of the FD&C Act, requires all manufacturers to submit lists of their drugs and thus provides the agency a complete inventory of all marketed products.

By the end of 1971, FDA had disposed of dozens of requests for hearings on the revocation of NDAs. In no instance had it found a manufacturer's supporting data sufficient to justify a hearing. One explanation for this striking consistency is that the agency's substantial evidence regulations embodied requirements for clinical investigations that few pre–1962 studies could meet. The drugs it initially selected for withdrawal—those evaluated by the NAS as "ineffective"—also presented the easiest targets. But it was becoming obvious that any manufacturer would have to make an overwhelming showing to persuade FDA to expend the resources even one hearing would require.

In 1972, three court rulings threatened to undermine FDA's basic approach. In *Hynson, Westcott & Dunning, Inc. v. Richardson,* 461 F.2d 215 (4th Cir. 1972), the Fourth Circuit held that the petitioner was statutorily entitled to a hearing on the effectiveness of its drug, Lutrexin, before its NDA could be withdrawn. In *Bentex Pharmaceuticals, Inc. v. Richardson,* 463 F.2d 363 (4th Cir. 1972), the same court ruled that FDA lacked jurisdiction to determine whether a product is a new drug, and that therefore the issue could be raised *de novo* by a declaratory judgment suit. And in *USV Pharmaceutical Corp. v. Richardson,* 461 F.2d 223 (4th Cir. 1972), the court held that the status of a me-too drug was not dependent on the status of the pioneer, even when the latter's NDA was withdrawn. FDA sought and obtained certiorari in all three cases and it supported the petition for certiorari in *Ciba–Geigy Corp. v. Richardson,* 446 F.2d 466 (2d Cir. 1971), which had upheld its summary order withdrawing approval of an NDA'd drug. In June 1973, in opinions reproduced below, the Supreme Court sustained FDA on all of the legal issues involved. *See* Hutt, *Views on Supreme Court/FDA Decisions,* 28 FDC L.J. 662 (1973). FDA later revised its summary judgment procedures, 38 Fed. Reg. 35024 (December 21, 1973), 39 Fed. Reg. 9750 (March 13, 1974), to reflect the Court's opinions.

The Supreme Court decisions did not end litigation nor resolve all of FDA's problems in implementing the 1962 Amendments. The Court concluded that Hynson itself had presented sufficient evidence to justify a hearing. Several subsequent agency denials of hearings have been upheld, but others have been reversed with instructions to hold a hearing. *Compare Agri–Tech, Inc. v. Richardson,* 482 F.2d 1148 (8th Cir. 1973); *North American Pharmacal, Inc. v. Department of HEW,* 491 F.2d 546 (8th Cir. 1973); *Cooper Laboratories, Inc. v. Commissioner,* 501 F.2d 772 (D.C. Cir. 1974); *Masti–Kure Products Co. v. Califano,* 587 F.2d 1099 (D.C. Cir. 1978), *with E.R. Squibb & Sons, Inc. v. Weinberger,* 483 F.2d 1382 (3d Cir. 1973); *Hess & Clark v. FDA,* 495 F.2d 975 (D.C. Cir. 1974); *Chemetron Corp. v. Department of HEW,* 495 F.2d 995 (D.C. Cir. 1974); *Sterling Drug, Inc. v. Weinberger,* 503 F.2d 675 (2d Cir. 1974) and 509 F.2d 1236 (2d Cir. 1975); *Edison Pharmaceutical Co. v. FDA,* 513 F.2d 1063 (D.C. Cir. 1975), *rehearing en banc denied,* 517 F.2d 164 (1975); *Smithkline Corp. v. FDA,* 587 F.2d 1107 (D.C. Cir. 1978); *American Cyanamid Co. v. FDA,* 606 F.2d 1307 (D.C. Cir. 1979); *Brandenfels v. Heckler,* 716 F.2d 553 (9th Cir. 1983).

Even before the Court vindicated its basic approach, some consumer groups had become impatient with FDA's slow progress in implementing the 1962 Amendments and sued to force prompter action. In

American Public Health Ass'n v. Veneman, 349 F.Supp. 1311 (D.D.C. 1972), p. 503 *infra,* the court held FDA's performance unlawful in several respects and issued a detailed order requiring it to complete the DESI process within four years. This ruling imposed a new and, as it developed, unfulfillable demand on the agency, a demand ironically inflated by FDA's own decision to extend the NAS findings to all pre–1962 me-too drugs.

FDA had difficulty developing a consistent approach to this facet of the problem. In May 1968, as noted p. 480 *supra,* it proposed a procedure for determining old drug status for some of these products, but never made this proposal final. The agency later determined that me-too drugs which had been found under the DESI program to be effective could be the subject of an "abbreviated" NDA which need contain only labeling and manufacturing information, but not data relating to safety and effectiveness. 34 Fed. Reg. 2673 (February 27, 1969), 35 Fed. Reg. 6574 (April 24, 1970). This approach rested on the theory that the active ingredients in such products have become generally recognized as safe and effective and thus FDA need only require assurance that individual versions were properly labeled and manufactured. When concern about the bioavailability and bioequivalence of these me-too drugs emerged, FDA issued separate regulations to address these issues, p. 576 *infra.* As the DESI program progressed, new abbreviated NDAs began to swamp the agency. By June 1975, it had received over 6000 abbreviated NDAs, of which roughly 1100 had been acted on. To meet this backlog, FDA informally adopted a policy of permitting the marketing of a me-too drug upon submission of an abbreviated NDA even before it was approved. This decision was destined to bring the agency into court once more.

In 40 Fed. Reg. 26142 (June 20, 1975), FDA proposed comprehensive regulations governing the status of me-too drugs. The agency had long planned to develop "old drug monographs" for pre–1962 prescription drugs. *See* McEniry, *Drug Monographs,* 29 FDC L.J. 166 (1974). In the June 1975 proposal the agency stated that it would soon propose a new procedure for establishing old drug monographs for drugs that had been found safe and effective through the DESI program. In summary, the agency stated that a drug determined to be effective under the DESI program would not require an NDA or abbreviated NDA if it presented no bioavailability, bioequivalence, or special manufacturing problem. And the agency announced that on an interim basis it would follow these criteria in its enforcement of the Act. *See* Spencer, *New Concepts in Abbreviated NDAs,* 30 FDC L.J. 426 (1975).

FDA's new approach was promptly challenged in *Hoffmann–La-Roche, Inc. v. Weinberger,* 425 F.Supp. 890 (D.D.C. 1975), p. 492 *infra.* The court ruled that FDA could not sanction the marketing of me-too drugs without an individualized determination of old drug status. The agency therefore withdrew its interim enforcement policy in 40 Fed. Reg. 43531 (September 22, 1975), 41 Fed. Reg. 9001 (March 2, 1976), but has never acted on the June 1975 proposal. Later, in 41 Fed. Reg.

41770 (September 23, 1976), FDA announced a policy codified in Compliance Policy Guide 7132c.02, implementing the *Hoffmann–LaRoche* decision, for bringing regulatory actions against me-too drugs without an approved NDA or abbreviated NDA.

This enforcement policy was in turn challenged by the manufacturers of generic me-too drugs. In two cases, *United States v. Articles of Drug ... Lannett Co.,* 585 F.2d 575 (3rd Cir. 1978), and *Premo Pharmaceutical Laboratories, Inc. v. United States,* 629 F.2d 795 (2d Cir. 1980), the courts split on the question whether a generic version of an approved pioneer drug was no longer a new drug and could therefore be marketed without an NDA or abbreviated NDA. In *United States v. Generix Drug Corp.,* 460 U.S. 453 (1983), the Supreme Court resolved this conflict, holding that the Act's definition of "drug" includes inactive as well as active ingredients and therefore that a generic version of a pioneer drug requires its own NDA or abbreviated NDA if it differs in any significant respect from the pioneer. The Court did not, however, reach the issue of what sorts of differences would be significant.

As the end of the 1970s approached, therefore, FDA had adopted the following enforcement policy with respect to generic drugs. First, the agency was prepared to approve an abbreviated NDA for any generic version of a pre–1962 pioneer drug that had been found effective under the DESI program. Second, it would initiate regulatory action against any generic drug on the market without an approved NDA or abbreviated NDA. Third, it would not approve an abbreviated NDA, but insisted on a full NDA, for a generic version of a post–1962 new drug. From 1938, FDA had consistently taken the position that each NDA was a individual license, and that the accompanying safety and effectiveness information constituted confidential commercial information that was not disclosable to the public or available for use by another applicant under section 301(j) of the FD&C Act, the Freedom of Information Act, or the Federal Trade Secrets Act, 18 U.S.C. § 1905. The proposed but never enacted Drug Regulation Reform Act, considered by Congress during 1977–1980, would have authorized abbreviated NDAs for post–1962 new drugs.

The agency thus found itself caught between two important and long-standing policies. It had been successful in requiring an NDA or abbreviated NDA for every prescription drug on the market. But it could not approve abbreviated NDAs for post–1962 new drugs without violating the confidentiality provisions of the law. In an attempt to break the impasse, in July 1978 the agency announced it would approve a "paper" NDA for a generic copy of a pioneer new drug, whether pre–1962 or post–1962, based upon the *published* scientific data on the pioneer's safety and effectiveness. In 45 Fed. Reg. 82052 (December 12, 1980), FDA denied a petition to withdraw this new policy, which was later upheld in the face of claims that it had not been adopted through informal rulemaking under the APA. *Burroughs Wellcome Co. v. Schweiker,* 649 F.2d 221 (4th Cir. 1981). *Upjohn Manufacturing Co. v.*

Schweiker, 681 F.2d 480 (6th Cir. 1982), sustained the policy's application to a specific drug product. Despite these victories, FDA recognized that its "paper NDA" policy could not apply to more than a small fraction of the ever-increasing number of post–1962 new drugs. For most post–1962 new drugs, the published literature contained inadequate data on animal toxicity and human clinical trials to justify approval of a paper NDA. *See, e.g.,* 49 Fed. Reg. 15824 (April 19, 1984).

After the collapse of efforts to amend the FD&C Act in the late 1970s, FDA in 1983 began to work on a proposed regulation to establish the basis for some form of abbreviated NDA procedure for post–1962 new drugs. When this proposal did not surface quickly, the National Association of Pharmaceutical Manufacturers, an association of generic drug manufacturers, brought suit seeking a declaratory judgment that the agency could lawfully approve abbreviated NDAs for post–1962 new drugs.

Meanwhile, makers of innovative new drugs had become increasingly concerned about the gradual diminution of the effective patent life for pioneer products once they completed the rigorous development and testing program and exited from the NDA approval process. *See* Hutt, *The Importance of Patent Term Restoration to Pharmaceutical Innovation,* 1 Health Affairs, No. 2, at 6 (Spring 1982). In 1984, Representative Henry Waxman introduced a proposal that combined patent term restoration with authority for FDA to approve abbreviated NDAs for post–1962 new drugs. This legislation was ultimately enacted as the Drug Price Competition and Patent Term Restoration Act of 1984, 98 Stat. 1585, thus breaking the two-decade old impasse over the marketing of generic versions of post–1962 drugs.

A final category of prescription drugs further complicated the picture that FDA confronted in 1962. A significant number of pre–1962 prescription drugs never came under the DESI program. Some of these were first marketed before 1938 and thus have never been the subject of an NDA. Others were covered by NDAs but were not reviewed by the NAS panels because their manufacturers did not respond to the agency's request for information. In 40 Fed. Reg. 53609 (November 19, 1979), FDA listed the NDAs involved, invited the submission of further data, and stated that the effectiveness of these drugs would be reviewed internally by the agency.

In early 1984 prescription drugs that had never been the subject of any form of NDA became a high priority for FDA. An intravenous vitamin E product marketed without an NDA produced serious adverse reactions that required a nationwide recall. *See* "E–Ferol Update," FDA Talk Paper No. T84–30 (April 27, 1984); "FDA's Regulation of the Marketing of Unapproved New Drugs: The Case of E–Ferol Vitamin E Aqueous Solution," Hearing before a Subcomm. of the House Comm. on Government Operations, 98th Cong., 2d Sess. (1984); "Deficiencies in FDA's Regulation of the Marketing of Unapproved New Drugs: The Case of E–Ferol," H.R. Rep. No. 98–1168, 98th Cong., 2d Sess. (1984).

Based on information obtained under the Drug Listing Act, FDA deduced that there were approximately 5000 prescription drugs marketed without an approved NDA of any kind. While some 1800 would eventually be subject to the DESI Program, approximately 2400 were never subject to the DESI Program. The remainder fell into a variety of additional categories. Lacking authority to require an NDA for these drugs, FDA promulgated a regulation requiring the maintenance of records and submission of reports of adverse drug reactions for all prescription drugs marketed without approved NDAs, 50 Fed. Reg. 11478 (March 21, 1985), 51 Fed. Reg. 24476 (July 3, 1986), codified in 21 C.F.R. § 310.305.

Throughout these events, FDA continued, albeit in desultory fashion, to press ahead to complete implementation of the DESI Review. Having missed the original four-year deadline imposed by the court in *American Public Health Association v. Veneman,* 349 F.Supp. 1311 (D.D.C. 1972), the agency entered into an agreement with the plaintiffs, *American Public Health Association v. Harris,* Food Drug Cosm. L. Rep. (CCH) ¶ 38,068 (D.D.C. 1980), establishing a new timetable. The semi-annual reports that FDA has submitted to the court confirm that the agency continues to be in violation of the new agreement as well as the 1972 order.

In response to court orders in specific cases and on its own initiative in others, FDA has held a number of hearings on the withdrawal of approval of pre–1962 pioneer NDAs. *See, e.g.,* 44 Fed. Reg. 11835 (March 2, 1979) (Alevaire); 44 Fed. Reg. 75718 (December 21, 1971) (oral proteolytic enzymes); 47 Fed. Reg. 23564 (May 28, 1982) (combination antibiotic and antifungal drugs); 49 Fed. Reg. 33173 (August 21, 1984) (Vioform HC); 49 Fed. Reg. 36439 (September 17, 1984) (Mycolog); 49 Fed. Reg. 36439 (September 17, 1984) (Marax); 49 Fed. Reg. 38363 (September 28, 1984) (Vasodilan); 49 Fed. Reg. 40212 (October 15, 1984) (Parafon Forte); 49 Fed. Reg. 40972 (October 18, 1984) (Cyclospasmol); 49 Fed. Reg. 50788 (December 31, 1984) (Mepergan Fortis); 51 Fed. Reg. 20551 (June 5, 1986) (Deprol). In no instance has the manufacturer prevailed before an Administrative Law Judge or the Commissioner. In the cases appealed to the courts the Commissioner's rulings have been sustained, *Warner–Lambert Co. v. Heckler,* 787 F.2d 147 (3d Cir. 1986) (oral proteolytic enzymes); *E.R. Squibb and Sons, Inc. v. Bowen,* 870 F.2d 678 (D.C. Cir. 1989) (mysteclin).

With all other avenues foreclosed, manufacturers have been left with only one plausible defense to an enforcement action challenging a prescription drug product on the ground that it is an illegal new drug marketed without an approved NDA—the claim is that the product is in fact generally recognized as safe and effective (GRAS and GRAE) and therefore does not require an approved NDA. Though such claims have routinely failed, they continue to be asserted. *See, e.g., United States v. An Article ... "Furestrol Vaginal Suppositories",* 415 F.2d 390 (5th Cir. 1969); *Tyler Pharmacal Distributors, Inc. v. U.S. Dept. of HEW,* 408 F.2d 95 (7th Cir. 1969); *Durovic v. Richardson,* 479 F.2d 242

(7th Cir. 1973); *United States v. 1,048,000 Capsules ... Afrodex*, 494 F.2d 1158 (5th Cir. 1974); *United States v. Mosinee Research Corp.*, 583 F.2d 930 (7th Cir. 1978); *United States v. X–Otag Plus Tablets*, 602 F.2d 1387 (10th Cir. 1979); *United States v. Articles of Drug ... 5,906 Boxes*, 745 F.2d 105 (1st Cir. 1984); *United States v. Articles of Drug ... Promise Toothpaste for Sensitive Teeth*, 826 F.2d 564 (7th Cir. 1987); *United States v. Atropine Sulfate 1.0 mg. (Article of Drug) Dey–Dose*, 843 F.2d 860 (5th Cir. 1988); *United States v. Undetermined Quantities of a Drug ... Anucort HC Suppositories*, 857 F.2d 1466 (3d Cir. 1988), *aff'g* 709 F.Supp. 511 (D.N.J. 1987); *United States v. 225 Cartons ... Fiorinal With Codeine No. 1*, 871 F.2d 409 (3d Cir. 1989); *Merritt Corp. v. Folsom*, 165 F.Supp. 418 (D.D.C. 1958); *United States v. Articles of Drug Labeled "Quick–O–Ver"*, 274 F.Supp. 443 (D. Md. 1967); *United States v. An Article of Drug ... "Wynn 30 Sustained–Medication Tablets Quinaglute*, 268 F.Supp. 245 (E.D. Mo. 1967); *United States v. An Article of Drug ... Excederin P.M.*, Food Drug Cosm. L. Rep. (CCH) ¶ 40,486 (E.D.N.Y. 1971); *United States v. An Article of Drug ... "Mykocert"*, 345 F.Supp. 571 (N.D. Ill. 1972); *United States v. Articles of Drug ... Colchicine*, 442 F.Supp. 1236 (S.D.N.Y. 1978), *aff'd without opinion sub nom. United States v. Consolidated Midland Corp.*, 603 F.2d 215 (2d Cir. 1979); *United States v. K–N Enterprises Inc.*, 461 F.Supp. 988 (N.D. Ill. 1978); *United States v. Sene X Eleemosynary Corp., Inc.*, 479 F.Supp. 970 (S.D. Fla. 1979), *aff'd*, Food Drug Cosm. L. Rep. (CCH) ¶ 38,207 (11th Cir. 1983); *United States v. Articles of Drug ... Hormonin*, 498 F.Supp. 424 (D.N.J. 1980); *United States v. 1,834/100 Capsule Bottles ... " New Formula Hauck G–2 Capsules*, Food Drug Cosm. L. Rep. (CCH) ¶ 38,058 (N.D. Ga. 1987); *United States v. 118/100 Tablet Bottles*, 662 F.Supp. 511 (W.D. La. 1987); *Lederle Laboratories v. Department of HHS*, Food Drug Cosm. L. Rep. (CCH) ¶ 38,088 (D.D.C. 1988); *United States v. 50 Boxes ... Cafergot P–B Suppositories*, 721 F.Supp. 1462 (D. Mass. 1989); *United States v. Seven Cardboard Cases.... "100 Capsules NDC, Esgic, with Codeine Capsules,"* 716 F.Supp. 1221 (E.D. Mo. 1989).

Of course, the new drug requirements also apply to post–1962 drugs. Indeed, all new prescription entities introduced since 1962 have gone through the new drug approval process. In this respect, the coverage of the law has not been an important issue. Nor, typically, has FDA confronted claims to procedural rights that challenged its implementation of the effectiveness or the safety standard. The controversial issues have involved the agency's internal processes for evaluating and acting on NDAs, and the impact of those requirements on the availability of drugs and the health of patients.

3. THE COVERAGE OF THE NEW DRUG PROVISIONS

With certain exceptions, the expansive authority conferred by the 1962 Amendments is confined to new drugs. Since both the scope of the FDA power and the costs, in terms of testing expense and marketing delay, of a manufacturer's compliance are thus dependent on a product's status as a new drug, the statutory definition has been the focus of continuous debate and litigation.

a. The General Standard

UNITED STATES v. ARTICLE OF DRUG ... "MYKOCERT"

United States District Court, Northern District of Illinois, 1972,
345 F. Supp. 571.

MAROVITZ, District Judge.

The Complaint alleges that the seized article of drug was misbranded while held for sale after shipment in interstate commerce within the meaning of the Act, 21 U.S.C. as follows:....

§ 352(f)(1) in that it is a drug and its labeling fails to bear adequate directions for use and it is not exempt from such requirement, under the regulations, 21 CFR 1.106(g), since the article is a new drug subject to the provisions of 21 U.S.C. § 355, and no approval of an application filed pursuant to 21 U.S.C. § 355(b) is effective with respect to such drug, and no notice of claimed investigational exemption under 21 U.S.C. § 355(i) and regulations 21 CFR 130.3 is on file for such drug....

The seeming complexity of this action diminishes, once the critical issue around which the entire case revolves is isolated. The drug here in question consists of a tampon impregnated with 14 mgs. of the chemical ingredient 9–aminoacridine hydrochloride and a "binder" of 14 mgs. of polyvinylpyrrolidone which Beutlich markets as a prescription drug for the alleviation of various vaginal infections....

The regulations in 21 CFR § 130.1(h) [now § 310.3(h)] ... indicate the various conceivable manifestations of "newness":

(h) The newness of a drug may arise by reason (among other reasons) of:

(1) The newness for drug use of any substance which composes such drug, in whole or in part, whether it be an active substance or a menstruum, excipient, carrier, coating, or other component.

(2) The newness for drug use of a combination of two or more substances, none of which is a new drug.

(3) The newness for drug use of the proportion of a substance in a combination, even though such combi-

nation containing such substance in other proportion is not a new drug.

(4) The newness of use of such drug in diagnosing, curing, mitigating, treating, or preventing a disease, or to affect a structure or function of the body, even though such drug is not a new drug when used in another disease or to affect another structure or function of the body.

(5) The newness of a dosage, or method or duration of administration or application, or other conditions of use prescribed, recommended, or suggested in the labeling of such drug, even though such drug when used in other dosage, or other method or duration of administration or application, or different condition, is not a new drug....

One indication that a drug is not generally recognized among qualified experts as safe and effective for its intended use, that some Courts have accepted, is the absence of any published medical or scientific literature relating to the usage of the drug since the lack of documented sources of information perforce curtails the widespread knowledge of the drug's effectiveness or safety. This test by itself has been recognized as determinative of "newness" by several cases especially in this district.

Other courts have searched for proof of general recognition in different, other directions and have required a higher degree of proof to establish non-recognition. The most common procedure is the disposition of the cause in drug cases of this nature on cross-motions for summary judgment which are accompanied by various affidavits attesting to the non-recognition or general recognition of the drug as the case may be. These affidavits must be directed not at the "safe and effective" portion of 21 U.S.C. § 321(p) but at the "generally recognized" portion and actual safety and effectiveness is not at issue under this test. Thus actual safety proven by a small sampling short of general recognition is not sufficient to cure violations of the regulations applying to new drugs.

Some difficulty has been encountered by the courts in determining precisely what degree of recognition both in quantity and quality constitutes "general recognition" under the statute and that task is rendered all the more difficult when it must be accomplished within the strict confines of the summary judgment rule on the basis of conflicting affidavits which all claim expertise in the field. Some cases have taken the position that the mere existence of conflict between qualified experts in supporting affidavits establishes a lack of general recognition as a matter of law (see *Merritt Corp. v. Folsom*, 165 F.Supp. 418 (D.D.C. 1958)) while other courts in dicta attempted to soften the mere conflict rule where a genuine difference of opinion exists since general recognition ought not mean unanimous recognition. *United States v. 7 Car-*

tons ... *Ferro–Lac*, 293 F.Supp. 660 (S.D. Ill. 1968); *AMP v. Gardner*, 389 F.2d 825 (2nd Cir. 1968).

In addition to the various rules that have evolved in regard to the weight given affidavits in such an action certain guidelines developed pertaining to the qualifications of the affiants and the content of the affidavits. Some courts have pointed out that the personal opinions of experts are not adequate to establish general recognition and that the affidavits should instead attest to the existence of the opinion or recognition in the general community. Furthermore the affiant expert must be one qualified by scientific training and experience to evaluate the safety and effectiveness of drugs and cannot simply be a medical practitioner whose only knowledge is based on prescribing the drug for his own patients.

... It must be noted that many of the problems encountered in determining general recognition are a result of the limitations of the summary judgment procedure. While we do not in any way dispute the validity of the absence-of-a-body-of-literature test, or express an opinion as to soundness of the mere conflict of affidavits test, or in any way cast doubt on the continuing viability of summary judgment disposition of drug cases where appropriate, it must be admitted that there is greater leeway available to the Court where it can decide subjective facts in addition to applying objective tests. The opportunity to decide facts as well as law allows for a broader range of information and evidence to be taken into consideration. . . .

Claimant's contention that Mykocert is not a new drug can only succeed if it is recognized by experts in the field as safe and effective. There are two possible alternatives that would substantiate claimant's assertions. Either a Mykocert type drug in its exact form, dosage, and application must be recognized by experts (even though that drug may be marketed under a different name) or each of the component parts of Mykocert must be recognized with the critical caveat that the combination of these parts does not in any way create a new drug under 21 CFR § 130(h). . . .

Literature on Mykocert in its exact form is virtually non-existent, no less a body of literature, and there is no expert opinion available as to the general recognition of a 14 mgs. dosage of 9–aminoacridine applied in a tampon form and claimant therefore cannot succeed with the contention that a Mykocert type drug itself is recognized. Without going into great detail the few affidavits that address themselves to Mykocert itself rather than to its component parts are inadequate, since they focus on safety and effectiveness rather than general recognition and furthermore are by practitioners prescribing the drug for patients rather than experts in the field.

In addition it is difficult for this court to acknowledge the general recognition of Mykocert when the chairmen of the Obstetrics and Gynecology Departments at Chicago Medical School; State University of New York, Downstate Medical Center; Northwestern University

Medical School; and Loyola University Medical Center all swear that Mykocert is not generally recognized. While we do not express an opinion as to whether a "mere" conflict in expert opinion constitutes lack of general recognition, it cannot be denied that the affidavits of five of the leading doctors in the field which deny general recognition creates more than a "mere" conflict. It is inconceivable that a drug such as this could be considered generally recognized in the face of such learned non-recognition.

Yet even if these experts claim that Mykocert is not generally recognized in its present state, claimants might still attempt to salvage Mykocert by using the other avenue available—that absence of recognition for Mykocert as such is irrelevant given the fact that its component parts are generally recognized. Claimant does in fact place great faith in this contention by directing a vast amount of literature to the effectiveness and recognition of tampons and aminoacridines generally for use on infections. In order for this argument to succeed Mykocert in its present state must be similar enough in form, dosage, purpose, and application to the general usage of aminoacridines so as to be within the genre "aminoacridine" and the general recognition attributed to that genre. If Mykocert deviates in any substantial degree from previous forms of aminoacridine usage then it cannot rely on the general recognition of its component parts. The regulations in fact indicate that combinations of "old" drugs may be a "new" drug as is stated in 21 CFR 130.1(h)(1) through (5).

Simply stated *under the drug laws the whole of a drug may be greater or "newer" than all of its parts.* How critical this factor becomes to our case is evidenced in the fact that the vast majority of claimants' affidavits and documents are directed at the recognition of the component parts of Mykocert rather than to the exact form and dosage of Mykocert.... [I]f we determine that Mykocert is more than just the component parts of tampons and aminoacridines, claimant is practically foreclosed from succeeding based on its almost total reliance on affidavits directed at the component parts rather than the whole.

In adding up the tampon and aminoacridine usage we do not come up with a total of Mykocert. In view of the fact that the 14 mgs. dosage of Mykocert is a much larger dosage than used in other aminoacridine medications for vaginal infections; given the tampon form of application which is unlike gell tablet and cream form of application of vaginal infection medication; that the element of polyvinylpyrrolidone is added as a chemical binder, we hold that Mykocert is a new drug as defined in 21 CFR § 130.1(h)(5)....

We believe that the new dosage and form of application creates greater risks and questions of safety and effectiveness than previously recognized forms of medication for vaginal infections and given the delicate area of its application—warrants a finding of "newness." ...

NOTES

1. *Summary Judgment. See Lemmon Pharmacal Co. v. Richardson,* 319 F.Supp. 375 (E.D. Pa. 1970), where the court observed:

> The cited cases, in my opinion, require a discriminating analysis of the affidavits submitted by the parties to determine whether there really is a triable issue as to general recognition. Not every conflict in medical opinion is necessarily adequate to negative general recognition....
>
> Plaintiff's affiants, Drs. Gordon and Danowski, both acknowledge that the medical educational community in this country does not teach the use of thyroid except for thyroid deficiency. This fact, coupled with the specific dangers pointed out by the government's affiants as being inherent in Obestat because of its thyroid content, and the non-responsiveness of the plaintiff's affidavits to these specific dangers, justifies the conclusion that no genuine issue of fact exists for trial....

The *Lemmon* case involved an FDA regulation, 21 C.F.R. § 250.11, that declared thyroid-containing drugs intended for the treatment of human obesity new drugs. The court implied that this determination lay properly within FDA's primary jurisdiction. The issue of who may determine whether a drug is a new drug for which marketing approval is required is considered at p. 506 *infra.*

2. *Evidence of General Recognition.* In 1973 the Supreme Court approved FDA's position that "general recognition" of safety and effectiveness must be based upon the same quantity and quality of scientific evidence that would be needed to obtain an NDA. *Weinberger v. Bentex Pharmaceuticals, Inc.,* 412 U.S. 645 (1973). *See Weinberger v. Hynson, Westcott & Dunning, Inc.,* 412 U.S. 609 (1973).

HOFFMANN–LaROCHE, INC. v. WEINBERGER

United States District Court, District of Columbia, 1975.
425 F. Supp. 890.

JUNE L. GREEN, District Judge.

Plaintiff, Hoffmann–LaRoche, Inc., has brought suit for declaratory and injunctive relief.... Specifically, Hoffmann–LaRoche challenges the FDA's policy of permitting the introduction of a new drug in interstate commerce without first approving a new drug application for such drug as required by 21 U.S.C. §§ 331, 355 (1970)....

... Hoffmann–LaRoche is the holder of three approved new drug applications for compounds which contain chlordiazepoxide or chlordiazepoxide hydrochloride (both hereafter referred to as "chlordiazepoxide"). Plaintiff markets these drugs under the trademark "Librium." Since 1959, when Hoffmann–LaRoche first filed a new drug application for chlordiazepoxide, Hoffmann–LaRoche has marketed the drug only after it has obtained approval by the FDA of its new drug applications.

On January 20, 1975, plaintiff filed suit in the United States District Court for the District of New Jersey against Zenith Laboratories, Inc. and its subsidiary, Paramount Supply Corp., alleging infringement of plaintiff's patent on chlordiazepoxide. During the course of pretrial discovery in that case, plaintiff learned from officials of the defendant companies that they had begun to ship chlordiazepoxide capsules in interstate commerce. In March 1973, Zenith filed an abbreviated new drug application with the FDA on chlordiazepoxide. On February 27, 1975, plaintiff field this action in district court. The FDA approved the new drug application submitted by Zenith Laboratories on March 7, 1975. . . .

The crux of this controversy is the use by the FDA of the new drug application procedure as a sort of administrative holding action to regulate the sale and manufacture of "me-too" drugs. Me-too drugs are drugs which are chemically equivalent to a pioneer drug for which a full new drug application is in effect. It is estimated that five to thirteen me-too drugs exist for every new drug that has a FDA approved new drug application. It is the present policy of the FDA, termed an interim policy, to require the filing of an abbreviated new drug application by the manufacturers of each me-too drug where the pioneer drug has a full new drug application approved pursuant to 21 U.S.C. § 355 (1970). The FDA's position is that marketing of these drugs may be permitted without the approval of each individual new drug application.

The FDA advances two principal arguments to justify its policy. First, it claims that its compliance resources are limited and must be concentrated primarily in those areas where a potential health problem exists. Thus, the FDA has directed its compliance activities toward those drug products which have been found ineffective rather than toward those which have been found effective. Second, for those drugs that the NAS/NRC have found effective and are widely recognized as safe and effective and no bioavailability or special manufacturing problem is known or suspected, the need to police their distribution is minimal. Additionally, the FDA claims that it would have a difficult time in court contending that a specific version is a new drug within the meaning of 21 U.S.C. § 321(p) (1970).

On the contrary, Hoffmann–LaRoche argues that the FDA's action is another example of its failure to follow the 1962 New Drug Amendments. Like the situation condemned in *American Public Health Assoc. v. Veneman,* the FDA is again acting contrary to the clear statutory directives of section 355. Plaintiff contends that the plain meaning of section 355 dictates that once the FDA requires a new drug application to be filed, then the approval process must be completed before such drug can be marketed. . . .

Reaching the merits of plaintiff's statutory argument, the Court holds that the FDA's policy of permitting new drugs to be marketed without an approved new drug application contravenes the clear statutory requirement of preclearance mandated by 21 U.S.C. § 355 (1970).

The FDA's choice of policy is not within the intendment of the 1962 New Drug Amendments and the legislative scheme they embody.

... The Court recognizes that the FDA is to be given the administrative flexibility to make regulations and to determine the new drug status of individual drugs or classes of drugs. Certainly it has the power to promulgate regulations that adopt a monograph procedure for human prescription drugs similar to that adopted for over-the-counter drugs whereby a drug or drugs may be declared to be no longer new drugs. See, 21 C.F.R. § 330.10 (1974). The FDA can regulate the bioequivalence and special manufacturing problems through its general rule-making power. However, the argument that the FDA lacks the administrative resources to insure compliance with section 355 cannot be permitted to postpone to some indefinite future date the implementation of the required preclearance approval of new drug applications....

Summary judgment will therefore be entered for the plaintiff.[6] Defendants will be permanently enjoined from implementing its policy which permits the introduction into interstate commerce without an approved new drug application of prescription drugs which the FDA has previously declared to be new drugs within the meaning of 21 U.S.C. § 321(p).

NOTES

1. *Abbreviated NDAs.* The FDA policy rejected by Judge Green represented an effort by FDA to assure that the abbreviated NDA requirement did not specially burden new manufacturers, who otherwise would have to delay marketing while the bureaucratic machinery ground its way through the flood of applications, while similar "yet to be approved" products remained on the market simply because these were there when the process began. FDA did not appeal Judge Green's ruling. *Compare Public Citizen v. Schmidt,* FDLI 1975–1977 Jud. Rec. 359 (D.D.C. 1976), which held that the new drug status of chloroform "was not an 'open and shut' case" and thus that FDA had authority to phase out its use through a rulemaking proceeding.

No court ruled on the legality of FDA's abbreviated NDA policy—a policy that permitted the agency to approve the marketing of a pre–1962 new drug without the submission of full reports of safety and effectiveness and without formal release of the safety and effectiveness data supporting the pioneer product—before the 1984 statute codified this policy.

2. *"Paper NDAs" for Post-1962 Drugs.* Prior to the enactment of the 1984 Drug Price competition and Patent Term Restoration Act, FDA refused to accept abbreviated NDAs for post–1962 drugs. The agency was, however, concerned that an approach that required redundant preclinical and clinical testing of generic equivalent products would not increase protection of consumers and would burden scarce testing facilities. In 1978, it announced the

6. Whatever the anticompetitive effects and secondary patent protection judgment for plaintiff will give to manufacturers with approved new drug applications, the overriding interest in insuring the health and safety of the public through compliance with section 355 requires the result reached here.

following "paper NDA" policy for approval of duplicates of post–1962 new drugs:

> A drug marketed for the first time after 1962 under an approved New Drug Application may be marketed by a second firm only after the second firm has received the approval of a full New Drug Application for that purpose. Current Agency policy does not permit ANDAs for this purpose. Present interpretation of the law is that no data in the NDA can be utilized to support another NDA without express permission of the original NDA holder. Thus, in the case of duplicate NDAs for already approved post–62 drugs, the Agency will accept published reports as the main supporting documentation for safety and effectiveness. The Agency will not interpret the "full reports of investigations" phrase in the law as requiring either case reports or an exhaustive review of all published reports on the drug. Depending upon the quality of the published data, selected preclinical and perhaps additional clinical studies may be required of the new sponsor prior to NDA approval.

Memorandum from Associate Director of New Drug Evaluation (July 31, 1978). This policy was upheld in *Burroughs Wellcome Co. v. Schweiker,* 649 F.2d 221 (4th Cir. 1981), and *Upjohn Manufacturing Co. v. Schweiker,* 681 F.2d 480 (6th Cir. 1982), and later revoked (as superseded) by the preamble to FDA's proposed regulations to implement the 1984 Act, 54 Fed. Reg. 28872, 28890 (July 10, 1989).

3. *Bioequivalence of Me–Too Drugs.* The driving force behind FDA's ultimately successful assertion that all prescription drugs must have an approved NDA or abbreviated NDA was the agency's need to be able to represent that all generic versions of a drug have been demonstrated to be bioequivalent and thus clinically interchangeable. *See* p. 576 *infra;* Benfield, *Life After Lannett: Open Season For "Me-too" Drugs?,* 34 FDC L.J. 212 (1979); Lambert, *Law, Power and Money: A Generic Trinity,* 35 FDC L.J. 306 (1980).

UNITED STATES v. GENERIX DRUG CORP.

Supreme Court of the United States, 1983.
460 U.S. 453.

JUSTICE STEVENS delivered the opinion of the Court.

The question presented is whether the statutory prohibition against the marketing of a "new drug" without the prior approval of the Food and Drug Administration (FDA) requires respondent Generix Drug Corp. to have approved new drug applications (NDA's) before it may market its generic drug products. In statutory terms, we are required to determine whether the term "drug" as used in the relevant sections of the Federal Food, Drug, and Cosmetic Act (Act), as amended, 21 U.S.C. § 301 *et seq.* (1976 ed. and Supp. V), refers only to the active ingredient in a drug product or to the entire product. We hold that Congress intended the word to have the broader meaning....

In examining this statutory definition [of the term "drug"], the Court of Appeals was persuaded that only active ingredients come within the terms of subsection (A). Unfortunately, the court [of Appeals] did not analyze the entire definition. If it had done so, it would have noted both that the terms of subsections (A), (B), and (C) are plainly broad enough to include more than just active ingredients, and that they *must* do so unless subsection (D) is to be superfluous. Because the definition is disjunctive, generic drug products are quite plainly drugs within the meaning of the Act.

The natural reading of this definition is corroborated by other sections of the Act.... The term "drug" is plainly intended throughout the Act to include entire drug products, complete with active and inactive ingredients....

In this case we are not required to determine what types of differences between drugs would be significant or insignificant under the statute. Respondent Generix argued only that its products are not new drugs under the theory that "drug" means "active ingredient"; it does not argue that its complete products—active ingredients and excipients together—are the same as previously approved products. The latter argument would, of course, have been unavailing on the facts before us; for the respondent has not questioned the District Court's finding of a reasonable possibility that its products are not bioequivalent to any previously approved products. We thus do not reach the issue of whether two demonstrably bioequivalent products, containing the same active ingredients but different excipients, might under some circumstances be the same "drug."

In summary, a generic drug product is a "drug" within the meaning of § 201(g)(1) of the Act. Such a product is therefore a "new drug," subject to the requirements of § 505, until the product (and not merely its active ingredient) no longer falls within the terms of § 201(p)....

NOTES

1. *Post–1962 Drugs.* This decision prompted FDA officials to begin development of a policy for approval of abbreviated NDAs for post–1962 generic drugs, and eventually provoked a suit by generic drug manufacturers to force the agency to issue such a policy. One year later, the legislation ultimately enacted as the Drug Price Competition and Patent Term Act of 1984 was introduced.

2. *Exceptions to Generix.* In *United States v. Atropine Sulfate 1.0 Mg. (Article of Drug)*, 843 F.2d 860 (5th Cir. 1988), the court rejected the claimant's argument that its generic product was "uniquely equivalent" to the pioneer new drug and thus fell within the exception left open by the Supreme Court in the *Generix* decision.

---

b. The "Grandfather" Clauses

When Congress first required that new drugs be proved safe for the conditions of their intended use, it specified in section 201(p)(1) that this requirement should not apply to any drug marketed under the 1906 Food and Drugs Act (*i.e.*, prior to 1938) as long as its labeling continued to contain "the same representations concerning the conditions of its use." This "grandfather" clause for pre–1938 drugs was not changed in 1962.

The 1962 Amendments contained their own so-called transitional provisions designed to provide either permanent or temporary exemption from the new effectiveness requirement for certain classes of drugs first marketed after 1938. These transitional provisions appeared in section 107(c) of the Amendments, but are not codified in the FD&C Act.

UNITED STATES v. ALLAN DRUG CORP.

United States Court of Appeals, Tenth Circuit, 1966.
357 F.2d 713.

MURRAH, Chief Judge.

In this consolidated libel action the Colorado District Court condemned as misbranded a drug labeled "Halsion, A Plan of Medication and Care for Acne and Pimples" and returned the seized articles to the intervening claimant to be brought into compliance with the drug law under the supervision of a representative of the Secretary of Health, Education and Welfare. This appeal is from an order of the court approving the relabeling and authorizing the marketing of the product as relabeled over the protest of the Federal Food, Drug and Cosmetic Administration. . . .

On trial of the case the Court found "That the labeling material in its net effect represented to prospective purchasers * * * that the 'Halsion Plan' in and of itself is an adequate and effective treatment for acne and pimples and would give lasting relief from these conditions . . . [and] that "These representations were misleading. . . ." Amenable to the requirements of § 334(d), the order return[ed] the seized articles for relabeling. . . .

In a letter responding to the [claimant's] proposed relabeling the Secretary took the position that the labeling did not comply with the Court's guidelines. . . . Finally, the Secretary took the position that the requirements of § 334(d) made it necessary to consider the marketing status of the Halsion tablets under the Drug Amendments of 1962. In that regard the Secretary contended that having shown to the satisfaction of the Court that the drug was not generally recognized by experts as effective for its intended uses, it cannot now be legally marketed unless its effectiveness has been established pursuant to a "New Drug application" in accordance with the statutory procedure. . . .

For reasons we shall attempt to demonstrate we are of the considered opinion that when, based on the facts, the trial court held the Halsion labeling false and misleading, hence misbranded, it became a "new drug" within the meaning of § 321(p)(1), as amended, and was subject to the administrative procedures prescribed in § 355 as amended. . . .

... The exception or the Grandfather Clause was perpetuated verbatim [by the 1962 Amendments] so that a drug not generally recognized as safe or effective on the date of the Amendment would not be deemed to be a new drug on that date if its labeling contained the same representations concerning the conditions of its use. Additionally, and under another and different section of the amending Act [107(c)(4)] pertaining to the effective dates of the Amendments, the Grandfather Clause was restated, "In the case of any drug which, on the day immediately preceding the enactment date (A) was commercially used or sold in the United States * * * the amendments to section 2901(p) * * * shall not apply to such drug when intended solely for the use under conditions prescribed, recommended, or suggested in labeling with respect to such drug on that day." While the exempting language of the basic Act and the Amendment is verbally different, they are undoubtedly intended to mean the same thing. . . .

The trial court construed the critical words "solely for use under conditions prescribed, recommended, or suggested in labeling" to mean that the Amendments should apply to a new or different area of use under conditions prescribed in the labeling. He did not think Congress intended the Amendments to apply to a mere change in the labeling after the effective date of the Act, thus imposing upon a drug manufacturer the onerous burden of the new drug procedures when, as in this case, the effect of the change in the labeling was merely to reduce the use of the drug under conditions prescribed or recommended in the labeling. . . .

Since we are dealing with a Grandfather Clause exception, we must construe it strictly against one who invokes it. . . . .

Judged in this context, we construe the critical language of the Grandfather Clauses to exempt drugs not generally recognized as effective if on the effective date of the Act the labeling contained the same representations concerning its use, and thus confine the exemption to drugs intended solely for use under conditions prescribed on the effective date of the Act. Given this interpretation, the condemned article loses the immunity of the Grandfather Clause and becomes a new drug subject to § 355. This is not to say that every change in labeling must necessarily result in the manufacturer filing a new drug application to reintroduce the article into interstate commerce. It may well be that a condemned drug may be brought into compliance with the provisions of the Drug Act under the supervision of the Secretary by relabeling the article for another use for which it is generally recognized as effective. . . . But, we need not speculate on the effective uses for which this article may be properly relabeled. It is enough to say that where, as here, an article has been condemned as mislabeled in fact and misbranded in law, it can be brought into compliance and reintroduced for the same or similar use only as a new drug under the procedures prescribed in § 355. . . .

[The dissenting opinion of Judge Seth is omitted.]

NOTE

In *United States v. An Article of Drug . . . "Bentex Ulcerine,"* (S.D. Tex. 1970, 1971), *aff'd*, 469 F.2d 875 (5th Cir. 1972), the district court rejected the claimant's contention that its drug was protected by the transitional provisions of the 1962 Amendments:

> The claimant's evidence shows De–Nol was distributed to only a very limited extent before October 9, 1962. Between 1958 and June 30, 1963, a total of only four thousand bottles were imported. . . .

> Claimant's evidence on this issue is not impressive. At best, it tends to show that the drug was used, prescribed and enthusiastically endorses by a few physicians in Memphis, Tennessee (including the importer); and sold to no more than perhaps 150 to 200 doctors in some two or three neighboring states.

> Bearing in mind that the test is whether the drug was *generally recognized* as safe on the date in question (not whether in fact it *was* safe), I am simply unable to find its use or reputation was sufficiently widespread at that time as to qualify.

See also United States v. Undetermined Quantities of an Article of Drug . . . Anucort HC Suppositories, 709 F.Supp. 511 (D.N.J. 1987), *aff'd without opinion,* 857 F.2d 1466 (3d Cir. 1988); *United States v. Articles of Drug . . . 5,906 Boxes,* 745 F.2d 105 (1st Cir. 1984); *United States v. 1,048,000 Capsules . . . "Afrodex,"* 494 F.2d 1158 (5th Cir. 1974), *aff'g* 347 F.Supp. 768 (S.D. Tex. 1972); *United States v. 675 Cases . . . "Damason–P,"* Food Drug Cosm. L. Rep. (CCH) ¶ 38,156 (C.D. Cal. 1989); *United States v. Articles of Drug . . . "Colchicine,"* 442 F.Supp. 1236 (S.D.N.Y. 1978). No drug has yet been judicially determined to fall within the 1938 or 1962 grandfather clause.

One of the important issues raised in the four Supreme Court cases in 1973 was whether the a pioneer drug's approved NDA "covered" generic "me-too" versions. A holding that they were "covered" would deny them the protection of the grandfather clause and subject them to the Act's proof of effectiveness requirement.

USV PHARMACEUTICAL CORP. v. WEINBERGER

Supreme Court of the United States, 1973.
412 U.S. 655.

Mr. Justice DOUGLAS delivered the opinion of the Court.

Petitioner sells a line of drugs containing, as a principal active ingredient, citrus bioflavonoid, which is an extract from fruit skins. The drugs are sold in capsules, syrup, and tablets. In the 1950's . . . [NDA's] were filed and became effective for seven of them; two, however, were sold without any NDA. In 1961 the ... [FDA] advised petitioner that two of the products, when distributed under the existing labels, were not new drugs. These drugs were recommended for a wide variety of ailments from bleeding, to hypertension, to ulcerative colitis.... [NAS–NRC] panels reviewed them. One panel on metabolic disorders concluded that the "use of these materials as hemostatic agents for capillary fragility is felt to be unjustifiable and not proved." A panel on hematologic disorders found there was no proof that these products were efficacious for any medical use.

Based upon the NAS–NRC reports and its own evaluation, FDA gave notice of opportunity for hearing on its proposal to withdraw approvals of NDA's for all drugs containing these compounds, alone or in combination with other drugs. Petitioner thereupon brought suit in the District Court.... The administrative proceedings went forward, FDA refusing a stay pending the judicial proceedings. Petitioner submitted no evidence of "adequate and well-controlled investigations" ... to support its claims of effectiveness. The Commissioner made findings and withdrew petitioner's NDA's.

The resolution of the questions presented turns essentially on the meaning of § 107(c)(4)....

... Without transitional protection all drugs—except those marketed prior to the 1938 Act whose labeling had not been changed and which were exempt from the "new drug" provision of § 201(p)—would have been in violation of the amended Act unless generally recognized as effective. Even NDA's which were outstanding would have become ineffective because FDA had not approved them under the new criteria. Section 107(c)(2) of the amendments therefore provides that applications which were effective on the day before the enactment date of the 1962 amendments should be deemed "approved." Section 107(c)(2) thus eliminated the necessity to review and approve every application already on file.

Section 107(c)(3) provides that drugs covered by NDA's already on file whose labeling remains unchanged are not affected by the amended provisions of § 505(b) or by approvals or refusals under § 505(d) insofar as the effectiveness of the drugs is concerned, so long as the application is not withdrawn or suspended under § 505(e). It also provides that the new effectiveness requirement in the withdrawal provision would not apply until two years after the amendments were adopted, or until the NDA approval[s] were withdrawn for reasons other than lack of the drug's effectiveness, whichever came first....

Section 107(c)(4) exempted drugs from the new effectiveness requirements so long as their composition and labeling remained unchanged. This exemption, however, applies only to a product that, on the day before the 1962 amendments became effective, (A) was used or sold commercially in the United States; (B) was generally recognized by the experts as safe; and (C) was not "covered" by an "effective" application.

The first question is, which "me-too" copies of an NDA drug are subject to the efficacy requirements to the same extent as the NDA product itself? Are only the "me-too's" of the same manufacturer "covered" by an effective application within the meaning of § 107(c)(4)(C) and thus not exempt from § 201(p) or are no "me-too's" exempt whoever manufactures them. It seems clear that § 107(c) was designed in general to make the new 1962 requirements applicable to drugs then on the market after a two-year grace period. Section 107(c)(4) created an exception from this general policy.... It is true that an NDA covers a particular product or products that it names and that § 505 when applied to an NDA is personal to the manufacturer who files it. Section 505, in other words, addresses itself to drugs as individual products. But we agree with the Government that "any drug" when used in § 107(c)(4) is used in the generic sense, which means that the "me-too's" whether products of the same or of different manufacturers "covered" by an "effective" NDA, are not exempt from the efficacy requirements of § 201(p). If that were not true, then, as the Court of Appeals said, the "me-too's" of one manufacturer covered by an NDA of another manufacturer would be exempt from regulation, while the "me-too's" of the manufacturer holding the NDA could be regulated. That seems to be a reading of § 107(c)(4) that is discriminatory and needlessly so. For it is avoided by taking "any drug" in that subsection as a generic term. The transitional nature of § 107(c) works in that direction. A reading to exclude all "me-too" drugs from the word "covered" as used in § 107(c)(4) would create a hiatus in the regulatory scheme for which there seems to be no cogent reason. We find no persuasive reason to resolve the ambiguities in favor of the manufacturers so that pre-existing pioneer drugs would be subject to the new efficacy requirements but the "me-too's" which often do equal service for them would escape the thrust of the 1962 amendments. That resolution of the ambiguities would largely leave pre–1962 drugs of unproved effectiveness untouched by the 1962 amendments and perpetuate a competitive contest in the marketing of ineffective pre–1962 drugs. FDA would, of course, have authority to pursue that category of drugs under the misbranding provisions of the Act. But that slow, cumbersome method is utterly unsuited to the needs. We decline to attribute such a self-defeating purpose to the Congress ...

Petitioner, focusing on prescription drugs, contends that the construction of § 107(c)(4) urged by the Government would make the exemption meaningless. Prescription drugs, as FDA points out, are not likely to have come on the market subsequent to 1938 without being a "new drug" for some time. But the over-the-counter (OTC) drugs, known as the proprietaries, are often made up of old, established ingredients. Such products, coming on the market for the first time between 1938 and 1962, might never have been subject to new drug regulation. If so, they would be entitled to the exemption provided by § 107(c)(4)....

It can be inferred ... that prescription drugs on the market were to be subjected to the efficacy requirements. If the 1962 amendments are to be comprehensively meaningful, we decline to read § 107(c)(4) so as to provide a loophole so that the manufacturers can go on marketing drugs previously subject to new drug regulation without demonstrating by the new statutory standards that they are effective as claimed.

The second question presented by this case is whether an applicant could have withdrawn or "deactivated" an NDA prior to the 1962 amendments so that its drug was no longer "covered by an effective application" and thus is now exempt from efficacy regulation by reason of § 107(c)(4). Petitioner in 1961 had stated in a letter to the Director of New Drug Branch of the Bureau of Medicine in FDA that "[i]t is our recollection that the C.V.P. class of products were no longer considered to be new drugs...." Petitioner in 1961 also stopped filing supplemental information as required by regulation with regard to the products for which NDA's had become effective. It claims that these acts were sufficient to withdraw the NDA's and to bring its products within the exemption.

Initially, we repeat that the legislative history indicates that it was Congress' purpose to exempt only those drugs that never had been subject to the new drug regulation. Quite obviously, any drug for which an NDA once had been effective does not fall within that category.

Congress rejected an approach that would have exempted from the efficacy requirements of the 1962 amendments all drugs then marketed which had become generally recognized as safe. It now would be irrational for us to construe § 107(c)(4) of the amendments to exempt a drug merely because the manufacturer had taken some formal steps totally unrelated to the drug's effectiveness to indicate that the drug was no longer a "new drug" under the pre–1962 standards. The result would be that some drugs for which an NDA had been filed would be subject to the efficacy requirements and some would not, even though one could not differentiate between the drugs on the grounds of effectiveness.... It would be totally inconsistent with the statutory scheme and the policy underlying the 1962 amendments, as well as patently unjust, to conclude that some manufacturers could continue to market their bioflavonoid products, but others could not. We cannot attribute such an intention to Congress and, accordingly, cannot agree with petitioner that its NDA's had been withdrawn prior to 1962 so that its bioflavonoid products were no longer "covered by an effective application."

Affirmed.

NOTE

USV prevailed in its appeal from FDA's denial of a hearing on the withdrawal of approval of the bioflavonoid NDAs. *USV Pharmaceutical Corp. v. Secretary of HEW,* 466 F.2d 455 (D.C. Cir. 1972). FDA thereafter published a notice of opportunity for hearing under its revised summary judgment procedures, 36 Fed. Reg. 24935 (July 8, 1974), and this time the company did not contest the withdrawal of the NDAs. 42 Fed. Reg. 10066 (February 18, 1977).

———

A decade after enactment of the 1962 Drug Amendments, and five years after the NAS had begun to submit its evaluations of pre–1962 new drugs, consumer organizations challenged FDA's procedure and timetable for implementing the Amendments.

AMERICAN PUBLIC HEALTH ASS'N v. VENEMAN

United States District Court, District of Columbia, 1972.
349 F. Supp. 1311.

BRYANT, District Judge.

In January, 1968, the FDA began implementation of the NAS–NRC reports. The procedure adopted has been to evaluate each report and to release it to the public only after the FDA evaluation is completed. When the FDA completes its evaluation of an NAS–NRC report, an announcement is made in the Federal Register that the FDA has concluded that the drugs involved are "effective," "probably effective," "possibly effective," or "lack substantial evidence of effectiveness." ...

After announcing the classification of a drug in the Federal Register, the FDA affords the drug manufacturer a period of time to provide additional data to the FDA in every case where the drug is classified as anything other than "effective." The manufacturer is given 12 months or 6 months where the drug is listed as probably or possibly effective, respectively, and 30 days where the drug is classified as lacking substantial evidence of effectiveness. During this time period, the manufacturer is permitted to continue marketing the drug. If, at the end of the interim period, no studies have been undertaken by the manufacturer, or if the studies do not provide substantial evidence of effectiveness, procedures are supposed to be instituted to withdraw approval of the drug pursuant to 21 U.S.C. § 355(e)....

First the plaintiffs assert that the FDA practice of granting manufacturers time to bolster the record regarding a drug's effectiveness, after the FDA has publicly concluded that a drug is less than effective, is a violation of the statutory mandate. The statute states unequivocably that

> The Secretary *shall.*. .withdraw approval of any application with respect to any drug under this section if the Secretary finds ... that there is a lack of substantial evidence that the drug will have the effect it purports or is represented to have under the conditions of use prescribed ... 21 U.S.C. § 355(3) [Emphasis added]. ...

Thus it could not be clear that the Secretary *must* begin the procedures to withdraw a drug when he concludes that there is no

substantial evidence of efficacy. The defendants contend that the
many announcements which have been published in the Federal Register regarding FDA conclusions about the efficacy of various drugs are
not findings by the agency and that the FDA is "not required by law to
notice the cases [where a drug has been found less than effective] or
press them to hearing immediately upon its announcement of the
NAS–NRC findings and its concurrence. It has discretion in the
selection of cases to notice for hearing." This argument is unpersuasive in view of the clear language of the statute and regulations and the
Congressional intent to rid the marketplace of ineffective drugs.[14]

The plaintiffs' second claim is that once the FDA commences the
procedure outlined in the statute or regulation for withdrawing a drug,
it fails to adhere to those procedures. Plaintiffs assert, and the defendants do not refute it, that for many drugs the FDA has published in
the Federal Register the required notice of an opportunity for a hearing
and that the manufacturers have failed to avail themselves of the
opportunity for the hearing within the required 30 days; nevertheless
the FDA has failed to withdraw these drugs from the market. In these
circumstances, the withdrawal is both required by the statute and
purely a ministerial duty, and failure to withdraw constitutes agency
action unlawfully withheld.

In addition, plaintiffs contend that where drug manufacturers have
requested a hearing, such hearings have been a long time in coming.
They cite as examples two drugs where no hearing had been scheduled
at the time the plaintiffs filed their memorandum, even though the
manufacturers had requested hearings one and a half years before....
As the court reads 21 C.F.R. § 130.14(b), a hearing on withdrawal of a
new drug application is to be scheduled as soon as practicable, and
while such a provision confers some agency discretion in scheduling the
hearing, interminable delay obviously is not contemplated....

In response to the court's inquiry the defendants advised the court
on February 2, 1972, that 814 reports still had not been evaluated by
the FDA. Of these outstanding reports, 327 had been returned to
NAS–NRC for further evaluation in early 1971 and were reported on by
NAS–NRC in October, 1971; they are presently being reevaluated by
the FDA. In addition, the FDA has advised that the 260 NAS–NRC
reports on over-the-counter drugs will not be rated by the FDA (and
hence will remain unpublished) because it has announced a new program with regard to over-the-counter drugs. The plaintiffs have protested that the proposed procedures are "enormously elaborate" and
will create extensive delay in applying the efficacy requirement to

14. The court feels compelled to state
that even if the statute and regulation did
not require immediate action by the FDA
to withdraw an ineffective drug, the court
would grant mandamus based upon not
only the statute, but also the failure of the
FDA to adhere to its regulation declaring
that a drug would be withdrawn at the end
of a 30 day, 6 month or 12 month period.
Furthermore, the court cannot understand
the solicitude of the FDA for the drug
manufacturers in giving additional time to
supplement the record when in all cases
the manufacturers have been on notice regarding the statute's efficacy requirement
for at least four or more years....

over-the-counter drugs. The court shares this concern, since over-the-counter drugs are purchased without medical advice in most cases, and an NAS–NRC report on over-the-counter drugs indicates that only 25% of all such drugs are effective....

At the very outset the Congress ... allowed a two-year grace period before the 1962 amendments were to become effective. When, as is the case here, the Congress has shown an awareness of a problem and has acted accordingly, it seems inappropriate for an agency to adopt procedures which extend the grace period far beyond that envisioned by the statute, and which effectively stay implementation of the Congressional mandate that drugs in the marketplace be both safe and effective.

Based upon the entire record in this case, the court concludes that there is no compelling reason why the remaining NAS–NRC reports should not be immediately released, that it would be an abuse of agency discretion to refuse to make such reports public, and that the court should set a deadline for the FDA to complete its evaluation of all drugs with regard to efficacy....

Counsel are directed to present an appropriate order.

NOTES

1. *Veneman Order.* FDA did not appeal this ruling because its top officials believed that judicial oversight could provide the leverage necessary to galvanize the agency into action. Judge Bryant subsequently entered an order, drafted by government counsel, which established a schedule for completion of the DESI Review. The order required agency action, in descending order of priority, on drugs rated by the NAS–NRC panels and FDA as "ineffective," "possible effective," and "probably effective." The entire task was to be finished by 1976. OTC drugs and medically important prescription drugs were exempted. FDA was required to file semi-annual progress reports with the court. *See* 37 Fed. Reg. 26623 (December 14, 1972).

2. *Paragraph XIV Drugs.* The order entered by Judge Bryant is in many significant respects inconsistent with the *Veneman* opinion, revealing that many practical problems in implementing the 1962 Amendments were not appreciated when the opinion was written. Paragraph XIV of the order—under which the marketing of drugs with important medical uses was allowed to continue until studies meeting contemporary standards could be conducted to verify their effectiveness—is an example. FDA's implementation of this provision can be traced through a series of notices, *e.g.,* 37 Fed. Reg. 26623 (December 14, 1972), 38 Fed. Reg. 18477 (July 11, 1973), 41 Fed. Reg. 32937 (August 6, 1976), 42 Fed. Reg. 43127 (August 26, 1977), 42 Fed. Reg. 44286 (September 2, 1977), 42 Fed. Reg. 56156 (October 21, 1977), 43 Fed. Reg. 7044 (February 17, 1978), 43 Fed Reg. 26489 (June 20, 1978), 44 Fed. Reg. 40933 (July 13, 1979), and 45 Fed. Reg. 4471 (January 22, 1980).

3. *Failure to Meet Schedule.* FDA failed to meet the mandated four-year schedule. By the end of 1976 it had largely completed work on the higher-rated drugs, by inducing manufacturers to revise label claims or, in some instances, by upgrading its own evaluation. It had revoked NDAs for drugs whose manufacturers had not submitted any additional evidence of effectiveness. But it had fallen behind in two areas. (1) It had not ruled on several requests for

formal hearings nor held any hearings because these tasks were the most labor-intensive and demanded the efforts of a relatively few knowledgeable employees. (2) As Judge Bryant's order permitted, it had created a substantial backlog of so-called Paragraph XIV drugs. In many instances clinical investigations had not commenced because FDA had been unable to devise appropriate testing protocols.

4. *Revised Order.* In March 1979, the *Veneman* plaintiffs moved to reopen the proceedings to seek further relief. In an agreement reached by the parties, *American Public Health Ass'n v. Harris,* Food Drug Cosm. L. Rep. (CCH) ¶ 38,068 (D.D.C. 1980), FDA agreed to "make a good faith effort to assure a more expeditious resolution of matters covered by the Court Order" of 1972 and to "attempt to achieve" specific new goals "to the maximum extent feasible." FDA continues to submit semiannual reports to the court on its progress. As of the December 1989 report, eight drugs still awaited final decision.

5. *Federal Reimbursement for Less–Than–Effective Drugs.* In 45 Fed. Reg. 37858 (June 5, 1980), HCFA proposed to prohibit the use of Federal funds to pay for any drug that FDA had, in a final administrative ruling, found to be less than effective. Before HCFA had an opportunity to promulgate a final regulation, Congress included in the Omnibus Budget Reconciliation Act of 1981, 95 Stat. 357, 787, an amendment to the Social Security Act prohibiting the expenditure of federal funds under Medicare and Medicaid for drugs for which FDA has published a notice of opportunity for hearing to withdraw approval of the NDA. That provision, codified in 42 U.S.C. § 1395y(c), was implemented by HCFA in 46 Fed. Reg. 48550 (October 1, 1981), 46 Fed. Reg. 51646 (October 21, 1981), 46 Fed. Reg. 53664, 54304 (October 30, 1981), codified in 42 C.F.R. § 405.232(c).

---

c. Jurisdiction to Determine New Drug Status
WEINBERGER v. BENTEX PHARMACEUTICALS, INC.
Supreme Court of the United States, 1973.
412 U.S. 645.

Mr. Justice DOUGLAS delivered the opinion of the Court.

In this case Bentex and some 20 other firms ... filed this suit for a declaratory judgment that their drugs containing pentylenetetrazol are generally recognized as safe and effective, and thus not "new drugs" within the meaning of § 201(p)(1).... They also sought exemption from the new effectiveness requirements by reason of § 107(c)(4) of the 1962 amendments....

... [T]hree separate National Academy of Sciences–National Research Council (NAS–NRC) panels reviewed the evidence concerning these drugs, and each concluded that the drug was "ineffective" for the indicated use. The Commissioner concluded there was a lack of substantial evidence that these drugs were effective for their intended uses and gave notice of his intention to initiate proceedings to withdraw approval of the new drug applications (NDA's). FDA had taken the position that withdrawal of approval of an NDA would operate to remove marketing approval for all drugs of similar composition, known as "me-too" drugs, whether or not they were expressly covered by an effective NDA. Accordingly, the notice invited the holders of the NDA's for drugs containing pentylenetetrazol, "and any interested person who might be adversely affected by their removal from the market," to submit "adequate and well-controlled studies" to establish the effectiveness of the drugs. Only one NDA holder submitted further evidence, which the Commissioner held did not satisfy the statutory standard. He thereupon gave notice of intent to issue an order withdrawing approval of the NDA's under § 505(e). Again, all those who might be adversely affected by withdrawal of the NDA's were given the opportunity to participate. Only one NDA holder requested a hearing but filed no data to support it. The Commissioner issued orders withdrawing approval of the three NDA's; no appeal was taken.... It appears that all of the parties to this suit market "me-too" drugs, none of which was expressly covered by an effective NDA.

The District Court held that although it could determine whether the drugs were "new" or "grandfathered" drugs, its jurisdiction was concurrent with that of FDA and that FDA should resolve the "new drug" issue in an administrative proceeding.... The Court of Appeals ... reversed and ... held that FDA has no jurisdiction, either primary or concurrent, to decide in an administrative proceeding what is a "new drug" for which an NDA is required. In its view the 1962 Act established two forums for the regulation of drugs: an administrative one for premarketing clearances for "new drugs" or withdrawal of previously approved NDA's, with the right of appeal; and, second, a judicial one for enforcement of the requirement that "new drugs" be cleared as safe and effective before marketing by providing the Government with judicial remedies of seizure, injunction, and criminal prosecution available solely in the District Court.

We reverse the Court of Appeals....

... While § 505(h) would appear to be the exclusive method of obtaining judicial review of FDA's order withdrawing an NDA covering the instant drugs, the Government apparently did not oppose the District Court's taking jurisdiction, or appeal from its action, and presents no objection to the exercise by the courts of jurisdiction in this case. It does, however, strenuously oppose the conclusions reached by the Court of Appeals.

... The line sought to be drawn by the Court of Appeals is FDA action on NDA's pursuant to § 505(d) and § 505(e), on the one hand, and the question of "new drug" determination on the other. We can discern no such jurisdictional line under the Act. The FDA, as already stated, may deny an NDA where there is a lack of "substantial evidence" of the drug's effectiveness, based, as we have outlined, on clinical investigation by experts. But the "new drug" definition under § 201(p) encompasses a drug "not generally recognized, among experts

qualified by scientific training and experience to evaluate the safety
and effectiveness of drugs, as safe and effective for use." Whether a
particular drug is a "new drug," depends in part on the expert knowledge and experience of scientists based on controlled clinical experimentation and backed by substantial support in scientific literature.
One function is not peculiar to judicial expertise, the other to administrative expertise. The two types of cases overlap and strongly suggest
that Congress desired that the administrative agency make both kinds
of determination. Even where no such administrative determination
has been made and the issue arises in a district court in enforcement
proceedings, it would be commonplace for the court to await an appropriate administrative declaration before it acted. It may, of course, be
true that in some cases general recognition that a drug is efficacious
might be made without the kind of scientific support necessary to
obtain approval of an NDA. But ... the reach of scientific inquiry
under both § 505(d) and § 201(p) is precisely the same.

We think that it is implicit in the regulatory scheme, not spelled
out *in haec verba,* that FDA has jurisdiction to decide with administrative finality, subject to the types of judicial review provided, the "new
drug" status of individual drugs or classes of drugs. The deluge of
litigation that would follow if "me-too" drugs and OTC drugs had to
receive *de novo* hearings in the courts would inure to the interests of
manufacturers and merchants in drugs, but not to the interests of the
public that Congress was anxious to protect by the 1962 amendments,
as well as OTC drugs and drugs covered by the 1972 [Drug Listing] Act.
We are told that FDA is incapable of handling a caseload of more than
perhaps 10 or 15 *de novo* judicial proceedings a year. Clearly, if FDA
were required to litigate, on a case-by-case basis, the "new drug" status
of each drug now marketed, the regulatory scheme of the Act would be
severely undermined. If not totally destroyed. Moreover, a case-by-
case approach is inherently unfair because it requires compliance by
one manufacturer while his competitors marketing similar drugs remain free to violate the Act....

... The determination whether a drug is generally recognized as
safe and effective within the meaning of § 201(p)(1) necessarily implicates complex chemical and pharmacological consideration. Threshold
questions within the peculiar expertise of an administrative agency are
appropriately routed to the agency, while the court stays its hand....

CIBA CORP. v. WEINBERGER
Supreme Court of the United States, 1973.
412 U.S. 640.

Mr. Justice DOUGLAS delivered the opinion of the Court.

Petitioner manufactures a drug called Ritonic Capsules for which it
filed a new drug application (NDA) that became effective in 1959....

A panel of the National Academy of Sciences–National Research Council (NAS–NRC) reviewed the claims made for Ritonic Capsules and found it "ineffective" for each of the claims. FDA concluded there was a lack of substantial evidence of its efficacy and gave notice of its intent to withdraw the NDA, offering petitioner an opportunity to submit the required kind of data bearing on the efficacy of the drug and stating that withdrawal of approval of the NDA would cause the Ritonic Capsules to be a "new drug" for which no NDA was in effect, thereby making future sales unlawful.

Petitioner responded, submitting data on the issue of efficacy and maintained that Ritonic Capsules was not a "new drug" for purposes of the Act as amended. FDA concluded that petitioner's evidence was insufficient to establish effectiveness and ... withdrew approval of the NDA on the ground that there was no substantial evidence that the drug was effective as claimed.... The Court of Appeals affirmed the withdrawal order. *CIBA–Geigy Corp. v. Richardson,* 446 F.2d 466.

Meanwhile, and prior to the issuance of the withdrawal order, petitioner brought suit in the District Court for the District of New Jersey seeking declaratory and injunctive relief. After hearing, the District Court granted the Government's motion to dismiss the complaint for lack of jurisdiction. On appeal, the Court of Appeals for the Third Circuit affirmed, 463 F.2d 225, holding that FDA was authorized to decide the jurisdictional question as an incident of its power to approve or withdraw approval for NDA's, that its decision on that issue was reviewable on direct appeal by a court of appeals, and since the Court of Appeals for the Second Circuit had ruled against petitioner on that appeal, the jurisdictional question could not be relitigated in a separate suit for a declaratory judgment. We affirm the Court of Appeals.

We have stated in *Weinberger v. Bentex Pharmaceuticals, Inc.,* our reasons for concluding that FDA has jurisdiction in an administrative proceeding to determine whether a drug product is a "new drug" within the meaning of § 201(p) of the Act....

It is, of course, true that the Act gives FDA a second line of defense—civil injunction proceedings, criminal penalties, and *in rem* seizure and condemnation. Those are sanctions to enforce the prohibition of the Act against the sale in commerce of any article in violation of § 505. But the Act does not create a dual system of control—one administrative, and the other judicial. Cases may arise where there has been no formal administrative determination of the "new drug" issue, it being first tendered to a district court. Even then, however, the district court might well stay its hand, awaiting an appropriate administrative determination of the threshold question. Where there is, however, an administrative determination, whether it be explicit or implicit in the withdrawal of an NDA, the tactic of "reserving" the threshold question (the jurisdictional issue) for later judicial determination is not tolerable. [P]etitioner, having an opportunity to litigate the "new drug" issue before FDA and to raise the issue on appeal to a court of appeals, may not relitigate the issue in another proceedings.

Affirmed.

NOTES

1. *Primary Jurisdiction.* The Supreme Court's holdings in *Bentex* and *CIBA* that FDA has "primary jurisdiction" to determine new drug status was a major victory for the agency. Ironically, though, the opinions have provided the pretext for challenges to FDA's use of its traditional court enforcement weapons to enforce the new drug requirements. *See* p. 1279 *infra.*

2. *Subsequent Proceedings.* Following the *Bentex* decision, FDA published a notice of opportunity for hearing in 41 Fed. Reg. 4625 (January 30, 1976). In 47 Fed. Reg. 19208 (May 4, 1982), the agency denied a hearing and withdrew approval of the NDAs for pentylenetetrazol. The denial of a hearing was overturned in *Boots Pharmaceuticals, Inc. v. Schweiker,* Food Drug Cosm. L. Rep. (CCH) § 38,200 (W.D. La. 1982), but this ruling was summarily reversed without opposition on appeal and no hearing was ever held.

---

d. The Practice of Pharmacy

Long before there were independent drug manufacturers, apothecaries, later called pharmacists, compounded drugs both for their own patients and in response to prescriptions of physicians. Companies engaged in manufacturing and distributing drugs did not emerge in the United States until the latter half of the 19th century. Today the vast majority of prescription drugs are produced in finished form by drug manufacturers and only dispensed by pharmacists, but the compounding of prescription drugs still occupies a distinctive place under the FD&C Act. The following FDA policy specifically refers to hospital pharmacies, but the principles it enunciates apply to all pharmacies.

COMPLIANCE POLICY GUIDE 7132.06
Food and Drug Administration.

1. Compounding in Hospitals—Registration

We interpret Section 510 of the Federal Food, Drug, and Cosmetic Act as not requiring registration by the hospital pharmacy that compounds medication for inpatient dispensing, outpatient dispensing (sale or free), mailing to a patient within the State or out of the State, or for transferral to another unit of the same hospital (within the State or in another State) for dispensing by that unit of the hospital. However, if the hospital pharmacy compounds medication which it sells to another hospital or a drugstore, such sale is not at "retail" and registration is required.

2. *Application of the "current good manufacturing practices" regulations to hospital pharmacies.*

Section 501(a)(2)(B) of the Act provides that a drug shall be deemed to be adulterated if "the methods used in, or the facilities or controls used for its manufacture, processing, packing, or holding do not conform to current good manufacturing practice ..." This section, through the operation of Section 301(k), is applicable to hospital pharmacies, as well as to manufacturers, whether or not the establishments are required to register with FDA under Section 510. However, the CGMP regulations set forth in 21 CFR 211 apply to those establishments which are both required to register under Section 510 and which prepare dosage forms. Therefore, if the hospital pharmacy is not required to register as described in paragraph one above, 21 CFR 211 does not apply. It is the policy of FDA not to routinely inspect such pharmacies for compliance with Section 501(a)(2)(B) if they operate within state or local laws governing the practice of pharmacy. However, when a hospital pharmacy is engaged in repacking or relabeling operations that are beyond the usual conduct of dispensing or selling drugs at retail, the exemptions in the Act cease to apply; the establishment is required to register and is subject to regular inspections under Section 704 of the Act.....

3. *Investigational drugs*

We do not believe that preparation of investigational drugs by a hospital pharmacy for use by an investigator in the hospital or in another hospital, requires registration under Section 510 of the Act. However, if the new drug has been or is to be shipped in interstate commerce for clinical trials, the "sponsor" of the investigation should file a "Notice of Claimed Investigational Exemption for a New Drug" before the shipment is made or the trials started. This "Notice" would necessarily include the name and address of the pharmacy and provide information regarding manufacture of the new drug by the pharmacy.....

4. *New drug applications*

We recognize that a physician may prescribe an unusual preparation that requires compounding by the pharmacy from drugs readily available for other uses and which is not generally regarded as safe and effective for the intended use. If the pharmacy merely acts to fill each individual prescription as received, it is our opinion that clearance under the "new drug" provisions of the Act is not required.

If the hospital prepares a bulk quantity of an unusual drug in anticipation of prescriptions from the physician who developed the formula, or from other physicians who have been induced to use the unusual medication, we believe the situation would then differ from the one described in the preceding paragraph. If such drug is shipped interstate or a major ingredient used in manufacturing the drug is received from an out-of-state supplier, we would regard the article as a "new drug" in interstate commerce and therefore subject to the investigational new drug regulations.

5. Prepacking

We do not believe that "prepackaging" by the hospital pharmacy for dispensing within the hospital, or for outpatient dispensing, or for transferral to another unit of the hospital, would require registration under Section 510 of the Act. However, repacking of a drug which is sold to another hospital, whether or not such other hospital is under the control of the same corporation, would require registration under Section 510.....

NOTES

1. *Judicial Support.* In *Cedars North Towers Pharmacy, Inc. v. United States,* 1978–1980 FDLI Jud. Rec. 668 (S.D. Fla. 1978), a pharmacy which prepared, packaged, and shipped to physicians throughout the country various drugs formulated by a physician, sought a declaratory judgment that these activities fell within the practice of pharmacy. The court held that the pharmacy was a drug manufacturer and that the drugs were new drugs under the FD&C Act. *See also United States v. Sene X Eleemosynary Corp., Inc.,* 479 F.Supp. 970 (S.D. Fla. 1979), *aff'd without opinion,* Food Drug Cosm. L. Rep. (CCH) ¶ 38,207 (11th Cir. 1983), rejecting a defense to an injunction action based upon the practice of pharmacy.

2. *Parenteral Nutrition.* Perhaps the most important application of the pharmacy exemption covers parenteral nutrition. FDA has long taken the position that any parenteral nutrition product is inherently a drug. *See, e.g.,* FDA Trade Correspondence 2–A (November 5, 1945); Nelson, *Amino Acid Preparations,* 1 FDC L.Q. 178 (1946). In 39 Fed. Reg. 39473 (November 7, 1974), 43 Fed. Reg. 58557 (December 15, 1978), FDA promulgated 21 C.F.R. § 310.509, which requires an NDA for any parenteral drug product in a plastic container. As part of the DESI Program, FDA reviewed the pre–1962 NDAs for parenteral nutrition products and, based upon guidelines prepared by the American Medical Association in December 1975, *see* American Medical ʼAssociation Department of Foods and Nutrition, *Multivitamin Preparations for Parenteral Use,* 3 Journal of Parenteral and Enteral Nutrition 258 (August 1979), FDA ultimately established criteria for safe and effective parenteral nutrition solutions in 37 Fed. Reg. 15027 (July 27, 1972), 37 Fed. Reg. 26623 (December 14, 1972), 44 Fed. Reg. 40933 (July 13, 1979), 47 Fed. Reg. 44022 (October 5, 1982), 48 Fed. Reg. 2835 (January 21, 1983), 49 Fed. Reg. 36446 (September 17, 1984), 50 Fed. Reg. 8193 (February 28, 1985). These standardized NDA'd nutritional solutions are shipped to a local pharmacy—usually owned by the pharmaceutical company that makes the solutions—where they are modified by adding nutrition components to meet the needs of an individual patient based upon the prescription of a physician.

3. *Compounding of Parenteral Nutrition Solutions.* As part of the practice of pharmacy, a parenteral nutrition solution may be modified to add one or more prescription drugs pursuant to the order of a physician for a particular patient. Beginning in the mid–1980s, one company undertook to perform this function in regional compounding centers rather than at local pharmacies, reasoning that this would reduce the possibility of compounding error and product contamination. However, *United States v. Baxter Healthcare Corp.,* 712 F.Supp. 1352 (N.D. Ill. 1989), *aff'd,* 901 F.2d 1401 (7th Cir. 1990), agreed that this was outside the practice of pharmacy and that, because the new drugs being added to the parenteral nutrition solutions were being used outside the approved NDAs, the practice violated the FD&C Act.

The district court pointed out that its sole role was "to apply the law, and leave policy differences to the critics."

> By their nature, written rules are not fluid. Events and technologies can outdistance them, which leads some to argue that rules—instead of bettering the lot of citizens—become downright unhelpful. Critics level probably more of these charges against the food and drug laws than they do against any other body of regulations.

FDA conducted a nationwide inspection of pharmacies manufacturing large volume parenteral solutions beginning in mid–1986 to determine that they were not exceeding the practice of pharmacy. *See* Memorandum from Center for Drugs and Biologics Consumer Safety Officer R.L. Sorensen to Regional Food and Drug Directors on Inspections of Pharmacies Manufacturing Large-Volume Parenterals, and Other Products (July 8, 1986).

4. · *Mail Order Pharmacy.* The FD&C Act does not distinguish among the various types of pharmacy practice, and thus embraces mail order pharmacy, an activity that community and hospital pharmacy organizations have gone to great efforts to discourage. *See, e.g., Federal Prescription Service, Inc., v. American Pharmaceutical Ass'n,* 663 F.2d 253 (D.C. Cir. 1981), *rev'g* 484 F.Supp. 1195 (D.D.C. 1980).

5. *Scope of Practice of Pharmacy.* In Regulatory Letter No. CHI–379–85 (June 27, 1985), FDA took the position that "compounding and dispensing prescription drug products specifically compounded on the basis of a valid prescription issued by a duly licensed practitioner for a specific patient" was within the practice of pharmacy, but that performing this function for other pharmacies falls outside the practice of pharmacy.

---

4. THE APPROVAL PROCESS FOR NEW DRUGS

a. Clinical Investigation

In order to market a new drug, a manufacturer must first obtain FDA approval of a new drug application (NDA). Before submitting an application the manufacturer must conduct, or arrange to be conducted, preclinical (animal) tests and clinical (human) studies designed to demonstrate that the drug is safe and effective under the criteria outlined in section 505(d). Usually this will require shipment of the drug in interstate commerce, *e.g.*, to researchers at medical schools across the country. But section 505(a) prohibits the shipment of any new drug for which FDA has not approved a new drug application. To enable sponsors of new drugs to carry out the testing necessary to support general marketing, Congress in section 505(i) permitted FDA to exempt a drug from this prohibition and certain other requirements of the Act for the limited purpose of conducting clinical investigations. While dispute persists over the status of some drugs marketed prior to 1962, all new chemical entities used in prescription drugs introduced in this country since that date have gone through the investigational new drug (IND) process outlined in the following materials.

THE FOOD AND DRUG ADMINISTRATION'S
PROCESS FOR APPROVING NEW DRUGS

Report of the Subcommittee on Science, Research and Technology
of the House Committee on Science and Technology
96th Congress, 2nd Session (1980).

In the U.S. the process from research to marketing approval for a new drug today, takes about 7 to 13 years and costs $30 million to $50 million. Both time and cost have increased dramatically in the last two decades. The total process to discover, develop, test and gain marketing approval for a new chemical entity (NCE) can be divided into three major stages:

		Years
1.	Preclinical research aimed at the discovery and identification of drug which is sufficiently promising to study in humans	1–4
2.	Clinical research to determine human efficacy and side effects (IND, Phases I, II, III)	4–6
3.	FDA evaluation and approval of a new drug application (NDA)	2–3
	Total	7–13

The total process is usually shorter for generic drugs and drugs which are simply a new formulation of an already approved drug. This is due mainly to shortening of the preclinical and the clinical research stages. However, the time FDA takes to review and approve a New Drug Application (NDA) does not seem to vary greatly for new chemical entities when compared with NDA review and approval requirements for new formulations or generics....

Most preclinical research takes place in industry.... With few exceptions, pharmaceutical industry research development and related decisionmaking activities involved in this process are not regulated directly by the FDA. FDA's requirements for NDA's do, however, affect the type and direction of research and other development activities which must be done once a new chemical entity is identified. The research process begins with a pharmacotherapeutic concept. The scientist must have a biological mechanism to regulate and/or a chemical lead to follow, either of which must be important to the particular target disease. Because of the resources needed, the state of the knowledge of a disease area and the probability of scientific and/or marketing success are evaluated before the research process proceeds.

Once a chemical lead is established, interesting compounds are prepared by chemists and are examined in detail by pharmacologists with sophisticated techniques in a broad range of test systems, from subcellular particles to laboratory animals. The best compounds with potential therapeutic applications are then submitted to toxicological examination which usually includes determinations of lethal doses in at least three species of animals and pathological studies for detection of organ toxicity. An estimate is made of a therapeutic ratio by comparing a presumed effective dose in a series of animal models with toxic doses in the same species.

Potentially useful compounds are considered for clinical pharmacology. This is a crucial period in the life of a new chemical entity, and only a few compounds of hundreds synthesized will be investigated in man. Decisions on which of several analogs to proceed with is extremely difficult. Judgments must be made both with regard to the estimated therapeutic index and, after consideration of a number of other factors including duration of effect, oral absorption, and cost of production.

Compounds chosen for human study must then undergo additional toxicological evaluations and pharmacokinetic studies to determine how the drug is metabolized and excreted in animals. Finally, the drug must be prepared in a form which is stable and bioavailable. Preclinical research data on the chemistry, pharmacology, and toxicology of the promising compound selected for human studies is then submitted to the FDA in a document called a "Claimed Exemption for an Investigational New Drug" (IND).

The Food, Drug and Cosmetic Act states that research on a new drug in human beings can be done only after a notice of claimed exemption for an IND (investigational new drug) has been submitted to the FDA and at least thirty days have expired without notification from the FDA that studies may not commence. The prime purpose of the IND is to protect the safety of investigational subjects while developing the data on safety of investigational subjects while developing the data on safety and effectiveness necessary to permit the marketing of the drug. A corollary responsibility of IND is to ensure the appropriateness and scientific design of studies under the IND so that the IND review process may efficiently anticipate and prevent problems which might arise in NDA review.

The considerations on which the FDA makes its decision to permit or restrict initial research include:

The protection of the human research subject.

The adequacy of animal studies already completed and analyzed.

The scientific merits of the research plan.

The qualifications of the investigator.

If the FDA does not reject the IND, and if Institutional Review Boards (IRBs) in the institutions in which the drug will be tested also approve, clinical studies in humans can begin according to three prescribed phases—Phase I, Phase II, and Phase III—as set forth in FDA regulations.

PHASE I

In this phase the clinical pharmacologist has the responsibility of administering the drug to a human volunteer for the first time. He must thoroughly review the preclinical data, and if more information is required additional pharmacological and toxicological investigations must be carried out.

After satisfactory completion of these studies, the drug is administered to a few volunteers, usually healthy subjects but also sometimes patients, in order to ascertain drug metabolism and excretion and also to estimate the potential of the drug for producing adverse effects. Drug administration begins at very low single doses and the dose is then increased very gradually. If single dose studies show no untoward effects, multiple dose studies will be initiated. Throughout all of these studies batteries of laboratory tests are also obtained. These investigations are concerned with detecting adverse effects and usually do not provide data concerning efficacy of the new drug in the disease state it is designed to treat. If adverse effects which would limit the use of the drug are found, the drug will be abandoned at this stage.

PHASE II

If there are no problems in human toleration of a drug the drug then enters phase II, and for the first time it is studied in patients with the disease which the drug is designed to treat. Relatively small numbers of patients are investigated intensively with specialized studies tailored to the type of drug and the disease to be treated. Again dosage protocols begin with single dose studies and then proceed to multiple dose studies. The objective is to determine whether the drug has the desired therapeutic effect, the dose range at which this effect occurs, and whether any adverse effects observed will limit the drug's usefulness. Lack of efficacy at this phase will result in drug abandonment. Drugs still considered to be effective and safe then enter phase III for more extensive clinical investigation.

PHASE III

In this phase hundreds and even thousands of patients are investigated. These studies take place in a clinical setting approximating the environment in which the drug will be used. Usually masked, comparative studies with placebo or a standard drug are carried out, and great care is taken to detect adverse reactions and potential interactions of the new drug with other medications. The clinical, pharmacological and toxicological data for a drug satisfactorily completing at least two adequate and well controlled phase III studies is then assembled in a New Drug Application and submitted for approval to the FDA's Bureau of Drugs. Only about one out of ten drugs for which an IND was filed will have sufficient merit to file an NDA.

NOTES

1. *Responsibility to Test.* The FD&C Act places responsibility for testing new drugs on the manufacturer who desires FDA approval for marketing.

Manufacturers in turn fund independent medical experts, most of whom are affiliated with teaching hospitals, to conduct these tests. Suspicion of manufacturer bias has prompted some critics of FDA and of the industry to advocate that responsibility for testing be removed from private hands and taken over by the government or some other independent testing institution.

2. *Consent of Test Subjects.* Section 505(i) requires that FDA's regulations shall condition the IND exemption upon assurance by the sponsor of an investigation that all investigators

> will inform any human beings to whom such drugs, or any controls used in connection therewith, are being administered, or their representatives, that such drugs are being used for investigational purposes and will obtain the consent of such human beings or their representatives, except where they deem it not feasible or, in their professional judgment, contrary to the best interests of such human beings.

Based upon this language, and the remainder of section 505(i), FDA has established an elaborate system of controls over the conduct of clinical drug investigations. The present regulations, which require written consent of test subjects in virtually all cases and the approval of a local institutional review board for any study conducted in an institutional setting, now appear at 21 C.F.R. Part 312. In 48 Fed. Reg. 26720 (June 9, 1983), 52 Fed. Reg. 8798 (March 19, 1987), FDA promulgated a comprehensive revision of the IND regulations which had been under consideration for a decade. In general, the new IND regulations codified existing practice and reorganized the old regulations to make them more easily understandable, but did little to reduce regulatory requirements or to speed up the investigation and approval of new drugs.

3. *Ambiguity of FDA Role.* There has long been controversy over FDA's role in reviewing an IND and, in particular, over whether the agency's responsibility is solely to protect the safety of human subjects or to assure that the clinical protocol is adequately designed to yield data that can support ultimate approval of an NDA. The revised IND regulations, 21 C.F.R. § 312.22(a), state:

> FDA's primary objectives in reviewing an IND are, in all phases of the investigation, to assure the safety and rights of subjects, and in Phase 2 and 3, to help assure that the quality of the scientific evaluation of drugs is adequate to permit an evaluation of the drug's effectiveness and safety.

This declaration notwithstanding, FDA reviewers often comment on the scientific adequacy of protocols for Phase I studies. Between 1980 and 1988, FDA placed between 5 and 15 percent of new commercial INDs on "clinical hold." Letter from R. Temple, M.D., Director of the Office of Drug Evaluation in the FDA Center for Drug Evaluation and Research to Dr. E. Stonehill, National Cancer Institute (September 28, 1989). In 55 Fed. Reg. 20802 (May 21, 1990), FDA proposed to expand its authority to impose clinical holds and to terminate an IND, for the stated purpose of exerting control over protocols for expanded use of investigational drugs in general and AIDS drugs in particular, *see* p. 554 *infra.*

4. *Institutional Review Boards.* Some observers have argued that Phase I studies should only require approval by a local IRB. This is the approach used for investigational studies of non-significant risk medical devices. *See* p. 756 *infra;* 21 C.F.R. § 812.2. Although it entertained this possibility in its preamble to the proposed revision of the IND regulations, 48 Fed. Reg. 26720, 26722

(June 9, 1983), FDA expressed the preliminary view that the other changes may make it unnecessary. In the preamble to the final regulations, 52 Fed. Reg. 8798, 8805–8806 (March 19, 1987), the agency concluded that the issue required additional study.

5. *Oversight of Clinical Investigators.* Because FDA has often encountered fraudulent reporting of clinical studies of investigational new drugs, the IND regulations in 21 C.F.R. § 312.70 provide for disqualification of clinical investigators. FDA has recommended criminal prosecution of several clinical investigators for violation of the False Reports to the Government Act, 18 U.S.C. § 1001. *See, e.g., United States v. Smith,* 740 F.2d 734 (9th Cir. 1984); "New Jersey Doctor Pleads Guilty to Drug Testing Fraud," FDA talk Paper No. P88–78 (October 25, 1988). The agency has also initiated prosecutions for fraudulent animal testing of new drugs. *See, e.g., United States v. Keplinger,* 776 F.2d 678 (7th Cir. 1985). In 47 Fed. Reg. 52228 (November 19, 1982), FDA published guidelines for reinstating previously disqualified clinical investigators.

6. *FDA Power to Mandate Testing.* FDA has no authority to require any person to investigate a new drug, however promising the drug may be, nor can any citizen compel FDA or the Federal government to undertake studies of a drug or to permit a drug to be made available for treatment. *See, e.g., DeVito v. HEM, Inc.,* 705 F.Supp. 1076 (M.D. Pa. 1988); *National Gay Rights Advocates v. United States Department of HHS,* Food Drug Cosm. L. Rep. (CCH) ¶ 38,080 (D.D.C. 1988); *Kulsar v. Ambach,* 598 F.Supp. 1124 (W.D.N.Y. 1984); *Marinoff v. Department of HEW,* 456 F.Supp. 1120 (S.D.N.Y. 1978). Patients are required to follow the same drug approval process as pharmaceutical companies. *Duncan v. United States,* 590 F.Supp. 39 (W.D. Okl. 1984).

7. *Protocol Guidelines.* Since enactment of the 1962 Drug Amendments, FDA has repeatedly stated that one of the major reasons for the length of time required for development and approval of new drugs has been the failure of the pharmaceutical industry and clinical investigators to utilize adequate protocols for clinical trials. The agency in the early 1970s began to develop model protocols for clinical trials for different therapeutic classes of drugs. To forestall concern that these model protocols would stifle innovation in clinical investigation, FDA issued the protocols as "guidelines." Under 21 C.F.R. § 10.90(b), an FDA guideline establishes principles or practices of general applicability that are binding only on the agency. Thus, conduct of a clinical trial in accordance with an FDA guideline assures that the results will be accepted by the agency as scientifically valid.

8. *Use of Investigational Drugs for Treatment.* Two statutory provisions authorize the use of investigational drugs for treatment purposes. Section 528 of the FD&C Act requires FDA to encourage the sponsor of an orphan drug to design "open protocols" for "persons with the disease or condition who need the drug to treat the disease or condition and who cannot be satisfactorily treated by available alternative drugs." The term "compassionate IND" is synonymous with an "open protocol." H.R. Rep. No. 97–840, 97th Cong. 2nd Sess, 11 (1982). Section 2312 of the Public Health Service Act, 42 U.S.C. § 300cc–12, provides that FDA shall encourage "an application to use the drug in the treatment of individuals" as part of the IND where "there is preliminary evidence that a new drug has effectiveness in humans with respect to the prevention or treatment of acquired immune deficiency syndrome."

9. *Government–Sponsored INDs.* The Federal government has a long history of supporting academic and industry scientists in the development of new drugs, and of licensing of new drugs to industry for commercialization. *See, e.g.,* Swann, *Biomedical Research and Government Support: The Case of Drug Development,* 31 Pharmacy In History, No. 3, at 103 (1989). The National Cancer Institute (NCI) has participated in the development of a number of important anticancer drugs. The National Technical Information Service (NTIS) of the Department of Commerce and the National Institutes of Health regularly publish notices in the Federal Register of the availability of Federal government patents on pharmaceutical products available for licensing, and of exclusive licenses subsequently granted to pharmaceutical companies to develop the drugs involved. The exclusive license for a particularly important anticancer drug was renewed, 48 Fed. Reg. 5313 (February 4, 1983), 48 Fed. Reg. 53177 (November 25, 1983) over the objections of competitors who argued that any license should be nonexclusive. NIH has made available a number of potential AIDS drugs for licensing, *e.g.,* 53 Fed. Reg. 40134 (October 13, 1988), 54 Fed. Reg. 39815 (September 28, 1989).

10. *Regulations Governing Drug Tests.* The agency proposed new regulations governing the responsibilities of sponsors and monitors of clinical investigations in 42 Fed. Reg. 49612 (September 17, 1977), and new regulations governing the obligations of clinical investigators in 43 Fed. Reg. 35210 (August 8, 1978), but they have never been promulgated in final form. A guideline for monitoring clinical investigators was made available in 53 Fed. Reg. 4723 (February 17, 1988). New regulations governing institutional review boards were promulgated in 43 Fed. Reg. 35186 (August 8, 1978), 44 Fed. Reg. 47713 (August 14, 1979), 46 Fed. Reg. 8942 (January 27, 1981), revising 21 C.F.R. Part 56. FDA also published good laboratory practice (GLP) regulations governing preclinical testing of food additives, human drugs, and animal drugs in 41 Fed. Reg. 51206 (November 19, 1976), 43 Fed. Reg. 59986 (December 22, 1978), 49 Fed. Reg. 43530 (October 29, 1984), and 52 Fed. Reg. 33768 (September 4, 1987), codified in 21 C.F.R. Part 58. In 43 Fed. Reg. 19417 (May 5, 1978), 45 Fed. Reg. 36386 (May 30, 1980) FDA issued regulations that sharply limit the use of prisoner volunteers in clinical testing of new drugs. *See generally* Kingham, *History of FDA Regulation of Clinical Research,* 22 Drug Info. J. 151 (1988).

---

b. The New Drug Application

THE FOOD AND DRUG ADMINISTRATION'S
PROCESS FOR APPROVING NEW DRUGS

Report of the Subcommittee on Science, Research and Technology
of the House Committee on Science and Technology.
96th Congress, 2nd Session (1980).

The NDA must contain all information, both favorable and unfavorable, the sponsor has obtained through investigations relating to both the safety and the effectiveness of the new drug. It must also contain information on the process by which the drug is made and how the quality of the drug will be assured. Each NDA consists of about 2 to 15 volumes of summary material accompanied by about 10 to 100 volumes (occasionally up to 400 volumes 100,000 to 200,000 pages) of raw data.

By law, the FDA has one hundred and eighty days in which to review the NDA and either approve or disapprove the application. The FDA may withhold final action on the NDA pending the compilation and submission of additional data, if the applicant agrees to the extension. The grounds for refusing to approve an application are specified in the Act and regulations. Where the FDA proposes to refuse to approve the NDA, the applicant is notified of an opportunity for a hearing on the question of whether or not the NDA is approvable. In this review, FDA determines whether the drug is safe and effective, whether the drug can be manufactured consistently and whether the benefits of the drug when used properly outweigh the risks. The FDA must also approve the description of the drug (package insert) which will be distributed to the prescribing physician before a drug can be marketed.

The time the agency takes to approve new drugs has been steadily increasing. FDA review and approval of the paper work associated with NDA's took 14 months in 1963, but has doubled since then. The agency's own estimates of average times to approve an NDA are shown on the following table (Table 1). Coupled with the increasing time and costs required to approve NDA's, it needs to be recognized that this stage in the drug approval process represents a fraction of the increasing time and costs required for other stages in the process, for example, the clinical trial stage in Phase III of the IND process.

TABLE 1

Fiscal year	NDA's approved	Average elapsed time for NDA's (months)[1]
1971	62	37.3
1972	57	25.9
1973	52	27.5
1974	85	27.3
1975	71	22.3
1976	72	20.0
Transition quarter	15	25.8
1977	91	26.3
1978	80	33.3
1979	90	35.2

[1] Elapsed time from receipt of original NDA to final approval by FDA.

NOTES

1. *NDA Regulations.* Following its success in the four Supreme Court cases in 1973, FDA planned to undertake a total revision of its IND and NDA regulations. This work was interrupted first by investigations growing out of allegations of improper FDA handling of new drug decisions during the fall of 1974, "Examination of the Pharmaceutical Industry, 1973–74," Joint Hearings Before the Subcomm. on Health of the Senate Comm. on Labor and Public Welfare and the Subcomm. on Administrative Practice and Procedure of the Senate Comm. on the Judiciary, 93rd Cong., 2nd Sess., Part 7 (1974), and later by Congressional consideration of the Drug Regulation Reform Act in 1977–1980. FDA promulgated new NDA regulations in 47 Fed. Reg. 46622 (October

19, 1982), 50 Fed. Reg. 7452 (February 22, 1985), completely revising 21 C.F.R. Part 314. Thereafter, FDA made available several guidelines on compliance with the new provisions. *See, e.g.,* 50 Fed. Reg. 26411 (June 26, 1985), 53 Fed. Reg. 39524 (October 7, 1988).

2. *NDA Filing.* An NDA is not "filed" when it is submitted to FDA. It becomes "filed" only after it has been reviewed and the agency concludes that it is complete enough to be acted on. This procedure, which dates back to 1938, was upheld in *Newport Pharmaceuticals International, Inc. v. Schweiker,* Food Drug. Cosm. L. Rep. (CCH) ¶ 38,148 (D.D.C. 1981).

3. *Data Supporting Approval.* In an unusual situation, one party to a joint venture to develop recombinant erythropoietin (EPO) for two separate indications sued the other to require that the data supporting both indications be submitted to FDA. *Ortho Pharmaceutical Corp. v. Amgen, Inc.,* 709 F.Supp. 504 (D. Del. 1989). The court granted the requested injunction, which was honored by the defendant, but the agency approved the drug for only one of the two requested indications.

4. *User Fees.* In 50 Fed. Reg. 31726 (August 6, 1985), pursuant to administration policy to raise additional funds without new taxes, FDA proposed to establish "user fees" in the amount of $126,200 for a full NDA, $16,400 for a supplemental NDA, and $9,900 for an abbreviated NDA. Since then user fees have been proposed for FDA as part of the HHS appropriations process, but Congress has consistently rejected them.

5. *Studies of NDA Process.* The new drug approval process has been the subject of dozens of studies and reports. *See* Hutt, *Investigations and Reports Respecting FDA Regulation of New Drugs,* 33 Clinical Pharmacology and Therapeutics 537 (Part I) and 674 (Part II) (1983). The early implementation of section 505 is discussed in Anderson, *The "New Drug" Section,* 1 FDC L.Q. 71 (1946); Nelson, *New Drug Requirements of the Federal Food, Drug and Cosmetic Act,* 3 FDC L.Q. 227 (1949); *Development of New Drugs,* 5 FDC L.J. 238 (1950); *Twelve Years of the New Drug Section,* 6 FDC L.J. 344 (1951); Stormont, *Application of the Federal Act to New Drugs,* 2 FDC L.Q. 490 (1947); Van Winkle, *The Safety of New Drugs,* 2 Stan. Med. Bull. 103 (August 1944); *Laboratory and Clinical Appraisal of New Drugs,* 126 J.A.M.A. 958 (December 9, 1946). *See also* the FDA testimony in "Drug Safety (Part 1)," Hearings before a Subcomm. of the House Comm. on Government Operations, 88th Cong., 2d Sess. (1964).

REGULATION OF ANTIBIOTIC DRUGS

The 1938 FD&C Act contained no provisions relating specifically to insulin or antibiotics. Congress added section 506 to provide for the certification of insulin, 55 Stat. 851 (1941), and section 507 to provide for certification of the first antibiotic drug, penicillin, in 59 Stat. 463 (1945). Thereafter, section 507 was amended to include streptomycin in 61 Stat. 11 (1947), aureomycin, chloramphenicol, and bacitracin in 63 Stat. 409 (1949), and to substitute chlortetracycline for aureomycin in 67 Stat. 389 (1953). The Drug Amendments of 1962, 76 Stat. 780, 785 amended section 705 to include all antibiotic drugs.

Because antibiotics are produced from microorganisms, individual batch certification was thought necessary to assure the identity, and thus the safety and effectiveness, of these drugs. Antibiotic drugs are subject to the same IND and NDA requirements under 21 C.F.R. Parts 312 and 314 as other new drugs.

Because of the high level of manufacturer compliance with antibiotic standards, FDA exempted all classes of antibiotic drugs from batch certification in 47 Fed. Reg. 19954 (May 7, 1982), 47 Fed. Reg. 39155 (September 7, 1982), codified in 21 C.F.R. § 433.1. *See* GAO, FDA SHOULD REDUCE EXPENSIVE ANTIBIOTIC TESTING AND CHARGE FEES WHICH MORE CLOSELY REFLECT COST OF CERTIFICATION, No. HRD–82–11 (October 28, 1981). Thus, antibiotic drugs are currently regulated in a manner that is virtually indistinguishable from nonantibiotic new drugs.

---

c. The Safety Standard

Section 505(d) specifies that the FDA shall withhold approval of a new drug unless the sponsor's evidence shows it to be safe "by all methods reasonably applicable to show whether or not such drug is safe for use under the conditions of use prescribed, recommended, or suggested" in the proposed labeling. The Act does not say how the agency shall assess safety, and FDA has never attempted to spell out in regulations the criteria that it employs. A revealing discussion of the agency's decisionmaking is the following testimony by FDA Commissioner George Larrick.

DRUG SAFETY
Hearings Before a Subcommittee of the House Committee on
Government Operations.
88th Congress 2d Session (1964).

The decisionmaking process can conveniently be regarded as a three-step operation.....

Step 1. Determine the benefit to be derived from the drug;

Step 2. Determine the risk; and

Step 3. Weigh the benefit against the risk and decide whether it is in the public interest to approve the drug for marketing or to withdraw approval if the product is already on the market....

The 1938 new drug section of the law did not require a manufacturer to prove that his new drug would yield the benefits claimed on its label. It spoke only of safety. Thus, many of the Government's decisions allowing drugs to be marketed had to be made without access to the full facts a physician would want in deciding whether to use the product....

Of course the question of benefit was an integral part of the safety question in dealing with a product to be used in a life-threatening disease such as pneumonia or in dealing with a drug presenting grave risks. We required information about effectiveness for such drugs in order to reach a decision about safety. But many fairly innocuous new drugs offered for ailments that were not life-threatening were presented to us for evaluation without evidence that they would do what the label claimed. We had no power in such case to require submission of efficacy data....

In evaluating risk we need, to the extent it is available, and in many of these areas the extent of the available science is quite deficient, information on such things as:

1. The interaction of the drug with body processes, including: hormonal, enzymic, metabolic, and reproductive processes.

2. The manner in which the drug is absorbed, distributed in body tissues, and inactivated or excreted.....

3. Whether active compounds arise from the metabolism of the drug by the body.

4. The influence of other chemicals, such as other drugs or even articles of food or drink upon the activity of the drug in question.

5. How the activity of the drug in animals compares with its activity in man....

No plan of clinical investigation, even the most expensive, can be expected to give all of the information that will be revealed by general marketing and use of a new drug.... General use involves more patients than can possibly be employed in clinical trial. Whereas the clinical trial may expose hundreds or at most thousands of people to a new product, general use may involve several million. Physicians who investigate a drug before it is marketed, even in the widespread tests just before marketing, are generally selected because of their specialized superior training and skill and because of their interest in clinical testing. After release the drug will be used by some physicians with less training, less skill, and less opportunity to make sure they are adhering to all of the suggestions in the labeling of the drug.

In fact, the early period following general marketing of a new drug must be regarded as a final step in the testing of the product. There is no way to duplicate fully in clinical trials the great variety of use conditions under which a new drug will be employed when it is finally approved....

The decision to approve a drug for marketing, or to withdraw an earlier approval requires a weighing of the benefit to be expected from use of the product against the risk inherent in its use.... The Government must make a judgment as to the hazards likely to be encountered when the drug is employed; by physicians of varying skills and abilities, in patients with a multitude of disease processes, many occurring concurrently, and in patients incorrectly diagnosed or inadequately tested with accepted laboratory procedures....

We seek to make decisions about drugs solely on the basis of scientific consideration. But over a period of time, the direction of Government's decisions will inevitably be influenced by public reaction.... The judgments of society are not necessarily consistent with scientific facts. Neither are they always logical. They can be and sometimes are arbitrary. Even so, neither the executive nor the legislative branches of government can long ignore them. If it should become the overwhelming public view that society should drastically limit the risk no matter how much good a drug can do, then we would be forced to remove from the market many drugs whose good far outweighs their harm. Carried too far, such developments would seriously impede the progress of medicine....

NOTES

1. *Approval of Drug Labeling.* See Merrill, *Compensation for Prescription Drug Injuries,* 59 Va. L. Rev. 1 (1973):

The FDA not only decides whether a drug may be marketed, it also determines how it may be promoted and sold. The agency approves, and for practical purposes prescribes, the labeling that the drug must bear. The label typically includes information concerning dosages, directions for administration, conditions for which the drug is effective, contraindications (disease conditions in which the drug may be harmful), and warnings about known or suspected side effects and adverse reactions. In this critical part of the approval process the FDA attempts to refine and articulate its initial weighing of hazards and benefits. It believes, and indeed tort law assumes, that the information conveyed by the labeling will effectively control the use of a drug and thereby limit risks and enhance benefits....

2. *Risk v. Benefit.* Professor Cavers, *The Legal Control of Clinical Investigation of Drugs: Some Political, Economic, and Social Questions,* 98 Daedalus 427 (1969), characterized the agency's analytical process as follows:

... [T]his evaluation does not call for a simple "yes" or "no" judgment. One dosage level may be safe, another questionable, but the safer dosage level may be of doubtful efficacy. A satisfactory answer may lie in between. Negotiation follows. The reports of clinical trials may include some evidence of hazard, but was the reported condition the consequence of the drug's administration or of other factors? There may have been side effects disclosed in the trials, but ought these merely to be listed as such or was their association with a given condition such as to require its listing in the labeling as a contraindication? The FDA must evaluate the sponsor's statistical work; it may have to decide whether a sponsor was justified in downgrading a side effect as "rare" or "infrequent."

3. *Procedures for Disapproval.* The most notable example of FDA disapproval of an NDA for a prescription drug on the ground of lack of safety is medroxyprogesterone acetate (Depo–Provera). FDA had already established patient package inserts for use of Depo–Provera as an injectable contraceptive in 39 Fed. Reg. 11680 (March 29, 1974), 39 Fed. Reg. 32907 (September 12, 1974), codified in 21 C.F.R. § 310.501a, in anticipation of approval of the NDA, when it learned that the drug presented a risk of cancer, 39 Fed. Reg. 38226 (October 30, 1974), 40 Fed. Reg. 12830 (March 21, 1975). In 43 Fed. Reg. 28555 (June 30, 1978), FDA published a notice of opportunity for hearing to disapprove the NDA, based on its carcinogenicity in beagle dogs. The applicant elected a hearing before a public board of inquiry 44 Fed. Reg. 44274 (July 27,

1979), which recommended in 49 Fed. Reg. 43507 (October 29, 1984) against approval of the NDA, Food Drug Cosm. L. Rep. (CCH) ¶ 39,291 (October 17, 1984). The company then withdrew its NDA in 51 Fed. Reg. 37651 (October 23, 1986). Subsequently, FDA proposed in 52 Fed. Reg. 13109 (April 21, 1987) to revoke the PPI for Depo–Provera.

---

d. The Effectiveness Standard

Section 505(d) also specifies that the FDA shall withhold approval of a new drug unless the sponsor provides "substantial evidence that the drug will have the effect it purports or as represented to have under the conditions of use prescribed, recommended, or suggested in the proposed labeling." The statute defines "substantial evidence" of effectiveness as

> evidence consisting of adequate and well-controlled investigations, including clinical investigations, by experts qualified by scientific training and experience to evaluate the effectiveness of the drug involved, on the basis of which it could fairly and responsibly be concluded by such experts that the drug will have the effect it purports or as represented to have under the conditions of use prescribed, recommended, or suggested in the labeling or proposed labeling thereof.

ADEQUATE AND WELL–CONTROLLED STUDIES
21 C.F.R. § 314.26.

(a) The purpose of conducting clinical investigations of a drug is to distinguish the effect of a drug from other influences, such as spontaneous change in the course of the disease, placebo effect, or biased observation.... Reports of adequate and well-controlled investigations provide the primary basis for determining whether there is "substantial evidence" to support the claims of effectiveness for new drugs and antibiotics. Therefore, the study report should provide sufficient details of study design, conduct, and analysis to allow critical evaluation and a determination of whether the characteristics of an adequate and well-controlled study are present.

(b) An adequate and well-controlled study has the following characteristics:

(1) There is a clear statement of the objectives of the investigation and a summary of the proposed or actual methods of analysis in the protocol for the study and in the report of its results....

(2) The study uses a design that permits a valid comparison with a control to provide a quantitative assessment of drug effect. The protocol for the study and report of results should describe the study design precisely; for example, duration of treatment periods, whether treat-

ments are parallel, sequential, or crossover, and whether the sample size is predetermined or based upon some interim analysis. Generally, the following types of control are recognized:

(i) *Placebo concurrent control.* The test drug is compared with an inactive preparation designed to resemble the test drug as far as possible....

(ii) *Dose-comparison concurrent control.* At least two doses of the drug are compared....

(iii) *No treatment concurrent control.* Where objective measurements of effectiveness are available and placebo effect is negligible, the test drug is compared with no treatment....

(iv) *Active treatment concurrent control.* The test drug is compared with known effective therapy; for example, where the condition treated is such that administration of placebo or no treatment would be contrary to the interest of the patient....

(v) *Historical control.* The results of treatment with the test drug are compared with experience historically derived from the adequately documented natural history of the disease or condition, or from the results of active treatment, in comparable patients or populations. Because historical control populations usually cannot be as well assessed with respect to pertinent variables as can concurrent control populations, historical control designs are usually reserved for special circumstances. Examples include studies of diseases with high and predictable mortality (for example, certain malignancies) and studies in which the effect of the drug is self-evident (general anesthetics, drug metabolism).

(3) The method of selection of subjects provides adequate assurance that they have the disease or condition being studied, or evidence of susceptibility and exposure to the condition against which prophylaxis is directed.

(4) The method of assigning patients to treatment and control groups minimizes bias and is intended to assure comparability of the groups with respect to pertinent variables such as age, sex, severity of disease, duration of disease, and use of drugs or therapy other than the test drug....

(5) Adequate measures are taken to minimize bias on the part of the subjects, observers, and analysts of the data....

(6) The methods of assessment of subjects' response are well-defined and reliable....

(7) There is an analysis of the results of the study adequate to assess the effects of the drug....

NOTES

1. *Meaning of Substantial Evidence.* The Senate Report on the 1962 Drug Amendments provides this description of the proof of effectiveness requirement:

When a drug has been adequately tested by qualified experts and has been found to have the effect claimed for it, this claim should be permitted even though there may be preponderant evidence to the contrary based upon equally reliable studies. There may also be a situation in which a new drug has been studied in a limited number of hospitals and clinics and its effectiveness established only to the satisfaction of a few investigators qualified to use it. There may be many physicians who deny the effectiveness simply on the basis of a disbelief growing out of their past experience with other drugs or with the diseases involved. Again the studies may show that the drug will help a substantial percentage of the patients in a given disease condition but will not be effective in other cases. What the committee intends is to permit the claim for this new drug to be made to the medical profession with a proper explanation of the basis on which it rests.

In such a delicate area of medicine, the committee wants to make sure that safe new drugs become available for use by the medical profession so long as they are supported as to effectiveness by a responsible body of opinion.

S. Rep. No. 1744, 87th Cong., 2nd Sess., Pt. 1 at 16 (1962).

2. *One or More Studies.* Section 505(d) refers to "investigations," including clinical "investigations." This raises the question whether there must be at least two clinical investigations to support approval of an NDA. The regulations FDA promulgated immediately following the 1962 Drug Amendments stated, in 28 Fed. Reg. 1449 (February 14, 1963), 28 Fed. Reg. 6377 (June 20, 1963), that "ordinarily" more than one clinical study would be required. In implementing the DESI program, however, FDA summarily withdrew approval of an NDA only where there was *no* adequate and well-controlled clinical study. In 39 Fed. Reg. 9750, 9755 (March 13, 1974), FDA declined to adopt a requirement that two, rather than just one, adequate and well-controlled clinical studies be identified in order to demonstrate a drug's effectiveness. When it revised the NDA regulations in 1985, FDA retained the provision that summary revocation of an NDA will not occur where at least one adequate and well-controlled clinical investigation has been identified, 21 C.F.R. § 314.200(g)(1). FDA officials testified that the agency has authority to approve an NDA on the basis of a single adequate and well-controlled clinical study. "Use of Advisory Committees by the Food and Drug Administration," Hearings Before a Subcomm. of the House Comm. on Government Operations, 93rd Cong., 2nd Sess. 122 (1974); "The Regulation of New Drugs by the Food and Drug Administration: The New Drug Review Process," Hearings Before a Subcomm. of the House Comm. on Government Operations, 97th Cong., 2nd Sess. 37 (1982). Nonetheless, for most NDA's FDA requires at least two adequate and well-controlled clinical studies.

3. *Clinical Testing Guidelines.* To advise manufacturers and investigators on testing protocols that will satisfy the agency's requirements for adequate and well-controlled clinical studies, FDA has issued clinical testing guidelines for several types of drugs, *e.g.*, 44 Fed. Reg. 20796 (April 6, 1979). Pursuant to 22 C.F.R. § 10.90(b), these guidelines are advisory only.

4. *Relative Efficacy.* The history of the 1962 Amendments clearly reveals Congress' intention that FDA not refuse to approve a drug on the ground of "relative efficacy," *i.e.*, that a more effective drug is available. While FDA has formally observed this mandate, it has taken other arguably inconsistent

actions. First, it has disapproved drugs on the ground of relative safety. *See, e.g.,* Ballin, *Who Makes the Therapeutic Decisions?* 242 J.A.M.A. 2875 (1979). Second, it has stated that the labeling of a less effective drug may be required to specify the drug of choice. Third, it has taken the position that, to be found "effective," a drug must be shown to have a clinically significant effect. *See* 44 Fed. Reg. 51512 (August 31, 1979).

5. *Combination Drugs.* FDA promulgated a policy on proving the effectiveness of combination prescription drugs, 21 C.F.R. § 300.50, in 36 Fed. Reg. 3126 (February 18, 1971), 36 Fed. Reg. 20037 (October 15, 1971). *See* Boggan, *The FDA's Combination Drug Policy,* 30 FDC L.J. 276 (1975).

6. *Assessing Efficacy.* For examples of the complex judgments involved in the evaluation of drug effectiveness, *see* Hood, *More on Sulfinpyrazone After Myocardial Infarction,* 306 N. Eng. J. Med. 988 (April 22, 1982), and the FDA reconsideration of the safety and effectiveness of Ilosone (erythromycin estolate) in 44 Fed. Reg. 69670 (December 4, 1979), 47 Fed. Reg. 22547 (May 25, 1982).

7. *Statistical Analysis.* To minimize bias and maximize statistical power, FDA emphasizes the use of the so-called "intent-to-treat" analysis of large clinical trials. Under this approach, all patients who are included in the control or treatment group, without exception, must be included in the ultimate analysis of the results, regardless of whether additional information reveals that they failed to follow the protocol instructions or otherwise do not represent appropriate subjects. For example, patients who are instructed to take the drug according to a specified regimen, but who fail to take it, are included in the analysis even though they obviously could not have exhibited any benefits from the drug. Accordingly, the results of an "intent-to-treat" analysis provide an average of those subjects who comply with the protocol and those who do not. Depending upon the extent of noncompliance with the protocol, the results may accurately reflect the effectiveness of the drug or may be seriously misleading. More accurate analysis can be obtained by stratifying the clinical data according to the level of patient compliance with the prescribed drug regimen. The physician package insert for Questran (cholestyramine), for example, provides information on the reduction in cholesterol in relation to the amount of the drug taken in a clinical trial, *i.e.,* the patient compliance with the drug regimen established in the protocol:

Packet Count	Total Cholesterol Lowering	Reduction in Coronary Heart Disease Risk
0–2	4.4%	10.9%
2–5	11.5%	26.1%
5–6	19.0%	39.3%

8. *Clinical Endpoints.* For drugs that are intended to treat serious and life-threatening disease, such as AIDS and cancer, an important issue is the "clinical end points" to be studied in order to determine effectiveness. The ultimate endpoint of interest is the survival of the patient. Clinical trials studying only patient survival may, however, require large numbers of subjects and take many years to complete. For that reason, researchers seek "surrogate" endpoints that will demonstrate, at a much earlier stage, whether the drug is effective. These surrogate endpoints are typically physiological param-

eters that correlate with the progress of the disease. *See, e.g.,* Wittes, *Antineo-plastic Agents and FDA Regulations: Square Pegs for Round Holes?,* 71 Cancer Treatment Reports 795 (September 1987). For some diseases, the correlation between particular physiological parameters and the disease is sufficiently well-established that they are accepted as surrogate endpoints. For example, reduction in serum cholesterol is now accepted as a surrogate endpoint to demonstrate the effectiveness of a drug in reducing the risk of coronary heart disease. For cancer and AIDS, however, there is substantial debate whether any surrogate endpoints have been sufficiently validated to permit approval of drugs for these indications without more direct evidence of their effect on morbidity and mortality.

9. *Exemptions.* The FDA regulations permit the agency to exempt a drug, in writing, from the requirement for controlled studies. One of these rare exemptions was granted by FDA for the approval of AZT for use in children with AIDS. *See* E. Cooper, *Remarks at Institute of Medicine Workshop on Drug Development for Pediatric HIV Infection and AIDS* (June 29, 1990).

---

e. Priority For Review

FDA has regularly accorded expedited consideration to applications for important new medicines. *See Providing a Breakthrough for Drugs With Promise,* 13 FDA Consumer, No. 6, at 25 (July–August 1979). In 1974, FDA formalized this logical, if not expressly authorized, practice by establishing a matrix to classify NDAs according to chemical type and therapeutic potential to determine their priority for review.

STAFF MANUAL GUIDE BD4820.3

Food and Drug Administration.

1. *PURPOSE.* This guide provides for the classification, by chemical type and therapeutic potential, of commercially sponsored INDs and NDAs. It also states FDA's policy concerning the review priorities for INDs and NDAs.

2. *BACKGROUND.* The IND/NDA classification system which appears in this section was devised to provide a convenient way of describing drug applications upon initial receipt and throughout the review process.

   This system also provides a basis for reporting the types of new drug products which are being approved or which are under review. The system will, in future years, permit retrospective searches of the files to identify trends in the new drug development and approval process. The classification assigned is a factor in determining which drugs will be submitted to advisory committee review and which will be candidates for "End of Phase II" conferences and priority review. Drugs which meet the criteria for priority review may make an early submission of NDA manufacturing and controls information.

3. IND/NDA CLASSIFICATION SYSTEM.....

b. Therapeutic Potential.

Type A—Important therapeutic gain—i.e., drug may provide effective therapy or diagnosis (by virtue of greatly increased effectiveness or safety) for a disease not adequately treated or diagnosed by any marketed drug, or provide improved treatment of a disease through improved effectiveness or safety (including decreased abuse potential).

Type B—Modest therapeutic gain—i.e., drug has a modest, but real, potential advantage over other available marketed drugs—e.g., greater patient convenience, elimination of an annoying but not dangerous adverse reaction, potential for large cost reduction, less frequent dosage schedule, useful in specific subpopulation of those with disease (e.g., those allergic to other available drugs), etc.

Type C—Little or no therapeutic gain—i.e., drug essentially duplicates in medical importance and therapeutic usage one or more already marketed drugs.

N.B. These types are mutually exclusive. Only one of these letters may be included in the overall classification number. ...

Other Information.

Type M—Drug already *marketed* in The United Kingdom, France, Germany, Italy, or Japan.

Type H—Orphan Drug

Type P—A very important feature of application is the *packaging* or container, not the drug itself.

Type R—Drug is subject to specific unique conditions of approval (e.g., additional studies) outlined in approvable or approval letter for NDA.

Type S—Application is *sensitive* by virtue of wide publicity, congressional interest, unusual request from firm, etc.

Type T—Important problem in *toxicity*—e.g., carcinogenic in animals. The toxicity problem exceeds or is unique from the drugs already approved for the same patients).

Type U—Drug is likely to be *used in children*.

N.B. These types are not mutually exclusive. All appropriate letters shall be included in the overall classification number.

4. *PRIORITY REVIEW POLICY.*

The Priority Review Policy recognizes the importance of prompt action to evaluate applications for new drugs which have the potential for important or modest therapeutic advances (A's and B's). When a reviewer is assigned an NDA with an A or B classification, review of that NDA will take precedence over an NDA that is identified as affording little or no therapeutic advance (C).... Should a reviewer receive two NDAs at the same time with different therapeutic classifications, the higher classification (i.e., A's first, C's lowest) will determine the review priority. Other work continues to be assigned while high priority NDAs are under review. A 30 day safety review for a newly submitted IND takes precedence over even a high priority NDA.....

5. *RESPONSIBILITIES AND PROCEDURES.*

  a. *Original INDs and NDAs.* The Drug Group Leader is responsible for determining the classification of each original commercially sponsored application. The Division Director is responsible for approving the classification....

  b. *IND AMENDMENTS.* The reviewing medical officer is responsible for recommending to the Group Leader changes in classification when justified on the basis of new information in IND amendments, the medical literature, advisory committee opinions, etc. The Group Leader approves or modifies the recommendation and the Division Director is responsible for approving the classification.....

NOTES

1. *Authority to Prioritize.* A priority review policy necessarily means that NDAs for drugs assigned a low classification will be reviewed more slowly than those with a higher classification, even though they may be economically important to the applicant. Section 505 makes no reference whatever to prioritizing NDAs for review; it does specify that FDA is to reach a final decision on any NDA within 180 days, a schedule the agency very rarely meets even for drugs of great therapeutic promise.

2. *Challenge to FDA Priorities.* FDA did not establish this priority classification system by public rulemaking, and the agency has not provided a procedure by which an applicant may dispute its initial classification of a drug. Nor has any applicant contested FDA's classification of its NDA or the agency's review in accordance with its priority classification.

---

f. FDA Approval or Denial

Section 505 does not require FDA to explain its approval of an NDA. In its Public Information Regulations, 39 Fed. Reg. 44602, 44635-36 (December 24, 1974), however, FDA announced that, beginning in July 1975, it would release a summary of the basis of approval (SBA) for every NDA rather than disclose internal agency memoranda prepared in the course of reaching its decision.

Only one FDA decision to *approve* a drug has been challenged in the courts. When FDA approved an NDA for an OTC version of ibuprofen, two competitors of the applicant challenged this action, *see* note 5, p. 417 *supra.* Neither was successful.

Perhaps surprisingly, court challenges to decisions denying approval are also rare. Manufacturers who anticipate denial almost invariably seek instead to persuade the agency to change its mind, realizing that recourse to judicial review of an adverse determination is likely to be futile.

UBIOTICA CORP. v. FDA

United States Court of Appeals, Sixth Circuit, 1970.
427 F.2d 376.

COMBS, Circuit Judge.

Petitioner originally filed its new drug application and claim for investigational exemption in June, 1963. The new drug is proposed for treatment of mongolism.....

In November, 1963, the Commissioner notified petitioner that, since certain conditions had not been met, the investigational exemption allowing clinical testing of the drug was terminated. Petitioner unsuccessfully sought to enjoin and vacate this order in *Turkel v. Food and Drug Administration,* 334 F.2d 844 (6th Cir. 1964). We held there that 21 U.S.C. § 355(h) does not permit review of the withdrawal of an investigational exemption except on appeal from a subsequent order of the Secretary refusing to approve a new drug application. However, prior to our decision in *Turkel,* petitioner withdrew the new drug application which it had submitted in June, 1963.

Then, in June, 1966 petitioner submitted a second new drug application which was designated as supplemental to the previously withdrawn new drug application. After extended correspondence, petitioner was notified that the Commissioner proposed to issue an order refusing approval of the new drug application. A hearing was held, and subsequently the order was issued which is the subject of this appeal. The record before us consists of numerous exhibits and in excess of 6,000 pages of transcript. On this appeal we are asked to review the Commissioner's action in refusing to approve the new drug application and also in terminating petitioner's investigational exemption....

In enacting section 355, Congress clearly placed on the applicant the burden of establishing that the drug proposed to be distributed in interstate commerce is both safe and effective for the intended use. Here, the hearing examiner properly phrased the issues in terms of the statutory grounds for rejection set forth in section 355(d), and the Government came forward with proof as to why petitioner had not satisfied the burden of proof required of a new drug applicant under section 355. The Commissioner adopted the findings of the hearing examiner and concluded that the new drug application should not be approved in that it was deficient in each of the five respects enumerated above under section 355(d). The question here is whether those findings are supported by substantial evidence. We conclude that they are and that the Commissioner properly refused to approve the new drug application....

... Relying on ... *Turkel,* the hearing examiner divided the subsequent hearing into two phases—one phase was devoted to a consideration of the refusal to approve the new drug application and the other to the termination of the investigational exemption. Following the hearing, the examiner concluded that the exemption had been properly terminated.

Our examination of the record convinces us that on the basis of the material submitted in 1963 in support of the claimed exemption, the Commissioner did not act arbitrarily in terminating the investigational exemption....

NOTES

1. *Exhaustion of FDA Procedures.* The ruling in *Turkel v. FDA,* reaffirmed in the principal case, that the sponsor of a clinical investigation whose IND is terminated may only obtain judicial review of that action by filing an NDA and seeking review of FDA's subsequent denial of approval seems questionable. Recent "exhaustion" cases suggest that it would not be followed today. *See Rosado v. Wyman,* 397 U.S. 397 (1970); *Leedom v. Kyne,* 358 U.S. 184 (1958); *Elmo Division of Drive-X Co. v. Dixon,* 348 F.2d 342 (D.C. Cir. 1965). *See also AMP Inc. v. Gardner,* 275 F.Supp. 410 (S.D.N.Y. 1967), *aff'd,* 389 F.2d 825 (2d Cir.1968).

2. *Judicial Review of FDA Decisions.* The perfunctory judicial scrutiny of FDA's denial of Ubiotica's NDA is paralleled in one of the two other court challenges to FDA's refusal to approve a drug. *See Unimed, Inc. v. Richardson,* 458 F.2d 787 (D.C. Cir. 1972), in which the court's full opinion, after describing the applicant's argument, consisted of the following paragraph:

> We have examined the record of the administrative hearing on this point with care, particularly with a view to grasping as best we can the nature of the divergences between the differing expert witnesses. Although the matter seems to us one not entirely free from doubt, we remind ourselves that our role in the Congressional scheme is not to give an independent judgment of our own, but rather to determine whether the expert agency entrusted with regulatory responsibility has taken an irrational or arbitrary view of the evidence assembled before it. We are unable to say that it has; and, accordingly, the petition for review is denied.

The third court challenge to FDA's refusal to approve a drug has a unique history. A physician, Dr. Murray Israel, developed an injectable drug, Cothyrobal, for hypercholesterolemia and hypothyroidism. Frustrated by the agency's skeptical and desultory handing of his NDA, he unsuccessfully sued the agency and a competitor, alleging a conspiracy to keep the drug off the market. *Israel v. Baxter Laboratories, Inc.,* 466 F.2d 272 (D.C. Cir. 1972). Following FDA's eventual denial of approval and its refusal to grant an administrative hearing, the court set aside the agency's decision and ordered it to hold an evidentiary hearing on the issue, *Edison Pharmaceutical Co., Inc. v. FDA,* 513 F.2d 1063 (D.C.Cir.1975), *rehearing en banc denied,* 517 F.2d 164. The agency's ultimate denial of the NDA, following the hearing, was upheld. *Edison Pharmaceutical Co., Inc. v. FDA,* 600 F.2d 831 (D.C. Cir. 1979).

Accordingly, judicial review of the new drug approval process has been not only casual, but infrequent. No sponsor has successfully sought reversal of an FDA refusal to approve its drug. The lesson has not been lost on the vast majority of applicants who understand that the only way to secure approval of an NDA is to satisfy the agency.

Challenges to FDA's final decisions under sections 505(d) and (e) must be filed in the court of appeals for the appropriate circuit. A district court thus lacks jurisdiction to order FDA to approve an NDA, but may entertain a case seeking to force FDA to rule on an NDA within a specified period of time. *IMS Limited v. Schweiker,* Food Drug Cosm. L. Rep. (CCH) ¶ 38, 104 (C.D. Cal. 1981).

3. *Grounds for Disapproval.* A 1980 FDA analysis of NDA approvals during the 1970s produced the surprising findings that 61 percent of the deficiencies cited in nonapproval letters during 1977 and 1978 related to the chemistry and manufacturing portions of the NDA, and that nearly 90 percent of such letters identified such deficiencies. Only 22 percent of the deficiencies related to the applicant's evidence of safety and effectiveness. Cook, *et al.,* APPROVALS AND NONAPPROVALS OF NEW DRUG APPLICATIONS DURING THE 1970s, FDA OPE Study No. 57 (December 1980). A 1988 FDA report examined the fate of 174 new chemical entity (NCE) drugs for which INDs were filed during 1976–1978. Nine percent had been discontinued before the commencement of Phase I studies; 20 percent had been discontinued during Phase I studies; 39 percent during Phase II studies; and 5 percent during Phase III studies. Twenty-seven percent had become the subject of a submitted NDA, of which nearly all—85 percent—ultimately gained approval. Tucker *et al.,* THE OUTCOME OF RESEARCH ON NEW MOLECULAR ENTITIES COMMENCING CLINICAL RESEARCH IN THE YEARS 1976–1978, FDA OPE Study No. 77 (May 1988).

4. *Radioactive Drugs.* Radioactive drugs have received distinctive treatment. Few of these drugs have been the subject of NDAs, and therefore it is not feasible to regulate all radioactive-tagged drugs through the new drug process. FDA has established an old drug monograph approach, 21 C.F.R. part 361, in cooperation with the Nuclear Regulatory Commission. *See* 37 Fed. Reg. 21026 (November 3, 1971), 39 Fed. Reg. 26143 (July 17, 1974), 39 Fed. Reg. 27538 (July 29, 1974), 40 Fed. Reg. 31298 (July 25, 1975), 41 Fed. Reg. 7747 (February 20, 1976), 41 Fed. Reg. 35171 (August 20, 1976), 41 Fed. Reg. 42947 (September 29, 1976), 42 Fed. Reg. 23161 (May 6, 1977), 43 Fed. Reg. 11208 (March 17, 1978), 44 Fed. Reg. 8242 (February 9, 1979), 45 Fed. Reg. 24920 (April 11, 1980), 46 Fed. Reg. 46403 (September 18, 1981), 49 Fed. Reg. 24949 (June 18, 1984). The NRC regulations governing licensing of individuals and institutions for medical use of radioactive material were overhauled in 50 Fed. Reg. 30616 (July 26, 1985), 51 Fed. Reg. 36932 (October 16, 1986), and are codified in 10 C.F.R. Part 35. The NRC has established training and experience criteria for physicians who request authorization to engage in nuclear medicine, 47 Fed. Reg. 3228 (January 22, 1982), 47 Fed. Reg. 54376 (December 2, 1982).

5. *NDA's Invited by FDA.* On rare occasions FDA has formally announced that it would approve NDAs for particular drugs if and when they were submitted. In 38 Fed. Reg. 26809 (September 26, 1973), 40 Fed. Reg. 5351 (February 5, 1975), FDA published a regulation, codified in 21 C.F.R. § 310.501(b), stating that NDAs would be approved for diethylstilbestrol (DES) as a postcoital contraceptive. FDA had hoped that this announcement would induce DES manufacturers to add postcoital contraception as an approved indication, but the plausible fear of liability has deterred every potential applicant. DES products approved for other uses thus continue to be prescribed for this still unapproved use as well. More recently FDA announced that it had approved two NDAs for potassium iodide as a thyroid-blocking agent for use in radiation emergencies, 45 Fed. Reg. 11912 (February 22, 1980). These NDAs were received after the agency, 43 Fed. Reg. 58798 (December 15, 1978), had invited manufacturers to seek approval as part of an emergency preparedness program for possible accidents at nuclear facilities. The agency announced the availability of draft recommendations for administering potassium iodide to the general public in a radiation emergency in 46 Fed. Reg. 30199 (June 5, 1981), 47 Fed. Reg. 28158 (June 29, 1982).

6. *FDA Control Over Packaging.* FDA control over the safety and effectiveness of a new drug extends to the packaging as well. *See* 49 Fed. Reg. 4040 (February 1, 1984), announcing the availability of a draft guideline on the documentation needed in an NDA to support the safety of drug packaging.

7. *Supplemental NDAs.* Once an NDA has been approved, 21 C.F.R. § 314.70 requires that a supplemental NDA be submitted and approved for each change in any condition established in the approved NDA, with limited exceptions. Because supplemental NDAs have a lower priority than original NDAs, the agency usually has a substantial backlog of such applications. Even minor changes in manufacturing procedures may be delayed for years until the agency approves a supplemental NDA authorizing their implementation.

8. *Publicity about NDA Approvals.* Section 301(*l*) of the FD&C Act prohibits any representation that FDA has approved an NDA for a drug. Despite plausible arguments that this provision is an anachronism, repeated attempts to repeal it have failed. *See, e.g.,* H.R. Rep. No. 98–431, 98th Cong., 1st Sess. (1983), H.R. Rep. No. 99–143, 99th Cong, 1st Sess. (1985).

9. *FDA Alert List.* Any drug establishment found by FDA inspection not to be in compliance with GMP regulations is placed by the agency on an "alert list." It is standard FDA procedure not to approve any NDA or ANDA of any firm which is on the alert list. FDA's immediate withdrawal of an ANDA it had approved on the same day an inspection resulted in placing the company on the alert list, was upheld in *American Therapeutics, Inc. v. Sullivan,* Food Drug Cosm. L. Rep. (CCH) ¶ 38,159 (D.D.C. 1990).

PRESCRIPTION DRUG CONTROLLED SUBSTANCES

Prior to 1970, Federal control of narcotic drugs, marijuana, and other drugs used for recreational and nonmedical purposes was shared among several agencies and rested on a haphazard cluster of laws enacted since 1900. For example, FDA was responsible for enforcement of the Drug Abuse Control Amendments of 1965, 79 Stat. 226, to prevent abuse of depressant and stimulant drugs, such as the amphetamines and barbiturates, which also have legitimate medical use. In 1970, Congress repealed the earlier statutes and enacted a new comprehensive law, the Controlled Substances Act, 84 Stat. 1236,

1242, codified in 21 U.S.C. § 801 *et seq.* Responsibility for enforcement of the Controlled Substances Act rests with the Drug Enforcement Administration (DEA) of the Department of Justice, which has the obligation to consult with FDA on the scheduling of controlled substances. FDA's recommendations are binding on scientific and medical matters, and DEA may not schedule a drug if FDA recommends against it.

The Controlled Substances Act establishes five schedules of controlled substances, which can be summarized as follows: Schedule I includes drugs with a high potential for abuse that have no currently accepted medical use (*e.g.*, heroin). Schedule II includes drugs with a high potential for abuse with a currently accepted medical use. Schedule III includes drugs with a moderate potential for abuse and accepted medical use. Schedule IV includes substances with a low potential for abuse and accepted medical use. Schedule V includes substances with the lowest potential for abuse and currently accepted medical use.

The Act bans domestic distribution of all Schedule I drugs. The controls used to regulate drugs on Schedules II–V are calibrated to the degree of danger. Because the controls over scheduled drugs increase with the schedule to which they are assigned, scheduling decisions are of major important to the pharmaceutical industry. *See, e.g., Grinspoon v. DEA,* 828 F.2d 881 (1st Cir. 1987); *Reckitt & Colman, Ltd. v. DEA,* 788 F.2d 22 (D.C. Cir. 1986); *Hoffmann-La Roche, Inc. v. Kleindienst,* 478 F.2d 1 (3d Cir. 1973); *United States v. Hovey,* 674 F. Supp. 161 (D. Del. 1987). DEA may also establish production quotas for Schedule I and Schedule II drugs. *Western Fher Laboratories v. Levi,* 529 F.2d 325 (1st Cir. 1976). Nonetheless, although, the requirements established under the Controlled Substances Act may impose extra burdens upon manufacturers, physicians, and pharmacists, they do not prevent FDA from approving an NDA for any controlled substance that has a legitimate medical use.

The efforts of the National Organization for the Reform of Marijuana Laws (NORML) are reflected in more than 15 years of administrative and judicial consideration of the appropriate scheduling of tetrahydrocannabinol (THC), the principal active ingredient in marijuana. DEA denied the first NORML petition to move marijuana from Schedule I to Schedule II in 37 Fed. Reg. 10897 (September 1, 1972), but the matter was remanded for an administrative hearing in *NORML v. Ingersoll,* 497 F.2d 654 (D.C. Cir. 1974). After a hearing, DEA again denied the NORML petition, 40 Fed. Reg. 44164 (September 25, 1975), but the court remanded the matter once more with instructions to refer the petition to the Secretary of HHS for medical and scientific evaluation, *NORML v. DEA,* 559 F.2d 735 (D.C. Cir. 1977). After receiving FDA's evaluation and recommendations through HHS, DEA again denied the NORMAL petition in 44 Fed. Reg. 36123 (June 20, 1979). And again the court disagreed, remanding with directions that FDA take into account new evidence concerning medical use of THC. *NORML v. DEA,* No. 79–1660 (D.C. Cir., October 16, 1980). In 47 Fed. Reg. 10080 (March 9, 1982), FDA recommended to the Department of HHS that THC remain in Schedule I until an NDA for THC was approved for medical purposes. In May 1985, FDA approved an NDA for a drug containing synthetic THC. In 51 Fed. Reg. 17476 (May 13, 1986), DEA classified this formulation in Schedule II. DEA then announced hearings on the NORML petition to reschedule marijuana in 51 Fed. Reg. 22946 (June 24, 1986). An administrative law judge recommended that marijuana be rescheduled from Schedule I to Schedule II, but the Administrator of DEA rejected this recommendation and denied the NORML petition in 54 Fed. Reg. 53767 (December

29, 1989). A previous constitutional challenge to the classification of marijuana in Schedule I failed, *NORML v. Bell*, 488 F.Supp. 123 (D.D.C. 1980); *Hartz v. Bensinger*, 461 F.Supp. 431 (E.D. Pa. 1978). *See also Productos Medix, S.A. v. U.S. Treasury Dept.*, Food Drug Cosm. L. Rep. (CCH) ¶ 38,131 (S.D. Tex. 1989), *aff'd*, 915 F.2d 1567 (5th Cir. 1990).

The use of otherwise banned Schedule I controlled substances as part of a religious ceremony has also provoked litigation. The plaintiff in *Peyote Way Church of God, Inc. v. Smith*, 556 F.Supp. 632 (N.D. Tex. 1983), 742 F.2d 193 (5th Cir. 1984), 698 F.Supp. 1342 (N.D. Tex. 1988), has thus far been unsuccessful in gaining permission to use peyote in its ceremonies despite its claims of discrimination because the Native American Church has obtained permission to use the drug. *See also Oregon Dept. of Human Resources v. Smith*, ___ U.S. ___, 110 S.Ct. 1595 (1990) (state is not barred by the First Amendment from prohibiting sacramental use of peyote); *Olsen v. DEA*, 878 F.2d 1458 (D.C. Cir. 1989) (rejecting a religious use exemption for marijuana).

----

g. Postapproval Requirements

Section 505(k) requires the holder of an NDA to establish and maintain such records, and make such reports, as FDA may require by general regulation or by specific order. Pursuant to this authority, FDA regulations require prompt reports of serious adverse reactions, 21 C.F.R. § 314.80, and periodic reports of all information relating to a drug's safety and effectiveness, 21 C.F.R. § 314.81.

NANCY MATTISON AND BARBARA W. RICHARD,
POSTAPPROVAL RESEARCH REQUESTED BY THE FDA AT
THE TIME OF NCE APPROVAL, 1970–1984

21 Drug Information Journal 309 (1987).

In 1970 the Food and Drug Administration for the first time granted marketing approval for a new drug on the condition that the sponsoring companies perform specific research after approval. The drug, levodopa, is indicated for treatment of Parkinson's disease. Although the agency was satisfied that clinical trials had proved the drug safe and effective, there was concern about the long-term effects of the drug in chronic use. At the same time, the FDA was reluctant to hold up approval of a drug it considered to be "one of the major drug discoveries of recent years" and one that could benefit up to a million Americans. As a compromise, FDA required that long-term studies be done after approval, thereby allowing the drug to be marketed 2 to 3 years earlier than would have been possible otherwise.

Between 1970 and 1984, the FDA requested postapproval research at the time of approval (PAR) for more than 50 new drugs. This research has been of two types: large postmarketing surveillance (PMS) studies and smaller postapproval research studies similar in design and focus to those performed as part of the preapproval drug development process.....

The FDA's authority to require research at or after approval is not stated unequivocally in the Food, Drug and Cosmetic Act (or its amendments). Beginning with levodopa, the agency has based its actions on section 505(e) and 505(k) of the law, which empower the Secretary ... to require the records and reports necessary after approval of a ... NDA to determine whether approval should be withdrawn. In response, it has been argued that these provisions were intended to apply only to data collected in the normal course of business and cannot be extended to cover special studies.

In some cases, the agency has officially stated its intention to require special studies, citing 505(e) and (k). It did so in a 1972 regulation providing for postapproval studies of drugs for chronic use. In 1977 the FDA announced that special studies would be required for inhalation anesthetics already approved. However, with the exception of two sets of studies for chronic use (levodopa and methadone), the FDA has not officially justified requiring PAR as a condition of approval.

Given this somewhat tenuous legal basis, the operation of this PAR system depends primarily on the voluntary cooperation of the sponsoring company.... However, this may suggest more willing compliance by the industry than is in fact the case. According to representatives of the industry, firms generally agree to PAR as an expediency—failure to do so, they believe, would result in long delays in approving the drug.

FDA considers the information collected by PAR to be an integral part of the data necessary to the proper use of a drug, but not essential to approval. The studies would be required as part of the NDA, however, if the alternative of requiring PAR was not available.... The particular PAR studies required depend on a variety of factors. Some are intended to deal with changes in policy without the delay that would be entailed by requiring additional preapproval studies. For example, when FDA increased its approval requirement from one to two carcinogenicity tests, it allowed the second test to be performed after approval for drugs that were close to approval.

The interests of individual reviewers and other FDA officials are also reflected in the PAR request. This is true of the studies in children that were required in the 1970s and of more recent studies refining dose information. The interests of FDA personnel, however, are not necessarily idiosyncratic; they often reflect the concerns of the wider medical scientific community.

Other PAR studies may be required because the agency or the firms overlooked the need for them earlier in the development process. The recently issued clinical guidelines are expected to minimize such omissions by offering a comprehensive checklist of studies to be done on each new drug.

Even with the new clinical guidelines, firms will not be able to predict with certainty what PAR may be required or whether a trade-off between PAR and earlier approval is possible. Decisions are made by the individual medical reviewers (or the division director) on a case-by-case basis. No written policy statement or guidelines exist or are contemplated.....

NOTES

1. *Commentary.* See also Richard *et al., Postapproval Research as a Condition of Approval: An Update, 1985–1986,* 3 J. Clin. Res. & Drug Dev. 247 (1989).

2. *FDA Regulations.* FDA issued general regulations governing post-marketing research in 35 Fed. Reg. 14784 (September 23, 1970), 37 Fed. Reg. 201 (January 7, 1972), codified in 21 C.F.R. § 310.303. The regulation prescribing postapproval studies of levodopa was issued at the same time but later repealed in 40 Fed. Reg. 54252 (November 21, 1975), 41 Fed. Reg. 9546 (March 5, 1976). FDA also established postapproval research requirements for methadone, which remain in 21 C.F.R. § 310.304(b). Since 1976 the agency has not used the procedure established in § 310.303.

3. *Postmarketing Toxicological Testing.* Whether to demand additional animal testing for a marketed drug is often a difficult scientific question. In 41 Fed. Reg. 14888 (April 8, 1976), 42 Fed. Reg. 37538 (July 22, 1977), FDA required additional animal studies on the potential of inhalation anesthetic drugs to cause cancer and reproductive toxicity. In response to a petition from the affected drug manufacturers, FDA stayed, 44 Fed. Reg. 11753 (March 2, 1979), and later revoked, the regulation. 46 Fed. Reg. 43465 (August 28, 1981), 47 Fed. Reg. 49014 (October 29, 1982).

h. Withdrawal of Marketing Approval

WEINBERGER v. HYNSON, WESTCOTT & DUNNING, INC.

Supreme Court of the United States, 1973.
412 U.S. 609.

Mr. Justice DOUGLAS delivered the opinion of the Court.

... Hynson, Westcott & Dunning, Inc., had filed an application under the 1938 Act for a drug called Lutrexin, recommended by Hynson for use in the treatment of premature labor, threatened and habitual abortion, and dysmenorrhea. FDA informed Hynson that Hynson's studies submitted with the application were not sufficiently well controlled to justify the claims of effectiveness and urged Hynson not to represent the drug as useful for threatened and habitual abortion. But FDA allowed the application to become effective, since the 1938 Act permitted evaluation of a new drug solely on the grounds of its *safety.* ... When the 1962 amendments became effective and NAS–NRC undertook to appraise the efficacy of drugs theretofore approved as safe, Hynson submitted a list of literature references, a copy of an unpublished study, and a representative sample testimonial letter on behalf of Lutrexin. The panel of NAS–NRC working in the relevant field reported to FDA that Hynson's claims for effectiveness of the drug were either inappropriate or unwarranted in the absence of submission of further appropriate documentation. At the invitation of the Commissioner of Food and Drugs, Hynson submitted additional data. But the Commissioner concluded that this additional information was inadequate and published notice of his intention to withdraw approval of the NDA's covering the drug, offering Hynson the opportunity for a prewithdrawal hearing [in accordance with section 505(e) of the Act]. Before the hearing could take place, Hynson brought suit in the District Court for a declaratory judgment that the drugs in question were exempt from the *efficacy* review provisions of the 1962 amendments or, alternatively, that there was no lack of substantial evidence of the drug's *efficacy*. The Government's motion to dismiss was granted, the District Court ruling that FDA had primary jurisdiction and that Hynson had failed to exhaust its administrative remedies.

While the District Court litigation was pending, FDA promulgated new regulations establishing minimal standards for "adequate and well-controlled investigations" and limiting the right to a hearing to those applicants who could proffer at least some evidence meeting those standards. Although Hynson maintained that it was not subject to the new regulations because its initial request for a hearing predated their issuance, it renewed its request and submitted the material which it claimed constituted "substantial evidence" of Lutrexin's effectiveness. The Commissioner denied the request for a hearing and withdrew the NDA for Lutrexin. He ruled that Lutrexin is not exempt from the 1962 amendments and that Hynson had not submitted adequate evidence that Lutrexin is not a new drug or is effective. The Court of Appeals reversed, holding that while the drug in question was not exempt, Hynson was entitled to a hearing on the substantial-evidence question.

Section 505(e) directs FDA to withdraw approval of an NDA if the manufacturer fails to carry the burden of showing there is "substantial evidence" respecting the *efficacy* of the drug.... The Act and the Regulations, in their reduction of that standard to detailed guidelines, make FDA's so-called administrative summary judgment procedure appropriate.

The general contours of "substantial evidence" are defined by § 505(d) of the Act to include "evidence consisting of adequate and well-controlled investigations, including clinical investigations, by experts qualified by scientific training and experience to evaluate the effectiveness of the drug involved, on the basis of which it could fairly and responsibly be concluded by such experts that the drug will have the effect it purports or is represented to have under the conditions of use prescribed, recommended, or suggested in the labeling or proposed labeling thereof." Acting pursuant to his "authority to promulgate regulations for the efficient enforcement" of the Act, § 701(a), the Commissioner has detailed the "principles ... recognized by the scientific community as the essentials of adequate and well-controlled clini-

cal investigations. They provide the basis for the determination whether there is 'substantial evidence' to support the claims of effectiveness
for 'new drugs'...." 21 CFR § 130.12(a)(5)(ii) [now
§ 314.111(a)(5)(ii)].... [T]he regulation provides that "[u]ncontrolled
studies or partially controlled studies are not acceptable as the sole
basis for the approval of claims of effectiveness. Such studies, carefully
conducted and documented, may provide corroborative support....
Isolated case reports, random experience, and reports lacking the
details which permit scientific evaluation will not be considered."

    ... [I]t is not disputed here that [these regulations] express well-es-
tablished principles of scientific investigation. Moreover, their strict
and demanding standards, barring anecdotal evidence indicating that
doctors "believe" in the efficacy of a drug, are amply justified by the
legislative history....

    To be sure, the Act requires FDA to give "due notice and opportuni-
ty for hearing to the applicant" before it can withdraw its approval of
an NDA. FDA, however, by regulation, requires any applicant who
desires a hearing to submit reasons "why the application ... should not
be withdrawn, together with a well-organized and full-factual analysis
of the clinical and other investigational data he is prepared to prove in
support of his opposition to the notice of opportunity for a hearing....
When it clearly appears from the data in the application and from the
reasons and factual analysis in the request for the hearing that there is
no genuine and substantial issue of fact ..., e.g., no adequate and
well-controlled clinical investigations to support the claims of effectiveness," the Commissioner may deny a hearing and enter an order
withdrawing the application based solely on these data. What the
agency has said, then, is that it will not provide a formal hearing where
it is apparent at the threshold that the applicant has not tendered *any*
evidence which *on its face* meets the statutory standards as particular-
ized by the regulations.

    The propriety of such a procedure was decided in *United States v.
Storer Broadcasting Co.*, 351 U.S. 192, and *FPC v. Texaco, Inc.*, 377 U.S.
33. We said in *Texaco:*

    "[T]he statutory requirement for a hearing under § 7 [of the
    Natural Gas Act] does not preclude the Commission from
    particularizing statutory standards through the rulemaking
    process and barring at the threshold those who neither mea-
    sure up to them nor show reasons why in the public interest
    the rule should be waived."

There can be no question that to prevail at a hearing an applicant must
furnish evidence stemming from "adequate and well-controlled investigations." We cannot impute to Congress the design of requiring, nor
does due process demand, a hearing when it appears conclusively from
the applicant's "pleadings" that the application cannot succeed.[17] ...

17. This applies, of course, only to those   regulations that are precise. For example,

Our conclusion that the summary judgment procedure of FDA is valid does not end the matter, for Hynson argues that its submission to FDA satisfied its threshold burden. In reviewing an order of the Commissioner denying a hearing, a court of appeals must determine whether the Commissioner's findings accurately reflect the study in question and if they do, whether the deficiencies he finds conclusively render the study inadequate or uncontrolled in light of the pertinent regulations. There is a contrariety of opinion within the Court concerning the adequacy of Hynson's submission. Since a majority are of the view that the submission was sufficient to warrant a hearing, we affirm the Court of Appeal on that phase of the case....

Regulatory agencies have by the requirements of particular statutes usually proceeded on a case-by-case basis, giving each person subject to regulation separate hearings. But there is not always a constitutional reason why that must be done.... The comprehensive, rather than the individual, treatment may indeed be necessary for quick effective relief. A generic drug—which is found to be unsafe and/or lacking in efficacy—may be manufactured by several persons or manufacturers. To require separate judicial proceedings to be brought against each, as if each were the owner of a Black Acre being condemned, would be to create delay where in the interests of public health there should be prompt action. A single administrative proceeding in which each manufacturer may be heard is constitutionally permissible measured by the requirements of procedural due process....

[FDA's] determination that a product is a "new drug" or a "me-too" drug is, of course, reviewable. But its jurisdiction to determine whether it has jurisdiction is as essential to its effective operation as is a court's like power....

The question then presented is whether FDA properly exercised its jurisdiction in this instance.... Finding that Hynson had failed to present any evidence of adequate and well-controlled investigations in support of Lutrexin's effectiveness, [the Commissioner] concluded that "there is no data based upon which experts can fairly and responsibly conclude that the safety and effectiveness of the drugs has been proven and is so well established that the drugs can be generally recognized among such experts as safe and effective for their intended uses." The

the plan or protocol for a study must include "[a] summary of the methods of analysis and an evaluation of data derived from the study, including any appropriate statistical methods." 21 CFR § 130.12(a) [314.111(a)(5)(ii)(a)(5)]. A mere reading of the study submitted will indicate whether the study is totally deficient in this regard. Some of the regulations, however, are not precise, as they call for the exercise of discretion or subjective judgment in determining whether a study is adequate and well-controlled. For example, § 130.12(a) [314.111(a)(5)(ii)(a)(2)(i)] requires that the plan or protocol for the study include a method of selection of the subjects that provide [sic] "*adequate* assurance that they are suitable for the purposes of the study." (Emphasis added.) The qualitative standards "adequate" and "suitable" do not lend themselves to clear-cut definition, and it may not be possible to tell from the face of a study whether the standards have been met. Thus, it might not be proper to deny a hearing on the ground that the study did not comply with this regulation.

Commissioner also held that Lutrexin is not exempt under § 107(c)(4) because its NDA, which had become effective in 1953, had not been withdrawn prior to the enactment of the 1962 amendments and thus was "covered by an effective application" within the meaning of § 107(c)(4)(C).... Although we agree that the Commissioner properly ruled that Lutrexin does not come within § 107(c)(4), we conclude that the Commissioner's order with respect to Lutrexin's "new drug" status must be vacated.

The thrust of § 201(p) is both qualitative and quantitative. The Act, however, nowhere defines what constitutes "general recognition" among experts. Hynson contends that the "lack of substantial evidence" is applicable only to proof of the *actual* effectiveness of drugs that fall within the definition of a new drug and not to the initial determination under § 201(p) whether a drug is "generally recognized" as effective. It would rely solely on the testimony of physicians and the extant literature, evidence that has been characterized as "anecdotal." We agree with FDA, however, that the statutory scheme and overriding purpose of the 1962 amendments compel the conclusion that the hurdle of "general recognition" of effectiveness requires at least "substantial evidence" of effectiveness for approval of an NDA....

Moreover, the interpretation of § 201(p) urged by Hynson is not consistent with the statutory scheme as it operates on a purely prospective basis. Under subsection (2), a drug cannot transcend "new drug" status until it has been used "to a material extent or for a material time." Yet, a drug cannot be marketed lawfully before an NDA has been approved by the Commissioner on the basis of "substantial evidence." As the Solicitor General argues, "the Act is designed so that drugs on the market, unless exempt, will have mustered the requisite scientifically reliable evidence of effectiveness long before they are in a position to drop out of active regulation by ceasing to be a 'new drug.'"

It is well established that our task in interpreting separate provisions of a single Act is to give the Act "the most harmonious, comprehensive meaning possible" in light of the legislative policy and purpose. We accordingly have concluded that a drug can be "generally recognized" by experts as effective for intended use within the meaning of the Act only when that expert consensus is founded upon "substantial evidence" as defined in § 505(d). We have held ... however, that the Commissioner was not justified in withdrawing Hynson's NDA without a prior hearing on whether Hynson had submitted "substantial evidence" of Lutrexin's effectiveness. Consequently, any ruling as to Lutrexin's "new drug" status is premature and must await the outcome of this hearing....

[The opinion of Mr. Justice Powell, concurring in part and concurring in the result in part, is omitted.]

NOTES

1. *Subsequent Proceedings.* Following this decision, FDA published a notice of hearing in 39 Fed. Reg. 15341 (May 2, 1974) and subsequently held a

formal evidentiary hearing. The Commissioner's decision withdrawing approval of the NDAs for Lutrexin, 41 Fed. Reg. 14406 (April 5, 1976), was not challenged.

2. *New Drug Status.* The *Hynson* decision effectively renders every new chemical entity introduced since 1962 a "new drug," for it holds that no drug can be generally recognized as effective in the absence of the "adequate and well-controlled" clinical studies that are required for approval of an NDA.

As the *Hynson* case illustrates, lack of substantial evidence of effectiveness was the chief reason for withdrawal of approval of many pre–1962 new drugs. For a number of effective drugs approved since 1962, however, the problem has been infrequent but serious adverse reactions that were only revealed with use in a large patient population.

STATEMENT OF JOSEPH F. SADUSK, JR., M.D*

Drug Safety Hearings Before the Intergovernmental Relations Subcommittee
of the House Committee on Government Operations.
89th Congress, 1st Session (1965).

Soon after the introduction of Parnate to the market [in 1961] a few cases of hypertensive reaction with headache were reported.... In the summer of 1961 the labeling was revised to call attention to this reaction. Approximately 1 year later another supplemental [new drug] application was processed to provide for further changes in the labeling which in part cautioned against the use of Parnate with other drugs....

It became apparent late in 1962 and early in 1963 that the number of severe reactions associated with the use of Parnate was increasing.... In a meeting of September 17, 1963, of FDA with representatives of the firm, the latter presented new information on adverse reactions and proposed to send a warning letter to physicians. .... By February 1964, approximately 400 cases of hypertensive reaction, including 50 cerebrovascular accidents with 16 deaths, had been reported....

... [A] meeting with representatives of the firm was held in the office of Commissioner Larrick on February 18, 1964. Following a general discussion of the situation the visitors were informed of our intention to issue a notice of hearing on a proposal to withdraw approval of the drug.... The proposal that a panel of experts be appointed to consider the matter was again made by the company. Mr. Larrick explained that FDA had already canvassed outside experts and for this reason would not be willing to substitute an advisory committee for the hearing procedure or to delay this procedure for the formation of an advisory committee.

* [FDA Medical Director.]

Six days following the meeting, Mr. Munns, president of Smith, Kline & French, informed Mr. Rankin by phone that the firm had decided to withdraw Parnate from the market, but not to voluntarily withdraw the NDA.... The action of FDA which resulted in withdrawal of Parnate from the market was followed by many letters from physicians, who had used the drug, protesting the action. Several were from psychiatrists of recognized eminence. The consensus of this correspondence was to the effect that Parnate was an effective antidepressant for certain patients, it was irreplaceable by other available drugs, and its adverse effects were outweighed by its value in converting invalidism to a useful life and in the prevention of suicides....

Our FDA studies up through the May–June 1964 period indicated that 38 strokes had been reported in the United States, among which 21 deaths resulted in patients who were on Parnate. A careful review of these cases by the Bureau of Medicine staff responsible for the analysis of these cases indicated that in only 6 of these 38 strokes would there appear to be a highly probably causal relationship between stroke and the use of Parnate, although the attending physicians involved in care of the patients considered 19 of the cases to be causal....

Our records reveal that up to August 1964 a total of 216 strokes were reported from both domestic and foreign sources in patients who were receiving Parnate before the labeling change. Of these 216 patients, 146 were from the United States. Most of these reports came in during the summer of 1964....

In final summary of the question of efficacy, it was our opinion that Parnate is an effective drug within the meaning of the 1962 Drug Amendments to the Federal Food, Drug, and Cosmetic Act. Consequently, I stated to the Commissioner that it was my carefully considered opinion that Parnate should be returned to the market under the condition of acceptance by Smith Kline & French of a drastic revision of their previous labeling....

... [T]he revised labeling called for a number of factors of safety....

1. Parnate is to be used only in cases of severe depression.

2. Parnate is to be used only in patients who are either hospitalized or in patients who are under close observation and in whom electroconvulsive therapy is not indicated or other medication had been found to be ineffective.

3. Parnate is not to be used in patients over 60 years of age or in patients in whom there is evidence of history of hypertension or other cardiovascular disease.

4. The maximum dosage of Parnate was to be significantly reduced, employing a recommended top level of 30 milligrams per day as compared to a top level of 60 milligrams per

day which was endorsed in the previous level of September 1963.

5. Parnate is not to be used in combination with many other potent drugs.

... Particular warning was also given to the need for the patient to abstain from cheese while on Parnate....

Subsequent to the time that Parnate reappeared on the market; namely, August 1, 1964, a careful analysis has been continued of severe adverse reactions reported to us from use of this drug. This analysis indicates that from August 1, 1964, through May 31, 1965 (a period of 9 months) there have been reported to FDA 18 strokes and 25 hypertensive reactions without serious sequela.... In the 18, there were 7 fatalities—4 from the United States, 3 from foreign sources. The four fatalities in this country involved use of the drug prior to August 1, 1964. There have been no reported deaths which have come to our attention involving the use of Parnate in the United States since Parnate was returned to the market with revised labeling....

NOTES

1. *Failure to Report Adverse Reactions.* During the Bureau of Medicine's reevaluation of Parnate in the summer of 1964, an agency toxicologist discovered "discrepancies" in the firm's original reporting of cerebrovascular lesions in animals to which the drug had been administered in preclinical tests. While acknowledging that the firm may have been attempting to avert concern about Parnate's safety, Dr. Sadusk adhered to his conclusion that the drug should be permitted back on the market. In a similar case, FDA sought to initiate proceedings to withdraw approval of the underlying NDA on the ground that the application had contained an "untrue statement of a material fact," 41 Fed. Reg. 45605 (October 15, 1976).

2. *Congressional Reactions.* The discovery of serious adverse reactions after a drug is marketed, and thus in wide use, is not an uncommon event, and its occurrence almost invariably prompts outraged reactions within Congress. *See, e.g.,* "Corporate Criminal Liability," Hearings before the Subcomm. on Crime of the House Comm. on the Judiciary, 96th Cong., 1st and 2nd Sess. (1980) (Selacryn); "The Regulation of New Drugs by the Food and Drug Administration: The New Drug Review Process," Hearings before a Subcomm. of the House Comm. on Government Operations, 97th Cong., 2d Sess. (1982), "Deficiencies in FDA's Regulation of the New Drug 'Oraflex'," H.R. Rep. No. 98–511, 98th Cong., 2d Sess. (1983); "The Regulation of New Drugs by the Food and Drug Administration: The New Drug Review Process," Hearings before a Subcomm. of the House Comm. on Government Operations, 97th Cong., 2d Sess. (1982) (Feldene); "FDA's Regulation of Zomax," H.R. Rep. No. 98–584, 98th Cong., 1st Sess. (1983); "Oversight of the New Drug Review Process and FDA's Regulation of Merital," Hearing before a Subcomm. of the House Comm. on Government Operations, 99th Cong., 2d Sess. (1986), "FDA's Regulation of the New Drug Merital," H.R. Rep. No. 100–206, 100th Cong., 1st Sess. (1987); FDA's Regulation of the New Drug Suprol," Hearings before a Subcomm. of the House Comm. on Government Operations, 100th Cong., 1st Sess. (1987); "FDA's Regulation of the New Drug Versed," Hearings before a Subcomm. of the House Comm. on Government Operations, 100th Cong., 2d Sess. (1988), "FDA's Defi-

cient Regulation of the New Drug Versed," H.R. Rep. No. 100–1086, 100th Cong., 2d Sess. (1988). In cases where marketing of the drug was suspended, the company acted voluntarily. In some instances, the agency has specifically requested the manufacturer to make the drug available for compassionate use when no effective alternative existed.

3. *Evaluating Adverse Reactions.* For a case study of the problems involved in assessing and responding to reports of postmarketing adverse reactions, *see* Shubin, *Triazure and Public Drug Policies,* Perspectives in Biology and Medicine 185 (Winter 1979); "FDA's Regulation of the Drug 'Triazure'," Hearing Before a Subcomm. of the House Comm. on Government Operations, 94th Cong., 2d Sess. (1976).

4. *Postmarketing Adverse Reactions.* Because an investigational new drug is tested in a relatively small number of patients before an NDA is approved, it is almost certain that low frequency adverse reactions will be discovered when use becomes widespread. In FDA DRUG REVIEW: POSTAPPROVAL RISKS 1976–85, PEMD–90–15 (1990), the General Accounting Office found that of 198 drugs approved by FDA during this period, about half had serious postapproval risks as evidenced by labeling changes or market withdrawal. All but six of the drugs studied were still being marketed in 1989, based upon the agency's determination that the benefits outweigh the risks.

---

i.   Immediate Ban of an "Imminent Hazard"
FORSHAM v. CALIFANO

United States District Court, District of Columbia, 1977.
442 F.Supp. 203.

CORCORAN, District Judge.

Plaintiffs are seven physicians who specialize in the treatment of diabetes and six diabetic patients taking phenformin hydrochloride (phenformin) prescribed by their physicians as part of their diabetic therapy. Phenformin is an orally administered drug designed to control blood sugar levels in patients with adult-onset diabetes who are not dependent on insulin and who cannot or will not reduce their daily caloric intake....

The defendant is the Secretary of Health, Education and Welfare (the Secretary) who, pursuant to Section 505(e) of the Federal Food, Drug and Cosmetic Act, has suspended new drug applications for phenformin on grounds that the drug poses an "imminent hazard." ...

In considering the likelihood of success on the merits, it should be noted at the outset that the review by this Court of the Secretary's decision to suspend phenformin pursuant to his authority under 21 U.S.C. § 355(e) is limited to a determination of whether that decision was arbitrary and capricious, an abuse of discretion, or otherwise not in accordance with the law.... In other words, [the plaintiffs] must demonstrate the substantial likelihood that the decision was "a clear error of judgment" by the Secretary and that he failed to articulate any rational connection between the facts submitted to him and the choice he made....

While acknowledging the existence of "conflicting testimony" on the incidence of lactic acidosis among phenformin patients and the view expressed by the manufacturers that labeling changes made in January, 1977 would reduce the incidence of phenformin-related lactic acidosis, the Secretary nonetheless deemed that the following factors necessitated his decision to suspend:

1. The discontinued marketing of phenformin in Norway and Canada based on the experience in those countries with phenformin related lactic acidosis cases.

2. Adverse reports of phenformin-related lactic acidosis in Finland, Sweden, New Zealand, and Australia.

3. The discontinued use of phenformin by several diabetes clinics in major U.S. hospitals.

4. The unanimous October, 1976 recommendation by the FDA Endocrinology and Metabolism Advisory Committee that phenformin be removed from the market.

5. The May 6, 1977 decision by the FDA's Bureau of Drugs to seek withdrawal of approval of NDA's for phenformin.

6. Calculations submitted by the FDA's Bureau of Drugs based on information it had received from phenformin manufacturers, research conducted in other countries, studies conducted in a group of university based medical centers and reports from individual hospitals. Those calculations indicated that:

a. Between 0.25 and four cases of lactic acidosis arose per 1,000 phenformin users per year with an approximate mortality rate of fifty per cent.

b. That the estimated incidence of death due to lactic acidosis in phenformin users is between 0.125 and 2 deaths annually per 1,000 patients—a rate 5 to 80 times higher than that of other widely used drugs known to cause fatalities even when properly used.

c. That between four and 60 patients would die each month from phenformin-induced lactic acidosis.

d. That final administrative action on withdrawal of the NDA's for phenformin could take from six to twelve months during which time anywhere from 10 to 700 people could die from phenformin associated lactic acidosis.

.... [P]laintiffs allege that the standards used by the Secretary in determining that phenformin posed an imminent hazard under the statute do not comport either with the standards dictated by Congress[4] or with those set forth in the FDA's own regulation.[5]

As recited in the Order, the criteria used by the Secretary to determine the imminence of the hazard included:

1. The severity of the harm that could be caused by the drug during the completion of customary administrative proceedings to withdraw the drug from the general market.

2. The likelihood that the drug will cause such harm to users while the administrative process is being completed.

3. The risk to patients currently taking the drug that might be occasioned by the immediate removal of the drug from the market taking into account the availability of other therapies and the steps necessary for patients to adjust to these other therapies.

4. The likelihood that after the customary administrative process is completed, the drug will be withdrawn from the general marketing.

5. The availability of other approaches to protect the public health.

Upon reviewing these criteria, the Court is not persuaded either that they improperly reflect the intent of Congress or are at substantial variance with the FDA regulation. And, even if there may exist some discrepancy between the Secretary's criteria and those set forth in 21 CFR § 2.5, we would note that the regulation was designed to guide the FDA Commissioner in making his *recommendations* to the Secretary with respect to the existence of an imminent hazard, and would not necessarily bind the Secretary in making his nondelegable decision to suspend. Further we are not inclined to adopt plaintiff's "crisis" interpretation of imminent hazard. Rather we are more persuaded by defendant's suggested analogy to cases interpreting the imminent hazard provisions of the Federal Insecticide, Fungicide and Rodenticide Act which caution "against any approach to the term imminent hazard ...

4. Plaintiffs cite the Senate Judiciary Report accompanying the 1962 Amendments ... which added the imminent hazard provision to the effect that the Secretary's power should be exercised "only in the exceptional case of an emergency which does not permit the Secretary to correct it by other means." S. Rep. No. 1744, Pt. 2, 87th Cong., 2d Sess. p. 7 (1962).

Reference is also made to the consideration of the amendments by the Senate where it was noted that the imminent hazard authority "should only be exercised under the most extreme conditions and with the utmost care." 108 Cong. Rec. 16304 (Aug. 23, 1962).

5. The FDA regulation defines imminent hazard as one, "(1) that should be corrected immediately to prevent injury and (2) that should not be permitted to continue while a hearing or other formal proceeding is being held. The 'imminent hazard' may be declared at any point in the chain of events which may ultimately result in harm to the public health. The occurrence of the final anticipated injury is not essential to establish that an 'imminent hazard' of such occurrence exists." 21 C.F.R. § 2.5(a).

The regulation also noted that in determining the existence of an imminent hazard, the number, nature, severity and duration of the injury will be considered.

that restricts it to a concept of crisis" and adopt the view that "It is enough that there is substantial likelihood that serious harm will be experienced during ... any realistic projection of the administrative process." *See Environmental Defense Fund v. Environmental Protection Agency,* 510 F.2d 1291 (1975) (E.D.F. II); *Environmental Defense Fund v. Environmental Protection Agency,* 465 F.2d 528 (1972) (E.D.F. I).

We decide accordingly that the Secretary's criteria for evaluating the existence of an imminent hazard were not improper. There remains to be determined whether a rational connection exists between the facts on which he relied and his decision to suspend. Keeping in mind that "invocation of this emergency power is a matter which is peculiarly one of judgment," this Court cannot say that the facts on which the Secretary relied, particularly the calculations provided by the Bureau of Drugs, do not adequately support his decision to suspend....

Assuming, as we must at this juncture, the validity of the Bureau of Drug's projection of between four and 60 phenformin related deaths each month, we cannot find that the Secretary's conclusion that labeling changes "cannot be expected to achieve a needed reduction in the usage of phenformin within any reasonable time frame ... with so many lives at stake," was either arbitrary or unreasonable. Nor was it made so by his decision to act first on phenformin rather than some other drug which may pose a hazard of similar magnitude....

... [P]laintiffs also object to what it alleges is the unprecedented and unlawful attempt by the Secretary to create within the suspension order a voluntary system of limited distribution to those small number of patients for whom it may be determined that phenformin's benefits outweigh its risks. Plaintiffs voice similar objections to the Secretary's 90 day delay in implementing his order. In view of the fact that the Secretary's power to suspend under Section 355(e) has never been exercised, it is obvious that any method of implementation used would be unprecedented.... It appears to us that the Secretary's dual concerns of an orderly withdrawal of the use of the drug from the majority of patients now using it, and of accommodating the small number of patients for whom the benefits outweighed the risks were eminently reasonable and that the power to deal with them in the manner in which he did could fairly be implied from his power to suspend.

... [T]he Court concludes that it must deny plaintiffs' Motion for a Preliminary Injunction....

NOTES

1. *Limited Distribution.* As the court notes, Secretary Califano's suspension of the NDAs for phenformin was the first time this nondelegable authority had ever been exercised. The action came in response to a petition and threatened lawsuit by the Health Research Group, and followed FDA's publication of a notice proposing to withdraw approval of the NDAs. 42 Fed. Reg. 23170 (May 6, 1977). Secretary Califano instructed FDA to attempt to negotiate an arrangement with the two manufacturers under which phenformin

could continue to be supplied to the relatively small number of patients for whom it was believed the therapy of choice. These negotiations failed, but the firms continued to distribute small quantities of phenformin under a compassionate IND.

2. *Standing to Challenge NDA Withdrawal.* After the District Court declined to overturn Secretary Califano's suspension order, a full evidentiary hearing was held on the proposed withdrawal of the NDAs, following which the Commissioner ordered the NDAs withdrawn. 43 Fed. Reg. 54995 (November 24, 1978). Forsham subsequently sought review of this order as well as review of the district court's original ruling. The court of appeals dismissed the latter appeal as moot, and ruled that Forsham and his co-plaintiffs, prescribing physicians and patients, lacked standing to seek review of the Commissioner's order under section 505(h) of the Act, 21 U.S.C. § 355(h): "[O]nly an 'applicant' may petition a Court of Appeals to review the . . . withdrawal of his approval of a new drug application." *Forsham v. Califano,* Food Drug Cosm. L. Rep. (CCH) ¶ 38,241 (D.C. Cir. 1979).

3. *Petition to Suspend Propoxyphene.* Secretary Califano's willingness to exercise the previously dormant "imminent hazard" authority prompted a similar petition a year later from the Health Research Group which this time sought suspension of the drug propoxyphene because of fatalities attributed to overdose. The Secretary denied the petition pending consideration of rescheduling of the drug under the Controlled Substances Act and strengthened label warnings, including patient labeling, against the risks of misuse. *In re Petition to Suspend New Drug Applications for Propoxyphene: Order of the Secretary Denying Petition* (February 15, 1979). After a public hearing on the safety and effectiveness of the drug, 44 Fed. Reg. 11837 (March 2, 1979), the company voluntarily agreed to revise the drug's labeling and distribute a PPI.

4. *Butazolidin, Tandearil, and Feldene.* In response to a petition to ban the nonsteroidal anti-inflammatory drugs Butazolidin (phenyllbutazone) and Tandearil (oxyphenbutazone), FDA conducted a hearing to develop recommendations for the HHS Secretary, 49 Fed. Reg. 1939 (January 16, 1984). On FDA's recommendation, the Secretary denied the petition. FDA Dkt No. 84N–0014 (August 7, 1984). In response to a petition to ban Feldene (prioxicam), FDA again conducted a public hearing, 51 Fed. Reg. 3658 (January 29, 1986), to develop recommendations for the Secretary. In this case, too, the Secretary adopted FDA's recommendation and denied the petition. FDA Dkt No. 86P–0023 (July 7, 1986). Three months later a second petition, to require stronger warnings for Feldene, was filed, FDA Dkt No. 86P–0450, but never acted upon.

5. *Accutane.* In May 1988 FDA, rather than HHS, was petitioned to declare Accutane (isotretinoin) an imminent hazard. The agency denied the petition. FDA Dkt No. 88P–0191/CP (May 2, 1989).

6. *Imminent Hazard Criteria.* FDA's definition of imminent hazard, 35 Fed. Reg. 18679 (December 9, 1970), 36 Fed. Reg. 12516 (July 1, 1971), is codified in 21 C.F.R. § 2.5. In 44 Fed. Reg. 48979 (August 12, 1979) the Secretary of HHS proposed new criteria and procedures for implementing the "imminent hazard" provisions of the Act, but as of June 30, 1990, no further action had been taken on this proposal.

5. THE AIDS REVOLUTION

For a quarter century, the victims of serious and life-threatening diseases have had to wait patiently while clinical trials were conducted and the results submitted to FDA for review and, in many cases, ultimate approval before effective drugs became widely available.

Acquired immune deficiency syndrome (AIDS) destroys the body's natural capacity to fight disease (the immune system) and thus leaves its victims vulnerable to life-threatening infections, cancer, and other diseases. AIDS was first identified as a distinct disease in 1979, only two years after the first case was diagnosed in the United States. An infectious disease, AIDS spread rapidly among homosexuals before its presence and methods of transmission were understood. Impatient with the customary IND/NDA process, members of the gay community mounted a campaign to speed up the availability of both investigational and approved new drugs to treat the victims of AIDS. Their persistence has brought about a revolution in the availability of investigational drugs to treat life-threatening diseases, in the early approval of new drugs for these diseases, and in the importation of wholly untested drugs. *See How the AIDS Crisis Made Drug Regulators Speed Up,* New York Times, September 24, 1989, p. E.5.

MORBIDITY AND MORTALITY WEEKLY REPORT
Volume 38, No. 32, August 18, 1988.

In June 1981, the first cases of the illness now known as acquired immunodeficiency syndrome (AIDS) were reported from Los Angeles in five young homosexual men diagnosed with *Pneumocystis carinii* pneumonia and other opportunistic infections. Since then, state and territorial health departments have reported >100,000 cases of AIDS and >59,000 AIDS-related deaths to CDC. AIDS is now a major cause of morbidity and mortality in children and young adults in the United States, ranking 15th among leading causes of death in 1988 and seventh among estimated years of potential life lost before age 65 in 1987. The first 50,000 cases of AIDS were reported to CDC from 1981 to 1987; the second 50,000 were reported between December 1987 and July 1989.....

The number of AIDS cases are one indication of the larger epidemic of HIV infection. An estimated 1–1.5 million persons are infected with HIV in the United States, with recent seroprevalence studies suggesting that the actual number is closer to the lower end of this range. A cohort study of homosexual/bisexual men in San Francisco suggests that 54% of infected persons will develop AIDS within 10 years of infection and that up to 99% will eventually develop AIDS. Therefore, the number of persons with AIDS and other severe manifestations of HIV infection will continue to increase.....

NOTE
The General Accounting Office has estimated a "realistic range" of from 300,000 to 480,000 cases of AIDS in the U.S. population through 1991. AIDS

FORECASTING: UNDERCOUNT OF CASES AND LACK OF KEY DATA
WEAKEN EXISTING ESTIMATES, No. B–230539 (June 1, 1989).

---

a. Use of Investigational Drugs in Patient Treatment

Since 1938, FDA has consistently taken the position that an unapproved new drug may be investigated in human subjects to obtain evidence to support an NDA, but may not lawfully be "commercialized" prior to approval. Before the 1962 Amendments, the agency's regulations specified that investigational drugs were to be made available "solely for investigational use by or under the direction of, an expert qualified by scientific training and experience to investigate the safety of such drug." 21 C.F.R. § 130.2(a)(2)(1962). Nonetheless, the use of investigational drugs for treatment, rather than for investigational purposes, was not specifically addressed in FDA publications or contemporary articles describing the new drug process. The original IND regulations, 27 Fed. Reg. 7990 (August 10, 1962), 28 Fed. Reg. 179 (January 8, 1963), provided that the sponsor shall not "commercially distribute nor test-market" the drug prior to approval and provided that an IND could be terminated if FDA found that the drug "is being or is to be sold or otherwise distributed for commercial purposes not justified by the requirements of the investigation." 21 C.F.R. 130.-3(a)(11) & 130.3(d)(8) (1964). The IND form itself, beginning in 1963, required that the sponsor provide

> [i]f the drug is to be sold, a full explanation why sale is required and should not be regarded as the commercialization of a new drug for which an application is not approved.

Thus, FDA embraced two related enforcement principles. First, investigational drugs were to be used solely for investigational purposes and not for treatment. Second, investigational drugs were to be made available without charge, except under unusual circumstances that were fully justified in the IND.

As new drugs began to be developed to treat serious diseases for which no alternative therapy was available, FDA discarded the rule that an investigational drug could not be used for treatment purposes. Although it did not amend the IND regulations to reflect this change in policy, the agency allowed the use of investigational drugs in patient treatment, while clinical trials were ongoing, on various terms. It frequently granted an emergency IND, usually by telephone, where a physician needed to use an investigational drug in a life-threatening situation. Under so-called "compassionate INDs" FDA approved protocols for treatment use of investigational drugs for all patients who met the protocol criteria. An "open label IND," similar to a compassionate IND, established specific patient criteria for general use of the drug not intended for life-threatening disease to obtain additional information on the safety and effectiveness. INDs also became vehicles for allowing treatment with orphan drugs and drugs for tropical diseases.

One goal of FDA's most recent revision of the IND regulations, 48 Fed. Reg. 26720 (June 9, 1983), 52 Fed. Reg. 8798 (March 19, 1987), was to rationalize these exceptions to the general ban on commercialization of an investigational drug. The agency's 1983 proposal contained new sections on "treatment use" and "emergency use" that did no more than codify existing agency practice. By the time the final regulation was promulgated in March 1987, however, the AIDS epidemic had forced FDA to reevaluate these provisions. The emergency use provision was retained, 21 C.F.R. § 313.36, but the treatment use provision was reproposed in more detailed form and promulgated just two months later as a final regulation.

INVESTIGATIONAL NEW DRUG, ANTIBIOTIC, AND BIOLOGICAL DRUG PRODUCT REGULATIONS: TREATMENT USE AND SALE
52 Federal Register 19466 (May 22, 1987).

In the FEDERAL REGISTER of March 19, 1987 (52 FR 8850), FDA published proposed regulations governing the conditions under which patients could obtain investigational drugs primarily for treatment use, and the conditions under which investigational drugs could be sold.....

Like the proposal, the final rule regarding treatment use provides general criteria for allowing an investigational new drug to be made available to desperately ill patients primarily for treatment use. Minor modifications have been made to these criteria to read as follows: (1) The drug is intended to treat a serious or immediately life-threatening disease; (2) there is no comparable or satisfactory alternative drug or other therapy available to treat that stage of the disease in the intended patient population; (3) the drug is under investigation in a controlled clinical trial under an IND in effect for the trial, or all clinical trials have been completed; and (4) the sponsor of the controlled clinical trial is actively pursuing marketing approval of the investigational drug with due diligence (§ 312.34(b)(1)).

In response to comments, FDA has revised the criteria for the granting of a treatment IND for drugs intended to treat immediately life-threatening diseases. In this situation, under the final rule, the Commissioner may deny a request for treatment use if the available scientific evidence, taken as a whole, fails to provide reasonable basis for concluding that the drug: (1) May be effective for its intended use in its intended patient population; or (2) would not expose the patients to whom the drug is to be administered to an unreasonable and significant additional risk of illness or injury (§ 312.34(b)(3)(i)(A) and (B).

FDA has also added into the regulation a definition of "immediately life-threatening" to mean a stage of a disease in which there is a reasonable likelihood that death will occur within a matter of months or in which premature death is likely without early treatment (§ 312.-34(b)(3)(ii)).....

Under the final rule, FDA would continue to presume that supplying investigational drugs to subjects participating in clinical trials without charge is part of the normal cost of doing business, and that FDA approval for charging would only be granted upon a showing of why charging is needed for the sponsor to undertake or continue the clinical trial (§ 312.7(d)(1)).

With respect to drugs provided under treatment IND's, the final rule has been revised to authorize sponsors to charge for investigational drugs provided there is adequate enrollment in the ongoing clinical investigations under the authorized IND. This provision is in addition to the three other conditions contained in the reproposal, namely, that the sale does not constitute commercial marketing of a new drug for which a marketing application has not been approved; the drug is not being commercially promoted or advertised; and the sponsor of the drug is actively pursuing marketing approval with due diligence (§ 312.-7(d)(2)).

In all cases, the final rule provides that the sponsor may not commercialize an investigational drug by charging a price larger than that necessary to recover costs of manufacture, research, development, and handling of the investigational drug (§ 312.7(d)(3)). This is the same standard currently applied to charging for investigational medical devices.....

NOTES

1. *Publication of Treatment INDs.* For several years FDA has periodically published a list of all drugs subject to treatment INDs. *See, e.g.,* "Treatment IND Update," FDA Talk Paper T90–14 (March 20, 1990). See generally Marlin, *Treatment INDs: A Faster Route to Drug Approval,* 39 Am. U. L. Rev. 171 (1989); Cocchetto, *Issues Regarding Compassionate Treatment With Investigational New Drugs,* 23 Drug Info. J. 87 (1989).

2. *Publication of AIDS INDs.* After publishing these regulations, FDA began to publish a list of all AIDS drugs in clinical trial under an IND. In the AIDS Amendments of 1988, enacted as part of the Health Omnibus Programs Extension of 1988, 102 Stat. 3048, 3062, 3072, codified in 42 U.S.C. § 300cc–17(d), (e), FDA was directed to establish, as part of a data bank on AIDS drugs, a registry of clinical trials on AIDS drugs conducted under an IND. The Department of HHS announced the availability of the data bank and IND registry in "AIDS Clinical Trials Lists Completed," HHS News No. P89–33 (July 18, 1989).

3. *The AIDS Amendments.* The AIDS Amendments of 1988 essentially ratified the treatment IND policy adopted by FDA. The Amendments, 102 Stat. at 3066–3067, codified at 42 U.S.C. § 300cc–12, require FDA to encourage submission of an IND for clinical trials, and submission of a treatment IND for the treatment of individuals not in clinical trials, for any investigational drug where there is "preliminary evidence that the drug has effectiveness in humans" in the prevention or treatment of AIDS. FDA is specifically authorized

to provide technical assistance, directly or through grants or contracts, to facilitate submission of INDs for these purposes.

4. *Continuing Demands.* These statutory and regulatory initiatives have not satisfied all the agency's critics. "FDA Responds to Act Up Demands," FDA Talk Paper No. T88–74 (October 5, 1988). Some have contended that the agency has applied the treatment IND regulations more restrictively than their wording had promised. Rather than allowing a treatment IND for any drug that "may" be effective for some AIDS victims, they have claimed, FDA has approved a treatment IND for a drug only after the sponsor has already submitted substantial evidence of safety and effectiveness of the drug, as a "bridge" to NDA approval. Many argue that treatment INDs should be granted much earlier, even if this should allow use of some drugs that are later found to be unsafe or ineffective. According to a news article:

> Even as the FDA was easing its rules, AIDS sufferers were still suffering for a cure on the black market for unapproved drugs. It was revealed last week that an underground network of doctors in four cities has been conducting a clandestine trial of a drug known as Compound Q. In test tubes, it can destroy cells infected with the AIDS virus, but it has not yet been proved to be safe and effective in humans. In the unofficial trial, 42 patients have received Compound Q, which is derived from a Chinese cucumber-like plant....

> The secret study, organized by a San Francisco-based group of AIDS activists called Project Inform, came to light after one of the patients died. He went into a coma, later awoke but then choked while vomiting—ten days after his first Compound–Q treatment. The FDA has launched an investigation of the study.

> The Compound–Q affair has heightened concern about the widespread use of unproven drugs. "There is always a tension between treatment of a patient and the need for solid drug testing," says Dr. Frank Young, the FDA commissioner. But AIDS has increased that tension.....

> Although FDA officials dispute the notion, some experts are concerned that the use of unproven medications may be getting out of control. So many AIDS patients are taking a pharmacological stew of approved and experimental drugs and potions that it is difficult to gauge the effectiveness of any single drug. Underground studies of experimental drugs, like the Compound–Q effort, confuse an already complex situation and frustrate scientists. "They're violating all the standards of safe testing of new compounds," says Dr. Paul Volberding, an AIDS specialist at the University of California at San Francisco. The haphazard use of experimental drugs may help some AIDS patients in the short run, but it will slow down the quest to discover the best ways to treat the many people who will contract the disease in the future.

Drugs from the Underground, Time Magazine, July 10, 1989, p. 49.

5. *Compassionate, Open Label, and Parallel Track INDs.* In addition to treatment INDs and emergency use INDs, formally sanctioned by its regulations, FDA continues to permit compassionate INDs and open label INDs on an ad hoc basis. Furthermore, at the suggestion of the Director of the National Institute of Allergy and Infectious Diseases, FDA has proposed in 55 Fed. Reg.

20856 (May 21, 1990) still another type of IND to permit the early treatment use of investigational drugs, called the "parallel track." A parallel track IND allows an investigational drug to be used for treatment purposes, but not to be sold, where it has been shown to be safe but not yet shown to be effective, and an adequate number of patients are enrolled in clinical trials. The parallel track IND can be used only for patients who do not meet the criteria for, or for some other reason are not able to participate in, a clinical trial, and for whom there is no satisfactory alternative drug. The parallel track IND is thus indistinguishable from, and perhaps a replacement for, a compassionate IND or open label IND, except that it is available earlier in the drug development process.

6. *Group C Cancer Drugs.* The National Cancer Institute (NCI) plays a major role in the discovery and development of anticancer drugs. *See, e.g.,* GAO, IMPROVEMENTS NEEDED IN CLINICAL TESTING OF ANTICANC-ER DRUGS, No. HRD–83–52 (September 26, 1983); "Oversight of Drug Development Program of the National Cancer Institute," Hearing before the Subcomm. on Investigations and General Oversight of the Senate Comm. on Labor and Human Resources, 97th Cong., 2d Sess. (1982). Since 1976, NCI has furnished qualified physicians the most promising investigational drugs, called "Group C" drugs, to treat their patients under a drug master file submitted to FDA. This program was incorporated in a Memorandum of Understanding between the two agencies published in 44 Fed. Reg. 25510 (May 1, 1979). Beginning in October 1980, Group C drugs were made eligible for Medicare reimbursement even though still investigational. In 1988 FDA's Center for Drug Evaluation and Research determined that NCI would continue to use the designation "Group C" for these drugs, that FDA would use the designation "treatment IND/Group C" for these drugs, and that FDA "will treat NCI applications for Group C status as treatment IND requests, no matter what name they come under, and utilize the standards that we would ordinarily use for such a request."

USE OF LAETRILE FOR CANCER

For more than a decade, from 1975 through 1987, cancer patients, often aided by producers, sought the same right to use unproven remedies that spokespersons for AIDS patients have now won. Their central focus was Laetrile (amygdalin), a poorly-characterized natural constituent of apricot kernels. FDA first seized quantities of Laetrile in 1960 at the Hoxsey Cancer Center in Dallas, Texas. Laetrile was one of a number of unproven drugs made and administered by Dr. Ernst T. Krebs of San Francisco, with whom FDA had engaged in litigation as early as the 1920s.

Unproven cancer remedies have been the focus of major FDA enforcement actions beginning in the early 1900s. Following enactment of the 1962 Drug Amendments, the new statutory requirements provided FDA with important new enforcement tools. For example, the agency successfully ended the marketing of Krebiozen on the ground that it was an illegal new drug. *Tutoki v. Celebrezze,* 375 F.2d 105 (7th Cir. 1967); *Rutherford v. American Medical Ass'n,* 379 F.2d 641 (7th Cir. 1967); *Durovic v. Richardson,* 479 F.2d 242 (7th Cir. 1973).

In 1975, two cancer victims sued to enjoin FDA from interfering with their personal use of Laetrile. The court determined that the plaintiffs were incapable of complying with the new drug approval requirements of FDA and thus were entitled to an injunction against the agency to preserve their free choice of treatment. *Rutherford v. United States,* 399 F.Supp. 1208 (W.D. Okl. 1975). On appeal, the Tenth Circuit (2–1) upheld the injunction pending a formal determination by FDA of Laetrile's regulatory status, 542 F.2d 1137 (10th Cir. 1976). The district court thereafter remanded the matter to FDA for preparation of an appropriate administrative record and meanwhile reaffirmed its injunction. 424 F.Supp. 105 (W.D. Okl. 1977). The district court later also certified the case as a class action, 429 F.Supp. 506 (W.D. Okl. 1977), a ruling FDA did not appeal.

Following a public hearing, 42 Fed. Reg. 10066 (February 18, 1977), the FDA Commissioner determined that Laetrile was not GRAS and GRAE and was not exempt from the new drug provisions of the FD&C Act under either grandfather clause, 42 Fed. Reg. 39768 (August 5, 1977). *See* "Banning of the Drug Laetrile from Interstate Commerce by FDA," Hearing before the Subcomm. on Health and Scientific Research of the Senate Comm. on Human Resources, 95th Cong., 1st Sess. (1977). When the dispute returned to court, the district judge held that Laetrile was grandfathered under the FD&C Act and concluded that in any case the plaintiffs had a constitutional right of privacy to use the drug in the treatment of their disease. 438 F.Supp. 1287 (W.D. Okl. 1977). On appeal, the Tenth Circuit held that, wholly apart from any constitutional issues, the new drug provisions of the FD&C Act have no application to terminally ill cancer patients:

> ... [W]hat can "generally recognized" as "safe" and effective" mean as to such persons who are so fatally stricken with a disease for which there is no known cure? What meaning can "effective" have in the absence of anything which may be used as a standard? Under this record Laetrile is as effective as anything else. What can "effective" mean if the person, by all prevailing standards, and under the position the Commission takes, is going to die of cancer regardless of what may be done. Thus there has been no standard here advanced by the Commission against which to measure the safeness or effectiveness of the drug as to the plaintiffs. Clearly the terms have no meaning under these circumstances, and certainly not the abstract meaning sought to be applied by the Commission....
>
> It would not seem difficult to define the group to which this determination of a legal issue applies. A licensed medical practitioner can express an opinion as to whether, under the present state of the art, a particular person is terminally ill with cancer, and to so certify.....
>
> We do not reach the constitutional aspects which were applied by the district court. We conclude, however, that the permanent injunction granted by the district court should be continued but be limited only to permit procurement of intravenous injections administered by a licensed medical practitioner to persons who are certified by a licensed medical practitioner to be terminally ill of cancer in some form.

582 F.2d 1234, 1237 (10th Cir. 1978). *Compare United States v. Mosinee Research Corp.,* 583 F.2d 930 (7th Cir. 1978). A unanimous Supreme Court reversed this decision, holding that the FD&C Act "makes no special provision for drugs used to treat terminally ill patients," 442 U.S. 544 (1979). The Court accepted FDA's arguments that it was important to protect individuals suffering from a potentially fatal disease from rejecting conventional therapy in favor

of a drug with no demonstrable curative properties, and to protect the public generally from "the vast range of self-styled panaceas that inventive minds can devise."

When the case returned to it, the Tenth Circuit rejected the district court's constitutional ruling:

> It is apparent in the context with which we are here concerned that the decision by the patient whether to have treatment or not is a protected right, but his selection of a particular treatment, or at least a medication, is within the area of governmental interests in protecting public health. The premarketing requirement of the Federal Food, Drug and Cosmetic Act, 21 U.S.C. § 355, is an exercise of Congressional authority to limit the patient's choice of medication.

616 F.2d 455 (10th Cir. 1980). *See also Carnohan v. United States,* 616 F.2d 1120 (9th Cir. 1980); *Judkins v. United States,* Food Drug Cosm. L. Rep. (CCH) ¶ 38,179 (D. Or. 1978).

But the battle was not ended. The district court dismissed the complaint and dissolved its injunctions in March 1984, 1983–1984 FDLI Jud. Rec. 173 (W.D. Okl. 1984), but two months later it granted a motion to reopen the case and in March 1985 entered an order determining that the consent order between the parties and the government must be enforced and that, because Laetrile is GRAS and GRAE for the reduction of cancer pain, the injunction against FDA interference in the use of Laetrile by cancer patients would be reinstated. Food Drug Cosm. L. Rep. (CCH) ¶ 38,312 (W.D. Okl. 1985). This time, the Tenth Circuit quickly reversed the district court, determined that the consent order had been dissolved, and ordered the district court to dismiss the action and dissolve all injunctions. 806 F.2d 1455 (10th Cir. 1986). On remand, the district court complied, finally bringing to a close a decade of litigation. Food Drug Cosm. L. Rep. ¶ 38,030 (W.D. Okl. 1987). *See* "Postscript on Laetrile," FDA Talk Paper No. T87–27 (June 18, 1987).

Throughout this judicial sparring, supporters of Laetrile also sought its legalization through state legislation. More than one-third of the states ultimately legalized use of the drug within their borders. *See also Wickwire v. New York State Dept. of Health,* Food Drug Cosm. L. Rep. (CCH) ¶ 38,166 (N.Y. 1978), allowing a patient to be treated with Laetrile over the objections of the Department of Health. Laetrile also remains available from foreign sources.

----

b. Expedited Approval of Life–Saving Drugs

As discussed p. 516 *supra,* FDA has consistently taken the position that, although ordinarily at least two adequate and well-controlled clinical trials are required for approval of an NDA, it may approve a drug on the basis of a single controlled clinical study. Faced with the AIDS epidemic FDA, for the first time, announced an official policy on expedited approval of new drugs for life-threatening and severely debilitating diseases.

INVESTIGATIONAL NEW DRUG, ANTIBIOTIC, AND BIOLOGICAL DRUG PRODUCT REGULATIONS: PROCEDURES FOR DRUGS INTENDED TO TREAT LIFE–THREATENING AND SEVERELY DEBILITATING ILLNESSES

53 Federal Register 41516 (October 21, 1988).

... The purpose of these new procedures (§ 312.80) is to expedite the development, evaluation, and marketing of new therapies intended to treat persons with life-threatening or severely-debilitating illnesses, especially where no satisfactory alternative therapies exist....

The scope of the new procedures (§ 312.81) will apply to new drugs, antibiotics, and biological products that are being studied for their safety and effectiveness in treating life-threatening or severely-debilitating illnesses. Within the context of these procedures, the term "life-threatening" is defined to include diseases where the likelihood of death is high unless the course of the disease is interrupted (e.g., AIDS and cancer), as well as diseases or conditions with potentially fatal outcomes where the end point of clinical trial analysis is survival (e.g., increased survival in persons who have had a stroke or heart attack). The term "severely-debilitating" refers to diseases or conditions that cause major irreversible morbidity (e.g., blindness or neurological degeneration).

A key component of the procedures is early consultation between FDA and drug sponsors (§ 312.82) to seek agreement on the design of necessary preclinical and clinical studies needed to gain marketing approval. Such consultation is intended to improve the efficiency of the process by preventing false starts and wasted effort that could otherwise result from studies that are flawed in design. Most important, at the end of early (phase 1) clinical testing, FDA and the sponsor will seek to reach agreement on the proper design of phase 2 controlled clinical trials, with the goal that such research will be adequate to provide sufficient data on the product's safety and effectiveness to support a decision on its approvability for marketing....

If the preliminary analysis of test results appears promising, FDA may ask the sponsor (§ 312.83) to submit a treatment protocol to be reviewed under the treatment IND regulations. Such a treatment protocol, if submitted and granted, would serve as a bridge between the completion of early stages of clinical trials and final marketing approval.

Once phase 2 testing and analysis is completed by the sponsor and a marketing application is submitted, FDA will evaluate the data utilizing a medical risk-benefit analysis (§ 312.84). As part of this evaluation, FDA will consider whether the benefits of the drug outweigh the known and potential risks of the drug and the need to answer remaining questions about risks and benefits of the drug, taking into consideration the severity of the disease and the absence of satisfactory alternative therapy. In making decisions on whether to grant marketing approval for products that have been the subject of an end-of-phase 1 meeting under this rule, FDA will usually seek the advice of outside expert scientific consultants or advisory committees.....

Finally, when approval or licensing of a product is being granted, FDA may seek agreement from the sponsor (§ 312.85) to conduct certain postmarketing (phase 4) studies to delineate additional information about the drug's risks, benefits, and optimal use. These studies could include, but would not be limited to, studying different doses or schedules of administration than were used in phase 2 studies, use of the drugs in other patient populations or other stages of the disease, and use of the drug over a longer period of time.

These procedures were modeled after the highly successful development, evaluation, and approval of zidovudine, the first drug approved to treat the AIDS virus. Close consultation between FDA, the sponsor, and the National Institutes of Health resulted in efficient preclinical animal testing (2 to 4 weeks in duration), focused phase 1 clinical testing, and a well-designed and conducted multi-center phase 2 clinical trial that provided dramatic evidence of increased survival in patients with advanced cases of AIDS. Given such evidence, FDA approved a treatment protocol in 5 days, and marketing approval in 107 days. Concurrent with approval, the sponsor agreed to conduct phase 4 research studying the effects of zidovudine in patients at an earlier stage of the disease. In total, the drug development and evaluation process, which takes an average of 8 years from initial human testing under an IND to final marketing approval, took only 2 years for zidovudine. Although the total development time will vary with different drugs, FDA believes that the approach contained in these new procedures has great potential for increasing significantly the efficiency of the drug development and evaluation process for the drugs affected.....

For the reasons described below, FDA is issuing these procedures as an interim rule, with an opportunity for public comment. Because of the urgency associated with life-threatening illnesses, the agency intends to begin implementation of these procedures immediately, but will consider modifications to them based on issues raised during the comment period and experience gained under the interim rule.

---

c. Importation of Unapproved New Drugs

Since 1977, the FDA Regulatory Procedures Manual provisions for mail importation (Chapt. 9–71–00) and personal baggage (Chapt. 9–72–00) have stated that FDA will not detain unapproved new drugs imported for personal use. At the same time, however, the Manual has continued to prohibit the importation of any "new drugs that are not covered by an approved NDA" and of any product subject to an Import Alert because of concerns about safety or fraud. Faced with a large number of unapproved AIDS drugs being imported for personal use, the agency issued the following guidance:

> Because of the desire to acquire articles for treatment of serious and life-threatening conditions like AIDS and cancer, individuals have been purchasing unapproved products from foreign sources.... Such products are often shipped to the purchaser by mail.

> Even though such products are subject to refusal, we may use our discretion to examine the background, risk, and purpose of these products before making a final decision.....

> 2. A product entered for personal use, which meets the criteria in item 4 below, may proceed without sampling or detention.

> 3. Products that are not identified, or are not accompanied by documentation of intended use, should be detained. Other reasons for detention may include: size of the shipment (amount inconsistent with personal use), fraudulent promotion or misrepresentation, or an unreasonable health risk due to either toxicity or possible contamination....

> 4. Following detention, shipments may be released to an individual if the following criteria can be satisfied and there is no safety risk or evidence of fraud:

>> • the product was purchased for personal use

>> • the product is not for commercial distribution and the amount of product is not excessive (i.e., 3 months supply of a drug)

>> • the intended use of the product is appropriately identified

>> • the patient seeking to import the product affirms in writing that it is for the patient's own use and provides the name and address of the doctor licensed in the U.S. responsible for his or her treatment with the product

> 5. If the district should encounter a situation suggesting promotional and/or commercial activity that falls within our health fraud guideline, the district should recommend that an Import Alert be

issued for the automatic detention of the product
and identification of the promoter involved.

"Pilot Guidance for Release of Mail Importations," Director, FDA Office
of Regional Operations, July 20, 1988.

NOTES

1. *Policy Interpretation.* In a letter from FDA Associate Commissioner for
Legislative Affairs H.C. Cannon to Representative John Dingell (August 19,
1988), FDA stated that the new importation policy applied whether the drugs
were approved or unapproved in the country of origin; included any drug for
the treatment of serious and life-threatening conditions; applied to both individuals and organizations; applied whether or not an IND has been submitted
to FDA; and permitted FDA to deny entry wherever there was an unreasonable risk to patients. In accordance with this policy, AIDS patients have
organized buying groups to purchase unapproved drugs from abroad.

2. *Drugs on Import Alert.* The FDA importation policy does not apply to
drugs that have been made the subject of an Import Alert. FDA has issued
some 40 Import Alerts for medical products that are unsafe or clearly fraudulent. "Policy on Importing Unapproved AIDS Drugs for Personal Use," FDA
Talk Paper No. T88–51 (July 27, 1988).

---

d. Enforcement Discretion

FDA has declined to initiate regulatory action against various
activities by organized nonprofit AIDS groups that would almost surely
trigger enforcement immediately if engaged in by commercial enterprises. For example, on July 23, 1988, in a speech to the Second
International Lesbian and Gay Health Conference & Aids Forum in
Boston, FDA Commissioner Frank Young declared:

> The absence of an effective AIDS therapy has led to
> promotion of a number of unproven remedies or unproven
> drugs. Most of these products will be cast aside as ineffective
> after they have been popular for awhile....

> Traditionally, FDA has not interfered with individuals
> that use unproven substances in self-treatment. Nor have we
> interfered, when doctors prescribed drugs for other than their
> approved use. On the other hand, we have acted against
> promoters or seized products when there was a fraudulent
> promotion, or when the product represented an unreasonable
> risk. FDA's new policy regarding self-help, nonprofit clinics is
> similar to our policy regarding the use of unproven substances
> in self-treatment—that is, not to interfere as long as patients
> are not being harmed, clinics do not promote unproven prod-
> ucts outside the clinic, and the clinic does not serve as a
> subterfuge for a commercial enterprise.

GINA KOLATA, AN ANGRY RESPONSE TO ACTIONS ON AIDS SPURS F.D.A. SHIFT

The New York Times, June 26, 1988, p. 1.

Ripples of fear and resentment spread among AIDS patients and their advocates last week as the Food and Drug Administration threatened to restrict access to a substance thousands of patients are taking in the hope it might help fight their disease. On Monday, without publicity, the agency acted to stop two companies from selling AL–721, a substance made from eggs and soybeans that is being marketed as a food but is widely used as a possible treatment against the AIDS virus on the basis of slim anecdotal evidence. Then, on Thursday, as spreading word of the actions led to protests, the agency partly reversed itself. It allowed the companies to continue selling AL–721 but warned them not to suggest in their marketing that it was a drug.....

As last week's action and retreat against the two companies suggested, F.D.A. officials feel AL–721 puts them in a quandary. The agency is struggling to balance its mandate to protect the public from useless and perhaps harmful drugs against the understandable demand by the AIDS community for freer access to possible treatments for those facing death from acquired immune deficiency syndrome.....

In the last two years the use of AL–721 by AIDS virus carriers and AIDS patients has soared, promoted and organized by an impressive network. As many as 19 buyers clubs have sprung up around the country, purchasing AL–721 in bulk and even testing shipments to be sure they are pure. While it may not be dangerous, the substance is not cost-free. Patients pay about $135 to $250 a month for it, and taking it disrupts their lives. AL–721 requires refrigeration and, according to some, should not be taken within two hours of a meal.

It was developed about three years ago by Dr. Meir Shinitzky and his colleagues at the Weizmann Institute of Science in Rehovot, Israel. Dr. Shinitzky explained in a telephone interview that the substance was composed of three lipids, fats found in egg yolks, soybeans and some other foods. The theory is that the compound reduces the level of cholesterol in the membranes of blood cells and the AIDS virus. This makes the membranes more fluid, which Dr. Shinitzky and others postulate hampers the ability of the AIDS virus to attach to and invade body cells.....

When Dr. Shinitzky began making claims for AL–721 about two years ago, AIDS patients flew to Israel for the substance. Then, some began making a version of it for themselves, extracting it from egg yolks with acetone heated to near boiling. Later, they discovered a supplier in Japan and imported the substance. And finally, in the last year, as many as a half dozen companies in this country began openly marketing AL–721 as a food, which allowed them to skirt F.D.A. regulations for licensing drugs.

Yet calling AL–721 a food is the thinnest of guises, AIDS patients and their advocates say. Everyone is winking and nodding as buyers clubs purchase huge amounts of the substance and sell it to people infected with the AIDS virus. In New York City, the People With AIDS Health Club, sells a ton of AL–721 a month—enough to treat nearly 1,000 people, according to Mr. Callen.

On Monday, New Jersey officials, acting at the request of the F.D.A., entered a warehouse in South Plainfield, N.J. and put an embargo on 41 cases of AL–721, made by the Ethigen Corporation of Los Angeles. Also on Monday, the agency sent a letter to Nutricology, Inc. of San Leandro, Calif., telling the company to stop selling its version of the substance, which it calls Pe 9+. In both instances, the agency felt that the companies were selling AL–721 as an AIDS drug, not food.

As word of the action spread through the AIDS community, people felt panicked and outraged. Almost immediately, lawyers for gay support groups called the agency, and some AIDS patients began stockpiling AL–721. By Thursday, the agency called off the embargo and informed Nutricology that if it would comply with agency regulations and stop implying that the substance is useful against AIDS, it could resume selling the product.

NOTES

1. *Compound Q.* In June 1989 FDA announced it was investigating the distribution of "Compound Q," another untested treatment for AIDS:

> Trichosanthin is a plant protein, which researchers think may be an effective agent against the AIDS virus. An FDA-sanctioned clinical study of GLQ–223, a refined form of trichosanthin, was started at San Francisco General Hospital in May 1989. This initial human study is designed to test the safety of this drug's use in treating AIDS patients, and particularly to determine at what dose levels the drug can be tolerated.
>
> According to media reports, Project Inform, a San Francisco-based AIDS activist group initiated distribution of a trichosanthin-based preparation imported from China, supposedly to test its efficacy in AIDS patients..... There have been several media reports that the death of one patient and the serious adverse reactions of other patients participating in this informal study have been either directly or indirectly linked to this trichosanthin-based product.....
>
> The agency feels that the concerns raised by this operation point out the need to conduct clinical studies in a scientific manner, that includes careful study design, institutional monitoring mechanisms and consistent reporting channels. Such studies assure the acquisition of good clinical data in the shortest possible time, and ensure the safety of patients.

"FDA Statement on Unauthorized AIDS Drug Study," FDA Talk Paper No. T89–40 (June 28, 1987).

2. *Commercial Cancer Clinics.* Compare FDA's action to its efforts to shut down for-profit cancer clinics using unproven cancer drugs. *United States v. Burzynski Cancer Research Institute,* 819 F.2d 1301 (5th Cir. 1987); *United States v. Hoxsey Cancer Clinic,* 198 F.2d 273 (5th Cir. 1952).

---

6. ORPHAN DRUGS - *Rare disease*

FDA's requirements for approval of a new drug present special difficulties for the development of drugs intended to treat rare diseases whose potential sales are not large enough to justify funding of the necessary animal and clinical tests. For several years, FDA kept many such drugs indefinitely in "orphan IND" status, contrary to the intent of section 505(i), while allowing them to be used for patient treatment. One goal of FDA's revision of the IND regulations in the late 1970s was to establish a formal regulatory status for these orphan INDs.

The report of a HHS interagency task force, SIGNIFICANT DRUGS OF LIMITED COMMERCIAL VALUE (June 1979), outlined new mechanisms for spurring the development of orphan drugs. Soon after, Congress enacted the Orphan Drug Act, 96 Stat. 2049 (1983), to provide two types of incentives for the development of orphan drugs. First, the Act amended the Internal Revenue Code to provide tax credits for expenditures for clinical testing. *See* 26 U.S.C. § 44H. Second, it added four new sections, 525–528, to the FD&C Act. These provisions require FDA to provide sponsors written recommendations for the animal and clinical investigations needed for approval of an NDA, authorize FDA to designate those drugs that qualify as orphan drugs, provide seven years of post-approval market exclusivity for any unpatentable orphan drug (during which even a full NDA for an identical drug cannot be approved by FDA), and direct the agency to encourage open label INDs for orphan drugs under which patients suffering from the disease can obtain the drug for treatment. The industry response to the 1983 Act surpassed expectations, in part because several orphan drugs had already been identified and were thus available for immediate development.

To provide additional incentives for manufacturers to expand research into new clinical areas, Congress made two other important changes to the FD&C Act. In the Health Promotion and Disease Prevention Amendments of 1984, 98 Stat. 2815, 2817, section 526(a)(2) was revised to define as a "rare disease or condition" any that affects fewer than 200,000 persons in the United States. This change greatly expanded the number of diseases that could be regarded as "rare" and thus the number of drugs that could qualify as orphan drugs. The Orphan Drug Amendments of 1985, 99 Stat. 387, expanded the provision for market exclusivity to include patented as well as unpatentable drugs.

GENENTECH, INC. v. BOWEN

United States District Court, District of Columbia, 1987.

676 F. Supp. 301.

STANLEY S. HARRIS, District Judge.....

This case revolves around certain elements of the FDA's implementation of the Orphan Drug Act.....

Human growth hormone (hGH) is a protein naturally produced and secreted by the human pituitary gland. In some children, between 6,000 and 15,000 in the United States, the pituitary gland does not produce enough hGH, resulting in stunted growth. Since 1958, the condition had been treated by supplementing a patient's natural hGH with hGH derived from the pituitary glands of human cadavers. However, in 1985, use of pituitary-derived hGH was effectively eliminated by the discovery that three hGH patients who had been treated with hGH provided by NHPP had developed Creutzfeldt–Jakob Disease, an extremely rare but fatal condition, apparently due to exposure to a pathogen transmitted by the pituitary-derived hGH. Although no cases of Creutzfeldt–Jakob Disease have ever been linked to hGH distributed by Serone or KabiVitrum, neither has distributed pituitary-derived hGH in the United States since 1985.

On October 17, 1985, the FDA granted Genentech, a pharmaceutical developer that specializes in the use of biotechnology (popularly known as "gene splicing"), marketing approval for a human growth product known commercially as Protropin. Genentech's product differs from pituitary-derived hGH in two important respects. First, it is synthesized through a recombinant DNA process utilizing *E. coli* bacteria, rather than produced in a human gland. Second, Genentech's "r-hGH" product includes an amino acid group not commonly found in pituitary-derived hGH. In terms of chemical structure, Genentech's r-hGH has the same sequence of 191 amino acids found in hGH, with an additional methionine amino acid group attached to one end of the molecule. Because Genentech's drug apparently does not present the risk of Creutzfeldt–Jakob Disease associated with pituitary-derived hGH, its approval in 1985 filled an important health need. On December 12, 1985, the FDA designated Protropin as an orphan drug, thus granting Genentech marketing exclusivity, pursuant to 21 U.S.C. § 360cc, until December 12, 1992. Genentech estimates that it invested approximately $45 million developing its r-hGH product.

On June 12, 1986, the FDA designated an r-hGH drug developed by intervenor-defendant Lilly as an orphan drug for the treatment of human growth hormone deficiency. Unlike Genentech's r-hGH product, the chemical structure of Lilly's product is identical to that of natural, pituitary-derived hGH; that is, Lilly's drug does not contain the additional methionyl group found in Protropin. On October 15, 1986, Lilly submitted to the FDA a New Drug Application (NDA) for its r-hGH product, seeking permission to market the drug commercially.

On November 3, 1986, Genentech submitted a "citizen petition" to the FDA. In it, Genentech took the position that Lilly's drug was, for the purposes of the Orphan Drug Act, the same as Protropin and therefore ineligible for marketing approval until 1992. Genentech asked the FDA to implement procedures under which the manufacturer of an orphan drug with marketing exclusivity would receive notice of, and the opportunity to contest, another manufacturer's claim that its drug was "different" for the purposes of Orphan Drug Act protection. Genentech also requested an administrative stay of approval of any new r-hGH products until Genentech received the proposed procedural opportunities, as well as an opportunity to seek judicial relief.

When Genentech learned that the FDA was preparing to approve the NDA for Lilly's methionyl-free r-hGH product, known commercially as Humatrope, Genentech sought an emergency stay from the FDA. When that request was denied, Genentech filed suit in this Court on March 6, 1987, seeking temporary, preliminary, and permanent injunctive relief, in addition to a declaratory judgment that the FDA's application of the Orphan Drug Act violated Genentech's statutory and constitutional rights.

The Court denied the plaintiff's request for a temporary restraining order on March 6, 1987. That same day, the FDA formally responded to Genentech's citizen petition, denying the requests for implementation of new procedures and for a stay. The FDA also informed Genentech and Serono by letters that their methionyl-free r-hGH products had been designated orphan drugs. On March 8, the FDA approved Lilly's NDA for Humatrope, thereby authorizing Lilly to market the drug commercially and triggering the orphan drug exclusivity provision of 21 U.S.C. § 360cc. Genentech and Nordisk have submitted NDAs for methionyl-free r-hGH products, but the FDA has not yet ruled on either NDA.....

Movants contend that Humatrope's orphan drug designation violated both the Orphan Drug Act and the FDA's binding regulations implementing the Act. Their argument is based on the contention that Humatrope and pituitary-derived hGH are the same drug. In light of the peculiar facts of this case, the Court cannot accept movants' contention, and therefore must uphold the Humatrope designation.

The dispute presented here involved the proper application of 21 U.S.C. § 360bb(a), the section of the Act governing orphan drug designations, which provides, in relevant part:

(1) The manufacturer or the sponsor of a drug may request the Secretary to designate the drug as a drug for a rare disease or condition. If the Secretary finds that a drug for which a request is submitted under this subsection is being or will be investigated for a rare disease or condition and—

(A) if an application for such drug is approved under section 355 of this title,

* * * * * * *

the approval ... would be for use of such disease or condition, the Secretary shall designate the drug as a drug for such disease or condition.

Movants read this section as requiring that the orphan drug designation of a particular drug occur prior to approval of an NDA for that drug. They then argue that the approval of NDAs for pituitary-approved hGH in the 1970's precluded the orphan drug designation of Humatrope in 1986. Assuming, without deciding, that movants' construction of § 360bb(a) is correct, the Court rejects their argument in this case because it is plain that Humatrope and pituitary-derived hGH are not the same drug for the purposes of § 360bb(a).

A review of the Act's legislative history, as all of the parties would agree, sheds no direct light on the question of how broadly or narrowly the word "drug" should be construed in § 360bb(a). . . .

Two related aspects of this particular case convince the Court that if Congress had been presented with the facts of this case, it would have considered Humatrope and pituitary-derived hGH different drugs for the purposes of § 360bb(a). First, Humatrope, by virtue of its synthetic origin, does not present the danger of contamination with the Creutzfeldt–Jakob prion that is associated with hGH obtained from human cadavers. While movants are correct in noting that none of the reported cases of Creutzfeldt–Jakob Disease has been linked to hGH marketed under the approved NDAs held by Serono and Kabi, it is also true that so little is known about the contamination process that no manufacturer can warrant that its product is free from contamination. Thus, any pituitary-derived hGH product presents a risk (albeit unquantifiable) of lethal side effects not associated with r-hGH products such as Protropin and Humatrope.

Second, the industry's response to the linking of Creutzfeldt–Jakob Disease to pituitary-derived hGH—withdrawal from the United States market—meant that regardless of the status of the Serono and Kabi NDAs, methionyl-free hGH would not be available to hGH-deficient children in this country. The legislative history is replete with references to the fundamental need to provide treatment for presently untreated patients; the fact that NDAs for pituitary-derived hGH were technically still valid would not have convinced Congress that growth hormone deficiency was not a condition in need of new treatments. One need only imagine a world without methionyl r-hGH (plaintiff's Protropin) to appreciate the unacceptable ramifications of movants' argument when applied to this case. Without Protropin, children in need of supplemental hGH would go without treatment, while movants offered assurances that no additional orphan drug designations were necessary because valid, but unused, NDAs remained in effect. In enacting the Orphan Drug Act, Congress clearly focused on the availability of treatments, not the existence of prior NDAs. The Court is satisfied that Congress would have considered Humatrope sufficiently "different" to justify orphan drug designation.[26]....

NOTES

1. *Implementing Regulations.* FDA published notices of the availability of interim guidelines to implement the Orphan Drug Act in 48 Fed. Reg. 40784 (September 9, 1983), 50 Fed. Reg. 19583 (May 9, 1985). In 1986 the agency published a notice of its intent to initiate rulemaking to implement the Act, 51 Fed. Reg. 4505 (February 5, 1986), and proposed regulations were published in 56 Fed.Reg. 3338 (January 29, 1991).

2. *Timing of Claim of Orphan Drug Status.* FDA initially concluded that a drug was eligible for orphan drug designation if a petition was received before the agency approved an NDA for use of the drug to treat the rare disease, 51 Fed. Reg. 4505 (February 5, 1986). The Orphan Drug Amendments of 1988, 102 Stat. 90, amended section 526 to require that a petition for orphan drug designation be made before the submission of an NDA for the orphan drug use.

3. *Roster of Orphan Drug Listing.* FDA periodically publishes a cumulative list of orphan drug designations. *See, e.g.,* 54 Fed. Reg. 16294 (April 21, 1989), 55 Fed. Reg. 11438 (March 28, 1990).

4. *Orphan Products Board.* As originally enacted, the Orphan Drug Act created an Orphan Products Board, comprised entirely of officials of the Department of HHS, to promote the development of drugs and devices for rare diseases and conditions. 96 Stat. 2049, 2052 (1983). The Orphan Drug Amendments of 1985 substituted a new National Commission on Orphan Diseases, with nongovernmental membership, to assess governmental and nongovernmental activities with respect to rare diseases. 99 Stat. 387, 388. FDA has generally heeded the recommendations of the National Commission. *See, e.g.,* "Orphan Product Development Policies," FDA Talk Paper No. T89–30 (May 8, 1989).

5. *Seven Year Exclusivity.* As illustrated in the *Genentech* case, the assurance of seven years of market exclusivity is of major commercial importance. An amendment to allow exceptions to this provision passed by Congress was vetoed by President Bush on the ground that it would undermine the commercial incentive to develop orphan drugs. 26 Weekly Comp. of Pres.Doc. 1796 (November 8, 1990).

6. *Commentary.* See Carter and Bennett, *Developments in Orphan Drugs,* 44 FDC L. J. 627 (1989); Grossman, *The Orphan Drug Act: Adoption or Foster*

---

26. The court also rejects two arguments advanced by movants which, if adopted, would represent amendment of the Orphan Drug Act through judicial fiat. First, movants contend that designation of Humatrope violates the spirit of the Act by granting orphan drug benefits to a profitable drug. This possibility was explicitly considered—and accepted—in 1984 when the definition of rare disease or condition was amended to include all diseases afflicting fewer than 200,000 people in the United States. *See supra* note 8. This Court does not sit to judge the wisdom of that policy choice. Second, movants argue that the Humatrope designation violates the spirit of the Act by granting benefits to a manufacturer that did not rely on the Act's incentives when deciding whether to invest in new drug development. Consequently, movants assert that Congress did not intend for Lilly to profit from orphan drug designation. To accept movants' argument, however, would be to write into the Act an effective date that Congress chose not to impose; Congress chose to make orphan drug benefits available immediately. The Court declines movants' invitation to impose an additional condition on the receipt of benefits under the Act.

Care?, 39 FDC L. J. 128 (1984); Hurwitz, *Legal and Ethical Issues in the Clinical Testing of Drugs for Rare Diseases*, 40 FDC L. J. 396 (1985); Kenney, *The Orphan Drug Act—Is it a Barrier to Innovation? Does it Create Unintended Windfalls?*, 43 FDC L. J. 667 (1988); O'Reilly, *Orphan Drugs: The Strange Case of "Baby M"*, 42 FDC L.J. 516 (1987).

7. THE ABBREVIATED NEW DRUG PROCESS

FDA's abbreviated NDA policy for pre–1962 new drugs and its paper NDA policy for post–1962 new drugs were codified and extended to all new drugs, together with patent term restoration, in the Drug Price Competition and Patent Restoration Act of 1984, 98 Stat. 1585.

PETER BARTON HUTT, LANDMARK PHARMACEUTICAL LAW ENACTED

1 Health Scan, No. 3, p. 11 (1984).

... [T]he Drug Price Competition and Patent Term Restoration Act of 1984 ... caps fifteen years of controversy about the procedures to be used by the Food and Drug Administration (FDA) in approving the marketing of *generic* drugs, and about the incentives for developing important new pioneer drugs, given the erosion of patent protection resulting from lengthy regulatory processes. The legislation applies to all drugs marketed in the United States and to all patents granted in the United States, regardless of whether the drug is imported, or the new drug application (NDA) or patent is owned abroad....

The new statute keeps abbreviated NDAs and paper NDAs separate, but applies the ... same rules to both. Because it is easier to obtain an abbreviated NDA than a paper NDA, however, it is anticipated that few if any of the latter will be submitted. Accordingly, the rest of this article refers only to abbreviated NDAs, but must be understood to encompass paper NDAs as well.

The statute amends the FD&C Act to establish a new procedure for abbreviated NDAs. Unlike a pioneer NDA, which must contain full animal and human data to establish the safety and effectiveness of the drug, an abbreviated NDA need only contain sufficient information to demonstrate that the generic version of the drug is bioavailable and is bioequivalent to the pioneer drug. In return, however, the statute provides three new statutory protections for manufacturers of pioneer new drugs; protection against release of safety and effectiveness information, protection against an abbreviated NDA becoming effective before all relevant product and use patents for the pioneer drug have expired, and protection against an abbreviated NDA becoming effective during specified periods of market exclusivity that are independent of the patent status of the pioneer drug.

Part of the disagreement about abbreviated NDAs for post–1962 drugs during the past several years has been a dispute about the status of the safety and effectiveness information submitted in the pioneer NDA. The FDA has consistently stated ... that this information constitutes trade secrets which cannot be released to the public or used to approve a generic drug. The new statute provides that such information will retain its trade secret status and cannot be released to the public at least up to the point where an abbreviated NDA for a generic version could be made effective by FDA. Thereafter, the status of such information continues to enjoy protection against disclosure as trade secrets or other confidential commercial information. Under all circumstances, however, such information—even if not disclosable to the public—can be used by FDA to approve an abbreviated NDA for a generic drug.

Although FDA can approve an abbreviated NDA for a patented pioneer drug, that approval cannot be made effective (and thus the generic version cannot be marketed) until all relevant product and use patents have expired. Thus, a patented product or use (but not a patented process) will be protected by FDA until the relevant patents expire, because FDA is precluded from making an abbreviated NDA for a generic drug effective during the life of those patents. This is an entirely new concept under the FD&C Act. Previously, FDA approved all forms of NDAs without any consideration of patent status.

The new statute does permit a generic company to challenge a product or use patent which the pioneer NDA holder identifies as precluding the marketing of generic versions. The generic company which wishes to initiate such a challenge must submit an abbreviated NDA to FDA certifying that any relevant patent is invalid or will not be infringed, must notify the patent owner of that certification, and must specify the legal and factual basis for it. If the patent owner takes no action within 45 days, FDA may proceed to handle the abbreviated NDA like any other abbreviated NDA and the patent owner remains free to initiate or not initiate any form of patent litigation once the drug is approved by FDA and marketed. If the patent owner chooses to challenge the certification of patent invalidity or noninfringement and keep the generic version off the market, however, it must bring suit within 45 days of receiving the generic company's notification. If that is done, FDA is precluded from making the abbreviated NDA effective for a period of 30 months while the matter is being litigated or until the trial court decides the matter. If at the end of that 30 months the litigation is not concluded, an approved abbreviated NDA will become effective, and the generic drug can be marketed subject to the outcome of the pending litigation, unless the court itself enjoins marketing.

In addition to protection of trade secret data and product and use patents, the statute sets specified time periods during which abbreviated NDAs for generic drugs cannot become effective and thus generic versions cannot be marketed....

• All pioneer drugs approved by FDA during 1962–1981 are subject to abbreviated NDAs immediately.

• Abbreviated NDAs for new chemical entity (NCE) drugs approved during 1982–1984 cannot become effective for ten years after the date of approval of the pioneer NDA.

• Abbreviated NDAs for non-NCE drugs approved during 1982–1984 cannot be made effective for two years following the date of enactment of the legislation.

• Abbreviated NDAs for post-enactment NCE drugs cannot be submitted to (or accepted by) FDA for five years following the date of approval of the pioneer NDA, except that an abbreviated NDA challenging a patent for a pioneer drug can be submitted after four years.

• Abbreviated NDAs for post-enactment, non-NCE drugs cannot become effective for three years following the date of approval of the pioneer NDA if the FDA approval of the pioneer NDA is based upon new clinical investigations.

• Abbreviated NDAs covering changes in pioneer NDAs (e.g., new uses, new dosages, or new processes) approved by FDA after the date of enactment cannot become effective for three years after such FDA approval if the supplemental NDA submitted by the pioneer NDA holder to obtain approval of those changes is based upon reports of new clinical investigations. All of these provisions also apply, as already noted, to paper NDAs. These time periods apply regardless of the status of any patents for the pioneer drug. If, at the end of the applicable period of market exclusivity, any product or use patent for the pioneer drug remains unexpired, however, no approval of an abbreviated NDA could be made effective by the FDA for that drug until the last such patent expires.

The biotechnology industry requested Congress to include in this legislation a specific provision prohibiting an abbreviated NDA for any pioneer NDA utilizing recombinant DNA technology for a period of ten years following approval of the pioneer NDA. This [proposal] was not accepted. Drugs made from recombinant DNA technology are therefore subject to the other provisions of the new law. If such a drug is an NCE drug, no abbreviated NDA may be submitted for five years after approval of the pioneer NDA (or four years, if a patent is being challenged). If it is a non-NCE drug, an abbreviated NDA cannot be made effective until three years after approval of the pioneer NDA.....

Under the new statute (which amends the patent law) the patent for any drug approved by FDA after the date of enactment is potentially eligible for patent term extension....

Any product, use, or process patent is potentially subject to extension. The patent may be a broad genus patent, or a narrow species patent. The decision as to which patent to extend is up to the patent owner. No patent may be extended more than once, and only one patent may be extended for any regulatory review. Moreover, the marketing or use of the product permitted by the regulatory review must represent the first permission for that marketing or use, and cannot previously have been permitted by an earlier regulatory review. The only exception to this rule is for a new process using recombinant DNA technology, where the production of the product permitted by an earlier regulatory review does not preclude the extension of a process patent for making the product through recombinant DNA technology as a result of a second regulatory review.

Patent term extension may be obtained for the length of the regulatory review period as defined in the statute, subject to three important limitations. The regulatory review period for a drug is defined as half the IND (human clinical study) time, plus the whole time during which FDA is reviewing the NDA. Thus, if the IND time is eight years and the NDA time is two years, the regulatory review period would be 6 years (half the 8–year IND time *plus* the full two-year NDA time).

The three important limitations to the length of patent term extension are as follows. First, under no circumstances may it exceed five years. For a "pipeline" drug, whose regulatory review period spans the enactment date of the legislation, this limitation is two years. Second, the total effective patent life (defined as the time from the date of the pioneer NDA approval to the conclusion of patent protection, including the extended patent term) may not exceed a total of fourteen years. Third, the regulatory review period is to be reduced by any amount of time during which the NDA applicant has not exerted "due diligence" in attempting to obtain FDA approval of the NDA. The statute defines "due diligence" in terms of usual industry practice and requires FDA to initiate a due diligence investigation only upon petition of an interested person showing good cause.

In order to obtain patent term restoration, the patent holder must submit an application to the Patent Office within sixty days of approval of the NDA. The Patent Office is directed to take action upon the application solely on the basis of information contained in the application, in order to reduce the burden placed on it by the legislation.

NOTES

1. *Implementing Regulations.* For a more detailed discussion of the 1984 statute, *see* Flannery and Hutt, *Balancing Competition and Patent Protection in the Drug Industry: The Drug Price Competition and Patent Term Restoration Act of 1984*, 40 FDC L.J. 269 (1985). FDA published detailed proposed regulations to implement the generic drug provisions of the statute in 54 Fed. Reg. 28872 (July 10, 1989).

2. *Eligibility for Abbreviated NDA.* Where a pioneer drug is withdrawn from marketing by its manufacturer for reason of safety, it is automatically withdrawn from the FDA approved drug list and can no longer be the subject of an abbreviated NDA. *See, e.g.,* 51 Fed. Reg. 21981 (June 17, 1986) (nomifensine maleate).

3. *Market Exclusivity.* The market exclusivity provisions of the 1984 statute have provoked extensive litigation. *See, e.g., Mead Johnson Pharmaceutical Group v. Bowen,* 838 F.2d 1332 (D.C. Cir. 1988); *Norwich Eaton Pharmaceuticals, Inc. v. Bowen,* 808 F.2d 486 (6th Cir. 1987); *Abbott Laboratories v. Young,* 691 F.Supp. 462 (D.D.C. 1988); *Burroughs Wellcome Co. v. Bowen,* 630 F.Supp. 787 (E.D.N.C. 1986); *Glaxo, Inc. v. Heckler,* 623 F.Supp. 69 (E.D.N.C. 1985); *Inwood Laboratories, Inc. v. Young,* 723 F.Supp. 1523 (D.D.C. 1989).

4. *Antibiotic Drugs.* Because Section 507 of the FD&C Act requires FDA to issue regulations for the certification of antibiotic drugs (as contrasted with the individual NDA licensing system for nonantibiotic new drugs), FDA determined that the statute authorized the agency to approve requests for certification for generic versions of antibiotic drugs without the need for additional safety and effectiveness data. Accordingly, although the patent term restoration portion of the Drug Price Competition and Patent Term Restoration Act of 1984 applied to antibiotic drugs, the abbreviated NDA provisions did not and thus the market exclusivity provisions also do not apply to antibiotic drugs.

5. *Patent Term Restoration.* The Patent and Trademark Office has promulgated regulations implementing the patent provisions of the 1984 statute in 51 Fed. Reg. 27205 (July 30, 1986), 52 Fed. Reg. 9386 (March 24, 1987), codified in 37 C.F.R. § 1.710 *et seq.* FDA promulgated regulations implementing the patent provisions of the 1984 statute for which it is responsible in 51 Fed. Reg. 25338 (July 11, 1986), 53 Fed. Reg. 7298 (March 7, 1988), codified in 21 C.F.R. Part 60. FDA and the Patent and Trademark Office entered into a Memorandum of Understanding in 52 Fed. Reg. 17830 (May 12, 1987) to coordinate implementation of these regulations. FDA regularly published in the Federal Register notices of the determinations of regulatory review periods for purposes of patent term extension.

6. *Eligibility for Extension.* In the first cases it has decided under the 1984 Act, the United States Court of Appeals for the Federal Circuit has held that 35 U.S.C. § 156(a)(5)(A) precludes patent term restoration for a second approved use after the new drug was initially approved for another use, and that the provisions in 35 U.S.C. § 271(e)(1) allow a manufacturer to test a patent-holder's device (or drug) to obtain information to support FDA approval of the product, prior to expiration of the patent. *Fisons plc v. Quigg,* 876 F.2d 99 (Fed. Cir. 1989); *Eli Lilly and Co. v. Medtronic, Inc.,* 872 F.2d 402 (Fed. Cir. 1989), *aff'd,* __ U.S. __, 110 S.Ct. 2683 (1990).

7. *Statutory Extensions.* In addition to the general statutory patent term restoration provided by the 1984 statute, specific patent term extensions have been granted by Congressional enactment for Forane in 97 Stat. 831, 832–833 (1983), Impro in 98 Stat. 3430 (1984), glyburide in 98 Stat. 3434 (1984), and Lopid in 102 Stat. 1107, 1569–1570 (1988).

8. *Economic Impact.* In the first two years after enactment of the 1984 statute, FDA approved some 520 abbreviated NDAs. The first analysis of the economic impact of the statute concluded that the generic drug industry made relatively greater gains than the pioneer drug industry, but that this balance could shift significantly when drugs now in development gain approval and receive up to five years of patent extension. Kaitin and Trimble, *Implementation of the Drug Price Competition and Patent Term Restoration Act of 1984: A Progress Report,* 1 J. Clin. Res. & Drug Dev. 263 (1987).

9. *Caseload.* As of October 1989, the Patent and Trademark Office had received 130 applications for patent term extension. Of these, 33 were with-

drawn or denied and 25 remain pending, while 72 were granted: 60 for human drugs, 11 for medical devices, and one for a food additive. In none of these instances has FDA determined, or has any interested person requested, a hearing to determine, that the applicant has failed to act with due diligence under 35 U.S.C. § 156(d)(2)(B). Van Horn and Boland, *Patent Laws and Biotechnology* 2 (October 13, 1989).

FDA REGULATION AND PROMOTION OF GENERIC DRUGS

The primary goal of the investigations begun by Senator Kefauver in 1959 was to reduce drug prices through increased competition in the pharmaceutical industry. Although the only element of Kefauver's proposed legislation that became part of the 1962 Drug Amendments was the requirement that drug labeling disclose the generic name, the Federal government's growing responsibility for drug purchases has led FDA to assume a role in promoting the use of generic drugs that extends beyond its narrow statutory mandate.

The Social Security Amendments of 1965, 79 Stat. 286 established Federal programs to provide medical benefits to the elderly and disabled (Medicare) and, in cooperation with the states, to the needy (Medicaid). Medicare covers the costs of medical care provided in two contexts. Part A primarily covers inpatient hospitalization services, including drugs. Part B is a voluntary program of supplemental medical insurance which includes drugs provided incidental to a physician's care that cannot be self-administered. Although each state has its own Medicaid rules, most cover outpatient prescription drugs for needy patients. The costs to both Federal and state governments for reimbursing prescription drug purchases have continued to increase, and accordingly the incentive to encourage price competition and contain costs has been substantial. *See, e.g.,* Giumarra, *Drug Amendments of 1962—Generic-Name Prescribing: Drug Price Panacea?,* 16 Stan. L. Rev. 649 (1964); Note, *Consumer Protection and Prescription Drugs: The Generic Drug Substitution Laws,* 67 Ky. L.J. 384 (1978–1979).

Soon after the NAS began to deliver its DESI reports to FDA in 1967, FDA devised the abbreviated NDA to secure control over, and at the same time allowed marketing of, pre–1962 prescription drugs. 34 Fed. Reg. 2673 (February 27, 1969). One requirement for approval of an abbreviated NDA was proof of "biological availability." Faced with competitors that had FDA approval, manufacturers of pioneer drugs questioned the quality, and thus the clinical effectiveness, of generic products. In DRUG BIOEQUIVALENCE (1974), the Office of Technology Assessment concluded that "current standards and regulatory practices do not insure bioequivalence for drug products" and that "present compendial standards and guidelines for Current Good Manufacturing Practice do not insure quality in uniform bioavailability for drug products."

Just as these questions were being raised, FDA encountered the first major bioavailability/bioequivalence problem with an important prescription drug, digoxin, versions of which were being marketed without approved NDAs. FDA promptly adopted stringent conditions for testing and labeling of digoxin drugs in 39 Fed. Reg. 2471 (January 22, 1974), now codified in 21 C.F.R. § 310.500. Following a public hearing 39 Fed. Reg. 9129, 9184 (March 8, 1974), it revised the labeling, 41 Fed. Reg. 43135 (September 30, 1976), and reimposed the requirement of an abbreviated NDA for all generic versions.

FDA promulgated general regulations governing drug bioavailability and bioequivalence in 38 Fed. Reg. 885 (January 5, 1973), 40 Fed. Reg. 26164 (June

20, 1975), 42 Fed. Reg. 1624 (January 7, 1977), 42 Fed. Reg. 42311 (August 23, 1977), codified in 21 C.F.R. Part 320. *See* Cabana, *Bioavailability/Bioequivalence* 32 FDC L.J. 512 (1977); Doluisio, *A Definition of Bioequivalence/Bioavailability and a Historical Perspective,* 32 FDC L.J. 506 (1977); Spencer, *Bioequivalence/Bioavailability—The FDA's Plans,* 31 FDC L.J. 32 (1976). 21 C.F.R. § 320.1 defines the critical terms as follows:

(a) "Bioavailability" means the rate and extent to which the active drug ingredient or therapeutic moiety is absorbed from a drug product and becomes available at the site of drug action.

(b) "Drug product" means a finished dosage form, e.g., tablet, capsule, or solution, that contains the active drug ingredient, generally, but not necessarily, in association with inactive ingredients.

(c) "Pharmaceutical equivalents" means drug products that contain identical amounts of the identical active drug ingredient, i.e., the same salt or ester of the same therapeutic moiety, in identical dosage forms, but not necessarily containing the same inactive ingredients, and that meet the identical compendial or other applicable standard of identity, strength, quality, and purity, including potency and, where applicable, content uniformity, disintegration times and/or dissolution rates.

(d) "Pharmaceutical alternatives" means drug products that contain the identical therapeutic moiety, or its precursor, but not necessarily in the same amount or dosage form or as the same salt or ester....

(e) "Bioequivalent drug products" means pharmaceutical equivalents or pharmaceutical alternatives whose rate and extent of absorption do not show a significant difference when administered at the same molar dose of the therapeutic moiety under similar experimental conditions, either single dose or multiple dose. Some pharmaceutical equivalents or pharmaceutical alternatives may be equivalent in the extent of their absorption but not in their rate of absorption and yet may be considered bioequivalent because such differences in the rate of absorption are intentional and are reflected in the labeling, are not essential to the attainment of effective body drug concentrations on chronic use, or are considered medically insignificant for the particular drug product studied.

FDA also set forth a procedure to establish bioequivalence requirements for specific drugs and proposed regulations for eleven drug clusters, the first for anticonvolusants, 42 Fed. Reg. 39675 (August 5, 1977), and the last for quinidine, 45 Fed. Reg. 72200 (October 31, 1980). The agency later determined simply to set bioequivalence requirements through the abbreviated NDA process rather than by regulations, 54 Fed. Reg. 28823, 28872, 28911 (July 10, 1989).

With greater assurance of the quality and clinical effectiveness of generic drugs, the Department of HEW in 39 Fed. Reg. 40302 (November 15, 1974), 40 Fed. Reg. 32284 (July 31, 1975), established procedures for fixing the maximum allowable cost (MAC) that the Federal government would reimburse for any multi-source drug dispensed to patients under Medicare and other programs. Under these procedures, a new body, the Pharmaceutical Reimbursement Board, would establish a "MAC" for a drug based on the "lowest unit price at which the drug is widely and consistently available from any formulator or labeler." The MAC did not apply where "the prescriber has certified in his own handwriting [that a particular brand] is medically necessary for that patient." For a single-source drug, reimbursement was based on the actual cost of the product. Though the MAC regulations withstood legal challenge, *American Medical Association v. Mathews*, 429 F.Supp. 1179 (N.D. Ill. 1977); *Hoffmann–LaRoche, Inc. v. Califano*, 453 F.Supp. 900 (D.D.C. 1978), 48 Fed. Reg. 35506 (August 4, 1983), HHS later revoked them, 51 Fed. Reg. 29560 (August 19, 1986), 51 Fed. Reg. 33086 (September 18, 1986), 52 Fed. Reg. 28648 (July 31, 1987), on the grounds that they had had little impact on drug costs and that alternative approaches to encouraging generic prescribing under Medicaid would be more cost-effective.

During the 1970s many states also sought to promote the use of generic drugs under Medicaid. To assist the states in developing formularies listing drugs appropriate for reimbursement, FDA initially disseminated lists of all drugs it had approved for marketing, 41 Fed. Reg. 5539 (February 5, 1976), 43 Fed. Reg. 28557 (June 30, 1978). Soon afterwards it prepared a list of "therapeutically equivalent drugs," including prices, and in 44 Fed. Reg. 2932 (January 12, 1979) proposed that it be distributed to all physicians and pharmacists to aid them to make comparisons among products containing the same generic active ingredients. Following an unsuccessful attempt to halt the rulemaking, *Pharmaceutical Manufacturers Association v. Kennedy*, 471 F.Supp. 1224 (D. Md. 1979), FDA issued a final regulation in 45 Fed. Reg. 72582 (October 31, 1980), codified in 21 C.F.R. § 20.117(a)(3), making available a list of all approved drugs together with "an evaluation of the therapeutic equivalence of the drug products covered by such applications." The Drug Price Competition and Patent Term Restoration Act of 1984 added section 505(j)(6) to the FD&C Act to require FDA to publish such a list as a way of identifying drugs eligible for abbreviated NDAs. In accordance with that provision, the agency publishes a yearly list of approved drugs, with monthly revisions, commonly referred to as the "Orange Book."

The Orange Book contains two types of therapeutic equivalence evaluations. A drug given an "A" rating is considered by FDA to be "therapeutically equivalent to other pharmaceutically equivalent products." Drugs that "FDA does not at this time consider to be therapeuticallly equivalent to other pharmaceutically equivalent products, *i.e.*, drug products for which actual or potential bioequivalence problems have not been resolved by adequate evidence of bioequivalence," are rated "B." FDA arrives at these ratings without consultation with manufacturers and without notice-and-comment rulemaking. When FDA considered changing the classification of a generic antihypertensive drug from "A" to "B" because of uncertainty about therapeutic equivalence, however, it first provided an opportunity for the manufacturer to respond. *See* "FDA to Propose Withdrawal of Bolar's Generic Antihypertensive," FDA Talk Paper No. T89–53 (August 28, 1989); "FDA Officially Changes Rating of Bolar's Antihypertensive," FDA Talk Paper No. T89–57 (September 28, 1989).

As the rate of applications for approval of generic versions of post–1962 new drugs rose following the Drug Price Competition and Patent Term Restoration Act, manufacturers of pioneer drugs amplified their criticisms of generic products. In 1986, FDA established a Bioequivalence Task Force and scheduled a public hearing on the subject in 51 Fed. Reg. 23476 (June 27, 1986). *See* 51 Fed. Reg. 46721 (December 24, 1986), 53 Fed. Reg. 6036 (February 29, 1988). One conclusion of the Task Force was that FDA should improve its procedures to detect and evaluate reports of drug product therapeutic failure that could be indicative of product inequivalence. In response FDA established a Therapeutic Inequivalence Act Coordinating Committee, 53 Fed. Reg. 35562 (September 14, 1988).

In 1988, the House Subcommittee on Oversight and investigations launched an investigation into allegations by some manufacturers of generic drugs that their applications were not being processed fairly or expeditiously by FDA. "Misconduct Allegations in Generic Drug Reviews," FDA Talk Paper No. T88–48 (July 6, 1988); "FDA's Generic Drug Approval Process (Parts 1–3)," Hearings before the Subcomm. on Oversight and Investigations of the House Comm. on Energy and Commerce, 101st Cong., 1st Sess. (1989). The Subcommittee found that some employees of the FDA Division of Generic Drugs of the Office of Drug Standards had accepted illegal gratuities from manufacturers, that some manufacturers conducted (and submitted) bioavailability and bioequivalence studies using the pioneer drug rather than their own generic products, and that significant discrepancies occurred in the testing and manufacture of some generic drugs. The agency employees and responsible officials of the implicated manufacturers were prosecuted, the suspect products were recalled and approval of their abbreviated NDAs withdrawn or proposed to be withdrawn, and FDA undertook investigations of manufacturing facilities and testing of products to verify the quality and clinical effectiveness of the generic drug supply. *See, e.g.,* "Vitarine Suspends Distribution of Drugs After Inquiry," FDA Talk Paper No. T89–36 (June 1, 1989); "Generics Firm Recalls Diuretic," FDA Talk Paper No. T89–47 (July 24, 1989); "FDA Testing Generics of Top Thirty Drugs," FDA Talk Paper No. T89–51 (August 16, 1989): "FDA Inspections of Makers of Generic Drugs," FDA Talk Paper No. T89–52 (August 23, 1989); 54 Fed. Reg. 35535 (August 28, 1989); 54 Fed. Reg. 40740 (October 3, 1989); 54 Fed. Reg. 42367 (October 16, 1989); 54 Fed. Reg. 48026 (November 20, 1989); 55 Fed. Reg. 5074 (February 13, 1990); 55 Fed. Reg. 8995 (March 9, 1990); 55 Fed. Reg. 9360 (March 13, 1990); 55 Fed. Reg. 21103 (May 22, 1990); 55 Fed. Reg. 25712 (June 22, 1990); 55 Fed.Reg. 24934 (June 19, 1990); 55 Fed.Reg. 25712 (June 22, 1990); 55 Fed.Reg. 46245 (November 2, 1990); 55 Fed.Reg. 47542 (November 14, 1990); 55 Fed.Reg. 47919 (November 16, 1990); 56 Fed.Reg. 2528 (January 23, 1991). FDA made management changes and upgraded the Division of Generic Drugs. "Temporary Changes Made In Generic Drugs Management," FDA Talk Paper No. T89–34 (May 15, 1989); 54 Fed. Reg. 32014 (August 3, 1989). On August 18, 1989, the Secretary of HHS and the FDA Commissioner issued statements announcing intensified analyses of generic drugs and their manufacturers, strengthened generic drug review procedures, and creation of an independent ombudsman to assure fairness in decisionmaking on product approval. FDA issued AN INTERIM REPORT ON GENERIC DRUGS (November 17, 1989), established an advisory committee on generic drugs in 55 Fed. Reg. 5838 (February 20, 1990), requested public comment on the generic drug program in 55 Fed.Reg. 6049 (February 21, 1990), held a public meeting on new policies and procedures for generic drugs announced in 55 Fed.Reg. 38583 (September 19, 1990), and established a public file with all pertinent records on the agency's generic drug policies in 55 Fed.Reg. 42654 (October 22, 1990), as part of its program to reassure the public about the safety and effectiveness of generic drugs. An interim regulation on retention of bioavailability and bioequivalence testing samples was promulgated in 55 Fed.Reg. 47034 (November 8, 1990).

Legislation was introduced in May 1990 to provide increased penalties, including debarment, against individuals and corporations who defrauded FDA in generic drug applications, H.R. 4810, 101st Cong., 2d Sess., but it did not pass because of controversy over whether it should cover NDAs and other premarket approval applications submitted to FDA as well. A study commissioned by the generic drug industry made recommendations for improving FDA regulation of the industry. Blue Ribbon Committee on Generic Medicines, GENERIC MEDICINES: RESTORING PUBLIC CONFIDENCE (November 15, 1990). By early 1991, five FDA employees had been convicted of bribery or perjury, eight generic drug companies had been found to have submitted applications to FDA containing fraudulent data, and investigations by both FDA and congressional oversight committees were continuing.

---

8. IMPACT OF THE 1962 DRUG AMENDMENTS

a. The "Drug Lag"

The seminal critique of FDA's regulation of new drugs is the study of the 1962 Drug Amendments by Professor Sam Peltzman. Peltzman summarized his study, published as REGULATION OF PHARMACEUTICAL INNOVATION (AEI, 1974), in congressional testimony.

STATEMENT OF SAM PELTZMAN

Before the Subcommittee on Monopoly of the Senate Small Business Committee.
93d Congress, 1st Session (1973).

[T]he benefits provided by the amendments seem clearly outweighed by the costs they have engendered.... As I hope to make clear, consumers could not have avoided losses under the most efficient and well-intentioned administration of the law....

It is beyond dispute that new drug innovation in the United States has declined since 1962. The 15 years prior to 1962 saw an average of 42 new chemical entities marketed per year compared to 16 in the subsequent decade. What is in dispute is the connection of this decline to the 1962 amendments. Innovation was declining from 1959 to 1962, and it is sometimes thought that the post–1962 experience might simply be a continuation of a previous trend. However, my research has led me to reject this explanation. I found that prior to 1962 there was a regular, highly predictable relationship between the rate of drug innovation in any year and previous growth in the market for drugs.... Subnormal growth in prescription sales led—with a lag of about two years, that being the average development time for new drugs—to subnormal innovation. That relationship held closely in the 1959–62 period and accounts fully for the decline in innovation: growth of the drug market peaked in the mid 1950's and declined to about 1960. However, unlike the pre–1962 period, the resumption of drug market growth in the early 1960s did not subsequently lead to increased innovation....

... [I]t appears that the Amendments are preventing development of something like 25 new chemical entities for the U.S. drug market annually. I will argue subsequently that only a small fraction of the sales of those drugs would likely prove ineffective.... [This] means that the amendments' proof of efficiency and clinical testing requirements impose costs on the drug development process which discourage new drug development. I have estimated that the R. & D. costs for developing a new chemical entity have been about doubled by the added testing and information requirements of the Amendments.... It is simply unreasonable to expect a cost increase of this magnitude not to discourage development of new drugs, effective as well as ineffective.... Even if an effective new drug could be developed, neither the FDA nor the consumer will hear of it if its prospective returns cannot defray added development costs....

... If the pre–1962 rate of innovation had been maintained, annual sales of new drugs in their initial full year of marketing would, given the larger size of today's drug market, approximate $125 million.... The comparable post–1962 figure is about $50 million.... [I]f one assumes that about 10 percent of the pre–1962 drug sales were for ineffective drugs ... and that none of the post–1962 drugs are ineffective ... then the decline in sales of effective new drugs due to the Amendments is over $60 million per year. My net benefit estimate of 50 percent of sales then applies a benefit loss exceeding $30 million on new drugs in their initial year of marketing. This loss will recur each year that new drugs remain on the market and sales remain $60 million lower ... [A]ssuming that these new drugs have level sales and a market life of 15 years ..., the total benefits sacrificed due to reduced innovation in a single year would exceed $450 million into a present value of about $250 million.... In addition ... because the amendments have been such an effective barrier to new competition for existing drugs, price rivalry in the drug market has been weakened. My estimate of the consumer cost of the resulting high prices for old and new drugs is about $50 million per year.

The benefits attributable to the Amendments must, of course, be set against this ... cost. I used two approaches to estimate the waste on ineffective new drugs prior to 1962. One was the test of the marketplace.... If a new drug is ineffective, one would expect some reduction in prescribing for it as physicians accumulate evidence ... of its ineffectiveness.... If the Amendments screened ineffective drugs out, one would then find sales of pre–1962 new drugs taken together growing more slowly over time than their post–1962 counterparts.... I will not burden the committee with this calculation, because the plain fact is that the difference in market acceptance between pre- and post–1962 drugs is trivial....

... I turned to drug evaluations by experts—specifically the AMA Council on Drugs. A highly skeptical layman's reading of their *Drug Evaluations* turned up 16 of 80 new chemical entities introduced 1960–62 which could be labeled either ineffective, or no more effective than a cheaper alternative. The total consumer waste on these drugs—expenditures on the eight ineffective drugs, and the price premium for the eight equally effective but more expensive drugs—scaled to the 1970 drug market was under $20 million annually.... [U]nlike most new drugs, sales of the ineffective drugs decline markedly over time.... Taking both this decline and the difference between present and future losses into account, I arrive at a present value of well under $100 million for the total waste imposed on consumers....

The extravagant potential costs of the risk-tradeoff in the Amendments can be illustrated by first examining its potential benefits in forestalling something like the thalidomide tragedy.... [T]he thalidomide tragedy was, in fact, forestalled in the United States without the Amendments. But if we ... consider what might have been, and ... assume that the thalidomide tragedy here might have been as widespread as it was in West Germany ... we could have expected the birth of about 20,000 phocomelic infants on a 1970 population base.... If we further make the extreme assumption that none of these infants would be at all productive in adulthood, I estimate the present value of the economic cost of this hypothetical event at between $150 and $500 million.... Now, if we are going to assume that the Amendments completely eliminate the potential for such tragedies, we must gauge the frequency with which such a tragedy could otherwise be expected to occur in order to evaluate the prospective benefits.... Since a tragedy as profound as thalidomide has in fact never occurred in the United States, this must be largely conjectural.... [W]e could attribute to the Amendments a potential for preventing something like 10,000 deaths or serious disabilities and an economic loss of something like $300 million perhaps once per decade....

NOTES

1. *FDA Risk Aversion.* Peltzman's study prompted Professor Milton Friedman to write in the January 8, 1973 issue of *Newsweek:*

Put yourself in the position of an FDA official charged with approving or disapproving a new drug. You can make two very different kinds of serious mistakes:

1. Approve a drug that turns out to have unanticipated side effects resulting in death or serious impairment of a sizable number of persons.

2. Refuse approval of a drug that is capable of saving many lives or relieving great distress and has no untoward side effects....

With visions of the thalidomide episode dancing in your head and the knowledge of the fame and acclaim that came to the woman who held up approval of thalidomide in the U.S., is there any doubt which mistake you will be more anxious to avoid? With the best will in the world, you will be led to reject or postpone approval of many a good drug in order to avoid even a remote possibility of approving a drug that will have newsworthy side effects....

2. *Drug Lag Literature.* The literature dealing with the "drug lag" is extensive, and the conclusions reached about the impact of FDA's implementation of the 1962 Amendments conflicting. For statements of both sides of the issue, *compare* Kennedy, *A Calm Look at "Drug Lag,"* 239 J.A.M.A. 423 (1978), *with* Wardell, *A Close Inspection of the "Calm Look,"* 239 J.A.M.A. 2004 (1978). In addition to Peltzman's work, *see* Wardell and Lasagna, REGULATION AND DRUG DEVELOPMENT (AEI, 1975). In June 1979 representatives of the General Accounting Office provided a prepublication look at a study it had undertaken, which concluded that Americans wait significantly longer than citizens of other developed countries for important new drugs to obtain approval. *See* "Review of the United States General Accounting Office of the Food and Drug Administration's Drug Approval Process," Subcomm. on Science, Research and Technology of the House Comm. on Science and Technology, 96th Cong., 1st Sess. (1979). The final GAO report expressed the same view. *See* FDA DRUG APPROVAL—A LENGTHY PROCESS THAT DELAYS THE AVAILABILITY OF IMPORTANT NEW DRUGS (1980). *See also* Berlin and Jonsson, *International Dissemination of New Drugs: A Comparative Study of Six Countries,* 7 Managerial & Decision Economics 235 (1986); Haas, *et al., A Historical Look at Drug Introductions on a Five-Country Market: A Comparison of the United States and Four European Countries* (1960–1981), FDA OPE Study No. 60 (March 1982); Lasagna, *The Development and Regulation of New Medications,* 200 Science 871 (1978); Mattison, *et al., New Drug Development in the United States, 1963 through 1984,* 43 Clin. Pharmacol. & Therapy. 290 (March 1988); Miller, *et al., Delays in the Drug Approval Process: Recent Trends,* 2 J. Clin. Res. & Drug Dev. 31 (1988); National Academy of Sciences, THE COMPETITIVE STATUS OF THE U.S. PHARMACEUTICAL INDUSTRY (1983); Parker, *Regulating Pharmaceutical Innovation: An Economist's View,* 32 FDC L.J. 160 (1977); Seidman, *The Politics of Policy Analysis: Protection or Overprotection in Drug Regulation?,* Regulation (July/August 1977) at 22; Shifrin and Tayan, *The Drug Lag: An Interpretive Review of the Literature,* 7 Int. J. of Health Serv. 359 (1977); Tadlow, *Competition and "Quality" in the Drug Industry: The 1962 Kefauver-Harris Drug Amendments as Barriers to Entry,* 5 Antitrust L. & Econ. Rev. 103 (Winter 1971–72); Wardell, *More Regulation or Better Therapies?,* Regulation (September/October 1979), at 25; Weimer, *Safe—And Available—Drugs,* in R.W. Poole, Jr., ed., INSTEAD OF REGULATION (1982); S.N. Wiggins, THE COST OF DEVELOPING A NEW DRUG (June 1987). Some critics have even urged that the Act should be amended to repeal the requirement that new drugs be proved effective. *See* Dorsey, *The Case of Deregulating Drug Efficacy,* 242 J.A.M.A. 1755 (1979).

3. *Impediments to Drug Research.* For a discussion of the political, social and regulatory (including liability) climate that inhibits contraceptive research in the United States, *see* Djerassi, *The Bitter Pill,* 245 Science 356 (July 28, 1989).

----

b. Impact on "Freedom of Choice"

Government control of market access for prescription drugs is designed to accomplish two objectives: (1) prevent distribution of drugs that may affirmatively harm some consumers, and (2) protect consumers against drugs that fail to perform as claimed. But these objectives are not achieved without costs to consumers.

TUTOKI v. CELEBREZZE

United States Court of Appeals, Seventh Circuit, 1967.
375 F.2d 105.

KILEY, Circuit Judge.

The original plaintiff, now deceased, was Geraldine Roy, a cancer patient residing in Arizona....

The gist of the various claims is that defendants, under color of the Federal Food, Drug and Cosmetic Act of 1938, prevented the interstate shipment of Krebiozen and are continuing to do so by their unconstitutional and unlawful acts, to the detriment of plaintiffs, who are cancer patients.... The plaintiffs allege that defendants, acting under color of law but beyond their authority, coerced Dr. Stevan Durovic, sponsor of the drug Krebiozen, into withdrawing his application for an exemption to ship Krebiozen interstate; that defendants have imposed discriminatory; harsh and severe standards in testing Krebiozen so that it cannot obtain approval and were predetermined to refuse Krebiozen an exemption; that as a result plaintiffs, advised by their physicians to receive treatment with Krebiozen, have been forced to leave their homes in other states of their residence and come to Illinois to receive the necessary treatment, which has benefited them; that as a result defendants by this conduct have subjected plaintiffs to irreparable injury through "cruel and unusual punishment," violated their constitutional rights and caused physiological, psychological and proprietary damage; and that plaintiffs have no adequate remedy at law.

In the first five counts plaintiffs seek a declaratory judgment with respect to their rights and defendants' liabilities, and a declaratory judgment that section 505 of the Act is unconstitutional as applied to them and to Krebiozen. They also seek an injunction to restrain defendants from enforcing the section 505(a) prohibition against interstate shipment of Krebiozen....

The present posture of Krebiozen vis-a-vis the Food and Drug Administration (FDA) is that it is not approved under or exempted from section 505. The FDA has promulgated no order with respect to the drug, and no application of plaintiffs is pending before the agency.

An essential element of proof by plaintiffs would be a showing that if the FDA has passed upon Krebiozen according to statutory and constitutional standards, it would have been approved or exempted. The relief sought by plaintiffs therefore presupposes a determination by the district court that Krebiozen should be approved for interstate shipment or exempted from the prohibition pursuant to the standards Congress enacted in the Food, Drug and Cosmetic Act. This determination is a matter within the primary jurisdiction of the FDA....

... We hold that the district court did not err in dismissing the complaint....

NOTE

See also Rutherford v. American Medical Ass'n, 379 F.2d 641 (7th Cir. 1967); *Durovic v. Richardson*, 479 F.2d 242 (7th Cir. 1973) (rejecting suits to restrain FDA from removing Krebiozen from commerce).

PETER BARTON HUTT, LAETRILE DECISION IGNORES CONSTITUTIONAL QUESTION

Legal Times of Washington, July 2, 1979.

Because of the obvious distasteful implications of an unproven cancer cure, it is all too easy to overlook the serious moral and ethical issues, and their constitutional implications, raised in the Laetrile litigation....[C]ommercialization of an unproven anticancer drug, raising false hopes in the terminally ill is unconscionable.

Preemptory denial of a cancer victim's last wishes, on the other hand, raises equally serious questions....

It would be possible for the courts to fashion, from long-established constitutional doctrines, a requirement that FDA adopt the least stringent requirements for control of Laetrile necessary to achieve the intended beneficial purposes of the 1938 Act and the 1962 Amendments, i.e., to prevent any commercialization of Laetrile or exploitation of cancer patients.....

... [T]he rigid approach taken by FDA with Laetrile thus far has had other serious ramifications. A number of States have enacted laws designed to legalize Laetrile within their borders. Because Laetrile can readily be prepared from apricot seeds at any location, the interstate commerce requirements of the FD&C Act can easily be avoided....

NOTES

1. *Right of Privacy. See People v. Privitera*, 23 Cal. 3d 697, 153 Cal. Rptr. 431, 591 P.2d 919 (1979), holding (5–2) that the constitutional right to privacy does not protect a cancer patient's desire to obtain and use Laetrile. In addition to the many cases brought against FDA to enjoin agency action against Laetrile, the agency itself mounted a vigorous enforcement effort against persons responsible for commercializing the drug. *See, e.g., United States v. Mosinee Research Corp.*, 583 F.2d 930 (7th Cir. 1978); *United States v. Spectro Foods Corp.*, 544 F.2d 1175 (3d Cir. 1976); *United States v. General Research Laboratories*, 397 F. Supp. 197 (C.D. Cal. 1975). In *Importation of Amygdalin* ..., FDA Consumer (December 1979–January 1980), at 40 (S.D. Cal. 1977), the court ordered FDA to permit the importation of Laetrile solely for use by an individual *"who, by conclusive proof, is shown to be terminally ill with cancer and unresponsive to any recognized treatment presently available in the United States."* (Emphasis in original.)

2. *Commentary. See* Block, *Laetrile: Individual Choice for Cancer Patients*, 7 NYU Rev. L. & Soc. Change 313 (1978); Cunite, *Freedom of Choice in Medical Treatment: Reconsidering the Efficacy Requirement of the FDCA*, 9 Loyola L.J. 205 (1977); Eddy, *The Laetrile Controversy: Background and Issues*,

20 Ariz. L. Rev. 825 (1978); Note, *Restrictions on Unorthodox Health Treatment in California: A Legal and Economic Analysis,* 24 U.C.L.A. L. Rev. 647 (1977); Note, *Laetrile: Statutory and Constitutional Limitations on the Regulation of Ineffective Drugs,* 127 U. Pa. L. Rev. 233 (1978). *See also* Jukes, *Laetrile on Trial,* 242 J.A.M.A. 719 (1979); Khandekar and Edelman, *Studies of Amygdalin (Laetrile) Toxicity in Rodents,* 242 J.A.M.A. 169 (1979); Regelson, *The 'Grand Conspiracy' Against the Cancer Cure,* 243 J.A.M.A. 337 (1980); Tius, *Constitutional and Legislative Challenges to the Federal Pre-market Proof of Drug Effectiveness Requirement,* 13 New Eng. L. Rev. 279 (1977).

RICHARD J. CROUT, THE NATURE OF REGULATORY CHOICES

33 Food Drug Cosmetic Law Journal 413 (1978).

There was a time, not very long ago, when I thought the quality of public discussion on our drug regulatory system in the United States was extraordinarily low. In those days it was typical for most critics of the FDA to cast all criticism into one of two models, depending upon their point of view. The first of these might be called the "political" model and is highly popular among physicians, clinical investigators, and the drug industry. According to this construct, the regulation of drugs is conducted by slow, unimaginative bureaucrats who are intent on disapproving drugs so as to avoid criticism by Congressional committees for approving anything with risks. By combining such qualities as lack of perspective, overconcern with safety, and inefficiency, they manage to bog down all of drug regulation into a mire of technicalities. Admirers of this model tend to see regulatory decisions as contests between science and politics, and they plead for an FDA which is "more scientific" and "more reasonable."

The other model might be called the "sellout" model and is particularly popular among consumer activists, certain congressional committees, and the press. According to this formulation, the Agency is also slow and bureaucratic—a point on which all critics seem to agree—but largely because it lacks commitment in enforcing the law. Because of personal allegiance to the medical profession and the drug industry, the regulator is seen as quick to approve new drugs without adequate evidence for safety or effectiveness but as slow and inept in withdrawing drugs from the market. The new effect is an industry-dominated Agency which fails to enforce the law....

Each of these models has the virtue of being readily understandable and is inherently plausible. It appeals to the biases of nearly everyone to view regulatory controversies as basically one-on-one contests between the virtuous and the untrustworthy....

If drug development is to move faster in this country, the public must come to accept the idea that less control over research is, in the long run, safer than the alternative, because freedom is essential to discovery and insight. This is a sophisticated concept, not easily explained to the public, and certainly not about to be readily accepted by those already suspicious of science and technology, and of physicians. The challenge to those concerned about the innovative process is to defend that point of view in public on its merits, not to promote some simplistic, extraneous "solution" such as repeal of the effectiveness requirement....

In contrast to those concerned about the effect of regulation on innovation, the laetrile supporters really do want, I suspect, simple repeal of the effectiveness requirement.... It may not be wise ... to continue the pretense that substances such as laetrile must either be accepted as therapeutic drugs or be suppressed. The drug regulatory law deals with science, and to risk its essential features in the political arena over relatively innocuous products is to court a serious long-term setback to the rational control of powerful chemicals in our society. We may well be better off to tolerate a few follies in the marketplace. But again the choice is between competing good values—do we want scientific rationality or personal freedom? And if we want the latter, are we willing to pay the price of a few frauds here and there?

MICHAEL KINSLEY,
THE FDA: TOO CAUTIOUS, NOT TOO BOLD

The Washington Post, August 10, 1989, p. A25.

In the early 1960s, popular magazines were full of complaints about the regulation of prescription drugs. Saturday Review demanded that "a disinterested agency" take charge of judging "the 'cures' that flood the market." Harper's warned of inadequate clinical testing, attacked lax standards and corruption at the Food and Drug Administration and expressed the hope that tighter regulation "may lead to a substantial reduction in the number of new preparations marketed every year."

The August 1989 Reader's Digest also has an article complaining about the regulation of prescription drugs. It's called, "Why Can't We Get the Medicine We Need?" Subtitle: "The Food and Drug Administration's foot-dragging could cost you your health, or even your life." Excessive bureaucracy and caution—even corruption—at the FDA are keeping vital drugs off the market, the author charges. She demands that Congress "repeal the agency's authority to review drug efficacy" because "the relative merits of drugs ... are ... personal decisions."....

America's elephantine drug approval policy is an example of our society's immature attitude toward risk. Life is inherently risky; reducing one risk often increases others, yet at any time we tend to focus on only one side of the equation. In order to reduce to absolute zero the risk of a Thalidomide catastrophe, we have created a system that denies sick people helpful medicines.

This happens in three ways. First, people suffer and die needlessly while medicines go through the FDA process. Until recently, the process took an average of eight years. Second, medicines that could meet FDA standards never get the chance because the process is too costly (typically $100 million). Third, the government's standards are simply too high. Once a drug is established as safe, why should it also have to be proven effective before people can get it? In the case of fatal diseases, why must a drug even be proven perfectly safe?....

And yet, these days, the above complaints are old-hat. At least in the case of AIDS drugs, virtually anybody can get into an experimental treatment program ... In short, the FDA is managing to get risky drugs to desperate patients without having to admit that it is lowering its standards. But obviously an elaborate testing program becomes superfluous if every potential customer gets to participate in the test.

By evading its own excessive standards instead of simply lowering them (or asking Congress to lower them), the FDA is helping us all to avoid making a sensible decision about the risk-benefit trade-off. It is still too hard to get a new medicine with a normal prescription, but it may be getting too easy to get one as part of an "experiment." Some day there will be another Thalidomide, and the public, which is now clamoring for increased access to new drugs, will clamor with equal passion for increased protection from them. I would not want to be the FDA commissioner forced to explain to a congressional subcommittee that the thousands of victims were simply voluntary participants in a massive testing program.

D. REGULATION OF OVER–THE–COUNTER DRUGS

From the enactment of the 1938 Act FDA has drawn clear distinctions between prescription and OTC drugs, although many requirements of the Act and regulations apply to both classes. This Part explores the special problems FDA has encountered in applying the new drug requirements, and specifically the 1962 effectiveness standard, to OTC drugs.

1. THE OTC DRUG REVIEW

Congress's mandate in the 1962 Drug Amendments to review all previously approved NDAs extended to OTC as well as prescription drugs. Many OTC drugs could not be considered "covered" by effective NDAs, however, and FDA concluded that case-by-case challenges to such products on the ground that they were "new drugs" marketed without approval would not assure their safety or effectiveness. In 1972, FDA proposed a new approach which featured expert advisory committees and relied on the agency's claim to primary jurisdiction to determine new drug status.

OVER-THE-COUNTER DRUGS: PROPOSAL ESTABLISHING RULE MAKING PROCEDURES FOR CLASSIFICATION

37 Federal Register 85 (January 5, 1972).

The NAS–NRC reviewed 420 OTC drugs which were broadly representative of the whole range of the OTC market. The NAS–NRC panels' conclusions, which were based upon supporting data submitted by manufacturers, were that approximately 25 percent of the drugs reviewed had an indication that was classifiable as effective.

Estimates of the number of OTC drug products on the market vary from 100,000 to one-half million. Extremely few of these drugs have been approved through the new-drug procedures set forth in section 505 of the act. Some OTC drugs may be excluded from the definition of a new drug by reasons of the so-called 1938 grandfather clause in section 201(p)(1) of the act, and others may be excluded from application of the Drug Amendments of 1962 by reason of the so-called 1962 grandfather clause in section 107(c) of those amendments. Any OTC drug excluded from new-drug status by reason of the 1938 or 1962 grandfather clause is, however, subject to other requirements for drugs in Chapter V of the act, and in particular may not be misbranded under section 502.

The Food and Drug Administration intends to require that all unapproved new drugs and misbranded drugs either be reformulated and/or relabeled to meet all requirements of the act or be removed from the market. In carrying out its responsibilities in this area, the Food and Drug Administration may either initiate a separate court action with respect to each violative OTC drug or deal with all OTC drugs through rulemaking by therapeutic classes on an industry wide basis. It has been determined that the latter approach should be pursued. In making this decision, the following factors were considered:

1. The limited resources of the Food and Drug Administration would be overwhelmed by attempting to review separately the labeling and the data on the safety and effectiveness for each OTC drug now on the market. . . .

2. Litigation to remove violative OTC preparations from the market would necessarily be on a drug-by-drug basis. . . . Such litigation is time-consuming and expensive and is sometimes ineffective because manufacturers may change the formulation of the drug in question and/or its labeling claims and reintroduce the product into the market, thus requiring still further litigation.

3. Litigation to delineate the precise scope of the 1938 and 1962 grandfather clauses in order to determine exactly

which of the thousands of OTC drugs on the market may validly claim exemption from new-drug status under those clauses and then to determine on a drug-by-drug basis which of those grandfathered claims and formulations are safe and effective under the prescribed, recommended, or suggested conditions of use, and thus not misbranded, would more than exhaust all present resources of the agency....

4. Of paramount concern is the inadequate consumer protection produced by a product-by-product review and case-by-case litigation against each drug....

5. It is impossible to proceed simultaneously by litigation against all manufacturers of similar preparations or their drugs....

6. Practically all of the thousands of OTC drugs now marketed are compounded from only an estimated 200 active ingredients which are used either alone or in varying combinations. Many thousands of these drugs are readily comparable in that the labeling is similar and the active ingredients are the same, or are essentially the same, but are present in slightly different dosages. Although each is a separate product, the same scientific and medical evidence is relevant in reviewing all OTC drugs within a given therapeutic class....

Accordingly, the Commissioner proposes to establish procedures for rule making which will result in classifying some OTC drugs as generally recognized among qualified experts as safe and effective and not misbranded under prescribed, recommended, or suggested conditions of use. Any OTC drug not meeting the requirements established for such drugs pursuant to this procedure will have to be the subject of an approved new-drug application prior to marketing. (Since a grandfathered drug that is found to be misbranded would be required to change its formulation and/or labeling and thus lose its grandfathered status, any such product must either meet the applicable monograph or be the subject of an approved new-drug application in order to be legally marketed.) A deviation from a monograph will be approved for an individual manufacturer through approval of a new-drug application justifying such a deviation. Shipment of a non-conforming OTC drug (one neither classified as generally recognized as safe and effective and not misbranded, nor subject to an approved NDA) in interstate commerce will be prohibited....

PROCEDURES FOR CLASSIFICATION OF OVER–THE–COUNTER DRUGS
37 Federal Register 9464 (May 11, 1972).

. . .

Some comments have contended that the Food and Drug Administration does not have the authority to regulate drugs by therapeutic

class, because the authority to do so has not been given by Congress
... These comments also argue that the category reviews are not
legally proper, since it is a subversion of the NDA procedures (21 U.S.C.
355), which call for a drug-by-drug review. The regulations however do
not state that the OTC drugs reviewed are new drugs which have been
approved, but instead provide for monographs which will include those
drugs that do not require an NDA. Nothing in the act prohibits the use
of the therapeutic category approach to defining those OTC drugs that
are generally recognized as safe and effective and misbranded....

There was also comment that the required proof of effectiveness is
far too rigorous and in effect adopts for OTC drugs a standard that
should apply only to prescription drugs.... There can be no question,
however, that the best possible data would consist of adequate and well
controlled clinical studies of the drug ..., and in any event the
regulation allows for a waiver where there is a showing that such
studies are unnecessary or inappropriate....

Comments argued that section 503(b) of the act determines prescription status and that this is not a question that should be asked of a
panel. This issue is fundamentally no different, however, from the
other issues being considered by the panels. Each panel is being asked
for its reviews on the safety and effectiveness of OTC drugs, and it may
well be that they will decide that a drug is generally recognized as safe
and effective but that because of adverse reaction or side effects it is not
safe and effective for OTC use....

... Although the data submitted by interested parties are to relate
only to OTC drugs, the panel is charged with making recommendations
with respect to all drugs that should be on OTC status. Any interested
person may, of course, submit data and views suggesting that a prescription drug be moved to OTC status....

Another comment objects to the statement ... that the proposed
monograph would specify a reasonable period of time within which
drugs falling within subdivision (iii) could be marketed while the data
necessary to evaluate the drug is being obtained for evaluation by the
Food and Drug Administration...There can be no justification to
allow the continued marketing of a drug when the Commissioner finds
it to be ineffective. On the other hand there is justification as provided
in subdivision (iii) for allowing an interested party time to prove a drug
safe and effective, if the evidence is insufficient for the Commissioner to
make a proper determination.... It is intended that reasonable time
will be provided as long as testing is in progress that is adequate to
resolve the medical issues raised by the panel and the Commissioner....

Almost every comment contended that the Food and Drug Administration lacks legal authority under the act to promulgate OTC drug
monographs that constitute binding substantive rules and that the

agency's authority is limited to issuing interpretive guidelines. Section 701(a) of the act expressly grants "the authority to promulgate regulations for the efficient enforcement of this Act." Numerous Supreme Court cases, interpreting comparable legislative authorization in other regulatory statutes, have upheld the right to proceed by substantive rule making rather than on a case-by-case basis, to particularize general statutory standards. ...

Some comments stated that, even if there were authority to issue substantive regulations, the proposed OTC drug procedures fail to meet Constitutional requirements, because they do not provide for an evidentiary hearing or cross-examination and there is no written record available for review. The regulations promulgated in this order governing the OTC review meet all of the requirements of the Administrative Procedure Act and of due process of law.... In the 'OTC drug review procedures, far greater procedural rights are granted than are required under the Administrative Procedure Act. Instead of a simple notice of proposed rule making giving the substance of the proposed rule, all interested persons have an opportunity, prior to any court review, to submit the data on which the proposed rule will be based and to request an oral hearing before the panel, to provide written comments and objections to the Commissioner, and to request an oral hearing before the Commissioner. In addition, interested organizations have an opportunity to recommend lists of experts to serve on the panels themselves....

The comments argued that, even if the Food and Drug Administration had the authority to determine by rule making which drugs are generally recognized as safe and effective, there is no authority to set a standard to determine which drugs are misbranded, because the statute specifically provides for court adjudication of this issue. The legal authority to utilize a rule making rather than a case-by-case adjudication approach with respect to misbranding stands on no different footing than the legal authority to exercise rule making with respect to new drug status. Both instances involve explication, particularization, and definition of general statutory requirements as they apply to large numbers of products now on the market....

Similarly, most comments argued that, even if the agency has the authority to establish binding substantive rules, the 1938 and 1962 grandfather clauses preclude review of OTC drugs protected by them. The grandfather clauses apply only to the new drug provisions of the act, however, and not to the adulteration or misbranding provisions. The review contained in these regulations is designed to particularize not just the new drug provisions of the act, but also the misbranding provisions.

OVER–THE–COUNTER HUMAN DRUGS
WHICH ARE GENERALLY RECOGNIZED AS SAFE
AND EFFECTIVE AND NOT MISBRANDED

21 C.F.R. Part 330.

§ 330.10 Procedures for classifying OTC drugs as generally recognized as safe and effective and not misbranded, and for establishing monographs

... (a) *Procedure for establishing OTC drug monographs.* (1) *Advisory review panels.* The Commissioner shall appoint advisory review panels of qualified experts to evaluate the safety and effectiveness of OTC drugs, to review OTC drug labeling, and to advise him on the promulgation of monographs establishing conditions under which OTC drugs are generally recognized as safe and effective and not misbranded.... The members of a panel ... may include persons from lists submitted by organizations representing professional, consumer, and industry interests....

(3) *Deliberations of an advisory review panel.* An advisory review panel will ... review the data submitted to it and to prepare a report containing its conclusions and recommendations to the Commissioner with respect to the safety and effectiveness of the drugs in a designated category of the OTC drugs. A panel may consult any individual or group. Any interested person may request an opportunity to present oral views to the panel; such request may be granted or denied by the panel.... Any interested person may present written data and views which shall be considered by the panel....

(4) *Standards for safety, effectiveness, and labeling.* The advisory review panel ... shall apply the following standards: ...

(i) Safety means a low incidence of adverse reactions or significant side effects under adequate directions for use and warnings against unsafe use as well as low potential for harm which may result from abuse under conditions of widespread availability. Proof of safety shall consist of adequate tests by methods reasonably applicable to show the drug is safe under the prescribed, recommended, or suggested conditions of use. This proof shall include results of significant human experience during marketing. General recognition of safety shall ordinarily be based upon published studies which may be corroborated by unpublished studies and other data.

(ii) Effectiveness means a reasonable expectation that, in a significant proportion of the target population, the pharmacological effect of the drug, when used under adequate directions for use and warnings against unsafe use, will provide clinically significant relief of the type claimed. Proof of effectiveness shall consist of controlled clinical investigations as defined in § 314.111(a)(5)(ii) of this chapter, unless this requirement is waived on the basis of a showing that it is not reasonably applicable to the drug or essential to the validity of the investigation and that an alternative method of investigation is adequate to substantiate effectiveness. Investigations may be corroborated by partially controlled or uncontrolled studies, documented clinical studies by qualified experts, and reports of significant human experience marketing.... General recognition of effectiveness shall ordinarily be based upon published studies which may be corroborated by unpublished studies and other data.

(iii) The benefit-to-risk ratio of a drug shall be considered in determining safety and effectiveness.

(iv) An OTC drug may combine two or more safe and effective active ingredients and may be generally recognized as safe and effective when each active ingredient makes a contribution to the claimed effect(s); when combining of the active ingredients does not decrease the safety or effectiveness of any of the individual active ingredients; and when the combination, when used under adequate directions for use and warnings against unsafe use, provides rational concurrent therapy for a significant proportion of the target population....

(5) *Advisory review panel report to the Commissioner.* ... Included within this report shall be:

(i) A recommended monograph or monographs covering the category of OTC drugs and establishing conditions under which the drugs involved are generally recognized as safe and effective and not misbranded (Category I)....

(ii) A statement of all active ingredients, labeling claims or other statements, or other conditions reviewed and excluded from the monograph on the basis of the panel's determination that they would result in the drug's not being generally recognized as safe and effective or would result in misbranding (Category II).

(iii) A statement of all active ingredients, labeling claims or other statements, or other conditions reviewed and excluded from the monograph on the basis of the panel's determination that the available data are insufficient to classify such condition under either paragraph (a)(5)(i) or (ii) of this section and for which further testing is therefore required (Category III)....

(6) *Proposed monograph.* After reviewing the conclusions and recommendations of the advisory review panel, the Commissioner shall publish in the FEDERAL REGISTER a proposed order containing:

(i) A monograph or monographs establishing conditions under which a category of OTC drugs is generally recognized as safe and effective and not misbranded (Category I).

(ii) A statement of the conditions excluded from the monograph on the basis of the Commissioner's determination that they would result in the drug's not being generally recognized as safe and effective or would result in misbranding (Category II).

(iii) A statement of the conditions excluded from the monograph on the basis of the Commissioner's determination that the available data are insufficient ... (Category III).

(iv) The full report(s) of the panel to the Commissioner....

(7) *Tentative final monograph.* After reviewing all comments and reply comments, the Commissioner shall publish ... a tentative order containing a monograph establishing conditions under which a category of OTC drugs is generally recognized as safe and effective and not misbranded. Within 30 days, any interested party may file ... written objections specifying with particularity the omissions or additions requested.... A request for an oral hearing may accompany such objections.

(8) *Oral hearing before the Commissioner.* After reviewing objections filed in response to the tentative final monograph, the Commissioner, if he finds reasonable grounds in support thereof, shall ... schedule an oral hearing....

(9) *Final monograph.* After reviewing the objections and considering the arguments made at any oral hearing, the Commissioner shall publish ... a final order containing a monograph establishing conditions under which a category of OTC drugs is generally recognized as safe and effective and not misbranded....

(11) *Court appeal.* The monograph contained in the final order constitutes final agency action from which appeal lies to the courts....

(b) *Regulatory action.* Any product which fails to conform to an applicable monograph after its effective date is liable to regulatory action.

NOTES

1. *Legality of OTC Drug Review.* Surprisingly, the legality of the OTC Drug Review was not challenged when the basic procedures were established in 1972. Several court opinions have referred approvingly to the Review. *See, e.g. Weinberger v. Bentex Pharmaceuticals, Inc.,* 412 U.S. 645 (1973); *Warner–Lambert Co. v. FTC,* 361 F.Supp. 948 (D.D.C. 1973); *United States v. Articles of Food and Drug ... Coli-Trol 80 Medicated,* 372 F.Supp. 915 (N.D. Ga. 1974). Two specific aspects of the OTC drug review procedures have been challenged. FDA's initial use of closed panel meetings, with confidential transcripts, was upheld by one court and declared unlawful by another before the issue was mooted by the enactment of the Federal Advisory Committee Act. *See* pp. 1286–94 *infra.* The agency's approval for continued marketing of Category III drugs was enjoined in *Cutler v. Kennedy,* p. 605 *infra.*

2. *FDA Request for Data.* Because FDA has no statutory power to require a manufacturer to submit any information to, or otherwise participate in, the

OTC Drug Review, the agency was concerned that companies might submit only favorable information. FDA's initial requests for data on specific drug categories therefore contained this language:

> ... If the submission is by a manufacturer, a statement signed by the person responsible for such submission, that to the best of his knowledge it includes unfavorable information, as well as any favorable information, known to him pertinent to an evaluation of the safety, effectiveness, and labeling of such a product. Thus, if any type of scientific data is submitted, a balanced submission of favorable and unfavorable data must be submitted....

See, e.g., 37 Fed. Reg. 26842 (December 16, 1972) (antimicrobial drugs).

3. *General Requirements for OTC Drugs.* The general conditions for all OTC drugs in 21 C.F.R. § 330.1 were promulgated in 38 Fed. Reg. 8714 (April 5, 1973), 38 Fed. Reg. 31258 (November 12, 1973), 39 Fed. Reg. 19880 (June 4, 1974), 40 Fed. Reg. 11717 (March 13, 1975).

4. *Combination OTC Drugs.* The conditions under which combination OTC drugs are permitted have long been in dispute. 21 C.F.R. § 330.10(a)(4)(iv) paraphrases the prescription combination drug regulation in 21 C.F.R. § 330.50. Because of the significant differences between OTC and Rx drugs, however, many more combinations have been permitted for OTC drugs. To promote uniformity among the several review panels, FTC issued a guideline for OTC combination drug products, 43 Fed. Reg. 55466 (November 28, 1978).

5. *Encouraged Reformulation.* FDA encouraged manufacturers to reformulate and relabel their products to conform to proposed monographs even before they are promulgated in final form. The agency adopted a regulation, 21 C.F.R. § 330.12(d), stating that it would not take action against such products, pending promulgation of a final monograph, if such changes resulted in loss of grandfather protection. FDA also persuaded the court in *American Public Health Ass'n v. Veneman,* 349 F.Supp. 1311 (D.D.C. 1972), p. 503 *supra,* to exempt all OTC drugs from its implementation order, 37 Fed. Reg. 26623, ¶ XV (December 14, 1972). *See* 37 Fed. Reg. 7807 (April 20, 1972), 39 Fed. Reg. 1580 (January 11, 1974).

6. *Homeopathic Drugs.* FDA decided to defer consideration of homeopathic drugs, for which there is scant evidence of effectiveness, because they represent such a small volume. *See* 37 Fed. Reg. 9464, 9466 (May 11, 1972). In the interim, *Meserey v. United States,* 447 F. Supp. 548 (D. Nev. 1977), confirmed that homeopathic drugs are subject to all the drug provisions of the FD&C Act. Compliance Policy Guide 7132.15 (May 31, 1988) sets forth FDA's policy on the conditions under which homeopathic drugs may be marketed.

7. *Inactive Ingredients.* FDA also deferred review of inactive ingredients used in OTC drug products until evaluation of all active ingredients was completed. In 42 Fed. Reg. 19156 (April 12, 1977), the agency proposed general conditions for use and labeling of inactive ingredients pending such review. No action had been taken on this proposal as of June 30, 1990. One proposed provision would have established a uniform approach to the voluntary declaration of inactive ingredients on OTC drug labels. In 1984, the nonprescription drug industry established its own voluntary program for the labeling of inactive ingredients on OTC drug labels. *See* Proprietary Association, GUIDELINES FOR DISCLOSURE OF INACTIVE INGREDIENTS IN OTC MEDICINES (1984).

8. *Outstanding NDAs.* In order to mesh the NDA procedures with the OTC Drug Review procedures, FDA withdrew all NDAs for OTC antacid drugs upon promulgation of the final antacid monograph. *See* 39 Fed. Reg. 19882 (June 4, 1974), 39 Fed. Reg. 39591 (November 8, 1974).

9. *FDA Enforcement Policy.* A well-understood premise of the OTC review was that FDA would not devote its resources to enforcement actions against individual OTC products even though they might technically be unapproved new drugs. In short, the agency would countenance continued marketing of most OTC products pending completion of the review. But FDA added two caveats. It would take action against an individual OTC product if it believed the product posed a significant health hazard or was likely to defraud consumers. *See* Compliance Policy Guide 7132b.15 (October 1, 1980). In addition, the agency made clear that it would not hesitate to act outside the scope and schedule of the review to deal with ingredients that were found by the panels, or otherwise demonstrated, to be health hazards. Thus FDA has dealt specially with hexachlorophene, an antimicrobial ingredient used in cleansing products, 37 Fed. Reg. 219 (January 7, 1972), 37 Fed. Reg. 20160 (September 27, 1972), codified at 21 C.F.R. § 250.250; TBS, an antibacterial ingredient, in 39 Fed. Reg. 33102 (September 13, 1974), 40 Fed. Reg. 50527 (October 30, 1975), codified in 21 C.F.R. § 310.508; zirconium, an antiperspirant ingredient 40 Fed. Reg. 24328 (June 5, 1975), 42 Fed. Reg. 41374 (August 16, 1977), codified at 21 C.F.R. § 310.510; chloroform, 41 Fed. Reg. 15026 (April 19, 1976), 41 Fed. Reg. 26842 (June 29, 1976), codified at 21 C.F.R. § 310.513; and methapyrilene, an ingredient of sleep-aid products found by the national Cancer Institute to be carcinogenic in animals.

10. *Daytime Sedatives.* In 44 Fed. Reg. 36378 (June 22, 1979), FDA issued a final order dealing with OTC daytime sedative products. The document set forth FDA's conclusion that "any ingredient when labeled for use as an over-the-counter daytime sedative is not generally recognized as safe and effective for this intended use." The agency's conclusion, which precludes the marketing of any OTC product for use as a daytime sedative, was based on findings that the ingredients used in such products were either ineffective at the dosages used (and potentially toxic at higher dosages) or only capable of rendering the user sleepy. The agency's ruling relied on concerns about potential societal abuse as a basis for its conclusion that no daytime OTC sedative can be generally recognized as safe and effective.

11. *Premature Marketing.* Once the nonprescription drug industry began to appreciate the commercial implications of and opportunities in the OTC drug review, companies closely followed each panel and anticipated the results of the review by marketing new products that previously were not permitted (*e.g.*, drugs previously limited to prescription status or marketed for a different indication or containing less of the active ingredient) even before the panel submitted its report. After FDA forced the nationwide recall of a new product marketed in anticipation of a panel conclusion with which it disagreed, p. 417 *supra*, the agency promulgated 21 C.F.R. § 330.13, 40 Fed. Reg. 56675 (December 4, 1975), 41 Fed. Reg. 32480 (August 4, 1976), governing the conditions under which manufacturers may safely follow the recommendations of an OTC drug panel before a final monograph has been promulgated. The FDA policy was amended in 47 Fed. Reg. 17738 (April 23, 1982) to provide that, where the Commissioner agrees that a new product meets all the requirements for Category I and provides notice of that determination in the Federal Register, marketing may begin before promulgation of a final monograph.

12. *New Combination Products.* Because most new OTC drug products utilize combinations of active ingredients, FDA has paid particular attention to the marketing of new combinations of active ingredients not explicitly recognized in an OTC drug monograph. In Compliance Policy Guide 7132b.16 (October 1, 1980), the agency took the position that no new OTC combination drug not on the market before May 11, 1972 may be marketed before it has been classified in Category I in a proposed monograph and the Commissioner has not dissented unless the agency has announced in the Federal Register that the combination is permitted. In the face of this guidance, a company unsuccessfully attempted to market a toothpaste containing both an anticaries active ingredient and a tooth desensitizer, a combination not sanctioned by the report of the OTC Dental Drug Panel. *See United States v. Articles of Drug ... Promise Toothpaste for Sensitive Teeth,* 826 F.2d 564 (7th Cir. 1987), *aff'g* 624 F.Supp. 766 (N.D. Ill. 1985). *See also Farquhar v. FDA,* 616 F.Supp. 190 (D.D.C. 1985).

13. *Warnings for OTC Drugs.* Prior to the OTC Drug Review, recommended and required warnings for OTC drugs were published in 21 C.F.R. Parts 201 and 369. The Review, however, has provided a vehicle for examining the needs for, and content of required warnings for all OTC drugs. In *Public Citizen Health Research Group v. Commissioner,* 740 F.2d 21 (D.C. Cir. 1984), the court declined to order FDA to require a warning on aspirin-containing products about the risk of Reye Syndrome. FDA ultimately did prescribe such a warning in 47 Fed. Reg. 57886 (December 28, 1982), 50 Fed. Reg. 51400 (December 17, 1985), 51 Fed. Reg. 8180 (March 7, 1986), 53 Fed. Reg. 1796 (January 22, 1988), 53 Fed. Reg. 21633 (June 9, 1988), codified in 21 C.F.R. § 201.314(h). Additional pregnancy warnings were promulgated for aspirin in 55 Fed. Reg. 27776 (July 5, 1990), and warnings were proposed for all OTC drugs containing water-soluble gums as active ingredients in 55 Fed.Reg. 45782 (October 30, 1990).

14. *NDA Deviations.* Once an OTC drug monograph has become final, a manufacturer may wish to deviate in some way from its provisions. 21 C.F.R. § 330.11 provides that an NDA may be submitted for any such deviation and include only information pertinent to the deviation requested.

15. *Professional Labeling.* Some OTC drugs have prescription as well as nonprescription indications. In such instances, the applicable monographs specifically provide for "professional labeling" containing these prescription indications. *See, e.g.,* 21 C.F.R. § 331.31, relating to peptic ulcer claims for antacid products, and 21 C.F.R. § 332.31, permitting postoperative gas pain claims for antiflatulent products.

16. *Reopening the OTC Drug Review.* In general, FDA has resisted reopening the OTC Drug Review to include additional ingredients. In 54 Fed. Reg. 50240 (December 5, 1989), however, the agency requested the submission of data for ingredients contained in eyewash drug products used for emergency first aid treatment of chemical burns of the eye, because these important products were missed by earlier panel reports. In 55 Fed.Reg. 38560 (September 19, 1990), FDA also reopened the Review to consider products for which dental plaque and gingivitis claims are made.

17. *Mailing OTC Drugs.* The Drug and Household Substance Mailing Act of 1990, 104 Stat. 1184, prohibits the mailing of a "household substance" (which includes OTC drugs) which does not comply with any special child-resistant

packaging requirements established for the product under the Poison Prevention Packaging Act of 1970.

18. *Commentary.* For analyses of the OTC drug review, *see* Ames & McCracken, *Framing Regulatory Standards to Avoid Formal Adjudication: The FDA as a Case Study,* 64 Calif. L. Rev. 14 (1976); Harlow, *The FDA's OTC Drug Review: The Development and Analysis of Some Aspects of the Procedure,* 32 FDC L.J. 248 (1977); Selmer, *FDA's Over–the–Counter Drug Review: Expeditious Enforcement By Rulemaking,* 11 Mich. J. of L. Reform 142 (1977).

---

2. THE OTC DRUG REVIEW AND FTC REGULATION OF DRUG ADVERTISING

Congress declined in 1938 to give FDA jurisdiction to regulate drug advertising and instead confirmed the advertising authority of the Federal Trade Commission. *See* Jackson, FOOD AND DRUG LEGISLATION IN THE NEW DEAL (1970); Cavers, *The Food, Drug, and Cosmetic Act of 1938: Its Legislative History and Its Substantive Provisions,* 6 Law & Contemp. Probs. 2 (1939); Note, *The FTC's Injunctive Authority Against False Advertising of Food and Drugs,* 75 Mich. L. Rev. 745 (1977). Congress created exceptions to this general allocation of jurisdiction by granting FDA authority to regulate advertising for prescription drugs under section 502(n) in the Drug Amendments of 1962, p. 454 *supra,* and for vitamins and minerals under sections 403(a)(2) and 707 in the Vitamin–Mineral Amendments of 1976, p. 454 *supra.* With respect to OTC drugs, however, FTC retains the jurisdiction that it was granted in 1938.

The two agencies are supposed to cooperate in the exercise of their abutting responsibilities. *See* FDA–FTC Memorandum of Understanding, 36 Fed. Reg. 18539 (September 16, 1971). FDA's commencement of the OTC Review promised new opportunities for collaboration. In determining what label claims for OTC drugs were supported by legally adequate evidence of effectiveness and would not render drugs misbranded, FDA would inevitably examine evidence that might be pertinent to a determination of whether advertising claims for a drug were deceptive. Both agencies hoped that the FTC would be able to make use of FDA's monographs in a fashion that would limit claims in advertising to those approved for labeling.

At the outset of the OTC Drug Review, FDA intended that the only label claims that could lawfully be made for an OTC drug were those specified in a final monograph for the class of drugs or approved by the agency in a new drug application. The agency took the position on several occasions that a manufacturer must use the precise terminology set forth in the monograph in describing the indications for use of a product or in providing warnings about misuse. *See* 38 Fed. Reg. 31260, ¶¶ 17, 49 (November 12, 1973); 39 Fed. Reg. 19868, ¶ 50 (June 4, 1974);

40 Fed. Reg. 11718 (March 13, 1975). This so-called "exclusivity" policy did not prevent the use of accurate and non-misleading descriptive phrases or adjectives, *e.g.*, "sparkling" antacid. 40 Fed. Reg. 11718 (March 13, 1975).

Based on this policy the FTC proposed a trade regulation rule under sections 5 and 12 of the Federal Trade Commission Act, 15 U.S.C. §§ 45, 52, that would translate FDA's OTC drug monographs into commensurate restrictions on advertising. 40 Fed. Reg. 52631 (November 11, 1975). Under the terms of the rule as proposed, it would be a violation of the FTC Act to disseminate an advertisement for an OTC drug in any drug category

> for which an applicable final monograph has been established by the Food and Drug Administration ... which advertisement makes any claim, directly or by implication, which the Commissioner of Food and Drugs has determined, in a final order accompanying such monograph, may not appear in the labeling of such drug.

As the FTC rulemaking progressed, it became evident that counsel supporting the proposed rule were seeking the broadest possible construction of FDA's monographs. They argued that in the course of approving label claims in a final monograph FDA necessarily concluded that other terminology would not convey the same message to consumers, and accordingly that drugs bearing other terminology would not be generally recognized as safe and effective and not misbranded. From this premise it was a small step to the conclusion that advertising using nonconforming terminology to describe a drug's performance would be deceptive.

The presiding officer's report largely rejected the staff position, 44 Fed. Reg. 1123 (January 4, 1979), and though the staff persevered, 44 Fed. Reg. 31241 (May 31, 1979), the full Commission in 46 Fed. Reg. 24584 (May 1, 1981) terminated the proceeding with the following explanation:

> The Commission has concluded that in advertising a drug for a permissible (i.e., FDA-approved) purpose, advertisers should not always be limited (as they would have been under the original proposed rule) to the labeling language approved by FDA.

The Commission declared that it would continue to review advertising for OTC drugs, in the light of FDA monographs, to determine whether further action is necessary.

NOTES

1. *Commentary.* For further discussion of the FTC "claims" TRR, *see* Altman, *Labeling and Advertising Trends,* 34 FDC L.J. 569 (1979); DiPrima, *Some Partisan Musings on the OTC Review and the Advertising TRRs,* 32 FDC L.J. 405 (1977); Herzog, *The FTC's Proposed Rule on OTC Drug Advertising,* 31 FDC L.J. 147 (1976).

2. *FDA Label Warnings.* The FTC proposed a second TRR to require that some of the label warnings required by the final FDA monograph for antacid drugs also appear in advertising, 41 Fed. Reg. 14534 (April 6, 1976), 43 Fed. Reg. 38851 (August 31, 1978). *See* DiPrima, *Advertising of OTC Drugs: Proposed TRR on Warnings,* 32 FDC L.J. 96 (1977); Dym, *Affirmative Disclosure of Warning Information in OTC Drug Advertising,* 34 FDC L.J. 564 (1979); Herzog, *The Antacid Warning—Rulemaking at the FTC,* 32 FDC L.J. 76 (1977). Following a public hearing, publication of the staff report, 48 Fed. Reg. 36273 (August 10, 1983), and an oral hearing before the Commissioners the FTC terminated this proceeding in 49 Fed. Reg. 46156 (November 23, 1984). The Commission concluded that the record did not support the staff's contention that antacid advertisements would be deceptive or unfair if they failed to contain warnings similar to those required by FDA in labeling.

3. *Defensive Use of OTC Panel Report.* For an unsuccessful attempt by a respondent before the FTC to use the tentative conclusions of an OTC Drug Review panel defensively, *see Warner-Lambert Co. v. FTC,* 562 F.2d 749 (D.C. Cir. 1977).

4. *Claim Substantiation.* In *Pfizer, Inc.,* 81 F.T.C. 23 (1972), the FTC enunciated the policy that it is unfair and deceptive for a manufacturer to make any affirmative drug product claims without having a "reasonable basis" for it. Relying on the prevailing view of experts in the field, the Commission has required at least two clinical studies to substantiate OTC drug advertising claims. *See Thompson Medical Co., Inc.* 104 F.T.C. 648 (1984), *aff'd,* 791 F.2d 189 (D.C. Cir. 1986); *Bristol Myers Co.,* 102 F.T.C. 21 (1983), *aff'd,* 738 F.2d 554 (2d Cir. 1984); *American Home Products Corp.,* 98 F.T.C. 136 (1981), *aff'd,* 695 F.2d 681 (3d Cir. 1982).

3. OTC DRUG INDICATIONS

When FDA began the OTC Drug Review, it took the position that the "indications" (uses) in the labeling of a drug must use the identical terminology set forth in the OTC drug monograph—the "exclusivity" rule on which the FTC based its since-abandoned TRR for OTC drug advertising. Manufacturers of OTC drugs continued to oppose FDA's position, arguing that greater flexibility should be permitted for both legal and policy reasons. After a public hearing, 47 Fed. Reg. 29002 (July 2, 1982), the agency published the following proposal.

LABELING OF DRUG PRODUCTS FOR OVER–THE COUNTER HUMAN USE
50 Federal Register 15810 (April 22, 1985).

The policy of limiting monograph labeling terminology to specific words and phrases considered and approved by FDA has been the subject of comment throughout the OTC drug review process. With the publication of the tentative final monograph for OTC antacid drug products in the Federal Register of November 12, 1973 (38 FR 31280), FDA responded to comments proposing that terms other than those specified in the monograph should be allowed in the product labeling. The agency concluded that the terms recommended by the panel fully met the intent of the regulation. The agency also stated that allowing each manufacturer to select words other than those set forth in the monograph would result in continued consumer confusion and deception (38 FR 31264)....

The notice of hearing defined the scope of the hearing broadly as encompassing all aspects, both practical and legal, of the exclusivity policy and its possible alternatives.... The inquiry was structured, however, to seek answers to the following questions (47 FR 29003):

(1) Does the government have a substantial interest in restricting the terminology used in the labeling of OTC drug products?

(2) If the government's interest is substantial, does restricting labeling to terminology approved by FDA in a final monograph directly advance this interest?

(3) Is the restriction imposed by the exclusivity policy more extensive than is necessary to serve that interest?

(4) By imposing such a restriction, does the agency exceed its authority under the Federal Food, Drug, and Cosmetic Act?

(5) Is the restriction a prior restraint on free speech that is prohibited by the Constitution?

(6) Should there be limitations on terminology used in the labeling of OTC drug products? If the current policy of exclusivity of labeling should be changed, what changes would be desirable from the standpoint of consumers and marketers?

The notice of hearing identified and solicited comments on the following possible alternatives to the exclusivity policy:

(1) Provide a separate list of approved synonyms maintained on file in the Dockets Management Branch.

The notice stated that this alternative would retain the exclusivity policy but provide a simpler and more expeditious means of obtaining additional acceptable language for use in labeling.

(2) Require specific information to be included in a designated area of a product's labeling without deviation from the approved language but permit manufacturers to use their own synonymous language outside the designated area.

The notice stated that this alternative would preserve the exclusivity policy with respect to claims made in the designated area, thus providing consumers with an FDA-approved source of information on the label itself, while at the same time allowing manufacturers the flexibility to employ reasonable truthful interpretative language elsewhere in the product's labeling. The notice also stated that the agency believed that this alternative represents a compromise that may incorporate the advantages of the exclusivity policy while avoiding some of its perceived rigidity.

(3) Allow manufacturers to interpret the claims included in a monograph in synonymous language.

The notice stated that this alternative would abandon the exclusivity policy. Manufacturers would still be required to employ accurate, nonmisleading terminology, but would not have to obtain FDA's prior approval for the language chosen.... The agency has decided ... that the present exclusivity policy, while legally supportable, should not be continued for policy reasons. FDA specifically rejects the assertions in the submitted comments that the present policy is legally deficient on constitutional grounds, is in violation of the Administrative Procedure Act (APA), or contrary to the Federal Food, Drug, and Cosmetic Act....

As discussed in detail below, the new labeling requirements would allow for a[n] alternative labeling of OTC drug products. The label and labeling would be required to contain, in a prominent and conspicuous location, either (1) within a boxed area that is designated "APPROVED USES" the specific wording set out in the indications for use section of an applicable OTC drug monograph, or (2) within a nonboxed area alternative wording relating to indications for use that is not false or misleading. As a third alternative, monograph language would be used in the boxed area and the label and labeling could contain elsewhere alternative wording describing indications for use, so long as the alternative wording was not false or misleading.

The agency believes that labeling established in an OTC drug monograph would continue to serve a vital purpose. It would represent the agency's determination, following extensive notice and comment rulemaking, of the specific indications for which an OTC drug product would be generally recognized as safe and effective, and not misbranded. Because the monographs would prove a definitive explanation of those uses a particular drug is good for, FDA would be able to determine whether nonmonograph language is an accurate description of a drug's properties....

The agency emphasizes, as described below in the discussion of the proposed regulation, that it will use the monograph language as a regulatory benchmark. FDA will carefully examine any alternative language to ensure that it does not go beyond the approved indications, thereby causing the drug to become a "new drug" or misbranded, or both, under the act. Language that is so nondescriptive as to be meaningless, or that indicates uses for a new indication, would cause the product to be misbranded, a new drug, or both....

NOTE

The final regulation, 51 Fed.Reg. 16258 (May 1, 1986), is codified in 21 C.F.R. § 330.1(c)(2). The regulation specifies that flexibility is allowed only for labeled "indications" and not for any other required features of OTC drug labeling.

4. LEGALITY OF CATEGORY III

Another controversial feature of the OTC Drug Review was the provision allowing continued marketing of products containing ingredients classified by final FDA monographs in Category III. Authorizing continued marketing of drugs for which available data are insufficient to permit a determination of general recognition of safety and effectiveness was thought necessary to persuade many drug manufacturers to accede to the basic concept of the Review. If FDA had insisted on taking immediate action against any product for which general recognition of safety and, particularly, effectiveness were not established by the agency's prevailing criteria, *see Weinberger v. Hynson, Westcott & Dunning, Inc.,* p. 539 *supra,* firms would have refused to participate in the process and taken their chances litigating the new drug status of their products.

More important, the agency concluded that it was not feasible to conduct a review of any group of already-marketed ingredients or products, under present standards of safety and effectiveness, without permitting some additional time for further testing, because those ingredients or products were marketed during an earlier era when the standards of safety and effectiveness were substantially less than they are today. All FDA review programs confront this reality. Accommodating it was even more important for OTC drugs, many of which were first marketed decades before the acceptance of scientific testing for safety and effectiveness.

FDA also hoped to avoid litigation over the status of individual OTC drug products under the 1938 and 1962 grandfather clauses. In its brief in *USV Pharmaceutical Corp. v. Weinberger,* p. 499 *supra,* FDA acknowledged that a significant number of OTC drug ingredients enjoyed grandfather status as long as no change in formulation or labeling occurred. By establishing a transitional category, FDA hoped to induce the manufacturers of these products to conduct further testing which would then permit a definitive determination of their safety and effectiveness.

Thus, Category III was designed as a bridge between the status quo and GRAS/GRAE status for ingredients for which the requisite evidence could be obtained. FDA's regulations originally made clear that the agency would not initiate enforcement action against such products prior to the expiration of the time specified for completion of the necessary studies. As the schedule for completion of the OTC Review lengthened, however, pressure on FDA to depart from its systematic approach or curtail the marketing of Category III ingredients mounted.

CUTLER v. KENNEDY

United States District Court, District of Columbia, 1979.
475 F. Supp. 838.

SIRICA, District Judge.....

In response to "numerous requests for clarification of the conditions under which Category III conditions could continue to be promoted and marketed pending further testing," the Commissioner proposed amendments to the OTC procedural regulations in October 1975. 40 Fed. Reg. 49097 (1975). Eventually, the FDA modified those regulations to provide more detailed procedures for amendment of monographs. This was coupled with a new provision authorizing continued marketing of Category III drugs and specifying the conditions under which such drugs may be marketed pending further testing. 42 Fed. Reg. 12137 (1977).

With regard to continued marketing of Category III products, the OTC regulations now provide:

> After publication of the final monograph, any product with a condition (e.g., ingredient, labeling claim, combination of ingredients) subject to paragraph (a)(6)(iii)(Category III) of this section may remain on the market, or may be introduced into the market, provided that the Food and Drug Administration receives notification that the number of studies specified in the applicable testing guidelines will be undertaken to obtain the data necessary to resolve the issues that resulted in such classification.

In short, in order to take advantage of a Category III classification, and in order to continue marketing the affected product without fear of "regulatory action," a manufacturer must agree to initiate testing under specified guidelines....

The 1977 amendments also added specific Category III provisions to the monograph amendment procedures. Petitions to amend a monograph to include conditions previously placed in Category III must be filed before the expiration date (the end of the testing period) of the condition. Where testing has been undertaken ... a petition to amend allows marketing of relevant drug products until disapproval of the petition or a decision to reclassify the affected conditions in Category II. Products placed in Category III may therefore be marketed indefinitely so long as the manufacturer agrees to perform the required testing and then petitions for an amendment of the pertinent monograph.

Plaintiffs Mimi Cutler, Pamela S. Ellsworth, and Stephen D. Annand are each consumers of various OTC drugs.... Plaintiffs' basic rationale can be quite simply stated. Under the OTC regulations, drugs are not placed in Category III unless there is insufficient evidence to determine that they are generally recognized as safe and effective. Given the *Hynson* case and the strict requirements for "general recognition," they say this means that Category III drugs lack substantial evidence of effectiveness, are necessarily new drugs, and, under the Act, cannot be marketed without an NDA....

Plaintiffs also apparently contend, although their papers are considerably less clear on this point, that once having concluded, in effect, that Category III drugs are not supported by substantial evidence of safety or efficacy, the Commissioner has a statutory *duty* to take action to remove such drugs from the market. In addition to asking the Court to avoid those aspects of the regulations which authorize continued marketing of Category III drugs, therefore, plaintiffs also request an order directing the Commissioner "to take appropriate steps to remove from the market Category III drugs for which there is no approved new drug application."

Defendants' basic position is equally straightforward. Only Category II, not Category III, contains drugs which the agency has finally determined to be not generally recognized as safe and effective. Category III, by comparison, contains conditions regarding which "the available data is insufficient to classify" the condition as either generally recognized or not generally recognized as safe and effective. Therefore, defendants argue, placement of a drug in Category III does not mean that it is a new drug, but only that the agency has decided to reserve a decision on its status until more information is available. The federal defendant also emphasizes that as a matter of practice Category III will only contain conditions regarding which there are questions of efficacy. All potential safety problems which have come to light, even at the panel stage, have been addressed by separate regulatory action outside the rulemaking process.

In addition, the Commissioner argued that the Category III system makes eminently good sense. It allows continued marketing, and encourages continued testing, of safe drugs which are capable of being shown effective, but which do not as yet meet the rigorous testing standards being established by the agency's experts as part of the OTC review process. It is also pointed out that a drug is in Category III even if it is safe and effective for most of its ingredients and recommended uses, but only safe and unclear on effectiveness as to others.

The question before the Court, however, is not whether the FDA has adopted a wise or reasonable policy, but rather whether that policy, as implemented through the OTC regulations and Drug Review Program, is one which is in harmony with the Federal Food, Drug, and Cosmetic Act.... Whatever the precise significance of a Category III determination, ... one point is abundantly clear. The Commissioner's OTC regulations formally authorize the continued marketing of Category III drug products in the absence of an administrative determination that those products are, today, generally recognized by experts as safe and effective. This flies in the face of the statutory scheme.

Under the Act, with very limited exceptions not here relevant, drugs can be lawfully marketed in only two ways. They are either new drugs which must be licensed, or they are generally recognized by experts as safe and effective, and are therefore not subject to active regulation. The goal of the Act is to insure that *every* marketed drug is both safe and effective. There are no other possibilities, no interim provisions under which safe, but only potentially effective drugs can be marketed pending testing. Even assuming that defendants are correct that Category III drugs are not *necessarily* unlawful new drugs, there is no question that they are *potentially* unlawful new drugs. To say that the Commissioner has the authority under the Act to affirmatively sanction the marketing of such drugs, effectively exempting them from the enforcement provisions of the Act for periods ranging from two to at least five years, is nothing less than a frontal assault on the premarket licensing scheme of the Food, Drug, and Cosmetic Act....

Finally, the challenged regulations, however well intentioned, are fundamentally at odds with Congressional intent as manifested by the specific transitional provisions for the new effectiveness requirements imposed in the 1962 Drug Amendments....In light of these comprehensive and detailed transitional provisions, the Commissioner's decision, over a decade later, to further cushion the impact of the efficacy requirements through a sort of Category III grace period cannot be reconciled with the clear intent of Congress to make those requirements immediately applicable to all but a limited class of OTC drugs. The Court concludes that the challenged regulations are unlawful to the extent they affirmatively sanction continued marketing of Category III drugs.

The question of appropriate relief raises an additional, and difficult, issue. As noted above, part of plaintiffs' requested relief is an order directing the Commissioner "to take all appropriate steps" to remove any Category III drug from the market which is not covered by an NDA. The assumption underlying this request is apparently that the Commissioner, in addition to exceeding his statutory authority by authorizing the marketing of Category III drugs, has violated a statutory duty or abused his discretion by not moving to do just the opposite—removing them from the market.

The Court is sympathetic to plaintiffs' frustrations with the history of enforcement of the Drug Amendments of 1962.... On balance, however, even assuming that placement of a drug in Category III, absent grandfather status or coverage by an NDA, is tantamount to a finding of illegality under the Act, the Court cannot agree with plaintiffs that the Commissioner must move to take such drugs off the market.

First, plaintiffs have not attempted to demonstrate that the Commissioner has a duty to seek enforcement action against every unlawfully marketed drug. Certainly, the statutory scheme and traditional notions of prosecutorial discretion would suggest just the opposite. Only new drugs must be reviewed by the Commissioner prior to marketing. With regard to drugs not subject to active regulation as

new drugs, the Act is not self-executing. The agency's ultimate remedy
is to request the Justice Department to bring enforcement actions in a
federal district court in the name of the United States. Congress did
cast certain of the Commissioner's drug review duties in mandatory,
nondiscretionary terms. But with regard to his duty to institute
enforcement proceedings, what little indication there is in the Act is to
the contrary. Section 306 of the Act, in fact, states that the Commissioner shall not be required "to report for prosecution, or for the
institution of libel or injunction proceedings, minor violations of this
chapter whenever he believes that the public interest will be adequately served by a suitable written notice or warning."

Second, and wholly apart from the question of the agency's discretion, the Court believes that the more extensive relief sought by
plaintiffs is unwarranted under traditional principles of equity. The
parties have identified only one drug product—Gaviscon—currently
being marketed pursuant to a Category III determination. With regard
to future Category III orders, the Court's decision to void the marketing
authorization feature of the challenged regulations will afford the FDA
an opportunity to amend its regulations in any way it sees fit. In these
circumstances, it would be unwise and injudicious to require the agency
to take steps immediately to remove Category III drugs from the
market as they are finally classified. The agency may prefer to revise
the system.

It should be emphasized, however, that the FDA may not lawfully
maintain Category III in any form in which drugs with Category III
conditions (as Category III conditions are presently defined) are exempted from enforcement action. Informally, of course, the FDA will be
free to exercise its discretion to seek enforcement actions or not to seek
enforcement actions. It may thus be argued that the Court's ruling
simply permits the agency to accomplish informally and indirectly
what it cannot accomplish in a formal order. But that is the system
Congress created....

NOTES

1. *Testing Category III Ingredients.* Prior to the *Cutler* decision, FDA was
forced to decide the conditions under which Category III active ingredients
could be tested. The agency concluded, 40 Fed. Reg. 49097 (October 21, 1975),
42 Fed. Reg. 19137 (April 12, 1977), that the manufacturer must make a
fundamental choice at the beginning of testing: either (1) discontinue marketing the ingredient, test it under an IND, and file an NDA to obtain approval of
its use; or (2) continue marketing the ingredient while testing is in progress, in
which case no NDA may be obtained and any approval will be in the form of an
amendment to the monograph.

2. *Subsequent Proceedings.* Neither FDA nor the industry intervenor
defendants appealed the *Cutler* decision. In 44 Fed. Reg. 61608 (October 26,
1979), 45 Fed. Reg. 31422 (May 13, 1980), 46 Fed. Reg. 47739 (September 29,
1981), FDA revised its regulations to comply with the decision. The revised
regulations deleted the authorization to market Category III ingredients after
publication of a final monograph and required testing of ingredients to be

completed prior to such publication in order to be eligible for Category I. At the same time, 46 Fed. Reg. 47740 (September 29, 1981), FDA published a policy statement announcing that it would welcome meetings with industry representatives to study protocols and test results for Category III ingredients, and promising to comment on the adequacy of study results to upgrade an ingredient while it is being separately considered as part of the monograph process. In substance, therefore, the *Cutler* decision resulted in Category III ingredients being tested and FDA decisions on those ingredients reached before, rather than after, publication of the final monograph.

---

5. COMPLETION OF THE OTC DRUG REVIEW

The OTC Drug Review has been one of the most complex and difficult rulemaking efforts undertaken by any government agency. As the Review has progressed, and manufacturers of OTC drugs have responded by reformulating and relabeling their products, often even before final monographs have been promulgated, the program's priority on FDA's agenda has fallen. See GAO, FDA'S APPROACH TO REVIEWING OVER–THE–COUNTER DRUGS IS REASONABLE, BUT PROGRESS IS SLOW, No. HRD–82–41 (April 26, 1982).

CUTLER v. HAYES
United States Court of Appeals, District of Columbia Circuit, 1987.
818 F.2d 879.

SPOTTSWOOD W. ROBINSON, III, Circuit Judge:

This case presents a challenge by consumers of over-the-counter (OTC) drugs to the program undertaken by the Food and Drug Administration (FDA) comprehensively to review these drugs for their safety and effectiveness. The consumers allege (1) that the regulations implementing this program violate the Food, Drug, and Cosmetic Act of 1938 (FDC Act), as amended by the Drug Amendments of 1962, pursuant to which they were promulgated; (2) that FDA's policy of nonenforcement of the efficacy requirement for marketing over-the-counter drugs in interstate commerce violates the agency's statutory duty; and (3) that FDA's lack of progress in completing the review program and the unlikelihood that the review will be completed in the near future infringes the provisions of the Administrative Procedure Act disapproving unreasonable agency delay. The District Court granted appellees' motion for summary judgment on all counts. While we affirm the District Court's judgment on appellants' first two claims, we vacate the judgment on the charge of unreasonable delay and remand the case to the District Court for reconsideration in accordance with this opinion.....

As we understand their argument, appellants assert that FDA has abdicated its statutory duty by (1) postponing enforcement of the Act's efficacy requirement and substantially limiting enforcement of the safety mandate until the completion of the OTC drug review program, and (2) then delaying completion of the program unreasonably.....

... The FDC Act imposes no clear duty upon FDA to bring enforcement proceedings to effectuate either the safety or the efficacy requirements of the Act. Without a doubt, FDA has a responsibility under the Act to identify drugs generally recognized as safe and effective and require premarketing clearance for all others. But Congress has not given FDA an inflexible mandate to bring enforcement actions against all violators of the Act....

Nor does FDA's policy of postponing enforcement of the efficacy requirement until after publication of final monographs afford a basis for intervention.... Particularly as an agency with limited resources, FDA reasonably may assign enforcement of a statutory requirement designed to prevent unnecessary consumer expense to a lower priority than that accorded one concerned with identifying and eliminating threats to human life. More importantly, until FDA issues a final monograph, the agency has yet to make a substantiated and conclusive determination that a drug is not generally recognized as effective; besides, prior to promulgation of a final monograph, the agency's conclusion that an OTC drug is ineffective is subject to reconsideration based on new information that may be submitted to FDA. It would be a futile act, as well as one financially disastrous for manufacturers of pharmaceuticals, were the agency to require removal of a potentially ineffective drug from interstate commerce only to find, on the basis of later unfolding information, that the drug should have been classified as generally recognized as effective. Given these rational justifications for postponing enforcement of the efficacy requirement, we hold that FDA's policy on that score does not amount to an abuse of discretion.

As we have already stated, the 1962 amendments to the FDC Act obligate FDA to review all nonexempt OTC drugs for their therapeutic efficacy as well as their safety. Concededly, FDA has broad discretion in deciding how to achieve this objective. The District Court erred, however, in equating the agency's freedom to exercise its discretion with voluntariness. Although FDA's discretion extends to review of OTC drugs by ingredient rather than by product—a choice implicitly approved by the Supreme Court in *Bentex Pharmaceuticals*—the agency lacks authority to simply do nothing to effectuate the purpose of the Act.

Once FDA elected to respond to its legislative directive by establishing the OTC drug review program, the APA imposed an obligation to proceed with reasonable dispatch. We have often intervened to compel an agency unreasonably delaying to speed up its activities, and our authority to do so in appropriate instances is not here in question. In rejecting appellants' delay argument, however, the District Court examined none of the factors that have traditionally guided assessments on the propriety of agency delay; rather, the court relied solely on a single precedent—*McIlwain v. Hayes* [p. _____ *supra*]—which involved a statutory scheme very different from the one before us today. The provisions governing marketing of food color additives contain a transitional mechanism allowing commercially-established additives to be marketed on an interim basis prior to a final determination on safety; as this court observed, it authorized FDA to postpone the closing date for submissions " 'for such period or periods as ... necessary to carry out the purpose of this section.' " Not only do the 1962 amendments of the FDC act lack an analogous provision, but the majority opinion in *McIlwain* took pains to distinguish the statutory arrangement in that case from the regime implicated here. It should also be noted that in the case at bar, initial research had indicated that a vast number of drugs on the market were ineffective, while none of the test data on the food additives at issue in *McIlwain* suggested that they were unsafe....

Since the District Court relied solely on *McIlwain* to support its award of summary judgment, we must remand for reconsideration in accordance with correct legal standards....

Any discussion of the standards relevant to the issue of delay must begin with recognition that an administrative agency is entitled to considerable deference in establishing a timetable for completing its proceedings. An agency has broad discretion to set its agenda and to first apply its limited resources to the regulatory tasks it deems most pressing. The agency's discretion is not unbounded, however, since the consequences of dilatoriness may be great.... "Quite simply, excessive delay saps the public confidence in an agency's ability to discharge its responsibilities and creates uncertainty for the parties, who must incorporate the potential effect of possible agency decisionmaking into future plans." Moreover, unjustifiable delay may undermine the statutory scheme and could inflict harm on individuals in need of final action. In some cases, agency delay may collide with the right to judicial review.

Our cases identify a number of factors that aid in determining whether an agency's foot-dragging constitutes unreasonable delay. First, the court should ascertain the length of time that has elapsed since the agency came under a duty to act, and should evaluate any prospect of early completion. Next, "[t]he reasonableness of the delay must be judged 'in the context of the statute' which authorizes the agency's action." This entails an examination of any legislative mandate in the statute and the degree of discretion given the agency by Congress. The court must also estimate the extent to which delay may be undermining the statutory scheme, either by frustrating the statutory goal or by creating a situation in which the agency is "losing its ability to effectively regulate at all."

Third, and perhaps most critically, the court must examine the consequences of the agency's delay. The deference traditionally accorded an agency to develop its own schedule is sharply reduced when injury likely will result from avoidable delay. Economic harm is clearly an important consideration and will, in some cases, justify court intervention, and "[d]elays that might be altogether reasonable in the sphere of economic regulation are less tolerable when human lives are at stake." Lack of alternative means of eliminating or reducing the hazard necessarily adds to unreasonableness of a delay.

The agency must justify its delay to the court's satisfaction. If the court determines that the agency delays in bad faith, it should conclude that the delay is unreasonable. If the court finds an absence of bad faith, it should then consider the agency's explanation, such as administrative necessity, insufficient resources, or the complexity of the task confronting the agency. Although complexity bears on avoidance in ascertaining reasonableness, it is not always sufficient to justify lengthy delays. And if an agency's failure to proceed expeditiously will result in harm or substantial nullification of a right conferred by statute, "the courts must act to make certain that what can be done is done." The court should weigh any plea of administrative error, administrative convenience, practical difficulty in carrying out a legislative mandate, or need to prioritize in the face of limited resources. Of course, these justifications become less persuasive as delay progresses, and must always be balanced against the potential for harm.....

Lastly, appellants attack as inconsistent with the FDC Act and the District Court's decision in *Cutler v. Kennedy,* the amendment to the OTC drug review regulations creating a period for comment on temporary final monographs. This amendment eliminated the marketing period for Category III drugs after formulation of the final monograph, but added a twelve-month period following publication of the tentative final monograph for interested persons to present "new data and information to support a condition excluded from the monograph in the tentative order." ...

Appellants argue that the newly-added twelve-month period for submitting additional information bearing on tentative final monographs serves only to delay implementation of the Act's safety and efficacy requirements by further postponing publication of final monographs, and, in effect, to sanction the impermissible marketing of Category III drugs at an earlier stage in the process....

We do not share appellants' expansive interpretation of *Cutler.* It is evident that there the first set of OTC regulations were condemned because they permitted continued marketing of Category III drugs after publication of final monographs. By eliminating this marketing authorization, however, FDA has overcome the difficulty that was fatal in *Cutler.*

Nor do we perceive the current regulations as arbitrary, capricious, or otherwise inconsistent with the FDC Act. The OTC review program in its present form does not sanction the marketing of OTC drugs during the twelve-month period for which the administrative record remains open. Moreover, until publication of a final monograph, FDA makes no conclusive determination of a drug's GRAS/E status; rather, panel recommendations and tentative conclusions remain subject to reconsideration in light of any additional information submitted in timely fashion to the agency. Moreover, the agency has presented reasonable justifications for adopting the twelve-month open-record period. FDA designed this procedure to facilitate gathering of supplemental information, including that which is often solicited by the agency from manufacturers. Leaving the record open for this period promotes efficiency since it eliminates the need to deal with the expectably large number of individual petitions to reopen the record, and allows the agency simultaneously to evaluate the public comments, objections, and requests for hearings tendered after publication of the tentative final monographs. We therefore conclude that FDA did not act arbitrarily or otherwise improperly when it amended its regulations on Category III drugs.

In 1962, Congress ordained that only those drugs generally recognized as safe and effective could be marketed without premarketing clearance. Because, a quarter-century later, this mandate has not yet been fully satisfied, close scrutiny must be paid to appellants' claim that FDA has unreasonably delayed its completion of the OTC drug review program. . . . .

NOTES

1. *Proceedings on Remand.* On remand, at the request of the district court FDA submitted A HISTORICAL EXAMINATION OF FDA'S REVIEW OF THE SAFETY AND EFFECTIVENESS OF OVER-THE-COUNTER DRUGS (September 22, 1987). The district court had taken no final action in the case as of January 1, 1991. In a memorandum submitted to the district court on September 25, 1989, plaintiffs complained that FDA was late in publishing many OTC Drug Review documents and thus that the current agency schedule, which projects completion in 1993, cannot be met.

2. *Progress of OTC Review.* FDA passed one landmark in the OTC Drug Review on October 7, 1983, when it published the last of the 58 reports prepared by the 17 advisory panels. The 17 panels held 508 meetings over 1,047 days and reviewed some 20,000 volumes of data on more than 700 active ingredients used in over 300,000 nonprescription drug products. See HHS News No. P83–22 (October 7, 1983). Because most OTC drugs are reformulated and relabeled to comply with the panel reports soon after, and sometimes even before, their publication, the major impact of the OTC Drug Review has already been reflected in the marketplace.

The OTC panels reviewed some 722 active ingredients for approximately 1,454 specific uses. They rated roughly 30 percent as Category I for the intended use, 34 percent as Category II, and 36 percent as Category III. The agency later upgraded many Category III active ingredients to Category I based upon new information. Gilbertson, THE PRESCRIPTION TO OTC SWITCH: FDA VIEW 5 (April 1986).

The progress of the OTC Drug Review can be monitored through FDA's Semiannual Regulatory Agenda. See, e.g., 52 Fed. Reg. 14314 (April 27, 1987), 52 Fed. Reg. 40309 (October 26, 1987), 53 Fed. Reg. 13804 (April 25, 1988), 53 Fed. Reg. 41925 (October 24, 1988), 54 Fed. Reg. 16653 (April 24, 1989), 54 Fed.

Reg. 44644 (October 30, 1989), 55 Fed. Reg. 16168 (April 23, 1990), 55 Fed.Reg. 44470 (October 29, 1990).

3. *Exclusion of Unimportant Ingredients.* To speed up completion of the OTC Drug Review FDA, in 55 Fed. Reg. 20434 (May 16, 1990), 55 Fed.Reg. 46914 (November 7, 1990), deleted from further consideration several Category II and III active ingredients on which the agency has received no public comment.

----

6. OTC DRUG PRODUCT TAMPERING

TAMPER–RESISTANT PACKAGING REQUIREMENTS FOR CERTAIN OVER–THE–COUNTER HUMAN DRUG AND COSMETIC PRODUCTS

47 Federal Register 50442 (November 5, 1982).

FDA is issuing final regulations to require tamper-resistant packaging for certain over-the-counter (OTC) drug and cosmetic products. OTC drug products subject to these regulations include all OTC drug products except dermatologics (i.e., products applied to the skin), dentifrices, and insulin. The OTC drug products that are covered by these regulations include oral (except dentifrices), nasal, otic, ophthalmic, rectal, and vaginal drug products. Cosmetic products covered by these regulations are liquids that are used orally, such as mouthwashes, gargles, breath fresheners, etc., and vaginal cosmetic products. The agency is requiring that the packaging of these products be capable of providing consumers with visible evidence of package tampering....

On September 30, 1982, FDA was advised that several persons living in the Chicago metropolitan area had died from cyanide poisoning after taking Extra–Strength Tylenol capsules. Capsules taken from bottles of Extra–Strength Tylenol in the possession of the victims were chemically analyzed by local authorities, and some of the capsules in these bottles were found to contain lethal amounts of potassium cyanide. By October 1, several more Chicago area residents had died from cyanide poisoning after ingesting Tylenol Extra–Strength capsules, bringing the total of deaths to seven.

On September 30, government authorities and the manufacturer of Tylenol, McNeil Consumer Products, Fort Washington, PA, began an investigation to determine the manner in which the capsules had become contaminated with cyanide. The capsules involved in the seven deaths were manufactured in two plants, one in Pennsylvania and one in Texas. FDA investigators immediately inspected both plants. Based on the plant inspections, FDA concluded that the contamination had not occurred at either plant, but rather was the result of tampering after the capsules had been shipped to distribution points and, most likely, after they had reached the retail shelves.....

Since the Tylenol poisonings, several cases of serious injuries have been reported resulting from the use of products that have been tampered with. These incidents, although not the initial impetus for these regulations, further demonstrate the need for their prompt implementation.

The poisoning fatalities make plain the gravity of the risk to which the nation's population is exposed from malicious tampering with drug products sold over-the-counter to the consumer. The Tylenol incident occurred in the Chicago area, but it was followed by others elsewhere in the country. Nor is the potential for such tampering confined to one manufacturer's products. Incidents of OTC drug product tampering have occurred in recent weeks. The combined incidents demonstrate that the need for adequate product security is national in scope and requires an industrywide response.....

The agency defines a tamper-resistant package as one having an indicator or barrier to entry which, if breached or missing, can reasonably be expected to provide visible evidence to consumers that tampering has occurred. Tamper-resistant packaging may involve immediate-container/closure systems or secondary-container/carton systems or any combination thereof intended to provide a visual indication of package integrity when handled in a reasonable manner during manufacture, distribution, and retail display. The visual indication is required to be accompanied by appropriate illustrations or precautionary statements to describe the safeguarding mechanism to the consumer. To reduce the possibility that the security mechanism can be restored after tampering, the agency is also requiring that either the tamper-resistant feature be designed from materials that are generally not readily available (e.g., an aerosol system) or that barriers made from readily obtainable material (e.g., plain tape, paper seals, clear plastic) carry a distinctive design or logo.

The agency stresses that tamper-*proof* packaging is not possible. Although the requirements in this final rule will reduce the potential for tampering, they cannot eliminate it. Neither the agency nor manufacturers can guarantee protection against malicious tampering but can only make tampering more difficult by making product packaging more *resistant* to tampering. For this reason, the agency will consider any labeling statement suggesting that the package is tamper-proof, as contrasted with tamper-resistant, to be false and misleading. Consumers must act to protect themselves from injury by inspecting the condition of the packages they buy, the tablets and capsules they take, and the liquids they drink.....

NOTES

1. *Anti-Tampering Act.* In response to the Chicago Tylenol poisonings, Congress enacted the Federal Anti-Tampering Act, 97 Stat. 831 (1983), codified in 18 U.S.C. § 1365, which makes it a crime to tamper with a consumer product with reckless disregard for the risk of persons or with intent to cause injury to a business. The Act also prohibits communication of false information that a

consumer product has been tainted and threats to tamper with a consumer product.

2. *Incidents of Tampering.* Despite the efforts of the agency and of Congress, however, tampering with FDA-regulated products has continued. In 1986, the agency acknowledged that reports of tampering had "decreased significantly" following the actions taken in 1982, but then recounted more recent incidents:

> In February 1986, FDA again received a report of a death linked to the tampering of Tylenol capsules with cyanide. In the following months, FDA has been embroiled in a widespread series of investigations of tampering incidents that include dozens of products such as Gerber baby food, Girl Scout cookies, Ac'cent flavor enhancer, and other OTC drugs including Contac, Teldrin, Dietac, Excedrin and Anacin-3.....

> ... FDA will continue to support the criminal investigation of tamperings and falsely reported tamperings. In addition, FDA, with assistance from the Proprietary Association and other industry and consumer groups, will continue to focus efforts on public education since investigation of tampering incidents shows that current packaging is indeed very tamper-evident and has usually offered a signal to users that the product has been tampered with. The report also says that FDA will work with the pharmaceutical industry to encourage and emphasize the rapid adoption of improved tamper-resistant packaging including the utilization of more than one tamper-resistant feature per package, phasing out weaker tamper-resistant packaging technologies such as glued cartons, and bringing uniformity to tamper-resistant packaging within the product lines of companies....

"Agency Report on Tampering Available," FDA Talk Paper No. 786–49 (July 9, 1986). The agency devoted $2.85 million to OTC drug tampering problems during fiscal year 1986. "Cost of Tampering and Other Emergencies," FDA Talk Paper No. T87–10 (February 18, 1987).

E. REGULATING PHYSICIAN PRESCRIBING
1. PHYSICIAN PRESCRIBING HABITS

By statutory definition, a prescription drug is a drug for which adequate directions for layperson use cannot be written, because such persons lack the scientific understanding needed to diagnose their disease or to use the drug in treating it. As we have suggested p. 418 *supra*, this rationale for restricting drugs to sale only by prescription drug is beginning to erode. With the spread of patient labeling and other educational materials, patients have become more knowledgeable about prescription drugs and often participate with their physicians in treatment decisions.

From its adoption of regulations in 1939 to create a mandatory category of prescription drugs, FDA has sought to protect users of these drugs in two distinct ways. First, it has attempted to assure through the new drug approval process and other regulatory controls that prescription drugs are safe and effective. Second, the agency has sought to provide prescribing physicians through package inserts containing increasingly detailed information about their use in patients. The physician package insert has now become a summary of all that is known about the safety and effectiveness of a drug. It represents a distillation of the results of testing arrived at through negotiations between agency officials and the drug's sponsor. Both FDA and pharmaceutical manufacturers assume that the physician package insert will influence the physician's use of the drug. The correctness of FDA's reliance upon the physician package insert thus depends on the validity of that assumption.

Without question, the physician package insert significantly influences how prescription drugs are used. But it is also clear that every prescription drug is sometimes, perhaps frequently, administered for conditions that fall outside the FDA-approved insert. There are several reasons for this. The physician package insert describes only those conditions that have been systematically studied, and not all possible conditions of use. Physicians who routinely confront the duty to care for seriously ill patients are impelled to try new methods of treatment. Medical need invariably outpaces controlled clinical evaluation. New uses of established drugs often gain acceptance before controlled studies are launched, supplemental NDAs submitted, and FDA approval obtained. On the other extreme, use of a drug for an unapproved indication can also represent poor judgment, failure to heed appropriate warnings, or inadequate medical training.

Thus, FDA is often faced with the following dilemma. Some unapproved uses represent sound medical care, sometimes even the only possible treatment. Other unapproved uses represent recklessness. Initially the agency took the position that only the information contained in the FDA-approved physician package insert represents reliable information about a new drug and cautioned physicians not to stray beyond it. When pressed, however, FDA backed away from the proposition that prescribing a new drug for an indication not approved in the FDA-approved physician package insert constituted a violation of the FD&C Act. Instead, the agency took the more limited position that the manufacturer may not promote an approved drug for unapproved uses.

2. FDA CONTROL OF PHYSICIAN PRESCRIBING

NEW DRUGS USED FOR NONAPPROVED PURPOSES (METHOTREXATE FOR PSORIASIS)

Hearings Before a Subcommittee of the House Committee
on Government Operations.
92d Congress, 1st Session (1971).

Mr. Rosenthal.... If you find ... that physicians who are not part of the IND studies are dispensing a drug improperly, is it also your attitude that nothing can be done?

Mr. Goodrich [FDA Chief Counsel]. We could have done more than we did. The problem here was the physicians were using the drug on the basis of literature reports. The company was saying that it was not promoting the drug. We examined the evidence; we thought they did.

... We found out that when a physician out in the prescribing territory asked the detail man about Methotrexate for psoriasis then that would be reported back to Lederle and Lederle would send the physician a letter and reprints. They would send a disclaimer that they were not promoting the drug for that purpose, but that they would supply the information that it had been used; it had been used successfully by simply reporting out of the literature, and they would give him some information about the dose.

Mr. Rosenthal. That was not legal, what they were doing?

Mr. Goodrich. No; it was not....

And Dr. Ley's approach, Mr. Rosenthal, was that it should be dealt with as an educational program with the profession. He encouraged the American Medical Association Journal to run an editorial on this....

Mr. Grant [Deputy FDA Commissioner].... Methotrexate is not the only drug that is being used for conditions for which it is not approved or labeled. Drugs approved for marketing for one purpose sometimes are found in ingenuity or by accident or have other uses....

Our problem in dealing with the use of drugs for conditions in which they are not approved involves both the manufacturer and the prescribing physician. We have direct control over the manufacturer. We can take legal and administrative actions to assure that any drug is labeled for all of the conditions for which it is intended to be used, whether that intent is openly expressed in the promotional literature and promotional practices, or whether it is demonstrated by the manufacturer supplying a drug for purposes not covered in the approved labeling.

As to the physician, no less a group than the Council on Drugs of the American Medical Association has taken the position that it is within the physician's sole discretion to choose and to prescribe a drug for his own patient. . . .

What physicians need to know is that when they prescribe outside the limits of safety and effectiveness that have been established through the adequate and well-controlled clinical investigations required by the new drug procedures, they are using the drug investigationally on their patients. If any untoward reaction or adverse effect occurs, the physician may well be called upon to defend the reasonableness of his therapy. . . .

LEGAL STATUS OF APPROVED LABELING FOR PRESCRIPTION DRUGS; PRESCRIBING FOR USES UNAPPROVED BY THE FOOD AND DRUG ADMINISTRATION: NOTICE OF PROPOSED RULE MAKING

37 Federal Register 16503 (August 15, 1972).

The widespread use of certain prescription drugs for conditions not named in the official labeling has led to questions concerning the legal responsibilities of the prescribing physicians and the position of the Food and Drug Administration with respect to such use. . . .

Section 505 of the Federal Food, Drug, and Cosmetic Act prohibits the introduction or delivery for introduction into interstate commerce of any new drug without the filing of an investigational new drug plan or approval of a new drug application. Unlike the adulteration and misbranding provisions of the Act, the new drug provisions apply only at the moment of shipment in interstate commerce and not to action taken subsequent to shipment in interstate commerce. In *United States v. Phelps Dodge Mercantile Co.,* 157 F.2d 453 (9th Cir. 1946) [p. 1070 *infra*] the court held that violations while products are held for sale after interstate shipment did not come within the jurisdiction of the Act. As a result of that decision, Congress enacted the Miller amendment of 1948 amending section 301(k) of the Act to extend the reach of the adulteration and misbranding provisions of the Act to violations after interstate shipment. The 1948 amendment did not, however, also extend the reach of the new drug provisions of the Act, which are separate from the adulteration and misbranding provisions, to action taken after interstate shipment.

The major objective of the drug provisions of the Federal Food, Drug, and Cosmetic Act is to assure that drugs will be safe and effective for use under the conditions of use prescribed, recommended, or suggested in the labeling thereof. . . . When a new drug is approved for marketing, the conditions of use that have been approved are required to be set forth in detail in the official labeling. This labeling must accompany the drug in interstate shipment and must contain adequate information for safe and effective use of the drug. . . . It presents a full disclosure summarization of drug use information, which the supplier of the drug is required to develop from accumulated clinical experience, and systematic drug trials consisting of preclinical investigations and adequate well-controlled clinical investigations that demonstrate the drug's safety and the effectiveness it purports or is represented to possess.

If an approved new drug is shipped in interstate commerce with the approved package insert, and neither the shipper nor the recipient intends that it be used for an unapproved purpose, the requirements of section 505 of the Act are satisfied. Once the new drug is in a local pharmacy after interstate shipment, the physician may, as part of the practice of medicine, lawfully prescribe a different dosage for his patient, or may otherwise vary the conditions of use from those approved in the package insert, without informing or obtaining the approval of the Food and Drug Administration.

This interpretation of the Act is consistent with congressional intent as indicated in the legislative history of the 1938 Act and the drug amendments of 1962.... In the 1938 Act and the 1962 amendments, however, Congress clearly required the Food and Drug Administration to control the availability of drugs for prescribing by the physicians..... As the law now stands, therefore, the Food and Drug Administration is charged with the responsibility of judging the safety and effectiveness of drugs and the truthfulness of their labeling. The physician is then responsible for making the final judgment as to which, if any, of the available drugs his patient will receive in the light of the information contained in their labeling and other adequate scientific data available to him.

Although the Act does not require a physician to file an investigational new drug plan before prescribing an approved drug for unapproved uses, or to submit to the Food and Drug Administration data concerning the therapeutic results and the adverse reactions obtained, it is sometimes in the best interests of the physician and the public that this be done. The physician should recognize that such use is investigational, and he should take account of the scientific principles, including the moral and ethical considerations, applicable to the safe use of investigational drugs in human patients....

Where the unapproved use of an approved new drug becomes widespread or endangers the public health, the Food and Drug Administration is obligated to investigate it thoroughly and to take whatever action is warranted to protect the public. Several alternative courses of action are available to the Food and Drug Administration under these circumstances, depending upon the specific facts of each case. These actions include: Requiring a change in the labeling to warn against or to approve the unapproved use, seeking substantial evidence to substantiate the use, restricting the channel of distribution, and even withdrawing approval of the drug and removing it from the market in extreme cases. When necessary, the Food and Drug Administration will not hesitate to take whatever action of this nature may be required to bring possible harmful use of an approved drug under control.

Section 1.106 of the regulations [now 21 C.F.R. § 201.5] requires the labeling to contain appropriate information with respect to all intended uses of the drugs. Thus, where a manufacturer or his representative, or any person in the chain of distribution, does anything that directly or indirectly suggests to the physician or to the patient that an approved drug may properly be used for unapproved uses for which it is neither labeled nor advertised, that action constitutes a direct violation of the Act and is punishable accordingly....

NOTES

1. *Subsequent Proceedings.* FDA has taken no further action on this proposal, but it continues to refer to this notice as its established policy, *e.g.,* "Use of Approved Drugs For Unlabeled Indications," 12 FDA Drug Bulletin 4 (April 1982). The preamble to FDA's proposed comprehensive revision of the IND regulations, 48 Fed. Reg. 26720 (June 9, 1983), reiterated the agency's August 1972 policy statement and, in addition, proposed to exempt even those clinical investigations using a marketed drug for unapproved purposes whose results are not intended to be submitted in support of a supplemental NDA. This language was retained in the final regulations, 52 Fed. Reg. 8798 (March 19, 1987), and is codified in 21 C.F.R. § 312.2(d).

2. *Commentary.* For a detailed analysis of the pertinent legislative history and the controversy that led to the August 1972 proposal, *see* Hutt, *Regulation of the Practice of Medicine under the Pure Food and Drug Laws,* 33 Q. Bull. Ass'n of Food & Drug Off., No. 1, at 3 (1969); *see also* Kessler, *Regulating the Prescribing of Human Drugs for Non-approved Uses under the Food, Drug, and Cosmetic Act,* 15 Harv. J. Legis. 693 (1978); McEniry and Willig, *The Federal Food, Drug, and Cosmetic Act and the Medical Practitioners,* 29 FDC L.J. 548 (1974); Shapiro, *Limiting Physician Freedom to Prescribe a Drug for any Purpose: The Need for FDA Regulation,* 73 Nw. L. Rev. 801 (1979).

3. *State Law.* A related issue is whether the unapproved use of an approved new drug complies with state law as well. Relying upon FDA's position, those states that have considered the matter have determined that the physician is not bound by the approved physician package insert. *See, e.g.,* Opinion of California Attorney General E.J. Younger, CV 76/212 and 77/236 (May 2, 1978); Opinion of California Legislative Counsel B.M. Gregory No. 8182 (May 26, 1981).

4. *Use of Anticancer Drugs in Combination.* No cancer drug has been approved by FDA with labeling that explicitly recommends its use in combination with any other cancer drug. The National Cancer Institute (NCI) not only recommends and makes available a number of Group C investigational cancer drugs for routine cancer therapy, *see* p. 557 *supra,* but also recommends that virtually all cancer drugs be used in various combination in order to achieve the most effective therapy. In distributing or referring to standard NCI materials, pharmaceutical manufacturers are thus clearly recommending their drugs for unapproved uses. For years FDA has taken no action to prevent this activity, but in early 1991 the agency issued a letter objecting to the practice. Letter from K.R. Feather, Acting Director of the Division of Drug Advertising and Labeling, to R.L. Gelb, Chairman of Bristol–Myers Squibb, January 25, 1991.

5. *Depo–Provera*. The Department of HHS has itself officially used approved drugs for unapproved purposes. The Indian Health Service has prescribed Depo–Provera for contraceptive use even after FDA specifically disapproved this indication as described in note 3, p. 524 *supra*. "Use of the Drug, Depo Provera, by the Indian Health Service," Oversight Hearing before the Subcomm. on General Oversight and Investigations of the House Comm. on Interior and Insular Affairs, 100th Cong., 1st Sess. (1987).

6. *Generic Drugs*. Relying upon the FDA policy, the Chairman of the Subcommittee on Health and the Environment of the House Committee on Energy and Commerce took the position that a generic drug may lawfully be prescribed for a use for which only the pioneer drug has been approved, without added risk of liability on the part of the pharmacist or the physician. *See* letter from Representative H.A. Waxman to F.S. Mayer (November 25, 1985).

7. *Reimbursement for Unapproved Uses*. Even though FDA has stated that a physician may lawfully prescribe a new drug for an unapproved use, reimbursement for such uses under Medicare, Medicaid, and private insurance programs remains unclear. *See also* Higgins, *Insurers Starting to Balk: Off-Label Rx*, 29 Medical World News, No. 20, at 22 (October 24, 1988).

8. *Physician Distribution*. Although a physician does not violate section 505 of the FD&C Act by *prescribing* an approved new drug for an unapproved use, physicians who *distribute* either approved or unapproved drugs for unapproved uses are fully subject to the requirements of section 505. *See, e.g., United States v. Sartori*, Food Drug Cosm. L. Rep. (CCH) ¶ 38,196 (D.Md. 1982). Where the requisite interstate commerce is lacking, misbranding or adulteration charges may properly be brought against the illegal drug.

9. *Diversion of Drugs Exempted for Studies in Animals*. FDA's August 1972 policy apparently does not provide a basis for prohibiting the diversion of experimental drugs from animal testing to human use. In 1983, FDA discovered that interferon, a biological drug which was being shipped for investigational use only in laboratory animals or in vitro studies, was being diverted to human use. The agency published a notice, 48 Fed. Reg. 52644 (November 21, 1983), warning that such diversion constituted a violation of section 351 of the Public Health Service Act.

10. *FTC Enforcement*. When physicians began to advertise unapproved uses of approved new drugs, however, government agencies took a different position. In 1975, the Federal Trade Commission sought to enjoin a weight reduction clinic from advertising human chorionic gonadotropin or any other unapproved drug for use in its treatment program. Citing FDA's August 1972 policy, however, the District Court ruled that advertising a treatment program that utilized an unapproved new drug did not violate the FD&C Act. *F.T.C. v. Simeon Management Corp.*, 391 F.Supp. 697 (N.D. Cal. 1975), *aff'd*, 532 F.2d 708 (9th Cir. 1976).

UNITED STATES v. AN ARTICLE OF DRUG ... DISO-TATE

United States District Court, Eastern District of Louisiana, 1976.
1975–1977 FDLI Jud. Rec. 239.

GORDON, J., District Judge.

This suit was originally instituted as a forfeiture action for the seizure and condemnation of the drug Disodium Edetate (EDTA), which is held for sale at Meadowbrook Hospital, on the ground that the drug was misbranded after shipment in interstate commerce..... However, as the prayer for injunctive relief indicates, the Government is now not only attempting to enjoin the misbranding of EDTA, but also its administration. The issuance of the injunction will avoid the necessity of the Government making multiple, and perhaps daily, seizures of EDTA in order to prevent the misbranding of EDTA.

The evidence is undisputed that the defendants have used EDTA in the treatment of arteriosclerosis and other circulatory diseases (chelation therapy).... [N]ot only does the labeling [of EDTA] fail to bear adequate direction for its use in the treatment of circulatory diseases, but also it is specifically contraindicated for that type of treatment....

Testimony at the injunction hearing established that Dr. Evers has held a press conference and distributed promotional literature advocating EDTA therapy for cardiovascular therapy, and that promotional literature of a same sort was distributed at a convention of the National Health Federation. It was shown that Dr. Evers continued to distribute chelation therapy advertising to prospective patients and both he and Meadowbrook Hospital enjoy a national reputation as employing EDTA in the treatment of arteriosclerosis.

Accordingly, it is this Court's conclusion that the intended use of EDTA at Meadowbrook Hospital is in the treatment of arteriosclerosis and that the failure of the drug's label to comply with 21 C.F.R. § 200.100 causes it to be misbranded within the meaning of 21 U.S.C.A. § 352(f)(1)....

As a general proposition, the Food and Drug Administration is charged with the responsibility of removing misbranded drugs from the market. Normally, this is done by seizure of the article in question. However, in the case at bar, the Government wishes to go one step further by enjoining the actual administration of EDTA by Dr. Evers and his employees at Meadowbrook Hospital. Initially, the Court expressed concern over the possibility that such an injunction would constitute an unwarranted interference with the practice of medicine. However, a closer analysis of the jurisprudence and the particular facts of this case reveal that the injunctive relief as requested by the Government is not only lawful but also compelled....

In the case at bar, the Court feels that the requested injunction is justified as the only possible means of removing the misbranded drugs from interstate commerce....

The Court is of the further opinion that such an injunction will not interfere with or regulate the practice of medicine in any degree greater than it is already regulated under the Food, Drug and Cosmetic Act. As noted above, the Food and Drug Administration is charged with the responsibility of removing misbranded drugs from the flow of interstate commerce. The injunction as prayed for by the Government is the only practical and equitable means of carrying out that responsibility in the case at bar.[3] . . .

UNITED STATES v. EVERS

United States District Court, Middle District of Alabama, 1978.
453 F. Supp. 1141.

VARNER, District Judge.

. . . The Plaintiff, the United States of America, spear-headed by the Federal Drug Administration, filed this proceeding against Dr. H. Ray Evers, a licensed physician in the State of Alabama, alleging (1) that Defendant has been engaged in promoting and administering calcium disodium versenate in treatment for arteriosclerosis; (2) that the labeling of the drug, commonly called the package insert, which is prescribed and approved by the Federal Drug Administration, indicates that the drug is recommended for treatment of heavy metal poisons but not for other things here relevant; (3) that patients being treated by the Defendant are subjected to an unwarranted risk of grave physical injury or death as a result of said treatment; and (4) that the promotion and administering of said drug, after having utilized interstate commerce in obtaining the same, amounts to a mislabeling of the drug under the provisions of Title 21, U.S.C. §§ 331(k) and 352(f)(1). . . .

The defense is that Defendant is not using the drug for other than treatment of metal poisoning, its recommended use, and that, in any event, the Defendant is a licensed physician in the State of Alabama and that licensed physicians have a right and a duty to use drugs in prescribing for their patients' usage in accordance with their best judgment as physicians and that the Federal Food and Drug Act does not prohibit a licensed physician's using a drug for a disease or weakness in a patient in any manner which is not contraindicated on the package insert. . . .

The legal issues presented by this cause, in the opinion of this court, place squarely before this court the question of whether a licensed physician may be enjoined from prescribing for his patient a

---

3. This is not to say that a licensed physician cannot utilize a drug for experimental or investigational uses, which would otherwise cause the drug to be misbranded. To use a drug in such a way, the physician is obligated to follow the procedure set forth at 21 U.S.C.A. § 355(i) and the complementing regulations found at 21 C.F.R. § 312.1. Suffice it to say that such procedures were not followed in this case.

drug of which the package insert is silent as to whether the drug is indicated or contraindicated for the patient's illness....

In response to Dr. Evers' contention that the Federal Drug Administration has no power to direct how he shall treat his own patients, the government relies upon *United States v. Hoxsey Cancer Clinic,* 198 F.2d 273 (5th Cir. 1952), in which a layman, Hoxsey, was advertising and shipping drugs in interstate commerce as a cancer cure and the court found that the literature distributed constituted mislabeling of the drugs within the meaning of the act because it contained misleading statements and therefore the drugs were misbranded and Hoxsey was enjoined from the continuation of such interstate commerce. The *Hoxsey* case is comparable to the instant case in that the Hoxsey Clinic was staffed by licensed physicians but Hoxsey was shipping the drugs in interstate commerce to other than his patients after having advertised them for unapproved usage while Dr. Evers, after having received a drug in interstate commerce, holds them for prescribed use on his patients....

The government also relies on the case of *United States of America v. An Article of Drug * * * Diso–Tate, Etc., H. Ray Evers, and Meadow-brook Hospital,* No. 75–1790 (E.D. La., Sept. 28, 1976) [p. 623 *supra*]....
In that case, Dr. Evers again was advertising in interstate commerce and receiving shipments of drugs to effect the chelation of patients as a treatment for arteriosclerosis. Two obvious differences appeared in that case as compared with the instant case. The drug used for chelation in Louisiana was contraindicated for arteriosclerosis on the label and Dr. Evers himself was not a licensed physician and was operating as a layman in Louisiana. That case, therefore, has limited authority in the instant case. It is notable, however, that that court expressed its concern about any unwarranted interference with the practice of medicine even though Dr. Evers was not licensed to practice in Louisiana at that time....

Perhaps the government's position is best exemplified by the explanation of the purposes of the Federal Food and Drug Administration's interest in practices such as those enjoyed by Dr. Evers in the Federal Register for August 15, 1972 (Vol. 37, No. 150, p. 16503). That position is that once a drug is in a local pharmacy, after interstate shipment, a physician may, as part of the practice of medicine, lawfully prescribe a different dosage for his patients or may vary the conditions of use from those approved in the package insert, without informing or obtaining the approval of the Food and Drug Administration. Congress did not intend the Food and Drug Administration to interfere with medical practice as between the physician and the patient. Congress recognized a patient's right to seek civil damages in the courts if there should be evidence of malpractice, and declined to provide any legislative restrictions upon the medical profession. It appears to this Court that such a restriction would exceed the powers of Congress. There is no federal prohibition of transportation of an approved drug in interstate shipment with the approved package insert when neither the shipper nor the recipient intends that it be used for an unapproved purpose. If the illegal purpose is devised after termination of interstate shipment, the matter passed from federal jurisdiction, but jurisdiction may well apply if the shipper or the recipient intends an illegal use at the time of the deposit of the shipment in interstate commerce. Then the act and the illegal contention may coincide so as to furnish federal jurisdiction over interstate commerce.....

It is well-recognized that a package insert may not contain the most up-to-date information about a drug and the physician must be free to use the drug for an indication not in the package insert when such usage is part of the practice of medicine and for the benefit of the patient. Hopefully the physician would welcome a well-documented package insert because he finds it useful because the information in it is supported by substantial documented evidence. However, the physician can ascertain from medical literature and from medical meetings new and interesting proposed uses for drugs marketed under package inserts not including the proposed usages. The package insert's most important educational value derives from the fact that it is a well-reviewed, authoritative document. New uses for drugs are often discovered, reported in medical journals and at medical meetings, and subsequently may be widely used by the medical profession. But the Federal Drug Administration does not permit the package insert to be amended to include such uses unless the manufacturer submits convincing evidence supporting the change. The manufacturer may not have sufficient commercial interests or financial wherewithal to warrant following the necessary procedures to obtain FDA approval for the additional use of the drug. When physicians go beyond the directions given in the package insert it does not mean they are acting illegally or unethically and Congress did not intend to empower the FDA to interfere with medical practice by limiting the ability of physicians to prescribe according to their best judgment....

This court is, therefore, of the opinion from the pleadings, the evidence and the authority presented to it that Dr. Evers is not misbranding the drug in question and that the relief prayed by the plaintiff should be denied. Judgment will enter in accordance with this memorandum opinion.

NOTE

Judge Varner later dismissed a suit by Evers against the FDA District Director, finding the latter was immune from liability for his actions in initiating the investigations that resulted in both of the above-described enforcement actions. *Evers v. White*, FDLI 1978–1980 Jud. Rec. 764 (M.D. Ala. 1979).

UNITED STATES v. EVERS

United States Court of Appeals, Fifth Circuit, 1981.
643 F.2d 1043.

RANDALL, Circuit Judge:

In this action the government charges a licensed Alabama physician with a violation of section 301(k) of the Federal Food, Drug, and Cosmetic Act. That section prohibits, *inter alia,* the misbranding of a drug which is held for sale after shipment in interstate commerce. The government charges that the drug at issue, which is a prescription drug, was misbranded under section 502(f)(1) of the Act, which deems a drug to be misbranded unless its labeling contains "adequate directions for use." In particular, the government alleges that the physician promoted and administered a drug for a use that is not approved by the Food and Drug Administration (the FDA), without providing adequate directions for such use to his patients. The district court found that the physician had indeed failed to provide adequate directions for the intended use of the drug, but held that the physician's actions were within "the practice of medicine" and therefore beyond the constitutional reach of federal power and beyond the intended reach of the Act....

We do not reach the issue on which the district court's opinion rests, for we find that the government has not established a violation of section 301(k) of the Act. Since prescription drugs are required by regulations promulgated pursuant to section 502(f)(1) of the Act to bear adequate information for use by physicians but not for use by patients, and since the physician charged in this case was administering the drug to his own patients but not distributing it to other physicians, we hold that Dr. Evers has not violated section 301(k) of the Act by his failure to provide such "adequate directions for use" as are required by section 502(f)(1) of the Act.....

A central part of Dr. Evers' approach to the treatment of degenerative diseases is his use of "chemo-endartectomy therapy." Dr. Evers explains this therapy as "a special treatment given by licensed doctors for the relief of poor circulation that has been caused by hardening of the arteries (arteriosclerosis, atherosclerosis)." ... The most important part of Dr. Evers' chemo-endartectomy therapy is his use of "chelation." Chelation is a chemical reaction which occurs between certain drugs and various harmful metals in a form which allows them to pass out of the body through the kidneys. Chelating drugs are ordinarily used for the treatment of heavy metal poisoning, particularly lead poisoning. According to Dr. Evers, however, this process also removes from blood vessels buildups of calcium which are blocking the vessels and causing hardening of the arteries....

Whether this process actually has this beneficial effect is a serious question. Dr. Evers' claims for his therapy are not generally accepted by the medical profession, and, as discussed below, the FDA has not approved any chelating drug for use in the treatment of circulatory disorders. Moreover, chelating drugs bear a serious danger: if too many heavy metals are passed into the kidneys within too short a period of time, the patient may suffer kidney failure and may die as a result. An additional danger, of course, is that patients who could benefit from a more traditional mode of treatment (probably heart by-pass surgery) will be convinced by Dr. Evers' alternative to postpone that treatment until it is too late.....

The government contends that Dr. Evers violated section 301(k) of the Act, which prohibits any act with respect to a drug which "is done while such [drug] is held for sale (whether or not the first sale) áfter shipment in interstate commerce and [which] results in such article being ... misbranded." The government must therefore establish two separate elements: (1) that the act in question occurred while the drug was held for sale after shipment in interstate commerce; and (2) that the act resulted in the article being misbranded. The focus of the government's case, as well as of Dr. Evers' defense and of the district court's opinion, is the second of these elements. In order to establish this element, that is, to demonstrate that Dr. Evers has "misbranded" Calcium EDTA, the government relies solely on section 502(f)(1) of the Act. That section deems a drug to be misbranded "unless its labeling bears ... adequate directions for use." In brief, the government contends that Dr. Evers failed to provide "adequate directions for use" when he promoted and prescribed Calcium EDTA for the treatment of circulatory disorders, a use for which the drug has not been approved by the FDA.

In response to this charge, Dr. Evers (as well as certain of his patients, as intervenors) argues that as a licensed physician he has a right to prescribe any lawful drug for any purpose, whether or not that purpose has been approved by the FDA. The district court agreed with Dr. Evers and held that no misbranding could result from a doctor's prescription of a lawful drug to his own patients....

However, the analysis urged by Dr. Evers and adopted by the district court misapprehends the thrust of the government's case against Dr. Evers, for the FDA has at no point contended, and the government does not argue on appeal, that the misbranding provisions of the Act prohibit a doctor from prescribing a lawful drug for a purpose for which the drug has not been approved by the FDA. To the contrary, the FDA has explicitly informed Dr. Evers that he could legally prescribe chelating drugs for the treatment of circulatory disorders.....

The object of the government's case against Dr. Evers is not, therefore, his *prescription* of Calcium EDTA for use in the treatment of circulatory disorders. Instead, the government seeks to challenge Dr. Evers' *promotion* and *advertising* of chelating drugs for that use. According to the government, Dr. Evers "misbranded" Calcium EDTA when he publicly advocated his use of chelating drugs for an unapproved purpose without providing "adequate directions" for such a use.....

When each of the two elements of the offense with which Dr. Evers is charged is examined individually, Dr. Evers does indeed seem to have violated the statute. A different picture emerges, however, when the two elements are considered together. Since Calcium EDTA is a prescription drug, the FDA can establish an act of misbranding under section 502(f)(1) of the Act only by proving that Dr. Evers did not provide adequate information *for use by physicians,* as is required by the exceptions to that section. The information provided by Dr. Evers to his patients is irrelevant to the question at hand, for according to FDA regulations there is *no* information which could have been provided about this prescription drug which would have constituted "adequate directions for [lay] use." However, the government argues that Dr. Evers "held [Calcium EDTA] for sale" within the meaning of section 301(k) because he maintained a supply of the drug for use *on his own patients;* the government does not contend that Dr. Evers was distributing Calcium EDTA to other licensed physicians. The government therefore must find itself in an awkward position: while the misbranding violation it urges is based on Dr. Evers' failure to provide adequate information to licensed physicians, it seeks to include his actions within the reach of section 301(k) of the Act by virtue of his distribution to patients.

The requirement which the FDA seeks to impose is nonsensical. Since Calcium EDTA is a prescription drug, the misbranding provision under which Dr. evers was charged requires him to provide adequate information for use by prescribing physicians. However, Dr. Evers was the only physician who used the Calcium EDTA in question. The government's application of the statute may therefore be reduced to the following proposition: Dr. Evers did not provide adequate information to himself. It is doubtful at best that this interpretation was intended by the drafters of the statute.

In more specific terms, the government's interpretation of the Act breaks down over its use of the phrase "held for sale after shipment in interstate commerce." Although Dr. Evers was holding Calcium EDTA for sale in the sense that he was distributing it *to his own patients,* he was not holding it for sale *to physicians.* Section 301(k) of the Act cannot reasonably be read to require a physician who is holding a drug for sale only to patients to provide adequate information to physicians to whom he is not distributing the drug. We think it clear that a single doctor may be holding drugs for sale to one group of purchasers but not to another. If the doctor is not holding the drug for sale to the party to whom he owes a statutory obligation of full disclosure (in this case other prescribing physicians), then it makes no sense to impose the requirements of the statute. No legitimate purpose is served when a statutory provision requiring disclosure to one particular group of purchasers is invoked on the basis of sales made to a different group. Since Dr. Evers was holding Calcium EDTA, a prescription drug, for sale only to his patients, and since section 502(f)(1) of the Act does not require any disclosure to patients regarding prescription drugs, we conclude that Dr. Evers did not violate section 301(k) of the Act.[16]

PHYSICIAN CIVIL LIABILITY FOR DEVIATING FROM THE PACKAGE INSERT

No court has held that a physician's deviation from the officially approved labeling—whether directions for use, warnings, contraindications, or statements of relative efficacy—is *per se* negligence. The practitioner who departs from the manufacturer's recommendations does not *necessarily* incur liability for any untoward effects which flow from a drug. Official statements of organized medicine indicate that doctors are aware of this negative conclusion. See AMA DRUG EVALUATIONS A–4 (1971); AMA Council on Drugs, *The Package Insert*, 207 J.A.M.A. 1342 (1969).

The threshold question in many cases is whether the package insert is admissible in court. Of course, this question is moot if the manufacturer is also a defendant. Most cases permit the introduction of the insert where the manufacturer is not a co-defendant, but the courts differ in the purposes for which such evidence may be received. Many courts admit the insert after finding it to be relevant and reliable evidence of the proper standard of care. *See Julien v. Barker*, 75 Idaho 413, 272 P.2d 718 (1954). Others attempt to place the insert within the "not for the truth therein" hearsay exception. *See Koury v. Follo*, 272 N.C. 366, 158 S.E.2d 548 (1968); *Sanzari v. Rosenfeld*, 34 N.J. 128, 167 A.2d 625 (1961).

Once the insert is admitted into evidence, courts differ on what they will permit the jury to infer from its contents. *Salgo v. Leland Stanford Jr. Univ. Bd. of Trustees*, 154 Cal.App.2d 560, 317 P.2d 170 (1957) held that a physician package insert constitutes evidence of the appropriate standard of care, but does not conclusively establish the applicable standard. *Mulder v. Parke Davis & Co.*, 288 Minn. 332, 181 N.W.2d 882 (1970), held that the physician package insert represents prima facie evidence of the standard of care. The *Mulder* case illustrates the potential impact of a holding which permits the jury to infer

---

16. One might argue that although Dr. Evers did not distribute Calcium EDTA to other physicians, he nevertheless "labeled" the drug to the medical community at large through his public promotional and advertising efforts, and that he therefore caused the drug to be "misbranded" because the drug's label did not meet the full disclosure requirements of the regulatory exception to section 502(f)(1) with respect to the new use advocated for the drug by Dr. Evers. This seems to be the theory on which the District Court for the Eastern District of Louisiana found a misbranding violation in the government's earlier suit against Dr. Evers. *See United States v. An Article of Drug ... Diso-tate.* This approach relies on the promotion *per se* of the drug, and seems to ignore altogether the fact that misbranding under section 301(k) of the Act can occur only with respect to particular drugs "held for sale after shipment in interstate commerce." At base, this theory equates *promotion* with sale, and therefore brings into question the legality of a physician's advocacy of any medical program involving drugs not approved for the advocated use by the FDA, even when the physician does not himself sell or even dispense the drug. But the Act was intended to regulate the distribution of drugs in interstate commerce, not to restrain physicians from public advocacy of medical opinions not shared by the FDA. We believe, therefore, that a doctor who merely advocates to other doctors a lawful prescription drug for a use not approved by the FDA, and does not distribute that drug to other doctors, is not holding that drug for sale within the meaning of the statute and therefore is not in violation of section 301(k) of the Act.

the standard of care from the insert alone. Mrs. Mulder died from aplastic anemia after extensive Chloromycetin therapy. The plaintiff alleged negligence in three particulars: prescribing Chloromycetin in the first place, giving an insufficient dose which needlessly prolonged therapy, and failing to make blood tests to determine whether the drug was inducing blood dyscrasias. The trial judge entered a directed verdict for the defendant because of the lack of evidence establishing a professional standard of care. In reversing, the Supreme Court of Minnesota made the following statement about the legal effect of a physician's departure from the manufacturer's recommendations:

> Where the dosage is prescribed by the manufacturer, testimony of the physician's failure to adhere to its recommendation is sufficient evidence to require him to explain the reason for his deviation. This is particularly true where the manufacturer's warning puts the doctor on notice of potentially lethal effects.

Does, therefore, a demonstrable departure from the manufacturer's recommendation establish a *prima facie* case of negligence?

Afraid, perhaps, that an affirmative answer to this question was precisely what the court intended, the Minnesota State Medical Association sought rehearing and a clarification of the court's position. The Association argued that a *prima facie* case was not made in the absence of expert testimony establishing that the manufacturer's recommendations were generally referred to and relied upon and testimony establishing that the physician had deviated from the standard of care normally observed in his community.

The Minnesota Supreme Court denied the petition for rehearing but appended to its previous opinion the following two paragraphs:

> Where a drug manufacturer recommends to the medical profession (1) the conditions under which its drug should be prescribed; (2) the disorders it is designed to relieve; (3) the precautionary measures which should be observed; and (4) warns of the dangers which are inherent in its use, a doctor's deviation from such recommendations is prima facie evidence of negligence if there is competent medical testimony that his patient's injury or death resulted from the doctor's failure to adhere to the recommendations.

> Under such circumstances, it is incumbent on the doctor to disclose his reasons for departing from the procedures recommended by the manufacturer. Although it will ordinarily be a jury question whether the doctor has justified or excused his deviation, there may be situations where as a matter of law the explanation exonerates him unless rebutted by other competent medical testimony.

For a comprehensive treatment of the subject, *see* Note, *Package Inserts for Prescription Drugs as Evidence in Medical Malpractice Suits,* 44 U. Chi. L. Rev. 398 (1977). *See also* Merrill, *Compensation for Prescription Drug Injuries,* 59 Va. L. Rev. 1 (1973).

3. CONTROLS OVER DISTRIBUTION

AMERICAN PHARMACEUTICAL ASS'N v. WEINBERGER

United States District Court, District of Columbia, 1974.
377 F.Supp. 824.

JOHN H. PRATT, District Judge.

... Plaintiffs challenge the validity of certain provisions of the Food and Drug Administration's methadone regulations.... [37 Fed. Reg. 6940 (April 6, 1972), 37 Fed.Reg. 26790 (December 15, 1972).] Specifically, plaintiffs object to those parts of the regulations which purport to restrict the distribution of methadone to direct shipments from the manufacturer to (a) approved maintenance treatment programs, (b) approved hospital pharmacies, and (c) in cases where hospital pharmacies are unavailable in a particular area, to selected community pharmacies. Plaintiffs include the American Pharmaceutical Association (APhA), a professional association of pharmacists with a membership in excess of 50,000, three individual professional pharmacists and an individual physician....

The drug methadone, a synthetic substitute for morphine, is a "new" drug within the meaning of section 201(p) of the Federal Food, Drug and Cosmetic Act and, as a new drug, requires FDA's approval of a NDA, filed with the Commissioner of Food and Drugs pursuant to section 505(b) of the Act. The drug was first approved by FDA in the 1950's as safe for use as an analgesic and antitussive agent as well as for short-term detoxification of persons addicted to heroin. Subsequently, investigation of methadone for use in long-term maintenance of narcotic addicts (methadone maintenance) was approved by FDA pursuant to its authority under 21 U.S.C. § 355(i), the investigational new-drug (IND) exemption.... [In 1972] FDA determined that "retention of the drug [methadone] solely on an investigational status appears to be no longer warranted" and published a notice of proposed rulemaking which resulted, with certain modifications, in the regulations now in question.

The final regulation gave notice that pursuant to FDA's authority under 21 U.S.C. § 355(c), the Commissioner was withdrawing approval of all outstanding NDA's because of "a lack of substantial evidence that methadone is safe and effective for detoxification, and analgesia, or antitussive use *under the conditions of use that presently exist.*" Having withdrawn all approved NDA's, the Commission's new regulatory scheme is presently the exclusive means of distribution for the drug methadone. The Commissioner has thereby created an admittedly unique classification for methadone since on the one hand he has determined that methadone should not be limited solely to investigational status while at the same time concluding that the drug is inappropriate for regular NDA approval....

The defendants point ... out that § 355(d) gives the Secretary the authority to refuse to approve an NDA where the reports of the investigations submitted do not include adequate tests showing whether the new drug is "safe for use under the conditions prescribed, recommended, or suggested in the proposed labeling thereof." Defendants argue that the term "safe" should be interpreted with reference not only to the inherent qualities of the drug under consideration but also in the sense of the drug's being secure from possible misuse. Such a broad interpretation would, according to defendants' theory, serve as the statutory foundation for FDA's exercise of authority in restricting methadone's channels of distribution because FDA's principal rationale for restricting distribution was "to help reduce the likelihood of diversion."

... As noted above, the term "safe" is used in conjunction with the phrase "for use under the conditions prescribed, recommended, or suggested in the proposed labeling thereof. When taken in this context, a determination of whether a drug is "safe" is premised on the drug's use in the "prescribed, recommended, or suggested" manner.... Thus ... the Court concludes that the term "safe" was intended to refer to a determination of the inherent safety or lack thereof of the drug under consideration when used for its intended purpose.[9] ...

In addition to being a "new" drug and thus within the jurisdiction of the FDA, methadone is a controlled substance within Schedule II of the Controlled Substances Act, 21 U.S.C. § 812. Under this Act the Attorney General is made responsible for the registration of any person who manufactures, distributes or dispenses any controlled substance....

The Court concludes that Congress intended to create two complementary institutional checks on the production and marketing of new drugs. At the production or pre-marketing stage, the FDA is given the primary responsibility in determining which new drugs should be permitted to enter the flow of commerce.... When an IND exemption is approved, the Commissioner may, of course, severely restrict the distribution of the exempted drug to bona fide researchers and clinicians. But once a drug is cleared for marketing by way of an NDA-approval, for whatever uses the Commissioner deems appropriate, the question of permissible distribution of the drug, when that drug is a controlled substance, is one clearly within the jurisdiction of the Justice Department.... To allow the challenged portions of the methadone regulations to stand, therefore, would be to abrogate the collective judgment of Congress with regard to the appropriate means of controlling unlawful drug diversion....

9. Even if the Court were to agree with defendant's interpretation of the term "safe," this alone would not provide a statutory basis for the regulations challenged herein. At most such an interpretation would authorize FDA to deny or withdraw any methadone NDA based on a finding that the drug could not be "safely" distributed. As outlined in the Court's opinion, FDA's discretion under the Act's NDA provisions is limited to either approving or denying NDA's and nowhere is FDA empowered to approve an NDA upon the condition that the drug be distributed only through specified channels.

NOTES

1. *Subsequent Proceedings.* On appeal, Judge Pratt's decision was affirmed *per curiam,* 530 F.2d 1054 (D.C. Cir. 1976). Though he concurred in the judgment, Judge McGowan was not content to adopt the lower court's opinion:

> ... The FDA contends that where there exists a documentary pattern of drug misuse contrary to the intended uses specified in the labelling, the drug is unsafe for approval unless controls over distribution are imposed. As a corollary, it asserts that for a drug such as methadone, for which there is substantial evidence of misuse, the FDA must have the power to restrict distribution to avoid the dilemma of either disapproving a drug with important therapeutic benefits or of placing on the market a drug likely to be misused....

> Although these arguments have some weight, I do not find them ultimately convincing. The word "safe" in section 355(d) is, to my mind, best interpreted as requiring the labelling to include the evidence from drug testing, and the inferences therefrom, indicating the therapeutic benefits, possible dangers, and uncertainties involved in use of a drug, as an aid to a conscientious physician in determining appropriate medical treatment. That view seems to me to accord with both the most reasonable interpretation of the statutory language and the common understanding of the FDA's mission. Thus, methadone is safe for its intended use notwithstanding the possibility that it will be employed in unintended fashions....

> There would be almost no limit to the FDA's authority were its view adopted. If, for example, it had concluded before 1970 that without restrictions on methadone of the sort now contained in the Controlled Substances Act the possibility of drug misuse remained high, there would be no barrier under its argument to its having established a regulatory scheme of the complexity of that ultimately adopted in that Act....

2. *Methadone Regulations.* FDA subsequently revised its methadone regulations in 41 Fed. Reg. 28261 (July 9, 1976) by deleting the restrictions on distribution to pharmacies. The regulations were recodified in 42 Fed. Reg. 46698 (September 16, 1977) and significant amendments were adopted in 41 Fed. Reg. 17926 (April 29, 1976), 42 Fed. Reg. 56897 (October 28, 1977), and 45 Fed. Reg. 62694 (September 19, 1980). Additional changes were adopted in 48 Fed. Reg. 41049 (September 13, 1983), 52 Fed. Reg. 37046 (October 2, 1987), 54 Fed. Reg. 8954 (March 2, 1989). Largely in response to the spread of AIDS among heroin users, FDA proposed further revisions in 54 Fed. Reg. 8973 (March 2, 1989), 54 Fed. Reg. 50226 (December 4, 1989). In light of the *American Pharmaceutical Ass'n* decision, can FDA justify retaining its restrictions on physician prescribing of methadone?

3. *Phenformin Precedent.* Can Secretary Califano's suspension of the NDA for phenformin and FDA's subsequent withdrawal of approval of the drug, p. 547 *supra,* be reconciled with the *American Pharmaceutical Ass'n* ruling?

4. *Distribution Restrictions.* For a discussion of several proposed control mechanisms to restrict drug distribution and prescribing, *see* Hutt, *The Legal Requirement That Drugs Be Proved Safe and Effective Before Their Use,* in Lasagna, CONTROVERSIES IN THERAPEUTICS 495 (1980). The Drug Regulation Reform Act of 1979, which passed the Senate but was never adopted by

the House, would have authorized FDA to restrict distribution of drugs. *See* S. Rep. No. 96–321, 96th Cong., 1st Sess. (1979).

5. *Voluntary Restrictions.* Although *American Pharmaceutical Ass'n* held that FDA may not restrict distribution as a condition of approving an NDA, the court did not state that a pharmaceutical manufacturer could not *voluntarily* limit distribution or that FDA could not approve labeling that incorporated such voluntary controls. In fact, FDA now routinely approves physician package inserts that contain various limitations on the type of pharmacy at which the drug will be available, the conditions under which pharmacies will be permitted to stock the drug, or the qualifications of the physicians who will be permitted to prescribe the drug. *See, e.g.,* the restrictions voluntarily imposed by Sandoz for clozapine (Clozaril) for use in schizophrenia, where the drug is not available through pharmacies and must be administered by trained home health care workers. *Clozapine for Schizophrenia,* 32 The Medical Letter 3 (January 12, 1990). As a result of pressure from pharmacists and state health care agencies, and following filing of an antitrust suit by several state attorneys general, Sandoz abandoned this plan in early 1991.

6. *Accutane Restrictions.* In addition to providing stringent warnings for Accutane (isotretinoin), p. 436 *supra,* to reduce potential side effects, the manufacturer engaged in an extensive physician education campaign and, in accordance with FDA directives, specified that physicians should obtain informed consent from patients. *See* Stern, *When A Uniquely Effective Drug is Teratogenic: The Case of Isotretinoin,* 320 N. Eng. J. Med. 1007 (April 13, 1989); 321 N. Eng. J. Med. 756 (September 14, 1989). FDA's Dermatologic Drugs Advisory Committee has reviewed the agency's handling of Accutane on eight occasions. "Accutane Update," FDA Talk paper No. T90–25 (May 22, 1990).

7. *Controlled Substances and Medical Devices.* Distribution of prescription drug controlled substances is subject to restriction under the Controlled Substances Act, p. 535 *supra.* The Medical Device Amendments of 1976 explicitly authorize FDA to limit distribution of a restricted device pursuant to section 520(e) of the FD&C Act.

Chapter IV
ANIMAL FEED AND DRUGS

A. GENERAL STATUTORY REQUIREMENTS

The provisions of the 1938 Act, like those of the 1906 Act, governing human food and human drugs, by statutory definition embrace *animal* feed and *animal* drugs as well. Thus, most of the requirements examined in Chapters II and III are potentially applicable to products marketed for use in livestock production or for feeding and treatment of household pets.

Food or drug. The elusive dichotomy between human food and human drugs divides animal feed and animal drugs as well. *See, e.g.,* FDA's ruling, 52 Fed. Reg. 25072 (July 2, 1987), that parenteral amino acids are new animal drugs.

Adulterated animal feed. Numerous seizure actions under the 1906 Act charged economic adulteration of animal feed. In *United States v. One Car Load of Corno Horse and Mule Feed,* 188 Fed. 453 (M.D.Ala. 1911), the court concluded that "oat feed" was not limited to ground or crushed whole oats but that it included the by-product of mills producing rolled oats or oatmeal for human food and thus could lawfully consist largely of the residual oat hulls. However, in *United States v. 154 Sacks of Oats,* 283 Fed. 985 (W.D. Va. 1922), oats containing 23 percent of foreign material, some intentionally added, were held to be adulterated. In *United States v. 800 Sacks Barley Mixed Oats,* 64 F.2d 678 (5th Cir. 1933), a mixture of barley and oats was held not to be adulterated by reason of 4 percent excess moisture.

In recent years, FDA has focused its attention on the safety of animal feed, particularly as the composition of feed administered to livestock may affect the safety of human food. For example, in 32 Fed. Reg. 4058 (March 15, 1967), codified at 21 C.F.R. § 500.35, FDA declared animal feed adulterated if it is contaminated with salmonella microorganisms. This statement of policy did nothing, however, to diminish growing economic incentives to make use of recycled animal waste in animal feed. After debating the health implications of this practice internally for several years, FDA published a notice containing background information in 42 Fed. Reg. 64662 (December 27, 1977), and requested information and views. But in 45 Fed. Reg. 86272 (December 30, 1980), the agency announced that it was leaving to the states the regulation of the use of recycled animal waste and was therefore revoking 21 C.F.R. § 500.35.

In 42 Fed. Reg. 49468 (September 27, 1977), FDA proposed to establish a new section of the regulations which would list all substances prohibited from use in animal feed or pet food. The agency proposed to list trichloroethylene as the first prohibited substance. This proposal was based upon a National Cancer Institute report that trichloroethylene is a carcinogen in test animals. As of June 30, 1990, however, no action had been taken on this proposal.

Misbranded animal feed. Several FDA enforcement actions charged misbranding of animal feed. In *United States v. 154 Sacks of Oats*, 294 Fed. 340 (W.D. Va. 1923), the court reconsidered its earlier conclusion respecting economic adulteration, p. 636 *supra*, and held that the oats were misbranded. In *United States v. Feeders' Supply & Mfg. Co.*, 15 F.Supp. 385 (W.D. Mo. 1936), the defendant was convicted for selling animal feed labeled as not less than 43 percent protein which actually contained not more than 38.56 percent protein. *See also United States v. Saunders Mills, Inc.*, 1938–1964 FDLI Jud. Rec. 454 (S.D. Ohio 1944).

Misbranded animal drugs. The 1906 Act's stringent "false and fraudulent" standard for misbranding of drugs, p. 390 *supra*, did not always defeat enforcement. *United States v. Dr. David Roberts Veterinary Co.*, 104 F.2d 785 (7th Cir. 1939), upheld a conviction for false curative or therapeutic claims for a variety of animal drugs. In *United States v. 14 105 Pound Bags ... Mineral Compound*, 118 F.Supp. 837 (D. Idaho 1953), a drug for the treatment of bloat in sheep and cattle was found misbranded under the 1938 Act. A drug represented as a treatment for poultry cannibalism was held ineffective in *United States v. 18 Cases ... "Barton's Cannibalism Remedy,"* 1938–1964 FDLI Jud. Rec. 1335 (D. Neb. 1956). *See also United States v. An Article of Drug ... "Misty Dog Food ... ."* 1969–1974 FDLI Jud. Rec. 108 (D.D.C. 1972); *United States v. An Article of Food ... "Medi–Matic Free Choice Poultry Formula (Medicated)"* 1965–1968 FDLI Jud. Rec. 1 (W.D. Ark. 1968). More recently FDA has relied on rulemaking rather than court enforcement to correct label deceptions. For example, in 39 Fed. Reg. 25229 (July 9, 1974), the agency promulgated a regulation, 21 C.F.R. § 500.52, governing use of terms such as "tonic," "toner," or "conditioner" in labeling of preparations intended for use in or on animals.

New animal drugs. Prior to the enactment of the Animal Drug Amendments in 1968, new drugs for animal use were subject to the same licensure requirements under section 505 as new drugs for human use. FDA often found itself enmeshed in protracted litigation over the "new drug" status of veterinary products. *See, e.g., United States v. 7 Cartons ... "Ferro–Lac Swine Formula Concentrate (Medicated),"* 293 F.Supp. 660 (S.D. Ill. 1968), *aff'd on other grounds*, 424 F.2d 1364 (7th Cir. 1970). New animal drugs approved for safety between 1938 and 1962 were subject to the 1966–1968 National Academy of Sciences review and the FDA drug efficacy study implementation (DESI) program examined in Chapter III.

Feed additives. Similarly, prior to 1968, substances added to animal feed, including new animal drugs, were subject to the same requirements as food additives for human food use. Thus, unless GRAS or prior sanctioned, an ingredient of animal feed required an approved food additive regulation under section 409 of the Act. *See, e.g., United States v. Seven Cartons ... "Ferro–Lac Swine Formula Concentrate,"* 424 F.2d 1364 (7th Cir. 1970). FDA established general regulations for banning substances as unsafe animal food additives and issued a tentative final regulation prohibiting deodorizer distillates in animal food or feed under section 402(a)(2)(C) in 45 Fed. Reg. 28316, 28349 (April 29, 1980).

Pet food. A unique unwritten understanding between FDA and state regulatory officials governs the regulation of pet food. Standards and labeling requirements for pet food are established and published by the Association of American Feed Control Officials, and are enforced by both FDA and state agencies. Pet food labels must, however, comply with the same labeling requirements under the FD&C Act as human food. Accordingly, when exemptions from these requirements are needed, FDA must be directly involved. *See* 48 Fed. Reg. 2136 (January 18, 1983), 51 Fed. Reg. 11456 (April 3, 1986), where FDA denied an industry request for the use of class or collective names for pet food ingredients, rather than the individual common or usual name for each ingredient; and 41 Fed. Reg. 15731 (April 14, 1976), where FDA denied an industry request to declare water at the end of the list of ingredients rather than in order of predominance.

B. THE ANIMAL DRUG AMENDMENTS OF 1968

To eliminate the overlapping regulatory requirements imposed by the food additive provisions of section 409, the new drug provisions of section 505, and the antibiotic drug provisions of section 507, Congress enacted the Animal Drug Amendments, 82 Stat. 342 (1968), which added section 512 to the Act. In basic outline the criteria and procedures for approval of new animal drugs remained similar to those for human drugs, but the 1968 Amendments introduced some important formal distinctions reflecting differences in the way animal drugs are manufactured, distributed, and administered. The following excerpt from the legislative history summarizes their chief goal and basic features.

ANIMAL DRUG AMENDMENTS
H.R. Rep. No. 875, 90th Cong., 1st Sess. (1967).

The bill would consolidate into one place in the law all of the principal provisions of the Federal Food, Drug, and Cosmetic Act which relate to premarketing clearance of new drugs for administration to animals, either directly or in their feed and water....

In many cases, the requirements for clearance of new drugs for administration to animals are more complicated than the clearance procedures for new human drugs. These complexities have in some instances led to long delays in the clearance of new animal drugs, and the purpose of the bill is to provide a single procedure for clearance of these drugs....

In the past 15 years the animal feed industry in the United States has been virtually revolutionized through the use of drugs and other additives in the feed of animals. Drugs are used to promote growth and combat disease, and as a result of the increasing use, animals today add more meat per pound to feed in a much shorter time than has ever been true in the past. This means that the price of meat and poultry is much less than it otherwise would be. For example, in 1950 broiler production was about 630 million birds whereas in 1965 it was well over 2 billion. The average retail price of broilers has dropped from 57 cents a pound in 1950 to approximately 39 cents today. This results from two factors. First, a few years ago, broiler producers had 15 to 20 percent of their chicks die before they reached maturity whereas today it is not unusual for broiler producers to raise 99 to 100 percent of the chicks started.

In addition, broilers are ready for market weeks earlier today than a few years ago, and they consume less feed per pound of added body weight than was true a few years ago. Similar developments have taken place in the beef producing industry and in the production of swine, lambs, and other animals.

... Yet the farmer even today suffers enormous losses in disease, parasites, and insects, losses estimated by the Department of Agriculture at $2.8 billion per year. These losses not only reduce farm income, but, by reducing the supply of food, affect the availability of meat, poultry, eggs, and milk and increase the cost of the basic foods to the consumer. Each delay in the clearance of safe and effective products for animal health perpetuates these losses. Every duplication of unnecessary controls adds to the ultimate cost of providing food for the consumer. Every lack of administrative coordination adds needlessly to the time required to provide the farmer with the resources he needs to feed an ever-growing population....

Subsection (a) of the proposed new section 512 provides in general that a new animal drug shall be considered as adulterated unless there is in effect an approval of an application with respect to the drug. In general, this subsection follows corresponding provisions in sections 409(a), 505, and 507 of the act.

Subsection (b) corresponds to section 505(b) of the act, and details the requirements for an application with respect to a new animal drug....

Subsection (i) requires publication of a notice in the Federal Register of information with respect to approved applications for use of new animal drugs in manufacture of animal feed. The application must refer to the regulation published pursuant to subsection (i) on which the application relies, together with other information....

In general, the procedure prescribed in this subsection for approval of an application is similar to that set out for approval of the basic application, and the same is true with respect to withdrawal of approval, except that an order granting approval for use of an animal drug in feed manufacture shall be disapproved automatically when the basic animal drug application is disapproved. Since disapproval of the basic application may occur only after notice and opportunity for a hearing, the feed manufacturer may intervene in that proceeding....

NOTES

1. *Animal Drug Effectiveness.* Since 1968 FDA has implemented the effectiveness requirement of section 512 in a fashion that parallels its implementation of section 505's effectiveness standard for new human drugs. *See, e.g., Masti–Kure Products Co. v. Califano,* 587 F.2d 1099 (D.C.Cir. 1978); *Agri–Tech, Inc. v. Richardson,* 482 F.2d 1148 (8th Cir. 1973); *Diamond Laboratories, Inc. v. Richardson,* 452 F.2d 803 (8th Cir. 1972); *Masti–Kure Products Co. v. Weinberger,* 1969–1974 FDLI Jud. Rec. 655 (D.D.C. 1974); *United States v. Articles of Food and Drug Coli-Trol 80 Medicated,* 372 F.Supp. 915 (N.D. Ga. 1974); *United States v. An Article of Drug.... "Entrol–C Medicated,"* 362 F.Supp. 424 (S.D. Cal. 1973).

2. *Substantial Evidence.* FDA has interpreted the substantial evidence of effectiveness standard in section 512(d)(3) in terms similar to those applicable to new human drugs. *See* 21 C.F.R. § 514.111(a)(5), 35 Fed. Reg. 7569 (May 15, 1970), 36 Fed. Reg. 18375 (September 14, 1971). FDA amended these terms in 44 Fed. Reg. 16007 (March 16, 1979).

3. *Combination Drugs.* The requirement that each active ingredient in a combination new animal drug be shown to contribute to the effect of the drug, 21 C.F.R. § 514.1(b)(8)(v), 35 Fed. Reg. 7569 (May 15, 1970), 36 Fed. Reg. 18375 (September 14, 1971), has been further explained in FDA guidelines announced in 43 Fed. Reg. 46375 (October 8, 1978), 48 Fed. Reg. 19472 (April 29, 1983), 48 Fed. Reg. 51537 (November 9, 1983). *See* Allera, *FDA's Combination Animal Drug Policy—Is It Feasible? Or Should Elsie be the Only One Getting Milked?* 33 FDC L.J. 267 (1978). In 46 Fed. Reg. 8741 (January 27, 1981), FDA denied a petition requesting that it approve a combination animal drug merely on the basis that each component was the subject of an approved NADA and insisted on proof that the combination itself was safe and effective. The agency's position was upheld in *International Nutrition, Inc. v. U.S. Dept. of HHS,* 676 F.2d 338 (8th Cir. 1982).

4. *Antibiotic Certification.* Section 507 of the FD&C Act, which was added to the statute in 1945 to require FDA to certify batches of penicillin and subsequently amended several times to include other antibiotics, did not distinguish between human and animal drugs. The 1968 Animal Drug Amendments incorporated the provisions of section 507 into new section 512. In the intervening years, FDA determined that batch-by-batch certification was no longer required to assure the safety of animal antibiotics, and revoked require-

ments for certification, *e.g.*, 47 Fed. Reg. 39155 (September 7, 1982). In the Generic Animal Drug and Patent Term Restoration Act of 1988, Congress repealed all antibiotic certification provisions for animal drugs, and FDA has accordingly revoked its remaining regulations, 54 Fed. Reg. 22741 (May 26, 1989).

5. *New Animal Drug Status.* The enactment of the 1968 Amendments did not stem litigation over the food additive and new drug status of particular products. *E.g., United States v. An Article of Drug Consisting of 4,680 Pails,* 725 F.2d 976 (5th Cir. 1984); *United States v. Undetermined Quantities of Various Articles of Drug ... Equidantin Nitrofurantoin Suspension,* 675 F.2d 994 (8th Cir. 1982); *United States v. Western Serum Company,* Inc., 666 F.2d 335 (9th Cir. 1982); *United States v. An Article of Drug ... "Cap–Chur–Sol,"* 661 F.2d 742 (9th Cir. 1981).

6. *Withdrawal of Approval.* Following a long history of GMP problems, FDA finally took the drastic action of withdrawing approval of all the NDAs and NADAs for sterile injectible products manufactured by Copanos and Kanasco, claiming that the manufacturing procedures were inadequate to assure the identity and quality of the drugs. The notice of opportunity for hearing was published in 52 Fed. Reg. 7318 (March 10, 1987) and the approvals were withdrawn and a hearing denied in 52 Fed. Reg. 29274 (August 6, 1987). FDA's actions were upheld on review. *John D. Copanos and Sons, Inc. v. Food and Drug Administration,* 854 F.2d 510 (D.C. Cir. 1988).

7. *Gentian Violet.* For more than ten years, FDA waged a long and frustrating war against the use of gentian violet as an ingredient in animal feed. Through the 1970s, the agency prevailed in a series of seizure actions against Naremco products containing gentian violet. *United States v. Articles of Food and Drug, Coli–Trol 80 Medicated,* 518 F.2d 743 (5th Cir. 1975), *aff'g* 372 F.Supp. 915 (N.D. Ga. 1974); *United States v. An Article of Drug ... Entrol–C Medicated,* 513 F.2d 1127 (9th Cir. 1975), *aff'g,* 362 F.Supp. 424 (S.D. Cal. 1973); *United States v. 41 Cases,* 420 F.2d 1126 (5th Cir. 1970); *United States v. Seven Cartons ... "Ferro–Lac Swine Formula Concentrate",* 424 F.2d 1364 (7th Cir. 1970), *aff'g in part and vacating in part* 293 F.Supp. 660 (S.D. Ill. 1968); *United States v. 14 Cases ... "Naremco Medi–Matic",* 374 F.Supp. 922 (W.D. Mo. 1974). In 1977 the agency obtained an injunction prohibiting any further use of gentian violet in animal feed or drugs. *United States v. Naremco, Inc.,* 553 F.2d 1138 (8th Cir. 1977).

Marshall Minerals then took up the cause of gentian violet. The company submitted a food additive petition to use the material in poultry feed and, at the same time, marketed it on the alternative theory that it was GRAS and thus did not require a food additive regulation. FDA initially declined to file the food additive petition on the ground that it was incomplete, but it was ordered by the District Court for the Middle District of Georgia to accept the petition and not to interfere with the Marshall Mineral's use of gentian violet. FDA grudgingly filed the petition, 43 Fed. Reg. 21727 (May 19, 1978), and successfully appealed only the other parts of the injunction prohibiting it from enforcement activities relating to gentian violet. *Southeastern Minerals, Inc. v. Harris,* 622 F.2d 758 (5th Cir. 1980). In the meantime, FDA denied the food additive petition, 44 Fed. Reg. 19035 (March 30, 1979), as well as a request for a hearing on the denial, 45 Fed. Reg. 20559 (March 28, 1980), only to be overruled, *Marshall Minerals, Inc. v. FDA,* 661 F.2d 409 (5th Cir. 1981). While the food additive petition was being contested, FDA also brought seizure actions against the products marketed by Marshall Minerals. The district court granted FDA summary judgment, *United States v. An Article of Food Consisting of 345/50–Pound Bags,* FDC L. Rep. (CCH) ¶ 38, 003 (N.D. Ga. 1979), but the court of appeals determined that there were genuine issues of fact to be tried. *United States v. An Article of Food,* 622 F.2d 768 (5th Cir. 1980). At trial, a jury determined that gentian violet is GRAS as a mold inhibitor at 8 ppm in poultry feed. *United States v. An Article of Food ... Gentian Violet,* Food Drug Cosm. L. Rep. (CCH) ¶ 38,139 (N.D. Ga. 1981). FDA announced that, though it did not agree with the decision, it would not appeal and, pending further scientific studies on gentian violet, would not take regulatory action against this use, 47 Fed. Reg. 32480 (July 27, 1982). The GAO later concluded that FDA's actions against gentian violet did not amount to harassment, FDA'S REGULATION OF GENTIAN VIOLET APPEARS REASONABLE, HRD–80–91 (August 15, 1980). Reopening the matter after a decade of inaction in 55 Fed. Reg. 5194 (February 13, 1990), the agency proposed to declare gentian violet to be unsafe for use in animal feed. This was followed by a notice of filing of a food additive petition, 55 Fed. Reg. 27304 (July 2, 1990), seeking approval for the safe use of gentian violet in poultry feed. In light of the pending rulemaking, the court in *Naremco, Inc.* v. *FDA,* Food Drug Cosm. L. Rep. (CCH) ¶ 38, 157 (W.D. Mo. 1990), declined to determine *de novo* whether gentian violet is GRAS or a food additive.

8. *FDA Determination of New Animal Drug Status.* FDA often issues notices determining the status of specific products or ingredients, ordinarily after affording an opportunity for written public comment. 21 C.F.R. § 510.455 prescribes the new animal drug requirements for medicated feed blocks and other "free-choice" feeds. *See* 38 Fed. Reg. 30746 (November 7, 1973), 41 Fed. Reg. 32213 (August 2, 1976), 42 Fed. Reg. 23149 (May 6, 1977), 44 Fed. Reg. 10790 (February 23, 1979), 49 Fed. Reg. 45593 (November 19, 1984), 51 Fed. Reg. 19826 & 19898 (June 3, 1986). 21 C.F.R. § 510.413 requires that any animal drug containing chloroform must be the subject of an approved new animal drug application. 41 Fed. Reg. 52482 (November 30, 1976), 42 Fed. Reg. 44225 (September 2, 1977). The difficulty of regulating both human and animal safety, as well as effectiveness in animals, is illustrated by FDA's requirements established for sulfonamide drugs, 49 Fed. Reg. 27543 (July 5, 1984).

9. *Review and Approval.* Approvals of new animal drugs, unlike approvals of new human drugs, are required by section 512 to be published in the Federal Register. Notices of such approval appear regularly and are codified in 21 C.F.R. Subchapter E. As it was done for human drugs, FDA has established a "fast track" classification for reviewing important new animal drugs, 45 Fed. Reg. 56919 (August 26, 1980).

10. *Release of Safety and Efficacy Data.* FDA has established guidelines for the preparation of a "Freedom of Information summary" of safety and effectiveness data which is to be made publicly available after an NADA is approved. 41 Fed. Reg. 21498 (May 26, 1976), 48 Fed. Reg. 37711 (August 19, 1983), 50 Fed. Reg. 33641 (August 20, 1985). The summary is drafted by the applicant but must be approved by FDA.

11. *Promotion of FDA Approval.* The FD&C Act does not expressly prohibit promotion of a new animal drug that truthfully states that FDA has approved an NADA for it. FDA has issued a compliance policy guide to assure that such statements are accurate and appropriate, 51 Fed. Reg. 28765 (August 11, 1986).

12. *Good Manufacturing Practice.* Animal feed and animal drugs are also subject to FDA's GMP regulations for food and for drugs. The agency has brought court enforcement action against animal products made in violation of these requirements and has withdrawn approval of NADAs for such products. *See United States v. Articles of Drug ... Manufactured or Labeled by Goshen Laboratories, Inc.,* Food Drug Cosm. L. Rep. (CCH) ¶ 38, 174 (S.D.N.Y. 1982); *United States v. Bronson Farms, Inc.,* Food Drug Cosm. L. Rep. (CCH) ¶ 38,354 (M.D. Fla. 1986). *See also* 52 Fed. Reg. 7311 (March 10, 1987), 52 Fed. Reg. 29274 (August 6, 1987).

13. *Minor Uses.* Concern has been voiced that there are "minor uses" of animal drugs for which development of full-blown NADAs cannot be justified economically. FDA has made available special guidelines to facilitate approval of such drugs, 21 C.F.R. § 514.1(d), 44 Fed. Reg. 42716 (July 20, 1979), 48 Fed. Reg. 1922 (January 14, 1983). It makes funds available for research on minor uses, *e.g.,* 49 Fed. Reg. 18359 (April 30, 1984), 50 Fed. Reg. 9718 (March 11, 1985), and establishes a public master file for use by any applicant for approval of an NADA, *e.g.,* 51 Fed. Reg. 12930 (April 16, 1986), 52 Fed. Reg. 4968 (February 18, 1987), 54 Fed. Reg. 6758 (February 14, 1989), 55 Fed. Reg. 9771 (March 15, 1990).

14. *Investigational Animal Drugs.* Under 21 C.F.R. Part 511, 35 Fed. Reg. 7569 (May 15, 1970), 36 Fed. Reg. 18375 (September 14, 1971), an investigational new animal drug application (INAD) is required only for field trials and not for laboratory animal research. Guidelines for reporting the details of a clinical trial under an INAD were announced in 42 Fed. Reg. 6002 (February 1, 1977).

15. *Animal Biological Drugs.* In 1913 Congress enacted a separate animal Virus, Serum, and Toxin Act to regulate animal biological drugs, 37 Stat. 832, 21 U.S.C. §§ 151 *et seq.* This statute is administered by USDA. To avoid regulatory duplication, 21 C.F.R. §§ 511.1(b)(5) and 510.4 exempt animal biologics from section 512 of the FD&C Act if they comply with the provisions of the 1913 statute. Because the 1913 statute applied only to the interstate shipment of finished products, FDA asserted jurisdiction over animal biological drugs that were not shipped in interstate commerce but contained components that were so shipped. *Animal Health Institute v. USDA,* 487 F.Supp. 376 (D. Colo. 1980); *Grand Laboratories, Inc. v. Harris,* 660 F.2d 1288 (8th Cir. 1981) (en banc), *rev'g* 644 F.2d 729 (8th Cir. 1981). FDA and USDA subsequently entered into a Memorandum of Understanding on their respective jurisdictions, 47 Fed. Reg. 26458 (June 18, 1982). The Food Security Act of 1985, 99 Stat. 1354, 1654 (1985), made both intrastate and exported animal biologics subject to the 1913 statute and strengthened USDA's enforcement authority, thus ousting FDA from jurisdiction over animal biological products. The USDA requirements allow time for unregulated products to phase into the new licensing system, 55 Fed. Reg. 18345 (May 2, 1990).

16. *Medicated Animal Feed.* Regulation of medicated animal feed has presented difficult problems chiefly because of the large number of feed mills throughout the country that are engaged in mixing medication with feed. For many years every mill was required to have an approval from FDA, a so-called Form 1800, for each different medicated feed that it mixed. In 43 Fed. Reg. 2526 (January 17, 1978), FDA proposed to revise the regulations, which had simply been recodified from human drug and food additive counterparts after enactment of the 1968 Amendments, to incorporate terminology more appropriate for products for animal use. An internal agency task force subsequently

published a report on FDA's current medicated feed program, 43 Fed. Reg. 58634 (December 15, 1978). FDA announced in 44 Fed. Reg. 12208 (March 6, 1979) that final action on the earlier proposal would be postponed until decisions were reached on the recommendations in the report. Proposed new regulations were published in 46 Fed. Reg. 2456 (January 9, 1981), and public workshops and meetings held, 46 Fed. Reg. 12211 (February 13, 1981). Tentative final regulations appeared in 48 Fed. Reg. 34574 (July 29, 1983) and final regulations in 51 Fed. Reg. 7382 (March 3, 1986). FDA later revised its interpretation of these regulations without proposing formal changes, 55 Fed. Reg. 25972 (June 26, 1990). *See Upjohn Co. v. FDA*, 811 F.2d 1583 (D.C. Cir. 1987); *United States v. Bronson Farms, Inc.*, Food Drug Cosm. L. Rep. (CCH) ¶ 38,354 (M.D. Fla. 1986). *See also United States v. URSA Farmers Coooperative Co.*, Food Drug Cosm. L. Rep. (CCH) ¶ 38,149 (C.D. Ill. 1981); *United States v. An Article of Drug and DeKalb A.G. Research, Inc.*, Food Drug Cosm. L. Rep. (CCH) ¶ 38,180 (N.D. Ill. 1978).

Under the new regulations, codified in 21 C.F.R. Part 558, animal drugs are divided into two categories (those for which no withdrawal period is required, and those for which a withdrawal period is required or a zero residue tolerance is imposed) and medicated feed is divided into three types. Using this matrix, FDA requires an NADA, a medicated feed application, or no advance approval at all, based upon the degree of control that it believes appropriate.

17. *Animal Feed Additives.* The 1968 Amendments did not eliminate the need for petitions requesting approval, under section 409, of non-drug additives to animal feed. Some have raised difficult issues of scientific and regulatory policy. *See, e.g.,* the food additive regulation for selenium, 21 C.F.R. § 573.920, 38 Fed. Reg. 10458 (April 27, 1973), 39 Fed. Reg. 1355 (January 8, 1974), 46 Fed. Reg. 43415 (August 28, 1981), 46 Fed. Reg. 49115 (October 6, 1981), 52 Fed. Reg. 10887 (April 6, 1987); the proposed food additive regulation for copper, 38 Fed. Reg. 25694 (September 14, 1973); and the notices discussing the legal status of vitamin K, 41 Fed. Reg. 35009 (August 18, 1976), 48 Fed Reg. 16748 (April 19, 1983). *See also Heterochemical Corp. v. FDA*, 644 F.Supp. 271 (E.D.N.Y. 1986).

18. *Animal Drugs and FIFRA.* There is substantial overlap between the new animal drug provisions of the FD&C Act and the pesticide registration provisions of the Federal Insecticide, Fungicide, and Rodenticide Act (FIFRA) administered by EPA. *See United States v. Articles of Drug in Possession of Nip–Co Mfg., Inc.*, Food Drug Cosm. L. Rep. (CCH) ¶ 38,233 (S.D.N.Y. 1979). The two agencies have entered into a Memorandum of Understanding to reduce duplication, 36 Fed. Reg. 24234 (December 22, 1971), 38 Fed. Reg. 24233 (September 6, 1973)). In 41 Fed. Reg. 26734 (June 29, 1976), FDA assumed exclusive jurisdiction of new animal drugs that are also pesticides. Nonetheless, EPA adopted a statement of policy, 44 Fed. Reg. 15768 (March 15, 1979), 44 Fed. Reg. 62940 (November 1, 1979), respecting the application of FIFRA to veterinarians who use or dispense pesticides in the course of their practice. A new MOU published in 48 Fed. Reg. 22799 (May 20, 1983) gave FDA exclusive jurisdiction over new animal drugs that are also pesticides, but it was stayed in 48 Fed. Reg. 37077 (August 16, 1983) and remained in limbo as of June 30, 1990.

19. *Commentary.* For contrasting evaluations of FDA's implementation of the 1968 Amendments, see Craig, *The Animal Drug Amendments of 1968—In Retrospect,* 34 FDC L.J. 228 (1979); Crawford, *Animal Drug Amendments—Ten Years After,* 34 FDC L.J. 196 (1979); Van Houweling, *Looking Back at the Animal Drug Amendments of the Act,* 34 FDC L.J. 199 (1979). 43 FDC L.J., No.

6 (1988) contains a 20–year retrospective of the 1968 Amendments. *See also* "Human Food Safety and the Regulation of Animal Drugs," H.R. Rep. No. 99–461, 99th Cong., 1st Sess. (1985).

C. GENERIC ANIMAL DRUG AND PATENT TERM RESTORATION ACT

During the 1980s, FDA approved abbreviated NADAs for generic versions of pre–1962 DESI animal drugs, *e.g.*, 46 Fed. Reg. 36254 (July 14, 1981), but did not adopt a written policy on abbreviated NADAs or paper NADAs for post–1962 generic animal drugs. The agency did, however, issue a guideline on bioequivalence studies for use "where bioequivalency data are acceptable to the bureau, in lieu of safety or efficacy data, for new animal drug approval," 48 Fed. Reg. 2207 (January 18, 1983), 50 Fed. Reg. 32641 (August 13, 1984). As congressional deliberations on the Drug Price Competition and Patent Term Restoration Act of 1984 reached their conclusion, the draftsmen excluded animal drugs.

Following enactment of the 1984 Act, p. ___ *supra*, FDA came under increasing pressure to adopt administratively a similar approach for regulating post–1962 generic animal drugs. One controversy lead to substantial litigation. Schering Corporation obtained an approved NADA for gentamicin sulfate. Tri–Bio Laboratories attempted to obtain approval of an abbreviated NADA for the same drug, but FDA declined to approve it for lack of the requisite safety and effectiveness data. Tri–Bio marketed the drug anyway, and FDA seized the product. FDA and Tri–Bio then entered into a consent agreement under which the agency would not initiate any further enforcement for 18 months and Tri–Bio would submit a citizens petition attempting to demonstrate that gentamicin sulfate is an old animal drug that does not require approval of an NADA. At that point, Schering brought suit against FDA to set aside the consent agreement. The district court's ruling that the issue was not yet ripe for judicial review was upheld on appeal. *Schering Corp. v. Heckler*, 779 F.2d 683 (D.C. Cir. 1985). Tri–Bio subsequently submitted its citizen petition, which FDA promptly denied, and Tri–Bio then brought an unsuccessful declaratory judgment action challenging FDA's determination that gentamicin sulfate is a new animal drug that requires approval of an NADA before marketing. *Tri–Bio Laboratories, Inc. v. United States*, 836 F.2d 135 (3d Cir. 1987). *See also United States v. Undetermined Quantities ... Equidantin Nitrofurantoin Suspension*, 675 F.2d 994 (8th Cir. 1982). Thus, the same sort of litigation that precipitated enactment of the Drug Price Competition and Patent Term Restoration Act of 1984 also led to the enactment of analogous animal drug legislation.

Under consideration from 1986, the Generic Animal Drug and Patent Term Restoration Act became law in November 1988, 102 Stat.

3971. *See* Geyer, *The Generic Animal Drug and Patent Term Restoration Act,* 44 FDC L.J. 537 (1989). Although modeled on the 1984 Act, the 1988 statute differed in several significant respects. The 1988 Act does not cover animal biological products that are regulated under the Animal Virus, Serum, and Toxin Act of 1913, which is administered by USDA, *see* note 15 p. 643 *supra.* Congress explicitly excluded from the 1988 Act any new animal drug primarily manufactured using biotechnology techniques. Numerous details of the two statutes also differ, reflecting both industry experience with the 1984 Act and the customary political compromises needed to secure enactment of any statute. These details apart, however, the 1988 Act embodies the same trade-off of reduced requirements for generic animal drug approval in return for longer patent protection for pioneer products that is reflected in the 1984 Act. FDA began to implement the 1988 Act by announcing the availability of policy letters, *e.g.,* 53 Fed. Reg. 50460 (December 15, 1988), 54 Fed. Reg. 26111 (June 21, 1989), 54 Fed. Reg. 35534 (August 28, 1989), 55 Fed. Reg. 3107 (January 30, 1990), 55 Fed. Reg. 24645 (June 18, 1990), and a list of new animal drugs previously approved for safety and effectiveness, 54 Fed. Reg. 6607 (February 13, 1989). For announcements of patent term extension for new animal drugs, *see* 55 Fed. Reg. 9773 (March 15, 1990), 55 Fed. Reg. 17821 (April 27, 1990).

D. ADMINISTRATION OF CARCINOGENIC DRUGS TO FOOD–PRODUCING ANIMALS

During the past three decades, FDA has devoted substantial attention to regulating carcinogenic animal drugs that are used in food-producing animals and thus may leave carcinogenic residues in human food derived from the animals. This effort has been an important component in the evolution of FDA's comprehensive regulatory approach for carcinogens, which is the subject of Chapter VIII.

E. ANTIBIOTICS IN ANIMAL FEED

For over two decades FDA officials have been evaluating claims that the subtherapeutic use of antibiotics in the feed of food-producing animals, such as cattle, swine, and poultry, a practice that is widespread in the United States and some other countries, poses a human health hazard. As the following materials demonstrate, the attempt to assess the risks posed by this practice has taken the agency to the frontiers of modern science. Regulatory action to restrict the use of these drugs would test the limits of the concept of "safety" in section 512 of the FD&C Act.

HAROLD C. HOPKINS, KEEPING THE KICK IN ANTIBIOTICS

FDA Papers (June 1972).

The dual use of antibiotics—at concentrated or therapeutic dosages in humans and animals to treat diseases, and at low levels in feeds to promote faster growth in food-producing animals—has been widely discussed in recent years. The problem is that some bacteria exposed to low levels of antibiotics for prolonged periods in animals develop a resistance to some of these drugs.... If the resistant bacteria find their way into the human system, they may successfully fight off antibiotic treatment, making it less effective for treatment of humans. Concern over this question increased after Japanese scientists in 1959 discovered a resistance phenomenon, now known as the "R factor," among some intestinal bacteria. The "R factor" is the capability of bacteria to transfer antibiotic resistance to the same or another species by simple contact. "R factor" transfer can involve resistance to several antibiotics even though only a single antibiotic is used. To those who are concerned ... the corollary is that the R factor will result in larger amounts of disease-causing bacteria in animals. Humans may become exposed to these large numbers of antibiotic-resistant bacteria from animals which are a major source of our food. After this resistance develops, antibiotic treatment may be less effective in humans....

ANTIBIOTIC AND SULFONAMIDE DRUGS IN ANIMAL FEEDS: PROPOSED STATEMENT OF POLICY

37 Federal Register 2444 (February 1, 1972).

In April, 1970 the Commissioner of Food and Drugs established a Task Force of scientists to undertake a comprehensive review of the use of antibiotic drugs in animal feeds.... The Task Force was established on the recommendation of the FDA Science Advisory Committee following its review of a report issued by the Government of Great Britain on the use of antibiotics in veterinary medicine and animal husbandry. The British study, known as the Swann Committee Report, recommended that antibiotics should be divided into "feed" antibiotics and "therapeutic" antibiotics and that only those antibiotics not used for treatment of diseases in man should be allowed in animal feeds at the so-called growth promotion level....

... [T]he Task Force concluded that:

1. Human illnesses and death have been reported due to both antibiotic-sensitive and antibiotic-resistant bacteria of animal origin. Food-producing animals constitute a major reservoir of certain bacteria (*e.g.*, Salmonella) pathogenic for man. Evidence suggests that the use of certain antibiotics in food-producing animals promotes an increase in the animal reser-

voir of Salmonella through promotion of cross-colonization and infection, prolongation of the carrier state, and relapse of disease. Furthermore, the use of some antibiotics in animals produces a marked increase in the prevalence of R-factor containing bacteria which may be transmissible to man's enteric flora. These observations lead to the logical conclusion, though not fully documented, that such practices give rise to a human health hazard.

2. The continuous feeding of certain antibiotics to animals has been reported to compromise the treatment of certain animal diseases. Additional information is needed to quantitate the extent of this problem....

3. The categorization of antibiotics into those for human and those for animal use ... must not result in compromising the availability of effective antimicrobials for humans or animals. However, it is the consensus of the Task Force that it would be highly desirable that in the future a group of antibacterial agents be reserved exclusively for human use.

4. Limiting the types of antibiotics permitted in animal feeds is a step toward controlling the numbers of micro-organisms resistant to antibiotics....

5. When drug withdrawal times are not adhered to, antibiotic residues may be present in meat and meat products....

... [I]t is proposed that [FDA regulations] be amended by adding thereto the following new section:

§ 135.109 [now § 558.15] Antibiotic and sulfonamide drugs in animal feeds.

(a) The Commissioner will propose to revoke currently permitted uses of subtherapeutic and/or growth promotant uses of antibacterial agents in feeds ... when such drugs are also used in human clinical medicine, unless data are submitted which establish their safety and effectiveness under specific criteria based on the guidelines contained in the Report of the FDA Task Force on the Use of Antibiotics in Animal Feeds.

(b) Within 30 days following the effective date of this regulation any person interested in retaining approval of tetracyclines, streptomycin, dihydrostreptomycin, sulfonamides, and penicillins for use in poultry after January 1, 1973, or in swine, cattle, and sheep after July 1, 1973, or of all other such approved antibiotics after December 31, 1973, shall satisfy the Commissioner in writing that studies adequate and appropriate to meet the prescribed criteria have been undertaken....

(c) Following implementation of the requirements of paragraphs (a) and (b) of this section:

(1) Those antibacterial drugs which fail to meet the prescribed criteria will be reserved for high-level, short-term use and shall be used only by or on the order of a licensed veterinarian....

ANTIBIOTIC AND SULFONAMIDE DRUGS IN THE FEED OF ANIMALS

38 Federal Register 9811 (April 20, 1973).

The commercial animal and poultry production practices used in this country today, including the use of medication in feed administered to the entire herd or flock, have made it possible to effectively concentrate large numbers of animals into small areas without serious losses in production efficiency. From such concentration and intensified production, benefits accrue in terms of efficient land usage, labor savings, and more efficient conversion of animal feed to animal protein, thereby making a major contribution to the abundance of food from animals.... Immediate and total withdrawal of these drugs from animal feeds could seriously disrupt the quality and quantity of an important portion of our total human diet....

... The concept of "safety" as used in the act does not require complete certainty of the absolute harmlessness of a drug, but rather the reasonable certainty in the minds of competent scientists that it is not harmful when balanced against the benefits to be obtained from the drug. Using these criteria, the Commissioner concludes, ... that these drugs have been shown to be safe under the conditions of use ... and thus that there is presently no basis for withdrawing any of these drugs solely on safety grounds under section 512(e) of the act.

The ... task force report recommended withdrawal of the drugs by certain specific target dates. Those target dates are not adopted in the final regulation for two reasons. First, establishment of the testing requirements to be imposed with respect to these drugs has been far more complex than the task force realized, and therefore has taken far longer than initially contemplated. Second, in the absence of a finding of a lack of proof of safety, or failure to submit required reports, there is no legal basis for a decision arbitrarily to withdraw these drugs from the market....

The Commissioner recognizes that difficult questions exist with respect to the benefit-risk analysis necessary in determining whether the safety evidence is sufficient to approve or insufficient to justify continued approval of the safety of any drug. Questions about potential and theoretical hazard, of the nature raised with respect to the use of antibacterials in animal feed for growth promotion purposes, continually arise and obviously deserve serious consideration. Where these questions indicate a serious health hazard, withdrawal should immediately be ordered. Where, as here, only a potential or theoretical hazard is raised, which does not show that the drug is not shown to be safe, it is the opinion of the Commissioner that the proper way to proceed is to require the submission of appropriate records and reports pursuant to section 512(e) of the act, to facilitate a determination whether there is a ground for withdrawing approval of the drug in question. . . .

It would be chaotic, and is clearly not feasible, to withdraw approval of all food or drug substances merely because new questions have arisen, new testing is considered scientifically appropriate, or new studies raise issues that require further exploration. That is the situation involved here. . . .

1. The antibacterial drugs commonly used in animal feed and which are recognized to cause transferable drug resistance and are commonly used to treat human and animal diseases include the tetracyclines, streptomycin, dihydrostreptomycin, the sulfonamides, and penicillin. The use of these drugs in feeds may also affect the reservoir of salmonella organisms in food animals. An assessment of the effect of subtherapeutic levels of these drugs in feed on the salmonella reservoir can be completed in a relatively short time. Therefore, continued marketing of products containing any of these named drugs will be dependent on completion of salmonella reservoir studies by no later than 1 year following the effective date of this order. A determination that the drug promotes a significant increase in the salmonella reservoir will be considered sufficient grounds for proceeding to withdrawal approval of that drug.

2. The approval for the use of antibiotic and sulfonamide drugs in animal feeds at subtherapeutic levels will be withdrawn, unless by no later than 2 years following the date of this order there has been submitted conclusive evidence demonstrating that no human or animal health hazard exists which can be attributed to such use. . . .

3. By no later than 2 years following the effective date of this order, all drug efficacy data shall be submitted for any feed-use combination product containing an antibiotic or sulfonamide drug and any feed-use single ingredient antibiotic or sulfonamide product not reviewed by the National Academy of Sciences–National Research Council drug efficacy study. . . .

This course of action and the criteria referred to have been reviewed in joint consultation between the agency and officers of the Canadian Health Protection Branch in order to facilitate the development of a policy generally applicable to both countries. . . . *

———

FDA withdrew all approvals held by firms that had not complied with the requirements of this regulation, 39 Fed. Reg. 28393 (August 6, 1974), 41 Fed. Reg. 8282 (February 25, 1976). A year later, in April

* [The final regulation is codified in 21 C.F.R. § 558.15].

1977, Donald Kennedy, Professor of Human Biology at Stanford University, became Commissioner of Food and Drugs. The first Commissioner in more than a decade who was not a physician, Kennedy was nonetheless intimately familiar with the scientific issues posed by the use of antibiotics in feed. Within a month of his appointment FDA published the following notice.

RESTRICTION OF SUBTHERAPEUTIC USE OF ANTIBACTERIALS IN ANIMAL FEEDS: INTENT TO PROPOSE RULES AND CALLS FOR ENVIRONMENTAL IMPACT DATA

42 Federal Register 27264 (May 27, 1977).

The Commissioner of Food and Drugs is announcing his intention to implement decisions reached after evaluating the information collected under § 558.15 *Antibiotic, nitrofuran, and sulfonamide drugs in the feed of animals* (21 CFR 558.15).... Although each step in the overall process has not yet been precisely defined, in general the Bureau of Veterinary Medicine will propose:

1. To terminate all subtherapeutic use of penicillin in all feed;

2. To restrict the use of the tetracyclines to situations where there are no viable alternatives;

3. To impose restrictions on the distribution and use of the remaining uses of penicillin and tetracycline; and

4. To expedite implementation of the drug efficacy study implementation (DESI) notices proposing to withdraw approval of all penicillin and tetracycline combination products that lack evidence of effectiveness....

Under the National Environmental Policy Act of 1968, the Commissioner is required to assess the environmental impact of the agency's major actions to determine whether is a significant effect on the quality of the human environment and decide if an environmental impact statement (EIS) is necessary.... Several factors in this case favor gathering information and preparing a comprehensive EIS on the general use of antibacterial drugs in animal feeds. Briefly, they are as follows:

1. The subtherapeutic use of antibacterials in animal feeds is widespread.

2. Although the presence of bacteria that are resistant to one or more antibacterials has been demonstrated, the importance of this is strongly debated. Further, the magnitude of any effects on the public health stemming from the development of drug-resistant bacteria in the environment is largely unknown but potentially significant.

3. Although some antibacterials, *e.g.*, tetracyclines, are primarily excreted intact by the target animal, the effect of

drug residues on soil microflora, including the possible development of drug-resistant nonenteric bacteria, is largely unknown.

4. The proposed actions may cause a shift in drug production and drug use to alternative antibacterials that are not extensively used today....

The agency has the authority to refuse to file or approve a new animal drug application (NADA) unless it is accompanied by an appropriate environmental impact assessment report (EIAR), and this requirement is being applied to all previously approved new animal drugs as appropriate supplemental NADA's are filed. Therefore, the Commissioner requests that all holders of NADA's for the above listed drugs who have never filed an EIAR for the subtherapeutic use of their product[s] submit such reports at this time. For holders who have previously submitted EIAR's, the Commissioner requests any additional environmental information gathered since the EIAR was filed....

NOTES

1. *Next Steps.* FDA published detailed notices of opportunity for hearing on subtherapeutic uses of penicillin and tetracycline in animal feed in 42 Fed. Reg. 29999 (June 10, 1977), 42 Fed. Reg. 43772 (August 30, 1977), 42 Fed. Reg. 56264 (October 21, 1977), and announced its intention to conduct hearings in 43 Fed. Reg. 53827 (November 17, 1978). The availability of FDA's draft environmental impact statement was announced in 43 Fed. Reg. 35108 (August 8, 1978).

2. *GAO Encouragement.* In 1977 the General Accounting Office issued a report criticizing FDA's failure to disapprove the marketing of a number of antibiotics for low level use in animal feed. NEED TO ESTABLISH SAFETY AND EFFECTIVENESS OF ANTIBIOTICS USED IN ANIMAL FEEDS, HRD–77–81. The Office of Technology Assessment, in a separate study, identified five congressional options for handling this matter. DRUGS IN LIVESTOCK FEED (1979).

3. *NAS Review.* The House Appropriations Committee later instructed FDA to delay regulatory action against the use of antibiotics in animal feed pending a study of the matter by the National Academy of Sciences. A public meeting of the NAS Committee to Study the Human Health Effects of Subtherapeutic Antibiotic Use in Animal Feeds was announced in 44 Fed. Reg. 36479 (June 22, 1979). The NAS concluded that it is not possible to conduct a single comprehensive epidemiological study to settle the issues, but suggested other studies that could provide useful information. National Academy of Sciences, THE EFFECTS ON HUMAN HEALTH OF SUBTHERAPEUTIC USE OF ANTIMICROBIALS IN ANIMAL FEED (1980). The House Appropriations Committee then instructed FDA to conduct the suggested studies.

4. *British Followup.* In May 1980, the British Medical Journal reported two episodes in which antibiotic-resistant infections in humans (nearly 300 in one case) could be traced to the development of resistant organisms in antibiotic-treated livestock. The publication attributed these signs of the failure of the Swann Report's recommendations to continued misuse of antibiotics by farmers, and to imprudent prescribing by both veterinarians and physicians. *Why Has Swann Failed?*, May 7, 1980.

5. *Postponement.* In July 1981, manufacturers of animal drugs requested that, until the matter is resolved, approvals of new uses and new combinations of antibiotics should be continued, and FDA agreed to do so, 48 Fed. Reg. 4490 and 4554 (February 1, 1983).

6. *NRDC Petition.* In November 1984, the Natural Resources Defense Council petitioned the Secretary of HHS to suspend the NADAs for all the drugs involved on the ground that their continued use constituted an imminent hazard to public health. After a public hearing, announced in 49 Fed. Reg. 49645 (December 31, 1984), the petition was denied. Surprisingly, the Secretary's denial was not challenged in court.

7. *Scientific Followup.* The Centers for Disease Control (CDC) continues to investigate and publish information suggesting a link between antibiotic resistant salmonella and the use of subtherapeutic antibiotics in animal feed. Holmberg, *et al.*, *Drug–Resistant Salmonella From Animals Feed Antimicrobials*, 311 N.E.J.M. 617 (September 6, 1984); Levy, *Playing Antibiotic Pool: Time to Tally the Score*, 311 N.E.J.M. 663 (September 6, 1984); Spika, *et al.*, *Chloramphenicol–Resistant Salmonella Newport Traced Through Hamburger to Dairy Farms: A Major Persisting Source of Human Salmonellosis in California*, 316 N.E.J.M. 565 (March 5, 1987).

8. *Institute of Medicine Review.* In February 1989, the Institute of Medicine of the NAS issued a new report on the subject, HUMAN HEALTH RISKS WITH THE SUBTHERAPEUTIC USE OF PENICILLIN OR TETRACYCLINES IN ANIMAL FEED (1988). The IOM panel concluded that it was "unable to find data directly implicating the subtherapeutic use of feed antimicrobials in human illness and that much of the available evidence was primarily circumstantial, often ambiguous, and sometimes conflicting" (p. 7), but developed a novel risk assessment model that estimated the possible number of excess deaths per year under a variety of assumptions. The panel's report recommended additional research to obtain better information on which more accurate predictions of human risk could be based. FDA requested public comment on the report in 54 Fed. Reg. 5549 (February 3, 1989).

9. *Private Challenge to Antibiotic Use.* In an unusual case, the Animal Legal Defense Fund of Boston sued a Wisconsin veal producer alleging that the defendant raised calves in confined pens, fed them iron-deprived diets, and gave them subtherapeutic doses of animal drugs that may be dangerous to humans, and that failing to tell consumers about these practices was unfair and deceptive under Massachusetts law. The court entered summary judgment for the defendant, finding that there is no private right of action under the Massachusetts animal cruelty statutes, that the Massachusetts unfair trade practice statute cannot be used to enforce the animal cruelty statutes, and that FDA regulation of animal drugs preempts Massachusetts law on this subject. *Animal Legal Defense Fund Boston, Inc. v. Provimi Veal Corp.*, 626 F.Supp. 278 (D. Mass. 1986), *aff'd without opinion*, 802 F.2d 440 (1st Cir. 1987).

10. *Sulfonamide Drugs.* The regulation of sulfonamide-containing drugs for use in food-producing animals has a lengthy history. Two decades ago, FDA required residue depletion data to permit the establishment of an adequate withdrawal period to assure that edible products from treated animals are safe for consumption, 35 Fed. Reg. 16538 (October 23, 1970), 21 C.F.R. § 510.450. Interim marketing was permitted while approved NADAs were being obtained for all sulfonamide-containing drugs, 38 Fed. Reg. 19404 (July 20, 1973), 39 Fed. Reg. 26633 (July 22, 1974), 42 Fed. Reg. 62211 (December 9, 1977), 43 Fed. Reg.

19385 (May 5, 1978). FDA ended interim marketing, and announced the requirement of an approved NADA, for these drugs in 49 Fed. Reg. 27543 (July 5, 1984) and proposed to remove the original interim marketing regulation in 53 Fed. Reg. 35833 (September 15, 1988). After sulfamethazine was found to be carcinogenic in both mice, 53 Fed. Reg. 9492 (March 23, 1988), and rats, 53 Fed. Reg. 17850 (May 18, 1988), FDA announced a public hearing in 53 Fed. Reg. 17852 (May 18, 1988) to determine a proper course of action. Following the hearing, FDA took action to prevent all further use of the drug in food-producing animals not on the specific ground of carcinogenicity but on the more general ground that the data were inadequate to support the safety of the drug either in animals or as a result of human consumption of edible products from treated animals, 53 Fed. Reg. 46050 (November 15, 1988), 53 Fed. Reg. 51950 (December 23, 1988), 54 Fed. Reg. 10725 (March 15, 1989), 54 Fed. Reg. 22015 (May 22, 1989), 54 Fed. Reg. 38442 (September 18, 1989). Illegal use of the drug in milk-producing cows dropped dramatically. Young, *A Lesson in Industry Education: Keeping Drug Residues Out of Milk,* 23 FDA Consumer, No. 2, at 7 (March 1989). Receipt of the carcinogenicity test results was announced in 54 Fed Reg. 29947 (July 17, 1989).

11. *Residue Monitoring.* USDA shares responsibility with FDA for monitoring the residues of animal drugs in livestock. *See* 49 Fed. Reg. 23602 (June 7, 1984), 50 Fed. Reg. 32162 (August 9, 1985), 52 Fed. Reg. 2101 (January 20, 1987), 53 Fed. Reg. 52177 (December 27, 1988), 55 Fed. Reg. 7472 (March 2, 1990), adding 9 C.F.R. § 310.21, relating to USDA post-mortem inspection of carcasses suspected of containing sulfamethazine and antibiotic residues; 45 Fed. Reg. 63930 (September 16, 1980), 50 Fed. Reg. 20796 (May 20, 1985), and 53 Fed. Reg. 52177 (December 27, 1988), recording FDA's and USDA's concern about the continuing occurrence of above-tolerance sulfamethazine residues in swine. *See also United States v. Nelson Farms, Inc.,* Food Drug Cosm. L. Rep. (CCH) ¶ 38,019 (D.Vt. 1987). Animal drug residues are a subject of constant FDA interest. In 52 Fed. Reg. 165 (January 2, 1987), FDA announced the availability of funds to support studies on the development and improvement of analytical methodologies for residues of high priority animal drugs in tissues. *See* Stefan, *FDA's Role in Combatting Animal Drug Residues,* 52 J. AFDO, no. 3., at 45 (July 1988). FDA, USDA, and EPA have a Memorandum of Understanding covering monitoring for, and control of, drug and pesticide residues in food, 50 Fed. Reg. 2304 (January 16, 1985).

12. *Bovine Spongiform Encephalopathy.* Beginning in late 1988, Britain was swept by fear that a newly-identified cattle disease, bovine spongiform encephalopathy (BSE), could be transmitted to humans through the milk of cows whose feed included bone meal from slaughtered sheep that had the disease. A working party established by the Department of Health and Ministry of Agriculture, Fisheries and Food issued a report that concluded that "the risk of transmission of BSE to humans appears remote," but that the possibility "cannot be entirely ruled out." REPORT OF THE WORKING PARTY ON BOVINE SPONGIFORM ENCEPHALOPATHY 14 (February 1989).

13. *EC Opposition to Hormone-fed Beef.* The recent confrontation between the United States and the European Community (EC) over the importation of hormone-fed American beef had its counterpart a century ago when Germany refused to allow imports of American pork because of fear of trichinosis. *Compare* "Prohibiting the Use in Livestock Farming of Certain Substances Having a Hormonal Action," EEC Council Directive 85/649/EEC,

Official Journal of the European Communities No. L. 382, P. 228 (December 31, 1985), *with* Nugent & Hoy, *Public Health or Protectionism: The German–American Pork War*, 1880–1891, 63 Bull. Hist. Med., No. 2, at 198 (June 1989), and "Hormones Used in Meat Are Safe," FDA Talk Paper No. T89–5 (January 23, 1989). Congress enacted several statutes during 1880–1899 to regulate the import and export of livestock and feed. Hutt & Hutt II, *A History of Government Regulation of Adulteration and Misbranding of Food,* 39 FDC L.J. 2, 45–46 (1984). *See also* Barents, *Hormones and the Growth of Community Agricultural Law: Some Reflections on the Hormone Judgment (Case 68/86),* 1988 Legal Issues of European Integration, No.1, at 1; Halpern, *The U.S.-EC Hormone Beef Controversy and the Standards Code: Implications for the Application of Health Regulations to Agricultural Trade,* 14 N.C. J. Int. L. & Comm. Reg. 135 (1989); Note, *The EC Hormone Ban Dispute and the Application of the Dispute Settlements Provisions of the Standards Code,* 10 Mich.J. Int'l L. 872 (1989).

F. PRESCRIPTION ANIMAL DRUGS

Prior to 1988, the FD&C Act's animal drug provisions did not contain a counterpart of section 503(b), which mandates prescription status for some human drugs (*see* pages 404–21 *et seq. supra*). However, FDA created a class of prescription animal drugs by regulation. After an initial setback, the agency's regulation was upheld as a valid interpretation of the statutory requirement in section 502(f)(1) for "adequate directions for use." *United States v. Colahan,* 635 F.2d 564 (6th Cir. 1980), *rev'g,* Food Drug Cosm. L. Rep. (CCH) ¶ 38,004 (N.D. Ohio 1979). *See also* Food Drug Cosm. L. Rep. (CCH) ¶ 38,015 (6th Cir. 1987).

The distinction between Rx and OTC status for animal drugs is more complex than for human drugs. The new drug provisions of the FD&C Act are violated only when a new human drug is shipped in commerce without an NDA. Thus, a physician who merely prescribes an approved drug for a use not sanctioned by the FDA-approved package insert does not violate the Act. The new animal drug provisions are, however, violated whenever an animal drug becomes adulterated, even after shipment in interstate commerce. Thus, a veterinarian who engages in "extra-label use" outside the FDA-approved label commits a violation of the Act.

FDA has had difficulty reconciling the professional status of veterinarians with the statutory controls over animal drugs. The problem is complicated by the fact that many lay persons in the animal husbandry industry are as knowledgeable and experienced as veterinarians in the use of prescription animal drugs. FDA published a draft guideline for veterinary prescriptions in 49 Fed. Reg. 30076 (July 26, 1984), designed to prevent sale of prescription animal drugs to lay persons for use in food-producing animals. After a public hearing and comments which protested the draft guideline, it was withdrawn with the following cryptic explanation.

DRAFT GUIDELINE FOR VETERINARY PRESCRIPTIONS AND OTHER ORDERS; DRAFT GUIDELINE WITHDRAWN.

50 Federal Register 19382 (May 8, 1985).

Withdrawal of the guideline, however, does not change: (1) The agency's position on the need for a veterinarian's prescription or other order in connection with the sale and use of a veterinary prescription drug; (2) the agency's position that a bona fide veterinarian/patient/client relationship must be involved in the distribution of veterinarial prescription drugs; and (3) the labeling and documentation requirements already imposed by statute and regulation, before the proposal of the draft guideline. For example, this action has no effect on the agency's enforcement of 21 CFR 201.110 or on FDA's policy that veterinarians and other dispensers of prescription veterinary drugs shall keep adequate written records of drugs they dispense. FDA will continue to pursue its efforts to control the illegal distribution of veterinary prescription drugs, especially when those drugs are intended for use in food animals.

In the interim, FDA had issued a compliance policy guide on extra-label use of new animal drugs in food-producing animals, stating that, except by a veterinarian under defined circumstances, such use was illegal even if no detectable residue resulted, 49 Fed. Reg. 20915 (May 17, 1984). The guide has since been twice revised, 49 Fed. Reg. 45930 (November 21, 1984), 51 Fed. Reg. 42656 (November 25, 1986).

FDA, COMPLIANCE POLICY GUIDE 7125.06

(November 1, 1986).

Concern over the extra-label use of drugs in treating food-producing animals and the possibility that human food may become adulterated with illegal drug residues from such misuse has prompted a revision in the Center for Veterinary Medicine (CVM) extra-label drug use policy. Under the revised policy, a finding of illegal drug residues no longer will be a prerequisite for initiating regulatory action based on extra-label drug use of drugs in food-producing animals.

For the purpose of this policy, "extra-label use" refers to the actual or intended use of a new animal drug in a food-producing animal in a manner that is not in accordance with the drug labeling. This includes, but is not limited to, use in species or for indications (disease or other conditions) not listed in the labeling, use at dosage levels higher than those stated in the labeling, and failure to observe the stated withdrawal time.

FDA in the past has not sanctioned extra-label uses of drugs in food-producing animals, but the agency has stated that it would refrain from instituting regulatory action against licensed veterinarians for using or prescribing in their practices any drugs they could legally obtain. Nevertheless, it has been FDA's position that veterinarians may be subject to regulatory action for any violative drug residues in human food resulting from their prescriptions, recommendations, or treatments contrary to label instructions. Similarly, *anyone* in the producing or marketing chain who could be shown to have caused illegal drug residues through extra-label use of drugs in food-producing animals has been subject to regulatory action.

POLICY

The use or intended use of new animal drugs in treating food-producing animals in any manner other than in accord with the approved labeling causes the drugs to be adulterated under the Federal Food, Drug, and Cosmetic Act (the Act) (sections 501(a)(5) and (6), 512(a)(1)(A) and (B), 512(a)(2)). The agency will consider regulatory action when such use or intended use is found, whether by a veterinarian, producer, or other person. Regulatory actions will also be considered against distributors and others who might cause adulteration of approved new animal drugs. Nevertheless, extra-label drug use in treating food-producing animals may be considered by a veterinarian when the health of animals is immediately threatened and suffering or death would result from failure to treat the affected animals. In instances of this nature regulatory action would not ordinarily be considered, provided all of the following criteria are met and precautions observed:

1. A careful medical diagnosis is made by an attending veterinarian within the context of a valid veterinarian-client-patient relationship **;

2. A determination is made that, (a) there is no marketed drug specifically labeled to treat the condition diagnosed, or (b) drug therapy at the dosage recommended by the labeling has been found clinically ineffective in the animals to be treated;

3. Procedures are instituted to assure that identity of the treated animals is carefully maintained; and

---

** A valid veterinarian-patient relationship, as defined by the American Veterinary Medical Association is the following:

"An appropriate veterinarian-client-patient relationship will exist when: (1) the veterinarian has assumed the responsibility for making medical judgements regarding the health of the animal(s) and the need for medical treatment, and the client (owner or other caretaker) has agreed to follow the instructions of the veterinarian; and when (2) there is sufficient knowledge of the animal(s) by the veterinarian to initiate at least a general or preliminary diagnosis of the medical condition of the animal(s). This means that the veterinarian has recently seen and is personally acquainted with the keeping and care of the animal(s) by virtue of an examination of the animal(s), and/or by medically appropriate and timely visits to the premises where the animal(s) are kept; and when (3) the practicing veterinarian is readily available for follow-up in case of adverse reactions or failure of the regimen of therapy."

4. Significantly extended time period is assigned for drug withdrawal prior to marketing meat, milk, or eggs; steps are taken to assure that the assigned time frames are met, and no illegal residues occur.

Extra-label use of drugs in treating food-producing animals may under this policy, therefore, be considered only in special circumstances. The "exempting" criteria do not include drug use in treating food-producing animals by the layman. Lay persons cannot be expected to have sufficient knowledge and understanding concerning animal diseases, pharmacology, toxicology, drug interactions, and other scientific parameters to use drugs in treating food-producing animals in any way other than as labeled.

Certain drugs may not be used in treating food-producing animals even under the cited criteria. This includes chloramphenicol. Extra-label uses of drugs in treating food-producing animals for improving rate of weight gain, feed efficiency, or other production purposes, or for routine disease prevention are inappropriate as is use for therapeutic purposes other than under the circumstances described above. Also, the criteria cited above do not sanction the sale and use, for any purpose, of new animal drugs that are not approved, such as diethylstilbestrol (DES). Furthermore, a drug (including a bulk drug) may not be mixed into feed for any use or at a potency level not specifically permitted by the regulations in 21 CFR Part 558, even if prescribed or ordered by a veterinarian.

REGULATORY GUIDANCE

The highest priorities for regulatory attention regarding extra-label use are:

· Instances where illegal residues occur.

· Use of chloramphenicol or diethylstilbestrol (DES) in food animals.

· Use of dimetridazole, ipronidazole or other nitroimidazoles in unapproved species such as swine.

· Manufacturers and distributors who promote extra-label use of drugs.

· The mixing of drugs into medicated feeds intended for extra-label use.

· Extra-label use by laymen at their own initiative.

NOTES

· 1. *Enforcement by FDA.* In *Cowdin v. Young,* 681 F. Supp. 366 (W.D.La. 1987), the court granted FDA's motion to dismiss a court action challenging the compliance policy guide on the grounds that the issues were not ripe and that veterinarians did not have standing to challenge the guide. In *United States v. Blease,* Food Drug Cosm. L. Rep. (CCH) ¶ 38,095 (D.N.J. 1988), FDA obtained an injunction, and in *United States v. Jacobs,* Food Drug Cosm. L. Rep. CCH ¶ 38,113 (E.D. Cal. 1989), the agency successfully opposed a motion to dismiss a criminal indictment, in cases involving extra-label use of new animal drugs.

2. *Chloramphenicol Withdrawal.* Because of evidence of widespread misuse in food-producing animals, FDA withdrew approval of the NADAs for chloramphenicol oral solution. The drug had been approved only for use in dogs because of its known human toxicity. 50 Fed. Reg. 27059 (July 1, 1985), 51 Fed. Reg. 1367 and 1441 (January 13, 1986).

3. *Shipment of Bulk Drugs.* FDA has long taken the position that unapproved bulk drugs for veterinary use may not be sold to veterinarians and may only be sold to holders of approved NADAs. After an internal task force report, made available in 48 Fed. Reg. 34512 (July 29, 1983), FDA proposed to adopt new procedures under which NADAs could be approved for bulk new animal drug substances that are to be compounded into finished dosage form by or on the prescription of licensed veterinarians for use in their professional practices, 50 Fed. Reg. 27016 (July 1, 1985). FDA withdrew this proposal in 54 Fed. Reg. 12454 (March 27, 1989) on the grounds, among others, that veterinarians may lack the necessary qualifications for compounding complex drug formulas and are not subject to GMP requirements. Two district courts initially held that a bulk animal drug supplied to veterinarians for use within the scope of the practice of their profession is not subject to the requirements for new animal drugs, but FDA prevailed upon appeal in both cases. *United States v. 9/1 KG. Containers, More or Less, of an Article of Drug for Veterinary Use,* 854 F.2d 173 (7th Cir. 1988), *rev'g* 674 F. Supp. 1344 (C.D. Ill. 1987); *United States v. Algon Chemical, Inc.,* 879 F.2d 1154 (3d Cir. 1989), *rev'g* 689 F. Supp. 394 (D.N.J. 1988). Accordingly, veterinarians have access only to approved prescription animal drugs and must ordinarily use those drugs within the confines of the FDA-approved label.

4. *Statutory Support for Prescription Status.* The Generic Animal Drug and Patent Term Restoration Act of 1988 added a new section 503(c) establishing criteria for prescription animal drugs. The new provision did not, however, address the authority of veterinarians to engage in extra-label use or to compound animal drugs from unapproved bulk sources.

5. *Rx to OTC Switch.* In 41 Fed. Reg. 51078 (November 19, 1976), FDA issued a notice of opportunity for hearing on a proposal to deny a supplemental NADA to switch a new animal drug from Rx to OTC status. After it denied a hearing in 42 Fed. Reg. 46595 (September 16, 1977), the agency was ordered by the court to grant a hearing on the issue. *American Cyanamid Co. v. FDA,* 606 F.2d 1307 (D.C. Cir. 1979). Following the hearing, announced in 45 Fed. Reg. 40236 (June 13, 1980), the Administrative Law Judge and subsequently the Commissioner upheld the initial decision, 49 Fed. Reg. 26311 (June 27, 1984), *aff'd, American Cyanamid Co. v. Young,* 770 F.2d 1213 (D.C. Cir. 1985). *See also* 46 Fed. Reg. 46396 (September 18, 1981), where FDA denied another petition to switch an animal drug from Rx to OTC status. The FDA Veterinary Medicine Advisory Committee recommended to FDA in October 1988 criteria for determining Rx and OTC status, and FDA has established an internal committee to reevaluate the matter. FDA Veterinarian 4 (March/April 1989).

Chapter V

BIOLOGICS AND BLOOD PRODUCTS

A. HISTORICAL AND STATUTORY BACKGROUND

Smallpox was once the most feared disease, with the highest mortality rate, in human history. Its devastating effects are widely chronicled. Near the end of the Middle Ages halting efforts began to prevent the disease. Based on the observation that victims who survived never got smallpox again, the practice arose in the Far East of inoculation with smallpox puss or scabs—called "variolation." By the 16th century this practice had spread to Europe. During a severe smallpox epidemic in Boston in 1721, Cotton Mather persuaded Dr. Zabdiel Boylston to use variolation for the first time in North America. Initially resisted by the medical profession, variolation eventually became common practice in this country too.

Observing that milkmaids rarely had smallpox, Edward Jenner inoculated first one boy, and then several children, in Gloucestershire, England, with cowpox taken from an infected milkmaid and then challenged them by inoculation with live smallpox. All displayed resistance to smallpox. Following publication of Jenner's results in 1798, Dr. Benjamin Waterhouse conducted confirmatory tests in Boston by inoculation with the cowpox vaccine and subsequent challenge with injection of live smallpox. Thereafter, the use of Jenner's vaccine spread rapidly. *See generally* F. Fenner *et al.*, SMALLPOX AND ITS ERADICATION (1988).

Inevitably, fake smallpox vaccine appeared in the market, and neither physicians nor the general public could distinguish the genuine product. A crusading Baltimore physician, James Smith, persuaded the Maryland legislature to establish a public lottery to raise funds so that he could distribute "genuine vaccine matter" free to everyone. L. Md., ch. 123 (1809). Smith later persuaded Congress to enact similar legislation. 2 Stat. 806 (1813). Under the Federal statute, the President was authorized to appoint a Vaccine Agent "to preserve the genuine vaccine matter, and to furnish the same to any citizen of the United States, whenever it may be applied for, through the medium of the postoffice...." Smith was appointed the first and only Vaccine Agent of the United States. Following an outbreak of smallpox in

660

North Carolina that was attributed to vaccine Smith had furnished, H.R. Rep. No. 48, 17th Cong., 1st Sess. (1822), H.R. Rep. No. 93, 17th Cong., 1st Sess. (1822), Congress repealed the 1813 Act on the premise that it was "better to commit the subject altogether to the local authorities...." 3 Stat. 677 (1822). Though investigations continued, H.R. Rep. No. 95, 19th Cong., 2d Sess. (1827), the true cause of the North Carolina incident was never confirmed. Thus, the first Federal experiment in drug regulation ended in tragedy and a reversion to state control.

By the late 19th century diphtheria had become the third most prevalent cause of death in the United States. The causative agent was identified, and through injection into animals who built up an immunity, an "antitoxin" was produced that provided immunity against diphtheria. In 1901, an outbreak of tetanus in Camden, New Jersey, was traced to contaminated smallpox vaccine. A year later an outbreak of tetanus in St. Louis was traced to contaminated diphtheria antitoxin. *See generally* J. Liebenau, MEDICAL SCIENCE AND MEDICAL INDUSTRY: THE FORMATION OF THE AMERICAN PHARMACEUTICAL INDUSTRY (1987). At the request of the Medical Society of the District of Columbia and spurred by these episodes, Congress enacted the law that today still underpins Federal regulation of biological products for human use, commonly called the Biologics Act, in 32 Stat. 728 (1902). The Biologics Act was reenacted in 1944 as part of the recodification of the Public Health Service Act, 58 Stat. 682, 702 (1944), and is now codified at 42 U.S.C. § 262.

ANNABEL HECHT, MAKING SURE BIOLOGICALS ARE SAFE
FDA Consumer, July–August 1977, at 21.

Vaccines are just one of a group of drug products that are called "biologics" because they are made from or with the aid of living organisms that are produced in man or animals. Biologics also include antitoxins used to protect children against diphtheria, tetanus, and whooping cough; serums for the treatment of disease; products to diagnose and treat allergies; and blood for transfusions and for other medical purposes.....

During its first 46 years the biologics control program was under the supervision of the director of the Hygienic Laboratory and its successor, the National Institutes of Health (NIH). In 1948 it was made a part of the National Microbiological Institute, a unit of NIH. In 1955, after some polio cases resulted from vaccine containing undetected live virus, the need for strengthening the program became clear and the Division of Biologics Standards was established. To improve regulatory control of biologics, the Division was transferred from the National Institutes of Health to FDA in 1972 and renamed the Bureau of Biologics....

When the Public Health Service Act was recodified in 1944 a major issue was the status of biological products under the FD&C Act. During hearings on the recodification bill the issue triggered the following testimony:

Mr. [Alanson W.] Willcox [Acting General Counsel, Federal Security Agency]. Senator, you have had considerable discussion in the past few weeks in regard to the section of this bill, No. 351, which incorporates and reenacts the old act passed in 1902.

Under that act the Public Health Service licenses and controls the manufacture of virus serums, toxins, and so on. That is in the main simply reenacted by this section....

This first suggestion ... is to strike out the word "efficaciousness." That does not appear in the present statute and that would make the line read:

> The continued safety, purity, potency of such products * * *.

The other change is [in] subsection (g) [which] provides:

> The persons and the products to which this section is applicable shall be subject also to the provisions of the Federal Food, Drug, and Cosmetic Act

and then it has the exception of one proviso.

That, I am convinced, is the present law, though there has been some difference of opinion on the subject. I have made a study on the point, and I should like to file for the record a brief statement of our reasons for being confident that is the present law....

The wording of that subsection [(g)] has caused some alarm in the industry for fear it would mean duplication of administrative control, which is the last thing we want or anybody else wants. I am going to suggest that subsection be revised to read this way:

> Nothing contained in this Act shall be construed as in any way affecting, modifying, repealing, or superseding the provisions of the Federal Food, Drug, and Cosmetic Act.

We are making that suggestion, only because we are confident that it does now apply. The controls which the Public Health Service exercises are, I think, very effective but there is also a possibility in anything of that sort that some product which is dangerous to life may inadvertently get out into the market. The Federal Food and Drug, unlike this act, contains seizure of power [sic]. We are very firmly of the opinion that the authority in law to pick up off the market any dangerous product that might have gotten out despite the most rigid controls should be continued and, as I say, it is only because of our confidence that this revised wording would continue that, that we are willing to suggest the revised wording....

I did want the record to show we do not suggest what we have conceived to be any change of the substantive law. We do feel very decidedly that legal authority should be preserved for use in emergency that may never happen, but against which we should be prepared....

Hearings before a Subcomm. of the Senate Comm. on Education and Labor, 78th Cong., 2d Sess. 48 (1944).

Section 351 of the Public Health Service Act, often referred to in these materials as the Biologics Act, now reads in material part as follows:

(a) No person shall sell, barter, or exchange, or offer for sale, barter, or exchange in the District of Columbia, or send, carry, or bring for sale, barter, or exchange from any State or possession into any other State or possession or into any foreign country, or from any foreign country into any State or possession, any virus, therapeutic serum, toxin, antitoxin, vaccine, blood, blood component or derivative, allergenic product, or analogous product, or arsphenamine or its derivatives (or any other trivalent organic arsenic compound), applicable to the prevention, treatment, or cure of diseases or injuries of man, unless (1) such ... product has been propagated or manufactured and prepared at an establishment holding an unsuspended and unrevoked license, issued by the Secretary as hereinafter authorized ...; and (2) each package of such ... product is plainly marked with the proper name of the article contained therein, the name, address, and license number of the manufacturer, and the date beyond which the contents cannot be expected beyond reasonable doubt to yield their specific results....

(b) No person shall falsely label or mark any package or container of any ... product aforesaid; nor alter any label or mark.

(c) Any officer, agent, or employee of the Department of Health, Education, and Welfare, authorized by the Secretary for the purpose, may during all reasonable hours enter and inspect any establishment for the propagation or manufacture and preparation of any ... product aforesaid for sale, barter, or exchange....

(d) Licenses for the maintenance of establishments for the propagation or manufacture and preparation of products described in subsection (a) of this section may be issued only upon a showing that the establishment and the products for which a

license is desired meet standards, designed to insure the continued safety, purity, and potency of such products, prescribed
in regulations ..., and licenses for new products may be issued
only upon a showing that they meet such standards. All such
licenses shall be issued, suspended, and revoked as prescribed
by regulations....

(f) Any person who shall violate, or aid or abet in violating,
any of the provisions of this section shall be punished upon
conviction by a fine not exceeding $500 or by imprisonment not
exceeding one year, or by both such fine and imprisonment, in
the discretion of the court.

(g) Nothing contained in this Act shall be construed as in any
way affecting, modifying, repealing, or superseding the provisions of the Federal Food, drug, and Cosmetic Act....

NOTES

1. *Veterinary Biologics.* Congress enacted a separate Animal Virus, Serum, and Toxin Act to regulate veterinary biological products as part of the
appropriations legislation for the U.S. Department of Agriculture Bureau of
Animal Industry for fiscal year 1914, 37 Stat. 828, 832–33, now codified in 21
U.S.C. § 151 *et seq. See* Chapter IV, note 15, p. 643 *supra.*

2. *Commercial Sale.* Unlike the FD&C Act, section 351 is limited to
commercial production or sale of these products. *See* 29 Op. Att'y Gen. 340, 343
(1912):

> ... [T]he language of the act [must be accepted] as final and limits
> the application thereof to persons who bring virus, etc., into the United
> States or one of the States for sale, barter, or exchange.... Congress
> may easily have intended to draw the line between the sale of these
> articles, which would lead to their indiscriminate dissemination, and
> their use in scientific and experimental research.

For that reason, investigational biologics are subject to the IND requirements of
section 505(i) of the FD&C Act prior to their licensure for marketing under
section 351. *See* 21 C.F.R. § 312.2(a).

3. *Institutional History.* The FDA Bureau of Biologics remained a separate administrative unit from the time of its transfer from NIH in 1972 until it
was merged with the Bureau of Drugs in 1982, 47 Fed. Reg. 26913 (June 22,
1982), and the combined unit named the National Center for Drugs and
Biologics, later shortened to the Center for Drugs and Biologics. The two units
were again separated in 1988, 52 Fed. Reg. 38275 (October 15, 1987), 53 Fed.
Reg. 8978 (March 18, 1988), and the biologics unit was renamed the Center for
Biologics Evaluation and Research.

4. *Biologics Compared to New Drugs.* The requirements for licensure
under the Biologics Act differ from the requirements for new drugs under the
FD&C Act. A producer of biologicals must obtain separate licenses both for the
manufacturing plant and for each individual product to be manufactured at
that plant. Once the specific plant has been approved, moreover, it is more
difficult to secure approval of an alternative manufacturing site for a biological
than for a new drug. Biological products are more difficult to identify and
characterize than chemical products, and accordingly it is more difficult to

provide assurance that the identity of the biological product remains unaltered under different manufacturing conditions. FDA has therefore customarily required confirmatory *clinical* testing of any product manufactured at a new site before it will license production there. To the extent that more modern biological products can be adequately characterized and identified by chemical analysis, however, it would appear both unnecessary and imprudent to require additional clinical testing as a condition of approval of additional manufacturing sites.

5. *Biological Standards.* Some biological products are regulated under standards established by public regulation rather than solely by private license, and FDA must consequently devote resources to their continuing review and revision. For example, the agency proposed a major revision of the standards for the live oral (Sabin) polio vaccine in 51 Fed. Reg. 16620 (May 5, 1986) and, after once extending the time for comments in 51 Fed. Reg. 25710 (July 16, 1986), reopened the comment period in 52 Fed. Reg. 1933 (January 16, 1987) to permit all issues to be debated publicly before an advisory committee.

6. *Exotic Biologics.* In *United States v. Miami Serpentarium Laboratories, Inc.,* Food Drug Cosm. L. Rep. (CCH) ¶ 38,164 (S.D. Fla. 1982), FDA obtained an injunction against interstate shipment of a snake venom product, for failure to obtain the required biological establishment and product licenses. *See* Cooper, *Snake Venom—Of Hope and the Scientific Method,* 38 FDC L.J. 13 (1983). Because an unproven biological "immuno-augmentative therapy" was used only intrastate, however, FDA had to be content to advise the public "to avoid this unproven nostrum." "Immuno–Augmenative Therapy," FDA Talk Paper No. T82–14 (March 2, 1982).

7. *Commentary.* *See* Banta, *Federal Regulation of Biologicals Applicable to the Diseases of Man,* 13 FDC L.J. 215 (1958); Burney, *Human Biological Drugs and Basic Drug Research,* 14 FDC L.J. 621 (1959); Hardin, *Poliomyelitis Vaccine—History, Regulations and Recommendations,* 40 FDC L.J. 145 (1985); Hopps, *The Bureau of Biologics: What It Is and What It Does,* 33 FDC L.J. 198 (1978); Meyer, *Biologicals and FDA,* FDA Consumer, Apr. 1973, at 12; Timm, *75 Years Compliance with Biological Product Regulations,* 33 FDC L.J. 225 (1978).

———

The difficulty of implementing the Biologics Act is illustrated by the regulatory and legal controversies in which it has been involved, which were chronicled in a series of articles that appeared in *Science* magazine in 1972.* The first major controversy followed the approval, by NIH's National Biological Institute, of the Salk vaccine made by Cutter Laboratories in 1955:

> In 1955 a newly developed vaccine against poliomyelitis was rushed onto the market and promptly caused among the vaccinees and their families ten deaths and 192 cases of paralytic polio. The Cutter "incident," as the scandal was named after the company that produced most of the bad vaccine, caused the resignation of a Secretary of Health, Education and

* Copyright 1972 by the American Association for the Advancement of Science.

Welfare, a Surgeon General, and a Director of the National
Institutes of Health. To ensure that such an incident should
not recur, the NIH laboratory charged with regulating vaccines was reorganized as the Division of Biologics Standards
(DBS), and the assistant chief of the laboratory, Dr. Roderick
Murray, was installed as the DBS director. For some 16 years
the DBS performed its regulatory activities in decent obscurity,
a dim companion of the pure research institutes on the NIH
campus at Bethesda, Maryland....

Wade, *Division of Biologics Standards: In the Matter of J. Anthony
Morris*, 175 Science 861 (1972).

The Cutter incident spawned more than sixty lawsuits against the
company, resulting in a precedent-setting finding of liability based on
breach of implied warranty. *See Gottsdanker v. Cutter Laboratories*,
182 Cal. App. 2d 602, 6 Cal. Rptr. 320 (1960). *See also* Baynes, *Liability
For Vaccine Related Injuries: Public Health Considerations and Some
Reflections on the Swine Flu Experience*, 21 St. Louis U.L.J. 44 (1977);
Hardin, *Poliomyelitis Vaccine—History, Regulations and Recommenda-
tions*, 40 FDC L.J. 145 (1985); Note, *The Cutter Polio Vaccine Incident:
A Case Study of Manufacturers' Liability Without Fault in Tort and
Warranty*, 65 Yale L.J. 262 (1955).

In the early 1970s a DBS scientist, Dr. Anthony Morris, charged
that the research and regulatory functions of the Division of Biologics
Standards created an inherent conflict of interests.

> The common theme of the ... charges is that in numerous
> instances, amounting to a "pattern of administrative insensi-
> tivity," the DBS management has suppressed or ignored scien-
> tific findings that would adversely affect the vaccine market.
> The motive for this alleged behavior is ascribed ... to a
> "passionate commitment to vaccine therapy" on the part of the
> DBS leadership....

Wade, *Division of Biologics Standards: Scientific Management Questioned*, 175 Science 966 (1972).

> ... Federal responsibility for vaccines does not rest solely
> on the DBS, but is diffused over a handful of committees with
> interlocking memberships. Thus, if the mass annual inocula-
> tions against influenza were indeed the "forcing on the public
> [of] a bogus situation.... The vaccine we were promoting was
> not having any beneficial effects," it is not too clear whether
> responsibility would lie with the DBS for certifying an ineffica-
> cious vaccine or with a second body, the Center for Disease
> Control's Advisory Committee on Immunization Practices
> (ACIP), whose function is to decide who should be vaccinated
> against what. Again, when the typhus vaccine shot into every
> U.S. Army recruit since World War II turned out in 1969 to be
> producing insufficient antibody even though it had regularly
> passed the DBS tests, it was unclear whether the DBS or the

Armed Forces Epidemiological Board (AFEB) should claim fatherhood of the fiasco. Federal responsibility for the development of new vaccines is notably imprecise....

Besides diffuseness of responsibility, the picture is also blurred by a reluctance among vaccine workers to discuss problems openly when they arise. This is because of the understandable fear that public confidence in vaccines—and vaccine authorities—will be eroded....

None of this implies that faults have been covered up or that the public has been conspired against in any way; but there are dangers that problems will be underemphasized in any system that discourages the fullest possible discussion, as some believe the DBS does.....

... [M]any of the most important decisions made by the DBS have been reached with the aid of large, often international, conferences. Murray says the licensing of live polio vaccine in 1961 was the hardest choice he has faced because there were three different virus strains from which to select, but he emphasizes that the decision was made on a collective basis, not by him alone.

Another important decision was the licensing of rubella vaccine in 1969, when again there was a choice of virus strains—one developed by three scientists in the DBS .... and another by ... the Wistar Institute. There is no reason to suppose that individual DBS scientists acted other than entirely honorably, but the DBS as an institution was put in a classic conflict of interest position in having to decide upon a vaccine it had itself developed.....

... The whole mechanism of biologics control should be reviewed in the light of consumer protection—the DBS should probably assume from the manufacturers the prime responsibility for conducting the more crucial tests of vaccine safety.... The director of the DBS should have responsibility for organizing the research program as well as the regulatory activities of the division.

In addition, federal responsibility for vaccine development should be clarified, in a way that ensures the DBS does not develop vaccines in-house. There should be some court of appeal against the director's decisions. Since the DBS acts, in effect, for the academic community on behalf of the public, there should be a stronger connection with the academic world than occasional ad hoc conferences and a rubber-stamp board of scientific counselors. Standing committees of scientists might be established—one to oversee research and another for regulations—so as to buttress the director's posture toward manufacturers. Problems with vaccines should be more openly discussed, and herd immunity should be sought by means other than treating the public as one....

Wade, *Division of Biologics Standards: The Boat That Never Rocked,* 175 Science 1225 (1972).

A contemporaneous General Accounting Office investigation resulted in accusations, and heated denials, of improper certification of influenza vaccine:

> ... The GAO investigators discovered that on the evidence of the DBS's own records, 130 of the 221 lots of influenza vaccine released by the DBS in 1966–68 failed to meet the standards of potency required by the agency's own regulations. One hundred and fifteen of these lots were subpotent according to the test results submitted to the DBS by the manufacturers themselves. Another 15 lots were potent according to the manufacturers' tests and failed the tests conducted by DBS scientists, yet were released for public use by the DBS management....

> According to Robert W. Berliner, NIH deputy director for science, the GAO report fails to make allowance for the variability of the test used to assess influenza vaccine potency. The vaccines the GAO describes as subpotent, Berliner told *Science,* were those that fell in the lower half of the statistical scatter about the mean and which may in fact have been potent. If the DBS had raised its potency standards significantly, the stronger vaccines in the statistical scatter would have caused unpleasant side effects. The DBS policy was thus reasonable scientifically, even though it contradicted the precise letter of the DBS's regulations.....

> The precise effect of the DBS policy of releasing subpotent vaccines is hard to estimate but probably some 67 million doses of influenza vaccine were used in the United States during the 3 years covered by the GAO report. If half of these vaccines failed the DBS's own standards, and the cost to each recipient was $1 a head (a conservative estimate), then the DBS has allowed citizens to spend more than $30 million on subpotent vaccines....

Wade, *DBS: Agency Contravenes Its Own Regulations,* 176 Science 34 (1972).

These disclosures culminated in the transfer on July 1, 1972, of responsibility for implementation of the Biologics Act from DBS to FDA, 37 Fed.Reg. 12865 (June 29, 1972). *See generally* "Consumer Safety Act of 1972," Hearings before the Subcomm. on Executive Reorganization and Government Research of the Senate Comm. on Government Operations, 92d Cong., 2d Sess. (1972). The DBS scientist whose charges precipitated this transfer was later removed by FDA. Osborn, *In the Matter of Witch Hunts,* 240 J.A.M.A. 1616 (October 6,

1978). The Federal Employee Appeals Authority sustained the agency's action in June 1977. A request to reopen the decision was remanded by the Appeals Review Board for a further hearing. An Administrative Law Judge then determined that the penalty of removal was warranted, stating that "Removal is especially justifiable when avoidance of peer review if combined with a performance of invalid scientific work which is used as the basis for alarming conclusions in the field of public health regulation." *In the Matter of Dr. J. Anthony Morris,* Merit Systems Protection Board Decision No. DC752B90251 (June 13, 1979). A subsequent GAO investigation, brought on by congressional suspicion of FDA's handling of the Morris case, failed to uncover any serious deficiencies in its regulation of biologics. ANSWERS TO QUESTIONS ON SELECTED FDA BUREAU OF BIOLOGICS' REGULATION ACTIVITIES, HRD–80–55 (1980).

NOTE

Working relationships have been established among the FDA units responsible for medical devices, radiological health, and biologics. The Bureau of Biologics has lead responsibility for the regulation of medical devices used in the processing or administration of biological products, 44 Fed. Reg. 24236 (April 24, 1979), 47 Fed. Reg. 15412 (April 9, 1982). Responsibility for biological in vitro diagnostic products was transferred to the Bureau of Medical Devices in 45 Fed. Reg. 51226 (August 1, 1980), 45 Fed. Reg. 58964 (September 5, 1980), 47 Fed. Reg. 34532 (August 10, 1982), 51 Fed. Reg. 37976 (October 27, 1986). A biological monoclonal antibody product prepared by hybridoma technology remains subject to biological licensing, however, whether it is intended for in vivo use or for in vitro testing of a licensed biological product, 48 Fed. Reg. 50795 (November 3, 1983). In 51 Fed. Reg. 33664 (September 22, 1986), FDA stated that products intended to determine whether an individual is allergic to a particular chemical, by oral challenge or by skin testing, is a biological product subject to the licensure provisions of the Biologics Act. FDA announced in 55 Fed. Reg. 5892 (February 20, 1990) that in vitro diagnostic products to detect total antibody to hepatitis B core antigen, previously regulated as medical devices, were in the future going to be regulated as biological products because their major use had changed from clinical diagnostic use to screening blood intended for transfusion. Under 21 C.F.R. § 312.140, an IND for a biological drug is submitted directly to the Center for Biologics, and under 21 C.F.R. § 314.440 an NDA for a drug that is to be handled by the Center for Biologics is to be sent directly there.

B. THE BIOLOGICS REVIEW

The GAO Report of March 1972 discussed above concluded that ineffective biologics had been licensed under the Biologics Act because of the failure to apply the requirements for proof of effectiveness added to the FD&C Act by the Drug Amendments of 1962:

> ... The GAO report states that according to Murray himself, 75 of the 263 products licensed by the DBS are

generally not recognized as effective by most of the medical profession. Only 32 of these products are currently on sale to the public.... The GAO report reveals that [DBS] ... was advised by HEW counsel in February 1969 that the DBS possessed authority under ... [the Drug Amendments of 1962] to enforce vaccine efficacy. Murray refused to use the [FD&C] act ... on the grounds that to do so would strengthen the argument of those who wished to merge the DBS with the FDA into a single control agency....

Wade, *DBS: Agency Contravenes Its Own Regulations,* 176 Science 34 (1972).

In anticipation of the GAO findings, the Secretary of HEW redelegated authority to administer the drug provisions of the FD&C Act for all biological products concurrently to FDA and DBS, 37 Fed. Reg. 4004 (February 25, 1972). NIH, DBS's, parent agency, then announced its intention to review the effectiveness of all licensed biologicals. The announcement called for manufacturers to submit "substantial evidence of effectiveness" of their products meeting the requirements of FDA's Bureau of Drugs, now codified in 21 C.F.R. § 314.126, or risk withdrawal of their licenses, 37 Fed. Reg. 5404 (March 15, 1972).

Following its assumption of responsibility for administering the Biologics Act and the formation of the Bureau of Biologics, FDA revoked NIH's March 15, 1972 notice and proposed detailed procedures for the review of the safety, effectiveness, and labeling of all licensed biologicals. The Biologics Review was closely patterned after the OTC Drug Review, but with significant differences that are described in the chartering documents.

BIOLOGICAL PRODUCTS: PROCEDURES FOR REVIEW OF SAFETY, EFFECTIVENESS, AND LABELING

37 Federal Register 16679 (August 18, 1972).

This proposal will establish a procedure under which the safety, effectiveness, and labeling of all biological products presently licensed under section 351 of the Public Health Service Act will be reviewed. Advisory review panels comprised of independent experts will provide their conclusions and recommendations to the Commissioner of Food and Drugs, who then will review and implement them....

The review procedure proposed in this notice relies for legal authority on both the Federal Food, Drug, and Cosmetic Act and section 351 of the Public Health Service Act. To the extent that licensed biological products are presently not required to comply with the provisions of the Federal Food, Drug, and Cosmetic Act, these regulations supersede any such exemptions....

The Commissioner of Food and Drugs is aware of the unique problems involved in applying the requirement of "substantial evidence of effectiveness" to biological products, under the Federal Food, Drug, and Cosmetic Act. Where adequate and well-controlled studies are not feasible, and acceptable alternative scientific methods of demonstrating effectiveness are available, the latter will be sufficient. The advisory review panels convened under the procedure proposed in this notice will initially develop the standard and methodology for effectiveness for a particular class of biological products, ... subject to review by the Commissioner of Food and Drugs.... Each review panel will determine those biological products that are and are not safe, effective, and not misbranded, as well as those for which further study is required. The applicable product licenses will then be confirmed, revoked, or permitted to remain in effect on an interim basis pending further study....

PROCEDURES FOR REVIEW OF SAFETY, EFFECTIVENESS AND LABELING
38 Federal Register 4319 (February 13, 1973).

Many comments stated that the proposed regulations combined the substance of the requirements of the Federal Food, Drug, and Cosmetic Act with the procedural requirements of the Public Health Service Act, by making the standards of safety and effectiveness set forth in the new drug provisions of section 505 of the Federal Food, Drug, and Cosmetic Act applicable to biological products through the employment of the licensing provisions of the Public Health Service Act. These comments contended that such a combination was not legally permissible. To the contrary, biological products, subject to regulation under section 351 of the Public Health Service Act, are also drugs, within the meaning of section 201(g)(1) of the Federal Food, Drug, and Cosmetic Act, and are therefore also subject to regulation under that act....

Some comments argued that the license of a biological product which is not a new drug within the meaning of section 505 of the Federal Food, Drug, and Cosmetic Act cannot be revoked solely because a product is lacking in substantial evidence of effectiveness.... Regardless of whether a particular biological product is a new drug, however, all biological products are subject to the misbranding provisions of both section 502 of the Federal Food, Drug, and Cosmetic Act and section 351(b) of the Public Health Service Act. A biological product whose label purports, represents, or suggests it to be effective and/or safe for certain intended uses, and which is not safe and effective for such uses, is misbranded within the meaning of both acts, and therefore should not and will not be licensed under section 351 of the Public Health Service Act.... The burden is on the prospective licensee, as it is upon a new drug applicant, to show a lack of misbranding to obtain a license or an approved new drug application, and this burden remains on the licensee or new drug applicant after the license or new drug application is issued and approved....

Many comments were received questioning the FDA's authority summarily to revoke a license for a biological product on the ground that the requested data and information were not submitted. The FDA has sufficient authority under section 351 of the Public Health Service Act to revoke a license for a willful failure to submit required safety and effectiveness data. Nevertheless, the Commissioner has determined to revise the procedures governing the treatment accorded licensees failing to submit safety and effectiveness data for their products. Licenses for such products will not be revoked until such time as the Commissioner has published the final order establishing standards for the safety, effectiveness, and labeling of the particular category of biological products, and the products for which no data have been submitted fail to meet those standards. This approach has been adopted so as to ensure that no person currently receiving a licensed biological product in a medical context will be deprived of any of the possible benefits of the product until an expert advisory panel has made a thorough evaluation of all available safety and effectiveness data concerning the product. . . .

NOTE

FDA issued requests for data and information relating to the eight classes of biologics under review in 37 Fed. Reg. 16690 (August 18, 1972) (bacterial vaccines and bacterial antigens with no U.S. standard of potency); 38 Fed. Reg. 5358 (February 28, 1973) (bacterial vaccines and toxoids with standards of potency); 38 Fed. Reg. 5359 (February 28, 1973) (viral and rickettsial vaccines); 39 Fed. Reg. 1082 (January 4, 1974) (allergenic biological products); 39 Fed. Reg. 7445 (February 26, 1974) (skin test antigens); 39 Fed. Reg. 21176 (June 19, 1974) (distributing remaining biological products among the existing panels); and 39 Fed. Reg. 43413 (December 13, 1974) (blood, blood components, and derivatives).

The report of the panel responsible for reviewing bacterial vaccines and antigens with no U.S. standard of potency was published in 42 Fed. Reg. 58266 (November 8, 1977). The FDA Commissioner adopted the entire report and proposed that the panel's recommendations be implemented without change. The agency soon after published a notice of opportunity for hearing on revocation of the licenses for products placed by the panel in Category II, 21 C.F.R. § 601.25(f)(2) (unsafe, ineffective, or misbranded), and in Category IIIB, 21 C.F.R. § 601.25(f)(3) (insufficient data for final classification coupled with a recommendation that the product should not be marketed pending the necessary further testing). 42 Fed. Reg. 62162 (December 9, 1977). On October 27, 1978, FDA announced its final actions based upon that notice of opportunity for hearing.

BACTERIAL VACCINES AND BACTERIAL ANTIGENS WITH NO U.S. STANDARD OF POTENCY: REVOCATION OF LICENSES AND RECLASSIFICATION

43 Federal Register 50247 (October 27, 1978).

The Commissioner has received numerous letters from patients and doctors expressing concern over the recommendation to revoke the license for the manufacture of V–677, Streptococcus Vaccines (Intravenous). Most letters provided testimonials in support of the effectiveness of the V–677 product for the treatment of arthritis. Some letters requested a formal hearing.

The Commissioner recognizes the concern and the sense of frustration some patients must feel regarding the proposed revocation. However, the law provides that the safety and effectiveness of biological drugs must be established by scientifically sound evidence. The expert panel evaluated all the bacterial vaccines, using the same criteria to establish safety and effectiveness.... The data submitted by Eli Lilly and Co. did not satisfy the criteria, and the panel and the Commissioner concluded that V–677 should be removed from the market pending the results of scientific studies to establish its safety and effectiveness. In addition, the testimonials submitted by individuals do not satisfy the statutory standard and do not support approval of a biological drug....

The Commissioner advises that a hearing may be requested only by a manufacturer whose license is the subject of the proposed revocation.... [I]f a licensee is given the opportunity to request a hearing but fails to demonstrate an interest in continuing to market the product by not requesting a hearing or submitting data, there is no hearing in which to participate.... Although anyone can apply for licensure, patients and-or doctors cannot compel a licensee to continue to produce or to take any particular action to protect its license. For this reason, the Commissioner is obliged to deny requests for a hearing from patients.... [Neither Lilly nor three other manufacturers requested a hearing on the commissioner's decision.]

Delmont Laboratories, Inc., requested a hearing and submitted data and information in support of its Staphage Lysate (SPL) type I, and types I and III combined. The Commissioner concludes that these data would not only justify a hearing but are adequate to justify reclassification at this time. The Commissioner finds that the potential benefits outweigh the potential risk in use of the product. Therefore, Staphage Lysate (SPL) type I, and types I and III combined, for Staphylococcal Disease (bacterial antigen made from staphylococcus) are reclassified from category IIIB to category IIIA (biological products for which available data are insufficient to classify their safety and effectiveness but which may remain in interstate commerce pending completion of testing). Because no hearing is necessary for a category IIIA product, the December notice is withdrawn for the product....

BACTERIAL VACCINES AND BACTERIAL ANTIGENS WITH "NO U.S. STANDARD OF POTENCY"

44 Federal Register 1544 (January 5, 1979).

In the FEDERAL REGISTER of November 8, 1977, the Commissioner of Food and Drugs published a proposal containing findings of the Panel on Review of Bacterial Vaccines and Bacterial Antigens with "No U.S. Standard of Potency." The Panel evaluated the safety and effectiveness of 32 bacterial vaccine and bacterial antigen products and recommended that: (a) no products be placed in Category I (those biological products determined to be safe, effective, and not misbranded); (b) three products be placed in Category II (those biological products determined to be unsafe, ineffective or misbranded); (c) seven products be placed in Category IIIA (those biological products for which available data are insufficient to classify their safety and effectiveness but which may remain in the interstate commerce pending completion of testing and conformance with the recommendations of the Panel); and (d) twenty-two products be placed in Category IIIB (those biological products for which available data are insufficient to classify their safety and effectiveness and which should not continue in interstate commerce)....

In addition, the November 1977 proposal contained the Commissioner's responses to other panel recommendations concerning the testing, content, and labeling of bacterial vaccines and antigens. In view of these recommendations, the Commissioner proposed two amendments to the biologics regulations: (1) in [21 C.F.R.] § 601.25(h) to require that the labeling for Category IIIA bacterial vaccines and antigens contain a prominent boxed statement referencing the Panel's findings of insufficient data on safety and effectiveness, that written informed consent be obtained from participants in the additional studies performed pursuant to § 601.25(h), and that a patient information insert be included with category IIIA products continued in interstate commerce.....

The Panel's report ... makes clear that the views of those persons who have submitted comments on the Commissioner's proposal have already been thoughtfully considered. In discussing its evaluation of safety, the Panel identified exactly those problems which establish the need for scientifically valid and controlled studies: the lack of an effective mandatory system for reporting adverse reactions, that a practicing physician sees only a limited number of patients and therefore will identify only adverse reactions that occur at a very high rate, that patients with severe reactions may not return to the same treatment situation, and that a causal relationship is difficult to discern due to the time and other events between the administration of a drug and the onset of the adverse reaction. The Panel's summary clearly shows that every effort was made to give all reasonable credit to significant human experience during marketing.

The Commissioner notes that nondeliberative portions of all meetings of the Panel were open to the public. Announcements of the meetings were published in the FEDERAL REGISTER before each meeting, and interested persons were given an opportunity to make presentations to the Panel. No person who requested an opportunity to appear and make a presentation was denied that request. In addition, as part of the process of nominating qualified experts to serve on the Panel, the Commissioner issued letters to approximately 35 medical and scientific associations and consumer groups advising them of the review of bacterial vaccines and bacterial antigen products. Ample opportunity was given for public participation in the proceedings, and manufacturers had adequate time and opportunity to present additional data in support of continued licensure for their products. For these reasons, the request that additional public hearings be provided to present a forum for those disagreeing with the Panel's recommendations and the Commissioner's conclusions is denied....

The Commissioner notes that there are numerous drugs other than V–677 which are marketed for the treatment of arthritis.... The Commissioner also notes that the classification of a product into Category IIIB does not preclude further studies. It requires only that the product not be marketed commercially while controlled studies are conducted in accordance with the IND provisions of the law. Those persons being treated with V–677 may serve as test subjects for the IND clinical trials. This mechanism provides for continued availability of a drug but only as part of a plan to study its safety and effectiveness. This mechanism also provides maximum protection to the test subjects. Thus, although the Eli Lilly and Co. licenses for ... V–677 have been revoked, the law does not prohibit investigational new drug use of either drug....

The Panel recommended that the Federal government sponsor some of the studies required to establish the safety and effectiveness of bacterial vaccines and bacterial antigen products.....The comments suggested that Federal support was necessary because the cost for the required studies would be prohibitive for small manufacturers. In view of the Panel's recommendation and the responses submitted, the Director, Bureau of Biologics, will notify the appropriate Federal agencies so that such studies may be considered and priorities assigned. The FDA budget does not provide for developmental research in support of marketed products because the law places this burden upon the proponent or manufacturer....

In conjunction with the proposal to place certain products in Category IIIA and in view of the Panel's conclusions concerning the effectiveness of Category IIIA drugs, the Commissioner proposed that (1) the circular and promotional material for these drugs must have a prominent boxed statement referencing the need for further data to fully establish effectiveness; (2) written informed consent be obtained from participants in the requisite additional studies, an explanation of the product and the purpose of the study be given to such participants, and a clear opportunity be provided to them to refuse to participate in the study; and (3) a printed patient insert be included with all Category IIIA Bacterial Vaccines and Bacterial Antigens which have been designated as having "No U.S. Standard of Potency" continued in interstate commerce....

As the Commissioner noted in the proposal, the conclusion by an expert panel that the data in support of the products' safety and effectiveness are currently insufficient is a material fact within the meaning of section 201(n) of the Federal Food, Drug, and Cosmetic Act and the failure to disclose this fact is misleading, resulting in the products being misbranded. Moreover, the Commissioner believes that it is essential that patients and physicians be aware of the lack of controlled studies in support of a product.... However, the Commissioner had decided that the adoption of the boxed warning and written informed consent for participants in studies conducted on Category IIIA products (§ 601.25(h)(4) and (5)) should be promulgated upon specific notice to those persons affected by the review of each category of biological products. Accordingly, this final order imposes these requirements for Bacterial Vaccines and Bacterial Antigens with "No U.S. Standard of Potency" only....

Three comments from manufacturers and manufacturer associations stated that § 610.25(h)(6) should not be amended to require a printed patient insert because the presence of a printed patient insert may result in the patient's refusal to take medications bearing such labeling. One comment stated that FDA has no legal authority to require such patient labeling....

These products are administered repeatedly and over long periods of time. The medical profession generally recognizes that other therapies are available for the conditions for which these products are used. There is no present assurance that persons treated with these products are being made aware of the potential for risk or of the availability of alternative modes of treatment....

The Commissioner notes, and concurs with the Panel's finding regarding, the specific characteristics of these products which distinguish them from other licensed biologics and from other drugs, and which therefore make it necessary, in the judgment of the Panel and the Commissioner, to provide information to prospective users....

NOTES

1. *Comparison to OTC Drug Review.* The procedures of the OTC Drug Review, 21 C.F.R. Part 330, make no provision for a Category IIIB, a box labeling statement for Category III products, or written informed consent for clinical investigations of Category III products, and they require an oral hearing before the Commissioner in addition to informal rulemaking on the agency's proposed implementation of the Review panels' recommendations. As

a result of legal challenges to its procedures for the OTC Drug Review, p. 605 *supra*, FDA revised the regulations governing the Biologics Review to provide for the reclassification of Category IIIA products into either Category I or Category II, 46 Fed. Reg. 4634 (January 16, 1981), 47 Fed. Reg. 44062 (October 5, 1982).

2. *Skin Test Antigens.* FDA's proposals based on the report of the panel on skin test antigens were published in 42 Fed. Reg. 52674 (September 30, 1977), and its final actions in 44 Fed. Reg. 40284 (July 10, 1979). FDA issued a notice of opportunity for hearing on revocation of product licenses in 42 Fed. Reg. 56800 (October 28, 1977), and published its final actions on those licenses in 43 Fed. Reg. 50250 (October 27, 1978). On the basis of further testing, one product was reclassified from Category IIIA to Category I, 46 Fed. Reg. 51036 (October 16, 1981).

3. *Viral and Rickettsial Vaccines.* FDA proposed implementation of the recommendations of the panel on viral and rickettsial vaccines in 45 Fed. Reg. 25652 (April 15, 1980). Final action was announced in 47 Fed. Reg. 24696 (June 8, 1982). Licenses were revoked in 45 Fed. Reg. 65675 (October 3, 1980), 46 Fed. Reg. 10014 (January 30, 1981).

4. *Bacterial Vaccines and Toxoids.* FDA proposed implementation of the report of the panel on bacterial vaccines and toxoids with a standard of potency in 50 Fed. Reg. 51002 (December 13, 1985), and published a notice of opportunity for hearing on the revocation of product licenses in 52 Fed. Reg. 11123 (April 7, 1987).

5. *Allergenic Extracts.* FDA proposed implementation of the report of the panel on allergenic extracts in 50 Fed. Reg. 3082 (January 23, 1985), and published a notice of opportunity for hearing on the revocation of product licenses in 50 Fed. Reg. 32314 (August 9, 1985).

6. *Blood Products.* FDA proposed implementation of the report of the panel on blood and blood derivatives in 50 Fed. Reg. 52602 (December 24, 1985).

7. *Investigational Biologics.* An investigational biological drug is subject to the investigational new drug provisions of section 505(i) of the FD&C Act, but IND submissions are made to the Center for Biologics Evaluation and Research. To avoid regulatory duplication, 21 C.F.R. § 310.4(a) provides that a biological drug that has been licensed under the Biologics Act need not also have an approved NDA under section 505 of the FD&C Act.

C. BLOOD AND BLOOD PRODUCTS

1. REGULATORY JURISDICTION

The court in *United States v. Calise*, 217 F.Supp. 705 (S.D.N.Y. 1962), addressed the central issue of the basis of Federal jurisdiction to regulate blood products:

> The voluminous eighty count indictment ... charges defendants ... with several types of violations of the Public Health Service Act and the Federal Food, Drug and Cosmetic Act, and a conspiracy to violate those statutes....
>
> The defendants ... allege that the indictment fails to state an offense against the United States in that 21 U.S.C. § 321(g)

is unconstitutional. It is claimed that the definition of "drugs" appearing therein is so "indefinite and uncertain that it contains no ascertainable standard of guilt thereby violating the first essential of due process of law." ... Section 312(g)(2) defines drugs as "articles intended for use in the diagnosis, cure, mitigation, treatment, or prevention of disease in man or other animals." There can be no question but that the defendants dealt in blood products for their use in the treatment of human disease. I, therefore, hold that the whole human blood referred to in the indictment would constitute a "drug" within the meaning of the statute. The language of Section 321(g)(2) clearly complies with the test of constitutionality. It gives adequate warning to ordinarily intelligent persons as to what manner of conduct is prohibited....

The defendants in *Calise* were not unique in attempting to confine federal jurisdiction over their activities to the provisions of the Public Health Service Act. In a case involving the purported cancer cure, Krebiozen, the drug's proponents argued unsuccessfully that it was a biological product and thus not subject to the FD&C Act. *Rutherford v. American Medical Ass'n,* 379 F.2d 641 (7th Cir. 1967).

Prior to 1970, the Biologics Act did not expressly include blood products, and two cases decided in the 1960s reached conflicting results on the issue. In *United States v. Steinschreiber,* 219 F.Supp. 373 (S.D.N.Y.1963), *aff'd per curiam,* 326 F.2d 759 (2d Cir.1964), the court held that human blood plasma is analogous to a therapeutic serum and is thus properly regulated under the Biologics Act. The court also concluded that processing and drying liquid blood constitute sufficient steps in the "manufacture" or "preparation" of the final product to subject the activities to the Act. *See also United States v. Steinschreiber,* 218 F.Supp. 426 (S.D.N.Y.1962). *Blank v. United States,* 400 F.2d 302 (5th Cir.1968), however, held that citrated whole blood (human) and packed red blood cells (human) are not analogous to a therapeutic serum. The court concluded that only immunological agents were covered by the Biologics Act, though it sustained the defendant's conviction under the FD&C Act for interstate shipment of a misbranded drug.

Following the decision in the *Blank* case, Congress amended the Biologics Act in 1970 specifically to include vaccines, blood, blood components or derivatives, and allergenic products, 84 Stat. 1297, 1308.

NOTES

1. *In Vitro Tests.* In 38 Fed. Reg. 1404 (January 12, 1973), FDA published a notice in which it concluded that the Biologics Act covers a lysate prepared from the circulating blood cells (amebocytes) of the horseshoe crab, which has been shown to be a sensitive indicator of the presence of bacterial endotoxins and thus is useful both as an *in vitro* test in detecting clinical endotoxemia and

for the detection of bacterial endotoxins (pyrogens) in biological products and other drugs or fluids for human parenteral administration.

2.   *Commentary.* For a discussion of the interrelationship between medical science and regulation in the licensing of just one blood product, *see* Swisher, *The Introduction of Adenine Fortified Blood Preservatives,* 17 Transfusion, No. 4, at 309 (1977).

---

2.   THE REGULATORY MECHANISM

MICHAEL RODELL,* OVERVIEW OF THE REGULATORY PROCESS IN THE MANUFACTURE OF PLASMA AND PLASMA DERIVATIVES

34 Food Drug Cosmetic Law Journal 208 (1979).

The production of plasma derivatives, such as Antihemophilic Factor, Normal Serum Albumin, and various Immune Globulins, is regulated by ... FDA under both the Federal Food, Drug, and Cosmetic Act and the Public Health Service Act....

As authorized by the Public Health Service Act, the Agency is empowered to grant and revoke Establishment Licenses and Product Licenses, both of which are required in order to manufacture and distribute biological products. Consequently, the FDA has a control mechanism available to itself, that is, license revocation, in biological product manufacture that is not available in the case of non-biological drug and device manufacture....

Obviously, the primary source material in the production of plasma derivatives is plasma. The great majority of plasma used by fractionators is obtained from plasmapheresis centers, who manufacture a licensed biological product, Source Plasma (Human). Thus, we have a unique situation in which a raw material is subject to many of the same regulatory requirements as is the final product. A significant quantity of plasma also is obtained from community blood banks as Recovered Plasma, that is, plasma separated from indate or outdate whole blood. This type of plasma may be obtained only if the manufacturer and the blood bank have executed a Short Supply Agreement, which effectively places a regulatory burden on the manufacturer to assure himself that plasma is collected in a satisfactory manner.

As mentioned earlier, no biological product can be distributed in interstate commerce unless the manufacturer holds a valid Establishment License and a Product License for the product involved. The Establishment License Application includes information relevant to the manufacturer's buildings and facilities, and delineates in detailed fashion those areas involved in each phase of manufacturing. It also

---

* [Then Director of Regulatory Affairs and
Clinical Development at the Highland Division, Travenol Labs, Inc.]

includes pertinent information regarding the Responsible Head of the Establishment, who is to exercise control of the Establishment in all matters relating to compliance with the regulations. The Responsible Head represents the Establishment in all pertinent matters with the Bureau, and must have authority to enforce or direct the enforcement of discipline and performance of activities by employees....

A Product License Application would include detailed information as to where and how a product is processed, tested, packaged and labeled. Data demonstrating product safety and efficacy would be submitted in support of the application, as would samples of the product itself. Major or significant changes in either type of application require advance filing of amendment requests; such changes generally cannot be implemented prior to receiving written approval from the Bureau of Biologics.

Each facility involved in the manufacture of biological products is inspected annually by members of the Bureau of Biologics, or, in the case of licensed blood banks and plasmapheresis centers, by FDA field personnel....

Unless specifically exempted, samples of each lot of biological product must be submitted to the Bureau of Biologics, along with a signed copy of test results, prior to the distribution of the lot.... Upon receipt of written notification of release, the manufacturer may then distribute the lot. Material not meeting the Bureau's standards is rejected, and may not be distributed.

The Product License files for biological products also include labeling, which is subject to review and approval by the Bureau of Biologics.... [A]ny proposed revision in product labeling must be submitted to and approved by the Agency prior to being used.

Another powerful control tool is the Bureau's authority to promulgate regulations and standards. Whereas regulations can cover a wide range of activities, from how a sterility or general safety test is performed to good manufacturing practices, standards are generally confined to an individual product or group of products and delineate acceptable criteria for such products. Standards may include potency and purity requirements for a product, and how to determine such parameters; they may include source material requirements; they may include required processing steps.....

One of the major effects of this rigorous control system is the loss of valuable and costly time in being able to distribute biological products.... It is not unusual to file a Product License Application or an amendment to an existing license, and have several months elapse before receiving any substantial response from the Agency, other than an assignment of a reference number. Labeling reviews may take 60 days or longer.... Most serious, however, are the problems associated with batch release of biological products. Under the best of conditions, release times may be as minimal as 3 weeks.... A great number of plasma derivative products experience 8 week release times; one product line has an average release time of 5 months. . . .

FD&C ACT REQUIREMENTS APPLICABLE TO
BLOOD PRODUCTS

Following the transfer of the Biologics Act to FDA on July 1, 1972, several provisions of the FD&C Act were applied to blood products as well as to other biological products:

1. *Establishment Registration and Inspection.* FDA required registration of blood establishments, 37 Fed. Reg. 17419 (August 26, 1972), 38 Fed. Reg. 2965 (January 31, 1973), 40 Fed. Reg. 52788 (November 12, 1975), 21 C.F.R. Part 607. *See also* 45 Fed. Reg. 19316 (March 25, 1980), 45 Fed. Reg. 64601 (September 30, 1980), 45 Fed. Reg. 85727 (December 30, 1980), 49 Fed. Reg. 34448 (August 31, 1984). The frequency of the inspection of blood establishments was changed from at least once every year to at least once every two years, 47 Fed. Reg. 32953 (July 30, 1982), 48 Fed. Reg. 26313 (June 7, 1983). Alternative procedures governing the regulation of blood and blood products were promulgated in 54 Fed. Reg. 30093 (July 18, 1989), 55 Fed. Reg. 10420 (March 21, 1990).

2. *Good Manufacturing Practice.* FDA promulgated regulations governing current good manufacturing practices (GMP) in the collection, processing, and storage of human blood and blood components, 39 Fed. Reg. 18614 (May 28, 1974), 40 Fed. Reg. 53532 (November 18, 1975). Additional record-keeping requirements were first proposed, 41 Fed. Reg. 18095 (April 30, 1976), then withdrawn as unnecessary, 43 Fed. Reg. 59098 (December 19, 1978). *See* 21 C.F.R. Part 606. By combining the jurisdictional and regulatory provisions of the Biologics Act and the FD&C Act, FDA brought all blood and blood products produced and used in the United States under uniform Federal requirements. FDA has extended its blood GMP regulations to apply to unlicensed blood products that are used as components of medical devices, 53 Fed. Reg. 23414 (June 22, 1988), 54 Fed. Reg. 24706 (June 9, 1989).

3. *Advertising of Biologicals.* In 39 Fed. Reg. 43654 (December 17, 1974), FDA advised that advertising for prescription biological products is subject to section 502(n) of the FD&C Act and the implementing regulations in 21 C.F.R. Part 202.

4. *Container Regulation.* Responsibility for regulation of containers for collection or processing of blood and blood components, with or without ingredients such as anticoagulant solutions, was established in 40 Fed. Reg. 33971 (August 13, 1975).

5. *Package Inserts.* In 1978, FDA announced a guideline for the physician package insert for Immune Serum Globulin (Human), to promote consistency in the format and content of package inserts. 43 Fed. Reg. 15779 (April 14, 1978).

6. *Adverse Reaction Reports.* In 44 Fed. Reg. 24233 (April 24, 1979), FDA announced the availability of a draft of a proposed regulation requiring records and reports of adverse reactions and product experiences involving licensed biological products, and a proposal and accompanying draft guideline modeled after the NDA requirements were published in 55 Fed. Reg. 11611 and 11655 (March 29, 1990). Regulations requiring the submission of error and accident reports by licensed and unlicensed blood establishments were proposed in 45 Fed. Reg. 52821 (August 8, 1980) but had not been promulgated as of June 30, 1990.

7. *Plasma Volume Expanders.* Responsibility for regulation of plasma volume expanders was established in the Bureau of Biologics in 44 Fed. Reg. 54043 (September 18, 1979).

8. *Plasma Exchange.* Plasma derived from therapeutic plasma exchange was subjected to FDA regulation in 48 Fed. Reg. 14048 (April 1, 1983).

9. *Investigational Blood Products.* FDA clarified the relationship between the Biologics Act and section 505(i) of the FD&C Act insofar as they relate to investigational products in 45 Fed. Reg. 73922 (November 7, 1980).

10. *Prescription Labeling.* FDA explicitly required the standard prescription legend to be included in the labeling of all prescription biological products, 46 Fed. Reg. 40212 (August 7, 1981), 47 Fed. Reg. 22518 (May 25, 1982).

SAFETY STANDARDS FOR BLOOD PRODUCTS

The complex relationship between modern medical science and FDA safety regulation is nowhere more evident than in many of the regulations for blood products promulgated during the past two decades:

1. *Platelet Concentrate.* Standards for Platelet Concentrate (Human): 36 Fed. Reg. 6835 (April 9, 1971), 39 Fed. Reg. 2008 (January 16, 1974), 40 Fed. Reg. 4300 (January 29, 1975), 42 Fed. Reg. 10982 (February 25, 1977), 45 Fed. Reg. 2852 (January 15, 1980), 45 Fed. Reg. 27926 (April 25, 1980), 45 Fed. Reg. 45924 (July 8, 1980), 47 Fed. Reg. 49017 (October 29, 1982).

2. *Serum Albumin and Plasma Protein Fraction.* Standards for Normal Serum Albumin (Human) and Plasma Protein Fraction (Human): 37 Fed. Reg. 12505, 12506 (June 24, 1972), 40 Fed. Reg. 7456 (February 20, 1975), 42 Fed. Reg. 27575 (May 31, 1977), 42 Fed. Reg. 44228 (September 2, 1977), 48 Fed. Reg. 19897 (May 3, 1983), 48 Fed. Reg. 34480 (July 29, 1983), 49 Fed. Reg. 1685 (January 13, 1984), 49 Fed. Reg. 2243 (January 19, 1984).

3. *Plasmapheresis.* FDA regulations for the collection and manufacture by plasmapheresis of plasma to be used in the preparation of products made by fractionation, and standards for a product defined as Source Plasma (Human): 37 Fed. Reg. 17419 (August 26, 1972), 38 Fed. Reg. 19362 (July 20, 1973), 39 Fed. Reg. 35187 (September 30, 1974), 41 Fed. Reg. 10762 (March 12, 1976), 42 Fed. Reg. 18129 (April 5, 1977), 42 Fed. Reg. 25381 (May 17, 1977). FDA amended its regulations to provide further protection to plasmapheresis donors, 39 Fed. Reg. 26161 (July 17, 1974), 41 Fed. Reg. 10762 (March 12, 1976). *See also* 42 Fed. Reg. 25339 (May 17, 1977), 43 Fed. Reg. 9804 (March 10, 1978), 45 Fed. Reg. 28359 (April 29, 1980), 45 Fed. Reg. 79092 (November 28, 1980), 45 Fed. Reg. 80500 (December 5, 1980), 46 Fed. Reg. 49204 (October 6, 1981), 46 Fed. Reg. 57480 (November 24, 1981), 47 Fed. Reg. 30968 (July 16, 1982). Guidelines for immunizing Source Plasma (Human) donors with Red Blood Cells (Human) were announced in 42 Fed. Reg. 25381 (May 17, 1977), and revised in 43 Fed. Reg. 19461 (May 5, 1978). The agency promulgated regulations to permit the preparation of Cryoprecipitated Antihemophilic Factor (Human) from plasma obtained by plasmapheresis, and to prescribe criteria for donor suitability, collection, and testing of source material to protect the donor and assure the integrity of the source material, 40 Fed. Reg. 41799 (September 9, 1975), 42 Fed. Reg. 21772 (April 29, 1977), 42 Fed. Reg. 37545 (July 22, 1977), 45 Fed. Reg. 22975 (April 4, 1980), 45 Fed. Reg. 28358 (April 29, 1980), 45 Fed. Reg. 45924 (July 8, 1980), 47 Fed. Reg. 15329 (April 9, 1982).

4. *Blood Grouping Serum.* Standards for Blood Grouping Serum: 38 Fed. Reg. 31312 (November 13, 1973), 40 Fed. Reg. 52623 (November 11, 1975), 42 Fed. Reg. 54534 (October 7, 1977), 42 Fed. Reg. 61257 (December 2, 1977), 43 Fed. Reg. 19844 (May 9, 1978), 46 Fed. Reg. 35122 (July 7, 1981), 47 Fed. Reg. 22519 (May 25, 1982), 50 Fed. Reg. 8743 (March 5, 1985), 53 Fed. Reg. 12760 (April 19, 1988).

5. *Single Donor Plasma.* Standards for Single Donor Plasma (Human) Products: 40 Fed. Reg. 52619 (November 11, 1975), 42 Fed. Reg. 59873 (November 22, 1977).

6. *Reagent Red Blood Cells.* Standards for Reagent Red Blood Cells: 40 Fed. Reg. 52621 (November 11, 1975), 43 Fed. Reg. 10554 (March 14, 1978), 50 Fed. Reg. 24542 (June 11, 1985).

7. *Additives to Whole Human Blood.* Addition of citrate phosphate dextrose adenine (CPDA) to the list of approved anticoagulants for Whole Blood (Human), and products derived from Whole Blood (Human): 43 Fed. Reg. 2890 (January 20, 1978), 43 Fed. Reg. 34457 (August 4, 1978), 45 Fed. Reg. 72422 (October 31, 1980), 48 Fed. Reg. 33494 (July 22, 1983).

8. *Blood Group Substances.* Standards for Blood Group Substances A, B, and AB: 43 Fed. Reg. 11716 (March 21, 1978), 44 Fed. Reg. 20673 (April 6, 1979), 45 Fed. Reg. 72422 (October 31, 1980), 48 Fed. Reg. 33494 (July 22, 1983).

9. *General FDA Regulations.* FDA proposed a complete reorganization and revision of all of its regulations for blood products in 45 Fed. Reg. 72422 (October 31, 1980) and reviewed all of the current blood regulations at a public meeting announced in 47 Fed. Reg. 12358 (March 23, 1982). It later withdrew the full proposal, 48 Fed. Reg. 33494 (July 22, 1983), and implemented only parts of it. FDA changed the "proper name" of various blood products in 50 Fed. Reg. 4128 (January 29, 1985) and revised its labeling requirements to clarify them and make them more uniform in 50 Fed. Reg. 35458 (August 30, 1985).

10. *Blood Bank Regulation.* FDA and HCFA executed a Memorandum of Understanding, published in 45 Fed. Reg. 19316 (March 25, 1980), to coordinate their inspection of blood banks and transfusion services. FDA exempted from its establishment registration requirements all transfusion services and clinical laboratories that are regulated by HCFA under Medicare, 45 Fed. Reg. 64601 (September 30, 1980), 45 Fed. Reg. 85727 (December 30, 1980). HCFA in turn adopted FDA's blood regulations, 46 Fed. Reg. 41059 (August 14, 1981), to assure uniform and efficient regulation of these facilities.

11. *Enforcement of FDA Regulations.* FDA has expended substantial efforts to enforce its regulations for blood products. *See, e.g.,* the notices revoking the establishment and product licenses for blood products in 42 Fed. Reg. 24328, 24329 (May 13, 1977), 43 Fed. Reg. 44887, 44888 (September 29, 1978), 43 Fed. Reg. 59905 (December 22, 1978), 44 Fed. Reg. 24235 (April 24, 1979), 45 Fed. Reg. 42376 (June 24, 1980), 44 Fed. Reg. 46317 (August 7, 1979), 47 Fed. Reg. 20192 (May 11, 1982), 47 Fed. Reg. 51626 (November 16, 1982), 48 Fed. Reg. 6780 (February 15, 1983), 49 Fed. Reg. 6573 (February 22, 1984), 49 Fed. Reg. 27626 (July 5, 1984), 50 Fed. Reg. 33415 (August 19, 1985), 52 Fed. Reg. 32845 (August 31, 1987), 53 Fed. Reg. 23453 (June 22, 1988), and 54 Fed. Reg. 22018 (May 22, 1989). Convictions for violating FDA's blood regulations were upheld in *United States v. Diaz,* 690 F.2d 1352 (11th Cir. 1982).

3. SAFETY OF DONATED BLOOD

WHOLE BLOOD AND RED BLOOD CELLS: LABEL STATEMENT TO DISTINGUISH VOLUNTEER FROM PAID BLOOD DONORS

40 Federal Register 53040 (November 14, 1975).

... [A] DHEW task force ... identified the major problem areas in the existing blood collection and distribution system and made recommendations that were incorporated into a National Blood Policy published in the FEDERAL REGISTER of March 8, 1974 (39 FR 9326)....

... The National Blood Policy recognizes that reliance upon commercial sources of blood and blood components for transfusion therapy has contributed to a significantly disproportionate incidence of hepatitis, since such blood is often collected from sectors of society in which transmissible hepatitis is more prevalent. For this reason, the National Blood Policy encourages efforts to bring into being an all-voluntary blood donation system and to eliminate commercialism in the acquisition of whole blood and whole blood components.... For over 25 years numerous health-related organizations have been committed to encouraging a voluntary blood donation system .....

Viral hepatitis, type B, is a disease marked by acute liver dysfunction with malaise, anorexia, nausea and vomiting, enlargement of the liver and jaundice, usually self-limited in course but sometimes leading to chronic liver disease and death. The disease may be transmitted to patients by transfusion of blood plasma or serum infected with hepatitis B virus. Hepatitis B surface Antigen (HB_SAg) is a component on the surface of the virus, and detection of HB_SAg in blood, plasma, or serum is a valid indication of the presence of hepatitis B virus. To reduce the risk of transmitting viral hepatitis, type B, [the] Food and Drug Administration has required, under § 610.40 (21 CFR 610.40), that each donation of human blood, plasma, or serum to be used in preparing a biological product be tested for the presence of HB_SAg. Section 610.41 (21 CFR 610.41) requires that those units found to be positive for HB_SAg cannot be used for manufacturing injectable biological products, including whole blood and red blood cells for transfusion, and donors who have tested positive may not serve as donors for any such products. Although there has been a continuing evolution of methodology towards more sensitive methods of detecting HB_SAg, the most sensitive methods presently available ... still do not detect the lowest level of HB_SAg in blood. Accordingly, the risk of transmitting viral hepatitis, type B, has been reduced but not eliminated.

The Commissioner is proposing labeling requirements for Whole Blood (Human) and Red Blood Cells (Human) that would distinguish blood from volunteer donors and blood from paid donors. The Commissioner concludes that the proposed labeling requirements will promote the use of blood from donors from sectors of society in which transmissible viral hepatitis, type B, is less prevalent, thereby reducing the risk of hepatitis associated with transfusion therapy. This finding is supported by the published data indicating that blood from donors from commercial blood banks is more likely to contain HB_SAg than blood from volunteer donors and that the incidence of posttransfusion hepatitis is significantly greater in recipients of blood from paid donors than from recipients of blood from volunteer donors.....

The proposed regulations require that the labeling for licensed and unlicensed whole blood and red blood cells distinguishes between paid and volunteer donors as the source of the blood and that the labels carry a warning regarding the higher risks of transmitting hepatitis from use of blood from paid donors. As has been shown, this information is a material fact about the quality of the blood and the potential adverse consequences of its use. Failure to reveal this fact would render the labeling misleading within the meaning of section 201(n) of the Federal Food, Drug, and Cosmetic Act and misbranded within the meaning of section 502(a).... Also, section 502(f) of the act requires adequate directions for use and adequate warnings. Blood from paid donors carries a greater risk of transmitting hepatitis than blood from volunteer donors, and a label statement is necessary to provide physicians adequate and clear warnings to be on sufficient notice of this fact.

The jurisdiction of the act is not limited to situations where the drug itself has been, or is to be, introduced into interstate commerce. Consistent with section 201(g)(1)(D) of the act, if one of the drug's essential components such as the anticoagulant solution has moved in interstate commerce, the entire drug is subject to the requirements of the act and the FDA may regulate the final drug product....

Pursuant to section 351(d) of the Public Health Service Act, regulations may be promulgated to assure proper labeling for many biological products, including licensed blood products such as Whole Blood (Human) and Red Blood Cells (Human). These proposed labeling requirements are authorized by this provision of the act.

In addition, section 351(b) of the Public Health Service Act prohibits the false labeling or marking of any package or container of any biological product, such as Whole Blood (Human) and Red Blood Cells (Human). The false labeling provisions of both acts were designed to accomplish substantially the same result, and the Commissioner concludes that they should be so interpreted and applied. Significantly, section 351(b) contains no interstate commerce requirement. It applies to all blood, whether or not it has moved or is offered for sale in interstate commerce. These statutory provisions also authorize standards for labeling for all whole blood and red blood cells in interstate and intrastate commerce. Blood from paid donors is more dangerous, in that it is more likely to result in post-transfusion hepatitis, than blood from volunteer donors. Accordingly, whole blood and red blood cells collected from paid donors are "falsely labeled or marked" when their labels do not contain explicit warnings and affirmative statements as to their collection from paid donors or volunteer donors.

Pursuant to section 361 of the Public Health Service Act (42 U.S.C. § 264) ... the Commissioner of Food and Drugs is authorized to promulgate regulations for any measures that, in his judgment, may be necessary to prevent the introduction, transmission, or spread of blood-related communicable disease from one state to another. Of necessity, this authority must be exercised upon the disease-causing substance within the state where it is collected, manufactured, or otherwise found. Thus, the Commissioner may promulgate regulations for intra-state blood labeling pursuant to the act, as hepatitis is a communicable disease....

After requesting information for use in the formulation of a definition for "paid" and "volunteer" blood donors, 41 Fed. Reg. 4955 (February 3, 1976), and conducting a public meeting, 41 Fed. Reg. 8523 (February 27, 1976), FDA issued a reproposal, 42 Fed. Reg. 11018 (February 25, 1977), and subsequently promulgated final regulations, which included the following introduction.

WHOLE BLOOD AND COMPONENTS OF WHOLE BLOOD INTENDED FOR TRANSFUSION; DONOR CLASSIFICATION LABELING REQUIREMENTS

43 Federal Register 2142 (January 13, 1978).

The February 1977 proposal differed from the November 1975 proposal in that it made the labeling requirements applicable to all blood components intended for transfusion rather than to only whole blood and red blood cells. The February 1977 proposal did not, however, repropose the warning statement concerning the increased risks of hepatitis from blood collected from paid donors....

Nineteen comments suggested that the term "paid" donor include a person who receives: (1) a large amount of time off from work, (2) additional vacation time, (3) rewards generally used as a motivation for donation, such as lotteries, giveaways, a chance interest in a prize with significant dollar value, or nonmonetary rewards associated with product promotion, (4) reduction or cancellation of hospital charges that are unrelated to the transfusion, and (5) the cancellation or refund of nonreplacement fees and blood assurance/insurance benefits.

... [T]he high risk of posttransfusion hepatitis associated with blood from paid donors primarily reflects the fact that direct monetary payment attracts and motivates donations from individuals in unfortunate socio-economic circumstances in whom transmissible hepatitis is particularly prevalent, including drug addicts who are in desperate need of money to purchase drugs. Benefits which are not readily convertible to cash such as those identified in the comments, are not likely to attract those groups in which transmissible hepatitis is prevalent. For this reason, the Commissioner concludes that donors receiving such benefits should not be classified as paid donors.....

... Some large institutional blood banks, such as hospitals and community blood banks, screen paid donors so that they have a lower incidence of HB_sAg than do some volunteer donor populations.....

Twelve comments suggested that the Commissioner require the donor classification statement to be changed to "first time donor" or "repeat donor" instead of "paid donor" or "volunteer donor" because the risk of hepatitis in blood from first time donors, whether paid or volunteer, is greater than the risk from repeat donors, whose blood has already been biologically tested, i.e., followup monitoring of the recipient has shown no hepatitis transmission....

The Commissioner recognizes that a small proportion of "paid donor" blood is being obtained from biologically tested donors whose hepatitis risk is as low as or lower than that from random volunteer donors. In those few situations, mechanisms are available for informing hospital administrators, physicians, and patients. The mechanisms include information in the package circular accompanying the blood unit and agreements between the blood bank and the purchasing hospitals and physicians.....

... If identification of donor source is required for both paid and volunteer donors, an unlabeled unit will not result in unjustified reliance, and the recipient will be on notice to check with the collecting facility. In addition, the affirmative disclosure of the donor source on blood labeling will serve to inform patient consumers, who are not as likely as hospital administrators and physicians to be current on Federal labeling laws for blood and blood products. The Commissioner reiterates his belief, stated in the preamble to the February 25, 1977 proposal, that any cost increase resulting from the proposed labeling requirement will be minimal. All whole blood products for transfusion must bear a label with significant information. The donor classification can be included on the labels along with the currently required information and incorporated as new labels are printed.....

Four States with effective blood labeling laws—Illinois, California, Georgia, and Florida—do not require an additional warning statement. The experiences in these States, particularly in Illinois where this law has been in effect for several years, support the necessity for only a brief descriptive term without an explicit warning of the probability of infection....

Twenty-nine comments suggested that the proposed labeling is unnecessary and should be withdrawn since (1) no scientific data have been presented to support the fact that a label will insure the safety of transfused blood, (2) no information has been presented to show that the labeling will significantly reduce the number of blood units which transmit disease, and (3) the rule is a superficial answer to a serious medical problem and therefore will not contribute to the solution.... The Commissioner disagrees with these comments. As a result of the 1973 Illinois law that all blood collected in or transported into the State must prominently display whether it was collected from paid or volunteer donors, the number of units of purchased blood infused decreased by 35.2 percent despite a 15 percent increase in the number of transfusions (fiscal 1974 to fiscal 1975). Furthermore, the percentage of outdated blood fell from 15.4 percent to 12.9 percent in the same period.

In a study conducted at the Hines Veterans' Administration Hospital, Chicago, Ill., 20.8 percent of transfused patients developed posttransfusion hepatitis from 1968–70, when 92 percent of the hospital blood supply was obtained from paid donors. However, the incidence of hepatitis decreased by 62 percent, to a rate of 7.9 percent of transfused patients, when 96 percent of the hospital's blood supply was obtained from volunteer donors. Similarly, in New Jersey, during a period in which the proportion of blood obtained from paid donors decreased from 31 percent (1970) to 9 percent (1973), the number of overt cases of posttransfusion hepatitis decreased from 424 (1 per 117 transfused patients) (1970) to 159 (1 per 284 transfused patients) (1973). In addition, during 1961–70 and 1971–73, the rate of fatalities resulting from posttransfusion hepatitis decreased from 12.9 percent to 7.2 percent, respectively. The Commissioner believes that these experiences, reported in November 1975, demonstrate that the paid and volunteer labeling significantly aids in reducing the incidence of posttransfusion hepatitis, and that it also promotes blood therapy safety and is therefore a valid, albeit partial, answer to the problem.....

Seven comments suggested that the proposed rules, if adopted, would make it more difficult to maintain adequate supplies of blood. This concern is based on the following assertions: (1) the 1973 Illinois blood labeling law forced that State to import volunteer blood while sending paid blood collected in Illinois to other States, (2) The General Accounting Office has reported (MWD–82) that the proposed labeling "could cause blood shortages," and (3) in Los Angeles, Calif., where a similar blood labeling law is in effect, hospitals in affluent areas meet their needs exclusively with volunteer blood, at the expense of hospitals serving areas of lower socio-economic status, which are forced to rely heavily on blood from less desirable sources. The comments postulated that in the absence of sufficient voluntary blood to replace the paid blood sources, hospitals will be faced with critical blood shortages and not be able to meet the total blood needs of the disadvantaged sections of society they serve....

Donor classification legislation is now effective in the states of Illinois, California, Florida, and Georgia. The longest experience with such legislation, in Illinois, does not support the contention that shortages in the blood supply will result because of the donor classification requirement. Indeed, the number of units collected from voluntary donors in Illinois increased sufficiently after the enactment of the donor classification legislation to provide adequately for all needs for blood within the State.

The cost-to-benefit balance of this regulation seems beyond serious question. . . .

NOTE

See generally A.W. Drake *et al.*, THE AMERICAN BLOOD SUPPLY (1982); R. Eckert and E.L. Wallace, SECURING A SAFER BLOOD SUPPLY: TWO VIEWS (1985); GAO, PROBLEMS IN CARRYING OUT THE NATIONAL BLOOD POLICY, HRD–77–150 (1979); OTA, BLOOD POLICY & TECHNOLO-GY, OTA–H–260 (January 1985). Even before the emergence of AIDS, regulation of the safety of the blood supply was a difficult challenge. *See* Donohue, *Blood and Blood Products: A Five Year Challenge,* 36 FDC L.J. 27 (1981).

4. PROTECTING THE BLOOD SUPPLY IN THE ERA OF AIDS

Acquired Immune Deficiency Syndrome (AIDS) destroys the body's natural ability to fight disease, leaving its victims vulnerable to dangerous infections, cancer, and other diseases. Although its origin remains uncertain, AIDS was identified as a distinct disease in 1979, and was first diagnosed in a patient in the United States in 1981. By 1983, it had become apparent that blood donated by AIDS patients spread the disease, and FDA advised plasma centers and blood banks throughout the country to screen out donors who were at increased risk from AIDS as an interim measure until specific laboratory tests could be developed to screen donated blood. HHS News No. P83–6 (March 25, 1983). As early as November 1983, blood products had to be withdrawn from the market because units of plasma used in the pool from which the products were manufactured had been obtained from a donor who subsequently died of AIDS. "Withdrawal of AHF—AIDS," FDA Talk Paper No. T83–44 (November 1, 1983).

After scientists at the National Cancer Institute and in France isolated the AIDS virus in April 1984, several companies began developing tests to screen blood to detect antibodies that would indicate exposure to the virus, known at that time as HTLV–III (for "human T-lymphotropic virus type III"). This terminology was later supplanted by "human immunodeficiency virus" (HIV), the term that is now used. Since discovery of a second AIDS virus in one U.S. patient in December 1987, this terminology has been further refined as HIV–1 and HIV–2. "HIV–2 Diagnosed in United States," FDA Talk Paper No. T88–10 (January 29, 1988).

NIH developed and patented a prototype screening test for antibodies to AIDS in April 1984 and, after soliciting applications in 49 Fed. Reg. 18899 (May 3, 1984), selected five companies in June 1984 to obtain FDA approval for and commercialize the test kits. The first tests used an enzyme-linked immunosorbent assay (ELISA) test. The first application for a biologics license was submitted to FDA in December 1984, and by March 1985 two licenses had been granted. HHS News No. P85–8 (March 4, 1985) and No. P85–9 (March 7, 1985). FDA immediately notified all blood facilities about the tests and scheduled a workshop on their use, 50 Fed. Reg. 28477 (July 12, 1985). It approved three more tests later in the year. "AIDS Antibody Test Approved," FDA Talk Paper No. T85–56 (October 21, 1985). Although these tests were developed to screen blood, they quickly began to be used to identify patients infected with AIDS.

In addition to these screening tests, a laboratory test, the Western Blot Assay, which employs a different technology, was used to confirm specimens found to be positive in the ELISA test. Initially a laboratory test, the Western Blot Assay was not subject to FDA approval at that time, "HTLV–III Antibody Test Licensing and Labeling—An Update," FDA Talk Paper No. T86–34 (May 13, 1986), but it was later approved by the agency to validate the results of the ELISA tests. "Update on AIDS Test Kits," FDA Talk Paper No. T87–48 (October 26, 1987).

By 1986, FDA concluded that it had sufficient experience with the new blood screening tests to propose testing of every unit of human blood and blood components intended for use in preparing any biological product. 51 Fed. Reg. 6362 (February 21, 1986). Regulations were not promulgated in final form until January 1988, 53 Fed. Reg. 111 (January 5, 1988), but use of the tests began with their initial availability in March 1985. In 1988 FDA reported:

> Since testing of the blood supply began, approximately 30 million units of whole blood have been screened for antibody to HIV. Several thousand infected donors have been identified using current test assays thus saving several thousand people who received blood and blood products from exposure to HIV.

"Study of Seven Donors of AIDS–Contaminated Blood," FDA Talk Paper No. T88–23 (February 25, 1988). In addition to requiring the use of blood screening tests, FDA has continued to work with blood banks to identify and screen out blood donors at increased risk of transmitting AIDS. *See, e.g.,* "New AIDS Blood Donor Guidelines," FDA Talk Paper No. T86–82 (November 21, 1986).

Not surprisingly, a market quickly developed for blood test kits for AIDS that could be used by laymen. FDA announced that no test kit had been approved for home use. "Unapproved AIDS Home Test Kits," FDA Talk Paper No. T87–35 (July 23, 1987). The agency announced that AIDS test kits would be approved "for professional use only," *i.e.,* that samples must be collected by authorized persons, a licensed screening test must be used, samples tested positive by a screening test must be confirmed by a Western Blot or comparable assay, and the result must be reported to a professional health care provider for interpretation and reporting to the person who was tested. "Status of AIDS

Home Test Kits," FDA Talk Paper No. T88–34 (May 10, 1988). Although home test kits are subject to regulation as medical devices, FDA concluded that the Center for Biologics should be responsible for their review when and if the agency permitted their use.

Following a number of recalls of blood and blood plasma in early 1988 because of possible AIDS contamination, FDA inspectors undertook in the following months to visit every registered United States blood bank and plasma center—2,424 establishments in all. Although 11 percent of the establishments were found to deviate to some degree from FDA regulations, no instance of transfusion with blood shown to contain the AIDS virus was found. "A Year of Blood Bank and Plasma Center Inspections," FDA Talk Paper No. T88–80 (November 1, 1988).

In 54 Fed. Reg. 24296 (June 6, 1989), FDA proposed to amend its blood regulations to require that every establishment or laboratory responsible for performing FDA-required HIV testing participate in an approved program to demonstrate proficiency in performing the test. Imposition of this requirement was one of the recommendations contained in the REPORT OF THE PRESIDENTIAL COMMISSION ON THE HUMAN IMMUNODEFICIENCY VIRUS EPIDEMIC 80–81 (June 1988), which President Reagan directed the Secretary of HHS to implement, 24 Week. Comp. of Pres. Doc. 1006 (1988). HCFA had previously proposed regulations for laboratories regulated under Medicare, Medicaid, and the Clinical Laboratories Improvement Act of 1967 (CLIA) to require uniform proficiency testing standards in 53 Fed. Reg. 29590 (August 5, 1988); the FDA proposal covered additional laboratories not covered by HCFA.

In 53 Fed. Reg. 46118 (November 16, 1988), FDA made available a draft "points to consider" regarding labeling and premarket submission of in vitro diagnostic devices for use in the home, and shortly thereafter, in 54 Fed. Reg. 7279 (February 17, 1989), announced an open public meeting to discuss whether FDA should approve blood collection kits and home test kits designed to detect the HIV antibody. The announcement reiterated the agency's position that none of these HIV antibody testing kits is "substantially equivalent" to any pre–1976 medical device and its policy that premarket approval would currently be granted only for professional use, subject to conditions previously announced. The public meeting was to consider whether this policy should be changed, and it provoked substantial controversy. *See* "Risks and Implications of AIDS–HIV testing in Nontraditional Laboratories and in the Home," Hearing before the Subcomm. on Regulation, Business Opportunities, and Energy of the House Comm. on Small Business, 101st Cong., 1st Sess. (1989). A year later, based upon the development of new technology, FDA announced that it would begin to review applications for approval of home test kits for AIDS. "Applications for AIDS Home test Kits," FDA Talk Paper No. T90–20 (April 30, 1990).

The ELISA diagnostic test licensed by FDA in 1984 to detect the presence of HIV actually detected the body's response to HIV, *i.e.*, the antibodies to the virus. In 54 Fed. Reg. 48943 (November 28, 1989), FDA issued draft "points to consider" in the manufacturer and clinical evaluation of in vitro diagnostic products to detect antibodies to HIV. In August 1989, FDA licensed the first diagnostic kit to detect the presence of HIV by directly detecting the proteins (antigens) of the virus itself. The product was approved to help physicians diagnose and treat HIV infected individuals, but not for use in screening blood. The theory that this test might detect the presence of HIV at an earlier point after infection was not borne out by extensive studies. "New AIDS Test Detects Antigens," FDA Talk Paper No. T89–49 (August 3, 1989).

The potential liability of participants in the blood collection and distribution system for transmission of AIDS to patients who receive blood transfusions has been a growing worry. *See, e.g.,* Sazama, *Legal and Regulatory Problems Facing Blood Suppliers,* 6 HealthSpan, No. 8, at 8 (September 1989). FDA has announced the availability of a guideline for collection of blood from high risk donors, for research and other special purposes, 55 Fed. Reg. 18030 (April 30, 1990).

Because FDA does not now regulate human organs or tissue except for blood, testing of prospective donors of transplantable materials for the presence of HIV antibody is not legally required. FDA and CDC have, however, recommended that such testing be undertaken before the use of any donated human materials. *Testing Donors of Organs, Tissue, and Semen for Antibody to Human T–Lymphotropic Virus Type III/Lymphadenopathy–Associated Virus,* 34 Morbidity and Mortality Weekly Report 294 (May 24, 1985); *Semen Banking, Organ and Tissue Transplantation, and HIV Antibody Testing,* 37 Morbidity and Mortality Weekly Report 57 (February 5, 1988).

In related actions OSHA has proposed regulations to control occupational exposure to bloodborne pathogens, including HIV, in 52 Fed. Reg. 45438 (November 27, 1987), 54 Fed. Reg. 23042 (May 30, 1989), and the Postal Service has undertaken to regulate the mailing of all etiologic agents, 53 Fed. Reg. 23775 (June 24, 1988), 54 Fed. Reg. 11970 (March 23, 1989), 54 Fed. Reg. 33523 (August 15, 1989).

D. ORGAN AND TISSUE TRANSPLANTS

The only human materials intended to be transferred from the body of one individual to another that are currently regulated by FDA (or, except by indirect funding restrictions, by any federal agency) are blood and its byproducts. Since 1960, however, transplantation of body organs (*e.g.,* heart, liver, and kidneys) and other human tissue (*e.g.,* skin, bone marrow, semen) has become common. In a statement submitted to a committee of Congress in 1983, but surprisingly not reprinted in the committee's published report, FDA officials explained why the agency does not seek to regulate these products.

STATEMENT BY THE FOOD AND DRUG ADMINISTRATION CONCERNING ITS LEGAL AUTHORITY TO REGULATE HUMAN ORGAN TRANSPLANTS AND TO PROHIBIT THEIR SALE

Hearing Before the Subcommittee on Investigations and Oversight,
House Committee on Science and Technology, 98th Congress, 1st Session (1983).

As technology has advanced in recent years, the transplantation of human organs has become more common and questions have arisen concerning the appropriateness of the commercialization of human organs and what role, if any, the government should play in the regulation of their sale and distribution. The Food and Drug Administration has never had occasion formally to address the issue of its authority to regulate the sale of human organs. This statement constitutes the FDA's first examination of that issue.

The Federal Food, Drug, and Cosmetic Act defines the term "drug" in part as "articles intended for use in the diagnosis, cure, mitigation, treatment, or prevention of disease in man ...;" and "articles (other than food) intended to affect the structure or any function of the body of man ... " 21 U.S.C. § 321(g)(1)(B) and (C). The Supreme Court has interpreted this definition to be " ... as broad as its literal language indicates—and ... broader than any strict medical definition might otherwise allow." *United States v. An Article of Drug ... Bacto–Unidisk,* 394 U.S. 784 (1968).

A human organ intended for use in transplantation arguably could be regulated as a drug because it falls within the literal language of these provisions. Although Congress could not have had human organ transplants in mind when it defined the term "drug" in 1938, the caselaw suggests that the definition is not limited to the types of substances used as drugs prior to 1938....

Although the caselaw has interpreted the term "drug" very broadly, no court has held that a human organ intended for use in transplantation is a drug. Such an interpretation, while arguably supportable, would extend the legal definition well beyond the traditional medical concept of the term "drug." The unprecedented nature of this interpretation necessarily means that considerable uncertainty would be associated with a conclusion by FDA that the definition of the term "drug" includes human organ transplants. Adding to this uncertainty is FDA's current administrative interpretation of the term "drug," which cannot be read to include human organs. That interpretation states: "[a] drug ... is a chemical or a combination of chemicals in liquid, paste, powder, or other drug dosage form that is ingested, or instilled into body orifices, or rubbed or poured onto the body in order to achieve its intended medical purpose." 47 FR 46139, (Oct. 15, 1982, Merck Sharp & Dohme Research Laboratories; Reclassification of Lacrisert as an Approved New Drug). Although this administrative interpretation would not be conclusive, it would be given deference by a reviewing court.

Section 201(h) of the FDC Act, as amended by the Medical Device Amendments of 1976, defines the term "device" as "an instrument, apparatus, implement, machine, contrivance, implant, in vitro reagent, or other similar or related article ... which is ... intended for use in the diagnosis of disease or other conditions, or in the cure, mitigation, treatment, or prevention of disease" or which is "intended to affect the structure or any function of the body," *and* "which does not achieve any of its principal intended purposes through chemical action within or on the body" or by "being metabolized." 21 U.S.C. 321(h). A human organ transplant could be regarded as within the literal language of the statute, for a transplanted organ is a type of "implant." If this interpretation were adopted, an organ transplant could be regulated as a device so long as the organ did not achieve any of its principal intended purposes through chemical action or by being metabolized.

On the other hand, the definition's list of things that are "devices" —"instrument, apparatus, implement, machine, contrivance, implant, in vitro reagent"—implies that Congress understood the term "device" to refer to the product of human artifice. Except for implants and in vitro reagents, the items in the list are man-made products that generally are constructed of materials such as metal or plastic. Although some devices regulated by FDA consist in part of organic material, the material is usually either a part of a man-made device, or it is treated to make it useful for its intended purpose rather than simply being substituted for its equivalent material in the human body. In vitro reagents often use organic material, but as part of a system designed to diagnose diseases or conditions. There are many man-made devices that are "implants." Cardiac pacemakers, artificial joints, and intraocular plastic lenses fall into this category. The legislative intent underlying the definition of "device" is, therefore, probably limited to artificial implants. This view is consistent with the principle of statutory construction that a word is known by the company it keeps (*noscitur a sociis*).

Further support for this view is found in the legislative history of the 1976 Amendments. The Amendments contain special provisions with respect to the classification of devices intended to be implanted into the human body. The legislative history of these provisions makes it plain that Congress had in mind man-made products, *e.g.*, heart pacemakers, intrauterine devices, and intraocular lenses. More generally, the legislative history of the 1976 Amendments reveals that Congress was well aware of the post-war revolution in biomedical technology that resulted in the introduction of a wide variety of sophisticated products, and meant to expand FDA's authority to regulate such man-made objects as devices; there is in the legislative history no indication that Congress gave any thought to whether a human organ intended for transplantation is a "device." Yet Congress surely was aware that human organs had been transplanted before 1976, when the Amendments became law, and also must have known that FDA did not regulate such organs as devices or drugs....

The Public Health Service Act, 42 U.S.C. 262, *et seq.,* ("the PHS Act") authorizes the licensure of a class of products that has come to be known as "biological products." Although the term is undefined, the Act includes the following as subject to licensure: " ... any virus, therapeutic serum, toxin, antitoxin, vaccine, blood, blood component or derivative, allergenic product, or analogous product ... applicable to the prevention, treatment, or cure of diseases or injuries of man...."

Whether a human organ transplant is a biological product depends on whether solid organs, such as the heart, liver, or kidneys, are "analogous" to blood or blood derivatives. If the term "analogous" is interpreted in its broadest sense, FDA arguably could regulate human organ transplants as biological products. Blood is essentially a liquid organ. Blood performs vital functions comparable to the functions performed by solid organs. Blood is composed of tissue cells, which are similar but not identical to the tissue cells of solid organs.

The legislative history of the PHS Act suggests, however, that a narrower interpretation of the term "analogous" would be more in keeping with the legislative design for the regulation of "biological products." The predecessor of the PHS Act, the Viruses, Serums, and Toxins Act of 1902 ("VSTA"), defined a biological product as "any virus, therapeutic serum, toxin, antitoxin, or analogous product." In 1970, Congress amended the VSTA by adding to the definition the terms "blood" and "blood component or derivative." The legislative history of the 1970 amendment states that Congress added these terms because " ... the products and processes involved in blood transfusions were not known in 1902 when the 'Virus–Toxin law,' which preceded section 351 [42 U.S.C. § 262(a)], was enacted ... [and] Congress [therefore] could not have intended that they be included." 116 Cong. Rec. 31017 (1970) (remarks of Sen. Dominick). Under this rationale, the definition of "analogous products" would be limited to those human organs for which transplantation had become known at the time of the enactment of the 1970 amendment to the VSTA. By 1970, kidney and bone marrow transplants had become fairly common and liver and heart transplants had been performed, but were still in the experimental stages.

Moreover, it is by no means clear that, by adding the words "blood, blood component or derivative," Congress intended to include as "analogous" products the entire range of human organs then known to be capable of transplantation. Kidney and bone marrow transplants were known to be a part of the developing field of organ transplants, yet those organs were not mentioned by name in the 1970 amendment. Furthermore, although as a matter of human physiology blood is correctly regarded as a "liquid organ," it seems improbable that those who drafted the amendment viewed blood as simply one of the several organs or organ systems that make up the human body. The more plausible assumption is that Congress believed that blood should be subject to regulation, and included it in the list of biological substances for which a license was required as a means of authorizing necessary governmental controls. Under this view, the term "analogous product" would include analogous blood products, not solid organs that are "analogous" because blood is also, in a broader sense, a human "organ," albeit a liquid organ....

Under an expansive legal interpretation, human organ transplants could possibly be regulated as drugs, devices, or biological products. It is, however, by no means clear that such an interpretation would be consistent with the legislative intent underlying the definitions or that it would withstand judicial challenge. Assuming that FDA were to assert jurisdiction, FDA's regulation of human organs would not result in a ban on their sale for profit. The statutes FDA administers are not intended to deal with the ethical issues that are involved in the sale of therapeutic products. There is thus in these statutes no express prohibition against the sale of an approved drug, device, or biological product, or any provision that governs the terms and conditions under which products are obtained or transferred to users.

NOTES

1. *Federal Legislation.* The National Organ Transplant Act, 98 Stat. 2339 (1984), established a task force on organ transplantation in the Department of HHS, provided assistance to qualified organ procurement organizations, and made it unlawful "for any person to knowingly acquire, receive, or otherwise transfer any human organ for valuable consideration for use in human transplantation if the transfer affects interstate commerce." The prohibition of organ purchases, codified in 42 U.S.C. § 274e, applies to the human kidneys, liver, heart, lung, pancreas, bone marrow, cornea, eye, bone, skin, and any other organ specified in regulations promulgated by the Secretary of HHS. The statute was designed to preserve a system of voluntary donation of these organs. *See generally* Cotton and Sandler, *The Regulation of Organ Procurement and Transplantation in the United States,* 7 J. Legal Med. 55 (1986); Note, *Regulating the Sale of Human Organs,* 71 Va. L. Rev. 1015 (1985).

2. *Autologous Blood.* FDA previously did not regulate, and it appears that the National Organ Transplant Act does not apply to, the collection, storage, and use of autologous blood, *i.e.,* blood that is taken from an individual, stored, and subsequently administered to the same individual. In memoranda dated March 15, 1989, and February 12, 1990, however, the agency instituted partial regulation of autologous blood but exempted intraoperative or postoperative red blood cell salvage.

3. *Non–Human Organs.* Transplantation between species is also increasingly feasible. *See* American Medical Association Council on Scientific Affairs, *Xenografts: Review of the Literature and Current Status,* 254 J. A.M.A. 3353 (Dec. 20, 1985). FDA has taken no action to regulate the animal organs and tissue that are used.

4. *Cultured Skin Tissue.* FDA has concluded that a human skin product made through the use of tissue culture technology entirely of human collagen and human cells is a medical device under the FD&C Act. *See* Letter from W.E. Gundaker, Director of the Office of Compliance of the FDA Center for Devices and Radiological Health to E. Bell, Organogenesis Inc. (April 23, 1986).

5. *Public Funding.* HCFA agreed to pay for heart transplantation under Medicare, almost exactly twenty years after Dr. Christiaan Barnard performed

the first heart transplantation, 51 Fed. Reg. 37164 (October 17, 1986), 52 Fed. Reg. 10935 (April 6, 1987). For an analysis of the issues surrounding this decision, *see, e.g.,* Casscells, *Heart Transplantation,* 315 New Eng. J. Med. 1365 (November 20, 1986). HCFA has also established general requirements for hospitals participating in the Medicare and Medicaid programs covering organ transplants in 52 Fed. Reg. 28666 (July 31, 1987), 53 Fed. Reg. 6526 (March 1, 1988).

6. *United Network for Organ Sharing.* The National Organ Transplant Act established the United Network for Organ Sharing, a private organization for the voluntary procurement of organs. All hospitals that perform organ transplants and all organ procurement organizations that participate in Medicare or Medicaid must be members of the Network and abide by its requirements.

7. *Ownership of Tissues Removed During Medical Treatment.* An individual's right to any cells taken from his or her body, and later used for commercial purposes, has become a major source of controversy. *See, e.g., Moore v. Regents of the University of California,* 252 Cal.Rptr. 816, 763 P.2d 479, *rev'd in part,* 51 Cal.3d 120, 271 Cal.Rptr. 146, 793 P.2d 479 (1990); Stone, *Cells for Sale,* 9 Discover, No. 8, at 33 (August 1988).

E. NATIONAL IMMUNIZATION POLICY

This section explores a subject that lies outside the traditional conception of FDA's regulatory responsibility—private liability for injuries caused by products that it regulates. The subject merits attention here because increasingly FDA decisions have been affected by, or taken cognizance of, developments in private liability litigation involving products that it regulates. In the field of biologics, many of which are designed for use in government supported disease prevention programs, decisions by public health authorities respecting the need for development and production of products are often influenced by private liability concerns, which in turn may have a direct impact on FDA's workload.

1. MANUFACTURER LIABILITY

Several court decisions have dramatically expanded the liability of manufacturers of vaccines used in mass public health immunization programs for injuries traceable to the use of their products. The following case is a landmark.

REYES v. WYETH LABORATORIES
United States Court of Appeals, Fifth Circuit, 1974.
498 F.2d 1264.

WISDOM, Circuit Judge:

Twenty or thirty years ago poliomyelitis was a dread disease that especially attacked the very young. In 1952 alone, there were 57,879 reported cases of polio in the United States; 21,269 of these resulted in crippling paralysis to the victims. By 1970, when Anita Reyes contracted polio, the number of those stricken by polio had diminished dramatically; she was one of just 33 individuals to be afflicted during that year. Credit for this precipitous decline must go primarily to the medical researchers who discovered the viral nature of the disease, and were able to isolate and reproduce the virus in an inactivated or an attenuated form....

On May 8, 1970, Anita Reyes was fed two drops of Sabin oral polio vaccine by eye-dropper at the Hidalgo County Department of Health clinic in Mission, Texas. The vaccine was administered to Anita by a registered nurse; there were no doctors present. Mrs. Reyes testified that she was not warned of any possible danger involved in Anita's taking the vaccine. Mrs. Reyes has a seventh grade education, but her primary language is Spanish. She signed a form releasing the State of Texas from "all liability in connection with immunization." The form contained no warning of any sort, and it is apparent from her testimony that she either did not read the form or lacked the linguistic ability to understand its significance. About fourteen days after the vaccine was administered, Anita Reyes became ill. On May 23, 1970, she was admitted to the McAllen (Texas) General Hospital, where her disease was diagnosed as Type I paralytic poliomyelitis. As a result of the polio, at the time of trial Anita was completely paralyzed from the waist down, her left arm had become atrophied, and she was unable to control her bladder or bowel movements.

The vaccine given Anita Reyes in the Mission clinic on May 8, 1970 was part of a "lot," No. 15509, prepared by Wyeth. Lot No. 15509 was trivalent oral polio vaccine that Wyeth had titered (mixed) from Types I, II, and III monovalent vaccine provided by Pfizer, Ltd. In response to an order placed by the Texas State Department of Health on December 23, 1969, Wyeth shipped 3500 vials of Lot No. 15509 vaccine to the State Health Department which in turn transferred 400 vials to the Hidalgo County Health Department. The jury found that vaccine from one of these vials was given to Anita Reyes. Included with every vial, each of which contained ten doses of vaccine, was a "package circular" provided by Wyeth which was intended to warn doctors, hospitals, or other purchasers of potential dangers in ingesting the vaccine. Mrs. Lenore Willey, the public health nurse who administered the vaccine to Anita Reyes, testified that she had read the directions on this package insert, but that it was not the practice of the nurses at the Mission Health Clinic to pass on the warnings to the vaccinees or to their guardians. She testified that she gave Mrs. Reyes no warning before she administered the vaccine to Anita....

... Our inquiry is bounded by the jury's finding that Wyeth's vaccine was the producing cause of Anita Reyes' polio, and by those principles of products liability law we conclude would be applied by the courts of Texas.... Basically, Section 402A [of the Restatement (Second) of Torts] subjects to liability the seller or manufacturer of a product sold "in a defective condition unreasonably dangerous" to an ultimate user or consumer whose person or property is physically harmed by the product.....

... It is clear ... that the vaccine was not itself defective. Wyeth Vaccine Lot No. 15509 was exactly what its makers and the Texas public health authorities intended it to be: trivalent live-virus Sabin oral polio vaccine....

Although the living virus in the vaccine does not make the vaccine defective, it does make it what the Restatement calls an "unavoidably unsafe product," one which cannot be made "safe" no matter how carefully it is manufactured. Such products are not necessarily "*unreasonably* dangerous," for as this Court has long recognized in wrestling with product liability questions, many goods possess both utility and danger. Rather, in evaluating the possible liability of a manufacturer for injuries caused by his inevitably hazardous products, a two-step analysis is required to determine first, whether the product is so unsafe that marketing it at all is "unreasonably dangerous per se," and, if not, whether the product has been introduced into the stream of commerce without sufficient safeguards and is thereby "unreasonably dangerous as marketed." ...

... Obviously, use of an unavoidably unsafe product always presents at least a minimal danger of harm, but only if the potential harmful effects of the product—both qualitative and quantitative—outweigh the legitimate public interest in its availability will it be declared unreasonably dangerous per se and the person placing it on the market held liable. Applying this standard here, the scales must tip in favor of availability. The evil to be prevented—poliomyelitis and its accompanying paralysis—is great. Although the danger that vaccinees may contract polio is qualitatively devastating, it is statistically miniscule. On balance then, marketing the vaccine is justified despite the danger....

... As comment k to Section 402A instructs, an unavoidably unsafe product is neither defective nor *unreasonably* dangerous if such a product is "properly prepared, and is accompanied by proper directions and warning."....

We cannot quarrel with the general proposition that where *prescription* drugs are concerned, the manufacturer's duty to warn is limited to an obligation to advise the prescribing physician of any potential dangers that may result from the drug's use.... Although there is no question that Sabin oral vaccine is licensed for sale only as a prescription drug, the district court, in its charge to the jury, noted that the vaccine was not administered as a prescription drug at the Mission Clinic. The court charged: "if you [the jury] find that a warning should have been given, the warning had to be given to Anita and her parents, not to Mrs. Wiley, that Public Health nurse, somebody, else.... The ultimate consumer is the one that had to be warned." The district court apparently based this instruction on the leading federal case in the area, *Davis v. Wyeth Laboratories,* 399 F.2d 121. In *Davis,* the plaintiff had allegedly contracted polio from Wyeth oral vaccine distributed at a public clinic. The Ninth Circuit held that where no individualized medical judgment intervenes between the manufacturer of a prescription drug and the ultimate consumer, "it is the responsibility of the manufacturer to see that warnings reach the consumer, either by giving warning itself or by obligating the purchaser to give warning." ...

Wyeth does not resist the Ninth Circuit's holding in *Davis,* but asserts that the instant case can be distinguished on four grounds. First, the appellant argues, Davis received his vaccine during a mass immunization program, whereas Anita Reyes ingested her vaccine at her parents' request. Second, Wyeth stresses the fact that Davis received his vaccine from a pharmacist, but Reyes' was administered by a public health nurse. Third, Wyeth's active participation in the mass immunization program involved in the *Davis* case is contrasted to its relatively passive role here. Finally, Wyeth urges that unlike the situation in *Davis,* here it had no knowledge that the vaccine would not be administered as a prescription drug.

None of these asserted grounds for distinguishing *Davis* justifies a different result here. The first two arguments are admittedly distinctions between *Davis* and the instant controversy, but they have no bearing on the *rationale* of the *Davis* opinion. Whether vaccine was received during a mass immunization or an on-going program, whether it was administered by nurse or pharmacist, it was, in both these cases, dispensed without the sort of individualized medical balancing of the risks to the vaccinee that is contemplated by the prescription drug exception. The third and fourth asserted bases for distinguishing *Davis* from this case are essentially the same: Wyeth took no active part in the vaccination process here, and did not know that its vaccine would be dispensed without procedures appropriate for distribution of prescription drugs.

Were we to conclude that Wyeth neither knew nor had reason to know that its vaccine would be dispensed without prescription drug safeguards, we might be required to hold that the *rationale* in *Davis* is inapplicable here. But Wyeth had ample reason to foresee the way in which its vaccine would be distributed.... Neal Nathanson, Professor of Epidemiology at the Johns Hopkins University School of Public Health and a witness for Wyeth testified that it was common knowledge in the drug industry that "a great majority" of vaccinees receive their Sabin vaccine in mass administrations or county clinics manned at least in part by volunteers.... These clinics, as Wyeth must be presumed to know, dispense Sabin vaccine to all comers in an "assembly line" fashion; there is often neither time nor personnel to make an "individualized medical judgment" of the vaccinee's needs or susceptibilities....

... The jury found that the defendant's polio vaccine caused Anita Reyes's polio. Testimony by her mother as to what she would have done, had proper warnings been provided, would have been both speculative and self-serving. Thus we turn to the ... presumption that a warning, had it been given, would have been heeded. Buttressing the presumption that Mrs. Reyes might have taken preventive steps is the testimony of Reyes' expert, Dr. Ramiro Casson, that some pediatricians in Hidalgo County, at least by the time of trial, had begun administering killed-virus vaccine to infants in order to build up their level of antibodies before feeding them the live-virus drug. Tending to rebut the presumption that Mrs. Reyes would have behaved differently had she been warned was the fact that she twice returned to the Mission Clinic for further doses of vaccine, even after Anita contracted polio. Yet it is patent from her testimony that Mrs. Reyes had not, even then, been informed of the danger of the polio vaccine, and did not in fact understand what medication Anita was to receive. The legal presumption ... thus operates here to provide the final element necessary to hold Wyeth Laboratories liable for Anita Reyes' poliomyelitis....

In closing, we feel that we should comment on the important policy considerations raised in the briefs of the amici curiae, the American Academy of Pediatrics [AAP] and the Conference of State and Territorial Epidemiologists [CSTE]. Both insist that the holding we reached is "dangerous" to the nation's preventive medicine programs and contravenes a strong public policy favoring large-scale participation in immunization efforts to combat infectious disease....

Citing a recent Texas statute which requires that all Texas schoolchildren receive polio vaccine, the AAP insists that this renders any warnings futile. This argument assumes, of course, that the only options available are to ingest the oral vaccine at the clinic or to eschew immunity. Obviously, however, one can choose to be innoculated with killed-virus Salk vaccine, either to provide complete immunity or as a precautionary prelude to ingesting oral vaccine. The AAP also insists that the warnings would be so complex or misleading as to confuse and frighten potential vaccinees. This is possible. Yet we believe that a warning advising a patron of a public health clinic of the relative risk of contracting polio from a "wild" source against the slight chance of contracting it from the vaccine would not be terrifying or confusing. Some would be sufficiently concerned to take the Salk vaccine innoculation. Others, perhaps those who, like the plaintiff in *Davis,* have as great a chance of contracting polio from the vaccine as contracting it from a wild source, will undoubtedly be deterred from immunization. The AAP's answer to this problem is to warn no one. That is no answer.

This position raises a policy consideration scarcely less urgent than the need for mass immunization from disease; the right of the individual to choose and control what risk he will take, in the absence of an individualized medical judgment by a physician familiar with his needs and susceptibilities. Recognition of this right counters the argument advanced in the CSTE's brief that once an epidemiological balancing of the risks of immunization has been made, no warning is required.... Here, the qualitative risk was great, the quantitative risk minute. The end sought to be achieved—immunization—is important both to the individual and society. Striking the balance in this case is difficult, but ... we conclude that a sufficient "true choice judgment" was involved here to lend strong policy support to our holding. First, the risk here was foreseeable statistically, although unknowable individually. Thus ... here there was a basis for rational choice. Second, a choice here, if given, had an opportunity to be efficacious, since reasonable alternatives to taking the oral vaccine were available. Therefore, the choice was not so clear cut that even offering the opportunity to choose was meaningless.

    ... Statistically predictable as are these rare cases of vaccine-induced polio, a strong argument can be advanced that the loss ought not lie where it falls (on the victim), but should be borne by the manufacturer as a foreseeable cost of doing business, and passed on to the public in the form of price increases to his customers.

    Contrary to the assertions of the AAP and the CSTE, we feel strongly that our holding is in accord with public policy considerations. We recognize both the essential role the city health clinic and the rural county clinic play in the nation's public health scheme, and the dangers that their depersonalized medical treatment pose. We do not then, lay down an absolute duty to warn all who receive medication at public clinics. Instead, we hold that in the case of a prescription drug which is unavoidably unsafe, and as to which there is a certain, though small, risk throughout the population, there must be *either* a warning—meaningful and complete so as to be understood by the recipient—*or* an individualized medical judgment that this treatment or medication is necessary and desirable for this patient....

    The judgment is affirmed.

NOTES

    1. *Bystander Recovery. Givens v. Lederle,* 556 F.2d 1341 (5th Cir. 1977), affirmed a jury verdict against the defendant manufacturer of Sabin oral live virus polio vaccine and in favor of an unvaccinated plaintiff, who contracted paralytic poliomyelitis after her infant daughter had been given the vaccine by a private pediatrician. The court found that the manufacturer's package insert failed to reach the consumer and warn of the risks of taking a live vaccine. Though in this case a private physician administered the dose, the court held that the language of the warning did not sufficiently alert even the physician of the risks.

    2. *Failure to Warn as Cause in Fact.* In *Cunningham v. Charles Pfizer & Co.,* 532 P.2d 1377 (Okl. 1974), the court reversed a verdict holding the manufacturer strictly liable for failure adequately to warn the plaintiff, who contracted polio after ingesting oral polio vaccine. The court remanded the case, requiring the plaintiff to establish that he would have refused the vaccine if he had been properly warned of the risks involved.

3. *Government Liability.* In *Hitchcock v. United States,* 479 F. Supp. 65 (D.D.C. 1979), the wife of a U.S. Foreign Service Officer was held entitled to damages from the government for paralysis resulting from the routine administration by a State Department nurse of an antirabies vaccine given as prophylaxis prior to foreign duty. No physician was present and the plaintiff received no information about the benefits or risks.

2. GOVERNMENT LIABILITY

As the *Reyes* case suggests, the national campaign to achieve near universal immunization against polio produced a small number of cases of polio attributable to the vaccine itself. In addition to seeking recovery from the manufacturer, victims of these "accidents" have sometimes sued the government itself.

BERKOVITZ v. UNITED STATES

Supreme Court of the United States, 1988.
486 U.S. 531.

JUSTICE MARSHALL delivered the opinion of the Court.

The question in this case is whether the discretionary function exception of the Federal Tort Claims Act (FTCA or Act), 28 U.S.C. § 2680(a), bars a suit based on the Government's licensing of an oral polio vaccine and on its subsequent approval of the release of a specific lot of that vaccine to the public.

I

On May 10, 1979, Kevan Berkovitz, then a 2–month–old infant, ingested a dose of Orimune, an oral polio vaccine manufactured by Lederle Laboratories. Within one month, he contracted a severe case of polio. The disease left Berkovitz almost completely paralyzed and unable to breathe without the assistance of a respirator. The Communicable Disease Center, an agency of the Federal Government, determined that Berkovitz had contracted polio from the vaccine.

Berkovitz, joined by his parents as guardians, subsequently filed suit against the United States in Federal District Court.[1] The complaint alleged that the United States was liable for his injuries under the FTCA, because the Division of Biologic Standards (DBS), then a part of the National Institutes of Health, had acted wrongfully in licensing Lederle Laboratories to produce Orimune and because the Bureau of Biologics of the Food and Drug Administration (FDA) had acted wrongfully in approving release to the public of the particular lot of vaccine containing Berkovitz's dose. According to petitioners, these actions

1. Petitioners also sued Lederle Laboratories in a separate civil action. That suit was settled before the instant case was filed.

violated federal law and policy regarding the inspection and approval of polio vaccines.

The Government moved to dismiss the suit for lack of subject-matter jurisdiction on the ground that the agency actions fell within the discretionary function exception of the FTCA. The District Court denied this motion, concluding that neither the licensing of Orimune nor the release of a specific lot of that vaccine to the public was a "discretionary function" within the meaning of the FTCA. At the Government's request, the District Court certified its decision for immediate appeal to the Third Circuit pursuant to 28 U.S.C. § 1292(b), and the Court of Appeals accepted jurisdiction.

A divided panel of the Court of Appeals reversed. 822 F.2d 1322 (CA3 1987). The court initially rejected the Government's argument that the discretionary function exception bars all claims arising out of the regulatory activities of federal agencies. The court stated that "the discretionary function exception is inapplicable to non-discretionary regulatory actions," and noted that employees of regulatory agencies have no discretion to violate the command of federal statutes or regulations. Contrary to petitioners' claim, however, the court held that federal law imposed no duties on federal agencies with respect to the licensing of polio virus vaccines or the approval of the distribution of particular vaccine lots to the public. [T]he court concluded that the licensing and release of polio vaccines were wholly discretionary actions and, as such, could not form the basis for suit against the United States. A dissenting judge argued that the relevant statutes and regulations obligated the DBS to require the submission of test data relating to a vaccine from the manufacturer and to deny a license when the test data showed that the vaccine failed to conform with applicable safety standards. Reading the complaint in this case as alleging a failure on the part of the DBS to act in accordance with these directives, the dissenting judge concluded that the discretionary function exception did not bar petitioners' suit.

We granted certiorari to resolve a conflict in the Circuits regarding the effect of the discretionary function exception on claims arising from the Government's regulation of polio vaccines. We now reverse the Third Circuit's judgment.

II

The determination of whether the discretionary function exception bars a suit against the Government is guided by several established principles. This Court stated in [United States v.] Varig [Airlines, 467 U.S. 797 (1984)] that "it is the nature of the conduct, rather than the status of the actor, that governs whether the discretionary function exception applies in a given case." In examining the nature of the challenged conduct, a court must first consider whether the action is a matter of choice for the acting employee. This inquiry is mandated by the language of the exception; conduct cannot be discretionary unless it involves an element of judgment or choice. Thus, the discretionary function exception will not apply when a federal statute, regulation, or policy specifically prescribes a course of action for an employee to follow. In this event, the employee has no rightful option but to adhere to the directive. And if the employee's conduct cannot appropriately be the product of judgment or choice then there is no discretion in the conduct for the discretionary function exception to protect....

Moreover, assuming the challenged conduct involves an element of judgment, a court must determine whether that judgment is of the kind that the discretionary function exception was designed to shield. The basis for the discretionary function exception was Congress' desire to "prevent judicial 'second-guessing' of legislative and administrative decisions grounded in social, economic, and political policy through the medium of an action in tort." The exception, properly construed, therefore protects only governmental actions and decisions based on considerations of public policy. In sum, the discretionary function exception insulates the Government from liability if the action challenged in the case involves the permissible exercise of policy judgment.

This Court's decision in *Varig Airlines* illustrates these propositions.... Congress had given the Secretary of Transportation broad authority to establish and implement a program for enforcing compliance with airplane safety standards. In the exercise of that authority, the FAA, as the Secretary's designee, had devised a system of "spot-checking" airplanes for compliance. This Court first held that the establishment of that system was a discretionary function within the meaning of the FTCA because it represented a policy determination as to how best to "accommodat[e] the goal of air transportation safety and the reality of finite agency resources." The Court then stated that the discretionary function exception also protected "the acts of FAA employees in executing the 'spot-check' program" because under this program the employees "were specifically empowered to make policy judgments regarding the degree of confidence that might reasonably be placed in a given manufacturer, the need to maximize compliance with FAA regulations, and the efficient allocation of agency resources." Thus, the Court held the challenged acts protected from liability because they were within the range of choice accorded by federal policy and law and were the results of policy determinations.

In restating and clarifying the scope of the discretionary function exception, we intend specifically to reject the Government's argument, pressed both in this Court and the Court of Appeals, that the exception precludes liability for any and all acts arising out of the regulatory programs of federal agencies.... The discretionary function exception applies only to conduct that involves the permissible exercise of policy judgment. The question in this case is whether the governmental activities challenged by petitioners are of this discretionary nature.

III

Petitioners' suit raises two broad claims. First, petitioners assert that the DBS violated a federal statute and accompanying regulations in issuing a license to Lederle Laboratories to produce Orimune. Second, petitioners argue that the Bureau of Biologics of the FDA violated federal regulations and policy in approving the release of the particular lot of Orimune that contained Kevan Berkovitz's dose. We examine each of these broad claims by reviewing the applicable regulatory scheme and petitioners' specific allegations of agency wrongdoing. Because the decision we review adjudicated a motion to dismiss, we accept all of the factual allegations in petitioners' complaint as true and ask whether, in these circumstances, dismissal of the complaint was appropriate.

Under federal law, a manufacturer must receive a product license prior to marketing a brand of live oral polio vaccine. In order to become eligible for such a license, a manufacturer must first make a sample of the vaccine product. This process begins with the selection of an original virus strain. The manufacturer grows a seed virus from this strain; the seed virus is then used to produce monopools, portions of which are combined to form the consumer-level product. Federal regulations set forth safety criteria for the original strain and the vaccine monopools. Under the regulations, the manufacturer must conduct a variety of tests to measure the safety of the product at each stage of the manufacturing process. Upon completion of the manufacturing process and the required testing, the manufacturer is required to submit an application for a product license to the DBS. In addition to this application, the manufacturer must submit data from the tests performed and a sample of the finished product.

In deciding whether to issue a license, the DBS is required to comply with certain statutory and regulatory provisions. The Public Health Service Act provides:

> "Licenses for the maintenance of establishments for the propagation or manufacture and preparation of products [including polio vaccines] may be issued only upon a showing that the establishment and the products for which a license is desired meet standards, designed to insure the continued safety, purity, and potency of such products, prescribed in regulations, and licenses for new products may be issued only upon a showing that they meet such standards. All such licenses shall be issued, suspended, and revoked as prescribed by regulations...." § 351(d), 58 Stat. 702–703, as amended, 42 U.S.C. § 262(d).

A regulation similarly provides that "[a] product license shall be issued only upon examination of the product and upon a determination that the product complies with the standards prescribed in the regulations...." In addition, a regulation states that "[a]n application for license shall not be considered as filed" until the DBS receives the information and data regarding the product that the manufacturer is required to submit. These statutory and regulatory provisions require the DBS, prior to issuing a product license, to receive all data the manufacturer is required to submit, examine the product, and make a determination that the product complies with safety standards.

Petitioners' first allegation with regard to the licensing of Orimune is that the DBS issued a product license without first receiving data that the manufacturer must submit showing how the product, at the various stages of the manufacturing process, matched up against regulatory safety standards. The discretionary function exception does not bar a cause of action based on this allegation. The statute and regulations described above require, as a precondition to licensing, that the DBS receive certain test data from the manufacturer relating to the product's compliance with regulatory standards. The DBS has no discretion to issue a license without first receiving the required test data; to do so would violate a specific statutory and regulatory directive. Accordingly, to the extent that petitioners' licensing claim is based on a decision of the DBS to issue a license without having received the required test data, the discretionary function exception imposes no bar.

Petitioners' other allegation regarding the licensing of Orimune is difficult to describe with precision. Petitioners contend that the DBS licensed Orimune even though the vaccine did not comply with certain regulatory safety standards.[9] This charge may be understood in any of three ways. First, petitioners may mean that the DBS licensed Orimune without first making a determination as to whether the vaccine complied with regulatory standards. Second, petitioners may intend to argue that the DBS specifically found that Orimune failed to comply with certain regulatory standards and nonetheless issued a license for the vaccine's manufacture. Third, petitioners may concede that the DBS made a determination of compliance, but allege that this determination was incorrect. Neither petitioners' complaint nor their briefs and argument before this Court make entirely clear their theory of the case.

If petitioners aver that the DBS licensed Orimune either without determining whether the vaccine complied with regulatory standards or after determining that the vaccine failed to comply, the discretionary function exception does not bar the claim. Under the scheme governing the DBS's regulation of polio vaccines, the DBS may not issue a

---

9. Petitioners point to two specific regulatory standards that the product allegedly failed to satisfy. First, petitioners claim that an original virus strain from which the vaccine was made did not comply with the requirement that the strain be "free of harmful effect upon administration in the recommended dosage to at least 100,000 people susceptible to poliomyelitis." Second, petitioners assert that the strain, a seed virus, a vaccine monopool, and the ultimate vaccine product failed to comply with the regulatory scheme's neurovirulence requirement. Neurovirulence is the capacity of an infectious agent to product pathologic effects on the central nervous system. In this context, it refers to the vaccine's ability to cause paralytic poliomyelitis. The neurovirulence of a vaccine product is tested by injecting the product into monkeys. The product meets the neurovirulence criterion only if a specified number of the animals survive and a "comparative analysis" demonstrates that the neurovirulence of the vaccine product "does not exceed" the neurovirulence of a reference product previously selected by the agency.

license except upon an examination of the product and a determination that the product complies with all regulatory standards. The agency has no discretion to deviate from this mandated procedure.[10] Petitioners' claim, if interpreted as alleging that the DBS licensed Orimune in the absence of a determination that the vaccine complied with regulatory standards, therefore does not challenge a discretionary function. Rather, the claim charges a failure on the part of the agency to perform its clear duty under federal law. When a suit charges an agency with failing to act in accord with a specific mandatory directive, the discretionary function exception does not apply.

If petitioners' claim is that the DBS made a determination that Orimune complied with regulatory standards, but that the determination was incorrect, the question of the applicability of the discretionary function exception requires a somewhat different analysis. In that event, the question turns on whether the manner and method of determining compliance with the safety standards at issue involves agency judgment of the kind protected by the discretionary function exception.[11] Petitioners contend that the determination involves the application of objective scientific standards, whereas the Government asserts that the determination incorporates considerable "policy judgment." In making these assertions, the parties have framed the issue appropriately; application of the discretionary function exception to the claim that the determination of compliance was incorrect hinges on whether the agency officials making that determination permissibly exercise policy choice. The parties, however, have not addressed this question in detail, and they have given us no indication of the way in which the DBS interprets and applies the regulations setting forth the criteria for compliance. Given that these regulations are particularly abstruse, we hesitate to decide the question on the scanty record before us. We therefore leave it to the District Court to decide, if petitioners choose to press this claim, whether agency officials appropriately exercise policy judgment in determining that a vaccine product complies with the relevant safety standards.

The regulatory scheme governing release of vaccine lots is distinct from that governing the issuance of licenses. The former set of regulations places an obligation on manufacturers to examine all vaccine lots prior to distribution to ensure that they comply with regulatory standards. These regulations, however, do not impose a corresponding duty on the Bureau of Biologics. Although the regulations empower the Bureau to examine any vaccine lot and prevent the distribution of a noncomplying lot, see 21 CFR § 610.2(a)(1978), they do not require the

---

10. Even the Government conceded at oral argument that the DBS has no discretion to issue a product license without an examination of the product and a determination that the product complies with regulatory standards....

11. ... [T]he regulatory standards that petitioners claim were not satisfied in this case are the neurovirulence criterion and the requirement that virus strains be free from harmful effect. The question presented is thus whether the determination that a vaccine product complies with each of these regulatory standards involves judgment of the kind that the discretionary function exception protects.

Bureau to take such action in all cases. The regulations generally allow the Bureau to determine the appropriate manner in which to regulate the release of vaccine lots, rather than mandating certain kinds of agency action. The regulatory scheme governing the release of vaccine lots is substantially similar in this respect to the scheme discussed in *United States v. Varig Airlines.*

Given this regulatory context, the discretionary function exception bars any claims that challenge the Bureau's formulation of policy as to the appropriate way in which to regulate the release of vaccine lots.... In addition, if the policies and programs formulated by the Bureau allow room for implementing officials to make independent policy judgments, the discretionary function exception protects the acts taken by those officials in the exercise of this discretion.... The discretionary function exception, however, does not apply if the acts complained of do not involve the permissible exercise of policy discretion. Thus, if the Bureau's policy leaves no room for an official to exercise policy judgment in performing a given act, or if the act simply does not involve the exercise of such judgment, the discretionary function exception does not bar a claim that the act was negligent or wrongful....

Viewed in light of these principles, petitioners' claim regarding the release of the vaccine lot from which Kevan Berkovitz received his dose survives the Government's motion to dismiss. Petitioners allege that, under the authority granted by the regulations, the Bureau of Biologics has adopted a policy of testing all vaccine lots for compliance with safety standards and preventing the distribution to the public of any lots that fail to comply. Petitioners further allege that notwithstanding this policy, which allegedly leaves no room for implementing officials to exercise independent policy judgment, employees of the Bureau knowingly approved the release of a lot that did not comply with safety standards. Thus, petitioners' complaint is directed at a governmental action that allegedly involved no policy discretion. Petitioners, of course, have not proved their factual allegations, but they are not required to do so on a motion to dismiss. If those allegations are correct—that is, if the Bureau's policy did not allow the official who took the challenged action to release a noncomplying lot on the basis of policy considerations—the discretionary function exception does not bar the claim. Because petitioners may yet show, on the basis of materials obtained in discovery or otherwise, that the conduct challenged here did not involve the permissible exercise of policy discretion, the invocation of the discretionary function exception to dismiss petitioners' lot release claim was improper.

NOTES

1. *Proceedings on Remand.* The court of appeals denied the government's motion to dismiss and remanded the case to the district court for a trial on the merits, 858 F.2d 122 (3d Cir.1988). Thereafter the case was consolidated with several other suits seeking damages for injuries resulting from the administra-

tion of Orimune. *In re Sabin Polio Vaccine Products Liability Litigation,* 743 F.Supp. 410 (D.Md.1990).

2. *Related Theory of Government Liability.* In *Griffin v. United States,* 500 F.2d 1059 (3d Cir. 1974), the court sustained recovery against the government for the severe injuries suffered following administration of a dose of Sabin polio vaccine that the Division of Biological Standards had licensed. The DBS had promulgated a regulation establishing specifications that its employees were to apply in determining nonvirulence of batches of the vaccine—specifications that many outside experts had criticized as unnecessarily stringent. The DBS had released the batch of vaccine administered to Mrs. Griffin even though it did not meet these specifications. The court disagreed with the government's contention that the decision whether to release the vaccine was discretionary and that the DBS regulation required a judgmental determination:

> We acknowledge that under DBS' construction of the regulation, the implementation called for a judgmental determination as to the degree to which each of the enumerated criteria indicated neurovirulence.... The judgment, however, was that of a professional measuring neurovirulence. It was not that of a policy-maker promulgating regulations by balancing competing policy considerations in determining the public interest.... At issue was a scientific, but not policy-making, determination as to whether each of the criteria listed ... was met and the extent to which each such factor accurately indicated neurovirulence. DBS' responsibility was limited to merely executing the policy judgments of the Surgeon General.....
>
> ... The Government's release of Lot 56 was predicated upon its reliance on a factor called "biological variation." Reliance on this factor, however, was not authorized by the regulations. We therefore conclude ... that DBS' activity was not immunized from judicial review.

---

3. FORMULATION OF A NATIONAL POLICY

EDWARD MORTIMER, IMMUNIZATION AGAINST INFECTIOUS DISEASE

200 Science 902 (1978).*

What is the importance of immunization, past and present, in the control of infectious disease? In the United States since the turn of the century life expectancy has increased remarkably. Expected duration of life for individuals born in 1900 was 47.3 years; in 1970 it was 70.9 years. The age-adjusted death rate in 1900 was 17.2 deaths per thousand population, whereas in 1970 it was 9.5 per thousand, a reduction in mortality of 45 percent....

Since the turn of the century the decrease in mortality has been most pronounced in younger age groups.... The mortality rate in

---

* Copyright 1978 by the American Association for the Advancement of Science.

children 1 to 4 years of age declined 96 percent between 1900 and 1970, whereas that in the population aged between 65 and 74 years declined by only a little more than a third.... [M]uch of this change in mortality in younger age groups is due to a decrease in deaths from certain infectious diseases, including the common contagious diseases of childhood, tuberculosis, meningitis, pneumonia, and epidemic diseases such as typhoid fever, plague, and smallpox ... [I]n children older than 1 year of age, approximately two-thirds of the decreased mortality can be attributed to a decline in deaths from the above-specified infectious diseases.

... Clearly, there are multiple reasons for the decline in mortality due to infectious diseases in the United States in this century, and in many instances it is impossible to determine the relative importance of different factors.... There is little question that the natural history of some infectious diseases has changed spontaneously over the years, for reasons not entirely clear..... To a considerable extent in some diseases, the decline in mortality can be attributed to man's intervention in terms of sanitary control of water supplies and refuse and proper food handling. An example of such a disease is typhoid fever.....

Control of nonhuman vectors has been responsible for much of the decline in mortality from some diseases, such as rabies, typhus fever, and malaria in the United States. Antimicrobial drugs effective against certain bacterial diseases have certainly contributed to the decline in mortality from infection since their development and widespread use during, and subsequent to, World War II. However, studies in Sweden have suggested that death rates from many bacterial diseases that declined subsequent to the development of antibiotic drugs were actually declining at the same rate prior to their use....

In view of the above, what has been the contribution of immunization to the decreased mortality from infectious disease in the United States? In the case of a number of diseases, immunization—though available and of some effect—has been of negligible importance. These diseases include typhoid fever, cholera, epidemic typhus fever, and plague.... The disappearance of mortality from one disease (smallpox) and the rarity of deaths from two others (tetanus and poliomyelitis) can be attributed almost entirely to active immunization.....

Vaccines are not perfect. Indeed, the protective efficacy of some, such as cholera and typhoid vaccines and BCG for tuberculosis, is such that control of the disease by epidemiologic and chemotherapeutic means is far more efficacious.... Even those vaccines employed for the routine immunization of children are not always 100 percent efficacious and are associated with some risk. Moreover, although these vaccines have been used for many years, data that prove efficacy for some are not adequate by 1978 standards....

The lack of visibility of vaccine-preventable diseases in the United States has ... resulted in a certain amount of complacency in both health professionals and the public. In 1975 only 116 deaths were reported from diseases against which children are routinely immunized. This has resulted in less than the optimum number of children being immunized. For example, in 1975 only 64.8 percent of 1 to 4–year–old children had received three or more doses of poliomyelitis vaccine, compared to 73.9 percent in 1965. The low was 1973 with 60.4 percent. Only 75.2 percent of 1 to 4–year–olds had received three or more doses of diphtheria and tetanus toxoids and pertussis vaccine, and 65.5 percent measles vaccine. This latter deficit resulted in localized outbreaks of measles with more than 41,000 cases in 1976; how small the proportions of the population immune to poliomyelitis and diphtheria must be before substantial outbreaks occur is unknown.....

Major problems with the potential of compromising immunization programs seriously are those of informed consent and litigation surrounding vaccine-related injures. Largely as a consequence of these closely related problems, the production of measles, rubella, mumps, and oral poliomyelitis vaccines is limited to one manufacturer in the United States. Six other producers of one or more of these vaccines have ceased providing them in recent years. Because of litigation and judgments awarded the victims of injury from vaccines, advocacy has developed for a system of public recompense for those individuals inadvertently injured by programs of accepted public health merit. The need for individual informed consent concerns many physicians; is it possible to fully and fairly inform patients and parents of the benefits and risks associated with a given vaccine, and do they have the background and perspective to make appropriate decisions? Should we combine a system of public recompense for vaccine injury with a system of public informed consent for mandatory immunization, rather than individual consent? If the public is to assume responsibility for those few permanently injured by a vaccine, should the public also accept responsibility for the individual who refused immunization and ended up permanently in an institution as a consequence of measles encephalitis? . . .

NOTE

For a review of diseases of importance in the United States and developing countries that could be addressed by new vaccines, *see* Institute of Medicine, NEW VACCINE DEVELOPMENT: ESTABLISHING PRIORITIES, Vols. I & II (1985, 1986).

REPORT AND RECOMMENDATIONS OF THE NATIONAL IMMUNIZATION WORK GROUPS ON LIABILITY
(DHEW, 1977).

The liability problem we now face is a much more difficult one than that of the summer of 1976.... Events of recent months have shown that the fears of the insurance companies were valid, however vaguely they were understood and however poorly they were defined....

... The basic liability problem for manufacturers centers on the shift of responsibility of the so-called duty to warn, as set forth in *Davis v. Wyeth Laboratories, Inc.*, and *Reyes v. Wyeth Laboratories, Inc.* From the manufacturer's standpoint, the difficulty with these decisions does not rest on the requirement that the vaccinee, his parent or guardian, be advised of the benefits and risks of the vaccine, but, rather, on the fact that the cases require the manufacturer to provide this information (i.e., for a manufacturer to assume the overall control of vaccination programs at the federal, state, and local levels). This ... is the proper responsibility of public health officials.... [S]uch a requirement is totally beyond the control and ability of the vaccine manufacturer....

Assigning the "duty to warn" to manufacturers has created considerable concern among public health agencies. This is largely due to its influence in interpositioning manufacturers in the usual flow of preventive medical services. Furthermore, public health agencies and health personnel ... have sensed, rightly or wrongly, that their personal liability in vaccine associated injury is also being called into question....

The Liability Work Group focused on two alternatives, the difference between the two approaches deriving from a consideration of whether both emergency mass immunization programs and routine mass immunization programs should be treated in the same way.

A. PROPOSAL FOR SEPARATE SYSTEMS

Liability exposures to emergency situations may vary from those found in routine programs in one or more of the following aspects:

- Size of population immunized
- Scope of population immunized (elderly, high risks, etc.)
- Experience with type of vaccine
- Accelerated testing and production time
- Public awareness due to mass programs and focus during pre-immunization debate of possible dangers.

These factors have created and will continue to create insurance availability problems. Accordingly, some believe that different approaches to the liability problems may well be considered....

1. Liability System for Routine Immunization Programs

It was proposed that all mass immunization programs will be deemed to be routine and handled in the following manner unless the President declares a program to be "emergency." In that instance it is proposed that one of the alternatives in (2) below would be more appropriate.

The proposal calls for:

(a) Enactment of federal legislation authorizing the DHEW to indemnify government contractors who supply, distribute, or administer vaccine for routine mass immunization programs against losses resulting from claims or suits based on injuries not caused by the contractor's failure to perform its obligations under the contract.

(b) Encouragement by the federal government of efforts to enact appropriate legislation in the states.

2. Liability System for Emergency Mass Immunization Programs

... [D]ifferent approaches should be considered as follows:

(a) *No-fault alternative.* This alternative is more fully explained in the single system approach.

(b) *Elimination of legal liability.* The rationale for this approach is that individuals have a societal obligation which, under unusual circumstances, transcends individual rights and expectations. When an emergency arises of a cataclysmic nature, requiring the immunization of great masses of people for the continued survival of a society, the extent of adverse reaction to such an immunization program may have to be accepted by each member of society. We reject this alternative for any except the most severe, cataclysmic situations....

B. PROPOSAL FOR A SINGLE SYSTEM

The rationale for proposing a single system approach is that it enunciates a point of view that people participating in any mass immunization program are potentially subject to injury which can be construed to have been incurred "in the public interest." Since any immunization program necessarily involves some risk to recipients, and because the public's perception[s] of risks and remedies are inevitably influenced by the most visible program, a single approach provides a more logical, consistent, and equitable remedy for those who suffer ill-effects from any mass immunization program.

This alternative approach requires the enactment of federal legislation.... This law ... should become operative upon declaration by the President that a grave public health interest exists applicable to the general population or important categories of individuals, characterized by age, health status, location, unusual vulnerability to disease or health hazard, or in need of special protection. The recommended major provisions of this statute are as follows:

1. Persons suffering a vaccine associated injury or disability which results in economic loss following receipt of an inoculation with a vaccine designated by the federal govern-

ment as being in the public interest, would be eligible for compensation by the United States.

2. All claims for vaccine associated injury or disability would be made only against the federal government (an exclusive remedy).

3. As provided in Public Law 94–380, the federal government should have discretion to bring an action against a program participant [for losses] resulting from negligent acts or omissions.

4. The federal government should be charged with responsibility for clearly and fully disclosing the relative risks and benefits of designated vaccines and the rights and remedies available to potential vaccinees.

5. In order to encourage widespread participation in programs using government designated vaccines, all individuals/organizations involved in manufacture, distribution, and administration of such vaccines should be immune from any legal action by inoculees or their representatives for injures/disabilities alleged to have resulted from receipt of such vaccine....

NOTE

For discussions of the liability question and proposals for possible solutions, *see* Institute of Medicine, EVALUATION OF POLIOMYELITIS VACCINES (1977); VACCINE SUPPLY AND INNOVATION (1985); DHEW, LIABILITY ARISING OUT OF IMMUNIZATION PROGRAMS, FINAL REPORT TO CONGRESS (1978); GAO, DISCUSSION OF SELECTED ISSUES AFFECTING FEDERAL IMMUNIZATION ACTIVITIES, HRD–80–52 (1980); OTA, REVIEW OF SELECTED FEDERAL VACCINE AND IMMUNIZATION POLICIES, OTA–H–96 (1979); COST EFFECTIVENESS OF INFLUENZA VACCINATION, OTA–H–152 (December 1981); Curran, *Public Warnings of the Risk in Oral Polio Vaccine*, 65 Am. J. Pub. Health 501 (1975); Franklin and Mais, *Tort Law and Mass Immunization Programs: Lessons from the Polio and Flu Episodes*, 65 Calif. L. Rev. 754 (1977); Herndon and Ballentine, *Vaccines: Precious Ounces of Prevention*, FDA Consumer, May 1983, at 20; Kitch, *The Vaccine Dilemma*, II Issues in Science and Technology, no. 2, at 108 (Winter 1986); Ladimer, *Legal and Regulatory Perspectives in Mass Immunization Programs*, 1976 Ins. L.J. 459; Comment, *Immunization Injuries: Proposed Compensatory Mechanisms—An Analysis*, 11 Conn. L. Rev. 147 (1978); Note, *Apportioning Liability in Mass Inoculations: A Comparison of Two Views and a Look at the Future*, 6 N.Y.U. Rev. L. & Soc. Change 239 (1977); Note, *Mass Immunization Cases: Drug Manufacturer's Liability for Failure to Warn*, 29 Vand. L. Rev. 235 (1976); Institute of Medicine, "Proceedings of a Workshop on Vaccine Innovation and Supply," Report for the use of the Subcomm. on Oversight and Investigations of the House Comm. on Energy and Commerce, 99th Cong., 2d Sess. (Comm. Print 1986); "Childhood Immunizations," Staff Report, Subcomm. on Health and the Environment of the House Comm. on Energy and Commerce, 99th Cong., 2d Sess. (Comm. Print 1986).

4. THE SWINE FLU ACT OF 1976

THOMAS BAYNES, LIABILITY FOR VACCINE RELATED INJURIES: PUBLIC HEALTH CONSIDERATIONS AND SOME REFLECTIONS ON THE SWINE FLU EXPERIENCE

21 St. Louis University Law Journal 44 (1977).

... Swine flu was a new major strain of influenza that was first isolated from soldiers at Fort Dix, New Jersey, but similar to a strain which caused a major epidemic from 1918 to 1920. It was suspected that should an outbreak of swine flu occur, a substantially higher percentage of those infected would die than in a normal influenza epidemic. It would cause a higher mortality rate in young adults by way of virus pneumonia which would not necessarily be treatable with antibiotics. The unique aspect of the swine flu situation was in the early warning of a possible epidemic. Nevertheless, skeptics questioned the need for such a large scale program, especially in view of its overall cost....

On March 24, 1976, President Ford requested Congress to appropriate funds for the development of a swine flu vaccine so that every citizen in the United States could be inoculated against this new influenza. In less than 30 days, $135 million had been provided to achieve that goal. The enabling legislation which would implement the mass immunization program was another matter.... Through the cooperation of four major drug manufacturers and public health officials, a swine flu vaccine was developed. Field trials were initiated to test the prototype vaccines. Over five thousand adults and children received the vaccines during the trials. Preliminary analysis proved favorable.....

About mid July, even though the vaccine was in production, a problem regarding the House bill developed between drug manufacturers and their insurors.... The insurance companies were unwilling to underwrite the drug companies' liability for vaccine related injuries, and manufacturers were not going to provide any vaccine to the federal government (the only purchaser) unless they had the insurance coverage.....

The impass continued throughout July, until the American Legion's National Convention in Philadelphia provided an unexpected stimulus. By August 3rd, the news media across the country were carrying stories of numerous deaths among the legionaries who had attended the convention. The "Legionaires Disease" was front page news in Washington during the entire week. Immediately the question was asked: Is it swine flu? ...

The liability protection demands of the insurance industry and the drug manufacturers baffled many members of Congress. The investigating subcommittee cited statistics of fewer than 20 claims against vaccine manufacturers out of a production of 70 million doses of flu vaccine over a five year period. With such a seemingly negligible risk, the fears of the insurers were difficult to understand. The concerns of the manufacturer's were not, however, predicated on the claims history of influenza vaccines. They were clearly linked to the warning requirement established in the *Davis* and *Reyes* decisions. The concern was not over the law of negligence, but of strict liability under § 402A of the Restatement of Torts. The solution arrived at under the swine influenza legislation only protected the manufacturers from the latter theory of liability.

     ... The final solution was an adaption of the federal tort claims concept.* The exclusive remedy for all injury claims arising out of the swine flu immunization program were to be brought against the United States Government.... The procedures to be followed were to be the same as those under the Federal Torts Claims Act but with three exceptions. First, the cause of action could be based on any theory of liability which was actionable under the law where the program participant's act or omission occurred. Secondly, the discretionary function immunity would not be available to the government as a defense against claims arising out of the actions of a program participant. Finally, the Claims Act's prejudice associated with the failure to file an administrative claim as a condition precedent to litigation was modified.... The term "program participant" is the focal point of the legislation's liability scheme. The term includes the manufacturers or distributors of the vaccine, public and private agencies, organizations, and medical personnel who provide swine flu innoculations without charge and who comply with the procedures for informing vaccinees of the risks and benefits of immunization....

     The legislation requires the Attorney General to defend all claims arising out of the immunization program against the federal government, its employees, or program participants and their insurors.... Where a program participant has been negligent or has violated its contractual obligations (not amounting to a negation of its protected status) the legislation creates a cause of action in the federal government....

     The swine flu mass immunization program, beset with difficulties from its inception, continued its troubled path through implementation. Before the program got underway, a Gallup Poll showed that 93% of the public were aware of the availability of the vaccine, but only 53% were planning to be innoculated. The concern over the safety of the vaccine was made more apparent when immediately after the program began three vaccinees died. Eight states temporarily suspended their programs. After a number of reports of suspected association between the swine flu vaccine and Guillian–Barre syndrome, the federal govern-

---

* The swine flu vaccination program was carried out under the National Swine Flu   Immunization Program of 1976, 90 Stat. 1113 (1976), 42 U.S.C. §§ 247b(j)-(*l*).

ment indefinitely halted the mass immunization program in December, 1976.

Subsequently, the program was reinstated on a limited basis. Public attitudes had been so adversely affected, however, that little hope remained for any significant demand for the immunization shots. In January, 1977, the Justice Department reported a steady influx of injury claims under the swine flu liability provisions. It was suggested in one report that upwards of ten thousand claims could be expected, and one claim alone alleged damages of 5.4 million dollars. The estimated costs of processing and defending these suits, apart from any judgments rendered, ranged in the millions of dollars...."

NOTES

1. *Critiques of Swine Flu Campaign.* For a highly critical examination of the decision making process concerning swine flu, undertaken at the request of Joseph Califano, the Secretary of HEW who made the ultimate decision to proceed, *see* R. Neustadt and H. Fineberg, THE SWINE FLU AFFAIR: DECISION–MAKING ON A SLIPPERY DISEASE (1978). *See also* A. Silverstein, PURE POLITICS AND IMPURE SCIENCE: THE SWINE FLU AFFAIR (1981).

2. *Constitutionality of Restrictions on Liability.* The constitutionality of the Swine Flu Act has been upheld in *Jones v. Wyeth Laboratories, Inc.,* 583 F.2d 1070 (8th Cir. 1978); *Ducharme v. Merrill–National Laboratories,* 574 F.2d 1307 (5th Cir. 1978).

3. *Claims Arising Out of Swine Flu Vaccination Campaign.* The refusal of the manufacturers of the swine flu vaccine, even in the face of substantial pressure, to proceed without government indemnification, proved prudent. By the time the statutory limitations period expired on December 16, 1978, nearly 3700 individuals had filed claims seeking more than $3.3 billion in damages. Gaskins, *Equity and Compensation: The Case of Swine Flu,* 10 Hastings Center Report, no. 1, at 5 (February 1980). The Judicial Panel on Multi-District Litigation transferred all actions to the District of Columbia for coordinated or consolidated pretrial proceedings, *In re Swine Flu Immunization Products Liability Litigation,* 446 F.Supp. 244 (J.P.M.D.L. 1978), 453 F.Supp. 648 (J.P.M. D.L. 1978), 464 F.Supp. 949 (J.P.M.D.L. 1979), and for award of attorneys' fees, 89 F.R.D. 695 (D.D.C. 1980). For representative decisions in individual cases, *see Petty v. United States,* 740 F.2d 1428 (8th Cir. 1984); *Unthank v. United States,* 732 F.2d 1517 (10th Cir. 1984); *Zeck v. United States,* 720 F.2d 534 (8th Cir. 1983); *Hasler v. United States,* 718 F.2d 202 (6th Cir. 1983); *Kynaston v. United States,* 717 F.2d 506 (10th Cir. 1983); *Daniels v. United States,* 704 F.2d 587 (11th Cir. 1983); *Freeman v. United States,* 704 F.2d 154 (5th Cir. 1983); *DiPippa v. United States,* 687 F.2d 14 (3d Cir. 1982); *Wallace v. United States,* 669 F.2d 947 (4th Cir. 1982); *Hunt v. United States,* 636 F.2d 580 (D.C. Cir. 1980); *Overton v. United States,* 619 F.2d 1299 (8th Cir. 1980).

5. NATIONAL CHILDHOOD VACCINE INJURY ACT OF 1986

Faced with the liability rules established in *Reyes* and other cases, and continually reminded by the swine flu episode of their enormous potential liability, fewer and fewer companies have been willing to engage in vaccine research and production. *See* Institute of Medicine, VACCINE SUPPLY AND INNOVATION (1985). In response to this withdrawal from the market, Congress enacted the National Childhood Vaccine Injury Act of 1986, 100 Stat. 3743, 3755, to establish a national program to encourage childhood vaccination and to provide government compensation for any injury resulting from administration of the vaccines listed in the statute. The program is codified in Title XXI of the Public Health Service Act, 42 U.S.C. § 300aa–1 *et seq.* The 1986 Act was funded in the Omnibus Budget Reconciliation Act of 1987, 101 Stat. 1330–327, by enacting a manufacturer's excise tax on vaccines and creating a vaccine injury compensation trust fund from which all claims of compensation are to be paid. The tax and trust fund provisions are codified in sections 4131 and 9510 of the Internal Revenue Code, 26 U.S.C. §§ 4131, 9510.

In substance, the Childhood Vaccine Injury Act creates a no-fault compensation system funded by an excise tax levied on product sales. Compensation is payable if a child experiences specified symptoms or reactions within stated time periods after vaccination and they persist for six months, unless the government can prove that the injury was caused by some other event. A claimant is not required to prove causation or negligence. All vaccine recipients who are injured after October 1, 1988 must participate in this program. If a claimant is not satisfied by the compensation awarded, he may reject the award and sue in tort under state law. The Act discourages such suits, however, by legislatively overruling the *Reyes* decision. The Act also provides that, in any such suit, a manufacturer is not liable for unavoidable side effects if the vaccine was properly prepared and was accompanied by the directions and warnings specified by FDA, unless it withheld information from FDA or otherwise violated the FD&C Act. Compliance with the FD&C Act is a defense to any claim for punitive damages. *See generally* Lenchek, *A Shot in the Arm: The National Childhood Vaccine Injury Act of 1986,* The Washington Lawyer, (March/Apr. 1989), at 24; Comment, *The National Childhood Vaccine Injury Act of 1986: A Solution to the Vaccine Liability Crisis?,* 63 Wash. L. Rev. 149 (1988). Interim procedures requiring reporting of adverse reactions to childhood vaccines were promulgated in 53 Fed. Reg. 10565 (October 13, 1988).

The 1986 Act thus appears to respond at least in part to the need for a Federal insurance program that will guarantee adequate compensation to persons who are injured, provide manufacturers reasonable certainty respecting their liability exposure, and thereby promote vaccination while encouraging development of new vaccines.

Chapter VI
MEDICAL DEVICES

FDA's regulation of medical devices has embraced two distinct phases. The first phase began with enactment of the 1938 Act and extended to the mid–1970s. The second and still evolving phase opened with enactment of the Medical Device Amendments of 1976. This Chapter reviews FDA's enforcement of the medical device provisions of the 1938 Act, explores the reasons why the 1976 Amendments were enacted, and examines the first decade of FDA's implementation of the new regulatory regime.

A. HISTORICAL BACKGROUND

Medical devices were made subject to the 1938 Act largely because of congressional concern about the growing number of fraudulent devices being marketed during the 1930s, but this problem was not new.

WALLACE F. JANSSEN, THE GADGETEERS
Chapter 16 of Barrett & Knight, THE HEALTH ROBBERS (1980).*

When Benjamin Franklin published his discoveries on electricity he also helped open the door for two of the most famous, frauds in medical history. . . . In 1784, while representing the United States in France, Franklin was appointed to a royal commission to investigate the hypnotist Antoine Mesmer, whose treatments had become the rage of Paris. Mesmer, clad in a lilac suit, carrying a metal wand and playing a harmonica, healed by what he called "animal magnetism." Patients sat around a huge vat or "battery," holding iron rods which were immersed in a solution. The treatments went on for hours, accompanied by shouts, hysterical laughter and convulsions. The Franklin commission, after conducting some experiments, reported no electricity in Mesmer's tub. Nor could they detect the current known as "animal magnetism." A royal decree banned further treatments, but Mesmer was allowed to take his winnings to England. . . .

Ten years later, Elisha Perkins, a mule trader turned physician, secured a patent for "Perkins Tractors." . . . The tractors, two pointed rods about three inches long, one gold-colored, the other silver, were simply drawn downward across the afflicted part of the anatomy, in a sort of scratching motion. This, it was theorized, would draw off the "noxious fluid" (electricity) which was alleged to cause disease. "Tractoration," of course, was universal therapy—good for everything. For a time, the Perkins treatment enjoyed amazing popularity. Ministers, college professors and Congressmen gave enthusiastic endorsement. The Chief Justice of the Supreme Court bought a pair and President Washington himself is supposed to have been a customer. The medical profession was initially impressed; but in 1796 the Connecticut Medical Society condemned the treatment as "gleaned from the miserable remains of animal magnetism." In the following year the Society expelled Dr. Perkins from membership. In 1799, Dr. Perkins voluntarily served in a yellow fever epidemic in New York, caught the disease, and died. Tractoration withered away.

But electrical health gadgetry marched on—through the 19th century and into the 20th.... In the 1920's, Albert Abrams, M.D., invented the system of diagnosis and healing he called "Radionics." Soon more than 3,000 local practitioners, mainly chiropractors, were sending dried blood specimens from patients to be inserted in Abrams' "Radioscope." The diagnosis would come back on a postcard, with recommended dial settings for treatment with other Abrams machines....

Albert Abrams had many imitators, among them Ruth Drown, a Los Angeles chiropractor. One of her many nonsensical inventions was the Drown Radio-therapeutic Instrument. With this little black box and *two* blood spots, Mrs. Drown claimed to be able to "tune in" specific organs of the body and treat a patient by remote control anywhere in the world! ...

Wilhelm Reich, M.D., one-time pupil of psychiatrist Sigmund Freud, claimed to have discovered "orgone energy," the most powerful force in the universe, and wrote extensively of its manifestations.... Soon after coming to the United States in 1934, Reich designed and built "orgone accumulators." Most of them were boxes of wood, metal and insulation board about the size of a telephone booth. Disease, he claimed, could be cured simply by sitting inside the box and absorbing the orgone. Hundreds of the boxes were sold or leased to practitioners and laymen for treatment of all kinds of diseases including cancer. Rentals were around $250 per month....

THEODORE H. COOPER *, DEVICE LEGISLATION

26 Food Drug Cosmetic Law Journal 165 (1971).

By 1937, there were 463 manufacturers of surgical, medical and dental instruments and supplies, and the value of their shipments was

* [Dr. Theodore Cooper, Director of the National Heart and Lung Institute, chaired the Department of HEW Study Group on Medical Devices in 1969–1970. He

a little over one million dollars. The industry grew rather slowly over the next decade. By 1947, the number of manufacturers picked up in the Census count had about doubled—to 980 establishments—while the value of shipments had more than tripled—to $372 million.

In the late 1950's and early 1960's, medical devices rapidly became both more numerous and more complex. Starting with the introduction of monitoring equipment into coronary care units, and automation into laboratories, electronics came to medicine. new implanted devices such as pacemakers, modern anesthetic equipment, and a myriad of diagnostic and therapeutic instruments began to appear. By 1963, there were over 1,300 manufacturers, and the value of shipments had grown to over $1 billion.... By 1967, comparable Census data showed almost 1,500 manufacturers with shipments valued at over $1.5 billion. Census estimates that the 1970 value of shipments was more than $2 billion, and that by 1975, the $2.8 billion, or almost the $3 billion mark will be reached. Census staff emphasize that all of these may be underestimates because of the characteristics of their accounting system.

Today, Census estimates that more than half of the total value of medical device shipments is accounted for in surgical appliances and supplies, including familiar consumable items such as sutures and dressings. Surgical and medical instruments—including X-ray machines and EKG machines—account for slightly less than one-third of the Census totals, with dental supplies and equipment coming in third....

NOTES

1. *History of Device Regulation.* For a comprehensive overview of device regulation, see Hutt, *A History of Government Regulation of Adulteration and Misbranding of Medical Devices,* 44 FDC L.J. 99 (1989).

2. *1938 Legislative History.* The key legislative history of the device provisions of the 1938 Act is summarized in *United States v. An Article of Drug ... Bacto–Unidisk,* 394 U.S. 784 (1969).

3. *Organizational Responsibility.* The same FDA unit was responsible for regulating drugs and medical devices under the 1938 Act until the device program was transferred from the Bureau of Drugs to the Office of the Associate Commissioner for Medical Affairs in 1971. Link and Pilot, *FDA's Medical Device Program,* FDA Papers, May 1972, at 24 (1972). In anticipation of the enactment of the Medical Device Amendments, it was transferred to a new Bureau of Medical Devices and Diagnostic Products in 39 Fed. Reg. 5812 (February 15, 1974), which in 1982 was in turn combined with the Bureau of Radiological Health to form the National Center for Devices and Radiological Health, 47 Fed. Reg. 44614 (October 8, 1982).

served as Assistant Secretary for Health from 1974 to 1976.]

B. THE 1938 ACT DEFINITION OF "DEVICE"

UNITED STATES v. 23 ... ARTICLES

United States Court of Appeals, Second Circuit, 1951.
192 F.2d 308.

WOODBURY, Circuit Judge.

The United States of America filed a libel ... seeking the seizure and condemnation of certain phonograph records, and various accompanying items of printed and graphic matter, all of which were moving or had moved in interstate commerce. The phonograph records were entitled in part "Time To Sleep," and their accompanying literature consists of (1) an album in part entitled, "De Luxe Records Presents Time To Sleep a Tested Method of Inducing Sleep Conceived and Transcribed by Ralph Slater," (2) a leaflet in part reading: "Sleep With This Amazing Record 'Time to Sleep,'" (3) a certificate entitled "Sleep Guaranteed," (4) display cards entitled "De Luxe Records Presents Time to Sleep," and (5) a poster headed "A 'Dream Girl' Shows a New Way to Dreamland." ...

Section 201(h) of the Act under consideration provides in material part that "[t]he term 'device' ... means instruments, apparatus, and contrivances, including their components, parts, and accessories, intended (1) for use in the diagnosis, cure, mitigation, treatment, or prevention of disease in man or other animals; or (2) to affect the structure or any function of the body of man or other animals."

Certainly a phonograph record, if not itself an instrument or an apparatus, is a contrivance. And moreover, it is without question a component, part or accessory of a phonograph, or like record playing machine, which in its turn is without any doubt at all an instrument, apparatus or contrivance. The real question therefore is whether the libeled records were intended for either of the uses described in (1) or (2) of § 201(h), supra. Obviously the records were intended for use in the cure, mitigation, treatment or perhaps prevention of insomnia. But the medical experts who testified at the trial were agreed that insomnia is not a disease, but is a symptom of a disease, usually although not necessarily a neurological one, or of an emotional disturbance of some kind. Thus it may be argued that the records do not fall within the coverage of (1) above.

However, all the expert witnesses who testified on the point were unanimous that sleep is a function of the body, or body and mind, of man and other animals, and this testimony brings the records within the terms of (2), supra, for their intended use was to affect that function, *i.e.* to induce sleep in those who needed it but had difficulty in obtaining enough. Without further laboring the point it will suffice to say that the records involved are "devices within the meaning of § 201(h)(2) of the Act....

In *United States v. Undetermined Quantities of ... Self–Hypnosis Tape Recordings,* 1981–1982 FDLI Jud. Rec. 94 (W.D. Mich. 1982), the court rejected the claimant's motion for summary judgment on the ground that tape recordings intended to provide self-hypnotic advice on a wide variety of medical matters were properly classified as medical devices. In the court's subsequent decision after trial, it faced the problem of distinguishing between health-related informational materials that do and do not fall within the definition of a device.

UNITED STATES v. UNDETERMINED QUANTITIES OF ARTICLE OF DEVICE

United States District Court, Western District of Michigan, 1982.
Med. Devices Rep. (CCH) ¶ 15,055.

This is an action by the United States, under the Federal Food, Drug and Cosmetic Act [the Act], 21 U.S.C. § 301 et seq., seeking the condemnation and forfeiture of thirty-two different tape recordings, marketed by the claimant, Potentials Unlimited, Inc. under various titles. These tape recordings were initially seized, pursuant to warrant, on January 6, 1981. The tapes sought to be condemned include:

1. "Relief of Back Pain" or "Back Pain"
2. "Removal of Warts"
3. "Bust Englargment" or "Natural Bust Englargment"
4. "Migraine Relief" or "Headaches"
5. "Pain Relief," "Pain," or "Pain Control"
6. "Freedom from Acne" or "Acne"
7. "Freedom from Allergies," "Removal of Allergies," "Elimination of Allergies," or "Allergies"
8. "Lower High Blood Pressure" or "Blood Pressure"
9. "Menstrual Problems" or "Monthly Cycle"
10. "Improving Vision" or "Vision"
11. "Stop Hair Loss" or "Hair Loss"
12. "Painless Dentistry," "Pleasant Dentistry," or "Dentistry"
13. "Psychic Healing" or "Psychiatric Healing"
14. "Hearing Loss" or "Hearing"
15. "Stop Bed–Wetting" or "Bed–Wetting"
16. "Gaining Weight" or "Weight Gain"
17. "Conception"
18. "Healthy Teeth and Gums" or "Teeth and Gums"
19. "Hyperactive Children"

20. "Operations: Before and After" or "Operations"
21. "Relaxation"
22. "Birth Separation"
23. "Stuttering"
24. "Up From Depression"
25. "Astral Sounds"
26. "Heal Your Bad Nerves (Good Health)" or "Good Health"
27. "Birth Control"
28. "Weight Loss"
29. "Arthritis Pain" or "Relieve Arthritis Pain"
30. "Insomnia"
31. "Stomach Problems"
32. "Tic," "Facial Tic," or "Stop Facial Tic"

Although the claimant disputes whether the labeling of the tapes is false or misleading and whether they lack adequate directions for use, it does not dispute that the tapes were manufactured in an unregistered establishment, that the tapes themselves are not registered as medical devices, or that there was no premarket notification of their manufacture and sale. It follows that if, in fact, the tapes are medical devices, they are in violation of the Act and are subject to forfeiture. Therefore, the resolution of this action turns upon one question; are these tapes medical devices within the meaning of the Act? . . . .

In January, 1981 Potentials Unlimited marketed over 100 tape recordings. Most of these are unrelated to health or medical problems, as evidenced by the fact that only 32 of the tapes are under seizure. The catalogue distributed by Potentials identifies many different "self-hypnosis" tapes with such titles as "Memory," "Good Study Habits," "Fear of Flying," "Stop Smoking," "Freedom from Guilt," "Jealousy," "Self–Confidence," "How to be Popular," "Be a Better Bowler," and "How to be a Great Golfer." Barrie Konicov wrote and recorded the master tape recordings for each of Potential's self-hypnosis tapes. The tapes are divided, by the catalogue, into several different "series." Most of the seized tapes fall under the "Health Series" although a few are listed under other categories.

The Potentials Unlimited catalogue comprises the most significant and detailed promotional literature used to market the tapes. . . . . The introduction refers to the tape recordings, at one point, as "learning"; however, read as a whole, the introduction leaves the impression that the positive suggestions contained on the tapes will act upon the "subconscious mind" to automatically bring about the changes which a person desires. Any teaching and learning aspects of the tapes are deemphasized or negated by the reference to "magic" and the implication that the tapes will work better, "without any interference from your conscious mind." Indeed, the introduction suggests that the tapes will be more beneficial if played during sleep, rather than actually being listened to and assimilated.

The catalogue distributed in 1981 contains a disclaimer on page 3, in small but easily legible print, which states:

> No therapeutic claims of any kind are made with regard to these tape programs. We believe cures or improvements are a matter of mind over matter and these tapes are not intended as a substitute for seeing your physician, or for medical treatment. Parental guidance is suggested for children's use.

An earlier version of this disclaimer was introduced into the catalogue sometime in 1980 after the FDA had begun investigating Potentials Unlimited in February of that year. In previous catalogues no such disclaimer was included.

The general introduction applies to all of the self-hypnosis tapes. The separate descriptive paragraphs contained in the catalogue refer by title and content to specific tapes and the specific problem or aspect of a person's life which that tape is designed to improve. The paragraphs are not specific regarding how the tapes work, instead they are anecdotal and conversational attempts to interest the reader in the specific tape. When combined with the general introduction, the individual descriptions generally leave the impression that the tapes will cure or treat the specific health-related problem indicated by the title of the tape.

Generally there is no dispute that the tapes purport to effect [sic] structures or functions of the body or to mitigate the effects of diseases. Several of the tapes are intended for use in the mitigation of pain. The claimant, although it introduced no evidence at trial, disputes whether pain is a function of the body. However, the medical testimony clearly established that pain is a physical warning signal produced by the body to indicate that a problem within the body exists. As such, it is a function of the body. Additionally, several of the tapes purport to alleviate the pain associated with particular diseases.

The tape "Weight Loss", based upon its content and the claims made in the catalogue, appears to be intended only to affect a person's eating habits. Although eating has a biological function, in modern society eating is more commonly considered a social activity, and overeating is considered a bad habit. Thus, the tape is listed in the catalogue under the "Habit Series" rather than as part of the health series. The "Weight Loss" tape does not purport to affect body structure except through a change in behavior.

The tape recordings themselves are very similar in style, structure, and content. They begin with brief instructions regarding the use and purpose of the particular tape, a standard hypnotic induction, and a series of statements, descriptions of visual images, and suggestions designed to influence the listener's thinking. Many of the images are repeated in more than one tape.

All of the tapes clearly convey a number of related ideas revolving around a central theme, *i.e.* that a person's thoughts can influence their health or physical characteristics. This central theme is developed through an emphasis on the benefits of relaxation, the elimination of negative feelings such as anger, hate and jealousy, the creation of a positive self-image, and the idea that reality is a reflection of one's own perceptions. Thus, according to the tapes, if a person thinks of himself in a particular, desired way, such as thin, free of allergies or pain, or generally healthy, the person will actually take on those desired characteristics. The tapes are clearly designed to communicate both this central tenet, and a method for putting it into practice.

The court does not find that the tapes themselves are, apart from the claims made in the catalogue, designed or intended to be used in the cure or treatment of the physical and mental conditions indicated by their titles. Each tape is designed to teach a method of mental therapy which it is claimed will have beneficial effects on a particular aspect of a person's life. Any therapeutic results flow from the listener's successful implementation of the lessons contained on the tape. The purported "treatment", therefore, consists of the new thought patterns, beliefs, and behaviors which the listener has learned and adopted. The lessons contained on the tapes are communicated linguistically, and can be understood as well by reading transcripts of the tapes as by listening to the tapes. The contents of the tapes could also be transmitted directly between two individuals, using speech, without the use of tape recording devices. Therefore, the court finds that the mechanical components of these tape recordings are not part of any medical treatment and are used only as a means of communicating the verbal ideas and methods found on the tapes.

The tapes use hypnosis and hypnotic suggestion to communicate the ideas which they contain. The American Medical Association has recognized hypnosis as a useful "modality" for medical treatment, when used in conjunction with other treatments, since 1957. There are controlled studies indicating that hypnosis techniques may be useful in the removal of warts, the treatment of asthma, the mitigation of all kinds of pain, the reduction of myopia (near-sightedness), and in enlarging the female bust. In addition, there are anecdotal reports of the successful use of hypnosis to cure or treat virtually every condition encompassed by the 32 self-hypnosis tapes under seizure. Scientific research regarding the use of hypnosis in treating these other conditions has generally been negative. No research has been done, specifically, regarding the use of hypnotic tape recordings....

The fundamental finding regarding hypnosis, as it impacts upon this case, is that hypnosis is an ill defined and little understood concept which it is at least possible to view as a special form of communication or as a teaching device. This finding is significant since the court has found that the tapes under seizure communicate several clearly identifiable ideas. Since hypnosis can be considered a form of communication, the fact that the tapes use hypnosis techniques, does not prevent their classification as communication or teaching devices. The court rejects Dr. Reyher's testimony that communication must be logical, rational, or objectively purposeful. His definition of communication, besides being outside his field of expertise (as he readily admitted) would exclude poetry, art, music, and drama from the area of communication. Whatever, the merits of such a restricted definition for some purposes, it does not comport with the ordinary concept of communication and is irrelevant for First Amendment purposes.

There is no evidence that the self-hypnosis tapes manufactured by Potential's Unlimited can actually achieve the results which are claimed in the Potential catalogue. The tapes could be harmful if they caused someone to delay seeking adequate medical care for a disease condition. Additionally, the uncontrolled use of hypnosis could be dangerous because persons could develop anxiety reactions to some of the suggestions contained on the tapes.

This case illustrates the difficulty which inevitably arises in balancing the ideal of philosophical and economic freedom against the practical need to protect unwary and vulnerable individuals from the claims of rapacious and unethical businessmen. The idea of freedom is represented by the testimony of Barrie Konicov in his February 18, 1982 deposition at pages 58–59:

Q Mr. Konicov, does your firm still market a tape called "Astro [sic] Sounds"?

A Yes, we do.

* * * *

Q How does it differ from the other tapes?

A It's just a bunch of loud, squeaky noises.

Q And what is it supposed to do?

A I don't know.

Q Why do you sell the tape if you don't know what it does or what it purports to do?

A Why?

Q Yes.

A To give people a choice to buy it or not to buy it.

Underlying this case, of course, is the fundamental question of whether consumers should be allowed the choice of buying Potentials Unlimited self-hypnosis tapes without the prior intervention and approval of the Federal government in the form of the Food and Drug Administration.

Representing the other side of the balancing dilemma is society's concern for the gullible or the desperate individual who is induced to forego necessary medical treatment by the fraudulent, or simply mistaken, claims of the purveyors of medical drugs and devices. Although the construction and fantastic claims made for many quack devices over the years often seem quite amusing, use of these devices can have serious health consequences. Whether sold to a consumer or a health professional, a device which does not perform as promised may pose a risk to health as well as an economic detriment to the purchaser. Reliance on unwarranted claims made for a device, recommending use in serious disease conditions, may induce the purchaser to forego seeking timely and appropriate medical treatment.

Fortunately, the court need not confront the problem presented in this case from the fundamental level of balancing the costs and benefits of the two competing perspectives suggested above. Congress has already engaged in such a balancing process and has determined that "medical devices" should be regulated by the FDA for the protection and benefit of the consuming public seeking medical treatment. In doing so, Congress has adopted a broad definition of medical device which is to be liberally construed in order to effectuate the purpose of the Act. *United States v. Bacto Unidisk*, 394 U.S. 784, (1969).

Essentially, the definition of medical device contained in the Act, establishes three characteristics which identifies [sic] an article as a device subject to regulation under the Act.

(1) It must be an instrument, apparatus, implement, machine, contrivance, implant, in vitro reagent, or other similar or related article, including any component, part, or accessory;

(2) It must be recognized in the National Formulary or United States Pharmacopeia, or it must be intended for use in the diagnosis, treatment, or prevention of disease, or it must be intended to affect the structure or function of the body; and

(3) It must not achieve its intended purposes through chemical action within or on the body and must not depend on metabolization in order to achieve its intended purposes.

There is no doubt that a tape recording is an implement, apparatus, or contrivance. However, a distinction must be made in this case between the tapes themselves, and the ideas that are contained on the tapes. Congress did not intend to regulate an article or device, the sole function of which is to serve as a means of communicating health related ideas or information. Had Congress had such an intent it would have expressly included books, the quintessential communication device, in the definition of "medical device." It did not do so.

The idea that a person can control and improve their health in general, or specific physical conditions, through the intervention of their thoughts, i.e. with their minds, is simply that, an idea, which anyone, including the claimant in this case, is free to believe, to disseminate, and, unless specifically prohibited, to act upon as they wish by virtue of the First Amendment. As found by the court, the tape recordings under seizure in this case are designed and intended to communicate and to teach certain ideas, beliefs, and mental processes which are claimed to have health benefits when adopted and practiced by the listener. Congress did not purport to regulate quack medical ideas or beliefs when it drafted the definition of medical device contained in the Act. By no stretch of language can an idea or a mental process be considered an instrument, apparatus, implement, machine, contrivance, implant, or in vitro reagent, or a similar or related article.

The "liberal interpretation" to be accorded the Act must yield somewhat when it comes into conflict with First Amendment freedoms.... Since ideas, beliefs and mental processes do not come within the statutory definition they are outside the jurisdiction of the FDA. Mechanical devices which do no more than communicate or expound such ideas, beliefs and mental processes are likewise outside the jurisdiction of the FDA. To include such devices within the definition would have grave First Amendment implications and would, by implication, bring health related books, magazines, and publications within the agency jurisdiction. That is a result Congress clearly did not contemplate or intend.

The fact that the tapes in issue do no more than communicate certain ideas using hypnosis as a tool in that communication does not end the inquiry into whether these tapes, as marketed by Potentials Unlimited, are subject to regulation as medical devices. Articles and devices which have no intended therapeutic qualities may be regulated if they are sold by the vendor accompanied by therapeutic claims. Thus, the seller's objective manifestation of a therapeutic intent brings otherwise medically benign articles within the purview of the Act.....

The therapeutic claims contained in promotional literature can convert the most innocent of articles into drugs or devices within the meaning of the Act ... The conduct of Potentials Unlimited in marketing these tapes as therapeutic medical devices is subject to regulation by Congress, even if the tapes themselves communicate ideas.

As stated in the court's findings of fact, the catalogue distributed by Potentials Unlimited tells the reader through its general introduction, that the self-hypnosis tapes will work "like magic," by "saturating the subconscious mind with positive suggestions." This language creates the expectation of an automatic and mechanical process by which suggestions will be implanted in the brain, much like a drug, and miraculous cures will result from the therapeutic effects of these suggestions. The whole introduction is designed to imply a therapeutic result from listening to the tapes, rather than a simple act of communication. Hypnosis is regarded, in the catalogue, as a treatment rather than a form of communication. Coupled with the titles of the seized tapes, an intended therapeutic use for the tapes is objectively manifested. This objective manifestation makes the tapes, as they are presently marketed, medical devices, to the extent they are used in treating disease or to affect body function.

The court has found that the "Weight Loss" tape is intended only to the claimed effect on body weight inherent in the title is based on the commonly accepted connection between eating behavior and body weight. Although the statutory language must be construed broadly to carry out the purposes of the Act, the court concludes that a tape purporting only to affect the habit of overeating is not intended to affect a "structure or function of the body" within the meaning of the Act. All of the other seized tapes are intended for use in the treatment of disease or to affect a structure or function of the body.

The petition for condemnation against the 32 tapes previously listed in this opinion is granted except as to the tapes "Weight Loss," "Psychic Healing," and "Astral Sounds."

UNITED STATES v. AN ARTICLE OF DRUG ... BACTO–UNIDISK

Supreme Court of the United States, 1969.
394 U.S. 784.

Mr. Chief Justice WARREN delivered the opinion of the court.

At issue here is the scope of the statutory definition of drug contained in the Federal Food, Drug, and Cosmetic Act and the extent of the Secretary of Health, Education, and Welfare's regulatory authority under that definition. The specific item involved in this definitional controversy is a laboratory aid known as an antibiotic sensitivity disc, used as a screening test for help in determining the proper antibiotic drug to administer to patients. If the article is a "drug" ... then the Secretary can subject it to pre-market clearance regulations promulgated pursuant to § 507 of the Act.... If, on the other hand, the article is merely a "device" under the Act, it is subject only to the misbranding and adulteration proscriptions of the Act and does not have to be pretested before marketing; and, of course, if the disc does not fall under either definition, the Act itself is totally inapplicable.....

At the outset, it is clear from § 201 that the word "drug" is a term of art for the purposes of the Act, encompassing far more than the strict medical definition of that word.....

The historical expansion of the definition of drug, and the creation of a parallel concept of devices, clearly show, we think, that Congress fully intended that the Act's coverage be as broad as its literal language indicates and equally clearly, broader than any strict medical definition might otherwise allow. Strong indications from legislative history that Congress intended the broad coverage the District Court thought "ridiculous" should satisfy us that the lower courts erred in refusing to apply the Act's language as written. But we are all the more convinced that we must give effect to congressional intent in view of the well-accepted principle that remedial legislation such as the Food, Drug, and Cosmetic Act is to be given a liberal construction consistent with the Act's overriding purpose to protect the public health, and specifically, § 507's purpose to ensure that antibiotic products marketed serve the public with "efficacy" and "safety."

Respondent's alternative contention, that even if its product does fall within the purview of the Act, it is plainly a "device" and therefore by definition necessarily not a "drug," must also be rejected, we believe, in light of the foregoing analysis. At the outset, it must be conceded that the language of the statute is of little assistance in determining precisely what differentiates a "drug" from a "device": to the extent that both are intended for use in the treatment, mitigation and cure of disease, the former is an "article" and the latter includes "instruments," "apparatus," and "contrivances." Despite the obvious areas of overlap in definition, we are not entirely without guidance in determining the propriety of the Secretary's decision below, given the overall goals of the Act and its legislative history.

More specifically, ... the "natural way" to draw the line "is in light of the statutory purpose." Since the patient will tend to derive less benefit and perhaps some harm from a particular antibiotic if, though the drug itself was properly batch-tested, it was not the proper antibiotic to use, it was entirely reasonable for the Secretary to determine that the discs, like the antibiotics they serve, are drugs and similarly subject to pre-clearance certification under § 507. An opposite conclusion might undercut the value of testing the antibiotics themselves, for such testing would be a useless exercise if the wrong drug were ultimately administered, even partially as the result of an unreliable disc. . . .

      Reversed.

NOTES

1. *"New Drug" Devices.* In *AMP, Inc. v. Gardner*, 389 F.2d 825 (2d Cir.1968), *cert. denied*, 393 U.S. 825 (1968), the court found the two products described below to be drugs:

> Both of the products are intended to be used in a new method of tying off, or ligating, severed blood vessels during surgery. The conventional ligating method is to hand-tie ligatures around severed vessels by means of a surgeon's knot (which is a reef knot). AMP's products both consist of a disposable applicator, a nylon ligature loop, and a nylon locking disk. . . . The ligature is applied by inserting the hemostat or tube into the body and placing the loop around the severed vessel, then tightening the loop and locking it in place with the disk. The excess nylon thread is cut off, and the disk and the rest of the thread remain in the patient's body.

2. *In Vitro Diagnostics.* Following the *Bacto–Unidisk* decision, FDA could have required the submission of NDAs for all in vitro diagnostic products. Instead, mindful of both the resources it would need and the impact on the industry and the public health, FDA explicitly declined to determine whether these products would be regulated as drugs or devices. Rather, the agency prescribed detailed labeling requirements to assure that users would have accurate and reliable information. 37 Fed. Reg. 819 (January 19, 1972), 37 Fed. Reg. 16613, (August 17, 1972), 38 Fed. Reg. 7096 (March 15, 1973), now codified in 21 C.F.R. Part 807 (1989). *See* Ringuette, *Regulatory Aspects of Reagents,* 27 FDC L.J. 557 (1972); *The Future of Diagnostic Kits and Reagents,* 29 FDC L.J.

246 (1974). Because of the importance of reliable diagnoses of gonorrhea and cancer, however, FDA announced that any diagnostic test for these diseases would require an approved NDA, 38 Fed. Reg. 10488 (April 27, 1973), 39 Fed. Reg. 3705 (January 29, 1974).

3. *Scope of Drug Definition.* After *Bacto–Unidisk,* FDA took the position that with medical products falling "in the middle ground or the grey area, where they are not clearly one or the other, [it had] complete discretion at this time to decide whether it will handle those products as drugs or devices. . . ." The agency suggested that these "grey area" products could be reclassified from drug status to device status by appropriate changes in the statutory definitions and thus that industry has "a stake in seeing that legislation is passed so that this type of appropriate classification can be carried out." Remarks by FDA Chief Counsel Peter Barton Hutt at the FDA Medical Device Conference of April 11, 1972, 34 FDC Reports (the "Pink Sheet"), No. 16, at 18–20 (April 17, 1972). The legislation then pending would not have amended the statutory definitions. The bill was subsequently changed and the enacted version did reclassify grey area medical products from drug to device status. *See* p. 751 *infra.*

4. *Commentary.* For discussion of the *AMP* and *Bacto–Unidisk* decisions, *see* Kleinfeld, *Surgical Implants: Drugs or Devices, and New Device Legislation,* 23 FDC L.J. 510 (1968); Styn, *A Dichotomy in Consumer Protection—The Drug–Device Definition Dilemma,* 44 Ind. L.J. 503 (1969); Weitzman, *Drug, Device, Cosmetic?* (pts. I–II), 24 FDC L.J. 226, 320 (1969).

**NEW DRUG STATUS OF
CERTAIN INTRAUTERINE DEVICES**

38 Federal Register 6137 (March 7, 1973).

On June 5, 1971, there was published in the FEDERAL REGISTER (36 FR 10983), a proposed policy statement regarding the new drug status of intrauterine devices incorporating heavy metals, drugs, or other substances used for the purpose of contraception. . . .

. . . [One] firm commented that the proposal did not define clearly enough those intrauterine devices that would require a new drug application and those that would not. . . . [T]he order has been revised to exclude from consideration as new drugs the following: (1) IUD's fabricated solely from inactive materials such as inactive plastics or metals and (2) IUD's with substances added to improve the physical characteristics if such substances do not contribute to contraception through chemical action on or within the body and are not dependent upon being metabolized for the achievement of the contraceptive purposes. . . .

§ 130.50 Certain intrauterine devices for human use for the purpose of contraception [now § 310.502(a)]

(a) The Food and Drug Administration has become aware of the increased clinical use for the purpose of contraception of intrauterine devices that incorporate heavy metals, drugs, or other active substances. The amount of local irritation caused by such active materials has been reported as being correlated, in animal studies, to the efficacy of such devices in achieving their contraceptive effect....

(b) Intrauterine devices used for the purpose of contraception and incorporating heavy metals, drugs, or other active substances to increase the contraceptive effect, to decrease adverse reactions, or to provide increased medical acceptability, are not generally recognized as safe and effective for contraception and are new drugs within the meaning of section 201(p) of the Federal Food, Drug, and Cosmetic Act.

REGULATION OF MEDICAL DEVICES
(INTRAUTERINE CONTRACEPTIVE DEVICES)

Hearings Before the Intergovernmental Relations Subcommittee of the
House Committee on Government Operations, 93d Congress, 1st Session (1973).

Mr. Fountain.... I believe it was developed yesterday through questioning that since there are no premarket clearance requirements for devices, the burden of proof is on the Government to establish in any given instance that a device is dangerous to health....

Would it have been unreasonable to hold these new products, for which there was no prior marketing clinical experience, to be new drugs?

Mr. Hutt.... If we had enough scientific evidence to state that ones already marketed were generally recognized as safe and effective, then, obviously, we could classify all IUD's as drugs and only the new ones as new drugs.

I think it is probably not the situation that we did have enough information that we could make that scientific distinction. What we would have been faced with [was] ... taking all IUD's off the market on the grounds that none of them were old drugs; that is, none of them were generally recognized as safe and effective. In short, without new legislation that would have specific transitional provisions that would allow us to say, all right, leave these drugs on the market pending the further testing for a specific period of time, without specific congressional authorization to do that, we would have been in a very difficult position to try to catch up with history in regulating these products....

Mr. Fountain. If there were no prior marketing clinical experience, it is your opinion it would have been unreasonable to hold them as new drugs? ...

Dr. Jennings.... The question was not only of the difficulty of sustaining the legal position, which Mr. Hutt has addressed, but also the question of resources to be devoted to calling such things as the lenses and the IUD's and heart valves, drugs.... [I]t was decided that we would make better use of our limited resources by following the "devices" provisions.

In addition, at that point in time there was the general feeling, based on what the committee had produced, that as a broad category, the IUD's did not represent a high degree of risk in the total spectrum of medical devices that were under our surveillance at that point in time. . . .

Mr. Hutt. . . . [Y]ou could not distinguish legally between one type of implant and another. That is, what I would call an inactive implant. If, for example, a heart valve or replacement for a bone or joint was inactive, then it would also be a drug, if an inactive IUD was a drug. There is no way to distinguish between them.

NOTE

Regulations prescribing professional and patient labeling for IUDs, 21 C.F.R. §§ 310.502 and 801.427 (1989), were proposed in 40 Fed. Reg. 27796 (July 1, 1975) and promulgated in 42 Fed. Reg. 23772 (May 10, 1977).

C. ENFORCEMENT OF THE 1938 ACT

MEDICAL DEVICE LEGISLATION—1975

House Committee on Interstate and Foreign Commerce.
94th Congress, 1st Session (1975).

The medical devices in use during the late 1930's and through the late 1940's were of relatively simple and basic design. Seizure and injunction actions by FDA were generally limited to actions against a persistent series of "quack" devices. Legitimate devices were generally only reviewed for the accuracy of labeling. Between 1939 and 1941, the FDA initiated roughly 100 seizure actions against devices. At that time, several dangerous devices, such as lead nipple shields which caused nursing infants to incur lead poisoning, contraceptives which often caused genital infection and injury, and vaporizers which caused sinus and eustachian tube infections were removed from the market. . . .

The post-war years brought forth a wide variety of "quack" devices utilizing colored lights, dangerous gases such as ozone and chlorine, radio waves, heat, and vibration with claims of treatment and cure for virtually every disease known to man. One such device was a simple galvanometer which was encased in an impressive box and purportedly could diagnose any illness known to man. But when tested by the FDA on a corpse, the device registered a reading. It cost only a few dollars to produce, yet sold for hundreds of dollars.

The post-war revolution in biomedical technology also resulted in the introduction of a wide variety of sophisticated but legitimate devices. New developments in the electronic, plastics, metallurgy, and ceramics industries, coupled with progress in design engineering, led to invention of the heart pacemaker, the kidney dialysis machine, defibrillators, cardiac and renal catheters, surgical implants, artificial vessels and heart valves, intensive care monitoring units, and a wide spectrum of diagnostic and therapeutic devices. The increased sophistication of medical devices coupled with a stronger authority to regulate drugs caused FDA to classify some of the new products as drugs. In general, during the 1950's and 1960's, FDA encountered increasing difficulty in proving why certain defective or ineffective medical devices should be removed from the market. This was due to an increasing number of medical device manufacturers who began to regularly challenge FDA actions in the courts. As a result of the increased sophistication of products, FDA has been forced to develop elaborate evidence to substantiate its proposed regulatory actions.

NOTES

1. *Enforcement Against Quack Devices.* Although most FDA device seizures have resulted in default or consent decrees, actions against so-called "quack" devices have often resulted in protracted litigation. *See, e.g., United States v. Urbuteit,* 335 U.S. 355 (1948); *United States v. Articles of Device ... "Kuf Diatherapuncteur ..."*, 481 F.2d 434 (10th Cir. 1973); *United States v. Ellis Research Laboratories, Inc.,* 300 F.2d 550 (7th Cir. 1962); *Drown v. United States,* 198 F.2d 999 (9th Cir. 1952), discussed in Klinger, *Conflict with Quackery,* 8 FDC L.J. 777 (1953); *United States v. Ghadiali,* 165 F.2d 957 (3d Cir. 1948); *United States v. One Device ... Colonic Irrigator,* 160 F.2d 194 (10th Cir. 1947); *United States v. Relaxacizor, Inc.,* 340 F.Supp. 943 (C.D. Cal. 1970); *United States v. 46 Devices Labeled "Dynatone,"* 315 F.Supp. 588 (D. Minn. 1970); *United States v. An Article of Device ... "Cameron Spitler Amblyo-Syntonizer ...,"* 261 F.Supp. 243 (D. Neb. 1966); *United States v. "2000 Plastic Tubular Cases ... Each Containing 2 Toothbrushes,"* 231 F.Supp. 236 (M.D. Pa. 1964); *United States v. 24 Devices ... "Sunflo Flowing Air Purifier,"* 202 F.Supp. 147 (D.N.J. 1962); *United States v. Article of Device ... "110 V Vapozone ...,"* 194 F.Supp. 332 (N.D. Cal. 1961); *United States v. 22 Devices ... Halox Therapeutic Generator,* 98 F.Supp. 914 (S.D. Cal. 1951); *United States v. 6 Devices, "Electreat Mechanical Heart,"* 38 F.Supp. 236 (W.D. Mo. 1941). *See also* FDA, RECENT ENFORCEMENT ACTIONS INVOLVING THERAPEUTIC DEVICES, JANUARY 1–DECEMBER 31, 1963 (1964).

2. *Diapulse Litigation.* In November 1965, FDA instituted its first seizure of a Diapulse, beginning litigation that lasted more than 20 years. The Diapulse was designed to produce a high frequency electrical pulse, similar to a conventional diathermy unit, but with lower output. FDA took the position that it was a misbranded device because it did not produce sufficient heat to provide the claimed therapeutic benefit. Although the government prevailed at trial, *United States v. An Article of Device ... Diapulse Manufacturing Corp. of Am.,* 269 F.Supp. 162 (D. Conn. 1967), and on appeal, 389 F.2d 612 (2d Cir. 1968), the violations continued. FDA therefore secured an injunction against further sales. *United States v. Diapulse Corp. of Am.,* 457 F.2d 25 (2d Cir. 1972). *See* Comment, *U.S. v. The Diapulse Corporation of America,* 8 New Eng. L. Rev. 111 (1972). In October 1973 FDA advised Congress: "The *Diapulse* cases require us to expend an inordinate amount of the resources allocated to device regulation, and thereby restrict investigative effort with respect to other

dangerous or useless devices." "Medical Devices," Hearings Before the Sub-comm. on Public Health and Environment of the House Comm. on Interstate and Foreign Commerce, 93d Cong., 1st Sess. 155 (1973).

The *Diapulse* litigation did not end with the Second Circuit's 1972 decision. FDA enforcement activities continued into 1976. FDA's criminal contempt action failed, but the injunction was strengthened. *United States v. Diapulse Corp. of Am.*, 365 F.Supp. 935 (E.D.N.Y. 1973), 514 F.2d 1097 (2d Cir. 1975). FDA then lost a seizure action in a district court, but won on appeal. *United States v. Articles of Device* ... *"Diapulse,"* 527 F.2d 1008 (6th Cir. 1976), *reh'g denied,* 532 F.2d 1056 (6th Cir. 1976). FDA again initiated seizures but, although it granted summary judgment to the agency, the district court allowed the devices to be relabeled over the agency's objections. The court of appeals ruled that the district court had incorrectly conducted a de novo trial on the validity of the claims. *United States v. An Article of Device* ... *Diapulse,* 650 F.2d 908 (7th Cir. 1981). On remand, the district court affirmed FDA's refusal to accept the Diapulse relabeling. *See United States v. An Article of Device* ... *Diapulse,* 768 F.2d 826 (7th Cir. 1985). In the interim, based upon FDA's approval of a similar device marketed by a competing company, the Diapulse Corporation persuaded the district court to modify the 1974 injunction to permit the marketing of an identical Diapulse device. That ruling against FDA was upheld on appeal. *United States v. Diapulse Corp. of Am.,* 748 F.2d 56 (2d Cir. 1984). The Diapulse Corporation later successfully sued to recover attorneys' fees under the Equal Access to Justice Act, 1985–1986 FDLI Jud. Rec. 413 (E.D.N.Y. 1985).

Rather than market a Diapulse identical to the higher-powered competitive device FDA ·had approved, however, the Diapulse Corporation persisted in research on its own lower-powered version. It ultimately obtained FDA's agreement to a narrower claim, "for adjunctive use in the palliative treatment of post-operative edema and pain in superficial tissues." 13 Medical Devices, Diagnostics & Instrumentation Rep. (the "Gray Sheet"), No. 16, at I & W–12 (April 20, 1987).

3. *Acupuncture Needles.* In an attempt to anticipate regulatory problems with acupuncture needles, FDA issued a notice in 38 Fed. Reg. 6419 (March 9, 1973), stating that it would consider any acupuncture needle to be misbranded unless it was labeled only for experimental use by or under the direct supervision of a licensed medical or dental practitioner, with the informed consent of the patient, and under an investigational protocol approved by an institutional review committee. FDA's seizure of two mislabeled electric acupuncture devices was upheld in *United States v. Articles of Device [Acuflex; Pro–Med]*, 426 F. Supp. 366 (W.D. Pa. 1977).

L. Ron Hubbard began his career writing about the new science of "dianetics," expanded it into a book, started the Hubbard Dianetic Research Foundation, and then established the Founding Church of Scientology. FDA enforcement of the 1938 Act against the Hubbard Electrometer, or E-meter, became complicated when the Founding Church of Scientology asserted that use of the E-meter plays an essential part in the practice of religion.

FOUNDING CHURCH OF SCIENTOLOGY v. UNITED STATES

United States Court of Appeals, District of Columbia Circuit, 1969.
409 F.2d 1146, *cert. denied,* 396 U.S. 963.

J. SKELLY WRIGHT, Circuit Judge.

This is an appeal from a judgment and decree of condemnation and destruction against several electrical instruments and a large quantity of literature owned by claimants-appellants, The Founding Church of Scientology of Washington, D.C. and various individual adherents of that organization. The instruments and literature were seized by the Food and Drug Administration as "devices" with accompanying "false and misleading labeling" subject to condemnation under the Food, Drug and Cosmetic Act. The Government further charged that the instruments were "devices" lacking "adequate directions for use," in further violation of the Act. After a jury trial, a general verdict "for the Government" was returned, and a judgment and decree of condemnation was entered.

Appellants contend that ... the proceedings interfered with the free exercise of their religion, and that the evidence was insufficient to sustain the verdict. Because we find that much of the literature relied on by the Government to establish misbranding was not "labeling" within the meaning of the statute as interpreted in the light of the First Amendment, we reverse....

... The Government has charged that the instruments seized, Hubbard Electrometers or "E-meters," are "devices" as defined in the Act, that the literature seized constitutes "labeling" of the device, in that it is "written, printed, or graphic matter * * * accompanying" the device; and that this "labeling" is false or misleading....

Appellants in this case, claimants to the seized materials, are individual and corporate adherents to the movement known as Scientology. The movement apparently rests almost entirely upon the writings of one man, L. Ron Hubbard, an American who maintained the headquarters of the movement in England at the time this action was brought. In the early 1950's, Hubbard wrote tracts elucidating what he called "Dianetics." Dianetics is a theory of the mind which sets out many of the therapeutic techniques now used by Scientologists, including techniques attacked by the Government in this case as false healing....

Dianetics is not presented as a simple description of the mind, but as a practical science which can cure many of the ills of man. It terms the ordinary person, encumbered by the "engrams" of his reactive mind, as a "preclear," by analogy to a computer from which previously programmed instructions have not been erased. The goal of Dianetics is to make persons "clear," thus freeing the rational and infallible analytical mind....

From the evidence developed at trial, it appears that a major activity of the Founding Church and its affiliated organizations in the District of Columbia is providing "auditing," at substantial fees (at the time of trial $500 for a 25–hour course), to persons interested in Scientology.... There is no membership in the Church as such; persons are accepted for auditing on the basis of their interest in Scientology (and presumably their ability to pay for its benefits).

The Hubbard Electrometer, or E-meter, plays an essential, or at least important, part in the process of auditing. The E-meter is a skin galvanometer, similar to those used in giving lie detector tests. The subject or "preclear" holds in his hands two tin soup cans, which are linked to the electrical apparatus. A needle on the apparatus registers changes in the electrical resistance of the subject's skin. The auditor asks questions of the subject, and the movement of the needle is apparently used as a check of the emotional reaction to the questions. According to complex rules and procedures set out in Scientology publications, the auditor can interpret the movements of the needle after certain prescribed questions are asked, and use them in diagnosing the mental and spiritual condition of the subject. The E-meters are sold for about $125, and are advertised in Scientology publications available at the Distribution Center adjoining the Church.....

In its legal arguments the Government has contended from the outset that whether or not Scientology is a religion, and whether or not auditing or processing is a practice of that religion, are entirely irrelevant to the case. Religious beliefs, it is argued, are entirely protected by the First Amendment, but action in the name of religion is susceptible to legal regulation under the same standards and to the same degree as it would be if entirely secular in purpose.

Appellants have argued from the first that the entire case must fall as an unconstitutional religious persecution. In their view, auditing or processing is a central practice of their religion, akin to confession in the Catholic Church, and hence entirely exempt from regulation or prohibition. They have made no attempt to contradict the expert testimony introduced by the Government. They have conceded that the E-meter is of no use in the diagnosis or treatment of disease as such, and have argued that it was never put forward as having such use. Auditing or processing, in their view, treats the spirit of man, not his body, though through the healing of the spirit the body can be affected....

The principles enunciated in [prior decisions of the Supreme Court] ... at least raise a constitutional doubt concerning the condemnation of instruments and literature apparently central to the practice of religion. That doubt becomes more serious when we turn to the decision of the Supreme Court in *United States v. Ballard,* 322 U.S. 78 (1944)....

... Here the E-meter has been condemned, not because it is itself harmful, but because the representations made concerning it are "false or misleading." And the largest part of those representations is contained in the literature of Scientology describing the process of auditing which appellants have claimed, without contest from the Government, is part of the doctrine of their religion and central to its exercise. Thus if their claims to religious status are accepted, a finding that the seized literature misrepresents the benefits from auditing is a finding that their religious doctrines are false. To construe the Food, Drug and Cosmetic Act to permit such a finding would ... present the gravest constitutional difficulties....

By far the greatest bulk of the material alleged to be "false labeling" of the E-meter consists of the general literature of Scientology, which presents in an integrated manner the theory sketched earlier concerning the human mind, the sources of various sorts of unhappiness, personality disorder and psychosomatic complaints, and the way in which he process of auditing can alleviate these ills.....

Were the literature here introduced clearly secular, we might well conclude that under existing law it constituted "labeling" for purposes of the Act.... However, such broad readings are not favored when they impinge upon constitutionally sensitive areas, especially in the absence of a showing of legislative intent to regulate these areas....

Finally, we come to the vexing question: is Scientology a religion? On the record as a whole, we find that appellants have made out a *prima facie* case that the Founding Church of Scientology is a religion.....

(1) We do not hold that the Founding Church is for all legal purposes a religion. Any *prima facie* case made out for religious status is subject to contradiction by a showing that the beliefs asserted to be religious are not held in good faith by those asserting them, and that forms of religious organization were erected for the sole purpose of cloaking a secular enterprise with the legal protections of religion.

(2) We do not hold that, even if Scientology is a religion, all literature published by it is religious doctrine immune from the Act.

(3) We do not hold that public health laws in general, or the Food, Drug and Cosmetic Act in particular, have no application to the activities of religion. For instance, it may well be that adulterated foods, drugs or devices used in religious practices can be condemned under the Act. It may be that a drug or device used in religion is subject to condemnation as "misbranded" if its labeling is found to lack, for instance, adequate directions for use, as was charged in this case. Our holding prevents only a finding of false labeling on the basis of doctrinal religious literature.

(4) Finally, we made no holding concerning the power of Congress to deal generally with the making of false claims by religions deemed injurious to the public health or welfare....

McGOWAN, Circuit Judge (dissenting):....

This proceeding did not involve an inquisition into the validity of any personal religious beliefs, or the infliction of a punishment upon any person for holding or disseminating such beliefs. It was a proceeding against property under a Congressional statute aimed at protecting the unsophisticated against not only wasting their money but, more importantly, endangering their lives by relying upon misbranded machines. There is, as the majority points out, a well-recognized distinction between the good faith holding of a religious belief, however bizarre, and unlimited freedom to implement that belief by conduct. I do not believe that the Government was required, at least in a statutory *in rem* proceeding of the kind here involved, to show that, over and above the misbranding of the device, the religious pretensions of its sponsors were fraudulent.

NOTES

1. *Subsequent Proceedings.* Upon retrial following the court of appeals' remand, the district court held that the Founding Church of Scientology had met its burden of establishing its status as a bona fide religion. It also found the E-meter to be misbranded. The court's decree returned the devices and literature to the church for use only in bona fide religious counseling. *United States v. An Article of Device... "Hubbard Electrometer,"* 333 F.Supp. 357 (D.D.C. 1971). Its order, designed to assure observance of this limitation, would have required the following statement to be affixed to every E-meter, and a similar version to be signed by every recipient of auditing services and to appear in the Church's E-meter literature:

> The E-meter is a device which has been condemned by Order of a Federal Court for misrepresentation and misbranding, in violation of the Federal Food, Drug, and Cosmetic Act. Use of the E-meter is permitted only as part of bona-fide religious activity. The E-meter is not medically or scientifically useful for the diagnosis, treatment, or prevention of any disease. It is not medically or scientifically capable of improving the health or bodily functions of anyone. Any person using, selling or distributing the E-meter is forbidden by law to represent, state or imply that the E-meter is useful in the diagnosis, treatment, or prevention of any disease.

1969–1974 FDLI Jud. Rec. 90 (D.D.C. 1971). Upon appeal once more, the court of appeals, per curiam, concluded that the district court order "would invoke the Government and the courts in an excessive entanglement with religion ... in circumstances in which the legitimate governmental interest in law enforcement can be protected by a narrower remedy." It therefore modified the order to read as follows:

> 1. E-meters shall be used or sold or distributed only for use in bona fide religious counseling.

> 2. Each E-meter shall bear the following warning, printed in 11-point leaded type, permanently affixed to the front of the E-meter so that it is clearly visible when the E-meter is used, sold, or distributed:

>> The E-meter is not medically or scientifically useful for the diagnosis, treatment, or prevention of any disease. It is not medically or scientifically capable of improving the health or bodily functions of anyone.

3. Any and all items of written, printed, or graphic matter which directly or indirectly refers [sic] to the E-meter or to Dianetics and/or Scientology and/or auditing or processing shall ... bear the following prominent printed warning ...:

WARNING

The device known as a Hubbard Electrometer, or E-meter, used in auditing, a process of Scientology and Dianetics, is not medically or scientifically useful for the diagnosis, treatment, or prevention of any disease. It is not medically or scientifically capable of improving the health or bodily functions of anyone.

1969–1974 FDLI Jud.Rec. 131 (D.C. Cir. 1973).

2. *Other E–Meter Litigation.* Courts in *Church of Scientology of California v. Richardson,* 437 F.2d 214 (9th Cir. 1971), and *Church of Scientology of Minnesota v. Department of HEW,* 459 F.2d 1044 (8th Cir. 1972), *aff'g* 341 F.Supp. 563 (D. Minn. 1971), upheld FDA's summary detention of imported E-meters based on charges, *inter alia* that their labeling failed to bear "adequate directions for use." Both decisions relied on the broad authority over imports granted to FDA by section 801(a) of the FD&C Act.

3. *Scientology's Tax Status.* The tax status of the Church of Scientology has also been a source of continuing litigation. *See, e.g., Church of Scientology v. Commissioner of Internal Revenue,* 823 F.2d 1310 (9th Cir. 1987); *Founding Church of Scientology v. United States,* 412 F.2d 1197 (Ct. Cl. 1969).

4. *Criminal Prosecution.* In October 1979, nine high officials of the Church of Scientology, including Hubbard's wife, were found guilty of a criminal conspiracy to break into, infiltrate, bug, and steal documents from government agencies and private organizations. These actions were taken in response to what Church officials viewed as harassment by government agencies and private groups. *United States v. Heldt,* 668 F.2d 1238 (D.C. Cir. 1981). *See also United States v. Hubbard,* 650 F.2d 293 (D.C. Cir. 1980); *United States v. Hubbard,* 686 F.2d 955 (D.C. Cir. 1982).

D. THE 1976 MEDICAL DEVICE AMENDMENTS

1. BACKGROUND

In 1976, after many years of consideration, Congress enacted comprehensive changes in the Federal law regulating medical devices.

MEDICAL DEVICE AMENDMENTS OF 1976
House Report No. 853, 94th Congress, 2d Session (1976).

FDA began focusing more attention on hazards from legitimate medical devices around 1960.... New developments in the electronic, plastic, metallurgy, and ceramics industries, coupled with progress in design engineering, led to invention of the heart pacemaker, the kidney dialysis machine, defibrillators, cardiac and renal catheters, surgical implants, artificial vessels and heart valves, intensive care monitoring units, and a wide spectrum of other diagnostic and therapeutic devices. Although many lives have been saved or improved by the new discoveries, the potential for harm to consumers has been heightened by the critical medical conditions in which sophisticated modern devices are used and by the complicated technology involved in their manufacture and use. In the search to expand medical knowledge, new experimental approaches have sometimes been tried without adequate premarket clinical testing, quality control in materials selected, or patient consent.

An example ... is the Dalkon Shield. In November 1970, the Dalkon Shield was introduced to the medical profession as a safe effective contraceptive device.... In less than two years the Shield had been adopted by 1,497 family planning clinics in the United States and was also being used in world population control programs. The manufacturer reported that more than one million Shields had been sold. In May of 1972, the Family Planning Digest, an official HEW publication, reported that, based on an eighteen month study of 937 patients in family planning programs in California, the pregnancy rate with the Shield was 5.1%, the removal rate for medical reasons was 26.4%, the infection rate was 5%, and the continuation rate after eighteen months was under 60%. By mid–1975 the Shield had been linked to sixteen deaths and twenty-five miscarriages. Presently, more than 500 lawsuits seeking compensatory and punitive damages totalling more than $400 million are pending against the manufacturer of the Shield, which is no longer being marketed....

Experience with two other types of devices further demonstrates the need for increased statutory authority. Significant defects in cardiac pacemakers have necessitated 34 voluntary recalls of pacemakers, involving 23,000 units, since 1972. A recent investigation in four states of eleven patients who experienced unusual eye infections following implantation of intraocular lenses revealed serious impairment of vision in all patients and the necessity to remove the eyes of five patients....

The bills considered by Congress in the late 1950s and early 1960s to modernize the drug provisions of the 1938 Act also addressed medical devices. To secure enactment of the 1962 Drug Amendments after the widespread publicity about thalidomide, however, FDA acquiesced in the deletion of coverage of medical devices. In the following years several proposals to broaden regulatory controls over medical devices were considered by Congress but no consensus emerged. In his 1969 Consumer Message to Congress, President Nixon ordered the Department of HEW to study the matter before proposing further legislation. The Study Group on Medical Devices issued its report in September 1970. *See* Cooper, *Device Legislation,* 26 FDC L.J. 165 (1971); Hutt, *A*

History of Government Regulation of Adulteration and Misbranding of Medical Devices, 44 FDC L.J. 99 (1989).

STUDY GROUP ON MEDICAL DEVICES, MEDICAL DEVICES: A LEGISLATIVE PLAN

(DHEW, 1970).

The variety of medical devices already in use are produced from an equally wide variety of materials. Moreover, the bases of scientific data range from almost pure empiricism to reasonably well systematized information. As a result, there are many scientific and technical issues involved in the evaluation of medical devices that require judgment by expert professionals all along the developmental continuum from research through development to testing, evaluation, and preparation for sale. Accordingly, unilateral decisions by government agencies without expert advice would be as unwise as unilateral decisions by developers or producers....

The study group agrees that definition and classification are important, and that there are inherent differences between drugs and devices—differences in the state of the art, and the size and scope of manufacture. Therefore, the study group believes that a new regulatory plan is needed, one which is specifically adapted to the needs of devices.... By drawing upon the advice of appropriate scientific organizations, the Department can determine an appropriate basis for decisions about which devices are so well recognized as safe and effective as to require neither standards nor pre-clearance. It can also identify devices or characteristics of devices for which *standards* should and can be developed and applied. With continuing assistance of the scientific and medical community, a system for *review of objective data prior to clinical application* can be devised for new and unproven critical devices that are at the leading edge of technological innovation and biomedical explorations to assure the safety and reliability of devices offered to the profession.

NOTES

1. *Pre-Enactment Implementation of Device Amendments.* FDA began to implement the recommendations of the Cooper Committee even before the 1976 Amendments were enacted. *See* Link, *Cooper Committee Report and Its Effect on Current FDA Medical Device Activities,* 27 FDC L.J. 624 (1972).

2. *Legislative History.* The House Report's explanation of the 1976 Amendments consumes 87 pages, H.R. Rep. No. 853, 94th Cong., 2d Sess. (1976). The legislation itself runs 45 pages, 90 Stat. 539 (1976); by contrast, the entire 1938 Act was 19 pages long.

3. *FDA Implementation Plan.* Seven days after President Ford signed the 1976 Amendments, FDA published a notice in 41 Fed. Reg. 22620 (June 4, 1976) summarizing its intended implementation of the new statute.

2. OVERVIEW OF THE 1976 AMENDMENTS

The 1976 Device Amendments added more than a dozen provisions to the 1938 Act, which together create a complex and novel system for regulating the development, introduction, and marketing of medical devices. The new regime can best be understood by focusing on six key features.

First, the Amendments revised the definition of a "device" to achieve two purposes. The new definition was intended to convert some medical products regulated as drugs to devices. The definition was also broadened to include products intended to diagnose physiological conditions that are not ordinarily regarded as diseases, such as pregnancy.

Second, the Amendments required FDA to classify or categorize all medical devices in accordance with the relative degree of assurance of their safety and effectiveness. Class I includes those devices for which neither a standard nor premarket approval is warranted because the general regulatory controls available under the FD&C Act are sufficient to assure safety and effectiveness. Class II includes those devices for which general controls are not sufficient and for which enough information exists to develop a performance standard. Class III includes those devices for which general controls are not sufficient to assure safety and effectiveness and there is not sufficient information to establish a performance standard. Class III also includes all devices introduced after the enactment of the 1976 Amendments (postenactment devices) that are not substantially equivalent to a device marketed prior to enactment (preenactment devices). FDA has authority to reclassify a device when the information available warrants doing so.

Third, the Amendments provide for comprehensive control over the market introduction of all medical devices, a system which operates independently of the classification scheme. After 1976, a device may lawfully be marketed in only one of three ways: (1) a device may be the subject of a premarket notification (PMN) to FDA under section 510(k) which demonstrates that it is "substantially equivalent" to a preenactment device; (2) it may be the subject of a premarket approval (PMA) application under Section 515; or (3) upon petition to FDA under section 513(f)(2)(A), it may be reclassified from class III to class II or I.

Fourth, two classes of preenactment medical devices are subject to special requirements under the 1976 Amendments. A class II medical device must comply with any performance standard established by FDA for that device under section 514. A class III device must be the subject of an application, eventually approved by FDA, demonstrating its safety and effectiveness and submitted once the agency promulgates a regulation requiring the submission of applications for that type of device.

Fifth, all medical devices, regardless of class and regardless of the manner of market introduction, are subject to the general regulatory controls established under the 1938 Act and amplified by the 1976 Amendments. These "general controls" include the basic adulteration and misbranding provisions as well as applicable good manufacturing practice (GMP) regulations, banned device regulations, and notification and repair, replacement, or refund requirements.

Sixth, Congress in the 1976 Amendments and in other legislation has enacted special rules for specific types of devices. Examples include requirements for custom devices, a registry of cardiac pacemaker uses, and provisions for extending the patent term for certain Class III devices.

NOTES

1. *Commentary.* See FDA, REQUIREMENTS OF LAWS AND REGULATIONS ENFORCED BY THE U.S. FOOD AND DRUG ADMINISTRATION, FDA-85-115, at 64 (1985); Foote, *Loops and Loopholes: Hazardous Device Regulation Under the 1976 Medical Device Amendments to the Food, Drug, and Cosmetic Act,* 7 Ecology L.Q. 101 (1978); Horton, *Medical Devices: Strengthening Consumer Protection,* FDA Consumer, October 1976, at 4; Villforth, *The Medical Device Amendments: 10 Years After,* 20 FDA Consumer, May 1986, at 28; Weigel and Raubicheck, *How to Comply With the New Medical Device Law,* 31 FDC L.J. 312 (1976).

2. *1990 Amendments.* The Safe Medical Devices Act of 1990, 104 Stat. 4511, made numerous adjustments in the 1976 structure but did modify the basic regulatory approach.

---

3. THE DEFINITION OF "DEVICE"

Compare the 1938 Act definition of "device," discussed earlier in this chapter, with the new version adopted by the 1976 Amendments.

PREGNANCY TEST KITS: TRANSFER OF RESPONSIBILITY FROM THE BUREAU OF BIOLOGICS TO THE BUREAU OF MEDICAL DEVICES

44 Federal Register 10133 (February 16, 1979).

The Medical Device Amendments of 1976 ... expanded the definition of "device" in section 201(h) of the act to include in vitro reagents and similar articles intended for use in the diagnosis of disease or other conditions. ...

... Although FDA believes that the *OVA II* decision is not a sound precedent for future cases because it adopts an unduly restrictive interpretation of the definition of "drug," the precise issue in that case, FDA's authority to regulate pregnancy test kits has been addressed by the Medical Device Amendments of 1976, which expanded the definition of "device" in section 201(h) of the Act to include in vitro products for the diagnosis of any "condition" as well as for the diagnosis of disease....

Because FDA has clear and adequate authority to regulate in vitro products for the determination of pregnancy as devices, FDA has concluded that Anti–HCG serum products for assisting in the determination of pregnancy will be regulated only under the device provisions of the Federal Food, Drug, and Cosmetic Act. Accordingly, by this notice, Anti–HCG serum intended for assisting in the determination of pregnancy is no longer subject to the licensing requirements of section 351 of the Public Health Service Act. All existing licenses for Anti–HCG serum intended for use in assisting in the determination of pregnancy are hereby revoked.

———

The case referred to in this document, *United States v. An Article of Drug ... Ova II*, 414 F.Supp. 660 (D. N.J. 1975), *aff'd without opinion*, 535 F.2d 1248 (3d Cir. 1976), was a seizure action against a pregnancy test kit sold for home use. The government claimed that this *in vitro* diagnostic product, consisting of vials of sodium hydroxide and hydrochloric acid, was a new drug under the Act. The trial court disagreed, concluding that it fell outside all three dimensions of the Act's definition of "drug." Though both its ingredients appear in the U.S. Pharmacopeia and the National Formulary, the Act's official compendia, "the OVA II kit is not a drug ... since it is not ... related to the diagnosis of disease," since "the existence or non-existence of pregnancy ... is not of itself a disease." Finally, the court held, because the product was to be used *in vitro* it was not a intended "to affect the structure or any function of the body."

Until the passage of the 1976 Amendments, the *OVA II* decision threatened to undermine FDA's efforts to assert control over the reliability, and thus the safety, of a host of *in vitro* diagnostics.

Congress' hope that the new definition would make the scope of the term "device" easier to comprehend has proved illusory, as the development of computer hardware and software illustrates.

DRAFT POLICY GUIDANCE FOR REGULATION OF COMPUTER PRODUCTS

52 Federal Register 36104 (September 25, 1987).

FDA is making available for public comment draft policy guidance for the regulation of computer products. The draft policy guidance clarifies how FDA would apply existing statutory requirements to the regulation of computer products (i.e., both hardware and software) when such products meet the definition of a medical device in the Medical Device Amendments of 1976....

Under the draft policy, FDA would not regard computer products used only for traditional "library" functions such as storage, retrieval, and dissemination of information—functions traditionally carried out through textbooks and journals—to be medical devices subject to regulation by the agency. Similarly, the policy notes that FDA's device regulations and authorities also would not apply to computer products used for general accounting or communications functions or solely for instructional purposes, rather than to diagnose or treat patients.

When a computer product is a "component, part, or accessory" of a product recognized as a medical device in its own right, the computer component is regulated according to the requirements for the parent device (unless the component of the device is separately classified).

Computer products which are medical devices, and not components, parts, or accessories of other articles which are themselves medical devices, are regulated with the least degree of control necessary to provide reasonable assurance of safety and effectiveness. For example, many software products known as "expert" or "knowledge based" systems that are not used with existing medical devices and that are intended to involve competent human intervention before any impact on human health occurs (e.g., where clinical judgment and experience can be used to check and interpret a system's output) are exempt from registration, listing, premarket notification, and premarket approval requirements. FDA is also not aware of any computer product that is not a component, part, or accessory of another device that would require an approval premarket approval (PMA) application before marketing.

The agency is cognizant of the need to safeguard First Amendment protections and recognizes that, in some cases, it may be difficult to make a clear distinction between software products that perform traditional "book" or "library" functions, and software products that fall within the definition of a medical device under the draft policy, based on their intended use in the diagnosis or management of health-related conditions. FDA believes flexible guidance is necessary for effective implementation of the medical devices law and specifically invites comments on the appropriateness of the approach taken in the draft policy.

NOTES

1. *Specific Products.* In FDA Regulatory Letter BOS–88–10 (June 23, 1988), FDA Boston District Director E. J. McDonnell took the position that a computerized blood bank and laboratory management system that takes data directly from automated blood analyzers and uses it as the basis for labeling blood and blood components is a medical device and subject to the premarket notification requirements of section 510(k). *United States v. 22 Rectangular or Cylindrical Devices ... "The Ster–O–Lizer MD–200",* 714 F.Supp. 1159 (D. Utah 1989), held that a surgical instrument sterilizer is a medical device. FDA determined in 55 Fed. Reg. 23985 (June 13, 1990) that an in vitro test procedure for the detection of use of drugs of abuse by hair analysis is a medical device that requires premarket approval. In 55 Fed. Reg. 5892 (February 20, 1990),

FDA announced that in vitro diagnostic test kits that are used to detect total antibody to hepatitis B core antigen in blood will be regulated as biologics rather than as medical devices, because the major use has changed from clinical diagnostic use to screening blood intended for transfusion. Under FDA Compliance Policy Guide 7124.28 (December 29, 1987), firms that recondition or rebuild medical devices are subject to the 1976 Amendments.

2. *Intended Use.* Although the 1976 Amendments revised the definition of "device," the legal touchstone remains an article's "intended" use. Accordingly, FDA has taken the position that exercise equipment used in recreational and sporting activities will be regulated as medical devices only where those products are intended for medical purposes and thus are properly classified as "therapeutic equipment." 48 Fed. Reg. 53032, 53043–44 (November 23, 1983). Similarly, the agency concluded that "electrostatic air cleaners are not inherently medical devices" because they have other uses as well, and that the fact that FDA regulates the emission of ozone from medical devices in 21 C.F.R. § 801.415 does not mean that all products emitting ozone are medical devices. Letter from FDA Chief Counsel R.M. Cooper to CPSC Assistant General Counsel S. Lemberg (May 14, 1979). FDA has declined to regulate attached cigarette filters, or detached cigarette filters for which no medical claims are made, as medical devices. 47 Fed. Reg. 31130, 31132 (July 16, 1982). Because of the decision in *Action on Smoking and Health v. Harris,* 655 F.2d 236 (D.C. Cir. 1980), p. 382 *supra,* the agency's ruling on cigarette filters was not challenged in the courts.

3. *Drug–Device Switch.* Even where an article is clearly subject to FDA jurisdiction, the new definition of "device" does not always indicate how it will be regulated. For example, barium sulfate, used as an X-ray contrast medium, was regulated as a drug prior to 1976; was switched to device status after the 1976 Amendments; and has now been returned to drug status even though it appears to fit squarely within the new device definition. "Reg Letter Shows How Firm Got Caught in Drug–Device Switch," 14 Devices & Diagnostics Letter, No. 45, at 5 (Nov. 6, 1987).

4. *Drug–Device Combinations.* Medical products that combine a drug and a device present special problems. Where the drug is being administered for a use approved by FDA, the combination will generally be regulated only as a device. *See, e.g.,* the FDA determination that a hemodialysis concentrate used in dialysis machines to remove waste from the bloodstream of patients suffering from kidney disease is properly regulated as a device. 21 C.F.R. § 876.5820; *United States v. Diversified Medical Services,* 1985–1986 FDLI Jud. Rec. 189 (C.D. Cal. 1985). Infusion pumps and nebulizers for use with approved drugs are regulated by FDA as devices. Where an approved device is marketed for use with a drug that has not been approved for that use, however, FDA has ruled that the device is misbranded. *See* FDA Regulatory Letter No. 89–HFD–313–26 (April 28, 1989), declaring that labeling for an approved infusion pump is unlawful because it promotes the use of the pump for the administration of several drug products for uses that are not covered by approved NDAs. Section 503(f), added by the Safe Medical Devices Act of 1990, 104 Stat. 4511, directs FDA to regulate combination products according to their "primary mode of action."

5. *Denture Repair Products.* FDA established detailed labeling requirements for denture repair products and related materials, 33 Fed. Reg. 5365 (April 4, 1968), 34 Fed. Reg. 14167 (September 9, 1969), codified in 21 C.F.R. § 801.405, without determining whether they would be regulated as drugs or

devices. After two decades of uncertainty about whether various types of denture products are to be considered drugs, devices, or even in some cases cosmetics, FDA determined that they would henceforth be regulated solely as medical devices. 53 Fed. Reg. 30872 (August 16, 1988).

6. *Dual Use Products.* In classifying medical devices, FDA has included the following statement for products that have both medical and nonmedical uses.

> FDA has also clarified several regulations classifying products that have both medical and nonmedical uses. FDA will regulate a multi-purpose product as a medical device if it is intended for a medical purpose ... FDA will determine the intended use of a product based upon the expressions of the person legally responsible for its labeling and by the circumstances surrounding its distribution. The most important factors the agency will consider in determining the intended use of a particular product are the labeling, advertising, and other representations accompanying the product. Products that have medical uses only are clearly intended for medical purposes, and, therefore, will be regulated as medical devices whether or not medical claims are made for them.

45 Fed. Reg. 60576, 60579 (September 12, 1980).

7. *1990 Amendments.* The 1990 Amendments amended the definitions of "drug" and "device". The exclusion of devices from the definition of a drug was removed, and the definition of a device was modified to state that an article is a device only if it does not achieve its "primary" purpose (rather than "any of its principal" purposes) through chemical action within or on the body or by being metabolized.

---

4. CLASSIFICATION AND RECLASSIFICATION

a. Classification

Even before passage of the 1976 Amendments, FDA undertook an inventory of existing medical devices on the market, established 14 panels of experts, and began the process of classifying medical devices under procedures announced in 40 Fed. Reg. 21848 (May 19, 1975). Classification reports were in fact issued by some of these panels before the new amendments became law. Following enactment, FDA promulgated new classification procedures to meet the requirements of section 513 of the 1976 Amendments. 42 Fed. Reg. 46028 (September 13, 1977), 43 Fed. Reg. 32988 (July 28, 1978), codified at 21 C.F.R. Part 860.

Classification of the diverse universe of devices took longer than either FDA or Congress had anticipated. By 1984, FDA had completed classification of 11 out of 19 categories (comprising about 1700 types) of devices and had issued proposed classifications for the other eight. Of these 1700 types, roughly 30 percent were placed in Class I, 60 percent in Class II, and 10 percent in Class III. Office of Technology Assessment, FEDERAL POLICIES AND THE MEDICAL DEVICES INDUS-

TRY, OTA–H–230, at 105–106 (Oct. 1984) [hereinafter OTA DEVICES REPORT]. FDA completed the classification process with a final rule, 53 Fed. Reg. 23856 (June 24, 1988), classifying general and plastic surgery devices. There have been no formal legal challenges to the results of this classification process, perhaps because, in the vast majority of cases, a device's classification does not control when and how it can be marketed.

NOTE

FDA's classification process has proved responsive to a wide variety of societal interests. For example, in response to comments questioning its proposal to place in Class II the electroconvulsive therapy device used in psychiatric patients and, voicing doubts about this method of treatment, the agency ultimately classified the device in Class III, 44 Fed. Reg. 51726 (September 4, 1979).

---

b. Reclassification

The opportunity provided by sections 513(e), (f)(2)(A), and 520(*l*)(2) for reclassification of a device from Class III to either Class II or Class I, is likely to prove important for two categories of devices.

The first category includes approximately a score of "transitional" devices that FDA had regulated as new drugs prior to enactment of the 1976 Amendments and that Congress, at the agency's urging, automatically assigned to Class III under section 520(k)(1). The agency identified these transitional devices in 42 Fed. Reg. 63472 (December 16, 1977). It took the position that these transitional devices and their postenactment counterparts remain in Class III by statute unless and until reclassified, and no postenactment device in this category can come on the market without FDA approval of a PMA application by taking advantage of the substantial equivalence thoroughfare in sections 513(f)(1)(A) and 515(b)(1). The 1990 Amendments added section 520(1)(5), requiring FDA to reconsider the classification of all Class III transitional devices, and to consider down-classifying them. Section 4(b)(3) of the 1990 Amendments, which is not codified, specifies that daily wear soft or daily wear nonhydrophilic plastic contact lenses must be down-classified unless FDA affirmatively rules otherwise.

The second category potentially includes any other class III device. Before the 1990 Amendments, reclassification was important only for the relatively small portion of postenactment devices that could not identify a substantially equivalent preenactment device to serve as a predicate for immediate marketing, or when FDA published a regulation requiring approval of applications for all Class III devices of that type. However, the 1990 Amendments added section 515(i), which requires FDA to reconsider the classification of all Class III preenactment devices and either to down-classify them or to commence rulemaking to require submission of premarket approval (PMA) applications.

NOTE

Section 513(e) authorizes FDA, upon the petition of any interested person, to change the classification of a device. In *Thompson v. Procter & Gamble Co.,* No. 80 Civ. 3711 (N.D. Cal.1982), the court dismissed a mandamus action against FDA seeking an order directing the agency to reclassify tampons because they are unsafe and should require premarket approval, on the ground that the plaintiffs had failed to exhaust their administrative remedies under section 513(e).

---

5. REGULATION OF MARKET INTRODUCTION

Since the enactment of the 1976 Amendments, there are only three ways a new medical device can lawfully be introduced: (1) as a device that is substantially equivalent to a preenactment device under sections 513(f)(1) and 515(b)(1) and for which a PMN has been submitted to FDA under section 510(k); (2) as a device for which a premarket approval (PMA) application has been submitted to FDA and approved by the agency under section 515; or (3) as a device that has been reclassified by FDA from Class III to Class II or Class I under section 513(f)(2). Since 1976, with FDA approval, more than 98 percent of new medical devices have entered the market with the filing of a PMN as substantial equivalents of a preenactment device. Of the less than two percent for which FDA has required premarket approval, approximately half have been contact lenses. OTA DEVICES REPORT 103–104; S. Rep. No. 588, 100th Cong., 2d Sess. 9 (1988). The number of devices initially marketed through the reclassification process has been negligible. Each of these three approaches is discussed below.

When FDA officials were engaged in drafting the legislation that became the 1976 Device Amendments, they faced a familiar issue in the design of new health and safety legislation—whether to impose the new statutory requirements for proof of safety and effectiveness only on postenactment devices (thus discriminating between old and new devices). Assuming that the same standards should in principle apply to both old and new devices, a related issue was how much time preenactment devices should be afforded to demonstrate compliance with the new standards. For a general discussion of the law's propensity to apply more stringent standards to new technologies, *see* Huber, *The Old–New Division in Risk Regulation,* 69 Va. L. Rev. 1025 (1983). FDA advocated and Congress endorsed the following policy.

For Class I devices the issue of discrimination never arises because they are subject only to the general regulatory controls of the FD&C Act. General controls apply to *all* medical devices, whatever the date of their introduction. Thus, the same requirements apply at the same time to both categories of Class I devices.

Nor does the issue of discrimination arise for Class II devices. A Class II device is subject only to the general regulatory controls unless FDA promulgates a standard. Once a standard for a type of device is promulgated, both preenactment and postenactment devices of that type are subject to its requirements in the same way, at the same time.

For Class III devices, the new requirements for proof of safety and efficacy would apply in discriminatory fashion if the statute were not written to avoid it. A preenactment Class III device would remain *on* the market while the manufacturer gathered and FDA evaluated evidence of safety and effectiveness. And a counterpart postenactment device would remain *off* the market while the same evidence was being obtained and evaluated. Furthermore, once the postenactment device was approved by FDA, it would enter the market to compete with preenactment counterparts whose safety and effectiveness FDA had not yet approved.

To avoid this result, the draftsmen included in sections 513(f)(1)(A) and 515(b)(1) language stating that a preenactment Class III device, and any postenactment Class III device that is substantially equivalent to a preenactment Class III device, need not secure FDA approval of safety and effectiveness until FDA promulgates a regulation triggering the approval requirement for the specific type of device. Thus, a postenactment Class III device that is substantially equivalent to a preenactment Class III device can go on the market immediately, with only the submission of a PMN. It will then be subject to the same general controls as its preenactment counterpart (and other medical devices). When FDA orders the submission of PMA applications for devices of that type, the requirement applies equally to both preenactment and postenactment products.

There appears to be only one exception to the general rule that a postenactment Class III device that is substantially equivalent to a preenactment Class III device may be marketed immediately. As noted above, the 1976 Amendments placed approximately 20 "transitional" devices in Class III because they had been regulated as new drugs prior to 1976. Although the statute is not clear on the point, FDA has taken the position that a postenactment device that is substantially equivalent to a preenactment "transition" device may not be marketed without approval of a PMA application unless the device has been reclassified. Congress addressed this arguable inequity in the 1990 Amendments by requiring FDA to reconsider its initial classification of all transitional devices.

a. Substantial Equivalence

The 1976 Amendments did not include a definition of "substantially equivalent." The legislative history, however, indicates that substantial equivalence is to be assessed not merely in terms of physical characteristics and intended use, but also in terms of safety and effectiveness:

> The term "substantially equivalent" is not intended to be so narrow as to refer only to devices that are identical to marketed devices nor so broad as to refer to devices which are intended to be used for the same purposes as marketed products. The Committee believes that the term should be construed narrowly where necessary to assure the safety and effectiveness of a device but not so narrowly where differences between a new device and a marketed device do not relate to safety and effectiveness. Thus, differences between "new" and marketed devices in materials, design, or energy source, for example, would have a bearing on the adequacy of information as to a new device's safety and effectiveness, and such devices should be automatically classified into Class III. On the other hand, copies of devices marketed prior to enactment, or devices whose variations are immaterial to safety and effectiveness would not necessarily fall under the automatic classification scheme.

H.R. Rep. No. 853, 94th Cong., 2d Sess. 36–37 (1976). Thus, the concept of substantial equivalence was left for FDA to interpret, but it was clearly intended to embrace some inquiry into the safety and effectiveness of a new device.

Congress also concluded that the manufacturer of a new device should not have the authority to resolve the issue of substantial equivalence unilaterally. Section 510(k) requires every person who plans to market a new device to submit to FDA a notification of such intent at least 90 days in advance. This premarket notification (PMN) is required to set forth the legal basis on which the device is being introduced. The House Report, at p. 37, provided the following explanation:

> The proposed Bill contains provisions designed to insure that manufacturers do not intentionally or unintentionally circumvent the automatic classification of "new" devices. These provisions, included in amendments to Section 510 of Act, would require all persons to advise the Secretary ninety days before they intend to begin marketing a device as to whether the device has been classified under Section 513. This provision will enable the Secretary to assure that "new" devices are not marketed until they comply with premarket approval requirements or are reclassified into Class I or II.

Accordingly, the regulatory structure created by the 1976 Amendments was predicated on three principles. First, a postenactment device that is substantially equivalent to a preenactment device should have to meet the same standards of safety and effectiveness, on the same schedule. Second, a postenactment device that has no preenactment counterpart should presumptively be approved by FDA for safety and effectiveness. Third, a mechanism such as section 510(k)'s PMN requirement should be established to allow FDA to review a manufacturer's decision to introduce a device and thereby prevent the introduction of novel devices that have not undergone official assessment.

This is the scheme that FDA attempted to implement prior to 1990. What neither the agency nor Congress foresaw, however, was how many postenactment devices for which PMNs were submitted might qualify as substantially equivalent and, thus, postpone compliance with any requirement for premarket approval. Between 1985 and March 1990 FDA received PMNs for 31,031 devices. The agency disputed the manufacturer's claim of substantial equivalence for 564 of these. In fiscal year 1989, FDA received 7,022 section 510(k) submissions and found all but 92 to be for devices "substantially equivalent" to preenactment products. *See* Leflar, *Public Accountability and Medical Device Regulation,* 2 Harv.J. of L. & Tech. 1 (1989).

NOTES

1. *PMN Regulations.* The regulations governing premarket notification were promulgated in 41 Fed. Reg. 37458 (September 3, 1976), 42 Fed. Reg. 42520 (August 23, 1977), and are codified in 21 C.F.R. § 807.81 *et seq.* Although the regulations do not explicitly require submission of safety and effectiveness data, manufacturers routinely include this information; a PMN that did not include such data would be likely to prompt questions and face delay from FDA.

2. *PMN Review Process.* In response to criticisms of its process for reviewing premarket notifications FDA established an internal task force and later issued GUIDANCE ON THE CENTER FOR DEVICES AND RADIOLOGICAL HEALTH'S PREMARKET NOTIFICATION REVIEW PROGRAM (June 30, 1986), which digests a decade of agency experience in implementing section 510(k).

3. *Equivalence "Creep".* FDA has taken the position that a new device, which is substantially equivalent to a marketed postenactment device that was in turn substantially equivalent to a preenactment device, may itself be considered substantially equivalent to that preenactment device. This concept has been termed "piggybacking," OTA MEDICAL DEVICE REPORT at 104, and it has drawn criticism from some quarters. *See, e.g.,* Leflar, *Public Accountability and Medical Device Regulation,* 2 Harv. J. L. & Tech. 1 (1989).

4. *PMN Exemptions.* After several years' experience, FDA concluded that there was no public health need to require a PMN for many common Class I devices. Accordingly, the agency adopted 21 C.F.R. § 862.9, establishing criteria for exemptions from the PMN requirement. 52 Fed. Reg. 16139 (May 1, 1987), 53 Fed. Reg. 21447 (June 8, 1988).

5. *Impact of AIDS Epidemic.* FDA has tightened its regulations of two important medical devices that help prevent the transmission of the AIDS

virus. In 52 Fed. Reg. 12605 (April 17, 1987), 53 Fed. Reg. 573 (January 8, 1988), the agency announced a strengthened inspection program, a more stringent defect standard, and a new labeling guideline for condoms. When FDA classified patient examination gloves in Class I, 45 Fed. Reg. 69678, 69723 (October 21, 1980), it exempted these devices both from the requirement of a PMN and from the GMP regulations, but following publication of "Recommendations for Prevention of HIV Transmission in Health–Care Settings," 36 Morbidity and Mortality Weekly Report, No. 2S (August 21, 1987), the agency revoked these exemptions, 54 Fed. Reg. 1602 (January 13, 1989), and promulgated new requirements, 54 Fed. Reg. 48218 (November 21, 1989), 54. Fed. Reg. 51254 (December 12, 1990).

   6. *Ratification by Congress.* The 1990 Amendments effectively incorporate FDA's approach directly into section 513(i) of the statute. A new device is regarded as substantially equivalent to a preenactment device if it has the same intended use and technological characteristics, or the same intended use and different technological characteristics but the PMN contains information demonstrating that the new device is as safe and effective as a lawfully marketed device and does not raise different questions of safety and effectiveness. The PMN must contain a summary of pertinent safety and effectiveness information or state that such information will be made available upon request by any person. "Piggybacking" is authorized.

---

b. Premarket Approval

   For postenactment Class III devices that have no preenactment counterpart, and thus represent new medical technologies, marketing can not begin until FDA has approved a PMA application under section 515.

Investigational Devices

   The statute and FDA regulations provide for the investigational use of an unapproved new postenactment Class III device in order to obtain the safety and effectiveness data required to support a PMA application. The arrangements resemble those for clinical testing of new drugs, with one major difference. Under section 520(g), which authorizes an investigational device exemption (IDE), FDA accepts approval of a proposed clinical investigation by a local institutional review board (IRB) in lieu of its own. FDA has implemented this provision by dividing investigational devices into two categories: those that represent a "significant risk" and those that do not. The IDE requirements for a device in the "significant risk" category are similar to those for new drugs. For a device in the second category, however, IRB approval will suffice; an IDE need not be submitted to FDA. 41 Fed. Reg. 35282 (August 20, 1976), 43 Fed. Reg. 20726 (May 12, 1978), 43 Fed. Reg. 25142 (June 9, 1978), 45 Fed. Reg. 3732 (January 18, 1980), codified in 21 C.F.R. Part 812. *See* Bozeman, *The Clinical Investigation of Medical Devices—A Preliminary Guide for Manufacturers,* 34 FDC L.J. 289 (1979).

The IDE system appears to have worked well for routine long term investigations of new devices, but it seems less well-suited to studies of devices that are deployed infrequently but usually in an emergency. For example, FDA had approved an IDE for the Jarvik–7 artificial heart, setting stringent protocol conditions, months before Dr. William DeVries implanted it in Dr. Barney Clark on December 1–2, 1982. After four permanent implants of the Jarvik–7 heart, however, an FDA advisory committee reviewed the program and recommended that "FDA should assume a more direct oversight role as the clinical trial proceeds, and should approve subsequent implants on a case-by-case basis." "FDA Sets New Requirements For Permanent Artificial Heart Program," FDA Talk Paper No. T86–3 (January 7, 1986).

In the interim, however, the exigencies of patient care overcame FDA's IDE requirements for another type of artificial heart.

CRISTINE RUSSELL, TEMPORARY HEART IMPLANTED: TUCSON OPERATION LACKED FDA APPROVAL

The Washington Post, Thursday, March 7, 1985, Page A–1.

Doctors at a University of Arizona teaching hospital yesterday implanted a new type of temporary artificial heart in a dying 32-year-old man while they tried to locate a human heart for transplant..... Dr. Allan Beigel, a university vice president and spokesman for the University Medical Center hospital, said last night that the mechanical device, designed by a Chinese dentist, "had not been tested in humans" and does not have government approval, but was implanted anyway because "the alternative was that the patient would die." The recipient, identified only as a Caucasian divorced father of two, had rejected a human heart transplant earlier in the day and had been placed on a heart-lung machine. Beigel said time was of the utmost concern because the patient was reaching the point where continued use of the machine risked causing irreparable damage.

The patient was reported in critical but stable condition after the three-hour implant procedure, which has not been approved by the federal Food and Drug Administration. Asked at a news briefing last night whether FDA approval was needed for the operation, Dr. Jack Copeland, head of the hospital's heart-transplant team, said: "Ideally, they should have, but you can't think of everything." Later, he added, "We did not set out to do a human experiment. We set out to do a heart transplant. We were faced with a patient who had no alternative except death."

The mechanical heart used, called the Phoenix heart, was developed at St. Luke's Hospital in Phoenix, where it has been under study for about two years, Beigel said. It was one of three devices—including the Jarvik–7 artificial heart, which has been implanted into three permanent artificial-heart recipients—rushed to Tucson when the patient's condition began deteriorating.

An FDA spokesman said last night that the agency had informed the university yesterday that federal permission was needed for human experimentation with unproven medical devices, but that the university failed to obtain the approval. University spokesman Mike Letson said "there was not time" to obtain permission, adding, "The legal ramifications will have to come along later."

FDA spokesman David Duarte said the agency "is waiting to hear the facts from the university." He said the FDA response could range from a reprimand to taking the matter to court.

After FDA completed an investigation of the episode, on May 10, 1985, John Villforth, Director of the Center for Devices and Radiological Health, wrote to the administrator of the University of Arizona's hospital:

> Based on the discussions ... and our review of the patient's records, we believe that:
>
> > (a) the implant was unanticipated in that Dr. Copeland did not plan to use the artificial heart until it became apparent that the first transplant was unsuccessful;
> >
> > (b) this situation was unusual because the donor heart failed in the patient so soon after the transplant;
> >
> > (c) the artificial heart was used only as a life-saving measure until another donor heart could be obtained; and
> >
> > (d) Dr. Copeland followed established practices at your institution for emergency procedures, e.g., consulting with another physician and notifying the IRB.
>
> FDA understands the situation that occurred at the University of Arizona Hospital and the reasons why Dr. Copeland took the actions he did to save the patient's life; however, we also believe that all of the patients who might benefit from such a device are best served when the device is used in a planned clinical investigation, where the device's safety and effectiveness can be studied....
>
> Although the Medical Device Amendments to the Food, Drug, and Cosmetic Act do not provide for the emergency use of unapproved devices, FDA has discretion to withhold consideration of regulatory action in appropriate circumstances. Because we believe that the situation at the University of Arizona Hospital constitutes such a circumstance, no further action by FDA is indicated and we consider the matter closed.
>
> We would be pleased to assist you in obtaining FDA approval for investigations of artificial hearts, should you wish to con-

duct such studies. We are now encouraging sponsors of investigations to include in their investigations therapeutic use of life-saving devices in situations where no alternative exists. We will permit these investigations provided that we have data that assure us the device is not unsafe, *e.g.,* in the case of an artificial heart, it does not produce thromboemboli that result in stroke or organ damage. This will allow physicians to have access to life-saving devices, while at the same time, ensuring that physicians participate in an approved investigation....

To govern future emergencies of this sort, FDA then published the following guidance.

GUIDANCE FOR THE EMERGENCY USE OF UNAPPROVED MEDICAL DEVICES; AVAILABILITY
50 Federal Register 42866 (October 25, 1985).

This guidance applies to the emergency use of an unapproved medical device. For the purpose of the guidance, an unapproved medical device is a device that is utilized for a purpose, condition, or use for which the device requires, but does not have, an approved application for premarket approval under section 515 ... or an approved Application for an Investigational Device Exemption (IDE) under section 520(g)....

An unapproved device may be used in human subjects only if it is approved for clinical testing under an IDE. An emergency need to use an unapproved device may occur when an IDE for the device does not exist, when a physician wants to use the device in a way not approved under the IDE, or when a physician or institution is not approved under the IDE.

In an orderly developmental process, the device's developer—a physician, scientist, or manufacturer—anticipates the need to conduct clinical studies and uses the IDE to ensure that adequate preclinical testing has been done, that the appropriate subjects will be selected, that subjects participate only after providing informed consent, that the device will be used properly, that subjects will be monitored adequately after the device is used, and that complete scientific data will be collected promptly. These data form the basis for subsequent marketing approval of the device.

The Food and Drug Administration (FDA) recognizes that even during the earliest phases of device design, development, and testing, emergencies arise where an unapproved device offers the only alternative for saving the life of a dying patient, but an IDE has not yet been approved for the device or the use, or an IDE has been approved but the physician who wishes to use the device is not an investigator under the IDE. Using its enforcement discretion, FDA will not object if a physician chooses to use an unapproved device in such an emergency, provided that the physician later justifies to FDA that an emergency actually existed.

Each of the following conditions should exist for a situation to be considered an emergency:

1. The patient is in a life-threatening condition that needs immediate treatment;

2. No generally acceptable alternative for treating the patient is available; and

3. Because of the immediate need to use the device, there is no time to use existing procedures to get FDA approval for the use.

FDA expects the physician to determine whether these criteria have been met, to assess the potential for benefits from the unapproved use of the device, and to have substantial reason to believe that benefits will exist. FDA further expects the physician not to conclude that an "emergency" situation exists in advance of the time when treatment may be needed based solely on the expectation that IDE approval procedures may require more time than remains. Physicians should be aware that FDA expects them to exercise reasonable foresight with respect to potential emergencies and to make appropriate arrangements under the IDE procedures far enough in advance to avoid creating a situation in which such arrangements are impracticable.

In the event that a device is used in circumstances meeting the criteria listed above, FDA would expect the physician to follow as many patient protection procedures as possible. These include obtaining:

1. An independent assessment by an uninvolved physician;

2. Informed consent from the patient or a legal representative;

3. Institutional clearance as specified by institutional policies;

4. The Institutional Review Board (IRB) chairperson's concurrence, and

5. Authorization from the sponsor, if an approved IDE for the device exists.

FDA would not object if an unapproved device were shipped without FDA approval to a physician who claims to be faced with, and describes, the kind of emergency situation discussed above. The person shipping the device should notify FDA—by telephone (302–427–8162)—immediately after shipment is made. An unapproved device may not be shipped in anticipation of an emergency.

After an unapproved device is used in an emergency, the physician should:

1. Notify the IRB and otherwise comply with provisions of the IRB regulations (21 CFR Part 56) and the informed consent regulations (21 CFR Part 50);

2.   Evaluate the likelihood of a similar need for the device in the future: If it is likely, immediately initiate efforts to obtain IRB approval and an approved IDE for the device's subsequent use;

3.   If an IDE exists, notify the sponsor of the emergency use of the device: The sponsor must comply with the reporting requirements of the IDE regulations; and

4.   If an IDE does not exist, notify FDA of the emergency use of the device and provide FDA with a written summary of the conditions constituting the emergency, patient protection measures, and any scientific results.

Subsequent use of the device in an emergency situation may not occur unless the physician or another person obtains approval of an IDE for the device and its use.   If an IDE application for subsequent use has been filed with FDA and FDA disapproves the IDE application, the device may not be used even if the circumstances constituting an emergency exist.   Developers of devices that could be used in emergencies should anticipate the likelihood of emergency uses and should obtain an approved IDE. FDA will consider taking regulatory action if an unapproved device is used in inappropriate situations.

CDRH developed this guidance in response to a situation concerning the emergency use of an unapproved cardiovascular device.   CDRH will apply this guidance to other types of potentially life-saving unapproved devices in emergency situations.   In all situations in which the use of an unapproved device would not meet the criteria for emergency use under this guidance, such unapproved device may not be used without an approved IDE.

NOTES

1.   *Feasibility Studies.*   Often only a limited "feasibility" study is conducted on a significant risk investigational device to determine whether a full investigation is warranted.   Because FDA's IDE regulations impose substantial obligations even for such a limited test, the American Society of Artificial Internal Organs petitioned the agency to reduce the requirements for such a "feasibility" investigation.   FDA published the petition for comment, 51 Fed. Reg. 11266 (April 1, 1986), and subsequently announced a comprehensive review of the IDE regulations, 51 Fed. Reg. 26830 (July 25, 1986).   FDA responded to the ASAIO petition by issuing guidance on May 17, 1989, adopting a flexible approach in the review of IDE applications for feasibility studies.

2.   *"Research Use Only" Exemption.*   An exemption from the IDE requirements in 21 C.F.R. § 812.2(c)(3) allows the sale of a diagnostic device labeled "For Research Use Only" if the testing is noninvasive, does not require an invasive sampling procedure that presents a significant risk or introduces energy into a subject, and is not used without confirmation by another established diagnostic product or procedure.   In a consent decree entered in *United States v. Centocor, Inc.,* Civ. No. 85–5613 (E.D. Pa.1986), 22 FDA Consumer, No. 7, at 44 (September 1989), the defendant agreed not only to label a diagnostic device "For Research Use Only" but also to obtain from each researcher a written agreement that the device will not be used for investigation involving clinical use, including diagnosis or monitoring, and that results of tests will not

be used in conjunction with any patient records or treatment. The consent decree prohibited shipment to any researcher before this agreement was executed. FDA has since used this consent decree as a model for regulating diagnostic products sold for research use only. *See also* 48 Fed. Reg. 52644 (November 21, 1983).

Premarket Approval Applications

After the sponsor of an investigational device has obtained the requisite safety and effectiveness data, it must submit a PMA application to FDA for review and approval. FDA has promulgated regulations governing the PMA process in 45 Fed. Reg. 81769 (Dec. 12, 1980), 51 Fed. Reg. 26342 (July 22, 1986), codified in 21 C.F.R. Part 814.

Based upon FDA's successful use of advisory committees to review the safety and effectiveness of nonprescription drugs and biological products during the early 1970s, *see* pp. 588, 669 *supra*, section 515(c)(2) provides the opportunity for advisory committee review of any PMA application. Under the 1990 Amendments, a PMA application is to be referred to an advisory committee either on FDA's own initiative or upon the request of the applicant unless the agency finds that the information in the application substantially duplicates information which has previously been reviewed by an advisory committee.

After it had initially denied approval for an antibiotic bone cement, FDA granted the applicant's petition for reconsideration before an advisory committee under section 515(g)(2)(A), 51 Fed. Reg. 19610 (May 30, 1986). The advisory committee, established in 52 Fed. Reg. 3865 (February 6, 1987), was given the following charge:

> The function of the committee is to provide to the Commissioner a report and recommendation on whether CDRH, in denying premarket approval for Surgical Simplex™ P Antibiotic Bone Cement, was correct in its determination in this case that an adequate and well-controlled investigation in humans is necessary to satisfy the safety and effectiveness requirements of section 515(d)(2)(A) and (B) of the act. The committee's report and recommendation should be based on consideration of the following questions:

> 1. Is a well-controlled clinical investigation in humans necessary in this case to demonstrate a reasonable assurance that the device is safe and effective as labeled?

> 2. Assuming that a well-controlled investigation in humans is necessary, what parameters should be investigated in such a study to demonstrate a reasonable assurance that the device will have the effect it purports or is represented to have under the conditions of use prescribed, recommended, or suggested in the device's labeling?

3. Can clinical studies in humans (reported in the literature or in an individual surgeon's case reports) of bone cement with concentrations of antibiotic different from the concentrations of antibiotic in the device subject to the PMA demonstrate a reasonable assurance of safety and effectiveness to support a PMA approval?

4. Does the PMA contain studies that adequately demonstrate that the device will fix prostheses to living bone in orthopedic surgical procedures in humans?

5. Does the PMA contain studies that adequately demonstrate that the leaching out of antibiotic from the bone cement will not adversely affect the cement's long-term function in humans?

6. Does the PMA contain studies or evidence that adequately demonstrate that when the product is used as recommended in the labeling, adequate amounts of antibiotic will be delivered to the operative site in humans to eliminate those bacteria commonly found to cause infections associated with implant surgery?

7. Does the PMA adequately demonstrate that a reasonable assurance of safety and effectiveness is present for those persons most likely to be exposed to the device (*e.g.*, the elderly) when the device is used as labeled?

In short, the task of the advisory committee is to decide whether CDRH's order is consistent with the scientific evidence that was before the Center at the time that it made the decision embodied in the order.

52 Fed. Reg. 10413 (April 1, 1987). The advisory committee's report endorsed the Center's decision, and the FDA Commissioner subsequently denied approval of the PMA application. *In the Matter of Howmedica Simplex P Antibiotic Bone Cement,* Med. Dev. Rep. (CCH) ¶ 15,101 (FDA Dkt. No. 84P–0346, March 28, 1988).

PMA applications for new devices can raise difficult ethical and economic issues as well as issues of medicine and science. For example, in 1978 FDA began to receive PMA applications for a number of alpha-fetoprotein (AFP) test kits, which were intended for use in screening pregnant women to aid in the diagnosis of neural tube defects (NTDs). NTDs are among the most common serious birth defects. The AFP test does not provide a definitive diagnosis; a positive result requires further diagnostic procedures, such as ultrasound and amniocentesis, to determine whether the fetus is defective. In 44 Fed. Reg. 45644 (August 3, 1979) FDA initially announced its intent to establish restrictions on the sale, distribution, and use of AFP tests. A consumer organization subsequently petitioned the agency to prohibit unrestricted marketing of the tests on the ground that their use could result in abortion of healthy fetuses if inadequate followup tests were not con-

ducted or laboratory results were inaccurately interpreted. "Alpha–Fe-
toprotein," FDA Talk Paper No. T79–36 (August 17, 1979). In 45 Fed.
Reg. 74158 (November 7, 1980), FDA proposed to restrict the sale, use,
and distribution of AFP test kits. Simultaneously, CDC and HCFA
proposed their own conditions for AFP testing under the Clinical
Laboratories Improvement Act and under Medicare. 45 Fed. Reg.
74174 (November 7, 1980). Following a public hearing, FDA withdrew
its proposal, explaining:

> The proposed rule was developed after several health pro-
> fessional and consumer organizations expressed concern to
> FDA about possible problems that could result from the unre-
> stricted use of AFP test kits. One concern was that there are
> insufficient ancillary services (ultrasonography, amniocentesis,
> genetic counseling) available to meet the demand for confirma-
> tory tests when AFP test results suggest the presence of NTD's
> in fetuses. Another concern was that these ancillary services
> might not be utilized in a timely manner. A third concern was
> that physicians are not adequately trained to interpret the
> results of AFP tests and that laboratories have not yet reached
> the level of expertise necessary to ensure satisfactory results.

> The proposed rule would have required that AFP testing
> be conducted only in a program headed by a coordinator. The
> coordinator would have been responsible for, among other
> things, ensuring the availability of a complying laboratory,
> providing ultrasonograph and amniocentesis testing, providing
> genetic counseling, and compiling information for the manufac-
> turer's quarterly and annual evaluation reports for submission
> to FDA. Laboratories, physicians, and ultrasonography and
> amniocentesis facilities would have been required to keep
> certain records, make periodic reports to manufacturers, and
> submit to FDA inspection. Laboratories also would have been
> required to participate in an FDA-approved proficiency testing
> program and to test a minimum of 50 maternal serum and
> amniotic fluid samples each week. Manufacturers of the kits
> would have been required to distribute physician, laboratory,
> and patient labeling, to submit quarterly and annual reports to
> FDA, and to maintain distribution records for each AFP test
> kit distributed.....

> After reviewing the comments received and testimony
> presented at the public hearing, FDA has concluded that the
> proposed restrictions are not necessary to provide reasonable
> assurance of the safety and effectiveness of AFP test kits and,
> therefore, that restrictions under 21 U.S.C. § 360j(e) are not
> appropriate. This conclusion is based on a number of consider-
> ations, including:

> *Safety and effectiveness of AFP test kits.* No evidence was
> submitted during the public comment period to demonstrate

that there might have been significant problems involving the safety or effectiveness of AFP test kits....

Postapproval study. FDA approval of any applications for premarket approval of any AFP test kits will establish certain conditions on the sale of AFP test kits. The manufacturers will be required to submit to FDA quarterly reports concerning postapproval experience with the device. These requirements will allow FDA to monitor future product performance.

Patient and physician education. The manufacturers also will be required to distribute FDA-approved physician, laboratory, and patient labeling....

Laboratory quality assurance. AFP test kits are not significantly different from other radioimmunoassay devices commonly used in clinical laboratories. Almost all laboratories are subject to the rules of State agencies as well as those of HCFA and CDC generally applicable to laboratories and diagnostic products. In addition, many laboratories voluntarily submit to proficiency testing by the College of American Pathologists and are subject to accreditation by the Joint Commission for Accreditation of Hospitals. FDA believes that these controls are adequate to assure the quality of laboratory testing.

Shortages. There are no demonstrated shortages of adequate facilities and qualified personnel for followup testing....

Costs and benefits. The proposed restrictions would have increased the cost of the AFP kit itself (estimated by one manufacturer to be 50 percent), would have imposed additional costs on the testing procedure by requiring a coordinator and clerical support for each AFP testing activity (two comments estimated salary costs from $30,000 to $110,000 per year in addition to office space, etc.), and would have established strict recordkeeping requirements. FDA has determined the increased costs are not warranted.

In sum, FDA has concluded that the proposed restrictions are not necessary to ensure the safety and effectiveness of AFP test kits when used as an aid in detecting NTD's and would not provide significant benefit to the public health.

48 Fed. Reg. 27780 (June 17, 1983).

This decision drew both praise and criticism. *E.g.,* Sun, *FDA Draws Criticism on Prenatal Test,* 221 Science 440 (July 29, 1983). Subsequently, FDA approved PMA applications for the test kit in 49 Fed. Reg. 6174 (February 17, 1984), 49 Fed. Reg. 30018 (July 25, 1984), 51 Fed. Reg. 21982 (June 17, 1986).

After FDA has approved a PMA application, any interested person, including any member of the public, may petition the agency for reconsideration. *See, e.g.,* 47 Fed. Reg. 7877 (February 23, 1982), announcing a public hearing on a petition to withdraw premarket approval of three gonorrhea antibody test kits. The petition to withdraw approval of the gonorrhea test kits was denied in 48 Fed. Reg. 335 (January 4, 1983) but resulted in a decision to establish criteria for evaluating future in vitro screening devices. In 49 Fed. Reg. 32258 (August 13, 1984), FDA announced that, based on experience with the AFP test kits, the Center for Devices and Radiological Health had prepared REPORT ON IN VITRO SCREENING DEVICES, which "discusses fundamental screening factors that CDRH considers when assessing the safety and effectiveness of in vitro screening devices, how a device's projected utility affects CDRH's consideration of the device's safety and effectiveness, and CDRH's views on development of standards for screening devices."

Where to draw the line between laboratory and home use of in vitro diagnostic devices has proved a difficult issue for FDA, which it has resolved on an ad hoc basis. In recognition of "the growing interest in home-use in vitro devices," FDA held a public meeting of the chairpersons and the consumer and industry representatives of four of its advisory committees to help develop "uniform evaluation criteria for home-use in vitro devices to help insure that these devices are regulated in a consistent fashion and that consumers are provided with reliable, adequately labeled products." 50 Fed. Reg. 32641 (August 13, 1985). The agency subsequently released a draft "points to consider" in formulating labeling and premarket submissions for home use in vitro diagnostic devices. Interest in this issue was heightened with the announcement in 54 Fed. Reg. 7279 (February 17, 1989) of the public meeting to consider whether AIDS test kits should be approved for home use.

NOTES

1. *Criteria for Approval.* Compare section 505(d), which requires proof that a new drug be proved both safe and effective, with the standard for approval of a Class II or Class III medical device under section 513(a)(2)(C), which provides that safety and effectiveness are to be determined by weighing the probable benefit to health against the probable risk of injury or illness. Does the more recent language represent a fundamental shift in congressional policy, or merely more sophisticated understanding of the criteria for assessing new medical technologies?

2. *Expedited Review.* In October 1989, the CDRH Office of Device Evaluation announced that it would provide expedited review of any IDE or PMA application for a life-threatening or severely debilitating illness for which no alternative product was available.

3. *Suspension of approval.* The 1990 Amendments added new section 515(e)(3), which authorizes FDA to suspend approval of a PMA application if, after providing an opportunity for an informal hearing, it determines there is reasonable probability that use of the device would cause serious adverse health consequences or death.

4. *Nose Clips. Lake v. FDA*, Med. Dev. Rep. (CCH) ¶ 15,117 (E.D. Pa. 1989), upheld FDA's refusal to approve a PMA application for a nose clip

represented to cure the common cold and allergies because of a lack of adequate evidence of safety and effectiveness.

5. *Intraocular Lenses.* Because in 41 Fed. Reg. 14570 (April 6, 1976) FDA had announced that intraocular lenses were new drugs, section 513(f)(1) of the 1976 Amendments automatically classified these products as transitional Class III devices. Regulatory requirements for these devices were announced in 42 Fed. Reg. 58874 (November 11, 1977), 42 Fed. Reg. 63472 (December 16, 1977), 43 Fed. Reg. 11759 (March 21, 1978). The agency has since granted approval for the marketing of individual intraocular lenses, *e.g.,* 46 Fed. Reg. 60650 (December 11, 1981), 51 Fed. Reg. 22135 (June 18, 1986).

6. *Implanted Devices.* Not surprisingly, FDA gives close scrutiny to any device intended to be implanted in the body. In 53 Fed. Reg. 5469 (February 24, 1988), FDA announced the availability of a guideline prepared jointly by regulatory officials in the United Kingdom, Canada, and the United States, on testing of medical devices to establish human biocompatibility. Because of continuing concern about the safety of breast prostheses, FDA in 54 Fed. Reg. 10729 (March 15, 1989) announced the development of "an educational program to assure that women considering surgical implantation of breast prostheses devices are fully informed of the benefits and risks associated with the devices before consenting to the surgical procedure."

7. *Postmarketing Restrictions.* FDA's regulations authorize the agency, in appropriate cases, to impose conditions on the approval of a device under sections 515(d)(1)(B)(ii), 519, or 520. For many Class III devices approved since 1976, the agency has required some form of additional postmarketing studies. These have included clinical studies, evaluation of explanted devices, patient followup, patient registries, and a variety of other similar requirements. G.R.W. Smith, POST–APPROVAL REQUIREMENTS FOR CLASS III MEDICAL DEVICES: A REVIEW (June 21, 1988).

8. *Devices Utilizing Radio Transmission.* The medical device industry obtained an exemption for specialized medical computing devices from the Federal Communications Commission's general regulations governing interference to radio and television reception by equipment utilizing digital electronics technology. 46 Fed. Reg. 44790 (September 8, 1981), 47 Fed. Reg. 31266 (July 19, 1982), codified in 47 C.F.R. § 15.801(c)(5). The FCC has also issued regulations permitting the emergency use of biomedical telemetry systems (diagnostic devices that transmit a patient's vital life signs by radio communication to a hospital where a physician can make a diagnosis and prescribe appropriate treatment) on VHF frequencies. 45 Fed. Reg. 53844 (August 13, 1980), 46 Fed. Reg. 22590 (April 20, 1981), codified in 47 C.F.R. § 90.53(b)(26).

CLINICAL LABORATORY IMPROVEMENT ACT OF 1967

The Clinical Laboratory Improvement Act of 1967 (CLIA), 81 Stat. 533, 536, codified in 42 U.S.C. § 263a *et seq.,* provides for federal licensure of clinical laboratories doing business in interstate commerce. The statute is administered by the Centers for Disease Control under regulations codified in 42 C.F.R. Part 74. To be eligible for payment for services provided to Medicare and Medicaid patients any laboratory must meet the minimum quality standards established by HCFA under 42 C.F.R. Part 405, subpart M. As of 1988, 1,520 laboratories were licensed under CLIA (of which 1,320 were Medicare-certified) and over 12,000 laboratories certified by Medicare. Because an estimated 100,000 laboratories located in the offices of physicians were not licensed or certified, Congress enacted the Clinical Laboratory Improvement Amendments of 1988, 102 Stat. 2903, to extend the CLIA to these laboratories as well. The 1988 Amendments also establish accreditation, quality control, and proficiency testing programs, and provide for inspection and other enforcement authority. S. Rep. No. 100–561, 100th Cong., 2d Sess. (1988). The CLIA regulations were revised and recodified in a new 21 C.F.R. Part 493, 53 Fed. Reg. 29590 (August 5, 1988), 55 Fed. Reg. 9538 (March 14,1990). Revisions to reflect the 1988 Amendments were proposed in 55 Fed. Reg. 20896 (May 21, 1990).

Product Development Protocols

At the urging of makers of cardiac pacemakers, in 1976 FDA acquiesced in the inclusion of section 515(f), which provides an alternative track for the consideration and approval of PMA applications, termed a "product development protocol" (PDP). Under this approach, FDA and the applicant agree in advance upon a testing program which, if completed with successful results, will result in marketing approval. Four years after enactment of the 1976 Amendments, FDA issued a guideline for PDPs.

MEDICAL DEVICES; PRODUCT DEVELOPMENT PROTOCOL AVAILABILITY OF GUIDELINES
45 Federal Register 62555 (September 19, 1980).

The purpose of a PDP is to encourage the development of innovative devices, to reduce development time and costs by combining the conventional two-step investigatory and premarket development procedure into one regulatory mechanism, to aid small manufacturers, and to provide sponsors greater certainty that a testing approach will be acceptable to FDA. The guideline is intended to assist persons submitting PDP's to the agency to meet these objectives.

PDP's are optional; FDA cannot require a sponsor to submit a PDP rather than a premarket approval application (PMA) when seeking approval for a device. However, a sponsor may gain major advantages in using a PDP. For example, a sponsor can obtain FDA assistance in designing the testing procedures and protocols. Also, the sponsor receives a commitment from FDA that if the testing is done under these approved procedures and protocols and the test results are satisfactory, the device will be approved by FDA for marketing. Small manufacturers are likely to benefit from FDA assistance particularly for products that are used in limited circumstances ...

There are five steps in the PDP process. Step I is a presubmission conference with FDA. The presubmission conference is designed to ensure that a PDP is appropriate for a particular device rather than an IDE and PMA (or reclassification of the device). Step II is FDA's determination that a PDP is appropriate. In this step, FDA formally determines whether a PDP that has been submitted by a sponsor is appropriate for the device. Step III is filing and approving a PDP. FDA will file a PDP if the PDP is suitable for submission to an advisory panel for review. To be suitable, the PDP must be designed to develop, or in fact contain, sufficient data to permit an evaluation of the device's safety and effectiveness. Upon filing of a suitable PDP, FDA will refer the PDP to an advisory panel for a recommendation. Subsequently, FDA will evaluate the PDP and the panel's recommendation and either approve or disapprove the PDP. Step IV is the submission of pre-clinical test results. After a PDP is approved, the sponsor may submit pre-clinical test data for FDA evaluation prior to beginning clinical trials. Although a PDP may be approved before pre-clinical testing, FDA will authorize the initiation of clinical trials only after reviewing the pre-clinical test results. After pre-clinical test results are evaluated, FDA will inform sponsors whether they may begin clinical tests with human subjects. This part of Step IV is similar to what happens when a sponsor seeks approval of an IDE. PDP sponsors must comply with the IDE requirements set forth in Part 812 including recordkeeping, institutional review board (IRB) review, and informed consent. Step V is the submission of clinical test results. This step is similar to what happens when a sponsor applies for approval of a PMA. FDA will review pre-clinical and clinical data together with manufacturing data and determine whether the device is suitable for marketing. After evaluating the data, FDA will declare the PDP "completed" or "not completed."

A significant difference between the PDP and IDE/PMA procedure is in the time schedules. A PDP must be approved or disapproved within 120 days of the date it is filed by FDA. An IDE, however, is deemed approved 30 days after receipt by FDA. There is no statutory time limit for FDA review of PDP preclinical data submitted to obtain FDA authorization to begin clinical trials.....

Despite early expectations, the product development protocol provision has so far proved an empty invitation. In the first fourteen years under the Device Amendments the mechanism has reportedly been employed only once.

FDA's implementation of the premarket approval provisions of the 1976 Amendments proved surprisingly uncontroversial until the late 1980s. The time required for FDA review of a PMA application was approximately half that for review of an NDA. No doubt the agency's prompt processing of PMAs was in part attributable to the relatively small number of Class III postenactment devices required to go through the premarket approval process. As this book went to press, however, these time frames had begun to lengthen significantly.

USE OF DATA IN ONE PMA APPLICATION TO APPROVE A SUBSEQUENT PMA APPLICATION

Under the 1976 Amendments, the data contained in a PMA application was considered confidential and thus could not be used by FDA or relied on by another applicant to support approval of a PMA application for an identical or similar device. The 1990 Amendments added new section 520(h)(4), which authorizes FDA to refer to clinical and preclinical data in a prior PMA application, but not descriptions of methods of manufacture and product composition, to approve a subsequent PMA application one year after a PMA application has been approved for the "fourth device of a kind," *i.e.*, if the "me too" device will be the fifth (or later) entrant into the market. FDA must publish an order in the Federal Register identifying the four devices and the date on which the data contained in the four PMA applications will be available for use in approving other devices.

---

c. Reclassification

Under section 513(f)(2)(A), the manufacturer of a Class III postenactment device that is not substantially equivalent to a preenactment device, and thus presumptively required to obtain premarket approval before it may be marketed, may instead petition FDA to reclassify the device in Class II or I. If reclassified, the device would no longer be subject to premarket approval and could immediately be marketed.

From the manufacturer's perspective the key question, of course, is whether the reclassification can be accomplished more speedily or will require less safety and effectiveness data than approval of a PMA application.

The first decade's experience under the 1976 Amendments suggested that reclassification offers no shortcut to the market. FDA denied several reclassification petitions, and rarely ruled expeditiously. By the late 1980s some observers detected changes in the pattern, 54 Fed. Reg. 30206 (July 19, 1989), 54 Fed. Reg. 48238 (November 22, 1989), 54 Fed. Reg. 50737 (December 11, 1989), but it remained doubtful that reclassification petitions under section 513(f)(2)(A) would become numerous or enjoy a high rate of success. *See generally* Kahan, *Medical Device Reclassification: The Evolution of FDA Policy*, 42 FDC L.J. 288 (1987). The difficulties presented by the reclassification process are illustrated in three cases and by the amendments to the process that Congress enacted in 1990.

Prior to the 1976 Amendments FDA classified all hard and soft contact lenses, except hard contact lenses made from polymethylmethacrylate (PMMA), as new drugs. 40 Fed. Reg. 44844 (September 30, 1975). Accordingly, these lenses were automatically classified as Class III transitional devices under section 520(k)(1). Under FDA's interpretation, this statutory classification precluded any finding of substantial equivalence to a postenactment product. Thus, a postenactment hard or soft lens could only be marketed with FDA approval of a PMA application or after reclassification to Class II or Class I.

In 1981, the Contact Lens Manufacturers Association petitioned FDA to reclassify contact lenses made from several materials. FDA initially indicated its agreement with the petition, 46 Fed. Reg. 57648 (November 24, 1981), 47 Fed. Reg. 53402 (November 26, 1982), but after a hearing the agency withdrew its proposal on the ground that the publicly available evidence was insufficient to support reclassification. 48 Fed. Reg. 56778 (December 23, 1983), 49 Fed. Reg. 17523 (April 24, 1984). In a challenge limited to rigid gas permeable (RGP) hard contact lenses, the D.C. Circuit Court of Appeals upheld FDA's decision. *Contact Lens Manufacturers Ass'n v. FDA,* 766 F.2d 592 (D.C. Cir. 1985). In a footnote the court summarily rejected any argument that the RGP lenses were substantially equivalent to the PMMA lenses. 766 F.2d at 598 n.6.

The second case involved a sweat inhibition device with the brand name "Drionic." FDA initially took the position that there was no equivalent preenactment device, and the device thus automatically fell in Class III. The manufacturer submitted a petition for reclassification, which FDA denied. 48 Fed. Reg. 24981 (June 3, 1983), 49 Fed. Reg. 18788 (May 2, 1984). In a separate lawsuit, the manufacturer elicited FDA's acknowledgment that the Drionic device was in fact substantially equivalent to a preenactment *prescription* product but not to a preenactment nonprescription device, and it thereupon sought review of the denial of its reclassification petition. Though critical of procedural lapses by FDA, the court upheld the agency's decision on the merits. *General Medical Co. v. FDA,* 770 F.2d 214 (D.C. Cir. 1985).

More recently, in *Lake v. FDA,* Med. Dev. Rep. (CCH) ¶ 15,117 (E.D. Pa. 1989), the plaintiff claimed that FDA had arbitrarily refused to reclassify from Class III its nose clip, represented to cure the common cold and allergies. The plaintiff argued that, because the device obviously presented no risk of illness or injury, it fell squarely within section 513(a)(1)(A)(ii)'s definition of a Class I device despite the lack of evidence of effectiveness. Acknowledging that this possibility had been raised by the opinion in *General Medical Co.,* 770 F.2d at 222, the *Lake* court rejected the plaintiff's literal interpretation of the statute:

> It could not have been the intent of Congress to allow the marketing of unproven medical devices about which no scientific evidence is available. To hold otherwise would allow people to market all manner of fraudulent devices. We are long passed the day when snake oil can be sold with impunity. Plaintiff's reading of the statute would shift the burden of proof to the FDA and that is not how our public health laws are designed to work. When there is no valid scientific evidence of efficacy, and the risks are unknown, the risk is unreasonable.

Because of the obstacles to reclassification and the relatively large number of devices placed in Class III under the 1976 law, the 1990 Amendments require FDA to reconsider the classification of all Class III devices, and either to down-classify them or begin rulemaking to require submission of safety and effectiveness data for preenactment and postenactment versions of unreclassified devices.

HUMANITARIAN DEVICE EXEMPTION

The 1990 Amendments added a new section 520(m) to encourage the discovery and use of devices intended to benefit patients in the treatment and diagnosis of diseases that affect fewer than 4,000 individuals in the United States. The new provision authorizes FDA to grant individual requests for an exemption for such devices from the effectiveness requirements of sections 514 and 515.

6. REQUIREMENTS FOR PREENACTMENT CLASS II AND CLASS III DEVICES

a. Performance Standards and Special Controls for Class II Devices

Prior to 1976 FDA had promulgated what it claimed to be a "standard" for impact-resistant lenses, and it had proposed the development of standards for in vitro diagnostic products. As enacted, section 514 of the 1976 Amendments provided that FDA "may" establish performance standards. One author of this book contends that this language was carefully chosen by FDA officials involved in drafting the original legislation to negate any implication that the agency was obligated to establish a performance standard for every Class II device or that it was obliged to adopt standards in accordance with any fixed schedule. It was their expectation that the provision for performance standards, like the requirement for approval of preenactment Class III devices, would be implemented in accordance with priorities to be determined in the future and in light of the resources then available to the agency. Some observers, however, have urged a much more restrictive interpretation of this provision. E.g., Leflar, *Public Accountability and Medical Device Regulation*, 2 Harv. J. L. & Tech. 1 (1989).

Shortly after passage of the 1976 Amendments, FDA described its activities to encourage and support the development of performance standards for devices by private organizations and associations.

MEDICAL DEVICES: PERFORMANCE STANDARDS ACTIVITIES
41 Federal Register 34099 (August 12, 1976).

For several years, FDA has been engaged in activities designed to encourage the development of voluntary performance standards for medical devices. These efforts have been aimed primarily at developing criteria for measuring the performance characteristics of certain currently marketed devices that may present an unusual or serious risk of injury to persons treated with such products. Prior to the passage of the recent device amendments, FDA contemplated the possibility of adopting such standards as legal requirements for specific devices, relying upon the general rule making authority conferred by section 701(a) of the act....

The Food and Drug Administration intends to continue to promote such voluntary efforts because they contribute to assuring the safety and effectiveness of marketed devices. Voluntary or privately recognized performance standards will not be a substitute for the formal promulgation of standards under section 514 of the act for any device that is classified in the performance standard category. However, voluntary or privately recognized standards can serve as informal standards prior to classification as well as during the development of formal standards for devices that are not candidates for immediate attention, and they may be the basis for subsequent formal FDA standards....

Four years later, FDA promulgated regulations establishing procedures for the development of device performance standards in 43 Fed. Reg. 32264 (July 25, 1978), 45 Fed. Reg. 7474 (February 1, 1980). Concluding that it lacked the resources to establish performance standards for all Class II devices, the agency simultaneously published the following notice proposing increased reliance on voluntary standards.

VOLUNTARY STANDARDS POLICY FOR MEDICAL DEVICES; REQUEST FOR COMMENTS

45 Federal Register 7490 (February 1, 1980).

FDA believes that endorsing adequate voluntary standards will (1) encourage manufacturers, voluntary standards organizations, and other interested persons to continue to develop performance standards in their areas of expertise, (2) result in a greater number of performance standards being established more rapidly with fewer FDA resources than if only mandatory standards were issued, and (3) permit FDA to concentrate on the development of standards for class II devices that are not the subject of adequate voluntary standards and are selected for their impact on the public health....

Mandatory standards offer one important advantage over voluntary standards—FDA can require compliance with a mandatory standard and can take regulatory action against manufacturers that fail to comply or devices that fail to conform to that standard. With voluntary standards, however, FDA can take regulatory action against manufacturers of devices that fail to meet a voluntary standard only if the devices' labeling or advertising claims to meet that standard....

FDA believes, however, that device manufacturers generally have a strong incentive to comply with voluntary standards, especially those endorsed by FDA. Hospitals and other device purchasers will be inclined to purchase devices that conform to FDA-endorsed voluntary standards because of their potential liability in the event that a patient or user is injured by a device that does not conform to an existing FDA-endorsed voluntary standard. Federal and State governments, major purchasers of medical devices, will be encouraged by FDA to purchase devices that conform to FDA-endorsed voluntary standards. In addition, FDA will encourage manufacturers of devices that conform to FDA-endorsed voluntary standards to label their devices as conforming.

FDA is thus changing its policy described in the FEDERAL REGISTER notice of August 12, 1976; the notice states "Voluntary or privately recognized performance standards will not be a substitute for the formal promulgation of standards under section 514 of the act for any device that is classified in the performance standard category." Under the policy that the agency now proposes, FDA will endorse particular voluntary standards, and, if voluntary conformance is adequate, defer development of mandatory standards....

FDA will notify the developer of a standard by letter of those provisions of the standard endorsed by FDA. The Bureau of Medical Devices will maintain a file of endorsement letters and endorsed standards. Copies of the letters only will be available to the public upon request. An address where requests may be sent will be published in the final notice implementing FDA's voluntary standards policy. In addition, FDA will publish periodically a notice in the FEDERAL REGISTER listing all FDA-endorsed voluntary standards. Copies of the endorsed standards may be obtained from the developer, at the address stated in the endorsement letter and published in the notice....

By 1985, however, FDA had again reversed its position and announced that it would proceed to establish mandatory performance standards for at least some Class II devices under section 514, rather than rely on voluntary standards.

POLICY STATEMENT; CLASS II MEDICAL DEVICES
50 Federal Register 43060 (October 23, 1985).

... The Food and Drug Administration (FDA) is announcing its policy for setting priorities for initiating proceedings to establish performance standards for medical devices classified into class II, a category of devices under the Medical Device Amendments for which FDA is required to establish performance standards. At this time, however, FDA does not have the resources to establish performance standards for all class II devices. Accordingly, the policy describes the factors the agency takes into account in establishing priorities for initiating standard-setting proceedings....

When setting priorities for initiating proceedings to establish performance standards for class II medical devices under section 514 of the act, FDA will consider the following factors: the seriousness of questions concerning a device's safety or effectiveness; the risks associated with the use of the device; the significance of the device to the public health; the present and projected use of the device; the recommendations of FDA's advisory committees; the impact of an FDA guideline or recommendation; the effect of a Federal standard or other regulatory controls under an authority other than the act; the impact of voluntary standards; the impact of activities authorized under the general controls provisions of the act; the effect of dissemination of information and educational efforts; the sufficiency of voluntary corrective actions; valid scientific evidence developed since classification; the existence of a petition for reclassification; and the impact of other factors that affect the device's safety or effectiveness such as the likelihood of developing an FDA guideline or adequate voluntary standard. The policy, set forth at the end of this notice, elaborates on these factors....

1. Several comments ... stated that under the policy the voluntary standard-writing process could have greater potential for significant participation by health care providers, small manufacturers, and consumers than could a proceeding to establish a performance standard under section 514 of the act. Other comments supported FDA's participation in the development of voluntary standards, and said that timely involvement by FDA in reviewing evolving standards was essential. A comment claimed that, especially in times of Federal budget constraints, FDA should make every effort to use the voluntary standards process.

The final policy on class II devices ... is different from the 1980 proposed policy in several major respects. The final policy identifies the factors FDA takes into account in setting priorities for initiating proceedings to establish performance standards under section 514 of the act. Among the factors FDA considers is the existence of an adequate, adhered to voluntary standard. The policy does not include a provision for endorsement of voluntary standards nor does it provide for promotion of such standards.

FDA eliminated the endorsement provision from the final policy primarily because the agency received many comments stating that the endorsement and promotion provisions of the 1980 proposed policy gave the appearance of substantive rulemaking. These comments argued that a voluntary standard endorsed and promoted by FDA would be perceived by manufacturers and consumers as mandatory. Although FDA did not intend that an endorsed standard would have the force and effect of law, FDA has been convinced that endorsement of a standard, taken together with FDA's promotion of the endorsed standard, could have misled manufacturers and consumers to believe the standard was mandatory.

The provisions of the 1980 proposed policy may have been misleading because the proposed policy appeared to state that the endorsement of voluntary standards might in some cases be a substitute for the establishment of performance standards under section 514 of the act, and suggested that the existence of an endorsed standard would alone be a basis for deferring initiation of a proceeding to establish a performance standard under section 514 of the act. Under the final policy, FDA will not conclude that a performance standard is unnecessary solely on the basis of the existence of an adequate, adhered to voluntary standard. Rather, under the final policy, the existence of an adequate, adhered to voluntary standard would be one of several factors that FDA takes into account in setting priorities for initiating a proceeding to establish a performance standard.

FDA now believes that it should focus its limited resources on setting priorities for, and initiating proceedings to establish, performance standards, rather than on endorsement and promotion of voluntary standards. FDA agrees, however, that the agency can play a valuable role in voluntary standards writing....

Participation in outside standard-setting activities by FDA employees is governed by § 10.95 of its administrative practices and procedures regulations (21 CFR 10.95). Such activities include the development of performance characteristics, testing methodology, manufacturing practices, scientific protocols, compliance criteria, ingredient specifications, labeling, and other technical or policy criteria. FDA will continue to encourage employee participation in outside standard-setting activities, subject to § 10.95 of its regulations, and the revised Office of Management and Budget (OMB) Circular A-119 "Federal Participation in the Development and Use of Voluntary Standards" (47 FR 49496; November 1, 1982).

NOTES

1. *Standards Under Development.* FDA has proceeded with the establishment of device performance standards in accordance with this policy statement. The agency began with cardiac monitors, 48 Fed. Reg. 31394 (July 8, 1983), 50 Fed. Reg. 48156 (November 21, 1985); vascular graft prostheses, 48 Fed Reg. 31395 (July 8, 1983), 51 Fed. Reg. 564 (January 6, 1986); and continuous ventilators, 48 Fed. Reg. 27723 (June 17, 1983), 48 Fed. Reg. 31393 (July 8, 1983), 51 Fed. Reg. 11516 (April 3, 1986). The agency also withdrew a proposal to establish a generic standard for all electromedical devices. 45 Fed. Reg. 58970 (September 5, 1980), 52 Fed. Reg. 38276 (October 15, 1987). The standard nearest promulgation is for the infant apnea monitor, 48 Fed. Reg. 31392 (July 8, 1983), 51 Fed. Reg. 6886 (February 26, 1986), 51 Fed. Reg. 23832 (July 1, 1986), 53 Fed. Reg. 13296 (April 22, 1988), for which FDA announced the availability of the first and second drafts in 54 Fed. Reg. 187 (January 4, 1989), 54 Fed. Reg. 50437 (December 6, 1989).

2. *Support for Standard Development.* FDA established requirements for persons who seek agency support to develop a proposed performance standard for any Class II medical device in 51 Fed. Reg. 23832 (July 1, 1986).

3. *Procedural Similarities to CPSA.* The original procedure for setting standards under section 514 resembled that prescribed in the Consumer Product Safety Act, 15 U.S.C. §§ 2056, 2058, for consumer product safety standards. The 1990 Amendments replaced this elaborate procedure with notice-and-comment rulemaking.

4. *Eyeglass Standards.* Before the 1976 Amendments FDA established a standard for impact-resistant lenses in eyeglasses and sunglasses, 35 Fed. Reg. 15402 (October 2, 1970), 36 Fed. Reg. 8939 (May 15, 1971), amended 36 Fed. Reg. 18871 (September 23, 1971), 37 Fed. Reg. 2503 (February 2, 1972), 43 Fed. Reg. 1106 (January 6, 1978), 44 Fed. Reg. 20676 (April 6, 1979), codified in 21 C.F.R. § 801.410.

5. *In Vitro Diagnostics.* In 1972, as part of its decision to regulate in vitro diagnostic products without ruling whether they are drugs or devices, FDA established a procedure for establishing standards for this group of products as well as detailed labeling requirements. *See* note 2, p. 732 *supra.* FDA published a request for data to establish a product class standard for detection or measurement of glucose or total sugars in 38 Fed. Reg. 13573 (May 23, 1973) and a notice of the availability of a draft standard in 41 Fed. Reg. 22394 (June 3, 1976), as well as notices requesting information to establish standards for other in vitro diagnostic products. Following enactment of the 1976 Amendments, the agency revoked the separate procedures for standards for in vitro diagnostic products, 45 Fed. Reg. 7474 (February 1, 1980), and withdrew the proposed glucose standard, 51 Fed. Reg. 13023 (April 17, 1986).

SPECIAL CONTROLS

Recognizing that not all Class II devices justify performance standards, the 1990 Amendments revise section 513(a)(1)(B) to expand Class II to include devices subject to so-called "special controls" as well as performance standards. Special controls are defined to include postmarket surveillance, patient registries, development and dissemination of guidelines, recommendations, and other appropriate action FDA deems necessary to assure safety and effectiveness.

---

b. Approval of Preenactment Class III Devices

Under section 515(b), FDA is empowered to promulgate regulations requiring that preenactment Class III devices and their postenactment equivalents undergo approval for safety and effectiveness. Because of concern that the agency would have inadequate resources to meet mandatory deadlines, the legislation was drafted without any time requirements for implementing this provision. Instead, section 513(d)(3) authorized the establishment of priorities for implementing section 515(b). FDA announced its intent to require premarket approval of 13 types of preenactment Class III devices in 48 Fed. Reg. 40272 (September 6, 1983), 52 Fed. Reg. 17732 (May 11, 1987), announced its intent to initiate proceedings to require approval for another 31 types of devices in 54 Fed. Reg. 550 (January 6, 1989), and has proposed or issued final regulations requiring approval of several other types of devices. Following reports of adverse effects from silicone breast implants, "FDA Seeks Panels Advice on Silicone Breast Implants," FDA Talk Paper No. T88–81 (November 3, 1988), FDA proposed to require premarket approval for these devices in 55 Fed. Reg. 20568 (May 17, 1990).

In response to criticism that FDA was not moving quickly enough to require submission of safety and effectiveness data for preenactment Class III devices and their post-enactment equivalents, Congress in 1990 added new section 515(i) to achieve two objectives. First, FDA is required to reconsider its classification of all Class III devices so that only those devices that warrant premarket approval remain in Class III. This process is to be completed by December 1, 1995. Second, for those devices that it retains in Class III, FDA must within 12 months promulgate a regulation requiring submission of premarket approval applications.

7. GENERAL REGULATORY CONTROLS FOR ALL DEVICES

All marketed devices, regardless of date of introduction or classification, are subject to the following general regulatory controls.

a. Adulteration and Misbranding

The adulteration and misbranding provisions that applied to medical devices under the 1938 Act continue to apply under the 1976 Amendments. For postenactment devices, section 510(k)'s requirement of a PMN has proved a potent regulatory weapon. FDA has acted to remove a number of products marketed after 1976 simply for failure to follow the section 510(k) requirement. *E.g., United States v. Clark Research and Development, Inc.*, Med. Dev. Rep. (CCH) ¶ 15,119 (E.D. La. 1989); *United States v. An Article of Device ... Stryker Shoulder 130–10 Dacron Ligament Prosthesis*, 607 F. Supp. 990 (W.D. Mich. 1985); *United States v. Undetermined Quantities of an Article of Device ... "Gendertest,"* 1985–1986 FDLI Jud. Rec. 30 (C.D. Cal. 1985); *United States v. An Article of Device ... Ovutron*, 1981–1982 FDLI Jud. Rec. 92 (D. Ariz. 1982). For preenactment devices, however, the agency has had to rely on conventional, and often difficult to prove, charges of adulteration or misbranding. *E.g., United States v. An Article of Device ... "Toftness Radiation Detector,"* 731 F.2d 1253 (7th Cir. 1984); *United States v. An Article of Device "Theramatic "*, 715 F.2d 1339 (9th Cir. 1983); *United States v. Torigian Laboratories, Inc.*, 577 F. Supp. 1514 (E.D.N.Y. 1984); *United States v. An Article or Device Consisting of ... Biotone Model 4 ... Muscle Stimulator*, 557 F. Supp. 141 (N.D. Ga. 1982); *United States v. An Article ... Acu–Dot*, 483 F. Supp. 1311 (N.D.

Ohio 1980); *United States v. Articles of Device ... Acuflex; Pro–Med,*
426 F. Supp. 366 (W.D. Pa. 1977).

ELECTRICAL MUSCLE STIMULATORS
FDA Talk Paper, January 15, 1982.

Medical devices known as electrical muscle stimulators are being
used—often inappropriately—in health spas and figure salons across
the United States. Not to be confused with simple massage devices, the
electrical muscle stimulators contract muscles by passing electric current through electrodes (contact pads) applied to the skin. Powered by
batteries or line current, they are similar to the Relaxacisor, an
electrical muscle stimulator sold without prescription until 1970, when
FDA won a court decision permanently prohibiting such sales. (During
the five-month trial, 40 witnesses testified they suffered varying degrees of injury while using the machine.)

FDA now regulates electrical muscle stimulators as prescription
medical devices to be used only by or on order of a licensed practitioner.
Medical experts agree that there are legitimate uses for these devices in
physical therapy for treating specific medical problems, such as relaxation of muscle spasms. They are also properly used to increase blood
circulation to a part of the body, prevent blood clots in the leg muscles
of bedridden patients after surgery, re-educate muscles after a stroke,
and increase or monitor the range of motion of an arm or leg.

When used in health spas, however, the devices are usually promoted for "slimming and trimming," "weight loss," "body shaping and
contouring," bust development, wrinkle removal, spot reducing and
"cellulite" removal.

FDA has not seen any evidence that electrical muscle stimulators
are safe and effective for these or any similar purposes. Indeed, FDA
considers muscle stimulators promoted or used for these purposes to be
misbranded and fraudulent, even if a physician or other licensed
practitioner is using the device.

Some states license cosmetologists to use electrical muscle stimulators. But FDA does not believe the devices are safe and effective for
use by cosmetologists, particularly since cosmetologists do not have the
training to diagnose medical conditions in which the stimulators might
cause harm.

AMERICAN SPEECH AND HEARING ASS'N v. CALIFANO
United States District Court, District of Columbia, 1977.
Civ. No. 77–1327.

GESELL, District Judge.

This is a suit by the American Speech and Hearing Association
(ASHA), a national association of audiologists and speech pathologists

... to declare illegal and to enjoin the operation of final rules promulgated by the Food and Drug Administration (FDA) governing the manufacture and distribution of hearing aid devices. The rules require a prior examination by a physician before a hearing aid is administered and preempt any less stringent state laws to the contrary....

The material facts are not in dispute. Prior to implementation of the challenged regulations, the marketing of hearing aid devices was regulated, if at all, by the states. Abuses were prevalent.... In some states an examination by a physician specializing in hearing disorders or an audiologist was required as a condition precedent to obtaining a hearing aid. Some states required no examination at all. Rules in some states applied only to certain age segments of the population.

In March 1974 the defendant Department of Health, Education and Welfare established a Task Force to study problems relating to the marketing of quality hearing aids throughout the United States.... As a result of the Task Force findings ... the FDA undertook to develop national rules. Proposed rules were published in the FEDERAL REGISTER on April 21, 1976, and a 60–day comment period was provided. 41 Fed. Reg. 16756 (1976).

Section 801.421(a) of the proposed rules required an examination, subject to waiver in certain instances, by a licensed physician prior to issuance of a hearing aid to a user. It also provided that "[s]tate and local governments may make more stringent conditions for sale of hearing aids." Thus, those state rules requiring an examination by an audiologist in addition to one by a physician were left intact.

On May 28, 1977, however, during the comment period for the proposed rules, Congress passed the Medical Device Amendments of 1976. The amendments mandate preemption of state and local requirements with respect to medical devices (including hearing aids) that are "different from, or in addition to" any requirements established by the FDA. The Amendments do allow the FDA, by regulation issued after notice and an opportunity for an oral hearing, to exempt a state or local medical device requirement from preemption under such conditions as the FDA may prescribe if the requirement is (1) more stringent than the federal requirements applicable to the device, or (2) required by compelling local conditions and compliance with it would not cause the device to be in violation of any other federal requirements....

The hearing aid rules were promulgated in final form on February 15, 1977.... 42 Fed. Reg. 9286 (1977). The requirement of prior examination by a physician was retained, but, due to the intervening enactment of the Medical Device Amendments, the allowance for differing state and local regulations was deleted.... Plaintiffs contend that the requirement that the pre-sale evaluation be conducted by a physician rather than by any practitioner licensed to administer hearing aid devices violates an express provision of the Medical Device Amendments and in any event is arbitrary and capricious.

At the very heart of the substantive dispute is the fact that FDA's requirement of examination by a physician as opposed to an audiologist has threatened an important facet of the audiologist's role in the hearing aid delivery system.... A clinical audiologist is a graduate-school-trained "individual qualified to provide professional assistance concerning communication problems associated with hearing impairment." Such assistance includes prevention, identification, evaluation, and rehabilitation of people with auditory disorders....

... Plaintiffs argue that the regulation in question is invalid under subsection (A) [of section 520(e)(1)] which, in plaintiffs' opinion, requires any regulation mandating pre-sale authorization by a licensed practitioner to apply equally to all licensed practitioners. In most states audiologists, physicians, and hearing aid dealers are all licensed practitioners within the meaning of the statute....

Plaintiffs' argument has several flaws. First, it is incorrect to characterize it as one of exclusion: neither audiologists nor dealers are barred from doing anything, nor are they deprived of their status as practitioners. Second, at least in the context of hearing aid sales, plaintiffs' construction of the term "practitioner" leaves subsection (A) devoid of meaning. Hearing aids are always sold by "licensed practitioners" who, by the very act of selling have "authorized" the sale. The type of restriction comprehended by plaintiffs' interpretation of subsection (A) imposes no restriction at all.... [T]he Court ... find[s] that subsection (A) permits the FDA to distinguish among different types of practitioners and thus to authorize the type of regulation at issue.

This result accords with plain sense. The purpose of the Amendments was to empower the Secretary or his designate to root out the abuses extant under state regulation of medical devices. The regulation at issue is so obviously directed toward that goal that the Court would have to ignore the most fundamental tenets of statutory interpretation to void it....

Plaintiffs argue that ... the regulation ... is nonetheless arbitrary and capricious and thus voidable under section 10 of the APA, 5 U.S.C. § 706(2)(A). Under the Amendments the regulation is valid only if "there cannot otherwise be reasonable assurance of [the] safety and effectiveness" of hearing aid devices. Yet if this is so is it not irrational to make the examination requirement waivable in a large number of cases? And is it not irrational to allow the required examination to be performed by any physician, a class that include podiatrists, gynecologists, and others with little familiarity with hearing disorders, yet at the same time exclude audiologists, whose expertise is in this area?

These are thoughtful questions. The record shows, however, that they were carefully considered by the FDA prior to enactment. The regulation is accompanied by detailed and conscientious findings of fact that justify the rule adopted. The seeming contradictions are actually the result of compromises between the competing demands of economy and safety. After extended and careful study, the FDA found a medical evaluation to be essential for proper diagnosis and treatment. It also found that audiologists were unable to "differentiate, diagnose, evaluate, and treat the medical cause or causes of a hearing impairment." Examinations were authorized by all physicians because of the scarcity of otologists, otolaryngologists, and other physicians specializing in hearing disorders. A required audiological examination in addition to that of a physician was rejected as too expensive and of dubious incremental benefit. The waiver provision was included to accommodate certain religious and personal beliefs as well as those with the most limited access to physicians. Those eligible to waive the examination may do so only upon signing a form strongly advising against waiver. The Court is far from convinced of the wisdom of the compromise adopted, but is mindful of the limited scope of its review and the deference due to the "informed experience and judgment of the agency to whom Congress delegated appropriate authority." Because the regulatory choice made in this case cannot be termed unconsidered, it is upheld....

FDA may invoke the Act's adulteration or misbranding provisions when it is not feasible to establish a performance standard and it believes that revised labeling can adequately protect consumers. Following discovery of the association between tampons and toxic shock syndrome (TSS), FDA mandated a strong label warning statement. 45 Fed. Reg. 69840 (October 21, 1980), 47 Fed. Reg. 26982 (June 22, 1982). After the American Society for Testing and Materials (ASTM) was unable to devise a performance standard for tampons, and the three principal manufacturers adopted differing approaches to providing label information about product absorbency, FDA proposed to establish a uniform test for absorbency and a uniform letter designation, from A (the lowest degree of absorbency) to F (the highest degree of absorbency), for purposes of product labeling. 53 Fed. Reg. 37250 (September 23, 1988). Comments from the public, however, caused the agency to revise this approach.

MEDICAL DEVICES; LABELING FOR MENSTRUAL TAMPONS; RANGES OF ABSORBENCY; REPROPOSED RULE

54 Federal Register 25076 (June 12, 1989).

... The Food and Drug Administration (FDA) is reproposing amendments to its tampon labeling regulation. The reproposed rule would require that manufacturers of menstrual tampons determine tampon absorbency using a test method specified in the reproposal, and, based on the results of that testing, express absorbency on tampon labeling by using one of six specified absorbency terms, each of which corresponds to a range of absorbency set forth in the reproposal. The reproposed rule would enable consumers to compare the absorbency of one brand and style of tampons with the absorbency of other brands and styles before purchasing them.....

FDA received many comments on the use of letters to designate ranges of absorbency. One manufacturer, one consumer group, and several individual consumers, opposing the use of letters, contended that their use would create confusion because consumers are accustomed to numbers, not letters, representing quantity or size, because the use of letters would require that consumers learn two systems (the letters and the numerical ranges to which they refer), and because consumers would not know whether "A" were high or low. A comment from an individual consumer argued that "A" commonly indicates "most desirable" and, thus, would be misinterpreted by consumers. By contrast, comments from two manufacturers, two consumer groups, and most individual consumers supported the use of letter designations. These comments supported the use of a labeling scheme that does not use numbers, arguing that letter designations would provide an accurate and simple labeling approach incorporating notions familiar to most consumers, and that, because consumers are accustomed to thinking that higher numbers are better in terms of increased protection or decreased risk (as with sunscreen labeling), any final rule should use a different system, one that would not encourage the use of higher absorbencies. Another consumer group stated that letter designations would be easy for women to accept, noting that letters are used by the pantyhose industry. Individual consumers, also supporting the use of letter designations, claimed that most people will believe that "A" offers the least amount of absorbency, and that a letter rating would make the categories more distinct and informative and would influence consumers to use less absorbent tampons.

Although the agency agrees that the use of sun protection factors on labeling for sunscreens is effective and appropriate, FDA believes that this is so because the public understands that the higher the number, the greater the blockage of ultraviolet radiation and the greater the health benefit. In the case of tampons and TSS, the reverse would be true: the higher the number the higher the risk of TSS and the lower the public health benefit. FDA, therefore, believes that the analogy to sunscreen labeling is unpersuasive. Also, the agency continues to believe that the use of single numbers to represent grams of fluid absorbed by tampons is not feasible at this time.

FDA agrees, however, with the comments that the use of letters representing numerical ranges might be confusing and that consumers might not be able to readily ascertain which letters represented high or low absorbency. For example, if consumers assumed that the letters represented a hierarchy similar to that commonly used in educational grading systems, consumers could select a "D" thinking it was a very low absorbency product, when, in fact, it is highly absorbent. The agency has tentatively concluded, therefore, that letter designations would not provide to consumers the clear, nonmisleading absorbency information that was intended in the proposed rule, and, accordingly, has removed letter designations from the reproposal.

FDA, however, also agrees that a numerical system, by itself, would pose the problems discussed in other comments. The agency has tentatively concluded that a system in which a new set of standardized, clear, nonmisleading terms of absorbency, corresponding to standardized nonoverlapping ranges of absorbency, would best facilitate interbrand comparison of tampon absorbencies and selection of the least absorbent tampon needed. Accordingly, FDA now proposes to further revise § 801.430(e)(1) to require the use of the following absorbency terms in lieu of letters: low absorbency, medium absorbency, medium-high absorbency, high absorbency, very high absorbency, and highest absorbency, each corresponding to one of the six nonoverlapping ranges provided for in the initial proposal. The applicable term, which must be on the principal display panel(s), would readily convey absorbency information to consumers. In addition, reproposed § 801.430(e)(2) would permit a manufacturer to include on tampon labeling the numerical range of absorbency corresponding to the applicable term of absorbency whenever the manufacturer used a term. . . .

Consumer groups and some individual consumers argued that all materials, additives, and fragrances should be listed on the product label so that consumers can choose the products they want to purchase or avoid them on the basis of which ingredients are known to be or suspected of being hazardous, as well as which ingredients have the potential for causing allergic reactions, sensitivity, or irritation. On the other hand, several individual consumers argued against ingredient labeling, some stating that there were no data of which they were aware suggesting the need, others maintaining that it was simply not as important as absorbency labeling. One group of consumers claimed that consumers probably would not use ingredient labeling because concerns about ingredients were not sufficiently important.

Two manufacturers argued that there was no legal requirement or current regulatory basis for mandating ingredient labeling of tampons. These comments noted, however, that manufacturers, in response to consumer interest, have voluntarily implemented an ingredient labeling system for tampons, and argued, on that basis as well, that there is no need for FDA to require such labeling in any final rule.

None of the comments favoring ingredient labeling cited, discussed, or submitted any data showing an association between any ingredient in any currently marketed tampon and any risk to health, including allergic reaction, sensitivity, or irritation, and FDA is unaware of any such data. Moreover, none of the comments provided any legal theory under which the agency could require ingredient labeling for tampons. Absent information indicating that the disclosure of tampon ingredients on package labeling is necessary for the safe or effective use of the product or that the omission of such information is material to the safe or effective use of tampons, FDA has tentatively concluded that it does not have the authority to require tampon manufacturers to list ingredient information on product labeling. . . .

NOTE

Following the decision in *Public Citizen Health Research Group v. Commissioner, Food and Drug Administration,* 724 F. Supp. 1013 (D.D.C. 1989), criticising FDA's seven-year delay in promulgating these regulations and ordering final regulations to be promulgated within two months, FDA published final regulations in 54 Fed. Reg. 43766 (October 26, 1989). The final regulations, codified in 21 C.F.R. § 801.430, once again changed the required absorbency terms, finally settling upon the terms actually used by the industry: junior absorbency, regular absorbency, super absorbency, and super plus absorbency.

---

b. Establishment Registration and Listing

FDA has promulgated regulations governing device establishment registration, 41 Fed. Reg. 37458 (September 3, 1976), 42 Fed. Reg. 42520 (August 23, 1977), and device listing, 42 Fed. Reg. 52808 (September 30, 1977), 43 Fed. Reg. 37990 (August 25, 1978), codified in 21 C.F.R. Part 807. As of June 30, 1990, approximately 13,000 domestic and 4,500 foreign medical device establishments were registered with FDA. Foreign establishment registration is voluntary. FDA lists approximately 100,000 device classification records, each of which represents a general type of device. Because related devices may be covered under a single record, the total number of devices on the market substantially exceeds 100,000.

---

c. Good Manufacturing Practice (GMP)

FDA has established regulations governing good manufacturing practices (GMP) for devices. 42 Fed. Reg. 11998 (March 1, 1977), 43 Fed. Reg. 31508 (July 21, 1978), codified in 21 C.F.R. Part 820. In 55 Fed. Reg. 24544 (June 15, 1990), the agency announced that it is considering revision of those regulations. The current regulations distinguish between "critical" and "noncritical" devices. A critical device is intended for surgical implant or to support or to sustain life, whose failure to perform properly can reasonably be expected to result in significant injury. The most rigorous GMP requirements apply only to critical devices. FDA has published an advisory list of critical devices in 53 Fed. Reg. 8854 (March 17, 1988), 54 Fed. Reg. 51496 (December 15, 1989). Guidelines for process validation were announced in 48 Fed. Reg. 13096 (March 29, 1983), 52 Fed. Reg. 17638 (May 11, 1987), and draft guidelines for in vitro diagnostic product GMPs were announced in 53 Fed. Reg. 11561 (April 7, 1986), 55 Fed. Reg. 14836 (April 19, 1990).

When concern was first raised about the potential carcinogenicity of ethylene oxide (ETO), FDA published a notice of its intent to propose maximum residue limits for medical devices in 43 Fed. Reg. 27474 (June 23, 1978). Because ETO is used to assure the sterility of many devices, FDA opposed any ban of this chemical. As of June 30, 1990, the agency has not published a proposal or taken any further action on ETO. Concerns about the toxicity, including the carcinogenicity, of ETO have been addressed by EPA in response to the recommendations of the Interagency Testing Committee under the Toxic Substances Control Act, 49 Fed. Reg. 200 (January 3, 1984), and by OSHA, 47 Fed. Reg. 3566 (January 26, 1982), 48 Fed. Reg. 17284 (April 21, 1983), 49 Fed. Reg. 36659 (September 19, 1984, 50 Fed. Reg. 64 (January 2, 1985). *See Public Citizen Health Research Group v. Tyson,* 796 F.2d 1479 (D.C.Cir.1986); *Public Citizen Health Research Group v. Brock,* 823 F.2d 626 (D.C.Cir.1987) (upholding OSHA's exposure limit for ETO); *see also* 53 Fed. Reg. 1724 (January 21, 1988), 53 Fed. Reg. 11414 (April 6, 1988).

When FDA initiated suit to enforce a draft guideline adopting a sterility assurance level of 0.1 percent, the court refused to recognize the draft guideline because it had not been formally adopted as part of the GMP regulations, and ruled that the evidence at trial did not independently establish the validity of a 0.1 percent sterility assurance level. *United States v. Bioclinical Systems, Inc.,* 666 F.Supp. 82 (D.Md. 1987).

Because of concern that device failures are due in large part to design and production deficiencies, Congress in 1990 amended section 520(f) to permit FDA to impose GMP requirements concerning "preproduction design validation (including a process to assess the performance of a device but not including an evaluation of the safety or effectiveness of a device)."

----

d. Restricted Devices

Section 520(e) authorizes FDA, by regulation, to require that a device be restricted to sale, distribution, or use only upon prescription, or upon such other conditions as FDA may require. A restricted device is thus analogous to a prescription drug. Under section 704, FDA inspectors are entitled to examine factory records for restricted devices, just as they may inspect prescription drug records.

Immediately after passage of the 1976 Amendments, before issuing regulations to implement section 520(e), FDA claimed authority to inspect records for devices that manufacturers had previously confined to prescription sale. The agency was rebuffed by the courts, which held that it was required to issue regulations designating specific devices as restricted before it could utilize the new inspection authority. *Becton, Dickinson and Coe v. FDA,* 589 F.2d 1175 (2d Cir. 1978); *In re Estab-*

lishment Inspection Portex, Inc., 595 F.2d 84 (1st Cir. 1979). *See generally* Kelleher, *FDA Inspection and Restricted Devices*, 33 FDC L.J. 331 (1978). FDA subsequently published a proposed regulation, 45 Fed. Reg. 65619 (October 3, 1980). But after its authority to inspect pacemaker records under sections 519 (records and reports) and 520(f) (GMP regulations) was upheld, *In the Matter of Establishment Inspection of Medtronic, Inc.*, 500 F. Supp. 536 (D. Minn. 1980), the agency withdrew this proposal, 46 Fed. Reg. 57569 (November 24, 1981). The agency reasoned that its pre–1976 regulation defining prescription devices (21 CF.R. § 801.109) was sufficient to distinguish between prescription and nonprescription devices and that its existing inspection powers would be adequate:

> FDA will use the inspectional authority available under 21 U.S.C. 374(e) for inspection of records required by the good manufacturing practice regulation (21 CFR Part 820) as well as the dispensing and labeling requirements of the present prescription devices regulation and other applicable regulations in regulating medical devices.

FDA has taken no further action to issue general regulations governing restricted devices. In promulgating premarket approval regulations, however, the agency provided that approval of a Class III device could be conditioned upon compliance with restrictions imposed under section 520(e). 21 C.F.R. § 814.44(e). Accordingly, the requirements for labeling and advertising for restricted devices under section 502(r) remain inoperative, except as FDA has made them conditions of approval of individual Class III devices.

---

e. Records and Reports

Section 519 authorizes FDA to promulgate regulations requiring makers and distributors of devices to maintain records and submit reports. FDA proposed regulations to require reports on adverse reactions to, or malfunctioning of, medical devices, 45 Fed. Reg. 76183 (November 18, 1980); placed this proposal in abeyance, 46 Fed. Reg. 57568 (November 24, 1981); issued a reproposal, 48 Fed. Reg. 24014 (May 27, 1983); and promulgated final regulations in 49 Fed. Reg. 36326 (September 14, 1984), codified in 21 C.F.R. Part 803. Under the final regulations, a manufacturer or importer must submit to FDA a report whenever it receives information that reasonably suggests that a medical device may have caused or contributed to a death or serious injury, or that a medical device has malfunctioned in a way that would be likely to cause or contribute to a death or serious injury. *See* Basile, *Medical Device Reporting: The Good, the Bad, and the Ugly*, 42 FDC L.J. 83 (1987). A bill to expand medical device reporting to hospitals and other medical service facilities, H.R. Rep. No. 100–782, 100th Cong., 2nd Sess. (1988), initially met criticism from both FDA and device makers and was not enacted, but the requirement was later enacted in 1990 as section 519(b). For critical reviews of the FDA device reporting regulations, *see* GAO, MEDICAL DEVICES: EARLY WARNING OF PROBLEMS IS HAMPERED BY SEVERE UNDERREPORTING, PEMD–87–1 (December 1986); MEDICAL DEVICES: FDA'S FORE-CAST OF PROBLEM REPORTS AND FTEs UNDER H.R. 4640, PEMD–88–30 (July 1988); MEDICAL DEVICES: FDA's IMPLEMEN-TATION OF THE MEDICAL DEVICE REPORTING REGULATION, PEMD–89–10 (February 1989).

f. Banned Devices

Section 516 authorizes FDA, by regulation, to ban a device that presents substantial deception or an unreasonable and substantial risk of illness or injury. It was included in the 1976 Amendments primarily to enable FDA to deal with the "quack" devices that occupied so much of its attention in the past. The agency has adopted procedural regulations to implement this provision. 42 Fed. Reg. 42000 (August 19, 1977), 44 Fed. Reg. 29214 (May 18, 1979), codified in 21 C.F.R. Part 895. In 48 Fed. Reg. 25126 (June 3, 1983), 49 Fed. Reg. 1177 (January 10, 1984), FDA promulgated its first and thus far only regulation under this provision, banning prosthetic hair fibers intended for implantation into the human scalp to simulate natural hair or conceal baldness.

g. Notification and Repair, Replacement, or Refund

Section 518 authorizes FDA to order a manufacturer to notify the public of an unreasonable risk of substantial harm from a marketed device and to repair or replace the device or refund the purchase price. This provision was patterned on similar grants of authority to the National Highway and Traffic Safety Administration, to the Consumer Product Safety Commission, and to FDA itself under the Radiation Control for Health and Safety Act. FDA considers section 518 self-exe-cuting and therefore has not promulgated implementing regulations. In 49 Fed. Reg. 11716 (March 27, 1984), however, FDA did make available for public comment a draft guideline on Medical Device Notification and Voluntary Safety Alert, which sets forth the procedure that it follows in implementing section 518.

FDA has invoked section 518 on several occasions, thus far without precipitating litigation. In 1978, when a manufacturer of a dangerous defective defibrillator refused to pay for repairs in units of the device that had already been distributed to hospitals, FDA ordered the manu-facturer to submit an adequate plan for repairing the defects in the distributed devices. Although the firm initially demanded a hearing on the agency's action, it subsequently submitted a plan which, after several changes, FDA accepted.

IN RE PROCTER & GAMBLE CO.: CONSENT AGREEMENT
U.S. Food and Drug Administration, September 26, 1980.

. . . .

2. Rely brand tampon ("Rely") is a device. . . .

3. Toxic Shock Syndrome ("TSS") is a recently recognized disease. The exact cause of and cure for TSS are not known, although *Staphylococcus aureus* may play an important role in the etiology of the disease. TSS is a rare disease which progresses rapidly and, in some instances, has resulted in death. The Food and Drug Administration ("FDA") believes that TSS is a significant public health problem. The Center for Disease Control ("CDC") and FDA believe there is an association between use of Rely and occurrence of TSS, a proposition which P&G vigorously disputes.

4. On September 23, 1980, FDA advised P&G that FDA was contemplating the possibility of invoking the provisions of 21 U.S.C. § 360h to compel the firm to engage in a notification and retrieval/refund program.

5. In settlement of actions contemplated by FDA under 21 U.S.C. § 360h, P&G and FDA enter into this Agreement, which constitutes a "requirement" for purposes of 21 U.S.C. § 352(t)(1).

6. P&G expressly denies that Rely is in any way defective or that the sale or distribution of Rely violated the Act or any other law. This agreement does not constitute an admission by P&G of any such violation.

7. By its acceptance of this Agreement, FDA does not waive any of its rights to initiate administrative or judicial enforcement under the Act or other applicable law against Rely, P&G, or any P&G officer, agent, attorney, or employee should FDA, in its discretion, determine that such action is appropriate.

Therefore, IT IS AGREED that P&G shall:

8. Discontinue all sale and commercial distribution of Rely.

9. Make every reasonable effort to withdraw from all media any advertisement for Rely placed prior to September 22, 1980.

10. Conduct the consumer notification program set forth and explained as follows. . . .

11. Conduct a retrieval/refund program as follows. . . .

12. P&G shall make available to FDA for review and copying all documents related to the notification and retrieval/refund programs. . . . .

13.   P&G shall retain the records relating to the notification and retrieval/refund programs according to the following schedule, except that P&G is not required to retain copies of records already submitted to FDA....

IT IS UNDERSTOOD that P&G has already commenced or completed certain of these undertakings prior to entering into this Agreement.

IT IS FURTHER AGREED that P&G shall advise FDA when all its undertakings and any other steps reasonably necessary to accomplish the purpose of these notification and retrieval/refund programs have been carried out. FDA will review P&G's actions and if it agrees that P&G's undertakings and the purpose of these programs have been carried out, shall notify P&G that these programs have been concluded. Thereafter, P&G shall continue to retrieve Rely and refund in accordance with the provisions of the retrieval/refund program to any consumers, distributors, or retailers who P&G learns has Rely.

IT IS FURTHER AGREED that P&G shall not reintroduce for commercial distribution nor export nor offer for export the products covered by this Agreement or identical products under any name without the prior written permission of the Director of FDA's Bureau of Medical Devices.

NOTES

1. *Medtronic Pacemakers.* On February 19, 1979, Medtronic submitted a PMN to FDA under section 510(k) for the Model 6972 bipolar pacemaker lead. On April 19, 1979, FDA concurred that the device was substantially equivalent to a preenactment device. Experience with the device, however, disclosed a high failure rate, which led to a full FDA investigation and a congressional hearing. "Failed Pacemaker Leads," Hearing before the Subcomm. on Oversight and Investigations of the House Comm. on Energy and Commerce, 98th Cong., 2nd Sess. (1984). After extensive deliberation, FDA decided not to pursue possible action under section 518(b) for repair, replacement, or refund.

> This decision is based on the absence here of any ongoing public health problem or concern which could be addressed by such an action. The pacemaker leads of concern are no longer being manufactured or sold, unimplanted leads have been recalled, and the firm has a program for reimbursement or elimination of out-of-pocket costs to patients who require surgery or increased monitoring because they rely on Model 6972 leads.

Memorandum from FDA Commissioner F.E. Young to CDRH Director J.C. Villforth (August 19, 1985).

2. *Dalkon Shield.* In *National Women's Health Network, Inc. v. A.H. Robins Co., Inc.*, 545 F. Supp. 1177 (D. Mass. 1982) the court dismissed a class action for injunctive relief to require a nationwide notification and refund program for the Dalkon Shield brought against the manufacturer of this IUD, on the grounds that the FD&C Act creates no private right of action and that any state cause of action would be preempted by the 1976 Amendments.

h. Administrative Detention

To implement its new authority under section 304(g) to detain illegal devices by administrative order for up to 30 days in order to initiate court enforcement action, FDA established procedural regulations in 42 Fed. Reg. 54574 (October 7, 1977), 44 Fed. Reg. 13234 (March 9, 1979), codified in 21 C.F.R. § 800.55.

---

i. Postmarketing Surveillance

The 1990 Amendments added section 522, which requires postmarket surveillance for any device that is a permanent implant the failure of which may cause serious adverse health consequences or death, or is intended for a use in supporting or sustaining human life, or potentially presents a serious risk to human health. FDA is also authorized to impose postmarket surveillance for any other device where necessary to protect the public health or to provide adequate safety or effectiveness data.

---

j. Mandatory Recalls

New section 518(e) requires FDA to order that the distribution of a device cease and that health professionals and device user facilities be notified if the agency finds that the device would cause serious adverse health consequences or death. The person subject to the order shall have the opportunity for an informal hearing.

---

k. Device Tracking

New section 519(e) requires that any manufacturer adopt a method of "device tracking" for any permanently implantable, life sustaining, or life supporting device, or any other device designated by FDA whose failure would be likely to have serious adverse health consequences.

---

l. Reports of Removals and Corrections

Under new section 519(f), added by the 1990 Amendments, FDA must promulgate regulations requiring the manufacturer, importer, or distributor of a device to report any correction or removal of a device undertaken to reduce a risk to health or to remedy a violation of the FD&C Act which may present a risk to health.

---

m. Civil Penalties

The 1990 Amendments added new section 303(f), which provides that any person who violates the device provisions of the FD&C Act may be liable for a civil penalty in an amount not to exceed $15,000 for each violation and $1 million for all such violations adjudicated in a single proceeding. FDA is given authority to assess civil penalties after affording the opportunity for a formal adjudicatory hearing under 5 U.S.C. § 554.

8. RULES FOR SPECIFIC MARKETED DEVICES

a. Custom Devices

Section 520(b) provides that the requirements of sections 514 and 515 do not apply to any device which, in order to comply with the order of an individual physician or dentist, necessarily deviates from an otherwise applicable performance standard or approved PMA application, if the device is not generally available for purchase in finished form, or to other physicians or dentists, and is intended for use by an individual patient or to meet the special needs of the physician or dentist.

In *Contact Lens Manufacturers Ass'n v. FDA*, 766 F.2d 592 (D.C. Cir. 1985), p. 771 *supra*, the manufacturers contended that soft lenses are custom devices and thus exempt from the classification scheme. The court upheld FDA's rejection of this claim on the ground that, though individually ground to doctors' specifications for specific patients, as a class soft lenses are generally available to or used by other physicians and most prescriptions are likely to be replicated. 766 F.2d at 598–99. In an advisory opinion, FDA Associate Commissioner for Regulatory Affairs J.P. Hile to B. Gersh, Dkt. No. 82A–0264 (March 7, 1983), FDA took the position that a custom device may not be a "standardized modification" of a marketed device, may not be "commercially distributed," and must be "made in a specific form for a patient named in the order of a physician or intended to meet the special needs of such physician in the course of his or her professional practice."

b. Cardiac Pacemaker Registry

A rider to the Deficit Reduction Act of 1984, 98 Stat. 494, 1068, codified at 42 U.S.C. § 1395y(h), requires FDA to establish a national registry of all cardiac pacemaker devices and leads implanted or removed with Medicare reimbursement. The registry is to assist HCFA in determining proper medical payments and aid FDA in assessing compliance with regulatory requirements. FDA's regulations for this registry, 51 Fed. Reg. 16792 (May 6, 1986), 52 Fed. Reg. 27756 (July 23, 1987), are codified in 21 C.F.R. Part 805. For criticism of the implementation of this statute by HCFA and FDA, *see* "Pacemakers Revisited: A Saga of Benign Neglect," Hearing before the Senate Special Comm. on Aging, 99th Cong., 1st Sess. (1985).

---

c. Patent Term Restoration

The Drug Price Competition and Patent Term Restoration Act of 1984, p. 571, *supra,* provided stronger protection for drug patents and easier entry of generic drugs into the market once the pioneer's patent and any period of market exclusivity has expired. The 1984 Act also offered patent term restoration of up to five years for medical devices subject to a regulatory review period that would otherwise reduce their effective patent life. Certain premarket approval devices have, in fact, been awarded extensions of their patent term under this statute. *E.g.,* 51 Fed. Reg. 34143 (September 25, 1986), 53 Fed. Reg. 32700 (August 26, 1988), 54 Fed. Reg. 32125 (August 4, 1989). *Eli Lilly & Co. v. Medtronic, Inc.,* 872 F.2d 402 (Fed. Cir. 1989), *aff'd,* ___ U.S. ___, 110 S.Ct. 2683 (1990), held that 35 U.S.C. § 271(e)(1), which states that research conducted with a patented drug to develop information for submission to FDA does not constitute infringement, applies to medical devices as well as to drugs.

---

d. Orphan Devices

Congress initially enacted the Orphan Drug Act of 1983, p. 566, *supra,* to provide additional incentives for investment in the development of drugs for rare diseases. The Orphan Drug Amendments of 1988, 102 Stat. 90, added medical devices to the provision of the 1983 Act that allows financial assistance to defray the cost of developing products for rare diseases or conditions. The 1988 Amendments also require the Department of HHS to conduct a study to determine whether the other statutory incentives that apply to orphan drugs should also be applied to orphan medical devices in order to encourage the development of such devices.

NOTES

1. *Export of Devices.* The export provisions of the 1976 Amendments are examined in detail at p. 1098 *infra.*

2. *Preemption of State Regulation.* The statutory preemption provision in section 521 and its interpretation by FDA are discussed at p. 1033 *infra.*

3. *Assessments of FDA Implementation.* The 1976 Amendments are lengthy and complex. Their implementation, particularly in an era of increasingly restricted governmental resources, has not been a simple matter. Most reviews of FDA's performance have generally agreed with its implementation strategy, while suggesting improvements that could be made. *E.g.*, GAO, FEDERAL REGULATION OF MEDICAL DEVICES—PROBLEMS STILL TO BE OVERCOME, HRD–83–53 (1983); GAO, MEDICAL DEVICES: FDA'S 510(K) OPERATIONS COULD BE IMPROVED, PEMD–88–14 (1988); OTA, FEDERAL POLICIES AND THE MEDICAL DEVICES INDUSTRY, OTA–H–229 (1984). One sharply critical report, "Medical Device Regulation: The FDA's Neglected Child," Report of the Subcomm. on Oversight and Investigations of the House Comm. on Energy and Commerce, 98th Cong., 1st Sess. (1983), was followed by proposed amendments to the Act that would have made regulation of medical devices significantly more stringent. *See* H.R. 4640 and H.R. Rep. No. 100–782, 100th Cong., 2nd Sess. (1988); H.R. 3095, 101st Cong., 1st Sess. (1989), 135 Cong. Rec. E2815 (daily ed. August 3, 1989). The 1990 Amendments, however, essentially confirmed FDA's approval.

4. *Medical Waste.* The discovery of used medical devices in waste washed up on public beaches in the Northeast led to the enactment of the Medical Waste Tracking Act of 1988, 102 Stat. 2950, 42 U.S.C. § 6992, an amendment to the Solid Waste Disposal Act, commonly referred to as the Resource Conservation and Recovery Act (RCRA). Pursuant to this Act, EPA has promulgated regulations establishing a demonstration tracking system for medical waste, 54 Fed. Reg. 12326 (March 24, 1989), 54 Fed. Reg. 24310 (June 6, 1989), 54 Fed. Reg. 35189 (August 24, 1989), and ATSDR has submitted a report to Congress on the health effects of medical waste, 55 Fed. Reg. 1770 (January 18, 1990). *See* GAO, MEDICAL WASTE REGULATION: HEALTH AND ENVIRONMENTAL RISKS NEED TO BE FULLY ASSESSED, RCED–90–86 (March 1990).

E. RADIATION CONTROL FOR HEALTH AND SAFETY ACT OF 1968

FDA's responsibility for assuring the safety and effectiveness of medical equipment is not confined to the device provisions of the FD&C Act. Under the Radiation Control for Health and Safety Act of 1968, 82 Stat. 1173, originally codified as 42 U.S.C. § 263b *et seq.*, and recodified by 104 Stat. 4511, 4529 (1990) as 21 U.S.C. § 530 *et seq.*, the agency is also responsible for regulating products that emit radiation, many of which fit the definition of a device. This responsibility was transferred to FDA in 1971, 36 Fed. Reg. 12803 (July 7, 1971), and combined with the medical devices program in 1982, note 3 p. 722 *supra*.

Because FDA's activities under the Radiation Act chiefly concern the design, manufacture, and use of medical instrumentation, it is logical to provide an introduction to the program here, but there is an additional justification for treating radiation-emitting products in this chapter. FDA's ability to minimize the risks of medical devices without nullifying their benefits depends in many instances on its power to control the ways in which they are put to use by medical professionals.

This theme of utilization review and control pervades the field of medical radiation.

This theme recurs in an altered form in Part F. As government pays an increasing share of the nation's total bill for health care, demands that these funds be expended wisely and that overall costs be controlled influence judgments about the development and use of new medical technologies. Efforts to evaluate the cost-effectiveness of innovative diagnostic and therapeutic procedures have often focused on medical devices, such as the CT scanner, or procedures that rely on them, such as mammography.

DIAGNOSTIC X–RAY SYSTEMS: PROPOSED AMENDMENT OF ASSEMBLY AND REASSEMBLY PROVISIONS

44 Federal Register 22755 (April 17, 1979).

The Federal performance standard for diagnostic x-ray systems and their major components ... published in the FEDERAL REGISTER of August 15, 1972 (37 FR 16461) ... contains performance requirements for specific x-ray system components and for diagnostic x-ray systems made up of these components. The standard also contains ... the requirement that manufacturers certify that all specified components manufactured after August 1, 1974, comply with the standard. After publication of the ... final rule, manufacturers posed a number of questions on how the standard would apply to the sale and installation of both new and used x-ray components....

... [T]wo notices of proposed rulemaking addressing these situations were published in the FEDERAL REGISTER of February 28, 1973 (38 FR 5349). After incorporating changes indicated by comments on the proposals, § 1000.16 (21 CFR 1000.16) was published as a final rule ... in the FEDERAL REGISTER of July 29, 1974 (39 FR 27432)....

Section 1000.16 provided for a 5–year transition period after the effective date of the standard, during which reassembly of any x-ray system was permitted, and the assembly of uncertified components was permitted as long as no certified component was involved in the system. However, the policy also provided that, after August 1, 1979, no uncertified components could be assembled into a system or reassembled when the reassembly was associated with a change of ownership and location.

The 5–year transition period permitted by § 1000.16 was intended to:

    (1) Prevent the downgrading of the radiation safety performance of certified components and systems containing certified components, by requiring that new, complete systems be composed of either all uncertified or all certified components, and by prohibiting replacement of a certified component in an x-ray system by an uncertified component (§ 1000.16(a)(1)).

(2) Promote the upgrading of systems containing uncertified components, by requiring that once a certified component has been installed into a system, all future components installed into the system must be certified (§ 1000.16(a)(2) and (3)).

(3) Allow the reassembly of systems that have been upgraded with one or more certified components (§ 1000.-16(a)(4))....

After August 1, 1979, § 1000.16 was intended to:

(1) Extend and tighten the provisions of § 1000.16(a) by requiring that all new systems contain only certified components and force the upgrading of uncertified systems when components of these systems are replaced due to wear and tear by requiring that all components added to any system be certified (§ 1000.16(c)).

(2) Prevent the reassembly of uncertified components by allowing only certified components to be reassembled, when a system is sold and relocated (§ 1000.16(d)).

Thus, no uncertified components or systems may be marketed and installed after August 1, 1979 under the current provisions of § 1000.16(c) and (d).

As part of a program of reevaluating the benefits and economic impact of regulations on diagnostic x-ray systems, FDA has completed a new cost-benefit analysis of the diagnostic x-ray performance standard and the policy on assembly and reassembly of components....

FDA ... believes that the Federal policy concerning used x-ray equipment as it is currently scheduled to be after August 1, 1979, is not appropriate. Controls are needed, however, after August 1, 1979, to preserve the radiation safety provided by certified systems and to promote the continued upgrading of uncertified x-ray systems when it may be done in a constructive, cost-effective manner. Therefore, the agency has examined modifications to § 1000.16 that would establish the desired controls at reasonable cost....

Section 1000.16(d) as currently constituted will prohibit the reassembly of uncertified x-ray components and systems after August 1, 1979, if the reassembly is associated with a change in ownership and location of the components or system. FDA proposes to revoke this section to permit the continued reassembly of uncertified x-ray equipment.

Because both a change in ownership and a relocation of the system are required, the effect of § 1000.16(d) is limited to a small percentage of the total number of x-ray systems. The agency's cost-benefit analysis estimates that, at the end of 1979, there would be about 100,000 uncertified systems in use. The analysis also estimates that 1,100 to 2,600 uncertified systems would be resold and relocated and thus would come under the provisions of § 1000.16(d) in the year following August 1, 1979. This represents an annual rate of 1 to 2 percent of the uncertified systems expected to be in use during that year. Furthermore, approximately 95 percent of these x-ray systems are less than 14 years old. Thus, in the first year after the effective date of § 1000.16(d), the large majority of systems entering the used equipment market will have been manufactured after 1965. These systems contain many of the features required by the Federal performance standard....

The economic impact of the additional cost of purchasing new equipment and the loss in resale value of used equipment under the current regulation has been estimated to be between 34 and 121 million dollars in 1980 and between 18 and 64 million dollars in 1985. Furthermore, the analysis reported a benefit/cost ratio for § 1000.16 after August 1, 1979, of 0.4 to 0.6 and a benefit/cost ratio for the diagnostic x-ray standard of 4.5. Thus, § 1000.16 as currently constituted is only 1/10 as cost effective as the x-ray standard....

Several current or contemplated agency action programs address the improvement in performance of all diagnostic x-ray systems, not just uncertified systems that enter the used equipment market. Although these programs involve voluntary compliance, participation by health care facilities is very high. The programs generally are designed to increase the quality of radiographs and lower radiation exposure....

Furthermore attrition is gradually reducing the available supply of uncertified components. As uncertified components wear out in older uncertified systems, they will generally be replaced by certified components because of the unavailability of suitable used uncertified components....

This proposal to revoke § 1000.16(d) would, therefore, trade the forced upgrading of a small number of uncertified x-ray systems by a non-cost-effective approach for a more gradual upgrading of all uncertified systems by methods that would make more efficient use of resources.

FDA has compared the relative effects of § 1000.16(a) and (c). Both paragraphs have the same effect, except that § 1000.16(c) prohibits the installation of an uncertified component into any existing system, while § 1000.16(a) allows the installation if all the components of the existing system are uncertified. The agency questions whether the more restrictive prohibition in § 1000.16(c) and its effective date of August 1, 1979, is necessary or desirable.

Replacing a single uncertified component in an uncertified system with a certified component does not provide as much performance improvement as replacing the uncertified component with a group of certified components. For example, the replacement of an uncertified tube-housing assembly by a certified component when the other components of the system are uncertified may not provide the same improvement in radiation protection performance as replacing both the tube-housing assembly and the beam-limiting device....

NOTES

1. *Suspension of Regulations.* In 44 Fed. Reg. 44843 (July 31, 1979), FDA suspended the assembly and reassembly provisions that were to become effective on August 1, and in 44 Fed. Reg. 49667 (August 24, 1979), those provisions were revoked.

2. *Review of Diagnostic X–Ray Standard.* FDA undertook a full review of the performance standard for diagnostic x-ray systems in 47 Fed. Reg. 51710 (November 16, 1982). As part of this review, the agency made available an overview of the costs and benefits of the standard in 49 Fed. Reg. 2918 (January 24, 1984) and issued a final report in 50 Fed. Reg. 46646 (November 12, 1985). Proposed amendments to the standard, based on this review, were published in 54 Fed. Reg. 42674 (October 17, 1989).

3. *CT Scanners.* As a result of the development and widespread use of computed tomography (CT) diagnostic x-ray systems, FDA revised the x-ray standard, 45 Fed. Reg. 72204 (October 31, 1980), 49 Fed. Reg. 34698 (August 31, 1984), to add a new standard in 21 C.F.R. § 1020.33 for this equipment.

4. *Civil Penalties.* Until the 1990 Amendments to the device provisions of the FD&C Act, p. 792 *supra,* the Radiation Act was the only statute administered by FDA that authorizes civil penalties. *See United States v. Hodges X-ray, Inc.,* 759 F.2d 557 (6th Cir. 1985), holding that a company's president, as well as the company, may be held liable for civil penalties for violations of the x-ray standard.

5. *Laser and Ultrasound Standards.* FDA has issued standards under the Radiation Act for laser products in 38 Fed. Reg. 34084 (December 10, 1973), 40 Fed. Reg. 32252 (July 31, 1975), 42 Fed. Reg. 17495 (April 1, 1977), 43 Fed. Reg. 55387 (November 28, 1978), 45 Fed. Reg. 74374 (November 7, 1980), 48 Fed. Reg. 54164 (November 30, 1983), 50 Fed. Reg. 33682 (August 20, 1985), codified in 21 C.F.R. § 1040.10; and for ultrasonic therapy products in 41 Fed. Reg. 23973 (June 14, 1976) 43 Fed. Reg. 7166 (February 17, 1978), codified in 21 C.F.R. § 1050.10.

6. *NMR Devices.* Before FDA approved nuclear magnetic resonance (NMR) devices, the agency made available a guideline for evaluating the radiation risk presented during investigation of the device under an IDE, 47 Fed. Reg. 11972 (March 19, 1982).

7. *Relationship to Device Statute.* The precise relationship between the standard-setting and premarket approval authority of the Medical Device Amendments and the Radiation Act's standard-setting authority is uncertain. It does seem clear that FDA is obligated to regulate radiation-emitting devices under the 1976 Amendments and has discretion to regulate them under the Radiation Act as well. Because all new radiation-emitting medical devices must be the subject of premarket approval under section 515, the agency may in the future have little occasion to establish performance standards under the Radiation Act.

8. *Variances.* Under general regulations that apply to all electronic product performance standards, FDA may grant variances in accordance with 21 C.F.R. § 1010.4. After 20 years of publishing those variances (most for laser light shows) in the Federal Register, FDA observed that it had never received comment on any of them and announced it was discontinuing publication, 53 Fed. Reg. 52683 (December 29, 1988).

9. *Commentary.* For an excellent discussion of the health benefits and risks from radiation, *see* Rados, *Primer on Radiation,* 13 FDA Consumer, No. 6, at 5 (July–August 1979). *See also* HEW, REPORT OF THE INTERAGENCY TASK FORCE ON THE HEALTH EFFECTS OF IONIZING RADIATION (1979); GAO, RADIATION CONTROL PROGRAMS PROVIDE LIMITED PROTECTION, HRD–80–25 (1979); National Academy of Sciences, FEDERAL RESEARCH ON THE BIOLOGICAL AND HEALTH EFFECTS OF IONIZING RADIATION (1981); THE EFFECTS ON POPULATIONS OF EXPOSURE TO LOW LEVELS OF IONIZING RADIATION (1972 and 1980); Steneck, *et al., The Origins of U.S. Safety Standards for Microwave Radiation,* 208 Science 1230 (1980); Villforth, *The X Raying of America,* 13 FDA Consumer No. 10, at 13 (December 1979–January 1980). *See also* "Unnecessary Exposure to Radiation from Medical and Dental X–Rays," Hearings before the Subcomm. on Oversight and Investigations of the House Comm. on Interstate and Foreign Commerce, 96th Cong., 1st Sess. (1979).

MEDICAL RADIATION EXPOSURE OF WOMEN OF CHILDBEARING AGE: ADVANCE NOTICE OF PROPOSED GUIDELINE PUBLICATION

40 Federal Register 58151 (December 15, 1975).

The FDA, through the Bureau of Radiological Health and under authority of the Radiation Control for Health and Safety Act of 1968, conducts and supports research, training, and operational activities to minimize unnecessary exposure of the public to electronic product radiation. In carrying out the purposes of the act, the Commissioner is authorized to make such recommendations relating to the control of electronic product radiation as he considers appropriate (section 356(b)(1)(A)). In this capacity and under the authority of section 301. . . . the Commissioner is considering the development of guidelines that would provide recommendations to health practitioners and others concerning the exposure of women of childbearing age to ionizing radiation for diagnostic purposes. These recommendations are intended to minimize unnecessary exposure of developing human embryos and fetuses to ionizing radiation that results from radiological examinations. . . .

These guidelines would be among several which will be proposed by the Commissioner concerning the hazards and control of electronic product radiation or radiation from other sources. Some of these guidelines may be established for areas or activities inappropriate for mandatory control. . . . These guidelines, which will provide guidance on techniques for reducing unnecessary exposure to electronic product or other sources of radiation such as nuclear medicine procedures, should be implemented through educational programs and cooperative activities with professional organizations and State health agencies. . . .

To assist the Commissioner in this study and the development of useful guidelines, detailed scientific and technical data, as well as comments or suggestions, supported by detailed rationale and justification are solicited on the following questions:

1. Is it advisable to schedule nonemergency radiological examinations of the abdomen of women of childbearing age only during the early part of the menstrual cycle? If such scheduling is appropriate, should this be done only when the examination could be deferred until term if a pregnancy is observed or suspected at the time the examination is scheduled to occur?

2. Is it feasible to modify radiological examinations of known or possibly pregnant women, *e.g.,* fewer views, different technique factors, to reduce exposure of the embryo or fetus? If so, under what circumstances? To what extent does this result in an unacceptable loss of diagnostic information?

3. Is it advisable to recommend to institutions that the physician ordering the examination indicate on the referral slip whether or not the patient is or could be pregnant?

4. Is it advisable to recommend to institutions that the physician ordering the examination indicate on the referral slip whether he would be satisfied with a limited study, *i.e.,* modified from the routine manner of performance, on a patient known or suspected to be pregnant?

5. For which abdominal x-ray examinations could fetal shielding be employed without compromising the diagnostic value of the radiograph?

6. To what extent do pelvimetry examinations affect decisionmaking in the management of delivery?

7. How much radiation exposure is received by the embryo or fetus from various diagnostic nuclear medicine procedures?

8. With what frequency are nuclear medicine diagnostic procedures performed on women of childbearing age?

9. How useful is nuclear medicine placental scanning in the medical management of pregnant women? ...

FDA GUIDELINES FOR RADIATION EXPOSURE

FDA has embarked upon a program of issuing recommendations and guidelines relating to safe exposure to radiation. Although these recommendations were initially codified in the Code of Federal Regulations, in 48 Fed. Reg. 1734 (January 14, 1983) FDA announced that they would no longer be published in full in the Federal Register. Their availability is now merely announced in the Federal Register but they are widely circulated throughout the medical profession.

1. *Maternal Exposure.* FDA published proposed recommendations for medical radiation exposure of women of childbearing potential in 44 Fed. Reg. 66616 (November 20, 1979).

2. *Gonad Shielding.* Recommendations for the use of gonad shields during x-ray were issued in 40 Fed. Reg. 42749 (September 16, 1975), 41 Fed. Reg. 30327 (July 23, 1976), codified in 21 C.F.R. § 1000.50.

3. *Quality Assurance.* Recommendations for quality assurance programs in diagnostic radiology facilities were issued in 43 Fed. Reg. 18207 (April 28, 1978), 44 Fed. Reg. 71728 (December 11, 1979), codified in 21 C.F.R. § 1000.55.

4. *Dental X–Rays.* Recommendations on insurance company requirements for dental x-ray examinations were issued in 44 Fed. Reg. 41486 (July 17, 1979), 45 Fed. Reg. 40976 (June 17, 1980), codified in 21 C.F.R. § 1000.60.

5. *Technician Qualifications.* FDA proposed recommended national standards for qualifications of medical radiation technologists in 44 Fed. Reg. 14637 (March 13, 1979), but since legislation delegating this responsibility to the Health Resources and Services Administration, note 1 p. 805 *infra,* it has not pursued this matter.

6. *Diagnostic Radiology.* FDA has developed recommendations on radiation exposure from diagnostic radiology examinations in 44 Fed. Reg. 48354 (August 17, 1979), 48 Fed. Reg. 34520 (July 29, 1983), 51 Fed. Reg. 6039 (February 19, 1986).

7. *Radiation for Benign Diseases.* FDA endorsed recommendations by the National Academy of Sciences on the use of radiation for the treatment of benign diseases in 45 Fed. Reg. 23068 (April 4, 1980).

8. *Nuclear Medicine.* FDA has offered recommendations on quality assurance in nuclear medicine facilities in 44 Fed. Reg. 48264 (August 17, 1979), 48 Fed. Reg. 1734 (January 14, 1983), 50 Fed. Reg. 20011 (May 13, 1985).

9. *Fetal Protection.* Recommendations to minimize diagnostic nuclear medicine exposure to the embryo, fetus, and infant were announced in 50 Fed. Reg. 28265 (July 11, 1985), 51 Fed. Reg. 6039 (February 19, 1986).

10. *Referral Criteria.* FDA began a program of preparing referral criteria for medical radiological examinations in order to reduce x-ray examinations that are not likely to affect patient management in 46 Fed. Reg. 30568 (June 9, 1981). Draft or final reports have been issued for pelvic x-ray in 46 Fed. Reg. 3069 (January 13, 1981); chest x-ray in 46 Fed. Reg. 30568 (June 9, 1981), 49 Fed. Reg. 13588 (April 5, 1984); skull x-ray in 49 Fed. Reg. 20556 (May 15, 1984); presurgical chest x-ray in 49 Fed. Reg. 28111 (July 10, 1984); and dental x-ray in 50 Fed. Reg. 29483 (July 19, 1985).

11. *PUVA Therapy.* In 45 Fed. Reg. 8870 (February 8, 1980), FDA issued a notice of intent to adopt safety performance recommendations for devices used as a radiation source in combination with a psoralen drug in treating psoriasis.

12. *State Regulations.* FDA has issued suggested state regulations for the control of radiation in 45 Fed. Reg. 28498 (April 29, 1980), 53 Fed. Reg. 29527 (August 5, 1988).

————

More than a decade ago FDA established a standard for sunlamps in 42 Fed. Reg. 65189 (December 30, 1977), 44 Fed. Reg. 65352 (November 9, 1979), codified in 21 C.F.R. § 1040.20. The rapid growth of commercial suntanning facilities led the agency to propose revisions in

the standard, 48 Fed. Reg. 22886 (May 20, 1983), to reflect the changes
in product technology and design.

SUNLAMP PRODUCTS; PERFORMANCE STANDARD

50 Federal Register 36548 (September 6, 1985).

FDA believes that irradiation of the skin with ultraviolet radiation
to induce skin tanning is hazardous. The performance standard for
sunlamp products was established to protect the consumer from acute
burns (as evidenced by erythema) and from exposure to hazardous
radiation that is unnecessary for skin tanning (in this case, UV radiation of wavelengths in air of less than 260 nanometers (nm)) and to
warn the consumer of the known adverse effects to the body after
exposure to ultraviolet radiation. FDA believes that the user of a
sunlamp product can take appropriate action when informed of the
possible adverse effects to the body from exposure to ultraviolet radiation, if the product is equipped with necessary safety performance
features. . . .

A comment suggested that the warning statement required by
§ 1040.20(d)(1)(i) should utilize the signal word "CAUTION" rather
than "DANGER." The comment contended that the word "DANGER"
implies an immediate and serious threat to life, a hazard not associated
with UVA sunlamp products, i.e., sunlamp products that operate in the
wavelength region of 320 to 400 nm. The comment stated that there is
a need for an appropriate warning label cautioning the user that
certain safeguards need to be observed to avoid injury and that prolonged use has long-term risk.

The agency believes that the word "DANGER" as used on the
warning statement is appropriate. Exposure to ultraviolet radiation
can be an immediate threat to life for people using photosensitizing
medications or cosmetics and for people with a medical condition that
causes them to be sensitive to ultraviolet radiation, for example, pho-
toallergies.

One comment urged that UVA lamps should be exempt from the
provisions of § 1040.20(d) that require the warning: "As with natural
sunlight, overexposure can cause eye and skin injury and allergic
reactions. Repeated exposure may cause premature aging of the skin
and skin cancer." The comment argued that radiation at wavelengths
in air longer than 320 nm cannot induce skin cancer and that only
radiation at wavelengths in air shorter than 320 nm is responsible for
premature skin aging. . . .

FDA disagrees that it has been proven that UVA does not cause
skin cancer or premature skin aging, or that UVA radiation can protect
humans against UVB radiation. Relatively few studies have been
carried out on the long-term biological effects of UVA radiation in
humans or in animals. Further studies are needed to establish clearly
the long-term biological effects of UVA radiation. There are, however,

reports that, under long-term continuous exposure, UVA radiation can induce skin cancer in test animals. Also, there is evidence that the incidence of skin tumors induced in animals by irradiation with a combination of UVB and UVA radiation can be increased by subsequent irradiation with UVA alone.

There is evidence that UVA radiation can enhance the photoreactivation of pyrimidine dimers in the DNA of human leukocytes. However, this effect has not been shown to provide humans protection against UVB radiation. The Task Force on Photobiology of the American Academy of Dermatology has expressed concerns about potential risks of tanning with UVA radiation.

Based on available evidence, FDA concludes that to exempt UVA lamps from the warning statement required by the standard would not promote the public health and safety.

One comment disagreed with the language of the warning statement set forth in § 1040.20(d)(1) of the proposed amendments and argued that the statement, "If you do not tan in the sun, you are unlikely to tan from the use of this product," would be inappropriate because it may confuse the sunlamp user. The comment argued that the action of direct exposure to the sun cannot be compared to that of exposure to either UVA or UVB suntanning equipment; that the current warnings already clearly and accurately provide the same information in more detail; and that the quoted statement would be redundant to the statement "Consult a physician before using lamp if taking any medication or if you believe yourself sensitive to sunlight.

The agency disagrees with the comment. The scientific literature clearly demonstrates that some people do not tan or that they tan only with great difficulty using either the sun or sunlamps. People who, when exposed to the sun, do not tan or tan only with great difficulty should be informed about the futility of exposures to potentially hazardous ultraviolet radiation. . . .

Therefore, under the Public Health Service Act, as amended by the Radiation Control for Health and Safety Act of 1968, Part 1040 is amended to read as follows: . . . .

2. By revising § 1040.20, to read as follows:

§ 1040.20 Sunlamp products and ultraviolet lamps intended for use in sunlamp products.

(d) *Label requirements*. . . .

(1) *Labels for sunlamp products.* Each sunlamp product shall have a label(s) which contains:

(i) A warning statement with the words "DANGER—Ultraviolet radiation. Follow instructions. Avoid overexposure. As with natural sunlight, overexposure can cause eye and skin injury and allergic reactions. Repeated exposure may cause premature aging of the skin and skin cancer. WEAR PROTECTIVE EYEWEAR; FAILURE TO

MAY RESULT IN SEVERE BURNS OR LONG-TERM INJURY TO THE EYES. Medications or cosmetics may increase your sensitivity to the ultraviolet radiation. Consult physician before using sunlamp if you are using medications or have a history of skin problems or believe yourself especially sensitive to sunlight. If you do not tan in the sun, you are unlikely to tan from the use of this product."

NOTES

1. *Violations of Sunlamp Standards.* In lengthy litigation, FDA successfully obtained an injunction and civil penalties for violations of the sunlamp standard in 47 separate suntanning booths. *Throneberry v. FDA,* 1983–1984 FDLI Jud. Rec. 242 (E.D. Tenn. 1983), 1983–1984 FDLI Jud. Rec. 382 (E.D. Tenn. 1984).

2. *TV and Microwave Standards.* FDA has also established performance standards under the Radiation Act for such common household articles as television receivers, 21 C.F.R. § 1020.10, and microwave ovens, 21 C.F.R. § 1030.10.

3. *Commentary.* For a review of potential other sources of radiation hazards, *see* Brodeur, *Annals of Radiation: The Hazards of Electromagnetic Fields,* The New Yorker, June 12, 19, and 26, 1989.

USE OF VIDEO DISPLAY TERMINALS BY PREGNANT WOMEN
FDA Talk Paper, February 7, 1983.

Over the past several months there have been accounts in the news media of "clusters" of adverse pregnancy outcomes among women who work at video display terminals (VDTs). Many of these reports have come from Canada. For example, there have been news accounts that since VDTs were installed in the offices of a Vancouver hospital in 1978, only one of six pregnancies among women working at the machines resulted in a normal, full-term birth. There were two miscarriages, one premature birth, one child with club foot and an eye defect requiring surgery and one with bronchitis. FDA has received inquiries as to whether such "clusters" could be caused by radiation from VDTs.

Over the past several years, FDA's National Center for Devices and Radiological Health (NCDRH) has tested more than 100 VDTs for radiation leakage and has a continuing program of routine testing to monitor radiation emissions from VDTs. An April 1981 *FDA Consumer* article about the original test results ("VDTs Pass Medical Tests") stated: "VDTs emit little or no harmful radiation under normal operation conditions; the emissions that are detectable are well below any existing national and international standards.." Results from NCDRH's current testing still support that conclusion.

Despite the recent reports of "clusters" of adverse pregnancy outcomes, FDA finds no evidence that the levels of radiation from VDTs are responsible. While exposure to ionizing radiation (such as X-rays) can cause birth defects and miscarriages at very high exposure levels, the levels necessary for such effects are at least a thousand times higher than those to which VDT operators might be exposed. In fact, the ionizing radiation levels from VDTs are so low that they are generally difficult to distinguish from natural background radiation. For non-ionizing radiation (such as radiofrequency, light and ultrasound), the difference between emission levels from VDTs and levels known to cause adverse effects in the developing embryo is also large.

Other health and scientific organizations have reached similar conclusions. A report of a symposium on VDTs sponsored by the National Research Council of the National Academy of Sciences states: "Even under conditions designed to maximize potential emissions, the levels of all types of electromagnetic radiation emitted are far below accepted occupational and environmental health and safety limits of exposure." In a study published in June 1981, the National Institute for Occupational Safety and Health concluded that "the VDT does not present a radiation hazard to the employees working at or near a terminal."

Epidemiologists and statisticians at the NCDRH and at the U.S. Centers for Disease Control have noted that some "clusters" of adverse pregnancy outcomes would normally be expected on the basis of chance alone. Indeed, evaluation of some of the reported "clusters" led to the conclusion that they did not establish a general pattern associating the use of VDTs with problem pregnancies.

The conclusion? The reported "clusters" of problem pregnancies among VDT users would be expected from chance alone; it is highly unlikely that they have been caused by the low radiation emissions from the machines.

OTHER RADIATION CONTROL PROGRAMS

Several Federal agencies in addition to FDA regulate exposure to radiation. While not exhaustive, this note describes some of these other authorities and their relationship to FDA's authority under the Radiation Act.

1. *HCFA.* Under the Consumer–Patient Radiation Health and Safety Act of 1981, 95 Stat. 357, 598, enacted as part of the Omnibus Budget Reconciliation Act of 1981, the Health Resources and Services Administration has promulgated regulations, 48 Fed. Reg. 31966 (July 12, 1983), 50 Fed. Reg. 50710 (December 11, 1985), codified in 42 C.F.R. Part 75, governing the accreditation of educational programs for, and the credentialing of, radiologic personnel. The standards are mandatory for Federal agencies and voluntary for the states.

2. *FCC.* The Federal Communications Commission considers the biological effects of radiofrequency (RF) radiation when authorizing the use of communications devices. *See* 47 Fed. Reg. 8214 (February 25, 1982).

3. *NRC.* The Nuclear Regulatory Commission, in addition to regulating the medical use of radioactive byproduct material, *see* note 4, p. 534 *supra*, regulates exposure to radioactive material in consumer products in 10 C.F.R. Part 32.

4. *EPA.* EPA has authority to advise the President and other agencies on the health hazards of radiation under 42 U.S.C. § 2021(h). EPA and FDA entered into a Memorandum of Understanding to coordinate their activities in this area in 42 Fed. Reg. 5123 (January 27, 1977). EPA and the Department of HEW then submitted joint recommendations on this subject to President Carter, who approved and published them in 43 Fed. Reg. 4377 (February 1, 1978). A multiagency Memorandum of Understanding, 44 Fed. Reg. 30306 (May 24, 1979), specifies the roles of all Federal agencies in responding to potential radioactive contamination from foreign nuclear detonations during peacetime. In 15 Weekly Comp. of Pres. Doc. 2006 (October 23, 1979), President Carter announced the establishment of a Radiation Policy Council, similar to the Federal Radiation Council originally established by 73 Stat. 688, to coordinate all Federal activities that use or control radiation, with EPA as the lead agency. EPA established a development plan for issuing guidance for airborne release of radioactivity to protect the general public under radiological accident conditions in 44 Fed. Reg. 75344 (December 19, 1979). In 44 Fed. Reg. 53785 (September 17, 1979), 52 Fed. Reg. 2822 (January 27, 1987), EPA developed and President Reagan issued to Federal agencies radiation protection guidance for occupational exposure. EPA has also published an advance notice of proposed radiation protection criteria for cleanup of land facilities contaminated with residual radioactive materials in 51 Fed. Reg. 22264 (June 18, 1986) and has published proposed recommendations for controlling public exposure to radiofrequency radiation in 47 Fed. Reg. 57338 (December 23, 1982), 48 Fed. Reg. 33345 (July 21, 1983), 49 Fed. Reg. 48221 (December 11, 1984), 51 Fed. Reg. 27318 (July 30, 1986).

F. ASSESSMENT OF MEDICAL DEVICE TECHNOLOGY

FDA has formal authority under the FD&C Act only to evaluate the safety and effectiveness of medical devices. But the contribution of new medical instrumentation to the raising cost of medical care has also raised questions about the cost-effectiveness of many devices, including some that, from the agency's frame of reference, are unquestionably both safe and efficacious.

SAMUEL O. THIER, NEW MEDICAL DEVICES AND HEALTH CARE

NEW MEDICAL DEVICES: INVENTION, DEVELOPMENT, AND USE.
(NAS–IOM 1988).

The problem in introducing new technology is an old one. For example, a newspaper editorial in 1834 said of a medical instrument: "That it will ever come into general use, notwithstanding its value, is extremely doubtful because its beneficial application requires much time and gives a good bit of trouble, both to the patient and the practitioner because its hue and character are foreign and opposed to all our habits and associations. There is something even ludicrous in the picture of a gray physician proudly listening through a long tube applied to the patient's thorax." That *London Times* editorial was criticizing the introduction of the stethoscope. New medical technologies since then have also been resisted, sometimes by the public, sometimes by the profession, sometimes by both. . . .

One of the tensions in the system is between the natural resistance to new technology and the fascinated attraction to it. That emotional ambivalence is an important reality. But there is a more important economic resistance: technology generally and devices particularly have become identified as culprits in the rise of health care costs. The general sense is that every time a new technology is introduced, the costs of care are driven up. That may be true if the technology is expensive and is used often.

However, technology also can lower costs in many health care circumstances. Sometimes the cost-cutting effect is direct and obvious. Other times it is indirect, measurable mainly in the quicker return of patients to a productive existence, which rarely is calculated in the costs of introducing medical technology.

Some of the stigma on technology as costly stems from its improper siting. Because of the health care reimbursement system, we have commonly put technology in the most expensive settings, where the support staff and overhead costs are the highest. Other blame attaches to our failure to ensure skilled use of the technology. The assumption that we could release technology on an unprepared medical profession and have it spread with appropriate skills throughout the nation is a delusion. That simply does not happen, and thus we have persons applying technologies who are prepared neither by skill nor by knowledge of the proper indications for use. A further problem relates to a system that pays practitioners more for technologic skills than for cognitive medical skills. When that happens, it drives the use of technology into inappropriate applications.

Something I wrote a few years ago puts it in perspective from the physician's standpoint.

It is a paradox of modern medicine that, as technology provides for greater precision in diagnosis and treatment, practicing physicians are becoming less critical and efficient in its use. The difficulties for the physician in practice are understandable. The last two to three decades have been historically unique in the rate at which new biomedical knowledge has been produced and applied. New insights into the basic mechanism of disease have been translated into new diagnostic tests and therapeutic modalities. . . . New technology is frequently introduced through journal articles, consultants' suggestions, conferences, postgraduate courses, and newsletters. Often there is inadequate perspective provided for the use of the technology and certainly inadequate perspective in a clinical circumstance or in relation to other existing technologies.

The physician, understandably, continues to use what has proven helpful in the past and merely adds new technology to established patterns. The result is a proliferation of technology rather than substitution of newer and better approaches for outdated ones.

What are we to do in response to burgeoning innovation? It does not permit for assimilation of the information that would enable us to make proper use of the technology and ensure that patients will benefit to the maximum extent possible from innovation. The way in which we deal with technology does not permit focused analysis of how good it is and how well it works, nor does it permit effective long-range monitoring of who uses it and how well they use it.

In the assessment of medical technology there are several perspectives that must be satisfied. The needs of somebody who is pondering reimbursement for a technology differ considerably from the needs of a hospital deciding whether it wishes to introduce the technology for the care of its patients. That information, in turn, differs from what physicians need to know to change their practice patterns and use the technology, and that differs from what a patient needs to know to ask proper questions of the doctor.

I would like to suggest a framework for introducing technology that will enable us to determine where that technology fits in the scheme of things and what its contribution to health care might be. The perspective is that of the health profession, the people conducting screening for, and prevention of, disease and employing diagnostic technology, therapeutic technology, and rehabilitative technology.

The development of health care in the past century first emphasized diagnosis, because it was something a physician could actually do. Much later came the methods of effective therapy that currently get so much attention. The discovery of, and investment in, good screening techniques and in major rehabilitative measures is recent, but it is probably much more important economically than the diagnostic and therapeutic modalities. The result of this developmental history is that the reimbursement system has been focused on diagnosis and therapy instead of screening and rehabilitation.

OFFICE OF TECHNOLOGY ASSESSMENT, DEVELOPMENT OF MEDICAL TECHNOLOGY: OPPORTUNITIES FOR ASSESSMENT

(1976).

The assessment of the potential social impacts of new medical technologies while they are still being developed might serve two important purposes:

- Information obtained from assessments could be used in formulating policies to insure that research-development funds are invested wisely. Once the benefits and drawbacks of a particular new technology are considered explicitly, its development might be expedited or constrained. Priority might be given to development of alternative forms of the technology that minimize drawbacks or maximize benefits. One specific issue, for example, concerns whether to invest funds to develop medical technologies that would benefit the greatest number of people, even though such technologies might take many years to develop, or whether to invest those funds in developing technologies in the immediate future that could provide great benefit to (or even save the lives of) relatively few people. Assessment could not, of course, resolve this dilemma, but it might better inform the decisionmaking process that must occur.

• Assessment might provide information that could improve the process of planning for the eventual introduction of new medical technologies into the medical service system. Societal changes that might be required for or result from introduction of a new technology might be anticipated.....

... In addition ... [e]ffective programs of assessment could—

• Encourage more effective education of and communication with the public on issues concerning medical technology;

• Allow opportunities for more effective public input to decisions dealing with the development and use of new medical technology;

• Improve technical input to political decisions about research policy; and

• Tap the resources of social responsibility already present in the scientific community....

INSTITUTE OF MEDICINE,
COMPUTED TOMOGRAPHIC SCANNING
(National Academy of Sciences, 1977).

Computed tomographic (CT) scanning is a recently developed technique which combines radiographic and computer techniques to produce cross-section images of the head and body. Whereas conventional x-ray films show internal structures superimposed upon each other and, therefore, are best suited to high contrast structures such as bone, the CT scanner can produce high quality images of soft tissue structures....

The first two CT scanning units in the United States were installed in mid–1973. Slightly less than four years after that introduction, it was estimated that at least 760 CT scanners were in operation or had been ordered by American hospitals, clinics, and physicians, posing a ratio of one machine for every 281,000 people in the nation.

Such swift and widespread adoption of this new medical technology has attracted the attention of planners, insurers, and investigators of health services. Their questions concern efficacy and expense. The long-term effects of CT scanning on medical care and its costs are not yet discernible, although there is little doubt that the technique represents a major improvement in diagnostic imaging. Head scanning became an accepted diagnostic tool before coordinated studies of its impact on diagnosis could be completed, and there are as yet few reports to indicate what the information from CT scanning of the head has meant for patient treatment methods or outcomes. Now, as CT is extended to other areas of the body, the same concerns apply.

As for medical care expenditures, scanners range in price from $300,000 to $700,000 each.... Operating costs for a unit are estimated to range from $259,000 to $371,000 per year. The real costs of CT scanning will depend not only on the number of units purchased and the number of scans performed, but also on the extent to which CT scanning replaces other diagnostic procedures and reduces hospitalization. There is not enough evidence now to enable measurement of these effects.

The rapid acceptance of CT scanning has also heightened concerns about other diagnostic technologies and even medical technology in general. Evidence is accumulating that the present organization of medical care and methods of financing and regulating that care in the United States have encouraged investment in beds and equipment beyond a socially efficient level. Competition among hospitals for medical staff, prestige, or revenues is often cited as a reason for overinvestment in capital equipment. The risk of losses from overinvestment has been reduced or eliminated by the retrospective, cost-based reimbursement systems that predominate today. Regulation designed to control large capital expenditures may have had a perverse effect itself; state certificate of need (CON) laws requiring institutions to obtain approval for purchasing expensive equipment like the CT scanner may have stimulated hospitals to adopt new technologies quickly—before the planning agency has sufficient facts to approve or deny the purchase....

Concurrent with the proliferation of equipment has been an increasing rate of use of diagnostic tests, including x-rays.... Changes in medical education have placed increasing emphasis on objective tests and precise measurement when less technologically advanced methods might still be adequate for diagnosis. Fear of malpractice litigation encourages "defensive" medical practice, usually expressed as over-utilization of services, particularly diagnostic tests. The growing share of personal health care expenditures covered by third-party reimbursement has reduced the incentives to control use, because the physician's decision to use services is separated from the patient's immediate expenses.

... Well designed studies of the efficacy of procedures are necessary to evaluate any technology, but the completion of such studies prior to the introduction of new technologies is very unusual. The application of new diagnostic or treatment techniques has typically been based on observational studies with inherent problems of observer bias, rather than on rigorous evidence that can only be gathered through well-designed clinical trials or the statistical analysis of large numbers of observations. Often an assessment of the broader implications of introducing new technologies is also needed. At present, such studies are not required or coordinated by any organization, public, or private, and no system exists to identify areas for evaluation of emerging technologies at an early age. . . .

Until better data are available, all attempts to recommend and implement policies on the use of new technologies must be viewed as tentative because of the inadequacies of our traditional approaches to acquisition and evaluation of clinical information. . . .

NOTES

1. *Merits of Technology Assessment.* There is debate over the validity and thus the utility of technology assessment. Some have contended that, because the true range of effectiveness and the efficiency of a medical device cannot be foreseen before its introduction and use, technology assessment stifles medical progress and impedes patient care. Using the CT scanner as an example, it has been argued that the assessments conducted in the late 1970s by the Institute of Medicine, *supra,* and by OTA, POLICY IMPLICATIONS OF THE COMPUTED TOMOGRAPHY (CT) SCANNER (1978), failed to anticipate its medical utility and that restriction of its dissemination, as some advocated at the time, would have harmed the public health. Others respond that society simply cannot afford all new medical technologies.

2. *Commentary.* The literature on technology assessment of medical devices continues to grow. Important reports include several by the Institute of Medicine, MEDICAL TECHNOLOGY AND THE HEALTH CARE SYSTEM (1979); EVALUATING MEDICAL TECHNOLOGIES IN CLINICAL USE (1981); ASSESSING MEDICAL TECHNOLOGIES (1985); NEW MEDICAL DEVICES: INVENTION, DEVELOPMENT, AND USE (1988); TECHNOLOGICAL INNOVATION: COMPARING DEVELOPMENT OF DRUGS, DEVICES, AND PROCEDURES IN MEDICINE (1989); and by OTA, DEVELOPMENT OF MEDICAL TECHNOLOGY: OPPORTUNITIES FOR ASSESSMENT, OTA-H-34 (1976); ASSESSING THE EFFICACY AND SAFETY OF MEDICAL TECHNOLOGIES, OTA-H-75 (1978); MEDICAL TECHNOLOGY UNDER PROPOSALS TO INCREASE COMPETITION IN HEALTH CARE, OTA-H-190 (1982); STRATEGIES FOR MEDICAL TECHNOLOGY ASSESSMENT, OTA-H-181 (1982); DIAGNOSIS RELATED GROUPS (DRGS) AND THE MEDICARE PROGRAM: IMPLICATIONS FOR MEDICAL TECHNOLOGY, OTA-TM-H-17 (1983). *See also* Hillman, *Government Health Policy and the Diffusion of New Medical Devices,* 21 Health Serv. Res. 681 (1986).

TECHNOLOGY ASSESSMENT BY FEDERAL AGENCIES

Medicare Coverage. Section 1862(a)(1) of the Social Security Amendments of 1965 (commonly known as the Medicare Act), 79 Stat. 286, 325, codified in 42 U.S.C. § 1395y(a)(1), provides that no payment shall be made for items or services, including medical devices, "which are not reasonable and necessary for the diagnosis or treatment of illness or injury or to improve the functioning of a malformed body member." In implementing this provision, the Health Care Financing Administration (HCFA) has denied Medicare coverage for "experimental" use of medical devices, and has required an independent assessment in addition to FDA clearance through a PMN or a PMA application before approving coverage. *See* 55 Fed. Reg. 21250 (May 23, 1990), proposing to limit Medicare coverage to intraocular lens that have an approved PMA application; Schatz, *Medicare Coverage of New Technologies: Initial Responses,* 6 HealthSpan, No. 5, at 3 (May 19, 1989). To resolve a major challenge to both its policy and procedures, HCFA proposed regulations, 54 Fed. Reg. 4302 (January 30, 1989), to establish clear rules for this process for the future. Under proposed section 405.380(b)(1)(vi), medical devices whose marketing FDA has allowed under section 510(k) in response to a PMN submitted with clinical data are considered reimbursable when used for the conditions set forth in the labeling, but not necessarily for other conditions. *See generally* Kave and Manoukian, *The effect of the Medicare Prospective Payment System on the Adoption of New Technology: The Case of Cochlear Implants,* 321 N.E.J.M. 1378 (November 16, 1989).

Prospective Payment and DRGs. The Social Security Amendments of 1983, 97 Stat. 65, 149, replaced Medicare's original cost-based reimbursement formula with a prospective payment system (PPS) based upon 470 diagnosis related groups (DRGs). Under PPS, the hospital receives a fixed payment for each Medicare patient in accordance with the applicable DRGs. PPS thus gives providers clear economic incentives to restrain the cost of medical technology. The legislation also created a Prospective Payment Assessment Commission (ProPac) to conduct or sponsor assessments of medical technology in order to advise HCFA on appropriate reimbursement rates for DRGs. *See* Foote, *Assessing Medical Technology Assessment: Past Present, and Future,* 65 Milbank Quarterly, no. 1, at 59 (1987); Garrison and Wilensky, *Cost Containment and Incentives for Technology,* 5 Health Affairs, no. 2, at 46 (Summer 1986).

Office of Health Technology Assessment. Pursuant to the Health Services Research, Health Statistics, and Health Care Technology Act of 1978, 92 Stat. 3443, 3445, the Department of HEW established a National Center for Health Technology and solicited views on its functions in 44 Fed. Reg. 51338 (August 31, 1979). In December 1981, however, funding expired and thus the Center ceased to exist. Perry, *The Brief Life of the National Center for Health Care Technology,* 307 N. Eng. J. Med. 1095 (October 21, 1982); Perry, *Technology Assessment: Continuing Uncertainty,* 314 N. Eng. J. Med. 240 (January 23, 1986). In response to a report by the Institute of Medicine, A CONSORTIUM FOR ASSESSING MEDICAL TECHNOLOGY (1983), recommending a private-public enterprise, Congress included two provisions in the Health Promotion and Disease Prevention Amendments of 1984, 98 Stat. 2815. First, it combined DHH's health services research and technology assessment functions into a single National Center for Health Services Research and Health Care Technology Assessment, 42 U.S.C. § 242n. Second, it authorized grants for a Council on Health Care Technology, 42 U.S.C. § 242n. The revitalized Office of Health Technology Assessment in the National Center for Health Services Research and Health Care Technology Assessment has periodically announced the proposed assessment of, and the availability of reports on, the use of specific medical devices in health care. The subjects covered include reuse of hemodialysis devices, 51 Fed. Reg. 12397 (April 10, 1986); lithotripsy procedures for treatment of kidney stones, 51 Fed. Reg. 15963 (April 29, 1986); use of the cardiointegram as a diagnostic and predictive cardiovascular test, 52 Fed. Reg. 7934 (March 13, 1987); pressure-limited respirators for breathing therapy, 53 Fed. Reg. 32941 (August 29, 1988); and electrostimulation of salivary production in the treatment of xerostomia, 54 Fed. Reg. 8829 (March 2, 1989). The Institute of Medicine has created the Council on Health Care Technology, with funding provided equally by Congress and the private sector. The Council does not conduct technology assessments but provides a forum for exchange of views among the estimated 100 groups involved in the technology assessment field.

State Certificate of Need Regulation. Beginning in 1964, most states enacted "certificate of need" (CON) statutes under which state agencies must review and approve new medical construction and medical equipment costing more than a specified threshold level. Under the National Health Planning and Resources Development Act of 1974, 88 Stat. 2225, 2246, the Public Health Service Act was amended to require national guidelines for health planning and to promote state health planning, including state CON programs. In the Health Planning and Resources Development Amendments of 1979, 93 Stat. 592, 614, states were required to conform their CON laws to minimum Federal standards in order to receive Federal funding. *See generally* OTA, FEDERAL POLICIES AND THE MEDICAL DEVICES INDUSTRY OTA-H-229 (1984). In 100 Stat. 3743, 3799 (1986), this entire Federal program was repealed.

5. *Antitrust Issues. See* Havighurst, *Applying Antitrust Law to Collaboration in the Production of Information: The Case of Medical Technology Assessment,* 51 L. and Contemp. Probs. 341 (1988).

Chapter VII
COSMETICS

A. HISTORICAL AND STATUTORY BACKGROUND

FDA first acquired authority to regulate cosmetics with enactment of the 1938 Act. The safety of cosmetics, however, had been a concern in Congress as early as 1881. H.R. Rep. No. 199, 46th Cong., 3d Sess. 2 (1881). Following the example of a Massachusetts statute (L. Mass. 1886, c. 171), Congress in 1898 amended the District of Columbia food and drug law to define the term "drug" to include cosmetics. 30 Stat. 246. The original 1897 bill to create a Federal law similarly "included cosmetics in the definition of drugs, but this portion was dropped in 1900 as partial payment for support from the National Pure Food and Drug Congress." Anderson, *Pioneer Statutes: The Pure Food and Drugs Act of 1906*, 13 J. Pub. L. 189, 195 (1964).

SENATE REPORT NO. 361
74th Congress, 1st Session (1935).

While the definition of the term cosmetic does not include devices, it is drawn in broad terms to include all substances and preparations, other than ordinary toilet or household soap, intended for cleansing, or altering the appearance of, or promoting the attractiveness of the person. Cosmetics may be used externally, orifically, or even internally as in the case of arsenic for clearing the complexion. The definition therefore must be sufficiently broad to cover potential abuses no matter how the substance or preparation is used. While soaps sold only for ordinary toilet or household use are specifically exempted from the definition of cosmetic and will not be subject to the definition of drug, soaps for which claims concerning disease are made or which are sold as pharmacopoeial articles will come within the definition of drug and will thus be subject to regulation. Likewise soaps intended for other than ordinary toilet or household use and represented, for instance, as beautifying agents, will come within the definition of cosmetic.....

Section [601] deals with adulterated cosmetics.... There are on the market a number of preparations, notably hair dyes, eyelash and eyebrow dyes, complexion bleaches and depilatories, which have caused serious impairment to the health of users and, in a number of instances, have resulted in such injuries as blindness and paralysis. These injuries have been caused by such toxic substances as certain coal-tar dyes and metals like lead, arsenic, mercury, and thallium, upon which the beautifying "action" of the preparations depends. Paragraph (a) is intended to protect the user against such hazards to health.

It will be noted that in drafting this paragraph the same general form has been used, to avoid complications arising from allergic reaction to wholesome products, as was employed in dealing with food under section [401](a)(2).... [O]nly those products are considered as adulterated which contain poisonous and deleterious substances, and then only when those substances are present in such quantity which may render the product injurious. This would not prevent the marketing of a face powder or cream or any other cosmetic which did not contain poisonous or deleterious ingredients, even though such cosmetics might contain ingredients to which a certain class of unfortunate people are allergic....

Paragraph (a) of ... section [602] is identical with the general misbranding provision on food.... Paragraphs (b) and (c) ... are merely an extension to cosmetics of provisions in the food and drug chapters....

NOTES

1. *Commentary.* For an entrancing treatment of cosmetic regulation in historical context, *see* Mock, *Cosmetic Law: History and Observation*, 1 FDC L.Q. 61 (1946). Accounts of the dangers of cosmetics which led to their inclusion in the 1938 Act may be found in A. Kallet and Schlink, 100,000,000 GUINEA PIGS ch. V. (1933); R. Lamb, AMERICAN CHAMBER OF HORRORS ch. 2 (1936). A defense of the industry was offered by E.G. McDonough, TRUTH ABOUT COSMETICS (1937).

2. *State Regulation.* The constitutionality of an early state law requiring the registration of cosmetic preparations was upheld in *Bourjois, Inc. v. Chapman*, 301 U.S. 183 (1937).

GEORGE P. LARRICK,* SOME CURRENT PROBLEMS IN THE REGULATION OF COSMETICS UNDER THE FEDERAL FOOD, DRUG, AND COSMETIC ACT

3 Food Drug Cosmetic Law Quarterly 570 (1948).

We do recognize that a great deal of progress has been made, but the principal object of this short talk is to emphasize the need for universal acceptance in the industry of the fact that a real scientific appraisal of the safety and suitability of materials used should be made

* [George Larrick was then Associate FDA Commissioner and later became Commissioner of Food and Drugs.]

before an ingredient is included in the composition of products designed to enhance the attractiveness of users. The same scientific approach should, of course, be followed in deciding what claims can legitimately be made....

There is still, in our opinion, too much secrecy concerning the precise composition of some ingredients of beautifying agents. We encounter instances wherein manufacturers or distributors of finished products do not know the composition of the preparations which they sell....

This situation encourages changes in composition of the basic ingredients without the knowledge of the cosmetic firm. Scarcities or price variations are sometimes an invitation to change these compositions without notice. Occasionally, these circumstances have led to the introduction of dangerous ingredients....

The Select Committee To Investigate the Use of Chemicals in Food Products, chaired by Representative James Delaney of New York, was established on June 20, 1950, pursuant to House Resolution 323, 81st Cong., 1st Sess. On October 15, 1951, the House extended the scope of the committee's authority to include "an investigation and study of the nature, extent, and effect of the use of chemicals, compounds, and synthetics in the production, processing, preparation, and packaging of cosmetics to determine the effect of the use of such chemicals, compounds, and synthetics upon the health and welfare of the Nation...." A year later the committee issued its final report.

INVESTIGATION OF THE USE OF CHEMICALS IN FOODS AND COSMETICS

House Report No. 2182, 82d Congress, 2d Session (1952).

... The partial regulation of cosmetics ... has appreciably decreased the incidence of serious harm, but insufficiently tested cosmetics still constitute a source of considerable annoyance, discomfort, and disability.

Under existing law, a dangerous cosmetic can be removed from the market by the institution of seizure proceedings. Unfortunately, the protection offered the public by this procedure is somewhat illusory. Before the government can avail itself of this remedy, data must first be assembled which will sustain the Government's burden of establishing to the satisfaction of a court and jury, by a preponderance of the evidence, that the cosmetic may cause injury to users.... It is clear that substances and combinations of substances have been used in cosmetics which, because of their injurious effects, would have been excluded if a law had existed requiring that adequate information concerning their safety be obtained before the cosmetics were sold to consumers....

There is probably no cosmetic ingredient which can be used with impunity by every human being. In the case of virtually every cosmetic preparation, some particular person or limited number of persons may experience an unfavorable reaction, although all others may suffer no ill effects. Allowance must necessarily be made, therefore, for some incidence of untoward effects....

1. Pretesting

Most of the representatives of the cosmetic industry took the position that existing legislation was adequate to protect the public fully.... The incongruity of the position of some industry representatives is exemplified by their testimony that the companies they represent conduct rigorous and exhaustive tests, and maintain strict controls over their products, as a necessary precaution to protect both themselves and the health of their customers. Nevertheless, they were opposed to a requirement that all cosmetic manufacturers observe essentially the same safety standards....

... Your committee recommends ... that the Federal Food, Drug, and Cosmetic Act be amended to require that cosmetics be subjected to essentially the same safety requirements as now apply to new drugs. Under such an amendment, data would not be required to be submitted to the Food and Drug Administration with respect to cosmetics which are generally recognized by qualified experts as safe under the conditions of use for which they are sold....

2. Soaps....

Soaps which have been on the market for years, and are generally recognized by competent authorities as being safe, would be unaffected by pretesting legislation. As indicated, however, inadequately tested hair shampoos have caused injury to the eye. There is an even greater possibility of injury from soaps containing new ingredients, for soaps are used to wash the face and, therefore, more readily make contact with the eye than do shampoos.... Your committee is of the opinion that the Federal Food, Drug, and Cosmetic Act is in need of amendment to bring soaps within the definition of cosmetics.

3. Labeling of Ingredients

... Physicians who specialize in the fields of allergy and dermatology testified that the labeling of cosmetic ingredients would be most helpful in their diagnosis and treatment of patients who may be suffering from the effects of some cosmetic ingredient.... Industry representatives testified, generally, in opposition to the labeling of ingredients, on the ground that cosmetics are composed of a large number of ingredients and that a long list affixed to the product would destroy the attractiveness of the package. The committee recognizes the importance of packaging attractiveness in the sale of cosmetics, and that in some instances it would be most difficult to set forth on the label of a cosmetic preparation a list of its numerous ingredients. It is the committee's view, however, that a list of ingredients need not in all cases by physically affixed to the cosmetic. Where the number of ingredients is quite large, the list can be contained, in most instances, in the cosmetic package in the form of an accompanying circular....

4. Coal–Tar Hair Dyes

Coal-tar hair dyes have long been a source of difficulty for cosmetic users. Paraphenylenediamine, a coal-tar color base for a large number of hair dyes, has a high sensitizing potential. There was considerable testimony that there have been reactions to this substance varying from slight dermatitis around the forehead, eyes, scalp, face, and neck, to generalized dermatitis requiring hospitalization....

Coal-tar hair dyes are permitted special privileges under [section 601(a)].... These provisions of the law have proven inadequate to provide the protection intended....

S.L. MAYHAM,* CHEMICALS IN COSMETICS

7 Food Drug Cosmetic Law Journal 184 (1952).

... The provisions of the present law, as they affect cosmetics, are entirely adequate to control any situation which is controllable with any type of law whatever....

... I have surveyed the 189 (and there are only 189) adjudicated cases on cosmetics since the enactment of the law in 1938. During those 13 years there have been 95 adjudicated cases brought under the adulteration provisions of the Act. One of these was won by the defendant, leaving 94 such cases. Of these 94 cases, only 59 were brought because of the presence of harmful or deleterious ingredients used in the manufacture of the cosmetics. The other 35 were because of the presence of filth, products being held under insanitary conditions, and for other reasons technically and legalistically classified as adulterations. Of these 59 which were brought because of the presence of a harmful ingredient, 22 came in the very early stages..... [L]et us be generous and say there were 34 cases where the presence of a chemical in a cosmetic was brought to court and proved to have done a harm.

This was over the period of 13 years since the law went into effect. During that time, the Toilet Goods Association has estimated that ... 26,301,000,000 packages of cosmetics [have been] sold and consumed in the United States. I contend that to find only 34 cases where harm has arisen from the presence of a poisonous ingredient in over 26 billion packages of cosmetics sold is not only *de minimis* but is really "much ado about nothing." ...

* [Then Executive Vice President of the Toilet Goods Association.]

The first [proposal] is to write into the cosmetic section of the present law something akin to the new-drug application provision of the present law..... From my observation of the industry, I would say that more than two thirds of the present cosmetic manufacturers do not have sufficient resources to file one single new-cosmetic application should there be such a provision in the law....

The second proposal ... is to list all ingredients of every cosmetic on the label.... Let us look at this proposal for a moment and consider how it would work. First, I have examined a great many cosmetic formulas. Few of them contain less than 15 ingredients and many of them contain 50 or more. Just where on the label or in the labeling would this list appear in distinguishable form? If you consider the perfume ingredients used in some of these products, you might well have to list 150 items on the label. The names of most of these would be completely unfamiliar to anyone who might want to read them.....

... [L]et us go back now for a moment to the lady who is allergic. She goes to a dermatologist who discovers that she is allergic possibly to lanolin, so she wants to avoid lanolin in cosmetics. If her dermatologist really knows his business he is aware of the fact that there are already a number of cosmetic manufacturers making hypo-allergenic cosmetics which exclude every possible known allergen and that these companies are willing to make up on special order at very, very reasonable prices cosmetics excluding the ingredients to which the individual may be allergic. So, the industry itself has made provision to take care of these cases of allergy and it would seem folly to insist on listing all the ingredients of a cosmetic, when absolutely nothing in the way of public protection would be accomplished by doing it....

... I would call attention to the record of the hearings of the Delaney Committee to date. Practically every industry witness who has appeared has shown how carefully he insists upon control of the product from the time of purchase of the raw material until the ultimate consumer actually uses it. He tests the raw materials, he tests the products in process, he tests the finished product and he does so without any great love for the public, but because he knows that if a manufacturer puts out something that is harmful and poisonous he will not stay in business....

A quarter of a century later the issues dividing proponents and opponents of new cosmetic legislation had not changed significantly.

U.S. GENERAL ACCOUNTING OFFICE, LACK OF AUTHORITY HAMPERS ATTEMPTS TO INCREASE COSMETIC SAFETY
(1978).

About 125 ingredients available for use in cosmetics are suspected of causing cancer, according to studies. In addition, about 25 are suspected of causing birth defects and 20 may cause adverse effects on the nervous system, including headaches, drowsiness, and convulsions.... Although many of the reported adverse effects have not been verified, 12 of the ingredients are known to cause cancer in humans or contain impurities known to cause cancer in humans. Another 18 ingredients have been found to cause cancer in animals.....

Although there is increasing evidence that some cosmetic products and ingredients may carry a significant risk of injury to consumers, the Food and Drug Administration does not have an effective program for regulating cosmetics.... The act ... does NOT authorize the Food and Drug Administration to require manufacturers to

- register their plants or products,
- file data on the ingredients in their products,
- file reports of cosmetic-related injuries, or
- test their products for safety....

... [I]n 1972 and 1973 the agency asked cosmetic manufacturers, packers, and distributors to register their plants and file information on the ingredients used in their products and the injuries reported from their use. As of December 1977, about 40 percent of the manufacturers and packers had registered their plants; less than 20 percent of the manufacturers, packers, and distributors had filed ingredient listings, and less than 4 percent had filed injury reports. A Food and Drug Administration regulation requires that labeling of cosmetics that have not been adequately tested for safety include a warning to that effect. This regulation cannot be effectively enforced because the agency is not authorized to require manufacturers to test their products for safety or to make their test available to the agency. In addition, many manufacturers have refused Food and Drug Administration inspectors access to manufacturing records, such as qualitative and quantitative formulas, sales or shipping records, and consumer complaint files. The agency lacks authority to require that such records be made available....

The Food and Drug Administration has not inspected most manufacturers' plants or sampled most of their products for compliance with the Federal Food, Drug, and Cosmetic Act. Only about half the cosmetic establishments were inspected between fiscal years 1969 and 1975. Since 1975 the agency identified about 1,000 additional manufacturers, which it had never inspected because they had been unknown to the agency. The Food and Drug Administration also has not established criteria to determine whether adequate methods, facilities, and controls are used in all phases of manufacturing and distribution of cosmetics. According to an agency official, about 75 percent of a sample of over 300 firms inspected since 1976 had deficiencies in their manufacturing practices. Between 1974 and 1976 Food and Drug Administration inspectors and laboratories identified over 400 violations of the cosmetic provisions of the act which they believed warranted some form of regulatory action. Yet only 141 regulatory actions were taken; 54 involved 1 violative product. No prosecutions were started.

Establishing regulations to prohibit or limit the use of an individual ingredient or requiring the use of a specific warning on the label is an effective way to increase consumer safety with regard to a specific product or class of products. However, as of January 1, 1978, the Food and Drug Administration had established regulations governing the use of only 11 ingredients used in cosmetics and had required precautionary labeling only on feminine deodorant sprays, aerosols containing chlorofluorocarbon propellants, and aerosol cosmetics in self-pressurized containers....

Although the Food and Drug Administration cannot require cosmetic manufacturers to test the safety of their products, it can establish regulations identifying appropriate tests which should be used by manufacturers in evaluating safety. The agency said that development of appropriate tests is both difficult and resource demanding.

Some coal tar hair dyes may pose a significant risk of cancer to consumers because they contain colors known to cause or suspected of causing cancer in humans or animals. However, exemptions granted to coal tar hair dyes under the Federal Food, Drug, and Cosmetic Act prevent the Food and Drug Administration from regulating hair dyes effectively.... The Congress should repeal these exemptions....

STATEMENT OF THE COSMETIC, TOILETRY AND FRAGRANCE ASSOCIATION, INC.

"Cancer–Causing Chemicals–Part 1 (Safety of Cosmetics and Hair Dyes),"
Hearings Before the Subcommittee on Oversight and Investigations
of the House Committee on Interstate and Foreign Commerce (January 26, 1978).

Cosmetic products have an enviable safety record. In September 1973, the panel on chemicals and health of the President's Science Advisory Committee issued a report published by the National Science Foundation which concluded with respect to cosmetics:

From what may be judged from human experience, the incidence of injury is small.

In the total pattern of environmental risks, those from cosmetics are both infrequent and slight.

While there are no formal pretesting or preclearance requirements for cosmetics, the total effect of individual and informal review—usually private rather than governmental— together with the innocuousness of most materials used, has made the injury rate fairly low by comparison with other widely prevalent sources of hazard.

It seems likely, though solid information is lacking, that the actual injury rate from cosmetics has declined, while the complaint rate has increased as a result of greater consumer awareness of the Food and Drug Administration as a regulatory agency, and of the existence of legal and insurance remedies.

Company records show that reactions to cosmetics are rarely serious and are almost invariably transient and reversible. We are unaware that any case of cancer has ever been shown to have been caused by any cosmetic....

The FDA regulation requiring ingredient labeling for cosmetics is effective. The regulation requires that all retail cosmetic packaging list the ingredients in descending order of predominance with the exception of flavor and fragrance. It is more informative than food ingredient labeling because it requires specific designation of color ingredients, and is far more informative than drug ingredient labeling which requires declaration only of active ingredients.

Any cosmetic which has not been adequately substantiated for safety prior to marketing is required by an FDA regulation to bear the warning statement that "the safety of this product has not been determined." ... CTFA strongly supports the concept of safety substantiation, firmly believing that it is the obligation of every manufacturer and distributor not to market any cosmetic which has not been substantiated for safety. CTFA has not challenged the legal authority of FDA to promulgate its regulation requiring safety substantiation, and has over the years established many programs designed to help industry meet its obligation to the public even before it became a legal requirement....

CTFA inaugurated its scientific program 30 years ago with the establishment of analytical standards for ingredients commonly used in cosmetics. In the past 10 years it has formed scientific committees of qualified experts to analyze and resolve scientific questions dealing with microbiology, pharmacology, and toxicology, quality assurance, color safety, hair coloring, ingredient nomenclature, and a wide variety of other subjects. CTFA regularly develops and disseminates standards for raw material specifications, testing methods, and ingredient descriptions, as well as technical guidelines to help insure the quality and safety of finished products.

CTFA initiated and submitted three major petitions to FDA, on the basis of which FDA has promulgated regulations governing voluntary registration of cosmetic product manufacturing plants, filing of cosmetic product formulas, and filing of cosmetic product experience reports. The following statistics reflect voluntary industry participation in these three programs as of September 30, 1977. About 900 cosmetic plants have been registered with FDA, representing about 85 percent of the volume of cosmetics sold in the United States. Some 23,500 cosmetic formulas have been submitted to FDA, representing about 80 percent of the volume of cosmetics sold in the United States. About 125 companies were participating in the product experience reporting program, representing about 50 percent of the volume of cosmetics sold in the United States....

CTFA has recently undertaken a major program to review the safety of cosmetic ingredients. All available published and unpublished data on individual ingredients will be compiled and submitted for review by an independent expert panel of eminent scientists. The expert panel members have been required to meet the same strict conflict-of-interest standards as are applied to members of Federal Government advisory committees. The review process is modeled directly after current FDA safety review programs, and includes a consumer liaison selected by consumer organizations, an industry liaison, and an FDA contact person....

NOTES

1. *Reprise.* The same debate was replayed a decade later. "Potential Health Hazards of Cosmetic Products," Hearings Before the Subcomm. on Regulation and Business Opportunities of the House Comm. on Small Business, 100th Cong., 2d Sess. (1988).

2. *Legislative Proposals.* Since 1938 many bills have been introduced in Congress to amend and strengthen the cosmetic provisions of the FD&C Act. *See, e.g.,* Kleinfeld, *Cosmetic Legislation: Benefit–Risk,* 29 FDC L.J. 308 (1974); *The Role of Government in the Field of Cosmetics,* 20 FDC L.J. 480 (1965); *What Kind of Cosmetic Legislation?,* 19 FDC L.J. 87 (1964); Levine, *Cosmetics: Is New Legislation Needed?,* 29 FDC L.J. 564 (1974); Page and Blackburn, *Behind the Looking Glass: Administrative, Legislative and Private Approaches to Cosmetic Safety Substantiation,* 24 UCLA L. Rev. 795 (1977). These proposals received serious consideration, however, only in the Senate in 1974 and 1975. *See* "Cosmetic Safety Act of 1974," Hearings Before the Subcomm. on Health of the Senate Comm. on Labor and Public Welfare, 93d Cong., 2d Sess. (1974); "Cosmetic Safety Amendments, 1975," Hearing Before the Subcomm. on Health of the Senate Comm. on Labor and Public Welfare, 94th Cong., 1st Sess. (1975). Cosmetic legislation was reported out of committee, S. Rep. No. 94–1047, 94th Cong., 2d Sess. (1976), and passed the Senate, 122 Cong. Rec. 24629 (July 30, 1976), but was never taken up by the House.

3. *Enforcement History.* For a summary of the 205 notices of judgment in legal actions by FDA against cosmetics between 1938 and 1959, *see* Munch and Munch, *Notices of Judgment—Cosmetics,* 14 FDC L.J. 399 (1959).

4. *Commentary.* For general discussions of the adequacy of FDA regulation of cosmetic safety, *see* Gilhooley, *Federal Regulation of Cosmetics: An Overview,* 33 FDC L.J. 231 (1978); Henteleff, *A Cosmetic Legal Update,* 33 FDC L.J. 252 (1978); McNamara, *FDA Regulation of Cosmetics in 1979: Industry Concerns,* 34 FDC L.J. 236 (1979).

B. DEFINITION OF "COSMETIC"

PETER BARTON HUTT, RECONCILING THE LEGAL, MEDICAL, AND COSMETIC CHEMIST APPROACH TO THE DEFINITION OF A "COSMETIC"

3 CTFA Cosmetic Journal, No. 3 (1971).

The first principle is that the intended use of the product, rather than its inherent properties, control[s] its classification.... [T]he controlling representations made by the manufacturer may appear in labeling, in advertising, or in any other form of oral or written communication. And an implicit representation is as controlling as an explicit one....

The second general principle is that the representations made for a product may properly classify it in more than one product category under the Act. If a product were represented both to treat a disease and to promote attractiveness, it would properly be classified as both a drug and cosmetic, and must meet the legal requirements for both categories....

The third, and final, general principle is that it is the initial and primary responsibility of the manufacturer or distributor of a product to determine the proper classification of his product, and to make certain that it meets all applicable legal requirements....

Attempting to formulate a hard and fast rule differentiating between cosmetic claims and drug claims is virtually impossible. Some cosmetics are intended merely to color some part of the body, in order to promote attractiveness, and present no problem of proper classification. And on the other end of the scale, some products are represented to effect a physiological change in the body, and these would clearly fall into the drug category as well as the cosmetic category. But in between these two extremes is the difficult area of judgment—the cosmetics that claim to promote attractiveness through a slight, and usually temporary, physical but not physiological, effect upon the skin.

The Food and Drug Administration attempted to deal with the proper legal classification of some of these various types of products in the advisory opinions contained in its Trade Correspondence during 1938–1946. The difficulty in resolving these matters on a purely rational basis is readily demonstrated by just three of those opinions. FDA stated that mercury preparations used to bleach or remove tan are drugs because they are intended to affect the structure and function of the body. On the other hand, an article represented solely to produce an even tan is regarded by FDA as a cosmetic. And a product intended not just to produce an even tan, but also to prevent sunburn, is a drug....

A further indication of the distinction between a product that does and does not affect a bodily structure or function may be found in the area of deodorants. A product that absorbs perspiration, or masks its odor, or prevents odor by germicidal or bacteriostatic agents that act upon odor-producing bacteria, is classified by the Food and Drug Administration as a cosmetic and not a drug. A product that is designed to reduce perspiration odor by reducing the perspiration itself, through a change in the sweat glands, is considered by the Food and Drug Administration to be a drug.

A cosmetic may properly be represented for use to mask or cover up the physical manifestations of a disease, without becoming a drug. Acne and dandruff are regarded as disease conditions, and any product represented to treat those conditions is classified as a drug. But products that claim merely to cover up manifestations of acne, or to wash away loose dandruff flakes, would properly be classified solely as cosmetics.

An analogous question is presented by "hypoallergenic" cosmetic products, which claim to have "screened out" most irritants. Since hypoallergenic foods have not been regarded as drugs it would appear that hypoallergenic cosmetics would similarly not be regarded as drugs absent specific claims that certain diseases will be treated or relieved by the product. . . .

A question frequently asked is whether any inclusion of an active ingredient in a cosmetic automatically classifies it as a drug. The answer is that classification depends upon the claims made, not upon the inclusion of the ingredient itself. . . .

Not long after enactment of the 1938 Act, the Food and Drug Administration stated in Trade Correspondence that such devices as rubber gloves represented to protect the housewife's hands against water, and paper napkins and facial tissues are not cosmetics. Since then, however, legal action has been taken against a number of cosmetic devices under the cosmetic provisions of the Act. Before the 1962 Amendments, such action was relatively rare, and involved articles like hair brushes, stockings, and tooth picks. Since 1962, however, the Food and Drug Administration has listed as cosmetics many different forms of electrical and mechanical beautifying devices. . . .

UNITED STATES v. AN ARTICLE . . . SUDDEN CHANGE

United States Court of Appeals, Second Circuit, 1969.
409 F.2d 734.

ANDERSON, Circuit Judge:

This is an appeal in a seizure action from an order of the United States District Court for the Eastern District of New York . . . granting summary judgment for the claimant. The seizure concerned 216 bottles of a cosmetic product called "Sudden Change" which is a clear liquid lotion consisting primarily of two ingredients: bovine albumen (15%) and distilled water (over 84%). It is meant to be applied externally to the surface of the facial skin, and it is claimed, *inter alia*, in its labeling and advertising that it will provide a "Face Lift Without Surgery." The court below described the effects of the product as follows:

> Allowed to dry on the skin, it leaves a film which (1) masks imperfections, making the skin look smoother and (2) acts mechanically to smooth and firm the skin by tightening the surface. Both effects are temporary. There is apparently no absorption by, or changes in, skin tissue resulting from its applications; it washes off.

The central issue presented in this appeal is whether Sudden Change is, within the meaning of the Federal Food, Drug and Cosmetic Act, 21 U.S.C. § 321(g)(1), a "drug."....

It is well settled that the intended use of a product may be determined from its label, accompanying labeling, promotional material, advertising and any other relevant source. Regardless of the actual physical effect of a product, it will be deemed a drug for purposes of the Act where the labeling and promotional claims show intended uses that bring it within the drug definition....

The mere statement of this rule poses a crucial issue: by what standards are these claims to be evaluated? Or, to put it another way, what degree of sophistication or vulnerability is to be ascribed to the hypothetical potential consumer in order to understand how these claims are understood by the buying public? .... [W]e conclude that the purposes of the Act will best be effected by postulating a consuming public which includes "the ignorant, the unthinking and the credulous * * *." ...

While it is not altogether clear what standard the court below applied, the reasoning appears to assume something like a "reasonable woman" standard. Thus, the District Court assumes that the "constant exposure to puffing and extravagant claims" has induced "some immunity in the beautifiers' hyperbole" which is such that the court "cannot believe" that the potential consumer of Sudden Change "expects anything other than a possibility that she may look better." We agree that certain claims which arguably would bring the product within § 321(g)(1)(C) have so drenched the potential consumer that even the "ignorant, the unthinking and the credulous" must be presumed able to discount their promises as typical of cosmetic advertising puffery. We cannot agree, however, with the conclusion that such immunity or skepticism somehow transfers to the promise to "lift out puffs" or give a "face lift without surgery." The references to "face lift" and "surgery" carry distinctly physiological connotations, suggesting, at least to the vulnerable consumer that the product will "affect the structure * * * of the body * * *" in some way other than merely temporarily altering the appearance. We do not accept the concept that skepticism toward familiar claims necessarily entails skepticism toward unfamiliar claims; the theory of the legislation is that someone might take the claim literally.

In other words, with the exception of those claims which have become so associated with the familiar exaggerations of cosmetics advertising that virtually everyone can be presumed to be capable of discounting them as puffery,[10] the question of whether a product is "intended to affect the structure * * * of the body of man * * * " is to be answered by considering, first, how the claim might be understood by the "ignorant, unthinking or credulous" consumer, and second, whether the claim as so understood may fairly be said to constitute a representation that the product will affect the structure of the body in some medical—or drug-type fashion, *i.e.,* in some way other than merely "altering the appearance."

We hold, therefore, that so long as Sudden Change is claimed to give a "face lift without surgery" and to "lift out puffs" it is to be deemed a drug within the meaning of 21 U.S.C. § 321(g)(*l*)(C). It should be understood, however, that if the claimant ceases to employ these promotional claims and avoids any others which may fairly be interpreted as claiming to affect the structure of the skin in some physiological, though temporary, way, then, assuming *arguendo* that no actual physical effect exists, the product will not be deemed a drug for purposes of the Act. While there may be merit in the cause of those who seek to require pretesting of new cosmetics, it is not for the courts to legislate such a requirement; rather it must rest in the hands of Congress to decide whether such an amendment to the statute should be enacted or not.....

MANSFIELD, District Judge (dissenting):....

In view of the existence of ample authority for regulation of cosmetics, it strikes me as unnecessary, in the absence of some imminent danger to public health—and none is suggested here—for the Court to adopt new standards of construction for the purpose of determining whether an article is intended as a "drug" rather than to follow time-proven rules. Yet that is exactly what the Court does here, with the result that it opens up a new—and in my view, unnecessary—avenue for regulation of cosmetics as drugs. If Congress believes that protection of the public requires pretesting and clearance of cosmetics by the Food and Drug Administration ... and that their components be listed on the label, it has the power to act. I do not think the Court should do so by a process of tortuous construction....

It may well be that the existence of fraud upon consumers of such products (whether drugs or cosmetics) should depend upon whether "the ignorant, the unthinking and credulous" would be deceived. The

---

10. ... We agree that the legislative history and the language of the Act require rejection of any rule which would convert all cosmetics into drugs. We believe, however, that the test which we have applied draws the necessary line while at the same time protecting the public. For example, promises that a product will "soften" or "moisturize" a woman's skin are so thor- oughly familiar that constant exposure can be presumed to have induced sufficient immunity even in our hypothetical vulnerable consumer (this assumes, *arguendo,* that these promises have exactly the same degree of drug-type connotations as the "face lift without surgery" claim—an assumption which we reject).

issue before us, however, is not whether consumers may be defrauded by the labelling and enclosures used in connection with the sale of "Sudden Change." The issue is whether the product must be classified as a "drug" which must be pre-tested, cleared and bear a label listing its components. Since that issue turns upon whether the article is "*intended* to affect the structure of the body" (emphasis added), it seems to me that the "gullible" woman standard is both irrelevant and unnecessary, and that the standard should be whether a reasonable person would construe the labeling and advertising as showing that the product was so intended....

NOTES

1. *Parallel Cases.* In *United States v. An Article ... "Line Away,"* 415 F.2d 369 (3d Cir. 1969), the court concluded that the promotional material for a similar product attributed drug characteristics to it:

> ... [T]he repeated statements that Line Away is made in a "pharmaceutical laboratory" and packaged under "biologically aseptic conditions" imply that the product itself is a pharmaceutical. Characterizing the lotion as "super-active" and "amazing," creating a "tingling sensation" when "at work," "tightening" the skin and "discouraging new wrinkles from forming" strongly reinforces the impression that this is a therapeutic product, the protein content of which has a tonic or otherwise wholesome physiological effect on the skin itself.... Even the denial that Line Away is a "hormone" or a "harmful drug," read in the context of the other representations, suggests that it is a harmless drug.
>
> Some "puffery" may not amount to representation of a cosmetic as a drug, but when "puffery" contains the strong therapeutic implications we find in the Line Away promotional material, we think the dividing line has been crossed.

But *United States v. An Article ... "Helene Curtis Magic Secret ...,"* 331 F. Supp. 912 (D. Md. 1971), held that Helene Curtis' very similar wrinkle smoother was a cosmetic and not a drug:

> ... The only two claims made for "Magic Secret" which even approach the magnitude of the claims made in *Line Away* and *Sudden Change* are that "Magic Secret" is a "pure protein" which causes an "astringent sensation." The promotional material does not emphasize these two claims and even the "ignorant, unthinking and credulous" consumer would not be led by these references to believe that "Magic Secret" would do other than alter their appearance. It is apparent that the promotional claims made for "Magic Secret" are less exaggerated than those reported in *Line Away* and *Sudden Change*. It cannot be said that they carry the same drug connotations as found by the Second and Third Circuits.

The court concluded that the product's promotional material would lead a prospective purchaser only to expect that she may look better, and not that the structure of the body would be affected.

2. *Current FDA Policy.* Beginning in April 1987, FDA sent regulatory letters to dozens of cosmetic manufacturers alleging that products for which "wrinkle remover" claims were made are illegal new drugs. "'Antiaging'

Creams Challenged," FDA Talk Paper No. T87–24 (May 14, 1987). A political Commentator had the following comment on this enforcement campaign:

> Wrinkle–Fighting potions are the loveliest delusion of our time. So, as might be expected, the Food and Drug Administration is attentively monitoring advertised hints that science has at last been successfully harnessed to the cause of eternally youthful skin.
>
> Ah, misguided FDA, are you so caught up on the truly worrisome problems of pills versus sickness that there's time to spare for America's harmless and futile quest to slow, maybe reverse, the facial signs of the passage of time?
>
> Never has so much done so little or produced such enduring hope.
>
> In a sensibly ordered society, could anything be less the business of government? Absolutely nothing.

Greenberg, "Federal Monitoring of Miracles," Baltimore Sun, June 10, 1986.

A series of meetings and correspondence between an industry coalition and FDA on this matter was abruptly terminated on November 19, 1987 by the following response of the FDA Associate Commissioner for Regulatory Affairs.

> We consider a claim that a product will affect the body in some physiological way to be a drug claim, even if the claim is that the effect is only temporary. Such a claim constitutes a representation that the product is intended to affect the structure or function of the body and thus makes the product a drug under 21 U.S.C. 321(g)(1)(C). Therefore, we consider most of the anti-aging and skin physiology claims that you outline in your letter to be drug claims. For example, claims that a product 'counteracts,' 'retards,' or 'controls' aging or the aging process, as well as claims that a product will 'rejuvenate,' 'repair,' or 'renew' the skin, are drug claims because they can be fairly understood as claims that a function of the body, or that the structure of the body, will be affected by the product. For this reason also, all of the examples that you use to allege an effect within the epidermis as the basis for a temporary beneficial effect on wrinkles, lines, or fine lines are unacceptable. A claim such as 'molecules absorb ... and expand, exerting upward pressure to 'lift' wrinkles 'upward' is a claim for an inner, structural change.

The Associate Commissioner did offer some guidelines for cosmetic claims:

> While we agree with your statements that wrinkles will not be reversed or removed by these products ... we would not object to claims that products will temporarily improve the appearance of such outward signs of aging. The label of such products should state that the product is intended to cover up the signs of aging, to improve the appearance by adding color or a luster to skin, or otherwise to affect the appearance through physical means....
>
> However, we would consider a product that claims to improve or to maintain temporarily the appearance or the feel of the skin to be a cosmetic. For example, a product that claims to moisturize or soften the skin is a cosmetic.

Although the FDA letter threatened prompt regulatory action, only one formal enforcement proceeding against any product or manufacturer had been initiated as of June 30, 1990. Meanwhile, negotiations between individual cosmetic manufacturers and FDA have continued. An attempt by one manufacturer to obtain clarification of the dividing line between cosmetic and drug claims for these products through a declaratory judgment action was thwarted when the court agreed with FDA's claim that the matter was not ripe for judicial review. *Estee Lauder, Inc. v. FDA,* 727 F. Supp. 1 (D.D.C. 1989).

3. *Commentary.* For additional discussion of the legal definition of a cosmetic, *see* Erlebacher, *When Is a "Cosmetic" Also a "Drug" Under the Federal Food, Drug and Cosmetic Act,* 27 FDC L.J. 740 (1972); Kleinfeld, *"Cosmetic" or "Drug"—The Minotaur's Labyrinth,* 22 FDC L.J. 376 (1967); McNamara, *Performance Claims for Skin Care Cosmetics,* 41 FDC L.J. 151 (1986); *Symposium on the Cosmetic-Drug Distinction,* 21 Drug Info. J. 377 (1987).

4. *Dermatologic Definition.* FDA scientists recognized very early that all cosmetics penetrate the skin and thus affect the body, as one wrote: "[T]here are few if any substances which are not absorbed through the intact skin, even though the idea is prevalent that the skin is a relatively effective barrier to its environment." Calvery, *Safeguarding Foods and Drugs in Wartime,* 32 American Scientist No. 2, at 103, 119 (1944). Some dermatologists have contended that, because all cosmetics necessarily affect the structure or function of the skin, the legal definition of a cosmetic should be changed to reflect biological reality. Kanof, *Cosmetic—A Definition in Law,* 6 Cutis 527 (1970); Editorial, *Cosmetic or Drug,* 212 J.A.M.A. 2255 (1970); *Cosmetic: Definition in Law,* 2 TGA Cosm. J., No. 4, at 20 (1970).

5. *Cosmetic/Drug Distinction.* A number of products fit both the cosmetic and the drug definitions. FDA has announced that mercury-containing cosmetics for use as skin-bleaching agents are also drugs, 21 C.F.R. § 700.13, 37 Fed. Reg. 12967 (June 30, 1972), 38 Fed. Reg. 853 (January 5, 1973). In proposing to recognize the second edition of the CTFA Cosmetic Ingredient Dictionary as a source for ingredient labeling, 42 Fed. Reg. 56757 (October 28, 1977), FDA listed 16 substances that the agency asserted were "generally recognized as drugs and are not known to be used as cosmetic ingredients" regardless of the claims made for them. Subsequently, the agency stated that the mere listing of "placental extract" on the labeling of a cosmetic would not necessarily constitute a drug claim. 45 Fed. Reg. 3574 (January 18, 1980).

When FDA published its tentative final monograph for topical OTC hormone drug products, 54 Fed. Reg. 40618 (October 2, 1989), determining that no product falling within this category is generally recognized as safe and effective, it specifically stated that:

> Skin care products that contained hormones are solely cosmetics if the claims in the labeling, promotional material, advertising, and other relevant materials are only cosmetic in nature (*e.g.,* to promote attractiveness), and no actual or implied therapeutic claims, or claims that the product will affect the structure or function of the body are made. The agency considers the use of the word "hormone" in the text of the labeling (*e.g.,* "This cream (or oil) is scientifically formulated to contain a hormone") or in the ingredient statement to be an implied drug claim.

The agency stated that the chemical name of the specific hormone could be included in the ingredient statement, or elsewhere in labeling, without converting the cosmetic into a drug. In FDA Compliance Program Guidance Manual 7329.001 (November 19, 1988), FDA took the position that sun products labeled with a specific sun protection factor (SPF), or containing sunscreen ingredients and making sunscreen claims, or listing a sunscreen ingredient as an active ingredient are drugs rather than cosmetics. No mention was made of the status of products containing sunscreen ingredients listed as inactive ingredients.

In *United States v. Articles of Drug for Veterinary Use ... Goshen Laboratories, Inc.*, FDA L. Rep. (CCH) ¶ 38,174 (S.D.N.Y. 1982), the claimant unsuccessfully argued that the veterinary products involved were "canine cosmetics" that are not subject to the FD&C Act and not animal drugs. When the new concept of "aroma therapy" was first advanced in the promotion of perfume, FDA announced that any specific claims for prevention or treatment of disease would result in the perfume becoming a drug. "Aroma Therapy," FDA Talk Paper No. T86–28 (April 23, 1986).

6. *OTC Drug Review.* The relationship between the Act's definitions of cosmetic and drug has frequently been at issue in the OTC Drug Review. In regulating hexachlorophene and TBS, *see* note 1, p. 838 *infra*, FDA promulgated identical but separate regulations covering cosmetic and drug use of these substances, thus obviating any consideration of the proper legal classification of particular products. For discussions of the various OTC drug monographs in which the cosmetic/drug distinction has been considered, *see* Gilbertson, *FDA OTC Drugs Standards Versus Cosmetic Standards*, 21 Drug Info. J. 379 (1987); McNamara, *The Food and Drug Administration Over-the-Counter Drug Review—Concerns of the Cosmetic Industry*, 38 FDC L. J. 289 (1983).

7. *Soap Exemption.* FDA has defined the scope of the soap exemption in 21 C.F.R. § 701.20, 23 Fed. Reg. 7483 (September 26, 1958). In *United States v. An Article of Cosmetic ... Beacon Castile Shampoo*, 1969–1974 FDLI Jud. Rec. 149 (N.D. Ohio 1973), the court held that the claimant had the burden of proving the product fell within the soap exemption. The court acknowledged that a shampoo made from soap would fall within that exemption, but concluded that the claimant's shampoo did not qualify because it contained a synthetic detergent.

8. *Food/Drug Distinction.* Compare the analogous issues raised by the relationship between the Act's definitions of food and drug, as exemplified by *National Nutritional Foods Ass'n v. FDA*, 504 F.2d 761 (2d Cir. 1974), p. 215 *supra*, and *National Nutritional Foods Ass'n v. Mathews*, 557 F.2d 325 (2d Cir. 1977), p. 29 *supra*.

C. ADULTERATED COSMETICS

UNITED STATES v. AN ARTICLE OF COSMETIC ... "BEACON CASTILE SHAMPOO ..."

United States District Court, Northern District of Ohio, 1974.
1969–1974 FDLI Jud. Rec. 160.

THE COURT:....

As the case was finally submitted to me for determination, the claim of the Government narrowed to a contention that the article of commerce is adulterated in that it contains deleterious substances, namely, potassium oleate and Neutronyx 600, which may render it injurious to users under such conditions of use as are customary or usual. Thus the claim is based on the wording of Section 361(a), which declares that "a cosmetic shall be deemed to be adulterated (A) if it bears or contains ... any deleterious substance which may render it injurious to users under the conditions of use prescribed in the labeling thereof, or under such conditions of use as are customary or usual."

Government's counsel has correctly noted that the meaning of the words "may render the deleterious substance injurious" actually bears the same meaning as given or interpreted by the United States Supreme Court in the case of *United States vs. Lexington Mill and Elevator Company* [p. 287 *supra*].... Further, I think it is correct and appropriate to observe and to determine here that the word "injurious" is understood to mean capable of causing physical harm when the cosmetic is rubbed or poured on or otherwise applied on the human body as intended. However, it is concluded that the physical harm which may result from the deleterious substance may be temporary as well as permanent.

However, if temporary, it should be objectively and medically demonstrable that it is damaging either externally or internally to a part of the body, including but not limited to the skin, tissues, or vessels of the body. It should be added that, as I construe the term, pain alone without objective injury would not be enough to establish the injurious character of the deleterious substance.

... Under the evidence in this case it develops that the potential harm of the subject Beacon Castile Shampoo relates to its full strength concentrate getting into the eyes of a human being. Hence it is essential to determine whether, within the second condition of 361(a), the Beacon Castile Shampoo is injurious to a user who is using the shampoo in a customary or usual manner. I, therefore, conclude that it is part of the government's burden of proof in this case to show that getting the full concentrate of shampoo into one's eyes would occur under a condition of use that is customary or usual.

There is no evidence in this record that shows exactly what condition of use is customary or usual in applying shampoo to the hair. But certainly the evidence in this record does not disclose any basis for inferring that one is likely to apply shampoo to the hair without water and, if so, that the full strength of the shampoo would trickle down undiluted into the eyes.... Similarly, I think there is no evidence here that it is a customary and usual use to apply the shampoo so closely to the eyes that it would enter the eye in a full concentrated condition.

But the Government's burden goes further. Assuming that full strength shampoo got into a user's eyes while washing his hair, it is my conclusion that it is the Government's further burden to show that the user would not then flush or wash out the eye in the customary and usual use of the shampoo.

The burden which I feel is imposed on the Government in this respect immediately takes us ... to the results of the Harris study..... [T]he Harris report shows, with reference to each of the instillations, whether it be quarter strength, half strength, or full strength, that there was ocular burning and irritation. Surely, in the customary and usual use of shampoo, if by accident some shampoo got into one's eye and caused ocular burning and irritation, the autonomic response of a human being would be to wash out his eye. Hence the Harris report, the keystone of the Government's case, fails to show that it was conducted under circumstances that represented the customary and usual use of the Beacon Castile Shampoo.

The significance of the omission of washing as a step in the protocol of the Harris human studies becomes quite apparent when the Marzulli studies are considered together with Dr. Marzulli's oral testimony of last Saturday. Dr. Marzulli's tests of March 25th, 1970, showed corneal epithelial damage to the eye of one of two rabbits where eyes were washed 30 seconds after the instillation of full strength Beacon, and significant iritis of the eyes of two rabbits washed after 30 seconds. It was quite clear in Dr. Marzulli's testimony of last Saturday that these findings were regarded by him as essential to his conclusions, for he testified in substance as follows—and these are my notes, but in substance this is the way I took down his testimony:

"We were concerned that shampoo that causes damage despite washing should not be marketed. If an eye is unwashed and produces injury to the cornea, that shampoo should not be marketed. If, in addition, flushing the eye 30 seconds after does not prevent injury, that shampoo should not be marketed." The absence of the washing step from the protocol of the Harris studies thus has this added result: It negatives the extrapolation of this key portion of the Marzulli rabbit studies, and thus the relevancy of the principal point in Dr. Marzulli's testimony is impaired.... Thus it is not the ocular burning that represents an injury.

There is also evidence in the human studies of mild-to-moderate injection of the conjunctiva; yet this is not deemed sufficient to constitute an injury within the contemplation of 361(a). Surely there are many soaps that might cause temporary redness to the conjunctiva, and yet I don't believe they would be subject to condemnation. Surely it is clear in the Harris studies that there is no injury to the iris of any of the 22 human subjects. And thus up to this point the human studies do not disclose any injury that I think would fall within the contemplation of 361(a).

There is, however, destruction of the corneal epithelium of Joan Hughes. This, it turned out, was a temporary destruction; and in accordance with the medical testimony that I received, the epithelium of Joan Hughes was reported by Dr. Harris as being restored in 72 hours. The evidence in the case seems to indicate that, when epithelium is destroyed, one third of it will be restored within the first 24 hours, the second third within the second 24 hours, and the third third within the third 24 hours.

This destruction of corneal epithelium is deemed to be and determined to be a sufficient injury to meet the meaning of the word "injurious" in 361(a), especially because there is certainly a basis for believing that there is a susceptibility to infection, though the evidence indicates that it is a very small possibility. And yet the possibility remains, and presumably within that very broad language of 361(a), the definition of "injurious," if there is a possibility of injury, this would constitute an injury within that term.

Then there were also two other persons of the 22 who had slight corneal staining, which is indicative of some slight corneal epithelial injury. But the significant point is that the injury of Joan Hughes occurred only when full strength shampoo was applied to her eye. And likewise, the slight corneal staining occurred only when the full strength Beacon shampoo was applied to the eyes of those two other subjects.... Thus the only evidence in this record that would sustain the Government's burden is the human studies as to the temporary injury that occurred to the cornea of Joan Hughes when full strength Beacon Castile Shampoo was applied to one of her eyes. Yet it is this full concentration that has previously not been proved by the Government, as I evaluate the evidence, as being shown to be a condition customary or usual in the use of a shampoo....

On the entire record, as I previously have shown, the Government has not proved that the use of the full concentrate in a manner that would get into the human eye while shampooing the hair represents a customary and usual use of the shampoo. In fact, that in the usual and customary use of this shampoo the full shampoo has not gotten into the eyes of the user is certainly a fair inference to draw from the facts set forth in the stipulation.

Those facts show that the Claimant, Consolidated Royal Chemical Company, has manufactured and sold over two million gallons of shampoo of this formulation from August 11th, 1958, to the date of seizure in January, 1971. Approximately eight to ten million bottles of this product have been sold, usually in 16, 32 and 64 ounce containers. During this period neither Claimant nor its insurers received any claim of injury to the eyes of a user.

And, therefore, on the entire record, I conclude and determine that the Government has failed to establish its requisite burden of proof....

NOTES

1. *Baby Shampoo.* On April 4, 1979, FDA's Associate Commissioner for Compliance sent the following letter to R. C. Stites, President of Johnson & Johnson Baby Product Company:

On June 17, 1978, you submitted a petition requesting that the Commissioner of Food and Drugs propose regulations ... defining the term "baby shampoo" for the purpose of cosmetic labeling and requiring that shampoos so designated comply with prescribed animal testing requirements to demonstrate ocular safety.... For the reasons stated below, the agency is denying your petition....

... Your petition contains no data to support the allegation that baby shampoos contain a deleterious substance that may render them injurious to babies' eyes under customary conditions of use. It simply notes society's emphasis upon the safety of products designed for use on babies and young children and asserts that baby shampoos should be subject to more stringent safety requirements. It is argued that baby shampoos may accidentally spill into babies' eyes. While this may be true, you have not submitted data to support your conclusion....

... You presented a 1976 consumer perception survey to support the allegation that a "baby shampoo" that is a potential eye irritant is misbranded because, to consumers, a "baby shampoo" is expected to be "more gentle and mild and less irritating to eyes and scalp than a product labeled 'shampoo.'" This comparative definition of the term "baby shampoo" is not adequately supported by the results of the survey. Furthermore, in our view, the survey results are undermined by the possibility of bias because an inherently comparison-oriented situation was used in conducting the survey....

Finally, we agree that a rabbit eye irritation test similar to the one you propose would be capable of distinguishing between moderately or strongly irritating shampoos and those which possess little or no potential for ocular irritancy. However, it is generally recognized that the rabbit eye irritation test is not capable of making fine distinctions between degrees of irritancy. Our understanding of the standard your petition sets forth includes the requirement that "baby shampoos" are, among other characteristics, free of stinging and burning qualities.... These characteristics cannot be measured by the rabbit eye irritation test....

21 CFR 10.30(e)(1) provides that the Commissioner shall review and rule upon a petition, taking into consideration, *inter alia,* the agency resources available to handle the category of subject matter involved and the priority assigned to the petition in relation both to the category of subject matter involved and the overall work of the agency.... This means that a petition such as yours must establish, by adequate supporting documentation, that a health problem exists which, in comparison with health problems that are currently being addressed by the agency, warrants the reallocation of FDA resources. Your petition fails to do this....

Johnson & Johnson submitted a new citizen petition (No. 80P-0139/CP) on April 8, 1980, with additional information supporting its request that all baby shampoos be required to pass a standard rabbit eye safety test, but FDA again denied the petition on October 5, 1981, concluding that there was no basis for requiring baby shampoos to be safer than other shampoos, that no evidence demonstrated that baby eyes are different than adult eyes, and that available data did not demonstrate a significant difference between babies and other age groups in injury frequency from shampoos.

2. *Cosmetic GMPs.* On the need for cosmetic GMP regulations, *see* Milardo, *Quality Assurance Guidelines—The Industry's Viewpoint,* 31 FDC L.J. 105

(1976); Pietrangelo, *Cosmetic Quality Assurance—Alias Cosmetic Good Manufacturing Practices*, 31 FDC L.J. 167 (1976); Wenninger, *Quality Assurance Procedures for the Cosmetic Industry—The FDA's Viewpoint*, 31 FDC L.J. 101 (1976).

CTFA, the cosmetic industry trade association, submitted a citizen petition (No. 77P–0315) to FDA on July 28, 1977, requesting the promulgation of cosmetic GMP regulations. No action was ever taken by FDA on this petition. FDA stated in October 1977 that it intended to propose GMP regulations with respect to preservative systems in mascara and other eye area cosmetic products, 42 Fed. Reg. 54837 (October 11, 1977), but no action was ever taken on this matter. Current FDA views with respect to cosmetic GMP are reflected in the yearly revisions to the cosmetic provisions of the FDA Inspection Operations Manual and Compliance Program Guidance Manual.

3. *GMPs for Cosmetic–Drugs.* In response to a CTFA comment urging that products that fall within both the cosmetic and the drug provisions of the Act be subject to different GMP requirements than other drug products, FDA defended the need for covering all drug products with the same GMP requirements:

> ... A number of comments, including a petition to the Commissioner, were received regarding the applicability of the proposed general CGMP regulations to a class of products identified as cosmetic-drug products and described as those which: (1) Meet the definitions of both "drug" and "cosmetic" under section 201 of the act; (2) represent a minimum health or safety risk; and (3) are marketed over-the-counter for regular and frequent consumer use without dosage limitations. Examples of these products are described as medicated skin creams, antibacterial soap, antiperspirants, and topical sunburn prevention products. Specifically, the comments requested separate CGMP regulations for this alleged class of drugs....
>
> The Commissioner has concluded that these regulations ... must apply to all products meeting the definition of drug products, whether the drug products are highly potent prescription drugs or are OTC drugs of the type described as "cosmetic-type." Past experience of the agency has demonstrated that the public has been put in a hazardous situation because of manufacturing errors in OTC products.... That many of the general CGMP regulations are applicable to and reasonable for the cosmetic-type drug products is evidenced by the fact that a majority of the specific suggestions submitted by the petitioner and others as applicable for cosmetic-type drug products duplicated in substance, a number of comments submitted by other OTC manufacturers and manufacturers of prescription drug products....

43 Fed. Reg. 45014, 45027–45028 (September 29, 1978).

4. *Commentary.* For an early FDA review of potential toxicity problems raised by cosmetics, *see* Lehman, *Toxicological Aspects of Certain Types of Cosmetics*, 15 FDC L.J. 399 (1960).

AEROSOL DRUG AND COSMETIC PRODUCTS
CONTAINING ZIRCONIUM

42 Federal Register 41374 (August 16, 1977).

... In the Federal Register of June 5, 1975 (40 FR 24328), the Commissioner proposed that any aerosol drug or cosmetic product containing zirconium is a new drug or an adulterated cosmetic....

The June 5, 1975 proposal was in response to a report submitted to the Commissioner by the over-the-counter (OTC) Panel on Review of Antiperspirant Drug Products. This panel concluded in their report that zirconium compounds have caused skin granulomas and toxic effects in the lungs and other organs of experimental animals and expressed concern about the potential toxicity of such compounds when used in humans over an extended period of time. Although extensive animal toxicity data were received, these data failed to provide a basis for establishment of a safe level for long-term use. The panel also concluded that the benefit likely to be derived from the use of zirconium-containing aerosol antiperspirants is unsupportable in view of the risks involved....

Therefore, the panel recommended that:

1. All zirconium-containing aerosol antiperspirants be placed in Category II (not generally recognized as safe), and

2. Because conclusive testing to establish the safety might take years to accomplish, the Commissioner should take immediate steps to remove these ingredients from interstate commerce until safety has been demonstrated.

The Commissioner ... adopted their position in the June 5, 1975 proposal. He further concluded that, based on this adverse benefit-to-risk ratio and the recommendation for prompt action, any delay in action regarding the use of these drug and cosmetic products was unjustified and contrary to the public interest.....

Because it appears that conclusive testing to establish the safety of zirconium-containing aerosol antiperspirants would take years to accomplish, and because during that time millions of consumers would be unnecessarily subjected to risk, the Commissioner has decided to stop movement of these agents in interstate commerce until safety testing adequate for approval of a new drug application has been done, as recommended in the proposed rule making.

Based on the estimates of outstanding stocks of zirconium-containing aerosol antiperspirants currently on the market, and in keeping with the conclusions presented in the proposed rule making that the major safety issue is attributable to prolonged use, the Commissioner does not at this time anticipate that a recall of previously marketed zirconium-containing aerosol drug and cosmetic products is necessary to protect the public health....

The available toxicological data indicate that zirconium compounds may be responsible for human skin granulomas as well as toxic effects in the lungs and other internal organs of test animals. Accordingly, these ingredients in aerosol formulations are not generally recognized as safe, and the Commissioner considers any drug product containing zirconium in aerosol form to be a new drug. Furthermore, the Commissioner believes that the available information is sufficient to show that aerosol cosmetic products containing zirconium may be injurious to users. The regulation as proposed stated that regulatory action was being taken with respect to cosmetic products "[b]ased upon the lack of toxicological data adequate to establish a safe level for use * * *." The final regulation relating to cosmetic products has been revised to delete this phrase, to identify the risks from zirconium use that are of concern, and to refer to the statutory test for determining when a product is adulterated....

§ 700.16 Use of aerosol cosmetic products containing zirconium

(a) Zirconium-containing complexes have been used as an ingredient in cosmetics and/or cosmetics that are also drugs, as, for example, aerosol antiperspirants. Evidence indicates that certain zirconium compounds have caused human skin granulomas and toxic effects in the lungs and other organs of experimental animals. When used in aerosol form, some zirconium will reach the deep portions of the lungs of users. The lung is an organ, like skin, subject to the development of granulomas. Unlike the skin, the lung will not reveal the presence of granulomatous changes until they have become advanced and, in some cases, permanent. It is the view of the Commissioner that zirconium is a deleterious substance that may render any cosmetic aerosol product that contains it injurious to users....

NOTES

1. *Banned Ingredients.* Other substances banned by FDA under the cosmetic adulteration provisions of the FD&C Act are listed at 21 C.F.R. §§ 700.11–700.23. Examples include hexachlorophene, 37 Fed. Reg. 219 (January 7, 1972), 37 Fed. Reg. 20160 (September 27, 1972); vinyl chloride, 39 Fed. Reg. 14215 (April 22, 1974), 39 Fed. Reg. 30830 (August 26, 1974); halogenated salicylanilides, 39 Fed. Reg. 33102 (September 13, 1974), 40 Fed. Reg. 50527 (October 30, 1975); chloroform, 41 Fed. Reg. 15026 (April 9, 1976), 41 Fed. Reg. 26842 (June 29, 1976); chlorofluorocarbon propellants, 41 Fed. Reg. 52070 (November 26, 1976), 42 Fed. Reg. 24536 (May 13, 1977), 43 Fed. Reg. 11301 (March 17, 1978); and methylene chloride, 54 Fed. Reg. 27328 (June 29, 1989).

FDA has also proposed to ban 2–mercaptoimidazoline, 39 Fed. Reg. 15306 (May 2, 1974), and trichloroethylene 42 Fed. Reg. 49467 (September 27, 1977). As of June 30, 1990, no further action had been taken on either proposal.

2. *OTC Drug Review.* The impact of the OTC Drug Review on the status of substances also used in cosmetic products is discussed in Giovacchini, *The Significance of the Over–the–Counter Drug Review with Respect to the Safety Considerations of Cosmetic Ingredients,* 30 FDC L.J. 223 (1975); Yingling, *The*

Effect of the FDA's OTC Drug Review Program on the Cosmetic Industry, 33 FDC L.J. 78 (1978).

3. *EC Regulation.* The European Community adopted Council Directive 76/768/EEC relating to cosmetic products, Official Journal of the European Communities No. L 262, p. 169 (July 27, 1976) which requires that cosmetic products "must not be liable to cause damage to human health when they are applied under normal conditions of use." In contrast to the United States, where the only cosmetic ingredients requiring approval before they may be used are color additives, the EC directive adopts a listing approach for all cosmetic ingredients. Thus, the EC has issued several annexes listing provisional, permanent, and restricted (including banned) substances, and substances left to regulation by individual countries.

NITROSAMINE–CONTAMINATED COSMETICS; CALL FOR INDUSTRY ACTION; REQUEST FOR DATA

44 Federal Register 21365 (April 10, 1979).

... Some nitrosamines are potent animal carcinogens. The carcinogenicity of NDELA at high dose levels has been established in two animal species....

A limited number of cosmetic products have been analyzed for NDELA in both private and FDA laboratories. A number of these products were found to be contaminated with NDELA. The contamination is believed to be caused by the chemical reaction between the amines used to formulate the products and a nitrosating agent.... Analytical methods for identifying nitrosamines such as NDELA at concentrations of parts per million (ppm) and parts per billion (ppb) are quite new.... Analyses were made of 29 cosmetics thought likely to contain such contamination. It was found that 27 of the 29 contained up to 48 ppm of NDELA....

Recent studies have also been conducted in FDA laboratories to determine whether NDELA penetrates the skin. The agency now has evidence that NDELA penetrates excised human skin from an aqueous vehicle. One study that has been completed demonstrated that NDELA penetrates the skin of live monkeys....

The Commissioner of Food and Drugs has therefore determined that cosmetics containing nitrosamines may be considered adulterated under section 601 of the Federal Food, Drug, and Cosmetic Act. Cosmetic manufacturers are put on notice that cosmetic products may be analyzed by FDA for nitrosamine contamination and that individual products could be subject to enforcement action. However, the Commissioner is still considering whether a compliance program is needed to reduce or eliminate nitrosamine contamination in cosmetics, and, if so, what the nature of the program should be. Three factors will influence the Commissioner's decision on how to proceed in this matter:

1. The results of FDA's continuing efforts to understand better the nature of the problem and the means of reducing or preventing it. . . .

2. The extent to which the public health risk is alleviated by industry reformulation of products.

3. The results of FDA's continuing efforts to determine the extent of the formation of, and human exposure to, nitrosamines in cosmetics. . . .

NOTES

1. *Nitrosamines.* FDA has continued to express concern about nitrosamines in cosmetics (as well as in food and drugs), but as of June 30, 1990 had not adopted a specific tolerance level or taken formal regulatory action against products containing nitrosamines.

2. *Enforcement History.* The following summary illustrates the variety of circumstances in which FDA has brought court enforcement action or requested recalls to protect consumers against unsafe cosmetics:

Early in 1978, FDA received about 50 complaints of hair breakage and scalp irritation associated with a hair straightener. An investigation disclosed that a compounding error had resulted in one batch of the product containing 60% more than the intended level of free caustic (sodium hydroxide). During the course of the FDA investigation the firm recalled the product.

In 1974 consumer complaints of fingernail injuries associated with the use of certain nail extenders led FDA to investigate the problem. It was determined that the methyl methacrylate monomer used in these products was causing the injuries. The FDA obtained a court order to seize the offending product. Similar products were voluntarily recalled by the distributors and some have since been reformulated. . . .

During 1976 and 1977, a number of consumer complaints that a nail hardener had caused serious allergic and irritant effects were received. An investigation and subsequent laboratory analyses demonstrated that the product contained formaldehyde at a potentially harmful concentration. The product was seized in August 1977.

Fifteen consumer complaints of axillary irritation from a new deodorant were received during 1976. During the course of the investigation of the problem, FDA was notified by the firm that distribution of the product had been terminated. The adverse experiences reported to FDA were not serious enough to warrant regulatory action.

During 1976–1978 an unusually large number of consumer complaints concerning one brand of suntan product were received. The ensuing investigation disclosed that the firm also had received many complaints. Many of the adverse experiences appeared to be a form of photocontact dermatitis. Research sponsored by the firm and investigations by FDA identified 6–methylcoumarin (6–MC), a fragrance ingredient in the suntan products, as a potent photocontact allergen.

When FDA learned that 6–MC was commonly used in suntan or sunscreen products, telegrams were sent to all known domestic firms which either market suntan/sunscreen products or distribute fragrance compounds to the cosmetics industry, requesting that they immediately terminate the use of 6–MC in all topical products and recall existing stocks of suntans or sunscreen products containing 6–MC....

Grief, *et al.*, "Cosmetics Regulation," 7 FDA By–Lines 331, 333–334 (September 1979).

3. *Child Resistant Packaging.* Because of a report of accidental poisoning from ingestion of a solvent product intended for use in the removal of sculptured nails, Caravati & Litovitz, *Pediatric Cyanide Intoxication and Death from an Acetonitrile–Containing Cosmetic,* 260 J.A.M.A. 3470 (December 16, 1988), CTFA submitted a petition and the Consumer Product Safety Commission promulgated a regulation requiring child-resistant packaging under the Poison Prevention Packaging Act to protect against accidental ingestion of acetonitrile contained in glue removers, 55 Fed. Reg. 1456 (January 16, 1990), 55 Fed. Reg. 5,897 (December 8, 1990). The Drug and Household Substance Mailing Act of 1990, 104 Stat. 1184, prohibits the mailing of any cosmetic that fails to comply with an applicable requirement for child-resistant packaging.

4. *Opposition to Animal Testing.* Paradoxically, at the same time that the public and FDA are demanding greater assurance of safety of all FDA-regulated products, animal rights activists are demanding an end to the type of animal testing used to evaluate product toxicity. The cosmetic industry has been a principal target of the animal rights proponents. For a discussion of the issues involved, *see* National Academy of Sciences, USE OF LABORATORY ANIMALS IN BIOMEDICAL AND BEHAVIORAL RESEARCH (1988); Office of Technology Assessment, ALTERNATIVES TO ANIMAL USE IN RESEARCH, TESTING, AND EDUCATION, OTA–BA–273 (1986).

Faced with these attacks, some cosmetic industry officials have promised to end animal testing, and some firms have promoted their products as not tested on animals (*e.g.,* "beauty without cruelty"). In a decision handed down in December 1988 by a Higher Regional Court in Frankfurt, Germany, however, the representation of "beauty without cruelty" was held to be misleading, and thus illegal, unless the manufacturer can demonstrate that neither the finished product nor any of the ingredients has *ever* been tested in animals by itself or by anyone else. Such a showing would be impossible for any ingredient in any consumer product.

5. *Mailing Fragrances.* The Drug and Household Substance Mailing Act of 1990, 104 Stat. 1184, prohibits the mailing of any fragrance advertising sample unless it is sealed or otherwise prepared to prevent individuals from being unknowingly or involuntarily exposed to the sample.

D. MISBRANDED COSMETICS
PRESERVATION OF COSMETICS COMING IN CONTACT WITH THE EYE: INTENT TO PROPOSE REGULATIONS AND REQUEST FOR INFORMATION
42 Federal Register 54837 (October 11, 1977).

... FDA has received several reports of corneal ulceration associated with the use of cosmetic mascaras containing pathogenic microorganisms.... Mascaras can become contaminated with various microorganisms when the consumer uses the product and re-inserts the applicator wand into the container after application of the mascara to the eye lashes. The re-insertion of the applicator wand into the mascara is part of the intended or customary conditions of use of the products. Without an adequate preservative system, microorganisms introduced into the mascara with the applicator wand can survive and multiply inside the container. When the mascara is used again, if the microorganisms on the applicator wand come into contact with a scratched or damaged cornea, the eye may become infected....

The reported incidents all involve mascaras in which the microorganism *Pseudomonas aeruginosa* has been found. *Pseudomonas aeruginosa* is an ubiquitous bacterium that may be present on the skin as a transient microorganism. It may readily grow in a cosmetic unless the cosmetic contains a preservative adequate to prevent contamination. *Pseudomonas aeruginosa* infections, if not recognized and treated immediately, can cause corneal ulceration that leads to partial or total blindness in the injured eye....

The Commissioner believes that the preservative systems used in mascara and other eye-contact products should be adequate not only to prevent the further growth of microorganisms introduced during use but also to reduce significantly the number of microorganisms introduced during use. The Commissioner expects to promulgate all-inclusive regulations delineating good manufacturing practice for cosmetics at some point, and he intends to propose regulations regarding microbial preservation of cosmetics coming in contact with the eye as a first step.....

The Commissioner also advises that he considers inadequately preserved cosmetics to be in violation of the Act. Under section 601 of the act, a cosmetic is considered adulterated if it is prepared under conditions whereby it may have been rendered injurious to health, as well as if it bears any poisonous or deleterious substance that may render it injurious to users under the conditions of use. Furthermore, under sections 201(n), 601, and 602 of the act and 21 CFR 740.10, the label must bear any warning statements that are necessary or appropriate to prevent a health hazard that may be associated with the product. Manufacturers and distributors should be advised that FDA.... does not intend to await the completion of the rule making proceeding announced in this notice of intent before taking needed regulatory action....

FOOD, DRUG, AND COSMETIC PRODUCTS:
WARNING STATEMENTS
40 Federal Register 8912 (March 3, 1975).

The Commissioner of Food and Drugs is establishing required warnings for certain food, drug, and cosmetic products. Products packaged in self-pressurized containers are required to bear warnings to ensure their safe use and storage. Aerosol products containing halocarbon or hydrocarbon propellants are required to bear warnings against the dangers of deliberate concentration and inhalation. Cosmetic products whose safety has not been adequately substantiated are required to warn of that fact on the label. . . .

The Commissioner concludes that section 201(n) of the act applies in those situations where abuse has become sufficiently frequent to constitute a hazard of widespread public concern. Section 201(n) of the act is applicable to require affirmative disclosures in the light of representations and also to reveal consequences of customary or usual conditions of use. The very act of representing a product for food, drug, or cosmetic use constitutes an inherent implied representation of its safety. Warnings to ensure safe use are therefore within the scope of section 201(n) of the act. Moreover, the customary or usual conditions of use of such products often involve little or no protection against their misuse, where no warning exists. Accordingly, section 201(n) of the act is applicable to assure that consumers will understand, and guard against, the potential consequences of inadvertent misuse under conditions of such customary or usual conditions of use. In addition, the Commissioner advises that "conditions of use" is not a narrow term limited to the active handling, operation, and application of a product, but rather includes the entire setting and circumstances in which a product is used. The usual conditions of use of aerosol products are, that once purchased, they are freely available to all members of a household. Thus, warnings against misuse of aerosol products may alert parents of adolescent children to take precautions to ensure that such products in the household are not misused. . . .

The availability of section 201(n) of the act to require an explicit warning against misuse was upheld in *United States v. 12 Bottles of Esterex* (E.D. Mo. 1946), reported in V. Kleinfeld C. Dunn, Federal Food, Drug and Cosmetic Act 1938–1949 at 523, 525. . . . .

The Commissioner advises that the safety of a product can be adequately substantiated through (a) reliance on already available toxicological test data on individual ingredients and on product formulations that are similar in composition to the particular cosmetic, and (b) performance of any additional toxicological and other tests that are appropriate in the light of such existing data and information. Although satisfactory toxicological data may exist for each ingredient of a cosmetic, it will still be necessary to conduct some toxicological testing with the complete formulation to assure adequately the safety of the finished cosmetic. . . .

The Commissioner recognizes that a manufacturer of a cosmetic ingredient cannot always foresee, much less control, the uses of the ingredient in cosmetic products, and therefore cannot be held responsible for the safety of the ingredient under every possible condition of use. The manufacturer is responsible, however, for the safety of the ingredient under the conditions of use recommended in its labeling as well as reasonably expected related uses, and the safety of the ingredient must be adequately substantiated for use under these conditions if the label does not bear the warning statement required by § 740.1.....

One comment argued that substantiation of safety amounts to premarketing review of cosmetics since the manufacturer would have to meet the "vague" standard of adequate substantiation for safety before his cosmetics could be marketed, and would bear the burden of meeting this standard in a court review.

... It is the manufacturer, not the Food and Drug Administration who is responsible for having his product in compliance with the act and regulations promulgated thereunder. The act necessarily contemplates that the manufacturer has assured itself of the safety of its product, but in no way does this imply Food and Drug Administration approval or review prior to marketing....

Part 740—Cosmetic Product Warning Statements

§ 740.1 Establishment of warning statements

(a) The label of a cosmetic product shall bear a warning statement whenever necessary or appropriate to prevent a health hazard that may be associated with the product.

(b) The Commissioner of Food and Drugs, either on his own initiative or on behalf of any interested person who has submitted a petition, may publish a proposal to establish or amend, under Subpart B of this part, a regulation prescribing a warning for a cosmetic.....

§ 740.10 Labeling of cosmetic products for which adequate substantiation of safety has not been obtained

(a) Each ingredient used in a cosmetic product and each finished cosmetic product shall be adequately substantiated for safety prior to marketing. Any such ingredient or product whose safety is not adequately substantiated prior to marketing is misbranded unless it contains the following conspicuous statement on the principal display panel:

Warning—The safety of this product has not been determined.

(b) An ingredient or product having a history of use in or as a cosmetic may at any time have its safety brought into question by new information that in itself is not conclusive. The warning required by paragraph (a) of this section is not required for such an ingredient or product if:

> (1) The safety of the ingredient or product had been adequately substantiated prior to development of the new information;

> (2) The new information does not demonstrate a hazard to human health; and

(3) Adequate studies are being conducted to determine expeditiously the safety of the ingredient or product.

(c) Paragraph (b) of this section does not constitute an exemption to the adulteration provisions of the act or to any other requirement in the act or this chapter.

§ 740.11 Cosmetics in self-pressurized containers

(a)(1) The label of a cosmetic packaged in a self-pressurized container and intended to be expelled from the package under pressure shall bear the following warning:

> *Warning*—Avoid spraying in eyes. Contents under pressure. Do not puncture or incinerate. Do not store in temperature above 120 F. Keep out of reach of children....

NOTES

1. *Judicial Affirmance.* FDA's aerosol warning was upheld in *Cosmetic, Toiletry, and Fragrance Ass'n, Inc. v. Schmidt*, 409 F. Supp. 57 (D.D.C. 1976).

2. *Feminine Deodorant Sprays.* At the same time, FDA prescribed a warning statement for feminine deodorant sprays, 21 C.F.R. § 740.12, 38 Fed. Reg. 16236 (June 21, 1973), 40 Fed. Reg. 8926 (March 3, 1975). FDA concluded that "the reported adverse reactions do not demonstrate a health hazard which is serious enough to justify removal of these products from the market" but agreed with comments that "these sprays offer no medical usefulness or hygienic benefits" and therefore stated that the use of the term "hygienic" would render the products misbranded under section 602(a).

3. *Talcum Powders.* A citizen petition (No. 83P–0404), submitted on December 2, 1983, requesting FDA to require a label warning for cosmetic talcum powders because of their potential asbestos content, was denied by FDA on July 21, 1986.

4. *Bubble Bath.* The need for a label warning for bubble bath products provoked dispute between FDA and the cosmetic industry for a full decade. FDA proposed a label warning about irritation of the skin and urinary tract from bubble bath products in 42 Fed. Reg. 5368 (January 28, 1977). Manufacturers commented that the incidence of problems was trivial. In 45 Fed. Reg. 55172 (August 19, 1980), however, FDA promulgated a final regulation requiring a warning, stating that the number of reported reactions was "sufficiently large enough to indicate a public hazard." In response to an industry petition, FDA stayed the regulation and requested further comment in 48 Fed. Reg. 7169 and 7203 (February 18, 1983). After further comment, FDA reinstated the warning in 51 Fed. Reg. 20471 (June 5, 1986), but excluded products labeled exclusively for adults. Industry again petitioned FDA for reconsideration but the petition was denied and the regulation has become effective.

5. *Disclosure to Dermatologists.* It is common practice for cosmetic companies to provide the components of their products to dermatologists to use in skin patch tests on patients to determine sensitivity to particular substances. *See, e.g.,* March, *Editorial: Cosmetic Formula Information*, 216 J.A.M.A. 1337 (May 24, 1971); CTFA, COSMETIC INDUSTRY ON CALL (1988). FDA encourages this practice, 21 C.F.R. § 720.4(b)(4). In 51 Fed. Reg. 33664 (September 22, 1986), FDA took the position that all skin patch test kits "intended for

commercial marketing" are drugs or biologics that require FDA approval. This would permit cosmetic companies to continue their present practice but would prohibit the marketing of commercial kits without FDA approval.

6. *Failure to Warn as Misbranding.* *See also* 16 C.F.R. § 1500.81(a), originally promulgated by FDA under the Federal Hazardous Substances Act before it was transferred to the Consumer Product Safety Commission, which provides that where a cosmetic "offers a substantial risk of injury or illness from any handling or use that is customary or usual it may be regarded as misbranded under the Federal Food, Drug, and Cosmetic Act because its label fails to reveal material facts with respect to consequences that may result from use of the article (21 U.S.C. 321(n)) when its label fails to bear information to alert the householder to this hazard."

ALMAY, INC. v. CALIFANO

United States Court of Appeals, District of Columbia Circuit, 1977.
569 F.2d 674.

MARKEY, Chief Judge, United States Court of Customs and Patent Appeals: . . . .

On February 25, 1974, appellee Food and Drug Administration (FDA) in accordance with 21 U.S.C. §§ 321(m), 362(a), and 371(a), initiated informal rulemaking proceedings by publishing a proposed regulation governing hypoallergenic cosmetics, under which:

> A cosmetic may be designated in its labeling by words that state or imply that the product of any ingredient thereof is "hypoallergenic" if it has been shown by scientific studies that the relative frequency of adverse reactions in human subjects from the test product is significantly less than the relative frequency of such reactions from each reference product(s). [39 F.R. 7291.]

The lynch-pin of the regulation was its requirement for employment of "comparison testing," *i.e.,* for testing the labeled product against "reference product(s)" defined in the regulation as "similar-use competitive products in the same cosmetic product category" and representing a market share of 10%. Adoption of the comparison testing method rested entirely on the Commissioner's adoption of a comparative definition: "the term 'hypoallergenic' means to the consumer that the product causes fewer adverse reactions than other, similar-type use products ... " and the feeling that, while use of "hypoallergenic" has expanded over the years, the difference between "hypoallergenic" cosmetics and those not so labeled has become less distinct.

Included in the preamble were comments of the Cosmetic, Toiletry and Fragrance Association (CFTA), the Bureau of Consumer Protection of the Federal Trade Commission (FTC), and appellant Almay Corporation (Almay). CFTA alleged that "there is no demonstrated need nor is it practicable for the minimizing of allergic reactions to be an overriding consideration in all aspects of production and marketing of every cosmetic product".... Almay objected to the comparison testing method because the composition of the selected reference products could not be predicted..... [T]he FTC filed the results of a consumer survey on hypoallergenic cosmetics, and ... comments thereon by the Director of FTC's Bureau of Consumer Protection.....

Comments were also submitted by a number of dermatologists, consumer groups, and individual consumers. Eight dermatologists favored testing in which a product would have to demonstrate an extremely low potential for allergic reaction to qualify as hypoallergenic. Seven dermatologists opposed the comparison test method, and one was non-committal. Four consumer groups took issue with the comparative definition as likely to cause confusion among users of hypoallergenic cosmetics. One consumer group was in general agreement with the FDA proposal.....

FDA justified its decision to define "hypoallergenic" as meaning less allergenic than some competing products on what it considered confusion in the use of the term..... The district court found the Commissioner's definition supported by two factors in the administrative record: (1) a significantly greater number of consumers believed that "hypoallergenic" meant "safer than competitors" rather than "very safe," and (2) a comparative definition would be more helpful to consumers because adverse reactions to cosmetic products are relatively rare today overall.....

Involved here is an informal rulemaking proceeding, in which no hearing is required. The scope of review is therefore governed by the "arbitrary or capricious" standards set out in the Administrative Procedure Act, 5 U.S.C. § 706(2)(A).....

The fact that an "arbitrary and capricious" standard applies to informal rulemaking, rather than a "substantial evidence" requirement, cannot mean that *nothing* of an evidentiary nature is needed in the administrative record to support an agency decision. On the contrary, there being no evidentiary hearing, informal rulemaking proceedings are much more susceptible to abuse, and it becomes all the more important that a rational basis for the agency's decision be found in the facts of record....

FDA relies first on the preamble to its own proposed regulation in support of the Commissioner's conclusion. Respecting the definition of "hypoallergenic," the preamble is conclusory. The only authorities cited are a dictionary which defines "hypo" to mean "under," "beneath," "down," "less than normal," of "the lowest position in a series of compounds;" and the statement of an AMA Committee on Cutaneous Health and Cosmetics that "the term 'hypoallergenic' as applied to cosmetics has outlived its usefulness, is misleading, and should be dropped from the labeling of cosmetic products."

... The dictionary definition clearly does not support the Commissioner's decision to define "hypoallergenic" as causing "fewer reactions than *some* [10% of the market] products."

... In light of the AMA report's conclusion that "hypoallergenic" should be dropped entirely, and of its further statement that "little distinction can be made between established cosmetic products as to their sensitization potential," it was inappropriate to cite the AMA report in support of any use whatever of "hypoallergenic," no matter how defined.

FDA relied also on the FTC survey.... In drawing inference from the FTC survey, the Commissioner failed to consider a relevant factor— the comments of the FTC's Director of the Bureau of Consumer Protection..... The Director ... stated on the record that the survey: (1) was limited in population sample and number of questions; (2) was silent in important respects; (3) lacked a breakdown between users and non-users; (4) lacked a tabulation; (5) established that consumers lacked medical knowledge sufficient to distinguish skin reactions; (6) produced results which should be used with caution; and (7) probably produced fewer "correct" definitions because it was not limited to consumers interested in the subject, *i.e.,* hypoallergenic cosmetic users. Finally, the survey defined the "correct" definition as "less likely to cause irritation than regular cosmetics," yet the Commissioner chose a different definition: "less likely to cause adverse reactions than some [10% of market] similar-use competitive products in the same category."

We are fully aware of the caveat that we must not substitute our judgment for that of the regulator, nor shall we. We are equally aware, however, of the need for rationality, in the interest not only of justice, our major concern, but in the interest of the continued viability and public acceptance of the federal regulatory scheme itself....

An aura of unreality surrounds the creation of a definition in the present case. In the apparent belief that most products are today non-allergenic, it may have been thought that producers could not find 10% of marketed products producing more reactions and that use of "hypoallergenic" would thereupon cease. If so, the cumbersome method here chosen to achieve that result is an irrational substitute for a direct prohibition of all use of "hypoallergenic." ...

NOTES

1. *Revocation of Regulation.* FDA revoked this regulation in 43 Fed. Reg. 10559 (March 14, 1978), and has not since initiated regulatory action against cosmetic products labeled as hypoallergenic.

2. *Misleading Claims.* For a list of cosmetic claims that FDA regarded as false or misleading in 1939, *see* FDA Trade Correspondence 10 (August 2, 1939), 1938–1949 FDLI Jud. Rec. at 566.

3. *"See Through" Labels.* FDA once proposed to ban, as misbranded, all "see-through" cosmetic labels (*i.e.,* labels that can be read only through the

container and its contents), 39 Fed. Reg. 25328 (July 10, 1974), but later relented, 44 Fed. Reg. 47547 (August 14, 1979).

E. COSMETIC INGREDIENT LABELING
VOLUNTARY INGREDIENT LABELING:
NOTICE TO COSMETIC MANUFACTURERS AND DISTRIBUTORS
37 Federal Register 16208 (August 11, 1972).

Regulatory initiatives. In the FEDERAL REGISTER of April 11, 1972 (37 F.R. 7151), the Commissioner of Food and Drugs ... announced that the Food and Drug Administration would give consideration to publishing a proposal under the Fair Packaging and Labeling Act for the labeling of ingredients....

Legislative initiatives. Title IV of S. 3419, passed by the Senate on June 21, 1972, would require cosmetic ingredient labeling. No comparable provision appears in the House version of this legislation (H.R. 15003) which was reported out of the House Committee on Interstate and Foreign Commerce on June 1, 1972....

Voluntary initiatives. The President's Special Assistant for Consumer Affairs ... and the Food and Drug Administration have received requests for clarification of the format in which cosmetic ingredient labeling should be presented if the manufacturer or distributor wishes to adopt the labeling declaration on a voluntary basis at this time.

The Commissioner has concluded that it is premature at this time, in view of the pending legislation, to promulgate a regulation requiring cosmetic ingredient labeling. Nevertheless, to encourage voluntary cosmetic ingredient labeling and to answer questions about the proper format for doing so, the Commissioner hereby advises manufacturers and distributors of cosmetics that the following format should be utilized by those manufacturers who wish to adopt cosmetic ingredient labeling on a voluntary basis in the interim....

FDA's suggested format for voluntary cosmetic ingredient labeling was soon supplanted by the mandatory format prescribed by the following regulation.

COSMETIC INGREDIENT LABELING
38 Federal Register 28912 (October 17, 1973).

In the FEDERAL REGISTER of February 7, 1973 (38 FR 3523), the Commissioner of Food and Drugs published two proposals concerning the labeling of cosmetic ingredients....

Several comments questioned the legal basis for the proposals, contending that [section 5(c) of] the Fair Packaging and Labeling Act grants authority to establish ingredient labeling only on a commodity-by-commodity basis, and only as necessary to prevent consumer deception or to facilitate value comparisons.

... For the purposes of ingredient labeling, the Commissioner concludes that all cosmetics are appropriately considered a single "commodity.".....

The Commissioner also concludes that cosmetic ingredient labeling is necessary to prevent the deception of consumers and to facilitate value comparisons. Ingredient labeling can be meaningful in preventing consumer deception by precluding product claims that are unreasonable in relation to the ingredients present and by providing consumers with additional information that can contribute to a knowledgeable judgment regarding the reasonableness of the price of the product. Furthermore, while ingredient identity may not be the sole determinant of a product's value to a consumer, it is one important criterion of a product's value in comparison with others. The presence of a substance to which a consumer is allergic or sensitive, for example, may render the product worthless to that consumer....

The Commissioner recognizes that section 5(c)(3) of the act does not grant authority for promulgating ingredient labeling regulations that require the divulgence of trade secrets. However, because quantitative formulas are not revealed, he does not agree that the mere listing of ingredients in descending order of their predominance is tantamount to the divulgence of a trade secret. Furthermore, the final regulation does not require declaration by name of flavors or fragrances, the two types of cosmetic ingredients which would be the most likely of any to create trade secret issues. Nevertheless, in consideration of the possibility that there may be some legitimate trade secret issues regarding the mere identity of other ingredients, the final regulation provides for an administrative review of any such claims of trade secret status and for exemption from label declaration by name for any legitimate trade secret identity.....

The Commissioner recognizes that many consumers may initially be unfamiliar with certain cosmetic ingredients, but concludes that increasing familiarity will be acquired. Certain ingredients have become known to consumers who, for example, are aware of their sensitivity to specific substances and who will quickly learn to utilize the ingredient statement. Ingredient labeling will have to be accompanied by the acquisition of additional information by consumers if they are to be fully informed. Ingredient labeling will, however, directly provide some of the necessary information and should help to motivate consumers to acquire the necessary additional information....

Therefore, pursuant to provisions of the Fair Packaging and Labeling Act and the Federal Food, Drug, and Cosmetic Act (sec. 701(e) ...), Part 1 is amended by adding the following new section:

§ 1.205 [now § 701.3] Cosmetics; labeling requirements; designation of ingredients

(a) The label on each package of a cosmetic shall bear a declaration of the name of each ingredient in descending order of predominance, except that fragrance or flavor, may be listed as fragrance or flavor. An ingredient which is both fragrance and flavor shall be designated by each of the functions it performs unless such ingredient is identified by name.... Where one or more ingredients is accepted by the Food and Drug Administration as exempt from public disclosure pursuant to the procedure established in § 172.9(a) [now § 720.8(a)] of this chapter, in lieu of label declaration of identity the phrase "and other ingredients" may be used at the end of the ingredient declaration.

(b) ... The declaration shall appear on any appropriate information panel in letters not less than 1/16 of an inch in height and without obscuring design, vignettes, or crowding. In the absence of sufficient space for such declaration on the package, or where the manufacturer or distributor wishes to use a decorative container, the declaration may appear on a firmly affixed tag, tape, or card. In those cases where there is insufficient space for such declaration on the package, and it is not practical to firmly affix a tag, tape, or card, the Commissioner may establish by regulation an acceptable alternate (*e.g.,* a smaller type size). A petition requesting such a regulation as an amendment to this paragraph shall be submitted to the Hearing Clerk in the form established in § 2.65 [now revoked and replaced by 21 C.F.R. § 10.30] of this chapter.

(c) A cosmetic ingredient shall be identified in the declaration of ingredients by:

(1) The name established by the Commissioner for that ingredient ... pursuant to paragraph (e) of this section;

(2) In the absence of such name, the name adopted ... in the following ... compendia, listed in order as the source to be utilized:

(i) CTFA (Cosmetic, Toiletry and Fragrance Association, Inc.) Cosmetic Ingredient Dictionary, First Ed., 1973.

(ii) United States Pharmacopeia, 18th Ed., 1970.

(iii) National Formulary, 13th Ed., 1970.

(iv) Food Chemicals Codex, Second Ed., 1972.

(v) United States Adopted Names (USAN 10) and the USP Dictionary of Drug Names, 1961–1971 cumulative list, and 1973 Supplement.

(3) In the absence of such a listing, the name generally recognized by consumers.

(4) In the absence of any of the above, the chemical or other technical name or description.

(d) Where a cosmetic product is also a drug, the declaration shall first declare the active drug ingredients as required under section 502(e) of the Federal Food, Drug, and Cosmetic Act, and shall then declare the cosmetic ingredients. . . .

Any person who will be adversely affected by the foregoing order may . . . file . . . written objections thereto. Objections shall show wherein the person filing will be adversely affected by the order, specify with particularity the provisions of the order deemed objectionable, and state the grounds for objections. . . .

NOTES

1. *Final Regulations.* FDA issued final cosmetic ingredient labeling regulations after a series of notices in which it attempted to accommodate all objections filed to the original final order and denied belated requests for a hearing, 39 Fed. Reg. 27181 (July 25, 1974), 40 Fed. Reg. 8918 and 8924 (March 3, 1975), 40 Fed. Reg. 23458 (May 30, 1975). The procedure followed by the agency in promulgating these regulations (since recodified as 21 C.F.R. § 701.3), without conducting an evidentiary hearing, was upheld by a divided court in *Independent Cosmetic Manufacturers & Distributors, Inc. v. Califano,* 574 F.2d 553 (D.C. Cir. 1978).

2. *Determination of Trade Secret Status.* The process used by FDA to determine whether a cosmetic ingredient represents a trade secret and is therefore exempt from required label declaration was challenged in *Zotos Intern., Inc. v. Kennedy,* 460 F. Supp. 268 (D.D.C. 1978). The district court ruled that the procedure, which did not afford an opportunity for a hearing or other form of "focused dialogue" with the agency, violated the due process clause of the Constitution. In *Carson Products Co. v. Califano,* 594 F.2d 453 (5th Cir. 1979), the court agreed with the *Zotos* decision but held that the procedures afforded Carson satisfied due process and that the facts justified FDA's conclusion that the ingredient involved was not a trade secret. The court in *Del Laboratories, Inc. v. United States,* 86 F.R.D. 676 (D.D.C. 1980), overturned FDA's preliminary refusal to recognize the trade secret status of an ingredient of the plaintiff's products. To remedy the deficiencies discovered by the courts, FDA established a new procedure for considering requests for confidentiality of cosmetic ingredient identity in 47 Fed. Reg. 38353 (August 31, 1982), 51 Fed. Reg. 11441 (April 3, 1986). Even following these new regulations, FDA had difficulty justifying its decisions. In the continuing *Zotos* litigation, FDA again rejected trade secret status after reconsideration under the new regulations, and the district court affirmed the FDA decision. However, the court of appeals reversed and remanded the matter for yet additional proceedings because the agency had given inconsistent reasons for its decision, *Zotos Intern., Inc. v. Young,* 830 F.2d 350 (D.C. Cir. 1987).

3. *Ingredient Names.* In 42 Fed. Reg. 56757 (October 28, 1977) and 45 Fed. Reg. 3574 (January 18, 1980), FDA recognized the second edition of the CTFA Cosmetic Ingredient Dictionary but refused to adopt the CTFA names for 34 listed substances and required the description of the chemical composition of 16 listed substances. Because of the Office of the Federal Register rule that federal regulation may not incorporate documents by prospective reference, the cosmetic ingredient labeling regulations must be revised whenever a new edition of or supplement to the CTFA Cosmetic Ingredient Dictionary is published. FDA has failed to respond promptly to CTFA petitions recognizing

these new editions and supplements but has agreed that industry may use new names added by these documents, but not changes in names from the specific edition recognized in the regulation, pending further FDA action.

4. *Color Additive Names.* In 50 Fed. Reg. 23815 (June 6, 1985), FDA permitted color additives to be designated in product labeling without their prefix, *i.e.,* "Yellow 5" rather than "FD&C Yellow No. 5," and proposed to change its regulations to reflect this policy.

5. *Commentary.* For differing views about the cosmetic ingredient labeling regulations, *see* Berdick, *Cosmetic Ingredient Labeling—The Nomenclature Problem,* 31 FDC L.J. 125 (1976); Byerley, *Cosmetic Ingredient Labeling—An FDA Chimera,* 31 FDC L.J. 109 (1976); Eiermann, *Cosmetic Ingredient Labeling Requirements,* 31 FDC L.J. 115 (1976); Gilhooley, *Status Report on Cosmetic Ingredient Labeling,* 31 FDC L.J. 121 (1976); Lambert, *Working Out Cosmetic Ingredient Labeling,* 30 FDC L.J. 228 (1975).

6. *Scope of Ingredient Labeling.* The FPLA applies only to retail packaging and contains no criminal enforcement sanctions. Ingredient labeling for cosmetics is thus required to appear only on the outside labeling and only on retail packages (and not on packages sold to beauty salons or institutions for use on the premises), and the requirement is enforceable only by civil action. Following congressional hearings that criticized this gap in ingredient labeling, note 1 p. 823 *supra,* on December 16, 1988 five cosmetic industry trade associations announced a voluntary program to provide ingredient information for all professional cosmetic products manufactured on or after December 31, 1989. Under this voluntary program, the ingredient information for professional cosmetic products may be provided on the product label or in accompanying labeling, and may be provided in descending order of predominance or in alphabetical order.

F. VOLUNTARY "REGULATION" OF COSMETICS

In response to petitions from the cosmetic industry, FDA has promulgated regulations governing the voluntary registration of cosmetic establishments (21 C.F.R. Part 710), voluntary filing of cosmetic product ingredient statements (21 C.F.R. Part 720), and voluntary filing of product experience reports (21 C.F.R. Part 730).

VOLUNTARY REGISTRATION OF COSMETIC PRODUCT ESTABLISHMENTS; VOLUNTARY FILING OF COSMETIC PRODUCT INGREDIENT AND COSMETIC RAW MATERIAL COMPOSITION STATEMENTS

37 Federal Register 7151 (April 11, 1972).

... [A] member of Congress urged that the registration and filing of ingredient statements by producers of cosmetics be mandatory [and] that foreign producers of cosmetics be subjected to the regulations.... Two other comments challenged the legality of establishing voluntary regulations under section 701(a) of the Federal Food, Drug, and Cosmetic Act and urged that the regulations issued be mandatory....

The Commissioner has considered these comments and concludes that under section 701(a) of the act he is authorized to accept the voluntary registration of cosmetic product establishments and the voluntary filing of cosmetic product ingredient statements and cosmetic raw material composition statements as set forth in the regulations established below. He also agrees that foreign producers should be included in this voluntary registration. He concludes however that promulgation of a mandatory regulation could result in lengthy litigation that would seriously delay FDA from obtaining the type of information expected as a result of this promulgation.....

A dermatologist commented that the proposed regulations ... did not go far enough, particularly in the provision for providing coded samples to physicians treating persons suffering from allergic reaction. He urged establishment of a "Register" that would list all ingredients of all cosmetic products used in the United States and would be made available to every practicing dermatologist. The Commissioner concludes that a "Register" of cosmetic ingredients goes beyond the scope of the proposal and cannot be implemented by these regulations. The Commissioner considers that promulgation of labeling requirements for cosmetic ingredients will substantially satisfy the need of dermatologists for this type of data....

VOLUNTARY FILING OF COSMETIC PRODUCT EXPERIENCES

38 Federal Register 28914 (October 17, 1973).

In the FEDERAL REGISTER of November 1, 1972 (37 FR 23344) a notice of proposed rulemaking ... included the text of regulations suggested in a petition filed by the Cosmetic, Toiletry, and Fragrance Association, Inc. (CTFA) ... as well as regulations proposed by the Commissioner....

A number of comments agreed with the FDA proposal that all complaints alleging bodily injury received by a manufacturer, packer, or distributor should be submitted to the Food and Drug Administration. The petitioner opposed the request for the submission of all complaints and suggested that provision be made for a manufacturer, packer, or distributor to use a screening procedure for determining reportable experiences and in the absence of such a procedure to submit all alleged injury complaints received.

The Commissioner of Food and Drugs concludes that the submission of complaints that have been screened by a procedure appropriately designed to eliminate any unfounded or spurious complaints would be more meaningful and, therefore, adopts the suggestion of the petitioner. However, in order to protect against the use of screening procedures which might eliminate valid experience reports, the regulation provides that any procedure used to screen such reports should be filed with the agency and that it will be subject to public inspection.....

Several comments argued for a broad definition of "reportable experience." It was asserted that any bodily injury resulting from the accidental or deliberate misuse of a cosmetic product is a valid reportable experience. The petitioner, on the other hand, opposed the inclusion of any experience not in association with the intended use of a cosmetic product.

The Commissioner is of the opinion that any information he can obtain in regard to injuries involving cosmetic products, including adverse reactions resulting from the accidental or deliberate misuse of cosmetic products, may be of use in protecting the public health, and therefore he has concluded that all such experiences should be considered reportable..... [T]he rules governing confidentiality granted to voluntarily submitted data on cosmetic product experiences should be the same as the rules governing confidentiality for other data submitted to the agency on a voluntary basis [set forth in 21 C.F.R. § 20.111].....

A public interest group requested that FDA obtain testing data on products for which complaints have been received. The regulation provides that the Commissioner may request additional information in response to reports received....

The Commissioner is of the opinion that statistical data obtained from the submission of reportable experiences will be meaningful only if the agency obtains sufficient information to relate the number of the reportable experiences in a product category to the total number of cosmetic product units sold in that particular product category. Such information by product categories can be obtained, however, without the need for filing a separate negative report for each product by brand name. The regulation now provides for the submission of a "Summary Report of Cosmetic Product Experience by Product Categories." The person submitting this report need not list products by brand name, but only the total number of product units in each product category estimated to have been distributed to consumers during the reporting period, together with the number and rate of reportable experiences in each category....

NOTES

1. *Confidentiality of Reports.* FDA subsequently issued final regulations under the Freedom of Information Act granting confidentiality to product experience reports, 21 C.F.R. § 730.7, promulgated in 39 Fed. Reg. 44602 (December 24, 1974).

2. *Simplification of Reporting Requirements.* In an effort to improve compliance with the voluntary reporting regulations, FDA reduced the reporting burdens in 45 Fed. Reg. 73960 (November 7, 1980), 46 Fed. Reg. 38073 (July

24, 1981), 50 Fed. Reg. 47760 (November 20, 1985), 51 Fed. Reg. 25687 (July 16, 1986). On May 15, 1989, CTFA submitted a citizen petition to FDA (No. 89P–0180) requesting that the voluntary filing of cosmetic formulas be simplified by eliminating the requirement for semi-quantitative information, thus permitting manufacturers to submit a simple list of ingredients. FDA proposed amendments to the regulations in accordance with this petition, 55 Fed.Reg. 42993 (October 29, 1990), and stated that they could be implemented immediately. The industry record of compliance with the voluntary reporting regulations was a subject of debate during the 1988 House hearings on cosmetic product safety, note 1 p. 823 *supra*. *See* GAO, COSMETICS REGULATION INFORMATION ON VOLUNTARY ACTIONS AGREED TO BY FDA AND THE INDUSTRY, HRD–90–58 (March 1990).

3. *Commentary.* For an FDA description of cosmetic experience reporting, *see* Wenninger, *Voluntary Cosmetic Product Experience Reporting—The FDA Viewpoint,* 30 FDC L.J. 204 (1975). For discussion of cosmetic industry concerns about product experience reporting, *see* Lambert, *Carrot and Stick: Product Experience Reporting and Cosmetic Ingredient Labeling,* 29 FDC L.J. 78 (1974); Pietrangelo, *Product Experience Reporting—An Industry View,* 30 FDC L.J. 219 (1975); Wolcott, *Cosmetics Workshop—Product Experience Reporting,* 29 FDC L.J. 284 (1974).

In 1976 the Cosmetic, Toiletry, and Fragrance Association undertook its own comprehensive review of the safety of ingredients used in cosmetic products.

ROBERT L. ELDER, THE COSMETIC INGREDIENT REVIEW—A SAFETY EVALUATION PROGRAM

11 Journal American Academy of Dermatology 1168 (1984).

The Cosmetic Ingredient Review (CIR) was established in 1976 by the Cosmetic, Toiletry and Fragrance Association to review and document information on the safety of ingredients as used in cosmetic products....

CTFA recognized that acceptance of the program and its results would depend on three major factors: (1) the safety review process had to be conducted with no cosmetic industry bias; (2) the Panel of Experts who would review the safety test data on each ingredient had to be given complete independence; and (3) the review process, the reports, and all of the data used in the safety evaluation had to be available for public and scientific scrutiny.

These three major requirements were codified into formal, written procedures that established CIR as an independent, nonprofit organizations. CIR staff and all consultants were to be separate from CTFA and the cosmetic industry and must pass the same conflict of interest requirements stipulated for special federal government employees. All reports were to be discussed and voted on in a public meeting before being released for a 90–day public comment period without prior industry review. And finally, all data, published or unpublished, used by the CIR Expert Panel would be available for public review.

Policy guidance for the CIR program is provided by a five-person Steering Committee chaired by the president of CTFA [and including two scientists] . . . appointed by the American Academy of Dermatology . . . [and] the Society of Toxicology. Two scientists from industry—the current chairman of CTFA's Scientific Advisory Committee and CTFA's senior vice-president for Science—also serve on the Committee. The Steering Committee has no input into the scientific evaluations of the CIR Expert Panel. One of the Steering Committee's major responsibilities is the selection of the seven-member CIR Expert Panel. This is done following a public announcement requesting nominees. . . .

Three nonvoting members assist the Expert Panel and attend the public meetings. These include a consumer representative (appointed by the Consumer Federation of America), an industry liaison, and a Food and Drug Administration (FDA) "contact person." . . .

The priority order of ingredient review is established by using a weighted formula that includes factors for: ingredient concentration in cosmetic products, number of products containing the ingredient, frequency of consumer use, area of use, use by sensitive population subgroups, biologic activity, estimate of penetration, and frequency of consumer complaints about products containing the ingredient. . . . Ingredients specifically regulated by the FDA, such as color additives, are exempt from CIR review. Any ingredient that is being evaluated by the FDA under the Over–The–Counter Drug Review (OTC) or for use as a Direct Food Additive is deferred until that review is completed. Fragrance materials are being evaluated separately in a program sponsored by the Research Institute for Fragrance Materials (RIFM) and are not included in the CIR review program. The CIR ingredient review list is developed as described and then issued for public comment before it is forwarded with all the comments to the Expert Panel for their review and approval. The Expert Panel may at any time add, delete, or change the order of ingredient review without requesting concurrence by the Steering Committee. . . .

. . . [T]he review of each ingredient goes through several stages. The staff of CIR prepares a Scientific Literature Review summarizing the published information and publicly requests any relevant published or unpublished data that the review does not already include.

Individually, ingredient suppliers and cosmetic manufacturers have tested ingredients, as well as formulations, for many years. Although much of these data have been published, a significant portion are in industry files and not available for public or scientific review. The collection of these data and the test protocols used to produce the data are critical to the success of the program. At the end of a 90–day public comment period, all submitted data are incorporated into a document for consideration by a subgroup (Team) of the Expert Panel. From 25% to 75% of the data included in the CIR reports has not been published previously. Teams meet in a series of closed working sessions to evaluate the report and determine whether there are sufficient data upon which to base a conclusion. A document reflecting those considerations is then prepared for review by the full Expert Panel. After discussion of this document in public meetings of the full Panel, a Tentative Report is issued with one of three conclusions: (1) that the ingredient is safe as currently used, (2) that the ingredient is unsafe, or (3) that there is insufficient information for the Panel to make a determination of safety. It is significant that CIR procedures require documented evidence giving reasonable assurance of safety before reaching the final determination. Lack of adverse information about an ingredient is not sufficient to justify a determination of safety.

The Tentative Report is then made available for a 90–day public comment period.... A Final Report, incorporating any substantive changes resulting from public comment, is then released by the Expert Panel....

STATEMENT OF ROBERT L. ELDER, SC.D.*

"Potential Hazards Of Cosmetic Products,"
Hearing Before the Subcommittee on Regulation and Business Opportunities
House Committee on Small Business (September 15, 1988).

The CTFA Ingredient Dictionary currently lists 5000 nonfragrance ingredients. These are ingredients that are offered for use by the cosmetic industry. Many are not used in a cosmetic at any given time. It is estimated that about 2300 of these nonfragrance ingredients are in actual use at any one time. Data from the FDA cosmetic voluntary reporting program indicate that approximately 700 of these 2300 ingredients have been reported to be used in 20 or more cosmetic formulations. The 700 ingredients whose reported frequency of use is greater than 20 are the ingredients that have thus far been prioritized for CIR review. Although we have prioritized only those cosmetic ingredients used in 20 or more formulations, in going through this process we have actually considered a much larger number of ingredients. We considered all ingredients in 10 or more formulations when we established the 1984 priority list, to make sure that important chemicals were not missed. And in 1987 FDA provided to the Expert Panel a list of all chemicals used in *any* cosmetic formulation, again to be sure that any important chemical was included. Thus, we have cast a wide net. One-third of these 700 ingredients are already regulated by FDA for use in food or drug products or as color additives....

As of August 1, 1988, the Expert Panel has issued 112 Final Reports covering 277 ingredients. In the course of completing these reports, the Expert Panel issued 22 Insufficient Data Announcements.

* [Director and Scientific Coordinator Cosmetic Ingredient Review (CIR)].

Thirteen of these announcements resulted in a response supplying the appropriate data required to make a decision on the safety of the ingredients, but nine did not. Of the 277 ingredients reviewed, the Expert Panel concluded that 237 are safe for use in cosmetics at the present practices of use. Use limitations have been included in the conclusions of 18 reports for 30 ingredients. For nine ingredients, reports have been released stating that there were insufficient data to judge safety. One report was released in which the Expert Panel found the ingredient, p-hydroxyanisole, unsafe for use in cosmetics. There are currently 32 reports on 49 ingredients at various stages of development and review.

The current CIR status of the 700 most frequently used cosmetic ingredients is as follows:

```
Already reviewed by CIR .......................... 39 percent (277)
Under review by CIR .............................. 9 percent (49)
Scheduled for review by CIR ...................... 15 percent (111)
Deferred, awaiting FDA OTC Report ............... 19 percent (133)
Exempt (RIFM ingredients) ....................... 2 percent (14)
Exempt (regulated by FDA) ....................... 16 percent (112)
```

NOTES

1. *Challenge to FDA's Role.* Before the CTFA review commenced, Consumers Union brought suit against FDA, contending that discussions between the association and FDA about plans for the program were advisory committee meetings that must comply with all of the requirements of the Federal Advisory Committee Act, *see* p. 1286 *infra*. In *Consumers Union of United States, Inc. v. Department of HEW*, 409 F.Supp. 473 (D.D.C. 1976), *aff'd without opinion*, 551 F.2d 466 (D.C.Cir. 1977), the court concluded that CTFA was not "advising" FDA but that "CTFA in its own discretion was ultimately to decide whether or not to initiate a testing program." The court observed that FDA "appears to lack statutory authority to require initiation of an ingredient testing program."

2. *Commentary.* The objectives of the cosmetic industry's self-regulation program are discussed in Berdick, *The Cosmetic Industry's Approach to Voluntary Regulation—Scientific Aspects*, 27 FDC L.J. 208 (1972); Edmondson, *Cosmetic Industry Self–Regulation*, 27 FDC L.J. 45 (1972). For contrasting assessments of the effectiveness of the cosmetic industry self-regulation program, *compare* Berdick, *Cosmetic Industry Initiatives*, 33 FDC L.J. 239 (1978), *with* Page and Blackburn, *Behind the Looking Glass: Administrative, Legislative And Private Approaches To Cosmetic Safety Substantiation*, 24 UCLA L. Rev. 795 (1977). *See also* Bergfeld, *et al., The Cosmetic Ingredient Review Self Regulatory Program*, 9 Dermatologist Clinics, No. 1, at 105 (January 1991). Estrin, *The Cosmetic Ingredient Review*, 21 Cutis 35 (1978); Beyer, *The Cosmetic Ingredient Review: A Status Report*, 4 Clin. Therapeutics 2 (1981).

G. COAL TAR HAIR DYES

The special treatment accorded coal tar hair dyes by section 601(a) of the 1938 Act has been a continuing source of frustration for FDA, which periodically has sought to circumvent the provision.

TOILET GOODS ASS'N v. FINCH

United States Court of Appeals, Second Circuit, 1969.

419 F.2d 21.

FRIENDLY, Circuit Judge:

Nine years ago Congress amended the Food, Drug, and Cosmetic Act by enacting the Color Additive Amendments of 1960. Nearly three years later, after appropriate rule-making proceedings, the Food and Drug Administration (FDA) published its Regulations thereunder, 28 F.R. 6439. This litigation about the validity of their provisions concerning diluents, finished cosmetics and hair-dyes has continued ever since.....

The Regulation held invalid by the district court, 21 C.F.R. § 8.1(u), provides:

> (u) The "hair-dye" exemption in section 601(a) of the act applies to those articles intended for use in altering the color of the hair and which are, or which bear or contain, color additives with the sensitization potential of causing skin irritation in certain individuals and possible blindness when used for dyeing the eyelashes or eyebrows. The exemption is permitted with the condition that the label of any such article bear conspicuously the statutory caution and adequate directions for preliminary patch-testing. If the poisonous or deleterious substance in the "hair dye" is one to which the caution is inapplicable and for which patch-testing provides no safeguard, the exemption does not apply; nor does the exemption extend to poisonous or deleterious diluents that may be introduced as wetting agents, hair conditioners, emulsifiers, or other components in a color shampoo, rinse, tint, or similar dual-purpose cosmetics that alter the color of the hair....

Taking first things first, we agree with the invalidation of so much of the Regulation as sought to deprive coal-tar hair dyes of the exemption conferred by § 361(a) in cases where, in the view of FDA, the coal-tar color ingredient carries a danger for which patch-testing provides no safeguard. The Government's argument should indeed be appealing to a legislator—what good is the warning to make a patch test if the test will not disclose the danger? But a court must take the statute as it is, and Congress wrote with great specificity....

It is equally plain that the exemption of § 361(a) does not apply to coloring ingredients in hair dyes not derived from coal-tar; indeed we do not read the decree as prohibiting a regulation which would make that clear. We likewise see no basis for invalidating the portion of the Regulation which says that the exemption does not apply to poisonous or deleterious diluents. It is inconceivable that Congress meant to deprive the FDA of its ordinary powers with respect to other ingredients simply because they are combined with a coal-tar dye.

We think the court also erred in excluding from § 361(e) color additives in hair dyes other than those made from coal tar. The 1938 Act applied only to coal-tar colors, and the exemption of hair dyes in subdivision (e) was logical since coal-tar colors were dealt with by subdivision (a) in a supposedly adequate fashion. The modification of subdivision (e) in 1960 was part of a program to regulate all colors, and not merely coal-tar colors. But, if the statute be read with entire literalness, the unaltered introductory provision in subsection (e) now would have the effect of excluding any sanction for the use in a hair dye of an unlisted or uncertified coloring ingredient although not within the proviso to § 361(a). In the absence of any legislative history indicating an intention to broaden the exemption in § 361(e), the most sensible construction is that, despite the retention of the introductory words "if it is not a hair dye," Congress did not mean to exempt non-coal-tar color additives used in hair dyes from the requirement of listing and certification....

NOTES

1. *Origin of Exemption.* The coal tar hair dye exemption in section 601(a) resulted from intensive lobbying during consideration of the 1983 Act by thousands of beauty shop operators and employees who were concerned that the pending legislation would require FDA to ban coal tar hair dye products and thus seriously injure their business. The allegation that some ingredients in coal tar hair dyes are carcinogenic prompted Congressional hearings in 1978 and 1979. "Cancer–Causing Chemicals—Part 1 (Safety of Cosmetics and Hair Dyes)," Hearings Before the Subcomm. on Oversight and Investigations of the House Comm. on Interstate and Foreign Commerce, 95th Cong., 2nd Sess. (1978); Safety of Hair Dyes and Cosmetic Products, Hearing before the Subcomm. on Oversight and Investigations of the House Comm. on Interstate and Foreign Commerce, 96th Cong., 1st Sess. (1979). FDA regulation of carcinogenic coal tar hair dye substances is considered in detail at p. 908 *infra.*

2. *Scope of Exemption.* The coal tar hair dye exemption extends only to products intended to dye the hair, and does not include products for the eyebrow and eyelash. *Byrd v. United States*, 154 F.2d 62 (5th Cir. 1946).

3. *Deletion of Caution.* FDA Trade Correspondence 103 (February 29, 1940), 1938–49 FDLI Jud. Rec. at 610, states that hair dyes containing harmless coal tar colors need not bear the caution statements specified in section 601(a) of the FD&C Act. Use of the statutory caution statement exempts a coal tar hair dye from section 601(a). Failure to use the statutory caution statement subjects a coal tar hair dye to section 601(a), but as long as the product does not contain any poisonous or deleterious substance it is not unlawful. Under section 601(e), a coal tar hair dye is exempt from the color additive requirements of section 706 regardless whether it bears the statutory caution statement.

4. *Roux Litigation.* FDA has been continually frustrated in efforts to establish that certain ingredients used in Roux Lash & Brow Tint Kits are hazardous color additives. Not long after enactment of the FD&C Act FDA seized this product, contending that it contained three poisonous or deleterious substances. The first jury to hear the case was unable to agree on a verdict. A

second jury returned a verdict for Roux. *See* Munch and Munch, *Notices of Judgment—Cosmetics*, 20 FDC L.J. 399, 400–401 (1959).

In 1968 FDA instituted another seizure of the product, charging that the three ingredients were unapproved color additives. The district court dismissed the case on the ground that it was controlled by the decision in *TGA v. Gardner*, 278 F. Supp. 786 (S.D.N.Y. 1968). This ruling was reversed on appeal and the case was remanded for trial. *United States v. Roux Laboratories, Inc.*, 437 F.2d 209 (9th Cir. 1971). The district court ultimately dismissed the action on the ground that a 1963 Federal Register notice exempted the substances from color additive requirements. *See Roux Lash & Brow Tints*, FDA Consumer, November 1974, p. 42.

In 1974 FDA brought yet another seizure, again alleging the use of unapproved color additives. The trial judge this time ruled that the 1963 Federal Register notice did not exempt the substances. Following trial of the factual question whether the ingredients were color additives or diluents, the jury returned a verdict for the claimant. *Roux Lash & Brow Tint Kits*, FDA Consumer, December 1977–January 1978, p. 37.

5. *Tattoos.* FDA does not regulate the dyes used in tattooing; a practice whose regulation varies widely among the states. Stauter, *Tattooing: The Protection of the Public Health*, 6 Health Matrix, No. 2 (1988).

Chapter VIII

REGULATION OF CARCINOGENS

A. HISTORICAL BACKGROUND

While cancer has gripped public attention and preoccupied regulatory officials only in this century, its existence as a discrete disease and the lack of effective treatments were recognized in ancient times. In the 4th century B.C. Hippocrates wrote: "It is better not to apply any treatment in cases of occult cancer; for, if treated, the patients die quickly; but if not treated, they hold out for a long time." II APHORISMS 256 (F. Adams translation, 1886). Four centuries later the Roman physician Celsus offered this pessimistic assessment of the progress of cancer:

> ... [G]enerally the first stage is what the Greeks call cacothese; then from that follows a carcinoma without ulceration; then ulceration, and from that a kind of wart. It is only the cacoethes which can be removed; the other stages are irritated by treatment; and the more so the more vigorous it is. Some have used caustic medicaments, some the cautery, some excision with a scalpel; but no medicament has ever given relief; the parts cauterized are excited immediately to an increase until they cause death. After excision, even when a scar has formed, none the less the disease has returned and caused death; while at the same time the majority of patients; though no violent measure are applied in the attempt to remove the tumor, but only mild applications in order to soothe it, attain to a ripe old age in spite of it. No one, however, except by time and experiment, can have the skill to distinguish a cacoethees which admits of being treated from a carcinoma which does not.

II DE MEDICINA, Book V, Chapter 28, pp. 129, 131 (W.G. Spencer translation, 1938). *See also* Riddle, *Ancient and Medieval Chemotherapy for Cancer,* 76 ISIS 319 (1985).

Though more is known each year about the causes of cancer in humans, complete understanding of the disease remains elusive. Percivall Pott, an English physician, published the first epidemiological report identifying one cause of cancer in 1775. Pott described what he termed "chimney-sweepers' cancer," a disease "which always makes its first attack on, and its first appearance in the inferior part of the scrotum...." He advocated immediate surgery upon discovery of the lesion "for when the disease has got head, it is rapid in its progress, painful in all its attacks, and most certainly destructive in its event." CHIRURGICAL OBSERVATIONS 64–68. Apart from Pott's prescient finding, however, knowledge about the causes, mechanisms, and treatments of cancer remained primitive throughout the 19th century. Only after scientists began using large colonies of inbred strains of rodents in toxicity studies in the early decades of this century did scientific investigation of the processes of carcinogenesis itself begin in earnest. Tests in experimental animals also provided a method—still the chief method—for evaluating the potential carcinogenicity of specific substances, including substances intended for use in food and drugs.

This chapter examines FDA's efforts to assess and regulate constituents of food and drugs that are suspected or known to be capable of causing cancer. The history of the agency's policy reveals the difficulty of these tasks at the same time as it mirrors the evolution in our understanding of the causes and processes of carcinogenesis.

B. FDA POLICY PRIOR TO 1960

Before this century determining the safety of foods and drugs was an exercise of observation and judgment; "risk assessment" depended largely on human trial and error.

Hippocrates is often called the "founder" of medicine because he related all disease to natural, rather than supernatural, causes. Many ancient Greek and Roman writers recognized that consumption of different amounts of the same substance had quite different effects. But it was Paracelsus, an enigmatic alchemist writing in the first half of the 16th century, who articulated the relationship between dose and response: "Poison is in everything, and nothing is without poison. The dosage makes it either a poison or a remedy." H.M. Pachter, MAGIC INTO SCIENCE: THE STORY OF PARACELSUS 86 (1951). Paracelsus' profound insight did not immediately advance social decisionmaking. He correctly pointed out that there is a line dividing safe from unsafe doses, but he offered no criteria for determining how to draw that line. It took several centuries before dose-response relationships assumed their present importance in regulatory risk assessment.

Systematic and controlled toxicity testing in laboratory animals made possible for the first time the formulation of an *operational* definition of safety. During the mid–1940s, FDA scientists adopted the rough rule of thumb that a safe human dose of a substance was 1/100th of the highest dose that produced no toxic effects (the "no effect level" or now the "no observed effect level" (NOEL)) in test animals.

ARNOLD LEHMAN, et al., PROCEDURES FOR THE APPRAISAL OF THE TOXICITY OF CHEMICALS IN FOODS

4 Food Drug Cosmetic Law Journal 412 (1949).

While it is not especially difficult to evaluate a set of pharmacological data which lead to the conclusion that the substance being investigated is a poison, it is extremely difficult to conclude that any chemical is safe for human consumption. It would be difficult, if not impossible, to set up a number of criteria which, if met, would automatically make the compound safe for use. Each chemical must be evaluated as a separate entity by individuals with adequate scientific background and experience....

The first consideration is the transference of animal data to what might be expected for man. Experience has shown that if *all* of the experimental data are correlated, a good estimate of the probable effect on man can be made. In some cases, it is possible to compare the effects of the chemical with a drug or compound which has a known history on both man and animals. In other cases, the comparative biochemistry of man and the various species of animals used will serve as a guide for evaluating the data obtained. Finally, there are compounds which produce effects in animals that are so alarming that one has no hesitation in excluding such compounds from further consideration. For example, if a chemical has been shown to possess carcinogenic properties, there would be no question in applying animal data to man....

The second factor that must be kept in mind is the apparent heterogeneity of man as compared with the relative homogeneity of experimental animals. Normally, laboratory animals exist under controlled conditions, are fed adequate diets, and are in good health. If a chemical is added to human food, however, it is eaten by all people, the young and old, those suffering from various pathological conditions, and those existing in borderline states of nutrition. Obviously, all of these conditions are not and cannot readily be duplicated in animal experiments. About the only compensation that can be made is the provision of an adequate margin of safety in establishing safe levels for the particular chemical in a food.

The third consideration which is all too often overlooked is the other sources of exposure to a given chemical. These other sources may include industrial exposure to the chemical, the natural occurrence of the chemical in drinking water or edible plants and animals, and existing or proposed uses of this chemical in other food products. Here also should be mentioned the possibilities that a chemical may act synergistically with other constituents of the diet, may alter intestinal absorption, may interfere with utilization of accessory food factors, and may increase the ease with which allergic conditions can be produced.

Since man is the ultimate consumer of the chemical to be added to foods, clinical trials are certainly to be desired.... Human volunteers even in moderate numbers are difficult to obtain; hence, considerable reliance must be placed on the results of animal experimentation, and this accounts for the emphasis placed on the objective of a 100–fold margin of safety.

As Dr. Lehman relates, however, a finding that a substance caused cancer in animals was regarded as so "alarming" as to exclude it from consideration for human exposure. Accordingly, FDA used (and continues to use) the 100:1 safety factor to set permissible exposure levels for substances that cause any toxic effects other than cancer. For cancer, however, no safety factor was ever used. The agency's goal was to prevent the use of carcinogens in human food or drugs.

This policy prevailed from the enactment of the 1938 Act. Under the provision requiring certification of coal tar colors used in food, drugs, and cosmetics, FDA immediately deleted from the permitted list of colors "the only two coal-tar colors known to be capable of producing carcinogenic manifestations." Calvery, *Coal–Tar Colors: Their Use in Foods, Drugs, and Cosmetics*, 114 Am. J. Pharm. 324, 334 (1942). When the agency discovered that one of these colors, Butter Yellow (dimethyl-amino-azobenzene), was still being used after being delisted in 1919, it launched a comprehensive enforcement campaign, including seizures, injunctions, and criminal prosecutions. 1945 FDA ANNUAL REPORT at 52. In 1950, FDA banned two nonnutritive sweeteners on the basis of animal experiments which showed them to be carcinogenic. 15 Fed. Reg. 321 (January 19, 1950). Four years later, it banned natural tonka beans and their constituent, coumarin, because coumarin was found to be carcinogenic. 19 Fed. Reg. 1239 (March 5, 1954).

Thus, twenty years before the enactment of the 1958 Food Additives Amendment FDA embraced a policy of prohibiting the addition of any carcinogen to food and drugs.

C. THE DELANEY CLAUSE
1. THE INCIDENCE OF HUMAN CANCER

Cancer primarily afflicts older people and its prevalence varies with the age of the population. In the early years of our nation, life expectancy was low. Shortly before the Civil War, for example, average life expectancies at birth in Boston and New York were 21.43 and 19.6 years. L. Shattuck, REPORT OF THE SANITARY COMMISSION OF MASSACHUSETTS 104 (1850). By 1900, as a result of the public health measures undertaken during the previous half century, life expectancy of Americans at birth in this country had risen to 47.3 years. Life expectancy has continued to rise and in 1988 it had reached 71.5 years for men and 78.3 years for women.

This dramatic rise in longevity in a little more than a century has been achieved chiefly through successful assaults on infectious diseases. The three leading causes of death in 1900 were pneumonia and influenza, tuberculosis, and diarrhea. Now, these diseases occur less frequently and rarely cause death. Today's two leading causes of death are heart disease and cancer. The sharp rise in the number of cancer fatalities is largely the result of successful attacks on infectious diseases, not of an increase in the incidence of cancer itself. Current mortality statistics indicate that the overall prevalence of cancer in this country remains steady. Some types of cancer have become more common while others have declined in frequency, but overall, the age-adjusted incidence does not appear to have changed significantly.

Based upon evidence of sharp variations in cancer frequency among different populations, epidemiologists have concluded that up to 90 percent of all cancers are "environmental" in origin. But this label can be misleading; "environmental causes" of cancer include not only air and water pollutants, but also lifestyle factors such as smoking, consumption of alcoholic beverages, and sexual habits. At a 1979 conference of the American Health Foundation, a group of cancer experts produced the following consensus ranking of cancer risk factors:

Factors in Cancer, as Summarized by the Conference on the Primary Promotion of Cancer, New York, 1979

	Men	Women
	Percent of Cancers Involving the Listed Factors	
Smoking	25–35	5–10
Alcohol	7	2
Occupation	6	2
Nutrition	30	30–50
Food contaminants	0	0
Drugs	1	1
Air pollution	0	0
Ionizing radiation	3	3
Ultraviolet radiation	(skin 50)[1]	(skin 50)[1]
Heredity	10–25	10–25
Viruses	1	1
Immunodeficiency	1	1

[1] Excluded from total cancers.

M. Shimkin, INDUSTRIAL AND LIFE–STYLE CARCINOGENS 10 (1980).

In a comprehensive study commissioned by the Office of Technology Assessment, two prominent British epidemiologists reached similar conclusions:

Proportions of Cancer Deaths Attributed to Various Different Factors

Factor or class of factors	Percent of all Cancer deaths	
	Best estimate	Range of acceptable estimates
Tobacco	30	25–40
Alcohol	3	2–4
Diet	35	10–70
Food additives	1	−5[1]–2
Reproductive and sexual behavior	7	1–13
Occupation	4	2–8
Pollution	2	1–5
Industrial products	1	1–2
Medicines and medical	1	0.5–3
Geophysical factors[2]	3	2–4
Infection	10?	1–?
Unknown	?	?

[1] Allowing for a possibly protective effect of antioxidants and other preservatives.
[2] Only about 1%, not 3%, could reasonably be described as "avoidable".

Doll & Peto, *The Causes of Cancer: Quantitative Estimates of Avoidable Risks of Cancer in The United States Today*, 66 J. Nat'l Cancer Inst. 1191, 1256 (1981).

While these tables represent estimates rather than measured frequencies, they have elicited agreement from other experts, and thus provide a fair picture of the major causes of cancer among Americans.

---

2. ENACTMENT OF THE 1958 DELANEY CLAUSE

As the number of people dying from cancer increased in the 1930s and 1940s, public concern about the disease grew. Inevitably, this concern stimulated congressional consideration of measures to reduce potential cancer risks. One result of this effort was the enactment of one of the most notorious and least frequently invoked passages in the FD&C Act—the Delaney Clause.

The Delaney Clause now appears in three provisions of the Act: the Food Additives Amendment of 1958 (section 409(c)(3)(A)), the Color Additive Amendments of 1960 (section 706(b)(5)(B)), and the Animal Drug Amendments of 1968 (section 512(d)(1)(H)). While the three versions differ slightly in their language, their basic thrust is similar— to prevent the addition to food of any substance that has been shown to induce cancer in man or laboratory animals. The language of section 409(c)(3)(A) is exemplary:

[N]o such regulation [authorizing use of a food additive] shall issue if a fair evaluation of the data before the Secretary—

(A) fails to establish that the proposed use of the food additive, under the conditions of use to be specified in the regulation, will be safe: *Provided,* That no additive shall be deemed to be safe if it is found to induce cancer when ingested by man or animal, or if it is found, after tests which are appropriate for the evaluation of the safety of food additives, to induce cancer in man or animal. . . .

The Delaney Clause was the product—we might even say the by-product—of broader public concern about the potential health effects of substances used in food production, coupled with an appreciation of the benefits that many new ingredients and packaging materials provided. While the clause commanded attention during congressional deliberations on the Food Additives Amendment and Color Additive Amendments, it was not the central focus of debate at either stage. The accompanying legislative history, therefore, while suggestive, can at the same time be frustrating for those who wish to divine Congress' contemporaneous understanding of the twin provisions that have excited so much interest since. It is fair to acknowledge here that there is no agreement on the proper interpretation of the key passages, which are quoted below. This lack of agreement has played an important role in FDA's continuing efforts to fashion a policy to regulate carcinogens. For the views of the authors on the Delaney Clause, *see, e.g.,* Hutt, *The Basis and Purpose of Government Regulation of Adulteration and Misbranding of Food,* 33 FDC L.J. 505 (1978); *Public Policy Issues in Regulating Carcinogens in Food,* 33 FDC L.J. 541 (1978); *Unresolved Issues in the Conflict Between Individual Freedom and Government Control of Food Safety,* 33 FDC L.J. 558 (1978); *FDA Can Handle Food Safety Issues Most Effectively,* Legal Times of Wash., April 27, 1981, at 28; Merrill, *FDA's Implementation of the Delaney Clause: Repudiation of Congressional Choice or Reasoned Adaptation to Scientific Progress?,* 5 Yale J. on Reg. 1 (1987); *FDA's "Erasure" of the Delaney Clause: A Case Study in Statutory Interpretation,* 50 AFDO Q. Bull. 199 (1986); *Regulating Carcinogens in Food: A Legislator's Guide to the Food Safety Provisions of the Federal Food, Drug and Cosmetic Act,* 77 Mich. L. Rev. 171 (1978). *Compare* Gilhooley, *Plain Meaning, Absurd Results and the Legislative Purpose: The Interpretation of the Delaney Clause,* 40 Admin. L. Rev. 267 (1988), *with* Cooper, *Stretching Delaney Til It Breaks,* Regulation, November/December 1985, at 11.

In 1950, the House of Representatives established a Select Committee to Investigate the Use of Chemicals in Food Products, chaired by Representative James J. Delaney (D., N.Y.). The reports of that committee did not make specific recommendations about carcinogens. No special consideration was given to carcinogens during the enactment of the Miller Pesticide Amendments of 1954, which added section 408 to the FD&C Act. Nor did the initial versions of the legislation which ultimately became the Food Additives Amendment of 1958 contain anticancer language. In 1957, however, as Congress began seriously to consider special requirements for food additives, Representative Delaney introduced a revised bill (H.R. 7798, 85th Cong., 1st Sess.), which contained the following clause:

> The Secretary shall not approve for use in food any chemical additive found to induce cancer in man, or, after tests, found to induce cancer in animals.

The Department of Health, Education, and Welfare initially objected to this provision on the following grounds:

> We, of course, agree that no chemical should be permitted to be used in food if, as so used, it may cause cancer. We assume that this, and no more, is the aim of the sponsor. No specific reference to carcinogens is necessary for that purpose, however, since the general requirements of this bill give assurance that no chemical additive can be cleared if there is reasonable doubt about its safety in that respect.
>
> On the other hand, the above-quoted provisions are so broadly phrased that they could be read to bar an additive from the food supply even if it can induce cancer only when used on test animals in a way having no bearing on the question of carcinogenicity for its intended use. This, we think, would not be in the public interest. Scientists, I am advised, can produce cancer in test animals by injecting sugar in a certain manner, and they can produce cancers by injections into test animals of cottonseed oil, olive oil, or tannic acid (a component of many foods). Probably they can do the same thing with other naturally occurring foods chemicals. We think that it would be unnecessary and undesirable to rule out of the food supply sugar, vegetable oils, or common table beverages simply because, by an extraordinary method of application never encountered at the dining table, it is possible to induce cancer by injecting the substances into the muscles of test animals.

"Food Additives," Hearings before a Subcomm. of the House Comm. on Interstate and Foreign Commerce, 85th Cong. 38–39 (1958).

In July 1958, the House Commerce Committee reported out a bill requiring premarketing clearance of food additives but containing no anticancer clause. Subsequent to the filing of the report, Representative Delaney urged the addition of the following anticancer language:

> *Provided,* That no additive shall be deemed to be safe if it is found to induce cancer when ingested by man or animal, or if it is found, after tests which are appropriate for the evaluation of the safety of food additives, to induce cancer in man or animal.

To assure enactment of the legislation, HEW agreed to this amendment, which became part of the statute. In a letter to the committee chairman the Department's spokesman, Assistant Secretary Elliot Richardson, at once embraced Delaney's goal and stated that the anticancer language would not change the bill's meaning:

> ... This Department is in complete accord with the intent of these suggestions—that no substance should be sanctioned for uses in food that might produce cancer in man. H.R. 13254, as approved by your committee, will accomplish this intent, since it specifically instructs the Secretary not to issue a regulation permitting use of an additive in food if a fair evaluation of the data before the Secretary fails to establish that the proposed use of the additive will be safe. The scientific tests that are adequate to establish the safety of an additive will give information about the tendency of an additive to produce cancer when it is present in food. Any indication that the additive may thus be carcinogenic would, under the terms of the bill, restrain the Secretary from approving the proposed use of the additive unless and until further testing shows to the point of reasonable certainty that the additive would not produce cancer and thus would be safe under the proposed conditions of use. This would afford good, strong public health protection.
>
> There are many serious conditions other than cancer that may be caused or aggravated by the improper use of chemicals. It is manifestly impracticable to itemize all of them in a bill. To single out one class of diseases for special mention would be anomalous and could be misinterpreted....
>
> At the same time, if it would serve to allay any lingering apprehension on the part of those who desire an explicit statutory mandate on this point, the Department would interpose no objection to appropriate mention of cancer in food additives legislation. If the specific disease were referred to in the law, it would however, be important for everyone to have a clear understanding that this would in no way restrict the Department's freedom in guarding against other harmful effects from food additives.

The HEW spokesman welcomed the amendment's reference to "appropriate tests," which it had urged:

> ... [T]he language suggested by some to bar carcinogenic additives would, if read literally, forbid the approval for use in food of any substance that causes any type of cancer in any test animal by any route of administration. This could lead to undesirable results which obviously were not intended by those who suggested the language. Concentrated sugar solution, lard, certain edible vegetable oils, and even cold water have been reported to cause a type of cancer at the site of injection when injected repeatedly by hypodermic needle into the same spot in a test animal. But scientists have not suggested that these same substances cause cancer when swallowed by mouth.

The enactment of a law which would seem to bar such common materials from the diet on the basis of the evidence described above, would place the agency that administered it in an untenable position. The agency would either have to try to enforce the law literally so as to keep these items out of the diet—evidently an impossible task—*or it would have to read between the lines of the law an intent which would make the law workable,* without a clear guide from Congress as to what was meant.

104 Cong. Rec. 17415 (August 13, 1958) (emphasis supplied). The bill was passed by the House with the revised amendment.

In the Senate, the House-passed bill was favorably reported without hearings. Commenting on the anticancer clause the Senate Report declared:

We applaud Congressman Delaney for having taken this, as he has every other opportunity, to focus our attention on the cancer-producing potentialities of various substances, but we want the record to show that in our opinion the bill is aimed at preventing the addition to the food our people eat of any substances the ingestion of which reasonable people would expect to produce not just cancer but any disease or disability. In short, we believe the bill reads and means the same with or without the inclusion of the clause referred to. This is also the view of the Food and Drug Administration.

S. Rep. No. 2422, 85th Cong., 2d Sess. 10–11 (1958). The bill passed the Senate and, after minor Senate amendments were agreed to by the House, was signed into law as the Food Additives Amendment of 1958.

---

3. LEGISLATIVE HISTORY OF THE COLOR ADDITIVES DELANEY CLAUSE

As recounted in Chapter II, not long after enactment of the Food Additives Amendment of 1958, the Supreme Court in the *Florida Citrus Exchange* case upheld FDA's interpretation of the existing coal tar color provisions which effectively disabled the agency from setting safe tolerances for any toxic color. Accordingly, both the agency and industry groups supported the enactment of legislation similar to the new food additives law to regulate the use of color additives.

The 1960 Color Additive Amendments contain a Delaney Clause similar in language and identical in principle to the clause that appears in section 409. For example, this clause precludes approval for food use of any color additive shown to induce cancer when ingested by experimental animals. Because the Amendments do not recognize a category of "generally recognized as safe" colors or exclude substances that were sanctioned or used prior to 1960, the Delaney Clause in section 706 applies to all food coloring agents except those that are only provisionally listed while further safety testing is being conducted.

The original House bill contained an anticancer clause; the bill initially introduced in the Senate was silent on the point. Both bills contained language comparable to the food additive legislation, requiring proof of the safety of a color before FDA could permanently list it. This requirement was not controversial and emerged in the final statute. The Senate bill was considered first and the Senate Committee on Labor and Public Welfare reported it favorably without an anticancer clause.

Just before Thanksgiving, 1959, HEW Secretary Flemming issued a statement advising the public about the possible contamination of substantial quantities of cranberries with a pesticide, aminotriazol, which FDA had recently determined was a carcinogen. Although the Act's pesticide residue provisions contain no anticancer clause, the agency determined that use of this pesticide could not be approved as safe, and that the public should be warned of the potential hazard. *See* Gellhorn, *Adverse Publicity by Administrative Agencies*, 86 Harv. L. Rev. 1380, 1408–10 (1973). During the same period, FDA determined that the previously-approved use of diethylstilbestrol (DES) in poultry resulted in detectable residues in liver and skin fat, *see* p. 877 *infra*. Although the 1958 Delaney Clause did not apply, because DES was subject to a prior sanction and therefore not a "food additive," FDA proposed to withdraw the new drug application for this use on the ground that the finding of residues confirmed that it was unsafe.

On the heels of these two episodes, HEW Secretary Flemming appeared before the House Commerce Committee in January 1960 to testify in support of the proposed color additive legislation. Because it was obvious that a major issue would be the desirability of including an anticancer clause, Flemming requested the National Cancer Institute to summarize the prevailing scientific knowledge about the etiology of cancer. The NCI summary concluded:

> No one at this time can tell how much or how little of a carcinogen would be required to produce cancer in any human being, or how long it would take the cancer to develop.

"Color Additives," Hearings Before the House Comm. on Interstate and Foreign Commerce, 86th Cong., 2d Sess. 45, 52 (1960).

After offering the NCI report for the record, Secretary Flemming testified:

> This is why we have no hesitancy in advocating the inclusion of the anticancer clause.

> Unless and until there is a sound scientific basis for the establishment of tolerances for carcinogens, I believe the Government has a duty to make clear—in law as well as in administrative policy—that it will do everything possible to

put persons in a position where they will not unnecessarily be adding residues of carcinogens to their diet. *Id.* at 61–62.

Flemming argued that the anticancer clause allowed greater room for scientific judgment than its critics claimed:

It has been suggested that once a chemical is shown to induce a tumor in a single rat, this forecloses further research and forever forbids the use of the chemical in food. This is not true. The conclusion that an additive "is found to induce cancer when ingested by man or animal" is a scientific one. The conclusion is reached by competent scientists using widely accepted scientific testing methods and critical judgment. An isolated and inexplicable tumor would not be a basis for concluding that the test substance produces cancer.....

This, I believe, is as far as our discretion should go in the light of present scientific knowledge. We have no basis for asking Congress to give us discretion to establish a safe tolerance for a substance which definitely has been shown to produce cancer when added to the diet of test animals. We simply have no basis on which such discretion could be exercised because no one can tell us with any assurance at all how to establish a safe dose of any cancer-producing substance.

Id. at 62. In a subsequent colloquy with Chairman Harris, Flemming returned to the distinction between the exercise of scientific judgment in identifying carcinogenic activity and the discretion to set tolerance levels for carcinogens:

When the time comes that our research reaches the place where that threshold can be identified, where a tolerance can be established that we know will not induce cancer in man, then we will come back and ask the Congress to give us authority to identify the threshold or to establish the tolerance. *Id.* at 95.

Even with Flemming's assurances, some feared that the Delaney Clause was too rigid. In early 1960, the President's Special Assistant for Science and Technology convened a panel of prominent scientists, chaired by the President of the National Academy of Sciences, to consider the regulation of carcinogens in food. The panel's report was released by the White House on May 14, 1960, just before the 1960 Amendments were to be voted on by the House and Senate. *See* President's Scientific Advisory Committee, REPORT OF THE PANEL ON FOOD ADDITIVES (May 1960), reprinted in 106 Cong. Rec. 15380 (July 1, 1960).

The report recounted the difficulties encountered in interpreting and administering the 1958 Delaney Clause:

The panel subscribes to the intent of the Congress in approving this Section of the Food Additives Amendment to protect the public from increasing cancer risks through the diet. However, there are certain difficulties in its practical application—difficulties which give rise to many uncertainties both on the part of the public and those whose responsibility it is to administer the law.

The report pointed out that trace amounts of carcinogens occur in common food products:

> In foodstuffs, as they occur in nature, one finds traces of chemicals which in larger amounts are generally accepted as carcinogenic, such as certain inorganic arsenic compounds, radium and selenium. It can be shown by methods of analysis now available that ordinary table salt derived from rock salt contains trace amounts of radium and that foodstuffs containing iron salts are contaminated by minute quantities of arsenic. Although it cannot be stated absolutely that these traces of carcinogenic materials have never induced cancer in any human, the available evidence has not directed suspicion to these trace amounts as significant to the over-all cancer morbidity.

The panel report concluded with this advice about regulatory policy:

> In applying the provisions of Section 409(c)(3) of the Food Additives Amendment ... the enforcing agency must employ the "rule of reason" based on scientific judgment in order to carry out the intent of the Congress to protect the public from the possibility of increasing cancer risks through the diet.
>
> The definition of a carcinogen implicit in the language of Section 409(c) requires discretion in its interpretation because so many variables enter into a judgment as to whether a particular substance is or is not carcinogenic.
>
> It is to be emphasized that the present difficulty in establishing whether there are permissible levels for certain possibly carcinogenic food additives is accentuated by the limited relevant scientific information available. From the experience obtained in animal experiments and study of humans who have been exposed to carcinogens in the course of their work such as cited above, the panel believes that the probability of cancer induction from a particular carcinogen in minute doses may be eventually assessed by weighing scientific evidence as it becomes available.
>
> The special emphasis placed by the Congress on the protection of the public from the dangers resulting from the addition of possible carcinogens to food calls for prudent administration of section 409(c).... Since an area of administrative discretion based on the rule of reason is unavoidable if the clause is to be workable, it is essential that this discretion be based on the most informed and expert scientific advice available. Until the causes of carcinogenesis are better understood, each situa-

tion must be judged in the light of all applicable evidence. In this way the protection of public health can best be assured.

> ... If existing legislation does not permit the Secretary of Health, Education, and Welfare to exercise discretion consistent with the recommendations of this report, it is recommended that appropriate modifications in the law be sought.

Id. at 8–9. This report was widely disseminated during the congressional debate on the 1960 Delaney Clause.

The House Commerce Committee, favorably reporting the bill ultimately enacted, H. R. Rep. No. 1761, 86th Cong., 2d Sess. 13–14 (1960), discussed several proposed amendments to the anticancer clause and explained why no changes were made:

> One industry witness objected to any anticancer clause. Another witness argued that it is possible to establish safe tolerance levels for substances that produce cancer when fed to test animals. Some would have the ban on cancer producers apply only to colors that induce cancer when ingested in an amount and under conditions reasonably related to their intended use. And another witness proposed that the cancer clause be taken out of its present position in the bill and added with material language changes to section 705(b)(5)(A) so that it would become simply one of the factors for the Secretary to consider in evaluating the safety of a color additive.

> It is evident that such proposed changes are intended to give the Secretary the right to establish tolerances for presumed safe levels of colors that produce cancer when tested under appropriate laboratory conditions. Thus, any of the proposals, if adopted, would weaken the present anticancer clause in the reported bill. For this reason all of the proposed changes were rejected by the committee.....

> Some of the panel members have suggested that despite these difficulties, in extraordinary cases, the Secretary of Health, Education, and Welfare should have the authority to decide that a minute amount of a cancer-producing chemical may be added to man's food after a group of scientists consider all the facts and conclude that the quantity to be tolerated is probably without hazard.....

> In view of the uncertainty surrounding the determination of safe tolerances for carcinogens, the committee decided that the Delaney anticancer provision in the reported bill should be retained without change.

The condition that any test demonstrating carcinogenicity be appropriate was incorporated in the enacted version of the anticancer clause. The clause contains two parts: A color additive that will or may result in ingestion is deemed unsafe if it is found to cause cancer when ingested or if it is found to cause cancer after tests "which are

appropriate for the evaluation of the safety of additives for use in food."
A color additive that will not be ingested, on the other hand, falls
within the proscription of the anticancer clause only if it is found to
cause cancer "after tests which are appropriate for the evaluation of
the safety of additives for such [non-ingestion] use, or after other
relevant exposure of man or animal to such additive."

For over a decade FDA applied either Delaney Clause on only two
occasions, both times to ban unimportant indirect food additives, 32
Fed. Reg. 5675 (April 7, 1967) (1,2–dihydro-2, 2, 4–trimethylquinoline,
polymerized), and 34 Fed. Reg. 19073 (December 2, 1968) (4,4–methylen-
ebis(2–choroanaline)). In that era few substances were systematically
tested for carcinogenicity, the customary test protocols were less rigorous than those now in use, and available analytical methods were not
sufficiently sensitive to detect trace amounts of known or suspected
carcinogens in consumer products. The 1970s, however, brought dramatic changes on several fronts.

D. REGULATION OF DIETHYLSTILBESTROL

While few substances have attracted as much attention from FDA,
Congress, or the public as diethylstilbestrol (DES), notoriety alone
would not justify an entire section. FDA's attempts to regulate DES,
however, illustrate several of the most difficult issues it has confronted
in regulating carcinogenic substances.

1. THE GENERAL SAFETY STANDARD
BELL v. GODDARD
United States Court of Appeals, Seventh Circuit, 1966.
366 F.2d 177.

SWYGERT, Circuit Judge.....

On December 10, 1959 the Secretary of Health, Education, and
Welfare announced that a recently completed re-examination of the use
of stilbestrol in the poultry industry had led him to the conclusion that
it was desirable to eliminate a potential cancer hazard to the consuming public occasioned by the ingestion of stilbestrol-treated poultry.
Shortly thereafter, this administrative proceeding was initiated by the
Commissioner of Food and Drugs..... [T]he Commissioner ... issued a
final order with findings of fact and conclusions of law suspending all
the new drug applications involved.... Thereafter the petitioner instituted this appeal....

The drug involved, Stilboserts, consists of pellets containing either
12 or 15 milligrams of diethylstilbestrol. The pellets, to be implanted
in live poultry, are designed to provide for the gradual release of DES
over a period of weeks. The labeling submitted with the new drug

application recommends the implantation of one tablet in chickens of any age four to six weeks before marketing, and two tablets in turkeys six weeks before marketing. Implantation is "under the loose skin just below the head." Stilboserts were recommended for poultry fattening and to produce tenderized, flavorized, upgraded poultry, and to improve feed efficiency.

DES is a synthetic estrogenic drug which was first used in medical practice in 1939; the use of natural estrogens in medicine dates to about 1920. The first new drug application for the use of DES in medicine was approved in 1941; a new drug application for use of DES in poultry production was first approved in 1947. The fact that oral administration of DES had been shown to produce cancer in test animals was known at that time, and DES was suspected of being carcinogenic to humans. It was believed, however, that no significant residue of the drug remained in the edible tissue of treated poultry.

Beginning in 1955, a team of scientists of the Food and Drug Administration headed by Dr. Ernest Umberger developed a bio-assay method of detecting and measuring the estrogenic residue remaining in edible tissues of poultry treated with drugs containing DES. . . . Dr. Umberger was able to calculate that the petitioner's product, Stilboserts, in 15 and 12 milligram doses, under the conditions of use in the petitioner's new drug application, results in [up to 50 ppb] residues of added DES four weeks after chickens are treated. . . .

DES is a synthetic organic compound which, when administered to man or animals, has all the biological effects of the naturally-occurring female sex hormones known as estrogens. Except for quantitative differences, the effects of DES or other estrogenic substances, on either humans or animals are identical, however administered. . . . On the basis of animal tests and clinical experience, experts have concluded that DES is a carcinogen to man. Prolonged exposure to small amounts of carcinogenic substances has been shown to be more dangerous than single or short term exposure to the same or larger quantities. There is no known threshold or safe level for DES, either as a cause or stimulator of cancer, and there is no known methodology by which such a level can be established.

Based upon these facts, the Commissioner determined that the addition of diethylstilbestrol to poultry, resulting in residues in the edible portions, was unsafe to the consuming public. . . .

The petitioner contends that the residues of DES found in the livers of caponettes which have been treated with Stilboserts are so miniscule as not to pose a health hazard, in other words, that Stilboserts were not shown to be "unsafe" within the meaning of section 355(e). He points to the evidence in the record that the caponette trade represented one per cent of the poultry market, an average of one caponette per year for every third family in the United States. Assuming residues of the order of forty-five parts per billion, as found by the examiner, this means, according to the petitioner, a total of six micrograms per caponette, a per capita exposure on the average of less than one microgram per year. The petitioner indicates that it is a common practice to apply a safety margin of 100 to 1. This would raise the exposure of DES in the diet per person to a maximum of 100 micrograms, which the petitioner says is an inconsequential, nonharmful residue of the drug in the diet. He further maintains that estrogen occurs in many natural foods and that, according to the evidence, the amount of estrogen exposure in the diet from a variety of common foodstuffs is greater than any exposure from caponette residues. The petitioner also points out that estrogen is produced naturally in the human body which has a regulatory mechanism that varies the amount produced, that this internal regulation in turn is affected by estrogen introduced by external sources, and that excess estrogen is detoxified and conjugated in the liver as a natural process, whatever its sources, natural or external. . . .

The answer to the petitioner's contentions in great part is that DES is a carcinogen. . . . It is true that the petitioner's expert witnesses disagreed, and testified that the small amount of DES found in caponette livers is safe and would not impose a risk. But this conflict in testimony does not mean that the Commissioner's ultimate finding that the petitioner's drug was not safe is without substantial evidentiary support.

Although the actual number or percentage of chickens treated with DES is unknown, it is a known fact that the consumption of caponettes is not evenly spread over the population. Therefore, attempting to assess the safety factor by averaging per capita consumption in order to show the lack of exposure and hazard, as the petitioner suggests, is not justified. Secondly, even though estrogen occurs naturally in certain foodstuffs, such as beef liver, eggs, and lettuce, there is as yet no knowledge of the amounts which are contained in such foods. The existence of natural estrogen in foodstuffs does not warrant the intake of DES by a deliberate means of exposure through the implantation of such drug in a chicken so as to make it tastier and to save feed costs. If estrogens are contained naturally in certain items of diet, there is no justification for adding more by an artificial method. Finally, the petitioner's contention that the DES residues found in caponettes create no hazard because the estrogen is detoxified and conjugated in the liver. of the person who ingests them finds little support in the record.

We hold that there is substantial evidentiary support for the Commissioner's order suspending the petitioner's new drug application for the product Stilboserts on the ground that the use of diethylstilbestrol according to the directions for use upon which the application became effective is unsafe within the meaning of section 505(e). . . .

---

2. THE DELANEY CLAUSE

DES had also been approved for use in cattle and sheep. Following enactment of the 1958 Food Additives Amendment, FDA took the position the Delaney Clause precluded it from approving any new DES uses or products. But the agency also concluded that it could not withdraw existing approvals because they constituted "prior sanctioned" uses that were exempt from the Act's definition of food additive and, thus, from the Delaney Clause as well. Faced with this discrepancy Congress enacted the so-called "DES proviso" as part of the Drug Amendments of 1962 to require FDA to resume approving DES for use in animals as long as no residue could be found in food produced from the animals. *See* 108 Cong. Rec. 21077–81 (September 27, 1962). The proviso appears in section 409(c)(3)(A) of the Act and reads as follows:

> [E]xcept that [the Delaney] proviso shall not apply with respect to the use of a substance as an ingredient of feed for animals which are raised for food production, if the Secretary finds (i) that, under the conditions of use and feeding specified in proposed labeling and reasonably certain to be followed in practice, such additive will not adversely affect the animals for which such feed is intended, and (ii) that no residue of the additive will be found (by methods of examination prescribed or approved by the Secretary by regulations, which regulations shall not be subject to subsections (f) and (g) of this section, in any edible portion of such animal after slaughter or in any food yielded by or derived from the living animal.

In the early 1970s, USDA monitoring of livers of slaughtered steers detected small residues of DES used in animal feed. FDA therefore promulgated a requirement that the withdrawal period for DES (*i.e.,* the time between the last use of DES in the feed of an animal and the date of slaughter) be extended from 48 hours to seven days. 36 Fed. Reg. 23292 (December 8, 1971). USDA simultaneously required written certification that this new withdrawal period was in fact followed. On March 11, 1972, FDA announced the opportunity for a hearing on a proposal to withdraw approval for use in liquid animal feed premixes, 37 Fed. Reg. 526 (January 13, 1972). Because of continuing reports of residues, the agency announced the opportunity for a hearing to determine whether *any* approvals for DES uses in animal feed or as implants could be continued, 37 Fed. Reg. 12251 (June 21, 1972).

Meanwhile, USDA undertook new analytic studies using a more sensitive radioactive tracer method to determine whether DES residues occurred only when the prescribed withdrawal period was ignored. When the test results showed residues even under the approved conditions of use, FDA concluded that the situation paralleled *Bell v. Goddard* and denied requests for a hearing and withdrew all approvals of DES for use in animal feed, 37 Fed. Reg. 26507 (December 9, 1972). Formal revocation of the applicable regulations was accomplished in 37 Fed. Reg. 26307 (December 9, 1972). The agency later obtained similar results from a study using radioactive tagged DES implants and therefore summarily withdrew approval of all NADAs for this use as well, 38 Fed. Reg. 10485 (April 27, 1973). A week later it also revoked the regulation prescribing the official method for detection of DES residues, 38 Fed. Reg. 10926 (May 3, 1973).

Various manufacturers of DES sought direct review of the agency's orders in the United States Court of Appeals for the District of Columbia Circuit. In response to a preliminary court order, additional requests for a hearing on the use of DES implants were filed. The agency once more denied a hearing, 38 Fed. Reg. 29510 (October 25, 1973).

HESS & CLARK, DIV. OF RHODIA, INC. v. FDA

United States District Court of Appeals, District of Columbia Circuit, 1974.
495 F.2d 975.

LEVENTHAL, Circuit Judge.

We set aside the Commissioner's orders and remand the case to the FDA for further proceedings..... The Commissioner bases his withdrawal of approval of the NADA for DES pellets on 21 U.S.C. § 360b(e)(1)(B). The Act provides that the Secretary may issue such an order only after "due notice and opportunity for hearing." The only bases for permitting withdrawal of approval for an NADA without a prior hearing are (1) the statutory proviso relating to emergency action in the fact of an imminent hazard to health, and (2) the provisions in the regulations for "summary judgment."....

In the instant case, there is no determination by the Secretary that there was an imminent hazard from DES implants to the health of man or animals....

... There is no doubt of the general validity of the agency's "summary judgment" regulations and procedure. But they must be applied consistently with basic fairness, and with the statutory requirement that the order may be issued only after "due notice and opportunity for hearing." Thus, the issue is whether the Commissioner gave adequate notice to the petitioners and then received responses insufficient to raise material issues of fact.....

The June, 1972, Notice did not and could not contain any of the data on which the FDA relied in withdrawing its approval of the petitioner's NADA's..... [U]ntil petitioners had notice of the test results, and of the FDA interpretation of those results, they cannot be said to have had due notice and opportunity for hearing....

Moreover, the Commissioner ... change[d] his theory. The June, 1972, Notice indicated that the Commissioner planned to withdraw his approval of the NADA's pursuant to 21 U.S.C. § 360b(e).... However, in the August, 1972, Order to the premix suppliers—which FDA now wishes to be reconstituted as a "notice" to the implant suppliers—the Commissioner stated that his action withdrawing approval of the premix NADA's was "required under the strict terms of section 512(d)(1)(H) and 512(e)(1)(B) of the Act." ... [T]he Commissioner's statement, fairly read, identifies a reliance on the Delaney Clause theory.... In this court, however, counsel for the Commissioner argue that the Commissioner's action was never based on the Delaney Clause.....

... [B]y April, 1973, in deciding whether to accord the petitioners a hearing, the FDA had before it the substantial data from the USDA testing program, the information contained in the NADA's that the petitioners had filed and that the FDA had approved in the 1950's, and the responses which the petitioners had made to the June 21, 1972, Notice. At that time, the specific information received from the USDA should have been transmitted by FDA to the petitioners with provision of opportunity to answer. Without such a submission of the basis on which he proposed to act, in a statement transmitted to petitioners prior to the cut-off date for a response, the Commissioner's use of summary judgment was invalid.....

... [T]he FDA can remove a drug from the market when new evidence indicates a violation of the Delaney Clause. If the FDA, using an approved test method, detected residues of DES in edible portions of slaughtered animals, then it could show a violation of the Delaney Clause.

In the instant case, however, despite references to the Delaney Clause, and despite continual reference in the briefs and at oral argument to the fact that DES is a carcinogen, the FDA has plainly not used the Delaney Clause theory. One possible reason for this election is that the detected residues may not be DES residues and hence the Delaney Clause may be inoperative. In any event, the USDA did not detect the residues while using an "approved" test method as required by the Delaney Clause. In it regulations, the FDA has approved only the "mouse-uterine" test. Using this test, no residues have been found in the tissues of slaughtered animals. Rather, the only method by which residues have been detected is the radioisotope tracer test, but that method has not been approved. For that reason, the Delaney Clause is plainly inapplicable, without regard to the composition of the residues.

The Commissioner relies on the alternative theory of the "general safety" clause of section 360b(e)(1)(B), contending that the new evidence from the USDA tests "shows that [DES] is not shown to be safe.".... The statute plainly places on the FDA an initial burden to adduce the "new evidence" and what that new evidence "shows." Only when the FDA has met this initial burden of coming forward with the new evidence is there a burden on the manufacturer to show that the drug is safe. Only at this later stage must the manufacturer produce "adequate tests" of safety.....

Because he is not using the Delaney Clause, it is not enough for the Commissioner merely to show that animal carcasses contain residues and that DES is a carcinogen. Instead, the FDA must show that two different issues are resolved in its favor before it can shift to petitioners the burden of showing safety: (1) whether the detected residues are related to the use of DES implants; (2) if so, whether the residues, because of their composition, and in the amounts present in the tissue, present some potential hazard to the public health.

Petitioners have submitted material supporting the assertion that the testing method itself produced the detected residues. The thrust of these submissions is that the residues resulted from the presence of impurities in the specially made "tagged" implants. Hess & Clark speculates that some of these impurity-caused residues may be so-called "pseudo-DES," while the composition of the remainder is unknown.

... This issue is quite material: if the residues are caused by the test, then the Commissioner could hardly maintain that their presence shows that commercial use of DES implants is not shown to be safe. Accordingly, we conclude that petitioner's submissions raise substantial and material issues of fact about the very premise of the FDA action, *i.e.* that commercial use of DES implants has caused harmful residues in human food. Even if the commercial use of DES implants causes the detected residues, petitioners further assert that a material issue exists whether implants are safe. The FDA argues that if the residues exist, and if the implants caused them, then the manufacturers have the burden of proving the safety of their products.....

This argument skimps FDA's responsibility. The ... statute requires the FDA to consider the relationship between a drug's safety and residues left in food because of use of the drug. The statute does not say that because a drug leaves residues, it is unsafe *per se*. We think it implicit in the statute that when the FDA proposes to withdraw an approval because new evidence shows the drug leaves residues, it has an initial burden of coming forward with some evidence of the relationship between the residue and safety to warrant shifting to the manufacturer the burden of showing safety. This is at least the case where, as here, the residues are of unknown composition.....

Even if the residues were "free DES" rather than DES conjugate, petitioner Vineland has submitted data indicating that such small amounts of DES are safe. So long as the Commissioner does not invoke the Delaney Clause, that issue is not foreclosed by a showing that larger amounts of DES are carcinogenic. The FDA routinely allows sale in limited quantities of drugs that would be lethal in substantial amounts, and it has acknowledged that small amounts of DES may present no danger to the consumer.[57]

Outside of the *per se* rule of the Delaney Clause, the typical issue for the FDA is not the absolute safety of a drug. Most drugs are unsafe

---

57. Hess & Clark's reply brief quotes testimony by Dr. Henry Simmons, then director of the FDA's Bureau of Drugs in which he stated that consumption of liver containing (presumably) 2 ppb of DES would pose a pregnant woman no hazard. Moreover, the agency has recently sanctioned the substantial ingestion of DES (albeit by a limited group of consumers) in

in some degree.[58] Rather, the issue for the FDA is whether to allow sale of the drug, usually under specific restrictions. Resolution of this issue inevitably means calculating whether the benefits which the drug produces outweigh the costs of its restricted use. In the present case, DES is asserted to be of substantial benefit in enhancing meat production, and this is not gainsaid by FDA. The FDA must consider, after hearing, whether DES pellets would be safe in terms of the amounts of residue consumed. Or the FDA might restrict such consumption by a ban on sale of liver, the only food material in which any residues have even been detected. . . .

Thus, as to the relationship of the residues and safety, there exist in this case at least three issues: (1) whether the detected residues are composed solely of DES conjugates, and whether that substance is harmful; (2) whether, if they consist of DES, the residues are nonetheless harmless; (3) whether, if the residues are harmful, the FDA should keep DES implants from the market, in light of their acknowledged value and of the possibility for meaningful restrictions on consumption of the residues.

NOTE

In *Chemetron Corp. v. United States Department of HEW*, 495 F.2d 995 (D.C. Cir. 1974), decided the same day as *Hess & Clark*, the Court of Appeals reversed FDA's withdrawal of the NADAs for DES premixes. Judge Leventhal ruled that the Commissioner's explicit reliance on the Delaney Clause as a basis for withdrawal was misplaced because the drug residues detected by USDA in animals fed DES had not been identified by the mouse uterine assay method previously approved by FDA.

In 39 Fed. Reg. 11323 (March 27, 1974), FDA reinstated the NADAs for DES and encouraged further precautions to reduce the possibility of residues. Simultaneously the agency took the first step toward final revocation of the NADAs by proposing to revoke the currently approved mouse uterine test method of detecting DES residues, 39 Fed. Reg. 11299 (March 27, 1974). For the next 22 months the matter was held in abeyance pending development of a general policy respecting the required sensitivity of methods of detecting residues of carcinogenic animal drugs, the subject of the next part. When that project could not be concluded expeditiously, FDA published a notice of opportunity for a hearing on a proposal to withdraw approval of all NADAs for DES, 41 Fed. Reg. 1804 (January 12, 1976), and later ordered a hearing with respect to those NADAs on which a hearing was requested, 41 Fed. Reg. 52105 (November 26, 1976).

After a lengthy evidentiary hearing FDA's Administrative Law Judge issued an Initial Decision concluding that the Delaney Clause did

the so called "morning after" pill. 38 Fed. Reg. 26,809 (September 26, 1973).

58. See R. Merrill, *Compensation for Prescription Drug Injuries,* 59 Va. L. Rev. 1, 2–29 (1973) (and sources cited therein).

not require withdrawal of the NADAs but that DES had not been shown to be safe. Food Drug Cosm. L. Rep. (CCH) ¶ 38,198 (September 21, 1978). This ruling was appealed to the Commissioner of Food and Drugs.

DIETHYLSTILBESTROL: WITHDRAWAL OF APPROVAL OF NEW ANIMAL DRUG APPLICATION

44 Federal Register 54852 (September 21, 1979).

As Commissioner of Food and Drugs, I am . . . ordering withdrawal of approval of new animal drug applications . . . for diethylstilbestrol (DES) implants and liquid and dry feed premixes for use in cattle and sheep. . . . .

. . . [This] Decision discusses what might at first appear to be very small amounts of DES in edible tissues of meat from treated animals. Yet, as a respected cancer expert has testified, we have no data upon which to base the conclusion that any amount of a carcinogen above the single-molecule level would not produce a response. The risk of cancer would, of course, be expected to be lower the smaller the number of molecules of a carcinogen that are ingested. . . . . [T]he risk associated with DES must be considered in light of the widespread consumption of DES-treated meat. In 1975, over 25 million head of DES-treated cattle (and over 7 million head of DES-treated sheep) were reported slaughtered.

. . . [A]lthough there is evidence, discussed below, that DES used as medication in pregnant women causes cancer in some of their female offspring, it is unlikely that any individual will ever be identified as having been afflicted with cancer because he or she consumed meat containing residues of DES in the range of parts per billion. . . . [B]ecause our population is inevitably exposed to a variety of carcinogens, it is generally impossible (in the absence of evidence of, for example, occupational exposure to carcinogenic chemicals) to attribute any specific cancer to any specific cause. Yet this record warrants a finding that a significant (though unquantifiable) number of the cancers that do occur in this country today are associated with the use of DES in food-producing animals. . . .

The Administrative Law Judge found that neither the approved analytical method for DES nor any other analytical method is adequate for use with DES. He was not, however, authorized to revoke the regulations setting out the approved analytical method for DES and did not purport to do so. Because, at the time of the Initial Decision, there was an approved method and no residues had been reported by that method, the Administrative Law Judge found that the Delaney Clause had not been shown to apply to DES.

. . . I am now revoking the analytical method for DES. My decision to do so is supported by the evidence in the record that no analytical method is acceptable for DES. Because there is now no approved method of analysis for DES, I conclude that the Delaney Clause applies to the drug. I therefore withdraw approval of the DES NADA's on that ground....

I have carefully considered whether the evidence in the record shows that use of DES as an animal drug results in DES residues in edible tissues.... I have found convincing evidence on this issue from two separate sets of data: the radiotracer studies and the results of the Department of Agriculture monitoring program....

... I find that DES is a carcinogen [in animals] and that the results of the Gass study do not demonstrate a no-effect level for the carcinogenicity of DES. The NCTR data are not complete and cannot be relied upon. The results of the NCTR study reported by Dr. Jukes would not, at any rate, justify a finding that there is a no-effect level for DES. These findings warrant a conclusion that DES has not been shown to be safe and that is it unsafe.....

... I find that evidence in the record concerning the incidence of clear cell adenocarcinoma in daughters of mothers treated with DES (the Herbst data) supports the conclusion (which may also be drawn from animal carcinogenicity data) that DES presents a human cancer risk. The evidence from the treatment of women with DES provides no basis for concluding that there is a no-effect level for DES with respect to cancer. These findings warrant the conclusions that DES has not been shown to be safe and that it is unsafe.....

... The Administrative Law Judge held that under 21 U.S.C. § 306b consideration of the alleged societal benefits of the use of DES is not an appropriate part of the decision whether approval of the new animal drug application should be withdrawn. This interpretation of the statute is supported by the legislative history of the statute, is consistent with positions the agency has taken previously on this issue, and reflects sound public policy. In *Hess & Clark, Division of Rhodia, Inc. v. FDA,* 495 F.2d 975 (D.C. Cir. 1974), however, the Court stated in *dictum* that the FDA should consider the benefits of the use of DES should it proceed under the "safety clause."

There is, of course, an obvious difference between the therapeutic benefits of a drug, which often alleviate a risk to the person to whom the drug is administered, and so-called "socio-economic" benefits associated with the use of a drug. The former are the *only* type of benefits that the FDA considers in determining whether a human drug is safe. The agency never considers socio-economic benefits in making that decision. Moreover, the consideration of risks and benefits with respect to human drugs is always based on the premise that before being exposed to risk, an individual patient will have the protection of either a physician's evaluation (in the case of a prescription drug) or adequate directions for use enabling the patient himself to decide whether to run the risk (in the case of an over-the-counter drug). No such protection is available to those exposed to the risk from residues of DES in meat.....

... Congress ... did not authorize or require consideration of the socio-economic benefits of an animal drug in determining its safety. Indeed, the language adopted by Congress, having its roots in the human drug and food additive provisions of the law, clearly reflects an intention that FDA definitely not consider socio-economic benefits in making decisions on the safety of animal drugs. I thus conclude that Congress has made the determination that an animal drug that poses a risk to humans can never be considered "safe" because it provides an economic or other social benefit to society.....

The manufacturing parties do quote from the preamble to regulations issued by the FDA in 1976 that deal not with animal drugs but rather with food additives. As first proposed in September of 1974, these regulations would have defined "safe" and "safety" to include consideration of, among other factors, "[t]he benefit contributed by the substance" (39 FR 34194 (September 23, 1974)). When the final regulations were issued, this consideration was deleted. In an apparent attempt to explain the agency's rationale for the original proposal, however, the preamble to the final regulation made the following statement (41 FR 53601; December 7, 1976):

> The Commissioner concludes that it is appropriate to recognize that the benefit contributed by a substance is inevitably a factor to be considered in determining whether a particular substance is "safe" (or generally recognized as "safe") for its intended use. The term "safe" is to be given its ordinary meaning, and in its common usage the term is understood to carry an assessment of benefits and risks. It is true, as the comment states, that minor food additives are not approved at levels that may present a hazard to the normal consumer. This result is required by the act because the benefit of a minor food additive is too small to justify the imposition of a known risk to normal consumers; use of such ingredient at levels that may present a hazard to the normal consumer would not be "safe." However, this result does not necessarily follow in the case of important food additives. For example, if it were found that a major food source such as meat or grain was associated with the development of chronic diseases in normal individuals, it would not necessarily follow that the food was unsafe within the meaning of the act. The ordinary understanding of the term "safe" would require some benefit-to-risk analysis in such circumstances.

> Another example relates to the incidence of allergic reactions to particular food ingredients. Adverse reactions caused by allergy are clearly a consideration in determining whether a food ingredient is safe. Ordinarily, the incidence of allergic reactions from a food additive cannot be considered because data and test protocols do not exist. When data exist, however, they may be considered, and an assessment of benefits and risks becomes relevant. For example, if it were deter-

mined that both a particular emulsifier and a particular fruit resulted in the same unusually high incidence of allergic reactions, one might reasonably conclude that the emulsifier was not safe but that the fruit was safe. Such conclusions would simply represent common understanding of the concept of safety * * *

The Commissioner has, however, deleted from the regulations the reference to consideration of benefits on the ground that this separate consideration is legitimately included within the concept of safety as used in the act. Furthermore, explicitly retaining the criterion of benefit in the regulations might be construed as requiring routine formal analysis of a factor that the agency will only occasionally need to take into account, because the agency's general guidelines will result in disapproval of food additives that may cause toxic effects in normal individuals.

This language is quoted in full because I am, on behalf of the FDA, disavowing it. It has never been the basis for an agency decision. As discussed, there is no justification for such a statement either in the statute itself or in its legislative history.....

... There are persuasive policy arguments against having an administrative agency such as the FDA make the kind of risk-benefit analysis sought by the manufacturing parties here. It may be that preliminary issues in this analysis are of the type that the FDA is qualified by experience and expertise to resolve. The agency is equipped, for instance, to evaluate calculations of the risk from a drug such as DES if the necessary data are available (they are not here). Once the risk and the benefits of an animal drug are determined, however, the ultimate issues require pure value judgments....

Here ... the manufacturing parties ask the FDA to weigh a risk of cancer and other serious adverse effects against an economic benefit. Arguably, the persons at risk also receive part of the economic benefit because the meat they purchase may be available at a lower price because of the use of DES. But much of the economic benefit, as evidenced by the tenacity with which the withdrawal of the DES NADA's has been fought, goes to parties other than the consumers of the meat products of DES-treated animals.

Perhaps society is willing to expose all of its meat-consuming members to a relatively small risk of cancer and other adverse effects in order to provide a small economic benefit to those consumers and a larger economic benefit to DES producers and, potentially, users. The FDA is not, however, qualified in any particular way to make that value judgment for society. The value judgment could not be supported by a record; a record could support only factual findings not value judgments. Nor could the value judgment be effectively reviewed by a court, which in general is limited to consideration of facts, law, and procedures. In a democratic system, the appropriate place for value judgments to be made is the legislature. Here, as discussed above, it is apparent that Congress has shouldered the responsibility for resolving this issue. It has decided that no economic benefit justifies use of an animal drug that presents an identifiable risk to the health of consumers.

NOTES

1. *Judicial Review.* In *Rhone–Poulenc, Inc. v. Food and Drug Administration,* 636 F.2d 750 (D.C. Cir. 1980), the Commissioner's withdrawal of the NADAs for DES was upheld. But the court of appeals declined to rule on the validity of his reliance on the Delaney Clause and went out of its way to reject his treatment of the court's earlier discussion of the role of benefits in evaluating the safety of animal drug residues.

2. *Subsequent Proceedings.* While the *Rhone–Poulenc* case was pending, FDA formally withdrew approval of the NADAs for DES in 44 Fed. Reg. 39387, 39388, and 39618 (July 6, 1979). While partial stays of the effective date of these regulations were granted, 44 Fed. Reg. 42679, 42781 (July 20, 1979), 44 Fed. Reg. 45618, 45764 (August 3, 1979), the ban of DES became effective on November 1, 1979, and USDA therefore also revoked its DES certification requirements, 44 Fed. Reg. 59498 (October 16, 1979).

3. *Continued Illegal Use.* The ban of DES was disregarded by many cattle growers. FDA determined that, even though continued use was illegal, "the public interest is not well served by the discard of a large number of food-producing animals that can be reconditioned" and it therefore established criteria in 45 Fed. Reg. 27014 (April 22, 1980) for allowing food from illegally treated cattle to be marketed. FDA subsequently revised its conditions for marketing in 45 Fed. Reg. 51921 (August 5, 1980). FDA prosecuted some producers that had illegally implanted DES, with mixed results. *See* "DES Update," FDA Talk Paper T81–11 (April 20, 1981); "DES Prosecutions," FDA Talk Paper T84–94 (December 24, 1984); *United States v. Cermiga,* 20 FDA Consumer, No. 7, at 40 (September 1986). The agency's seizure of illegal supplies of DES was upheld, *United States v. Articles of Drug Containing Dicthylstilbestrol,* FDC L. Rep. (CCH) ¶ 38,145 (D. Neb. 1981). When the government attempted to condemn carcasses of cattle that had been illegally implanted, however, the court ruled that it failed to prove that the beef contained an added poisonous or deleterious substance that could render the food injurious to health. *United States v. 2,116 Boxes of Boned Beef,* 516 F. Supp. 321 (D. Kan. 1981). The government did not appeal this ruling.

4. *DES for Human Use.* At the same time FDA was pursuing withdrawal of approval of DES for animal use, the agency promulgated a regulation stating its willingness to approve NDAs for use of DES as a postcoital human contraceptive under carefully controlled conditions. 40 Fed. Reg. 5351 (February 5, 1975). *See* 21 C.F.R. § 310.501(b), including the requirement that manufacturers supply a package insert for the patients given the drug. As of June 30, 1990, no manufacturers of human dosage forms of DES had sought approval in accordance with the terms of this regulation.

5. *Proposed Statutory Bans.* The United States Senate twice passed legislation to forbid the approval of DES use in animals or in humans. *See* S. Rep. No. 1088, 92d Cong., 2d Sess. (1972), 118 Cong. Rec. 31537–50 (1972); S. Rep. No. 264, 94th Cong., 1st Sess. (1975), 121 Cong. Rec. 27851–82 and 28155–80 (1975). On both occasions the House failed to act.

6. *Commentary.* For a lively debate on the DES controversy, *see Public Policy Panel: FDA—Diethylstilbestrol,* in Hiatt, Watson and Winsten, ORIGINS OF HUMAN CANCER, Vol. C, at 1651–82 (1977).

7. *Nitrofurans.* FDA has also taken action to revoke the NADAs for animal drugs containing nitrofurans on the ground that they are carcinogenic. FDA initially proposed to withdraw approval of the NADAs under the general safety requirements of the FD&C Act in 36 Fed. Reg. 5926 (March 31, 1971), 36 Fed. Reg. 14343 (August 4, 1971), then invoked the Delaney Clause as well, 41 Fed. Reg. 19907 (May 13, 1976), announced a hearing on both of these issues in 49 Fed. Reg. 34965, 34967, 34971 (September 4, 1984), and began the hearing in 1985. The Administrative Law Judge handed down his Initial Decision in favor of the agency on November 12, 1986 and the manufacturer appealed to the Commissioner. As of January 1, 1991, the Commissioner had not issued his decision.

E. QUANTITATIVE RISK ASSESSMENT

Prior to 1972, the possibility that the magnitude of the risk presented by a carcinogen could be estimated had been discussed in the scientific literature but had not received serious attention from regulatory agencies. In reaction to its problems with DES, however, FDA turned to quantitative risk assessment as a tool for regulating carcinogenic animal drugs. By the end of the decade the agency was relying on quantitative risk estimates in arriving at decisions on carcinogenic constituents in food, drugs, medical devices, and cosmetics. Other Federal health and safety agencies also embraced this technique in evaluating carcinogens.

Quantitative risk assessment is the mathematical extrapolation of data from high-dose animal feeding studies to derive statistical estimates of the cancer risk associated with the much smaller amounts of a carcinogenic substance to which humans typically are exposed under actual conditions of use. Risk assessment involves four steps: identifying a hazard, generally on the basis of animal studies; extrapolating from the high animal doses to predict human response at lower doses; assessing the degree of human exposure to the substance; and characterizing the risk to humans on the basis of the computed dose-response curve, human exposure, and all other relevant information. *See generally* National Academy of Sciences, RISK ASSESSMENT IN THE FEDERAL GOVERNMENT: MANAGING THE PROCESS (1983).

Because of uncertainties in the risk assessment process, assumptions must be made to fill gaps in underlying scientific knowledge. It is standard practice among regulators and many scientists to rely on highly conservative assumptions at each stage of the process. For example, it is assumed that laboratory animals are appropriate models for human risk; data from the most sensitive sex of the most sensitive animal species are chosen; benign are equated with malignant tumors; the relationship between dose and response is assumed to be linear rather than to decrease more rapidly at low doses, as biological models and studies would often suggest; human exposure and absorption rates are overestimated; and the uncertainties at each stage of the process are assumed away at the next stage. In all, risk assessment generally produces "worst-case" estimates that may be orders of magnitude higher than the actual risk.

1. CARCINOGENIC ANIMAL DRUGS

Section 512(d)(1)(H) of the FD&C Act—the so-called "DES proviso" —allows FDA to approve a carcinogenic new animal drug for use in food-producing animals if it concludes that, when used in accordance with its label directions, "no residue" will be found in the food derived from the animals using the detection method prescribed by FDA. Obviously, the sensitivity of the detection method FDA prescribes will determine the likelihood of finding residues. An extremely sensitive method will detect minute residues. A method that is not very sensitive may fail to detect residues that pose a significant risk.

For more than a decade FDA had no uniform criteria for determining the level of sensitivity it should require for detection methods. Sometimes it simply approved the best method available. More often it insisted that a drug's sponsor submit a method capable of measuring a specified level of residues, typically 2 ppb. In 1973 FDA chose to rely on quantitative risk assessment to determine the sensitivity of the detection method required to allow approval of any carcinogenic animal drug. In short, the agency decided to key the required level of detection sensitivity to the risk posed by residues that might escape detection.

The key to FDA's "sensitivity of method" (SOM) approach is the performance of a quantitative risk assessment for the animal drug under consideration. In proposed regulations published in 38 Fed. Reg. 19226 (July 19, 1973), the agency prescribed a modified version of the Mantel–Bryan method as the appropriate mathematical extrapolation model. It allowed adjustments to account for differences between animals and humans, and it specified that a one in 100 million lifetime individual risk of cancer could be considered "acceptable." Using the agency's proposed formula, it was possible to calculate the level of drug residues which, were it to occur in the food derived from the animal, would be regarded as "safe." The drug's sponsor would then be required to submit a detection method capable of measuring residues at or below this level.

FDA issued final regulations, 42 Fed. Reg. 10412 (February 22, 1977), which adopted a 1975 refinement of the Mantel–Bryan mathematical extrapolation model and revised the acceptable risk level to one in one million. The regulations were then challenged on both procedural and substantive grounds. In *Animal Health Institute v. FDA*, Food Drug Cosm. L. Rep. (CCH) ¶ 38,154 (D.D.C. 1978), the court concluded that changes FDA had made in the extrapolation model between the proposal and the final order were substantial enough to require a remand to the agency for consideration whether to supplement the record or to allow another opportunity for public comment. FDA subsequently revoked the 1977 regulations, 43 Fed. Reg. 22675 (May 26, 1978), and published a new "sensitivity of method" proposal.

CHEMICAL COMPOUNDS IN FOOD–PRODUCING ANIMALS: CRITERIA AND PROCEDURES FOR EVALUATING ASSAYS FOR CARCINOGENIC RESIDUES

44 Federal Register 17070 (March 20, 1979).

These proposed regulations would provide an operational definition of the no-residue requirement of the so-called "DES proviso" to the anticancer clauses. The regulations also propose to establish criteria for accepting assays and procedures for establishing suitable postadministration withdrawal periods to prevent the occurrence of carcinogenic residues in edible animal products....

Based on experience with the principles outlined in the [1973] proposal, gained through several years of regulating these chemicals on a case-by-case basis, the Commissioner believes that they have potential applicability for regulating all compounds covered by the act. Moreover, due to the extensive interest in the issues, the Commissioner now believes that the time is ripe for formulating a comprehensive approach for regulating all chemical carcinogens..... Because an error in selecting the basic principles could lead to a future tragedy, the principles adopted at this time must be reasonable and must not underestimate the potential risks associated with the use of chemicals. Accordingly, the Commissioner is proposing to adopt principles that some may consider too "conservative."....

Two interpretations of the [DES] proviso are, in theory, possible. The first interpretation, which in the Commissioner's judgment is the less probable, is that Congress intended to allow FDA to approve the use of a carcinogenic compound in food-producing animals only if the agency could be absolutely positive that no traces whatever—no matter how small—would remain in edible tissues.

This interpretation presents several difficulties, all stemming from the fact that any introduction of a compound, whether or not carcinogenic, is likely to leave in edible tissues minute residues, which are below the level of detection of any known or likely to be developed method of analysis, i.e., assay.... Although different assays may have different lowest limits of measurement, all assays are subject to the same type of limitation. Thus, when a tissue is examined with an assay having a lowest limit of measurement of 1 ppb and no interpretable response is observed, the analyst can conclude only that the compound under analysis is not present at a level of 1 ppb or above. It can never be concluded that the compound is "not present" in the absolute sense. It is thus impossible to determine the conditions under which edible tissues derived from food-producing animals that have received a carcinogen will contain no residue if the phrase "no residue" is to be interpreted literally....

This interpretation would thus render the DES proviso a "Catch–22." The proviso would permit the Commissioner to approve carcinogenic drugs for animals only when certain that no residues whatever would remain, but since the Commissioner could conclude only that some trace might well remain, no such drug could ever be approved....

... [T]he "absolutely no molecules" interpretation seems, at the very least, an improbable interpretation of an amendment enacted by Congress precisely because it wanted to relieve animal drugs from the rigid strictures of the anticancer clauses. Moreover, any interpretation of a statutory provision that would render it totally inoperative should be rejected unless considerations of overwhelming persuasiveness require that interpretation.....

A second, and in the Commissioner's view more plausible, interpretation of the DES proviso accepts the words of the amendment and focuses on the ... language, "no residue of such drug will be found * * * by methods of examination prescribed or approved by the Secretary by regulations * * *." Under this interpretation, a sponsored compound that is carcinogenic may be approved for use in animals if examination of edible tissues by an assay approved by FDA reveals no residues.....

The Commissioner believes that the criteria to be applied in evaluating assays for carcinogenic residues in the edible tissue of food-producing animals must further the congressional intent to minimize public exposure to carcinogens, without nullifying the decision reflected in the DES proviso, as the first interpretation of the proviso would do. As explained more fully below, the criteria set forth in these regulations for evaluating assays for carcinogenic residues are minimum requirements. They are designed to identify assays that are (1) reliable and practical for use by a regulatory agency and (2) capable of measuring residues at levels that have been determined, on the basis of animal toxicity tests, to present no significant increase in human risk of cancer. An assay that does not meet both criteria cannot be approved.....

... [W]ith two possible exceptions not applicable here (establishment of tolerances for unavoidable contaminants under section 406 and for pesticides under 408(h)), the Federal Food, Drug, and Cosmetic Act contains no provisions requiring the Commissioner to consider costs or technical feasibility in making any safety decision, including any decision involving cancer-causing chemicals. The distinction between the statutory provisions applicable to food additives, color additives, and animal drugs and those applicable to pesticides and unavoidable contaminant tolerances demonstrates Congress' decision to make costs and technical feasibility relevant to some public health matters but not to others. Nevertheless, in light of the court's remand order, the Commissioner recognized the agency's obligations to review this element of the proposal. Based on the act's legislative history, the case law, and the agency's public protection function, the Commissioner concludes that the procedures used to designate requirements for assays can be technology-forcing if necessary.....

..... By enacting and twice re-enacting the Delaney clause, Congress made clear its willingness to ban entirely from the human food supply food additives, color additives, and animal drugs that present a carcinogenic risk to man. It enacted the DES proviso with the intent and expectation that the provision that "no residue * * * will be found" would sufficiently protect the human food supply from any significant cancer risk from food additives, color additives, and animal drugs. Thus, in enacting the DES proviso, Congress did not change in any way the policy of the Delaney clause to protect the human food supply from carcinogenic additives and animal drugs; it merely eliminated an application of the clause that it considered unnecessary to the complete achievement of that policy.

From this statutory structure and language, it is evident that any consideration of feasibility and costs is subsidiary to the overriding congressional purpose to permit no additional human cancer risk from food additives, color additives, or animal drugs. The Commissioner's discretion to establish "methods of examination" for detecting residues is to be exercised so as to carry out that congressional purpose. The factor that determines the acceptable level of measurement of an assay method is protection of the human food supply from carcinogenic risks. If, on the basis of toxicological considerations, the Commissioner determines that a certain level of assay measurement is necessary to prevent a significant human cancer risk from use of a carcinogenic substance in food animals, then a method having that level of measurement is necessary to carry out the congressional purpose. If no such method is feasible, or if it is too costly to develop or apply one, then the choice is between refusing to permit the use of the substance altogether and permitting its use despite the fact there is no method of examination that can prevent the use of the substance from presenting a significant human cancer risk. Under the general safety clause and the Delaney clause, that choice can be resolved in only one way: by refusing to permit the use of the substance.....

It is true that these proposed regulations will permit the approval, for use in animal feed or for use as animal drugs, of carcinogenic compounds that are likely to leave residues below the lowest level of reliable measurement of any assay meeting all the criteria of the regulation. Indeed, as a result of Congress' enacting the DES proviso, the agency will not have any certainty that these residues, in amounts below the level of detectability, are not always present. This result makes sense in practical terms, however, for a regulatory agency cannot effectively control residues—of any compound—that are so small that they escape measurement by every available assay.....

If it has been determined that a sponsored compound when administered to food-producing animals has the potential to contaminate edible tissue with residues whose consumption may pose a risk of human carcinogenesis, the agency cannot approve the sponsored compound unless it can be demonstrated that conditions of use can be established that ensure that the no-residue requirement of the act will be met. To establish those conditions of use and to provide a means for ascertaining whether these conditions are met in actual practice, some operational definition of "no residue" is necessary....

The Commissioner has considered three basic alternative approaches to an operational definition of the phrase. Under one approach, the term "no residue" might be operationally defined as satisfied when the levels of residues fall below those that can be measured by available analytical methodology. A second approach would be to establish some low finite level (*e.g.*, 1 part per billion) as a "practical zero" and to require assays that can reliably measure this zero, and to insist on the development of new assays if available assays are not adequate. Finally, "no residue" might be operationally defined on the basis of quantitative carcinogenicity testing of residues and the extrapolation of test data using one of a number of available procedures to arrive at levels that are safe in the total diet of test animals and that would, if they occurred, be considered safe in the total diet of man. Under this approach, the Commissioner would require assays that can reliably measure that safe level in edible tissues. For the reasons discussed below in this preamble, the Commissioner has concluded that alternative 3 should be adopted.....

By adopting this approach to implementing the no-residue standard, the Commissioner has assumed that: (i) The dose-response relationship between chemical compounds and carcinogenesis can be quantified, and (ii) a dietary level of a carcinogen can be identified at which no significant human risk of carcinogenesis would derive from consuming food containing residues below this level.

The dose-response relationships between compounds and carcinogenesis can be determined by testing in experimental animals, although the determinations are subject to known limitations inherent in every measuring device or system. The second assumption, that residue levels representing no significant human risk of carcinogenesis can be assigned, protects the public from the potential and real dangers inherent in the interpretations of the "no-residue" standard of the act discussed as alternatives one and two.....

In the period 1973 through 1977, the Commissioner extensively reviewed the known procedures that may be used to derive an operational definition of the no-residue standards of the act from animal carcinogenesis data. This review persuaded the Commissioner that the same scientific and technical limitations are common to all. Specifically, because the mechanism of chemical carcinogenesis is not sufficiently understood, none of the procedures has a fully adequate biological

rationale. All require extrapolation of risk-dose relations from responses in the observable range to that segment of the dose-response curve
where the responses are not observable. Matters are further complicated by the fact that the risk-dose relations assumed by the various
procedures are practically indistinguishable in the observable range of
risk ... but diverge substantially in their projections of risks in the
unobservable range.....

... Of the three general procedures recommended by the comments or available in the literature (the curvilinear models, linear
extrapolation and the Mantel and Bryan procedure), the Commissioner
has now decided that for purposes of this regulation, linear extrapolation best meets the above criteria:

(1) Of the available procedures, the linear procedure is
least likely to underestimate risk. That is, at the level of
acceptable risk (1 in 1 million over a lifetime), the maximum
permissible dose of residues calculated by use of the linear
extrapolation is usually lower than that obtained by the use of
the other procedures.

(2) Linear extrapolation does not require the use of complicated mathematical procedures and can be carried out without
the aid of complex computer programs....

(3) No arbitrary selection of slope is required to carry out
linear extrapolation.....

For the above reasons the Commissioner now proposes to adopt
linear extrapolation for regulating compounds subject to these regulations....

The 1973 proposal suggested that an acceptable level of risk for test
animals, and thus for man, could be 1 in 100 million over a lifetime.
Many comments argued that this level of risk was unnecessarily
conservative in light of the many other cumulative, conservative restrictions already in the proposed regulations. In the February notice
the Commissioner concluded that the 1 in 100 million level of risk was
unduly limiting without substantial compensation in terms of public
health. Consequently, the notice established the maximum risk to be
used in the Mantel–Bryan calculation as 1 in 1 million.....

In the Commissioner's opinion, the acceptable risk level should (1)
not significantly increase the human cancer risk and (2) subject to that
constraint, be as high as possible in order to permit the use of carcinogenic animal drugs and food additives as decreed by Congress..... In
addition to protecting the public health and satisfying the congressional
directive, the Commissioner believes the selected level of risk should be
consistent with acceptable levels of risk for other materials that are
considered safe, and should prevent any false sense of security in the
calculations. After reviewing data on acceptable levels of risk and
knowing the limitations on the procedures, the Commissioner has

concluded that a level of risk of 1 in 1 million over a lifetime satisfies all of these criteria. . . .

NOTES

1. *Translating Risk Estimates.* The end product of any quantitative risk assessment for a carcinogen is the correlation of a level of risk with a given dose. This risk level is usually stated in terms of the lifetime risk of cancer of an exposed individual and in terms of the increased number of cancers that would occur annually in the United States population. An individual risk of one in 100,000 means that an exposed individual has that additional risk of developing cancer from this exposure alone during his lifetime. Roughly 4,000,000 persons are born each year in the United States. An individual lifetime risk of one in 100,000 associated with exposure to a substance would mean that 40 of these might develop cancer at some point in their lifetimes if they do not die of other causes—including cancers with other causes—first. Assuming an average lifetime of 70 years, this cohort would experience an average maximum risk of 4/7 of one cancer case each year.

2. *"Acceptable" Risk.* The level of risk that a regulatory agency ought to consider "acceptable" or "insignificant" is, as could be expected, controversial. The level of risk considered "acceptable," moreover, must be keyed to a specified mathematical extrapolation model. The more conservative the model, the higher the risk it will project for a given level of exposure. For example, it has been estimated that the risk projected by the Mantel–Bryan procedure may differ from the risk estimated by the linear model by an order of magnitude (*i.e.*, a factor of 10). It should be noted, however, that any of the mathematical extrapolation models provides the so-called "upper bound" risk, and does not purport to predict the number of cancers that will occur. Each of these mathematical models incorporates so many conservative assumptions that it is unlikely that the actual number of cancers would approach the upper-bound "worst case." For that reason, the result of a risk assessment is often depicted as a range of potential risk from zero to the number given by the quantitative risk assessment.

3. *Criticisms of Quantitative Risk Assessment.* There remains considerable disagreement about the validity of this approach. A number of scientists oppose any quantitative risk assessment on the ground that the methodology is still too imprecise and, in any event, the available toxicological data often are insufficient to justify basing regulatory decisions on such calculations. Probably a majority of scientists recognize the uncertainties and limitations of quantitative risk assessment but consider the technique more reliable and useful for regulatory decisionmaking than the use of arbitrary safety factors, which provide no scientific basis for regulating carcinogens.

4. *Estradiol.* After initially concluding to withdraw approval of a carcinogenic animal drug, estradiol, 44 Fed. Reg. 1462, 1463 (January 5, 1979), FDA reversed itself and approved the drug for steers and heifers, concluding that the residues of the drug in human food represent an insignificant risk of cancer and thus are safe. 46 Fed. Reg. 24694 (May 1, 1981), 47 Fed. Reg. 51108 (November 12, 1982), 48 Fed. Reg. 48659 (October 20, 1983), 49 Fed. Reg. 13872 (April 9, 1984), 49 Fed. Reg. 29777 (July 24, 1984). The agency approved the drug even though the sponsor failed to meet the explicit statutory requirement that there be a "regulatory method" to detect the residue in food. It concluded that the drug "is likely to leave a safe level of residue of carcinogenic endogenous hormones in the edible tissue" and thus it is "unreasonable to disapprove that

product because a post slaughter method (*i.e.*, 'regulatory method') capable of monitoring such small amounts of residues has not been developed." 46 Fed. Reg. at 24696. Because no comparable data were submitted to justify use of the drug in chickens, however, FDA withdrew approval for that use. 53 Fed. Reg. 4214 (February 12, 1988), 53 Fed. Reg. 15885 (May 4, 1988).

5. *Commentary.* For a scientific discussion of the SOM approach, *see* Perez, *Human Safety Data Collection and Evaluation for the Approval of New Animal Drugs*, 3 J. Toxicol. & Envt'l Health 837 (1977). *See also* Gass, *A Discussion of Assay Sensitivity Methodology and Carcinogenic Potential*, 30 FDC L.J. 111 (1975); Salsburg, *Mantel–Bryan—Its Faults and Alternatives Available After Thirteen More Years of Experimentation*, 30 FDC L.J. 116 (1975); Zimbelman, *Biological Perspectives on Approaches to Sensitivity of Analytical Methods for Tissue Residues*, 30 FDC L.J. 124 (1975). For illustrations of the application of the SOM approach to individual animal drugs, *see* the notices of opportunity for hearing on proposals to withdraw approval of various NADAs in 41 Fed. Reg. 19907 (May 13, 1976), 41 Fed. Reg. 34891, 34899, 34908 (August 17, 1976), 44 Fed. Reg. 1463 (January 5, 1979).

6. *Risk Perception and Communication.* The field of risk assessment has grown up with the discipline of risk perception and communication, whose proponents deal with public education relating to risk and the need for accurate and simplified communication techniques in order to help the public understand whatever risks it may face. For an overview, *see* Slovic, *Perception of Risk*, 236 Science 280 (April 17, 1987); National Academy of Sciences, IMPROVING RISK COMMUNICATION (1989).

7. *Risk Comparisons.* Analysts have compared the risks of different occupations and other activities, and the risks of various natural and synthetic substances. So long as the distinction is made between actuarial risks, *i.e.*, measured frequencies, and calculated or estimates risks, these comparisons can be enlightening. *See, e.g.*, E. Crouch and R. Wilson, RISK/BENEFIT ANALYSIS 173 (1982); B. Fischoff, *et al.*, ACCEPTABLE RISK *(1981); C. R. Richmond,* et al., *eds.*, HEALTH RISK ANALYSIS *(1980); J. Urquhart and K. Heilmann, RISK WATCH: THE ODDS OF LIFE (1984); Allman,* Staying Alive in the 20th Century, *6 Science 85 at 31 (October 1985); Cohen and Lee,* A Catalog of Risks, *36 Health Physics 707 (1979); Cothern and Marcus,* Estimating Risk for Carcinogenic Environmental Contaminants and its Impact on Regulatory Decisionmaking, *4 Regul. Toxicol. & Pharmacol. 265 (1984); Crouch and Wilson,* Inter–Risk Comparisons, *in J. Rodricks and R. Tardiff, eds.,* ASSESSMENT AND MANAGEMENT OF CHEMICAL RISKS *97 (1984); Leigh,* Estimates of the Probability of Job–Related Death in 347 Occupations, *29 J. Occup. Med. 510 (June 1987); Miller,* Comparative Data on Life–Threatening Risks, *5 Toxic Substances J. 3 (Summer 1983); Morrall,* A Review of the Record, *Regulation 25 (November/December 1986); Perera and Boffetta,* Perspectives on Comparing Risks of Environmental Carcinogens, *80 J.N.C.I. 1282 (October 19, 1988); Pochin,* Estimates of Industrial and Other Risks, *12 J. Royal Coll. Physn's 210 (1978); Spilker and Cuatrecasas,* Assessing Risks, *2 DN&P, No. 2, at 69 (March 1969); Wilson,* Analyzing the Daily Risks of Life, *81 Tech. Rev. 41 (1979); Wilson,* Measuring and Comparing Risks to Establish a De Minimis Risk Level, *8 Reg. Toxicol. & Pharmcol. 267 (1988).*

After reviewing comments on its 1979 proposal, and taking account of continuing advances in risk assessment methodology, FDA withdrew the document and published a revised proposal in 1985.

SPONSORED COMPOUNDS IN FOOD–PRODUCING ANIMALS; CRITERIA AND PROCEDURES FOR EVALUATING THE SAFETY OF CARCINOGENIC RESIDUES

50 Federal Register 45530 (October 31, 1985).

A. The Level of Risk. . . .

. . . The selection of an insignificant level of risk is a choice which, although susceptible to being posed as a question of fact, cannot be answered solely by science or currently available information. It is, instead, a policy question that must be answered by weighing a number of subjective considerations.

No comments on the 1979 proposal were received that disagreed with FDA's decision that the 1 in 1 million level presents an insignificant risk to the public. No comments at all, however, were received from the general public. All comments were from regulated industry. These comments contended that the 1 in 1 million level represented an insignificant risk but that higher levels might also represent insignificant risks. The comments, however, as discussed below, failed to demonstrate that any higher level satisfied FDA's responsibility under the statute to protect the public health. FDA has carefully studied the submitted comments, the suggested alternatives, and other available information on risk assessment and has concluded that the 1 in 1 million level represents an insignificant level of risks.

FDA emphasizes that the 1 in 1 million level of risk adopted for these regulations does not mean that 1 in every 1 million people will contract cancer as a result of this regulation. Rather, as far as can be determined, in all probability no one will contact cancer as a result of this regulation. The 1 in 1 million level represents a (1) 1 in 1 million increase in risk over the normal risk of cancer and (2) a lifetime—not annual—risk. Furthermore, because of a number of assumptions used in the risk assessment procedure and the extrapolation model used, FDA expects that the actual risk to an individual will be between 1 in 1 million and some much lower, but indeterminable, level.

Some comments on the 1979 proposal suggested, without support, that no specific level of risk should be adopted for general use, but that a level of risk should be chosen for each compound on an individual basis. FDA disagrees. Under the suggested procedure sponsors would receive no guidance about the likelihood of approval of a compound during the expensive stage of drug development or about the factors consider in determining whether the compound should be approved. This unstructured ad hoc approach would be contrary to the interests of the public health and would result in inequitable treatment of sponsors.

Comments argued that FDA could determine a level of insignificant risk by comparing risks presented from carcinogens in food with risks individuals voluntarily assume from using their occupation, from common forms of transportation, from leisure activities, and the like. Comments also contended that FDA could similarly use involuntary risks. Accordingly, comments argued that because risks of a magnitude of 1 in 15,000 over a lifetime (1 in 1 million yearly) do not concern (that is, are "accepted by") most people, FDA should adopt that level of risk for these regulations. Other comments used similar reasoning to support a 1 in 100,000 risk level.

The comments overlook the fact that when FDA approves the use of a carcinogenic compound, FDA affirmatively allows a risk to be imposed on the public. The public is not "accepting" that risk because (1) The public has no information on the risk presented by carcinogenic compounds in its food, and (2) the public has no way of avoiding that risk assuming it wishes to continue to eat meat, milk, or eggs. Furthermore, these comments do not address the growing evidence that group attitudes and group choices do not follow the same patterns as individual choices. Reliance on group preference, therefore, might cause the imposition of a risk that is unacceptable to many individuals.

In the final analysis, the comments and information regarding public perception of risk at best allow FDA to infer the increment of risk of cancer that certain members of society would consider unavoidable, tolerable, or unnoticeable. Although FDA has considered the comments and information provided, FDA concludes that the sole use of social preferences and the magnitude of involuntary risks to select an insignificant level of risk provides an incomplete basis for determining the level of risk to which the public should be exposed by substances permitted in the food supply. FDA also concludes that an increase in the level of risk to 1 in 15,000 might significantly increase the risk of cancer to people, and, until better information is provided, such a level must be viewed as unacceptable in light of current knowledge and legal standards.

... The question that logically follows is whether a level of 1 in 100,000 presents a significant risk to people. If FDA were to propose 1 in 100,000 as the insignificant level of risk, the permitted concentration of residue would increase by a factor of 10.... Whether the 1 in 100,000 level would pose a significant increase in the risk of cancer to people is, however, the critical question. It is not a question which can be unequivocally answered, and it calls for a difficult decision by FDA: for no matter what arguments are made and no matter what numbers are used, the actual risk of cancer to people remains unquantifiable.

The 1 in 100,000 level does not carry with it the degree of concern presented by the 1 in 15,000 level. Similarly, it is not as insignificant as the 1 in 1 million level. The approval of a carcinogenic sponsored compound, at any level of risk, does not include consideration of the potential interaction or synergy between an approved compound and any other substance or substances to which people are exposed. Certainly, the more approved carcinogenic compounds that are marketed the greater is the likelihood of cancer induction in people.

In the presence of these uncertainties, FDA cannot, with assurance, state that the 1 in 100,000 level would pose an insignificant level of risk of cancer to people. FDA can state, and comments agree, that the 1 in 1 million level presents an insignificant level of risk of cancer to people. Furthermore, FDA has developed confidence in the merit of the 1 in 1 million level because in recent years the agency has considered that level as its benchmark in evaluating the safety of carcinogenic compounds administered to food-producing animals. Under these circumstances, the agency believes that the most reasonable level of risk to apply in these regulations is the 1 in 1 million level. . . .

B. Uncertainties in Quantitative Risk Assessment

... Pervasive uncertainty is the primary analytical difficulty in making a risk assessment that involves trying to define the human health effects of exposure to harmful residues. Although the risk assessment procedures proposed for these regulations draw extensively on science, which has developed a basis for linking exposure to residues to potential chronic health effects, there is uncertainty in types, probability, and magnitude of the health effects that will be associated with a given compound and its residues. These problems have no immediate solutions because of the many gaps in FDA's ability to ascertain the nature or extent of the effects associated with specific exposures. Where science fails to provide solutions, FDA applies conservative assumptions to ensure that its decisions will not adversely affect the public health.

For example, FDA relies upon the results of animal bioassays on a given substance to make a regulatory decision. FDA recognizes the inherent limitations and uncertainties in such bioassays, but relies on their results because there is scientific consensus that the bioassay is the best way currently available of determining the carcinogenicity of a compound. However, if one were to conduct a superb bioassay in which 1,000 animals were placed at risk and no tumors were detected, one could not conclude that the compound was not a carcinogen, but only that at the 99 percent confidence level the lifetime risk of cancer to the test animal was less than approximately 1 in 200. In such circumstances, FDA would regulate the compound under the general food safety requirements of the act for risks other than cancer and would apply a safety factor of 100 to the dose giving no observed effect in the bioassay. Thus, assuming a superb bioassay and assuming that the highest dose used in the bioassay is also the dose that gives no observed toxicological effect, FDA may be imposing a maximum lifetime risk of cancer of 1 in 20,000 on the public. FDA allows marketing of the compound because there is a scientific consensus that the results of such an assay are sufficient to create a rebuttable presumption that the compound is not carcinogenic.

On the other hand, if FDA concludes that the bioassay shows that the sponsored compound or its residues are carcinogenic, there are uncertainties in the estimate of risk to people from the compound's residues in edible products of target animals. These uncertainties exist because people are exposed to much lower residue levels than are experimental animals and because it had not been determined whether the potency of a carcinogen is proportionately the same at that lower level. The scientific community has not reached a consensus on the procedure for making this extrapolation of risk.

The risk assessment procedure used by FDA requires that the upper 95 percent confidence limit on the tumor incidence data be used to estimate the carcinogenic potency of a substance. Assuming a typical bioassay conducted on a sponsored compound (e.g., 50 animals per sex per dose) and a 20 percent incidence of tumors, this requirement causes an overestimate of the most probable potency by a factor of two. In addition, data from the most sensitive species and the most sensitive sex are used, resulting in an overestimate of the most probable potency by a factor of one to four.

The risk assessment procedure used by FDA assumes that each residue is as potent as the most potent compound detected in the bioassay. This is unlikely to be true, but in the absence of a bioassay on each residue and of knowledge of the quantity of each residue in the tissue, the effect on risk to the consuming public cannot be quantified.....

The risk assessment procedure used by FDA assumes that a lower frequency of dosing has no effect on carcinogenic potency. This is unlikely to be true. Because the animals used in the bioassay receive a constant and daily dose, but people will most likely be exposed to sporadic doses, the carcinogenic potency to people is most likely overestimated. However, FDA has no data that will allow a reliable prediction of the magnitude of this overestimate.....

The risk assessment procedure used by FDA includes a calculation of the upper limit of carcinogenic potency at low dose, a dose representative of what people are exposed to....

The risk assessment procedure used by FDA assumes a one to one correspondence between the carcinogenic potency of the compound in the test animals and in people. The available, but extremely limited, data submitted in a comment suggest that carcinogenic potency of a specific chemical in rodents and people may vary by an order of magnitude, but is as likely to be high as low.

The risk assessment procedure used by FDA assumes that the concentration of residue in the edible product is at the permitted concentration, that consumption of that edible product by all people is equal to the consumption by the 90th percentile eater, and that all marketed animals are treated with the carcinogen (market penetration of 100 percent). These assumptions may overestimate risk. The extent of the overestimation cannot be quantified.

For the comments, the assumptions and requirements discussed above are multiple conservatisms; for FDA, each of these assumptions and requirements is a matter of prudence dictated by the lack of scientific consensus and FDA's responsibility under the statute to ensure to a reasonable certainty that the public will not be harmed.

NOTES

1. *Conservatism in Assessing Risks.* FDA has repeatedly emphasized that the mathematical extrapolation procedures used in its quantitative risk assessments are "extremely conservative statistical analyses," 51 Fed. Reg. 28331, 28344, 28346, 28360, (August 7, 1986), that greatly overstate real risk:

> [B]y using certain conservative extrapolation models it is possible to estimate an upper limit of risk. * * * The estimate of risk may be exaggerated by these conservative extrapolation models. Because the estimated risk will not be understated, however, such risk assessment techniques can be used with confidence to determine whether ... there is a reasonable certainty that no harm will result from the intended use of an additive....

47 Fed. Reg. 14464, 14466 (April 2, 1982). FDA has utilized these conservative quantitative risk assessment procedures to determine that carcinogenic substances in food and cosmetics are safe under their actual conditions of use:

> The estimate of the risk is likely to be exaggerated because the extrapolation models used are designed to estimate the maximum risk consistent with the data. For this reason, the estimate can be used with confidence to conclude that a substance is safe under specific conditions of use....

49 Fed. Reg. 36635, 36638 (September 19, 1984).

2. *One in One Million Risk.* The agency has emphasized that a one in one million level of risk, calculated by these procedures, is an "extremely small, perhaps non-existent, theoretical risk" that "represents a calculated statistical upper bound estimate of a conservative model" and "does not represent a documented experience of a real expectation." Letter from FDA Acting Commissioner Novitch to Representative Weiss (December 28, 1983) at 9, 10. According to the agency, a one in one million level of risk over a lifetime "imposes no additional risk of cancer to the public," 44 Fed. Reg. 17070, 17093 (March 20, 1979), and "is consistent with the likelihood that no cancers will result," 46 Fed. Reg. 15500, 15501 (March 6, 1981), 47 Fed. Reg. 49628, 49631 (November 2, 1982).

> This computed level of risk is an upper bound level. It is not an actuarial risk. An actuarial risk is the risk determined by the actual incidence of an event. In contrast, the computed risk is a projection based on certain assumptions that enable the agency to estimate a risk that is too small to actually be measured. The agency uses conservative assumptions to ensure that the computation does not understate the risk.

50 Fed. Reg. 51551, 51557 (December 18, 1985).

The agency has variously characterized a one in one million risk as "represent[ing] no significant carcinogenic burden in the total diet of man," 42 Fed. Reg. 10412, 10422 (February 22, 1977); "for all practical purposes, zero," 50 Fed. Reg. 51551, 51557 (December 18, 1985); "the functional equivalent of no risk at all," 51 Fed. Reg. 28331, 28344 (August 7, 1986); "so low as to be effectively no risk," *id.;* assuring that "in all probability no one will contract cancer," 50 Fed. Reg. 45530, 45541 (October 31, 1985); and "so low that there is a reasonable certainty of no harm." 51 Fed. Reg. 4173, 4174 (February 3, 1986).

3. *Refusal to Reduce Risk Level.* FDA has declined to reduce its one in one million criterion of "insignificant" risk.

> In summary, the Commissioner has concluded that a risk level of 1 in 1 million over a lifetime imposes no additional risk of cancer to the public. A lower risk would not significantly increase the public health protection....

44 Fed. Reg. 17070, 17093 (March 20, 1979). "[A]ny 'gain' from removing [a risk of this magnitude] from the market would be trivial or of no value." Letter from FDA Commissioner Young to S.M. Wolfe, FDA Dkt. No. 84P–0429 (June 21, 1985). *See also* 50 Fed. Reg. 51551, 51557 (December 18, 1985).

---

2. CARCINOGENIC CONTAMINANTS OF FOOD

AFLATOXINS IN SHELLED PEANUTS AND PEANUT PRODUCTS USED AS HUMAN FOODS: PROPOSED TOLERANCE

39 Federal Register 42748 (December 6, 1974).

Aflatoxins may contaminate foods whenever the producing molds grow on foods under favorable conditions of temperature and humidity.... Corn, barley, copra, cassava, tree nuts, cottonseed, peanuts, rice, wheat, and grain sorghum are subject to natural aflatoxin contamination. In the United States, aflatoxins have been detected only in corn, figs, grain sorghum, cottonseed, certain tree nuts, and peanuts. Aflatoxins are present in peanuts and peanut products because of these contaminating molds. They are, therefore, added substances within the meaning of [section 402(a)(1) of the] Act....

The Commissioner has a two-fold concern with aflatoxins. First, animals fed aflatoxins are subject to acute toxic effects. Second, and of primary concern, data which indicate that these substances, particularly aflatoxin B_1, in some species of test animals are among the most potent liver carcinogens known.....

Epidemiological studies bearing on the possible effects of aflatoxin in man have been performed on specific population groups in Southeast Asia and Africa, where there is a known high incidence of primary liver cancer.... The result of these studies is an indication of a general correlation between the incidence of primary liver cancer in humans and the exposure to aflatoxins.

No epidemiological studies of these types have been carried out in the United States. However, primary liver cancer is a minor form of cancer in the United States, accounting for about 0.7 percent of all cancer cases. In addition, cancer rates in those areas of the United States where climatic conditions are most conducive to aflatoxin contamination (i.e., the southeastern states) do not differ significantly from other areas....

Thus, while it is not certain that aflatoxins are a cause of primary liver cancer in the United States, the Commissioner concludes that the observations of severe carcinogenic effects in experimental animals and positive correlations between dietary aflatoxins and primary human liver cancer seen in other parts of the world are sufficient justification to regard aflatoxins as poisonous or deleterious substances and to take actions to hold the human exposure to aflatoxins in the United States to the lowest level possible.... In 1965, the FDA established an informal action level of 30 ppb total aflatoxins. In 1969, it was reduced to the current level of 20 ppb total aflatoxins.....

Fungicides, crop rotational practices, and other good agronomic practices can ameliorate the problem to an extent. It is impossible at this time totally to eliminate all of the breakdowns that can occur in the total process of growing, harvesting, and storing peanuts.... Processors of shelled nuts can eliminate some contaminated material by using a number of standard manual, mechanical, and electronic sorting procedures....

Survey data ... indicate that since 1971 an average of 93 percent of sampled peanut products contained aflatoxins below the 20 ppb level. The Commissioner concludes that current agricultural and manufacturing technology is capable of meeting a level below that which it is now being asked to meet. Although the immediate result of lowering the level may be the loss of a small percentage of the peanut supply, improved producer practices should compensate for any short-run loss.

Obviously, for complete protection, aflatoxins should be eliminated from food, but this is not presently feasible. Therefore, it is necessary for the Commissioner to weigh the consequences of possible levels above zero.

Setting a level at 5 or 10 ppb was considered by the Commissioner. Eleven of the 12 major U.S. manufacturers of peanut butter could meet a 10 ppb level in 90 percent of their products. The Canadian government survey of 1972 indicated that 95 percent of the samples of peanut butter could meet this standard. However, there is year-to-year variability in aflatoxin contamination of the peanut crop. The FDA survey of 1973 evidenced the fact that only 89 percent of the peanut butter samples and 82 percent of the establishments surveyed met a 10 ppb level. Of the 12 largest establishments surveyed, only seven met a 5 ppb limit in 90 percent of their samples. There are also data showing that in some years only about 60 percent of the peanut butter produced met a 5 ppb level. One bad crop year could effectively eliminate a large percentage of peanut products from the market. Thus, a move to a 5 or 10 ppb could result in significant losses to producers, manufacturers, and consumers alike. These increased losses of food would result in much higher prices or in unavailability of what is generally considered a highly nutritious and useful food.

Another important consideration concerns setting a tolerance at a level at which manufacturers have the capability to monitor their products during processing and to ensure that the finished product complies with the tolerance.... Setting a tolerance level of 5 or 10 ppb for aflatoxins in peanut products would have the effect of requiring manufacturers to employ an analytical limit of less than 1 to 5 ppb for quality control purposes. Because present sampling and analytical methodologies have considerable error at the 1–5 ppb range, analytical results obtained for such quality control samples would not accurately represent the production lot from which the sample was drawn. Therefore, the capability of manufacturers to control their production at these levels is extremely questionable, and to guard against the release of products containing levels of aflatoxins in excess of 5 or 10 ppb is not possible.....

In addition, because there is no direct evidence that aflatoxins cause cancer in man or of what may be the level of no effect, the Commissioner cannot conclude that there is any tangible gain from lowering the permissible level to either 10 or 5 ppb. Such uncertain benefit to the public health must be weighed against the clear loss of food that would result.....

The Commissioner has considered promulgating the present proposal as an action level.... The Commissioner is unaware of any new or anticipated developments that would affect the proposed 15 ppb level in the near future. There are no new procedures pending, either agronomic or technical, that will alter the present unavoidability of aflatoxins. Furthermore, it is unlikely that any new pertinent information will become available in the near future. Therefore, it is the Commissioner's preliminary conclusion that the most reasonable approach to regulating aflatoxin, in shelled peanuts and peanut products, would be a formal tolerance established under section 406.

NOTES

1. *Risk Assessment for Aflatoxins.* FDA later released a formal assessment of the risk posed by aflatoxin in peanuts. 43 Fed. Reg. 8808 (March 3, 1978). The agency's estimate of the human risk of liver cancer based on animal test data using the less conservative Mantel–Bryan mathematical model (rather than the linear model) substantially exceeded the reported incidence of liver cancer in the United States from all causes. FDA speculated that "possible explanations for these differences are: (1) the level of human exposure to aflatoxin has been overestimated; (2) the Mantel–Bryan extrapolation procedure is overly conservative in this case; and/or (3) rats may not be an appropriate model for predicting aflatoxin-induced primary liver cancer in humans." FDA, ASSESSMENT OF ESTIMATED RISK RESULTING FROM AFLATOXINS IN CONSUMER PEANUT PRODUCTS AND OTHER FOOD COMMODITIES (1978).

2. *Variability in Contamination.* FDA's concern about the variability of aflatoxin contamination proved correct. Severe contamination problems in 1977–78 led FDA to issue an action level for aflatoxin in milk, 42 Fed. Reg. 61630 (December 6, 1977), and to permit "blending" of aflatoxin-contaminated

corn, 43 Fed. Reg. 14122 (April 4, 1978), p. 256, *supra*. In *United States v. Boston Farm Center, Inc.*, 590 F.2d 149 (5th Cir. 1979), the court overturned a lower court ruling allowing up to 100 ppb aflatoxin in corn and upheld FDA's 20 ppb action level.

In 1980, the corn crop in southeastern United States contained a higher than usual level of aflatoxin due to an unusual combination of early drought and late rains. At the request of the States of South Carolina, North Carolina, and Virginia, FDA agreed to an exemption raising the action level for aflatoxin in corn for use solely as feed for mature nonlactating livestock and poultry from 20 ppb to 100 ppb, 46 Fed. Reg. 7447 (January 23, 1981). The Community Nutrition Institute challenged this decision, on both procedural grounds discussed p. 1254 *infra*, and the substantive grounds that the higher level of aflatoxin was unsafe and that the FDA policy of permitting farmers to blend corn containing high levels of aflatoxin with corn containing lower levels was illegal. In *Community Nutrition Institute v. Novitch*, 583 F.Supp. 294 (D.D.C. 1984), the 100 ppb level was upheld as "safe for consumption" and the FDA authorization for blending was held to be lawful. Following the Supreme Court's decision on the legality of action levels, the court of appeals held that the intentional blending of contaminated corn constitutes adulteration but, citing the *Chaney* case, p. 1057, *infra*, upheld FDA's discretion not to initiate enforcement proceedings. *Community Nutrition Institute v. Young*, 818 F.2d 943 (D.C. Cir. 1987). In 54 Fed. Reg. 22622 (May 25, 1989), FDA issued revised action levels for aflatoxin and its enforcement policy with respect to the blending of contaminated and noncontaminated corn from the 1988 harvest.

3. *Other Contaminants.* FDA has established tolerances and action levels for other carcinogenic contaminants of food under section 406 of the Act. The only formal section 406 tolerances ever established permit PCBs in food and food packaging. 37 Fed. Reg. 5705 (March 18, 1972), 38 Fed. Reg. 18096 (July 6, 1973), 41 Fed. Reg. 8409 (February 26, 1976), 42 Fed. Reg. 17487 (April 1, 1977), 44 Fed. Reg. 38330 (June 29, 1979), 47 Fed. Reg. 10079 (March 9, 1982), 48 Fed. Reg. 37020 (August 16, 1983), 48 Fed. Reg. 45544 (October 6, 1983), 49 Fed. Reg. 21514 (May 22, 1984), codified at 21 C.F.R. § 109.30. Action levels have been set for carcinogenic nitrosamines in malt beverages, 45 Fed. Reg. 39341 (June 10, 1980), barley malt contaminated with nitrosamines, 46 Fed. Reg. 39218 (July 31, 1981); and rubber baby bottle nipples contaminated with nitrosamines, 48 Fed. Reg. 57014 (December 27, 1983), 49 Fed. Reg. 26149 (June 26, 1984), 49 Fed. Reg. 50789 (December 31, 1984); FDA Compliance Policy Guide No. 7117.11 (June 28, 1988). Action levels have been established for residues of a variety of carcinogenic pesticides in foods, *e.g.*, 52 Fed. Reg. 18025 (May 13, 1987). With regard to 2,3,7,8–TCDD (dioxin), which it has characterized as "the most carcinogenic substance known to science," FDA has stated that fish containing more than 50 ppt should not be consumed at all, fish containing 25–50 ppt should not be consumed more than twice each month, and that below 25 ppt there is "no public health problem." "Dioxin—The Impact on Human Health," Hearings before the Subcomm. on Natural Resources, Agriculture Research and Environment of the House Comm. on Science and Technology, 98th Cong., 1st Sess. 78, 79, 81 (1983). FDA's refusal to issue a tolerance or action level for dioxin in fish and other food was upheld in *National Wildlife Federation v. Secretary of Health and Human Services*, 808 F.2d 12 (6th Cir. 1986).

4. *Acrylonitrile.* In 1978 FDA banned acrylonitrile for use in formulating plastic bottles because of the possibility that some small amount could migrate from the bottle wall to the food it contained. In *Monsanto Co. v. Kennedy,* 613 F.2d 947 (D.C. Cir. 1979), the court overturned this ban because FDA had not considered the possibility that the risk involved might be *de minimis.* The court stated that:

> [T]here is latitude inherent in the statutory scheme to avoid literal application of the statutory definition of "food additive" in those *de minimis* situations that, in the informed judgment of the Commissioner, clearly present no public health or safety concerns.

Id. at 954. Upon reconsideration, FDA determined that the human cancer risk was 1 in 3 million and therefore approved the use of acrylonitrile in plastic bottles for food use, 49 Fed. Reg. 36635 (September 19, 1984), and for alcoholic beverage use, 52 Fed. Reg. 33802 (September 8, 1987). In 55 Fed. Reg. 8476 (March 8, 1990), however, FDA requested information on existing uses of acrylonitrile in order to determine whether additional restrictions should be imposed.

5. *Polyvinyl Chloride.* After concluding that vinyl chloride monomer (VCM) was carcinogenic, FDA banned the use of vinyl chloride in aerosol cosmetic products in 1975, 39 Fed. Reg. 30830 (August 26, 1974), and proposed to ban or severely restrict the use of polyvinyl chloride (PVC) in food packaging, 40 Fed. Reg. 40529 (September 3, 1975). Following the decision in *Monsanto,* however, the agency reassessed its position, withdrew the 1975 proposal, 51 Fed. Reg. 4173 (February 3, 1986), and published a new proposal to set limits on the use of PVC in food packaging that would assure a cancer risk from VCM of less than one in 10 million, 51 Fed. Reg. 4177 (February 3, 1986). FDA announced its intent to prepare an Environmental Impact Statement on that proposal in 53 Fed. Reg. 47264 (November 22, 1988).

3.　CARCINOGENIC COAL TAR HAIR DYES

Although FDA began using quantitative risk assessment to regulate carcinogenic animal drug residues in 1973 and to control environmental contaminants in food shortly thereafter, the agency was slow to apply this new tool in other areas of its jurisdiction. In 43 Fed. Reg. 1101 (January 6, 1978), the agency proposed to require a cancer warning on labels of, and on posters at beauty shops that used, any hair dye containing the coal tar ingredient 4–MMPD (also known as 2,4–DAA). The warning, based on an NCI-sponsored study that demonstrated the ingredient caused cancer in laboratory animals, was to read:

> WARNING. Contains an ingredient that can penetrate your skin and has been determined to cause cancer in laboratory animals.

Following public comment, the agency issued the following regulation.

COSMETIC PRODUCT WARNING STATEMENTS:
COAL TAR HAIR DYES CONTAINING 4–MMPD

44 Federal Register 59509 (October 16, 1979).

FDA [concedes that it] does not have the statutory authority to prohibit the interstate distribution of hair dyes containing 4–MMPD....

Several comments maintained that FDA has no authority to require the proposed warning due to the statutory exemptions for coal tar hair dyes found in sections 601(a) and (e) and 602(e) of the FD&C Act. According to the comments, coal tar hair dyes bearing the caution and "patch test" statements provided for in section 601(a) of the FD&C Act are "totally exempt" from the statute....

FDA disagrees. Congress exempted coal tar hair dyes bearing the patch test caution statement from the provisions of the FD&C Act that prohibit cosmetics from containing any substance that may be injurious to users (section 601(a)) and from containing any unsafe color additive (section 601(e)); but Congress did not exempt the dyes from the misbranding provisions of sections 201(n) and 602(a) of the FD&C Act, which require truthful labeling....

Generally, when dealing with questions about the carcinogenicity of ingredients intentionally added to products within its jurisdiction, FDA has relied upon the strength of the evidence showing whether or not the ingredient is a carcinogen, without reference to "degree of risk." That is, once it is established that the deliberate addition of an ingredient to a food or cosmetic results in a potential human cancer risk, the agency then has a basis for regulatory action, without having to establish the particular level of that risk (see, for example, 21 CFR 189.145 (dulcin)). Although FDA often makes rough estimates of the relative size or the level of a cancer risk, such estimations have been used by FDA for secondary purposes, such as establishing priorities. (FDA has also proposed the use of risk assessment procedures as the basis for regulating cancer-causing compounds used in food-producing animals, but that proposal relates to the DES proviso in 21 U.S.C. § 360b(d)(1)(H), which is not relevant here.) In general, however, the presence in an FDA regulated product of any level of human risk from a deliberately added carcinogenic ingredient is not only material, but is a decisive factor in FDA's decisionmaking on whether to permit the addition of an ingredient to products.

FDA has adhered to this policy in dealing with cosmetic ingredients. FDA will not permit the deliberate addition to cosmetics of any ingredient that is a potential human carcinogen. For example, vinyl chloride and chloroform have been prohibited as cosmetic ingredients due to the risk of cancer associated with their use (21 CFR 700.14, 700.18). FDA's policy of prohibiting deliberately added carcinogenic ingredients has fostered a reasonable expectation by consumers that this policy applies to all cosmetic ingredients....

In fact, but for the statutory provision preventing it, FDA would have applied this policy here and banned 4–MMPD in hair dyes. The general effect of the act's adulteration provisions, and the Delaney anticancer clause governing food additives and color additives, in preventing the deliberate addition of carcinogens to foods and cosmetics is well known. The provisions of section 601(a) and (e) that prevent FDA from banning 4–MMPD are anomalous when viewed against the background of other provisions in the FD&C Act that prohibit the deliberate addition to foods and cosmetics of carcinogenic ingredients. As a result of more than 20 years of experience with (and in recent years much controversy and publicity about) the Delaney Clause, the public is unlikely to expect cosmetics regulated by FDA under the FD&C Act to contain a deliberately added carcinogen. Thus, it is a material fact that a cosmetic product contains an ingredient consumers could reasonably expect to be banned from cosmetics....

It has not been necessary in the past to require warning statements for cosmetics containing deliberately added carcinogens because FDA has prohibited the use of these ingredients under section 601(a) of the FD&C Act. The use of the misbranding provisions in this case is both necessary and appropriate.....

It should be noted, that, under the more conservative estimates of risk included in one comment, the dark shades of hair dye having the highest concentration of 4–MMPD pose lifetime risks in excess of one-in-a-million, which is one of the benchmarks for acceptable risks cited in the comment. Moreover, ... FDA does not have the authority to inspect records and to obtain data about cosmetics that the agency would need to have if it were to use risk assessments for cosmetics for the purposes advocated in the comment. Such records would include data on product consumption and human exposure.....

FDA did not compare the risk from 4–MMPD in cosmetics with a variety of other risks, as these comments suggest be done. Some of the suggested benchmark risks, like natural disasters, are beyond the government's ability to regulate; others, like sports, have not been a major focus of government safety regulation; and still others, like occupational safety hazards and automobile traffic hazards, are subject to Federal regulation under statutory criteria that call for a consideration of the feasibility or practicability of regulatory standards. In motorcycle racing, rock climbing, automobile driving, and some of the other activities cited in the comments, the risks are obvious and are voluntarily assumed. In contrast, hair dyes are assumed by users to be safe, and the cancer risks will not be apparent to users unless the labeling brings the risk to their attention. Moreover, the fact that some people "accept" some high risks in some aspects of their lives does not mean that they or others are willing to accept risks in other aspects of their lives. The fact that some users of hair dyes engage in dangerous sports does not entail that they are prepared to disregard even small risks from hair dyes. In sum, FDA believes that the activities cited in the comment that are not under FDA's jurisdiction involve diverse considerations and are not directly relevant in determining FDA's responsibilities under the FD&C Act for judging the materiality of risks from cosmetics for deciding when to bring such risks to the attention of consumers....

It was asserted in the comments that it is inconsistent to require a warning on hair dyes containing 4–MMPD yet require no warning on other products within FDA's jurisdiction that also contain carcinogens.... [M]any of the other specific substances cited by the comments are not analogous to 4–MMPD in hair dyes in terms of the appropriateness of a warning. The agency has previously explained, for example, its rationale for believing that selenium and beverage alcohol do not present a risk of cancer when consumed at levels below those that induce hepatotoxic effect (38 FR 10458 (April 27, 1973) and 39 FR 1355 (January 8, 1974)). Some of the substances cited in the comments are inherent rather than added substances in food, and the statutory standard for prohibiting these substances may warrant a different policy with respect to warnings (21 U.S.C. §342(a)(1)). Some of the activities listed in the comments involve matters for which labeling presents practical difficulties. In the case of charcoal broiled steaks, for example, the warning would have to be directed at a manner of cooking meat, a product with respect to which FDA's authority is limited under section 902(b) of the FD&C Act. Any regulation by FDA of substances in drinking water would have to take account of the responsibilities vested in the Environmental Protection Agency under the Safe Drinking Water Act.....

In regulating aflatoxins, FDA has been primarily concerned with the aflatoxin level above which foods with aflatoxin should be prohibited. FDA has not considered requiring a label warning. Aflatoxins are unintentional contaminants, and they do not appear in every unit of peanuts, corn, and milk, or the foods containing these ingredients. Thus, any warning on these products would have to be considered in light of the fact that no detectable levels of aflatoxin may be present in some foods affected by the warning.... Moreover, given the prevalence of foods containing milk, corn and peanuts in some form, it may be impractical and confusing to require a warning on all the foods that may be affected. Indeed, a requirement for warnings on all foods that may contain an inherent carcinogenic ingredient or a carcinogenic contaminant (in contrast to a deliberately added carcinogenic substance) would apply to many, perhaps most, foods in a supermarket. Such warnings would be so numerous they would confuse the public, would not promote informed consumer decisionmaking, and would not advance the public health. Warnings concerning deliberately added, unbannable carcinogens do not present this difficulty. If interested persons believe, however, that a warning should appear on foods containing aflatoxins or other substances, they should file a citizen petition with adequate supporting data, to request the agency to require a warning.....

One comment ... described the risk from the brown and blond shades that have lower concentrations of 4–MMPD as being "disproportionately small," in comparison with black shades and as posing a risk under a linear model for brown shades of 1 in 6.2 million and for blond shades of 1 in 62 million.

This preamble has already discussed the general reasons for rejecting the position that the risk of cancer from hair dyes is too small to warrant a warning to consumers. Moreover, FDA's authority and resources for its cosmetics program are too limited to attempt to place varying restrictions on the amounts of a substance and tailor a regulatory policy to changing patterns of cosmetics use.....

One comment averred that if FDA insists on requiring the warning statements verbatim, as proposed, or in any event without adequate information accurately describing the potential risk involved, cosmetic manufacturers have a First Amendment right to prepare an informative and accurate package insert to provide hair dye consumers with the factual information they need to assess intelligently the possible risk of using hair dyes containing 4–MMPD.

FDA advises that manufacturers do not have a First Amendment right to make misleading statement[s] (see *Virginia State Bd. v. Virginia Citizens' Consumer Council, Inc.,* 425 U.S. 748, 771, 772, n.24 (1976)). Furthermore, manufacturers do not have a constitutional right to contradict or discount on a label a warning that is required by a regulation promulgated in accordance with applicable legal standards and procedures. Under the FD&C Act and the APA, there is an established public procedure for determining the content of health-related information on labels. Once a label warning has been adopted by that procedure (which can culminate in judicial review), the text of the warning cannot be modified, added to, or subtracted from by a firm or by FDA without going through the same procedure again. FDA's position that manufacturers may not include a statement of difference of opinion with respect to any required warnings is stated in 21 CFR 1.21(c)....

The comments pointed out that FDA advised in the preamble to 21 CFR 1.21(c)(1) that "the degree of scientific uncertainty about a possible hazard, or its frequency of occurrence, or other similar related information may, of course, accompany or be part of a warning," and that it is common "to point out that the relationship between adverse animal findings and human consequences has not yet been determined" (see the Federal Register of September 16, 1974 at 39 FR 33232). In giving this advice, the agency's attention was focused on additional information given to a physician about drugs....

Because most consumers are not experts in the evaluation of toxicological information, there is a considerable potential that they will be misled by information about a hazard that would not be misleading to a physician or expert in the field. For example, those commenting believe that the labeling should provide information on the degree of risk in terms of "maximum" lifetime risk from the substance, and on a comparison with other risks consumers commonly face every-day. However, due to the lack of validation, the risk assessments cannot predict with certainty the maximum degree of risk to which consumers are exposed in absolute terms.... Risk assessment can be useful on a comparative basis, but even if the limited comparative use were pointed out to consumers in labeling, there is a considerable possibility that consumers would interpret the comparative figures as predictions of the absolute degree of risk.

It is conceivable that the misleading potential of the labeling statements contemplated in the comments might be corrected by a balanced presentation of all the relevant information on these matters, including FDA's reasons, as discussed elsewhere in this document, for disagreeing with many of the contentions in the comments. The presentation would have to be fairly done; and FDA believes that such a presentation is likely to be so complex, and necessitate so much explanation of difficult scientific, statutory, and policy matters, that it could not feasibly be done in labeling in a way that consumers would understand. Thus, FDA believes that the full debate about these issues should occur in a more appropriate forum than labeling. This notice-and-comment proceeding is such a forum.....

FDA does not agree that the text of the proposed warning state-ment is false or misleading. As discussed in this preamble and in the proposal, the text reflects the facts that 4–MMPD penetrates human skin and causes cancer in animals..... Like the text of the warning prescribed by Congress to alert the consumer to the risks of saccharin in food, the warning indicates the existence of a possible risk without attempting to indicate how certain or probable the risk is. There is no reason to expect that consumers will interpret a warning that concerns the *nature* of a risk and that is phrased in general terms—as is the warning required here—as conveying information on the *size* of the risk in absolute terms or in comparison to other risks. Warning labels—in-cluding those for cigarettes and saccharin—simply do not purport to provide, and are not understood by the public as providing, that kind of information. There is always some possibility that consumers may misunderstand the text of any warning, but further public debate on cancer issues generally may help eliminate or reduce confusion in this instance.

NOTES

1. *Relative Risk of 4–MMPD.* It was clear from FDA's own statements, and from estimates prepared by its staff that became part of the rulemaking record, that the risk posed by 4–MMPD is very low, at least for persons to whose hair the dyes are applied. Many comments cited these estimates to dramatize the apparent disparities between the agency's proposed approach to hair dyes and its ostensibly more casual treatment of other, larger risks.

2. *Court Challenge to 4–MMPD Warning.* The cosmetic industry challenged FDA's regulation as arbitrary and capricious. *Carson Products Co. v. Department of Health and Human Services,* Food Drug Cosm. L. Rep. (CCH) ¶ 38,071 (S.D. Ga. 1980). A consent order ending the litigation contained the following terms:

> The regulation is remanded to FDA for reconsideration and further rulemaking as necessary. In connection with any rulemaking undertaken pursuant to this remand, FDA agrees to propose the utilization of scientifically accepted procedures of risk assessment and to raise the issue as to whether, in view of those procedures, hair dyes containing 4–MMPD present a generally recognized level of insignificant risk to human health. Any rule proposed by FDA may address any other matter that the Agency deems relevant. The issuance of any final regulation will be the result of the Agency's exercise of discretion in considering all relevant matters submitted in the course of the proceeding.

> This Order does not determine whether or not 4–MMPD does or can cause a risk to humans. The Order also makes no determination whether or not any aspect of the stayed regulation is valid. Plaintiffs reserve their right to challenge the regulation and any new or modified regulation which FDA promulgates on remand.

FDA stayed its regulation, 47 Fed. Reg. 7829 (February 23, 1982), and as of June 30, 1990, had not reopened the matter. Nor has the agency since proposed to ban, or to require a cancer warning for, a substance that poses less than a one in one million risk of cancer.

3. *Coal Tar Hair Dyes.* Though several other coal tar substances used in hair dyes have been shown to be carcinogenic in National Toxicology Program bioassays, FDA has not taken action to regulate any of them. *E.g.,* 43 Fed. Reg. 45645 (October 3, 1978) (4–amino–2–nitro–phenol); 51 Fed. Reg. 31376 (September 3, 1986) (C.I. Disperse Blue 1); 51 Fed. Reg. 10576 (March 27, 1986) (HC Red No. 3); 53 Fed. Reg. 25213 (July 5, 1988) (2–amino–t–nitrophenol); 53 Fed. Reg. 51322 (December 21, 1988) (2–amino–4–nitrophenol).

4. *Phenylenediamines.* Phenylenediamines are essential components of coal tar hair dyes. Under the Toxic Substances Control Act, (TSCA), EPA has engaged in rulemaking to consider whether testing of these chemical substances should be required, 45 Fed. Reg. 35897 (May 28, 1980), 47 Fed. Reg. 973 (January 8, 1982), 47 Fed. Reg. 26992 (June 22, 1982), 47 Fed. Reg. 38780 (September 2, 1982), 50 Fed. Reg. 4267 (January 30, 1985), 51 Fed. Reg. 472 (January 6, 1986), 53 Fed. Reg. 913 (January 14, 1988). Because FDA-regulated products are exempt from TSCA, EPA emphasized that this action was being taken in respect to uses not regulated by FDA, 47 Fed. Reg. at 979.

5. *Hair Dye Risks.* For evaluations of the carcinogenic risk posed by hair dyes, *see* Cordle and Thompson, *An Epidemiologic Assessment of Hair Dye Use,* 1 Regul. Toxicol. & Pharm. 388 (1981); Wilson, *Risks Posed By Various Components of Hair Dyes,* 278 Arch. Dermatol. Res. 165 (1985). *Compare* "Cancer–Causing Chemicals—Part I: Safety of Cosmetics and Hair Dyes," Hearings before the Subcomm. on Oversight and Investigations of the House Comm. on Interstate and Foreign Commerce, 95th Cong., 2nd Sess. (1978); "Safety of Hair Dyes and Cosmetic Products." Hearing before the Subcomm. on Oversight and Investigations of the House Comm. on Interstate and Foreign Commerce, 96th Cong., 1st Sess. (1979).

6. *Methylene Chloride.* FDA banned methylene chloride as an ingredient in cosmetic products after determining that the upper bound lifetime cancer risk significantly exceeded one in one million. 50 Fed. Reg. 51551 (December 18, 1985), 54 Fed. Reg. 27328 (June 29, 1989), codified in 21 C.F.R. § 700.19.

---

4. CARCINOGENIC CONSTITUENTS OF COLOR AND FOOD ADDITIVES

It should be obvious that the Delaney Clause is not self-implementing. In addition to issues presented by its language in cases to which the clause concededly applies, questions of coverage lurk around many corners. For example, how (if at all) does the Delaney Clause apply to a naturally-occurring carcinogenic constituent of a raw agricultural commodity. In a report prepared in response to a request from the House Appropriations Committee, FDA offered the following analysis:

> ... [T]he detection of a trace amount of a known carcinogenic substance naturally present in a food, or unavoidably added to a food in the course of its manufacture or processing, does not invoke the anticancer clauses. It has been pointed out, for example, that there are small amounts of estrogenic substances, which are regarded as carcinogenic, naturally present in many foods. The anticancer clauses would be applicable, however, only if the food itself (containing the naturally-occurring substance) were, upon feeding to test animals or some other appropriate test, found to induce cancer. If this were to happen, the food itself would then be prohibited for use as a "food additive"—*i.e.*, for any use other than as an unprocessed raw agricultural commodity....

"Agriculture–Environmental and Consumer Protection Appropriations for 1975," Hearings before a Subcomm. of the House Comm. on Appropriations, 93d Cong., 2d Sess. (1974).

By contrast, for many years the agency followed a more cautious policy toward carcinogenic impurities of synthetic food and color additives, as the next excerpt reveals.

POLICY FOR REGULATING CARCINOGENIC CHEMICALS IN FOOD AND COLOR ADDITIVES: ADVANCE NOTICE OF PROPOSED RULEMAKING

47 Federal Register 14464 (April 2, 1982).

... [N]o food additive or color additive can be produced absolutely pure. Each additive, even a highly purified one, consists of an array of chemical entities, both functional and nonfunctional. For example, a color additive may contain one primary and a number of secondary colors, all of which are somewhat functional in the final additive. A polymer resin used in food packaging may contain a continuum of chemicals from monomer and dimer to high molecular weight polymers, only some of which are functional. Finally, all chemical substances, including those used as additives, contain numerous impurities such as residual reactants, intermediates, manufacturing aids, and products of side reactions and degradation.....

During the two decades that FDA has administered the food and color additive provisions, the agency has, with a few exceptions, interpreted the Food and Color Additive Amendments to ban the use of any additive that was found to contain or was suspected of containing minor amounts of carcinogenic chemicals, even if the additive as a whole had not been found to cause cancer (noncarcinogenic additives).

For example, FDA terminated the provisional listings of carbon black (41 FR 41857; September 23, 1976) and graphite (42 FR 60734; November 29, 1977) because the agency suspected that these colors could contain polynuclear aromatic hydrocarbons (PNA's), some of which are carcinogenic. The agency removed Ext. D&C Yellow No. 1 from the provisional list (42 FR 62478; December 13, 1977) because of the possibility that it might contain as impurities 4–aminobiphenyl and benzidine, both of which have been shown to be carcinogenic in humans. FDA terminated the provisional listing of D&C Red Nos. 10, 11, 12, and 13 because the agency suspected that they might contain low levels of [beta]-naphthylamine, a known human carcinogen (42 FR 62475; December 13, 1977).

The agency has also proposed to restrict the uses of polyvinyl chloride (PVC) materials in contact with food (40 FR 40529; September 3, 1975) because of a finding that vinyl chloride monomer, a known human carcinogen, could migrate in small amounts into food from PVC bottles.

The agency has approved the use of food and color additives that contain or may contain minor amounts of lead and arsenic, proven carcinogens. Those chemicals are ubiquitous environmental contaminants, routinely found in food and water as well as in chemicals used to manufacture food and color additives. Their pervasiveness is such that no food or color additive can realistically be manufactured without the possibility of some lead or arsenic contamination. Thus, because the alternative would be to prohibit the use of all additives, the agency has minimized the amount of the chemicals and thus the risk attendant to the use of such additives by setting specifications for lead and arsenic in many food and color additive regulations. FDA does not regard these exceptional situations as constituting a true departure from its traditional regulatory approach described in the examples listed above .....

Recent scientific and legal developments have convinced FDA that it may now be necessary and appropriate for the agency to reconsider how it determines whether there has been an adequate demonstration of the safety of a food additive or color additive that contains a carcinogenic constituent but that is not itself carcinogenic.

Over the past 20 years, there have been rapid developments in analytical capabilities that make it possible to decrease by orders of magnitude the levels at which the components of a substance such as a food additive or color additive are detectable and identifiable.... Coupled with this development has been a large increase in the number of substances that have been studied for carcinogenicity in animal bioassays. For example, Tomatis has reported that 828 chemical substances were under test for cancer throughout the world in 1975. Many of these bioassays have resulted in positive findings for carcinogenesis. The Occupational Safety and Health Administration has reported that about 17 percent of 7,000 test chemicals on a Public Health Service list are tumorigenic. Griesmer and Cueto have reported that 52 percent of the chemicals that have been studied in the National Cancer Institute (NCI) bioassay program are carcinogenic. A National Toxicology Program report indicated that 41 percent of 95 tests completed showed that the tested substances are carcinogenic.

As the number of chemicals that are found to cause cancer in animals has grown, and as scientists' ability to detect the components of a substance has become more acute, the chances that a food additive or color additive will be found to contain a carcinogenic chemical entity increase. It is the agency's frank expectation that a growing number of additives will be found to contain a carcinogenic chemical in future years. If FDA continues to implement the regulatory approach that it has followed in recent years, it will be forced to refuse to approve or to terminate the approval of the use of each of these additives, even though they themselves may be safe.

However, the agency believes that there are alternatives to its current policy that will adequately protect the public health. Not all of the additives that have been or will be found to contain carcinogenic chemicals will themselves be shown to induce cancer in appropriate tests (*e.g.* D&C Green No. 6). The agency believes that a distinction can be drawn between additives that contain a carcinogenic chemical but that have not themselves been shown to be carcinogenic. Two recent developments support the agency's belief that such a distinction is appropriate.

One development was the 1979 decision by the United States Court of Appeals for the District of Columbia in *Monsanto Co. v. Kennedy*, 613 F.2d 947 (D.C. Cir. 1979). In discussing whether a substance that migrates into food is a food additive, that court expressed the view that there is "administrative discretion, inherent in the statutory scheme, to deal appropriately with *de minimis* situations." If FDA has discretion to disregard low-level migration into food of substances in indirect additives because the migration of the particular additive presents no public health concern, then the agency may also disregard, after appropriate tests, a carcinogenic chemical in a noncarcinogenic food additive or color additive, if FDA determines that there is a reasonable certainty of no harm from the chemical.

Second, the agency is now confident that it possesses the capacity, through the use of extrapolation procedures, to assess adequately the upper level of risk presented by the use of a non-carcinogenic additive that contains a carcinogenic chemical....Many theoretical models have been developed to extrapolate from animal experimental data to the relatively low levels of possible human exposure, but they can vary widely in the risk values that they predict. Thus, knowledge of the true risk at relatively low exposures is elusive.

Nevertheless, even though there is an inadequate scientific basis for confidence in the accuracy of predictions of actual risk by these procedures, there has been a growing recognition in the scientific community that by using certain conservative extrapolation models it is possible to estimate an upper limit of risk. The estimate of the risk may be exaggerated by these conservative extrapolation models. Because the estimated risk will not be understated, however, such risk assessment techniques can be used with confidence to determine whether, under the general safety clause, there is a reasonable certainty that no harm will result from the intended use of an additive.

In the decision on D&C Green No. 6 published elsewhere in this issue of the FEDERAL REGISTER, FDA is approving a color additive that has not been shown to be a carcinogen in appropriate tests, even though it contains a carcinogenic impurity. In this advance notice of proposed rulemaking, FDA is announcing its intent to formally adopt the principles on which that decision is based as the general policy of the agency....

The policy consist of three elements:

1. Clarifying exactly what an "additive" is;

2. Interpreting the Delaney Clause to apply only when the additive itself has been shown to cause cancer; and

3. Using risk assessment as one of the tools for determining whether the additive is safe under the general safety clause.....

Conceivably, each chemical in the complex mixture that constitutes a food additive could itself be considered to be a food additive. Each of these chemicals in some sense becomes a component of the food of which the additive is a part. For example, in the case of an indirect food additive used in food packaging or the like, any chemical impurity that migrates from the indirect additive into food could be considered to be an additive. In the *Monsanto* case, the agency argued that the food additive definition applied to the residual acrylonitrile monomer used to fabricate the final bottle, as well as to the bottle itself, because the monomer was intended for use and was used to manufacture the copolymer bottle. However, the *Monsanto* court held that the statute does not compel the Commissioner of Food and Drugs to declare that each chemical in an additive is itself an additive.....

The Delaney Clause requires the disapproval of any food additive that has been shown to be a carcinogen in appropriate testing....

However, it does not state that an additive shall not be deemed safe if the additive "or any of the chemicals present in the additive" is found to induce cancer.... A natural reading of the language that does appear in the statute establishes that the Delaney Clause does not apply any carcinogenic chemical in a food additive absent a finding, after appropriate tests, that the additive as a whole induces cancer. Similar reasoning would apply to the Delaney Clause in the color additive provisions of the act.

The legislative histories of the Food Additives Amendment and Color Additive Amendments are silent on this question. However, the agency's contemporaneous interpretation of the Color Additive Amendments supports the interpretation of the Delaney Clause set forth above, as explained in the preamble to the D&C Green No. 6 regulation.

... FDA believes that risk assessment may be appropriately used to determine whether, under the general safety clause, there is a reasonable certainty that no harm will result from the proposed use of the additive.....

Once FDA has determined a maximum acceptable level of exposure to a carcinogenic chemical, the agency would then consider whether the amount of actual exposure to the chemical from food additives and color additives is within the acceptable level. If necessary, the agency would develop specifications for such chemicals in individual additive regulations, taking into account total estimated exposures.

... The risk assessment procedures discussed in this advance notice would not modify currently applied requirements under the general safety clause other than to provide a procedure for determining whether a noncarcinogenic additive that contains minor amounts of a proven carcinogenic chemical is safe. The risk assessment procedure would provide a method for estimating the levels of such chemicals that meet the general safety clause standard of safety. The upper limit of acceptable exposure would be determined by carcinogenic potency and risk extrapolation by the best current scientific methods available. FDA believes that any risk assessment procedure should yield such low acceptable levels that nothing but minor levels of carcinogenic chemicals would be able to pass the screen.....

FDA believes that this general policy is a sensible, scientific means of limiting the circumstances in which it will be necessary for the government to act to ban the use of a food additive or color additive, without compromising the public health protection afforded by the act. This policy, if finally adopted, is intended to be implemented solely in those instances (*e.g.*, in the case of D&C Green No. 6) where data demonstrate that there is a reasonable certainty that no harm will result from the use of an additive that contains a carcinogenic chemical.....

Although the Natural Resources Defense Council submitted objections to FDA's approval of D&C Red No. 6, when the agency rejected them and denied a hearing, 48 Fed. Reg. 34463 (July 29, 1983), NRDC did not appeal the matter to the courts. FDA's reliance on this "constituents policy" to approve a second color additive, D&C Green No. 5, 47 Fed. Reg. 14138 (April 2, 1982), 47 Fed. Reg. 24278 (June 4, 1982), however, did trigger a court challenge.

SCOTT v. FOOD AND DRUG ADMINISTRATION

United States Court of Appeals, Sixth Circuit, 1984.
728 F.2d 322.

PER CURIAM.

Petitioner, acting pro se, seeks judicial review of 21 C.F.R. 74.1205, a regulation issued by the Food and Drug Administration (FDA) authorizing the permanent listing and therefore the continued use of a color additive, D&C Green No. 5, in drugs and cosmetics....

D&C Green No. 5 contains another color additive, D&C Green No. 6, manufactured through the use of p-toluidine, which has been proven to be a carcinogenic when tested separately, and which is present in minute quantities as a chemical impurity in D&C Green No. 5. After extensive tests, the FDA determined that D&C Green No. 5, as a whole, did not cause cancer in test animals. It also determined that p-toluidine was not itself a color additive. It concluded, therefore, that the Delaney Clause ... did not bar the permanent listing of D&C Green No. 5.....

The FDA first ... determined that the maximum life-term average individual exposure to p-toluidine from use of D&C Green No. 5 would be 50 nanograms per day. The FDA then extrapolated from the level of risk found in animal bioassays to the conditions of probable exposure for humans using two different risk assessment procedures. Under the first procedure, the upper limit individual's life time risk of contracting cancer from exposure to 50 nanograms per day of p-toluidine through the use of D&C Green No. 5 was 1 in 30 million; the second procedure resulted in a calculation of a 1 in 300 million risk. The agency concluded "that there is a reasonable certainty of no harm from the exposure of p-toluidine that results from the use of D&C Green No. 5."

... Petitioner does not contest the validity of the tests employed by the FDA in determining that D&C Green No. 5 was safe for its intended uses but rather asserts that the Delaney Clause, as a matter of law, prohibits approval of a color additive when it contains a carcinogenic impurity in any amount and that the FDA has no discretion to find D&C Green No. 5 "safe" under the General Safety Clause because "[it is not] possible to establish a safe level of exposure to a carcinogen."....

We affirm the judgment of the Food and Drug Administration.....
The FDA's finding that the Delaney Clause is inapplicable to the

instant case because D&C Green No. 5 does not cause cancer in humans is in accordance with the law. In its final order, the FDA stated its rationale for its conclusion, and it was fully mindful of the Delaney Clause in making its decision:

> [T]he Agency does not believe that it is disregarding the Delaney Clause. In drafting the Delaney Clause, Congress implicitly recognized that known carcinogens might be present in color additives as intermediaries or impurities but at levels too low to trigger a response in conventional test systems. Congress apparently concluded that the presence of these intermediaries or impurities at these low levels was acceptable. This legislative judgment accounts for the absence of any requirement in the Delaney Clause that the impurities and intermediaries in a color additive, rather than the additive as a whole, be tested or otherwise evaluated for safety. Thus, Congress drew a rough, quantitative distinction between a color additive that is deemed unsafe under the Delaney Clause because it causes cancer, and an additive that is not subject to the Delaney Clause because it does not cause cancer even though one of its constituents does. FDA's decision on D&C Green No. 5 is consistent with this distinction.

This interpretation of the Delaney Clause case is a reasonable one, and it is consistent with its legislative history. Congress distinguished between "pure dye" and its "impurities" in its list of factors for the FDA to consider under the General Safety Clause, but omitted "impurities" as a factor under the Delaney Clause. Although the Agency's regulatory interpretation of the Delaney Clause contains the words, "color additive *including its components*," it is clear that this regulation was aimed only at those additives containing impurities that produced cancer when tested together. . . .

Since in the instant case it was determined by the FDA that D&C Green No. 5, after testing as a whole, did not cause cancer in test animals, under the plain language of the Delaney Clause and the FDA's interpretation of that Clause, the FDA was not prohibited from permanently listing D&C Green No. 5.

The FDA's conclusion that the risk levels ascertained after testing D&C Green No. 5 by isolating p-toluidine were so low as to preclude a reasonable harm from exposure to the additive, within the meaning of the General Safety Clause, is also in accordance with the law. . . . This finding is consistent with the holding in *Monsanto v. Kennedy,* 613 F.2d 947 (D.C. Cir. 1979). . . .

. . . We agree with the FDA's conclusion that since it "has discretion to find that low-level migration into food of substances in indirect additives is so insignificant as to present no public health or safety concern . . . it can make a similar finding about a carcinogenic constituent or impurity that is present in a color additive." Accordingly, we hold that the FDA did not abuse its discretion under the General Safety

Clause in determining that the presence of p-toluidine in D&C Green No. 5 created no unreasonable risk of harm to individuals exposed to the color additive.

NOTES

1. *Approval of Other Carcinogenic "Constituents."* Although FDA has periodically announced that it intends to publish the constituents policy as a proposed regulation, it had not done so as of June 30, 1990. Nonetheless, since the decision in *Scott* the agency has approved more than 30 color additives and indirect food additives containing a variety of trace carcinogenic constituents. *E.g.,* 48 Fed. Reg. 37615 (August 19, 1983), 49 Fed. Reg. 13018 (April 2, 1984), 50 Fed. Reg. 49684 (December 4, 1985) (dibutyltin diacetate); 50 Fed. Reg. 4643 (February 1, 1985) (dimethylnitrosamine); 50 Fed. Reg. 20406 (May 16, 1985) (C.I. Vat Yellow 4); 50 Fed. Reg. 35774 (September 4, 1985) (4-aminoazobenzene, 4-aminobiphenyl, aniline, azobenzene, benzidine, and 1,3-dephenyltriazene); 51 Fed. Reg. 28930 (August 13, 1986) (1,4-dioxane and ethylene oxide); 52 Fed. Reg. 19722 (May 27, 1987) (methylene chloride); 52 Fed. Reg. 29178 (August 6, 1987) (hydrazine); 52 Fed. Reg. 39508 (October 22, 1987) (ethylenimine and 1,2-dichloroethane); 53 Fed. Reg. 31832 (August 22, 1988) (1,2-dichloroethane, epichlorohydrin, 2,4-toluenediisocyanate, and 2,4-toluenediamine).

2. *Carbon Black and Orange B.* In 41 Fed. Reg. 41857 (September 23, 1976), FDA terminated the provisional listing of carbon black because it may contain carcinogenic constituents. Two years later, in 43 Fed. Reg. 45611 (October 3, 1978), FDA proposed to revoke the permanent listing of Orange B for use in food because of the possible presence of a carcinogenic constituent, beta-naphthylamine. FDA has taken no further action on Orange B, and the cosmetic industry has petitioned for approval of carbon black, 52 Fed. Reg. 7933 (March 13, 1987).

3. *Indirect Additives.* FDA in 43 Fed. Reg. 56247 (December 1, 1978) proposed to ban the use of 2-nitropropane as an indirect additive for use in food packaging because of its carcinogenicity. No further action has been taken on that proposal, but the agency has approved another indirect food additive, 2-amino-2-methyl-1-proponol which contains 2-nitropropane as a constituent, 52 Fed. Reg. 29665 (August 11, 1987).

---

5. CARCINOGENIC COLOR AND FOOD ADDITIVES

FDA's ban of the nonnutritive sweetener, cyclamate, on the ground that it had been shown to be carcinogenic in animal tests, 34 Fed. Reg. 17063 (October 21, 1969), caused major disruption in the diet food industry. The agency's initial effort to soften the blow by reclassifying cyclamate-containing dietary foods as drugs, and therefore not subject to the Delaney Clause, proved politically infeasible and was subsequently abandoned. 34 Fed. Reg. 19547 (December 11, 1969), 34 Fed. Reg. 20426 (December 31, 1969), 35 Fed. Reg. 2774 (February 10, 1970), 35 Fed. Reg. 5008 (March 24, 1970), 35 Fed. Reg. 11177 (July 11, 1970), 35 Fed. Reg. 13644 (August 27, 1970). Periodic attempts to persuade the agency to reapprove cyclamate have so far failed. 41 Fed. Reg. 43754 (October 4, 1976), 42 Fed. Reg. 12515 (March 4, 1977), 44 Fed. Reg. 47620 (August 14, 1979), 45 Fed. Reg. 61474 (September 16, 1980), 49 Fed. Reg. 24953 (June 18, 1984). In 1985 FDA's Cancer Assessment Committee concluded that cyclamate is not a carcinogen, but a report by the National Academy of Sciences stating that cyclamate may be a tumor promoter or co-carcinogen led to yet another reassessment. *See* "Cyclamate Update," FDA Talk paper T89–35 (May 16, 1989).

Meanwhile, a review panel convened by the United States Claims Court pursuant to Senate Resolution No. 225, 95th Cong., 1st Sess. (1977), in accordance with 28 U.S.C. §§ 1492 and 2509, reversed a hearing officer's report which would have awarded $6.4 million to food canners who suffered losses following FDA's original ban. The court found that "there was no wrongdoing on the part of government officials and employees"; it concluded, therefore, that the industry "does not have a legal or equitable claim against the government and that any award would be a gratuity." *California Canners & Growers Association v. United States,* 9 Cl.Ct. 774 (1986).

Following cyclamate's removal from the market in 1970, saccharin remained the only nonnutritive sweetener approved in the U.S.

In 1972, FDA had before it the results of two animal studies which indicated that saccharin was a carcinogen. With candor that cannot be expected of any government official while still in office Dr. Charles Edwards, the Commissioner who had decided against banning saccharin in 1972, later explained his reasons for that decision:

> Technically, I could have banned saccharin immediately under the Delaney Clause, in early 1972, on the basis of those animal studies. I did not take that step because, once again, it was clear to me that the law should not be interpreted to yield absurd results. Saccharin was, at that time, the only remaining nonnutritive sweetener on the market. American consumers demand the availability of diet food products. It is irrelevant whether these diet products produce quantifiable health benefits or whether consumers simply like them. The point is that saccharin, like nitrite and many other important food substances, has come to be accepted and expected by the American public, and any law which does not recognize this simply will not work.

"Oversight of Food Safety, 1983," Hearings Before the Senate Comm. on Labor and Human Resources, 98th Cong., 1st Sess. 20–21 (1983). In early 1977 a third chronic feeding study conducted by the Canadian government confirmed that saccharin was a carcinogen in rats.

SACCHARIN AND ITS SALTS:
PROPOSED RULE MAKING

42 Federal Register 19996 (April 15, 1977).

... Approximately 6 to 7.6 million pounds of saccharin were used in the United States in 1976.... Food and beverage uses are by far the most extensive, accounting for over 70 percent of the saccharin used.

The soft drink industry accounts for about 74 percent of the saccharin consumed in food and beverages in the United States. Other dietary uses, which account for 14 percent of the saccharin consumed, include powdered juices and drinks, other beverages, sauces and dressings, canned fruits, dessert toppings, cookies, gums, jams, candies, ice cream and puddings. About 12 percent of the saccharin consumed is as a sweetener in place of nutritive sweeteners (*e.g.*, sugar) in coffee and tea and on cereal.....

... In 1972, because of the questions about the safety of saccharin, FDA removed saccharin from the list of substances generally recognized as safe (GRAS) and imposed limits on the use of saccharin to discourage general use by consumers and to inhibit an increase in its use by the general population. At that time, FDA also issued an interim food additive regulation to permit continued limited use of saccharin pending completion of studies to resolve the questions concerning the safety of saccharin.....

The results of the Canadian study have been evaluated by expert pathologists, including scientists from FDA and other institutions in the United States, from Great Britain, and from other European countries, as well as from Canada. The findings indicate unequivocally that saccharin causes bladder tumors in the test animals.....

An important question raised about the animal studies on saccharin is their relevance to human beings. Public reaction to recent publicity about the Canadian study suggests considerable misunderstanding about the nature of toxicity testing in animals and the interpretation of results. For example, it has been widely publicized that the dose of saccharin found to be carcinogenic in rats is about 1,000 times that ingested by a human in a single diet beverage (when both doses are adjusted for the difference in body weight between rats and humans). Since this amount of saccharin would clearly never be ingested chronically by any person, some have suggested that these results have no pertinence whatsoever to human risk. In the judgment of FDA, this conclusion is not valid.....

Current scientific methods are not capable of determining the exact risk to humans of a chemical found to be carcinogenic in animals. However, techniques are available for estimating the upper limits of the risk. The Food and Drug Administration estimates that the lifetime ingestion of the amount of saccharin in one diet beverage per day results in a risk to the individual of somewhere between zero and 4 in

10,000 of developing a cancer of the bladder. If this risk is transposed to the population at large and if everyone in the United States drank one such beverage a day, this would result in somewhere between zero and 1,200 additional cases of bladder cancer each year....

In the Canadian study, a 24 percent incidence of bladder tumors (12 of 50) was noted in the second generation male rats fed saccharin in a dose of 5 percent of the diet. This was the most sensitive group in the study to the carcinogenic effect of saccharin. Thus, in the absence of evidence that factors involved in its sensitivity are not relevant to the human population, this group is used to estimate the upper limit of human risk. There were no bladder tumors in an untreated control group of comparable size. Although the observed incidence of bladder tumors was 24 percent, the upper limit of risk in this study at the 95 percent confidence level is 36 percent. A 5 percent dietary level of saccharin in the rat is equivalent to 2,500 milligrams/kilogram/day of saccharin. If a 60–kilogram human (approximately 132 pounds) were to ingest 150 milligrams/day of saccharin (*i.e.*, 2.5 milligrams/kilogram/day) over a lifetime, he or she would thus receive the equivalent of one one-thousandth of the rat dose per day. This dose is approximately that contained in one large diet beverage drink (12–1/2 ounces) per day.

Since rats fed 2,500 milligrams/kilogram/day may have as high as a 36 percent incidence of bladder tumors, ingestion by rats of one one-thousandth of that dose could yield, by linear extrapolation, an incidence of 0.036 percent or 4 cases per 10,000. The lifetime risk of bladder cancer in humans in the United States is 1.5 percent; that is, of every 10,000 persons, it is expected that 150 will develop bladder cancer sometime during their lives. Extrapolating from the Canadian rat study, and if one assumes a direct correlation between the estimate of maximum risk of saccharin in rats and in humans, if a human ingests 150 milligrams/day of saccharin for a lifetime, he could increase the risk of bladder cancer by 0.036 percent, for a total risk of approximately 1.54 percent. That is, of every 10,000 persons, 154 might develop bladder cancer (if they all use 150 milligrams/day of saccharin) and if the assumptions are valid.....

The estimated increase in risk from this moderate use of saccharin cannot be detected in human epidemiological studies. Such studies usually can only detect increased risks of 200 to 300 percent (*i.e.*, 2 to 3 times the baseline rate) or greater. Even the best feasible epidemiologic study is not likely to detect an increased risk of only 2 to 4 percent over background incidence..... The Food and Drug Administration thus considers the animal data and the human epidemiological data on saccharin to be compatible....

Press reports of the announcement of FDA's intention to withdraw approval of saccharin as an ingredient in foods and beverages have given the impression that the Commissioner is acting reluctantly, based exclusively on the Delaney anticancer clause.....

The discussion in the previous section makes clear that the human risk of cancer indicated by these findings is significant and cannot be ignored. The Commissioner believes that conscientious protection of the public health is not consistent with continued general use in foods of a compound shown to present the kind of risk of cancer that has been demonstrated for saccharin—regardless of the asserted benefits of its use for some individuals in the population.

Section 409(c) of the act requires that any food additive must be found to be safe for human consumption before it can be approved or, in case of an additive already approved, continue to be used in foods. Based on the accumulated evidence of hazard associated with ingestion of saccharin, culminated by the Canadian study, the Commissioner concludes that the finding required by the statute can no longer be made.....

Therefore, under both the general safety requirement of the Food Additives Amendment of 1958 and the Delaney anticancer clause, the Commissioner concludes that saccharin may no longer be approved as a food additive.... He feels constrained to point out ... that the wisdom of the Delaney clause is not at issue in this proceeding. FDA could not ignore that provision even if the Commissioner were persuaded that the risks to human health were less than they appear. He further notes that under the provisions of the law relating to food additives, FDA is not empowered to take into account the asserted benefits of any food additive in applying the basic safety standard of the act.

The Commissioner does recognize, however, the potential medical value of permitting saccharin to remain available for individuals who may depend on a nonnutritive sweetener to maintain a diet free from sugar, provided such products can meet the standards of the drug provisions of the act.....

NOTES

1. *Congress' Response.* Following publication of FDA's 1977 proposal to ban saccharin, it became apparent that Congress would not permit the ban to become effective. In November 1977, Congress passed and the President signed the Saccharin Study and Labeling Act, 91 Stat. 1451, which forbade FDA, for a period of 18 months, to take any action to prohibit or restrict the sale of saccharin sweetened foods, and instructed the Department of HEW to conduct or arrange for studies of the health benefits and risks of saccharin, and of the current national food safety policy. The legislation added to the FD&C Act sections 403(o) and (p), which require that warnings about the risk of cancer be placed on all food containing saccharin and in all retail stores selling food containing saccharin. 42 Fed. Reg. 59119 (November 15, 1977), 42 Fed. Reg. 62209 (December 9, 1977) (guidelines for labeling warning); 42 Fed. Reg. 62160 (December 9, 1977), 43 Fed. Reg. 8793 (March 3, 1978), 21 C.F.R. § 101.11 (retail store warning); 43 Fed. Reg. 5851 (February 10, 1978), 43 Fed. Reg. 45613 (October 3, 1978) (decision not to require warning on vending machines). In *Jackson v. H.R. Nicholson Co.,* Food Drug Cosm. L. Rep. (CCH) ¶ 38,180 (D.D.C., July 19, 1982), the court held that the defendant manufacturer of an imitation grape beverage base containing saccharin had no duty directly to

warn an inmate who consumed the beverage in a prison as long as the label contained the required statutory warning.

2. *NAS Studies.* The congressionally mandated studies were completed early in 1979. *See* National Academy of Sciences, Committee for a Study on Saccharin and Food Safety Policy, SACCHARIN: TECHNICAL ASSESSMENT OF RISKS AND BENEFITS (Part One, 1978); FOOD SAFETY POLICY: SCIENTIFIC AND SOCIETAL CONSIDERATIONS (Part Two, 1979). *See also,* OTA, ASSESSMENT OF TECHNOLOGIES FOR DETERMINING CANCER RISKS FROM THE ENVIRONMENT, OTA–H–138 (June 1981); Merrill and Taylor, *Saccharin: A Case Study of Government Regulation of Environmental Carcinogens,* 5 Va. J. Nat. Res. L. 1 (1985).

3. *Authority to Phase Out Use of Carcinogenic Additives.* In March 1979 the Attorney General advised the Secretaries of HEW and Agriculture, p. 1189 *infra*, that under the FD&C Act FDA could not gradually phase out the use of nitrite in bacon if it were determined to be a carcinogen.

4. *Proposals to Amend the Delaney Clause.* While Congress was considering legislation to forestall FDA's proposed ban against saccharin, there were also numerous proposals before it that would revise fundamentally the general standards for approval of food additives. A bill that drew the support of several members of the House, H.R. 5166, 95th Cong., 1st Sess. (1977), would have permitted FDA to approve the use of a carcinogenic additive upon a finding that its benefits outweighed the risks:

(B)(i) [Such] a finding ... may be made only after the Secretary has received and considered the recommendations respecting such finding submitted by an advisory committee appointed by the Secretary from (I) individuals who are qualified by scientific training and experience to evaluate the carcinogenic effect of the food additive with respect to which such finding would be made and to evaluate the other effects of the use of such additive, (II) persons representative of the interests of consumers and the food additive industry affected, and (III) nutritionists, economists, scientists, and lawyers. The Secretary shall also provide reasonable opportunity for interested persons to comment on such a finding, and such a finding shall not take effect until the expiration of one hundred and twenty days after it is published in the Federal Register.

(ii) In making such a finding with respect to a food additive, the Secretary shall consider and in the finding—

(I) evaluate the intake level at which the food additive causes cancer in animals in relation to the reasonably expected intake level of the additive by humans,

(II) evaluate the quality of any test data and the validity of any tests which may have been performed on the food additive.

(III) assess human epidemiological and exposure data respecting the food additive and statistical data on human consumption of it,

(IV) evaluate any known biological mechanism of the carcinogenic effect of the food additive,

(V) evaluate the means available to minimize human exposure to the risks presented by the food additive and the adequacy of the data available on such means, and

(VI) evaluate the probable effects of prohibiting the use of the food additive and evaluate the probable effects of permitting its use, such evaluations to be made in accordance with the following priorities: first, health risks and benefits; second, nutritional needs and benefits and the effects on the nutritional value, cost, availability, and acceptability of food; third, environmental effects; and fourth, the interests of the general public.

A comprehensive revision of the food safety provisions of the FD&C Act, incorporating quantitative risk assessment, proposed in S. 1442, 97th Cong., 1st Sess. (1981), was the subject of congressional hearings, "Oversight of Food Safety, 1983," Hearings before the Senate Comm. on Labor and Human Resources, 98th Cong., 1st Sess. (1983), and in substantially contracted form continues to be considered, *e.g.*, S. 2468, 100th Cong., 2nd Sess. (1988), 134 Cong. Reg. S7185 (June 6, 1988). *See* GAO, REGULATION OF CANCER–CAUSING FOOD ADDITIVES—TIME FOR A CHANGE?, HRD–82–3 (December 11, 1981).

5. *Studies of Saccharin.* An epidemiologic study by the National Cancer Institute of 9,000 people found no overall added risk from the use of nonnutritive sweeteners, but did find the possibility of a slightly increased risk to some subgroups. FDA took the position that this study and two others were consistent with its judgment, based on the animal studies, that saccharin is a weak carcinogen. "Saccharin Studies," FDA Talk Paper T80–12 (March 7, 1980). A congressional report observed that most epidemiological studies are only capable of detecting increased risks of 200 to 300 percent and concluded that the available studies of the effects of saccharin would probably fail to detect an additional 20,000 cases of cancer per year. H.R. Rep. No. 348, 96th Cong., 1st Sess. 27–28 (1979).

6. *Saccharin Ban Moratorium.* The moratorium enacted by Congress in 1977 has been extended several times. 94 Stat. 536 (1980), 98 Stat. 173 (1983), 99 Stat. 81 (1985), 101 Stat. 391, 431 (1987).

LEAD ACETATE; LISTING AS A COLOR ADDITIVE IN COSMETICS THAT COLOR THE HAIR ON THE SCALP
45 Federal Register 72112 (October 31, 1980).

Lead acetate is a metallic salt color additive which had been used in cosmetic hair dyes before the enactment of the Amendments.....

By 1978, it was settled scientifically that lead acetate used as a hair dye would present no risk to the public health from the standpoint of classical lead toxicity (lead poisoning) (43 FR 8791; March 3, 1978). However, it had been established conclusively through animal feeding testing in the 1950's and 1960's that lead acetate was an animal carcinogen in two species, the mouse and the rat. Yet, because the limited human epidemiological data were considered equivocal, a definitive conclusion whether lead was a human carcinogen could not be reached.

In addition, the scientific evidence did not establish conclusively whether lead acetate hair dyes would be absorbed through the scalp.... Because lead is ubiquitous in the environment, the major problem inherent in determining the likelihood of percutaneous absorption of lead is the variable "background" level that is always present in humans. Humans are exposed to lead from numerous sources, including lead found unavoidably in the food, the water, and the air. As a result of the variation of lead in these sources, human lead intakes have not been precisely defined.... The question of percutaneous absorption of lead presented difficulties because it required a determination of what level of increase over the "background" must be detectable to permit a scientific conclusion that no significant absorption would occur from the use of lead acetate as a hair dye....

Under section 706(b)(4) of the Amendments, a color additive cannot be permanently listed unless the evidence establishes that it is "safe." This is referred to as the "general safety clause" for color additives. In addition to passing muster under the general safety clause, a color additive must also pass the test laid down by the color additive anticancer (Delaney) clause in section 706(b)(5)(B) of the Amendments.... The applicable provision is the second section of the color additive Delaney Clause (section 706(b)(5)(B)(ii) of the Amendments), which states that a color additive:

> * * * shall be deemed unsafe, and shall not be listed, for any use which will not result in ingestion of any part of such additive, if, after tests which are appropriate for the evaluation of the safety of additives for such use or after other relevant exposure of man or animal to such additive, it is found by the Secretary to induce cancer in man or animal.

....[T]he "non-ingestion clause," does not make an animal ingestion study demonstrating carcinogenicity an absolute bar to the approval of a petition for a non-ingested color additive. Instead, it requires the agency to make one of two additional findings:

1. That the tests relied upon to conclude that the substance is an animal or human carcinogen are "appropriate for the evaluation of the safety of additives" for the particular use under review; or,

2. That other exposure of man or animal "relevant" to the substance shows it to be a carcinogen.

... [T]o interpret the non-ingestion color additive Delaney Clause to mean that a positive animal feeding study is a per se bar to the permanent listing of a non-ingested color additive would eliminate the criteria of "appropriateness" and "relevance" from the statute itself.... As discussed below, after a thorough evaluation of all available scientific evidence relevant to the issue, the agency cannot find that the animal feeding studies are either "appropriate" or "relevant" for making the safety determination for lead acetate hair dyes under section 706(b)(5)(B)(ii) of the Amendments. This conclusion is based upon the unusual combination of scientific facts peculiar to lead acetate in hair dyes, a combination which will rarely, if ever, be presented again in this context.

1. The Combe, Inc. radioactive tracer skin absorption study, in attempting to identify whether systemic absorption of lead occurred following the application of the hair dye, demonstrated that on an average only 0.5 *ug* of lead per application penetrates the skin. Conventional analytical methods could not detect so small an amount of lead. Indeed, the agency believed prior to the performance of the study that absorption would not be considered significant, in an analytical sense, unless found to be greater than 1 *ug*. On the basis of that study, it is estimated that frequent users of lead acetate hair dyes who might apply the hair dye as often as twice per week, could have an average daily absorption of lead from that source of 0.3 *ug* (3/10 of one millionth of a gram).... [T]his compares to an average human absorption of lead from air, food, and water of approximately 35 *ug*/per day. Thus, the average user of lead acetate hair dye might increase his or her body lead burden by less than 1 percent. Such an increase of absorbed lead from hair dyes over the normal human "background" levels of lead does not augment the existing risk of acute or chronic lead toxicity, including cancer, in any clearly discernible, much less significant, manner.

2. The scientific data submitted to FDA concerning the issue of whether lead is a human carcinogen are not sufficient for substantiating a direct correlation between lead exposure and human carcinogenicity. However, even if a direct correlation could be made, the human cancer risk from the use of lead acetate hair dye would be a clearly insignificant one. In the course of the safety evaluation of this petition, FDA considered risk assessments prepared by FDA staff personnel and Dr. Richard Wilson of Harvard University on behalf of Combe, Inc. These assessments were performed independently; yet they reached very similar conclusions. Using "worst case" risk estimates extrapolated from the animal toxicity data (*i.e.*, assuming carcinogenicity), the agency calculated that the upper limit of lifetime cancer risk from the use of lead acetate in hair dyes was approximately two in ten million lifetimes. Dr. Wilson's risk assessment calculated that the upper limit lifetime cancer risk from lead acetate in hair dyes was about one in eighteen and one half million lifetimes. The disparity in the upper limit lifetime risk derived by these assessments can be attributed to slight differences in the assumptions underlying each assessment. These very conservative risk assessments support a conclusion that any risk likely to result from use of lead acetate hair dye cannot be considered significant in terms of public health protection.

Having considered the trivial amount of lead absorption in relation to the ever present normal lead "background" in humans and recognizing that, even if a human cancer risk exists from the use of lead acetate hair dyes, such an added risk would be minute. FDA concludes that lead acetate, by any reasonable standard, is safe for use in hair dyes. Because FDA regards this use of lead acetate to be safe, the agency is unable to conclude that the studies showing lead acetate to be an animal carcinogen are "appropriate" or "relevant" for the purpose of applying the non-ingested color additive Delaney Clause.

The reasoning that leads FDA to conclude that lead acetate is safe and that the Delaney Clause cannot be invoked also justifies the conclusion that lead acetate hair dyes satisfy the general safety provisions under section 706(b)(5)(A)(i) through (iv) of the Amendments.

NOTES

1. *Denial of Hearing.* Six months later, FDA confirmed the effective date of the permanent listing of lead acetate and rejected, as inadequate to justify an evidentiary hearing, the objections filed by several consumer groups, 46 Fed. Reg. 15500 (March 6, 1981). The agency concluded that the objectors had misconstrued its assessment of the cancer risk faced by lead acetate-based hair dyes:

> The objection stated "if the risk is 1 in a million and if more than 1 million persons use hair dyes with lead acetate, then at least 1 person will die as a direct consequence of the FDA's decision." This conclusion reflects a misunderstanding of the risk estimation that FDA performed, and of the meaning and use of risk estimates in determining whether a substance is safe.

> Upper limit estimates of risk using "worst case" assumptions cannot be used to predict with mathematical precision what will actually occur. Yet, because risk estimates take into account the risk resulting from incomplete information, extreme assumptions of overuse, abuse, and over application, etc., (hence, "worst case estimates"), are factored in to reach a conclusion with reasonable certainty of what will not occur. The agency's conclusion that less than 1 out of 5 million persons would be at risk from the use of this color additive in hair dyes based upon the "worst case estimates" is consistent with the likelihood that no cancers will result from the topical use of this color additive. Thus, in terms of the public health protection, this additive presents no significant safety or health concerns and is, therefore, safe....

2. *Press Reaction.* The lead acetate decision was not challenged in the courts. Noting that "there is a healthy new skepticism about how far regulators should go without first proving the extent of risk or the value of a ban," the New York Times editorialized that "The F.D.A.'s restraint in this case is welcome", and suggested that "an important precedent has been set." "The agency has edged away from its previous inclination to ban any product that contained any amount of a carcinogen. To cling to such an extreme position would only have weakened confidence in the regulators and eroded their power to protect the public against real dangers." "A Carcinogen Passes," New York Times, November 9, 1980, p. 18E.

LISTING OF D&C ORANGE NO. 17 FOR USE IN EXTERNALLY APPLIED DRUGS AND COSMETICS

51 Federal Register 28331 (August 7, 1986).

In the FEDERAL REGISTER of April 1, 1983 (48 FR 13976), FDA announced that the provisional listing of the use of D&C Orange No. 17 for coloring ingested drugs and cosmetics had expired (48 FR 13976) and denied that portion of the petition that requested the listing of D&C Orange No. 17 for ingested drug and cosmetic uses (48 FR 14045). FDA took the latter action because it concluded, on the basis of the animal experiments that had been performed as a condition of the provisional listing of D&C Orange No. 17, that the color additive was carcinogenic when administered in the diet of laboratory animals.... D&C Orange No. 17 remained provisionally listed for use in externally applied drugs and cosmetics.

... [T]he petitioner continued to seek permanent listing for the use of this color additive in external cosmetic and drug products that are not subject to incidental ingestion. On March 22, 1983, CTFA submitted preliminary results of a percutaneous absorption study of D&C Orange No. 17. Another CTFA submission, dated April 15, 1983, included a review and analysis of scientific studies, including an assessment of the risk from the use of D&C Orange No. 17 in external cosmetic and drug products, a final report on percutaneous absorption of D&C Orange No. 17, and a discussion of the legal issues raised by external use of this color additive....

In ... (50 FR 26377, June 26, 1985), FDA announced that the Commissioner had established a scientific review panel (panel) of Public Health Service scientists to evaluate data and report on the risk assessment issues.... In the report, the panel concluded that the risk assessments submitted by the petitioner for several of the color additives, including D&C Orange No. 17, are consistent with current acceptable usages in risk assessment. The panel concluded that the range of lifetime risk presented by external exposure to D&C Orange No. 17 was extremely low. The report of the panel was also submitted to peer review and subsequently published in *Risk Analysis,* 6:2:117–154, 1986, thereby broadly providing the risk analysis assessment to the scientific community.....

FDA has evaluated all the available evidence regarding the safety of D&C Orange No. 17. Based upon this evaluation, FDA finds that the use of D&C Orange No. 17 in externally applied drugs and cosmetics is safe. Although the external uses involve, based on conservative statistical analysis, a theoretical carcinogenic risk, the agency finds that this risk is so trivial as to be effectively no risk at all. For these reasons, the agency has decided to permanently list these uses of D&C Orange No. 17.....

CTFA calculated both the "best conservative estimate" and the "upper bound estimates" of risk from the use of D&C Orange No. 17 in externally applied cosmetics and drugs, using currently accepted methods of risk assessment.... It was standard procedure by CTFA to make highly conservative "worst case" assumptions at each step, so that the final estimates likely overstated the actual risks by large factors. In its report, CTFA presented both "best conservative estimate" and "upper bound estimate" calculations to illustrate the range of potential risk. The "best conservative estimate" was based upon the extrapolation curve that best fits the experimental data, but also included such highly conservative "worst case" elements as the assumption that an individual'consumer will be in the upper 90th percentile for frequency of use of all cosmetic products and will use only those cosmetic products that contain D&C Orange No. 17 at the maximum concentration. The "upper bound estimate" includes all "worst case" assumptions.

The CTFA risk assessment combined adenomas and carcinomas from the mouse liver tumor data and used the "worst case" maximum projections of human exposure and skin penetration. The multistage extrapolation model using the "worst case" maximum human exposure provides a "best conservative estimate" of potential lifetime risk to humans of 4×10^{-11} (1 in 25 billion), and an "upper bound estimate" of 7×10^{-11} (1 in 14 billion). For the rat liver tumors, CTFA again combined both adenomas and carcinomas in order to provide a very conservative "worst case" estimate of potential risk to humans. The multistage extrapolation model using the "worst case" maximum human exposure provided a "best conservative estimate" of potential lifetime risk to humans of 1.1×10^{-19} (1 in 10 sextillion), and an "upper bound estimate" of 2.1×10^{-10} (1 in 4.8 billion).....

The panel evaluated the possibility of performing a scientifically valid carcinogenic risk assessment on D&C Orange No. 17 for externally applied drug and cosmetic uses. The panel did not consider risk assessments for other toxic endpoints—indeed, it was not necessary to do so because no safety concerns other than carcinogenicity have been associated with the external uses of D&C Orange No. 17....

The panel's revised risk estimates are as follows:

	Risk (CTFA/ 90)*	Risk/90	Risk/Rea
Rat	2.1×10^{-10}	5.1×10^{-11}	1.5×10^{-11}
Mouse	0.7×10^{-10}	1.7×10^{-11}	0.5×10^{-11}

*Note that CTFA does not give an average exposure estimate for D-&-C Orange No. 17. Risk (CTFA/90) is the CTFA risk estimate at the upper 90th percentile of exposure. Risk/90 is the risk estimate based on the panel's calculation at the 90th percentile of exposure.
Risk (REA) is the risk estimate based on the panel's calculation of a more reasonable estimate of exposure.

The above risk estimates are based on the reasonable estimates of exposure, whenever the panel believed that it was possible to make such an estimate. In situations where available data would allow for a choice between "degrees of reasonable estimate," the panel consistently selected the estimate associated with the higher risk.....

In the past, because the data and information show that D&C Orange No. 17 is a carcinogen when ingested by laboratory animals, FDA in all likelihood would have terminated the provisional listing and denied CTFA's petition for the externally applied uses of D&C Orange No. 17 without any further discussion. In the present instance, however, CTFA has presented arguments that this color additive can be regulated for safe use in externally applied drugs and cosmetics....

FDA agrees with the panel that CTFA's risk estimates on the use of D&C Orange No. 17 in externally applied drugs and cosmetics, as modified in the panel's report, represent a reliable upper bound risk and that those risk estimates can be used to evaluate the proposed external uses of D&C Orange No. 17....

Because FDA considers D&C Orange No. 17 to be a carcinogen when ingested by laboratory animals, ... the Delaney Clause (section 706(b)(5)(B)(i) of the act) is applicable. A strictly literal application of the Delaney Clause would prohibit FDA from finding that D&C Orange No. 17 is safe and, therefore, prohibit FDA from permanently listing the color for externally applied uses in drugs and cosmetics. However, as seen from CTFA's and the panel's risk estimates, the calculated risk for these uses of D&C Orange No. 17 is extremely low. In fact, the level is three to four orders of magnitude lower than that level of risk which the agency accepts in other areas concerning carcinogens; for example, its procedures and criteria for permitting carcinogenic food additive residues in animal tissues under section 512(d)(1)(H) of the act, the DES proviso to the Delaney Clause.... With such a negligible risk, there is no gain to the public and the statutory purpose is not implemented or served by an agency action delisting the substance.

Under these circumstances, FDA concludes that it should not interpret the Delaney Clause to require a ban on this use of D&C Orange No. 17. Therefore, FDA has decided to exercise its inherent authority under the *de minimis* doctrine and concludes that the Delaney Clause does not require a ban in the case of the externally applied uses of D&C Orange No. 17. Because there are no other safety problems with this use of D&C Orange No. 17, FDA finds that the externally applied uses are safe.

In its April 15, 1983, submission, CTFA argued that the applicable statutory authority under the act and judicial precedent authorize FDA to apply a *de minimis* interpretation of the Delaney Clause for a carcinogenic color additive that presents an insignificant risk of cancer. CTFA also argued that the Delaney Clause does not apply to the external uses of D&C Orange No. 17 because the tests on D&C Orange No. 17 are not appropriate for the evaluation of the substance.

FDA agrees with the former position and in the following section of this notice discusses the applicability of the *de minimis* doctrine to D&C Orange No. 17. The agency, however, disagrees with CTFA's latter argument, one that draws heavily on the agency's decision to list the color additive lead acetate. CTFA's studies show that a portion of the radiolabeled material in the D&C Orange No. 17 used for percutaneous study penetrated the skin and entered the circulatory system. Under these circumstances, in the absence of any metabolic or other data suggesting that ingestion studies are inapplicable, ingestion studies are appropriate as a basis for risk assessment of the external uses of D&C Orange No. 17.....

Two conditions must apply to justify an agency's exercise of its authority to interpret a legal requirement as not requiring action in *de minimis* situations. First, it must be consistent with the legislative design for the agency to find that a situation is trivial and, therefore, one that need not be regulated. *Alabama Power Co. v. Costle,* 636 F.2d 333, 360 (D.C. Cir. 1979). Second, it must be clear that the situation is in fact trivial, and that no real benefit will flow from regulating the particular situation. Both conditions apply here.

1. The establishment of a *de minimis* exception to the Delaney Clause is consistent with the legislative design.

In *Alabama Power Co. v. Costle, supra,* the court stated that the implication of *de minimis* authority is consistent with most statutes. The court stated that unless Congress has been extraordinarily rigid, there is likely a basis for an implication of such authority....

The clearest statement of the congressional intent for the Delaney Clause is in the legislative history of the Color Additive Amendments of 1960. The Senate considered that the calculation of risk would permit interpretation of the Delaney Clause to allow color additives producing a negligible risk. This is clear from a colloquy on the Senate floor initiated by Senator Jacob Javits in debate on his motion to reconsider the vote to approve the Color Additive Amendments. Senator Javits, focusing on the Delaney Clause, made the record clear in discussion with Republican leader Senator Dirksen and committee chairman Senator Hill that the Senate had agreed to pass the Color Additive Amendments with the Delaney Clause based upon its understanding that the authority conferred by that clause "should be used and applied within the 'rule of reason.'"[1] Both Senator Dirksen and Senator Hill agreed that the "rule of reason" was to be applied in interpreting the Delaney Clause. On that basis, Senator Javits did not pursue his motion to reconsider.

The term "rule of reason" was taken from a report to the President from the President's Science Advisory Committee and from the Departments of Agriculture and of Health, Education, and Welfare (the predecessor to the Department of Health and Human Services) that

---

1. More recently, Senator Javits reviewed this discussion. On July 10, 1985, he sent Margaret Heckler, Secretary of the Department of Health and Human Services, a letter stating that his views had not changed since 1960. He stated that it was his continuing understanding that the rule of reason "would dictate that where the danger to the public is negligible in using products with such color additives, then use should not be prohibited." A copy of Senator Javits' letter to Secretary Heckler is included in the record of this rulemaking.

analyzed the effect of the Delaney Clause that is applicable to food additives.

This report on implementation of the food additive provision, relied upon by the Senators as illustrating their understanding of the types of circumstances in which the "rule of reason" would appropriately be applied, accurately predicted the advent of the science of risk assessment. The report stated that: "From the experience obtained in animal experiments and study of humans who have been exposed to carcinogens in the course of their work the panel believes that the probability of cancer induction from a particular carcinogen in minute doses may be eventually assessed by weighing scientific evidence as it becomes available."

Thus, the Senate agreed to adopt the color additive Delaney Clause only with the understanding that the clause would be administered with "a rule of reason," premised on the expectation that scientists would be able to determine the "probability of cancer induction." Thus, far from having been "extraordinarily rigid," Congress clearly contemplated that those administering the Delaney Clause would have discretion to implement that provision in a reasonable way.[2]

This interpretation of the Delaney Clause finds support in recent case law. In *Monsanto v. Kennedy,* the court held that not all chemicals that become components of food need be considered food additives.... [T]he *Monsanto* decision is important to the agency's present action even though that case involved the definition of "food additive" and not the application of the Delaney Clause, and even though FDA, when it issued the order that was ultimately reviewed by the court, had not made a final determination as to the carcinogenicity of the chemical at issue, acrylonitrile monomer.

The court also held in *Monsanto* that the "*de minimis*" concept, applied to the threshold "food additive" definition, could be utilized to allow the marketing of a substance that presents no real public health risk. Thus, the court's decision in *Monsanto* has the practical effect of shielding substances that present effectively no carcinogenic risk from the Delaney Clause. Although the court did not explicitly interpret the Delaney Clause as inapplicable to such substances, the court presumably knew that if a carcinogenic chemical was disregarded as *de minimis* in relation to the food additive definition, the chemical would not be subject to the Delaney Clause, which applies only when that definition is met. Necessarily, therefore, the court regarded this consequence as legally warranted.

Moreover, in *Scott v. FDA,* the Sixth Circuit upheld the so-called constituents policy....

2. This grant of discretion is not inconsistent with the fact that Congress clearly intended to prevent the imposition of a tolerance for a carcinogen. Where the probability of harm is so small as to be of no practical significance, it is reasonable and appropriate to apply the "*de minimis* concept. And, doing so does not in any way reflect an intent to set a tolerance.

In addition to the foregoing precedents, the state of scientific knowledge about cancer when the Delaney Clause was passed also supports the implication of *de minimis* authority under the Delaney Clause and the fact that the provision could not possibly have been meant to be "extraordinarily rigid." In 1958, there were only four substances that were known to induce cancer in humans: soot, radiation, tobacco smoke, and *beta*-naphthylamine. Only 20 years later, scientists had identified 37 human carcinogens and over 500 animal carcinogens.

With the advent of sensitive chemical analytical methodologies, scientists have been able to find carcinogens throughout the food supply in extremely small quantities....

There is no indication that in 1958 Congress foresaw the likelihood that, within less than 30 years after the Delaney Clause was enacted, science would have progressed so far as to be able to document the widespread presence of trace amounts of proven carcinogens in food. There is no indication that Congress anticipated the extent to which substances, then regarded either as absent from foods or as noncarcinogenic on the basis of less adequate technology, would later prove to be carcinogenic. In short, the scientific knowledge about carcinogens was much more limited in 1958 than it is today. The solution Congress decided upon in 1958 for handling added carcinogens, given that state of knowledge, was not extraordinarily rigid but was entirely reasonable, *i.e.*, a few substances, present at levels then detectable, would be banned; most food would be unaffected.

Under these circumstances, it would not be consistent with the legislative design for FDA, today, to attempt to prohibit all added carcinogens from the food supply provided the risks presented by permitted levels are trivial. Permitting merely a *de minimis* level of risk from such carcinogens is not only sound regulatory policy but is also consistent with the underlying purpose of the Delaney Clause as enacted in 1958—the assurance that the food supply will be free from any meaningful risk of cancer presented by substances added to food....

2. The risk from the use of D&C Orange No. 17 in externally applied drugs and cosmetics is, in fact, so trivial as to be effectively no risk.

According to the panel's revised risk estimates, the highest lifetime level of risk presented by the external uses of D&C Orange No. 17 is 1 in 19 billion, *i.e.*, 5.1×10^{-11} .... The risk from the use of D&C Orange No. 17 in externally applied drugs and cosmetics will not exceed 1 in 19 billion and is likely to be somewhere between that level and zero. The 1 in 19 billion level represents a 1 in 19 billion increase in risk over the normal risk of cancer in a lifetime—not annual—risk. FDA emphasizes that the 1 in 19 billion level of risk does not mean that 1 in every 19 billion people will contract cancer as a result. Rather, in all likelihood, no one will contract cancer as a result of this exposure. In light of the level of risk presented by the external uses of D&C Orange No. 17, FDA finds that the uses are safe, that they impose no additional risk of cancer to the public, and that any risk they may present is of no public health consequence.

. . . [I]n a notice published in the FEDERAL REGISTER of December 18, 1985 (50 FR 51551), the agency proposed that methylene chloride when used to decaffeinate coffee is safe, in light of the fact that the potential risk posed by permitted levels of methylene chloride residue in coffee does not exceed 1 in 1 million. In that notice, the agency also suggested that the lifetime risk for this use of methylene chloride to decaffeinate coffee is *de minimis.*

Other Federal agencies have also used a 1 in 1 million level as a basis for regulatory decisionmaking permitting human exposure to carcinogens. In fact, they have sometimes made regulatory decisions that have allowed a cancer risk greater than 1 in 1 million. . . .

For example, under the Occupational Safety and Health Act (OSH Act) (29 U.S.C. 651 *et seq.*), OSHA issues health standards for the workplace. . . . In the FEDERAL REGISTER of January 14, 1983 (48 FR 1864), OSHA established a new permissible exposure limit for inorganic arsenic after determining the risk of lung cancer death associated with such a level would be 8 cases per 1,000 workers exposed over a working lifetime. The standard was upheld by the Ninth Circuit Court of Appeals in *ASARCO v. OSHA,* 746 F.2d 483 (9th Cir. 1984). In a similar action in the FEDERAL REGISTER of June 22, 1984 (49 FR 25734), OSHA published a final rule establishing a new permissible exposure limit for ethylene oxide. The new 1 part per million permissible exposure limit represented a risk of 12 to 23 excess deaths per 10,000 workers exposed over a working lifetime.

The Environmental Protection Agency (EPA) in recent years has also relied upon the 1 in 1 million lifetime level as a reasonable criterion for separating high risk problems from low risk problems presented by the wide ranging environmental contaminants EPA must regulate. . . . For example, under the Safe Drinking Water Act (42 U.S.C. 300f et seq.), EPA sets drinking water standards that contain maximum contaminant levels for toxicants, including carcinogens. Maximum contaminant levels for carcinogens that have been promulgated or proposed to date by EPA generally fall into lifetime risk ranges of 1 in 10,000 to 1 in 1 million. Similarly, EPA recently proposed to establish the 1 in 1 million level as the "point of departure" in determining the level of control for all known and possible carcinogenic constituents compounds resulting from hazardous waste contamination (51 FR 1602, 1635; January 14, 1986). . . .

Although comparisons between the safety decisions made by OSHA and EPA with those made by FDA must be tempered by the fact that the decisions are made under different statutory frameworks, the decisions support the consensus proportion that a lifetime level of 1 in 1 million presents an extremely small risk.

FDA's ruling on Orange No. 17 was immediately challenged by a consumer organization. In the course of preparing the government's brief, the Department of Justice expressed reluctance to defend FDA's decision on the grounds originally advanced. Before the government's brief was filed, FDA published the following clarification.

CORRECTION OF LISTING OF D&C ORANGE NO. 17 FOR USE IN EXTERNALLY APPLIED DRUGS AND COSMETICS

52 Federal Register 5081 (February 19, 1987).

On August 7, 1986, FDA published the permanent listing of D&C Orange No. 17 as a color additive for use in externally applied drugs and cosmetics. . . .

After summarizing the animal toxicity studies for this color additive as part of its explanation of this conclusion, FDA observed that the "data and information regarding the safety of D&C Orange No. 17 support FDA's conclusion that the substance induces cancer when tested in laboratory animals." (51 FR 28341, August 7, 1986). This clarification of the Final Rule is being published to make clear that FDA was not, by this observation, concluding that this additive induces cancer in animals within the meaning of the Delaney Clause. As explained in the permanent listing document, in calculating the risk to man presented by the expected use of D&C Orange No. 17, FDA concluded that absorption of the color additive through the human skin was essentially the same as oral exposure in the rat. By virtue of this essentially one-to-one correspondence in absorption between rodent and man, a conclusion for purposes of the Delaney Clause that a substance at a given level poses a *de minimis* risk to humans implicitly includes the conclusion that a *de minimis* level of risk at a comparable level of exposure is presented to animals. Accordingly, D&C Orange No. 17 can not be said to induce cancer in animals, as well as in man, within the meaning of the Delaney Clause. When a substance causes only a *de minimis* level of risk in animals, it cannot be said to induce cancer in animals within the meaning of the Delaney Clause.

. . . [T]he Delaney Clause, at the very least, gives to the Secretary the same ability to exercise judgment in fulfilling his responsibilities under that statute as other regulatory statutes give to other administrative decision-makers. That is, the Secretary can exercise his expert judgment to conclude that an item has such a *de minimis* impact on public health or welfare as to not trigger the regulatory structures set out by Congress.

In more explicit Delaney Clause terms, this means that FDA can conclude that a particular food or color additive poses no more than a *de minimis* risk of cancer to man or animal and that such an additive is, consequently, safe both in fact and within the meaning of the law. The words "induce cancer in man or animal" as used in the Delaney Clause are terms of art intended to convey a regulatory judgment that is something more than a scientific observation that an additive is carcinogenic in laboratory animals. To limit this judgment to such a simple observation would be to arbitrarily exclude from FDA's consideration developing sophisticated testing and analytical methodologies, leaving FDA with only the most primitive techniques for its use in this important endeavor to protect public health. Certainly the language of the Delaney Clause itself cannot be read to mandate such a counterproductive limit on FDA's discharge of its responsibilities. Moreover, nothing in the legislative history indicates that Congress intended to impose such a scientifically anachronistic meaning on the words of the statute, stopping the technological clock and relegating FDA's expert regulatory judgment to outdated analytical tools.

The need for this clarification stems from the failure of the preamble to the Final Rule to rigorously and unambiguously reserve the expression "to induce cancer" to the meaning conveyed by the statutory term of art.....

Clearly, though D&C Orange No. 17 is carcinogenic when administered in very high doses up to the maximum tolerated dose in animal toxicity studies, those same studies indicate that this additive is not a highly potent carcinogen. Moreover, when real life use is examined, the increased risk of cancer posed by this substance is so trivial as to be nearly meaningless. Similarly, it cannot be said that D&C Orange No. 17 poses anything more than a *de minimis* risk of cancer to animals. Accordingly, FDA has concluded, and clarifies the preamble to the amendments of 21 CFR 74.1267, 81.1, 81.27 and 82.1267 published at 51 FR 28346 on August 7, 1986 to explicitly state, that D&C Orange No. 17 does not induce cancer in man or animal within the meaning of the Delaney Clause.

PUBLIC CITIZEN v. YOUNG

United States Court of Appeals, District of Columbia Circuit, 1987.
831 F.2d 1108.

WILLIAMS, Circuit Judge:

... Assuming that the quantitative risk assessments are accurate, as we do for these purposes, it seems altogether correct to characterize these risks as trivial. For example, CTFA notes that a consumer would run a one-in-a-million lifetime risk of cancer if he or she ate *one* peanut with the FDA-permitted level of aflatoxins once every *250* days (liver cancer). Another activity posing a one-in-a-million lifetime risk is spending 1,000 minutes (less than 17 hours) every year in the city of Denver—with its high elevation and cosmic radiation levels—rather than in the District of Columbia. Most of us would not regard these as high-risk activities. Those who indulge in them can hardly be thought of as living dangerously. Indeed, they are risks taken without a second thought by persons whose economic position allows them a broad range of choice.

According to the risk assessments here, the riskier dye poses one ninth as much risk as the peanut or Colorado hypothetical; the less risky one poses only one 19,000th as much. It may help put the one-in-a-million lifetime risk in perspective to compare it with a concededly dangerous activity, in which millions nonetheless engage, cigarette smoking. Each one-in-a-million risk amounts to less than one *200,000th* the lifetime risk incurred by the average male smoker. Thus, a person would have to be exposed to more than 2,000 chemicals bearing the one-in-a-million lifetime risk, at the rates assumed in the risk assessment, in order to reach 100th the risk involved in smoking. To reach that level of risk with chemicals equivalent to the less risky dye (Orange No. 17) he would have to be exposed to more than 40 million such chemicals.

The Delaney Clause of the Color Additive Amendments provides as follows:

> a color additive ... (ii) shall be deemed unsafe, and shall not be listed, for any use which will not result in ingestion of any part of such additive, if, after tests which are appropriate for the evaluation of the safety of additives for such use, or after other relevant exposure of man or animal to such additive, it is found by the Secretary to induce cancer in man or animal.... 21 U.S.C. § 376(b)(5)(B).

The natural—almost inescapable—reading of this language is that if the Secretary finds the additive to "induce" cancer in animals, he must deny listing. Here, of course, the agency made precisely the finding that Orange No. 17 and Red. No. 19 [a second color additive approved by FDA on the similar grounds] "induce[ ] cancer when tested in laboratory animals." ...

Courts (and agencies) are not, of course, helpless slaves to literalism. One escape hatch, invoked by the government and CTFA here, is the *de minimis* doctrine, shorthand for *de minimis non curat lex* ("the law does not concern itself with trifles"). The doctrine—articulated in recent times in a series of decisions by Judge Leventhal—serves a number of purposes. One is to spare agency resources for more important matters. But that is a goal of dubious relevance here. The finding of trivial risk necessarily followed not only the elaborate animal testing, but also the quantitative risk assessment process itself; indeed, application of the doctrine required additional expenditure of agency resources.

More relevant is the concept that "notwithstanding the 'plain meaning' of a statute, a court must look beyond the words to the purpose of the act where its literal terms lead to 'absurd or futile results.' " Imposition of pointless burdens on regulated entities is obviously to be avoided if possible, especially as burdens on them almost invariably entail losses for their customers: here, obviously, loss of access to the colors made possible by a broad range of dyes.

... Assuming as always the validity of the risk assessments, we believe that the risks posed by the two dyes would have to be characterized as "acceptable." Accordingly, if the statute were to permit a *de minimis* exception, this would appear to be a case for its application.

Moreover, failure to employ a *de minimis* doctrine may lead to regulation that not only is "absurd or futile" in some general cost-benefit sense but also is directly contrary to the *primary* legislative goal.... In a certain sense, precisely that may be the effect here. The primary goal of the Act is human safety, but literal application of the Delaney Clause may in some instances increase risk. No one contends that the Color Additive Amendments impose a zero-risk standard for non-carcinogenic substances; if they did, the number of dyes passing muster might prove minuscule. As a result, makers of drugs and cosmetics who are barred from using a carcinogenic dye carrying a one–in–20–million lifetime risk may use instead a noncarcinogenic, but toxic, dye carrying, say, a one–in–10–million lifetime risk. The substitution appears to be a clear loss for safety.

Judge Leventhal articulated the standard for application of *de minimis* as virtually a presumption in its favor: "Unless Congress has been extraordinarily rigid, there is likely a basis for an implication of *de minimis* authority to provide [an] exemption when the burdens of regulation yield a gain of trivial or no value." But the doctrine obviously is not available to thwart a statutory command; it must be interpreted with a view to "implementing the legislative design." Nor is an agency to apply it on a finding merely that regulatory costs exceed regulatory benefits.

Here, we cannot find that exemption of exceedingly small (but measurable) risks tends to implement the legislative design of the color additive Delaney Clause. The language itself is rigid; the context—an alternative design admitting administrative discretion for all risks other than carcinogens—tends to confirm that rigidity.....

[The court then examined to the legislative history of the 1960 Color Additive Amendments, searching for indications that Congress might not have intended the Delaney Clause to be applied literally in all cases.]

Like all legislative history, this is hardly conclusive. But short of an explicit declaration in the statute barring use of *de minimis* exception, this is perhaps as strong as it is likely to get. Facing the explicit claim that the Clause was "extraordinarily rigid," a claim well supported by the Clause's language in contrast with the bill's grant of discretion elsewhere, Congress persevered.

Moreover, our reading of the legislative history suggests some possible explanations for Congress's apparent rigidity. One is that Congress, and the nation in general (at least as perceived by Congress), appear to have been truly alarmed about the risks of cancer. This concern resulted in a close focus on substances increasing cancer threats and a willingness to take extreme steps to lessen even small risks. Congress hoped to reduce the incidence of cancer by banning carcinogenic dyes, and may also have hoped to lessen public fears by demonstrating strong resolve.

A second possible explanation for Congress's failure to authorize greater administrative discretion is that it perceived color additives as lacking any great value.... It is true that the legislation as a whole implicitly recognizes that color additives are of value, since one of its purposes was to allow tolerances for certain dyes—harmful but not carcinogenic—that would have been banned under the former law.... Nevertheless, there is evidence that Congress thought the public could get along without carcinogenic colors, especially in view of the existence of safer substitutes. Thus the legislators may have estimated the costs of an overly protective rule as trivial.

So far as we can determine, no one drew the legislators' attention to the way in which the Delaney Clause, interacting with the flexible standard for determining safety of non-carcinogens, might cause manufacturers to substitute more dangerous toxic chemicals for less dangerous carcinogens. But the obviously more stringent standard for carcinogens may rest on a view that cancer deaths are in some way more to be feared than others.

Finally, as we have already noted, the House committee (or its amanuenses) considered the possibility that its no-threshold assumption might prove false and contemplated a solution: renewed consideration by Congress.

Considering these circumstances—great concern over a specific health risk, the apparently low cost of protection, and the possibility of remedying any mistakes—Congress's enactment of an absolute rule seems less surprising.

Apart from their contentions on legislative history, the FDA and CTFA assert two grounds for a *de minimis* exception: an analysis of two cases applying *de minimis* concepts in the food and drug regulation context, and contentions that, because of scientific advances since enactment, the disallowance of *de minimis* authority would have preposterous results in related areas of food and drug law....

Monsanto Co. v. Kennedy, considered whether acrylonitrile in beverage containers, was a "food additive" within the meaning of the Food, Drug and Cosmetic Act's definition of that term.....

By operation of the second law of thermodynamics, any substance, obviously including acrylonitrile, will migrate in minute amounts from a bottle into a beverage within the bottle. Questions had been raised about its safety. The court found the FDA's decision to ban its use sufficiently well considered. In remanding the case for reconsideration, the court emphasized the FDA Commissioner's discretion to exclude a chemical from the statutory definition of food additives if "the level of migration into food ... is so negligible as to present no public health or safety concerns." The opinion makes no suggestion that anyone supposed acrylonitrile to be carcinogenic, or that the Delaney Clause governing food additives, was in any way implicated. Thus the case cannot support a view that the food additive Delaney Clause (or, obviously, the color additive one) admits of a *de minimis* exception.

Scott v. Food and Drug Administration involved the color additive Delaney Clause, but is nonetheless distinguishable.... Application of a *de minimis* exception for *constituents* of a color additive ... seems to us materially different from use of such a doctrine for the color additive itself. As the *Scott* court noted, the FDA's action was completely consistent with the plain language of the statute, as there was no finding that the *dye* caused cancer in animals. Here, as we have observed, application of a *de minimis* exception requires putting a gloss on the statute qualifying its literal terms.

Monsanto and *Scott* demonstrate that the *de minimis* doctrine is alive and well in the food and drug context, even on the periphery of the Delaney Clauses. But no case has applied it to limit the apparent meaning of any of those Clauses in their core operation.

The CTFA also argues that in a number of respects scientific advance has rendered obsolete any inference of congressional insistence on rigidity.... If the color additive Delaney Clause has no *de minimis* exception, it follows (they suggest) that the food additive one must be equally rigid. The upshot would be to deny the American people access to a healthy food supply.

As a historical matter, the argument is overdrawn: the House committee was clearly on notice that certain common foods and nutrients were suspected carcinogens. Beyond that, it is not clear that an interpretation of the food additive Delaney Clause identical with our interpretation of the color additive clause would entail the feared consequences. The food additive *definition* contains an exception for substances "generally recognized" as safe (known as the "GRAS" exception), an exception that has no parallel in the color additive definition. That definition may permit a *de minimis* exception at a stage that logically precedes the FDA's ever reaching the food additive Delaney Clause. Indeed, *Monsanto* so holds—though, as we have noted, in a case not trenching upon the food additive Delaney Clause. Moreover, the GRAS exception itself builds in special protection for substances used in food prior to January 1, 1958, which may be shown to be safe "through either scientific procedures or experience based on common use in food." Indeed, the Kistiakowsky Report, filed with the [1960] House committee, stated that the grandfathering provision of the food additives Delaney Clause "considerably narrows [its] effect ... on industry and the public."

The relationship of the GRAS exception and the food additive Delaney Clause clearly poses a problem: if the food additive definition allows the FDA to classify as GRAS substances carrying trivial risks ... but the food additive Delaney Clause is absolute, then Congress has adopted inconsistent provisions.... On the other hand, if (1) the GRAS exception does not encompass substances with trivial carcinogenic effect (especially if its special provision for substances used before 1958 does not do so for long-established substances), and (2) the food additive Delaney Clause is as rigid as we find the color additive clause to be, conceivably the consequences identified by the CTFA, or some of them, may follow. All these are difficult questions, but they are neither before us nor is their answer foreordained by our decision here.

Moreover, we deal here only with the color additive Delaney Clause, not the one for food additives. Although the clauses have almost identical wording, the context is clearly different. Without having canvassed the legislative history of the food additive Delaney Clause, we may safely say that its proponents could not have regarded as trivial the social cost of banning those parts of the American diet that CTFA argues are at risk.

Finally, even a court decision construing the food additive provisions to require a ban on dietary essentials would not, in fact, bring about such a ban. As Secretary Flemming noted, in words selected by the *House Report* for quotation, the FDA could bring critical new discoveries to Congress's attention. If the present law would lead to the consequences predicted, we suppose that the FDA would do so, and that Congress would respond.

After Public Citizen initiated the litigation, the FDA published a notice embellishing the preamble to its initial safety determinations. These notices effectively apply quantitative risk assessment at the stage of determining whether a substance "induce[s] cancer in man or animal." They assert that even where a substance does cause cancer in animals in the conventional sense of the term, the FDA may find that it does not "induce cancer in man or animal" within the meaning of 21 U.S.C. § 376(b)(5)(B). It is not crystal clear whether such a negative finding would flow simply from a quantitative risk assessment finding the risk to be trivial for humans under conditions of intended use, or whether it would require a projection back to the laboratory animal: *i.e.,* an assessment that the risk would be trivial for animals exposed to the substance in quantities proportional to the exposure hypothesized for human risk assessment purposes. (Perhaps the distinction is without a difference.)....

The notices acknowledged that the words "to induce cancer" had not been "rigorously and unambiguously" so limited in the previous notices. This is a considerable understatement. The original determinations were quite unambiguous in concluding that the colors induced cancer in animals in valid tests. . . .

The plain language of the Delaney Clause covers all animals exposed to color additives, including laboratory animals exposed to high doses. It would be surprising if it did not. High-dose exposures are standard testing procedure, today just as in 1960; such high doses are justified to offset practical limitations on such tests: compared to expected exposure of millions of humans over long periods, the time periods are short and the animals few. Many references in the legislative history reflect awareness of reliance on animal testing, and at least the more sophisticated participants must have been aware that this meant high-dose testing. A few so specified.

All this indicates to us that Congress did not intend the FDA to be able to take a finding that a substance causes only trivial risk in humans and work back from that to a finding that the substance does not "induce cancer in . . . animals." This is simply the basic question— is the operation of the clause automatic once the FDA makes a finding of carcinogenicity in animals?—in a new guise. The only new argument offered in the notices is that, without the new interpretation, only "primitive techniques" could be used. In fact, of course, the agency is clearly free to incorporate the latest breakthroughs in animal testing; indeed, here it touted the most recent animal tests as "state of the art." The limitation on techniques is only that the agency may not, once a color additive is found to induce cancer in test animals in the conventional sense of the term, undercut the statutory consequence. As we find the FDA's construction "contrary to clear congressional intent" we need not defer to it.

In sum, we hold that the Delaney Clause of the Color Additive Amendments does not contain an implicit *de minimis* exception for carcinogenic dyes with trivial risks to humans. We based this decision on our understanding that Congress adopted an "extraordinarily rigid" position, denying the FDA authority to list a dye once it found it to "induce cancer in . . . animals" in the conventional sense of the term. We believe that, in the color additive context, Congress intended that if this rule produced unexpected or undesirable consequences, the agency should come to it for relief. That moment may well have arrived, but we cannot provide the desired escape.

NOTES

1. *Subsequent Proceedings.* Following this court decision, and a denial of certiorari by the Supreme Court, FDA disapproved the color additives involved in the litigation and two other color additives that had been approved on the same basis in the interim, 53 Fed. Reg. 26766, 26768, 26881, 26884, 26885 (July 15, 1988).

2. *De Minimis Filth in Food.* Compare the court decisions applying the *de minimis* doctrine to filth in food, pp. 235–36 *supra,* under section 402(a)(3)'s language prohibiting food that contains "any" filthy substance.

3. *FDA Discretion.* In 1987, a former FDA Chief Counsel suggested that the agency erred when it attempted to reinterpret the legal meaning of the Delaney Clause rather than taking its language at face value and reaching the same result by exercising the scientific judgment inherent in "induces cancer" to treat

> tumor development in experimental animals dosed at the level of maximum tolerated dose as insufficient to prove that the additive induces cancer when ingested. The observation of tumors, even malignant ones, at this extreme boundary of the experiment should have been regarded only as part of the total scientific evidence about carcinogenicity of the color additive, and a rule of reason judgment should have been reached that the colors do not fall within the ban of the Delaney Clause. I do not believe that FDA has ever had a policy of basing a judgment on the issue of cancer causation upon the results of a study in only one strain, gender, and species, at one dose in one experiment. Indeed, that is what Secretary Flemming warned against.

Letter from W. W. Goodrich to D. W. Sigelman, Counsel to the Human Resources and Intergovernmental Relations Subcomm., House Comm. on Government Operations (September 11, 1987).

4. *D&C Red No. 36.* Shortly after disapproving D&C Orange No. 17, and D&C Red No. 19, FDA approved D&C Red No. 36, 53 Fed. Reg. 29024 (August 2, 1988). When Red No. 36 was tested in rodents, it was not found to be carcinogenic. Because that testing revealed other toxic effects similar to those produced by D&C Red No. 9 (which was found to be carcinogenic and thus banned), and because the two color additives were tested in different strains of rodents, the agency had to decide whether to require that Red No. 36 be tested in the same strain of rodents used to test Red No. 9. FDA declined to mandate further testing, explaining:

> The assessment shows that even assuming that D&C Red No. 36 was carcinogenic if subjected to further testing in a strain of rat other than the Sprague–Dawley, the theoretical, upper-bound, lifetime risk associated with the exaggerated use exposure to the compound would be extremely small, that is, less than 8×10^{-8} [*i.e.,* one in 12.5 million] ...

This explanation provoked no objections and the agency confirmed its approval in 54 Fed. Reg. 9200 (March 6, 1989).

5. *Dimethyl Dicarbonate.* In 53 Fed. Reg. 41325 (October 21, 1988), FDA approved the use of dimethyl dicarbonate for direct use as a yeast inhibitor in wines. FDA noted that the additive could react with naturally occurring ammonia in wine to form trace amounts of methyl carbamate, a carcinogen in rats, but concluded that the risk was less than one in 42 million and thus that the additive was safe.

6. *Methylene Chloride.* At the same time that FDA proposed to ban the use of methylene chloride in cosmetics, p. 838 *supra,* it announced that it was not proposing to revoke the existing food additive regulation, 21 C.F.R. § 173.255, authorizing the use of methylene chloride for decaffination of coffee because the residue of the additive in coffee represents less than a one in one million risk, 50 Fed. Reg. 51551 (December 18, 1985). In *Public Citizen v. Bowen,* 833 F.2d 364 (D.C. Cir. 1987), the court determined that this decision was not ripe for judicial review. In its preamble to the final regulation

banning methylene chloride from cosmetics, 54 Fed. Reg. 27328, 27330 (June 29, 1989), FDA stated:

> The agency expects that it will take a substantial amount of time for it to consider what effect, if any, the court decision in *Public Citizen v. Young* will have on FDA's regulation of food additives, including methylene chloride.

No further action has been taken on this matter as of June 30, 1990.

7. *Ethylene Oxide.* Ethylene oxide (ETO) is currently the subject of a food additive regulation in 21 C.F.R. § 193.200, permitting its use as a fumigant for the control of microorganisms and insect infestation in spices. Because it was listed as a carcinogen in Department of HHS, FOURTH ANNUAL REPORT ON CARCINOGENS (1985), EPA received a petition, announced in 52 Fed. Reg. 47753 (December 16, 1987), requesting that the food additive regulation be revoked under the Delaney Clause. *See generally* "Use and Control of Ethylene Oxide (ETO)," Hearing before the Subcomm. on Labor Standards of the House Comm. on Education and Labor, 98th Cong., 1st Sess. (1983).

8. *Coverage of Delaney Clause.* Section 409 empowers FDA to promulgate a food additive regulation under two circumstances. First, the agency is required by section 409(c) to act on any petition submitted by an interested person under section 409(b). Second, under section 409(d) FDA may promulgate a food additive regulation on its own initiative. The Delaney Clause appears in section 409(c) and not in section 409(d). No similar distinction exists in section 706.

9. *Color Additive Advisory Committee.* Section 706(b)(5)(C) provides a unique opportunity for the petitioner or any person adversely affected to trigger advisory committee review of any question involving application of the Delaney Clause to a color additive. FDA has issued regulations governing this procedure, 21 C.F.R. § 14.140 *et seq. See* Becker, *The Scientific Advisory Committee and the Administration of Color Additives,* 15 FDC L.J. 801 (1960).

---

6. CARCINOGENIC NATURAL FOODS

A significant number of natural foods have been found to be carcinogenic in laboratory animals. *See, e.g.,* Toth & Erickson, *Cancer Induction in Mice by Feeding of the Uncooked Cultivated Mushroom of Commerce, Agaricus bisporue,* 46 Cancer Res. 4007 (August 1986):

> The cultivated mushroom of commerce in the Western hemisphere, *Agaricus bisporus,* was given p.o. to randomly bred Swiss mice for three days and was followed by semisynthetic diet for 4 days each week for life.... As a result of treatment, tumors were induced in the bone, forestomach, liver, and lungs.... The investigation thus proves the carcinogenicity of uncooked *Agaricus bisporus.*

In addition, many chemicals found to be carcinogenic in laboratory animals are constituents in important foods. For example, the NTP announced in 48 Fed. Reg. 4557 (February 1, 1983) that allyl isothiocyanate, which was shown to be a carcinogen, is:

the major component in volatile oil of mustard, a flavoring agent prepared from seed of black mustard.

Allyl isothiocyanate may be present in syrups, meats, condiments, baked goods, candy, ice cream and ices, and nonalcoholic beverages. Allyl isothiocyanate is found in cabbage, broccoli, kale, cauliflower and horseradish.

In 55 Fed. Reg. 26016 (June 26, 1990), NTP announced clear evidence of the carcinogenicity of d-Limonene, "a naturally occurring monoterpene found in many volatile oils, especially citrus oils which are used as a flavor and fragrance additive for food ... " *See also* Ames, *et al., Ranking Possible Carcinogenic Hazards,* 236 Science 271 (April 17, 1987); *Dietary Carcinogens and Anticarcinogens,* 221 Science 1256 (September 23, 1983).

FDA scientists have pointed out that traditional methods of cooking and preserving food often contaminate food with carcinogens. For example, charbroiling and smoking contaminate food with polynuclear aromatic hydrocarbons, and pickling produces nitrosamines.

This is just the tip of the iceberg. The spectrum of natural carcinogenic contaminants at low levels in food is far larger than these two examples can suggest. These "added" carcinogens are officially ignored because the exposures are ubiquitous and they would be extraordinarily difficult if not impossible to control and regulate.

Scheuplein, *et al., New Approaches to the Regulation of Carcinogens in Foods: The Food and Drug Administration,* in Melman and Weisburger, eds., HANDBOOK OF CARCINOGEN TESTING 556, 563 (1985). *See also* Prival, *Carcinogens and Mutagens Present as Natural Components of Food or Induced by Cooking,* 6 Nutr. Cancer 236 (1985). The Director of the Office of Toxicological Sciences in FDA's Center for Food Safety and Applied Nutrition has concluded that, although "we should continue to minimize exposure to carcinogens from any major source," the data suggest that almost 98% of the cancer risk from food is natural in origin, and thus

even a modestly effective attempt to lessen the dietary risk of natural carcinogens would probably be enormously more useful to human health than regulatory efforts devoted to eliminating traces of pesticide residues or contaminants. The risk from natural carcinogens appears to be so much greater that just reducing it a few percent ... promises a greater decrease in absolute cancer risk than the total elimination of the lesser risks.

Scheuplein, *Perspectives on Toxicological Risk: An Example: Food–Borne Carcinogenic Risk* 25 (1989) (unpublished manuscript).

As early as 1954 FDA banned the use of natural tonka beans as food because of the carcinogenicity of a constituent, corumarin, 19 Fed. Reg. 1239 (March 5, 1954). FDA published an order banning the use of safrole and oil of sassafras in 25 Fed. Reg. 12412 (December 2, 1960) based on animal studies demonstrating carcinogenicity. This ban was extended to include natural sassafras bark marketed for use in making sassafras tea in the home in 38 Fed. Reg. 20040 (July 26, 1973), 39 Fed. Reg. 26748 (July 23, 1974), 39 Fed. Reg. 34172 (September 23, 1974), 41 Fed. Reg. 19207 (May 11, 1976), 21 C.F.R. § 189.180. Although a 1973 seizure of sassafras bark was initially contested, the claimant subsequently withdrew the claim and thus the validity of FDA's position was not litigated. *United States v. Articles of Food ... Select Natural Herb Tea, Sassafras, etc.*, Civ. No. 73–1370–RF (C.D. Cal., June 15, 1973). Since then, the agency has not sought to ban natural food products containing carcinogenic constituents. Although FDA has quietly ignored carcinogenicity studies relating to long-established food products, it has consistently taken the position that a substance found to be carcinogenic in test animals *cannot* be regarded as GRAS, although a substance containing a carcinogenic constituent *can* be regarded as GRAS, *e.g.*, "Agriculture, Rural Development and Related Agencies Appropriations for 1984," Hearings Before a Subcomm. of the House Comm. on Appropriations, 98th Cong., 1st Sess., Part 4, at 475 (1983).

On occasion, FDA has banned synthetic chemicals that are identical to natural constituents of food. After determining that cinnamyl anthranilate, a food additive used for flavoring, was carcinogenic, FDA proposed to ban its use but concluded that no recall would be required because the risk was less than one in one million. 47 Fed. Reg. 22545 (May 25, 1982). Cinnamyl anthranilate is a synthetic chemical that is identical to a natural flavor constituent in food. In the final order banning this additive, FDA stated that the initial risk assessment was conducted only to assess the need for a recall. It asserted that information was insufficient to conduct a full risk assessment that there was in any case no reason to do so because manufacture and use of the additive had ceased. 50 Fed. Reg. 42929 (October 23, 1985).

The suggestion has been made, though the issue has not been settled, that a naturally occurring substance is properly regulated only under the "ordinarily" injurious to health standard because it is not an "added substance" within the meaning of section 402(a)(1).

---

7. CARCINOGENIC DRUGS AND DEVICES

The provisions of the FD&C Act governing human drugs and devices contain no anticancer clause; they contemplate that FDA will balance risks against benefits. Even so, the risk of cancer can generate uniquely intense concern in this context as well. In 44 Fed. Reg. 19034 (March 30, 1979), FDA announced a draft guideline on the decisionmaking criteria to be used when a drug is identified as a known or possible carcinogen. FDA instituted a general policy of requiring, with some exceptions, that new human drugs undergo testing for carcinogenicity following congressional criticism that it was not sufficiently attentive to cancer risks. "FDA's Regulation of Zomax," Hearings before a Subcomm. of the House Comm. on Government Operations, 98th Cong., 1st Sess. (1983); "FDA's Regulation of Zomax," H.R. Rep. No. 98–584, 98th Cong., 1st Sess. (1983). Another oversight hearing on the agency's approval of a contraceptive sponge centered on the risk of carcinogenic contaminants. "FDA's Approval of the Today Contraceptive Sponge," Hearing before a Subcomm. of the House Comm. on Government Operations, 98th Cong., 1st Sess. (1983). Evidence that a prescription drug is a human or animal carcinogen triggers a requirement to include a warning in the physician package insert, 21 C.F.R. § 201.57(e)(5).

---

8. CHARACTERIZATION AND CLASSIFICATION OF CARCINOGENS

Current FDA policy is binary: a substance is characterized either as carcinogenic or not carcinogenic in test animals. Any substance found to be carcinogenic in test animals is presumed by FDA to be a human carcinogen. FDA has not reviewed its policy governing the characterization and classification of substances as carcinogenic since 1970. *See* Food and Drug Administration Advisory Committee on Protocols for Safety Evaluation, Panel on Carcinogenesis, *Report on Cancer Testing in the Safety Evaluation of Food Additives and Pesticides,* 20 Toxicol. & Appl. Pharmacol. 419 (1971). In the two ensuing decades, however, other U.S. and international agencies have adopted more subtle and elaborate criteria for distinguishing among different levels of animal data and their potential relevance to human health.

The International Agency for Research on Cancer (IARC) recognizes four categories or tiers of animal evidence of carcinogenicity: (1) sufficient evidence, (2) limited evidence, (3) inadequate evidence, and (4) evidence suggesting lack of carcinogenicity. IARC MONOGRAPHS ON THE EVALUATION OF CARCINOGENIC RISKS TO HUMANS, IARC Internat. Tech. Rep. No. 87/001, at 30–31 (1987). The National Toxicology Program (NTP) has adopted a five-tier system for describing the "strength of evidence" of the experimental findings from its animal carcinogenicity studies, 51 Fed. Reg. 2579 (January 17, 1986), 51 Fed. Reg. 11843 (April 7, 1986). The five categories are: (1) clear evidence, (2) some evidence, (3) no evidence, (4) equivocal evidence, and (5) inadequate study. The first two categories (clear evidence and some evidence) represent positive results.

Based upon the "weight" of the animal evidence, as well as any relevant human or in vitro data, NTP then classifies a substance as "known" or as "reasonably anticipated" to be a human carcinogen. NTP's refusal to consider the mechanism of action for an animal carcinogen in making these determinations for purposes of the required annual report under 42 U.S.C. § 241(b)(4) was upheld in *Synthetic*

Organic Chemical Mfrs. Ass'n v. Secretary, Dept of HHS, 720 F.Supp. 1244 (W.D. La. 1989). IARC classifies substances according to carcinogenic potential under four headings: Group 1 (substances carcinogenic to humans), Group 2A (substances probably carcinogenic to humans), Group 2B (substances possibly carcinogenic to humans), and Group 3 (substances not classifiable). IARC, *supra,* at 31–32. Like NTP, IARC ignores evidence relating to mechanism of action. In 1986 EPA adopted a similar system, which includes an additional category: Group A (human carcinogens), Group B (probable human carcinogens), Group C (possible human carcinogens), Group D (not classifiable as to human carcinogenicity), and Group E (evidence of noncarcinogenicity for humans), 51 Fed. Reg. 33992 (September 24, 1986). Only for substances in Group A and Group B will EPA undertake a quantitative risk assessment.

When a government panel reviewed the safety of various color additives, it commented on the discrepancy between the FDA system and the IARC/NTP/EPA systems:

> [T]he Panel did not evaluate the weight of evidence for human carcinogenicity since it understood that it was FDA policy to consider an agent which is carcinogenic in some experimental paradigm, in any species, as a suspect human carcinogen. If the weight of evidence would have been evaluated, there is the possibility that one or more of the colors would not have fulfilled some accepted criteria (*e.g.,* IARC criteria) to be considered human carcinogens.

Hart, *et al., Final Report of the Color Additive Scientific Review Panel,* 6 Risk Analysis 117, 119 (1986).

NOTES

1. *Qualitative Evaluation of Carcinogenicity.* FDA approved FD&C Blue No. 2 in 48 Fed. Reg. 5252 (February 4, 1983), in the face of a statistically significant increase in tumors in test animals, on the ground that the biological evidence that the color additive was not carcinogenic outweighed the statistical evidence. Though contested at a hearing, this decision was upheld by the Administrative Law Judge and by the Commissioner, 52 Fed. Reg. 8113 (March 16, 1987). On judicial review, the objectors abandoned this issue, and the Commissioner's decision was affirmed. *Simpson v. Young,* 854 F.2d 1429 (D.C. Cir. 1988).

2. *Formaldehyde.* Following a major scientific consensus workshop conducted by FDA's National Center for Toxicological Research, 47 Fed. Reg. 55034 (December 7, 1982), 48 Fed. Reg. 36201 (August 9, 1983), FDA determined that inhalation studies demonstrating that formaldehyde was carcinogenic in rodents were not scientifically "appropriate" under the Delaney Clause to demonstrate a hazard from oral ingestion. *See also* 49 Fed. Reg. 6672, 6679 (February 22, 1984) (formaldehyde from aspartame); 49 Fed. Reg. 47480 (December 5, 1984) (formaldehyde from acetone formaldehyde condensate); 52 Fed. Reg. 4492, 4493 (February 12, 1987) (formaldehyde from polyoxymethylene copolymer).

3. *Appropriateness of Animal Models.* FDA has occasionally determined that a finding of carcinogenicity in a particular animal species was not relevant to human risk because the species was not an appropriate model. For example, FDA explained:

> The agency has required non-rodent animal models for carcinogenic testing of steroid contraceptives because the rodent was felt to be physiologically too divergent from the human to be a reliable test animal.

Letter from Acting FDA Commissioner M. Novitch to T. Weiss, Chairman of the Subcomm. on Intergovernmental Relations and Human Resources, House Comm. on Government Operations (December 28, 1983), at 2. Although butylated hydroxyanisole (BHA), a widely used food preservative, was shown by Japanese researchers to be associated with the occurrence of squamous cell tumors in the rat forestomach, FDA has so far taken no action, apparently reasoning that this is not an appropriate model for humans, who do not have forestomachs. Food Chemical News (June 27, 1983) at 17; Food Chemical News (March 7, 1983) at 3. The agency also questioned the relevance to humans of studies showing that lead is a carcinogen in laboratory animals, 44 Fed. Reg. 51233 (August 31, 1979).

---

9. USE OF QUANTITATIVE RISK ASSESSMENT BY OTHER GOVERNMENT AGENCIES

Government–Wide Policies. In 1977, the four principal health regulatory agencies (FDA, EPA, CPSC, and OSHA) established the Interagency Regulatory Liaison Group (IRLG) to develop common approaches to the regulation of toxic chemicals. One of the IRLG's first projects was the establishment of a Work Group on Risk Assessment. The efforts of the Work Group were complicated by interagency policy differences. Although FDA and EPA strongly supported quantitative risk assessment for carcinogens and had been using this technique for some years, OSHA had recently proposed an approach to classifying carcinogens that explicitly refrained from giving weight to carcinogenic potency or risk assessment, 42 Fed. Reg. 54148 (October 4, 1977). The final IRLG report, 44 Fed. Reg. 39858 (July 6, 1979), was therefore a relatively muted document. While recognizing its limitations, the report nevertheless endorsed the use of quantitative risk assessment.

On February 1, 1979, the Office of Science and Technology Policy (OSTP) of the Executive Office of the President issued a staff paper, IDENTIFICATION, CHARACTERIZATION, AND CONTROL OF POTENTIAL HUMAN CARCINOGENS: A FRAMEWORK FOR FEDERAL DECISION–MAKING, which strongly advocated use of quantitative risk assessment. The now-defunct Regulatory Council likewise issued a statement on regulation of chemical carcinogens in 44 Fed. Reg. 60038 (October 17, 1979), which declared that, except where a statute "explicitly indicates which substances are to be controlled and how, every regulatory proposal will be accompanied by some form of risk assessment." The statement went on to say that all carcinogens "will be considered capable of causing or contributing to the development of cancer even at the lowest doses of exposure."

Several years later, OSTP convened an Interagency Staff Group on Chemical Carcinogenesis, and prepared a comprehensive review of the science and associated principles governing the assessment of chemical carcinogens, 49 Fed. Reg. 21594 (May 22, 1984), 50 Fed. Reg. 10372 (March 14, 1985).

A review of 132 agency decisions on carcinogenic chemicals found that every one with an estimated individual risk greater than 4 in 1000 was subjected to regulation and that, with the exception of FDA's decision to regulate dimethylnitrosamine in baby bottle nipples, no action was taken to reduce individual lifetime risk levels below one in one million. Travis, *et al.*, *Cancer Risk Management*, 21 Environ. Sci. Technol. 415 (1987).

EPA Regulation of Carcinogens. EPA published interim guidelines for quantitative risk assessment of carcinogens in 1976, 41 Fed. Reg. 21403 (May 25, 1976). EPA's current guidelines for carcinogen risk assessment were published in 51 Fed. Reg. 33992 (September 24, 1986). The agency has since announced its intent to review and update those guidelines, 53 Fed. Reg. 32656 (August 26, 1988), 54 Fed. Reg. 16403 (April 24, 1989), 54 Fed. Reg. 25619 (June 16, 1989).

Many court decisions have discussed and often implied approval for EPA reliance on quantitative risk assessment. *E.g., Natural Resources Defense Council, Inc. v. Environmental Protection Agency,* 824 F.2d 1211 (D.C. Cir. 1987); *Natural Resources Defense Council, Inc. v. U.S. Environmental Protection Agency,* 824 F.2d 1146 (D.C. Cir. 1987); *American Mining Congress v. Thomas,* 772 F.2d 617, 640 (10th Cir. 1985); *American Petroleum Institute v. Costle,* 665 F.2d 1176 (D.C. Cir. 1981); *Lead Industries Association, Inc. v. Environmental Protection Agency,* 647 F.2d 1130 (D.C. Cir. 1980); *Environmental Defense Fund v. Environmental Protection Agency,* 598 F.2d 62 (D.C. Cir. 1978).

The Federal Insecticide, Fungicide, and Rodenticide Act (FIFRA) requires EPA to register a pesticide if it determines that it does not present an "unreasonable" risk. Thus, the agency may approve the use of carcinogenic pesticides on food crops if it determines that the benefits outweigh the risks. For any pesticide registered for food use under FIFRA, a tolerance for any residue in or on the raw agricultural commodity must also be established under section 408 of the FD&C Act. That provision directs EPA to consider both economic factors and consumer safety and it contains no Delaney Clause.

Under section 402(a)(2)(C), the residue in processed food of a pesticide lawfully used on a raw agricultural commodity does not require a separate food additive regulation *if* the residue has been reduced to the extent possible in good manufacturing practice and the level in the food when ready to eat does not exceed the tolerance established for the raw agricultural commodity. By virtue of this complicated arrangement, the Delaney Clause does not apply to a carcinogenic pesticide residue in processed food if these two conditions are met. If either is not met, however, the pesticide residue in the processed food is unlawful unless it is GRAS, subject to a prior sanction, or allowed by a food additive regulation promulgated under section 409. Section 409, however, contains the original Delaney Clause, which precludes issuance of a food additive regulation for any carcinogen.

In summary, the FD&C Act allows a carcinogenic pesticide residue in a raw agricultural commodity that is consumed as such, and in processed food where the residue is not concentrated, but it ostensibly prohibits any carcinogenic residue that concentrates in processed food. A committee of the National Academy of Sciences concluded that this set of rules both failed to protect consumer health and inhibited introduction of new, safer food-use pesticides. It recommended that EPA regulate carcinogenic residues using an across-the-board negligible risk standard. NAS, RELATING PESTICIDES IN FOOD: THE DELANEY PARADOX (1987). EPA has announced plans to implement this recommendation without additional legislation, 53 Fed. Reg. 41104 (October 19, 1988), 53 Fed. Reg. 41126 (October 19, 1988), 56 Fed. Reg. 7751 (February 25, 1991).

EPA has registered dozens of carcinogenic pesticides for food use. *See, e.g.,* 53 Fed. Reg. 41104, 41119–41123 (October 19, 1988). Nationwide controversy and alarm has been raised when individual states have stepped in to regulate food residues of ethylene dibromide (EDB) and daminozide (Alar) during the 1980s. *See, e.g., National Coalition Against the Misuse of Pesticides v. Thomas,* 809 F.2d 875, 815 F.2d 1579 (D.C. Cir. 1987).

OSHA Regulation of Carcinogens. The Occupational Safety and Health Administration (OSHA) initially declined to employ quantitative risk assessment in regulating carcinogens under the Occupational Safety and Health Act. Instead, it formulated a complex policy, 42 Fed. Reg. 54148 (October 4, 1977), 45 Fed. Reg. 5002 (January 22, 1980), which committed the agency to reduce worker exposure to any carcinogen to the lowest technologically achievable level, regardless of the magnitude of risk. Following the Supreme Court's decision in *Industrial Union Department, AFL–CIO v. American Petroleum Institute,* 448 U.S. 607 (1980), which required the agency to demonstrate that existing levels of worker exposure to benzene posed a significant risk before it could regulate, OSHA amended its carcinogen policy, 46 Fed. Reg. 5878 (January 21, 1981), and later announced that it was reconsidering the entire approach, 47 Fed. Reg. 187 (January 5, 1982), 48 Fed. Reg. 241 (January 4, 1983). While OSHA has taken no further steps to revise its 1980 regulation, its subsequent standards for carcinogens reflect explicit reliance on quantitative risk assessment. *E.g., International Union, United Automobile, Aerospace and Agricultural Implement Workers of America v. Pendergrass,* 878 F.2d 389 (D.C. Cir. 1989); *Building and Construction Trades Department, AFL–CIO v. Brock,* 838 F.2d 1258 (D.C. Cir. 1988); *Public Citizen Health Research Group v. Tyson,* 796

F.2d 1479 (D.C.Cir.1986); *ASARCO, Inc. v. Occupational Safety and Health Administration*, 746 F.2d 483 (9th Cir. 1984); *Asbestos Information Association/North America v. Occupational Safety and Health Administration*, 727 F.2d 415 (5th Cir. 1984).

CPSC Regulation of Carcinogens. Of the four principal federal health and safety agencies, the Consumer Product Safety Commission (CPSC) has had the least experience regulating carcinogens. On the one occasion it explicitly relied on quantitative risk assessment to justify action, a ban of urea-formaldehyde foam insulation, the Commission's action was set aside. *Gulf South Insulation v. U.S. Consumer Product Safety Commission*, 701 F.2d 1137 (5th Cir. 1983). *See generally* Merrill, CPSC Regulation of Cancer Risks in Consumer Products: 1972–1981, 67 Va.L.Rev. 1261 (1981).

Risk Assessments in Civil Litigation. Some plaintiffs seeking to recover for cancer have introduced quantitative assessments, typically based on human studies, to support their claims of causation. In other cases, plaintiffs have used such assessments to support claims of increased risk or fear of cancer. *See, e.g., In re "Agent Orange" Product Liability Litigation*, 597 F.Supp. 740, 781–783 (E.D.N.Y. 1984); *Sterling v. Velsicol Chemical Corp.* 855 F.2d 1188 (6th Cir. 1988). *See generally* Walker, *Quantitative Risk Assessments As Evidence in Civil Litigation*, 8 Risk Analysis 605 (1988).

F. SECONDARY CARCINOGENS

SELENIUM IN ANIMAL FEED;
PROPOSED FOOD ADDITIVE REGULATION

38 Federal Register 10458 (April 27, 1973).

The Commissioner of Food and Drugs ... proposes that the food additive regulations should be amended as set forth below to provide for the safe use of selenium as a nutrient in the feed of chickens, turkeys, and swine.....

Selenium is an element essential for normal growth and metabolism in animals. The minimum dietary requirements for selenium in poultry and swine range from 0.1 to 0.2 p/m of available selenium in the form of sodium selenite or sodium selenate. A dietary intake of less than these quantities of available selenium may result in a variety of debilitating conditions....

It has been estimated that 70 percent of domestic basic feedstuffs (corn and soybeans) contain less selenium than that required to meet the animals' nutritional needs.....

The applicability of the anticancer clause (sec. 409(c)(3)(A)) of the act to the addition of selenium to animal feed has been thoroughly considered.... Available data have been evaluated by the Food and

Drug Administration and the National Cancer Institute. Based on these evaluations, it has been concluded that the judicious administration of selenium derivatives to domestic animals would not constitute a carcinogenic risk. In three of the six studies available on the subject, test animals were found to have developed neoplastic lesions. These lesions were concluded to be a consequence of the liver cirrhosis produced by frank selenium toxicity. Further evaluation of the results of these three studies was complicated by the unusually high levels of selenium that had been administered, faulty experimental design, and, or infectious conditions present in the animal colonies used. Results of the remaining three studies, all of which were well controlled investigations, were negative for carcinogenic activity.

Selenium at high dietary levels (above 2 p/m for experimental animals) is a proven hepatotoxic agent. Early studies at dietary levels of 5, 7, and 10 p/m showed liver damage and regeneration in rats and an increased incidence of hepatoma in treated animals as compared with controls. Hepatoma did not occur in the absence of severe hepatotoxic phenomena. In more recent studies, hepatotoxicity was observed in rats fed selenium at 2 p/m. At 16 p/m, more severe liver damage was observed but was not associated with hepatoma. No hepatotoxic effects were noted at 0.5 p.m or below.

In this respect, selenium is no different from a number of foods and drugs available in the marketplace today. Beverage alcohol, for example, is associated with a higher incidence of liver cirrhosis, which, in turn, is associated with a higher incidence of liver cancer.

The Commissioner is of the opinion that these foods and drugs are not, by reason of their capacity to induce liver damage when abused by being consumed at high levels, properly classified as carcinogenic because of their potential association with a higher rate of liver cancer. The various anticancer clauses contained in the act were predicated on the theory that, since we do not know the mechanisms of carcinogenesis, even one molecule of a carcinogen should not be allowed into the food supply. The anticancer clauses do not apply in the case of an agent that (1) occurs naturally in practically all foods, (2) is used in a manner such that the natural level in food is not increased, (3) has a definite hepatotoxic effect/no-effect level, and (4) has a possible carcinogenic effect which is associated only with the hepatotoxic effect.

Accordingly, the Commissioner has concluded that: (1) The available information does not support classification of selenium or its compounds as having carcinogenic activity, (2) the use of selenium as set forth below constitutes no carcinogenic risk, and (3) the limitations set forth below, while satisfying the animals' dietary need for selenium, will assure safety to animals treated with sodium selenite or sodium selenate and to consumers of edible products of such treated animals.

NOTES

1. *Subsequent Proceedings.* The environmental concerns about selenium are examined in 54 Fed. Reg. 29019 (July 11, 1989).

2. *FD&C Red No. 3.* In 52 Fed. Reg. 29728 (August 11, 1987), FDA released a report by a panel of government scientists the agency had convened to evaluate the color additive, FD&C Red No. 3. This color has been shown to cause cancer in experimental animals, but the proponents of listing sought to persuade FDA that its mechanism of carcinogenic action posed no cancer risk for humans who might ingest it. The panel summarized its findings as follows:

[The Panel] ... was directed to make an inquiry into whether the data indicated that FD&C Red No. 3(R–3) had a secondary mechanism of carcinogenesis, whether the potential human risk of the color could be determined, and whether additional studies to address important questions in determining risk should be performed....

1. R–3 is a rat oncogen with equivocal evidence of carcinogenicity and with some evidence for causing benign thyroid tumors.

2. The tumorigenic effect of R–3 on rats is more likely to be the result of an indirect (secondary) mechanism.

3. It is likely, not certain, that the tumorigenic effect of R–3 is attributable to its iodine component present in part as an impurity.

4. There is insufficient evidence to support the assumption that R–3 is tumorigenic to humans, but this possibility cannot be ruled out.

5. The average per capita exposure to R–3 through food and internal drugs is estimated at 1.41 mg/d.

6. If it is assumed that R–3 poses a tumorigenic risk to humans, the risk from ingesting R–3 containing food and drugs is small, that is, the number of people with R–3 induced tumors would be too small to be observed by epidemiologic or other human studies.....

8. Two options have been offered as a basis for setting any human exposure level: the use of biologically-based mathematical models or the NOEL approach.

After digesting this report, FDA announced that it would not extend the provisional listing of Red No. 3 to allow further testing to demonstrate whether the color additive is a primary or a secondary carcinogen. 54 Fed. Reg. 27640 (June 30, 1980). Within days, however, the House Appropriations Committee included a statement in its report recommending the agency's budget that it expected FDA to continue the provisional listing until additional testing is completed. 135 Cong. Rec. H3836 (daily ed., July 19, 1989).

In 1984 the Director of FDA's Center for Food Safety and Applied Nutrition summarized the questions the agency would have to resolve before it could approve Red No. 3:

Even if sufficient evidence of a secondary mechanism is developed, the agency would still need to consider other scientific questions in deciding on the safety of this color additive. Among the relevant questions are: (a) whether valid scientific data demonstrate that the cancer caused by the color additive has a clearly established threshold below which cancer will not be induced; (b) whether there is an adequate margin of safety between that threshold and expected consumption levels; and (c) whether FD&C Red No. 3 has otherwise been shown to be safe for its uses.

"The Regulation by the Department of Health and Human Services of Carcinogenic Color Additives," Hearing Before a Subcomm. of the House Comm. on Government Operations, 98th Cong., 2d Sess. 84–85 (1984) (Letter from Sanford A. Miller, Ph.D., to National Food Processors Association (April 16, 1984)). Contemporaneously, *id.* at 379, the Center's Deputy Director told Congress that a secondary carcinogen with a demonstrated threshold could be approved notwithstanding the Delaney Clause because humans would not be exposed to any risk of cancer:

> There is a possibility [for FD&C Red. No. 3] that there might be a conclusion that the secondary mechanism is, in fact, obtainable and that, if a secondary mechanism is obtainable, then some specification can be written for the color that would preclude a carcinogenic result when ingested by man.

In 55 Fed. Reg. 3516 (February 1, 1990), however, FDA terminated the provisional listing of the color additive for cosmetics, external drugs, and lakes, stating that industry had failed to prove the hypothesis that it is a secondary carcinogen. As of June 30, 1990, FDA has not taken action to revoke the permanent listing of FD&C Red No. 3 for food and ingested drug use.

3. *Butylated Hydroxyanisole.* Butylated hydroxyanisole (BHA), a widely-used food preservative that is credited with *reducing* human cancer, has been listed by both IARC and NTP as a carcinogen. FDA unsuccessfully opposed both actions in the belief that BHA is a secondary carcinogen that at low doses poses no human risk.

4. *Dioxin.* There has been continuing controversy whether 2,3,7,8–TCDD (dioxin) is a primary or secondary carcinogen. FDA and EPA have determined that it has not yet been satisfactorily shown to be a secondary carcinogen and have continued to regulate it as a no-threshold carcinogen, relying on quantitative risk assessment. Members of the EC have accepted the evidence of a secondary mechanism and thus have set dioxin exposure limits based on safety factors. In consequence, there is a 1000–fold difference between U.S. limits on exposure to dioxin and those observed in Europe. *See* Gough, *Science Policy Choices and the Estimation of Cancer Risk Associated with Exposure to TCDD,* 8 Risk Analysis 337 (1988). In the interim, the paper industry reduced dioxin contamination to an insignificant level. "Progress in Eliminating Dioxin from Packaging," FDA Talk Paper T90–21 (April 30, 1990).

5. *Other Secondary Carcinogens.* FDA found that the scientific evidence is insufficient to characterize either chloroform or methylene chloride as a secondary carcinogen, 41 Fed. Reg. 26842, 26843 (June 29, 1976), 54 Fed. Reg. 27328, 27333 (June 29, 1989). On the other hand, FDA, like EPA, has agreed that melamine is a secondary carcinogen, 49 Fed. Reg. 18120 (April 27, 1984), 53 Fed. Reg. 23128 (June 20, 1988), 54 Fed. Reg. 12912 (March 29, 1989). Other determinations by FDA that a substance is a secondary carcinogen that poses no human risk are likely to be reflected in internal memoranda that have not become a matter of public record.

6. *FDA Policy.* On October 7, 1985, FDA Commissioner Young provided the Acting Assistant Secretary for Health the following delphic summary of the agency's approach:

[T]he present regulatory strategy and structure utilized by the Food and Drug Administration evaluates potential substances on the basis of whether or not they are a complete carcinogen. This leaves to debate the role of the substance as a promoter, as a co-carcinogen, as an enhancer of carcinogenicity, or as a secondary carcinogen. Within this issue is the question of having enough information upon which to regulate; if the information does exist, how should we use it to develop a risk assessment for the substance.

See also Connery, ed., REPORT OF THE EPA WORKSHOP ON THE DEVELOPMENT OF RISK ASSESSMENT METHODOLOGIES FOR TUMOR PROMOTORS (EPA, June 1987).

G. FUTURE ISSUES

PETER BARTON HUTT, FOOD AND DRUG LAW: A STRONG AND CONTINUING TRADITION

37 Food Drug Cosmetic Law Journal 123 (1982).

By 1900 ... life expectancy at birth in this country was 47.3 years. In 1940, when the present Federal Food, Drug, and Cosmetic Act was in place, it had reached 62.9 years. In 1960, at the time Congress enacted the Food Additives Amendment, the Color Additive Amendments, and the Drug Amendments, it stood at 69.7 years. In 1978 ... it reached 73.3 years....

... Although the precise contribution of food and drug regulation to the public health movement cannot be quantified, it obviously has been a major component. Without question, these regulatory efforts represent one of the most successful government programs in history. But it is equally important to recognize that the success of these programs in the past cannot be sustained at the same pace indefinitely. Neither public health programs in general, nor food and drug regulation in particular, can add another 26 years to our national life expectancy in the next 75 years or, indeed, in the foreseeable future.....

Food and drug regulation was designed, from its inception, to deal with the acute causes of death.... The 1906 Act was directed against poisons in food and food-borne disease. Regulatory strategy dictated elimination of dangerous ingredients and contaminating microorganisms. It was a sound strategy then, it remained a sound strategy when the law was modernized in 1938, and it continues to be a sound strategy today. Food-borne disease has not been, and by its very nature cannot be, completely eliminated in the same way that smallpox has now been eradicated.....

... [T]raditional regulatory strategy involves elimination of dangerous substances from the food and drug supply. This clearly works for such substances as salmonella, botulism, and other pathogenic microorganisms. It works equally well for frank poisons that can produce demonstrable injury, such as diethylene glycol and thalidomide. The question being raised today, however, is whether that regulatory strategy applies equally well to protect the public health against the causes of chronic disease.....

The burden of demonstrating safety has changed for some categories of substances but not for others. For food and color additives, and new human and animal drugs, the burden of demonstrating safety has been shifted to the regulated industry. For many other ingredients used in food and drugs, however, the burden of demonstrating a lack of safety remains on the government, where it has been for centuries. This change in strategy, however, does not seem at all related to any attempt to prevent chronic disease. There is no evidence whatever that the principal causes of heart disease and cancer fall into those categories that now require premarket approval rather than into those categories that are exempt from premarket approval. One can persuasively argue, indeed, that the reverse is likely to be true. Heart disease and cancer have existed for centuries. To the extent that these diseases are attributable to any particular substances, therefore, those substances are more likely to be in the categories of old substances that are exempt from premarket approval than in the categories of new substances that now require premarket approval. ....

The credibility of regulatory agencies has been severely damaged by the mounting evidence that some of the most popular items in our food supply are carcinogenic by some form of scientific test. The public is not prepared to give up charcoal-broiled steak and hamburgers, pepper, nutmeg, mustard, and coffee, much less the essential nutrients that have been implicated by this scientific evidence. The failure of traditional regulatory techniques to deal with these problems was definitively demonstrated when regulatory action was threatened against artificially sweetened food containing saccharin and cured meat containing nitrites. The government quickly learned that the public simply did not intend the food and drug laws to be applied literally when it meant the elimination of important items from the food supply.

Evidence mounts that to reduce either heart disease or cancer there must be major lifestyle changes. Where this is true, it radically alters the prospects for regulatory intervention. Regulation can require some modifications in individual items in the food supply, but it cannot reform the entire American diet. If it is the way we eat and live that is associated with cancer, rather than specific substances in our environment, the traditional approaches of a regulatory agency are obviously inappropriate.....

In such instances, FDA must temper its customary regulatory strategy with respect for the desire and the ability of the public to make its own decisions. Increased reliance upon the alternative regulatory tool of labeling, as contrasted with banning, must be considered. Public health will remain foremost, but it will be achieved by public education and information as much as it will by direct government intervention.....

Perhaps most devastating, the eradication of cancer and heart disease would have a much smaller impact on longevity than is commonly assumed. If all cancer, from all sources, were eliminated from the United States, average life expectancy at birth would still be increased by only 2.5 years. If a 30% reduction in cancer were achieved—an obviously more realistic but still extremely difficult goal—average life expectancy at birth would be increased by 0.71 year. A 30% reduction in major cardiovascular disease would produce an increase in average life expectancy at birth of 1.98 years. Application of the same 30% reduction to the working ages, 15 to 70 years, would result in a gain for them of 0.43 year from major cardiovascular disease and 0.26 year from cancer.....

The question, then, is whether the heroic personal, societal, and regulatory measures that would be required to make a substantial reduction in cancer—assuming that they would be effective, an assumption that is entirely conjectural—would be worth an additional 0.26 to 0.71 year added to the end of our lives. The smallest part of the sacrifice necessary to make that effort would entail the economic cost of regulation. Much more important would be the foregone pleasures of life-style, dietary habits, and individual food items that we have all learned to enjoy.

NOTES

1. *Life Style Changes.* Fries, *et al.*, *Health Promotion and the Compression of Morbidity*, Lancet 481 (March 4, 1989), point out that the substantial increase in life expectancy, and our lack of ability to achieve overall life extension, require "a change of focus from quantity to quality of life—'Add Life to Your Years, Not Years to Your Life':

> As life-style practices continue to improve and as mortality rates at advanced years decline more slowly, there may be disillusionment about the link between risk factors and health. It is critically important to recognize that the dividends of prevention are mainly in reduction of the population illness burden and enhancement of the quality of life, and that these are very large dividends indeed.... The primary purpose of population interventions, risk assessment, and risk reduction in developed societies is to compress morbidity and to improve the quality and vigour of life.

2. *More Carcinogens.* Of 86 chronic bioassays conducted by NTP and reported between July 1981 and July 1984, exactly half showed carcinogenic effects. Haseman, *et al.*, *Results From 86 Two–Year Carcinogenicity Studies Conducted By the National Toxicology Program*, 14 J. Tox. & Environ. Health 621, 634 (1984). FDA has stated that the sensitivity of analytical detection methodology increased in the period from 1958 to 1979 "between two and five orders of magnitude," 44 Fed. Reg. 17070, 17075 (March 20, 1979), *i.e.*, between 100 and 100,000 times. The increase in the number of chemicals found to be carcinogenic in test animals, their easy detection, and the heavy expenditures required to remove or control them have led some respected cancer experts to suggest that the strategy of regulatory control has been overemphasized. *See,*

e.g., Higginson, *Changing Concepts in Cancer Prevention: Limitations and Implications for Future Research in Environmental Carcinogenesis*, 48 Cancer Res. 1381 (March 15, 1988).

3. *Costs of Regulation.* The Office of Management and Budget (OMB) has expressed concern about the cost-effectiveness efforts to regulate small risks:

> In deciding whether—or how much—to regulate, a regulatory official must look not only at total risks but also at the risk *reduction* that could be achieved and the cost of doing so. Balancing these factors is the challenge of risk management.

OMB went on to question the cumulative impact of conservative assumptions used in quantitative risk assessment.

> Often each conservative assumption is made by a different scientist or analyst responsible for a portion of the risk assessment. Each may think that erring on the side of caution or conservatism is reasonable. However, the effect of these individual conservative assumptions is compounded in the final estimate of risk presented to the decisionmaker. For example, if at each of two different steps in an analysis, estimates are chosen that have a 5 percent chance of being less than the true risk, then the final risk estimate will have only a 0.25 percent chance of being less than the true risk (0.05 x 0.05 = 0.0025). That is, the risk estimate will have a 99.75 percent chance of being greater than the true risk. If there were 5 steps in the analysis instead of 2 and a conservative estimate at the 5 percent level were chosen for each step then the final risk estimate would have a 0.00003 percent (0.05^5) chance of being less than the true risk, or 3 chances in 10 million. In other words, the estimate has a 99.99997 percent chance of overstating the true risk.
>
> In practice, there may be as many as 20 distinct stages in a risk assessment where conservative assumptions are made. A typical risk assessment would probably contain about 10. The final risk estimate derived from these compounded conservative assumptions may be more than a million times greater than the best estimate and may, thus, have a probability of being accurate that is virtually zero....

OMB, REGULATORY PROGRAM OF THE UNITED STATES GOVERNMENT April 1, 1986–March 31, 1987, xx & xxv (1987).

4. *Proposition 65.* On November 4, 1986, by a large majority the voters of California enacted Proposition 65 as an initiative measure under Article II, Section 8 of the California Constitution. Codified in California Health and Safety Code §§ 25249.5–25249.13, Proposition 65 requires the governor to publish, and periodically revise, a list of natural and synthetic chemicals "known to the state to cause cancer ..." Any listed chemical is presumed to be a health hazard, and any individual exposed to a listed chemical must be given a "clear and reasonable warning" about the exposure by the person responsible for the exposure unless that person can prove that the exposure represents "no significant risk," assuming lifetime exposure at the level in question. More than 370 natural and synthetic chemicals have now been listed as carcinogens, including some essential nutrients and many natural constituents of food. The impact of this experiment in risk communication is discussed in Hutt, *Application of Proposition 65 to Food, Drugs, Medical Devices, and Cosmetics,* in National Legal Center for the Public Interest, CLEAN WATER AND TOXIC WASTE: AT WHAT COST FOR WHAT GAIN? 23 (1989); Kuryla, *California Proposition 65 and the Chemical Hazard Warning: Risk Management Under the New Code of Popular Outrage,* 8 Va. J. Nat. Res. L. 103 (1988).

Chapter IX
REGULATION OF BIOTECHNOLOGY

A. HISTORICAL AND TECHNICAL BACKGROUND

In 1953, James Watson and Francis Crick discovered and described the double-helix structure of deoxyribonucleic acid (DNA), and thus opened the field of molecular biology. In the early 1970s, scientists developed the techniques for cutting DNA molecules with a restriction enzyme, inserting foreign DNA, placing the recombined (recombinant) DNA into a host microorganism, and then replicating (cloning) the recombined DNA through fermentation of the microorganism. These remarkable technical achievements laid the foundations for commercial biotechnology.

The techniques of biotechnology have broad implications for many industries, but perhaps promise the greatest innovations in the production of products regulated by FDA. Like many other powerful new technologies, however, biotechnology may carry risks as well as benefits, and several of its applications have engendered fervent emotional reactions and raised serious ethical concerns. In this chapter we explore some of these issues as they are presented by the application of biotechnology in the production of products regulated by FDA.

OFFICE OF TECHNOLOGY ASSESSMENT, COMMERCIAL BIOTECHNOLOGY: AN INTERNATIONAL ANALYSIS
(1984)

The novel technologies used in biotechnology are extremely powerful because they allow a large amount of control over biological systems. Recombinant DNA technology ... allows direct manipulation of the genetic material of individual cells. The ability to direct which genes are used by cells permits more control over the production of biological molecules than ever before. Recombinant DNA technology can be used in a wide range of industrial sectors to develop micro-organisms that produce new products, existing products more efficiently, or large quantities of otherwise scarce products. This technology can also be used to develop organisms that themselves are useful, such as micro-organisms that degrade toxic wastes or new strains of agriculturally important plants.

Cell fusion, the artificial joining of cells, combines the desirable characteristics of different types of cells into one cell. This technique has been used recently to incorporate in one cell the traits for immortality and rapid proliferation from certain cancer cells and the ability to produce useful antibodies from specialized cells of the immune system. The cell line resulting from such a fusion, known as hybridoma, produces large quantities of *monoclonal antibodies (MAbs),* so called because they are produced by the progeny, or clones, of a single hybridoma cell. MAbs can potentially be used for many purposes, including the diagnosis and treatment of disease and the purification of proteins.

The commercial success of specific industrial applications of rDNA and cell fusion techniques will hinge on advances in bioprocess engineering. *Bioprocess technology,* though not a novel genetic technique, allows the adaptation of biological methods of production to large-scale industrial use. Most industrial biological syntheses at present are carried out in single batches, and a small amount of product is recovered from large quantities of cellular components, nutrients, wastes, and water. Recent improvements in techniques for immobilizing cells or enzymes and in bioreactor design, for example, are helping to increase production and facilitate recovery of many substances. Additionally, new genetic techniques can aid in the design of more efficient bioreactors, sensors, and recovery systems.....

Biotechnology could potentially affect any current industrial biological process or any process in which a biological catalyst could replace a chemical one....

The industrial sector in which the earliest applications of new biotechnology have occurred is the pharmaceutical sector. Reasons for the rapid diffusion of the new techniques into the pharmaceutical sector include the following:

- Recombinant DNA and MAb technologies were developed with public funds directed toward biomedical research. The first biotechnology products, such as rDNA-produced human insulin, interferon, and MAb diagnostic kits, are a direct result of the biomedical nature of the basic research that led to these new technologies.

- Pharmaceutical companies have had years of experience with biological production methods, and this experience has enabled them to take advantage of the new technologies.

- Pharmaceutical products are high value-added and can be priced to recover costs incurred during R & D, so the pharmaceutical sector is a good place to begin the costly process of developing a new technology.....

The following figure illustrates the basic processes involved in manufacturing a product (in the illustration, a drug) through recombinant DNA techniques.

Hutt & Merrill Food & Drug Law 2nd Ed. UCB—23

The Product Development Process *

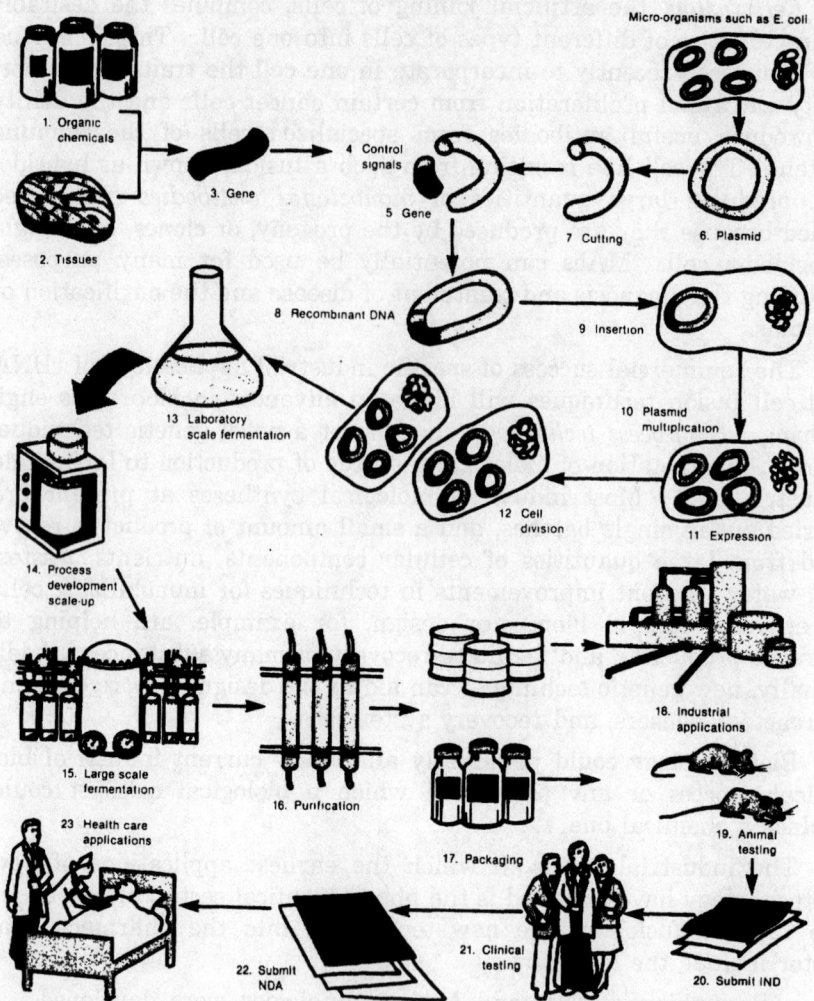

The development process begins by obtaining DNA either through organic synthesis (1) or derived from biological sources such as tissues (2). The DNA obtained from one or both sources is tailored to form the basic "gene" (3) which contains the genetic information to "code" for a desired product, such as human interferon or human insulin. Control signals (4) containing instructions are added to this gene (5). Circular DNA molecules called plasmids (6) are isolated from micro-organisms such as *E. coli*; cut open (7) and spliced back (8) together with genes and control signals to form "recombinant DNA" molecules. These molecules are then introduced into a host cell (9).

Each plasmid is copied many times in a cell (10). Each cell then translates the information contained in these plasmids into the desired product, a process called "expression" (11). Cells divide (12) and pass on to their offspring the same genetic information contained in the parent cell.

Fermentation of large populations of genetically engineered micro-organisms is first done in shaker flasks (13), and then in small fermenters (14) to determine growth conditions, and eventually in larger fermentation tanks (15). Cellular extract obtained from the fermentation process is then separated, purified (16), and packaged (17) either for industrial use (18) or health care applications.

Health care products are first tested in animal studies (19) to demonstrate a product's pharmacological activity and safety. In the United States, an investigational new drug application (20) is submitted to begin human clinical trials to establish safety and efficacy. Following clinical testing (21), a new drug application (NDA) (22) is filed with the Food and Drug Administration (FDA). When the NDA has been reviewed and approved by the FDA the product may be marketed in the United States (23).

SOURCE: Genentech, Inc.

* From Office of Technology Assessment, IMPACTS OF APPLIED GENETICS: MICROORGANISMS, PLANTS, AND ANIMALS 6 (1981).

STEVE OLSON, BIOTECHNOLOGY: AN INDUSTRY COMES OF AGE

(National Academy Press 1986).

Human beings rely on the earth's bountiful supply of life for a wide variety of essential substances. We survive by consuming the edible portions of plants and animals, and our clothes and homes are composed at least in part of biologically derived materials. Microorganisms are used to make bread, to convert milk into cheese, and to brew alcoholic beverages. Common substances like vinegar, vitamins, and monosodium glutamate are manufactured using microbial "factories." Antibiotics are extracted from various strains of molds and bacteria.

Over the course of time, human ingenuity has gradually worked to improve these organisms. People have selected plants, animals, and microorganisms with the most useful characteristics from among those found wild in the environment. They have bred individuals from the same or closely related species to produce offspring with new, more desirable combinations of traits. Among the results of this genetic husbandry have been improved varieties of crops and livestock, industrial microbes that are hardier and more efficient, and novel antibiotics.

. . . The techniques of genetic engineering, and in particular recombinant DNA, have made it possible to manipulate genetic material on the smallest possible scale—individual genes. The effect on molecular biology, immunology, and other scientific disciplines has been little short of revolutionary. . . . .

But genetic engineering has done more than give researchers the ability to understand the genetic structure of living things; it has also given them the ability to change that structure. It is now possible to move genetic material in a functional form from one organism to another, creating genetic constructs that have never before existed in nature. For instance, the gene that produces a protein in a human cell can be isolated and inserted into a bacterium. That bacterium can then be reproduced or cloned, creating many identical copies of the gene. If the gene can be coaxed to manufacture the same protein in bacteria that it does in humans, large quantities of the protein can be produced for pharmaceutical applications. And bacteria are not the only possible recipients of new genetic material. Functional genes can be inserted into the cells of plants, animals, and even humans. . . . .

Any technology that deals so directly with the basic processes of life inevitably raises compelling questions. The early debates about the safety of recombinant DNA research have quieted, but new issues have taken their place. Will the release of genetically engineered organisms into the environment pose threats to human health or to natural ecosystems? How should the ability to alter the genetic makeup of human beings be managed? Is new legislation necessary to regulate the products that are likely to be manufactured with genetic engineering? Should the U.S. government be encouraging the development of the American biotechnology industry in light of the considerable competition expected from biotechnology companies abroad? ...

The Molecular and Microbial Products of Biotechnology

Most of the products being developed in biotechnology fall into one of two very broad categories: chemical substances that can be made using genetically engineered organisms, and genetically engineered organisms themselves.

Included in the first category are the wide variety of compounds that have drawn the attention of pharmaceutical manufacturers. Genetically engineered microorganisms can be used to produce hormones like insulin and growth hormone, other biological response modifiers such as interferons and neuropeptides, blood products like clotting and antishock factors, vaccines against previously unpreventable diseases, new antibiotics, and many other kinds of biologically active molecules....

The ability of genetically engineered microorganisms to produce valuable chemical compounds will also lead to applications in many other industries, including the food processing, chemicals, and energy industries. Among the numerous substances whose production could be affected by biotechnology are alcohol, enzymes, amino acids, vitamins, high-grade oils, adhesives, and dyes....

The use of biological processes in industry places special demands on manufacturing. Generally, biological conversions entail a fermentation process. Nutrients and raw materials are supplied to living cells in a reactor vessel; the cells convert the raw materials into products; and the products are withdrawn, separated, and purified. These bioconversions must be carefully monitored and controlled. Indeed, the development of economical fermentation equipment and methods is one of the greatest challenges facing biotechnology today.

But not all genetically engineered microorganisms will be used in fermentation processes. Some are being designed for use in the environment. Many of these will have agricultural applications, but others might be used to degrade wastes or toxic substances, to leach or concentrate minerals from ores, or to increase the extraction of oil from wells.

An important subset of the molecular products of biotechnology are the proteins known as monoclonal antibodies. These are produced not through recombinant DNA techniques but through the fusion of a tumor cell with an antibody-producing white blood cell. The result is a virtually immortal clone of cells producing antibodies that are chemically identical. Monoclonal antibodies have already found a wide range of uses in research, because of their remarkable ability to attach to specific molecular configurations. They are also being used in a number of in vitro diagnostic tests to detect the presence of disease or other conditions. At the same time, investigators are examining their possible uses within the body to expose diseased areas to scanning instruments, to confer passive immunity against disease, or to carry biologically active agents to diseased tissues.

Many of the products being developed for use in human health care have agricultural analogs. New or cheaper drugs, vaccines, and diagnostics will all cut the toll of disease and lost productivity that continues to be a major concern in agriculture. Furthermore, genetically engineered microorganisms will be used to produce feed additives, growth enhancers, and other compounds that will boost agricultural yields.

But biotechnology has a fundamentally different capability in agriculture. It can potentially be used to change the genetic constitution of microorganisms, plants, and animals to make them more productive, more resistant to disease or environmental stress, or more nutritious....

Probably the first application of this type will involve the genetic engineering of microorganisms. Researchers are working to produce microorganisms that will supply plants or animals with essential nutrients, protect them from insects or disease, or provide them with compounds that influence their growth. A central concern of this work is the competitiveness of the genetically engineered microorganisms in agricultural environments, since the microorganisms will generally have to survive and multiply to perform their functions.

The genetic engineering of plants and animals is a far more daunting technical task than the genetic engineering of microorganisms, but this is where the greatest potential benefits lie. Researchers have already succeeded in inserting functional genes into plant cells, in regenerating whole plants that express the gene, and in having the gene passed on to offspring. In this way, they hope to eventually be able to transfer into plants such traits as resistance to pesticides, tolerance to environmental conditions such as salinity or toxic metals, greater nutritive value or productivity, or perhaps even the ability to fix nitrogen from the atmosphere. However, major technical barriers still prohibit the genetic engineering of most of the agriculturally important food crops. For instance, the majority of desirable agricultural traits are likely to arise from the interaction of many different genes, making it difficult to transfer these traits between plants. A major current limitation on research in this area is the paucity of basic biochemical knowledge about plants....

Genes have also been inserted into the sex cells of animals in such a way that they are reproduced in the cells of the mature animal, function in those cells, and are passed on to offspring. For instance, researchers have introduced growth hormone genes into several kinds of agriculturally important animals in an attempt to make the animals grow faster, larger, or leaner. It remains to be seen whether this genetic modification will upset the animals' metabolic balance, causing harmful long-term effects on their health.

Human Gene Therapy

Just as genes can be inserted in a functional form into the cells of animals, so they can be inserted into human cells. There is an important distinction between the genetic engineering of animals and humans, however. For the foreseeable future, genes will be introduced only into limited subsets of a patient's somatic cells. Because the new genes will be reproduced only in that population of cells, they will not be passed on to offspring....

The first attempts at human gene therapy will involve the insertion of genes into bone marrow cells extracted from patients with severe genetic disorders. The transformed bone marrow cells will be reinserted into the patient's body, where, if the procedure is successful, they will multiply and alleviate the patient's disease. This type of treatment is essentially similar to other kinds of medical procedures, such as transplants, and it raises no new ethical problems.

The technical and ethical problems associated with germline gene therapy are far more formidable. First, the procedures used with animals so damage most of the treated cells that they never develop into live animals. Second, only a fraction of the treated cells that do grow contain the foreign gene. Third, the insertion of a gene can cause severe and often lethal mutations in the cell. Finally, germline gene therapy would alter the genetic pool of the human species, raising fundamental questions about tampering with humanity's genetic heritage.

Ethical considerations are also associated with the use of genetic engineering to enhance a human characteristic, as opposed to replacing a defective gene. In certain cases the issues are clear-cut, as in the condemnation of any attempt to insert a growth hormone gene into an otherwise normal person. But other cases are less well resolved. For instance, it may eventually be possible through human gene therapy to reduce a person's susceptibility to various diseases.....

The Release of Genetically Engineered Organisms into the Environment

Another issue that has generated considerable public discussion in recent years has been the approach of the first field tests of genetically engineered organisms in the environment. It is very difficult to predict exactly what influence a novel organism will exert on an ecosystem, and history is replete with examples of organisms introduced into an environment from elsewhere in the world that had unanticipated, and occasionally devastating, effects. By the same token, conventional breeding techniques have been used throughout history to create new varieties of plants and animals without undue consequences.

To calculate the environmental risk of genetically engineered organisms, five questions must be answered. Will the organism be released into the environment? Will it survive once it is released? Will the organism multiply? Will it move from the place where it is released to a place where it has an effect? And what will that effect be? Furthermore, a genetically engineered organism can sexually or asexually transfer part of its DNA to another organism, which generates a similar string of questions for the organism receiving the DNA.

The chance that a genetically engineered organism will have a detrimental effect on the environment is the product of the five factors listed above. In any given case, the probability that the answer to one or more of these questions will be "yes" is likely to be low, which makes the overall probability of a harmful effect even lower. But it is not zero, and the harmful consequences of a low-probability event could be substantial. . . .

FOOD BIOTECHNOLOGY

A Scientific Status Summary by the Institute of Food
Technologists' Expert Panel on Food Safety & Nutrition
Food Technology, January 1988, p. 133.

Biotechnology has been broadly defined as the utilization of biologically derived molecules, structures, cells, or organisms to carry out a specific process. This is true of many established food processes—for example, cheesemaking and brewing. The beauty of modern biotechnology lies in its specificity. The biotechnologist can target only one or two protein molecules for change in an organism containing thousands of proteins. This seemingly minor alteration can have profound effects. The amount of an important flavor, color, or enzyme may be increased manyfold. It can allow crops to grow under marginal or poor conditions. With a few exceptions, most short-term results of modern biotechnology applied to food production will be invisible to the consumer's eye. However, indirect effects on existing products, such as cost savings and product improvements, will be far-reaching. . . .

NOTES

1. *Commentary.* The literature on biotechnology is enormous. Additional useful sources include J.W. Evans and A. Hollaender, eds., GENETIC ENGINEERING OF ANIMALS (1985); National Academy of Sciences, GENETIC ENGINEERING OF PLANTS: AGRICULTURAL RESEARCH OPPORTUNITIES AND POLICY CONCERNS (1984); National Academy of Sciences, RESEARCH WITH RECOMBINANT DNA (1977); S. Panem, ed., BIOTECHNOLOGY IMPLICATIONS FOR PUBLIC POLICY (1985); *Symposium on Biotechnology and the Law: Recombinant DNA and the Control of Scientific Research,* 51 S. Cal. L. Rev. 969 *et seq.* (1978). For accounts of the scientific discoveries that opened this field, *see* S.S. Hall, INVISIBLE FRONTIERS (1987); H.F. Judson, THE EIGHTH DAY OF CREATION (1979).

2. *Ethical Issues.* For analysis of the technical and ethical dimensions of genetic engineering, *see* President's Commission for the Study of Ethical Problems in Medicine and Biomedical and Behavioral Research, SPLICING LIFE: THE SOCIAL AND ETHICAL ISSUES OF GENETIC ENGINEERING WITH HUMAN BEINGS (1982); *see also* OTA, HUMAN GENE THERAPY: BACKGROUND PAPER (1984).

3. *Food Applications.* In February 1988 the FDA Office of Planning and Evaluation and the Center for Food Safety and Applied Nutrition reported that during the previous two years 155 firms were applying the new scientific principles of biotechnology to the improvement of food or food sources. Experts consulted by FDA identified more than 1200 examples of future food biotechnology advances, most of which were expected to be technically feasible by 1990. FDA, FOOD BIOTECHNOLOGY: PRESENT AND FUTURE, Vol. I (PB88–177–993), Vol. II (PB88–178–009) (February 1988). FDA and USDA have sponsored a conference on scientific issues associated with the development of transgenic plants intended for food use, 53 Fed.Reg. 28674 (July 29, 1988), and FDA has contracted with the Federation of American Societies for Experimental Biology (FASEB) to establish criteria for determining the regulatory status of food and food ingredients produced by new technologies, 53 Fed. Reg. 33182 (August 30, 1988).

B. NIH REGULATION OF RECOMBINANT DNA RESEARCH

As the implications of the rapid advances in molecular biology during the early 1970s became evident, many scientists themselves voiced concerns about the potential risks of their research. In September 1973, a majority of the participants at a research conference voted to send a letter to the President of the National Academy of Sciences requesting that the risks of biotechnology be studied. In July 1974, eleven of the leading researchers in the field, acting for the Academy, made the unprecedented recommendation that there be a voluntary moratorium on certain types of recombinant DNA experimentation until appropriate review and guidelines could be developed. Guidelines were developed and approved by scientists attending a closed meeting in February 1975 at the Asilomar Conference Center in California.

At the same time, the National Institutes of Health began to prepare its own research guidelines, which quickly became the controlling requirements. After a public hearing in February 1976, NIH published final guidelines in 41 Fed. Reg. 27902 (July 7, 1976). As a formal matter, the NIH Guidelines applied only to recombinant DNA research conducted under NIH grants or contracts. Other government funding agencies immediately adopted the NIH Guidelines, however, and industry representatives announced that privately-funded research would follow them as well. Although Congress initially considered special legislation, the existence of the NIH Guidelines and the intensive lobbying of the scientific community averted enactment.

NOTES

1. *Historical Background.* The history of the initial moratorium, the Asilomar Conference, the NIH Guidelines, and subsequent attempts to enact legislation restricting recombinant DNA research, is documented in J.D. Watson & J. Tooze, THE DNA STORY: A DOCUMENTARY HISTORY OF GENE CLONING (1981).

2. *NIH Guidelines.* NIH has periodically published revised versions of its guidelines in the Federal Register, but none has been codified in the Code of Federal Regulations. The guidelines remain in effect, however, and they constitute binding requirements for all NIH-funded research. Furthermore, they carry the endorsement of all other government funding agencies, and continue to be followed in privately-funded research as well. NIH has published a series of volumes containing all documents relating to the NIH Guidelines from 1975 to the present.

3. *Statutory Authority.* During the debate over the need for new legislation to support regulation of recombinant DNA research, one of the authors of this casebook contended that section 361 of the Public Health Service Act, which authorizes action necessary "to prevent the introduction, transmission, or spread of communicable diseases," 42 U.S.C. § 264, is broad enough to allow regulation of any hazard from recombinant DNA research. Letter from P.B. Hutt to NIH Director S. Fredrickson (February 20, 1976), reprinted in Watson & Tooze, note 1 *supra*, at 156; Hutt, *Research on Recombinant DNA Molecules: The Regulatory Issues*, 51 S. Cal. L. Rev. 1435, 1443–44 (1978). Neither that law nor any other statute has ever been invoked to justify the NIH Guidelines, but neither has their legality ever been challenged in court.

C. REGULATING THE PRODUCTS OF BIOTECHNOLOGY

Once biotechnology moves beyond the research stage, its applications are potentially subject to the array of existing statutes designed to protect health and safety.

PETER BARTON HUTT, EXISTING REGULATORY AUTHORITY TO CONTROL THE PROCESSES AND PRODUCTS OF BIOTECHNOLOGY

B. Fields, et al., eds., GEMETICALLY ALTERED VIRUSES AND THE ENVIRONMENT, Banbury Report No. 22 (1985).

There are two general kinds of federal regulatory statutes to protect the public health and safety: those that regulate particular products ... and those that regulate industrial processes....

The principal statute enacted by Congress to regulate all "chemical substances" is the Toxic Substances Control Act (TSCA) of 1976, administered by EPA. TSCA provides a full range of regulatory control over both old and new chemicals. EPA is authorized to impose any testing requirement or limitations upon manufacture or use that may be justified to prevent an unreasonable risk to health or the environment. TSCA covers both the chemical itself and the byproducts of the manufacturing process.... EPA has now taken the position that the products of biotechnology are fully covered by TSCA.

USDA has authority to prevent harm to plants and animals through a broad variety of statutes. The Organic Act of 1944 authorizes USDA to cooperate with states and other organizations to detect and control the spread of plant pests. The Federal Plant Pest Act prohibits the importation or interstate commerce of any plant product which may contain a plant disease or pest. The Noxious Weed Act regulates the importation or interstate movement of all noxious weeds and related plant material. USDA has authority to regulate seeds under the Federal Seed Act. Thus, USDA has plenary authority to regulate the development and introduction of new plants and plant pests.

Existing federal statutes also grant similar authority with respect to animals. Quarantine and related laws provide strong authority to regulate the importation and interstate movement of animals and to prevent the introduction or spread of communicable disease among animals. Special authority is also given under the Federal Meat Inspection Act, the Poultry Products Inspection Act, and the Egg Inspection Act.

The Endangered Species Act of 1973 authorizes the Department of the Interior, and other federal agencies as well, to protect all species of fish, wildlife, and plants listed by DOI as endangered. Under a statute authorizing DOI to regulate the importation of injurious animals and other legislative authority, the President has issued an executive order to restrict the importation and introduction of exotic species of plants or animals into natural ecosystems in the United States and abroad.

... Food, drugs, medical devices, cosmetics, and animal food and drugs, are regulated by FDA under the Federal Food, Drug, and Cosmetic Act of 1938. Human biological drugs are regulated under the Biologics Act of 1902 and animal biological drugs are regulated under the Virus Serum Toxin Act of 1913. All forms of pesticides and related products are regulated by EPA under the Federal Insecticide, Fungicide, and Rodenticide Act....

The principal statute enacted by Congress to assure a safe workplace is the Occupational Safety and Health Act. The OSH Act contains a general duty clause requiring all employers to maintain working conditions that will protect employees from harm, and authorizes OSHA to issue standards to protect workers from any significant risk of material health impairment. In addition to this broad authority, the product-specific statutes already discussed above also provide separate authority for other agencies to protect workers from hazard. OSHA has published guidelines stating that the OSH Act applies fully to all aspects of the field of biotechnology.

Several broad environmental statutes, all of which are administered by EPA, are available to regulate the byproducts of industrial processes in order to assure a healthy and unpolluted environment: the Clean Air Act, the Water Pollution Control Act (commonly known as the Clean Water Act), the Safe Water Drinking Act, the Resource Conservation and Recovery Act (RCRA) (including the Solid Waste Disposal Act), the Comprehensive Environmental Response, Compensation, and Liability Act (Superfund Act), and the Marine Protection, Research, and Sanctuaries Act....

The Hazardous Materials Transportation Act, administered by the Department of Transportation, authorizes DOT to regulate the packing, labeling, and routing of the shipment of any hazardous materials, and empowers DOT to halt any shipment which is an imminent hazard. Under Section 361 of the Public Health Service Act, the Centers for Disease Control also regulates the shipment of all etiologic agents.

... [A]dditional general controls have been enacted that can be used to regulate any aspect of biotechnology. Section 361 of the Public Health Service Act broadly authorizes the Public Health Service to adopt any controls over intrastate or interstate commerce to prevent the spread of any communicable disease. The National Environmental Policy Act (NEPA) ... has been used, in particular, to require that adequate attention be given to the environmental impact of research on recombinant DNA molecules. The Department of Commerce also has plenary authority under the Export Administration Act to restrict exportation of confidential technical information for reasons of foreign policy or national security.

Even this very brief characterization of the important regulatory statutes available to control biotechnology demonstrates their extraordinary breadth and depth. Rather than raising concern about whether these statutes are adequate to control this emerging new technology, they instead raise concern about whether existing regulatory controls may impose such restrictions that the scientific potential offered by biotechnology, for the future benefit of the public, may not be realized as quickly or efficiently as could be done without such regulation....

NOTE

For other references to statutes available to control biotechnology, *see* 49 Fed. Reg. 50856, 50859–50877 (December 31, 1984); 50 Fed. Reg. 47174, 47177–47195 (November 14, 1985); McChesney and Adler, *Biotechnology Released from the Lab: The Environmental Regulatory Framework*, 13 Envtl. L. Rep. 10366 (November 1983). For a skeptical assessment of the adequacy of this battery of health and safety laws to control the hazards of biotechnology, *see* Jaffee, *Inadequacies in the Federal Regulation of Biotechnology*, 11 Harv. Envtl. L. Rev. 491 (1987). *See also* Shapiro, *Biotechnology and the Design of Regulation*, 17 Ecology L.Q. 1 (1990) (supporting recommendations of the U.S. Administrative Conference, 54 Fed. Reg. 53493 (December 29, 1989)).

In 1978 FDA announced its intention to propose regulations requiring that all recombinant DNA research on, and production of, any product for which a submission was to be made to FDA must be conducted in compliance with the NIH Guidelines, 43 Fed. Reg. 60134 (December 22, 1978). The agency later abandoned this approach, however, and instead began to issue "points to consider" for the guidance of industry in the development of biotechnology products, 49 Fed. Reg. 1138 (January 9, 1984), 49 Fed. Reg. 23456 (June 6, 1984), 53 Fed. Reg. 5468 (February 24, 1984). FDA established general requirements for cell lines used for manufacturing biological products in 49 Fed. Reg. 27622 (December 6, 1984), 51 Fed. Reg. 44451 (December 10, 1986). The agency requested comment on its "points to consider" document in 54 Fed. Reg. 46305 (November 2, 1989).

In 1984, the Executive Office of the President's Cabinet Council on Natural Resources and the Environment established an Interagency Working Group on Biotechnology, chaired by the Office of Science and Technology Policy (OSTP). The initial report of the Working Group contemplated a closely managed regulation of biotechnology by all federal regulatory agencies under OSTP oversight, 49 Fed. Reg. 50856 (December 31, 1984). In response to comments that this would add yet another layer of regulation and hinder commercialization of biotechnology, the White House reduced the OSTP role to one of general liaison and coordination through a new Biotechnology Science Coordinating Committee (BSCC) within the Federal Coordinating Council for Science, Engineering, and Technology, 50 Fed. Reg. 47174 (November 14, 1985), 51 Fed. Reg. 23302 (June 26, 1986). *See* Miller, *et al., The U.S. Coordinated Framework for the Regulation of Biotechnology: Protection of Human Health*, 38 Int'l Dig. Health Legis. 644 (1987). As part of the effort of the Working Group, FDA issued a statement of policy summarizing its general approach to the regulation of products within its jurisdiction.

STATEMENT OF POLICY FOR REGULATING
BIOTECHNOLOGY PRODUCTS
51 Federal Register 23309 (June 26, 1986).

Although there are no statutory provisions or regulations that address biotechnology specifically, the laws and regulations under which the agency approves products place the burden of proof of safety as well as effectiveness of products on the manufacturer. The agency possesses extensive experience with these regulatory mechanisms and applies them to the products of biotechnological processes. In this notice, FDA proposes no new procedures or requirements for regulated industry or individuals. Rather, the administrative review of products using biotechnology is based on the intended use of each product on a case-by-case basis.

The marketing of new drugs and biologics for human use, and new animal drugs, requires prior approval of an appropriate new drug application (NDA), biological product license, or new animal drug application (NADA). For new medical devices, including diagnostic devices for human use, either a premarket approval application (PMA) or reclassification petition is required. If the device is determined to be substantially equivalent to an already marketed device, a premarket notification under section 510(k) ... is required. For food products, section 409 of the act requires preclearance of food additives including those prepared using biotechnology. Section 706 ... requires preclearance of color additives. The implementing regulations for food and color additive petitions and for affirming generally recognized as safe (GRAS) food substances are sufficiently comprehensive to apply to those involving new biotechnology.

Genetic manipulations of plants or animals may enter FDA's jurisdiction in other ways; for example, the introduction into a plant of a gene coding for a pesticide or growth factor may constitute adulteration of foodstuff derived from the plant, or the use of a new microorganism found in a food such as yogurt could be considered a food additive. Such situations will be evaluated case-by-case and in cooperation with the U.S. Department of Agriculture (USDA), where appropriate.

Congress has provided FDA authority under the Act and the Public Health Service (PHS) Act to regulate products regardless of how they are manufactured. Each request for product approval will be considered using the appropriate statutory and regulatory criteria....

General Requirements for New Drugs and Biologics for Human Use ....

Manufacturers of new drugs and biologics must operate in conformance with current good manufacturing practice (CGMP) regulations. These regulations require adequately equipped manufacturing facilities, adequately trained personnel, stringent control over the manufacturing process, and appropriate finished product examination....

The sponsor's process techniques are also considered in FDA's reviews and communications for the development of appropriate information on which the submission of an NDA, ANDA, or biological product license application would be based. For example, the use of recombinant DNA technology to manufacture new drugs or biological products may result in products that differ from similar products manufactured with conventional methods. Determination of the extent of testing required will depend upon the nature of the particular product. In some instances the molecular structure of the product may differ from the structure of the active molecule in nature. For example, the first human growth hormone manufactured using recombinant microorganisms has an extra amino acid, an amino-terminal methionine; hence, it is an analogue of the native hormone. Such differences could affect the drug's activity or immunogenicity and, consequently, could affect the extent of testing required.

Another consideration in the review of new drugs or biological products produced by recombinant techniques is whether the manufacturing process includes adequate quality controls. For example, the occurrence of mutations in the coding sequence of the cloned gene during fermentation could give rise to a subpopulation of molecules with an anomalous primary structure and altered activity. This is a potential problem inherent in the production of polypeptides in any fermentation process. As with conventionally produced products, assurance of adequate processing techniques and controls is important in the manufacturing of any biotechnology-produced new drug or biological product. Review of the production of human viral vaccines routinely involves a number of considerations including the purity of the media and the serum used to grow the cell substrate, the nature of the cell substrate, and the characterization of the virus. In the case of live viral vaccine, the final product is biologically active and is intended to replicate in the recipient. Therefore, the composition, concentration, subtype, immunogenicity, reactivity, and nonpathogenicity of the vaccine preparation are all considerations in the final review, whatever the techniques employed in "engineering" the virus. However, special considerations may arise based upon the specific technology employed. For example, a hepatitis B vaccine produced in yeast (via recombinant DNA techniques) would be monitored for yeast cell contaminants, while distinctly different contaminants would be of concern in a similar vaccine produced from the plasma of infected patients.

Nucleic acids or viruses used for human gene therapy will be subject to the same requirements as other biological drugs. It is possible that scientific reviews of these products will also be performed by the National Institutes of Health.

To provide guidance to current or prospective manufacturers of drugs and biological products, the FDA has developed a series of documents describing points that manufacturers might wish to consider in the production and testing of products....

General Requirements for Animal Food Additives and Drugs

Animal food additives and drugs are subject to similar mandatory requirements of the act as the like products for use in humans. Animal biologics, however, are licensed by the U.S. Department of Agriculture (USDA) under the authority of the Virus–Serum–Toxin Act of 1913. Questions as to whether a product is an animal biological subject to USDA licensure, or a new animal drug to be regulated by FDA, are referred to a standing committee of representatives from USDA and FDA.

... Substances that are used in animal feeds, other than drugs, and that are produced by recombinant DNA technology, are considered to be food additives and require approval of a separate food additive petition (FAP), even though a similar substance is currently approved as a food additive.

There have been questions about the requirement of an original application for a biotechnology product, even when the product is identical to a currently approved animal drug held by the same applicant. FDA's Center for Veterinary Medicine (CVM) has determined that, when the new substance produced by biotechnology is identical or virtually identical to an approved substance produced by conventional technology, only a supplemental application is necessary. Of course, in this instance the sponsor of the biotechnology product must also be the sponsor of the conventionally produced product. If, on the other hand, the new substance produced by biotechnology is significantly different from that produced by conventional means, an original application will be needed.

Two examples, each involving the adoption of rDNA technology as an alternative means of producing a substance that is currently the subject of an approved NADA, will illustrate. In the first example, the drug is (or appears to be) unchanged by the new production method. Under the current regulations, such a departure in manufacturing procedure requires a supplemental application which requires approval before implementation.... However, in accordance with the CVM's supplemental policy the underlying safety and effectiveness data supporting the original NADA usually would not be reviewed (for compliance with contemporary standards) since there is likely no increased risk of human exposure to the drug. Data may be required to demonstrate the new animal drug product is essentially biologically equivalent to the drug product for which approval has already been granted....

In the second example, a new method of manufacture changes the molecular structure or chemical composition of the active ingredient. Such a change in the identity of the new animal drug normally will require an original new animal drug application and subsequent publication of a notice of approval in the Federal Register. Ordinarily, an original NADA requires complete safety and effectiveness studies meeting contemporary standards. However, reference to data in another NADA sometimes suffices to support a separate NADA approval; where the existing NADA is owned by the applicant of the new NADA, or where the new applicant obtains authorization to refer to another NADA. In this case, reference might be made to data contained in the NADA supporting approval of the drug as produced by conventional means.....

Thus, regardless of the type of application required, there is no legal requirement for the generation of new safety and effectiveness data if the applicant has access to previously submitted data, and there is no scientific need.....

General Requirements for Foods

... No particular statutory provision or regulation deals expressly with food produced by new biotechnology. Accordingly, when confronted by an issue concerning the regulation of food produced by new biotechnology, the Agency will apply the relevant statutory or regulatory provisions. Most issues concerning the safety of a food will involve the application of either section 402(a)(1) or section 409 of the Act.

... For example, if a food produced by new biotechnology contains a higher level of a substance than it might ordinarily have, then that level "may be injurious to health" and the agency could regulate the product under section 402(a)(1). Similarly, if a food produced by new biotechnology contains, as a result of the production process, a harmful or deleterious substance not contained ordinarily in the food, the food could be in violation of the section.....

Comments questioned whether a substance (including microbes) that is GRAS could lose its GRAS status solely because it was produced or modified by new biotechnology. The answer is yes, if the substance (and its contaminants) has been altered in such a way that it can no longer be generally recognized by qualified experts to be safe. In this instance, the substance would be a food additive and the provisions of section 409 would apply....

FDA anticipates that the techniques of new biotechnology used in producing food will, for the most part, involve rDNA and microbial isolation. The agency applies certain general principles that it will follow in determining the safety of foods produced by such techniques.

When determining the safety of food produced by rDNA techniques, the agency takes into consideration, but is not restricted to, whether:

    1. The cloned DNA as well as the vector used are properly identified;

    2. The details of the construction of the production organism are available;

    3. There is information documenting that the inserted DNA is well-characterized and free from sequences that code for harmful products, and

    4. The food produced is purified, characterized, and standardized.

When determining the safety of food produced by microbial isolation, the agency will take into consideration, but is not restricted to, whether:

    1. The microbial isolate used for production is identified taxonomically, and if the strain of the isolate has been genetically manipulated, whether each strain contributing genetic information to the production strain is identified;

    2. The cultural purity and genetic stability of isolate have been maintained;

    3. Fermentation has been performed with a pure culture and monitored for purity;

4. The microbial isolate used for production also produces antibiotics or toxins;

5. The isolates are pathogenic; and

6. Viable cells of the production strain are present in the final product.

As a general rule, the extent of testing required on a food product produced by biotechnology will depend upon many factors, including the novelty of the substances used to produce the food . . ., the purity of the resulting product, and the estimated consumption of the product.

The agency will require that the final product intended for commercialization be the article tested. . . .

Obligations Under the National Environmental Policy Act

All premarketing approvals of FDA-regulated products are subject to the requirements of the National Environmental Policy Act (NEPA), as defined by the Council on Environmental Quality's regulations (40 CFR Parts 1500–1508) and as further described by FDA's NEPA-implementing procedures (21 CFR Part 25, final rule published April 26, 1985, 50 FR 16636). For new products or major new uses for existing products, these procedures ordinarily require the preparation of an environmental assessment. An environmental impact statement is required if the manufacture, use, or disposal of the product is anticipated to cause significant environmental impacts. . . . .

NOTES

1. *Commentary. See generally* Note, *An Overview of FDA Regulation of Biotechnology Derived Products: Dealing with the Collision of Science and Society,* 11 Rutgers Computer & Tech. L.J. 501 (1985).

2. *Food Applications.* In 51 Fed. Reg. 10571 (March 27, 1986), FDA published a notice of a GRAS affirmation petition for alpha-analyse enzyme made from recombinant DNA techniques, for use as an ingredient of human food. The first food substance made from recombinant DNA processes that FDA has approved is chymosin, an enzyme for use in making cheese and other food products, which the agency affirmed as GRAS in 53 Fed. Reg. 3792 (February 9, 1988), 55 Fed. Reg. 10932 (March 23, 1990), 21 C.F.R. § 184.1685. *See also* 53 Fed. Reg. 5319 (February 23, 1988), 53 Fed. Reg. 16191 (May 5, 1988), 54 Fed. Reg. 20203 (May 10, 1989), 55 Fed. Reg. 10113 (March 19, 1990). *See generally,* Ausubel, *Federal Regulation of Genetically Engineered Food Additives and Pesticides,* 4 High Tech. L.J. 114 (1989); Bonk, *FDA Regulation of Biotechnology,* 43 FDC L.J. 67 (1988); Clausi, *Interfaces of the Food Industry with Biotechnology,* 40 FDC L.J. 259 (1985); Gibbs & Kahan, *Federal Regulation of Food and Food Additive Biotechnology,* 38 Admin. L. Rev. 1 (1986); Jones, *Commercialization of Gene Transfer in Food Organisms: A Science-Based Regulatory Model,* 40 FDC L.J. 477 (1985); Jones, *Genetic Engineering in Domestic Food Animals: Legal and Regulatory Considerations,* 38 FDC L.J. 273 (1983); McNamara, *FDA Regulation of Food Substances Produced by New Techniques of Biotechnology,* 42 FDC L.J. 50 (1987); Mahinka & Sanzo, *Biotechnology Litigation and Federal Regulation: Status and Implications,* 42 FDC L.J.

500 (1987); Note, *Regulation of Genetically Engineered Foods Under the Federal Food, Drug, and Cosmetic Act,* 33 Am. U.L. Rev. 899 (1984)

3. *Agriculture Applications.* Virtually every plant or animal that is used as a source of human food is subject to genetic manipulation using recombinant DNA technology. Recognizing this, USDA has exercised its authority to promulgate regulations, 51 Fed. Reg. 23352 (June 26, 1986), 52 Fed. Reg. 22892 (June 16, 1987), 7 C.F.R. Part 340, governing all genetically engineered plants. USDA has published a guide to environmental experimentation in this area, AGRICULTURAL BIOTECHNOLOGY: INTRODUCTION TO FIELD TEST-ING (March 1990). *See also* Bastian, *Biotechnology and the United States Department of Agriculture: Problems of Regulation in a Promotional Agency,* 17 Ecology L. Q. 413 (1990).

4. *Drug Applications.* FDA has approved several NDAs for new drugs made by recombinant DNA technology, including Humalin (insulin), Protropin and Humatrope (human growth factor), Intron A and Rofron–A (treatment of hairy cell leukemia), Orthoclone OKT–3 (a monoclonal antibody for treatment of renal transplant rejection), Recombivax HB (hepatitis B vaccine), Activase (a tissue plasminogen activator (TPA) for the management of acute myocardial infarction), and Epogen (erythropoietin, for treatment of kidney disease). Following FDA approval of recombinant insulin, the agency had to establish new certification standards for the product, 50 Fed. Reg. 14296 (April 11, 1985). *See generally* Miller, *The Impact of New Technology on Regulation by the FDA: Recombinant DNA Technology,* 36 FDC L.J. 348 (1981); Nightingale, *Emerging Technologies and FDA Policy Formulation: The Impact of Government Regulation on Developing Drugs from New Technologies,* 37 FDC L.J. 212 (1982); Zoon, *The Impact of New Biotechnology on the Regulation of Drugs and Biologics,* 41 FDC L.J. 429 (1986). These NDAs have been approved far more rapidly than the median approval time for all NDAs.

5. *Monoclonal Antibodies.* FDA has sanctioned the marketing of more than 200 in vitro diagnostic products using monoclonal antibodies, most through the section 510(k) notification process, *e.g.,* "The Pink Sheet," FDC Repts, October 19, 1981, at T + G–4, but a few through premarket approval, *e.g.,* 51 Fed. Reg. 12211 (April 9, 1986), 52 Fed. Reg. 16316 (May 4, 1987), 53 Fed. Reg. 48730 (December 2, 1988). *See generally* Miller, *FDA and the Growth of Biotechnology,* 6 Pharmaceutical Engineering, no. 5, at 28 (September 1986); Young, *DNA Probes: Fruits of the New Biotechnology,* 258 J.A.M.A. 2404 (1987). In 48 Fed. Reg. 50795 (November 3, 1983), FDA determined that any monoclonal antibody used in humans, or to test a licensed biological product, would be regulated as a biological rather than as a medical device.

6. *Human Growth Hormone.* Legislation has been proposed to place human growth hormones produced by recombinant DNA technology under Schedule II of the Controlled Substances Act. H.R. 5653, 99th Cong., 2d Sess. (1986), 132 Cong. Rec. E3453 (daily ed. October 7, 1986).

7. *Bovine Sematotropin.* The development of bovine sematotropin, a bovine growth hormone that could increase a cow's milk production by 10–40 percent, has engendered considerable controversy, including a citizen petition to FDA (promptly denied by the agency) requesting preparation of an environmental impact statement and denial of the NADA, and a congressional hearing on the implications of this product for the dairy industry. *See, e.g.,* "Review of Status and Potential Impact of Bovine Growth Hormone," Hearing before the Subcomm. on Livestock, Dairy, and Poultry of the House Comm. on Agricul-

ture, 99th Cong., 2d Sess. (1986); G. Becker and S. Taylor, BOVINE GROWTH HORMONE (SOMATOTROPIN): AGRICULTURAL AND REGULATORY ISSUES, Lib. Cong., Cong. Res. Serv. (November 20, 1986); Rauch, *Drug on the Market,* 19 Nat'l J. 818 (April 4, 1987).

8. *Animal Biologicals.* The licensure under the VS&T Act of an animal vaccine produced through recombinant DNA technology was the subject of a congressional hearing into whether USDA and the company had acted properly. "USDA Licensing of a Genetically Altered Veterinary Vaccine," Joint Hearing Before the Subcomm. on Investigations and Oversight of the House Comm. on Science and Technology and the Subcomm. on Department Operations, Research, and Foreign Agriculture of the House Comm. on Agriculture, 99th Cong., 2nd Sess. (1986). USDA has undertaken public reviews of genetically engineered animal vaccines in 54 Fed. Reg. 161 (January 4, 1989), 54 Fed. Reg. 9241 (March 6, 1989).

9. *Other Agencies.* In addition to FDA and USDA, other agencies have published policies for regulating biotechnology products: EPA, in 49 Fed. Reg. 50880 (December 31, 1984), 51 Fed. Reg. 23313 (June 26, 1986), 54 Fed. Reg. 7027 (February 15, 1989); OSHA, in 50 Fed. Reg. 14468 (April 12, 1985), 51 Fed. Reg. 23347 (June 26, 1986).

10. *Environmental Release.* Most of the public concern about biotechnology has focused on so-called "deliberate release" of new organisms. *E.g.,* GAO, BIOTECHNOLOGY: MANAGING THE RISKS OF FIELD TESTING GENETICALLY ENGINEERED ORGANISMS, RCED–88–27 (June 1988); Note, *The Rutabaga that Ate Pittsburgh: Federal Regulation of Free Release Biotechnology,* 72 Va. L. Rev. 1529 (1986). All FDA-regulated products are, of course, deliberately released into the environment. As many have noted, moreover, biotechnology began centuries ago with fermentation of new food products like beer, and has continued with the development of numerous hybrid plants and animals used for human food. The major development would therefore appear to be not biotechnology itself, but the degree of precise control possible with the new techniques of molecular biology. A National Academy of Sciences panel has concluded that "there is no evidence that unique hazards exist either in the use of R–DNA techniques or in the movement of genes between unrelated organisms." INTRODUCTION OF RECOMBINANT DNA–ENGINEERED ORGANISMS INTO THE ENVIRONMENT: KEY ISSUES 22 (1987).

Other commentators are not persuaded that current statutes provide the government adequate authority to control the multi-dimensional, if uncertain, hazards of biotechnology. Dr. Margaret Mellon, Director of the National Biotechnology Policy Center at the National Wildlife Federation, argues:

> The federal coordinated framework is an unsatisfactory vehicle for the regulation of the products of the emerging genetic technology....
> [A]lthough some elements are sound, the framework as a whole is flawed and full of gaps, many of which are attributable to the fact that our existing laws were promulgated or enacted to deal with other problems.....
>
> Looking at the regulatory framework as a whole, we conclude that it is seriously flawed. Among its major deficiencies are the following:
>
> 1. *Incomplete coverage of genetically novel organisms, particularly animals*

The existing statutes, regulations, and guidelines arbitrarily exclude important classes of engineered organisms, the most important of which is genetically novel animals, ranging from rats and fish and oysters to insects. For the most part, the release of engineered animals from commercial facilities is entirely unregulated. Another important gap in jurisdiction is created by the narrow restriction of the NIH Guidelines and Plant Pest Act pre-release review programs to organisms produced by one modern genetic technology—recombinant DNA techniques—which excludes genetically novel organisms created by more recently developed techniques like chemical and electroporation.

Yet another important gap concerns genetically engineered plants, including crops engineered to contain pesticides. Again the gap is caused by the restriction of the Plant Pest Act to organisms that are plant pests. Since very few plants are themselves plant pests, most plants are brought under USDA jurisdiction only if they fall in the category of plants constructed with vectors (plasmids or viruses) that are, or come from, plant pests. . . .

2. *Confusing, overlapping and incomplete coverage of research activities*

The coverage of the research activities is one of the most confusing under the existing legal framework governing genetic engineering. It now appears that industry and university researchers (often not distinct categories) involved with releases will have to contend with at least the NIH guidelines, EPA's FIFRA and TSCA programs, and USDA research guidelines. . . . [T]here is little hope that the profusion of regulatory regimes applicable to industry and university researchers will result in the streamlined, efficient, and effective review process.

3. *Inappropriate statutory mandates*

The environmental implications of the release of engineered organisms should be regulated by agencies possessing a statutory mandate to protect the environment. USDA lacks such a mandate. For the most part its statutes are intended to protect the agroeconomy rather than the environment as a whole. . . .

BIOTECHNOLOGY AND THE ENVIRONMENT 45–49 (1988).

11. *Patentability of Microorganisms.* In *Diamond v. Chakrabarty,* 447 U.S. 303 (1980), the Supreme Court held that man-made microorganisms may be patented. On April 7, 1987, the Patent and Trademark Office extended this ruling to include all "multicellular living organisms, including animals." Its announcement provoked the amendment of pending supplemental appropriations legislation in both houses to impose a moratorium on animal patenting, 133 Cong. Rec. S7268 (daily ed. May 28, 1987), which was deleted in conference. H.R. Rep. No. 100–888, 100th Cong., 2d Sess. (1988), S. 2111, 100th Cong., 2d Sess. (1988). *See* Hendricks, *Patenting of Biotechnology,* 80 J.N.C.I. 553 (1988); Note, *Altering Nature's Blueprints for Profit: Patenting Multicellular Animals,* 74 Va. L. Rev. 1327 (1988).

12. *NEPA.* The Foundation on Economic Trends, an organization opposed to any uses of biotechnology that may present the potential for public hazard, has been partially successful in suits to force both research and regulatory agencies to adhere to the procedural requirements of NEPA, but

unsuccessful in preventing the underlying experimentation or product approval. *E.g., Foundation on Economic Trends v. Lyng,* 817 F.2d 882 (D.C. Cir. 1987); *Foundation on Economic Trends v. Heckler,* 756 F.2d 143 (D.C. Cir. 1985); *Foundation on Economic Trends v. Thomas,* 661 F. Supp. 713 (D.D.C. 1986); *Foundation on Economic Trends v. Johnson,* 661 F. Supp. 107 (D.D.C. 1986).

13. *Congressional Hearings.* Committees of both the Senate and the House have conducted hearings on numerous facets of biotechnology. A sampling of relevant recent hearings includes "Biotechnology: Vaccine Development," Subcomm. on Oversight and Investigations of the House Comm. on Energy and Commerce, 99th Cong., 1st Sess. (1985); "Biotechnology and Agriculture," "The Use of Human Biological Materials in the Development of Biomedical Products," and "Planned Releases of Genetically–Altered Organisms: The Status of Government Research and Regulation," Subcomm. on Investigations and Oversight, House Comm. on Science and Technology, 99th Cong., 1st Sess. (1985); "'Ice–Minus': A Case Study of EPA's Review of Genetically Engineered Microbial Pesticides," and "The Biotechnology Science Coordination Act of 1986," Subcomm. on Oversight and Investigations, House Comm. on Science and Technology, 99th Cong., 2d Sess. (1986); "Coordinated Framework for Regulation of Biotechnology," Subcomm. on Investigations and Oversight, on Natural Resources, Agriculture Research and Environment, and on Science, Research and Technology, House Comm. on Science and Technology, 99th Cong., 2d Sess. (1986); "USDA Licensing of a Genetically Altered Veterinary Vaccine," Joint Hearing before the Subcomm. on Investigations and Oversight, House Comm. on Science and Technology, and the Subcomm. on Department Operations, Research, and Foreign Agriculture, House Comm. on Agriculture, 99th Cong., 2d Sess. (1986); "The Commercial Development of Medical Biotechnology," Technology Policy Task Force, House Comm. on Science, Space, and Technology, 100th Cong., 1st Sess. (1987); "The Use and Regulation of Biotechnology in Agriculture," Joint Hearing Before the Senate Comm. on Agriculture, Nutrition, and Forestry and the Subcomm. on Technology and the Law of the Senate Comm. on the Judiciary, 100th Cong., 1st Sess. (1987); "Federal Oversight of Biotechnology," Subcomm. on Hazardous Wastes and Toxic Substances of the Senate Comm. on Environment and Public Works, 100th Cong., 1st Sess. (1987); "Field Testing Genetically–Engineered Organisms," Subcomm. on Natural Resources, Agricultural Research and Environment of the House Comm. on Science, Space, and Technology, 100th Cong., 2nd Sess. (1988). For a general summary of issues from the congressional perspective, *see* "Issues in the Federal Regulation of Biotechnology: From Research to Release," Report Prepared by the Subcomm. on Investigations and Oversight of the House Comm. on Science and Technology, 99th Cong., 2d Sess. (1986).

Chapter X

STATE LAWS AND
THEIR RELATION TO FEDERAL LAW

An important and continuing chapter in the history of U.S. food and drug regulation is the relationship between Federal and state laws and regulations. Space does not permit examination of the substantive law of even one of the states, much less a survey of them all. This chapter instead examines the persistent issues surrounding the scope of state authority and the doctrines of implied and explicit Federal preemption.

A. HISTORICAL BACKGROUND
PETER BARTON HUTT, THE BASIS AND PURPOSE OF GOVERNMENT REGULATION OF ADULTERATION AND MISBRANDING OF FOOD
33 Food Drug Cosmetic Law Journal 505 (1978).

It was not until the establishment of the Department of Agriculture in 1862 that any segment of the agriculture industry in this country received much consideration in Congress, and even after that it was at least another 25 years before most members of Congress were willing to consider agricultural problems as national rather than local in nature. The following excerpt from a debate in the House of Representatives in 1884 on a resolution to allow the Committee on Public Health to investigate adulteration of food, drink, and medicine, is indicative of the attitude prevalent at that time:

"Mr. Cox, of New York. * * * We are omniverous [sic]. We are taking in everything. We are now discussing a matter of health—a local matter—and after a while we will have a committee sent out to investigate how much sand the grocer puts into his sugar or how much water is put into the milk.

Mr. Adams, of Illinois. This resolution covers that now.

Mr. Cox, of New York. Of course it covers it, State rights and all. Why can not we keep within the purview of our Federal power? Why this investigation? Is it to investigate oleomargarine? What is it? Is it to help the farmer? If it is, let the States do it. That is within their ordinary functions. It is a

local matter belonging to the States. Let us keep our hands
out of it." 15 Cong. Rec. 2427 (March 31, 1884)....

The 1906 Act and its successor, the Federal Food, Drug, and
Cosmetic Act of 1938, were a reflection of the emerging nationwide food
marketing system in this country. Nonetheless, in spite of a 70–year
tradition of a single federal statute governing the food supply, and a
marketing system that knows no political bounds, there remain today
the persistent vestiges of inconsistent state and local laws and regulations reflecting the piecemeal approach to food regulation that characterized the 1800's....

NOTES

1. *Drive for Uniformity.* It may surprise some readers to learn that state
and local officials have long been concerned about lack of uniformity among
food and drug laws. The original 1884 constitution of the Association of
Official Agricultural Chemists (now the Association of Official Analytical
Chemists) stated that the objectives were "to secure, as far as possible, uniformity in legislation ... and uniformity and accuracy in the methods and results"
of analysis. K. Helrich, THE GREAT COLLABORATION: THE FIRST ONE
HUNDRED YEARS OF THE ASSOCIATION OF OFFICIAL ANALYTICAL
CHEMISTS 9 (1984). In 1897, representatives from ten states met "for the
purpose of forming a national Association ... with the end in view of producing, as nearly as conditions and laws would permit, uniformity of action in the
enforcement of such [food and drug] laws." The constitution of the resulting
organization, adopted in 1897, stated that the purpose was

> to promote and foster such legislation as would tend to protect public
> health and prevent deception ...—also to promote uniformity in
> legislation and rulings....

Reindollar, *The Association of Food and Drug Officials,* 6 FDC L.J. 52, 53, 54
(1951). That organization, now the Association of Food and Drug Officials
(AFDO), includes as members regulatory officials from Federal, state, county,
and local governments.

2. *AFDO Support for Uniformity.* The following excerpt illustrates the
consistent AFDO position over many years:

> There are too many selfish individuals and communities, too many
> greedy interests—posing as public-spirited citizens, progressive commu-
> nities, and high-minded enterprise seeking advantage through the
> enactment of discriminatory legislation, often represented as "regula-
> tory" and "inspectional," and predicated on the police power of the
> state, the real reason for which is the elimination of competition from
> other states....

> Food and Drug Officials can render a national service, make
> regulatory work easier and more forceful, compliance simpler, and at
> the same time promote expansion of industry and commerce if they
> will:

> > 1. Discourage the enactment of laws that make it impossible
> > for legitimate industry of one state to engage in trade in another
> > state under conditions which are fair and equitable.

2. Seek the repeal of discriminatory laws that now retard commerce between the states, discourage legitimate trade, prevent expansion and complicate the problem of policing industry; all to the detriment of legitimate enterprises and with no consequent benefit to the consumer.

3. Encourage the enactment of uniform laws and the adoption of uniform regulations looking toward honest protection of the consumer. If the honest consumer is adequately protected, the dishonest industry cannot prosper.

Editorial, 5 Q.Bull. AFDO No. 1, at 2 (1941). Association resolutions favoring uniform Federal, state, and local food and drug laws and regulations have appeared repeatedly in AFDO's Quarterly Bulletin: 4 Q. Bull., No. 1, at 3 (1940); 5 Q. Bull., No. 1, at 8 (1941); 9 Q. Bull., No. 1, at 44 (1945); 31 Q. Bull., No. 1, at 73 (1967); 33 Q. Bull., No. 1, at 46 (1969); 37 Q. Bull., No. 1, at 19 (1973).

3. *Uniform State Laws.* AFDO has sponsored the development of uniform state legislation under both the 1906 Act and the 1938 Act, and has periodically revised this legislation to reflect changes in the Federal law. Salthe, *State Food, Drug and Cosmetic Legislation and its Administration,* 6 L. & Contemp. Probs. 165, 167 (1939); Wiemann, *Report on Revision of the Uniform State Food, Drug and Cosmetic Bill,* 17 FDC L.J. 218 (1962). The current version of the Uniform State Food, Drug and Cosmetic Bill may be found in Food Drug Cosm. L. Rep. (CCH) ¶ 10,100. Earlier versions under the 1938 Act may be found in "Consumer Protection Activities of State Governments," H.R. Rep. No. 445, 88th Cong., 1st Sess. 88, 104 (1963). State officials have admonished their colleagues to work for adoption of this legislation, and to administer state and local laws in a manner consistent with Federal interpretations. *E.g.,* Cobb, *Eliminating Duplication and Promoting Uniformity—A State Viewpoint,* 44 Q. Bull.AFDO 40 (1980); Fisher, *Federal/State Concurrent Regulations,* 29 FDC L.J. 20 (1974); Lakey, *Uniform State Food Laws and Amendments,* 14 FDC L.J. 179 (1959); Randall, *Factors Affecting the States' Adoption of the Food–Additives Law as Well as Other Recent Amendments to the Federal Food, Drug, and Cosmetic Act,* 14 FDC L.J. 172 (1959); Sullivan, *The Desirability of Uniformity Between State and Federal Laws on Food Additives,* 16 FDC L.J. 34 (1961); Sullivan, *Uniform State Laws and the Impact of Federal Amendments,* 14 FDC L.J. 167 (1959); Sullivan, *The Effect of Uniform Legislation on State Control,* 3 FDC L.Q. 444 (1948); Trichter, *The Federal Food, Drug and Cosmetic Act and the New York City Sanitary Code,* 11 FDC L.J. 86 (1956). The AFDO President's address in 1971 accurately noted that "No presidential address would be complete without the subject of uniformity, uniformity of laws and regulations, uniformity of interpretation, and uniformity of endorsement," and acknowledged that "we still have considerable work to be done."

4. *Conforming State Regulations.* Section 24 of the Uniform State Food, Drug, and Cosmetic Bill authorizes the state authority "to make the regulations promulgated under this Act conform, insofar as practicable, with those promulgated under the Federal Act." Most state laws contain a provision that requires or urges uniformity with the FD&C Act and FDA regulations. Enforcing compliance with these provisions, however, has not proved easy. In *American Grain Products Processing Institute v. Department of Public Health,* 467 N.E.2d 455 (Mass. 1984), the court decided (4–3) that, even though a state statute provided that any state standard or tolerance must conform to the Federal standard or tolerance, Massachusetts need not follow the Federal "action level"

for ethylene dibromide (EDB) in food because EDB had been exempted from the requirement of a tolerance and thus no finite tolerance had been set. In *Processed Apples Institute, Inc. v. Department of Public Health,* 402 Mass. 392, 522 N.E.2d 965 (1988), the court held (5–1) that the same statute was intended to set a floor and not a ceiling and that Massachusetts could "conform" to the Federal tolerance by imposing a more stringent limit on residues of the pesticide daminozide on apple products.

FDA, STATE PROGRAMS AND SERVICES IN FOOD AND DRUG CONTROL

(1978).

No State has a single agency responsible for all program areas of food and drug control.... The extent to which the States have divided their food and drug control responsibilities varies from two to four or more agencies with the majority of States having three agencies involved....

... [T]he variability of organizational structures complicates the problems of many of the individual State agencies in accomplishing their program goals because of overlapping responsibilities and the lack of a clear delineation of responsibilities. For example, it is not uncommon to find authority granted to two agencies for some divided program segments of a single program category (*e.g.,* milk, shellfish). Frequently, two or more independent agencies of relatively equal rank are charged with enforcement of portions of the same general food and drug law. In still other States, there is no central State control over the food and drug programs. In these instances, the State agency has an unclear role as an advisor or consultant to the local government. However, the local agency may not be legally bound to follow the advice and/or direction that may be suggested by the State agency. Nevertheless, while the survey reports reveal a vast and complex organizational profile of State actions in food and drug control, they also show that State agencies have strong program components and nationally represent a strong collective strength with substantial food and drug control resources.....

... Basic State food and drug laws are patterned in varying degrees after Federal food and drug laws at different stages in their evolution or after the Uniform State Food, Drug and Cosmetic Bill of the Association of Food and Drug Officials. Currently, 42 States have enacted food provisions based on the 1938 Federal FD&C Act. Approximately half of the States have updated the food provisions to include such major amendments as the Food and Color Additives Amendment and the Pesticide Amendment.... Forty one States have enacted drug provisions based upon the 1938 Federal FD&C Act. Less than a third of the States have modernized their drug legislation by the inclusion of the modern new drug amendments (Kefauver–Harris Legislation). The uniform device provisions have been enacted by 38 States and 43 have its cosmetic requirements.... Twenty four States have adopted the 1970 Model Feed Bill with eighteen States operating under adopted provisions of the 1958 Model Feed Bill. Ten States have adopted laws for control of blood banks. Forty seven States and the Commonwealth of Puerto Rico have enacted specific laws for the regulation of ionizing radiation with sixteen having approved legislation for the regulation of nonionizing radiation....

MELVIN HINICH & RICHARD STAELIN, REGULATION OF THE U.S. FOOD INDUSTRY

Appendix, VI Study on Federal Regulation,
S. Doc. No. 14, 96th Congress, 1st Session (1978).

Why does food regulation differ among the states? We suggest two factors: local special interest groups use their influence in state legislatures to secure a competitive advantage, and special features exist between differing locales, leading to a heterogeneity of preferences across regions. In other words the economic and social forces which affect food regulation at the national level are also present at the state and even local level. Just as U.S. producers profit from Federal regulations which raise the costs of foreign producers, local producers profit from regulations which give them a competitive edge over their competitors in other regions. The consumers pay for any profits which result from constraints on free trade, although they also get the benefits of being protected by the regulatory actions of the Government. Not all the profits, however, go to the producers; labor unions and local suppliers can also benefit at the expense of others. Since there are fewer special interest groups in a state or local region as compared to the nation as a whole, it is probably easier for these groups to organize to exert effective pressure for restrictive regulations....

Arguments made for uniformity of legislation stress the desirability of modernizing food laws, regulations, and standards. Uniform legislation is said to be needed to protect consumers' health, assure high quality food, and eliminate objectionable trade barriers.....

Another argument for uniformity of state food laws by the food industry is that concerning productivity. Non-uniform statutes are said to necessitate additional production lines for the same product to meet different requirements, thereby reducing productivity. Some other arguments for uniformity stress that the legal interpretation of acts in state courts are unpredictable—adding more uncertainty to the business. With uniform legislation, a state can coordinate state enforcement efforts with the FDA (*e.g.* supplementing field forces, exchange of laboratory results, and use of FDA resources where expert testimony is needed). State scientific resources can be devoted to enforcement of federally established standards, revising them as special circumstances or doubt arise.

While there is general support for uniformity, this does not necessarily translate into proof that Federal pre-emption of state food and drug law is best for the consumer. States have provided much impetus for food and drug legislation and uniformity in law and regulation, have played a crucial part in enforcing Federal pre-emptive legislation, and have shown a willingness to adopt uniform regulations (*e.g.*, the Interstate Milk Shippers Program). Moreover, without any say, state legislators may be more reluctant to appropriate state funds to enforce Federal laws and regulations. Also, states have expressed a desire to retain the authority to require nutritional standards and maintain enforcement ability over and above that of the Federal government. Differing regulations also allow for different sensibilities among geographic areas in regard to ingredients in meat or other products.

Clearly regulation which is intended to restrain trade and thus protect local interest groups should be discontinued. This would imply the use of uniform national safety regulations. However, the question is not quite that clear-cut since economic special interests are not alone in wanting local laws. Consumers may also want food standards which are stronger or weaker than the federal ones.....

As with Federal agencies, state and local units can regulate either by banning or providing information. In our opinion it seems reasonable for a local government, whose citizens have very different risk preferences from the rest of the nation, to exercise its judgment and ban a product from its region, since this does not impose costs on other consumer groups. Jurisdictional duplication and conflict about product labeling, on the other hand, cause economic losses to everyone, since there normally exist economies of scale in production and marketing which are unrealized if labeling regulations vary by region. For example, if label requirements vary by area, major food producers can not advantageously use the low cost mass distribution systems now available. This implies a significant economic advantage for a uniform national labeling code which would allow firms to market their products without having to worry about specific labels for individual areas....

NOTES

1. *Costs of Lack of Uniformity.* For reports and analyses documenting the adverse economic impact of nonuniform state and Federal regulation of food and drug laws, *see* "An Inquiry Into Conflicting and Duplicative Regulatory Requirements Affecting Selected Industries and Sectors," 96th Cong., 2d Sess. (Joint Comm. Print 1980); R.E. Jenkins, A COMPARATIVE STUDY OF STATE FOOD AND DRUG REGULATORY PROGRAMS, Ohio State University Ph.D. Dissertation (1976); REPORT ON THE WHITE HOUSE CONFERENCE ON FOOD, NUTRITION AND HEALTH, *Panel III–2: New Foods* (1969); National Commission on Food Marketing, FOOD FROM FARMER TO CONSUMER (1966); REPORT OF PUBLIC ADMINISTRATION SERVICE ON A STUDY OF STATE AND LOCAL FOOD AND DRUG PROGRAMS (1965);

"Consumer Protection Activities of State Governments," H.R. Rep. No. 445, 88th Cong., 1st Sess (1963); H.R. Rep. No. 921, 88th Cong., 1st Sess. (1963); and USDA, BARRIERS TO INTERNAL TRADE IN FARM PRODUCTS (1939).

2. *State Dependence on FDA.* In 1974, an Indiana food and drug official acknowledged the deficiencies of state regulation and local dependence on FDA, but argued against federal preemption:

> *First,* the states have for many years provided much of the impetus for food and drug legislation.... The present system, while certainly not perfect, is working reasonably well.

> *Second,* in much of the recent federal preemptive legislation, the enforcing agency has found that it is necessary to enlist the aid of state agencies for proper enforcement....

> *Third,* state legislators are becoming more and more reluctant to appropriate state funds to enforce federal laws and regulations. This reluctance also extends to state laws which are required to be equal to or identical with federal legislation....

> *Fourth,* it is readily understandable that state officials are not eager to enforce regulations in which they had no input....

> *Fifth,* states are capable of adopting uniform regulations and indeed have done so. Even though an occasional maverick raises his head, on the whole, the record is good....

Fisher, *Federal/State Concurrent Regulations,* 29 FDC L.J. 20, 24–25 (1974).

H. THOMAS AUSTERN,
FEDERALISM IN CONSUMER PROTECTION:
CONFLICT OR COORDINATION?

29 Bulletin of the Association of Food & Drug Officials of U.S., No. 4, at 148 (1965).

... I should like to analyze with you the pragmatic problem of coordinating Federal and State action in the regulation of food and drugs in the consumer interest. Two principles, I suggest, should control that inquiry.

The first is that there is a place, indeed an important place, for State activity, and that effective consumer protection requires that there be fully deployed the corps of dedicated State and local regulatory officials who have devoted their careers to that end....

The second controlling principle is that there should be no barriers to the free interstate movement of foods and drugs. As a corollary, the sophistication of modern food and drug production, and the delicacy of present-day techniques for determining pesticide residues, food additive safety, and drug efficacy, require both uniformity and the avoidance of costly duplication of research....

In my approach to the problem of distribution of regulatory functions between State and Federal agencies, as well as the desirable coordination and relative emphasis, I divide the area of needed regulatory activity into four parts. . . .

. . . [A]s to environmental sanitation. That covers not only food and drug manufacture, but also distribution and retail sale, as well as fundamental sanitation in local restaurants and food stores. Here the State and local health inspectors and health officials should play the dominant role. They can achieve the greatest degree of protection for the consuming public. . . .

Turning to the second area—the *safety* of composition of foods and drugs—the lines of responsibility begin to blend. Present-day sophistication of food manufacture and of drug technology impose too great a burden on the scientific resources of individual State agencies. . . .

When one leaves the area of environmental or compositional safety, and enters the third area of *economic* regulation, the national interest in freedom of the movement of goods usually should stay the hand of the State. . . . Interstate dealing, as well as the cost economies of mass production, dictate that there be a uniform package and label for all interstate distribution along with a trademark that can be nationally advertised. . . .

Turning, finally, to the economic regulation of food composition by standardization, one finds the most discomforting area of chaos and perhaps plain rivalry. . . . It is not too much to hope that in this area of economic control over composition of food products, the States will yield to Federal standardization, and at the same time that the FDA will develop better and more responsive mechanisms for consultation and consideration of the views of State officials. . . .

NOTES

1. *Pre–1906 State Laws.* Surveys of state food and drug laws before enactment of the 1906 Act may be found in Bigelow, *Foods and Food Control,* USDA Bu. Chem. Bull. No. 69, Pts. I–V (1902); Wedderburn, *Special Report on the Extent and Character of Food Adulteration,* USDA Div. Chem. Bull. No. 32, at 87 (1892). *See also* Bigelow, *Officials Charged with the Enforcement of Food Laws in the United States and Canada,* USDA Bur. Chem. Circ. No. 16 (1904).

2. *State Laws in 1938.* The status of state legislation at the time of enactment of the 1938 Act was reviewed in detail in Salthe, *State Food, Drug and Cosmetic Legislation and its Administration,* 6 Law & Contemp. Probs. 165 (1939). The results of a detailed survey of state food regulation were reported in House Comm. on Government Operations, "Consumer Protection Activities of State Governments: Part 2—The Regulation of Foods and Related Products," H.R. Rep. No. 921, 88th Cong., 1st Sess. (1963).

3. *Proposed Expansion of State Control.* During the Eisenhower Administration consideration was given to transferring responsibility for control of local food and drug law problems from FDA to state and local authorities. *See* Stapleton, *Administration and Enforcement of State Food and Drug Laws,* 10 FDC L.J. 794 (1955), which opposed this approach.

4. *Prospective Adoption of Federal Regulations.* One obstacle to uniform Federal and state food and drug law requirements is the prohibition, in some

states, against prospective adoption of Federal regulations. In these states, the legislature may incorporate by reference only those FDA regulations in effect at the time it enacts legislation. *See* Christopher, *May a State Adopt Prospective Federal Regulations,* 15 FDC L.J. 373 (1960).

5. *Federal–State Compacts.* For arguments in favor of Federal-state compacts as an alternative to Federal preemption, *see* Engdahl, *Consolidation by Compact: A Remedy for Preemption of State Food and Drug Laws,* 14 J. of Pub. L. 276 (1965).

6. *Commentary.* The literature dealing with statutory uniformity and Federal preemption is abundant. *See, e.g.,* Barmak, *State Legislative Impact on the Drug Industry,* 33 FDC L.J. 641 (1978); Burditt, *The Importance of Uniformity Among State Food and Drug Laws,* 26 FDC L.J. 96 (1971); *The Challenge of Uniformity,* 48 AFDO Quart. Bull. 233 (1984); Christopher, *Conflicts Between State and Federal Food and Drug Laws,* 16 FDC L.J. 164 (1961); Downey, *Laboratories or Puppets? The Challenge of Federal Preemption of State Legislation,* 34 FDC L.J. 334 (1979); Engdahl, *Consolidating State and Federal Regulatory Power over Foods and Drugs,* 20 FDC L.J. 587 (1965); Goodrich, *The Applicability of the Federal Food, Drug, and Cosmetic Act to Intrastate Commerce,* 3 FDC L.Q. 332 (1948), *Uniformity in Federal–State Food Regulations,* 17 FDC L.J. 305 (1962); Heckman, *California's Proposition 65: A Federal Supremacy and States' Rights Conflict in the Health and Safety Arena,* 43 FDC L.J. 269 (1988); Hensel, *Federal–State Uniformity and Cooperation on Meat Products,* 29 Q. Bull.AFDO 143 (1965); *Importance of Uniformity in the Weights and Measures Field,* 19 FDC L.J. 274 (1964); Hooker, *The Impossible Dream: Maximum Uniformity with Maximum Freedom,* 48 J. AFDO, No. 2, at 74 (April 1984); Manelli, *State Legislation and the Regulation of OTC Drugs,* 33 FDC L.J. 650 (1978); Markel, *Federal Pre-emption,* 17 FDC L.J. 453 (1962); McLaughlin and Corrigan, *Federal Preemption—A Possible Route to Uniformity in the Food, Drug and Cosmetic Law Area,* 28 Bus. Law 785 (1973); Miller, *Uniform Food Laws,* 6 FDC L.J. 924 (1951); Mitchell, *State Regulation and Federal Preemption of Food Labeling,* 45 FDC L.J. 123 (1990); Nedelman, *Uniformity in the Regulation of Food,* 54 J. AFDO, No. 1, at 47 (January 1990); Prentice, *Uniform Food Laws,* 4 FDC L.Q. 502 (1949); Reindollar, *The Association of Food and Drug Officials,* 6 FDC L.J. 52 (1951); Schipa, *The Desirability of Uniform Food Laws,* 3 FDC L.Q. 518 (1948); Silverglade, *Preemption—The Consumer Viewpoint,* 45 FDC L.J. 143 (1990); Smith, *What Hath* Rath *Wrought? Federal Preemption in Food Labeling,* 33 FDC L.J. 28 (1978); Taylor, *Federal Preemption and Food and Drug Regulation: The Practical Modern Meaning of an Ancient Doctrine,* 38 FDC L.J. 306 (1983).

B. THE 1906 ACT

In the late 19th century, the Supreme Court first dealt with the constitutional authority of the states to regulate food products marketed interstate.

PLUMLEY v. MASSACHUSETTS

Supreme Court of the United States, 1894.
155 U.S. 461.

Mr. Justice HARLAN delivered the opinion of the court.

Plumley, the plaintiff in error, was convicted in the Municipal Court of Boston upon the charge of having sold in that city on the 6th day of October, 1891, in violation of the law of Massachusetts, a certain article, product and compound known as oleomargarine, made partly of fats, oils and oleaginous substances and compounds thereof, not produced from unadulterated milk or cream but manufactured in imitation of yellow butter produced from pure unadulterated milk and cream.

The prosecution was based upon a statute of that Commonwealth approved March 10, 1891, Mass. Stats. 1891, c. 58, p. 695, entitled "An act to prevent deception in the manufacture and sale of imitation butter." ...

The vital question in this case is ... whether, as contended by the petitioner, the statute under examination in its application to sales of oleomargarine brought into Massachusetts from other States is in conflict with the clause of the Constitution of the United States investing Congress with power to regulate commerce among the several States....

It will be observed that the statute of Massachusetts which is alleged to be repugnant to the commerce clause of the Constitution does not prohibit the manufacture or sale of all oleomargarine, but only such as is colored in imitation of yellow butter produced from pure unadulterated milk or cream of such milk. If free from coloration or ingredient that "causes it to look like butter," the right to sell it "in a separate and distinct form, and in such manner as will advise the consumer of its real character," is neither restricted nor prohibited. It appears, in this case, that oleomargarine, in its natural condition, is of "a light-yellowish color," and that the article sold by the accused was artificially colored "in imitation of yellow butter." ... If any one thinks that oleomargarine, not artificially colored so as to cause it to look like butter, is as palatable or as wholesome for purposes of food as pure butter he is, as already observed, at liberty under the statute of Massachusetts to manufacture it in that State or to sell it there in such manner as to inform the customer of its real character. He is only forbidden to practice, in such matters, a fraud upon the general public. The statute seeks to suppress false pretenses and to promote fair dealing in the sale of an article of food. It compels the sale of oleomargarine for what it really is, by preventing its sale for what it is not. Can it be that the Constitution of the United States secures to any one the privilege of manufacturing and selling an article of food in such manner as to induce the mass of people to believe that they are buying something which, in fact, is wholly different from that which is offered for sale? Does the freedom of commerce among the States demand a recognition of the right to practice a deception upon the public in the sale of any articles, even those that may have become the subject of trade in different parts of the country? ...

If there be any subject over which it would seem the States ought to have plenary control, and the power to legislate in respect to which it ought not to be supposed was intended to be surrendered to the general government, it is the protection of the people against fraud and deception in the sale of food products. Such legislation may, indeed, indirectly or incidentally affect trade in such products transported from one State to another State. But that circumstance does not show that laws of the character alluded to are inconsistent with the power of Congress to regulate commerce among the States....

[The dissenting opinion of Chief Justice Fuller, joined by Justices Field and Brewer, is omitted.]

THE INTENDED IMPACT OF THE 1906 ACT

In January 1879, Dr. E.R. Squibb delivered a major address to the Medical Society of the State of New York, proposing enactment of a nationwide food and drug law. He began his remarks with:

> It is self-evident that a law to be most effective in preventing the adulteration of food and medicine should be general or national in order to secure universality and uniformity of action....

E.R. Squibb, PROPOSED LEGISLATION ON THE ADULTERATION OF FOOD AND MEDICINE 3 (1879). Only ten days later, the first comprehensive Federal legislation was introduced in Congress. H.R. 5916, 45th Cong., 3d Sess. (1879). Because of strong feelings in Congress that this was properly a matter for state and local regulation, *see* p. 987 *supra*, Federal legislation was debated in Congress from 1879 to 1906. Throughout this time, the need for national uniformity in regulation of food and drugs was an important argument in favor of the legislation. The Chief of the USDA Food Laboratory argued for national legislation because "[b]y no other means can we hope to secure laws uniform in their scope, requirements and penalties among ourselves...." Bigelow, *The Development of Pure Food Legislation,* 7 Science 505, 512 (April 15, 1898). The Chief of the USDA Bureau of Chemistry stated that legislation was necessary "to secure uniformity in the composition of drugs...." Wiley, *Drugs and Their Adulteration and The Laws Relating Thereto,* 2 Washington Medical Annals 205 (1903). The Director of the Bureau of Chemistry of the New York State Department of Health noted that

> it is very certain that the widely differing statutes relating to our food supply in the different States have worked much mischief, been the cause of much confusion, and seriously embarrassed some useful industries. I think all who have studied the matter will be inclined to admit that uniformity in our food laws is much to be desired....

W.G. Tucker, FOOD ADULTERATION: ITS NATURE AND EXTENT, AND HOW TO DEAL WITH IT 21 (1903).

Consistent with this recurrently expressed concern, the House Report on the 1906 Act stated that

[t]he laws and regulations of the different States are diverse, confusing, and often contradictory. What one State now requires the adjoining State may forbid. Our food products are not raised principally in the States of their consumption.

State boundary lines are unknown in our commerce, except by reason of local regulations and laws, such as State pure-food laws. It is desirable, as far as possible, that the commerce between the States be unhindered. One of the hoped-for good results of a national law on the subject of pure foods is the bringing about of a uniformity of laws and regulations on the part of the States within their own several borders.

The House bill that eventually became the 1906 Act contained a provision expressly preserving state power to regulate food and drugs, H.R. Rep. No. 2118, 59th Cong., 1st Sess. 5 (1906), but it was deleted in conference with the following cryptic explanation:

Omitted from the bill, as reported by the conferees, is ... also section 12 of the House amendment, providing that articles complying with the provisions of the act shall not be interfered with by the several States so long as they remain in original unbroken packages.

H.R. Rep. No. 5056, 59th Cong., 1st Sess. 8–9 (1906). The 1906 Act, however, did not establish the basis for a comprehensive national regulatory scheme. It applied only to unbroken packages in interstate commerce, and only to the actual label of the product.

SAVAGE v. JONES

Supreme Court of the United States, 1912.
225 U.S. 501.

Mr. Justice HUGHES ... delivered the opinion of the court.

The principal contention in support of this appeal is that the statute of Indiana (Acts 1907, chapter 206) ... is an unconstitutional interference with the complainant's right to engage in interstate commerce.... The question of its constitutional validity may be considered in two aspects, (1) independently of the operation and effect of the act of Congress of June 30, 1906, known as "The Food and Drugs Act," and (2) in the light of this Federal enactment.

First. The statute relates to the sale of various sorts of food, for domestic animals, embraced in the term "concentrated commercial feeding stuff" as defined in the act. It requires the filing of a statement and a sworn certificate, the affixing of a label bearing certain information, and a stamp....

The evident purpose of the statute is to prevent fraud and imposition in the sale of food for domestic animals, a matter of great importance to the people of the State.... It was not aimed at interstate commerce, but without discrimination sought to promote fair dealing in the described articles of food.... The bill complains of the injury to manufacturers if they are forced to reveal their secret formu-

998 STATE LAWS AND THEIR RELATION TO FEDERAL LAW Ch. 10

las and processes. We need not here express an opinion upon this question, in the breadth suggested, as the statute does not compel a disclosure of formulas or manner of combination. It does demand a statement of the ingredients, and also of the minimum percentage of crude fat and crude protein and of the maximum percentage of crude fiber, a requirement of obvious propriety in connection with substances purveyed as feeding stuffs.

... [W]hen the local police regulation has real relation to the suitable protection of the people of the State, and is reasonable in its requirements, it is not invalid because it may incidentally affect interstate commerce, provided it does not conflict with legislation enacted by Congress pursuant to its constitutional authority....

Second. The question remains whether the statute of Indiana is in conflict with ... the Food and Drugs Act of June 30, 1906.... It will be observed that in its enumeration of the acts, which constitute a violation of the statute, Congress has not included the failure to disclose the ingredients of the article....

Congress has thus limited the scope of its prohibitions. It has not included that at which the Indiana statute aims. Can it be said that Congress, nevertheless, has denied to the State, with respect to the feeding stuffs coming from another State and sold in the original packages, the power the State otherwise would have to prevent imposition upon the public by making a reasonable and nondiscriminatory provision for the disclosure of ingredients, and for inspection and analysis? If there be such denial it is not to be found in any express declaration to that effect....

... [T]he intent to supersede the exercise by the State of its police power as to matters not covered by the Federal legislation is not to be inferred from the mere fact that Congress has seen fit to circumscribe its regulation and to occupy a limited field. In other words, such intent is not to be implied unless the act of Congress fairly interpreted is in actual conflict with the law of the State. This principle has had abundant illustration....

... The requirements, the enforcement of which the bill seeks to enjoin, are not in any way in conflict with the provisions of the Federal act. They may be sustained without impairing in the slightest degree its operation and effect. There is no question here of conflicting standards, or of opposition of state to Federal authority. It follows that the complainant's bill in this aspect of the case was without equity....

McDERMOTT v. WISCONSIN
Supreme Court of the United States, 1913.
228 U.S. 115.

Mr. Justice DAY delivered the opinion of the court.

The facts are that the plaintiffs in error were retail merchants in Oregon, Dane County, Wisconsin; that before the filing of the complaints against them each had bought for himself for resale as such merchant from wholesale grocers in Chicago and had received by rail from that city twelve half gallon tin cans or pails of the articles designated in the complaints, each shipment being made in wooden boxes containing the cans, and that when the goods were received at their stores the respective plaintiffs in error took the cans from the boxes, placed them on the shelves for sale at retail, and destroyed the boxes in which the goods were shipped to them, as was customary in such cases. From their nature, the articles thus canned and offered to be sold, instead of being labeled as they were, if labeled in accordance with the state law, would have been branded with the words "Glucose flavored with Refiner's Syrup," and, as the statute provides that the mixtures or syrups offered for sale shall have upon them no designation or brand which represents or contains the name of a saccharine substance other than that required by the state law, the labels upon the cans must be removed, if the state authority is recognized.

Plaintiffs in error contend that the cans were labeled in accordance with the Food and Drugs Act passed by Congress, June 30, 1906.... And it is insisted that the Federal Food and Drugs Act passed under the authority of the Constitution has taken possession of this field of regulation and that the state act is a wrongful interference with the exclusive power of Congress over interstate commerce, in which, it appears, the goods in question were shipped. The case presents, among other questions, the constitutional question whether the state act in permitting the sale of this article only when labeled according to the state law is open to the objection just indicated....

... [I]t is essential to a legal exercise of possession of and traffic in such goods under the state law that labels which presumably meet with the requirements of the Federal law and for the determination of the correctness of which Congress has provided effectual means, shall be removed from the packages before the first sale by the importer. In this connection it might be noted that as a practical matter, at least, the first time the opportunity of inspection by the Federal authorities arises in cases like the present is when the goods, after having been manufactured, put up in package form and boxed in one State and having been transported in interstate commerce, arrive at their destination, are delivered to the consignee, unboxed, and placed by him upon the shelves of his store for sale. Conceding to the State the authority to make regulations consistent with the Federal law for the further protection of its citizens against impure and misbranded food and drugs, we think to permit such regulation as is embodied in this statute is to permit a State to discredit and burden legitimate Federal regulations of interstate commerce, to destroy rights arising out of the Federal statute which have accrued both to the Government and the shipper, and to impair the effect of a Federal law which has been enacted under the Constitutional power of Congress over the subject.

To require the removal or destruction before the goods are sold of the evidence which Congress has, by the Food and Drugs Act, as we shall see, provided may be examined to determine the compliance or noncompliance with the regulations of the Federal law, is beyond the power of the State. The Wisconsin act which permits the sale of articles subject to the regulations of interstate commerce only upon condition that they contain the exclusive labels required by the statute is an act in excess of its legitimate power.

It is insisted, however, that, since at the time when the state act undertook to regulate the branding of these goods, namely, when in the possession of the plaintiffs in error and held upon their shelves for sale, the cans had been removed from the boxes in which they were shipped in interstate commerce, they had therefore passed beyond the jurisdiction of Congress, and their regulation was exclusively a matter for state legislation. This assertion is based upon the original package doctrine as it is said to have been laid down in the former decisions of this court. . . .

Congress having made adulterated and misbranded articles contraband of interstate commerce, in the manner we have already pointed out, provides in § 10 of the act that such articles may be proceeded against and seized for confiscation and condemnation while being transported from one State, Territory, district, or insular possession to another for sale, or, having been transported, remaining "unloaded, unsold, or in original unbroken packages," and the subsequent provisions of the section regulate the disposition of the articles seized. . . . It is enough, by the terms of the act, if the articles are *unsold,* whether in original packages or not. . . . The legislative means provided in the Federal law for its own enforcement may not be thwarted by state legislation having a direct effect to impair the effectual exercise of such means.

For the reasons stated, the statute of Wisconsin, in forbidding all labels other than the one it prescribed, is invalid. . . .

NOTES

1. *Early Cases Upholding State Regulation.* In *Price v. Illinois,* 238 U.S. 446 (1915), the Supreme Court upheld an Illinois statute which prohibited the marketing of a food preservative containing boric acid—a product lawful under Federal law. After rejecting a contention that the statute exceeded the state's police power, the Court turned to the appellant's claim that it unconstitutionally burdened interstate commerce:

> . . . [N]o question is presented in the present case as to the power of Congress to make provision with respect to the immediate containers (as well as the larger receptacle in which the latter are shipped) of articles prepared in one State and transported to another, so as suitably to enforce its regulations as to interstate trade. *McDermott v. Wisconsin.* It does not appear that the state law as here applied is in conflict with any Federal rule.

In *Armour & Co. v. North Dakota,* 240 U.S. 510 (1916) the Supreme Court unanimously upheld a North Dakota law requiring lard sold at retail to be packaged in specified sizes, although Federal law permitted it to be sold in any size package so long as the net weight was stated on the label:

> It is objected that the law violates the commerce clause of the Constitution. This is certainly not true of the sale to Lard. It was distinctly by retail and in the package of retail, not in the package of importation. . . .

> Nor do we think that the law is repugnant to the Pure Food and Drugs Act. . . . That act is directed against the adulteration and misbranding of articles of food transported in interstate commerce. The state statute has no such purpose; it is directed to the manner of selling at retail, which is in no way repugnant to the Federal Law and the operation of that law is in no way displaced or interfered with.

Weigle v. Curtice Bros. Co., 248 U.S. 285 (1919), required the Court again to examine the scope of state power to regulate foods which met the requirements of Federal law. A Wisconsin statute prohibited the sale within the state of any food containing benzoic acid or benzoates. The plaintiff, who shipped fruit preserved with sodium benzoate in glass jars, packed in wooden crates, from New York, brought suit to enjoin enforcement of the state law, contending that "under the Food and Drugs Act and the Commerce Clause, [it] was invalid even as applied to domestic retail sales of single bottles. . . ." The plaintiff's argument, in substance, was that since the individual bottles were still subject to the misbranding requirements of the Federal Act, they were immune from Wisconsin law:

> . . . For reasons stated in *McDermott v. Wisconsin,* if the State could require the label to be removed while the bottles remained in the importer's hands unsold, it could interfere with the means reasonably adopted by Congress to make its regulations obeyed. But all this has nothing to do with the question when interstate commerce is over and the articles carried in it have come under the general power of the State. The law upon that point has undergone no change.

> . . . The fact that a food or drug might be condemned by Congress if it passed from State to State, does not carry an immunity of foods or drugs, making the same passage, that it does not condemn. . . . When objects of commerce get within the sphere of state legislation the State may exercise its independent judgment and prohibit what Congress did not see fit to forbid. . . .

See also Hebe Co. v. Shaw, 248 U.S. 297 (1919), in which the Court sustained an Ohio statute regulating condensed milk as construed to prohibit the sale of labeled condensed skim milk containing coconut oil. Justice Holmes declared: "The cases are the original packages so far as the present question is concerned, although no doubt, as shown by *McDermott v. Wisconsin,* the power of Congress to regulate interstate commerce would extend for some purposes to the cans."

In *Corn Products Refining Co. v. Eddy,* 249 U.S. 427 (1919), the Court held that a Kansas law requiring that a proprietary syrup mixture be labeled "compound" did not violate the equal protection clause of the Fourteenth Amendment or burden interstate commerce. The fact that the Kansas statute closely followed the Federal definition of "misbranded" was not dispositive on the question of whether Congress has preempted the field:

It is argued that the present case is controlled rather by *McDermott v. Wisconsin,* and in effect that this case must be taken as overruling *Savage v. Jones.* The contention is unfounded.... The Wisconsin statute was held to be in conflict because it required that ... the label that showed compliance with the act of Congress ... be removed from the package before the first sale by the importer, and while the goods remained still subject to federal inspection....

In *Hygrade Provision Co. v. Sherman,* 266 U.S. 497 (1925), the Court upheld without dissent a New York law prohibiting any false representation that meat is kosher:

> ... It is enough to say that the statutes now assailed are not aimed at interstate commerce, do not impose a direct burden upon such commerce, make no discrimination against it, are fairly within the range of the police power of the State, bear a reasonable relation to the legitimate purpose of the enactments, and do not conflict with any congressional legislation....

In *Bourjois, Inc. v. Chapman,* 301 U.S. 183 (1937), the Court upheld a 1935 Maine law requiring registration of all cosmetic preparations against attack under the commerce clause.

2. *USDA Promotion of Uniformity.* Following enactment of the 1906 Act, the USDA Bureau of Chemistry made major efforts to implement the congressional intent of national uniformity in the regulation of food and drugs. The 1914 Annual Report of the Bureau of Chemistry reported cooperative efforts with state officials "for the purpose of fixing working standards for foods and drugs" that "should serve as a uniform guide in the enforcement of the food and drug laws throughout the country" and thus "should very largely overcome the lack of uniformity." 1914 Annual Report at 1. A report on the progress achieved by the Bureau of Chemistry during the first ten years under the 1906 Act, contained in the 1917 Annual Report, related attempts to deal with "much confusion and apparent conflict between the local and Federal laws and the local and Federal administration of the laws," resulting in "extra cost, which naturally was passed on to the ultimate consumer." 1917 Annual Report at 12–13. The 1921 Annual Report similarly recounted that "both officials and manufacturers complained greatly of the lack of uniformity in the exercise of food control by the Federal and State Governments":

> Lack of uniformity increases the costs of doing business, and the increased cost is usually passed on to the consumer. It arises not merely from differences in the various laws but also from differences in the interpretation of the laws by the officials and in the application by them of different standards to the same product in different jurisdictions.

1921 Annual Report at 7. In 1924, an attempt was made to devise "a uniform method of procedure" for regulation under both federal and state food and drug laws. 1924 Annual Report at 26. FDA has continued to deal with this persistent problem of nonuniform food and drug laws in the years since. *See, e.g.,* Pearson, *Uniform State Food Laws,* 14 FDC L.J. 183 (1959); Hile, *Remarks on Eliminating Duplication and Promoting Uniformity,* 44 Q. Bull. AFDO 37 (1980); Silver, *What is Holding Up the Golden Age of Inter–Agency Coordination?,* 53 J. AFDO 34 (1989).

C. THE 1938 ACT

The 1906 Act's limitations on Federal jurisdiction were removed by Congress in 1938, but the 1938 Act's legislative history reflects considerable interest in preserving or promoting uniformity between Federal and state food and drug laws. In the Senate report on the final bill, that interest was reflected in a debate over the desirability of amending the existing statute rather than enacting an entirely new law:

> One of the innumerable objections originating with those who are opposed to any new food and drug legislation is that the bill is in the form of a revision rather than amendments to the present law. It is urged that by appropriate amendments court decisions under the old law will be preserved and that uniformity with existing State laws will be promoted....
>
> It is true that many State laws are modeled after the existing Federal law. But the problem of uniformity is not more easily solved by amendment than by revision. The contrary is true. In bringing their own laws in line with modern requirements the States would encounter the same difficulties your committee has found in efforts to amend. The States have unanimously urged the Federal Government to take leadership in modernizing existing law. Greater uniformity can be guaranteed by the logical, orderly form of this bill than by a confusion of amendments.

S. Rep. No. 361, 74th Cong., 1st Sess. 2–3 (1935). However, the committee minority, *id.,* Pt. 2, at 2–3, took a different view of the matter:

> It is not disputed that the present law is an effectual statute in its existing scope and extent. The criticism of it, advanced in support of new legislation, is that it requires strengthening and extension or, in the President's words, "practical improvements." That is quite possible without discarding the statute in its entirety and, with one stroke, wiping out the clarity and certainty that exist under the court decisions and the uniformity in Federal and State statutes.

In *United States v. Phelps Dodge Mercantile Co.,* 157 F.2d 453 (9th Cir. 1946), *cert. denied,* 330 U.S. 818 (1947), p. 1070 *supra,* the Court of Appeals for the Ninth Circuit sharply restricted FDA's enforcement authority under the 1938 Act. The court affirmed a district court order dismissing the libel brought by the United States against cartons of macaroni and spaghetti held for two years in the defendant's Arizona warehouse. Release of the food was appropriate because the plaintiff did not prove that it "was adulterated when introduced into or while in interstate commerce," even though the food was adulterated while held in the original packages. Within a year Congress amended sections 301(k) and 304(a) of the Act, 52 Stat. 582 (1948), to reach products that become adulterated or misbranded after shipment in interstate commerce. The House report on these amendments, H.R. Rep. No. 807, 80th Cong., 1st Sess. 6 (1947), addressed their impact on state laws:

> The enactment of the proposed amendments would not have the effect of excluding State authority in the same field (*Savage v. Jones,* 225 U.S. 501 (1912)). The Food and Drug Administration has worked cooperatively with the States, and the amendments are not intended to disturb that relationship.

The 1948 amendments did not forestall litigation over the relation between state and Federal food and drug laws, as the following cases illustrate.

CLOVERLEAF BUTTER CO. v. PATTERSON

Supreme Court of the United States, 1942.
315 U.S. 148.

Mr. Justice REED delivered the opinion of the Court.

The petitioner, Cloverleaf Butter Company, is engaged at Birmingham, Alabama, in the manufacture of process or renovated butter from packing stock butter. It obtains 25% of its supplies of packing stock butter from the farmers and country merchants of Alabama and 75% from those of other states, and it ships interstate 90% of its finished product. The production of renovated butter is taxed and regulated by the United States. . . .

The respondents, Alabama officials charged with the duty of enforcing the Alabama laws in regard to renovated butter, entered petitioner's factory and, in a little more than a year, seized on sixteen separate occasions a total of over twenty thousand pounds of packing stock butter, the material from which the finished product is made. Defendants also seized some butter moving to the factory in interstate commerce. . . . .

The test to be applied to the action of the state in seizing material intended solely for incorporation into a product prepared for interstate commerce is the effect of that action upon the national regulatory policy declared by the federal statute. . . . The rule is clear that state action may be excluded by clear implication or inconsistency. Its application to individual cases creates difficulties. The differentiation between cases where the assumption of federal power is exclusive and where it admits state action is narrow. . . . .

Coming finally to the query whether the state's claim interferes or conflicts with the purpose or provisions of the federal legislation, we determine that it does. The manufacture and distribution in interstate and foreign commerce of process and renovated butter is a substantial industry which, because of its multi-state activity, cannot be effectively regulated by isolated competing states. Its wholesome and successful functioning touches farm producers and city consumers. Science made possible the utilization of large quantities of packing stock butter which fell below the standards of public demand and Congress undertook to regulate the production in order that the resulting commodity might be free of ingredients deleterious to health. It left the states free to act on the packing stock supplies prior to the time of their delivery into the hands of the manufacturer and to regulate sales of the finished product within their borders. But, once the material was definitely marked for commerce by acquisition of the manufacturer, it passed into the domain of federal control.

Inspection of the factory and of the material was provided for explicitly. Confiscation of the finished product was authorized upon a finding of its unsuitability for food through the use of unhealthful or unwholesome materials, a finding that might be based upon visual or delicate laboratory tests, or upon observation of the use of such materials in the process of manufacture. By the statutes and regulations, the Department of Agriculture has authority to watch the consumer's interest throughout the process of manufacture and distribution. It sees to the sanitation of the factories in such minutiae as the clean hands of the employees and the elimination of objectionable odors, inspects the materials used, including air for aerating the oils, and confiscates the finished product when materials which would be unwholesome if utilized are present after manufacture. Confiscation by the state of material in production nullifies federal discretion over ingredients....

Mr. Chief Justice STONE....

The decision of the Court appears to me to depart radically from the salutary principle that Congress, in enacting legislation within its constitutional authority, will not be deemed to have intended to strike down a state statute designed to protect the health and safety of the public unless the act, in terms or in its practical administration, conflicts with the act of Congress or plainly and palpably infringes its policy....

... [N]ot only is there a complete want of conflict between the two statutes and their administration, but it seems plain that the Alabama statute, both by its terms and in its practical administration, aids and supplements the federal regulation and policy. Consequently there is no room for any inference that Congress, by its enactment, sought to stay the hands of the state in the exercise of a power with which the federal act does not conflict. The basic and identical concern of both governments is to protect the consuming public from contaminated butter. If the state seizes unfit packing stock, the federal authorities are relieved of the necessity of detecting it and of seizing the renovated product which it contaminates....

FLORIDA LIME & AVOCADO GROWERS, INC. v. PAUL

Supreme Court of the United States, 1963.

373 U.S. 132.

Mr. Justice BRENNAN delivered the opinion of the Court.

Section 792 of California's Agricultural Code, which gauges the maturity of avocados by oil content, prohibits the transportation or sale in California of avocados which contain "less than 8 per cent of oil, by weight ... excluding the skin and seed." In contrast, federal marketing orders approved by the Secretary of Agriculture gauge the maturity of avocados grown in Florida by standards which attribute no significance to oil content. This case presents the question of the constitutionality of the California statute insofar as it may be applied to exclude from California markets certain Florida avocados which, although certified to be mature under the federal regulations, do not uniformly meet the California requirement of 8% of oil....

... In adopting his calendar test of maturity for the varieties grown in South Florida the Secretary expressly rejected physical and chemical tests as insufficiently reliable guides for gauging the maturity of the Florida fruit.

... Whether a State may constitutionally reject commodities which a federal authority has certified to be marketable depends upon whether the state regulation "stands as an obstacle to the accomplishment and execution of the full purposes and objectives of Congress," *Hines v. Davidowitz*, 312 U.S. 52, 67 (1941). By that test, we hold that § 792 is not such an obstacle; there is neither such actual conflict between the two schemes of regulation that both cannot stand in the same area, nor evidence of a congressional design to preempt the field....

A holding of federal exclusion of state law is inescapable and requires no inquiry into congressional design where compliance with both federal and state regulations is a physical impossibility for one engaged in interstate commerce.... No such impossibility of dual compliance is presented on this record, however. As to those Florida avocados of the hybrid and Guatemalan varieties which were actually rejected by the California test, the District Court indicated that the Florida growers might have avoided such rejections by leaving the fruit on the trees beyond the earliest picking date permitted by the federal regulations, and nothing in the record contradicts that suggestion....

The issue under the head of the Supremacy Clause is narrowed then to this: Does either the nature of the subject matter, namely the maturity of avocados, or any explicit declaration of congressional design to displace state regulation, require § 792 to yield to the federal marketing orders? The maturity of avocados seems to be an inherently unlikely candidate for exclusive federal regulation.... On the contrary, the maturity of avocados is a subject matter of the kind this Court has traditionally regarded as properly within the scope of state superintendence. Specifically, the supervision of the readying of foodstuffs for market has always been deemed a matter of peculiarly local concern....

It is true that more recently we sustained a federal statute broadly regulating the production of renovated butter. But we were scrupulous in pointing out that a State might nevertheless—at least in the absence of an express contrary command of Congress—confiscate or exclude from market the processed butter which had complied with all the federal *processing* standards, "because of a higher standard demanded by a state for its consumers." A state regulation so purposed was, we affirmed, "permissible under all the authorities." *Cloverleaf Butter Co. v. Patterson,* 315 U.S. 148, 162 (1942). That distinction is a fundamental one, which illumines and delineates the problem of the present case. Federal regulation by means of minimum standards of the picking, processing, and transportation of agricultural commodities, however comprehensive *for those purposes* that regulation may be, does not of itself import displacement of state control over the distribution and retail sale of those commodities in the interests of the *consumers* of the commodities within the State. Thus, while Florida may perhaps not prevent the exportation of federally certified fruit by superimposing a higher maturity standard, nothing in *Cloverleaf* forbids California to regulate their marketing. Congressional regulation of one end of the stream of commerce does not, *ipso facto,* oust all state regulation at the other end. Such a displacement may not be inferred automatically from the fact that Congress has regulated production and packing of commodities for the interstate market....

... While it is conceded that the California statute is not a health measure, neither logic nor precedent invites any distinction between state regulations designed to keep unhealthful or unsafe commodities off the grocer's shelves, and those designed to prevent the deception of consumers....

Since no irreconcilable conflict with the federal regulation requires a conclusion that § 792 was displaced, we turn to the question whether Congress has nevertheless ordained that the state regulation shall yield.... [W]e conclude that Congress has not attempted to oust or displace state powers to enact the regulation embodied in § 792....

[Justice Brennan concluded that the record was inadequate to permit a judgment about whether the California statute unreasonably burdened interstate commerce. Justice White, in a dissenting opinion joined by Justices Black, Douglas, and Clark, concluded that California's statute was inconsistent with, and thus preempted by, federal law.]

NOTES

1. *Displacement of State Regulation.* In *Gorolin Corp. v. City of New York,* Food Drug Cosm. L. Rep. (CCH) ¶ 7116 (S.D.N.Y. 1949), the plaintiff Illinois corporation manufactured Lastone, a coal tar hair dye, and shipped it in interstate commerce to New York City. There officials seized the product for violation of a local law which prohibited the sale unless the coal tar ingredients

were from a certified batch or unless the package bore a cautionary label describing instructions for a patch test. The court held that enforcement of the city law conflicted with the FD&C Act, which the court concluded would apply to the plaintiff's product even after its arrival in New York. Citing *McDermott*, the court declined to permit enforcement of the New York law.

Borden Co. v. Liddy, 239 F. Supp. 289 (S.D. Iowa 1965), held that the misbranding provisions of an Iowa law, which required 12% milkfat in ice cream compared with FDA's standard of 10%, could not be enforced against Borden's 10% product shipped from outside the state but that the identical adulteration provisions of that law could be enforced. *Compare People v. Breen*, 326 Mich. 720, 40 N.W.2d 778 (1950), which upheld a Michigan law prohibiting the sale of yellow margarine even though the FDA standard of identity for margarine permitted artificial coloring. *See also Pepperidge Farm, Inc. v. Foust*, 117 N.E.2d 724 (Ohio Ct. C. P. 1953) (FDA standard of identity defining rolls as units weighing less than 8 ounces did not preempt an Ohio regulation setting 3 ounce maximum for rolls).

Dean Foods Co. v. Wisconsin Dept. of Agriculture, 478 F. Supp. 224 (W.D. Wis. 1979), enjoined enforcement against a "pasteurized chocolate flavored drink" of a statute prohibiting any food that "purports to be" milk and that contains any fat or oil other than milkfat, concluding that the state should explore less draconian ways of protecting its interest.

2. *Meat, Poultry, Eggs.* Congress has included prohibitions against any "additional" or "different" state requirement in the Federal Meat Inspection Act, 21 U.S.C. § 678, the Poultry Products Inspection Act, 21 U.S.C. § 467e, and the Egg Products Inspection Act, 21 U.S.C. § 1052. Following enactment of 21 U.S.C. § 678 in 1967, the meat industry waged a successful 14–year war to have the courts invalidate the Michigan Comminuted Meat Law, which established ingredient requirements for various meat products that differed from the USDA requirements. After a district court held that the matter should first be decided in a state court, *Armour & Co. v. Ball*, 337 F. Supp. 938 (W.D. Mich. 1971), the court of appeals reversed, determined that declaratory judgment was appropriate, and concluded that the Federal law preempted the state law. 468 F.2d 76 (6th Cir. 1972). Michigan then amended its statute to require grocery stores and restaurants that sell meat products whose ingredients do not meet the Michigan standards to notify consumers of that fact by a placard "clearly visible to a consumer" or by a printed notice on menus. The district court first ruled that these mandated notices did not constitute "labeling" and were thus not preempted, 520 F. Supp. 929 (W.D. Mich. 1981), but after trial determined that the Michigan law violated the Commerce Clause. 550 F. Supp. 285 (W.D. Mich. 1982), *aff'd sub nom. American Meat Institute v. ·Pridgeon*, 724 F.2d 45 (6th Cir. 1984). *Mario's Butcher Shop and Food Center, Inc. v. Armour and Co.*, 574 F. Supp. 653 (N.D. Ill. 1983), held that state consumer fraud statutes are also preempted. *Chicago–Midwest Meat Association v. City of Evanston*, 589 F.2d 278 (7th Cir. 1978), however, held that a municipal ordinance authorizing the inspection of meat delivery vehicles did not violate either 21 U.S.C. § 678 or the Commerce Clause.

JONES v. RATH PACKING CO.

Supreme Court of the United States, 1977.
430 U.S. 519.

Mr. Justice MARSHALL delivered the opinion of the Court.

Petitioner Jones is Director of the Department of Weights and Measures in Riverside County, Cal. In that capacity he ordered removed from sale bacon packaged by respondent Rath Packing Co. and flour packaged by three millers, respondents General Mills, Inc., Pillsbury Co., and Seaboard Allied Milling Corp. (hereafter millers). Jones acted after determining by means of procedures set forth in 4 Cal. Admin. Code c. 8, Art. 5, that the packages were contained in lots whose average net weight was less than the net weight stated on the packages. The removal orders were authorized by Cal. Bus. & Prof. Code § 12211 (West Supp. 1977)....

In its present posture, this litigation contains no claim that the Constitution alone denies California power to enact the challenged provisions. We are required to decide only whether the federal laws which govern respondents' packing operations preclude California from enforcing § 12211, as implemented by Art. 5....

Section 12211 ... applies to both Rath's bacon and the millers' flour. The standard it establishes is straightforward: "[T]he average weight or measure of the packages or containers in a lot of any ... commodity sampled shall not be less, at the time of sale or offer for sale, than the net weight or measure stated upon the package." ...

Rath's bacon is produced at plants subject to federal inspection under the Federal Meat Inspection Act (FMIA or Act).... Among the requirements imposed on federally inspected plants, and enforced by Department of Agriculture inspectors, are standards of accuracy in labeling. On the record before us, we may assume that Rath's bacon complies with these standards....

The Secretary of Agriculture has used his discretionary authority [under 21 U.S.C. § 601(n)(5)(B)] to permit "reasonable variations" in the accuracy of the required statement of quantity:

> "The statement [of net quantity of contents] as it is shown on a label shall not be false or misleading and shall express an accurate statement of the quantity of contents of the container exclusive of wrappers and packing substances. Reasonable variations caused by loss or gain of moisture during the course of good distribution practices or by unavoidable deviations in good manufacturing practice will be recognized. Variations from stated quantity of contents shall not be unreasonably large." 9 CFR § 317.2(h)(2) (1976).

Thus, the FMIA, as implemented by statutorily authorized regulations, requires the label of a meat product accurately to indicate the net weight of the contents unless the difference between stated and actual weights is reasonable and results from the specified causes.

Section 408 of the FMIA prohibits the imposition of "[m]arking, labeling, packaging, or ingredient requirements in addition to, or different than, those made under" the Act. This explicit pre-emption provision dictates the result in the controversy between Jones and Rath. California's use of a statistical sampling process to determine the average net weight of a lot implicitly allows for variation from stated weight caused by unavoidable deviations in the manufacturing process. But California makes no allowance for loss of weight resulting from moisture loss during the course of good distribution practice. Thus, the state law's requirement—that the label accurately state the net weight, with implicit allowance only for reasonable manufacturing variations— is "different than" the federal requirement, which permits manufacturing deviations *and* variations caused by moisture loss during good distribution practice.... We therefore conclude that with respect to Rath's packaged bacon, § 12211 and Art. 5 are pre-empted by federal law.

The federal law governing net-weight labeling of the millers' flour is contained in two statutes, the Federal Food, Drug, and Cosmetic Act (FDCA) and the Fair Packaging and Labeling Act (FPLA), 15 U.S.C. §§ 1451–1461. For the reasons stated below, we conclude that the federal weight-labeling standard for flour is the same as that for meat.

... [The net weight labeling requirement in section 403(e)] is identical to the parallel provision in the FMIA, except that the FDCA mandates rather than allows the promulgation of implementing regulations. The regulation issued in response to this statutory mandate is also substantially identical to its counterpart under the FMIA:

> "The declaration of net quantity of contents shall express an accurate statement of the quantity of contents of the package. Reasonable variations caused by loss or gain of moisture during the course of good distribution practice or by unavoidable deviations in good manufacturing practice will be recognized. Variations from stated quantity of contents shall not be unreasonably large." 21 CFR § 1.8b(q) (1976).

Since flour is a food under the FDCA, its manufacture is also subject to the provisions of the FPLA.... [T]he FPLA bans the distribution in commerce of any packaged commodity unless it complies with regulations

> "which shall provide that—

> "(2) The net quantity of contents (in terms of weight, measure, or numerical count) shall be separately and accurately stated in a uniform location upon the principal display panel of [the required] label." § 1453(a).

The FPLA also contains a saving clause which specifies that nothing in the FPLA "shall be construed to repeal, invalidate, or supersede" the FDCA. § 1460. Nothing in the FPLA explicitly permits any variation between stated weight and actual weight.

The *amici* States contend that since the FPLA does not allow any variations from stated weight, there is no difference between federal law governing labeling of flour and California law. The Court of Appeals, however, held that because of the saving clause, compliance with the FDCA, which does allow reasonable variations, satisfies the requirements of the FPLA.... We can only conclude that under the FPLA, as under the FDCA, a manufacturer of food is not subject to enforcement action for violation of the net-weight labeling requirements if the label accurately states the net weight, with allowance for the specified reasonable variations.

The FDCA contains no pre-emptive language. The FPLA, on the other hand, declares that

> "it is the express intent of Congress to supersede any and all laws of the States or political subdivisions thereof insofar as they may now or hereafter provide for the labeling of the net qua[nt]ity of contents of the package of any consumer commodity covered by this chapter which are less stringent than or require information different from the requirements of section 1453 of this title or regulations promulgated pursuant thereto." 15 U.S.C. § 1461....

The basis for the Court of Appeals' holding is unclear.... [T]he Court of Appeals may have found California's approach less stringent because the State takes no enforcement action against lots whose average net weight *exceeds* the weight stated on the label, even if that excess is not a reasonable variation attributable to a federally allowed cause.

We have some doubt that by pre-empting less stringent state laws, Congress intended to compel the States to expend scarce enforcement resources to prevent the sale of packages which contain more than the stated net weight. We do not have to reach that question, however, because in this respect California law apparently differs not at all from federal law, as applied.... Since neither jurisdiction is concerned with overweighting in the administration of its weights and measures laws, we cannot say that California's statutory lack of concern for that "problem" makes its laws less stringent than the federal.

... Respondents attribute to the ban on requiring different information a broad meaning, similar in scope to the pre-emption provision of the FMIA. They contend that since California law requires the label to state the minimum net weight, it requires "information different from" the federal laws, which demand an accurate statement with allowance for the specified reasonable variations. The legislative history, however, suggests that the statute expressly pre-empts as requiring "different information" only state laws governing net quantity labeling which impose requirements inconsistent with those imposed by federal law. Since it would be possible to comply with the state law without triggering federal enforcement action we conclude that the state requirement is not inconsistent with federal law. We therefore hold that

15 U.S.C. § 1461 does not pre-empt California's § 12211 as implemented by Art. 5.

That holding does not, however, resolve this case, for we still must determine whether the state law "stands as an obstacle to the accomplishment and execution of the full purposes and objectives of Congress." As Congress clearly stated, a major purpose of the FPLA is to facilitate value comparisons among similar products. Obviously, this goal cannot be accomplished unless packages that bear the same indicated weight in fact contain the same quantity of the product for which the consumer is paying. The significance of this requirement for our purposes results from the physical attributes of flour. . . .

The moisture content of flour does not remain constant after milling is completed. If the relative humidity of the atmosphere in which it is stored is greater than 60%, flour will gain moisture, and if the humidity is less than 60%, it will lose moisture. The federal net-weight labeling standard permits variations from stated weight caused by this gain or loss of moisture.

Packages that meet the federal labeling requirements and that have the same stated quantity of contents can be expected to contain the same amount of flour solids. Manufacturers will produce flour with a moisture content fixed by the requirements of the milling process. Since manufacturers have reason not to pack significantly more than is required and federal law prohibits underpacking, they will pack the same amount of this similarly composed flour into packages of any given size. Despite any changes in weight resulting from changes in moisture content during distribution, the packages will contain the same amount of flour solids when they reach the consumer. This identity of contents facilitates consumer value comparisons.

The State's refusal to permit reasonable weight variations resulting from loss of moisture during distribution produces a different effect. In order to be certain of meeting the California standard, a miller must ensure that loss of moisture during distribution will not bring the weight of the contents below the stated weight. Local millers, which serve a limited area, could do so by adjusting their packing practices to the specific humidity conditions of their region. For example, a miller in an area where the humidity is typically higher than 60% would not need to overpack at all. By contrast, a miller with a national marketing area would not know the destination of its flour when it was packaged and would therefore have to assume that the flour would lose weight during distribution. The national manufacturer, therefore, would have to overpack.

Similarly, manufacturers who distributed only in States that followed the federal standard would not be concerned with compensating for possible moisture loss during distribution. National manufacturers who did not exclude the nonconforming States from their marketing area, on the other hand, would have to overpack. Thus, as a result of the application of the California standard, consumers throughout the country who attempted to compare the value of identically labeled packages of flour would not be comparing packages which contained identical amounts of flour solids. Value comparisons which did not account for this difference—and there would be no way for the consumer to make the necessary calculations—would be misleading.

We therefore conclude that with respect to the millers' flour, enforcement of § 12211, as implemented by Art. 5, would prevent "the accomplishment and execution of the full purposes and objectives of Congress" in passing the FPLA. Under the Constitution, that result is impermissible, and the state law must yield to the federal. . . .

Mr. Justice REHNQUIST, with whom Mr. Justice STEWART joins, concurring in part and dissenting in part.

I agree that with respect to Rath's packaged bacon, § 12211 of the Cal. Bus. & Prof. Code and Art. 5 of 4 Cal. Admin. Code, c. 8, are pre-empted by the express pre-emptive provision of the Federal Meat Inspection Act. . . . I am unable to agree, however, with the implicit pre-emption the Court finds with respect to the flour. . . . .

. . . It is virtually impossible to say, as the Court does, that "neither the State nor the Federal Government is concerned with overweighting," and yet conclude that state-induced overweighting conflicts with a "value comparison" purpose, while, presumably, other overweighting does not. In viewing such a purpose to be sufficient to require pre-emption while the very purpose is ignored in practice by the administering federal agency reverses the normal presumption against finding pre-emption. The reasoning process which leads the Court to conclude that there is no express pre-emption leads me to conclude that there is no implied pre-emption. . . .

Similarly defective is the reasoning process by which the majority concludes that local millers could adjust their packaging practices to specific humidity conditions, while national millers could not, since the national millers "would not know the destination of [their] flour when it was packaged and would therefore have to assume that the flour would lose weight during distribution." This assumption, too, is unsupported by the record. We simply have no basis for concluding that national distributors do not know, or could not know through the exertion of some modicum of effort, where their flour will end up. . . .

The assumptions in the Court's opinion not only are insufficient to compel a finding of implied pre-emption, they suggest an approach to the question of pre-emption wholly at odds with that enunciated in *Florida Lime & Avocado Growers, Inc. v. Paul,* 373 U.S. 132 (1963). There, this Court . . . rejected a test which looked to the similarity of purposes, and noted instead that a manufacturer could have complied with both statutes by modifying procedures somewhat, which demonstrated that there was "no inevitable collision between the two schemes of regulation, despite the dissimilarity of the standards." Nothing has been shown to demonstrate that this conclusion is not equally justified in the instant case. . . .

NOTES

1. *General Mills.* In *General Mills, Inc. v. Furness,* 398 F. Supp. 151 (S.D.N.Y. 1974), *aff'd without opinion,* 508 F.2d 836 (2d Cir. 1975), the court upheld the practice by New York State officials of issuing a notice of violation for flour packages found underweight at the point of sale and allowing the company to defend by showing that the difference in weight was caused by moisture loss or some other unavoidable condition.

2. *Applicability of 1906 Act Precedents.* In an *amicus* brief in the *Rath* case, the Grocery Manufacturers of America contended that the cases decided under the 1906 Act were irrelevant to the issue of preemption under the 1938 FD&C Act:

> In several of the decisions, the Court upheld state requirements that applied only to foods held for retail sale and not contained in original unbroken packages that had been shipped in interstate commerce. These decisions were based in part on the jurisdictional provisions of the 1906 Act (which reached only goods that remained "unloaded, unsold, or in original unbroken packages" after interstate shipment) and on the limited concept of the Commerce power from which those provisions were derived. That jurisdictional limitation was eliminated in the 1938 Act....
>
> In *McDermott v. Wisconsin,* the Court invalidated a state regulation that affected an aspect of food labeling that was affirmatively regulated by the 1906 Act.... The Court's decision cannot be explained as an example of irreconcilable conflict between state and federal law, since the labeling requirement imposed by state law was also permitted under the federal statute....
>
> The *Savage* and *Corn Products* decisions ... rested on a determination that the 1906 Act did not "cover the entire field" of food labeling, and that states remained free to regulate those aspects of food labeling not touched by the federal law. The *McDermott* decision recognized, however, that, as to those aspects of food labeling for which the federal statute established an affirmative regulatory scheme, it left no room for supplementary state requirements, even though they might not conflict irreconcilably with requirements imposed under federal law.
>
> ... [T]he 1938 Act represented a major departure from the essentially "negative" regulatory scheme adopted by the 1906 Act. The 1938 Act established the basis for a comprehensive system of federal regulations that "cover the entire ground" of food labeling. No "gaps" remain for supplementary state regulations that do not in some manner interfere with the federal system....

COSMETIC, TOILETRY AND FRAGRANCE ASS'N, INC. v. MINNESOTA

United States District Court, District of Minnesota, 1977.
440 F. Supp. 1216, *aff'd per curiam,* 575 F.2d 1256.

DEVITT, Chief Judge.

The challenged statute, enacted on May 21, 1977, requires that any pressurized container employing a saturated chlorofluorocarbon propellant sold at wholesale within Minnesota on or after October 31, 1977 shall display on its front panel the following warning:

> Warning: Contains a chlorofluorocarbon that may harm the public health and environment by reducing ozone in the upper atmosphere.

This warning is a preparatory step toward the total [state] ban of such propellants effective July 1, 1979. This procedure parallels that taken by the United States Food and Drug Administration (FDA) in its attempt to regulate chlorofluorocarbon propellants for cosmetics under the authority of the Food, Drug, and Cosmetic Act of 1938. On April 26, 1977, the FDA promulgated a regulation which requires a warning identical to that required by the challenged statute, 42 F.R. 22033 (1977), and on May 10, 1977 proposed a rule banning such propellants after April 15, 1979, 42 F.R. 24541 (1977)....

The most important distinctions between the FDA regulation and the challenged statute are with regard to the placement of the warning. The federal rule requires that the warning ".... appear on an appropriate panel with such prominence and conspicuousness as to render it likely to be read and understood by ordinary individuals under normal conditions of purchase." The Minnesota statute unequivocally states that the warning shall appear on the front panel. Furthermore, the regulation takes the functional approach of allowing the warning to be placed where it will most effectively trigger purchaser awareness, while the statute stipulates that the warning appear on the immediate container....

Plaintiffs base their constitutional attack on two separate theories —(1) that state legislation in the area of aerosol product labeling has been pre-empted by federal regulation in this field and is therefore unconstitutional under the Supremacy Clause of the United States Constitution; and (2) that the statute effects an unreasonable burden on interstate commerce violative of the Commerce Clause. U.S. Const., art. I, § 8, cl. 3.... [N]either party has been able to point to any aspect of the statute or to any legislative history which sheds light on the question of congressional intent to pre-empt state regulation in the enactment of the Food, Drug, and Cosmetic Act of 1938....

Historically, except in rather limited circumstances, the FDA has enforced the requirements of the Food, Drug, and Cosmetic Act by promulgating non-binding interpretative regulations to be applied on a case-by-case, adjudicatory basis. Only in recent years has the agency begun to issue substantive regulations under its rule-making authority.... In fact, the FDA's authority to issue such regulations has been clearly recognized only very recently.

This history of case-by-case enforcement reasonably leads to the inference that in 1938, Congress viewed pre-emption in the food, drug, and cosmetic field, if it thought about it at all, as a rather limited doctrine. That is, pre-emption would occur in a situation where the FDA was seeking to enforce an interpretative rule against a particular product in a specific administrative adjudicatory proceeding while a state was attempting to enforce its rules against the same product. This is a far cry from the type of pre-emption at issue here—that by virtue of legislative rules promulgated by the FDA, state activity in the area regulated is barred. It is only in recent years that this species of "administrative pre-emption" has become possible. Thus, the court concludes that a determination of whether preemptive intent existed in 1938 is irrelevant to the case at bar. . . .

. . . This court is not prepared to say that sovereigns other than the federal government are barred from regulating product labeling in general, that a state or locality cannot require labels or warnings regarding problems which have not been addressed by the federal government. However, when federal agencies have perceived a specific risk and have required labeling to alleviate that risk, the court feels that a state's freedom to require other than identical labeling with respect to that risk is precluded. This is precisely what has occurred in this case. . . .

. . . [A] court must specifically delineate the contours of the operative field of federal regulation in examining the pervasiveness question. In this instance, the court defines the field generally as that of consumer product labeling with the caveat that pre-emption problems do not arise until the responsible federal agencies act with respect to a specific regulatory goal. For the foregoing reasons, the court finds that in the area of ozone deterioration warnings, federal action has been so pervasive as to resolve this factor in favor of a preliminary finding of pre-emption. . . .

Next, the court must consider whether the nature of consumer product labeling requires exclusive federal regulation in order to achieve uniformity vital to national interests. Plaintiffs quote several statements by the Commissioner of the FDA which emphasize the need for a uniform national warning of the ozone deterioration risk posed by the use of chlorofluorocarbons. 42 F.R. 22026 (1977). These statements support the common sense notion that in an economy where goods are distributed on a national level, a subordinate unit of government should not be able to require that an interstate producer create special packaging or manufacture a special product for a limited distribution area once the federal government has acted with regard to the interest sought to be furthered by the subordinate entity's action. . . . Therefore, the court concludes that uniformity in labeling is required to meet the dual national goal of the most effective warning at the least possible cost.

. . . When the aerosol container appears on the retail shelves within a larger package, the statute's requirement that the warning appear on the immediate container as opposed to the regulations' mandate that it be placed on the container's package raises a practical and philosophical conflict. This conflict is not merely textual, it appears to be the product of differing policy goals—use awareness and purchase awareness. A consumer who purchases a packaged container with only the container bearing the warning is not aware of the chlorofluorocarbon risk until the container is removed for use. The same consumer will become aware of the risk at the point of purchase if the product conforms to the federal requirement of conspicuousness to the normal purchaser. It is no answer to say that the manufacturer can comply with both goals and both requirements by placing a warning on the package and on the container. The responsible administrative agency has determined that the federal policy is purchase awareness and that a policy of use awareness " . . . would require more time and expense and thus cause more disruption." The court concludes that Minnesota's container labeling requirement is an obstacle to full effectuation of the federal purpose.

When the statutory front labeling requirement is considered apart from the immediate container requirement, different considerations emerge. Frontal warnings on aerosol products which are not retailed in a larger package would effectuate the federal policy of purchase awareness. However, the FDA considered the advisability of front labeling and in its informed discretion, rejected such a standard in favor of its functionally oriented requirement. Defendants' suggestion that both mandates can be fulfilled by placing the warning on the front of the container is contrary to this administrative determination. An attempt by this court to "second guess" the FDA's decision, as defendants seemingly desire, would violate the judicial function in resolving the pre-emption question. The FDA presumably analyzed the countervailing policy considerations and expressly rejected the alternative proposed by defendants. That action was part of a concerted and pervasive federal regulatory scheme and was in furtherance of a federal interest requiring uniformity. The court's inquiry can go no further. . . .

For the foregoing reasons, the court finds that plaintiffs have demonstrated a substantial probability of success at trial with regard to their contention that Minnesota Laws 1977, ch. 373, § 1, subd. 2 is unconstitutional under the Supremacy Clause of the United States Constitution. . . .

PREEMPTION UNDER THE FHSA

In *Chemical Specialties Mfrs. Ass'n, Inc. v. Clark,* 482 F.2d 325 (5th Cir. 1973), a Dade County, Florida, ordinance requiring that any detergent bear a label listing the ingredients in descending order of predominance was held expressly preempted by section 18 of the Federal Hazardous Substances Act, 15 U.S.C. § 1261, even though there was no conflict between requirements. *Compare Procter & Gamble Co. v. City of Chicago,* 509 F.2d 69 (7th Cir.), *cert. denied,* 421 U.S. 978 (1975) (upholding a Chicago ordinance banning phosphate detergents).

GROCERY MFRS. OF AMERICA, INC. v. GERACE

United States Court of Appeals, Second Circuit, 1985.
755 F.2d 993.

MESKILL, Circuit Judge:

This is an appeal from a judgment entered in the United States District Court for the Southern District of New York, Duffy, J., granting the motion of plaintiff-appellee Grocery Manufacturers of America (GMA) for preliminary and permanent injunctive relief. The district court, in a decision reported at 581 F. Supp. 658 (S.D.N.Y. 1984), enjoined the enforcement of N.Y. Agric. & Mkts. Law § 63 (section 63), which it found invalid on federal preemption and Commerce Clause grounds. We affirm in part and reverse in part.

This litigation involves state and federal regulatory schemes that require descriptive labeling of cheese alternatives: products composed wholly or partly of food that looks, smells and tastes like cheese, but is not, in fact, cheese. The major focus of the dispute concerns the use and meaning of the modifier "imitation" as applied to these products. A brief discussion of cheese-making is in order.

Real cheese is made from milk with its milkfat content intact. Cheese alternatives may be made in two ways. One method begins with either milk from which the milkfat has been removed or casein, natural milk protein extracted from milk. The altered milk or casein is then combined with vegetable oil, which substitutes for milkfat. This type of alternative cheese is lower in calories and cholesterol than real cheese. It sells at prices fifty to sixty percent lower than real cheese. The other type of alternative cheese is chemically similar to real cheese but is made wholly or in part with substitute dairy products. This is presumably even less expensive to manufacture than the former. Vitamins and minerals may be added to raise the nutritional level of alternative cheese.

Alleging that New York's imitation cheese law was in conflict with federal labeling requirements and with the Commerce Clause, GMA commenced this litigation.... New York counterclaimed and ... sought to have 21 C.F.R. § 101.3 (1984), the federal regulation that defines the term "imitation" for purposes of food package labeling, declared invalid.

The text of New York's section 63, enacted in 1982, ... requires that alternative cheese products feature labels that display prominently the descriptive term "imitation." It also directs that anyone who sells prepared foods containing cheese alternatives, whether for carry out or for consumption on the premises, must display a sign that discloses in three inch letters those foods that contain "imitation cheese." Further, it provides that restaurant menus must append the words "contains imitation cheese" to the item designation of any offering containing alternative cheese. And, finally, alternative cheese products available for use by customers on the premises—as, for example, something resembling grated parmesan—must be conspicuously labeled as "imitation cheese." Section 63 does not define imitation. The regulations promulgated pursuant to the statute define "imitation cheese" as any food simulating "cheese" as described or standardized by regulation but failing to meet that description or standard. Neither the statute nor any of its regulations is concerned with nutritional values.

The federal scheme implicated here, which establishes the requisite information content of package labels for foods shipped in interstate commerce, involves three federal statutes and two federal agencies.... [The court summarized the FDA and USDA requirements for labeling substitute and imitation foods, pp. 149–54 *supra*.]

The preemptive effect of the FDCA depends entirely on whether the FDA's definition of imitation is valid and therefore entitled to our deference. Characterizing 21 C.F.R. § 101.3(e) as an attempt to administratively amend the FDCA, New York argues that we should disregard the regulation and give the word imitation its ordinary meaning.... New York correctly notes that the FDA's regulatory definition of imitation is at odds with the judicial gloss placed on the term....

If we were addressing the validity of the FDA regulation in or about 1973, the year of its promulgation, we might be inclined to reject it. But the regulation has been in effect for eleven years. Congress' failure during this period to alter the relevant statutory language or to otherwise condemn the regulatory definition, while not a fail-safe guide, allows us at least to infer that it has acquiesced in the FDA's construction.... The FDA's definition of imitation is entitled to our deference.

Thus, as applied to alternative cheese, the New York labeling scheme is in direct conflict with its federal counterpart. Including the term "imitation" on the label of a nutritionally superior alternative cheese in order to comply with New York law, would render the product misbranded under federal law. Compliance with both the state and federal requirements is impossible. To the extent that it attempts to regulate the labeling of alternative cheese, the New York law is preempted.

Whether the New York law as applied to meat and poultry products that contain alternative cheese is also preempted requires us to determine whether the reach of the preemption provisions of the [Federal Meat Inspection Act] and the [Poultry Products Inspection Act] extends to the New York labeling requirements.....

Even if it should be classified as an interpretive rule or a statement of general policy, rather than as a formal rule adopted via adjudication, the USDA's practice of following the FDA definition of imitation when reviewing meat and poultry product labels is valid. The distinctions between formal rules and interpretive rules or general statements of policy are often vague. But we need not explore the nuances. If the USDA's practice is merely interpretive, it is a reasonable interpretation and therefore entitled to judicial respect.... Consequently, the New

York requirements are "different from" the federal requirements, as administered, and they are therefore preempted.

Notwithstanding the conflict created by its use of "imitation," the New York law imposes other labeling requirements that are "in addition to[ ] or different than" the federal requirements.... New York's section 63 mandates the precise size of the letters in and relative location of the word "imitation" on package labels. These requirements do not comport exactly with the federal specifications. Therefore, the state requirements are preempted.

Our preemption holdings make it unnecessary for us to determine whether the New York labeling provisions are invalid under the Commerce Clause as well. Accordingly, we direct our Commerce Clause analysis only to the New York sign, menu and container provisions, subsections 3, 4 and 5 of section 63....

The district court correctly determined that the New York law regulates evenhandedly. The state requirements do not distinguish between alternative cheese products from in-state manufacturers and those from out-of-state manufacturers. And, to the extent that they indirectly advantage the dairy industry, that effect is not necessarily limited to in-state dairy producers.

Further, the local interest which the New York scheme was designed to protect is a legitimate one. States have traditionally acted to protect consumers by regulating foods produced and/or marketed within their borders. Under federal law, foods packaged for wholesale or retail marketing are labeled to indicate that they fit into one of three categories: real cheese, alternative cheese that meets or exceeds federal nutritional guidelines or alternative cheese that falls below nutritional guidelines. New York has determined that patrons of food service establishments and restaurants—heretofore wholly uninformed as to the composition of any cheese-like substance served to them—are entitled to know at least whether they are buying real cheese or a cheese alternative. The record shows that health and nutrition professionals strongly disagree about the intrinsic value of the federal nutritional guidelines applied to alternative cheese products.... The very existence of this controversy persuades us that New York's nutritional concerns are not unreasonable. In addition to promoting those concerns, the state requirements are intended to prevent deception and unfair competition, to promote honesty and fair dealing and to permit consumers to clearly discern whether they are buying real cheese or not. We believe that the sign, menu and container provisions effectuate a legitimate, local public purpose.

The final step of our Commerce Clause analysis requires us to balance the local interest served against the burden imposed on interstate commerce by the disputed sections. Interestingly, the federal government did not join in GMA's challenge to the sign, menu and container provisions. Neither did the operators of any restaurants or food service establishments, though they are surely the persons most directly affected by these provisions....

The New York sign, menu and container provisions do not produce such an inaccurate or misleading result that they fail to serve a legitimate state purpose. And although complying with the sign posting requirement will certainly not enhance the decor of most restaurants, that negative is not a violation of the Commerce Clause. Indeed, consumers seeking low cholesterol foods may be benefited by the prominence of the signs. The disputed provisions here are the result of legislative choices. The arguments against the provisions "relate[ ] to the wisdom of the statute, not to its burden on commerce." That wisdom is better reconsidered in Albany than Foley Square.....

NOTES

1. *California Proposition 65.* In a letter dated August 28, 1987 FDA Commissioner Young urged California Governor George Deukmejian to interpret Proposition 65, Note 4 p. 963 *supra*, to recognize that FDA-regulated products present no significant risk and thus are exempt from the state's warning requirement. In the alternative, Commissioner Young importuned:

> [W]e urge you to consider implementing the warning requirements through means appropriate to sale only within California, rather than requiring warnings on the products themselves which would directly affect interstate commerce as well. In this way, California consumers could be notified of the presence of even trace amounts of carcinogens or reproductive toxicants without requiring that firms doing business in interstate commerce create special labels just for products sold in California. We are concerned that creation of such special labels could cause a serious logistical problem that also might create serious public health problems. For example, the consumer may be confused when confronted by warning labels on large numbers of products and may be less likely to heed those warnings that have been carefully designed by FDA, Congress, and your State to protect against more significant and possibly more immediate harm.

2. *Other Recent Cases. Lever Brothers Co. v. Maurer,* 712 F. Supp. 645 (S.D. Ohio 1989), invalidated, as preempted by the FD&C Act and the Commerce Clause, a state statute precluding use of the word "butter" in the labeling of any substitute for butter. In *Committee for Accurate Labeling and Marketing v. Brownback,* 665 F. Supp. 880 (D. Kan. 1987), the court held that the Kansas Artificial Dairy Products Act, which required any "artificial" dairy product to be labeled as such, was preempted under the Supremacy Clause because it stood as an obstacle to the accomplishment of the FDA regulation of food labeling generally and the definition of an imitation food in particular. *Compare Grocery Mfrs. of America, Inc. v. Department of Public Health,* 379 Mass. 70, 393 N.E.2d 881 (1979), which held that a state law requiring food labels to disclose "last date of use" or "pull date" was not preempted because the FD&C Act contained no provision relating to open date labeling and meat products were specifically excluded from the state requirement. In an unusual case, an animal welfare organization brought suit against a veal producer to require that retail consumers be informed about the assertedly cruel manner in which veal calves are raised. The court held that the plaintiff's claims were preempted by FDA's and USDA's comprehensive Federal regulation of animal

feed, animal drugs, and meat. *Animal Legal Defense Fund Boston, Inc. v. Provimi Veal Corp.*, 626 F. Supp. 278 (D. Mass.), *aff'd without opinion*, 802 F.2d 440 (1st Cir. 1986).

3. *Pennsylvania Bakery Product Legend.* One of the best-known food labeling provisions in the United States is 43 Pennsylvania Statutes § 405, which requires every "bakery product" to bear the well-recognized "Registered with Pennsylvania Department of Agriculture" legend in full text or an approved abbreviated form. Enacted in 1933, this statute has never been judicially challenged. What would happen if all 50 states followed Pennsylvania's example?

4. *FDA Diffidence.* Because FDA works closely with state food and drug officials and often depends upon their resources to enforce the law, the agency has traditionally avoided any public position on Federal preemption. Only in *Rath Packing*, p. 1009 *supra*, and in *Gerace*, p. 1018 *supra*, has FDA participated urging preemption.

5. *Commentary.* For an insightful analysis of the relative roles of Federal and state food regulation during the early 1980s, *see* Cobb, *Federal–State–Local Food Regulation: View from a Chameleon*, 49 Q. Bull. AFDO 85 (1985).

6. *Uniformity in Australia.* In Australia, regulation of food and drugs has traditionally been the prerogative of the six states rather than the federal government. Convinced at last of "the considerable problems that this fragmented state food regulation system has caused," Australian authorities have recently undertaken a program to adopt uniform national regulatory standards. Wright, *The Development of Food Standards in Australia—An Aussie Recipe for Cooperative Federalism*, 44 FDC L.J. 251 (1989).

HILLSBOROUGH COUNTY v. AUTOMATED MEDICAL LABORATORIES, INC.

Supreme Court of the United States, 1985.
471 U.S. 707.

JUSTICE MARSHALL delivered the opinion of the Court.

The question presented is whether the federal regulations governing the collection of blood plasma from paid donors pre-empt certain local ordinances. Appellee Automated Medical Laboratories, Inc., is a Florida corporation that operates, through subsidiaries, eight blood plasma centers in the United States. One of the centers, Tampa Plasma Corporation (TPC), is located in Hillsborough County, Florida. Appellee's plasma centers collect blood plasma from donors by employing a procedure called plasmapheresis.... Appellee sells the plasma to pharmaceutical manufacturers.

Vendors of blood products, such as TPC, are subject to federal supervision. Under § 351(a) of the Public Health Service Act, such vendors must be licensed by the Secretary of Health and Human Services (HHS). Licenses are issued only on a showing that the vendor's establishment and blood products meet certain safety, purity, and potency standards established by the Secretary. HHS is authorized to inspect such establishments for compliance. Pursuant to § 351 of the Act, the Food and Drug Administration (FDA), as the designee of the Secretary, has established standards for the collection of plasma....

In 1980, Hillsborough County adopted Ordinances 80–11 and 80–12.... Ordinance 80–12 establishes a countywide identification system, which requires all potential donors to obtain from the County Health Department an identification card, valid for six months, that may be used only at the plasmapheresis center specified on the card. The ordinance incorporates by reference the FDA's blood plasma regulations, but also imposes donor testing and recordkeeping requirements beyond those contained in the federal regulations. Specifically, the ordinance requires that donors be tested for hepatitis prior to registration, that they donate at only one center, and that they be given a breath analysis for alcohol content before each plasma donation....

In December 1981, appellee filed suit in the United States District Court for the Middle District of Florida, challenging the constitutionality of the ordinances and their implementing regulations. Appellee argued primarily that the ordinances violated the Supremacy Clause, the Commerce Clause, and the Fourteenth Amendment's Equal Protection Clause.....

In arguing that the Hillsborough County ordinances and regulations are pre-empted, appellee faces an uphill battle. The first hurdle that appellee must overcome is the FDA's statement, when it promulgated the plasmapheresis regulations in 1973, that it did not intend its regulations to be exclusive. In response to comments expressing concern that the regulations governing the licensing of plasmapheresis facilities "would pre-empt State and local laws governing plasmapheresis," the FDA explained in a statement accompanying the regulations that "[t]hese regulations are not intended to usurp the powers of State or local authorities to regulate plasmapheresis procedures in their localities."

The question whether the regulation of an entire field has been reserved by the Federal Government is, essentially, a question of ascertaining the intent underlying the federal scheme. In this case, appellee concedes that neither Congress nor the FDA expressly pre-empted state and local regulation of plasmapheresis. Thus, if the county ordinances challenged here are to fail they must do so either because Congress or the FDA *implicitly* pre-empted the whole field of plasmapheresis regulation, or because particular provisions in the local ordinances conflict with the federal scheme. According to appellee, two separate factors support the inference of a federal intent to pre-empt the whole field: the pervasiveness of the FDA's regulations and the dominance of the federal interest in this area. Appellee also argues that the challenged ordinances reduce the number of plasma donors, and that this effect conflicts with the congressional goal of ensuring an adequate supply of plasma.

The FDA's statement is dispositive on the question of implicit intent to pre-empt unless either the agency's position is inconsistent with clearly expressed congressional intent, or subsequent developments reveal a change in that position. Given appellee's first argument for implicit pre-emption—that the comprehensiveness of the FDA's regulations evinces an intent to pre-empt—any pre-emptive effect must result from the change since 1973 in the comprehensiveness of the federal regulations. To prevail on its second argument for implicit pre-emption—the dominance of the federal interest in plasmapheresis regulation—appellee must show either that this interest became more compelling since 1973, or that, in 1973, the FDA seriously underestimated the federal interest in plasmapheresis regulation.

The second obstacle in appellee's path is the presumption that state or local regulation of matters related to health and safety is not invalidated under the Supremacy Clause. Through the challenged ordinances, Hillsborough County has attempted to protect the health of its plasma donors by preventing them from donating too frequently. It also has attempted to ensure the quality of the plasma collected so as to protect, in turn, the recipients of such plasma. "Where ... the field that Congress is said to have pre-empted has been traditionally occupied by the States 'we start with the assumption that the historic police powers of the States were not to be superseded by the Federal Act unless that was the clear and manifest purpose of Congress.'" Of course, the same principles apply where, as here, the field is said to have been pre-empted by an agency, acting pursuant to congressional delegation. Appellee must thus present a showing of implicit pre-emption of the whole field, or of a conflict between a particular local provision and the federal scheme, that is strong enough to overcome the presumption that state and local regulation of health and safety matters can constitutionally coexist with federal regulation.

Given the clear indication of the FDA's intention *not to pre-empt* and the deference with which we must review the challenged ordinances, we conclude that these ordinances are not pre-empted by the federal scheme.

We reject the argument that an intent to pre-empt may be inferred from the comprehensiveness of the FDA's regulations at issue here.... The FDA has not indicated that the new regulations affected its disavowal in 1973 of any intent to pre-empt state and local regulation, and the fact that the federal scheme was expanded to reach other uses of plasma does not cast doubt on the continued validity of that disavowal. Indeed, even in the absence of the 1973 statement, the comprehensiveness of the FDA's regulations would not justify pre-emption....

We are even more reluctant to infer pre-emption from the comprehensiveness of regulations than from the comprehensiveness of statutes. As a result of their specialized functions, agencies normally deal with problems in far more detail than does Congress. To infer pre-emption whenever an agency deals with a problem comprehensively is virtually tantamount to saying that whenever a federal agency decides to step into a field, its regulations will be exclusive. Such a rule, of course, would be inconsistent with the federal-state balance embodied in our Supremacy Clause jurisprudence.

Moreover, because agencies normally address problems in a detailed manner and can speak through a variety of means, including regulations, preambles, interpretive statements, and responses to comments, we can expect that they will make their intentions clear if they intend for their regulations to be exclusive. Thus, if an agency does not speak to the question of pre-emption, we will pause before saying that the mere volume and complexity of its regulations indicate that the agency did in fact intend to pre-empt. Given the presumption that state and local regulation related to matters of health and safety can normally coexist with federal regulations, we will seldom infer, solely from the comprehensiveness of federal regulations, an intent to pre-empt in its entirety a field related to health and safety....

Appellee's second argument for pre-emption of the whole field of plasmapheresis regulation is that an intent to pre-empt can be inferred from the dominant federal interest in this field. We are unpersuaded by the argument. Undoubtedly, every subject that merits congressional legislation is, by definition, a subject of national concern. That cannot mean, however, that every federal statute ousts all related state law. Neither does the Supremacy Clause require us to rank congressional enactments in order of "importance" and hold that, for those at the top of the scale, federal regulation must be exclusive.

Instead, we must look for special features warranting pre-emption. Our case law provides us with clear standards to guide our inquiry in this area. For example, in the seminal case of *Hines v. Davidowitz,* the Court inferred an intent to pre-empt from the dominance of the federal interest in foreign affairs because "the supremacy of the national power in the general field of foreign affairs ... is made clear by the Constitution," and the regulation of that field is "intimately blended and intertwined with responsibilities of the national government." Needless to say, those factors are absent here. Rather, as we have stated, the regulation of health and safety matters is primarily, and historically, a matter of local concern.

There is also no merit in appellee's reliance on the National Blood Policy as an indication of the dominance of the federal interest in this area. Nothing in that policy takes plasma regulation out of the health-and-safety category and converts it into an area of overriding national concern.

Appellee's final argument is that even if the regulations are not comprehensive enough and the federal interest is not dominant enough to pre-empt the entire field of plasmapheresis regulation, the Hillsborough County ordinances must be struck down because they conflict with the federal scheme. Appellee argues principally that the challenged ordinances impose on plasma centers and donors requirements more stringent than those imposed by the federal regulations, and therefore that they present a serious obstacle to the federal goal of ensuring an "adequate supply of plasma." We find this concern too speculative to support pre-emption.... More importantly, even if the Hillsborough County ordinances had, in fact, reduced the supply of plasma in that county, it would not necessarily follow that they interfere with the federal goal of maintaining an adequate supply of plasma....

Finally, the FDA possesses the authority to promulgate regulations pre-empting local legislation that imperils the supply of plasma and can do so with relative ease. Moreover, the agency can be expected to monitor, on a continuing basis, the effects on the federal program of local requirements. Thus, since the agency has not suggested that the county ordinances interfere with federal goals, we are reluctant in the absence of strong evidence to find a threat to the federal goal of ensuring sufficient plasma.

Our analysis would be somewhat different had Congress not delegated to the FDA the administration of the federal program. Congress, unlike an agency, normally does not follow, years after the enactment of federal legislation, the effects of external factors on the goals that the federal legislation sought to promote. Moreover, it is more difficult for Congress to make its intentions known—for example by amending a statute—than it is for an agency to amend its regulations or to otherwise indicate its position.

In summary, given the findings of the District Court, the lack of any evidence in the record of a threat to the "adequacy" of the plasma supply, and the significance that we attach to the lack of a statement by the FDA, we conclude that the Hillsborough County requirements do not imperil the federal goal of ensuring sufficient plasma....

NOTES

1. *State Regulation of Blood Products.* On remand, the Hillsborough ordinances were upheld. *Immuno International, A.G. v. Hillsborough County, Florida*, 775 F. 2d 1430 (11th Cir. 1985). *Compare State v. Interstate Blood Bank, Inc.*, 65 Wis.2d 482, 222 N.W.2d 912 (1974), which overturned the defendant's conviction for unlawfully operating a commercial blood bank, declaring Wisconsin's statute unconstitutional under the Commerce and Supremacy Clauses. While conceding that protecting the health of both donors and recipients was a legitimate objective of the police power, the court held that the statute unduly burdened interstate commerce, because other similarly federally licensed blood banks relied on defendant to supply blood interstate and the purpose of federal regulations was also to insure the safety, purity and potency of the product.

> ... [W]hen the federal government has undertaken a comprehensive regulatory and licensing system of an occupation engaged in interstate commerce for a particular purpose, *i.e.*, to insure the safety, potency, and purity of a particular product, the states are preempted

from prohibiting the same occupation as a means of accomplishing the same purposes.

See also Samuels v. Health & Hospital Corp. of the City of New York, 432 F. Supp. 1283 (S.D.N.Y. 1977), holding that classification of blood as a "drug" under the FD&C Act does not preempt a different classification for purposes of state product liability law.

2. *Agency Intention.* In other opinions the Supreme Court has emphasized that, relying upon *United States v. Shimer,* 367 U.S. 374 (1961), an agency's intent to preempt state regulation will usually be decisive. *E.g., City of New York v. FCC,* 486 U.S. 57, 64 (1988); *Capital Cities Cable, Inc. v. Crisp,* 467 U.S. 691, 698–700 (1984); *Fidelity Federal Savings & Loan Association v. de la Cuesta,* 458 U.S. 141, 152–54 (1982).

3. *Scope of Agency Preemption.* Professor Susan Bartlett Foote argues that Federal agencies like FDA should preempt only product design/performance standards, minimum safety requirements, and requirements applicable to interstate packaging, and should leave the states free to impose more stringent safety requirements, local labeling requirements and other conditions of sale, and restrictions on use (including a ban). Foote, *Administrative Preemption: An Experiment in Regulatory Federalism,* 70 Va. L. Rev. 1429 (1984). If FDA embraced this approach and every state were to adopt the permitted controls, what would be the impact on national marketing of food and drugs?

4. *Pursuing Uniformity in the EC.* While the United States tolerates substantial local variation in the regulation of food and drugs, the European Community has taken major steps to require uniform regulation among its member countries by 1992. To break down historical impediments to free trade among member nations, the EC has launched an impressive number of programs to eliminate physical, technical, and fiscal barriers by 1992. EC, COMPLETING THE INTERNAL MARKET: A WHITE PAPER FROM THE COMMISSION TO THE EUROPEAN COUNCIL (June 1985). If the EC succeeds, it will achieve a fully unified internal market that will comprise some 320 million people.

In March 1987, the EC Court of Justice invalidated West German legislation that required all imported beer to meet its beer purity standard, derived from a German Royal Decree of 1516, as an illegal restriction on trade under the EEC Treaty of Rome. *See* Note, *The Free Movement of Goods and Regulation for Public Health and Consumer Protection in the EEC: The West German "Beer Purity" Case,* 28 Va. J. Int'l L. 753 (1988), which discusses EC Court of Justice decisions relating to food and drug regulation.

5. *Preemption in Other Contexts.* For analyses of the application of preemption principles in other areas of Federal regulation, *see* Hill, *Preemption of State Common Law Remedies by Federal Environmental Statutes:* International Paper Co. v. Ouellette, 14 Ecology L.Q. 541 (1987); Howarth, *Preemption and Punitive Damages: The Conflict Continues under FIFRA,* 136 U. Pa. L. Rev. 1301 (1988); Pierce, *Regulation, Deregulation, Federalism, and Administrative Law: Agency Power to Preempt State Regulation,* 46 U. Pitt. L. Rev. 607 (1985); Note, *The Extent of OSHA Preemption of State Hazard Reporting Requirements,* 88 Colum. L. Rev. 630 (1988); Note, *Getting Away with Murder: Federal OSHA Preemption of State Criminal Prosecutions for Industrial Accidents,* 101 Harv. L. Rev. 535 (1987).

D. ADMINISTRATIVE PREEMPTION BY FDA

Beginning in the late 1970s, the California Department of Health proposed to require that all nonprescription drugs include a warning that the safety of the drug during pregnancy or nursing is unknown, unless the manufacturer secured an exemption by submitting substantial evidence that the warning was not needed. On four occasions, FDA opposed issuance of the proposed regulation. The California Office of Administrative Law disapproved the regulation, but California Governor Brown overruled that decision in October 1981. The matter was then resolved in California by the enactment of an amendment to Section 10381 of the California Health and Safety Code which requires any nonprescription drug intended for systemic absorption into the human body to include the following warning on the label:

> Caution: If pregnant or nursing a baby, consult your physician or pharmacist before using this product.

The effective date of this statute was November 18, 1982.

In 47 Fed. Reg. 39470 (September 7, 1982), FDA proposed a similar warning for all systemically absorbed nonprescription drugs. The agency's preamble invited comments on the preemptive effect the proposed warning should have on state labeling requirements such as the California law. Three months later, FDA issued the following final regulation.

PREGNANT OR NURSING WOMEN; AMENDMENT OF LABELING REQUIREMENTS FOR OVER–THE COUNTER HUMAN DRUGS

47 Federal Register 54750 (December 3, 1982).

The Food and Drug Administration (FDA) is amending the general drug labeling provisions to include a warning concerning the use by pregnant or nursing women of over-the-counter (OTC) drugs intended for systemic absorption....

Several comments that were submitted in response to the agency's invitation for comments on the preemptive effect the FDA warning would have on the California and other similar State OTC drug labeling requirements supported FDA's view that a Federal pregnancy-nursing warning requirement would preempt State pregnancy-nursing warnings.... Some comments took a more expansive view of the preemptive effects of the proposal, stating that all State OTC drug labeling requirements of any type either already were preempted by virtue of FDA's pervasive regulation of OTC drugs or could be preempted were FDA to issue a statement of its intention to preempt.

A comment submitted by the California Department of Health Services, however, opposed the statements in the proposal on the preemptive effects of the FDA warning on general legal and policy grounds.... The Federal Food, Drug, and Cosmetic Act does not expressly preempt State activity relating to OTC drug labeling. Therefore, in determining whether FDA's pregnancy-nursing warning preempts California's warning, the doctrine of implied preemption must be applied. As stated in the proposed rule, a single national pregnancy-nursing warning with a specified text is necessary to ensure that OTC drugs are used safely and for their intended purposes. A single national warning will help ensure that consumers receive clear, unambiguous, and consistent information on the labeling of OTC drugs concerning use by pregnant or nursing women. Differing State requirements could conflict with the Federal warning, cause confusion to consumers, and otherwise weaken the Federal warning. FDA believes that differing State OTC drug pregnancy-nursing warning requirements would prevent accomplishment of the full purpose and objectives of the agency in issuing the regulation and that, under the doctrine of implied preemption, these State requirements are preempted by the regulation as a matter of law.

As noted in the proposal, the California warning allows for the use of pregnancy-nursing warnings that are "substantially similar" to the California requirement. In view of comments made by the California Department of Health Services, the FDA warning would appear to meet the California "substantially similar" exception. Therefore, under these circumstances, the issue appears to be academic: manufacturers who use the FDA warning would also be in compliance with the California requirement.

FDA shares the concerns of the comments that States may elect to regulate aspects of OTC drug labeling other than pregnancy-nursing warnings. The agency is concerned that a proliferation of such State requirements may weaken FDA's efforts to develop comprehensive national labeling and other requirements for OTC drugs. The current regulation, however, is intended to apply only to one aspect of OTC drug labeling: pregnancy-nursing warnings. FDA will monitor future State labeling requirements to determine whether further action is necessary.

The California warning requirement becomes effective on November 18, 1982. FDA regards the California requirement as preempted as of the date of publication of this regulation....

NOTES

1. *Tamper-Resistant Packaging.* After FDA published its proposal but before it promulgated this final regulation, the agency was forced to confront the need for tamper-resistant packaging requirements as a result of the purposeful cyanide contamination of Extra-Strength Tylenol capsules in Chicago. The agency promulgated its tamper-resistant packaging requirements in final form, together with the following determination:

FDA intends that the regulations issued in this document preempt State and local packaging requirements that are not identical to it in all respects, including those relating to the use of alternative tamper-resistant packaging systems, the coverage of the regulations within the product categories addressed, the label statement alternating [sic] consumers, exemptions, and effective dates.

47 Fed. Reg. 50442, 50447–48 (November 5, 1982).

2. *Reye Syndrome Warning.* In 50 Fed. Reg. 51400 (December 17, 1985), FDA proposed to require that the labeling of oral nonprescription aspirin products bear a warning about the risk of Reye syndrome. In response to comments, the agency announced in the preamble to the final regulation that "FDA intends that the regulations issued in this document preempt State and local packaging requirements that are not identical to it." 51 Fed. Reg. 8180, 8181 (March 7, 1986).

3. *Administrative Conference Recommendations.* In 1984 the Administrative Conference of the United States issued a report, 49 Fed. Reg. 49837 (December 24, 1984), which made the following recommendations:

1. Congress should address foreseeable preemption issues clearly and explicitly when it enacts a statute affecting regulation or deregulation of an area of conduct.

2. Each federal agency should establish procedures to ensure consideration of the need to preempt state laws or regulations that harm federally protected interests in the areas of regulatory responsibility delegated to that agency by Congress, and each agency should clearly and explicitly address preemption issues in the course of regulatory decision-making. . . .

3. When a federal agency foresees the possibility of a conflict between a state law or regulation and federally protected interests within the federal agency's area of regulatory responsibility, the agency should, when practicable, engage in informal dialogue with state authorities in an effort to avoid such a conflict.

4. When a federal agency proposes to act through agency adjudication or rulemaking to preempt a state law or regulation, the agency should attempt to provide all affected states, as well as other affected interests, notice and an opportunity for appropriate participation in the proceedings.

4. *Reagan Era Federalism.* During the early 1980s President Reagan, under the banner of "New Federalism," pursued and encouraged efforts to return responsibility for many governmental activities to the States. Counsel to Vice President Bush, Boyden Gray, wrote that the President recognized

that state and local administration of regulatory programs may conflict in some instances with other goals of regulatory relief or with other important federal interests. For example, individual states may operate specific programs more effectively than the federal government, but the combined effect of disparate state regulatory standards may intolerably burden interstate commerce, thus requiring uniform federal regulation.

Acknowledging "the need for a strong central government to promote commerce and other federal interests," Gray distinguished between those activities that are primarily local and those that involve such "burdens on interstate commerce" that national uniformity is required. *Regulation and Federalism,* 1

Yale J. Reg. 93, 95–96 (1983). The FINAL REPORT OF THE PRESIDENTIAL TASK FORCE ON REGULATORY RELIEF 51 (August 11, 1983) declared:

> [R]egulating the safety of drugs and food additives is appropriate to the federal government, since the products being regulated are usually marketed on a nationwide basis, differing state standards could impose large costs on interstate commerce, and benefits of multiple approaches to screening new drugs are small.

In 52 Fed. Reg. 41685 (October 30, 1987), President Reagan issued Executive Order No. 12612 on Federalism. The order encouraged "healthy diversity" in the public policies among the several states. Federal action limiting the policy making discretion of the states is to be taken only where "the national activity is necessitated by the presence of a problem of national scope." Agencies were directed to preempt local regulation "only when the statute contains an express preemption provision or there is some other firm and palpable evidence compelling the conclusion that the Congress intended preemption of State law, or when the exercise of State authority directly conflicts with the exercise of Federal authority under the Federal statute." *See also* President Bush's "Memorandum on Federalism" 26 Week. Comp. Pres. Doc. 264 (February 16, 1990).

5. *Alcohol in Confectionery.* Section 402(d)(2), as amended in 100 Stat. 30, 35 (1986), represents a new approach to federal-state uniformity. Prior to 1986, confectionery was not permitted to contain alcohol in excess of 0.5 percent derived solely from flavoring. The 1986 Amendment legalized the use of alcohol in confectionery if it is intended for sale only in states that have legalized the sale of such products.

6. *Prescription Drug Marketing Act.* The Prescription Drug Marketing Act of 1987, 102 Stat. 95, which added section 503(e)(2), requires that all state licensing of wholesale prescription drug distributors must comply with FDA guidelines. In signing this legislation, President Reagan stated that this provision is "contrary to fundamental principles of federalism" and urged Congress to repeal it, 24 Week. Comp. Pres. Doc. 519 (April 25, 1988). To date Congress has not responded.

E. PREEMPTION UNDER THE 1962 DRUG AMENDMENTS

During the debates on the bill that eventually became the Drug Amendments of 1962, 108 Cong. Rec. 21083 (September 27, 1962), the House of Representatives adopted a specific preemption provision, following this brief exchange:

> Mr. Smith of Virginia. Mr. Chairman, I offer an amendment. . . .
>
> "Sec. 203. Nothing in the Federal Food, Drug, and Cosmetic Act, as amended, shall be construed as invalidating any provision of State law which would be valid in the absence of such Act unless there is a direct and positive conflict between such Act and such provision of State law." . . .

Mr. Harris. Mr. Chairman, earlier in the debate today I was asked the question by one of our colleagues about the preemption of State laws and made the categorical statement that this legislation did not preempt any State laws and was not so intended. The gentleman was kind enough to call to my attention his amendment, prior to this time.... I think it is in line with the statement that I made previously on the floor of the House....

Mr. Schenck. Mr. Chairman, as the gentleman will recall in my statement on the floor I pointed out that there are many instances where State laws in the area of food and drugs and health are even stronger than some of the Federal laws. I pointed out also that the Federal law should not preempt in those fields. I would like to assure the gentleman from Virginia that I have no objection to his amendment....

The House–Senate conference revised Representative Smith's provision to make it applicable only to the Drug Amendments of 1962 and not to the entire FD&C Act. H.R. Rep. No. 2526, 87th Cong., 2d Sess. 15 (1962).

The provision ultimately enacted, 76 Stat. 793 (1962), states:

Sec. 202. Nothing in the amendments made by this Act to the Federal Food, Drug, and Cosmetic Act shall be construed as invalidating any provision of State law which would be valid in the absence of such amendments unless there is a direct and positive conflict between such amendments and such provision of State law.

NOTES

1. *Proposed Preemption of State Drug Regulation.* The proposed Drug Regulation Reform Act of 1979, S. 1075, 96th Cong., 1st Sess. (1979), contained an explicit prospective statutory preemption. S. Rep. No. 321, 96th Cong., 1st Sess. 45–46 (1979).

2. *Preemption and Tort Liability.* A line of cases holds that the new drug and new animal drug requirements of the FD&C Act do not preempt state tort law. *E.g., Hill v. Searle Laboratories,* 884 F.2d 1064 (8th Cir. 1989); *Osburn v. Anchor Laboratories, Inc.* 825 F.2d 908 (5th Cir. 1987); *Kociemba v. G.D. Searle & Co.,* 707 F. Supp. 1517 (D. Minn. 1989); *Brown v. McNeil Laboratories, Inc.,* Food Drug Cosm. L. Rep. (CCH) ¶ 38,096 (W.D. Mich. 1988); *Stephens v. G.D. Searle & Co.,* 602 F. Supp. 379 (E.D. Mich. 1985); *Feldman v. Lederle Laboratories,* 97 N.J. 429, 479 A.2d 374 (1984). Those decisions were predicated on the conclusion that the FDA regulations then in effect allowed a manufacturer, without prior FDA approval, to add warnings as soon as information indicated they were appropriate. In *Feldman v. Lederle Laboratories,* 314 Pa.Super. 539, 561 A. 2d 288 (1983), by contrast, the court held that the 1962–1963 labeling requirements for antibiotic drugs preempted a state failure to warn verdict because they explicitly forbade any change in labeling without agency approval.

3. *Vaccine Policy and Tort Liability.* Early rulings that Federal vaccine policy preempted recovery under state law for injuries caused by vaccine

products were subsequently reversed. *Morris v. Parke, Davis & Co.*, 573 F. Supp. 1324 (C.D. Cal. 1983), *rev'd*, 667 F. Supp. 1332 (C.D. Cal. 1987); *Hurley v. Lederle Laboratories*, 651 F. Supp. 993 (E.D. Tex. 1986), *rev'd*, 851 F.2d 1536 (5th Cir.), *superseded*, 863 F.2d 1173 (1988); *Abbot v. American Cyanamid Co.*, 844 F.2d 1108 (4th Cir. 1988).

4. *Mail Order Prescription Drugs.* The Attorney General of Nebraska has advised that any state requirements on out-of-state pharmacies that mail prescription drugs into Nebraska would be preempted under the FD&C Act. Op. No. 88007, FDC L. Rep. (CCH) ¶ 38,073 (February 10, 1988).

F. WAIVERS OF PREEMPTION UNDER THE 1976 MEDICAL DEVICE AMENDMENTS

IN THE MEDICAL DEVICE AMENDMENTS OF 1976, CONGRESS ATTEMPTED TO DEFINE WITH SOME PRECISION THE FEDERAL AND STATE ROLES IN THE REGULATION OF MEDICAL INSTRUMENTATION. THE RESULT IS SECTION 521 OF THE ACT, WHICH READS:

SEC. 521(A) EXCEPT AS PROVIDED IN SUBSECTION (B), NO STATE OR POLITICAL SUBDIVISION OF A STATE MAY ESTABLISH OR CONTINUE IN EFFECT WITH RESPECT TO A DEVICE INTENDED FOR HUMAN USE ANY REQUIREMENT—

(1) which is different from, or in addition to, any requirement applicable under this Act to the device, and

(2) which relates to the safety or effectiveness of the device or to any other matter included in a requirement applicable to the device under this Act.

(b) Upon application of a State or a political subdivision thereof, the Secretary may, by regulation promulgated after notice and opportunity for an oral hearing, exempt from subsection (a), under such conditions as may be prescribed in such regulation, a requirement of such State or political subdivision applicable to a device intended for human use if—

(1) the requirement is more stringent than a requirement under this Act which would be applicable to the device if an exemption were not in effect under this subsection; or

(2) the requirement—

(A) is required by compelling local conditions, and

(B) compliance with the requirement would not cause the device to be in violation of any applicable requirement under this Act.

MEDICAL DEVICE AMENDMENTS OF 1976
HOUSE REPORT NO. 94–853.
94th Congress, 2d Session (1976).

The Committee recognizes that if a substantial number of differing requirements applicable to a medical device are imposed by jurisdictions other than the Federal government, interstate commerce would be unduly burdened....

In the absence of effective Federal regulation of medical devices, some States have established their own programs. The most comprehensive State regulation of which the Committee is aware is that of California, which in 1970 adopted the Sherman Food, Drug, and Cosmetic Law. This law requires premarket approval of all new medical devices, requires compliance of device manufacturers with good manufacturing practices and authorizes inspection of establishments which manufacture devices. Implementation of the Sherman Law has resulted in the requirement that intrauterine devices are subject to premarket clearance in California.

Because there are some situations in which regulation of devices by States and localities would constitute a useful supplement to Federal regulation, the reported bill authorizes a State or political subdivision thereof to petition the Secretary for exemptions from the bill's general prohibition of non-Federal regulation....

In the Committee's view, requirements imposed under the California statute serve as an example of requirements that the Secretary should authorize to be continued (provided any application submitted by a State meets requirements pursuant to the reported bill)....

Pursuant to section 521 FDA proposed, 42 Fed. Reg. 30383 (June 14, 1977), and later promulgated, regulations governing exemptions from Federal preemption of state and local device requirements.

EXEMPTIONS FROM FEDERAL PREEMPTION OF STATE AND LOCAL DEVICE REQUIREMENTS
43 Federal Register 18661 (May 2, 1978).

Many comments stated that there is no basis in the act or in the legislative history to justify the interpretation of section 521 of the act set forth in the first sentence of proposed § 808.1(d). That sentence stated that State and local requirements are preempted only when FDA has established specific counterpart regulations or there are other specific requirements applicable to a particular device under the act, thereby making any existing divergent State or local requirements applicable to the device different from, or in addition to, the specific FDA requirements....

... [F]rom a plain reading of section 521 of the act it is clear that the scope of preemption is limited to instances where there are specific FDA requirements applicable to a particular device or class of devices. As noted in the preamble to the proposal, a prime example is the preemption of divergent State or local requirements relating to hearing aid labeling and conditions for sale, which occurred when the new FDA hearing aid regulations took effect on August 25, 1977. Here, only requirements relating to labeling and conditions for sale were preempted, not all State or local requirements regulating other facets of hearing aid distribution....

... [I]nterpretations urged by the comments would provide less public protection from unsafe and ineffective medical devices because State and local regulation of medical devices would be reduced or eliminated before compensating FDA regulations could become effective. For example, many States have laws governing labeling and conditions for sale of hearing aids. Under the theory espoused in the comments, these laws were preempted on May 28, 1976, although the FDA regulations on hearing aids did not become effective until August 25, 1977. In the interim, presumably, hearing aids were regulated neither by the States nor FDA. In the absence of a specific Congressional directive to this effect, however, the Commissioner will not adopt such a position.

The Commissioner also believes that the interpretation expressed in the regulation will not cause an undue burden on interstate commerce because it merely allows State and local requirements to continue in effect until FDA establishes a national policy on the regulation of specific devices. Thus, since there is no duplication between FDA and State programs, there is no greater burden on interstate commerce than if the Amendments had not been enacted.

Several comments stated that there is no basis in the act or in the legislative history for the statement in proposed § 808.1(d)(2) that section 521(a) does not preempt State or local requirements that are equal to, or substantially identical to, requirements imposed by or under the Act.... The Commissioner believes that a common sense reading of section 521 of the act supports the "substantially identical" concept in § 808.1(d)(2). Thus, while a State or local requirement may differ in some nonessential manner from an FDA requirement, if it is substantially identical to an FDA requirement it is not "different from" the FDA requirement within the meaning of section 521, and therefore not preempted....

The Commissioner also cannot accept the argument that an identical State or local requirement is preempted because it is "in addition to" the FDA requirement. Such an interpretation of section 521 renders meaningless the "different from" language of section 521 because under this theory any State and local requirement would be preempted whether or not it was actually "different from" an FDA requirement....

The Commissioner believes that State laws relating to inspection, registration, and licensing usually are not requirements "with respect to a device" within the meaning of section 521 of the act because they generally pertain either to persons who manufacture or distribute devices or to places where devices are manufactured, and not directly to devices. In order for a State provision to be a requirement with respect to a device within the meaning of section 521 of the act—and thereby a candidate for preemption—it must relate to the device itself....

NOTES

1. *FDA Regulations.* FDA's general regulations governing exemptions from Federal preemption of state medical device laws, and the specific exemptions that have been granted, are codified in 21 C.F.R. Part 808.

2. *California Exemption Application.* FDA received an application from California for an exemption from section 521's preemption of its medical device requirements and in 42 Fed. Reg. 9186 (February 15, 1977) published a proposal to grant the application, with one exception. After holding a public hearing, 42 Fed. Reg. 25919 (May 20, 1977), FDA reproposed its regulation responding to the California petition in 44 Fed. Reg. 19438 (April 3, 1979) and in 45 Fed. Reg. 67321 (October 10, 1980) promulgated final regulations, granting some exemptions and denying others.

3. *Hearing Aid Controls.* FDA proposed a regulation responding to the applications of Massachusetts and Rhode Island for exemptions from preemption of hearing aid requirements in 44 Fed. Reg. 22119 (April 13, 1979) and after a public hearing, 44 Fed. Reg. 47105 (August 10, 1979), promulgated final regulations in 45 Fed. Reg. 67325 (October 10, 1980). Massachusetts challenged FDA's denial of its application for an exemption for two provisions of its statute governing the sale of hearing aids, contending that the agency's published criteria for exemptions were invalid because they permit, in 21 C.F.R. § 808.25(g)(3), broad consideration of "the best interest of public health, taking into account the potential burden on interstate commerce." FDA's criteria for exemptions from preemption and its action on the Massachusetts application were both approved in *Commonwealth of Massachusetts v. Hayes,* 691 F.2d 57 (1st Cir. 1982). For a discussion of the circumstances under which state hearing aid requirements are not preempted, see 55 Fed. Reg. 23984 (June 13, 1990). State hearing aid requirements were upheld in *Smith v. Pingree,* 651 F.2d 1021 (5th Cir. 1981); *New Jersey Guild of Hearing Aid Dispensers v. Long,* 75 N.J. 544, 384 A.2d 795 (1978).

4. *Suntanning Equipment.* In response to a request for an advisory opinion on whether a city may ban the use of indoor commercial tanning equipment, the agency said it had to consider both section 521 of the FD&C Act and the preemption provisions applicable to electronic products under section 360F of the Public Health Service Act, 42 U.S.C. § 263n. FDA advised that section 521 does not preempt the city ordinance because the agency has not promulgated any requirements under the FD&C Act applicable to the use of sun tanning equipment, and that section 360F does not preempt because the ordinance does not establish a standard applicable to the performance of sun tanning equipment. Letter from J. M. Taylor to D. R. Kalins, FDA Dkt. No. 87A–0201 (June 20, 1988).

KIEVLAN v. DAHLBERG ELECTRONICS

Court of Appeal, First District, Division 4, 1978.
78 Cal. App. 3d 951, 144 Cal. Rptr. 585, *appeal dismissed,* 440 U.S. 951.

CALDECOTT, Presiding Justice.

Dahlberg Electronics, Inc., and Detection Sciences, Inc., defendants ... appeal from a judgment permanently enjoining them "from advertising their hearing aids in California by representing that said hearing aids have any effect on diseases or disorders of the ear, or auditory apparatus, including hearing loss and deafness."....

Defendants have appealed from the judgment on the grounds (1) the trial court erred in its construction and application of section 26463 of the Health and Safety Code; (2) that the statute is unconstitutional; and (3) that state regulation of hearing aid advertising has been preempted by federal law and regulation....

[The court rejected the defendants' first two arguments in portions of the opinion not reproduced here.]

Defendants' third contention is that state regulation of hearing aid advertising has been preempted by federal law and regulation. On May 28, 1976, the Medical Device Amendments of 1976 were enacted.... Implementing regulations concerning hearing aid devices were approved by the Food and Drug Administration on February 10, 1977, and became effective August 15, 1977. According to the language of section 360k [section 521 of the Act], the preemptive effect of the act upon state action, with respect to hearing aids, is to be determined by the three-way test (1) whether the state action is a "requirement" and, if it is, (2) whether it is "different from, or in addition to" any requirement of the act on that subject *and* (3) whether it "relates to the ... effectiveness" of hearing aids. Because the three factors appear in a conjunctive context, all three must appear before a court may declare that the act preempts Health and Safety Code section 26463, subdivision (m), in the hearing aid business.

Section 26463, subdivision (m), meets the third test to the categorical extent that it "relates to the ... effectiveness" of hearing aids by prohibiting representations on this subject in copy which advertises them for sale. But, because it does this and no more, it fails the first test of preemption because it is a flat *prohibition:* it is not a "requirement."

If it may be treated as a "requirement," its effect is nevertheless limited to the *advertising* of hearing aids for sale. The federal act reaches the subject of advertising, but of "restricted devices" only. By the act's terms, "restricted devices" are those which the Secretary of Health, Education and Welfare determines, by regulation, may be sold upon licensed-practitioner prescription only....

Defendants have not shown that the secretary has classified hearing aids as "restricted devices." The federal act itself thus includes no "requirement" concerning the advertising of hearing aids. No such "requirement" appears in the implementing regulations adopted by the secretary, which have nothing to do with advertising. Health and Safety Code section 26463, subdivision (m), cannot be "different from, or in addition to," a "requirement" of the act which does not exist. The second test of its preemption by the act therefore fails as well. Thus, section 26463 is not preempted by federal law....

NOTES

1. *Commentary.* See Downey, *Laboratories or Puppets? The Challenge of Federal Preemption of State Legislation,* 34 FDC L.J. 334 (1979).

2. *Preemption of State Tort Claims.* Some courts have held that section 521(a)'s preemption of different or additional state "requirements" bars imposition of civil liability for personal injuries caused by a medical device. *E.g., Rinehart v. International Playtex, Inc.,* 688 F. Supp. 475 (S.D. Ind. 1988); *Edmondson v. International Playtex, Inc.,* 678 F. Supp. 1571 (N.D. Ga. 1987); *Stewart v. International Playtex, Inc.,* 672 F. Supp. 907 (D.S.C. 1987). As interpreted by FDA, section 521(a) preempts state requirements only in those areas where FDA has specifically regulated the device. Accordingly, FDA requirements for tampon labeling with respect to toxic shock syndrome preempt state tort claims based upon failure to warn but not claims based upon a design defect. *See Moore v. Kimberly–Clark Corp., 867 F.2d 243 (5th Cir. 1989); Rinehart v. International Playtex, Inc., supra.* In *O'Gilvie v. International Playtex, Inc.,* 821 F.2d 1438 (10th Cir. 1987), the court upheld civil recovery against the manufacturer of a medical device without considering the preemption issue. Because FDA regulated the copper IUD as a new drug rather than as a medical device, claims that suits for injuries caused by these products are preempted have had no success. *E.g., Spychala v. G.D. Searle & Co.,* 705 F. Supp. 1024 (D. N.J. 1988); *Kociemba v. G.D. Searle & Co.,* 680 F. Supp. 1293 (D. Minn. 1988). The court in *Callan v. G.D. Searle & Co.,* 709 F.Supp. 662 (D. Md. 1989), in allowing a state tort action against a maker of the copper IUD because FDA had regulated the product as a drug, also stated that it would have reached the same result if the agency had regulated it as a device.

3. *State Enforcement Remedies.* FDA has issued an advisory opinion stating that section 521 of the FD&C Act does not preempt application of state law injunctive remedies to medical devices generally or to IUDs in particular. Letter from FDA Associate Commissioner for Regulatory Affairs J.P. Hile to National Women's Health Network, Dkt. No. 83A–0140/AP (March 8, 1984). The advisory opinion explained that section 521 preempts only state requirements that relate specifically to medical devices, and that there is no indication that Congress intended to preempt the application of general state law remedies that only incidentally apply to devices. *But see National Women's Health Network, Inc. v. A.H. Robins Co., Inc.,* 545 F.Supp. 1177 (D. Mass. 1982), holding that state action to require a national notification and recall campaign for IUDs would be preempted by the FD&C Act.

G. PREEMPTION UNDER THE 1990 FOOD LABELING AMENDMENTS

The Nutrition Labeling and Education Act of 1990, 104 Stat. 2353, expressly prohibits any state or local government from directly or indirectly establishing any food labeling requirement of the type governed by sections 403(b)–(k), (q), and (r) of the FD&C Act that is not identical to FDA requirements. This preemption provision becomes effective in four stages. (1) It is effective immediately upon enactment for food standards. (2) It is effective one year after enactment for imitation labeling, declaration of ingredients, declaration of net quantity of contents, and the name and address of the manufacturer. (3) State requirements for nutrition labeling, nutrient descriptors, and disease prevention claims become preempted when FDA regulations implementing the new authorities of sections 403(q) and (r) become effective. (4) The remainder of the Act's food labeling provisions become subject to preemption, after a study required to be conducted by FDA, 24–30 months after enactment.

NOTES

1. *Preemption of Indirect Requirements.* In response to concerns raised by the food industry that states might enact legislation designed to accomplish indirectly what they could no longer do directly, as Michigan attempted for comminuted meat, Note 2, page 1008 *supra*, the prohibition against indirect requirements was added to the law.

2. *Restaurant and Retail Food.* Because food consumed in restaurants and food prepared in retail stores (*e.g.*, bread baked on the premises in a grocery store) are exempt from the food labeling requirements of sections 403(q) and (r), state and local requirements governing such food were excluded from preemption.

3. *State Petitions.* A state or local agency may petition FDA to exempt a specific requirement from preemption. FDA may grant the petition if the state or local requirement would not cause any food to be in violation of the FD&C Act, would not unduly burden interstate commerce, and is designed to address a particular need for information which is not met by the FD&C Act.

4. *Safety Warnings.* Congress declined to preempt state or local safety warnings for food (of the sort epitomized by California Proposition 65) but went out of its way to make clear that it did not intend to influence the outcome of any litigation challenging the constitutionality of such warnings under the Commerce Clause or Supremacy Clause.

Chapter XI
FDA ENFORCEMENT

A. PROHIBITED ACTS
1. SECTION 301

Section 301, which enumerates the acts prohibited by the statute, is the heart of the enforcement provisions of the FD&C Act. These prohibitions are in turn enforceable by the judicial remedies provided elsewhere in the Act and by other mechanisms. Broadly speaking, section 301 prohibits the violation of any of the substantive proscriptions or requirements of the Act. One or more provisions of section 301 is thus involved in *every* enforcement case initiated by FDA, and extensive treatment of each of these provisions would be redundant.

One feature of section 301 deserves separate consideration. The section's opening phrase provides that the "causing" of any prohibited act, as well as the act itself, is prohibited. Neither the legislative history of the Act nor any judicial opinion discusses the scope of this provision. The provision had no counterpart in the 1906 Act, and Congress gave no reason for its inclusion in the 1938 Act. The provision is most often cited in holding corporate officers criminally liable for violations of the Act, although such liability had also been sustained under the 1906 Act. *See* p. 1150 *infra*. *See generally* Harding, *The "Causing" Provision and Jurisdictional Limits*, 6 FDC L.J. 594 (1951). In *United States v. Industrial Laboratories Co.*, 456 F.2d 908 (10th Cir. 1972), it was assumed without discussion that a consulting laboratory that failed to perform proper tests on a drug "caused" the adulteration of the product. Presumably any person involved in a violation is brought within the Act under this provision. *See, e.g., United States v. International Exterminator Corp.*, 294 F.2d 270 (5th Cir. 1961), involving the liability of a pest control service for causing the introduction of contaminated food into interstate commerce.

NOTES

1. *Enforcement History*. For analyses of FDA enforcement actions under the 1906 Act, *see* Munch and Munch, *Notices of Judgment—The First Thousand*, 10 FDC L.J. 219 (1955); *Notices of Judgment—Nos. 1001 to 5000*, 11 FDC L.J. 17 (1956); *Notices of Judgment—Nos. 5001 to 15,000*, 11 FDC L.J. 196 (1956); *Notices of Judgment—Nos. 15,001 to 31,157*, 13 FDC L.J. 178 (1958). For a similar series under the 1938 Act, *see* Munch and Munch, *Notices of*

Judgment—Cosmetics: C.N.J.'s Nos. 1 to 205, 14 FDC L.J. 399 (1959); *Notices of Judgment—Foods: F.N.J.'s Nos. 1 to 23,400,* 14 FDC L.J. 402 (1959). Many of the early drug and device notices of judgment under the 1938 Act are summarized in Munch, *A Half–Century of Drug Control,* 11 FDC L.J. 305 (1956). Colorful examples of early enforcement activities can be found in White, *Enforcing the 1938 Food, Drug, and Cosmetic Act: The Class of '39,* 52 J. AFDO, No. 4, at 10 (October 1988); Young, *From Oysters to After–Dinner Mints: The Role of the Early Food and Drug Inspector,* 42 J. Hist. Med. and Allied Sci. 30 (1987).

2. *Judicial Interpretation.* Numerous Supreme Court opinions have stated that the 1906 and 1938 Acts should be construed broadly in order to achieve their intended purpose. *See, e.g., United States v. Lexington Mill & Elevator Co.,* 232 U.S. 399 (1914); *United States v. Dotterweich,* 320 U.S. 277 (1943); *United States v. Sullivan,* 332 U.S. 689 (1948); *United States v. An Article of Drug ... Bacto–Unidisk,* 394 U.S. 784 (1969); *United States v. Park,* 421 U.S. 658 (1975).

3. *Commentary. See generally* Lee, *The Enforcement Provisions of the Food, Drug, and Cosmetic Act,* 6 Law & Contemp. Probs. 70 (1939); *Developments in the Law—The Federal Food, Drug, and Cosmetic Act,* 67 Harv. L. Rev. 632 (1954).

---

2. FDA REGULATORY PHILOSOPHY AND COMPLIANCE POLICY

PETER BARTON HUTT, PHILOSOPHY OF REGULATION UNDER THE FEDERAL FOOD, DRUG AND COSMETIC ACT

28 Food Drug Cosmetic Law Journal 177 (1973).

... Congress chose for the most part to express its mandate in broad and general terms, rather than in narrow and specific terms.... Congress obviously knew in 1938 that it could not foresee future developments, and that it must proceed primarily by establishing general principles, permitting implementation within broad parameters, if regulation in this important area was to be effective.

In this respect, the Act must be regarded as a constitution. It establishes a set of fundamental objectives—safe, effective, wholesome, and truthfully-labeled products—without attempting to specify every detail of regulation. The mission of the Food and Drug Administration is to implement these objectives through the most effective and efficient controls that can be devised.

This does not mean that the Act provides unfettered discretion for the Agency to do whatever it wishes in pursuing these objectives. We may not and do not ignore the statute. In some areas, Congress did lay down very specific rules which, until changed must control.....

But the fact that Congress simply has not considered or spoken on a particular issue certainly is no bar to the Food and Drug Administration exerting initiative and leadership in the public interest. Except where expressly prohibited, I believe the Food and Drug Administration is obligated to develop whatever innovative and creative regulatory programs are reasonable and are most appropriate to achieve the fundamental objectives laid down by Congress. And in spite of the diversity of the Agency's new programs, I am not at all certain that the Food and Drug Administration has yet begun to explore the full reaches of existing statutory authority....

H. THOMAS AUSTERN, PHILOSOPHY OF REGULATION: A REPLY TO MR. HUTT

28 Food Drug Cosmetic Law Journal 189 (1973).

... Despite some semantic obeisance to "unfettered discretion," the premise is that *except* where specifically prohibited by Congress, the FDA is free, and indeed is *obligated,* to develop whatever innovative and creative regulatory programs *it* believes are most appropriate to implement the fundamental objectives it finds in the Act.

Mr. Hutt grants that FDA cannot override Congress by administrative fiat, but he insists that simply because Congress has *not spoken* on a particular issue there is no bar to FDA exercising new authority....

Some might urge that that view is contrary to experience, that on the many amendments since 1938 Congress had never objected to being bothered, or had thought that under what Mr. Hutt calls "the FDA constitution," FDA should have made new law itself rather than through careful Congressional deliberation that would strike a *legislative* balance.

It is no distortion, I hope, of his basic approach to read it as meaning: Everything *we* want to do that is not specifically prohibited can be made mandatory if we think it is in the public interest. Well, as Mr. Justice Cardozo once observed: "That is delegation running riot."....

We do not often indulge in government by decree or in regulation by fiat. I agree that regulation becomes futile, if not impossible, absent *enforcement*. But as a lawyer I look at Section 301 to see what Congress has specifically made a prohibited act, backed by the sanctions of seizure, injunction, and criminal penalties....

FDA COMPLIANCE PHILOSOPHY
May 6, 1971

TO: Associate and Assistant Commissioners
      Bureau and Office Directors
      Directors of Offices of Compliance
      Regional Food and Drug Directors
      Deputy Regional Food and Drug Directors

FROM: Charles C. Edwards, M.D., Commissioner of Food and Drugs

... [A]ll FDA managers and employees in the various headquarters and field offices should be guided by the following statement of general principles in carrying out our mandated responsibilities in consumer protection:

a. The Food and Drug Administration is a scientifically oriented law enforcement agency. Our mission is to provide consumer protection through judicious enforcement of the various laws which have been entrusted to our administration.

b. We encourage industry self regulation and will participate in cooperative programs designed to inform industry how to meet the requirements of the law and to promote voluntary compliance through preventive measures designed to keep unsafe, unfit or ineffective products from reaching the consumer, or to remove expeditiously such products from the market when found.

c. We also will fully utilize formal enforcement procedures, including the punitive provisions of the various laws under which we operate, when dealing with those sections of the regulated industry which may have chosen not to comply, or which may have been unable to comply with the requirements of the law.....

e. All violations of the law which come to our attention through our own activities or through other sources will be evaluated as to how best the consumer can be served, in consideration of the seriousness of the observed problem and our available resources and other priorities.

f. We will use all available compliance measures to achieve optimum consumer protection. This may include the release of information to the general public and/or professional groups; administrative action; the institution of recall; or seizure, injunction, or prosecution action.

COMPLIANCE POLICY GUIDE 7150.10
52 Federal Register 27731 (July 23, 1987).

SUBJECT: Health Fraud—Factors in Considering Regulatory Action

BACKGROUND
Health Fraud products are articles of unproven effectiveness that are promoted to improve health, well being, or appearance. They can be drugs, devices, foods or cosmetics for animal or human use.....

DEFINITIONS
A health fraud product presents a direct health hazard if it is likely to cause injury, death or other serious adverse effect when used as directed or in a customary manner.

A health fraud product presents an indirect health hazard if, as a result of reliance on the product, the consumer is likely to delay or discontinue appropriate medical treatment. The health hazard is indirect when it does no direct harm to the person as a result of its use, but rather denies, delays, or interferes with effective treatment. Consumers who purchase these products are misled by exaggerated or false claims that are made for the products.

POLICY

Products that pose a direct health hazard to the user shall receive the agency's highest priority attention, regardless of whether they are health fraud products.... Health fraud products for which there is not a documented direct health hazard (*i.e.*, indirect health hazard products) will still be considered for regulatory action but on a lower priority.

In evaluating regulatory actions against indirect health hazard products, the following factors should be considered by districts and the centers:

1. Whether the therapeutic claims, or conditions to be treated are significant as interpreted by the appropriate center;

2. Whether there are scientific data or specific information to support the safety or effectiveness of the product for its intended or customary use;

3. The degree of vulnerability of the prospective user group, *e.g.*, the elderly, persons with illnesses for which there is no recognized effective treatment;

4. The availability of other administrative or regulatory alternatives to bring the product or firm into compliance, *e.g.*, education, referral or cooperation with local, state or other federal agencies;

5. The amount of agency resources required and whether they are sufficient to pursue the action to its conclusion.

6. The source of the product, size of the industry distributing the same or similar products, and the impact of the action on that source and industry;

7. The cost of the product, the economic impact of this cost on the target user group, as well as the profit (per sale) realized from the sale of the product;

8. The amount (dollar and volume) of product sold, and the geographical scope of its distribution;

In most cases, the seriousness of the therapeutic claims and the nature of the indirect hazard will be obvious. We recognize that when a product with unproven therapeutic claims is first introduced, it is difficult to predict its economic impact because, whether or not a regulatory action is taken, the product may not be accepted in the marketplace. Generally, new health fraud products with undetermined economic impact and limited health significance should result in a Notice of Adverse Findings Letter to the promoter. Regulatory action should be considered for products of limited health significance when it appears there is a growing national or substantial regional market for them. The office of compliance in each center will designate a contact and a back-up person for primary consultation on health fraud action.....

---

3. INDUSTRY–WIDE ENFORCEMENT

It is well established that a regulatory agency has discretion to initiate enforcement action against fewer than all of the firms engaged in similar unlawful conduct, and to appraise and discount the impact on competition of case-by-case enforcement. *See Moog Industries, Inc. v. FTC,* 355 U.S. 411 (1958); *see also FTC v. Universal–Rundle Corp.,* 387 U.S. 244 (1967). Yet there are strong arguments favoring a more comprehensive approach to regulation.

PETER BARTON HUTT, PHILOSOPHY OF REGULATION UNDER THE FEDERAL FOOD, DRUG AND COSMETIC ACT

28 Food Drug Cosmetic Law Journal 177 (1973).

... Standing alone, institution of legal enforcement action, resulting in costly and time-consuming litigation on a case-by-case basis, is an inadequate method of regulation. It fails to inform the regulated industry of its obligations, it involves years of delay, and the end results are often uncertain. Worst of all, it inevitably results in invidious selective enforcement, whereby one or two individuals or companies must be singled out as the test cases while the rest of the industry is left alone. By contrast, the promulgation of regulations informs an entire industry of all applicable requirements and has proved to be far more likely to induce widespread compliance. Litigation in many instances represents the failure of effective regulation.

This past year has seen more new regulatory programs undertaken by detailed substantive and procedural regulations published in the FEDERAL REGISTER than at any other time in the history of the Food and Drug Administration. Indeed, those in industry who formerly complained that they could not determine what the Food and Drug Administration expected of them are now complaining that [FDA is] spelling out those requirements all too clearly.....

OVER–THE–COUNTER DRUGS: PROPOSAL
ESTABLISHING RULE MAKING
PROCEDURES FOR CLASSIFICATION

37 Federal Register 85 (January 5, 1972).

The Food and Drug Administration intends to require that all unapproved new drugs and misbranded drugs either be reformulated and/or relabeled to meet all requirements of the act or be removed from the market. In carrying out its responsibilities in this area, the Food and Drug Administration may either initiate a separate court action with respect to each violative OTC drug or deal with all OTC drugs through rulemaking by therapeutic classes on an industrywide basis. It has been determined that the latter approach should be pursued.....

Litigation to remove violative OTC preparations from the market would necessarily be on a drug-by-drug basis.... Such litigation is time-consuming and expensive and is sometimes ineffective because manufacturers may change the formulation of the drug in question and/or its labeling claims and reintroduce the product into the market, thus requiring still further litigation....

Of paramount concern is the inadequate consumer protection produced by a product-by-product review and case-by-case litigation against each drug. It is not unreasonable to expect that a very large number of violative drugs would remain on the market for long periods of time because of the limited resources of the agency to evaluate and proceed against such drugs and the delays inherent in complicated litigation through trial and appellate courts.

It is impossible to proceed simultaneously by litigation against all manufacturers of similar preparations or their drugs. The situation will arise, as it has before, that preparations similar to those proceeded against will remain on the market long after their less fortunate counterparts have been removed. This situation must be avoided for two reasons. First, and most important, the public is not sufficiently protected when violative drugs remain on the market. Second, equitable enforcement of the law requires that the agency proceed against all manufacturers of similar preparations, since those not proceeded against would have an unfair competitive advantage.

Practically all of the thousands of OTC drugs now marketed are compounded from only an estimated 200 active ingredients which are used either alone or in varying combinations.... [T]he same scientific and medical evidence is relevant in reviewing all OTC drugs within a given therapeutic class....

NOTES

1. *Supreme Court Support.* In *Weinberger v. Bentex Pharmaceuticals, Inc.,* 412 U.S. 645 (1973), the Supreme Court endorsed FDA's approach to implementation of the 1962 effectiveness standard:

FDA must be Evenhanded

... The deluge of litigation that would follow if "me-too" drugs and OTC drugs had to receive *de novo* hearings in the courts would inure to the interests of manufacturers and merchants in drugs, but not to the interests of the public that Congress was anxious to protect by the 1962 amendments, as well as OTC drugs and drugs covered by the 1972 [Drug Listing] Act. We are told that FDA is incapable of handling a caseload of more than perhaps 10 or 15 *de novo* judicial proceedings in a year. Clearly, if FDA were required to litigate, on a case-by-case basis, the "new drug" status of each drug now marketed, the regulatory scheme of the Act would be severely undermined, if not totally destroyed. Moreover, a case-by-case approach is inherently unfair because it requires compliance by one manufacturer while his competitors marketing similar drugs remain free to violate the Act....

2. *Limits on Even-handed Enforcement.* In *United States v. Articles ... Coli–Trol 80 Medicated*, 372 F.Supp. 915 (N.D. Ga. 1974), the claimant contested FDA's seizure of its OTC veterinary products as arbitrary and discriminatory:

... This argument is based on the fact that the Commissioner ... has proposed a policy of taking no enforcement action against OTC drugs for human use where lack of efficacy is the issue, pending a category-by-category review of those drugs ... while he has not done the same for OTC drugs for veterinary use....

The FDA ... explained why OTC drugs for veterinary use were not being treated in a similar manner, to wit:

"... It is undoubtedly true that OTC veterinary drugs should be reviewed in the same way as OTC human drugs. Because of limited resources, however, it is impractical at this time to review OTC veterinary drugs, the higher priority must be given to a review of OTC human drugs." ...

As a general rule laws are to some extent inherently unequal. Almost every statute or governmental regulation involves some disparity in treatment; few statutes affect everyone in the country in the same manner.... The only constitutional requirement is that any disparity in treatment caused by such classification be *reasonable*. ...

... The FDA's distinguishing OTC drugs for human use from OTC drugs for veterinary use appears to the court to be entirely reasonable, rational, and in keeping with the public interest whose health and welfare the agency is charged to protect....

NORTH AMERICAN PHARMACAL, INC. v. DEPARTMENT OF HEW

United States Court of Appeals, Eighth Circuit, 1973.
491 F.2d 546.

GIBSON, Circuit Judge.....

... [On] February 12, 1973, the FDA published in 38 Fed. Reg. 4279 its intention to withdraw NDA's covering combination amphetamine products and sent statutorily required notices to the holders of NDA's, including Petitioner Eastern Research Laboratories. The notices and conclusions on the safety and efficacy of these drugs were also, pursuant to 21 C.F.R. § 130.40 [now § 310.6], directed to and affected the Petitioners as manufacturers of the so-called "me-too" drugs, drugs similar in content and formulation to the previously approved new-drugs, which approval the FDA proposed to withdraw. Manufacturers, who had submitted NDA's were notified by certified mail and other interested parties were notified of an opportunity for hearing by the Federal Register publication, provided they submitted a well-organized and full factual analysis of data in support of their opposition to withdrawal. Although five requests for a hearing were filed by other manufacturers, none of the Petitioners in this case requested a hearing during the time allowed.

March 30, 1973, the FDA published in 38 Fed. Reg. 8290 a "Notice of Withdrawal of Approval of New Drug Applications" that withdrew approval of NDA's for combination amphetamine drugs, except those for which hearings had been requested. No request for a hearing was filed by Petitioners. Subsequently, they were notified by certified mail that their products were included in the withdrawal order and were told these products could no longer be manufactured or shipped in interstate commerce, and were requested to recall all such products in the chain of distribution....

Petitioners argue that they were deprived of due process by the FDA's failure to give them personal notice of their opportunity for hearing before a withdrawal of the NDA's covering combination amphetamines....

We are of the view that publication in the Federal Register gives "me-too" manufacturers sufficient opportunity to be heard.....

Since the "me-toos" are riding on the backs of the NDA's and thus vicariously receive the benefits of the NDA's approval, it is incumbent upon the "me-too" drug manufacturers to keep advised of the status and the validity of the NDA's that form the basis for the manufacture and distribution of their "me-too" product. The "me-too" rights to distribute in interstate commerce should certainly be no greater than the rights of the NDA's to so distribute. Notice in the Federal Register is calculated to reach all such "me-too" manufacturers who, because of their dependence for validity upon the NDA's, should be required, both as a matter of self-interest and of law, to keep abreast of the FDA regulations affecting their products. Under these circumstances, it should not be incumbent upon the FDA to ferret out the "me-too" manufacturers....

NOTE

In 41 Fed. Reg. 35741 (August 24, 1976), FDA denied the hearing previously requested by the holders of NDA's for combination amphetamine products. The agency's order was overturned in *Smithkline Corp. v. FDA*, 587 F.2d 1107 (D.C. Cir. 1978), in an opinion that strongly suggested a hearing was warranted. A notice of hearing was published in 44 Fed. Reg. 53574 (September 14, 1979).

Just as the hearing began Smithkline entered into an agreement by which it withdrew its request for a hearing on the understanding that FDA would not take action against any lots of the products involved that were introduced into interstate commerce before April 30, 1980.

FDA's original decision to withdraw the NDA's for which no hearing was requested, as well as those drugs for which no NDA had ever been submitted, thus resulted in a situation in which one firm's products remained on the market for seven years after those of all of its competitors were removed. Was there a better way for the agency to proceed?

IVY–REED CO., INC.: STEER–OID; OPPORTUNITY FOR HEARING

44 Federal Register 1462 (January 5, 1979).

The Director of the Bureau of Veterinary Medicine of the Food and Drug Administration (FDA) is issuing a notice of opportunity for hearing on a proposed refusal to approve new animal drug application (NADA) No. 110–315 submitted by Ivy–Reed Co., Inc. for Steer-oid, a product containing 20 milligrams (mg) of estradiol benzoate in combination with 200 mg of progesterone per dose implanted subcutaneously in the ear of cattle for growth promotion and feed efficiency....

Elsewhere in this issue of the FEDERAL REGISTER the Director is issuing a notice of opportunity for hearing on the proposal to withdraw approval of approved NADA 9–576 for a product (Synovex S, the generic equivalent of Steer-oid)....

Ivy–Reed Co., Inc. submitted its NADA for Steer-oid on June 3, 1977.... Ivy–Reed did not submit any data to demonstrate that use of the drug will not result in unsafe residues in human food. Accordingly, its NADA for Steer-oid was found incomplete under § 514.100(g) of the regulations, and the firm was so notified by letters dated February 1, and May 18, 1978. Ivy–Reed never requested the issuance of a notice of opportunity for hearing, as permitted by § 514.100(g), but instead sought FDA permission to market Steer-oid, pending the development of data either by Syntex or Ivy–Reed to demonstrate the use of the drug will not result in unsafe residues in human food. By letters dated June 27, and August 21, 1978, the Deputy Commissioner of Food and Drugs rejected Ivy–Reed's proposal and announced the agency's intention to issue notices of opportunity for hearing proposing to refuse to approve Ivy–Reed's NADA for Steer-oid and to withdraw approval of Syntex's NADA for Synovex S.... Thereafter, Ivy–Reed brought suit in the United States District Court for the District of New Jersey (*Ivy–Reed Co., Inc. v. FDA*, Civ. A. No. 78–2658) seeking an order directing FDA to approve its NADA for Steer-oid. On December 7, 1978, the Court refused to issue the order requested by Ivy–Reed and ordered FDA to issue the notice required by section 512(c) of the act either approving the aplication or giving the applicant notice of opportunity for a hearing.

... [N]either Ivy–Reed nor Syntex Laboratories has submitted data to demonstrate that the use of this drug in food-producing animals will not result in unsafe residues in human food. Without such information, Ivy–Reed's NADA is not approvable. The Director is incorporating by reference into this notice Sections II through V of the companion notice published elsewhere in this issue concerning Syntex Laboratories' NADA 9–576 for Synovex S as the basis for refusing to approve Ivy–Reed's NADA 110–315 for Steer-oid....

NOTES

1. *Incumbents v. New Entrants.* See *Barr Laboratories, Inc. v. Harris,* Food Drug Cosm. L. Rep. (CCH) ¶ 38,012 (D.D.C. 1979), where the court declined to enjoin preliminarily FDA's decision not to certify batches of an antibiotic for a new entrant into the market while it was in the process of withdrawing approval of the pioneer product: "The Act's purpose is to protect public health, not ensure or enhance equitable economic circumstances." The court subsequently dismissed the complaint. 482 F. Supp. 1183 (D.D.C. 1980).

2. *Consistency Over Time.* Although slavish consistency is not required of administrative agencies, reviewing courts demand convincing explanations for departures from long-standing practice or the adoption of policies that seem clearly discriminatory in their impact. *See Greater Boston Television Corp. v. FCC,* 444 F.2d 841 (D.C. Cir. 1970), *cert. denied,* 403 U.S. 923 (1971). Thus, *Rhodia, Inc. v. FDA,* 608 F.2d 1376 (D.C. Cir. 1979), held that FDA could not reject a supplemental NDA on a ground inconsistent with its prior practice.

UNITED STATES v. UNDETERMINED QUANTITIES OF AN ARTICLE OF DRUG LABELED AS EXACHOL

United States District Court, Southern District of New York, 1989.
716 F. Supp. 787.

SWEET, District Judge....

Health Club manufactures and sells a product which until April 1987 was known as the Atherex Institute Formula and thereafter was distributed under the name "Exachol." Exachol is comprised of lecithin, phosphatidyl ethanolamine, phosphatidyl choline, lethicon, phosphatidyl inositol, extract of chondrus crispus, carrageenan extract, silicon, niacin, and "compounded plant extract," all apparently natural products found in food.... According to Health Club, the ingredients used in Exachol are commonly available as food supplements for which scientific data as to their effectiveness is publicly available.

In 1985, 1986 and 1987, the FDA received complaints and inquiries from physicians, consumers, and state health departments about literature being distributed by Health Club stating that Exachol is useful for the prevention and treatment of coronary disease. According to the

FDA, an inspection conducted on December 8, 1986, revealed that the labelling and promotion of Exachol asserts that Exachol is effective in the prevention and treatment of coronary thrombosis, arteriosclerosis, atherosclerosis and angina. . . .

According to Health Club, each package for sale is accompanied by an instructional brochure which explains the purpose and use of the comprehensive Exachol three-way plan. The three steps of the plan are: (1) proper eating; (2) moderate exercise; and (3) inclusion of the Exachol supplement. The instructions state that:

> Exachol is a nutritional, dietary supplement, invaluable for the maintenance and protection of health and nutrition.

Health Club solicits orders through a mail order brochure which states in part:

> The Exachol Program is a preventive plan designed to help you keep your cholesterol under control by a combined approach including moderate exercise, proper eating and Exachol capsules. It is not intended as a substitute for any medical treatment your medical condition may require.

On April 9, 1987, FDA sent Health Club a regulatory letter which stated that Exachol was a drug within Section 201(g) of the Federal Food, Drug and Cosmetic Act. . . . .

. . . The FDA has also sent regulatory letters to sixty-four fish oil supplement manufacturers which were promoted for use "in the treatment and prevention of heart disease, and the lowering of cholesterol and triglyceride levels."

On August 4, 1987, the FDA published the Health Claims for Food Policy in the form of a Notice of Proposed Rulemaking concerning the content of health-related claims or information placed on food labelling and the criteria applied to evaluate the propriety of such labelling. Pending the rulemaking proceeding, the FDA decided to apply the proposed criteria to any questioned labelling:

> (1) Information on the labelling must be truthful and not misleading to the consumer

> (2) The claims should be supported by valid, reliable, scientific evidence that is publicly available (prior to any health related claim being made)

> (3) The claims must be consistent with generally recognized medical and nutritional principles.

> (4) Food labels containing a health-related claim must also contain the nutrition labelling information required by 21 CFR § 101.9.

The FDA also indicated that it would apply the same criteria to dietary supplements, noting that it may be more difficult for dietary supplements to meet the criteria.

The FDA's policy and application of the Health Claims for Food Policy to at least two products is relevant here. In 1984, the Kellogg Company ("Kellogg") began to promote its All–Bran cereal ("All–Bran") with labelling that recommended in connection with the prevention of cancer that consumers "eat high fiber foods, eat foods low in fat, eat fresh fruits and vegetables, eat a well-balanced diet and avoid being overweight." The FDA drafted a regulatory letter to Kellogg's suggesting that the labelling could be misleading and that the label promotes All–Bran as a product effective and adequate in the prevention of cancer. The letter charged Kellogg's with violations of both the food and drug provisions of the Act. However, the letter was never sent, and there was no action taken against Kellogg's regarding the All–Bran product.

On February 12, 1988, Congressman Theodore Weiss made a request for an assessment of whether the Kellogg labelling met the standards of the FDa's health claims proposal. The FDA responded that it would wait until it had developed a single standard for considering health related information or food labels before determining whether Kellogg's claims were misleading. The FDA contended that All–Bran is both a food and a drug and that, as is its right, it will decline to treat All–Bran as a drug and will not prosecute Kellogg on the basis of scientific evidence which indicates that the labelling is not misleading.

With respect to the fish oil products the FDA advised the manufacturers to identify those claims each would remove from the labels and to propose the appropriate claims they would include. On June 1, 1988 the FDA advised the Council for Responsible Nutrition ("CRN"), an agency which had responded on behalf of the manufacturers, that the FDA was reviewing the scientific basis for the fish oil labelling claims and would not initiate any proceeding until it had completed such review. This letter further stated that the labelling would be judged by the criteria contained in FDA's health messages proposal and that the FDA would give the industry a fair opportunity to complete its submission of scientific evidence substantiating the health benefits of fish oils and ninety days after the completion of the guidelines to bring their labelling into compliance. FDA reserved its right to bring enforcement action against those companies making therapeutic claims for fish oils that would not be permitted under the health messages proposal no matter how well substantiated.....

... [T]he initial issue to address is whether the Exachol product can be regulated as a drug.....

The claims clearly identify a product which is intended to prevent cholesterol deposits and thereby to mitigate the possibility of coronary thrombosis. Avoidance and prevention are synonymous here for lowering one's cholesterol level which both prevents and avoids heart disease. Here the Health Club is not advocating simply complete or partial avoidance of cholesterol intake, but the use of Exachol pills to prevent the build up of cholesterol on arterial walls. Thus, Health

Club's therapeutic and preventive claims indicate that the FDA could properly classify Exachol as a drug.

It therefore follows that Exachol could be considered a "new drug" within the meaning of 21 U.S.C. § 321(p) and the Health Club has failed to file a new drug application under 21 U.S.C. § 355(a) or notice of investigational exemption under 21 U.S.C. § 331(d). However, the Health Club has chosen not to file as a "new drug." Instead, Exachol seeks treatment as a "special dietary food" under the Health Claims for Food policy. Similarly, Exachol seeks to avoid the FDA claim of misbranding under 21 U.S.C. § 334(a)(1) on the basis that its labelling is not misleading under the same policy.

Health Club does not maintain that Exachol is a food within the definition of 21 U.S.C. § 321(f). Exachol is, however, a special dietary food. 21 U.S.C. § 350(c)(A) applies the term "special dietary use" to a food which purports to be used by man to supply "a special dietary need that exists by reason of a physical, physiological, pathological or other condition, including but not limited to the condition of disease, convalescence, pregnancy, lactation, infancy, allergic hypersensitivity to food, underweight, overweight, or the need to control the intake of sodium."
. . .

In the past, the FDA has considered foods for a special dietary use as those which are to be used by people who already suffer from a disease or disorder such as obesity or diabetes. The products are produced and marketed particularly for those consumers and not for the general public. Similarly, Exachol is targeted to people who already have a heart condition or a high cholesterol level as evidenced by its claims that Exachol "helps to get the cholesterol level in your blood under control." The product does address a special dietary need that a person with a high cholesterol content has. It is therefore a food for special dietary use within the definition of 21 U.S.C. § 350(c)(3)(A).

Under the health claims policy, a company is permitted to label its food or food supplement with appropriate health related messages without the product being rendered "misbranded" or a "drug" under the Act.....

According to the FDA, this policy is inapplicable to Exachol because Exachol is a drug. The correct inquiry, however, is whether the labelling accompanying Exachol is consistent with the criteria discussed by FDA for the type of health claim which does not trigger the drug provisions of the Act.

Health Club claims that other companies such as the Kellogg Company, Mazola and Fleischmann are distributing products bearing labels with claims linking diet, nutrition, exercise and their products with health and avoidance of disease conditions. Specifically the FDA's application of the health claims rule to Kellogg's All Bran and various fish oil products before determining whether they will be regulated as drugs indicates that Health Club has been treated in a manner inconsistent with the FDA's established policy.

Health Club has shown that Exachol was similarly situated to the other two products. All–Bran is a food within the definition of 21 U.S.C. § 321(f) since it is used by man for food. Exachol too is a food, for a special dietary use. Like All–Bran, Exachol can be regulated as a drug as well. The FDA has declined to regulate All–Bran as a drug until it has developed and applied one standard for considering health related information on food labels. As a result, the Health Claims for Food Policy, which applies to foods, should be applied to both products since the effect of the current labelling of each is virtually indistinguishable.

The FDA claims that Health Club has not submitted evidence similar to Kellogg's scientific evidence upon which the FDA based its decision indicating that its labels were not misleading. However, this did not constitute grounds for the prosecution of the fish oil manufacturers. The FDA has withheld review of the scientific evidence submitted by the fish oil manufacturers and classification of the fish oil products until after the health claims policy is applied. Further the FDA has given the fish oil manufacturers additional time to compile their evidence despite the fact that at the time the regulatory letters were written to the fish oil manufacturers, the FDA was "unaware of any history of fish oil use as a food supplement" of that there was any evidence to indicate that the product was approved as safe. The FDA was also aware of scientific studies indicating possible adverse effects of prolonged consumption of the fish oil products.

The FDA has not indicated any knowledge of scientific evidence that suggests Exachol will have adverse effects upon its consumers. The FDA has apparently already reviewed Exachol's scientific evidence without awaiting the formalization of the health claims policy. There is no evidence offered here that the fish oil companies are compiling scientific data that will substantiate their claims of the health benefits of fish oils any more than the evidence which Health Club may present to substantiate its claims. Further the FDA has given no indication that the scientific evidence which Kellogg submitted, characterized in a letter responding to Congressman Weiss's request for an assessment of the Kellogg labelling, as "some epidemiological data [which] support the statements being made [and] other data, including animal and clinical studies [which] are less conclusive," will significantly differ from that which Health Club has provided or may provide. Because the FDA makes no clear distinction between the scientific evidence presented for each product it has not sufficiently disputed health Club's claim that Exachol is similarly situated to All–Bran and the fish oil products.

Finally the FDA has not set forth its criteria for distinguishing which products are similar to Exachol and which are not. The Health Club has made a sufficient showing of its similarity to products to be considered under the Health Claims for Food Policy against which judicial action was not taken.

Courts reviewing administrative action require consistency from the government—whether the context be the denial of a regulatory exemption; the denial of a license; or the issuance of a cease and desist order. In every context, the overriding principle of fairness is always the same: the government must govern with an even hand.

In *United States v. Diapulse Corp. of America,* 748 F.2d 56 (2d Cir. 1984), the same standard of evenhandedness was required. There, the Diapulse Corporation of America sought to modify an injunction issued several years earlier in an enforcement action by the FDA, which prohibited Diapulse from marketing one of its products. Diapulse had moved to modify the injunction because the FDA has subsequently approved the same product for sale by a different company. Despite FDA objection, the district court agreed to a modification of the injunction. This decision was affirmed by the Second Circuit.

In explaining its affirmance, the Second Circuit declared that the government must act "evenhandedly" and that it could "not 'grant to one person the right to do that which it denies to another similarly situated.'" In the future, the Court instructed, the government could not continue "to treat like cases differently," and "must apply to [Diapulse] the same scientific and legal standards it applies to [Diapulse's] competitors."

Because the FDA has not treated Exachol under its Health Claims for Food Policy, it has applied an uneven regulatory policy, requiring denial of the requested summary judgment.....

---

4. FDA DISCRETION TO ENFORCE THE FD&C ACT

PETER BARTON HUTT,
FDA REDUCES ECONOMIC REGULATION OF FOOD INDUSTRY

Legal Times of Washington, August 30, 1981, at 31.

In the past ... FDA resources have generally been sufficient to permit policing of the act's economic provisions to forestall widespread industry violations. Throughout its history, the FDA has occasionally declined to take regulatory action against specific economic violations, but it has usually found sufficient resources to bring appropriate action against flagrant violations and violations that threaten to engulf an entire segment of the industry.

In the early 1970s, faced with increasing demands for enforcement activities involving health and safety questions, the agency began to search for new and less resource-intensive techniques to achieve enforcement objectives. In some areas, regulations were made more specific and detailed, and less judgmental, so that enforcement would be "cut and dried" and thus involve fewer disputes. For example, the type size for the mandatory information on food labels was specified as one-sixteenth of an inch, rather than leaving to the judgment of the industry and the FDA inspector whether the information was displayed "prominently" with "conspicuousness" as required by the FDCA.

Following a study showing that 99.7 percent of all FDA formal seizure actions brought in the courts did not proceed to litigation, the agency also determined to shift one of its enforcement activities from court to a less formal negotiation process. The agency therefore undertook to send a "regulatory letter," which provides the recipient an opportunity to correct the violation. If it is not corrected, the FDA is committed to bring legal action in the courts. In most instances, the company is all too happy to promise to correct the violation without formal court action. Regulatory letters were initially devised to handle economic violations of the act, and they have largely been used in this area.

Within the recent past, however, the FDA has cut back drastically on its regulatory activity regarding economic violations of the [FD&C Act]. Industry requests that the FDA enforce the act's economic provisions have been met with a standard FDA response, both orally and in writing, that the agency's limited resources simply do not permit enforcement activities in this area.

Perhaps in an effort to justify budget increases (or at least to prevent further budget cuts), the agency has forthrightly stated that it simply will not enforce certain parts of the act. Even flagrant and widespread violations have been included within the new policy. Those who have been rebuffed by the FDA in their attempt to obtain enforcement against economic violations have sought recourse in two places: Congress and the courts.

Attempts to bring pressure on the FDA through individual members of Congress have been, in general, to no avail. The FDA has responded to congressional letters on behalf of constituents in much the same was it is has responded to the food industry in general. But the agency is clearly responsive to its congressional appropriations committees. In the Senate report on the FDA's fiscal 1981 appropriations, the committee expressed its concern "that adulterated frozen concentrated orange juice in retail containers and adulterated orange juice from concentrate is being produced and sold at an increasing rate in a number of areas in the country." The committee report noted that this has an "adverse impact on the consumer" and "works an economic hardship on growers and processors who produce a pure product." Thus, the committee stated its belief that the FDA "should pursue a vigorous enforcement policy with respect to any violations of Federal standards of identity for orange juice," and directed the agency to submit a report of its plan for enforcement within three months of the appropriations bill's enactment. (S. Rep. No. 96–1030, at 100 (1980).)

The result has been predictable, of course. Last month, the FDA instituted its first enforcement action against the economic adulteration of orange juice, bringing a formal seizure action against 800

55–gallon drums of a product that violated the standard of identity. Thus, the pressure brought by the orange juice industry, through Congress, has proved to be quite effective.

Another industry group, frustrated with the FDA's unwillingness to bring action against what the group regards as unfair labeling has resorted to the courts. The National Milk Producers Federation (NMPF) has actively opposed FDA regulations regarding the requirements for "imitation" labeling, particularly as they apply to substitute dairy products. The NMPF brought to the attention of the FDA two substitute cheese product labels it regarded as violative. The agency responded that at "the present time economic violations generally are considered low priority." ...

> Our high priorities are health hazards, filth, and nutrition. Our lowest priorities are food economics and food standards. Thus we expect no actions in the near future concerning the cheese substitute products indicated in your letters.

The NMPF brought suit in November 1979 to compel the FDA to take appropriate regulatory action. In June 1980, the district court granted summary judgment for the FDA. The court determined that the NMPF

> cited no authority holding that the FDA's duty to enforce the Act is a ministerial duty compelled by law. Where enforcement proceedings are discretionary, a mandamus action will not lie.

NMPF v. Harris, Food Drug Cos. L. Rep. (CCH) ¶ 38,045 (D. Minn. 1980) [*aff'd,* 653 F.2d 339 (8th Cir. 1981)].

> ... [T]he FDA's continuing failure to enforce the FDCA's economic provisions invites serious problems both for consumers and for the regulated industry. Such a policy encourages less responsible manufacturers to flaunt the law and can force even the most responsible members of the industry to cut corners in order to meet competition.

HECKLER v. CHANEY

Supreme Court of the United States, 1985.
470 U.S. 821.

JUSTICE REHNQUIST delivered the opinion of the Court.

This case presents the question of the extent to which a decision of an administrative agency to exercise its "discretion" not to undertake certain enforcement actions is subject to judicial review under the Administrative Procedure Act, 5 U.S.C. § 501 *et seq.* (APA). Respondents are several prison inmates convicted of capital offenses and sentenced to death by lethal injection of drugs. They petitioned the Food and Drug Administration (FDA), alleging that under the circumstances the use of these drugs for capital punishment violated the

Federal Food, Drug, and Cosmetic Act, 52 Stat. 1040, as amended, 21 U.S.C. § 301 *et seq.* (FDCA), and requesting that the FDA take various enforcement actions to prevent these violations. The FDA refused their request. We review here a decision of the Court of Appeals for the District of Columbia Circuit, which held the FDA's refusal to take enforcement actions both reviewable and an abuse of discretion, and remanded the case with directions that the agency be required "to fulfill its statutory function." 718 F.2d 1174, 1191 (1983).....

The Court of Appeals' decision addressed three questions: (1) whether the FDA had jurisdiction to undertake the enforcement actions requested, (2) whether if it did have jurisdiction its refusal to take those actions was subject to judicial review, and (3) whether if reviewable its refusal was arbitrary, capricious, or an abuse of discretion. In reaching our conclusion that the Court of Appeals was wrong, however, we need not and do not address the thorny question of the FDA's jurisdiction. For us, this case turns on the important question of the extent to which determinations by the FDA *not to exercise* its enforcement authority over the use of drugs in interstate commerce may be judicially reviewed. That decision in turn involves the construction of two separate but necessarily interrelated statutes, the APA and the FDCA.

The APA's comprehensive provisions for judicial review of "agency actions" are contained in 5 U.S.C. §§ 701–706. Any person "adversely affected or aggrieved" by agency action, *see* § 702, including a "failure to act," is entitled to "judicial review thereof," as long as the action is a "final agency action for which there is no other adequate remedy in a court," *see* § 704. The standards to be applied on review are governed by the provisions of § 706. But before any review at all may be had, a party must first clear the hurdle of § 701(a). That section provides that the chapter on judicial review "applies, according to the provisions thereof, except to the extent that (1) statutes preclude judicial review; or (2) agency action is committed to agency discretion by law." Petitioner urges that the decision of the FDA to refuse enforcement is an action "committed to agency discretion by law" under § 701(a)(2).....

This Court first discussed § (a)(2) in *Citizens to Preserve Overton Park v. Volpe,* 401 U.S. 402 (1971)....

[*Overton Park*] answers several of the questions raised by the language of § 701(a), although it raises others. First, it clearly separates the exception provided by § (a)(1) from the § (a)(2) exception. The former applies when Congress has expressed an intent to preclude judicial review. The latter applies in different circumstances; even where Congress has not affirmatively precluded review, review is not to be had if the statute is drawn so that a court would have no meaningful standard against which to judge the agency's exercise of discretion. In such a case, the statute ("law") can be taken to have "committed" the decisionmaking to the agency's judgment absolutely. This construction avoids conflict with the "abuse of discretion" standard of review in § 706—if no judicially manageable standards are available for judging how and when an agency should exercise its discretion, then it is impossible to evaluate agency action for "abuse of discretion." In addition, this construction satisfies the principle of statutory construction mentioned earlier, by identifying a separate class of cases to which § 701(a)(2) applies.....

Overton Park did not involve an agency's refusal to take requested enforcement action. It involved an affirmative act of approval under a statute that set clear guidelines for determining when such approval should be given. Refusals to take enforcement steps generally involve precisely the opposite situation, and in that situation we think the presumption is that judicial review is not available. This Court has recognized on several occasions over many years that an agency's decision not to prosecute or enforce, whether through civil or criminal process, is a decision generally committed to an agency's absolute discretion. This recognition of the existence of discretion is attributable in no small part to the general unsuitability for judicial review of agency decisions to refuse enforcement.

The reasons for this general unsuitability are many. First, an agency decision not to enforce often involves a complicated balancing of a number of factors which are peculiarly within its expertise. Thus, the agency must not only assess whether a violation has occurred, but whether agency resources are best spent on this violation or another, whether the agency is likely to succeed if it acts, whether the particular enforcement action requested best fits the agency's overall policies, and, indeed, whether the agency has enough resources to undertake the action at all. An agency generally cannot act against each technical violation of the statute it is charged with enforcing. The agency is far better equipped than the courts to deal with the many variables involved in the proper ordering of its priorities. Similar concerns animate the principles of administrative law that courts generally will defer to an agency's construction of the statute it is charged with implementing, and to the procedures it adopts for implementing that statute.

In addition to these administrative concerns, we note that when an agency refuses to act it generally does not exercise its *coercive* power over an individual's liberty or property rights, and thus does not infringe upon areas that courts often are called upon to protect....

We of course only list the above concerns to facilitate understanding of our conclusion that an agency's decision not to take enforcement action should be presumed immune from judicial review under § 701(a)(2). For good reasons, such a decision has traditionally been "committed to agency discretion," and we believe that the Congress enacting the APA did not intend to alter that tradition. In so stating, we emphasize that the decision is only presumptively unreviewable; the presumption may be rebutted where the substantive statute has provided guidelines for the agency to follow in establishing its enforcement powers. Thus, in establishing this presumption in the APA, Congress did not set agencies free to disregard legislative direction in the statutory scheme that the agency administers. Congress may limit an agency's exercise of enforcement power if it wishes, either by setting substantive priorities, or by otherwise circumscribing an agency's power to discriminate among issues or cases it will pursue.....

To enforce the various substantive prohibitions contained in the FDCA, the Act provides for injunctions, 21 U.S.C. § 332, criminal sanctions, §§ 333 and 335, and seizure of any offending food, drug, or cosmetic article, § 334. The Act's general provision for enforcement, § 372, provides only that "[t]he Secretary is *authorized* to conduct examinations and investigations ... " (emphasis added).... § 332 gives no indication of when an injunction should be sought, and § 334, providing for seizures, is framed in the permissive—the offending food, drug, or cosmetic "shall be liable to be proceeded against." The section on criminal sanctions states baldly that any person who violates the Act's substantive prohibitions "shall be imprisoned ... or fined." Respondents argue that this statement mandates criminal prosecution of every violator of the Act but they adduce no indication in case law or legislative history that such was Congress' intention in using this language, which is commonly found in the criminal provisions of Title 18 of the United States Code. We are unwilling to attribute such a sweeping meaning to this language, particularly since the Act charges the Secretary only with recommending prosecution; any criminal prosecutions must be instituted by the Attorney General. The Act's enforcement provisions thus commit complete discretion to the Secretary to decide how and when they should be exercised.

Respondents nevertheless present three separate authorities that they claim provide the courts with sufficient indicia of an intent to circumscribe enforcement discretion. Two of these may be dealt with summarily. First, we reject respondents' argument that the Act's substantive prohibitions of "misbranding" and the introduction of "new drugs" absent agency approval supply us with "law to apply." These provisions are simply irrelevant to the agency's discretion to refuse to initiate proceedings.

We also find singularly unhelpful the agency "policy statement" on which the Court of Appeals placed great reliance [37 Fed. Reg. 16503 (August 15, 1972), p. 619 *supra*.]. We would have difficulty with this statement's vague language even if it were a properly adopted agency rule.... But in any event the policy statement was attached to a rule that was never adopted. Whatever force such a statement might have, and leaving to one side the problem of whether an agency's rules might under certain circumstances provide courts with adequate guidelines

---

4. We do not have in this case a refusal by the agency to institute proceedings based solely on the belief that it lacks jurisdiction. Nor do we have a situation where it could justifiably be found that the agency has "consciously and expressly adopted a general policy" that is so extreme as to amount to an abdication of its statutory responsibilities....

for informed judicial review of decisions not to enforce, we do not think the language of the agency's "policy statement" can plausibly be read to override the agency's express assertion of unreviewable discretion contained in the above rule.

Respondents' third argument, based upon § 306 of the FDCA, merits only slightly more consideration. That section provides:

> "Nothing in this chapter shall be construed as requiring the Secretary to report for prosecution, or for the institution of libel or injunction proceedings, minor violations of this chapter whenever he believes that the public interest will be adequately served by a suitable written notice or ruling."

Respondents seek to draw from this section the negative implication that the Secretary is *required* to report for prosecution all "major" violations of the Act, however, those might be defined, and that it therefore supplies the needed indication of an intent to limit agency enforcement discretion. We think that this section simply does not give rise to the negative implication which respondents seek to draw from it. The section is not addressed to agency proceedings designed to discover the existence of violations, but applies only to a situation where a violation has already been established to the satisfaction of the agency. We do not believe the section speaks to the criteria which shall be used by the agency for investigating *possible* violations of the Act.

We therefore conclude that the presumption that agency decisions not to institute proceedings are unreviewable under 5 U.S.C. § 701(a)(2) is not overcome by the enforcement provisions of the FDCA. The FDA's decision not to take the enforcement actions requested by respondents is therefore not subject to judicial review under the APA.... In so holding, we essentially leave to Congress, and not to the courts, the decision as to whether an agency's refusal to institute proceedings should be judicially reviewable. No colorable claim is made in this case that the agency's refusal to institute proceedings violated any constitutional rights of respondents, and we do not address the issue that would be raised in such a case. The fact that the drugs involved in this case are ultimately to be used in imposing the death penalty must not lead this Court or other courts to import profound differences of opinion over the meaning of the Eighth Amendment to the United States Constitution into the domain of administrative law.

The judgment of the Court of Appeals is

Reversed.

[The concurring opinions of Justice Brennan and Justice Marshall are omitted.]

NOTE

In *Heterochemical Corp. v. FDA*, 644 F. Supp. 271 (E.D.N.Y. 1986), the plaintiff petitioned FDA to take regulatory action against three competitors who sold vitamin K for use in animal feed without FDA approval. After publishing the petition in 41 Fed. Reg. 35009 (August 18, 1976), the agency denied it seven years later in 48 Fed. Reg. 16748 (April 19, 1983), and the plaintiff sought judicial review. FDA took the position that *Chaney* was dispositive. The court refused to dismiss the action, however, holding that the Supreme Court had excluded from FDA's unreviewable discretion those situations where the agency had already determined that there was a violation of the FD&C Act, particularly where FDA regulations themselves established a required course of agency action. The court later held that the plaintiff had to make its case for abuse of discretion on the basis of the formal administrative record and could not supplement that record or obtain further information about the agency's deliberative process through discovery or deposition. Food Drug Cosm. L. Rep. (CCH) ¶ 38,074 (E.D.N.Y. 1987).

---

5. ROLE OF THE JUSTICE DEPARTMENT

Like most other Federal agencies, FDA must rely on the Department of Justice and local U.S. Attorneys to initiate suits to enforce the FD&C Act.

FOOD AND DRUG ADMINISTRATION ACT

Hearings on H.R. 15315 Before the Subcommittee on Public
Health and Environment of the House Committee on Interstate
and Foreign Commerce, 92d Cong., 2d Sess. (1972).

Mr. Hastings [Republican Congressman from New York].... There have been many charges by many people—responsibly or not, I won't comment on—that the prosecutions of FDA violations have in fact not been as diligent or successful as they possibly could be....

Mr. Kurzman [DHEW Assistant Secretary for Legislation].... The answer to your particular question, Mr. Hastings, is that we have made a very rapid survey which is not as yet complete, in part as a result of the chairman's letter within the last couple of days to Commissioner Edwards, of the number of cases for which FDA has sought remedies, both criminal and civil, and the results of those cases....

(The following tables were received for the record:)

FDA Civil Cases——Jan. 1, 1968, Through June 1, 1972

Calendar Year	Seizure Cases Recommended	Seizure Cases Declined to File	Total Seizure [1]	Seizure Cases [2]
1968	537	4	88	9
1969	545	1	62	8
1970	692	1	75	12
1971 [3]	856	0	44 [4]	13
1972 [3]	325	0	—[5]	—[5]
Total	2,955	6	269	42

[1]. Total seizure cases dismissed because product no longer available.
[2]. Seizure cases dismissed because product no longer available and delay in filing over 1 month.
[3]. 1st 6 months only.
[4]. The disposition of many of these cases is still pending.
[5]. Unavailable.

Criminal Cases Recommended by FDA
to Department of Justice—
Jan. 1, 1968, Through June 12, 1972

Calendar Year	Number of Cases Recommended	No Action Yet Taken by D/J	Cases Filed	Filing Declined	Cases Disposed of Over Objection by FDA	
					Dismissed After Filing	One or More Defendants Dropped Before or After Filing
1968	86	0	75	12	3	14
1969	31	0	21	10	1	6
1970	44	0	36	8	2	4
1971 [1]	60	3	52	4	1	10
1972 [1]	32	10	18	3	1	5
Total	253	13	202	37	8	39

[1.] The disposition of many of these cases is still pending.

Note: The total of 84 cases disposed of over objection by FDA involved 101 individual defendants dropped.

Mr. Hutt [FDA Chief Counsel].... [A]s far as we can determine, in roughly 30 to 35 percent of the criminal cases brought, the Department of Justice has either declined to file the case or has dismissed the case over the Food and Drug Administration's objection, or has dismissed one or more individuals over the Food and Drug Administration's objection:....

Mr. Kurzman.... There have historically been [exceptions] where Congress has given or sought to give one or more agencies the power to go to court independently of the Department of Justice, either wholly independently.... I believe all administrations have resisted this kind of splitting up of the litigating power....

As an ex-assistant U.S. attorney myself, I am very much aware of how our current arrangement of U.S. attorney offices is designed to bring to the Federal Government the same kind of effectiveness that private attorneys often seek.... It is wise to have, from the point of view of not only efficiency but success, attorneys on the scene who are residents of the district involved and know well the way the particular judges of that court operate and the way juries react to particular types of cases, who can assess the workload of that particular court and can make the most effective judgment as to whether they are likely to win the case asking for the particular remedy involved....

I recall making judgments of that sort, myself. It is the ultimate test of the use of court sanctions for the enforcement of the Congress' will, and I think that judgment has been wisely delegated to attorneys on the spot. So the administration, like previous administrations, prefers to keep that unitary judgment in the Department of Justice and with the U.S. attorneys' offices around the country. As I pointed out, there are 62 independent agencies, all reporting to the President, and if subagencies were to be given this power as well as all those departments, you can just imagine the duplication of effort and the tremendous fragmentation and weakening of the Government's posture before these courts and these juries if there were helter-skelter enforcement sought by attorneys out of the Washington offices of each independent agency or indeed certainly if each agency felt called upon to set up its own satellite U.S. attorney offices in the most heavily trafficked districts....

Mr. Rogers. I am concerned, too, because I have a letter from the former counsel of HEW for Food and Drug and we wanted his experience in this area....

Dear Mr. Chairman: ... I am writing about the proposal now before your Subcommittee, H.R. 15315, which includes a provision authorizing the Agency's counsel to represent it in Court. This is an issue on which I have strong feelings arising out of my own experience as FDA's Chief Counsel. I am convinced that FDA requires a very knowledgeable and fully effective advocate in the courtroom to uphold and to enforce the laws committed to its administration....

The outside interests with whom FDA litigates are able to select their own expert counsel—both trial and appellate counsel—from the best of the Nation's practitioners. Fairness to the public interest calls for an equal expertise of representation in any area involving a complex statutory scheme such as the Federal Food, Drug, and Cosmetic Act. This expertise comes from close association with, and participation in, FDA's programs as they develop....

Recently, the representation of FDA within the Department of Justice was transferred to the Antitrust Division, away from the Criminal Division that had been responsible for at least 30 years. It became more difficult, and in many cases impossible, for the Agency's counsel to make arrangements to speak for it in Court contests. This arrangement has the disadvantage of requiring trial and appellate counsel to be brought into cases after they have fully developed in the administrative agency, and does not permit Agency counsel closest to the case to represent its interest in Court except through Department of Justice counsel. Even where the Department of Justice takes the lead in the Court case, it is necessary to supply Agency counsel because of his better knowledge of the facts and the law. Duplication of legal services is both costly and unnecessary.

Moreover, the Congress holds FDA and its Commissioner responsible for the efficient administration of these laws. Your Committee, the Appropriations Committee, and the Government Operations Committee have emphasized this point. Yet the Department of Justice has taken a role in deciding when to prosecute enforcement actions and how to settle them once they have been initiated....

I think the FDA should have the right to speak through its own chosen counsel when it considers this necessary (as where the Department of Justice fails or refuses to act), and it should have the right to press any case that the Commissioner considers vital to the achievement of his program purposes.

Respectfully, William M. Goodrich....

Mr. Kurzman.... Let me comment briefly, though, on two points.... I know that in the southern district of New York, which probably accounts for an enormous proportion of regulatory cases filed by all agencies because it is the headquarters of so much of American industry, the U.S. attorney office there at the time I was there in the late 1950's and early 1960's was specialized in this regard. It did have assistant U.S. attorneys who handled nothing but FDA cases and who had developed over the years enormous expertise comparable, I am sure, to what the agency itself develops....

NOTE

Compare McConachie, *The Role of the Department of Justice in Enforcing the Federal Food, Drug and Cosmetic Act,* 31 FDC L.J. 333 (1976), *with* Cooper, *Litigating Authority in the Federal Government: An Agency View* (Unpublished, 1979).

---

6. THE EMERGING ROLE OF THE HHS INSPECTOR GENERAL

In 90 Stat. 2429 (1976), Congress created the Office of Inspector General in the Department of HEW, for the purpose of "preventing and detecting fraud and abuse" in departmental programs and operations. Two years later, in the Inspector General Act of 1978, 92 Stat. 1101, 5 U.S.C. App. 3, Congress created an Office of Inspector General in other departments and agencies as well. As part of the Inspector General Act Amendments of 1988, 102 Stat. 2515, the 1976 statute was repealed, and the HHS Office of Inspector General was made subject to the 1978 statute.

A GAO report, FOOD AND DRUG ADMINISTRATION: HHS INSPECTOR GENERAL SHOULD BE INVOLVED IN CRIMINAL INVESTIGATIONS, HRD–88–8 (November 19, 1987), acknowledged that the HHS Inspector General was not intended to replace the FDA regulatory function, but still recommended that the Inspector General be involved in FDA criminal investigations. Following that report, the Office of Legal Counsel in the Department of Justice issued an opinion that under the 1978 statute inspectors general do not have authority to investigate violations of regulatory statutes but rather are limited to investigating the employees and operations of a department and its contractors, grantees, and other recipients of federal funds in order to "root out waste and fraud." Memorandum from Assistant Attorney General D.W. Kmiec to Department of Labor Acting Solicitor J.G. Thorn (March 9, 1989), reprinted in 3 Corporate Crime Reporter, No. 32, at 18 (August 14, 1989).

Nonetheless, on the heels of the generic drug scandal, p. 579 *supra,* the HHS Inspector General was delegated "the responsibility for conducting investigations of criminal violations of the Federal Food, Drug and Cosmetic Act for which the penalty is a felony," excluding "any program inspection or examination authority" and any other matters that "should remain a function of the Food and Drug Administration." Memorandum from HHS Secretary L.W. Sullivan to HHS Inspector General R.P. Kusserow (July 24, 1989). This action was reported to have precipitated the resignation of the FDA Chief Counsel. Himelstein, *Top FDA Lawyer Resigns Over Policy Dispute,* XII Legal Times of Washington, No. 11, at 6 (August 7, 1989). Although the Inspector General and FDA attempted to limit the delegation to situations where there was "fraud by or upon employees of the FDA," Memorandum from HHS Inspector General R.P. Kusserow to HHS General Counsel M.J. Astrue and Commissioner of Food and Drugs F.E. Young (October 2, 1989), and to situations "when FDA requests their assistance," "Statement by the Commissioner of Food and Drugs," HHS News (August 18, 1989), the delegation continued to attract substantial criticism. Secretary Sullivan rescinded the delegation on December 28, 1989 on the stated basis that the generic drug "emergency" was over and its need had "passed." *See* "Naked Reverse: Secretary Sullivan's Recission of his Delegation of Investigative Authority to the Inspector General," Staff Report Prepared for the Use of the Subcomm. on Oversight and Investigations of the House Comm. on Energy and Commerce, 101st Cong., 2d Sess., Comm. Print 101–S (1990).

B. ENFORCEMENT JURISDICTION

1. INTRODUCTION INTO INTERSTATE COMMERCE

UNITED STATES v. 7 BARRELS ... SPRAY DRIED WHOLE EGG

United States Circuit Court of Appeals, Seventh Circuit, 1944.
141 F.2d 767.

SPARKS, Circuit Judge.

The Government appeals from a judgment dismissing its libel for want of jurisdiction. The libel, alleging adulteration, had been filed against one lot of seven barrels of dried eggs which it sought to condemn under the provisions of § 304(a) of the Federal Food, Drug, and Cosmetic Act. The claimant ... interposed two defenses, first, that the libel failed to state facts indicating that the article seized was introduced into or was in interstate commerce, at the time of the seizure....

The subject of the libel was part of 150 barrels of spray-dried whole eggs tendered by appellee to the Federal Surplus Commodities Corporation in part performance of a contract between the parties....

Appellant contends that the contract was a transaction in interstate commerce; that the barrels were marked and set aside as the property to be used in fulfillment of the contract, thus being brought within the exclusive dominion of the out-of-state purchaser, and thereby introduced into commerce within the meaning of the statute. It further contends that the subsequent rejection of the eggs did not remove them from the jurisdiction of the Act or divest them of their interstate character.

We are not in accord with these contentions. It is clear that the contract is quite conditional in its character. It consists of an accepted offer to deliver at appellee's plant, on or before a certain date, a prescribed amount of eggs of a described character. The eggs here libeled were part of a lot intended for delivery, if accepted, within the time, and at the place named in the contract, in part performance thereof. True, they were marked and set aside in seller's plant. However, they were not thus segregated as the property to be used in fulfillment of the contract, but for inspection and testing to determine whether they complied with the required specifications. This was necessary before there could be an acceptance of the delivery, and before acceptance there could be no dominion of the FSCC over the property.

The contract provided that the product should be considered ready for delivery on the date the inspection certificate was issued, and not sooner.... It seems to us that the only reasons for the required preliminary marking and segregation of the barrels before the inspection and test was [sic] that actual delivery might be expedited after the acceptance, and the probability of substitution for any part of the tendered produce, without the knowledge of the FSCC, would be greatly minimized.

It is quite apparent that the object of the statute is to prevent adulterated articles of food from entering interstate commerce. That object seems to have been fully accomplished long before this libel suit was filed. After the inspection certificate was issued neither party insisted upon a delivery of the seven barrels, and that was as early as a delivery could be made under Article 7 of the contract. Appellee thereupon substituted seven other barrels in their stead and the FSCC accepted them, whereupon the State of Indiana placed an embargo upon the rejected barrels, the effect of which was to prevent their removal from the plant. Hence they could never become a part of interstate commerce.

We recognize the legal principle that goods may become a part of interstate commerce before transportation begins, and may remain such after transportation ends. The cases bearing on the former enunciate the rule that where goods are purchased in one State for transportation to another, the commerce includes the purchase quite as much as it does the transportation. . . .

In the instant case, however, the contract did not provide, nor did the parties intend that the eggs segregated and marked prior to the test would then and there become a part of interstate commerce, or that such acts would amount to a sale or delivery of them. . . . We are convinced that if appellee had sold and shipped, or contracted to ship, the seven barrels of eggs to customers in another state it would be held to have engaged in interstate commerce. However, our conclusion is that appellee never sold nor shipped, nor did it contract to sell or ship, to customers in another state the seven barrels of eggs in question.

Affirmed.

NOTE

See also *Hipolite Egg Co. v. United States,* 220 U.S. 45 (1911) (1906 Act applies to the shipment of food for use in the manufacture of another food product); *United States v. 52 Drums of Maple Syrup,* 110 F.2d 914 (2d Cir. 1940) (adulterated food shipped in commerce is illegal even though intended for processing to bring it into compliance).

UNITED STATES v. SANDERS

United States Court of Appeals, Tenth Circuit, 1952.
196 F.2d 895.

HUXMAN, Circuit Judge.

On October 17, 1951, an injunction was entered against appellee . . . enjoining him from directly or indirectly introducing or causing to be introduced, and delivering or causing to be delivered, for introduction into interstate commerce, in violation of 21 U.S.C. § 331(a), a drug which was misbranded. . . . Thereafter this action was filed in the nature of an application for an order to show cause why he should not be prosecuted for criminal contempt for a violation of the injunction. . . .

It is admitted that the drug in question was misbranded. Appellee's position adopted by the court is that his activities do not constitute interstate commerce as prohibited by the injunction. . . .

The application for the order to show cause among others alleged that since the issuance of the injunction appellee had . . . on January 24, 1951 . . . sold and delivered to Loyd Mangan of Garden City,

Kansas, for introduction into interstate commerce two one quart jars of said misbranded drug, with the knowledge that Mangan intended to and would return to Garden City, Kansas, with said article or drug. The complaint alleged five other specific sales made to out of state customers and alleged that all of said sales were made with the knowledge that the purchaser was from out of the state and intended to and would return to his place of residence out of the state with said drugs....

... The Act must be given a reasonable construction to effectuate its salutary purposes. It prohibits not only the introduction into interstate commerce of adulterated articles but also the delivery thereof for introduction into commerce. One is as much a violation of the Act as the other. There is a long line of cases beginning with *In re Dahnke–Walker Milling Co. v. Bondurant,* 257 U.S. 282 (1921), holding that where one purchases goods in one state for transportation to another the interstate commerce transaction includes the purchase as well as the transportation.... The decisions, however, make it clear that whether delivery for transportation is made to a common carrier, a private carrier, or even to the purchaser for transportation by himself is immaterial.

To be guilty of violating the Act, it was not necessary that appellee be engaged in interstate commerce with respect to a misbranded drug. It was sufficient if he was engaged in delivering such a drug for introduction into interstate commerce. If appellee knowingly and regularly sold misbranded drugs and delivered them, knowing that they were purchased for transportation in interstate commerce, and solicited customers to return for future purchases and deliveries, he was guilty of a violation of the Act....

NOTES

1. *Supporting Authority.* See *Drown v. United States,* 198 F.2d 999 (9th Cir. 1952) (sale to buyer known to be returning to Illinois constituted delivery for introduction into interstate commerce).

2. *Dispensing of Rx Drugs.* Compare Trade Correspondence No. 183 (March 15, 1940), in which FDA provided the following reply to a physician who treated patients in several states:

> With reference to medicines given to your patients at your hospital and transported by them to their homes in some other states for use by themselves, it is our opinion that such a transaction is not interstate commerce as that term is defined in Section 201(b) of the Act. We are still of the opinion, however, that the shipment of drugs by you to patients in other states, whether by mail, express, messenger, or otherwise, is interstate commerce, and that products so shipped are required by the statute to comply with its terms.

3. *Holding Prior to Shipment.* See *United States v. International Exterminator Corp.,* 294 F.2d 270 (5th Cir. 1961):

> ... [T]he defendants operate an exterminator and pest-control service for establishments such as warehouses, mills and dryers which

store and sell foods such as beans, rice, flour, sugar, meal, salt, bakery supplies and also animal and poultry feed. In so doing, it is averred, the defendants are causing quantities of a poisonous liquid known as compound 1080 to be placed in the establishments in uncovered paper bait cups in close proximity to the foods. This, the complaint alleged, results in the foods being adulterated within the meaning of the Act "because of being held under insanitary conditions whereby they may have been rendered injurious to health prior to being introduced or delivered for introduction into interstate commerce." . . .

There seems to us no question but that the complaint brings the case within the interstate commerce requirements of the Act.

---

2. HELD FOR SALE AFTER SHIPMENT IN INTER-STATE COMMERCE

UNITED STATES v. PHELPS DODGE MERCANTILE CO.

United States Court of Appeals, Ninth Circuit, 1946.
157 F.2d 453.

MATHEWS, Circuit Judge.

. . . [T]he United States, proceeded against 175 cartons of food (150 cartons of spaghetti and 25 cartons of macaroni) in possession of appellee, Phelps Dodge Mercantile Company, in the District of Arizona. . . .

. . . [T]he libel stated . . . that on September 28, 1945—more than two years after it was shipped in interstate commerce—the food was adulterated. The libel did not state that the food was adulterated when introduced into or while in interstate commerce. Instead, the libel stated . . . that the food was adulterated while held in original packages by appellee at its warehouse in Douglas, Arizona. Thus it appeared that the adulteration of the food occurred after it ended its interstate journey and came to rest at appellee's warehouse.

Appellant contends that the fact that the food was adulterated while held in original packages was sufficient to warrant its condemnation. We do not agree. . . . 21 U.S.C. § 334(a), under which this proceeding was brought, provides for the condemnation of "Any article of food * * * that is adulterated * * * when introduced into or while in interstate commerce." It says nothing about original packages. The terms "interstate commerce" and "original packages" are not synonymous. Articles may be in interstate commerce without being in original packages. They may be in original packages without being in interstate commerce. They may be in both interstate commerce and original packages and, if in both, may cease to be in interstate commerce and yet remain in original packages. Hence the fact that the food was adulterated while held in original packages did not show that it was adulterated when introduced into or while in interstate commerce....

UNITED STATES v. SULLIVAN

Supreme Court of the United States, 1948.
332 U.S. 689.

Mr. Justice BLACK delivered the opinion of the Court.

Respondent, a retail druggist in Columbus, Georgia, was charged in two counts of an information with a violation of § 301(k) of the Federal Food, Drug, and Cosmetic Act of 1938. That section prohibits "the doing of any ... act with respect to, a ... drug ... if such act is done while such article is held for sale after shipment in interstate commerce and results in such article being misbranded." Section 502(f) of the Act declares a drug "to be misbranded ... unless its labeling bears (1) adequate directions for use; and (2) such adequate warnings against use ... dangerous to health, or against unsafe dosage ... as are necessary for the protection of users." ...

The facts alleged are these: A laboratory had shipped in interstate commerce from Chicago, Illinois, to a consignee at Atlanta, Georgia, a number of bottles, each containing 1,000 sulfathiazole tablets. These bottles had labels affixed to them, which, as required by § 502(f)(1) and (2) of the Act, set out adequate directions for the use of the tablets and adequate warnings to protect ultimate consumers from dangers incident to this use. Respondent bought one of these properly labeled bottles of sulfathiazole tablets from the Atlanta consignee, transferred it to his Columbus, Georgia, drugstore, and there held the tablets for resale. On two separate occasions twelve tablets were removed from the properly labeled and branded bottle, placed in pill boxes, and sold to customers. These boxes were labeled "sulfathiazole." They did not contain the statutorily required adequate directions for use or warnings of danger.

Respondent's motion to dismiss the information was overruled, a jury was waived, evidence was heard, and respondent was convicted under both counts.

The Circuit Court of Appeals reversed. 161 F.2d 629. The court thought that as a result of respondent's action the sulfathiazole became "misbranded" within the meaning of the Federal Act, and that in its "broadest possible sense" the Act's language "may include what happened." However, it was also of the opinion that the Act ought not be taken so broadly "but held to apply only to the holding for the first sale by the importer after interstate shipment." ...

... When we seek the meaning of § 301(k) from its language we find that the offense it creates and which is here charged requires the doing of some act with respect to a drug (1) which results in its being misbranded, (2) while the article is held for sale "after shipment in interstate commerce." Respondent has not seriously contended that the "misbranded" portion of § 301(k) is ambiguous. Section 502(f), as has been seen, provides that a drug is misbranded unless the labeling contains adequate directions and adequate warnings. The labeling here did not contain the information which § 502(f) requires. . . .

Furthermore, it would require great ingenuity to discover ambiguity in the additional requirement of § 301(k) that the misbranding occur "while such article is held for sale after shipment in interstate commerce." The words accurately describe respondent's conduct here. He held the drugs for sale after they had been shipped in interstate commerce from Chicago to Atlanta. It is true that respondent bought them over six months after the interstate shipment had been completed by their delivery to another consignee. But the language used by Congress broadly and unqualifiedly prohibits misbranding articles held for sale after shipment in interstate commerce, without regard to how long after the shipment the misbranding occurred, how many intrastate sales had intervened, or who had received the articles at the end of the interstate shipment. Accordingly, we find that the conduct of the respondent falls within the literal meaning of § 301(k).

. . . Given the meaning that we have found the literal language of § 301(k) to have, it is thoroughly consistent with the general aims and purposes of the Act. . . . Its purpose was to safeguard the consumer by applying the Act to articles from the moment of their introduction into interstate commerce all the way to the moment of their delivery to the ultimate consumer. Section 301(a) forbids the "introduction or delivery for introduction into interstate commerce" of misbranded or adulterated drugs; § 301(b) forbids the misbranding or adulteration of drugs while "in interstate commerce"; and § 301(c) prohibits the "receipt in interstate commerce" of any misbranded or adulterated drug, and "the delivery or proffered delivery thereof for pay or otherwise." But these three paragraphs alone would not supply protection all the way to the consumer. The words of paragraph (k) "while such article is held for sale after shipment in interstate commerce" apparently were designed to fill this gap and to extend the Act's coverage to every article that had gone through interstate commerce until it finally reached the ultimate consumer. . . .

Reversed.

Mr. Justice FRANKFURTER, dissenting.

. . . [A]n article is "misbranded" only if there is "adulteration, mutilation, destruction, obliteration, or removal of the whole or any part of the labeling of, or the doing of any act with respect to, a food, drug, device, or cosmetic." Here there was no "alteration, mutilation, destruction, obliteration, or removal" of any part of the label. The decisive question is whether taking a unit from a container and putting it in a bag, whether it be food, drug or cosmetic, is doing "any other act" in the context in which that phrase is used in the setting of the Federal Food, Drug, and Cosmetic Act and particularly of § 301(k).

As bearing upon the appropriate answer to this question, it cannot be that a transfer from a jar, the bulk container, to a small paper bag, without transferring the label of the jar to the paper bag, is "any other act" when applied to a drug, but not "any other act" when applied to candies or cosmetics. Before we reach the possible discretion that may be exercised in prosecuting a certain conduct, it must be determined whether there is anything to prosecute....

It is this inescapable conjunction of food, drugs and cosmetics in the prohibition of § 301(k) that calls for a consideration of the phrase "or the doing of any other act," in the context of the rest of the sentence and with due regard for the important fact that the States are also deeply concerned with the protection of the health and welfare of their citizens or transactions peculiarly within local enforcing powers. So considered, "the doing of any other act" should be read with the meaning which radiates to that loose phrase from the particularities that precede it, namely "alteration, mutilation, destruction, obliteration, or removal" of any part of the label.... There is nothing in the legislative history of the Act ... to give the slightest basis for inferring that Congress contemplated what the Court now finds in the statute. The statute in its entirety was of course intended to protect the ultimate consumer. This is no more true in regard to the requirements pertaining to drugs than of those pertaining to food. As to the reach of the statute—the means by which its ultimate purpose is to be achieved—the legislative history sheds precisely the same light on the provisions pertaining to food as on the provisions pertaining to drugs. If differentiations are to be made in the enforcement of the Act and in the meaning which the ordinary person is to derive from the Act, such differentiations are interpolations of construction. They are not expressions by Congress.

In the light of this approach to the problem of construction presented by this Act, I would affirm the judgment below....

NOTES

1. *Legislative Overruling of Phelps Dodge.* In reaction to the *Phelps Dodge* decision, Congress revised sections 301(k) and 304(a) of the Act in 62 Stat. 582 (1948). The House Report, H.R. Rep. No. 807, 80th Cong., 1st Sess. (1947), explained the changes:

> Section 301(k) of the present law, which is enforceable by criminal and injunction proceedings, prohibits the doing of any act with respect to an article of food, drug, device, or cosmetic, while it is "held for sale" after shipment in interstate commerce, if such act results in the article being misbranded. The first section of the bill amends this subsection by inserting "(whether or not the first sale)" after the words quoted above, so as to make it clear that the subsection is not limited to the case where the act occurs while the article is held for first sale after interstate shipment. This section also extends the coverage of the

subsection to acts which result in adulteration, as well as those resulting in misbranding.

Section 304(a) now authorizes, among other things, seizure and condemnation of any article of food, drug, device, or cosmetic that is adulterated or misbranded when introduced into or "while in interstate commerce." Section 2 of the bill amends this provision by inserting after the words "while in interstate commerce" the words "or while held for sale (whether or not the first sale) after shipment in interstate commerce." The language being added, except for the parenthetical expression, is identical with language now contained in section 301(k). . . .

. . . The 1906 act authorized seizure of foods and drugs that became adulterated or misbranded after interstate movement had ceased if they remained unloaded, unsold, or in original unbroken packages. Thousands of shipments of foods and drugs that became filthy, debased, or deteriorated after interstate transportation were seized and condemned under this provision and thereby were prevented from reaching the consuming public. The authority to make seizures in such circumstances was never challenged by court contest. . . .

From time to time seizures have been made of foods contaminated with toxins produced by bacteria. Frequently it is impossible to tell whether the toxin developed before or after the end of the interstate journey. The toxins of different organisms cause illnesses of varying degrees of seriousness. That caused by the toxin of the botulinus organism is of high mortality. Such dangerous products do not appear frequently, but when they are found it is vital that there be adequate legal authority to apprehend them. The great bulk of the commodities involved in this problem are those which become contaminated by rodents, insects, and other vermin.

The insertion of the parenthetical wording "(whether or not the first sale)" in section 301(k) is not designed to change the original intended meaning of the section but would simply make it entirely clear that "held for sale" includes the first sale and any subsequent sale. As a result of a decision on May 12, 1947, by the Circuit Court of Appeals for the Fifth Circuit, in the case of *Jordan J. Sullivan v. United States,* doubts have arisen as to the ultimate judicial interpretation of the present language. . . .

The committee's recommendation that section 301(k) be amended so as to cover adulteration as well as misbranding will make this subsection coextensive with section 304(a). . . .

2. *Goods in Possession of Ultimate Consumer.* *United States v. Olsen,* 161 F.2d 669 (9th Cir. 1947), reversed the dismissal of the government's seizure of a device. The undisputed facts indicated that the article was misbranded when introduced into interstate commerce, even though seizure had occurred in appellee's private home:

It is immaterial, if true, that appellee had purchased and paid for the article, had it in his home, was satisfied with it and desired to keep it; that the article was not inherently dangerous or harmful; that appellee did not intend to use it commercially or permits its use by persons other than himself and his mother and brothers. . . .

On this reasoning, the court in *United States v. One Article of Device Labeled Spectrochrome,* 77 F. Supp. 50 (D. Or. 1948), reluctantly upheld a subsequent seizure order but deplored the adoption of a country-wide "policy of entering private homes to seize articles ... [as] governmental madness."

UNITED STATES v. WIESENFELD WAREHOUSE CO.

Supreme Court of the United States, 1964.
376 U.S. 86.

Mr. Justice STEWART delivered the opinion of the Court.

... The question presented by this appeal is whether a criminal information which alleges the holding of food by a public storage warehouseman (after interstate shipment and before ultimate sale) under insanitary conditions in a building accessible to rodents, birds, and insects, where it may have become contaminated with filth, charges an offense under § 301(k)....

In arriving at its construction of the statute, the District Court reasoned that § 301(k) "as it is presently written, is too vague and indefinite to apply to the mere act of 'holding' goods." Accordingly, "in an effort to uphold the statute as constitutional," the court applied the rule of *ejusdem generis* to limit the words "the doing of any other act" in § 301(k) to acts of "the same general nature" as those specifically enumerated in the subsection, *i.e.,* acts relating to the alteration, mutilation, destruction, obliteration, or removal of the labeling of articles. We find such reliance on the rule *ejusdem generis* misplaced; its application to § 301(k) is contrary to both the text and legislative history of the subsection, and unnecessary to a constitutionally permissible construction of the statute.

The language of § 301(k) unambiguously defines two distinct offenses with respect to food held for sale after interstate shipment. As originally enacted in 1938, the subsection prohibited "[t]he alteration, mutilation, destruction, obliteration, or removal" of the label, or "the doing of any other act" with respect to the product which "results in such article being misbranded." The section was amended in 1948 to prohibit additionally the "doing of any other act" with respect to the product which "results in such article being adulterated." The acts specifically enumerated in the original enactment relate to the offense of misbranding through labeling or the lack thereof. The separate offense of adulteration, on the other hand, is concerned solely with deterioration or contamination of the commodity itself. For the most part, acts resulting in misbranding and acts resulting in adulteration are wholly distinct. Consequently, since the enumerated label-defacing offenses bear no textual or logical relation to the scope of the general language condemning acts of product adulteration, application of the rule of *ejusdem generis* to limit the words "the doing of any other act" resulting in product adulteration in § 301(k) to acts of the same general character as those specifically enumerated with respect to misbranding is wholly inappropriate.

Moreover, the legislative history makes plain that no such application of the rule was intended....

Finally, the appellee attempts to uphold the dismissal of the information on a ground not relied on by the District Court. The appellee says that it was a bailee of the food, not a seller, and that it was not holding the food for sale within the meaning of § 301(k). Both the language and the purpose of the statute refute this construction. The language of § 301(k) does not limit its application to one holding title to the goods, and since the danger to the public from insanitary storage of food is the same regardless of the proprietary status of the person storing it, the purpose of the legislation—to safeguard the consumer from the time the food is introduced into the channels of interstate commerce to the point that it is delivered to the ultimate consumer—would be substantially thwarted by such an unwarranted reading of the statutory language....

Reversed and remanded.

Purpose of act would be thwarted, if Act ct. was kept

UNITED STATES v. 40 CASES ... "PINOCCHIO BRAND 75% CORN, PEANUT OIL AND SOYA BEAN OIL BLENDED WITH 25% PURE OLIVE OIL"

United States Court of Appeals, Second Circuit, 1961.
289 F.2d 343.

LUMBARD, Chief Judge.

The single question before us on this appeal is whether § 304(a) of the Federal Food, Drug, and Cosmetic Act authorizes the United States to proceed against and seize mislabeled or adulterated cans of blended vegetable oils mixed entirely within the State of New York from various oils shipped under proper labels from other states and foreign countries.... The district judge held that the blended oil was a "new product" and therefore not the same as those shipped in interstate commerce....

The United States did not in the district court or here challenge the truth of the company's assertion that the blending process was done entirely within the State of New York, nor did it claim that the blended oil was carried across any state line. It is also undisputed that the various oils from which the blend was made had been shipped under proper labels from New Jersey, Illinois and Georgia, and that olive oil had been transported to the company's plant in Ozone Park, New York, from Spain, Italy and Tunisia. The United States contends that although the component oils were correctly labeled when shipped interstate, the misbranding or adulteration which occurred during or after the blending of the oils brought them within the compass of the federal act as articles of food held for sale after interstate shipment.

. . . Had the company in this case not mixed the oils it received from various sources but instead pasted new misleading labels on the containers in which they were shipped in interstate commerce or otherwise adulterated the oils, seizure would have been authorized. The appellee would have us hold here that the blending of the oils which had been transported in interstate commerce took the final product out from under federal regulation although each of its separate components was being held for sale after shipment in interstate commerce. We do not agree. . . .

. . . Congress sought to fill the gap in the regulatory scheme pointed out in *United States v. Phelps Dodge Mercantile Co., supra,* by subjecting to condemnation food which had been adulterated or misbranded after coming to rest within a state but before being sold to a consumer. The interest of the federal government in ensuring that such food meets minimum standards of purity and is not misbranded arises out of its supervisory function over interstate commerce. The House and Senate reports both referred expressly to the Congressional desire to protect the integrity of interstate products so as not to depress the demand for goods that must travel across state lines. This interest surely extends to products such as olive oil, which a New York consumer would probably recognize as out-of-state or foreign in origin.

Moreover, in this case all the components of the oil blend had been transported in interstate commerce, and the completed mixture was being held for sale as "oil"—the very same type of food which had traveled across the state line. This is not a case in which oil which was transported interstate was used as one of many ingredients in a finished product which in no way resembled the food which had crossed state lines. Oil may come in many varieties, but to the unsophisticated consumer one oil blend is much like another. We would be undermining the remedial legislative purpose of consumer protection were we to deny the power to seize misbranded articles on the ground that such foods as corn oil, peanut oil, soya bean oil and olive oil when mixed constitute a "different product" from a blend of less than all or from a pure measure of any one of them. . . .

NOTES

1. *Supporting Authority.* For other cases holding that shipment of product ingredients in interstate commerce is sufficient to confer jurisdiction on FDA, *see United States v. An Article of Food . . . Coco Rico,* 752 F.2d 11 (1st Cir. 1985); *United States v. Dianovin Pharmaceuticals, Inc.,* 475 F.2d 100 (1st Cir. 1973); *United States v. Cassaro, Inc.,* 443 F.2d 153 (1st Cir. 1971); *Palmer v. United States,* 340 F.2d 48 (5th Cir. 1964); *United States v. Detroit Vital Foods, Inc.,* 330 F.2d 78 (6th Cir. 1964); *United States v. Allbrook Freezing & Cold Storage,* 194 F.2d 937 (5th Cir. 1952); *United States v. Miami Serpentarium Laboratories, Inc.,* Food Drug Cosm. L. Rep. (CCH) ¶ 38,164 (S.D. Fla. 1982); *United States v. 14 Cases . . . Naremco Medi-Matic Free Choice Poultry Formula,*

374 F. Supp. 922 (W.D. Mo. 1974); *United States v. 39 Cases ... "Korleen Tablets,"* 192 F.Supp. 51 (E.D. Mich. 1961).

2. *Device Components.* In *United States v. An Article or Device ... "Gonsertron Corp.,"* 180 F. Supp. 52 (E.D. Mich. 1959), the government attempted to seize a device constructed in Michigan from mechanical parts shipped from other states, none of which was made to the specifications of the claimant. The court dismissed its libel:

> The Government agrees that the manufactured device was not introduced in interstate commerce or held for sale in interstate commerce. It contends, however, that Sec. 321(h) of 21 U.S.C. defines device to mean "instruments, apparatus and contrivances, including their components, parts, and accessories," and therefore concludes that since some of the components used in the manufacture of the device were transported in interstate commerce, the device must also be considered to have been introduced in interstate commerce. Sec. 321(h) merely provides that if a device is subject to libel, all the component parts and accessories are also subject to libel. Neither the language of Sec. 321(h) nor the cases cited by the Government support the construction of Sec. 321(h) that the Government urges....

3. *Proof of Shipment.* Archambault v. United States, 224 F.2d 925 (10th Cir. 1955), held that interstate commerce could be proved simply by the fact that a drug produced in one State was subsequently found in another.

4. *Use in Patient Treatment.* In *United States v. An Article of Device ... "Cameron Spitler Amblyo–Syntonizer,"* 261 F.Supp. 243 (D. Neb. 1966), the court granted summary judgment for the libelant:

> Although the claimant never sold the devices in the commercial sense, the device was used in the claimant's treatment of patients. In *United States v. 10 Cartons of Black Tablets,* 152 F. Supp. 360 (W.D. Pa. 1957), the articles were not sold to patients but used as part of the treatment in the cancer clinic. The court held that such use was within the scope of the "holding for sale."

Other rulings that "held for sale" includes any use other than personal consumption include *United States v. Diapulse Corp. of America,* 514 F.2d 1097 (2d Cir. 1975); *United States v. Bronson Farms, Inc.,* Food Drug Cosm. L. Rep. (CCH) ¶ 38,354 (M.D. Fla., 1986); *United State v. Articles of Drug ... "Hydralazine HCL,"* 568 F. Supp. 29 (D.N.J. 1983); *United States v. Article of Animal Drug Containing Diethylstilbestrol,* 528 F. Supp. 202 (D. Neb. 1981); *United States v. Articles of Device [Acuflex, Pro–Med],* 426 F. Supp. 366 (W.D. Pa. 1977); *United States v. Article of Device ... Cameron Spitler,* 261 F. Supp. 243 (D. Neb. 1966); *United States v. 10 Cartons ... "Hoxsey",* 152 F. Supp. 360 (W.D. Pa. 1957).

4. *Commentary.* See generally Goodrich, *The Applicability of the Federal Food, Drug, and Cosmetic Act to Interstate Commerce,* 3 FDC L.Q. 332 (1948); Kemker, *The Commerce Clause and the Federal Food, Drug, and Cosmetic Act,* 10 FDC L.J. 389 (1955).

FDA JURISDICTION OVER RESTAURANTS

In a 1975 report, FEDERAL SUPPORT FOR RESTAURANT SANITATION FOUND LARGELY INEFFECTIVE, the General Accounting Office criticized sanitary conditions in American restaurants:

At GAO's request, the Food and Drug Administration ... inspected, from January through March 1974, 185 restaurants selected at random from 14,736 restaurants in 9 metropolitan cities. On the basis of the inspection results, GAO estimates that about 90 percent of the 14,736 restaurants were insanitary. Since these inspections were made ... sanitation conditions in restaurants have not greatly improved....

The Federal Food, Drug, and Cosmetic Act prohibits the adulteration of food shipped in interstate commerce, including food held in restaurants. The Food and Drug Administration ... relies on State and local governments to regulate restaurants. To help State governments carry out their regulatory activities, the agency has established an advisory and voluntary food service sanitation program that ... is not effectual. The Food and Drug Administration's assistance includes encouraging States to adopt uniform sanitation ordinances and codes, evaluating the effectiveness of State programs, and certifying State sanitation officers. Its role has been to advise States that want help on improving their regulatory programs. The States in turn guide and assist local governments wishing to improve the effectiveness of their food service sanitation programs. However, local governments generally have been ineffective in regulating restaurant sanitation and, generally, the States' monitoring of these programs has been minimal....

FDA anticipated this report by publishing proposed regulations governing sanitation in food service establishments. 39 Fed. Reg. 35438 (October 1, 1974). The agency's preamble explained:

Over the past 40 years, the Public Health Service has provided assistance to State and local health agencies in the establishment and maintenance of food sanitation programs for food service establishments within their jurisdiction, pursuant to the provisions of the Public Health Service Act....

The Federal Food, Drug, and Cosmetic Act also obligates the Food and Drug Administration (FDA) to regulate food held for sale after shipment in interstate commerce. The FDA has recognized the primary jurisdiction of State and local governments over food service establishments and has therefore concentrated its regulatory efforts on assuring the safety and sanitation of food up to the point when it reaches such establishments.

It is estimated that there are approximately 600,000 food service establishments in the United States serving about 150 million meals daily. It is apparent that the FDA could neither inspect nor regulate more than an insigificant portion of these establishments. The primary burden for regulation of food service establishments must therefore remain with State and local agencies.....

The purpose of the proposed regulations and model ordinance is to provide food service establishments with standards, and State and local governments with a comprehensive model law for the regulation of food service sanitation....

In response to opposition from state officials to its proposed codification of food service requirements in Federal regulations, and following reevaluation of its own enforcement priorities, FDA abandoned this proposal, 42 Fed. Reg. 15428 (March 22, 1977). *See* FDA Cooperative Food Sanitation Programs, p. 266 *supra*.

---

3. OLEOMARGARINE

The Oleomargarine Act of 1950, 64 Stat. 20 (1950), which added section 407 to the FD&C Act, applies to all margarine sold at retail or used in public eating places, whether or not it has been shipped in interstate commerce.

REPEALING THE TAXES ON OLEOMARGARINE
Senate Report No. 309, 81st Congress, 1st Session (1949).

The act of August 2, 1886 (24 Stat. 209) defined "butter" and "oleomargarine" and imposed the following taxes on oleomargarine: Manufacturers, $600; wholesalers, $480; retailers, $48; domestic oleomargarine, 2 cents per pound; and imported oleomargarine, 15 cents per pound. This tax statute contained packaging and labeling provisions and, in addition to providing for the forfeiture of unstamped oleomargarine, it provided for the forfeiture of oleomargarine which was adjudged to be deleterious to the public health. It was clear from its inception that this exercise of the taxing power was primarily designed to achieve certain regulatory effects in the field of competition between oleomargarine and butter....

The present difference in tax treatment between yellow oleomargarine and other oleomargarine was inserted in the law by the act of May 9, 1902 (32 Stat. 193). The purpose of this differential tax treatment was to regulate further the competition of oleomargarine and butter. This act imposed a 10-cents-per-pound tax on oleomargarine artificially colored to look like butter. By the act of March 4, 1931 (46 Stat. 1549), the 10-cent tax was made to apply to all oleomargarine which met a statutory definition of "yellow," whether or not colored artificially....

The House bill (H.R. 2023) repeals the internal-revenue taxes on oleomargarine and permits the oleomargarine interests to sell their product in harmless colors of their own choice in free competition with butter unhindered by the burden of discriminatory Federal taxation. However, the bill eliminates any possibility that the consumer of table spreads will not know what he is getting. The competition between the two principal table spreads for consumer preference is to be free of confusion as to identity. At the present time oleomargarine which has moved in interstate commerce is required to meet the exacting requirements of the Federal Food, Drug, and Cosmetic Act with respect to labeling. There is little danger that the consumer of interstate oleomargarine will be confused as to the product he obtains. There remain however two principal levels at which confusion of identity may occur: One is at the restaurant level where the applicability of the Federal Food, Drug, and Cosmetic Act is uncertain, and the other exists with respect to oleomargarine produced and sold in the same State. The House bill (H.R. 2023) brings the regulation of colored oleomargarine squarely within the Federal Food, Drug, and Cosmetic Act, irrespective of the source of the oleomargarine, and specifically regulates the restaurant transaction of serving colored oleomargarine. Thus, intrastate colored oleomargarine would be held to the same standards respecting purity and labeling as colored oleomargarine which is shipped in interstate channels....

NOTE

The legislation described in the Senate Report was enacted on March 16, 1950. Section 407(a) requires prominent label disclosure on all packages of colored oleomargarine or margarine produced and sold interstate or intrastate and requires restaurants serving colored margarine to serve it only in triangular portions or to disclose their practice by a prominent placard or menu statement. *See United States v. Rutstein,* 163 F. Supp. 71 (S.D.N.Y. 1958) (1950 Act applies only to retail packages). *See also* Christopher, *The Oleomargarine Amendment,* 5 FDC L.J. 279 (1950). For a vivid account of the butter-margarine wars, *see Miller, Public Choice at the Dawn of Special Interest State: The Story of Butter and Margarine,* 77 Calif. L. Rev. 83 (1989).

---

4. MEDICAL DEVICES

The Medical Device Amendments of 1976 amended the Act to authorize seizure (but not criminal penalties or injunctive action) against misbranded or adulterated devices without proof of interstate commerce.

UNITED STATES v. UNDETERMINED QUANTITIES OF AN ARTICLE OF DEVICE ... "DEPILATRON EPILATOR"

United States District Court, Southern District of New York, 1979.
473 F. Supp. 913.

SAND, District Judge.

This action is an *in rem* proceeding ... for forfeiture and condemnation of a depilatory device. Claimant has moved to dismiss the complaint on the grounds that 21 U.S.C. § 334(a)(2) "is unconstitutional on its face as a violation of the commerce clause of the United States Constitution." ...

Section 334(a) provides for the seizure of, *inter alia,* adulterated or misbranded devices. Prior to 1976, it was a requirement of such seizures that the device in question have been introduced into interstate commerce. Subsection 334(a) was amended in 1976, however, so as to include adulterated or misbranded devices in the class of articles which are "liable to be proceeded against at any time on libel of information" without regard to interstate commerce.

Claimant concedes that "Congress may regulate not only interstate commerce, but also those wholly intrastate activities which it concludes have an affect [sic] upon interstate commerce." Claimant's contention is, rather, that where Congress seeks to regulate intrastate activities, "a proper nexus to interstate commerce must be made by Congress in order to justify [the] departure from the Commerce Clause", and that Congress has failed to make the required findings.

The legislative history of the 1976 amendment contains no express consideration of the impact of the intrastate sale and distribution of medical devices on interstate commerce. It was, however, the clear intent of Congress

> to authorize the seizure of devices which are distributed wholly in intrastate commerce. This provision will be applicable to all devices and will assist enforcement by doing away with the cumbersome and time consuming task of establishing interstate shipment. This provision will be particularly useful against quack devices....

The Government argues that § 334(a)(2) is a valid exercise of Congress' power under the Commerce Clause, and that its legislative history "plainly implies [that] effective protection of the public health and safety would be sacrificed were Congress to have required that the source and destination of all allegedly adulterated or misbranded devices be determined in seizure cases." Moreover, the Government argues that

> [w]ith respect to the absence of express legislative history regarding the impact of the intrastate sale and distribution of medical devices on interstate commerce, it is enough that this Court perceive a basis upon which Congress could have predicated a judgment that such a nexus exists....

We agree that the absence of formal findings as to the nexus between intrastate sale and distribution of medical devices and interstate commerce is not fatal, as long as Congress had a rational basis for finding such a nexus. Congress alluded to the proliferation of medical devices and to the danger posed by unsafe and ineffective devices to the public health and safety. In light of the extensive hearings held by Congress with respect to the 1976 legislation, we find that Congress did have a sufficient basis for concluding that the regulation of the intrastate sale and distribution of medical devices was necessary for the proper regulation of interstate commerce....

NOTE

In addition to permitting FDA to seize misbranded or adulterated devices without proving interstate commerce, the Device Amendments added a new section 709 to the Act, which provides: "In *any* action to enforce the requirements of this Act respecting a device the connection with interstate commerce required for jurisdiction in such action shall be presumed to exist." (Emphasis added.) This provision was intended to relieve FDA of the burden of demonstrating a connection with interstate commerce in criminal and injunction proceedings. *See* H.R. Rep. No. 94–853, 94th Cong., 2nd Sess. 15 (1976).

---

5. BIOLOGICS

UNITED STATES v. CALISE

United States District Court, Southern District of New York, 1962.
217 F. Supp. 705.

CASHIN, District Judge.

The voluminous eighty count indictment in the above entitled action charges defendants, John P. Calise and Westchester Blood Service, Inc., with several types of violations of the Public Health Service Act and the Federal Food, Drug and Cosmetic Act, and a conspiracy to violate those statutes. . . .

The defendants further assert that counts . . . alleging violations of the mislabeling provisions of 42 U.S.C. § 262(b), are not within the jurisdiction of this court because the acts complained of occurred entirely within the boundaries of the State of New York. The subsection reads as follows:

> "(b) No person shall falsely label or mark any package or container of any virus, serum, toxin, antitoxin, or other product aforesaid; nor alter any label or mark on any package or container of any virus, serum, toxin, antitoxin, or other product aforesaid so as to falsify such label or mark."

The language in subsection (b) does not indicate that Congress intended the effect of the statute to be confined merely to products moving in interstate commerce. The restrictive interpretation of subdivision (b) which the defendants urge is not persuasive, in view of the fact that Congress could very easily have expressed such an intention in the Public Health Service act, as it was cautious to do in 21 U.S.C. § 331(k) where such an intention actually existed. Furthermore, the manner in which Congress separated the mislabeling ban of Section 262(b) from the labeling requirements of Section 262(a)(2) would seem to be indicative of an intention that Section 262(b) was to reach further in its scope from Section 262(a). To restrict Section 262(b) exclusively to products moving in interstate commerce would also be inconsistent with the general purpose of the Public Health Service Act as a whole, because such an interpretation would encourage unscrupulous distributors to sell falsely labeled products on the local market which have been marked so as to apparently meet federal standards, but which do not meet those standards. This would grant such distributors a definite advantage in competing with those who sell interstate products which fulfill the licensing and labeling requirements of 42 U.S.C. § 262(a)....

NOTES

1. *Joint Reliance on FD&C Act and Biologics Act.* In the preambles to its proposed and final GMP regulations for the collection, processing, and storage of human blood and blood components, 39 Fed. Reg. 18614 (May 28, 1974), 40 Fed. Reg. 53532 (November 18, 1975), FDA invoked both the FD&C and the Biologics Act, thus exerting regulatory control over both intrastate and inter-state blood banks.

2. *Turtle Ban. State of Louisiana v. Mathews,* 427 F. Supp. 174 (E.D. La. 1977), upheld FDA's ban on intrastate as well as interstate commerce in small turtles to prevent the spread of communicable disease under section 361 of the Public Health Service Act.

C. REGULATION OF FOREIGN COMMERCE
1. IMPORTATION INTO THE UNITED STATES

SUGARMAN v. FORBRAGD

United States Court of Appeals, Ninth Circuit, 1968.
405 F.2d 1189.

MERRILL, Circuit Judge:

Appellant seeks by suit for injunction to review an order of the Food and Drug Administration excluding from import as adulterated certain damaged coffee beans. In entering its order the Food and Drug Administration was acting ... pursuant to the terms of the Food, Drug and Cosmetic Act, 21 U.S.C. § 381(a). The question presented is wheth-er (absent arbitrary or capricious action which clearly is lacking here) such an order excluding material from import under § 381(a) is subject to judicial review. The District Court held that it was not. We agree.

Appellant contends that the Administrative Procedure Act applies to require agency notice and hearing and provide judicial review. By the terms of that Act, § 701(a)(2), it is not to apply where "agency action is committed to agency discretion by law." In our judgment that is the situation here; by 21 U.S.C. § 381(a) exclusion from import as there provided is committed to the discretion of the Secretary of Health, Education and Welfare.

We note that the prescribed procedure suggests final discretionary authority in the Secretary. His judgment must be accepted and acted upon by the Secretary of the Treasury. Further, the language of the section "if it appears" suggests discretion to be tested by a standard of arbitrariness rather than error. These suggestions in our view are compellingly borne out by the fact that the Secretary's judgment may be founded solely upon his examination of the material in question. While the superficiality of tests and inspections or an arbitrary refusal to accept their results may be appropriate subjects for judicial review, a dispute as to what an examination has established or disclosed is more appropriately left to agency expertise.

The material in question was determined to be adulterated under the statutory definition for the reason that it was found to be "unfit for food." Appellant contends that to preclude arbitrary action the Secretary should promulgate regulations spelling out fitness for food. The administration here determined from its examination that due to its damage the material in question was wholly lacking in recognized food values. A determination of unfitness under these facts cannot, in our judgment, be regarded as arbitrary even in absence of more explicit definition by regulation.

Judgment affirmed.

L & M INDUSTRIES, INC. v. KENTER

United States Court of Appeals, Second Circuit, 1972.
458 F.2d 968.

WATERMAN, Circuit Judge:

The defendant is a Food and Drug Officer employed by the U.S. Food and Drug Administration, who had obtained a sampling of a shipment from Europe which plaintiff was seeking to import, and had then detained the shipment because of an alleged misbranding. L & M had sought the issuance of an order restraining the defendant from any further detention of plaintiff's goods and requiring the F.D.A. to act upon L & M's Application for Authorization to Relabel and to release the detained goods belonging to it. . . .

. . . We are convinced that the appellee here has acted beyond the scope of his statutory authority in failing to provide a meaningful opportunity for the plaintiff-appellant to appear before the Secretary of Health, Education and Welfare and introduce testimony relating to the key issue of whether the goods are adulterated, an opportunity provided for by 21 U.S.C. § 381(a). We reserve the judgment and order below and remand with instructions to proceed in accordance with the disposition expressed in this opinion. . . .

After an examination of the product, the Food and Drug Administration issued on October 28, 1970 a Notice of Detention and hearing informing the appellant that it had been concluded that a shipment comprised of 720 cartons of Herbal Yeast Food Supplement appeared to be misbranded within the meaning of several sections of the Federal Food, Drug, and Cosmetic Act. . . .

On November 4, 1970, a hearing was held pursuant to 21 C.F.R. 1.318 [now 21 C.F.R. § 1.94] during which the appellant apparently was told that the complete quantitative formula and a complete description of the manufacturing processes would have to be submitted along with the Application for Authorization to Relabel as required by 21 C.F.R. 1.319(a) [now 21 C.F.R. § 1.95(a)].... [A]ppellant submitted the application on the day following the hearing, November 5, 1970, but the statement concerning the formula and the manufacturing processes was not presented until January 26, 1971. On the basis of this information, plaintiff was advised by the F.D.A. on February 17 that the article could not be relabeled so as to bring it into compliance with the law within the meaning of 21 U.S.C. § 381, and a Notice of Refusal was issued.

The central factor in the F.D.A.'s determination was its finding that " ... the Bio–Strath product must be classified as adulterated under Section 402(a)(2)(C)." It determined that the substrate of herbs upon which the yeast was grown was " . . . not generally recognized as safe...." L & M was thereafter informed that a food additive regulation would have to be issued to legalize the use of the product, but, in the meantime, while the importer petitioned for such a regulation, the merchandise would have to be either exported or destroyed.

Obviously the Agency correctly reasoned that if the product were adulterated no amount of relabeling could bring the product into conformity with the law. We do not believe, however, that the manner by which the F.D.A. arrived at its conclusion that the product was adulterated, or appeared to be adulterated, is justified by a reading of 21 U.S.C. § 381....

Clearly, Section 381 and the regulation implementing that section envision some participation by the owner of the product in the decision-making process relating to the product's admissibility. The section enables the owner to be heard and to present evidence bearing upon the issues involved in the administrative decision as to the admissibility of his product. Implicit in "the right to introduce testimony" is the right to know what the issues are that the testimony is to relate to. Thus a reasonable interpretation of the language of Section 381 requires that in the notice prescribed by that section there be included a statement of the grounds upon which the article may be refused admission....

Here appellant was notified that its product was subject to refusal of admission because of misbranding. It is disingenuous, however, for the Food and Drug Administration to argue that misbranding was the reason for the Notice of Refusal. It is clear that its refusal to admit the yeast product was predicated on the determination that it was adulterated within the meaning of 21 U.S.C. § 342(a)(2)(C). L & M was effectively denied the opportunity to be heard or to introduce testimony as to this central issue for it never received a Section 381 notice that adulteration was in question. Therefore, we find that the F.D.A. exceeded its statutory authority when it determined Bio–Strath Elixir to be adulterated without first providing the appellant with the opportunity to be heard on that issue....

NOTE

The procedure under which FDA has regulated imported food and drugs has been sharply questioned in three separate cases. In *Caribbean Produce Exchange, Inc. v. Secretary of HHS,* Food Drug Cosm. L. Rep. (CCH) ¶ 38,100 & ¶ 38,110 (D.P.R. 1988), *rev'd,* 893 F.2d 3 (1st Cir. 1989), the district court enjoined the FDA detention procedure for imported garlic because its requirements had not been established through rulemaking. The court of appeals, however, remanded the case for an evidentiary hearing. In *Bellarno International Ltd. v. FDA,* 678 F. Supp. 410 (E.D.N.Y. 1988), the court invalidated an FDA "import alert" that provided for automatic detention of drugs that had been exported and then reimported, because of the agency's failure to engage in notice-and-comment rulemaking. In *United States v. Articles of Drugs Consisting of 203 Paper Bags,* 634 F. Supp. 435 (N.D. Ill. 1985), *vacated,* 818 F.2d 569 (7th Cir. 1987), the district court allowed reexportation of illegal animal drugs, over FDA's protest, because the agency had failed to establish its requirements for imported drugs through rulemaking. The court of appeals vacated this decision as moot after the drugs had been reexported.

GOODWIN v. UNITED STATES

United States District Court, Southern District of California, 1972.
371 F. Supp. 433.

WALLACE, District Judge.

Plaintiff is an American citizen who for the past two and one-half years has been engaged in the regular importation of live clams into the United States from Mexican waters in the Gulf of California....

During the two and one-half years of operation, plaintiff's live clams have been frequently tested by the Food & Drug Administration for presence of E. Coli bacteria and have been allowed to be released in the open market for sale for human consumption. Between September 22, 1971, and November 2, 1971, the United States Food & Drug Administration issued notices of detention pursuant to 21 U.S.C. § 381 against five lots of live clams offered for import by plaintiff Donald G. Goodwin. The basis for each detention was that the clams were prepared, packed or held under insanitary conditions whereby they may have been contaminated with filth and were adulterated within the meaning of 21 U.S.C. § 342(a)(4) in that they came from uncertified waters.

The Food & Drug Administration, during the summer of 1971, informally established a policy, which was implemented in this area in September, 1971, which bars the importation of shellfish from any waters of a foreign country which are not from "certified" waters.... United States, Japan, and Canada have entered into reciprocal certification programs whereby waters within those territorial boundaries are subject to testing and certification, which comply with federal standards as set forth by the National Shellfish Sanitation Program. Waters of nations who do not participate in this program are regarded as uncertified waters.

Live clams can be carriers of certain diseases. There are now established tests which can determine the presence of E. coli bacteria in said live clams. The presence of a high level of E. coli bacteria in laboratory tests of live clams may indicate that the clams have been grown under insanitary conditions in waters which were contaminated with human fecal material....

Of the five loads of live clams initially detained by the Food & Drug Administation in September of 1971, one lot, which was sampled by the Food & Drug Administration, was found to contain too high a count of E. coli bacteria to meet the former standards of the Food & Drug Administration....

There is no known test to determine whether shellfish, including clams, are carriers of infectious hepatitis or typhoid. There are tests which can be performed to determine whether shellfish, including clams, are carriers of salmonellosis and possibly typhoid, but these tests do not provide a feasible approach to protection in that they are costly, incomplete and/or destroy the marketability of the product.... There have been serious outbreaks of infectious hepatitis, typhoid, and gastroenteritis, associated with the consumption of contaminated shellfish, which outbreaks have been documented in the scientific literature....

The importation and commercial distribution of clams from foreign uncertified waters creates a substantial possible public health danger to the American consumer....

From the foregoing findings of fact, the Court makes the following conclusions of law.

1. The United States Food & Drug Administration has authority to bar the importation of all shellfish (including clams) which appear from examination of such shellfish, or otherwise, to have been manufactured, processed, or packed under insanitary conditions, or to be adulterated in that they may be injurious to health.

2. The Food & Drug Administration is not required to find that each shellfish is actually contaminated prior to barring its importation from a foreign country; rather, it is sufficient that the shellfish appear to have been grown or processed under insanitary conditions, which conclusion may be derived from an examination of the shellfish or otherwise....

4. This Court has jurisdiction to review the issue of whether the Food & Drug Administration acted arbitrarily or capriciously in deciding to bar the importation of all shellfish from foreign uncertified waters. *Sugarman v. Forbragd,* 405 F.2d 1189 (9th Cir. 1968)....

7. In this case, from the combined factors of (1) the presence of E. coli bacteria in the detained loads showing that the beds from which plaintiff's clams are harvested are in proximity to possible fecal contamination, (2) the general lack of sanitary conditions and the high

incidence of gastroenteritic diseases and of viral hepatitis in Mexico, and (3) the uncertainty as to a potential of danger because the waters are not certified, I cannot hold that it was an arbitrary or capriciouis determination that it "appears" the clams in question were grown under insanitary conditions or were "adulterated" pursuant to 21 U.S.C. § 381(a). . . .

NOTES

1. *Supporting Authority.* See also *Seabrook International Foods, Inc. v. Harris,* 501 F. Supp. 1086 (D.D.C. 1980); *Meserey v. United States,* 447 F. Supp. 548 (D. Nev. 1977); *Canadian Memorial Chiropractic College v. Shumate,* 1965–1968 FDLI Jud. Rec. 379 (W.D.N.Y. 1967); *Viliamarin (Prieto) and A.C.L. Haase Co. v. Sestric,* 1965–1968 FDLI Jud. Rec. 467 (E.D. Mo. 1963); *The James J. Hill,* 65 F. Supp. 265 (D. Md. 1946).

2. *Entry into Interstate Commerce.* Once imported food is admitted into the United States, and thus has passed from the control of the customs officials, it becomes part of interstate commerce and is subject to all of the provisions of the FD&C Act that apply to domestic food. *See Otis McAllister & Co. v. United States,* 194 F.2d 386 (5th Cir. 1952); *230 Boxes . . . Fish v. United States,* 168 F.2d 361 (6th Cir. 1948); *United States v. 231 Boxes . . . Frozen Tullibees,* 1938–1964 FDLI Jud. Rec. 841 (S.D. Cal. 1949).

3. *Coordination with Customs Service.* FDA performs import sampling services and refuses entry to violative products for the Customs Service pursuant to a Memorandum of Understanding published in 44 Fed. Reg. 53577 (September 14, 1979).

4. *Products Under Bond.* Products entering the United States under bond pursuant to 19 U.S.C. § 1553 are exempt from customs duties but are subject to FDA jurisdiction. *United States v. Articles of Drug,* Food Drug Cosm. L. Rep. (CCH) ¶ 38,131 (S.D. Calif. 1981); *United States v. An Article of Drug . . . K.H. 3 Geriatricum–Schwarzhaupt,* 520 F. Supp. 467 (S.D. Tex. 1981); *United States v. 300 Oz. Gerovital Lotion,* 492 F. Supp. 114 (C.D. Cal. 1980).

5. *USDA Powers.* In *Ganadera Industrial, S.A. v. Block,* 727 F.2d 1156 (D.C. Cir. 1984), the court upheld a USDA decision to ban the importation of meat by the plaintiff Costa Rican company until the chairman of the board and controlling stockholder, who had been indicted in the United States for criminal violations of the Federal Meat Inspection Act, was removed from his management position and from control of the company through a voting trust.

6. *GAO Oversight.* The General Accounting Office has been a frequent critic of FDA's enforcement against imported products. *See, e.g.,* FOOD AND DRUG ADMINISTRATION'S PROGRAM FOR REGULATING IMPORTED PRODUCTS NEEDS IMPROVING, No. HRD–77–72 (July 5, 1977); BETTER REGULATION OF PESTICIDE EXPORTS AND PESTICIDE RESIDUES IN IMPORTED FOOD IS ESSENTIAL, No. CED–79–43 (June 22, 1979); ENFORCEMENT OF U.S. IMPORT ADMISSIBILITY REQUIREMENTS: BETTER MANAGEMENT COULD SAVE WORK, REDUCE DELAYS, AND IMPROVE SERVICE AND IMPORTER'S COMPLIANCE, No. GGD–82–12 (January 25, 1982); PESTICIDES: FDA'S INVESTIGATION OF IMPORTED APPLE JUICE CONCENTRATE, No. RCED–86–214FS (August 1986); IMPORTED MEAT AND LIVESTOCK: CHEMICAL RESIDUE DETECTION AND THE ISSUE OF LABELING, No. RCED–87–142 (September 1987); ADP SYSTEMS: FDA CAN REDUCE DEVELOPMENT RISKS FOR ITS IMPORT INFORMA-

TION SYSTEM, No. IMTEC–88–42 (September 1988); IMPORTED FOODS: OPPORTUNITIES TO IMPROVE FDA'S INSPECTION PROGRAM, No. HRD–89–88 (April 1989); FOOD SAFETY AND QUALITY: FIVE COUNTRIES' EFFORTS TO MEET U.S. REQUIREMENTS ON IMPORTED PRODUCE, No. RCED–90–55 (March 1990).

7. *GATT Coverage.* The General Agreement on Tariffs and Trade (GATT), 61 Stat. A3 (1947), has governed international trade in agricultural, consumer, and industrial products for more than 40 years. Because GATT permits each country to enact its own health and safety laws, however, food and drug regulatory requirements remain trade barriers throughout the world.

8. *Commentary.* *See generally* KIllingsworth, *Import Control Under Federal Laws,* 2 FDC L.Q. 498 (1947), 5 FDC L.J. 205 (1950), and 8 FDC L.J. 117 (1953); Smith, *Detention and Seizure of Imports by the Food and Drug Administration,* 33 FDC L.J. 726 (1978).

---

2. EXPORTATION FROM THE UNITED STATES

Over the years, FDA has adopted a progressively narrower interpretation of the export provisions in section 801(d) of the Act.

UNITED STATES v. KENT FOOD CORP.

United States Circuit Court of Appeals, Second Circuit, 1948.
168 F.2d 632.

CLARK, Circuit Judge.

This appeal presents the question whether food condemned as adulterated in interstate commerce under the prohibition of the Federal Food, Drug, and Cosmetic Act, § 304, may be released to the owners for export to another country. The district court, in an endeavor to conserve food available for human consumption and relying upon a provision of the Act exempting food products intended for export, § 801(d), held in favor of the claimant owners. The United States has appealed, contending that such action is beyond the court's power....

... [T]he language of ... section [801(d)] deals with a subject matter entirely apart from that of condemnation under § 334. Here we have the statement of an exemption from the operation of the Act. Sec. 334 deals, however, with the consequences of a violation of the Act by introducing an adulterated article into interstate commerce; and subd. (d) sets forth sanctions and remedies for such violation. Thus the part of the section which deals with release to the owner expressly provides either for destruction of the article or for its being brought into compliance with the provisions of the Act. It is further made clear that the article is not to be sold contrary to the provisions either of the Act or the laws of the jurisdiction in which it is sold. There is no provision for a sanction by way of a delayed exemption for export purposes, such as might have been secured had the articles been originally intended for such purposes.... The court thought it had discretion to resort, even after the articles had been condemned, to the special exemption granted by the statute.

In this we think the court was in error. The power specifically given to the court to do only certain things upon condemnation of the articles excludes the possibility of according them a status they might originally have had, had they never been introduced into interstate commerce for the purpose of domestic sale....

Reversed and remanded.   *NO - once in IC, you fucked it its bad.*

UNITED STATES v. AN ARTICLE ... ENRICHED RICE

United States District Court, Southern District of Texas. 1975.
FDA Consumer, October 1976, at 36.

Claimant's motion is premised upon its argument that the seized goods are not subject to condemnation pursuant to 21 U.S.C. § 334 because they are not intended for domestic consumption but are destined to be exported....

The Court does not find that, in order to establish subject matter jurisdiction in this action, it is necessary for the Government to plead and prove that the goods to be seized do not fall within the statutory exemption provided for exports.... It is the general rule that one who seeks the benefits of a statutory exemption has the burden of proving that he falls within its perimeters....

Alternatively, claimant argues that it has met its burden of proving the applicability of the exemption provided by § 381(d) because the evidence it has submitted in support of the motion demonstrates that the export of the seized product would not be in violation of the laws of Chile. In view of the fact that disposition of this argument will require a consideration of facts outside of the pleadings, the Court will consider the motion to dismiss as a motion for summary judgment pursuant to Rule 56, Fed. R. Civ. P.

There appears to be little dissention between both parties that the applicable provisions of the law of Chile may be summarized as follows: (1) the importation of foodstuffs requires notification of the proper governmental authorities who may then inspect the product upon its arrival and thereafter take appropriate action in accepting, rejecting or altering the condition of the imported goods; (2) all imported foodstuffs must be accompanied by a sanitation certificate issued by a competent authority of the exporting country; (3) the manufacture, sale, storage for sale of altered, contaminated, adulterated or falsified foods with risk to the health of men or animals is prohibited.

Insofar as items (1) and (2) are concerned, the Court does not find that these would prohibit the application of the export exemption to the seized goods in question here. Claimant had secured the necessary sanitation certificate prior to the seizure of the article of food in question here. Furthermore, it must be presumed that claimant will comply with the provisions requiring notice to be given to appropriate Chilean authorities in the absence of any evidence to the contrary. However, item (3) does prohibit the sale or storage for sale of altered food products. It is clearly the intention of claimant to export the seized goods for sale.... [T]he sale and shipment of the goods seized in this action, if altered within the meaning of Chilean law, will conflict with the laws of the receiving country.

Thus, it will be necessary for the Court to hear further evidence with respect to the Government's contention that the seized goods are in fact adulterated under the laws of the United States. It will be necessary thereafter for the claimant to demonstrate that, even if the goods are adulterated under our laws, they are not altered or adulterated within the meaning of these provisions of the Chilean law. Because the above questions present issues of fact that cannot be determined on the basis of the record now before the Court, claimant's motion for summary judgment will be denied and this matter set for hearing at a later date.

COMPLIANCE POLICY GUIDE NO. 7127.02

Subject: Uncertified or Delisted Colors in Foods for Export (*e.g.* FD&C Red No. 2)....

Policy: Colors such as FD&C Red No. 2, which have been delisted, can be used in lots of food specifically manufactured for export to a country in which its use is legal, provided all the requirements of section 801(d) of the Act are followed and provided further, that a control system is followed which insures that there is no possibility of diversion by mistake or otherwise to domestic channels, of the food containing the color. Proper control can be achieved by following the procedure set forth below:

1. Prior to start of production and for each lot produced a separate order, letter from the purchaser and letter from an official of the country must be obtained.

The order from the purchaser must state the exact amount desired by the foreign purchaser and must state on the order or be accompanied by a letter from the purchaser stating that he desires that FD&C Red No. 2 or other specific color be used in the lot and that he is aware of its illegality in the United States. The letter from a responsible official of the country to which the lot is to be shipped shall state that the use of the color is legal in his country. Since the laws and regulations of countries are subject to change, a continuing order or letter will not be satisfactory.

2.   The stock of the color to be used for export production must be kept locked up at all times, except when actually being used. Complete records must be kept accounting for all use.

3.   During all stages of production, manufacture, processing and packing the lot must be kept segregated from all other production and must be clearly marked that it is "for export only."

The outside of each shipping package of the lot must be labeled to show it is for export.

4.   All records, pertaining to such lots, including orders and letters, must be kept for at least three years and made available to any Food and Drug Administration inspector upon oral or written request.

NOTE

See also United States v. 182 Bags ... Cocoa Beans ... Robusta, Food Drug Cosm. L. Rep. (CCH) ¶ 38,247 (E.D. Pa. 1978). *See generally* Williams, *Regulation of Exports Under the Federal Food, Drug, and Cosmetic Act,* 3 FDC L.Q. 382 (1948).

CARL BORCHSENIUS CO. v. GARDNER

United States District Court, Eastern District of Louisiana, 1968.
282 F.Supp. 396.

CASSIBRY, District Judge.

The shipment of 5,000 bags of coffee, weighing 665,000 pounds with an estimated invoice value of $227,000, arrived at the Port of New Orleans from Paranagua, Brazil aboard the Mario D'Almeida on November 21, 1967. . . .

A wharf examination of the shipment by a United States Food and Drug Inspector on December 1 disclosed damp, moldy coffee in four of the six samples taken in the inspection. Approximately 1,500 bags were wet and some contained moldy coffee. The entire shipment of 5,000 bags was detained by the Food and Drug Administration. . . .

On December 1, plaintiff filed an application for authorization pursuant to 21 U.S.C. § 381(b) to attempt to bring the 5,000 bags of coffee into compliance with the Act by the procedure of "skimming the coffee to remove molded beans" and "drying the coffee out to remove wet beans." This authorization was given on December 4. . . .

Of the 5,000 bags, examination showed 2,325 to be sound, and upon request of plaintiff's representatives these bags were released under a partial release of the shipment on December 8. . . .

On December 26, the defendant C. C. Freeman, Acting Director of the Food and Drug Administration for this District, advised the plaintiff's representative by letter that a "Release Notice" on the 1,730 bags made sound would be issued upon receipt of proof of destruction of the remaining 270 bags of poor skims, 231 bags of sweepings and 1,053 bags of moldy coffee in original bags.   The plaintiff had no objection to destruction of the 270 bags of poor skims and the 231 bags of sweepings, but it representative requested on January 2, 1968 that the 1,730 bags of "made sound" coffee be released for import and that it be allowed to burnish, rebag and export the 1,053 bags which had not been reconditioned.   The request to burnish, rebag and export was denied by Acting Director Freeman by letter of January 3....

The only issue before the Court is whether the defendants acted within the limits of their statutory authority in this case, and to resolve that issue the Court must determine whether the defendants have the discretion under 21 U.S.C. § 381(b) to require destruction of articles offered for import, which are rejected because they cannot be brought into compliance with the Act, without giving the applicant an opportunity to export the rejected articles.

The defendants agree that the owner or consignee could choose to export articles refused admission under the language in subsection (a) that "The Secretary of the Treasury shall *cause the destruction of any such article refused admission unless such article is exported, * * *,*" and they agree that had the plaintiff in this case not chosen to attempt to bring the coffee into compliance under subsection (b), it would have had the choice of exporting the entire shipment of 5,000 bags.   (Italics here and elsewhere mine).   They argue that such a choice is not available to an owner or consignee as to rejected articles from the attempt at compliance under the language of subsection (b) that "the Secretary of Health, Education and Welfare may, in accordance with regulations authorize the applicant to perform such relabeling or other action specified in such authorization (*including destruction nor export of rejected articles or portions thereof,* as may be specified in the Secretary's authorization)," and that the rejected articles may be ordered destroyed at their discretion.

This contention of defendants as to their discretion under 381(b) is not only at variance with the policy set by Congress as to the disposition of articles rejected for admission set out in 381(a), but is at variance with a continuing policy of Congress as to the disposition of articles refused admission for import....

There is nothing in 381(b) to indicate that the taking advantage of the opportunity to bring articles into compliance with standards for import makes those rejected from the compliance operation products involved in illegal import activity.   Interpreting that statute as giving administrative discretion to destroy rejected articles would be a radical departure from the policy of Congress on this matter, and such a major change in policy could hardly be expected to appear as a parenthetical insertion in a statute.   I find nothing from policy considerations to support the argument of defendants that Congress intended when a consignee elects to avail himself of the compliance provisions of 381(b) to deprive him of the choice under 381(a) to export rejected articles. From this viewpoint the contention of plaintiff that 381(a) and (b) should be read together, and that the parenthetical phrase regarding disposition of rejecting articles in (b) was not intended to depart from the disposition provision of (a) and deprive the consignee of the choice of export is logical and persuasive....

The Court concludes that the defendants do not have the discretion under 381(b) to require the destruction of articles offered for import, which are rejected because they cannot be brought into compliance with the Act, without giving the applicant an opportunity to export the rejected articles upon compliance with the applicable statutes; therefore, the action in this case in refusing to grant the request for permission to export the rejected coffee, and in requiring its destruction as a condition of release of the sound coffee, was beyond their statutory authority. Judgment is rendered in accordance with these views granting to plaintiff the relief prayed for.

NOTE

Compare United States v. 484 Bags, More or Less, 423 F.2d 839 (5th Cir. 1970), p. 233 *supra,* in which the court refused to permit reexport of imported moldy coffee seized under section 402(a)(3):

> If the coffee is found to be adulterated it must be destroyed. Disposition of it is controlled by the first sentence of § 334(d). The exception to that subsection, adopted by amendment in 1957, authorized under limited and prescribed conditions the export of articles condemned under § 334. Those conditions are not met in this instance, since the adulteration occurred after the coffee was imported. The language of the statute and the legislative history permit no other conclusion....

UNITED STATES v. 76,552 POUNDS OF FROG LEGS

United States District Court, Southern District of Texas, 1976.
423 F. Supp. 329.

GARZA, Chief Judge.

Agent Gene Nicko, of the United States Customs Service, received information from a confidential informer that certain frog leg shippers were engaged in illegal activity. He was told that frog leg importers are forced to sell, at depressed prices, all contaminated frog legs that had been refused importation entry into the United States. Salvage buyers, who bought this food product at reduced prices, would subsequently illegally reintroduce this food into the United States at regular prices....

... When it was discovered that Progressive had in fact sold contaminated frog legs in domestic commerce when they should have been under bond but were not, both the Secretary of the Treasury and the Secretary of Health, Education and Welfare decided to seek forfeiture of the food for various violations of ... the Food and Drug Act....

The statutory import-export exemption in 21 U.S.C. § 381 does not apply to claimant's, Progressive Sea Products, Inc., frog legs. The clear wording of the statute provides that articles intended for export under the provisions of the statute are not exempt if such article is sold or offered for sale in domestic commerce. The record establishes that some of the frog legs in the shipments under seizure were sold and offered for sale in domestic commerce. The statute further provides that the Secretary shall seek condemnation if the article is not exported within 90 days and an extension is not granted under the appropriate regulations. The record establishes that the frog legs, if ever intended for export, were not exported within 90 days and an extension was not granted....

This Court holds that the claimant is not entitled to the benefits of the statutory exemption, 21 U.S.C. § 381, allowing the exportation of adulterated frog legs which have been refused entry. This Court further holds the Secretary of Health, Education and Welfare, through the F.D.A., did not abuse its discretionary power to revoke claimant's import-export privilege under § 381 and seek condemnation....

Having determined that the frog legs should be condemned, this Court must next determine whether to order the frog legs destroyed or to allow the claimant conditional repossession. This Court has discretionary power to permit the claimant's attempt to salvage a potentially valuable food regardless of the claimant's mala fides....

This Court holds the claimant is not entitled to the benefit of the import-export provisions found in 21 U.S.C. § 334(d)(1).... Section 334(d)(1) is not available where food is condemned because it is injurious to health. This is necessary to prevent adulterated food from being commingled with good lots of the same food and again offered for import under conditions that would make the adulteration difficult to detect....

---

3. EXPORT OF NEW DRUGS, NEW ANIMAL DRUGS, BIOLOGICAL PRODUCTS, AND MEDICAL DEVICES

a. New Human and Animal Drugs Prior to 1986

When section 505 was added to the Act just prior to enactment in 1938, the export provisions of section 801 were not modified to permit exportation of unapproved new drugs. Accordingly, FDA took the position that no new drug may be exported without an IND or an approved NDA.

UNITED STATES v. AN ARTICLE OF DRUG ...
ETHIONAMIDE–INH

United States District Court, Eastern District of New York, 1967.
1965–1968 FDLI Jud. and Ad. Rec. 16.

DOOLING, District Judge.

The government seized a large quantity of tablets of Ethionamide–INH in the possession of Amfre–Grant, Inc. on the ground that it was a "new drug" ... and that no approval of an application ... was effective for the drug....

... The drug in question is a combination of equal quantities (125 mg.) of ethionamide and isoniazid or isononicotinic acid hydrazide (INH).... While use of ethionamide in conjunction with INH is known in the literature, it is not contended that the particular Amfre–Grant combination has been approved for use in the manner recommended in the insert included in the completed packages, or that it could qualify as not a "new drug" because it was generally recognized by qualified persons to be safe and effective for use as recommended.

Amfre–Grant has supplied the drug to Vietnam, where it has been approved for sale, in 1966 and early 1967, and the Agency for International Development has approved the drug for Vietnamese sale, and authorized the use of AID funds to pay for it. The packaging for the drug is entirely in French, and the package displays the Vietnamese registration number; the insertion sheet is in French and Vietnamese. The package indicates that the drug is to be sold on prescription only....

... Section 381(d) took its present form in the 1938 Act, and the legislative history is invoked to show that the primary concern of the Congress was to safeguard residents of the United States, and that the narrow focus of that concern resulted in the rejection of amendments to Section 381(d) that would have required exports to be in compliance with some but not all of the standards of the Act. It is argued that the "new drug" provisions of 21 U.S.C. Sec. 355 were introduced late in the transit of the bill through the Congress, that no hearings and little debate accompanied the addition of Section 355 to the Senate Bill in the House, and that the section was added under the goad of concern over deaths caused in 1937 by using "antifreeze," diethylene glycol, as the carrier in "Elixir Sulfanilamide." ...

The argument must yield to the language of the statute. The exemption of Section 381(d) applies to what would otherwise be "adulterated or misbranded" within the other sections of the Act. On those words hinge the operation of the Act as it applies to foods and drugs that are not "new drugs." The "new drug" provisions, although solidly embedded in the Act, operate separately, and it is not a necessary, nor even a probable, inference that the policy considerations that led to the enactment of Section 381(d) would extend to the new drug provisions. . . .

NOTES

1. *Supporting Authority.* See *United States v. Yaron Laboratories, Inc.,* 365 F. Supp. 917 (N.D. Cal. 1972).

2. *Drug Intermediates.* 21 C.F.R. § 310.3(g) defines "new drug substance" to exclude "intermediates used in the synthesis of such substance." Such intermediates may therefore be exported without an IND or NDA.

3. *Pesticides.* Compare the export requirements for unregistered pesticides enacted in the Federal Pesticide Act of 1978, 92 Stat. 819 (1978), 7 U.S.C. § 136o, and EPA's proposed statement of policy, 44 Fed. Reg. 41955 (July 18, 1979).

4. *New Animal Drugs.* When Congress enacted the Animal Drug Amendments, it amended section 801(d) to adopt explicitly the same export policy that had implicitly been adopted for new drugs in 1938. Proposed regulations governing export of new animal drugs for investigational use, 43 Fed. Reg. 1100 (January 6, 1978), 49 Fed. Reg. 44766 (November 9, 1984), became moot upon enactment of the Drug Export Amendments Act of 1986.

----

b. Medical Devices

The Medical Device Amendments of 1976 embody a different approach to the export of products that have not met requirements for domestic marketing.

MEDICAL DEVICE AMENDMENTS OF 1976
Conference Report No. 94–1090,
94th Congress, 2d Session (1976).

The conference substitute … retains the provisions of existing section 801(d) of the Act relating to the export of food, drugs, devices, cosmetics and new animal drugs (with nonsubstantive drafting changes), and authorizes the export of devices which do not comply with applicable requirements relating to performance standards or premarket approval, or are exempt from such requirements because they are in investigational use, or are banned only if (1) they meet the requirements of existing section 801(d) of the Act, (2) the Secretary has determined that the exportation of such devices is not contrary to public health and safety, and (3) the Secretary has determined that such devices have the approval of the countries to which they are intended for export.

NOTE

Under 21 C.F.R. § 812.18(b), FDA requires that a person exporting an investigational device subject to an investigational device exemption (IDE) must also obtain approval of an export application under section 801(d)(2) of the

FD&C Act. *See* Cole, *Import and Export of Medical Devices*, 34 FDC L.J. 140 (1979).

---

c. A Revised Export Policy for Drugs
STATEMENT OF HEW SECRETARY JOSEPH A. CALIFANO, JR.

Hearings on H.R. 11611 Before the Subcommittee on Health
and the Environment of the House Committee on Interstate
and Foreign Commerce, Part 1, 95th Congress, 2d Session (1978).

... [I]n 1976 Congress adopted an export policy that permits the export of medical devices that are not approved for use in the United States. This policy reflects the fact that the benefits an risks of a medical device may vary from one country to another, depending on physical conditions in the country, health related characteristics of the population, the nature and extent of the health care delivery system, and the types of health problems with which that system must deal. These same considerations apply to drugs. A drug which has an unfavorable benefit/risk ratio in the U.S. and therefore is not approved for use here may, due to differences in circumstances, have a very favorable benefit/risk ratio in another country and therefore may be entirely appropriate for use in that country.

The bill builds on and refines the export policy for medical devices. Unapproved drugs may be exported to meet the health needs of foreign countries, if certain requirements are met. The government of the foreign country must be informed of the regulatory status of the drug in the U.S., and must signify that it does not object to importation of the drug. An exported drug must meet the same manufacturing and quality standards that apply to drugs used in the U.S. FDA would retain authority to prohibit the export of a drug if the export would be contrary to the public health of the foreign country or of the U.S. (An export could be contrary to the public health of the U.S. if, for example, a drug of abuse were to be exported to a nearby country and then smuggled back into the U.S.; or if a drug with a mechanism of administration potentially harmful to the world population (*e.g.*, using chlorofluorocarbons) were exported.)

This export policy will give due respect to the health decisions of foreign countries, while fulfilling America's obligation not to dump dangerous drugs overseas. It will also encourage drug manufacturing in the U.S., and thereby help increase jobs and ease our balance of payments problems.

NOTE

For a full discussion of this proposal, *see* Kennedy, *Food and Drug Administration and Pharmaceuticals for Developing Countries*, in Institute of Medicine, PHARMACEUTICALS FOR DEVELOPING COUNTRIES (NAS 1979). *See*

"Export of Products Banned by U.S. Regulatory Agencies," H.R. Rep. No. 95–1686, 95th Cong., 2d Sess. (1978):

> In 1977, U.S. exports to foreign countries totaled $120.1 billion. Among the vast numbers of American products exported annually are millions of dollars worth of consumer products, drugs, pesticides, devices, and chemicals which a U.S. regulatory agency has determined to be unsafe for domestic consumption. The Federal role in relation to banned items has, in recent years, taken on greater significance since a greater number of products are now affected by regulatory actions.
>
> The question of what U.S. policy in this area should be is not easily resolved. Factors which play a role in the determination of whether to allow the export of a banned product include the type of product, the nature of the hazard, the importing country, the availability of alternatives, and the state of the scientific and technological art in a particular area. However, there is no disagreement that the current approach to resolving the issues raised in this area has been unsatisfactory and requires change. In some cases, dangerous products are exported without agency awareness and without proper notice to the importing country. In other cases, the product cannot be exported even though benefits may outweigh the risk to a foreign country....

See also Schulberg, *United States Export of Products Banned for Domestic Use,* 20 Harv. Int'l L.J. 331 (1979).

THE DRUG EXPORT AMENDMENTS ACT OF 1986

The Drug Export Amendments Act of 1986, 100 Stat. 3743, which added section 802 to the FD&C Act and section 351(h) to the PHS Act, authorizes the limited export of unapproved new human and animal drugs and new biological products, unapproved drugs for the treatment or prevention of tropical diseases, and partially processed biological products.

Unapproved new human and animal drugs and biological products. Under section 802, FDA may approve an export application for an unapproved new human drug, animal drug, or biological product if (a) there is an active IND or INAD for the product, (b) approval is being actively pursued in the United States, (c) the product is exported to one or more of 21 listed countries, (d) the product is currently approved and marketed in the receiving country, (e) FDA has not disapproved the product, (f) the product is manufactured in conformity with GMP and is not adulterated, (g) the product's labeling lists the countries to which FDA has permitted it to be exported, (h) FDA has not determined that domestic manufacture of the drug for export is contrary to the public health and safety of the United States, and (i) the product complies with section 801(d). An application for export approval, setting forth compliance with these requirements, must be filed with FDA, and notice of filing must then be published in the Federal Register. Following approval, the applicant remains obligated to submit to FDA any information that could justify withdrawal of approval. Approval may be withdrawn if any of the criteria for approval is no longer met. FDA may also revoke its approval for export to a specific importer if the agency determines that the importer has transshipped the drug to a country other than one of the 21 listed countries.

Unapproved drugs for the treatment or prevention of tropical diseases. The Act establishes separate statutory requirements for products intended for tropical diseases because such diseases do not occur in the United States and thus drugs for their treatment cannot be approved here. Section 802(f) therefore provides that FDA will approve an export application if (a) the agency finds that the product is safe and effective in the country to which it is to be exported, (b) it is manufactured in conformity with GMP and is not adulterated, (c) its labeling bears a list of the countries to which export is approved, (d) it is not the subject of a notice by FDA determining that the domestic manufacture of the drug for export is contrary to the public health and safety of the United States, and (e) the product complies with section 801(d).

Partially processed biological products. Under section 351(h) of the PHS Act, FDA may approve an export application for a partially processed biological product which is not in a form applicable to the prevention, treatment, or cure of disease and which is intended for further manufacture into final dosage form in one of the 21 listed countries if (a) FDA determines that the product is manufactured in conformity with GMP, (b) the label lists the countries to which it may lawfully be exported, and (c) FDA does not determine that prohibiting the export of the product is necessary for protection of the public health in the United States or in the country to which it is to be exported.

From 1938 to 1986, American pharmaceutical manufacturers commonly built manufacturing facilities abroad in order to be certain that, if foreign approvals for new products preceded United States approvals, they could lawfully supply foreign markets. This practice became increasingly important after the Drug Amendments of 1962, when United States approval became more difficult to obtain. The result was that the domestic pharmaceutical industry was forced to "export" the manufacture of many of its most important drugs.

It had been hoped that enactment of export legislation would reverse this trend. However, because of the restrictions contained in the 1986 Act, including the limitation on the countries to which an unapproved drug may be exported for marketing and the threat that FDA approval may be revoked if the product is found in an unlisted country, the 1986 Act has not yet had a significant impact.

As of January 1, 1991, FDA has issued no regulations implementing the 1986 Act. Information on the required contents of an export application is available from FDA, which has published notices stating where applications should be submitted, 52 Fed. Reg. 10633 (April 2, 1987), 54 Fed. Reg. 10587 (March 14, 1989). Notice of export applications are published periodically in the Federal Register.

EXPORT OF ANTIBIOTIC DRUGS

Because an antibiotic drug that lacks approval under section 507 of the FD&C Act is adulterated and misbranded, unapproved antibiotic drugs *can* lawfully be exported under section 801(d). Accordingly, the 1986 Act does not apply to antibiotic drugs. *See* Cook, *The U.S. Export of "Pipeline" Therapeutic Drugs,* 12 Col. J. Environ. L. 39 (1987).

D. FACTORY INSPECTION

The 1906 Act contained no provision authorizing FDA to inspect the establishments in which food and drugs were manufactured, processed, or stored. Section 704 of the 1938 Act therefore represented a major increase in the agency's enforcement authority.

1. CONSTITUTIONAL LIMITATIONS

UNITED STATES v. CARDIFF

Supreme Court of the United States, 1952.
344 U.S. 174.

Mr. Justice DOUGLAS delivered the opinion of the Court.

Respondent was convicted of violating § 301(f) of the Federal Food, Drug, and Cosmetic Act [which] ... prohibits "The refusal to permit entry or inspection as authorized by section 704." Section 704 authorizes the federal officers or employees "after first making request and obtaining permission of the owner, operator, or custodian" of the plant or factory "to enter" and "to inspect" the establishment, equipment, materials and the like "at reasonable times."

Respondent is president of a corporation which processes apples at Yakima, Washington, for shipment in interstate commerce. Authorized agents applied to respondent for permission to enter and inspect his factory at reasonable hours. He refused permission, and it was that refusal which was the basis of the information filed against him and under which he was convicted and fined....

The Department of Justice urges us to read § 301(f) as prohibiting a refusal to permit entry or inspection at any reasonable time. It argues that that construction is needed if the Act is to have real sanctions and if the benign purposes of the Act are to be realized. It points out that factory inspection has become the primary investigative device for enforcement of this law, that it is from factory inspections that about 80 percent of the violations are discovered, that the small force of inspectors makes factory inspections, rather than random sampling of finished goods, the only effective method of enforcing the Act.

All that the Department says may be true. But it does not enable us to make sense out of the statute. Nowhere does the Act say that a factory manager must allow entry and inspection at a reasonable hour. Section 704 makes entry and inspection conditioned on "making request and obtaining permission." It is that entry and inspection which § 301(f) backs with a sanction. It would seem therefore on the face of the statute that the Act prohibits the refusal to permit inspection only if permission has been previously granted. Under that view the Act makes illegal the revocation of permission once given, not the failure to give permission. But that view would breed a host of problems. Would revocation of permission once given carry the criminal penalty no matter how long ago it was granted and no matter if it had no relation to the inspection demanded? Or must the permission granted and revoked relate to the demand for inspection on which the prosecution is based? Those uncertainties make that construction pregnant with danger for the regulated business. The alternative construction pressed on us is equally treacherous because it gives conflicting commands. It makes inspection dependent on consent and makes refusal to allow inspection a crime. However we read § 301(f) we think it is not fair warning to the factory manager that if he fails to give consent, he is a criminal.... We cannot sanction taking a man by the heels for refusing to grant the permission which this Act on its face apparently gave him the right to withhold. That would be making an act criminal without fair and effective notice....

NOTE

In response to the *Cardiff* decision Congress reenacted section 704 of the Act in its present form. 67 Stat. 476 (1953). Thereafter FDA announced revised procedures for conducting inspections:

Commissioner of Food and Drugs Charles W. Crawford said that FDA inspections are now giving written notice of intention to inspect at the time when they present their credentials to the owner, operator, or agent in charge of the plant....

Inspectors are also leaving written reports on conditions or practices which indicate that any products in the establishment contain filth or decomposition or have been prepared, packed or held under insanitary conditions....

In compliance with other provisions of the new law, inspectors are now giving written receipts for all samples taken in connection with an inspection. District offices of the Food and Drug Administration will report promptly to the management of food plants the results of analyses of food samples....

In connection with these actions Commissioner Crawford said that while some phases of FDA inspections are now clearly on a mandatory basis, there are others which Congress apparently intended to be put on a voluntary basis....

"Modern production and distribution are carried on to a large extent through the medium of written instructions and records. The legislative history indicates Congress did not intend to include prescription files, formula files, complaint files, and personnel files within the scope of required inspections. FDA interprets this to mean that inspection of these records will be on a voluntary basis....

"The inspector may state reasons for asking to examine a particular record or file but will not otherwise press the owner, operator or agent for permission to see it...."

FDA Press Release (August 27, 1953). *See* Rhyne and Mullin, *Inspect What? A Study in Legislative History,* 9 FDC L.J. 18 (1954).

UNITED STATES v. JAMIESON–McKAMES
PHARMACEUTICALS, INC.

United States Court of Appeals, Eighth Circuit, 1981.

651 F.2d 532.

ARNOLD, Circuit Judge....

Jamieson–McKames Pharmaceuticals, Inc. (Jamieson–McKames) is a Missouri corporation with its principal place of business in St. Louis, Missouri. The company manufactured, purchased, packaged, labeled, distributed, and sold drugs from before June 1972 until November 1975.....

On October 29, 30, and 31, and November 3, 1975, federal and state agents entered and searched the premises of Jamieson–McKames Pharmaceuticals, Inc., and Pharmacare, Inc.... Samples of drugs were taken, documents were taken, quantities of drugs were embargoed, the premises and contents photographed, and machinery seized..... Thereafter, on May 12, 1977, defendants were charged in an 11–count indictment with counterfeiting, adulterating, and misbranding drugs and conspiracy to counterfeit, adulterate, and misbrand drugs. The indictment also charged that the defendants committed all of these acts with the intent to defraud and mislead, rendering such felonies punishable under 21 U.S.C. § 333(b). The appellants contend that their Fourth Amendment rights were violated by the failure of the court to suppress evidence seized by government agents from the defendants' business premises....

The seizures at the Wentzville pharmacy were conducted on the authority of a notice to inspect authorized by 21 U.S.C. § 374(a). The employee in charge was given a copy of the notice to inspect, but no warrant to inspect was obtained.

The Supreme Court has held that warrantless searches are generally unreasonable, and that commercial premises as well as homes are within the Fourth Amendment's protection. *Marshall v. Barlow's, Inc.,* 436 U.S. 307 (1978). An exception from the search-warrant requirement has, however, been delineated for industries "long subject to close supervision and inspection," *Colonnade Catering Corp. v. United States,* 397 U.S. 72 (1970), and "pervasively regulated business[es]," *United States v. Biswell,* 406 U.S. 311 (1972). *Colonnade* involved the liquor industry, and *Biswell* the interstate sale of firearms. The threshold question therefore is whether the drug-manufacturing industry should be included within this class of closely regulated businesses.

The appellants argue that the drug-manufacturing industry is no more closely regulated than any number of industries involved in interstate commerce, and that therefore the rule of *Marshall v. Barlow's, Inc., supra,* requiring a warrant in the absence of consent before an administrative search can take place, should apply. In *Barlow's,* the Supreme Court held that warrantless searches authorized by § 8(a) of the Occupational Safety and Health Act violated the Fourth Amendment. There, however, the government sought to inspect work areas not open to the public on the premises of an electrical and plumbing contractor. In *Barlow's* the argument that all businesses involved in interstate commerce had "long been subject to close supervision" of working conditions was urged by the Secretary of Labor but explicitly rejected by the Court. In rejecting this argument and others the Court specifically preserved the *Colonnade–Biswell* exception to the warrant requirement. The Court indicated that there were other industries, covered by regulatory schemes applicable only to them, where regulation might be so pervasive that a *Colonnade–Biswell* exception to the warrant requirement could apply. Such warrantless searches are upheld because "when an entrepreneur embarks on such a business, he has chosen to subject himself to a full arsenal of governmental regulation," and " 'in effect consents to the restrictions placed on him.' " Further, in the face of a long history of government scrutiny, such a proprietor has no "reasonable expectation of privacy."

We think the drug-manufacturing industry is properly within the *Colonnade–Biswell* exception to the warrant requirement. The drug-manufacturing industry has a long history of supervision and inspection. The present Food, Drug, and Cosmetic Act has its origins in the Food and Drug Act of 1906. . . .

The *Biswell* Court acknowledged that the history of regulation of interstate firearms traffic was "not as deeply rooted" as the history of liquor regulation, but included firearms within the warrant exception because their regulation was of "central importance to federal efforts to prevent violent crime and to assist the states in regulating the firearms traffic within their borders." This passage teaches that the nature of the federal or public interest sought to be furthered by the regulatory scheme is important to our analysis. It is difficult to overstate the urgent nature of the public-health interests served by effective regulation of our nation's drug-manufacturing industry. Furthermore, virtually every phase of the drug industry is heavily regulated, from packaging, labeling, and certification of expiration dates, to prior FDA approval before new drugs can be marketed. The regulatory burdens on the drug-manufacturing industry are weighty, and that weight indicates that the drug manufacturer accepts the burdens as well as the benefits of the business and "consents to the regulations placed on him." *Marshall v. Barlow's, Inc.*, 436 U.S,. at 313.

The final lesson of *Barlow's* is that the reasonableness of warrantless searches is dependent on the "specific enforcement needs and privacy guarantees of each statute." In *Barlow's* the Court was unconvinced that requiring OSHA officials to obtain administrative warrants when consent to inspect was withheld would cripple the effectiveness of the enforcement scheme. . . .

Regulation of the drug industry differs from the OSHA situation in another significant way. The class sought to be protected by OSHA regulation of safety of work areas is made up of employees, who are in the work place itself and free to report violations at any time. The protected class in the area of drug manufacturing is the consuming public, which has no way of learning of violations short of illness resulting from the consumption of defective drug products. In this sense the enforcement needs of drug-industry regulation are considerably more critical than those before the Court in *Barlow's*.....

In sum, the authorizing statute now before the Court was not painted with so broad a brush as the one rejected in *Barlow's*, the enforcement needs are more critical in the drug-manufacturing field, and the interests of the general public are more urgent. We hold that inspections authorized by § 374 are "reasonable" and therefore not inconsistent with the Fourth Amendment. Thus, this case falls within the "carefully defined classes of cases" which are an exception to the search-warrant requirement. We share, to a degree, the fears expressed by appellants that many businesses are thoroughly regulated by the United States, and that an undue extension of our rationale might obliterate much of the Fourth Amendment's protection. On balance, however, we are persuaded that the capacity for good or ill of the manufacture of drugs for human consumption is so great that Congress had power to enact § 374(a).

Having concluded that drug manufacturing is a "pervasively regulated" industry does not end our inquiry, but establishes only that Congress has broad authority to place restrictions on that industry that might otherwise violate the Fourth amendment. A question remains as to whether the conduct of the government in this case conforms with the statutory scheme provided by the Congress.....

The Federal Food, Drug, and Cosmetic Act contains provisions, similar to those addressed in *Colonnade* which punish refusals to permit inspections by imprisonment up to one year, or a fine of not more than $1,000, or both. It follows, therefore, as in *Colonnade*, that an inspection pursuant to a § 374 notice to inspect is authorized only when there is a valid consent. If consent is withheld, a separate violation of the Act occurs, and the FDA inspectors are required to obtain a warrant before the inspection can proceed.....

We add a word of clarification as to the meaning of the term "consent" as we intend it in this context. We do not mean, by imposing a requirement of "consent," to require a factual determination as to whether appellants, with respect to the Wentzville site, knowingly and understandingly relinquished a known right. The question is whether appellants refused to permit entry or inspection, thereby violating 21 U.S.C. § 331(f). If they did so refuse, then FDA was obliged to obtain an administrative warrant in order to effect the inspection, and could also seek a separate criminal prosecution for the refusal itself. If appellants did not refuse to permit entry or inspection, then they "consented" to the search and seizure, as we use that term here. This formulation, while it may not answer every question that may arise with respect to searches and seizures pursuant to § 374 notices of inspection, seems to us to be the most logical way to harmonize *Biswell* and *Colonnade*.....

Appellants next argue that the inspections were part of an ongoing criminal investigation, and that therefore a warrant issued on less than criminal probable cause was not sufficient to authorize a search. It is our view that a warrant based on an administrative showing of probable cause is valid in this pervasively regulated industry. To hold otherwise would be inconsistent with our conclusion, already expressed, that warrantless entry under a notice of inspection does not violate the Fourth Amendment in the drug-manufacturing field. Probable-cause standards are relaxed because the business person engaged in this industry has a lesser expectation of privacy.....

Appellants next argue that certain statements made by the defendants to FDA agents during the searches were inadmissible at trial because *Miranda* warnings were not given. The district court held that *Miranda* was not applicable because "the evidence failed to establish that defendants ... were in a custodial situation, subject to arrest."

Evidence presented at trial showed that FDA agents are without authority to make arrests, that the defendants' movements were not restricted during the time of the search, and that there were no threats or coercion. Evidence also indicated that appellants' employees were free to go about their business, and that consultation with attorneys was not limited. There is ample evidence to support the district court's finding, and the statements were therefore properly admitted at trial.....

NOTES

1. *Supporting Authority.* See also *United States v. Del Campo Baking Mfg. Co.,* 345 F. Supp. 1371 (D. Del. 1972); compare *United States v. Litvin,* 353 F. Supp. 1333 (D.D.C. 1973).

2. *Records Access.* In *United States v. Stanack Sales Co.,* 387 F.2d 849 (3d Cir. 1968), defendants permitted FDA inspectors to enter and inspect their premises but refused access to their business records. The court held that, by granting access to the premises, defendants did not waive their constitutional right to require a search warrant or subpoena before opening their records.

3. *Clinical Investigators.* In *New York v. Burger,* 482 U.S. 691 (1987), the Supreme Court upheld the warrantless inspection of an automobile junkyard under a statute regulating such businesses on the grounds that (1) the government had a substantial interest in regulating junkyards, (2) warrantless inspections were necessary to further the regulatory scheme, and (3) in certainty and regularity of its application, the statutory inspection program provided a constitutionally adequate substitute for a warrant. Applying these criteria, the court in *United States v. Fogari,* 1987–1988 FDLI Jud. Rec. 144 (D.N.J. 1988), upheld a warrantless inspection of a physician who was conducting clinical investigations whose results were to be submitted to FDA.

4. *Physician Exemption.* Section 704(a)(2)(B) explicitly exempts from FDA inspection any practitioner licensed by law to prescribe or administer drugs and who manufactures those drugs solely for use in his professional practice. In

United States v. Jacobs, Food Drugs Cosm. L. Rep. (CCH) ¶ 38,123 (E.D. Cal. 1989), the court ruled that the failure of an FDA inspector either to request the defendant physician's permission to inspect records or to inform the defendant that his inspection authority did not extend to the records of a licensed physician did not require the suppression of the evidence obtained. Because the defendant had not objected to the inspection, the court concluded that he consented.

5. *Criminal Investigation.* An argument that FDA used its section 704 inspection authority to gather evidence for a criminal prosecution was rejected in *United States v. Gel Spice Co., Inc.,* 773 F.2d 427 (2d Cir. 1985), for lack of evidence of bad faith. The court held that the mere fact that FDA was pursuing criminal enforcement of the FD&C Act at the same time that it conducted a section 704 inspection did not evidence bad faith because the agency has concurrent civil and criminal enforcement responsibilities.

6. *Inspection Warrants. See In re Mallard Beauty Products, Inc.,* Food Drug Cosn. L. Rep. (CCH) ¶ 38,232 (S.D. Ala. 1979), and *United States v. Roux Laboratories, Inc.,* 456 F. Supp. 973 (M.D. Fla. 1978), holding companies in civil contempt for failure to comply with an administrative warrant for inspection obtained by FDA. *But see United States v. Undetermined Quantities of Various Articles of Drugs ... Morton Pharmaceuticals,* 1978–1980 FDLI Jud. Rec. 23 (W.D. Tenn. 1978), holding an FDA seizure invalid because it was accomplished without a court-awarded warrant.

7. *Search warrants.* FDA officials are authorized to request the issuance of a search warrant under Rule 41 of the Federal Rules of Criminal Procedure pursuant to 28 C.F.R. § 60.3(a)(3), promulgated in 44 Fed. Reg. 21785 (April 12, 1979).

8. *Commentary. See generally* Allera, *Warrantless Inspections of the Food Industry,* 34 FDC L.J. 260 (1979); Safir, *Establishment Inspections: The Risk of Refusal,* 33 FDC L.J. 680 (1978). A number of articles have been written on the history and interpretation of section 704 and on the practical aspects of an FDA factory inspection. In addition to those already cited, *see* Basile, *The Law of Inspections,* 34 FDC L.J. 20 (1979); Celeste, *The Inevitable FDA Inspection,* 34 FDC L.J. 32 (1979); Clark, *Inspecting Food Processing Plants,* 18 FDC L.J. 365 (1963); Horton, *Warrantless Inspections Under the Federal Food, Drug, and Cosmetic Act,* 42 Geo. Wash. L. Rev. 1089 (1974); Hutt, *Factory Inspection Authority—The Statutory Viewpoint,* 22 FDC L.J. 667 (1967); Jackson, *FDA Inspectional Records and Freedom of Information,* 33 FDC L.J. 692 (1978); Neely, *FDA Inspectional Authority—Is There an Outer Limit?,* 33 FDC L.J. 710 (1978); Shupack, *The Inspectional Process—A Statutory Overview,* 33 FDC L.J. 697 (1978); Wharton, *Original Federal Food and Drugs Act of June 30, 1906— Its Inspection Evolution,* 1 FDC L.Q. 348 (1946); Papers Presented at the 21st Annual Educational Conference of the Food and Drug Law Institute, Inc., 33 FDC L.J. 100–160 (1975).

UNITED STATES v. THRIFTIMART, INC.

United States Court of Appeals, Ninth Circuit, 1970.
429 F.2d 1006.

MERRILL, Circuit Judge:

Appellants have been convicted of violations of the Federal Food, Drug & Cosmetic Act, 21 U.S.C. § 331(k) and § 333(a). Upon inspection, food in four company warehouses had been found to be infested with insects..... The inspectors testified that on arrival at the warehouses they approached the managers, filled out and presented their notices of inspection, requested permission to inspect and in each case were told, "Go ahead" or words of similar import....

... The precise issue raised is whether the informal and casual consent to search given by the warehouse managers made it unnecessary to secure a search warrant. Appellants argue that a waiver of search warrant "cannot be conclusively presumed from a verbal expression of assent. The court must determine from all the circumstances whether the verbal assent reflected an understanding, uncoerced, and unequivocal election to grant officers a license which the person knows may be freely and effectively withheld." Since the managers were not warned that they had a right to refuse entry and since there was no proof that they knew they had such a right, appellants argue that the consent was not effective to remove the need for a search warrant....

It is clear ... that the administrative search is to be treated differently than the criminal search. The issue in this case is whether the body of law that has grown up around the definition of consent to a search in the criminal area should mechanically be applied to the inspection of a warehouse. In a criminal search the inherent coercion of the badge and the presence of armed police make it likely that the consent to criminal search is not voluntary....

... Food inspections occur with regularity. As here, the judgment as to consent to access is often a matter of company policy rather than of local managerial decision. FDA inspectors are unarmed and make their inspections during business hours. Also, the consent to an inspection is not only not suspect but is to be expected. The inspection itself is inevitable. Nothing is to be gained by demanding a warrant except that the inspectors have been put to trouble—an unlikely aim for the businessman anxious for administrative good will.

... Here, the managers were asked for permission to inspect; the request implied an option to refuse and presented an opportunity to object to the inspection in an atmosphere uncharged with coercive elements. The fact that the inspectors did not warn the managers of their right to insist upon a warrant and the possibility that the managers were not aware of the precise nature of their rights under the Fourth Amendment did not render their consent unknowing or involuntary. They, as representatives of Thriftimart, Inc., were presented with a clear opportunity to object to the inspection and were asked if they had any objection. Their manifestation of assent, no matter how casual, can reasonably be accepted as waiver of warrant.

In conclusion, we hold that in the context of the exclusionary rule a warrantless inspectorial search of business premises is reasonable when entry is gained not by force or misrepresentation, but is, with knowledge of its purpose afforded by manifestation of assent. Lack of warrant under these circumstances did not render the inspections unreasonable under the Fourth Amendment....

NOTES

1. *Supporting Authority.* See also *United States v. Alfred M. Lewis, Inc.,* 431 F.2d 303 (9th Cir. 1970); *United States v. Hammond Milling Co.,* 413 F.2d 608 (5th Cir. 1969); *United States v. Stanack Sales Co.,* 387 F.2d 849 (3d Cir. 1968); *United States v. Crescent–Kelvan Co.,* 164 F.2d 582 (3d Cir. 1948); *United States v. Jamieson–McKames Pharmaceutical, Inc.,* Food Drug Cos. L. Rep. (CCH) ¶ 38,248 (E.D. Mo. 1979); *United States v. General Pharmacal Co.,* 205 F. Supp. 692 (D.N.J. 1962); *United States v. Arnold's Pharmacy, Inc.,* 116 F. Supp. 310 (D.N.J. 1953).

2. *Lack of Consent.* United States v. J. B. Kramer Grocery Co., Inc., 418 F.2d 987 (8th Cir. 1969), held that the trial court properly suppressed evidence obtained by an FDA inspector during a warrantless inspection of defendant's warehouse where the evidence indicated that the inspector had so harassed and intimidated the defendant that his consent to the inspection could not be considered voluntary. *See also United States v. I.D. Russell Laboratories,* 439 F. Supp. 711 (W.D. Mo. 1977), which relied upon *Kramer* to uphold the defendants' right to refuse to permit a warrantless FDA inspection.

3. *Authority to Consent.* In *United States v. Maryland Baking Co.,* 81 F. Supp. 560 (N.D. Ga. 1948) the court held that under section 704 consent must be given by the "owner, operator, or custodian" and not by a subordinate employee.

4. *Oral Statements during Inspection.* In *United States v. Dudgeon,* 279 F. Supp. 300 (D. Mass. 1967), the defendant, claiming support from *Miranda v. Arizona,* 384 U.S. 436 (1966), unsuccessfully sought to suppress statements he had given during the course of a consensual inspection on the ground that the inspectors had not warned him that anything he said could be introduced in evidence against him:

> ... [W]hen defendant was interrogated by McDonnell, he was neither in custody, under arrest nor under any detention imposed by the inspector. No coercion was employed by McDonnell in eliciting the statements from the defendant or examining the invoices. He was not compelled to answer any inquiries directed to him by McDonnell or to exhibit the invoices.... Hence, the evidence is not subject to exclusion on the grounds that it was elicited through or is the fruit of a custodial interrogation of the kind ruled unconstitutional in the cases cited.

See also United States v. Thriftimart, Inc., 429 F.2d 1006 (9th Cir. 1970); *United States v. Del Campo Baking Mfg. Co.,* 345 F. Supp. 1371 (D. Del. 1972).

MECHANICAL REQUIREMENTS OF INSPECTION

1. *Duration of Inspection.* In *United States v. Durbin,* 373 F. Supp. 1136 (E.D. Okl. 1974), the court observed: "[D]efendant's interpretation of 21 U.S.C. § 374(a) as requiring a separate notice for each day of a multiple day inspection is incorrect.... [T]he Notice was dated May 31, 1973 and was effective until the inspection was completed and the required Report submitted."

2. *Time of Day.* In re Establishment Inspection of New England Medical Center Hospital, 1969–1974 FDLI Jud. Rec. 622 (D. Mass. 1974), authorized FDA

investigators and a local medical examiner to enter the hospital any time except between 6:00 A.M. and 1:00 P.M. in order to determine what caused a radiation therapy stretcher assembly to rise and crush a patient against the ceiling. The judge concluded that the investigation could proceed more rapidly if access to the device were not limited and could continue in a closed room without disturbing other patients.

3. *Probable Cause.* In 1973, FDA prepared its customary general warrant of arrest for a diathermy machine and accompanying leaflets in the possession of a neurosurgeon. The clerk of the district court routinely signed the warrant of arrest, and the United States Marshal executed the warrant by entering the office of the neurosurgeon and seizing the device. The Ninth Circuit in *United States v. An Article of Device . . . "Theramatic,"* 641 F.2d 1289 (9th Cir. 1981), held that this procedure violated the Fourth Amendment:

> We hold that absent exigent circumstances, entrance into homes and offices to seize items alleged to violate the Food, Drug, and Cosmetic Act must comply with the basic requirements of the Fourth Amendment: the verified complaint on which the warrant authorizing seizure is based must provide probable cause to believe that the article to be seized violates the act, and the complaint must be scrutinized by a detached, independent official empowered to decide whether probable cause does exist, before the warrant is issued.

The court acknowledged that two other circuits had reached the contrary conclusion. *Founding Church of Scientology v. United States,* 409 F.2d 1146 (D.C. Cir. 1969); *United States v. Articles of Hazardous Substance,* 588 F.2d 39 (4th Cir. 1978). *United States v. Articles of Drug . . . Wans,* 526 F.Supp. 703 (D.P.R. 1981), also declined to follow the *Thematic* decision.

4. *Specificity and Scope. See In Re Administrative Warrant . . . Regarding Portex, Inc.,* 585 F.2d 1152 (1st Cir. 1978); *In the Matter of Establishment Inspection of Medtronic, Inc.,* 500 F.Supp. 536 (D. Minn. 1980).

---

2. SCOPE OF SECTION 704 INSPECTIONS

Neither as enacted nor as revised in 1953 did section 704 generally empower FDA to inspect establishment records. However, FDA has required producers of low acid and acidified food to disclose processing records as a condition for avoiding the imposition of emergency permit controls. 21 C.F.R. § 108.35(c)(3)(iii) and (h). In addition the Drug Amendments of 1962 and the Device Amendments of 1976 amended section 704 to authorize FDA to inspect "records, files, papers, processes, controls, and facilities," except for "financial data, sales data other than shipment data, pricing data, personnel data . . . and research data" for prescription drugs and restricted devices. *United States v. Diapulse Corp.,* 514 F.2d 1097 (2d Cir. 1975), approved FDA inspection of medical device records prior to the Medical Device Amendments of 1976. *See* Elson, *Inspection of Records,* 5 FDC L.J. 755 (1950); McKray, *Record Inspection 1906–1963,* 18 FDC L.J. 301 & 380

(1963). *See also* Young, *From Oysters to After–Dinner Mints: The Role of the Early Food and Drug Inspector,* 42 J. Hist. Med. & Allied Sci. 30 (1987).

The absence of explicit records inspection authority has not prevented FDA inspectors from requesting access to pertinent establishment records, and often getting it.

UNITED STATES v. 75 CASES ... PEANUT BUTTER, LABELED ... "TOP NOTCH BRAND"
United States Circuit Court of Appeals, Fourth Circuit, 1944.
146 F.2d 124.

DOBIE, Circuit Judge.

The Old Dominion Peanut Corporation (hereinafter referred to as claimant) is a corporation with its place of business in Norfolk, Virginia, engaged in manufacturing peanut butter and peanut candies. On or about October 15, 1943, one Rankin, an inspector for the Food and Drug Administration, went to claimant's plant for the purpose of making an inspection of the factory, under authority of Section 374 of the Act. He saw Stubbs, claimant's president, and revealed the purpose of his visit. Stubbs made no objection. An inspection of the factory was made and Rankin found rodent pellets and refuse in and around the food products. Chapman, claimant's plant superintendent, secured containers for Rankin and samples of the food products were taken.

After the completion of the factory inspection, Rankin asked to see the company invoices for the purpose of ascertaining where shipments of these food products were being made. Mizzell, the claimant's sales manager, produced the invoices for Rankin's inspection. No objection whatever was made by either Stubbs or Mizzell....

The District Court found, and we agree with this finding, that permission to inspect the factory was fully and freely given. Further findings were made to the effect that permission was given to Rankin to inspect the claimant's invoices; but the District Court held that this permission was secured by a method that "smacks of surprise, if not of actual misrepresentation." This finding was predicated on the Court's interpretation of the requirements of Section 373 [§ 703] of the Act, and was, we think, clearly erroneous....

The Court below has taken the position, that since Section 373 "meticulously" sets out the method by which information as to interstate shipments is to be obtained, should the Government choose to avail itself of any other method, it must make a full and complete disclosure to the claimant and make sure that claimant's consent is not due in any respect to a failure to understand the fullest use to which the records might be put by the Government.

While we agree that in no case should the Government be permitted to use fraudulent methods in obtaining evidence, we think that the District Court has here placed an unduly narrow construction on this statute. No such interpretation is warranted, either by the words of the Act, by its purpose, or by its legislative history. . . .

Claimant contends here, as it did below, that since the Act provides that the records of carriers and receivers may be examined, this excludes the examination of the claimant's records. We agree with the District Court that the prescribing of certain compulsory methods of investigation does not exclude permissive investigation. The affidavit filed by Stubbs clearly shows the unfortunate result which would follow from a contrary view. The affiant there states that one of the interstate shipments involved was moved by the purchaser in his own truck. Such an instance reveals the difficulties confronted by those administering the Act, should permissive examination of the shipper's records be denied. In such cases there would be no common carrier's records to be examined. Such a view would clearly not be in conformity with the purposes of the Act.

Reversed and remanded.

NOTES

1. *Voluntary Disclosure.* In *United States v. Arnold's Pharmacy, Inc.,* 116 F. Supp. 310 (D.N.J. 1953), the defendants were convicted of dispensing prescription drugs without a physician's authorization. The government's evidence included the pharmacy's shipping and prescription records, which the defendant had voluntarily shown to FDA inspectors. At trial, the defendants sought to suppress its evidence on the ground that it had been "obtained under" section 703 of the Act and therefore could not be used to support their prosecution. The court rejected this claim:

> . . . [T]he purpose of the provision here in question was to close an earlier loophole in the enforcement provisions of the act, which handicapped its enforcement, this handicap being caused by the refusal of certain carriers, if not others, to permit the copying of essential records. In other words, where, as was generally the case, these records were willingly made available to the Government, so that the Act could readily be enforced, the previous law was effective. But, in cases where this access and copying was refused, the section in question would apply to overcome such refusal, and eliminate such "handicap to its (the Act's) enforcement." . . .

> Since the evidence here was voluntarily turned over to the Government by its owners, the conditions for the applicability of the statutory provision in question did not exist, and the statute does not apply. And since the evidence was not obtained unconstitutionally, defendant's motion for the suppression, impounding and return of the evidence, is denied.

For other cases holding that section 703 applies only where the person refused to provide the requested records voluntarily and FDA requests them in writing, see *United States v. Herold,* 136 F. Supp. 15 (E.D.N.Y. 1955); *United States v. Lyon Drug Co.,* 122 F. Supp. 597 (E.D. Wis. 1954). As a result of these decisions FDA rarely makes a written request for records under section 703.

2. *Contract Laboratories.* Where a contract research organization assumed responsibilities for clinical trials regulated by FDA, the court held in *Leo*

Winter Associates, Inc. v. Department HHS, 497 F. Supp. 429 (D.D.C. 1980), that the organization was subject to FDA inspection.

    3. *Purpose of Inspection.* In *R.T. French Co. v. Commissioner of Food and Drugs,* Food Drug Cosm. L. Rep. (CCH) ¶ 38,258 (D. Idaho 1984), the court held that an investigatory inspection to gather information from which FDA intended to promulgate microbiological standards for the potato industry was lawful under section 704.

    4. *Inspection Costs.* In *United States v. Tri–Bio Laboratories, Inc.* 700 F. Supp. 223 (M.D. Pa. 1988), the court held that it has inherent equitable power to order defendants to bear the cost of FDA inspection to enforce an injunction, but declined to exercise that authority under the circumstances of this case which showed no reasonable likelihood of future violations.

TRIANGLE CANDY CO. v. UNITED STATES

United States Circuit Court of Appeals, Ninth Circuit, 1944.
144 F.2d 195.

DENMAN, Circuit Judge.

    This is an appeal by defendants and appellants, Triangle Candy Company, a corporation, and Bernard G. Kennepohl, from judgments rendered against them after appellants were found guilty on six counts of violation of the Federal Food, Drug, and Cosmetic Act....

    There were seven counts in the information. The adulteration charge was twofold in character in all but the first count. Alleged in each count was adulteration under 21 U.S.C. § 342(a)(4), providing that a food shall be deemed adulterated "if it has been prepared, packed, or held under insanitary conditions whereby it may have become contaminated with filth, or whereby it may have been rendered injurious to health." In all counts save the first it was additionally alleged that there was adulteration of the candy involved under 21 U.S.C. § 342(a)(3), providing that a food shall be deemed to be adulterated "if it consists in whole or in part of any filthy, putrid, or decomposed substance, or if it is otherwise unfit for food."

    The sample provision requirement of the Act [section 702(b), provides that, when FDA inspectors collect a sample for analysis, a portion shall be provided to the owner upon request. FDA regulations, 21 C.F.R. § 2.10(b), reflect this requirement and recognize] ... a list of seven exceptions, none of them pertinent to the facts of this case....

    The only testimony regarding the amount of the samples left after analysis was not from any collector but from the government's chief chemist of the Los Angeles station to whom the collector sent the collected samples. He nowhere testified that double the amount deemed needed for analysis was received, plus enough to use at the trial. All he testified to is that "the reason why samples were not furnished which the candy company requested was because all the samples at the Los Angeles station were used in the course of the analyses by the chemists involved; that there was no candy left over after the analyses [which] could be sent to them."

It is thus apparent that the government, failing to supply the demanded samples, has not brought itself within the exceptions of the regulations created under the statute. The problem thus becomes one of the effect of such failure to obey the mandate that the Administrator "shall * * * provide" the samples. . . .

We hold that the provision is not merely directory—for the guidance of the Administrator—but mandatorily gives the right to samples to the accused manufacturers, unless the Administrator brings himself within the excepting regulations. . . .

. . . If those accused under the Act are not given a portion of the sample, their power to make a complete defense is substantially curtailed. Intent is no part of the crime with which they are charged. If they have introduced the food into interstate commerce, and if it is adulterated, they are guilty, regardless of their intent or lack of knowledge as to adulteration. It may frequently happen that the single factual issue is that of adulteration. Without access to a portion of the sample, they are confronted by a government analysis of that sample which they cannot refute but at best, and with difficulty, impeach by challenging the government's method of sampling and testing.

Section 372(b), then, must have been intended to provide defendants with an opportunity for independent analysis; and it is clear that the results of such analysis may be among the most important pieces of evidence defendants can offer in their own behalf. Deprival of the chance to make this test . . . prejudices defendants' substantial rights. This consideration, added to the statute's mandatory wording, and the analogy of cases under other acts, lead us to the conclusion that provision of a portion of the sample, save in properly excepted cases, is a condition precedent to prosecution. . . .

NOTES

1. *Sample Size.* In *United States v. Roux Laboratories, Inc.*, 456 F. Supp. 973 (M.D. Fla. 1978), the court rejected the contention that FDA inspectors' demand for an eight-ounce total sample of expensive cosmetic ingredients was unreasonable. The court also rejected Roux's claim that the agency should be required to disclose in advance what tests it intended to conduct.

2. *FDA Analysis.* The defendant in *United States v. Durbin*, 373 F. Supp. 1136 (E.D. Okl. 1974), owner of a wholesale grocery business, asked for both a reserve sample and the FDA analysis of its samples. The court responded:

. . . [T]he Plaintiff acknowledges that Defendant is entitled to a part of the samples but resists Defendant's request for a copy of an analysis of the samples. Though it may be arguable whether Defendant is entitled to a copy of said analysis pursuant to 21 U.S.C. § 374(d) because he is not a manufacturer, processor, or packer, it appears to the Court that such analysis would be a scientific test under Rule 16(a)(2), Federal Rules of Criminal Procedure, and is therefore discoverable under said Rule.

3. *Agency Practice. See also United States v. Gnome Bakers, Inc.*, 135 F. Supp. 273 (S.D.N.Y. 1955), which held that the requirement that FDA furnish a receipt for any sample does not apply where the agency buys the product at retail. FDA has issued regulations respecting samples in 21 C.F.R. § 2.10.

UNITED STATES v. ACRI WHOLESALE GROCERY CO.

United States District Court, Southern District of Iowa, 1976.
409 F. Supp. 529.

HANSON, Chief Judge.

The scope of review by a district court following a conviction before a magistrate is "the same as on appeal from a judgment of a district court to a court of appeals." Rule 8(d), Title 18, United States Code....

The relevant facts are as follows: In July and October of 1973, inspectors from the Federal Drug Administration (FDA) conducted extensive inspections of the Acri Wholesale Grocery Company warehouse in Des Moines, Iowa. The inspections were conducted during normal business hours. At both inspections, the FDA inspectors presented credentials and a written notice of inspection to Anthony Acri. Further, all indications pointed to routine inspections for contaminated or adulterated foodstuffs. The inspectors were occasionally accompanied by Anthony Acri or other employees on inspection tours of the warehouse. Photographs were taken by the inspectors at both inspections and a stroboscopic light source was utilized for photographs of the warehouse interior. No clandestine measures were taken by the inspectors to hide their photographic activities. The photographs depicted conditions existing inside and immediately adjacent to the exterior of the warehouse, including areas from which the inspectors obtained testing samples. These samples were taken from food substances, usually flour and sugar, which appeared to the inspectors to be contaminated by rodents. Receipts for all samples taken by the inspectors were given to Anthony Acri; and written reports of warehouse conditions, as observed and recorded by the inspectors, were given to Anthony Acri following both inspections....

The defendants initially contend the trial [magistrate] ... erred in admitting into evidence photographs taken during the inspections.... Pursuant to Section 374(a), a flexible standard of "reasonableness" defines the contours of an FDA inspection. The Court believes, under the circumstances present in this case, the photographing of warehouse conditions by FDA agents was not unreasonable. The agents were in the warehouse pursuant to lawful authority and following all procedural requirements mandated under Section 374, *supra*. Further, although it is an unnecessary basis for an inspection, the defendants fully consented to the inspections by FDA. The photographs were taken as part of the inspection, and the inspectors made no efforts to conceal the fact that photographs were being taken. Moreover, in this case the photographs introduced into evidence at trial were merely cumulative of the inspectors' testimony regarding the insanitary conditions in the warehouse....

... Assuming *arguendo,* the photographing of evidence in this case is a "search and seizure" under the Fourth Amendment, the Court believes that once the validity of the inspection is established, the propriety of a photographic "search" is co-extensive with the validity of the inspection. The Court therefore finds that the inspection was conducted pursuant to proper authority, and that no illegal or unwarranted intrusion resulted from the photographic activities.....

NOTES

1. *Supporting Authority.* See *United States v. Jamieson–McKames Pharmaceutical, Inc.,* Food Drug Cos.L Rep. (CCH) ¶ 38,248 (E.D. Mo. 1979). *Cf. Durovic v. Palmer,* 342 F.2d 634 (7th Cir. 1965). For a contrary view, *see* Winston, *Does "Inspection" Include the Right to Take Photographs,* 9 FDC L.J. 544 (1954).

2. *Guidance to FDA Inspectors.* Prior to July 1986, section 523.1 of the FDA Inspection Operations Manual instructed inspectors not to request permission to take photographs but to "proceed on the assumption that they can be taken." The inspectors were told to put away their cameras if management objects and, after an explanation of FDA's need for the photographs, "still insists photos not be taken." Following the *Acri* decision and the Supreme Court decision in *Dow Chemical Co. v. United States,* 476 U.S. 227 (1986), upholding EPA's aerial photography of open and visible areas of business premises, FDA revised its Inspection Operations Manual. If plant management objects to the taking of photographs, agency inspectors are to:

Advise management that the U.S. Courts have held that photographs may lawfully be taken as part of an inspection.....

If management refuses, advise your district so that legal remedies may be sought to allow you to take photographs, if appropriate. If you have already taken some photos, do not surrender these to management. They may obtain copies [of] photos [taken by FDA] under the Freedom of Information Act.

Pursuant to these instructions, FDA inspectors have routinely insisted on taking photographs and, where refused, have in some instances successfully sought warrant approval for this practice.

3. *Tape Recording.* In *American Dietaids Co. v. Celebrezze,* 317 F.2d 658 (2d Cir. 1963), the court declined to rule on the legality of FDA inspectors' surreptitious use of tape recorders, concluding that there was no showing that the agency intended soon to reinspect the plaintiff's premises using recorders. The use of tape recorders and other electronic surveillance equipment by FDA inspectors was the subject of three days of congressional hearings, during which a number of FDA cases involving such equipment were discussed in detail. "Invasions of Privacy (Government Agencies)," Hearings on S. Res. 39 Before the Subcomm. on Administrative Practice and Procedure of the Senate Comm. on the Judiciary, Part 2, 89th Cong., 1st Sess. (1965). The agency has since adopted a policy against any use of tape recorders during an inspection.

3. MODE OF INSPECTION

The FDA method of intermittent random factory inspections, coupled with occasional "for cause" inspections, differs markedly from the continuous factory inspection by resident inspectors conducted by USDA under the Federal Meat Inspection Act and the Poultry Products Inspection Act.

REPORT ON THE WHITE HOUSE CONFERENCE ON FOOD, NUTRITION AND HEALTH

Panel III–2, New Foods (1969).

... The policy of continuous inspection ... was established at a time when this was the only means available to assure the wholesomeness of meat and poultry products. Continuous inspection of this type is extraordinarily costly. The expense is borne by the consumer in the form of higher taxes and higher meat and poultry prices. Although continuous inspection is still merited for ante mortem and post mortem inspection of fresh meat and poultry, modern methods of inspection, already in use for other foods, are now available to replace this method of inspection for plants making food products derived from or utilizing inspection meat with the same or grater degree of confidence that the end product will be wholesome....

Continuous inspection of plants making food products derived from or utilizing inspected meat and poultry products should be replaced by modern inspection and quality control techniques, including statistical sampling, in orderly and deliberate steps consistent with protection of the public health. Information currently available on quality control and inspection in other industries, and as applied to other food products that are often manufactured in the same plants, should be brought to bear n the virtually identical problems with respect to processed and fabricated meat and poultry products....

NOTES

1. *Commentary.* See "Regulatory Organization," V Study on Federal Regulation, Senate Comm. on Governmental Affairs, 95th Cong., 1st Sess. (1977); Booz, Allen, & Hamilton, STUDY OF THE FEDERAL MEAT AND POULTRY INSPECTION SYSTEM (June 1977); GAO, A BETTER WAY FOR THE DEPARTMENT OF AGRICULTURE TO INSPECT MEAT AND POULTRY PROCESSING PLANTS, No. B–163450 (December 1977). USDA has proposed a voluntary approach to the use of quality control systems in meat and poultry plants in lieu of continuous factory inspection. 44 Fed. Reg. 53526 (September 14, 1979)

2. *Program Integrity.* In addition to their cost, USDA's continuous inspection programs have from time to time been vulnerable to compromise by inspected firms. The relationship between resident inspectors and employees

of inspected establishments imposes strains on both parties. *See United States v. Seuss,* 474 F.2d 385 (1st Cir. 1973). The REPORT OF THE USDA FOOD SAFETY AND QUALITY SERVICE TASK FORCE ON PROGRAM QUALITY (October 1979) concluded that continuous factory inspection "because of its structure and functions is inherently vulnerable to corruption," and recommended a new "integrity program" to combat this problem.

3. *Fish Inspection.* Despite criticisms of continuous factory inspection, Congress has seriously entertained proposals to require this approach for fish during hearings conducted in 1967–1968 and in 1989. *Compare* "Fishery Products Protection Act of 1967," Hearings before the Consumer Subcomm. of the Senate Comm. on Commerce, 90th Cong., 1st Sess (1967); "Wholesome Fish and Fishery Products Act and Assistance Needed to Implement It," Hearings before the Consumer Subcomm. of the Senate Comm. on Commerce, 90th Cong., 2nd Sess. (1968), *with* "Seafood Safety," Hearing before the Subcomm. on Oversight and Investigations of the House Comm. on Energy and Commerce, 101st Cong., 1st Sess. (1989); "Fish and Fish Product Safety Act," Hearing before the Subcomm. on Health and the Environment of the House Comm. on Energy and Commerce, 101st Cong., 1st Sess. (1989); "Seafood Inspection System," Hearing before the Subcomm. on Fisheries and Wildlife Conservation and the Environment of the House Comm. on Merchant Marine and Fisheries, 101st Cong., 1st Sess. (1989); "Seafood Inspection Legislation," Hearing before the Subcomm. on Fisheries and Wildlife Conservation and the Environment of the House Comm. on Merchant Marine and Fisheries, 101st Cong., 1st Sess. (1989).

INNOVATIONS IN FACTORY INSPECTION

FDA. In the late 1960s FDA began an Intensified Drug Inspection Program (IDIP) and in the early 1970's it instituted a food factory inspection program based upon Hazard Analysis and Critical Control Point (HACCP), concepts described by Hile, *Food and Drug Administration Inspections—A New Approach,* 29 FDC L.J. 101 (1974):

... Those of you familiar with the drug industry will remember our Intensified Drug Inspection Program or the IDIP. Under this program, a nationally uniform intensive inspection approach was used to determine whether a firm was complying with the drug Good Manufacturing Practices (GMP's) or could be brought into compliance with them. Some plants got tired of seeing the FDA inspectors, but there were major overall improvements in the industry. At approximately the same time, a management consultant firm, which had studied the FDA field operations, recommended the planned national use of limited inspections. Part of the approach included a series of in-depth inspections to determine critical points or "key indicators" in the process. These "key indicators" could later be used to direct limited inspections....

"HACCP" is defined as the Hazard Analysis Critical Control point Investigational Technique. "Critical" in this sense denotes a point where lack of control may present a potential danger to health in the product.

... The inspection technique can be simply divided into three parts: The first part consists of a traditional inspection of the plant covering the processing of the day together with a flow charting of the process and the identification of the critical control points in that process. The second part is to determine the extent of the firm's own quality control program covering these critical points. And the third part is to document the extent to which the firm is adhering to its own quality control program. The approach is designed to give FDA an insight into how the firm is running 365 days a year, particularly when an inspector is not there. It is designed to rather precisely identify the potential problems associated with the product and it provides a clear definition of what needs to be done to correct objectionable conditions and procedures....

In the late 1960s FDA also began a Comparative Quality Assurance Program of "self-certification' of compliance in the food industry in order to reduce the need for agency-conducted inspections, but after 10 years, it abandoned the experiment. Food Chemical News, March 27, 1978, at 58.

The General Accounting Office has made a number of recommendations to improve FDA factory inspection. *See* FOOD INSPECTIONS: FDA SHOULD RELY MORE ON STATE AGENCIES, No. HRD–86–2 (February 18, 1986); FOOD AND DRUG ADMINISTRATION: LABORATORY ANALYSIS OF PRODUCT SAMPLES NEEDS TO BE MORE TIMELY, No. HRD–86–102 (September 19, 1986); IMPORTED FOODS: OPPORTUNITIES TO IMPROVE FDA'S INSPECTION PROGRAM, No. HRD–89–88 (April 28, 1989); DOMESTIC FOOD SAFETY: FDA COULD IMPROVE INSPECTION PROGRAM TO MAKE BETTER USE OF RESOURCES, No. HRD–89–125 (September 27, 1989).

USDA. In the last decade USDA has begun to experiment with different forms of "continuous" inspection for meat and poultry. In 45 Fed. Reg. 54310 (August 15, 1980), the agency adopted a total quality control (TQC) system under which meat and poultry establishments became eligible to assume more responsibility to control their own production through a quality control program. In effect, the TQC system adopted the HACCP concept and required industry to verify compliance, under USDA supervision. This program was expanded in 50 Fed. Reg. 33348 (August 19, 1985), 51 Fed. Reg. 32301 (September 11, 1986). In 48 Fed. Reg. 55490 (December 13, 1983), USDA announced an intensified regulatory enforcement program for plants identified as chronically operating on an unacceptable level.

USDA has experimented with various types of continuous inspection for poultry for the past 20 years, under statutory authority that is more flexible than the laws applicable to meat. The history and applicability of the systems now authorized in 9 C.F.R. § 381.76 are discussed in 51 Fed. Reg. 3569 (January 29, 1986), 53 Fed. Reg. 46855 (November 21, 1988). A streamlined inspection system (SIS) has also been proposed for cattle in 53 Fed. Reg. 48262 (November 30, 1988).

As part of the Processed Products Inspection Improvement Act of 1986, 100 Stat. 3556, 3567, Congress amended the Federal Meat Inspection Act to permit examination and inspection of meat food products "with such frequency and in such manner as the Secretary considers necessary, as provided in rules and regulations issued by the Secretary, taking into account such factors as the Secretary considers to be appropriate." The Poultry Products Improvement Act already contained similar language permitting inspection flexibility. USDA promptly began to implement a change to a "discretionary inspection" system based upon public health criteria, by authorizing experimental programs in 52 Fed. Reg. 10028 (March 30, 1987), 52 Fed. Reg. 48084 (December 18,

1987). The National Academy of Sciences conducted two studies for USDA to assist the efforts to improve meat and poultry inspection: MEAT AND POUL- TRY INSPECTION: THE SCIENTIFIC BASIS OF THE NATION'S PROGRAM (1985); POULTRY INSPECTION: THE BASIS FOR A RISK–ASSESSMENT APPROACH (1987). After proposing comprehensive regulations to implement the new statutory provision in the form of an "improved processing inspection" (IPI) program in 53 Fed. Reg. 44818 (November 4, 1988), USDA withdrew the proposal in 54 Fed. Reg. 22300 (Mary 23, 1989) in response to comment.

To implement the United States–Canada Free Trade Agreement Implemen- tation Act of 1988, 102 Stat. 1851, USDA adopted an interim streamlined inspection procedure for meat and poultry products imported from Canada in 54 Fed. Reg. 273 (January 5, 1989) and proposed to exempt Canadian meat from reinspection and other requirements in 55 Fed. Reg. 26695 (June 29, 1990).

E. SEIZURE

1. GOVERNING PRINCIPLES

FOUR HUNDRED AND FORTY–THREE CANS OF FROZEN EGG PRODUCT v. UNITED STATES

Supreme Court of the United States, 1912.
226 U.S. 172.

Mr. Justice DAY delivered the opinion of the court.

The United States filed its libel alleging that four hundred and forty-three cans of frozen egg product, in the possession of the Mer- chants' Refrigerating Company at Jersey City, New Jersey, consisted in whole or in part of a "filthy, decomposed and putrid animal, to wit, egg substance," and praying for their condemnation....

We are met at the outset with a question of jurisdiction. Section 10 of the [1906] Pure Food Act provides:

"That any article of food ... that is adulterated or misbranded within the meaning of this Act, and is being transported from ne State ... to another for sale, ... shall be liable to be proceeded against in any district court of the United States within the district where the same if is found, and seized for confiscation by a process of libel for condemnation.... The proceedings of such libel cases shall conform, as near as may be, to the proceedings in admiralty, except that either party may demand trial by jury of any issue of fact joined in such case, and all such proceedings shall be at the suit of and in the name of the United States." ...

These proceedings for the seizure and condemnation of property which is impure or adulterated are intended to be in a sense summary, and yet the statute as we have construed it gives the owner a right to a hearing in a court of record with a right of review upon questions of law by writ of error in the Circuit Court of Appeals, and ... finally in this court....

We do not think it was intended to liken the proceedings to those in admiralty beyond the seizure of the property by process *in rem,* then giving the case the character of a law action, with trial by jury if demanded and with the review already obtaining in actions at law. It is true that, if the action is tried in the District Court without a jury, the Circuit Court of Appeals is limited to a consideration of such questions of law as may have been presented by the record proper, independently of the special finding. But the party on jury trial may reserve his exceptions, take a bill of exceptions and have a review upon writ of error in the manner we have pointed out. . . .

NOTES

1. *Seizure of Labeling.* The power of seizure extends to product labeling as well as to the article itself. *See, e.g., United States v. 8 Cartons, Containing "Plantation 'The Original' . . . Molasses,"* 103 F.Supp. 626 (W.D.N.Y. 1951). But *United States v. Vitasafe Corp.,* 345 F.2d 864 (3d Cir. 1965), held that labeling for an illegal product could not be condemned unless it had "accompanied" the product in interstate commerce.

2. *Counterfeiting Equipment.* Under section 304(a)(2) of the Act, any equipment used in counterfeiting a drug may also be confiscated. *United States v. All Equipment Including, But Not Limited to, an Encapsulating Machine,* 475 F. Supp. 39 (E.D. Mo. 1979).

3. *Removal of Labeling. Lee v. United States,* 187 F.2d 1005 (10th Cir. 1951), held that once a device is misbranded it is subject to seizure, and removal of the illegal labeling does not render it immune from condemnation.

4. *Products Under Bond.* Where an article is refused import by FDA, but it has technically entered interstate commerce under customs bond, FDA may either require that the article be exported or may seize it. *E.g., United States v. Ravi Club Frozen Shrimp,* Food Drug Cosm. L. Rep. (CCH) ¶ 38,064 (S.D. Tex. 1980); *United States v. 76,552 Pounds of Frog Legs,* 423 F.Supp. 329 (S.D. Tex. 1976); *230 Boxes, More or Less, of Fish v. United States,* 168 F.2d 361 (6th Cir. 1948).

5. *Re-export.* An article imported into the United States and subsequently found to be illegal may be exported if the importer had no cause to believe that it was illegal when it was imported. *United States v. Articles of Drug . . . 203 Paper Bags,* 634 F.Supp. 435 (N.D. Ill. 1985). But as *United States v. An Article of Food . . . "Basmati Rice,"* Food Drug Cosm. L. Rep. ¶ 38,009 (N.D. Calif. 1986), illustrates, a claimant has a heavy burden to prove it lacked cause to believe that the product was illegal.

6. *Specificity of Warrant.* For contrasting views about the specificity needed in the warrant of seizure, *compare United States v. An Article of Food . . . "Sof–T–Salt Meat Curing General Purpose Salt,"* Food Drug Cosm. L. Rep. (CCH) ¶ 38,325 (N.D. Ala. 1985), *with United States v. Articles of Drug . . . Ru–Vert,* Food Drug Cosm. L. Rep. (CCH) ¶ 38,201 (W.D. La. 1982).

7. *New drugs.* As discussed at pp. 619–30 *supra,* FDA has predicated its conclusion that the FD&C Act does not apply to a physician who prescribes an approved drug for an unapproved use on the narrower interstate commerce requirement that is applicable to new drugs. This necessarily means that the mere shipment of raw materials (including the active ingredient) in interstate commerce is insufficient to confer jurisdiction on FDA. On occasion, FDA loses

sight of its own construction of the FD&C Act and seizes products as illegal new drugs that have not themselves been shipped in commerce. *E.g., United States v. Articles of Drug ... Wans,* 526 F. Supp. 703 (D.P.R. 1981).

UNITED STATES v. 893 ONE–GALLON CANS ... LABELED BROWN'S INHALANT

United States District Court, District of Delaware, 1942.
45 F. Supp. 467.

LEAHY, District Judge.

A libel was filed which sought seizure and condemnation of certain cans containing poultry medicine.... The claimants, who were in possession of the articles, filed an answer denying the property was misbranded. The manufacturer, Edgar W. Brown, an individual engaged in business under the name of "Brown's Poultry Products Co.," in Lancaster, Pennsylvania, was permitted to intervene on May 21, 1942, to defend the labeling on his own behalf. In the order permitting the intervention, there was a provision directing that the property be discharged from seizure and delivered to the claimant upon the claimant's filing bond; and that the claimant should not sell said property unless and until the labels were removed.... On May 26, 1942, the Government moved to amend the precipitous order of May 21, 1942, by striking out those portions which permitted a return of the seized property.

In opposing the Government's motion, both the manufacturer and claimant assert that as this is a cause in Admiralty, they should be allowed to have possession of the property before final hearing and decree by filing an appropriate bond in view of the fact that the statute provides that the procedure under Section 304(b) "shall conform, as nearly as may be, to the procedure in admiralty; * * * " ... The Government contends that there can be no release of seized property under the statute until "after entry of the [final] decree" of condemnation....

Not only is the legislative history of Section 304 helpful in determining its meaning, but a mere examination of the statute makes it clear that (1) an article may be proceeded against by libel when it is adulterated or misbranded; (2) once such an article is seized the issue of adulteration or misbranding must be determined by the Court; (3) if the article is neither adulterated nor misbranded, it is released to the claimant; but (4) if it is adulterated or misbranded it may be disposed of only as provided by Section 304(d). Destruction or release may only be had after decree....

NOTES

1. *Supporting Authority. See United States v. Article of Device ... "110 V Vapozone ... ",* 194 F. Supp. 332 (N.D. Cal. 1961), holding that seized product should not be returned to the claimant *pendente lite.*

2. *Release of Seized Articles.* For differing views on whether a court may permit seized articles to be released for lawful use prior to a decision on their legality *compare United States v. Alcon Laboratories,* 636 F.2d 876 (1st Cir. 1981), *with United States v. Undetermined Quantities of Drugs,* 675 F. Supp. 1113 (N.D. Ill. 1987).

3. *Perishable Commodities.* Seizure of perishable commodities may result in the destruction or loss of value of the articles even if the claimant ultimately prevails. For example, although the claimant prevailed in a seizure of beef containing DES, *United States v. 2,116 Boxes of Boned Beef,* 516 F. Supp. 321 (D. Kan. 1981), *aff'd,* 726 F.2d 1481 (10th Cir. 1984), the claimant's attempt to recover the lost value of the food under the Tucker Act, 28 U.S.C. § 1491(a)(1), was rejected because the Tenth Circuit determined that the seizure was reasonable. *Jarboe–Lackey Feedlots, Inc. v. United States,* 7 Cl. Ct. 329 (1985).

UNITED STATES v. 3 UNLABELED 25–POUND BAGS DRIED MUSHROOMS

United States Circuit Court of Appeals, Seventh Circuit, 1946.
157 F.2d 722.

MINTON, Circuit Judge.

... The court found the mushrooms were adulterated within the meaning of the Act, and on July 13, 1945 entered a decree that the mushrooms be condemned, forfeited, and destroyed.

The claimant filed a motion to vacate this judgment and for a new trial. This motion was overruled on the 11th day of October, 1945, at which time the claimant gave notice of appeal. In the meantime, no stay of the court's order or decree having been entered, the Marshall destroyed the mushrooms. Therefore, the subject matter of the libel and of this action is no longer in existence.

The continued existence of the mushrooms is essential to our right to proceed against the things themselves. The action is an action in rem. In such a proceeding, there is no party defendant. The goods stand to answer....

Counsel for the Government readily admits the matter is moot here and counsel for the claimant reluctantly admits it is moot, but both parties ask us to decide the issue between them. This we decline to do. If we were to affirm the judgment, the District Court could not destroy the mushrooms. They have already been destroyed. If we reversed the judgment, there would be no mushrooms to restore to the claimant. The cause is clearly moot. We are not authorized to decide arguments but only "cases and controversies." ...

NOTES

1. *Appeal from Seizure.* An appeal by a claimant from an adverse district court decision must await a final decree of condemnation and an order dispos-

ing of the articles. *See United States v. 38 Cases ... "Mr. Enzyme",* 369 F.2d 399 (3d Cir. 1966).

2. *Compensation for Seized Goods.* In *United States v. An Article of Food ... 55 Gallons ... Honey,* Adm. 78–6–D (D.N.H., May 15, 1979), the court awarded custody of the condemned honey to the New Hampshire Department of Fish and Game to "constructively destroy the substance in the drums by using it as bear bait" but ruled that the claimant had no right to compensation for the use of the condemned goods.

3. *Jurisdiction Over Claimant.* In *United States v. An Article of Drug ... Neo–Terramycin Soluble Powder Concentrate,* 540 F.Supp. 363 (N.D. Tex. 1982), the court held that, even if the seized article is removed from the jurisdiction, the court retains *in personam* jurisdiction once a claim has been filed.

4. *Mootness.* In *United States v. Articles of Drug Consisting of 203 Paper Bags,* 818 F.2d 569 (7th Cir. 1987), after the district court allowed illegal new animal drugs to be reexported, the court of appeals vacated all of the district court orders on the ground that the matter was now moot.

5. *Costs of Litigation.* Where a claim for seized articles is withdrawn prior to judgment, the claimant is nonetheless properly charged for costs, as provided in section 304(e) of the FD&C Act. *United States v. 374 100 Pound Burlap Bags ... Cocoa Beans,* Food Drug Cosm. L. Rep. (CCH) ¶ 38,119 (E.D. Pa. 1989); *United States v. An Article of Food ... "COJM Grade A,"* Food Drug Cosm. L. Rep. (CCH) ¶ 38,179 (N.D. Ill. 1982). *See United States v. An Article of Food ... Raisins,* Food Drug Cosm.L. Rep. (CCH) ¶ 38,002 (E.D. Tenn. 1979).

6. *Personal Jurisdiction.* If seized goods are claimed, the claimant submits to the personal jurisdiction of the court and FDA may then move to amend the complaint to add a request for an injunction.

7. *Commentary. See generally* Kleinfeld, *The Seizure Section of the Federal Food, Drug, and Cosmetic Act,* 2 FDC L.Q. 21 (1947); Taylor, *Seizures and Injunctions: Their Role in FDA's Enforcement Program,* 33 FDC L.J. 596 (1978).

---

2. MULTIPLE SEIZURES

EWING v. MYTINGER & CASSELBERRY, INC.

Supreme Court of the United States, 1950.
339 U.S. 594.

Mr. Justice DOUGLAS delivered the opinion of the Court.

This is an appeal from a three-judge District Court specially constituted on appellee's application for an injunction to restrain enforcement of a portion of an Act of Congress for repugnance to the Due Process Clause of the Fifth Amendment.....

Appellee is the exclusive national distributor of Nutrilite Food Supplement, an encapsulated concentrate of alfalfa, water cress, parsley, and synthetic vitamins combined in a package with mineral tablets. There is no claim that the ingredients of the preparation are harmful or dangerous to health. The sole claim is that the labeling was, to use the statutory words, "misleading to the injury or damage of the purchaser or consumer" and that therefore the preparation was "misbranded" when introduced into interstate commerce.

This was indeed the administrative finding behind eleven seizures resulting in that number of libel suits, between September and December, 1948.... Shortly thereafter the present suit was instituted to have the multiple seizure provision of § 304(a) declared unconstitutional and to dismiss all libel cases except the first one instituted. The District Court held that appellants had acted arbitrarily and capriciously in violation of the Fifth Amendment in instituting multiple libel suits without first affording the appellee a hearing on the probable cause issue; that the multiple seizure provision of § 304(a) was unconstitutional under the Due Process Clause of the Fifth Amendment; and that appellants should be permanently enjoined from instituting any action raising a claim that the booklet accompanying the preparation was a misbranding since it was not fraudulent, false, or misleading.

First. The administrative finding of probable cause required by § 304(a) is merely the statutory prerequisite to the bringing of the lawsuit. When the libels are filed the owner has an opportunity to appear as a claimant and to have a full hearing before the court. This hearing, we conclude, satisfies the requirements of due process....

It is said that these multiple seizure decisions of the Administrator can cause irreparable damage to a business. And so they can. The impact of the initiation of judicial proceedings is often serious.... Yet it has never been held that the hand of government must be stayed until the courts have an opportunity to determine whether the government is justified in instituting suit in the courts. Discretion of any official may be abused. Yet it is not a requirement of due process that there be judicial inquiry before discretion can be exercised. It is sufficient, where only property rights are concerned, that there is at some stage an opportunity for a hearing and a judicial determination....

Second. The District Court had no jurisdiction to review the administrative determination of probable cause.

The determination of probable cause in and of itself had no binding legal consequence.... It took the exercise of discretion on the part of the Attorney General, as we have pointed out above, to bring it into play against appellee's business. Judicial review of such a preliminary step in a judicial proceeding is so unique that we are not willing easily to infer that it exists....

The purpose of the multiple seizure provision is plain. It is to arrest the distribution of an article that is dangerous, or whose labeling is fraudulent or misleading, pending a determination of the issue of adulteration or misbranding. The public therefore has a stake in the jurisdictional issue before us. If the District Court can step in, stay the institution of seizures, and bring the administrative regulation to a halt until it hears the case, the public will be denied the speedy protection which Congress provided by multiple seizures. It is not enough to say that the vitamin preparation in the present case is not dangerous to health. This preparation may be relatively innocuous. But the statutory scheme treats every "misbranded article" the same in this respect—whether it is "dangerous to health," or its labeling is "fraudulent," or materially "misleading to the injury or damage of the purchaser or consumer.".... Congress weighed the potential injury to the public from misbranded articles against the injury to the purveyor of the article from a temporary interference with its distribution and decided in favor of the speedy, preventive device of multiple seizures. We would impair or destroy the effectiveness of that device if we sanctioned the interferences which a grant of jurisdiction to the District Court would entail....

Reversed.

Mr. Justice JACKSON, dissenting....

The trial court of three judges wrote no opinion but made forty-three detailed findings of fact.... The substance of these is to find that the Government instituted a multiplicity of court actions, with seizures in widely separated parts of the country, with a purpose to harass appellee and its dealers and intending that these actions and the attendant publicity would injure appellee's business *before any of the issues in such cases could be tried.* This, the court held, was justified by no emergency, the product being, at worst, harmless and having been marketed for years with knowledge of the Department.

Assuming as I do that the Act on its face is not constitutionally defective, the question remains whether it has been so misused by refusal of administrative hearing, together with such irreparable injury in anticipation of judicial hearing, as to deny appellee due process of law or to amount to an abuse of process of the courts.

The Government has sought and received from this Court protection against a multiplicity of suits under circumstances where injury was less apparent than in this. The holding of the court below and the contention of the appellee here that the Government is not entitled to so apply the statute as to bring multiple actions designed to destroy a business before it can be heard in its own defense is not frivolous, to say the least. I am constrained to withhold assent to a decision that passes in silence what I think presents a serious issue.

PARKE, DAVIS & CO. v. CALIFANO

United States Court of Appeals, Sixth Circuit, 1977.
564 F.2d 1200.

LIVELY, Circuit Judge.

The question in this case is whether the district court properly enjoined enforcement actions by the Food and Drug Administration

1128 FDA ENFORCEMENT Ch. 11

(FDA) which were instituted as libels for the seizure of drugs in warehouses of the plaintiff, Parke, Davis & Company (Parke Davis)....
The district court found that the FDA's threat to initiate enforcement actions against Parke Davis under the circumstances of this case was a "final agency action for which there is no other adequate remedy in a court ... " and subject to judicial review pursuant to 5 U.S.C. § 704. The district court further found that it was necessary in order to prevent an irreparable injury to Parke Davis to grant injunctive relief pending review of the agency action, as authorized by 5 U.S.C. § 705.

The dispute in the case concerns the right of Parke Davis to market as an antitussive (cough inhibitor) a nonprescription, over-the-counter drug product containing diphenhydramine hydrochloride (DPH). [The court related that in 1948 FDA approved Parke Davis' NDA for this product for prescription use. Parke Davis subsequently pursued two approaches to "switch" the product from Rx to OTC status, through the OTC drug review and by submitting a supplemental NDA. In 1975, after the OTC Cough–Cold Panel agreed to recommend that the product should be available OTC and FDA's Associate Chief Counsel wrote Parke Davis indicating that the agency was extremely unlikely to initiate enforcement action, the firm marketed an OTC version of the product. In September 1976 FDA disapproved the supplemental NDA and stated that it would not accept the review panel's recommendation. Ed.] ...

The present action was filed in the United States District Court for the Eastern District of Michigan on November 29, 1976. Three days prior thereto FDA personnel had been instructed to prepare draft complaints for seizure of Benylin Cough Syrup in 13 districts and letters to the United States attorneys in those districts recommending institution of seizure actions pursuant to 21 U.S.C. § 334. On November 30 and December 1, 1976 complaints were filed and seizures of Benylin Cough Syrup were effected in the Northern District of Texas, the Northern District of Illinois and the District of Minnesota. The district court in the present action issued a temporary restraining order on December 1, 1976 and, after hearings on December 3rd and 8th, issued a preliminary injunction on that latter date. Shortly thereafer the district court filed a memorandum opinion setting forth its reasons for granting the injunction.....

When this action was filed in the district court Parke Davis had taken the necessary steps to obtain a final decision on its right to market Benylin over the counter by protesting the ruling that its supplemental NDA was not approvable. A hearing will be held before a final decision is rendered on that application, and the decision will be subject to judicial review by the appropriate court of appeals pursuant to 21 U.S.C. § 371(f)(1).

We conclude that the district court had no jurisdiction to review the decision of the FDA to initiate enforcement actions. That decision is indistinguishable from the finding of probable cause which the Supreme Court has held may not be challenged in a separate action.

Parke Davis argues in this court that the district court did more than review the decision of the commissioner to initiate enforcement proceedings. It contends that the district court acted properly under the Administrative Procedure Act to prevent irreparable injury from an arbitrary and capricious action of the commissioner in seizing drug products which were being distributed over the counter as a matter of right following publication of the preliminary monograph without dissent. Parke Davis relies primarily on *Upjohn Co. v. Finch,* 303 F.Supp. 241 (W.D. Mich. 1969). In *Upjohn* the FDA revoked a certificate for marketing an antibiotic which had been approved for 12 years. No enforcement action was pending and no hearing was provided prior to revocation. *Upjohn* is distinguishable in at least two respects. First, the drug in question had been approved for sale—this was not in dispute. In the present case Benylin has never received final approval as an over-the-counter drug. The "switch-over" proceedings are still in progress, and a hearing is scheduled. The OTC Review was concluded with a decision adverse to Parke Davis. Secondly, in this case enforcement proceedings were pending in other jurisdictions when the district court issued its injunctive orders. Every issue raised in this case, including the question of whether the OTC Review regulations deprived Parke Davis of due process rights by failing to provide for a hearing and failing to contain guidelines for the commissioner in determining whether to accept or dissent from a panel monograph, could have been raised in the enforcement proceedings.

Thus Parke Davis had an adequate remedy, and the district court erred in holding that it did not. Parke Davis had the same remedy which was available to the distributor in *Ewing*—the statutory right to contest the seizure of its property in the libels, four of which had been filed before the injunction was entered in the present action.... Though the district court had jurisdiction under the Administrative Procedure Act to consider the complaint of Parke Davis, insofar as it questioned the regulations and procedures of the FDA as contrasted with the mere decision to initiate enforcement proceedings, it was an abuse of discretion to enjoin the FDA in the circumstances of this case where pending enforcement actions provided an opportunity for a full hearing before a court....

NOTES

1. *Supporting Authority. See Merritt Corp. v. Folsom,* 165 F. Supp. 418 (D.D.C. 1958). In *Dainty–Maid, Inc. v. United States,* 216 F.2d 668 (6th Cir. 1954), claimant sought dismissal of multiple seizures for misbranding, on the ground that the labeling involved was not identical to the labeling held illegal in an earlier default judgment. The court refused, holding that whether the new labeling involved the same misbranding as the earlier judgment was a factual question for the district court.

2. *Ripeness for Review.* In *Natick Paperboard Corp. v. Weinberger*, 498 F.2d 125 (1st Cir. 1974), the court was called upon to reconcile the holding in *Ewing* that a seizure may not be enjoined with the holding in *Abbott Laboratories,* p. 1258 *infra,* permitting preenforcement review:

> We think the best accommodation of these conflicting policies is to construe § 334 as not precluding district court jurisdiction to decide the definitional question within the context of an action solely for declaratory relief. At the same time, we want to make clear that the existence of this limited jurisdiction does not permit the district court to halt in any way the seizure of appellants' food-packaging materials while the definitional issue is being resolved. . . .

See also United States v. Alcon Laboratories, 636 F.2d 876 (1st Cir. 1981); *Gemini Pharmaceutical v. HHS,* Food Drug Cosm. L. Rep. (CCH) ¶ 38,248 (E.D. N.Y. 1983).

3. *Commentary. See* Lev, *The Multiple Seizure Bludgeon,* 5 FDC L.J. 535 (1950); Swire, *FDA's Multiple Seizure Powers: A Time for Equity,* 34 FDC L.J. 244 (1979).

---

3. PROOF REQUIRED FOR CONDEMNATION

In a civil seizure action the government must prove its case by a preponderance of the evidence. *See, e.g., United States v. 60 28–Capsule Bottles* . . . *"Unitrol,"* 325 F.2d 513 (3d Cir. 1963); *United States v. 4 Cases * * * Slim–Mint Chewing Gum,* 300 F.2d 144 (7th Cir. 1962); *United States v. 449 Cases, Containing Tomato Paste,* 212 F.2d 567 (2d Cir. 1954).

UNITED STATES v. 43½ GROSS RUBBER PROPHYLACTICS LABELED IN PART "XCELLO'S PROPHYLACTICS"

United States District Court, District of Minnesota, 1946.
65 F. Supp. 534.

NORDBYE, District Judge.

The government inspection has established that the devices tested were defective in the number indicated, and there can be no serious doubt that the strength and quality of these particular defective articles fell below that which they purported or were represented to possess. . . .

The problem presented, however, pertains to the right of the Government to condemn the entire shipment. . . . The Government took two samples—a pre-seizure and a post-seizure. While the method by which the first sample was taken is not entirely clear in the record, it does appear that, in taking the post-seizure samples, the Government took one dozen articles from each of the 36 gross cartons of Xcellos, and from the three gross so selected 72 samples were taken at random. . . . The average defects, therefore, of all the tests is approximately 7.37 per cent. But of the entire shipment seized a fraction of one per cent is definitely shown to be defective, and claimant contends that the Government has failed to sustain the burden of proof which rests on it in these proceedings in its attempt to condemn the entire shipment. It should be pointed out that apparently the only practical tests which the government representatives are able to make with the facilities available to them results in the article's being rendered useless after the test has been made. Concededly, the burden of proof rests upon the Government. But it does not follow that each individual article in the shipment must be tested. Inspection and condemnation on the basis of samples tested is clearly contemplated by the Act. . . . No serious question is raised in this proceeding as to the samples taken being representative. But claimant contends that the Court cannot order the condemnation of good articles, and concededly some of the remaining articles are in all probability free from defects. However, in urging this contention, claimant fails to distinguish between condemnation and the confiscation or sale of goods. Condemnation only sustains the Government's position that the good as they were composed in interstate shipment violate the provision and purpose of the Federal Food, Drug, and Cosmetic Act. After the decree, the claimant can separate the good from the defective if it posts a bond, and thereby will be able to retain the balance of the goods. . . . [T]he Court is not required or permitted to establish any formulas as to what tolerance of defects should be allowed, if any, in every type of libel proceeding before it determines that the Government has sustained the burden of proof as to any particular shipment. Suffice it to say that, on the state of the facts herein, and assuming that the same ratio of defectives would be found in the entire shipment, it would follow that over 1,500 defective articles would be found in this shipment. Such a number, if sold on the market, would constitute a potential menace to public health, and, in view of the claimed purpose and object of the devices, that is, the prevention of disease, are sufficient to sustain the libel proceedings herein. . . .

NOTES

1. *Standard for Condemnation.* If the government proves *any* charge of illegality the product must be condemned:

> . . . [I]n view of the disposition of the motion as it relates to the other diseases, the factual allegations, admissions and denials as to cancer, heart disease, defective birth of offspring and loss of teeth need not be considered. For the Government to prevail, it is not necessary that all the representations in the labeling are false; if any single claim in the labeling is false or misleading, the device is misbranded under § 352(a). . . .

United States v. 2000 Plastic Tubular Cases . . . Toothbrushes, 231 F.Supp. 236, 240 (M.D.Pa. 1964) (and cases cited therein). *See also Buticaps, Inc. v. United States,* 252 F.2d 634 (D.C. Cir. 1958).

2. *FDA Expenses.* In *United States v. Article of Drug,* 428 F. Supp. 278 (E.D. Tenn. 1976), the court denied the government's motion to order the claimant to pay its expenses in proving that the seized articles were "new

animal drugs," which the claimant refused to admit when requested to do so. They court found that the claimant had a reasonable basis for believing it might prevail on the issue.

---

4. TRANSFER OF PROCEEDINGS

CLINTON FOODS, INC. v. UNITED STATES

United States Court of Appeals, Fourth Circuit, 1951.
188 F.2d 289.

PARKER, Chief Judge.

... In April 1950 the United States instituted a condemnation proceeding ... in the United States District Court for the Southern District of West Virginia against 630 cases of orangeade found within the District, on the ground that the orangeade was both misbranded and adulterated within the prohibition of the statute. Clinton Foods, Inc., intervened as owner in the condemnation proceeding and filed answer denying the charges of misbranding and adulteration. It subsequently made a motion that the case be transferred for trial to the District of Maryland; but this was denied by the District Judge on the ground that he had no power to order the transfer. Appeal was taken from this denial of the motion and, in addition, Clinton Foods has filed a petition in this court asking a writ of mandamus against the District Judge on the ground that he had power to grant the motion and should have exercised his discretion in passing upon it.....

Assuming without deciding that in a proper case this court has power to issue a writ of mandamus ... we think it clear that this is not a case in which the writ should be granted, as the District Judge was clearly right in holding that he had no power to transfer the case to the District of Maryland....

28 U.S.C. § 1404(a) provides: "(a) For the convenience of parties and witnesses, in the interest of justice, a district court may transfer any civil action to any other district or division where it might have been brought." The condemnation proceeding against the 630 cases of orangeade could not have been brought in any district other than the Southern District of West Virginia, for it was there that the property sought to be condemned was situate. It is well settled that a proceeding in rem against specific property is local in character and must be brought where the property is subject to seizure under process of the court. Since the suit for condemnation of the 630 cases of orangeade could not have been brought in any other district than that in which they were seized, it is clear that it may not be transferred from that district under the provisions of 28 U.S.C. § 1404(a)....

Nothing in 21 U.S.C. § 334(a) authorizes the transfer asked. That section requires condemnation proceedings under the Food, Drug and Cosmetic Act for adulteration or misbranding to be brought within the district where the article is found. The proviso, which applies only to libels on account of misbranding, authorizes the limitation to a single proceeding of the proceedings which may be brought for misbranding and the removal for trial of such proceeding. It is significant that the proviso makes no such provision where condemnation is sought on the ground of adulteration, which is ordinarily more serious than mis-branding and is more often the basis of a forfeiture of the property. There is no authority in the district court to remove a case under this proviso, as distinguished from consolidating a multiplicity of cases under sec. 334(b), where adulteration is charged. *United States v. 74 cases etc. of Oysters*, 55 F. Supp. 745. And the rule is not different because adulteration along with misbranding is charged in a single libel. *United States v. 11 Cases etc. Ido–Pheno–Chon*, 94 F. Supp. 925.

For the reasons stated, the appeal will be dismissed and the petition for writ of mandamus will be denied.

NOTE

Where multiple seizures are filed in different jurisdictions they may be consolidated in a district of reasonable proximity to the claimant's place of business pursuant to section 304(b). *See, e.g., United States v. 91 Packages ... Nutrilite Food Supplement*, 93 F. Supp. 763 (D.N.J. 1950). *See generally* Kleinfeld and Dickerman, *Removal and Consolidation in Condemnation Proceedings*, 2 FDC L.Q. 197 (1947).

5.　SALVAGING

UNITED STATES v. 1322 CANS ... OF BLACK RASPBERRY PUREE

United States District Court, Northern District of Ohio, 1946.
68 F.Supp. 881.

Jones, District Judge.

... The decree provides for the condemnation of the black raspberry puree because it was adulterated and upon bond allows the reconditioning by distillation or reprocessing for making cordials, brandies or jellies but subject to the approval of the Food and Drug Administration.... The claimant wants to reprocess the puree by filtration and make jelly of it. The Food and Drug Administration objects to this method and refuses to supervise a reconditioning process of the filtration type because, as it says, such process would not produce a product which it would approve for human consumption....

... After a product has been condemned its reprocess is a permissive matter within the discretion of the court as indicated by the use of the word "may" in the statute. The statute also provides that the reconditioned puree may be brought into compliance with the provisions of the Pure Food and Drug law under the supervision of the

Administration. Where several methods of reprocessing are enumerated, as in this decree, the question of who shall determine the one to be used and which, when used, will bring the reconditioned puree into compliance with the statute seems to be the only question for decision. . . .

The Food and Drug Administration has determined that distillation is the only process which would recondition this puree for human consumption and which it would approve. I see no abuse of discretion in making this determination nor can the court interfere with that determination. To interfere would be substituting the judgment of the court for that of the Food and Drug Administration upon a matter which it is better able to decide and upon an issue which I think is not properly joined in this case.

NOTE

In *338 Cartons . . . of Butter v. United States,* 165 F.2d 728 (4th Cir. 1947), the court declined to overrule the lower court's refusal to permit the claimant to recondition insect contaminated butter for human consumption, although it held that the judgment was an appealable final decision. *See also United States v. 1,638 Cases of Adulterated Alcoholic Beverages,* 624 F.2d 900 (9th Cir. 1980); *United States v. 76,552 Pounds of Frog Legs,* 423 F. Supp. 329 (S.D. Tex. 1976); *United States v. An Article of Drug for Veterinary Use,* Food Drug Cosm. L. Rep. (CCH) ¶ 38,112 (W.D. Mo. 1989); *United States v. An Article of Food . . . Purporting to be Honey,* Food Drug Cosm. L. Rep. (CCH) ¶ 38,216 (D.N.H. 1978); *United States v. Various Cases of Adulterated Alcoholic Beverages,* 421 F. Supp. 1 (D. Alaska 1976). The seized product must be condemned before reconditioning may begin. *See In re United States,* 140 F.2d 19 (5th Cir. 1943). Violation of a court decree permitting salvaging after condemnation will result in forfeiture of the bond posted by the claimant. *See Stinson Canning Co. v. United States,* 170 F.2d 764 (4th Cir. 1948); *Fresh Grown Preserve Corp. v. United States,* 143 F.2d 191 (6th Cir. 1944). *See generally* Jacobs, *An Analysis of the Application of the Salvaging Provision of the Food, Drug, and Cosmetic Act of 1938,* 26 FDC L.J. 240 (1971); Kleinfeld, *The Salvaging of Products Condemned Under the Federal Food, Drug, and Cosmetic Act,* 2 FDC L.Q. 335 (1947).

BUTICAPS, INC. v. UNITED STATES

United States Court of Appeals, District of Columbia Circuit, 1958.
252 F.2d 634.

PER CURIAM.

The libel in this case was filed to condemn certain articles of drug (a claimed skin conditioner) in accordance with the Federal Food, Drug and Cosmetic Act. It was claimed that the articles were misbranded within the meaning of said Act in that: (1) as alleged in paragraph 3 of the libel a leaflet . . . contained statements which were false and misleading; and (2) as alleged in paragraph 4 of the libel the aforementioned articles were further misbranded in that the designations of certain vitamins and proteins appearing on the package labels were false and misleading. Thereafter, the libel was amended by adding paragraph 3(a) to allege that the name "buticaps" on the package labels, leaflet and booklet represents and implies that the articles will beautify the skin of the user, which is false and misleading since the articles will not beautify the skin of the user.

After answer by libelee admitting the allegations in paragraphs 3 and 4 of the libel but denying the allegations in paragraph 3(a) as to the use of the word "buticaps," the Government filed motion for judgment on the pleadings. This motion was not opposed but, in the answer thereto, libelee [claimed] urged: "If this Motion is granted, claimant's pleading with regard to the name 'Buticaps' must be taken as true."

The District Court filed a memorandum announcing that it would grant the motion for judgment on the pleadings but would exercise its discretion in not ordering the articles destroyed, as it had a right to do, and would release the seized articles for relabeling.... [O]n May 21, 1957, the court entered its order, reciting, among other things, that because of libelee's insistence upon the use of the name "Buticaps," further efforts to relabel would be fruitless; and the court directed that the articles seized be destroyed by the United States Marshal. This appeal followed.

We think this ruling of the District Court was erroneous. The judgment on the pleadings was limited, of necessity, to the admitted facts. We believe that the refusal of the Department of Health, Education and Welfare to allow relabeling unless the word "Buticaps" was eliminated was unauthorized, and that libelee was entitled to a *judicial* hearing and ruling on the question of the alleged misuse of the word.

We agree that, as the Government contends, "[b]y violating the law and introducing a misbranded drug into interstate commerce, the owner of the article, after there has been a judicial determination that the article violates the law, loses any *right* to repossess his property" and that "[h]e regains the property upon such terms and conditions as to the trial court seem just and proper, within the confines of the powers conferred by Section 304(d)" of the Act. But the terms and conditions are to be fixed by the *court* and not by the Department of Health, Education and Welfare. Libelee is entitled to judicial due process.

It is no answer, as urged by libelant, to say that the name "Buticaps" itself implies that the article will impart beauty. It may be that, on hearing, the court, on evidence, could determine that the use of the name "Buticaps" is misleading.....

———————

6. EFFECTIVENESS OF SEIZURES

PETER BARTON HUTT, PHILOSOPHY OF REGULATION UNDER THE FEDERAL FOOD, DRUG AND COSMETIC ACT

28 Food Drug Cosmetic Law Journal 177 (1973).

... [A] seizure represents a substantial expenditure of governmental resources.... Many seizures, involving relatively minor violations, include only a small amount of the total goods involved. During the past ten years 13% of our seizure recommendations were never executed because the product had been moved or consumed during the time taken to complete these procedures. And during this same period, 99.7% of all seizures were adjudicated by default or consent, and were not litigated through to trial....

There is no question that, in many instances, the traditional seizure mechanism remains very useful. Where an entire carload or grain elevator of food is found adulterated, seizure obviously does accomplish its intended purpose. In an unfortunately large number of instances, however, seizure is a wholly ineffective and inappropriate remedy that needs to be supplemented by more efficient approaches. One particularly disturbing aspect is that, as any food and drug lawyer knows, the impact of a single seizure of a small amount of a product can be effectively blunted simply by filing a claim and engaging in the usual pre-trial discovery. The inventory of the offending product can then be relabeled, or exhausted without change, and at that point a consent decree can be accepted or the claim withdrawn and the case forfeited. In the meantime, the public is subjected to the illegal product, and the entire purpose of the seizure is substantially delayed and subverted.

There is no easy solution to these problems. Whether or not statutory changes occur, it is clear that the Food and Drug Administration will continue its use of recall and detention, in lieu of seizure, where this is the most appropriate means of enforcement available. Another approach that I favor is the increased use of a regulatory letter to a company under section 306 of the Act where relatively minor violations are involved (*e.g.*, FPLA violations, some misbranding charges, and perhaps instances of esthetic adulteration), requiring compliance with the law within a specified period of time. Failure to comply would then be subject to injunction and/or criminal action, and in some instances also seizure....

NOTE

In the early 1970s, FDA began to use regulatory letters frequently in lieu of seizures, particularly in cases involving no danger to health. The agency proposed regulations to codify this approach in 43 Fed. Reg. 27498 (June 23, 1978), p. 1192 *infra*, but later withdrew that proposal in 45 Fed. Reg. 60449 (September 12, 1980) and issued guidelines in Chapters 8–10 of the REGULATORY PROCEDURES MANUAL instead.

7. ADMINISTRATIVE DETENTION

To prevent illegal articles from being moved or consumed while it is taking the steps necessary to accomplish a seizure, FDA often requests state officials to use their statutory powers to embargo or detain the articles by administrative order. The agency shares with USDA the authority to detain by administrative order meat, poultry, and egg products under 21 U.S.C. §§ 679(b), 467f(b), and 1052(d). For USDA regulations implementing this authority, *see* 9 C.F.R. Part 329. The Medical Device Amendments also provided FDA with administrative detention authority for medical devices under section 304(g). *See* 21 C.F.R. § 800.55; *Life Design Systems, Inc. v. Sullivan*, Civ. No. CA3–90–701–D (N.D. Tex. 1990). FDA has often asked Congress to enact administrative detention authority for all of the products it regulates. The Senate included such authority for drugs when it passed S. 1075, the Drug Regulation Reform Act of 1979, S. Rep. No. 96–321, 96th Cong., 1st Sess. (1979), and for foods when it passed the Consumer Food Act of 1976, S. Rep. No. 94–684, 94th Cong., 2d Sess. (1976). Neither bill was acted on by the House. *See* GAO, LEGISLATIVE CHANGES AND ADMINISTRATIVE IMPROVEMENTS SHOULD BE CONSIDERED FOR FDA TO BETTER PROTECT THE PUBLIC FROM ADULTERATED FOOD PRODUCTS, HRD–84–61 (September 26, 1984).

F. INJUNCTIONS

The 1906 Act did not authorize FDA to seek injunctive relief against violators. The legislative history of the 1938 Act reveals various reasons for including injunction authority. During Senate hearings an early version of the legislation, FDA Chief Campbell testified:

> The next section ... provides for the suppression of repetitious offenses. In the present circumstances there is no way by which that can be done effectively. If an article is misbranded or adulterated the manufacturer can continue for a protracted period its production and shipment in interstate commerce because of the delay incident to the conclusion of a prosecution. Even though a conviction were obtained, it would be impossible to bring the matter at issue to a definite determination without the lapse of an inordinate period. This section by expediting action and suppressing continued offenses is for the more adequate protection of the public....

"Food, Drugs, and Cosmetics," Hearings Before a Subcomm. of the Senate Comm. on Commerce, 73d Cong., 2d Sess. 78 (1933).

FOOD, DRUG, AND COSMETIC ACT

House Report No. 2139, 75th Congress, 3d Session (1938).

Section 302 provides a new enforcement procedure for food and drug legislation by authorizing the courts to enjoin violations. This procedure will be particularly advantageous in border-line cases that cannot be settled without litigation. In many such cases it is unfair to the manufacturer to subject him to criminal trial and likewise unfair to the public to have the issue determined under the restrictions necessarily prevailing in criminal procedure. This remedy should reduce litigation. In some cases it should avoid the hardship and expense to litigants in seizure cases.... A seizure case finally decided in favor of a defendant leaves him without recourse for his losses, including court costs, storage, and other charges.

NOTES

1. *Jury Trial.* A defendant is not entitled to a jury trial in an injunction suit under the Act. *See United States v. Ellis Research Laboratories, Inc.*, 300 F.2d 550 (7th Cir. 1962). Under section 302(b), however, a charge of violation of an injunction is triable to a jury. *See United States v. Lit Drug Co.*, 333 F. Supp. 990 (D.N.J. 1971).

2. *Commentary. See generally* Barrett, *Injunction Power Under the Food, Drug, and Cosmetic Act,* 5 FDC L.J. 788 (1950); Buckley, *Injunction Proceedings,* 6 FDC L.J. 515 (1951); Burditt, *The Trial of an Injunction Suit,* 25 FDC L.J. 238 (1970); Morey, *Handling FDA Injunction Actions,* 31 FDC L.J. 366 (1976).

UNITED STATES v. ODESSA UNION WAREHOUSE CO–OP

United States Court of Appeals, Ninth Circuit, 1987.
833 F.2d 172.

CANBY, Circuit Judge:....

In April 1986, the government conducted extensive inspections of thirteen grain elevators operated by Odessa in eastern and central Washington. The inspections revealed violations of the food contamination and adulteration standards of the FDCA. The condition of Odessa's wheat at the time of the FDA inspection is uncontested. The wheat in the Odessa-operated elevators was moldy and contaminated with live and dead insect, insect larvae and rodent excreta. Various structural defects allowed for entry of rodents and birds at six of the storage stations.

Prior FDA inspections of Odessa facilities had also revealed unsanitary conditions. In May 1985, inspections showed live insect infestation at each of seven facilities. Two stations contained rodent excreta

on the grain-conveying equipment. In 1983 and 1984, the Washington
State Department of Agriculture, under contract with the FDA, inspected Odessa's storage facilities and discovered significant sanitary problems. As a result of these inspections, the FDA had imposed embargoes
on thousands of bushels of wheat under Odessa's control.

As a result of the April 1986 inspections, the government sought a
preliminary injunction to enjoin the sale and movement of wheat held
in Odessa's elevators until Odessa complied with FDCA standards. In
response to the filing of the injunction action by the government, and
prior to the September 1986 district court hearing, Odessa took action
to improve the sanitation at its facilities. Odessa's general manager
testified that Odessa cleaned and fumigated the wheat, removed rodent
and bird excreta from the wheat's surface, destroyed rodent tunnels,
and sealed the elevators to prevent future infestation. In addition,
Odessa hired a sanitation expert to recommend additional sanitation
policy and procedures.

The district court, applying a standard we will set forth below,
denied the government's motion for a preliminary injunction.....

The factors we traditionally consider in determining whether to
grant a preliminary injunction in this circuit are (1) the likelihood of
plaintiff's success on the merits; (2) the possibility of plaintiff's suffering irreparable injury if relief is not granted; (3) the extent to which
the balance of hardships favors the respective parties; and (4) in
certain cases, whether the public interest will be advanced by the
provision of preliminary relief. To obtain a preliminary injunction, the
moving party must show either (1) a combination of probable success on
the merits and the possibility of irreparable injury or (2) that serious
questions are raised and the balance of hardships tips in its favor.
These two formulations represent two points on a sliding scale in which
the required degree of irreparable harm increases as the probability of
success decreases.

The motion for preliminary injunction in this action was brought
by the government pursuant to the FDCA. That fact unquestionably
affects the balance of factors that determines whether an injunction
should be granted. The function of a court in deciding whether to issue
an injunction authorized by a statute of the United States to enforce
and implement Congressional policy is a different one from that of the
court when weighing claims of two private litigants. This is not to say
that the violation of a federal statute automatically requires a district
court to issue an injunction.... However, the fact that a federal
statute is being enforced by the agency charged with that duty may
alter the burden of proof of a particular element necessary to obtain
injunctive relief. Once Congress, exercising its delegated powers, has
decided the order of priorities in a given area, it is for the courts to
enforce them when asked.

The district court in this case applied neither the conventional
balancing test ... nor the glosses on that test that arise from the fact

that a federal agency is seeking to enforce an act of Congress. Instead, the district court announced the following standard:

> "The teachings of the appellate courts list several of these conditions, but Federal judges being an independent group, this Court has developed his own list of conditions and feels that a preliminary injunction should issue only when the circumstances truly permit no other course, when the crisis is current or at least appears to be recurrent, that the response of the respondent is recalcitrant and clearly so, and that the total impact of the Order must be assessed."

Applying this standard, the district court denied the preliminary injunction on the grounds that Odessa was making improvements in its unsanitary conditions and that the granting of injunctive relief might put Odessa out of business and adversely affect the local agricultural economy.

The standard announced and applied by the district court is far too restrictive, compared with the standards for statutory injunctions set forth above....

To obtain a preliminary injunction, the movant must ordinarily show that there exists a significant threat of irreparable injury. The district court may have imposed a variant of this requirement in insisting upon the existence of a "crisis." Whether or not the variant is a sufficient substitute is beside the point because the requirement itself is inapplicable to this case. Where an injunction is authorized by statute, and the statutory conditions are satisfied as in the facts presented here, the agency to whom the enforcement of the right has been entrusted is not required to show irreparable injury. No specific or immediate showing of the precise way in which violation of the law will result in public harm is required. The district court accordingly should have presumed that the government would suffer irreparable injury from a denial of its motion.

A second element of the test for issuance of a preliminary injunction is the moving party's probable success on the merits.... Because irreparable injury must be presumed in a statutory enforcement action, the district court needed only to find some chance of probable success on the merits. The record indicates that there is a substantial likelihood of success on the merits in this action given the uncontested evidence that Odessa remained in violation of the FDCA up until the September 1986 hearing, despite its efforts to improve sanitary conditions. Had the district court applied the correct standard, the government's likelihood of success on the merits and the presumptive finding of irreparable injury would have met the first test for issuance of a preliminary injunction.....

... Because the district court erroneously applied its own set of conditions in denying the government's motion, and because the record indicates that the government may qualify for a preliminary injunction under this circuit's standards, the district court's order must be reversed and remanded for reevaluation under the correct standards.

NOTE

In *United States v. Nutrition Service, Inc.*, 227 F. Supp. 375 (W.D. Pa. 1964), the court enjoined distribution of a drug, Mucorhicin, which FDA claimed to be ineffective, observing:

> It is true that the evidence presented at this hearing did not show that the use of Mucorhicin by anyone or the administering of it to any person produced any harmful effects. But that does not mean that because such evidence has not been introduced, that the hope held out by the producers of Mucorhicin to the medically aidable patients may not induce them to delay medical treatment by competent doctors to the extent where they become less capable or incapable of being aided, and so cause irreparable public injury.... Congress intended that all persons in the national domain be protected against any such injury and this is reason enough for preventing any irreparable injury existing or threatening the public.... I am, however, persuaded by something more.....
>
> There is sufficient showing, where as here, the Government presents evidence of violations of the provisions of a statute enacted for the protection of the public. Nor is it necessary to demonstrate the precise way in which violations of the law might result in injury to the public interest. It is sufficient to show only that the threatened act is within the declared prohibition of Congress....

See also United States v. Diapulse Corp., 457 F.2d 25 (2d Cir. 1972); *United States v. Sene X Eleemosynary Corp., Inc.*, 479 F. Supp. 970 (S.D. Fla. 1979).

UNITED STATES v. CHATTANOOGA BAKERY, INC.

United States District Court, Eastern District, of Tennessee, 1949.
1938–1964 FDLI Jud. Rec. 975.

DARR, District Judge.

The action is brought by the United States under Section 302(a) of the Federal Food, Drug, and Cosmetic Act, claiming that the defendants introduced or delivered for introduction in interstate commerce food products that were adulterated.

Inspections over a period of three or four years are claimed wherein improper conditions were pointed out to the defendants from time to time and that while some improvement has been made as a result of said complaints, the conditions have not been completely rectified. In 1948 an action was brought in the United States District Court against the corporate defendant on account of the breaches of the Act, to which action a plea of *nolo contendre* was made and a fine of $800.00 imposed....

The latest inspection of the Government Inspectors appears to have been made on July 29, 1949 as a result of which the Acting Chief,

Cincinnati District, Food and Drug Administration, submits an affidavit outlining numerous insanitary conditions and numerous filthy substances which were found in the manufactured products as well as in the raw materials found on the premises.... The Government Inspectors indicate that the defendants have shown a cooperative attitude, have made many improvements in the sanitary conditions, and have in many ways fully complied with the suggestions or requests made by the Inspectors....

The Inspectors representing the Tennessee Department of Health and the Chattanooga–Hamilton County Health Department affirm that insanitary conditions and improper operating conditions observed by them from time to time have been fully rectified by the defendants, and as of July 1, 1949, two Inspectors report that the condition of the plant and the operating materials were found to be in satisfactory condition....

The question for immediate consideration is whether the Court should grant a preliminary injunction in advance of hearing the full facts on a trial of the case. The injunction sought is only for a compliance with the Act. Normally there would be no hardship in requiring such compliance. Persons are expected to comply with the law. But, in view of the conflicting opinions of the Inspectors, whose affidavits are before the Court, it would seem difficult to determine, in advance and without hearing the full facts, whether the defendants are in compliance with the Act.....

The granting of an injunction is discretionary and not mandatory in the case of clear violations of the law, even in cases involving the public interest brought under statutory authority. While it might be more imperative to issue an injunction in public interest where the statute directs, yet the equities are somewhat the same as in ordinary injunction actions....

The Court cannot say, under the facts submitted, that the defendants are complying with the Act, but the extent to which they may be remiss or what additional precautions, if any, should be taken, is not clear. The Court is of the opinion that in view of the expressed desire and efforts of the defendants to comply with the law that it is unnecessary and perhaps improper, *in advance of a hearing on the merits,* to grant an injunction.

NOTES

1. *Injunction Denied.* The court denied a preliminary injunction in *United States v. Cargill, Inc.,* 1938–1964 FDLI Jud. Rec. 2081 (N.D.N.Y. 1963), because "there was no showing of existent danger or the probability of future violations":

> There is no need shown for injunction, and the safeguards promised to the government by Cargill, Inc. in the future to alleviate and insure against undesirable conditions of storage at the Port of Albany are recommendable and persuasive in the record.... The government has

gained its goal and the public health interest and pocketbook have been efficiently protected. Common sense often makes good law.

In *United States v. Sars of Louisiana*, 324 F. Supp. 307, 310 (E.D. La. 1971), the court denied an injunction. Though the defendants did not dispute that when inspected in 1968 and 1970 their animal food product contained Salmonella microorganisms, by the time the case came to trial they had complied with all the recommendations of FDA inspectors.

Thus, the critical determination in this case is whether or not it is reasonable to expect that the defendants will commit violative acts in the future. It is the conclusion of this Court, from the evidence at trial, that there is simply no showing that such violations are likely to reoccur....

See also *United States v. Nelson Farms, Inc.*, Food Drug Cosm. L. Rep. (CCH) ¶ 38,019 (D. Vt. 1987); *United States v. Lacy Feed Co.*, Food Drug Cosm. L. Rep. (CCH) ¶ 38,335 (W.D. Tex. 1985); *United States v. Flea–Tabs, Inc.*, Food Drug Cosm. L. Rep. (CCH) ¶ 38,123 (C.D. Cal. 1981); *United States v. W.F. Morgan & Sons*, 155 F. Supp. 40 (E.D. Va. 1957); *United States v. Cowley Pharmaceuticals, Inc.*, 1938–1964 FDLI Jud. Rec. 473 (D. Mass. 1948).

2. *Injunction Granted.* Compare *United States v. Mosinee Research Corp.*, 583 F.2d 930 (7th Cir. 1978); *United States v. Wilson Williams, Inc.*, 277 F.2d 535 (2d Cir. 1960); *United States v. Algon Chemical, Inc.*, Food Drug Cosm. L. Rep. (CCH) ¶ 38,167 (D.N.J. 1990); *United States v. Bronson Farms, Inc.*, Food Drug Cosm. L. Rep. (CCH) ¶ 38,354 (M.D. Fla. 1986); *United States v. Tomahara Enterprises, Ltd.*, Food Drug Cosm. L. Rep. (CCH) ¶ 38,217 (N.D.N.Y. 1983); *United States v. Lazere*, 56 F. Supp. 730 (N.D. Iowa 1944).

3. *Consent Decree.* For a typical FDA consent decree of permanent injunction, *see United States v. Manhattan Bakery*, Food Drug Cosm. L. Rep. (CCH) ¶ 38,163 (N.D. Ga. 1982).

UNITED STATES v. LIT DRUG CO.

United States District Court, District of New Jersey, 1971.
333 F. Supp. 990.

COOLAHAN, District Judge.

The government filed its complaint for an injunction restraining defendants from their alleged illegal activities on July 27, 1971. This lengthy prayer for relief, supported by several detailed affidavits, charged defendants with manufacturing and holding for sale adulterated and misbranded drugs ... and with the unlawful introduction of these drugs into interstate commerce.... This Court granted the government's request for a Temporary Restraining Order which enjoined further interstate shipment of drugs by defendant until certain conditions had been fulfilled. First, the methods, facilities and controls for manufacturing, processing, packaging, and labeling of defendants' drugs were to be brought in conformity with the current good manufacturing practices, as defined in 21 C.F.R. § 133.1–14 [now 21 C.F.R. Parts 210 and 211].... As a second condition upon future interstate commerce, defendants were required to grant duly authorized Food and Drug Administration inspectors access to defendants' plant for the purpose of inspecting defendants' records, materials, equipment and labeling in order to insure, to the satisfaction of the government, that defendants had in fact realigned the operation of the plant in conformity with current good manufacturing practices. Third and finally, all the drugs on hand at defendants' plant site were to be subject to examination by officials of the Food and Drug Administration, assays were to be made in order to assure the safety, identity, purity, strength and quality of these drugs, and recalls were to be made of any line of drug determined to be adulterated or misbranded.....

Defendants vigorously oppose what they regard as a loosely worded order. The complaint is that "current good manufacturing practices" presents no ascertainable standard of performance assuming defendants make a good faith effort to cooperate with FDA officials in complying with the sanctions with which it has no quarrel....

... [S]pecificity, as demanded by Rule 65(d) and as envisioned by scholars like Professor Moore, is a matter relative to each case. Where, as here, the defendants have been engaged in an overt, long standing, schematic and unpenitent thwarting of the law, particularly a law enacted for the protection of an otherwise helpless consumer public, the specificity which defendants can respectfully demand under Rule 65(d) can hardly compare to that which might be afforded were there only a single, isolated infraction....

... While misbranding is an obvious threat to public health, the prohibition against misbranding is certainly not as susceptible to repeated violations as in the case of adulteration. In misbranding cases, it is a relatively simple matter for the court to fashion an order which shall proscribe the false or misleading material. Supervising compliance is also relatively easy. The facts in this case alone are excellent proof that a narrowly worded order enjoining adulteration, on the other hand, can hardly curb the reckless infractions of a highly culpable drug manufacturer, whether his adulterating tactics are ingenious or ingenuous. Similarly, considering the multifaceted imperfections of the Lit Drug plant operation, and considering also the innumerable possible defects which may be located in the future, it would be extremely impractical to ask the FDA, which must supervise compliance to bring a new action for each added infraction detected, no matter how small or no matter how closely incident to past violations.

The danger of overbreadth ... is missing in this case. Unlike misbranding, "current good manufacturing practices" is a term of art within the industry. The drug industry is well aware of what is meant by current good manufacturing practices, and there is every reason to believe that reputable manufacturers have welcomed the efforts of the FDA in defining that phrase by regulations promulgated by the Secretary of Health, Education and Welfare under the Act. Misbranding, on the other hand, is nowhere defined so elaborately in regulations, but is only incidentally defined by scattered references or examples. By and large, the metes and bounds of misbranding are delineated in case law. . . .

Defendants contest that part of the proposed order which restrains Lit Drug from engaging in interstate commerce until FDA officials have made a thorough plant inspection of all equipment, materials, labels, containers and procedures and are satisfied that such are in compliance with current good manufacturing practices. Defendants attack this as pre-screening not authorized by the Food, Drug and Cosmetic Act, and take the view that this Court under 21 U.S.C. § 332 may only enjoin illegal activities and leave defendants to risk a contempt citation in the event of non-compliance. This narrow construction of § 332 is not only unjustified but plainly hostile to the intent of Congress in enacting the Food, Drug and Cosmetic Act. Effective deterrence as a weightier and more beneficial weapon against drug adulteration than criminal sanctions is a message that pervades the legislative history of this Act. Congressional concern for the *manner* in which a drug is produced, aside from a consideration of the composition of the drug, is apparent in the new language of 21 U.S.C. § 351(a)(2) by which a drug is deemed adulterated if it has been processed, packed or held under unsanitary conditions, or if any manufacturing, packing or holding method does not conform to current good manufacturing practice. Thus a drug may be pharmaceutically perfect in content but still be regarded as adulterated under the law. Congress preferred this approach rather than rely upon governmental intervention once the injurious drugs had entered the stream of commerce. . . .

Defendants complain against that part of the order which forbids interstate commerce until the FDA has had an opportunity to examine and assay all of the drugs presently being held at the Lit Drug plant and to recall those assayed lots which prove to be adulterated. Defendants do not quarrel with the government demand for a recall of drugs which the plant inspection reveals to be adulterated, but they do argue that this procedure is not related to the future production of drugs, inasmuch as the government has adequate safeguards in those parts of the injunction which direct defendants to make specific corrections. Insofar as the defendants argue that such procedure is not authorized by the Act their argument must fall for the reasons already assigned by this Court in the preceding discussion. . . . Here . . . the time during which interstate commerce is restricted is clearly related to a valid objective. It may well be that the FDA has not yet uncovered all infractions of which defendants are guilty. At least in these extreme circumstances, where defendants have stipulated its marketing of drugs defective with innumerable adulterations, the facts give rise to this presumption. Hence, it is totally reasonable that the FDA should have an opportunity to examine and assay given lots both within the plant and from those drugs recalled, in order to assure the complete safety of defendants' future operations. Seen in this light, the examination and assay of drugs already manufactured is not so unrelated to the future production of drugs as defendants argue.....

NOTE

In *Hygrade Food Products Corp. v. United States*, 160 F.2d 816 (8th Cir. 1947), the court modified the trial court's two-year injunction against interstate shipment of any cheese products manufactured by the defendant. It found the injunction to be overbroad in light of improvements made in sanitary conditions and plant management:

> The injunction here absolutely closes the door of the court on the defendant for an arbitrary period of two years regardless of what changes may be brought about during that time. Defendant can not even ask the court to modify the injunction. This is true for a period of two years even though the grounds for which it was granted no longer exist by reason of a change in the controlling facts on which the injunction rested.

See also *United States v. Diapulse Corp. of America*, 748 F.2d 56 (2d Cir. 1984); *United States v. Spectro Foods Corp.*, 544 F.2d 1175 (3d Cir. 1976).

UNITED STATES v. 184 BARRELS DRIED WHOLE EGGS

United States District Court, Eastern District of Wisconsin, 1943.
53 F. Supp. 652.

DUFFY, District Judge.

At the commencement of the trial, after the court had expressed doubt on the jurisdictional question of interstate commerce, plaintiff's attorney moved that the prayer for condemnation be amended by the addition of an alternate prayer for injunctive relief, in the event that the prayer for condemnation were denied on jurisdictional grounds.... Both prayers for relief grew out of the same transaction. The basic issues of adulteration were identical. If the court ruled adversely to the government on the jurisdictional question, it would have been necessary to start a new action for injunctive relief, in which the same testimony would have been presented. The government and the Wisconsin Dried Egg Company would be parties to both actions. As the plaintiff well states the situation, "Both prayers for relief involve the same transaction, the same res, the same parties, the same court, the same evidence, and the same issues, save that the amendment injected one additional issue as to the appropriateness of issuing a statutory injunction." The issuance of an injunction is authorized under Sec. 302(a) of the act. It was believed that time and expense would be saved to all concerned by proceeding with the trial, and withholding a ruling on the motion to amend; and this was done. Claimant objected to the amendment on the ground it changed an in rem action to one in personam. It did not ask for an extension of time and after its objection was overruled, it presented evidence on the merits.

There can be no doubt that while the seizure action was pending, a separate suit for injunctive relief could have been commenced in this court. It would then have been appropriate for the court to have ordered a consolidation.

Where a party is before the court in an in rem proceeding the court has the power to render an in personam judgment against him. It has likewise been held that the distinction between the proceedings in rem and in personam have no proper relation to the question of jurisdiction. While the court may refrain from exercising such power if by so doing it would impair substantial rights, yet where it will further the ends of justice and eliminate multiplicity of action and save expense to the parties, it should be invoked....

UNITED STATES v. 47 BOTTLES
JENASOL RJ FORMULA '60'

United States Court of Appeals, Third Circuit, 1963.
320 F.2d 564.

BIGGS, Chief Judge.

This is an appeal from an order of the court below entered February 21, 1962, directing the condemnation of a drug and enjoining the claimant, Marvin Schere, doing business as Jenasol Company (Jenasol), from re-introducing the drug into interstate commerce as labeled or as accompanied with certain labeling materials.....

In its opinion, filed on December 14, 1961, the court found as a fact that the literature was false and misleading as to the efficacy of the drug, concluded that the literature constituted "labeling" within the meaning of 21 U.S.C. § 321(m), and stated that a decree of condemnation would be issued.... The United States moved to amend the libel to include a prayer for injunctive relief against the claimant. In a second opinion, filed February 6, 1962, the court specifically found that the labeling was false and misleading in all respects, deemed the libel amended to include a prayer for injunctive relief in accordance with the motion of the United States and granted the injunction against Jenasol. An order of condemnation and injunction against the claimant was issued on February 21, 1962.....

We think that in the case at bar the trial judge did not properly exercise his legal discretion in granting leave to amend the prayer for relief at such a late stage in the proceedings. Assuming *arguendo* that the court below had jurisdiction over the person of the claimant so as to have the power to grant injunctive *in personam* relief, an issue we need not and therefore do not decide, we nonetheless think it unfair and substantially prejudicial to permit the injection of a new and different prayer for relief after trial at the very end of the case as was allowed here. But for the brief oral argument on the motion, Jenasol had no opportunity to raise and assert, through evidence or otherwise, equitable considerations by way of defense to an injunction or other possible mitigating factors....

Accordingly, the judgment of the District Court will be affirmed as to the decree of condemnation but will be reversed as to the injunctive relief granted.

NOTE

Violation of an injunction may lead to a suit for contempt under section 302(b) of the Act. *Colgrove v. United States*, 176 F.2d 614 (9th Cir. 1949), affirmed a judgment holding appellants in criminal contempt for violation of injunctions issued under 21 U.S.C. § 332(a). The government in numerous past actions had condemned the appellants' product, "Coluso Natural Oil," when introduced in interstate commerce, as having no value in the treatment of skin diseases. The appellants consented to the permanent injunction prohibiting advertising the product as a remedy for skin diseases for which the label contained inadequate directions for use. Though appellant devised a new label emphasizing use of the product as a remedy for four specific diseases, the advertising testimonials still endorsed the product for other skin conditions. The court found ample authority to issue the injunction and disallowed appellants' collateral attack: "It is settled law that unless an injunction is void its propriety must be tested by appeal and not by disobedience." Whether FDA must prove intent to sustain a charge of criminal contempt of an injunction has not been resolved. *Compare United States v. Schlicksup Drug Co., Inc.*, 206 F. Supp. 801 (S.D. Ill. 1962), *with United States v. I. D. Russell Laboratories*, 439 F. Supp. 711 (W.D. Mo. 1977). *See also United States v. M.T. Products, Ltd.*, 1987–1988 FDLI Jud. Rec. 132 (10th Cir. 1988); *United States v. Spectro Foods Corp.*, 544 F.2d 1175 (3d Cir. 1976); *United Pharmacal Corp. v. United States*, 306 F.2d 515 (1st Cir. 1962); *Reich v. United States*, 239 F.2d 134 (1st Cir. 1956); *United States v. Sanders*, 196 F.2d 895 (10th Cir. 1952); *United States v. Jacobs*, Food Drug Cosm. L. Rep. (CCH) ¶¶ 38,113, 38,123 (E.D. Cal. 1989); *United States v. K–N Enterprises, Inc.*, Food Drug Cosm. L. Rep. (CCH) ¶ 38,133 (N.D. Ill. 1981); *United States v. Sherwood*, 175 F. Supp. 480 (S.D.N.Y. 1959).

For discussion of some of the more technical aspects of section 302(b), *see United States v. Dean Rubber Mfg. Co.*, 72 F. Supp. 819 (W.D. Mo. 1947); *United States v. Diapulse Corp.*, 365 F. Supp. 935 (E.D.N.Y. 1973).

G. CRIMINAL LIABILITY

1. PHILOSOPHY OF PROSECUTION

ARTHUR KALLET & F.J. SCHLINK, 100,000,000 GUINEA PIGS

(1933).

... The Act's authorizing that goods be seized or confiscated for condemnation was clearly intended to permit the summary and forcible removal from the market of dangerous, adulterated, poisonous, or misbranded goods which were a menace to public health and which, in emergency, might need to be acted against so urgently that a punitive proceeding, only, against a manufacturer or dealer, with its long course of appeals to court above court, might be too slow to serve the public's necessity. This action against the goods instead of against the offender is now used for a very different purpose by the Administration. By the use of this provision, the prosecuting officers run no risk of the offender's receiving at the hands of the court the more unpleasant penalty of fine or imprisonment for second, third, and tenth offenses against the Act.... If the owner of the goods loses the action at bar, the worst that can happen is loss of the value of the shipment, crate, or carton of confiscated goods which were adulterated or misbranded. Often he does not suffer even that ridiculously inadequate penalty....

Thus it comes about that only one man has ever served a jail sentence for a Food and Drugs Act offense. Clearly, it is not the intent of the Administration to punish business crimes by even a very short prison sentence, no matter how many be poisoned or die.... [N]o corporation officer need fear the exaction of the penalties of the law for any crime of adulteration, community poisoning, or large-scale swindle by misbranding that he may commit....

SAM D. FINE,* THE PHILOSOPHY OF ENFORCEMENT

31 Food Drug Cosmetic Law Journal 324 (1976).

... FDA, of necessity, must depend upon the entire regulated industry for a great amount of self-regulation. With its limited resources, the Agency can never hope to monitor completely the massive industries subject to its legislative mandates.... Can all of the FDA's enforcement be by self-regulation? I believe we can all agree that the answer is no.... I am persuaded that prosecution of firms can have an important and dramatic impact on their peers....

In considering whether or not prosecution action should be forwarded to the next reviewing authority, and eventually to a United States Attorney, one or more of the following general conditions must exist. In most cases, more than one of the conditions does exist.

(1) The violations ordinarily are shown to be of a continuing nature; that is, previous inspections or documented incidents indicate management of the firm is aware of the problem and has failed to take steps to correct the violations. This situation requires a showing of awareness....

(2) The violation is so gross that any reasonable person would conclude management must have known of the conditions. Examples include a heavily insect or rodent-infested warehouse or an obvious fraud....

(3) The violations are such that it is obvious that normal attention by management could have prevented them; for example, those situa-

* [Mr. Fine was FDA Associate Commissioner for Compliance.]

tions where violations develop because management delegates authority and does not exercise normal care....

(4) The violations are such that they are life-threatening or injuries have occurred; for example, botulism in improperly prepared products or serious drug mix-ups....

(5) The violations are deliberate attempts to circumvent the law; for instance, submission of false data, falsification of records, or deliberate short weight or subpotency....

What this means is that continuation or repetition of violations over a period of time, or a single gross or deliberate violation, generally will trigger consideration for prosecution....

NOTE

See also Austern, *Sanctions in Silhouette: An Inquiry Into the Enforcement of the Federal Food, Drug, and Cosmetic Act,* 51 Calif. L. Rev. 38 (1963); Depew, *The Philosophy of Enforcement of the Federal Food, Drug and Cosmetic Act,* 18 FDC L.J. 185 (1963); Hoffman, *Enforcement Trends Under the Federal Food, Drug and Cosmetic Act—A View From Outside,* 31 FDC L.J. 338 (1976).

---

2. STANDARD OF LIABILITY

Most violations of the FD&C Act potentially carry criminal penalties. The Act's standard of criminal liability differs from the standard customarily imposed by American criminal law and has proved one of the most controversial features of the statute.

UNITED STATES v. DOTTERWEICH

Supreme Court of the United States, 1943.
320 U.S. 277.

Mr. Justice FRANKFURTER delivered the opinion of the Court.

This was a prosecution begun by two informations, consolidated for trial, charging Buffalo Pharmacal Company, Inc., and Dotterweich, its president and general manager, with violations of the ... Federal Food, Drug, and Cosmetic Act. The Company, a jobber in drugs, purchased them from their manufacturers and shipped them, repacked under its own label, in interstate commerce.... Three counts went to the jury— two, for shipping misbranded drugs in interstate commerce, and a third, for so shipping an adulterated drug. The jury disagreed as to the corporation and found Dotterweich guilty on all three counts. We start with the finding of the Circuit Court of Appeals that the evidence was adequate to support the verdict of adulteration and misbranding.

Two other questions which the Circuit Court of Appeals decided against Dotterweich call only or summary disposition to clear the path for the main question before us. He invoked § 305 of the Act requiring the Administrator, before reporting a violation for prosecution by a United States Attorney, to give the suspect an "opportunity to present his views." We agree with the Circuit Court of Appeals that the giving of such an opportunity, which was not accorded to Dotterweich, is not a prerequisite to prosecution.... Equally baseless is the claim of Dotterweich that, having failed to find the corporation guilty, the jury could not find him guilty. Whether the jury's verdict was the result of carelessness or compromise or a belief that the responsible individual should suffer the penalty instead of merely increasing, as it were, the cost of running the business of the corporation, is immaterial. Juries may indulge in precisely such motives or vagaries.

And so we are brought to our real problem. The Circuit Court of Appeals, one judge dissenting, reversed the conviction on the ground that only the corporation was the "person" subject to prosecution unless, perchance, Buffalo Pharmacal was a counterfeit corporation serving as a screen for Dotterweich....

The court below drew its conclusion not from the provisions defining the offenses on which this prosecution was based (§§ 301(a) and 303(a)), but from the terms of § 303(c). That section affords immunity from prosecution if certain conditions are satisfied. The condition relevant to this case is a guaranty from the seller of the innocence of his product....

The Circuit Court of Appeals found it "difficult to believe that Congress expected anyone except the principal to get such a guaranty, or to make the guilt of an agent depend upon whether his employer had gotten one." And so it cut down the scope of the penalizing provisions of the Act to the restrictive view, as a matter of language and policy, it took of the relieving effect of a guaranty.

The guaranty clause cannot be read in isolation.... The purposes of this legislation thus touch phases of the lives and health of people which, in the circumstances of modern industrialism, are largely beyond self-protection. Regard for these purposes should infuse construction of the legislation if it is to be treated as a working instrument of government and not merely as a collection of English words. The prosecution to which Dotterweich was subjected is based on a now familiar type of legislation whereby penalties serve as effective means of regulation. Such legislation dispenses with the conventional requirement for criminal conduct—awareness of some wrongdoing. In the interest of the larger good it puts the burden of acting at hazard upon a person otherwise innocent but standing in responsible relation to a public danger....

The Act is concerned not with the proprietory relation to a misbranded or an adulterated drug but with its distribution. In the case of a corporation such distribution must be accomplished, and may be furthered, by persons standing in various relations to the incorporeal proprietor.... To read the guaranty section, as did the court below, so as to restrict liability for penalties to the only person who normally would receive a guaranty—the proprietor—disregards the admonition that "the meaning of a sentence is to be felt rather than to be proved." It also reads an exception to an important provision safeguarding the public welfare with a liberality which more appropriately belongs to enforcement of the central purpose of the Act.

The Circuit Court of Appeals was evidently tempted to make such a devitalizing use of the guaranty provision through fear that an enforcement of § 301(a) as written might operate too harshly by sweeping within its condemnation any person however remotely entangled in the proscribed shipment. But that is not the way to read legislation. Literalism and evisceration are equally to be avoided. To speak with technical accuracy, under § 301 a corporation may commit an offense and all persons who aid and abet its commission are equally guilty. Whether an accused shares responsibility in the business process resulting in unlawful distribution depends on the evidence produced at the trial and its submission—assuming the evidence warrants it—to the jury under appropriate guidance. The offense is committed, unless the enterprise which they are serving enjoys the immunity of a guaranty, by all who do have such a responsible share in the furtherance of the transaction which the statute outlaws, namely, to put into the stream of interstate commerce adulterated or misbranded drugs. Hardship there doubtless may be under a statute which thus penalizes the transaction though consciousness of wrongdoing be totally wanting. Balancing relative hardships, Congress has preferred to place it upon those who have at least the opportunity of informing themselves of the existence of conditions imposed for the protection of consumers before sharing in illicit commerce, rather than to throw the hazard on the innocent public who are wholly helpless.

It would be too treacherous to define or even to indicate by way of illustration the class of employees which stands in such a responsible relation. To attempt a formula embracing the variety of conduct whereby persons may responsibly contribute in furthering a transaction forbidden by an Act of Congress, to wit, to send illicit goods across state lines, would be mischievous futility. In such matters the good sense of prosecutors, the wise guidance of trial judges, and the ultimate judgment of juries must be trusted. Our system of criminal justice necessarily depends on "conscience and circumspection in prosecuting officers," even when the consequences are far more drastic than they are under the provision of law before us. For present purpose it suffices to say that in what the defense characterized as "a very fair charge" the District Court properly left the question of the responsibility of Dotterweich for the shipment to the jury, and there was sufficient evidence to support its verdict.

Reversed.

Mr. Justice MURPHY, dissenting.

... There is no evidence in this case of any personal guilt on the part of the respondent. There is no proof or claim that he ever knew of the introduction into commerce of the adulterated drugs in question, much less that he actively participated in their introduction. Guilt is imputed to the respondent solely on the basis of his authority and responsibility as president and general manager of the corporation.

It is fundamental principle of Anglo–Saxon jurisprudence that guilt is personal and that it ought not lightly to be imputed to a citizen who, like the respondent, has no evil intention or consciousness of wrongdoing. It may be proper to charge him with responsibility to the corporation and the stockholders for negligence and mismanagement. But in the absence of clear statutory authorization it is inconsistent with established canons of criminal law to rest liability on an act in which the accused did not participate and of which he had no personal knowledge. Before we place the stigma of a criminal conviction upon any such citizen the legislative mandate must be clear and unambiguous. . . .

The dangers inherent in any attempt to create liability without express Congressional intention or authorization are illustrated by this case. Without any legislative guides, we are confronted with the problem of determining precisely which officers, employees and agents of a corporation are to be subject to his Act by our fiat. To erect standards of responsibility is a difficult legislative task and the opinion of this Court admits that it is "too treacherous" and a "mischievous futility" for us to engage in such pursuits. But the only alternative is a blind resort to "the good sense of prosecutors, the wise guidance of trial judges, and the ultimate judgment of juries." Yet that situation is precisely what our constitutional system sought to avoid. Reliance on the legislature to define crimes and criminals distinguishes our form of jurisprudence from certain less desirable ones. The legislative power to restraint the liberty and to imperil the good reputation of citizens must not rest upon the variable attitudes and opinions of those charged with the duties of interpreting and enforcing the mandates of the law. I therefore cannot approve the decision of the Court in this case.

Mr. Justice ROBERTS, Mr. Justice REED and Mr. Justice RUTLEDGE join in this dissent.

NOTES

1. *Impossibility.* In *United States v. Weisenfeld Warehouse Co.,* 376 U.S. 86 (1964), p. 1075 *supra,* the Court confronted the contention that the defendant was immune from prosecution because it was impossible for him to comply with the requirements of the 1938 Act:

> It is argued, nevertheless, that the Government in this case is seeking to impose criminal sanctions upon one "who is, by the very nature of his business powerless" to protect against this kind of contamination, however high the standard of care exercised. Whatever the truth of this claim, it involves factual proof to be raised defensively at a trial on the merits. We are here concerned only with the construction of the statute as it relates to the sufficiency of the information. . . .

In *United States v. Certified Grocers Co–Op,* 1968–1974 FDLI Jud. Rec. 299 (W.D. Wis. 1974), the court denied defendants' motion to dismiss the information charging violation of the Act by the holding and contamination of foods in a rodent infested warehouse. The court refused to accept the defense of impossibility even though the prosecution stipulated that the defendant was doing everything possible to maintain sanitary conditions in that warehouse. The court reasoned that the defendants were helpless only for as long as they continued to use that particular warehouse.

2. *Lack of knowledge.* United States v. Parfait Powder Puff Co., 163 F.2d 1008 (7th Cir. 1947), affirmed the defendant's conviction for introducing an adulterated cosmetic product into interstate commerce. The defendant, a cosmetics company, had entered into a contract with Helfrich Laboratories under which Helfrich would manufacture and distribute hair lacquer pads with the Parfait Powder Puff Company label. Defendant tested the first sample submitted by Helfrich and found it satisfactory. When shellac supplies became difficult to obtain, however, Helfrich made a substitution in the lacquer formula without the defendant's knowledge. Subsequently, the defendant learned of the substitution and immediately forbade its use. The defendant's argument that Helfrich was an independent contractor for whose acts it was not responsible was rejected by the court of appeals, which reasoned that the defendant incurred liability when it voluntarily selected Helfrich to manufacture and distribute a product it knew would become part of interstate commerce.

3. *Responsible Officer.* A district court's revocation of a suspended sentence for violation of the Act was sustained in *United States v. Shapiro,* 491 F.2d 335 (6th Cir. 1974). The defendant, convicted for operating the Tasty Cookie Company under unsanitary conditions, was given a probated sentence contingent upon his rectifying those conditions before continuing production. The defendant also agreed to sell the plant as soon as a buyer could be found. Following the trial court's order, the plant was temporarily closed for cleaning. Within several months the defendant entered into a formal "operations and management" agreement giving the newly found buyer complete production control until the final closing. Several days prior to that closing, FDA inspected the plant and found it infested with vermin. Acting upon the FDA's petition, the trial court revoked probation and imposed a 6–month sentence. The court was unpersuaded by the defendant's arguments that he was no longer the responsible officer because equitable title and plant control had passed to his purchaser. The court of appeals found that the trial judge had not abused his discretion in revoking probation under these circumstances because the defendant still had legal title at the time of inspection.

4. *Interaction of Civil and Criminal Proceedings.* In *United States v. Kordel,* 397 U.S. 1 (1970), FDA instituted a seizure, served interrogatories and then issued a notice under section 305 of the Act that the agency also contemplated criminal prosecution. The defendant objected to answering the interrogatories while the possibility of a criminal action existed, but ultimately complied and supplied the answers which were then used in the criminal prosecution. The Supreme Court held that this did not violate the privilege against self-incrimination or basic standards of fairness, concluding that FDA should not be required to choose between civil and criminal enforcement proceedings. *See also United States v. Gel Spice Co., Inc.,* 773 F.2d 427 (2d Cir. 1985).

UNITED STATES v. PARK

Supreme Court of the United States, 1975.

421 U.S. 658.

Mr. Chief Justice BURGER delivered the opinion of the Court.

Acme Markets, Inc., is a national retail food chain with approximately 36,000 employees, 874 retail outlets, 12 general warehouses, and four special warehouses. Its headquarters, including the office of the president, respondent Park, who is chief executive officer of the corporation, are located in Philadelphia, Pa. In a five-count information filed in the United States District Court for the District of Maryland, the Government charged Acme and respondent with violations of the Federal Food, Drug, and Cosmetic Act. Each count of the information alleged that the defendants had received food that had been shipped in interstate commerce and that, while the food was being held for sale in Acme's Baltimore warehouse following shipment in interstate commerce, they caused it to be held in a building accessible to rodents and to be exposed to contamination by rodents. These acts were alleged to have resulted in the food's being adulterated within the meaning of 21 U.S.C. §§ 342(a)(3) and (4)....

Acme pleaded guilty to each count of the information. Respondent pleaded not guilty. The evidence at trial demonstrated that in April 1970 the Food and Drug Administration (FDA) advised respondent by letter of insanitary conditions in Acme's Philadelphia warehouse. In 1971 the FDA found that similar conditions existed in the firm's Baltimore warehouse. An FDA consumer safety officer testified concerning evidence of rodent infestation and other insanitary conditions discovered during a 12–day inspection of the Baltimore warehouse in November and December 1971. He also related that a second inspection of the warehouse had been conducted in March 1972. On that occasion the inspectors found that there had been improvement in the sanitary conditions, but that "there was still evidence of rodent activity in the building and in the warehouses and we found some rodent-contaminated lots of food items."

The Government also presented testimony by the Chief of Compliance of the FDA's Baltimore office, who informed respondent by letter of the conditions at the Baltimore warehouse after the first inspection. There was testimony by Acme's Baltimore division vice president, who had responded to the letter on behalf of Acme and respondent and who described the steps taken to remedy the insanitary conditions discovered by both inspections. The Government's final witness, Acme's vice president for legal affairs and assistant secretary, identified respondent as the president and chief executive officer of the company and read a bylaw prescribing the duties of the chief executive officer. He testified that respondent functioned by delegating "normal operating duties," including sanitation, but that he retained "certain things, which are the big, broad, principles of the operation of the company," and had "the responsibility of seeing that they all work together." ...

Respondent was the only defense witness. He testified that, although all of Acme's employees were in a sense under his general direction, the company had an "organizational structure for responsibilities for certain functions" according to which different phases of its operation were "assigned to individuals who, in turn, have staff and departments under them." He identified those individuals responsible for sanitation, and related that upon receipt of the January 1972 FDA letter, he had conferred with the vice president for legal affairs, who informed him that the Baltimore division vice president "was investigating the situation immediately and would be taking corrective action and would be preparing a summary of the corrective action to reply to the letter." Respondent stated that he did not "believe there was anything [he] could have done more constructively than what [he] found was being done."

On cross-examination, respondent conceded that providing sanitary conditions for food offered for sale to the public was something that he was "responsible for in the entire operation of the company," and he stated that it was one of many phases of the company that he assigned to "dependable subordinates." Respondent was asked about and, over the objections of his counsel, admitted receiving the April 1970 letter addressed to him from the FDA regarding insanitary conditions at Acme's Philadelphia warehouse. He acknowledged that, with the exception of the division vice president, the same individuals had responsibility for sanitation in both Baltimore and Philadelphia. Finally, in response to questions concerning the Philadelphia and Baltimore incidents, respondent admitted that the Baltimore problem indicated the system for handling sanitation "wasn't working perfectly" and that as Acme's chief executive officer he was responsible for "any result which occurs in our company."

At the close of the evidence, respondent's renewed motion for a judgment of acquittal was denied. The relevant portion of the trial judge's instructions to the jury challenged by respondent is set out in the margin.[9] Respondent's counsel objected to the instructions on the

---

9. "In order to find the Defendant guilty on any count of the Information, you must find beyond a reasonable doubt on each count....

"Thirdly, that John R. Park held a position of authority in the operation of the business of Acme Markets, Incorporated.

" ... The main issue for your determination is only with the third element, whether the Defendant held a position of authority and responsibility in the business of Acme Markets....

"The statute makes individuals, as well as corporations, liable for violations. An individual is liable if it is clear, beyond a reasonable doubt, that ... the individual had a responsible relation to the situation, even though he may not have participated personally.

"The individual is or could be liable under the statute, even if he did not consciously do wrong. However, the fact that the Defendant is pres[id]ent and is a chief executive officer of the Acme Markets does not require a finding of guilt. Though, he need not have personally participated in the situation, he must have had a responsible relationship to the issue. The issue

ground that they failed fairly to reflect our decision in *United States v. Dotterweich,* and to define " 'responsible relationship.' " The trial judge overruled the objection. The jury found respondent guilty on all counts of the information, and he was subsequently sentenced to pay a fine of $50 on each count.

The Court of Appeals reversed the conviction and remanded for a new trial.... The Court of Appeals concluded that the trial judge's instructions "might well have left the jury with the erroneous impression that Park could be found guilty in the absence of 'wrongful action' on his part," and that proof of this element was required by due process. It ... directed that on retrial the jury be instructed as to "wrongful action,' which might be "gross negligence and inattention in discharging ... corporate duties and obligations or any of a host of other acts of commission or omission which would 'cause' the contamination of food."

The Court of Appeals also held that the admission in evidence of the April 1970 FDA warning to respondent was error warranting reversal, based on its conclusion that, "as this case was submitted to the jury and in light of the sole issue presented," there was no need for the evidence and thus that its prejudicial effect outweighed its relevancy....

We granted certiorari because of an apparent conflict among the Courts of Appeals with respect to the standard of liability of corporate officers under the Federal Food, Drug, and Cosmetic Act as construed in *United States v. Dotterweich,* and because of the importance of the question to the Government's enforcement program. We reverse....

The rationale of the interpretation given the Act in *Dotterweich,* as holding criminally accountable the persons whose failure to exercise the authority and supervisory responsibility reposed in them by the business organization resulted in the violation complained of, has been confirmed in our subsequent cases. Thus, the Court has reaffirmed the proposition that "the public interest in the purity of its food is so great as to warrant the imposition of the highest standard of care on distributors." ... Similarly, in cases decided after *Dotterweich,* the Courts of Appeals have recognized that those corporate agents vested with the responsibility, and power commensurate with that responsibility, to devise whatever measures are necessary to ensure compliance with the Act bears a "responsible relationship" to, or have a "responsible share" in, violations.

Thus *Dotterweich* and the cases which have followed reveal that in providing sanctions which reach and touch the individuals who execute the corporate mission—and this is by no means necessarily confined to a single corporate agent or employee—the Act imposes not only a positive duty to seek out and remedy violations when they occur but

is, in this case, whether the Defendant, John R. Park, by virtue of his position in the company, had a position of authority and responsibility in the situation out of which these charges arose."

Hutt & Merrill Food & Drug Law 2nd Ed. UCB—27

also, and primarily, a duty to implement measures that will insure that violations will not occur. The requirements of foresight and vigilance imposed on responsible corporate agents are beyond question demanding, and perhaps onerous, but they are no more stringent than the public has a right to expect of those who voluntarily assume positions of authority in business enterprises whose services and products affect the health and well-being of the public that supports them.[15]

The Act does not, as we observed in *Dotterweich*, make criminal liability turn on "awareness of some wrongdoing" or "conscious fraud." The duty imposed by Congress on responsible corporate agents is, we emphasize, one that requires the highest standard of foresight and vigilance, but the Act, in its criminal aspect, does not require that which is objectively impossible. The theory upon which responsible corporate agents are held criminally accountable for "causing" violations of the Act permits a claim that a defendant was "powerless" to prevent or correct the violation to "be raised defensively at a trial on the merits." *United States v. Wiesenfeld Warehouse Co.*, 376 U.S. 86, 91 (1964). If such a claim is made, the defendant has the burden of coming forward with evidence, but this does not alter the Government's ultimate burden of proving beyond a reasonable doubt the defendant's guilt, including his power, in light of the duty imposed by the Act, to prevent or correct the prohibited condition. Congress has seen fit to enforce the accountability of responsible corporate agents dealing with products which may affect the health of consumers by penal sanctions cast in rigorous terms, and the obligation of the courts is to give them effect so long as they do not violate the Constitution.

We cannot agree with the Court of Appeals that it was incumbent upon the District Court to instruct the jury that the Government had the burden of establishing "wrongful action" in the sense in which the Court of Appeals used that phrase. The concept of a "responsible relationship" to, or a "responsible share" in, a violation of the Act indeed imports some measure of blameworthiness; but it is equally clear that the Government establishes a prima facie case when it introduces evidence sufficient to warrant a finding by the trier of the facts that the defendant had, by reason of his position in the corporation, responsibility and authority either to prevent in the first instance, or promptly to correct, the violation complained of, and that he failed to do so. The failure thus to fulfill the duty imposed by the interaction of the corporate agent's authority and the statute furnishes a sufficient causal link. The considerations which prompted the imposition of this duty, and the scope of the duty, provide the measure of culpability....

Our conclusion ... suggests as well our disagreement with that court concerning the admissibility of evidence demonstrating that respondent was advised by the FDA in 1970 of insanitary conditions in

---

15. We note that in 1948 the Senate passed an amendment to § 303(a) of the Act to impose criminal liability only for violations committed "willfully or as a result of gross negligence." 94 Cong. Rec. 6760–6761 (1948). However, the amendment was subsequently stricken in conference. Id., at 8551, 8838.

Acme's Philadelphia warehouse. We are satisfied that the Act imposes the highest standard of care and permits conviction of responsible corporate officials who, in light of this standard of care, have the power to prevent or correct violations of its provisions. . . .

Respondent testified in his defense that he had employed a system in which he relied upon his subordinates, and that he was ultimately responsible for this system. He testified further that he had found these subordinates to be "dependable" and had "great confidence" in them. By this and other testimony respondent evidently sought to persuade the jury that, as the president of a large corporation, he had no choice but to delegate duties to those in whom he reposed confidence, that he had no reason to suspect his subordinates were failing to insure compliance with the Act, and that, once violations were unearthed, acting through those subordinates he did everything possible to correct them.

Although we need not decide whether this testimony would have entitled respondent to an instruction as to his lack of power, had he requested it, the testimony clearly created the "need" for rebuttal evidence. That evidence was not offered to show that respondent had a propensity to commit criminal acts or that the crime charged had been committed; its purpose was to demonstrate that respondent was on notice that he could not rely on his system of delegation to subordinates to prevent or correct insanitary conditions at Acme's warehouses, and that he must have been aware of the deficiencies of this system before the Baltimore violations were discovered. The evidence was therefore relevant since it served to rebut respondent's defense that he had justifiably relied upon subordinates to handle sanitation matters. And, particularly in light of the difficult task of juries in prosecutions under the Act, we conclude that its relevance and persuasiveness outweighed any prejudicial effect.

Reversed.

Mr. Justice STEWART, with whom Mr. Justice MARSHALL and Mr. Justice POWELL join, dissenting.

Although agreeing with much of what is said in the Court's opinion, I dissent from the opinion and judgment, because the jury instructions in this case were not consistent with the law as the Court today expounds it.

As I understand the Court's opinion, it holds that in order to sustain a conviction under § 301(k) of the Federal Food, Drug, and Cosmetic Act the prosecution must at least show that by reason of an individual's corporate position and responsibilities, he had a duty to use care to maintain the physical integrity of the corporation's food products. A jury may then draw the inference that when the food is found to be in such condition as to violate the statute's prohibitions, that condition was "caused" by a breach of the standard of care imposed upon the responsible official. This is the language of negligence, and I agree with it. . . .

The trial judge instructed the jury to find Park guilty if it found beyond a reasonable doubt that Park "had a responsible relation to the situation.... The issue is, in this case, whether the Defendant, John R. Park, by virtue of his position in the company, had a position of authority and responsibility in the situation out of which these charges arose." Requiring, as it did, a verdict of guilty upon a finding of "responsibility," this instruction standing alone could have been construed as a direction to convict if the jury found Park "responsible" for the condition in the sense that his position as chief executive officer gave him formal responsibility within the structure of the corporation. But the trial judge went on specifically to caution the jury not to attach such a meaning to his instruction, saying that "the fact that the Defendant is pres[id]ent and is a chief executive officer of the Acme Markets does not require a finding of guilt." "Responsibility" as used by the trial judge therefore had whatever meaning the jury in its unguided discretion chose to give it.

The instructions therefore, expressed nothing more than a tautology. They told the jury: "You must find the defendant guilty if you find that he is to be held accountable for this adulterated food." In other words: "You must find the defendant guilty if you conclude that he is guilty." ...

... The instructions given by the trial court in this case ... were a virtual nullity, a mere authorization to convict if the jury thought it appropriate. Such instructions—regardless of the blameworthiness of the defendant's conduct, regardless of the social value of the Food, Drug, and Cosmetic Act, and regardless of the importance of convicting those who violate it—have no place in our jurisprudence.

The *Dotterweich* case stands for two propositions, and I accept them both. First, "any person" within the meaning of 21 U.S.C. § 333 may include any corporate officer or employee "standing in responsible relation" to a condition or transaction forbidden by the Act. Second, a person may be convicted of a criminal offense under the Act even in the absence of "the conventional requirement for criminal conduct—awareness of some wrongdoing."

But before a person can be convicted of a criminal violation of this Act, a jury must find—and must be clearly instructed that it must find—evidence beyond a reasonable doubt that he engaged in wrongful conduct amounting at least to common-law negligence. There were no such instructions, and clearly, therefore, no such finding in this case....

NOTES

1. *Prosecutory Discretion.* The government's brief in *Park,* at pp. 30–32, offered the following account of the agency's exercise of enforcement discretion under the FD&C Act:

In enacting the 1938 Act Congress recognized that the strict standards of liability created might operate harshly, or even unfairly.

Congress therefore expressed its concern that minor violations of the Act should not be subjected to criminal prosecutions. Thus, Section 306 of the Act provides that:

> Nothing in this chapter shall be construed as requiring the Secretary to report for prosecution, or for the institution of libel or injunction proceedings, minor violations of this chapter whenever he believes that the public interest will be adequately served by a suitable written notice or warning.

This provision indicates that FDA was expected to exercise reasonable discretion in invoking the Act's criminal sanctions....

In exercising the reasonable prosecutorial discretion contemplated by Congress and this Court, FDA has applied criteria which do not result in criminal prosecutions for every violation of the statute's strict standard of criminal liability. The government is interested in the prevention and correction of conditions potentially dangerous to the public health and welfare, not in prosecution for its own sake. Accordingly, FDA's standards for reference of cases to the Department of Justice for prosecution embrace the following categories: continuing violations of law (*e.g.*, continuing insanitary conditions in a food plant); violations of an obvious and flagrant nature (*e.g.*, food warehouse overrun with rodents, birds and insects, which contains plainly contaminated products); and intentionally false or fraudulent violations.

The standard for prosecution of individual corporate officials, as distinguished from the prosecution of their corporations, is based on the reasonable relationship criterion of *Dotterweich*. The government's policy is to prosecute only those individuals who are in a position and who have an opportunity to prevent or correct violations, but fail to do so. Officials who lack authority to prevent or correct violations, or who were totally unaware of any problem and could not have been expected to be aware of it in the reasonable exercise of their corporate duties, are not the subject of criminal action. Even if investigation discloses the elements of liability, and indicates that an official bears a responsible relationship to them, the agency will not ordinarily recommend prosecution unless that official, after becoming aware of possible violations, often (as with Park) as a result of notification by FDA, has failed to correct them or to change his managerial system so as to prevent further violations. In those instances where prosecution is brought, it is brought for past, as well as the most recent, violations.....

See also FDA, REGULATORY PROCEDURES MANUAL ch. 8–50.

2. *Subsequent Authority.* The Ninth Circuit, applying the *Park* standard of "foresight and vigilance," upheld the convictions of corporate officers in two cases decided the same day in 1976. By *per curiam* opinion in *United States v. Y. Hata & Co., Ltd.*, 535 F.2d 508 (9th Cir. 1976), the court rejected the defense tendered by the company's president that he had done everything possible to correct the unsanitary warehouse conditions. Having discovered the violations months before FDA inspection, the company had attempted unsuccessfully to prevent access of birds to stored food. At the time of inspection, the company was awaiting shipment of materials with which it would correct the problem. The court concluded that since the final solution of caging the storage area off

from infesting birds was neither novel nor impossible, the defendant was not excused.

Rodent infestation and contamination of stored food resulted in the conviction of the corporation's secretary-treasurer in *United States v. Starr,* 535 F.2d 512 (9th Cir. 1976). The court rejected the defendant's two-pronged argument of objective impossibility. The defendant's contention, that he was helpless to prevent contamination resulting from the natural flow of rodents seeking sanctuary from the plowing of a nearby field, was rejected. The claim, that the janitor was instructed to correct the situation and had deliberately failed to do so, was rejected in part because the defendant worked in close proximity to the scene of the violations and was therefore in a position to observe for himself whether the necessary corrections were being made. *See also United States v. Gel Spice Co., Inc.,* 773 F.2d 427 (2d Cir. 1985).

The court in *United States v. New England Grocers Supply Co.,* 488 F. Supp. 230 (D. Mass. 1980), set aside a magistrate's finding of guilt because the magistrate had not found beyond a reasonable doubt that the defendant corporate officers were not powerless to prevent the charged violations. The magistrate subsequently found the defendants not guilty because FDA did not present evidence to prove beyond a reasonable doubt that they could, by the use of extraordinary care, correct or prevent the violations involved, *United States v. New England Grocer Supply,* 1978–1980 FDLI Jud. Rec. 233 (D. Mass. 1980).

3. *Other Cases.* Decisions construing the criminal provisions in the FD&C Act are far too numerous to list. The more important cases in addition to those cited elsewhere in this section include *United States v. Crescent–Kelvan Co.,* 164 F.2d 582 (3d Cir. 1948); *Pasadena Research Laboratories v. United States,* 169 F.2d 375 (9th Cir. 1948), *cert. denied,* 335 U.S. 853 (1948); *United States v. Kaadt,* 171 F.2d 600 (7th Cir. 1948); *Golden Grain Macaroni Co. v. United States,* 209 F.2d 166 (9th Cir. 1953); *United States v. H. Wool & Sons, Inc.,* 215 F.2d 95 (2d Cir. 1954); *Lelles v. United States,* 241 F.2d 21 (9th Cir. 1957); *United States v. Hohensee,* 243 F.2d 367 (3d Cir. 1957); *V.E. Irons, Inc. v. United States,* 244 F.2d 34 (1st Cir. 1957); *United States v. Ellis Research Laboratories, Inc.,* 300 F.2d 550 (7th Cir. 1962); *United States v. Taller,* 394 F.2d 435 (2d Cir. 1968); *United States v. Thriftimart, Inc.,* 429 F.2d 1006 (9th Cir. 1970); *United States v. Cassaro, Inc.,* 443 F.2d 153 (1st Cir. 1971); *United States v. Industrial Laboratories Co.,* 456 F.2d 908 (10th Cir. 1972); *United States v. H.B. Gregory Co.,* 502 F.2d 700 (7th Cir. 1974), *United States v. Torigian Laboratories, Inc.,* 577 F. Supp. 1514 (E.D.N.Y. 1984), *aff'd without opinion,* 751 F.2d 373 (2d Cir. 1984); *United States v. Corbi,* Food Drug Cosm. L. Rep. (CCH) ¶ 38,040 (C.D. Cal. 1980).

4. *Record of Conviction.* Where individual defendants were acquitted on all charges of intent to violate the FD&C Act, but were convicted under the *Park* doctrine that intent is not required, the court reluctantly denied the defendants' motion to expunge their criminal records in *United States v. Purity Condiments, Inc.,* Food Drug Cosm. L. Rep. (CCH) ¶ 38,276 (S.D. Fla. 1984). The court concluded that the rationale underlying the FD&C Act and the applicable precedent left no choice but to deny the motions for expungement, but characterized this lack of discretionary power as amounting to "an unreasonable and impermissible restraint on judicial authority."

5. *Felony Violations.* The court in *United States v. Bradshaw,* 840 F.2d 871 (11th Cir. 1988), held that the requirement of intent to make a violation a felony under section 303(d) includes the intent to defraud or mislead state and

Federal government enforcement agencies and not merely ultimate consumers. *See also United States v. Cattle King Packing Co.*, 793 F.2d 232 (10th Cir. 1986).

6. *Venue for Trial.* The Sixth Amendment to the Constitution provides that a criminal defendant has the right to be tried in the "district wherein the crime shall have been committed." The court in *United States v. Beach–Nut Nutrition Corp.*, 871 F.2d 1181 (2d Cir. 1989), reversed convictions for adulteration of orange juice because the adulteration did not occur in the district where the trial was held. *Compare United States v. Taller*, 394 F.2d 435 (2d Cir. 1968).

7. *Separate Violations.* FDA may bring a separate criminal charge for each illegal action, even if they all arose out of a single transaction. *See United States v. H. B. Gregory Co.*, 502 F.2d 700 (7th Cir. 1974); *Akin Distributors of Florida, Inc. v. United States*, 399 F.2d 306 (5th Cir. 1968); *V.E. Irons, Inc. v. United States*, 244 F.2d 34 (1st Cir. 1957).

8. *Unsuccessful Prosecutions.* The criminal cases that FDA has lost at trial have rarely been reported. Most appear only in the FDA notices of judgment, which are required to be published by section 705(a) of the Act and are currently listed in issues of FDA Consumer. *See, e.g., United States v. White*, FDA Consumer, No. 5, at 43 (June 1990); *United States v. CPC International*, 16 FDA Consumer, No. 7, at 33, (September 1982); *United States v. Bass*, 10 FDA Consumer, No. 10, at 38 (December 1976–January 1977); *United States v. Scientific Associates, Inc.*, 4 FDA Papers, No. 10, at 40 (December 1970–January 1971); *United States v. Abbott Laboratories*, 3 FDA Papers, No. 1, at 36 (March 1969).

9. *Commentary. See, e.g.*, Burditt, *The Park Case in Perspective*, 31 FDC L.J. 137 (1976); O'Keefe, *Criminal Liability: Park Update*, 32 FDC L.J. 392 (1977); O'Keefe and Isley, *Dotterweich Revisited—Criminal Liability Under the Federal Food, Drug, and Cosmetic Act*, 31 FDC L.J. 69 (1976); O'Keefe and Shapiro, *Personal Criminal Liability Under the Federal Food, Drug, and Cosmetic Act: The Dotterweich Doctrine*, 30 FDC L.J. 5 (1975); Merrill, *The Park Case*, 30 FDC L.J. 683 (1975); Rodwin, *A Violation of the Federal Food, Drug, and Cosmetic Act—A Crime in Search of a Criminal*, 31 FDC L.J. 616 (1976); Sethi and Katz, *The Expanding Scope of Personal Criminal Liability of Corporate Executives—Some Implications of United States v. Park*, 32 FDC L.J. 544 (1977).

PROPOSALS TO CHANGE THE CRIMINAL LIABILITY STANDARD

The Supreme Court's decision in *Park* rekindled efforts to relax the FD&C Act's criminal liability standard. In 1976, the Senate passed the Consumer Food Act, S. 641, 94th Cong., 2d Sess., which incorporated compromise language altering that standard. As reported from committee the bill would have required the Government to show that a violation had occurred "knowingly, willfully, or negligently." S. Rep. No. 94–684, 94th Cong., 2d Sess. (1976). The Department of HEW and FDA both opposed any weakening of the strict liability standard. Increasing the government's burden of proof, FDA argued, would impair its meager enforcement program. The agency reasoned that the fear of criminal sanctions generated by the strict liability standard encouraged self-regulation of the food industry. That standard, by placing compliance responsibility at the top levels of corporate organization, insured that all precautions necessary to protect food safety would be taken.

During the floor debate on S. 641, the Senate amended the committee version upon the motion of Senators Hathaway and Durkin. The Hathaway amendment altered the liability standard recommended by the committee by substituting the following language for "negligently":

> ... with the care, skill, prudence, and diligence under the circumstances then prevailing that a prudent man acting in a like capacity and familiar with such matters would use in the conduct of an enterprise of a like character.

122 Cong. Rec. 7219 (March 18, 1976). Senator Hathaway contended that the negligence standard would have required the government to prove wanton or reckless behavior—a too demanding standard to protect the public. Although passed overwhelmingly in the Senate, S. 641 was never acted upon by the House.

Debate over the *Park* standard surfaced again during consideration of drug reform legislation in 1978 and 1979. By this time, however, the Department of HEW had altered its position on the issue. The identical bills introduced in the House and Senate, H.R. 1161 and S.2755, 95th Cong., 2d Sess. (1978), would have incorporated language similar to that of the 1976 Hathaway amendment. The bills used the term "negligence," but defined it to mean:

> ... acting without the care, skill, prudence, or diligence, under the circumstances then prevailing, that a prudent person would use if acting in a like capacity and familiar with the matters with which a prudent person in like capacity would be familiar.

124 Cong. Rec. 7203 (March 16, 1978). In testimony supporting the drug reform legislation, HEW Secretary Califano endorsed the change. HEW and, reluctantly, FDA justified their new position in terms of both fairness and efficacy. The *Park* standard was characterized as unfair because it could result in imposition of criminal liability for actions or omissions without any showing of fault. The agency also conceded that infrequent prosecution under the *Park* standard was not the most effective way of protecting the consumer. Instead, the agency supported the less draconian but more flexible and potentially more complete enforcement tools of expanded investigatory authority and administratively imposed civil penalties. The proposed drug legislation did not emerge from committee in either body in 1978.

The Drug Regulation Reform Act of 1979, S. 1075, which passed the Senate but was not considered in the House, similarly adopted a civil rather than criminal negligence standard for criminal liability. See S. Rep. No. 96–321, 96th Cong., 1st Sess. (1979). The past decade saw no revival of legislative efforts to amend the Act's criminal liability standard.

AUTHORIZED CRIMINAL PENALTIES

Section 303 provides criminal penalties of $1,000 or up to one year in jail for any violation of the Act and $10,000 or up to three years in jail for a second offense or a violation with the intent to defraud or mislead. Although the provision's format was modified by the Comprehensive Drug Abuse Prevention and Control Act of 1970, 84 Stat. 1236, 1281, its substance has remained unchanged.

In the Sentencing Reform Act of 1984, 98 Stat. 1837, 1995, Congress enacted new criminal fines in 18 U.S.C. § 3571, which were made applicable to any offense under any Federal statute by 18 U.S.C. § 3551. These provisions impose maximum fines for individuals of $25,000 for a misdemeanor and $250,000 for a felony, and for corporations and organizations of $100,000 for a misdemeanor and $500,000 for a felony. To complicate matters, less than three weeks later Congress enacted the Criminal Fine Enforcement Act, 98 Stat. 3134, 3137 (1984), adding new maximum fines under 18 U.S.C. § 3623, which was a part of chapter 229. Because the earlier Sentencing Reform Act repealed all of chapter 229 effective as of November 1, 1987, 18 U.S.C. § 3623 is now repealed and the fines authorized by 18 U.S.C. § 3571 apply to the FD&C Act.

The Anti–Drug Abuse Act of 1988, 102 Stat. 4181, 4230, added section 303(e) to the FD&C Act increasing the penalties for distribution of any anabolic steroids to a minor under 18 years of age up to six years imprisonment and to any other person up to three years imprisonment. Any conviction involving an anabolic steroid or a human growth hormone triggers application of 21 U.S.C. § 853, which provides for forfeiture of all property used to support the illegal distribution or purchased with the profits.

The Prescription Drug Marketing Act of 1987, 102 Stat. 95, 99 added section 303(b)(1), which establishes criminal penalties of not more than 10 years imprisonment or a fine of $250,000 for violation of the prescription drug sample requirements in that statute. Under section 303(b)(5), moreover, a "bounty hunter" who provides information leading to the arrest and conviction of a person for a violation is entitled to one-half of the criminal fine but not more than $125,000.

3.　THE GUARANTY CLAUSE

Under section 303(c) of the Act, a person who in good faith merely receives and later delivers an illegal article is exempt from criminal liability. And a person who introduces an illegal article into commerce is also exempt from liability if he has received the article in good faith and obtained a written guaranty that it is not in violation of the Act. In turn, the giving of a false guaranty is prohibited by section 301(h) and is thus a criminal offense.

UNITED STATES v. CROWN RUBBER SUNDRIES CO.

United States District Court, Northern District of Ohio, 1946.
67 F.Supp. 92.

FREED, District Judge.

Crown Rubber Sundries Co., a partnership, and one of the partners, individually, Joseph Lader, were charged in eight counts of an information alleging violation ... in the shipment and sale of rubber prophylactics which were, in fact, ineffective for prophylactic purposes because of the presence of holes and perforations in the devices.... The defendants rely solely upon the claim that they are free from guilt because they received a guaranty given them by the L. E. Shunk Latex Products, Inc., the manufacturer, warranting that all the merchandise compiled with the provisions of the Pure Food, Drug and Cosmetic Act, and authorizing them to make the same guaranty to their distributees.

The undisputed facts show that the defendants received the merchandise in bulk, that they repacked the prophylactics in individual containers bearing their own labels and shipped them to their own customers. There was some evidence tending to show that the merchandise was acquired by the purchase of a wholesale business which had in stock the prophylactics which the original owner had purchased from the Shunk company.

Since the purchase was not made directly from the manufacturer, it is questioned whether the guaranty made to these defendants could inure to their benefit. It is urged by the Government that the guaranty which affords a defense is only one which is made to him who purchases directly from the guarantor. Although the court is of the opinion that the Government's contention in this regard is correct, the real issue is whether the defense of the guaranty, as a matter of law, can be made under the state of the evidence which is not in dispute. Assuming, for the purpose of the instant case, that the defendants did have a right to rely upon a guaranty received from someone other than the person from whom they purchased the merchandise, the question remains whether the guaranty affords a defense under the statute. . . .

It is the judgment of this court that no person may rely upon any guaranty unless, in introducing the product into interstate commerce, he has acted merely as a conduit through which the merchandise reaches the consumer. . . . The guaranty can be received in good faith, within the meaning of the statute, only if the shipper passes the product on in the same form as he received it, without repacking it or subjecting it to any new hazards of adulteration or failure which were not present when the original guaranty upon which he relies was given.

The facts in this case show the prophylactics were purchased by the defendants in bulk and that they repackaged and relabeled them. They shipped them in cartons bearing their own trade name.

When this state of facts appears, in the judgment of the court, as a matter of law, the defense of the guaranty no longer is available to the defendants. . . .

UNITED STATES v. BALANCED FOODS, INC.

United States District Court, Southern District of New York, 1955.
146 F. Supp. 154.

REEVES, District Judge.

The defendants are charged in two counts with having shipped a misbranded food product in interstate commerce in different periods during the year 1953. . . .

. . . At the trial of the case the defendants submitted a guaranty from a responsible producer, as contemplated by the several sections of the statutes, and the defendants strongly asserted their good faith in receiving said product because of said guaranty. Before the shipments in question were made, the defendants were advised of the contention made by government agents and agents of the City of New York, that the product was misbranded and in fact some of the merchandise held by the defendants was seized by said agents. The defendants communicated these facts to the guarantor and were given assurances that the charge was a mistake and that, if necessary, a slight change would be made in the labels as well as in the company's literature, so as to satisfy the government through its agents. With these assurances the defendants continued to deal in the product and to make shipments....

... The defendants in the transaction of their business handling, as the testimony indicated, from 1,500 to 2,000 different products, would undoubtedly have a right, with such assurances as were given in this case, to proceed in the transaction of their business until there was such an adjudication or authoritative determination that the merchandise was misbranded as to bring home to them definite knowledge of the fact that by such shipments they were in fact violating the law....

The evidence justifies the court in believing that the personal defendant, who acted for the corporate defendant at all times in receiving the product, was actually in an attitude of trust and confidence, and in such trust and confidence the shipments complained against were made. It would follow that the motion for an order directing acquittal should be sustained, and it is so ordered.

UNITED STATES v. WALSH

Supreme Court of the United States, 1947.
331 U.S. 432.

Mr. Justice MURPHY delivered the opinion of the Court.

Appellee does business in San Diego, California, under the name of Kelp Laboratories. An information has been filed, charging appellee with having given a false guaranty in violation of § 301(h). The following facts have been alleged: In February 1943, appellee gave a continuing guaranty to Richard Harrison Products, of Hollywood, California, stating that no products thereafter shipped to the latter would be adulterated or misbranded within the meaning of the Act. On February 24, 1945, while the guaranty was in full force and effect, appellee consigned to Richard Harrison Products, at Hollywood, a shipment of vitamin products which were allegedly adulterated and misbranded—thereby making the guaranty false in respect of that shipment....

Appellee moved to dismiss the information on the ground that it did not state an offense. The argument was that § 301(h) applies only to a guaranty that is false relative to an interstate shipment, whereas the alleged shipment here was to a consignee within California, the state of origin, and there was no allegation that the consignee purchased the order for someone outside California or that it intended to sell the products in its interstate rather than its intrastate business. The District Court gave an oral opinion sustaining appellee's contention and granting the motion to dismiss. The case is here on direct appeal by the United States. . . .

. . . § 301(h), with which we are concerned, does not speak specifically in interstate terms. It prohibits the "giving of a guaranty or undertaking referred to in section 303(c)(2), which guaranty or undertaking is false". . . . Nothing on the face of the section limits its application to guaranties relating to articles introduced or delivered for introduction into interstate commerce. . . .

We thus conclude that § 301(h) definitely proscribes the giving of a false guaranty to one engaged wholly or partly in an interstate business irrespective of whether that guaranty leads in any particular instance to an illegal shipment in interstate commerce. Such a construction is entirely consistent with the interstate setting of the Act. A manufacturer or processor ordinarily has no way of knowing whether a dealer, whose business includes making interstate sales, will redistribute a particular shipment in interstate or intrastate commerce. But if he guarantees that his product is not adulterated or misbranded within the meaning of the Act, he clearly intends to assure the dealer that the latter may redistribute the product in interstate commerce without incurring any of the liabilities of the Act. And the dealer is thereby more likely to engage in interstate shipment by such a dealer is strong enough to make reasonable the prohibition of all false guaranties to him, even though some of them may actually result only in intrastate distribution. . . .

So construed, § 301(h) raises no constitutional difficulties. The commerce clause of the Constitution is not to be interpreted so as to deny to Congress the power to make effective its regulation of interstate commerce. . . .

[The dissenting opinion of Mr. Justice Jackson is omitted.]

NOTE

See also Barnes v. United States, 142 F.2d 648 (9th Cir. 1944), *United States v. Santoro & Sons, Inc.*, 1965–1968 FDLI Jud. & Admin. Rec. 277 (E.D.N.Y. 1965); *United States v. Colosse Cheese & Butter Co.*, 133 F. Supp. 953 (N.D.N.Y. 1955).

4. SECTION 305 HEARINGS

ENFORCEMENT POLICY, PRACTICES, AND PROCEDURES: INFORMAL HEARING BEFORE REPORT ON CRIMINAL VIOLATION

41 Federal Register 14769 (April 7, 1976).

Section 305 of the act provides that "Before any violation of this Act is reported by the Secretary to any United States attorney for institution of a criminal proceeding, the person against whom such proceeding is contemplated shall be given appropriate notice and an opportunity to present his views, either orally or in writing, with regard to such contemplated proceeding." ...

... Congress recognized when it enacted the 1938 act that not all violations would warrant prosecution. Accordingly, the act included section 306, which provides that when the Secretary of Health, Education, and Welfare believes the public interest would be adequately served by a suitable written notice or warning, he need not report minor violations for the institution of prosecution, seizure, or injunction. Many violations, including most minor violations, can be readily corrected if brought promptly to the attention of the person responsible. To deal with such violations, FDA in the past used an administrative procedure known as "citation for warning." Over the years, this practice was used for many types of violations that, in the agency's judgment, appeared to fall somewhere between those that are subject to an informal hearing before report of a criminal violation and those that are subject to section 306 of the act.

Although the practice of citation for warning frequently achieved correction of violations, it also had an undesirable consequence. Because it was often used to deal with violations for which the agency was not prepared to recommend prosecution, citation for warning diluted the significance of section 305 hearings in situations in which prosecution was clearly appropriate. This practice has therefore been abandoned.... [S]ection 305 hearings are no longer used to deal with those types of violations in which some sort of warning is a proper first step. Instead, section 305 hearings are used as Congress originally intended. FDA accordingly will schedule a hearing only when criminal prosecution is seriously contemplated.

It must be recognized, however, that the failure to provide an opportunity for a section 305 hearing is not a bar to prosecution of persons who violate the act.... [H]owever, the Commissioner will dispense with the section 305 hearing procedure only in compelling circumstances. This would occur so infrequently, if ever, that it is not prudent to attempt to illustrate the "compelling circumstances" standard by examples....

Response to a Notice of Hearing, in writing or in person, is entirely voluntary. A person who receives a Notice of Hearing may elect not to respond, may respond in writing, may respond through a designated representative, or may appear personally with or without the aid of counsel. Failure by any person to respond to the Notice of Hearing will not prejudice the agency's final determination. A decision whether the matter will be referred to a United States attorney will be made solely on the evidence in the agency's possession. The Commissioner notes, however, that the opportunity for presentation of views may be important where the person who received the Notice of Hearing believes he is not responsible for the alleged violations. . . .

Sharp differences frequently appear between FDA's views as set forth in the Charge Sheet and the respondents' views expressed during the section 305 hearing. It is important that the summary of the hearing that is prepared be accurate and fairly reflect the views of the respondents. Accordingly, the proposed procedures adopt current agency practice under which the hearing officer dictates a summary of the hearing in the presence of the respondents and affords them an opportunity to make any necessary corrections or additions. Furthermore, although a section 305 hearing is not a formal hearing, either the respondent or the agency may arrange for the preparation of a verbatim transcript. The proposed regulations also permit a respondent to supplement the record of his personal appearance following the hearing. . . .

After reviewing all relevant information, FDA may conclude not to recommend prosecution of one or more persons named in a Notice of Hearing. Whenever FDA and the United States attorney both decide not to prosecute all persons names in a Notice of Hearing for the offenses charged, the Commissioner will undertake to notify such persons. No individual named in the Notice of Hearing will be notified of a decision not to seek prosecution until determination has been made that such notification will not prejudice the prosecution of any other person. . . .

NOTES

1. *FDA regulations.* Final regulations governing section 305 hearings were promulgated in 42 Fed. Reg. 6801 (February 4, 1977) and codified in 21 C.F.R. § 7.84 *et seq.* Subsequently, in 43 Fed. Reg. 20508 (May 12, 1978), FDA proposed to revise the regulations:

Section 305 of the act, by its terms, applies only when the agency has determined that "a violation" of the act has occurred and the agency intends to refer the case to a United States attorney for a "criminal proceeding" that is, prosecution. A request for a grand jury investigation does not constitute the reporting of a violation for prosecution. Accordingly, the revised regulation, in § 7.85(a), makes clear that the agency need not hold a section 305 hearing when it is considering recommending a grand jury investigation instead of a criminal prosecution based on the evidence then available. . . .

Since a 305 notice alerts a prospective defendant that prosecution may be imminent, it may result in the alteration or destruction of potentially incriminating evidence. . . . When FDA has reason to believe that such alteration or destruction will occur, or that a potential defendant will flee, a 305 notice need not be issued.

. . . FDA's current practice is to reference in the 305 notice other Federal statutes violated by the same conduct that violates the Federal Food, Drug, and Cosmetic Act. This practice is retained in revised § 7.84(c). However, if the agency does not contemplate proceeding with a recommendation under the Federal Food, Drug, and Cosmetic Act, no 305 hearing will be held with regard to the violation of other statutes.

The revisions resulting from this proposal were promulgated in 44 Fed. Reg. 12164 (March 5, 1979); FDA, REGULATORY PROCEDURES MANUAL ch. 8–40.

2. *Commentary.* For further treatment of hearings under section 305, *see* McMurray, *Section 305 Hearings—Defense Considerations*, 31 FDC L.J. 386 (1976); Pfeifer, *Section 305 Hearings and Criminal Prosecutions*, 31 FDC L.J. 376 (1976); Wilmoth, *Criminal Prosecutions, Inspections and Section 305 Hearings*, 33 FDC L.J. 360 (1978).

OTHER STATUTES INVOKED IN CRIMINAL ENFORCEMENT OF THE FD&C ACT

Several provisions in Title 18 of the United States Code are potentially applicable for ancillary enforcement of the FD&C Act:

Conspiracy, 18 U.S.C. § 371. United States v. Beech–Nut Nutrition Corp., 871 F.2d 1181 (2d Cir. 1989), *United States v. Automated Medical Laboratories, Inc.,* 770 F.2d 399 (4th Cir. 1985); *United States v. General Nutrition, Inc.,* 638 F. Supp. 556 (W.D.N.Y. 1986); *United States v. Haga,* 1985–1986 FDLI Jud. Rec. 146 (N.D.Tex. 1986); *United States v. Velsicol Chemical Chemical Corp.,* 498 F. Supp. 1255 (D.D.C. 1980).

False Reports, 18 U.S.C. § 1001. United States v. Keplinger, 776 F.2d 678 (7th Cir. 1985); *United States v. Automated Medical Laboratories, Inc.,* 770 F.2d 399 (4th Cir.1985); *United States v. Smith,* 740 F.2d 734 (9th Cir. 1984); *United States v. Velsicol Chemical Corp.,* 498 F. Supp. 1255 (D.D.C. 1980).

Mail Fraud, 18 U.S.C. § 1341. United States v. Beech–Nut Nutrition Corp., 871 F.2d 1181 (2d Cir. 1989); *United States v. Taller,* 394 F.2d 435 (2d Cir. 1968).

Perjury, 18 U.S.C. § 1623. United States v. Lighte, 782 F.2d 367 (2d Cir. 1986).

H. CIVIL PENALTIES

The 1938 Act contained no civil money penalty provisions. Although several more recent regulatory statutes contain civil money penalty provisions and the U.S. Administrative Conference has recommended that the FD&C Act be amended to allow imposition of civil penalties, 49 Fed. Reg. 9904 (March 16, 1984), 49 Fed. Reg. 29937 (July 25, 1984), Congress has enacted civil penalties only in the Safe Medical Devices Act of 1990, p. 792 *supra.* FDA currently administers two other statutes that include civil penalty provisions.

1. THE RADIATION CONTROL FOR HEALTH AND SAFETY ACT OF 1968

Former section 360C(b) of the Public Health Service Act, 42 U.S.C. § 263k(b), now recodified as section 539 of the FD&C Act, authorizes FDA to seek the imposition of civil penalties for violations of the Radiation Act. Orders imposing civil penalties under section 360C(b) are enforceable in U.S. district courts.

UNITED STATES v. HODGES X–RAY, INC.

United States Court of Appeals, Sixth Circuit, 1985.
759 F.2d 557.

KRUPANSKY, Circuit Judge.

Defendants Hodges X–Ray, Inc. and James J. Hodges appealed from the grant of summary judgment in favor of the United States, wherein the court assessed $20,500 in civil penalties against each defendant for violations of certain Food and Drug Administration (FDA) regulations. The assessments were predicated upon the finding of the court below that x-ray equipment manufactured by the defendants failed to comply with 21 C.F.R. § 1020.31(a)(1), which requires a display of exposure time on the control panel in seconds, and 21 C.F.R. § 1020.31(a)(2), which mandates that each machine terminated exposure at a preset time.

Hodges commenced manufacturing its "Trace–Ray III" x-ray units in 1976. The control panel calibrated exposure time in "pulses" rather than the traditional increments of seconds. According to industry standards, one "pulse" is equivalent to 1/120 of a second. The equipment was distributed to dentists, chiropractors and veterinarians throughout the United States.

In a telegram transmitted on March 17, 1977, the FDA notified Hodges of the failure of some units to terminate exposure at the present time interval. In a follow-up letter to Hodges on April 25, 1977, the FDA asserted a defect in the failure of the units to (1) correctly terminate exposure and (2) to indicate exposure time in increments of seconds. These violations are the subject of the instant appeal.

In further correspondence to Hodges dated July 5, 1977, the FDA recommended certain corrective procedures to alleviate the asserted violations, namely, the failure of the units to display exposure time in seconds. The FDA requested that Hodges supply each Trace Ray III purchaser with a self-adhesive label on the unit, which would explain that one pulse was equal to 1/120 of a second, with instructions to the purchaser to attach the label to the control panel of each unit in a prominent place.. . . .

In October, 1977, Hodges, X-ray, Inc. was sold to Western States, but James Hodges was retained as "consultant" to the new owners. In this capacity, Hodges notified the FDA that the corrective procedures had come to fruition. According to the declaration submitted by Robert G. Britain, the deputy director of the Office of Medical Devices in the FDA's National Center for Devices and Radiological Health, however, the corrections were not made to the FDA's satisfaction. Britain further explained that the FDA notified Hodges in August, 1979, of its intent to take regulatory action unless Hodges undertook additional corrective measures. Hodges responded by stating that the firm's assets had been sold and thus it could not carry out the corrective modifications.

In September, 1979, the FDA decided to initiate more stringent action because, according to Britain, "in conjunction with the danger to health, some units were being redistributed or considered for export, while others were being repaired inadequately or without adequate supervision." Thus, the FDA instituted seizure proceedings against all known Trace–Ray III machines, including about 115 manufactured by Hodges X-ray, Inc. Britain also averred that "[a]lmost all of the Tracer-ay [sic] III machines have been condemned, and either released for reconditioning under FDA's approval or destroyed. Those seizures are one of the largest multiple seizures in FDA's history and required a major commitment of agency resources."

As a result of the foregoing, the government filed its complaint for civil penalties on October 7, 1981. The complaint alleged that Hodges violated the Radiation Control for Health and Safety Act of 1958 (RCHSA) by: (1) introducing into interstate commerce sixty-six diagnostic X-ray machines that failed to comply with two applicable performance standards promulgated pursuant to RCHSA, 42 U.S.C. § 263j(a)(1); and (2) certifying that the machines complied with all performance standards when in fact the machines did not comply, 42 U.S.C. § 263j(a)(5).....

As a threshold issue, Hodges urged that he could not be held individually liable for the statutory violations asserted in the government's complaint. More specifically, Hodges argued that he was not a "manufacturer' within the meaning of 42 U.S.C. § 263j. However, this argument is not persuasive for several reasons. First, 42 U.S.C. § 263c(3) defines the term "manufacturer" as "any *person* engaged in the business of manufacturing, assembling, or importing of electronic products." (emphasis added). Since Hodges was the major shareholder and president of Hodges X-ray, Inc., the conclusion that he was included in this definition is self-evident. Secondly, in an analogous situation litigated under the Federal Food, Drug & Cosmetic Act (FDCA), the Supreme Court decided that corporate officers could be held individually liable for violations of public health legislation.

Although the *Park* and *Dotterweich* cases were premised upon the FDCA, the RCHSA is undeniably in the same class of public welfare statutes and thus the conclusions of those cases are equally applicable here.

Hodges attempted to distinguish *Park* and *Dotterweich* with the argument that they applied to criminal, rather than civil liability. However, the rationale for holding corporate offices criminally responsible for acts of the corporation, which could lead to incarceration, is even more persuasive where only civil liability is involved, which at most would result in a monetary penalty. The fact that a corporate officer could be subjected to criminal punishment upon a showing of a responsible relationship to the acts of a corporation that violate health and safety statutes renders *civil* liability appropriate as well. Therefore, the district court's determination that Hodges could be held individually liable for RCHSA violations should not be disturbed on appeal.....

Hodges' final argument charged that the district court improperly assessed the amount of civil penalties without a hearing. However, a hearing for the purpose of determining the amount of civil penalties is not mandatory. Moreover, the record contained sufficient evidence from which to ascertain the amount of penalties to be assessed. (The statute provides a maximum $1,000 penalty for each violation.) Further, a number of equitable factors were before the district court, which, though irrelevant to the imposition of liability, were appropriate for consideration in determining the proper amount of penalties. These included the sale of Hodges' assets to another corporation and Hodges' attempts to take corrective action. Finally, the RCHSA provides that the civil penalty assessed by the court "may on application be remitted or mitigated by the Secretary [of the U.S. Department of Health and Human Services]." Thus, the statute explicitly provides Hodges with an opportunity to seek reduction of the civil penalties by the administrative agency. In view of this remedy provided by statute, Hodges' argument that the district court is required to hold a separate hearing on the amount of civil penalties is without merit....

NOTES

1. *Supporting Authority. See also Throneberry* v. *FDA*, 1983–1984 FDLI Jud. Rec. 242, 382 (E.D. Tenn. 1983), imposing civil penalties for failure to give adequate warnings of the dangers of exposure to ultraviolet radiation in 47 separate sun tanning booths.

2. *Compliance Policy.* The FDA civil penalties policy under the Radiation Act is set forth in Compliance Policy Guide No. 7133.23 (March 1, 1983).

2. THE PRESCRIPTION DRUG MARKETING ACT OF 1987

New section 303(b) authorizes civil penalties for violation of the drug sample provisions of the FD&C Act. In addition to criminal penalties, a manufacturer or distributor is subject to a civil penalty of not more than $50,000 for each of the first two violations resulting in a conviction in any 10–year period and for not more than $1 million for each violation resulting in a conviction after the second conviction in any 10–year period. The failure to report to FDA a conviction under state law is also subject to a civil penalty of not more than $100,000. These civil penalties are imposed by a Federal district court, not by FDA. As of June 30, 1990, no civil penalties under this authority have been imposed.

I. RESTITUTION

UNITED STATES v. PARKINSON

United States Court of Appeals, Ninth Circuit, 1956.
240 F.2d 918.

JAMES ALGER FEE, Circuit Judge.

This cause was brought at the instance of Food and Drug Administration ... against the individuals named as defendants, praying that these latter be restrained from introducing into interstate commerce certain misbranded drugs and requiring defendants to make restitution to purchasers thereof, present and past. The claimed misbranding related to relief from male sexual weakness and impotence and to rapid sexual rejuvenation.... [A]fter the grant of preliminary injunction, there was entered a judgment by which defendants were permanently enjoined and restrained from doing acts in violation of § 301(a) of the Federal Food, Drug, and Cosmetic Act with respect to all these drugs enumerated, "or other similar drugs, or other drugs offered for similar purposes." This portion of the judgment was entered by consent. There was also submitted to the court by stipulation the question whether restitution could be required....

It is difficult indeed to see how any relief could be granted in this case. The supposition is that there were purchasers because there were allegations in the complaint of sales in interstate commerce. But no purchaser was named as a party to the action. The United States did not sue as a representative of any purchaser. There is a suggestion in the prayer only that relief be granted by way of restitution. The body of the complaint contains no allegations upon which the suggestion could be supported. There was no evidence introduced either as to identity of purchasers or as to the amount of drugs unlawfully sold. No judgment could be entered for such refunds, if found in favor of the purchasers themselves, because none was a party to the proceeding. No judgment could be entered in their behalf in favor of the United States or the agency....

In a sound and able opinion ... [the] District Judge analyzed the problem, reviewed the statutes and determined that the particular enactment did not confer jurisdiction upon the United States District

Courts to make such an order. With this opinion we agree, and the conclusions thereof we affirm....

The Congress granted three specific powers by this Act. The first was the power to bring criminal prosecutions for violations. The second permitted seizure of drugs proscribed in interstate commerce. The third empowered the courts to restrain violations. Ordinarily, grant of such specific powers would be indicia of the denial of more extensive authority....

... Those who drafted the law and secured passage thereof were fully cognizant of the evils at which it was aimed. Unquestionably, there was a subsidiary purpose to protect the purses of the public and to prevent the vending of alleged remedies, which at best were useless, to fatten the pockets of the exploiter. The agents of the government ... emphasize the persistence of the individual defendants here, notwithstanding criminal convictions, decrees of restraint and seizure of drugs, in finding new drugs to exploit by false advertising in order to reap a golden harvest for a short time.

But advertisements of nostrums for restoration of "Lost Manhood" have appeared in the daily newspapers for at least fifty years in the past. The drafters of the bill and those who engineered its adoption were cognizant of the persistence of those who desired to make money by such means.

The record of the past few decades is replete with examples of the tendency of executive agencies to expand their field of operations. A passion and a zeal to crusade affects their operations. Strong public opinion may temporarily encourage excesses in zeal.... These are warning signs that zeal for the noblest causes should not be translated into uncontrolled power of suppression of the contraries. The courts are charged with the duty of compelling restraint.

It is particularly urged upon us that a court of equity has power to fashion remedies to meet situations and to compel compliance with decrees. To a certain extent this is correct in litigation between private individuals. But Chancery has ceased for long ages to issue new writs whereby supposed wrongs could be cured. Such objectives are modernly to be accomplished only by legislation....

... The use of the extraordinary remedies of equity in governmental litigation should never be permitted by the courts unless clearly authorized by the statute in express terms. Anything which savors of a penalty should not be permitted unless Congress has expressly so provided, since the spirit of equity abhorred such punitive measures. Here it is apparently contemplated that a judgment be entered in favor of the United States for a definite sum of money for "restitution." If the agency were unable or did not give the moneys to the purchasers, it would be covered into the Treasury of the United States.

The collection of moneys not held in trust or earmarked from an individual by an executive department without limitation in amount and without detailed means outlined for disbursement to persons supposed to have paid them constitutes a penalty for violation of a regulation. Indeed, it is with great difficulty, as suggested above, that either the remedy or the word "restitution" can be twisted or tortured to cover the relief which the agency seeks in this case.

The holding of the Court is that neither the statute nor any other legislation gives the District Court jurisdiction to grant the relief sought. . . .

NOTES

1. *Other Authority.* The first case in which FDA relied on the Act's injunction authority to seek a court order directing the manufacturer of a misbranded product to reimburse purchasers was *United States v. Mytinger & Casselberry, Inc.,* 1938–1964 FDLI Jud. Rec. 1208 (S.D. Cal. 1951). That case was resolved by a consent decree that did not include a provision for restitution but it generated a substantial literature on the issue of legal authority. For the views of opposing counsel in that case, *compare* Levine, *Restitution—A New Enforcement Sanction,* 6 FDC L.J. 503 (1951), *with* Rhyne, *Penalty Through Publicity: FDA's Restitution Gambit,* 7 FDC L.J. 666 (1952). *See also* Williams, *If This Be Equity,* 10 FDC L.J. 92 (1955); Note, *Restitution in Food and Drug Enforcement,* 4 Stan. L. Rev. 519 (1952).

2. *FDA Practice.* FDA has not sought court-ordered restitution since the *Parkinson* decision. *See also Voluntary Recall Under Way on Over-Counter Sleeping Pills,* Wash. Post, June 9, 1979, § A, at 3, col. 5: " . . . Wayne Pines, a spokesman for the Food and Drug Administration, said it will be up to individual companies whether to reimburse consumers who have the drugs in their home medicine cabinets." *See generally* Wade and Kamenshine, *Restitution for Defrauded Consumers: Making the Remedy Effective Through Suit by Government Agency,* 37 Geo. Wash. L. Rev. 1031 (1969).

3. *Restitution under the Medical Device Amendments and the Radiation Act.* The Medical Device Amendments of 1976, in section 518 of the Act, gave FDA restitution authority respecting medical devices. *See* pp. 788–89 *supra.* Former section 359 of the Public Health Service Act, 42 U.S.C. § 263g, now recodified as section 535 of the FD&C Act, requires manufacturers of electronic products to notify purchasers of those products when safety defects are discovered and to repair the defect, replace the product, or refund the cost. Regulations implementing this provision appear in 21 C.F.R. Part 1004.

4. *Restitution by Other Agencies. Heater v. FTC,* 503 F.2d 321 (9th Cir. 1974), denied the FTC authority to order restitution. *See also* Sebert, *Obtaining Monetary Redress for Consumers Through Action by the Federal Trade Commission,* 57 Minn. L. Rev. 225 (1972). On the reasoning in *Heater,* authority to order restitution has also been denied to the CPSC under the Flammable Fabrics Act. *Congoleum Industries, Inc. v. CPSC,* 602 F.2d 220 (9th Cir. 1979). However, the CPSC has specific statutory restitution authority under the Federal Hazardous Substances Act, 15 U.S.C. § 1274, and the Consumer Product Safety Act, 15 U.S.C. § 2064.

5. *Animal Biologics.* The Animal Virus, Serum, and Toxin Act (VS&T Act), 21 U.S.C. § 151 *et seq.,* which was enacted in 1913, contains criminal penalties but no authority for injunctions. *Impro Products, Inc. v. Block,* 722

F.2d 845 (D.C. Cir. 1983), declined to find an "implied" civil remedy under the VS&T Act.

J. RECALLS

Since before passage of the 1938 Act FDA has used its own resources, and encouraged manufacturers, to recall illegal products from the market. The recall of the infamous Elixir Sulfanilamide accounted for 99.2 percent of the product manufactured. In 1947 the agency explained its practice:

> As soon as the [Food and Drug] Administration learns that a potentially injurious product has been distributed, its efforts to retrieve the suspect batches are abated only when every unit is accounted for. As far as possible this is accomplished through instigating adequate recalls by the shippers and checking upon their effectiveness and the safe disposition of the returned goods. When necessary, the goods are removed from consumer channels by individual visits to wholesale houses, retail drug stores, hospitals, and other consignees, with the very real assistance of State and local enforcement agencies whose efforts have been an important factor in the success of every major round-up. After the dangerous drugs have been accounted for, the firm involved is cited to a hearing with a view to criminal prosecution if the error was one which could have been avoided by good manufacturing practice or could have been corrected at an earlier stage.

FEDERAL SECURITY AGENCY, ANNUAL REPORT 525 (1947).

The Act itself, however, says nothing about recalls. FDA's prevailing practice, upon learning about an illegal product in commercial distribution, is to encourage the manufacturer to recall it from commercial channels, sometimes implying a threat of court enforcement. In a few cases, the agency has sought a court order to recall an illegal product.

UNITED STATES v. C. E. B. PRODUCTS, INC.
United States District Court, Northern District of Illinois, 1974.
380 F. Supp. 664.

DECKER, District Judge.

This suit was instituted on May 30, 1974, by the filing of a complaint and a motion for a temporary restraining order. The complaint alleges that defendants, a corporation and two of its officers, are engaged in causing the manufacture of an article of cosmetic ... designated by the name "Long Nails." Said cosmetic is claimed to be adulterated within the definition of 21 U.S.C. § 361(a) in that the

article contains a ("poisonous or deleterious substance")—methyl methacrylate monomer—"which may render it injurious to users under the
conditions of use prescribed in the labeling thereof, or under such
conditions of use as are customary or usual." ...

The Government's prayer for relief [in addition to seeking an
injunction against further distribution of the product] also requested
that the court order defendants to notify, all persons, down to the retail
level, to whom any of the cosmetic had been distributed, that the
product contained a poisonous or deleterious substance and to "direct
all such persons to return the article to the defendants." All parties,
and the court, have viewed that paragraph as a demand for a judicially-
ordered "recall" of those packages of Long Nails which may still be
sitting on store or warehouse shelves. Defendants strenuously object to
this demand, arguing that the court is without authority under the
Federal Food, Drug, and Cosmetic Act to order a recall, and that even if
such authority exists, the court should decline to enter such an order as
a matter of discretion....

The Government brought this suit for injunction pursuant to
section 302(a) of the Act.... A careful review of the FDCA in its
entirety reveals that this is the sole authorization for equitable relief.
And it is clear that nowhere in section 302(a) is recall specifically
mentioned. The section appears to contemplate only negative injunctions prohibiting statutory violations, rather than any sort of mandatory or affirmative relief.... Thus, no explicit statutory authorization
for either administrative or judicial recalls exists. The legislative
remedy of the Act apparently contains no reference to the recall
remedy. Indeed, the legislative background is of relatively minimal
assistance in determining congressional intent with respect to the
injunctive provision at all; section 302 caused little discussion.

Initially, it is noteworthy that the Federal Food and Drugs Act of
1906 contained no injunctive provision.... Thus, there existed no
injunctive precedent which Congress could be deemed to have approved
in section 302(a) or which could have guided Congress in shaping that
provision. Secondly, the scant legislative history which does exist
suggests, if anything, that Congress was concerned with the harshness
of the remedies upon manufacturers... [T]he House, at least, considered seizure to be the most severe remedy and that injunctive
proceedings were viewed as a means to alleviate the hardships seizures
might cause to manufacturers. Given this orientation, and the potential difficulties concomitant to a recall, it is difficult to conclude that
Congress intended section 302(a) to authorize judicial recalls.

Despite this congressional silence, recalls have played an increasingly significant role in the FDA's enforcement of the Act. Approximately 18 years ago, the agency initiated procedures for the voluntary
recall of violative products, as an alternative to seizures, prosecution,
and injunctive actions. In March, 1971, a subcommittee of the House
of Representatives Committee on Government Operations held a hear-

ing on these recall practices. Hearing on Recall Procedures of the Food and Drug Administration Before a Subcomm. of the House Comm. on Gov't Operations, 92d Cong., 1st Sess. (1971). Questioning of senior FDA officials made clear that neither the members of the subcommittee nor the FDA considered the Act to authorize judicial or administrative recalls. . . .

Only two cases have been discovered in the official reporters wherein recall was judicially sanctioned in litigation arising under section 302(a). In neither instance, however, did the court address the question at issue here. In *United States v. Lanpar Co.*, 293 F. Supp. 147 (N.D. Tex. 1968), the court merely entered findings of fact and conclusions of law and ordered the defendant drug company to recall and destroy certain reports, bulletins, and leaflets, and drugs containing combinations of digitalis and thyroid. The second case, *United States v. Lit Drug Co.*, 333 F. Supp. 990 (D.N.J. 1971), had been preceded by a history of 15 voluntary recalls of adulterated drugs by defendants. Significantly, the court expressly noted that "[d]efendants do not quarrel with the government demand for a recall of drugs. . . ."

In a somewhat analogous case to this one, *United States v. Parkinson*, [135 F.Supp. 208], heavily relied upon by defendant, the court determined that it lacked authority under section 302(a) to order the manufacturer of an adulterated product to make *restitution* to the purchasers of the product. (Both parties seem to agree that "restitution" and "recall" are different labels for essentially the same result.). .

It is clear that the FDCA establishes a specific, threefold enforcement scheme of injunctions, seizure, and criminal prosecutions. This system provides adequate before and after the fact remedies. Injunctive suits are appropriate for preventive relief, and criminal and seizure proceedings are available after the allegedly offending article has begun movement in interstate commerce. In seeking this recall, the government is asking for judicial sanction of an additional arrow for its already well-equipped bow. Although the institution of multiple seizure actions may be more burdensome than a single recall to the government, that alternative remains as a valid and frequently-used enforcement tool. Moreover, after studying the FDA's voluntary recall program, the aforementioned House subcommittee indicated its view on the efficacy of seizure by its statement that "the statute appears to provide *adequate authority to clear the market* of potentially dangerous or fraudulent products by seizure alone. . . ."

No Hobson's choice . . . is involved in the FDCA procedures. Congress may have considered the probability that the adulterated nature of a cosmetic may not become known until after its distribution in interstate commerce and its use by consumers, as appears to have been the case with "Long Nails." Furthermore, when the public danger is clear, the literature indicates that manufacturers are willing to institute their own recalls or to cooperate with the FDA in a recall effort.

Hobsons choice?

Thus, this court cannot conclude that "effective enforcement [of the Act] could ... only be expected," by interpreting section 302(a), or the statute in general and the circumstances surrounding its enactment, to allow the court to exercise its equitable powers to order a recall of adulterated products already on the market. This court is convinced that such an interpretation would constitute an unjustifiable judicial amendment of the FDCA....

However, even assuming that the statutory language and policy and the legislative history supported a judicially-ordered recall under section 302(a) or inherent equitable jurisdiction, this court, in the exercise of its equitable discretion, would decline to enter such an order. A balancing of the parties' interests, plus due regard for the public welfare, does not support recall relief. Although two hearings have been held in this matter, the case is still in a preliminary stage. A full trial on the merits remains for the future. With the case in this posture, a mandatory injunction should be issued only in exceptional circumstances.

Defendants have presented evidence to cast serious doubt upon the wisdom of ordering a recall. The uncontroverted testimony of the president of defendant C.E.B. Products, Inc., established that a recall would render the company insolvent and necessitate bankruptcy proceedings.... The injuries suffered by consumers, upon which proof was presented—nails splitting and falling off, redness, soreness, nail disfigurement, and infection—albeit serious and uncomfortable, are not of that severity and proportion to warrant the extraordinary remedy sought by the Government. It appears in most cases that the harm can be treated....

UNITED STATES v. K–N ENTERPRISES, INC.
United States District Court, Northern District of Illinois, 1978.
461 F. Supp. 988.

McMILLEN, District Judge.....

The Second Amended Complaint was filed pursuant to the civil enforcement provision of the Federal Food, Drug and Cosmetic Act. It seeks to preclude the manufacture and distribution of certain specified drugs and devices until the requirements of the statute and the Food and Drug Administration regulations have been satisfied. Defendants have voluntarily agreed to cease distribution of the drugs until further notice, but they have not agreed to cease distribution of the devices nor to recall any drugs or devices which have already been distributed. We find and conclude that the drugs covered by the Second Amended Complaint should be recalled and not further distributed or manufactured until the F.D.A. regulations have been complied with, but that further proceedings may be necessary to determine what specific types of compliance are necessary.....

The remaining contested issue concerns whether or not this court has the power to order the defendants to recall the two drugs which have not been properly approved or certified. There is no specific authority in the statute for requiring recalls. We are, however, granted the specific jurisdiction "to restrain violations of section 331." 21 U.S.C. § 332(a). The word "restrain" in our opinion is broad enough to cover affirmative or mandatory relief. . . .

More significantly, we believe that our general equity jurisdiction suffices for the authority to order a recall, since the statute by which we are given jurisdiction over this controversy does not preclude such relief. In *Porter v. Warner Holding Co.*, 328 U.S. 395 (1946), the court stated:

> . . . the court may go beyond the matters immediately underlying its equitable jurisdiction and decide whatever other issues and give whatever other relief may be necessary under the circumstances. Only in that way can equity do complete rather than truncated justice. . . .
>
> Moreover, the comprehensiveness of this equitable jurisdiction is not to be denied or limited in the absence of a clear and valid legislative command. Unless a statute in so many words, or by a necessary and inescapable inference restricts the court's jurisdiction in equity, the full scope of that jurisdiction is to be recognized and applied. . . .

Since we have no doubt that this court has the power to require defendants to recall the drugs, the remaining question is whether this equitable relief should be granted under the present circumstances. The potential harm to the public in consuming drugs which have not been approved or certified in accordance with the law is self-evident. . . . The damage possibly sustained by the defendants because of an improper recall is outweighed by this threatened harm and by their undisputed violation of §§ 351(a)(2), 355(a), and 357 of the Act.

The government is authorized by § 334(a) of the Act to seize the products; recall is considerably less burdensome to the government and hardly more burdensome to the manufacturer, who contends that few or any drugs remain in commerce. These considerations were lacking in *United States v. C. E. B. Products, Inc.*, in which recall was denied not solely because of lack of power in the District Court but also because of a failure to find that the public and not the defendant would be irreparably damaged. We find not only irreparable damage to the public in the case at bar, but also that the damage to the public greatly outweighs the potential damage to the defendants. . . .

NOTES

1. *Supporting Authority.* In *United States v. X–Otag Plus Tablets*, 441 F. Supp. 105 (D.Colo. 1977), the court agreed with the *C.E.B. Products* decision and held that it had no authority to order a recall of marketed drugs. The government did not challenge that holding on appeal, 602 F.2d 1387 (10th Cir.

1979). FDA was also denied a recall order in *United States v. Superpharm Corp.*, 530 F. Supp. 408 (E.D.N.Y. 1981), where the court concluded that the "statutory remedies provide for sufficient means to enforce the act, and the legislative history and the Act itself manifest a reluctance to expand enforcement powers to the point where they are punitive." The court stated that "no resort to, or expansion of, the court's equitable power is needed to remove these drugs from interstate commerce."

2. *Consent Devices.* Courts have included recall requirements in other injunctions sought by FDA without challenge by the defendants. *See, e.g., United States v. Lit Drug Co.*, 333 F. Supp. 990 (D.N.J. 1971); *United States v. Lanpar Co.*, 293 F. Supp. 147 (N.D. Tex. 1968); *Reich v. United States*, 239 F.2d 134 (1st Cir. 1956). In *United States v. Spectro Foods Corp.*, 544 F.2d 1175 (3d Cir. 1976), the Third Circuit found it unnecessary to decide whether the Act authorizes a recall order because, in that case, the recall order was not supported by specific findings of irreparable injury.

In 36 Fed. Reg. 11514 (June 15, 1971), FDA issued its first formal statement of policy on product recalls. That statement was withdrawn in 38 Fed. Reg. 27592 (October 5, 1973). The agency's recall policy was subsequently published in both its REGULATORY PROCEDURES MANUAL and COMPLIANCE POLICY GUIDE, as announced in 41 Fed. Reg. 8408 (February 26, 1976), pending development of comprehensive recall regulations.

ENFORCEMENT POLICY, PRACTICES AND PROCEDURES: RECALL POLICY AND PROCEDURES

41 Federal Register 26924 (June 30, 1976).

Most manufacturers and distributors of products subject to the jurisdiction of FDA have long recognized their responsibility to market safe and properly labeled products and to take measures to protect the public from adulterated and misbranded products that have already reached the marketplace. Indeed, it is not unusual for a firm, when it learns that a distributed product is defective, to take steps to correct the situation by removing the product from commerce or by remedying the defect. The Commissioner generally regards such responsible, voluntary action as an acceptable alternative to an agency-initiated seizure of the defective product.

Most firms honor FDA requests to recall violative foods, drugs, devices, cosmetics, or biologics. . . . Thus, the recall policy and procedures of FDA are, in part, founded upon the cooperation of firms and their willingness to remove violative products from the marketplace. While the act does not explicitly mention recalls, the statutory sanctions available to FDA have a vital role in a firm's willingness to recall and support the development of recall as a major FDA regulatory tool. In those cases where a firm refuses to undertake a recall when requested to do so by FDA or where the agency has reason to believe that a recall would not be effective, FDA may initiate seizure and/or seek an injunction. Criminal prosecution may also be initiated. Therefore, protection of public health and welfare, which is the purpose of recalls, is not predicated solely on the principle of industry cooperation....

The Commissioner is proposing these regulations to define more clearly FDA recall policy and procedures and to provide guidance to the regulated industry so that firms may more effectively discharge their responsibility to remove or correct violative products in commerce. The proposed regulations are authorized by section 701(a) of the Federal Food, Drug, and Cosmetic Act ... and sections 301, 351, and 361 of the Public Health Service Act (42 U.S.C. §§ 241, 262, and 264) relating to cooperative programs for the protection of the public health, to biological products, and to interstate quarantine. The provisions of the proposed regulations that describe responsibilities of recalling firms consist of guidelines rather than enforceable requirements. In this respect, the proposed regulations do not exhaust the authority of FDA to prevent the introduction of violative products into commercial channels, facilitate recalls by manufacturers, and enable the agency to monitor recalls. If experience under the final regulations proves that mandatory requirements are necessary, the Commissioner will propose appropriate revisions.

Product recall has evolved over the years as the most expeditious and effective method of removing violative products from the marketplace, particularly those that present a danger to health....

Public notification of recalls became routine in 1967 through the initiation of the weekly "FDA Enforcement Report," formally titled the "Food and Drug Administration Weekly Report of Seizures, Prosecutions, Injunctions, Field Corrections and Recalls." When this report was published, all product removal actions were considered to be recalls, regardless of the seriousness of the violation involved or whether a violation actually existed. Consequently, the number of recalls increased greatly, and it became increasingly difficult for the agency to monitor recalls effectively. In addition, the public's sense of urgency that should be associated with certain recalls was diminished because of the lack of a clear differentiation between recalls that involved health hazards or other significant violations, and those that did not....

... [A]nother problem with recall procedures was [later] identified. Over the years, FDA had frequently found it necessary to assume part or all of the burden of implementing recalls. This sometimes imposed extremely heavy and unwarranted drains on the agency's resources....

FDA-initiated recalls. There are two types of FDA-initiated recalls. First, when the agency determines that a marketed product violates the law and so informs the responsible firm, a later recall of the product by that firm is considered an "FDA-initiated recall," even though such action has not been specifically requested by the agency. Second, when use of the product presents a danger to health or significant consumer deception and immediate action is necessary, the Commissioner or his designee will formally notify the firm of this determination and of the need to begin immediately a recall of the product. Because the latter type of FDA-initiated recall is an urgent matter and must be used judiciously, the decision to request a recall shall be made only by the Commissioner or his designee.

Firm-initiated recall. A firm may, for a variety of reasons, on its own initiative remove, correct or otherwise dispose of an illegal product that it has distributed in commerce. FDA has clear authority to require notification that a firm has initiated a recall of new drugs, new animal drugs, biologics, foods subject to emergency permit control, electronic products subject to the Radiation Control for Health and Safety Act, and articles subject to interstate quarantine regulations. However, the Commissioner also believes it serves the public interest for firms to notify FDA when a recall of any other FDA-regulated product is initiated....

The proposed regulations also provide that the Commissioner will continue the policy of making available to the public information on all recalls by routinely issuing the weekly "FDA Enforcement Report." ... The report is not, however, intended to serve, nor is it used by the agency, as a form of public warning or as a means of seeking publicity in the news media....

A recall involves several separate but related steps that are taken by recalling firms and by FDA. These include: evaluation of the health hazard associated with the product being recalled or being considered for recall; developing and following a recall strategy (described below in this preamble); recall communications to a firm's customers; periodic reports on the progress of the recall; and finally, termination of the recall and proper disposition or correction of the violative product. The combined purpose of these steps is to assure that a recall is conducted in a manner that achieves the orderly removal or correction of a violative product to the extent necessary to protect public health....

Recall strategy. Each recall, whether FDA-initiated or firm-initiated, requires devising a specific course of action to implement the recall....

1. Depth of recall. This element refers to the level of product distribution to which the recall is to extend. There are three basic options: (1) Consumer or user level (which may vary with product); (2) retail level; or (3) wholesale level....

2. Public warnings. This element of the recall strategy refers to FDA-issued warnings to the public about a product in consumer channels that is being recalled. The purpose of a public warning is to alert consumers or users that a product presents a serious hazard to health....

3. Effectiveness checks. The third element of recall strategy involves verification that consignees (recipients of a product being

recalled) have been notified of the recall and have taken appropriate action ... [which is] a vital part of the overall responsibility of recalling firms. For FDA to routinely carry out industry's task of assuring recall effectiveness would represent misuse of public funds. However ... FDA will monitor the efforts of a firm to effect a recall, and where necessary, will initiate its own effectiveness checks....

Because the Commissioner considers recalls to be primarily the responsibility of manufacturers and distributors of regulated products, this notice describes ways in which they should carry out this responsibility, which can be summarized in the following steps:

1.   Develop a contingency plan for a recall.

2.   Develop the capability of tracing product distribution and identifying the product being recalled.

3.   Promptly notify FDA when products are being removed or corrected ... and provide the agency with pertinent information on these actions.

4.   Initiate a recall when it is requested by FDA.

5.   Develop and follow a recall strategy for handling any recall situation.

6.   Assume the responsibility and expense of conducting all aspects of a recall, including effectiveness checks.

7.   Notify all consignees of initiated recalls.

8.   Evaluate the circumstances causing the violation and take steps to prevent recurrence of violations and future recalls.

9.   Provide periodic reports to FDA on the progress of the recall.

10.   When a recall is completed, certify to FDA that the recall has been effective and that final disposition of the recalled product has been made....

NOTES

1.   *Recall Regulations.* FDA's final recall regulations, 43 Fed. Reg. 26202 (June 16, 1978), are codified in 21 C.F.R. §§ 7.40 et seq. The detailed FDA policy regarding product recall is set forth in chapter 5–00 of the agency's REGULATORY PROCEDURES MANUAL.

2.   *Infant Formula Recalls.* The Infant Formula Act of 1980, 94 Stat. 1190, included a provision in section 412 of the FD&C Act directing FDA to prescribe the scope and extent of recalls of infant formulas necessary and appropriate for the degree of risk to human health. In accordance with this provision, FDA established infant formula recall requirements in 47 Fed. Reg. 2231 (January 15, 1982), 47 Fed. Reg. 18832 (April 30, 1982). The 1980 statute was further strengthened by the Alcohol and Drug Abuse Amendments of 1986, 100 Stat. 3207, 3207, which added the provision now found in section 412(e)(1) requiring a manufacturer to take all actions necessary to recall an infant formula if FDA determines that it presents a risk to human health. Following passage of the 1986 statute, FDA promulgated additional recall regulations in

52 Fed. Reg. 30171 (August 13, 1987), 54 Fed. Reg. 4006 (January 27, 1989), 54 Fed. Reg. 11518 (March 21, 1989), codified in 21 C.F.R. Part 107.

3. *USDA Recall Policy.* FDA and USDA have entered into a Memorandum of Understanding to coordinate their responsibilities for food recalls, published in 40 Fed. Reg. 25079 (June 12, 1975). USDA subsequently announced in 44 Fed. Reg. 56732 (October 2, 1979) the availability of its own internal directive concerning recalls.

4. *Commentary.* There is an extensive literature on FDA recall authority and policy. *See, e.g.,* Bozeman, *Recalls—On Making the Best of a Bad Thing,* 33 FDC L.J. 342 (1978); Harkins, *Product Recall,* 31 FDC L.J. 383 (1976); Kasperson, *Recalls Revisited,* 29 Bus. Law. 631 (1974); Papers Presented at the 27th Annual Meeting of the Food, Drug and Cosmetic Law Section of the New York State Bar Association, reprinted in 27 FDC L.J. 332–354 (1972); A Symposium on the Recall of Food Products presented at the 32nd Annual Meeting of the Institute of Food Technologists, reprinted in 27 FDC L.J. 660–736 (1972).

GENERAL ACCOUNTING OFFICE, LACK OF AUTHORITY LIMITS CONSUMER PROTECTION: PROBLEMS IN IDENTIFYING AND REMOVING FROM THE MARKET PRODUCTS WHICH VIOLATE THE LAW

Report No. B–16 4031(2) (1972).

FDA has had difficulties in removing defective products from markets because it lacks the authority to:

• obtain access to records needed to identify, examine, and remove products suspected or known to be defective ...;

• detain products from interstate shipment until determination can be made whether they should be removed from the market; and

• take steps required to withdraw them....

Methods available to FDA for removing from the market products suspected or known to be defective—called seizures and recalls—often are not effective....

A food firm found that some of its canned products contained botulism, a deadly poison. Had FDA been required to seize the product at each location, over 25,000 separate seizure actions would have been needed. The firm agreed to recall the product, and there was responsive cooperation from other concerned public and private interests in removing the product from the market. However, because of financial problems, the firm believed it could not honor the agreement. FDA found it necessary to seize the product at 100 different places.

... Voluntary recalls ... have a disadvantage in that there is no law requiring such removal actions. Because FDA cannot enforce recalls, they are a matter of negotiation between industry and FDA and can be delayed or ineffectively carried out by the companies involved.

GAO's review of 106 recalls requested by three FDA district offices during fiscal year 1971 showed that an average of 15 days passed before the firm acted on FDA's request. Of the recalls, 23 percent required more than 25 days to initiate. In these cases GAO found that an average of 38 percent of the product was sold during the delay. A firm produced a prescription drug that did not meet Federal standards for dissolution. After FDA notified the company of the defective product, the firm took 55 days to initiate the recall. During this period, about 75,000 of the defective tablets were sold.

FDA should have authority to order recalls when products are found to be defective....

NOTES

1. *Device Recalls.* GAO was critical of FDA's medical device recalls in MEDICAL DEVICE RECALLS: AN OVERVIEW AND ANALYSIS 1983–88, PEMD–89–15BR (August 1989); MEDICAL DEVICE RECALLS: EXAMINATION OF SELECTED CASES, PEMD–90–6 (October 1989). In 55 Fed. Reg. 21108 (May 22, 1990), FDA announced the availability of a report analyzing device quality problems that led to recalls during 1983–1988, to help identify areas where additional control should be emphasized.

2. *Statutory Recall Authority.* FDA has never vigorously sought legislation giving it power to order recalls administratively, fearing that such authority would almost certainly be encumbered by procedural requirements that would effectively frustrate its exercise. The U.S. Administrative Conference, however, has recommended that Congress give FDA additional enforcement tools to detain products administratively prior to filing a seizure, to seek court-ordered recalls, and to seek civil penalties. 49 Fed. Reg. 9904 (March 16, 1984); 49 Fed. Reg. 29937 (July 25, 1984). *See also* Note, *The Food and Drug Administration's Recall Power After United States v. C.E.B. Products, Inc.: The Need to Amend the Food, Drug, and Cosmetic Act,* 69 Nw. U. L. Rev. 936 (1975).

3. *GAO Advice.* For specific suggestions regarding FDA recall procedures, *see* GAO, LEGISLATIVE CHANGES AND ADMINISTRATIVE IMPROVEMENTS SHOULD BE CONSIDERED FOR FDA TO BETTER PROTECT THE PUBLIC FROM ADULTERATED FOOD PRODUCTS, No. HRD–84–61 (September 26, 1984); FDA'S OVERSIGHT OF THE 1982 CANNED SALMON RECALLS, No. HRD–84–77 (September 12, 1984).

K. INFORMAL ENFORCEMENT

Section 306 of the Act permits FDA to decline to institute formal enforcement proceedings for "minor violations of this Act whenever [it] believes that the public interest will be adequately served by a suitable written notice or warning." The Supreme Court has cited section 306 in rejecting arguments against literal interpretation of the Act's broader provisions. *See, e.g., United States v. Dotterweich,* 320 U.S. 277 (1943); *United States v. Sullivan,* 332 U.S. 689 (1948); *United States v. Park,* 421 U.S. 658 (1975); *Heckler v. Chaney,* 470 U.S. 821 (1985).

Defendants have invoked it as the basis for challenging FDA's initiation of enforcement proceedings. The Court in *United States v. Hunter Pharmacy, Inc.,* 213 F. Supp. 323 (S.D.N.Y. 1963), responded to such an argument as follows:

> The defendants claim that the failure of the administrative agency to implement section 306 of the Act is denial of due process.... The determination of whether a violation is of such a nature as not to require criminal prosecution to vindicate the public interest is entrusted to the judgment of the Secretary. In the instant case, the reference of the matter to the United States Attorney for prosecution is indication that he deems the offenses as other than "minor," or that he believes the public interest will not be adequately safeguarded by a warning. The statute nowhere commands, with respect to this section, that he establish rules and regulations for procedures to determine whether a warning instead of a prosecution of injunction serves to vindicate the public interest. The statute itself indicates the matter rests in his discretion.

FDA has cited section 306 as authority for the issuance of informal tolerances for filth and other contaminants in food. *See United States v. 900 Cases ... Peaches,* 390 F. Supp. 1006 (E.D.N.Y. 1975), *aff'd without opinion sub nom. United States v. Noroian,* 556 F.2d 562 (2d Cir. 1977); *United States v. Ewig Bros. Co.,* 502 F.2d 715 (7th Cir. 1974); *United States v. Goodman,* 486 F.2d 847 (7th Cir. 1973); *United States v. 484 Bags, More or Less,* 423 F.2d 839 (5th Cir. 1970); *Dean Rubber Mfg. Co. v. United States,* 356 F.2d 161 (8th Cir. 1966); *United States v. 1,500 Cases, More or Less, Tomato Paste,* 236 F.2d 208 (7th Cir. 1956); *United States v. 449 Cases, Containing "Tomato Paste,"* 212 F.2d 567 (2d Cir. 1954); *Caribbean Produce Exchange, Inc. v. Department of HHS,* Food Drug Cosm. L. Rep. (CCH) ¶ 38,110 (D.P.R. 1988), *rev'd on other grounds,* 893 F.2d 3 (1st Cir. 1989); *United States v. 233 Tins ... "Grove Brand Whole Blakemore Strawberries,"* 175 F. Supp. 694 (W.D. Ark. 1959).

There are, however, limits to FDA's discretion under section 306 to refrain from initiating enforcement against violations of the Act. In March 1979 in response to an inquiry from the Secretaries of HEW and Agriculture, the Attorney General provided the following opinion on FDA's discretion in regulating nitrite in foods.

MEMORANDUM FOR THE ATTORNEY GENERAL
Re: Proposed Phasing Out of Nitrites in Foods
43 Opinions of the Attorney General No. 19 (March 30, 1979).

The Secretary of HEW, acting through the Commissioner of FDA, proposes, should he finally determine that the addition of nitrites adulterates foods under his jurisdiction within the meaning of the Food and Drug Act, to exercise enforcement discretion to permit nitrites to be added to these foods over the period of gradual and indefinite phasing out of their use....

... We are informed that FDA intends, based on the evidence of the carcinogenicity of nitrites, to initiate proceedings to revoke existing food additive regulations authorizing their addition in certain products. If it determines as a result of this process that nitrites are an unsafe food additive, FDA, to implement the proposed phasing out of nitrites, would replace these food additives regulations with regulations specifying the schedule and details of the suggested "phase-out" of the use of nitrites, which, in effect will permit the continued addition of nitrites until a feasible substitute is developed. These regulations would not be food additive regulations, but a formalization of FDA's enforcement policy.... The "phase-out" regulations, as prepared by FDA, would be designed to permit the addition of nitrites up to the levels deemed necessary to prevent the development of *Clostridium botulinum* until the time that feasible alternative methods of prevention are developed.

For the reasons that follow, we do not believe that the proposed phasing out through the withholding of enforcement is consistent with the Secretary's obligations under the Act....

The proposed regulations withholding enforcement for an indefinite and probably extended period of time with respect to the addition of nitrites up to a certain level would, according to FDA, be issued pursuant to 21 U.S.C. § 371(a) (1976), which authorizes the Secretary of HEW to issue regulations for the "efficient enforcement" of the Food and Drug Act. But a grant of authority such as this is only "the power to adopt regulations to carry into effect the will of Congress as expressed by the statute." ... The regulations proposed here would ignore the statutory requirement of a finding to a reasonable certainty that no harm will result from the addition of a food additive and constitute the establishment of a tolerance in direct contravention of the evident congressional judgment that there should be no tolerance for substances found, after appropriate tests, to induce cancer in man or animal. Such regulations would therefore not be consistent with the Food and Drug Act or further its "efficient enforcement."

FDA suggests, however, that while the Delaney Clause states an unequivocal standard with respect to the approval or disapproval of a food additive, it establishes no particular time frame or other requirements or procedures for the implementation or enforcement of a ban of a substance found to cause cancer....

We do not believe that the scope of the Commissioner's implementation and enforcement discretion may be so readily divorced from the substantive provisions he is implementing and enforcing. The evident purpose of the Delaney Clause is to prohibit the *use* of additives which induce cancer in test animals, not merely to furnish a procedural guidepost for the Commissioner in issuing or revoking regulations....

We may assume that section 348(f)(3) does grant the Commissioner some discretion to establish a reasonable effective date for a final order revoking an existing food additive regulation, and that a delayed effective date therefore might result in the continued use of an unsafe additive prior to that date. It would be a considerable leap, however, to conclude that this statutory language providing that an order may not go into effect for 90 days authorizes the Commissioner to permit continued use of a substance over a period of years....

... The phasing out proposal would apparently involve the final revocation of existing food additive regulations and substitution of other regulations setting forth the levels of nitrite which will not trigger enforcement by FDA. This, it is suggested, would constitute a permissible exercise of enforcement discretion. We disagree....

We may assume that faithful execution of the laws ordinarily does permit the exercise of judgment in deciding how best to implement the law in the myriad of factual situations with which an agency is confronted.... There are, for example, particular cases arising under any statutory scheme in which an alleged violation is merely minor and technical or difficult of proof or in which the prudent allocation of resources or equitable factors weigh against the initiation of administrative, civil, or criminal proceedings, even where it appears there may have been a violation of the literal terms of the statute....

Congress expressly sanctioned at least a degree of this type of discretion in ... [section 306].... The purpose of this provision was described by the Senate Committee as follows:

> Violations of the law sometimes occur which are of technical or formal nature only and which do not result in deception or other imposition on public welfare. Usually such violations are inadvertent and their correction can be promptly effected by calling them to the attention of the manufacturer. This section would authorize the enforcing agency to follow this course. It is not intended that this procedure should apply where the violation is more than merely technical and becomes one of substance rather than form. In no event is the conventional legal procedure denied if such action is necessary to effect compliance.

S. Rep. No. 361, 74th Cong., 1st Sess. 28–29 (1935)....

The FDA has informed you that it would not regard the deliberate, continued additions of a carcinogenic substance to food—even at a controlled level—as minor violations within the meaning of 21 U.S.C. § 336 (1976). This conclusion is compatible with the legislative history of the Delaney Clause expressing a clear congressional purpose to prevent the establishment of *any* tolerance level for a substance found to cause cancer when ingested by man or animals. Such violations would appear to be one of "substance rather than form" for which enforcement "action is necessary to effect compliance." Therefore, the proposed phasing out of nitrite use does not conform to the scope of enforcement discretion contemplated by the Congress when it enacted the Food and Drug Act....

The proposed phasing out of nitrites through the withholding of enforcement ... would not be a mere formalization of FDA policy on the allocation of scarce enforcement resources, an identification of minor violations, or an effort to give content or limits to a vague statute. The effect of the policy—indeed its purpose—would be to authorize the continued use of nitrites in certain products under circumstances that would concededly constitute non-minor violations of the specific terms of the Food and Drug Act....

The public health considerations underlying the desire to permit the continued addition of nitrites and nitrates to certain foods are clearly important. But the balancing of these competing health risks is a matter for the Congress in determining whether to amend the Food and Drug Act, not for the Secretary in administering the law....

NOTE

For discussion of FDA discretion to enforce the FD&C Act, *see Heckler v. Chaney,* 470 U.S. 821 (1985); *United States v. Undetermined Quantities of an Article of Drug Labeled as Exachol,* 716 F. Supp. 787 (S.D.N.Y. 1989); *Heterochemical Corp. v. FDA,* 644 F. Supp. 271 (E.D.N.Y. 1986).

Historically, FDA relied primarily upon seizure and other formal court proceedings to enforce the FD&C Act. Beginning in the early 1970s, however, the agency developed regulatory letters and other informal compliance correspondence as alternatives to court enforcement.

ENFORCEMENT POLICY FOR CERTAIN COMPLIANCE CORRESPONDENCE

43 Federal Register 27498 (June 23, 1978).

If FDA had unlimited resources, it would seek to pursue all violations vigorously. Practically, of course, unlimited resources are not available. Consequently, decisions must be made regarding the relative priority of industry-wide compliance programs. Similar decisions must be made as to which individual offenders and violative products should be proceeded against and the type of regulatory action to be taken. In some cases it may be sufficient simply to notify individuals and firms that they are in violation of the law. In other cases it may be necessary to invoke administrative and/or judicial sanctions. The Commissioner believes that in enacting section 306 of the act (21 U.S.C. 336), Congress fully intended the FDA exercise such judgment....

Notification of violations is given in several ways. Probably the most important is the use of letters to bring adverse findings to the attention of management. In addition, the agency published regulations, holds instructional workshops and meetings, works with individual firms in identifying critical areas in production and quality control, provides written guidance through advisory opinions, publishes various instructional materials and aids, and publicizes requirements for compliance.

Since 1972, the agency has used two types of letters: The Regulatory Letter and the Report of Inspectional Finding (also known as Information Letter). While the primary purpose of both letters was to solicit prompt correction by management, neither letter was intended to commit the agency to take legal action if the necessary remedial measures were not undertaken.... The agency's current regulatory philosophy ... provides that seizure and/or injunction would be obviated by adequate voluntary corrective action, but that correction would not necessarily preclude criminal prosecution, or civil penalties....

The Commissioner has reviewed the agency's current policy and procedures relating to Regulatory and Information Letters and has concluded that they should be clarified and modified. Therefore, the Commissioner is proposing to redefine and establish new nomenclature for correspondence designed to stimulate voluntary remedial action. Notices of Adverse Findings will generally replace Information Letters; the terminology for Regulatory Letters will remain the same. Under the new policy, when the agency issues a Regulatory Letter and voluntary corrective action is not promptly taken, judicial and/or administrative proceedings will generally be instituted....

... It is the policy of the agency that, once uncovered, a violation should be promptly brought to the attention of management officials responsible for the unlawful practice, condition, or product. Although the first notification may be a seizure, injunction, or publication of a FEDERAL REGISTER notice (*e.g.*, notice of opportunity for hearing), it is most often conveyed to responsible management by means of official correspondence. It is important, therefore, that responsible individuals understand that a Notice of Adverse Findings indicates FDA's awareness of a violation that must be corrected. It also indicates that the agency is requesting voluntary correction without having made any final decision on whether to commence administrative or legal action....

A Notice of Adverse Findings leaves the agency with flexibility in determining whether or not to proceed with administrative or legal action.... [A] Regulatory Letter represents a "promise to sue" on the part of FDA. Regulatory Letters are most likely to be issued to bring about prompt correction of violations posing a hazard to health and violations involving economic deception. A Regulatory Letter will not be issued when the agency has reason to believe the violation is intentional, flagrant, part of a history of similar or substantially similar conduct, or indicates a callous disregard for potential consequences to the health or safety of the consumer. In these instances, the agency will move immediately to institute administrative action and/or request court enforcement action....

NOTES

1. *Evolution of Agency Policy.* FDA later withdrew this proposal, 45 Fed. Reg. 60449 (September 12, 1980), and established its policy on compliance correspondence in chapters 8–10 of the REGULATORY PROCEDURES MANUAL instead. When FDA devised regulatory letters they were intended to represent final statements of enforcement policy subject to court challenge. The agency has since characterized regulatory letters as informal correspondence, which do not constitute final agency action, and the courts have agreed. *E.g., Biotics Research Corp. v. Heckler,* 710 F.2d 1375 (9th Cir. 1983); pp. 1261–62 *infra.* This policy change occurred because the Office of Chief Counsel has no control over the issuance of regulatory letters and thus is not prepared routinely to defend them in court.

2. *Commentary. See* Lambert, *Recalls, Regulatory Letters and Publicity— Quasi–Statutory Remedies,* 31 FDC L.J. 360 (1976); Pines, *Regulatory Letters, Publicity and Recalls,* 31 FDC L.J. 352 (1976).

L. PUBLICITY

ARTHUR KALLET & F.J. SCHLINK, 100,000,000 GUINEA PIGS

(1933).

We, as citizens and victims of poisonous and fraudulently labeled food and medicine, have a right to know exactly what goes on and under what pressures and influences. We have a right to demand an instant reversal of the policy set down in a letter of the chief of drug control:

> "The Administration cannot with propriety discuss products manufactured by other concerns with representatives *other than those of the company.* [Italics ours.] We are authorized to publish notices of judgment after court action has been caused [*completed* is evidently the meaning] giving the Government's analysis and the findings of the court."

... Director Campbell of the Administration is quoted as saying, in explaining the adoption of the newer corrective and educational as against the punitive policy which the law provides, that "the pure food laws provide for such mild penalties that a manufacturer could pay the fines imposed the same as he pays insurance and continue to do wrong." ... Mr. Campbell says that they do not fear the small fine; it is the publicity they fear. But the Department often does not give publicity at all, or only so long after the case is brought that all current news significance with respect to the adulteration or misbranding practices of a manufacturer is lost. Clearly, under this line of meaning, the manufacturers have precisely nothing to fear. The fines actually assessed are too small, and the dreaded publicity which is "the real punishment" does not take place....

Unlike many regulatory laws, which leave the matter to implication, the FD&C Act in section 705 expressly authorizes the issuance of information to the public. Moreover, section 301(b) of the PHS Act, 42 U.S.C. § 242o, provides:

> From time to time the Secretary shall issue information related to public health, in the form of publications or otherwise, for the use of the public, and shall publish weekly reports of health conditions in the United States and other countries and other pertinent health information for the use of persons and institutions concerned with health services.

HOXSEY CANCER CLINIC v. FOLSOM

United States District Court, District of Columbia, 1957.
155 F. Supp. 376.

HOLTZOFF, District Judge.

The Food and Drug Administration has issued a circular, copies of which are being posted in post offices throughout the country, warning the public that the so-called Hoxsey cancer treatment has been found worthless insofar as internal cancer is concerned. It also warns those afflicted with cancer not to be misled by the false promise that the Hoxsey cancer treatment will cure or alleviate their condition. This action is brought by Harry M. Hoxsey who claims to have treated patients afflicted with cancer, to enjoin the Secretary of the Department of Health, Education, and Welfare, and the Commissioner of the Food and Drug Administration, against the dissemination of this poster.

The defendants claim that they are acting pursuant to the authority of [Section 705(b) of the FD&C Act]. . . .

It is claimed in behalf of the plaintiff that the statute to which reference has just been made is unconstitutional as a denial of due process or law in that it does not provide for any notice or hearing, administrative or otherwise, before the Secretary disseminates information of the type described in the statute. It is elementary law, of course, that an order of an administrative agency adjudicating rights or directing someone to do or refrain from doing something must be based on a hearing after due notice. Here, however, the situation is entirely different. The defendants have made no order; they are issuing no directions. What they are doing is disseminating information and warning the public against the use of certain medicines and of a certain treatment for internal cancer. There is no basis for requiring a hearing before information can be disseminated.

But beyond that, even in the absence of this statute there would be nothing to prevent the defendants from disseminating information to the public. . . . The defendants are performing a public duty when they are urging the use of certain treatments or warning the public against the use of certain treatments. The only purpose of this statute is to place within the express scope of the duties of the Secretary something that was one of his implied functions.

If, however, the contents of the poster were erroneous then the question might arise whether they were libelous. It is a well settled rule of equity that equity does not enjoin a libel or slander, and that the only remedy for libel or slander is an action for damages if the libelous character of a statement to which objection is made can be established.... Naturally in a libel suit the question would arise whether there is absolute or conditional privilege, and those questions are not before the Court at this time....

AJAY NUTRITION FOODS, INC. v. FDA

United States District Court, District of New Jersey, 1974.
378 F. Supp. 210, *aff'd*, 523 F.2d 625.

COOLAHAN, District Judge.

This is an action against the Food and Drug Administration ... brought as a class action by the corporate plaintiffs, who are engaged in the sale and distribution of health food products.... Plaintiffs sue to enjoin defendants from issuing certain press releases and public announcements that are alleged to be damaging to their businesses, and ask the Court to award damages totaling $500 million....

The action centers on events contemporaneous with publication by the FDA of regulations affecting the health food "industry." ...

Specifically, plaintiffs state that certain "press releases, public announcements and other communications" issued by the FDA "have resulted in the deprivation of property without due process of law and the wrongful and unlawful interference with the rights of the plaintiffs and the other members of the class to carry on a business." Plaintiffs allege that the class has been referred to as "nutrition quacks," "food faddists," "health quacks," and that the products that are produced have been referred to as "shotgun mixtures." Further, plaintiffs claim that the FDA has sought to discredit certain fastly held tenets of health food enthusiasts. Lastly, plaintiffs allege that the FDA statements "are knowingly and maliciously false and untrue and not justified by any fair balance of competing social interest ... [they are] not factual, but rather represent character attacks by the defendants." ...

The Government's position is that the *Barr v. Mateo* doctrine [360 U.S. 564 (1959)] compels a judgment for the defendants in the case at bar. The Government relies heavily upon the fact that the issuance of press releases to the public is a duty of the Commissioner of the FDA that is mandated by Congress....

The plaintiffs have sought to diminish the legal effect of defendant's § 375 mandate by arguing that "the damage claim is not only based on libel and slander, but ... is also grounded on the wrongful actions of the defendants which deprived the plaintiffs of property without due process of law and which interfered with their right to seek effective judicial review." The plaintiffs have, in the view of this court, advanced this argument because of their failure to overcome *Barr v. Matteo* in respect to plaintiff's accusations grounded in libel. A due process claim separate from a claim of libel is possible only if plaintiffs are prepared to allege that the statements of the FDA, *even if true,* would be a violation of defendants' executive authority. If this is in fact the plaintiffs' contention, the proper forums for resolution of the issue are the United States Courts of Appeals under the authority of Courts of Appeals to rule on the validity of administrative regulations in an administrative law context.

Plaintiffs further aver that § 375(b) did not afford a mandate to the defendants here "because the type of references to plaintiffs and other members of the class set forth in the complaint can hardly represent the dissemination of ... information contemplated by Congress. It is submitted that the health food industry, taken as a whole, does not involve gross deception of the consumer nor imminent danger to health." To counter this argument the Government has demonstrated that the press release statements that plaintiffs have found so objectionable stem directly from the published tentative orders. This Court is satisfied that the Government's contentions in respect to this issue are correct; the statements in the press release are consistent with and stem from the same investigations that led to the proposed regulations. A challenge to the press release as broad as that presented by the plaintiffs here is in effect a challenge on the proposed regulations.

But, even if the press release were not related to the proposed administrative regulations, the plaintiffs' complaint would still necessitate dismissal.... The *Barr v. Matteo* privilege exists as long as a press release constitutes "standard agency practice." Plaintiffs' complaint fails to allege that there has been a deviation from recognized agency practice, unless it can be shown that use of the words "quacks," "faddists," and "shotgun mixtures" constitutes a deviation. While the Government contends in its brief that such words were never used, for purposes of this motion the Court must assume those allegations to be true.

The Court holds that the alleged "defamation" of the "health food industry" through use by the Government of the terms "quacks," "faddists," and "shotgun mixtures," is not actionable under common law principles even were the *Barr v. Matteo* doctrine not available to the Government here. While it is true that a corporation may have a cause of action in defamation, this Court holds that an entire industry, such as the health food processing industry, cannot sue on grounds of defamation....

... The class involved, in plaintiffs' words, "so numerous that it is impracticable to bring [all members] before the Court," is much too broad to require the protection of a court order, particularly in view of the legitimate function of Government to inform the public of business abuses.

For the foregoing reasons the Government's motion to dismiss should be granted....

Based upon Gellhorn, *Adverse Publicity By Administrative Agencies*, 86 Harv. L. Rev. 1380 (1973), the U.S. Administrative Conference adopted recommendations respecting the use of publicity by regulatory agencies. The primary recommendation was that agencies should adopt regulations describing the circumstances and appropriate content of agency publicity, particularly that related to pending administrative or judicial proceedings, and providing a procedure for retraction or correction of erroneous publicity. *See* Recommendation 73–1: Adverse Agency Publicity, 38 Fed. Reg. 16839 (June 27, 1973).

The Department of HEW responded to the Conference's recommendation by adopting regulations, proposed in 39 Fed. Reg. 28643 (August 9, 1974) and codified at 45 C.F.R. Part 17, which apply to FDA as well as other departmental components. The preamble to the final regulations, 41 Fed. Reg. 2 (January 2, 1976), stated:

> ... It is ... Department policy to avoid issuance of statements by an agency or its personnel which invite public attention to an agency's action which may adversely affect persons or organizations where a reasonable and *equally* effective alternative is available. The Department also realizes that when it is necessary to warn of a danger to public health or safety, the balance between the need to serve the public interest adequately and to observe the rights of persons or organizations affected may appropriately be weighted in favor of the public interest....
>
> ... The Secretary does not agree that the regulation will have an adverse impact on any enforcement activity. The regulation specifically permits release of adverse information when necessary to protect public health or safety. The Food and Drug Administration ... may also publish rules not inconsistent with this regulation addressing its particular problems....

ADMINISTRATIVE PRACTICES AND PROCEDURES: PUBLICITY POLICY

42 Federal Register 12436 (March 4, 1977).

... Every citizen is affected by how FDA carries out its responsibilities to ensure the safety and nondeceptive labeling of the nation's supply of foods, drugs, devices, and cosmetics.... The Food and Drug Administration believes it has an affirmative obligation to see that the public knows about and understands the agency's actions and has an opportunity to participate in decisions affecting the public health and the honest marketing of products. Issuing publicity is important to FDA fulfillment of this commitment....

... The Food and Drug Administration seeks publicity for several purposes, among which are:

1. To warn against the use of marketed products that may be hazardous.

2. To warn against gross economic deception.

3. To encourage public comment on proposed regulations or actions and other public participation in FDA activities.

4. To report to the public on adjudicated court proceedings.

5. To present to the public FDA's views on matters of public interest.

6. To report on studies or investigations that may form the basis for an FDA regulatory action.

Despite these positive objectives of publicity, there are occasions when publicity can have a negative or adverse effect. For example, an excess of negative information could make the public indifferent or insensitive to important warnings about a potentially dangerous product. Adverse publicity may prejudice a defendant's right to a fair trial in a criminal prosecution, or might improperly influence civil litigation. Under certain circumstances, the issuance of publicity could create a greater hazard than that posed by particular violation by causing a panic-type reaction. Adverse publicity can cause economic harm to both individuals and firms....

The Food and Drug Administration recognizes a clear distinction between publicity that involves the mass media and materials issued to inform and/or educate the public. Considerable information about FDA and its activities is contained in publications or audio-visual materials produced by the agency....

The Food and Drug Administration does not issue any of these publications or provide any of this information for the purpose of seeking publicity in the news media. For purposes of this regulation, these publications are not considered to be publicity. Similarly, public appearances by FDA employees at public meetings are not considered to be publicity. The Commissioner or a representative often is called to testify before congressional committees, and such appearances customarily are covered by the news media. These appearances and any subsequent release, by the committee or its staff, of materials provided to support such testimony are not publicity within the scope of these regulations....

The Administrative Conference also recommended that disparaging terminology should be avoided in the issuance of adverse publicity. The Commissioner believes there is no way that such terminology can be entirely avoided when the purpose of the publicity is to warn of a threat to the public health or to report to the public about an action taken by FDA against a firm or product. The agency agrees that personally disparaging or gratuitously critical remarks, not required in reporting the facts of a situation, should be and will be avoided.

Issuance of information that may be adverse to an individual, firm, or product is justifiable when it is needed to fulfill the agency's primary mission. Adverse publicity also may be an unavoidable consequence of information issued for an appropriate agency purpose. In issuing press releases relating to actions of a general nature (such as rule making), specific persons, firms, or products will be named only if the Commissioner determines it is necessary to explain fully the background or consequences of the action being discussed....

The Food and Drug Administration will continue to seek publicity, when appropriate, even if there is the possibility that the information may be ignored, misinterpreted, oversimplified, overstated, or misunderstood by the media or by the public....

... FDA—on behalf of the public—has an interest in assuring that no information is issued that may endanger its ability to pursue a warranted prosecution or other appropriate enforcement action. It also has an interest in guarding against injury from unwarranted publicity about agency charges of law violations prior to the completion of administrative proceedings to resolve disputes related to the validity of the charges....

The proposed provisions relating to publicity about litigation, administrative hearings, and related investigations would not in any way restrict the issuance of warnings to protect the public health or to avoid substantial economic harm, even if there is a possibility the publicity might prejudice a pending or future criminal trial or other proceeding. The Commissioner believes that his obligations to protect the public are paramount. If publicity were in fact prejudicial, it might be possible to cure its effects by impaneling a jury unaffected by the publicity or by other measures; but the Commissioner believes that, if need be, he must risk dismissal of a prosecution because of the impact of publicity, rather than fail to issue a warning that he believes is needed to protect the public....

The proposed regulations ... also define what is actually meant by "advance notice." The release of the actual text of a press release to the affected firm or individual, without making the text available upon request to all persons, would be inconsistent with the principle of equal access to public information followed by the Commissioner in administering the Freedom of Information Act.... To make the actual text available to the firm or individual and the mass media simultaneously would defeat the practical difficulties in making the exact text available in advance. The proposed regulations attempt to solve this dilemma by providing notice to a firm or individual that publicity on a given subject is to issue without providing the exact text. Because of the varying degrees of public hazard that may exist in different situations, specific time frames for advance notice are not proposed.

Advance notice of FDA's plans to seek publicity that may be adverse is appropriate when needed to enable affected persons to make a timely response of their own to the press. Advance notice of publicity usually will not be given to selected persons or firms regarding the agency's initiation of proposed rule making.... Advance notice of the initiation by FDA of enforcement action in the courts is not appropriate since it would require a prior notification about the underlying action. Disclosure of those plans in some instances might lead to the removal of products about to be seized or to the destruction or loss of evidence relating to an imminent injunction....

The fifth and final specific recommendation by the Administrative Conference calls for a retraction or correction of adverse agency publicity where it is shown to be erroneous or misleading, and when a person named in the publicity requests a retraction or correction. The Food and Drug Administration concurs in this recommendation, and both the HEW regulations and the proposed regulations provide for such corrections or retractions....

NOTES

1. *Agency Policy Still Pending.* As of June 30, 1990, FDA had not taken action to finalize its proposed regulations, and had issued no other guidelines governing agency publicity.

2. *Press Release Policy.* On April 15, 1986, FDA Commissioner Young responded to an inquiry from Senator John Heinz who sought an explanation of the agency's use of press releases:

> In issuing publicity about potential risks of products we regulate, we attempt to choose a level of alert appropriate to the nature and scope of the problem. We also take into account the publicity and notifications issued by the manufacturer. Our goal is to assure that appropriate warnings are conveyed to health professionals and consumers without creating undue alarm.
>
> Often in the past we have utilized press releases and *FDA Talk Papers* to alert the public about product withdrawals. Generally, a press release is issued when we feel that the scope of the problem warrants more widespread publicity. A *Talk Paper*, on the other hand, is generally used when we believe the problem to be of a narrower scope. Although *Talk Papers* are not normally distributed to the press, they are available to the press and are often used as a source for news stories.

3. *Judicial Treatment of FDA Publicity.* See *United States v. An Article of Device ... Diapulse Mfg. Corp.,* 262 F. Supp. 728 (D. Conn. 1967); *Durovic v. Palmer,* Food Drug Cosm. L. Rep. (CCH) ¶ 40,099 (N.D. Ill. 1964), *aff'd,* 342 F.2d 634 (7th Cir. 1965). In *Sperling & Schwartz, Inc. v. United States,* Food Drug Cosm. L. Rep. (CCH) ¶ 38,140 (Ct. Cl. 1977), the plaintiff challenged FDA's

issuance of a press release warning consumers to avoid using certain imported dinnerware because of its high lead content. The Court of Claims concluded that the press release was not libelous and that the plaintiff had no claim for damages against the United States. *Compare Bristol–Myers Co. v. FTC*, 424 F.2d 935 (D.C. Cir. 1970); *FTC v. Cinderella Career & Finishing Schools, Inc.*, 404 F.2d 1308 (D.C. Cir. 1968). *See also Impro Products, Inc. v. Block*, 722 F.2d 845 (D.C. Cir. 1983).

4. *Commentary.* A series of articles describes FDA's public information function, *see* Janssen, *Public Information Under the Federal Food, Drug, and Cosmetic Act*, pts. I–IV, 12 FDC L.J. 57, 93, 229,566 (1957). Other articles describe the effects and debate the propriety of this function. Fisher, *Publicity and the FDA*, 28 FDC L.J. 436 (1973); Goodrich, *Cranberries, Chickens and Charcoal*, 15 FDC L.J. 87 (1960); Morey, *Publicity as a Regulatory Tool*, 30 FDC L.J. 469 (1975); Smith, *The Cranberry Scare and Cabinet Immunity*, 16 FDC L.J. 209 (1961).

5. *Departmental Regulations.* The Department of HHS proposed to revise its regulations in 45 Fed. Reg. 10820 (February 19, 1980), but no final action had been taken on this proposal as of June 30, 1990.

UNITED STATES v. ABBOTT LABORATORIES

United States Court of Appeals, Fourth Circuit, 1974.
505 F.2d 565.

WINTER, Circuit Judge.

In December, 1970, the Center for Disease Control (CDC) of the United States Public Health Service investigated an increase in the incidence of blood poisoning among hospital patients. CDC concluded that between October, 1970, and March 1, 1971, one hundred fifty cases of blood poisoning and nine deaths had occurred in eight hospitals among patients who had received intravenous fluid therapy employing intravenous fluids and intravenous fluid systems manufactured by Abbott.... The report of these findings received national media coverage describing the illnesses and deaths and isolation of the "guilty germ" in the cap liner of Abbott bottles. On March 22, 1971, Abbott issued a nationwide recall of its intravenous solutions.

FDA recommended to the Department of Justice that Abbott and those of its employees "responsible" for distribution of the allegedly contaminated intravenous solutions be prosecuted. The matter was presented to a grand jury in a district in which Abbott manufactures intravenous solutions, and the indictment was returned on May 29, 1973. As soon as the indictment was returned, the United States Attorney for the Eastern District of North Carolina notified the news media that he had a press release concerning the indictment. The news department of a Raleigh television station requested an interview with him. The request was granted and the interview held at about 2:00 p.m. in his office. Two special prosecutors from the Justice Department and an attorney from FDA were also present....

During the pretaping interrogation, the correspondent asked whether any deaths or illnesses were attributed to the misbranded drugs. One of the special prosecutors replied that "the Center for Disease Control in Atlanta previously reported that nine deaths occurred in 1971." During the subsequent taping session, the correspondent asked the same question of the U.S. Attorney. Not expecting this question to be asked, he replied that the indictment had nothing to do with any deaths. Following the taped interview, the correspondent continued to ask questions concerning deaths attributable to Abbott's intravenous solution. The answers, in substance, provided the same information as the answer quoted above.

On the six o'clock news that day, the Raleigh TV station broadcast a news report concerning the indictment, which contained the following statements:

Nine deaths and four hundred illnesses have been attributed to contaminated drugs made by a North Carolina company.... The drugs were manufactured by the Abbott Laboratories Hospital Products Division of Rocky Mount.

The taped interview was also broadcast on this program, but the U.S. Attorney's statement that the indictment had nothing to do with any deaths was omitted.

On the same day, United Press International (UPI) ran a story citing sources in the Justice Department in Washington, containing the following statement:

A federal grand jury has returned criminal indictments against Abbott Laboratories, Inc. and five of its present or former employees on charges involving allegedly contaminated intravenous fluid linked to nine deaths and hundreds of injuries, the Justice Department announced Tuesday.

The circumstances make it clear that the remarks of those present at the interview in the U.S. Attorney's office in Raleigh were *not* the source of this news release. Nothing further is apparently known about the actual source of this release than that which appears on its face. This UPI release received the wide publication that could be expected in the case of a wire service of this type.

On May 29, 1973, some hours after the indictment was handed down, the FDA issued a press release in Washington, D.C., containing the following statements:

Five present or former officials of the company also were named in the indictment for interstate shipment of intravenous drugs that were unsterile and dangerous to public health.

The Center for Disease Control, at Atlanta, Georgia, reported fifty deaths from four hundred and twelve patient episodes during late 1970 and early 1972 from septicemias (blood poisonings) which CDC determined to be associated with the use of contaminated Abbott intravenous solutions. . . .

These individuals held positions of responsibility with respect to the adulteration and misbranding for the intravenous drugs named in the indictment.

Both the UPI "nine deaths" release and the FDA "fifty deaths" release received wide coverage throughout the nation in the television, radio and printed media at the time of the indictment. The "nine deaths" story arising out of the interview with the U.S. Attorney reached the viewers of WRAL–TV of Raleigh, North Carolina, who are spread throughout many of the counties of the Eastern District of North Carolina.

The proof shows that the death or possible death of persons who had received Abbott's intravenous solutions was mentioned before the grand jury in three separate instances. . . .

Defendants sought dismissal of the indictment by two motions. On July 13, 1973, they moved to dismiss the indictment on the grounds that the prejudicial publicity engendered by the "nine deaths" story arising out of the WRAL–TV interview with the prosecutor and, independently, out of the UPI release in Washington, and by the FDA's "fifty deaths" release prevented the defendants from receiving a fair trial. On October 3, 1973, the defendants moved that the indictment be dismissed on the ground that the statements made by the special prosecutor before the grand jury concerning the deaths allegedly caused by Abbott's intravenous solutions were highly prejudicial and deliberately inflammatory. . . . On December 13, 1973, the district court entered an order dismissing the indictment as to all defendants both on the ground that prejudicial publicity precluded a fair trial and on the ground that prosecutorial misconduct before the grand jury invalidated the indictment. . . . The district court made no finding of whether the charges in the "nine deaths" and "fifty deaths" stories were true.

We accept, without question, that the pretrial publicity in this case was prejudicial and highly inflammatory. . . . Irrespective of the outcome of this case, we join in the district court's condemnation of this conduct and express our strongest disapproval that highly placed legal officers would make a statement of this import with regard to a pending criminal prosecution, and even more so that FDA, which had referred the matter to the Department of Justice, would issue a press release containing such prejudicial material. We are presented, however, with the question of whether this misconduct on the part of the government was so prejudicial to the defendants' right to a fair trial that it should be redressed by dismissal of the indictment. . . .

No case of which we are aware, nor any to which we have been referred, holds that, without resort to the traditional means of effective protection of a defendant's right to a fair trial, *i.e.,* voir dire, change of venue, continuance, pretrial publicity has been so inflammatory and prejudicial that a fair trial is absolutely precluded and an indictment should be dismissed without an initial attempt, by the use of one or more of the procedures mentioned, to see if an impartial jury can be impanelled.... [T]he district court's finding that a fair trial was impossible and its legal conclusion that the indictment should be dismissed cannot stand, since voir dire was not employed.

Because of what we have concluded with respect to voir dire, elaborate discussion of the curative devices of change of venue and continuance is unnecessary....

We disagree that the indictment should be dismissed because of irrelevant prejudicial and inflammatory information brought to the attention of the grand jury which indicted defendants. Our disagreement follows from our conclusion that the "nine deaths" and "fifty deaths" data was relevant.

The grand jury was investigating possible violations of the federal drug laws. Defendants were indicted, *inter alia,* for a violation of 21 U.S.C. § 352(j); whether it had been violated was certainly within the scope of the grand jury's investigation. That statute seems a drug "misbranded" if it is "dangerous to health when used in the dosage, or with the frequency or duration prescribed, recommended, or suggested in the labeling thereof." Evidence that use of Abbott's intravenous solutions may have been the cause of deaths which occurred manifestly would establish that the solutions were "dangerous to health." ...

The district court found that the primary purpose of references to deaths before the grand jury was to influence the jurors and arouse their prejudice against defendants. We think this finding clearly erroneous. The record is devoid of direct evidence to support it....

NOTE

See also Marshall v. United States, 360 U.S. 310 (1959), a prosecution for unlawfully dispensing controlled drugs without a prescription, in which news reports of the defendant's past convictions arising out of his prescribing dangerous drugs under the pretense he was a physician were held inadmissible.

M. FDA ENFORCEMENT STATISTICS

Activity	1939	1951	1963	1976	1989
Criminal Prosecution	626	347	248	43	16
Seizure	1,861	1,341	1,049	317	144
Injunction	0	4	30	39	13
Regulatory Letters	N.A.	N.A.	N.A.	982	370
Recalls	0	54	101	837	2,183
Factory Inspections	N.A.	13,357	36,639	39,870	17,740
Import Inspections	16,352	39,942	30,985	N.A.	N.A.
Samples	39,746	40,853	103,166	57,495	71,932
Personnel	565	1,000	3,210	6,683	7,395
Appropriations ($ millions)	2.226	5.467	29.065	201.805	487.344

Activity	1939	1951	1963	1976	1989
National Income ($ billions)	41.6	77.8	91.7	170.5	371.3
U.S. Population (thousands)	130,880	154,287	189,242	218,035	248,500 (est.)
Federal Budget ($ billions)	N.A.	N.A.	106.6	298.1	490.7

N.A. = Not Available

N. RES JUDICATA AND RELATED DOCTRINES

1. RES JUDICATA IN FDA CASES

UNITED STATES v. 17 CASES ... OF NUE–OVO

United States District Court, Northern District of Illinois, 1949.
1938–1964 FDLI Jud. Rec. 858.

CAMPBELL, District Judge.

This is a consolidation of six cases, all involving the same subject matter. The proceedings are brought pursuant to libels alleging misbranding, under 21 U.S.C. § 352(a), of a certain product known as Nue–Ovo, which is manufactured by the claimant, Research Laboratories, Inc.... It is the contention of the Government that the [labeling] statement in each case is false and misleading, in that its ultimate effect is to represent and suggest that the article is effective in the treatment of arthritis and rheumatism, whereas the article is not so effective.

Libellant now moves for summary judgment on the basis of estoppel by judgment, *i.e.*, that judgments have previously been rendered in favor of the libellant in the United States District Court of the Western District of Washington.... Claimant opposes the motion on the ground that different issues of law and fact exist in the present cases.

Although the claimant admits the wording set forth on the shipping cases and circulars, it cites the language of the back bottle label in support of its contention:

"IMPORTANT

"Many users believe NUE–OVO has brought them relief, but experts differ as to its merits. It is prescribed by some doctors although not generally accepted by the medical profession. If it does not relieve you after a fair trial in accordance with the directions, discontinue its use. Any guarantee to induce the purchase of NUE–OVO is unauthorized."

It is claimant's position, therefore, that the present consolidated actions present the issues of whether (1) the labeling represents that there is a difference of medical opinion as to the effectiveness of the product in the treatment of arthritis and rheumatism, and (2) there is in fact such a difference of medical opinion, whereas in the previous actions it had only to be determined whether the product was represented to be effective in the treatment of those diseases and whether it was so effective.

Claimant's argument is untenable. In effect, the supposedly new issues were presented to and disposed of by the Court of Appeals of the Ninth Circuit in *Research Laboratories v. United States,* 167 F.2d 410....

Since, therefore, the juries in the previous cases determined that the product was ineffective in the treatment of arthritis and rheumatism, they must necessarily have rejected as valueless the testimony of the witnesses appearing on behalf of the claimant. In other words, a finding that there was not an honest difference of opinion as to effectiveness, was an essential ingredient of the conclusion that the product was ineffective....

It still remains, however, to be decided whether all issues presented in this litigation are *res judicata.* ... Each of the articles involved in these consolidated cases bears an identical label. This label lists ... ingredients ... identical with the ingredients of the article which was involved in [the prior ... cases].... This element, combined with the determinations, both direct and necessarily implied, of the juries in the previous cases as to effectiveness, clearly brings the instant action within the doctrine of *res judicata.* ...

The entire history of the manufacture and sale of Nue–Ovo is marked by questionable promotional methods. This most recent mode of labeling is merely another subtle maneuver adopted for the purpose of avoiding the dictates of the Food and Drugs Act and inducing a gullible public to purchase a worthless product for the cure of rheumatism and arthritis....

Accordingly, therefore, the Government's motion for summary judgment is granted....

RES JUDICATA BASED ON PRIOR CIVIL ACTIONS

In *598 Cases ... Tomatoes v. United States,* 211 F.2d 249 (7th Cir. 1954), the court declined to hold that an earlier injunction decree obtained by FDA was res judicata in a subsequent seizure action because of an unresolved factual issue as to whether the same food was involved in the two proceedings. *See also United States v. Nysco Laboratories, Inc.,* 318 F.2d 817 (2d Cir. 1963); *United States v. An Article of Food ... "Schmidt's Blue Ribbon,"* 1969–1974 FDLI Jud. Rec. 166 (D. Md. 1974); *United States v. 4 Cans ... Master Liquid,* 127 F. Supp. 243 (N.D. Iowa 1955); *United States v. 14 105 Pound Bags ... Mineral Compound,* 118 F. Supp. 837 (D. Idaho 1953).

In *United States v. Five Cases ... Capon Springs Water,* 156 F.2d 493 (2d Cir. 1946), the court held that a decision for the claimant in a civil misbranding action under the 1906 Act was not res judicata in a subsequent civil misbranding action under the 1938 Act because the 1906 Act required proof of fraud.

In *George H. Lee Co. v. United States,* 41 F.2d 460 (9th Cir. 1930), the court held the government estopped from bringing this action against Lee's Lice Killer, because previous proceedings against a different shipment of the same product culminated in a decree in favor of the owner.

Where plaintiffs unsuccessfully sued to prevent FDA from interfering with their use of Laetrile in *Rutherford v. United States,* 582 F.2d 1234 (10th Cir. 1978), a subsequent action by some of those plaintiffs was dismissed in *Keene v. United States,* Food Drug Cosm. L. Rep. (CCH) ¶ 38,233 (S.D. W.Va. 1979), because the plaintiffs, the defendants, and the cause of action were the same. Where the court held in *Cutler v. Kennedy,* 475 F. Supp. 838 (D.D.C. 1979), that plaintiff consumers had standing to challenge the legality of the FDA OTC Drug Review, that jurisdictional determination was held to be binding in a second suit involving the same parties challenging the OTC Drug Review. *Cutler v. Hayes,* 818 F.2d 879 (D.C. Cir. 1987).

A court's initial classification of an article as a food or drug is not res judicata when the labeling is changed, *United States v. Articles of Drug ... Neptone,* 568 F.Supp. 1182 (N.D. Cal. 1983), since proper classification "rests entirely on the pattern of promotion used by claimant in the several years immediately preceding the instant seizure."

Where FDA obtained judgment against one version of a drug as an illegal new drug, *United States v. 225 Cartons ... "Fiorinal With Codeine No. 1",* 871 F.2d 409 (3d Cir. 1989), the court in a second seizure of a related drug determined that the claimant was collaterally estopped from relitigating the new drug issue, *United States v. Sandoz Pharmaceuticals Corp.,* 894 F.2d 825 (6th Cir. 1990). An adverse judgment in an FDA civil case may also be res judicata in a subsequent private civil case for damages. *See Smith v. Great Atlantic & Pacific Tea Co.,* 170 F.2d 474 (8th Cir. 1948); *Sussex Drug Products Co. v. Kanasco, Ltd.,* Food Drug Cosm. L. Rep. (CCH) ¶ 38,103 (D.N.J. 1988).

In *FTC v. Raladam Co.,* 316 U.S. 149 (1942), the Supreme Court overturned a court of appeals order vacating an FTC order prohibiting the promotion of Marmola as a remedy for overweight. In 1929, in a similar case against Raladam, the Court had affirmed dismissal of a Commission order on the ground of inadequate proof on the record. However, the Court concluded that the latter action brought in 1935 against the same product on a different set of facts and a different record was not barred by res judicata. *See also Porter & Dietsch, Inc. v. FTC,* 605 F.2d 294 (7th Cir. 1979) which held that two earlier Postal Service decisions do not bar a later FTC decision where there is a "clear and convincing need for a new determination of the issue .... [b]ecause of the potential impact of the determination on the public interest", *Kurzon v. United States Postal Service,* 539 F.2d 788 (1st Cir. 1976); *Exposition Press, Inc. v. FTC,* 295 F.2d 869 (2d Cir. 1961), *cert. denied,* 370 U.S. 917 (1962).

UNITED STATES v. GRAMER

United States Court of Appeals, Ninth Circuit, 1951.
191 F.2d 741.

STEPHENS, Circuit Judge.

A criminal action brought by the United States ... charged Gramer, claimant herein, with the introduction into interstate commerce of misbranded drugs in violation of the Federal Food, Drug, and Cosmetic Act. After a plea of not guilty was entered a trial on the merits was had and the district judge, sitting without a jury, adjudged claimant not guilty.

In January, 1950, two libels were filed by the government in the U.S. District Court for the Western District of Washington, against separate subsequent shipments of the same preparation of drugs as was involved in the Minnesota federal district court, for seizure and condemnation pursuant to provisions of the same act. The cases were consolidated since the articles proceeded against and the charges were the same in both cases. It was undisputed that the contents of the bottles, the accompanying literature, the labeling, and all of the material issues except criminality, raised were the same as those involved in the prior 1949 criminal action. Claimant's motion for summary judgment was granted for the reason that the issues raised by the government in the cause were adjudicated in favor of Gramer in the prior criminal action. . . .

. . . [N]either the judicial doctrine of *res judicata* nor the constitutional mandate against double jeopardy operates to prevent the action here involved.

Res judicata. Where a right, question or fact has been put in issue and determined by a court of competent jurisdiction, as a ground of recovery, it cannot again be disputed in a subsequent suit between the same parties or their privies. But the Supreme Court has held that neither the doctrine of *res judicata* nor the rule of the *Coffey* case [116 U.S. 436 (1886)] has application to a situation where there has been an acquittal on a criminal charge followed by a civil action requiring a different degree of proof.

Hence, since the prior action by the government was criminal in nature, while the cause before us is civil, the doctrine of *res judicata* does not operate to make the acquittal a bar.

Double jeopardy. . . . Since it is admitted that the libels filed herein did not seek to condemn the same shipment of preparation which was involved in the prior criminal action it is immediately apparent that there is no question of double jeopardy involved. . . .

RES JUDICATA BASED ON PRIOR CRIMINAL CASE

See *United States v. Certain Bottles of Lee's "Save the Baby,"* 37 F.2d 137 (D. Conn. 1929); *United States v. 38 Cases . . . Figlia Mia Brand*, 99 F. Supp. 460 (S.D.N.Y. 1951); Dickerman, *Res Judicata—An Acquittal in a Criminal Case Does Not Bar Subsequent Seizure Action*, 7 FDC L.J. 293 (1952). *Compare Stanley v. United States*, 111 F.2d 898 (6th Cir. 1940), holding that prior dismissal of a criminal charge of misbranding, on the ground that label statements did not claim a curative effect, barred a seizure action based on the same labeling. See also *United States v. 119 Packages . . . Z–G Herbs, XXX No. 17, Double Strength*, 15 F. Supp. 327 (S.D.N.Y. 1936). In *Keene v. United States*, 81 F.R.D. 653 (S.D. W.Va. 1979), the district court gave res judicata effect to the earlier decisions of the Western District of Oklahoma in *Rutherford v. United*

States, 399 F. Supp. 1208 (W.D. Okl. 1975), 429 F. Supp. 506 (W.D. Okl. 1977), granting cancer patients access to Laetrile, but on the condition that they submit evidence of terminal illness.

Although the issue apparently has never been litigated, it is likely that a criminal conviction for violation of the FD&C Act would be res judicata in a subsequent FDA civil action. *See Developments in the Law: The Federal Food, Drug, and Cosmetic Act,* 67 Harv. L. Rev. 632 (1954). *See generally* Bohon, *Res Judicata as a Weapon of Enforcement of the Federal Food Drug, and Cosmetic Act,* 9 FDC L.J. 256 (1954).

RES JUDICATA BASED ON ASSOCIATION SUITS

On occasion FDA has prevailed in a declaratory judgment action brought by a trade association, and later been confronted by attempts by individual association members to relitigate the same issue in other suits. In several cases involving other agencies, courts have refused to permit a second action where the association was found to have the same interests as its members. *See, e.g., Expert Electric, Inc. v. Levine,* 554 F.2d 1227 (2d Cir. 1977); *Aluminum Co. of America v. Admiral Merchants Motor Freight, Inc.,* 486 F.2d 717 (7th Cir. 1973); *Acree v. Air Line Pilots Ass'n,* 390 F.2d 199 (5th Cir. 1968); *Proctor & Gamble Co. v. Byers Transportation Co.,* 355 F. Supp. 547 (W.D. Mo. 1973). *But see Spring Mills, Inc. v. Consumer Product Safety Com'n,* 434 F. Supp. 416 (D.S.C. 1977). Dictum in *National Automatic Laundry and Cleaning Council v. Shultz,* 443 F.2d 689 (D.C. Cir. 1971), states that a court may dismiss an action brought by an organization if it is not brought as a class action reasoning that "the Government should be able to offset the diversion of enforcement resources required to defend a pre-enforcement review action by the assurance that the determination in such a litigation will have a reasonably broad *res judicata* effect."

In 1975, FDA proposed a regulation stating that it would treat participation by a trade association in an administrative proceeding as binding all members who did not expressly decline to be represented and would attempt to have court challenges by trade associations converted into class actions and otherwise seek to bar duplicate suits by association members. 40 Fed. Reg. 40682, 40698, 40732 (September 3, 1975). The agency later withdrew the portion of the proposal addressed to agency proceedings. 42 Fed. Reg. 4680, 4696 (January 25, 1977). *See* 21 C.F.R. § 10.105. It unsuccessfully sought dismissal of a trade association suit because it was not brought as a class action in *American Frozen Food Institute v. Mathews,* 413 F.Supp. 548 (D.D.C. 1976).

---

2. EFFECT OF SUITS BY OTHER AGENCIES

UNITED STATES v. WILLARD TABLET CO.

United States Circuit Court of Appeals, Seventh Circuit, 1944.
141 F.2d 141.

MAJOR, Circuit Judge.

The United States (libelant) instituted this proceeding for condemnation of a quantity of Willard's Tablets shipped in interstate commerce on the ground that the labeling thereof was false, in violation of the Food, Drug, and Cosmetic Act, and the articles were therefore subject to seizure and confiscation.... The lower court sustained the claimant's defense of res judicata, based upon a prior proceeding before the Federal Trade Commission, and dismissed the action....

The government urges as a basis for overruling the lower court's holding that: (1) the issues herein involved were not determined by the Federal Trade Commission; (2) unaffirmed decisions of the Federal Trade Commission do not have the finality necessary to constitute res judicata; (3) there is no mutuality of estoppel; (4) the lower court's holding would impair the enforcement of the Food, Drug, and Cosmetic Act; and (5) the District Court improperly dismissed the amended libel as to that part alleging that the directions for use on the labeling were inadequate.

The facts as stipulated and adopted by the lower court effectively dispose of the government's first contention. The stipulation disclosed: (1) that the statements relied upon by the government to uphold the charge of misbranding are identical with those approved by the Federal Trade Commission; (2) that the fundamental issue of fact as to whether the Willard Tablets would give the relief claimed was considered by the Federal Trade Commission. We, therefore, have the incongruous situation of one branch of the government approving the method now pursued by the claimant and another branch seeking to condemn. That is, to say the least, placing claimant in an embarrassing situation and should be avoided if possible.....

The government's second contention seems to rest solely upon the provisions of the Federal Trade Commission Act that the Commission may, under certain conditions, modify its order after the expiration of time for appeal. Therefore, the contention is that such power of modification leaves an unappealed order without that finality essential to invoke the doctrine of res judicata. With this contention we do not agree....

We agree with appellee's contention that mutuality of estoppel is not herein involved. We have held that the facts found by the Federal Trade Commission are conclusive and binding upon the District Court. The same result would obtain if the government were depending upon these findings to sustain its charge of misbranding....

What we have heretofore said sufficiently disposes of the argument that the decisions of the Federal Trade Commission should not be allowed to impair the enforcement of the Food, Drug, and Cosmetic Act. Under the facts stipulated herein and to which this decision is limited, there can be no impairment of the enforcement of the aforementioned Act....

NOTES

1. *FTC Proceedings. See George H. Lee Co. v. FTC,* 113 F.2d 583 (8th Cir. 1940), holding that a decision in a prior FDA civil action is res judicata in a subsequent FTC civil action. *See also United States v. 14 Cartons ... "Ayds*

*Candy....,"*1938–1964 FDLI Jud. Rec. 182 (E.D. Mo. 1946), holding that an earlier decision that the advertising claims for a reducing aid did not violate the Federal Trade Commission Act, *Carlay Co. v. FTC,* 153 F.2d 493 (7th Cir. 1946), barred an FDA seizure action alleging misbranding. In *Sekov Corp. v. United States,* 139 F.2d 197 (5th Cir. 1943), the court declined to invoke res judicata on the ground that the issues in the earlier FTC proceeding were different from those in the subsequent FDA seizure. *See also United States v. Five Cases ... Capon Springs Water,* 156 F.2d 493 (2d Cir. 1946). In *United States v. An Article of Drug ... Ova II,* 414 F. Supp. 660 (D.N.J. 1975), FDA withdrew a claim that the claimant's pregnancy test kit was falsely labeled in order not to prejudice a possible future proceeding by the FTC under section 5 of the Federal Trade Commission Act.

2. *Mail Fraud Proceedings.* A decision in an action under the Mail Fraud Act, 18 U.S.C. § 1341, has been held not to be res judicata with respect to any subsequent FDA action because the Mail Fraud Act requires proof of fraudulent purpose and intent to deceive. *See United States v. 3963 Bottles ... " Enerjol Double Strength,* 265 F.2d 332 (7th Cir. 1959); *United States v. Kaadt,* 171 F.2d 600 (7th Cir. 1948). In *United States v. 42 Jars ... "Bee Royale Capsules,"* 264 F.2d 666 (3d Cir. 1959), the court declined to apply a broader concept of "res administrata":

> ... A benevolent Uncle Sam is, as the cartoons show him, to be treated as a unified individual with the addition of a degree of omniscience not accorded to him by anyone before. Furthermore, all his citizens, both natural and corporate, are included in the family of his children thus to create privity, or something akin to it, between them.
>
> It is hardly necessary to add that a court cannot swallow any such broad proposition as this.... [W]hile there may be cases where the administrative process works hardship, this is not one of them. As indicated above, there is not a single fibril to connect these two pieces of Government procedure except certain claims made on behalf of that product known as Bee Royale jelly....

See Kurzon v. United States Postal Service, 539 F.2d 788 (1st Cir. 1976), holding that a decision for the government in an earlier FDA civil action did not bar a later action under the Mail Fraud Act. In *Aycock v. O'Brien,* 28 F.2d 817 (9th Cir. 1928), the court held an acquittal in an FDA criminal action not to be res judicata in a civil case brought 11 years later under the Mail Fraud Act involving the same products because the parties were different and because during the lapse of time medical knowledge may have changed.

3. *State Proceedings.* In *United States v. Depilatron Epilator,* 473 F. Supp. 913 (S.D.N.Y. 1979), FDA brought a seizure action against misleading labeling of a medical device after a state court in California had determined that the labeling was not misleading. The district court held that, although FDA and the FTC had participated in the California state action, that participation was "minimal" and thus FDA was not collaterally estopped from bringing its own action.

4. *Commentary. See* Bohon, *Res Judicata as a Weapon of Enforcement of the Federal Food, Drug, and Cosmetic Act,* 9 FDC L.J. 256 (1954); Note, *Res Judicata and Two Coordinate Federal Agencies,* 95 U. Pa. L. Rev. 388 (1947); Annot., 152 A.L.R. 1198 (1944).

3. SIMULTANEOUS GOVERNMENT PROCEEDINGS

WARNER–LAMBERT CO. v. FEDERAL TRADE COMMISSION

United States District Court, District of Columbia, 1973.

361 F. Supp. 948.

JOHN H. PRATT, District Judge.

This action seeks to restrain the Federal Trade Commission from undertaking further proceedings in FTC Docket No. 8891, and to restrain the Secretary of Health, Education and Welfare and the Commissioner of Food and Drugs from further proceeding with its review of over-the-counter cold remedies, unless and until the two federal agencies take appropriate action to prevent the conduct of two simultaneous proceedings with regard to the cold and sore throat claims of Listerine Antiseptic. . . .

Plaintiff is the respondent in an adjudicative proceeding presently pending before the FTC under FTC Docket 8891. . . .

The complaint, in general, alleges Warner–Lambert, in its advertising, offering for sale, sale and distribution of the mouthwash preparation Listerine to retailers for resale to the public, has misrepresented by false, deceptive and misleading statements the effect of the product in the prevention, cure, treatment and mitigation of colds and sore throats. . . . Warner–Lambert, on August 30, 1972, filed an answer, denying the substantive averments of the FTC complaint. Hearings before the Administrative Law Judge have been scheduled to commence on September 24, 1973.

. . . Because of the inadequacy, great cost, and burden on the courts of proceeding against individual drugs on a case-by-case basis, the Commissioner of Food and Drugs, on December 30, 1971, proposed new regulations setting up a procedure for a thorough and complete review of all over-the-counter drugs. . . .

. . . With respect to cold remedies, Listerine is one of many products to be reviewed. No monograph has yet been proposed. An invitation for all interested persons to submit data bearing on the safety and effectiveness of the ingredients of cough-cold remedies was published on August 9, 1972. As a nonprescription cough and cold remedy, Listerine will be subject to the requirements of any monograph issued by FDA pursuant to the rulemaking proceedings.

Plaintiff argues the two proceedings complained of are unlawful in that they violate a "rule" of both agencies. The "rule" which plaintiff asserts is binding upon defendants in a "Memorandum of Understanding" issued jointly by FTC and FDA and published at 36 Fed. Reg. 18539 (1971). Plaintiff's contention is erroneous. Even assuming, arguendo, the "rule" is binding on defendants, it is clear it does not apply to the proceedings in issue. . . .

As far as the proceedings themselves are concerned, it is the Court's opinion they are quite different. As has been pointed out previously, the proceeding before the Federal Trade Commission is an adversary proceeding. It is an adjudicatory proceeding. It involves only Warner–Lambert.

The proceeding before the Food and Drug Administration is a rulemaking proceeding. It involves thousands of manufacturers of over-the-counter products, including cold remedies. It is a proceeding which individual companies can participate in or decline to participate in, at their option, recognizing it may also be to their possible disadvantage. . . .

The Supreme Court has long held that the same issues and parties may be proceeded against simultaneously by more than one agency. . . . These same principles apply to the concurrent actions of FDA and FTC which may involve the same parties or issues. The propriety of simultaneous FDA–FTC proceedings involving the same issues does not, as claimant would have this Court believe, present a novel legal issue. For in at least three cases, the courts, including this Court, have held that concurrent FDA–FTC proceedings involving the same or similar matters are proper, and that the statutory remedies of the two agencies are cumulative and not mutually exclusive. . . .

NOTE

The FTC subsequently issued a cease and desist order against Listerine advertising which was upheld in *Warner–Lambert Co. v. FTC,* 562 F.2d 749 (D.C. Cir. 1977). FDA also proposed a monograph relating to OTC cough-cold drugs in 41 Fed. Reg. 38312 (September 9, 1976). In upholding the FTC order the court of appeals stated: "Since the FDA did not consider the extensive record compiled in the FTC proceeding, its conclusion that there is insufficient data about the ingredients of Listerine to justify classifying it as effective or ineffective is not necessarily inconsistent with the FTC's conclusion that Listerine's advertising claims are deceptive." For other cases recognizing the propriety of concurrent FDA–FTC proceedings, *see United States v. 1 Dozen Bottles . . . Boncquet Tablets,* 146 F.2d 361 (4th Cir. 1944); *United States v. Research Laboratories, Inc.,* 126 F.2d 42 (9th Cir. 1942); *United States v. Various Quantities . . . "Instant Alberty Food,"* 83 F. Supp. 882 (D.D.C. 1949); *United States v. Paddock,* 67 F. Supp. 819 (W.D. Mo. 1946).

4. ESTOPPEL AGAINST THE GOVERNMENT

UNITED STATES v. 354 BULK CARTONS ...
TRIM REDUCING–AID CIGARETTES

United States District Court, District of New Jersey, 1959.
178 F. Supp. 847.

WORTENDYKE, District Judge.

... [L]ibelant contends that the articles seized consisted of a drug shipped in interstate commerce, misbranded in violation of 21 U.S.C. § 334(a), when introduced therein, and constituting a new drug with respect to which an effective new drug application was not on file, as required by 21 U.S.C. § 355(a)....

Respecting the requirement of 21 U.S.C. § 355(a) that no person shall introduce into interstate commerce any new drug unless an application filed pursuant to subsection (b) of that section is effective with respect to such drug, claimant's president admits in his affidavit that no such application was filed before the commencement of the sale of Trim cigarettes. He would, however, explain such failure to file such an application by the statement that it was orally excused, by telephone, by Dr. Ralph G. Smith, of the Medical Division of the Federal Drug Administration. Abbott says that before the execution of the contract between claimant and Riggio Tobacco Corporation, for the manufacture by the latter of Trim cigarettes, counsel for the manufacturer insisted that the Administration be contacted for the purpose of ascertaining whether there was anything dangerous to human beings in their proposed ingredients.... Abbott's affidavit states that Dr. Smith advised that it was unnecessary for a new drug application to be filed since the ingredients of the cigarette disclosed to him were all well-known and harmless for human use in the form prescribed. The amount of tartaric acid in the formula which Abbott sets forth in his affidavit is 0.0005 gram per cigarette.... In his affidavit, Dr. Smith admits that his business diary reveals his receipt of a telephone call from claimant's attorney, on the date mentioned by Abbott, with reference to a cigarette containing flavoring and tartaric acid, but that this diary "does not reveal" that he advised the attorney that a new drug application would be unnecessary for the product, but the doctor expresses the opinion that the use of tartaric acid in cigarettes is not generally recognized among experts qualified to evaluate the safety of drugs, as safe for use in a recurring condition such as obesity. Assuming that Dr. Smith, a Government employee, told claimant's attorney that it would be unnecessary for claimant to file a new drug application with the Administration, claimant's failure to comply with the statute in that regard cannot be excused under the theory of estoppel against the Government....

NOTE

For other cases holding that FDA is not estopped from initiating regulatory action by prior contradictory statements of agency employees, *see Bentex*

Pharmaceuticals, Inc. v. Richardson, 463 F.2d 363 (4th Cir. 1972), *rev'd on other grounds,* 412 U.S. 645 (1973); *AMP, Inc. v. Gardner,* 389 F.2d 825 (2d Cir. 1968); *United States v. 154 Sacks of Oats,* 294 Fed. 340 (W.D. Va. 1923); *United States v. 60 28–Capsule Bottles ... "Unitrol,"* 211 F. Supp. 207 (D.N.J. 1962). In *United States v. Articles of Food ... Clover Club Potato Chips,* 67 F.R.D. 419 (D. Idaho 1975), the court stated that the validity of an alleged agreement by FDA not to seize the existing inventory of illegal food labeling in return for the company changing all future labeling "depends upon the authority of the official" at FDA who made that agreement.

FDA has by regulation provided for the issuance of formal advisory opinions and guidelines that are binding upon the agency and thus would presumably estop contrary action. 21 C.F.R. §§ 10.85 and 10.-90(b), promulgated in 42 Fed. Reg. 4680 (January 25, 1977). The preamble to the agency's 1975 proposal explained these provisions.

ADMINISTRATIVE PRACTICES AND PROCEDURES: NOTICE OF PROPOSED RULE MAKING

40 Federal Register 40682 (September 3, 1975).

Throughout its history, the Food and Drug Administration has issued advisory opinions in various forms. Early advisory opinions, between 1938 and 1946, were issued as trade correspondence (TC's). More recently, advisory opinions have been codified in the agency's Compliance Policy Guides manual, which is available from the Public Records and Documents Center, in other documents designated as "advisory opinions," and in preambles to FEDERAL REGISTER documents. The proposed regulations recognizing the continuing status of these prior documents as advisory opinions except to the extent that they are revoked....

Prior Food and Drug Administration policy has not distinguished between formal advisory opinions and informal oral advice and correspondence. As a result, confusion and uncertainty has been engendered both within the agency and outside as to whether opinions expressed in correspondence or orally carry the weight of the agency or only of the individual agency employee involved.

Absent specific regulations to the contrary, the statements of a government employee do not bind the government. Accordingly, because of the lack of any agency regulations on this matter, none of the correspondence or oral advice previously issued by the agency has had any binding legal effect.... The Commissioner would resolve the present uncertainty by the proposal of regulations that would clearly and explicitly recognize the difference between the informal opinion of an individual in the agency, which represents his best information and advice, and the formal opinion of the agency, which represents a position of the Food and Drug Administration that is binding and commits the agency to the views expressed until they are formally modified or revoked ...

Under [§ 10.85 as codified], a request for a formal advisory opinion would be made pursuant to a specified form. The resulting advisory opinion would have to be followed by the agency until it is amended or revoked. Amendment or revocation of an advisory opinion would be required to be made with the same degree of public dissemination as adoption of the original advisory opinion, or by publishing notice of such revocation in the FEDERAL REGISTER, which by statute constitutes adequate public notice. An advisory opinion would, however, have to be explicitly revoked....

All statements or advice given by a Food and Drug Administration employee orally or in writing, but which did not constitute an advisory opinion, would represent informal communications that contain the best information and opinion available to that employee at that time, but would not have the same binding effect as an advisory opinion. Accordingly, such informal communications would in no way obligate or commit the agency to the views expressed....

Ordinarily, an advisory opinion would commit the Food and Drug Administration to the position stated in the opinion, until it is amended or revoked. In unusual situations involving an immediate and significant danger to health, however, the Commissioner could take appropriate civil enforcement action contrary to an advisory opinion prior to amending or revoking it....

O. PRIVATE ENFORCEMENT OF THE FD&C ACT

1. IMPLIED PRIVATE CAUSES OF ACTION

FLORIDA EX REL. BROWARD COUNTY v. ELI LILLY & CO.

United States District Court, Southern District of Florida, 1971.
329 F. Supp. 364.

ATKINS, District Judge.

... [T]he State of Florida ... brought suit on its own behalf and on behalf of class of consumers and purchasers against the defendants to recover damages allegedly sustained in connection with the purchase, administration and use of certain fixed-ratio combination drugs claimed to have been manufactured and sold by the defendants. In essence, the Florida complaint charged that the defendants fraudulently induced the plaintiff to purchase drugs by falsely representing their effectiveness and side effects and by failing to provide adequate directions for and warnings against their use. Such conduct was claimed to be actionable under provisions of the Federal Food, Drug, and Cosmetic

Act. The complaint also charged the defendants with common law fraud, negligence and breach of warranty....

The defendants moved to dismiss the First Amended Complaint. Specifically, the defendants argued that the claims of the plaintiff could not be brought under the Federal Food, Drug, and Cosmetic Act....

The Federal Food, Drug, and Cosmetic Act does not create a private right of action and the claims pleaded in the First Amended Complaint do not, therefore, arise under federal law. Section 307 of the Act provides that "all" proceedings for the enforcement or to restrain violations of the Act shall be brought by the United States. Section 302(a) limits the jurisdiction of district courts under the Act to injunctive proceedings involving purely prospective relief. The legislative history of the Act indicates that an express provision for a private right of action for damages was included in an early version of the bill but was omitted from all later versions after being attacked on the ground that it would create an unnecessary federal action duplicative of state remedies. Thus, the terms and legislative history of the statute compel the conclusion that Congress did not intend to allow private rights of action for damages under the statute.

This conclusion is reinforced by the decisions of the only two other courts that have squarely faced this issue. *Clairol, Inc. v. Suburban Cosmetics, Inc.,* 278 F. Supp. 859 (N.D. Ill. 1968), *Wells v. Wells,* 240 F. Supp. 282 (W.D. Ky. 1965), and by the several other federal decisions which, in viewing the relationship between the Federal Food, Drug, and Cosmetic Act and applicable state remedies, have clearly indicated that violations of the Act do not constitute an independent basis for federal question jurisdiction. *Orthopedic Equipment Co. v. Eutsler,* 276 F.2d 455 (4th Cir. 1960), *Herman v. Smith, Kline & French Laboratories,* 286 F.Supp. 694 (E.D. Wis. 1968).

Plaintiff's reliance upon cases arising under other federal regulatory statutes is misplaced. First, the federal statutes involved in those cases had neither provisions requiring all actions to be brought by the United States nor ones restricting federal district court jurisdiction to injunctive actions. Secondly, those decisions did not deal with legislative history like that of the Food, Drug and Cosmetic Act, showing an explicit rejection by Congress of a provision for private actions. Finally, such decisions typically involve claims for which no corresponding civil remedies are available in state courts....

NOTES

1. *FD&C Act Cases. See also Fiedler v. Clark,* 714 F.2d 77 (9th Cir. 1983); *Gelley v. Astra Pharmaceutical Products, Inc.,* 466 F. Supp. 182 (D. Minn.), *aff'd,* 610 F.2d 558 (8th Cir. 1979), p. 1224 *infra; Raye v. Medtronic Corp.,* 696 F. Supp. 1273 (D. Minn. 1988); *Griffin v. O'Neal, Jones & Feldman, Inc.,* 604 F. Supp. 717 (S.D. Ohio 1985); *Munson v. Eli Lilly and Co.,* 1987–1988 FDLI Jud. Rec. 760 (D. Minn. 1987); *National Women's Health Network, Inc. v. A.H. Robins Co., Inc.,* 545 F. Supp. 1177 (D. Mass. 1982); *American Home Products Corp. v. Johnson and Johnson,* 436 F. Supp. 785 (S.D.N.Y. 1977); *Powell v. Kull,*

329 F. Supp. 193 (M.D. Pa. 1971). Violation of the FD&C Act that leads to abrogation of a contract can also be the subject of a private damage action. *See, e.g., Gerber Products Co. v. Fisher Tank Co.*, 833 F.2d 505 (4th Cir. 1987); *Burke Pest Control, Inc. v. Joseph Schlitz Brewing Co.*, 438 So. 2d 95 (Fla. App. 1983), involving allegations that contamination of food packaging resulted in damage to the plaintiffs. For discussion of private suits under the FD&C Act, *see* Cole & Shapiro, *Private Litigation Under the Federal Food, Drug, and Cosmetic Act: Should the Right to Sue be Implied?*, 30 FDC L.J. 576 (1975); Sales, *Does the FDC Act Create a Private Right of Action?*, 28 FDC L.J. 501 (1973).

In *Merrell Dow Pharmaceuticals, Inc. v. Thompson*, 478 U.S. 804 (1986), the Supreme Court held (5–4) that a complaint alleging a violation of the FD&C Act as an element of a state cause of action could not be brought in a Federal court. The majority and dissenting opinions both assumed that the FD&C Act does not create a private right of action in favor of individuals injured by conduct in violation of the Act.

2. *Private Suits Under Other Statutes.* In *Pacific Trading Co. v. Wilson & Co., Inc.*, 547 F.2d 367 (7th Cir. 1976), the court held that no private cause of action may be implied under the Packers and Stockyards Act, the United States Warehouse act, the FD&C Act, or the Federal Meat Inspection Act. A private cause of action under the Federal Meat Inspection Act was also rejected in *Shoultz v. Monfort of Colorado, Inc.*, 754 F.2d 318 (10th Cir. 1985); *Mario's Butcher Shop and Food Center, Inc. v. Armour and Co.*, 574 F. Supp. 653 (N.D. Ill. 1983). *Cross v. Board of Supervisors of San Mateo County*, 326 F. Supp. 634 (N.D. Cal. 1968), rejected private claims based on the Federal Trade Commission Act, the Federal Hazardous Substances Act, and the FD&C Act. *Holloway v. Bristol–Myers Corp.*, 485 F.2d 986 (D.C. Cir. 1973), and *Carlson v. Coca–Cola Co.*, 483 F.2d 279 (9th Cir. 1973), denied a private cause of action under the Federal Trade Commission Act. *See* Note, *Judicial Refusal to Imply a Private Right of Action Under the FTCA*, 1974 Duke L.J. 506 (1974). No private right of action is provided by the Federal Insecticide, Fungicide, and Rodenticide Act, *Fiedler v. Clark*, 714 F.2d 77 (9th Cir. 1983); *In re "Agent Orange" Product Liability Litigation*, 635 F.2d 987 (2d Cir. 1980).

3. *Supreme Court Jurisprudence.* In *Cort v. Ash*, 422 U.S. 66 (1975), the Court enunciated four criteria for determining whether a private cause of action will be implied under Federal regulatory statutes; more recent decisions have made clear that the central inquiry has become whether Congress, expressly or impliedly, intended to permit private enforcement. The Court's contemporary treatment of implied private rights is illustrated in *Transamerica Mortgage Advisers, Inc. v. Lewis*, 440 U.S. 943 (1979); *Touche Ross & Co. v. Redington*, 442 U.S. 560 (1979); *Cannon v. University of Chicago*, 441 U.S. 677 (1979) (dissenting opinion).

4. *State Statutes.* Violation of a state food and drug law may allow an independent private cause of action or may in any event give rise to a cause of action under other state statutes. *Compare Committee on Children's Television, Inc. v. General Foods Corp.*, 197 Cal.Rptr. 783, 673 P.2d 660 (1983), *with National Women's Health Network, Inc. v. A.H. Robins Co., Inc.*, 545 F. Supp. 1177 (D.Mass. 1982).

2. THE EFFECT OF THE 1938 ACT ON COMMON LAW SUITS

ORTHOPEDIC EQUIPMENT CO. v. EUTSLER

United States Court of Appeals, Fourth Circuit, 1960.
276 F.2d 455.

SOBELOFF, Chief Judge.

... On March 30, 1956, the twenty-one year old plaintiff was helping his father take down a tree on a farm near Orange, Virginia. He was injured by the tree falling upon him. At the University of Virginia Hospital, it was found that he had sustained a fracture of the leg and other injuries. In the judgment of the surgeons, the treatment indicated for the fracture was an operation known as intramedullary nailing by use of a Kuntscher Cloverleaf Intramedullary Nail. This involves the insertion of a long metal rod or nail into the medullary canal (containing the marrow) of the femur (or thigh bone), in order to stabilize the broken fragments. The advantage sought by this method is an early union and weight-bearing without the necessity of a plaster cast.

A team of orthopedists, experienced in this technique, operated on April 3, 1956. Having prepared the canal by use of a 9mm. medullary reamer or drill, the surgeons began to insert into the medullary canal a Kuntscher Cloverleaf intramedullary nail manufactured by the defendant. These Kuntscher nails usually have imprinted upon them two figures signifying their dimensions, *e.g.*, 9 x 40, 10 x 42, but the imprint or label does not explain the meaning of these figures. It is agreed by the parties that the larger figure is understood to represent the length of the nail in centimeters. According to the plaintiff's expert witnesses, the interpretation placed upon the smaller figure by orthopedists is that the nail will fit into a hole having a width or diameter corresponding in millimeters to the figure on the nail.... Furthermore, plaintiff's experts testified, orthopedic surgeons invariably rely upon the figures imprinted on the nail when there are figures imprinted, without making independent measurements. Thus, according to the surgeon, they relied in this instance too on the accuracy of the marking, "OEC 9 x 40," in selecting the nail.

As the nail was driven down the canal of the upper fragment of the thigh bone, the surgeons at first met normal resistance. When it penetrated further, however, greater resistance was encountered. Nevertheless, the doctors did not regard this as unusual, since they knew that they had used a 9mm. reamer and the nail was marked to indicate 9mm.; they concluded that it must merely have met some slight obstruction which, as in past operations, would be passed or overcome without difficulty. Accordingly, as was customary in such cases, two or three slightly heavier blows were then struck.

Because the nail would progress no further even after these heavier blows, the surgeons decided to remove it. However, when persistent efforts to dislodge the nail proved unavailing, the portion of the nail protruding below the canal of the upper fragment was cut off, the wound closed, and a plaster cast applied in the hope that in a few weeks the bones would atrophy sufficiently to loosen the nail and permits its withdrawal.

About a month later, on May 4, the surgeons again tried to extract the nail, but were unsuccessful. Thereupon, one of the doctors designed a new instrument, and by its use removal of the nail was finally accomplished in a third operation on June 5. Measurements of cross-sections of the nail, as testified to by a machinist, varied from a minimum of 9.27mm to a maximum of 10.12mm. Due to the nail's impaction, incurable osteomyelitis or bone infection resulted. The Plaintiff has permanently lost the use of his leg, and its ultimate amputation is expected.

This action was brought against defendant for alleged "negligent manufacture, labelling and launching on the market of said nail * * *," plaintiff presumably at first intending to charge ordinary common law negligence only. Later, however, it was stipulated by counsel that, without formal amendment, the complaint should also be regarded as alleging a violation of the Federal Food, Drug, and Cosmetic Act. . . .

Having determined that the Federal Food, Drug, and Cosmetic Act applies in the instant case, and that there was sufficient evidence of misbranding, we turn now to the effect of a violation of the Act. The Federal Food, Drug, and Cosmetic Act does not expressly provide a civil remedy for injured consumers. However, the statute imposes an absolute duty on manufacturers not to misbrand their products, and the breach of this duty may give rise to civil liability.

The basic question is whether a violation of the strict duty created by the Act shall be deemed negligence per se under Virginia law, assuming as we must from the submission made to the jury and from its verdict, that the violation was the proximate cause of the plaintiff's injury. The majority of American courts which have passed on this question, in cases arising under state laws resembling the Federal Act, have held violations to be negligence per se. . . .

Since Virginia law seems to regard violation of motor vehicle statutes as negligence per se, again assuming from the jury's verdict here that the violation was found to be a proximate cause of the injury, and in light of the decisions in other states passing on this question, we think that a violation of the Federal Food, Drug, and Cosmetic Act is negligence per se in Virginia, and that the District Judge correctly based his charge on that premise. . . .

NOTE

Stanton v. Astra Pharmaceutical Products, Inc., 718 F.2d 553 (3d Cir. 1983), sustained a jury award to an injured consumer based upon the company's failure to submit adverse reaction reports to FDA. *See Toole v. Richardson-Merrell Inc.*, 251 Cal. App. 2d 689, 60 Cal. Rptr. 398 (1967). *See also* Kaplan,

Variations on a Single Theme—The Impact of the Pure–Food Statutes on Civil Liability, 13 FDC L.J. 11 (1958); Woods, *The Effect of the Food, Drug and Cosmetic Act on Private Litigation,* 8 FDC L.J. 511 (1953).

---

3. SUITS AGAINST THE GOVERNMENT

RICHARD A. MERRILL, COMPENSATION FOR PRESCRIPTION DRUG INJURIES

59 Virginia Law Review 1 (1973).

... One might expect the increasing judicial willingness to impose liability without fault on manufacturers of harmful consumer products to have led to a similar expansion of government liability beyond negligence.... The courts have uniformly held that the Tort Claims Act does not permit recovery based upon absolute liability, strict liability, or other non-fault theories....

The Act's waiver of immunity is further qualified by several exceptions in section 2680 [of 28 U.S.C.], which provide the government numerous affirmative defenses to liability. For example, section 2680(a) excepts any claim based upon the "act or omission of an employee of the Government, exercising due care, in the execution of a statute or regulation, whether or not such statute or regulation be valid...." Congress intended this exception to preclude review by tort action of the legality of statutes and regulations. Therefore, an agency is immune from suit for any harm resulting from the adoption of a regulation or from the conduct of an employee utilizing "due care" in its execution.

Perhaps more important in the present context, the government is also immune from liability for "any claim ... based upon the exercise or performance or the failure to exercise or perform a discretionary function or duty ... whether or not the discretion involved be abused." ...

Not surprisingly, it is difficult to determine which activities or decisions are discretionary. The Supreme Court has stated broadly that "where there is room for policy judgment and decision there is discretion," and has additionally attempted to distinguish "discretionary" functions by questioning whether the decision that caused harm was made at a "planning" or an "operational" level.....

A third statutory exception that could limit the FDA's potential liability is the exclusion in section 2680(h) of "any claim arising out of ... misrepresentation...." This provision ... has been most frequently invoked to avoid liability for financial loss incurred by private individuals who bought or sold property based on an erroneous representation of a government employee or agency. For example, this preemption precluded recovery by a company that purchased tomato paste in reliance on an erroneous FDA certification that it was marketable. . . .

***

GRAY v. UNITED STATES

United States District Court, Southern District of Texas, 1978.
445 F. Supp. 337.

STERLING, District Judge.

This is a civil damage suit brought by the plaintiff, Beverly Ann Gray (Gray), against a drug company, Eli Lilly and Company (Lilly), and the United States. Plaintiff alleges that she has been harmed by a drug diethylstilbestrol (DES), taken by her mother during Gray's period of gestation. The pleadings and affidavits indicate that DES was dispensed by physicians in the early 1950's to pregnant women with histories of miscarriages in order to avoid problem pregnancies. It was not until 1971 that the medical community recognized that DES caused cancer in women whose mothers took the drug. This is the basis of Gray's complaint. In essence this is a products liability case. . . .

In her original complaint, plaintiff alleges that the United States government, through its agent, the Food and Drug Administration (FDA), was negligent in failing properly to test DES, in failing to warn of the adverse effects of DES, and in approving DES and representing that it was safe. . . .

The issue thus is whether the FDA's evaluation and issuance of new drug applications for DES by 1953 constituted a discretionary function within the ambit of 28 U.S.C. § 2680(a). . . . Gray has argued strenuously that the FDA's action was one of perfunctory scientific deduction and not that of making discretionary policy decisions. The government on the other hand places the FDA in a more paternal position with great latitude to decide what is safe for the public. . . .

The discretionary acts sought to be exonerated by § 2680(a) must be conduct that brings to bear policy judgments, the balancing of a risk-benefit formulae. It is in those problem areas where the public imposes upon its decision makers both a duty and an unrestrained liberty to consider and construct a solution, that the results of such deliberations should be protected. Otherwise the threat of future litigation might intimidate the creativity of those decision makers burdened with the duty of working out a problem. Such is the situation before this court. The FDA was given a general statutory mandate to assure the public that a marketed drug is safe to use. No broader standard of duty is imposed upon the FDA than the three words, safe for use. There are no particular scientific tests or measuring sticks by which the FDA must qualify a new drug. Instead the FDA is given the liberty to consider all factors it deems relevant in its own determination of a drug's safety for the public. The severity of the task delegated to the FDA demands that such an agency be given the freedom effectively to exercise its expertise. Congress has chosen the FDA to be the decision maker in this area, and its judgments in approving a drug as safe for use must be beyond private scrutiny and litigation.....

In light of the above reasons, this Court is of the opinion that the conduct of the FDA was discretionary within the terms of 28 U.S.C. § 2680(a), and therefore the plaintiff Gray's suit against the government is barred....

FEDERAL TORT CLAIMS ACT CASES

See Gelley v. Astra Pharmaceutical Prods., Inc., 466 F. Supp. 182 (D.Minn. 1979), *aff'd,* 610 F.2d 558 (8th Cir. 1979), where the plaintiffs sought to escape the holding of the principal case:

Generally, plaintiff's theory of liability against the government is that the FDA negligently failed to withdraw its prior approval of xylocaine and negligently failed to enforce the provisions of the Food, Drug and Cosmetic Act and its own regulations relating to information collection and labeling changes, thereby allowing xylocaine to remain in interstate commerce in a misbranded and/or adulterated condition....

... [A]s the Federal Tort Claims Act makes explicit, the law of the place where the act or omission occurred which gives rise to the claim is the foundation upon which federal governmental liability is predicated.... The law of the District of Columbia does not impose a tort duty on private persons to perform activities required by the FDA regulatory scheme. Regulatory activity engaged in by FDA personnel simply has no counterpart in private activity and thus cannot give rise to liability under the common law of the District of Columbia or elsewhere.... The result of the plaintiff's argument, if accepted, would be to impose liability on the federal government for the failure of its regulatory employees to protect the public in general against third party violations of federal law. This result would cast the federal government in the role of an insurer against violations of regulatory law, certainly a result not contemplated by Congress in enacting the Federal Tort Claims act.

But see Berkovitz v. United States, 486 U.S. 531 (1988), pp. 703–10 *supra,* where the Supreme Court outlined the circumstances in which the government could be liable for injuries resulting from FDA's decision to release lots of oral polio vaccine. While this decision may be limited in its impact to the special functions that FDA performs in the regulation of biological products, for which it assesses both the safety and efficacy of the "prototype" and the contents of individual product lots, Justice Marshall's language surely represents a narrowing of the discretionary function exemption.

FDA has been held to be immune from suit under the FTCA for the assertedly negligent approval of a new drug, *Bailey v. Eli Lilly Co., Inc.,* 607 F. Supp. 660 (M.D. Pa. 1985), for wrongful refusal to approve a new drug, *Hogan v. FDA,* 1965–1968 FDLI Jud. Rec. 376 (S.D. Cal. 1965), and for allegedly negligent inspection, *Anglo–American and Overseas Corp. v. United States,* 242 F.2d 236 (2d Cir. 1957). In *Schindler v. United States,* Civ. No. 77–72707 (E.D. Mich., September 18, 1979), the court dismissed an action against the United States based upon FDA's licensing of a vaccine, which it held to be a discretionary function. It distinguished *Griffin*, p. 710 supra, as involving nondiscretionary physical testing of a licensed product.

MIZOKAMI v. UNITED STATES

United States Court of Claims, 1969.
414 F.2d 1375.

PER CURIAM.

Plaintiffs, partners in Mizokami Brothers Produce, growers and shipper of fresh vegetables, are the largest growers of summer spinach in the United States. From their main location at Blanca, Colorado, plaintiffs ship most of their summer spinach crop to the eastern United States, where it is washed, graded, and made in 10–20–ounce packages ready for household use by firms in the prepackaged vegetable industry.

Between July 16 and August 17, 1962, agents of the Food and Drug Administration (FDA) took samples from 10 cars of spinach shipped by plaintiffs to various customers to check for possible violations of the Federal Food, Drug, and Cosmetic Act. As to eight of the cars, plaintiffs were advised that no unallowable pesticide contamination had been found. By means of paper chromatographic testing, however, FDA determined that two shipments to Muller Foods Company of Jersey City, New Jersey, were contaminated with heptachlor, a pesticide for which FDA regulations allowed no human tolerance on spinach.... On August 14, 1962, defendant filed a libel of seizure and condemnation against the 418 bushels of spinach in the United States District Court for New Jersey on grounds that it was contaminated or adulterated within the meaning of 21 U.S.C. §§ 342(a)(2)(B) and 346a(a)....

Plaintiffs took numerous steps to check the accuracy of the FDA finding and to investigate potential sources of contamination after hearing of the finding from the Muller Foods Company on August 10, 1962.... Tests ... proved negative as to the presence of heptachlor. On August 30, 1962, plaintiff Mike Mizokami and counsel appeared at an FDA hearing in Denver, denying ever having used heptachlor, and presenting results of their fruitless search for a source of contamination.

At this juncture, the FDA sent a sample of the condemned spinach to Washington for analysis by gas chromatography, a procedure considerably more sensitive than paper chromatography. By letter of September 24, 1962, the Deputy Commissioner of FDA admitted to plaintiffs that the original analysis by paper chromatography was in error and that the gas chromatographic analysis had not confirmed the presence of heptachlor.

Plaintiffs now claim damages resulting from FDA action in the amount of $543,879.96....

Plaintiffs are before the court under Priv. L. No. 88–346 (1964) which provides as follows:

> * * * That jurisdiction is hereby conferred on the United States Court of Claims to hear, determine, and render judgment on the claims of ... Mizokami Brothers Produce, of Blanca, Colorado, based upon damages and losses allegedly sustained as the result of erroneous determinations by the Food and Drug Administration in 1962 that spinach ... was contaminated by the pesticide heptachlor. Suit upon such claims may be instituted any time within one year of the date of approval of this Act....

It is clear that Priv. L. No. 88–346 constitutes a waiver of the sovereign immunity which defendant could otherwise claim in this case. In the absence of the special act, any suit on the above-stated facts under the Federal Tort Claims Act would be precluded by 28 U.S.C. § 2680(h), which expressly excepts from the Tort Claims Act waiver of sovereign immunity "[a]ny claim arising out of * * * misrepresentation * * *." ...

It thus seems certain that the sovereign immunity bar was lifted by the provision that "jurisdiction is hereby conferred" on this court to "hear, determine, and render judgment" on plaintiffs' claims. To hold otherwise would be to presume that Congress passed the bill in question merely to send plaintiffs to this forum for a ritual ... dismissal of their petition.

It is concluded, however, that Congress has gone one step further and conceded liability for the actions of the FDA. The committee report in each House contains the following crucial wording: ...

> * * * The committee finds that it must disagree with the conclusion of the Department of Health, Education, and Welfare that relief should not be extended in this case. * * *
>
> It is not enough to say that a mistake by the Government should be borne by the individual harmed in the absence of general legislation. * * * The Congress has the power to grant relief and it seems only right that a remedy should be provided. However, this committee feels that questions concerning the quantum of damages and whether a sufficient connection can be proven between the Government's action and the alleged losses are most properly determined by a court. Under a jurisdictional bill, these matters must be proven by competent evidence in accordance with the rules and procedures of the Court of Claims.

Though perhaps it could more clearly have so provided, it thus appears that Congress has left the factual and legal questions relating to causation and damages, matters especially appropriate for judicial determination, for this court, having first determined liability it-self.....

NOTE

In two other cases, brought without the aid of special legislation, the Court of Claims denied recovery for damages resulting from alleged improper action by FDA. *California Canners & Growers Ass'n v. United States*, 7 Cl. Ct. 69 (1984), *rev'd*, 9 Cl. Ct. 774 (1986); *Sperling & Schwartz, Inc. v. United States*, Food Drug Cosm. L. Rep. (CCH) ¶ 38,140 (Cl. Ct. 1977).

---

4. SUITS UNDER THE LANHAM ACT

a. Prior to 1988

The Lanham Act, 60 Stat. 427 (1946), represented a comprehensive revision of the United States law of trademarks. Section 43(a) of the Act, 15 U.S.C. § 1125(a), provides a private civil cause of action for damages or an injunction for any false representation made in connection with any goods or services. Until 1988, it read as follows:

> Any person who shall affix, apply, or annex, or use in connection with any goods or services, or any container or containers for goods, a false designation of origin, or any false description or representation, including words or other symbols tending falsely to describe or represent the same, and shall cause such goods or services to enter into commerce, and any person who shall with knowledge of the falsity of such designation of origin or description or representation cause or procure the same to be transported or used in commerce or deliver the same to any carrier to be transported or used, shall be liable to a civil action by any person doing business in the locality falsely indicated as that of origin or in the region of which said locality is situated, or by any person who believes that he is or is likely to be damaged by the use of any such false description or representation.

POTATO CHIP INSTITUTE v. GENERAL MILLS, INC.

United States Court of Appeals, Eighth Circuit, 1972.
461 F.2d 1088.

PER CURIAM.

Appellants Potato Chip Institute and Weaver Potato Chip Co. filed this suit seeking an injunction to prevent General Mills Co. from advertising as potato chips its product called Chipos. The complaint is premised upon § 43(a) of the Lanham Act....

Judge Urbom, after a five-day hearing, concluded that "the past experience of the consumer so shades the term with a raw potato overlay ... " that it would mislead the public to advertise Chipos as potato chips without any further explanation. However, he also concluded "that the phrase 'potato chip,' standing alone, is a generic term which is capable of including both chips made of raw potatoes and chips made of dehydrated potatoes." He also found that defendant's practice of adding to its label the descriptive words "fashioned from dried potato granules," would, if displayed properly, prevent misleading the public because the label would not then misdescribe or misrepresent the product. Accordingly, Judge Urbom declined to enjoin General Mills from calling Chipos "potato chips," but he did permanently enjoin General Mills from advertising Chipos as potato chips "without an accompanying prominent declaration that CHIPOS are made from dried or dehydrated potatoes."

Appellants contention on appeal is that the phrase potato chip has only one meaning, to wit: a thin slice of *raw* potato fried in deep fat; and therefore that the qualifying phrase does not remove the confusion because it is contradictory rather than explanatory. However, it is well settled that if the contested phrase is susceptible to two meanings so that an explanatory phrase will preclude deception, it is sufficient to require the addition of the explanation rather than prohibit using the ambiguous phrase.

... We are satisfied that the findings of the district court are responsive to substantial evidence, and that the ultimate judgment was not induced by a misconception of the applicable law....

PROCTER & GAMBLE CO. v. CHESEBROUGH–POND'S INC.

United States Court of Appeals, Second Circuit, 1984.
747 F.2d 114.

MANSFIELD, Circuit Judge:

Comparative television advertising on a national scale by manufacturers claiming superiority for their products over competing brands has magnified the risk of competitive harm from false advertising and has led to the proliferation of suits by competitors alleging violations of § 43(a) of the Lanham Act. These consolidated appeals represent another example of efforts to use the courts as a means of policing this relatively new practice, raising issues as to the scope of the Lanham Act and the court's role in evaluating tests relied upon as support for claims of product superiority.

Each of two giants in the soap and toilet goods market, Chesebrough–Pond's Inc. ("Chesebrough") and The Procter & Gamble Company ("P & G"), appeals from an order of the Southern District of New York, 588 F. Supp. 1082, Gerard L. Goettel, *Judge*, denying preliminary relief in its action to enjoin the other from using alleged false claims of superiority or equality for its product. We affirm the denial of preliminary injunctive relief in both actions.

The products forming the basis of the two actions are widely advertised and distributed hand and body lotions. P & G's "New Wondra" and versions thereof and Chesebrough's "Vaseline Intensive care Lotion" ("VICL") and variations of it. Beginning in November 1983, P & G began advertising New Wondra on TV and in print as superior to other leading lotions in the therapeutic treatment of dry skin. . . . P & G advertised, for instance, (1) that "New Wondra beats the leading lotions"; (2) that it is "[b]etter than any top lotion"; (3) that it "relieves dry skin better than any leading lotion"; (4) that "[d]ermatologists proved it in clinical tests. New Wondra improves the condition of rough dry skin better"; and (5) that New Wondra "works better than any other leading lotion at turning rough dry hands soft and smooth." At about the same time, Chesebrough began to run television commercials and advertisements making a somewhat less extravagant claim that P & G's assertion of superiority. Chesebrough claimed parity for VICL, *i.e.*, that it was equal in effectiveness to any other leading brand. According to the ads "[w]hen it comes to relieving dry skin, no leading lotion beats Vaseline Intensive Care Lotion" and "you can't buy better lotions to heal winter dry skin." . . . .

Judge Goettel, after reviewing in detail the tests made by P & G and Chesebrough, concluded that, although P & G's tests were not worthless, they "were far from perfect and are subject to various infirmities." Chesebrough's tests, he found, were "more questionable than P & G's," but he noted that they had been used only to support a lesser claim of parity rather than a claim of superiority such as that asserted by P & G for New Wondra. Although some of the weaknesses in each party's tests and analytical methods were noted, none was found sufficiently significant to call for outright rejection of the test results. . . . .

Although a plaintiff need not prove obviousness or bad faith and although proof of good faith does not immunize a defendant, each plaintiff bears the burden of showing that the challenged advertisement is false and misleading, not merely that it is unsubstantiated by acceptable tests or other proof. The mere fact that one party's evidence in support of the truth of its advertisements was unpersuasive would not *ipso facto* entitle the other party to relief. In the present case, for instance, regardless of the weaknesses of the tests made and relied on by Chesebrough to support its parity claims, P & G would be entitled to relief against Chesebrough only upon adducing evidence that the Chesebrough ads were false. Conversely, even if P & G did not prevail on its claim, Chesebrough could obtain an injunction against P & G only by establishing that the latter's advertising claim of test-proven superiority was false. To prove such falsity Chesebrough assumed the burden of showing that the tests referred to by P & G were not sufficiently reliable to permit one to conclude with reasonable certainty that they established the proposition for which they were cited. The fact-finder's judgment should consider all relevant circumstances, including the state of the testing art, the existence and feasibility of superior procedures, the objectivity and skill of the persons conducting the tests, the accuracy of their reports, and the results of other pertinent tests.

The issuance of preliminary injunctive relief in the present two cases therefore turns mainly on issues of fact rather than of law, *i.e.,* the weight to be given by the district court to the evidence about the comparison tests conducted by the parties. If a party fails to show a likelihood of success by adducing through tests or other evidence that the other's claim of superiority or parity is probably false, the district judge's exercise of his broad discretion to deny relief must be upheld.....

McNEILAB, INC. v. AMERICAN HOME PRODUCTS CORP.

United States Court of Appeals, Second Circuit, 1988.
848 F.2d 34.

IRVING R. KAUFMAN, Circuit Judge:

The ongoing competition between McNeilab, Inc. (McNeil), a wholly owned subsidiary of Johnson & Johnson, Inc., and American Home Products Corporation (AHP), rival pain reliever manufacturers, has brought anything but relief to the federal courts. Instead, repeated and protracted litigation has created a substantial headache....

Plaintiff-appellee McNeil manufactures Tylenol, the leading aspirin-free over-the-counter (OTC) pain reliever. The active ingredient in Tylenol is acetaminophen. Defendant-appellant American Home Products manufactures Advil, a competing product. The active ingredient in Advil is ibuprofen. Tylenol and Advil compete directly, along with aspirin, in the lucrative OTC internal analgesic market. To distinguish their products in consumers' minds, each manufacturer stresses the diverse qualities of its drug's ingredients, particularly with respect to safety and effectiveness.

Ibuprofen has been available in the United States as a prescription drug since 1974. The Food and Drug Administration approved it for over-the-counter distribution in 1984. Like aspirin, ibuprofen is a nonsteroidal anti-inflammatory drug that inhibits the body's production of prostaglandins. Prostaglandins sensitize nerve endings to pain and inflamed joints; thus these drugs prevent pain and swelling. Because prostaglandins also protect the stomach lining, however, impeding their production may lead to stomach irritation or ulcers. Ibuprofen is less likely to cause these side effects than aspirin. Acetaminophen, on the other hand, does not affect prostaglandin production; it reduces suffering by raising the pain threshold. Consequently, acetaminophen is relatively free of adverse gastrointestinal side effects.

AHP introduced Advil in 1984. McNeil, perceiving a threat to its market position, responded with heavy promotion of Tylenol. It distributed innumerable free samples to physicians and engaged in widespread print and television advertising. The competition swiftly turned bitter, however, as AHP filed suit in the United States District Court for the Southern District of New York, charging McNeil with false advertising. The principal target of AHP's claim was a safety profile McNeil provided physicians visually linking ibuprofen to aspirin in a comparative display. The effect, AHP asserted, was to suggest that ibuprofen shared aspirin's high propensity to irritate the stomach. McNeil counterclaimed, raising allegations that AHP's multi-media advertising campaign concealed its product's side effects.

In April 1987, after a lengthy trial, Judge Conner held that both parties had violated section 43(a) of the Lanham Act, 15 U.S.C. § 1125(a) (1982). *American Home Products Corp. v. Johnson & Johnson,* 654 F. Supp. 568 (S.D.N.Y. 1987) (*Advil I*). Specifically, he found McNeil had falsely equated ibuprofen's risks with aspirin's and had exaggerated acetaminophen's safety superiority over ibuprofen. AHP, he determined, misled consumers by claiming ibuprofen was less susceptible than acetaminophen to adverse reactions with other drugs....

Within days, AHP launched a new televised campaign proclaiming, "if you worry about the discomfort of stomach upset as I do, I find that *nothing is better than Advil. Not even Tylenol.*" (emphasis added). AHP also introduced a commercial stating that "*like Tylenol, Advil doesn't upset my stomach.*" (emphasis added). Thus, AHP linked Advil directly to Tylenol. In response, McNeil brought this Lanham Act claim, seeking damages and injunctive relief.

McNeil charged the slogans would mislead and confuse consumers by falsely representing that Advil and Tylenol cause stomach upset with the same frequency. McNeil also alleged the commercials contradicted Judge Conner's determination in *Advil I* that Advil is more likely than Tylenol to cause *severe* side effects. AHP responded that the comparisons were neither false nor misleading because ibuprofen and acetaminophen produce similar *minor* side effects. Consumers, AHP contended, would not interpret "stomach upset" to include serious gastrointestinal injury, but, rather, would distinguish between subjective and objective stomach problems. Accordingly, the decision in this case depended upon consumer understanding of the phrase "stomach upset."....

Judge Conner convened a second evidentiary hearing in October to consider McNeil's challenge to the adjusted language. McNeil supplemented the record of the first hearing with three new surveys indicating consumer confusion from the updated advertisements. It also adduced testimony from a prominent gastroenterologist that his patients used the phrase "stomach upset" in a generic fashion to describe all types of stomach ailments, whether subjective or objective. Moreover, McNeil introduced testimony that the television networks were initially reluctant to air the modified commercials due, at least in part, to a propensity to confuse viewers. As a result, Judge Conner preliminarily enjoined AHP's claim that Advil is "like Tylenol" with regard to "minor" or "occasional" stomach upset, *McNeilab, Inc. v. American Home Products Corp.,* 675 F. Supp. 819 (S.D.N.Y. 1987) (*Advil II*), and this appeal ensued.....

AHP's challenges raise serious questions related to the usefulness of McNeil's research....

Judge Conner recognized the surveys' deficiencies but determined that the evidence was relevant despite its flaws. The results, he concluded, were "supported by the other evidence adduced by McNeil and by common sense." We have previously upheld reliance on disputed survey data that were supported by testimony. And, although AHP's objections undermine the precision of the surveys, they do not deplete them of all value. The district court, therefore, had ample basis to find the research relevant, and did not abuse its discretion in admitting the evidence.....

One further issue merits discussion. The district court wrote, "Where false or misleading advertising in violation of the Lanham Act is shown, irreparable harm is presumed." The case it relied upon for this proposition, however, states: "The likelihood of injury and causation will *not* be presumed, but must be demonstrated in some manner." *Coca–Cola* [*v. Tropicana Products*], 690 F.2d 312 at 316 (emphasis added); *see also Johnson & Johnson v. Carter–Wallace, Inc.,* 631 F.2d 186, 189–90 (2d Cir. 1980). This apparent confusion need not detain us; an important distinction must be drawn between the instant case and *Coca–Cola* and *Johnson & Johnson.*

Both *Coca–Cola* and *Johnson & Johnson* involved misleading, non-comparative commercials which touted the benefits of the product advertised but made no direct reference to any competitor's product. The injury in such cases accrues equally to all competitors; none is more likely to suffer from the offending broadcasts than any other. The Lanham Act, however, only authorizes actions by one "who believes that he is or is likely to be damaged." 15 U.S.C. § 1125(a). Thus, we required some indication of actual injury and causation to satisfy Lanham Act standing requirements and to ensure a plaintiff's injury was not speculative.

This case, by contrast, presents a false comparative advertising claim. Thus, the concerns voiced in *Coca–Cola* and *Johnson & Johnson* regarding speculative injury do not arise. A misleading comparison to a specific competing product necessarily diminishes that product's value in the minds of the consumer. By falsely implying that Advil is as safe as Tylenol in all respects, AHP deprived McNeil of a legitimate competitive advantage and reduced consumers' incentive to select Tylenol rather than Advil.... Consequently, the district court did not err in presuming harm from a finding of false or misleading advertising.

The decision of the district court is affirmed.

NOTES

1. *Consumer Suits. See Florida ex rel. Broward County v. Eli Lilly & Co.,* p. 1217 *supra,* where the court also dismissed the claim based on the Lanham Act with the following statement: "The commentators agree that members of the general public, as consumers, have no right of action under the Lanham Act."

2. *FDA-Regulated Products.* Litigation under the Lanham Act with respect to FDA-regulated products has increased sharply since 1970. *See, e.g., Alpo Petfoods, Inc. v. Ralston Purina Co.,* 913 F.2d 958 (D.C.Cir.1990); *Sandoz Pharmaceuticals Corp. v. Richardson-Vicks, Inc.,* 902 F.2d 222 (3d Cir.1990); *Johnson & Johnson v. GAC International, Inc.,* 862 F.2d 975 (2d Cir. 1988); *Coca-Cola Co. v. Procter & Gamble Co.,* 822 F.2d 28 (6th Cir. 1987); *Coca-Cola Co. v. Tropicana Products, Inc.,* 690 F.2d 312 (2d Cir. 1982); *Vidal Sassoon, Inc. v. Bristol-Myers Co.,* 661 F.2d 272 (2d Cir. 1981); *Johnson & Johnson v. Carter-Wallace, Inc.,* 631 F.2d 186 (2d Cir. 1980); *American Home Products Corp. v. Johnson & Johnson,* 577 F.2d 160 (2d Cir. 1978); *Bernard Food Industries, Inc. v. Dietene Co.,* 415 F.2d 1279 (7th Cir. 1969); *Grove Fresh Distributors, Inc. v. Flavor Fresh Foods, Inc.,* 720 F.Supp. 714 (N.D. Ill. 1989); *Ciba-Geigy Corp. v. Thompson Medical Co., Inc.,* 672 F. Supp. 679 (S.D.N.Y. 1985); *American Home Products Corp. v. Johnson & Johnson,* 672 F. Supp. 135 (S.D.N.Y. 1987); *McNeilab, Inc. v. Bristol-Myers Co.,* 656 F. Supp. 88 (E.D. Pa. 1986); *Grant Airmass Corp. v. Gaymar Industries, Inc.,* 645 F. Supp. 1507 (S.D.N.Y. 1986); *Thompson Medical Co. v. Ciba-Geigy Corp.,* 643 F.Supp. 1190 (S.D.N.Y. 1986); *Upjohn Co. v. Riahom Corp.,* 641 F. Supp. 1209 (D.Del. 1986); *Upjohn Co. v. American Home Products Corp.,* 598 F. Supp. 550 (S.D.N.Y. 1984); *American Home Products Corp. v. Abbott Laboratories,* 522 F. Supp. 1035 (S.D.N.Y. 1981); *McNeilab, Inc. v. American Home Products Corp.,* 501 F. Supp. 517 (S.D.N.Y. 1980); *Sherrell Perfumers, Inc. v. Revlon, Inc.,* 483 F. Supp. 188 (S.D.N.Y. 1980); *Johnson & Johnson v. Quality Pure Mfg., Inc.,* 484 F. Supp. 975 (D.N.J. 1979).

3. *FDA Access to Evidence.* Evidence obtained in connection with a suit under section 43(a) of the Lanham Act is potentially subject to subpoena by FDA for use in an action brought by the agency to enforce the FD&C Act. *United States v. Hoyvald,* Food Drug Cosm. L. Rep. (CCH) ¶ 38,061 (E.D.N.Y. 1987).

---

b. 1988 Revision of the Lanham Act

As part of the Trademark Law Revision Act of 1988, 102 Stat. 3935, 3946, section 43(a) of the Lanham Act was amended to read:

> Any person who, on or in connection with any goods or services, or any container for goods, uses in commerce any word, term, name, symbol, or device, or any combination thereof, or any false designation of origin, false or misleading description of fact, or false or misleading representation of fact, which—
>
> (1) is likely to cause confusion, or to cause mistake, or to deceive as to the affiliation, connection, or association of

such person with another person, or as to the origin, sponsorship, or approval of his or her goods, services, or commercial activities by another person, or

(2) in commercial advertising or promotion, misrepresents the nature, characteristics, qualities, or geographic origin of his or her or another person's goods, services, or commercial activities,

shall be liable in a civil action by any person who believes that he or she is or is likely to be damaged by such act.

This revision effected two changes in the 1946 statute. First, section 43(a) was expanded to impose liability when a person makes a false or misleading representation of fact about another person's goods, services, or commercial activities. Before 1988, liability attached only to false or misleading representations made by the defendant about its own goods or services. Second, the 1988 legislation amended sections 34–36 of the Act to make explicit that all remedies available for infringement of a registered trademark are also available for violation of section 43(a) with respect to an unregistered trademark. These remedies include injunctive relief, damages, recovery of profits, destruction of infringing materials, and, in exceptional cases, attorneys fees.

SUITS UNDER RICO

The Racketeer Influenced and Corrupt Organization (RICO) Act was enacted in 84 Stat. 922, 941 as part of the Organized Crime Control Act of 1970, and is codified in 18 U.S.C. § 1961 *et seq.* Section 1962 makes it unlawful for any person (a) to use or invest income derived from a pattern of racketeering activity to acquire an interest in an enterprise, (b) to acquire or maintain through a pattern of racketeering activity an interest or control over an enterprise, (c) to conduct or participate in the affairs of an enterprise through a pattern of racketeering activity, and (d) to conspire to commit any of the prior three offenses. Section 1964(c) allows any person injured in its business or property to sue and recover treble damages, court costs, and reasonable attorneys fees.

Attempts by injured plaintiffs to use RICO in product liability actions have uniformly failed because of lack of evidence of any pattern of racketeering activity, lack of injury to business or property, and a lack of the required interaction between a person and an enterprise. *E.g., Raye v. Medtronic Corp.,* 696 F. Supp. 1273 (D. Minn. 1988); *Munson v. Eli Lilly and Co.,* 1987–1988 FDLI Jud. Rec. 760 (D. Minn. 1987); *Griffin v. O'Neal, Jones & Feldman, Inc.,* 604 F. Supp. 717 (S.D.Ohio 1985). A RICO action brought by a company against a former employee and others alleging a fraudulent scheme to misappropriate trade secrets relating to medical devices was dismissed on the grounds that there was no showing of a pattern of racketeering activity or of an enterprise distinct from the persons named, *Medical Inc. v. Angicor Ltd,* 677 F. Supp. 1000 (D. Minn. 1988). *See also Grove Fresh Distributors, Inc. v. Flavor Fresh Foods, Inc.,* 720 F.Supp. 714 (N.D. Ill. 1989). Creative plaintiffs nonetheless may yet be able to allege RICO violations that will survive scrutiny under the statute. For example, competitors have charged RICO violations against companies involved in the generic drug scandal, p. 579 *supra,* alleging damages resulting from their pattern of unlawful activity.

P. STATE ENFORCEMENT OF THE FD&C ACT

Since 1938, section 702(a) of the FD&C Act has authorized FDA to conduct examinations and investigations using state employees who have been "commissioned" as FDA officers. Under the Nutrition Labeling and Education Act of 1990, 104 Stat. 2353, states were for the first time authorized directly to enforce particular food labeling provisions of the FD&C Act in Federal courts. All of the food labeling provisions that are subject to Federal preemption under section 403A of the FD&C Act are also subject to state enforcement under section 307(b) of the FD&C Act.

Section 307(b) is limited to civil actions brought within the geographical area of the state. A state is precluded from bringing any such action until 30 days after it provides notice to FDA of its intent to do so. If FDA commences formal or informal regulatory action relating to the matter the state must wait an additional 90 days. If at the end of that 90 days FDA is diligently prosecuting the matter in court or has settled it, the state is foreclosed from bringing any action in Federal court.

Because the state may in any event bring any such action in its own state court without FDA agreement, it is unclear why a state would ever wish to face these procedural obstacles in order to bring the same action in a Federal court.

Chapter XII

FDA PRACTICE AND PROCEDURE

A. FDA'S APPROACH TO REGULATION

1. OVERVIEW

The experience of most government agencies suggests that the number and length of their regulations increase with time. FDA fits this pattern. The agency's regulations occupied about 250 pages in the Code of Federal Regulations in 1948, increased to 585 pages in 1956, and ballooned from 1718 pages in 1969 to 2951 pages in 1979. By 1989 they totalled 3793 pages.

The proliferation of FDA regulations reflects the major change in the agency's approach to enforcing the FD&C Act. Prior to 1970, FDA relied on court enforcement as its main method for assuring compliance. This approach was feasible, and indeed appropriate, because the issues facing the agency were typically less complex and its objectives were less ambitious. As one example, in the area of food labeling, FDA was only expected to enforce explicit mandatory labeling requirements (the name of the food, the name and address of the manufacturer, the net quantity of contents, and the statement of ingredients) and the Act's general prohibition against false or misleading statements. Now, FDA is expected to establish labeling requirements that will allow consumers to evaluate the composition and nutritional quality of food. While court enforcement fulfilled FDA's former role, it could not suffice as public and congressional perceptions of the agency's role changed.

For the past generation FDA has interpreted and applied the FD&C Act primarily through regulations. It has continued to rely on court enforcement to deal with traditional problems of filth in food or fraudulent labeling, and to assure compliance with promulgated regulations. But new substantive law is rarely made through court action. The agency's modern approach has had judicial support:

> [O]ver the last decade rule-making has been increasingly substituted for adjudication as a regulatory technique, with the support and encouragement of courts, at least where the regulation involves specialized scientific knowledge. Where the objective is essentially legislative, i.e., to establish rules or principles by which an entire industry may be governed, the case-by-case adversary proceeding, in which the agency con-

fronts a single alleged offender selected for suit with respect to a specific factual situation, has frequently proved to be an unsuitable method of enforcing the law, since it often resolves narrow issues of importance only to the immediate adversaries rather than broad questions of interest to the industry or the public. The rule-making proceeding, on the other hand, provides the agency with an opportunity first to receive a wide spectrum of views proffered by all segments affected by the proposed rule (*e.g.,* manufacturers, vendors, doctors, consumers) and then in a legislative fashion to consider and choose from several alternatives or options rather than limit its decisions to narrow issues controlling a particular case. Furthermore, once binding regulations are promulgated, the industry and public are put on notice and may be guided accordingly rather than speculate as to the outcome of a seizure or enforcement suit.

National Nutritional Foods Ass'n v. Weinberger, 512 F.2d 688 (2d Cir. 1975).

FDA has pioneered rulemaking as a regulatory technique. Like other government agencies, it has issued regulations to particularize specific substantive requirements of the FD&C Act. An example is the regulation establishing the required type, size and location for mandatory information on food labels, 38 Fed. Reg. 2124 (January 19, 1973), 38 Fed. Reg. 6950 (March 14, 1973). Previously, FDA had relied on court action to enforce the requirement of section 403(f) that this information appear "prominently" and "with such conspicuousness (as compared with other words, statements, designs, or devices in the labeling) and in such terms as to render it likely to be read and understood by the ordinary individual under customary conditions of purchase and use." By mandating a specific type size and establishing rules for placement of this information on the label, FDA eliminated uncertainty and dispute and thus obviated court action except against firms that do not follow the prescribed standards. *See generally* McNamara, *The New Age of FDA Rule–Making,* 31 FDC L.J. 393 (1976); Merrill, *Administrative Rule–Making,* 30 FDC L.J. 478 (1975).

In addition to such traditional rulemaking, FDA has issued regulations to establish a variety of nonstatutory mechanisms for resolving broad issues that were not foreseen when the FD&C Act was passed. A good example of this use of rulemaking is the OTC Drug Review, p. 588 *supra.* The FD&C Act does not explicitly authorize FDA either to establish advisory committees to review the safety, effectiveness, and labeling of OTC drugs, or to promulgate regulations that determine which OTC drugs are safe, effective, and properly labeled.

FDA is the only agency that has issued comprehensive regulations specifying how it will interpret and apply other Federal laws of government-wide applicability, such as the Freedom of Information Act, the National Environmental Policy Act, and the Federal Advisory Committee Act. FDA's Public Information Regulations, for example, p. 1299 *infra*, list all of the numerous types of documents in its files and specify exactly how each type will be dealt with under the FOIA. *See* Hutt, *Granting Access By Policy Regulation*, in Department of Justice, INTER-AGENCY SYMPOSIUM ON IMPROVED ADMINISTRATION OF THE FREEDOM OF INFORMATION ACT 132 (November 29, 1973). Finally, FDA has codified most of its administrative practices and procedures in regulations. For a discussion of the use of rulemaking to particularize statutory requirements previously enforced only by court action, *see* Coleman, *The Use of Regulations to Enforce Statutory Quality Assurance Requirements*, 31 FDC L.J. 96 (1976).

2. FDA'S PROCEDURAL REGULATIONS

In 40 Fed. Reg. 22950 (May 27, 1975), FDA published comprehensive regulations governing the agency's administrative practices and procedures. The regulations, consisting of 34 pages of preamble and 62 pages of codified rules, were made effective 60 days later, without time for comment, on the premise that as procedural regulations they were exempt from the rulemaking requirements of 5 U.S.C. § 533. Suit was promptly brought seeking a declaration that the regulations were unlawful because of the agency's failure to provide notice and an opportunity for public comment. *American College of Neuropsychopharmacology v. Weinberger,* Food Drug Cosm. L. Rep. (CCH) ¶ 38,025 (D.D.C. 1975), held that the regulations, even though procedural, had substantial impact and thus could not lawfully be issued without complying with 5 U.S.C. § 553. 40 Fed. Reg. 33063 (August 6, 1975).

Following this ruling, FDA republished the entire document as a proposal, 40 Fed. Reg. 40682 (September 3, 1975). After receiving comments, the agency promulgated final regulations in stages: 41 Fed. Reg. 26636 (June 28, 1976), 41 Fed. Reg. 48258 (November 2, 1976), 41 Fed. Reg. 51706 (November 23, 1976), 41 Fed. Reg. 52148 (November 26, 1976), 42 Fed. Reg. 4680 (January 25, 1977). Within two months the entire regulations were reorganized and recodified, with different section numbers. 42 Fed. Reg. 15553 (March 22, 1977). Later, as part of HEW's "operation common sense," FDA promulgated revisions to "incorporate editorial changes" and to make them "more concise and readable," 53 Fed. Reg. 51966 (November 7, 1978), 44 Fed. Reg. 22318 (April 13, 1979).

Because of the broad scope of the regulations, it is not feasible to summarize even the important issues with which they deal. The following paragraphs provide pertinent references, arranged by subject matter.

1. FDA's general administrative practices and procedures are set out in 21 C.F.R. Part 10, 42 Fed. Reg. 4680 (January 25, 1977). *See*

Pape, *Meetings and Correspondence, Including FOI Considerations,* 32 FDC L.J. 226 (1977); Peskoe, *Submissions and Petitions Under the FDA's Procedural Regulations,* 32 FDC L.J. 216 (1977); Van Brunt, *Advisory Opinions,* 32 FDC L.J. 304 (1977).

2.   Regulations governing formal evidentiary public hearings appear at 21 C.F.R. Part 12, 41 Fed. Reg. 51706 (November 23, 1976), 53 Fed. Reg. 2767 (February 1, 1988), 53 Fed. Reg. 29453 (August 5, 1988).

3.   Regulations governing advisory committees appear at 21 C.F.R. Part 14, 41 Fed. Reg. 52148 (November 26, 1976).

4.   Regulations governing legislative-type hearings appear at 21 C.F.R. Part 15, 41 Fed. Reg. 48258 (November 2, 1976).   *See* Bennett, *Committee or Commissioner,* 32 FDC L.J. 323 (1977).

5.   Regulations governing informal regulatory hearings appear at 21 C.F.R. Part 16, 41 Fed. Reg. 48258 (November 2, 1976), 51 Fed. Reg. 43217 (December 1, 1986), 53 Fed. Reg. 4613 (February 17, 1988).   *See* Greene, *Informal FDA Hearings,* 32 FDC L.J. 354 (1977).

6.   Regulations prescribing standards of conduct and defining conflicts of interest appear at 21 C.F.R. Part 19, 41 Fed. Reg. 48258 (November 2, 1976).

See generally Greenberger, *A Consumer Advocate's View of the FDA's Procedures and Practices,* 32 FDC L.J. 293 (1977); Hoffman, *The FDA's New Forms of Public Hearing—Choosing Among the Alternatives,* 32 FDC L.J. 330 (1977); Rothschild, *The FDA's Regulations—A Model for the Future?,* 32 FDC L.J. 344 (1977); Thompson, *Public Hearings—A View from the Bar,* 32 FDC L.J. 312 (1977).

---

3. PLANNING AND PRIORITIES

Beginning in the early 1970s, FDA has engaged in a yearly planning process that establishes the agency priorities and budgets the time of all field and headquarters personnel accordingly.   *See* Barkdoll, *Making Planning Relevant to Public Agency Management,* Long Range Planning 59 (February 19, 1976).   Beginning in the mid–1970s, FDA extended its planning process to involve consumers, industry, health professionals, and state regulatory officials.   *See* Barkdoll, *Involving Constituents in Agency Priority Setting: A Case Study,* 6 Evaluation and Program Planning 31 (1983).   Each year during the 1970s, these activities produced a comprehensive plan for the agency as well as periodic long range plans, with specific goals and objectives.   Beginning in the mid–1980s, these yearly plans were augmented by three additional "action plans," established in July 1985, May 1987, and May 1989, establishing agency goals in highly visible areas that affect the public health.

Efforts to plan and set priorities cannot, however, evade the central reality—FDA lacks the resources to implement all of the missions delegated to it by Congress. The agency therefore budgets its resources on the basis of three principles. First, it must devote *some* resources to every aspect of the FD&C Act, to avoid criticism that some activities are completely unregulated. Second, it must devote the vast bulk of its resources to those problems that receive the greatest public attention and that can have the greatest public health impact, recognizing that these may not be the same. Third, it must be prepared at any moment to reorder or abandon its priorities to respond to public health emergencies, such as a product tampering crisis.

USER FEES

Under 31 U.S.C. § 9701, a Federal agency may charge for services it provides when those services confer a special benefit upon an identifiable recipient. User charges collected pursuant to this provision go into the general treasury and are not added to the funds appropriated for the agency. For example, charges made for providing records under the Freedom of Information Act could not be used by the agency to support FOI Act activities prior to enactment of section 711 as part of the Food and Drug Administration Revitalization Act, 104 Stat. 4583 (1990).

For more than 20 years, user charges have been considered for a variety of FDA activities. *E.g.,* GAO, FEES NOT CHARGED FOR PROCESSING APPLICATIONS FOR NEW DRUGS, No. B–164031 (2) (November 4, 1971); THE CONGRESS SHOULD CONSIDER EXPLORING OPPORTUNITIES TO EXPAND AND IMPROVE THE APPLICATION OF USER CHARGES BY FEDERAL AGENCIES, No. PAD–80–25 (March 28, 1980). Regulated firms have opposed user charges by FDA on the grounds that FDA action is designed to protect the public generally and not to provide a special benefit to an identifiable recipient, that user fees would constitute a hidden tax on industry, and that in any case imposition of user fees would not increase the resources available to FDA because they would be paid into the general treasury. FDA officials generally opposed user charges until President Reagan endorsed them. In 50 Fed. Reg. 31726 (August 6, 1985), the agency proposed to establish user fees for NDAs. The House and Senate Appropriations Committees have historically opposed user charges by FDA, however, and as of June 30, 1990, there has been no final action on the proposed regulation or on any other form of user charges or registration fees.

4. FDA, REGULATED FIRMS, AND THE PUBLIC

Throughout FDA's history there has been controversy over the relationship that does, or should, prevail between the agency and private individuals or organizations, particularly regulated firms. Years ago political scientists formulated the so-called "capture" model of regulatory behavior in which the regulated industry increasingly dominates the agency established by Congress to regulate it. By contrast, relations between FDA and the industries it regulates have been more adversarial, often contentious. Because compliance with the FD&C Act necessarily requires voluntary action by regulated firms, however, frequent informal communication is essential to make the process work. When occasional breaches of the public trust by employees of FDA or regulated firms have been uncovered, there have been demands for a more formal relationship, and Commissioners have issued memoranda (none ever codified) prescribing arms-length dealing.

For example, in August 1974 eleven employees of the then Bureau of Drugs testified at a Senate hearing that FDA officials had harassed them when they made decisions adverse to pharmaceutical manufacturers. "Examination of the Pharmaceutical Industry, 1973–74," Joint Hearings Before the Subcomm. on Health of the Senate Comm. on Labor and Public Welfare and the Subcomm. on Administrative Practice and Procedure of the Senate Comm. on the Judiciary, 93rd Cong., 1st & 2nd Sess., Pt. 7 (1974). One month later, the Commissioner denied the charges and defended the integrity of the new drug approval process. "Regulation of New Drug R&D By the Food and Drug Administration, 1974," 93rd Cong., 2nd Sess. (1974). An outside review panel was later appointed by HEW Secretary David Mathews to conduct an independent investigation.

REVIEW PANEL ON NEW DRUG REGULATION, FINAL REPORT
(HEW 1977).

... FDA's communications with the sponsors of new drugs are largely informal. FDA employees and industry representatives frequently discuss INDs and NDAs in telephone conversations and at meetings. Industry representatives also make numerous unscheduled visits to FDA reviewers to drop off materials, chat, and check on the status of their companies' applications....

FDA employees and industry representatives have stated that oral communications are essential because many scientific issues are not easily resolved through written correspondence. Nevertheless, such a system has led to questions about the influence exerted by the pharmaceutical industry on agency decisions, especially in light of FDA's trade secrets policy.

The Panel's investigations of relationships between FDA and the pharmaceutical industry did not uncover a pattern of undue industry influence. Furthermore, the Panel agrees that non-written communication at times can be a more efficient means of resolving complex scientific questions than written communication.... However, the Panel found no justification for much of the informal, non-written contact which takes place between FDA staff and industry representatives....

... Because the system is *ad hoc,* Bureau procedures for communicating with industry vary from division to division and sometimes from reviewer to reviewer. Although FDA staff are required to prepare memoranda of their communications with industry representatives, the Panel found that reviewers differed in the extent to which they documented such contacts and in the amount of detail they provided in memoranda. In some cases, this resulted in an incomplete written record of FDA decision-making....

The Panel recommends that FDA institute a more formalized system of contact, in which written correspondence is the preferred means of communication. Such a system, using a minimum of oral, informal communications, is appropriate for FDA to assure both its regulatees and the public that it is performing its function fairly and objectively. It also is necessary to produce a well-documented record of FDA decision-making. Finally, written correspondence is consistent with the Bureau of Drugs' duty to approve or disapprove new drugs solely on the basis of the scientific data presented....

Over a decade later a committee chartered by the President's Cancer Panel, at the request of President Bush, to identify ways to expedite the development and approval of important new drugs, offered a contrasting assessment.

FINAL REPORT OF THE NATIONAL COMMITTEE TO REVIEW PROCEDURES FOR APPROVAL OF NEW DRUGS FOR CANCER AND AIDS

(HHS 1990).

If the drug development and approval process is to proceed expeditiously, it is essential that there be free and open communication between FDA and drug sponsors at all times. The relationship between FDA reviewers and drug sponsors must be informal, highly interactive, and foster a spirit of mutual cooperation. An atmosphere of arms-length formality will slow down the process, raise artificial barriers to drug development and approval, and seriously harm the public health. The development and approval of AIDS and cancer drugs depends upon helpful cooperation, not adversarial isolation. Communications should most frequently be by telephone, fax, and computer, to provide current information, quick responses to important questions, and a feeling of genuine partnership. The artificial barriers that have been erected through years of criticism on the part of both the regulators and the regulated have created a serious threat to rapid development and approval of new drugs, and can no longer be tolerated.

NOTE

1. *Commentary. See* Hutt, *Balanced Government Regulation of Consumer Products,* 31 FDC L.J. 592 (1976):

... Consumer groups have argued that the FDA is dominated by the food industry, and the food industry has responded with equal vehemence that consumer advocates have undue influence over the Agency.... Neither group is as effective as the other believes, or even as the group itself believes. It would be refreshing, even though unexpected, if both agreed to a truce on this relatively trivial issue, and instead dealt with the important and difficult matters pending before the Agency on their merits. . . .

2. *Agency Regulations.* FDA's regulations, 21 C.F.R. §§ 10.65, 10.70, and 10.80, permit essentially unlimited contact between agency employees and the public but require that all significant contacts be summarized and disclosed. If a draft regulation is made available to any outside person, it is available to everyone. *See, e.g.,* 37 Fed. Reg. 24117 (November 14, 1972), 40 Fed. Reg. 12535 (March 19, 1975). All memoranda summarizing meetings or telephone conversations are available to the public and are required to be made part of the pertinent administrative record. *Cf. Home Box Office, Inc. v. FCC,* 567 F.2d 9 (D.C. Cir. 1977). The only published guidance for communications between FDA and the pharmaceutical industry is contained in Center for Drug Evaluation and Research, STAFF MANUAL GUIDE BD 4800.3 (May 29, 1981), which depicts a rather formal mode. But this guide has no official status and thus is not enforced with respect to either FDA or industry personnel.

3. *Generic Drug Scandal.* For a discussion of the most recent scandal involving bribes by some generic drug manufacturer to induce FDA employees to act favorably on their applications, p. 579 *supra, see* "FDA's Generic Drug Approval Process (Parts 1 and 2)," Hearings Before the Subcomm. on Oversight and Investigations of the House Comm. on Energy and Commerce, 101st Cong., 1st Sess. (1989).

---

5. FDA AND OTHER FEDERAL REGULATORY AGENCIES

Since 1970, proliferation of new Federal regulatory statutes and agencies has enlarged the need for FDA to coordinate activities with other agencies. Some memoranda of understanding (MOU) and interagency agreements (IAG) have been published in the Federal Register and some have not. All are compiled in FDA, COMPLIANCE POLICY GUIDES MANUAL. FDA proposed to exempt MOUs with state agencies from Federal Register publication in 51 Fed. Reg. 19851 (June 3, 1986).

Mutually Exclusive Jurisdiction. FDA-regulated products are often explicitly excluded from other regulatory statues. For example, the Toxic Substances Control Act (TSCA), 15 U.S.C. § 2602(2)(B)(vi), excludes FDA-regulated products and EPA has interpreted this exclusion as extending to all aspects of these products, including raw materials, *e.g.,* 42 Fed. Reg. 13130 (March 9, 1977), 42 Fed. Reg. 64572 (December 23, 1977), 43 Fed. Reg. 11318 (March 17, 1978). Because jurisdictional lines are not always easy to draw, however, FDA has on occasion entered into agreements with other regulatory agencies to allocate responsibilities. For example, FDA and the Consumer Product Safety Commission (CPSC) have agreed that, to the extent that food containers and utensils that do not become components of food present a hazard, they are subject to regulation by CPSC, 41 Fed. Reg. 34342 (August 13, 1976).

Overlapping Jurisdiction. In other instances FDA-regulated products are not exempt from other regulatory statutes. Early statutes regulating other products often addressed the jurisdictional issue ambiguously or not at all. For example, the jurisdictional divisions between USDA and FDA for meat, p. 34 *supra,* and between BATF and FDA for alcoholic beverages, p. 34 *supra,* have been the subject of intense controversy and not even now definitively resolved. Following the creation of EPA by Executive Order in 1970, to guide agency officials and regulated firms FDA and EPA entered into a series of agreements regarding matters of mutual responsibility in 36 Fed. Reg. 24234 (December 22, 1971), 38 Fed. Reg. 24233 (September 6, 1973), 40 Fed. Reg. 25078 (June 12, 1975). An attempt to explain the joint regulation of pesticides that are also new animal drugs, 48 Fed. Reg. 22799 (May 20, 1983), was stayed in 48 Fed. Reg. 37077 (August 16, 1983). FDA and BATF have entered into an MOU defining their responsibilities for adulterated alcoholic beverages in 52 Fed. Reg. 45502 (November 30, 1987). FDA and the Patent and Trademark Office (PTO) have entered into an MOU establishing procedures for their mutual responsibilities under the Drug Price Competition and Patent Term Restoration Act of 1984 in 52 Fed. Reg. 17830 (May 12, 1987).

Concurrent Jurisdiction. FDA and the Customs Service of the Department of Treasury, which jointly enforce the import provisions of the FD&C Act, have established a working relationship on sampling and refusal of imports in 44 Fed. Reg. 53577 (September 14, 1979). FDA has entered into an MOU with the Interstate Shellfish Sanitation Conference in 49 Fed. Reg. 12751 (March 30, 1984), which was one factor in FDA's recision of a proposed national shellfish safety program, 50 Fed. Reg. 7797 (February 26, 1985).

Service To Other Agencies. Even where jurisdiction is not overlapping or concurrent, FDA has agreed to provide services to other agencies as a part of its regulatory activities. For example, FDA has agreed to inspect toxicology testing laboratories for compliance with EPA's GLP requirements, 43 Fed. Reg. 14124 (April 4, 1978), and has assumed the responsibility to assure that drugs and biologics procured by Department of Defense are of appropriate quality, FDA Compliance Policy Guide No. 7155d.02 (October 1, 1980).

B. SECTION 701(a) RULEMAKING

The FD&C Act contains two grants of rulemaking authority. Section 701(e) empowers FDA to promulgate regulations to implement enumerated substantive sections of the Act. Rulemaking under section

701(e) is subject to special procedures, including the opportunity for a formal evidentiary hearing of the type described in sections 556 and 557 of the Administrative Procedure Act, 5 U.S.C. §§ 556 and 557. Section 701(e) rules have always been recognized as having the force of law.

Section 701(a) of the Act empowers FDA "to promulgate regulations for the efficient enforcement of this Act." Because Congress did not specify what procedures were to be followed in exercising this authority, rulemaking pursuant to section 701(a) is subject only to the informal "notice-and-comment" procedures of 5 U.S.C. § 553.

1. HHS AND OMB SUPERVISION OF FDA RULE-MAKING

The authority to administer the FD&C Act is expressly lodged in the Secretary of HHS. Neither FDA nor the Commissioner of Food and Drugs was mentioned in the Act before 1988. When FDA was formally established by statute in the Food and Drug Administration Act of 1988, 102 Stat. 3048, 3120, which added section 903 to the FD&C Act, the delegation of authority to implement the Act was not modified.

Prior to 1981 the Secretary of HHS formally delegated authority to implement the FD&C Act to the Commissioner. This implicitly included the authority to propose and promulgate regulations without HHS approval. As a practical matter, successive Commissioners kept Secretaries and their staffs informed about important FDA actions, including regulations, but there was no process of formal HHS review and approval. The extent of HHS supervision over FDA regulations largely depended on the desires of the individual Secretary. For example, there was closer supervision of FDA regulations during the last half of the 1970s under HEW Secretary Califano than had occurred during the first half of the decade.

In 46 Fed. Reg. 26052 (May 11, 1981), HHS Secretary Schweiker promulgated a regulation, codified in 21 C.F.R. § 5.11, stating that "the Secretary reserves the authority to approve regulations of the Food and Drug Administration" which establish general rules applicable to a class of products or present highly significant public issues. Regulations promulgated under section 701(e) were excluded from this reservation of authority. In 47 Fed. Reg. 16010 (April 14, 1982), the regulation was modified to permit, but not require, the Secretary to approve regulations promulgated through formal rulemaking as well. Accordingly, since 1981, all significant FDA proposed and final regulations have been reviewed and approved by HHS.

At the same time, the Executive Office of the President, through the Office of Management and Budget (OMB), also put in place a system for close supervision of most Federal agency rulemaking. Executive Order 11821, 39 Fed. Reg. 41501 (November 29, 1974), required that every Federal agency proposing a "major" regulation must evaluate its potential inflation impact and prepare an inflation impact statement

(IIS). The Office of the Federal Register required that the inflation impact analysis be referenced in the preamble to every proposed or final regulation, 40 Fed. Reg. 26312 (June 23, 1975), 40 Fed. Reg. 48979 (October 20, 1975), 41 Fed. Reg. 43476 (October 1, 1976).

President Jimmy Carter, whose election platform promised regulatory reform, issued Executive Order 12044, 43 Fed. Reg. 12661 (March 24, 1978), requiring a regulatory analysis of significant regulations and a review of existing regulations, and Executive Order 12174, 44 Fed. Reg. 69609 (December 4, 1979), requiring a reduction in the paperwork burden imposed by the Federal government. Based upon these two executive orders, Congress enacted the Regulatory Flexibility Act, 94 Stat. 1164 (1980), requiring each agency to publish a semiannual regulatory agenda, to perform regulatory flexibility analysis for each proposed and final regulation, and to conduct periodic reviews of regulations; and the Paperwork Reduction Act of 1980, 94 Stat. 2812, which created the OMB Office of Information and Regulatory Affairs (OIRA) with authority to reduce the Federal paperwork burden.

Extending the examples of his predecessors, President Reagan issued Executive Order 12291, 46 Fed. Reg. 13193 (February 19, 1981) and Executive Order 12498, 50 Fed. Reg. 1036 (January 8, 1985), requiring a regulatory impact analysis for each major proposed and final regulation, a yearly regulatory program from each agency, and OMB review of all of these documents. Operating under these executive orders, OMB has had a major impact on FDA regulations. *See, e.g.,* "Office of Management and Budget Influence on Agency Regulations," Senate Comm. on Environment and Public Works, 99th Cong., 2nd Sess. S. Comm. Print. 99–156 (1986); "FDA's Continuing Failure to Regulate Health Claims for Foods," Hearings Before the Human Resources and Intergovernmental Relations Subcomm. of the House Comm. on Government Operations, 101st Cong., 1st Sess. (1989). An attempt under the Freedom of Information Act to obtain records that would reveal the status of FDA regulations under review in HHS and OMB was denied in *Wolfe v. Department of HHS,* 839 F.2d 768 (D.C. Cir. 1988) (en banc). *See also* GAO, REGULATORY REVIEW: INFORMATION ON OMB'S REVIEW PROCESS, No. GGD–89–101FS (July 1989).

OMB promulgated regulations to implement the Paperwork Reduction Act in 45 Fed. Reg. 2586 (January 11, 1980), 47 Fed. Reg. 39515 (September 8, 1982), 48 Fed. Reg. 13666 (March 31, 1983), 52 Fed. Reg. 27768 (July 23, 1987), and 53 Fed. Reg. 16618 (May 10, 1988), codified in 5 C.F.R. Part 1320. *See* GAO, IMPLEMENTING THE PAPERWORK REDUCTION ACT: SOME PROGRESS, BUT MANY PROBLEMS REMAIN, No. GGD–83–35 (April 20, 1983). In a decision that has obvious implications for FDA, the Supreme Court held in *Dole v. United Steel Workers of America,* 110 S. Ct. 929 (1990), that the Paperwork Reduction Act does not grant OMB authority to review and approve regulations mandating disclosures by private enterprises directly to their employees or to the public.

In accordance with these statutory and executive order requirements, FDA has undertaken reviews of its regulations, 46 Fed. Fed.
Reg. 36333 (July 14, 1981), 47 Fed. Reg. 29004 (July 2, 1982), and
regularly published a semiannual regulatory agenda. HHS published
policies and procedures to implement Executive Order 12291 in 47 Fed.
Reg. 1426 (January 13, 1982).

------

2. INFORMAL RULEMAKING REQUIREMENTS

Most FDA regulations are promulgated pursuant to the authority
of section 701(a) of the FD&C Act. 5 U.S.C. § 553(b) describes the
procedures that agencies must observe in informal rulemaking of the
type authorized by section 701(a). These include: (1) publication of a
notice of proposed rulemaking which sets forth either the terms or
substance of the proposed regulation or a description of the subjects and
issues involved; (2) an opportunity for interested persons to comment,
either orally or in writing; and (3) publication of a concise statement of
the basis and purpose with any final rule. In the last two decades
reviewing courts have interpreted these basic requirements as imposing
significant obligations on agencies to expose the premises of their policy
choices to factual contest and observe other safeguards previously
associated with more formal proceedings. The following FDA case,
involving a regulation promulgated by FDA before the agency began its
practice of explanatory preambles, is illustrative.

UNITED STATES v. NOVA SCOTIA
FOOD PRODUCTS CORP.
United States Court of Appeals, Second Circuit, 1977.
568 F.2d 240.

GURFEIN, Circuit Judge:

This appeal involving a regulation of the Food and Drug Administration is not here upon a direct review of agency action. It is an
appeal from a judgment of the District Court for the Eastern District of
New York ... enjoining the appellants, after a hearing, from processing hot smoked whitefish except in accordance with time-temperature-
salinity (T–T–S) regulations contained in 21 C.F.R. Part 122 (1977)....

The regulations cited above require that hot-process smoked fish be
heated by a controlled heat process that provides a monitoring system
positioned in as many strategic locations in the oven as necessary to
assure a continuous temperature through each fish of not less than 180
F° for a minimum of 30 minutes for fish which have been brined to
contain 3.5% water phase salt or at 150 F° for a minimum of 30
minutes if the salinity was at 5% water phase. Since *each* fish must
meet these requirements, it is necessary to heat an entire batch of fish

to even higher temperatures so that the lowest temperature for *any* fish will meet the minimum requirements.....

[The health rationale for the regulations and the authority of FDA to issue them pursuant to section 402(a)(4) are discussed in portions of the opinion reproduced at p. 269 *supra.*]

The Commissioner thereafter issued the final regulations [35 Fed. Reg. 17401 (November 13, 1970)] in which he adopted certain suggestions made in the comments, including a suggestion by the National Fisheries Institute, Inc.... the intervenor herein. The original proposal provided that the fish would have to be cooked to a temperature of 180 F° for at least 30 minutes, if the fish have been brined to contain 3.5% water phase salt, with no alternative. In the final regulation, an alternative suggested by the intervenor "that the parameter of 150 F° for 30 minutes and 5% salt in the water phase be established as an alternate procedure to that stated in the proposed regulation for an interim period until specific parameters can be established" was accepted, but as a permanent part of the regulation rather than for an interim period....

The Commissioner did not answer the suggestion by the Bureau of Fisheries that nitrite and salt as additives could safely lower the high temperature otherwise required, a solution which the FDA had accepted in the case of chub. Nor did the Commissioner respond to the claim of Nova Scotia through its trade association .... that "[t]he proposed process requirements suggested by the FDA for hot processed smoked fish are neither commercially feasible nor based on sound scientific evidence obtained with the variety of smoked fish products to be included under this regulation."

Nova Scotia, in its own comment, wrote to the Commissioner that "the heating of certain types of fish to high temperatures will completely destroy the product." ...

When, after several inspections and warnings, Nova Scotia failed to comply with the regulation, an action by the United States Attorney for injunctive relief was filed on April 7, 1976, six years later and resulted in the judgment here on appeal....

Appellants contend that there is an inadequate administrative record upon which to predicate judicial review, and that the failure to disclose to interested persons the factual material upon which the agency was relying vitiates the element of fairness which is essential to any kind of administrative action. Moreover, they argue that the "concise general statement of ... basis and purpose" by the Commissioner was inadequate.

... The extent of the administrative record required for judicial review of informal rulemaking is largely a function of the scope of judicial review. Even when the standard of review is whether the promulgation of the rule was "arbitrary, capricious, an abuse of discretion, or otherwise not in accordance with law," as specified in 5 U.S.C.

§ 706(2)(A), judicial review must, nevertheless, be based on the "whole record" (id.)....

No contemporaneous record was made or certified.[13] When, during the enforcement action, the basis for the regulation was sought through pretrial discovery, the record was created by searching the files of the FDA and the memories of those who participated in the process of rulemaking. This resulted in what became Exhibit D at the trial of the injunction action. Exhibit D consists of (1) Tab A containing the comments received from outside parties during the administrative "notice and comment" proceedings and (2) Tabs B through L consisting of scientific data and the like upon which the Commissioner now says he relied but which were not made known to the interested parties.

Appellants object to the exclusion of evidence in the District Court "aimed directly at showing that the scientific evidence relied upon by the FDA was inaccurate and not based upon a realistic appraisal of the true facts. Appellants attempted to introduce scientific evidence to demonstrate that in fixing the processing parameters FDA relied upon tests in which ground fish were injected with many millions of botulism [sic] spores and then tested for outgrowth at various processing levels whereas the spore levels in nature are far less and outgrowth would have been prevented by far less stringent processing parameters." The District Court properly excluded the evidence.

In an enforcement action, we must rely exclusively on the record made before the agency to determine the validity of the regulation. The exception to the exclusivity of that record is that "there may be independent judicial fact-finding when issues that are not before the agency are raised in a proceeding to *enforce* non-adjudicatory agency action."

Though this is an enforcement proceeding and the question is close, we think that the "issues" *were* fairly before the agency and hence that *de novo* evidence was properly excluded by Judge Dooling. Our concern is, rather, with the manner in which the agency treated the issues tendered.

The keys issues were (1) whether, in the light of the rather scant history of botulism in whitefish, that species should have been considered separately rather than included in a general regulation which failed to distinguish species from species; (2) whether the application of the proposed T–T–S requirements for smoked whitefish made the whitefish commercially unsaleable; and (3) whether the agency recognized that prospect, but nevertheless decided that the public health needs should prevail even if that meant commercial death for the whitefish industry. The procedural issues were whether, in the light of these key questions, the agency procedure was inadequate because (i) it failed to

---

13. A practice developed in the early years of the APA of not making a formal contemporaneous record, but rather, when challenged, to put together a historical record of what had been available for agency consideration at the time the regulation was promulgated....

disclose to interested parties the scientific data and the methodology upon which it relied; and (ii) because it failed utterly to address itself to the pertinent question of commercial feasibility....

Interested parties were not informed [in FDA's notice of proposed rulemaking] of the scientific data, or at least of a selection of such data deemed important by the agency, so that comments could be addressed to the data. Appellants argue that unless the scientific data relied upon by the agency are spread upon the public records, criticism of the methodology used or the meaning to be inferred from the data is rendered impossible.....

We think that the scientific data should have been disclosed to focus on the proper interpretation of "insanitary conditions." When the basis for a proposed rule is a scientific decision, the scientific material which is believed to support the rule should be exposed to the view of interested parties for their comment. One cannot ask for comment on a scientific paper without allowing the participants to read the paper. Scientific research is sometimes rejected for diverse inadequacies of methodology; and statistical results are sometimes rebutted because of a lack of adequate gathering technique or of supportable extrapolation. Such is the stuff of scientific debate. To suppress meaningful comment by failure to disclose the basic data relied upon is akin to rejecting comment altogether....

Appellants additionally attack the "concise general statement" required by [the] APA as inadequate. We think that, in the circumstances, it was less than adequate. It is not in keeping with the rational process to leave vital questions, raised by comments which are of cogent materiality, completely unanswered. The agencies certainly have a good deal of discretion in expressing the basis of a rule, but the agencies do not have quite the prerogative of obscurantism reserved to legislatures....

The Secretary was squarely faced with the question whether it was necessary to formulate a rule with specific parameters that applied to all species of fish, and particularly whether lower temperatures with the addition of nitrite and salt would not be sufficient. Though this alternative was suggested by an agency of the federal government, its suggestion, though acknowledged, was never answered.

Moreover, the comment that to apply the proposed T–T–S requirements to whitefish would destroy the commercial product was neither discussed nor answered. We think that to sanction silence in the face of such vital questions would be to make the statutory requirement of a "concise general statement" less than an adequate safeguard against arbitrary decision-making....

One may recognize that even commercial infeasibility cannot stand in the way of an overwhelming public interest. Yet the administrative process should disclose, at least, whether the proposed regulation is considered to be commercially feasible, or whether other considerations prevail even if commercial unfeasibility is acknowledged. This kind of forthright disclosure and basic statement was lacking in the formulation of the T–T–S standard made applicable to whitefish....

We cannot, on this appeal, remand to the agency to allow further comments by interested parties, addressed to the scientific data now disclosed at the trial below. We hold in this enforcement proceeding, therefore, that the regulation, as it affects non-vacuum-packed hot-smoked whitefish, was promulgated in an arbitrary manner and is invalid....

INFORMAL RULEMAKING PROCEDURES

Rationale. FDA's current regulations, 21 C.F.R. § 10.40(b)(1), require essentially the procedures that are mandated by the APA. Yet it is apparent that in the late 1960s the practice of many Federal agencies, including FDA, did not meet this standard. Writing more than a decade ago, Professor (now Justice) Scalia offered an explanation for the insistence of reviewing courts that agencies engaged in informal rulemaking provide procedural safeguards beyond the bare essentials historically associated with section 553:

> 1. Not until 1956 was it established that an agency charged with issuing and denying licenses in adjudicatory hearings could establish generic disqualifying factors in informal rulemaking, thereby avoiding adversarial procedures on those issues. Not until 1968 was it established that a major rate-making agency (the FPC) had implicit authority to fix rates on an areawide basis rather than company by company, enabling the avoidance of constitutional and statutory requirements for an adjudicatory hearing. And not until 1973 was it judicially determined that the FTC, one of the oldest of the regulatory agencies, had authority to prohibit unfair trade practices by rule, as opposed to operating exclusively through individual "cease-and-desist" proceedings.

> Decisions such as these have facilitated what is perhaps the most notable development in federal government administration during the past two decades: "The contrivance of more expeditious administrative methods"—that is, the constant and accelerating flight away from individualized, adjudicatory proceedings to generalized disposition through rulemaking....

> 2. Another post-APA development of monumental importance was the establishment in 1967 of the principle that rules could be challenged in court directly rather than merely in the context of an adjudicatory enforcement proceeding against a particular individual, combined with the doctrine (clearly enunciated in 1973) that "the focal point for judicial review should be the administrative record already in existence, not some new record made initially in the reviewing court." By reason of these holdings—and of a large number of new statutes which explicitly provided for direct court-of-appeals review of rulemaking—the validity of rules was increasingly decided on briefs in a court of appeals, or before a district court which could take no new evidence.

> The cumulative effect of these developments was that by the mid-1970s vast numbers of issues of the sort which in 1946 would have been resolved in a formal adjudicatory context before the agency, or even in an adjudicatory judicial proceeding, were being resolved in

informal rulemaking and informal adjudication; that the courts were expected to provide, in the words of one of the Supreme Court's more expansive descriptions (which it probably now regrets), "a thorough, probing, in-depth review" of that agency action, but taking the agency record as it was and without conducting any additional evidentiary proceedings. . . .

Scalia, *Vermont Yankee: The APA, The D.C. Circuit, and the Supreme Court,* 1978 Sup. Ct. Rev. 345 (1979).

Need for reproposal. When an agency contemplates major changes in a proposed regulation, it may be obligated to provide an additional opportunity for public comment. *Compare Chocolate Mfrs Ass'n of the United States v. Block,* 755 F.2d 1098 (4th Cir. 1985), and *Animal Health Inst. v. FDA,* Food Drug Cosm. L. Rep. (CCH) ¶ 38,154 (D.D.C. 1978), p. 480 *supra, with Pharmaceutical Mfrs. Ass'n v. Gardner,* 381 F.2d 271 (D.C. Cir. 1967).

Exceptions to 5 U.S.C. § 553. Section 553(b) ostensibly permits an agency to dispense with public rulemaking when issuing an interpretive or procedural rule or a statement of policy. Court rulings, however, have significantly narrowed these exceptions. *See, e.g., National Nutritional Foods Ass'n v. Kennedy,* 572 F.2d 377 (2d Cir. 1978); *American College of Neuropsychopharmacology v. Weinberger,* Food Drug Cosm. L. Rep. (CCH) ¶ 38,025 (D.D.C. 1975). FDA's regulations, 21 C.F.R. § 10.40(d) and (e), further limit the situations in which the agency will invoke any of these exemptions.

Statement of basis and purpose. Anticipating rulings such as *Nova Scotia,* FDA has for some time required that the preamble to a final regulation "summarize each type of comment submitted on the proposal" and "contain a thorough and comprehensible articulation of the Commissioner's decision on each issue." 21 C.F.R. § 10.40(c)(3).

Record for judicial review. In *Nova Scotia,* FDA successfully argued that review of its smoked fish regulations should be confined to the record of its original rulemaking, a position also reflected in the agency's regulations. 21 C.F.R. § 10.45(f). *See also Heterochemical Corp. v. FDA,* Food Drug Cosm. L. Rep. (CCH) ¶ 38,074 (E.D.N.Y. 1987). When an agency's reasoning on a critical issue is not apparent from the rulemaking record, a reviewing court ordinarily will remand the matter to the agency for elaboration or reopening of the record. On rare occasions, however, a district court will permit the submission of additional testimony or affidavits to clarify the agency's position. *See National Nutritional Foods Ass'n v. Mathews,* 557 F.2d 325 (2d Cir. 1977), p. 29 *supra. Compare Almay, Inc. v. Califano,* 569 F.2d 674 (D.C. Cir. 1977).

Standard for review. Section 701(a) regulations are subject to the judicial review standards established in 5 U.S.C. § 706(2)(A), *i.e.,* they will be upheld unless the court determines they are "arbitrary, capricious, an abuse of discretion, or otherwise not in accordance with law." *But see National Nutritional Foods Ass'n v. Weinberger,* 512 F.2d 688 (2d Cir. 1975), where Judge Lumbard suggested that an agency abuses its discretion even in informal rulemaking "if its actions are not supported by substantial evidence."

Exhaustion of remedies. In *Bradley v. Weinberger,* 483 F.2d 410 (1st Cir. 1973), the court vacated an injunction against FDA on the ground that the plaintiffs had failed to exhaust their administrative remedies, and remanded the matter to the agency. The plaintiffs had relied in court on arguments that they had omitted to bring to FDA's attention during the administrative process.

See also Public Citizen Health Research Group v. Commissioner, 740 F.2d 21 (D.C.Cir. 1984); *National Nutritional Foods Ass'n v. Califano,* 603 F.2d 327 (2d Cir. 1979); *Public Citizen v. Goyan,* 496 F. Supp. 364 (D.D.C. 1980).

Forum for review. 21 C.F.R. § 10.45(g) requests that all suits challenging an FDA regulation be filed in a single district court, and states that FDA will take appropriate action to avoid multiple challenges in various jurisdictions. In *Abbott Laboratories,* Justice Harlan identified several ways in which courts can respond to duplicative suits. *See also National Health Federation v. Weinberger,* 518 F.2d 711 (7th Cir. 1975); *Pharmaceutical Mfrs. Ass'n v. FDA,* Food Drug Cosm. L. Rep. (CCH) ¶ 38,130 (D. Del. 1977).

Effective date. Since 1973, FDA has established a uniform effective date for all food labeling regulations adopted within a specified time period to avoid repeated costly labeling changes. *See, e.g.,* 43 Fed. Reg. 44830 (September 29, 1978), 55 Fed. Reg. 276 (January 4, 1990). FDA's choice of wording in specifying the effective date can be critical to firms which must comply. A regulation may make a new requirement effective for all products that are "manufactured," or that are "introduced into interstate commerce," or that are "initially introduced into interstate commerce" or that are "labeled" after the specified date. Each of these formulations has a different impact on product inventories, and the choice among them usually reflects a calculated policy judgment by FDA. Section 6(d) of the Fair Packaging and Labeling Act, 15 U.S.C. § 1455(d), provides that no FPLA regulation shall "preclude the orderly disposal of packages in inventory or with the trade as of the effective date of such regulation." In *Public Citizen v. Schmidt,* Food Drug Cosm. L. Rep. (CCH) § 38,075 (D.D.C. 1976), the court upheld a delayed effective date for a ban of a carcinogen, chloroform, on the ground that "a precipitous ban on chloroform was both impractical and unenforceable."

Impact of Regulations on Existing Product Approvals. FDA regulations may alter the conditions of a product approval, even though the FD&C Act ostensibly requires an opportunity for a formal hearing before the agency may revoke or amend product approvals. In *Upjohn Co. v. FDA,* 811 F.2d 1583 (D.C. Cir. 1987), the court upheld an FDA regulation revoking all medicated feed application exemptions for a class of new animal drugs.

Interpretation of the FD&C Act. Where the intent of Congress is not clear, the courts will uphold the FDA's "permissible" and "reasonable" construction of the Act. *See, e.g., Young v. Community Nutrition Institute,* 476 U.S. 974 (1986), relying upon *Chevron U.S.A., Inc. v. Natural Resources Defense Council, Inc.,* 467 U.S. 837 (1984).

FDA Reversal of a Prior Decision. Even before *Motor Vehicle Mfrs. Ass'n v. State Farm Mutual Automobile Insurance Co.,* 463 U.S. 29 (1983), FDA realized that a decision to rescind a regulation imposes a heavy burden to supply a reasoned analysis. *See, e.g.,* the agency's extensive justification when it revoked the patient package insert (PPI) regulation, pp. 446–50 *supra.* Although a consortium of consumer organizations sued when FDA stayed the regulation, no challenge was brought to contest FDA's final decision to rescind the regulation.

Unreasonable Delay. Courts may scrutinize FDA's response to a petition to initiate rulemaking, or its progress in rulemaking, to assure that the agency is not guilty of unreasonable delay. *See, e.g., Cutler v. Hayes,* 818 F.2d 879 (D.C. Cir. 1987); *Public Citizen Health Research Group v. Commissioner,* 740 F.2d 21

(D.C. Cir. 1984); *Public Citizen v. Heckler*, 602 F. Supp. 611 (D.D.C. 1985); *American Public Health Ass'n v. Veneman*, 349 F. Supp. 1311 (D.D.C. 1972).

Discretion Not to Promulgate Regulations. See, e.g., National Wildlife Federation v. Secretary of HHS, 808 F.2d 12 (6th Cir. 1986); *Center for Science in the Public Interest v. Novitch*, Food Drug Cosm. L. Rep. (CCH) ¶ 38,275 (D.D.C. 1984). The only cases in which a court has required FDA to promulgate a regulation were *Public Citizen v. Heckler*, 602 F. Supp. 611 (D.D.C. 1985), 653 F. Supp. 1229 (D.D.C. 1986), pp. 263–66 *supra*, and *Public Citizen Health Research Group v. Commissioner, FDA*, 724 F.Supp. 1013 (D.D.C.1989).

---

3. FAILURE TO PROMULGATE REGULATIONS

FDA has discretion to enforce the FD&C Act either by bringing court enforcement action or by promulgating regulations. Where it does not wish to expend the resources necessary to develop regulations, the agency may adopt guidelines for initiating court enforcement action. In such cases, the agency must independently prove that the articles involved do in fact violate the statute. When FDA claims that an article violates the Act because it does not comply with an internal guideline, however, the question arises whether FDA must first comply with the rulemaking requirements of the APA.

Following the decision in the Supreme Court that FDA has the authority to enforce the food safety provisions in sections 402(a)(1) and 406 through action levels rather than substantive rules, *Young v. Community Nutrition Institute*, 476 U.S. 974 (1986), the court of appeals faced the question on remand of the proper administrative procedure for establishing action levels.

COMMUNITY NUTRITION INSTITUTE v. YOUNG

United States Court of Appeals, District of Columbia Circuit, 1987.
818 F.2d 943.

PER CURIAM:....

Under the APA, agency rules may be issued only after the familiar notice-and-comment procedures enumerated in the statute are completed. It is undisputed that the action level at issue here was promulgated *sans* those procedures. FDA, however, argues that notice-and-comment requirements do not apply by virtue of subsection (b)(3)(A) of section 553, which carves out an exception for "interpretative rules [and] general statements of policy." According to the FDA, action levels represent nothing more than nonbinding statements of agency enforcement policy. CNI, on the other hand, argues that the action levels restrict enforcement discretion to such a degree as to constitute legislative rules.....

... [W]e are persuaded that the FDA action levels are legislative rules and thus subject to the notice-and-comment requirements of section 553. While FDA now characterizes the action levels as policy statements, a variety of factors indicate otherwise.

First. The language employed by FDA in creating and describing action levels suggests that those levels both have a present effect and are binding. Specifically, the agency's regulations on action levels explain an action level in the following way:

> [A]n action level for an added poisonous or deleterious substance ... may be established to define the level of contamination at which food *will be deemed to be adulterated.* An action level may *prohibit any detectable amount of substance in food.* (emphasis added).

This language, speaking as it does of an action level "defin[ing]" the acceptable level and "prohibit[ing]" substances, clearly reflects an interpretation of action levels as presently binding norms. This type of mandatory, definitive language is a powerful, even potentially dispositive, factor suggesting that action levels are substantive rules....

Second. This view of action levels—as having a present, binding effect—is confirmed by the fact that FDA considers it necessary for food producers to secure *exceptions* to the action levels. A specific regulatory provision allows FDA to "exempt from regulatory action and permit the marketing of any food that is unlawfully contaminated with a poisonous or deleterious substance" if certain conditions exist. This language implies that in the absence of an exemption, food with aflatoxin contamination over the action level is "unlawful." This putatively unlawful status can derive only from the action level, which, again, indicates that the action level is a presently binding norm. If, as the agency would have it, action levels did indeed "not bind courts, food producers or FDA," it would scarcely be necessary to require that "exceptions" be obtained.

Third. On several occasions, in authorizing blending of adulterated with unadulterated corn, the FDA has made statements indicating that action levels establish a binding norm. For example, in a telegram to the Commissioner of the South Carolina Department of Agriculture, in which it indicated its approval of a blending plan, the FDA stated that "[a]ny shipments made independent of this plan *would,* if found to exceed the 20 ppb level, *be considered adulterated and subject to condemnation.*" But we need not resort to informal communications, where precision of draftsmanship may understandably be wanting. For, in a formal notice published in the Federal Register of a decision to permit blending and interstate shipment, FDA wrote:

> Any food that contains aflatoxin in excess of 20 ppb ... *is considered by FDA to be adulterated* under section 402(a) of the Federal Food, Drug, and Cosmetic Act (21 U.S.C. 342(a)(1), and *therefore may not be shipped in interstate commerce.* (emphasis added).

Both statements, one informal and the other elaborately formal, indicate that action levels constitute substantive rules. The agency's own words strongly suggest that action levels are not musing about what the FDA might do in the future but rather that they set a precise level of aflatoxin contamination that FDA has presently deemed permissible. Action levels inform food producers what this level is; indeed, that is their very purpose.

We are not unmindful that in a suit to enjoin shipment of allegedly contaminated corn, it appears that FDA would be obliged to prove that the corn is "adulterated," within the meaning of the FDC Act, rather than merely prove non-compliance with the action level. The action level thus does not bind food producers in the sense that producers are automatically subject to enforcement proceedings for violating the action level. This factor, accordingly, points in favor of the agency's characterization. But the fact that action levels do not completely bind food producers as would a more classic legislative rule (where the only issue before the court would be if the agency rule were in fact violated) is not determinative of the issue. For here, we are convinced that FDA has bound itself. As FDA conceded at oral argument, it would be daunting indeed to try to convince a court that the agency could appropriately prosecute a producer for shipping corn with less than 20 ppb aflatoxin. And this type of cabining of an agency's prosecutorial discretion can in fact rise to the level of a substantive, legislative rule. That is exactly what has happened here.

In sum, consideration of a variety of factors leads us to conclude that the FDA's action levels are not within the section 553(b)(3)(A) exception to notice-and-comment requirements. Since all agree that those procedures were not followed, the action level at issue here cannot stand.

We pause to observe that nothing in our decision today generally precludes FDA from proceeding by way of informal action levels. The Supreme Court has, of course, decided that such a course is permissible under the FDC Act. Our limited holding is that the current action levels are treated as substantive rules by FDA and, as such, can only be permitted if notice-and-comment procedures are employed. If it so chooses, FDA could proceed by action levels that are pure policy statements. But in order to do so, FDA must avoid giving action levels the kind of substantive significance that it now so plainly attaches to them.

We add one additional caveat. Our holding today in no way indicates that agencies develop written guidelines to aid their exercise of discretion only at the peril of having a court transmogrify those guidelines into binding norms. We recognize that such guidelines have the not inconsiderable benefits of apprising the regulated community of the agency's intentions as well as informing the exercise of discretion by agents and officers in the field. It is beyond question that many such statements are non-binding in nature and would thus be characterized by a court as interpretative rules or policy statements. We are persuaded that courts will appropriately reach an opposite conclusion only where, as here, the *agency* itself has given its rules substantive effect.

In sum, our holding today is narrow. We conclude that in the circumstances of this case, FDA by virtue of its own course of conduct has chosen to limit its discretion and promulgated action levels which it gives a present, binding effect. Having accorded such substantive significance to action levels, FDA is compelled by the APA to utilize notice-and-comment procedures in promulgating them....

STARR, Circuit Judge, concurring in part and dissenting in part:....

The abiding characteristic of a legislative rule is that it is law. It defines a standard of conduct that regulated individuals or entities ignore at their peril, in the face of possible enforcement action. Significantly, the only issue in any such proceeding is whether the rule applies to the facts at hand. "The underlying policy embodied in the rule is not generally subject to challenge before the agency."....

... [I]n crafting the APA, Congress directed that courts should recognize certain exceptions to the statute's notice-and-comment requirements. Specifically, Congress recognized that not all agency pronouncements, even those of considerable moment, rise to the dignity of law. Thus, the APA excepts, as the panel opinion recounts, interpretative rules and general statements of policy from the general notice-and-comment requirements. While it is no doubt true, and indeed is frequently recognized, that such agency pronouncements may have a direct effect on the regulated community, and may even be judicially reviewable, these pronouncements still lack the dignity of "law." Before that status can be achieved, the agency must run its policies through the notice-and-comment gantlet. [sic] Perhaps in part because the agency here has avoided testing its pronouncements in this way, it must in any future proceeding defend and justify its chosen standard in the face of a challenge to that standard.

The majority is quite correct when it chronicles the difficulty courts have found in attempting to fathom the distinction between legislative or substantive rules on one hand, and interpretative rules or policy statements on the other.....

... Action levels offer guidance to the regulated community with respect to what products FDA deems adulterated within the meaning of the FDC Act. But in an enforcement proceeding in which FDA seeks either to impose sanctions for shipment of an adulterated product or to enjoin shipment of an adulterated product, the agency must prove the product is "adulterated." That is, FDA cannot merely show that the product at issue fails to comply with the action level. Rather, FDA must offer scientific or other probative evidence to support its contention that the product is adulterated. Thus, the action level does not have the force of law in the subsequent proceeding. Indeed, it has no "force" at all......

NOTES

1. *Subsequent Proceedings.* Following this decision, FDA acquiesced and promulgated the regulations discussed p. 306 *supra*, stating that action levels constitute only prosecutorial guidance and not substantive requirements. 53 Fed. Reg. 5043 (February 19, 1988).

2. *Supporting Authority.* The courts have often invalidated, or refused to enforce, FDA guidelines that have not been subjected to notice-and-comment. *See, e.g., Caribbean Produce Exchange, Inc. v. Secretary of HHS,* Food Drug Cosm. L. Rep. (CCH) ¶¶ 38,100 and 38,110 (Puerto Rico 1988), *rev'd and remanded,* 893 F.2d 3 (1st Cir. 1989); *Bellarno International Ltd. v. FDA,* 678 F. Supp. 410 (E.D.N.Y. 1988); *United States v. Bioclinical Systems, Inc.,* 666 F. Supp. 82 (D.Md. 1987); *United States v. Articles of Drugs Consisting of 203 Paperbags,* 634 F. Supp. 435 (N.D. Ill. 1985), *vacated,* 818 F.2d 569 (7th Cir. 1987). In *Upjohn Mfg. Co. v. Schweiker,* 681 F.2d 480 (6th Cir. 1982), and *Burroughs Wellcome Co. v. Schweiker,* 649 F.2d 221 (4th Cir. 1981), however, the courts determined that the FDA "paper NDA" policy, p. 484 *supra,* could be implemented through an internal agency memorandum.

---

4. RIPENESS FOR JUDICIAL REVIEW

For several years following enactment of the FD&C Act, section 701(a) was regarded as permitting FDA to adopt only "interpretive" regulations. Interpretations of the statute by the agency, whether set out in letters or adopted through rulemaking under section 701(a), were not considered to have the force of law. In the following landmark case, pharmaceutical manufacturers sought a declaratory judgment that FDA regulations issued under section 701(a) were unlawful. FDA countered that the regulations could be challenged only by way of defense in a court enforcement action brought by the government. The Supreme Court held that the regulations constituted final agency action and thus were immediately reviewable under the Administrative Procedure Act, and so holding implied that valid section 701(a) regulations had the force of law.

ABBOTT LABORATORIES v. GARDNER
Supreme Court of the United States, 1967.
387 U.S. 136.

Mr. Justice HARLAN delivered the opinion of the Court.

In 1962 Congress amended the Federal Food, Drug, and Cosmetic Act to require manufacturers of prescription drugs to print the "established name" of the drug "prominently and in type at least half as large as that used thereon for any proprietary name or designation for such drug," on labels and other printed material.... After inviting and considering comments submitted by interested parties the Commissioner promulgated the following regulation for the "efficient enforcement" of the Act, § 701(a):

> "If the label or labeling of a prescription drug bears a proprietary name or designation for the drug or any ingredient thereof, the established name, if such there be, corresponding to such proprietary name or designation, shall accompany each appearance of such proprietary name or designation."

A similar rule was made applicable to advertisements for prescription drugs.

The present action was brought by a group of 37 individual drug manufacturers and by the Pharmaceutical Manufacturers Association, of which all the petitioner companies are members, and which includes manufacturers of more than 90% of the Nation's supply of prescription drugs. They challenged the regulations on the ground that the Commissioner exceeded his authority under the statute by promulgating an order requiring labels, advertisements, and other printed matter relating to prescription drugs to designate the established name of the particular drug involved every time its trade name is used anywhere in such material.

... The Court of Appeals for the Third Circuit ... held first that under the statutory scheme provided by the Federal Food, Drug, and Cosmetic act pre-enforcement review of these regulations was unauthorized and therefore beyond the jurisdiction of the District Court....

The first question we consider is whether Congress by the Federal Food, Drug, and Cosmetic Act intended to forbid pre-enforcement review of this sort of regulation promulgated by the Commissioner. The question is phrased in terms of "prohibition" rather than "authorization" because a survey of our cases shows that judicial review of a final agency action by an aggrieved person will not be cut off unless there is persuasive reason to believe that such was the purpose of Congress....

... [W]e are wholly unpersuaded that the statutory scheme in the food and drug area excludes this type of action. The Government relies on no explicit statutory authority for its argument that pre-enforcement review is unavailable, but insists instead that because the statute includes a specific procedure for such review of certain enumerated kinds of regulations, not encompassing those of the kind involved here, other types were necessarily meant to be excluded from any pre-enforcement review. The issue, however, is not so readily resolved; we must go further and inquire whether in the context of the entire legislative scheme the existence of that circumscribed remedy evinces a congressional purpose to bar agency action not within its purview from judicial review....

In this case the Government has not demonstrated such a purpose; indeed, a study of the legislative history shows rather conclusively that the specific review provisions were designed to give an additional remedy and not to cut down more traditional channels of review.....

We conclude that nothing in the Food, Drug, and Cosmetic Act itself precludes this action.

A further inquiry must, however, be made. The injunctive and declaratory judgment remedies are discretionary, and courts traditionally have been reluctant to apply them to administrative determinations unless these arise in the context of a controversy "ripe" for judicial resolution. Without undertaking to survey the intricacies of the ripeness doctrine it is fair to say that its basic rationale is to prevent the courts, through avoidance of premature adjudication, from entangling themselves in abstract disagreements over administrative policies, and also to protect the agencies from judicial interference until an administrative decision has been formalized and its effects felt in a concrete way by the challenging parties. The problem is best seen in a twofold aspect, requiring us to evaluate both the fitness of the issues for judicial decision and the hardship to the parties of withholding court consideration.

As to the former factor, we believe the issues presented are appropriate for judicial resolution at this time. First, all parties agree that the issue tendered is a purely legal one: whether the statute was properly construed by the Commissioner to require the established name of the drug to be used *every time* the proprietary name is employed.... It is suggested that the justification for this rule might vary with different circumstances, and that the expertise of the Commissioner is relevant to passing upon the validity of the regulation. This of course it true, but the suggestion overlooks the fact that both sides have approached this case as one purely of congressional intent, and that the Government made no effort to justify the regulation in factual terms.

Second, the regulations in issue we find to be "final agency action" within the meaning of § 10 of the Administrative Procedure Act, 5 U.S.C. § 704, as construed in judicial decisions. An "agency action includes any "rule," defined by the Act as "an agency statement of general or particular applicability and future effect designed to implement, interpret, or prescribe law or policy, §§ 2(c), 2(g). The cases dealing with judicial review of administrative actions have interpreted the "finality" element in a pragmatic way....

... The regulation challenged here, promulgated in a formal manner after announcement in the Federal Register and consideration of comments by interested parties is quite clearly definitive. There is no hint that this regulation is informal, or only the ruling of a subordinate official, or tentative. It was made effective upon publication, and the Assistant General Counsel for Food and Drugs stated in the District Court that compliance was expected.

The Government argues, however, that the present case can be distinguished on the ground that in [prior cases] ... the agency involved could implement its policy directly, while here the Attorney General must authorize criminal and seizure actions for violations of the statute. In the context of this case, we do not find this argument persuasive. These regulations are not meant to advise the Attorney General, but purport to be directly authorized by the statute. Thus, if within the Commissioner's authority, they have the status of law and violations of them carry heavy criminal and civil sanctions. Also, there is no representation that the Attorney General and the Commissioner disagree in this area; the Justice Department is defending this very suit. It would be adherence to a mere technicality to give any credence to this contention. Moreover, the agency does have direct authority to enforce this regulation in the context of passing upon applications for clearance of new drugs, § 505, or certification of certain antibiotics, § 507.

This is also a case in which the impact of the regulations upon the petitioners is sufficiently direct and immediate as to render the issue appropriate for judicial review at this stage. These regulations purport to give an authoritative interpretation of a statutory provision that has a direct effect on the day-to-day business of all prescription drug companies; its promulgation puts petitioners in a dilemma that it was the very purpose of the Declaratory Judgment Act to ameliorate.... The regulations are clear-cut, and were made effective immediately upon publication; as noted earlier the agency's counsel represented to the District Court that immediate compliance with their terms was expected. If petitioners wish to comply they must change all their labels, advertisements, and promotional materials; they must destroy stocks of printed matter; and they must invest heavily in new printing type and new supplies. The alternative to compliance—continued use of material which they believe in good faith meets the statutory requirements, but which clearly does not meet the regulation of the Commissioner—may be even more costly. That course would risk serious criminal and civil penalties for the unlawful distribution of "misbranded" drugs.....

NOTES

1. *Companion Cases.* Two companion cases were decided by the Court the same day as *Abbott Laboratories.* In *Toilet Goods Ass'n v. Gardner,* 387 U.S. 158 (1967), a regulation authorizing FDA to suspend color additive certification if its inspectors were refused free access to manufacturing facilities, processes, and formulae of cosmetic producers was held not ripe for review prior to implementation. In *Gardner v. Toilet Goods Ass'n,* 387 U.S. 167 (1967), however, the Court permitted preenforcement review of other regulations implementing the Color Additive Amendments of 1960.

2. *Regulatory Letters.* When FDA first used regulatory letters as an alternative to court enforcement, it intended that they represent the agency's definitive position and thus final action that could be the subject of a declaratory judgment action. The agency has since retreated from this position, arguing that regulatory letters are only advisory. And the courts have accordingly held that they are not subject to preenforcement review. *See, e.g., Biotics Research*

Co. v. Heckler, 710 F.2d 1375 (9th Cir. 1983); *Estee Lauder, Inc. v. FDA*, 727 F. Supp. 1 (D.D.C. 1989); *IMS Ltd. v. Califano*, 453 F. Supp. 157 (C.D. Cal. 1977). The courts had previously held that other forms of FDA correspondence could not be directly challenged in court. *See Helco Products Co. v. McNutt*, 137 F.2d 681 (D.C. Cir. 1943); *Wilmington Chemical Corp. v. Celebrezze*, 229 F. Supp. 168 (N.D. Ill. 1964). *See also Stauffer Chemical Co. v. FDA*, 670 F.2d 106 (9th Cir. 1982).

3. *Other Authority.* In *Tyson Foods, Inc. v. USDA*, Food Drug Cosm. L. Rep. (CCH) ¶ 38,249 (W.D. Ark. 1979), the court dismissed a suit seeking a declaratory judgment of the "prior sanction" status of sodium nitrite in poultry products on the grounds that there had been no final administrative determination or regulation on the matter and that jurisdiction to review any food additive regulation lay only in the courts of appeals. *See also Hoffmann–La Roche, Inc. v. Harris*, 484 F. Supp. 58 (D.D.C. 1979), where the court held that the plaintiff must first petition FDA to change the administrative practice to which it objected (the approval of so-called "paper NDAs") before the matter would be ripe for judicial review. In *Pharmaceutical Manufacturers Ass'n v. Kennedy*, 471 F. Supp. 1224 (D. Md., 1979), the court held that FDA's publication of a list of therapeutically equivalent drugs was not "agency action" reviewable under the APA.

4. *Patient Suits.* Individual patients have challenged FDA policies toward new drugs with mixed success. *Rutherford v. United States*, 399 F. Supp. 1208 (W.D. Okl. 1975), *aff'd*, 542 F.2d 1137 (10th Cir. 1976), held that plaintiffs were entitled to a full FDA administrative determination of the new drug status of Laetrile. In *National Gay Rights Advocates v. Department of HHS*, Food Drugs Cosm. L. Rep. (CCH) ¶ 38,080 (D.D.C. 1988), and *Breitmeyer v. Califano*, 463 F. Supp. 810 (E.D. Mich. 1978), however, the courts denied declaratory relief on the ground that the plaintiffs had failed to exhaust their administrative remedies.

5. *FDA Policy.* 21 C.F.R. § 10.45(d) provides that, after final administrative action on any issue, the agency will take the position that the issue is ripe for judicial review prior to enforcement and that any interested person is affected and thus has standing to obtain review. This has not prevented the Department of Justice from asserting a contrary position in court. *See, e.g., Bradley v. Weinberger*, 483 F.2d 410, 413 n.1 (1st Cir. 1973).

6. *Equal Access to Justice Act.* Under the Equal Access to Justice Act, 28 U.S.C. § 2412, the courts are empowered to award attorneys' fees to a party who successfully challenges Federal agency action unless the court finds that the government's position was substantially justified or that special circumstances make an award unjust. *See Center for Science in the Public Interest v. Regan*, 802 F.2d 518 (D.C. Cir. 1986); *United States v. 2,116 Boxes of Boned Beef*, 726 F.2d 1481 (10th Cir. 1984); *Public Citizen Health Research Group v. Young*, 700 F. Supp. 581 (D.D.C. 1988).

---

5. EFFECT OF SECTION 701(a) REGULATIONS

Despite the early uncertainty about the scope of FDA's rulemaking authority under section 701(a), it is now clear that regulations adopted pursuant to this power, and implementing other substantive requirements of the FD&C Act, have the force of law. A series of judicial decisions cumulatively demonstrate that the "interpretative"-"substantive" debate is dead. One of the most influential opinions was that of the Second Circuit in *National Nutritional Foods Ass'n v. Weinberger*, 512 F.2d 688 (2d Cir. 1975), where the court wrote:

> Congress did not expressly spell out the authoritative effect that should be given to regulations promulgated under §§ 701(a) and 701(e). This naturally leads one to wonder, in view of the care with which Congress spelled out the elaborate § 701(e) procedure, whether it intended any limits on the apparently expansive delegation of rule-making power granted by § 701(a), and specifically whether (as appellants urge) the latter was meant merely to grant authority to issue interpretive, non-binding advisory opinions with respect to matters of lesser importance. . . .

> A court may well consider it within its power to review the legality of some types of regulations which seek at length to flesh out the terms of a broad statute, especially when the regulations themselves are rather imprecise. In such cases a court in an enforcement proceeding will in any event be forced to develop a considerable factual record to determine whether there has been a violation of the regulation. But, as Judge Frankel observed, attempts to draw a hard and fast line between "interpretive" and "substantive" regulations have been rather unrewarding. The line of demarcation between the two is often far from clear. . . . We have come to recognize that, if the administrative process is to be practically effective, specific regulations promulgated pursuant to a general statutory delegation of authority must be treated as authoritative, whether labelled "substantive" or "interpretive", especially in areas where the agency possesses expertise not shared by the courts. In that event its views are unlikely to be disturbed by the court in an enforcement proceeding. Where once we may have demanded proof of specific delegation of legislative authority to an agency purporting to promulgate substantive rules we have learned from experience to accept a general delegation as sufficient in certain areas of expertise.

> Whatever doubts might have been entertained regarding the FDA's power under § 701(a) to promulgate binding regulations were dispelled by the Supreme Court's recent decision in *Weinberger v. Hynson, Westcott & Dunning, Inc.*, and its companion cases. . . . .

> Our attention has not been directed to anything in the legislative history of §§ 701(a) and (e) that militates against these conclusions. On the contrary, over the last decade rulemaking has been increasingly substituted for adjudication as a regulatory technique, with the support and encourage-

ment of courts, at least where the regulation involves specialized scientific knowledge.... Where the objective is essentially legislative, *i.e.*, to establish rules or principles by which an entire industry may be governed, the case-by-case adversary proceeding, in which the agency confronts a single alleged offender selected for suit with respect to a specific factual situation, has frequently proved to be an unsuitable method of enforcing the law, since it often resolves narrow issues of importance only to the immediate adversaries rather than broad questions of interest to the industry or the public. The rule-making proceeding, on the other hand, provides the agency with an opportunity first to receive a wide spectrum of views proffered by all segments affected by the proposed rule (*e.g.*, manufacturers, vendors, doctors, consumers) and then in a legislative fashion to consider and choose from several alternatives or options rather than limit its decisions to narrow issues controlling a particular case. Furthermore, once binding regulations are promulgated, the industry and public are put on notice and may be guided accordingly rather than speculate as to the outcome of a seizure or enforcement suit....

NOTES

1. *Effect of Abbott Laboratories.* The Supreme Court's ruling in *Abbott* that section 701(a) regulations could be challenged in a preenforcement suit led logically to the conclusion that review should be based on the rulemaking record compiled by the agency. The posture of a preenforcement suit makes it virtually impossible for a court to visualize the impact of a regulation in the numerous contexts to which it might apply. The question presented, essentially, is whether the regulation is authorized by law and supported by the facts relied on by the agency. Focused in this fashion, it is difficult for a reviewing court to conclude that the regulation is invalid unless the agency committed some procedural error or made an obvious error in judgment. The regulation is thus likely to be upheld, and thereby given "substantive" effect, even though it might later be applied in some contexts where a court—were it any longer free to do so—might consider it "arbitrary or capricious." *See* Merrill, *FDA and the Effects of Substantive Rules*, 35 FDC L.J. 270 (1980).

2. *Supporting Authority.* Numerous subsequent cases have considered the effect of section 701(a) regulations. None suggests that FDA lacks substantive rulemaking power. *See National Ass'n of Pharmaceutical Mfrs. v. FDA*, 637 F.2d 877 (2d Cir. 1981); *National Nutritional Foods Ass'n v. Califano*, 603 F.2d 327 (2d Cir. 1979); *National Confectioners Ass'n v. Califano*, 569 F.2d 690 (D.C. Cir. 1978).

3. *Commentary.* For contrary views, *see* Bass, *Is the Substantive–Interpretative Issue Really Dead?*, 30 FDC L.J. 448 (1975); Cody, *Authoritative Effect of FDA Regulations*, 24 Bus. Law. 479 (1969).

C. FORMAL RULEMAKING AND ADJUDICATION

Section 701(e) and several other provisions of the FD&C Act provide that certain types of regulations (*e.g.*, special dietary food labeling requirements, the grant or denial of food additive and color additive petitions) and adjudicatory orders (*e.g.,* the approval, disapproval, or revocation of new drug and new animal drug applications) may only be issued after affording an opportunity for a trial-type hearing. Any hearing held pursuant to these provisions must comply with the applicable provisions of the Administrative Procedure Act, 5 U.S.C. §§ 556 and 557. Historically, most formal hearings at FDA involved food standards. The Nutrition Labeling and Education Act, 104 Stat. 2353, removed food standards from section 701(e), except for amendments to the standards for maple sirup and dairy products.

---

1. JUSTIFICATION FOR AN EVIDENTIARY HEARING

DYESTUFFS AND CHEMICALS, INC. v. FLEMMING

United States Court of Appeals, Eighth Circuit, 1959.
271 F.2d 281.

VOGEL, Circuit Judge.

Petitioner is a producer of food colors, including certain coal tar colors known as FD&C Yellows 3 and 4 which have been widely used in the coloring of edible fat products, principally butter and oleomargarine. FD&C Yellows 3 and 4 have been certified by the respondent and his predecessors under § 346(b) as safe for such use for approximately the past 40 years. On January 24, 1957, the Deputy Commissioner of Food and Drugs published in the Federal Register a notice of his proposal to amend the Food and Drug Administration regulations by removing FD&C Yellow Nos. 1, 2, 3 and 4 from the approved list for unrestricted use. . . . After receiving comments, including those of the Certified Color Industry Committee of which petitioner is a member, the Commissioner on May 4, 1957, published an order removing the colors in question from the approved list, because they "are not harmless and suitable for use within the meaning of" 21 U.S.C. § 346(b). . . . On May 27, 1957, within the time provided by law, the Certified Color Industry Committee filed objections to the order and requested a hearing thereon in accordance with the provisions of 21 U.S.C. § 371(e)(2, 3). The objections . . . were mainly on the ground that the term "harmless" had long been judicially and administratively construed to mean "harmless and suitable for use in food" *under the intended conditions of their use* and that petitioner's product could so qualify *when used within certain stated tolerances.* . . .

On February 6, 1959, the Deputy Commissioner, without a hearing as provided for in 21 U.S.C. § 371(e)(2, 3), published the final order delisting the colors in question. The order explained the failure to grant a hearing as follows:

"The Supreme Court's (*Flemming v. Florida Citrus Exchange* [p. 358, *supra*] . . .) decision having established the proper construction of the law, the objection of the Certified

Color Industry Committee to the delisting of FD&C Yellow Nos. 1, 2, 3, and 4 is without substance, and no purpose could be served by holding a public hearing. The Department has no authority to certify colors that are themselves toxic, as is the case with FD&C Yellow Nos. 1, 2, 3, and 4, and the Department has no authority to establish a tolerance for such a color, as requested by the Industry Committee." ...

... Petitioner contends that [Sections 701(e)(2) and (3)] ... constitute an unconditional statutory requirement for a hearing upon the filing of objections and that they were wholly disregarded by the order deleting the colors from the harmless list, with the result that no chance was afforded petitioner and others to raise any objections that might be available or to question and refute the pharmacological evidence referred to in the Secretary's order.

Respondent counters by claiming that the grounds set forth in petitioner's objections were wholly insufficient to warrant a hearing in that they sought the promulgation of regulations that were beyond the Department's authority. Petitioner's "grounds for objection" were four in number. The first asserted that, "The colors affected by the order serve a useful and desirable purpose in coloring food and drugs," and that they had been so used for many years, principally with margarine and butter. Objection No. 2 alleged:

"The evidence of potential injury from the use of FD&C Yellow Nos. 1, 2, 3 and 4 is inadequate to justify the order...."

Objection No. 3 asserted that:

"The reasonably anticipated uses of the four yellow colors do not justify any fear of injury from their use. * * *"

Objection No. 4:

" * * * urges that the Commissioner take action to prohibit such excessive concentrations, rather than to bar the proper and harmless use now being made of the colors."

It seems to us obvious, as it did to the respondent, that under the holding of the Supreme Court in *Flemming v. Florida Citrus Exchange,* each of the objections set forth by the petitioner must be held inadequate to prevent the removal of the coal tar colors in question from the "harmless" list. Objection No. 1 merely asserts usefulness and desirability. While No. 2 alleges that the evidence of potential injury is inadequate to justify the order, it is based upon the contention that "the 'no-harm' level thus shown (500–1,000 ppm) is so far in excess of the level of actual use in the human diet that those results do not afford any basis for the order." No. 3 asserts that the reasonably anticipated uses do not justify fear of injury; and No. 4 suggests that the Commissioner do what the Supreme Court held he had no authority to do in *Flemming v. Florida Citrus Exchange.* ... We thus conclude that the four grounds set forth in the petitioner's objections to the order were legally insufficient and turn next to the question of whether a hearing must be held even though the prerequisite objections fail to state valid or legal grounds for the requested action.

It will be noted that 21 U.S.C. § 371(e)(2) provides that objections may be filed " * * * stating the grounds therefor, and requesting a public hearing upon such objections * * * " and (3) " * * * the Secretary, after due notice, *shall hold such a public hearing for the purpose of receiving evidence relevant and material to the issues raised by such objections."* (Emphasis supplied.) It is only after filing objections and " * * * stating the grounds therefor, and requesting a public hearing upon such objections * * *"" that an interested party is entitled to a hearing. The hearing is solely for the purpose of receiving evidence "relevant and material to the issues raised by such objections." Certainly, then, the objections, in order to be effective and necessitate the hearing requested, must be legally adequate so that, if true, the order complained of could not prevail. The objections must raise "issues." The issues must be material to the question involved; that is, the legality of the order attacked. They may not be frivolous or inconsequential. Where the objections stated and the issues raised thereby are, even if true, legally insufficient, their effect is a nullity and no objections have been stated. Congress did not intend the governmental agencies created by it to perform useless or unfruitful tasks. If it is perfectly clear that petitioner's appeal for a hearing contains nothing material and the objections stated do not abrogate the legality of the order attacked, no hearing is required by law....

REGULATIONS FOR THE ENFORCEMENT OF THE FEDERAL FOOD, DRUG, AND COSMETIC ACT, AND THE FAIR PACKAGING AND LABELING ACT: RULING ON OBJECTIONS

32 Federal Register 13276 (September 20, 1967).

After consideration of the more than 300 comments received in response to the proposal in this matter published in the FEDERAL REGISTER of March 17, 1967 (32 F.R. 4172), the Commissioner of Food and Drugs published an order July 21, 1967 (32 F.R. 10729), which provided in accordance with section 701(e) of the Federal Food, Drug, and Cosmetic Act for the filing within 30 days of objections and requests for a public hearing. Almost 50 communications were received in response to the order either expressing objections, offering comments, or asking questions. Some of those submitting objections also requested that their objections be the subject of a public hearing....

Several objections were received to the requirement of § 1.8a(b) that the corporate name of the manufacturer, packer, or distributor be declared even when a division of the corporation is also designated. Since this involves a question of law—is the corporation name necessary to meet the provision of section 403(e)(1) of the Federal Food, Drug, and Cosmetic Act and section 4(a)(1) of the Fair Packaging and Labeling Act—it is not properly a subject for consideration at a public hearing.

Several objections involved the provision of § 1.8b(f) specifying that the statement of net contents is to appear in the lower 30 percent of the label, which area was selected to meet the requirement of section 4(a)(2) of the Fair Packaging and Labeling Act that the statement "be separately and accurately stated in a uniform location upon the principal display panel." these objections represent that the selection of the lower 30 percent by the Commissioner is not in accord with the present location of the net quantity statement on some labels in use by the objectors and that this is not the best location that could have been chosen in the interest of consumers. The Commissioner does not dispute that other placement provisions could have been adopted. It was impossible for the Commissioner to select a single location that would be agreeable to all parties for all food labels on the market. The law requires the Commissioner to select a single location that would be agreeable to all parties for all food labels on the market. The law requires the Commissioner to select a uniform location for this information that would be conspicuous and suitable. A public hearing as to the best location is not required, nor would a hearing of opinions on other places where this information might be placed change the situation. Such opinions have already been presented to the Commissioner at great length. Since the statute provides that the selection of the uniform location shall be made by the Commissioner and not by popular vote, and since no substantial objection to his selection has been offered, it is found that there is no basis for a public hearing on this issue. . . .

Objections were received with reference to the size of type selected by the Commissioner and to the dividing points for the different sizes of type. Here again, the situation called for the Commissioner to designate the size of type for different sizes of packages. It is recognized that the sizes selected would not necessarily meet the sizes now in use by some manufacturers and distributors; similarly it is recognized that no matter what dividing lines were selected, there would be those who would desire different dividing lines to meet their own particular problems. Since this was a matter that the Commissioner had to decide, it is not considered as one warranting a public hearing. . . .

Therefore, the Commissioner finds that none of the objections received during the statutory period warrant a stay of the effective date of the subject order or the holding of a public hearing, and hereby announces that the regulations as published in the FEDERAL REGISTER of July 21, 1967 (32 F.R. 10729), including the clarifying changes hereinafter set forth, are final. . . .

NOTES

1. *Commentary.* For a critical analysis of the FDA ruling denying a hearing on the regulations implementing the FPLA, a ruling that was not

challenged in court, *see* Forte, *Fair Hearing in Administrative Rule–Making: A Recent Experience Under the Federal Food, Drug and Cosmetic and Fair Packaging and Labeling Acts,* 1968 Duke L.J. 1.

2. *FDA Regulations.* 21 C.F.R. § 12.24(b), proposed in 40 Fed. Reg. 40682 (September 3, 1975) and promulgated in 41 Fed. Reg. 51706 (November 23, 1976) (as subsequently edited), specifies the following criteria for determining whether a hearing is justified on objections to a regulation that is subject to section 701(e):

(b) A request for a hearing will be granted if the material submitted shows the following:

(1) There is a genuine and substantial issue of fact for resolution at a hearing. A hearing will not be granted on issues of policy or law.

(2) The factual issue can be resolved by available and specifically identified reliable evidence. A hearing will not be granted on the basis of mere allegations or denials or general descriptions of positions and contentions.

(3) The data and information submitted, if established at a hearing, would be adequate to justify resolution of the factual issue in the way sought by the person. A hearing will be denied if the Commissioner concludes that the data and information submitted are insufficient to justify the factual determination urged, even if accurate.

(4) Resolution of the factual issue in the way sought by the person is adequate to justify the action requested. A hearing will not be granted on factual issues that are not determinative with respect to the action requested, *e.g.,* if the Commissioner concludes that the action would be the same even if the factual issue were resolved in the way sought, or if a request is made that a final regulation include a provision not reasonably encompassed by the proposal. A hearing will be granted upon proper objection and request when a food standard or other regulation is shown to have the effect of excluding or otherwise affecting a product or ingredient.

(5) The action requested is not inconsistent with any provision in the act or any regulation in this chapter particularizing statutory standards. The proper procedure in those circumstances is for the person requesting the hearing to petition for an amendment or waiver of the regulation involved.

3. *CPSC Practice. Pactra Industries, Inc. v. Consumer Product Safety Com'n,* 555 F.2d 677 (9th Cir. 1977), overturned a rule banning vinyl chloride propellants in consumer products issued by the CPSC under the Hazardous Substances Act, which incorporates the formal rulemaking requirements of the FD&C Act. The Commission had declined to hold a hearing on objections to its "final" rule, concluding in substance that there were no facts the objectors could prove which would alter its judgment. The court of appeals rejected the Commission's reasoning:

We hold that section 371(e) leaves the agency no discretion to rule on the quality and validity of the objections prior to the formal hearing, so long as they are made in good faith and draw in question in a material way the underpinnings of the regulation at issue. It is inconsistent with the statutory scheme to require the objecting party to allege anything more.

The Commission's summary procedure may be justified where, as was the case in *Dyestuffs*, the issues raised by the objecting party have been authoritatively determined to be legally irrelevant. But a different case is presented where, merely because the agency has concluded that the scientific evidence is adequate to support its order, a hearing is denied on the assumption that it would serve no purpose....

But see Seacoast Anti–Pollution League v. Costle, 572 F.2d 872 (1st Cir. 1978), upholding EPA's summary judgment procedure patterned after 21 C.F.R. § 12.24(b).

4. *Denial of Hearing.* In *Community Nutrition Institute v. Young*, 773 F.2d 1356 (D.C. Cir. 1985), the court upheld FDA's approval of beverage uses of aspartame without a formal hearing. *See also Pineapple Growers Ass'n of Hawaii v. FDA*, 673 F.2d 1083 (9th Cir. 1982). In *Cook Chocolate Co. v. Miller*, 72 F. Supp. 573 (D.D.C. 1947), 1938–1964 FDLI Jud. Rec. 985 (D.D.C. 1949), a food processor petitioned to amend a food standard and, when FDA declined to hold a hearing on the matter, brought suit contending that he had demonstrated the statutorily required "reasonable grounds" for a hearing. After conducting a trial on the issue, the district court concluded that the evidence failed to show that FDA had abused its discretion. *But see Marshall Minerals, Inc. v. FDA*, 661 F.2d 409 (5th Cir. 1981), overturning FDA's denial of a request for a public hearing on a food additive petition.

5. *Section 701(e) Procedures.* Under section 701(e), attention to detail is essential. Failure to object to a regulation will bar judicial review. *Nader v. EPA*, 859 F.2d 747 (9th Cir. 1988). Furthermore, jurisdiction to review the agency's action lies only in a court of appeals. *Community Nutrition Institute v. Young*, 773 F.2d 1356 (D.C. Cir. 1985). In *Scott v. Califano*, Food Drug Cosm. L. Rep. (CCH) ¶ 38,135 (D.D.C. 1977), the court dismissed an action to require publication of a proposed regulation under section 701(e) because the petitioner had sought court review before the expiration of the 180 days provided by FDA in 21 C.F.R. § 10.30(e)(2) for a reply to petitions. *Compare Committee for Hand Gun Control, Inc. v. CPSC*, 388 F. Supp. 216 (D.D.C. 1974).

6. *Finality.* Ordinarily a court will not interfere with an agency proceeding while it is still in progress. *See, e.g., National Nutritional Foods Ass'n v. FDA*, 491 F.2d 1141 (2d Cir. 1974). In *Abbott Laboratories v. Harris*, 481 F. Supp. 74 (N.D. Ill. 1979), however, the court allowed the plaintiff discovery against the agency, while FDA was still considering its petition to approve cyclamate, to explore whether non-statutory factors had been decisive in the agency's six-year delay in reaching a final decision.

7. *Right to Hearing and to Review.* Because an NDA is a private license, the FD&C Act permits only the applicant to request a hearing on an adverse agency action. FDA has declared, for example, that "a physician has no legal right to a hearing to contest withdrawal of approval of a new drug," 40 Fed. Reg. 22950, 22967 (May 27, 1975). *See also Rutherford v. Medical Ass'n*, 379 F.2d 641 (7th Cir. 1967); *Tutoki v. Celebrezze*, 375 F.2d 105 (7th Cir. 1967) (cancer patients have no standing to contest FDA prohibition of Krebiozen except by filing their own new drug application and appealing from its denial).

The issue of *who* could be "adversely affected" within the meaning of sections 701(e) and (f) and thus could demand a hearing and seek subsequent court review arose soon after FDA first began to promulgate food standards. *See Reade v. Ewing*, 205 F.2d 630 (2d Cir. 1953) (consumer of food may be adversely affected by a food standard); *United States Cane Sugar Refiners' Ass'n v. McNutt*, 138 F.2d 116 (2d Cir. 1943) (ingredient supplier is not adversely affected by a food standard that excludes an ingredient it markets); *Land O'Lakes Creameries, Inc. v. McNutt*, 132 F.2d 653 (8th Cir. 1943) (producer of a competitive product has standing to seek review of a food standard); *A.E. Staley Mfg. Co. v. Secretary of Agriculture*, 120 F.2d 258 (7th Cir. 1941) (food processor is adversely affected by a food standard that excludes an ingredient he uses).

8. *Review Jurisdiction.* *National Nutritional Foods Ass'n v. FDA*, 504 F.2d 761 (2nd Cir. 1974), p. 215 *supra*, held that where FDA issue regulations under the authority of both sections 701(e) and (a), the section 701(a) regulations could be reviewed by the court of appeals under the doctrine of pendent jurisdiction.

9. *Funding for Participation.* FDA established procedures to fund members of the public to participate in agency hearings in 41 Fed. Reg. 35855 (August 25, 1976), 44 Fed. Reg. 23044 (April 17, 1979), 44 Fed. Reg. 59174 (October 12, 1979), 44 Fed. Reg. 72585 (December 14, 1979). It employed these procedures to assist participants in hearings on Dexamyl, Aspartame, and Depo–Provera, 44 Fed. Reg. 72585 (December 14, 1979), and the withdrawal of NDAs for oral proteolytic enzymes, 45 Fed. Reg. 2909 (January 15, 1980). Following a ruling that it lacked authority to spend public funds for public participation in agency proceedings, *Pacific Legal Foundation v. Goyan*, 664 F.2d 1221 (4th Cir. 1981), however, FDA revoked these regulations in 47 Fed. Reg. 12951 (March 26, 1982).

---

2. HEARING PROCEDURES

Many of the formal evidentiary hearings conducted by FDA since 1938 have been lengthy, and some proceedings have been cited as evidence of the need to reform or abandon formal rulemaking. President Carter once stated that "It should not have taken 12 years and a hearing record of over 100,000 pages for the FDA to decide what percentage of peanuts there ought to be in peanut butter.... I would have used that example even if I had grown soybeans and wheat, by the way." 15 Weekly Comp. of Pres. Doc. 482, 484 (March 25, 1979).The most cogent criticisms of the FDA experience include Fisher, *Procedural Techniques in Food and Drug Administration Proceedings*, 17 FDC L.J. 724 (1962); Hamilton, *Rulemaking on A Record by the Food and Drug Administration*, 50 Tex. L. Rev. 1132 (1972); Note, *FDA Rulemaking Hearings: A Way Out of the Peanut Butter Quagmire*, 40 Geo. Wash. L. Rev. 726 (1972). *See also* Administrative Conference of the United States, Recommendation No. 71–7, 2 RECOMMENDATIONS AND REPORTS OF THE ADMINISTRATIVE CONFERENCE OF THE UNITED STATES 42 (1973); Austern, *Is Government by Exhortation Desir-*

able?, *22 FDC L.J. 647 (1967); Goodrich,* A Reply to Professor Hamilton's Comments and Recommendations for Procedural Reform, *26 FDC L.J. 639 (1971); Hamilton,* Procedures for the Adoption of Rules of General Applicability: The Need for Procedural Innovation in Administrative Rulemaking, *60 Calif. L. Rev. 1276 (1972); Hoffman,* Some Suggestions for Improvements in the Hearing and Rulemaking Procedures of the Food and Drug Administration, *23 FDC L.J. 465 (1968); Levine,* Separation of Functions in FDA Administrative Proceedings, *23 FDC L.J. 132 (1968); Pendergast,* The Nature of Section 701 Hearings and Suggestions for Improving the Procedures for the Conduct of Such Hearings, *24 FDC L.J. 527 (1969);* FDA Procedures, *25 FDC L.J. 191 (1970).*

Some reforms in the procedures for formal hearings can be implemented without amending the FD&C Act or 5 U.S.C. §§ 556 & 557, but many require legislative authorization. Thus, it is not surprising that formal hearings continue to provoke controversy.

a. Limits on Cross Examination

On the premise that repetitive cross examination of witnesses has been a major cause of the length of formal hearings, FDA attempted to limit cross examination to the full extent permitted by the Administrative Procedure Act, 40 Fed. Reg. 40682 (September 3, 1975), 41 Fed. Reg. 51706 (November 23, 1976) (as subsequently edited).

§ 12.87 Purpose; oral and written testimony; burden of proof.

(a) The objective of a formal evidentiary hearing is the fair determination of relevant facts consistent with the right of all interested persons to participate and the public interest in promptly settling controversial matters affecting the public health and welfare.

(b) Accordingly, the evidence at a hearing is to be developed to the maximum extent through written submissions, including written direct testimony, which may be in narrative or in question-and-answer form.

(1) In a hearing, the issues may have general applicability and depend on general facts that do not concern particular action of a specific party, *e.g.,* the safety or effectiveness of a class of drug products, the safety of a food or color additive, or a definition and standard of identity for a food; or the issues may have specific applicability to past action and depend upon particular facts concerning only that party, *e.g.,* the applicability of a grandfather clause to a particular brand of a drug or the failure of a particular manufacturer to meet required manufacturing and processing specifications or other general standards.

(i) If the proceeding involves general issues, direct testimony will be submitted in writing, except on a showing that written direct testimony is insufficient for a full and true disclosure of relevant facts and that the participant will be prejudiced if unable to present oral direct testimony. If the proceeding involves particular issues, each party may determine whether, and the extent to which, each wishes to present direct testimony orally or in writing.

(ii) Oral cross-examination of witnesses will be permitted if it appears that alternative means of developing the evidence are insufficient for a full and true disclosure of the facts and that the party requesting oral cross-examination will be prejudiced by denial of the request or that oral cross-examination is the most effective and efficient means to clarify the matters at issue.

(2) Witnesses shall give testimony under oath.

(c) Except as provided in paragraph (d) of this section, in a hearing involving issuing, amending, or revoking a regulation or order, the originator of the proposal or petition or of any significant modification will be, within the meaning of 5 U.S.C. 556(d), the proponent of the regulation or order, and will have the burden of proof. A participant who proposes to substitute a new provision for a provision objected to has the burden of proof in relation to the new provision.

(d) At a hearing involving issuing, amending, or revoking a regulation or order relating to the safety or effectiveness of a drug, antibiotic, device, food additive, or color additive, the participant who is contending that the product is safe or effective or both and who is requesting approval or contesting withdrawal of approval has the burden of proof in establishing safety or effectiveness or both and thus the right to approval. The burden of proof remains on that participant in an amendment or revocation proceeding.

NOTES

1. *Implementation.* Implementation of these provisions is left to the presiding administrative law judge. Anderson, *An Overview of Recent Regulatory Developments—The Case for Evidentiary Hearings,* 31 FDC L.J. 159, 165 (1976), agrees that cross examination has been abused but cautions that "the elimination of cross-examination is likely to encourage generality, foster imprecision and have a generally negative effect on the factual integrity of any Agency action."

2. *Judicial Review.* The most recent judicial examinations of FDA formal rulemaking are *E.R. Squibb and Sons, Inc. v. Bowen,* 870 F.2d 678 (D.C. Cir. 1989); *Warner–Lambert Co. v. Heckler,* 787 F.2d 147 (3d Cir. 1986); *National Nutrition Foods Ass'n v. FDA,* 504 F.2d 761 (2d Cir. 1974). No party who has contested an FDA action subject to section 701(e) has wholly prevailed before the ALJ, the Commissioner, or in court.

---

b. Alternative Informal Hearings

Recognizing that it could not repeal the Act's provisions for formal hearings and that legislation authorizing major reform in procedures was unlikely. FDA promulgated 21 C.F.R. § 12.32, which authorizes the parties to any proceeding that is subject to a formal hearing to agree to an informal hearing instead. The regulation offers three alternatives to a formal hearing: a board of inquiry, an advisory committee, or a legislative-type hearing before the FDA.

ADMINISTRATIVE PRACTICES AND PROCEDURES

40 Federal Register 40682 (September 3, 1975).

... [T]he Commissioner has recognized that, in those situations where complex scientific and medical issues are involved, a searching scientific inquiry conducted by independent experts may well be more appropriate to resolve the matters involved than a formal evidentiary public hearing. Use of a public hearing before a Board of Inquiry pursuant to [21 C.F.R. Part 13] or a public hearing before a public advisory committee pursuant to [21 C.F.R. Part 14] would therefore be authorized....

There has been substantial concern expressed in recent years about the need for development of more appropriate procedures than trial-type hearing for resolving difficult scientific issues. The Commissioner believes that a Public Board of Inquiry or a public advisory committee represents a feasible approach to this problem, combining the features of traditional scientific inquiry with the need of the law to develop a full record on which to base the Commissioner's decision and subsequent judicial review....

... Proposed § 2.117 [now 21 C.F.R. § 12.32] would provide that a person who had a right to an opportunity for a formal evidentiary hearing could waive that opportunity and, in lieu thereof, request a public hearing before a Public Board of Inquiry ..., a public hearing before a public advisory committee ..., or a public hearing before the Commissioner.... Such a waiver could, but would not have to, be conditioned upon the grant of one of these alternative forms of hearing. Such a request could be on his own initiative or at the suggestion of the Commissioner....

... [T]he proposed regulations would establish, as an alternative to a formal evidentiary public hearing, an informal public hearing before a Public Board of Inquiry that would be conducted in the form of a scientific inquiry rather than as a legal trial.... Proposed § 2.202 [now 21 C.F.R. § 13.10] would require that the members of a Board have medical, technical, scientific, or other qualifications relevant to the issues to be considered at the hearing. The members would be special government employees and thus subject to the conflict of interest rules applicable to such employees....

Within 30 days after the notice of the hearing before the Board was published in the FEDERAL REGISTER, each of the parties to the proceeding and any person whose petition was the subject of the hearing would submit a list of five nominees for members of the Board. Such persons could agree upon a single list of nominees. Following receipt of such lists, such persons could submit comments on the other lists submitted. The Commissioner would then review the lists and comments and select one member of the Board from the lists submitted by the director of the agency bureau involved and any person whose petition was the subject of the hearing, one member from the lists submitted by the other parties, and one member of his own choosing from any source whatever who would serve as the Chairman of the Board. Thus, although the parties would have a right to participate in the selection of the members of the Board, the Commissioner would have the final determination on this matter.

In lieu of the nomination procedure set out above, the parties to such a proceeding and any person whose petition was the subject of the hearing could meet and agree upon any other method of selection that was reasonable, and subject to the approval of the Commissioner. For example, any standing advisory committee of the agency could be utilized as the Board for a particular proceeding....

Proposed § 2.206(a) [now 21 C.F.R. § 13.30] would make it clear that the purpose of a Board is to review complex technical issues in a reasonably short time by using the informal approach of a scientific inquiry rather than the formal procedures of a legal trial. Accordingly, it is anticipated that there will be little, if any, need for participation by attorneys in the proceeding....

The Chairman of the Board would determine the order in which the parties and participants make their presentations. Such order of presentation could well be the subject of a prior agreement. Each participant could then proceed with his presentation, which would be made without interruptions and without objection or other legalistic procedures. At the conclusion of a participant's presentation, each of the other participants could briefly state questions or criticism and suggest further questioning with respect to specific matters. The members of the Board could interrupt a participant at any time to ask questions, and could conduct further questioning at the conclusion of the participant's full presentation either on their own initiative or at the suggestion of the other participants. The exact nature of the proceeding would largely be in the discretion of the Chairman, who would be the presiding officer and would have all of the powers necessary to conduct a fair and expeditious hearing.

In addition to hearing the views of the participants, the Board could independently consult with any other person who it concluded may have useful information. All such consultation would have to be at an announced hearing of the Board unless all participants agreed that it could be done in writing. Moreover, any participant in the proceeding could submit to the Board a request that it consult with specific persons who could have useful information. The Board could accept or deny such a request, in its discretion....

The administrative record of the public hearing would constitute the exclusive record for decision on the matter.....

NOTE

1. *Objections to Alternative Procedures.* The final regulations governing hearings before a board of inquiry were promulgated at 41 Fed. Reg. 26636 (June 28, 1976) without significant change. One comment argued that, where a third party objects to the granting of a petition (*e.g.*, a food additive petition) and asks for an alternative form of hearing, FDA must also obtain the consent of the person whose petition is at issue before the alternative form of hearing may be used. In 41 Fed. Reg. 51706 (November 23, 1976), FDA rejected this argument, concluding that under such circumstances the successful petitioner has no legal right to determine the form of the hearing.

2. *Experience with Public Boards of Inquiry.* FDA has used boards of inquiry in two proceedings, 44 Fed. Reg. 31716 (June 1, 1979) (aspartame) and 44 Fed. Reg. 44274 (July 27, 1979) (Depo Provera). Following a cautiously favorable assessment of these two proceedings, Shapiro, *Scientific Issues and the Function of Hearing Procedures: Evaluating the FDA's Public Board of Inquiry,* 1986 Duke L. J. 288, the U.S. Administrative Conference recommended "continued experimentation with alternative types of hearing procedures for the resolution of scientific issues" and suggested specific improvements in the approach used by FDA, 50 Fed. Reg. 52893 (December 27, 1985).

D. PRIMARY JURISDICTION

1. INTRODUCTION

PETER BARTON HUTT, FDA COURT ACTIONS AND RECENT LEGAL DEVELOPMENTS.

39 Quarterly Bulletin Association of Food & Drug Officials 11 (1975).

... [T]he *Bentex, Hynson, Wescott & Dunning, USV,* and *Ciba* cases .... involved the status of new drugs under the Act. However, in briefing those cases, we went far beyond the specific issues they raised. We briefed, for example, the entire legality of our over-the-counter drug review procedures. We put before the Court the proposition that our nutrition labeling program, our regulation of in vitro diagnostic products, the biologics review, the GRAS list review, and virtually every program that we have undertaken in the last two or three years, directly rested on the agency's primary jurisdiction, and that these four court cases would determine whether we would continue our course of action or whether we would have to adopt some new way of proceeding in the future....

The principle of primary jurisdiction, in my opinion, was the most important issue at stake in those cases. These unanimous decisions, therefore, represent a major strengthening of the agency's legal authority, and may well be the most important court decisions we have ever obtained....

---

2. SUITS AGAINST FDA

IMS, LTD. v. CALIFANO,

United States District Court, Central District of California, 1977.
453 F.Supp. 157.

KELLEHER, District Judge.

On June 13, 1977, the District Director for the Los Angeles District of the FDA sent plaintiff drug manufacturer a letter which stated that a recent inspection of plaintiff's firm indicated that plaintiff was in violation of § 505 of the Act in that the furosemide plaintiff was found to be importing was a "new drug" as to which plaintiff had failed to file and obtain approval of an NDA. The letter requested plaintiff to contact the FDA within ten days, stating the action plaintiff proposed to take to correct the violation, and threatened the invocation of regulatory sanctions should plaintiff fail to respond.

Apparently plaintiff's response was to file this lawsuit. Plaintiff contends that furosemide is not subject to the § 505 premarketing clearance procedures in that it is not a "new drug" within the meaning of § 201(p)....

The FDA filed the instant motion to dismiss or, alternatively, for summary judgment on September 12, 1977.

The motion is granted, without prejudice. The basis for this disposition is primary jurisdiction of the FDA to resolve the jurisdictional question (*i.e.*, whether plaintiff's product constitutes a "new drug" requiring filing and approval of an NDA), absence of final agency action so as to permit district court review under the Administrative Procedure Act (APA), and failure of plaintiff to exhaust administrative remedies....

Plaintiff claims that the June 13, 1977 letter from the District Director of the Los Angeles District of the FDA constitutes "final agency action" for purposes of APA and that plaintiff has exhausted its administrative remedies, as required by *Hynson*. While having a certain superficial appeal, the contentions are without merit.... It seems clear that the type of informal letter issued by the FDA, apparently without having first conducted any tests, does not constitute the kind of formal or final agency action the Supreme Court had in mind. Moreover, the agency's regulations expressly state that meetings and correspondence do not constitute final administrative action which is subject to judicial review. 21 C.F.R. § 10.65(a). Finally, as pointed out above, it is incorrect for plaintiff to state that it has no intra-agency avenue of review to test the District Director's demand and that therefore it has exhausted its administrative remedies. Under 21 C.F.R. § 10.25(a), plaintiff may "petition the Commissioner to issue, amend, or revoke a regulation or order, or to take or refrain from taking any other form of administrative action...." And the petition may, at plaintiff's option, take the form of a citizen's petition under 21 C.F.R. § 10.30, which rebuts plaintiff's claim that to require plaintiff to file an NDA in order to test the question of the very need to file an NDA is self-defeating. Primary jurisdiction to determine whether plaintiff's product is a "new drug" lies with the FDA, with review of its formal determination available in the district court under APA....

NOTES

1. *Supporting Authority. Carolina Brown, Inc. v. Weinberger,* 365 F. Supp. 310 (D.S.C. 1973), and *National Ethical Pharmaceutical Ass'n v. Weinberger,* 365 F. Supp. 735 (D.S.C. 1973), *aff'd per curiam,* 503 F.2d 1051 (4th Cir. 1974), dismissed suits seeking a declaration of a drug's status on the ground that this issue lay within FDA's primary jurisdiction and that judicial review should be available only after a ruling by the agency.

2. *Laetrile.* Recognition of FDA's primary jurisdiction may require the agency to conduct an administrative proceeding that it had not planned in order to document its position on an issue. In *Rutherford v. United States,* 542 F.2d 1137 (10th Cir. 1976), FDA was instructed to hold an administrative hearing to compile a record supporting its announced view that Laetrile is a new drug that requires formal agency approval before it may lawfully be shipped in interstate commerce. The plaintiff in *Rutherford* was a cancer patient who sought a judicial ruling that the agency's position was inconsistent with the statute and violated the Constitutional rights of cancer patients. The district court ruled in the plaintiff's favor, enjoining FDA from interfering with his right to obtain Laetrile for his personal use. The Tenth Circuit refused to set aside the lower court's injunction pending FDA's exercise of its primary jurisdiction to determine new drug status:

> The FDA has argued that they have not issued any regulation or rule which specifically or positively forbids the administration of Laetrile. This is true. However, the FDA has made an administrative determination that Laetrile is a new drug and this places the plaintiff in a position in which he has to admit that it is a new drug in order to get the FDA to move. As a result he could not be heard to say that they have not effectively stymied the use of this drug. The FDA has done this without citing any facts whatsoever....

> From what has been said it is obvious that we are not in agreement with the trial court's opinion that the FDA has to approve or disapprove any new drug even in the absence of an application that satisfies the statutory mandate.... It follows that the FDA was not compelled to pursue this new drug procedure in the Laetrile situation in the absence of an application.

> We are unable, however, to see how the FDA can escape the obligation of producing an administrative record to support its determination of the first and more fundamental issue that Laetrile is a *new* drug, for it is not a new drug merely because they said it is.... To support its determination the FDA in the case at bar would have to present substantial evidence to support the proposition that Laetrile is not generally recognized among qualified experts as "safe and effective," and that Laetrile is not grandfathered by either of the exemptions discussed above.

> It seems doubtful that the FDA has in fact developed an administrative record adequate under 5 U.S.C. § 554(c) and hence there is probably nothing which is presently available for a court to review.

Nothing in the record suggests that the FDA has dealt with Laetrile in a rule-making proceeding under Section 701 of the Act. Hence, if this is true the appropriate procedure for the district court is to remand the case back to the FDA for proceedings adequate to develop a record supportive of the agency's determination; the proceedings should give Laetrile proponents an opportunity to express their views....

The district court thereupon returned the issue to FDA to assemble an administrative record, *Rutherford v. United States*, 424 F. Supp. 105 (W.D. Okl. 1977), and certified the case as a class action, 429 F.Supp. 506 (W.D. Okl. 1977). FDA held a legislative-style hearing and subsequently ruled that Laetrile may not lawfully be marketed as a food or drug. 42 Fed. Reg. 39768 (August 5, 1977). That decision was in turn challenged in court. *See* pp. 557–59 *supra*.

---

3. FDA ENFORCEMENT SUITS

Following the Supreme Court's holding in *Weinberger v. Bentex Pharmaceuticals, Inc.*, 412 U.S. 645 (1973), p. 506 *supra*, that "the District Court's referral of the 'new drug' ... issues to FDA was appropriate, as these are the kinds of issues peculiarly suited to initial determination by the FDA," and the Tenth Circuit's *Rutherford* ruling, defendants in several civil enforcement actions have claimed that the agency must first document its administrative determination of illegality before initiating enforcement proceedings.

UNITED STATES v. ALCON LABS

United States Court of Appeals, First Circuit, 1981.
636 F.2d 876.

LEVIN H. CAMPBELL, Circuit Judge....

Alcon manufactures and markets in suppository dosage a prescription antiemetic drug called "WANS." The drug contains pyrilamine maleate (an antihistamine) and pentobarbital sodium (a barbituate) and comes in three dosage strengths, WANS No. 1, WANS No. 2 and WANS Children. WANS has been used under medical supervision for approximately 25 years, and did not become an object of FDA concern until 1978....

On March 17, 1978, the FDA sent Alcon a regulatory letter informing it of a report received from the agency's Neurological Drugs Advisory Committee "that children aged 6 months to seven years who were treated for nausea and vomiting with drugs containing pyrilamine maleate and pentobarbital, experienced severe and sometimes fatal reactions." The Committee had concluded, the letter went on, "that there is no evidence of safety and efficacy for drugs containing pyrilamine maleate with or without a barbiturate in the treatment of nausea and vomiting." Based on the Committee's report, "and because [the FDA was] unaware of substantial scientific evidence which demonstrates that a combination of these ingredients is generally recognized as safe and effective for the treatment of nausea and vomiting," the FDA advised Alcon that it considered Alcon's marketing of WANS to be in violation of the "new drug" provision of the Federal Food, Drug, and Cosmetic Act, 21 U.S.C. § 355. The letter stated that under FDA regulatory policy as formulated in Compliance Policy Guide 7132c.08, WANS had become subject to immediate regulatory action outside the agency's ordinary enforcement priorities "because of new information concerning the safety and efficacy of these drugs." Alcon was told to reply within ten days, and was warned that failure to discontinue marketing WANS would expose the company to seizure and injunction actions.....

Alcon continued to manufacture WANS and on September 21, 1978 the FDA instituted a seizure action in federal district court alleging that the drug was a "new drug" being marketed in violation of Section 505 of the Act, 21 U.S.C. § 355..... On March 21, 1979 ... Alcon moved the district court to remand to the FDA....

No further action was taken in the case until January 28, 1980. On that date the FDA instituted a second seizure against WANS. Large quantities of the drug were again confiscated. A month later, on February 27, 1980, the district court consolidated the latest seizure action with the pending actions, and ordered the entire case to be,

> "remanded to the Food and Drug Administration (FDA) with instructions to defer regulatory action against the WANS preparations involved in this matter or against defendants based upon the alleged 'new drug' status of WANS until FDA holds a hearing pursuant to 5 U.S.C. § 554 and thereafter makes an administrative determination of the new drug status of WANS in conformity with the enforcement priorities enunciated in FDA's Compliance Policy Guide 7132c.08....."

The district court premised its decision to remand to the FDA on interrelated procedural and substantive grounds. The court was troubled by the agency's failure to conduct "a formal administrative determination of the 'new drug' status of WANS" before instituting suit against Alcon. In the absence of such a determination, the court felt that an FDA internal regulation—Compliance Policy Guide 7132c.08— precluded enforcement action against WANS unless the agency possessed "significant new information which questions the safety of the drug." However, the court characterized itself as ill-suited to decide the "new drug" status of WANS or to determine whether "significant new information" existed that questioned WANS' safety. Citing lack of jurisdiction, the doctrine of primary agency jurisdiction and prudential considerations, the court decided that these questions were better left to "the Agency entrusted by Congress with the necessary expertise to make a responsible determination." Accordingly, it ordered the action "remanded to the Food and Drug Administration to hold a formal administrative hearing pursuant to 5 U.S.C. 554 on the issue as to whether WANS is a 'new drug' in conformity with the enforcement priorities enunciated in FDA's Compliance Policy Guide 7132c.08."

The court's concern over summary institution of enforcement proceedings is shared by some in the drug industry, but the imposition of a pre-enforcement hearing requirement (coupled with preliminary relief, as, to be meaningful, it would have to be) is at odds with the language and intent of the Act.... The district court's concern that the FDA might be proceeding in violation of its own internal regulatory guidelines was also in error.....

Finally, we turn to the district court's belief that it lacked, or should not have exercised, jurisdiction over the "new drug" and "grandfather clause" questions in this case. The court's declaration that "[i]t is not within the jurisdiction of this Court to determine whether the drug in issue is or is not a new drug" is plainly incorrect. Jurisdiction over the new drug issue is shared by the FDA, and the federal district courts.

Further, the district court's invocation of the doctrine of "primary jurisdiction" to justify its refusal to exercise its own jurisdiction is not persuasive. As we have elsewhere stated, deference to an agency's primary jurisdiction makes little sense in the context of an enforcement proceeding initiated by the agency. This is especially true where, as here, a party remains subject to the agency's regulatory efforts despite the remand. We have held above that a district court lacks the power to require the FDA to defer seizures *pendente lite* or to order release of seized drugs prior to a determination of the merits of the agency's claims. The effect of a remand to the agency thus would hardly be beneficial to the product's manufacturer. Without the relief afforded by the other aspects of the district court's order, Alcon would be deprived of a judicial remedy in return for an administrative procedure of uncertain duration before an unsympathetic agency. We would be surprised if either Alcon or the district court would be content with a remand under such circumstances. With this consideration in mind, and in view of the fact that the FDA's current position on the "new drug" status of WANS is already clear; that the FDA carried the burden of proving its position at trial; and that the agency has no duty to hold a pre-enforcement hearing or to justify its action under its Compliance Policy Guide, we do not see what would be gained in this case by a remand. At least it can be said that two fundamental purposes of deference to agency jurisdiction—"coordinating administrative and judicial machinery" and assuring uniformity of regulation, would not be served by the district court's order.

This is not to say that a remand in the context of enforcement proceedings might never be appropriate. In *Bentex Pharmaceuticals,* 412 U.S. 645, the Supreme Court upheld the power of a district court to refer to the FDA "new drug" and "grandfather clause" issues initially presented to the court in a declaratory judgment action instituted by drug manufacturers. The Court went on to note that a court could stay its hand "[e]ven where no ... administrative determination has been made and the issue arises in a district court in enforcement proceedings. ..." This observation, however, should be understood in relation to the situation in *Bentex*, where some 21 drug manufacturers had requested declaratory relief. There the court was in essence being asked to issue, without benefit of prior administrative proceedings, a decision upon whether a substantial portion of an industry was complying with the Act. Here the district court is being asked only to decide whether a single drug manufactured by a single company is being marketed illegally. The agency's view of the question is clear and will have to be substantiated for the agency to prevail in court. We therefore conclude that under *Bentex* this is not an appropriate case for a remand.

As the district court recognized, a third purpose of the doctrine of primary jurisdiction—taking advantage "of agencies' special expertise," weighs in favor of a remand, but not, we think, decisively. The Supreme Court has described the "new drug" and "grandfather clause" issues as "the kinds of issues peculiarly suited to initial determination by the FDA." Nevertheless, contrary to the Court's suggestion it has not been "commonplace" for courts to await an appropriate administrative declaration in enforcement proceedings, lower courts continue to hear and decide the "new drug" status of drugs challenged by the FDA in seizure and injunction actions. The government asserts, and we have found nothing to the contrary, that of the hundreds of enforcement actions brought by the FDA under section 505 since 1938, none save the present has been remanded to the agency. Returning issues in an enforcement action to the FDA imposes an administrative burden for which the Act makes no provision, and insofar as the procedure delays adjudication of the regulatory status of a drug, may work to the disadvantage not only of the agency and public, but also of the manufacturer. In such circumstances the power to remand must be used sparingly. Had the trial set for May 1979 been held, WANS' status would long since have been laid to rest. In deciding the case, the FDA's expertise would have been available to the court, in that to sustain its burden the agency would have had to present expert evidence establishing its claims regarding WANS. We therefore conclude that the district court erred in remanding the case to the FDA.

NOTES

1. *Supporting Authority.* See also *United States v. Western Serum Co., Inc.*, 666 F.2d 335 (9th Cir. 1982); *Premo Pharmaceutical Laboratories, Inc. v. United States*, 629 F.2d 795 (2d Cir. 1980); *United States v. An Article of Drug ... "Tutag Pharmaceuticals ... X–Otag Plus Tablets,"* 602 F.2d 1387 (10th Cir. 1979); *United States v. Mosinee Research Corp.*, 583 F.2d 930 (7th Cir. 1978); *United States v. 118/100 Tablet Bottles*, 662 F. Supp. 511 (W.D. La. 1987); *United States v. 1,834/100 Capsule Bottles ... "New Formula Hauck G–2 Capsules,"* Food Drug Cosm. L. Rep. (CCH) ¶ 38,058 (N.D. Ga. 1987); *United*

States v. The Upjohn Co., Food Drug Cosm. L. Rep. (CCH) ¶ 38,302 (W.D. Mich. 1985); *United States v. Articles of Hazardous Substance,* 588 F.2d 39 (4th Cir. 1978); *United States v. An Article of Drug ... "Beuthanasia–D Regular,"* Food Drug Cosm. L. Rep. (CCH) ¶ 38,265 (D. Neb. 1979).

2. *Spontaneous Primary Jurisdiction.* FDA has occasionally sought to resolve an enforcement action by invoking its primary jurisdiction. In March 1983, FDA brought a seizure action against a generic new animal drug that had been marketed without an approved NADA. After the seizure went by default, the generic manufacturer filed a declaratory judgment action seeking a court determination that the drug was not a new animal drug and therefore that a NADA was not required. FDA and the generic manufacturer then entered into a stipulation of voluntary dismissal, under which the generic manufacturer agreed to file a citizen petition with FDA seeking an administrative determination that the drug is not a new animal drug, and FDA agreed not to initiate any enforcement litigation until 18 months, or 30 days after any denial of the citizen petition, whichever was later. The pioneer manufacturer, which had an approved NADA, sought unsuccessfully to overturn this settlement in *Schering Corp. v. Heckler,* 779 F.2d 683 (D.C. Cir. 1985). Following FDA's denial of its citizen petition, the generic manufacturer unsuccessfully renewed its suit for declaratory judgment, *Tri–Bio Laboratories, Inc. v. United States,* 836 F.2d 135 (3d Cir. 1987).

3. *Private Litigation.* Suits between private parties may frequently raise issues that fall within FDA's special competence. In *Purdue Frederick Co. v. Acme United Corp.,* Civ. No. N–74–115 (D. Conn., January 30, 1975), the plaintiff alleged violation of the false advertising provision of the Lanham Act and unfair competition. It claimed that the defendant's antiseptic drug, formulated in a novel fashion, should not be marketed under the same generic name as its own product. It suggested that FDA be asked for its views on a series of questions, most of which revolved around the issue of whether the defendant's drug was lawfully marketed under the FD&C Act. The trial court declined to refer the matter to FDA because it appeared clear that the agency's OTC Drug Review had several years to run, but it invited the agency to submit answers to specific questions respecting the bioequivalence of the defendant's formulation. The agency answered those questions. The matter was subsequently settled out of court.

4. *Agency Response.* Following this experience, FDA adopted a regulation, 21 C.F.R. § 10.25(c), 40 Fed. Reg. 40682 (September 3, 1975), 42 Fed. Reg. 4680 (January 25, 1977), providing that it will institute an administrative proceeding whenever a court holds in abeyance or refers to the agency any matter for an administrative determination, and the agency concludes that an administrative determination on the matter "is feasible in light of agency priorities and resources." Reference of issues in private litigation to FDA can be important in product liability suits, where the status of a product or ingredient under the FD&C Act is often in dispute. *See, e.g., Hoffman v. Sterling Drug, Inc.,* 485 F.2d 132 (3d Cir. 1973).

E. ADVISORY COMMITTEES
1. FDA RELIANCE ON ADVISORY COMMITTEES
STATEMENT OF
COMMISSIONER ALEXANDER M. SCHMIDT, M.D.

"Use of Advisory Committees By the Food and Drug Administration,"
Hearings Before a Subcommittee of the House Committee on Government
Operations, 93d Congress, 2d Session (1974).

... [W]hile the responsibilities of the Food and Drug Administration have expanded markedly in recent years, the expansion in scientific information with which we must cope has been even greater. In addition, we are being asked, almost on a daily basis, to increase the involvement of the sciences, the professions, and the public in our fact-finding and decisionmaking process....

To enable us to make the best possible judgments, we have and will continue to use advisory committees to provide us with information, interpretation and advice which will supplement that generated internally. The important point is that we use advisory committees *in addition to,* not in lieu of, FDA staff. The functions of two committee categories, the Over–the–Counter (OTC) Drug Panels and the Biologics Efficacy Review Panels, demonstrate the increasingly important role of broadly constituted scientific advisory bodies as integral parts of our regulatory process....

There are a number of advantages of the use of advisory committees, both to the Food and Drug Administration and to the public:

1. The Agency gains access to highest levels of scholarship in the scientific community and in Federal agencies other than the FDA. Professional, trade, and consumer organizations are urged to suggest qualified experts conversant with the distinctive requirements, usages, problems, and sensitivities recognized by these dissimilar groups. State-of-the-art knowledge is contributed by individuals engaged in research or clinical practice.

2. Regulatory decisions are recognized by affected parties as having the backing of leaders in the medical, academic, and scientific communities, all of whom are visible and accountable.

3. Participation by the scientific community improves the credibility and acceptability of Agency decisions because the public recognizes that professional competence and balanced considerations are paramount in the formulation of public policy.

4. In areas where the Agency lacks intramural competence to deal with a matter in a definitive fashion, participation of selected technical committees or panels permits a prompt and responsive effort.

5. The rotation nature of committee memberships promotes the availability of individuals who are in the forefront of their fields.

6. Exposure of consultants and committee members to the Agency's deliberations and problems promotes a desirable dissemination of information which might otherwise be confined to official circles....

7. The incorporation of advisory committees into the review process aids decisionmaking by providing a formal setting for comprehensive review of data, scientific discussion, and resolution of problems....

In sum, advisory committees are used to obtain the best possible advice on scientific and regulatory matters.... Each of those from whom we obtain advice is expected to be a leader in his profession and fully conversant with the most advanced expression of its scientific basis, clinical or technical applications, and societal implications. Since authorities in any field are rarely unanimous on all subjects which may come under consideration, a diligent effort is made to obtain the services of authorities who represent broad-ranging viewpoints so that interpretations which derive from any given set of facts may be examined from multiple points of view....

NOTES

1. *Agency Advisory Committees.* FDA created 17 new advisory committees during 1972 and 29 new advisory committees during 1973, as part of the program described by Dr. Schmidt. Sixteen additional committees were established to implement the Medical Device Amendments of 1976.

2. *Commentary.* For views from differing perspectives on FDA's expanded use of advisory committees, *see* Hickman, *Advisory Committees at FDA—A Legal Perspective,* 29 FDC L.J. 395 (1974); Kanig, *Advisory Committees: An Expanding Concept in the Field of Drug Regulation—The Perspective of a Liaison Representative,* 29 FDC L.J. 353 (1974); Walters, *Use of FDA Advisory Committees: Present and Future,* 29 FDC L.J. 348 (1974).

3. *External Review Panels.* On two occasions FDA has contracted with outside independent scientific organizations to conduct comprehensive scientific reviews of ingredients or products for regulatory purposes. The National Academy of Sciences reviewed the effectiveness of new drugs approved prior to 1962. The Federation of American Societies of Experimental Biology conducted the review of food substances on FDA's list of GRAS food substances. Both organizations utilized expert committees. FDA has also often sought the advice of outside organizations on specific issues, such as the safety of cyclamate and saccharin.

4. *Uses of Agency Advisory Committees.* FDA relies heavily on technical advisory committees for advice on such issues as the approval of new drugs or the adequacy of clinical test designs. 21 C.F.R. § 14.160 *et seq.* Throughout the 1970s and 1980s, the agency used these advisory committees to hold public hearings on a wide variety of issues, including proposed approvals, or denials of approval, of new products. The committees have also reviewed proposed approval or denial of new uses for existing products, or new warnings, or even

revocation of prior approvals. *See, e.g.,* 46 Fed. Reg. 14355 (February 27, 1981), announcing an advisory committee hearing on the proposed revocation of erythromycin estolate, which FDA had approved more than 20 years earlier. *See* Brown and Richard, *Advisory Committees and the Drug Approval Process,* 2 J. Clin. Res. & Drug Dev. 15 (1988). *See also* Burack, *Of Reliable Science: Scientific Peer Review, Federal Regulatory Agencies and the Courts,* 7 Va. J. of Nat. Res. Law 27 (1987).

With the exception of the Board of Tea Experts, as of December 31, 1990, no committee advised FDA on issues involving food or cosmetics. The Center for Food Safety and Applied Nutrition has instead entered into contracts with the Federation of American Societies for Experimental Biology (FASEB) to provide independent advice. *See* 52 Fed. Reg. 27588 (July 22, 1987).

5. *Statutory Committees.* A minority of FDA advisory committees are statutorily mandated. These include the Technical Electronic Product Radiation Safety Standards Committee, 42 U.S.C. § 263t(f)(1)(A); the Board of Tea Experts, 21 U.S.C. § 42; color additive advisory committees, 21 U.S.C. § 376(b)(5)(C)(D); the Device Good Manufacturing Practice Advisory Committee, 21 U.S.C. § 360j(f)(3); and the advisory review panels for medical devices, 21 U.S.C. § 360c(b).

6. *Consumer Representatives.* A novel innovation by FDA has been the inclusion of a consumer liaison and an industry liaison on most advisory committees. 21 C.F.R. § 14.84. Congress mandated this approach in the Medical Device Amendments of 1976, 21 U.S.C. §§ 360c(b)(2) and 360d(g)(5).

7. *Power to Create Committees.* All current FDA advisory committees have been established by the Secretary of HHS. However, Section 903(c) of the FD&C Act, as added by the Food and Drug Administration Act of 1988, 102 Stat. 3048, 3120, and amended by the Food and Drug Administration Revitalization Act, 104 Stat. 4583 (1990), explicitly empowers the FDA Commissioner to "establish such technical and scientific review groups as are needed to carry out the functions" of FDA. This provision, permits FDA to appoint the members of its technical advisory committees without review or approval by the Department of HHS.

8. *Video Coverage.* FDA has published a guideline on videotaping of agency proceedings in general, and advisory committee meetings in particular, 48 Fed. Reg. 37709 (August 19, 1983), 49 Fed. Reg. 14723 (August 13, 1984), codified in 21 C.F.R. § 10.200 et seq.

---

2. THE FEDERAL ADVISORY COMMITTEE ACT

In 1972 Congress enacted the Federal Advisory Committee Act (FACA), 86 Stat. 770, to regulate the establishment and operations of committees advising Federal agencies. Other aims were to limit the number of committees and confine their role to that of providing advice.

a. Coverage of FACA

Questions about the coverage of FACA have generated more controversy than have its basic procedural requirements for established committees with well-recognized functions. *Food Chemical News, Inc. v. Davis,* 378 F. Supp. 1048 (D.D.C. 1974), held the Act applicable to a series of meetings that the Director of the Bureau of Alcohol, Tobacco and Firearms had scheduled separately with consumer and industry groups to discuss proposals for alcoholic beverage labeling. The aim of the plaintiff, a weekly trade journal, was to forces BATF to open the meetings to the public. A similar objective inspired the plaintiff in the following suit challenging meetings between an industry group and FDA officials.

CONSUMERS UNION OF UNITED STATES, INC.
v. DEPARTMENT OF HEW

United States District Court, District of Columbia, 1976.
409 F. Supp. 473, *aff'd without opinion,* 551 F.2d 466.

JOHN LEWIS SMITH, Jr. District Judge.

This case involves a relatively narrow legal question: Were the meetings held on April 9 and September 17, 1975 between Food and Drug Administration (FDA) officials and representatives of the Cosmetic, Toiletry and Fragrance Association, Inc. (CTFA, Intervenor) advisory committee meetings within the meaning of the Federal Advisory Committee Act? If so, they were invalidly held since under FACA the meetings should have been open to the public and the "advising" group authorized through administrative approval and chartering....

The FDA has considered the desirability of labeling and of testing cosmetic ingredients since 1960. The initiative in these areas has moved back and forth from agency to industry, with industry representatives (acting at times to forestall pending legislation) proposing certain voluntary programs and FDA calling for refinements and clarifications in procedures. There now exist procedures for voluntary registration of cosmetic product establishments, for voluntary filing of cosmetic product ingredients, and for voluntary filing of cosmetic product experiences....

In the area of testing cosmetic ingredients, FDA–CTFA efforts have increased in the past two years. Speaking at CTFA's annual meeting on February 27, 1974, FDA Commissioner Schmidt discussed the need for establishment of an ingredient review program. Another FDA official, Dr. Mark Novitch, stated: "Certainly, this kind of approach [*i.e.,* cosmetic ingredient safety substantiation paralleling the drug review process] is something you should consider and we *will* consider in our common effort to increase our mutual assurance and the public's confidence in the safety of our cosmetic products." (Emphasis in original.) CTFA had been developing a safety review program since 1972, and planning and consultation moved forward rapidly. After three exploratory meetings between FDA and CTFA representatives in 1974 and two briefing meetings in early 1975, CTFA requested a meeting with FDA to discuss CTFA's draft proposal. This meeting was held on April 9, 1975, and detailed minutes were kept for the session.

Plaintiff's counsel subsequently requested permission to attend or participate in future FDA–CTFA meetings on the ingredient review proposal, invoking the Federal Advisory Committee Act. Commissioner Schmidt denied the request on grounds that these were private, CTFA-initiated meetings. Following the filing of this lawsuit, a second meeting was held on September 17, 1975 to discuss CTFA's revised proposal. Minutes were also kept for this meeting.

Resolution of the issues in this case requires a careful examination of FACA and its administrative and judicial construction. The Federal Advisory Committee Act was aimed at eliminating useless advisory committees, strengthening the independence of remaining advisory committees, and preventing advisory groups from becoming self-serving. The Act defines advisory committee in a general, open-ended fashion. For purposes of this action, the term includes "any committee, board, commission, council, conference, panel, task force, or other similar group ... which is ... established or utilized by one or more agencies, in the interest of obtaining advice or recommendations for ... [such] agencies...." The legislative history does not clarify the meaning of the words "utilized by" an agency. This language was added in conference and the intent was not clarified either in the report or on the floor....

Several recent cases have interpreted FACA and afford some guidance to the Court in determining what constitutes an advisory committee under the Act. In *Nader v. Baroody,* 396 F. Supp. 1231 (D.D.C. 1975), the court held that certain bi-weekly meetings with various constituent and interest groups at the White House did not come within FACA's reach. The meetings were found to be of a random nature, without formally organized groups, without presidential request for policy recommendations, and without any continuity or follow-up. Further, to have applied the Act so as to impinge upon the effective discharge of the President's business might have raised serious constitutional questions.

In *Food Chemical News, Inc. v. Davis,* 378 F. Supp. 1048 (D.D.C. 1974), the court held as subject to FACA an agency's informal meetings with consumer and distilled spirits industry representatives relative to drafting proposed ingredient labeling regulations....

The matter before the Court involves a factual situation different from the above-mentioned cases. The meetings complained of here were not ad hoc, amorphous or casual group meetings as in *Nader v. Baroody, supra.* The FDA–CTFA conferences were the culmination of many months of planning, consulting, and revising. On the other hand—and unlike *Food Chemical News, supra*—the two meetings were not called to consider proposals dealing with impending agency action. They are essentially consultations concerning the *group's own* proposal. This is a crucial factor for determining the group's status under the Act.

At the April 9 and September 17, 1975 meetings, the FDA was primarily responding and reacting to a CTFA-initiated, CTFA-administered program....The mechanics of the review process were probed and certain weaknesses pointed out by FDA, such as potential conflicts of interest in the expert panel and lack of interest in the expert panel and lack of public involvement. The agency also explored its role in the program, i.e., "how the proposed program would interface with the FDA regulatory process." ...

Based on the record, the Court finds that CTFA was not advising the FDA about the cosmetic ingredient testing program. CTFA was presenting a voluntary, industry-sponsored proposal and seeking the FDA's comments and advice. For a variety of reasons including budget limitations, statutory authority, and other important priorities, the FDA had been unable either to develop or to require a cosmetic testing program. Under these circumstances CTFA took the initiative. This is the converse of *Food Chemical News,* where the agency, acting under clear regulatory authority, solicited industry and consumer viewpoints on amendments which the agency itself was preparing. Granting that FDA had frequently expressed its concern for cosmetic ingredient testing, the Court finds that planning had evolved beyond agency control. CTFA in its own discretion was ultimately to decide whether or not to initiate a testing program. Such a relationship of agency and group does not rise to the level of a FACA "advisory" relationship.

NOTE

In subsequently adopted regulations, 40 Fed. Reg. 40682 (September 3, 1975), 41 Fed. Reg. 52148 (November 26, 1976) (as edited), FDA explained its interpretation of the scope of the Advisory Committee Act:

§ 14.1 **Scope**....

(b) In determining whether a group is a "public advisory committee" ... the following guidelines will be used:

(1) An advisory committee may be a standing advisory committee or an ad hoc advisory committee....

(2) An advisory committee may be a policy advisory committee or a technical advisory committee....

(3) An advisory committee includes any of its subgroups when the subgroup is working on behalf of the committee....

(4) A committee composed entirely of full-time Federal Government employees is not an advisory committee.

(5) An advisory committee ordinarily has a fixed membership, a defined purpose of providing advice to the agency on a particular subject, regular or periodic meetings, and an organizational structure, for example, a chairman and staff, and serves as a source of independent expertise and advice rather than as a representative of or advocate for any particular interest. The following groups are not advisory committees:

(i) A group of persons convened on an ad hoc basis to discuss a matter of current interest to FDA, but which has no continuing function or organization and does not involve substantial special preparation.

     (ii) A group of two or more FDA consultants meeting with the agency on an ad hoc basis.

     (iii) A group of experts who are employed by a private company or a trade association which has been requested by FDA to provide its views on a regulatory matter pending before FDA.

     (iv) A consulting firm hired by FDA to provide advice regarding a matter.

(6) An advisory committee that is utilized by FDA is subject to this subpart even though it was not established by FDA. In general, a committee is "utilized" when FDA requests advice or recommendations from the committee on a specific matter in order to obtain an independent review and consideration of the matter, and not when FDA is merely seeking the comments of all interested persons or of persons who have a specific interest in the matter.

NATIONAL NUTRITIONAL FOODS ASS'N v. CALIFANO

United States Court of Appeals, Second Circuit, 1979.
603 F.2d 327.

FRIENDLY, Circuit Judge.

This is an appeal from an order of the District Court for the Southern District of New York, 457 F. Supp. 275 (1978), in an action by two trade associations whose members manufacture and sell protein supplements.... The action concerns FDA rulemaking designed to require warnings for protein supplements and other preparations that may be used as the sole or primary source of calories in order to lose weight....

Liquid protein products have been available for direct retail sale to the consuming public for at least 12 years. Within the last five years new medical research has suggested the usefulness of a modified fasting diet, supplemented by protein, vitamins and minerals, in alleviating obesity. Prominent in this "Protein Sparing Modified Fast" (PSMF) research was Dr. George L. Blackburn of the Harvard University Medical School, who is Director of the Center for Nutritional Research in Boston....

The controversy was heated by the publication in late 1976 of "The Last Chance Diet" by Robert Linn, a doctor of osteopathy, which popularized the use of liquid protein products for diet control. The ASBP [American Society of Bariatric Physicians] attacked the new widespread and uncontrolled use of PSMF programs and urged its members to help with the problem, through such means as writing letters to newspapers....

Primary responsibility in the FDA for products such as those manufactured and sold by plaintiffs lay in Dr. Allan Forbes, Acting

Associate Director for Nutrition and Consumer Sciences in the Bureau of Foods. In the spring of 1977 he and Dr. Blackburn had various conversations about Dr. Linn's book and the consequent popularity of liquid food protein products, including Dr. Blackburn's attempts to dissuade Dr. Linn from publishing. In a letter to Dr. Forbes dated May 25, 1977, Dr. Blackburn suggested that the Bureau of Foods might become involved. During the summer of 1977, the FDA received a report of a death believed to be associated with the use of liquid protein products in dieting; a second death was reported in September. At a conference of FDA officials held on or before October 3, 1977, it was decided, among other things, "to obtain the advice of experts in the field of obesity research among whom are Dr. George L. Blackburn, Dr. Theodore B. Van Itallie, and Dr. Sanford A. Miller." ...

Later in October, Dr. Forbes learned that a conference on obesity was scheduled to take place on October 20–22, 1977, at the National Institutes of Health in Bethesda, Md., near the FDA's headquarters. Between October 18 and 22 he communicated with five clinicians who were attending the conference and arranged for them to meet with him and six other FDA officials.... The memorandum recites that the "ultimate purpose for the meeting" was to assist the FDA in selecting the best course of action "for regulating the production and promotion of [protein products used for weight reduction] and/or informing the public of their hazard potential." It described the five physicians as an "ad hoc advisory group." ... The memorandum concluded by saying:

> The members of the ad hoc advisory group have graciously agreed to provide further assistance to FDA as the need may arise.

On November 9, 1977 the Commissioner of Food and Drugs held a press conference and issued a press release on the subject of protein supplements used to fight obesity. He declared the FDA was aware of 16 reported deaths and a number of severe illnesses possibly associated with the use of such products and expressed special concern about the "liquid protein diets now so popular," which were being promoted in the new media and in books such as Dr. Linn's. He said that his statements reflected not only the views of the FDA but also "the information provided by the Center for Disease Control and advice given us by leading experts in obesity and obesity control," two of whom, Drs. Blackburn and Van Itallie, were present and could answer questions.

As should have been expected, this publicity resulted in a drastic decline in the sale of protein products for use in weight reduction. On December 2, 1977, the FDA gave notice of a proposed rule, 42 F.R. 61285, whereby protein supplements intended for use in weight reduction or maintenance programs would be required to bear the following warning:

> *Warning.* Very low calorie protein diets may cause serious illness or death. DO NOT USE FOR WEIGHT REDUCTION

OR MAINTENANCE WITHOUT MEDICAL SUPERVISION. Do not use for any purpose without medical advice if you are taking medication. Not for use by infants, children, or pregnant or nursing women.

The notice relied heavily on the October 20 meeting with the ad hoc advisory group, which was described in detail, and the memorandum of the meeting was placed on file with the Hearing Clerk.....

Appellants contend that the meeting of October 20, 1977, was of an advisory committee as defined in FACA and did not comply with the Act and the FDA's regulations thereunder, 21 C.F.R. §§ 14.1 *et seq.,* in several respects. The FDA gave no notice of the meeting as required by 21 C.F.R. § 14.20 and § 10(a)(2) of the Act. No advisory committee charter was filed as required by § 9(c). The meeting was not open to the public, nor were interested persons given any opportunity to appear before the committee or file statements with it, as required by § 10(a)(1) and (3). Most important, appellants claim that appointment of a group composed solely of physicians, understandably leaning in favor of medical supervision of the use of protein supplements to conquer obesity, did not comply with § 5(b)(2) and (3), made applicable to agencies by § 5(c), which require that membership of an advisory committee "be fairly balanced in terms of the points of view represented and the functions to be performed" and that suitable provision be made to assure that advice and recommendations "will not be inappropriately influenced ... by any special interest." The FDA's principal answer is that the group convened on October 20 was not an advisory committee within the meaning of FACA....

In the long run the Government's argument that the October 20 meeting was not within FACA rests mainly on what it conceives to be common sense. An agency dealing with technical matters ought to be able to get the advice of highly qualified technicians in the private sector before it even initiates proceedings or takes other action, and to get this speedily and informally. Yet the OMB guidelines require that before creating a new advisory committee, an agency must first consult with the OMB secretariat and, if the OMB concurs, a process that may be time consuming, must publish in the Federal Register a certification of need and a description of the nature and purpose of the committee at least 15 days (unless that period is shortened by the OMB secretariat) before the filing of the committee's charter, 39 F.R. 12389, which under § 9(c) of the Act, is a precondition to the committee's meeting. Congress, the Government argues, could not have intended to place such obstacles in the way of what proved to be a one-time meeting, even though there may have been an intention to hold more....

... [W]e find *Food Chemical News* to be more nearly in point. One factor weighing heavily with us is that the Commissioner leaned so strongly on the advisory group in his press release and, even more so, in his proposed regulation. If an agency wishes to rely publicly on the backing of an advisory committee it must do what the statute commands. Such a situation directly implicates the concern Congress addressed in § 5(c)(2) and (3) of the Act, that agency action might be dominated by one particular viewpoint. Some two months elapsed between the initial plan for the meeting and the publication of the proposal, in which the advisory group was mentioned on four occasions. Even if the calling of the meeting without reference to FACA was a pardonable inadvertence, there was ample time for compliance before December 7. All things considered, we believe this to be a situation wherein Congress meant FACA to apply. If the straitjacket is too tight, Congress is free to loosen it.

The question of remedy remains. So far as we are aware, no court has held that a violation of FACA would invalidate a regulation adopted under otherwise appropriate procedures, simply because it stemmed from the advisory committee's recommendations, or even that pending rulemaking must be aborted and a fresh start made. We perceive no sound basis for doing so. Applicable rulemaking procedures afford ample opportunity to correct infirmities resulting from improper advisory committee action prior to the proposal.... We likewise cannot fault the district judge for concluding that, in light of the Government's agreement not to reconvene this particular group, there was no need for an injunction. Whether it was proper to deny declaratory relief is a closer question.... In any event this opinion gives appellants substantially the same relief as a declaratory order....

NOTES

1. *Judicial Reflections.* Commenting on this ruling Judge Friendly later wrote:

> No one seems even to have considered that in seeking to cure one trouble by imposing procedural requirements, the statute would create others. Just what is an advisory committee? In a recent opinion, where the FDA had consulted with a number of physicians who were attending a meeting of the nearby National Institute of Health, I regretfully found it impossible to accept the Government's position that simply by keeping things informal an agency can escape from a statute whose very purpose is to require formality.

> Against this a judge would scarcely wish to say that if on the night of Three Mile Island the NRC wanted to telephone a few eminent atomic scientists, it could not legally have done so. Assuming that a talk with one scientist would not have been subject to FACA, what about a conference call with five? What about a couple of meetings in Harrisburg during the next few days? Beyond this the statute necessitates additional staff in each agency and in the Office of Management and Budget. Would we not have been better off with a bit more trust and less law?

Friendly, *Should We Be Turning Back the Law Flood?,* Legal Times of Washington, October 8, 1979, at 7. FDA issued its final regulation prescribing a warning for liquid protein products at 45 Fed. Reg. 22904 (April 4, 1980).

2. *Application to Nongovernmental Bodies.* FACA has been held not to apply to committees formed by independent scientific bodies, like the National

Academy of Sciences, providing advice to the Federal government. *Food Chemical News v. Young*, 900 F.2d 328 (D.C. Cir. 1990), *rev'g* 709 F. Supp. 5 (D.D.C. 1989), on the authority of *Public Citizen v. United States Department of Justice*, 491 U.S. 440 (1989); *Lombardo v. Handler*, 397 F. Supp. 792 (D.D.C. 1975), *aff'd without opinion*, 546 F.2d 1043 (D.C. Cir. 1976). FDA's requirements for such committees appear at 21 C.F.R. § 14.15. *See also* Scarlett, *The FDA's Regulatory Proposals for the Management of Advisory Committees*, 30 FDC L.J. 503 (1975); McGrew, *How to Let in the Sunshine Without Getting Burned: Protecting Your Rights Before Advisory Committees*, 30 FDC L.J. 536 (1975).

3. *FDA Regulations.* In addition to interpreting the scope of FACA, FDA's regulations, 21 C.F.R. Part 14, contain comprehensive rules governing the establishment and operation of agency advisory committees. The two main issues raised by these regulations involve public access to advisory committee meetings and sanctions for violation FACA. 21 C.F.R. § 14.7 provides for an administrative appeal and remedies for noncompliance with FACA. If FDA concludes that the FACA has been violated, it "shall grant any appropriate relief and shall take appropriate steps to prevent its recurrence in the future."

4. *Open Meetings.* For the first three years of their existence the OTC Drug Review panels began each meeting with an open session and then conducted their deliberations in closed session. Transcripts of closed meetings were made but were not released to the public. This approach was proposed for all FDA advisory committees in 40 Fed. Reg. 40682 (September 3, 1975). FDA's policy of withholding meeting transcripts was initially upheld in *Smart v. FDA*, Civ. No. C–73–118–RHS (N.D. Cal., April 24, 1974), but was subsequently held to contravene the Freedom of Information Act in *Wolfe v. Weinberger*, 403 F. Supp. 238 (D.D.C. 1975). Because the *Wolfe* decision did not consider FACA, FDA did not appeal but expressly declined to accept the decision as binding on all agency advisory committees, 40 Fed. Reg. 58165 (December 15, 1975).

In mid–1976 FDA reversed its policy and opened the deliberative portions of all advisory committee meetings to public attendance. On September 13, 1976, Congress enacted the Government in the Sunshine Act, 90 Stat. 1241, which amended the FACA to narrow the circumstances under which an advisory committee may be closed. FDA promulgated final advisory committee regulations in 41 Fed. Reg. 52148 (November 26, 1976), 21 C.F.R. §§ 14.25 and 14.27, providing that all advisory committee meetings would be open except during consideration of trade secrets, investigatory files, sensitive internal documents, or matters involving personal privacy.

5. *Draft Reports.* In *Bristol Meyers Co. v. Kennedy*, Food Drug Cosm. L. Rep. (CCH) ¶ 38,224 (D.D.C. 1979), plaintiff sought the transcripts of the 1972–1976 closed sessions of an OTC drug panel and all drafts of the proposed monograph, and argued that the closed sessions violated the FACA and thus invalidated the panel's report. FDA provided the requested transcripts but not the panel drafts. The court held that the drafts as a whole reflected the deliberative process of the panel and thus were exempt from public disclosure. The court also ruled that any FACA violation was mooted by the release of the transcripts of the closed sessions and would in any event not be ripe for judicial review until a final regulation was promulgated.

6. *GSA Guidelines.* The General Services Administration has promulgated regulations containing policies and guidelines to be followed by Federal agencies in the administration of FACA in 41 C.F.R. Part 101–6.

b. Composition Of Advisory Committees

PUBLIC CITIZEN v. NATIONAL ADVISORY COMMITTEE

United States Court of Appeals, District of Columbia Circuit, 1989.
886 F.2d 419.

PER CURIAM:

This is an appeal from a judgment of the United States District Court for the District of Columbia dismissing a complaint filed by public interest organizations that challenge, as violating the Federal Advisory Committee Act, the composition of a federal advisory committee.

The members of the panel are divided about the correct disposition of the case. Judge Silberman concludes that the appellants do not have standing to maintain the suit and that their claims are not justiciable. Judge Friedman is of the view that the district court correctly rejected the challenges to the advisory committee. Judge Edwards concludes that the appellants have standing and raise justiciable claims, and that the appellants have shown that the composition of the advisory committee violates the Act. The result of these divergent views of the members of the panel is that the judgment of the district court is affirmed, with Judge Edwards concurring in part and dissenting in part....

Opinion, concurring in the judgment, filed by Circuit Judge FRIEDMAN.

In November 1987, the United States Department of Agriculture (Department) announced plans to establish a National Advisory Committee on Microbiological Criteria for Foods (Committee). The purpose of the Committee was to provide advice and recommendations to the Secretaries of Agriculture and Health and Human Services (HHS) on the development of microbiological criteria by which the safety and wholesomeness of food could be assessed.

The Committee's mandate was primarily technical and scientific. Developing microbiological criteria for foods requires an understanding of the complex science in the area and an appropriate background and training.....

The Committee membership .... consisted of two university professors, one state agriculture department official, one state department of agriculture and consumer services official, two persons employed by food research firms, six persons employed by federal agencies, and six persons employed by private food companies....

The Committee held its first meeting on April 5, 1988. By letter dated May 12, 1988, the appellants requested the Secretary of Agriculture to "take immediate action to appoint consumer representatives with public health expertise to membership" on the Committee, and, further, offered to "recommend ... individuals with appropriate credentials in public health and consumer concerns.".... The Assistant Secretary replied:

> Although the Committee is composed of scientific experts, the consumer perspective is also brought to the Committee, by its membership. In particular, Dr. Martha Rhodes, Assistant Commissioner of the Florida Department of Agriculture and Consumer Services, was selected for the Committee because of her expertise in microbiology, public health, and consumer affairs, as well as her involvement with State governmental matters. If you would like to recommend others for membership on the Committee, we will be happy to review their qualifications and consider them when there is a vacancy.....

The appellants then filed the present action in the district court seeking declaratory and injunctive relief against the government's alleged violation of the Federal Advisory Committee Act. They also sought a preliminary injunction against the Committee acting until it was "in compliance with the requirements" of the Act.....

The appellants originally contended that because the Committee's recommendations will directly affect the interest of consumers, the Act requires that the Committee contain representatives of consumers, and that the Committee lacks such representation because "not a single member of the Committee works for, or is associated with, a consumer or public health organization, despite the fact that there are such individuals who have expertise and backgrounds in the very issues to be scrutinized by the Committee."

Section 5 [of FACA], however, "confers no cognizable personal right to an advisory committee appointment." Thus, none of the individuals the appellants have recommended is entitled to a position on the Committee. Moreover, the appellants have not pointed to any provision of the Act, and I know of none, that requires that the Committee must include individuals who work for, or are associated with, a consumer or public health organization.

The appropriate inquiry in determining whether the Committee's membership satisfies the "fairly balanced" standard in section 5(b)(2) is whether the Committee's members "represent a fair balance of viewpoints given the functions to be performed." Since the Committee's function in this case involves highly technical and scientific studies and recommendations, a "fair balance" of viewpoints can be achieved even though the Committee does not have any members who are consumer advocates or proponents of consumer interests.

The statutory directive that membership of the Committee be "fairly balanced" does not mean that such balance can be provided only by individuals who work for, or are associated with, a consumer or public health organization.....

The determination of how the "fairly balanced" membership of an advisory committee ... is to be achieved, necessarily lies largely within the discretion of the official who appoints the committee. In my view, the membership of the Committee that the Secretary of Agriculture appointed did not violate the "fairly balanced" requirement of the Act, and the secretary did not abuse his discretion by failing to include on the Committee direct representatives of consumer organizations....

The appellants have not shown that the original Committee was dominated or "inappropriately influenced" by food industry representatives. Only six of the 18 members were employed by the food industry. The appellants' contention that four other members of the Committee— the two employees of independent food research firms and the two university professors—represent food industry interests is unconvincing. The mere fact that the individuals employed by independent food research firms have food company clients or that the professors have performed some consulting work for food companies in the past, does not demonstrate that they are a part of "special interest groups [that] may use their membership on [advisory committees] to promote their private concerns,"....

Opinion, concurring in the judgment, filed by Circuit Judge SILBERMAN.

... For any claim under section 5(b)(2) of the FACA to be justiciable under the APA, we must first conclude that Congress provided "a meaningful standard against which to judge the agency's exercise of discretion." Where no such meaningful standard exists, "the statute ('law') can be taken to have 'committed' the decisionmaking to the agency's judgment absolutely," thereby precluding judicial review under 5 U.S.C. § 701(a)(2). I cannot discern any meaningful standard that is susceptible of judicial application in the formulation "fairly balanced in terms of the points of view represented and the functions to be performed." Therefore, I believe that judicial review is unavailable.....

... Appellants would divide the world of those interested in microbiological food contamination into three "classes" (government, industry, and consumers), each of which it alleges must have representation on the Committee. But there surely are other appropriate divisions, and choosing the best one is a political task not properly undertaken by life-tenured, unelected federal judges. On the other hand, to examine a member's relevant policy views—which brings one back to "points of view" which the direct interest proxy was designed to avoid—the court must somehow determine whether the views of a particular committee member are sufficiently close to those of the appellants to deem them "representative." Again, I see no principled way to decide such a question. Would the court rule, for instance, that when two parties agree on a certain percentage (what percentage?) of issues (which issues?) one may be deemed "representative" of the other? Neither the statutory language nor the appellants' proffered "standard," therefore, offers us effective guidance to determine whether an advisory committee is "fairly balanced in terms of the points of view represented."....

The instant case illustrates powerfully, in my view, the kind of arbitrary judgments courts would have to make to adjudicate claims under FACA's "fairly balanced" requirement. Appellants assert that, at minimum, *consumers* are affected by the work of this Committee and therefore *consumers* must have "some" representation on it. Undeniably, consumers will be directly affected by the work of the Committee since it advises the Department of Agriculture on the desirable form and extent of federal regulation of food products, but I hardly think that proposition helps appellants' case. Everyone in the entire United states is a consumer of food products, so I do not understand why *any* American—including all those who have already been appointed to the Committee—would not legitimately be considered a consumer representative. Whatever else he or she may do, that hypothetical person is a consumer.

Appellants' brief defines a consumer representative as one who "works for or is associated with a consumer or public health organization." But why should an organization that labels itself a representative of consumers have any greater legal claim to placement on the Advisory Committee than any other individual American or organization who buys or eats food? Indeed, at oral argument, counsel for petitioner conceded that the name of an organization could not be determinative in judging whether an organization qualified as a consumer representative, thus implying that we as a court would have to determine which organizations or individuals qualified as bona fide "consumer representatives."

I think it rather obvious that appellants thereby wish the court either to decide, or simply to assume the resolution of a major political question of our time. Appellants represent one philosophical, ideological, and political view of consumer welfare. I think it fair to describe that view as one that typically urges greater governmental regulation of the production of goods or services in the marketplace. But that view is hardly the only one that claims to maximize consumer welfare. At the other end of the political-ideological spectrum are those individuals or organizations who generally oppose government regulation since the cost incurred translates into higher prices for consumers and they believe those higher prices exceed the benefits that regulation is likely to afford. This debate is one key element in the division between the two major political parties in the United states. As such, it is hardly open to a federal court to express its view on such an issue by determining which kind of organization or individual legitimately represents consumers.....

EDWARDS, Circuit Judge, concurring in part and dissenting in part:....

The Committee at issue in this case is charged with recommending regulations for a broad range of food products. These decisions have health and safety implications that directly affect consumers. Recommendations regarding these regulations involve complex policy choices, not merely—or even primarily—technical determinations. For these reasons, especially in light of the legislative history of section 5, I disagree with Judge Friedman's opinion that the Committee's mandate in this instance was "primarily technical and scientific," and I conclude that a fair balance of viewpoints cannot be achieved without representation of consumer interests.....

The Government argues that consumers are represented by Dr. Martha Rhodes, the Assistant Commissioner of Agriculture for the Florida Department of Agriculture and Consumer Affairs, and by Dr. Mitchell Cohen of the Centers for Disease Control. Both of these persons, however, are government employees with a variety of regulatory responsibilities. One of the dangers that Congress specifically identified in adopting FACA was the risk that governmental officials would be unduly influenced by industry leaders. That is, it is precisely the lack of representatives of the public interest independent of *both* government *and* industry that prompted Congress to enact the "fairly balanced" provision. The fact that Dr. Rhodes and Dr. Cohen are state rather than federal government officials does not demonstrate that they will be less amenable to influence by industry representatives. This is not to impugn the integrity of either individual. Rather, it is to say that it is unnecessary for the court to assess the individual viewpoints of Dr. Rhodes and Dr. Cohen in order to find that their presence does not mitigate the lack of consumer representation. I, thus, conclude that, on the record before us, the Committee does not include any representative of consumer interests and, consequently, that it is not "fairly balanced" as required by section 5 of FACA.....

F. PUBLIC ACCESS TO FDA RECORDS

1. OVERVIEW

In 1966, Congress enacted the Freedom of Information Act (FOIA), 80 Stat. 250, since frequently amended and now codified in 5 U.S.C. § 552. The Act was intended to expand public access to government records dramatically, but its impact was felt only gradually. Today, however, FDA receives an enormous number of requests for documents under FOIA, more than any other agency except the FBI.

PETER BARTON HUTT, PUBLIC INFORMATION
AND PUBLIC PARTICIPATION IN
THE FOOD AND DRUG ADMINISTRATION
36 Quarterly Bulletin of the Ass'n of Food and Drug Officials 212 (1972).

... The Food and Drug Administration is the largest repository of private scientific research in the world. [It] receive[s] mountains of important data and information on the safety, effectiveness, and functionality of foods and drugs, and undoubtedly will soon be receiving the same type of information for devices and cosmetics, that is available nowhere else. Since 1938, virtually none of it has been divulged. It is now proposed, however, that most of it will become available for public disclosure upon request.

The [May 5, 1972] proposal takes precautions to protect the confidentiality of information that genuinely can be regarded as a trade secret, in that its disclosure would destroy the competitive advantage of the person who has submitted it. The safety and effectiveness data for a new drug or a new animal drug would not be released, for example, because to do so would destroy the competitive advantage obtained from that data by the holders of the NDA or the NADA. Once those products become subject to abbreviated applications or become old drugs, however, that competitive advantage no longer exists, and it is therefore proposed that the data would promptly be released to the public upon request. Similarly, since food additives, color additives, and antibiotics are subject to public regulations rather than private licenses, and thus permit any person to engage in the their manufacture, it is proposed that the scientific data underlying those regulations would promptly be released to the public upon request the moment that the regulation is promulgated.

In an area ... involving inspectional and other regulatory efforts, equally important changes in policy are proposed....[A]n FDA inspector provides a Form 483 to an establishment upon completion of an inspection, to inform them of significant violations. the inspector then prepares an Establishment Inspection Report (EIR), which is retained for our own files, and in many instances writes a top official in the company to bring to his personal attention any violations of the law. Samples may be taken, and later analyzed, and other evidence may be accumulated....

... [The agency] propose[s] to make available to the public, upon request, the Form 483 and any correspondence with the company or the individual involved. These documents are in the nature of an informal warning, rather than an investigatory file for law enforcement purposes, and thus would not be exempt from disclosure. The remaining information, such as the EIR, sample analyses, and so forth would be retained as confidential until the file is closed or a decision is made not to pursue legal action....

A third area of interest is the Agency's general correspondence with the outside world. The proposal adopts the position that all such documents would be released unless they fall within a specific exemption. Thus, correspondence with members of Congress, complaints from consumers, minutes of meetings with trade associations, summaries of scientific conferences, and similar documents would be available upon request....

NOTES

1. *FDA Regulations.* FDA's public information regulations were proposed in 37 Fed. Reg. 9128 (May 5, 1972) and were implemented immediately. The final regulations, which also took account of the Freedom of Information Act Amendments of 1974, 88 Stat. 1561, were promulgated in 39 Fed. Reg. 44602 (December 24, 1974). An additional 60 days were provided for public comment, after which further amendments were adopted in 41 Fed. Reg. 9317 (March 4, 1976), 42 Fed. Reg. 3094 (January 14, 1977). The regulations are codified in 21 C.F.R. Part 20.)

The Department of HHS FOIA regulations, codified in 45 C.F.R. Part 5, also apply to FDA.

2. *Fees.* Pursuant to the Freedom of Information Reform Act of 1986, 100 Stat. 3207, OMB has promulgated regulations in 5 C.F.R. Part 1303 setting a uniform schedule of fees applicable to all Federal agencies. Section 7:1 of the FD & C Act authorizes FDA to retain FOI fees to help fund the agency's FOI activities.

3. *Agency Records.* The FOIA applies only to documents actually in the possession of FDA, and does not include material, such as the records of clinical investigators, to which the agency has the right of access but of which it does not have custody. *Forsham v. Harris,* 445 U.S. 169 (1980).

---

2. TRADE SECRETS

The most controversial issues raised by FDA's public information policy revolve around the definition of, and protection accorded to, trade secrets. Particular attention has been focused on the status of scientific data submitted to the agency in support of new drug applications and other requests for marketing approval. Prior to 1972, FDA took the position that all such scientific data constituted trade secret information that could not be released to the public under both section 301(j) of the FD&C Act and the general prohibition against disclosure of trade secrets, 18 U.S.C. § 1905. In 37 Fed. Reg. 9128 (May 5, 1972), the agency refined its position to state that scientific data needed to obtain a private license for a product (*e.g.*, a new drug) would be kept confidential, but that scientific data relating to a product which did not need a private license (*e.g.*, an "old" drug) or relating to public regulation under which any firm could market its own product (*e.g.*, a food additive, color additive, or antibiotic) provide no competitive advantage and thus could not be regarded as trade secret information. The status of NDA safety and efficacy data was at the time at issue in *Morgan v. FDA,* 495 F.2d 1075 (D.C. Cir. 1974), which did not produce a definitive ruling. The debate was resolved by the enactment of the Drug Price Competition and Patent Term Restoration Act of 1984, p. 571 *supra,* and note 3 p. 1303 *infra.*

FDA's final FOIA regulations, 39 Fed. Reg. 44602 (December 24, 1974), continued to protect the confidentiality of NDA data but provided for release of summaries of the data and the agency's reasons for approving the NDA.

a. The Definition of "Trade Secret"

Relying the RESTATEMENT OF TORTS (SECOND), FDA arrived at the following definitions of trade secrets and confidential commercial information:

> **§ 20.61   Trade secrets and commercial or financial information which is privileged or confidential.**
>
> (a) A trade secret may consist of any formula, pattern, device, or compilation of information which is used in one's business and which gives him an opportunity to obtain an advantage over competitors who do not know or use it.
>
> (b) Commercial or financial information that is privileged or confidential means valuable data or information which is used in one's business and is of a type customarily held in strict confidence or regarded as privileged and not disclosed to any member of the public by the person to whom it belongs.
>
> (c) Data and information submitted or divulged to the Food and Drug Administration which fall within the definitions of a trade secret or confidential commercial or financial information are not available for public disclosure.

In *Public Citizen Health Research Group v. FDA*, 704 F.2d 1280 (D.C. Cir. 1983), the court of appeals offered its own definitions. The court defined a trade secret as "a secret, commercially valuable plan, formula, process, or device that is used for the making, preparing, compounding, or processing of trade commodities and that can be said to be the end product of either innovation or substantial effort." It held that commercial information could be accorded confidentiality if its disclosure would either "(1) . . . impair the Government's ability to obtain necessary information in the future; or (2) . . . cause substantial harm to the competitive position of the person from whom the information was obtained." This decision did not prompt FDA to amend 21 C.F.R. § 20.61.

NOTES

1. *Confidentiality of NDA Data.* In *Tri–Bio Laboratories, Inc. v. United States*, 836 F.2d 135 (3d Cir. 1987), the court held that the manufacturer of a generic new animal drug could not rely upon the safety and effectiveness data submitted by the manufacturer of the pioneer drug, upholding FDA's position that unpublished safety and effectiveness data may not be disclosed until a determination is made that they are no longer needed to support FDA approval of the product. *See also Webb v. Department of HHS*, 696 F.2d 101 (D.C. Cir. 1982).

2. *Confidentiality of Device Data.* The same issue arose during debate over the Medical Device Amendments of 1976. Section 520(c) prohibits FDA

from disclosing trade secret information or using trade secret information to approve or reclassify a class III device. This provision prevented the reclassification of contact lenses, p. 770 *supra*, but has been modified by the Safe Medical Devices Act of 1990, 104 Stat. 4511.

3. *Access by Makers of Generic Drugs.* During consideration of the Drug Price Competition and Patent Term Amendments of 1984, the issue arose as to the continuing trade secret status of data submitted for the pioneer drug after generic versions are permitted. In a letter for the record the FDA Commissioner wrote that safety and effectiveness data would be made public following approval of generic versions of a pioneer drug unless "extraordinary circumstances" were shown. The Commissioner explained this would require a demonstration that the data continued to represent trade secret or confidential commercial or financial information. 130 Cong. Rec. 24977–78 (September 12, 1984). This position is now reflected in 21 C.F.R. § 314.430(f).

4. *Adverse Reaction Reports.* The issue in *Public Citizen Health Research Group v. FDA*, 704 F.2d 1280 (D.C. Cir. 1983), involved disclosure of reports of adverse reactions to intraocular lens. On remand, using the court of appeals definitions, the district court determined that company-specific adverse reaction rates could be withheld but averaged adverse reaction data had to be disclosed. *See also Kennedy v. FDA*, 1985–1986 FDLI Jud. Rec. 471 (N.D. Ohio 1986), upholding FDA's refusal to disclose company-specific adverse reaction reports on intraocular lenses to a plaintiff suing the company.

5. *Product Ingredients.* For examples of the difficulties involved in determining what constitutes a "trade secret," *see Zotos International, Inc. v. Kennedy*, 460 F. Supp. 268 (D.D.C. 1978); *Zotos International, Inc. v. Young*, 830 F.2d 350 (D.C. Cir. 1987).

---

b. Predisclosure Notification

PHARMACEUTICAL MANUFACTURERS ASS'N v. WEINBERGER

United States District Court, District of Columbia, 1975.
401 F. Supp. 444.

SIRICA, District Judge.

This action was instituted by the plaintiff, an association of drug companies, on May 7, 1975, when a complaint seeking declaratory and injunctive relief was filed. The motion for a preliminary injunction was filed the same day seeking to prohibit the defendants, the Secretary of the Department of H.E.W. and the Commissioner of Food and Drugs, from applying and enforcing certain regulations published by the Commissioner.... Specifically, plaintiff seeks to require the F.D.A. to provide notice to an affected drug company of any proposed release of information pursuant to Freedom of Information Act (hereinafter F.O.I.A.) requests, in order to provide an opportunity for the affected company to consult with the F.D.A. concerning the propriety of the release of said information, and to provide an opportunity for judicial review of the F.D.A.'s decision.

... F.D.A. freely admits that the drug manufacturers do maintain a property interest in certain sensitive information which is supplied to it. If such information were to be disclosed, a substantial loss could be incurred by the drug company which supplied the information.

The importance of maintaining the confidentiality of such information is reflected in two statutes which prohibit disclosure of certain information by the F.D.A. The Food, Drug and Cosmetic Act itself expressly prohibits revealing to any person outside the Department of H.E.W. or the courts "any information acquired under authority of [the F.D.A.] concerning any method or process which as a trade secret is entitled to protection." 21 U.S.C. § 331(j). Also applicable to the F.D.A.—as well as to all federal agencies—is 18 U.S.C. § 1905 which provides criminal punishment for any government employee who

> publishes, divulges, discloses, or makes known in any manner or to any extent not authorized by law any information coming to him ... which ... concerns or relates to trade secrets, processes, operations, style of work, or apparatus, or to the identity, confidential statistical data, amount or source of income, profits, losses or expenditures of any person, firm, partnership, corporation or association....

However, the F.O.I.A. also applies to the F.D.A. It provides that "each agency ... on request for identifiable records ... shall make the records promptly available to any person." 5 U.S.C. § 552(a)(3). Recent amendments to the F.O.I.A. emphasize the necessity for an agency to provide the requested information expeditiously. But the disclosure requirements of the F.O.I.A. do not apply to information that falls within any of its nine exemptions.... The fourth exemption, 5 U.S.C. § 552(b)(4) exempts "trade secrets and commercial or financial information obtained from a person and privileged or confidential." ...

The regulations here in controversy were enacted by the F.D.A. to implement the F.O.I.A. by setting up the procedures whereby the public may obtain the information from the F.D.A. and whereby the agency can deal with requests for information from the public. In promulgating these regulations the F.D.A. not only interpreted the F.O.I.A. from the standpoint of an agency obligated with implementing the legislation, but also interpreted and construed 21 U.S.C. § 331(j) which directly concerns the realm of its special expertise and administrative experience....

The plaintiff argues that the notice provision of the new regulations does not satisfy due process or the confidentiality requirement of the nondisclosure statutes and exemption four; ... [T]he principal thrust of the motion for a preliminary injunction is that the F.D.A. must provide for some notice to affected drug companies before it releases any material from its files....

The Court first notes that the regulations here disputed do provide for prior notice of the possible release of exempt material and judicial review of the same:

§ 4.45 [now 21 C.F.R. § 20.45]. In situations where the confidentiality of data or information is uncertain and there is a request for public disclosure, the Food and Drug Administration will consult with the person who has submitted or divulged the data or information or who would be affected by disclosure before determining whether or not such data or information is available for public disclosure.

§ 4.46 [now 21 C.F.R. § 20.46]. Where the Food and Drug Administration consults with a person who will be affected by a proposed disclosure of data or information contained in Food and Drug Administration records pursuant to § 4.45 and rejects the person's request that part or all of the records not be made available for public disclosure, the decision constitutes final agency action that is subject to judicial review pursuant to 5 U.S.C. chapter 7. The person affected will be permitted 5 days after receipt of notification of such decision within which to institute suit in a United States District Court to enjoin release of the records involved. If suit is brought, the Food and Drug Administration will not disclose the records involved until the matter and all related appeals have been concluded.

However, what plaintiff claims is constitutionally and legally required is that the F.D.A. must notify the drug companies of the proposed release of any and all information which they submitted or which concerns them before it is actually released. Plaintiff argues that the F.D.A. will not always know when the confidentiality of information is uncertain. Two or three incidents are noted in which allegedly confidential, nondisclosable, F.O.I.A.-exempt information was inadvertently released by the F.D.A. pursuant to F.O.I.A. requests. In those cases the affected drug companies were not notified, consulted, or given the opportunity for judicial review before the information was disclosed. . . .

The existence of such statutes as the one involved in *American Sumatra* [v. SEC, 93 F.2d 236 (D.C. Cir. 1937)] implies that general constitutional principles do not provide for the relief that the plaintiff here seeks, and that legislative action is needed if such procedures are to be assured. When Congress is persuaded that such measures are necessary in light of the disclosure provisions of the F.O.I.A., it has specifically acted to insure that sensitive information is not disclosed under F.O.I.A. requests. Indeed, counsel for the defendants has notified the court that there is presently pending before Congress legislation that would, in certain cases involving the F.D.A., create a right to prior notice and judicial review comparable to that which the plaintiff seeks to obtain by injunction here.

Recent cases have implied that individuals do not have a right under the F.O.I.A. to block disclosure of information that falls within the exemptions to the F.O.I.A. because those exemptions permit, rather than require, nondisclosure. If there is no right to nondisclosure under the F.O.I.A., the Court does not perceive how there could be a right, under the F.O.I.A., to notice before a decision regarding nondisclosure is made. . . .

Furthermore, it appears that the regulations here disputed were properly promulgated, with public notice, opportunity for public comment, etc. Thus, to the extent that it could be said that the plaintiff is deprived of property rights by operation of the regulations, at least it has been afforded due process by the considered and proper manner in which the regulations have been promulgated.

Moreover, if the regulations do not provide for the absolute right to notice before the disclosure of F.D.A. information, they do provide for substantial notice and opportunity for judicial review. §§ 4.45, 4.46. Indeed, those provisions can be interpreted as providing for notice and opportunity for judicial review any time the issue of confidentiality reasonably arises under a request for F.O.I.A. information. The regulation provides that the notice provisions will be applied whenever the confidentiality of information is "uncertain." The Commissioner implies that only when the material is "clearly disclosable under law" will notice not be given. The Court may assume, absent a contrary showing, that those regulations will be generously and liberally interpreted.

The plaintiff here is not seeking to prevent the disclosure of specific information which has been requested under F.O.I.A. provisions. Rather, what it seeks to prevent is some type of speculative future harm—the possibility of accidental disclosure in the future of unidentified confidential information. The threat of harm alleged, then, is not specific or certain, rather it is conjectural and speculative. Nor is it certain that the injury, if it did occur, would be irreparable injury. . . .

Ordered that the plaintiff's motion for a preliminary injunction be, and the same hereby is, denied.

NOTES

1. *Subsequent Proceedings.* In subsequently granting summary judgment to FDA in this case, the court noted that:

> "[T]he FDA apparently has one of the largest FOIA dockets in the government, averaging 1500 to 1800 requests per month. Broad, categorical regulations are therefore imperative. Ad hoc inquiries or item by item consultations would not only be impracticable but also undercut the open disclosure policy of the FOIA and the FDA regulations.

Pharmaceutical Mfrs. Ass'n v. Weinberger, 411 F. Supp. 576 (D.D.C. 1976).

2. *Cost of Processing FOIA Requests.* Food Chemical News, February 5, 1979, at 27 reported that:

> The Food and Drug Administration has calculated that operation of its Freedom of Information program in 1978 cost the government $1,807,-000—with the total costs incurred at $1,962,000 and the amount received in fees at $155,000.

In its annual report on FOI activities, FDA estimated that a total of 95.68 staff-years were expended on the program. The report indicated that 85% of the FOI requests came from industry or its representatives.

The FOI operation, which is now in FDA's Office of Public Affairs, is being beefed up to wipe out the backlog of requests. Some staffers have been added to the program, and FDA-ers say the average processing time for an FOI request is now 15 days, with 95% of them processed within 11 days. The agency is starting processing of FOI requests the day they are received, so there is expected to be no backlog.

Of 32,852 FOI requests received by FDA during 1978, there were 577 denials. . . .

In 1988, the agency's cost of processing FOIA requests was $5.6 million, for which $451,000 was received in fees. The work consumed 125 staff years. Over 90 percent of all requests were from or on behalf of regulated firms. "Agriculture, Rural Development, and Related Agencies Appropriations for Fiscal Year 1990," Hearings before a Subcomm. of the Senate Comm. on Appropriations, 101st Cong., 1st Sess. 429 (1989).

3. *Defending Nondisclosure.* Where a request for commercial information is made to FDA, the company that submitted it almost always invariably steps forward to defend its confidentiality. If FDA refuses disclosure and is sued, the submitting company typically intervenes as a party or participates as amicus curiae. *See, e.g., Washington Post v. Department of Justice,* 863 F.2d 96 (D.C. Cir. 1988); *Greenberg v. FDA,* 803 F.2d 1213 (D.C. Cir. 1986); *Public Citizen Health Research Group v. FDA,* 704 F.2d 1280 (D.C. Cir. 1983); *Webb v. Department of HHS,* 696 F.2d 101 (D.C. Cir. 1982); *Campbell v. Department of HHS,* 682 F.2d 256 (D.C. Cir. 1982); *Lederle Laboratories v. Department of HHS,* Food Drug Cosm. L. Rep. (CCH) ¶ 38,088 (D.D.C. 1988); *Johnson v. Department of HEW,* 462 F. Supp. 336 (D.D.C. 1978). FDA's regulations also provide an opportunity for the submitting company to bring a reverse FOIA action if the agency determines that the contested information should be disclosed. Reverse FOIA suits to challenge confidential commercial information were sanctioned in *Chrysler Corp. v. Brown,* 441 U.S. 281 (1979).

4. *Disclosure to Other Agencies.* Section 301(j) of the FD&C Act prohibits disclosure of trade secret information to any person outside the Department of HHS. Because this appeared to bar FDA from sharing such information with a contractor engaged to assist FDA (*e.g.,* to review an NDA), the Medical Device Amendments of 1976 added section 708 to permit such disclosures to contractors under appropriate safeguards. The Attorney General has determined that section 301(j) prohibits FDA from disclosing trade secret information to committees of Congress. "Federal Food, Drug and Cosmetic Act—Prohibition on Disclosure of Trade Secret Information to a Congressional Committee," 43 Op. Atty. Gen., No. 21 (September 8, 1978). FDA amended its regulations in 47 Fed. Reg. 10804 (March 12, 1982) to clarify that information subject to section 301(j) may not be disclosed to any other Federal agency. The House version of 1989 budget reconciliation legislation contained language exempting congressional committees from section 301(j), but the enacted legislation inadvertently omitted this provision. Section 301(j) was ultimately amended in the Omnibus Budget Reconciliation Act of 1990, 104 Stat. 1388, 1388–210.

5. *An Alternative to Discovery.* The FOIA has become an important new
method of discovery in FDA enforcement actions. *See, e.g., Parke, Davis & Co.
v. Califano,* 623 F.2d 1 (6th Cir. 1980); *Grand Laboratories, Inc. v. Department
of HHS,* Food Drug Cosm. L. Rep. (CCH) ¶ 38,171 (D.D.C. 1982); *Sterling Drug,
Inc. v. Harris,* 488 F. Supp. 1019 (S.D.N.Y. 1980); *California Canners & Growers
Ass'n v. United States,* FDLI 1978–1980 Jud. Rec. 990 (Ct. Cl. 1980); *Church of
Scientology v. Califano,* FDLI 1978–1980 Jud. Rec. 922 (D.D.C. 1978); *Morton-
Norwich Products, Inc. v. Mathews,* 415 F. Supp. 78 (D.D.C. 1976).

FREEDOM OF INFORMATION ACT REQUESTS FOR
BUSINESS DATA AND REVERSE–FOIA LAWSUITS

House Report No. 95–1382, 95th Congress, 2d Session (1978).

Understandably, firms that submit confidential documents to Federal agencies have expressed concerned about their release. While
competitively harmful business information may be withheld under the
Freedom of Information Act, other data may legitimately be sought and
publicly released. Business's concern is not merely theoretical—numerous disputes and court cases have arisen over the release of such
information.

The committee concludes that the major problem in handling the
disclosure of business information concerns the procedure by which
agencies decide what data to release or withhold. This report is thus
primarily concerned with the process of identifying and separating
confidential information. . . .

Notice to the submitter. It is consistent with basic notions of
fairness that a corporate submitter be given some form of notice about
the pending release of information it supplied the Government. Notice
permits a submitter to explain the need for confidential treatment of
data, and allows an opportunity to challenge the release in court. The
committee recommends that each agency select and formally adopt a
method of predisclosure notification to submitters most suitable to the
agency's own circumstances, records, and FOIA caseload. Notice does
not necessarily have to be provided each time a request is received for
business records. . . .

Identification confidential information by the submitter. A requirement that confidential records be marked by the submitter at the
time they are filed with the Government may help agencies narrow the
amount of data whose confidentiality is later called into dispute. A
submitter's confidentiality marking would not be binding on an agency
but would clearly identify those portions that are not confidential and
that could be publicly released without further review. . . .

*Determination of confidentiality by agencies at the time of submis-
sion.* Some agencies have adopted a limited practice of ruling on the
confidentiality of a business's records at the time of submission. The
committee does not recommend the use of this procedure because

information loses its confidential nature over time, and it is rarely possible to adequately determine confidentiality in advance of the receipt of an actual Freedom of Information Act request. Advance determinations may also waste agency resources and bypass the FOIA's requirements that disclosable portions of records be segregated from nondisclosable parts....

Substantive disclosure rules. The committee recommends that agencies review their experience with FOIA requests for business documents in order to identify classes of documents that do not contain confidential information. Agencies should formally adopt substantive rules providing for the disclosure of such documents.... Because of the difficulty of deciding in advance whether it is appropriate to grant confidential treatment, however, no rules should be issued providing that specified categories of business documents are automatically exempt from disclosure....

Agency proceedings. The committee recommends that agencies institute an informal proceeding consisting of written pleadings and affidavits for FOIA requests involving records that may be confidential under exemption 4. Such a proceeding will permit the compilation of a record of the agency decision that can be used if the submitter later sues to block a disclosure determination. A proceeding will also allow the submitter a more complete opportunity to justify the need for confidentiality....

NOTE

For the FDA testimony on these issues, *see* "Business Record Exemption of the Freedom of Information Act: Hearings Before a Subcomm. of the House Comm. on Government Operations," 95th Cong., 1st Sess. (1977). *See also* Brown, *Disclosure of Business Secrets Under FOIA: A Business Perspective,* 34 FDC L.J. 148 (1979). Although this legislation was not enacted, a decade later President Reagan issued Executive Order 12600, 52 Fed. Reg. 23781 (June 25, 1987), establishing predisclosure notification procedures for confidential commercial information. FDA has not found it necessary to amend its FOIA regulations in order to comply with these requirements.

G.   ENVIRONMENTAL CONSIDERATIONS

The National Environmental Policy Act (NEPA), 83 Stat. 852 (1969), requires all Federal agencies to consider the environmental impact of any major action they take that may significantly affect the quality of the environment. FDA has adopted regulations, 37 Fed. Reg. 13636 (July 12, 1972), 38 Fed. Reg. 7001 (March 15, 1973), to implement this requirement. 21 C.F.R. Part 25. Initially, the agency took the position that NEPA required it to consider the environmental impact of every important action including, for example, the approval of a new drug or a food additive. Later, faced with the impracticality of implementing this policy, FDA announced, 40 Fed. Reg. 16662 (April 14, 1975), that it had no statutory authority to approve or disapprove new drugs or food additives on any ground other than those specified in the FD&C Act, hoping to precipitate a judicial challenge that would clarify its obligations under NEPA.

ENVIRONMENTAL DEFENSE FUND, INC. v. MATHEWS

United States District Court, District of Columbia, 1976.
410 F.Supp. 336.

JOHN H. PRATT, District Judge.....

NEPA was enacted in 1969 as a mandate to the agencies of the Federal Government to take environmental considerations into account in their planning and decision-making "to the fullest extent possible." 42 U.S.C. § 4332.... NEPA does not supersede other statutory duties, but, to the extent that it is reconcilable with those duties, it supplements them. Full compliance with its requirements cannot be avoided unless such compliance directly conflicts with other existing statutory duties.

In 1973, FDA promulgated regulations implementing its obligations under NEPA. In recognition of the breadth of the NEPA mandate, the Commissioner declared that

> ... [T]he National Environmental Policy Act, as interpreted by the courts, amends the Federal Food, Drug and Cosmetic Act to the extent that it requires the FDA to give full consideration without restrictions of time to all environmental issues relevant to FDA approval of food additive petitions, new drugs and new animal drugs.

In April, 1975, FDA promulgated an amendment to this regulation which is the subject of this action. Said amendment reads:

> A determination of adverse environmental impact has no legal or regulatory effect and does not authorize the Commissioner to take or refrain from taking any action under the laws he administers. The Commissioner may take or refrain from taking action on the basis of a determination of an adverse environmental impact only to the extent that such action is independently authorized by the laws he administers.

In effect, the amending regulation limits the grounds on which the Commissioner of FDA can base any action to those expressly provided for in the Food, Drug and Cosmetic Act or in other statutes which FDA administers. He is prohibited from acting solely on the basis of environmental considerations not identified in those statutes. This limitation of the agency's discretion to act in accordance with environmental considerations directly contravenes the mandate of NEPA to all Federal agencies to consider the environmental effects of their actions "to the fullest extent possible." [1]

Defendants contend that FDA's statutes, particularly the FDCA, dictate that it act only in accordance with specifically expressed criteria, and that to the extent that NEPA demands consideration of additional criteria, it is in direct conflict with those statutes. Accordingly, they maintain that such a direct statutory conflict exempts FDA from full compliance with NEPA.

It appears clear to us that, contrary to defendants' contention, FDA's existing statutory duties under the FDCA and its other statutes are not in direct conflict with its duties under NEPA. The FDCA does not state that the listed considerations are the only ones which the Commissioner may take into account in reaching a decision. Nor does it explicitly require that product applications be granted if the specified grounds are met. It merely lists criteria which the Commissioner must consider in reaching his decision. In the absence of a clear statutory provision excluding consideration of environmental factors, and in light of NEPA's broad mandate that all environmental considerations be taken into account, we find that NEPA provides FDA with supplementary authority to base its substantive decisions on all environmental considerations including those not expressly identified in the FDCA and FDA's other statutes. This conclusion finds support in the legislative history, the precise statutory language, the holdings of the courts, and the construction adopted by other Federal agencies.

This is not to say that NEPA requires FDA's substantive decisions to favor environment protection over other relevant factors. Rather, it means that NEPA requires FDA to *consider* environmental factors in its decision-making process and supplements its existing authority to permit it to act on those considerations. It permits FDA to base a decision upon environmental factors, when balanced with other relevant considerations. Since the contested regulation prohibits FDA from acting on the basis of such environmental considerations, it is directly contrary to the letter and spirit of NEPA. . . .

Accordingly, plaintiff's motion for summary judgment is granted. . . .

NOTES

1. *FDA Response.* Following this decision FDA revoked the contested amendment to its NEPA regulations in 41 Fed. Reg. 21768 (Mary 28, 1976). Since enactment of NEPA, however, the agency has not taken an action in which it has identified any environmental effects not involving risks to health as an influential consideration. When FDA denied a food additive petition on the ground that the environmental impact analysis report was insufficient, the

---

1. The Council on Environmental Quality, one of whose primary functions is to monitor and promote agency compliance with NEPA, advised FDA that it believes that the amending regulation is in violation of NEPA. The Environmental Protection Agency notified FDA that it concurs in the opinion expressed by CEQ. The FDA's obduracy in the face of these authoritative expressions has caused this suit to be filed.

court in *Marshall Minerals, Inc. v. FDA,* 661 F.2d 409 (5th Cir. 1981), reversed, holding that this raised no issue beyond the human safety questions previously considered, that Marshall Minerals had complied with all environmental analysis requirements, and that no separate environmental concerns prevented approval of the petition. More recently, however, FDA has announced its intention to prepare an environmental impact statement on the use of polyvinyl chloride and other chlorinated polymers, 53 Fed. Reg. 47264 (November 22, 1988), and published its tentative responses to environmental concerns about raising the permitted level of selenium in animal feed, 54 Fed. Reg. 29019 (July 11, 1989).

2. *Plastic Bottles.* FDA initiated an inquiry into the environmental impact of food additive regulations for plastic beverage containers in 38 Fed. Reg. 24391 (September 7, 1973). A draft environmental impact statement (EIS) was later made available, 40 Fed. Reg. 16708 (April 14, 1975), and a final EIS was issued, 41 Fed. Reg. 43944 (October 5, 1976). In 42 Fed. Reg. 9227 (February 15, 1977), the agency stated that, in acting on food additive petitions, environmental considerations "carry no greater weight than the factors required to be considered in section 409 of the act." It concluded that "the adverse environmental effects of the action, to some extent offset by the potential beneficial effects, are not of sufficient magnitude to justify limitation or revocation of food additive regulations permitting plastic bottles for carbonated beverages and beer."

3. *Agency Regulations.* To comply with guidelines issued by the Council on Environmental Quality (CEQ), FDA promulgated changes in its regulations, 39 Fed. Reg. 13742 (April 16, 1974), 42 Fed. Reg. 19986 (April 15, 1977), 44 Fed. Reg. 71742 (December 11, 1979), 50 Fed. Reg. 16636 (April 26, 1985). FDA announced the availability of a technical handbook providing guidance in preparing environmental assessments in 52 Fed. Reg. 37372 (October 6, 1987).

4. *Objections to FDA Omission of Environmental Assessment.* NEPA has occasionally been invoked by parties opposing FDA action. *See Calorie Control Council, Inc. v. Department of HEW,* Food Drug Cosm. L. Rep. (CCH) ¶ 38,124 (D.D.C. 1977), in which the court refused to enjoin FDA's proposed ban of saccharin on the ground that the agency had failed to file an environmental impact statement:

> The principal concern of NEPA is "the physical environmental resources of the nation." The Act requires consideration of factors other than those directly related to the physical environment, but "only where there [is] a primary impact on the physical environment."
>
> The public health consequences which Calorie Control Council foresees in FDA's proposed rulemaking are insufficient to trigger the applicability of NEPA absent an indication of a potential primary impact on the physical environment. No such primary impact is evident in this case, and none has been alleged....

The court later dismissed the action in *Calorie Control Council, Inc. v. Department of HEW,* Food Drug Cosm. L. Rep. (CCH) ¶ 38,218 (D.D.C. 1978). Other cases rejecting NEPA-based objections to FDA action include *Rhone–Poulenc, Inc. v. FDA,* 636 F.2d 750 (D.C. Cir. 1980); *National Pork Producers Council v. Bergland,* 631 F.2d 1353 (8th Cir. 1980); *American Meat Institute v. Bergland,* 459 F. Supp. 1308 (D.D.C. 1978). FDA denied a petition that it prepare an environmental impact statement with respect to the pending approval of bovine growth hormone. "Response to Bovine Growth Hormone Petition," FDA Talk Paper No. T86–72 (October 2, 1986).

H. REGULATORY REFORM

Demands for "regulatory reform" are almost as old as the pressures to create regulatory agencies. Proposals for reform have taken a variety of forms, ranging from suggestions to abandon government intervention in some areas to recommendations for improvements in agency procedure. The enactment of the Federal Register Act in 1936, the Report of the Attorney General's Committee on Administrative Procedure in 1941, and the subsequent enactment of the Administrative Procedure Act in 1946 were early expressions of the latter type of concern. As the size and power of administrative agencies have grown, more fundamental problems have been perceived. *See, e.g.,* S. Breyer, REGULATION AND ITS REFORM (1982); Cramton, *Causes and Cures of Administrative Delay,* 58 A.B.A.J. 937 (1972); Gellhorn, *Administrative Procedure Reform: Hardy Perennial,* 48 A.B.A.J. 243 (1962). It is only in recent years, however, that regulatory performance has become the subject of broad public interest and serious congressional study. In some fields, such as transportation, Congress has actively pursued deregulation. Health and safety regulatory programs, however, have so far largely escaped this thrust of reform, although pressures to weigh the costs of regulation and seek the lowest-cost safeguards have begun to grow.

During the past generation FDA has taken steps to reform its approach to regulation in two principal ways. First, the agency has in some areas adopted new requirements that are designed to reduce restrictions on regulated firms. Examples include the adoption of "common or usual names" for some foods rather than standards of identity; the revision of "recipe" food standards to permit any safe and suitable ingredients; and the use of class monographs for OTC drugs instead of requiring NDAs for each individual product. Second, FDA has fashioned alternative procedures for resolving disputed technical issues with the objective of strengthening the scientific basis and reducing the time required for decision. Examples include its increased reliance on expert advisory committees and the creation of a board of inquiry as a substitute for a trial-type adjudicatory hearing. There are, however, limitations on the extent to which any optional reforms can speed up the administrative process, make it fairer, or reduce the economic impact of regulation in the absence of basic changes in the FD&C Act.

Government regulation can affect both the pace and direction of industrial activity. The precise effects on private activity are significantly influenced by the form regulation takes, *e.g.,* product standards, premarket approval, disclosure to users. Yet, until recently, concern about the impact of regulation on new product development played almost no role in FDA's choice of regulatory approaches. Indeed, before the passage of the Medical Device Amendments of 1976, concerns about such effects were seldom voiced in congressional debates on the agency's performance or statutory powers.

The initial, and primary, determinant of regulatory form is the statute in which Congress creates an agency and authorizes it to operate. Thus, *Congress* chose in 1962 to authorize FDA to require new drugs to be submitted for approval of their safety and effectiveness prior to marketing. Congress—or individual members—can also influence the form regulation takes through the budget approval and oversight processes. And of course the agency which is given responsibility for implementing a regulatory statute can significantly influence its shape and form—notwithstanding the specific terms of the statute under which it operates. Even the most carefully designed statute affords opportunities for administrative innovation.

Agency officials influence the contours of regulation in many obvious ways. Administrators differ in intelligence, vigor, and resourcefulness. Successive heads of the same agency often possess sharply differing views about their role; one may assume a "tough cop" posture while another will espouse "cooperation" with regulated firms. An agency's program can be altered by a shift of funding or the retirement or transfer of experienced administrators or scientists.

Other factors, too, are important. The configuration of an industry will influence not only the shape of legislation but also how the agency administers it. There can be little doubt that, prior to the advent of biotechnology, FDA's Center for Biologics Evaluation and Research could use techniques in communicating with—and in regulating—the relatively small number of readily identified manufacturers of vaccines that simply were not available to the Center for Food Safety and Applied Nutrition, which is responsible for an unknown number of products made by thousands of manufacturers, many of them anonymous. Vulnerability to public disclosures of product hazards makes one industry amenable to negotiated settlement of agency charges, while producers of other products may be prepared to litigate a claim of hazard until the agency grows tired or obsolescence occurs.

An industry's sensitivity to publicity often mirrors the political scrutiny of the responsible agency. This scrutiny can fundamentally alter the focus of regulatory programs. Congressional hearings are often a precursor to new regulatory initiatives, sometimes supported by new budgetary authorizations, but very often unaccompanied by any revision of the agency's basic statutory authority. For example, in the mid–1970s FDA undertook a major effort to monitor the performance of preclinical (*i.e.,* animal) tests that are routinely conducted on drugs, food additives, and similar products to evaluate their safety. The additional appropriations and the program itself were the result of a series of intensely critical hearings chaired by Senator Edward Kennedy in 1975 and 1976 which attracted wide television coverage.

FDA's response to this issue illustrates, first, the often fragile tie between statutory design and the form of regulation and, second, the substantial influence of administrative initiative on the form of government regulation. The scope of FDA's authority to regulate the design of preclinical tests is, at best, unclear. Nothing in the FD&C Act says in so many words that the agency may prescribe how to conduct the tests it ultimately requires for safety assessments. Its authority to inspect many of the facilities where these tests are conducted—university laboratories and private laboratories which do not produce products subject to FDA regulation—is problematic. The agency does possess the authority to reject products for which the tests are insufficient to support the statutorily-mandated finding of safety. But simply turning down inadequately tested products would be inefficient in many ways. Even a series of product disapprovals might provide only weak signals to testing laboratories about the deficiencies the agency found. Furthermore, the approach would depend on the discovery of obvious deficiencies or fraud. It would inevitably lead to protracted litigation with the manufacturers of regulated products. And it would reach only tests that manufacturers chose to submit.

Thus, FDA concluded that a different approach, one that emphasized prophylaxis, was necessary. It therefore prescribed regulations governing "Good Laboratory Practices" (GLP), which specify in detail the features that must or should characterize the well-conducted preclinical study. 21 C.F.R. Part 58. And it established a force of inspectors to visit the establishments that conduct such tests to ensure compliance with the regulations. FDA also created—by regulation—a system for "disqualifying" laboratories that persistently fail to meet its standards.

This example contains several lessons about how government regulators operate. These patterns reflect the work of individuals who care deeply about getting their job done. And in this case, "their job" is to assure that preclinical tests of drugs and food additives are well-designed, properly conducted, and carefully and honestly reported. The FDA architects of this program were not indifferent to its costs for the private sector, *see* 41 Fed. Reg. 51206 (November 19, 1976), but their primary concern, dramatized by the Congressional oversight hearings and echoed by the FD&C Act, was to devise a system that promotes reliable safety judgments and is easy to enforce.

PETER BARTON HUTT, SAFETY REGULATION IN THE REAL WORLD
28 Food Drug Cosmetic Law Journal 460 (1973).

The Food and Drug Administration's decision-making process on safety issues, and the public perception of it, are hampered by five basic obstacles. No one of these obstacles is critical, but their combined impact can at times be severe....

First, the scientific data base is seldom adequate to make a definitive safety judgment on any food or drug.....

Second, even when substantial safety data are available on a particular substance, there is seldom scientific agreement on the meaning or significance of that information.....

Third, even assuming that an adequate scientific data base were available, together with scientific agreement on the meaning and significance of the data, there appears to be no public or scientific consensus today on the risk or uncertainty acceptable to justify the marketing of any substance as a food or drug.

To some, who favor a return to more simple days, no risk or uncertainty whatever is justified for any addition of a chemical to food. They would, indeed, require a showing of some greater benefit to society before any ingredient is permitted. To others, who see enormous progress in food technology and nutrition from the use of food additives, the usual risks associated with technological innovation are regarded as entirely reasonable.... We must recognize that this type of issue presents fundamental differences in philosophical principles, not simply a narrow dispute on technical details. It raises the most basic questions of personal beliefs and human values—the degree of risk or uncertainty that any individual is willing to accept in his daily life. Attempts to resolve it on the basis of rigorous scientific testing or analytical discourse, therefore, simply miss the point....

Fourth, there is enormous and continuing public pressure for the Food and Drug Administration to resolve whatever may be the latest current safety issue promptly and decisively.

Delay and indecision weaken public confidence and intensify fear and concern. Industrial representatives, faced with potential harm to their economic interests, demand reassurance, that the public need fear no danger. Consumer activists, sensing a further victory in their war against unsafe products, intensify the public campaign to discredit the suspect product. Congress, reacting to the legitimate concern of their constituencies, demand[s] a prompt resolution. The media, recognizing a story of interest to the entire public, does not fail to give it ample prominence. Thus, regardless of the uncertainties and imponderables, a decision must frequently be reached immediately, on the basis of whatever meager information may exist....

Fifth, regardless of the outcome of the decision, those who disagree with it will continue to pursue the matter through all available channels, while those who agree with it will inevitably remain silent, preparing themselves for the next issue.....

LOUIS ROTHSCHILD, THE NEWEST REGULATORY AGENCY IN WASHINGTON

33 Food Drug Cosmetic Law Journal 86 (1978).

Many of you lived through the decade of deliberation on vitamins and minerals and special dietary foods. The Food and Drug Administration (FDA) proposed a revision of the special dietary food regulations along with a food standard for fortified foods.... The upshot of the matter, of course, was that Congress invalidated the whole thing.... Congress adopted Senator Proxmire's bill to take the FDA out of the vitamin-mineral business. Congress in its wisdom had invalidated all of the lengthy expensive procedures it had mandated....

... Because of the dangers of microbiological contamination, the FDA proposed issuing shellfish sanitation regulations to replace the voluntary system under which shellfish had been monitored. The Agency received many lengthy comments criticizing the proposal. However, before it could be revised by the FDA, Congress acted to postpone the proposal....

I am not criticizing the right of any segment of the population to take its troubles to Capitol Hill, for hearings to be held, or for members of Congress to express their views. However, I am disturbed by the threat of legislation to cut the ground out from under the FDA if it does not do what isolated Congressmen or a powerful Congressional subcommittee tells it to do, even though it may conflict with the Agency's stated policy or Congressional mandate.

... In response to an industry proposal, the FDA amended the ice cream standard to permit use of "safe and suitable" optional ingredients.... No one objected, until the dairy industry expressed the view that it might be hurt by imports of caseinates used in ice cream under the revised standard. There have been Congressional hearings and abusive letters to the FDA from members of Congress regarding ice cream. The upshot was legislation pitting the United States Department of Agriculture (USDA) against the FDA in this day of supposed coordination and cooperation between government agencies....

... [S]accharin ... is another example of Congress interceding in the operation of the regulatory agencies, and this time in the area of safety rather than in the area of economics....

The FDA has proposed banning low-level uses of penicillin and some low-level uses of tetracyclines in animal feeds because of the possibility of resistance and transfer of resistance.... Pro-antibiotic and anti-antibiotic Congressmen and Senators immediately started a marathon round of hearings on animal drugs in feeds.....If Congress— sparked by the powerful agricultural lobby—should act to reverse the FDA as it did in the case of shellfish sanitation and saccharin, the position of all the regulatory agencies would be jeopardized. The principle would be established: Enforce the law as it is written except in cases in which Congress is subjected to pressure from the folks back home.

. . . If Congress is going to regulate such specific matters as dietary supplements, shellfish sanitation, laetrile, baked goods, ice cream, and saccharin, we really have little need of any other regulatory agencies. Abolition of all of them would really be regulatory reform with a vengeance. . . .

STATEMENT OF ALEXANDER M. SCHMIDT, M.D., COMMISSIONER OF FOOD AND DRUGS

"Regulation of New Drug R. & D. By the Food.
And Drug Administration,"
Joint Hearings Before the Subcomm. on Health of the Senate Comm.
on Labor and Public Welfare and the Subcomm. on Administrative Practice and
Procedure of the Senate Comm. on the Judiciary, 93d Congress, 2d Session (1974).

By far the greatest pressure that the Bureau of Drugs or the Food and Drug Administration receives with respect to the new drug approval process is brought to bear through Congressional hearings. In all of our history, we are unable to find one instance where a Congressional hearing investigated the failure of FDA to approve a new drug. The occasions on which hearings have been held to criticize approval of a new drug have been so frequent in the past ten years that we have not even attempted to count them.

At both the staff level and managerial level, the message conveyed by this situation could not be clearer. Whenever a difficult or controversial issue is resolved by approval, the Agency and the individuals involved will be publicly investigated. Whenever it is resolved by disapproval, no inquiry will be made. The Congressional pressure for negative action is therefore intense, and ever increasing.

This can be remedied only by Congressional recognition that the failure to approve an important new drug may well be extremely detrimental to the public health. Congress should be as willing to investigate charges that FDA is not approving important new therapeutic advances, as it is to hear charges that we resolve close issues in favor of approval. Until perspective is brought to the legislative oversight function, the pressure from Congress for FDA to disapprove new drugs will continue to be felt, and could be a major factor in health care in this country. . . .

NOTE

See also Hutt, *Balanced Government Regulation of Consumer Products,* 31 FDC L.J. 592 (1976); Green and Waitzman, BUSINESS WAR ON THE LAW: AN ANALYSIS OF THE BENEFITS OF FEDERAL HEALTH/SAFETY ENFORCEMENT 131a (1979) (1978 estimated $.4 billion cost of regulation under the FD&C Act estimated to yield $1.4 billion in public benefits); Mashaw, *Regulation, Logic and Ideology,* Regulation (November/December 1979) at 44.

COMPLIANCE WITH STATUTORY DEADLINES

Several provisions of the FD&C Act prescribe time limits for agency action. Like many other agencies, FDA has had little success meeting these deadlines.

Time limits for agency action. Section 409(b)(5) of the FD&C Act requires FDA to publish a notice within 30 days after the "filing" of a food additive petition, and section 409(c)(2) requires the agency to act on the petition within 90 days after the date of filing unless it extends that period for another 90 days "to investigate and study the petition." Similar statutory time limits are imposed by sections 505(c) (new drug applications), 512(c) (new animal drug applications), 515(d)(1)(A) (device premarket approval applications), and 706(d)(1) (color additive petitions). Yet FDA has almost never acted within the specified period.

It has been standard practice for FDA to conduct a preliminary review of any application for approval, and then to notify the applicant that it is "incomplete" and thus not eligible for "filing." Although FDA regulations sometimes require that an "incomplete" letter be sent within 15 days of receipt of the application, often it is sent just before the end of the period set by statute for review of the application. FDA thereby avoids "filing" the application and, on its theory, the statutory time limit does not begin to run. The initial submission of an application is therefore only the beginning of a negotiation process between the applicant and agency reviewers leading ultimately toward official "filing" several months or sometimes even years later.

Often the questions raised by FDA prior to "filing" are entirely legitimate, though they customarily relate to the substantive criteria for approval, rather than formal adequacy of the application. And in some instances they may reflect concerns that are beyond the scope of the agency's legal authority. Applicants for marketing approval have almost uniformly been unwilling to contest the legality of this process out of fear that a court challenge might precipitate a premature negative decision on the merits, delay even further ultimate FDA approval, or prejudice the agency's attitude toward other pending or future applications in which the applicant is interested.

One of the rare legal challenges to FDA's failure to meet a statutory deadline is *Southeastern Minerals, Inc. v. Califano,* (M.D. Ga., January 31, 1978). Southeastern Minerals, a manufacturer of medicated feed premixes for livestock, in 1976 began adding gentian violet to several of its products. The firm apparently took the position that gentian violet was GRAS, and therefore did not require a food additive regulation. When the firm realized that FDA officials took a different view and were likely to initiate enforcement proceedings against its products, it grudgingly submitted a food additive petition on August 18, 1977. Two months later FDA replied by letter that the petition was under review, but the agency did not publish a notice of filing within 30 days of receiving the petition. Discussions between the firm and FDA eventually resulted in suspension of production, but threatened enforcement action against existing stocks, coupled with the agency's inaction, led Southeastern, approximately 120 days after submitting its petition, to bring suit against FDA for failure to comply with the statutory deadlines. On January 30, 1978, the firm received an "incomplete" letter from FDA, but at no time did the agency formally extend the 90–day period for review of the petition.

The district judge interpreted the Act as imposing mandatory time limits for action on FDA:

The evidence in this case shows that the Plaintiffs have done everything within their power to cooperate and work with the Defendants, going so far in these efforts as to subordinate their own good faith interpretations and contentions to the requests and demands of the Defendants. The Defendants have reciprocated with bureaucratic arrogance. . . .

The Defendants in this case on the one hand have failed and refused to perform the duties cast upon them by the Federal Food, Drug and Cosmetic Act in failing to act upon the Plaintiffs' petition and at the same time have used their failure against the Plaintiffs in having Plaintiffs' product detained by the states and subsequently seized all upon the theory that it is an "unapproved" feed additive. It is the opinion of this Court that such conduct both in the failure and refusal to act upon the petition while simultaneously detaining the product on the basis that it is an unapproved feed additive constitutes a clear denial of the rights of Plaintiffs and effectively takes their property without due process.[2] . . .

The court enjoined FDA from interfering with the firm's marketing of gentian violet until final action on its food additive petition, including judicial review if sought. The petition was subsequently denied in 44 Fed. Reg. 19035 (March 30, 1979), and the petitioner's request for a hearing was subsequently rejected on the ground that no genuine issues of material fact had been raised, 45 Fed. Reg. 20559 (March 28, 1980). When these actions were reviewed, the court of appeals dissolved the district court injunction against action by FDA but agreed that the agency had demonstrated "a bureaucratic hubris that confuses abusive power with reason." The court declared that the agency's disregard of the statutory 180–day limit "is equally regrettable and inexcusable," *Southeastern Minerals, Inc. v. Harris,* 622 F.2d 758 (5th Cir. 1980). The court later overturned FDA's denial of a hearing on the food additive petition. *Marshall Minerals, Inc. v. FDA,* 661 F.2d 409 (5th Cir. 1981).

Each year the Food Chemical News reports the status of the various types of petitions and proposed regulations relating to the food additive provisions of the FD&C act. As of December 31, 1979, 91 GRAS proposals, 37 GRAS affirmation petitions, and 165 food additive petitions (92 of which involved pesticides and thus were under EPA jurisdiction) were pending. Only 64 of the 165 food additive petitions had been pending for less than one year. The oldest pending matters extended back to 1962. *See* Food Chemical News, January 14, 1980, at 3. As of December 31, 1979, FDA had a backlog of 50 food standard matters that had seen no action for the preceding six months. Of those, 44 had been dormant for longer than a year, and the last action on one dated as far back as 1968. In addition, there were 16 pending common or usual name proposals and 7 pending nutritional quality guidelines. *See id.* January 21, 1980, at 3.

---

2. During the hearing on this matter the Defendants took the position that the reason that they had not acted on the petition was because the petition had never been filed. When the Court observed that in August, 1977 the Defendants acknowledged that the petition had been received and that it had been given a file number and later by another letter assured the Plaintiffs that the petition was being reviewed, the Defendants resorted to a play on words, suggesting that there is a difference between "filed" and "received." It is noted however that eventually, to his credit, Defendants' counsel frankly admitted that the Defendants' delay in responding to the petition was unjustified. . . .

Ten years later the situation had not improved. As of December 31, 1989, 87 GRAS proposals, 53 GRAS affirmation petitions, 141 FDA food additive petitions, and 190 EPA pesticide food additive petitions were pending before FDA. Only 48 of the 141 FDA food additive petitions had been pending for less than one year. The oldest pending matter dated from 1962. *See Food Chemical News*, January 15, 1990, at 3; January 22, 1990, at 3; January 29, 1990, at 3. As of December 31, 1989, the agency also had a backlog of 46 food standard issues. On 42 of these no action had been taken for more than a year, and on one the most recent action occurred in 1968. In addition, six common or usual name proposals were pending. *See id.*, February 12, 1990, at 3.

In an October 1979 announcement on programs to encourage industrial innovation, President Carter stated that "all administrators of Federal executive agencies responsible for clearance of new products will be directed to develop and implement an expedited process for projects having a strong innovative impact or exceptional social benefit, and to do so without jeopardizing the quality of the review process." 15 Weekly Comp. of Pres. Doc. 2069 (October 31, 1979). In response, FDA began a program under which food additive and color additive petitions are reviewed and, if facially complete, are "filed" shortly after receipt and thus are the subject of a notice published in the Federal Register. This formality has not, however, succeeded in reducing the time for ultimate approval.

FDA has voluntarily established a six-month deadline for responding to citizen petitions, 21 C.F.R. § 10.30(e)(2). In practice, however, this deadline is seldom met, and when it is the agency's initial response often states simply that a substantive determination is not yet feasible.

FDA generally takes more than 12 months to promulgate a final regulation following publication of the proposal. For a list of 36 drug regulations for which this occurred during the 1970s, *see* "Drug Regulation Reform Act of 1978," Hearings on H.R. 11611 Before the Subcomm. on Health and the Environment of the House Comm. on Interstate and Foreign Commerce, Part II, 95th Cong., 2d Sess. (1978). FDA has also experienced difficulty in meeting time limits it has imposed on itself voluntarily.

Statutory deadlines. In the Food Additives Amendments of 1958, the Color Additive Amendments of 1960, the Drug Amendments of 1962, the Medical Device Amendments of 1976, and the Drug Price Competition and Patent Term Restoration Act of 1984. Congress specified several statutory deadlines within which specific regulations were to be issued or programs were to be completed. Most of these deadlines, as well, have not been met.

(a) Section 6 of the Food Additives Amendment of 1958 provided for a transition period of 30 months within which all food additives were to be subject to a food additive regulation. Because FDA could not meet that deadline, the Food Additives Transitional Provisions Amendment of 1961 was enacted to extend it to June 30, 1964 and the Food Additives Transitional Provisions Amendment of 1964 further extended it to December 31, 1965. This later deadline was met only because the majority of food ingredients were exempted from the requirement of a regulation on the ground that they were GRAS or subject to a prior sanction.

(b) More than thirty years will have elapsed by the time the 1960 Color Additive Amendments are fully implemented. *See* p. 368 *supra.*

(c) Section 107(c)(3) of the Drug Amendments of 1962 provided a two-year "grace period" before the new proof of effectiveness requirement could be applied to new drugs for which NDA's became effective during the period 1938–1962. In *American Public Health Ass'n v. Veneman,* 349 F. Supp. 1311 (D.D.C. 1972), p. 503 *supra,* the court concluded that FDA had failed to implement the Amendments as rapidly as Congress had mandated, and issued a detailed order requiring staged implementation by October 10, 1976. *See* 37 Fed. Reg. 26623 (December 14, 1972). FDA has not yet completed its implementation of the 1962 Amendments. *See* "Drug Regulation Reform Act of 1978, Part I, Hearings before the Subcomm. on Health and the Environ. of the House Comm. on Interstate and Foreign Commerce, 95th Cong., 2d Sess. (1978).

(d) Section 520(g)(2)(A) of the Act, added by the 1976 Medical Device Amendments, required FDA to promulgate regulations governing investigational use of medical devices within 120 days after the date of enactment of that provision, which was May 28, 1976. The 1976 Amendments also mandated a comment period of at least 60 days on all proposed device regulations. Implementing regulations were proposed in 41 Fed. Reg. 35282 (August 20, 1976), provoking critical comments from manufacturers, clinicians, and consumer groups. A tentative final order was published in 43 Fed. Reg. 20726 (May 12, 1978), on which a public hearing was held. Final investigational device regulations were promulgated in 45 Fed. Reg. 3732 (January 18, 1980).

Because of its unhappy experience with statutory deadlines under other statutes, FDA successfully opposed the inclusion in the 1976 Amendments of any mandatory time period for which all Class II or III devices marketed prior to 1976 must be subject to a standard or an approved application. Instead, Congress required FDA to set priorities for these actions and then to work on them as resources permit. In the Safe Medical Devices Act of 1990, however, Congress did impose deadlines for beginning the process of reviewing preenactment Class III devices.

(e) Section 105(a) of the Drug Price Competition and Patent Term Restoration Act of 1984 required that implementing regulations be promulgated within one year of the date of enactment. Proposed regulations were published by FDA in 54 Fed. Reg. 28872 (July 10, 1989), but final regulations had not appeared by June 30, 1990.

(f) FDA met a statutory deadline when it adopted regulations to implement the Drug Listing Act of 1972, 37 Fed. Reg. 26431 (December 12, 1972), 38 Fed. Reg. 6258 (March 7, 1973), prior to the effective date of that statute. Computerization of the drug listing information received under section 510 of the Act proceeded very slowly, however, and the entire system did not become operational until the 1980s.

(g) Examples of the failure of other agencies to comply with statutory time periods are also abundant:

Section 8(a) of the Toxic Substances Control Act required EPA to promulgate regulations governing the submission of inventory reports within 180 days of the effective date of the Act (i.e., no later than July 1, 1977) and Section 8(b) required that the actual inventory be published within 315 days of the effective date of the Act (i.e., no later than October 15, 1977). In fact, the inventory regulations were promulgated in 42 Fed.Reg. 64572 (December 23, 1977), the publication of the "initial" inventory was announced as of June 1, 1979, in 44 Fed.Reg. 28558 (May 15, 1979), and the final "revised" inventory in 45 Fed.Reg. 50544 (July 29, 1980).

The statutory time limits specified in Section 4 of the Federal Environmental Pesticide Control Act of 1972 (which amended the Federal Insecticide, Fungicide, and Rodenticide Act) have proved to be meaningless. Not one of those statutory time limits has been met by EPA. In recognition of the futility of setting any deadline for reregistration Congress subsequently amended FIFRA to repeal the statutory deadline and to replace it with a requirement that "the Administrator shall accomplish the reregistration of all pesticides in the most expeditious manner practicable." 92 Stat. 820 (1978), 72 U.S.C.A. § 136a(g).

For judicial treatment of EPA's obligation to meet statutory deadlines, see *NRDC v. Train,* 510 F.2d 692 (D.C. Cir. 1974); *NRDC v. EPA,* 475 F.2d 968 (D.C. Cir. 1973). In *Hercules, Inc. v. EPA,* 598 F.2d 91 (D.C. Cir. 1978), the omission of a tentative decision, required by 5 U.S.C.A. § 557(b) in formal evidentiary proceedings, was held to be justified by the need to meet deadlines imposed by a statute and a consent decree.

(h) In 1978, the U.S. Administrative Conference adopted the following recommendation, 1 C.F.R. § 305.78–3:

> Congressional expectations that statutory time limits would be effective have remained largely unfulfilled.... Agency officials often view statutory timetables as unrealistically rigid demands that disregard the agency's need to adjust to changing circumstances. Practical experience at diverse agencies lends support to this appraisal.
>
> Statutory time limits tend to undermine an agency's ability to establish priorities and to control the course of its proceedings. Such limits also enable outside interests to impose their priorities on an agency through suit or threat of suit to enforce them. When asked to enforce statutory time limits, courts have recognized that an agency's observance of the prescribed limits may conflict with other requirements of law (*e.g.,* the requirements of sound decision-making). Judges have, therefore, treated the enforcement of statutory time limits as a matter lying within their own equitable discretion despite the precisely measured language of the statutes....

Recommendation

1. Reasonable timetables or deadlines can help reduce administrative delay. Generally, it is preferable that such limits be established by the agencies themselves, rather than by statute....

3. Whether or not required to do so by statute, each agency should adopt time limits or guidelines for the prompt disposition of its adjudicatory and rulemaking actions, either by announcing schedules for particular agency proceedings or by adopting regulations that contain general timetables for dealing with categories of the agency's proceedings....

5. Congress ordinarily should not impose statutory time limits on rulemaking proceedings. Purely as a practical matter, modern rulemaking proceedings are too complex and varied, and involve too many stages, to permit fixing unyielding time frames for agency decision-making. Strict time limits, moreover, may foreclose the use of procedural techniques that can be valuable in enhancing the degree of public participation and insuring completeness of information....

7. If a statutory time limit is imposed, Congress should expressly state whether affected persons may enforce the time limit through judicial action and, if so, the nature of the relief available for this purpose. In cases where the time limit is intended only as a norm by which the agency's performance is to be measured, a requirement that the agency report deviations form the time limit to Congress may be a desirable means of assuring oversight of its performance.

See generally Tomlinson, *Report on the Experience of Various Agencies with Statutory Time Limits Applicable to Licensing or Clearance Functions and to Rulemaking,* Administrative Conference of the U.S. (1978), on which this recommendation was based.

(i) Most recently, Congress included provisions in the Nutrition Labeling and Education Act of 1990 and the Safe Medical Devices Act of 1990 which set deadlines for the publication of proposed and final regulations and specified that the proposed regulations automatically become final if the agency has not completed rulemaking by the statutory deadline.

INTERAGENCY COORDINATION

FDA has for many years had close working relationships, and in some instances a formal liaison agreement or a "memorandum of understanding" (MOU), with other Federal, state, and foreign agencies. These agreements and memoranda are public documents and most are published in the Federal Register as they are executed, in accordance with FDA policy as announced in 39 Fed. Reg. 35697 (October 3, 1974). They are collected in the FDA COMPLIANCE POLICY GUIDES MANUAL.

In an attempt to improve coordination of Federal efforts to regulate environmental hazards to human health, FDA, EPA, CPSC, and OSHA formed the Interagency Regulatory Liaison Group (IRLG) in 1977, 42 Fed. Reg. 54856 (October 11, 1977). The Food Safety and Quality Service (FSQS) of USDA joined the IRLG two years later, 44 Fed. Reg. 34648 (June 15, 1979). For reports of its progress and activities, *see* 44 Fed. Reg. 29822 (May 22, 1979), 44 Fed. Reg. 39858 (July 6, 1979), 45 Fed. Reg. 6276 (January 25, 1980). During the Reagan Administration, however, this experiment in interagency coordination was abandoned.

Another part of President Carter's regulatory reform program was the establishment of the Regulatory Council, 14 Weekly Comp. of Pres. Doc. 1905 (October 31, 1978). The Council was comprised of 35 Federal departments and agencies, and was responsible for coordinating Federal regulatory activities and expanding efforts to manage the regulatory process more effectively. One function of the Regulatory Council was to assist implementation of Executive Order 12044, published in 43 Fed. Reg. 12661 (March 24, 1978).

The Carter Administration also attempted to foster and coordinate Federal consumer programs in the wake of the defeat of legislation that would have established a specific consumer advocacy office. *See* Executive Order 12160, "Providing for Enhancement and Coordination of Federal Consumer Programs," 15 Weekly Comp. of Pres. Doc. 1761 (September 26, 1979), 44 Fed. Reg. 55787 (September 28, 1979). The work of the Consumer Affairs Council, and the requirements for development of "consumer programs" by all departments and agencies, were described in 44 Fed. Reg. 71103 (December 10, 1979).

As regularly happens when the Presidency changes parties, the Reagan Administration swept away the experiments of the Carter Administration, and instituted in its own programs. For a description of the several executive orders through which President Reagan sought to reform regulation by extending OMB control over agency rulemaking, *see* pp. 1245–47 *supra*.

The Department of HEW announced the establishment of a National Toxicology Program in 43 Fed. Reg. 53060 (November 15, 1978) in order to strengthen the Department's activities in the testing of chemicals of public health concern and in the development and validation of better test methods. Participating in NTP are FDA, NCI, CDC/NIOSH, and NIEHS. The first NTP annual plan was announced in 45 Fed. Reg. 8888 (February 8, 1980), and subsequent plans and reports have periodically been announced, *e.g.*, 54 Fed. Reg. 42570 (October 17, 1989), 55 Fed. Reg. 11059 (March 26, 1990).

*

APPENDIX A

LAWS APPLICABLE TO PRODUCERS OF FOOD, DRUGS, COSMETICS, AND MEDICAL DEVICES

The Food and Drugs Act of 1906 was the first Federal legislation designed to regulate a broad range of consumer products. Only a handful of similar statutes were enacted in this early period of Congressional activity—the Biologics Act of 1902, the Meat Inspection Acts of 1906 and 1907, and the Insecticide Act of 1910. Between 1910 and 1970, Congress addressed only hazardous household products, controlled by the Caustic Poison Act of 1927 and the Federal Hazardous Substances Act of 1960 and its subsequent amendments, although of course it began an intermittent process of legislating to protect the environment.

In the 1970s, Congress enacted more health, safety, and environmental statutes than in the previous several decades. As it enlarged the body of health protection legislation, Congress confronted the difficult problem of meshing new statutes with existing laws, including the FD&C Act. In some instances, Congress made clear the intended relationship between new laws and the Act, but in other instances this relationship was left to the responsible agencies, and ultimately the courts, to resolve.

In the 1980s Congress passed more than twenty laws affecting FDA or FDA-regulated products. Some of these laws, such as the Medical Waste Tracking Act, the Infant Formula Act, and the Federal Anti-Tampering Act, were reactions to widely publicized scandals. Others, such as the Clinical Laboratories Improvement Act and the Processed Products Inspection Improvement Act involved mostly internal administrative changes arising out of the decade's climate of deregulation. Also, Congress began focusing more closely on economic factors affecting the development and availability of important new drugs and technology. The Drug Price Competition and Patent Term Restoration Act and the Orphan Drug Act and its subsequent amendments illustrate Congressional concern with balancing the affordability to the public of new innovations with protecting the economic incentives of firms to conduct the costly research needed to develop new technology.

The following summary illustrates the current range and complexity of federal regulatory requirements applicable to persons and firms regulated by FDA.

1. Advertising and Labeling Practices.

The Federal Trade Commission Act, 38 Stat. 717 (1914), as amended, 15 U.S.C. §§ 41 et seq., empowers the FTC to prevent any unfair methods of competition or other unfair or deceptive acts or practices. This authority has long been recognized as encompassing false or misleading advertising, labeling, or other promotional practices for FDA-regulated products.

The Wheeler–Lea Act, 52 Stat. 111 (1938), added sections 12–17 to the FTC Act, 15 U.S.C. §§ 52–55, specifically to allow the FTC to seek court injunctions against false advertisements for food, drugs, devices, or cosmetics.

The Kefauver–Harris Amendments of 1962, 76 Stat. 780 (1962), which added section 502(n) to the FD&C Act, 21 U.S.C. § 352(n), exempted prescription drug advertising from sections 12–17 of the FTC Act.

The Magnuson–Moss Warranty–Federal Trade Commission Improvement Act, 88 Stat. 2183 (1975), 15 U.S.C. §§ 2301 et seq., authorizes the FTC to regulate written warranties for consumer products, which include FDA-regulated products. See 16 C.F.R. Parts 701–703.

Title V of the Health Research and Health Services Amendments of 1976, 90 Stat. 401 (1976), 21 U.S.C. §§ 350, 378, which added sections 411 and 707 to the FD&C Act restraining regulation of vitamin-mineral products, explicitly mandates coordination between FDA and FTC in this area.

The Medical Device Amendments of 1976, 90 Stat. 539 (1976) (codified at various sections of 21 U.S.C.), which added section 502(r) to the FD&C Act, 21 U.S.C. § 352(r), exempted advertising for restricted devices from sections 12–17 of the FTC Act.

2. Alcoholic Beverages.

The Federal Alcohol Administration Act, 49 Stat. 977 (1935) as amended, 27 U.S.C. §§ 201 et seq., grants comprehensive regulatory control of alcoholic beverages to the Treasury Department. This power has been delegated to the Bureau of Alcohol, Tobacco and Firearms. Although products subject to this Act are not explicitly exempt from the FD & C Act, the adulteration and food safety provisions of the Act do apply. One court has held that FDA lacks authority to regulate the labeling of alcoholic beverages, *Brown–Forman Distillers v. Mathews* 435 F.Supp. 5 (W.D.Ky.1976). The Court of Appeals for the District of Columbia Circuit has ruled that although BATF may, at its discretion, require ingredient labeling for alcoholic beverages, the FAA Act itself does not require such labeling. *Center for Science in the Public Interest v. Department of Treasury* 797 F.2d 995 (D.C.Cir.1986).

The Alcoholic Beverage Labeling Amendments of 1988, 102 Stat. 4181 (1988), 27 U.S.C. §§ 213 et seq., imposed warning lable requirements on alcoholic beverages and authorized the Secretary of the Treasury to implement and enforce the provisions.

3. Anabolic Steroids and Human Growth Hormones.

The Anti–Drug Abuse Act of 1988, 102 Stat. 4181 (1988), 21 U.S.C. §§ 333(e), 333a, amended the FD&C Act to prohibit the possession or distribution of anabolic steroids for any use other than treatment of disease under a doctor's supervision, subject to penalties under the Comprehensive Drug Abuse Prevention and Control Act of 1970, 84 Stat. 1236, as amended, 21 U.S.C. §§ 801 *et seq.*

4. Animal Welfare.

The Animal Welfare Act, 80 Stat. 350 (1966), as amended, 7 U.S.C. §§ 2131 *et seq.,* required USDA to promulgate standards regarding the human handling of animals used in research. The Animal Welfare Amendments of 1985, 99 Stat. 1354, 1645 (1985), 7 U.S.C. §§ 2132, 2143–2146, expanded the coverage of the act's provisions to any facility receiving federal aid for research using animals. The Amendments also require each facility to create a semi-independent research committee to monitor the health and treatment of research animals and report its findings annually to USDA. Section 2143 requires each facility to ensure that established training requirements for animal research employees are met, which training each facility may be required to provide. Section 2145 specifically requires the Secretary of Agriculture to consult with the Secretary of HHS before issuing any regulations under these provisions.

5. Biological Animal Drugs.

The Animal Virus, Serum, and Toxin Act, 37 Stat. 828 (1913), 21 U.S.C. §§ 151 *et seq.,* authorizes USDA to regulate biological animal drugs. Section 902(c) of the FD & C Act specifically provides that the FD&C Act does not in any way affect the 1913 Act. Although biological animal drugs are not explicitly exempted from the FD & C Act, FDA does not regulate them and has by regulation exempted them from the new animal drug provisions. *See* 21 C.F.R. § 510.4.

6. Biological Human Drugs.

The Biologics Act, 32 Stat. 728 (1902), as amended, 42 U.S.C. § 262, authorizes DHHS to regulate biological human drugs. The Secretary was given power to recall dangerous batches of biological products by the Drug Export Amendments Act of 1986, 100 Stat 3743 (1986), 42 U.S.C. § 262(d)(2), which also set civil penalties for violations of such recall orders. This Act also added § 262(h) allowing the exportation to approved countries of partially processed biological products intended for further refinement in the country of destination. Section 902(c) of the FD&C Act specifically provides that the Act does not in any way affect these provisions. The relationship between these laws is discussed at pages [662, 671–72] *supra*.

The National Childhood Vaccine Injury Act of 1986, 100 Stat. 3743, 3755 (1986), 42 U.S.C. §§ 300aa *et seq.*, amended the Public Health Service Act by establishing a comprehensive compensation program whereby awards are paid out of a trust fund, and claims are adjudicated by special masters subject to court supervision. Limitations on liability are established to protect manufacturers from excessive judgements arising from injuries caused by unavoidable side effects and reactions to vaccines manufactured according to established regulations.

7. Clinical Laboratories.

The Clinical Laboratories Improvement Act of 1967, 81 Stat. 533 (1967), 42 U.S.C. § 263a, regulates the licensing of clinical laboratories. The Clinical Laboratories Improvement Amendments of 1988, 102 Stat. 2903, substantially changed this area of regulation. The new provisions, which are scheduled to become fully implemented by 1991, replace the old licensing scheme with a certification program relying in large part on private independent accreditation bodies which have the authority to monitor compliance and make certification applications for their member labs. DHHS will monitor the enforcement of the accreditation bodies through spot checks of member labs.

8. Consumer Products.

The Federal Caustic Poison Act, 44 Stat. 1406 (1927), as amended, 15 U.S.C. §§ 401 *et seq.*, provides for labeling of dangerous caustic or corrosive substances. Section 12(a) provides that it shall apply to all products subject to the FD&C Act. Section 19 of the Hazardous Substances Act repeals the Federal Caustic Poison Act insofar as it applied to products regulated by the FD&C Act and exempt from the FHSA.

The Federal Hazardous Substances Labeling Act, 74 Stat. 372 (1960), as amended, 15 U.S.C. §§ 1261 *et seq.*, provides for the regulation of hazardous substances used in or around the household. Section 2(f)(3) exempts food, drugs, and cosmetics, but not medical devices.

The Flammable Fabrics Act, 67 Stat. 111 (1953), as amended, 15 U.S.C. §§ 1191 *et seq.*, authorizes regulation of wearing apparel and fabrics that are flammable. It does not exempt products subject to FDA regulation, some of which may be medical devices.

The Poison Prevention Packaging Act of 1970, 84 Stat. 1670 as amended, 15 U.S.C. §§ 1471 *et seq.*, authorizes special packaging to protect children from dangerous household substances. All FDA-regulated products are subject to the PPPA and many drugs are subject to additional special packaging requirements. *See* 16 C.F.R. Parts 1700–1704.

The Consumer Products Safety Act, 86 Stat. 1207 (1972), as amended, 15 U.S.C. §§ 2051 *et seq.*, empowers the Consumer Product Safety Commission to prevent unreasonable risks of injury from consumer products. Section 2052(a)(1)(H) and (I) exempts drugs, devices, cosmetics and food. Under a memorandum of understanding published at 41 Fed.Reg. 34342 (August 13, 1976), FDA and CPSC have agreed that CPSC may exert jurisdiction over food containers that present a physical hazard and do not migrate to food.

The Federal Anti–Tampering Act, 97 Stat. 831 (1983), 18 U.S.C. § 1365, makes it a felony to tamper with packaged consumer products such as foods, drugs, cosmetics and devices. FDA is given investigatory authority where products within its jurisdiction are involved.

9. Drinking Water.

The Safe Drinking Water Act, 88 Stat. 1660 (1974), as amended, 42 U.S.C. §§ 300f *et seq.*, establishes federal programs to assure the safety of public water systems. The Act transferred to EPA, from FDA, jurisdiction over national drinking water standards, but added section 410 to the FD&C Act to retain in FDA the jurisdiction over bottled drinking water. FDA and EPA have entered into Memoranda of Understanding on the regulation of water used on interstate carrier conveyances, 43 Fed.Reg. 43072 (September 22, 1978), and on control of direct and indirect additives to drinking water, 44 Fed.Reg. 42775 (July 20, 1979).

10. Drugs for Rare Diseases.

The Orphan Drug Act of 1983, 96 Stat. 2049 (1983), as amended, 21 U.S.C. §§ 360aa *et seq.*, allows development of patented drugs for rare ("orphan") diseases by non-patent holders when the patent holder cannot insure an adequate supply of the drug. Also, tax credits are given to manufacturers who test and develop orphan drugs in order to insure their availability. The Act established the Office of Orphan Products Development which reviews applications for orphan drug status. A list of designated orphan drugs, which is updated quarterly, can be found at 54 Fed.Reg. 16294 (April 21, 1989). Orphan drugs are discussed at pp. [566–71] *supra.*

11. Etiological Agents.

Section 361 of the Public Health Service Act, 58 Stat. 682, 703 (1944), 42 U.S.C. § 264, authorizes DHHS to take appropriate action to prevent the spread of communicable disease. Regulations promulgated pursuant to this authority may be found at 21 C.F.R. Part 1240 *et seq.*

The spread of communicable diseases through interstate transportation is jointly regulated by DHHS (sanitation of interstate conveyances, 21 C.F.R. Part 1250 *et seq.*) and the Center for Disease Control (interstate transportation of etiological agents, *see* note 25 *infra,* this appendix).

12. Fish.

In accordance with the provisions of the Agricultural Marketing Act of 1946, 60 Stat. 1082, as amended, 7 U.S.C. § 1622, relating to promotion of agricultural products, the National Marine Fisheries Service of the Department of Commerce conducts a voluntary inspection, grading and certification service for fish products. Regulations governing this program, and establishing names and standards for grades of fish, are codified in 50 C.F.R. Parts 260–266. A memorandum of understanding between the two agencies appears at 40 Fed.Reg. 3025 (January 17, 1975).

In 1990 Congress began consideration of bills to establish a mandatory seafood inspection system. The major obstacle to compromise was disagreement over which agency or agencies would assume primary responsibility for the new program. Two bills called for the Department of Agriculture to take primary responsibility over a mandatory inspection program, but differed over the roles to be played by FDA and NMFS. The Bush administration supported a stronger, but still voluntary inspection system to be run primarily by FDA with support from the National Marine Fisheries Service.

The FDA and NMFS published an Advance Notice of Proposed Rulemaking to announce their intention to establish a voluntary inspection program to be financed by fees paid by participating producers. 55 Fed.Reg. 26334 (June 27, 1990). As this book went to press, debate over the form and location of federal fish inspection was continuing in Congress.

13. Inspector General.

Congress established in HEW an Inspector General to monitor and make recommendations concerning the "economy and efficiency" of agency run programs and to detect and prevent fraud and abuse within the agency and by certain outside entities, such as health care providers reimbursed under federal medicare and medicaid programs. 90 Stat. 2429 (1976). In 1978, offices of Inspectors General were established in other federal agencies, 92 Stat. 1101, and in 1988 the Inspector General Act Amendments of 1988, 102 Stat. 2515, repealed the 1976 Act and made the HHS Inspector General subject to the provisions of the 1978 Act.

The Inspector General for HHS has been delegated certain additional powers by the Secretary to investigate and prosecute fraud and other criminal activities of both agency employees and grantees or recipients of agency funds. *See* 43 Fed.Reg. 50508 (Oct. 30, 1978).

In the late 1980s, the generic drug scandal, *see* pages [579–80] *supra*, prompted debate within DHHS over the role of the Inspector General to investigate criminal violations of the FD&C Act. *See* pages [1065–66] *supra*. As this book went to press, dispute over the I.G.'s role had not been conclusively settled.

14. Mail Fraud.

The postal fraud statutes, 18 U.S.C. §§ 1341–1343 and 39 U.S.C. § 3005, which date back to 1872, prohibit any fraud involving use of the mails. These statutes include any fraud involving FDA–regulated products. The Seventh Circuit recently upheld a mail fraud conviction arising out of falsified test data mailed to FDA as part of a product safety approval application. *See United States v. Keplinger* 776 F.2d 678 (7th Cir.1985).

15. Meat, Poultry, and Eggs.

Meat, poultry and eggs are subject to comprehensive regulation by USDA under the Federal Meat Inspection Act, 34 Stat. 674 (1906), 34 Stat. 1260 (1907), as amended by the Wholesome Meat Act, 81 Stat. 584 (1967), and by the Processed Products Inspection Improvement Act of 1986, 100 Stat. 3556, 21 U.S.C. §§ 601 *et seq.;* The Poultry Products Inspection Act, 71 Stat. 441 (1957), as modernized by the Wholesome Poultry Products Act, 82 Stat. 791 (1968), 21 U.S.C. §§ 451 *et seq.;* and the Egg Products Inspection Act, 84 Stat. 1620 (1970), 21 U.S.C. §§ 1031 *et seq.* These statutes and section 902(c) of the FD&C Act attempt to define their intended relationship. For a thorough discussion of the statutory provisions and the problems they present, *see* "Food Regulation: A Case Study of USDA and FDA," V Study on Federal Regulation, Senate Comm. on Governmental Affairs, 95th Cong., 1st Sess. (1977). USDA and FDA have entered into a number of Memoranda of Understanding. *See e.g.,* 37 Fed.Reg. 2686 (February 4, 1972) (egg products); 40 Fed.Reg. 16228 (April 10, 1975) (drug, pesticide, and industrial chemical residues in animal feeds, meat and poultry); and 40 Fed.Reg. 25079 (June 12, 1975) (recall and disposition of contaminated products).

16. Milk.

The Filled Milk Act, 42 Stat. 1486 (1923), 21 U.S.C. §§ 61 *et seq.,* prohibits interstate shipment of filled milk. Section 902(c) of the FD& C Act specifically provides that the FD&C Act does not affect the Filled Milk Act. *See* p. [116] *supra* for discussion of the current status of the Filled Milk Act.

The Import Milk Act, 44 Stat. 1101 (1927), 21 U.S.C. §§ 141 *et seq.,* authorizes DHHS to exercise special controls over imported milk. Section 902(c) of the FD&C Act specifically provides that the FD&C Act does not affect the Import Milk Act. *See* 21 C.F.R. Part 1210.

17. Occupational Safety and Health.

The Occupational Safety and Health Act of 1970, 84 Stat. 1590, 29 U.S.C. §§ 651 *et seq.,* authorizes the Occupational Safety and Health Administration (OSHA) to establish standards to reduce hazards to worker health and safety. All establishments in which products subject to FDA jurisdiction are manufactured or processed are also subject to regulation by OSHA.

18. Pesticides.

The Federal Insecticide, Fungicide, and Rodenticide Act, 61 Stat. 163 (1947), as modernized by the Federal Environmental Pesticide Control Act of 1972, 86 Stat. 973, 7 U.S.C. §§ 135 *et seq.,* authorizes EPA to register and otherwise regulate all pesticides; 7 U.S.C. § 136(t) defines "pest" and explicitly exempts from the definition any virus, bacteria, or other micro-organisms in or on living man or living animals. Section 136(k) exempts from the definition of "pest", any fungus on or in living man or other animals and those on or in processed food, beverages or pharmaceuticals. The FIFRA Amendments of 1988, 102 Stat. 2654, amended § 136(u) to extend the exemption to animal drugs. An EPA regulation, 40 C.F.R. §§ 152.5(d), mirrors this exemption and extends it to cosmetics.

When EPA was created by executive order under Reorganization Plan No. 3 of 1970, 35 Fed.Reg. 15623 (Oct. 6, 1970), authority to establish tolerances for pesticides in food under sections 408 and 409 of the FD&C Act was transferred to it from FDA. *See* section 2(a)(4) of Reorganization Plan No. 3 of 1970, (84 Stat. 2086 (1970)). FDA retains enforcement authority under these provisions, and establishes informal defect action levels when no formal tolerance exists. *See* page [307] *supra.*

The Pesticide Monitoring Improvements Act of 1988, 102 Stat. 1107, 1411 (1988), 21 U.S.C. §§ 1401–1403, requires FDA to expand and improve its pesticide monitoring and enforcement program for imported fruits and vegetables.

19. Public Health Education and Protection.

The Public Health Service Act, 58 Stat. 682 (1944), as amended, 42 U.S.C. §§ 201 *et seq.,* contains hundreds of provisions authorizing DHHS to engage in a wide variety of activities to promote the public health. Authority under some of these provisions has been delegated to FDA for use in its regulatory activities, *see* 21 C.F.R. § 5.10, but the majority are administered elsewhere in DHHS.

20. Radiological Products.

The Radiological Control for Health and Safety Act of 1968, 82 Stat. 1173, authorizes DHHS to regulate electronic product radiation.

This Act, which is administered by FDA and now recodified at 21 U.S.C. § 530 *et seq.*, applies to products regulated under the FD & C Act, such as medical devices. *See* p. [794] *supra.*

21. Solid Waste.

The Solid Waste Disposal Act, 90 Stat. 2795 (1976), as amended, 42 U.S.C. §§ 6901 *et seq.*, which consolidated and revised many Congressional enactments, authorizes a wide variety of federal controls and programs respecting disposal of solid waste. FDA-regulated firms and products are fully subject to its provisions.

The Medical Waste Tracking Act of 1988, 102 Stat. 2950, 42 U.S.C. §§ 6992 *et seq.*, amended the Solid Waste Disposal Act by establishing a two-year test program in several eastern states to classify and track the disposal of medical waste, especially items exposed to infectious agents. Any organization in the affected states that handles potentially infectious wastes (e.g. hospitals, laboratories and drug manufacturers) is subject to this program. Compliance will be monitored through mandatory recordkeeping provisions and violators face civil and criminal penalties.

22. Statutory Food Standards.

The Butter Standards Act, 42 Stat. 1500 (1923), 21 U.S.C. § 321a, establishes a statutory standard of identity for butter. Section 902(a) of the FD&C Act provides that this law shall remain in force and effect and be applicable to the provisions of the FD&C Act. The Dry Milk Solids Act, 58 Stat. 108 (1944), as amended, 21 U.S.C. § 321c, establishes a statutory standard for nonfat dry milk for purposes of the FD&C Act.

The Infant Formula Act of 1980, 94 Stat. 1190, 21 U.S.C. § 350(a), which added section 412 to the FD&C Act, regulates the manufacturing of prepared Infant Formulas, and establishes their minimum nutritional requirements.

23. Tea.

The Tea Importation Act, 29 Stat. 604 (1897), as amended, 21 U.S.C. §§ 41 *et seq.*, authorizes DHHS to enforce quality standards for all imported tea. The FDA regulations implementing this law are set out at 21 C.F.R. Part 1220.

24. Toxic Substances.

The Toxic Substances Control Act, 90 Stat. 2003 (1976), 15 U.S.C. §§ 2601 *et seq.*, empowers EPA to regulate unreasonable risks of injury to health or the environment from new and existing chemicals. Section 3(2)(B)(iv) of TSCA exempts any food, food additive, drug, cosmetic, or device.

25. Transportation of Hazardous Materials.

The Hazardous Materials Transportation Act, 88 Stat. 2156 (1974), 49 U.S.C. §§ 1801 *et seq.,* authorized the Department of Transportation to regulate the transportation of any substance which may pose an unreasonable risk to health, safety, or property. FDA-regulated products may be subject to these provisions. Also, the Center for Disease Control has promulgated additional regulations affecting the interstate transportation of etiological agents in 42 C.F.R. Part 72.

26. USDA Food Grading.

Under the Agricultural Marketing Act of 1946, 60 Stat. 1082 (1946), as amended, 7 U.S.C. § 1622, the Agricultural Marketing Service of the USDA conducts a voluntary inspection, grading, and certification service for agricultural products (except fish). Regulations governing this program, and establishing standards for grades of agricultural products, are codified in various parts of 7 C.F.R.. FDA and USDA have entered into Memoranda of Understanding to coordinate their functions respecting these products. *See, e.g.,* 39 Fed.Reg. 18695 (May 29, 1974) (grain, rice, and pulses), 40 Fed.Reg. 8846 (March 3, 1975) (salmonella in dry milk), and 42 Fed.Reg. 20350 (April 19, 1977) (inspection and grading of all food products).

APPENDIX B

DELEGATIONS OF AUTHORITY TO THE COMMISSIONER OF FOOD AND DRUGS

None of the statutes administered by the Food and Drug Administration expressly delegates authority to the Commissioner of Food and Drugs or to the agency. Most, including the FD&C Act, authorize action by the Secretary of Health and Human Services. A handful confer power directly on the President.

Historically, Secretaries of HHS (or, previously, Health, Education, and Welfare) have delegated the Secretary's powers, or subdelegated the President's authority, to the FDA Commissioner. They of course excepted those few powers, such as the authority to suspend the approval of a NDA for a drug judged to present an "imminent hazard." But with respect to the remainder, the vast majority of powers conferred by legislation, the Secretarial delegation was unqualified: the Commissioner stood in the shoes of the Secretary and the Commissioner's decision on a matter represented the decision of the Department (and the Administration). For most of the period since World War II, the Commissioner's delegated powers included the authority to propose and promulgate regulations. In this respect, the FDA Commissioner occupied a unique position in the Department.

The FDA Commissioner's official authority to act definitively, without departmental or presidential approval, did not of course mean that occupants of the office did not frequently consult with the Secretary or occasionally even with the President. Very often they did so on their own initiative, but no Commissioner would have considered it inappropriate to be asked by the Secretary or by the White House to consult about an important decision before it was taken. Consultation and oversight were by no means routine, however, and accordingly it should be no surprise that steps taken during the Reagan Administration to make all regulations issued by executive agencies subject to review in the Office of Management and Budget *did* engender suspicion within FDA. An even more important change, however, was HHS Secretary Schweiker's withdrawal from the Commissioner of authority to issue regulations without departmental review and approval in 1981.

This appendix sets forth the current delegations of authority to the Commissioner of Food and Drugs to administer laws that repose power in the Secretary of HHS (or the President) and Secretary Schweiker's revocation of the Commissioner's authority with respect to the promulgation of certain regulations.

21 C.F.R.

Subpart A—Delegations of Authority to the Commissioner of Food and Drugs

§ 5.10 Delegations from the Secretary, the Assistant Secretary for Health, and Public Health Service Officials.

(a) The Assistant Secretary for Health has redelegated to the Commissioner of Food and Drugs, with authority to redelegate except when specifically prohibited, all authority delegated to the Assistant Secretary for Health by the Secretary of Health and Human Services, as follows:

(1) Functions vested in the Secretary under the Federal Food, Drug, and Cosmetic Act (21 U.S.C. 301 et seq.), the Filled Milk Act (21 U.S.C. 61–63), the Federal Import Milk Act (21 U.S.C. 141 et seq.), the Tea Importation Act (21 U.S.C. 41 et seq.), the Federal Caustic Poison Act (44 Stat. 1406), and The Fair Packaging and Labeling Act (15 U.S.C. 1451 et seq.), pursuant to section 12 of Reorganization Plan No. IV and Reorganization Plan No. 1 of 1953, including authority to administer oaths vested in the Secretary of Agriculture by 7 U.S.C. 2217.

(2) Functions vested in the Secretary under section 301 (Research and Investigations); section 307 (International Cooperation); and section 311 (Federal–State Cooperation) of the Public Health Service Act (42 U.S.C. 241, 242*l*, 243), as amended, which relate to the functions of the Food and Drug Administration.

(3) Functions vested in the Secretary under sections 354 through 360F of the Public Health Service Act (42 U.S.C. 263b through 263n), as amended, which relate to electronic product radiation control.

(4) Functions vested in the Secretary under section 361 of the Public Health Service Act (42 U.S.C. 264), as amended, which relate to the law enforcement functions of the Food and Drug Administration concerning the following products and activities: biologicals (including blood and blood products); interstate travel sanitation (except interstate transportation of etiologic agents under 42 CFR 72); food (including milk and food service sanitation and shellfish sanitation); and drugs, devices, cosmetics, electronic products, and other items or products regulated by the Food and Drug Administration.

(5) Functions vested in the Secretary under sections 351 and 352 of Part F, Subpart 1 of the Public Health Service Act (42 U.S.C. 262 and 263), as amended, Biological Products, insofar as they relate to the functions assigned to the Food and Drug Administration.

(6) Functions vested in the Secretary under section 302(a) of the Public Health Service Act (42 U.S.C. 242(a)), as amended, which relate to the determination and reporting requirements with respect to the

medicinal and scientific requirements of the United States for controlled substances.

(7) Functions vested in the Secretary under section 303 of the Public Health Service Act (42 U.S.C. 242a), as amended, which relate to the authorization of persons engaged in research on the use and effect of drugs to protect the identity of their research subjects with respect to drugs scheduled under Pub.L. 91–513 for which an investigational new drug application is filed with the Food and Drug Administration and with respect to all drugs not scheduled under Pub.L. 91–513.

(8) Functions vested in the Secretary pertaining to section 4 of the Comprehensive Drug Abuse Prevention and Control Act of 1970 (84 Stat. 1241) which relate to the determination of the safety and effectiveness of drugs or to approve new drugs to be used in the treatment of narcotic addicts.

(9) Functions vested in the Secretary pertaining to section 303(f) of the Controlled Substances Act (21 U.S.C. 823(f)) which relate to the determination of the qualifications and competency of practitioners wishing to conduct research with controlled substances listed in Schedule I of the Act, and the merits of the research protocol.

(10) Functions vested in the Secretary pertaining to provisions of the Controlled Substances Act (21 U.S.C. 801 et seq.) which relate to administration of the Federal Food, Drug, and Cosmetic Act (21 U.S.C. 301 et seq.).

(11) Functions vested in the Secretary under section 409(b) of the Federal Meat Inspection Act (21 U.S.C. 679(b)) which relate to the detention of any carcass, part thereof, meat, or meat product of cattle, sheep, swine, goats, or equines.

(12) Functions vested in the Secretary under section 24(b) of the Poultry Products Inspection Act (21 U.S.C. 467f(b)) which relate to the detention of any poultry carcass, part thereof, or poultry product.

(13) Functions vested in the Secretary under the Egg Products Inspection Act (21 U.S.C. 1031 et seq.).

(14) Functions vested in the Secretary by amendments to the foregoing statutes subsequent to Reorganization Plan No. 1 of 1953.

(15) Function of issuing all regulations of the Food and Drug Administration, except as provided in § 5.11. The reservation of authority contained in Chapter 2–000 of the Department Organization Manual shall not apply.

(16) Functions vested in the Secretary under section 1103 of Executive Order 11490, as amended by Executive Order 11921, which relate to emergency health functions as they pertain to the operations and functional responsibilities assigned to the agency. This authority shall be exercised in accordance with section 102 and pertinent sections of Part 30 of Executive Order 11490 and guidelines promulgated by the Federal Preparedness Agency of the General Services Administration;

Office of the Secretary, HHS; and Office of the Assistant Secretary for Health.

(17) Function vested in the Secretary of authorizing and approving miscellaneous and emergency expenses of enforcement activities.

(18) Function vested in the Secretary under the Federal Advisory Committee Act, Pub.L. 92–463, to make determinations that advisory committee meetings are concerned with matters listed in 5 U.S.C. 552(b) and therefor may be closed to the public for those committees under the administrative jurisdiction of the Commissioner of Food and Drugs. This authority may not be redelegated. This authority is to be exercised in accordance with the requirements of the Act and only with respect to the following:

(i) Meetings, to the extent that they directly involve review, discussion or consideration of records of the Department which are exempt from disclosure under 5 U.S.C. 552(b)(4), (6), and (7), namely, (a) records containing trade secrets and commercial or financial information obtained from a person and privileged or confidential; (b) personnel, medical and similar files the disclosure of which would constitute a clearly unwarranted invasion of personal privacy; and (c) investigatory files compiled for law enforcement purposes;

(ii) Meetings to the extent that they involve the review, discussion, and evaluation of specific drugs and devices regulated by FDA which are intended to result in recommendations for regulatory decisions under the Federal Food, Drug, and Cosmetic Act and which are concerned with matters listed in 5 U.S.C. 552(b)(4), (5), and (7);

(iii) Meetings held for the sole purpose of considering and formulating advice which the committee will give or any final report it will render, *Provided:*

(a) The meetings will involve solely the internal expression of views and judgments of the members and it is essential to close the meeting or portions thereof to protect the free exchange of such views and avoid undue interference with agency or committee operations, and such views if reduced to writing would be protected from mandatory disclosure under 5 U.S.C. 552(b);

(b) The meeting is closed for the shortest time necessary, summarizing the work of the committee during the closed session, and a report, prepared by the executive secretary will be made available promptly to the public.

(c) When feasible, the public is given a timely opportunity to present relevant information and views to the committee; and

(d) Concurrence for closing the meetings for such purpose is obtained from the Office of the General Counsel and the Office of Public Affairs.

(19) Functions vested in the Secretary under the second sentence of section 310(a) and under section 310(b) (Health Conferences and Health

Education Information) of the Public Health Service Act (42 U.S.C. 242o), as amended, to call for a conference and invite as many health authorities and officials of State or local public or private agencies or organizations as deemed necessary or proper on subjects related to the functions of the Food and Drug Administration, and to issue information related to health for the use of the public and other pertinent health information for the use of persons and institutions concerned with health services when such information is related to the functions of the Food and Drug Administration.

(20) Functions vested in the Secretary under section 2101 of the Public Health Service Act (42 U.S.C. 219) as amended, to accept offers of gifts, excluding the acceptance of gifts of real property. Only the authority to accept unconditional gifts of personal property valued at $5,000 or less may be redelegated.

(21) Functions vested in the Secretary under section 362 of the Public Health Service Act (42 U.S.C. 265), as amended, which relate to the prohibition of the introduction of foods, drugs, devices, cosmetics, electronic products, and other items or products regulated by the Food and Drug Administration into the United States when it is determined that it is required in the interest of public health when such functions relate to the law enforcement functions of the Food and Drug Administration.

(22) Functions vested in the Secretary under section 1003(b)(3), Title X, of the Public Works and Economic Development Act of 1965 (42 U.S.C. 3246b(b)(3)) to waive any matching requirements for programs or projects of State and local governments funded under Title X of that act where it is determined that State or local governments concerned cannot reasonably obtain any non-Federal contributions.

(23) Functions vested in the Secretary under section 401(a) of the Lead–Based Paint Poisoning Prevention Act, as amended by Pub.L. 94–317 (42 U.S.C. 4831(a)) relating to the prohibition of the application of lead-based paint to cooking, drinking, or eating utensils.

(24) Functions vested in the Secretary for the health information and health promotion program under Title XVII of the Public Health Service Act (42 U.S.C. 300u et seq.), as amended, insofar as the authorities pertain to functions assigned to the Food and Drug Administration. The delegation includes, but is not limited to, the authorities under: section 1702(a)(1) and (3) and section 1704(1), (2), and (6). The delegation excludes the authority to select all Senior Executive Service, supergrade and equivalent, and Schedule C (GS–12 and above) positions; promulgate regulations; and submit reports to the President.

(25) To administer a Small Business Innovation Research Program under section 9 of the Small Business Act (15 U.S.C. 638), as amended. The delegation excludes the authority to promulgate regulations, establish advisory councils and committees, appoint members to advisory councils and committees, and submit reports to Congress.

(26) Functions vested in the Secretary under sections 982 and 983 of the Consumer–Patient Radiation Health and Safety Act of 1981 (42 U.S.C. 10007 and 10008), as amended. The delegation excludes the authority to promulgate regulations and submit reports to Congress. The authority delegated under section 983 of the Act may only be exercised as it relates to functions assigned to the Food and Drug Administration.

(27) Functions vested in the Secretary under section 156 of title 35 of the U.S.Code (35 U.S.C. 156), as amended, which allows for the extension of patent terms for human drug products, medical devices, food additives, and color additives subject to the Federal Food, Drug, and Cosmetic Act. These authorities may be redelegated except the authority to make due diligence determinations under section 156(d)(2)(B), which may not be redelegated to an Office below the Office of the Commissioner of Food and Drugs.

(28) Functions vested in the Secretary under section 1862(h)(1), (2)(A), and (3) of the Social Security Act (42 U.S.C. 1395y(h)(1), (2)(A), and (3)), as amended, which provides for a registry of all cardiac pacemaker devices and pacemaker leads for which payment was made under this title. The approval and issuance of regulations under that section are reserved to the Secretary, as provided in 21 CFR 5.11.

(29) Functions vested in the Secretary under the Stevenson–Wydler Technology Innovation Act of 1980 (15 U.S.C. 3701 et seq.) (the Act), as amended, and under Executive Order No. 12591 of April 10, 1987, as they pertain to the functions of the Food and Drug Administration. The delegation excludes the authority to promulgate regulations and submit reports to Congress; under section 11(a)(2) of the Act (15 U.S.C. 3710a(a)(2)) to approve agreements and contracts with invention management organizations; and under section 11(c)(3)(B) of the Act (15 U.S.C. 3710a(c)(3)(B)) to propose necessary statutory changes regarding conflict of interest.

(i) The authorities under sections 11(c)(5)(A) and (B) of the Act (15 U.S.C. 3710a(c)(5)(A) and (B)) to disapprove or require the modification of cooperative research and development agreements and licensing agreements after the agreement is presented to the Commissioner of Food and Drugs by the head of the laboratory concerned, and to transmit written explanation of such disapproval or modification to the head of the laboratory concerned, may be redelegated only to a senior official in the immediate office of the Commissioner.

(ii) The following authorities may not be redelegated: the authority under section 11(b)(3) of the Act (15 U.S.C. 3710a(b)(3)) to waive a right of ownership which the Federal Government may have to an invention made under a cooperative research and development agreement; the authority under section 11(b)(4) of the Act (15 U.S.C. 3710a(b)(4)) to permit employees or former employees to participate in efforts to commercialize inventions they made while in the service of the United States; the authority under section 11(c)(3)(A) of the Act (15

U.S.C. 3710a(c)(3)(A)) to review employee standards of conduct for resolving potential conflicts of interest; the authority under section 13(a)(1) of the Act (15 U.S.C. 3710c(a)(1)) to retain any royalties or other income, except as provided in section 13(a)(2) of the Act (15 U.S.C. 3710c(a)(2)); and the authority under section 13(a)(1)(A)(i) of the Act (15 U.S.C. 3710c(a)(1)(A)(i)) to pay royalties or other income the agency receives on account of an invention to the inventor if the inventor was an employee of the agency at the time the invention was made.

(iii) Any authorities under paragraph (a)(29) of this section delegated by the Commissioner of Food and Drugs may not be further redelegated.

(30) Functions vested in the Secretary under sections 4702, 4703, and 4704 of the Pesticide Monitoring Improvements Act of 1988 (21 U.S.C. 1401–1403) which relate to pesticide monitoring and enforcement information, foreign pesticide information, and pesticide analytical methods. The delegation excludes the authority to submit reports to Congress.

(31) Functions vested in the Secretary under the Government Patent Policy Act of 1980 as amended by the Federal Court Reorganization Act of 1984, as they pertain to the functions of the Food and Drug Administration (FDA). The delegated authorities, to be exercised in compliance with all existing rules and regulations regarding patent and invention rights and responsibilities, are restricted to the extent that 35 U.S.C. 203, as amended, may not be redelegated and that under 35 U.S.C. 207(a), the Assistant Secretary for Health is to be notified of any significant invention, patent, or license, so that the Assistant Secretary for Health may decide whether or not documentation concerning any such invention, patent, or license should be submitted to the Assistant Secretary for Health for signature. All other authorities may be redelegated to officials at the level equivalent to bureau and institute directors.

(i) Disposition of rights, 35 U.S.C. 202(c)(7), as amended: The authority to permit a nonprofit organization to assign the rights to a subject invention in the United States to organizations which do not have as one of their primary functions the management of inventions.

(ii) Disposition of rights, 35 U.S.C. 202(d), as amended: The authority to permit a contractor to grant requests for retention of rights by the inventor.

(iii) Disposition of rights, 35 U.S.C. 202(e), as amended: The authority to transfer or assign whatever rights FDA may acquire in the subject invention in any case when an agency employee is a coinventor of any invention made under a funding agreement with a nonprofit organization or small business firm. Such rights may be transferred or assigned from the FDA employee to the contractor subject to the conditions set forth in this chapter.

(iv) March-in-rights, 35 U.S.C. 203, as amended: The authority to require the contractor to grant nonexclusive, partially exclusive, or exclusive licenses to responsible applicant(s), or the authority for FDA to grant such licenses, provided such action would be in the best interest of FDA, in accordance with all provisions of this section.

(v) Preference for United States industry, 35 U.S.C. 204, as amended: The authority to waive the preference for U.S. industry requirement.

(vi) Domestic and foreign protection of federally owned inventions, 35 U.S.C. 207(a) as amended, the authority to:

(A) Apply for, obtain, and maintain patents or other forms of protection in the United States and in foreign countries on inventions in which the Federal Government owns a right, title, or interest;

(B) Grant nonexclusive, exclusive, or partially exclusive licenses under federally owned patent applications, patents, or other forms of protection obtained, royalty-free or for royalties or other consideration, and on such terms and conditions, including the grant to the licensee of the right of enforcement pursuant to the provisions of chapter 29 of title 35 as determined appropriate in the public interest;

(C) Undertake all other suitable and necessary steps to protect and administer rights to federally owned inventions on behalf of the Federal Government either directly or through contract; and

(D) Transfer custody and administration, in whole or in part, to another Federal agency, of the right, title, or interest in any federally owned invention.

(vii) Determination as to domestic rights and notice to employee of determination, 45 CFR 7.3 and 7.7, as amended, authority to:

(A) Leave title to invention in the FDA employee inventor where the Government has insufficient interest in an invention to obtain the entire domestic right, title, and interest therein; and

(B) Notify the FDA employee inventor of the determination in writing.

(b) The Assistant General Counsel in charge of the Food and Drug Division has been authorized to report apparent violations to the Department of Justice for the institution of criminal proceedings, pursuant to section 305 of the Federal Food, Drug, and Cosmetic Act, section 4 of the Federal Import Milk Act, and section 9(b) of the Federal Caustic Poison Act.

(c) The Director, Office of Management, Public Health Service, has redelegated to the Commissioner of Food and Drugs, with authority to redelegate, the authority to certify true copies of any books, records, or other documents on file within the Food and Drug Administration or extracts from such; to certify that true copies are true copies of the entire file of the Administration; to certify the complete original record or to certify the nonexistence of records on file within the Administration; and to cause the Seal of the Department of be affixed to such certifications and to agreements, awards, citations, diplomas, and similar documents.

(d) The Executive Officer, Public Health Service, has redelegated to the Commissioner of Food and Drugs appeal authority to take final action upon an individual's appeal of a refusal to correct or amend the individual's record when the appeal has been made by the individual under Privacy Act regulations (Part 21 of this chapter and 45 CFR Part 5b). The authority may not be redelegated.

(e) [Reserved]

(f) The Secretary of Health and Human Services has redelegated to the Commissioner of Food and Drugs, or his designee, the authority to take final action on matters pertaining to section 203 of the Equal Access to Justice Act (5 U.S.C. 504), and to develop procedures and regulations where necessary to supplement the Department's regulations, 45 CFR Part 13.

[42 FR 15560, Mar. 22, 1977]

§ 5.11 Reservation of authority.

(a) Notwithstanding provisions of § 5.10 or any previous delegations of authority to the contrary, the Secretary reserves the authority to approve regulations of the Food and Drug Administration, except regulations to which sections 556 and 557 of Title 5 of the United States Code apply, which:

(1) Establish procedural rules applicable to a general class of foods, drugs, cosmetics, medical devices, or other subjects of regulation; or

(2) Present highly significant public issues involving the quality, availability, marketability, or cost of one or more foods, drugs, cosmetics, medical devices, or other subjects of regulation.

(b) Nothing in this section precludes the Secretary from approving a regulation, or being notified in advance of an action, to which sections 556 and 557 of Title 5 of the United States Code apply, which meets one of the criteria in paragraph (a) of this section.

(c) This reservation of authority is intended only to improve the internal management of the Department of Health and Human Services, and is not intended to create any right or benefit, substantive or procedural, enforceable at law by a party against the United States, the Department of Health and Human Services, the Food and Drug Administration, any agency, officer, or employee of the United States, or any person. Regulations issued by the Food and Drug Administration without the approval of the Secretary are to be conclusively viewed as falling outside the scope of this reservation of authority.

*

INDEX

References are to Pages

---

†